INDIANA RULES OF COURT: KEYRULES

VOLUME IIIA - LOCAL

2014

THOMSON REUTERS™

Mat #41258957

ISBN: 978-0-314-65399-4

PREFACE

Indiana Rules of Court: KeyRules provides the practitioner with a comprehensive "single source" procedural guide for civil practice in state courts, combining applicable provisions of both statewide and local rules of civil procedure with relevant analytical materials.

This book consists of outlines of the applicable rules of practice, timing requirements, filing and service requirements, format requirements, hearing requirements, checklists and other pertinent documents related to pleadings, motions, requests, notices, and applications in selected Indiana courts.

The selected Indiana Circuit and Superior Courts include the following counties: Allen County, Hamilton County, Lake County, Marion County, and St. Joseph County.

THE PUBLISHER

December 2013

ADDITIONAL INFORMATION OR RESEARCH ASSISTANCE

For additional information or research assistance call the West reference attorneys at 1-800-REF-ATTY (1-800-733-2889). Contact West's editorial department directly with your questions and suggestions by e-mail at west.editor@thomson.com.

Courts Covered

*

Table of Contents

ALLEN COUNTY

HAMILTON COUNTY

TABLE OF CONTENTS

ST. JOSEPH COUNTY

APPENDIX - RELATED COURT DOCUMENTS

*

ALLEN COUNTY

Pleadings
Complaint

Document Last Updated October 2013

A. **Applicable Rules**

1. *State rules*

   a. Commencement of an action. IN ST TRIAL P Rule 3.

   b. Appearance. IN ST TRIAL P Rule 3.1.

   c. Process. IN ST TRIAL P Rule 4.

   d. Service. IN ST TRIAL P Rule 4.1; IN ST TRIAL P Rule 4.2; IN ST TRIAL P Rule 4.3; IN ST TRIAL P Rule 4.4; IN ST TRIAL P Rule 4.5; IN ST TRIAL P Rule 4.6; IN ST TRIAL P Rule 4.7; IN ST TRIAL P Rule 4.8; IN ST TRIAL P Rule 4.9; IN ST TRIAL P Rule 4.10; IN ST TRIAL P Rule 4.11; IN ST TRIAL P Rule 4.12; IN ST TRIAL P Rule 4.13; IN ST TRIAL P Rule 4.14; IN ST TRIAL P Rule 4.15; IN ST TRIAL P Rule 5.

   e. Time. IN ST TRIAL P Rule 6.

   f. Pleadings allowed; Form of motion. IN ST TRIAL P Rule 7.

   g. Rules of pleading. IN ST TRIAL P Rule 8; IN ST TRIAL P Rule 9; IN ST TRIAL P Rule 9.1; IN ST TRIAL P Rule 9.2.

   h. Form of pleading. IN ST TRIAL P Rule 10.

   i. Signing and verification of pleadings. IN ST TRIAL P Rule 11.

   j. Joinder. IN ST TRIAL P Rule 18; IN ST TRIAL P Rule 19.

   k. Jury trial of right. IN ST TRIAL P Rule 38.

   l. Evidence. IN ST TRIAL P Rule 43.

   m. Determination of foreign law. IN ST TRIAL P Rule 44.1.

   n. Judgment on the evidence (directed verdict). IN ST TRIAL P Rule 50.

   o. Findings by the court. IN ST TRIAL P Rule 52.

   p. Summary judgment. IN ST TRIAL P Rule 56.

   q. Motion to correct error. IN ST TRIAL P Rule 59.

   r. Relief from judgment or order. IN ST TRIAL P Rule 60.

   s. Trial court and clerks. IN ST TRIAL P Rule 72.

   t. Uniform case numbering system; Access to court records. IN ST ADMIN Rule 8; IN ST ADMIN Rule 9.

   u. Paper size. IN ST ADMIN Rule 11.

   v. Facsimile transmission. IN ST ADMIN Rule 12.

   w. Electronic filing and electronic service pilot projects. IN ST ADMIN Rule 16.

   x. Alternative dispute resolution. IN ST ADR Rule 1.1; IN ST ADR Rule 1.6; IN ST ADR Rule 8.8.

   y. Manner of service. IN ST 34-33-2-1.

   z. Privacy and confidentiality. IN ST 5-2-9-6; IN ST 5-14-3-4; IN ST 5-14-3-5.5; IN ST 6-4.1-5-10; IN ST 6-4.1-12-12; IN ST 6-8.1-7-1; IN ST 11-13-1-8; IN ST 12-23-14-13; IN ST 16-39-3-10; IN ST 16-41-8-1; IN ST 22-4-19-6; IN ST 31-11-1-6; IN ST 31-19-5-23; IN ST 31-19-13-2; IN ST

31-19-19-1; IN ST 31-33-18-1; IN ST 31-39-1-1; IN ST 31-39-1-2; IN ST 33-23-16-16; IN ST 35-34-2-4; IN ST 35-38-1-13; IN ST 35-38-9-1; IN ST ADR Rule 2.11; IN ST ADR Rule 4.4; IN ST ADR Rule 5.6; IN ST JURY Rule 10.

2. *Local rules*

   a. Applicability and citation of rules. IN ST ALLEN SUPER AND CIR CT CIV Rule AR00-1.

   b. Appearances. IN ST ALLEN SUPER AND CIR CT CIV Rule 3.1-1.

   c. Service of process. IN ST ALLEN SUPER AND CIR CT CIV Rule 4-1.

   d. Consent to alternate service. IN ST ALLEN SUPER AND CIR CT CIV Rule 5-1.

   e. Preparation of pleadings. IN ST ALLEN SUPER AND CIR CT CIV Rule 8-1.

   f. Filing. IN ST ALLEN SUPER AND CIR CT CIV Rule 77-1.

B. Timing

1. *Filing.* A civil action is commenced by filing with the court a complaint or such equivalent pleading or document as may be specified by statute, by payment of the prescribed filing fee or filing an order waiving the filing fee, and, where service of process is required, by furnishing to the clerk as many copies of the complaint and summons as are necessary. IN ST TRIAL P Rule 3. The claimant typically bears the burden of commencing an action within the applicable statute of limitations. 22B INPRAC 3:1; Huff v. Huff, 892 N.E.2d 1241 (Ind.Ct.App. 2008).

2. *Service.* The trial rules require a party to exercise due diligence in securing service of process. 1 INPRAC R 4; Geiger and Peters, Inc. v. American Fletcher Nat. Bank & Trust Co., 428 N.E.2d 1279 (Ind.Ct.App. 1981). If person seeking service of process fails without cause for sixty (60) days or more to provide clerk with required summons for issuance or with other information necessary to effectuate service, person has failed to exercise due diligence in securing service of process. Geiger and Peters, Inc. v. American Fletcher Nat. Bank & Trust Co., 428 N.E.2d 1279, 1281 (Ind.Ct.App. 1981).

3. *Computation of time*

   a. *Generally; Days excluded.* In computing any period of time prescribed or allowed by the Indiana Rules of Trial Procedure, by order of the court, or by any applicable statute, the day of the act, event, or default from which the designated period of time begins to run shall not be included. The last day of the period so computed is to be included unless it is:

      i. A Saturday,

      ii. A Sunday,

      iii. A legal holiday as defined by state statute, or

      iv. A day the office in which the act is to be done is closed during regular business hours. IN ST TRIAL P Rule 6(A).

   b. *Short periods.* In any event, the period runs until the end of the next day that is not a Saturday, a Sunday, a legal holiday, or a day on which the office is closed. When the period of time allowed is less than seven (7) days, intermediate Saturdays, Sundays, legal holidays, and days on which the office is closed shall be excluded from the computations. IN ST TRIAL P Rule 6(A).

   c. *Additional time after service by United States mail.* Whenever a party has the right or is required to do some act or take some proceedings within a prescribed period after the service of a notice or other paper upon him and the notice or paper is served upon him by United States mail, three (3) days shall be added to the prescribed period. IN ST TRIAL P Rule 6(E).

   d. *Enlargement of time.* When an act is required or allowed to be done at or within a specific time by the Indiana Rules of Trial Procedure, the court may at any time for cause shown:

      i. Order the period enlarged, with or without motion or notice, if request therefor is made before the expiration of the period originally prescribed or extended by a previous order; or

      ii. Upon motion made after the expiration of the specific period, permit the act to be done where the failure to act was the result of excusable neglect; but, the court may not extend the time for taking any action for judgment on the evidence under IN ST TRIAL P Rule 50(A), amendment of findings and judgment under IN ST TRIAL P Rule 52(B), to correct errors under IN ST TRIAL P Rule 59(C), statement in opposition to motion to correct error under IN ST TRIAL P Rule 59(E), or to obtain relief from final judgment under IN ST TRIAL P Rule 60(B), except to the extent and under the conditions stated in those rules. IN ST TRIAL P Rule 6(B).

C. General Requirements

1. *Pleading, generally*

    a. *Pleadings to be concise.* Each averment of a pleading shall be simple, concise, and direct. No technical forms of pleading or motions are required. All fictions in pleading are abolished. IN ST TRIAL P Rule 8(E)(1).

    b. *Pleading in the alternative.* A pleading may set forth two (2) or more statements of a claim or defense alternatively or hypothetically, either in one (1) count or defense or in separate counts or defenses. When two (2) or more statements are made in the alternative and one (1) of them if made independently would be sufficient, the pleading is not made insufficient by the insufficiency of one or more of the alternative statements. A pleading may also state as many separate claims or defenses as the pleader has regardless of consistency and whether based on legal or equitable grounds. All statements shall be made subject to the obligations set forth in IN ST TRIAL P Rule 11. IN ST TRIAL P Rule 8(E)(2).

    c. *Motions and pleadings, joint and several.* All motions and pleadings of any kind addressed to two (2) or more paragraphs of any pleading, or filed by two (2) or more parties, shall be taken and construed as joint, separate, and several motions or pleadings to each of such paragraphs and by and against each of such parties. All motions or pleadings containing two (2) or more subject-matters shall be taken and construed as separate and several as to each subject-matter. All objections to rulings made by two (2) or more parties shall be taken and construed as the joint, separate, and several objections of each of such parties. IN ST TRIAL P Rule 8(E)(3).

        i. A complaint filed by or against two (2) or more plaintiffs shall be taken and construed as joint, separate, and several as to each of said plaintiffs. IN ST TRIAL P Rule 8(E).

    d. *Construction of pleadings.* All pleadings shall be so construed as to do substantial justice, lead to disposition on the merits, and avoid litigation of procedural points. IN ST TRIAL P Rule 8(F).

2. *Contents of the complaint*

    a. *Pleading for relief; Notice pleading.* Indiana is a "notice pleading" jurisdiction. 22B INPRAC 8:1; State v. American Family Voices, Inc., 898 N.E.2d 293 (Ind. 2008). Notice pleading replaces the technical and complex method of pleading which existed prior to 1970. Notice pleading is grounded in due process of law and must provide a defendant with reasonable notice of the plaintiff's claim or an opponent's defense. 22B INPRAC 8:1; Noblesville Redevelopment Com'n v. Noblesville Associates Ltd. Partnership, 674 N.E.2d 558 (Ind. 1996). Notice pleading does not require that the plaintiff state all elements or facts essential to a cause of action. 22B INPRAC 8:1; State v. American Family Voices, Inc., 898 N.E.2d 293 (Ind. 2008). Instead, the complaint must state "a short and plain statement of the claim" showing an entitlement to relief, and a demand for relief. 22B INPRAC 8:1; Trail v. Boys and Girls Clubs of Northwest Indiana, 845 N.E.2d 130 (Ind. 2006).

    b. *Claims for relief.* To state a claim for relief, whether an original claim, counterclaim, cross-claim, or third-party claim, a pleading must contain:

        i. A short and plain statement of the claim showing that the pleader is entitled to relief, and

        ii. A demand for relief to which the pleader deems entitled. Relief in the alternative or of several different types may be demanded. However, in any complaint seeking damages for personal injury or death, or seeking punitive damages, no dollar amount or figure shall be included in the demand. IN ST TRIAL P Rule 8(A).

    c. *Res ipsa loquitur.* Res ipsa loquitur or a similar doctrine may be pleaded by alleging generally that the facts connected with the action are unknown to the pleader and are within the knowledge of the opposing party. IN ST TRIAL P Rule 9.1(B).

d. *Bona fide purchaser.* When the rights of a person depend upon his status as a bona fide purchaser for value or upon similar requirements, such status must be pleaded and proved by the person asserting it, but it may be pleaded in general terms. Once it is established that the person has given any required value, unless such value is commercially unreasonable, and that he has met any requirements of recordation, filing, possession, or perfection, the trier of fact must find that such value was given or such perfection was made in accordance with any requirements of good faith, lack of knowledge, or lack of notice unless and until evidence is introduced which would support a finding of its non-existence. IN ST TRIAL P Rule 9.1(D).

e. *Presumption; Matters of judicial notice.* Neither presumptions of law nor matters of which judicial notice may be taken need be stated in a pleading. IN ST TRIAL P Rule 9.1(E).

   i. *Presumption of jurisdiction.* Jurisdiction is presumed in Indiana. 22B INPRAC 8:2. Consequently, there is no requirement to affirmatively plead the existence of jurisdiction in the complaint, unless the action involves a special proceeding requiring such an allegation. 22B INPRAC 8:2; Cardinal Industries, Inc. v. Schwartz, 483 N.E.2d 458 (Ind.Ct.App. 1985). The plaintiff bears no burden to prove jurisdiction unless and until it is challenged by the defendant. 22B INPRAC 8:2; Brokemond v. Marshall Field & Co., 612 N.E.2d 143 (Ind.Ct.App. 1993).

f. *Equitable and legal claims in multi-count actions.* In multi-count actions, the inclusion of an equitable claim, standing alone, will not automatically draw the entire action into equity. Something more than the presence of an equitable claim is required, and the court must examine the claims at issue. 22B INPRAC 38:1 COMMENT; Lucas v. U.S. Bank, N.A., 953 N.E.2d 457 (Ind. 2011). Factors the court may consider in evaluating the nature of the underlying substantive claims include: the substance and central character of the complaint, the rights and interests at issue, the relief demanded, and any issues arising out of discovery. 22B INPRAC 38:1 COMMENT; Songer v. Civitas Bank, 771 N.E.2d 61 (Ind. 2002).

3. *Pleading special matters*

   a. *Capacity.* It is not necessary to aver the capacity of a party to sue or be sued, the authority of a party to sue or be sued in a representative capacity, or the legal existence of an organization that is made a party. The burden of proving lack of such capacity, authority, or legal existence shall be upon the person asserting lack of it, and shall be pleaded as an affirmative defense. IN ST TRIAL P Rule 9(A).

   b. *Fraud, mistake, condition of the mind.* In all averments of fraud or mistake, the circumstances constituting fraud or mistake shall be specifically averred. Malice, intent, knowledge, and other conditions of mind may be averred generally. IN ST TRIAL P Rule 9(B).

   c. *Conditions precedent.* In pleading the performance or occurrence of promissory or non-promissory conditions precedent, it is sufficient to aver generally that all conditions precedent have been performed, have occurred, or have been excused. A denial of performance or occurrence shall be made specifically and with particularity, and a denial of excuse generally. IN ST TRIAL P Rule 9(C).

   d. *Official document or act.* In pleading an official document or official act it is sufficient to aver that the document was issued or the act done in compliance with law. IN ST TRIAL P Rule 9(D).

   e. *Judgment.* In pleading a judgment or decision of a domestic or foreign court, judicial or quasi-judicial tribunal, or of a board or officer, it is sufficient to aver the judgment or decision without setting forth matter showing jurisdiction to render it. IN ST TRIAL P Rule 9(E).

   f. *Time and place.* For the purpose of testing the sufficiency of a pleading, averments of time and place are material and shall be considered like all other averments of material matter. However, time and place need be stated only with such specificity as will enable the opposing party to prepare his defense. IN ST TRIAL P Rule 9(F).

   g. *Special damages; Damages where no answer.* When items of special damage are claimed, they shall be specifically stated. The relief granted to the plaintiff, if there be no answer, cannot exceed the relief demanded in his complaint; but, in any other case, the court may grant him any relief consistent with the facts or matters pleaded. IN ST TRIAL P Rule 9(G).

4. *Joinder*

   a. *Of claims.* A party asserting a claim for relief as an original claim, counterclaim, cross-claim, or

4

third-party claim, may join, either as independent or as alternate claims, as many claims, whether legal, equitable, or statutory as he has against an opposing party. IN ST TRIAL P Rule 18(A).

b. *Of remedies; Fraudulent conveyances.* Whenever a claim is one heretofore cognizable only after another claim has been prosecuted to a conclusion, the two (2) claims may be joined in a single action; but the court shall grant relief in that action only in accordance with the relative substantive rights of the parties. In particular, a plaintiff may state a claim for money and a claim to have set aside a conveyance fraudulent as to him, without first having obtained a judgment establishing the claim for money. IN ST TRIAL P Rule 18(B).

c. *Of persons needed for just adjudication.* A person who is subject to service of process shall be joined as a party in the action if:

   i. In his absence complete relief cannot be accorded among those already parties; or

   ii. He claims an interest relating to the subject of the action and is so situated that the disposition of the action in his absence may:

   - As a practical matter impair or impede his ability to protect that interest, or

   - Leave any of the persons already parties subject to a substantial risk of incurring double, multiple, or otherwise inconsistent obligations by reason of his claimed interest. IN ST TRIAL P Rule 19(A).

   iii. If he has not been so joined, the court shall order that he be made a party. If he should join as a plaintiff but refuses to do so, he may be made a defendant. IN ST TRIAL P Rule 19(A).

5. *Trial by jury; Demand*

   a. *Causes triable by court and by jury.* Issues of law and issues of fact in causes that prior to the eighteenth day of June, 1852, were of exclusive equitable jurisdiction shall be tried by the court; issues of fact in all other causes shall be triable as the same are now triable. In case of the joinder of causes of action or defenses which, prior to said date, were of exclusive equitable jurisdiction with causes of action or defenses which, prior to said date, were designated as actions at law and triable by jury—the former shall be triable by the court, and the latter by a jury, unless waived; the trial of both may be at the same time or at different times, as the court may direct. IN ST TRIAL P Rule 38(A).

   b. *Demand.* Any party may demand a trial by jury of any issue triable of right by a jury by filing with the court and serving upon the other parties a demand therefor in writing at any time after the commencement of the action and not later than ten (10) days after the first responsive pleading to the complaint, or to a counterclaim, crossclaim or other claim if one properly is pleaded; and if no responsive pleading is filed or required, within ten (10) days after the time such pleading otherwise would have been required. Such demand is sufficient if indorsed upon a pleading of a party filed within such time. IN ST TRIAL P Rule 38(B).

   c. *Same; Specification of issues.* In his demand a party may specify the issues which he wishes so tried; otherwise he shall be deemed to have demanded trial by jury for all issues triable as of right by jury. Any other party must file a demand for jury trial to preserve his right to trial by jury:

      i. Of issues for which a right to trial by jury was not requested by another party; and

      ii. In case a request by another party was improper. But if a proper request for a trial by jury upon issues triable by jury as of right on his behalf is made by any party, such request shall be deemed to have been made on behalf of all parties entitled to a jury trial upon such issues. IN ST TRIAL P Rule 38(C).

   d. *Waiver.* The failure of a party to appear at the trial, and the failure of a party to serve a demand as required by IN ST TRIAL P Rule 38 and to file it as required by IN ST TRIAL P Rule 5(E) constitute waiver by him of trial by jury. A demand for trial by jury made as provided in IN ST TRIAL P Rule 38 may not be withdrawn without the consent of the other party or parties. IN ST TRIAL P Rule 38(D).

      i. The trial court shall not grant a demand for a trial by jury filed after the time fixed in IN ST TRIAL P Rule 38(B) has elapsed except upon the written agreement of all of the parties to the action, which agreement shall be filed with the court and made a part of the record. If such agreement is filed then the court may, in its discretion, grant a trial by jury in which event the grant of a trial by jury may not be withdrawn except by the agreement of all of the parties. IN ST TRIAL P Rule 38(D).

e. *Arbitration.* Nothing in the Indiana Rules of Trial Procedure shall deny the parties the right by contract or agreement to submit or to agree to submit controversies to arbitration made before or after commencement of an action thereon or deny the courts power to specifically enforce such agreements. IN ST TRIAL P Rule 38(E).

f. *Equitable and legal claims in multi-count actions.* In multi-count actions, the inclusion of an equitable claim, standing alone, will not automatically draw the entire action into equity. Something more than the presence of an equitable claim is required, and the court must examine the claims at issue. 22B INPRAC 38:1 COMMENT; Lucas v. U.S. Bank, N.A., 953 N.E.2d 457 (Ind. 2011). Factors the court may consider in evaluating the nature of the underlying substantive claims include: the substance and central character of the complaint, the rights and interests at issue, the relief demanded, and any issues arising out of discovery. 22B INPRAC 38:1 COMMENT; Songer v. Civitas Bank, 771 N.E.2d 61 (Ind. 2002).

6. *Use of alternative dispute resolution.* Except as provided by the Indiana Rules for Alternative Dispute Resolution, a presiding judge may order any civil or domestic relations proceeding or selected issues in such proceedings referred to mediation, non-binding arbitration or mini-trial. The selection criteria which should be used by the court are defined under the Indiana Rules for Alternative Dispute Resolution. Binding arbitration and a summary jury trial may be ordered only upon the agreement of the parties as consistent with provisions in the Indiana Rules for Alternative Dispute Resolution which address each method. IN ST ADR Rule 1.6. For information on Indiana's ADR process refer to IN ST ADR Rule 1.1 through IN ST ADR Rule 8.8.

D. Documents

1. *Required documents*

   a. *Summons.* Contemporaneously with the filing of the complaint or equivalent pleading, the person seeking service or his attorney shall furnish to the clerk as many copies of the complaint and summons as are necessary. IN ST TRIAL P Rule 4(B).

   b. *Complaint.* Refer to the General Requirements section of this document for information on the contents of a complaint.

   c. *Appearance form.* At the time an action is commenced, the party initiating the proceeding shall file with the clerk of the court an appearance form setting forth the following information:

      i. Name, address and telephone number of the initiating party or parties filing the appearance form;

      ii. Name, address, attorney number, telephone number, FAX number, and e-mail address of any attorney representing the party, as applicable;

      iii. The case type of the proceeding [see IN ST ADMIN Rule 8];

      iv. A statement that the party will or will not accept service by fax or by e-mail from:

         • Other parties and/or

         • The court under IN ST TRIAL P Rule 72(D);

      v. In domestic relations, Uniform Reciprocal Enforcement of Support (URESA), paternity, delinquency, Child in Need of Services (CHINS), guardianship, and any other proceedings in which support may be an issue, the Social Security Identification Number of all family members;

      vi. The caption and case number of all related cases;

      vii. Such additional matters specified by state or local rule required to maintain the information management system employed by the court;

      viii. In a proceeding involving a protection from abuse order, a workplace violence restraining order, or a no-contact order, the initiating party shall provide to the clerk a public mailing address for purposes of legal service. The initiating party may use the Attorney General Address Confidentiality program established by statute; and

    ix. In a proceeding involving a mental health commitment, except seventy-two (72) hour emergency detentions, the initiating party shall provide the full name of the person with respect to whom commitment is sought and the person's state of residence. In addition, the initiating party shall provide at least one of the following identifiers for the person:

- Date of birth;
- Social Security Number;
- Driver's license number with state of issue and date of expiration;
- Department of Correction number;
- State ID number with state of issue and date of expiration; or
- FBI number. IN ST TRIAL P Rule 3.1; IN ST ALLEN SUPER AND CIR CT CIV Rule 3.1-1(A).

    x. For information on specific local requirements for filing an appearance, refer to IN ST ALLEN SUPER AND CIR CT CIV Rule 3.1-1.

2. *Supplemental documents*

    a. *Proof of written instrument.* When any pleading allowed by the Indiana Rules of Trial Procedure is founded on a written instrument, the original, or a copy thereof, must be included in or filed with the pleading. Such instrument, whether copied in the pleadings or not, shall be taken as part of the record. When any pleading allowed by the Indiana Rules of Trial Procedure is founded on an account, an Affidavit of Debt, in a form substantially similar to that which is provided in IN ST TRIAL P App. A-2, shall be attached. IN ST TRIAL P Rule 9.2(A).

    b. *Notice of intent to use foreign law.* A party who intends to raise an issue concerning the law of a foreign country shall give notice in his pleadings or other reasonable written notice. The court, in determining foreign law, may consider any relevant material or source, including testimony, whether or not submitted by a party or admissible under IN ST TRIAL P Rule 43. The court's determination shall be treated as a ruling on a question of law. It shall be made by the court and not the jury and shall be reviewable. IN ST TRIAL P Rule 44.1(A).

    c. *Praecipe.* Affidavits, requests, and any other information relating to the summons and its service as required or permitted by the Indiana Rules of Trial Procedure shall be included in a praecipe attached to or entered upon the summons. Such praecipe shall be deemed to be a part of the summons for purposes of the Indiana Rules of Trial Procedure. Separate or additional summons shall, as provided by the Indiana Rules of Trial Procedure, be issued by the clerk at any time upon proper request of the person seeking service or his attorney. IN ST TRIAL P Rule 4(B).

    d. *Facsimile cover sheet.* Any document sent to the Clerk of the Circuit Court by electronic facsimile transmission shall be accompanied by a cover sheet which states the title of the document, case number, number of pages, identity and voice telephone number of the sending party and instructions for filing. The cover sheet shall contain the signature of the attorney or party, pro se, authorizing the filing. IN ST ADMIN Rule 12(D).

    e. *Additional copies for service*

        i. *By mail.* When service by certified mail is requested, the party shall not prepare envelopes, but shall furnish for each party to be served, the originals and three (3) copies of prepared summons, complaints, notices or subpoenas to the Clerk, who shall prepare the envelopes using the addresses furnished. Proper postage and return receipt request card will be furnished by the Clerk. Upon receipt of the return, the Clerk shall insert the return with the pleadings in the packet. IN ST ALLEN SUPER AND CIR CT CIV Rule 4-1(A)(1).

        ii. *By Sheriff.* When Sheriff service is requested, the party shall furnish for each party to be served, the original and three (3) copies of prepared summons, complaints, notices or subpoenas to the

Clerk, who will forward the documents to the Sheriff for proper service. IN ST ALLEN SUPER AND CIR CT CIV Rule 4-1(A)(2).

E. Format

1. *Form of pleadings*

   a. *Caption; Names of parties.* Every pleading shall contain a caption setting forth the name of the court, the title of the action, the file number, and a designation as in IN ST TRIAL P Rule 7(A). In the complaint the title of the action shall include the names of all the parties, but in other pleadings it is sufficient to state the name of the first party on each side with an appropriate indication of other parties. IN ST TRIAL P Rule 10(A).

   b. *Paragraphs; Separate statements.* All averments of a claim or defense shall be made in numbered paragraphs, the contents of each of which shall be limited as far as practicable to a statement of a single set of circumstances, and a paragraph may be referred to by number in all succeeding pleadings. Each claim founded upon a separate transaction or occurrence and each defense other than denials may be stated in a separate count or defense whenever a separation facilitates the clear presentation of the matters set forth. IN ST TRIAL P Rule 10(B).

   c. *Adoption by reference; Exhibits.* Statements in a pleading may be adopted by reference in a different part of the same pleading or in another pleading or in any motion. A copy of any written instrument which is an exhibit to a pleading is a part thereof for all purposes. IN ST TRIAL P Rule 10(C).

   d. *Citation.* Allen County Superior and Circuit court rules may be cited as L.R. _____. The Indiana Rules of Trial Procedure are hereinafter referred to as T.R. _____. IN ST ALLEN SUPER AND CIR CT CIV Rule AR00-1(B).

   e. *Paper.* All pleadings must be printed on white paper. IN ST ALLEN SUPER AND CIR CT CIV Rule 8-1(A).

   f. *Spacing.* The lines shall be double spaced except for quotations, which shall be indented and single-spaced. IN ST ALLEN SUPER AND CIR CT CIV Rule 8-1(A).

   g. *Photocopies.* Photocopies are acceptable if legible. IN ST ALLEN SUPER AND CIR CT CIV Rule 8-1(A).

   h. *Margins and binding.* Margins shall be one to one and one-half (1-1 1/2) inches on the left side and one-half (1/2) inch on the right. IN ST ALLEN SUPER AND CIR CT CIV Rule 8-1(B).

      i. Binding or stapling shall be at the top left and at no other place. IN ST ALLEN SUPER AND CIR CT CIV Rule 8-1(B).

      ii. Covers or backing shall not be used. IN ST ALLEN SUPER AND CIR CT CIV Rule 8-1(B).

   i. *Flat filing.* The files of the Clerk of the Court shall be kept under the "flat filing" system. All pleadings presented for filing with the Clerk or Court shall be flat and unfolded. Only the original of any pleading shall be placed in the Court file. IN ST ALLEN SUPER AND CIR CT CIV Rule 77-1(A).

   j. *Handwritten pleadings.* Handwritten pleadings may be accepted for filing in the discretion of the Court. IN ST ALLEN SUPER AND CIR CT CIV Rule 8-1(A).

2. *Size of papers for filing.* Effective January 1, 1992, all pleadings, copies, motions and documents filed with any trial court or appellate level court, typed or printed, with the exception of exhibits and existing wills, shall be prepared on eight and one-half by eleven inch (8 1/2" x 11") size paper. IN ST ADMIN Rule 11.

3. *Signature requirements*

   a. *Signature of attorney.* Every pleading or motion of a party represented by an attorney shall be signed by at least one (1) attorney of record in his individual name, whose address, telephone number, and attorney number shall be stated, except that this provision shall not apply to pleadings and motions made and transcribed at the trial or a hearing before the judge and received by him in such form. IN ST TRIAL P Rule 11(A). All pleadings to be signed by an attorney shall contain the written signature of the individual attorney, the attorney's printed name, Supreme Court Attorney Number, the name of the attorney's law firm, the attorney's address, telephone number, and a designation of the party for whom the attorney appears. IN ST ALLEN SUPER AND CIR CT CIV Rule 8-1(C). For the recommended signature format, refer to IN ST ALLEN SUPER AND CIR CT CIV Rule 8-1(C).

 i. The signature of an attorney constitutes a certificate by him that he has read the pleadings; that to the best of his knowledge, information, and belief, there is good ground to support it; and that it is not interposed for delay. IN ST TRIAL P Rule 11(A).

 ii. If a pleading or motion is not signed or is signed with intent to defeat the purpose of the rule, it may be stricken as sham and false and the action may proceed as though the pleading had not been served. IN ST TRIAL P Rule 11(A).

 iii. For a willful violation of IN ST TRIAL P Rule 11 an attorney may be subjected to appropriate disciplinary action. Similar action may be taken if scandalous or indecent matter is inserted. IN ST TRIAL P Rule 11(A).

 iv. Neither printed signatures, nor facsimile signatures shall be accepted on original documents. IN ST ALLEN SUPER AND CIR CT CIV Rule 8-1(C).

 v. Facsimile signatures are permitted on copies. IN ST ALLEN SUPER AND CIR CT CIV Rule 8-1(C).

b. *Signature of unrepresented party.* A party who is not represented by an attorney shall sign his pleading and state his address. IN ST TRIAL P Rule 11(A).

c. *Verification not generally required.* Except when specifically required by rule, pleadings or motions need not be verified or accompanied by affidavit. The rule in equity that the averments of an answer under oath must be overcome by the testimony of two (2) witnesses or of one (1) witness sustained by corroborating circumstances is abolished. IN ST TRIAL P Rule 11(A).

d. *Verification by affirmation or representation.* When in connection with any civil or special statutory proceeding it is required that any pleading, motion, petition, supporting affidavit, or other document of any kind, be verified, or that an oath be taken, it shall be sufficient if the subscriber simply affirms the truth of the matter to be verified by an affirmation or representation. IN ST TRIAL P Rule 11(B). IN ST TRIAL P Rule 11(B) states that the affirmation or representation should be in substantially the following language: "I (we) affirm, under the penalties for perjury, that the foregoing representation(s) is (are) true. (Signed) _____."

 i. Any person who falsifies an affirmation or representation of fact shall be subject to the same penalties as are prescribed by law for the making of a false affidavit. IN ST TRIAL P Rule 11(B).

e. *Verified pleadings, motions, and affidavits as evidence.* Pleadings, motions and affidavits accompanying or in support of such pleadings or motions when required to be verified or under oath shall be accepted as a representation that the signer had personal knowledge thereof or reasonable cause to believe the existence of the facts or matters stated or alleged therein; and, if otherwise competent or acceptable as evidence, may be admitted as evidence of the facts or matters stated or alleged therein when it is so provided in the Indiana Rules of Trial Procedure, by statute or other law, or to the extent the writing or signature expressly purports to be made upon the signer's personal knowledge. When such pleadings, motions and affidavits are verified or under oath they shall not require other or greater proof on the part of the adverse party than if not verified or not under oath unless expressly provided otherwise by the Indiana Rules of Trial Procedure, statute or other law. Affidavits upon motions for summary judgment under IN ST TRIAL P Rule 56 and in denial of execution under IN ST TRIAL P Rule 9.2 shall be made upon personal knowledge. IN ST TRIAL P Rule 11(C).

4. *Information excluded from public access.* Every document filed in a case shall separately identify information excluded from public access pursuant to IN ST ADMIN Rule 9(G)(1) as follows:

a. Whole documents that are excluded from public access pursuant to IN ST ADMIN Rule 9(G)(1) shall be tendered on light green paper or have a light green coversheet attached to the document, marked "Not for Public Access" or "Confidential." IN ST TRIAL P Rule 5(G)(1).

b. When only a portion of a document contains information excluded from public access pursuant to IN

ST ADMIN Rule 9(G)(1), said information shall be omitted [or redacted] from the filed document, and set forth on a separate accompanying document on light green paper conspicuously marked "Not for Public Access" or "Confidential" and clearly designated [or identifying] the caption and number of the case and the document and location within the document to which the redacted material pertains. IN ST TRIAL P Rule 5(G)(2).

c. With respect to documents filed in electronic format, the trial court, by local rule, may provide for compliance with IN ST TRIAL P Rule 5 in manner that separates and protects access to information excluded from public access. IN ST TRIAL P Rule 5(G)(3).

d. IN ST TRIAL P Rule 5(G) does not apply to a record sealed by the court pursuant to IN ST 5-14-3-5.5 or otherwise, nor to records, documents, or information filed in cases to which public access is prohibited pursuant to IN ST ADMIN Rule 9(G). IN ST TRIAL P Rule 5(G)(4).

e. The following information in case records is excluded from public access and is confidential:

   i. Information that is excluded from public access pursuant to federal law;

   ii. Information that is excluded from public access as declared confidential by Indiana statute or other court rule, including without limitation:

   - All adoption records created after July 8, 1941, as declared confidential by IN ST 31-19-19-1, et seq., except those specifically declared open by IN ST 31-19-13-2(2);

   - All records relating to chancroid, chlamydia, gonorrhea, hepatitis, human immunodeficiency virus (HIV), Lymphogranuloma venereum, syphilis, tuberculosis, as declared confidential by IN ST 16-41-8-1, et seq.;

   - All records relating to child abuse as declared confidential by IN ST 31-33-18-1, et seq.;

   - All records relating to drug tests as declared confidential by IN ST 5-14-3-4(a)(9);

   - Records of grand jury proceedings as declared confidential by IN ST 35-34-2-4;

   - Records of juvenile proceedings as declared confidential by IN ST 31-39-1-2, except those specifically open under statute;

   - All paternity records created after July 1, 1941 as declared confidential by IN ST 31-14-11-15, IN ST 31-19-5-23, IN ST 31-39-1-1 and IN ST 31-39-1-2 [Editor's note: IN ST 31-14-11-15 was repealed effective May 9, 2013];

   - All pre-sentence reports as declared confidential by IN ST 35-38-1-13;

   - Written petitions to permit marriages without consent and orders directing the Clerk of Court to issue a marriage license to underage persons, as declared confidential by IN ST 31-11-1-6;

   - Only those arrest warrants, search warrants, indictments and informations ordered confidential by the trial judge, prior to return of duly executed service as declared confidential by IN ST 5-14-3-4(b)(1);

   - All medical, mental health, or tax records unless determined by law or regulation of any governmental custodian not to be confidential, released by the subject of such records, or declared by a court of competent jurisdiction to be essential to the resolution of litigation as declared confidential by IN ST 16-39-3-10, IN ST 6-4.1-5-10, IN ST 6-4.1-12-12, and IN ST 6-8.1-7-1;

   - Personal information relating to jurors or prospective jurors, other than for the use of the parties and counsel, pursuant to IN ST JURY Rule 10;

   - Information relating to protection from abuse orders, no-contact orders and workplace violence restraining orders as declared confidential by IN ST 5-2-9-6, et seq.;

   - Mediation proceedings pursuant to IN ST ADR Rule 2.11, Mini-Trial proceedings pursuant to IN ST ADR Rule 4.4(C), and Summary Jury Trials pursuant to IN ST ADR Rule 5.6;

   - Information in probation files pursuant to the Probation Standards promulgated by the Judicial Conference of Indiana pursuant to IN ST 11-13-1-8(b);

- Information deemed confidential pursuant to the Rules for Court Administered Alcohol and Drug Programs promulgated by the Judicial Conference of Indiana pursuant to IN ST 12-23-14-13;
- Information deemed confidential pursuant to the Problem-Solving Court Rules promulgated by the Judicial Conference of Indiana pursuant to IN ST 33-23-16-16;
- All records of the Department of workforce Development as declared confidential by IN ST 22-4-19-6;
- Information regarding interception of electronic communications that is sealed or deemed confidential as set forth in IN ST 35-33.5-2-1, et seq.

iii. Information excluded from public access by specific court order;

iv. Complete Social Security Numbers of living persons;

v. With the exception of names, information such as addresses, phone numbers, and dates of birth which explicitly identifies:

- Natural persons who are witnesses or victims (not including defendants) in criminal, domestic violence, stalking, sexual assault, juvenile, or civil protection order proceedings, provided that juveniles who are victims of sex crimes shall be identified by initials only;
- Places of residence of judicial officers, clerks and other employees of courts and clerks of court, unless the person or persons about whom the information pertains waives confidentiality;

vi. Complete account numbers of specific assets, loans, bank accounts, credit cards, and personal identification numbers (PINs);

vii. All orders of expungement entered in criminal or juvenile proceedings, orders to restrict access to criminal history information pursuant to IN ST 35-38-5-5.5 or IN ST 35-38-8-5 and records excluded from public access by such orders, and information related to infractions that is excluded from public access pursuant to IN ST 34-28-5-15 or IN ST 34-28-5-16 [Editor's note: IN ST 35-38-5-5.5, IN ST 35-38-8-5 and IN ST 34-28-5-16 were repealed effective July 1, 2013; for information on orders restricting access to criminal history, refer to IN ST 35-38-9-1, et seq.];

viii. All personal notes and e-mail, and deliberative material, of judges, jurors, court staff and judicial agencies, and information recorded in personal data assistants (PDA's) or organizers and personal calendars. IN ST ADMIN Rule 9(G)(1).

5. *Form of the summons*

a. *Required contents of summons.* The summons shall contain:

i. The name and address of the person on whom the service is to be effected;

ii. The name, street address, and telephone number of the court and the cause number assigned to the case;

iii. The title of the case as shown by the complaint, but, if there are multiple parties, the title may be shortened to include only the first named plaintiff and defendant with an appropriate indication that there are additional parties;

iv. The name, address, and telephone number of the attorney for the person seeking service;

v. The time within which the Indiana Rules of Trial Procedure require the person being served to respond, and a clear statement that in case of his failure to do so, judgment by default may be rendered against him for the relief demanded in the complaint. IN ST TRIAL P Rule 4(C).

b. *Additional contents of summons.* The summons may also contain any additional information which will facilitate proper service. IN ST TRIAL P Rule 4(C).

F. Filing and Service Requirements

1. *Filing requirements.* A civil action is commenced by filing with the court a complaint or such equivalent

pleading or document as may be specified by statute, by payment of the prescribed filing fee or filing an order waiving the filing fee, and, where service of process is required, by furnishing to the clerk as many copies of the complaint and summons as are necessary. IN ST TRIAL P Rule 3. An action may be commenced by E-filing only in a court which has adopted a pilot project plan approved by the Division of State Court Administration pursuant to IN ST ADMIN Rule 16. IN ST ADMIN Rule 16(F).

  a. *Filing with the court defined.* The filing of pleadings, motions, and other papers with the court as required by the Indiana Rules of Trial Procedure shall be made by one of the following methods:

    i. Delivery to the clerk of the court;

    ii. Sending by electronic transmission under the procedure adopted pursuant to IN ST ADMIN Rule 12;

    iii. Mailing to the clerk by registered, certified or express mail return receipt requested;

    iv. Depositing with any third-party commercial carrier for delivery to the clerk within three (3) calendar days, cost prepaid, properly addressed;

    v. If the court so permits, filing with the judge, in which event the judge shall note thereon the filing date and forthwith transmit them to the office of the clerk; or

    vi. Electronic filing, as approved by the Division of State Court Administration pursuant to IN ST ADMIN Rule 16. IN ST TRIAL P Rule 5(F).

    vii. Filing by registered or certified mail and by third-party commercial carrier shall be complete upon mailing or deposit. IN ST TRIAL P Rule 5(F).

  b. *Facsimile filing*

    i. *Generally.* In counties where a majority of judges of the courts of record, by posted local rule, have authorized electronic facsimile filing and designated a telephone number to receive such transmissions, pleadings, motions, and other papers may be sent to the Clerk of Circuit Court by electronic facsimile transmission for filing in any case, provided:

      • Such matter does not exceed ten (10) pages, including the cover sheet;

      • Such matter does not require the payment of fees other than the electronic facsimile transcription fee set forth in IN ST ADMIN Rule 12(E);

      • The sending party creates at the time of transmission a machine generated log for such transmission; and

      • The original document and the transmission log are maintained by the sending party for the duration of the litigation. IN ST ADMIN Rule 12(B).

    ii. *Time of filing.* During normal, posted business hours, the time of filing shall be the time the duplicate document is produced in the office of the Clerk of the Circuit Court. Duplicate documents received at all other times shall be filed as of the next normal business day. IN ST ADMIN Rule 12(C).

      • If the receiving fax machine endorses its own time and date stamp upon the transmitted documents and the receiving machine produces a delivery receipt which is electronically created and transmitted to the sending party, the time of filing shall be the date and time recorded on the transmitted document by the receiving fax machine. IN ST ADMIN Rule 12(C).

  c. *Proof of filing.* Any party filing any paper by any method other than personal delivery to the clerk shall retain proof of filing. IN ST TRIAL P Rule 5(F).

2. *Service requirements.* The court acquires jurisdiction over a party or person who under the Indiana Rules of Trial Procedure commences or joins in the action, is served with summons or enters an appearance, or who is subjected to the power of the court under any other law. IN ST TRIAL P Rule 4(A).

  a. *Designation of method of service of the summons.* The person seeking service or his attorney may designate the manner of service upon the summons. If not so designated, the clerk shall cause service to be made by mail or other public means provided the mailing address of the person to be served is indicated in the summons or can be determined. If a mailing address is not furnished or cannot be determined or if service by mail or other public means is returned without acceptance, the complaint and summons shall promptly be delivered to the sheriff or his deputy who, unless otherwise directed, shall serve the summons. IN ST TRIAL P Rule 4(D).

b. *Summons and complaint to be served together.* The summons and complaint shall be served together unless otherwise ordered by the court. When service of summons is made by publication, the complaint shall not be published. When jurisdiction over a party is dependent upon service of process by publication or by his appearance, summons and complaint shall be deemed to have been served at the end of the day of last required publication in the case of service by publication, and at the time of appearance in jurisdiction acquired by appearance. Whenever the summons and complaint are not served or published together, the summons shall contain the full, unabbreviated title of the case. IN ST TRIAL P Rule 4(E); IN ST ALLEN SUPER AND CIR CT CIV Rule 4-1(B).

c. *Territorial limits and service under special order*

   i. *Territorial limits of effective service.* Process may be served anywhere within the territorial limits of this state and outside the state as provided in the Indiana Rules of Trial Procedure. IN ST TRIAL P Rule 4.14(A).

   ii. *Service under special order of court.* Upon application of any party the court in which any action is pending may make an appropriate order for service in a manner not provided by the Indiana Rules of Trial Procedure or statutes when such service is reasonably calculated to give the defendant actual knowledge of the proceedings and an opportunity to be heard. IN ST TRIAL P Rule 4.14(B).

d. *Return of service.* The person making service shall promptly make his return upon or attach it to a copy of the summons which shall be delivered to the clerk. The return shall be signed by the person making it, and shall include a statement:

   i. That service was made upon the person as required by law and the time, place, and manner thereof;

   ii. If service was not made, the particular manner in which it was thwarted in terms of fact or in terms of law;

   iii. Such other information as is expressly required by the Indiana Rules of Trial Procedure. IN ST TRIAL P Rule 4.15(A).

3. *Methods of service of the summons and complaint*

   a. *In general*

      i. *Methods of service.* Service may be made upon an individual, or an individual acting in a representative capacity, by:

         • Sending a copy of the summons and complaint by registered or certified mail or other public means by which a written acknowledgment of receipt may be requested and obtained to his residence, place of business or employment with return receipt requested and returned showing receipt of the letter; or

         • Delivering a copy of the summons and complaint to him personally; or

         • Leaving a copy of the summons and complaint at his dwelling house or usual place of abode; or

         • Serving his agent as provided by rule, statute or valid agreement. IN ST TRIAL P Rule 4.1(A).

         • Refer to the Documents section of this document for information on additional copies required for service by registered mail and/or service by sheriff.

      ii. *Copy service to be followed with mail.* Whenever service is made under IN ST TRIAL P Rule 4.1(A)(3) [by leaving a copy at dwelling or usual place of abode] or IN ST TRIAL P Rule 4.1(A)(4) [by service of agent], the person making the service also shall send by first class mail, a copy of the summons without the complaint to the last known address of the person being served, and this fact shall be shown upon the return. IN ST TRIAL P Rule 4.1(B).

    iii. *Service by fax or e-mail.* A party who has consented to service by fax or e-mail may be served as follows:

- Service by e-mail shall be made by attaching the document being served in PDF format. Discovery documents must also be served in accordance with IN ST TRIAL P Rule 26(A).

- Service by fax shall be deemed complete upon generation of a transmission record indicating the successful transmission of the entire document, except as provided in IN ST TRIAL P Rule 5(B)(3)(d).

- Service by e-mail shall be deemed complete upon transmission, except as provided in IN ST TRIAL P Rule 5(B)(3)(d).

- Service by fax or e-mail that occurs on a Saturday, Sunday, legal holiday, or day the court or agency in which the matter is pending is closed or after 5:00 PM local time of the recipient shall be deemed complete the next day that is not a Saturday, Sunday, legal holiday, or day that the court or agency in which the matter is pending is not closed. IN ST TRIAL P Rule 5(B)(3).

    iv. *Consent to alternate service.* Any Allen County Attorney or any Allen County law firm may, without charge, maintain an assigned Courthouse box in the library of the Allen County Courthouse for receipt of notices, pleadings, process orders, or other communications from the Court, the Clerk, and other attorneys or law firms. IN ST ALLEN SUPER AND CIR CT CIV Rule 5-1(A). For more information concerning the use of courthouse boxes, refer to IN ST ALLEN SUPER AND CIR CT CIV Rule 5-1.

b. *Proof of service.* Certificates of service or proof of mailing of pleadings concerning any case shall be deemed sufficient proof of service if such pleadings were mailed to the last known address of a party or attorney noted upon the chronological case summary of a case. IN ST ALLEN SUPER AND CIR CT CIV Rule 3.1-1(E).

c. *Service upon infants or incompetents*

    i. *Service upon infants.* Service upon an individual known to be an infant shall be made upon his next friend or guardian ad litem, if service is with respect to the same action in which the infant is so represented. If there is no next friend or guardian ad litem, service shall be made upon his court-appointed representative if one is known and can be served within this state. If there is no court-appointed representative, service shall be made upon either parent known to have custody of the infant, or if there is no parent, upon a person known to be standing in the position of custodian or parent. The infant shall also be served if he is fourteen (14) years of age or older. In the event that service, as provided above, is not possible, service shall be made on the infant. IN ST TRIAL P Rule 4.2(A).

    ii. *Service upon incompetents.* Service upon an individual who has been adjudged to be of unsound mind, otherwise incompetent or who is believed to be such shall be made upon his next friend or guardian ad litem, if service is with respect to the same action in which the incompetent is so represented. If there is no next friend or guardian ad litem, service shall be made upon his court-appointed representative if one is known and can be served within this state. If there is no court-appointed representative, then upon the named party and also upon a person known to be standing in the position of custodian of his person. IN ST TRIAL P Rule 4.2(B).

    iii. *Duty to inform court; Appearance.* Nothing herein is intended to affect the duty of a party to inform the court that a person is an infant or incompetent. An appearance by a court-appointed guardian, next friend or guardian ad litem or his attorney shall correct any defect in service under IN ST TRIAL P Rule 4.2 unless such defect be challenged. IN ST TRIAL P Rule 4.2(C).

d. *Service upon institutionalized persons.* Service of summons upon a person who is imprisoned or restrained in an institution shall be made by delivering or mailing a copy of the summons and complaint to the official in charge of the institution. It shall be the duty of said official to immediately deliver the summons and complaint to the person being served and allow him to make provisions for adequate representation by counsel. The official shall indicate upon the return whether the person has received the summons and been allowed an opportunity to retain counsel. IN ST TRIAL P Rule 4.3.

e. *Service upon individuals whose acts serve as basis for jurisdiction.* A person subject to the jurisdiction of the courts of this state under IN ST TRIAL P Rule 4.4 may be served with summons:

  i. As provided by IN ST TRIAL P Rule 4.1 (service on individuals), IN ST TRIAL P Rule 4.5 (service upon resident who cannot be found or served within the state), IN ST TRIAL P Rule 4.6 (service upon organizations), IN ST TRIAL P Rule 4.9 (in rem actions); or

  ii. The person shall be deemed to have appointed the Secretary of State as his agent upon whom service of summons may be made as provided in IN ST TRIAL P Rule 4.10. IN ST TRIAL P Rule 4.4(B).

f. *Service upon resident who cannot be found or served within the state.* When the person to be served is a resident of this state who cannot be served personally or by agent in this state and either cannot be found, has concealed his whereabouts or has left the state, summons may be served in the manner provided by IN ST TRIAL P Rule 4.9 (summons in in rem actions). IN ST TRIAL P Rule 4.5.

g. *Service upon organizations*

  i. *Persons to be served.* Service upon an organization may be made as follows:

     • In the case of a domestic or foreign organization upon an executive officer thereof, or if there is an agent appointed or deemed by law to have been appointed to receive service, then upon such agent. IN ST TRIAL P Rule 4.6(A)(1).

     • In the case of a partnership, upon a general partner thereof. IN ST TRIAL P Rule 4.6(A)(2).

     • In the case of a state governmental organization upon the executive officer thereof and also upon the Attorney General. IN ST TRIAL P Rule 4.6(A)(3).

     • In the case of a local governmental organization, upon the executive thereof and upon the attorney for the local governmental organization. IN ST TRIAL P Rule 4.6(A)(4).

     • When, in IN ST TRIAL P Rule 4.6(A)(3) and IN ST TRIAL P Rule 4.6(A)(4), a governmental representative is named as a party in his individual name or in such name along with his official title, then also upon such representative. IN ST TRIAL P Rule 4.6(A)(5).

  ii. *Manner of service.* Service under IN ST TRIAL P Rule 4.6(A) shall be made on the proper person in the manner provided by the Indiana Rules of Trial Procedure for service upon individuals, but a person seeking service or his attorney shall not knowingly direct service to be made at the person's dwelling house or place of abode, unless such is an address furnished under the requirements of a statute or valid agreement, or unless an affidavit on or attached to the summons states that service in another manner is impractical. IN ST TRIAL P Rule 4.6(B).

  iii. *Service at organization's office.* When shown upon an affidavit or in the return, that service upon an organization cannot be made as provided in IN ST TRIAL P Rule 4.6(A) or IN ST TRIAL P Rule 4.6(B), service may be made by leaving a copy of the summons and complaint at any office of such organization located within this state with the person in charge of such office. IN ST TRIAL P Rule 4.6(C).

h. *Summons; Service upon agent named by statute or agreement.* Whenever an agent (other than an agent appointed to receive service for a governmental organization of this state) has been designated by or pursuant to statute or valid agreement to receive service for the person being served, service may be made upon such agent as follows:

  i. If the agent is a governmental organization or officer designated by or pursuant to statute, service shall be made as provided in IN ST TRIAL P Rule 4.10. IN ST TRIAL P Rule 4.7(1).

  ii. If the agent is one other than that described in IN ST TRIAL P Rule 4.7(1), service shall be made upon him as provided in IN ST TRIAL P Rule 4.1 (service upon individuals) or IN ST TRIAL P Rule 4.6 (service upon organizations). If service cannot be made upon such agent, because there is no address furnished as required by statute or valid agreement or his whereabouts in this state are unknown, then his principal shall be deemed to have appointed the Secretary of State as a replacement for the agent and service may be made upon the Secretary of State as provided in IN ST TRIAL P Rule 4.10. IN ST TRIAL P Rule 4.7(2).

i. *Summons; Service of pleadings or summons on Attorney General.* Service of a copy of the summons and complaint or any pleading upon the Attorney General under the Indiana Rules of Trial Procedure or any statute shall be made by personal service upon him, a deputy or clerk at his office, or by mail or other public means to him at such office in the manner provided by IN ST TRIAL P Rule 4.1(A)(1), and by IN ST TRIAL P Rule 4.11 to the extent applicable. IN ST TRIAL P Rule 4.8.

j. *Summons; In rem actions*

   i. *In general.* In any action involving a res situated within this state, service may be made as provided in IN ST TRIAL P Rule 4.9. The court may render a judgment or decree to the extent of its jurisdiction over the res. IN ST TRIAL P Rule 4.9(A).

   ii. *Manner of service.* Service under IN ST TRIAL P Rule 4.9 may be made as follows:

   • By service of summons upon a person or his agent pursuant to the Indiana Rules of Trial Procedure; or

   • By service of summons outside this state in a manner provided by IN ST TRIAL P Rule 4.1 (service upon individuals) or by publication outside this state in a manner provided by IN ST TRIAL P Rule 4.13 (service by publication) or outside this state in any other manner as provided by the Indiana Rules of Trial Procedure; or

   • By service by publication pursuant to IN ST TRIAL P Rule 4.13. IN ST TRIAL P Rule 4.9(A).

k. *Summons; Service upon Secretary of State or other governmental agent.* Whenever, under the Indiana Rules of Trial Procedure or any statute, service is made upon the Secretary of State or any other governmental organization or officer, as agent for the person being served, service may be made upon such agent as provided in IN ST TRIAL P Rule 4.10. IN ST TRIAL P Rule 4.10(A).

   i. The person seeking service or his attorney shall:

   • Submit his request for service upon the agent in the praecipe for summons, and state that the governmental organization or officer is the agent of the person being served;

   • State the address of the person being served as filed and recorded pursuant to a statute or valid agreement, or if no such address is known, then his last known mailing address, and, if no such address is known, then such shall be stated;

   • Pay any fee prescribed by statute to be forwarded together with sufficient copies of the summons, affidavit and complaint, to the agent by the clerk of the court. IN ST TRIAL P Rule 4.10(A)(1).

   ii. Upon receipt thereof the agent shall promptly:

   • Send to the person being served a copy of the summons and complaint by registered or certified mail or by other public means by which a written acknowledgment of receipt may be obtained;

   • Complete and deliver to the clerk an affidavit showing the date of the mailing, or if there was no mailing, the reason therefor;

   • Send to the clerk a copy of the return receipt along with a copy of the summons;

   • File and retain a copy of the return receipt. IN ST TRIAL P Rule 4.10(A)(2).

l. *Summons; Registered or certified mail.* Whenever service by registered or certified mail or other public means by which a return receipt may be requested is authorized, the clerk of the court or a governmental agent under IN ST TRIAL P Rule 4.10 shall send the summons and complaint to the person being served at the address supplied upon the summons, or furnished by the person seeking service. In his return the clerk of the court or the governmental agent shall show the date and place of mailing, a copy of the mailed or electronically-transmitted return receipt if and when received by him showing whether the mailing was accepted or returned, and, if accepted, by whom. The return along with the receipt shall be promptly filed by the clerk with the pleadings and become a part of the record. If a mailing by the clerk of the court is returned without acceptance, the clerk shall reissue the summons and complaint for service as requested, by the person seeking service. IN ST TRIAL P Rule 4.11.

m. *Summons; Service by sheriff or other officer*

   i. *In general.* Whenever service is made by delivering a copy to a person personally or by leaving a copy at his dwelling house or place of employment as provided by IN ST TRIAL P Rule 4.1, summons shall be issued to and served by the sheriff, his deputy, or some person specially or regularly appointed by the court for that purpose. Service shall be effective if made by a person not otherwise authorized by the Indiana Rules of Trial Procedure, but proof of service by such a person must be made by him as a witness or by deposition without allowance of expenses therefor as costs. The person to whom the summons is delivered for service must act promptly and exercise reasonable care to cause service to be made. IN ST TRIAL P Rule 4.12(A).

   ii. *Special service by police officers.* A sheriff, his deputy, or any full-time state or municipal police officer may serve summons in any county of this state if he agrees or has agreed to make the service. When specially requested in the praecipe for summons, the complaint and summons shall be delivered to such officer by the clerk or the attorney for the person seeking service. No agreement with the sheriff or his deputy for such service in the sheriff's own county shall be permitted. In no event shall any expenses agreed upon under this provision be assessed or recovered as costs or affect court costs otherwise imposed for regular service. IN ST TRIAL P Rule 4.12(B).

   iii. *Service in other counties.* A summons may be served in any county in this state. If service is to be made in another county, the summons may be issued by the clerk for service therein to the sheriff of such county or to a person authorized to make service by the Indiana Rules of Trial Procedure. IN ST TRIAL P Rule 4.12(C).

   iv. *Service outside the state.* Personal service, when permitted by the Indiana Rules of Trial Procedure to be made outside the state, may be made there by any disinterested person or by the attorney representing the person seeking such service. The expenses of such person may be assessed as costs only if they are reasonable and if service by mail or other public means cannot be made or is not successful. IN ST TRIAL P Rule 4.12(D).

n. *Summons; Service by publication*

   i. *Praecipe for summons by publication.* In any action where notice by publication is permitted by the Indiana Rules of Trial Procedure or by statute, service may be made by publication. Summons by publication may name all the persons to be served, and separate publications with respect to each party shall not be required. The person seeking such service, or his attorney, shall submit his request therefor upon the praecipe for summons along with supporting affidavits that diligent search has been made that the defendant cannot be found, has concealed his whereabouts, or has left the state, and shall prepare the contents of the summons to be published. The summons shall be signed by the clerk of the court or the sheriff in such manner as to indicate that it is made by his authority. IN ST TRIAL P Rule 4.13(A).

   ii. *Contents of summons by publication.* The summons shall contain the following information:

- The name of the person being sued, and the person to whom the notice is directed, and, if the person's whereabouts are unknown or some or all of the parties are unknown, a statement to that effect;
- The name of the court and cause number assigned to the case;
- The title of the case as shown by the complaint, but if there are multiple parties, the title may be shortened to include only the first named plaintiff and those defendants to be served by publication with an appropriate indication that there are additional parties;
- The name and address of the attorney representing the person seeking service;
- A brief statement of the nature of the suit, which need not contain the details and particulars of the claim. A description of any property, relationship, or other res involved in the action, and a statement that the person being sued claims some interest therein;
- A clear statement that the person being sued must respond within thirty (30) days after the last notice of the action is published, and in case he fails to do so, judgment by default may

be entered against him for the relief demanded in the complaint. IN ST TRIAL P Rule 4.13(B).

iii. *Publication of summons.* The summons shall be published three (3) times by the clerk or person making it, the first publication promptly and each two (2) succeeding publications at least seven (7) and not more than fourteen (14) days after the prior publication, in a newspaper authorized by law to publish notices, and published in the county where the complaint or action is filed, where the res is located, or where the defendant resides or where he was known last to reside. If no newspaper is published in the county, then the summons shall be published in the county in this state nearest thereto in which any such paper may be printed, or in a place specially ordered by the court. The person seeking the service or his attorney may designate any qualified newspaper, and if he fails to do so, the selection may be made by the clerk. IN ST TRIAL P Rule 4.13(C).

iv. *By whom made or procured.* Service of summons by publication shall be made and procured by the clerk, by a person appointed by the court for that purpose, or by the clerk or sheriff of another county where publication is to be made. IN ST TRIAL P Rule 4.13(D).

v. *Return.* The clerk or person making the service shall prepare the return and include the following:

- Any supporting affidavits of the printer containing a copy of the summons which was published;
- An information or statement that the newspaper and the publication meet all legal requirements applicable to such publication;
- The dates of publication. IN ST TRIAL P Rule 4.13(E).
- The return and affidavits shall be filed with the pleadings and other papers in the case and shall become a part of the record as provided in the Indiana Rules of Trial Procedure. IN ST TRIAL P Rule 4.13(E).

o. *Service on agent of nonresident corporation.* In an action commenced in a court of general jurisdiction in Indiana by or against any corporation incorporated under the laws of Indiana, in which one (1) or more of the directors of the corporation is: (1) a necessary or proper party; and (2) a nonresident of Indiana; service of summons upon a director for the purpose of obtaining jurisdiction of the person of the director in the action is obtained by serving the summons on the resident agent of the corporation. IN ST 34-33-2-1.

G. Hearings

1. The Indiana rules do not contemplate a hearing regarding the service of the summons and complaint.

H. Forms

1. Official Complaint Forms for Indiana

a. Affidavit of debt. IN ST TRIAL P App. A-2.

b. Appearance by attorney in civil case. IN ST TRIAL P App. B.

2. Complaint Forms for Indiana

a. Caption; Generally. 5 INPRAC § 3:1.1.

b. Caption; Multiple parties. 5 INPRAC § 3:1.2.

c. Single count. 5 INPRAC § 3:1.3.

d. Multiple counts; Single defendant. 5 INPRAC § 3:1.4.

e. Multiple counts; Multiple defendants. 5 INPRAC § 3:1.5.

f. Signature; By party. 5 INPRAC § 3:1.6.

g. Signature; By attorney. 5 INPRAC § 3:1.7.

h. Verification. 5 INPRAC § 3:1.8.

i. Individual defendant. 5 INPRAC § 3:2.1.

   j. Resident agent of corporation. 5 INPRAC § 3:2.2.

   k. Attorney general. 5 INPRAC § 3:2.3.

   l. City attorney. 5 INPRAC § 3:2.4.

   m. Certificate; Personal service. 5 INPRAC § 3:2.5.

   n. Certificate; First class mail. 5 INPRAC § 3:2.6.

   o. Certificate; Registered mail. 5 INPRAC § 3:2.7.

   p. Certificate; Dwelling house. 5 INPRAC § 3:2.8.

   q. Clerk's certificate of mailing. 5 INPRAC § 3:2.9.

   r. Clerk's certificate of mailing; Acceptance by defendant. 5 INPRAC § 3:2.10.

   s. Clerk's return on service of summons by mail; Not accepted by defendant. 5 INPRAC § 3:2.11.

   t. Sheriff's return; Service of summons. 5 INPRAC § 3:2.12.

   u. Motion to appoint person to serve process. 5 INPRAC § 3:2.13.

   v. Published notice; Text. 5 INPRAC § 3:2.14.

   w. Affidavit of publisher. 5 INPRAC § 3:2.15.

   x. Clerk's return on service by publication. 5 INPRAC § 3:2.16.

   y. Complaint; Single count. 9 INPRAC § 2.3.

   z. Appearance by party initiating action; Form. 9 INPRAC § 6.3.

 3. Official Complaint Forms for Allen County

   a. Consent to alternate service. IN ST ALLEN SUPER AND CIR CT CIV App. A.

I. Checklist

 (I) ❑ Matters to be considered by the plaintiff

  (a) ❑ Required documents

   (1) ❑ Summons

   (2) ❑ Complaint

   (3) ❑ Appearance form

  (b) ❑ Supplemental documents

   (1) ❑ Proof of written instrument

   (2) ❑ Notice of intent to use foreign law

   (3) ❑ Praecipe

   (4) ❑ Facsimile cover sheet

   (5) ❑ Additional copies for service

  (c) ❑ Timing

   (1) ❑ The claimant typically bears the burden of commencing an action within the applicable statute of limitations

   (2) ❑ If person seeking service of process fails without cause for sixty (60) days or more to provide clerk with required summons for issuance or with other information necessary to effectuate service, person has failed to exercise due diligence in securing service of process

 (II) ❑ Matters to be considered by the defendant

  (a) ❑ Required documents

   (1) ❑ Answer

   (2) ❑ Appearance form

   (3) ❑ Certificate of service

(b) ❑ Supplemental documents

   (1) ❑ Admission of service

   (2) ❑ Proof of written instrument

   (3) ❑ Notice of intent to use foreign law

   (4) ❑ Facsimile cover sheet

(c) ❑ Timing

   (1) ❑ A responsive pleading required under the Indiana Rules of Trial Procedure, shall be served within twenty (20) days after service of the prior pleading

   (2) ❑ The service of a motion permitted under IN ST TRIAL P Rule 12 alters the time for service of responsive pleadings as follows, unless a different time is fixed by the court:

     (i) ❑ If the court does not grant the motion, the responsive pleading shall be served in ten (10) days after notice of the court's action;

     (ii) ❑ If the court grants the motion and the corrective action is allowed to be taken, it shall be taken within ten (10) days, and the responsive pleading shall be served within ten (10) days thereafter

Pleadings
Amended Complaint

Document Last Updated October 2013

A. Applicable Rules

1. *State rules*

   a. Appearance. IN ST TRIAL P Rule 3.1.

   b. Process. IN ST TRIAL P Rule 4.

   c. Service of the summons. IN ST TRIAL P Rule 4.1; IN ST TRIAL P Rule 4.2; IN ST TRIAL P Rule 4.3; IN ST TRIAL P Rule 4.4; IN ST TRIAL P Rule 4.5; IN ST TRIAL P Rule 4.6; IN ST TRIAL P Rule 4.7; IN ST TRIAL P Rule 4.8; IN ST TRIAL P Rule 4.9; IN ST TRIAL P Rule 4.10; IN ST TRIAL P Rule 4.11; IN ST TRIAL P Rule 4.12; IN ST TRIAL P Rule 4.13; IN ST TRIAL P Rule 4.14; IN ST TRIAL P Rule 4.15; IN ST 34-33-2-1.

   d. Service and filing of pleadings and other papers. IN ST TRIAL P Rule 5.

   e. Time. IN ST TRIAL P Rule 6.

   f. Pleadings. IN ST TRIAL P Rule 7 IN ST TRIAL P Rule 8; IN ST TRIAL P Rule 9; IN ST TRIAL P Rule 9.1; IN ST TRIAL P Rule 9.2; IN ST TRIAL P Rule 10.

   g. Signing and verification of pleadings. IN ST TRIAL P Rule 11.

   h. Amended and supplemental pleadings. IN ST TRIAL P Rule 15.

   i. Joinder. IN ST TRIAL P Rule 18; IN ST TRIAL P Rule 19.

   j. Evidence. IN ST TRIAL P Rule 43.

   k. Determination of foreign law. IN ST TRIAL P Rule 44.1.

   l. Judgment on the evidence (directed verdict). IN ST TRIAL P Rule 50.

   m. Findings by the court. IN ST TRIAL P Rule 52.

   n. Summary judgment. IN ST TRIAL P Rule 56.

   o. Motion to correct error. IN ST TRIAL P Rule 59.

   p. Relief from judgment or order. IN ST TRIAL P Rule 60.

   q. Access to court records. IN ST ADMIN Rule 9.

r. Paper size. IN ST ADMIN Rule 11.

s. Facsimile transmission. IN ST ADMIN Rule 12.

t. Electronic filing and electronic service pilot projects. IN ST ADMIN Rule 16.

u. Privacy and confidentiality. IN ST 5-2-9-6; IN ST 5-14-3-4; IN ST 5-14-3-5.5; IN ST 6-4.1-5-10; IN ST 6-4.1-12-12; IN ST 6-8.1-7-1; IN ST 11-13-1-8; IN ST 12-23-14-13; IN ST 16-39-3-10; IN ST 16-41-8-1; IN ST 22-4-19-6; IN ST 31-11-1-6; IN ST 31-19-5-23; IN ST 31-19-13-2; IN ST 31-19-19-1; IN ST 31-33-18-1; IN ST 31-39-1-1; IN ST 31-39-1-2; IN ST 33-23-16-16; IN ST 35-34-2-4; IN ST 35-38-1-13; IN ST 35-38-9-1; IN ST ADR Rule 2.11; IN ST ADR Rule 4.4; IN ST ADR Rule 5.6; IN ST JURY Rule 10.

2. *Local rules*

a. Applicability and citation of rules. IN ST ALLEN SUPER AND CIR CT CIV Rule AR00-1.

b. Appearances. IN ST ALLEN SUPER AND CIR CT CIV Rule 3.1-1.

c. Consent to alternate service. IN ST ALLEN SUPER AND CIR CT CIV Rule 5-1.

d. Preparation of pleadings. IN ST ALLEN SUPER AND CIR CT CIV Rule 8-1.

e. Filing. IN ST ALLEN SUPER AND CIR CT CIV Rule 77-1.

B. Timing

1. *Filing an amended pleading*

a. *As a matter of course.* A party may amend his pleading once as a matter of course at any time before a responsive pleading is served or, if the pleading is one to which no responsive pleading is permitted, and the action has not been placed upon the trial calendar, he may so amend it at any time within thirty (30) days after it is served. IN ST TRIAL P Rule 15(A).

b. *With leave of court.* Otherwise a party may amend his pleading only by leave of court or by written consent of the adverse party; and leave shall be given when justice so requires. IN ST TRIAL P Rule 15(A). Refer to the Indiana KeyRules Motion for Leave to Amend document for more information.

2. *Computation of time*

a. *Generally; Days excluded.* In computing any period of time prescribed or allowed by the Indiana Rules of Trial Procedure, by order of the court, or by any applicable statute, the day of the act, event, or default from which the designated period of time begins to run shall not be included. The last day of the period so computed is to be included unless it is:

i. A Saturday,

ii. A Sunday,

iii. A legal holiday as defined by state statute, or

iv. A day the office in which the act is to be done is closed during regular business hours. IN ST TRIAL P Rule 6(A).

b. *Short periods.* In any event, the period runs until the end of the next day that is not a Saturday, a Sunday, a legal holiday, or a day on which the office is closed. When the period of time allowed is less than seven (7) days, intermediate Saturdays, Sundays, legal holidays, and days on which the office is closed shall be excluded from the computations. IN ST TRIAL P Rule 6(A).

c. *Additional time after service by United States mail.* Whenever a party has the right or is required to do some act or take some proceedings within a prescribed period after the service of a notice or other paper upon him and the notice or paper is served upon him by United States mail, three (3) days shall be added to the prescribed period. IN ST TRIAL P Rule 6(E).

d. *Enlargement of time.* When an act is required or allowed to be done at or within a specific time by the Indiana Rules of Trial Procedure, the court may at any time for cause shown:

i. Order the period enlarged, with or without motion or notice, if request therefor is made before the expiration of the period originally prescribed or extended by a previous order; or

ii. Upon motion made after the expiration of the specific period, permit the act to be done where

the failure to act was the result of excusable neglect; but, the court may not extend the time for taking any action for judgment on the evidence under IN ST TRIAL P Rule 50(A), amendment of findings and judgment under IN ST TRIAL P Rule 52(B), to correct errors under IN ST TRIAL P Rule 59(C), statement in opposition to motion to correct error under IN ST TRIAL P Rule 59(E), or to obtain relief from final judgment under IN ST TRIAL P Rule 60(B), except to the extent and under the conditions stated in those rules. IN ST TRIAL P Rule 6(B).

C. General Requirements

1. *Amending pleadings.* The purpose of an amended pleading is to include matters that occurred before the filing of the original pleading but which were either overlooked by the pleader or unknown to him at the time. It is a substitute for the original and relates to the facts that existed when the original pleading was filed. An amended pleading supercedes the original as to those portions amended. 10 INPRAC § 46.1.

   a. *Amendments liberally allowed.* Amendments to pleadings are to be liberally allowed in order that all issues are presented in one action. 10 INPRAC § 46.1; Pinnacle Media, LLC v. Metropolitan Dev. Com'n of Marion County, 868 N.E.2d 894 (Ind.Ct.App. 2007).

   b. *Amendments to conform to the evidence.* When issues not raised by the pleadings are tried by express or implied consent of the parties, they shall be treated in all respects as if they had been raised in the pleadings. Such amendment of the pleadings as may be necessary to cause them to conform to the evidence and to raise these issues may be made upon motion of any party at any time, even after judgment, but failure so to amend does not affect the result of the trial of these issues. If evidence is objected to at the trial on the ground that it is not within the issues made by the pleadings, the court may allow the pleadings to be amended and shall do so freely when the presentation of the merits of the action will be subserved thereby and the objecting party fails to satisfy the court that the admission of such evidence would prejudice him in maintaining his action or defense upon the merits. The court may grant a continuance to enable the objecting party to meet such evidence. IN ST TRIAL P Rule 15(B).

   c. *Relation back of amendments*

      i. Whenever the claim or defense asserted in the amended pleading arose out of the conduct, transaction, or occurrence set forth or attempted to be set forth in the original pleading, the amendment relates back to the date of the original pleading. An amendment changing the party against whom a claim is asserted relates back if the foregoing provision is satisfied and, within one hundred and twenty (120) days of commencement of the action, the party to be brought in by amendment:

         • Has received such notice of the institution of the action that he will not be prejudiced in maintaining his defense on the merits; and

         • Knew or should have known that but for a mistake concerning the identity of the proper party, the action would have been brought against him. IN ST TRIAL P Rule 15(C).

      ii. The requirement of IN ST TRIAL P Rule 15(C)(1) and IN ST TRIAL P Rule 15(C)(2) with respect to a governmental organization to be brought into the action as defendant is satisfied:

         • In the case of a state or governmental organization by delivery or mailing of process to the attorney general or to a governmental executive [IN ST TRIAL P Rule 4.6(A)(3)]; or

         • In the case of a local governmental organization, by delivery or mailing of process to its attorney as provided by statute, to a governmental executive thereof [IN ST TRIAL P Rule 4.6(A)(4)], or to the officer holding the office if suit is against the officer or an office. IN ST TRIAL P Rule 15(C).

   d. *Amendment by leave.* Amendments, other than an amendment by right, may be made only by leave of court or by written consent of the opposing party. 2 INPRAC R 15(15.2). Refer to the Indiana KeyRules Motion for Leave to Amend document for more information on amending with leave of court.

2. *Pleading, generally*

   a. *Pleadings to be concise.* Each averment of a pleading shall be simple, concise, and direct. No technical forms of pleading or motions are required. All fictions in pleading are abolished. IN ST TRIAL P Rule 8(E)(1).

b. *Pleading in the alternative.* A pleading may set forth two (2) or more statements of a claim or defense alternatively or hypothetically, either in one (1) count or defense or in separate counts or defenses. When two (2) or more statements are made in the alternative and one (1) of them if made independently would be sufficient, the pleading is not made insufficient by the insufficiency of one or more of the alternative statements. A pleading may also state as many separate claims or defenses as the pleader has regardless of consistency and whether based on legal or equitable grounds. All statements shall be made subject to the obligations set forth in IN ST TRIAL P Rule 11. IN ST TRIAL P Rule 8(E)(2).

c. *Motions and pleadings, joint and several.* All motions and pleadings of any kind addressed to two (2) or more paragraphs of any pleading, or filed by two (2) or more parties, shall be taken and construed as joint, separate, and several motions or pleadings to each of such paragraphs and by and against each of such parties. All motions or pleadings containing two (2) or more subject-matters shall be taken and construed as separate and several as to each subject-matter. All objections to rulings made by two (2) or more parties shall be taken and construed as the joint, separate, and several objections of each of such parties. IN ST TRIAL P Rule 8(E)(3).

    i. A complaint filed by or against two (2) or more plaintiffs shall be taken and construed as joint, separate, and several as to each of said plaintiffs. IN ST TRIAL P Rule 8(E).

d. *Construction of pleadings.* All pleadings shall be so construed as to do substantial justice, lead to disposition on the merits, and avoid litigation of procedural points. IN ST TRIAL P Rule 8(F).

3. *Contents of the complaint*

a. *Pleading for relief; Notice pleading.* Indiana is a "notice pleading" jurisdiction. 22B INPRAC 8:1; State v. American Family Voices, Inc., 898 N.E.2d 293 (Ind. 2008). Notice pleading replaces the technical and complex method of pleading which existed prior to 1970. Notice pleading is grounded in due process of law and must provide a defendant with reasonable notice of the plaintiff's claim or an opponent's defense. 22B INPRAC 8:1; Noblesville Redevelopment Com'n v. Noblesville Associates Ltd. Partnership, 674 N.E.2d 558 (Ind. 1996). Notice pleading does not require that the plaintiff state all elements or facts essential to a cause of action. 22B INPRAC 8:1; State v. American Family Voices, Inc., 898 N.E.2d 293 (Ind. 2008). Instead, the complaint must state "a short and plain statement of the claim" showing an entitlement to relief, and a demand for relief. 22B INPRAC 8:1; Trail v. Boys and Girls Clubs of Northwest Indiana, 845 N.E.2d 130 (Ind. 2006).

b. *Claims for relief.* To state a claim for relief, whether an original claim, counterclaim, cross-claim, or third-party claim, a pleading must contain:

    i. A short and plain statement of the claim showing that the pleader is entitled to relief, and

    ii. A demand for relief to which the pleader deems entitled. Relief in the alternative or of several different types may be demanded. However, in any complaint seeking damages for personal injury or death, or seeking punitive damages, no dollar amount or figure shall be included in the demand. IN ST TRIAL P Rule 8(A).

c. *Res ipsa loquitur.* Res ipsa loquitur or a similar doctrine may be pleaded by alleging generally that the facts connected with the action are unknown to the pleader and are within the knowledge of the opposing party. IN ST TRIAL P Rule 9.1(B).

d. *Bona fide purchaser.* When the rights of a person depend upon his status as a bona fide purchaser for value or upon similar requirements, such status must be pleaded and proved by the person asserting it, but it may be pleaded in general terms. Once it is established that the person has given any required value, unless such value is commercially unreasonable, and that he has met any requirements of recordation, filing, possession, or perfection, the trier of fact must find that such value was given or such perfection was made in accordance with any requirements of good faith, lack of knowledge, or lack of notice unless and until evidence is introduced which would support a finding of its non-existence. IN ST TRIAL P Rule 9.1(D).

e. *Presumption; Matters of judicial notice.* Neither presumptions of law nor matters of which judicial notice may be taken need be stated in a pleading. IN ST TRIAL P Rule 9.1(E).

   i. *Presumption of jurisdiction.* Jurisdiction is presumed in Indiana. 22B INPRAC 8:2. Consequently, there is no requirement to affirmatively plead the existence of jurisdiction in the complaint, unless the action involves a special proceeding requiring such an allegation. 22B INPRAC 8:2; Cardinal Industries, Inc. v. Schwartz, 483 N.E.2d 458 (Ind.Ct.App. 1985). The plaintiff bears no burden to prove jurisdiction unless and until it is challenged by the defendant. 22B INPRAC 8:2; Brokemond v. Marshall Field & Co., 612 N.E.2d 143 (Ind.Ct.App. 1993).

f. *Equitable and legal claims in multi-count actions.* In multi-count actions, the inclusion of an equitable claim, standing alone, will not automatically draw the entire action into equity. Something more than the presence of an equitable claim is required, and the court must examine the claims at issue. 22B INPRAC 38:1 COMMENT; Lucas v. U.S. Bank, N.A., 953 N.E.2d 457 (Ind. 2011). Factors the court may consider in evaluating the nature of the underlying substantive claims include: the substance and central character of the complaint, the rights and interests at issue, the relief demanded, and any issues arising out of discovery. 22B INPRAC 38:1 COMMENT; Songer v. Civitas Bank, 771 N.E.2d 61 (Ind. 2002).

4. *Pleading special matters*

   a. *Capacity.* It is not necessary to aver the capacity of a party to sue or be sued, the authority of a party to sue or be sued in a representative capacity, or the legal existence of an organization that is made a party. The burden of proving lack of such capacity, authority, or legal existence shall be upon the person asserting lack of it, and shall be pleaded as an affirmative defense. IN ST TRIAL P Rule 9(A).

   b. *Fraud, mistake, condition of the mind.* In all averments of fraud or mistake, the circumstances constituting fraud or mistake shall be specifically averred. Malice, intent, knowledge, and other conditions of mind may be averred generally. IN ST TRIAL P Rule 9(B).

   c. *Conditions precedent.* In pleading the performance or occurrence of promissory or non-promissory conditions precedent, it is sufficient to aver generally that all conditions precedent have been performed, have occurred, or have been excused. A denial of performance or occurrence shall be made specifically and with particularity, and a denial of excuse generally. IN ST TRIAL P Rule 9(C).

   d. *Official document or act.* In pleading an official document or official act it is sufficient to aver that the document was issued or the act done in compliance with law. IN ST TRIAL P Rule 9(D).

   e. *Judgment.* In pleading a judgment or decision of a domestic or foreign court, judicial or quasi-judicial tribunal, or of a board or officer, it is sufficient to aver the judgment or decision without setting forth matter showing jurisdiction to render it. IN ST TRIAL P Rule 9(E).

   f. *Time and place.* For the purpose of testing the sufficiency of a pleading, averments of time and place are material and shall be considered like all other averments of material matter. However, time and place need be stated only with such specificity as will enable the opposing party to prepare his defense. IN ST TRIAL P Rule 9(F).

   g. *Special damages; Damages where no answer.* When items of special damage are claimed, they shall be specifically stated. The relief granted to the plaintiff, if there be no answer, cannot exceed the relief demanded in his complaint; but, in any other case, the court may grant him any relief consistent with the facts or matters pleaded. IN ST TRIAL P Rule 9(G).

5. *Joinder*

   a. *Of claims.* A party asserting a claim for relief as an original claim, counterclaim, cross-claim, or third-party claim, may join, either as independent or as alternate claims, as many claims, whether legal, equitable, or statutory as he has against an opposing party. IN ST TRIAL P Rule 18(A).

   b. *Of remedies; Fraudulent conveyances.* Whenever a claim is one heretofore cognizable only after another claim has been prosecuted to a conclusion, the two (2) claims may be joined in a single action; but the court shall grant relief in that action only in accordance with the relative substantive rights of the parties. In particular, a plaintiff may state a claim for money and a claim to have set aside a conveyance fraudulent as to him, without first having obtained a judgment establishing the claim for money. IN ST TRIAL P Rule 18(B).

c. *Of persons needed for just adjudication.* A person who is subject to service of process shall be joined as a party in the action if:

    i. In his absence complete relief cannot be accorded among those already parties; or

    ii. He claims an interest relating to the subject of the action and is so situated that the disposition of the action in his absence may:

- As a practical matter impair or impede his ability to protect that interest, or
- Leave any of the persons already parties subject to a substantial risk of incurring double, multiple, or otherwise inconsistent obligations by reason of his claimed interest. IN ST TRIAL P Rule 19(A).

    iii. If he has not been so joined, the court shall order that he be made a party. If he should join as a plaintiff but refuses to do so, he may be made a defendant. IN ST TRIAL P Rule 19(A).

6. *Trial by jury; Demand*

a. *Causes triable by court and by jury.* Issues of law and issues of fact in causes that prior to the eighteenth day of June, 1852, were of exclusive equitable jurisdiction shall be tried by the court; issues of fact in all other causes shall be triable as the same are now triable. In case of the joinder of causes of action or defenses which, prior to said date, were of exclusive equitable jurisdiction with causes of action or defenses which, prior to said date, were designated as actions at law and triable by jury—the former shall be triable by the court, and the latter by a jury, unless waived; the trial of both may be at the same time or at different times, as the court may direct. IN ST TRIAL P Rule 38(A).

b. *Demand.* Any party may demand a trial by jury of any issue triable of right by a jury by filing with the court and serving upon the other parties a demand therefor in writing at any time after the commencement of the action and not later than ten (10) days after the first responsive pleading to the complaint, or to a counterclaim, crossclaim or other claim if one properly is pleaded; and if no responsive pleading is filed or required, within ten (10) days after the time such pleading otherwise would have been required. Such demand is sufficient if indorsed upon a pleading of a party filed within such time. IN ST TRIAL P Rule 38(B).

c. *Same; Specification of issues.* In his demand a party may specify the issues which he wishes so tried; otherwise he shall be deemed to have demanded trial by jury for all issues triable as of right by jury. Any other party must file a demand for jury trial to preserve his right to trial by jury:

    i. Of issues for which a right to trial by jury was not requested by another party; and

    ii. In case a request by another party was improper. But if a proper request for a trial by jury upon issues triable by jury as of right on his behalf is made by any party, such request shall be deemed to have been made on behalf of all parties entitled to a jury trial upon such issues. IN ST TRIAL P Rule 38(C).

d. *Waiver.* The failure of a party to appear at the trial, and the failure of a party to serve a demand as required by IN ST TRIAL P Rule 38 and to file it as required by IN ST TRIAL P Rule 5(E) constitute waiver by him of trial by jury. A demand for trial by jury made as provided in IN ST TRIAL P Rule 38 may not be withdrawn without the consent of the other party or parties. IN ST TRIAL P Rule 38(D).

    i. The trial court shall not grant a demand for a trial by jury filed after the time fixed in IN ST TRIAL P Rule 38(B) has elapsed except upon the written agreement of all of the parties to the action, which agreement shall be filed with the court and made a part of the record. If such agreement is filed then the court may, in its discretion, grant a trial by jury in which event the grant of a trial by jury may not be withdrawn except by the agreement of all of the parties. IN ST TRIAL P Rule 38(D).

e. *Arbitration.* Nothing in the Indiana Rules of Trial Procedure shall deny the parties the right by contract or agreement to submit or to agree to submit controversies to arbitration made before or after commencement of an action thereon or deny the courts power to specifically enforce such agreements. IN ST TRIAL P Rule 38(E).

D. Documents

1. *Required documents*

   a. *Amended complaint.* Refer to the General Requirements section of this document for information on the contents of an amended complaint.

   b. *Certificate of service.* An attorney or unrepresented party tendering a document to the Clerk for filing shall certify that service has been made, list the parties served, and specify the date and means of service. The certificate of service shall be placed at the end of the document and shall not be separately filed. The separate filing of a certificate of service, however, shall not be grounds for rejecting a document for filing. The Clerk may permit documents to be filed without a certificate of service but shall require prompt filing of a separate certificate of service. IN ST TRIAL P Rule 5(C).

2. *Supplemental documents*

   a. *Proof of written instrument.* When any pleading allowed by the Indiana Rules of Trial Procedure is founded on a written instrument, the original, or a copy thereof, must be included in or filed with the pleading. Such instrument, whether copied in the pleadings or not, shall be taken as part of the record. When any pleading allowed by the Indiana Rules of Trial Procedure is founded on an account, an Affidavit of Debt, in a form substantially similar to that which is provided in IN ST TRIAL P App. A-2, shall be attached. IN ST TRIAL P Rule 9.2(A).

   b. *Notice of intent to use foreign law.* A party who intends to raise an issue concerning the law of a foreign country shall give notice in his pleadings or other reasonable written notice. The court, in determining foreign law, may consider any relevant material or source, including testimony, whether or not submitted by a party or admissible under IN ST TRIAL P Rule 43. The court's determination shall be treated as a ruling on a question of law. It shall be made by the court and not the jury and shall be reviewable. IN ST TRIAL P Rule 44.1(A).

   c. *Facsimile cover sheet.* Any document sent to the Clerk of the Circuit Court by electronic facsimile transmission shall be accompanied by a cover sheet which states the title of the document, case number, number of pages, identity and voice telephone number of the sending party and instructions for filing. The cover sheet shall contain the signature of the attorney or party, pro se, authorizing the filing. IN ST ADMIN Rule 12(D).

3. Refer to the Indiana KeyRules Complaint document for the required and supplemental documents for filing and serving an amended complaint against a new party.

E. Format

1. *Form of pleadings*

   a. *Caption; Names of parties.* Every pleading shall contain a caption setting forth the name of the court, the title of the action, the file number, and a designation as in IN ST TRIAL P Rule 7(A). In the complaint the title of the action shall include the names of all the parties, but in other pleadings it is sufficient to state the name of the first party on each side with an appropriate indication of other parties. IN ST TRIAL P Rule 10(A).

   b. *Paragraphs; Separate statements.* All averments of a claim or defense shall be made in numbered paragraphs, the contents of each of which shall be limited as far as practicable to a statement of a single set of circumstances, and a paragraph may be referred to by number in all succeeding pleadings. Each claim founded upon a separate transaction or occurrence and each defense other than denials may be stated in a separate count or defense whenever a separation facilitates the clear presentation of the matters set forth. IN ST TRIAL P Rule 10(B).

   c. *Adoption by reference; Exhibits.* Statements in a pleading may be adopted by reference in a different part of the same pleading or in another pleading or in any motion. A copy of any written instrument which is an exhibit to a pleading is a part thereof for all purposes. IN ST TRIAL P Rule 10(C).

   d. *Citation.* Allen County Superior and Circuit court rules may be cited as L.R. _____. The Indiana Rules of Trial Procedure are hereinafter referred to as T.R. _____. IN ST ALLEN SUPER AND CIR CT CIV Rule AR00-1(B).

   e. *Paper.* All pleadings must be printed on white paper. IN ST ALLEN SUPER AND CIR CT CIV Rule 8-1(A).

f. *Spacing.* The lines shall be double spaced except for quotations, which shall be indented and single-spaced. IN ST ALLEN SUPER AND CIR CT CIV Rule 8-1(A).

g. *Photocopies.* Photocopies are acceptable if legible. IN ST ALLEN SUPER AND CIR CT CIV Rule 8-1(A).

h. *Margins and binding.* Margins shall be one to one and one-half (1-1 1/2) inches on the left side and one-half (1/2) inch on the right. IN ST ALLEN SUPER AND CIR CT CIV Rule 8-1(B).

   i. Binding or stapling shall be at the top left and at no other place. IN ST ALLEN SUPER AND CIR CT CIV Rule 8-1(B).

   ii. Covers or backing shall not be used. IN ST ALLEN SUPER AND CIR CT CIV Rule 8-1(B).

i. *Flat filing.* The files of the Clerk of the Court shall be kept under the "flat filing" system. All pleadings presented for filing with the Clerk or Court shall be flat and unfolded. Only the original of any pleading shall be placed in the Court file. IN ST ALLEN SUPER AND CIR CT CIV Rule 77-1(A).

j. *Handwritten pleadings.* Handwritten pleadings may be accepted for filing in the discretion of the Court. IN ST ALLEN SUPER AND CIR CT CIV Rule 8-1(A).

2. *Size of papers for filing.* Effective January 1, 1992, all pleadings, copies, motions and documents filed with any trial court or appellate level court, typed or printed, with the exception of exhibits and existing wills, shall be prepared on eight and one-half by eleven inch (8 1/2" x 11") size paper. IN ST ADMIN Rule 11.

3. *Signature requirements*

   a. *Signature of attorney.* Every pleading or motion of a party represented by an attorney shall be signed by at least one (1) attorney of record in his individual name, whose address, telephone number, and attorney number shall be stated, except that this provision shall not apply to pleadings and motions made and transcribed at the trial or a hearing before the judge and received by him in such form. IN ST TRIAL P Rule 11(A). All pleadings to be signed by an attorney shall contain the written signature of the individual attorney, the attorney's printed name, Supreme Court Attorney Number, the name of the attorney's law firm, the attorney's address, telephone number, and a designation of the party for whom the attorney appears. IN ST ALLEN SUPER AND CIR CT CIV Rule 8-1(C). For the recommended signature format, refer to IN ST ALLEN SUPER AND CIR CT CIV Rule 8-1(C).

      i. The signature of an attorney constitutes a certificate by him that he has read the pleadings; that to the best of his knowledge, information, and belief, there is good ground to support it; and that it is not interposed for delay. IN ST TRIAL P Rule 11(A).

      ii. If a pleading or motion is not signed or is signed with intent to defeat the purpose of the rule, it may be stricken as sham and false and the action may proceed as though the pleading had not been served. IN ST TRIAL P Rule 11(A).

      iii. For a willful violation of IN ST TRIAL P Rule 11 an attorney may be subjected to appropriate disciplinary action. Similar action may be taken if scandalous or indecent matter is inserted. IN ST TRIAL P Rule 11(A).

      iv. Neither printed signatures, nor facsimile signatures shall be accepted on original documents. IN ST ALLEN SUPER AND CIR CT CIV Rule 8-1(C).

      v. Facsimile signatures are permitted on copies. IN ST ALLEN SUPER AND CIR CT CIV Rule 8-1(C).

   b. *Signature of unrepresented party.* A party who is not represented by an attorney shall sign his pleading and state his address. IN ST TRIAL P Rule 11(A).

   c. *Verification not generally required.* Except when specifically required by rule, pleadings or motions need not be verified or accompanied by affidavit. The rule in equity that the averments of an answer under oath must be overcome by the testimony of two (2) witnesses or of one (1) witness sustained by corroborating circumstances is abolished. IN ST TRIAL P Rule 11(A).

   d. *Verification by affirmation or representation.* When in connection with any civil or special statutory

proceeding it is required that any pleading, motion, petition, supporting affidavit, or other document of any kind, be verified, or that an oath be taken, it shall be sufficient if the subscriber simply affirms the truth of the matter to be verified by an affirmation or representation. IN ST TRIAL P Rule 11(B). IN ST TRIAL P Rule 11(B) states that the affirmation or representation should be in substantially the following language: "I (we) affirm, under the penalties for perjury, that the foregoing representation(s) is (are) true. (Signed) _____."

    i. Any person who falsifies an affirmation or representation of fact shall be subject to the same penalties as are prescribed by law for the making of a false affidavit. IN ST TRIAL P Rule 11(B).

    e. *Verified pleadings, motions, and affidavits as evidence.* Pleadings, motions and affidavits accompanying or in support of such pleadings or motions when required to be verified or under oath shall be accepted as a representation that the signer had personal knowledge thereof or reasonable cause to believe the existence of the facts or matters stated or alleged therein; and, if otherwise competent or acceptable as evidence, may be admitted as evidence of the facts or matters stated or alleged therein when it is so provided in the Indiana Rules of Trial Procedure, by statute or other law, or to the extent the writing or signature expressly purports to be made upon the signer's personal knowledge. When such pleadings, motions and affidavits are verified or under oath they shall not require other or greater proof on the part of the adverse party than if not verified or not under oath unless expressly provided otherwise by the Indiana Rules of Trial Procedure, statute or other law. Affidavits upon motions for summary judgment under IN ST TRIAL P Rule 56 and in denial of execution under IN ST TRIAL P Rule 9.2 shall be made upon personal knowledge. IN ST TRIAL P Rule 11(C).

4. *Information excluded from public access.* Every document filed in a case shall separately identify information excluded from public access pursuant to IN ST ADMIN Rule 9(G)(1) as follows:

    a. Whole documents that are excluded from public access pursuant to IN ST ADMIN Rule 9(G)(1) shall be tendered on light green paper or have a light green coversheet attached to the document, marked "Not for Public Access" or "Confidential." IN ST TRIAL P Rule 5(G)(1).

    b. When only a portion of a document contains information excluded from public access pursuant to IN ST ADMIN Rule 9(G)(1), said information shall be omitted [or redacted] from the filed document, and set forth on a separate accompanying document on light green paper conspicuously marked "Not for Public Access" or "Confidential" and clearly designated [or identifying] the caption and number of the case and the document and location within the document to which the redacted material pertains. IN ST TRIAL P Rule 5(G)(2).

    c. With respect to documents filed in electronic format, the trial court, by local rule, may provide for compliance with IN ST TRIAL P Rule 5 in manner that separates and protects access to information excluded from public access. IN ST TRIAL P Rule 5(G)(3).

    d. IN ST TRIAL P Rule 5(G) does not apply to a record sealed by the court pursuant to IN ST 5-14-3-5.5 or otherwise, nor to records, documents, or information filed in cases to which public access is prohibited pursuant to IN ST ADMIN Rule 9(G). IN ST TRIAL P Rule 5(G)(4).

    e. The following information in case records is excluded from public access and is confidential:

      i. Information that is excluded from public access pursuant to federal law;

      ii. Information that is excluded from public access as declared confidential by Indiana statute or other court rule, including without limitation:

- All adoption records created after July 8, 1941, as declared confidential by IN ST 31-19-19-1, et seq., except those specifically declared open by IN ST 31-19-13-2(2);
- All records relating to chancroid, chlamydia, gonorrhea, hepatitis, human immunodeficiency virus (HIV), Lymphogranuloma venereum, syphilis, tuberculosis, as declared confidential by IN ST 16-41-8-1, et seq.;
- All records relating to child abuse as declared confidential by IN ST 31-33-18-1, et seq.;
- All records relating to drug tests as declared confidential by IN ST 5-14-3-4(a)(9);
- Records of grand jury proceedings as declared confidential by IN ST 35-34-2-4;

- Records of juvenile proceedings as declared confidential by IN ST 31-39-1-2, except those specifically open under statute;
- All paternity records created after July 1, 1941 as declared confidential by IN ST 31-14-11-15, IN ST 31-19-5-23, IN ST 31-39-1-1 and IN ST 31-39-1-2 [Editor's note: IN ST 31-14-11-15 was repealed effective May 9, 2013];
- All pre-sentence reports as declared confidential by IN ST 35-38-1-13;
- Written petitions to permit marriages without consent and orders directing the Clerk of Court to issue a marriage license to underage persons, as declared confidential by IN ST 31-11-1-6;
- Only those arrest warrants, search warrants, indictments and informations ordered confidential by the trial judge, prior to return of duly executed service as declared confidential by IN ST 5-14-3-4(b)(1);
- All medical, mental health, or tax records unless determined by law or regulation of any governmental custodian not to be confidential, released by the subject of such records, or declared by a court of competent jurisdiction to be essential to the resolution of litigation as declared confidential by IN ST 16-39-3-10, IN ST 6-4.1-5-10, IN ST 6-4.1-12-12, and IN ST 6-8.1-7-1;
- Personal information relating to jurors or prospective jurors, other than for the use of the parties and counsel, pursuant to IN ST JURY Rule 10;
- Information relating to protection from abuse orders, no-contact orders and workplace violence restraining orders as declared confidential by IN ST 5-2-9-6, et seq.;
- Mediation proceedings pursuant to IN ST ADR Rule 2.11, Mini-Trial proceedings pursuant to IN ST ADR Rule 4.4(C), and Summary Jury Trials pursuant to IN ST ADR Rule 5.6;
- Information in probation files pursuant to the Probation Standards promulgated by the Judicial Conference of Indiana pursuant to IN ST 11-13-1-8(b);
- Information deemed confidential pursuant to the Rules for Court Administered Alcohol and Drug Programs promulgated by the Judicial Conference of Indiana pursuant to IN ST 12-23-14-13;
- Information deemed confidential pursuant to the Problem-Solving Court Rules promulgated by the Judicial Conference of Indiana pursuant to IN ST 33-23-16-16;
- All records of the Department of workforce Development as declared confidential by IN ST 22-4-19-6;
- Information regarding interception of electronic communications that is sealed or deemed confidential as set forth in IN ST 35-33.5-2-1, et seq.

iii. Information excluded from public access by specific court order;

iv. Complete Social Security Numbers of living persons;

v. With the exception of names, information such as addresses, phone numbers, and dates of birth which explicitly identifies:

- Natural persons who are witnesses or victims (not including defendants) in criminal, domestic violence, stalking, sexual assault, juvenile, or civil protection order proceedings, provided that juveniles who are victims of sex crimes shall be identified by initials only;
- Places of residence of judicial officers, clerks and other employees of courts and clerks of court, unless the person or persons about whom the information pertains waives confidentiality;

vi. Complete account numbers of specific assets, loans, bank accounts, credit cards, and personal identification numbers (PINs);

vii. All orders of expungement entered in criminal or juvenile proceedings, orders to restrict access

to criminal history information pursuant to IN ST 35-38-5-5.5 or IN ST 35-38-8-5 and records excluded from public access by such orders, and information related to infractions that is excluded from public access pursuant to IN ST 34-28-5-15 or IN ST 34-28-5-16 [Editor's note: IN ST 35-38-5-5.5, IN ST 35-38-8-5 and IN ST 34-28-5-16 were repealed effective July 1, 2013; for information on orders restricting access to criminal history, refer to IN ST 35-38-9-1, et seq.];

    viii. All personal notes and e-mail, and deliberative material, of judges, jurors, court staff and judicial agencies, and information recorded in personal data assistants (PDA's) or organizers and personal calendars. IN ST ADMIN Rule 9(G)(1).

F. Filing and Service Requirements

1. *Filing requirements.* Except as otherwise provided in IN ST TRIAL P Rule 5(E)(2), all pleadings and papers subsequent to the complaint which are required to be served upon a party shall be filed with the Court either before service or within a reasonable period of time thereafter. IN ST TRIAL P Rule 5(E)(1).

   a. *Filing with the court defined.* The filing of pleadings, motions, and other papers with the court as required by the Indiana Rules of Trial Procedure shall be made by one of the following methods:

       i. Delivery to the clerk of the court;

       ii. Sending by electronic transmission under the procedure adopted pursuant to IN ST ADMIN Rule 12;

       iii. Mailing to the clerk by registered, certified or express mail return receipt requested;

       iv. Depositing with any third-party commercial carrier for delivery to the clerk within three (3) calendar days, cost prepaid, properly addressed;

       v. If the court so permits, filing with the judge, in which event the judge shall note thereon the filing date and forthwith transmit them to the office of the clerk; or

       vi. Electronic filing, as approved by the Division of State Court Administration pursuant to IN ST ADMIN Rule 16. IN ST TRIAL P Rule 5(F).

       vii. Filing by registered or certified mail and by third-party commercial carrier shall be complete upon mailing or deposit. IN ST TRIAL P Rule 5(F).

   b. *Facsimile filing*

       i. *Generally.* In counties where a majority of judges of the courts of record, by posted local rule, have authorized electronic facsimile filing and designated a telephone number to receive such transmissions, pleadings, motions, and other papers may be sent to the Clerk of Circuit Court by electronic facsimile transmission for filing in any case, provided:

   - Such matter does not exceed ten (10) pages, including the cover sheet;

   - Such matter does not require the payment of fees other than the electronic facsimile transcription fee set forth in IN ST ADMIN Rule 12(E);

   - The sending party creates at the time of transmission a machine generated log for such transmission; and

   - The original document and the transmission log are maintained by the sending party for the duration of the litigation. IN ST ADMIN Rule 12(B).

       ii. *Time of filing.* During normal, posted business hours, the time of filing shall be the time the duplicate document is produced in the office of the Clerk of the Circuit Court. Duplicate documents received at all other times shall be filed as of the next normal business day. IN ST ADMIN Rule 12(C).

   - If the receiving fax machine endorses its own time and date stamp upon the transmitted documents and the receiving machine produces a delivery receipt which is electronically created and transmitted to the sending party, the time of filing shall be the date and time recorded on the transmitted document by the receiving fax machine. IN ST ADMIN Rule 12(C).

    c. *Proof of filing.* Any party filing any paper by any method other than personal delivery to the clerk shall retain proof of filing. IN ST TRIAL P Rule 5(F).

2. *Service requirements.* Unless otherwise provided by the Indiana Rules of Trial Procedure or an order of the court, each party and special judge, if any, shall be served with: (1) every order required by its terms to be served; (2) every pleading subsequent to the original complaint; (3) every written motion except one which may be heard ex parte; (4) every brief submitted to the trial court; (5) every paper relating to discovery required to be served upon a party; and (6) every written notice, appearance, demand, offer of judgment, designation of record on appeal, or similar paper. IN ST TRIAL P Rule 5(A).

    a. *Methods of service*

        i. *Personal service.* Whenever a party is represented by an attorney of record, service shall be made upon such attorney unless service upon the party himself is ordered by the court. Service upon the attorney or party shall be made by delivering or mailing a copy of the papers to the last known address or where an attorney or party has consented to service by fax or e-mail, as provided in IN ST TRIAL P Rule 3.1(A)(4), by faxing or e-mailing a copy of the documents to the fax number or e-mail address set out in the appearance form or correction as required by IN ST TRIAL P Rule 3.1(E). IN ST TRIAL P Rule 5(B). Delivery of a copy within IN ST TRIAL P Rule 5 means:

- Offering or tendering it to the attorney or party and stating the nature of the papers being served. Refusal to accept an offered or tendered document is a waiver of any objection to the sufficiency or adequacy of service of that document;

- Leaving it at his office with a clerk or other person in charge thereof, or if there is no one in charge, leaving it in a conspicuous place therein; or

- If the office is closed, by leaving it at his dwelling house or usual place of abode with some person of suitable age and discretion then residing therein; or,

- Leaving it at some other suitable place, selected by the attorney upon whom service is being made, pursuant to duly promulgated local rule. IN ST TRIAL P Rule 5(B)(1).

        ii. *Service by mail.* If service is made by mail, the papers shall be deposited in the United States mail addressed to the person on whom they are being served, with postage prepaid. Service shall be deemed complete upon mailing. Proof of service of all papers permitted to be mailed may be made by written acknowledgment of service, by affidavit of the person who mailed the papers, or by certificate of an attorney. It shall be the duty of attorneys when entering their appearance in a cause or when filing pleadings or papers therein, to have noted in the Chronological Case Summary or said pleadings or papers so filed the address and telephone number of their office. Service by delivery or by mail at such address shall be deemed sufficient and complete. IN ST TRIAL P Rule 5(B)(2).

        iii. *Service by fax or e-mail.* A party who has consented to service by fax or e-mail may be served as follows:

- Service by e-mail shall be made by attaching the document being served in .pdf format. Discovery documents must also be served in accordance with IN ST TRIAL P Rule 26(A). IN ST TRIAL P Rule 5(B)(3)(a).

- Service by fax shall be deemed complete upon generation of a transmission record indicating the successful transmission of the entire document, except as provided in IN ST TRIAL P Rule 5(B)(3)(d). IN ST TRIAL P Rule 5(B)(3)(b).

- Service by e-mail shall be deemed complete upon transmission, except as provided in IN ST TRIAL P Rule 5(B)(3)(d). IN ST TRIAL P Rule 5(B)(3)(c).

- Service by fax or e-mail that occurs on a Saturday, Sunday, legal holiday, or day the court or agency in which the matter is pending is closed or after 5:00 PM local time of the recipient shall be deemed complete the next day that is not a Saturday, Sunday, legal holiday, or day that the court or agency in which the matter is pending is not closed. IN ST TRIAL P Rule 5(B)(3)(d).

       iv.   *Consent to alternate service.* Any Allen County Attorney or any Allen County law firm may, without charge, maintain an assigned Courthouse box in the library of the Allen County Courthouse for receipt of notices, pleadings, process orders, or other communications from the Court, the Clerk, and other attorneys or law firms. IN ST ALLEN SUPER AND CIR CT CIV Rule 5-1(A). For more information concerning the use of courthouse boxes, refer to IN ST ALLEN SUPER AND CIR CT CIV Rule 5-1.

    b. *Serving numerous defendants.* In any action in which there are unusually large numbers of defendants, the court, upon motion or of its own initiative, may order:

       i.   That service of the pleadings of the defendants and replies thereto need not be made as between the defendants;

- That any cross-claim, counterclaim, or matter constituting an avoidance or affirmative defense contained therein shall be deemed to be denied or avoided by all other parties; and

- That the filing of any such pleading and service thereof upon the plaintiff constitutes due notice of it to the parties. IN ST TRIAL P Rule 5(D).

       ii. A copy of every such order shall be served upon the parties in such manner and form as the court directs. IN ST TRIAL P Rule 5(D).

    c. *Service on parties in default for failure to appear.* No service need be made on parties in default for failure to appear, except that pleadings asserting new or additional claims for relief against them shall be served upon them in the manner provided by service of summons in IN ST TRIAL P Rule 4. IN ST TRIAL P Rule 5(A).

    d. *Proof of service.* Certificates of service or proof of mailing of pleadings concerning any case shall be deemed sufficient proof of service if such pleadings were mailed to the last known address of a party or attorney noted upon the chronological case summary of a case. IN ST ALLEN SUPER AND CIR CT CIV Rule 3.1-1(E).

3. *Service requirements if adding a new party by amendment.* Refer to the Indiana KeyRules Complaint document for information on serving a new party added by amendment.

G. Hearings

1. The Indiana rules do not contemplate a hearing regarding the filing and service of an amended complaint.

H. Forms

1. Official Amended Complaint Forms for Indiana

    a. Affidavit of debt. IN ST TRIAL P App. A-2.

2. Amended Complaint Forms for Indiana

    a. Motion to file amended complaint. 5 INPRAC § 3:5.1.

    b. Motion to file amended complaint; Another form. 5 INPRAC § 3:5.2.

    c. Objections to motion to file amended complaint. 5 INPRAC § 3:5.3.

    d. Motion to amend pleading to conform to evidence. 5 INPRAC § 3:5.4.

    e. Amendment by stipulation. 10 INPRAC § 46.11.

    f. Caption; Generally. 5 INPRAC § 3:1.1.

    g. Caption; Multiple parties. 5 INPRAC § 3:1.2.

    h. Single count. 5 INPRAC § 3:1.3.

    i. Multiple counts; Single defendant. 5 INPRAC § 3:1.4.

    j. Multiple counts; Multiple defendants. 5 INPRAC § 3:1.5.

    k. Signature; By party. 5 INPRAC § 3:1.6.

    l. Signature; By attorney. 5 INPRAC § 3:1.7.

    m. Verification. 5 INPRAC § 3:1.8.

n. Individual defendant. 5 INPRAC § 3:2.1.

o. Resident agent of corporation. 5 INPRAC § 3:2.2.

p. Attorney general. 5 INPRAC § 3:2.3.

q. City attorney. 5 INPRAC § 3:2.4.

r. Certificate; Personal service. 5 INPRAC § 3:2.5.

s. Certificate; First class mail. 5 INPRAC § 3:2.6.

t. Certificate; Registered mail. 5 INPRAC § 3:2.7.

u. Certificate; Dwelling house. 5 INPRAC § 3:2.8.

v. Clerk's certificate of mailing. 5 INPRAC § 3:2.9.

w. Clerk's certificate of mailing; Acceptance by defendant. 5 INPRAC § 3:2.10.

x. Clerk's return on service of summons by mail; Not accepted by defendant. 5 INPRAC § 3:2.11.

y. Sheriff's return; Service of summons. 5 INPRAC § 3:2.12.

z. Motion to appoint person to serve process. 5 INPRAC § 3:2.13.

3. Official Amended Complaint Forms for Allen County

a. Consent to alternate service. IN ST ALLEN SUPER AND CIR CT CIV App. A.

I. Checklist

(I) ❏ Matters to be considered by the party filing the amended complaint

(a) ❏ Required documents if amending as matter of course

(1) ❏ Amended complaint

(2) ❏ Certificate of service

(b) ❏ Supplemental documents

(1) ❏ Proof of written instrument

(2) ❏ Notice of intent to use foreign law

(3) ❏ Facsimile cover sheet

(c) ❏ Timing

(1) ❏ As a matter of course before a responsive pleading is served, or, if the pleading is one to which no responsive pleading is permitted, within thirty (30) days after it is served

(2) ❏ At any time with leave of court

Pleadings
Answer

Document Last Updated October 2013

A. Applicable Rules

1. *State rules*

a. Appearance. IN ST TRIAL P Rule 3.1.

b. Process. IN ST TRIAL P Rule 4.

c. Service. IN ST TRIAL P Rule 4.15; IN ST TRIAL P Rule 4.16; IN ST TRIAL P Rule 5.

d. Time. IN ST TRIAL P Rule 6.

e. Pleadings. IN ST TRIAL P Rule 7; IN ST TRIAL P Rule 8; IN ST TRIAL P Rule 9; IN ST TRIAL P Rule 9.1; IN ST TRIAL P Rule 9.2; IN ST TRIAL P Rule 10.

f. Signing and verification of pleadings. IN ST TRIAL P Rule 11.

g. Defenses and objections; When and how presented; By pleading or motion; Motion for judgment on the pleadings. IN ST TRIAL P Rule 12.

h. Counterclaim and cross-claim. IN ST TRIAL P Rule 13.

i. Third-party practice. IN ST TRIAL P Rule 14.

j. Amended and supplemental pleadings. IN ST TRIAL P Rule 15.

k. Parties plaintiff and defendant; Capacity. IN ST TRIAL P Rule 17.

l. Joinder. IN ST TRIAL P Rule 19; IN ST TRIAL P Rule 20.

m. Jury trial of right. IN ST TRIAL P Rule 38.

n. Consolidation; Separate trials. IN ST TRIAL P Rule 42.

o. Evidence. IN ST TRIAL P Rule 43.

p. Determination of foreign law. IN ST TRIAL P Rule 44.1.

q. Judgment. IN ST TRIAL P Rule 50; IN ST TRIAL P Rule 52; IN ST TRIAL P Rule 54; IN ST TRIAL P Rule 56; IN ST TRIAL P Rule 59; IN ST TRIAL P Rule 60.

r. Venue requirements. IN ST TRIAL P Rule 75.

s. Alternative dispute resolution. IN ST ADR Rule 1.1; IN ST ADR Rule 1.6; IN ST ADR Rule 8.8.

t. Uniform case numbering system. IN ST ADMIN Rule 8.

u. Access to court records. IN ST ADMIN Rule 9.

v. Paper size. IN ST ADMIN Rule 11.

w. Facsimile transmission. IN ST ADMIN Rule 12.

x. Electronic filing and electronic service pilot projects. IN ST ADMIN Rule 16.

y. Privacy and confidentiality. IN ST 5-2-9-6; IN ST 5-14-3-4; IN ST 5-14-3-5.5; IN ST 6-4.1-5-10; IN ST 6-4.1-12-12; IN ST 6-8.1-7-1; IN ST 11-13-1-8; IN ST 12-23-14-13; IN ST 16-39-3-10; IN ST 16-41-8-1; IN ST 22-4-19-6; IN ST 31-11-1-6; IN ST 31-19-5-23; IN ST 31-19-13-2; IN ST 31-19-19-1; IN ST 31-33-18-1; IN ST 31-39-1-1; IN ST 31-39-1-2; IN ST 33-23-16-16; IN ST 35-34-2-4; IN ST 35-38-1-13; IN ST 35-38-9-1; IN ST ADR Rule 2.11; IN ST ADR Rule 4.4; IN ST ADR Rule 5.6; IN ST JURY Rule 10.

2. *Local rules*

a. Applicability and citation of rules. IN ST ALLEN SUPER AND CIR CT CIV Rule AR00-1.

b. Appearances. IN ST ALLEN SUPER AND CIR CT CIV Rule 3.1-1.

c. Consent to alternate service. IN ST ALLEN SUPER AND CIR CT CIV Rule 5-1.

d. Preparation of pleadings. IN ST ALLEN SUPER AND CIR CT CIV Rule 8-1.

e. Filing. IN ST ALLEN SUPER AND CIR CT CIV Rule 77-1.

B. Timing

1. *Time to serve answer.* A responsive pleading required under the Indiana Rules of Trial Procedure, shall be served within twenty (20) days after service of the prior pleading. IN ST TRIAL P Rule 6(C).

a. *Effect of IN ST TRIAL P Rule 12 motions.* The service of a motion permitted under IN ST TRIAL P Rule 12 alters the time for service of responsive pleadings as follows, unless a different time is fixed by the court:

i. If the court does not grant the motion, the responsive pleading shall be served in ten (10) days after notice of the court's action;

ii. If the court grants the motion and the corrective action is allowed to be taken, it shall be taken within ten (10) days, and the responsive pleading shall be served within ten (10) days thereafter. IN ST TRIAL P Rule 6(C).

2. *Responding to amended complaint.* A party shall plead in response to an amended pleading within the

time remaining for response to the original pleading or within twenty (20) days after service of the amended pleading, whichever period may be the longer, unless the court otherwise orders. IN ST TRIAL P Rule 15(A).

3. *Filing.* All pleadings and papers subsequent to the complaint which are required to be served upon a party shall be filed with the Court either before service or within a reasonable period of time thereafter. IN ST TRIAL P Rule 5(E)(1).

4. *Filing of third-party complaint.* The third-party plaintiff must file the third-party complaint with his original answer or by leave of court thereafter with good cause shown. IN ST TRIAL P Rule 14(A).

5. *Computation of time*

    a. *Generally; Days excluded.* In computing any period of time prescribed or allowed by the Indiana Rules of Trial Procedure, by order of the court, or by any applicable statute, the day of the act, event, or default from which the designated period of time begins to run shall not be included. The last day of the period so computed is to be included unless it is:

        i. A Saturday,

        ii. A Sunday,

        iii. A legal holiday as defined by state statute, or

        iv. A day the office in which the act is to be done is closed during regular business hours. IN ST TRIAL P Rule 6(A).

    b. *Short periods.* In any event, the period runs until the end of the next day that is not a Saturday, a Sunday, a legal holiday, or a day on which the office is closed. When the period of time allowed is less than seven (7) days, intermediate Saturdays, Sundays, legal holidays, and days on which the office is closed shall be excluded from the computations. IN ST TRIAL P Rule 6(A).

    c. *Additional time after service by United States mail.* Whenever a party has the right or is required to do some act or take some proceedings within a prescribed period after the service of a notice or other paper upon him and the notice or paper is served upon him by United States mail, three (3) days shall be added to the prescribed period. IN ST TRIAL P Rule 6(E).

    d. *Enlargement of time.* When an act is required or allowed to be done at or within a specific time by the Indiana Rules of Trial Procedure, the court may at any time for cause shown:

        i. Order the period enlarged, with or without motion or notice, if request therefor is made before the expiration of the period originally prescribed or extended by a previous order; or

        ii. Upon motion made after the expiration of the specific period, permit the act to be done where the failure to act was the result of excusable neglect; but, the court may not extend the time for taking any action for judgment on the evidence under IN ST TRIAL P Rule 50(A), amendment of findings and judgment under IN ST TRIAL P Rule 52(B), to correct errors under IN ST TRIAL P Rule 59(C), statement in opposition to motion to correct error under IN ST TRIAL P Rule 59(E), or to obtain relief from final judgment under IN ST TRIAL P Rule 60(B), except to the extent and under the conditions stated in those rules. IN ST TRIAL P Rule 6(B).

C. General Requirements

1. *Pleading, generally*

    a. *Pleadings to be concise.* Each averment of a pleading shall be simple, concise, and direct. No technical forms of pleading or motions are required. All fictions in pleading are abolished. IN ST TRIAL P Rule 8(E)(1).

    b. *Pleading in the alternative.* A pleading may set forth two (2) or more statements of a claim or defense alternatively or hypothetically, either in one (1) count or defense or in separate counts or defenses. When two (2) or more statements are made in the alternative and one (1) of them if made independently would be sufficient, the pleading is not made insufficient by the insufficiency of one or more of the alternative statements. A pleading may also state as many separate claims or defenses as the pleader has regardless of consistency and whether based on legal or equitable grounds. All statements shall be made subject to the obligations set forth in IN ST TRIAL P Rule 11. IN ST TRIAL P Rule 8(E)(2).

c. *Motions and pleadings, joint and several.* All motions and pleadings of any kind addressed to two (2) or more paragraphs of any pleading, or filed by two (2) or more parties, shall be taken and construed as joint, separate, and several motions or pleadings to each of such paragraphs and by and against each of such parties. All motions or pleadings containing two (2) or more subject-matters shall be taken and construed as separate and several as to each subject-matter. All objections to rulings made by two (2) or more parties shall be taken and construed as the joint, separate, and several objections of each of such parties. IN ST TRIAL P Rule 8(E)(3).

   i. A complaint filed by or against two (2) or more plaintiffs shall be taken and construed as joint, separate, and several as to each of said plaintiffs. IN ST TRIAL P Rule 8(E).

d. *Construction of pleadings.* All pleadings shall be so construed as to do substantial justice, lead to disposition on the merits, and avoid litigation of procedural points. IN ST TRIAL P Rule 8(F).

2. *Contents of the answer*

   a. *Defenses which may be raised by answer or motion.* Every defense, in law or fact, to a claim for relief in any pleading, whether a claim, counterclaim, cross-claim, or third-party claim, shall be asserted in the responsive pleading thereto if one is required; except that at the option of the pleader, the following defenses may be made by motion:

      i. Lack of jurisdiction over the subject matter;

      ii. Lack of jurisdiction over the person;

      iii. Incorrect venue under IN ST TRIAL P Rule 75, or any statutory provision. The disposition of this motion shall be consistent with IN ST TRIAL P Rule 75;

      iv. Insufficiency of process;

      v. Insufficiency of service of process;

      vi. Failure to state a claim upon which relief can be granted, which shall include failure to name the real party in interest under IN ST TRIAL P Rule 17;

      vii. Failure to join a party needed for just adjudication under IN ST TRIAL P Rule 19;

      viii. The same action pending in another state court of this state. IN ST TRIAL P Rule 12(B).

      ix. A motion making any of these defenses shall be made before pleading if a further pleading is permitted or within twenty (20) days after service of the prior pleading if none is required. If a pleading sets forth a claim for relief to which the adverse party is not required to serve a responsive pleading, any of the defenses in section IN ST TRIAL P Rule 12(B)(2), IN ST TRIAL P Rule 12(B)(3), IN ST TRIAL P Rule 12(B)(4), IN ST TRIAL P Rule 12(B)(5) or IN ST TRIAL P Rule 12(B)(8) is waived to the extent constitutionally permissible unless made in a motion within twenty (20) days after service of the prior pleading. No defense or objection is waived by being joined with one (1) or more other defenses or objections in a responsive pleading or motion. IN ST TRIAL P Rule 12(B).

   b. *Waiver or preservation of certain defenses*

      i. A defense of lack of jurisdiction over the person, improper venue, insufficiency of process, insufficiency of service of process, or the same action pending in another state court of this state is waived to the extent constitutionally permissible:

         • If omitted from a motion in the circumstances described in IN ST TRIAL P Rule 12(G),

         • If it is neither made by motion under IN ST TRIAL P Rule 12 nor included in a responsive pleading or an amendment thereof permitted by IN ST TRIAL P Rule 15(A) to be made as a matter of course. IN ST TRIAL P Rule 12(H)(1).

      ii. A defense of failure to state a claim upon which relief can be granted, a defense of failure to join an indispensable party under IN ST TRIAL P Rule 19(B), and an objection of failure to state a legal defense to a claim may be made in any pleading permitted or ordered under IN ST TRIAL P Rule 7(A) or by motion for judgment on the pleadings, or at the trial on the merits. IN ST TRIAL P Rule 12(H)(2).

c. *Defenses; Form of denials*

    i. A responsive pleading shall state in short and plain terms the pleader's defenses to each claim asserted and shall admit or controvert the averments set forth in the preceding pleading. If in good faith the pleader intends to deny all the averments in the preceding pleading, he may do so by general denial subject to the provisions of IN ST TRIAL P Rule 11. If he does not intend a general denial, he may:

        • Specifically deny designated averments or paragraphs; or

        • Generally deny all averments except such designated averments and paragraphs as he expressly admits. IN ST TRIAL P Rule 8(B).

    ii. If he lacks knowledge or information sufficient to form a belief as to the truth of an averment, he shall so state and his statement shall be considered a denial. If in good faith a pleader intends to deny only a part or a qualification of an averment, he shall specify so much of it as is true and material and deny the remainder. All denials shall fairly meet the substance of the averments denied. IN ST TRIAL P Rule 8 shall have no application to uncontested actions for divorce, or to answers required to be filed by clerks or guardians ad litem. IN ST TRIAL P Rule 8(B).

d. *Affirmative defenses.* A responsive pleading shall set forth affirmatively and carry the burden of proving: accord and satisfaction, arbitration and award, discharge in bankruptcy, duress, estoppel, failure of consideration, fraud, illegality, injury by fellow servant, laches, license, payment, release, res judicata, statute of frauds, statute of limitations, waiver, lack of jurisdiction over the subject-matter, lack of jurisdiction over the person, improper venue, insufficiency of process or service of process, the same action pending in another state court of this state, and any other matter constituting an avoidance, matter of abatement, or affirmative defense. A party required to affirmatively plead any matters, including matters formerly required to be pleaded affirmatively by reply, shall have the burden of proving such matters. The burden of proof imposed by this or any other provision of the Indiana Rules of Trial Procedure is subject to the rules of evidence or any statute fixing a different rule. If the pleading mistakenly designates a defense as a counterclaim or a counterclaim as a defense, the court shall treat the pleading as if there had been a proper designation. IN ST TRIAL P Rule 8(C).

    i. An affirmative defense, generally, must be affirmatively stated by the party who seeks its benefit. 1A INPRAC R 8(8.5); Rice v. Grant County Bd. of Com'rs, 472 N.E.2d 213 (Ind.Ct.App. 1984). If that party does not raise the affirmative defense, then it is waived. 1A INPRAC R 8(8.5); Piskorowski v. Shell Oil Co., 403 N.E.2d 838, 847 (Ind.Ct.App. 1980).

    ii. It is clear that the list of affirmative defenses found in IN ST TRIAL P Rule 8 is not exhaustive. The question comes: when is a defense to be treated as an affirmative defense, with all of the attending consequences? 1A INPRAC R 8(8.5). The "determination of whether a defense is affirmative depends on whether it controverts an element of the plaintiff's prima facie case or raises matter outside the scope of the prima facie case." 1A INPRAC R 8(8.5); Molargik v. West Enterprises, Inc., 605 N.E.2d 1197, 1198 (Ind.Ct.App. 1993).

e. *Defense of contributory negligence or assumed risk.* In all claims alleging negligence, the burden of pleading and proving contributory negligence, assumption of risk, or incurred risk shall be upon the defendant who may plead such by denial of the allegation. IN ST TRIAL P Rule 9.1(A).

f. *Res ipsa loquitur.* Res ipsa loquitur or a similar doctrine may be pleaded by alleging generally that the facts connected with the action are unknown to the pleader and are within the knowledge of the opposing party. IN ST TRIAL P Rule 9.1(B).

g. *Consideration.* When an action or defense is founded upon a written contract or release, lack of consideration for the promise or release is an affirmative defense, and the party asserting lack of it carries the burden of proof. IN ST TRIAL P Rule 9.1(C).

h. *Bona fide purchaser.* When the rights of a person depend upon his status as a bona fide purchaser for value or upon similar requirements, such status must be pleaded and proved by the person asserting it, but it may be pleaded in general terms. Once it is established that the person has given any required value, unless such value is commercially unreasonable, and that he has met any requirements of recordation, filing, possession, or perfection, the trier of fact must find that such value was given or such perfection was made in accordance with any requirements of good faith, lack of knowledge, or lack of notice unless and until evidence is introduced which would support a finding of its non-existence. IN ST TRIAL P Rule 9.1(D).

i. *Presumption; Matters of judicial notice.* Neither presumptions of law nor matters of which judicial notice may be taken need be stated in a pleading. IN ST TRIAL P Rule 9.1(E).

j. *Property distrained; Sufficient answer.* In an action to recover the possession of property distrained while doing damage, an answer that the defendant, or person by whose command he acted, was lawfully possessed of the real property upon which the distress was made, and that the property distrained was at the time doing damage thereon, shall be good without setting forth the title of such real property. IN ST TRIAL P Rule 9.1(F).

k. *Effect of failure to deny.* Averments in a pleading to which a responsive pleading is required, except those pertaining to amount of damages, are admitted when not denied in the responsive pleading. Averments in a pleading to which no responsive pleading is required or permitted shall be taken as denied or avoided. IN ST TRIAL P Rule 8(D).

l. *Effect of admission.* When a rhetorical paragraph or allegation is admitted, the effect in Indiana is to remove it from trial. Such an admission is a "judicial admission", and the claim or issue which is admitted cannot be denied later by the trier of the facts. Further, this admitted fact does not require evidence to "prove it"; it is established. It becomes, in short, controlling and indisputable in the litigation, unless the trial court permits an amendment to the pleading which might remove the controlling effect of the admission, and permit it to become another fact or item of evidence in the case. 1A INPRAC R 8(8.4); Aylesworth v. McKesson, 421 N.E.2d 422 (Ind.Ct.App. 1981).

3. *Pleading special matters*

a. *Capacity.* It is not necessary to aver the capacity of a party to sue or be sued, the authority of a party to sue or be sued in a representative capacity, or the legal existence of an organization that is made a party. The burden of proving lack of such capacity, authority, or legal existence shall be upon the person asserting lack of it, and shall be pleaded as an affirmative defense. IN ST TRIAL P Rule 9(A).

b. *Fraud, mistake, condition of the mind.* In all averments of fraud or mistake, the circumstances constituting fraud or mistake shall be specifically averred. Malice, intent, knowledge, and other conditions of mind may be averred generally. IN ST TRIAL P Rule 9(B).

c. *Conditions precedent.* In pleading the performance or occurrence of promissory or non-promissory conditions precedent, it is sufficient to aver generally that all conditions precedent have been performed, have occurred, or have been excused. A denial of performance or occurrence shall be made specifically and with particularity, and a denial of excuse generally. IN ST TRIAL P Rule 9(C).

d. *Official document or act.* In pleading an official document or official act it is sufficient to aver that the document was issued or the act done in compliance with law. IN ST TRIAL P Rule 9(D).

e. *Judgment.* In pleading a judgment or decision of a domestic or foreign court, judicial or quasi-judicial tribunal, or of a board or officer, it is sufficient to aver the judgment or decision without setting forth matter showing jurisdiction to render it. IN ST TRIAL P Rule 9(E).

f. *Time and place.* For the purpose of testing the sufficiency of a pleading, averments of time and place are material and shall be considered like all other averments of material matter. However, time and place need be stated only with such specificity as will enable the opposing party to prepare his defense. IN ST TRIAL P Rule 9(F).

g. *Special damages; Damages where no answer.* When items of special damage are claimed, they shall be specifically stated. The relief granted to the plaintiff, if there be no answer, cannot exceed the relief demanded in his complaint; but, in any other case, the court may grant him any relief consistent with the facts or matters pleaded. IN ST TRIAL P Rule 9(G).

4. *Counterclaim and cross-claim*

a. *Compulsory counterclaims.* A pleading shall state as a counterclaim any claim which at the time of serving the pleading the pleader has against any opposing party, if it arises out of the transaction or occurrence that is the subject-matter of the opposing party's claim and does not require for its adjudication the presence of third parties of whom the court cannot acquire jurisdiction. But the pleader need not state the claim if:

    i.   At the time the action was commenced the claim was the subject of another pending action; or

    ii.   The opposing party brought suit upon his claim by attachment or other process by which the court did not acquire jurisdiction to render a personal judgment on that claim, and the pleader is not stating any counterclaim under IN ST TRIAL P Rule 13. IN ST TRIAL P Rule 13(A).

b.   *Permissive counterclaims.* A pleading may state as a counterclaim any claim against an opposing party not arising out of the transaction or occurrence that is the subject-matter of the opposing party's claim. IN ST TRIAL P Rule 13(B).

c.   *Counterclaim exceeding opposing claim.* A counterclaim may or may not diminish or defeat the recovery sought by the opposing party. It may claim relief exceeding in amount or different in kind from that sought in the pleading of the opposing party. IN ST TRIAL P Rule 13(C).

d.   *Counterclaim against state.* IN ST TRIAL P Rule 13 shall not be construed to enlarge any right to assert a claim against the state. IN ST TRIAL P Rule 13(D).

e.   *Counterclaim maturing or acquired after pleading.* A claim which either matured or was acquired by the pleader after serving his pleading may, with the permission of the court, be presented as a counterclaim by supplemental pleading. A counterclaim or cross-claim which is not due may be asserted against a party who is insolvent or the representative of a party who has been subjected to insolvency proceedings, if recovery thereon will be impaired because of such party's insolvency. IN ST TRIAL P Rule 13(E).

f.   *Omitted counterclaim.* When a pleader fails to set up a counterclaim through oversight, inadvertence, or excusable neglect, or when justice requires, he may by leave of court set up the counterclaim by amendment. IN ST TRIAL P Rule 13(F).

g.   *Cross-claim against co-party.* A pleading may state as a cross-claim any claim by one party against a co-party. IN ST TRIAL P Rule 13(G).

h.   *Joinder of additional parties.* Persons other than those made parties to the original action may be made parties to a counterclaim or cross-claim in accordance with the provisions of IN ST TRIAL P Rule 14, IN ST TRIAL P Rule 19 and IN ST TRIAL P Rule 20. IN ST TRIAL P Rule 13(H).

i.   *Separate trials; Separate judgments*

    i.   If the court orders separate trials as provided in IN ST TRIAL P Rule 42(B), judgment on a counterclaim or cross-claim may be rendered in accordance with the terms of IN ST TRIAL P Rule 54(B) when the court has jurisdiction so to do, even if the claims of the opposing party have been dismissed or otherwise disposed of. In determining whether or not separate trial of a cross-claim shall be ordered, the court shall consider whether the cross-claim:

- Arises out of the transaction or occurrence or series of transactions or occurrences that is the subject-matter either of the original action or of a counterclaim therein;

- Relates to any property or contract that is the subject-matter of the original action; or

- Claims that the person against whom it is asserted is liable to the cross-claimant for all or part of plaintiff's claim against him. IN ST TRIAL P Rule 13(I).

    ii.   In addition, the court may consider any other relevant factors. IN ST TRIAL P Rule 13(I).

j.   *Effect of statute of limitations and other discharges at law.* The statute of limitations, a nonclaim statute or other discharge at law shall not bar a claim asserted as a counterclaim to the extent that:

    i.   It diminishes or defeats the opposing party's claim if it arises out of the transaction or occurrence that is the subject-matter of the opposing party's claim, or if it could have been asserted as a counterclaim to the opposing party's claim before it (the counterclaim) was barred; or

    ii.   It or the opposing party's claim relates to payment of or security for the other. IN ST TRIAL P Rule 13(J).

k. *Counterclaim by and against transferees and successors.* A counterclaim may be asserted by or against the transferee or successor of a claim subject to the following provisions:

    i.   A successor who is a guardian, representative of a decedent's estate, receiver or assignee for the benefit of creditors, trustee or the like may interpose a claim to which he succeeds against claims or proceedings brought in or outside the court of administration. A claim owing by his predecessor may be interposed against any claim brought by such successor in or outside the court of administration without the necessity of filing such claim or cause of action in the administration proceedings. IN ST TRIAL P Rule 13(K)(1).

    ii.   A transferee or successor of a claim takes it subject to any defense or counterclaim that is the subject-matter of the opposing party's claim; or that is available to the obligor at the time of the assignment or before the obligor received notice of the assignment. IN ST TRIAL P Rule 13(K)(2).

    iii.   A surety or party with total or partial recourse upon a claim upon which he is being sued may interpose as a counterclaim:

- Any claim of his own; and

- Any claim owned by the person against whom he has recourse who either has notice of the suit, is a party to the suit, is insolvent, has assigned his claim to the surety or party asserting it, or cannot be found. IN ST TRIAL P Rule 13(K)(3).

- A counterclaim under IN ST TRIAL P Rule 13(K)(3)(b) must tend to diminish or defeat the opposing party's claim, or it or the opposing claim must relate to payment of or security for the other, unless the person against whom recourse may be had is a party to the suit or the counterclaim has been assigned to the party asserting it; and if recovery on the counterclaim exceeds the opposing party's claim, any excess recovered shall be held in trust for such person against whom there is a right of recourse. IN ST TRIAL P Rule 13(K)(3).

    iv.   IN ST TRIAL P Rule 13(K)(1), IN ST TRIAL P Rule 13(K)(2), and IN ST TRIAL P Rule 13(K)(3), are subject to subdivision IN ST TRIAL P Rule 13(L). IN ST TRIAL P Rule 13(K)(4).

l. *Counterclaim and cross-claim subject to substantive law principles.* Counterclaim and cross-claims are subject to restrictions imposed by other statutes and principles of substantive common law and equity, including rules of commercial law, agency, estoppel, contract and the like. In appropriate cases the court may impose terms or conditions upon its judgment or decree and may enter conditional or noncanceling cross judgments to satisfy such restrictions. This provision is intended to deny or limit counterclaims or cross-claims:

    i.   Where a creditor will receive an unfair priority because a claim is assigned after insolvency proceedings, or assigned before such proceedings if it results in an unlawful preference;

    ii.   Where an unfair priority will be allowed if a surety interposing a claim owned in his own right against the creditor suing on the principal's obligation when the principal is solvent and the creditor is not;

    iii.   Where a claim by or against a representative, such as a guardian, receiver, representative of a decedent's estate, assignee for the benefit of creditors, trustee or the like in his individual capacity is asserted against a claim owing or owed by the estate he represents;

    iv.   Where a claim by or against a partnership or two (2) or more obligors is opposed against or by a claim of an individual to the extent that the individual will be allowed unfairly to profit or if it will adversely affect the rights of creditors; or

    v.   Where a claim is cut off by a holder in due course or a transferee who is protected under principles of commercial law, estoppel, or contract. IN ST TRIAL P Rule 13(L).

m. *Satisfaction of judgment.* Satisfaction of a judgment or credits thereon may be ordered, for sufficient cause, upon notice and motion. "Credits" include any counterclaim which tends to diminish or defeat the judgment, or any counterclaim where it or the opposing claim relates to payment of or security for the other. IN ST TRIAL P Rule 13(M).

5. *Third-party practice*

    a. *When defendant may bring in third party.* A defending party, as a third-party plaintiff, may cause a summons and complaint to be served upon a person not a party to the action who is or may be liable to him for all or part of the plaintiff's claim against him. IN ST TRIAL P Rule 14(A). The person served with the summons and the third-party complaint, hereinafter called the third-party defendant, as provided in IN ST TRIAL P Rule 12 and IN ST TRIAL P Rule 13 may make:

        i. His defenses, cross-claims and counterclaims to the third-party plaintiff's claims;

        ii. His defenses, counterclaims and cross-claims against any other defendants or third-party defendants;

        iii. Any defenses or claims which the third-party plaintiff has to the plaintiff's claim which are available to the third-party defendant against the plaintiff; and

        iv. Any defenses or claims which the third-party defendant has as against the plaintiff. IN ST TRIAL P Rule 14(A).

        v. The plaintiff may assert any claim against the third-party defendant who thereupon may assert his defenses, counterclaims and cross-claims, as provided in IN ST TRIAL P Rule 12 and IN ST TRIAL P Rule 13. A third-party defendant may proceed under IN ST TRIAL P Rule 14 against any person not a party to the action who is or may be liable to him for all or part of the claim made in the action against the third-party defendant. IN ST TRIAL P Rule 14(A).

    b. *When plaintiff may bring in third party.* When a counterclaim or other claim is asserted against a plaintiff, he may cause a third party to be brought in under circumstances, which, under IN ST TRIAL P Rule 14, would entitle a defendant to do so. IN ST TRIAL P Rule 14(B).

    c. *Severance; Parties improperly impleaded.* With his responsive pleading or by motion prior thereto, any party may move for severance of a third-party claim or ensuing claim as provided in IN ST TRIAL P Rule 14 or for a separate trial thereon. If the third-party defendant is a proper party to the proceedings under any other rule relating to parties, the action shall continue as in other cases where he is made a party. IN ST TRIAL P Rule 14(C).

6. *Trial by jury; Demand*

    a. *Causes triable by court and by jury.* Issues of law and issues of fact in causes that prior to the eighteenth day of June, 1852, were of exclusive equitable jurisdiction shall be tried by the court; issues of fact in all other causes shall be triable as the same are now triable. In case of the joinder of causes of action or defenses which, prior to said date, were of exclusive equitable jurisdiction with causes of action or defenses which, prior to said date, were designated as actions at law and triable by jury—the former shall be triable by the court, and the latter by a jury, unless waived; the trial of both may be at the same time or at different times, as the court may direct. IN ST TRIAL P Rule 38(A).

    b. *Demand.* Any party may demand a trial by jury of any issue triable of right by a jury by filing with the court and serving upon the other parties a demand therefor in writing at any time after the commencement of the action and not later than ten (10) days after the first responsive pleading to the complaint, or to a counterclaim, crossclaim or other claim if one properly is pleaded; and if no responsive pleading is filed or required, within ten (10) days after the time such pleading otherwise would have been required. Such demand is sufficient if indorsed upon a pleading of a party filed within such time. IN ST TRIAL P Rule 38(B).

    c. *Same; Specification of issues.* In his demand a party may specify the issues which he wishes so tried; otherwise he shall be deemed to have demanded trial by jury for all issues triable as of right by jury. Any other party must file a demand for jury trial to preserve his right to trial by jury:

        i. Of issues for which a right to trial by jury was not requested by another party; and

        ii. In case a request by another party was improper. But if a proper request for a trial by jury upon issues triable by jury as of right on his behalf is made by any party, such request shall be deemed to have been made on behalf of all parties entitled to a jury trial upon such issues. IN ST TRIAL P Rule 38(C).

d. *Waiver.* The failure of a party to appear at the trial, and the failure of a party to serve a demand as required by IN ST TRIAL P Rule 38 and to file it as required by IN ST TRIAL P Rule 5(E) constitute waiver by him of trial by jury. A demand for trial by jury made as herein provided may not be withdrawn without the consent of the other party or parties. IN ST TRIAL P Rule 38(D).

    i. The trial court shall not grant a demand for a trial by jury filed after the time fixed in IN ST TRIAL P Rule 38(B) has elapsed except upon the written agreement of all of the parties to the action, which agreement shall be filed with the court and made a part of the record. If such agreement is filed then the court may, in its discretion, grant a trial by jury in which event the grant of a trial by jury may not be withdrawn except by the agreement of all of the parties. IN ST TRIAL P Rule 38(D).

e. *Arbitration.* Nothing in the Indiana Rules of Trial Procedure shall deny the parties the right by contract or agreement to submit or to agree to submit controversies to arbitration made before or after commencement of an action thereon or deny the courts power to specifically enforce such agreements. IN ST TRIAL P Rule 38(E).

f. *Equitable and legal claims in multi-count actions.* In multi-count actions, the inclusion of an equitable claim, standing alone, will not automatically draw the entire action into equity. Something more than the presence of an equitable claim is required, and the court must examine the claims at issue. 22B INPRAC 38:1 COMMENT; Lucas v. U.S. Bank, N.A., 953 N.E.2d 457 (Ind. 2011). Factors the court may consider in evaluating the nature of the underlying substantive claims include: the substance and central character of the complaint, the rights and interests at issue, the relief demanded, and any issues arising out of discovery. 22B INPRAC 38:1 COMMENT; Songer v. Civitas Bank, 771 N.E.2d 61 (Ind. 2002).

7. *Use of alternative dispute resolution.* Except as provided by the Indiana Rules for Alternative Dispute Resolution, a presiding judge may order any civil or domestic relations proceeding or selected issues in such proceedings referred to mediation, non-binding arbitration or mini-trial. The selection criteria which should be used by the court are defined under the Indiana Rules for Alternative Dispute Resolution. Binding arbitration and a summary jury trial may be ordered only upon the agreement of the parties as consistent with provisions in the Indiana Rules for Alternative Dispute Resolution which address each method. IN ST ADR Rule 1.6. For information on Indiana's ADR process refer to IN ST ADR Rule 1.1 through IN ST ADR Rule 8.8.

D. Documents

1. *Required documents*

a. *Answer.* Refer to the General Requirements section of this document for information on the contents of an answer.

b. *Appearance form.* At the time the responding party or parties first appears in a case, the attorney representing such party or parties or the party or parties, if not represented by an attorney, shall file an appearance form setting forth the information set out in IN ST TRIAL P Rule 3.1(A). IN ST TRIAL P Rule 3.1(B). The appearance form shall set forth the following information:

    i. Name, address and telephone number of the initiating party or parties filing the appearance form;

    ii. Name, address, attorney number, telephone number, FAX number, and e-mail address of any attorney representing the party, as applicable;

    iii. The case type of the proceeding [IN ST ADMIN Rule 8(B)(3)];

    iv. A statement that the party will or will not accept service by fax or by e-mail from:

        • Other parties and/or

        • The court under IN ST TRIAL P Rule 72(D);

    v. In domestic relations, Uniform Reciprocal Enforcement of Support (URESA), paternity, delinquency, Child in Need of Services (CHINS), guardianship, and any other proceedings in which support may be an issue, the Social Security Identification Number of all family members;

vi.   The caption and case number of all related cases;

vii.   Such additional matters specified by state or local rule required to maintain the information management system employed by the court;

viii.   In a proceeding involving a protection from abuse order, a workplace violence restraining order, or a no-contact order, the initiating party shall provide to the clerk a public mailing address for purposes of legal service. The initiating party may use the Attorney General Address Confidentiality program established by statute; and

ix.   In a proceeding involving a mental health commitment, except seventy-two (72) hour emergency detentions, the initiating party shall provide the full name of the person with respect to whom commitment is sought and the person's state of residence. In addition, the initiating party shall provide at least one of the following identifiers for the person:

- Date of birth;
- Social Security Number;
- Driver's license number with state of issue and date of expiration;
- Department of Correction number;
- State ID number with state of issue and date of expiration; or
- FBI number. IN ST TRIAL P Rule 3.1(A); IN ST ALLEN SUPER AND CIR CT CIV Rule 3.1-1(A).

c.   *Certificate of service.* An attorney or unrepresented party tendering a document to the Clerk for filing shall certify that service has been made, list the parties served, and specify the date and means of service. The certificate of service shall be placed at the end of the document and shall not be separately filed. The separate filing of a certificate of service, however, shall not be grounds for rejecting a document for filing. The Clerk may permit documents to be filed without a certificate of service but shall require prompt filing of a separate certificate of service. IN ST TRIAL P Rule 5(C).

2.   *Supplemental documents*

a.   *Admission of service.* A written admission stating the date and place of service, signed by the person being served, may be filed with the clerk who shall file it with the pleadings. Such admission shall become a part of the record, constitute evidence of proper service, and shall be allowed as evidence in any action or proceeding. IN ST TRIAL P Rule 4.15(D).

i.   It shall be the duty of every person being served under the Indiana Rules of Trial Procedure to cooperate, accept service, comply with the provisions of the Indiana Rules of Trial Procedure, and, when service is made upon him personally, acknowledge receipt of the papers in writing over his signature. IN ST TRIAL P Rule 4.16(A).

- Offering or tendering the papers to the person being served and advising the person that he or she is being served is adequate service. IN ST TRIAL P Rule 4.16(A)(1).

- A person who has refused to accept the offer or tender of the papers being served thereafter may not challenge the service of those papers. IN ST TRIAL P Rule 4.16(A)(2).

b.   *Proof of written instrument.* When any pleading allowed by the Indiana Rules of Trial Procedure is founded on a written instrument, the original, or a copy thereof, must be included in or filed with the pleading. Such instrument, whether copied in the pleadings or not, shall be taken as part of the record. When any pleading allowed by the Indiana Rules of Trial Procedure is founded on an account, an Affidavit of Debt, in a form substantially similar to that which is provided in IN ST TRIAL P App. A-2, shall be attached. IN ST TRIAL P Rule 9.2(A).

c.   *Notice of intent to use foreign law.* A party who intends to raise an issue concerning the law of a foreign country shall give notice in his pleadings or other reasonable written notice. The court, in determining foreign law, may consider any relevant material or source, including testimony, whether or not submitted by a party or admissible under IN ST TRIAL P Rule 43. The court's determination shall be treated as a ruling on a question of law. It shall be made by the court and not the jury and shall be reviewable. IN ST TRIAL P Rule 44.1(A).

d. *Facsimile cover sheet.* Any document sent to the Clerk of the Circuit Court by electronic facsimile transmission shall be accompanied by a cover sheet which states the title of the document, case number, number of pages, identity and voice telephone number of the sending party and instructions for filing. The cover sheet shall contain the signature of the attorney or party, pro se, authorizing the filing. IN ST ADMIN Rule 12(D).

E. Format

1. *Form of pleadings*

   a. *Caption; Names of parties.* Every pleading shall contain a caption setting forth the name of the court, the title of the action, the file number, and a designation as in IN ST TRIAL P Rule 7(A). In the complaint the title of the action shall include the names of all the parties, but in other pleadings it is sufficient to state the name of the first party on each side with an appropriate indication of other parties. IN ST TRIAL P Rule 10(A).

   b. *Paragraphs; Separate statements.* All averments of a claim or defense shall be made in numbered paragraphs, the contents of each of which shall be limited as far as practicable to a statement of a single set of circumstances, and a paragraph may be referred to by number in all succeeding pleadings. Each claim founded upon a separate transaction or occurrence and each defense other than denials may be stated in a separate count or defense whenever a separation facilitates the clear presentation of the matters set forth. IN ST TRIAL P Rule 10(B).

   c. *Adoption by reference; Exhibits.* Statements in a pleading may be adopted by reference in a different part of the same pleading or in another pleading or in any motion. A copy of any written instrument which is an exhibit to a pleading is a part thereof for all purposes. IN ST TRIAL P Rule 10(C).

   d. *Citation.* Allen County Superior and Circuit court rules may be cited as L.R. _____. The Indiana Rules of Trial Procedure are hereinafter referred to as T.R. _____. IN ST ALLEN SUPER AND CIR CT CIV Rule AR00-1(B).

   e. *Paper.* All pleadings must be printed on white paper. IN ST ALLEN SUPER AND CIR CT CIV Rule 8-1(A).

   f. *Spacing.* The lines shall be double spaced except for quotations, which shall be indented and single-spaced. IN ST ALLEN SUPER AND CIR CT CIV Rule 8-1(A).

   g. *Photocopies.* Photocopies are acceptable if legible. IN ST ALLEN SUPER AND CIR CT CIV Rule 8-1(A).

   h. *Margins and binding.* Margins shall be one to one and one-half (1-1 1/2) inches on the left side and one-half (1/2) inch on the right. IN ST ALLEN SUPER AND CIR CT CIV Rule 8-1(B).

      i. Binding or stapling shall be at the top left and at no other place. IN ST ALLEN SUPER AND CIR CT CIV Rule 8-1(B).

      ii. Covers or backing shall not be used. IN ST ALLEN SUPER AND CIR CT CIV Rule 8-1(B).

   i. *Flat filing.* The files of the Clerk of the Court shall be kept under the "flat filing" system. All pleadings presented for filing with the Clerk or Court shall be flat and unfolded. Only the original of any pleading shall be placed in the Court file. IN ST ALLEN SUPER AND CIR CT CIV Rule 77-1(A).

   j. *Handwritten pleadings.* Handwritten pleadings may be accepted for filing in the discretion of the Court. IN ST ALLEN SUPER AND CIR CT CIV Rule 8-1(A).

2. *Size of papers for filing.* Effective January 1, 1992, all pleadings, copies, motions and documents filed with any trial court or appellate level court, typed or printed, with the exception of exhibits and existing wills, shall be prepared on eight and one-half by eleven inch (8 1/2" x 11") size paper. IN ST ADMIN Rule 11.

3. *Signature requirements*

   a. *Signature of attorney.* Every pleading or motion of a party represented by an attorney shall be signed by at least one (1) attorney of record in his individual name, whose address, telephone number, and attorney number shall be stated, except that this provision shall not apply to pleadings and motions

made and transcribed at the trial or a hearing before the judge and received by him in such form. IN ST TRIAL P Rule 11(A). All pleadings to be signed by an attorney shall contain the written signature of the individual attorney, the attorney's printed name, Supreme Court Attorney Number, the name of the attorney's law firm, the attorney's address, telephone number, and a designation of the party for whom the attorney appears. IN ST ALLEN SUPER AND CIR CT CIV Rule 8-1(C). For the recommended signature format, refer to IN ST ALLEN SUPER AND CIR CT CIV Rule 8-1(C).

    i. The signature of an attorney constitutes a certificate by him that he has read the pleadings; that to the best of his knowledge, information, and belief, there is good ground to support it; and that it is not interposed for delay. IN ST TRIAL P Rule 11(A).

    ii. If a pleading or motion is not signed or is signed with intent to defeat the purpose of the rule, it may be stricken as sham and false and the action may proceed as though the pleading had not been served. IN ST TRIAL P Rule 11(A).

    iii. For a willful violation of IN ST TRIAL P Rule 11 an attorney may be subjected to appropriate disciplinary action. Similar action may be taken if scandalous or indecent matter is inserted. IN ST TRIAL P Rule 11(A).

    iv. Neither printed signatures, nor facsimile signatures shall be accepted on original documents. IN ST ALLEN SUPER AND CIR CT CIV Rule 8-1(C).

    v. Facsimile signatures are permitted on copies. IN ST ALLEN SUPER AND CIR CT CIV Rule 8-1(C).

b. *Signature of unrepresented party.* A party who is not represented by an attorney shall sign his pleading and state his address. IN ST TRIAL P Rule 11(A).

c. *Verification not generally required.* Except when specifically required by rule, pleadings or motions need not be verified or accompanied by affidavit. The rule in equity that the averments of an answer under oath must be overcome by the testimony of two (2) witnesses or of one (1) witness sustained by corroborating circumstances is abolished. IN ST TRIAL P Rule 11(A).

d. *Verification by affirmation or representation.* When in connection with any civil or special statutory proceeding it is required that any pleading, motion, petition, supporting affidavit, or other document of any kind, be verified, or that an oath be taken, it shall be sufficient if the subscriber simply affirms the truth of the matter to be verified by an affirmation or representation. IN ST TRIAL P Rule 11(B). IN ST TRIAL P Rule 11(B) states that the affirmation or representation should be in substantially the following language: "I (we) affirm, under the penalties for perjury, that the foregoing representation(s) is (are) true. (Signed) _____."

    i. Any person who falsifies an affirmation or representation of fact shall be subject to the same penalties as are prescribed by law for the making of a false affidavit. IN ST TRIAL P Rule 11(B).

e. *Verified pleadings, motions, and affidavits as evidence.* Pleadings, motions and affidavits accompanying or in support of such pleadings or motions when required to be verified or under oath shall be accepted as a representation that the signer had personal knowledge thereof or reasonable cause to believe the existence of the facts or matters stated or alleged therein; and, if otherwise competent or acceptable as evidence, may be admitted as evidence of the facts or matters stated or alleged therein when it is so provided in the Indiana Rules of Trial Procedure, by statute or other law, or to the extent the writing or signature expressly purports to be made upon the signer's personal knowledge. When such pleadings, motions and affidavits are verified or under oath they shall not require other or greater proof on the part of the adverse party than if not verified or not under oath unless expressly provided otherwise by the Indiana Rules of Trial Procedure, statute or other law. Affidavits upon motions for summary judgment under IN ST TRIAL P Rule 56 and in denial of execution under IN ST TRIAL P Rule 9.2 shall be made upon personal knowledge. IN ST TRIAL P Rule 11(C).

4. *Information excluded from public access.* Every document filed in a case shall separately identify information excluded from public access pursuant to IN ST ADMIN Rule 9(G)(1) as follows:

a. Whole documents that are excluded from public access pursuant to IN ST ADMIN Rule 9(G)(1) shall be tendered on light green paper or have a light green coversheet attached to the document, marked "Not for Public Access" or "Confidential." IN ST TRIAL P Rule 5(G)(1).

b. When only a portion of a document contains information excluded from public access pursuant to IN ST ADMIN Rule 9(G)(1), said information shall be omitted [or redacted] from the filed document, and set forth on a separate accompanying document on light green paper conspicuously marked "Not for Public Access" or "Confidential" and clearly designated [or identifying] the caption and number of the case and the document and location within the document to which the redacted material pertains. IN ST TRIAL P Rule 5(G)(2).

c. With respect to documents filed in electronic format, the trial court, by local rule, may provide for compliance with IN ST TRIAL P Rule 5 in manner that separates and protects access to information excluded from public access. IN ST TRIAL P Rule 5(G)(3).

d. IN ST TRIAL P Rule 5(G) does not apply to a record sealed by the court pursuant to IN ST 5-14-3-5.5 or otherwise, nor to records, documents, or information filed in cases to which public access is prohibited pursuant to IN ST ADMIN Rule 9(G). IN ST TRIAL P Rule 5(G)(4).

e. The following information in case records is excluded from public access and is confidential:

  i. Information that is excluded from public access pursuant to federal law;

  ii. Information that is excluded from public access as declared confidential by Indiana statute or other court rule, including without limitation:

  - All adoption records created after July 8, 1941, as declared confidential by IN ST 31-19-19-1, et seq., except those specifically declared open by IN ST 31-19-13-2(2);

  - All records relating to chancroid, chlamydia, gonorrhea, hepatitis, human immunodeficiency virus (HIV), Lymphogranuloma venereum, syphilis, tuberculosis, as declared confidential by IN ST 16-41-8-1, et seq.;

  - All records relating to child abuse as declared confidential by IN ST 31-33-18-1, et seq.;

  - All records relating to drug tests as declared confidential by IN ST 5-14-3-4(a)(9);

  - Records of grand jury proceedings as declared confidential by IN ST 35-34-2-4;

  - Records of juvenile proceedings as declared confidential by IN ST 31-39-1-2, except those specifically open under statute;

  - All paternity records created after July 1, 1941 as declared confidential by IN ST 31-14-11-15, IN ST 31-19-5-23, IN ST 31-39-1-1 and IN ST 31-39-1-2 [Editor's note: IN ST 31-14-11-15 was repealed effective May 9, 2013];

  - All pre-sentence reports as declared confidential by IN ST 35-38-1-13;

  - Written petitions to permit marriages without consent and orders directing the Clerk of Court to issue a marriage license to underage persons, as declared confidential by IN ST 31-11-1-6;

  - Only those arrest warrants, search warrants, indictments and informations ordered confidential by the trial judge, prior to return of duly executed service as declared confidential by IN ST 5-14-3-4(b)(1);

  - All medical, mental health, or tax records unless determined by law or regulation of any governmental custodian not to be confidential, released by the subject of such records, or declared by a court of competent jurisdiction to be essential to the resolution of litigation as declared confidential by IN ST 16-39-3-10, IN ST 6-4.1-5-10, IN ST 6-4.1-12-12, and IN ST 6-8.1-7-1;

  - Personal information relating to jurors or prospective jurors, other than for the use of the parties and counsel, pursuant to IN ST JURY Rule 10;

  - Information relating to protection from abuse orders, no-contact orders and workplace violence restraining orders as declared confidential by IN ST 5-2-9-6, et seq.;

  - Mediation proceedings pursuant to IN ST ADR Rule 2.11, Mini-Trial proceedings pursuant to IN ST ADR Rule 4.4(C), and Summary Jury Trials pursuant to IN ST ADR Rule 5.6;

- Information in probation files pursuant to the Probation Standards promulgated by the Judicial Conference of Indiana pursuant to IN ST 11-13-1-8(b);

- Information deemed confidential pursuant to the Rules for Court Administered Alcohol and Drug Programs promulgated by the Judicial Conference of Indiana pursuant to IN ST 12-23-14-13;

- Information deemed confidential pursuant to the Problem-Solving Court Rules promulgated by the Judicial Conference of Indiana pursuant to IN ST 33-23-16-16;

- All records of the Department of workforce Development as declared confidential by IN ST 22-4-19-6;

- Information regarding interception of electronic communications that is sealed or deemed confidential as set forth in IN ST 35-33.5-2-1, et seq.

  iii. Information excluded from public access by specific court order;

  iv. Complete Social Security Numbers of living persons;

  v. With the exception of names, information such as addresses, phone numbers, and dates of birth which explicitly identifies:

- Natural persons who are witnesses or victims (not including defendants) in criminal, domestic violence, stalking, sexual assault, juvenile, or civil protection order proceedings, provided that juveniles who are victims of sex crimes shall be identified by initials only;

- Places of residence of judicial officers, clerks and other employees of courts and clerks of court, unless the person or persons about whom the information pertains waives confidentiality;

  vi. Complete account numbers of specific assets, loans, bank accounts, credit cards, and personal identification numbers (PINs);

  vii. All orders of expungement entered in criminal or juvenile proceedings, orders to restrict access to criminal history information pursuant to IN ST 35-38-5-5.5 or IN ST 35-38-8-5 and records excluded from public access by such orders, and information related to infractions that is excluded from public access pursuant to IN ST 34-28-5-15 or IN ST 34-28-5-16 [Editor's note: IN ST 35-38-5-5.5, IN ST 35-38-8-5 and IN ST 34-28-5-16 were repealed effective July 1, 2013; for information on orders restricting access to criminal history, refer to IN ST 35-38-9-1, et seq.];

  viii. All personal notes and e-mail, and deliberative material, of judges, jurors, court staff and judicial agencies, and information recorded in personal data assistants (PDA's) or organizers and personal calendars. IN ST ADMIN Rule 9(G)(1).

F. Filing and Service Requirements

1. *Filing requirements.* Except as otherwise provided in IN ST TRIAL P Rule 5(E)(2), all pleadings and papers subsequent to the complaint which are required to be served upon a party shall be filed with the Court either before service or within a reasonable period of time thereafter. IN ST TRIAL P Rule 5(E)(1).

  a. *Filing with the court defined.* The filing of pleadings, motions, and other papers with the court as required by the Indiana Rules of Trial Procedure shall be made by one of the following methods:

    i. Delivery to the clerk of the court;

    ii. Sending by electronic transmission under the procedure adopted pursuant to IN ST ADMIN Rule 12;

    iii. Mailing to the clerk by registered, certified or express mail return receipt requested;

    iv. Depositing with any third-party commercial carrier for delivery to the clerk within three (3) calendar days, cost prepaid, properly addressed;

    v. If the court so permits, filing with the judge, in which event the judge shall note thereon the filing date and forthwith transmit them to the office of the clerk; or

    vi. Electronic filing, as approved by the Division of State Court Administration pursuant to IN ST ADMIN Rule 16. IN ST TRIAL P Rule 5(F).

    vii. Filing by registered or certified mail and by third-party commercial carrier shall be complete upon mailing or deposit. IN ST TRIAL P Rule 5(F).

  b. *Facsimile filing*

    i. *Generally.* In counties where a majority of judges of the courts of record, by posted local rule, have authorized electronic facsimile filing and designated a telephone number to receive such transmissions, pleadings, motions, and other papers may be sent to the Clerk of Circuit Court by electronic facsimile transmission for filing in any case, provided:

- Such matter does not exceed ten (10) pages, including the cover sheet;

- Such matter does not require the payment of fees other than the electronic facsimile transcription fee set forth in IN ST ADMIN Rule 12(E);

- The sending party creates at the time of transmission a machine generated log for such transmission; and

- The original document and the transmission log are maintained by the sending party for the duration of the litigation. IN ST ADMIN Rule 12(B).

    ii. *Time of filing.* During normal, posted business hours, the time of filing shall be the time the duplicate document is produced in the office of the Clerk of the Circuit Court. Duplicate documents received at all other times shall be filed as of the next normal business day. IN ST ADMIN Rule 12(C).

- If the receiving fax machine endorses its own time and date stamp upon the transmitted documents and the receiving machine produces a delivery receipt which is electronically created and transmitted to the sending party, the time of filing shall be the date and time recorded on the transmitted document by the receiving fax machine. IN ST ADMIN Rule 12(C).

  c. *Proof of filing.* Any party filing any paper by any method other than personal delivery to the clerk shall retain proof of filing. IN ST TRIAL P Rule 5(F).

2. *Service requirements.* Unless otherwise provided by the Indiana Rules of Trial Procedure or an order of the court, each party and special judge, if any, shall be served with: (1) every order required by its terms to be served; (2) every pleading subsequent to the original complaint; (3) every written motion except one which may be heard ex parte; (4) every brief submitted to the trial court; (5) every paper relating to discovery required to be served upon a party; and (6) every written notice, appearance, demand, offer of judgment, designation of record on appeal, or similar paper. IN ST TRIAL P Rule 5(A).

  a. *Methods of service*

    i. *Personal service.* Whenever a party is represented by an attorney of record, service shall be made upon such attorney unless service upon the party himself is ordered by the court. Service upon the attorney or party shall be made by delivering or mailing a copy of the papers to the last known address or where an attorney or party has consented to service by fax or e-mail, as provided in IN ST TRIAL P Rule 3.1(A)(4), by faxing or e-mailing a copy of the documents to the fax number or e-mail address set out in the appearance form or correction as required by IN ST TRIAL P Rule 3.1(E). IN ST TRIAL P Rule 5(B). Delivery of a copy within IN ST TRIAL P Rule 5 means:

- Offering or tendering it to the attorney or party and stating the nature of the papers being served. Refusal to accept an offered or tendered document is a waiver of any objection to the sufficiency or adequacy of service of that document;

- Leaving it at his office with a clerk or other person in charge thereof, or if there is no one in charge, leaving it in a conspicuous place therein; or

- If the office is closed, by leaving it at his dwelling house or usual place of abode with some person of suitable age and discretion then residing therein; or,

- Leaving it at some other suitable place, selected by the attorney upon whom service is being made, pursuant to duly promulgated local rule. IN ST TRIAL P Rule 5(B)(1).

    ii. *Service by mail.* If service is made by mail, the papers shall be deposited in the United States mail addressed to the person on whom they are being served, with postage prepaid. Service shall be deemed complete upon mailing. Proof of service of all papers permitted to be mailed may be made by written acknowledgment of service, by affidavit of the person who mailed the papers, or by certificate of an attorney. It shall be the duty of attorneys when entering their appearance in a cause or when filing pleadings or papers therein, to have noted in the Chronological Case Summary or said pleadings or papers so filed the address and telephone number of their office. Service by delivery or by mail at such address shall be deemed sufficient and complete. IN ST TRIAL P Rule 5(B)(2).

    iii. *Service by fax or e-mail.* A party who has consented to service by fax or e-mail may be served as follows:

- Service by e-mail shall be made by attaching the document being served in .pdf format. Discovery documents must also be served in accordance with IN ST TRIAL P Rule 26(A). IN ST TRIAL P Rule 5(B)(3)(a).

- Service by fax shall be deemed complete upon generation of a transmission record indicating the successful transmission of the entire document, except as provided in IN ST TRIAL P Rule 5(B)(3)(d). IN ST TRIAL P Rule 5(B)(3)(b).

- Service by e-mail shall be deemed complete upon transmission, except as provided in IN ST TRIAL P Rule 5(B)(3)(d). IN ST TRIAL P Rule 5(B)(3)(c).

- Service by fax or e-mail that occurs on a Saturday, Sunday, legal holiday, or day the court or agency in which the matter is pending is closed or after 5:00 PM local time of the recipient shall be deemed complete the next day that is not a Saturday, Sunday, legal holiday, or day that the court or agency in which the matter is pending is not closed. IN ST TRIAL P Rule 5(B)(3)(d).

    iv. *Consent to alternate service.* Any Allen County Attorney or any Allen County law firm may, without charge, maintain an assigned Courthouse box in the library of the Allen County Courthouse for receipt of notices, pleadings, process orders, or other communications from the Court, the Clerk, and other attorneys or law firms. IN ST ALLEN SUPER AND CIR CT CIV Rule 5-1(A). For more information concerning the use of courthouse boxes, refer to IN ST ALLEN SUPER AND CIR CT CIV Rule 5-1.

b. *Serving numerous defendants.* In any action in which there are unusually large numbers of defendants, the court, upon motion or of its own initiative, may order:

    i. That service of the pleadings of the defendants and replies thereto need not be made as between the defendants;

- That any cross-claim, counterclaim, or matter constituting an avoidance or affirmative defense contained therein shall be deemed to be denied or avoided by all other parties; and

- That the filing of any such pleading and service thereof upon the plaintiff constitutes due notice of it to the parties. IN ST TRIAL P Rule 5(D).

    ii. A copy of every such order shall be served upon the parties in such manner and form as the court directs. IN ST TRIAL P Rule 5(D).

c. *Service on parties in default for failure to appear.* No service need be made on parties in default for failure to appear, except that pleadings asserting new or additional claims for relief against them shall be served upon them in the manner provided by service of summons in IN ST TRIAL P Rule 4. IN ST TRIAL P Rule 5(A).

d. *Proof of service.* Certificates of service or proof of mailing of pleadings concerning any case shall be deemed sufficient proof of service if such pleadings were mailed to the last known address of a party or attorney noted upon the chronological case summary of a case. IN ST ALLEN SUPER AND CIR CT CIV Rule 3.1-1(E).

G. Hearings

1. The Indiana rules do not contemplate a hearing regarding the filing and service of an answer.

H. Forms

  1. Official Answer Forms for Indiana

    a. Affidavit of debt. IN ST TRIAL P App. A-2.

    b. Appearance by attorney in civil case. IN ST TRIAL P App. B.

  2. Answer Forms for Indiana

    a. Appearance; By responding party. 9 INPRAC § 39.3.

    b. Answer; Form and content. 9 INPRAC § 41.1.

    c. Answer; General form. 9 INPRAC § 41.3.

    d. Answer; Another form. 9 INPRAC § 41.4.

    e. Answer; Another form. 9 INPRAC § 41.5.

    f. General denial. 9 INPRAC § 41.6.

    g. Specific denial of designated paragraph. 9 INPRAC § 41.7.

    h. Specific admission of designated paragraph. 9 INPRAC § 41.8.

    i. Denial of knowledge or information to form belief. 9 INPRAC § 41.9.

    j. Denial of knowledge or information to form belief; Another form. 9 INPRAC § 41.10.

    k. Partial denial and partial admission of designated paragraph. 9 INPRAC § 41.11.

    l. Denial of designated paragraph for reason that document speaks for itself. 9 INPRAC § 41.12.

    m. Adoption of admissions or denials by co-defendant's answer. 9 INPRAC § 41.13.

    n. Denial of execution of instrument filed with pleading. 9 INPRAC § 41.14.

    o. Answer to cross-claim. 9 INPRAC § 41.15.

    p. Answer to third-party complaint. 9 INPRAC § 41.16.

    q. Accord and satisfaction. 9 INPRAC § 41.21.

    r. Answer. 5 INPRAC § 3:3.3.

    s. Answer; Another form. 5 INPRAC § 3:3.4.

    t. Certificate of service; Personal service. 9 INPRAC § 5.7.

    u. Certificate of service; First class mail. 9 INPRAC § 5.8.

    v. Signature; By party. 9 INPRAC § 4.5.

    w. Signature; Attorney. 9 INPRAC § 4.6.

    x. Signature; Attorney; Another form. 9 INPRAC § 4.7.

    y. Signature; Attorney; Another form. 9 INPRAC § 4.8.

    z. Verification; Official form. 9 INPRAC § 4.9.

  3. Official Answer Forms for Allen County

    a. Consent to alternate service. IN ST ALLEN SUPER AND CIR CT CIV App. A.

I. Checklist

  (I) ❑ Matters to be considered by the plaintiff

    (a) ❑ Required documents

      (1) ❑ Summons

      (2) ❑ Complaint

      (3) ❑ Appearance form

    (b) ❑ Supplemental documents

      (1) ❑ Proof of written instrument

(2) ❑ Notice of intent to use foreign law

(3) ❑ Praecipe

(4) ❑ Facsimile cover sheet

(5) ❑ Additional copies for service

(c) ❑ Timing

(1) ❑ The claimant typically bears the burden of commencing an action within the applicable statute of limitations

(2) ❑ If person seeking service of process fails without cause for sixty (60) days or more to provide clerk with required summons for issuance or with other information necessary to effectuate service, person has failed to exercise due diligence in securing service of process

(II) ❑ Matters to be considered by the defendant

(a) ❑ Required documents

(1) ❑ Answer

(2) ❑ Appearance form

(3) ❑ Certificate of service

(b) ❑ Supplemental documents

(1) ❑ Admission of service

(2) ❑ Proof of written instrument

(3) ❑ Notice of intent to use foreign law

(4) ❑ Facsimile cover sheet

(c) ❑ Timing

(1) ❑ A responsive pleading required under the Indiana Rules of Trial Procedure, shall be served within twenty (20) days after service of the prior pleading

(2) ❑ The service of a motion permitted under IN ST TRIAL P Rule 12 alters the time for service of responsive pleadings as follows, unless a different time is fixed by the court:

(i) ❑ If the court does not grant the motion, the responsive pleading shall be served in ten (10) days after notice of the court's action;

(ii) ❑ If the court grants the motion and the corrective action is allowed to be taken, it shall be taken within ten (10) days, and the responsive pleading shall be served within ten (10) days thereafter

Pleadings
Amended Answer

Document Last Updated October 2013

A. Applicable Rules

1. *State rules*

   a. Summons. IN ST TRIAL P Rule 4.

   b. Appearance. IN ST TRIAL P Rule 3.1.

   c. Filing and service. IN ST TRIAL P Rule 4.6; IN ST TRIAL P Rule 5.

   d. Time. IN ST TRIAL P Rule 6.

   e. Pleadings. IN ST TRIAL P Rule 7; IN ST TRIAL P Rule 8; IN ST TRIAL P Rule 9; IN ST TRIAL P Rule 9.1; IN ST TRIAL P Rule 9.2; IN ST TRIAL P Rule 10; IN ST TRIAL P Rule 11.

f. Defenses and objections; When and how presented; By pleading or motion; Motion for judgment on the pleadings. IN ST TRIAL P Rule 12.

g. Counterclaim and cross-claim. IN ST TRIAL P Rule 13.

h. Third-party practice. IN ST TRIAL P Rule 14.

i. Amended and supplemental pleadings. IN ST TRIAL P Rule 15.

j. Parties plaintiff and defendant; Capacity. IN ST TRIAL P Rule 17.

k. Joinder. IN ST TRIAL P Rule 19; IN ST TRIAL P Rule 20.

l. Consolidation; Separate trials. IN ST TRIAL P Rule 42.

m. Evidence. IN ST TRIAL P Rule 43.

n. Determination of foreign law. IN ST TRIAL P Rule 44.1.

o. Judgment on the evidence (directed verdict). IN ST TRIAL P Rule 50.

p. Findings by the court. IN ST TRIAL P Rule 52.

q. Judgment; Costs. IN ST TRIAL P Rule 54.

r. Summary judgment. IN ST TRIAL P Rule 56.

s. Motion to correct error. IN ST TRIAL P Rule 59.

t. Relief from judgment or order. IN ST TRIAL P Rule 60.

u. Venue requirements. IN ST TRIAL P Rule 75.

v. Access to court records. IN ST ADMIN Rule 9.

w. Paper size. IN ST ADMIN Rule 11.

x. Facsimile transmission. IN ST ADMIN Rule 12.

y. Electronic filing and electronic service pilot projects. IN ST ADMIN Rule 16.

z. Privacy and confidentiality. IN ST 5-2-9-6; IN ST 5-14-3-4; IN ST 5-14-3-5.5; IN ST 6-4.1-5-10; IN ST 6-4.1-12-12; IN ST 6-8.1-7-1; IN ST 11-13-1-8; IN ST 12-23-14-13; IN ST 16-39-3-10; IN ST 16-41-8-1; IN ST 22-4-19-6; IN ST 31-11-1-6; IN ST 31-19-5-23; IN ST 31-19-13-2; IN ST 31-19-19-1; IN ST 31-33-18-1; IN ST 31-39-1-1; IN ST 31-39-1-2; IN ST 33-23-16-16; IN ST 35-34-2-4; IN ST 35-38-1-13; IN ST 35-38-9-1; IN ST ADR Rule 2.11; IN ST ADR Rule 4.4; IN ST ADR Rule 5.6; IN ST JURY Rule 10.

2. *Local rules*

   a. Applicability and citation of rules. IN ST ALLEN SUPER AND CIR CT CIV Rule AR00-1.

   b. Appearances. IN ST ALLEN SUPER AND CIR CT CIV Rule 3.1-1.

   c. Consent to alternate service. IN ST ALLEN SUPER AND CIR CT CIV Rule 5-1.

   d. Preparation of pleadings. IN ST ALLEN SUPER AND CIR CT CIV Rule 8-1.

   e. Filing. IN ST ALLEN SUPER AND CIR CT CIV Rule 77-1.

B. Timing

1. *Filing an amended pleading*

   a. *As a matter of course.* A party may amend his pleading once as a matter of course at any time before a responsive pleading is served or, if the pleading is one to which no responsive pleading is permitted, and the action has not been placed upon the trial calendar, he may so amend it at any time within thirty (30) days after it is served. IN ST TRIAL P Rule 15(A).

   b. *With leave of court.* Otherwise a party may amend his pleading only by leave of court or by written consent of the adverse party; and leave shall be given when justice so requires. IN ST TRIAL P Rule 15(A). Refer to the Indiana KeyRules Motion for Leave to Amend document for more information.

2. *Computation of time*

   a. *Generally; Days excluded.* In computing any period of time prescribed or allowed by the Indiana

Rules of Trial Procedure, by order of the court, or by any applicable statute, the day of the act, event, or default from which the designated period of time begins to run shall not be included. The last day of the period so computed is to be included unless it is:

   i.   A Saturday,

   ii. A Sunday,

   iii. A legal holiday as defined by state statute, or

   iv. A day the office in which the act is to be done is closed during regular business hours. IN ST TRIAL P Rule 6(A).

  b. *Short periods.* In any event, the period runs until the end of the next day that is not a Saturday, a Sunday, a legal holiday, or a day on which the office is closed. When the period of time allowed is less than seven (7) days, intermediate Saturdays, Sundays, legal holidays, and days on which the office is closed shall be excluded from the computations. IN ST TRIAL P Rule 6(A).

  c. *Additional time after service by United States mail.* Whenever a party has the right or is required to do some act or take some proceedings within a prescribed period after the service of a notice or other paper upon him and the notice or paper is served upon him by United States mail, three (3) days shall be added to the prescribed period. IN ST TRIAL P Rule 6(E).

  d. *Enlargement of time.* When an act is required or allowed to be done at or within a specific time by the Indiana Rules of Trial Procedure, the court may at any time for cause shown:

   i.   Order the period enlarged, with or without motion or notice, if request therefor is made before the expiration of the period originally prescribed or extended by a previous order; or

   ii. Upon motion made after the expiration of the specific period, permit the act to be done where the failure to act was the result of excusable neglect; but, the court may not extend the time for taking any action for judgment on the evidence under IN ST TRIAL P Rule 50(A), amendment of findings and judgment under IN ST TRIAL P Rule 52(B), to correct errors under IN ST TRIAL P Rule 59(C), statement in opposition to motion to correct error under IN ST TRIAL P Rule 59(E), or to obtain relief from final judgment under IN ST TRIAL P Rule 60(B), except to the extent and under the conditions stated in those rules. IN ST TRIAL P Rule 6(B).

C. General Requirements

1. *Amending pleadings.* The purpose of an amended pleading is to include matters that occurred before the filing of the original pleading but which were either overlooked by the pleader or unknown to him at the time. It is a substitute for the original and relates to the facts that existed when the original pleading was filed. An amended pleading supercedes the original as to those portions amended. 10 INPRAC § 46.1.

  a. *Amendments liberally allowed.* Amendments to pleadings are to be liberally allowed in order that all issues are presented in one action. 10 INPRAC § 46.1; Pinnacle Media, LLC v. Metropolitan Dev. Com'n of Marion County, 868 N.E.2d 894 (Ind.Ct.App. 2007).

  b. *Amendments to conform to the evidence.* When issues not raised by the pleadings are tried by express or implied consent of the parties, they shall be treated in all respects as if they had been raised in the pleadings. Such amendment of the pleadings as may be necessary to cause them to conform to the evidence and to raise these issues may be made upon motion of any party at any time, even after judgment, but failure so to amend does not affect the result of the trial of these issues. If evidence is objected to at the trial on the ground that it is not within the issues made by the pleadings, the court may allow the pleadings to be amended and shall do so freely when the presentation of the merits of the action will be subserved thereby and the objecting party fails to satisfy the court that the admission of such evidence would prejudice him in maintaining his action or defense upon the merits. The court may grant a continuance to enable the objecting party to meet such evidence. IN ST TRIAL P Rule 15(B).

  c. *Relation back of amendments*

   i.   Whenever the claim or defense asserted in the amended pleading arose out of the conduct, transaction, or occurrence set forth or attempted to be set forth in the original pleading, the amendment relates back to the date of the original pleading. An amendment changing the party against whom a claim is asserted relates back if the foregoing provision is satisfied and, within one hundred and twenty (120) days of commencement of the action, the party to be brought in by amendment:

- Has received such notice of the institution of the action that he will not be prejudiced in maintaining his defense on the merits; and

- Knew or should have known that but for a mistake concerning the identity of the proper party, the action would have been brought against him. IN ST TRIAL P Rule 15(C).

ii. The requirement of subsections IN ST TRIAL P Rule 15(C)(1) and IN ST TRIAL P Rule 15(C)(2) with respect to a governmental organization to be brought into the action as defendant is satisfied:

- In the case of a state or governmental organization by delivery or mailing of process to the attorney general or to a governmental executive [IN ST TRIAL P Rule 4.6(A)(3)]; or

- In the case of a local governmental organization, by delivery or mailing of process to its attorney as provided by statute, to a governmental executive thereof [IN ST TRIAL P Rule 4.6(A)(4)], or to the officer holding the office if suit is against the officer or an office. IN ST TRIAL P Rule 15(C).

d. *Amendment by leave.* Amendments, other than an amendment by right, may be made only by leave of court or by written consent of the opposing party. 2 INPRAC R 15(15.2). Refer to the Indiana KeyRules Motion for Leave to Amend document for more information on amending with leave of court.

2. *Pleading, generally*

a. *Pleadings to be concise.* Each averment of a pleading shall be simple, concise, and direct. No technical forms of pleading or motions are required. All fictions in pleading are abolished. IN ST TRIAL P Rule 8(E)(1).

b. *Pleading in the alternative.* A pleading may set forth two (2) or more statements of a claim or defense alternatively or hypothetically, either in one (1) count or defense or in separate counts or defenses. When two (2) or more statements are made in the alternative and one (1) of them if made independently would be sufficient, the pleading is not made insufficient by the insufficiency of one or more of the alternative statements. A pleading may also state as many separate claims or defenses as the pleader has regardless of consistency and whether based on legal or equitable grounds. All statements shall be made subject to the obligations set forth in IN ST TRIAL P Rule 11. IN ST TRIAL P Rule 8(E)(2).

c. *Motions and pleadings, joint and several.* All motions and pleadings of any kind addressed to two (2) or more paragraphs of any pleading, or filed by two (2) or more parties, shall be taken and construed as joint, separate, and several motions or pleadings to each of such paragraphs and by and against each of such parties. All motions or pleadings containing two (2) or more subject-matters shall be taken and construed as separate and several as to each subject-matter. All objections to rulings made by two (2) or more parties shall be taken and construed as the joint, separate, and several objections of each of such parties. IN ST TRIAL P Rule 8(E)(3).

i. A complaint filed by or against two (2) or more plaintiffs shall be taken and construed as joint, separate, and several as to each of said plaintiffs. IN ST TRIAL P Rule 8(E).

d. *Construction of pleadings.* All pleadings shall be so construed as to do substantial justice, lead to disposition on the merits, and avoid litigation of procedural points. IN ST TRIAL P Rule 8(F).

3. *Contents of the answer*

a. *Defenses which may be raised by answer or motion.* Every defense, in law or fact, to a claim for relief in any pleading, whether a claim, counterclaim, cross-claim, or third-party claim, shall be asserted in the responsive pleading thereto if one is required; except that at the option of the pleader, the following defenses may be made by motion:

i. Lack of jurisdiction over the subject matter;

ii. Lack of jurisdiction over the person;

iii. Incorrect venue under IN ST TRIAL P Rule 75, or any statutory provision. The disposition of this motion shall be consistent with IN ST TRIAL P Rule 75;

iv. Insufficiency of process;

v. Insufficiency of service of process;

vi. Failure to state a claim upon which relief can be granted, which shall include failure to name the real party in interest under IN ST TRIAL P Rule 17;

vii. Failure to join a party needed for just adjudication under IN ST TRIAL P Rule 19;

viii. The same action pending in another state court of this state. IN ST TRIAL P Rule 12(B).

ix. A motion making any of these defenses shall be made before pleading if a further pleading is permitted or within twenty (20) days after service of the prior pleading if none is required. If a pleading sets forth a claim for relief to which the adverse party is not required to serve a responsive pleading, any of the defenses in section IN ST TRIAL P Rule 12(B)(2), IN ST TRIAL P Rule 12(B)(3), IN ST TRIAL P Rule 12(B)(4), IN ST TRIAL P Rule 12(B)(5) or IN ST TRIAL P Rule 12(B)(8) is waived to the extent constitutionally permissible unless made in a motion within twenty (20) days after service of the prior pleading. No defense or objection is waived by being joined with one (1) or more other defenses or objections in a responsive pleading or motion. IN ST TRIAL P Rule 12(B).

b. *Waiver or preservation of certain defenses*

i. A defense of lack of jurisdiction over the person, improper venue, insufficiency of process, insufficiency of service of process, or the same action pending in another state court of this state is waived to the extent constitutionally permissible:

- If omitted from a motion in the circumstances described in IN ST TRIAL P Rule 12(G),

- If it is neither made by motion under IN ST TRIAL P Rule 12 nor included in a responsive pleading or an amendment thereof permitted by IN ST TRIAL P Rule 15(A) to be made as a matter of course. IN ST TRIAL P Rule 12(H)(1).

ii. A defense of failure to state a claim upon which relief can be granted, a defense of failure to join an indispensable party under IN ST TRIAL P Rule 19(B), and an objection of failure to state a legal defense to a claim may be made in any pleading permitted or ordered under IN ST TRIAL P Rule 7(A) or by motion for judgment on the pleadings, or at the trial on the merits. IN ST TRIAL P Rule 12(H)(2).

c. *Defenses; Form of denials*

i. A responsive pleading shall state in short and plain terms the pleader's defenses to each claim asserted and shall admit or controvert the averments set forth in the preceding pleading. If in good faith the pleader intends to deny all the averments in the preceding pleading, he may do so by general denial subject to the provisions of IN ST TRIAL P Rule 11. If he does not intend a general denial, he may:

- Specifically deny designated averments or paragraphs; or

- Generally deny all averments except such designated averments and paragraphs as he expressly admits. IN ST TRIAL P Rule 8(B).

ii. If he lacks knowledge or information sufficient to form a belief as to the truth of an averment, he shall so state and his statement shall be considered a denial. If in good faith a pleader intends to deny only a part or a qualification of an averment, he shall specify so much of it as is true and material and deny the remainder. All denials shall fairly meet the substance of the averments denied. IN ST TRIAL P Rule 8 shall have no application to uncontested actions for divorce, or to answers required to be filed by clerks or guardians ad litem. IN ST TRIAL P Rule 8(B).

d. *Affirmative defenses.* A responsive pleading shall set forth affirmatively and carry the burden of proving: accord and satisfaction, arbitration and award, discharge in bankruptcy, duress, estoppel, failure of consideration, fraud, illegality, injury by fellow servant, laches, license, payment, release, res judicata, statute of frauds, statute of limitations, waiver, lack of jurisdiction over the subject-matter, lack of jurisdiction over the person, improper venue, insufficiency of process or service of process, the same action pending in another state court of this state, and any other matter constituting an avoidance, matter of abatement, or affirmative defense. A party required to affirmatively plead any matters, including matters formerly required to be pleaded affirmatively by reply, shall have the burden of proving such matters. The burden of proof imposed by this or any other provision of the Indiana Rules of Trial Procedure is subject to the rules of evidence or any statute fixing a different rule. If the pleading mistakenly designates a defense as a counterclaim or a counterclaim as a defense, the court shall treat the pleading as if there had been a proper designation. IN ST TRIAL P Rule 8(C).

    i. An affirmative defense, generally, must be affirmatively stated by the party who seeks its benefit. 1A INPRAC R 8(8.5); Rice v. Grant County Bd. of Com'rs, 472 N.E.2d 213 (Ind.Ct.App. 1984). If that party does not raise the affirmative defense, then it is waived. 1A INPRAC R 8(8.5); Piskorowski v. Shell Oil Co., 403 N.E.2d 838, 847 (Ind.Ct.App. 1980).

    ii. It is clear that the list of affirmative defenses found in IN ST TRIAL P Rule 8 is not exhaustive. The question comes: when is a defense to be treated as an affirmative defense, with all of the attending consequences? 1A INPRAC R 8(8.5). The "determination of whether a defense is affirmative depends on whether it controverts an element of the plaintiff's prima facie case or raises matter outside the scope of the prima facie case." 1A INPRAC R 8(8.5); Molargik v. West Enterprises, Inc., 605 N.E.2d 1197, 1198 (Ind.Ct.App. 1993).

e. *Defense of contributory negligence or assumed risk.* In all claims alleging negligence, the burden of pleading and proving contributory negligence, assumption of risk, or incurred risk shall be upon the defendant who may plead such by denial of the allegation. IN ST TRIAL P Rule 9.1(A).

f. *Res ipsa loquitur.* Res ipsa loquitur or a similar doctrine may be pleaded by alleging generally that the facts connected with the action are unknown to the pleader and are within the knowledge of the opposing party. IN ST TRIAL P Rule 9.1(B).

g. *Consideration.* When an action or defense is founded upon a written contract or release, lack of consideration for the promise or release is an affirmative defense, and the party asserting lack of it carries the burden of proof. IN ST TRIAL P Rule 9.1(C).

h. *Bona fide purchaser.* When the rights of a person depend upon his status as a bona fide purchaser for value or upon similar requirements, such status must be pleaded and proved by the person asserting it, but it may be pleaded in general terms. Once it is established that the person has given any required value, unless such value is commercially unreasonable, and that he has met any requirements of recordation, filing, possession, or perfection, the trier of fact must find that such value was given or such perfection was made in accordance with any requirements of good faith, lack of knowledge, or lack of notice unless and until evidence is introduced which would support a finding of its non-existence. IN ST TRIAL P Rule 9.1(D).

i. *Presumption; Matters of judicial notice.* Neither presumptions of law nor matters of which judicial notice may be taken need be stated in a pleading. IN ST TRIAL P Rule 9.1(E).

j. *Property distrained; Sufficient answer.* In an action to recover the possession of property distrained while doing damage, an answer that the defendant, or person by whose command he acted, was lawfully possessed of the real property upon which the distress was made, and that the property distrained was at the time doing damage thereon, shall be good without setting forth the title of such real property. IN ST TRIAL P Rule 9.1(F).

k. *Effect of failure to deny.* Averments in a pleading to which a responsive pleading is required, except those pertaining to amount of damages, are admitted when not denied in the responsive pleading. Averments in a pleading to which no responsive pleading is required or permitted shall be taken as denied or avoided. IN ST TRIAL P Rule 8(D).

l. *Effect of admission.* When a rhetorical paragraph or allegation is admitted, the effect in Indiana is to remove it from trial. Such an admission is a "judicial admission", and the claim or issue which is admitted cannot be denied later by the trier of the facts. Further, this admitted fact does not require evidence to "prove it"; it is established. It becomes, in short, controlling and indisputable in the

AMENDED ANSWER

litigation, unless the trial court permits an amendment to the pleading which might remove the controlling effect of the admission, and permit it to become another fact or item of evidence in the case. 1A INPRAC R 8(8.4); Aylesworth v. McKesson, 421 N.E.2d 422 (Ind.Ct.App. 1981).

4. *Pleading special matters*

   a. *Capacity.* It is not necessary to aver the capacity of a party to sue or be sued, the authority of a party to sue or be sued in a representative capacity, or the legal existence of an organization that is made a party. The burden of proving lack of such capacity, authority, or legal existence shall be upon the person asserting lack of it, and shall be pleaded as an affirmative defense. IN ST TRIAL P Rule 9(A).

   b. *Fraud, mistake, condition of the mind.* In all averments of fraud or mistake, the circumstances constituting fraud or mistake shall be specifically averred. Malice, intent, knowledge, and other conditions of mind may be averred generally. IN ST TRIAL P Rule 9(B).

   c. *Conditions precedent.* In pleading the performance or occurrence of promissory or non-promissory conditions precedent, it is sufficient to aver generally that all conditions precedent have been performed, have occurred, or have been excused. A denial of performance or occurrence shall be made specifically and with particularity, and a denial of excuse generally. IN ST TRIAL P Rule 9(C).

   d. *Official document or act.* In pleading an official document or official act it is sufficient to aver that the document was issued or the act done in compliance with law. IN ST TRIAL P Rule 9(D).

   e. *Judgment.* In pleading a judgment or decision of a domestic or foreign court, judicial or quasi-judicial tribunal, or of a board or officer, it is sufficient to aver the judgment or decision without setting forth matter showing jurisdiction to render it. IN ST TRIAL P Rule 9(E).

   f. *Time and place.* For the purpose of testing the sufficiency of a pleading, averments of time and place are material and shall be considered like all other averments of material matter. However, time and place need be stated only with such specificity as will enable the opposing party to prepare his defense. IN ST TRIAL P Rule 9(F).

   g. *Special damages; Damages where no answer.* When items of special damage are claimed, they shall be specifically stated. The relief granted to the plaintiff, if there be no answer, cannot exceed the relief demanded in his complaint; but, in any other case, the court may grant him any relief consistent with the facts or matters pleaded. IN ST TRIAL P Rule 9(G).

5. *Counterclaim and cross-claim*

   a. *Compulsory counterclaims.* A pleading shall state as a counterclaim any claim which at the time of serving the pleading the pleader has against any opposing party, if it arises out of the transaction or occurrence that is the subject-matter of the opposing party's claim and does not require for its adjudication the presence of third parties of whom the court cannot acquire jurisdiction. But the pleader need not state the claim if:

      i. At the time the action was commenced the claim was the subject of another pending action; or

      ii. The opposing party brought suit upon his claim by attachment or other process by which the court did not acquire jurisdiction to render a personal judgment on that claim, and the pleader is not stating any counterclaim under IN ST TRIAL P Rule 13. IN ST TRIAL P Rule 13(A).

   b. *Permissive counterclaims.* A pleading may state as a counterclaim any claim against an opposing party not arising out of the transaction or occurrence that is the subject-matter of the opposing party's claim. IN ST TRIAL P Rule 13(B).

   c. *Counterclaim exceeding opposing claim.* A counterclaim may or may not diminish or defeat the recovery sought by the opposing party. It may claim relief exceeding in amount or different in kind from that sought in the pleading of the opposing party. IN ST TRIAL P Rule 13(C).

   d. *Counterclaim against state.* IN ST TRIAL P Rule 13 shall not be construed to enlarge any right to assert a claim against the state. IN ST TRIAL P Rule 13(D).

   e. *Counterclaim maturing or acquired after pleading.* A claim which either matured or was acquired by the pleader after serving his pleading may, with the permission of the court, be presented as a counterclaim by supplemental pleading. A counterclaim or cross-claim which is not due may be asserted against a party who is insolvent or the representative of a party who has been subjected to insolvency proceedings, if recovery thereon will be impaired because of such party's insolvency. IN ST TRIAL P Rule 13(E).

f. *Omitted counterclaim.* When a pleader fails to set up a counterclaim through oversight, inadvertence, or excusable neglect, or when justice requires, he may by leave of court set up the counterclaim by amendment. IN ST TRIAL P Rule 13(F).

g. *Cross-claim against co-party.* A pleading may state as a cross-claim any claim by one party against a co-party. IN ST TRIAL P Rule 13(G).

h. *Joinder of additional parties.* Persons other than those made parties to the original action may be made parties to a counterclaim or cross-claim in accordance with the provisions of IN ST TRIAL P Rule 14, IN ST TRIAL P Rule 19 and IN ST TRIAL P Rule 20. IN ST TRIAL P Rule 13(H).

i. *Separate trials; Separate judgments*

  i. If the court orders separate trials as provided in IN ST TRIAL P Rule 42(B), judgment on a counterclaim or cross-claim may be rendered in accordance with the terms of IN ST TRIAL P Rule 54(B) when the court has jurisdiction so to do, even if the claims of the opposing party have been dismissed or otherwise disposed of. In determining whether or not separate trial of a cross-claim shall be ordered, the court shall consider whether the cross-claim:

   • Arises out of the transaction or occurrence or series of transactions or occurrences that is the subject-matter either of the original action or of a counterclaim therein;

   • Relates to any property or contract that is the subject-matter of the original action; or

   • Claims that the person against whom it is asserted is liable to the cross-claimant for all or part of plaintiff's claim against him. IN ST TRIAL P Rule 13(I).

  ii. In addition, the court may consider any other relevant factors. IN ST TRIAL P Rule 13(I).

j. *Effect of statute of limitations and other discharges at law.* The statute of limitations, a nonclaim statute or other discharge at law shall not bar a claim asserted as a counterclaim to the extent that:

  i. It diminishes or defeats the opposing party's claim if it arises out of the transaction or occurrence that is the subject-matter of the opposing party's claim, or if it could have been asserted as a counterclaim to the opposing party's claim before it (the counterclaim) was barred; or

  ii. It or the opposing party's claim relates to payment of or security for the other. IN ST TRIAL P Rule 13(J).

k. *Counterclaim by and against transferees and successors.* A counterclaim may be asserted by or against the transferee or successor of a claim subject to the following provisions:

  i. A successor who is a guardian, representative of a decedent's estate, receiver or assignee for the benefit of creditors, trustee or the like may interpose a claim to which he succeeds against claims or proceedings brought in or outside the court of administration. A claim owing by his predecessor may be interposed against any claim brought by such successor in or outside the court of administration without the necessity of filing such claim or cause of action in the administration proceedings. IN ST TRIAL P Rule 13(K)(1).

  ii. A transferee or successor of a claim takes it subject to any defense or counterclaim that is the subject-matter of the opposing party's claim; or that is available to the obligor at the time of the assignment or before the obligor received notice of the assignment. IN ST TRIAL P Rule 13(K)(2).

  iii. A surety or party with total or partial recourse upon a claim upon which he is being sued may interpose as a counterclaim:

   • Any claim of his own; and

   • Any claim owned by the person against whom he has recourse who either has notice of the suit, is a party to the suit, is insolvent, has assigned his claim to the surety or party asserting it, or cannot be found. IN ST TRIAL P Rule 13(K)(3).

AMENDED ANSWER

- A counterclaim under IN ST TRIAL P Rule 13(K)(3)(b) must tend to diminish or defeat the opposing party's claim, or it or the opposing claim must relate to payment of or security for the other, unless the person against whom recourse may be had is a party to the suit or the counterclaim has been assigned to the party asserting it; and if recovery on the counterclaim exceeds the opposing party's claim, any excess recovered shall be held in trust for such person against whom there is a right of recourse. IN ST TRIAL P Rule 13(K)(3).

    iv. IN ST TRIAL P Rule 13(K)(1), IN ST TRIAL P Rule 13(K)(2), and IN ST TRIAL P Rule 13(K)(3), are subject to subdivision IN ST TRIAL P Rule 13(L). IN ST TRIAL P Rule 13(K)(4).

l. *Counterclaim and cross-claim subject to substantive law principles.* Counterclaim and cross-claims are subject to restrictions imposed by other statutes and principles of substantive common law and equity, including rules of commercial law, agency, estoppel, contract and the like. In appropriate cases the court may impose terms or conditions upon its judgment or decree and may enter conditional or noncanceling cross judgments to satisfy such restrictions. This provision is intended to deny or limit counterclaims or cross-claims:

    i. Where a creditor will receive an unfair priority because a claim is assigned after insolvency proceedings, or assigned before such proceedings if it results in an unlawful preference;

    ii. Where an unfair priority will be allowed if a surety interposing a claim owned in his own right against the creditor suing on the principal's obligation when the principal is solvent and the creditor is not;

    iii. Where a claim by or against a representative, such as a guardian, receiver, representative of a decedent's estate, assignee for the benefit of creditors, trustee or the like in his individual capacity is asserted against a claim owing or owed by the estate he represents;

    iv. Where a claim by or against a partnership or two (2) or more obligors is opposed against or by a claim of an individual to the extent that the individual will be allowed unfairly to profit or if it will adversely affect the rights of creditors; or

    v. Where a claim is cut off by a holder in due course or a transferee who is protected under principles of commercial law, estoppel, or contract. IN ST TRIAL P Rule 13(L).

m. *Satisfaction of judgment.* Satisfaction of a judgment or credits thereon may be ordered, for sufficient cause, upon notice and motion. "Credits" include any counterclaim which tends to diminish or defeat the judgment, or any counterclaim where it or the opposing claim relates to payment of or security for the other. IN ST TRIAL P Rule 13(M).

6. *Third-party practice*

a. *When defendant may bring in third party.* A defending party, as a third-party plaintiff, may cause a summons and complaint to be served upon a person not a party to the action who is or may be liable to him for all or part of the plaintiff's claim against him. IN ST TRIAL P Rule 14(A). The person served with the summons and the third-party complaint, hereinafter called the third-party defendant, as provided in IN ST TRIAL P Rule 12 and IN ST TRIAL P Rule 13 may make:

    i. His defenses, cross-claims and counterclaims to the third-party plaintiff's claims;

    ii. His defenses, counterclaims and cross-claims against any other defendants or third-party defendants;

    iii. Any defenses or claims which the third-party plaintiff has to the plaintiff's claim which are available to the third-party defendant against the plaintiff; and

    iv. Any defenses or claims which the third-party defendant has as against the plaintiff. IN ST TRIAL P Rule 14(A).

    v. The plaintiff may assert any claim against the third-party defendant who thereupon may assert his defenses, counterclaims and cross-claims, as provided in IN ST TRIAL P Rule 12 and IN ST TRIAL P Rule 13. A third-party defendant may proceed under IN ST TRIAL P Rule 14 against any person not a party to the action who is or may be liable to him for all or part of the claim made in the action against the third-party defendant. IN ST TRIAL P Rule 14(A).

b. *When plaintiff may bring in third party.* When a counterclaim or other claim is asserted against a plaintiff, he may cause a third party to be brought in under circumstances, which, under IN ST TRIAL P Rule 14, would entitle a defendant to do so. IN ST TRIAL P Rule 14(B).

c. *Severance; Parties improperly impleaded.* With his responsive pleading or by motion prior thereto, any party may move for severance of a third-party claim or ensuing claim as provided in IN ST TRIAL P Rule 14 or for a separate trial thereon. If the third-party defendant is a proper party to the proceedings under any other rule relating to parties, the action shall continue as in other cases where he is made a party. IN ST TRIAL P Rule 14(C).

7. *Trial by jury; Demand*

   a. *Causes triable by court and by jury.* Issues of law and issues of fact in causes that prior to the eighteenth day of June, 1852, were of exclusive equitable jurisdiction shall be tried by the court; issues of fact in all other causes shall be triable as the same are now triable. In case of the joinder of causes of action or defenses which, prior to said date, were of exclusive equitable jurisdiction with causes of action or defenses which, prior to said date, were designated as actions at law and triable by jury—the former shall be triable by the court, and the latter by a jury, unless waived; the trial of both may be at the same time or at different times, as the court may direct. IN ST TRIAL P Rule 38(A).

   b. *Demand.* Any party may demand a trial by jury of any issue triable of right by a jury by filing with the court and serving upon the other parties a demand therefor in writing at any time after the commencement of the action and not later than ten (10) days after the first responsive pleading to the complaint, or to a counterclaim, crossclaim or other claim if one properly is pleaded; and if no responsive pleading is filed or required, within ten (10) days after the time such pleading otherwise would have been required. Such demand is sufficient if indorsed upon a pleading of a party filed within such time. IN ST TRIAL P Rule 38(B).

   c. *Same; Specification of issues.* In his demand a party may specify the issues which he wishes so tried; otherwise he shall be deemed to have demanded trial by jury for all issues triable as of right by jury. Any other party must file a demand for jury trial to preserve his right to trial by jury:

      i. Of issues for which a right to trial by jury was not requested by another party; and

      ii. In case a request by another party was improper. But if a proper request for a trial by jury upon issues triable by jury as of right on his behalf is made by any party, such request shall be deemed to have been made on behalf of all parties entitled to a jury trial upon such issues. IN ST TRIAL P Rule 38(C).

   d. *Waiver.* The failure of a party to appear at the trial, and the failure of a party to serve a demand as required by IN ST TRIAL P Rule 38 and to file it as required by IN ST TRIAL P Rule 5(E) constitute waiver by him of trial by jury. A demand for trial by jury made as provided in IN ST TRIAL P Rule 38 may not be withdrawn without the consent of the other party or parties. IN ST TRIAL P Rule 38(D).

      i. The trial court shall not grant a demand for a trial by jury filed after the time fixed in IN ST TRIAL P Rule 38(B) has elapsed except upon the written agreement of all of the parties to the action, which agreement shall be filed with the court and made a part of the record. If such agreement is filed then the court may, in its discretion, grant a trial by jury in which event the grant of a trial by jury may not be withdrawn except by the agreement of all of the parties. IN ST TRIAL P Rule 38(D).

   e. *Arbitration.* Nothing in the Indiana Rules of Trial Procedure shall deny the parties the right by contract or agreement to submit or to agree to submit controversies to arbitration made before or after commencement of an action thereon or deny the courts power to specifically enforce such agreements. IN ST TRIAL P Rule 38(E).

D. Documents

1. *Required documents*

   a. *Amended answer.* Refer to the General Requirements section of this document for information on the contents of an amended answer.

b. *Certificate of service.* An attorney or unrepresented party tendering a document to the Clerk for filing shall certify that service has been made, list the parties served, and specify the date and means of service. The certificate of service shall be placed at the end of the document and shall not be separately filed. The separate filing of a certificate of service, however, shall not be grounds for rejecting a document for filing. The Clerk may permit documents to be filed without a certificate of service but shall require prompt filing of a separate certificate of service. IN ST TRIAL P Rule 5(C).

2. *Supplemental documents*

a. *Proof of written instrument.* When any pleading allowed by the Indiana Rules of Trial Procedure is founded on a written instrument, the original, or a copy thereof, must be included in or filed with the pleading. Such instrument, whether copied in the pleadings or not, shall be taken as part of the record. When any pleading allowed by the Indiana Rules of Trial Procedure is founded on an account, an Affidavit of Debt, in a form substantially similar to that which is provided in IN ST TRIAL P App. A-2, shall be attached. IN ST TRIAL P Rule 9.2(A).

b. *Notice of intent to use foreign law.* A party who intends to raise an issue concerning the law of a foreign country shall give notice in his pleadings or other reasonable written notice. The court, in determining foreign law, may consider any relevant material or source, including testimony, whether or not submitted by a party or admissible under IN ST TRIAL P Rule 43. The court's determination shall be treated as a ruling on a question of law. It shall be made by the court and not the jury and shall be reviewable. IN ST TRIAL P Rule 44.1(A).

c. *Facsimile cover sheet.* Any document sent to the Clerk of the Circuit Court by electronic facsimile transmission shall be accompanied by a cover sheet which states the title of the document, case number, number of pages, identity and voice telephone number of the sending party and instructions for filing. The cover sheet shall contain the signature of the attorney or party, pro se, authorizing the filing. IN ST ADMIN Rule 12(D).

E. Format

1. *Form of pleadings*

a. *Caption; Names of parties.* Every pleading shall contain a caption setting forth the name of the court, the title of the action, the file number, and a designation as in IN ST TRIAL P Rule 7(A). In the complaint the title of the action shall include the names of all the parties, but in other pleadings it is sufficient to state the name of the first party on each side with an appropriate indication of other parties. IN ST TRIAL P Rule 10(A).

b. *Paragraphs; Separate statements.* All averments of a claim or defense shall be made in numbered paragraphs, the contents of each of which shall be limited as far as practicable to a statement of a single set of circumstances, and a paragraph may be referred to by number in all succeeding pleadings. Each claim founded upon a separate transaction or occurrence and each defense other than denials may be stated in a separate count or defense whenever a separation facilitates the clear presentation of the matters set forth. IN ST TRIAL P Rule 10(B).

c. *Adoption by reference; Exhibits.* Statements in a pleading may be adopted by reference in a different part of the same pleading or in another pleading or in any motion. A copy of any written instrument which is an exhibit to a pleading is a part thereof for all purposes. IN ST TRIAL P Rule 10(C).

d. *Citation.* Allen County Superior and Circuit court rules may be cited as L.R. _____. The Indiana Rules of Trial Procedure are hereinafter referred to as T.R. _____. IN ST ALLEN SUPER AND CIR CT CIV Rule AR00-1(B).

e. *Paper.* All pleadings must be printed on white paper. IN ST ALLEN SUPER AND CIR CT CIV Rule 8-1(A).

f. *Spacing.* The lines shall be double spaced except for quotations, which shall be indented and single-spaced. IN ST ALLEN SUPER AND CIR CT CIV Rule 8-1(A).

g. *Photocopies.* Photocopies are acceptable if legible. IN ST ALLEN SUPER AND CIR CT CIV Rule 8-1(A).

h. *Margins and binding.* Margins shall be one to one and one-half (1-1 1/2) inches on the left side and one-half (1/2) inch on the right. IN ST ALLEN SUPER AND CIR CT CIV Rule 8-1(B).

   i. Binding or stapling shall be at the top left and at no other place. IN ST ALLEN SUPER AND CIR CT CIV Rule 8-1(B).

   ii. Covers or backing shall not be used. IN ST ALLEN SUPER AND CIR CT CIV Rule 8-1(B).

i. *Flat filing.* The files of the Clerk of the Court shall be kept under the "flat filing" system. All pleadings presented for filing with the Clerk or Court shall be flat and unfolded. Only the original of any pleading shall be placed in the Court file. IN ST ALLEN SUPER AND CIR CT CIV Rule 77-1(A).

j. *Handwritten pleadings.* Handwritten pleadings may be accepted for filing in the discretion of the Court. IN ST ALLEN SUPER AND CIR CT CIV Rule 8-1(A).

2. *Size of papers for filing.* Effective January 1, 1992, all pleadings, copies, motions and documents filed with any trial court or appellate level court, typed or printed, with the exception of exhibits and existing wills, shall be prepared on eight and one-half by eleven inch (8 1/2" x 11") size paper. IN ST ADMIN Rule 11.

3. *Signature requirements*

a. *Signature of attorney.* Every pleading or motion of a party represented by an attorney shall be signed by at least one (1) attorney of record in his individual name, whose address, telephone number, and attorney number shall be stated, except that this provision shall not apply to pleadings and motions made and transcribed at the trial or a hearing before the judge and received by him in such form. IN ST TRIAL P Rule 11(A). All pleadings to be signed by an attorney shall contain the written signature of the individual attorney, the attorney's printed name, Supreme Court Attorney Number, the name of the attorney's law firm, the attorney's address, telephone number, and a designation of the party for whom the attorney appears. IN ST ALLEN SUPER AND CIR CT CIV Rule 8-1(C). For the recommended signature format, refer to IN ST ALLEN SUPER AND CIR CT CIV Rule 8-1(C).

   i. The signature of an attorney constitutes a certificate by him that he has read the pleadings; that to the best of his knowledge, information, and belief, there is good ground to support it; and that it is not interposed for delay. IN ST TRIAL P Rule 11(A).

   ii. If a pleading or motion is not signed or is signed with intent to defeat the purpose of the rule, it may be stricken as sham and false and the action may proceed as though the pleading had not been served. IN ST TRIAL P Rule 11(A).

   iii. For a willful violation of IN ST TRIAL P Rule 11 an attorney may be subjected to appropriate disciplinary action. Similar action may be taken if scandalous or indecent matter is inserted. IN ST TRIAL P Rule 11(A).

   iv. Neither printed signatures, nor facsimile signatures shall be accepted on original documents. IN ST ALLEN SUPER AND CIR CT CIV Rule 8-1(C).

   v. Facsimile signatures are permitted on copies. IN ST ALLEN SUPER AND CIR CT CIV Rule 8-1(C).

b. *Signature of unrepresented party.* A party who is not represented by an attorney shall sign his pleading and state his address. IN ST TRIAL P Rule 11(A).

c. *Verification not generally required.* Except when specifically required by rule, pleadings or motions need not be verified or accompanied by affidavit. The rule in equity that the averments of an answer under oath must be overcome by the testimony of two (2) witnesses or of one (1) witness sustained by corroborating circumstances is abolished. IN ST TRIAL P Rule 11(A).

d. *Verification by affirmation or representation.* When in connection with any civil or special statutory proceeding it is required that any pleading, motion, petition, supporting affidavit, or other document of any kind, be verified, or that an oath be taken, it shall be sufficient if the subscriber simply affirms the truth of the matter to be verified by an affirmation or representation. IN ST TRIAL P Rule 11(B). IN ST TRIAL P Rule 11(B) states that the affirmation or representation should be in substantially the

following language: "I (we) affirm, under the penalties for perjury, that the foregoing representation(s) is (are) true. (Signed) _____."

    i. Any person who falsifies an affirmation or representation of fact shall be subject to the same penalties as are prescribed by law for the making of a false affidavit. IN ST TRIAL P Rule 11(B).

  e. *Verified pleadings, motions, and affidavits as evidence.* Pleadings, motions and affidavits accompanying or in support of such pleadings or motions when required to be verified or under oath shall be accepted as a representation that the signer had personal knowledge thereof or reasonable cause to believe the existence of the facts or matters stated or alleged therein; and, if otherwise competent or acceptable as evidence, may be admitted as evidence of the facts or matters stated or alleged therein when it is so provided in the Indiana Rules of Trial Procedure, by statute or other law, or to the extent the writing or signature expressly purports to be made upon the signer's personal knowledge. When such pleadings, motions and affidavits are verified or under oath they shall not require other or greater proof on the part of the adverse party than if not verified or not under oath unless expressly provided otherwise by the Indiana Rules of Trial Procedure, statute or other law. Affidavits upon motions for summary judgment under IN ST TRIAL P Rule 56 and in denial of execution under IN ST TRIAL P Rule 9.2 shall be made upon personal knowledge. IN ST TRIAL P Rule 11(C).

4. *Information excluded from public access.* Every document filed in a case shall separately identify information excluded from public access pursuant to IN ST ADMIN Rule 9(G)(1) as follows:

  a. Whole documents that are excluded from public access pursuant to IN ST ADMIN Rule 9(G)(1) shall be tendered on light green paper or have a light green coversheet attached to the document, marked "Not for Public Access" or "Confidential." IN ST TRIAL P Rule 5(G)(1).

  b. When only a portion of a document contains information excluded from public access pursuant to IN ST ADMIN Rule 9(G)(1), said information shall be omitted [or redacted] from the filed document, and set forth on a separate accompanying document on light green paper conspicuously marked "Not for Public Access" or "Confidential" and clearly designated [or identifying] the caption and number of the case and the document and location within the document to which the redacted material pertains. IN ST TRIAL P Rule 5(G)(2).

  c. With respect to documents filed in electronic format, the trial court, by local rule, may provide for compliance with IN ST TRIAL P Rule 5 in manner that separates and protects access to information excluded from public access. IN ST TRIAL P Rule 5(G)(3).

  d. IN ST TRIAL P Rule 5(G) does not apply to a record sealed by the court pursuant to IN ST 5-14-3-5.5 or otherwise, nor to records, documents, or information filed in cases to which public access is prohibited pursuant to IN ST ADMIN Rule 9(G). IN ST TRIAL P Rule 5(G)(4).

  e. The following information in case records is excluded from public access and is confidential:

    i. Information that is excluded from public access pursuant to federal law;

    ii. Information that is excluded from public access as declared confidential by Indiana statute or other court rule, including without limitation:

- All adoption records created after July 8, 1941, as declared confidential by IN ST 31-19-19-1, et seq., except those specifically declared open by IN ST 31-19-13-2(2);

- All records relating to chancroid, chlamydia, gonorrhea, hepatitis, human immunodeficiency virus (HIV), Lymphogranuloma venereum, syphilis, tuberculosis, as declared confidential by IN ST 16-41-8-1, et seq.;

- All records relating to child abuse as declared confidential by IN ST 31-33-18-1, et seq.;

- All records relating to drug tests as declared confidential by IN ST 5-14-3-4(a)(9);

- Records of grand jury proceedings as declared confidential by IN ST 35-34-2-4;

- Records of juvenile proceedings as declared confidential by IN ST 31-39-1-2, except those specifically open under statute;

- All paternity records created after July 1, 1941 as declared confidential by IN ST

31-14-11-15, IN ST 31-19-5-23, IN ST 31-39-1-1 and IN ST 31-39-1-2 [Editor's note: IN ST 31-14-11-15 was repealed effective May 9, 2013];

- All pre-sentence reports as declared confidential by IN ST 35-38-1-13;

- Written petitions to permit marriages without consent and orders directing the Clerk of Court to issue a marriage license to underage persons, as declared confidential by IN ST 31-11-1-6;

- Only those arrest warrants, search warrants, indictments and informations ordered confidential by the trial judge, prior to return of duly executed service as declared confidential by IN ST 5-14-3-4(b)(1);

- All medical, mental health, or tax records unless determined by law or regulation of any governmental custodian not to be confidential, released by the subject of such records, or declared by a court of competent jurisdiction to be essential to the resolution of litigation as declared confidential by IN ST 16-39-3-10, IN ST 6-4.1-5-10, IN ST 6-4.1-12-12, and IN ST 6-8.1-7-1;

- Personal information relating to jurors or prospective jurors, other than for the use of the parties and counsel, pursuant to IN ST JURY Rule 10;

- Information relating to protection from abuse orders, no-contact orders and workplace violence restraining orders as declared confidential by IN ST 5-2-9-6, et seq.;

- Mediation proceedings pursuant to IN ST ADR Rule 2.11, Mini-Trial proceedings pursuant to IN ST ADR Rule 4.4(C), and Summary Jury Trials pursuant to IN ST ADR Rule 5.6;

- Information in probation files pursuant to the Probation Standards promulgated by the Judicial Conference of Indiana pursuant to IN ST 11-13-1-8(b);

- Information deemed confidential pursuant to the Rules for Court Administered Alcohol and Drug Programs promulgated by the Judicial Conference of Indiana pursuant to IN ST 12-23-14-13;

- Information deemed confidential pursuant to the Problem-Solving Court Rules promulgated by the Judicial Conference of Indiana pursuant to IN ST 33-23-16-16;

- All records of the Department of workforce Development as declared confidential by IN ST 22-4-19-6;

- Information regarding interception of electronic communications that is sealed or deemed confidential as set forth in IN ST 35-33.5-2-1, et seq.

   iii.   Information excluded from public access by specific court order;

   iv.   Complete Social Security Numbers of living persons;

   v.   With the exception of names, information such as addresses, phone numbers, and dates of birth which explicitly identifies:

- Natural persons who are witnesses or victims (not including defendants) in criminal, domestic violence, stalking, sexual assault, juvenile, or civil protection order proceedings, provided that juveniles who are victims of sex crimes shall be identified by initials only;

- Places of residence of judicial officers, clerks and other employees of courts and clerks of court, unless the person or persons about whom the information pertains waives confidentiality;

   vi.   Complete account numbers of specific assets, loans, bank accounts, credit cards, and personal identification numbers (PINs);

   vii.   All orders of expungement entered in criminal or juvenile proceedings, orders to restrict access to criminal history information pursuant to IN ST 35-38-5-5.5 or IN ST 35-38-8-5 and records excluded from public access by such orders, and information related to infractions that is excluded from public access pursuant to IN ST 34-28-5-15 or IN ST 34-28-5-16 [Editor's note:

IN ST 35-38-5-5.5, IN ST 35-38-8-5 and IN ST 34-28-5-16 were repealed effective July 1, 2013; for information on orders restricting access to criminal history, refer to IN ST 35-38-9-1, et seq.];

viii. All personal notes and e-mail, and deliberative material, of judges, jurors, court staff and judicial agencies, and information recorded in personal data assistants (PDA's) or organizers and personal calendars. IN ST ADMIN Rule 9(G)(1).

F. Filing and Service Requirements

1. *Filing requirements.* Except as otherwise provided in IN ST TRIAL P Rule 5(E)(2), all pleadings and papers subsequent to the complaint which are required to be served upon a party shall be filed with the Court either before service or within a reasonable period of time thereafter. IN ST TRIAL P Rule 5(E)(1).

   a. *Filing with the court defined.* The filing of pleadings, motions, and other papers with the court as required by the Indiana Rules of Trial Procedure shall be made by one of the following methods:

      i. Delivery to the clerk of the court;

      ii. Sending by electronic transmission under the procedure adopted pursuant to IN ST ADMIN Rule 12;

      iii. Mailing to the clerk by registered, certified or express mail return receipt requested;

      iv. Depositing with any third-party commercial carrier for delivery to the clerk within three (3) calendar days, cost prepaid, properly addressed;

      v. If the court so permits, filing with the judge, in which event the judge shall note thereon the filing date and forthwith transmit them to the office of the clerk; or

      vi. Electronic filing, as approved by the Division of State Court Administration pursuant to IN ST ADMIN Rule 16. IN ST TRIAL P Rule 5(F).

      vii. Filing by registered or certified mail and by third-party commercial carrier shall be complete upon mailing or deposit. IN ST TRIAL P Rule 5(F).

   b. *Facsimile filing*

      i. *Generally.* In counties where a majority of judges of the courts of record, by posted local rule, have authorized electronic facsimile filing and designated a telephone number to receive such transmissions, pleadings, motions, and other papers may be sent to the Clerk of Circuit Court by electronic facsimile transmission for filing in any case, provided:

         • Such matter does not exceed ten (10) pages, including the cover sheet;

         • Such matter does not require the payment of fees other than the electronic facsimile transcription fee set forth in IN ST ADMIN Rule 12(E);

         • The sending party creates at the time of transmission a machine generated log for such transmission; and

         • The original document and the transmission log are maintained by the sending party for the duration of the litigation. IN ST ADMIN Rule 12(B).

      ii. *Time of filing.* During normal, posted business hours, the time of filing shall be the time the duplicate document is produced in the office of the Clerk of the Circuit Court. Duplicate documents received at all other times shall be filed as of the next normal business day. IN ST ADMIN Rule 12(C).

         • If the receiving fax machine endorses its own time and date stamp upon the transmitted documents and the receiving machine produces a delivery receipt which is electronically created and transmitted to the sending party, the time of filing shall be the date and time recorded on the transmitted document by the receiving fax machine. IN ST ADMIN Rule 12(C).

   c. *Proof of filing.* Any party filing any paper by any method other than personal delivery to the clerk shall retain proof of filing. IN ST TRIAL P Rule 5(F).

2. *Service requirements.* Unless otherwise provided by the Indiana Rules of Trial Procedure or an order of

the court, each party and special judge, if any, shall be served with: (1) every order required by its terms to be served; (2) every pleading subsequent to the original complaint; (3) every written motion except one which may be heard ex parte; (4) every brief submitted to the trial court; (5) every paper relating to discovery required to be served upon a party; and (6) every written notice, appearance, demand, offer of judgment, designation of record on appeal, or similar paper. IN ST TRIAL P Rule 5(A).

a. *Methods of service*

    i. *Personal service.* Whenever a party is represented by an attorney of record, service shall be made upon such attorney unless service upon the party himself is ordered by the court. Service upon the attorney or party shall be made by delivering or mailing a copy of the papers to the last known address or where an attorney or party has consented to service by fax or e-mail, as provided in IN ST TRIAL P Rule 3.1(A)(4), by faxing or e-mailing a copy of the documents to the fax number or e-mail address set out in the appearance form or correction as required by IN ST TRIAL P Rule 3.1(E). IN ST TRIAL P Rule 5(B). Delivery of a copy within IN ST TRIAL P Rule 5 means:

- Offering or tendering it to the attorney or party and stating the nature of the papers being served. Refusal to accept an offered or tendered document is a waiver of any objection to the sufficiency or adequacy of service of that document;

- Leaving it at his office with a clerk or other person in charge thereof, or if there is no one in charge, leaving it in a conspicuous place therein; or

- If the office is closed, by leaving it at his dwelling house or usual place of abode with some person of suitable age and discretion then residing therein; or,

- Leaving it at some other suitable place, selected by the attorney upon whom service is being made, pursuant to duly promulgated local rule. IN ST TRIAL P Rule 5(B)(1).

    ii. *Service by mail.* If service is made by mail, the papers shall be deposited in the United States mail addressed to the person on whom they are being served, with postage prepaid. Service shall be deemed complete upon mailing. Proof of service of all papers permitted to be mailed may be made by written acknowledgment of service, by affidavit of the person who mailed the papers, or by certificate of an attorney. It shall be the duty of attorneys when entering their appearance in a cause or when filing pleadings or papers therein, to have noted in the Chronological Case Summary or said pleadings or papers so filed the address and telephone number of their office. Service by delivery or by mail at such address shall be deemed sufficient and complete. IN ST TRIAL P Rule 5(B)(2).

    iii. *Service by fax or e-mail.* A party who has consented to service by fax or e-mail may be served as follows:

- Service by e-mail shall be made by attaching the document being served in .pdf format. Discovery documents must also be served in accordance with IN ST TRIAL P Rule 26(A). IN ST TRIAL P Rule 5(B)(3)(a).

- Service by fax shall be deemed complete upon generation of a transmission record indicating the successful transmission of the entire document, except as provided in IN ST TRIAL P Rule 5(B)(3)(d). IN ST TRIAL P Rule 5(B)(3)(b).

- Service by e-mail shall be deemed complete upon transmission, except as provided in IN ST TRIAL P Rule 5(B)(3)(d). IN ST TRIAL P Rule 5(B)(3)(c).

- Service by fax or e-mail that occurs on a Saturday, Sunday, legal holiday, or day the court or agency in which the matter is pending is closed or after 5:00 PM local time of the recipient shall be deemed complete the next day that is not a Saturday, Sunday, legal holiday, or day that the court or agency in which the matter is pending is not closed. IN ST TRIAL P Rule 5(B)(3)(d).

    iv. *Consent to alternate service.* Any Allen County Attorney or any Allen County law firm may, without charge, maintain an assigned Courthouse box in the library of the Allen County Courthouse for receipt of notices, pleadings, process orders, or other communications from the

Court, the Clerk, and other attorneys or law firms. IN ST ALLEN SUPER AND CIR CT CIV Rule 5-1(A). For more information concerning the use of courthouse boxes, refer to IN ST ALLEN SUPER AND CIR CT CIV Rule 5-1.

b. *Serving numerous defendants.* In any action in which there are unusually large numbers of defendants, the court, upon motion or of its own initiative, may order:

   i. That service of the pleadings of the defendants and replies thereto need not be made as between the defendants;

   • That any cross-claim, counterclaim, or matter constituting an avoidance or affirmative defense contained therein shall be deemed to be denied or avoided by all other parties; and

   • That the filing of any such pleading and service thereof upon the plaintiff constitutes due notice of it to the parties. IN ST TRIAL P Rule 5(D).

   ii. A copy of every such order shall be served upon the parties in such manner and form as the court directs. IN ST TRIAL P Rule 5(D).

c. *Service on parties in default for failure to appear.* No service need be made on parties in default for failure to appear, except that pleadings asserting new or additional claims for relief against them shall be served upon them in the manner provided by service of summons in IN ST TRIAL P Rule 4. IN ST TRIAL P Rule 5(A).

d. *Proof of mailing.* Certificates of service or proof of mailing of pleadings concerning any case shall be deemed sufficient proof of service if such pleadings were mailed to the last known address of a party or attorney noted upon the chronological case summary of a case. IN ST ALLEN SUPER AND CIR CT CIV Rule 3.1-1(E).

G. Hearings

1. The Indiana rules do not contemplate a hearing regarding the filing and service of an amended answer.

H. Forms

1. Official Amended Answer Forms for Indiana

   a. Affidavit of debt. IN ST TRIAL P App. A-2.

2. Amended Answer Forms for Indiana

   a. Amendment by stipulation. 10 INPRAC § 46.11.

   b. Amended answer by interlineations. 10 INPRAC § 46.12.

   c. Answer; Form and content. 9 INPRAC § 41.1.

   d. Answer; General form. 9 INPRAC § 41.3.

   e. Answer; Another form. 9 INPRAC § 41.4.

   f. Answer; Another form. 9 INPRAC § 41.5.

   g. General denial. 9 INPRAC § 41.6.

   h. Specific denial of designated paragraph. 9 INPRAC § 41.7.

   i. Specific admission of designated paragraph. 9 INPRAC § 41.8.

   j. Denial of knowledge or information to form belief. 9 INPRAC § 41.9.

   k. Denial of knowledge or information to form belief; Another form. 9 INPRAC § 41.10.

   l. Partial denial and partial admission of designated paragraph. 9 INPRAC § 41.11.

   m. Denial of designated paragraph for reason that document speaks for itself. 9 INPRAC § 41.12.

   n. Adoption of admissions or denials by co-defendant's answer. 9 INPRAC § 41.13.

   o. Denial of execution of instrument filed with pleading. 9 INPRAC § 41.14.

   p. Answer to cross-claim. 9 INPRAC § 41.15.

   q. Answer to third-party complaint. 9 INPRAC § 41.16.

r. Accord and satisfaction. 9 INPRAC § 41.21.

s. Answer. 5 INPRAC § 3:3.3.

t. Answer; Another form. 5 INPRAC § 3:3.4.

u. Certificate of service; Personal service. 9 INPRAC § 5.7.

v. Certificate of service; First class mail. 9 INPRAC § 5.8.

w. Signature; By party. 9 INPRAC § 4.5.

x. Signature; Attorney. 9 INPRAC § 4.6.

y. Signature; Attorney; Another form. 9 INPRAC § 4.7.

z. Signature; Attorney; Another form. 9 INPRAC § 4.8.

3. **Official Amended Answer Forms for Allen County**

    a. Consent to alternate service. IN ST ALLEN SUPER AND CIR CT CIV App. A.

I. Checklist

(I) ❑ Matters to be considered by the party filing the amended answer

    (a) ❑ Required documents if amending as matter of course

        (1) ❑ Amended answer

        (2) ❑ Certificate of service

    (b) ❑ Supplemental documents

        (1) ❑ Proof of written instrument

        (2) ❑ Notice of intent to use foreign law

        (3) ❑ Facsimile cover sheet

    (c) ❑ Timing

        (1) ❑ As a matter of course before a responsive pleading is served, or, if the pleading is one to which no responsive pleading is permitted, within thirty (30) days after it is served

        (2) ❑ At any time with leave of court

Motions, Oppositions and Replies
Motion to Strike

Document Last Updated October 2013

A. Applicable Rules

1. *State rules*

    a. Appearance. IN ST TRIAL P Rule 3.1.

    b. Process. IN ST TRIAL P Rule 4.

    c. Service and filing of pleadings and other papers. IN ST TRIAL P Rule 5.

    d. Time. IN ST TRIAL P Rule 6.

    e. Pleadings. IN ST TRIAL P Rule 7; IN ST TRIAL P Rule 8; IN ST TRIAL P Rule 9.2; IN ST TRIAL P Rule 10; IN ST TRIAL P Rule 11.

    f. Defenses and objections; When and how presented; By pleading or motion; Motion for judgment on the pleadings. IN ST TRIAL P Rule 12.

    g. Amended and supplemental pleadings. IN ST TRIAL P Rule 15.

    h. Joinder of person needed for just adjudication. IN ST TRIAL P Rule 19.

    i. Evidence. IN ST TRIAL P Rule 43.

j. Judgment on the evidence (directed verdict). IN ST TRIAL P Rule 50.

k. Findings by the court. IN ST TRIAL P Rule 52.

l. Summary judgment. IN ST TRIAL P Rule 56.

m. Motion to correct error. IN ST TRIAL P Rule 59.

n. Relief from judgment or order. IN ST TRIAL P Rule 60.

o. Trial court and clerks. IN ST TRIAL P Rule 72.

p. Hearing of motions. IN ST TRIAL P Rule 73.

q. Access to court records. IN ST ADMIN Rule 9.

r. Paper size. IN ST ADMIN Rule 11.

s. Facsimile transmission. IN ST ADMIN Rule 12.

t. Electronic filing and electronic service pilot projects. IN ST ADMIN Rule 16.

u. Sealing of certain records by court; Hearing; Notice. IN ST 5-14-3-5.5.

v. Privacy and confidentiality. IN ST 5-2-9-6; IN ST 5-14-3-4; IN ST 6-4.1-5-10; IN ST 6-4.1-12-12; IN ST 6-8.1-7-1; IN ST 11-13-1-8; IN ST 12-23-14-13; IN ST 16-39-3-10; IN ST 16-41-8-1; IN ST 22-4-19-6; IN ST 31-11-1-6; IN ST 31-19-5-23; IN ST 31-19-13-2; IN ST 31-19-19-1; IN ST 31-33-18-1; IN ST 31-39-1-1; IN ST 31-39-1-2; IN ST 33-23-16-16; IN ST 35-34-2-4; IN ST 35-38-1-13; IN ST 35-38-9-1; IN ST ADR Rule 2.11; IN ST ADR Rule 4.4; IN ST ADR Rule 5.6; IN ST JURY Rule 10.

2. *Local rules*

a. Applicability and citation of rules. IN ST ALLEN SUPER AND CIR CT CIV Rule AR00-1.

b. Proposed orders. IN ST ALLEN SUPER AND CIR CT CIV Rule TR00-1.

c. Appearances. IN ST ALLEN SUPER AND CIR CT CIV Rule 3.1-1.

d. Consent to alternate service. IN ST ALLEN SUPER AND CIR CT CIV Rule 5-1.

e. Motions in civil court. IN ST ALLEN SUPER AND CIR CT CIV Rule 7-1.

f. Preparation of pleadings. IN ST ALLEN SUPER AND CIR CT CIV Rule 8-1.

g. Filing. IN ST ALLEN SUPER AND CIR CT CIV Rule 77-1.

B. Timing

1. *Motion to strike.* Upon motion made by a party before responding to a pleading, or, if no responsive pleading is permitted by Indiana Rules of Trial Procedure, upon motion made by a party within twenty (20) days after the service of the pleading upon him or at any time upon the court's own initiative, the court may order stricken from any pleading any insufficient claim or defense or any redundant, immaterial, impertinent, or scandalous matter. IN ST TRIAL P Rule 12(F).

a. *Time to file a responsive pleading.* A responsive pleading required under the Indiana Rules of Trial Procedure, shall be served within twenty (20) days after service of the prior pleading. IN ST TRIAL P Rule 6(C).

b. *Filing.* All pleadings and papers subsequent to the complaint which are required to be served upon a party shall be filed with the Court either before service or within a reasonable period of time thereafter. IN ST TRIAL P Rule 5(E)(1).

2. *Service.* A written motion, other than one which may be heard ex parte, and notice of the hearing thereof shall be served not less than five (5) days before the time specified for the hearing, unless a different period is fixed by the Indiana Rules of Trial Procedure or by order of the court. IN ST TRIAL P Rule 6(D).

a. *Of supporting affidavits.* When a motion is supported by affidavit, the affidavit shall be served with the motion. IN ST TRIAL P Rule 6(D).

3. *Service of opposition.* Except as otherwise provided in IN ST TRIAL P Rule 59(D), opposing affidavits may be served not less than one (1) day before the hearing, unless the court permits them to be served at some other time. IN ST TRIAL P Rule 6(D).

4. *Computation of time*

    a. *Generally; Days excluded.* In computing any period of time prescribed or allowed by the Indiana Rules of Trial Procedure, by order of the court, or by any applicable statute, the day of the act, event, or default from which the designated period of time begins to run shall not be included. The last day of the period so computed is to be included unless it is:

       i. A Saturday,

       ii. A Sunday,

       iii. A legal holiday as defined by state statute, or

       iv. A day the office in which the act is to be done is closed during regular business hours. IN ST TRIAL P Rule 6(A).

    b. *Short periods.* In any event, the period runs until the end of the next day that is not a Saturday, a Sunday, a legal holiday, or a day on which the office is closed. When the period of time allowed is less than seven (7) days, intermediate Saturdays, Sundays, legal holidays, and days on which the office is closed shall be excluded from the computations. IN ST TRIAL P Rule 6(A).

    c. *Additional time after service by United States mail.* Whenever a party has the right or is required to do some act or take some proceedings within a prescribed period after the service of a notice or other paper upon him and the notice or paper is served upon him by United States mail, three (3) days shall be added to the prescribed period. IN ST TRIAL P Rule 6(E).

    d. *Enlargement of time.* When an act is required or allowed to be done at or within a specific time by the Indiana Rules of Trial Procedure, the court may at any time for cause shown:

       i. Order the period enlarged, with or without motion or notice, if request therefor is made before the expiration of the period originally prescribed or extended by a previous order; or

       ii. Upon motion made after the expiration of the specific period, permit the act to be done where the failure to act was the result of excusable neglect; but, the court may not extend the time for taking any action for judgment on the evidence under IN ST TRIAL P Rule 50(A), amendment of findings and judgment under IN ST TRIAL P Rule 52(B), to correct errors under IN ST TRIAL P Rule 59(C), statement in opposition to motion to correct error under IN ST TRIAL P Rule 59(E), or to obtain relief from final judgment under IN ST TRIAL P Rule 60(B), except to the extent and under the conditions stated in those rules. IN ST TRIAL P Rule 6(B).

C. General Requirements

1. *Motions, generally.* Unless made during a hearing or trial, or otherwise ordered by the court, an application to the court for an order shall be made by written motion. The motion shall state the grounds therefor and the relief or order sought. IN ST TRIAL P Rule 7(B).

    a. *Motions as distinct from pleadings.* Motions and responses to motions are not pleadings, and allegations contained in a motion are not admissions of a party. 22B INPRAC 7:2; Wachstetter v. County Properties, LLC, 832 N.E.2d 574 (Ind.Ct.App. 2005); Scott County Family YMCA, Inc. v. Hobbs, 817 N.E.2d 603 (Ind.Ct.App. 2004).

    b. *Unopposed motions generally granted.* It is common for a trial court to grant procedural motions, such as motions for enlargement of time, discovery motions, or motions for continuance, unless an objection is filed. 21 INPRAC § 13.8.

2. *Motion to strike*

    a. *Grounds generally.* Upon motion the court may order stricken from any pleading any insufficient claim or defense or any redundant, immaterial, impertinent, or scandalous matter. IN ST TRIAL P Rule 12(F).

       i. *Redundant.* Redundant matter refers to the needless repetition of immaterial factual allegations. 9 INPRAC § 42.20.

       ii. *Immaterial and impertinent.* Immaterial and impertinent matter consists of allegations that have no relevant or important relationship to plaintiff's claim. 9 INPRAC § 42.20.

       iii. *Scandalous.* Scandalous matter includes unnecessary allegations that are derogatory to the party referred to in the pleading. 9 INPRAC § 42.20.

b. *Contents and form of motion to strike.* Subject to IN ST TRIAL P Rule 12(F), every motion to insert new matter or to strike out any part or parts of any pleading, deposition, report, order or other document in a case shall be made in writing and shall set forth the words sought to be inserted or stricken. IN ST ALLEN SUPER AND CIR CT CIV Rule 7-1(F).

    i. Each set of words to be inserted or stricken shall be in a separate specification and each specification shall be numbered consecutively. IN ST ALLEN SUPER AND CIR CT CIV Rule 7-1(F).

c. *Availability and use of motion to strike.* A motion to strike redundant, immaterial, impertinent or scandalous matter is available to plaintiff and defendant alike, and may be employed against any pleading. 9 INPRAC § 42.20. Indiana's use of a motion to strike includes all of the uses which are found in federal practice plus the expanded use of the motion under Indiana's rule. Accordingly, a nonexclusive list of the uses of this motion will recognize that it is available:

    i. To strike matter which is immaterial, impertinent or scandalous;

    ii. To provide the plaintiff with a means by which to test the sufficiency of a defense;

    iii. To strike any insufficient claim or defense;

    iv. To strike a bad faith, or inadequate response to an order or rule; or

    v. To strike a response to an order or rule which introduces new material or allegations not previously made and which are not introduced pursuant to a right to amend a pleading. 1A INPRAC R 12(12.18).

d. *Trial court's discretion.* The trial court is given broad discretion to decide a motion to strike. 1A INPRAC R 12(12.18); City of Mishawaka v. Kvale, 810 N.E.2d 1129 (Ind.Ct.App. 2004).

e. *Not a method to challenge timeliness.* Language in IN ST TRIAL P Rule 12(F) which permits the trial court to strike any "insufficient" claim or defense refers to the legal insufficiency of the content or substance of the claim or defense, not the untimeliness of a pleading. 1A INPRAC R 12(12.18); Dreyer & Reinbold v. AutoXchange.com., Inc., 771 N.E.2d 764, 765 (Ind.Ct.App. 2002). Rather, the proper mechanism for challenging the timeliness of a pleading is IN ST TRIAL P Rule 55, which governs default judgments. 1A INPRAC R 12(12.18).

3. *Consolidation and waiver*

a. *Consolidation of defenses in motion.* A party who makes a motion under IN ST TRIAL P Rule 12 may join with it any other motions herein provided for and then available to him. If a party makes a motion under IN ST TRIAL P Rule 12 but omits therefrom any defense or objection then available to him which IN ST TRIAL P Rule 12 permits to be raised by motion, he shall not thereafter make a motion based on the defense or objection so omitted. He may, however, make such motions as are allowed under IN ST TRIAL P Rule 12(H)(2). IN ST TRIAL P Rule 12(G).

b. *Waiver or preservation of certain defenses.* No defense or objection is waived by being joined with one or more other defenses or objections in a responsive pleading or motion. IN ST TRIAL P Rule 12(B).

D. Documents

1. *Required documents*

a. *Motion and notice.* The requirement of notice is satisfied by service of the motion. IN ST TRIAL P Rule 7(B). Refer to the General Requirements section of this document for information on the content of a motion to strike.

b. *Proposed order.* Unless local practice provides differently, a party should submit a proposed order with its written motion to be signed by the judge once the motion has been granted. 21 INPRAC § 13.8.

    i. *Copies of proposed orders.* All proposed orders shall be submitted in an original plus a number of copies equal to one (1) more than the number of pro se parties and attorneys of record contained in the prepared proof of notice under IN ST TRIAL P Rule 72(D). IN ST ALLEN SUPER AND CIR CT CIV Rule TR00-1(C).

ii. *Proof of notice.* The proposed order shall also include a prepared proof of notice, under IN ST TRIAL P Rule 72(D). IN ST ALLEN SUPER AND CIR CT CIV Rule TR00-1(B).

iii. Refer to the Format section of this document for information on the form and content of the proposed order and the proof of notice.

c. *Certificate of service.* An attorney or unrepresented party tendering a document to the Clerk for filing shall certify that service has been made, list the parties served, and specify the date and means of service. The certificate of service shall be placed at the end of the document and shall not be separately filed. The separate filing of a certificate of service, however, shall not be grounds for rejecting a document for filing. The Clerk may permit documents to be filed without a certificate of service but shall require prompt filing of a separate certificate of service. IN ST TRIAL P Rule 5(C).

2. *Supplemental documents*

a. *Supporting evidence.* When a motion is based on facts not appearing of record the court may hear the matter on affidavits presented by the respective parties, but the court may direct that the matter be heard wholly or partly on oral testimony or depositions. IN ST TRIAL P Rule 43(B).

b. *Brief or memorandum.* If a party desires to file a brief or memorandum in support of any motion, such brief or memorandum shall be filed simultaneously with the motion, and a copy shall be promptly served upon the adverse party. IN ST ALLEN SUPER AND CIR CT CIV Rule 7-1(E).

c. *Facsimile cover sheet.* Any document sent to the Clerk of the Circuit Court by electronic facsimile transmission shall be accompanied by a cover sheet which states the title of the document, case number, number of pages, identity and voice telephone number of the sending party and instructions for filing. The cover sheet shall contain the signature of the attorney or party, pro se, authorizing the filing. IN ST ADMIN Rule 12(D).

E. Format

1. *Form of motions.* The rules applicable to captions, and the signing and form of pleadings (IN ST TRIAL P Rule 8 through IN ST TRIAL P Rule 11), apply to all motions and other papers provided under the Indiana Rules of Trial Procedure. 22B INPRAC 7:2.

2. *Form of pleadings*

a. *Caption; Names of parties.* Every pleading shall contain a caption setting forth the name of the court, the title of the action, the file number, and a designation as in IN ST TRIAL P Rule 7(A). In the complaint the title of the action shall include the names of all the parties, but in other pleadings it is sufficient to state the name of the first party on each side with an appropriate indication of other parties. IN ST TRIAL P Rule 10(A).

b. *Paragraphs; Separate statements.* All averments of a claim or defense shall be made in numbered paragraphs, the contents of each of which shall be limited as far as practicable to a statement of a single set of circumstances, and a paragraph may be referred to by number in all succeeding pleadings. Each claim founded upon a separate transaction or occurrence and each defense other than denials may be stated in a separate count or defense whenever a separation facilitates the clear presentation of the matters set forth. IN ST TRIAL P Rule 10(B).

c. *Adoption by reference; Exhibits.* Statements in a pleading may be adopted by reference in a different part of the same pleading or in another pleading or in any motion. A copy of any written instrument which is an exhibit to a pleading is a part thereof for all purposes. IN ST TRIAL P Rule 10(C).

d. *Citation.* Allen County Superior and Circuit court rules may be cited as L.R. _____. The Indiana Rules of Trial Procedure are hereinafter referred to as T.R. _____. IN ST ALLEN SUPER AND CIR CT CIV Rule AR00-1(B).

e. *Paper.* All pleadings must be printed on white paper. IN ST ALLEN SUPER AND CIR CT CIV Rule 8-1(A).

f. *Spacing.* The lines shall be double spaced except for quotations, which shall be indented and single-spaced. IN ST ALLEN SUPER AND CIR CT CIV Rule 8-1(A).

g. *Photocopies.* Photocopies are acceptable if legible. IN ST ALLEN SUPER AND CIR CT CIV Rule 8-1(A).

h. *Margins and binding.* Margins shall be one to one and one-half (1-1 1/2) inches on the left side and one-half (1/2) inch on the right. IN ST ALLEN SUPER AND CIR CT CIV Rule 8-1(B).

    i. Binding or stapling shall be at the top left and at no other place. IN ST ALLEN SUPER AND CIR CT CIV Rule 8-1(B).

    ii. Covers or backing shall not be used. IN ST ALLEN SUPER AND CIR CT CIV Rule 8-1(B).

i. *Flat filing.* The files of the Clerk of the Court shall be kept under the "flat filing" system. All pleadings presented for filing with the Clerk or Court shall be flat and unfolded. Only the original of any pleading shall be placed in the Court file. IN ST ALLEN SUPER AND CIR CT CIV Rule 77-1(A).

j. *Handwritten pleadings.* Handwritten pleadings may be accepted for filing in the discretion of the Court. IN ST ALLEN SUPER AND CIR CT CIV Rule 8-1(A).

3. *Size of papers for filing.* Effective January 1, 1992, all pleadings, copies, motions and documents filed with any trial court or appellate level court, typed or printed, with the exception of exhibits and existing wills, shall be prepared on eight and one-half by eleven inch (8 1/2" x 11") size paper. IN ST ADMIN Rule 11.

4. *Form of proposed orders*

a. *Form, caption, and title.* Any proposed order shall be a document that is separate and apart from the motion or application to which it relates and shall contain a caption showing the name of the court, the case number assigned to the case and the title of the case as shown by the complaint. IN ST ALLEN SUPER AND CIR CT CIV Rule TR00-1(B). If there are multiple parties, the title may be shortened to include only the first name plaintiff and defendant with appropriate indication that there are additional parties. IN ST ALLEN SUPER AND CIR CT CIV Rule TR00-1(B).

b. *Paper.* The proposed order shall be on white paper, eight and one half by eleven inches (8 1/2" x 11") in size, and each page shall be numbered. IN ST ALLEN SUPER AND CIR CT CIV Rule TR00-1(B).

c. *Signature line.* On the last page of the proposed order there shall be a line for the signature of the judge under which shall be typed "Judge, Allen Superior Court" or "Judge, Allen Circuit Court", whichever is applicable, to the left of which shall be the following: "Dated _____". IN ST ALLEN SUPER AND CIR CT CIV Rule TR00-1(B).

d. *Allowance of space for clerk.* To allow space for the Clerk to make entries on the proposed order to show compliance with the notice requirements of IN ST TRIAL P Rule 72(D), the lower four (4) inches of the last page of the proposed order shall be left blank. IN ST ALLEN SUPER AND CIR CT CIV Rule TR00-1(B).

e. *Proof of notice required.* The proposed order shall also include a prepared proof of notice, under IN ST TRIAL P Rule 72(D). The proof of notice shall conform to the format show in IN ST ALLEN SUPER AND CIR CT CIV Rule TR00-1(B). IN ST ALLEN SUPER AND CIR CT CIV Rule TR00-1(B).

5. *Signature requirements*

a. *Signature of attorney.* Every pleading or motion of a party represented by an attorney shall be signed by at least one (1) attorney of record in his individual name, whose address, telephone number, and attorney number shall be stated, except that this provision shall not apply to pleadings and motions made and transcribed at the trial or a hearing before the judge and received by him in such form. IN ST TRIAL P Rule 11(A). All pleadings to be signed by an attorney shall contain the written signature of the individual attorney, the attorney's printed name, Supreme Court Attorney Number, the name of the attorney's law firm, the attorney's address, telephone number, and a designation of the party for whom the attorney appears. IN ST ALLEN SUPER AND CIR CT CIV Rule 8-1(C). For the recommended signature format, refer to IN ST ALLEN SUPER AND CIR CT CIV Rule 8-1(C).

    i. The signature of an attorney constitutes a certificate by him that he has read the pleadings; that to the best of his knowledge, information, and belief, there is good ground to support it; and that it is not interposed for delay. IN ST TRIAL P Rule 11(A).

ii. If a pleading or motion is not signed or is signed with intent to defeat the purpose of the rule, it may be stricken as sham and false and the action may proceed as though the pleading had not been served. IN ST TRIAL P Rule 11(A).

iii. For a willful violation of IN ST TRIAL P Rule 11 an attorney may be subjected to appropriate disciplinary action. Similar action may be taken if scandalous or indecent matter is inserted. IN ST TRIAL P Rule 11(A).

iv. Neither printed signatures, nor facsimile signatures shall be accepted on original documents. IN ST ALLEN SUPER AND CIR CT CIV Rule 8-1(C).

v. Facsimile signatures are permitted on copies. IN ST ALLEN SUPER AND CIR CT CIV Rule 8-1(C).

b. *Signature of unrepresented party.* A party who is not represented by an attorney shall sign his pleading and state his address. IN ST TRIAL P Rule 11(A).

c. *Verification not generally required.* Except when specifically required by rule, pleadings or motions need not be verified or accompanied by affidavit. The rule in equity that the averments of an answer under oath must be overcome by the testimony of two (2) witnesses or of one (1) witness sustained by corroborating circumstances is abolished. IN ST TRIAL P Rule 11(A).

d. *Verification by affirmation or representation.* When in connection with any civil or special statutory proceeding it is required that any pleading, motion, petition, supporting affidavit, or other document of any kind, be verified, or that an oath be taken, it shall be sufficient if the subscriber simply affirms the truth of the matter to be verified by an affirmation or representation. IN ST TRIAL P Rule 11(B). IN ST TRIAL P Rule 11(B) states that the affirmation or representation should be in substantially the following language: "I (we) affirm, under the penalties for perjury, that the foregoing representation(s) is (are) true. (Signed) _____."

i. Any person who falsifies an affirmation or representation of fact shall be subject to the same penalties as are prescribed by law for the making of a false affidavit. IN ST TRIAL P Rule 11(B).

e. *Verified pleadings, motions, and affidavits as evidence.* Pleadings, motions and affidavits accompanying or in support of such pleadings or motions when required to be verified or under oath shall be accepted as a representation that the signer had personal knowledge thereof or reasonable cause to believe the existence of the facts or matters stated or alleged therein; and, if otherwise competent or acceptable as evidence, may be admitted as evidence of the facts or matters stated or alleged therein when it is so provided in the Indiana Rules of Trial Procedure, by statute or other law, or to the extent the writing or signature expressly purports to be made upon the signer's personal knowledge. When such pleadings, motions and affidavits are verified or under oath they shall not require other or greater proof on the part of the adverse party than if not verified or not under oath unless expressly provided otherwise by the Indiana Rules of Trial Procedure, statute or other law. Affidavits upon motions for summary judgment under IN ST TRIAL P Rule 56 and in denial of execution under IN ST TRIAL P Rule 9.2 shall be made upon personal knowledge. IN ST TRIAL P Rule 11(C).

6. *Information excluded from public access.* Every document filed in a case shall separately identify information excluded from public access pursuant to IN ST ADMIN Rule 9(G)(1) as follows:

a. Whole documents that are excluded from public access pursuant to IN ST ADMIN Rule 9(G)(1) shall be tendered on light green paper or have a light green coversheet attached to the document, marked "Not for Public Access" or "Confidential." IN ST TRIAL P Rule 5(G)(1).

b. When only a portion of a document contains information excluded from public access pursuant to IN ST ADMIN Rule 9(G)(1), said information shall be omitted [or redacted] from the filed document, and set forth on a separate accompanying document on light green paper conspicuously marked "Not for Public Access" or "Confidential" and clearly designated [or identifying] the caption and number of the case and the document and location within the document to which the redacted material pertains. IN ST TRIAL P Rule 5(G)(2).

c. With respect to documents filed in electronic format, the trial court, by local rule, may provide for compliance with IN ST TRIAL P Rule 5 in manner that separates and protects access to information excluded from public access. IN ST TRIAL P Rule 5(G)(3).

d. IN ST TRIAL P Rule 5(G) does not apply to a record sealed by the court pursuant to IN ST 5-14-3-5.5 or otherwise, nor to records, documents, or information filed in cases to which public access is prohibited pursuant to IN ST ADMIN Rule 9(G). IN ST TRIAL P Rule 5(G)(4).

e. The following information in case records is excluded from public access and is confidential:

   i. Information that is excluded from public access pursuant to federal law;

   ii. Information that is excluded from public access as declared confidential by Indiana statute or other court rule, including without limitation:

   • All adoption records created after July 8, 1941, as declared confidential by IN ST 31-19-19-1, et seq., except those specifically declared open by IN ST 31-19-13-2(2);

   • All records relating to chancroid, chlamydia, gonorrhea, hepatitis, human immunodeficiency virus (HIV), Lymphogranuloma venereum, syphilis, tuberculosis, as declared confidential by IN ST 16-41-8-1, et seq.;

   • All records relating to child abuse as declared confidential by IN ST 31-33-18-1, et seq.;

   • All records relating to drug tests as declared confidential by IN ST 5-14-3-4(a)(9);

   • Records of grand jury proceedings as declared confidential by IN ST 35-34-2-4;

   • Records of juvenile proceedings as declared confidential by IN ST 31-39-1-2, except those specifically open under statute;

   • All paternity records created after July 1, 1941 as declared confidential by IN ST 31-14-11-15, IN ST 31-19-5-23, IN ST 31-39-1-1 and IN ST 31-39-1-2 [Editor's note: IN ST 31-14-11-15 was repealed effective May 9, 2013];

   • All pre-sentence reports as declared confidential by IN ST 35-38-1-13;

   • Written petitions to permit marriages without consent and orders directing the Clerk of Court to issue a marriage license to underage persons, as declared confidential by IN ST 31-11-1-6;

   • Only those arrest warrants, search warrants, indictments and informations ordered confidential by the trial judge, prior to return of duly executed service as declared confidential by IN ST 5-14-3-4(b)(1);

   • All medical, mental health, or tax records unless determined by law or regulation of any governmental custodian not to be confidential, released by the subject of such records, or declared by a court of competent jurisdiction to be essential to the resolution of litigation as declared confidential by IN ST 16-39-3-10, IN ST 6-4.1-5-10, IN ST 6-4.1-12-12, and IN ST 6-8.1-7-1;

   • Personal information relating to jurors or prospective jurors, other than for the use of the parties and counsel, pursuant to IN ST JURY Rule 10;

   • Information relating to protection from abuse orders, no-contact orders and workplace violence restraining orders as declared confidential by IN ST 5-2-9-6, et seq.;

   • Mediation proceedings pursuant to IN ST ADR Rule 2.11, Mini-Trial proceedings pursuant to IN ST ADR Rule 4.4(C), and Summary Jury Trials pursuant to IN ST ADR Rule 5.6;

   • Information in probation files pursuant to the Probation Standards promulgated by the Judicial Conference of Indiana pursuant to IN ST 11-13-1-8(b);

   • Information deemed confidential pursuant to the Rules for Court Administered Alcohol and Drug Programs promulgated by the Judicial Conference of Indiana pursuant to IN ST 12-23-14-13;

   • Information deemed confidential pursuant to the Problem-Solving Court Rules promulgated by the Judicial Conference of Indiana pursuant to IN ST 33-23-16-16;

   • All records of the Department of workforce Development as declared confidential by IN ST 22-4-19-6;

- Information regarding interception of electronic communications that is sealed or deemed confidential as set forth in IN ST 35-33.5-2-1, et seq.

iii. Information excluded from public access by specific court order;

iv. Complete Social Security Numbers of living persons;

v. With the exception of names, information such as addresses, phone numbers, and dates of birth which explicitly identifies:

- Natural persons who are witnesses or victims (not including defendants) in criminal, domestic violence, stalking, sexual assault, juvenile, or civil protection order proceedings, provided that juveniles who are victims of sex crimes shall be identified by initials only;

- Places of residence of judicial officers, clerks and other employees of courts and clerks of court, unless the person or persons about whom the information pertains waives confidentiality;

vi. Complete account numbers of specific assets, loans, bank accounts, credit cards, and personal identification numbers (PINs);

vii. All orders of expungement entered in criminal or juvenile proceedings, orders to restrict access to criminal history information pursuant to IN ST 35-38-5-5.5 or IN ST 35-38-8-5 and records excluded from public access by such orders, and information related to infractions that is excluded from public access pursuant to IN ST 34-28-5-15 or IN ST 34-28-5-16 [Editor's note: IN ST 35-38-5-5.5, IN ST 35-38-8-5 and IN ST 34-28-5-16 were repealed effective July 1, 2013; for information on orders restricting access to criminal history, refer to IN ST 35-38-9-1, et seq.];

viii. All personal notes and e-mail, and deliberative material, of judges, jurors, court staff and judicial agencies, and information recorded in personal data assistants (PDA's) or organizers and personal calendars. IN ST ADMIN Rule 9(G)(1).

F. Filing and Service Requirements

1. *Filing requirements.* Except as otherwise provided in IN ST TRIAL P Rule 5(E)(2), all pleadings and papers subsequent to the complaint which are required to be served upon a party shall be filed with the Court either before service or within a reasonable period of time thereafter. IN ST TRIAL P Rule 5(E)(1).

   a. *Filing with the court defined.* The filing of pleadings, motions, and other papers with the court as required by the Indiana Rules of Trial Procedure shall be made by one of the following methods:

      i. Delivery to the clerk of the court;

      ii. Sending by electronic transmission under the procedure adopted pursuant to IN ST ADMIN Rule 12;

      iii. Mailing to the clerk by registered, certified or express mail return receipt requested;

      iv. Depositing with any third-party commercial carrier for delivery to the clerk within three (3) calendar days, cost prepaid, properly addressed;

      v. If the court so permits, filing with the judge, in which event the judge shall note thereon the filing date and forthwith transmit them to the office of the clerk; or

      vi. Electronic filing, as approved by the Division of State Court Administration pursuant to IN ST ADMIN Rule 16. IN ST TRIAL P Rule 5(F).

      vii. Filing by registered or certified mail and by third-party commercial carrier shall be complete upon mailing or deposit. IN ST TRIAL P Rule 5(F).

   b. *Facsimile filing*

      i. *Generally.* In counties where a majority of judges of the courts of record, by posted local rule, have authorized electronic facsimile filing and designated a telephone number to receive such transmissions, pleadings, motions, and other papers may be sent to the Clerk of Circuit Court by electronic facsimile transmission for filing in any case, provided:

         - Such matter does not exceed ten (10) pages, including the cover sheet;

- Such matter does not require the payment of fees other than the electronic facsimile transcription fee set forth in IN ST ADMIN Rule 12(E);
- The sending party creates at the time of transmission a machine generated log for such transmission; and
- The original document and the transmission log are maintained by the sending party for the duration of the litigation. IN ST ADMIN Rule 12(B).

  ii. *Time of filing.* During normal, posted business hours, the time of filing shall be the time the duplicate document is produced in the office of the Clerk of the Circuit Court. Duplicate documents received at all other times shall be filed as of the next normal business day. IN ST ADMIN Rule 12(C).

- If the receiving fax machine endorses its own time and date stamp upon the transmitted documents and the receiving machine produces a delivery receipt which is electronically created and transmitted to the sending party, the time of filing shall be the date and time recorded on the transmitted document by the receiving fax machine. IN ST ADMIN Rule 12(C).

  c. *Proof of filing.* Any party filing any paper by any method other than personal delivery to the clerk shall retain proof of filing. IN ST TRIAL P Rule 5(F).

2. *Service requirements.* Unless otherwise provided by the Indiana Rules of Trial Procedure or an order of the court, each party and special judge, if any, shall be served with: (1) every order required by its terms to be served; (2) every pleading subsequent to the original complaint; (3) every written motion except one which may be heard ex parte; (4) every brief submitted to the trial court; (5) every paper relating to discovery required to be served upon a party; and (6) every written notice, appearance, demand, offer of judgment, designation of record on appeal, or similar paper. IN ST TRIAL P Rule 5(A).

  a. *Methods of service*

    i. *Personal service.* Whenever a party is represented by an attorney of record, service shall be made upon such attorney unless service upon the party himself is ordered by the court. Service upon the attorney or party shall be made by delivering or mailing a copy of the papers to the last known address or where an attorney or party has consented to service by fax or e-mail, as provided in IN ST TRIAL P Rule 3.1(A)(4), by faxing or e-mailing a copy of the documents to the fax number or e-mail address set out in the appearance form or correction as required by IN ST TRIAL P Rule 3.1(E). IN ST TRIAL P Rule 5(B). Delivery of a copy within IN ST TRIAL P Rule 5 means:

- Offering or tendering it to the attorney or party and stating the nature of the papers being served. Refusal to accept an offered or tendered document is a waiver of any objection to the sufficiency or adequacy of service of that document;
- Leaving it at his office with a clerk or other person in charge thereof, or if there is no one in charge, leaving it in a conspicuous place therein; or
- If the office is closed, by leaving it at his dwelling house or usual place of abode with some person of suitable age and discretion then residing therein; or,
- Leaving it at some other suitable place, selected by the attorney upon whom service is being made, pursuant to duly promulgated local rule. IN ST TRIAL P Rule 5(B)(1).

    ii. *Service by mail.* If service is made by mail, the papers shall be deposited in the United States mail addressed to the person on whom they are being served, with postage prepaid. Service shall be deemed complete upon mailing. Proof of service of all papers permitted to be mailed may be made by written acknowledgment of service, by affidavit of the person who mailed the papers, or by certificate of an attorney. It shall be the duty of attorneys when entering their appearance in a cause or when filing pleadings or papers therein, to have noted in the Chronological Case Summary or said pleadings or papers so filed the address and telephone number of their office. Service by delivery or by mail at such address shall be deemed sufficient and complete. IN ST TRIAL P Rule 5(B)(2).

iii. *Service by fax or e-mail.* A party who has consented to service by fax or e-mail may be served as follows:

- Service by e-mail shall be made by attaching the document being served in .pdf format. Discovery documents must also be served in accordance with IN ST TRIAL P Rule 26(A). IN ST TRIAL P Rule 5(B)(3)(a).

- Service by fax shall be deemed complete upon generation of a transmission record indicating the successful transmission of the entire document, except as provided in IN ST TRIAL P Rule 5(B)(3)(d). IN ST TRIAL P Rule 5(B)(3)(b).

- Service by e-mail shall be deemed complete upon transmission, except as provided in IN ST TRIAL P Rule 5(B)(3)(d). IN ST TRIAL P Rule 5(B)(3)(c).

- Service by fax or e-mail that occurs on a Saturday, Sunday, legal holiday, or day the court or agency in which the matter is pending is closed or after 5:00 PM local time of the recipient shall be deemed complete the next day that is not a Saturday, Sunday, legal holiday, or day that the court or agency in which the matter is pending is not closed. IN ST TRIAL P Rule 5(B)(3)(d).

iv. *Consent to alternate service.* Any Allen County Attorney or any Allen County law firm may, without charge, maintain an assigned Courthouse box in the library of the Allen County Courthouse for receipt of notices, pleadings, process orders, or other communications from the Court, the Clerk, and other attorneys or law firms. IN ST ALLEN SUPER AND CIR CT CIV Rule 5-1(A). For more information concerning the use of courthouse boxes, refer to IN ST ALLEN SUPER AND CIR CT CIV Rule 5-1.

b. *Serving numerous defendants.* In any action in which there are unusually large numbers of defendants, the court, upon motion or of its own initiative, may order:

i. That service of the pleadings of the defendants and replies thereto need not be made as between the defendants;

- That any cross-claim, counterclaim, or matter constituting an avoidance or affirmative defense contained therein shall be deemed to be denied or avoided by all other parties; and

- That the filing of any such pleading and service thereof upon the plaintiff constitutes due notice of it to the parties. IN ST TRIAL P Rule 5(D).

ii. A copy of every such order shall be served upon the parties in such manner and form as the court directs. IN ST TRIAL P Rule 5(D).

c. *Service on parties in default for failure to appear.* No service need be made on parties in default for failure to appear, except that pleadings asserting new or additional claims for relief against them shall be served upon them in the manner provided by service of summons in IN ST TRIAL P Rule 4. IN ST TRIAL P Rule 5(A).

G. Hearings

1. *Hearing on motion.* Unless local conditions make it impracticable, each judge shall establish regular times and places, at intervals sufficiently frequent for the prompt dispatch of business, at which motions requiring notice and hearing may be heard and disposed of; but the judge at any time or place and on such notice, if any, as he considers reasonable may make order for the advancement, conduct, and hearing of actions. To expedite its business the court may direct the submission and determination of motions without oral hearing upon brief written statements of reasons in support and opposition, or direct or permit hearings by telephone conference call with all attorneys or other similar means of communication. IN ST TRIAL P Rule 73(A).

a. *Setting motions for hearing.* Except for the motions described in IN ST ALLEN SUPER AND CIR CT CIV Rule 7-1(E), all motions shall be set for hearing. IN ST ALLEN SUPER AND CIR CT CIV Rule 7-1(A). [Editor's note: While IN ST ALLEN SUPER AND CIR CT CIV Rule 7-1(A) refers to IN ST ALLEN SUPER AND CIR CT CIV Rule 7-1(E) as relating to hearings on motions, that reference is likely intended to be to IN ST ALLEN SUPER AND CIR CT CIV Rule 7-1(D).]

i. It shall be the responsibility of the moving party to request the date of such hearing from the

Judicial Assistant, or if the case has already been assigned to a Judge, from the Judicial Law Clerk of the assigned Judge. IN ST ALLEN SUPER AND CIR CT CIV Rule 7-1(A).

b. *Responsibility for notice of hearing.* It shall be the responsibility of the moving party to give notice to all other parties of hearings scheduled on motions. IN ST ALLEN SUPER AND CIR CT CIV Rule 7-1(I).

H. Forms

1. Motion to Strike Forms for Indiana

a. Motion to strike pleading not signed. 9 INPRAC § 4.18.

b. Motion to strike pleading as sham and false. 9 INPRAC § 4.19.

c. Motion to strike; Entire pleading. 9 INPRAC § 42.21.

d. Motion to strike; Portions of pleading. 9 INPRAC § 42.22.

e. Motion to strike; Insufficient defense in answer. 9 INPRAC § 42.23.

f. Motion to strike; Pleading that was not timely filed. 9 INPRAC § 42.24.

g. Motion to strike; Attorney fees claim. 9 INPRAC § 42.25.

h. Motion to strike; General denial in answer. 9 INPRAC § 42.26.

i. Motion to strike; Impertinent and scandalous material. 9 INPRAC § 42.27.

j. Motion to strike answer; Matter repleaded contrary to prior ruling. 9 INPRAC § 42.28.

k. Motion to strike; Failure to plead performance of conditions precedent. 9 INPRAC § 42.29.

l. Motion to strike; Appearance of defendant's attorney. 9 INPRAC § 42.30.

m. Certificate of service; Personal service. 9 INPRAC § 5.7.

n. Certificate of service; First class mail. 9 INPRAC § 5.8.

2. Official Motion to Strike Forms for Allen County

a. Consent to alternate service. IN ST ALLEN SUPER AND CIR CT CIV App. A.

I. Checklist

(I) ❑ Matters to be considered by moving party

   (a) ❑ Required documents

      (1) ❑ Motion and notice

      (2) ❑ Proposed order

      (3) ❑ Certificate of service

   (b) ❑ Supplemental documents

      (1) ❑ Supporting evidence

      (2) ❑ Brief or memorandum

      (3) ❑ Facsimile cover sheet

   (c) ❑ Timing

      (1) ❑ Upon motion made by a party before responding to a pleading, or, if no responsive pleading is permitted by Indiana Rules of Trial Procedure, upon motion made by a party within twenty (20) days after the service of the pleading upon him or at any time upon the court's own initiative, the court may order stricken from any pleading any insufficient claim or defense or any redundant, immaterial, impertinent, or scandalous matter

      (2) ❑ A written motion, other than one which may be heard ex parte, and notice of the hearing thereof shall be served not less than five (5) days before the time specified for the hearing, unless a different period is fixed by the Indiana Rules of Trial Procedure or by order of the court

(3) ❑ All pleadings and papers subsequent to the complaint which are required to be served upon a party shall be filed with the Court either before service or within a reasonable period of time thereafter

(II) ❑ Matters to be considered by the responding party

(a) ❑ Required documents

(1) ❑ Opposition

(2) ❑ Certificate of service

(b) ❑ Supplemental documents

(1) ❑ Supporting evidence

(2) ❑ Brief or memorandum

(3) ❑ Proposed order

(4) ❑ Facsimile cover sheet

(c) ❑ Timing

(1) ❑ Except as otherwise provided in IN ST TRIAL P Rule 59(D), opposing affidavits may be served not less than one (1) day before the hearing, unless the court permits them to be served at some other time

Motions, Oppositions and Replies
Motion to Dismiss for Improper Venue

Document Last Updated October 2013

A. Applicable Rules

1. *State rules*

a. Appearance. IN ST TRIAL P Rule 3.1.

b. Process. IN ST TRIAL P Rule 4.

c. Service and filing of pleadings and other papers. IN ST TRIAL P Rule 5.

d. Time. IN ST TRIAL P Rule 6.

e. Pleadings. IN ST TRIAL P Rule 7; IN ST TRIAL P Rule 8; IN ST TRIAL P Rule 9.2; IN ST TRIAL P Rule 10.

f. Signing and verification of pleadings. IN ST TRIAL P Rule 11.

g. Defenses and objections; When and how presented; By pleading or motion; Motion for judgment on the pleadings. IN ST TRIAL P Rule 12.

h. Amended and supplemental pleadings. IN ST TRIAL P Rule 15.

i. Joinder of person needed for just adjudication. IN ST TRIAL P Rule 19.

j. Misjoinder and non-joinder of parties; Venue and jurisdiction over the subject-matter. IN ST TRIAL P Rule 21.

k. Evidence. IN ST TRIAL P Rule 43.

l. Judgment on the evidence (directed verdict). IN ST TRIAL P Rule 50.

m. Findings by the court. IN ST TRIAL P Rule 52.

n. Summary judgment. IN ST TRIAL P Rule 56.

o. Motion to correct error. IN ST TRIAL P Rule 59.

p. Relief from judgment or order. IN ST TRIAL P Rule 60.

q. Trial court and clerks. IN ST TRIAL P Rule 72.

  r. Hearing of motions. IN ST TRIAL P Rule 73.

  s. Venue requirements. IN ST TRIAL P Rule 75.

  t. Interlocutory appeals. IN ST RAP Rule 14.

  u. Access to court records. IN ST ADMIN Rule 9.

  v. Paper size. IN ST ADMIN Rule 11.

  w. Facsimile transmission. IN ST ADMIN Rule 12.

  x. Electronic filing and electronic service pilot projects. IN ST ADMIN Rule 16.

  y. Sealing of certain records by court; Hearing; Notice. IN ST 5-14-3-5.5.

  z. Privacy and confidentiality. IN ST 5-2-9-6; IN ST 5-14-3-4; IN ST 6-4.1-5-10; IN ST 6-4.1-12-12; IN ST 6-8.1-7-1; IN ST 11-13-1-8; IN ST 12-23-14-13; IN ST 16-39-3-10; IN ST 16-41-8-1; IN ST 22-4-19-6; IN ST 31-11-1-6; IN ST 31-19-5-23; IN ST 31-19-13-2; IN ST 31-19-19-1; IN ST 31-33-18-1; IN ST 31-39-1-1; IN ST 31-39-1-2; IN ST 33-23-16-16; IN ST 35-34-2-4; IN ST 35-38-1-13; IN ST 35-38-9-1; IN ST ADR Rule 2.11; IN ST ADR Rule 4.4; IN ST ADR Rule 5.6; IN ST JURY Rule 10.

 2. *Local rules*

  a. Applicability and citation of rules. IN ST ALLEN SUPER AND CIR CT CIV Rule AR00-1.

  b. Proposed orders. IN ST ALLEN SUPER AND CIR CT CIV Rule TR00-1.

  c. Appearances. IN ST ALLEN SUPER AND CIR CT CIV Rule 3.1-1.

  d. Consent to alternate service. IN ST ALLEN SUPER AND CIR CT CIV Rule 5-1.

  e. Motions in civil court. IN ST ALLEN SUPER AND CIR CT CIV Rule 7-1.

  f. Preparation of pleadings. IN ST ALLEN SUPER AND CIR CT CIV Rule 8-1.

  g. Filing. IN ST ALLEN SUPER AND CIR CT CIV Rule 77-1.

B. Timing

 1. *Motion to dismiss for improper venue.* A motion making the defense of incorrect venue under IN ST TRIAL P Rule 75, or any statutory provision, shall be made before pleading if a further pleading is permitted or within twenty (20) days after service of the prior pleading if none is required. IN ST TRIAL P Rule 12(B); IN ST TRIAL P Rule 75(A).

  a. *Time to file a responsive pleading.* A responsive pleading required under the Indiana Rules of Trial Procedure, shall be served within twenty (20) days after service of the prior pleading. IN ST TRIAL P Rule 6(C).

  b. *Waiver of certain IN ST TRIAL P Rule 12(B) defenses.* If a pleading sets forth a claim for relief to which the adverse party is not required to serve a responsive pleading, any of the defenses in IN ST TRIAL P Rule 12(B)(2), IN ST TRIAL P Rule 12(B)(3), IN ST TRIAL P Rule 12(B)(4), IN ST TRIAL P Rule 12(B)(5) or IN ST TRIAL P Rule 12(B)(8) is waived to the extent constitutionally permissible unless made in a motion within twenty (20) days after service of the prior pleading. IN ST TRIAL P Rule 12(B).

  c. *Filing.* All pleadings and papers subsequent to the complaint which are required to be served upon a party shall be filed with the Court either before service or within a reasonable period of time thereafter. IN ST TRIAL P Rule 5(E)(1).

 2. *Service.* A written motion, other than one which may be heard ex parte, and notice of the hearing thereof shall be served not less than five (5) days before the time specified for the hearing, unless a different period is fixed by the Indiana Rules of Trial Procedure or by order of the court. IN ST TRIAL P Rule 6(D).

  a. *Of supporting affidavits.* When a motion is supported by affidavit, the affidavit shall be served with the motion; and,

 3. *Service of opposition.* Except as otherwise provided in IN ST TRIAL P Rule 59(D), opposing affidavits may be served not less than one (1) day before the hearing, unless the court permits them to be served at some other time. IN ST TRIAL P Rule 6(D).

4. *Computation of time*

    a. *Generally; Days excluded.* In computing any period of time prescribed or allowed by the Indiana Rules of Trial Procedure, by order of the court, or by any applicable statute, the day of the act, event, or default from which the designated period of time begins to run shall not be included. The last day of the period so computed is to be included unless it is:

        i. A Saturday,

        ii. A Sunday,

        iii. A legal holiday as defined by state statute, or

        iv. A day the office in which the act is to be done is closed during regular business hours. IN ST TRIAL P Rule 6(A).

    b. *Short periods.* In any event, the period runs until the end of the next day that is not a Saturday, a Sunday, a legal holiday, or a day on which the office is closed. When the period of time allowed is less than seven (7) days, intermediate Saturdays, Sundays, legal holidays, and days on which the office is closed shall be excluded from the computations. IN ST TRIAL P Rule 6(A).

    c. *Additional time after service by United States mail.* Whenever a party has the right or is required to do some act or take some proceedings within a prescribed period after the service of a notice or other paper upon him and the notice or paper is served upon him by United States mail, three (3) days shall be added to the prescribed period. IN ST TRIAL P Rule 6(E).

    d. *Enlargement of time.* When an act is required or allowed to be done at or within a specific time by the Indiana Rules of Trial Procedure, the court may at any time for cause shown:

        i. Order the period enlarged, with or without motion or notice, if request therefor is made before the expiration of the period originally prescribed or extended by a previous order; or

        ii. Upon motion made after the expiration of the specific period, permit the act to be done where the failure to act was the result of excusable neglect; but, the court may not extend the time for taking any action for judgment on the evidence under IN ST TRIAL P Rule 50(A), amendment of findings and judgment under IN ST TRIAL P Rule 52(B), to correct errors under IN ST TRIAL P Rule 59(C), statement in opposition to motion to correct error under IN ST TRIAL P Rule 59(E), or to obtain relief from final judgment under IN ST TRIAL P Rule 60(B), except to the extent and under the conditions stated in those rules. IN ST TRIAL P Rule 6(B).

C. General Requirements

1. *Motions, generally.* Unless made during a hearing or trial, or otherwise ordered by the court, an application to the court for an order shall be made by written motion. The motion shall state the grounds therefor and the relief or order sought. IN ST TRIAL P Rule 7(B).

    a. *Motions as distinct from pleadings.* Motions and responses to motions are not pleadings, and allegations contained in a motion are not admissions of a party. 22B INPRAC 7:2; Wachstetter v. County Properties, LLC, 832 N.E.2d 574 (Ind.Ct.App. 2005); Scott County Family YMCA, Inc. v. Hobbs, 817 N.E.2d 603 (Ind.Ct.App. 2004).

    b. *Unopposed motions generally granted.* It is common for a trial court to grant procedural motions, such as motions for enlargement of time, discovery motions, or motions for continuance, unless an objection is filed. 21 INPRAC § 13.8.

2. *Motion to dismiss for improper venue.* Every defense, in law or fact, to a claim for relief in any pleading, whether a claim, counterclaim, cross-claim, or third-party claim, shall be asserted in the responsive pleading thereto if one is required; except that at the option of the pleader, incorrect venue under IN ST TRIAL P Rule 75, or any statutory provision may be made by motion. IN ST TRIAL P Rule 12(B)(3). The disposition of this motion shall be consistent with IN ST TRIAL P Rule 75. IN ST TRIAL P Rule 12(B)(3). This means that, in almost every instance in which a motion is made under IN ST TRIAL P Rule 12(B)(3) or another statute, the action shall not be dismissed but transferred, consistent with IN ST TRIAL P Rule 75. 1A INPRAC R 12(12.7).

    a. *Venue.* Any case may be venued, commenced and decided in any court in any county, except, that upon the filing of a pleading or a motion to dismiss allowed by IN ST TRIAL P Rule 12(B)(3), the court, from allegations of the complaint or after hearing evidence thereon or considering affidavits or documentary evidence filed with the motion or in opposition to it, shall order the case transferred to a county or court selected by the party first properly filing such motion or pleading if the court determines that the county or court where the action was filed does not meet preferred venue requirements or is not authorized to decide the case and that the court or county selected has preferred venue and is authorized to decide the case. IN ST TRIAL P Rule 75(A).

b. *Preferred venue.* Preferred venue lies in:

i. The county where the greater percentage of individual defendants included in the complaint resides, or, if there is no such greater percentage, the place where any individual defendant so named resides; or

ii. The county where the land or some part thereof is located or the chattels or some part thereof are regularly located or kept, if the complaint includes a claim for injuries thereto or relating to such land or such chattels, including without limitation claims for recovery of possession or for injuries, to establish use or control, to quiet title or determine any interest, to avoid or set aside conveyances, to foreclose liens, to partition and to assert any matters for which in rem relief is or would be proper; or

iii. The county where the accident or collision occurred, if the complaint includes a claim for injuries relating to the operation of a motor vehicle or a vehicle on railroad, street or interurban tracks; or

iv. The county where either the principal office of a defendant organization is located or the office or agency of a defendant organization or individual to which the claim relates or out of which the claim arose is located, if one or more such organizations or individuals are included as defendants in the complaint; or

v. The county where either one or more individual plaintiffs reside, the principal office of a governmental organization is located, or the office of a governmental organization to which the claim relates or out of which the claim arose is located, if one or more governmental organizations are included as defendants in the complaint; or

vi. The county or court fixed by written stipulations signed by all the parties named in the complaint or their attorneys and filed with the court before ruling on the motion to dismiss; or

vii. The county where the individual is held in custody or is restrained, if the complaint seeks relief with respect to such individual's custody or restraint upon his freedom; or

viii. The county where a claim in the plaintiff's complaint may be commenced under any statute recognizing or creating a special or general remedy or proceeding; or

ix. The county where all or some of the property is located or can be found if the case seeks only judgment in rem against the property of a defendant being served by publication; or

x. The county where either one or more individual plaintiffs reside, the principal office of any plaintiff organization or governmental organization is located, or the office of any such plaintiff organization or governmental organization to which the claim relates or out of which the claim arose is located, if the case is not subject to the requirements of IN ST TRIAL P Rule 75(A)(1) through IN ST TRIAL P Rule 75(A)(9) or if all the defendants are nonresident individuals or nonresident organizations without a principal office in the state. IN ST TRIAL P Rule 75(A).

c. *Claim or proceeding filed in improper court*

i. Whenever a claim or proceeding is filed which should properly have been filed in another court of this state, and proper objection is made, the court in which such action is filed shall not then dismiss the action, but shall order the action transferred to the court in which it should have been filed. IN ST TRIAL P Rule 75(B)(1).

ii. The person filing the action shall, within twenty (20) days, pay such costs as are chargeable upon a change of venue and the papers and records shall be certified to the court of transfer in like manner as upon change of venue and the action shall be deemed commenced as of the date of filing the action in the original court. IN ST TRIAL P Rule 75(B)(2).

iii. If the party filing the action does not pay the costs of transfer within twenty (20) days of the order transferring venue, the original court shall dismiss the action without prejudice and shall order payment of reasonable attorney fees to the party making proper objection. IN ST TRIAL P Rule 75(B)(3).

d. *Assessment of costs, traveling expenses and attorneys' fees in resisting venue.* When the case is ordered transferred under the provisions of IN ST TRIAL P Rule 75 or IN ST TRIAL P Rule 21(B) the court shall order the parties or persons filing the complaint to pay the filing costs of refiling the case in the proper court and pay mileage expenses reasonably incurred by the parties and their attorneys in resisting the venue; and if it appears that the case was commenced in the wrong county by sham pleading, in bad faith or without cause, the court shall order payment of reasonable attorneys' fees incurred by parties successfully resisting the venue. IN ST TRIAL P Rule 75(C).

e. *Other venue statutes superseded by IN ST TRIAL P Rule 75.* Any provision of the Indiana Rules of Trial Procedure and any special or general statute relating to venue, the place of trial or the authority of the court to hear the case shall be subject to IN ST TRIAL P Rule 75, and the provisions of any statute fixing more stringent rules thereon shall be ineffective. No statute or rule fixing the place of trial shall be deemed a requirement of jurisdiction. IN ST TRIAL P Rule 75(D).

f. *Appeal.* An order transferring or refusing to transfer a case under IN ST TRIAL P Rule 75 shall be an interlocutory order appealable pursuant to IN ST RAP Rule 14(A)(8); provided, however, that the appeal of an interlocutory order under IN ST TRIAL P Rule 75 shall not stay proceedings in the trial court unless the trial court or the Court of Appeals so orders. IN ST TRIAL P Rule 75(E).

3. *Consolidation and waiver*

a. *Consolidation of defenses in motion.* A party who makes a motion under IN ST TRIAL P Rule 12 may join with it any other motions herein provided for and then available to him. If a party makes a motion under IN ST TRIAL P Rule 12 but omits therefrom any defense or objection then available to him which IN ST TRIAL P Rule 12 permits to be raised by motion, he shall not thereafter make a motion based on the defense or objection so omitted. He may, however, make such motions as are allowed under IN ST TRIAL P Rule 12(H)(2). IN ST TRIAL P Rule 12(G).

b. *Waiver or preservation of certain defenses.* No defense or objection is waived by being joined with one or more other defenses or objections in a responsive pleading or motion. IN ST TRIAL P Rule 12(B).

D. Documents

1. *Required documents*

a. *Motion and notice.* The requirement of notice is satisfied by service of the motion. IN ST TRIAL P Rule 7(B). Refer to the General Requirements section of this document for information on the content of a motion to dismiss for improper venue.

b. *Proposed order.* Unless local practice provides differently, a party should submit a proposed order with its written motion to be signed by the judge once the motion has been granted. 21 INPRAC § 13.8. Prior to entry by the Court of orders granting motions or applications, the moving party or applicant (or his or her attorney) shall, unless the Court directs otherwise, furnish the Court with proposed orders of a motion for dismissal. IN ST ALLEN SUPER AND CIR CT CIV Rule TR00-1(A)(5).

i. *Copies of proposed orders.* All proposed orders shall be submitted in an original plus a number of copies equal to one (1) more than the number of pro se parties and attorneys of record contained in the prepared proof of notice under IN ST TRIAL P Rule 72(D). IN ST ALLEN SUPER AND CIR CT CIV Rule TR00-1(C).

ii. *Proof of notice.* The proposed order shall also include a prepared proof of notice, under IN ST TRIAL P Rule 72(D). IN ST ALLEN SUPER AND CIR CT CIV Rule TR00-1(B).

iii. Refer to the Format section of this document for information on the form and content of the proposed order and the proof of notice.

c. *Certificate of service.* An attorney or unrepresented party tendering a document to the Clerk for filing shall certify that service has been made, list the parties served, and specify the date and means of service. The certificate of service shall be placed at the end of the document and shall not be separately filed. The separate filing of a certificate of service, however, shall not be grounds for rejecting a document for filing. The Clerk may permit documents to be filed without a certificate of service but shall require prompt filing of a separate certificate of service. IN ST TRIAL P Rule 5(C).

2. *Supplemental documents*

 a. *Supporting evidence.* When a motion is based on facts not appearing of record the court may hear the matter on affidavits presented by the respective parties, but the court may direct that the matter be heard wholly or partly on oral testimony or depositions. IN ST TRIAL P Rule 43(B).

 b. *Brief or memorandum.* If a party desires to file a brief or memorandum in support of any motion, such brief or memorandum shall be filed simultaneously with the motion, and a copy shall be promptly served upon the adverse party. IN ST ALLEN SUPER AND CIR CT CIV Rule 7-1(E).

 c. *Facsimile cover sheet.* Any document sent to the Clerk of the Circuit Court by electronic facsimile transmission shall be accompanied by a cover sheet which states the title of the document, case number, number of pages, identity and voice telephone number of the sending party and instructions for filing. The cover sheet shall contain the signature of the attorney or party, pro se, authorizing the filing. IN ST ADMIN Rule 12(D).

E. Format

1. *Form of motions.* The rules applicable to captions, and the signing and form of pleadings (IN ST TRIAL P Rule 8 through IN ST TRIAL P Rule 11), apply to all motions and other papers provided under the Indiana Rules of Trial Procedure. 22B INPRAC 7:2.

2. *Form of pleadings*

 a. *Caption; Names of parties.* Every pleading shall contain a caption setting forth the name of the court, the title of the action, the file number, and a designation as in IN ST TRIAL P Rule 7(A). In the complaint the title of the action shall include the names of all the parties, but in other pleadings it is sufficient to state the name of the first party on each side with an appropriate indication of other parties. IN ST TRIAL P Rule 10(A).

 b. *Paragraphs; Separate statements.* All averments of a claim or defense shall be made in numbered paragraphs, the contents of each of which shall be limited as far as practicable to a statement of a single set of circumstances, and a paragraph may be referred to by number in all succeeding pleadings. Each claim founded upon a separate transaction or occurrence and each defense other than denials may be stated in a separate count or defense whenever a separation facilitates the clear presentation of the matters set forth. IN ST TRIAL P Rule 10(B).

 c. *Adoption by reference; Exhibits.* Statements in a pleading may be adopted by reference in a different part of the same pleading or in another pleading or in any motion. A copy of any written instrument which is an exhibit to a pleading is a part thereof for all purposes. IN ST TRIAL P Rule 10(C).

 d. *Citation.* Allen County Superior and Circuit court rules may be cited as L.R. _____. The Indiana Rules of Trial Procedure are hereinafter referred to as T.R. _____. IN ST ALLEN SUPER AND CIR CT CIV Rule AR00-1(B).

 e. *Paper.* All pleadings must be printed on white paper. IN ST ALLEN SUPER AND CIR CT CIV Rule 8-1(A).

 f. *Spacing.* The lines shall be double spaced except for quotations, which shall be indented and single-spaced. IN ST ALLEN SUPER AND CIR CT CIV Rule 8-1(A).

 g. *Photocopies.* Photocopies are acceptable if legible. IN ST ALLEN SUPER AND CIR CT CIV Rule 8-1(A).

 h. *Margins and binding.* Margins shall be one to one and one-half (1-1 1/2) inches on the left side and one-half (1/2) inch on the right. IN ST ALLEN SUPER AND CIR CT CIV Rule 8-1(B).

  i. Binding or stapling shall be at the top left and at no other place. IN ST ALLEN SUPER AND CIR CT CIV Rule 8-1(B).

ii. Covers or backing shall not be used. IN ST ALLEN SUPER AND CIR CT CIV Rule 8-1(B).

i. *Flat filing.* The files of the Clerk of the Court shall be kept under the "flat filing" system. All pleadings presented for filing with the Clerk or Court shall be flat and unfolded. Only the original of any pleading shall be placed in the Court file. IN ST ALLEN SUPER AND CIR CT CIV Rule 77-1(A).

j. *Handwritten pleadings.* Handwritten pleadings may be accepted for filing in the discretion of the Court. IN ST ALLEN SUPER AND CIR CT CIV Rule 8-1(A).

3. *Size of papers for filing.* Effective January 1, 1992, all pleadings, copies, motions and documents filed with any trial court or appellate level court, typed or printed, with the exception of exhibits and existing wills, shall be prepared on eight and one-half by eleven inch (8 1/2" x 11") size paper. IN ST ADMIN Rule 11.

4. *Form of proposed orders*

a. *Form, caption, and title.* Any proposed order shall be a document that is separate and apart from the motion or application to which it relates and shall contain a caption showing the name of the court, the case number assigned to the case and the title of the case as shown by the complaint. IN ST ALLEN SUPER AND CIR CT CIV Rule TR00-1(B). If there are multiple parties, the title may be shortened to include only the first name plaintiff and defendant with appropriate indication that there are additional parties. IN ST ALLEN SUPER AND CIR CT CIV Rule TR00-1(B).

b. *Paper.* The proposed order shall be on white paper, eight and one half by eleven inches (8 1/2" x 11") in size, and each page shall be numbered. IN ST ALLEN SUPER AND CIR CT CIV Rule TR00-1(B).

c. *Signature line.* On the last page of the proposed order there shall be a line for the signature of the judge under which shall be typed "Judge, Allen Superior Court" or "Judge, Allen Circuit Court", whichever is applicable, to the left of which shall be the following: "Dated _____". IN ST ALLEN SUPER AND CIR CT CIV Rule TR00-1(B).

d. *Allowance of space for clerk.* To allow space for the Clerk to make entries on the proposed order to show compliance with the notice requirements of IN ST TRIAL P Rule 72(D), the lower four (4) inches of the last page of the proposed order shall be left blank. IN ST ALLEN SUPER AND CIR CT CIV Rule TR00-1(B).

e. *Proof of notice required.* The proposed order shall also include a prepared proof of notice, under IN ST TRIAL P Rule 72(D). The proof of notice shall conform to the format show in IN ST ALLEN SUPER AND CIR CT CIV Rule TR00-1(B). IN ST ALLEN SUPER AND CIR CT CIV Rule TR00-1(B).

5. *Signature requirements*

a. *Signature of attorney.* Every pleading or motion of a party represented by an attorney shall be signed by at least one (1) attorney of record in his individual name, whose address, telephone number, and attorney number shall be stated, except that this provision shall not apply to pleadings and motions made and transcribed at the trial or a hearing before the judge and received by him in such form. IN ST TRIAL P Rule 11(A). All pleadings to be signed by an attorney shall contain the written signature of the individual attorney, the attorney's printed name, Supreme Court Attorney Number, the name of the attorney's law firm, the attorney's address, telephone number, and a designation of the party for whom the attorney appears. IN ST ALLEN SUPER AND CIR CT CIV Rule 8-1(C). For the recommended signature format, refer to IN ST ALLEN SUPER AND CIR CT CIV Rule 8-1(C).

i. The signature of an attorney constitutes a certificate by him that he has read the pleadings; that to the best of his knowledge, information, and belief, there is good ground to support it; and that it is not interposed for delay. IN ST TRIAL P Rule 11(A).

ii. If a pleading or motion is not signed or is signed with intent to defeat the purpose of the rule, it may be stricken as sham and false and the action may proceed as though the pleading had not been served. IN ST TRIAL P Rule 11(A).

iii. For a willful violation of IN ST TRIAL P Rule 11 an attorney may be subjected to appropriate

disciplinary action. Similar action may be taken if scandalous or indecent matter is inserted. IN ST TRIAL P Rule 11(A).

    iv. Neither printed signatures, nor facsimile signatures shall be accepted on original documents. IN ST ALLEN SUPER AND CIR CT CIV Rule 8-1(C).

    v. Facsimile signatures are permitted on copies. IN ST ALLEN SUPER AND CIR CT CIV Rule 8-1(C).

b. *Signature of unrepresented party.* A party who is not represented by an attorney shall sign his pleading and state his address. IN ST TRIAL P Rule 11(A).

c. *Verification not generally required.* Except when specifically required by rule, pleadings or motions need not be verified or accompanied by affidavit. The rule in equity that the averments of an answer under oath must be overcome by the testimony of two (2) witnesses or of one (1) witness sustained by corroborating circumstances is abolished. IN ST TRIAL P Rule 11(A).

d. *Verification by affirmation or representation.* When in connection with any civil or special statutory proceeding it is required that any pleading, motion, petition, supporting affidavit, or other document of any kind, be verified, or that an oath be taken, it shall be sufficient if the subscriber simply affirms the truth of the matter to be verified by an affirmation or representation. IN ST TRIAL P Rule 11(B). IN ST TRIAL P Rule 11(B) states that the affirmation or representation should be in substantially the following language: "I (we) affirm, under the penalties for perjury, that the foregoing representation(s) is (are) true. (Signed) _____."

    i. Any person who falsifies an affirmation or representation of fact shall be subject to the same penalties as are prescribed by law for the making of a false affidavit. IN ST TRIAL P Rule 11(B).

e. *Verified pleadings, motions, and affidavits as evidence.* Pleadings, motions and affidavits accompanying or in support of such pleadings or motions when required to be verified or under oath shall be accepted as a representation that the signer had personal knowledge thereof or reasonable cause to believe the existence of the facts or matters stated or alleged therein; and, if otherwise competent or acceptable as evidence, may be admitted as evidence of the facts or matters stated or alleged therein when it is so provided in the Indiana Rules of Trial Procedure, by statute or other law, or to the extent the writing or signature expressly purports to be made upon the signer's personal knowledge. When such pleadings, motions and affidavits are verified or under oath they shall not require other or greater proof on the part of the adverse party than if not verified or not under oath unless expressly provided otherwise by the Indiana Rules of Trial Procedure, statute or other law. Affidavits upon motions for summary judgment under IN ST TRIAL P Rule 56 and in denial of execution under IN ST TRIAL P Rule 9.2 shall be made upon personal knowledge. IN ST TRIAL P Rule 11(C).

6. *Information excluded from public access.* Every document filed in a case shall separately identify information excluded from public access pursuant to IN ST ADMIN Rule 9(G)(1) as follows:

a. Whole documents that are excluded from public access pursuant to IN ST ADMIN Rule 9(G)(1) shall be tendered on light green paper or have a light green coversheet attached to the document, marked "Not for Public Access" or "Confidential." IN ST TRIAL P Rule 5(G)(1).

b. When only a portion of a document contains information excluded from public access pursuant to IN ST ADMIN Rule 9(G)(1), said information shall be omitted [or redacted] from the filed document, and set forth on a separate accompanying document on light green paper conspicuously marked "Not for Public Access" or "Confidential" and clearly designated [or identifying] the caption and number of the case and the document and location within the document to which the redacted material pertains. IN ST TRIAL P Rule 5(G)(2).

c. With respect to documents filed in electronic format, the trial court, by local rule, may provide for compliance with IN ST TRIAL P Rule 5 in manner that separates and protects access to information excluded from public access. IN ST TRIAL P Rule 5(G)(3).

d. IN ST TRIAL P Rule 5(G) does not apply to a record sealed by the court pursuant to IN ST 5-14-3-5.5 or otherwise, nor to records, documents, or information filed in cases to which public access is prohibited pursuant to IN ST ADMIN Rule 9(G). IN ST TRIAL P Rule 5(G)(4).

e. The following information in case records is excluded from public access and is confidential:

   i. Information that is excluded from public access pursuant to federal law;

   ii. Information that is excluded from public access as declared confidential by Indiana statute or other court rule, including without limitation:

- All adoption records created after July 8, 1941, as declared confidential by IN ST 31-19-19-1, et seq., except those specifically declared open by IN ST 31-19-13-2(2);

- All records relating to chancroid, chlamydia, gonorrhea, hepatitis, human immunodeficiency virus (HIV), Lymphogranuloma venereum, syphilis, tuberculosis, as declared confidential by IN ST 16-41-8-1, et seq.;

- All records relating to child abuse as declared confidential by IN ST 31-33-18-1, et seq.;

- All records relating to drug tests as declared confidential by IN ST 5-14-3-4(a)(9);

- Records of grand jury proceedings as declared confidential by IN ST 35-34-2-4;

- Records of juvenile proceedings as declared confidential by IN ST 31-39-1-2, except those specifically open under statute;

- All paternity records created after July 1, 1941 as declared confidential by IN ST 31-14-11-15, IN ST 31-19-5-23, IN ST 31-39-1-1 and IN ST 31-39-1-2 [Editor's note: IN ST 31-14-11-15 was repealed effective May 9, 2013];

- All pre-sentence reports as declared confidential by IN ST 35-38-1-13;

- Written petitions to permit marriages without consent and orders directing the Clerk of Court to issue a marriage license to underage persons, as declared confidential by IN ST 31-11-1-6;

- Only those arrest warrants, search warrants, indictments and informations ordered confidential by the trial judge, prior to return of duly executed service as declared confidential by IN ST 5-14-3-4(b)(1);

- All medical, mental health, or tax records unless determined by law or regulation of any governmental custodian not to be confidential, released by the subject of such records, or declared by a court of competent jurisdiction to be essential to the resolution of litigation as declared confidential by IN ST 16-39-3-10, IN ST 6-4.1-5-10, IN ST 6-4.1-12-12, and IN ST 6-8.1-7-1;

- Personal information relating to jurors or prospective jurors, other than for the use of the parties and counsel, pursuant to IN ST JURY Rule 10;

- Information relating to protection from abuse orders, no-contact orders and workplace violence restraining orders as declared confidential by IN ST 5-2-9-6, et seq.;

- Mediation proceedings pursuant to IN ST ADR Rule 2.11, Mini-Trial proceedings pursuant to IN ST ADR Rule 4.4(C), and Summary Jury Trials pursuant to IN ST ADR Rule 5.6;

- Information in probation files pursuant to the Probation Standards promulgated by the Judicial Conference of Indiana pursuant to IN ST 11-13-1-8(b);

- Information deemed confidential pursuant to the Rules for Court Administered Alcohol and Drug Programs promulgated by the Judicial Conference of Indiana pursuant to IN ST 12-23-14-13;

- Information deemed confidential pursuant to the Problem-Solving Court Rules promulgated by the Judicial Conference of Indiana pursuant to IN ST 33-23-16-16;

- All records of the Department of workforce Development as declared confidential by IN ST 22-4-19-6;

- Information regarding interception of electronic communications that is sealed or deemed confidential as set forth in IN ST 35-33.5-2-1, et seq.

    iii. Information excluded from public access by specific court order;

    iv. Complete Social Security Numbers of living persons;

    v. With the exception of names, information such as addresses, phone numbers, and dates of birth which explicitly identifies:

- Natural persons who are witnesses or victims (not including defendants) in criminal, domestic violence, stalking, sexual assault, juvenile, or civil protection order proceedings, provided that juveniles who are victims of sex crimes shall be identified by initials only;

- Places of residence of judicial officers, clerks and other employees of courts and clerks of court, unless the person or persons about whom the information pertains waives confidentiality;

    vi. Complete account numbers of specific assets, loans, bank accounts, credit cards, and personal identification numbers (PINs);

    vii. All orders of expungement entered in criminal or juvenile proceedings, orders to restrict access to criminal history information pursuant to IN ST 35-38-5-5.5 or IN ST 35-38-8-5 and records excluded from public access by such orders, and information related to infractions that is excluded from public access pursuant to IN ST 34-28-5-15 or IN ST 34-28-5-16 [Editor's note: IN ST 35-38-5-5.5, IN ST 35-38-8-5 and IN ST 34-28-5-16 were repealed effective July 1, 2013; for information on orders restricting access to criminal history, refer to IN ST 35-38-9-1, et seq.];

    viii. All personal notes and e-mail, and deliberative material, of judges, jurors, court staff and judicial agencies, and information recorded in personal data assistants (PDA's) or organizers and personal calendars. IN ST ADMIN Rule 9(G)(1).

F. Filing and Service Requirements

1. *Filing requirements.* Except as otherwise provided in IN ST TRIAL P Rule 5(E)(2), all pleadings and papers subsequent to the complaint which are required to be served upon a party shall be filed with the Court either before service or within a reasonable period of time thereafter. IN ST TRIAL P Rule 5(E)(1).

    a. *Filing with the court defined.* The filing of pleadings, motions, and other papers with the court as required by the Indiana Rules of Trial Procedure shall be made by one of the following methods:

        i. Delivery to the clerk of the court;

        ii. Sending by electronic transmission under the procedure adopted pursuant to IN ST ADMIN Rule 12;

        iii. Mailing to the clerk by registered, certified or express mail return receipt requested;

        iv. Depositing with any third-party commercial carrier for delivery to the clerk within three (3) calendar days, cost prepaid, properly addressed;

        v. If the court so permits, filing with the judge, in which event the judge shall note thereon the filing date and forthwith transmit them to the office of the clerk; or

        vi. Electronic filing, as approved by the Division of State Court Administration pursuant to IN ST ADMIN Rule 16. IN ST TRIAL P Rule 5(F).

        vii. Filing by registered or certified mail and by third-party commercial carrier shall be complete upon mailing or deposit. IN ST TRIAL P Rule 5(F).

    b. *Facsimile filing*

        i. *Generally.* In counties where a majority of judges of the courts of record, by posted local rule, have authorized electronic facsimile filing and designated a telephone number to receive such transmissions, pleadings, motions, and other papers may be sent to the Clerk of Circuit Court by electronic facsimile transmission for filing in any case, provided:

- Such matter does not exceed ten (10) pages, including the cover sheet;

- Such matter does not require the payment of fees other than the electronic facsimile transcription fee set forth in IN ST ADMIN Rule 12(E);

- The sending party creates at the time of transmission a machine generated log for such transmission; and

- The original document and the transmission log are maintained by the sending party for the duration of the litigation. IN ST ADMIN Rule 12(B).

ii. *Time of filing.* During normal, posted business hours, the time of filing shall be the time the duplicate document is produced in the office of the Clerk of the Circuit Court. Duplicate documents received at all other times shall be filed as of the next normal business day. IN ST ADMIN Rule 12(C).

- If the receiving fax machine endorses its own time and date stamp upon the transmitted documents and the receiving machine produces a delivery receipt which is electronically created and transmitted to the sending party, the time of filing shall be the date and time recorded on the transmitted document by the receiving fax machine. IN ST ADMIN Rule 12(C).

c. *Proof of filing.* Any party filing any paper by any method other than personal delivery to the clerk shall retain proof of filing. IN ST TRIAL P Rule 5(F).

d. *Copies of proposed orders.* All proposed orders shall be submitted in an original plus a number of copies equal to one (1) more than the number of pro se parties and attorneys of record contained in the prepared proof of notice under IN ST TRIAL P Rule 72(D). IN ST ALLEN SUPER AND CIR CT CIV Rule TR00-1(C).

2. *Service requirements.* Unless otherwise provided by the Indiana Rules of Trial Procedure or an order of the court, each party and special judge, if any, shall be served with: (1) every order required by its terms to be served; (2) every pleading subsequent to the original complaint; (3) every written motion except one which may be heard ex parte; (4) every brief submitted to the trial court; (5) every paper relating to discovery required to be served upon a party; and (6) every written notice, appearance, demand, offer of judgment, designation of record on appeal, or similar paper. IN ST TRIAL P Rule 5(A).

a. *Methods of service*

i. *Personal service.* Whenever a party is represented by an attorney of record, service shall be made upon such attorney unless service upon the party himself is ordered by the court. Service upon the attorney or party shall be made by delivering or mailing a copy of the papers to the last known address or where an attorney or party has consented to service by fax or e-mail, as provided in IN ST TRIAL P Rule 3.1(A)(4), by faxing or e-mailing a copy of the documents to the fax number or e-mail address set out in the appearance form or correction as required by IN ST TRIAL P Rule 3.1(E). IN ST TRIAL P Rule 5(B). Delivery of a copy within IN ST TRIAL P Rule 5 means:

- Offering or tendering it to the attorney or party and stating the nature of the papers being served. Refusal to accept an offered or tendered document is a waiver of any objection to the sufficiency or adequacy of service of that document;

- Leaving it at his office with a clerk or other person in charge thereof, or if there is no one in charge, leaving it in a conspicuous place therein; or

- If the office is closed, by leaving it at his dwelling house or usual place of abode with some person of suitable age and discretion then residing therein; or,

- Leaving it at some other suitable place, selected by the attorney upon whom service is being made, pursuant to duly promulgated local rule. IN ST TRIAL P Rule 5(B)(1).

ii. *Service by mail.* If service is made by mail, the papers shall be deposited in the United States mail addressed to the person on whom they are being served, with postage prepaid. Service shall be deemed complete upon mailing. Proof of service of all papers permitted to be mailed may be made by written acknowledgment of service, by affidavit of the person who mailed the papers, or by certificate of an attorney. It shall be the duty of attorneys when entering their appearance in a cause or when filing pleadings or papers therein, to have noted in the Chronological Case Summary or said pleadings or papers so filed the address and telephone number of their office. Service by delivery or by mail at such address shall be deemed sufficient and complete. IN ST TRIAL P Rule 5(B)(2).

    iii. *Service by fax or e-mail.* A party who has consented to service by fax or e-mail may be served as follows:

- Service by e-mail shall be made by attaching the document being served in .pdf format. Discovery documents must also be served in accordance with IN ST TRIAL P Rule 26(A). IN ST TRIAL P Rule 5(B)(3)(a).

- Service by fax shall be deemed complete upon generation of a transmission record indicating the successful transmission of the entire document, except as provided in IN ST TRIAL P Rule 5(B)(3)(d). IN ST TRIAL P Rule 5(B)(3)(b).

- Service by e-mail shall be deemed complete upon transmission, except as provided in IN ST TRIAL P Rule 5(B)(3)(d). IN ST TRIAL P Rule 5(B)(3)(c).

- Service by fax or e-mail that occurs on a Saturday, Sunday, legal holiday, or day the court or agency in which the matter is pending is closed or after 5:00 PM local time of the recipient shall be deemed complete the next day that is not a Saturday, Sunday, legal holiday, or day that the court or agency in which the matter is pending is not closed. IN ST TRIAL P Rule 5(B)(3)(d).

    iv. *Consent to alternate service.* Any Allen County Attorney or any Allen County law firm may, without charge, maintain an assigned Courthouse box in the library of the Allen County Courthouse for receipt of notices, pleadings, process orders, or other communications from the Court, the Clerk, and other attorneys or law firms. IN ST ALLEN SUPER AND CIR CT CIV Rule 5-1(A). For more information concerning the use of courthouse boxes, refer to IN ST ALLEN SUPER AND CIR CT CIV Rule 5-1.

  b. *Serving numerous defendants.* In any action in which there are unusually large numbers of defendants, the court, upon motion or of its own initiative, may order:

    i. That service of the pleadings of the defendants and replies thereto need not be made as between the defendants;

- That any cross-claim, counterclaim, or matter constituting an avoidance or affirmative defense contained therein shall be deemed to be denied or avoided by all other parties; and

- That the filing of any such pleading and service thereof upon the plaintiff constitutes due notice of it to the parties. IN ST TRIAL P Rule 5(D).

    ii. A copy of every such order shall be served upon the parties in such manner and form as the court directs. IN ST TRIAL P Rule 5(D).

  c. *Service on parties in default for failure to appear.* No service need be made on parties in default for failure to appear, except that pleadings asserting new or additional claims for relief against them shall be served upon them in the manner provided by service of summons in IN ST TRIAL P Rule 4. IN ST TRIAL P Rule 5(A).

G. Hearings

1. *Hearing on motion.* Unless local conditions make it impracticable, each judge shall establish regular times and places, at intervals sufficiently frequent for the prompt dispatch of business, at which motions requiring notice and hearing may be heard and disposed of; but the judge at any time or place and on such notice, if any, as he considers reasonable may make order for the advancement, conduct, and hearing of actions. To expedite its business the court may direct the submission and determination of motions without oral hearing upon brief written statements of reasons in support and opposition, or direct or permit hearings by telephone conference call with all attorneys or other similar means of communication. IN ST TRIAL P Rule 73(A).

  a. *Setting motions for hearing.* Except for the motions described in IN ST ALLEN SUPER AND CIR CT CIV Rule 7-1(E), all motions shall be set for hearing. IN ST ALLEN SUPER AND CIR CT CIV Rule 7-1(A). [Editor's note: While IN ST ALLEN SUPER AND CIR CT CIV Rule 7-1(A) refers to

IN ST ALLEN SUPER AND CIR CT CIV Rule 7-1(E) as relating to hearings on motions, that reference is likely intended to be to IN ST ALLEN SUPER AND CIR CT CIV Rule 7-1(D).]

    i. It shall be the responsibility of the moving party to request the date of such hearing from the Judicial Assistant, or if the case has already been assigned to a Judge, from the Judicial Law Clerk of the assigned Judge. IN ST ALLEN SUPER AND CIR CT CIV Rule 7-1(A).

  b. *Responsibility for notice of hearing.* It shall be the responsibility of the moving party to give notice to all other parties of hearings scheduled on motions. IN ST ALLEN SUPER AND CIR CT CIV Rule 7-1(I).

H. Forms

1. Official Motion to Dismiss for Improper Venue Forms for Allen County

  a. Consent to alternate service. IN ST ALLEN SUPER AND CIR CT CIV App. A.

2. Indiana Motion to Dismiss for Improper Venue Forms

  a. Incorrect venue. 9 INPRAC § 42.5.

  b. Motion to dismiss; Improper venue under contract. 9 INPRAC § 42.18.1.

  c. Motion to transfer from improper venue. 11 INPRAC § 111.2.

  d. Motion to transfer from improper venue. 5 INPRAC § 3:11.1.

  e. Motion for change of venue from county; For cause. 5 INPRAC § 3:11.2.

  f. Certificate of service; Personal service. 9 INPRAC § 5.7.

  g. Certificate of service; First class mail. 9 INPRAC § 5.8.

I. Checklist

(I) ❑ Matters to be considered by moving party

  (a) ❑ Required documents

    (1) ❑ Motion and notice

    (2) ❑ Proposed order

    (3) ❑ Certificate of service

  (b) ❑ Supplemental documents

    (1) ❑ Supporting evidence

    (2) ❑ Brief or memorandum

    (3) ❑ Facsimile cover sheet

  (c) ❑ Timing

    (1) ❑ A motion making the defense of incorrect venue under IN ST TRIAL P Rule 75, or any statutory provision, shall be made before pleading if a further pleading is permitted or within twenty (20) days after service of the prior pleading if none is required

    (2) ❑ A written motion, other than one which may be heard ex parte, and notice of the hearing thereof shall be served not less than five (5) days before the time specified for the hearing, unless a different period is fixed by the Indiana Rules of Trial Procedure or by order of the court

    (3) ❑ All pleadings and papers subsequent to the complaint which are required to be served upon a party shall be filed with the Court either before service or within a reasonable period of time thereafter

(II) ❑ Matters to be considered by the responding party

  (a) ❑ Required documents

    (1) ❑ Opposition

    (2) ❑ Certificate of service

(b) ❑ Supplemental documents

    (1) ❑ Supporting evidence

    (2) ❑ Brief or memorandum

    (3) ❑ Proposed order

    (4) ❑ Facsimile cover sheet

(c) ❑ Timing

    (1) ❑ Except as otherwise provided in IN ST TRIAL P Rule 59(D), opposing affidavits may be served not less than one (1) day before the hearing, unless the court permits them to be served at some other time

Motions, Oppositions and Replies
Motion for Leave to Amend

Document Last Updated October 2013

A. Applicable Rules

1. *State rules*

    a. Appearance. IN ST TRIAL P Rule 3.1.

    b. Summons. IN ST TRIAL P Rule 4; IN ST TRIAL P Rule 4.6.

    c. Service and filing of pleadings and other papers. IN ST TRIAL P Rule 5.

    d. Time. IN ST TRIAL P Rule 6.

    e. Pleadings and other papers. IN ST TRIAL P Rule 7; IN ST TRIAL P Rule 8; IN ST TRIAL P Rule 9.2; IN ST TRIAL P Rule 10.

    f. Signing and verification of pleadings. IN ST TRIAL P Rule 11.

    g. Amended and supplemental pleadings. IN ST TRIAL P Rule 15.

    h. Evidence. IN ST TRIAL P Rule 43.

    i. Judgment on the evidence (directed verdict). IN ST TRIAL P Rule 50.

    j. Findings by the court. IN ST TRIAL P Rule 52.

    k. Summary judgment. IN ST TRIAL P Rule 56.

    l. Motion to correct error. IN ST TRIAL P Rule 59.

    m. Relief from judgment or order. IN ST TRIAL P Rule 60.

    n. Trial court and clerks. IN ST TRIAL P Rule 72.

    o. Hearing of motions. IN ST TRIAL P Rule 73.

    p. Access to court records. IN ST ADMIN Rule 9.

    q. Paper size. IN ST ADMIN Rule 11.

    r. Facsimile transmission. IN ST ADMIN Rule 12.

    s. Electronic filing and electronic service pilot projects. IN ST ADMIN Rule 16.

    t. Sealing of certain records by court; Hearing; Notice. IN ST 5-14-3-5.5.

    u. Privacy and confidentiality. IN ST 5-2-9-6; IN ST 5-14-3-4; IN ST 6-4.1-5-10; IN ST 6-4.1-12-12; IN ST 6-8.1-7-1; IN ST 11-13-1-8; IN ST 12-23-14-13; IN ST 16-39-3-10; IN ST 16-41-8-1; IN ST 22-4-19-6; IN ST 31-11-1-6; IN ST 31-19-5-23; IN ST 31-19-13-2; IN ST 31-19-19-1; IN ST 31-33-18-1; IN ST 31-39-1-1; IN ST 31-39-1-2; IN ST 33-23-16-16; IN ST 35-34-2-4; IN ST 35-38-1-13; IN ST 35-38-9-1; IN ST ADR Rule 2.11; IN ST ADR Rule 4.4; IN ST ADR Rule 5.6; IN ST JURY Rule 10.

2. *Local rules*

   a. Applicability and citation of rules. IN ST ALLEN SUPER AND CIR CT CIV Rule AR00-1.

   b. Proposed orders. IN ST ALLEN SUPER AND CIR CT CIV Rule TR00-1.

   c. Appearances. IN ST ALLEN SUPER AND CIR CT CIV Rule 3.1-1.

   d. Consent to alternate service. IN ST ALLEN SUPER AND CIR CT CIV Rule 5-1.

   e. Motions in civil court. IN ST ALLEN SUPER AND CIR CT CIV Rule 7-1.

   f. Preparation of pleadings. IN ST ALLEN SUPER AND CIR CT CIV Rule 8-1.

   g. Filing. IN ST ALLEN SUPER AND CIR CT CIV Rule 77-1.

B. Timing

1. *Time for amending pleadings*

   a. *As a matter of course.* A party may amend his pleading once as a matter of course at any time before a responsive pleading is served or, if the pleading is one to which no responsive pleading is permitted, and the action has not been placed upon the trial calendar, he may so amend it at any time within thirty (30) days after it is served. IN ST TRIAL P Rule 15(A). Refer to the Indiana KeyRules Amended Complaint and Amended Answer documents for additional information on amending pleadings as a matter of course.

   b. *With leave of court.* Otherwise a party may amend his pleading only by leave of court or by written consent of the adverse party; and leave shall be given when justice so requires. IN ST TRIAL P Rule 15(A).

   c. *Filing.* All pleadings and papers subsequent to the complaint which are required to be served upon a party shall be filed with the Court either before service or within a reasonable period of time thereafter. IN ST TRIAL P Rule 5(E)(1).

2. *Service.* A written motion, other than one which may be heard ex parte, and notice of the hearing thereof shall be served not less than five (5) days before the time specified for the hearing, unless a different period is fixed by the Indiana Rules of Trial Procedure or by order of the court. IN ST TRIAL P Rule 6(D).

   a. *Of supporting affidavits.* When a motion is supported by affidavit, the affidavit shall be served with the motion. IN ST TRIAL P Rule 6(D).

3. *Service of opposition.* Except as otherwise provided in IN ST TRIAL P Rule 59(D), opposing affidavits may be served not less than one (1) day before the hearing, unless the court permits them to be served at some other time. IN ST TRIAL P Rule 6(D).

4. *Computation of time*

   a. *Generally; Days excluded.* In computing any period of time prescribed or allowed by the Indiana Rules of Trial Procedure, by order of the court, or by any applicable statute, the day of the act, event, or default from which the designated period of time begins to run shall not be included. The last day of the period so computed is to be included unless it is:

     i. A Saturday,

     ii. A Sunday,

     iii. A legal holiday as defined by state statute, or

     iv. A day the office in which the act is to be done is closed during regular business hours. IN ST TRIAL P Rule 6(A).

   b. *Short periods.* In any event, the period runs until the end of the next day that is not a Saturday, a Sunday, a legal holiday, or a day on which the office is closed. When the period of time allowed is less than seven (7) days, intermediate Saturdays, Sundays, legal holidays, and days on which the office is closed shall be excluded from the computations. IN ST TRIAL P Rule 6(A).

   c. *Additional time after service by United States mail.* Whenever a party has the right or is required to do some act or take some proceedings within a prescribed period after the service of a notice or other paper upon him and the notice or paper is served upon him by United States mail, three (3) days shall be added to the prescribed period. IN ST TRIAL P Rule 6(E).

d. *Enlargement of time.* When an act is required or allowed to be done at or within a specific time by the Indiana Rules of Trial Procedure, the court may at any time for cause shown:

    i. Order the period enlarged, with or without motion or notice, if request therefor is made before the expiration of the period originally prescribed or extended by a previous order; or

    ii. Upon motion made after the expiration of the specific period, permit the act to be done where the failure to act was the result of excusable neglect; but, the court may not extend the time for taking any action for judgment on the evidence under IN ST TRIAL P Rule 50(A), amendment of findings and judgment under IN ST TRIAL P Rule 52(B), to correct errors under IN ST TRIAL P Rule 59(C), statement in opposition to motion to correct error under IN ST TRIAL P Rule 59(E), or to obtain relief from final judgment under IN ST TRIAL P Rule 60(B), except to the extent and under the conditions stated in those rules. IN ST TRIAL P Rule 6(B).

C. General Requirements

1. *Motions, generally.* Unless made during a hearing or trial, or otherwise ordered by the court, an application to the court for an order shall be made by written motion. The motion shall state the grounds therefor and the relief or order sought. IN ST TRIAL P Rule 7(B).

    a. *Motions as distinct from pleadings.* Motions and responses to motions are not pleadings, and allegations contained in a motion are not admissions of a party. 22B INPRAC 7:2; Wachstetter v. County Properties, LLC, 832 N.E.2d 574 (Ind.Ct.App. 2005); Scott County Family YMCA, Inc. v. Hobbs, 817 N.E.2d 603 (Ind.Ct.App. 2004).

    b. *Unopposed motions generally granted.* It is common for a trial court to grant procedural motions, such as motions for enlargement of time, discovery motions, or motions for continuance, unless an objection is filed. 21 INPRAC § 13.8.

2. *Motion for leave to amend.* The purpose of an amended pleading is to include matters that occurred before the filing of the original pleading but which were either overlooked by the pleader or unknown to him at the time. It is a substitute for the original and relates to the facts that existed when the original pleading was filed. An amended pleading supercedes the original as to those portions amended. 10 INPRAC § 46.1.

    a. *Content of motion; Attorney certification.* All motions to amend pleadings shall contain a written representation of the moving party's attorney that said attorney advised opposing counsel of the substance of the motion and that opposing counsel either consents or objects to the motion or that the motion may be submitted for ruling by the Court without hearing or briefing. IN ST ALLEN SUPER AND CIR CT CIV Rule 7-1(C).

    b. *Amendments liberally allowed.* Amendments to pleadings are to be liberally allowed in order that all issues are presented in one action. 10 INPRAC § 46.1; Pinnacle Media, LLC v. Metropolitan Dev. Com'n of Marion County, 868 N.E.2d 894 (Ind.Ct.App. 2007).

    c. *Amendments to conform to the evidence.* When issues not raised by the pleadings are tried by express or implied consent of the parties, they shall be treated in all respects as if they had been raised in the pleadings. Such amendment of the pleadings as may be necessary to cause them to conform to the evidence and to raise these issues may be made upon motion of any party at any time, even after judgment, but failure so to amend does not affect the result of the trial of these issues. If evidence is objected to at the trial on the ground that it is not within the issues made by the pleadings, the court may allow the pleadings to be amended and shall do so freely when the presentation of the merits of the action will be subserved thereby and the objecting party fails to satisfy the court that the admission of such evidence would prejudice him in maintaining his action or defense upon the merits. The court may grant a continuance to enable the objecting party to meet such evidence. IN ST TRIAL P Rule 15(B).

    d. *Relation back of amendments*

        i. Whenever the claim or defense asserted in the amended pleading arose out of the conduct, transaction, or occurrence set forth or attempted to be set forth in the original pleading, the amendment relates back to the date of the original pleading. An amendment changing the party against whom a claim is asserted relates back if the foregoing provision is satisfied and, within one hundred and twenty (120) days of commencement of the action, the party to be brought in by amendment:

- Has received such notice of the institution of the action that he will not be prejudiced in maintaining his defense on the merits; and

- Knew or should have known that but for a mistake concerning the identity of the proper party, the action would have been brought against him. IN ST TRIAL P Rule 15(C).

ii. The requirement of IN ST TRIAL P Rule 15(C)(1) and IN ST TRIAL P Rule 15(C)(2) with respect to a governmental organization to be brought into the action as defendant is satisfied:

- In the case of a state or governmental organization by delivery or mailing of process to the attorney general or to a governmental executive [IN ST TRIAL P Rule 4.6(A)(3)]; or

- In the case of a local governmental organization, by delivery or mailing of process to its attorney as provided by statute, to a governmental executive thereof [IN ST TRIAL P Rule 4.6(A)(4)], or to the officer holding the office if suit is against the officer or an office. IN ST TRIAL P Rule 15(C).

e. *Amendment by leave.* Amendments, other than an amendment by right, may be made only by leave of court or by written consent of the opposing party. 2 INPRAC R 15(15.1).

f. *Factors considered.* In deciding whether to permit a party to amend his pleading, the court must consider a number of factors: (1) undue delay, (2) bad faith or dilatory motive on the part of the movant, (3) repeated failure to cure deficiencies by amendments previously allowed, (4) undue prejudice to the opposing party by virtue of allowance of the amendment, and (5) the futility of the amendment. 10 INPRAC § 46.1; Crawford v. City of Muncie, 655 N.E.2d 614 (Ind.Ct.App. 1995); Selvia v. Reitmeyer, 156 Ind.App. 203, 295 N.E.2d 869 (Ind.Ct.App. 1973).

D. Documents

1. *Required documents*

a. *Motion and notice.* The requirement of notice is satisfied by service of the motion. IN ST TRIAL P Rule 7(B). Refer to the General Requirements section of this document for information on the content of a motion for leave to amend.

b. *Copy of amended pleading.* A copy of the proposed amendment should be attached to the motion for leave to amend, along with a proposed order by the court which permits the amendment. 2 INPRAC R 15.

c. *Proposed order.* Unless local practice provides differently, a party should submit a proposed order with its written motion to be signed by the judge once the motion has been granted. 21 INPRAC § 13.8.

i. *Copies of proposed orders.* All proposed orders shall be submitted in an original plus a number of copies equal to one (1) more than the number of pro se parties and attorneys of record contained in the prepared proof of notice under IN ST TRIAL P Rule 72(D). IN ST ALLEN SUPER AND CIR CT CIV Rule TR00-1(C).

ii. *Proof of notice.* The proposed order shall also include a prepared proof of notice, under IN ST TRIAL P Rule 72(D). IN ST ALLEN SUPER AND CIR CT CIV Rule TR00-1(B).

iii. Refer to the Format section of this document for information on the form and content of the proposed order and the proof of notice.

d. *Certificate of service.* An attorney or unrepresented party tendering a document to the Clerk for filing shall certify that service has been made, list the parties served, and specify the date and means of service. The certificate of service shall be placed at the end of the document and shall not be separately filed. The separate filing of a certificate of service, however, shall not be grounds for rejecting a document for filing. The Clerk may permit documents to be filed without a certificate of service but shall require prompt filing of a separate certificate of service. IN ST TRIAL P Rule 5(C).

2. *Supplemental documents*

a. *Supporting evidence.* When a motion is based on facts not appearing of record the court may hear the matter on affidavits presented by the respective parties, but the court may direct that the matter be heard wholly or partly on oral testimony or depositions. IN ST TRIAL P Rule 43(B).

b. *Brief or memorandum.* If a party desires to file a brief or memorandum in support of any motion, such brief or memorandum shall be filed simultaneously with the motion, and a copy shall be promptly served upon the adverse party. IN ST ALLEN SUPER AND CIR CT CIV Rule 7-1(E).

c. *Facsimile cover sheet.* Any document sent to the Clerk of the Circuit Court by electronic facsimile transmission shall be accompanied by a cover sheet which states the title of the document, case number, number of pages, identity and voice telephone number of the sending party and instructions for filing. The cover sheet shall contain the signature of the attorney or party, pro se, authorizing the filing. IN ST ADMIN Rule 12(D).

E. Format

1. *Form of motions.* The rules applicable to captions, and the signing and form of pleadings (IN ST TRIAL P Rule 8 through IN ST TRIAL P Rule 11), apply to all motions and other papers provided under the Indiana Rules of Trial Procedure. 22B INPRAC 7:2.

2. *Form of pleadings*

   a. *Caption; Names of parties.* Every pleading shall contain a caption setting forth the name of the court, the title of the action, the file number, and a designation as in IN ST TRIAL P Rule 7(A). In the complaint the title of the action shall include the names of all the parties, but in other pleadings it is sufficient to state the name of the first party on each side with an appropriate indication of other parties. IN ST TRIAL P Rule 10(A).

   b. *Paragraphs; Separate statements.* All averments of a claim or defense shall be made in numbered paragraphs, the contents of each of which shall be limited as far as practicable to a statement of a single set of circumstances, and a paragraph may be referred to by number in all succeeding pleadings. Each claim founded upon a separate transaction or occurrence and each defense other than denials may be stated in a separate count or defense whenever a separation facilitates the clear presentation of the matters set forth. IN ST TRIAL P Rule 10(B).

   c. *Adoption by reference; Exhibits.* Statements in a pleading may be adopted by reference in a different part of the same pleading or in another pleading or in any motion. A copy of any written instrument which is an exhibit to a pleading is a part thereof for all purposes. IN ST TRIAL P Rule 10(C).

   d. *Citation.* Allen County Superior and Circuit court rules may be cited as L.R. _____. The Indiana Rules of Trial Procedure are hereinafter referred to as T.R. _____. IN ST ALLEN SUPER AND CIR CT CIV Rule AR00-1(B).

   e. *Paper.* All pleadings must be printed on white paper. IN ST ALLEN SUPER AND CIR CT CIV Rule 8-1(A).

   f. *Spacing.* The lines shall be double spaced except for quotations, which shall be indented and single-spaced. IN ST ALLEN SUPER AND CIR CT CIV Rule 8-1(A).

   g. *Photocopies.* Photocopies are acceptable if legible. IN ST ALLEN SUPER AND CIR CT CIV Rule 8-1(A).

   h. *Margins and binding.* Margins shall be one to one and one-half (1-1 1/2) inches on the left side and one-half (1/2) inch on the right. IN ST ALLEN SUPER AND CIR CT CIV Rule 8-1(B).

      i. Binding or stapling shall be at the top left and at no other place. IN ST ALLEN SUPER AND CIR CT CIV Rule 8-1(B).

      ii. Covers or backing shall not be used. IN ST ALLEN SUPER AND CIR CT CIV Rule 8-1(B).

   i. *Flat filing.* The files of the Clerk of the Court shall be kept under the "flat filing" system. All pleadings presented for filing with the Clerk or Court shall be flat and unfolded. Only the original of any pleading shall be placed in the Court file. IN ST ALLEN SUPER AND CIR CT CIV Rule 77-1(A).

   j. *Handwritten pleadings.* Handwritten pleadings may be accepted for filing in the discretion of the Court. IN ST ALLEN SUPER AND CIR CT CIV Rule 8-1(A).

3. *Size of papers for filing.* Effective January 1, 1992, all pleadings, copies, motions and documents filed with any trial court or appellate level court, typed or printed, with the exception of exhibits and existing wills, shall be prepared on eight and one-half by eleven inch (8 1/2" x 11") size paper. IN ST ADMIN Rule 11.

4. *Form of proposed orders*

   a. *Form, caption, and title.* Any proposed order shall be a document that is separate and apart from the motion or application to which it relates and shall contain a caption showing the name of the court, the case number assigned to the case and the title of the case as shown by the complaint. IN ST ALLEN SUPER AND CIR CT CIV Rule TR00-1(B). If there are multiple parties, the title may be shortened to include only the first name plaintiff and defendant with appropriate indication that there are additional parties. IN ST ALLEN SUPER AND CIR CT CIV Rule TR00-1(B).

   b. *Paper.* The proposed order shall be on white paper, eight and one half by eleven inches (8 1/2" x 11") in size, and each page shall be numbered. IN ST ALLEN SUPER AND CIR CT CIV Rule TR00-1(B).

   c. *Signature line.* On the last page of the proposed order there shall be a line for the signature of the judge under which shall be typed "Judge, Allen Superior Court" or "Judge, Allen Circuit Court", whichever is applicable, to the left of which shall be the following: "Dated _____". IN ST ALLEN SUPER AND CIR CT CIV Rule TR00-1(B).

   d. *Allowance of space for clerk.* To allow space for the Clerk to make entries on the proposed order to show compliance with the notice requirements of IN ST TRIAL P Rule 72(D), the lower four (4) inches of the last page of the proposed order shall be left blank. IN ST ALLEN SUPER AND CIR CT CIV Rule TR00-1(B).

   e. *Proof of notice required.* The proposed order shall also include a prepared proof of notice, under IN ST TRIAL P Rule 72(D). The proof of notice shall conform to the format show in IN ST ALLEN SUPER AND CIR CT CIV Rule TR00-1(B). IN ST ALLEN SUPER AND CIR CT CIV Rule TR00-1(B).

5. *Signature requirements*

   a. *Signature of attorney.* Every pleading or motion of a party represented by an attorney shall be signed by at least one (1) attorney of record in his individual name, whose address, telephone number, and attorney number shall be stated, except that this provision shall not apply to pleadings and motions made and transcribed at the trial or a hearing before the judge and received by him in such form. IN ST TRIAL P Rule 11(A). All pleadings to be signed by an attorney shall contain the written signature of the individual attorney, the attorney's printed name, Supreme Court Attorney Number, the name of the attorney's law firm, the attorney's address, telephone number, and a designation of the party for whom the attorney appears. IN ST ALLEN SUPER AND CIR CT CIV Rule 8-1(C). For the recommended signature format, refer to IN ST ALLEN SUPER AND CIR CT CIV Rule 8-1(C).

      i. The signature of an attorney constitutes a certificate by him that he has read the pleadings; that to the best of his knowledge, information, and belief, there is good ground to support it; and that it is not interposed for delay. IN ST TRIAL P Rule 11(A).

      ii. If a pleading or motion is not signed or is signed with intent to defeat the purpose of the rule, it may be stricken as sham and false and the action may proceed as though the pleading had not been served. IN ST TRIAL P Rule 11(A).

      iii. For a willful violation of IN ST TRIAL P Rule 11 an attorney may be subjected to appropriate disciplinary action. Similar action may be taken if scandalous or indecent matter is inserted. IN ST TRIAL P Rule 11(A).

      iv. Neither printed signatures, nor facsimile signatures shall be accepted on original documents. IN ST ALLEN SUPER AND CIR CT CIV Rule 8-1(C).

      v. Facsimile signatures are permitted on copies. IN ST ALLEN SUPER AND CIR CT CIV Rule 8-1(C).

   b. *Signature of unrepresented party.* A party who is not represented by an attorney shall sign his pleading and state his address. IN ST TRIAL P Rule 11(A).

c. *Verification not generally required.* Except when specifically required by rule, pleadings or motions need not be verified or accompanied by affidavit. The rule in equity that the averments of an answer under oath must be overcome by the testimony of two (2) witnesses or of one (1) witness sustained by corroborating circumstances is abolished. IN ST TRIAL P Rule 11(A).

d. *Verification by affirmation or representation.* When in connection with any civil or special statutory proceeding it is required that any pleading, motion, petition, supporting affidavit, or other document of any kind, be verified, or that an oath be taken, it shall be sufficient if the subscriber simply affirms the truth of the matter to be verified by an affirmation or representation. IN ST TRIAL P Rule 11(B). IN ST TRIAL P Rule 11(B) states that the affirmation or representation should be in substantially the following language: "I (we) affirm, under the penalties for perjury, that the foregoing representation(s) is (are) true. (Signed) _____."

   i. Any person who falsifies an affirmation or representation of fact shall be subject to the same penalties as are prescribed by law for the making of a false affidavit. IN ST TRIAL P Rule 11(B).

e. *Verified pleadings, motions, and affidavits as evidence.* Pleadings, motions and affidavits accompanying or in support of such pleadings or motions when required to be verified or under oath shall be accepted as a representation that the signer had personal knowledge thereof or reasonable cause to believe the existence of the facts or matters stated or alleged therein; and, if otherwise competent or acceptable as evidence, may be admitted as evidence of the facts or matters stated or alleged therein when it is so provided in the Indiana Rules of Trial Procedure, by statute or other law, or to the extent the writing or signature expressly purports to be made upon the signer's personal knowledge. When such pleadings, motions and affidavits are verified or under oath they shall not require other or greater proof on the part of the adverse party than if not verified or not under oath unless expressly provided otherwise by the Indiana Rules of Trial Procedure, statute or other law. Affidavits upon motions for summary judgment under IN ST TRIAL P Rule 56 and in denial of execution under IN ST TRIAL P Rule 9.2 shall be made upon personal knowledge. IN ST TRIAL P Rule 11(C).

6. *Information excluded from public access.* Every document filed in a case shall separately identify information excluded from public access pursuant to IN ST ADMIN Rule 9(G)(1) as follows:

   a. Whole documents that are excluded from public access pursuant to IN ST ADMIN Rule 9(G)(1) shall be tendered on light green paper or have a light green coversheet attached to the document, marked "Not for Public Access" or "Confidential." IN ST TRIAL P Rule 5(G)(1).

   b. When only a portion of a document contains information excluded from public access pursuant to IN ST ADMIN Rule 9(G)(1), said information shall be omitted [or redacted] from the filed document, and set forth on a separate accompanying document on light green paper conspicuously marked "Not for Public Access" or "Confidential" and clearly designated [or identifying] the caption and number of the case and the document and location within the document to which the redacted material pertains. IN ST TRIAL P Rule 5(G)(2).

   c. With respect to documents filed in electronic format, the trial court, by local rule, may provide for compliance with IN ST TRIAL P Rule 5 in manner that separates and protects access to information excluded from public access. IN ST TRIAL P Rule 5(G)(3).

   d. IN ST TRIAL P Rule 5(G) does not apply to a record sealed by the court pursuant to IN ST 5-14-3-5.5 or otherwise, nor to records, documents, or information filed in cases to which public access is prohibited pursuant to IN ST ADMIN Rule 9(G). IN ST TRIAL P Rule 5(G)(4).

   e. The following information in case records is excluded from public access and is confidential:

      i. Information that is excluded from public access pursuant to federal law;

      ii. Information that is excluded from public access as declared confidential by Indiana statute or other court rule, including without limitation:

         • All adoption records created after July 8, 1941, as declared confidential by IN ST 31-19-19-1, et seq., except those specifically declared open by IN ST 31-19-13-2(2);

         • All records relating to chancroid, chlamydia, gonorrhea, hepatitis, human immunodefi-

ciency virus (HIV), Lymphogranuloma venereum, syphilis, tuberculosis, as declared confidential by IN ST 16-41-8-1, et seq.;

- All records relating to child abuse as declared confidential by IN ST 31-33-18-1, et seq.;
- All records relating to drug tests as declared confidential by IN ST 5-14-3-4(a)(9);
- Records of grand jury proceedings as declared confidential by IN ST 35-34-2-4;
- Records of juvenile proceedings as declared confidential by IN ST 31-39-1-2, except those specifically open under statute;
- All paternity records created after July 1, 1941 as declared confidential by IN ST 31-14-11-15, IN ST 31-19-5-23, IN ST 31-39-1-1 and IN ST 31-39-1-2 [Editor's note: IN ST 31-14-11-15 was repealed effective May 9, 2013];
- All pre-sentence reports as declared confidential by IN ST 35-38-1-13;
- Written petitions to permit marriages without consent and orders directing the Clerk of Court to issue a marriage license to underage persons, as declared confidential by IN ST 31-11-1-6;
- Only those arrest warrants, search warrants, indictments and informations ordered confidential by the trial judge, prior to return of duly executed service as declared confidential by IN ST 5-14-3-4(b)(1);
- All medical, mental health, or tax records unless determined by law or regulation of any governmental custodian not to be confidential, released by the subject of such records, or declared by a court of competent jurisdiction to be essential to the resolution of litigation as declared confidential by IN ST 16-39-3-10, IN ST 6-4.1-5-10, IN ST 6-4.1-12-12, and IN ST 6-8.1-7-1;
- Personal information relating to jurors or prospective jurors, other than for the use of the parties and counsel, pursuant to IN ST JURY Rule 10;
- Information relating to protection from abuse orders, no-contact orders and workplace violence restraining orders as declared confidential by IN ST 5-2-9-6, et seq.;
- Mediation proceedings pursuant to IN ST ADR Rule 2.11, Mini-Trial proceedings pursuant to IN ST ADR Rule 4.4(C), and Summary Jury Trials pursuant to IN ST ADR Rule 5.6;
- Information in probation files pursuant to the Probation Standards promulgated by the Judicial Conference of Indiana pursuant to IN ST 11-13-1-8(b);
- Information deemed confidential pursuant to the Rules for Court Administered Alcohol and Drug Programs promulgated by the Judicial Conference of Indiana pursuant to IN ST 12-23-14-13;
- Information deemed confidential pursuant to the Problem-Solving Court Rules promulgated by the Judicial Conference of Indiana pursuant to IN ST 33-23-16-16;
- All records of the Department of workforce Development as declared confidential by IN ST 22-4-19-6;
- Information regarding interception of electronic communications that is sealed or deemed confidential as set forth in IN ST 35-33.5-2-1, et seq.

iii. Information excluded from public access by specific court order;

iv. Complete Social Security Numbers of living persons;

v. With the exception of names, information such as addresses, phone numbers, and dates of birth which explicitly identifies:

- Natural persons who are witnesses or victims (not including defendants) in criminal, domestic violence, stalking, sexual assault, juvenile, or civil protection order proceedings, provided that juveniles who are victims of sex crimes shall be identified by initials only;

- Places of residence of judicial officers, clerks and other employees of courts and clerks of court, unless the person or persons about whom the information pertains waives confidentiality;

vi. Complete account numbers of specific assets, loans, bank accounts, credit cards, and personal identification numbers (PINs);

vii. All orders of expungement entered in criminal or juvenile proceedings, orders to restrict access to criminal history information pursuant to IN ST 35-38-5-5.5 or IN ST 35-38-8-5 and records excluded from public access by such orders, and information related to infractions that is excluded from public access pursuant to IN ST 34-28-5-15 or IN ST 34-28-5-16 [Editor's note: IN ST 35-38-5-5.5, IN ST 35-38-8-5 and IN ST 34-28-5-16 were repealed effective July 1, 2013; for information on orders restricting access to criminal history, refer to IN ST 35-38-9-1, et seq.];

viii. All personal notes and e-mail, and deliberative material, of judges, jurors, court staff and judicial agencies, and information recorded in personal data assistants (PDA's) or organizers and personal calendars. IN ST ADMIN Rule 9(G)(1).

F. Filing and Service Requirements

1. *Filing requirements.* Except as otherwise provided in IN ST TRIAL P Rule 5(E)(2), all pleadings and papers subsequent to the complaint which are required to be served upon a party shall be filed with the Court either before service or within a reasonable period of time thereafter. IN ST TRIAL P Rule 5(E)(1).

   a. *Filing with the court defined.* The filing of pleadings, motions, and other papers with the court as required by the Indiana Rules of Trial Procedure shall be made by one of the following methods:

      i. Delivery to the clerk of the court;

      ii. Sending by electronic transmission under the procedure adopted pursuant to IN ST ADMIN Rule 12;

      iii. Mailing to the clerk by registered, certified or express mail return receipt requested;

      iv. Depositing with any third-party commercial carrier for delivery to the clerk within three (3) calendar days, cost prepaid, properly addressed;

      v. If the court so permits, filing with the judge, in which event the judge shall note thereon the filing date and forthwith transmit them to the office of the clerk; or

      vi. Electronic filing, as approved by the Division of State Court Administration pursuant to IN ST ADMIN Rule 16. IN ST TRIAL P Rule 5(F).

      vii. Filing by registered or certified mail and by third-party commercial carrier shall be complete upon mailing or deposit. IN ST TRIAL P Rule 5(F).

   b. *Facsimile filing*

      i. *Generally.* In counties where a majority of judges of the courts of record, by posted local rule, have authorized electronic facsimile filing and designated a telephone number to receive such transmissions, pleadings, motions, and other papers may be sent to the Clerk of Circuit Court by electronic facsimile transmission for filing in any case, provided:

         - Such matter does not exceed ten (10) pages, including the cover sheet;

         - Such matter does not require the payment of fees other than the electronic facsimile transcription fee set forth in IN ST ADMIN Rule 12(E);

         - The sending party creates at the time of transmission a machine generated log for such transmission; and

         - The original document and the transmission log are maintained by the sending party for the duration of the litigation. IN ST ADMIN Rule 12(B).

      ii. *Time of filing.* During normal, posted business hours, the time of filing shall be the time the duplicate document is produced in the office of the Clerk of the Circuit Court. Duplicate

documents received at all other times shall be filed as of the next normal business day. IN ST ADMIN Rule 12(C).

- If the receiving fax machine endorses its own time and date stamp upon the transmitted documents and the receiving machine produces a delivery receipt which is electronically created and transmitted to the sending party, the time of filing shall be the date and time recorded on the transmitted document by the receiving fax machine. IN ST ADMIN Rule 12(C).

c. *Proof of filing.* Any party filing any paper by any method other than personal delivery to the clerk shall retain proof of filing. IN ST TRIAL P Rule 5(F).

2. *Service requirements.* Unless otherwise provided by the Indiana Rules of Trial Procedure or an order of the court, each party and special judge, if any, shall be served with: (1) every order required by its terms to be served; (2) every pleading subsequent to the original complaint; (3) every written motion except one which may be heard ex parte; (4) every brief submitted to the trial court; (5) every paper relating to discovery required to be served upon a party; and (6) every written notice, appearance, demand, offer of judgment, designation of record on appeal, or similar paper. IN ST TRIAL P Rule 5(A).

a. *Methods of service*

   i. *Personal service.* Whenever a party is represented by an attorney of record, service shall be made upon such attorney unless service upon the party himself is ordered by the court. Service upon the attorney or party shall be made by delivering or mailing a copy of the papers to the last known address or where an attorney or party has consented to service by fax or e-mail, as provided in IN ST TRIAL P Rule 3.1(A)(4), by faxing or e-mailing a copy of the documents to the fax number or e-mail address set out in the appearance form or correction as required by IN ST TRIAL P Rule 3.1(E). IN ST TRIAL P Rule 5(B). Delivery of a copy within IN ST TRIAL P Rule 5 means:

- Offering or tendering it to the attorney or party and stating the nature of the papers being served. Refusal to accept an offered or tendered document is a waiver of any objection to the sufficiency or adequacy of service of that document;

- Leaving it at his office with a clerk or other person in charge thereof, or if there is no one in charge, leaving it in a conspicuous place therein; or

- If the office is closed, by leaving it at his dwelling house or usual place of abode with some person of suitable age and discretion then residing therein; or,

- Leaving it at some other suitable place, selected by the attorney upon whom service is being made, pursuant to duly promulgated local rule. IN ST TRIAL P Rule 5(B)(1).

   ii. *Service by mail.* If service is made by mail, the papers shall be deposited in the United States mail addressed to the person on whom they are being served, with postage prepaid. Service shall be deemed complete upon mailing. Proof of service of all papers permitted to be mailed may be made by written acknowledgment of service, by affidavit of the person who mailed the papers, or by certificate of an attorney. It shall be the duty of attorneys when entering their appearance in a cause or when filing pleadings or papers therein, to have noted in the Chronological Case Summary or said pleadings or papers so filed the address and telephone number of their office. Service by delivery or by mail at such address shall be deemed sufficient and complete. IN ST TRIAL P Rule 5(B)(2).

   iii. *Service by fax or e-mail.* A party who has consented to service by fax or e-mail may be served as follows:

- Service by e-mail shall be made by attaching the document being served in .pdf format. Discovery documents must also be served in accordance with IN ST TRIAL P Rule 26(A). IN ST TRIAL P Rule 5(B)(3)(a).

- Service by fax shall be deemed complete upon generation of a transmission record indicating the successful transmission of the entire document, except as provided in IN ST TRIAL P Rule 5(B)(3)(d). IN ST TRIAL P Rule 5(B)(3)(b).

- Service by e-mail shall be deemed complete upon transmission, except as provided in IN ST TRIAL P Rule 5(B)(3)(d). IN ST TRIAL P Rule 5(B)(3)(c).

- Service by fax or e-mail that occurs on a Saturday, Sunday, legal holiday, or day the court or agency in which the matter is pending is closed or after 5:00 PM local time of the recipient shall be deemed complete the next day that is not a Saturday, Sunday, legal holiday, or day that the court or agency in which the matter is pending is not closed. IN ST TRIAL P Rule 5(B)(3)(d).

iv. *Consent to alternate service.* Any Allen County Attorney or any Allen County law firm may, without charge, maintain an assigned Courthouse box in the library of the Allen County Courthouse for receipt of notices, pleadings, process orders, or other communications from the Court, the Clerk, and other attorneys or law firms. IN ST ALLEN SUPER AND CIR CT CIV Rule 5-1(A). For more information concerning the use of courthouse boxes, refer to IN ST ALLEN SUPER AND CIR CT CIV Rule 5-1.

b. *Serving numerous defendants.* In any action in which there are unusually large numbers of defendants, the court, upon motion or of its own initiative, may order:

i. That service of the pleadings of the defendants and replies thereto need not be made as between the defendants;

- That any cross-claim, counterclaim, or matter constituting an avoidance or affirmative defense contained therein shall be deemed to be denied or avoided by all other parties; and

- That the filing of any such pleading and service thereof upon the plaintiff constitutes due notice of it to the parties. IN ST TRIAL P Rule 5(D).

ii. A copy of every such order shall be served upon the parties in such manner and form as the court directs. IN ST TRIAL P Rule 5(D).

c. *Service on parties in default for failure to appear.* No service need be made on parties in default for failure to appear, except that pleadings asserting new or additional claims for relief against them shall be served upon them in the manner provided by service of summons in IN ST TRIAL P Rule 4. IN ST TRIAL P Rule 5(A).

G. Hearings

1. *Hearing on motion.* Unless local conditions make it impracticable, each judge shall establish regular times and places, at intervals sufficiently frequent for the prompt dispatch of business, at which motions requiring notice and hearing may be heard and disposed of; but the judge at any time or place and on such notice, if any, as he considers reasonable may make order for the advancement, conduct, and hearing of actions. To expedite its business the court may direct the submission and determination of motions without oral hearing upon brief written statements of reasons in support and opposition, or direct or permit hearings by telephone conference call with all attorneys or other similar means of communication. IN ST TRIAL P Rule 73(A).

a. *Setting motions for hearing.* Except for the motions described in IN ST ALLEN SUPER AND CIR CT CIV Rule 7-1(E), all motions shall be set for hearing. IN ST ALLEN SUPER AND CIR CT CIV Rule 7-1(A). [Editor's note: While IN ST ALLEN SUPER AND CIR CT CIV Rule 7-1(A) refers to IN ST ALLEN SUPER AND CIR CT CIV Rule 7-1(E) as relating to hearings on motions, that reference is likely intended to be to IN ST ALLEN SUPER AND CIR CT CIV Rule 7-1(D).]

i. It shall be the responsibility of the moving party to request the date of such hearing from the Judicial Assistant, or if the case has already been assigned to a Judge, from the Judicial Law Clerk of the assigned Judge. IN ST ALLEN SUPER AND CIR CT CIV Rule 7-1(A).

b. *Responsibility for notice of hearing.* It shall be the responsibility of the moving party to give notice to all other parties of hearings scheduled on motions. IN ST ALLEN SUPER AND CIR CT CIV Rule 7-1(I).

2. *Motions to amend pleadings.* Upon being advised of opposing counsel's objection per IN ST ALLEN SUPER AND CIR CT CIV Rule 7-1(C), the moving party's attorney shall request a date for hearing, as prescribed in IN ST ALLEN SUPER AND CIR CT CIV Rule 7-1(A). IN ST ALLEN SUPER AND CIR CT CIV Rule 7-1(C).

3. *Motions not likely to require hearing.* At the time of filing, the following motions, along with the court packet, shall be brought to the attention of the Judicial Assistant or Law Clerk of the Judge.

   a. Motion to Dismiss complaint by Plaintiff when no answer has been filed;

   b. Motion to Dismiss Counterclaim by Defendant when no reply has been filed;

   c. Motion to amend any pleading. IN ST ALLEN SUPER AND CIR CT CIV Rule 7-1(D).

   d. Such motions shall be summarily granted or denied ex parte unless the assigned Judge, determines that a hearing should be scheduled. IN ST ALLEN SUPER AND CIR CT CIV Rule 7-1(D).

H. Forms

1. Motion for Leave to Amend Forms for Indiana

   a. Motion to file amended complaint. 5 INPRAC § 3:5.1.

   b. Motion to file amended complaint; Another form. 5 INPRAC § 3:5.2.

   c. Motion to amend pleading to conform to evidence. 5 INPRAC § 3:5.4.

   d. Motion to amend complaint to compel joinder of defendant. 5 INPRAC § 3:7.2.

   e. Motion to amend caption. 9 INPRAC § 3.41.

   f. Affidavit in support of motion to amend caption. 9 INPRAC § 3.42.

   g. Motion for leave to amend complaint following dismissal. 9 INPRAC § 42.16.

   h. Motion for leave to file amended complaint against third party defendant. 10 INPRAC § 44.8.

   i. Motion to file amended complaint. 10 INPRAC § 46.7.

   j. Motion to amend complaint which has been dismissed; Filed more than 10 days after notice of dismissal. 10 INPRAC § 46.8.

   k. Motion to amend pleading; Another form. 10 INPRAC § 46.9.

   l. Order granting leave to amend complaint. 10 INPRAC § 46.10.

   m. Amendment by stipulation. 10 INPRAC § 46.11.

   n. Amended answer by interlineation. 10 INPRAC § 46.12.

   o. Objections to motion to amend complaint. 10 INPRAC § 46.13.

   p. Motion to amend pleading to conform to evidence. 10 INPRAC § 46.14.

   q. Motion for leave to change defendant after statute of limitations. 10 INPRAC § 46.16.

   r. Motion for leave to add party after statute of limitations. 10 INPRAC § 46.17.

   s. Motion to substitute real party in interest; Assignee of interest. 10 INPRAC § 47.10.

   t. Motion to amend complaint to compel joinder of defendant. 10 INPRAC § 49.3.

   u. Certificate of service; Personal service. 9 INPRAC § 5.7.

   v. Certificate of service; First class mail. 9 INPRAC § 5.8.

2. Official Motion for Leave to Amend Forms for Allen County

   a. Consent to alternate service. IN ST ALLEN SUPER AND CIR CT CIV App. A.

I. Checklist

   (I) ❑ Matters to be considered by moving party

      (a) ❑ Required documents

        (1) ❑ Motion and notice

        (2) ❑ Copy of amended pleading

        (3) ❑ Proposed order

        (4) ❑ Certificate of service

    (b) ❏ Supplemental documents

       (1) ❏ Supporting evidence

       (2) ❏ Brief or memorandum

       (3) ❏ Facsimile cover sheet

    (c) ❏ Timing

       (1) ❏ A party may amend his pleading once as a matter of course at any time before a responsive pleading is served or, if the pleading is one to which no responsive pleading is permitted, and the action has not been placed upon the trial calendar, he may so amend it at any time within thirty (30) days after it is served

       (2) ❏ Otherwise a party may amend his pleading only by leave of court or by written consent of the adverse party; and leave shall be given when justice so requires

       (3) ❏ A written motion, other than one which may be heard ex parte, and notice of the hearing thereof shall be served not less than five (5) days before the time specified for the hearing, unless a different period is fixed by the Indiana Rules of Trial Procedure or by order of the court

       (4) ❏ All pleadings and papers subsequent to the complaint which are required to be served upon a party shall be filed with the Court either before service or within a reasonable period of time thereafter

(II) ❏ Matters to be considered by the responding party

    (a) ❏ Required documents

       (1) ❏ Opposition

       (2) ❏ Certificate of service

    (b) ❏ Supplemental documents

       (1) ❏ Supporting evidence

       (2) ❏ Objection to written advisory

       (3) ❏ Brief or memorandum

       (4) ❏ Proposed order

       (5) ❏ Facsimile cover sheet

    (c) ❏ Timing

       (1) ❏ Except as otherwise provided in IN ST TRIAL P Rule 59(D), opposing affidavits may be served not less than one (1) day before the hearing, unless the court permits them to be served at some other time

Motions, Oppositions and Replies
Motion for Summary Judgment

Document Last Updated October 2013

A. Applicable Rules

  1. *State rules*

    a. Appearance. IN ST TRIAL P Rule 3.1.

    b. Process. IN ST TRIAL P Rule 4.

    c. Service and filing of pleadings and other papers. IN ST TRIAL P Rule 5.

    d. Time. IN ST TRIAL P Rule 6.

    e. Pleadings. IN ST TRIAL P Rule 7; IN ST TRIAL P Rule 8; IN ST TRIAL P Rule 9.2; IN ST TRIAL P Rule 10.

    f.   Signing and verification of pleadings. IN ST TRIAL P Rule 11.

    g.   Evidence. IN ST TRIAL P Rule 43.

    h.   Judgment on the evidence (directed verdict). IN ST TRIAL P Rule 50.

    i.   Findings by the court. IN ST TRIAL P Rule 52.

    j.   Summary judgment. IN ST TRIAL P Rule 56.

    k.   Motion to correct error. IN ST TRIAL P Rule 59.

    l.   Relief from judgment or order. IN ST TRIAL P Rule 60.

    m.   Trial court and clerks. IN ST TRIAL P Rule 72.

    n.   Hearing of motions. IN ST TRIAL P Rule 73.

    o.   Access to court records. IN ST ADMIN Rule 9.

    p.   Paper size. IN ST ADMIN Rule 11.

    q.   Facsimile transmission. IN ST ADMIN Rule 12.

    r.   Electronic filing and electronic service pilot projects. IN ST ADMIN Rule 16.

    s.   Sealing of certain records by court; Hearing; Notice. IN ST 5-14-3-5.5.

    t.   Privacy and confidentiality. IN ST 5-2-9-6; IN ST 5-14-3-4; IN ST 6-4.1-5-10; IN ST 6-4.1-12-12; IN ST 6-8.1-7-1; IN ST 11-13-1-8; IN ST 12-23-14-13; IN ST 16-39-3-10; IN ST 16-41-8-1; IN ST 22-4-19-6; IN ST 31-11-1-6; IN ST 31-19-5-23; IN ST 31-19-13-2; IN ST 31-19-19-1; IN ST 31-33-18-1; IN ST 31-39-1-1; IN ST 31-39-1-2; IN ST 33-23-16-16; IN ST 35-34-2-4; IN ST 35-38-1-13; IN ST 35-38-9-1; IN ST ADR Rule 2.11; IN ST ADR Rule 4.4; IN ST ADR Rule 5.6; IN ST JURY Rule 10.

2. *Local rules*

    a.   Applicability and citation of rules. IN ST ALLEN SUPER AND CIR CT CIV Rule AR00-1.

    b.   Proposed orders. IN ST ALLEN SUPER AND CIR CT CIV Rule TR00-1.

    c.   Appearances. IN ST ALLEN SUPER AND CIR CT CIV Rule 3.1-1.

    d.   Consent to alternate service. IN ST ALLEN SUPER AND CIR CT CIV Rule 5-1.

    e.   Motions in civil court. IN ST ALLEN SUPER AND CIR CT CIV Rule 7-1.

    f.   Preparation of pleadings. IN ST ALLEN SUPER AND CIR CT CIV Rule 8-1.

    g.   Filing. IN ST ALLEN SUPER AND CIR CT CIV Rule 77-1.

B. Timing

1. *Time for moving for summary judgment*

    a.   *For claimant.* A party seeking to recover upon a claim, counterclaim, or cross-claim or to obtain a declaratory judgment may, at any time after the expiration of twenty (20) days from the commencement of the action or after service of a motion for summary judgment by the adverse party, move with or without supporting affidavits for a summary judgment in his favor upon all or any part thereof. IN ST TRIAL P Rule 56(A).

    b.   *For defending party.* A party against whom a claim, counterclaim, or cross-claim is asserted or a declaratory judgment is sought may, at any time, move with or without supporting affidavits for a summary judgment in his favor as to all or any part thereof. IN ST TRIAL P Rule 56(B).

    c.   *Filing.* All pleadings and papers subsequent to the complaint which are required to be served upon a party shall be filed with the Court either before service or within a reasonable period of time thereafter. IN ST TRIAL P Rule 5(E)(1).

2. *Service.* A written motion, other than one which may be heard ex parte, and notice of the hearing thereof shall be served not less than five (5) days before the time specified for the hearing, unless a different period is fixed by the Indiana Rules of Trial Procedure or by order of the court. IN ST TRIAL P Rule 6(D).

    a.   *Of supporting affidavits.* When a motion is supported by affidavit, the affidavit shall be served with the motion. IN ST TRIAL P Rule 6(D).

3. *Service of opposition.* An adverse party shall have thirty (30) days after service of the motion to serve a response and any opposing affidavits. IN ST TRIAL P Rule 56(C).

   a. Except as otherwise provided in IN ST TRIAL P Rule 59(D), opposing affidavits may be served not less than one (1) day before the hearing, unless the court permits them to be served at some other time. IN ST TRIAL P Rule 6(D).

4. *Computation of time*

   a. *Generally; Days excluded.* In computing any period of time prescribed or allowed by the Indiana Rules of Trial Procedure, by order of the court, or by any applicable statute, the day of the act, event, or default from which the designated period of time begins to run shall not be included. The last day of the period so computed is to be included unless it is:

      i. A Saturday,

      ii. A Sunday,

      iii. A legal holiday as defined by state statute, or

      iv. A day the office in which the act is to be done is closed during regular business hours. IN ST TRIAL P Rule 6(A).

   b. *Short periods.* In any event, the period runs until the end of the next day that is not a Saturday, a Sunday, a legal holiday, or a day on which the office is closed. When the period of time allowed is less than seven (7) days, intermediate Saturdays, Sundays, legal holidays, and days on which the office is closed shall be excluded from the computations. IN ST TRIAL P Rule 6(A).

   c. *Additional time after service by United States mail.* Whenever a party has the right or is required to do some act or take some proceedings within a prescribed period after the service of a notice or other paper upon him and the notice or paper is served upon him by United States mail, three (3) days shall be added to the prescribed period. IN ST TRIAL P Rule 6(E).

   d. *Enlargement of time.* When an act is required or allowed to be done at or within a specific time by the Indiana Rules of Trial Procedure, the court may at any time for cause shown:

      i. Order the period enlarged, with or without motion or notice, if request therefor is made before the expiration of the period originally prescribed or extended by a previous order; or

      ii. Upon motion made after the expiration of the specific period, permit the act to be done where the failure to act was the result of excusable neglect; but, the court may not extend the time for taking any action for judgment on the evidence under IN ST TRIAL P Rule 50(A), amendment of findings and judgment under IN ST TRIAL P Rule 52(B), to correct errors under IN ST TRIAL P Rule 59(C), statement in opposition to motion to correct error under IN ST TRIAL P Rule 59(E), or to obtain relief from final judgment under IN ST TRIAL P Rule 60(B), except to the extent and under the conditions stated in those rules. IN ST TRIAL P Rule 6(B).

C. General Requirements

1. *Motions, generally.* Unless made during a hearing or trial, or otherwise ordered by the court, an application to the court for an order shall be made by written motion. The motion shall state the grounds therefor and the relief or order sought. IN ST TRIAL P Rule 7(B).

   a. *Motions as distinct from pleadings.* Motions and responses to motions are not pleadings, and allegations contained in a motion are not admissions of a party. 22B INPRAC 7:2; Wachstetter v. County Properties, LLC, 832 N.E.2d 574 (Ind.Ct.App. 2005); Scott County Family YMCA, Inc. v. Hobbs, 817 N.E.2d 603 (Ind.Ct.App. 2004).

   b. *Unopposed motions generally granted.* It is common for a trial court to grant procedural motions, such as motions for enlargement of time, discovery motions, or motions for continuance, unless an objection is filed. 21 INPRAC § 13.8.

2. *Motion for summary judgment.* Summary judgment is a procedure by which the trial court is asked to enter judgment when there are no genuine issues of material fact and the moving party is entitled to judgment as a matter of law. A summary judgment proceeding is not a trial, and is not intended to be a substitute for factual determinations where the facts are in dispute. Rather, summary judgment should be

used to terminate litigation about which there is no factual dispute and which may be determined as a matter of law. 11 INPRAC § 90.1; LeBrun v. Conner, 702 N.E.2d 754 (Ind.Ct.App. 1998).

a. *Burden.* The judgment sought shall be rendered forthwith if the designated evidentiary matter shows that there is no genuine issue as to any material fact and that the moving party is entitled to a judgment as a matter of law. IN ST TRIAL P Rule 56(C).

   i. A "genuine" issue of material fact exists if the trier of fact must resolve the opposing party's differing version of the underlying facts or if the undisputed facts support conflicting reasonable inferences. A fact is "material" if it might affect the outcome of a case by helping to prove or disprove an essential element of a claim or defense, or it facilitates a resolution of an issue in the case. 22B INPRAC 56:1; Williams v. Tharp, 914 N.E.2d 756 (Ind. 2009).

   ii. Summary judgment shall not be granted as of course because the opposing party fails to offer opposing affidavits or evidence, but the court shall make its determination from the evidentiary matter designated to the court. IN ST TRIAL P Rule 56(C).

   iii. The trial court must evaluate the evidence in favor of the non-moving party. 22B INPRAC 56:1.

   iv. Although Indiana courts are not consistent in describing the amount of proof required to sustain the moving party's initial burden, and IN ST TRIAL P Rule 56 is silent on the matter, a number of cases require "prima facie" proof. 22B INPRAC 56:5; DeHahn v. CSX Transp., Inc., 925 N.E.2d 442 (Ind.Ct.App. 2010). Once the moving party demonstrates the requirements for summary judgment, the burden shifts to the non-moving party to designate each material issue of fact which he asserts precludes entry of summary judgment and the evidence relevant to each designated fact. 22B INPRAC 56:5; Booth v. Wiley, 839 N.E.2d 1168 (Ind. 2005).

b. *When motion not required.* When any party has moved for summary judgment, the court may grant summary judgment for any other party upon the issues raised by the motion although no motion for summary judgment is filed by such party. IN ST TRIAL P Rule 56(B).

c. *Judgment on less than all issues or claims.* A summary judgment may be rendered upon less than all the issues or claims, including without limitation the issue of liability or damages alone although there is a genuine issue as to damages or liability as the case may be. IN ST TRIAL P Rule 56(C).

   i. *Partial judgment not entered; Exceptions.* A summary judgment upon less than all the issues involved in a claim or with respect to less than all the claims or parties shall be interlocutory unless the court in writing expressly determines that there is no just reason for delay and in writing expressly directs entry of judgment as to less than all the issues, claims or parties. IN ST TRIAL P Rule 56(C).

   ii. *Designation of specific findings.* The court shall designate the issues or claims upon which it finds no genuine issue as to any material facts. IN ST TRIAL P Rule 56(C).

   iii. *Case not fully adjudicated on motion.* If on motion under IN ST TRIAL P Rule 56 judgment is not rendered upon the whole case or for all the relief asked and a trial is necessary, the court at the hearing of the motion, by examining the pleadings and the evidence before it and by interrogating counsel, shall if practicable ascertain what material facts exist without substantial controversy and what material facts are actually and in good faith controverted. It shall thereupon make an order specifying the facts that appear without substantial controversy, including the extent to which the amount of damages or other relief is not in controversy, and directing such further proceedings in the action as are just. Upon the trial of the action the facts so specified shall be deemed established, and the trial shall be conducted accordingly. IN ST TRIAL P Rule 56(D).

d. *Form of affidavits; Further testimony; Defense required.* Supporting and opposing affidavits shall be made on personal knowledge, shall set forth such facts as would be admissible in evidence, and shall show affirmatively that the affiant is competent to testify to the matters stated therein. IN ST TRIAL P Rule 56(E).

   i. Sworn or certified copies not previously self-authenticated of all papers or parts thereof referred to in an affidavit shall be attached thereto or served therewith. IN ST TRIAL P Rule 56(E).

   ii. The court may permit affidavits to be supplemented or opposed by depositions, answers to interrogatories, or further affidavits. IN ST TRIAL P Rule 56(E).

iii. When a motion for summary judgment is made and supported as provided in IN ST TRIAL P Rule 56, an adverse party may not rest upon the mere allegations or denials of his pleading, but his response, by affidavits or as otherwise provided in IN ST TRIAL P Rule 56, must set forth specific facts showing that there is a genuine issue for trial. If he does not so respond, summary judgment, if appropriate, shall be entered against him. Denial of summary judgment may be challenged by a motion to correct errors after a final judgment or order is entered. IN ST TRIAL P Rule 56(E).

e. *When affidavits are unavailable.* Should it appear from the affidavits of a party opposing the motion that he cannot for reasons stated present by affidavit facts essential to justify his opposition, the court may refuse the application for judgment or may order a continuance to permit affidavits to be obtained or depositions to be taken or discovery to be had or may make such other order as is just. IN ST TRIAL P Rule 56(F).

f. *Affidavits made in bad faith.* Should it appear to the satisfaction of the court at any time that any of the affidavits presented pursuant to IN ST TRIAL P Rule 56 are presented in bad faith or solely for the purpose of delay, the court shall forthwith order the party employing them to pay to the other party the amount of the reasonable expenses which the filing of the affidavits caused him to incur, including reasonable attorney's fees, and any offending party or attorney may be adjudged guilty of contempt. IN ST TRIAL P Rule 56(G).

g. *Party opposing the motion.* A party opposing the motion shall also designate to the court each material issue of fact which that party asserts precludes entry of summary judgment and the evidence relevant thereto. IN ST TRIAL P Rule 56(C).

h. *Appeal; Reversal.* No judgment rendered on the motion shall be reversed on the ground that there is a genuine issue of material fact unless the material fact and the evidence relevant thereto shall have been specifically designated to the trial court. IN ST TRIAL P Rule 56(H).

D. Documents

1. *Required documents*

   a. *Motion and notice.* The requirement of notice is satisfied by service of the motion. IN ST TRIAL P Rule 7(B). Refer to the General Requirements section of this document for information on the content of a motion for summary judgment.

   b. *Supporting evidence.* At the time of filing the motion or response, a party shall designate to the court all parts of pleadings, depositions, answers to interrogatories, admissions, matters of judicial notice, and any other matters on which it relies for purposes of the motion. IN ST TRIAL P Rule 56(C).

      i. The party moving for judgment must designate sufficient evidence to establish that there is no genuine issue of material fact and that judgment is proper as a matter of law. 22B INPRAC 56:4; Jarboe v. Landmark Community Newspapers of Indiana, Inc., 644 N.E.2d 118 (Ind. 1994).

   c. *Proposed order.* Unless local practice provides differently, a party should submit a proposed order with its written motion to be signed by the judge once the motion has been granted. 21 INPRAC § 13.8.

      i. *Proposed orders on motions for summary judgment.* Proposed orders on motions for summary judgment may contain the language called for in IN ST TRIAL P Rule 56(C) that there is not just reason for delay and directs entry of final judgment as to less than all the issues, claims or parties. IN ST ALLEN SUPER AND CIR CT CIV Rule TR00-1(D).

      ii. *Copies of proposed orders.* All proposed orders shall be submitted in an original plus a number of copies equal to one (1) more than the number of pro se parties and attorneys of record contained in the prepared proof of notice under IN ST TRIAL P Rule 72(D). IN ST ALLEN SUPER AND CIR CT CIV Rule TR00-1(C).

      iii. *Proof of notice.* The proposed order shall also include a prepared proof of notice, under IN ST TRIAL P Rule 72(D). IN ST ALLEN SUPER AND CIR CT CIV Rule TR00-1(B).

      iv. Refer to the Format section of this document for information on the form and content of the proposed order and the proof of notice.

    d. *Certificate of service.* An attorney or unrepresented party tendering a document to the Clerk for filing shall certify that service has been made, list the parties served, and specify the date and means of service. The certificate of service shall be placed at the end of the document and shall not be separately filed. The separate filing of a certificate of service, however, shall not be grounds for rejecting a document for filing. The Clerk may permit documents to be filed without a certificate of service but shall require prompt filing of a separate certificate of service. IN ST TRIAL P Rule 5(C).

2. *Supplemental documents*

    a. *Additional supporting evidence.* When a motion is based on facts not appearing of record the court may hear the matter on affidavits presented by the respective parties, but the court may direct that the matter be heard wholly or partly on oral testimony or depositions. IN ST TRIAL P Rule 43(B).

    b. *Brief or memorandum.* If a party desires to file a brief or memorandum in support of any motion, such brief or memorandum shall be filed simultaneously with the motion, and a copy shall be promptly served upon the adverse party. IN ST ALLEN SUPER AND CIR CT CIV Rule 7-1(E).

    c. *Facsimile cover sheet.* Any document sent to the Clerk of the Circuit Court by electronic facsimile transmission shall be accompanied by a cover sheet which states the title of the document, case number, number of pages, identity and voice telephone number of the sending party and instructions for filing. The cover sheet shall contain the signature of the attorney or party, pro se, authorizing the filing. IN ST ADMIN Rule 12(D).

E. Format

1. *Form of motions.* The rules applicable to captions, and the signing and form of pleadings (IN ST TRIAL P Rule 8 through IN ST TRIAL P Rule 11), apply to all motions and other papers provided under the Indiana Rules of Trial Procedure. 22B INPRAC 7:2.

2. *Form of pleadings*

    a. *Caption; Names of parties.* Every pleading shall contain a caption setting forth the name of the court, the title of the action, the file number, and a designation as in IN ST TRIAL P Rule 7(A). In the complaint the title of the action shall include the names of all the parties, but in other pleadings it is sufficient to state the name of the first party on each side with an appropriate indication of other parties. IN ST TRIAL P Rule 10(A).

    b. *Paragraphs; Separate statements.* All averments of a claim or defense shall be made in numbered paragraphs, the contents of each of which shall be limited as far as practicable to a statement of a single set of circumstances, and a paragraph may be referred to by number in all succeeding pleadings. Each claim founded upon a separate transaction or occurrence and each defense other than denials may be stated in a separate count or defense whenever a separation facilitates the clear presentation of the matters set forth. IN ST TRIAL P Rule 10(B).

    c. *Adoption by reference; Exhibits.* Statements in a pleading may be adopted by reference in a different part of the same pleading or in another pleading or in any motion. A copy of any written instrument which is an exhibit to a pleading is a part thereof for all purposes. IN ST TRIAL P Rule 10(C).

    d. *Citation.* Allen County Superior and Circuit court rules may be cited as L.R. _____. The Indiana Rules of Trial Procedure are hereinafter referred to as T.R. _____. IN ST ALLEN SUPER AND CIR CT CIV Rule AR00-1(B).

    e. *Paper.* All pleadings must be printed on white paper. IN ST ALLEN SUPER AND CIR CT CIV Rule 8-1(A).

    f. *Spacing.* The lines shall be double spaced except for quotations, which shall be indented and single-spaced. IN ST ALLEN SUPER AND CIR CT CIV Rule 8-1(A).

    g. *Photocopies.* Photocopies are acceptable if legible. IN ST ALLEN SUPER AND CIR CT CIV Rule 8-1(A).

    h. *Margins and binding.* Margins shall be one to one and one-half (1-1 1/2) inches on the left side and one-half (1/2) inch on the right. IN ST ALLEN SUPER AND CIR CT CIV Rule 8-1(B).

      i. Binding or stapling shall be at the top left and at no other place. IN ST ALLEN SUPER AND CIR CT CIV Rule 8-1(B).

     ii.   Covers or backing shall not be used. IN ST ALLEN SUPER AND CIR CT CIV Rule 8-1(B).

  i.   *Flat filing.* The files of the Clerk of the Court shall be kept under the "flat filing" system. All pleadings presented for filing with the Clerk or Court shall be flat and unfolded. Only the original of any pleading shall be placed in the Court file. IN ST ALLEN SUPER AND CIR CT CIV Rule 77-1(A).

  j.   *Handwritten pleadings.* Handwritten pleadings may be accepted for filing in the discretion of the Court. IN ST ALLEN SUPER AND CIR CT CIV Rule 8-1(A).

3.   *Size of papers for filing.* Effective January 1, 1992, all pleadings, copies, motions and documents filed with any trial court or appellate level court, typed or printed, with the exception of exhibits and existing wills, shall be prepared on eight and one-half by eleven inch (8 1/2" x 11") size paper. IN ST ADMIN Rule 11.

4.   *Form of proposed orders*

  a.   *Form, caption, and title.* Any proposed order shall be a document that is separate and apart from the motion or application to which it relates and shall contain a caption showing the name of the court, the case number assigned to the case and the title of the case as shown by the complaint. IN ST ALLEN SUPER AND CIR CT CIV Rule TR00-1(B). If there are multiple parties, the title may be shortened to include only the first name plaintiff and defendant with appropriate indication that there are additional parties. IN ST ALLEN SUPER AND CIR CT CIV Rule TR00-1(B).

  b.   *Paper.* The proposed order shall be on white paper, eight and one half by eleven inches (8 1/2" x 11") in size, and each page shall be numbered. IN ST ALLEN SUPER AND CIR CT CIV Rule TR00-1(B).

  c.   *Signature line.* On the last page of the proposed order there shall be a line for the signature of the judge under which shall be typed "Judge, Allen Superior Court" or "Judge, Allen Circuit Court", whichever is applicable, to the left of which shall be the following: "Dated _____". IN ST ALLEN SUPER AND CIR CT CIV Rule TR00-1(B).

  d.   *Allowance of space for clerk.* To allow space for the Clerk to make entries on the proposed order to show compliance with the notice requirements of IN ST TRIAL P Rule 72(D), the lower four (4) inches of the last page of the proposed order shall be left blank. IN ST ALLEN SUPER AND CIR CT CIV Rule TR00-1(B).

  e.   *Proof of notice required.* The proposed order shall also include a prepared proof of notice, under IN ST TRIAL P Rule 72(D). The proof of notice shall conform to the format show in IN ST ALLEN SUPER AND CIR CT CIV Rule TR00-1(B). IN ST ALLEN SUPER AND CIR CT CIV Rule TR00-1(B).

5.   *Signature requirements*

  a.   *Signature of attorney.* Every pleading or motion of a party represented by an attorney shall be signed by at least one (1) attorney of record in his individual name, whose address, telephone number, and attorney number shall be stated, except that this provision shall not apply to pleadings and motions made and transcribed at the trial or a hearing before the judge and received by him in such form. IN ST TRIAL P Rule 11(A). All pleadings to be signed by an attorney shall contain the written signature of the individual attorney, the attorney's printed name, Supreme Court Attorney Number, the name of the attorney's law firm, the attorney's address, telephone number, and a designation of the party for whom the attorney appears. IN ST ALLEN SUPER AND CIR CT CIV Rule 8-1(C). For the recommended signature format, refer to IN ST ALLEN SUPER AND CIR CT CIV Rule 8-1(C).

     i.   The signature of an attorney constitutes a certificate by him that he has read the pleadings; that to the best of his knowledge, information, and belief, there is good ground to support it; and that it is not interposed for delay. IN ST TRIAL P Rule 11(A).

     ii.   If a pleading or motion is not signed or is signed with intent to defeat the purpose of the rule, it may be stricken as sham and false and the action may proceed as though the pleading had not been served. IN ST TRIAL P Rule 11(A).

     iii.   For a willful violation of IN ST TRIAL P Rule 11 an attorney may be subjected to appropriate

disciplinary action. Similar action may be taken if scandalous or indecent matter is inserted. IN ST TRIAL P Rule 11(A).

    iv. Neither printed signatures, nor facsimile signatures shall be accepted on original documents. IN ST ALLEN SUPER AND CIR CT CIV Rule 8-1(C).

    v. Facsimile signatures are permitted on copies. IN ST ALLEN SUPER AND CIR CT CIV Rule 8-1(C).

b. *Signature of unrepresented party.* A party who is not represented by an attorney shall sign his pleading and state his address. IN ST TRIAL P Rule 11(A).

c. *Verification not generally required.* Except when specifically required by rule, pleadings or motions need not be verified or accompanied by affidavit. The rule in equity that the averments of an answer under oath must be overcome by the testimony of two (2) witnesses or of one (1) witness sustained by corroborating circumstances is abolished. IN ST TRIAL P Rule 11(A).

d. *Verification by affirmation or representation.* When in connection with any civil or special statutory proceeding it is required that any pleading, motion, petition, supporting affidavit, or other document of any kind, be verified, or that an oath be taken, it shall be sufficient if the subscriber simply affirms the truth of the matter to be verified by an affirmation or representation. IN ST TRIAL P Rule 11(B). IN ST TRIAL P Rule 11(B) states that the affirmation or representation should be in substantially the following language: "I (we) affirm, under the penalties for perjury, that the foregoing representation(s) is (are) true. (Signed) _____."

    i. Any person who falsifies an affirmation or representation of fact shall be subject to the same penalties as are prescribed by law for the making of a false affidavit. IN ST TRIAL P Rule 11(B).

e. *Verified pleadings, motions, and affidavits as evidence.* Pleadings, motions and affidavits accompanying or in support of such pleadings or motions when required to be verified or under oath shall be accepted as a representation that the signer had personal knowledge thereof or reasonable cause to believe the existence of the facts or matters stated or alleged therein; and, if otherwise competent or acceptable as evidence, may be admitted as evidence of the facts or matters stated or alleged therein when it is so provided in the Indiana Rules of Trial Procedure, by statute or other law, or to the extent the writing or signature expressly purports to be made upon the signer's personal knowledge. When such pleadings, motions and affidavits are verified or under oath they shall not require other or greater proof on the part of the adverse party than if not verified or not under oath unless expressly provided otherwise by the Indiana Rules of Trial Procedure, statute or other law. Affidavits upon motions for summary judgment under IN ST TRIAL P Rule 56 and in denial of execution under IN ST TRIAL P Rule 9.2 shall be made upon personal knowledge. IN ST TRIAL P Rule 11(C).

6. *Information excluded from public access.* Every document filed in a case shall separately identify information excluded from public access pursuant to IN ST ADMIN Rule 9(G)(1) as follows:

a. Whole documents that are excluded from public access pursuant to IN ST ADMIN Rule 9(G)(1) shall be tendered on light green paper or have a light green coversheet attached to the document, marked "Not for Public Access" or "Confidential." IN ST TRIAL P Rule 5(G)(1).

b. When only a portion of a document contains information excluded from public access pursuant to IN ST ADMIN Rule 9(G)(1), said information shall be omitted [or redacted] from the filed document, and set forth on a separate accompanying document on light green paper conspicuously marked "Not for Public Access" or "Confidential" and clearly designated [or identifying] the caption and number of the case and the document and location within the document to which the redacted material pertains. IN ST TRIAL P Rule 5(G)(2).

c. With respect to documents filed in electronic format, the trial court, by local rule, may provide for compliance with IN ST TRIAL P Rule 5 in manner that separates and protects access to information excluded from public access. IN ST TRIAL P Rule 5(G)(3).

d. IN ST TRIAL P Rule 5(G) does not apply to a record sealed by the court pursuant to IN ST 5-14-3-5.5 or otherwise, nor to records, documents, or information filed in cases to which public access is prohibited pursuant to IN ST ADMIN Rule 9(G). IN ST TRIAL P Rule 5(G)(4).

e. The following information in case records is excluded from public access and is confidential:

    i. Information that is excluded from public access pursuant to federal law;

    ii. Information that is excluded from public access as declared confidential by Indiana statute or other court rule, including without limitation:

- All adoption records created after July 8, 1941, as declared confidential by IN ST 31-19-19-1, et seq., except those specifically declared open by IN ST 31-19-13-2(2);

- All records relating to chancroid, chlamydia, gonorrhea, hepatitis, human immunodeficiency virus (HIV), Lymphogranuloma venereum, syphilis, tuberculosis, as declared confidential by IN ST 16-41-8-1, et seq.;

- All records relating to child abuse as declared confidential by IN ST 31-33-18-1, et seq.;

- All records relating to drug tests as declared confidential by IN ST 5-14-3-4(a)(9);

- Records of grand jury proceedings as declared confidential by IN ST 35-34-2-4;

- Records of juvenile proceedings as declared confidential by IN ST 31-39-1-2, except those specifically open under statute;

- All paternity records created after July 1, 1941 as declared confidential by IN ST 31-14-11-15, IN ST 31-19-5-23, IN ST 31-39-1-1 and IN ST 31-39-1-2 [Editor's note: IN ST 31-14-11-15 was repealed effective May 9, 2013];

- All pre-sentence reports as declared confidential by IN ST 35-38-1-13;

- Written petitions to permit marriages without consent and orders directing the Clerk of Court to issue a marriage license to underage persons, as declared confidential by IN ST 31-11-1-6;

- Only those arrest warrants, search warrants, indictments and informations ordered confidential by the trial judge, prior to return of duly executed service as declared confidential by IN ST 5-14-3-4(b)(1);

- All medical, mental health, or tax records unless determined by law or regulation of any governmental custodian not to be confidential, released by the subject of such records, or declared by a court of competent jurisdiction to be essential to the resolution of litigation as declared confidential by IN ST 16-39-3-10, IN ST 6-4.1-5-10, IN ST 6-4.1-12-12, and IN ST 6-8.1-7-1;

- Personal information relating to jurors or prospective jurors, other than for the use of the parties and counsel, pursuant to IN ST JURY Rule 10;

- Information relating to protection from abuse orders, no-contact orders and workplace violence restraining orders as declared confidential by IN ST 5-2-9-6, et seq.;

- Mediation proceedings pursuant to IN ST ADR Rule 2.11, Mini-Trial proceedings pursuant to IN ST ADR Rule 4.4(C), and Summary Jury Trials pursuant to IN ST ADR Rule 5.6;

- Information in probation files pursuant to the Probation Standards promulgated by the Judicial Conference of Indiana pursuant to IN ST 11-13-1-8(b);

- Information deemed confidential pursuant to the Rules for Court Administered Alcohol and Drug Programs promulgated by the Judicial Conference of Indiana pursuant to IN ST 12-23-14-13;

- Information deemed confidential pursuant to the Problem-Solving Court Rules promulgated by the Judicial Conference of Indiana pursuant to IN ST 33-23-16-16;

- All records of the Department of workforce Development as declared confidential by IN ST 22-4-19-6;

- Information regarding interception of electronic communications that is sealed or deemed confidential as set forth in IN ST 35-33.5-2-1, et seq.

iii. Information excluded from public access by specific court order;

iv. Complete Social Security Numbers of living persons;

v. With the exception of names, information such as addresses, phone numbers, and dates of birth which explicitly identifies:

- Natural persons who are witnesses or victims (not including defendants) in criminal, domestic violence, stalking, sexual assault, juvenile, or civil protection order proceedings, provided that juveniles who are victims of sex crimes shall be identified by initials only;

- Places of residence of judicial officers, clerks and other employees of courts and clerks of court, unless the person or persons about whom the information pertains waives confidentiality;

vi. Complete account numbers of specific assets, loans, bank accounts, credit cards, and personal identification numbers (PINs);

vii. All orders of expungement entered in criminal or juvenile proceedings, orders to restrict access to criminal history information pursuant to IN ST 35-38-5-5.5 or IN ST 35-38-8-5 and records excluded from public access by such orders, and information related to infractions that is excluded from public access pursuant to IN ST 34-28-5-15 or IN ST 34-28-5-16 [Editor's note: IN ST 35-38-5-5.5, IN ST 35-38-8-5 and IN ST 34-28-5-16 were repealed effective July 1, 2013; for information on orders restricting access to criminal history, refer to IN ST 35-38-9-1, et seq.];

viii. All personal notes and e-mail, and deliberative material, of judges, jurors, court staff and judicial agencies, and information recorded in personal data assistants (PDA's) or organizers and personal calendars. IN ST ADMIN Rule 9(G)(1).

F. Filing and Service Requirements

1. *Filing requirements.* Except as otherwise provided in IN ST TRIAL P Rule 5(E)(2), all pleadings and papers subsequent to the complaint which are required to be served upon a party shall be filed with the Court either before service or within a reasonable period of time thereafter. IN ST TRIAL P Rule 5(E)(1).

    a. *Filing with the court defined.* The filing of pleadings, motions, and other papers with the court as required by the Indiana Rules of Trial Procedure shall be made by one of the following methods:

       i. Delivery to the clerk of the court;

       ii. Sending by electronic transmission under the procedure adopted pursuant to IN ST ADMIN Rule 12;

       iii. Mailing to the clerk by registered, certified or express mail return receipt requested;

       iv. Depositing with any third-party commercial carrier for delivery to the clerk within three (3) calendar days, cost prepaid, properly addressed;

       v. If the court so permits, filing with the judge, in which event the judge shall note thereon the filing date and forthwith transmit them to the office of the clerk; or

       vi. Electronic filing, as approved by the Division of State Court Administration pursuant to IN ST ADMIN Rule 16. IN ST TRIAL P Rule 5(F).

       vii. Filing by registered or certified mail and by third-party commercial carrier shall be complete upon mailing or deposit. IN ST TRIAL P Rule 5(F).

    b. *Facsimile filing*

       i. *Generally.* In counties where a majority of judges of the courts of record, by posted local rule, have authorized electronic facsimile filing and designated a telephone number to receive such transmissions, pleadings, motions, and other papers may be sent to the Clerk of Circuit Court by electronic facsimile transmission for filing in any case, provided:

          - Such matter does not exceed ten (10) pages, including the cover sheet;

          - Such matter does not require the payment of fees other than the electronic facsimile transcription fee set forth in IN ST ADMIN Rule 12(E);

- The sending party creates at the time of transmission a machine generated log for such transmission; and

- The original document and the transmission log are maintained by the sending party for the duration of the litigation. IN ST ADMIN Rule 12(B).

    ii. *Time of filing.* During normal, posted business hours, the time of filing shall be the time the duplicate document is produced in the office of the Clerk of the Circuit Court. Duplicate documents received at all other times shall be filed as of the next normal business day. IN ST ADMIN Rule 12(C).

- If the receiving fax machine endorses its own time and date stamp upon the transmitted documents and the receiving machine produces a delivery receipt which is electronically created and transmitted to the sending party, the time of filing shall be the date and time recorded on the transmitted document by the receiving fax machine. IN ST ADMIN Rule 12(C).

  c. *Proof of filing.* Any party filing any paper by any method other than personal delivery to the clerk shall retain proof of filing. IN ST TRIAL P Rule 5(F).

2. *Service requirements.* Unless otherwise provided by the Indiana Rules of Trial Procedure or an order of the court, each party and special judge, if any, shall be served with: (1) every order required by its terms to be served; (2) every pleading subsequent to the original complaint; (3) every written motion except one which may be heard ex parte; (4) every brief submitted to the trial court; (5) every paper relating to discovery required to be served upon a party; and (6) every written notice, appearance, demand, offer of judgment, designation of record on appeal, or similar paper. IN ST TRIAL P Rule 5(A).

  a. *Methods of service*

    i. *Personal service.* Whenever a party is represented by an attorney of record, service shall be made upon such attorney unless service upon the party himself is ordered by the court. Service upon the attorney or party shall be made by delivering or mailing a copy of the papers to the last known address or where an attorney or party has consented to service by fax or e-mail, as provided in IN ST TRIAL P Rule 3.1(A)(4), by faxing or e-mailing a copy of the documents to the fax number or e-mail address set out in the appearance form or correction as required by IN ST TRIAL P Rule 3.1(E). IN ST TRIAL P Rule 5(B). Delivery of a copy within IN ST TRIAL P Rule 5 means:

- Offering or tendering it to the attorney or party and stating the nature of the papers being served. Refusal to accept an offered or tendered document is a waiver of any objection to the sufficiency or adequacy of service of that document;

- Leaving it at his office with a clerk or other person in charge thereof, or if there is no one in charge, leaving it in a conspicuous place therein; or

- If the office is closed, by leaving it at his dwelling house or usual place of abode with some person of suitable age and discretion then residing therein; or,

- Leaving it at some other suitable place, selected by the attorney upon whom service is being made, pursuant to duly promulgated local rule. IN ST TRIAL P Rule 5(B)(1).

    ii. *Service by mail.* If service is made by mail, the papers shall be deposited in the United States mail addressed to the person on whom they are being served, with postage prepaid. Service shall be deemed complete upon mailing. Proof of service of all papers permitted to be mailed may be made by written acknowledgment of service, by affidavit of the person who mailed the papers, or by certificate of an attorney. It shall be the duty of attorneys when entering their appearance in a cause or when filing pleadings or papers therein, to have noted in the Chronological Case Summary or said pleadings or papers so filed the address and telephone number of their office. Service by delivery or by mail at such address shall be deemed sufficient and complete. IN ST TRIAL P Rule 5(B)(2).

    iii. *Service by fax or e-mail.* A party who has consented to service by fax or e-mail may be served as follows:

- Service by e-mail shall be made by attaching the document being served in .pdf format.

Discovery documents must also be served in accordance with IN ST TRIAL P Rule 26(A). IN ST TRIAL P Rule 5(B)(3)(a).

- Service by fax shall be deemed complete upon generation of a transmission record indicating the successful transmission of the entire document, except as provided in IN ST TRIAL P Rule 5(B)(3)(d). IN ST TRIAL P Rule 5(B)(3)(b).

- Service by e-mail shall be deemed complete upon transmission, except as provided in IN ST TRIAL P Rule 5(B)(3)(d). IN ST TRIAL P Rule 5(B)(3)(c).

- Service by fax or e-mail that occurs on a Saturday, Sunday, legal holiday, or day the court or agency in which the matter is pending is closed or after 5:00 PM local time of the recipient shall be deemed complete the next day that is not a Saturday, Sunday, legal holiday, or day that the court or agency in which the matter is pending is not closed. IN ST TRIAL P Rule 5(B)(3)(d).

 iv. *Consent to alternate service.* Any Allen County Attorney or any Allen County law firm may, without charge, maintain an assigned Courthouse box in the library of the Allen County Courthouse for receipt of notices, pleadings, process orders, or other communications from the Court, the Clerk, and other attorneys or law firms. IN ST ALLEN SUPER AND CIR CT CIV Rule 5-1(A). For more information concerning the use of courthouse boxes, refer to IN ST ALLEN SUPER AND CIR CT CIV Rule 5-1.

 b. *Serving numerous defendants.* In any action in which there are unusually large numbers of defendants, the court, upon motion or of its own initiative, may order:

  i. That service of the pleadings of the defendants and replies thereto need not be made as between the defendants;

- That any cross-claim, counterclaim, or matter constituting an avoidance or affirmative defense contained therein shall be deemed to be denied or avoided by all other parties; and

- That the filing of any such pleading and service thereof upon the plaintiff constitutes due notice of it to the parties. IN ST TRIAL P Rule 5(D).

  ii. A copy of every such order shall be served upon the parties in such manner and form as the court directs. IN ST TRIAL P Rule 5(D).

 c. *Service on parties in default for failure to appear.* No service need be made on parties in default for failure to appear, except that pleadings asserting new or additional claims for relief against them shall be served upon them in the manner provided by service of summons in IN ST TRIAL P Rule 4. IN ST TRIAL P Rule 5(A).

G. Hearings

1. *Hearing on motion.* Unless local conditions make it impracticable, each judge shall establish regular times and places, at intervals sufficiently frequent for the prompt dispatch of business, at which motions requiring notice and hearing may be heard and disposed of; but the judge at any time or place and on such notice, if any, as he considers reasonable may make order for the advancement, conduct, and hearing of actions. To expedite its business the court may direct the submission and determination of motions without oral hearing upon brief written statements of reasons in support and opposition, or direct or permit hearings by telephone conference call with all attorneys or other similar means of communication. IN ST TRIAL P Rule 73(A).

 a. *Setting motions for hearing.* Except for the motions described in IN ST ALLEN SUPER AND CIR CT CIV Rule 7-1(E), all motions shall be set for hearing. IN ST ALLEN SUPER AND CIR CT CIV Rule 7-1(A). [Editor's note: While IN ST ALLEN SUPER AND CIR CT CIV Rule 7-1(A) refers to IN ST ALLEN SUPER AND CIR CT CIV Rule 7-1(E) as relating to hearings on motions, that reference is likely intended to be to IN ST ALLEN SUPER AND CIR CT CIV Rule 7-1(D).]

  i. It shall be the responsibility of the moving party to request the date of such hearing from the Judicial Assistant, or if the case has already been assigned to a Judge, from the Judicial Law Clerk of the assigned Judge. IN ST ALLEN SUPER AND CIR CT CIV Rule 7-1(A).

 b. *Responsibility for notice of hearing.* It shall be the responsibility of the moving party to give notice

to all other parties of hearings scheduled on motions. IN ST ALLEN SUPER AND CIR CT CIV Rule 7-1(I).

2. *Hearing on summary judgment.* The court may conduct a hearing on the motion. However, upon motion of any party made no later than ten (10) days after the response was filed or was due, the court shall conduct a hearing on the motion which shall be held not less than ten (10) days after the time for filing the response. IN ST TRIAL P Rule 56(C).

H. Forms

1. Motion for Summary Judgment Forms for Indiana

    a. Notice of motion for summary judgment. 11 INPRAC § 90.2.

    b. Motion for summary judgment. 11 INPRAC § 90.3.

    c. Motion for summary judgment; Another form. 11 INPRAC § 90.4.

    d. Motion for summary judgment; Another form. 11 INPRAC § 90.5.

    e. Designation of materials relied upon in support of motion for summary judgment. 11 INPRAC § 90.6.

    f. Designation of material issues of fact that preclude entry of summary judgment. 11 INPRAC § 90.7.

    g. Response to statement of material issues of fact that preclude entry of summary judgment. 11 INPRAC § 90.8.

    h. Order granting motion for summary judgment. 11 INPRAC § 90.9.

    i. Order denying motion for summary judgment. 11 INPRAC § 90.10.

    j. Motion for partial summary judgment as to liability. 11 INPRAC § 90.11.

    k. Order for partial summary judgment as to liability. 11 INPRAC § 90.12.

    l. Order denying summary judgment and specifying issues. 11 INPRAC § 90.15.

    m. Affidavit in support of motion for summary judgment. 11 INPRAC § 90.16.

    n. Submission of proposed findings of fact, conclusions of law and proposed summary judgment. 11 INPRAC § 90.17.

    o. Findings of fact and conclusions of law in support of motion for summary judgment. 11 INPRAC § 90.18.

    p. Motion for hearing on motion for summary judgment. 11 INPRAC § 90.27.

    q. Certificate of service; Personal service. 9 INPRAC § 5.7.

    r. Certificate of service; First class mail. 9 INPRAC § 5.8.

2. Official Motion for Summary Judgment Forms for Allen County

    a. Consent to alternate service. IN ST ALLEN SUPER AND CIR CT CIV App. A.

I. Checklist

(I) ❑ Matters to be considered by moving party

    (a) ❑ Required documents

        (1) ❑ Motion and notice

        (2) ❑ Supporting evidence

        (3) ❑ Proposed order

        (4) ❑ Certificate of service

    (b) ❑ Supplemental documents

        (1) ❑ Additional supporting evidence

        (2) ❑ Brief or memorandum

        (3) ❑ Facsimile cover sheet

   (c) ❏ Timing

      (1) ❏ A party seeking to recover upon a claim, counterclaim, or cross-claim or to obtain a declaratory judgment may, at any time after the expiration of twenty (20) days from the commencement of the action or after service of a motion for summary judgment by the adverse party, move with or without supporting affidavits for a summary judgment in his favor upon all or any part thereof

      (2) ❏ A party against whom a claim, counterclaim, or cross-claim is asserted or a declaratory judgment is sought may, at any time, move with or without supporting affidavits for a summary judgment in his favor as to all or any part thereof

      (3) ❏ A written motion, other than one which may be heard ex parte, and notice of the hearing thereof shall be served not less than five (5) days before the time specified for the hearing, unless a different period is fixed by the Indiana Rules of Trial Procedure or by order of the court

      (4) ❏ All pleadings and papers subsequent to the complaint which are required to be served upon a party shall be filed with the Court either before service or within a reasonable period of time thereafter

(II) ❏ Matters to be considered by the responding party

   (a) ❏ Required documents

      (1) ❏ Opposition

      (2) ❏ Opposing evidence

      (3) ❏ Certificate of service

   (b) ❏ Supplemental documents

      (1) ❏ Additional evidence

      (2) ❏ Brief or memorandum

      (3) ❏ Proposed order

      (4) ❏ Facsimile cover sheet

   (c) ❏ Timing

      (1) ❏ An adverse party shall have thirty (30) days after service of the motion to serve a response and any opposing affidavits

      (2) ❏ Except as otherwise provided in IN ST TRIAL P Rule 59(D), opposing affidavits may be served not less than one (1) day before the hearing, unless the court permits them to be served at some other time

Motions, Oppositions and Replies
Motion for Sanctions

Document Last Updated October 2013

A. Applicable Rules

1. *State rules*

   a. Appearance. IN ST TRIAL P Rule 3.1.

   b. Process. IN ST TRIAL P Rule 4.

   c. Service and filing of pleadings and other papers. IN ST TRIAL P Rule 5.

   d. Time. IN ST TRIAL P Rule 6.

   e. Pleadings. IN ST TRIAL P Rule 7; IN ST TRIAL P Rule 8; IN ST TRIAL P Rule 9.2; IN ST TRIAL P Rule 10.

    f.   Signing and verification of pleadings. IN ST TRIAL P Rule 11.

    g.   General recovery rule. IN ST 34-52-1-1.

    h.   Evidence. IN ST TRIAL P Rule 43.

    i.   Judgment on the evidence (directed verdict). IN ST TRIAL P Rule 50.

    j.   Findings by the court. IN ST TRIAL P Rule 52.

    k.   Summary judgment. IN ST TRIAL P Rule 56.

    l.   Motion to correct error. IN ST TRIAL P Rule 59.

    m.   Relief from judgment or order. IN ST TRIAL P Rule 60.

    n.   Trial court and clerks. IN ST TRIAL P Rule 72.

    o.   Hearing of motions. IN ST TRIAL P Rule 73.

    p.   Access to court records. IN ST ADMIN Rule 9.

    q.   Paper size. IN ST ADMIN Rule 11.

    r.   Facsimile transmission. IN ST ADMIN Rule 12.

    s.   Electronic filing and electronic service pilot projects. IN ST ADMIN Rule 16.

    t.   Sealing of certain records by court; Hearing; Notice. IN ST 5-14-3-5.5.

    u.   Privacy and confidentiality. IN ST 5-2-9-6; IN ST 5-14-3-4; IN ST 6-4.1-5-10; IN ST 6-4.1-12-12; IN ST 6-8.1-7-1; IN ST 11-13-1-8; IN ST 12-23-14-13; IN ST 16-39-3-10; IN ST 16-41-8-1; IN ST 22-4-19-6; IN ST 31-11-1-6; IN ST 31-19-5-23; IN ST 31-19-13-2; IN ST 31-19-19-1; IN ST 31-33-18-1; IN ST 31-39-1-1; IN ST 31-39-1-2; IN ST 33-23-16-16; IN ST 35-34-2-4; IN ST 35-38-1-13; IN ST 35-38-9-1; IN ST ADR Rule 2.11; IN ST ADR Rule 4.4; IN ST ADR Rule 5.6; IN ST JURY Rule 10.

  2. *Local rules*

    a.   Applicability and citation of rules. IN ST ALLEN SUPER AND CIR CT CIV Rule AR00-1.

    b.   Proposed orders. IN ST ALLEN SUPER AND CIR CT CIV Rule TR00-1.

    c.   Appearances. IN ST ALLEN SUPER AND CIR CT CIV Rule 3.1-1.

    d.   Consent to alternate service. IN ST ALLEN SUPER AND CIR CT CIV Rule 5-1.

    e.   Motions in civil court. IN ST ALLEN SUPER AND CIR CT CIV Rule 7-1.

    f.   Preparation of pleadings. IN ST ALLEN SUPER AND CIR CT CIV Rule 8-1.

    g.   Filing. IN ST ALLEN SUPER AND CIR CT CIV Rule 77-1.

B. Timing

  1. *Motion for sanctions.* There are no specific time requirements for when a party may file a motion for sanctions.

    a.   *Filing.* All pleadings and papers subsequent to the complaint which are required to be served upon a party shall be filed with the Court either before service or within a reasonable period of time thereafter. IN ST TRIAL P Rule 5(E)(1).

  2. *Service.* A written motion, other than one which may be heard ex parte, and notice of the hearing thereof shall be served not less than five (5) days before the time specified for the hearing, unless a different period is fixed by the Indiana Rules of Trial Procedure or by order of the court. IN ST TRIAL P Rule 6(D).

    a.   *Of supporting affidavits.* When a motion is supported by affidavit, the affidavit shall be served with the motion. IN ST TRIAL P Rule 6(D).

  3. *Service of opposition.* Except as otherwise provided in IN ST TRIAL P Rule 59(D), opposing affidavits may be served not less than one (1) day before the hearing, unless the court permits them to be served at some other time. IN ST TRIAL P Rule 6(D).

  4. *Computation of time*

    a.   *Generally; Days excluded.* In computing any period of time prescribed or allowed by the Indiana

Rules of Trial Procedure, by order of the court, or by any applicable statute, the day of the act, event, or default from which the designated period of time begins to run shall not be included. The last day of the period so computed is to be included unless it is:

    i.   A Saturday,

    ii.   A Sunday,

    iii.   A legal holiday as defined by state statute, or

    iv.   A day the office in which the act is to be done is closed during regular business hours. IN ST TRIAL P Rule 6(A).

b.   *Short periods.* In any event, the period runs until the end of the next day that is not a Saturday, a Sunday, a legal holiday, or a day on which the office is closed. When the period of time allowed is less than seven (7) days, intermediate Saturdays, Sundays, legal holidays, and days on which the office is closed shall be excluded from the computations. IN ST TRIAL P Rule 6(A).

c.   *Additional time after service by United States mail.* Whenever a party has the right or is required to do some act or take some proceedings within a prescribed period after the service of a notice or other paper upon him and the notice or paper is served upon him by United States mail, three (3) days shall be added to the prescribed period. IN ST TRIAL P Rule 6(E).

d.   *Enlargement of time.* When an act is required or allowed to be done at or within a specific time by the Indiana Rules of Trial Procedure, the court may at any time for cause shown:

    i.   Order the period enlarged, with or without motion or notice, if request therefor is made before the expiration of the period originally prescribed or extended by a previous order; or

    ii.   Upon motion made after the expiration of the specific period, permit the act to be done where the failure to act was the result of excusable neglect; but, the court may not extend the time for taking any action for judgment on the evidence under IN ST TRIAL P Rule 50(A), amendment of findings and judgment under IN ST TRIAL P Rule 52(B), to correct errors under IN ST TRIAL P Rule 59(C), statement in opposition to motion to correct error under IN ST TRIAL P Rule 59(E), or to obtain relief from final judgment under IN ST TRIAL P Rule 60(B), except to the extent and under the conditions stated in those rules. IN ST TRIAL P Rule 6(B).

C. General Requirements

1.   *Motions, generally.* Unless made during a hearing or trial, or otherwise ordered by the court, an application to the court for an order shall be made by written motion. The motion shall state the grounds therefor and the relief or order sought. IN ST TRIAL P Rule 7(B).

a.   *Motions as distinct from pleadings.* Motions and responses to motions are not pleadings, and allegations contained in a motion are not admissions of a party. 22B INPRAC 7:2; Wachstetter v. County Properties, LLC, 832 N.E.2d 574 (Ind.Ct.App. 2005); Scott County Family YMCA, Inc. v. Hobbs, 817 N.E.2d 603 (Ind.Ct.App. 2004).

b.   *Unopposed motions generally granted.* It is common for a trial court to grant procedural motions, such as motions for enlargement of time, discovery motions, or motions for continuance, unless an objection is filed. 21 INPRAC § 13.8.

2.   *Motion for sanctions*

a.   *Signature and certification.* Every pleading or motion of a party represented by an attorney shall be signed by at least one (1) attorney of record in his individual name, whose address, telephone number, and attorney number shall be stated, except that this provision shall not apply to pleadings and motions made and transcribed at the trial or a hearing before the judge and received by him in such form. A party who is not represented by an attorney shall sign his pleading and state his address. IN ST TRIAL P Rule 11(A).

    i.   The signature of an attorney constitutes a certificate by him that he has read the pleadings; that to the best of his knowledge, information, and belief, there is good ground to support it; and that it is not interposed for delay. IN ST TRIAL P Rule 11(A).

    ii.   If a pleading or motion is not signed or is signed with intent to defeat the purpose of the rule, it

       may be stricken as sham and false and the action may proceed as though the pleading had not been served. IN ST TRIAL P Rule 11(A).

    iii.   For a willful violation of IN ST TRIAL P Rule 11 an attorney may be subjected to appropriate disciplinary action. Similar action may be taken if scandalous or indecent matter is inserted. IN ST TRIAL P Rule 11(A).

  b. *Frivolous claims.* A claim or defense is "frivolous, unreasonable or groundless" if it has been asserted primarily for the purpose of harassment, if the attorney is unable to make a good faith and rational argument on the merits of the action, or if the lawyer is unable to support the action by good faith and a rational argument for extension, modification, or reversal of existing law. 9 INPRAC § 4.3; Garage Doors of Indianapolis, Inc. v. Morton, 682 N.E.2d 1296 (Ind.Ct.App. 1997).

    i.   *Bad faith pleading.* For information on sanctions for bad faith pleading, refer to IN ST 34-52-1-1.

  c. *Factors for determining reasonableness.* Five factors are relevant to determine whether a litigant's conduct is "unreasonable":

    i.   The amount of time the attorney had to investigate facts, research the law and prepare documents;

    ii.   The extent to which the attorney had to rely upon his client for the factual foundation;

    iii.   The complexity of the facts and legal issues;

    iv.   The ability to conduct a pre-filing investigation; and

    v.   The plausibility of the arguments advanced by a party, including good faith efforts to extend or modify the law. 9 INPRAC § 4.3; General Collections, Inc. v. Decker, 545 N.E.2d 18 (Ind.Ct.App. 1989).

  d. *Determination of sanction.* The determination of a reasonable attorney fee requires the consideration of all relevant matters including but not limited to the attorney's experience and reputation, the nature of the employment, and the responsibility involved and the results obtained. A contingency fee agreement should not be used as the basis for determining a reasonable fee to be paid by a nonparty to that agreement. 9 INPRAC § 4.3; Mason v. Mason, 561 N.E.2d 809 (Ind.Ct.App. 1990).

D. Documents

1. *Required documents*

  a. *Motion and notice.* The requirement of notice is satisfied by service of the motion. IN ST TRIAL P Rule 7(B). Refer to the General Requirements section of this document for information on the content of a motion for sanctions.

  b. *Proposed order.* Unless local practice provides differently, a party should submit a proposed order with its written motion to be signed by the judge once the motion has been granted. 21 INPRAC § 13.8.

    i.   *Copies of proposed orders.* All proposed orders shall be submitted in an original plus a number of copies equal to one (1) more than the number of pro se parties and attorneys of record contained in the prepared proof of notice under IN ST TRIAL P Rule 72(D). IN ST ALLEN SUPER AND CIR CT CIV Rule TR00-1(C).

    ii.   *Proof of notice.* The proposed order shall also include a prepared proof of notice, under IN ST TRIAL P Rule 72(D). IN ST ALLEN SUPER AND CIR CT CIV Rule TR00-1(B).

    iii.   Refer to the Format section of this document for information on the form and content of the proposed order and the proof of notice.

  c. *Certificate of service.* An attorney or unrepresented party tendering a document to the Clerk for filing shall certify that service has been made, list the parties served, and specify the date and means of service. The certificate of service shall be placed at the end of the document and shall not be separately filed. The separate filing of a certificate of service, however, shall not be grounds for rejecting a document for filing. The Clerk may permit documents to be filed without a certificate of service but shall require prompt filing of a separate certificate of service. IN ST TRIAL P Rule 5(C).

2. *Supplemental documents*

    a. *Supporting evidence.* When a motion is based on facts not appearing of record the court may hear the matter on affidavits presented by the respective parties, but the court may direct that the matter be heard wholly or partly on oral testimony or depositions. IN ST TRIAL P Rule 43(B).

    b. *Brief or memorandum.* If a party desires to file a brief or memorandum in support of any motion, such brief or memorandum shall be filed simultaneously with the motion, and a copy shall be promptly served upon the adverse party. IN ST ALLEN SUPER AND CIR CT CIV Rule 7-1(E).

    c. *Facsimile cover sheet.* Any document sent to the Clerk of the Circuit Court by electronic facsimile transmission shall be accompanied by a cover sheet which states the title of the document, case number, number of pages, identity and voice telephone number of the sending party and instructions for filing. The cover sheet shall contain the signature of the attorney or party, pro se, authorizing the filing. IN ST ADMIN Rule 12(D).

E. Format

1. *Form of motions.* The rules applicable to captions, and the signing and form of pleadings (IN ST TRIAL P Rule 8 through IN ST TRIAL P Rule 11), apply to all motions and other papers provided under the Indiana Rules of Trial Procedure. 22B INPRAC 7:2.

2. *Form of pleadings*

    a. *Caption; Names of parties.* Every pleading shall contain a caption setting forth the name of the court, the title of the action, the file number, and a designation as in IN ST TRIAL P Rule 7(A). In the complaint the title of the action shall include the names of all the parties, but in other pleadings it is sufficient to state the name of the first party on each side with an appropriate indication of other parties. IN ST TRIAL P Rule 10(A).

    b. *Paragraphs; Separate statements.* All averments of a claim or defense shall be made in numbered paragraphs, the contents of each of which shall be limited as far as practicable to a statement of a single set of circumstances, and a paragraph may be referred to by number in all succeeding pleadings. Each claim founded upon a separate transaction or occurrence and each defense other than denials may be stated in a separate count or defense whenever a separation facilitates the clear presentation of the matters set forth. IN ST TRIAL P Rule 10(B).

    c. *Adoption by reference; Exhibits.* Statements in a pleading may be adopted by reference in a different part of the same pleading or in another pleading or in any motion. A copy of any written instrument which is an exhibit to a pleading is a part thereof for all purposes. IN ST TRIAL P Rule 10(C).

    d. *Citation.* Allen County Superior and Circuit court rules may be cited as L.R. _____. The Indiana Rules of Trial Procedure are hereinafter referred to as T.R. _____. IN ST ALLEN SUPER AND CIR CT CIV Rule AR00-1(B).

    e. *Paper.* All pleadings must be printed on white paper. IN ST ALLEN SUPER AND CIR CT CIV Rule 8-1(A).

    f. *Spacing.* The lines shall be double spaced except for quotations, which shall be indented and single-spaced. IN ST ALLEN SUPER AND CIR CT CIV Rule 8-1(A).

    g. *Photocopies.* Photocopies are acceptable if legible. IN ST ALLEN SUPER AND CIR CT CIV Rule 8-1(A).

    h. *Margins and binding.* Margins shall be one to one and one-half (1-1 1/2) inches on the left side and one-half (1/2) inch on the right. IN ST ALLEN SUPER AND CIR CT CIV Rule 8-1(B).

        i. Binding or stapling shall be at the top left and at no other place. IN ST ALLEN SUPER AND CIR CT CIV Rule 8-1(B).

        ii. Covers or backing shall not be used. IN ST ALLEN SUPER AND CIR CT CIV Rule 8-1(B).

    i. *Flat filing.* The files of the Clerk of the Court shall be kept under the "flat filing" system. All pleadings presented for filing with the Clerk or Court shall be flat and unfolded. Only the original of any pleading shall be placed in the Court file. IN ST ALLEN SUPER AND CIR CT CIV Rule 77-1(A).

j. *Handwritten pleadings.* Handwritten pleadings may be accepted for filing in the discretion of the Court. IN ST ALLEN SUPER AND CIR CT CIV Rule 8-1(A).

3. *Size of papers for filing.* Effective January 1, 1992, all pleadings, copies, motions and documents filed with any trial court or appellate level court, typed or printed, with the exception of exhibits and existing wills, shall be prepared on eight and one-half by eleven inch (8 1/2" x 11") size paper. IN ST ADMIN Rule 11.

4. *Form of proposed orders*

   a. *Form, caption, and title.* Any proposed order shall be a document that is separate and apart from the motion or application to which it relates and shall contain a caption showing the name of the court, the case number assigned to the case and the title of the case as shown by the complaint. IN ST ALLEN SUPER AND CIR CT CIV Rule TR00-1(B). If there are multiple parties, the title may be shortened to include only the first name plaintiff and defendant with appropriate indication that there are additional parties. IN ST ALLEN SUPER AND CIR CT CIV Rule TR00-1(B).

   b. *Paper.* The proposed order shall be on white paper, eight and one half by eleven inches (8 1/2" x 11") in size, and each page shall be numbered. IN ST ALLEN SUPER AND CIR CT CIV Rule TR00-1(B).

   c. *Signature line.* On the last page of the proposed order there shall be a line for the signature of the judge under which shall be typed "Judge, Allen Superior Court" or "Judge, Allen Circuit Court", whichever is applicable, to the left of which shall be the following: "Dated _____". IN ST ALLEN SUPER AND CIR CT CIV Rule TR00-1(B).

   d. *Allowance of space for clerk.* To allow space for the Clerk to make entries on the proposed order to show compliance with the notice requirements of IN ST TRIAL P Rule 72(D), the lower four (4) inches of the last page of the proposed order shall be left blank. IN ST ALLEN SUPER AND CIR CT CIV Rule TR00-1(B).

   e. *Proof of notice required.* The proposed order shall also include a prepared proof of notice, under IN ST TRIAL P Rule 72(D). The proof of notice shall conform to the format show in IN ST ALLEN SUPER AND CIR CT CIV Rule TR00-1(B). IN ST ALLEN SUPER AND CIR CT CIV Rule TR00-1(B).

5. *Signature requirements*

   a. *Signature of attorney.* Every pleading or motion of a party represented by an attorney shall be signed by at least one (1) attorney of record in his individual name, whose address, telephone number, and attorney number shall be stated, except that this provision shall not apply to pleadings and motions made and transcribed at the trial or a hearing before the judge and received by him in such form. IN ST TRIAL P Rule 11(A). All pleadings to be signed by an attorney shall contain the written signature of the individual attorney, the attorney's printed name, Supreme Court Attorney Number, the name of the attorney's law firm, the attorney's address, telephone number, and a designation of the party for whom the attorney appears. IN ST ALLEN SUPER AND CIR CT CIV Rule 8-1(C). For the recommended signature format, refer to IN ST ALLEN SUPER AND CIR CT CIV Rule 8-1(C).

      i. Neither printed signatures, nor facsimile signatures shall be accepted on original documents. IN ST ALLEN SUPER AND CIR CT CIV Rule 8-1(C).

      ii. Facsimile signatures are permitted on copies. IN ST ALLEN SUPER AND CIR CT CIV Rule 8-1(C).

      iii. Refer to the General Requirements section of this document for information on sanctions.

   b. *Signature of unrepresented party.* A party who is not represented by an attorney shall sign his pleading and state his address. IN ST TRIAL P Rule 11(A).

   c. *Verification not generally required.* Except when specifically required by rule, pleadings or motions need not be verified or accompanied by affidavit. The rule in equity that the averments of an answer under oath must be overcome by the testimony of two (2) witnesses or of one (1) witness sustained by corroborating circumstances is abolished. IN ST TRIAL P Rule 11(A).

   d. *Verification by affirmation or representation.* When in connection with any civil or special statutory

proceeding it is required that any pleading, motion, petition, supporting affidavit, or other document of any kind, be verified, or that an oath be taken, it shall be sufficient if the subscriber simply affirms the truth of the matter to be verified by an affirmation or representation. IN ST TRIAL P Rule 11(B). IN ST TRIAL P Rule 11(B) states that the affirmation or representation should be in substantially the following language: "I (we) affirm, under the penalties for perjury, that the foregoing representation(s) is (are) true. (Signed) _____."

    i.   Any person who falsifies an affirmation or representation of fact shall be subject to the same penalties as are prescribed by law for the making of a false affidavit. IN ST TRIAL P Rule 11(B).

   e.   *Verified pleadings, motions, and affidavits as evidence.* Pleadings, motions and affidavits accompanying or in support of such pleadings or motions when required to be verified or under oath shall be accepted as a representation that the signer had personal knowledge thereof or reasonable cause to believe the existence of the facts or matters stated or alleged therein; and, if otherwise competent or acceptable as evidence, may be admitted as evidence of the facts or matters stated or alleged therein when it is so provided in the Indiana Rules of Trial Procedure, by statute or other law, or to the extent the writing or signature expressly purports to be made upon the signer's personal knowledge. When such pleadings, motions and affidavits are verified or under oath they shall not require other or greater proof on the part of the adverse party than if not verified or not under oath unless expressly provided otherwise by the Indiana Rules of Trial Procedure, statute or other law. Affidavits upon motions for summary judgment under IN ST TRIAL P Rule 56 and in denial of execution under IN ST TRIAL P Rule 9.2 shall be made upon personal knowledge. IN ST TRIAL P Rule 11(C).

6. *Information excluded from public access.* Every document filed in a case shall separately identify information excluded from public access pursuant to IN ST ADMIN Rule 9(G)(1) as follows:

   a.   Whole documents that are excluded from public access pursuant to IN ST ADMIN Rule 9(G)(1) shall be tendered on light green paper or have a light green coversheet attached to the document, marked "Not for Public Access" or "Confidential." IN ST TRIAL P Rule 5(G)(1).

   b.   When only a portion of a document contains information excluded from public access pursuant to IN ST ADMIN Rule 9(G)(1), said information shall be omitted [or redacted] from the filed document, and set forth on a separate accompanying document on light green paper conspicuously marked "Not for Public Access" or "Confidential" and clearly designated [or identifying] the caption and number of the case and the document and location within the document to which the redacted material pertains. IN ST TRIAL P Rule 5(G)(2).

   c.   With respect to documents filed in electronic format, the trial court, by local rule, may provide for compliance with IN ST TRIAL P Rule 5 in manner that separates and protects access to information excluded from public access. IN ST TRIAL P Rule 5(G)(3).

   d.   IN ST TRIAL P Rule 5(G) does not apply to a record sealed by the court pursuant to IN ST 5-14-3-5.5 or otherwise, nor to records, documents, or information filed in cases to which public access is prohibited pursuant to IN ST ADMIN Rule 9(G). IN ST TRIAL P Rule 5(G)(4).

   e.   The following information in case records is excluded from public access and is confidential:

     i.   Information that is excluded from public access pursuant to federal law;

    ii.   Information that is excluded from public access as declared confidential by Indiana statute or other court rule, including without limitation:

- All adoption records created after July 8, 1941, as declared confidential by IN ST 31-19-19-1, et seq., except those specifically declared open by IN ST 31-19-13-2(2);

- All records relating to chancroid, chlamydia, gonorrhea, hepatitis, human immunodeficiency virus (HIV), Lymphogranuloma venereum, syphilis, tuberculosis, as declared confidential by IN ST 16-41-8-1, et seq.;

- All records relating to child abuse as declared confidential by IN ST 31-33-18-1, et seq.;

- All records relating to drug tests as declared confidential by IN ST 5-14-3-4(a)(9);

- Records of grand jury proceedings as declared confidential by IN ST 35-34-2-4;

- Records of juvenile proceedings as declared confidential by IN ST 31-39-1-2, except those specifically open under statute;

- All paternity records created after July 1, 1941 as declared confidential by IN ST 31-14-11-15, IN ST 31-19-5-23, IN ST 31-39-1-1 and IN ST 31-39-1-2 [Editor's note: IN ST 31-14-11-15 was repealed effective May 9, 2013];

- All pre-sentence reports as declared confidential by IN ST 35-38-1-13;

- Written petitions to permit marriages without consent and orders directing the Clerk of Court to issue a marriage license to underage persons, as declared confidential by IN ST 31-11-1-6;

- Only those arrest warrants, search warrants, indictments and informations ordered confidential by the trial judge, prior to return of duly executed service as declared confidential by IN ST 5-14-3-4(b)(1);

- All medical, mental health, or tax records unless determined by law or regulation of any governmental custodian not to be confidential, released by the subject of such records, or declared by a court of competent jurisdiction to be essential to the resolution of litigation as declared confidential by IN ST 16-39-3-10, IN ST 6-4.1-5-10, IN ST 6-4.1-12-12, and IN ST 6-8.1-7-1;

- Personal information relating to jurors or prospective jurors, other than for the use of the parties and counsel, pursuant to IN ST JURY Rule 10;

- Information relating to protection from abuse orders, no-contact orders and workplace violence restraining orders as declared confidential by IN ST 5-2-9-6, et seq.;

- Mediation proceedings pursuant to IN ST ADR Rule 2.11, Mini-Trial proceedings pursuant to IN ST ADR Rule 4.4(C), and Summary Jury Trials pursuant to IN ST ADR Rule 5.6;

- Information in probation files pursuant to the Probation Standards promulgated by the Judicial Conference of Indiana pursuant to IN ST 11-13-1-8(b);

- Information deemed confidential pursuant to the Rules for Court Administered Alcohol and Drug Programs promulgated by the Judicial Conference of Indiana pursuant to IN ST 12-23-14-13;

- Information deemed confidential pursuant to the Problem-Solving Court Rules promulgated by the Judicial Conference of Indiana pursuant to IN ST 33-23-16-16;

- All records of the Department of workforce Development as declared confidential by IN ST 22-4-19-6;

- Information regarding interception of electronic communications that is sealed or deemed confidential as set forth in IN ST 35-33.5-2-1, et seq.

iii. Information excluded from public access by specific court order;

iv. Complete Social Security Numbers of living persons;

v. With the exception of names, information such as addresses, phone numbers, and dates of birth which explicitly identifies:

- Natural persons who are witnesses or victims (not including defendants) in criminal, domestic violence, stalking, sexual assault, juvenile, or civil protection order proceedings, provided that juveniles who are victims of sex crimes shall be identified by initials only;

- Places of residence of judicial officers, clerks and other employees of courts and clerks of court, unless the person or persons about whom the information pertains waives confidentiality;

vi. Complete account numbers of specific assets, loans, bank accounts, credit cards, and personal identification numbers (PINs);

vii. All orders of expungement entered in criminal or juvenile proceedings, orders to restrict access

to criminal history information pursuant to IN ST 35-38-5-5.5 or IN ST 35-38-8-5 and records excluded from public access by such orders, and information related to infractions that is excluded from public access pursuant to IN ST 34-28-5-15 or IN ST 34-28-5-16 [Editor's note: IN ST 35-38-5-5.5, IN ST 35-38-8-5 and IN ST 34-28-5-16 were repealed effective July 1, 2013; for information on orders restricting access to criminal history, refer to IN ST 35-38-9-1, et seq.];

    viii. All personal notes and e-mail, and deliberative material, of judges, jurors, court staff and judicial agencies, and information recorded in personal data assistants (PDA's) or organizers and personal calendars. IN ST ADMIN Rule 9(G)(1).

F. Filing and Service Requirements

1. *Filing requirements.* Except as otherwise provided in IN ST TRIAL P Rule 5(E)(2), all pleadings and papers subsequent to the complaint which are required to be served upon a party shall be filed with the Court either before service or within a reasonable period of time thereafter. IN ST TRIAL P Rule 5(E)(1).

   a. *Filing with the court defined.* The filing of pleadings, motions, and other papers with the court as required by the Indiana Rules of Trial Procedure shall be made by one of the following methods:

       i. Delivery to the clerk of the court;

       ii. Sending by electronic transmission under the procedure adopted pursuant to IN ST ADMIN Rule 12;

       iii. Mailing to the clerk by registered, certified or express mail return receipt requested;

       iv. Depositing with any third-party commercial carrier for delivery to the clerk within three (3) calendar days, cost prepaid, properly addressed;

       v. If the court so permits, filing with the judge, in which event the judge shall note thereon the filing date and forthwith transmit them to the office of the clerk; or

       vi. Electronic filing, as approved by the Division of State Court Administration pursuant to IN ST ADMIN Rule 16. IN ST TRIAL P Rule 5(F).

       vii. Filing by registered or certified mail and by third-party commercial carrier shall be complete upon mailing or deposit. IN ST TRIAL P Rule 5(F).

   b. *Facsimile filing*

       i. *Generally.* In counties where a majority of judges of the courts of record, by posted local rule, have authorized electronic facsimile filing and designated a telephone number to receive such transmissions, pleadings, motions, and other papers may be sent to the Clerk of Circuit Court by electronic facsimile transmission for filing in any case, provided:

   - Such matter does not exceed ten (10) pages, including the cover sheet;

   - Such matter does not require the payment of fees other than the electronic facsimile transcription fee set forth in IN ST ADMIN Rule 12(E);

   - The sending party creates at the time of transmission a machine generated log for such transmission; and

   - The original document and the transmission log are maintained by the sending party for the duration of the litigation. IN ST ADMIN Rule 12(B).

       ii. *Time of filing.* During normal, posted business hours, the time of filing shall be the time the duplicate document is produced in the office of the Clerk of the Circuit Court. Duplicate documents received at all other times shall be filed as of the next normal business day. IN ST ADMIN Rule 12(C).

   - If the receiving fax machine endorses its own time and date stamp upon the transmitted documents and the receiving machine produces a delivery receipt which is electronically created and transmitted to the sending party, the time of filing shall be the date and time recorded on the transmitted document by the receiving fax machine. IN ST ADMIN Rule 12(C).

c. *Proof of filing.* Any party filing any paper by any method other than personal delivery to the clerk shall retain proof of filing. IN ST TRIAL P Rule 5(F).

2. *Service requirements.* Unless otherwise provided by the Indiana Rules of Trial Procedure or an order of the court, each party and special judge, if any, shall be served with: (1) every order required by its terms to be served; (2) every pleading subsequent to the original complaint; (3) every written motion except one which may be heard ex parte; (4) every brief submitted to the trial court; (5) every paper relating to discovery required to be served upon a party; and (6) every written notice, appearance, demand, offer of judgment, designation of record on appeal, or similar paper. IN ST TRIAL P Rule 5(A).

   a. *Methods of service*

     i. *Personal service.* Whenever a party is represented by an attorney of record, service shall be made upon such attorney unless service upon the party himself is ordered by the court. Service upon the attorney or party shall be made by delivering or mailing a copy of the papers to the last known address or where an attorney or party has consented to service by fax or e-mail, as provided in IN ST TRIAL P Rule 3.1(A)(4), by faxing or e-mailing a copy of the documents to the fax number or e-mail address set out in the appearance form or correction as required by IN ST TRIAL P Rule 3.1(E). IN ST TRIAL P Rule 5(B). Delivery of a copy within IN ST TRIAL P Rule 5 means:

- Offering or tendering it to the attorney or party and stating the nature of the papers being served. Refusal to accept an offered or tendered document is a waiver of any objection to the sufficiency or adequacy of service of that document;

- Leaving it at his office with a clerk or other person in charge thereof, or if there is no one in charge, leaving it in a conspicuous place therein; or

- If the office is closed, by leaving it at his dwelling house or usual place of abode with some person of suitable age and discretion then residing therein; or,

- Leaving it at some other suitable place, selected by the attorney upon whom service is being made, pursuant to duly promulgated local rule. IN ST TRIAL P Rule 5(B)(1).

     ii. *Service by mail.* If service is made by mail, the papers shall be deposited in the United States mail addressed to the person on whom they are being served, with postage prepaid. Service shall be deemed complete upon mailing. Proof of service of all papers permitted to be mailed may be made by written acknowledgment of service, by affidavit of the person who mailed the papers, or by certificate of an attorney. It shall be the duty of attorneys when entering their appearance in a cause or when filing pleadings or papers therein, to have noted in the Chronological Case Summary or said pleadings or papers so filed the address and telephone number of their office. Service by delivery or by mail at such address shall be deemed sufficient and complete. IN ST TRIAL P Rule 5(B)(2).

     iii. *Service by fax or e-mail.* A party who has consented to service by fax or e-mail may be served as follows:

- Service by e-mail shall be made by attaching the document being served in .pdf format. Discovery documents must also be served in accordance with IN ST TRIAL P Rule 26(A). IN ST TRIAL P Rule 5(B)(3)(a).

- Service by fax shall be deemed complete upon generation of a transmission record indicating the successful transmission of the entire document, except as provided in IN ST TRIAL P Rule 5(B)(3)(d). IN ST TRIAL P Rule 5(B)(3)(b).

- Service by e-mail shall be deemed complete upon transmission, except as provided in IN ST TRIAL P Rule 5(B)(3)(d). IN ST TRIAL P Rule 5(B)(3)(c).

- Service by fax or e-mail that occurs on a Saturday, Sunday, legal holiday, or day the court or agency in which the matter is pending is closed or after 5:00 PM local time of the recipient shall be deemed complete the next day that is not a Saturday, Sunday, legal holiday, or day that the court or agency in which the matter is pending is not closed. IN ST TRIAL P Rule 5(B)(3)(d).

    iv. *Consent to alternate service.* Any Allen County Attorney or any Allen County law firm may, without charge, maintain an assigned Courthouse box in the library of the Allen County Courthouse for receipt of notices, pleadings, process orders, or other communications from the Court, the Clerk, and other attorneys or law firms. IN ST ALLEN SUPER AND CIR CT CIV Rule 5-1(A). For more information concerning the use of courthouse boxes, refer to IN ST ALLEN SUPER AND CIR CT CIV Rule 5-1.

  b. *Serving numerous defendants.* In any action in which there are unusually large numbers of defendants, the court, upon motion or of its own initiative, may order:

    i. That service of the pleadings of the defendants and replies thereto need not be made as between the defendants;

- That any cross-claim, counterclaim, or matter constituting an avoidance or affirmative defense contained therein shall be deemed to be denied or avoided by all other parties; and

- That the filing of any such pleading and service thereof upon the plaintiff constitutes due notice of it to the parties. IN ST TRIAL P Rule 5(D).

    ii. A copy of every such order shall be served upon the parties in such manner and form as the court directs. IN ST TRIAL P Rule 5(D).

  c. *Service on parties in default for failure to appear.* No service need be made on parties in default for failure to appear, except that pleadings asserting new or additional claims for relief against them shall be served upon them in the manner provided by service of summons in IN ST TRIAL P Rule 4. IN ST TRIAL P Rule 5(A).

G. Hearings

  1. *Hearing on motion.* Unless local conditions make it impracticable, each judge shall establish regular times and places, at intervals sufficiently frequent for the prompt dispatch of business, at which motions requiring notice and hearing may be heard and disposed of; but the judge at any time or place and on such notice, if any, as he considers reasonable may make order for the advancement, conduct, and hearing of actions. To expedite its business the court may direct the submission and determination of motions without oral hearing upon brief written statements of reasons in support and opposition, or direct or permit hearings by telephone conference call with all attorneys or other similar means of communication. IN ST TRIAL P Rule 73(A).

  a. *Setting motions for hearing.* Except for the motions described in IN ST ALLEN SUPER AND CIR CT CIV Rule 7-1(E), all motions shall be set for hearing. IN ST ALLEN SUPER AND CIR CT CIV Rule 7-1(A). [Editor's note: While IN ST ALLEN SUPER AND CIR CT CIV Rule 7-1(A) refers to IN ST ALLEN SUPER AND CIR CT CIV Rule 7-1(E) as relating to hearings on motions, that reference is likely intended to be to IN ST ALLEN SUPER AND CIR CT CIV Rule 7-1(D).]

    i. It shall be the responsibility of the moving party to request the date of such hearing from the Judicial Assistant, or if the case has already been assigned to a Judge, from the Judicial Law Clerk of the assigned Judge. IN ST ALLEN SUPER AND CIR CT CIV Rule 7-1(A).

  b. *Responsibility for notice of hearing.* It shall be the responsibility of the moving party to give notice to all other parties of hearings scheduled on motions. IN ST ALLEN SUPER AND CIR CT CIV Rule 7-1(I).

H. Forms

  1. Motion for Sanctions Forms for Indiana

    a. Signature; By party. 9 INPRAC § 4.5.

    b. Signature; Attorney. 9 INPRAC § 4.6.

    c. Signature; Attorney; Another form. 9 INPRAC § 4.7.

    d. Signature; Attorney; Another form. 9 INPRAC § 4.8.

    e. Motion to impose sanctions on defendant; Improper answer. 9 INPRAC § 4.20.

    f. Certificate of service; Personal service. 9 INPRAC § 5.7.

g.   Certificate of service; First class mail. 9 INPRAC § 5.8.

2.   **Official Motion for Sanctions Forms for Allen County**

a.   Consent to alternate service. IN ST ALLEN SUPER AND CIR CT CIV App. A.

I.   **Checklist**

(I)   ❑ Matters to be considered by moving party

(a)   ❑ Required documents

(1)   ❑ Motion and notice

(2)   ❑ Proposed order

(3)   ❑ Certificate of service

(b)   ❑ Supplemental documents

(1)   ❑ Supporting evidence

(2)   ❑ Brief or memorandum

(3)   ❑ Facsimile cover sheet

(c)   ❑ Timing

(1)   ❑ There are no specific time requirements for when a party may file a motion for sanctions

(2)   ❑ A written motion, other than one which may be heard ex parte, and notice of the hearing thereof shall be served not less than five (5) days before the time specified for the hearing, unless a different period is fixed by the Indiana Rules of Trial Procedure or by order of the court

(3)   ❑ All pleadings and papers subsequent to the complaint which are required to be served upon a party shall be filed with the Court either before service or within a reasonable period of time thereafter

(II)   ❑ Matters to be considered by the responding party

(a)   ❑ Required documents

(1)   ❑ Opposition

(2)   ❑ Certificate of service

(b)   ❑ Supplemental documents

(1)   ❑ Supporting evidence

(2)   ❑ Brief or memorandum

(3)   ❑ Proposed order

(4)   ❑ Facsimile cover sheet

(c)   ❑ Timing

(1)   ❑ Except as otherwise provided in IN ST TRIAL P Rule 59(D), opposing affidavits may be served not less than one (1) day before the hearing, unless the court permits them to be served at some other time

Motions, Oppositions and Replies
Motion to Compel Discovery

Document Last Updated October 2013

A.   **Applicable Rules**

1.   *State rules*

a.   Appearance. IN ST TRIAL P Rule 3.1.

b. Summons. IN ST TRIAL P Rule 4.

c. Service and filing of pleadings and other papers. IN ST TRIAL P Rule 5.

d. Time. IN ST TRIAL P Rule 6.

e. Pleadings. IN ST TRIAL P Rule 7; IN ST TRIAL P Rule 8; IN ST TRIAL P Rule 9.2; IN ST TRIAL P Rule 10.

f. Signing and verification of pleadings. IN ST TRIAL P Rule 11.

g. General provisions regarding discovery. IN ST TRIAL P Rule 26.

h. Methods of discovery. IN ST TRIAL P Rule 27; IN ST TRIAL P Rule 30; IN ST TRIAL P Rule 31; IN ST TRIAL P Rule 33; IN ST TRIAL P Rule 34; IN ST TRIAL P Rule 36.

i. Failure to make or cooperate in discovery; Sanctions. IN ST TRIAL P Rule 37.

j. Evidence. IN ST TRIAL P Rule 43.

k. Judgment on the evidence (directed verdict). IN ST TRIAL P Rule 50.

l. Findings by the court. IN ST TRIAL P Rule 52.

m. Summary judgment. IN ST TRIAL P Rule 56.

n. Motion to correct error. IN ST TRIAL P Rule 59.

o. Relief from judgment or order. IN ST TRIAL P Rule 60.

p. Trial court and clerks. IN ST TRIAL P Rule 72.

q. Hearing of motions. IN ST TRIAL P Rule 73.

r. Access to court records. IN ST ADMIN Rule 9.

s. Paper size. IN ST ADMIN Rule 11.

t. Facsimile transmission. IN ST ADMIN Rule 12.

u. Electronic filing and electronic service pilot projects. IN ST ADMIN Rule 16.

v. Sealing of certain records by court; Hearing; Notice. IN ST 5-14-3-5.5.

w. Privacy and confidentiality. IN ST 5-2-9-6; IN ST 5-14-3-4; IN ST 6-4.1-5-10; IN ST 6-4.1-12-12; IN ST 6-8.1-7-1; IN ST 11-13-1-8; IN ST 12-23-14-13; IN ST 16-39-3-10; IN ST 16-41-8-1; IN ST 22-4-19-6; IN ST 31-11-1-6; IN ST 31-19-5-23; IN ST 31-19-13-2; IN ST 31-19-19-1; IN ST 31-33-18-1; IN ST 31-39-1-1; IN ST 31-39-1-2; IN ST 33-23-16-16; IN ST 35-34-2-4; IN ST 35-38-1-13; IN ST 35-38-9-1; IN ST ADR Rule 2.11; IN ST ADR Rule 4.4; IN ST ADR Rule 5.6; IN ST JURY Rule 10.

2. *Local rules*

a. Applicability and citation of rules. IN ST ALLEN SUPER AND CIR CT CIV Rule AR00-1.

b. Proposed orders. IN ST ALLEN SUPER AND CIR CT CIV Rule TR00-1.

c. Appearances. IN ST ALLEN SUPER AND CIR CT CIV Rule 3.1-1.

d. Consent to alternate service. IN ST ALLEN SUPER AND CIR CT CIV Rule 5-1.

e. Motions in civil court. IN ST ALLEN SUPER AND CIR CT CIV Rule 7-1.

f. Preparation of pleadings. IN ST ALLEN SUPER AND CIR CT CIV Rule 8-1.

g. Filing. IN ST ALLEN SUPER AND CIR CT CIV Rule 77-1.

B. Timing

1. *Motion to compel discovery.* There are no specific timing requirements for filing a motion to compel discovery. The moving party must provide reasonable notice of his intention to file a motion to compel with the other litigants and all affected persons. 10 INPRAC § 58.51.

a. *Filing.* All pleadings and papers subsequent to the complaint which are required to be served upon a party shall be filed with the Court either before service or within a reasonable period of time thereafter. IN ST TRIAL P Rule 5(E)(1).

2. *Service.* A written motion, other than one which may be heard ex parte, and notice of the hearing thereof shall be served not less than five (5) days before the time specified for the hearing, unless a different period is fixed by the Indiana Rules of Trial Procedure or by order of the court. IN ST TRIAL P Rule 6(D).

   a. *Of supporting affidavits.* When a motion is supported by affidavit, the affidavit shall be served with the motion. IN ST TRIAL P Rule 6(D).

3. *Service of opposition.* Except as otherwise provided in IN ST TRIAL P Rule 59(D), opposing affidavits may be served not less than one (1) day before the hearing, unless the court permits them to be served at some other time. IN ST TRIAL P Rule 6(D).

4. *Computation of time*

   a. *Generally; Days excluded.* In computing any period of time prescribed or allowed by the Indiana Rules of Trial Procedure, by order of the court, or by any applicable statute, the day of the act, event, or default from which the designated period of time begins to run shall not be included. The last day of the period so computed is to be included unless it is:

      i.   A Saturday,

      ii. A Sunday,

      iii. A legal holiday as defined by state statute, or

      iv. A day the office in which the act is to be done is closed during regular business hours. IN ST TRIAL P Rule 6(A).

   b. *Short periods.* In any event, the period runs until the end of the next day that is not a Saturday, a Sunday, a legal holiday, or a day on which the office is closed. When the period of time allowed is less than seven (7) days, intermediate Saturdays, Sundays, legal holidays, and days on which the office is closed shall be excluded from the computations. IN ST TRIAL P Rule 6(A).

   c. *Additional time after service by United States mail.* Whenever a party has the right or is required to do some act or take some proceedings within a prescribed period after the service of a notice or other paper upon him and the notice or paper is served upon him by United States mail, three (3) days shall be added to the prescribed period. IN ST TRIAL P Rule 6(E).

   d. *Enlargement of time.* When an act is required or allowed to be done at or within a specific time by the Indiana Rules of Trial Procedure, the court may at any time for cause shown:

      i. Order the period enlarged, with or without motion or notice, if request therefor is made before the expiration of the period originally prescribed or extended by a previous order; or

      ii. Upon motion made after the expiration of the specific period, permit the act to be done where the failure to act was the result of excusable neglect; but, the court may not extend the time for taking any action for judgment on the evidence under IN ST TRIAL P Rule 50(A), amendment of findings and judgment under IN ST TRIAL P Rule 52(B), to correct errors under IN ST TRIAL P Rule 59(C), statement in opposition to motion to correct error under IN ST TRIAL P Rule 59(E), or to obtain relief from final judgment under IN ST TRIAL P Rule 60(B), except to the extent and under the conditions stated in those rules. IN ST TRIAL P Rule 6(B).

C. General Requirements

1. *Motions, generally.* Unless made during a hearing or trial, or otherwise ordered by the court, an application to the court for an order shall be made by written motion. The motion shall state the grounds therefor and the relief or order sought. IN ST TRIAL P Rule 7(B).

   a. *Motions as distinct from pleadings.* Motions and responses to motions are not pleadings, and allegations contained in a motion are not admissions of a party. 22B INPRAC 7:2; Wachstetter v. County Properties, LLC, 832 N.E.2d 574 (Ind.Ct.App. 2005); Scott County Family YMCA, Inc. v. Hobbs, 817 N.E.2d 603 (Ind.Ct.App. 2004).

   b. *Unopposed motions generally granted.* It is common for a trial court to grant procedural motions, such as motions for enlargement of time, discovery motions, or motions for continuance, unless an objection is filed. 21 INPRAC § 13.8.

2. *Motion to compel discovery.* Motions under IN ST TRIAL P Rule 37 are intended secure compliance with

discovery requests and orders, ensure that one party will not profit from a failure to comply, and provide a general deterrence to discovery abuses. 22B INPRAC 37:1; Fifth Third Bank v. PNC Bank, 885 N.E.2d 52 (Ind.Ct.App. 2008).

a. *Appropriate court.* An application for an order to a party may be made to the court in which the action is pending, or alternately, on matters relating to a deposition or an order under IN ST TRIAL P Rule 34, to the court in the county where the deposition is being taken or where compliance is to be made under IN ST TRIAL P Rule 34. An application for an order to a deponent who is not a party shall be made to the court in the county where the deposition is being taken. IN ST TRIAL P Rule 37(A)(1).

b. *Motion.* If a party refuses to allow inspection under IN ST TRIAL P Rule 9.2(E), or if a deponent fails to answer a question propounded or submitted under IN ST TRIAL P Rule 30 or IN ST TRIAL P Rule 31, or an organization, including without limitation a governmental organization or a partnership, fails to make designation under IN ST TRIAL P Rule 30(B)(6) or IN ST TRIAL P Rule 31(A), or a party fails to answer an interrogatory submitted under IN ST TRIAL P Rule 33, or if a party or witness or other person, in response to a request submitted under IN ST TRIAL P Rule 34, fails to respond that inspection will be permitted as requested or fails to permit inspection as requested, the discovering party may move for an order compelling an answer, or a designation, or an order compelling inspection in accordance with the request. When taking a deposition on oral examination, the proponent of the question may complete or adjourn the examination before he applies for an order. IN ST TRIAL P Rule 37(A)(2).

    i. *Evasive or incomplete answer.* For purposes of IN ST TRIAL P Rule 37(A) an evasive or incomplete answer is to be treated as a failure to answer. IN ST TRIAL P Rule 37(A)(3).

c. *Content of motion.* A motion to compel discovery should state the history of the discovery dispute, evidence that the opposing party was properly served with the discovery request, the position taken by the parties, the grounds for the motion with supporting authority, and the relief sought. In addition, the motion should include a statement demonstrating compliance with the informal dispute resolution requirements of IN ST TRIAL P Rule 26(F). 10 INPRAC § 58.51.

d. *Request for relief.* A motion to compel, filed under IN ST TRIAL P Rule 37, may request the following relief:

    i. An order compelling a discovery response;

    ii. Sanctions under IN ST TRIAL P Rule 37(D) (this rule incorporates by reference the sanctions available to a trial court to punish a party who has refused to comply with a discovery order); and

    iii. An award of attorney fees and expenses incurred to obtain an order compelling discovery. 10 INPRAC § 58.51.

e. *Effect of granting or denial of the motion*

    i. *Denied in whole or in part.* If the court denies the motion in whole or in part, it may make such protective order as it would have been empowered to make on a motion made pursuant to IN ST TRIAL P Rule 26(C). IN ST TRIAL P Rule 37(A)(2).

    ii. *Granted in part and denied in part.* If the motion is granted in part and denied in part, the court may apportion the reasonable expenses incurred in relation to the motion among the parties and persons in a just manner. IN ST TRIAL P Rule 37(A)(4).

    iii. *Motion denied.* If the motion is denied, the court shall, after opportunity for hearing, require the moving party or the attorney advising the motion or both of them to pay to the party or deponent who opposed the motion the reasonable expenses incurred in opposing the motion, including attorney's fees, unless the court finds that the making of the motion was substantially justified or that other circumstances make an award of expenses unjust. IN ST TRIAL P Rule 37(A)(4).

    iv. *Motion granted.* If the motion is granted, the court shall, after opportunity for hearing, require the party or deponent whose conduct necessitated the motion or the party or attorney advising such conduct or both of them to pay to the moving party the reasonable expenses incurred in obtaining the order, including attorney's fees, unless the court finds that the opposition to the motion was substantially justified or that other circumstances make an award of expenses unjust. IN ST TRIAL P Rule 37(A)(4). Refer to the Indiana KeyRules Motion for Discovery Sanctions document for more information.

f.   *Expenses; Burden on non-prevailing party.* The non-prevailing party has the burden of proving that the reimbursement of expenses should not be awarded. 10 INPRAC § 58.51.

g.   *Discovery dispute motions.* The Court expects complete compliance with IN ST TRIAL P Rule 26(F). IN ST ALLEN SUPER AND CIR CT CIV Rule 7-1(H).

h.   *Opposition to motion to compel; Information not reasonably accessible.* On motion to compel discovery or for a protective order, the party from whom discovery is sought must show that the information is not reasonably accessible because of undue burden or cost. If that showing is made, the court may nonetheless order discovery from such sources if the requesting party shows good cause. The court may specify conditions for the discovery. IN ST TRIAL P Rule 26(C)(9).

D.   Documents

1.   *Required documents*

a.   *Motion and notice.* The requirement of notice is satisfied by service of the motion. IN ST TRIAL P Rule 7(B). Refer to the General Requirements section of this document for information on the content of a motion to compel discovery.

b.   *Disputed discovery.* In addition, the motion should attach a copy of the disputed discovery in accordance with the requirements of IN ST TRIAL P Rule 5(D). 10 INPRAC § 58.51.

c.   *Attorney certification.* Before any party files any motion or request to compel discovery pursuant to IN ST TRIAL P Rule 37, or any motion for protection from discovery pursuant to IN ST TRIAL P Rule 26(C), or any other discovery motion which seeks to enforce, modify, or limit discovery, that party shall:

   i.   Make a reasonable effort to reach agreement with the opposing party concerning the matter which is the subject of the motion or request; and

   ii.   Include in the motion or request a statement showing that the attorney making the motion or request has made a reasonable effort to reach agreement with the opposing attorney(s) concerning the matter(s) set forth in the motion or request. This statement shall recite, in addition, the date, time and place of this effort to reach agreement, whether in person or by phone, and the names of all parties and attorneys participating therein. If an attorney for any party advises the court in writing that an opposing attorney has refused or delayed meeting and discussing the issues covered in IN ST TRIAL P Rule 26(F), the court may take such action as is appropriate. IN ST TRIAL P Rule 26(F).

   iii.   The court may deny a discovery motion filed by a party who has failed to comply with the requirements of IN ST TRIAL P Rule 26(F). IN ST TRIAL P Rule 26(F).

d.   *Proposed order.* Unless local practice provides differently, a party should submit a proposed order with its written motion to be signed by the judge once the motion has been granted. 21 INPRAC § 13.8.

   i.   *Proposed order of a motion to compel discovery.* Prior to entry by the Court of orders granting motions or applications, the moving party or applicant (or his or her attorney) shall, unless the Court directs otherwise, furnish the Court with proposed orders of a motion to compel discovery. IN ST ALLEN SUPER AND CIR CT CIV Rule TR00-1(A)(4).

   ii.   *Copies of proposed orders.* All proposed orders shall be submitted in an original plus a number of copies equal to one (1) more than the number of pro se parties and attorneys of record contained in the prepared proof of notice under IN ST TRIAL P Rule 72(D). IN ST ALLEN SUPER AND CIR CT CIV Rule TR00-1(C).

   iii.   *Proof of notice.* The proposed order shall also include a prepared proof of notice, under IN ST TRIAL P Rule 72(D). IN ST ALLEN SUPER AND CIR CT CIV Rule TR00-1(B).

   iv.   Refer to the Format section of this document for information on the form and content of the proposed order and the proof of notice.

e. *Certificate of service.* An attorney or unrepresented party tendering a document to the Clerk for filing shall certify that service has been made, list the parties served, and specify the date and means of service. The certificate of service shall be placed at the end of the document and shall not be separately filed. The separate filing of a certificate of service, however, shall not be grounds for rejecting a document for filing. The Clerk may permit documents to be filed without a certificate of service but shall require prompt filing of a separate certificate of service. IN ST TRIAL P Rule 5(C).

2. *Supplemental documents*

a. *Supporting evidence.* When a motion is based on facts not appearing of record the court may hear the matter on affidavits presented by the respective parties, but the court may direct that the matter be heard wholly or partly on oral testimony or depositions. IN ST TRIAL P Rule 43(B).

b. *Briefs and memoranda regarding motions.* If a party desires to file a brief or memorandum in support of any motion, such brief or memorandum shall be filed simultaneously with the motion, and a copy shall be promptly served upon the adverse party. IN ST ALLEN SUPER AND CIR CT CIV Rule 7-1(E).

c. *Facsimile cover sheet.* Any document sent to the Clerk of the Circuit Court by electronic facsimile transmission shall be accompanied by a cover sheet which states the title of the document, case number, number of pages, identity and voice telephone number of the sending party and instructions for filing. The cover sheet shall contain the signature of the attorney or party, pro se, authorizing the filing. IN ST ADMIN Rule 12(D).

E. Format

1. *Form of motions.* The rules applicable to captions, and the signing and form of pleadings (IN ST TRIAL P Rule 8 through IN ST TRIAL P Rule 11), apply to all motions and other papers provided under the Indiana Rules of Trial Procedure. 22B INPRAC 7:2.

2. *Form of pleadings*

a. *Caption; Names of parties.* Every pleading shall contain a caption setting forth the name of the court, the title of the action, the file number, and a designation as in IN ST TRIAL P Rule 7(A). In the complaint the title of the action shall include the names of all the parties, but in other pleadings it is sufficient to state the name of the first party on each side with an appropriate indication of other parties. IN ST TRIAL P Rule 10(A).

b. *Paragraphs; Separate statements.* All averments of a claim or defense shall be made in numbered paragraphs, the contents of each of which shall be limited as far as practicable to a statement of a single set of circumstances, and a paragraph may be referred to by number in all succeeding pleadings. Each claim founded upon a separate transaction or occurrence and each defense other than denials may be stated in a separate count or defense whenever a separation facilitates the clear presentation of the matters set forth. IN ST TRIAL P Rule 10(B).

c. *Adoption by reference; Exhibits.* Statements in a pleading may be adopted by reference in a different part of the same pleading or in another pleading or in any motion. A copy of any written instrument which is an exhibit to a pleading is a part thereof for all purposes. IN ST TRIAL P Rule 10(C).

d. *Citation.* Allen County Superior and Circuit court rules may be cited as L.R. _____. The Indiana Rules of Trial Procedure are hereinafter referred to as T.R. _____. IN ST ALLEN SUPER AND CIR CT CIV Rule AR00-1(B).

e. *Paper.* All pleadings must be printed on white paper. IN ST ALLEN SUPER AND CIR CT CIV Rule 8-1(A).

f. *Spacing.* The lines shall be double spaced except for quotations, which shall be indented and single-spaced. IN ST ALLEN SUPER AND CIR CT CIV Rule 8-1(A).

g. *Photocopies.* Photocopies are acceptable if legible. IN ST ALLEN SUPER AND CIR CT CIV Rule 8-1(A).

h. *Margins and binding.* Margins shall be one to one and one-half (1-1 1/2) inches on the left side and one-half (1/2) inch on the right. IN ST ALLEN SUPER AND CIR CT CIV Rule 8-1(B).

i. Binding or stapling shall be at the top left and at no other place. IN ST ALLEN SUPER AND CIR CT CIV Rule 8-1(B).

    ii.   Covers or backing shall not be used. IN ST ALLEN SUPER AND CIR CT CIV Rule 8-1(B).

  i. *Flat filing.* The files of the Clerk of the Court shall be kept under the "flat filing" system. All pleadings presented for filing with the Clerk or Court shall be flat and unfolded. Only the original of any pleading shall be placed in the Court file. IN ST ALLEN SUPER AND CIR CT CIV Rule 77-1(A).

  j. *Handwritten pleadings.* Handwritten pleadings may be accepted for filing in the discretion of the Court. IN ST ALLEN SUPER AND CIR CT CIV Rule 8-1(A).

3. *Size of papers for filing.* Effective January 1, 1992, all pleadings, copies, motions and documents filed with any trial court or appellate level court, typed or printed, with the exception of exhibits and existing wills, shall be prepared on eight and one-half by eleven inch (8 1/2" x 11") size paper. IN ST ADMIN Rule 11.

4. *Form of proposed orders*

  a. *Form, caption, and title.* Any proposed order shall be a document that is separate and apart from the motion or application to which it relates and shall contain a caption showing the name of the court, the case number assigned to the case and the title of the case as shown by the complaint. IN ST ALLEN SUPER AND CIR CT CIV Rule TR00-1(B). If there are multiple parties, the title may be shortened to include only the first name plaintiff and defendant with appropriate indication that there are additional parties. IN ST ALLEN SUPER AND CIR CT CIV Rule TR00-1(B).

  b. *Paper.* The proposed order shall be on white paper, eight and one half by eleven inches (8 1/2" x 11") in size, and each page shall be numbered. IN ST ALLEN SUPER AND CIR CT CIV Rule TR00-1(B).

  c. *Signature line.* On the last page of the proposed order there shall be a line for the signature of the judge under which shall be typed "Judge, Allen Superior Court" or "Judge, Allen Circuit Court", whichever is applicable, to the left of which shall be the following: "Dated _____". IN ST ALLEN SUPER AND CIR CT CIV Rule TR00-1(B).

  d. *Allowance of space for clerk.* To allow space for the Clerk to make entries on the proposed order to show compliance with the notice requirements of IN ST TRIAL P Rule 72(D), the lower four (4) inches of the last page of the proposed order shall be left blank. IN ST ALLEN SUPER AND CIR CT CIV Rule TR00-1(B).

  e. *Proof of notice required.* The proposed order shall also include a prepared proof of notice, under IN ST TRIAL P Rule 72(D). The proof of notice shall conform to the format show in IN ST ALLEN SUPER AND CIR CT CIV Rule TR00-1(B). IN ST ALLEN SUPER AND CIR CT CIV Rule TR00-1(B).

5. *Signature requirements*

  a. *Signature of attorney.* Every pleading or motion of a party represented by an attorney shall be signed by at least one (1) attorney of record in his individual name, whose address, telephone number, and attorney number shall be stated, except that this provision shall not apply to pleadings and motions made and transcribed at the trial or a hearing before the judge and received by him in such form. IN ST TRIAL P Rule 11(A). All pleadings to be signed by an attorney shall contain the written signature of the individual attorney, the attorney's printed name, Supreme Court Attorney Number, the name of the attorney's law firm, the attorney's address, telephone number, and a designation of the party for whom the attorney appears. IN ST ALLEN SUPER AND CIR CT CIV Rule 8-1(C). For the recommended signature format, refer to IN ST ALLEN SUPER AND CIR CT CIV Rule 8-1(C).

    i.   The signature of an attorney constitutes a certificate by him that he has read the pleadings; that to the best of his knowledge, information, and belief, there is good ground to support it; and that it is not interposed for delay. IN ST TRIAL P Rule 11(A).

    ii.   If a pleading or motion is not signed or is signed with intent to defeat the purpose of the rule, it may be stricken as sham and false and the action may proceed as though the pleading had not been served. IN ST TRIAL P Rule 11(A).

    iii.   For a willful violation of IN ST TRIAL P Rule 11 an attorney may be subjected to appropriate

disciplinary action. Similar action may be taken if scandalous or indecent matter is inserted. IN ST TRIAL P Rule 11(A).

    iv.   Neither printed signatures, nor facsimile signatures shall be accepted on original documents. IN ST ALLEN SUPER AND CIR CT CIV Rule 8-1(C).

    v.   Facsimile signatures are permitted on copies. IN ST ALLEN SUPER AND CIR CT CIV Rule 8-1(C).

b.   *Signature of unrepresented party.* A party who is not represented by an attorney shall sign his pleading and state his address. IN ST TRIAL P Rule 11(A).

c.   *Verification not generally required.* Except when specifically required by rule, pleadings or motions need not be verified or accompanied by affidavit. The rule in equity that the averments of an answer under oath must be overcome by the testimony of two (2) witnesses or of one (1) witness sustained by corroborating circumstances is abolished. IN ST TRIAL P Rule 11(A).

d.   *Verification by affirmation or representation.* When in connection with any civil or special statutory proceeding it is required that any pleading, motion, petition, supporting affidavit, or other document of any kind, be verified, or that an oath be taken, it shall be sufficient if the subscriber simply affirms the truth of the matter to be verified by an affirmation or representation. IN ST TRIAL P Rule 11(B). IN ST TRIAL P Rule 11(B) states that the affirmation or representation should be in substantially the following language: "I (we) affirm, under the penalties for perjury, that the foregoing representation(s) is (are) true. (Signed) _____."

    i.   Any person who falsifies an affirmation or representation of fact shall be subject to the same penalties as are prescribed by law for the making of a false affidavit. IN ST TRIAL P Rule 11(B).

e.   *Verified pleadings, motions, and affidavits as evidence.* Pleadings, motions and affidavits accompanying or in support of such pleadings or motions when required to be verified or under oath shall be accepted as a representation that the signer had personal knowledge thereof or reasonable cause to believe the existence of the facts or matters stated or alleged therein; and, if otherwise competent or acceptable as evidence, may be admitted as evidence of the facts or matters stated or alleged therein when it is so provided in the Indiana Rules of Trial Procedure, by statute or other law, or to the extent the writing or signature expressly purports to be made upon the signer's personal knowledge. When such pleadings, motions and affidavits are verified or under oath they shall not require other or greater proof on the part of the adverse party than if not verified or not under oath unless expressly provided otherwise by the Indiana Rules of Trial Procedure, statute or other law. Affidavits upon motions for summary judgment under IN ST TRIAL P Rule 56 and in denial of execution under IN ST TRIAL P Rule 9.2 shall be made upon personal knowledge. IN ST TRIAL P Rule 11(C).

6.   *Information excluded from public access.* Every document filed in a case shall separately identify information excluded from public access pursuant to IN ST ADMIN Rule 9(G)(1) as follows:

a.   Whole documents that are excluded from public access pursuant to IN ST ADMIN Rule 9(G)(1) shall be tendered on light green paper or have a light green coversheet attached to the document, marked "Not for Public Access" or "Confidential." IN ST TRIAL P Rule 5(G)(1).

b.   When only a portion of a document contains information excluded from public access pursuant to IN ST ADMIN Rule 9(G)(1), said information shall be omitted [or redacted] from the filed document, and set forth on a separate accompanying document on light green paper conspicuously marked "Not for Public Access" or "Confidential" and clearly designated [or identifying] the caption and number of the case and the document and location within the document to which the redacted material pertains. IN ST TRIAL P Rule 5(G)(2).

c.   With respect to documents filed in electronic format, the trial court, by local rule, may provide for compliance with IN ST TRIAL P Rule 5 in manner that separates and protects access to information excluded from public access. IN ST TRIAL P Rule 5(G)(3).

d.   IN ST TRIAL P Rule 5(G) does not apply to a record sealed by the court pursuant to IN ST 5-14-3-5.5 or otherwise, nor to records, documents, or information filed in cases to which public access is prohibited pursuant to IN ST ADMIN Rule 9(G). IN ST TRIAL P Rule 5(G)(4).

e. The following information in case records is excluded from public access and is confidential:

i. Information that is excluded from public access pursuant to federal law;

ii. Information that is excluded from public access as declared confidential by Indiana statute or other court rule, including without limitation:

- All adoption records created after July 8, 1941, as declared confidential by IN ST 31-19-19-1, et seq., except those specifically declared open by IN ST 31-19-13-2(2);

- All records relating to chancroid, chlamydia, gonorrhea, hepatitis, human immunodeficiency virus (HIV), Lymphogranuloma venereum, syphilis, tuberculosis, as declared confidential by IN ST 16-41-8-1, et seq.;

- All records relating to child abuse as declared confidential by IN ST 31-33-18-1, et seq.;

- All records relating to drug tests as declared confidential by IN ST 5-14-3-4(a)(9);

- Records of grand jury proceedings as declared confidential by IN ST 35-34-2-4;

- Records of juvenile proceedings as declared confidential by IN ST 31-39-1-2, except those specifically open under statute;

- All paternity records created after July 1, 1941 as declared confidential by IN ST 31-14-11-15, IN ST 31-19-5-23, IN ST 31-39-1-1 and IN ST 31-39-1-2 [Editor's note: IN ST 31-14-11-15 was repealed effective May 9, 2013];

- All pre-sentence reports as declared confidential by IN ST 35-38-1-13;

- Written petitions to permit marriages without consent and orders directing the Clerk of Court to issue a marriage license to underage persons, as declared confidential by IN ST 31-11-1-6;

- Only those arrest warrants, search warrants, indictments and informations ordered confidential by the trial judge, prior to return of duly executed service as declared confidential by IN ST 5-14-3-4(b)(1);

- All medical, mental health, or tax records unless determined by law or regulation of any governmental custodian not to be confidential, released by the subject of such records, or declared by a court of competent jurisdiction to be essential to the resolution of litigation as declared confidential by IN ST 16-39-3-10, IN ST 6-4.1-5-10, IN ST 6-4.1-12-12, and IN ST 6-8.1-7-1;

- Personal information relating to jurors or prospective jurors, other than for the use of the parties and counsel, pursuant to IN ST JURY Rule 10;

- Information relating to protection from abuse orders, no-contact orders and workplace violence restraining orders as declared confidential by IN ST 5-2-9-6, et seq.;

- Mediation proceedings pursuant to IN ST ADR Rule 2.11, Mini-Trial proceedings pursuant to IN ST ADR Rule 4.4(C), and Summary Jury Trials pursuant to IN ST ADR Rule 5.6;

- Information in probation files pursuant to the Probation Standards promulgated by the Judicial Conference of Indiana pursuant to IN ST 11-13-1-8(b);

- Information deemed confidential pursuant to the Rules for Court Administered Alcohol and Drug Programs promulgated by the Judicial Conference of Indiana pursuant to IN ST 12-23-14-13;

- Information deemed confidential pursuant to the Problem-Solving Court Rules promulgated by the Judicial Conference of Indiana pursuant to IN ST 33-23-16-16;

- All records of the Department of workforce Development as declared confidential by IN ST 22-4-19-6;

- Information regarding interception of electronic communications that is sealed or deemed confidential as set forth in IN ST 35-33.5-2-1, et seq.

    iii. Information excluded from public access by specific court order;

    iv. Complete Social Security Numbers of living persons;

    v. With the exception of names, information such as addresses, phone numbers, and dates of birth which explicitly identifies:

- Natural persons who are witnesses or victims (not including defendants) in criminal, domestic violence, stalking, sexual assault, juvenile, or civil protection order proceedings, provided that juveniles who are victims of sex crimes shall be identified by initials only;

- Places of residence of judicial officers, clerks and other employees of courts and clerks of court, unless the person or persons about whom the information pertains waives confidentiality;

    vi. Complete account numbers of specific assets, loans, bank accounts, credit cards, and personal identification numbers (PINs);

    vii. All orders of expungement entered in criminal or juvenile proceedings, orders to restrict access to criminal history information pursuant to IN ST 35-38-5-5.5 or IN ST 35-38-8-5 and records excluded from public access by such orders, and information related to infractions that is excluded from public access pursuant to IN ST 34-28-5-15 or IN ST 34-28-5-16 [Editor's note: IN ST 35-38-5-5.5, IN ST 35-38-8-5 and IN ST 34-28-5-16 were repealed effective July 1, 2013; for information on orders restricting access to criminal history, refer to IN ST 35-38-9-1, et seq.];

    viii. All personal notes and e-mail, and deliberative material, of judges, jurors, court staff and judicial agencies, and information recorded in personal data assistants (PDA's) or organizers and personal calendars. IN ST ADMIN Rule 9(G)(1).

F. Filing and Service Requirements

  1. *Filing requirements.* Except as otherwise provided in IN ST TRIAL P Rule 5(E)(2), all pleadings and papers subsequent to the complaint which are required to be served upon a party shall be filed with the Court either before service or within a reasonable period of time thereafter. IN ST TRIAL P Rule 5(E)(1).

    a. *Filing with the court defined.* The filing of pleadings, motions, and other papers with the court as required by the Indiana Rules of Trial Procedure shall be made by one of the following methods:

      i. Delivery to the clerk of the court;

      ii. Sending by electronic transmission under the procedure adopted pursuant to IN ST ADMIN Rule 12;

      iii. Mailing to the clerk by registered, certified or express mail return receipt requested;

      iv. Depositing with any third-party commercial carrier for delivery to the clerk within three (3) calendar days, cost prepaid, properly addressed;

      v. If the court so permits, filing with the judge, in which event the judge shall note thereon the filing date and forthwith transmit them to the office of the clerk; or

      vi. Electronic filing, as approved by the Division of State Court Administration pursuant to IN ST ADMIN Rule 16. IN ST TRIAL P Rule 5(F).

      vii. Filing by registered or certified mail and by third-party commercial carrier shall be complete upon mailing or deposit. IN ST TRIAL P Rule 5(F).

    b. *Facsimile filing*

      i. *Generally.* In counties where a majority of judges of the courts of record, by posted local rule, have authorized electronic facsimile filing and designated a telephone number to receive such transmissions, pleadings, motions, and other papers may be sent to the Clerk of Circuit Court by electronic facsimile transmission for filing in any case, provided:

- Such matter does not exceed ten (10) pages, including the cover sheet;

- Such matter does not require the payment of fees other than the electronic facsimile transcription fee set forth in IN ST ADMIN Rule 12(E);

- The sending party creates at the time of transmission a machine generated log for such transmission; and

- The original document and the transmission log are maintained by the sending party for the duration of the litigation. IN ST ADMIN Rule 12(B).

    ii. *Time of filing.* During normal, posted business hours, the time of filing shall be the time the duplicate document is produced in the office of the Clerk of the Circuit Court. Duplicate documents received at all other times shall be filed as of the next normal business day. IN ST ADMIN Rule 12(C).

- If the receiving fax machine endorses its own time and date stamp upon the transmitted documents and the receiving machine produces a delivery receipt which is electronically created and transmitted to the sending party, the time of filing shall be the date and time recorded on the transmitted document by the receiving fax machine. IN ST ADMIN Rule 12(C).

    c. *Proof of filing.* Any party filing any paper by any method other than personal delivery to the clerk shall retain proof of filing. IN ST TRIAL P Rule 5(F).

2. *Service requirements.* Unless otherwise provided by the Indiana Rules of Trial Procedure or an order of the court, each party and special judge, if any, shall be served with: (1) every order required by its terms to be served; (2) every pleading subsequent to the original complaint; (3) every written motion except one which may be heard ex parte; (4) every brief submitted to the trial court; (5) every paper relating to discovery required to be served upon a party; and (6) every written notice, appearance, demand, offer of judgment, designation of record on appeal, or similar paper. IN ST TRIAL P Rule 5(A).

    a. *Methods of service*

        i. *Personal service.* Whenever a party is represented by an attorney of record, service shall be made upon such attorney unless service upon the party himself is ordered by the court. Service upon the attorney or party shall be made by delivering or mailing a copy of the papers to the last known address or where an attorney or party has consented to service by fax or e-mail, as provided in IN ST TRIAL P Rule 3.1(A)(4), by faxing or e-mailing a copy of the documents to the fax number or e-mail address set out in the appearance form or correction as required by IN ST TRIAL P Rule 3.1(E). IN ST TRIAL P Rule 5(B). Delivery of a copy within IN ST TRIAL P Rule 5 means:

- Offering or tendering it to the attorney or party and stating the nature of the papers being served. Refusal to accept an offered or tendered document is a waiver of any objection to the sufficiency or adequacy of service of that document;

- Leaving it at his office with a clerk or other person in charge thereof, or if there is no one in charge, leaving it in a conspicuous place therein; or

- If the office is closed, by leaving it at his dwelling house or usual place of abode with some person of suitable age and discretion then residing therein; or,

- Leaving it at some other suitable place, selected by the attorney upon whom service is being made, pursuant to duly promulgated local rule. IN ST TRIAL P Rule 5(B)(1).

        ii. *Service by mail.* If service is made by mail, the papers shall be deposited in the United States mail addressed to the person on whom they are being served, with postage prepaid. Service shall be deemed complete upon mailing. Proof of service of all papers permitted to be mailed may be made by written acknowledgment of service, by affidavit of the person who mailed the papers, or by certificate of an attorney. It shall be the duty of attorneys when entering their appearance in a cause or when filing pleadings or papers therein, to have noted in the Chronological Case Summary or said pleadings or papers so filed the address and telephone number of their office. Service by delivery or by mail at such address shall be deemed sufficient and complete. IN ST TRIAL P Rule 5(B)(2).

        iii. *Service by fax or e-mail.* A party who has consented to service by fax or e-mail may be served as follows:

- Service by e-mail shall be made by attaching the document being served in .pdf format.

Discovery documents must also be served in accordance with IN ST TRIAL P Rule 26(A). IN ST TRIAL P Rule 5(B)(3)(a).

- Service by fax shall be deemed complete upon generation of a transmission record indicating the successful transmission of the entire document, except as provided in IN ST TRIAL P Rule 5(B)(3)(d). IN ST TRIAL P Rule 5(B)(3)(b).

- Service by e-mail shall be deemed complete upon transmission, except as provided in IN ST TRIAL P Rule 5(B)(3)(d). IN ST TRIAL P Rule 5(B)(3)(c).

- Service by fax or e-mail that occurs on a Saturday, Sunday, legal holiday, or day the court or agency in which the matter is pending is closed or after 5:00 PM local time of the recipient shall be deemed complete the next day that is not a Saturday, Sunday, legal holiday, or day that the court or agency in which the matter is pending is not closed. IN ST TRIAL P Rule 5(B)(3)(d).

    iv.   *Consent to alternate service.* Any Allen County Attorney or any Allen County law firm may, without charge, maintain an assigned Courthouse box in the library of the Allen County Courthouse for receipt of notices, pleadings, process orders, or other communications from the Court, the Clerk, and other attorneys or law firms. IN ST ALLEN SUPER AND CIR CT CIV Rule 5-1(A). For more information concerning the use of courthouse boxes, refer to IN ST ALLEN SUPER AND CIR CT CIV Rule 5-1.

  b. *Serving numerous defendants.* In any action in which there are unusually large numbers of defendants, the court, upon motion or of its own initiative, may order:

    i.   That service of the pleadings of the defendants and replies thereto need not be made as between the defendants;

- That any cross-claim, counterclaim, or matter constituting an avoidance or affirmative defense contained therein shall be deemed to be denied or avoided by all other parties; and

- That the filing of any such pleading and service thereof upon the plaintiff constitutes due notice of it to the parties. IN ST TRIAL P Rule 5(D).

    ii.   A copy of every such order shall be served upon the parties in such manner and form as the court directs. IN ST TRIAL P Rule 5(D).

  c. *Service on parties in default for failure to appear.* No service need be made on parties in default for failure to appear, except that pleadings asserting new or additional claims for relief against them shall be served upon them in the manner provided by service of summons in IN ST TRIAL P Rule 4. IN ST TRIAL P Rule 5(A).

G. Hearings

1. *Hearing on motion.* Unless local conditions make it impracticable, each judge shall establish regular times and places, at intervals sufficiently frequent for the prompt dispatch of business, at which motions requiring notice and hearing may be heard and disposed of; but the judge at any time or place and on such notice, if any, as he considers reasonable may make order for the advancement, conduct, and hearing of actions. To expedite its business the court may direct the submission and determination of motions without oral hearing upon brief written statements of reasons in support and opposition, or direct or permit hearings by telephone conference call with all attorneys or other similar means of communication. IN ST TRIAL P Rule 73(A).

  a. *Setting motions for hearing.* Except for the motions described in IN ST ALLEN SUPER AND CIR CT CIV Rule 7-1(E), all motions shall be set for hearing. IN ST ALLEN SUPER AND CIR CT CIV Rule 7-1(A). [Editor's note: While IN ST ALLEN SUPER AND CIR CT CIV Rule 7-1(A) refers to IN ST ALLEN SUPER AND CIR CT CIV Rule 7-1(E) as relating to hearings on motions, that reference is likely intended to be to IN ST ALLEN SUPER AND CIR CT CIV Rule 7-1(D).]

    i.   It shall be the responsibility of the moving party to request the date of such hearing from the Judicial Assistant, or if the case has already been assigned to a Judge, from the Judicial Law Clerk of the assigned Judge. IN ST ALLEN SUPER AND CIR CT CIV Rule 7-1(A).

  b. *Responsibility for notice of hearing.* It shall be the responsibility of the moving party to give notice

to all other parties of hearings scheduled on motions. IN ST ALLEN SUPER AND CIR CT CIV Rule 7-1(I).

H. Forms

1. Motion to Compel Discovery Forms for Indiana

a. Notice. 5 INPRAC § 4:6.10.

b. Motion to compel. 5 INPRAC § 4:6.20.

c. Motion to compel; Failure to respond. 5 INPRAC § 4:6.30.

d. Motion to compel answers to interrogatories. 5 INPRAC § 4:6.40.

e. Motion to compel production of documents. 5 INPRAC § 4:6.50.

f. Motion to dismiss as sanction for failure to comply with court ordered discovery. 5 INPRAC § 4:6.60.

g. Notice of intention to file motion to compel discovery. 10 INPRAC § 58.54.

h. Motion to compel discovery; General form. 10 INPRAC § 58.55.

i. Order compelling requested discovery. 10 INPRAC § 58.56.

j. Order denying motion to compel discovery. 10 INPRAC § 58.57.

k. Motion to compel discovery; For failure to respond to discovery requests. 10 INPRAC § 58.58.

l. Motion to compel; Physician to release medical records. 10 INPRAC § 58.59.

m. Motion to compel plaintiff to execute medical records release. 10 INPRAC § 58.60.

n. Motion to compel; Production of surveillance videotape. 10 INPRAC § 58.61.

o. Motion for order that matters be taken as established. 10 INPRAC § 58.62.

p. Motion for order precluding litigation of issues. 10 INPRAC § 58.63.

q. Motion to compel; Failure to permit inspection of original documents. 10 INPRAC § 58.65.

r. Motion to compel; Answer to deposition questions. 10 INPRAC § 58.66.

s. Certificate of service; Personal service. 9 INPRAC § 5.7.

t. Certificate of service; First class mail. 9 INPRAC § 5.8.

2. Official Motion to Compel Discovery Forms for Allen County

a. Consent to alternate service. IN ST ALLEN SUPER AND CIR CT CIV App. A.

I. Checklist

(I) ❑ Matters to be considered by moving party

   (a) ❑ Required documents

      (1) ❑ Motion and notice

      (2) ❑ Disputed discovery

      (3) ❑ Attorney certification

      (4) ❑ Proposed order

      (5) ❑ Certificate of service

   (b) ❑ Supplemental documents

      (1) ❑ Supporting evidence

      (2) ❑ Brief or memorandum

      (3) ❑ Facsimile cover sheet

   (c) ❑ Timing

      (1) ❑ The moving party must provide reasonable notice of his intention to file a motion to compel with the other litigants and all affected persons

(2) ❑ A written motion, other than one which may be heard ex parte, and notice of the hearing thereof shall be served not less than five (5) days before the time specified for the hearing, unless a different period is fixed by the Indiana Rules of Trial Procedure or by order of the court

(3) ❑ All pleadings and papers subsequent to the complaint which are required to be served upon a party shall be filed with the Court either before service or within a reasonable period of time thereafter

(II) ❑ Matters to be considered by the responding party

    (a) ❑ Required documents

        (1) ❑ Opposition

        (2) ❑ Proposed order

        (3) ❑ Certificate of service

    (b) ❑ Supplemental documents

        (1) ❑ Supporting evidence

        (2) ❑ Brief or memorandum

        (3) ❑ Facsimile cover sheet

    (c) ❑ Timing

        (1) ❑ Except as otherwise provided in IN ST TRIAL P Rule 59(D), opposing affidavits may be served not less than one (1) day before the hearing, unless the court permits them to be served at some other time

Motions, Oppositions and Replies
Motion for Protective Order

Document Last Updated October 2013

A. Applicable Rules

1. *State rules*

    a. Appearance. IN ST TRIAL P Rule 3.1.

    b. Process. IN ST TRIAL P Rule 4.

    c. Service and filing of pleadings and other papers. IN ST TRIAL P Rule 5.

    d. Time. IN ST TRIAL P Rule 6.

    e. Pleadings. IN ST TRIAL P Rule 7; IN ST TRIAL P Rule 8; IN ST TRIAL P Rule 9.2; IN ST TRIAL P Rule 10.

    f. Signing and verification of pleadings. IN ST TRIAL P Rule 11.

    g. General provisions governing discovery. IN ST TRIAL P Rule 26.

    h. Methods of discovery. IN ST TRIAL P Rule 27; IN ST TRIAL P Rule 30; IN ST TRIAL P Rule 31; IN ST TRIAL P Rule 33; IN ST TRIAL P Rule 34; IN ST TRIAL P Rule 36.

    i. Failure to make or cooperate in discovery; Sanctions. IN ST TRIAL P Rule 37.

    j. Evidence. IN ST TRIAL P Rule 43.

    k. Judgment on the evidence (directed verdict). IN ST TRIAL P Rule 50.

    l. Findings by the court. IN ST TRIAL P Rule 52.

    m. Summary judgment. IN ST TRIAL P Rule 56.

    n. Motion to correct error. IN ST TRIAL P Rule 59.

    o. Relief from judgment or error. IN ST TRIAL P Rule 60.

p. Trial court and clerks. IN ST TRIAL P Rule 72.

q. Hearing of motions. IN ST TRIAL P Rule 73.

r. Access to court records. IN ST ADMIN Rule 9.

s. Paper size. IN ST ADMIN Rule 11.

t. Facsimile transmission. IN ST ADMIN Rule 12.

u. Electronic filing and electronic service pilot projects. IN ST ADMIN Rule 16.

v. Sealing of certain records by court; Hearing; Notice. IN ST 5-14-3-5.5.

w. Privacy and confidentiality. IN ST 5-2-9-6; IN ST 5-14-3-4; IN ST 6-4.1-5-10; IN ST 6-4.1-12-12; IN ST 6-8.1-7-1; IN ST 11-13-1-8; IN ST 12-23-14-13; IN ST 16-39-3-10; IN ST 16-41-8-1; IN ST 22-4-19-6; IN ST 31-11-1-6; IN ST 31-19-5-23; IN ST 31-19-13-2; IN ST 31-19-19-1; IN ST 31-33-18-1; IN ST 31-39-1-1; IN ST 31-39-1-2; IN ST 33-23-16-16; IN ST 35-34-2-4; IN ST 35-38-1-13; IN ST 35-38-9-1; IN ST ADR Rule 2.11; IN ST ADR Rule 4.4; IN ST ADR Rule 5.6; IN ST JURY Rule 10.

x. Trade secrets. IN ST 24-2-3-1; IN ST 24-2-3-2.

2. *Local rules*

a. Applicability and citation of rules. IN ST ALLEN SUPER AND CIR CT CIV Rule AR00-1.

b. Proposed orders. IN ST ALLEN SUPER AND CIR CT CIV Rule TR00-1.

c. Appearances. IN ST ALLEN SUPER AND CIR CT CIV Rule 3.1-1.

d. Consent to alternate service. IN ST ALLEN SUPER AND CIR CT CIV Rule 5-1.

e. Motions in civil court. IN ST ALLEN SUPER AND CIR CT CIV Rule 7-1.

f. Preparation of pleadings. IN ST ALLEN SUPER AND CIR CT CIV Rule 8-1.

g. Filing. IN ST ALLEN SUPER AND CIR CT CIV Rule 77-1.

B. Timing

1. *Motion for protective order.* There are no specific timing requirements for filing a motion for a protective order.

   a. *Filing.* All pleadings and papers subsequent to the complaint which are required to be served upon a party shall be filed with the Court either before service or within a reasonable period of time thereafter. IN ST TRIAL P Rule 5(E)(1).

2. *Service.* A written motion, other than one which may be heard ex parte, and notice of the hearing thereof shall be served not less than five (5) days before the time specified for the hearing, unless a different period is fixed by the Indiana Rules of Trial Procedure or by order of the court. IN ST TRIAL P Rule 6(D).

   a. *Of supporting affidavits.* When a motion is supported by affidavit, the affidavit shall be served with the motion. IN ST TRIAL P Rule 6(D).

3. *Service of opposition.* Except as otherwise provided in IN ST TRIAL P Rule 59(D), opposing affidavits may be served not less than one (1) day before the hearing, unless the court permits them to be served at some other time. IN ST TRIAL P Rule 6(D).

4. *Computation of time*

   a. *Generally; Days excluded.* In computing any period of time prescribed or allowed by the Indiana Rules of Trial Procedure, by order of the court, or by any applicable statute, the day of the act, event, or default from which the designated period of time begins to run shall not be included. The last day of the period so computed is to be included unless it is:

      i. A Saturday,

      ii. A Sunday,

      iii. A legal holiday as defined by state statute, or

      iv. A day the office in which the act is to be done is closed during regular business hours. IN ST TRIAL P Rule 6(A).

b. *Short periods.* In any event, the period runs until the end of the next day that is not a Saturday, a Sunday, a legal holiday, or a day on which the office is closed. When the period of time allowed is less than seven (7) days, intermediate Saturdays, Sundays, legal holidays, and days on which the office is closed shall be excluded from the computations. IN ST TRIAL P Rule 6(A).

c. *Additional time after service by United States mail.* Whenever a party has the right or is required to do some act or take some proceedings within a prescribed period after the service of a notice or other paper upon him and the notice or paper is served upon him by United States mail, three (3) days shall be added to the prescribed period. IN ST TRIAL P Rule 6(E).

d. *Enlargement of time.* When an act is required or allowed to be done at or within a specific time by the Indiana Rules of Trial Procedure, the court may at any time for cause shown:

    i. Order the period enlarged, with or without motion or notice, if request therefor is made before the expiration of the period originally prescribed or extended by a previous order; or

    ii. Upon motion made after the expiration of the specific period, permit the act to be done where the failure to act was the result of excusable neglect; but, the court may not extend the time for taking any action for judgment on the evidence under IN ST TRIAL P Rule 50(A), amendment of findings and judgment under IN ST TRIAL P Rule 52(B), to correct errors under IN ST TRIAL P Rule 59(C), statement in opposition to motion to correct error under IN ST TRIAL P Rule 59(E), or to obtain relief from final judgment under IN ST TRIAL P Rule 60(B), except to the extent and under the conditions stated in those rules. IN ST TRIAL P Rule 6(B).

C. General Requirements

1. *Motions, generally.* Unless made during a hearing or trial, or otherwise ordered by the court, an application to the court for an order shall be made by written motion. The motion shall state the grounds therefor and the relief or order sought. IN ST TRIAL P Rule 7(B).

a. *Motions as distinct from pleadings.* Motions and responses to motions are not pleadings, and allegations contained in a motion are not admissions of a party. 22B INPRAC 7:2; Wachstetter v. County Properties, LLC, 832 N.E.2d 574 (Ind.Ct.App. 2005); Scott County Family YMCA, Inc. v. Hobbs, 817 N.E.2d 603 (Ind.Ct.App. 2004).

b. *Unopposed motions generally granted.* It is common for a trial court to grant procedural motions, such as motions for enlargement of time, discovery motions, or motions for continuance, unless an objection is filed. 21 INPRAC § 13.8.

2. *Motion for protective order*

a. *Forms of protective order.* Upon motion by any party or by the person from whom discovery is sought, and for good cause shown, the court in which the action is pending or alternatively, on matters relating to a deposition, the court in the county where the deposition is being taken, may make any order which justice requires to protect a party or person from annoyance, embarrassment, oppression, or undue burden or expense, including one or more of the following:

    i. That the discovery not be had;

    ii. That the discovery may be had only on specified terms and conditions, including a designation of the time or place;

    iii. That the discovery may be had only by a method of discovery other than that selected by the party seeking discovery;

    iv. That certain matters not be inquired into, or that the scope of the discovery be limited to certain matters;

    v. That discovery be conducted with no one present except the parties and their attorneys and persons designated by the court;

    vi. That a deposition after being sealed be opened only by order of the court;

    vii. That a trade secret or other confidential research, development, or commercial information not be disclosed or be disclosed only in a designated way;

    viii. That the parties simultaneously file specified documents or information enclosed in sealed envelopes to be opened as directed by the court;

    ix.   That a party need not provide discovery of electronically stored information from sources that the party identifies as not reasonably accessible because of undue burden or cost. IN ST TRIAL P Rule 26(C).

b. *List in IN ST TRIAL P Rule 26(C) not exhaustive.* A court is not limited to the eight specified types of orders. A court may be as inventive as the case and the conditions require. A party or a nonparty may thus obtain any kind of protective order against any kind of discovery which is sought in the case, if "good cause" is shown. So also, however, if a protective order is sought and denied, the trial court may go further and issue an order to provide for or to permit the discovery. 2A INPRAC R 26(26.20).

c. *Trade secrets.* A protectable trade secret has four characteristics: (1) information, (2) which derives independent economic value, (3) is not generally known, or readily ascertainable by proper means by other persons who can obtain economic value from its disclosure or use, and (4) the subject of efforts reasonable under the circumstances to maintain its secrecy. 2A INPRAC R 26(26.23.1).

    i.   *Nature of determination.* The determination of whether information is a trade secret is a fact sensitive determination. 2A INPRAC R 26(26.23.1).

    ii. *Burden of proof.* The burden of proof is on the party asserting the trade secret to show that it is included in the categories of protectable trade secret information listed in the trade secrets statute. 2A INPRAC R 26(26.23.1); Northern Elec. Co., Inc. v. Torma, 819 N.E.2d 417 (Ind.Ct.App. 2004).

    iii. *Uniform trade secrets act.* The application of IN ST TRIAL P Rule 26 to trade secrets should be informed by Indiana's enactment of the Uniform Trade Secrets Act (UTSA) (refer to IN ST 24-2-3-1, et seq.), which provides states with a common legal framework for protecting trade secrets from misappropriation. 2A INPRAC R 26(26.23.1(C)).

    iv. *Trade secret defined.* "Trade secret" means information, including a formula, pattern, compilation, program, device, method, technique, or process, that:

- Derives independent economic value, actual or potential, from not being generally known to, and not being readily ascertainable by proper means by, other persons who can obtain economic value from its disclosure or use; and

- Is the subject of efforts that are reasonable under the circumstances to maintain its secrecy. IN ST 24-2-3-2.

d. *Information not reasonably accessible.* On motion to compel discovery or for a protective order, the party from whom discovery is sought must show that the information is not reasonably accessible because of undue burden or cost. If that showing is made, the court may nonetheless order discovery from such sources if the requesting party shows good cause. The court may specify conditions for the discovery. IN ST TRIAL P Rule 26(C)(9).

    i.   When filing a motion for protective order under IN ST TRIAL P Rule 26(C), the movant, whether a party or non-party, must allege and prove good cause for his request for protective order. The court is empowered to make any order which "justice requires to protect a party or person from annoyance, embarrassment, oppression, or undue burden or expense." Typically, this protection means that discovery will be denied altogether, or limited in scope or to specific terms. 10 INPRAC § 58.20.

e. *Party justified in resisting discovery.* A litigant is substantially justified in seeking to compel or resist discovery if reasonable persons could conclude that genuine issue existed as to whether person was bound to comply with requested discovery. 10 INPRAC § 58.20; Munsell v. Hambright, 776 N.E.2d 1272 (Ind.Ct.App. 2002).

f. *Award of expenses of motion.* If the motion for a protective order is denied in whole or in part, the court may, on such terms and conditions as are just, order that any party or person provide or permit discovery. The provisions of IN ST TRIAL P Rule 37(A)(4) apply to the award of expenses incurred in relation to the motion. IN ST TRIAL P Rule 26(C).

g. *Discovery dispute motions.* The Court expects complete compliance with IN ST TRIAL P Rule 26(F). IN ST ALLEN SUPER AND CIR CT CIV Rule 7-1(H).

D. Documents

1. *Required documents*

   a. *Motion and notice.* The requirement of notice is satisfied by service of the motion. IN ST TRIAL P Rule 7(B). Refer to the General Requirements section of this document for information on the content of a motion for a protective order.

   b. *Attorney certification.* Before any party files any motion or request to compel discovery pursuant to IN ST TRIAL P Rule 37, or any motion for protection from discovery pursuant to IN ST TRIAL P Rule 26(C), or any other discovery motion which seeks to enforce, modify, or limit discovery, that party shall:

      i. Make a reasonable effort to reach agreement with the opposing party concerning the matter which is the subject of the motion or request; and

      ii. Include in the motion or request a statement showing that the attorney making the motion or request has made a reasonable effort to reach agreement with the opposing attorney(s) concerning the matter(s) set forth in the motion or request. This statement shall recite, in addition, the date, time and place of this effort to reach agreement, whether in person or by phone, and the names of all parties and attorneys participating therein. If an attorney for any party advises the court in writing that an opposing attorney has refused or delayed meeting and discussing the issues covered in IN ST TRIAL P Rule 26(F), the court may take such action as is appropriate. IN ST TRIAL P Rule 26(F).

      iii. The court may deny a discovery motion filed by a party who has failed to comply with the requirements of IN ST TRIAL P Rule 26(F). IN ST TRIAL P Rule 26(F).

   c. *Proposed order.* Unless local practice provides differently, a party should submit a proposed order with its written motion to be signed by the judge once the motion has been granted. 21 INPRAC § 13.8.

      i. *Copies of proposed orders.* All proposed orders shall be submitted in an original plus a number of copies equal to one (1) more than the number of pro se parties and attorneys of record contained in the prepared proof of notice under IN ST TRIAL P Rule 72(D). IN ST ALLEN SUPER AND CIR CT CIV Rule TR00-1(C).

      ii. *Proof of notice.* The proposed order shall also include a prepared proof of notice, under IN ST TRIAL P Rule 72(D). IN ST ALLEN SUPER AND CIR CT CIV Rule TR00-1(B).

      iii. Refer to the Format section of this document for information on the form and content of the proposed order and the proof of notice.

   d. *Certificate of service.* An attorney or unrepresented party tendering a document to the Clerk for filing shall certify that service has been made, list the parties served, and specify the date and means of service. The certificate of service shall be placed at the end of the document and shall not be separately filed. The separate filing of a certificate of service, however, shall not be grounds for rejecting a document for filing. The Clerk may permit documents to be filed without a certificate of service but shall require prompt filing of a separate certificate of service. IN ST TRIAL P Rule 5(C).

2. *Supplemental documents*

   a. *Supporting evidence.* When a motion is based on facts not appearing of record the court may hear the matter on affidavits presented by the respective parties, but the court may direct that the matter be heard wholly or partly on oral testimony or depositions. IN ST TRIAL P Rule 43(B).

   b. *Brief or memorandum.* If a party desires to file a brief or memorandum in support of any motion, such brief or memorandum shall be filed simultaneously with the motion, and a copy shall be promptly served upon the adverse party. IN ST ALLEN SUPER AND CIR CT CIV Rule 7-1(E).

   c. *Facsimile cover sheet.* Any document sent to the Clerk of the Circuit Court by electronic facsimile transmission shall be accompanied by a cover sheet which states the title of the document, case number, number of pages, identity and voice telephone number of the sending party and instructions for filing. The cover sheet shall contain the signature of the attorney or party, pro se, authorizing the filing. IN ST ADMIN Rule 12(D).

E. Format

1. *Form of motions.* The rules applicable to captions, and the signing and form of pleadings (IN ST TRIAL P Rule 8 through IN ST TRIAL P Rule 11), apply to all motions and other papers provided under the Indiana Rules of Trial Procedure. 22B INPRAC 7:2.

2. *Form of pleadings*

   a. *Caption; Names of parties.* Every pleading shall contain a caption setting forth the name of the court, the title of the action, the file number, and a designation as in IN ST TRIAL P Rule 7(A). In the complaint the title of the action shall include the names of all the parties, but in other pleadings it is sufficient to state the name of the first party on each side with an appropriate indication of other parties. IN ST TRIAL P Rule 10(A).

   b. *Paragraphs; Separate statements.* All averments of a claim or defense shall be made in numbered paragraphs, the contents of each of which shall be limited as far as practicable to a statement of a single set of circumstances, and a paragraph may be referred to by number in all succeeding pleadings. Each claim founded upon a separate transaction or occurrence and each defense other than denials may be stated in a separate count or defense whenever a separation facilitates the clear presentation of the matters set forth. IN ST TRIAL P Rule 10(B).

   c. *Adoption by reference; Exhibits.* Statements in a pleading may be adopted by reference in a different part of the same pleading or in another pleading or in any motion. A copy of any written instrument which is an exhibit to a pleading is a part thereof for all purposes. IN ST TRIAL P Rule 10(C).

   d. *Citation.* Allen County Superior and Circuit court rules may be cited as L.R. _____. The Indiana Rules of Trial Procedure are hereinafter referred to as T.R. _____. IN ST ALLEN SUPER AND CIR CT CIV Rule AR00-1(B).

   e. *Paper.* All pleadings must be printed on white paper. IN ST ALLEN SUPER AND CIR CT CIV Rule 8-1(A).

   f. *Spacing.* The lines shall be double spaced except for quotations, which shall be indented and single-spaced. IN ST ALLEN SUPER AND CIR CT CIV Rule 8-1(A).

   g. *Photocopies.* Photocopies are acceptable if legible. IN ST ALLEN SUPER AND CIR CT CIV Rule 8-1(A).

   h. *Margins and binding.* Margins shall be one to one and one-half (1-1 1/2) inches on the left side and one-half (1/2) inch on the right. IN ST ALLEN SUPER AND CIR CT CIV Rule 8-1(B).

      i. Binding or stapling shall be at the top left and at no other place. IN ST ALLEN SUPER AND CIR CT CIV Rule 8-1(B).

      ii. Covers or backing shall not be used. IN ST ALLEN SUPER AND CIR CT CIV Rule 8-1(B).

   i. *Flat filing.* The files of the Clerk of the Court shall be kept under the "flat filing" system. All pleadings presented for filing with the Clerk or Court shall be flat and unfolded. Only the original of any pleading shall be placed in the Court file. IN ST ALLEN SUPER AND CIR CT CIV Rule 77-1(A).

   j. *Handwritten pleadings.* Handwritten pleadings may be accepted for filing in the discretion of the Court. IN ST ALLEN SUPER AND CIR CT CIV Rule 8-1(A).

3. *Size of papers for filing.* Effective January 1, 1992, all pleadings, copies, motions and documents filed with any trial court or appellate level court, typed or printed, with the exception of exhibits and existing wills, shall be prepared on eight and one-half by eleven inch (8 1/2" x 11") size paper. IN ST ADMIN Rule 11.

4. *Form of proposed orders*

   a. *Form, caption, and title.* Any proposed order shall be a document that is separate and apart from the motion or application to which it relates and shall contain a caption showing the name of the court, the case number assigned to the case and the title of the case as shown by the complaint. IN ST ALLEN SUPER AND CIR CT CIV Rule TR00-1(B). If there are multiple parties, the title may be shortened to include only the first name plaintiff and defendant with appropriate indication that there are additional parties. IN ST ALLEN SUPER AND CIR CT CIV Rule TR00-1(B).

b. *Paper.* The proposed order shall be on white paper, eight and one half by eleven inches (8 1/2" x 11") in size, and each page shall be numbered. IN ST ALLEN SUPER AND CIR CT CIV Rule TR00-1(B).

c. *Signature line.* On the last page of the proposed order there shall be a line for the signature of the judge under which shall be typed "Judge, Allen Superior Court" or "Judge, Allen Circuit Court", whichever is applicable, to the left of which shall be the following: "Dated _____". IN ST ALLEN SUPER AND CIR CT CIV Rule TR00-1(B).

d. *Allowance of space for clerk.* To allow space for the Clerk to make entries on the proposed order to show compliance with the notice requirements of IN ST TRIAL P Rule 72(D), the lower four (4) inches of the last page of the proposed order shall be left blank. IN ST ALLEN SUPER AND CIR CT CIV Rule TR00-1(B).

e. *Proof of notice required.* The proposed order shall also include a prepared proof of notice, under IN ST TRIAL P Rule 72(D). The proof of notice shall conform to the format show in IN ST ALLEN SUPER AND CIR CT CIV Rule TR00-1(B). IN ST ALLEN SUPER AND CIR CT CIV Rule TR00-1(B).

5. *Signature requirements*

a. *Signature of attorney.* Every pleading or motion of a party represented by an attorney shall be signed by at least one (1) attorney of record in his individual name, whose address, telephone number, and attorney number shall be stated, except that this provision shall not apply to pleadings and motions made and transcribed at the trial or a hearing before the judge and received by him in such form. IN ST TRIAL P Rule 11(A). All pleadings to be signed by an attorney shall contain the written signature of the individual attorney, the attorney's printed name, Supreme Court Attorney Number, the name of the attorney's law firm, the attorney's address, telephone number, and a designation of the party for whom the attorney appears. IN ST ALLEN SUPER AND CIR CT CIV Rule 8-1(C). For the recommended signature format, refer to IN ST ALLEN SUPER AND CIR CT CIV Rule 8-1(C).

   i. The signature of an attorney constitutes a certificate by him that he has read the pleadings; that to the best of his knowledge, information, and belief, there is good ground to support it; and that it is not interposed for delay. IN ST TRIAL P Rule 11(A).

   ii. If a pleading or motion is not signed or is signed with intent to defeat the purpose of the rule, it may be stricken as sham and false and the action may proceed as though the pleading had not been served. IN ST TRIAL P Rule 11(A).

   iii. For a willful violation of IN ST TRIAL P Rule 11 an attorney may be subjected to appropriate disciplinary action. Similar action may be taken if scandalous or indecent matter is inserted. IN ST TRIAL P Rule 11(A).

   iv. Neither printed signatures, nor facsimile signatures shall be accepted on original documents. IN ST ALLEN SUPER AND CIR CT CIV Rule 8-1(C).

   v. Facsimile signatures are permitted on copies. IN ST ALLEN SUPER AND CIR CT CIV Rule 8-1(C).

b. *Signature of unrepresented party.* A party who is not represented by an attorney shall sign his pleading and state his address. IN ST TRIAL P Rule 11(A).

c. *Verification not generally required.* Except when specifically required by rule, pleadings or motions need not be verified or accompanied by affidavit. The rule in equity that the averments of an answer under oath must be overcome by the testimony of two (2) witnesses or of one (1) witness sustained by corroborating circumstances is abolished. IN ST TRIAL P Rule 11(A).

d. *Verification by affirmation or representation.* When in connection with any civil or special statutory proceeding it is required that any pleading, motion, petition, supporting affidavit, or other document of any kind, be verified, or that an oath be taken, it shall be sufficient if the subscriber simply affirms the truth of the matter to be verified by an affirmation or representation. IN ST TRIAL P Rule 11(B). IN ST TRIAL P Rule 11(B) states that the affirmation or representation should be in substantially the

following language: "I (we) affirm, under the penalties for perjury, that the foregoing representation(s) is (are) true. (Signed) _____."

    i. Any person who falsifies an affirmation or representation of fact shall be subject to the same penalties as are prescribed by law for the making of a false affidavit. IN ST TRIAL P Rule 11(B).

e. *Verified pleadings, motions, and affidavits as evidence.* Pleadings, motions and affidavits accompanying or in support of such pleadings or motions when required to be verified or under oath shall be accepted as a representation that the signer had personal knowledge thereof or reasonable cause to believe the existence of the facts or matters stated or alleged therein; and, if otherwise competent or acceptable as evidence, may be admitted as evidence of the facts or matters stated or alleged therein when it is so provided in the Indiana Rules of Trial Procedure, by statute or other law, or to the extent the writing or signature expressly purports to be made upon the signer's personal knowledge. When such pleadings, motions and affidavits are verified or under oath they shall not require other or greater proof on the part of the adverse party than if not verified or not under oath unless expressly provided otherwise by the Indiana Rules of Trial Procedure, statute or other law. Affidavits upon motions for summary judgment under IN ST TRIAL P Rule 56 and in denial of execution under IN ST TRIAL P Rule 9.2 shall be made upon personal knowledge. IN ST TRIAL P Rule 11(C).

6. *Information excluded from public access.* Every document filed in a case shall separately identify information excluded from public access pursuant to IN ST ADMIN Rule 9(G)(1) as follows:

a. Whole documents that are excluded from public access pursuant to IN ST ADMIN Rule 9(G)(1) shall be tendered on light green paper or have a light green coversheet attached to the document, marked "Not for Public Access" or "Confidential." IN ST TRIAL P Rule 5(G)(1).

b. When only a portion of a document contains information excluded from public access pursuant to IN ST ADMIN Rule 9(G)(1), said information shall be omitted [or redacted] from the filed document, and set forth on a separate accompanying document on light green paper conspicuously marked "Not for Public Access" or "Confidential" and clearly designated [or identifying] the caption and number of the case and the document and location within the document to which the redacted material pertains. IN ST TRIAL P Rule 5(G)(2).

c. With respect to documents filed in electronic format, the trial court, by local rule, may provide for compliance with IN ST TRIAL P Rule 5 in manner that separates and protects access to information excluded from public access. IN ST TRIAL P Rule 5(G)(3).

d. IN ST TRIAL P Rule 5(G) does not apply to a record sealed by the court pursuant to IN ST 5-14-3-5.5 or otherwise, nor to records, documents, or information filed in cases to which public access is prohibited pursuant to IN ST ADMIN Rule 9(G). IN ST TRIAL P Rule 5(G)(4).

e. The following information in case records is excluded from public access and is confidential:

    i. Information that is excluded from public access pursuant to federal law;

    ii. Information that is excluded from public access as declared confidential by Indiana statute or other court rule, including without limitation:

- All adoption records created after July 8, 1941, as declared confidential by IN ST 31-19-19-1, et seq., except those specifically declared open by IN ST 31-19-13-2(2);

- All records relating to chancroid, chlamydia, gonorrhea, hepatitis, human immunodeficiency virus (HIV), Lymphogranuloma venereum, syphilis, tuberculosis, as declared confidential by IN ST 16-41-8-1, et seq.;

- All records relating to child abuse as declared confidential by IN ST 31-33-18-1, et seq.;

- All records relating to drug tests as declared confidential by IN ST 5-14-3-4(a)(9);

- Records of grand jury proceedings as declared confidential by IN ST 35-34-2-4;

- Records of juvenile proceedings as declared confidential by IN ST 31-39-1-2, except those specifically open under statute;

- All paternity records created after July 1, 1941 as declared confidential by IN ST

31-14-11-15, IN ST 31-19-5-23, IN ST 31-39-1-1 and IN ST 31-39-1-2 [Editor's note: IN ST 31-14-11-15 was repealed effective May 9, 2013];

- All pre-sentence reports as declared confidential by IN ST 35-38-1-13;

- Written petitions to permit marriages without consent and orders directing the Clerk of Court to issue a marriage license to underage persons, as declared confidential by IN ST 31-11-1-6;

- Only those arrest warrants, search warrants, indictments and informations ordered confidential by the trial judge, prior to return of duly executed service as declared confidential by IN ST 5-14-3-4(b)(1);

- All medical, mental health, or tax records unless determined by law or regulation of any governmental custodian not to be confidential, released by the subject of such records, or declared by a court of competent jurisdiction to be essential to the resolution of litigation as declared confidential by IN ST 16-39-3-10, IN ST 6-4.1-5-10, IN ST 6-4.1-12-12, and IN ST 6-8.1-7-1;

- Personal information relating to jurors or prospective jurors, other than for the use of the parties and counsel, pursuant to IN ST JURY Rule 10;

- Information relating to protection from abuse orders, no-contact orders and workplace violence restraining orders as declared confidential by IN ST 5-2-9-6, et seq.;

- Mediation proceedings pursuant to IN ST ADR Rule 2.11, Mini-Trial proceedings pursuant to IN ST ADR Rule 4.4(C), and Summary Jury Trials pursuant to IN ST ADR Rule 5.6;

- Information in probation files pursuant to the Probation Standards promulgated by the Judicial Conference of Indiana pursuant to IN ST 11-13-1-8(b);

- Information deemed confidential pursuant to the Rules for Court Administered Alcohol and Drug Programs promulgated by the Judicial Conference of Indiana pursuant to IN ST 12-23-14-13;

- Information deemed confidential pursuant to the Problem-Solving Court Rules promulgated by the Judicial Conference of Indiana pursuant to IN ST 33-23-16-16;

- All records of the Department of workforce Development as declared confidential by IN ST 22-4-19-6;

- Information regarding interception of electronic communications that is sealed or deemed confidential as set forth in IN ST 35-33.5-2-1, et seq.

iii. Information excluded from public access by specific court order;

iv. Complete Social Security Numbers of living persons;

v. With the exception of names, information such as addresses, phone numbers, and dates of birth which explicitly identifies:

- Natural persons who are witnesses or victims (not including defendants) in criminal, domestic violence, stalking, sexual assault, juvenile, or civil protection order proceedings, provided that juveniles who are victims of sex crimes shall be identified by initials only;

- Places of residence of judicial officers, clerks and other employees of courts and clerks of court, unless the person or persons about whom the information pertains waives confidentiality;

vi. Complete account numbers of specific assets, loans, bank accounts, credit cards, and personal identification numbers (PINs);

vii. All orders of expungement entered in criminal or juvenile proceedings, orders to restrict access to criminal history information pursuant to IN ST 35-38-5-5.5 or IN ST 35-38-8-5 and records excluded from public access by such orders, and information related to infractions that is excluded from public access pursuant to IN ST 34-28-5-15 or IN ST 34-28-5-16 [Editor's note:

IN ST 35-38-5-5.5, IN ST 35-38-8-5 and IN ST 34-28-5-16 were repealed effective July 1, 2013; for information on orders restricting access to criminal history, refer to IN ST 35-38-9-1, et seq.];

    viii.   All personal notes and e-mail, and deliberative material, of judges, jurors, court staff and judicial agencies, and information recorded in personal data assistants (PDA's) or organizers and personal calendars. IN ST ADMIN Rule 9(G)(1).

F. Filing and Service Requirements

1. *Filing requirements.* Except as otherwise provided in IN ST TRIAL P Rule 5(E)(2), all pleadings and papers subsequent to the complaint which are required to be served upon a party shall be filed with the Court either before service or within a reasonable period of time thereafter. IN ST TRIAL P Rule 5(E)(1).

    a.   *Filing with the court defined.* The filing of pleadings, motions, and other papers with the court as required by the Indiana Rules of Trial Procedure shall be made by one of the following methods:

        i.   Delivery to the clerk of the court;

        ii.   Sending by electronic transmission under the procedure adopted pursuant to IN ST ADMIN Rule 12;

        iii.   Mailing to the clerk by registered, certified or express mail return receipt requested;

        iv.   Depositing with any third-party commercial carrier for delivery to the clerk within three (3) calendar days, cost prepaid, properly addressed;

        v.   If the court so permits, filing with the judge, in which event the judge shall note thereon the filing date and forthwith transmit them to the office of the clerk; or

        vi.   Electronic filing, as approved by the Division of State Court Administration pursuant to IN ST ADMIN Rule 16. IN ST TRIAL P Rule 5(F).

        vii.   Filing by registered or certified mail and by third-party commercial carrier shall be complete upon mailing or deposit. IN ST TRIAL P Rule 5(F).

    b.   *Facsimile filing*

        i.   *Generally.* In counties where a majority of judges of the courts of record, by posted local rule, have authorized electronic facsimile filing and designated a telephone number to receive such transmissions, pleadings, motions, and other papers may be sent to the Clerk of Circuit Court by electronic facsimile transmission for filing in any case, provided:

- Such matter does not exceed ten (10) pages, including the cover sheet;

- Such matter does not require the payment of fees other than the electronic facsimile transcription fee set forth in IN ST ADMIN Rule 12(E);

- The sending party creates at the time of transmission a machine generated log for such transmission; and

- The original document and the transmission log are maintained by the sending party for the duration of the litigation. IN ST ADMIN Rule 12(B).

        ii.   *Time of filing.* During normal, posted business hours, the time of filing shall be the time the duplicate document is produced in the office of the Clerk of the Circuit Court. Duplicate documents received at all other times shall be filed as of the next normal business day. IN ST ADMIN Rule 12(C).

- If the receiving fax machine endorses its own time and date stamp upon the transmitted documents and the receiving machine produces a delivery receipt which is electronically created and transmitted to the sending party, the time of filing shall be the date and time recorded on the transmitted document by the receiving fax machine. IN ST ADMIN Rule 12(C).

    c.   *Proof of filing.* Any party filing any paper by any method other than personal delivery to the clerk shall retain proof of filing. IN ST TRIAL P Rule 5(F).

2. *Service requirements.* Unless otherwise provided by the Indiana Rules of Trial Procedure or an order of

the court, each party and special judge, if any, shall be served with: (1) every order required by its terms to be served; (2) every pleading subsequent to the original complaint; (3) every written motion except one which may be heard ex parte; (4) every brief submitted to the trial court; (5) every paper relating to discovery required to be served upon a party; and (6) every written notice, appearance, demand, offer of judgment, designation of record on appeal, or similar paper. IN ST TRIAL P Rule 5(A).

a. *Methods of service*

    i. *Personal service.* Whenever a party is represented by an attorney of record, service shall be made upon such attorney unless service upon the party himself is ordered by the court. Service upon the attorney or party shall be made by delivering or mailing a copy of the papers to the last known address or where an attorney or party has consented to service by fax or e-mail, as provided in IN ST TRIAL P Rule 3.1(A)(4), by faxing or e-mailing a copy of the documents to the fax number or e-mail address set out in the appearance form or correction as required by IN ST TRIAL P Rule 3.1(E). IN ST TRIAL P Rule 5(B). Delivery of a copy within IN ST TRIAL P Rule 5 means:

- Offering or tendering it to the attorney or party and stating the nature of the papers being served. Refusal to accept an offered or tendered document is a waiver of any objection to the sufficiency or adequacy of service of that document;

- Leaving it at his office with a clerk or other person in charge thereof, or if there is no one in charge, leaving it in a conspicuous place therein; or

- If the office is closed, by leaving it at his dwelling house or usual place of abode with some person of suitable age and discretion then residing therein; or,

- Leaving it at some other suitable place, selected by the attorney upon whom service is being made, pursuant to duly promulgated local rule. IN ST TRIAL P Rule 5(B)(1).

    ii. *Service by mail.* If service is made by mail, the papers shall be deposited in the United States mail addressed to the person on whom they are being served, with postage prepaid. Service shall be deemed complete upon mailing. Proof of service of all papers permitted to be mailed may be made by written acknowledgment of service, by affidavit of the person who mailed the papers, or by certificate of an attorney. It shall be the duty of attorneys when entering their appearance in a cause or when filing pleadings or papers therein, to have noted in the Chronological Case Summary or said pleadings or papers so filed the address and telephone number of their office. Service by delivery or by mail at such address shall be deemed sufficient and complete. IN ST TRIAL P Rule 5(B)(2).

    iii. *Service by fax or e-mail.* A party who has consented to service by fax or e-mail may be served as follows:

- Service by e-mail shall be made by attaching the document being served in .pdf format. Discovery documents must also be served in accordance with IN ST TRIAL P Rule 26(A). IN ST TRIAL P Rule 5(B)(3)(a).

- Service by fax shall be deemed complete upon generation of a transmission record indicating the successful transmission of the entire document, except as provided in IN ST TRIAL P Rule 5(B)(3)(d). IN ST TRIAL P Rule 5(B)(3)(b).

- Service by e-mail shall be deemed complete upon transmission, except as provided in IN ST TRIAL P Rule 5(B)(3)(d). IN ST TRIAL P Rule 5(B)(3)(c).

- Service by fax or e-mail that occurs on a Saturday, Sunday, legal holiday, or day the court or agency in which the matter is pending is closed or after 5:00 PM local time of the recipient shall be deemed complete the next day that is not a Saturday, Sunday, legal holiday, or day that the court or agency in which the matter is pending is not closed. IN ST TRIAL P Rule 5(B)(3)(d).

    iv. *Consent to alternate service.* Any Allen County Attorney or any Allen County law firm may, without charge, maintain an assigned Courthouse box in the library of the Allen County Courthouse for receipt of notices, pleadings, process orders, or other communications from the

Court, the Clerk, and other attorneys or law firms. IN ST ALLEN SUPER AND CIR CT CIV Rule 5-1(A). For more information concerning the use of courthouse boxes, refer to IN ST ALLEN SUPER AND CIR CT CIV Rule 5-1.

b. *Serving numerous defendants.* In any action in which there are unusually large numbers of defendants, the court, upon motion or of its own initiative, may order:

    i. That service of the pleadings of the defendants and replies thereto need not be made as between the defendants;

        • That any cross-claim, counterclaim, or matter constituting an avoidance or affirmative defense contained therein shall be deemed to be denied or avoided by all other parties; and

        • That the filing of any such pleading and service thereof upon the plaintiff constitutes due notice of it to the parties. IN ST TRIAL P Rule 5(D).

    ii. A copy of every such order shall be served upon the parties in such manner and form as the court directs. IN ST TRIAL P Rule 5(D).

c. *Service on parties in default for failure to appear.* No service need be made on parties in default for failure to appear, except that pleadings asserting new or additional claims for relief against them shall be served upon them in the manner provided by service of summons in IN ST TRIAL P Rule 4. IN ST TRIAL P Rule 5(A).

G. Hearings

1. *Hearing on motion.* Unless local conditions make it impracticable, each judge shall establish regular times and places, at intervals sufficiently frequent for the prompt dispatch of business, at which motions requiring notice and hearing may be heard and disposed of; but the judge at any time or place and on such notice, if any, as he considers reasonable may make order for the advancement, conduct, and hearing of actions. To expedite its business the court may direct the submission and determination of motions without oral hearing upon brief written statements of reasons in support and opposition, or direct or permit hearings by telephone conference call with all attorneys or other similar means of communication. IN ST TRIAL P Rule 73(A).

a. *Setting motions for hearing.* Except for the motions described in IN ST ALLEN SUPER AND CIR CT CIV Rule 7-1(E), all motions shall be set for hearing. IN ST ALLEN SUPER AND CIR CT CIV Rule 7-1(A). [Editor's note: While IN ST ALLEN SUPER AND CIR CT CIV Rule 7-1(A) refers to IN ST ALLEN SUPER AND CIR CT CIV Rule 7-1(E) as relating to hearings on motions, that reference is likely intended to be to IN ST ALLEN SUPER AND CIR CT CIV Rule 7-1(D).]

    i. It shall be the responsibility of the moving party to request the date of such hearing from the Judicial Assistant, or if the case has already been assigned to a Judge, from the Judicial Law Clerk of the assigned Judge. IN ST ALLEN SUPER AND CIR CT CIV Rule 7-1(A).

b. *Responsibility for notice of hearing.* It shall be the responsibility of the moving party to give notice to all other parties of hearings scheduled on motions. IN ST ALLEN SUPER AND CIR CT CIV Rule 7-1(I).

H. Forms

1. Motion for Protective Order Forms for Indiana

a. Pending motion. 5 INPRAC § 4:5.1.

b. Relevancy. 5 INPRAC § 4:5.2.

c. Unduly burdensome. 5 INPRAC § 4:5.3.

d. Privileged. 5 INPRAC § 4:5.4.

e. Mental impressions and legal conclusions. 5 INPRAC § 4:5.5.

f. Expert reports and papers. 5 INPRAC § 4:5.6.

g. Quash subpoena duces tecum. 5 INPRAC § 4:5.7.

h. Quash subpoena duces tecum; Non-party. 5 INPRAC § 4:5.8.

i. Trade secrets and confidential information. 5 INPRAC § 4:5.9.

j. Motion to lift protective order. 5 INPRAC § 4:5.10.

k. Motion for protective order; Discovery not be had; Protection against disclosure of expert report and papers. 10 INPRAC § 58.22.

l. Motion for protective order; Discovery not relevant to subject matter of action. 10 INPRAC § 58.23.

m. Motion for protective order; Discovery unduly burdensome; Alternative request for deposition. 10 INPRAC § 58.24.

n. Motion for protective order; Challenging date and time of deposition. 10 INPRAC § 58.25.

o. Motion for protective order; Challenging place of deposition. 10 INPRAC § 58.26.

p. Motion for protective order; To prevent the disclosure of trade secrets and confidential research and development. 10 INPRAC § 58.27.

q. Motion for protective order; To preclude further deposition of corporate officer. 10 INPRAC § 58.28.

r. Motion for protective order; To preclude taking expert deposition; Failure to obtain court order or to disclose expert opinions. 10 INPRAC § 58.30.

s. Motion for protective order; To preclude disclosure of privileged matters. 10 INPRAC § 58.31.

t. Motion for protective order; To have plaintiff's attorney and physician present during plaintiff's physical examination; Request to tape record physical examination. 10 INPRAC § 58.32.

u. Motion for protective order; To preclude defendant's attorney from conducting an informal interview of plaintiff's treating physician. 10 INPRAC § 58.33.

v. Motion for protective order; To produce documents at responding party's place of business. 10 INPRAC § 58.34.

w. Motion for protective order; Discovery limited to certain matter until court rules on pending motion. 10 INPRAC § 58.35.

x. Motion for protective order; Answers to discovery to be sealed to protect confidential commercial information. 10 INPRAC § 58.36.

y. Certificate of service; Personal service. 9 INPRAC § 5.7.

z. Certificate of service; First class mail. 9 INPRAC § 5.8.

2. Official Motion for Protective Order Forms for Allen County

a. Consent to alternate service. IN ST ALLEN SUPER AND CIR CT CIV App. A.

I. Checklist

(I) ❏ Matters to be considered by moving party

(a) ❏ Required documents

(1) ❏ Motion and notice

(2) ❏ Attorney certification

(3) ❏ Proposed order

(4) ❏ Certificate of service

(b) ❏ Supplemental documents

(1) ❏ Supporting evidence

(2) ❏ Brief or memorandum

(3) ❏ Facsimile cover sheet

(c) ❏ Timing

(1) ❏ There are no specific timing requirements for filing a motion for a protective order

(2) ❏ A written motion, other than one which may be heard ex parte, and notice of the hearing

thereof shall be served not less than five (5) days before the time specified for the hearing, unless a different period is fixed by the Indiana Rules of Trial Procedure or by order of the court

    (3) ❑ All pleadings and papers subsequent to the complaint which are required to be served upon a party shall be filed with the Court either before service or within a reasonable period of time thereafter

(II) ❑ Matters to be considered by the responding party

    (a) ❑ Required documents

        (1) ❑ Opposition

        (2) ❑ Certificate of service

    (b) ❑ Supplemental documents

        (1) ❑ Supporting evidence

        (2) ❑ Brief or memorandum

        (3) ❑ Proposed order

        (4) ❑ Facsimile cover sheet

    (c) ❑ Timing

        (1) ❑ Except as otherwise provided in IN ST TRIAL P Rule 59(D), opposing affidavits may be served not less than one (1) day before the hearing, unless the court permits them to be served at some other time

Motions, Oppositions and Replies
Motion for Discovery Sanctions

Document Last Updated October 2013

A. Applicable Rules

1. *State rules*

    a. Appearance. IN ST TRIAL P Rule 3.1.

    b. Process. IN ST TRIAL P Rule 4.

    c. Service and filing of pleadings and other papers. IN ST TRIAL P Rule 5.

    d. Time. IN ST TRIAL P Rule 6.

    e. Pleadings. IN ST TRIAL P Rule 7; IN ST TRIAL P Rule 8; IN ST TRIAL P Rule 9.2; IN ST TRIAL P Rule 10.

    f. Signing and verification of pleadings. IN ST TRIAL P Rule 11.

    g. General provisions governing discovery. IN ST TRIAL P Rule 26.

    h. Methods of discovery. IN ST TRIAL P Rule 27; IN ST TRIAL P Rule 30; IN ST TRIAL P Rule 31; IN ST TRIAL P Rule 33; IN ST TRIAL P Rule 34; IN ST TRIAL P Rule 35; IN ST TRIAL P Rule 36.

    i. Failure to make or cooperate in discovery; Sanctions. IN ST TRIAL P Rule 37.

    j. Evidence. IN ST TRIAL P Rule 43.

    k. Judgment on the evidence (directed verdict). IN ST TRIAL P Rule 50.

    l. Findings by the court. IN ST TRIAL P Rule 52.

    m. Summary judgment. IN ST TRIAL P Rule 56.

    n. Motion to correct error. IN ST TRIAL P Rule 59.

    o. Relief from judgment or order. IN ST TRIAL P Rule 60.

p. Trial court and clerks. IN ST TRIAL P Rule 72.

q. Hearing of motions. IN ST TRIAL P Rule 73.

r. Access to court records. IN ST ADMIN Rule 9.

s. Paper size. IN ST ADMIN Rule 11.

t. Facsimile transmission. IN ST ADMIN Rule 12.

u. Electronic filing and electronic service pilot projects. IN ST ADMIN Rule 16.

v. Sealing of certain records by court; Hearing; Notice. IN ST 5-14-3-5.5.

w. Privacy and confidentiality. IN ST 5-2-9-6; IN ST 5-14-3-4; IN ST 6-4.1-5-10; IN ST 6-4.1-12-12; IN ST 6-8.1-7-1; IN ST 11-13-1-8; IN ST 12-23-14-13; IN ST 16-39-3-10; IN ST 16-41-8-1; IN ST 22-4-19-6; IN ST 31-11-1-6; IN ST 31-19-5-23; IN ST 31-19-13-2; IN ST 31-19-19-1; IN ST 31-33-18-1; IN ST 31-39-1-1; IN ST 31-39-1-2; IN ST 33-23-16-16; IN ST 35-34-2-4; IN ST 35-38-1-13; IN ST 35-38-9-1; IN ST ADR Rule 2.11; IN ST ADR Rule 4.4; IN ST ADR Rule 5.6; IN ST JURY Rule 10.

2. *Local rules*

a. Applicability and citation of rules. IN ST ALLEN SUPER AND CIR CT CIV Rule AR00-1.

b. Proposed orders. IN ST ALLEN SUPER AND CIR CT CIV Rule TR00-1.

c. Appearances. IN ST ALLEN SUPER AND CIR CT CIV Rule 3.1-1.

d. Consent to alternate service. IN ST ALLEN SUPER AND CIR CT CIV Rule 5-1.

e. Motions in civil court. IN ST ALLEN SUPER AND CIR CT CIV Rule 7-1.

f. Preparation of pleadings. IN ST ALLEN SUPER AND CIR CT CIV Rule 8-1.

g. Filing. IN ST ALLEN SUPER AND CIR CT CIV Rule 77-1.

B. Timing

1. *Motion for discovery sanctions.* There are no specific timing requirements for filing a motion for discovery sanctions.

   a. *Filing.* All pleadings and papers subsequent to the complaint which are required to be served upon a party shall be filed with the Court either before service or within a reasonable period of time thereafter. IN ST TRIAL P Rule 5(E)(1).

2. *Service.* A written motion, other than one which may be heard ex parte, and notice of the hearing thereof shall be served not less than five (5) days before the time specified for the hearing, unless a different period is fixed by the Indiana Rules of Trial Procedure or by order of the court. IN ST TRIAL P Rule 6(D).

   a. *Of supporting affidavits.* When a motion is supported by affidavit, the affidavit shall be served with the motion. IN ST TRIAL P Rule 6(D).

3. *Service of opposition.* Except as otherwise provided in IN ST TRIAL P Rule 59(D), opposing affidavits may be served not less than one (1) day before the hearing, unless the court permits them to be served at some other time. IN ST TRIAL P Rule 6(D).

4. *Computation of time*

   a. *Generally; Days excluded.* In computing any period of time prescribed or allowed by the Indiana Rules of Trial Procedure, by order of the court, or by any applicable statute, the day of the act, event, or default from which the designated period of time begins to run shall not be included. The last day of the period so computed is to be included unless it is:

      i. A Saturday,

      ii. A Sunday,

      iii. A legal holiday as defined by state statute, or

      iv. A day the office in which the act is to be done is closed during regular business hours. IN ST TRIAL P Rule 6(A).

    b.   *Short periods*. In any event, the period runs until the end of the next day that is not a Saturday, a Sunday, a legal holiday, or a day on which the office is closed. When the period of time allowed is less than seven (7) days, intermediate Saturdays, Sundays, legal holidays, and days on which the office is closed shall be excluded from the computations. IN ST TRIAL P Rule 6(A).

    c.   *Additional time after service by United States mail*. Whenever a party has the right or is required to do some act or take some proceedings within a prescribed period after the service of a notice or other paper upon him and the notice or paper is served upon him by United States mail, three (3) days shall be added to the prescribed period. IN ST TRIAL P Rule 6(E).

    d.   *Enlargement of time*. When an act is required or allowed to be done at or within a specific time by the Indiana Rules of Trial Procedure, the court may at any time for cause shown:

        i.   Order the period enlarged, with or without motion or notice, if request therefor is made before the expiration of the period originally prescribed or extended by a previous order; or

        ii.   Upon motion made after the expiration of the specific period, permit the act to be done where the failure to act was the result of excusable neglect; but, the court may not extend the time for taking any action for judgment on the evidence under IN ST TRIAL P Rule 50(A), amendment of findings and judgment under IN ST TRIAL P Rule 52(B), to correct errors under IN ST TRIAL P Rule 59(C), statement in opposition to motion to correct error under IN ST TRIAL P Rule 59(E), or to obtain relief from final judgment under IN ST TRIAL P Rule 60(B), except to the extent and under the conditions stated in those rules. IN ST TRIAL P Rule 6(B).

C. General Requirements

1.   *Motions, generally*. Unless made during a hearing or trial, or otherwise ordered by the court, an application to the court for an order shall be made by written motion. The motion shall state the grounds therefor and the relief or order sought. IN ST TRIAL P Rule 7(B).

    a.   *Motions as distinct from pleadings*. Motions and responses to motions are not pleadings, and allegations contained in a motion are not admissions of a party. 22B INPRAC 7:2; Wachstetter v. County Properties, LLC, 832 N.E.2d 574 (Ind.Ct.App. 2005); Scott County Family YMCA, Inc. v. Hobbs, 817 N.E.2d 603 (Ind.Ct.App. 2004).

    b.   *Unopposed motions generally granted*. It is common for a trial court to grant procedural motions, such as motions for enlargement of time, discovery motions, or motions for continuance, unless an objection is filed. 21 INPRAC § 13.8.

2.   *Motion for discovery sanctions*

    a.   *Related to a motion to compel; Award of sanctions on motion*

        i.   *Motion granted*. If the motion is granted, the court shall, after opportunity for hearing, require the party or deponent whose conduct necessitated the motion or the party or attorney advising such conduct or both of them to pay to the moving party the reasonable expenses incurred in obtaining the order, including attorney's fees, unless the court finds that the opposition to the motion was substantially justified or that other circumstances make an award of expenses unjust. IN ST TRIAL P Rule 37(A)(4).

        ii.   *Motion denied*. If the motion is denied, the court shall, after opportunity for hearing, require the moving party or the attorney advising the motion or both of them to pay to the party or deponent who opposed the motion the reasonable expenses incurred in opposing the motion, including attorney's fees, unless the court finds that the making of the motion was substantially justified or that other circumstances make an award of expenses unjust. IN ST TRIAL P Rule 37(A)(4).

        iii.   *Granted in part and denied in part*. If the motion is granted in part and denied in part, the court may apportion the reasonable expenses incurred in relation to the motion among the parties and persons in a just manner. IN ST TRIAL P Rule 37(A)(4).

        iv.   Refer to the Indiana KeyRules Motion to Compel Discovery document for more information.

    b.   *Failure to comply with order*. The trial court may impose sanctions upon a party who fails to obey an order regarding discovery. 22 INPRAC § 27.7. The first step to invoking sanctions under IN ST TRIAL P Rule 37(B) is to file a motion to compel discovery under IN ST TRIAL P Rule 37(A) and obtain an order from the court requiring the opposing party to take a specific action in discovery. If the opposing party then fails to take the action mandated by the trial court's discovery order, the second step is to return to the trial court and file a motion for sanctions under IN ST TRIAL P Rule 37(B). 22 INPRAC § 27.7.

i. *Sanctions by court in county where deposition is taken.* If a deponent fails to be sworn or to answer a question after being directed to do so by the court in the county in which the deposition is being taken, the failure may be considered a contempt of that court. IN ST TRIAL P Rule 37(B)(1).

ii. *Sanctions by court in which action is pending.* If a party or an officer, director, or managing agent of a party or an organization, including a governmental organization, or a person designated under IN ST TRIAL P Rule 30(B)(6) or IN ST TRIAL P Rule 31(A) to testify on behalf of a party or an organization, including a governmental organization, fails to obey an order to provide or permit discovery, including an order made under IN ST TRIAL P Rule 37(A) or IN ST TRIAL P Rule 35, the court in which the action is pending may make such orders in regard to the failure as are just, and among others the following:

- An order that the matters regarding which the order was made or any other designated facts shall be taken to be established for the purposes of the action in accordance with the claim of the party obtaining the order;

- An order refusing to allow the disobedient party to support or oppose designated claims or defenses, or prohibiting him from introducing designated matters in evidence;

- An order striking out pleadings or parts thereof, or staying further proceedings until the order is obeyed, or dismissing the action or proceeding or any part thereof, or rendering a judgment by default against the disobedient party;

- In lieu of any of the foregoing orders or in addition thereto, an order treating as a contempt of court the failure to obey any orders except an order to submit to a physical or mental examination under IN ST TRIAL P Rule 35;

- Where a party has failed to comply with an order under IN ST TRIAL P Rule 35(A) requiring him to produce another for examination, such orders as are listed in IN ST TRIAL P Rule 37(B)(2)(a), IN ST TRIAL P Rule 37(B)(2)(b), and IN ST TRIAL P Rule 37(B)(2)(c), unless the party failing to comply shows that he is unable to produce such person for examination. IN ST TRIAL P Rule 37(B)(2).

- In lieu of any of the foregoing orders or in addition thereto, the court shall require the party failing to obey the order or the attorney advising him or both to pay the reasonable expenses, including attorney's fees, caused by the failure, unless the court finds that the failure was substantially justified or that other circumstances make an award of expenses unjust. IN ST TRIAL P Rule 37(B)(2).

c. *Expenses on failure to admit.* If a party fails to admit the genuineness of any document or the truth of any matter as requested under IN ST TRIAL P Rule 36, and if the party requesting the admissions thereafter proves the genuineness of the document or the truth of the matter, he may apply to the court for an order requiring the other party to pay him the reasonable expenses incurred in making that proof, including reasonable attorney's fees. The court shall make the order unless it finds that:

i. The request was held objectionable pursuant to IN ST TRIAL P Rule 36(A), or

ii. The admission sought was of no substantial importance, or

iii. The party failing to admit had reasonable ground to believe that he might prevail on the matter, or

iv. There was other good reason for the failure to admit. IN ST TRIAL P Rule 37(C).

d. *Failure of party to attend at own deposition or serve answers to interrogatories or respond to requests for inspection*

i. *Court order for failure to provide discovery.* If a party or an officer, director, or managing agent of a party or an organization, including without limitation a governmental organization, or a person designated under IN ST TRIAL P Rule 30(B)(6) or IN ST TRIAL P Rule 31(A) to testify on behalf of a party or an organization, including without limitation a governmental organization, fails (1) to appear before the officer who is to take his deposition, after being served with a proper notice, or (2) to serve answers or objections to interrogatories submitted under IN ST TRIAL P Rule 33, after proper service of the interrogatories, or (3) to serve a written response to a request for inspection submitted under IN ST TRIAL P Rule 34, after proper service of the request, the court in which the action is pending on motion may make such orders in regard to the failure as are just, and among others it may take any action authorized under IN ST TRIAL P Rule 37(B)(2)(a), IN ST TRIAL P Rule 37(B)(2)(b), and IN ST TRIAL P Rule 37(B)(2)(c). IN ST TRIAL P Rule 37(D).

ii. *Attorney fees against party failing to provide discovery.* In lieu of any order or in addition thereto, the court shall require the party failing to act or the attorney advising him or both to pay the reasonable expenses, including attorney's fees, caused by the failure, unless the court finds that the failure was substantially justified or that other circumstances make an award of expenses unjust. IN ST TRIAL P Rule 37(D)

iii. *Failure not excused for objectionable requests.* The failure to act described in IN ST TRIAL P Rule 37(D) may not be excused on the ground that the discovery sought is objectionable unless the party failing to act has applied for a protective order as provided by IN ST TRIAL P Rule 26(C). IN ST TRIAL P Rule 37(D). Refer to the Indiana KeyRules Motion for Protective Order document for more information.

iv. *Showing required.* To invoke the sanctions under IN ST TRIAL P Rule 37(D), it is sufficient that notice of the deposition or other discovery request was properly served upon the non-responding party, but no response was provided. 22 INPRAC § 27.8.

e. *Sanctions for spoliation of evidence.* In some cases a duty arises imposing an affirmative obligation to avoid the destruction or loss of documents and materials that are relevant and discoverable to claims and defenses that either have been or may be asserted in an action. The destruction, mutilation, alteration or concealment of such materials is called "spoliation." 3 INPRAC R 37(37.2.2); Glotzbach v. Froman, 854 N.E.2d 337 (Ind. 2006).

i. *Spoliation generally.* Spoliation typically presents itself in one of two ways:
- A party to litigation destroys materials that are relevant and discoverable in an action; or
- A non-party destroys materials that may be discoverable in an action to which that entity or individual will not be a party. 3 INPRAC R 37(37.2.2).

ii. *Duty to maintain evidence must exist.* A key component of a spoliation claim is that the party who destroyed the materials must have had a duty not to do so. A duty may arise in a number of ways: imposed by statute or case law, imposed by contract or some third party beneficiary arrangement, or imposed by the actions of the parties by which one party assumes a duty in law or equity toward another. When duty arises from the conduct of the parties as opposed to one established by statute or contract, the Indiana courts have identified three primary factors to determine whether a duty exists:
- The relationship between the parties,
- The reasonable foreseeability of harm to the injured litigant, and
- The public policy promoted by recognizing an enforceable duty. 3 INPRAC R 37(37.2.2); Webb v. Jarvis, 575 N.E.2d 992 (Ind. 1991).
- This balancing test is particularly useful where the element of duty has not already been established between the parties. 3 INPRAC R 37(37.2.2); Northern Indiana Public Service Co. v. Sharp, 790 N.E.2d 462 (Ind. 2003).

iii. *Factors to be considered by the court.* Even where the court finds an intentional spoliation, it is not mandatory that sanctions be imposed. Rather, the trial court should implement an approach by which it balances the nature of the offense against the harm suffered by the non-offending party because lost evidence is not available. 22 INPRAC § 27.9; Gribben v. Wal-Mart Stores, Inc., 824 N.E.2d 349 (Ind. 2005). Factors the court may consider include:

- The culpability of the spoliating party;
- The prejudice to the non-offending party;
- The degree of interference with the judicial process;
- Whether lesser sanctions are available to remedy any harm and deter future acts of spoliation;
- The amount of time lapsing from the date the spoliating party took possession of the evidence and the date of its loss or destruction;
- Protocols adopted, and followed, by the spoliating party to prevent the loss of evidence, such as a document retention policy;
- Whether evidence has been irretrievably lost and, if so, the circumstances of that loss;
- The existence of available alternatives that would allow the non-offending party to prove its case without the lost evidence;
- And whether sanctions will unfairly punish a party for the misconduct or mistake of his attorney or expert. 22 INPRAC § 27.9.

f. *No sanctions for good-faith loss of electronically stored information.* Absent exceptional circumstances, a court may not impose sanctions under the Indiana Rules of Trial Procedure these rules on a party for failing to provide electronically stored information lost as a result of the routine, good faith operation of an electronic information system. IN ST TRIAL P Rule 37(E).

g. *Discovery dispute motions.* The Court expects complete compliance with IN ST TRIAL P Rule 26(F). IN ST ALLEN SUPER AND CIR CT CIV Rule 7-1(H).

D. Documents

1. *Required documents*

a. *Motion and notice.* The requirement of notice is satisfied by service of the motion. IN ST TRIAL P Rule 7(B). Refer to the General Requirements section of this document for information on the content of a motion for discovery sanctions.

b. *Attorney certification.* Before any party files any motion or request to compel discovery pursuant to IN ST TRIAL P Rule 37, or any motion for protection from discovery pursuant to IN ST TRIAL P Rule 26(C), or any other discovery motion which seeks to enforce, modify, or limit discovery, that party shall:

i. Make a reasonable effort to reach agreement with the opposing party concerning the matter which is the subject of the motion or request; and

ii. Include in the motion or request a statement showing that the attorney making the motion or request has made a reasonable effort to reach agreement with the opposing attorney(s) concerning the matter(s) set forth in the motion or request. This statement shall recite, in addition, the date, time and place of this effort to reach agreement, whether in person or by phone, and the names of all parties and attorneys participating therein. If an attorney for any party advises the court in writing that an opposing attorney has refused or delayed meeting and discussing the issues covered in IN ST TRIAL P Rule 26(F), the court may take such action as is appropriate. IN ST TRIAL P Rule 26(F).

iii. The court may deny a discovery motion filed by a party who has failed to comply with the requirements of IN ST TRIAL P Rule 26(F). IN ST TRIAL P Rule 26(F).

c. *Proposed order.* Unless local practice provides differently, a party should submit a proposed order with its written motion to be signed by the judge once the motion has been granted. 21 INPRAC § 13.8.

i. *Copies of proposed orders.* All proposed orders shall be submitted in an original plus a number of copies equal to one (1) more than the number of pro se parties and attorneys of record contained in the prepared proof of notice under IN ST TRIAL P Rule 72(D). IN ST ALLEN SUPER AND CIR CT CIV Rule TR00-1(C).

    ii.   *Proof of notice.* The proposed order shall also include a prepared proof of notice, under IN ST TRIAL P Rule 72(D). IN ST ALLEN SUPER AND CIR CT CIV Rule TR00-1(B).

    iii.   Refer to the Format section of this document for information on the form and content of the proposed order and the proof of notice.

  d. *Certificate of service.* An attorney or unrepresented party tendering a document to the Clerk for filing shall certify that service has been made, list the parties served, and specify the date and means of service. The certificate of service shall be placed at the end of the document and shall not be separately filed. The separate filing of a certificate of service, however, shall not be grounds for rejecting a document for filing. The Clerk may permit documents to be filed without a certificate of service but shall require prompt filing of a separate certificate of service. IN ST TRIAL P Rule 5(C).

2. *Supplemental documents*

  a. *Supporting evidence.* When a motion is based on facts not appearing of record the court may hear the matter on affidavits presented by the respective parties, but the court may direct that the matter be heard wholly or partly on oral testimony or depositions. IN ST TRIAL P Rule 43(B).

  b. *Brief or memorandum.* If a party desires to file a brief or memorandum in support of any motion, such brief or memorandum shall be filed simultaneously with the motion, and a copy shall be promptly served upon the adverse party. IN ST ALLEN SUPER AND CIR CT CIV Rule 7-1(E).

  c. *Facsimile cover sheet.* Any document sent to the Clerk of the Circuit Court by electronic facsimile transmission shall be accompanied by a cover sheet which states the title of the document, case number, number of pages, identity and voice telephone number of the sending party and instructions for filing. The cover sheet shall contain the signature of the attorney or party, pro se, authorizing the filing. IN ST ADMIN Rule 12(D).

E. Format

1. *Form of motions.* The rules applicable to captions, and the signing and form of pleadings (IN ST TRIAL P Rule 8 through IN ST TRIAL P Rule 11), apply to all motions and other papers provided under the Indiana Rules of Trial Procedure. 22B INPRAC 7:2.

2. *Form of pleadings*

  a. *Caption; Names of parties.* Every pleading shall contain a caption setting forth the name of the court, the title of the action, the file number, and a designation as in IN ST TRIAL P Rule 7(A). In the complaint the title of the action shall include the names of all the parties, but in other pleadings it is sufficient to state the name of the first party on each side with an appropriate indication of other parties. IN ST TRIAL P Rule 10(A).

  b. *Paragraphs; Separate statements.* All averments of a claim or defense shall be made in numbered paragraphs, the contents of each of which shall be limited as far as practicable to a statement of a single set of circumstances, and a paragraph may be referred to by number in all succeeding pleadings. Each claim founded upon a separate transaction or occurrence and each defense other than denials may be stated in a separate count or defense whenever a separation facilitates the clear presentation of the matters set forth. IN ST TRIAL P Rule 10(B).

  c. *Adoption by reference; Exhibits.* Statements in a pleading may be adopted by reference in a different part of the same pleading or in another pleading or in any motion. A copy of any written instrument which is an exhibit to a pleading is a part thereof for all purposes. IN ST TRIAL P Rule 10(C).

  d. *Citation.* Allen County Superior and Circuit court rules may be cited as L.R. _____. The Indiana Rules of Trial Procedure are hereinafter referred to as T.R. _____. IN ST ALLEN SUPER AND CIR CT CIV Rule AR00-1(B).

  e. *Paper.* All pleadings must be printed on white paper. IN ST ALLEN SUPER AND CIR CT CIV Rule 8-1(A).

  f. *Spacing.* The lines shall be double spaced except for quotations, which shall be indented and single-spaced. IN ST ALLEN SUPER AND CIR CT CIV Rule 8-1(A).

g. *Photocopies.* Photocopies are acceptable if legible. IN ST ALLEN SUPER AND CIR CT CIV Rule 8-1(A).

h. *Margins and binding.* Margins shall be one to one and one-half (1-1 1/2) inches on the left side and one-half (1/2) inch on the right. IN ST ALLEN SUPER AND CIR CT CIV Rule 8-1(B).

   i. Binding or stapling shall be at the top left and at no other place. IN ST ALLEN SUPER AND CIR CT CIV Rule 8-1(B).

   ii. Covers or backing shall not be used. IN ST ALLEN SUPER AND CIR CT CIV Rule 8-1(B).

i. *Flat filing.* The files of the Clerk of the Court shall be kept under the "flat filing" system. All pleadings presented for filing with the Clerk or Court shall be flat and unfolded. Only the original of any pleading shall be placed in the Court file. IN ST ALLEN SUPER AND CIR CT CIV Rule 77-1(A).

j. *Handwritten pleadings.* Handwritten pleadings may be accepted for filing in the discretion of the Court. IN ST ALLEN SUPER AND CIR CT CIV Rule 8-1(A).

3. *Size of papers for filing.* Effective January 1, 1992, all pleadings, copies, motions and documents filed with any trial court or appellate level court, typed or printed, with the exception of exhibits and existing wills, shall be prepared on eight and one-half by eleven inch (8 1/2" x 11") size paper. IN ST ADMIN Rule 11.

4. *Form of proposed orders*

a. *Form, caption, and title.* Any proposed order shall be a document that is separate and apart from the motion or application to which it relates and shall contain a caption showing the name of the court, the case number assigned to the case and the title of the case as shown by the complaint. IN ST ALLEN SUPER AND CIR CT CIV Rule TR00-1(B). If there are multiple parties, the title may be shortened to include only the first name plaintiff and defendant with appropriate indication that there are additional parties. IN ST ALLEN SUPER AND CIR CT CIV Rule TR00-1(B).

b. *Paper.* The proposed order shall be on white paper, eight and one half by eleven inches (8 1/2" x 11") in size, and each page shall be numbered. IN ST ALLEN SUPER AND CIR CT CIV Rule TR00-1(B).

c. *Signature line.* On the last page of the proposed order there shall be a line for the signature of the judge under which shall be typed "Judge, Allen Superior Court" or "Judge, Allen Circuit Court", whichever is applicable, to the left of which shall be the following: "Dated _____". IN ST ALLEN SUPER AND CIR CT CIV Rule TR00-1(B).

d. *Allowance of space for clerk.* To allow space for the Clerk to make entries on the proposed order to show compliance with the notice requirements of IN ST TRIAL P Rule 72(D), the lower four (4) inches of the last page of the proposed order shall be left blank. IN ST ALLEN SUPER AND CIR CT CIV Rule TR00-1(B).

e. *Proof of notice required.* The proposed order shall also include a prepared proof of notice, under IN ST TRIAL P Rule 72(D). The proof of notice shall conform to the format show in IN ST ALLEN SUPER AND CIR CT CIV Rule TR00-1(B). IN ST ALLEN SUPER AND CIR CT CIV Rule TR00-1(B).

5. *Signature requirements*

a. *Signature of attorney.* Every pleading or motion of a party represented by an attorney shall be signed by at least one (1) attorney of record in his individual name, whose address, telephone number, and attorney number shall be stated, except that this provision shall not apply to pleadings and motions made and transcribed at the trial or a hearing before the judge and received by him in such form. IN ST TRIAL P Rule 11(A). All pleadings to be signed by an attorney shall contain the written signature of the individual attorney, the attorney's printed name, Supreme Court Attorney Number, the name of the attorney's law firm, the attorney's address, telephone number, and a designation of the party for whom the attorney appears. IN ST ALLEN SUPER AND CIR CT CIV Rule 8-1(C). For the recommended signature format, refer to IN ST ALLEN SUPER AND CIR CT CIV Rule 8-1(C).

   i. The signature of an attorney constitutes a certificate by him that he has read the pleadings; that

to the best of his knowledge, information, and belief, there is good ground to support it; and that it is not interposed for delay. IN ST TRIAL P Rule 11(A).

    ii.   If a pleading or motion is not signed or is signed with intent to defeat the purpose of the rule, it may be stricken as sham and false and the action may proceed as though the pleading had not been served. IN ST TRIAL P Rule 11(A).

    iii.   For a willful violation of IN ST TRIAL P Rule 11 an attorney may be subjected to appropriate disciplinary action. Similar action may be taken if scandalous or indecent matter is inserted. IN ST TRIAL P Rule 11(A).

    iv.   Neither printed signatures, nor facsimile signatures shall be accepted on original documents. IN ST ALLEN SUPER AND CIR CT CIV Rule 8-1(C).

    v.   Facsimile signatures are permitted on copies. IN ST ALLEN SUPER AND CIR CT CIV Rule 8-1(C).

b.   *Signature of unrepresented party.* A party who is not represented by an attorney shall sign his pleading and state his address. IN ST TRIAL P Rule 11(A).

c.   *Verification not generally required.* Except when specifically required by rule, pleadings or motions need not be verified or accompanied by affidavit. The rule in equity that the averments of an answer under oath must be overcome by the testimony of two (2) witnesses or of one (1) witness sustained by corroborating circumstances is abolished. IN ST TRIAL P Rule 11(A).

d.   *Verification by affirmation or representation.* When in connection with any civil or special statutory proceeding it is required that any pleading, motion, petition, supporting affidavit, or other document of any kind, be verified, or that an oath be taken, it shall be sufficient if the subscriber simply affirms the truth of the matter to be verified by an affirmation or representation. IN ST TRIAL P Rule 11(B). IN ST TRIAL P Rule 11(B) states that the affirmation or representation should be in substantially the following language: "I (we) affirm, under the penalties for perjury, that the foregoing representation(s) is (are) true. (Signed) _____."

    i.   Any person who falsifies an affirmation or representation of fact shall be subject to the same penalties as are prescribed by law for the making of a false affidavit. IN ST TRIAL P Rule 11(B).

e.   *Verified pleadings, motions, and affidavits as evidence.* Pleadings, motions and affidavits accompanying or in support of such pleadings or motions when required to be verified or under oath shall be accepted as a representation that the signer had personal knowledge thereof or reasonable cause to believe the existence of the facts or matters stated or alleged therein; and, if otherwise competent or acceptable as evidence, may be admitted as evidence of the facts or matters stated or alleged therein when it is so provided in the Indiana Rules of Trial Procedure, by statute or other law, or to the extent the writing or signature expressly purports to be made upon the signer's personal knowledge. When such pleadings, motions and affidavits are verified or under oath they shall not require other or greater proof on the part of the adverse party than if not verified or not under oath unless expressly provided otherwise by the Indiana Rules of Trial Procedure, statute or other law. Affidavits upon motions for summary judgment under IN ST TRIAL P Rule 56 and in denial of execution under IN ST TRIAL P Rule 9.2 shall be made upon personal knowledge. IN ST TRIAL P Rule 11(C).

6.   *Information excluded from public access.* Every document filed in a case shall separately identify information excluded from public access pursuant to IN ST ADMIN Rule 9(G)(1) as follows:

a.   Whole documents that are excluded from public access pursuant to IN ST ADMIN Rule 9(G)(1) shall be tendered on light green paper or have a light green coversheet attached to the document, marked "Not for Public Access" or "Confidential." IN ST TRIAL P Rule 5(G)(1).

b.   When only a portion of a document contains information excluded from public access pursuant to IN ST ADMIN Rule 9(G)(1), said information shall be omitted [or redacted] from the filed document, and set forth on a separate accompanying document on light green paper conspicuously marked "Not for Public Access" or "Confidential" and clearly designated [or identifying] the caption and number of the case and the document and location within the document to which the redacted material pertains. IN ST TRIAL P Rule 5(G)(2).

c. With respect to documents filed in electronic format, the trial court, by local rule, may provide for compliance with IN ST TRIAL P Rule 5 in manner that separates and protects access to information excluded from public access. IN ST TRIAL P Rule 5(G)(3).

d. IN ST TRIAL P Rule 5(G) does not apply to a record sealed by the court pursuant to IN ST 5-14-3-5.5 or otherwise, nor to records, documents, or information filed in cases to which public access is prohibited pursuant to IN ST ADMIN Rule 9(G). IN ST TRIAL P Rule 5(G)(4).

e. The following information in case records is excluded from public access and is confidential:

   i. Information that is excluded from public access pursuant to federal law;

   ii. Information that is excluded from public access as declared confidential by Indiana statute or other court rule, including without limitation:

   - All adoption records created after July 8, 1941, as declared confidential by IN ST 31-19-19-1, et seq., except those specifically declared open by IN ST 31-19-13-2(2);

   - All records relating to chancroid, chlamydia, gonorrhea, hepatitis, human immunodeficiency virus (HIV), Lymphogranuloma venereum, syphilis, tuberculosis, as declared confidential by IN ST 16-41-8-1, et seq.;

   - All records relating to child abuse as declared confidential by IN ST 31-33-18-1, et seq.;

   - All records relating to drug tests as declared confidential by IN ST 5-14-3-4(a)(9);

   - Records of grand jury proceedings as declared confidential by IN ST 35-34-2-4;

   - Records of juvenile proceedings as declared confidential by IN ST 31-39-1-2, except those specifically open under statute;

   - All paternity records created after July 1, 1941 as declared confidential by IN ST 31-14-11-15, IN ST 31-19-5-23, IN ST 31-39-1-1 and IN ST 31-39-1-2 [Editor's note: IN ST 31-14-11-15 was repealed effective May 9, 2013];

   - All pre-sentence reports as declared confidential by IN ST 35-38-1-13;

   - Written petitions to permit marriages without consent and orders directing the Clerk of Court to issue a marriage license to underage persons, as declared confidential by IN ST 31-11-1-6;

   - Only those arrest warrants, search warrants, indictments and informations ordered confidential by the trial judge, prior to return of duly executed service as declared confidential by IN ST 5-14-3-4(b)(1);

   - All medical, mental health, or tax records unless determined by law or regulation of any governmental custodian not to be confidential, released by the subject of such records, or declared by a court of competent jurisdiction to be essential to the resolution of litigation as declared confidential by IN ST 16-39-3-10, IN ST 6-4.1-5-10, IN ST 6-4.1-12-12, and IN ST 6-8.1-7-1;

   - Personal information relating to jurors or prospective jurors, other than for the use of the parties and counsel, pursuant to IN ST JURY Rule 10;

   - Information relating to protection from abuse orders, no-contact orders and workplace violence restraining orders as declared confidential by IN ST 5-2-9-6, et seq.;

   - Mediation proceedings pursuant to IN ST ADR Rule 2.11, Mini-Trial proceedings pursuant to IN ST ADR Rule 4.4(C), and Summary Jury Trials pursuant to IN ST ADR Rule 5.6;

   - Information in probation files pursuant to the Probation Standards promulgated by the Judicial Conference of Indiana pursuant to IN ST 11-13-1-8(b);

   - Information deemed confidential pursuant to the Rules for Court Administered Alcohol and Drug Programs promulgated by the Judicial Conference of Indiana pursuant to IN ST 12-23-14-13;

   - Information deemed confidential pursuant to the Problem-Solving Court Rules promulgated by the Judicial Conference of Indiana pursuant to IN ST 33-23-16-16;

- All records of the Department of workforce Development as declared confidential by IN ST 22-4-19-6;
- Information regarding interception of electronic communications that is sealed or deemed confidential as set forth in IN ST 35-33.5-2-1, et seq.

iii. Information excluded from public access by specific court order;

iv. Complete Social Security Numbers of living persons;

v. With the exception of names, information such as addresses, phone numbers, and dates of birth which explicitly identifies:

- Natural persons who are witnesses or victims (not including defendants) in criminal, domestic violence, stalking, sexual assault, juvenile, or civil protection order proceedings, provided that juveniles who are victims of sex crimes shall be identified by initials only;
- Places of residence of judicial officers, clerks and other employees of courts and clerks of court, unless the person or persons about whom the information pertains waives confidentiality;

vi. Complete account numbers of specific assets, loans, bank accounts, credit cards, and personal identification numbers (PINs);

vii. All orders of expungement entered in criminal or juvenile proceedings, orders to restrict access to criminal history information pursuant to IN ST 35-38-5-5.5 or IN ST 35-38-8-5 and records excluded from public access by such orders, and information related to infractions that is excluded from public access pursuant to IN ST 34-28-5-15 or IN ST 34-28-5-16 [Editor's note: IN ST 35-38-5-5.5, IN ST 35-38-8-5 and IN ST 34-28-5-16 were repealed effective July 1, 2013; for information on orders restricting access to criminal history, refer to IN ST 35-38-9-1, et seq.];

viii. All personal notes and e-mail, and deliberative material, of judges, jurors, court staff and judicial agencies, and information recorded in personal data assistants (PDA's) or organizers and personal calendars. IN ST ADMIN Rule 9(G)(1).

F. Filing and Service Requirements

1. *Filing requirements.* Except as otherwise provided in IN ST TRIAL P Rule 5(E)(2), all pleadings and papers subsequent to the complaint which are required to be served upon a party shall be filed with the Court either before service or within a reasonable period of time thereafter. IN ST TRIAL P Rule 5(E)(1).

   a. *Filing with the court defined.* The filing of pleadings, motions, and other papers with the court as required by the Indiana Rules of Trial Procedure shall be made by one of the following methods:

      i. Delivery to the clerk of the court;

      ii. Sending by electronic transmission under the procedure adopted pursuant to IN ST ADMIN Rule 12;

      iii. Mailing to the clerk by registered, certified or express mail return receipt requested;

      iv. Depositing with any third-party commercial carrier for delivery to the clerk within three (3) calendar days, cost prepaid, properly addressed;

      v. If the court so permits, filing with the judge, in which event the judge shall note thereon the filing date and forthwith transmit them to the office of the clerk; or

      vi. Electronic filing, as approved by the Division of State Court Administration pursuant to IN ST ADMIN Rule 16. IN ST TRIAL P Rule 5(F).

      vii. Filing by registered or certified mail and by third-party commercial carrier shall be complete upon mailing or deposit. IN ST TRIAL P Rule 5(F).

   b. *Facsimile filing*

      i. *Generally.* In counties where a majority of judges of the courts of record, by posted local rule, have authorized electronic facsimile filing and designated a telephone number to receive such

transmissions, pleadings, motions, and other papers may be sent to the Clerk of Circuit Court by electronic facsimile transmission for filing in any case, provided:

- Such matter does not exceed ten (10) pages, including the cover sheet;
- Such matter does not require the payment of fees other than the electronic facsimile transcription fee set forth in IN ST ADMIN Rule 12(E);
- The sending party creates at the time of transmission a machine generated log for such transmission; and
- The original document and the transmission log are maintained by the sending party for the duration of the litigation. IN ST ADMIN Rule 12(B).

    ii. *Time of filing.* During normal, posted business hours, the time of filing shall be the time the duplicate document is produced in the office of the Clerk of the Circuit Court. Duplicate documents received at all other times shall be filed as of the next normal business day. IN ST ADMIN Rule 12(C).

- If the receiving fax machine endorses its own time and date stamp upon the transmitted documents and the receiving machine produces a delivery receipt which is electronically created and transmitted to the sending party, the time of filing shall be the date and time recorded on the transmitted document by the receiving fax machine. IN ST ADMIN Rule 12(C).

  c. *Proof of filing.* Any party filing any paper by any method other than personal delivery to the clerk shall retain proof of filing. IN ST TRIAL P Rule 5(F).

2. *Service requirements.* Unless otherwise provided by the Indiana Rules of Trial Procedure or an order of the court, each party and special judge, if any, shall be served with: (1) every order required by its terms to be served; (2) every pleading subsequent to the original complaint; (3) every written motion except one which may be heard ex parte; (4) every brief submitted to the trial court; (5) every paper relating to discovery required to be served upon a party; and (6) every written notice, appearance, demand, offer of judgment, designation of record on appeal, or similar paper. IN ST TRIAL P Rule 5(A).

  a. *Methods of service*

    i. *Personal service.* Whenever a party is represented by an attorney of record, service shall be made upon such attorney unless service upon the party himself is ordered by the court. Service upon the attorney or party shall be made by delivering or mailing a copy of the papers to the last known address or where an attorney or party has consented to service by fax or e-mail, as provided in IN ST TRIAL P Rule 3.1(A)(4), by faxing or e-mailing a copy of the documents to the fax number or e-mail address set out in the appearance form or correction as required by IN ST TRIAL P Rule 3.1(E). IN ST TRIAL P Rule 5(B). Delivery of a copy within IN ST TRIAL P Rule 5 means:

- Offering or tendering it to the attorney or party and stating the nature of the papers being served. Refusal to accept an offered or tendered document is a waiver of any objection to the sufficiency or adequacy of service of that document;
- Leaving it at his office with a clerk or other person in charge thereof, or if there is no one in charge, leaving it in a conspicuous place therein; or
- If the office is closed, by leaving it at his dwelling house or usual place of abode with some person of suitable age and discretion then residing therein; or,
- Leaving it at some other suitable place, selected by the attorney upon whom service is being made, pursuant to duly promulgated local rule. IN ST TRIAL P Rule 5(B)(1).

    ii. *Service by mail.* If service is made by mail, the papers shall be deposited in the United States mail addressed to the person on whom they are being served, with postage prepaid. Service shall be deemed complete upon mailing. Proof of service of all papers permitted to be mailed may be made by written acknowledgment of service, by affidavit of the person who mailed the papers, or by certificate of an attorney. It shall be the duty of attorneys when entering their appearance in a cause or when filing pleadings or papers therein, to have noted in the

Chronological Case Summary or said pleadings or papers so filed the address and telephone number of their office. Service by delivery or by mail at such address shall be deemed sufficient and complete. IN ST TRIAL P Rule 5(B)(2).

   iii.   *Service by fax or e-mail.* A party who has consented to service by fax or e-mail may be served as follows:

- Service by e-mail shall be made by attaching the document being served in .pdf format. Discovery documents must also be served in accordance with IN ST TRIAL P Rule 26(A). IN ST TRIAL P Rule 5(B)(3)(a).

- Service by fax shall be deemed complete upon generation of a transmission record indicating the successful transmission of the entire document, except as provided in IN ST TRIAL P Rule 5(B)(3)(d). IN ST TRIAL P Rule 5(B)(3)(b).

- Service by e-mail shall be deemed complete upon transmission, except as provided in IN ST TRIAL P Rule 5(B)(3)(d). IN ST TRIAL P Rule 5(B)(3)(c).

- Service by fax or e-mail that occurs on a Saturday, Sunday, legal holiday, or day the court or agency in which the matter is pending is closed or after 5:00 PM local time of the recipient shall be deemed complete the next day that is not a Saturday, Sunday, legal holiday, or day that the court or agency in which the matter is pending is not closed. IN ST TRIAL P Rule 5(B)(3)(d).

   iv.   *Consent to alternate service.* Any Allen County Attorney or any Allen County law firm may, without charge, maintain an assigned Courthouse box in the library of the Allen County Courthouse for receipt of notices, pleadings, process orders, or other communications from the Court, the Clerk, and other attorneys or law firms. IN ST ALLEN SUPER AND CIR CT CIV Rule 5-1(A). For more information concerning the use of courthouse boxes, refer to IN ST ALLEN SUPER AND CIR CT CIV Rule 5-1.

  b.   *Serving numerous defendants.* In any action in which there are unusually large numbers of defendants, the court, upon motion or of its own initiative, may order:

   i.   That service of the pleadings of the defendants and replies thereto need not be made as between the defendants;

- That any cross-claim, counterclaim, or matter constituting an avoidance or affirmative defense contained therein shall be deemed to be denied or avoided by all other parties; and

- That the filing of any such pleading and service thereof upon the plaintiff constitutes due notice of it to the parties. IN ST TRIAL P Rule 5(D).

   ii.   A copy of every such order shall be served upon the parties in such manner and form as the court directs. IN ST TRIAL P Rule 5(D).

  c.   *Service on parties in default for failure to appear.* No service need be made on parties in default for failure to appear, except that pleadings asserting new or additional claims for relief against them shall be served upon them in the manner provided by service of summons in IN ST TRIAL P Rule 4. IN ST TRIAL P Rule 5(A).

G. Hearings

1. *Hearing on motion.* Unless local conditions make it impracticable, each judge shall establish regular times and places, at intervals sufficiently frequent for the prompt dispatch of business, at which motions requiring notice and hearing may be heard and disposed of; but the judge at any time or place and on such notice, if any, as he considers reasonable may make order for the advancement, conduct, and hearing of actions. To expedite its business the court may direct the submission and determination of motions without oral hearing upon brief written statements of reasons in support and opposition, or direct or permit hearings by telephone conference call with all attorneys or other similar means of communication. IN ST TRIAL P Rule 73(A).

  a.   *Setting motions for hearing.* Except for the motions described in IN ST ALLEN SUPER AND CIR CT CIV Rule 7-1(E), all motions shall be set for hearing. IN ST ALLEN SUPER AND CIR CT CIV Rule 7-1(A). [Editor's note: While IN ST ALLEN SUPER AND CIR CT CIV Rule 7-1(A) refers to

IN ST ALLEN SUPER AND CIR CT CIV Rule 7-1(E) as relating to hearings on motions, that reference is likely intended to be to IN ST ALLEN SUPER AND CIR CT CIV Rule 7-1(D).]

    i. It shall be the responsibility of the moving party to request the date of such hearing from the Judicial Assistant, or if the case has already been assigned to a Judge, from the Judicial Law Clerk of the assigned Judge. IN ST ALLEN SUPER AND CIR CT CIV Rule 7-1(A).

  b. *Responsibility for notice of hearing.* It shall be the responsibility of the moving party to give notice to all other parties of hearings scheduled on motions. IN ST ALLEN SUPER AND CIR CT CIV Rule 7-1(I).

2. *Hearings generally held before imposition of discovery sanctions.* As a general matter, most courts will conduct a hearing prior to imposing discovery sanctions, although IN ST TRIAL P Rule 37 and Indiana case law do not expressly require a court to do so. 22 INPRAC § 27.7.

H. Forms

1. Motion for Discovery Sanctions Forms for Indiana

  a. Motion to dismiss as sanction for failure to comply with court ordered discovery. 5 INPRAC § 4:6.60.

  b. Motion to dismiss action as sanction; For party's failure to comply with court ordered discovery. 10 INPRAC § 58.38.

  c. Motion for order precluding litigation of issues. 10 INPRAC § 58.63.

  d. Motion for judgment by default; As sanction for failure to comply with court order. 10 INPRAC § 58.64.

  e. Motion to exclude expert witness at trial. 10 INPRAC § 70.24

  f. Certificate of service; Personal service. 9 INPRAC § 5.7.

  g. Certificate of service; First class mail. 9 INPRAC § 5.8.

2. Official Motion for Discovery Sanctions Forms for Allen County

  a. Consent to alternate service. IN ST ALLEN SUPER AND CIR CT CIV App. A.

I. Checklist

(I) ❑ Matters to be considered by moving party

  (a) ❑ Required documents

    (1) ❑ Motion and notice

    (2) ❑ Attorney certification

    (3) ❑ Proposed order

    (4) ❑ Certificate of service

  (b) ❑ Supplemental documents

    (1) ❑ Supporting evidence

    (2) ❑ Brief or memorandum

    (3) ❑ Facsimile cover sheet

  (c) ❑ Timing

    (1) ❑ There are no specific timing requirements for filing a motion for discovery sanctions

    (2) ❑ A written motion, other than one which may be heard ex parte, and notice of the hearing thereof shall be served not less than five (5) days before the time specified for the hearing, unless a different period is fixed by the Indiana Rules of Trial Procedure or by order of the court

    (3) ❑ All pleadings and papers subsequent to the complaint which are required to be served upon a party shall be filed with the Court either before service or within a reasonable period of time thereafter

(II) ❑ Matters to be considered by the responding party

    (a) ❑ Required documents

        (1) ❑ Opposition

        (2) ❑ Certificate of service

    (b) ❑ Supplemental documents

        (1) ❑ Supporting evidence

        (2) ❑ Brief or memorandum

        (3) ❑ Proposed order

        (4) ❑ Facsimile cover sheet

    (c) ❑ Timing

        (1) ❑ Except as otherwise provided in IN ST TRIAL P Rule 59(D), opposing affidavits may be served not less than one (1) day before the hearing, unless the court permits them to be served at some other time

Motions, Oppositions and Replies
Motion for Preliminary Injunction

Document Last Updated October 2013

A. Applicable Rules

  1. *State rules*

    a. Appearance. IN ST TRIAL P Rule 3.1.

    b. Process. IN ST TRIAL P Rule 4.

    c. Service and filing of pleadings and other papers. IN ST TRIAL P Rule 5.

    d. Time. IN ST TRIAL P Rule 6.

    e. Pleadings. IN ST TRIAL P Rule 7; IN ST TRIAL P Rule 8; IN ST TRIAL P Rule 9.2; IN ST TRIAL P Rule 10.

    f. Signing and verification of pleadings. IN ST TRIAL P Rule 11.

    g. Evidence. IN ST TRIAL P Rule 43.

    h. Judgment on the evidence (directed verdict). IN ST TRIAL P Rule 50.

    i. Findings by the court. IN ST TRIAL P Rule 52.

    j. Summary judgment. IN ST TRIAL P Rule 56.

    k. Motion to correct error. IN ST TRIAL P Rule 59.

    l. Relief from judgment or order. IN ST TRIAL P Rule 60.

    m. Injunctions. IN ST TRIAL P Rule 65; IN ST 34-26-1-7; IN ST 34-26-1-8.

    n. Security; Proceedings against sureties. IN ST TRIAL P Rule 65.1.

    o. Trial court and clerks. IN ST TRIAL P Rule 72.

    p. Hearing of motions. IN ST TRIAL P Rule 73.

    q. Access to court records. IN ST ADMIN Rule 9.

    r. Paper size. IN ST ADMIN Rule 11.

    s. Facsimile transmission. IN ST ADMIN Rule 12.

    t. Electronic filing and electronic service pilot projects. IN ST ADMIN Rule 16.

    u. Sealing of certain records by court; Hearing; Notice. IN ST 5-14-3-5.5.

    v.   Privacy and confidentiality. IN ST 5-2-9-6; IN ST 5-14-3-4; IN ST 6-4.1-5-10; IN ST 6-4.1-12-12; IN ST 6-8.1-7-1; IN ST 11-13-1-8; IN ST 12-23-14-13; IN ST 16-39-3-10; IN ST 16-41-8-1; IN ST 22-4-19-6; IN ST 31-11-1-6; IN ST 31-19-5-23; IN ST 31-19-13-2; IN ST 31-19-19-1; IN ST 31-33-18-1; IN ST 31-39-1-1; IN ST 31-39-1-2; IN ST 33-23-16-16; IN ST 35-34-2-4; IN ST 35-38-1-13; IN ST 35-38-9-1; IN ST ADR Rule 2.11; IN ST ADR Rule 4.4; IN ST ADR Rule 5.6; IN ST JURY Rule 10.

2. *Local rules*

    a.   Applicability and citation of rules. IN ST ALLEN SUPER AND CIR CT CIV Rule AR00-1.

    b.   Proposed orders. IN ST ALLEN SUPER AND CIR CT CIV Rule TR00-1.

    c.   Appearances. IN ST ALLEN SUPER AND CIR CT CIV Rule 3.1-1.

    d.   Consent to alternate service. IN ST ALLEN SUPER AND CIR CT CIV Rule 5-1.

    e.   Motions in civil court. IN ST ALLEN SUPER AND CIR CT CIV Rule 7-1.

    f.   Preparation of pleadings. IN ST ALLEN SUPER AND CIR CT CIV Rule 8-1.

    g.   Filing. IN ST ALLEN SUPER AND CIR CT CIV Rule 77-1.

B. Timing

1. *Motion for preliminary injunction.* The injunction may be granted at the time of commencing the action, or at any time afterwards before judgment is rendered in the proceeding. IN ST 34-26-1-7. IN ST TRIAL P Rule 65 does not state when notice must be given. 4 INPRAC R 65(65.2).

    a.   *Filing.* All pleadings and papers subsequent to the complaint which are required to be served upon a party shall be filed with the Court either before service or within a reasonable period of time thereafter. IN ST TRIAL P Rule 5(E)(1).

2. *Service.* A written motion, other than one which may be heard ex parte, and notice of the hearing thereof shall be served not less than five (5) days before the time specified for the hearing, unless a different period is fixed by the Indiana Rules of Trial Procedure or by order of the court. IN ST TRIAL P Rule 6(D).

    a.   *Of supporting affidavits.* When a motion is supported by affidavit, the affidavit shall be served with the motion. IN ST TRIAL P Rule 6(D).

3. *Service of opposition.* Except as otherwise provided in IN ST TRIAL P Rule 59(D), opposing affidavits may be served not less than one (1) day before the hearing, unless the court permits them to be served at some other time. IN ST TRIAL P Rule 6(D).

4. *Computation of time*

    a.   *Generally; Days excluded.* In computing any period of time prescribed or allowed by the Indiana Rules of Trial Procedure, by order of the court, or by any applicable statute, the day of the act, event, or default from which the designated period of time begins to run shall not be included. The last day of the period so computed is to be included unless it is:

        i.   A Saturday,

        ii.   A Sunday,

        iii.   A legal holiday as defined by state statute, or

        iv.   A day the office in which the act is to be done is closed during regular business hours. IN ST TRIAL P Rule 6(A).

    b.   *Short periods.* In any event, the period runs until the end of the next day that is not a Saturday, a Sunday, a legal holiday, or a day on which the office is closed. When the period of time allowed is less than seven (7) days, intermediate Saturdays, Sundays, legal holidays, and days on which the office is closed shall be excluded from the computations. IN ST TRIAL P Rule 6(A).

    c.   *Additional time after service by United States mail.* Whenever a party has the right or is required to do some act or take some proceedings within a prescribed period after the service of a notice or other paper upon him and the notice or paper is served upon him by United States mail, three (3) days shall be added to the prescribed period. IN ST TRIAL P Rule 6(E).

    d. *Enlargement of time.* When an act is required or allowed to be done at or within a specific time by the Indiana Rules of Trial Procedure, the court may at any time for cause shown:

        i. Order the period enlarged, with or without motion or notice, if request therefor is made before the expiration of the period originally prescribed or extended by a previous order; or

        ii. Upon motion made after the expiration of the specific period, permit the act to be done where the failure to act was the result of excusable neglect; but, the court may not extend the time for taking any action for judgment on the evidence under IN ST TRIAL P Rule 50(A), amendment of findings and judgment under IN ST TRIAL P Rule 52(B), to correct errors under IN ST TRIAL P Rule 59(C), statement in opposition to motion to correct error under IN ST TRIAL P Rule 59(E), or to obtain relief from final judgment under IN ST TRIAL P Rule 60(B), except to the extent and under the conditions stated in those rules. IN ST TRIAL P Rule 6(B).

C. General Requirements

1. *Motions, generally.* Unless made during a hearing or trial, or otherwise ordered by the court, an application to the court for an order shall be made by written motion. The motion shall state the grounds therefor and the relief or order sought. IN ST TRIAL P Rule 7(B).

    a. *Motions as distinct from pleadings.* Motions and responses to motions are not pleadings, and allegations contained in a motion are not admissions of a party. 22B INPRAC 7:2; Wachstetter v. County Properties, LLC, 832 N.E.2d 574 (Ind.Ct.App. 2005); Scott County Family YMCA, Inc. v. Hobbs, 817 N.E.2d 603 (Ind.Ct.App. 2004).

    b. *Unopposed motions generally granted.* It is common for a trial court to grant procedural motions, such as motions for enlargement of time, discovery motions, or motions for continuance, unless an objection is filed. 21 INPRAC § 13.8.

2. *Motion for preliminary injunction.* The general purpose of a temporary restraining order and a preliminary injunction is to maintain and preserve the status quo until the merits of the case can be heard. The status quo is the last actual, peaceful and noncontested status which preceded the pending controversy. 4 INPRAC R 65(65.1); Rees v. Panhandle Eastern Pipe Line Co., 176 Ind.App. 597, 377 N.E.2d 640 (Ind.Ct.App. 1978). An injunction does not create or enlarge the rights of a party, it merely protects existing rights and prevents harm to the aggrieved party that cannot be corrected by a final judgment. 22B INPRAC 65:1; Franke v. Honeywell, Inc., 516 N.E.2d 1090 (Ind.Ct.App. 1987); Indiana & Michigan Elec. Co. v. Whitley County Rural Elec. Membership Corp., 161 Ind.App. 492, 316 N.E.2d 584 (Ind.Ct.App. 1974); AGS Capital Corp., Inc. v. Product Action Intern., LLC, 884 N.E.2d 294 (Ind.Ct.App. 2008).

    a. *Injunctions in general.* Whether or not a preliminary injunction should issue rests in the sound discretion of the trial court. Discretion to grant or deny a preliminary injunction is measured by the following factors and the burden lies with the movant to prove each element by a preponderance of the evidence. 4 INPRAC R 65(65.1); Crossmann Communities, Inc. v. Dean, 767 N.E.2d 1035, 1040 (Ind.Ct.App. 2002); Mercho-Roushdi Corp. v. Blatchford, 742 N.E.2d 519, 524 (Ind.Ct.App. 2001).

        i. If the movant fails to prove any of these requirements, the trial court's grant of an injunction is an abuse of discretion. 4 INPRAC R 65(65.1); Ind. Family and Soc. Servs. Admin. v. Walgreen Co., 769 N.E.2d 158, 161 (Ind. 2002):

- Whether the plaintiff's remedies at law are inadequate and the plaintiff will suffer irreparable harm pending the resolution of the substantive action if the injunction does not issue;

- Whether the plaintiff has demonstrated at least a reasonable likelihood of success at trial by establishing a prima facie case;

- Whether the threatened injury to the plaintiff outweighs the threatened harm the grant of the injunction may inflict on the defendant; and

- Whether the public interest would be disserved if the injunction is granted. 4 INPRAC R 65(65.1); Ind. Family and Soc. Servs. Admin. v. Walgreen Co., 769 N.E.2d 158, 161 (Ind. 2002); Daugherty v. Allen, 729 N.E.2d 228, 232 (Ind.Ct.App. 2000);

    ii.   Two (2) sweeping statements about the preliminary injunction often appear:

- Economic injury alone will not warrant the granting of a preliminary injunction. 4 INPRAC R 65(65.1); Wells v. Auberry, 429 N.E.2d 679 (Ind.Ct.App. 1982), and

- Injunctive relief is not appropriate if a remedy for damages is an adequate remedy and the defendant is solvent. 4 INPRAC R 65(65.1); Gaslight and Coke Company v. City of New Albany, 139 Ind. 660, 39 N.E. 462 (1894).

  b. *Consolidation of hearing with trial on merits.* Before or after the commencement of the hearing of an application for a preliminary injunction, the court may order the trial of the action on the merits to be advanced and consolidated with the hearing of the application. Even when this consolidation is not ordered, any evidence received upon an application for a preliminary injunction which would be admissible upon the trial on the merits becomes part of the record on the trial and need not be repeated upon the trial. IN ST TRIAL P Rule 65(A)(2).

    i.   The power of the court to order advancement and consolidation under IN ST TRIAL P Rule 65 is tempered by the due process requirements of fair notice and an opportunity to be heard. 4 INPRAC R 65(65.3); University of Texas v. Camenisch, 451 U.S. 390, 101 S.Ct. 1830, 68 L.Ed.2d 175 (1981). The court is required to give clear notice that consolidation of the trial on the merits with the hearing on the motion for preliminary injunction will be ordered, and the notice must be given at a time which will afford the parties a full opportunity to present their respective cases. 4 INPRAC R 65(65.3); Paris v. U.S. Department of Housing & Urban Dev., 713 F.2d 1341, 1345, (7th Cir. 1983).

  c. *Assignment of cases; Judge to act promptly.* Assignment of cases shall not be affected by the fact that a temporary restraining order or preliminary injunction is sought, but such case shall be assigned promptly and the judge regularly assigned to the case shall act upon and hear all matters relating to temporary restraining orders and preliminary injunctions. The judge shall make himself readily available to consider temporary restraining orders, conduct hearings, fix the manner of giving notice and the time and place for hearings under IN ST TRIAL P Rule 65, and shall act and require the parties to act promptly. IN ST TRIAL P Rule 65(A)(3).

    i.   If the party seeking relief or his attorney by affidavit establishes that the judge assigned to the case is not available or cannot be found to consider an application for a restraining order, to conduct a hearing, or to fix the manner of giving notice and the time and place for a hearing under IN ST TRIAL P Rule 65, he may apply to any other judge in the circuit who shall take all further action with respect to any temporary restraining order or preliminary injunction. If the affidavit establishes that no other judge in the circuit is available or to be found, he may apply to the judge of any adjoining circuit. Unless an order is entered within ten (10) days after the hearing upon the granting, modifying or dissolving of a temporary or preliminary injunction, the relief sought shall be subject to the provisions of IN ST TRIAL P Rule 53.1. IN ST TRIAL P Rule 65(A)(3).

  d. *Modification of orders; Responsive pleadings.* Upon the court's own motion or the motion of any party, orders granting or denying temporary restraining orders or preliminary injunctions may be dissolved, modified, granted or reinstated. Responsive pleadings shall not be required in response to any pleadings or motions relating to temporary restraining orders or preliminary injunctions. IN ST TRIAL P Rule 65(A)(4).

  e. *Form of order by judge.* Every order granting temporary injunction and every restraining order shall include or be accompanied by findings as required by IN ST TRIAL P Rule 52; shall be specific in terms; shall describe in reasonable detail, and not by reference to the complaint or other document, the act or acts sought to be restrained; and is binding only upon the parties to the action, their officers, agents, servants, employees, and attorneys, and upon those persons in active concert or participation with them who receive actual notice of the order by personal service or otherwise. IN ST TRIAL P Rule 65(D).

3. *Security*

  a. *Security requirement.* No restraining order or preliminary injunction shall issue except upon the giving of security by the applicant, in such sum as the court deems proper, for the payment of such costs and damages as may be incurred or suffered by any party who is found to have been wrongfully enjoined or restrained. No such security shall be required of a governmental organization, but such governmental organization shall be responsible for costs and damages as may be incurred or suffered by any party who is found to have been wrongfully enjoined or restrained. IN ST TRIAL P Rule 65(C).

  i. The provisions of IN ST TRIAL P Rule 65.1 apply to a surety upon a bond or undertaking under IN ST TRIAL P Rule 65. IN ST TRIAL P Rule 65(C).

 b. *Proceedings against sureties.* Whenever the Indiana Rules of Trial Procedure or other laws require or permit the giving of security by a party to a court action or proceeding, and security is given in the form of a bond or stipulation or other undertaking with one or more sureties, each surety submits himself to the jurisdiction of the court and irrevocably appoints the clerk of the court as his agent upon whom any papers affecting his liability on the bond or undertaking may be served. His liability may be enforced on motion without the necessity of an independent action. The motion and such notice of the motion as the court prescribes may be served on the clerk of the court, who shall forthwith mail copies to the sureties if their addresses are known. IN ST TRIAL P Rule 65.1 applies to bonds or security furnished on appeal, and enforcement shall be in the court to which the case is returned after appeal. IN ST TRIAL P Rule 65.1.

 c. *Bond generally used as security.* IN ST TRIAL P Rule 65(C) speaks only of the giving of security and does not expressly require a surety on a bond. In practice, however, the giving of a bond with an insurance company as surety in the amount set by the court is typically the device used to satisfy this section. 4 INPRAC R 65(65.6).

D. Documents

1. *Required documents*

 a. *Motion and notice.* No preliminary injunction shall be issued without an opportunity for a hearing upon notice to the adverse party. IN ST TRIAL P Rule 65(A)(1). The requirement of notice is satisfied by service of the motion. IN ST TRIAL P Rule 7(B). Refer to the General Requirements section of this document for information on the content of a motion for preliminary injunction.

 b. *Affidavit.* In all applications for an injunction, the complaint or as much of the complaint as pertains to the acts or proceedings to be enjoined, must be verified by affidavit. IN ST 34-26-1-7.

 c. *Security.* No restraining order or preliminary injunction shall issue except upon the giving of security by the applicant, in such sum as the court deems proper, for the payment of such costs and damages as may be incurred or suffered by any party who is found to have been wrongfully enjoined or restrained. IN ST TRIAL P Rule 65(C). Refer to the General Requirements section of this document for more information.

 d. *Proposed order.* Unless local practice provides differently, a party should submit a proposed order with its written motion to be signed by the judge once the motion has been granted. 21 INPRAC § 13.8.

  i. *Copies of proposed orders.* All proposed orders shall be submitted in an original plus a number of copies equal to one (1) more than the number of pro se parties and attorneys of record contained in the prepared proof of notice under IN ST TRIAL P Rule 72(D). IN ST ALLEN SUPER AND CIR CT CIV Rule TR00-1(C).

  ii. *Proof of notice.* The proposed order shall also include a prepared proof of notice, under IN ST TRIAL P Rule 72(D). IN ST ALLEN SUPER AND CIR CT CIV Rule TR00-1(B).

  iii. Refer to the Format section of this document for information on the form and content of the proposed order and the proof of notice.

 e. *Certificate of service.* An attorney or unrepresented party tendering a document to the Clerk for filing shall certify that service has been made, list the parties served, and specify the date and means of service. The certificate of service shall be placed at the end of the document and shall not be separately filed. The separate filing of a certificate of service, however, shall not be grounds for rejecting a document for filing. The Clerk may permit documents to be filed without a certificate of service but shall require prompt filing of a separate certificate of service. IN ST TRIAL P Rule 5(C).

2. *Supplemental documents*

    a. *Supporting evidence.* When a motion is based on facts not appearing of record the court may hear the matter on affidavits presented by the respective parties, but the court may direct that the matter be heard wholly or partly on oral testimony or depositions. IN ST TRIAL P Rule 43(B).

    b. *Brief or memorandum.* If a party desires to file a brief or memorandum in support of any motion, such brief or memorandum shall be filed simultaneously with the motion, and a copy shall be promptly served upon the adverse party. IN ST ALLEN SUPER AND CIR CT CIV Rule 7-1(E).

    c. *Facsimile cover sheet.* Any document sent to the Clerk of the Circuit Court by electronic facsimile transmission shall be accompanied by a cover sheet which states the title of the document, case number, number of pages, identity and voice telephone number of the sending party and instructions for filing. The cover sheet shall contain the signature of the attorney or party, pro se, authorizing the filing. IN ST ADMIN Rule 12(D).

E. Format

1. *Form of motions.* The rules applicable to captions, and the signing and form of pleadings (IN ST TRIAL P Rule 8 through IN ST TRIAL P Rule 11), apply to all motions and other papers provided under the Indiana Rules of Trial Procedure. 22B INPRAC 7:2.

2. *Form of pleadings*

    a. *Caption; Names of parties.* Every pleading shall contain a caption setting forth the name of the court, the title of the action, the file number, and a designation as in IN ST TRIAL P Rule 7(A). In the complaint the title of the action shall include the names of all the parties, but in other pleadings it is sufficient to state the name of the first party on each side with an appropriate indication of other parties. IN ST TRIAL P Rule 10(A).

    b. *Paragraphs; Separate statements.* All averments of a claim or defense shall be made in numbered paragraphs, the contents of each of which shall be limited as far as practicable to a statement of a single set of circumstances, and a paragraph may be referred to by number in all succeeding pleadings. Each claim founded upon a separate transaction or occurrence and each defense other than denials may be stated in a separate count or defense whenever a separation facilitates the clear presentation of the matters set forth. IN ST TRIAL P Rule 10(B).

    c. *Adoption by reference; Exhibits.* Statements in a pleading may be adopted by reference in a different part of the same pleading or in another pleading or in any motion. A copy of any written instrument which is an exhibit to a pleading is a part thereof for all purposes. IN ST TRIAL P Rule 10(C).

    d. *Citation.* Allen County Superior and Circuit court rules may be cited as L.R. _____. The Indiana Rules of Trial Procedure are hereinafter referred to as T.R. _____. IN ST ALLEN SUPER AND CIR CT CIV Rule AR00-1(B).

    e. *Paper.* All pleadings must be printed on white paper. IN ST ALLEN SUPER AND CIR CT CIV Rule 8-1(A).

    f. *Spacing.* The lines shall be double spaced except for quotations, which shall be indented and single-spaced. IN ST ALLEN SUPER AND CIR CT CIV Rule 8-1(A).

    g. *Photocopies.* Photocopies are acceptable if legible. IN ST ALLEN SUPER AND CIR CT CIV Rule 8-1(A).

    h. *Margins and binding.* Margins shall be one to one and one-half (1-1 1/2) inches on the left side and one-half (1/2) inch on the right. IN ST ALLEN SUPER AND CIR CT CIV Rule 8-1(B).

        i. Binding or stapling shall be at the top left and at no other place. IN ST ALLEN SUPER AND CIR CT CIV Rule 8-1(B).

        ii. Covers or backing shall not be used. IN ST ALLEN SUPER AND CIR CT CIV Rule 8-1(B).

    i. *Flat filing.* The files of the Clerk of the Court shall be kept under the "flat filing" system. All pleadings presented for filing with the Clerk or Court shall be flat and unfolded. Only the original of any pleading shall be placed in the Court file. IN ST ALLEN SUPER AND CIR CT CIV Rule 77-1(A).

j. *Handwritten pleadings.* Handwritten pleadings may be accepted for filing in the discretion of the Court. IN ST ALLEN SUPER AND CIR CT CIV Rule 8-1(A).

3. *Size of papers for filing.* Effective January 1, 1992, all pleadings, copies, motions and documents filed with any trial court or appellate level court, typed or printed, with the exception of exhibits and existing wills, shall be prepared on eight and one-half by eleven inch (8 1/2" x 11") size paper. IN ST ADMIN Rule 11.

4. *Form of proposed orders*

   a. *Form, caption, and title.* Any proposed order shall be a document that is separate and apart from the motion or application to which it relates and shall contain a caption showing the name of the court, the case number assigned to the case and the title of the case as shown by the complaint. IN ST ALLEN SUPER AND CIR CT CIV Rule TR00-1(B). If there are multiple parties, the title may be shortened to include only the first name plaintiff and defendant with appropriate indication that there are additional parties. IN ST ALLEN SUPER AND CIR CT CIV Rule TR00-1(B).

   b. *Paper.* The proposed order shall be on white paper, eight and one half by eleven inches (8 1/2" x 11") in size, and each page shall be numbered. IN ST ALLEN SUPER AND CIR CT CIV Rule TR00-1(B).

   c. *Signature line.* On the last page of the proposed order there shall be a line for the signature of the judge under which shall be typed "Judge, Allen Superior Court" or "Judge, Allen Circuit Court", whichever is applicable, to the left of which shall be the following: "Dated _____". IN ST ALLEN SUPER AND CIR CT CIV Rule TR00-1(B).

   d. *Allowance of space for clerk.* To allow space for the Clerk to make entries on the proposed order to show compliance with the notice requirements of IN ST TRIAL P Rule 72(D), the lower four (4) inches of the last page of the proposed order shall be left blank. IN ST ALLEN SUPER AND CIR CT CIV Rule TR00-1(B).

   e. *Proof of notice required.* The proposed order shall also include a prepared proof of notice, under IN ST TRIAL P Rule 72(D). The proof of notice shall conform to the format show in IN ST ALLEN SUPER AND CIR CT CIV Rule TR00-1(B). IN ST ALLEN SUPER AND CIR CT CIV Rule TR00-1(B).

5. *Signature requirements*

   a. *Signature of attorney.* Every pleading or motion of a party represented by an attorney shall be signed by at least one (1) attorney of record in his individual name, whose address, telephone number, and attorney number shall be stated, except that this provision shall not apply to pleadings and motions made and transcribed at the trial or a hearing before the judge and received by him in such form. IN ST TRIAL P Rule 11(A). All pleadings to be signed by an attorney shall contain the written signature of the individual attorney, the attorney's printed name, Supreme Court Attorney Number, the name of the attorney's law firm, the attorney's address, telephone number, and a designation of the party for whom the attorney appears. IN ST ALLEN SUPER AND CIR CT CIV Rule 8-1(C). For the recommended signature format, refer to IN ST ALLEN SUPER AND CIR CT CIV Rule 8-1(C).

      i. The signature of an attorney constitutes a certificate by him that he has read the pleadings; that to the best of his knowledge, information, and belief, there is good ground to support it; and that it is not interposed for delay. IN ST TRIAL P Rule 11(A).

      ii. If a pleading or motion is not signed or is signed with intent to defeat the purpose of the rule, it may be stricken as sham and false and the action may proceed as though the pleading had not been served. IN ST TRIAL P Rule 11(A).

      iii. For a willful violation of IN ST TRIAL P Rule 11 an attorney may be subjected to appropriate disciplinary action. Similar action may be taken if scandalous or indecent matter is inserted. IN ST TRIAL P Rule 11(A).

      iv. Neither printed signatures, nor facsimile signatures shall be accepted on original documents. IN ST ALLEN SUPER AND CIR CT CIV Rule 8-1(C).

    v.   Facsimile signatures are permitted on copies. IN ST ALLEN SUPER AND CIR CT CIV Rule 8-1(C).

b. *Signature of unrepresented party.* A party who is not represented by an attorney shall sign his pleading and state his address. IN ST TRIAL P Rule 11(A).

c. *Verification not generally required.* Except when specifically required by rule, pleadings or motions need not be verified or accompanied by affidavit. The rule in equity that the averments of an answer under oath must be overcome by the testimony of two (2) witnesses or of one (1) witness sustained by corroborating circumstances is abolished. IN ST TRIAL P Rule 11(A).

d. *Verification by affirmation or representation.* When in connection with any civil or special statutory proceeding it is required that any pleading, motion, petition, supporting affidavit, or other document of any kind, be verified, or that an oath be taken, it shall be sufficient if the subscriber simply affirms the truth of the matter to be verified by an affirmation or representation. IN ST TRIAL P Rule 11(B). IN ST TRIAL P Rule 11(B) states that the affirmation or representation should be in substantially the following language: "I (we) affirm, under the penalties for perjury, that the foregoing representation(s) is (are) true. (Signed) _____."

    i.   Any person who falsifies an affirmation or representation of fact shall be subject to the same penalties as are prescribed by law for the making of a false affidavit. IN ST TRIAL P Rule 11(B).

e. *Verified pleadings, motions, and affidavits as evidence.* Pleadings, motions and affidavits accompanying or in support of such pleadings or motions when required to be verified or under oath shall be accepted as a representation that the signer had personal knowledge thereof or reasonable cause to believe the existence of the facts or matters stated or alleged therein; and, if otherwise competent or acceptable as evidence, may be admitted as evidence of the facts or matters stated or alleged therein when it is so provided in the Indiana Rules of Trial Procedure, by statute or other law, or to the extent the writing or signature expressly purports to be made upon the signer's personal knowledge. When such pleadings, motions and affidavits are verified or under oath they shall not require other or greater proof on the part of the adverse party than if not verified or not under oath unless expressly provided otherwise by the Indiana Rules of Trial Procedure, statute or other law. Affidavits upon motions for summary judgment under IN ST TRIAL P Rule 56 and in denial of execution under IN ST TRIAL P Rule 9.2 shall be made upon personal knowledge. IN ST TRIAL P Rule 11(C).

6. *Information excluded from public access.* Every document filed in a case shall separately identify information excluded from public access pursuant to IN ST ADMIN Rule 9(G)(1) as follows:

a. Whole documents that are excluded from public access pursuant to IN ST ADMIN Rule 9(G)(1) shall be tendered on light green paper or have a light green coversheet attached to the document, marked "Not for Public Access" or "Confidential." IN ST TRIAL P Rule 5(G)(1).

b. When only a portion of a document contains information excluded from public access pursuant to IN ST ADMIN Rule 9(G)(1), said information shall be omitted [or redacted] from the filed document, and set forth on a separate accompanying document on light green paper conspicuously marked "Not for Public Access" or "Confidential" and clearly designated [or identifying] the caption and number of the case and the document and location within the document to which the redacted material pertains. IN ST TRIAL P Rule 5(G)(2).

c. With respect to documents filed in electronic format, the trial court, by local rule, may provide for compliance with IN ST TRIAL P Rule 5 in manner that separates and protects access to information excluded from public access. IN ST TRIAL P Rule 5(G)(3).

d. IN ST TRIAL P Rule 5(G) does not apply to a record sealed by the court pursuant to IN ST 5-14-3-5.5 or otherwise, nor to records, documents, or information filed in cases to which public access is prohibited pursuant to IN ST ADMIN Rule 9(G). IN ST TRIAL P Rule 5(G)(4).

e. The following information in case records is excluded from public access and is confidential:

    i.   Information that is excluded from public access pursuant to federal law;

ii. Information that is excluded from public access as declared confidential by Indiana statute or other court rule, including without limitation:

- All adoption records created after July 8, 1941, as declared confidential by IN ST 31-19-19-1, et seq., except those specifically declared open by IN ST 31-19-13-2(2);

- All records relating to chancroid, chlamydia, gonorrhea, hepatitis, human immunodeficiency virus (HIV), Lymphogranuloma venereum, syphilis, tuberculosis, as declared confidential by IN ST 16-41-8-1, et seq.;

- All records relating to child abuse as declared confidential by IN ST 31-33-18-1, et seq.;

- All records relating to drug tests as declared confidential by IN ST 5-14-3-4(a)(9);

- Records of grand jury proceedings as declared confidential by IN ST 35-34-2-4;

- Records of juvenile proceedings as declared confidential by IN ST 31-39-1-2, except those specifically open under statute;

- All paternity records created after July 1, 1941 as declared confidential by IN ST 31-14-11-15, IN ST 31-19-5-23, IN ST 31-39-1-1 and IN ST 31-39-1-2 [Editor's note: IN ST 31-14-11-15 was repealed effective May 9, 2013];

- All pre-sentence reports as declared confidential by IN ST 35-38-1-13;

- Written petitions to permit marriages without consent and orders directing the Clerk of Court to issue a marriage license to underage persons, as declared confidential by IN ST 31-11-1-6;

- Only those arrest warrants, search warrants, indictments and informations ordered confidential by the trial judge, prior to return of duly executed service as declared confidential by IN ST 5-14-3-4(b)(1);

- All medical, mental health, or tax records unless determined by law or regulation of any governmental custodian not to be confidential, released by the subject of such records, or declared by a court of competent jurisdiction to be essential to the resolution of litigation as declared confidential by IN ST 16-39-3-10, IN ST 6-4.1-5-10, IN ST 6-4.1-12-12, and IN ST 6-8.1-7-1;

- Personal information relating to jurors or prospective jurors, other than for the use of the parties and counsel, pursuant to IN ST JURY Rule 10;

- Information relating to protection from abuse orders, no-contact orders and workplace violence restraining orders as declared confidential by IN ST 5-2-9-6, et seq.;

- Mediation proceedings pursuant to IN ST ADR Rule 2.11, Mini-Trial proceedings pursuant to IN ST ADR Rule 4.4(C), and Summary Jury Trials pursuant to IN ST ADR Rule 5.6;

- Information in probation files pursuant to the Probation Standards promulgated by the Judicial Conference of Indiana pursuant to IN ST 11-13-1-8(b);

- Information deemed confidential pursuant to the Rules for Court Administered Alcohol and Drug Programs promulgated by the Judicial Conference of Indiana pursuant to IN ST 12-23-14-13;

- Information deemed confidential pursuant to the Problem-Solving Court Rules promulgated by the Judicial Conference of Indiana pursuant to IN ST 33-23-16-16;

- All records of the Department of workforce Development as declared confidential by IN ST 22-4-19-6;

- Information regarding interception of electronic communications that is sealed or deemed confidential as set forth in IN ST 35-33.5-2-1, et seq.

iii. Information excluded from public access by specific court order;

iv. Complete Social Security Numbers of living persons;

    v.   With the exception of names, information such as addresses, phone numbers, and dates of birth which explicitly identifies:

- Natural persons who are witnesses or victims (not including defendants) in criminal, domestic violence, stalking, sexual assault, juvenile, or civil protection order proceedings, provided that juveniles who are victims of sex crimes shall be identified by initials only;

- Places of residence of judicial officers, clerks and other employees of courts and clerks of court, unless the person or persons about whom the information pertains waives confidentiality;

    vi.   Complete account numbers of specific assets, loans, bank accounts, credit cards, and personal identification numbers (PINs);

    vii.   All orders of expungement entered in criminal or juvenile proceedings, orders to restrict access to criminal history information pursuant to IN ST 35-38-5-5.5 or IN ST 35-38-8-5 and records excluded from public access by such orders, and information related to infractions that is excluded from public access pursuant to IN ST 34-28-5-15 or IN ST 34-28-5-16 [Editor's note: IN ST 35-38-5-5.5, IN ST 35-38-8-5 and IN ST 34-28-5-16 were repealed effective July 1, 2013; for information on orders restricting access to criminal history, refer to IN ST 35-38-9-1, et seq.];

    viii.   All personal notes and e-mail, and deliberative material, of judges, jurors, court staff and judicial agencies, and information recorded in personal data assistants (PDA's) or organizers and personal calendars. IN ST ADMIN Rule 9(G)(1).

F. Filing and Service Requirements

1. *Filing requirements.* Except as otherwise provided in IN ST TRIAL P Rule 5(E)(2), all pleadings and papers subsequent to the complaint which are required to be served upon a party shall be filed with the Court either before service or within a reasonable period of time thereafter. IN ST TRIAL P Rule 5(E)(1).

    a.   *Filing with the court defined.* The filing of pleadings, motions, and other papers with the court as required by the Indiana Rules of Trial Procedure shall be made by one of the following methods:

        i.   Delivery to the clerk of the court;

        ii.   Sending by electronic transmission under the procedure adopted pursuant to IN ST ADMIN Rule 12;

        iii.   Mailing to the clerk by registered, certified or express mail return receipt requested;

        iv.   Depositing with any third-party commercial carrier for delivery to the clerk within three (3) calendar days, cost prepaid, properly addressed;

        v.   If the court so permits, filing with the judge, in which event the judge shall note thereon the filing date and forthwith transmit them to the office of the clerk; or

        vi.   Electronic filing, as approved by the Division of State Court Administration pursuant to IN ST ADMIN Rule 16. IN ST TRIAL P Rule 5(F).

        vii.   Filing by registered or certified mail and by third-party commercial carrier shall be complete upon mailing or deposit. IN ST TRIAL P Rule 5(F).

    b.   *Facsimile filing*

        i.   *Generally.* In counties where a majority of judges of the courts of record, by posted local rule, have authorized electronic facsimile filing and designated a telephone number to receive such transmissions, pleadings, motions, and other papers may be sent to the Clerk of Circuit Court by electronic facsimile transmission for filing in any case, provided:

- Such matter does not exceed ten (10) pages, including the cover sheet;

- Such matter does not require the payment of fees other than the electronic facsimile transcription fee set forth in IN ST ADMIN Rule 12(E);

- The sending party creates at the time of transmission a machine generated log for such transmission; and

- The original document and the transmission log are maintained by the sending party for the duration of the litigation. IN ST ADMIN Rule 12(B).

ii. *Time of filing.* During normal, posted business hours, the time of filing shall be the time the duplicate document is produced in the office of the Clerk of the Circuit Court. Duplicate documents received at all other times shall be filed as of the next normal business day. IN ST ADMIN Rule 12(C).

- If the receiving fax machine endorses its own time and date stamp upon the transmitted documents and the receiving machine produces a delivery receipt which is electronically created and transmitted to the sending party, the time of filing shall be the date and time recorded on the transmitted document by the receiving fax machine. IN ST ADMIN Rule 12(C).

c. *Proof of filing.* Any party filing any paper by any method other than personal delivery to the clerk shall retain proof of filing. IN ST TRIAL P Rule 5(F).

2. *Service requirements.* Unless otherwise provided by the Indiana Rules of Trial Procedure or an order of the court, each party and special judge, if any, shall be served with: (1) every order required by its terms to be served; (2) every pleading subsequent to the original complaint; (3) every written motion except one which may be heard ex parte; (4) every brief submitted to the trial court; (5) every paper relating to discovery required to be served upon a party; and (6) every written notice, appearance, demand, offer of judgment, designation of record on appeal, or similar paper. IN ST TRIAL P Rule 5(A).

a. *Methods of service*

i. *Personal service.* Whenever a party is represented by an attorney of record, service shall be made upon such attorney unless service upon the party himself is ordered by the court. Service upon the attorney or party shall be made by delivering or mailing a copy of the papers to the last known address or where an attorney or party has consented to service by fax or e-mail, as provided in IN ST TRIAL P Rule 3.1(A)(4), by faxing or e-mailing a copy of the documents to the fax number or e-mail address set out in the appearance form or correction as required by IN ST TRIAL P Rule 3.1(E). IN ST TRIAL P Rule 5(B). Delivery of a copy within IN ST TRIAL P Rule 5 means:

- Offering or tendering it to the attorney or party and stating the nature of the papers being served. Refusal to accept an offered or tendered document is a waiver of any objection to the sufficiency or adequacy of service of that document;

- Leaving it at his office with a clerk or other person in charge thereof, or if there is no one in charge, leaving it in a conspicuous place therein; or

- If the office is closed, by leaving it at his dwelling house or usual place of abode with some person of suitable age and discretion then residing therein; or,

- Leaving it at some other suitable place, selected by the attorney upon whom service is being made, pursuant to duly promulgated local rule. IN ST TRIAL P Rule 5(B)(1).

ii. *Service by mail.* If service is made by mail, the papers shall be deposited in the United States mail addressed to the person on whom they are being served, with postage prepaid. Service shall be deemed complete upon mailing. Proof of service of all papers permitted to be mailed may be made by written acknowledgment of service, by affidavit of the person who mailed the papers, or by certificate of an attorney. It shall be the duty of attorneys when entering their appearance in a cause or when filing pleadings or papers therein, to have noted in the Chronological Case Summary or said pleadings or papers so filed the address and telephone number of their office. Service by delivery or by mail at such address shall be deemed sufficient and complete. IN ST TRIAL P Rule 5(B)(2).

iii. *Service by fax or e-mail.* A party who has consented to service by fax or e-mail may be served as follows:

- Service by e-mail shall be made by attaching the document being served in .pdf format. Discovery documents must also be served in accordance with IN ST TRIAL P Rule 26(A). IN ST TRIAL P Rule 5(B)(3)(a).

- Service by fax shall be deemed complete upon generation of a transmission record indicating the successful transmission of the entire document, except as provided in IN ST TRIAL P Rule 5(B)(3)(d). IN ST TRIAL P Rule 5(B)(3)(b).

- Service by e-mail shall be deemed complete upon transmission, except as provided in IN ST TRIAL P Rule 5(B)(3)(d). IN ST TRIAL P Rule 5(B)(3)(c).

- Service by fax or e-mail that occurs on a Saturday, Sunday, legal holiday, or day the court or agency in which the matter is pending is closed or after 5:00 PM local time of the recipient shall be deemed complete the next day that is not a Saturday, Sunday, legal holiday, or day that the court or agency in which the matter is pending is not closed. IN ST TRIAL P Rule 5(B)(3)(d).

 iv. *Consent to alternate service.* Any Allen County Attorney or any Allen County law firm may, without charge, maintain an assigned Courthouse box in the library of the Allen County Courthouse for receipt of notices, pleadings, process orders, or other communications from the Court, the Clerk, and other attorneys or law firms. IN ST ALLEN SUPER AND CIR CT CIV Rule 5-1(A). For more information concerning the use of courthouse boxes, refer to IN ST ALLEN SUPER AND CIR CT CIV Rule 5-1.

b. *Serving numerous defendants.* In any action in which there are unusually large numbers of defendants, the court, upon motion or of its own initiative, may order:

 i. That service of the pleadings of the defendants and replies thereto need not be made as between the defendants;

- That any cross-claim, counterclaim, or matter constituting an avoidance or affirmative defense contained therein shall be deemed to be denied or avoided by all other parties; and

- That the filing of any such pleading and service thereof upon the plaintiff constitutes due notice of it to the parties. IN ST TRIAL P Rule 5(D).

 ii. A copy of every such order shall be served upon the parties in such manner and form as the court directs. IN ST TRIAL P Rule 5(D).

c. *Service on parties in default for failure to appear.* No service need be made on parties in default for failure to appear, except that pleadings asserting new or additional claims for relief against them shall be served upon them in the manner provided by service of summons in IN ST TRIAL P Rule 4. IN ST TRIAL P Rule 5(A).

G. Hearings

1. *Hearing on motion.* Unless local conditions make it impracticable, each judge shall establish regular times and places, at intervals sufficiently frequent for the prompt dispatch of business, at which motions requiring notice and hearing may be heard and disposed of; but the judge at any time or place and on such notice, if any, as he considers reasonable may make order for the advancement, conduct, and hearing of actions. To expedite its business the court may direct the submission and determination of motions without oral hearing upon brief written statements of reasons in support and opposition, or direct or permit hearings by telephone conference call with all attorneys or other similar means of communication. IN ST TRIAL P Rule 73(A).

a. *Setting motions for hearing.* Except for the motions described in IN ST ALLEN SUPER AND CIR CT CIV Rule 7-1(E), all motions shall be set for hearing. IN ST ALLEN SUPER AND CIR CT CIV Rule 7-1(A). [Editor's note: While IN ST ALLEN SUPER AND CIR CT CIV Rule 7-1(A) refers to IN ST ALLEN SUPER AND CIR CT CIV Rule 7-1(E) as relating to hearings on motions, that reference is likely intended to be to IN ST ALLEN SUPER AND CIR CT CIV Rule 7-1(D).]

 i. It shall be the responsibility of the moving party to request the date of such hearing from the Judicial Assistant, or if the case has already been assigned to a Judge, from the Judicial Law Clerk of the assigned Judge. IN ST ALLEN SUPER AND CIR CT CIV Rule 7-1(A).

b. *Responsibility for notice of hearing.* It shall be the responsibility of the moving party to give notice to all other parties of hearings scheduled on motions. IN ST ALLEN SUPER AND CIR CT CIV Rule 7-1(I).

2. *Presentation of evidence.* On the hearing of an application for a restraining order or temporary injunction, each party may read affidavits or documentary or record evidence. IN ST 34-26-1-8.

H. Forms

1. Motion for Preliminary Injunction Forms for Indiana

a. Prayer in complaint; For preliminary injunction. 5 INPRAC § 3:13.20.

b. Motion for preliminary injunction. 5 INPRAC § 3:13.40.

c. Notice of motion for preliminary injunction. 11 INPRAC § 97.14.

d. Undertaking as security to support granting of injunction. 11 INPRAC § 97.14.1.

e. Findings of fact in support of injunction. 11 INPRAC § 97.14.2.

f. Motion to dissolve temporary restraining order. 11 INPRAC § 97.14.3.

g. Motion for contempt for violation of injunction. 11 INPRAC § 97.14.4.

h. Motion for preliminary injunction. 11 INPRAC § 97.15.

i. Preliminary injunction. 11 INPRAC § 97.16.

j. Motion to vacate preliminary injunction; Failure to post bond. 11 INPRAC § 97.17.

k. Motion to vacate preliminary injunction; Another form. 11 INPRAC § 97.18.

l. Certificate of service; Personal service. 9 INPRAC § 5.7.

m. Certificate of service; First class mail. 9 INPRAC § 5.8.

2. Official Motion for preliminary Injunction Forms for Allen County

a. Consent to alternate service. IN ST ALLEN SUPER AND CIR CT CIV App. A.

I. Checklist

(I) ❑ Matters to be considered by moving party

   (a) ❑ Required documents

      (1) ❑ Motion and notice

      (2) ❑ Affidavit

      (3) ❑ Security

      (4) ❑ Proposed order

      (5) ❑ Certificate of service

   (b) ❑ Supplemental documents

      (1) ❑ Supporting evidence

      (2) ❑ Brief or memorandum

      (3) ❑ Facsimile cover sheet

   (c) ❑ Timing

      (1) ❑ The injunction may be granted at the time of commencing the action, or at any time afterwards before judgment is rendered in the proceeding

      (2) ❑ A written motion, other than one which may be heard ex parte, and notice of the hearing thereof shall be served not less than five (5) days before the time specified for the hearing, unless a different period is fixed by the Indiana Rules of Trial Procedure or by order of the court

      (3) ❑ All pleadings and papers subsequent to the complaint which are required to be served upon a party shall be filed with the Court either before service or within a reasonable period of time thereafter

(II) ❑ Matters to be considered by the responding party

    (a) ❑ Required documents

        (1) ❑ Opposition

        (2) ❑ Certificate of service

    (b) ❑ Supplemental documents

        (1) ❑ Supporting evidence

        (2) ❑ Brief or memorandum

        (3) ❑ Proposed order

        (4) ❑ Facsimile cover sheet

    (c) ❑ Timing

        (1) ❑ Except as otherwise provided in IN ST TRIAL P Rule 59(D), opposing affidavits may be served not less than one (1) day before the hearing, unless the court permits them to be served at some other time

Motions, Oppositions and Replies
Motion to Dismiss for Failure to State a Claim

Document Last Updated October 2013

A. Applicable Rules

  1. *State rules*

    a. Appearance. IN ST TRIAL P Rule 3.1.

    b. Process. IN ST TRIAL P Rule 4.

    c. Service and filing of pleadings and other papers. IN ST TRIAL P Rule 5.

    d. Time. IN ST TRIAL P Rule 6.

    e. Pleadings. IN ST TRIAL P Rule 7; IN ST TRIAL P Rule 8; IN ST TRIAL P Rule 9.2; IN ST TRIAL P Rule 10; IN ST TRIAL P Rule 11.

    f. Defenses and objections; When and how presented; By pleading or motion; Motion for judgment on the pleadings. IN ST TRIAL P Rule 12.

    g. Amended and supplemental pleadings. IN ST TRIAL P Rule 15.

    h. Joinder of person needed for just adjudication. IN ST TRIAL P Rule 19.

    i. Evidence. IN ST TRIAL P Rule 43.

    j. Judgment on the evidence (directed verdict). IN ST TRIAL P Rule 50.

    k. Findings by the court. IN ST TRIAL P Rule 52.

    l. Summary judgment. IN ST TRIAL P Rule 56.

    m. Motion to correct error. IN ST TRIAL P Rule 59.

    n. Relief from judgment or order. IN ST TRIAL P Rule 60.

    o. Trial court and clerks. IN ST TRIAL P Rule 72.

    p. Hearing of motions. IN ST TRIAL P Rule 73.

    q. Access to court records. IN ST ADMIN Rule 9.

    r. Paper size. IN ST ADMIN Rule 11.

    s. Facsimile transmission. IN ST ADMIN Rule 12.

    t. Electronic filing and electronic service pilot projects. IN ST ADMIN Rule 16.

u. Sealing of certain records by court; Hearing; Notice. IN ST 5-14-3-5.5.

v. Privacy and confidentiality. IN ST 5-2-9-6; IN ST 5-14-3-4; IN ST 6-4.1-5-10; IN ST 6-4.1-12-12; IN ST 6-8.1-7-1; IN ST 11-13-1-8; IN ST 12-23-14-13; IN ST 16-39-3-10; IN ST 16-41-8-1; IN ST 22-4-19-6; IN ST 31-11-1-6; IN ST 31-19-5-23; IN ST 31-19-13-2; IN ST 31-19-19-1; IN ST 31-33-18-1; IN ST 31-39-1-1; IN ST 31-39-1-2; IN ST 33-23-16-16; IN ST 35-34-2-4; IN ST 35-38-1-13; IN ST 35-38-9-1; IN ST ADR Rule 2.11; IN ST ADR Rule 4.4; IN ST ADR Rule 5.6; IN ST JURY Rule 10.

2. *Local rules*

  a. Proposed orders. IN ST ALLEN SUPER AND CIR CT CIV Rule TR00-1.

  b. Applicability and citation of rules. IN ST ALLEN SUPER AND CIR CT CIV Rule AR00-1.

  c. Appearances. IN ST ALLEN SUPER AND CIR CT CIV Rule 3.1-1.

  d. Consent to alternate service. IN ST ALLEN SUPER AND CIR CT CIV Rule 5-1.

  e. Motions in civil court. IN ST ALLEN SUPER AND CIR CT CIV Rule 7-1.

  f. Preparation of pleadings. IN ST ALLEN SUPER AND CIR CT CIV Rule 8-1.

  g. Filing. IN ST ALLEN SUPER AND CIR CT CIV Rule 77-1.

B. Timing

1. *Timing of motion to dismiss for failure to state a claim.* A motion making any of the defenses listed in IN ST TRIAL P Rule 12(B) shall be made before pleading if a further pleading is permitted or within twenty (20) days after service of the prior pleading if none is required. IN ST TRIAL P Rule 12(B).

  a. *Time to file a responsive pleading.* A responsive pleading required under the Indiana Rules of Trial Procedure, shall be served within twenty (20) days after service of the prior pleading. IN ST TRIAL P Rule 6(C).

  b. *Filing.* All pleadings and papers subsequent to the complaint which are required to be served upon a party shall be filed with the Court either before service or within a reasonable period of time thereafter. IN ST TRIAL P Rule 5(E)(1).

2. *Service.* A written motion, other than one which may be heard ex parte, and notice of the hearing thereof shall be served not less than five (5) days before the time specified for the hearing, unless a different period is fixed by the Indiana Rules of Trial Procedure or by order of the court. IN ST TRIAL P Rule 6(D).

  a. *Of supporting affidavits.* When a motion is supported by affidavit, the affidavit shall be served with the motion; and,

3. *Service of opposition.* Except as otherwise provided in IN ST TRIAL P Rule 59(D), opposing affidavits may be served not less than one (1) day before the hearing, unless the court permits them to be served at some other time. IN ST TRIAL P Rule 6(D).

4. *Computation of time*

  a. *Generally; Days excluded.* In computing any period of time prescribed or allowed by the Indiana Rules of Trial Procedure, by order of the court, or by any applicable statute, the day of the act, event, or default from which the designated period of time begins to run shall not be included. The last day of the period so computed is to be included unless it is:

    i. A Saturday,

    ii. A Sunday,

    iii. A legal holiday as defined by state statute, or

    iv. A day the office in which the act is to be done is closed during regular business hours. IN ST TRIAL P Rule 6(A).

  b. *Short periods.* In any event, the period runs until the end of the next day that is not a Saturday, a Sunday, a legal holiday, or a day on which the office is closed. When the period of time allowed is less than seven (7) days, intermediate Saturdays, Sundays, legal holidays, and days on which the office is closed shall be excluded from the computations. IN ST TRIAL P Rule 6(A).

c. *Additional time after service by United States mail.* Whenever a party has the right or is required to do some act or take some proceedings within a prescribed period after the service of a notice or other paper upon him and the notice or paper is served upon him by United States mail, three (3) days shall be added to the prescribed period. IN ST TRIAL P Rule 6(E).

d. *Enlargement of time.* When an act is required or allowed to be done at or within a specific time by the Indiana Rules of Trial Procedure, the court may at any time for cause shown:

i. Order the period enlarged, with or without motion or notice, if request therefor is made before the expiration of the period originally prescribed or extended by a previous order; or

ii. Upon motion made after the expiration of the specific period, permit the act to be done where the failure to act was the result of excusable neglect; but, the court may not extend the time for taking any action for judgment on the evidence under IN ST TRIAL P Rule 50(A), amendment of findings and judgment under IN ST TRIAL P Rule 52(B), to correct errors under IN ST TRIAL P Rule 59(C), statement in opposition to motion to correct error under IN ST TRIAL P Rule 59(E), or to obtain relief from final judgment under IN ST TRIAL P Rule 60(B), except to the extent and under the conditions stated in those rules. IN ST TRIAL P Rule 6(B).

C. General Requirements

1. *Motions, generally.* Unless made during a hearing or trial, or otherwise ordered by the court, an application to the court for an order shall be made by written motion. The motion shall state the grounds therefor and the relief or order sought. IN ST TRIAL P Rule 7(B).

a. *Motions as distinct from pleadings.* Motions and responses to motions are not pleadings, and allegations contained in a motion are not admissions of a party. 22B INPRAC 7:2; Wachstetter v. County Properties, LLC, 832 N.E.2d 574 (Ind.Ct.App. 2005); Scott County Family YMCA, Inc. v. Hobbs, 817 N.E.2d 603 (Ind.Ct.App. 2004).

b. *Unopposed motions generally granted.* It is common for a trial court to grant procedural motions, such as motions for enlargement of time, discovery motions, or motions for continuance, unless an objection is filed. 21 INPRAC § 13.8.

2. *Motion to dismiss for failure to state a claim.* Every defense, in law or fact, to a claim for relief in any pleading, whether a claim, counterclaim, cross-claim, or third-party claim, shall be asserted in the responsive pleading thereto if one is required; except that at the option of the pleader, the defense of failure to state a claim upon which relief can be granted, which shall include failure to name the real party in interest under IN ST TRIAL P Rule 17, may be made by motion. IN ST TRIAL P Rule 12(B)(6). A motion under IN ST TRIAL P Rule 12(B)(6) is intended to test the legal sufficiency of a claim rather than the facts supporting that claim. 1A INPRAC R 12(12.9); Meyers v. Meyers, 861 N.E.2d 704 (Ind. 2007).

a. *How motion made.* A defense of failure to state a claim upon which relief can be granted, a defense of failure to join an indispensable party under IN ST TRIAL P Rule 19(B), and an objection of failure to state a legal defense to a claim may be made in any pleading permitted or ordered under IN ST TRIAL P Rule 7(A) or by motion for judgment on the pleadings, or at the trial on the merits. IN ST TRIAL P Rule 12(H)(2).

b. *Claim admitted for purpose of motion.* A motion to dismiss for failure to state a claim admits, for the purpose of the motion, the existence of the claim as stated in the complaint, but challenges the plaintiff's right to relief. 9 INPRAC § 42.10; Mills v. American Playground Device Co., 427 N.E.2d 1130 (Ind.Ct.App. 1981). Motions to dismiss under IN ST TRIAL P Rule 12 are disfavored because they undermine the policy that favors deciding cases on their merits. 22 INPRAC § 15.19; Droscha v. Shepherd, 931 N.E.2d 882 (Ind.Ct.App. 2010).

c. *Motion decided on factual allegations of complaint.* The trial court should grant a motion to dismiss under IN ST TRIAL P Rule 12(B)(6) if the facts alleged in the complaint are incapable of supporting relief under any set of circumstances. 1A INPRAC R 12(12.9); McPeek v. McCardle, 888 N.E.2d 171 (Ind. 2008). In determining whether the facts alleged in the complaint are incapable of supporting relief, the court must look only to the complaint and may not resort to any other evidence in the record. When ruling on a motion to dismiss under IN ST TRIAL P Rule 12(B)(6), the court should consider all of the allegations in the complaint to be true and resolve all inferences in favor of the non-moving party. 1A INPRAC R 12(12.9); State v. American Family Voices, Inc., 898 N.E.2d 293 (Ind. 2008); Curtis v. Roob, 891 N.E.2d 577 (Ind.Ct.App. 2008).

d.   *Notice pleading and motions to dismiss.* Although notice pleading requirements under IN ST TRIAL P Rule 8(A) are fairly straightforward, and are well-grounded in Indiana jurisprudence, the mechanism for testing the legal sufficiency of the complaint, IN ST TRIAL P Rule 12(B)(6), has, over time, become somewhat limited because Indiana courts are instructed to dismiss an action under IN ST TRIAL P Rule 12(B)(6) only where the if the alleged facts do not support a claim for relief under any set of circumstances. 1A INPRAC R 12(12.9). Trial judges do not like to grant IN ST TRIAL P Rule 12(B)(6) motions where the claim is an inadequately pleaded complaint, which means a defendant's first meaningful opportunity to challenge a plaintiff's claim is the motion for summary judgment. 1A INPRAC R 12(12.9).

e.   *Conversion to motion for summary judgment.* A motion to dismiss under IN ST TRIAL P Rule 12(B)(6) for failure to state a claim upon which relief and Motion for Judgment on the Pleadings under IN ST TRIAL P Rule 12(C) will be converted into a motion for summary judgment under IN ST TRIAL P Rule 56 if the court considers matters outside the pleadings in deciding those motions. 11 INPRAC § 90.1; Duran v. Komyatte, 490 N.E.2d 388 (Ind.Ct.App. 1986). In such case, all parties shall be given reasonable opportunity to present all material made pertinent to such a motion by IN ST TRIAL P Rule 56. IN ST TRIAL P Rule 12(B).

f.   *Effect of granting of the motion.* When a motion to dismiss is sustained for failure to state a claim under IN ST TRIAL P Rule 12(B)(6) the pleading may be amended once as of right pursuant to IN ST TRIAL P Rule 15(A) within ten (10) days after service of notice of the court's order sustaining the motion and thereafter with permission of the court pursuant to such rule. IN ST TRIAL P Rule 12(B).

3.   *Consolidation and waiver*

a.   *Consolidation of defenses in motion.* A party who makes a motion under IN ST TRIAL P Rule 12 may join with it any other motions herein provided for and then available to him. If a party makes a motion under IN ST TRIAL P Rule 12 but omits therefrom any defense or objection then available to him which IN ST TRIAL P Rule 12 permits to be raised by motion, he shall not thereafter make a motion based on the defense or objection so omitted. He may, however, make such motions as are allowed under IN ST TRIAL P Rule 12(H)(2). IN ST TRIAL P Rule 12(G).

b.   *Waiver or preservation of certain defenses.* No defense or objection is waived by being joined with one or more other defenses or objections in a responsive pleading or motion. IN ST TRIAL P Rule 12(B).

D.   Documents

1.   *Required documents*

a.   *Motion and notice.* The requirement of notice is satisfied by service of the motion. IN ST TRIAL P Rule 7(B). Refer to the General Requirements section of this document for information on the content of a motion to dismiss to dismiss for failure to state a claim.

b.   *Proposed order.* Unless local practice provides differently, a party should submit a proposed order with its written motion to be signed by the judge once the motion has been granted. 21 INPRAC § 13.8.

  i.   *Proposed orders of a motion for dismissal.* Prior to entry by the Court of orders granting motions or applications, the moving party or applicant (or his or her attorney) shall, unless the Court directs otherwise, furnish the Court with proposed orders of a motion for dismissal. IN ST ALLEN SUPER AND CIR CT CIV Rule TR00-1(A)(5).

  ii.   *Copies of proposed orders.* All proposed orders shall be submitted in an original plus a number of copies equal to one (1) more than the number of pro se parties and attorneys of record contained in the prepared proof of notice under IN ST TRIAL P Rule 72(D). IN ST ALLEN SUPER AND CIR CT CIV Rule TR00-1(C).

  iii.   *Proof of notice.* The proposed order shall also include a prepared proof of notice, under IN ST TRIAL P Rule 72(D). IN ST ALLEN SUPER AND CIR CT CIV Rule TR00-1(B).

      iv.   Refer to the Format section of this document for information on the form and content of the proposed order and the proof of notice.

  c. *Certificate of service.* An attorney or unrepresented party tendering a document to the Clerk for filing shall certify that service has been made, list the parties served, and specify the date and means of service. The certificate of service shall be placed at the end of the document and shall not be separately filed. The separate filing of a certificate of service, however, shall not be grounds for rejecting a document for filing. The Clerk may permit documents to be filed without a certificate of service but shall require prompt filing of a separate certificate of service. IN ST TRIAL P Rule 5(C).

2. *Supplemental documents*

  a. *Brief or memorandum.* If a party desires to file a brief or memorandum in support of any motion, such brief or memorandum shall be filed simultaneously with the motion, and a copy shall be promptly served upon the adverse party. IN ST ALLEN SUPER AND CIR CT CIV Rule 7-1(E).

  b. *Facsimile cover sheet.* Any document sent to the Clerk of the Circuit Court by electronic facsimile transmission shall be accompanied by a cover sheet which states the title of the document, case number, number of pages, identity and voice telephone number of the sending party and instructions for filing. The cover sheet shall contain the signature of the attorney or party, pro se, authorizing the filing. IN ST ADMIN Rule 12(D).

E. Format

1. *Form of motions.* The rules applicable to captions, and the signing and form of pleadings (IN ST TRIAL P Rule 8 through IN ST TRIAL P Rule 11), apply to all motions and other papers provided under the Indiana Rules of Trial Procedure. 22B INPRAC 7:2.

2. *Form of pleadings*

  a. *Caption; Names of parties.* Every pleading shall contain a caption setting forth the name of the court, the title of the action, the file number, and a designation as in IN ST TRIAL P Rule 7(A). In the complaint the title of the action shall include the names of all the parties, but in other pleadings it is sufficient to state the name of the first party on each side with an appropriate indication of other parties. IN ST TRIAL P Rule 10(A).

  b. *Paragraphs; Separate statements.* All averments of a claim or defense shall be made in numbered paragraphs, the contents of each of which shall be limited as far as practicable to a statement of a single set of circumstances, and a paragraph may be referred to by number in all succeeding pleadings. Each claim founded upon a separate transaction or occurrence and each defense other than denials may be stated in a separate count or defense whenever a separation facilitates the clear presentation of the matters set forth. IN ST TRIAL P Rule 10(B).

  c. *Adoption by reference; Exhibits.* Statements in a pleading may be adopted by reference in a different part of the same pleading or in another pleading or in any motion. A copy of any written instrument which is an exhibit to a pleading is a part thereof for all purposes. IN ST TRIAL P Rule 10(C).

  d. *Citation.* Allen County Superior and Circuit court rules may be cited as L.R. _____. The Indiana Rules of Trial Procedure are hereinafter referred to as T.R. _____. IN ST ALLEN SUPER AND CIR CT CIV Rule AR00-1(B).

  e. *Paper.* All pleadings must be printed on white paper. IN ST ALLEN SUPER AND CIR CT CIV Rule 8-1(A).

  f. *Spacing.* The lines shall be double spaced except for quotations, which shall be indented and single-spaced. IN ST ALLEN SUPER AND CIR CT CIV Rule 8-1(A).

  g. *Photocopies.* Photocopies are acceptable if legible. IN ST ALLEN SUPER AND CIR CT CIV Rule 8-1(A).

  h. *Margins and binding.* Margins shall be one to one and one-half (1-1 1/2) inches on the left side and one-half (1/2) inch on the right. IN ST ALLEN SUPER AND CIR CT CIV Rule 8-1(B).

    i. Binding or stapling shall be at the top left and at no other place. IN ST ALLEN SUPER AND CIR CT CIV Rule 8-1(B).

      ii.   Covers or backing shall not be used. IN ST ALLEN SUPER AND CIR CT CIV Rule 8-1(B).

    i.   *Flat filing.* The files of the Clerk of the Court shall be kept under the "flat filing" system. All pleadings presented for filing with the Clerk or Court shall be flat and unfolded. Only the original of any pleading shall be placed in the Court file. IN ST ALLEN SUPER AND CIR CT CIV Rule 77-1(A).

    j.   *Handwritten pleadings.* Handwritten pleadings may be accepted for filing in the discretion of the Court. IN ST ALLEN SUPER AND CIR CT CIV Rule 8-1(A).

3.   *Size of papers for filing.* Effective January 1, 1992, all pleadings, copies, motions and documents filed with any trial court or appellate level court, typed or printed, with the exception of exhibits and existing wills, shall be prepared on eight and one-half by eleven inch (8 1/2" x 11") size paper. IN ST ADMIN Rule 11.

4.   *Form of proposed orders*

    a.   *Form, caption, and title.* Any proposed order shall be a document that is separate and apart from the motion or application to which it relates and shall contain a caption showing the name of the court, the case number assigned to the case and the title of the case as shown by the complaint. IN ST ALLEN SUPER AND CIR CT CIV Rule TR00-1(B). If there are multiple parties, the title may be shortened to include only the first name plaintiff and defendant with appropriate indication that there are additional parties. IN ST ALLEN SUPER AND CIR CT CIV Rule TR00-1(B).

    b.   *Paper.* The proposed order shall be on white paper, eight and one half by eleven inches (8 1/2" x 11") in size, and each page shall be numbered. IN ST ALLEN SUPER AND CIR CT CIV Rule TR00-1(B).

    c.   *Signature line.* On the last page of the proposed order there shall be a line for the signature of the judge under which shall be typed "Judge, Allen Superior Court" or "Judge, Allen Circuit Court", whichever is applicable, to the left of which shall be the following: "Dated _____". IN ST ALLEN SUPER AND CIR CT CIV Rule TR00-1(B).

    d.   *Allowance of space for clerk.* To allow space for the Clerk to make entries on the proposed order to show compliance with the notice requirements of IN ST TRIAL P Rule 72(D), the lower four (4) inches of the last page of the proposed order shall be left blank. IN ST ALLEN SUPER AND CIR CT CIV Rule TR00-1(B).

    e.   *Proof of notice required.* The proposed order shall also include a prepared proof of notice, under IN ST TRIAL P Rule 72(D). The proof of notice shall conform to the format show in IN ST ALLEN SUPER AND CIR CT CIV Rule TR00-1(B). IN ST ALLEN SUPER AND CIR CT CIV Rule TR00-1(B).

5.   *Signature requirements*

    a.   *Signature of attorney.* Every pleading or motion of a party represented by an attorney shall be signed by at least one (1) attorney of record in his individual name, whose address, telephone number, and attorney number shall be stated, except that this provision shall not apply to pleadings and motions made and transcribed at the trial or a hearing before the judge and received by him in such form. IN ST TRIAL P Rule 11(A). All pleadings to be signed by an attorney shall contain the written signature of the individual attorney, the attorney's printed name, Supreme Court Attorney Number, the name of the attorney's law firm, the attorney's address, telephone number, and a designation of the party for whom the attorney appears. IN ST ALLEN SUPER AND CIR CT CIV Rule 8-1(C). For the recommended signature format, refer to IN ST ALLEN SUPER AND CIR CT CIV Rule 8-1(C).

      i.   The signature of an attorney constitutes a certificate by him that he has read the pleadings; that to the best of his knowledge, information, and belief, there is good ground to support it; and that it is not interposed for delay. IN ST TRIAL P Rule 11(A).

      ii.   If a pleading or motion is not signed or is signed with intent to defeat the purpose of the rule, it may be stricken as sham and false and the action may proceed as though the pleading had not been served. IN ST TRIAL P Rule 11(A).

      iii.   For a willful violation of IN ST TRIAL P Rule 11 an attorney may be subjected to appropriate

disciplinary action. Similar action may be taken if scandalous or indecent matter is inserted. IN ST TRIAL P Rule 11(A).

    iv. Neither printed signatures, nor facsimile signatures shall be accepted on original documents. IN ST ALLEN SUPER AND CIR CT CIV Rule 8-1(C).

    v. Facsimile signatures are permitted on copies. IN ST ALLEN SUPER AND CIR CT CIV Rule 8-1(C).

b. *Signature of unrepresented party.* A party who is not represented by an attorney shall sign his pleading and state his address. IN ST TRIAL P Rule 11(A).

c. *Verification not generally required.* Except when specifically required by rule, pleadings or motions need not be verified or accompanied by affidavit. The rule in equity that the averments of an answer under oath must be overcome by the testimony of two (2) witnesses or of one (1) witness sustained by corroborating circumstances is abolished. IN ST TRIAL P Rule 11(A).

d. *Verification by affirmation or representation.* When in connection with any civil or special statutory proceeding it is required that any pleading, motion, petition, supporting affidavit, or other document of any kind, be verified, or that an oath be taken, it shall be sufficient if the subscriber simply affirms the truth of the matter to be verified by an affirmation or representation. IN ST TRIAL P Rule 11(B). IN ST TRIAL P Rule 11(B) states that the affirmation or representation should be in substantially the following language: "I (we) affirm, under the penalties for perjury, that the foregoing representation(s) is (are) true. (Signed) _____."

    i. Any person who falsifies an affirmation or representation of fact shall be subject to the same penalties as are prescribed by law for the making of a false affidavit. IN ST TRIAL P Rule 11(B).

e. *Verified pleadings, motions, and affidavits as evidence.* Pleadings, motions and affidavits accompanying or in support of such pleadings or motions when required to be verified or under oath shall be accepted as a representation that the signer had personal knowledge thereof or reasonable cause to believe the existence of the facts or matters stated or alleged therein; and, if otherwise competent or acceptable as evidence, may be admitted as evidence of the facts or matters stated or alleged therein when it is so provided in the Indiana Rules of Trial Procedure, by statute or other law, or to the extent the writing or signature expressly purports to be made upon the signer's personal knowledge. When such pleadings, motions and affidavits are verified or under oath they shall not require other or greater proof on the part of the adverse party than if not verified or not under oath unless expressly provided otherwise by the Indiana Rules of Trial Procedure, statute or other law. Affidavits upon motions for summary judgment under IN ST TRIAL P Rule 56 and in denial of execution under IN ST TRIAL P Rule 9.2 shall be made upon personal knowledge. IN ST TRIAL P Rule 11(C).

6. *Information excluded from public access.* Every document filed in a case shall separately identify information excluded from public access pursuant to IN ST ADMIN Rule 9(G)(1) as follows:

a. Whole documents that are excluded from public access pursuant to IN ST ADMIN Rule 9(G)(1) shall be tendered on light green paper or have a light green coversheet attached to the document, marked "Not for Public Access" or "Confidential." IN ST TRIAL P Rule 5(G)(1).

b. When only a portion of a document contains information excluded from public access pursuant to IN ST ADMIN Rule 9(G)(1), said information shall be omitted [or redacted] from the filed document, and set forth on a separate accompanying document on light green paper conspicuously marked "Not for Public Access" or "Confidential" and clearly designated [or identifying] the caption and number of the case and the document and location within the document to which the redacted material pertains. IN ST TRIAL P Rule 5(G)(2).

c. With respect to documents filed in electronic format, the trial court, by local rule, may provide for compliance with IN ST TRIAL P Rule 5 in manner that separates and protects access to information excluded from public access. IN ST TRIAL P Rule 5(G)(3).

d. IN ST TRIAL P Rule 5(G) does not apply to a record sealed by the court pursuant to IN ST 5-14-3-5.5 or otherwise, nor to records, documents, or information filed in cases to which public access is prohibited pursuant to IN ST ADMIN Rule 9(G). IN ST TRIAL P Rule 5(G)(4).

e. ` The following information in case records is excluded from public access and is confidential:

i. Information that is excluded from public access pursuant to federal law;

ii. Information that is excluded from public access as declared confidential by Indiana statute or other court rule, including without limitation:

- All adoption records created after July 8, 1941, as declared confidential by IN ST 31-19-19-1, et seq., except those specifically declared open by IN ST 31-19-13-2(2);

- All records relating to chancroid, chlamydia, gonorrhea, hepatitis, human immunodeficiency virus (HIV), Lymphogranuloma venereum, syphilis, tuberculosis, as declared confidential by IN ST 16-41-8-1, et seq.;

- All records relating to child abuse as declared confidential by IN ST 31-33-18-1, et seq.;

- All records relating to drug tests as declared confidential by IN ST 5-14-3-4(a)(9);

- Records of grand jury proceedings as declared confidential by IN ST 35-34-2-4;

- Records of juvenile proceedings as declared confidential by IN ST 31-39-1-2, except those specifically open under statute;

- All paternity records created after July 1, 1941 as declared confidential by IN ST 31-14-11-15, IN ST 31-19-5-23, IN ST 31-39-1-1 and IN ST 31-39-1-2 [Editor's note: IN ST 31-14-11-15 was repealed effective May 9, 2013];

- All pre-sentence reports as declared confidential by IN ST 35-38-1-13;

- Written petitions to permit marriages without consent and orders directing the Clerk of Court to issue a marriage license to underage persons, as declared confidential by IN ST 31-11-1-6;

- Only those arrest warrants, search warrants, indictments and informations ordered confidential by the trial judge, prior to return of duly executed service as declared confidential by IN ST 5-14-3-4(b)(1);

- All medical, mental health, or tax records unless determined by law or regulation of any governmental custodian not to be confidential, released by the subject of such records, or declared by a court of competent jurisdiction to be essential to the resolution of litigation as declared confidential by IN ST 16-39-3-10, IN ST 6-4.1-5-10, IN ST 6-4.1-12-12, and IN ST 6-8.1-7-1;

- Personal information relating to jurors or prospective jurors, other than for the use of the parties and counsel, pursuant to IN ST JURY Rule 10;

- Information relating to protection from abuse orders, no-contact orders and workplace violence restraining orders as declared confidential by IN ST 5-2-9-6, et seq.;

- Mediation proceedings pursuant to IN ST ADR Rule 2.11, Mini-Trial proceedings pursuant to IN ST ADR Rule 4.4(C), and Summary Jury Trials pursuant to IN ST ADR Rule 5.6;

- Information in probation files pursuant to the Probation Standards promulgated by the Judicial Conference of Indiana pursuant to IN ST 11-13-1-8(b);

- Information deemed confidential pursuant to the Rules for Court Administered Alcohol and Drug Programs promulgated by the Judicial Conference of Indiana pursuant to IN ST 12-23-14-13;

- Information deemed confidential pursuant to the Problem-Solving Court Rules promulgated by the Judicial Conference of Indiana pursuant to IN ST 33-23-16-16;

- All records of the Department of workforce Development as declared confidential by IN ST 22-4-19-6;

- Information regarding interception of electronic communications that is sealed or deemed confidential as set forth in IN ST 35-33.5-2-1, et seq.

iii. Information excluded from public access by specific court order;

iv. Complete Social Security Numbers of living persons;

v. With the exception of names, information such as addresses, phone numbers, and dates of birth which explicitly identifies:

- Natural persons who are witnesses or victims (not including defendants) in criminal, domestic violence, stalking, sexual assault, juvenile, or civil protection order proceedings, provided that juveniles who are victims of sex crimes shall be identified by initials only;

- Places of residence of judicial officers, clerks and other employees of courts and clerks of court, unless the person or persons about whom the information pertains waives confidentiality;

vi. Complete account numbers of specific assets, loans, bank accounts, credit cards, and personal identification numbers (PINs);

vii. All orders of expungement entered in criminal or juvenile proceedings, orders to restrict access to criminal history information pursuant to IN ST 35-38-5-5.5 or IN ST 35-38-8-5 and records excluded from public access by such orders, and information related to infractions that is excluded from public access pursuant to IN ST 34-28-5-15 or IN ST 34-28-5-16 [Editor's note: IN ST 35-38-5-5.5, IN ST 35-38-8-5 and IN ST 34-28-5-16 were repealed effective July 1, 2013; for information on orders restricting access to criminal history, refer to IN ST 35-38-9-1, et seq.];

viii. All personal notes and e-mail, and deliberative material, of judges, jurors, court staff and judicial agencies, and information recorded in personal data assistants (PDA's) or organizers and personal calendars. IN ST ADMIN Rule 9(G)(1).

F. Filing and Service Requirements

1. *Filing requirements.* Except as otherwise provided in IN ST TRIAL P Rule 5(E)(2), all pleadings and papers subsequent to the complaint which are required to be served upon a party shall be filed with the Court either before service or within a reasonable period of time thereafter. IN ST TRIAL P Rule 5(E)(1).

   a. *Filing with the court defined.* The filing of pleadings, motions, and other papers with the court as required by the Indiana Rules of Trial Procedure shall be made by one of the following methods:

      i. Delivery to the clerk of the court;

      ii. Sending by electronic transmission under the procedure adopted pursuant to IN ST ADMIN Rule 12;

      iii. Mailing to the clerk by registered, certified or express mail return receipt requested;

      iv. Depositing with any third-party commercial carrier for delivery to the clerk within three (3) calendar days, cost prepaid, properly addressed;

      v. If the court so permits, filing with the judge, in which event the judge shall note thereon the filing date and forthwith transmit them to the office of the clerk; or

      vi. Electronic filing, as approved by the Division of State Court Administration pursuant to IN ST ADMIN Rule 16. IN ST TRIAL P Rule 5(F).

      vii. Filing by registered or certified mail and by third-party commercial carrier shall be complete upon mailing or deposit. IN ST TRIAL P Rule 5(F).

   b. *Facsimile filing*

      i. *Generally.* In counties where a majority of judges of the courts of record, by posted local rule, have authorized electronic facsimile filing and designated a telephone number to receive such transmissions, pleadings, motions, and other papers may be sent to the Clerk of Circuit Court by electronic facsimile transmission for filing in any case, provided:

         - Such matter does not exceed ten (10) pages, including the cover sheet;

         - Such matter does not require the payment of fees other than the electronic facsimile transcription fee set forth in IN ST ADMIN Rule 12(E);

- The sending party creates at the time of transmission a machine generated log for such transmission; and

- The original document and the transmission log are maintained by the sending party for the duration of the litigation. IN ST ADMIN Rule 12(B).

 ii. *Time of filing*. During normal, posted business hours, the time of filing shall be the time the duplicate document is produced in the office of the Clerk of the Circuit Court. Duplicate documents received at all other times shall be filed as of the next normal business day. IN ST ADMIN Rule 12(C).

- If the receiving fax machine endorses its own time and date stamp upon the transmitted documents and the receiving machine produces a delivery receipt which is electronically created and transmitted to the sending party, the time of filing shall be the date and time recorded on the transmitted document by the receiving fax machine. IN ST ADMIN Rule 12(C).

 c. *Proof of filing*. Any party filing any paper by any method other than personal delivery to the clerk shall retain proof of filing. IN ST TRIAL P Rule 5(F).

2. *Service requirements*. Unless otherwise provided by the Indiana Rules of Trial Procedure or an order of the court, each party and special judge, if any, shall be served with: (1) every order required by its terms to be served; (2) every pleading subsequent to the original complaint; (3) every written motion except one which may be heard ex parte; (4) every brief submitted to the trial court; (5) every paper relating to discovery required to be served upon a party; and (6) every written notice, appearance, demand, offer of judgment, designation of record on appeal, or similar paper. IN ST TRIAL P Rule 5(A).

 a. *Methods of service*

  i. *Personal service*. Whenever a party is represented by an attorney of record, service shall be made upon such attorney unless service upon the party himself is ordered by the court. Service upon the attorney or party shall be made by delivering or mailing a copy of the papers to the last known address or where an attorney or party has consented to service by fax or e-mail, as provided in IN ST TRIAL P Rule 3.1(A)(4), by faxing or e-mailing a copy of the documents to the fax number or e-mail address set out in the appearance form or correction as required by IN ST TRIAL P Rule 3.1(E). IN ST TRIAL P Rule 5(B). Delivery of a copy within IN ST TRIAL P Rule 5 means:

- Offering or tendering it to the attorney or party and stating the nature of the papers being served. Refusal to accept an offered or tendered document is a waiver of any objection to the sufficiency or adequacy of service of that document;

- Leaving it at his office with a clerk or other person in charge thereof, or if there is no one in charge, leaving it in a conspicuous place therein; or

- If the office is closed, by leaving it at his dwelling house or usual place of abode with some person of suitable age and discretion then residing therein; or,

- Leaving it at some other suitable place, selected by the attorney upon whom service is being made, pursuant to duly promulgated local rule. IN ST TRIAL P Rule 5(B)(1).

  ii. *Service by mail*. If service is made by mail, the papers shall be deposited in the United States mail addressed to the person on whom they are being served, with postage prepaid. Service shall be deemed complete upon mailing. Proof of service of all papers permitted to be mailed may be made by written acknowledgment of service, by affidavit of the person who mailed the papers, or by certificate of an attorney. It shall be the duty of attorneys when entering their appearance in a cause or when filing pleadings or papers therein, to have noted in the Chronological Case Summary or said pleadings or papers so filed the address and telephone number of their office. Service by delivery or by mail at such address shall be deemed sufficient and complete. IN ST TRIAL P Rule 5(B)(2).

  iii. *Service by fax or e-mail*. A party who has consented to service by fax or e-mail may be served as follows:

- Service by e-mail shall be made by attaching the document being served in .pdf format.

Discovery documents must also be served in accordance with IN ST TRIAL P Rule 26(A). IN ST TRIAL P Rule 5(B)(3)(a).

- Service by fax shall be deemed complete upon generation of a transmission record indicating the successful transmission of the entire document, except as provided in IN ST TRIAL P Rule 5(B)(3)(d). IN ST TRIAL P Rule 5(B)(3)(b).

- Service by e-mail shall be deemed complete upon transmission, except as provided in IN ST TRIAL P Rule 5(B)(3)(d). IN ST TRIAL P Rule 5(B)(3)(c).

- Service by fax or e-mail that occurs on a Saturday, Sunday, legal holiday, or day the court or agency in which the matter is pending is closed or after 5:00 PM local time of the recipient shall be deemed complete the next day that is not a Saturday, Sunday, legal holiday, or day that the court or agency in which the matter is pending is not closed. IN ST TRIAL P Rule 5(B)(3)(d).

    iv. *Consent to alternate service.* Any Allen County Attorney or any Allen County law firm may, without charge, maintain an assigned Courthouse box in the library of the Allen County Courthouse for receipt of notices, pleadings, process orders, or other communications from the Court, the Clerk, and other attorneys or law firms. IN ST ALLEN SUPER AND CIR CT CIV Rule 5-1(A). For more information concerning the use of courthouse boxes, refer to IN ST ALLEN SUPER AND CIR CT CIV Rule 5-1.

  b. *Serving numerous defendants.* In any action in which there are unusually large numbers of defendants, the court, upon motion or of its own initiative, may order:

    i. That service of the pleadings of the defendants and replies thereto need not be made as between the defendants;

- That any cross-claim, counterclaim, or matter constituting an avoidance or affirmative defense contained therein shall be deemed to be denied or avoided by all other parties; and

- That the filing of any such pleading and service thereof upon the plaintiff constitutes due notice of it to the parties. IN ST TRIAL P Rule 5(D).

    ii. A copy of every such order shall be served upon the parties in such manner and form as the court directs. IN ST TRIAL P Rule 5(D).

  c. *Service on parties in default for failure to appear.* No service need be made on parties in default for failure to appear, except that pleadings asserting new or additional claims for relief against them shall be served upon them in the manner provided by service of summons in IN ST TRIAL P Rule 4. IN ST TRIAL P Rule 5(A).

G. Hearings

1. *Hearing on motion.* Unless local conditions make it impracticable, each judge shall establish regular times and places, at intervals sufficiently frequent for the prompt dispatch of business, at which motions requiring notice and hearing may be heard and disposed of; but the judge at any time or place and on such notice, if any, as he considers reasonable may make order for the advancement, conduct, and hearing of actions. To expedite its business the court may direct the submission and determination of motions without oral hearing upon brief written statements of reasons in support and opposition, or direct or permit hearings by telephone conference call with all attorneys or other similar means of communication. IN ST TRIAL P Rule 73(A).

  a. *Setting motions for hearing.* Except for the motions described in IN ST ALLEN SUPER AND CIR CT CIV Rule 7-1(E), all motions shall be set for hearing. IN ST ALLEN SUPER AND CIR CT CIV Rule 7-1(A). [Editor's note: While IN ST ALLEN SUPER AND CIR CT CIV Rule 7-1(A) refers to IN ST ALLEN SUPER AND CIR CT CIV Rule 7-1(E) as relating to hearings on motions, that reference is likely intended to be to IN ST ALLEN SUPER AND CIR CT CIV Rule 7-1(D).]

    i. It shall be the responsibility of the moving party to request the date of such hearing from the Judicial Assistant, or if the case has already been assigned to a Judge, from the Judicial Law Clerk of the assigned Judge. IN ST ALLEN SUPER AND CIR CT CIV Rule 7-1(A).

  b. *Responsibility for notice of hearing.* It shall be the responsibility of the moving party to give notice

to all other parties of hearings scheduled on motions. IN ST ALLEN SUPER AND CIR CT CIV Rule 7-1(I).

H. Forms

1. Motion to Dismiss for Failure to State a Claim Forms for Indiana

    a. General form. 5 INPRAC § 3:4.1.

    b. Failure to state a claim upon which relief can be granted. 5 INPRAC § 3:4.5.

    c. Motion to dismiss plaintiff's complaint; General form. 9 INPRAC § 42.2.

    d. Motion to dismiss; Failure to state a claim upon which relief can be granted. 9 INPRAC § 42.10.

    e. Certificate of service; Personal service. 9 INPRAC § 5.7.

    f. Certificate of service; First class mail. 9 INPRAC § 5.8.

    g. Statute of limitations. 9 INPRAC § 42.12.

    h. Application for hearing and preliminary determination of motion to dismiss. 9 INPRAC § 42.15.

2. Official Motion to Dismiss for Failure to State a Claim Forms for Allen County

    a. Consent to alternate service. IN ST ALLEN SUPER AND CIR CT CIV App. A.

I. Checklist

(I) ❑ Matters to be considered by moving party

    (a) ❑ Required documents

        (1) ❑ Motion and notice

        (2) ❑ Proposed order

        (3) ❑ Certificate of service

    (b) ❑ Supplemental documents

        (1) ❑ Brief or memorandum

        (2) ❑ Facsimile cover sheet

    (c) ❑ Timing

        (1) ❑ A motion to dismiss for failure to state a claim shall be made before pleading if a further pleading is permitted or within twenty (20) days after service of the prior pleading if none is required

        (2) ❑ A written motion, other than one which may be heard ex parte, and notice of the hearing thereof shall be served not less than five (5) days before the time specified for the hearing, unless a different period is fixed by the Indiana Rules of Trial Procedure or by order of the court

        (3) ❑ All pleadings and papers subsequent to the complaint which are required to be served upon a party shall be filed with the Court either before service or within a reasonable period of time thereafter

(II) ❑ Matters to be considered by the responding party

    (a) ❑ Required documents

        (1) ❑ Opposition

        (2) ❑ Certificate of service

    (b) ❑ Supplemental documents

        (1) ❑ Supporting evidence

        (2) ❑ Proposed order

        (3) ❑ Brief or memorandum

        (4) ❑ Facsimile cover sheet

(c) ❑ Timing

    (1)   ❑ Except as otherwise provided in IN ST TRIAL P Rule 59(D), opposing affidavits may be served not less than one (1) day before the hearing, unless the court permits them to be served at some other time

Motions, Oppositions and Replies
Motion to Dismiss for Lack of Subject Matter Jurisdiction

Document Last Updated October 2013

A. Applicable Rules

1. *State rules*

    a. Appearance. IN ST TRIAL P Rule 3.1.

    b. Process. IN ST TRIAL P Rule 4.

    c. Service and filing of pleadings and other papers. IN ST TRIAL P Rule 5.

    d. Time. IN ST TRIAL P Rule 6.

    e. Pleadings. IN ST TRIAL P Rule 7; IN ST TRIAL P Rule 8; IN ST TRIAL P Rule 9.2; IN ST TRIAL P Rule 10; IN ST TRIAL P Rule 11.

    f. Defenses and objections; When and how presented; By pleading or motion; Motion for judgment on the pleadings. IN ST TRIAL P Rule 12.

    g. Amended and supplemental pleadings. IN ST TRIAL P Rule 15.

    h. Joinder of person needed for just adjudication. IN ST TRIAL P Rule 19.

    i. Evidence. IN ST TRIAL P Rule 43.

    j. Judgment on the evidence (directed verdict). IN ST TRIAL P Rule 50.

    k. Findings by the court. IN ST TRIAL P Rule 52.

    l. Summary judgment. IN ST TRIAL P Rule 56.

    m. Motion to correct error. IN ST TRIAL P Rule 59.

    n. Relief from judgment or order. IN ST TRIAL P Rule 60.

    o. Trial court and clerks. IN ST TRIAL P Rule 72.

    p. Hearing of motions. IN ST TRIAL P Rule 73.

    q. Access to court records. IN ST ADMIN Rule 9.

    r. Paper size. IN ST ADMIN Rule 11.

    s. Facsimile transmission. IN ST ADMIN Rule 12.

    t. Electronic filing and electronic service pilot projects. IN ST ADMIN Rule 16.

    u. Sealing of certain records by court; Hearing; Notice. IN ST 5-14-3-5.5.

    v. Privacy and confidentiality. IN ST 5-2-9-6; IN ST 5-14-3-4; IN ST 6-4.1-5-10; IN ST 6-4.1-12-12; IN ST 6-8.1-7-1; IN ST 11-13-1-8; IN ST 12-23-14-13; IN ST 16-39-3-10; IN ST 16-41-8-1; IN ST 22-4-19-6; IN ST 31-11-1-6; IN ST 31-19-5-23; IN ST 31-19-13-2; IN ST 31-19-19-1; IN ST 31-33-18-1; IN ST 31-39-1-1; IN ST 31-39-1-2; IN ST 33-23-16-16; IN ST 35-34-2-4; IN ST 35-38-1-13; IN ST 35-38-9-1; IN ST ADR Rule 2.11; IN ST ADR Rule 4.4; IN ST ADR Rule 5.6; IN ST JURY Rule 10.

2. *Local rules*

    a. Applicability and citation of rules. IN ST ALLEN SUPER AND CIR CT CIV Rule AR00-1.

    b. Proposed orders. IN ST ALLEN SUPER AND CIR CT CIV Rule TR00-1.

    c. Appearances. IN ST ALLEN SUPER AND CIR CT CIV Rule 3.1-1.

d. Consent to alternate service. IN ST ALLEN SUPER AND CIR CT CIV Rule 5-1.

e. Motions in civil court. IN ST ALLEN SUPER AND CIR CT CIV Rule 7-1.

f. Preparation of pleadings. IN ST ALLEN SUPER AND CIR CT CIV Rule 8-1.

g. Filing. IN ST ALLEN SUPER AND CIR CT CIV Rule 77-1.

B. Timing

1. *Timing of motion to dismiss for failure lack of subject matter jurisdiction.* A motion making any of the defenses listed in IN ST TRIAL P Rule 12(B) shall be made before pleading if a further pleading is permitted or within twenty (20) days after service of the prior pleading if none is required. IN ST TRIAL P Rule 12(B). Usually, the issue is raised in a motion that is filed before an Answer is filed; or the issue might be consolidated in the Answer. If it is not raised by the parties, it will be raised by the court, and an appellate court may raise the question sua sponte. 1A INPRAC R 12(12.5); Decatur County Rural Elec. Membership Corp. v. Public Serv. Co., 150 Ind.App. 193, 275 N.E.2d 857 (Ind.App. 1971).

   a. *Time to file a responsive pleading.* A responsive pleading required under the Indiana Rules of Trial Procedure, shall be served within twenty (20) days after service of the prior pleading. IN ST TRIAL P Rule 6(C).

   b. *Filing.* All pleadings and papers subsequent to the complaint which are required to be served upon a party shall be filed with the Court either before service or within a reasonable period of time thereafter. IN ST TRIAL P Rule 5(E)(1).

2. *Service.* A written motion, other than one which may be heard ex parte, and notice of the hearing thereof shall be served not less than five (5) days before the time specified for the hearing, unless a different period is fixed by the Indiana Rules of Trial Procedure or by order of the court. IN ST TRIAL P Rule 6(D).

   a. *Of supporting affidavits.* When a motion is supported by affidavit, the affidavit shall be served with the motion. IN ST TRIAL P Rule 6(D).

3. *Service of opposition.* Except as otherwise provided in IN ST TRIAL P Rule 59(D), opposing affidavits may be served not less than one (1) day before the hearing, unless the court permits them to be served at some other time. IN ST TRIAL P Rule 6(D).

4. *Computation of time*

   a. *Generally; Days excluded.* In computing any period of time prescribed or allowed by the Indiana Rules of Trial Procedure, by order of the court, or by any applicable statute, the day of the act, event, or default from which the designated period of time begins to run shall not be included. The last day of the period so computed is to be included unless it is:

      i. A Saturday,

      ii. A Sunday,

      iii. A legal holiday as defined by state statute, or

      iv. A day the office in which the act is to be done is closed during regular business hours. IN ST TRIAL P Rule 6(A).

   b. *Short periods.* In any event, the period runs until the end of the next day that is not a Saturday, a Sunday, a legal holiday, or a day on which the office is closed. When the period of time allowed is less than seven (7) days, intermediate Saturdays, Sundays, legal holidays, and days on which the office is closed shall be excluded from the computations. IN ST TRIAL P Rule 6(A).

   c. *Additional time after service by United States mail.* Whenever a party has the right or is required to do some act or take some proceedings within a prescribed period after the service of a notice or other paper upon him and the notice or paper is served upon him by United States mail, three (3) days shall be added to the prescribed period. IN ST TRIAL P Rule 6(E).

   d. *Enlargement of time.* When an act is required or allowed to be done at or within a specific time by the Indiana Rules of Trial Procedure, the court may at any time for cause shown:

      i. Order the period enlarged, with or without motion or notice, if request therefor is made before the expiration of the period originally prescribed or extended by a previous order; or

    ii. Upon motion made after the expiration of the specific period, permit the act to be done where the failure to act was the result of excusable neglect; but, the court may not extend the time for taking any action for judgment on the evidence under IN ST TRIAL P Rule 50(A), amendment of findings and judgment under IN ST TRIAL P Rule 52(B), to correct errors under IN ST TRIAL P Rule 59(C), statement in opposition to motion to correct error under IN ST TRIAL P Rule 59(E), or to obtain relief from final judgment under IN ST TRIAL P Rule 60(B), except to the extent and under the conditions stated in those rules. IN ST TRIAL P Rule 6(B).

C. General Requirements

1. *Motions, generally.* Unless made during a hearing or trial, or otherwise ordered by the court, an application to the court for an order shall be made by written motion. The motion shall state the grounds therefor and the relief or order sought. IN ST TRIAL P Rule 7(B).

    a. *Motions as distinct from pleadings.* Motions and responses to motions are not pleadings, and allegations contained in a motion are not admissions of a party. 22B INPRAC 7:2; Wachstetter v. County Properties, LLC, 832 N.E.2d 574 (Ind.Ct.App. 2005); Scott County Family YMCA, Inc. v. Hobbs, 817 N.E.2d 603 (Ind.Ct.App. 2004).

    b. *Unopposed motions generally granted.* It is common for a trial court to grant procedural motions, such as motions for enlargement of time, discovery motions, or motions for continuance, unless an objection is filed. 21 INPRAC § 13.8.

2. *Motion to dismiss for lack of subject matter jurisdiction.* Every defense, in law or fact, to a claim for relief in any pleading, whether a claim, counterclaim, cross-claim, or third-party claim, shall be asserted in the responsive pleading thereto if one is required; except that at the option of the pleader, the defense of lack of jurisdiction over the subject matter may be made by motion. IN ST TRIAL P Rule 12(B)(1). Subject-matter jurisdiction refers to the power of the court or tribunal to entertain the general class of cases or disputes to which a pending case belongs. It means that the legislature or other authority, such as, perhaps, a supreme court, has invested the court with judicial power with which to entertain a case or controversy, and to hear the litigation and dispute. 1A INPRAC R 12(12.5).

    a. *Objection not waivable.* Subject-matter jurisdiction cannot be created by the parties to the litigation. Either it is there or it is not, quite independent of the conduct or the consent of the parties to the action. As such, the absence of subject-matter jurisdiction is never waivable and there is a positive duty on a court, whether trial or appellate, to raise the question of subject-matter jurisdiction whenever it might appear, if the parties have failed to present the question. 1A INPRAC R 12(12.5); Schoffstall v. Failey, 180 Ind.App. 528, 389 N.E. 361 (Ind.Ct.App. 1979).

    b. *Motion not to be made as one for summary judgment.* A motion to dismiss under IN ST TRIAL P Rule 12(B)(1) may not be presented in the form of a motion for summary judgment. 9 INPRAC § 42.3.

    c. *Precedence of subject matter jurisdiction.* Dismissal for lack of subject matter jurisdiction takes precedence over the determination of and action upon other substantive and procedural rights of the parties. 9 INPRAC § 42.3; Young v. Estate of Sweeney, 808 N.E.2d 1217 (Ind.Ct.App. 2004).

    d. *Issues examined separately; Jurisdiction over one claim as jurisdiction over case.* In order to determine whether a case is properly before the trial court, the court should examine each issue presented. If at least one of the issues is within the jurisdiction of the trial court, the entire case falls within the court's jurisdiction. Where at least one issue or claim is a proper matter for judicial determination or resolution, a trial court is not ousted of subject matter jurisdiction by the presence in a case of one or more issues which arguably are within the jurisdiction of administrative or regulatory agency. 9 INPRAC § 42.3; Alexander v. Cottey, 801 N.E.2d 651 (Ind.Ct.App. 2004).

    e. *Factual matters in determining subject matter jurisdiction.* The trial court considering a motion to dismiss for lack of subject matter jurisdiction has wide latitude to devise procedures to discover the facts relevant to jurisdiction and in weighing the evidence to resolve factual disputes affecting the jurisdictional challenge. 9 INPRAC § 42.3.

    f. *Failure to exhaust administrative remedies.* The doctrine of exhaustion of administrative remedies provides that a trial court will not acquire subject matter jurisdiction until the aggrieved party has exhausted all available remedies before the administrative agency. 9 INPRAC § 41.44; Indiana Dept. of Environmental Management v. NJK Farms, Inc., 921 N.E.2d 834 (Ind.Ct.App. 2010).

    i.   *Dismissal of workers' compensation cases.* A trial court must dismiss a matter for lack of subject matter jurisdiction pursuant to Indiana IN ST TRIAL P Rule 12(B)(1) where injuries claimed in the Plaintiff's complaint fall squarely within the Indiana Workers Compensation Act. 9 INPRAC § 42.3; ATFH Real Property, LLC v. Stewart, 879 N.E.2d 1184 (Ind.Ct.App. 2008).

    g.   *Leave to amend complaint if motion granted.* A dismissal for lack of subject matter jurisdiction is not an adjudication on the merits nor is it res judicata. If action is dismissed, plaintiff may file amended complaint as permitted by IN ST TRIAL P Rule 6(C). 9 INPRAC § 42.3; Hart v. Webster, 894 N.E.2d 1032 (Ind.Ct.App. 2008).

    h.   *Effect of judgment entered by court lacking subject matter jurisdiction.* A judgment entered by a court that lacks subject matter jurisdiction is void and may be attacked at any time. 9 INPRAC § 42.3; Roberson v. State, 903 N.E.2d 1009 (Ind.Ct.App. 2009).

3.   *Consolidation and waiver*

    a.   *Consolidation of defenses in motion.* A party who makes a motion under IN ST TRIAL P Rule 12 may join with it any other motions herein provided for and then available to him. If a party makes a motion under IN ST TRIAL P Rule 12 but omits therefrom any defense or objection then available to him which IN ST TRIAL P Rule 12 permits to be raised by motion, he shall not thereafter make a motion based on the defense or objection so omitted. He may, however, make such motions as are allowed under IN ST TRIAL P Rule 12(H)(2). IN ST TRIAL P Rule 12(G).

    b.   *Waiver or preservation of certain defenses.* No defense or objection is waived by being joined with one or more other defenses or objections in a responsive pleading or motion. IN ST TRIAL P Rule 12(B).

D. Documents

1.   *Required documents*

    a.   *Motion and notice.* The requirement of notice is satisfied by service of the motion. IN ST TRIAL P Rule 7(B). Refer to the General Requirements section of this document for information on the content of a motion to dismiss for lack of subject matter jurisdiction.

    b.   *Proposed order.* Unless local practice provides differently, a party should submit a proposed order with its written motion to be signed by the judge once the motion has been granted. 21 INPRAC § 13.8.

        i.   *Proposed orders of a motion for dismissal.* Prior to entry by the Court of orders granting motions or applications, the moving party or applicant (or his or her attorney) shall, unless the Court directs otherwise, furnish the Court with proposed orders of a motion for dismissal. IN ST ALLEN SUPER AND CIR CT CIV Rule TR00-1(A)(5).

        ii.   *Copies of proposed orders.* All proposed orders shall be submitted in an original plus a number of copies equal to one (1) more than the number of pro se parties and attorneys of record contained in the prepared proof of notice under IN ST TRIAL P Rule 72(D). IN ST ALLEN SUPER AND CIR CT CIV Rule TR00-1(C).

        iii.   *Proof of notice.* The proposed order shall also include a prepared proof of notice, under IN ST TRIAL P Rule 72(D). IN ST ALLEN SUPER AND CIR CT CIV Rule TR00-1(B).

        iv.   Refer to the Format section of this document for information on the form and content of the proposed order and the proof of notice.

    c.   *Certificate of service.* An attorney or unrepresented party tendering a document to the Clerk for filing shall certify that service has been made, list the parties served, and specify the date and means of service. The certificate of service shall be placed at the end of the document and shall not be separately filed. The separate filing of a certificate of service, however, shall not be grounds for rejecting a document for filing. The Clerk may permit documents to be filed without a certificate of service but shall require prompt filing of a separate certificate of service. IN ST TRIAL P Rule 5(C).

2. *Supplemental documents*

    a. *Supporting evidence.* When a motion is based on facts not appearing of record the court may hear the matter on affidavits presented by the respective parties, but the court may direct that the matter be heard wholly or partly on oral testimony or depositions. IN ST TRIAL P Rule 43(B).

    b. *Brief or memorandum.* If a party desires to file a brief or memorandum in support of any motion, such brief or memorandum shall be filed simultaneously with the motion, and a copy shall be promptly served upon the adverse party. IN ST ALLEN SUPER AND CIR CT CIV Rule 7-1(E).

    c. *Facsimile cover sheet.* Any document sent to the Clerk of the Circuit Court by electronic facsimile transmission shall be accompanied by a cover sheet which states the title of the document, case number, number of pages, identity and voice telephone number of the sending party and instructions for filing. The cover sheet shall contain the signature of the attorney or party, pro se, authorizing the filing. IN ST ADMIN Rule 12(D).

E. Format

1. *Form of motions.* The rules applicable to captions, and the signing and form of pleadings (IN ST TRIAL P Rule 8 through IN ST TRIAL P Rule 11), apply to all motions and other papers provided under the Indiana Rules of Trial Procedure. 22B INPRAC 7:2.

2. *Form of pleadings*

    a. *Caption; Names of parties.* Every pleading shall contain a caption setting forth the name of the court, the title of the action, the file number, and a designation as in IN ST TRIAL P Rule 7(A). In the complaint the title of the action shall include the names of all the parties, but in other pleadings it is sufficient to state the name of the first party on each side with an appropriate indication of other parties. IN ST TRIAL P Rule 10(A).

    b. *Paragraphs; Separate statements.* All averments of a claim or defense shall be made in numbered paragraphs, the contents of each of which shall be limited as far as practicable to a statement of a single set of circumstances, and a paragraph may be referred to by number in all succeeding pleadings. Each claim founded upon a separate transaction or occurrence and each defense other than denials may be stated in a separate count or defense whenever a separation facilitates the clear presentation of the matters set forth. IN ST TRIAL P Rule 10(B).

    c. *Adoption by reference; Exhibits.* Statements in a pleading may be adopted by reference in a different part of the same pleading or in another pleading or in any motion. A copy of any written instrument which is an exhibit to a pleading is a part thereof for all purposes. IN ST TRIAL P Rule 10(C).

    d. *Citation.* Allen County Superior and Circuit court rules may be cited as L.R. _____. The Indiana Rules of Trial Procedure are hereinafter referred to as T.R. _____. IN ST ALLEN SUPER AND CIR CT CIV Rule AR00-1(B).

    e. *Paper.* All pleadings must be printed on white paper. IN ST ALLEN SUPER AND CIR CT CIV Rule 8-1(A).

    f. *Spacing.* The lines shall be double spaced except for quotations, which shall be indented and single-spaced. IN ST ALLEN SUPER AND CIR CT CIV Rule 8-1(A).

    g. *Photocopies.* Photocopies are acceptable if legible. IN ST ALLEN SUPER AND CIR CT CIV Rule 8-1(A).

    h. *Margins and binding.* Margins shall be one to one and one-half (1-1 1/2) inches on the left side and one-half (1/2) inch on the right. IN ST ALLEN SUPER AND CIR CT CIV Rule 8-1(B).

        i. Binding or stapling shall be at the top left and at no other place. IN ST ALLEN SUPER AND CIR CT CIV Rule 8-1(B).

        ii. Covers or backing shall not be used. IN ST ALLEN SUPER AND CIR CT CIV Rule 8-1(B).

    i. *Flat filing.* The files of the Clerk of the Court shall be kept under the "flat filing" system. All pleadings presented for filing with the Clerk or Court shall be flat and unfolded. Only the original of any pleading shall be placed in the Court file. IN ST ALLEN SUPER AND CIR CT CIV Rule 77-1(A).

j. *Handwritten pleadings.* Handwritten pleadings may be accepted for filing in the discretion of the Court. IN ST ALLEN SUPER AND CIR CT CIV Rule 8-1(A).

3. *Size of papers for filing.* Effective January 1, 1992, all pleadings, copies, motions and documents filed with any trial court or appellate level court, typed or printed, with the exception of exhibits and existing wills, shall be prepared on eight and one-half by eleven inch (8 1/2" x 11") size paper. IN ST ADMIN Rule 11.

4. *Form of proposed orders*

   a. *Form, caption, and title.* Any proposed order shall be a document that is separate and apart from the motion or application to which it relates and shall contain a caption showing the name of the court, the case number assigned to the case and the title of the case as shown by the complaint. IN ST ALLEN SUPER AND CIR CT CIV Rule TR00-1(B). If there are multiple parties, the title may be shortened to include only the first name plaintiff and defendant with appropriate indication that there are additional parties. IN ST ALLEN SUPER AND CIR CT CIV Rule TR00-1(B).

   b. *Paper.* The proposed order shall be on white paper, eight and one half by eleven inches (8 1/2" x 11") in size, and each page shall be numbered. IN ST ALLEN SUPER AND CIR CT CIV Rule TR00-1(B).

   c. *Signature line.* On the last page of the proposed order there shall be a line for the signature of the judge under which shall be typed "Judge, Allen Superior Court" or "Judge, Allen Circuit Court", whichever is applicable, to the left of which shall be the following: "Dated _____". IN ST ALLEN SUPER AND CIR CT CIV Rule TR00-1(B).

   d. *Allowance of space for clerk.* To allow space for the Clerk to make entries on the proposed order to show compliance with the notice requirements of IN ST TRIAL P Rule 72(D), the lower four (4) inches of the last page of the proposed order shall be left blank. IN ST ALLEN SUPER AND CIR CT CIV Rule TR00-1(B).

   e. *Proof of notice required.* The proposed order shall also include a prepared proof of notice, under IN ST TRIAL P Rule 72(D). The proof of notice shall conform to the format show in IN ST ALLEN SUPER AND CIR CT CIV Rule TR00-1(B). IN ST ALLEN SUPER AND CIR CT CIV Rule TR00-1(B).

5. *Signature requirements*

   a. *Signature of attorney.* Every pleading or motion of a party represented by an attorney shall be signed by at least one (1) attorney of record in his individual name, whose address, telephone number, and attorney number shall be stated, except that this provision shall not apply to pleadings and motions made and transcribed at the trial or a hearing before the judge and received by him in such form. IN ST TRIAL P Rule 11(A). All pleadings to be signed by an attorney shall contain the written signature of the individual attorney, the attorney's printed name, Supreme Court Attorney Number, the name of the attorney's law firm, the attorney's address, telephone number, and a designation of the party for whom the attorney appears. IN ST ALLEN SUPER AND CIR CT CIV Rule 8-1(C). For the recommended signature format, refer to IN ST ALLEN SUPER AND CIR CT CIV Rule 8-1(C).

      i. The signature of an attorney constitutes a certificate by him that he has read the pleadings; that to the best of his knowledge, information, and belief, there is good ground to support it; and that it is not interposed for delay. IN ST TRIAL P Rule 11(A).

      ii. If a pleading or motion is not signed or is signed with intent to defeat the purpose of the rule, it may be stricken as sham and false and the action may proceed as though the pleading had not been served. IN ST TRIAL P Rule 11(A).

      iii. For a willful violation of IN ST TRIAL P Rule 11 an attorney may be subjected to appropriate disciplinary action. Similar action may be taken if scandalous or indecent matter is inserted. IN ST TRIAL P Rule 11(A).

      iv. Neither printed signatures, nor facsimile signatures shall be accepted on original documents. IN ST ALLEN SUPER AND CIR CT CIV Rule 8-1(C).

      v. Facsimile signatures are permitted on copies. IN ST ALLEN SUPER AND CIR CT CIV Rule 8-1(C).

b. *Signature of unrepresented party.* A party who is not represented by an attorney shall sign his pleading and state his address. IN ST TRIAL P Rule 11(A).

c. *Verification not generally required.* Except when specifically required by rule, pleadings or motions need not be verified or accompanied by affidavit. The rule in equity that the averments of an answer under oath must be overcome by the testimony of two (2) witnesses or of one (1) witness sustained by corroborating circumstances is abolished. IN ST TRIAL P Rule 11(A).

d. *Verification by affirmation or representation.* When in connection with any civil or special statutory proceeding it is required that any pleading, motion, petition, supporting affidavit, or other document of any kind, be verified, or that an oath be taken, it shall be sufficient if the subscriber simply affirms the truth of the matter to be verified by an affirmation or representation. IN ST TRIAL P Rule 11(B). IN ST TRIAL P Rule 11(B) states that the affirmation or representation should be in substantially the following language: "I (we) affirm, under the penalties for perjury, that the foregoing representation(s) is (are) true. (Signed) _____."

   i. Any person who falsifies an affirmation or representation of fact shall be subject to the same penalties as are prescribed by law for the making of a false affidavit. IN ST TRIAL P Rule 11(B).

e. *Verified pleadings, motions, and affidavits as evidence.* Pleadings, motions and affidavits accompanying or in support of such pleadings or motions when required to be verified or under oath shall be accepted as a representation that the signer had personal knowledge thereof or reasonable cause to believe the existence of the facts or matters stated or alleged therein; and, if otherwise competent or acceptable as evidence, may be admitted as evidence of the facts or matters stated or alleged therein when it is so provided in the Indiana Rules of Trial Procedure, by statute or other law, or to the extent the writing or signature expressly purports to be made upon the signer's personal knowledge. When such pleadings, motions and affidavits are verified or under oath they shall not require other or greater proof on the part of the adverse party than if not verified or not under oath unless expressly provided otherwise by the Indiana Rules of Trial Procedure, statute or other law. Affidavits upon motions for summary judgment under IN ST TRIAL P Rule 56 and in denial of execution under IN ST TRIAL P Rule 9.2 shall be made upon personal knowledge. IN ST TRIAL P Rule 11(C).

6. *Information excluded from public access.* Every document filed in a case shall separately identify information excluded from public access pursuant to IN ST ADMIN Rule 9(G)(1) as follows:

a. Whole documents that are excluded from public access pursuant to IN ST ADMIN Rule 9(G)(1) shall be tendered on light green paper or have a light green coversheet attached to the document, marked "Not for Public Access" or "Confidential." IN ST TRIAL P Rule 5(G)(1).

b. When only a portion of a document contains information excluded from public access pursuant to IN ST ADMIN Rule 9(G)(1), said information shall be omitted [or redacted] from the filed document, and set forth on a separate accompanying document on light green paper conspicuously marked "Not for Public Access" or "Confidential" and clearly designated [or identifying] the caption and number of the case and the document and location within the document to which the redacted material pertains. IN ST TRIAL P Rule 5(G)(2).

c. With respect to documents filed in electronic format, the trial court, by local rule, may provide for compliance with IN ST TRIAL P Rule 5 in manner that separates and protects access to information excluded from public access. IN ST TRIAL P Rule 5(G)(3).

d. IN ST TRIAL P Rule 5(G) does not apply to a record sealed by the court pursuant to IN ST 5-14-3-5.5 or otherwise, nor to records, documents, or information filed in cases to which public access is prohibited pursuant to IN ST ADMIN Rule 9(G). IN ST TRIAL P Rule 5(G)(4).

e. The following information in case records is excluded from public access and is confidential:

   i. Information that is excluded from public access pursuant to federal law;

   ii. Information that is excluded from public access as declared confidential by Indiana statute or other court rule, including without limitation:

      • All adoption records created after July 8, 1941, as declared confidential by IN ST 31-19-19-1, et seq., except those specifically declared open by IN ST 31-19-13-2(2);

- All records relating to chancroid, chlamydia, gonorrhea, hepatitis, human immunodeficiency virus (HIV), Lymphogranuloma venereum, syphilis, tuberculosis, as declared confidential by IN ST 16-41-8-1, et seq.;

- All records relating to child abuse as declared confidential by IN ST 31-33-18-1, et seq.;

- All records relating to drug tests as declared confidential by IN ST 5-14-3-4(a)(9);

- Records of grand jury proceedings as declared confidential by IN ST 35-34-2-4;

- Records of juvenile proceedings as declared confidential by IN ST 31-39-1-2, except those specifically open under statute;

- All paternity records created after July 1, 1941 as declared confidential by IN ST 31-14-11-15, IN ST 31-19-5-23, IN ST 31-39-1-1 and IN ST 31-39-1-2 [Editor's note: IN ST 31-14-11-15 was repealed effective May 9, 2013];

- All pre-sentence reports as declared confidential by IN ST 35-38-1-13;

- Written petitions to permit marriages without consent and orders directing the Clerk of Court to issue a marriage license to underage persons, as declared confidential by IN ST 31-11-1-6;

- Only those arrest warrants, search warrants, indictments and informations ordered confidential by the trial judge, prior to return of duly executed service as declared confidential by IN ST 5-14-3-4(b)(1);

- All medical, mental health, or tax records unless determined by law or regulation of any governmental custodian not to be confidential, released by the subject of such records, or declared by a court of competent jurisdiction to be essential to the resolution of litigation as declared confidential by IN ST 16-39-3-10, IN ST 6-4.1-5-10, IN ST 6-4.1-12-12, and IN ST 6-8.1-7-1;

- Personal information relating to jurors or prospective jurors, other than for the use of the parties and counsel, pursuant to IN ST JURY Rule 10;

- Information relating to protection from abuse orders, no-contact orders and workplace violence restraining orders as declared confidential by IN ST 5-2-9-6, et seq.;

- Mediation proceedings pursuant to IN ST ADR Rule 2.11, Mini-Trial proceedings pursuant to IN ST ADR Rule 4.4(C), and Summary Jury Trials pursuant to IN ST ADR Rule 5.6;

- Information in probation files pursuant to the Probation Standards promulgated by the Judicial Conference of Indiana pursuant to IN ST 11-13-1-8(b);

- Information deemed confidential pursuant to the Rules for Court Administered Alcohol and Drug Programs promulgated by the Judicial Conference of Indiana pursuant to IN ST 12-23-14-13;

- Information deemed confidential pursuant to the Problem-Solving Court Rules promulgated by the Judicial Conference of Indiana pursuant to IN ST 33-23-16-16;

- All records of the Department of workforce Development as declared confidential by IN ST 22-4-19-6;

- Information regarding interception of electronic communications that is sealed or deemed confidential as set forth in IN ST 35-33.5-2-1, et seq.

iii. Information excluded from public access by specific court order;

iv. Complete Social Security Numbers of living persons;

v. With the exception of names, information such as addresses, phone numbers, and dates of birth which explicitly identifies:

- Natural persons who are witnesses or victims (not including defendants) in criminal, domestic violence, stalking, sexual assault, juvenile, or civil protection order proceedings, provided that juveniles who are victims of sex crimes shall be identified by initials only;

- Places of residence of judicial officers, clerks and other employees of courts and clerks of court, unless the person or persons about whom the information pertains waives confidentiality;

vi. Complete account numbers of specific assets, loans, bank accounts, credit cards, and personal identification numbers (PINs);

vii. All orders of expungement entered in criminal or juvenile proceedings, orders to restrict access to criminal history information pursuant to IN ST 35-38-5-5.5 or IN ST 35-38-8-5 and records excluded from public access by such orders, and information related to infractions that is excluded from public access pursuant to IN ST 34-28-5-15 or IN ST 34-28-5-16 [Editor's note: IN ST 35-38-5-5.5, IN ST 35-38-8-5 and IN ST 34-28-5-16 were repealed effective July 1, 2013; for information on orders restricting access to criminal history, refer to IN ST 35-38-9-1, et seq.];

viii. All personal notes and e-mail, and deliberative material, of judges, jurors, court staff and judicial agencies, and information recorded in personal data assistants (PDA's) or organizers and personal calendars. IN ST ADMIN Rule 9(G)(1).

F. Filing and Service Requirements

1. *Filing requirements.* Except as otherwise provided in IN ST TRIAL P Rule 5(E)(2), all pleadings and papers subsequent to the complaint which are required to be served upon a party shall be filed with the Court either before service or within a reasonable period of time thereafter. IN ST TRIAL P Rule 5(E)(1).

   a. *Filing with the court defined.* The filing of pleadings, motions, and other papers with the court as required by the Indiana Rules of Trial Procedure shall be made by one of the following methods:

      i. Delivery to the clerk of the court;

      ii. Sending by electronic transmission under the procedure adopted pursuant to IN ST ADMIN Rule 12;

      iii. Mailing to the clerk by registered, certified or express mail return receipt requested;

      iv. Depositing with any third-party commercial carrier for delivery to the clerk within three (3) calendar days, cost prepaid, properly addressed;

      v. If the court so permits, filing with the judge, in which event the judge shall note thereon the filing date and forthwith transmit them to the office of the clerk; or

      vi. Electronic filing, as approved by the Division of State Court Administration pursuant to IN ST ADMIN Rule 16. IN ST TRIAL P Rule 5(F).

      vii. Filing by registered or certified mail and by third-party commercial carrier shall be complete upon mailing or deposit. IN ST TRIAL P Rule 5(F).

   b. *Facsimile filing*

      i. *Generally.* In counties where a majority of judges of the courts of record, by posted local rule, have authorized electronic facsimile filing and designated a telephone number to receive such transmissions, pleadings, motions, and other papers may be sent to the Clerk of Circuit Court by electronic facsimile transmission for filing in any case, provided:

         - Such matter does not exceed ten (10) pages, including the cover sheet;

         - Such matter does not require the payment of fees other than the electronic facsimile transcription fee set forth in IN ST ADMIN Rule 12(E);

         - The sending party creates at the time of transmission a machine generated log for such transmission; and

         - The original document and the transmission log are maintained by the sending party for the duration of the litigation. IN ST ADMIN Rule 12(B).

      ii. *Time of filing.* During normal, posted business hours, the time of filing shall be the time the duplicate document is produced in the office of the Clerk of the Circuit Court. Duplicate

documents received at all other times shall be filed as of the next normal business day. IN ST ADMIN Rule 12(C).

- If the receiving fax machine endorses its own time and date stamp upon the transmitted documents and the receiving machine produces a delivery receipt which is electronically created and transmitted to the sending party, the time of filing shall be the date and time recorded on the transmitted document by the receiving fax machine. IN ST ADMIN Rule 12(C).

   c. *Proof of filing.* Any party filing any paper by any method other than personal delivery to the clerk shall retain proof of filing. IN ST TRIAL P Rule 5(F).

2. *Service requirements.* Unless otherwise provided by the Indiana Rules of Trial Procedure or an order of the court, each party and special judge, if any, shall be served with: (1) every order required by its terms to be served; (2) every pleading subsequent to the original complaint; (3) every written motion except one which may be heard ex parte; (4) every brief submitted to the trial court; (5) every paper relating to discovery required to be served upon a party; and (6) every written notice, appearance, demand, offer of judgment, designation of record on appeal, or similar paper. IN ST TRIAL P Rule 5(A).

   a. *Methods of service*

      i. *Personal service.* Whenever a party is represented by an attorney of record, service shall be made upon such attorney unless service upon the party himself is ordered by the court. Service upon the attorney or party shall be made by delivering or mailing a copy of the papers to the last known address or where an attorney or party has consented to service by fax or e-mail, as provided in IN ST TRIAL P Rule 3.1(A)(4), by faxing or e-mailing a copy of the documents to the fax number or e-mail address set out in the appearance form or correction as required by IN ST TRIAL P Rule 3.1(E). IN ST TRIAL P Rule 5(B). Delivery of a copy within IN ST TRIAL P Rule 5 means:

- Offering or tendering it to the attorney or party and stating the nature of the papers being served. Refusal to accept an offered or tendered document is a waiver of any objection to the sufficiency or adequacy of service of that document;

- Leaving it at his office with a clerk or other person in charge thereof, or if there is no one in charge, leaving it in a conspicuous place therein; or

- If the office is closed, by leaving it at his dwelling house or usual place of abode with some person of suitable age and discretion then residing therein; or,

- Leaving it at some other suitable place, selected by the attorney upon whom service is being made, pursuant to duly promulgated local rule. IN ST TRIAL P Rule 5(B)(1).

     ii. *Service by mail.* If service is made by mail, the papers shall be deposited in the United States mail addressed to the person on whom they are being served, with postage prepaid. Service shall be deemed complete upon mailing. Proof of service of all papers permitted to be mailed may be made by written acknowledgment of service, by affidavit of the person who mailed the papers, or by certificate of an attorney. It shall be the duty of attorneys when entering their appearance in a cause or when filing pleadings or papers therein, to have noted in the Chronological Case Summary or said pleadings or papers so filed the address and telephone number of their office. Service by delivery or by mail at such address shall be deemed sufficient and complete. IN ST TRIAL P Rule 5(B)(2).

    iii. *Service by fax or e-mail.* A party who has consented to service by fax or e-mail may be served as follows:

- Service by e-mail shall be made by attaching the document being served in .pdf format. Discovery documents must also be served in accordance with IN ST TRIAL P Rule 26(A). IN ST TRIAL P Rule 5(B)(3)(a).

- Service by fax shall be deemed complete upon generation of a transmission record indicating the successful transmission of the entire document, except as provided in IN ST TRIAL P Rule 5(B)(3)(d). IN ST TRIAL P Rule 5(B)(3)(b).

- Service by e-mail shall be deemed complete upon transmission, except as provided in IN ST TRIAL P Rule 5(B)(3)(d). IN ST TRIAL P Rule 5(B)(3)(c).

- Service by fax or e-mail that occurs on a Saturday, Sunday, legal holiday, or day the court or agency in which the matter is pending is closed or after 5:00 PM local time of the recipient shall be deemed complete the next day that is not a Saturday, Sunday, legal holiday, or day that the court or agency in which the matter is pending is not closed. IN ST TRIAL P Rule 5(B)(3)(d).

    iv. *Consent to alternate service.* Any Allen County Attorney or any Allen County law firm may, without charge, maintain an assigned Courthouse box in the library of the Allen County Courthouse for receipt of notices, pleadings, process orders, or other communications from the Court, the Clerk, and other attorneys or law firms. IN ST ALLEN SUPER AND CIR CT CIV Rule 5-1(A). For more information concerning the use of courthouse boxes, refer to IN ST ALLEN SUPER AND CIR CT CIV Rule 5-1.

  b. *Serving numerous defendants.* In any action in which there are unusually large numbers of defendants, the court, upon motion or of its own initiative, may order:

    i. That service of the pleadings of the defendants and replies thereto need not be made as between the defendants;

- That any cross-claim, counterclaim, or matter constituting an avoidance or affirmative defense contained therein shall be deemed to be denied or avoided by all other parties; and

- That the filing of any such pleading and service thereof upon the plaintiff constitutes due notice of it to the parties. IN ST TRIAL P Rule 5(D).

    ii. A copy of every such order shall be served upon the parties in such manner and form as the court directs. IN ST TRIAL P Rule 5(D).

  c. *Service on parties in default for failure to appear.* No service need be made on parties in default for failure to appear, except that pleadings asserting new or additional claims for relief against them shall be served upon them in the manner provided by service of summons in IN ST TRIAL P Rule 4. IN ST TRIAL P Rule 5(A).

G. Hearings

1. *Hearing on motion.* Unless local conditions make it impracticable, each judge shall establish regular times and places, at intervals sufficiently frequent for the prompt dispatch of business, at which motions requiring notice and hearing may be heard and disposed of; but the judge at any time or place and on such notice, if any, as he considers reasonable may make order for the advancement, conduct, and hearing of actions. To expedite its business the court may direct the submission and determination of motions without oral hearing upon brief written statements of reasons in support and opposition, or direct or permit hearings by telephone conference call with all attorneys or other similar means of communication. IN ST TRIAL P Rule 73(A).

  a. *Setting motions for hearing.* Except for the motions described in IN ST ALLEN SUPER AND CIR CT CIV Rule 7-1(E), all motions shall be set for hearing. IN ST ALLEN SUPER AND CIR CT CIV Rule 7-1(A). [Editor's note: While IN ST ALLEN SUPER AND CIR CT CIV Rule 7-1(A) refers to IN ST ALLEN SUPER AND CIR CT CIV Rule 7-1(E) as relating to hearings on motions, that reference is likely intended to be to IN ST ALLEN SUPER AND CIR CT CIV Rule 7-1(D).]

    i. It shall be the responsibility of the moving party to request the date of such hearing from the Judicial Assistant, or if the case has already been assigned to a Judge, from the Judicial Law Clerk of the assigned Judge. IN ST ALLEN SUPER AND CIR CT CIV Rule 7-1(A).

  b. *Responsibility for notice of hearing.* It shall be the responsibility of the moving party to give notice to all other parties of hearings scheduled on motions. IN ST ALLEN SUPER AND CIR CT CIV Rule 7-1(I).

H. Forms

1. **Motion to Dismiss for Lack of Subject Matter Jurisdiction Forms for Indiana**

  a. General form. 5 INPRAC § 3:4.1.

    b.   Lack of subject matter jurisdiction. 5 INPRAC § 3:4.2.

    c.   Motion to dismiss plaintiff's complaint; General form. 9 INPRAC § 42.2.

    d.   Lack of jurisdiction over the subject matter. 9 INPRAC § 42.3.

    e.   Certificate of service; Personal service. 9 INPRAC § 5.7.

    f.   Certificate of service; First class mail. 9 INPRAC § 5.8.

2.   **Official Motion to Dismiss for Lack of Subject Matter Jurisdiction Forms for Allen County**

    a.   Consent to alternate service. IN ST ALLEN SUPER AND CIR CT CIV App. A.

I. Checklist

(I) ❑ Matters to be considered by moving party

    (a) ❑ Required documents

        (1) ❑ Motion and notice

        (2) ❑ Proposed order

        (3) ❑ Certificate of service

    (b) ❑ Supplemental documents

        (1) ❑ Supporting evidence

        (2) ❑ Brief or memorandum

        (3) ❑ Facsimile cover sheet

    (c) ❑ Timing

        (1) ❑ A motion to dismiss for lack of subject matter jurisdiction shall be made before pleading if a further pleading is permitted or within twenty (20) days after service of the prior pleading if none is required

        (2) ❑ A written motion, other than one which may be heard ex parte, and notice of the hearing thereof shall be served not less than five (5) days before the time specified for the hearing, unless a different period is fixed by the Indiana Rules of Trial Procedure or by order of the court

        (3) ❑ All pleadings and papers subsequent to the complaint which are required to be served upon a party shall be filed with the Court either before service or within a reasonable period of time thereafter

(II) ❑ Matters to be considered by the responding party

    (a) ❑ Required documents

        (1) ❑ Opposition

        (2) ❑ Certificate of service

    (b) ❑ Supplemental documents

        (1) ❑ Supporting evidence

        (2) ❑ Proposed order

        (3) ❑ Brief or memorandum

        (4) ❑ Facsimile cover sheet

    (c) ❑ Timing

        (1) ❑ Except as otherwise provided in IN ST TRIAL P Rule 59(D), opposing affidavits may be served not less than one (1) day before the hearing, unless the court permits them to be served at some other time

Motions, Oppositions and Replies
Motion to Dismiss for Lack of Personal Jurisdiction

Document Last Updated October 2013

A. Applicable Rules

1. *State rules*

   a. Appearance. IN ST TRIAL P Rule 3.1.

   b. Process. IN ST TRIAL P Rule 4.

   c. Service and filing of pleadings and other papers. IN ST TRIAL P Rule 5.

   d. Time. IN ST TRIAL P Rule 6.

   e. Pleadings. IN ST TRIAL P Rule 7; IN ST TRIAL P Rule 8; IN ST TRIAL P Rule 9.2; IN ST TRIAL P Rule 10; IN ST TRIAL P Rule 11.

   f. Defenses and objections; When and how presented; By pleading or motion; Motion for judgment on the pleadings. IN ST TRIAL P Rule 12.

   g. Amended and supplemental pleadings. IN ST TRIAL P Rule 15.

   h. Joinder of person needed for just adjudication. IN ST TRIAL P Rule 19.

   i. Evidence. IN ST TRIAL P Rule 43.

   j. Judgment on the evidence (directed verdict). IN ST TRIAL P Rule 50.

   k. Findings by the court. IN ST TRIAL P Rule 52.

   l. Summary judgment. IN ST TRIAL P Rule 56.

   m. Motion to correct error. IN ST TRIAL P Rule 59.

   n. Relief from judgment or order. IN ST TRIAL P Rule 60.

   o. Trial court and clerks. IN ST TRIAL P Rule 72.

   p. Hearing of motions. IN ST TRIAL P Rule 73.

   q. Access to court records. IN ST ADMIN Rule 9.

   r. Paper size. IN ST ADMIN Rule 11.

   s. Facsimile transmission. IN ST ADMIN Rule 12.

   t. Electronic filing and electronic service pilot projects. IN ST ADMIN Rule 16.

   u. Sealing of certain records by court; Hearing; Notice. IN ST 5-14-3-5.5.

   v. Privacy and confidentiality. IN ST 5-2-9-6; IN ST 5-14-3-4; IN ST 6-4.1-5-10; IN ST 6-4.1-12-12; IN ST 6-8.1-7-1; IN ST 11-13-1-8; IN ST 12-23-14-13; IN ST 16-39-3-10; IN ST 16-41-8-1; IN ST 22-4-19-6; IN ST 31-11-1-6; IN ST 31-19-5-23; IN ST 31-19-13-2; IN ST 31-19-19-1; IN ST 31-33-18-1; IN ST 31-39-1-1; IN ST 31-39-1-2; IN ST 33-23-16-16; IN ST 35-34-2-4; IN ST 35-38-1-13; IN ST 35-38-9-1; IN ST ADR Rule 2.11; IN ST ADR Rule 4.4; IN ST ADR Rule 5.6; IN ST JURY Rule 10.

2. *Local rules*

   a. Applicability and citation of rules. IN ST ALLEN SUPER AND CIR CT CIV Rule AR00-1.

   b. Proposed orders. IN ST ALLEN SUPER AND CIR CT CIV Rule TR00-1.

   c. Appearances. IN ST ALLEN SUPER AND CIR CT CIV Rule 3.1-1.

   d. Consent to alternate service. IN ST ALLEN SUPER AND CIR CT CIV Rule 5-1.

   e. Motions in civil court. IN ST ALLEN SUPER AND CIR CT CIV Rule 7-1.

   f. Preparation of pleadings. IN ST ALLEN SUPER AND CIR CT CIV Rule 8-1.

   g. Filing. IN ST ALLEN SUPER AND CIR CT CIV Rule 77-1.

B. Timing

1. *Timing of motion to dismiss for failure lack of personal matter jurisdiction.* A motion making any of the defenses listed in IN ST TRIAL P Rule 12(B) shall be made before pleading if a further pleading is permitted or within twenty (20) days after service of the prior pleading if none is required. IN ST TRIAL P Rule 12(B).

   a. *Time to file a responsive pleading.* A responsive pleading required under the Indiana Rules of Trial Procedure, shall be served within twenty (20) days after service of the prior pleading. IN ST TRIAL P Rule 6(C).

   b. *Waiver of certain IN ST TRIAL P Rule 12(B) defenses.* If a pleading sets forth a claim for relief to which the adverse party is not required to serve a responsive pleading, any of the defenses in IN ST TRIAL P Rule 12(B)(2), IN ST TRIAL P Rule 12(B)(3), IN ST TRIAL P Rule 12(B)(4), IN ST TRIAL P Rule 12(B)(5) or IN ST TRIAL P Rule 12(B)(8) is waived to the extent constitutionally permissible unless made in a motion within twenty (20) days after service of the prior pleading. IN ST TRIAL P Rule 12(B).

   c. *Filing.* All pleadings and papers subsequent to the complaint which are required to be served upon a party shall be filed with the Court either before service or within a reasonable period of time thereafter. IN ST TRIAL P Rule 5(E)(1).

2. *Service.* A written motion, other than one which may be heard ex parte, and notice of the hearing thereof shall be served not less than five (5) days before the time specified for the hearing, unless a different period is fixed by the Indiana Rules of Trial Procedure or by order of the court. IN ST TRIAL P Rule 6(D).

   a. *Of supporting affidavits.* When a motion is supported by affidavit, the affidavit shall be served with the motion. IN ST TRIAL P Rule 6(D).

3. *Service of opposition.* Except as otherwise provided in IN ST TRIAL P Rule 59(D), opposing affidavits may be served not less than one (1) day before the hearing, unless the court permits them to be served at some other time. IN ST TRIAL P Rule 6(D).

4. *Computation of time*

   a. *Generally; Days excluded.* In computing any period of time prescribed or allowed by the Indiana Rules of Trial Procedure, by order of the court, or by any applicable statute, the day of the act, event, or default from which the designated period of time begins to run shall not be included. The last day of the period so computed is to be included unless it is:

      i.   A Saturday,

      ii. A Sunday,

      iii. A legal holiday as defined by state statute, or

      iv. A day the office in which the act is to be done is closed during regular business hours. IN ST TRIAL P Rule 6(A).

   b. *Short periods.* In any event, the period runs until the end of the next day that is not a Saturday, a Sunday, a legal holiday, or a day on which the office is closed. When the period of time allowed is less than seven (7) days, intermediate Saturdays, Sundays, legal holidays, and days on which the office is closed shall be excluded from the computations. IN ST TRIAL P Rule 6(A).

   c. *Additional time after service by United States mail.* Whenever a party has the right or is required to do some act or take some proceedings within a prescribed period after the service of a notice or other paper upon him and the notice or paper is served upon him by United States mail, three (3) days shall be added to the prescribed period. IN ST TRIAL P Rule 6(E).

   d. *Enlargement of time.* When an act is required or allowed to be done at or within a specific time by the Indiana Rules of Trial Procedure, the court may at any time for cause shown:

      i. Order the period enlarged, with or without motion or notice, if request therefor is made before the expiration of the period originally prescribed or extended by a previous order; or

      ii. Upon motion made after the expiration of the specific period, permit the act to be done where the failure to act was the result of excusable neglect; but, the court may not extend the time for taking any action for judgment on the evidence under IN ST TRIAL P Rule 50(A), amendment of findings and judgment under IN ST TRIAL P Rule 52(B), to correct errors under IN ST TRIAL P Rule 59(C), statement in opposition to motion to correct error under IN ST TRIAL P Rule 59(E), or to obtain relief from final judgment under IN ST TRIAL P Rule 60(B), except to the extent and under the conditions stated in those rules. IN ST TRIAL P Rule 6(B).

C. General Requirements

1. *Motions, generally.* Unless made during a hearing or trial, or otherwise ordered by the court, an application to the court for an order shall be made by written motion. The motion shall state the grounds therefor and the relief or order sought. IN ST TRIAL P Rule 7(B).

   a. *Motions as distinct from pleadings.* Motions and responses to motions are not pleadings, and allegations contained in a motion are not admissions of a party. 22B INPRAC 7:2; Wachstetter v. County Properties, LLC, 832 N.E.2d 574 (Ind.Ct.App. 2005); Scott County Family YMCA, Inc. v. Hobbs, 817 N.E.2d 603 (Ind.Ct.App. 2004).

   b. *Unopposed motions generally granted.* It is common for a trial court to grant procedural motions, such as motions for enlargement of time, discovery motions, or motions for continuance, unless an objection is filed. 21 INPRAC § 13.8.

2. *Motion to dismiss for lack of personal jurisdiction.* Every defense, in law or fact, to a claim for relief in any pleading, whether a claim, counterclaim, cross-claim, or third-party claim, shall be asserted in the responsive pleading thereto if one is required; except that at the option of the pleader, the defense of lack of jurisdiction over person may be made by motion. IN ST TRIAL P Rule 12(b)(2). If personal jurisdiction is not present, then that party against whom jurisdiction is asserted must raise the question. 1A INPRAC R 12(12.6).

   a. *Presumption of jurisdiction.* Jurisdiction is presumed and, therefore, the defense of lack of personal jurisdiction may be asserted by motion under IN ST TRIAL P Rule 12(B)(2), or in the defendant's answer as an affirmative defense. 22 INPRAC § 15.16; Adsit Co., Inc. v. Gustin, 874 N.E.2d 1018 (Ind.Ct.App. 2007); Keesling v. Winstead, 858 N.E.2d 996 (Ind.Ct.App. 2006). Refer to the Indiana KeyRules Answer document for more information.

   b. *Personal jurisdiction.* The Due Process Clause of the Fourteenth Amendment requires that before a state may exercise jurisdiction over a defendant, the defendant must have certain minimum contacts with the state such that the maintenance of the suit does not offend traditional notions of fair play and substantial justice. 1A INPRAC R 12(12.6).

      i. *General jurisdiction.* If the defendant's contacts with the state are so continuous and systematic that the defendant should reasonably anticipate being haled into the courts of that state for any matter, then the defendant is subject to general jurisdiction, even in causes of action unrelated to the defendant's contacts with the forum state. 1A INPRAC R 12(12.6).

      ii. *Specific jurisdiction.* In cases where a defendant is not subject to general jurisdiction in a forum state, specific jurisdiction may be asserted if the controversy is related to or arises out of the defendant's contacts with the forum state. Specific jurisdiction requires that the defendant purposefully availed itself of the privilege of conducting activities within the forum state so that the defendant reasonably anticipates being haled into court there. A single contact with the forum state may be sufficient to establish specific jurisdiction over a defendant, if it creates a substantial connection with the forum state and the suit is related to that connection. 1A INPRAC R 12(12.6).

      iii. *Due process; Reasonableness.* A defendant cannot be haled into a jurisdiction solely as a result of random, fortuitous, or attenuated contacts or of the unilateral activity of another party or a third person. Once either general or specific jurisdiction has been established, due process requires that the assertion of personal jurisdiction over the defendant is reasonable. The assertion of personal jurisdiction will rarely be found unreasonable if minimum contacts are found. Five factors are used in determining reasonableness:

      - The burden on the defendant;
      - The forum State's interest in adjudicating the dispute;

- The plaintiff's interest in obtaining convenience and effective relief;
- The interstate judicial system's interest in obtaining the most efficient resolution of controversies; and
- The shared interest of the several States in furthering fundamental substantive social policies. 1A INPRAC R 12(12.6).

  iv. *Jurisdiction presumed.* Indiana state trial courts are courts of general jurisdiction and jurisdiction is presumed. The party contesting jurisdiction bears the burden of proving the lack of personal jurisdiction by a preponderance of the evidence, unless the lack of jurisdiction is apparent on the face of the complaint. A determination of the existence of personal jurisdiction is entitled to de novo review. 1A INPRAC R 12(12.6); Foley v. Schwartz, 943 N.E.2d 371 (Ind.Ct.App. 2011).

c. *Challenge to jurisdiction in first response to complaint.* The defendant may challenge the Indiana court's jurisdiction over him, without submitting to that jurisdiction, so long as the defense is asserted in the first response to the plaintiff's complaint and the defendant does not request affirmative relief from the court prior to asserting that defense. 22 INPRAC § 15.16.

d. *Burden shifting.* After the plaintiff establishes that there are minimum contacts between defendant and forum state to exercise personal jurisdiction without violating Due Process Clause, the defendant then carries the burden of proving that asserting jurisdiction is unfair and unreasonable. 1A INPRAC R 12(12.6); JPMorgan Chase Bank, N.A. v. Desert Palace, Inc., 882 N.E.2d 743 (Ind.Ct.App. 2008).

e. *Effect of granting of motion.* The dismissal of a complaint for lack of jurisdiction over the person is not an adjudication on the merits and does not prejudice the plaintiff's right to file another complaint if the court can obtain jurisdiction over the defendant. 9 INPRAC § 42.4.

3. *Consolidation and waiver*

a. *Consolidation of defenses in motion.* A party who makes a motion under IN ST TRIAL P Rule 12 may join with it any other motions herein provided for and then available to him. If a party makes a motion under IN ST TRIAL P Rule 12 but omits therefrom any defense or objection then available to him which IN ST TRIAL P Rule 12 permits to be raised by motion, he shall not thereafter make a motion based on the defense or objection so omitted. He may, however, make such motions as are allowed under IN ST TRIAL P Rule 12(H)(2). IN ST TRIAL P Rule 12(G).

b. *Waiver or preservation of certain defenses.* No defense or objection is waived by being joined with one or more other defenses or objections in a responsive pleading or motion. IN ST TRIAL P Rule 12(B).

D. Documents

1. *Required documents*

a. *Motion and notice.* The requirement of notice is satisfied by service of the motion. IN ST TRIAL P Rule 7(B). Refer to the General Requirements section of this document for information on the content of a motion to dismiss for lack of personal jurisdiction.

b. *Proposed order.* Unless local practice provides differently, a party should submit a proposed order with its written motion to be signed by the judge once the motion has been granted. 21 INPRAC § 13.8.

  i. *Proposed orders of a motion for dismissal.* Prior to entry by the Court of orders granting motions or applications, the moving party or applicant (or his or her attorney) shall, unless the Court directs otherwise, furnish the Court with proposed orders of a motion for dismissal. IN ST ALLEN SUPER AND CIR CT CIV Rule TR00-1(A)(5).

  ii. *Copies of proposed orders.* All proposed orders shall be submitted in an original plus a number of copies equal to one (1) more than the number of pro se parties and attorneys of record contained in the prepared proof of notice under IN ST TRIAL P Rule 72(D). IN ST ALLEN SUPER AND CIR CT CIV Rule TR00-1(C).

  iii. *Proof of notice.* The proposed order shall also include a prepared proof of notice, under IN ST TRIAL P Rule 72(D). IN ST ALLEN SUPER AND CIR CT CIV Rule TR00-1(B).

    iv.   Refer to the Format section of this document for information on the form and content of the proposed order and the proof of notice.

  c. *Certificate of service.* An attorney or unrepresented party tendering a document to the Clerk for filing shall certify that service has been made, list the parties served, and specify the date and means of service. The certificate of service shall be placed at the end of the document and shall not be separately filed. The separate filing of a certificate of service, however, shall not be grounds for rejecting a document for filing. The Clerk may permit documents to be filed without a certificate of service but shall require prompt filing of a separate certificate of service. IN ST TRIAL P Rule 5(C).

2. *Supplemental documents*

  a. *Supporting evidence.* When a motion is based on facts not appearing of record the court may hear the matter on affidavits presented by the respective parties, but the court may direct that the matter be heard wholly or partly on oral testimony or depositions. IN ST TRIAL P Rule 43(B).

  b. *Brief or memorandum.* If a party desires to file a brief or memorandum in support of any motion, such brief or memorandum shall be filed simultaneously with the motion, and a copy shall be promptly served upon the adverse party. IN ST ALLEN SUPER AND CIR CT CIV Rule 7-1(E).

  c. *Facsimile cover sheet.* Any document sent to the Clerk of the Circuit Court by electronic facsimile transmission shall be accompanied by a cover sheet which states the title of the document, case number, number of pages, identity and voice telephone number of the sending party and instructions for filing. The cover sheet shall contain the signature of the attorney or party, pro se, authorizing the filing. IN ST ADMIN Rule 12(D).

E. Format

1. *Form of motions.* The rules applicable to captions, and the signing and form of pleadings (IN ST TRIAL P Rule 8 through IN ST TRIAL P Rule 11), apply to all motions and other papers provided under the Indiana Rules of Trial Procedure. 22B INPRAC 7:2.

2. *Form of pleadings*

  a. *Caption; Names of parties.* Every pleading shall contain a caption setting forth the name of the court, the title of the action, the file number, and a designation as in IN ST TRIAL P Rule 7(A). In the complaint the title of the action shall include the names of all the parties, but in other pleadings it is sufficient to state the name of the first party on each side with an appropriate indication of other parties. IN ST TRIAL P Rule 10(A).

  b. *Paragraphs; Separate statements.* All averments of a claim or defense shall be made in numbered paragraphs, the contents of each of which shall be limited as far as practicable to a statement of a single set of circumstances, and a paragraph may be referred to by number in all succeeding pleadings. Each claim founded upon a separate transaction or occurrence and each defense other than denials may be stated in a separate count or defense whenever a separation facilitates the clear presentation of the matters set forth. IN ST TRIAL P Rule 10(B).

  c. *Adoption by reference; Exhibits.* Statements in a pleading may be adopted by reference in a different part of the same pleading or in another pleading or in any motion. A copy of any written instrument which is an exhibit to a pleading is a part thereof for all purposes. IN ST TRIAL P Rule 10(C).

  d. *Citation.* Allen County Superior and Circuit court rules may be cited as L.R. _____. The Indiana Rules of Trial Procedure are hereinafter referred to as T.R. _____. IN ST ALLEN SUPER AND CIR CT CIV Rule AR00-1(B).

  e. *Paper.* All pleadings must be printed on white paper. IN ST ALLEN SUPER AND CIR CT CIV Rule 8-1(A).

  f. *Spacing.* The lines shall be double spaced except for quotations, which shall be indented and single-spaced. IN ST ALLEN SUPER AND CIR CT CIV Rule 8-1(A).

  g. *Photocopies.* Photocopies are acceptable if legible. IN ST ALLEN SUPER AND CIR CT CIV Rule 8-1(A).

h. *Margins and binding.* Margins shall be one to one and one-half (1-1 1/2) inches on the left side and one-half (1/2) inch on the right. IN ST ALLEN SUPER AND CIR CT CIV Rule 8-1(B).

    i. Binding or stapling shall be at the top left and at no other place. IN ST ALLEN SUPER AND CIR CT CIV Rule 8-1(B).

    ii. Covers or backing shall not be used. IN ST ALLEN SUPER AND CIR CT CIV Rule 8-1(B).

i. *Flat filing.* The files of the Clerk of the Court shall be kept under the "flat filing" system. All pleadings presented for filing with the Clerk or Court shall be flat and unfolded. Only the original of any pleading shall be placed in the Court file. IN ST ALLEN SUPER AND CIR CT CIV Rule 77-1(A).

j. *Handwritten pleadings.* Handwritten pleadings may be accepted for filing in the discretion of the Court. IN ST ALLEN SUPER AND CIR CT CIV Rule 8-1(A).

3. *Size of papers for filing.* Effective January 1, 1992, all pleadings, copies, motions and documents filed with any trial court or appellate level court, typed or printed, with the exception of exhibits and existing wills, shall be prepared on eight and one-half by eleven inch (8 1/2" x 11") size paper. IN ST ADMIN Rule 11.

4. *Form of proposed orders*

a. *Form, caption, and title.* Any proposed order shall be a document that is separate and apart from the motion or application to which it relates and shall contain a caption showing the name of the court, the case number assigned to the case and the title of the case as shown by the complaint. IN ST ALLEN SUPER AND CIR CT CIV Rule TR00-1(B). If there are multiple parties, the title may be shortened to include only the first name plaintiff and defendant with appropriate indication that there are additional parties. IN ST ALLEN SUPER AND CIR CT CIV Rule TR00-1(B).

b. *Paper.* The proposed order shall be on white paper, eight and one half by eleven inches (8 1/2" x 11") in size, and each page shall be numbered. IN ST ALLEN SUPER AND CIR CT CIV Rule TR00-1(B).

c. *Signature line.* On the last page of the proposed order there shall be a line for the signature of the judge under which shall be typed "Judge, Allen Superior Court" or "Judge, Allen Circuit Court", whichever is applicable, to the left of which shall be the following: "Dated _____". IN ST ALLEN SUPER AND CIR CT CIV Rule TR00-1(B).

d. *Allowance of space for clerk.* To allow space for the Clerk to make entries on the proposed order to show compliance with the notice requirements of IN ST TRIAL P Rule 72(D), the lower four (4) inches of the last page of the proposed order shall be left blank. IN ST ALLEN SUPER AND CIR CT CIV Rule TR00-1(B).

e. *Proof of notice required.* The proposed order shall also include a prepared proof of notice, under IN ST TRIAL P Rule 72(D). The proof of notice shall conform to the format show in IN ST ALLEN SUPER AND CIR CT CIV Rule TR00-1(B). IN ST ALLEN SUPER AND CIR CT CIV Rule TR00-1(B).

5. *Signature requirements*

a. *Signature of attorney.* Every pleading or motion of a party represented by an attorney shall be signed by at least one (1) attorney of record in his individual name, whose address, telephone number, and attorney number shall be stated, except that this provision shall not apply to pleadings and motions made and transcribed at the trial or a hearing before the judge and received by him in such form. IN ST TRIAL P Rule 11(A). All pleadings to be signed by an attorney shall contain the written signature of the individual attorney, the attorney's printed name, Supreme Court Attorney Number, the name of the attorney's law firm, the attorney's address, telephone number, and a designation of the party for whom the attorney appears. IN ST ALLEN SUPER AND CIR CT CIV Rule 8-1(C). For the recommended signature format, refer to IN ST ALLEN SUPER AND CIR CT CIV Rule 8-1(C).

    i. The signature of an attorney constitutes a certificate by him that he has read the pleadings; that to the best of his knowledge, information, and belief, there is good ground to support it; and that it is not interposed for delay. IN ST TRIAL P Rule 11(A).

ii. If a pleading or motion is not signed or is signed with intent to defeat the purpose of the rule, it may be stricken as sham and false and the action may proceed as though the pleading had not been served. IN ST TRIAL P Rule 11(A).

iii. For a willful violation of IN ST TRIAL P Rule 11 an attorney may be subjected to appropriate disciplinary action. Similar action may be taken if scandalous or indecent matter is inserted. IN ST TRIAL P Rule 11(A).

iv. Neither printed signatures, nor facsimile signatures shall be accepted on original documents. IN ST ALLEN SUPER AND CIR CT CIV Rule 8-1(C).

v. Facsimile signatures are permitted on copies. IN ST ALLEN SUPER AND CIR CT CIV Rule 8-1(C).

b. *Signature of unrepresented party.* A party who is not represented by an attorney shall sign his pleading and state his address. IN ST TRIAL P Rule 11(A).

c. *Verification not generally required.* Except when specifically required by rule, pleadings or motions need not be verified or accompanied by affidavit. The rule in equity that the averments of an answer under oath must be overcome by the testimony of two (2) witnesses or of one (1) witness sustained by corroborating circumstances is abolished. IN ST TRIAL P Rule 11(A).

d. *Verification by affirmation or representation.* When in connection with any civil or special statutory proceeding it is required that any pleading, motion, petition, supporting affidavit, or other document of any kind, be verified, or that an oath be taken, it shall be sufficient if the subscriber simply affirms the truth of the matter to be verified by an affirmation or representation. IN ST TRIAL P Rule 11(B). IN ST TRIAL P Rule 11(B) states that the affirmation or representation should be in substantially the following language: "I (we) affirm, under the penalties for perjury, that the foregoing representation(s) is (are) true. (Signed) _____."

i. Any person who falsifies an affirmation or representation of fact shall be subject to the same penalties as are prescribed by law for the making of a false affidavit. IN ST TRIAL P Rule 11(B).

e. *Verified pleadings, motions, and affidavits as evidence.* Pleadings, motions and affidavits accompanying or in support of such pleadings or motions when required to be verified or under oath shall be accepted as a representation that the signer had personal knowledge thereof or reasonable cause to believe the existence of the facts or matters stated or alleged therein; and, if otherwise competent or acceptable as evidence, may be admitted as evidence of the facts or matters stated or alleged therein when it is so provided in the Indiana Rules of Trial Procedure, by statute or other law, or to the extent the writing or signature expressly purports to be made upon the signer's personal knowledge. When such pleadings, motions and affidavits are verified or under oath they shall not require other or greater proof on the part of the adverse party than if not verified or not under oath unless expressly provided otherwise by the Indiana Rules of Trial Procedure, statute or other law. Affidavits upon motions for summary judgment under IN ST TRIAL P Rule 56 and in denial of execution under IN ST TRIAL P Rule 9.2 shall be made upon personal knowledge. IN ST TRIAL P Rule 11(C).

6. *Information excluded from public access.* Every document filed in a case shall separately identify information excluded from public access pursuant to IN ST ADMIN Rule 9(G)(1) as follows:

a. Whole documents that are excluded from public access pursuant to IN ST ADMIN Rule 9(G)(1) shall be tendered on light green paper or have a light green coversheet attached to the document, marked "Not for Public Access" or "Confidential." IN ST TRIAL P Rule 5(G)(1).

b. When only a portion of a document contains information excluded from public access pursuant to IN ST ADMIN Rule 9(G)(1), said information shall be omitted [or redacted] from the filed document, and set forth on a separate accompanying document on light green paper conspicuously marked "Not for Public Access" or "Confidential" and clearly designated [or identifying] the caption and number of the case and the document and location within the document to which the redacted material pertains. IN ST TRIAL P Rule 5(G)(2).

c. With respect to documents filed in electronic format, the trial court, by local rule, may provide for compliance with IN ST TRIAL P Rule 5 in manner that separates and protects access to information excluded from public access. IN ST TRIAL P Rule 5(G)(3).

d. IN ST TRIAL P Rule 5(G) does not apply to a record sealed by the court pursuant to IN ST 5-14-3-5.5 or otherwise, nor to records, documents, or information filed in cases to which public access is prohibited pursuant to IN ST ADMIN Rule 9(G). IN ST TRIAL P Rule 5(G)(4).

e. The following information in case records is excluded from public access and is confidential:

  i. Information that is excluded from public access pursuant to federal law;

  ii. Information that is excluded from public access as declared confidential by Indiana statute or other court rule, including without limitation:

  - All adoption records created after July 8, 1941, as declared confidential by IN ST 31-19-19-1, et seq., except those specifically declared open by IN ST 31-19-13-2(2);

  - All records relating to chancroid, chlamydia, gonorrhea, hepatitis, human immunodeficiency virus (HIV), Lymphogranuloma venereum, syphilis, tuberculosis, as declared confidential by IN ST 16-41-8-1, et seq.;

  - All records relating to child abuse as declared confidential by IN ST 31-33-18-1, et seq.;

  - All records relating to drug tests as declared confidential by IN ST 5-14-3-4(a)(9);

  - Records of grand jury proceedings as declared confidential by IN ST 35-34-2-4;

  - Records of juvenile proceedings as declared confidential by IN ST 31-39-1-2, except those specifically open under statute;

  - All paternity records created after July 1, 1941 as declared confidential by IN ST 31-14-11-15, IN ST 31-19-5-23, IN ST 31-39-1-1 and IN ST 31-39-1-2 [Editor's note: IN ST 31-14-11-15 was repealed effective May 9, 2013];

  - All pre-sentence reports as declared confidential by IN ST 35-38-1-13;

  - Written petitions to permit marriages without consent and orders directing the Clerk of Court to issue a marriage license to underage persons, as declared confidential by IN ST 31-11-1-6;

  - Only those arrest warrants, search warrants, indictments and informations ordered confidential by the trial judge, prior to return of duly executed service as declared confidential by IN ST 5-14-3-4(b)(1);

  - All medical, mental health, or tax records unless determined by law or regulation of any governmental custodian not to be confidential, released by the subject of such records, or declared by a court of competent jurisdiction to be essential to the resolution of litigation as declared confidential by IN ST 16-39-3-10, IN ST 6-4.1-5-10, IN ST 6-4.1-12-12, and IN ST 6-8.1-7-1;

  - Personal information relating to jurors or prospective jurors, other than for the use of the parties and counsel, pursuant to IN ST JURY Rule 10;

  - Information relating to protection from abuse orders, no-contact orders and workplace violence restraining orders as declared confidential by IN ST 5-2-9-6, et seq.;

  - Mediation proceedings pursuant to IN ST ADR Rule 2.11, Mini-Trial proceedings pursuant to IN ST ADR Rule 4.4(C), and Summary Jury Trials pursuant to IN ST ADR Rule 5.6;

  - Information in probation files pursuant to the Probation Standards promulgated by the Judicial Conference of Indiana pursuant to IN ST 11-13-1-8(b);

  - Information deemed confidential pursuant to the Rules for Court Administered Alcohol and Drug Programs promulgated by the Judicial Conference of Indiana pursuant to IN ST 12-23-14-13;

  - Information deemed confidential pursuant to the Problem-Solving Court Rules promulgated by the Judicial Conference of Indiana pursuant to IN ST 33-23-16-16;

  - All records of the Department of workforce Development as declared confidential by IN ST 22-4-19-6;

- Information regarding interception of electronic communications that is sealed or deemed confidential as set forth in IN ST 35-33.5-2-1, et seq.

iii. Information excluded from public access by specific court order;

iv. Complete Social Security Numbers of living persons;

v. With the exception of names, information such as addresses, phone numbers, and dates of birth which explicitly identifies:

- Natural persons who are witnesses or victims (not including defendants) in criminal, domestic violence, stalking, sexual assault, juvenile, or civil protection order proceedings, provided that juveniles who are victims of sex crimes shall be identified by initials only;

- Places of residence of judicial officers, clerks and other employees of courts and clerks of court, unless the person or persons about whom the information pertains waives confidentiality;

vi. Complete account numbers of specific assets, loans, bank accounts, credit cards, and personal identification numbers (PINs);

vii. All orders of expungement entered in criminal or juvenile proceedings, orders to restrict access to criminal history information pursuant to IN ST 35-38-5-5.5 or IN ST 35-38-8-5 and records excluded from public access by such orders, and information related to infractions that is excluded from public access pursuant to IN ST 34-28-5-15 or IN ST 34-28-5-16 [Editor's note: IN ST 35-38-5-5.5, IN ST 35-38-8-5 and IN ST 34-28-5-16 were repealed effective July 1, 2013; for information on orders restricting access to criminal history, refer to IN ST 35-38-9-1, et seq.];

viii. All personal notes and e-mail, and deliberative material, of judges, jurors, court staff and judicial agencies, and information recorded in personal data assistants (PDA's) or organizers and personal calendars. IN ST ADMIN Rule 9(G)(1).

F. Filing and Service Requirements

1. *Filing requirements.* Except as otherwise provided in IN ST TRIAL P Rule 5(E)(2), all pleadings and papers subsequent to the complaint which are required to be served upon a party shall be filed with the Court either before service or within a reasonable period of time thereafter. IN ST TRIAL P Rule 5(E)(1).

   a. *Filing with the court defined.* The filing of pleadings, motions, and other papers with the court as required by the Indiana Rules of Trial Procedure shall be made by one of the following methods:

      i. Delivery to the clerk of the court;

      ii. Sending by electronic transmission under the procedure adopted pursuant to IN ST ADMIN Rule 12;

      iii. Mailing to the clerk by registered, certified or express mail return receipt requested;

      iv. Depositing with any third-party commercial carrier for delivery to the clerk within three (3) calendar days, cost prepaid, properly addressed;

      v. If the court so permits, filing with the judge, in which event the judge shall note thereon the filing date and forthwith transmit them to the office of the clerk; or

      vi. Electronic filing, as approved by the Division of State Court Administration pursuant to IN ST ADMIN Rule 16. IN ST TRIAL P Rule 5(F).

      vii. Filing by registered or certified mail and by third-party commercial carrier shall be complete upon mailing or deposit. IN ST TRIAL P Rule 5(F).

   b. *Facsimile filing*

      i. *Generally.* In counties where a majority of judges of the courts of record, by posted local rule, have authorized electronic facsimile filing and designated a telephone number to receive such transmissions, pleadings, motions, and other papers may be sent to the Clerk of Circuit Court by electronic facsimile transmission for filing in any case, provided:

         - Such matter does not exceed ten (10) pages, including the cover sheet;

- Such matter does not require the payment of fees other than the electronic facsimile transcription fee set forth in IN ST ADMIN Rule 12(E);

- The sending party creates at the time of transmission a machine generated log for such transmission; and

- The original document and the transmission log are maintained by the sending party for the duration of the litigation. IN ST ADMIN Rule 12(B).

    ii. *Time of filing.* During normal, posted business hours, the time of filing shall be the time the duplicate document is produced in the office of the Clerk of the Circuit Court. Duplicate documents received at all other times shall be filed as of the next normal business day. IN ST ADMIN Rule 12(C).

- If the receiving fax machine endorses its own time and date stamp upon the transmitted documents and the receiving machine produces a delivery receipt which is electronically created and transmitted to the sending party, the time of filing shall be the date and time recorded on the transmitted document by the receiving fax machine. IN ST ADMIN Rule 12(C).

  c. *Proof of filing.* Any party filing any paper by any method other than personal delivery to the clerk shall retain proof of filing. IN ST TRIAL P Rule 5(F).

2. *Service requirements.* Unless otherwise provided by the Indiana Rules of Trial Procedure or an order of the court, each party and special judge, if any, shall be served with: (1) every order required by its terms to be served; (2) every pleading subsequent to the original complaint; (3) every written motion except one which may be heard ex parte; (4) every brief submitted to the trial court; (5) every paper relating to discovery required to be served upon a party; and (6) every written notice, appearance, demand, offer of judgment, designation of record on appeal, or similar paper. IN ST TRIAL P Rule 5(A).

  a. *Methods of service*

    i. *Personal service.* Whenever a party is represented by an attorney of record, service shall be made upon such attorney unless service upon the party himself is ordered by the court. Service upon the attorney or party shall be made by delivering or mailing a copy of the papers to the last known address or where an attorney or party has consented to service by fax or e-mail, as provided in IN ST TRIAL P Rule 3.1(A)(4), by faxing or e-mailing a copy of the documents to the fax number or e-mail address set out in the appearance form or correction as required by IN ST TRIAL P Rule 3.1(E). IN ST TRIAL P Rule 5(B). Delivery of a copy within IN ST TRIAL P Rule 5 means:

- Offering or tendering it to the attorney or party and stating the nature of the papers being served. Refusal to accept an offered or tendered document is a waiver of any objection to the sufficiency or adequacy of service of that document;

- Leaving it at his office with a clerk or other person in charge thereof, or if there is no one in charge, leaving it in a conspicuous place therein; or

- If the office is closed, by leaving it at his dwelling house or usual place of abode with some person of suitable age and discretion then residing therein; or,

- Leaving it at some other suitable place, selected by the attorney upon whom service is being made, pursuant to duly promulgated local rule. IN ST TRIAL P Rule 5(B)(1).

    ii. *Service by mail.* If service is made by mail, the papers shall be deposited in the United States mail addressed to the person on whom they are being served, with postage prepaid. Service shall be deemed complete upon mailing. Proof of service of all papers permitted to be mailed may be made by written acknowledgment of service, by affidavit of the person who mailed the papers, or by certificate of an attorney. It shall be the duty of attorneys when entering their appearance in a cause or when filing pleadings or papers therein, to have noted in the Chronological Case Summary or said pleadings or papers so filed the address and telephone number of their office. Service by delivery or by mail at such address shall be deemed sufficient and complete. IN ST TRIAL P Rule 5(B)(2).

    iii. *Service by fax or e-mail.* A party who has consented to service by fax or e-mail may be served as follows:

- Service by e-mail shall be made by attaching the document being served in .pdf format. Discovery documents must also be served in accordance with IN ST TRIAL P Rule 26(A). IN ST TRIAL P Rule 5(B)(3)(a).

- Service by fax shall be deemed complete upon generation of a transmission record indicating the successful transmission of the entire document, except as provided in IN ST TRIAL P Rule 5(B)(3)(d). IN ST TRIAL P Rule 5(B)(3)(b).

- Service by e-mail shall be deemed complete upon transmission, except as provided in IN ST TRIAL P Rule 5(B)(3)(d). IN ST TRIAL P Rule 5(B)(3)(c).

- Service by fax or e-mail that occurs on a Saturday, Sunday, legal holiday, or day the court or agency in which the matter is pending is closed or after 5:00 PM local time of the recipient shall be deemed complete the next day that is not a Saturday, Sunday, legal holiday, or day that the court or agency in which the matter is pending is not closed. IN ST TRIAL P Rule 5(B)(3)(d).

    iv. *Consent to alternate service.* Any Allen County Attorney or any Allen County law firm may, without charge, maintain an assigned Courthouse box in the library of the Allen County Courthouse for receipt of notices, pleadings, process orders, or other communications from the Court, the Clerk, and other attorneys or law firms. IN ST ALLEN SUPER AND CIR CT CIV Rule 5-1(A). For more information concerning the use of courthouse boxes, refer to IN ST ALLEN SUPER AND CIR CT CIV Rule 5-1.

  b. *Serving numerous defendants.* In any action in which there are unusually large numbers of defendants, the court, upon motion or of its own initiative, may order:

    i. That service of the pleadings of the defendants and replies thereto need not be made as between the defendants;

- That any cross-claim, counterclaim, or matter constituting an avoidance or affirmative defense contained therein shall be deemed to be denied or avoided by all other parties; and

- That the filing of any such pleading and service thereof upon the plaintiff constitutes due notice of it to the parties. IN ST TRIAL P Rule 5(D).

    ii. A copy of every such order shall be served upon the parties in such manner and form as the court directs. IN ST TRIAL P Rule 5(D).

  c. *Service on parties in default for failure to appear.* No service need be made on parties in default for failure to appear, except that pleadings asserting new or additional claims for relief against them shall be served upon them in the manner provided by service of summons in IN ST TRIAL P Rule 4. IN ST TRIAL P Rule 5(A).

G. Hearings

1. *Hearing on motion.* Unless local conditions make it impracticable, each judge shall establish regular times and places, at intervals sufficiently frequent for the prompt dispatch of business, at which motions requiring notice and hearing may be heard and disposed of; but the judge at any time or place and on such notice, if any, as he considers reasonable may make order for the advancement, conduct, and hearing of actions. To expedite its business the court may direct the submission and determination of motions without oral hearing upon brief written statements of reasons in support and opposition, or direct or permit hearings by telephone conference call with all attorneys or other similar means of communication. IN ST TRIAL P Rule 73(A).

  a. *Setting motions for hearing.* Except for the motions described in IN ST ALLEN SUPER AND CIR CT CIV Rule 7-1(E), all motions shall be set for hearing. IN ST ALLEN SUPER AND CIR CT CIV Rule 7-1(A). [Editor's note: While IN ST ALLEN SUPER AND CIR CT CIV Rule 7-1(A) refers to IN ST ALLEN SUPER AND CIR CT CIV Rule 7-1(E) as relating to hearings on motions, that reference is likely intended to be to IN ST ALLEN SUPER AND CIR CT CIV Rule 7-1(D).]

    i. It shall be the responsibility of the moving party to request the date of such hearing from the

Judicial Assistant, or if the case has already been assigned to a Judge, from the Judicial Law Clerk of the assigned Judge. IN ST ALLEN SUPER AND CIR CT CIV Rule 7-1(A).

b. *Responsibility for notice of hearing.* It shall be the responsibility of the moving party to give notice to all other parties of hearings scheduled on motions. IN ST ALLEN SUPER AND CIR CT CIV Rule 7-1(I).

H. Forms

1. Motion to Dismiss for Lack of Personal Jurisdiction Forms for Indiana

a. General form. 5 INPRAC § 3:4.1.

b. Lack of personal jurisdiction. 5 INPRAC § 3:4.3.

c. Certificate of service; Personal service. 9 INPRAC § 5.7.

d. Certificate of service; First class mail. 9 INPRAC § 5.8.

e. Motion to dismiss plaintiff's complaint; General form. 9 INPRAC § 42.2.

f. Lack of personal jurisdiction. 9 INPRAC § 42.4.

2. Official Motion to Dismiss for Lack of Personal Jurisdiction Forms for Allen County

a. Consent to alternate service. IN ST ALLEN SUPER AND CIR CT CIV App. A.

I. Checklist

(I) ❑ Matters to be considered by moving party

  (a) ❑ Required documents

    (1) ❑ Motion and notice

    (2) ❑ Proposed order

    (3) ❑ Certificate of service

  (b) ❑ Supplemental documents

    (1) ❑ Supporting evidence

    (2) ❑ Brief or memorandum

    (3) ❑ Facsimile cover sheet

  (c) ❑ Timing

    (1) ❑ A motion to dismiss for lack of personal jurisdiction shall be made before pleading if a further pleading is permitted or within twenty (20) days after service of the prior pleading if none is required

    (2) ❑ A written motion, other than one which may be heard ex parte, and notice of the hearing thereof shall be served not less than five (5) days before the time specified for the hearing, unless a different period is fixed by the Indiana Rules of Trial Procedure or by order of the court

    (3) ❑ All pleadings and papers subsequent to the complaint which are required to be served upon a party shall be filed with the Court either before service or within a reasonable period of time thereafter

(II) ❑ Matters to be considered by the responding party

  (a) ❑ Required documents

    (1) ❑ Opposition

    (2) ❑ Certificate of service

  (b) ❑ Supplemental documents

    (1) ❑ Supporting evidence

    (2) ❑ Proposed order

(3) ❏ Brief or memorandum

(4) ❏ Facsimile cover sheet

(c) ❏ Timing

(1) ❏ Except as otherwise provided in IN ST TRIAL P Rule 59(D), opposing affidavits may be served not less than one (1) day before the hearing, unless the court permits them to be served at some other time

Requests, Notices and Applications
Interrogatories

Document Last Updated October 2013

A. Applicable Rules

1. *State rules*

a. Appearance. IN ST TRIAL P Rule 3.1.

b. Process. IN ST TRIAL P Rule 4.

c. Service and filing of pleadings and other papers. IN ST TRIAL P Rule 5.

d. Time. IN ST TRIAL P Rule 6.

e. Pleadings. IN ST TRIAL P Rule 7; IN ST TRIAL P Rule 9.2; IN ST TRIAL P Rule 10.

f. Signing and verification of pleadings. IN ST TRIAL P Rule 11.

g. General provisions governing discovery. IN ST TRIAL P Rule 26.

h. Methods of discovery. IN ST TRIAL P Rule 27; IN ST TRIAL P Rule 29; IN ST TRIAL P Rule 30; IN ST TRIAL P Rule 31; IN ST TRIAL P Rule 33; IN ST TRIAL P Rule 34; IN ST TRIAL P Rule 35; IN ST TRIAL P Rule 36.

i. Failure to make or cooperate in discovery; Sanctions. IN ST TRIAL P Rule 37.

j. Judgment on the evidence (directed verdict). IN ST TRIAL P Rule 50.

k. Findings by the court. IN ST TRIAL P Rule 52.

l. Summary judgment. IN ST TRIAL P Rule 56.

m. Motion to correct error. IN ST TRIAL P Rule 59.

n. Relief from judgment or order. IN ST TRIAL P Rule 60.

o. Access to court records. IN ST ADMIN Rule 9.

p. Paper size. IN ST ADMIN Rule 11.

q. Facsimile transmission. IN ST ADMIN Rule 12.

r. Electronic filing and electronic service pilot projects. IN ST ADMIN Rule 16.

s. Sealing of certain records by court; Hearing; Notice. IN ST 5-14-3-5.5.

t. Privacy and confidentiality. IN ST 5-2-9-6; IN ST 5-14-3-4; IN ST 6-4.1-5-10; IN ST 6-4.1-12-12; IN ST 6-8.1-7-1; IN ST 11-13-1-8; IN ST 12-23-14-13; IN ST 16-39-3-10; IN ST 16-41-8-1; IN ST 22-4-19-6; IN ST 31-11-1-6; IN ST 31-19-5-23; IN ST 31-19-13-2; IN ST 31-19-19-1; IN ST 31-33-18-1; IN ST 31-39-1-1; IN ST 31-39-1-2; IN ST 33-23-16-16; IN ST 35-34-2-4; IN ST 35-38-1-13; IN ST 35-38-9-1; IN ST ADR Rule 2.11; IN ST ADR Rule 4.4; IN ST ADR Rule 5.6; IN ST JURY Rule 10.

2. *Local rules*

a. Applicability and citation of rules. IN ST ALLEN SUPER AND CIR CT CIV Rule AR00-1.

b. Admissions, stipulations and agreements. IN ST ALLEN SUPER AND CIR CT CIV Rule TR00-2.

c. Appearances. IN ST ALLEN SUPER AND CIR CT CIV Rule 3.1-1.

    d.   Consent to alternate service. IN ST ALLEN SUPER AND CIR CT CIV Rule 5-1.

    e.   Preparation of pleadings. IN ST ALLEN SUPER AND CIR CT CIV Rule 8-1.

    f.   Filing. IN ST ALLEN SUPER AND CIR CT CIV Rule 77-1.

B. Timing

1. *Service of interrogatories.* Interrogatories may, without leave of court, be served upon the plaintiff after commencement of the action and upon any other party with or after service of the summons and complaint upon that party. IN ST TRIAL P Rule 33(A).

2. *Service of responses to interrogatories.* The party upon whom the interrogatories have been served shall serve a copy of the answers and objections within a period designated by the party submitting the interrogatories, not less than thirty (30) days after the service thereof or within such shorter or longer time as the court may allow. IN ST TRIAL P Rule 33(C).

3. *Computation of time*

    a.   *Generally; Days excluded.* In computing any period of time prescribed or allowed by the Indiana Rules of Trial Procedure, by order of the court, or by any applicable statute, the day of the act, event, or default from which the designated period of time begins to run shall not be included. The last day of the period so computed is to be included unless it is:

        i.   A Saturday,

        ii.   A Sunday,

        iii.   A legal holiday as defined by state statute, or

        iv.   A day the office in which the act is to be done is closed during regular business hours. IN ST TRIAL P Rule 6(A).

    b.   *Short periods.* In any event, the period runs until the end of the next day that is not a Saturday, a Sunday, a legal holiday, or a day on which the office is closed. When the period of time allowed is less than seven (7) days, intermediate Saturdays, Sundays, legal holidays, and days on which the office is closed shall be excluded from the computations. IN ST TRIAL P Rule 6(A).

    c.   *Additional time after service by United States mail.* Whenever a party has the right or is required to do some act or take some proceedings within a prescribed period after the service of a notice or other paper upon him and the notice or paper is served upon him by United States mail, three (3) days shall be added to the prescribed period. IN ST TRIAL P Rule 6(E).

    d.   *Enlargement of time.* When an act is required or allowed to be done at or within a specific time by the Indiana Rules of Trial Procedure, the court may at any time for cause shown:

        i.   Order the period enlarged, with or without motion or notice, if request therefor is made before the expiration of the period originally prescribed or extended by a previous order; or

        ii.   Upon motion made after the expiration of the specific period, permit the act to be done where the failure to act was the result of excusable neglect; but, the court may not extend the time for taking any action for judgment on the evidence under IN ST TRIAL P Rule 50(A), amendment of findings and judgment under IN ST TRIAL P Rule 52(B), to correct errors under IN ST TRIAL P Rule 59(C), statement in opposition to motion to correct error under IN ST TRIAL P Rule 59(E), or to obtain relief from final judgment under IN ST TRIAL P Rule 60(B), except to the extent and under the conditions stated in those rules. IN ST TRIAL P Rule 6(B).

C. General Requirements

1. *Scope of discovery.* Unless otherwise limited by order of the court in accordance with the Indiana Rules of Trial Procedure, the scope of discovery is as follows:

    a.   *In general.* Parties may obtain discovery regarding any matter, not privileged, which is relevant to the subject-matter involved in the pending action, whether it relates to the claim or defense of the party seeking discovery or the claim or defense of any other party, including the existence, description, nature, custody, condition and location of any books, documents, or other tangible things and the identity and location of persons having knowledge of any discoverable matter. It is not ground for objection that the information sought will be inadmissible at the trial if the information sought appears reasonably calculated to lead to the discovery of admissible evidence. IN ST TRIAL P Rule 26(B)(1).

   i. *Limiting discovery upon court determination.* The frequency or extent of use of the discovery methods otherwise permitted under the Indiana Rules of Trial Procedure and by any local rule shall be limited by the court if it determines that:

- The discovery sought is unreasonably cumulative or duplicative, or is obtainable from some other source that is more convenient, less burdensome, or less expensive;

- The party seeking discovery has had ample opportunity by discovery in the action to obtain the information sought or;

- The burden or expense of the proposed discovery outweighs its likely benefit, taking into account the needs of the case, the amount in controversy, the parties' resources, the importance of the issues at stake in the litigation, and the importance of the proposed discovery in resolving the issues. IN ST TRIAL P Rule 26(B)(1).

- The court may act upon its own initiative after reasonable notice or pursuant to a motion under IN ST TRIAL P Rule 26(C). IN ST TRIAL P Rule 26(B)(1). Refer to the Indiana KeyRules Motion for Protective Order document for more information.

   ii. *Relevancy in the discovery context.* When the word "relevancy" is used in IN ST TRIAL P Rule 26(B), it does not mean "relevancy" as that word in used to determine the admissibility of evidence in a trial court. It is much broader. It means "relevancy" to the "subject matter" of the litigation or pending action and it may relate to the claim or defense of any party. Pretrial discovery is available as to any nonprivileged matter relevant to the subject matter of the lawsuit or to obtain information reasonably calculated to lead to admissible evidence. 2A INPRAC R 26(26.4); Kaufmann v. Credithrift Financial, Inc., 465 N.E.2d 207, 210 (Ind.Ct.App. 1984).

   iii. *Tests for relevance.* Indiana case law has developed two (2) additional tests in this area. 2A INPRAC R 26(26.4).

- The first test determines when a document or a request for information is actually relevant to the subject matter in the pending action. A document [or discovery request] is relevant to discovery if there is the possibility the information sought may be relevant to the subject matter of the action. 2A INPRAC R 26(26.4); CIGNA-INA/Aetna v. Hagerman-Shambaugh, 473 N.E.2d 1033, 1036 (Ind.Ct.App. 1985).

- The second test speaks to appellate review of the trial court's determination that a document or discovery request is relevant to the subject matter of the pending action. The appellate court sees its review of the trial court's decision on relevancy to subject matter as being very limited. The court states: "Our review of the trial court's conclusion that the documents are relevant is limited. A trial court is vested with discretion in its rulings on discovery issues." 2A INPRAC R 26(26.4); Costanzi v. Ryan, 175 Ind.App. 257, 370 N.E.2d 1333 (Ind.Ct.App. 1978).

b. *Insurance agreements.* A party may obtain discovery of the existence and contents of any insurance agreement under which any person carrying on an insurance business may be liable to satisfy part or all of a judgment which may be entered in the action or to indemnify or reimburse for payments made to satisfy the judgment. Information concerning the insurance agreement is not by reason of disclosure admissible in evidence at trial. For purposes of IN ST TRIAL P Rule 26(B)(2), an application for insurance shall not be treated as part of an insurance agreement. IN ST TRIAL P Rule 26(B)(2).

c. *Trial preparation; Materials.* Subject to the provisions of IN ST TRIAL P Rule 26(B)(4), a party may obtain discovery of documents and tangible things otherwise discoverable under IN ST TRIAL P Rule 26(B)(1) and prepared in anticipation of litigation or for trial by or for another party or by or for that other party's representative (including his attorney, consultant, surety, indemnitor, insurer, or agent) only upon a showing that the party seeking discovery has substantial need of the materials in the preparation of his case and that he is unable without undue hardship to obtain the substantial equivalent of the materials by other means. In ordering discovery of such materials when the required showing has been made, the court shall protect against disclosure of the mental impressions, conclusions, opinions, or legal theories of an attorney or other representative of a party concerning the litigation. IN ST TRIAL P Rule 26(B)(3).

i.   A party may obtain without the required showing a statement concerning the action or its subject matter previously made by that party. Upon request, a person not a party may obtain without the required showing a statement concerning the action or its subject matter previously made by that person. If the request is refused, the person may move for a court order. The provisions of IN ST TRIAL P Rule 37(A)(4) apply to the award of expenses incurred in relation to the motion. For purposes of IN ST TRIAL P Rule 26(B)(3), a statement previously made is:

- A written statement signed or otherwise adopted approved by the person making it, or

- A stenographic, mechanical, electrical, or other recording, or a transcription thereof, which is a substantially verbatim recital of an oral statement by the person making it and contemporaneously recorded. IN ST TRIAL P Rule 26(B)(3).

ii. The protection of IN ST TRIAL P Rule 26(B)(3) extends to material prepared or collected before litigation actually commences, but that some possibility of litigation must actually exist before the privilege and IN ST TRIAL P Rule 26(B)(3) become operative. 2A INPRAC R 26(26.9); CIGNA-INA/Aetna v. Hagerman-Shambaugh, 473 N.E.2d 1033, 1037 (Ind.Ct.App. 1985).

d. *Trial preparation; Experts.* Discovery of facts known and opinions held by experts, otherwise discoverable under the provisions of IN ST TRIAL P Rule 26(B)(1) and acquired or developed in anticipation of litigation or for trial, may be obtained as follows:

i.   A party may through interrogatories require any other party to identify each person whom the other party expects to call as an expert witness at trial, to state the subject matter on which the expert is expected to testify, and to state the substance of the facts and opinions to which the expert is expected to testify and a summary of the grounds for each opinion. IN ST TRIAL P Rule 26(B)(4)(a)(i).

ii. Upon motion, the court may order further discovery by other means, subject to such restrictions as to scope and such provisions, pursuant to IN ST TRIAL P Rule 26(B)(4)(c), concerning fees and expenses as the court may deem appropriate. IN ST TRIAL P Rule 26(B)(4)(a)(ii).

iii. A party may discover facts known or opinions held by an expert who has been retained or specially employed by another party in anticipation of litigation or preparation for trial and who is not expected to be called as a witness at trial, only as provided in IN ST TRIAL P Rule 35(B) or upon a showing of exceptional circumstances under which it is impracticable for the party seeking discovery to obtain facts or opinions on the same subject by other means. IN ST TRIAL P Rule 26(B)(4)(b).

iv. Unless manifest injustice would result,

- The court shall require that the party seeking discovery pay the expert a reasonable fee for time spent in responding to discovery under IN ST TRIAL P Rule 26(B)(4)(a)(ii) and IN ST TRIAL P Rule 26(B)(4)(b); and

- With respect to discovery obtained under IN ST TRIAL P Rule 26(B)(4)(a)(ii) the court may require, and with respect to discovery obtained under IN ST TRIAL P Rule 26(B)(4)(b) the court shall require, the party seeking discovery to pay the other party a fair portion of the fees and expenses reasonably incurred by the latter party in obtaining facts and opinions from the expert. IN ST TRIAL P Rule 26(B)(4)(c).

e. *Claims of privilege or protection*

i.   *Information withheld.* When a party withholds information otherwise discoverable under the Indiana Rules of Trial Procedure by claiming that it is privileged or subject to protection as trial preparation material, the party shall make the claim expressly and shall describe the nature of the documents, communications, or things not produced or disclosed in a manner that, without revealing information itself privileged or protected, will enable other parties to assess the applicability of the privilege or protection. IN ST TRIAL P Rule 26(B)(5)(a).

ii. *Information produced.* If information is produced in discovery that is subject to a claim of privilege or protection as trial-preparation material, the party making the claim may notify any party that received the information of the claim and the basis for it. After being notified, a party must promptly return, sequester, or destroy the specified information and any copies it has and may not use or disclose the information until the claim is resolved. A receiving party may promptly present the information to the court under seal for a determination of the claim. If the receiving party disclosed the information before being notified, it must take reasonable steps to retrieve it. The producing party must preserve the information until the claim is resolved. IN ST TRIAL P Rule 26(B)(5)(b).

iii. *Waiver.* The law of discovery has developed some holdings which indicate that "waiver" of a privileged communication in a discovery setting might be more exacting than "waiver" of a privileged communication when the only question at hand is an interpretation of the privilege itself. Thus, in litigation in which several documents are in issue, and some are released inadvertently, there is strong case law that holds that the "inadvertent production" of a privileged document does not constitute a waiver of the attorney-client privilege. 2A INPRAC R 26(26.5); Transamerica Computer Co. v. International Business Machines Corp., 573 F.2d 646 (9th Cir. 1978). Such a rule should be measured against the usual rule which suggests that a voluntary disclosure to a third person will generally suffice to show a waiver of the attorney-client privilege. 2A INPRAC R 26(26.5).

f. *Use not limited.* Unless the court orders otherwise under IN ST TRIAL P Rule 26(C), the frequency of use of the methods listed in IN ST TRIAL P Rule 26(A) is not limited. IN ST TRIAL P Rule 26(A).

g. *Sequence of discovery.* Unless the court upon motion, for the convenience of parties and witnesses and in the interests of justice, orders otherwise, methods of discovery may be used in any sequence and the fact that a party is conducting discovery, whether by deposition or otherwise, shall not operate to delay any other party's discovery. IN ST TRIAL P Rule 26(D).

2. *Interrogatories.* Parties may obtain discovery by written interrogatories. IN ST TRIAL P Rule 26(A)(2). An interrogatory is a written question served upon another party which requires a written response under oath. 22 INPRAC § 23.1. Any party may serve upon any other party written interrogatories to be answered by the party served or, if the party served is an organization including a governmental organization, or a partnership, by any officer or agent, who shall furnish such information as is available to the party. IN ST TRIAL P Rule 33(A).

a. *Subject of interrogatories.* Interrogatories may relate to any matters which can be inquired into under IN ST TRIAL P Rule 26(B), and the answers may be used to the extent permitted by the rules of evidence. IN ST TRIAL P Rule 33(D).

i. This includes:

- The existence, description, nature, custody, condition and location of books, documents, or other tangible things; and
- The identity and location of persons having knowledge of relevant facts. 10 INPRAC § 65.1.

ii. Interrogatories cannot be objected to on the ground that the information sought will be inadmissible at trial if the discovery appears reasonably calculated to lead to the discovery of admissible evidence. 10 INPRAC § 65.1.

b. *Available for parties only.* Interrogatories may not be served on non-parties. 10 INPRAC § 65.1. There is no requirement that the party served shall be an "adverse" party. 2A INPRAC R 33(33.2).

c. *Submission to personal jurisdiction.* Under the current trial rules, discovery is self-executing and interrogatories are not filed with the court, but retained by the originating party until a discovery dispute arises or the discovery is needed for proceedings before the court. As such, Indiana courts have had to revisit the issue of whether a party's mere service of interrogatories constitutes a waiver of an objection to the court's personal jurisdiction over that party. 22 INPRAC § 23.14.

    i.   In Alberts v. Mack Trucks, Inc., the defendant served interrogatories before asserting a challenge to the court's personal jurisdiction. In ruling that serving interrogatories did not constitute a waiver of personal jurisdiction, the Indiana Court of Appeals noted the amendments to the Indiana Rules of Trial Procedure, which no longer require a party to file interrogatories with the court. Accordingly, the court held: By sending interrogatories to Alberts' counsel, NSC did not submit to the personal jurisdiction of the court. Jurisdiction will not be found to be waived until a party affirmatively uses the court's procedure, such as in a motion to compel answers to interrogatories. 22 INPRAC § 23.14; Alberts v. Mack Trucks, Inc., 540 N.E.2d 1268, 1271-72 (Ind.Ct.App. 1989).

    ii.   Therefore, merely serving interrogatories upon an opposing party before challenging the court's personal jurisdiction over a defendant should not result in a waiver of the jurisdictional issue unless the party otherwise affirmatively uses the court's resources. 22 INPRAC § 23.14.

  d. *Motion to compel discovery.* The party submitting the interrogatories may move for an order under IN ST TRIAL P Rule 37(A) with respect to any objection to or other failure to answer an interrogatory. IN ST TRIAL P Rule 33(C). Refer to the Indiana KeyRules Motion to Compel Discovery document for more information.

3. *Response to interrogatories*

  a. *Form of objections.* Answers or objections to interrogatories shall include the interrogatory which is being answered or to which an objection is made. The interrogatory which is being answered or objected to shall be placed immediately preceding the answer or objection. IN ST TRIAL P Rule 33(B).

  b. *Form of answer.* Each interrogatory shall be answered separately and fully in writing under oath, unless it is objected to, in which event the reasons for objections shall be stated in lieu of an answer. The answers are to be signed by the person making them, and the objections signed by the attorney making them. IN ST TRIAL P Rule 33(B).

  c. *Objections.* In addition to the objection that the matter is privileged, interrogatories may be objected to on the ground that they are not within the scope of discovery which is defined in IN ST TRIAL P Rule 26(B) because they seek information that is not relevant to the subject matter in the pending litigation, or that the requisite showing under IN ST TRIAL P Rule 26(B) has not been made, or that the information is held by experts and it is not discoverable except as permitted under IN ST TRIAL P Rule 26(B)(4). 2A INPRAC R 33(33.4). Objections to interrogatories must be specific. Common objections include (1) relevancy; (2) vague and ambiguous; (3) unduly burdensome; and (4) excessive in number. 10 INPRAC § 65.2.

    i.   *Objections to form.* The party upon whom the interrogatories have been served may object to the failure to follow the Format requirements in IN ST TRIAL P Rule 33(B) by returning the interrogatories to the party who caused them to be served. If this objection is to be made, the interrogatories shall be returned to the party who caused them to be served not later than the seventh (7th) day after they were received. If the interrogatories are not returned in that time, then this objection is waived. IN ST TRIAL P Rule 33(C).

    ii.   *Information not available.* If the objecting party takes the position that the information is not available, it is that party's burden to show that it is not available. 2A INPRAC R 33(33.4).

- As a general rule, a party may not refuse to answer an interrogatory on the ground that the information is not in his possession, in the sense that the party would have to consult books and records in order to answer. 2A INPRAC R 33(33.4); Flour Mills of America, Inc. v. Pace, 75 F.R.D. 676, 680 (E.D.Okl. 1977).

- An interrogatory seeking information in the possession of the party's employee is not objectionable if the questions call for answers which could be readily obtained by the person answering the interrogatory. 2A INPRAC R 33(33.4); Ballard v. Allegheny Airlines, Inc., 54 F.R.D. 67 (E.D.Pa. 1972).

iii. *Broad, burdensome, numerous.* An objection is permitted if the interrogatory is too broad, or too burdensome, or too many in the number and kinds of questions which are asked. 2A INPRAC R 33(33.4); Flour Mills of America, Inc. v. Pace, 75 F.R.D. 676, 680 (E.D.Okl. 1977); In re U.S. Financial Securities Litigation, 74 F.R.D. 497 (S.D.Cal. 1975).

iv. *Other objections.* An interrogatory otherwise proper is not objectionable merely because an answer to the interrogatory involves an opinion, contention, or legal conclusion, but the court may order that such an interrogatory be answered at a later time, or after designated discovery has been completed, or at a pre-trial conference. IN ST TRIAL P Rule 33(D).

- However, a party may not be forced to prepare his opponent's case for him. If the interrogatory would require a party to make extensive investigations, research, or compilation of data, it is an improper interrogatory, and it is burdensome and should be disallowed in a motion for a protective order. 2A INPRAC R 33(33.4); Halder v. International Telephone & Telegraph Co., 75 F.R.D. 657 (E.D.N.Y. 1977). Refer to the Indiana KeyRules Motion for Protective Order document for more information.

d. *Signature of responses.* The party served shall answer and sign the answer, and the attorney for the party served shall sign the objections. Both are then returned to the party taking the interrogatory. 2A INPRAC R 33(33.8).

i. An unsigned and unverified response does not qualify as an answer to an interrogatory and generally may not be used as such. 22 INPRAC § 23.6; Cabales v. U.S., 51 F.R.D. 498 (S.D.N.Y. 1970).

e. *Option to produce business records.* Where the answer to an interrogatory may be derived or ascertained from the business records of the party upon whom the interrogatory has been served or from an examination, audit or inspection of such business records, including a compilation, abstract or summary thereof, and the burden of deriving or ascertaining the answer is substantially the same for the party serving the interrogatory as for the party served, it is a sufficient answer to such interrogatory to specify the records from which the answer may be derived or ascertained and to afford to the party serving the interrogatory reasonable opportunity to examine, audit or inspect such records and to make copies, compilations, abstracts or summaries. A specification shall be in sufficient detail to permit the interrogating party to locate and to identify, as readily as can the party served, the records from which the answer may be ascertained. IN ST TRIAL P Rule 33(E).

f. *Supplementation of responses.* A party who has responded to a request for discovery with a response that was complete when made is under no duty to supplement his response to include information thereafter acquired, except as follows:

i. A party is under a duty seasonably to supplement his response with respect to any question directly addressed to:

- The identity and location of persons having knowledge of discoverable matters, and
- The identity of each person expected to be called as an expert witness at trial, the subject-matter on which he is expected to testify, and the substance of his testimony. IN ST TRIAL P Rule 26(E)(1).

ii. A party is under a duty seasonably to amend a prior response if he obtains information upon the basis of which:

- He knows that the response was incorrect when made, or
- He knows that the response though correct when made is no longer true and the circumstances are such that a failure to amend the response is in substance a knowing concealment. IN ST TRIAL P Rule 26(E)(2).

iii. A duty to supplement responses may be imposed by order of the court, agreement of the parties, or at any time prior to trial through new requests for supplementation of prior responses. IN ST TRIAL P Rule 26(E)(3).

iv. The duty seasonably to supplement a discovery response is absolute and is not predicated on a court order. "It is a breach of a litigant's duty reasonably to supplement if the litigant postpones supplementing its response by not obtaining from its experts the information which is to be supplied in answer to interrogatories." 2A INPRAC R 26(26.27); Lucas v. Dorsey Corp., 609 N.E.2d 1191, 1196 (Ind.Ct.App. 1993).

D. Documents

1. *Required documents*

   a. *Interrogatories.* Refer to the General Requirements section of this document for information on the scope and content of interrogatories.

   b. *Certificate of service.* An attorney or unrepresented party tendering a document to the Clerk for filing shall certify that service has been made, list the parties served, and specify the date and means of service. The certificate of service shall be placed at the end of the document and shall not be separately filed. The separate filing of a certificate of service, however, shall not be grounds for rejecting a document for filing. The Clerk may permit documents to be filed without a certificate of service but shall require prompt filing of a separate certificate of service. IN ST TRIAL P Rule 5(C).

2. *Supplemental documents*

   a. *Stipulation regarding discovery procedure.* Unless the court orders otherwise, the parties may by written stipulation:

      i. Provide that depositions may be taken before any person, at any time or place, upon any notice, and in any manner and when so taken may be used like other depositions, and

      ii. Modify the procedures provided by the Indiana Rules of Trial Procedure for other methods of discovery. IN ST TRIAL P Rule 29.

      iii. Admissions, stipulations and agreements concerning the proceedings in a case will not be enforced, unless submitted in writing or made of record. IN ST ALLEN SUPER AND CIR CT CIV Rule TR00-2.

   b. *Facsimile cover sheet.* Any document sent to the Clerk of the Circuit Court by electronic facsimile transmission shall be accompanied by a cover sheet which states the title of the document, case number, number of pages, identity and voice telephone number of the sending party and instructions for filing. The cover sheet shall contain the signature of the attorney or party, pro se, authorizing the filing. IN ST ADMIN Rule 12(D).

E. Format

1. *Format of interrogatories.* The rules applicable to captions, and the signing and form of pleadings (IN ST TRIAL P Rule 8 through IN ST TRIAL P Rule 11), apply to all motions and other papers provided under the Indiana Rules of Trial Procedure. 22B INPRAC 7:2. A party who serves written interrogatories under IN ST TRIAL P Rule 33 shall provide, after each interrogatory, a reasonable amount of space for a response or an objection. IN ST TRIAL P Rule 33(B).

   a. An interrogatory should pose a single direct question phrased in a manner that will advise the responding party what information is requested of him. 22 INPRAC § 23.5.

   b. An interrogatory may be divided into separate paragraphs and subparagraphs. The paragraphs should be identified as "1," "2," or "3"; or as "Interrogatory No. 1," "Interrogatory No. 2," etc. 22 INPRAC § 23.5.

2. *Form of pleadings*

   a. *Caption; Names of parties.* Every pleading shall contain a caption setting forth the name of the court, the title of the action, the file number, and a designation as in IN ST TRIAL P Rule 7(A). In the complaint the title of the action shall include the names of all the parties, but in other pleadings it is sufficient to state the name of the first party on each side with an appropriate indication of other parties. IN ST TRIAL P Rule 10(A).

   b. *Paragraphs; Separate statements.* All averments of a claim or defense shall be made in numbered paragraphs, the contents of each of which shall be limited as far as practicable to a statement of a single set of circumstances, and a paragraph may be referred to by number in all succeeding pleadings. Each claim founded upon a separate transaction or occurrence and each defense other

than denials may be stated in a separate count or defense whenever a separation facilitates the clear presentation of the matters set forth. IN ST TRIAL P Rule 10(B).

c. *Adoption by reference; Exhibits.* Statements in a pleading may be adopted by reference in a different part of the same pleading or in another pleading or in any motion. A copy of any written instrument which is an exhibit to a pleading is a part thereof for all purposes. IN ST TRIAL P Rule 10(C).

d. *Citation.* Allen County Superior and Circuit court rules may be cited as L.R. _____. The Indiana Rules of Trial Procedure are hereinafter referred to as T.R. _____. IN ST ALLEN SUPER AND CIR CT CIV Rule AR00-1(B).

e. *Paper.* All pleadings must be printed on white paper. IN ST ALLEN SUPER AND CIR CT CIV Rule 8-1(A).

f. *Spacing.* The lines shall be double spaced except for quotations, which shall be indented and single-spaced. IN ST ALLEN SUPER AND CIR CT CIV Rule 8-1(A).

g. *Photocopies.* Photocopies are acceptable if legible. IN ST ALLEN SUPER AND CIR CT CIV Rule 8-1(A).

h. *Margins and binding.* Margins shall be one to one and one-half (1-1 1/2) inches on the left side and one-half (1/2) inch on the right. IN ST ALLEN SUPER AND CIR CT CIV Rule 8-1(B).

   i. Binding or stapling shall be at the top left and at no other place. IN ST ALLEN SUPER AND CIR CT CIV Rule 8-1(B).

   ii. Covers or backing shall not be used. IN ST ALLEN SUPER AND CIR CT CIV Rule 8-1(B).

i. *Flat filing.* The files of the Clerk of the Court shall be kept under the "flat filing" system. All pleadings presented for filing with the Clerk or Court shall be flat and unfolded. Only the original of any pleading shall be placed in the Court file. IN ST ALLEN SUPER AND CIR CT CIV Rule 77-1(A).

j. *Handwritten pleadings.* Handwritten pleadings may be accepted for filing in the discretion of the Court. IN ST ALLEN SUPER AND CIR CT CIV Rule 8-1(A).

3. *Size of papers for filing.* Effective January 1, 1992, all pleadings, copies, motions and documents filed with any trial court or appellate level court, typed or printed, with the exception of exhibits and existing wills, shall be prepared on eight and one-half by eleven inch (8 1/2" x 11") size paper. IN ST ADMIN Rule 11.

4. *Signature requirements*

a. *Signature of attorney.* Every pleading or motion of a party represented by an attorney shall be signed by at least one (1) attorney of record in his individual name, whose address, telephone number, and attorney number shall be stated, except that this provision shall not apply to pleadings and motions made and transcribed at the trial or a hearing before the judge and received by him in such form. IN ST TRIAL P Rule 11(A). All pleadings to be signed by an attorney shall contain the written signature of the individual attorney, the attorney's printed name, Supreme Court Attorney Number, the name of the attorney's law firm, the attorney's address, telephone number, and a designation of the party for whom the attorney appears. IN ST ALLEN SUPER AND CIR CT CIV Rule 8-1(C). For the recommended signature format, refer to IN ST ALLEN SUPER AND CIR CT CIV Rule 8-1(C).

   i. The signature of an attorney constitutes a certificate by him that he has read the pleadings; that to the best of his knowledge, information, and belief, there is good ground to support it; and that it is not interposed for delay. IN ST TRIAL P Rule 11(A).

   ii. If a pleading or motion is not signed or is signed with intent to defeat the purpose of the rule, it may be stricken as sham and false and the action may proceed as though the pleading had not been served. IN ST TRIAL P Rule 11(A).

   iii. For a willful violation of IN ST TRIAL P Rule 11 an attorney may be subjected to appropriate disciplinary action. Similar action may be taken if scandalous or indecent matter is inserted. IN ST TRIAL P Rule 11(A).

   iv. Neither printed signatures, nor facsimile signatures shall be accepted on original documents. IN ST ALLEN SUPER AND CIR CT CIV Rule 8-1(C).

    v.   Facsimile signatures are permitted on copies. IN ST ALLEN SUPER AND CIR CT CIV Rule 8-1(C).

b.   *Signature of unrepresented party.* A party who is not represented by an attorney shall sign his pleading and state his address. IN ST TRIAL P Rule 11(A).

c.   *Verification not generally required.* Except when specifically required by rule, pleadings or motions need not be verified or accompanied by affidavit. The rule in equity that the averments of an answer under oath must be overcome by the testimony of two (2) witnesses or of one (1) witness sustained by corroborating circumstances is abolished. IN ST TRIAL P Rule 11(A).

d.   *Verification by affirmation or representation.* When in connection with any civil or special statutory proceeding it is required that any pleading, motion, petition, supporting affidavit, or other document of any kind, be verified, or that an oath be taken, it shall be sufficient if the subscriber simply affirms the truth of the matter to be verified by an affirmation or representation. IN ST TRIAL P Rule 11(B). IN ST TRIAL P Rule 11(B) states that the affirmation or representation should be in substantially the following language: "I (we) affirm, under the penalties for perjury, that the foregoing representation(s) is (are) true. (Signed) _____."

    i.   Any person who falsifies an affirmation or representation of fact shall be subject to the same penalties as are prescribed by law for the making of a false affidavit. IN ST TRIAL P Rule 11(B).

e.   *Verified pleadings, motions, and affidavits as evidence.* Pleadings, motions and affidavits accompanying or in support of such pleadings or motions when required to be verified or under oath shall be accepted as a representation that the signer had personal knowledge thereof or reasonable cause to believe the existence of the facts or matters stated or alleged therein; and, if otherwise competent or acceptable as evidence, may be admitted as evidence of the facts or matters stated or alleged therein when it is so provided in the Indiana Rules of Trial Procedure, by statute or other law, or to the extent the writing or signature expressly purports to be made upon the signer's personal knowledge. When such pleadings, motions and affidavits are verified or under oath they shall not require other or greater proof on the part of the adverse party than if not verified or not under oath unless expressly provided otherwise by the Indiana Rules of Trial Procedure, statute or other law. Affidavits upon motions for summary judgment under IN ST TRIAL P Rule 56 and in denial of execution under IN ST TRIAL P Rule 9.2 shall be made upon personal knowledge. IN ST TRIAL P Rule 11(C).

5.   *Information excluded from public access.* Every document filed in a case shall separately identify information excluded from public access pursuant to IN ST ADMIN Rule 9(G)(1) as follows:

a.   Whole documents that are excluded from public access pursuant to IN ST ADMIN Rule 9(G)(1) shall be tendered on light green paper or have a light green coversheet attached to the document, marked "Not for Public Access" or "Confidential." IN ST TRIAL P Rule 5(G)(1).

b.   When only a portion of a document contains information excluded from public access pursuant to IN ST ADMIN Rule 9(G)(1), said information shall be omitted [or redacted] from the filed document, and set forth on a separate accompanying document on light green paper conspicuously marked "Not for Public Access" or "Confidential" and clearly designated [or identifying] the caption and number of the case and the document and location within the document to which the redacted material pertains. IN ST TRIAL P Rule 5(G)(2).

c.   With respect to documents filed in electronic format, the trial court, by local rule, may provide for compliance with IN ST TRIAL P Rule 5 in manner that separates and protects access to information excluded from public access. IN ST TRIAL P Rule 5(G)(3).

d.   IN ST TRIAL P Rule 5(G) does not apply to a record sealed by the court pursuant to IN ST 5-14-3-5.5 or otherwise, nor to records, documents, or information filed in cases to which public access is prohibited pursuant to IN ST ADMIN Rule 9(G). IN ST TRIAL P Rule 5(G)(4).

e.   The following information in case records is excluded from public access and is confidential:

    i.   Information that is excluded from public access pursuant to federal law;

ii. Information that is excluded from public access as declared confidential by Indiana statute or other court rule, including without limitation:

- All adoption records created after July 8, 1941, as declared confidential by IN ST 31-19-19-1, et seq., except those specifically declared open by IN ST 31-19-13-2(2);

- All records relating to chancroid, chlamydia, gonorrhea, hepatitis, human immunodeficiency virus (HIV), Lymphogranuloma venereum, syphilis, tuberculosis, as declared confidential by IN ST 16-41-8-1, et seq.;

- All records relating to child abuse as declared confidential by IN ST 31-33-18-1, et seq.;

- All records relating to drug tests as declared confidential by IN ST 5-14-3-4(a)(9);

- Records of grand jury proceedings as declared confidential by IN ST 35-34-2-4;

- Records of juvenile proceedings as declared confidential by IN ST 31-39-1-2, except those specifically open under statute;

- All paternity records created after July 1, 1941 as declared confidential by IN ST 31-14-11-15, IN ST 31-19-5-23, IN ST 31-39-1-1 and IN ST 31-39-1-2 [Editor's note: IN ST 31-14-11-15 was repealed effective May 9, 2013];

- All pre-sentence reports as declared confidential by IN ST 35-38-1-13;

- Written petitions to permit marriages without consent and orders directing the Clerk of Court to issue a marriage license to underage persons, as declared confidential by IN ST 31-11-1-6;

- Only those arrest warrants, search warrants, indictments and informations ordered confidential by the trial judge, prior to return of duly executed service as declared confidential by IN ST 5-14-3-4(b)(1);

- All medical, mental health, or tax records unless determined by law or regulation of any governmental custodian not to be confidential, released by the subject of such records, or declared by a court of competent jurisdiction to be essential to the resolution of litigation as declared confidential by IN ST 16-39-3-10, IN ST 6-4.1-5-10, IN ST 6-4.1-12-12, and IN ST 6-8.1-7-1;

- Personal information relating to jurors or prospective jurors, other than for the use of the parties and counsel, pursuant to IN ST JURY Rule 10;

- Information relating to protection from abuse orders, no-contact orders and workplace violence restraining orders as declared confidential by IN ST 5-2-9-6, et seq.;

- Mediation proceedings pursuant to IN ST ADR Rule 2.11, Mini-Trial proceedings pursuant to IN ST ADR Rule 4.4(C), and Summary Jury Trials pursuant to IN ST ADR Rule 5.6;

- Information in probation files pursuant to the Probation Standards promulgated by the Judicial Conference of Indiana pursuant to IN ST 11-13-1-8(b);

- Information deemed confidential pursuant to the Rules for Court Administered Alcohol and Drug Programs promulgated by the Judicial Conference of Indiana pursuant to IN ST 12-23-14-13;

- Information deemed confidential pursuant to the Problem-Solving Court Rules promulgated by the Judicial Conference of Indiana pursuant to IN ST 33-23-16-16;

- All records of the Department of workforce Development as declared confidential by IN ST 22-4-19-6;

- Information regarding interception of electronic communications that is sealed or deemed confidential as set forth in IN ST 35-33.5-2-1, et seq.

iii. Information excluded from public access by specific court order;

iv. Complete Social Security Numbers of living persons;

v. With the exception of names, information such as addresses, phone numbers, and dates of birth which explicitly identifies:

- Natural persons who are witnesses or victims (not including defendants) in criminal, domestic violence, stalking, sexual assault, juvenile, or civil protection order proceedings, provided that juveniles who are victims of sex crimes shall be identified by initials only;

- Places of residence of judicial officers, clerks and other employees of courts and clerks of court, unless the person or persons about whom the information pertains waives confidentiality;

vi. Complete account numbers of specific assets, loans, bank accounts, credit cards, and personal identification numbers (PINs);

vii. All orders of expungement entered in criminal or juvenile proceedings, orders to restrict access to criminal history information pursuant to IN ST 35-38-5-5.5 or IN ST 35-38-8-5 and records excluded from public access by such orders, and information related to infractions that is excluded from public access pursuant to IN ST 34-28-5-15 or IN ST 34-28-5-16 [Editor's note: IN ST 35-38-5-5.5, IN ST 35-38-8-5 and IN ST 34-28-5-16 were repealed effective July 1, 2013; for information on orders restricting access to criminal history, refer to IN ST 35-38-9-1, et seq.];

viii. All personal notes and e-mail, and deliberative material, of judges, jurors, court staff and judicial agencies, and information recorded in personal data assistants (PDA's) or organizers and personal calendars. IN ST ADMIN Rule 9(G)(1).

F. Filing and Service Requirements

1. *Filing requirements.* Except as otherwise provided in IN ST TRIAL P Rule 5(E)(2), all pleadings and papers subsequent to the complaint which are required to be served upon a party shall be filed with the Court either before service or within a reasonable period of time thereafter. IN ST TRIAL P Rule 5(E)(1).

a. *Non-filing of discovery until necessary*

i. *Non-filing of discovery; Exceptions.* No deposition or request for discovery or response thereto under IN ST TRIAL P Rule 27, IN ST TRIAL P Rule 30, IN ST TRIAL P Rule 31, IN ST TRIAL P Rule 33, IN ST TRIAL P Rule 34 or IN ST TRIAL P Rule 36 shall be filed with the Court unless:

- A motion is filed pursuant to IN ST TRIAL P Rule 26(C) or IN ST TRIAL P Rule 37 and the original deposition or request for discovery or response thereto is necessary to enable the Court to rule; or

- A party desires to use the deposition or request for discovery or response thereto for evidentiary purposes at trial or in connection with a motion, and the Court, either upon its own motion or that of any party, or as a part of any pre-trial order, orders the filing of the original. IN ST TRIAL P Rule 5(E)(2).

ii. *Custody of original and period of retention*

- The original of a deposition shall, subject to the provisions of IN ST TRIAL P Rule 30(E), be delivered by the reporter to the party taking it and shall be maintained by that party until filed with the Court pursuant to IN ST TRIAL P Rule 5(E)(2) or until the later of final judgment, agreed settlement of the litigation or all appellate rights have been exhausted. IN ST TRIAL P Rule 5(E)(3)(a).

- The original or any request for discovery or response thereto under IN ST TRIAL P Rule 27, IN ST TRIAL P Rule 30, IN ST TRIAL P Rule 31, IN ST TRIAL P Rule 33, IN ST TRIAL P Rule 34 and IN ST TRIAL P Rule 36 shall be maintained by the party originating the request or response until filed with the Court pursuant to IN ST TRIAL P Rule 5(E)(2) or until the later of final judgment, agreed settlement or all appellate rights have been exhausted. IN ST TRIAL P Rule 5(E)(3)(b).

iii. *Original unavailable; Copies.* In the event it is made to appear to the satisfaction of the Court that the original of a deposition or request for discovery or response thereto cannot be filed with

the Court when required, the Court may allow use of a copy instead of the original. IN ST TRIAL P Rule 5(E)(4).

    iv. *Filing as publication.* The filing of any deposition shall constitute publication. IN ST TRIAL P Rule 5(E)(5).

b. *Filing with the court defined.* The filing of pleadings, motions, and other papers with the court as required by the Indiana Rules of Trial Procedure shall be made by one of the following methods:

    i. Delivery to the clerk of the court;

    ii. Sending by electronic transmission under the procedure adopted pursuant to IN ST ADMIN Rule 12;

    iii. Mailing to the clerk by registered, certified or express mail return receipt requested;

    iv. Depositing with any third-party commercial carrier for delivery to the clerk within three (3) calendar days, cost prepaid, properly addressed;

    v. If the court so permits, filing with the judge, in which event the judge shall note thereon the filing date and forthwith transmit them to the office of the clerk; or

    vi. Electronic filing, as approved by the Division of State Court Administration pursuant to IN ST ADMIN Rule 16. IN ST TRIAL P Rule 5(F).

    vii. Filing by registered or certified mail and by third-party commercial carrier shall be complete upon mailing or deposit. IN ST TRIAL P Rule 5(F).

c. *Facsimile filing*

    i. *Generally.* In counties where a majority of judges of the courts of record, by posted local rule, have authorized electronic facsimile filing and designated a telephone number to receive such transmissions, pleadings, motions, and other papers may be sent to the Clerk of Circuit Court by electronic facsimile transmission for filing in any case, provided:

- Such matter does not exceed ten (10) pages, including the cover sheet;
- Such matter does not require the payment of fees other than the electronic facsimile transcription fee set forth in IN ST ADMIN Rule 12(E);
- The sending party creates at the time of transmission a machine generated log for such transmission; and
- The original document and the transmission log are maintained by the sending party for the duration of the litigation. IN ST ADMIN Rule 12(B).

    ii. *Time of filing.* During normal, posted business hours, the time of filing shall be the time the duplicate document is produced in the office of the Clerk of the Circuit Court. Duplicate documents received at all other times shall be filed as of the next normal business day. IN ST ADMIN Rule 12(C).

- If the receiving fax machine endorses its own time and date stamp upon the transmitted documents and the receiving machine produces a delivery receipt which is electronically created and transmitted to the sending party, the time of filing shall be the date and time recorded on the transmitted document by the receiving fax machine. IN ST ADMIN Rule 12(C).

d. *Proof of filing.* Any party filing any paper by any method other than personal delivery to the clerk shall retain proof of filing. IN ST TRIAL P Rule 5(F).

2. *Service requirements.* Unless otherwise provided by the Indiana Rules of Trial Procedure or an order of the court, each party and special judge, if any, shall be served with: (1) every order required by its terms to be served; (2) every pleading subsequent to the original complaint; (3) every written motion except one which may be heard ex parte; (4) every brief submitted to the trial court; (5) every paper relating to discovery required to be served upon a party; and (6) every written notice, appearance, demand, offer of judgment, designation of record on appeal, or similar paper. IN ST TRIAL P Rule 5(A).

a. *Methods of service*

    i. *Personal service.* Whenever a party is represented by an attorney of record, service shall be

made upon such attorney unless service upon the party himself is ordered by the court. Service upon the attorney or party shall be made by delivering or mailing a copy of the papers to the last known address or where an attorney or party has consented to service by fax or e-mail, as provided in IN ST TRIAL P Rule 3.1(A)(4), by faxing or e-mailing a copy of the documents to the fax number or e-mail address set out in the appearance form or correction as required by IN ST TRIAL P Rule 3.1(E). IN ST TRIAL P Rule 5(B). Delivery of a copy within IN ST TRIAL P Rule 5 means:

- Offering or tendering it to the attorney or party and stating the nature of the papers being served. Refusal to accept an offered or tendered document is a waiver of any objection to the sufficiency or adequacy of service of that document;

- Leaving it at his office with a clerk or other person in charge thereof, or if there is no one in charge, leaving it in a conspicuous place therein; or

- If the office is closed, by leaving it at his dwelling house or usual place of abode with some person of suitable age and discretion then residing therein; or,

- Leaving it at some other suitable place, selected by the attorney upon whom service is being made, pursuant to duly promulgated local rule. IN ST TRIAL P Rule 5(B)(1).

ii. *Service by mail.* If service is made by mail, the papers shall be deposited in the United States mail addressed to the person on whom they are being served, with postage prepaid. Service shall be deemed complete upon mailing. Proof of service of all papers permitted to be mailed may be made by written acknowledgment of service, by affidavit of the person who mailed the papers, or by certificate of an attorney. It shall be the duty of attorneys when entering their appearance in a cause or when filing pleadings or papers therein, to have noted in the Chronological Case Summary or said pleadings or papers so filed the address and telephone number of their office. Service by delivery or by mail at such address shall be deemed sufficient and complete. IN ST TRIAL P Rule 5(B)(2).

b. *Serving numerous defendants.* In any action in which there are unusually large numbers of defendants, the court, upon motion or of its own initiative, may order:

i. That service of the pleadings of the defendants and replies thereto need not be made as between the defendants;

- That any cross-claim, counterclaim, or matter constituting an avoidance or affirmative defense contained therein shall be deemed to be denied or avoided by all other parties; and

- That the filing of any such pleading and service thereof upon the plaintiff constitutes due notice of it to the parties. IN ST TRIAL P Rule 5(D).

ii. A copy of every such order shall be served upon the parties in such manner and form as the court directs. IN ST TRIAL P Rule 5(D).

iii. *Service by fax or e-mail.* A party who has consented to service by fax or e-mail may be served as follows:

- Service by e-mail shall be made by attaching the document being served in .pdf format. Discovery documents must also be served in accordance with IN ST TRIAL P Rule 26(A). IN ST TRIAL P Rule 5(B)(3)(a).

- Service by fax shall be deemed complete upon generation of a transmission record indicating the successful transmission of the entire document, except as provided in IN ST TRIAL P Rule 5(B)(3)(d). IN ST TRIAL P Rule 5(B)(3)(b).

- Service by e-mail shall be deemed complete upon transmission, except as provided in IN ST TRIAL P Rule 5(B)(3)(d). IN ST TRIAL P Rule 5(B)(3)(c).

- Service by fax or e-mail that occurs on a Saturday, Sunday, legal holiday, or day the court or agency in which the matter is pending is closed or after 5:00 PM local time of the recipient shall be deemed complete the next day that is not a Saturday, Sunday, legal holiday, or day that the court or agency in which the matter is pending is not closed. IN ST TRIAL P Rule 5(B)(3)(d).

iv. *Additional service of electronic discovery.* In addition to service under Rule IN ST TRIAL P Rule 5(B) or a .pdf format electronic copy, a party propounding or responding to interrogatories, requests for production or requests for admission shall comply with IN ST TRIAL P Rule 26(A.1)(a) or IN ST TRIAL P Rule 26(A.1)(b). IN ST TRIAL P Rule 26(A.1).

- The party shall serve the discovery request or response in an electronic format (either on a disk or as an electronic document attachment) in any commercially available word processing software system. If transmitted on disk, each disk shall be labeled, identifying the caption of the case, the document, and the word processing version in which it is being submitted. If more than one (1) disk is used for the same document, each disk shall be labeled and also shall be sequentially numbered. If transmitted by electronic mail, the document must be accompanied by electronic memorandum providing the forgoing identifying information; or

- The party shall serve the opposing party with a verified statement that the attorney or party appealing pro se lacks the equipment and is unable to transmit the discovery as required by IN ST TRIAL P Rule 26(A.1). IN ST TRIAL P Rule 26(A.1).

v. *Consent to alternate service.* Any Allen County Attorney or any Allen County law firm may, without charge, maintain an assigned Courthouse box in the library of the Allen County Courthouse for receipt of notices, pleadings, process orders, or other communications from the Court, the Clerk, and other attorneys or law firms. IN ST ALLEN SUPER AND CIR CT CIV Rule 5-1(A). For more information concerning the use of courthouse boxes, refer to IN ST ALLEN SUPER AND CIR CT CIV Rule 5-1.

c. *Service on parties in default for failure to appear.* No service need be made on parties in default for failure to appear, except that pleadings asserting new or additional claims for relief against them shall be served upon them in the manner provided by service of summons in IN ST TRIAL P Rule 4. IN ST TRIAL P Rule 5(A).

G. Hearings

1. The Indiana rules do not contemplate a hearing related to the filing and service of interrogatories.

H. Forms

1. Interrogatory Forms for Indiana

a. General form. 5 INPRAC § 4:2.10.

b. Motion to enlarge time to answer. 5 INPRAC § 4:2.20.

c. Answers and objections; General form. 5 INPRAC § 4:2.30.

d. Answer; General form with standard objections. 5 INPRAC § 4:2.40.

e. Answer; Offer to produce business records. 5 INPRAC § 4:2.50.

f. Sample interrogatories relating to electronically stored information. 5 INPRAC § 4:2.60.

g. Motion to seal answers to interrogatories. 10 INPRAC § 65.6.1.

h. Interrogatories; General form. 10 INPRAC § 65.7.

i. Interrogatories; Another form. 10 INPRAC § 65.8.

j. Interrogatory preliminary instructions; Comprehensive form. 10 INPRAC § 65.9.

k. Interrogatory preliminary instructions; Abbreviated form. 10 INPRAC § 65.10.

l. Interrogatory definitions. 10 INPRAC § 65.11.

m. Motion to enlarge time to answer interrogatories. 10 INPRAC § 65.12.

n. Motion for enlargement of time; Response due after discovery completed. 10 INPRAC § 65.13.

o. Motion to shorten time to respond to interrogatories. 10 INPRAC § 65.15.

p. Motion to strike interrogatories; Excessive number under local rules. 10 INPRAC § 65.16.

q. Interrogatories to determine minimum contacts with state. 10 INPRAC § 65.20.

r.   Answers and objections to interrogatories; General form. 10 INPRAC § 65.30.

s.   Answers and objections to interrogatories; Another form. 10 INPRAC § 65.31.

t.   Standard objections to interrogatories; General form. 10 INPRAC § 65.32.

u.   Standard objections to interrogatories. 10 INPRAC § 65.33.

v.   Answer of interrogatory by offering to produce business records. 10 INPRAC § 65.34.

w.   Motion to compel answers to interrogatories. 10 INPRAC § 65.35.

x.   Attorney's signature as to objections; Alternate forms. 10 INPRAC § 65.36.

y.   Conversion; Plaintiff's interrogatories. 10 INPRAC § 66.27.

z.   Medical malpractice action. 10 INPRAC § 66.37.

2. **Official Interrogatory Forms for Allen County**

a.   Consent to alternate service. IN ST ALLEN SUPER AND CIR CT CIV App. A.

I. Checklist

(I)   ❑ Matters to be considered by the party serving the interrogatories

(a)   ❑ Required documents

(1)   ❑ Interrogatories

(2)   ❑ Certificate of service

(b)   ❑ Supplemental documents

(1)   ❑ Stipulation regarding discovery procedure

(2)   ❑ Facsimile cover sheet

(c)   ❑ Timing

(1)   ❑ Interrogatories may, without leave of court, be served upon the plaintiff after commencement of the action and upon any other party with or after service of the summons and complaint upon that party

(II)   ❑ Matters to be considered by the responding party

(a)   ❑ Required documents

(1)   ❑ Response to interrogatories

(2)   ❑ Certificate of service

(b)   ❑ Supplemental documents

(1)   ❑ Business records

(2)   ❑ Stipulation regarding discovery procedure

(3)   ❑ Facsimile cover sheet

(c)   ❑ Timing

(1)   ❑ The party upon whom the interrogatories have been served shall serve a copy of the answers and objections within a period designated by the party submitting the interrogatories, not less than thirty (30) days after the service thereof or within such shorter or longer time as the court may allow

Requests, Notices and Applications
Request for Production of Documents

Document Last Updated October 2013

A. Applicable Rules

1. *State rules*

   a. Appearance. IN ST TRIAL P Rule 3.1.

   b. Process. IN ST TRIAL P Rule 4.

   c. Service and filing of pleadings and other papers. IN ST TRIAL P Rule 5.

   d. Time. IN ST TRIAL P Rule 6.

   e. Pleadings. IN ST TRIAL P Rule 7; IN ST TRIAL P Rule 9.2; IN ST TRIAL P Rule 10.

   f. Signing and verification of pleadings. IN ST TRIAL P Rule 11.

   g. General provisions governing discovery. IN ST TRIAL P Rule 26.

   h. Methods of discovery. IN ST TRIAL P Rule 27; IN ST TRIAL P Rule 29; IN ST TRIAL P Rule 30; IN ST TRIAL P Rule 31; IN ST TRIAL P Rule 33; IN ST TRIAL P Rule 34; IN ST TRIAL P Rule 35; IN ST TRIAL P Rule 36.

   i. Failure to make or cooperate in discovery; Sanctions. IN ST TRIAL P Rule 37.

   j. Subpoena. IN ST TRIAL P Rule 45.

   k. Judgment on the evidence (directed verdict). IN ST TRIAL P Rule 50.

   l. Findings by the court. IN ST TRIAL P Rule 52.

   m. Summary judgment. IN ST TRIAL P Rule 56.

   n. Motion to correct error. IN ST TRIAL P Rule 59.

   o. Relief from judgment or order. IN ST TRIAL P Rule 60.

   p. Access to court records. IN ST ADMIN Rule 9.

   q. Paper size. IN ST ADMIN Rule 11.

   r. Facsimile transmission. IN ST ADMIN Rule 12.

   s. Electronic filing and electronic service pilot projects. IN ST ADMIN Rule 16.

   t. Sealing of certain records by court; Hearing; Notice. IN ST 5-14-3-5.5.

   u. Privacy and confidentiality. IN ST 5-2-9-6; IN ST 5-14-3-4; IN ST 6-4.1-5-10; IN ST 6-4.1-12-12; IN ST 6-8.1-7-1; IN ST 11-13-1-8; IN ST 12-23-14-13; IN ST 16-39-3-10; IN ST 16-41-8-1; IN ST 22-4-19-6; IN ST 31-11-1-6; IN ST 31-19-5-23; IN ST 31-19-13-2; IN ST 31-19-19-1; IN ST 31-33-18-1; IN ST 31-39-1-1; IN ST 31-39-1-2; IN ST 33-23-16-16; IN ST 35-34-2-4; IN ST 35-38-1-13; IN ST 35-38-9-1; IN ST ADR Rule 2.11; IN ST ADR Rule 4.4; IN ST ADR Rule 5.6; IN ST JURY Rule 10.

2. *Local rules*

   a. Applicability and citation of rules. IN ST ALLEN SUPER AND CIR CT CIV Rule AR00-1.

   b. Admissions, stipulations and agreements. IN ST ALLEN SUPER AND CIR CT CIV Rule TR00-2.

   c. Appearances. IN ST ALLEN SUPER AND CIR CT CIV Rule 3.1-1.

   d. Consent to alternate service. IN ST ALLEN SUPER AND CIR CT CIV Rule 5-1.

   e. Preparation of pleadings. IN ST ALLEN SUPER AND CIR CT CIV Rule 8-1.

   f. Filing. IN ST ALLEN SUPER AND CIR CT CIV Rule 77-1.

B. Timing

1. *Time for service of request for production of documents*

    a. *Service on parties.* The request may, without leave of court, be served upon the plaintiff after commencement of the action and upon any other party with or after service of the summons and complaint upon that party. IN ST TRIAL P Rule 34(B).

    b. *Service on non-parties.* Neither a request nor subpoena to produce or permit as permitted by IN ST TRIAL P Rule 34 shall be served upon a non-party until at least fifteen (15) days after the date on which the party intending to serve such request or subpoena serves a copy of the proposed request and subpoena on all other parties. Provided, however, that if such request or subpoena relates to a matter set for hearing within such fifteen (15) day period or arises out of a bona fide emergency, such request or subpoena may be served upon a non-party one (1) day after receipt of the proposed request or subpoena by all other parties. IN ST TRIAL P Rule 34(C)(2)

2. *Time for service of the response to the request for production of documents.* The party upon whom the request is served shall serve a written response within a period designated in the request, not less than thirty (30) days after the service thereof or within such shorter or longer time as the court may allow. IN ST TRIAL P Rule 34(B).

3. *Computation of time*

    a. *Generally; Days excluded.* In computing any period of time prescribed or allowed by the Indiana Rules of Trial Procedure, by order of the court, or by any applicable statute, the day of the act, event, or default from which the designated period of time begins to run shall not be included. The last day of the period so computed is to be included unless it is:

        i. A Saturday,

        ii. A Sunday,

        iii. A legal holiday as defined by state statute, or

        iv. A day the office in which the act is to be done is closed during regular business hours. IN ST TRIAL P Rule 6(A).

    b. *Short periods.* In any event, the period runs until the end of the next day that is not a Saturday, a Sunday, a legal holiday, or a day on which the office is closed. When the period of time allowed is less than seven (7) days, intermediate Saturdays, Sundays, legal holidays, and days on which the office is closed shall be excluded from the computations. IN ST TRIAL P Rule 6(A).

    c. *Additional time after service by United States mail.* Whenever a party has the right or is required to do some act or take some proceedings within a prescribed period after the service of a notice or other paper upon him and the notice or paper is served upon him by United States mail, three (3) days shall be added to the prescribed period. IN ST TRIAL P Rule 6(E).

    d. *Enlargement of time.* When an act is required or allowed to be done at or within a specific time by the Indiana Rules of Trial Procedure, the court may at any time for cause shown:

        i. Order the period enlarged, with or without motion or notice, if request therefor is made before the expiration of the period originally prescribed or extended by a previous order; or

        ii. Upon motion made after the expiration of the specific period, permit the act to be done where the failure to act was the result of excusable neglect; but, the court may not extend the time for taking any action for judgment on the evidence under IN ST TRIAL P Rule 50(A), amendment of findings and judgment under IN ST TRIAL P Rule 52(B), to correct errors under IN ST TRIAL P Rule 59(C), statement in opposition to motion to correct error under IN ST TRIAL P Rule 59(E), or to obtain relief from final judgment under IN ST TRIAL P Rule 60(B), except to the extent and under the conditions stated in those rules. IN ST TRIAL P Rule 6(B).

C. General Requirements

1. *Scope of discovery.* Unless otherwise limited by order of the court in accordance with the Indiana Rules of Trial Procedure, the scope of discovery is as follows:

    a. *In general.* Parties may obtain discovery regarding any matter, not privileged, which is relevant to the subject-matter involved in the pending action, whether it relates to the claim or defense of the party seeking discovery or the claim or defense of any other party, including the existence, description, nature, custody, condition and location of any books, documents, or other tangible things and the identity and location of persons having knowledge of any discoverable matter. It is not ground for objection that the information sought will be inadmissible at the trial if the information sought appears reasonably calculated to lead to the discovery of admissible evidence. IN ST TRIAL P Rule 26(B)(1).

i. *Limiting discovery upon court determination.* The frequency or extent of use of the discovery methods otherwise permitted under the Indiana Rules of Trial Procedure and by any local rule shall be limited by the court if it determines that:

- The discovery sought is unreasonably cumulative or duplicative, or is obtainable from some other source that is more convenient, less burdensome, or less expensive;

- The party seeking discovery has had ample opportunity by discovery in the action to obtain the information sought or;

- The burden or expense of the proposed discovery outweighs its likely benefit, taking into account the needs of the case, the amount in controversy, the parties' resources, the importance of the issues at stake in the litigation, and the importance of the proposed discovery in resolving the issues. IN ST TRIAL P Rule 26(B)(1).

- The court may act upon its own initiative after reasonable notice or pursuant to a motion under IN ST TRIAL P Rule 26(C). IN ST TRIAL P Rule 26(B)(1). Refer to the Indiana KeyRules Motion for Protective Order document for more information.

ii. *Relevancy in the discovery context.* When the word "relevancy" is used in IN ST TRIAL P Rule 26(B), it does not mean "relevancy" as that word in used to determine the admissibility of evidence in a trial court. It is much broader. It means "relevancy" to the "subject matter" of the litigation or pending action and it may relate to the claim or defense of any party. Pretrial discovery is available as to any nonprivileged matter relevant to the subject matter of the lawsuit or to obtain information reasonably calculated to lead to admissible evidence. 2A INPRAC R 26(26.4); Kaufmann v. Credithrift Financial, Inc., 465 N.E.2d 207, 210 (Ind.Ct.App. 1984).

iii. *Tests for relevance.* Indiana case law has developed two (2) additional tests in this area. 2A INPRAC R 26(26.4).

- The first test determines when a document or a request for information is actually relevant to the subject matter in the pending action. A document [or discovery request] is relevant to discovery if there is the possibility the information sought may be relevant to the subject matter of the action. 2A INPRAC R 26(26.4); CIGNA-INA/Aetna v. Hagerman-Shambaugh, 473 N.E.2d 1033, 1036 (Ind.Ct.App. 1985).

- The second test speaks to appellate review of the trial court's determination that a document or discovery request is relevant to the subject matter of the pending action. The appellate court sees its review of the trial court's decision on relevancy to subject matter as being very limited. The court states: "Our review of the trial court's conclusion that the documents are relevant is limited. A trial court is vested with discretion in its rulings on discovery issues." 2A INPRAC R 26(26.4); Costanzi v. Ryan, 175 Ind.App. 257, 370 N.E.2d 1333 (Ind.Ct.App. 1978).

b. *Insurance agreements.* A party may obtain discovery of the existence and contents of any insurance agreement under which any person carrying on an insurance business may be liable to satisfy part or all of a judgment which may be entered in the action or to indemnify or reimburse for payments made to satisfy the judgment. Information concerning the insurance agreement is not by reason of disclosure admissible in evidence at trial. For purposes of IN ST TRIAL P Rule 26(B)(2), an application for insurance shall not be treated as part of an insurance agreement. IN ST TRIAL P Rule 26(B)(2).

c. *Trial preparation; Materials.* Subject to the provisions of IN ST TRIAL P Rule 26(B)(4), a party may obtain discovery of documents and tangible things otherwise discoverable under IN ST TRIAL P Rule 26(B)(1) and prepared in anticipation of litigation or for trial by or for another party or by or for that other party's representative (including his attorney, consultant, surety, indemnitor, insurer, or agent) only upon a showing that the party seeking discovery has substantial need of the materials in the preparation of his case and that he is unable without undue hardship to obtain the substantial equivalent of the materials by other means. In ordering discovery of such materials when the required showing has been made, the court shall protect against disclosure of the mental impressions, conclusions, opinions, or legal theories of an attorney or other representative of a party concerning the litigation. IN ST TRIAL P Rule 26(B)(3).

i. A party may obtain without the required showing a statement concerning the action or its subject matter previously made by that party. Upon request, a person not a party may obtain without the required showing a statement concerning the action or its subject matter previously made by that person. If the request is refused, the person may move for a court order. The provisions of IN ST TRIAL P Rule 37(A)(4) apply to the award of expenses incurred in relation to the motion. For purposes of IN ST TRIAL P Rule 26(B)(3), a statement previously made is:

- A written statement signed or otherwise adopted approved by the person making it, or

- A stenographic, mechanical, electrical, or other recording, or a transcription thereof, which is a substantially verbatim recital of an oral statement by the person making it and contemporaneously recorded. IN ST TRIAL P Rule 26(B)(3).

ii. The protection of IN ST TRIAL P Rule 26(B)(3) extends to material prepared or collected before litigation actually commences, but that some possibility of litigation must actually exist before the privilege and IN ST TRIAL P Rule 26(B)(3) become operative. 2A INPRAC R 26(26.9).

d. *Trial preparation; Experts.* Discovery of facts known and opinions held by experts, otherwise discoverable under the provisions of IN ST TRIAL P Rule 26(B)(1) and acquired or developed in anticipation of litigation or for trial, may be obtained as follows:

i. A party may through interrogatories require any other party to identify each person whom the other party expects to call as an expert witness at trial, to state the subject matter on which the expert is expected to testify, and to state the substance of the facts and opinions to which the expert is expected to testify and a summary of the grounds for each opinion. IN ST TRIAL P Rule 26(B)(4)(a)(i).

ii. Upon motion, the court may order further discovery by other means, subject to such restrictions as to scope and such provisions, pursuant to IN ST TRIAL P Rule 26(B)(4)(c), concerning fees and expenses as the court may deem appropriate. IN ST TRIAL P Rule 26(B)(4)(a)(ii).

iii. A party may discover facts known or opinions held by an expert who has been retained or specially employed by another party in anticipation of litigation or preparation for trial and who is not expected to be called as a witness at trial, only as provided in IN ST TRIAL P Rule 35(B) or upon a showing of exceptional circumstances under which it is impracticable for the party seeking discovery to obtain facts or opinions on the same subject by other means. IN ST TRIAL P Rule 26(B)(4)(b).

iv. Unless manifest injustice would result,

- The court shall require that the party seeking discovery pay the expert a reasonable fee for time spent in responding to discovery under IN ST TRIAL P Rule 26(B)(4)(a)(ii) and IN ST TRIAL P Rule 26(B)(4)(b); and

- With respect to discovery obtained under IN ST TRIAL P Rule 26(B)(4)(a)(ii) the court may require, and with respect to discovery obtained under IN ST TRIAL P Rule 26(B)(4)(b) the court shall require, the party seeking discovery to pay the other party a fair portion of the fees and expenses reasonably incurred by the latter party in obtaining facts and opinions from the expert. IN ST TRIAL P Rule 26(B)(4).

e. *Claims of privilege or protection*

i. *Information withheld.* When a party withholds information otherwise discoverable under the

Indiana Rules of Trial Procedure by claiming that it is privileged or subject to protection as trial preparation material, the party shall make the claim expressly and shall describe the nature of the documents, communications, or things not produced or disclosed in a manner that, without revealing information itself privileged or protected, will enable other parties to assess the applicability of the privilege or protection. IN ST TRIAL P Rule 26(B)(5)(a).

    ii.   *Information produced.* If information is produced in discovery that is subject to a claim of privilege or protection as trial-preparation material, the party making the claim may notify any party that received the information of the claim and the basis for it. After being notified, a party must promptly return, sequester, or destroy the specified information and any copies it has and may not use or disclose the information until the claim is resolved. A receiving party may promptly present the information to the court under seal for a determination of the claim. If the receiving party disclosed the information before being notified, it must take reasonable steps to retrieve it. The producing party must preserve the information until the claim is resolved. IN ST TRIAL P Rule 26(B)(5)(b).

    iii.   *Waiver.* The law of discovery has developed some holdings which indicate that "waiver" of a privileged communication in a discovery setting might be more exacting than "waiver" of a privileged communication when the only question at hand is an interpretation of the privilege itself. Thus, in litigation in which several documents are in issue, and some are released inadvertently, there is strong case law that holds that the "inadvertent production" of a privileged document does not constitute a waiver of the attorney-client privilege. 2A INPRAC R 26(26.5); Transamerica Computer Co. v. International Business Machines Corp., 573 F.2d 646 (9th Cir. 1978). Such a rule should be measured against the usual rule which suggests that a voluntary disclosure to a third person will generally suffice to show a waiver of the attorney-client privilege. 2A INPRAC R 26(26.5).

  f.   *Use not limited.* Unless the court orders otherwise under IN ST TRIAL P Rule 26(C), the frequency of use of the methods listed in IN ST TRIAL P Rule 26(A) is not limited. IN ST TRIAL P Rule 26(A).

  g.   *Sequence of discovery.* Unless the court upon motion, for the convenience of parties and witnesses and in the interests of justice, orders otherwise, methods of discovery may be used in any sequence and the fact that a party is conducting discovery, whether by deposition or otherwise, shall not operate to delay any other party's discovery. IN ST TRIAL P Rule 26.

2. *Request for production of documents*

  a.   *Content of the request.* The request shall set forth the items to be inspected either by individual item or by category, and describe each item and category with reasonable particularity. The request may specify the form or forms in which electronically stored information is to be produced. The request shall specify a reasonable time, place, and manner of making the inspection and performing the related acts. Service is dispensed with if the whereabouts of the parties is unknown. IN ST TRIAL P Rule 34(B).

    i.   *Reasonable particularity.* A recurring issue appears among cases. It is whether a request is adequate or describes the items sought with "reasonable particularity" as stated in IN ST TRIAL P Rule 34(B). The essence of this matter is found in these words: "When the party seeking discovery issues a `shotgun' request that is unduly general, the court may avoid wading through documents by finding the items to be inspected not set forth with reasonable particularity, as required by IN ST TRIAL P Rule 34(B). 3 INPRAC R 34(34.1); Ray v. St. John's Health Care Corp., 582 N.E.2d 464, 474 (Ind.Ct.App. 1991); Richey v. Chappell, 572 N.E.2d 1338, 1339 (Ind.Ct.App. 1991).

  b.   *Requesting documents in specific form.* If a request for electronically stored information does not specify the form or forms of production, a responding party must produce the information in a form or forms in which it is ordinarily maintained or in a form or forms that are reasonably usable. IN ST TRIAL P Rule 34(B).

  c.   *Scope.* Any party may serve on any other party a request:

    i.   To produce and permit the party making the request, or someone acting on the requester's behalf, to inspect and copy, any designated documents or electronically stored information (including, without limitation, writings, drawings, graphs, charts, photographs, sound recordings, images and other data or data compilations from which information can be obtained or translated, if necessary, by the respondent into reasonably usable form) or to inspect and copy, test, or sample any designated tangible things which constitute or contain matters within the scope of IN ST TRIAL P Rule 26(B) and which are in the possession, custody or control of the party upon whom the request is served; or

ii. To permit entry upon designated land or other property in the possession or control of the party upon whom the request is served for the purpose of inspection and measuring, surveying, photographing, testing, or sampling the property or any designated object or operation thereon, within the scope of IN ST TRIAL P Rule 26(B). IN ST TRIAL P Rule 34(A).

d. *Application to non-parties.* A witness or person other than a party may be requested to produce or permit the matters allowed by IN ST TRIAL P Rule 34(A). Such request shall be served upon other parties and included in or with a subpoena served upon such witness or person. IN ST TRIAL P Rule 34(C)(1).

   i. *Content of request to non-parties*

   • The request shall contain the matter provided in IN ST TRIAL P Rule 34(B). IN ST TRIAL P Rule 34(C)(3).

   • It shall also state that the witness or person to whom it is directed is entitled to security against damages or payment of damages resulting from such request and may respond to such request by submitting to its terms, by proposing different terms, by objecting specifically or generally to the request by serving a written response to the party making the request within thirty (30) days, or by moving to quash as permitted by IN ST TRIAL P Rule 45(B). IN ST TRIAL P Rule 34(C)(3).

   ii. *Service of responses on other parties required.* A party receiving documents from a non-party pursuant to IN ST TRIAL P Rule 34(C) shall serve copies on all other parties within fifteen (15) days of receiving the documents. If the documents are voluminous and service of a complete set of copies is burdensome, the receiving party shall notify all parties within fifteen (15) days of receiving the documents that the documents are available for inspection at the location of their production by the non-party, or at another location agreed to by the parties. The parties shall agree to arrangements for copying, and any party desiring copies shall bear the cost of reproducing them. IN ST TRIAL P Rule 34(C)(4).

e. *Exception to best evidence rule.* When a party or witness in control of a writing or document subject to examination under IN ST TRIAL P Rule 34 or IN ST TRIAL P Rule 9.2(E) refuses or is unable to produce it, evidence thereof shall be allowed by other parties without compliance with the rule of evidence requiring production of the original document or writing as best evidence. IN ST TRIAL P Rule 34(D).

3. *Response to request for production of documents*

a. *Content of the response.* The response shall state, with respect to each item or category, that inspection and related activities will be permitted as requested, unless it is objected to, including an objection to the requested form or forms for producing electronically stored information, stating in which event the reasons for objection shall be stated. If objection is made to part of an item or category, the part shall be specified. IN ST TRIAL P Rule 34(B).

b. *Types of responses.* There are several responses that a party may make to a IN ST TRIAL P Rule 34 discovery request:

   i. Agree to produce the requested item or permit inspection at the time and place suggested by the discovering party. 10 INPRAC § 67.2.

   ii. Agree to production, but suggest another time and place. 10 INPRAC § 67.2.

   iii. Move for a protective order under IN ST TRIAL P Rule 26(C). 10 INPRAC § 67.2.

   iv. Object to the request. Common grounds for objection include:

   • The item sought does not exist. 10 INPRAC § 67.2.

- Respondent does not have possession, custody or control of the item requested. 10 INPRAC § 67.2.

- The request does not describe documents to be produced with reasonable particularity, or by individual item or category. 10 INPRAC § 67.2.

- The document requested fails to specify a reasonable time, place and manner of production. 10 INPRAC § 67.2.

- The discovery requested is privileged or constitutes work product (mental impressions, conclusions, opinions or legal theories of party or party's attorney). 10 INPRAC § 67.2.

- The discovery requested is not relevant to the subject matter of the litigation and not reasonably calculated to lead to the discovery of admissible evidence. 10 INPRAC § 67.2.

- The discovery requests documents prepared in anticipation of litigation when the requesting party does not have a substantial need of the materials in preparation of the case and is able to obtain the substantial equivalent of the materials without undue hardship and by other means. 10 INPRAC § 67.2.

- Nonparty's statement was prepared in anticipation of litigation and there has been no showing that the non-party's statement cannot be obtained without undue hardship by other means. 10 INPRAC § 67.2.

- The discovery requested contains opinions and facts of an expert who was retained and specially employed in anticipation of litigation or trial preparation and who is not expected to be called as a witness at trial and no exceptional circumstances exist which make it impracticable for the party seeking discovery to obtain the facts and opinions by other means. 10 INPRAC § 67.2.

- The requesting party refuses to pay a fair portion of costs incurred by responding party to produce documents. 10 INPRAC § 67.2.

- The testing procedure requested will destroy or materially alter the document or thing. 10 INPRAC § 67.2.

- The discovery requested is burdensome, oppressive or unduly expensive. 10 INPRAC § 67.2.

c. *Objection.* If objection is made to the requested form or forms for producing electronically stored information—or if no form was specified in the request—the responding party must state the form or forms it intends to use. The party submitting the request may move for an order under IN ST TRIAL P Rule 37(A) with respect to any objection to or other failure to respond to the request or any part thereof, or any failure to permit inspection as requested. IN ST TRIAL P Rule 34(B).

d. *Claims of privilege.* A blanket claim of privilege is not favored, and that the party who seeks to avoid discovery has the burden of establishing the essential elements of the privilege which is invoked. 3 INPRAC R 34(34.2); Ray v. St. John's Health Care Corp., 582 N.E.2d 464 (Ind.Ct.App. 1991).

e. *Electronically stored information; Production in multiple formats.* A party need not produce the same electronically stored information in more than one form. IN ST TRIAL P Rule 34(B).

f. *Response by a non-party.* Any party, or any witness or person upon whom the request properly is made may respond to the request as provided in IN ST TRIAL P Rule 34(B). If the response of the witness or person to whom it is directed is unfavorable, if he moves to quash, if he refuses to cooperate after responding or fails to respond, or if he objects, the party making the request may move for an order under IN ST TRIAL P Rule 37(A) with respect to any such response or objection. IN ST TRIAL P Rule 34(C)(3).

   i. In granting an order under IN ST TRIAL P Rule 34(C)(3) and IN ST TRIAL P Rule 37(A)(2) the court shall condition relief upon the prepayment of damages to be proximately incurred by the witness or person to whom the request is directed or require an adequate surety bond or other indemnity conditioned against such damages. Such damages shall include reasonable attorneys' fees incurred in reasonable resistance and in establishing such threatened damage or damages. IN ST TRIAL P Rule 34(C)(3).

  ii. Refer to the Indiana KeyRules Motion to Compel Discovery document more information.

 g. *Supplementation of responses.* A party who has responded to a request for discovery with a response that was complete when made is under no duty to supplement his response to include information thereafter acquired, except as follows:

  i. A party is under a duty seasonably to supplement his response with respect to any question directly addressed to:

- The identity and location of persons having knowledge of discoverable matters, and
- The identity of each person expected to be called as an expert witness at trial, the subject-matter on which he is expected to testify, and the substance of his testimony. IN ST TRIAL P Rule 26(E)(1).

  ii. A party is under a duty seasonably to amend a prior response if he obtains information upon the basis of which:

- He knows that the response was incorrect when made, or
- He knows that the response though correct when made is no longer true and the circumstances are such that a failure to amend the response is in substance a knowing concealment. IN ST TRIAL P Rule 26(E)(2).

  iii. A duty to supplement responses may be imposed by order of the court, agreement of the parties, or at any time prior to trial through new requests for supplementation of prior responses. IN ST TRIAL P Rule 26(E)(3).

  iv. The duty seasonably to supplement a discovery response is absolute and is not predicated on a court order. "It is a breach of a litigant's duty reasonably to supplement if the litigant postpones supplementing its response by not obtaining from its experts the information which is to be supplied in answer to interrogatories." 2A INPRAC R 26(26.27); Lucas v. Dorsey Corp., 609 N.E.2d 1191, 1196 (Ind.Ct.App. 1993).

D. Documents

1. *Required documents*

 a. *Request for production.* Refer to the General Requirements section of this document for information on the scope and content of a request for production of documents.

 b. *Certificate of service.* An attorney or unrepresented party tendering a document to the Clerk for filing shall certify that service has been made, list the parties served, and specify the date and means of service. The certificate of service shall be placed at the end of the document and shall not be separately filed. The separate filing of a certificate of service, however, shall not be grounds for rejecting a document for filing. The Clerk may permit documents to be filed without a certificate of service but shall require prompt filing of a separate certificate of service. IN ST TRIAL P Rule 5(C).

2. *Supplemental documents*

 a. *Stipulation regarding discovery procedure.* Unless the court orders otherwise, the parties may by written stipulation:

  i. Provide that depositions may be taken before any person, at any time or place, upon any notice, and in any manner and when so taken may be used like other depositions, and

  ii. Modify the procedures provided by the Indiana Rules of Trial Procedure for other methods of discovery. IN ST TRIAL P Rule 29.

  iii. Admissions, stipulations and agreements concerning the proceedings in a case will not be enforced, unless submitted in writing or made of record. IN ST ALLEN SUPER AND CIR CT CIV Rule TR00-2.

 b. *Subpoena.* Requests upon non-parties shall be included in or with a subpoena served upon such witness or person. IN ST TRIAL P Rule 34(C)(1).

 c. *Facsimile cover sheet.* Any document sent to the Clerk of the Circuit Court by electronic facsimile transmission shall be accompanied by a cover sheet which states the title of the document, case number, number of pages, identity and voice telephone number of the sending party and instructions for filing. The cover sheet shall contain the signature of the attorney or party, pro se, authorizing the filing. IN ST ADMIN Rule 12(D).

E. Format

1. *Form of documents produced.* The rules applicable to captions, and the signing and form of pleadings (IN ST TRIAL P Rule 8 through IN ST TRIAL P Rule 11), apply to all motions and other papers provided under the Indiana Rules of Trial Procedure. 22B INPRAC 7:2. Unless the parties otherwise agree, or the court otherwise orders, a party who produces documents for inspection shall produce them as they are kept in the usual course of business or shall organize and label them to correspond with the categories in the request. IN ST TRIAL P Rule 34(B).

2. *Form of pleadings*

   a. *Caption; Names of parties.* Every pleading shall contain a caption setting forth the name of the court, the title of the action, the file number, and a designation as in IN ST TRIAL P Rule 7(A). In the complaint the title of the action shall include the names of all the parties, but in other pleadings it is sufficient to state the name of the first party on each side with an appropriate indication of other parties. IN ST TRIAL P Rule 10(A).

   b. *Paragraphs; Separate statements.* All averments of a claim or defense shall be made in numbered paragraphs, the contents of each of which shall be limited as far as practicable to a statement of a single set of circumstances, and a paragraph may be referred to by number in all succeeding pleadings. Each claim founded upon a separate transaction or occurrence and each defense other than denials may be stated in a separate count or defense whenever a separation facilitates the clear presentation of the matters set forth. IN ST TRIAL P Rule 10(B).

   c. *Adoption by reference; Exhibits.* Statements in a pleading may be adopted by reference in a different part of the same pleading or in another pleading or in any motion. A copy of any written instrument which is an exhibit to a pleading is a part thereof for all purposes. IN ST TRIAL P Rule 10(C).

   d. *Citation.* Allen County Superior and Circuit court rules may be cited as L.R. _____. The Indiana Rules of Trial Procedure are hereinafter referred to as T.R. _____. IN ST ALLEN SUPER AND CIR CT CIV Rule AR00-1(B).

   e. *Paper.* All pleadings must be printed on white paper. IN ST ALLEN SUPER AND CIR CT CIV Rule 8-1(A).

   f. *Spacing.* The lines shall be double spaced except for quotations, which shall be indented and single-spaced. IN ST ALLEN SUPER AND CIR CT CIV Rule 8-1(A).

   g. *Photocopies.* Photocopies are acceptable if legible. IN ST ALLEN SUPER AND CIR CT CIV Rule 8-1(A).

   h. *Margins and binding.* Margins shall be one to one and one-half (1-1 1/2) inches on the left side and one-half (1/2) inch on the right. IN ST ALLEN SUPER AND CIR CT CIV Rule 8-1(B).

      i. Binding or stapling shall be at the top left and at no other place. IN ST ALLEN SUPER AND CIR CT CIV Rule 8-1(B).

      ii. Covers or backing shall not be used. IN ST ALLEN SUPER AND CIR CT CIV Rule 8-1(B).

   i. *Flat filing.* The files of the Clerk of the Court shall be kept under the "flat filing" system. All pleadings presented for filing with the Clerk or Court shall be flat and unfolded. Only the original of any pleading shall be placed in the Court file. IN ST ALLEN SUPER AND CIR CT CIV Rule 77-1(A).

   j. *Handwritten pleadings.* Handwritten pleadings may be accepted for filing in the discretion of the Court. IN ST ALLEN SUPER AND CIR CT CIV Rule 8-1(A).

3. *Size of papers for filing.* Effective January 1, 1992, all pleadings, copies, motions and documents filed with any trial court or appellate level court, typed or printed, with the exception of exhibits and existing wills, shall be prepared on eight and one-half by eleven inch (8 1/2" x 11") size paper. IN ST ADMIN Rule 11.

4. *Signature requirements*

   a. *Signature of attorney.* Every pleading or motion of a party represented by an attorney shall be signed by at least one (1) attorney of record in his individual name, whose address, telephone number, and attorney number shall be stated, except that this provision shall not apply to pleadings and motions made and transcribed at the trial or a hearing before the judge and received by him in such form. IN ST TRIAL P Rule 11(A). All pleadings to be signed by an attorney shall contain the written signature of the individual attorney, the attorney's printed name, Supreme Court Attorney Number, the name of the attorney's law firm, the attorney's address, telephone number, and a designation of the party for whom the attorney appears. IN ST ALLEN SUPER AND CIR CT CIV Rule 8-1(C). For the recommended signature format, refer to IN ST ALLEN SUPER AND CIR CT CIV Rule 8-1(C).

      i. The signature of an attorney constitutes a certificate by him that he has read the pleadings; that to the best of his knowledge, information, and belief, there is good ground to support it; and that it is not interposed for delay. IN ST TRIAL P Rule 11(A).

      ii. If a pleading or motion is not signed or is signed with intent to defeat the purpose of the rule, it may be stricken as sham and false and the action may proceed as though the pleading had not been served. IN ST TRIAL P Rule 11(A).

      iii. For a willful violation of IN ST TRIAL P Rule 11 an attorney may be subjected to appropriate disciplinary action. Similar action may be taken if scandalous or indecent matter is inserted. IN ST TRIAL P Rule 11(A).

      iv. Neither printed signatures, nor facsimile signatures shall be accepted on original documents. IN ST ALLEN SUPER AND CIR CT CIV Rule 8-1(C).

      v. Facsimile signatures are permitted on copies. IN ST ALLEN SUPER AND CIR CT CIV Rule 8-1(C).

   b. *Signature of unrepresented party.* A party who is not represented by an attorney shall sign his pleading and state his address. IN ST TRIAL P Rule 11(A).

   c. *Verification not generally required.* Except when specifically required by rule, pleadings or motions need not be verified or accompanied by affidavit. The rule in equity that the averments of an answer under oath must be overcome by the testimony of two (2) witnesses or of one (1) witness sustained by corroborating circumstances is abolished. IN ST TRIAL P Rule 11(A).

   d. *Verification by affirmation or representation.* When in connection with any civil or special statutory proceeding it is required that any pleading, motion, petition, supporting affidavit, or other document of any kind, be verified, or that an oath be taken, it shall be sufficient if the subscriber simply affirms the truth of the matter to be verified by an affirmation or representation. IN ST TRIAL P Rule 11(B). IN ST TRIAL P Rule 11(B) states that the affirmation or representation should be in substantially the following language: "I (we) affirm, under the penalties for perjury, that the foregoing representation(s) is (are) true. (Signed) _____."

      i. Any person who falsifies an affirmation or representation of fact shall be subject to the same penalties as are prescribed by law for the making of a false affidavit. IN ST TRIAL P Rule 11(B).

   e. *Verified pleadings, motions, and affidavits as evidence.* Pleadings, motions and affidavits accompanying or in support of such pleadings or motions when required to be verified or under oath shall be accepted as a representation that the signer had personal knowledge thereof or reasonable cause to believe the existence of the facts or matters stated or alleged therein; and, if otherwise competent or acceptable as evidence, may be admitted as evidence of the facts or matters stated or alleged therein when it is so provided in the Indiana Rules of Trial Procedure, by statute or other law, or to the extent the writing or signature expressly purports to be made upon the signer's personal knowledge. When such pleadings, motions and affidavits are verified or under oath they shall not require other or greater proof on the part of the adverse party than if not verified or not under oath unless expressly provided otherwise by the Indiana Rules of Trial Procedure, statute or other law. Affidavits upon motions for summary judgment under IN ST TRIAL P Rule 56 and in denial of execution under IN ST TRIAL P Rule 9.2 shall be made upon personal knowledge. IN ST TRIAL P Rule 11(C).

5. *Information excluded from public access.* Every document filed in a case shall separately identify information excluded from public access pursuant to IN ST ADMIN Rule 9(G)(1) as follows:

   a. Whole documents that are excluded from public access pursuant to IN ST ADMIN Rule 9(G)(1) shall be tendered on light green paper or have a light green coversheet attached to the document, marked "Not for Public Access" or "Confidential." IN ST TRIAL P Rule 5(G)(1).

   b. When only a portion of a document contains information excluded from public access pursuant to IN ST ADMIN Rule 9(G)(1), said information shall be omitted [or redacted] from the filed document, and set forth on a separate accompanying document on light green paper conspicuously marked "Not for Public Access" or "Confidential" and clearly designated [or identifying] the caption and number of the case and the document and location within the document to which the redacted material pertains. IN ST TRIAL P Rule 5(G)(2).

   c. With respect to documents filed in electronic format, the trial court, by local rule, may provide for compliance with IN ST TRIAL P Rule 5 in manner that separates and protects access to information excluded from public access. IN ST TRIAL P Rule 5(G)(3).

   d. IN ST TRIAL P Rule 5(G) does not apply to a record sealed by the court pursuant to IN ST 5-14-3-5.5 or otherwise, nor to records, documents, or information filed in cases to which public access is prohibited pursuant to IN ST ADMIN Rule 9(G). IN ST TRIAL P Rule 5(G)(4).

   e. The following information in case records is excluded from public access and is confidential:

      i. Information that is excluded from public access pursuant to federal law;

      ii. Information that is excluded from public access as declared confidential by Indiana statute or other court rule, including without limitation:

      • All adoption records created after July 8, 1941, as declared confidential by IN ST 31-19-19-1, et seq., except those specifically declared open by IN ST 31-19-13-2(2);

      • All records relating to chancroid, chlamydia, gonorrhea, hepatitis, human immunodeficiency virus (HIV), Lymphogranuloma venereum, syphilis, tuberculosis, as declared confidential by IN ST 16-41-8-1, et seq.;

      • All records relating to child abuse as declared confidential by IN ST 31-33-18-1, et seq.;

      • All records relating to drug tests as declared confidential by IN ST 5-14-3-4(a)(9);

      • Records of grand jury proceedings as declared confidential by IN ST 35-34-2-4;

      • Records of juvenile proceedings as declared confidential by IN ST 31-39-1-2, except those specifically open under statute;

      • All paternity records created after July 1, 1941 as declared confidential by IN ST 31-14-11-15, IN ST 31-19-5-23, IN ST 31-39-1-1 and IN ST 31-39-1-2 [Editor's note: IN ST 31-14-11-15 was repealed effective May 9, 2013];

      • All pre-sentence reports as declared confidential by IN ST 35-38-1-13;

      • Written petitions to permit marriages without consent and orders directing the Clerk of Court to issue a marriage license to underage persons, as declared confidential by IN ST 31-11-1-6;

      • Only those arrest warrants, search warrants, indictments and informations ordered confidential by the trial judge, prior to return of duly executed service as declared confidential by IN ST 5-14-3-4(b)(1);

      • All medical, mental health, or tax records unless determined by law or regulation of any governmental custodian not to be confidential, released by the subject of such records, or declared by a court of competent jurisdiction to be essential to the resolution of litigation as declared confidential by IN ST 16-39-3-10, IN ST 6-4.1-5-10, IN ST 6-4.1-12-12, and IN ST 6-8.1-7-1;

      • Personal information relating to jurors or prospective jurors, other than for the use of the parties and counsel, pursuant to IN ST JURY Rule 10;

- Information relating to protection from abuse orders, no-contact orders and workplace violence restraining orders as declared confidential by IN ST 5-2-9-6, et seq.;

- Mediation proceedings pursuant to IN ST ADR Rule 2.11, Mini-Trial proceedings pursuant to IN ST ADR Rule 4.4(C), and Summary Jury Trials pursuant to IN ST ADR Rule 5.6;

- Information in probation files pursuant to the Probation Standards promulgated by the Judicial Conference of Indiana pursuant to IN ST 11-13-1-8(b);

- Information deemed confidential pursuant to the Rules for Court Administered Alcohol and Drug Programs promulgated by the Judicial Conference of Indiana pursuant to IN ST 12-23-14-13;

- Information deemed confidential pursuant to the Problem-Solving Court Rules promulgated by the Judicial Conference of Indiana pursuant to IN ST 33-23-16-16;

- All records of the Department of workforce Development as declared confidential by IN ST 22-4-19-6;

- Information regarding interception of electronic communications that is sealed or deemed confidential as set forth in IN ST 35-33.5-2-1, et seq.

iii. Information excluded from public access by specific court order;

iv. Complete Social Security Numbers of living persons;

v. With the exception of names, information such as addresses, phone numbers, and dates of birth which explicitly identifies:

- Natural persons who are witnesses or victims (not including defendants) in criminal, domestic violence, stalking, sexual assault, juvenile, or civil protection order proceedings, provided that juveniles who are victims of sex crimes shall be identified by initials only;

- Places of residence of judicial officers, clerks and other employees of courts and clerks of court, unless the person or persons about whom the information pertains waives confidentiality;

vi. Complete account numbers of specific assets, loans, bank accounts, credit cards, and personal identification numbers (PINs);

vii. All orders of expungement entered in criminal or juvenile proceedings, orders to restrict access to criminal history information pursuant to IN ST 35-38-5-5.5 or IN ST 35-38-8-5 and records excluded from public access by such orders, and information related to infractions that is excluded from public access pursuant to IN ST 34-28-5-15 or IN ST 34-28-5-16 [Editor's note: IN ST 35-38-5-5.5, IN ST 35-38-8-5 and IN ST 34-28-5-16 were repealed effective July 1, 2013; for information on orders restricting access to criminal history, refer to IN ST 35-38-9-1, et seq.];

viii. All personal notes and e-mail, and deliberative material, of judges, jurors, court staff and judicial agencies, and information recorded in personal data assistants (PDA's) or organizers and personal calendars. IN ST ADMIN Rule 9(G)(1).

F. Filing and Service Requirements

1. *Filing requirements.* Except as otherwise provided in IN ST TRIAL P Rule 5(E)(2), all pleadings and papers subsequent to the complaint which are required to be served upon a party shall be filed with the Court either before service or within a reasonable period of time thereafter. IN ST TRIAL P Rule 5(E)(1).

   a. *Non-filing of discovery until necessary*

      i. *Non-filing of discovery; Exceptions.* No deposition or request for discovery or response thereto under IN ST TRIAL P Rule 27, IN ST TRIAL P Rule 30, IN ST TRIAL P Rule 31, IN ST TRIAL P Rule 33, IN ST TRIAL P Rule 34 or IN ST TRIAL P Rule 36 shall be filed with the Court unless:

         - A motion is filed pursuant to IN ST TRIAL P Rule 26(C) or IN ST TRIAL P Rule 37 and the original deposition or request for discovery or response thereto is necessary to enable the Court to rule; or

- A party desires to use the deposition or request for discovery or response thereto for evidentiary purposes at trial or in connection with a motion, and the Court, either upon its own motion or that of any party, or as a part of any pre-trial order, orders the filing of the original. IN ST TRIAL P Rule 5(E)(2).

ii. *Custody of original and period of retention*

- The original of a deposition shall, subject to the provisions of IN ST TRIAL P Rule 30(E), be delivered by the reporter to the party taking it and shall be maintained by that party until filed with the Court pursuant to IN ST TRIAL P Rule 5(E)(2) or until the later of final judgment, agreed settlement of the litigation or all appellate rights have been exhausted. IN ST TRIAL P Rule 5(E)(3)(a).

- The original or any request for discovery or response thereto under IN ST TRIAL P Rule 27, IN ST TRIAL P Rule 30, IN ST TRIAL P Rule 31, IN ST TRIAL P Rule 33, IN ST TRIAL P Rule 34 and IN ST TRIAL P Rule 36 shall be maintained by the party originating the request or response until filed with the Court pursuant to IN ST TRIAL P Rule 5(E)(2) or until the later of final judgment, agreed settlement or all appellate rights have been exhausted. IN ST TRIAL P Rule 5(E)(3)(b).

iii. *Original unavailable; Copies.* In the event it is made to appear to the satisfaction of the Court that the original of a deposition or request for discovery or response thereto cannot be filed with the Court when required, the Court may allow use of a copy instead of the original. IN ST TRIAL P Rule 5(E)(4).

iv. *Filing as publication.* The filing of any deposition shall constitute publication. IN ST TRIAL P Rule 5(E)(5).

b. *Filing with the court defined.* The filing of pleadings, motions, and other papers with the court as required by the Indiana Rules of Trial Procedure shall be made by one of the following methods:

i. Delivery to the clerk of the court;

ii. Sending by electronic transmission under the procedure adopted pursuant to IN ST ADMIN Rule 12;

iii. Mailing to the clerk by registered, certified or express mail return receipt requested;

iv. Depositing with any third-party commercial carrier for delivery to the clerk within three (3) calendar days, cost prepaid, properly addressed;

v. If the court so permits, filing with the judge, in which event the judge shall note thereon the filing date and forthwith transmit them to the office of the clerk; or

vi. Electronic filing, as approved by the Division of State Court Administration pursuant to IN ST ADMIN Rule 16. IN ST TRIAL P Rule 5(F).

vii. Filing by registered or certified mail and by third-party commercial carrier shall be complete upon mailing or deposit. IN ST TRIAL P Rule 5(F).

c. *Facsimile filing*

i. *Generally.* In counties where a majority of judges of the courts of record, by posted local rule, have authorized electronic facsimile filing and designated a telephone number to receive such transmissions, pleadings, motions, and other papers may be sent to the Clerk of Circuit Court by electronic facsimile transmission for filing in any case, provided:

- Such matter does not exceed ten (10) pages, including the cover sheet;

- Such matter does not require the payment of fees other than the electronic facsimile transcription fee set forth in IN ST ADMIN Rule 12(E);

- The sending party creates at the time of transmission a machine generated log for such transmission; and

- The original document and the transmission log are maintained by the sending party for the duration of the litigation. IN ST ADMIN Rule 12(B).

ii. *Time of filing.* During normal, posted business hours, the time of filing shall be the time the duplicate document is produced in the office of the Clerk of the Circuit Court. Duplicate documents received at all other times shall be filed as of the next normal business day. IN ST ADMIN Rule 12(C).

- If the receiving fax machine endorses its own time and date stamp upon the transmitted documents and the receiving machine produces a delivery receipt which is electronically created and transmitted to the sending party, the time of filing shall be the date and time recorded on the transmitted document by the receiving fax machine. IN ST ADMIN Rule 12(C).

d. *Proof of filing.* Any party filing any paper by any method other than personal delivery to the clerk shall retain proof of filing. IN ST TRIAL P Rule 5(F).

2. *Service requirements.* Unless otherwise provided by the Indiana Rules of Trial Procedure or an order of the court, each party and special judge, if any, shall be served with: (1) every order required by its terms to be served; (2) every pleading subsequent to the original complaint; (3) every written motion except one which may be heard ex parte; (4) every brief submitted to the trial court; (5) every paper relating to discovery required to be served upon a party; and (6) every written notice, appearance, demand, offer of judgment, designation of record on appeal, or similar paper. IN ST TRIAL P Rule 5(A).

a. *Methods of service*

i. *Personal service.* Whenever a party is represented by an attorney of record, service shall be made upon such attorney unless service upon the party himself is ordered by the court. Service upon the attorney or party shall be made by delivering or mailing a copy of the papers to the last known address or where an attorney or party has consented to service by fax or e-mail, as provided in IN ST TRIAL P Rule 3.1(A)(4), by faxing or e-mailing a copy of the documents to the fax number or e-mail address set out in the appearance form or correction as required by IN ST TRIAL P Rule 3.1(E). IN ST TRIAL P Rule 5(B). Delivery of a copy within IN ST TRIAL P Rule 5 means:

- Offering or tendering it to the attorney or party and stating the nature of the papers being served. Refusal to accept an offered or tendered document is a waiver of any objection to the sufficiency or adequacy of service of that document;

- Leaving it at his office with a clerk or other person in charge thereof, or if there is no one in charge, leaving it in a conspicuous place therein; or

- If the office is closed, by leaving it at his dwelling house or usual place of abode with some person of suitable age and discretion then residing therein; or,

- Leaving it at some other suitable place, selected by the attorney upon whom service is being made, pursuant to duly promulgated local rule. IN ST TRIAL P Rule 5(B)(1).

ii. *Service by mail.* If service is made by mail, the papers shall be deposited in the United States mail addressed to the person on whom they are being served, with postage prepaid. Service shall be deemed complete upon mailing. Proof of service of all papers permitted to be mailed may be made by written acknowledgment of service, by affidavit of the person who mailed the papers, or by certificate of an attorney. It shall be the duty of attorneys when entering their appearance in a cause or when filing pleadings or papers therein, to have noted in the Chronological Case Summary or said pleadings or papers so filed the address and telephone number of their office. Service by delivery or by mail at such address shall be deemed sufficient and complete. IN ST TRIAL P Rule 5(B)(2).

iii. *Service by fax or e-mail.* A party who has consented to service by fax or e-mail may be served as follows:

- Service by e-mail shall be made by attaching the document being served in .pdf format. Discovery documents must also be served in accordance with IN ST TRIAL P Rule 26(A). IN ST TRIAL P Rule 5(B)(3)(a).

- Service by fax shall be deemed complete upon generation of a transmission record indicating the successful transmission of the entire document, except as provided in IN ST TRIAL P Rule 5(B)(3)(d). IN ST TRIAL P Rule 5(B)(3)(b).

- Service by e-mail shall be deemed complete upon transmission, except as provided in IN ST TRIAL P Rule 5(B)(3)(d). IN ST TRIAL P Rule 5(B)(3)(c).

- Service by fax or e-mail that occurs on a Saturday, Sunday, legal holiday, or day the court or agency in which the matter is pending is closed or after 5:00 PM local time of the recipient shall be deemed complete the next day that is not a Saturday, Sunday, legal holiday, or day that the court or agency in which the matter is pending is not closed. IN ST TRIAL P Rule 5(B)(3)(d).

iv. *Additional service of electronic discovery.* In addition to service under Rule IN ST TRIAL P Rule 5(B) or a .pdf format electronic copy, a party propounding or responding to interrogatories, requests for production or requests for admission shall comply with IN ST TRIAL P Rule 26(A.1)(a) or IN ST TRIAL P Rule 26(A.1)(b). IN ST TRIAL P Rule 26(A.1).

- The party shall serve the discovery request or response in an electronic format (either on a disk or as an electronic document attachment) in any commercially available word processing software system. If transmitted on disk, each disk shall be labeled, identifying the caption of the case, the document, and the word processing version in which it is being submitted. If more than one (1) disk is used for the same document, each disk shall be labeled and also shall be sequentially numbered. If transmitted by electronic mail, the document must be accompanied by electronic memorandum providing the forgoing identifying information; or

- The party shall serve the opposing party with a verified statement that the attorney or party appealing pro se lacks the equipment and is unable to transmit the discovery as required by IN ST TRIAL P Rule 26(A.1). IN ST TRIAL P Rule 26(A.1).

v. *Consent to alternate service.* Any Allen County Attorney or any Allen County law firm may, without charge, maintain an assigned Courthouse box in the library of the Allen County Courthouse for receipt of notices, pleadings, process orders, or other communications from the Court, the Clerk, and other attorneys or law firms. IN ST ALLEN SUPER AND CIR CT CIV Rule 5-1(A). For more information concerning the use of courthouse boxes, refer to IN ST ALLEN SUPER AND CIR CT CIV Rule 5-1.

b. *Serving numerous defendants.* In any action in which there are unusually large numbers of defendants, the court, upon motion or of its own initiative, may order:

i. That service of the pleadings of the defendants and replies thereto need not be made as between the defendants;

- That any cross-claim, counterclaim, or matter constituting an avoidance or affirmative defense contained therein shall be deemed to be denied or avoided by all other parties; and

- That the filing of any such pleading and service thereof upon the plaintiff constitutes due notice of it to the parties. IN ST TRIAL P Rule 5(D).

ii. A copy of every such order shall be served upon the parties in such manner and form as the court directs. IN ST TRIAL P Rule 5(D).

c. *Service on parties in default for failure to appear.* No service need be made on parties in default for failure to appear, except that pleadings asserting new or additional claims for relief against them shall be served upon them in the manner provided by service of summons in IN ST TRIAL P Rule 4. IN ST TRIAL P Rule 5(A).

G. Hearings

1. The Indiana rules do not contemplate a hearing related to the filing and service of requests for production.

H. Forms

1. Request for Production of Documents Forms for Indiana

a. Request for production of documents. 5 INPRAC § 4:3.1.

b. Request for production of documents; Insurance company. 5 INPRAC § 4:3.2.

c. Request for production of documents; Medical records. 5 INPRAC § 4:3.3.

d. Request for production of documents; Non-party. 5 INPRAC § 4:3.4.

e. Motion to enlarge time to respond to request for production of documents. 5 INPRAC § 4:3.5.

f. Response to request for production of documents; General form with objections. 5 INPRAC § 4:3.6.

g. Request for production of documents; General form. 10 INPRAC § 67.6.

h. Request for entry upon land for inspection. 10 INPRAC § 67.7.

i. Request for production of documents; Products liability; Plaintiff to manufacturer. 10 INPRAC § 67.8.

j. Request for production of documents; Products liability; Property loss; Defendant. 10 INPRAC § 67.9.

k. Request for production of documents; Products liability; Vehicle; Plaintiff. 10 INPRAC § 67.10.

l. Products liability; Defendant to plaintiff regarding accident and injuries. 10 INPRAC § 67.11.

m. Request for production of documents; Action against insurance company. 10 INPRAC § 67.13.

n. Request for production of documents; Action against nursing home; Plaintiff. 10 INPRAC § 67.14.

o. Request for production of documents; Action against nursing home; Defendant. 10 INPRAC § 67.15.

p. Request for production of documents; Medical records. 10 INPRAC § 67.17.

q. Request for production of documents; To obtain corporate records. 10 INPRAC § 67.18.

r. Request for production of handwriting exemplars. 10 INPRAC § 67.19.

s. Response to request for production of documents; General form with objections. 10 INPRAC § 67.30.

t. Response to request for permission to enter upon land. 10 INPRAC § 67.31.

u. Motion to shorten time to respond to request for production. 10 INPRAC § 67.32.

v. Motion to enlarge time to respond to request for production. 10 INPRAC § 67.33.

w. Request for production of documents to nonparty; General form. 10 INPRAC § 67.40.

x. Request for production of documents to nonparty; Another form. 10 INPRAC § 67.41.

y. Request for production of documents to nonparty; Production of bank and financial records. 10 INPRAC § 67.42.

z. Request for production of documents to nonparty; Request that employer produce records relating to employee making personal injury claim. 10 INPRAC § 67.43.

2. **Official Request for Production of Documents Forms for Allen County**

a. Consent to alternate service. IN ST ALLEN SUPER AND CIR CT CIV App. A.

I. Checklist

(I) ❏ Matters to be considered by the party serving the request for production

    (a) ❏ Required documents

        (1) ❏ Request for production of documents

        (2) ❏ Certificate of service

    (b) ❏ Supplemental documents

        (1) ❏ Stipulation regarding discovery procedure

        (2) ❏ Subpoena

        (3) ❏ Facsimile cover sheet

(c) ❑ Timing

    (1) ❑ On parties: The request may, without leave of court, be served upon the plaintiff after commencement of the action and upon any other party with or after service of the summons and complaint upon that party

    (2) ❑ On non-parties: Neither a request nor subpoena to produce or permit as permitted by IN ST TRIAL P Rule 34 shall be served upon a non-party until at least fifteen (15) days after the date on which the party intending to serve such request or subpoena serves a copy of the proposed request and subpoena on all other parties

        (i) ❑ Provided, however, that if such request or subpoena relates to a matter set for hearing within such fifteen (15) day period or arises out of a bona fide emergency, such request or subpoena may be served upon a non-party one (1) day after receipt of the proposed request or subpoena by all other parties

(II) ❑ Matters to be considered by the responding party

    (a) ❑ Required documents

        (1) ❑ Response to request for production of documents

        (2) ❑ Certificate of service

    (b) ❑ Supplemental documents

        (1) ❑ Business records

        (2) ❑ Stipulation regarding discovery procedure

        (3) ❑ Facsimile cover sheet

    (c) ❑ Timing

        (1) ❑ The party upon whom the request is served shall serve a written response within a period designated in the request, not less than thirty (30) days after the service thereof or within such shorter for longer time as the court may allow

Requests, Notices and Applications
Request for Admissions

Document Last Updated October 2013

A. Applicable Rules

1. *State rules*

    a. Appearance. IN ST TRIAL P Rule 3.1.

    b. Process. IN ST TRIAL P Rule 4.

    c. Service and filing of pleadings and other papers. IN ST TRIAL P Rule 5.

    d. Time. IN ST TRIAL P Rule 6.

    e. Pleadings. IN ST TRIAL P Rule 7; IN ST TRIAL P Rule 9.2; IN ST TRIAL P Rule 10.

    f. Signing and verification of pleadings. IN ST TRIAL P Rule 11.

    g. Pre-trial procedure; Formulating issues. IN ST TRIAL P Rule 16.

    h. General provisions governing discovery. IN ST TRIAL P Rule 26.

    i. Methods of discovery. IN ST TRIAL P Rule 27; IN ST TRIAL P Rule 29; IN ST TRIAL P Rule 30; IN ST TRIAL P Rule 31; IN ST TRIAL P Rule 33; IN ST TRIAL P Rule 34; IN ST TRIAL P Rule 35; IN ST TRIAL P Rule 36.

    j. Failure to make or cooperate in discovery; Sanctions. IN ST TRIAL P Rule 37.

    k. Judgment on the evidence (directed verdict). IN ST TRIAL P Rule 50.

    l. Findings by the court. IN ST TRIAL P Rule 52.

m. Summary judgment. IN ST TRIAL P Rule 56.

n. Motion to correct error. IN ST TRIAL P Rule 59.

o. Relief from judgment or order. IN ST TRIAL P Rule 60.

p. Access to court records. IN ST ADMIN Rule 9.

q. Paper size. IN ST ADMIN Rule 11.

r. Facsimile transmission. IN ST ADMIN Rule 12.

s. Electronic filing and electronic service pilot projects. IN ST ADMIN Rule 16.

t. Sealing of certain records by court; Hearing; Notice. IN ST 5-14-3-5.5.

u. Privacy and confidentiality. IN ST 5-2-9-6; IN ST 5-14-3-4; IN ST 6-4.1-5-10; IN ST 6-4.1-12-12; IN ST 6-8.1-7-1; IN ST 11-13-1-8; IN ST 12-23-14-13; IN ST 16-39-3-10; IN ST 16-41-8-1; IN ST 22-4-19-6; IN ST 31-11-1-6; IN ST 31-19-5-23; IN ST 31-19-13-2; IN ST 31-19-19-1; IN ST 31-33-18-1; IN ST 31-39-1-1; IN ST 31-39-1-2; IN ST 33-23-16-16; IN ST 35-34-2-4; IN ST 35-38-1-13; IN ST 35-38-9-1; IN ST ADR Rule 2.11; IN ST ADR Rule 4.4; IN ST ADR Rule 5.6; IN ST JURY Rule 10.

2. *Local rules*

a. Applicability and citation of rules. IN ST ALLEN SUPER AND CIR CT CIV Rule AR00-1.

b. Admissions, stipulations and agreements. IN ST ALLEN SUPER AND CIR CT CIV Rule TR00-2.

c. Appearances. IN ST ALLEN SUPER AND CIR CT CIV Rule 3.1-1.

d. Consent to alternate service. IN ST ALLEN SUPER AND CIR CT CIV Rule 5-1.

e. Preparation of pleadings. IN ST ALLEN SUPER AND CIR CT CIV Rule 8-1.

f. Filing. IN ST ALLEN SUPER AND CIR CT CIV Rule 77-1.

B. Timing

1. *Time for service of request for admissions.* The request may, without leave of court, be served upon the plaintiff after commencement of the action and upon any other party with or after service of the summons and complaint upon that party. IN ST TRIAL P Rule 36(A).

2. *Time for service of response.* The matter is admitted unless, within a period designated in the request, not less than thirty (30) days after service thereof or within such shorter or longer time as the court may allow, the party to whom the request is directed serves upon the party requesting the admission a written answer or objection addressed to the matter. IN ST TRIAL P Rule 36(A).

3. *Computation of time*

a. *Generally; Days excluded.* In computing any period of time prescribed or allowed by the Indiana Rules of Trial Procedure, by order of the court, or by any applicable statute, the day of the act, event, or default from which the designated period of time begins to run shall not be included. The last day of the period so computed is to be included unless it is:

    i. A Saturday,

    ii. A Sunday,

    iii. A legal holiday as defined by state statute, or

    iv. A day the office in which the act is to be done is closed during regular business hours. IN ST TRIAL P Rule 6(A).

b. *Short periods.* In any event, the period runs until the end of the next day that is not a Saturday, a Sunday, a legal holiday, or a day on which the office is closed. When the period of time allowed is less than seven (7) days, intermediate Saturdays, Sundays, legal holidays, and days on which the office is closed shall be excluded from the computations. IN ST TRIAL P Rule 6(A).

c. *Additional time after service by United States mail.* Whenever a party has the right or is required to do some act or take some proceedings within a prescribed period after the service of a notice or other paper upon him and the notice or paper is served upon him by United States mail, three (3) days shall be added to the prescribed period. IN ST TRIAL P Rule 6(E).

    d. *Enlargement of time.* When an act is required or allowed to be done at or within a specific time by the Indiana Rules of Trial Procedure, the court may at any time for cause shown:

        i. Order the period enlarged, with or without motion or notice, if request therefor is made before the expiration of the period originally prescribed or extended by a previous order; or

        ii. Upon motion made after the expiration of the specific period, permit the act to be done where the failure to act was the result of excusable neglect; but, the court may not extend the time for taking any action for judgment on the evidence under IN ST TRIAL P Rule 50(A), amendment of findings and judgment under IN ST TRIAL P Rule 52(B), to correct errors under IN ST TRIAL P Rule 59(C), statement in opposition to motion to correct error under IN ST TRIAL P Rule 59(E), or to obtain relief from final judgment under IN ST TRIAL P Rule 60(B), except to the extent and under the conditions stated in those rules. IN ST TRIAL P Rule 6(B).

C. General Requirements

1. *Scope of discovery.* Unless otherwise limited by order of the court in accordance with the Indiana Rules of Trial Procedure, the scope of discovery is as follows:

    a. *In general.* Parties may obtain discovery regarding any matter, not privileged, which is relevant to the subject-matter involved in the pending action, whether it relates to the claim or defense of the party seeking discovery or the claim or defense of any other party, including the existence, description, nature, custody, condition and location of any books, documents, or other tangible things and the identity and location of persons having knowledge of any discoverable matter. It is not ground for objection that the information sought will be inadmissible at the trial if the information sought appears reasonably calculated to lead to the discovery of admissible evidence. IN ST TRIAL P Rule 26(B)(1).

        i. *Limiting discovery upon court determination.* The frequency or extent of use of the discovery methods otherwise permitted under the Indiana Rules of Trial Procedure and by any local rule shall be limited by the court if it determines that:

- The discovery sought is unreasonably cumulative or duplicative, or is obtainable from some other source that is more convenient, less burdensome, or less expensive;

- The party seeking discovery has had ample opportunity by discovery in the action to obtain the information sought or;

- The burden or expense of the proposed discovery outweighs its likely benefit, taking into account the needs of the case, the amount in controversy, the parties' resources, the importance of the issues at stake in the litigation, and the importance of the proposed discovery in resolving the issues. IN ST TRIAL P Rule 26(B)(1).

- The court may act upon its own initiative after reasonable notice or pursuant to a motion under IN ST TRIAL P Rule 26(C). IN ST TRIAL P Rule 26(B)(1). Refer to the Indiana KeyRules Motion for Protective Order document for more information.

        ii. *Relevancy in the discovery context.* When the word "relevancy" is used in IN ST TRIAL P Rule 26(B), it does not mean "relevancy" as that word in used to determine the admissibility of evidence in a trial court. It is much broader. It means "relevancy" to the "subject matter" of the litigation or pending action and it may relate to the claim or defense of any party. Pretrial discovery is available as to any nonprivileged matter relevant to the subject matter of the lawsuit or to obtain information reasonably calculated to lead to admissible evidence. 2A INPRAC R 26(26.4); Kaufmann v. Credithrift Financial, Inc., 465 N.E.2d 207, 210 (Ind.Ct.App. 1984).

        iii. *Tests for relevance.* Indiana case law has developed two (2) additional tests in this area. 2A INPRAC R 26(26.4).

- The first test determines when a document or a request for information is actually relevant to the subject matter in the pending action. A document [or discovery request] is relevant to discovery if there is the possibility the information sought may be relevant to the subject matter of the action. 2A INPRAC R 26(26.4); CIGNA-INA/Aetna v. Hagerman-Shambaugh, 473 N.E.2d 1033, 1036 (Ind.Ct.App. 1985).

- The second test speaks to appellate review of the trial court's determination that a document or discovery request is relevant to the subject matter of the pending action. The appellate court sees its review of the trial court's decision on relevancy to subject matter as being very limited. The court states: "Our review of the trial court's conclusion that the documents are relevant is limited. A trial court is vested with discretion in its rulings on discovery issues." 2A INPRAC R 26(26.4); Costanzi v. Ryan, 175 Ind.App. 257, 370 N.E.2d 1333 (Ind.Ct.App. 1978).

b. *Insurance agreements.* A party may obtain discovery of the existence and contents of any insurance agreement under which any person carrying on an insurance business may be liable to satisfy part or all of a judgment which may be entered in the action or to indemnify or reimburse for payments made to satisfy the judgment. Information concerning the insurance agreement is not by reason of disclosure admissible in evidence at trial. For purposes of IN ST TRIAL P Rule 26(B)(2), an application for insurance shall not be treated as part of an insurance agreement. IN ST TRIAL P Rule 26(B)(2).

c. *Trial preparation; Materials.* Subject to the provisions of IN ST TRIAL P Rule 26(B)(4), a party may obtain discovery of documents and tangible things otherwise discoverable under IN ST TRIAL P Rule 26(B)(1) and prepared in anticipation of litigation or for trial by or for another party or by or for that other party's representative (including his attorney, consultant, surety, indemnitor, insurer, or agent) only upon a showing that the party seeking discovery has substantial need of the materials in the preparation of his case and that he is unable without undue hardship to obtain the substantial equivalent of the materials by other means. In ordering discovery of such materials when the required showing has been made, the court shall protect against disclosure of the mental impressions, conclusions, opinions, or legal theories of an attorney or other representative of a party concerning the litigation. IN ST TRIAL P Rule 26(B)(3).

  i. A party may obtain without the required showing a statement concerning the action or its subject matter previously made by that party. Upon request, a person not a party may obtain without the required showing a statement concerning the action or its subject matter previously made by that person. If the request is refused, the person may move for a court order. The provisions of IN ST TRIAL P Rule 37(A)(4) apply to the award of expenses incurred in relation to the motion. For purposes of IN ST TRIAL P Rule 26(B)(3), a statement previously made is:

    - A written statement signed or otherwise adopted approved by the person making it, or
    - A stenographic, mechanical, electrical, or other recording, or a transcription thereof, which is a substantially verbatim recital of an oral statement by the person making it and contemporaneously recorded. IN ST TRIAL P Rule 26(B)(3).

  ii. The protection of IN ST TRIAL P Rule 26(B)(3) extends to material prepared or collected before litigation actually commences, but that some possibility of litigation must actually exist before the privilege and IN ST TRIAL P Rule 26(B)(3) become operative. 2A INPRAC R 26(26.9); CIGNA-INA/Aetna v. Hagerman-Shambaugh, 473 N.E.2d 1033, 1037 (Ind.Ct.App. 1985).

d. *Trial preparation; Experts.* Discovery of facts known and opinions held by experts, otherwise discoverable under the provisions of IN ST TRIAL P Rule 26(B)(1) and acquired or developed in anticipation of litigation or for trial, may be obtained as follows:

  i. A party may through interrogatories require any other party to identify each person whom the other party expects to call as an expert witness at trial, to state the subject matter on which the expert is expected to testify, and to state the substance of the facts and opinions to which the expert is expected to testify and a summary of the grounds for each opinion. IN ST TRIAL P Rule 26(B)(4)(a)(i).

  ii. Upon motion, the court may order further discovery by other means, subject to such restrictions as to scope and such provisions, pursuant to IN ST TRIAL P Rule 26(B)(4)(c), concerning fees and expenses as the court may deem appropriate. IN ST TRIAL P Rule 26(B)(4)(a)(ii).

  iii. A party may discover facts known or opinions held by an expert who has been retained or specially employed by another party in anticipation of litigation or preparation for trial and who is not expected to be called as a witness at trial, only as provided in IN ST TRIAL P Rule 35(B) or upon a showing of exceptional circumstances under which it is impracticable for the party seeking discovery to obtain facts or opinions on the same subject by other means. IN ST TRIAL P Rule 26(B)(4)(b).

    iv. Unless manifest injustice would result,

- The court shall require that the party seeking discovery pay the expert a reasonable fee for time spent in responding to discovery under IN ST TRIAL P Rule 26(B)(4)(a)(ii) and IN ST TRIAL P Rule 26(B)(4)(b); and

- With respect to discovery obtained under IN ST TRIAL P Rule 26(B)(4)(a)(ii) the court may require, and with respect to discovery obtained under IN ST TRIAL P Rule 26(B)(4)(b) the court shall require, the party seeking discovery to pay the other party a fair portion of the fees and expenses reasonably incurred by the latter party in obtaining facts and opinions from the expert. IN ST TRIAL P Rule 26(B)(4)(c).

e. *Claims of privilege or protection*

    i. *Information withheld.* When a party withholds information otherwise discoverable under the Indiana Rules of Trial Procedure by claiming that it is privileged or subject to protection as trial preparation material, the party shall make the claim expressly and shall describe the nature of the documents, communications, or things not produced or disclosed in a manner that, without revealing information itself privileged or protected, will enable other parties to assess the applicability of the privilege or protection. IN ST TRIAL P Rule 26(B)(5)(a).

    ii. *Information produced.* If information is produced in discovery that is subject to a claim of privilege or protection as trial-preparation material, the party making the claim may notify any party that received the information of the claim and the basis for it. After being notified, a party must promptly return, sequester, or destroy the specified information and any copies it has and may not use or disclose the information until the claim is resolved. A receiving party may promptly present the information to the court under seal for a determination of the claim. If the receiving party disclosed the information before being notified, it must take reasonable steps to retrieve it. The producing party must preserve the information until the claim is resolved. IN ST TRIAL P Rule 26(B)(5)(b).

    iii. *Waiver.* The law of discovery has developed some holdings which indicate that "waiver" of a privileged communication in a discovery setting might be more exacting than "waiver" of a privileged communication when the only question at hand is an interpretation of the privilege itself. Thus, in litigation in which several documents are in issue, and some are released inadvertently, there is strong case law that holds that the "inadvertent production" of a privileged document does not constitute a waiver of the attorney-client privilege. 2A INPRAC R 26(26.5); Transamerica Computer Co. v. International Business Machines Corp., 573 F.2d 646 (9th Cir. 1978). Such a rule should be measured against the usual rule which suggests that a voluntary disclosure to a third person will generally suffice to show a waiver of the attorney-client privilege. 2A INPRAC R 26(26.5).

f. *Use not limited.* Unless the court orders otherwise under IN ST TRIAL P Rule 26(C), the frequency of use of the methods listed in IN ST TRIAL P Rule 26(A) is not limited. IN ST TRIAL P Rule 26(A).

g. *Sequence of discovery.* Unless the court upon motion, for the convenience of parties and witnesses and in the interests of justice, orders otherwise, methods of discovery may be used in any sequence and the fact that a party is conducting discovery, whether by deposition or otherwise, shall not operate to delay any other party's discovery. IN ST TRIAL P Rule 26(D).

2. *Request for admissions.* A request for admission is a method of discovery which allows a party to establish facts and information during the discovery stage of the action so that evidence on those matters will not be required at trial. 22 INPRAC § 26.1; Walker v. Employers Ins. of Wausau, 846 N.E.2d 1098 (Ind.Ct.App. 2006); Brown v. Dobbs, 691 N.E.2d 907 (Ind.Ct.App. 1998). Requests for admission under IN ST TRIAL P Rule 36 are designed to simplify and clarify the issues, to cut trial preparation time, and to encourage settlement. 10 INPRAC § 69.1.

a. *Request for admissions generally.* A party may serve upon any other party a written request for the admission, for purposes of the pending action only, of the truth of any matters within the scope of IN ST TRIAL P Rule 26(B) set forth in the request, including the genuineness of any documents described in the request. IN ST TRIAL P Rule 36(A).

b. *Mutually known matters.* Requests for admissions as to matters within the mutual knowledge of both parties are proper. The function of IN ST TRIAL P Rule 36 is to establish admissions that will obviate the necessity of proof and expedite the trial, or to transform "mutual knowledge" into the established facts of a case. 3 INPRAC R 36(36.5).

c. *Requests to be carefully drafted.* The burden on the requesting party is to carefully and artfully draft the statement of fact contained in the request for admission. The statement must be precise, unambiguous, and in no way mislead the answering party. 3 INPRAC R 36(36.2).

   i. Fairness demands that any error arising out of inartful drafting be borne by the requesting party. The burden imposed on the answering party is unfairly "increased when the request for admission propounds a statement of fact which lacks clarity, is ambiguous, or which otherwise might mislead the answering party." 3 INPRAC R 36(36.2); F.W. Means & Co. v. Carstens, 428 N.E.2d 251, 257 (Ind.Ct.App. 1981).

d. *Admissions by the requestor.* Propounding of requests for admissions admits nothing as to the requesting party. 3 INPRAC R 36(36.2); Indiana Construction Service v. Amoco Oil Company, 533 N.E.2d 1300 (Ind.Ct.App. 1989). This party in the action made an admission in the text of or during the request, to which the receiving party, of course, agreed. But it was not binding, as to the requesting party, the court held. Such a request is binding as to the party admitting the fact in response to a request. 3 INPRAC R 36(36.2); Indiana Construction Service v. Amoco Oil Company, 533 N.E.2d 1300 (Ind.Ct.App. 1989).

e. *Motion to compel.* The party who has requested the admissions may move for an order with respect to the answers or objections. Unless the court determines that an objection is justified, it shall order that an answer be served. If the court determines that an answer does not comply with the requirements of IN ST TRIAL P Rule 36, it may order either that the matter is admitted or that an amended answer be served. The court may, in lieu of these orders, determine that final disposition of the request be made at a pre-trial conference or at a designated time prior to trial. IN ST TRIAL P Rule 36(A).

   i. The provisions of IN ST TRIAL P Rule 37(A)(4) apply to the award of expenses incurred in relation to the motion. IN ST TRIAL P Rule 36(A).

   ii. Refer to the Indiana KeyRules Motion to Compel Discovery document for more information.

3. *Response to request for admissions.* The matter is admitted unless, within a period designated in the request, not less than thirty (30) days after service thereof or within such shorter or longer time as the court may allow, the party to whom the request is directed serves upon the party requesting the admission a written answer or objection addressed to the matter, signed by the party or by his attorney. IN ST TRIAL P Rule 36(A).

a. *Methods of response.* IN ST TRIAL P Rule 36 recognizes at least four (4) responses. The party:

   i. May not respond, thereby admitting the request; or

   ii. Answer; or

   iii. Object to the request; or

   iv. File a qualified response. 3 INPRAC R 36(36.4).

b. *Effect of admission.* Any matter admitted under IN ST TRIAL P Rule 36 is conclusively established unless the court on motion permits withdrawal or amendment of the admission. IN ST TRIAL P Rule 36(B).

   i. Any admission made by a party under IN ST TRIAL P Rule 36 is for the purpose of the pending action only and is not an admission by him for any other purpose nor may it be used against him in any other proceeding. IN ST TRIAL P Rule 36(B).

c. *Denials.* The answer shall specifically deny the matter or set forth in detail the reasons why the answering party cannot truthfully admit or deny the matter. A denial shall fairly meet the substance of the requested admission, and when good faith requires that a party qualify his answer or deny only a part of the matter of which an admission is requested, he shall specify so much of it as is true and qualify or deny the remainder. IN ST TRIAL P Rule 36(A).

d. *Lack of information or knowledge.* An answering party may not give lack of information or knowledge as a reason for failure to admit or deny unless he states that he has made reasonable inquiry and that the information known or readily obtainable by him is insufficient to enable him to admit or deny or that the inquiry would be unreasonably burdensome. IN ST TRIAL P Rule 36(A).

e. *Objections.* If objection is made, the reasons therefor shall be stated. IN ST TRIAL P Rule 36(A).

   i. A party who considers that a matter of which an admission has been requested presents a genuine issue for trial may not, on that ground alone, object to the request; he may, subject to the provisions of IN ST TRIAL P Rule 37(C), deny the matter or set forth reasons why he cannot admit or deny it. IN ST TRIAL P Rule 36(A).

   ii. An objectionable request may not be properly attacked by a motion to strike, to dismiss, or to suppress. The party served must respond to the request and serve admissions or denials of all matters not deemed objectionable. 3 INPRAC R 36(36.4).

f. *Withdrawal or amendment of admissions.* Subject to the provisions of IN ST TRIAL P Rule 16 governing amendment of a pre-trial order, the court may permit withdrawal or amendment when the presentation of the merits of the action will be subserved thereby and the party who obtained the admission fails to satisfy the court that withdrawal or amendment will prejudice him in maintaining his action or defense on the merits. IN ST TRIAL P Rule 36(B).

   i. It is within sound discretion of trial court to permit or deny amendment of pretrial order, but trial court should amend or modify pretrial order when requested if modification is necessary to prevent manifest injustice. 2 INPRAC R 16(7); Hacienda Mexican Restaurant of Kalamazoo Corp. v. Hacienda Franchise Group, Inc., 641 N.E.2d 1036 (Ind.Ct.App. 1994).

g. *Supplementation of responses.* A party who has responded to a request for discovery with a response that was complete when made is under no duty to supplement his response to include information thereafter acquired, except as follows:

   i. A party is under a duty seasonably to supplement his response with respect to any question directly addressed to:

      • The identity and location of persons having knowledge of discoverable matters, and

      • The identity of each person expected to be called as an expert witness at trial, the subject-matter on which he is expected to testify, and the substance of his testimony. IN ST TRIAL P Rule 26(E)(1).

   ii. A party is under a duty seasonably to amend a prior response if he obtains information upon the basis of which:

      • He knows that the response was incorrect when made, or

      • He knows that the response though correct when made is no longer true and the circumstances are such that a failure to amend the response is in substance a knowing concealment. IN ST TRIAL P Rule 26(E)(2).

   iii. A duty to supplement responses may be imposed by order of the court, agreement of the parties, or at any time prior to trial through new requests for supplementation of prior responses. IN ST TRIAL P Rule 26(E)(3).

   iv. The duty seasonably to supplement a discovery response is absolute and is not predicated on a court order. "It is a breach of a litigant's duty reasonably to supplement if the litigant postpones supplementing its response by not obtaining from its experts the information which is to be supplied in answer to interrogatories." 2A INPRAC R 26(26.27); Lucas v. Dorsey Corp., 609 N.E.2d 1191, 1196 (Ind.Ct.App. 1993).

256

D. Documents

1. *Required documents*

   a. *Request for admissions.* Refer to the General Requirements section of this document for information on the scope and content of a request for admissions.

   b. *Copies of documents.* Copies of documents shall be served with the request unless they have been or are otherwise furnished or made available for inspection and copying. IN ST TRIAL P Rule 36(A).

   c. *Certificate of service.* An attorney or unrepresented party tendering a document to the Clerk for filing shall certify that service has been made, list the parties served, and specify the date and means of service. The certificate of service shall be placed at the end of the document and shall not be separately filed. The separate filing of a certificate of service, however, shall not be grounds for rejecting a document for filing. The Clerk may permit documents to be filed without a certificate of service but shall require prompt filing of a separate certificate of service. IN ST TRIAL P Rule 5(C).

2. *Supplemental documents*

   a. *Stipulation regarding discovery procedure.* Unless the court orders otherwise, the parties may by written stipulation:

      i. Provide that depositions may be taken before any person, at any time or place, upon any notice, and in any manner and when so taken may be used like other depositions, and

      ii. Modify the procedures provided by the Indiana Rules of Trial Procedure for other methods of discovery. IN ST TRIAL P Rule 29.

      iii. Admissions, stipulations and agreements concerning the proceedings in a case will not be enforced, unless submitted in writing or made of record. IN ST ALLEN SUPER AND CIR CT CIV Rule TR00-2.

   b. *Facsimile cover sheet.* Any document sent to the Clerk of the Circuit Court by electronic facsimile transmission shall be accompanied by a cover sheet which states the title of the document, case number, number of pages, identity and voice telephone number of the sending party and instructions for filing. The cover sheet shall contain the signature of the attorney or party, pro se, authorizing the filing. IN ST ADMIN Rule 12(D).

E. Format

1. *Form of requests for admissions.* The rules applicable to captions, and the signing and form of pleadings (IN ST TRIAL P Rule 8 through IN ST TRIAL P Rule 11), apply to all motions and other papers provided under the Indiana Rules of Trial Procedure. 22B INPRAC 7:2. Each matter of which an admission is requested shall be separately set forth. IN ST TRIAL P Rule 36(A).

2. *Form of pleadings*

   a. *Caption; Names of parties.* Every pleading shall contain a caption setting forth the name of the court, the title of the action, the file number, and a designation as in IN ST TRIAL P Rule 7(A). In the complaint the title of the action shall include the names of all the parties, but in other pleadings it is sufficient to state the name of the first party on each side with an appropriate indication of other parties. IN ST TRIAL P Rule 10(A).

   b. *Paragraphs; Separate statements.* All averments of a claim or defense shall be made in numbered paragraphs, the contents of each of which shall be limited as far as practicable to a statement of a single set of circumstances, and a paragraph may be referred to by number in all succeeding pleadings. Each claim founded upon a separate transaction or occurrence and each defense other than denials may be stated in a separate count or defense whenever a separation facilitates the clear presentation of the matters set forth. IN ST TRIAL P Rule 10(B).

   c. *Adoption by reference; Exhibits.* Statements in a pleading may be adopted by reference in a different part of the same pleading or in another pleading or in any motion. A copy of any written instrument which is an exhibit to a pleading is a part thereof for all purposes. IN ST TRIAL P Rule 10(C).

   d. *Citation.* Allen County Superior and Circuit court rules may be cited as L.R. _____. The Indiana Rules of Trial Procedure are hereinafter referred to as T.R. _____. IN ST ALLEN SUPER AND CIR CT CIV Rule AR00-1(B).

e. *Paper.* All pleadings must be printed on white paper. IN ST ALLEN SUPER AND CIR CT CIV Rule 8-1(A).

f. *Spacing.* The lines shall be double spaced except for quotations, which shall be indented and single-spaced. IN ST ALLEN SUPER AND CIR CT CIV Rule 8-1(A).

g. *Photocopies.* Photocopies are acceptable if legible. IN ST ALLEN SUPER AND CIR CT CIV Rule 8-1(A).

h. *Margins and binding.* Margins shall be one to one and one-half (1-1 1/2) inches on the left side and one-half (1/2) inch on the right. IN ST ALLEN SUPER AND CIR CT CIV Rule 8-1(B).

    i. Binding or stapling shall be at the top left and at no other place. IN ST ALLEN SUPER AND CIR CT CIV Rule 8-1(B).

    ii. Covers or backing shall not be used. IN ST ALLEN SUPER AND CIR CT CIV Rule 8-1(B).

i. *Flat filing.* The files of the Clerk of the Court shall be kept under the "flat filing" system. All pleadings presented for filing with the Clerk or Court shall be flat and unfolded. Only the original of any pleading shall be placed in the Court file. IN ST ALLEN SUPER AND CIR CT CIV Rule 77-1(A).

j. *Handwritten pleadings.* Handwritten pleadings may be accepted for filing in the discretion of the Court. IN ST ALLEN SUPER AND CIR CT CIV Rule 8-1(A).

3. *Size of papers for filing.* Effective January 1, 1992, all pleadings, copies, motions and documents filed with any trial court or appellate level court, typed or printed, with the exception of exhibits and existing wills, shall be prepared on eight and one-half by eleven inch (8 1/2" x 11") size paper. IN ST ADMIN Rule 11.

4. *Signature requirements*

a. *Signature of attorney.* Every pleading or motion of a party represented by an attorney shall be signed by at least one (1) attorney of record in his individual name, whose address, telephone number, and attorney number shall be stated, except that this provision shall not apply to pleadings and motions made and transcribed at the trial or a hearing before the judge and received by him in such form. IN ST TRIAL P Rule 11(A). All pleadings to be signed by an attorney shall contain the written signature of the individual attorney, the attorney's printed name, Supreme Court Attorney Number, the name of the attorney's law firm, the attorney's address, telephone number, and a designation of the party for whom the attorney appears. IN ST ALLEN SUPER AND CIR CT CIV Rule 8-1(C). For the recommended signature format, refer to IN ST ALLEN SUPER AND CIR CT CIV Rule 8-1(C).

    i. The signature of an attorney constitutes a certificate by him that he has read the pleadings; that to the best of his knowledge, information, and belief, there is good ground to support it; and that it is not interposed for delay. IN ST TRIAL P Rule 11(A).

    ii. If a pleading or motion is not signed or is signed with intent to defeat the purpose of the rule, it may be stricken as sham and false and the action may proceed as though the pleading had not been served. IN ST TRIAL P Rule 11(A).

    iii. For a willful violation of IN ST TRIAL P Rule 11 an attorney may be subjected to appropriate disciplinary action. Similar action may be taken if scandalous or indecent matter is inserted. IN ST TRIAL P Rule 11(A).

    iv. Neither printed signatures, nor facsimile signatures shall be accepted on original documents. IN ST ALLEN SUPER AND CIR CT CIV Rule 8-1(C).

    v. Facsimile signatures are permitted on copies. IN ST ALLEN SUPER AND CIR CT CIV Rule 8-1(C).

b. *Signature of unrepresented party.* A party who is not represented by an attorney shall sign his pleading and state his address. IN ST TRIAL P Rule 11(A).

c. *Verification not generally required.* Except when specifically required by rule, pleadings or motions need not be verified or accompanied by affidavit. The rule in equity that the averments of an answer under oath must be overcome by the testimony of two (2) witnesses or of one (1) witness sustained by corroborating circumstances is abolished. IN ST TRIAL P Rule 11(A).

    d. *Verification by affirmation or representation.* When in connection with any civil or special statutory proceeding it is required that any pleading, motion, petition, supporting affidavit, or other document of any kind, be verified, or that an oath be taken, it shall be sufficient if the subscriber simply affirms the truth of the matter to be verified by an affirmation or representation. IN ST TRIAL P Rule 11(B). IN ST TRIAL P Rule 11(B) states that the affirmation or representation should be in substantially the following language: "I (we) affirm, under the penalties for perjury, that the foregoing representation(s) is (are) true. (Signed) _____."

        i. Any person who falsifies an affirmation or representation of fact shall be subject to the same penalties as are prescribed by law for the making of a false affidavit. IN ST TRIAL P Rule 11(B).

    e. *Verified pleadings, motions, and affidavits as evidence.* Pleadings, motions and affidavits accompanying or in support of such pleadings or motions when required to be verified or under oath shall be accepted as a representation that the signer had personal knowledge thereof or reasonable cause to believe the existence of the facts or matters stated or alleged therein; and, if otherwise competent or acceptable as evidence, may be admitted as evidence of the facts or matters stated or alleged therein when it is so provided in the Indiana Rules of Trial Procedure, by statute or other law, or to the extent the writing or signature expressly purports to be made upon the signer's personal knowledge. When such pleadings, motions and affidavits are verified or under oath they shall not require other or greater proof on the part of the adverse party than if not verified or not under oath unless expressly provided otherwise by the Indiana Rules of Trial Procedure, statute or other law. Affidavits upon motions for summary judgment under IN ST TRIAL P Rule 56 and in denial of execution under IN ST TRIAL P Rule 9.2 shall be made upon personal knowledge. IN ST TRIAL P Rule 11(C).

5. *Information excluded from public access.* Every document filed in a case shall separately identify information excluded from public access pursuant to IN ST ADMIN Rule 9(G)(1) as follows:

    a. Whole documents that are excluded from public access pursuant to IN ST ADMIN Rule 9(G)(1) shall be tendered on light green paper or have a light green coversheet attached to the document, marked "Not for Public Access" or "Confidential." IN ST TRIAL P Rule 5(G)(1).

    b. When only a portion of a document contains information excluded from public access pursuant to IN ST ADMIN Rule 9(G)(1), said information shall be omitted [or redacted] from the filed document, and set forth on a separate accompanying document on light green paper conspicuously marked "Not for Public Access" or "Confidential" and clearly designated [or identifying] the caption and number of the case and the document and location within the document to which the redacted material pertains. IN ST TRIAL P Rule 5(G)(2).

    c. With respect to documents filed in electronic format, the trial court, by local rule, may provide for compliance with IN ST TRIAL P Rule 5 in manner that separates and protects access to information excluded from public access. IN ST TRIAL P Rule 5(G)(3).

    d. IN ST TRIAL P Rule 5(G) does not apply to a record sealed by the court pursuant to IN ST 5-14-3-5.5 or otherwise, nor to records, documents, or information filed in cases to which public access is prohibited pursuant to IN ST ADMIN Rule 9(G). IN ST TRIAL P Rule 5(G)(4).

    e. The following information in case records is excluded from public access and is confidential:

        i. Information that is excluded from public access pursuant to federal law;

       ii. Information that is excluded from public access as declared confidential by Indiana statute or other court rule, including without limitation:

- All adoption records created after July 8, 1941, as declared confidential by IN ST 31-19-19-1, et seq., except those specifically declared open by IN ST 31-19-13-2(2);

- All records relating to chancroid, chlamydia, gonorrhea, hepatitis, human immunodeficiency virus (HIV), Lymphogranuloma venereum, syphilis, tuberculosis, as declared confidential by IN ST 16-41-8-1, et seq.;

- All records relating to child abuse as declared confidential by IN ST 31-33-18-1, et seq.;

- All records relating to drug tests as declared confidential by IN ST 5-14-3-4(a)(9);

- Records of grand jury proceedings as declared confidential by IN ST 35-34-2-4;
- Records of juvenile proceedings as declared confidential by IN ST 31-39-1-2, except those specifically open under statute;
- All paternity records created after July 1, 1941 as declared confidential by IN ST 31-14-11-15, IN ST 31-19-5-23, IN ST 31-39-1-1 and IN ST 31-39-1-2 [Editor's note: IN ST 31-14-11-15 was repealed effective May 9, 2013];
- All pre-sentence reports as declared confidential by IN ST 35-38-1-13;
- Written petitions to permit marriages without consent and orders directing the Clerk of Court to issue a marriage license to underage persons, as declared confidential by IN ST 31-11-1-6;
- Only those arrest warrants, search warrants, indictments and informations ordered confidential by the trial judge, prior to return of duly executed service as declared confidential by IN ST 5-14-3-4(b)(1);
- All medical, mental health, or tax records unless determined by law or regulation of any governmental custodian not to be confidential, released by the subject of such records, or declared by a court of competent jurisdiction to be essential to the resolution of litigation as declared confidential by IN ST 16-39-3-10, IN ST 6-4.1-5-10, IN ST 6-4.1-12-12, and IN ST 6-8.1-7-1;
- Personal information relating to jurors or prospective jurors, other than for the use of the parties and counsel, pursuant to IN ST JURY Rule 10;
- Information relating to protection from abuse orders, no-contact orders and workplace violence restraining orders as declared confidential by IN ST 5-2-9-6, et seq.;
- Mediation proceedings pursuant to IN ST ADR Rule 2.11, Mini-Trial proceedings pursuant to IN ST ADR Rule 4.4(C), and Summary Jury Trials pursuant to IN ST ADR Rule 5.6;
- Information in probation files pursuant to the Probation Standards promulgated by the Judicial Conference of Indiana pursuant to IN ST 11-13-1-8(b);
- Information deemed confidential pursuant to the Rules for Court Administered Alcohol and Drug Programs promulgated by the Judicial Conference of Indiana pursuant to IN ST 12-23-14-13;
- Information deemed confidential pursuant to the Problem-Solving Court Rules promulgated by the Judicial Conference of Indiana pursuant to IN ST 33-23-16-16;
- All records of the Department of workforce Development as declared confidential by IN ST 22-4-19-6;
- Information regarding interception of electronic communications that is sealed or deemed confidential as set forth in IN ST 35-33.5-2-1, et seq.

iii. Information excluded from public access by specific court order;

iv. Complete Social Security Numbers of living persons;

v. With the exception of names, information such as addresses, phone numbers, and dates of birth which explicitly identifies:

- Natural persons who are witnesses or victims (not including defendants) in criminal, domestic violence, stalking, sexual assault, juvenile, or civil protection order proceedings, provided that juveniles who are victims of sex crimes shall be identified by initials only;
- Places of residence of judicial officers, clerks and other employees of courts and clerks of court, unless the person or persons about whom the information pertains waives confidentiality;

vi. Complete account numbers of specific assets, loans, bank accounts, credit cards, and personal identification numbers (PINs);

vii. All orders of expungement entered in criminal or juvenile proceedings, orders to restrict access to criminal history information pursuant to IN ST 35-38-5-5.5 or IN ST 35-38-8-5 and records excluded from public access by such orders, and information related to infractions that is excluded from public access pursuant to IN ST 34-28-5-15 or IN ST 34-28-5-16 [Editor's note: IN ST 35-38-5-5.5, IN ST 35-38-8-5 and IN ST 34-28-5-16 were repealed effective July 1, 2013; for information on orders restricting access to criminal history, refer to IN ST 35-38-9-1, et seq.];

viii. All personal notes and e-mail, and deliberative material, of judges, jurors, court staff and judicial agencies, and information recorded in personal data assistants (PDA's) or organizers and personal calendars. IN ST ADMIN Rule 9(G)(1).

F. Filing and Service Requirements

1. *Filing requirements.* Except as otherwise provided in IN ST TRIAL P Rule 5(E)(2), all pleadings and papers subsequent to the complaint which are required to be served upon a party shall be filed with the Court either before service or within a reasonable period of time thereafter. IN ST TRIAL P Rule 5(E)(1).

   a. *Non-filing of discovery until necessary*

      i. *Non-filing of discovery; Exceptions.* No deposition or request for discovery or response thereto under IN ST TRIAL P Rule 27, IN ST TRIAL P Rule 30, IN ST TRIAL P Rule 31, IN ST TRIAL P Rule 33, IN ST TRIAL P Rule 34 or IN ST TRIAL P Rule 36 shall be filed with the Court unless:

         • A motion is filed pursuant to IN ST TRIAL P Rule 26(C) or IN ST TRIAL P Rule 37 and the original deposition or request for discovery or response thereto is necessary to enable the Court to rule; or

         • A party desires to use the deposition or request for discovery or response thereto for evidentiary purposes at trial or in connection with a motion, and the Court, either upon its own motion or that of any party, or as a part of any pre-trial order, orders the filing of the original. IN ST TRIAL P Rule 5(E)(2).

      ii. *Custody of original and period of retention*

         • The original of a deposition shall, subject to the provisions of IN ST TRIAL P Rule 30(E), be delivered by the reporter to the party taking it and shall be maintained by that party until filed with the Court pursuant to IN ST TRIAL P Rule 5(E)(2) or until the later of final judgment, agreed settlement of the litigation or all appellate rights have been exhausted. IN ST TRIAL P Rule 5(E)(3)(a).

         • The original or any request for discovery or response thereto under IN ST TRIAL P Rule 27, IN ST TRIAL P Rule 30, IN ST TRIAL P Rule 31, IN ST TRIAL P Rule 33, IN ST TRIAL P Rule 34 and IN ST TRIAL P Rule 36 shall be maintained by the party originating the request or response until filed with the Court pursuant to IN ST TRIAL P Rule 5(E)(2) or until the later of final judgment, agreed settlement or all appellate rights have been exhausted. IN ST TRIAL P Rule 5(E)(3)(b).

      iii. *Original unavailable; Copies.* In the event it is made to appear to the satisfaction of the Court that the original of a deposition or request for discovery or response thereto cannot be filed with the Court when required, the Court may allow use of a copy instead of the original. IN ST TRIAL P Rule 5(E)(4).

      iv. *Filing as publication.* The filing of any deposition shall constitute publication. IN ST TRIAL P Rule 5(E)(5).

   b. *Filing with the court defined.* The filing of pleadings, motions, and other papers with the court as required by the Indiana Rules of Trial Procedure shall be made by one of the following methods:

      i. Delivery to the clerk of the court;

      ii. Sending by electronic transmission under the procedure adopted pursuant to IN ST ADMIN Rule 12;

      iii. Mailing to the clerk by registered, certified or express mail return receipt requested;

iv. Depositing with any third-party commercial carrier for delivery to the clerk within three (3) calendar days, cost prepaid, properly addressed;

v. If the court so permits, filing with the judge, in which event the judge shall note thereon the filing date and forthwith transmit them to the office of the clerk; or

vi. Electronic filing, as approved by the Division of State Court Administration pursuant to IN ST ADMIN Rule 16. IN ST TRIAL P Rule 5(F).

vii. Filing by registered or certified mail and by third-party commercial carrier shall be complete upon mailing or deposit. IN ST TRIAL P Rule 5(F).

c. *Facsimile filing*

  i. *Generally.* In counties where a majority of judges of the courts of record, by posted local rule, have authorized electronic facsimile filing and designated a telephone number to receive such transmissions, pleadings, motions, and other papers may be sent to the Clerk of Circuit Court by electronic facsimile transmission for filing in any case, provided:

  - Such matter does not exceed ten (10) pages, including the cover sheet;

  - Such matter does not require the payment of fees other than the electronic facsimile transcription fee set forth in IN ST ADMIN Rule 12(E);

  - The sending party creates at the time of transmission a machine generated log for such transmission; and

  - The original document and the transmission log are maintained by the sending party for the duration of the litigation. IN ST ADMIN Rule 12(B).

  ii. *Time of filing.* During normal, posted business hours, the time of filing shall be the time the duplicate document is produced in the office of the Clerk of the Circuit Court. Duplicate documents received at all other times shall be filed as of the next normal business day. IN ST ADMIN Rule 12(C).

  - If the receiving fax machine endorses its own time and date stamp upon the transmitted documents and the receiving machine produces a delivery receipt which is electronically created and transmitted to the sending party, the time of filing shall be the date and time recorded on the transmitted document by the receiving fax machine. IN ST ADMIN Rule 12(C).

d. *Proof of filing.* Any party filing any paper by any method other than personal delivery to the clerk shall retain proof of filing. IN ST TRIAL P Rule 5(F).

2. *Service requirements.* Unless otherwise provided by the Indiana Rules of Trial Procedure or an order of the court, each party and special judge, if any, shall be served with: (1) every order required by its terms to be served; (2) every pleading subsequent to the original complaint; (3) every written motion except one which may be heard ex parte; (4) every brief submitted to the trial court; (5) every paper relating to discovery required to be served upon a party; and (6) every written notice, appearance, demand, offer of judgment, designation of record on appeal, or similar paper. IN ST TRIAL P Rule 5(A).

a. *Methods of service*

  i. *Personal service.* Whenever a party is represented by an attorney of record, service shall be made upon such attorney unless service upon the party himself is ordered by the court. Service upon the attorney or party shall be made by delivering or mailing a copy of the papers to the last known address or where an attorney or party has consented to service by fax or e-mail, as provided in IN ST TRIAL P Rule 3.1(A)(4), by faxing or e-mailing a copy of the documents to the fax number or e-mail address set out in the appearance form or correction as required by IN ST TRIAL P Rule 3.1(E). IN ST TRIAL P Rule 5(B). Delivery of a copy within IN ST TRIAL P Rule 5 means:

  - Offering or tendering it to the attorney or party and stating the nature of the papers being served. Refusal to accept an offered or tendered document is a waiver of any objection to the sufficiency or adequacy of service of that document;

- Leaving it at his office with a clerk or other person in charge thereof, or if there is no one in charge, leaving it in a conspicuous place therein; or

- If the office is closed, by leaving it at his dwelling house or usual place of abode with some person of suitable age and discretion then residing therein; or,

- Leaving it at some other suitable place, selected by the attorney upon whom service is being made, pursuant to duly promulgated local rule. IN ST TRIAL P Rule 5(B)(1).

    ii. *Service by mail.* If service is made by mail, the papers shall be deposited in the United States mail addressed to the person on whom they are being served, with postage prepaid. Service shall be deemed complete upon mailing. Proof of service of all papers permitted to be mailed may be made by written acknowledgment of service, by affidavit of the person who mailed the papers, or by certificate of an attorney. It shall be the duty of attorneys when entering their appearance in a cause or when filing pleadings or papers therein, to have noted in the Chronological Case Summary or said pleadings or papers so filed the address and telephone number of their office. Service by delivery or by mail at such address shall be deemed sufficient and complete. IN ST TRIAL P Rule 5(B)(2).

b. *Serving numerous defendants.* In any action in which there are unusually large numbers of defendants, the court, upon motion or of its own initiative, may order:

    i. That service of the pleadings of the defendants and replies thereto need not be made as between the defendants;

- That any cross-claim, counterclaim, or matter constituting an avoidance or affirmative defense contained therein shall be deemed to be denied or avoided by all other parties; and

- That the filing of any such pleading and service thereof upon the plaintiff constitutes due notice of it to the parties. IN ST TRIAL P Rule 5(D).

    ii. A copy of every such order shall be served upon the parties in such manner and form as the court directs. IN ST TRIAL P Rule 5(D).

    iii. *Service by fax or e-mail.* A party who has consented to service by fax or e-mail may be served as follows:

- Service by e-mail shall be made by attaching the document being served in .pdf format. Discovery documents must also be served in accordance with IN ST TRIAL P Rule 26(A). IN ST TRIAL P Rule 5(B)(3)(a).

- Service by fax shall be deemed complete upon generation of a transmission record indicating the successful transmission of the entire document, except as provided in IN ST TRIAL P Rule 5(B)(3)(d). IN ST TRIAL P Rule 5(B)(3)(b).

- Service by e-mail shall be deemed complete upon transmission, except as provided in IN ST TRIAL P Rule 5(B)(3)(d). IN ST TRIAL P Rule 5(B)(3)(c).

- Service by fax or e-mail that occurs on a Saturday, Sunday, legal holiday, or day the court or agency in which the matter is pending is closed or after 5:00 PM local time of the recipient shall be deemed complete the next day that is not a Saturday, Sunday, legal holiday, or day that the court or agency in which the matter is pending is not closed. IN ST TRIAL P Rule 5(B)(3)(d).

    iv. *Additional service of electronic discovery.* In addition to service under Rule IN ST TRIAL P Rule 5(B) or a .pdf format electronic copy, a party propounding or responding to interrogatories, requests for production or requests for admission shall comply with IN ST TRIAL P Rule 26(A.1)(a) or IN ST TRIAL P Rule 26(A.1)(b). IN ST TRIAL P Rule 26(A.1).

- The party shall serve the discovery request or response in an electronic format (either on a disk or as an electronic document attachment) in any commercially available word processing software system. If transmitted on disk, each disk shall be labeled, identifying the caption of the case, the document, and the word processing version in which it is being submitted. If more than one (1) disk is used for the same document, each disk shall be labeled and also shall be sequentially numbered. If transmitted by electronic mail, the document must be accompanied by electronic memorandum providing the forgoing identifying information; or

- The party shall serve the opposing party with a verified statement that the attorney or party appealing pro se lacks the equipment and is unable to transmit the discovery as required by IN ST TRIAL P Rule 26(A.1). IN ST TRIAL P Rule 26(A.1).

    v. *Consent to alternate service.* Any Allen County Attorney or any Allen County law firm may, without charge, maintain an assigned Courthouse box in the library of the Allen County Courthouse for receipt of notices, pleadings, process orders, or other communications from the Court, the Clerk, and other attorneys or law firms. IN ST ALLEN SUPER AND CIR CT CIV Rule 5-1(A). For more information concerning the use of courthouse boxes, refer to IN ST ALLEN SUPER AND CIR CT CIV Rule 5-1.

  c. *Service on parties in default for failure to appear.* No service need be made on parties in default for failure to appear, except that pleadings asserting new or additional claims for relief against them shall be served upon them in the manner provided by service of summons in IN ST TRIAL P Rule 4. IN ST TRIAL P Rule 5(A).

G. Hearings

1. The Indiana rules do not contemplate a hearing related to the filing and service of requests for admissions.

H. Forms

1. Request for Admissions Forms for Indiana

  a. Request for admission. 5 INPRAC § 4:4.1.

  b. Response to request for admission. 5 INPRAC § 4:4.2.

  c. Response to request for admission; Alternative form. 5 INPRAC § 4:4.3.

  d. Motion for order that matter be deemed admitted. 5 INPRAC § 4:4.4.

  e. Requests for admission; General form. 10 INPRAC § 69.6.

  f. Requests for admission; Genuineness of document. 10 INPRAC § 69.7.

  g. Requests for admission; Specific document and matters related thereto; Insurance contract. 10 INPRAC § 69.8.

  h. Requests for admission; Action against bank. 10 INPRAC § 69.9.

  i. Requests for admission; Automobile accident. 10 INPRAC § 69.10.

  j. Requests for admission; Automobile accident; Respondeat superior. 10 INPRAC § 69.11.

  k. Requests for admission; Action on account stated. 10 INPRAC § 69.12.

  l. Requests for admission; Action to foreclose on mortgage. 10 INPRAC § 69.13.

  m. Requests for admission; Action for attorney malpractice. 10 INPRAC § 69.14.

  n. Requests for admission; Products liability action; Defective hair products; Defendants. 10 INPRAC § 69.15.

  o. Response to requests for admission; General form. 10 INPRAC § 69.20.

  p. Alternative responses to requests for admission. 10 INPRAC § 69.21.

  q. Motion for enlargement of time to respond to requests for admission. 10 INPRAC § 69.22.

  r. Motion to withdraw and amend response to requests for admission. 10 INPRAC § 69.23.

  s. Order granting motion to withdraw and amend responses. 10 INPRAC § 69.24.

  t. Motion for order that matter be deemed admitted. 10 INPRAC § 69.25.

  u. Motion for order requiring party to pay expenses for refusal to admit matters. 10 INPRAC § 69.26.

2. Official Request for Admissions Forms for Allen County

  a. Consent to alternate service. IN ST ALLEN SUPER AND CIR CT CIV App. A.

I. Checklist

(I) ❑ Matters to be considered by the party serving the request

    (a) ❑ Required documents

        (1) ❑ Request for admissions

        (2) ❑ Copies of documents

        (3) ❑ Certificate of service

    (b) ❑ Supplemental documents

        (1) ❑ Stipulation regarding discovery procedure

        (2) ❑ Facsimile cover sheet

    (c) ❑ Timing

        (1) ❑ The request may, without leave of court, be served upon the plaintiff after commencement of the action and upon any other party with or after service of the summons and complaint upon that party

(II) ❑ Matters to be considered by the responding party

    (a) ❑ Required documents

        (1) ❑ Response to request for admissions

        (2) ❑ Certificate of service

    (b) ❑ Supplemental documents

        (1) ❑ Stipulation regarding discovery procedure

        (2) ❑ Facsimile cover sheet

    (c) ❑ Timing

        (1) ❑ The matter is admitted unless, within a period designated in the request, not less than thirty (30) days after service thereof or within such shorter or longer time as the court may allow, the party to whom the request is directed serves upon the party requesting the admission a written answer or objection addressed to the matter

Requests, Notices and Applications
Notice of Deposition

Document Last Updated October 2013

A. Applicable Rules

1. *State rules*

    a. Appearance. IN ST TRIAL P Rule 3.1.

    b. Process. IN ST TRIAL P Rule 4.

    c. Service and filing of pleadings and other papers. IN ST TRIAL P Rule 5.

    d. Time. IN ST TRIAL P Rule 6.

    e. Pleadings. IN ST TRIAL P Rule 7; IN ST TRIAL P Rule 9.2; IN ST TRIAL P Rule 10.

    f. Signing and verification of pleadings. IN ST TRIAL P Rule 11.

    g. Parties plaintiff and defendant; Capacity. IN ST TRIAL P Rule 17.

    h. General provisions governing discovery. IN ST TRIAL P Rule 26.

    i. Discovery methods. IN ST TRIAL P Rule 27; IN ST TRIAL P Rule 28; IN ST TRIAL P Rule 29; IN ST TRIAL P Rule 30; IN ST TRIAL P Rule 31; IN ST TRIAL P Rule 32; IN ST TRIAL P Rule 33; IN ST TRIAL P Rule 34; IN ST TRIAL P Rule 35; IN ST TRIAL P Rule 36.

j.   Failure to make or cooperate in discovery; Sanctions. IN ST TRIAL P Rule 37.

k.   Evidence. IN ST TRIAL P Rule 43.

l.   Subpoena. IN ST TRIAL P Rule 45.

m.   Judgment on the evidence (directed verdict). IN ST TRIAL P Rule 50.

n.   Findings by the court. IN ST TRIAL P Rule 52.

o.   Summary judgment. IN ST TRIAL P Rule 56.

p.   Motion to correct error. IN ST TRIAL P Rule 59.

q.   Relief from judgment or order. IN ST TRIAL P Rule 60.

r.   Trial court and clerks. IN ST TRIAL P Rule 72.

s.   Recording machines; Court reports; Stenographic report or transcript as evidence. IN ST TRIAL P Rule 74.

t.   Access to court records. IN ST ADMIN Rule 9.

u.   Paper size. IN ST ADMIN Rule 11.

v.   Facsimile transmission. IN ST ADMIN Rule 12.

w.   Electronic filing and electronic service pilot projects. IN ST ADMIN Rule 16.

x.   Privacy and confidentiality. IN ST 5-2-9-6; IN ST 5-14-3-4; IN ST 6-4.1-5-10; IN ST 6-4.1-12-12; IN ST 6-8.1-7-1; IN ST 11-13-1-8; IN ST 12-23-14-13; IN ST 16-39-3-10; IN ST 16-41-8-1; IN ST 22-4-19-6; IN ST 31-11-1-6; IN ST 31-19-5-23; IN ST 31-19-13-2; IN ST 31-19-19-1; IN ST 31-33-18-1; IN ST 31-39-1-1; IN ST 31-39-1-2; IN ST 33-23-16-16; IN ST 35-34-2-4; IN ST 35-38-1-13; IN ST 35-38-9-1; IN ST ADR Rule 2.11; IN ST ADR Rule 4.4; IN ST ADR Rule 5.6; IN ST JURY Rule 10.

y.   Sealing of certain records by court; Hearing; Notice. IN ST 5-14-3-5.5.

2. *Local rules*

a.   Applicability and citation of rules. IN ST ALLEN SUPER AND CIR CT CIV Rule AR00-1.

b.   Proposed orders. IN ST ALLEN SUPER AND CIR CT CIV Rule TR00-1.

c.   Admissions, stipulations and agreements. IN ST ALLEN SUPER AND CIR CT CIV Rule TR00-2.

d.   Appearances. IN ST ALLEN SUPER AND CIR CT CIV Rule 3.1-1.

e.   Consent to alternate service. IN ST ALLEN SUPER AND CIR CT CIV Rule 5-1.

f.   Preparation of pleadings. IN ST ALLEN SUPER AND CIR CT CIV Rule 8-1.

g.   Filing. IN ST ALLEN SUPER AND CIR CT CIV Rule 77-1.

B. Timing

1. *Time for notice of deposition*

a.   *Depositions upon oral examination.* After commencement of the action, any party may take the testimony of any person, including a party, by deposition upon oral examination. IN ST TRIAL P Rule 30(A).

  i.   A party desiring to take the deposition of any person upon oral examination shall give reasonable notice in writing to every other party to the action. IN ST TRIAL P Rule 30(B)(1).

  •   The party who gives notice of taking a deposition must do so in a way which is sufficiently timely to permit the party who receives the notice to make arrangements to travel to the place where the deposition is to be taken, and the notice which is given must be in sufficient time to permit the party to seek a protective order under IN ST TRIAL P Rule 30(D) and IN ST TRIAL P Rule 26(C), if necessary. 2A INPRAC R 30(30.2).

  ii.   Leave of court, granted with or without notice, must be obtained only if the plaintiff seeks to take a deposition prior to the expiration of twenty (20) days after service of summons and complaint upon any defendant except that leave is not required:

- If a defendant has served a notice of taking deposition or otherwise sought discovery; or
- If special notice is given as provided in IN ST TRIAL P Rule 30(B)(2). IN ST TRIAL P Rule 30(A).

   iii. The court may for cause shown enlarge or shorten the time for taking the deposition. IN ST TRIAL P Rule 30(B)(3).

b. *Depositions upon written questions.* After commencement of the action, any party may take the testimony of any person, including a party, by deposition upon written questions. IN ST TRIAL P Rule 31(A).

   i. *Service of cross questions.* Within twenty (20) days after the notice and written questions are served, a party may serve cross questions upon all other parties. IN ST TRIAL P Rule 31(A).

   ii. *Service of redirect questions.* Within ten (10) days after being served with cross questions, a party may serve redirect questions upon all other parties. IN ST TRIAL P Rule 31(A).

   iii. *Service of recross questions.* Within ten (10) days after being served with redirect questions, a party may serve recross questions upon all other parties. IN ST TRIAL P Rule 31(A).

   iv. *Time to respond.* The court may for cause shown enlarge or shorten the time. IN ST TRIAL P Rule 31(A).

c. *For deposition before action.* At least twenty (20) days before the date of hearing the notice shall be served in the manner provided in IN ST TRIAL P Rule 4 for service of summons; but if such service cannot with due diligence be made upon any expected adverse party named in the petition, the court may make such order as is just for service by publication or otherwise, and shall appoint, for persons not served in the manner provided in IN ST TRIAL P Rule 4, an attorney who shall represent them, and, in case they are not otherwise represented, shall cross-examine the deponent. If any expected adverse party is a minor or incompetent the provisions of IN ST TRIAL P Rule 17(C) apply. IN ST TRIAL P Rule 27(A)(2).

   i. Refer to the Indiana KeyRules Complaint document for information regarding service under IN ST TRIAL P Rule 4.

d. *For deposition pending appeal.* The party who desires to perpetuate the testimony may make a motion in the court for leave to take the depositions, upon the same notice and service thereof as if the action was pending in the court. IN ST TRIAL P Rule 27(B).

   i. *Filing.* All pleadings and papers subsequent to the complaint which are required to be served upon a party shall be filed with the Court either before service or within a reasonable period of time thereafter. IN ST TRIAL P Rule 5(E)(1).

   ii. *Service.* A written motion, other than one which may be heard ex parte, and notice of the hearing thereof shall be served not less than five (5) days before the time specified for the hearing, unless a different period is fixed by the Indiana Rules of Trial Procedure or by order of the court. IN ST TRIAL P Rule 6(D).

- *Of supporting affidavits.* When a motion is supported by affidavit, the affidavit shall be served with the motion. IN ST TRIAL P Rule 6(D).

2. *Computation of time*

a. *Generally; Days excluded.* In computing any period of time prescribed or allowed by the Indiana Rules of Trial Procedure, by order of the court, or by any applicable statute, the day of the act, event, or default from which the designated period of time begins to run shall not be included. The last day of the period so computed is to be included unless it is:

   i. A Saturday,

   ii. A Sunday,

   iii. A legal holiday as defined by state statute, or

iv. A day the office in which the act is to be done is closed during regular business hours. IN ST TRIAL P Rule 6(A).

b. *Short periods.* In any event, the period runs until the end of the next day that is not a Saturday, a Sunday, a legal holiday, or a day on which the office is closed. When the period of time allowed is less than seven (7) days, intermediate Saturdays, Sundays, legal holidays, and days on which the office is closed shall be excluded from the computations. IN ST TRIAL P Rule 6(A).

c. *Additional time after service by United States mail.* Whenever a party has the right or is required to do some act or take some proceedings within a prescribed period after the service of a notice or other paper upon him and the notice or paper is served upon him by United States mail, three (3) days shall be added to the prescribed period. IN ST TRIAL P Rule 6(E).

d. *Enlargement of time.* When an act is required or allowed to be done at or within a specific time by the Indiana Rules of Trial Procedure, the court may at any time for cause shown:

i. Order the period enlarged, with or without motion or notice, if request therefor is made before the expiration of the period originally prescribed or extended by a previous order; or

ii. Upon motion made after the expiration of the specific period, permit the act to be done where the failure to act was the result of excusable neglect; but, the court may not extend the time for taking any action for judgment on the evidence under IN ST TRIAL P Rule 50(A), amendment of findings and judgment under IN ST TRIAL P Rule 52(B), to correct errors under IN ST TRIAL P Rule 59(C), statement in opposition to motion to correct error under IN ST TRIAL P Rule 59(E), or to obtain relief from final judgment under IN ST TRIAL P Rule 60(B), except to the extent and under the conditions stated in those rules. IN ST TRIAL P Rule 6(B).

C. General Requirements

1. *Scope of discovery.* Unless otherwise limited by order of the court in accordance with the Indiana Rules of Trial Procedure, the scope of discovery is as follows:

a. *In general.* Parties may obtain discovery regarding any matter, not privileged, which is relevant to the subject-matter involved in the pending action, whether it relates to the claim or defense of the party seeking discovery or the claim or defense of any other party, including the existence, description, nature, custody, condition and location of any books, documents, or other tangible things and the identity and location of persons having knowledge of any discoverable matter. It is not ground for objection that the information sought will be inadmissible at the trial if the information sought appears reasonably calculated to lead to the discovery of admissible evidence. IN ST TRIAL P Rule 26(B)(1).

i. *Limiting discovery upon court determination.* The frequency or extent of use of the discovery methods otherwise permitted under the Indiana Rules of Trial Procedure and by any local rule shall be limited by the court if it determines that:

- The discovery sought is unreasonably cumulative or duplicative, or is obtainable from some other source that is more convenient, less burdensome, or less expensive;

- The party seeking discovery has had ample opportunity by discovery in the action to obtain the information sought or;

- The burden or expense of the proposed discovery outweighs its likely benefit, taking into account the needs of the case, the amount in controversy, the parties' resources, the importance of the issues at stake in the litigation, and the importance of the proposed discovery in resolving the issues. IN ST TRIAL P Rule 26(B)(1).

- The court may act upon its own initiative after reasonable notice or pursuant to a motion under IN ST TRIAL P Rule 26(C). IN ST TRIAL P Rule 26(B)(1). Refer to the Indiana KeyRules Motion for Protective Order document for more information.

ii. *Relevancy in the discovery context.* When the word "relevancy" is used in IN ST TRIAL P Rule 26(B), it does not mean "relevancy" as that word in used to determine the admissibility of evidence in a trial court. It is much broader. It means "relevancy" to the "subject matter" of the litigation or pending action and it may relate to the claim or defense of any party. Pretrial discovery is available as to any nonprivileged matter relevant to the subject matter of the lawsuit or to obtain information reasonably calculated to lead to admissible evidence. 2A INPRAC R 26(26.4); Kaufmann v. Credithrift Financial, Inc., 465 N.E.2d 207, 210 (Ind.Ct.App. 1984).

iii. *Tests for relevance.* Indiana case law has developed two (2) additional tests in this area. 2A INPRAC R 26(26.4).

- The first test determines when a document or a request for information is actually relevant to the subject matter in the pending action. A document [or discovery request] is relevant to discovery if there is the possibility the information sought may be relevant to the subject matter of the action. 2A INPRAC R 26(26.4); CIGNA-INA/Aetna v. Hagerman-Shambaugh, 473 N.E.2d 1033, 1036 (Ind.Ct.App. 1985).

- The second test speaks to appellate review of the trial court's determination that a document or discovery request is relevant to the subject matter of the pending action. The appellate court sees its review of the trial court's decision on relevancy to subject matter as being very limited. The court states: "Our review of the trial court's conclusion that the documents are relevant is limited. A trial court is vested with discretion in its rulings on discovery issues." 2A INPRAC R 26(26.4); Costanzi v. Ryan, 175 Ind.App. 257, 370 N.E.2d 1333 (Ind.Ct.App. 1978).

b. *Insurance agreements.* A party may obtain discovery of the existence and contents of any insurance agreement under which any person carrying on an insurance business may be liable to satisfy part or all of a judgment which may be entered in the action or to indemnify or reimburse for payments made to satisfy the judgment. Information concerning the insurance agreement is not by reason of disclosure admissible in evidence at trial. For purposes of IN ST TRIAL P Rule 26(B)(2), an application for insurance shall not be treated as part of an insurance agreement. IN ST TRIAL P Rule 26(B)(2).

c. *Trial preparation; Materials.* Subject to the provisions of IN ST TRIAL P Rule 26(B)(4), a party may obtain discovery of documents and tangible things otherwise discoverable under IN ST TRIAL P Rule 26(B)(1) and prepared in anticipation of litigation or for trial by or for another party or by or for that other party's representative (including his attorney, consultant, surety, indemnitor, insurer, or agent) only upon a showing that the party seeking discovery has substantial need of the materials in the preparation of his case and that he is unable without undue hardship to obtain the substantial equivalent of the materials by other means. In ordering discovery of such materials when the required showing has been made, the court shall protect against disclosure of the mental impressions, conclusions, opinions, or legal theories of an attorney or other representative of a party concerning the litigation. IN ST TRIAL P Rule 26(B)(3).

i. A party may obtain without the required showing a statement concerning the action or its subject matter previously made by that party. Upon request, a person not a party may obtain without the required showing a statement concerning the action or its subject matter previously made by that person. If the request is refused, the person may move for a court order. The provisions of IN ST TRIAL P Rule 37(A)(4) apply to the award of expenses incurred in relation to the motion. For purposes of IN ST TRIAL P Rule 26(B)(3), a statement previously made is:

- A written statement signed or otherwise adopted approved by the person making it, or

- A stenographic, mechanical, electrical, or other recording, or a transcription thereof, which is a substantially verbatim recital of an oral statement by the person making it and contemporaneously recorded. IN ST TRIAL P Rule 26(B)(3).

ii. The protection of IN ST TRIAL P Rule 26(B)(3) extends to material prepared or collected before litigation actually commences, but that some possibility of litigation must actually exist before the privilege and IN ST TRIAL P Rule 26(B)(3) become operative. 2A INPRAC R 26(26.9).

d. *Trial preparation; Experts.* Discovery of facts known and opinions held by experts, otherwise discoverable under the provisions of IN ST TRIAL P Rule 26(B)(1) and acquired or developed in anticipation of litigation or for trial, may be obtained as follows:

i. A party may through interrogatories require any other party to identify each person whom the

other party expects to call as an expert witness at trial, to state the subject matter on which the expert is expected to testify, and to state the substance of the facts and opinions to which the expert is expected to testify and a summary of the grounds for each opinion. IN ST TRIAL P Rule 26(B)(4)(a)(i).

ii.   Upon motion, the court may order further discovery by other means, subject to such restrictions as to scope and such provisions, pursuant to IN ST TRIAL P Rule 26(B)(4)(c), concerning fees and expenses as the court may deem appropriate. IN ST TRIAL P Rule 26(B)(4)(a)(ii).

iii. A party may discover facts known or opinions held by an expert who has been retained or specially employed by another party in anticipation of litigation or preparation for trial and who is not expected to be called as a witness at trial, only as provided in IN ST TRIAL P Rule 35(B) or upon a showing of exceptional circumstances under which it is impracticable for the party seeking discovery to obtain facts or opinions on the same subject by other means. IN ST TRIAL P Rule 26(B)(4)(b).

iv.   Unless manifest injustice would result,

- The court shall require that the party seeking discovery pay the expert a reasonable fee for time spent in responding to discovery under IN ST TRIAL P Rule 26(B)(4)(a)(ii) and IN ST TRIAL P Rule 26(B)(4)(b); and

- With respect to discovery obtained under IN ST TRIAL P Rule 26(B)(4)(a)(ii) the court may require, and with respect to discovery obtained under IN ST TRIAL P Rule 26(B)(4)(b) the court shall require, the party seeking discovery to pay the other party a fair portion of the fees and expenses reasonably incurred by the latter party in obtaining facts and opinions from the expert. IN ST TRIAL P Rule 26(B)(4).

e. *Claims of privilege or protection*

i.   *Information withheld.* When a party withholds information otherwise discoverable under the Indiana Rules of Trial Procedure by claiming that it is privileged or subject to protection as trial preparation material, the party shall make the claim expressly and shall describe the nature of the documents, communications, or things not produced or disclosed in a manner that, without revealing information itself privileged or protected, will enable other parties to assess the applicability of the privilege or protection. IN ST TRIAL P Rule 26(B)(5)(a).

ii. *Information produced.* If information is produced in discovery that is subject to a claim of privilege or protection as trial-preparation material, the party making the claim may notify any party that received the information of the claim and the basis for it. After being notified, a party must promptly return, sequester, or destroy the specified information and any copies it has and may not use or disclose the information until the claim is resolved. A receiving party may promptly present the information to the court under seal for a determination of the claim. If the receiving party disclosed the information before being notified, it must take reasonable steps to retrieve it. The producing party must preserve the information until the claim is resolved. IN ST TRIAL P Rule 26(B)(5)(b).

iii. *Waiver.* The law of discovery has developed some holdings which indicate that "waiver" of a privileged communication in a discovery setting might be more exacting than "waiver" of a privileged communication when the only question at hand is an interpretation of the privilege itself. Thus, in litigation in which several documents are in issue, and some are released inadvertently, there is strong case law that holds that the "inadvertent production" of a privileged document does not constitute a waiver of the attorney-client privilege. 2A INPRAC R 26(26.5); Transamerica Computer Co. v. International Business Machines Corp., 573 F.2d 646 (9th Cir. 1978). Such a rule should be measured against the usual rule which suggests that a voluntary disclosure to a third person will generally suffice to show a waiver of the attorney-client privilege. 2A INPRAC R 26(26.5).

f. *Use not limited.* Unless the court orders otherwise under IN ST TRIAL P Rule 26(C), the frequency of use of the methods listed in IN ST TRIAL P Rule 26(A) is not limited. IN ST TRIAL P Rule 26(A).

g. *Sequence of discovery.* Unless the court upon motion, for the convenience of parties and witnesses

and in the interests of justice, orders otherwise, methods of discovery may be used in any sequence and the fact that a party is conducting discovery, whether by deposition or otherwise, shall not operate to delay any other party's discovery. IN ST TRIAL P Rule 26(D).

2. *Depositions upon oral examination.* IN ST TRIAL P Rule 30 provides for the pre-trial deposition on oral examination of a party, or a witness who is not a party. 2A INPRAC R 30(30.1).

   a. *Generally.* The deposition may be used to narrow issues, or to create and enlarge them. It will eliminate matters that are not disputed among the parties; it might introduce new issues and questions which become disputed. The range and purpose of the deposition's use is almost limitless, as long as it is taken consistent with IN ST TRIAL P Rule 26 and IN ST TRIAL P Rule 30 and the principles of IN ST TRIAL P Rule 32. The deposition may obtain evidence that is admissible at trial; it may go quite beyond admissibility at trial if the area of investigation is relevant to the subject matter of the case under IN ST TRIAL P Rule 26. It can disclose the existence and availability of facts that may lead to evidence which may be used at trial. 2A INPRAC R 30(30.1).

   b. *Notice*

      i. *Contents of notice.* The notice shall state the time and place for taking the deposition and the name and address of each person to be examined, if known, and if the name is not known, a general description sufficient to identify him or the particular class or group to which he belongs. If a subpoena duces tecum is to be served on the person to be examined, a designation of the materials to be produced thereunder shall be attached to or included in the notice. IN ST TRIAL P Rule 30(B)(1).

      ii. *Circumstances where leave of court required.* Leave of court, when required by IN ST TRIAL P Rule 30(A) is not required for the taking of a deposition by plaintiff if the notice:

        • States that the person to be examined is about to go out of the state or will be unavailable for examination unless his deposition is taken before expiration of the twenty (20) day period; and

        • Sets forth facts to support the statement. IN ST TRIAL P Rule 30(B)(2).

      iii. *Signature on notice.* The plaintiff's attorney shall sign the notice, and his signature constitutes a certification by him that to the best of his knowledge, information, and belief the statement and supporting facts are true. The sanctions provided by IN ST TRIAL P Rule 11 are applicable to the certification. IN ST TRIAL P Rule 30(B).

      iv. *Manner of recording.* If a party taking a deposition wishes to have the testimony recorded other than in a manner provided in IN ST TRIAL P Rule 74, the notice shall specify the manner of recording and preserving the deposition. The court may require stenographic taking or make any other order to assure that the recorded testimony will be accurate and trustworthy. IN ST TRIAL P Rule 30(B)(4).

      v. *Organization as deponent; Designation.* A party may in his notice name as the deponent an organization, including without limitation a governmental organization, or a partnership and designate with reasonable particularity the matters on which examination is requested. The organization so named shall designate one or more officers, directors, or managing agents, executive officers, or other persons duly authorized and consenting to testify on its behalf. The persons so designated shall testify as to matters known or available to the organization. IN ST TRIAL P Rule 30(B)(6) does not preclude taking a deposition by any other procedure authorized in the Indiana Rules of Trial Procedure. IN ST TRIAL P Rule 30(B)(6).

   c. *Improper service of notice.* If any party shows that when he was served with notice under IN ST TRIAL P Rule 30(B)(2) he was unable through the exercise of diligence to obtain counsel to represent him at the taking of the deposition, the deposition may not be used against him. IN ST TRIAL P Rule 30(B).

   d. *Examination and cross-examination; Record of examination; Oath; Objections.* Examination and cross-examination of witnesses may proceed as permitted at the trial under the provisions of IN ST TRIAL P Rule 43(B). The officer before whom the deposition is to be taken shall put the witness on oath and shall personally, or by someone acting under his direction and in his presence, record the testimony of the witness. The testimony shall be taken stenographically or recorded by any other means designated in accordance with IN ST TRIAL P Rule 30(B)(4). If requested by one of the parties, the testimony shall be transcribed. IN ST TRIAL P Rule 30(C).

   i.   *Objections*

- All objections made at the time of the examination to the qualifications of the officer taking the deposition, or to the manner of taking it, or to the evidence presented, or to the conduct of any party, and any other objection to the proceedings, shall be noted by the officer upon the deposition. IN ST TRIAL P Rule 30(C).

- When there is an objection to a question, the objection and reason therefor shall be noted, and the question shall be answered unless the attorney instructs the deponent not to answer, or the deponent refuses to answer, in which case either party may have the question certified by the Reporter, and the question with the objection thereto when so certified shall be delivered to the party requesting the certification who may then proceed under IN ST TRIAL P Rule 37(A). IN ST TRIAL P Rule 30(C).

- In lieu of participating in the oral examination, parties may serve written questions on the party taking the deposition and require him to transmit them to the officer, who shall propound them to the witness and record the answers verbatim. IN ST TRIAL P Rule 30(C).

e.   *Motion to terminate or limit examination.* At any time during the taking of the deposition, on motion of any party or of the deponent and upon a showing that the examination is being conducted in bad faith or in such manner as unreasonably to annoy, embarrass, or oppress the deponent or party, the court in which the action is pending or the court in the county where the deposition is being taken may order the officer conducting the examination to cease forthwith from taking the deposition, or may limit the scope and manner of the taking of the deposition as provided in IN ST TRIAL P Rule 26(C). IN ST TRIAL P Rule 30(D).

   i.   If the order made terminates the examination, it shall be resumed thereafter only upon the order of the court in which the action is pending. IN ST TRIAL P Rule 30(D).

   ii.   Upon demand of the objecting party or deponent the taking of the deposition shall be suspended for the time necessary to make a motion for an order. The provisions of IN ST TRIAL P Rule 37(A)(4) apply to the award of expenses incurred in relation to the motion. IN ST TRIAL P Rule 30(D).

   iii.   Refer to the Indiana KeyRules Motion for Protective Order and Motion for Discovery Sanctions documents for more information.

f.   *Submission to witness; Changes; Signing*

   i.   When the testimony is fully transcribed, the deposition shall be submitted to the witness for reading and signing and shall be read to or by him, unless such reading and signing have been waived by the witness and by each party. "Submitted to the witness" as used in IN ST TRIAL P Rule 30(E)(1) shall mean:

- Mailing of written notification by registered or certified mail to the witness and each attorney attending the deposition that the deposition can be read and examined in the office of the officer before whom the deposition was taken, or

- Mailing the original deposition, by registered or certified mail, to the witness at an address designated by the witness or his attorney, if requested to do so by the witness, his attorney, or the party taking the deposition. IN ST TRIAL P Rule 30(E)(1).

   ii.   If the witness desires to change any answer in the deposition submitted to him, each change, with a statement of the reason therefor, shall be made by the witness on a separate form provided by the officer, shall be signed by the witness and affixed to the original deposition by the officer. A copy of such changes shall be furnished by the officer to each party. IN ST TRIAL P Rule 30(E)(2).

   iii.   If the reading and signing have not been waived by the witness and by each party the deposition shall be signed by the witness and returned by him to the officer within thirty (30) days after it is submitted to the witness. If the deposition has been returned to the officer and has not been signed by the witness, the officer shall execute a certificate of that fact, attach it to the original deposition and deliver it to the party taking it. In such event, the deposition may be used by any party with the same force and effect as though it had been signed by the witness. IN ST TRIAL P Rule 30(E)(3).

    iv.   In the event the deposition is not returned to the officer within thirty (30) days after it has been submitted to the witness, the reporter shall execute a certificate of that fact and cause the certificate to be delivered to the party taking it. In such event, any party may use a copy of the deposition with the same force and effect as though the original had been signed by the witness. IN ST TRIAL P Rule 30(E)(4).

g.   *Certification and filing; Exhibits; Copies*

    i.   The officer shall certify on the deposition that the witness was duly sworn by him and that the deposition is a true record of the testimony given by the witness. He shall then securely seal the deposition in an envelope endorsed with the title of the action and marked "Deposition of (here insert name of witness)" and shall promptly deliver it to the party taking the deposition. IN ST TRIAL P Rule 30(F)(1). Documents and things, unless objection is made to their production for inspection during the examination of the witness, shall be marked for identification and annexed to and returned with the deposition, and may be inspected and copied by any party, except that:

- The person producing the materials may substitute copies to be marked for identification, if he affords to all parties fair opportunity to verify the copies by comparison with the originals; and

- If the person producing the materials requests their return the officer shall mark them, give each party an opportunity to inspect and copy them, and return them to the person producing them, and the materials may then be used in the same manner as if annexed to and returned with the deposition. IN ST TRIAL P Rule 30(F)(1).

    ii.   Upon payment of reasonable charges therefor, the officer shall furnish a copy of the deposition to any party or the deponent. IN ST TRIAL P Rule 30(F)(2).

    iii.   The officer taking the deposition shall give prompt notice to all parties of its delivery to the party taking the deposition. IN ST TRIAL P Rule 30(F)(3).

    iv.   The filing of depositions shall be in accordance with the provisions of IN ST TRIAL P Rule 5(E). IN ST TRIAL P Rule 30(F)(4).

h.   *Failure to attend or to serve subpoena; Expenses*

    i.   If the party giving the notice of the taking of a deposition fails to attend and proceed therewith and another party attends in person or by attorney pursuant to the notice, the court may order the party giving the notice to pay to such other party the amount of the reasonable expenses incurred by him and his attorney in so attending, including reasonable attorney's fees. IN ST TRIAL P Rule 30(G)(1).

    ii.   If the party giving the notice of the taking of a deposition of a witness other than a party fails to serve a subpoena upon him and the witness because of such failure does not attend, and if another party attends in person or by attorney because he expects the deposition of that witness to be taken, the court may order the party giving the notice to pay to such other party the amount of the reasonable expenses incurred by him and his attorney in so attending, including reasonable attorney's fees. IN ST TRIAL P Rule 30(G)(2).

i.   *Depositions of prisoners.* The deposition of a person confined in prison may be taken only by leave of court on such terms as the court prescribes. IN ST TRIAL P Rule 30(A).

j.   *Cost of deposition.* In Indiana the rule is that the party who initiates a deposition pays for the cost necessarily incurred as a result of the deposition. Those costs are: (1) the stenographic reporter's fees, (2) the transcription and filing fees, and (3) transportation costs and perhaps other costs which might naturally arise in a particular situation. 2A INPRAC R 30(30.8); Briggs v. Clinton County Bank & Trust Co. of Frankfort, Ind., 452 N.E.2d 989, 1009 (Ind.Ct.App. 1983).

3. *Deposition upon written questions.* The use of written questions under IN ST TRIAL P Rule 31 is often not as effective as taking a deposition on oral examination, and is generally, as a practical matter, not suitable for complicated cases or where cross-examination is necessary, as in the case of a reluctant or hostile witness. Written questions are, however, an inexpensive device where simple or formal facts are sought. 2A INPRAC R 31(31.1).

   a. *Notice.* A party desiring to take a deposition upon written questions shall serve them upon every other party with a notice stating:

      i. The name and address of the person who is to answer them, if known, and if the name is not known, a general description sufficient to identify him or the particular class or group to which he belongs; and

      ii. The name or descriptive title and address of the officer before whom the deposition is to be taken. IN ST TRIAL P Rule 31(A).

   b. *Depositions of specific persons*

      i. *Prisoners.* The deposition of a person confined in prison may be taken only by leave of court on such terms as the court prescribes. IN ST TRIAL P Rule 31(A).

      ii. *Organization.* A deposition upon written questions may be taken of an organization, including a governmental organization, or a partnership in accordance with the provisions of IN ST TRIAL P Rule 30(B)(6). IN ST TRIAL P Rule 31(A).

   c. *Officer to take responses and prepare record.* A copy of the notice and copies of all questions served shall be delivered by the party taking the deposition to the officer designated in the notice, who shall proceed promptly, in the manner provided by IN ST TRIAL P Rule 30(C), IN ST TRIAL P Rule 30(E), and IN ST TRIAL P Rule 30(F), to take the testimony of the witness in response to the questions and to prepare, certify, and deliver the deposition, attaching thereto the copy of the notice and the questions received by him, in accordance with IN ST TRIAL P Rule 5(E). IN ST TRIAL P Rule 31(B).

   d. *Notice of filing.* When the deposition is filed the party taking it shall promptly give notice thereof to all other parties. IN ST TRIAL P Rule 31(C).

4. *Depositions before action or pending appeal*

   a. *Use of deposition to perpetuate testimony.* IN ST TRIAL P Rule 27 does not exist to provide a method of discovery to determine whether a cause of action exists. Rather, the rule is intended to be used to "memorialize" evidence that is already known. Accordingly, a trial court should not grant a motion to perpetuate testimony by deposition on the mere possibility that witnesses may be transferred or leave current employment. 2A INPRAC R 27(27.2). IN ST TRIAL P Rule 27 is available for use "when a certain witness' testimony might become unavailable over time, and not to provide a method of discovery to determine whether a cause of action exits." 2A INPRAC R 27(27.2); Petition of Gary Construction, Inc., 96 F.R.D. 432 (D.C.Colo. 1983); Petition of Gurnsey, 223 F.Supp. 359 (D.D.C. 1963).

   b. *Before action; Petition required*

      i. *Petition.* A person who desires to perpetuate his own testimony or that of another person regarding any matter that may be cognizable in any court in which the action may be commenced, may file a verified petition in any such court of this state. IN ST TRIAL P Rule 27(A)(1). The petition shall be entitled in the name of the petitioner and shall state facts showing:

         • That the petitioner expects to be a party to an action cognizable in a court of this or another state;

         • The subject-matter of the expected action and his interest therein;

         • The facts which he desires to establish by the proposed testimony and his reasons for desiring to perpetuate it;

- The names or a description of the persons he expects will be adverse parties and their addresses so far as known; and

- The names and addresses of the persons to be examined and the substance of the testimony which he expects to elicit from each, and shall ask for an order authorizing the petitioner to take the depositions of the persons to be examined named in the petition, for the purpose of perpetuating their testimony. IN ST TRIAL P Rule 27(A)(1).

ii. *Notice and service.* The petitioner shall thereafter serve a notice upon each person named in the petition as an expected adverse party, together with a copy of the petition, stating that the petitioner will apply to the court, at a time and place named therein, for the order described in the petition. IN ST TRIAL P Rule 27(A)(2).

iii. *Order and examination.* If the court is satisfied that the perpetuation of the testimony may prevent a failure or delay of justice, it shall make an order designating or describing the persons whose depositions may be taken and specifying the subject-matter of the examination or written interrogatories. The depositions may then be taken in accordance with the Indiana Rules of Trial Procedure; and the court may make orders of the character provided for by IN ST TRIAL P Rule 34 and IN ST TRIAL P Rule 35. For the purpose of applying the Indiana Rules of Trial Procedure to depositions for perpetuating testimony, each reference therein to the court in which the action is pending shall be deemed to refer to the court in which the petition for such deposition was filed. IN ST TRIAL P Rule 27(A)(3).

iv. *Use of deposition.* If a deposition to perpetuate testimony is taken under the Indiana Rules of Trial Procedure or if, although not so taken, it would be admissible in evidence in the court of the state in which it is taken, it may be used in any action involving the same subject-matter subsequently brought in a court of this state in accordance with the provision of IN ST TRIAL P Rule 32. IN ST TRIAL P Rule 27(A)(3).

c. *Pending appeal.* If an appeal has been taken from a judgment of any court or before the taking of an appeal if the time therefor has not expired, the court in which the judgment was rendered may allow the taking of the depositions of witnesses to perpetuate their testimony for use in the event of further proceedings in such court. In such case the party who desires to perpetuate the testimony may make a motion in the court for leave to take the depositions, upon the same notice and service thereof as if the action was pending in the court. IN ST TRIAL P Rule 27(B).

i. The motion shall show:

- The names and addresses of the persons to be examined and the substance of the testimony which he expects to elicit from each;

- The reasons for perpetuating their testimony. IN ST TRIAL P Rule 27(B).

ii. If the court finds that the perpetuation of the testimony is proper to avoid a failure or delay of justice, it may make an order allowing the depositions to be taken and may make orders of the character provided for by IN ST TRIAL P Rule 34 and IN ST TRIAL P Rule 35, and thereupon the depositions may be taken and used in the same manner and under the same conditions as are prescribed in the Indiana Rules of Trial Procedure for depositions taken in actions pending in the court. IN ST TRIAL P Rule 27(B).

d. *Perpetuation by action.* IN ST TRIAL P Rule 27 does not limit the power of a court to entertain an action to perpetuate testimony. IN ST TRIAL P Rule 27(C).

e. *Filing deposition.* The filing or custody of any deposition or evidence obtained under IN ST TRIAL P Rule 27 shall be in accordance with IN ST TRIAL P Rule 5(E). IN ST TRIAL P Rule 27(D).

5. *Persons before whom depositions may be taken; Discovery across state lines; Before administrative agencies; And after judgment*

a. *Within the United States.* Within the United States or within a territory or insular possession subject to the dominion of the United States, depositions shall be taken before an officer authorized to administer oaths by the laws of the United States, or of the state of Indiana, or of the place where the examination is held, or before a person appointed by the court in which the action is pending. A person so appointed has power to administer oaths and take testimony. IN ST TRIAL P Rule 28(A).

b. *In foreign countries*

   i. In a foreign country, depositions may be taken:

- On notice before a person authorized to administer oaths in the place in which the examination is held, either by the law thereof or by the law of the United States; or

- Before a person commissioned by the court, and a person so commissioned shall have the power by virtue of his commission to administer any necessary oath and take testimony; or

- Pursuant to a letter rogatory. IN ST TRIAL P Rule 28(B).

   ii. A commission or a letter rogatory shall be issued on application and notice and on terms that are just and appropriate. It is not requisite to the issuance of a commission or a letter rogatory that the taking of the deposition in any other manner is impracticable or inconvenient; and both a commission and a letter rogatory may be issued in proper cases. A notice or commission may designate the person before whom the deposition is to be taken either by name or descriptive title. A letter rogatory may be addressed "To the Appropriate Authority in (here name the country)." Evidence obtained in response to a letter rogatory need not be excluded merely for the reason that it is not a verbatim transcript or that the testimony was not taken under oath or for any similar departure from the requirements for depositions taken within the United States under the Indiana Rules of Trial Procedure. IN ST TRIAL P Rule 28(B).

c. *Disqualification for interest.* Unless otherwise permitted by the Indiana Rules of Trial Procedure, no deposition shall be taken before a person who is a relative or employee or attorney or counsel of any of the parties, or is a relative or employee of such attorney or counsel, or is financially interested in the action. IN ST TRIAL P Rule 28(C).

   i. Disqualification of the person before whom the deposition is taken is one of the matters which is waived under IN ST TRIAL P Rule 32(D)(3) unless objection is made as soon as the disqualification is known or could have been known by reasonable diligence. 2A INPRAC R 28(28.3).

d. *Scope of discovery outside state; Protective and enforcement orders.* A deposition may be taken outside the state as provided in IN ST TRIAL P Rule 28(A) and IN ST TRIAL P Rule 28(B), and the deponent may be requested to produce documents and things, and may also be requested to allow inspections and copies as provided in IN ST TRIAL P Rule 34 to submit to examination under IN ST TRIAL P Rule 35. Protective orders may be granted by the court in which the action is pending and by the court where discovery is being made. Enforcement orders may be made by the court where the discovery is sought, and enforcement orders and sanctions may be made by the court where the action is pending as against parties and as against witnesses subject to the jurisdiction of the court. When no action is pending, a court of this state may authorize a deposition to be taken outside this state of any person and upon any matters allowed by IN ST TRIAL P Rule 27. IN ST TRIAL P Rule 28(D).

e. *Assistance to tribunals and litigants outside this state.* A court of this state may order a person who is domiciled or is found within this state to give his testimony or statement or to produce documents or other things, allow inspections and copies and permit physical and mental examinations for use in a proceeding in a tribunal outside this state. The order may be made upon the application of any interested person or in response to a letter rogatory and may prescribe the practice and procedure, which may be wholly or in part the practice and procedure of the tribunal outside this state, for taking the testimony or statement or producing the documents or other things. To the extent that the order does not prescribe otherwise, the practice and procedure shall be in accordance with that of the court of this state issuing the order. The order may direct that the testimony or statement be given, or document or other thing produced, before a person appointed by the court. The person appointed shall have power to administer any necessary oath. A person within this state may voluntarily give his testimony or statement or produce documents or other things allowing inspections and copies and permit physical and mental examinations for use in a proceeding before a tribunal outside this state. IN ST TRIAL P Rule 28(E).

f. *Discovery proceedings before administrative agencies.* Whenever an adjudicatory hearing, including any hearing in any proceeding subject to judicial review, is held by or before an administrative agency, any party to that adjudicatory hearing shall be entitled to use the discovery provisions of IN ST TRIAL P Rule 26 through IN ST TRIAL P Rule 37. Such discovery may include any relevant matter in the custody and control of the administrative agency. IN ST TRIAL P Rule 28(F).

    i. Protective and other orders shall be obtained first from the administrative agency, and if enforcement of such orders or right of discovery is necessary, it may be obtained in a court of general jurisdiction in the county where discovery is being made or sought, or where the hearing is being held. IN ST TRIAL P Rule 28(F).

g. *Applicability of other laws.* IN ST TRIAL P Rule 28 does not repeal or modify any other law of this state permitting another procedure for obtaining discovery for use in this state or in a tribunal outside this state, except as expressly provided in the Indiana Rules of Trial Procedure. IN ST TRIAL P Rule 28(G).

h. *Discovery after judgment.* Discovery after judgment may be had in proceedings to enforce or to challenge the judgment. IN ST TRIAL P Rule 28(H).

6. *Supplementation of responses.* A party who has responded to a request for discovery with a response that was complete when made is under no duty to supplement his response to include information thereafter acquired, except as follows:

a. A party is under a duty seasonably to supplement his response with respect to any question directly addressed to:

    i. The identity and location of persons having knowledge of discoverable matters, and

    ii. The identity of each person expected to be called as an expert witness at trial, the subject-matter on which he is expected to testify, and the substance of his testimony. IN ST TRIAL P Rule 26(E)(1).

b. A party is under a duty seasonably to amend a prior response if he obtains information upon the basis of which:

    i. He knows that the response was incorrect when made, or

    ii. He knows that the response though correct when made is no longer true and the circumstances are such that a failure to amend the response is in substance a knowing concealment. IN ST TRIAL P Rule 26(E)(2).

c. A duty to supplement responses may be imposed by order of the court, agreement of the parties, or at any time prior to trial through new requests for supplementation of prior responses. IN ST TRIAL P Rule 26(E)(3).

d. The duty seasonably to supplement a discovery response is absolute and is not predicated on a court order. "It is a breach of a litigant's duty reasonably to supplement if the litigant postpones supplementing its response by not obtaining from its experts the information which is to be supplied in answer to interrogatories." 2A INPRAC R 26(26.27); Lucas v. Dorsey Corp., 609 N.E.2d 1191, 1196 (Ind.Ct.App. 1993).

D. Documents

1. *Deposition upon oral examination*

a. *Required documents*

    i. *Notice of deposition.* Refer to the General Requirements section of this document for information on the content of a notice of deposition.

    ii. *Certificate of service.* An attorney or unrepresented party tendering a document to the Clerk for filing shall certify that service has been made, list the parties served, and specify the date and means of service. The certificate of service shall be placed at the end of the document and shall not be separately filed. The separate filing of a certificate of service, however, shall not be grounds for rejecting a document for filing. The Clerk may permit documents to be filed without a certificate of service but shall require prompt filing of a separate certificate of service. IN ST TRIAL P Rule 5(C).

b. *Supplemental documents*

    i. *Subpoena/subpoena duces tecum.* The attendance of witnesses may be compelled by the use of subpoena as provided in IN ST TRIAL P Rule 45. IN ST TRIAL P Rule 30(A).

- Proof of service of a notice to take a deposition as provided in IN ST TRIAL P Rule 30(B) and IN ST TRIAL P Rule 31(A) constitutes a sufficient authorization for the issuance by the clerk of court for the county in which the deposition is to be taken of subpoenas for the persons named or described therein. The subpoena may command the person to whom it is directed to produce designated books, papers, documents, or tangible things which constitute or contain matters within the scope of the examination permitted by IN ST TRIAL P Rule 26(B), but in that event the subpoena will be subject to the provisions of IN ST TRIAL P Rule 26(C) and IN ST TRIAL P Rule 45(B). IN ST TRIAL P Rule 45(D)(1).

- An individual may be required to attend an examination only in the county wherein he resides or is employed or transacts his business in person, or at such other convenient place as is fixed by an order of court. A nonresident of the state may be required to attend only in the state and county wherein he is served with a subpoena, or within forty (40) miles from the place of service, or at such other convenient place as is fixed by an order of court. A non-resident plaintiff may be required to attend at his own expense an examination in the county of this state where the action is commenced or in a county fixed by the court. IN ST TRIAL P Rule 45(D)(2).

    ii. *Request for production.* The notice to a deponent may be accompanied by a request made in compliance with IN ST TRIAL P Rule 34 for the production of documents and tangible things at the taking of the deposition. IN ST TRIAL P Rule 30(B)(5).

    iii. *Stipulation regarding discovery procedure.* Unless the court orders otherwise, the parties may by written stipulation:

- Provide that depositions may be taken before any person, at any time or place, upon any notice, and in any manner and when so taken may be used like other depositions, and

- Modify the procedures provided by the Indiana Rules of Trial Procedure for other methods of discovery. IN ST TRIAL P Rule 29.

- Admissions, stipulations and agreements concerning the proceedings in a case will not be enforced, unless submitted in writing or made of record. IN ST ALLEN SUPER AND CIR CT CIV Rule TR00-2.

    iv. *Facsimile cover sheet.* Any document sent to the Clerk of the Circuit Court by electronic facsimile transmission shall be accompanied by a cover sheet which states the title of the document, case number, number of pages, identity and voice telephone number of the sending party and instructions for filing. The cover sheet shall contain the signature of the attorney or party, pro se, authorizing the filing. IN ST ADMIN Rule 12(D).

2. *Deposition upon written questions*

  a. *Required documents*

    i. *Notice of deposition.* Refer to the General Requirements section of this document for information on the content of a notice of deposition.

    ii. *Certificate of service.* An attorney or unrepresented party tendering a document to the Clerk for filing shall certify that service has been made, list the parties served, and specify the date and means of service. The certificate of service shall be placed at the end of the document and shall not be separately filed. The separate filing of a certificate of service, however, shall not be grounds for rejecting a document for filing. The Clerk may permit documents to be filed without a certificate of service but shall require prompt filing of a separate certificate of service. IN ST TRIAL P Rule 5(C).

  b. *Supplemental documents*

    i. *Subpoena.* The attendance of witnesses may be compelled by the use of subpoena as provided in IN ST TRIAL P Rule 45. IN ST TRIAL P Rule 31(A).

- Proof of service of a notice to take a deposition as provided in IN ST TRIAL P Rule 30(B) and IN ST TRIAL P Rule 31(A) constitutes a sufficient authorization for the issuance by the clerk of court for the county in which the deposition is to be taken of subpoenas for the persons named or described therein. The subpoena may command the person to whom it is directed to produce designated books, papers, documents, or tangible things which constitute or contain matters within the scope of the examination permitted by IN ST TRIAL P Rule 26(B), but in that event the subpoena will be subject to the provisions of IN ST TRIAL P Rule 26(C) and IN ST TRIAL P Rule 45(B). IN ST TRIAL P Rule 45(D)(1).

- An individual may be required to attend an examination only in the county wherein he resides or is employed or transacts his business in person, or at such other convenient place as is fixed by an order of court. A nonresident of the state may be required to attend only in the state and county wherein he is served with a subpoena, or within forty (40) miles from the place of service, or at such other convenient place as is fixed by an order of court. A non-resident plaintiff may be required to attend at his own expense an examination in the county of this state where the action is commenced or in a county fixed by the court. IN ST TRIAL P Rule 45(D)(2).

    ii. *Stipulation regarding discovery procedure.* Unless the court orders otherwise, the parties may by written stipulation:

- Provide that depositions may be taken before any person, at any time or place, upon any notice, and in any manner and when so taken may be used like other depositions, and

- Modify the procedures provided by the Indiana Rules of Trial Procedure for other methods of discovery. IN ST TRIAL P Rule 29.

- Admissions, stipulations and agreements concerning the proceedings in a case will not be enforced, unless submitted in writing or made of record. IN ST ALLEN SUPER AND CIR CT CIV Rule TR00-2.

    iii. *Facsimile cover sheet.* Any document sent to the Clerk of the Circuit Court by electronic facsimile transmission shall be accompanied by a cover sheet which states the title of the document, case number, number of pages, identity and voice telephone number of the sending party and instructions for filing. The cover sheet shall contain the signature of the attorney or party, pro se, authorizing the filing. IN ST ADMIN Rule 12(D).

3. *Deposition before action*

  a. *Required documents*

    i. *Notice of deposition.* Refer to the General Requirements section of this document for information on the contents of a notice of deposition.

    ii. *Petition.* Refer to the General Requirements section of this document for information on the content of a petition.

    iii. *Certificate of service.* An attorney or unrepresented party tendering a document to the Clerk for filing shall certify that service has been made, list the parties served, and specify the date and means of service. The certificate of service shall be placed at the end of the document and shall not be separately filed. The separate filing of a certificate of service, however, shall not be grounds for rejecting a document for filing. The Clerk may permit documents to be filed without a certificate of service but shall require prompt filing of a separate certificate of service. IN ST TRIAL P Rule 5(C).

  b. *Supplemental documents*

    i. *Stipulation regarding discovery procedure.* Unless the court orders otherwise, the parties may by written stipulation:

- Provide that depositions may be taken before any person, at any time or place, upon any notice, and in any manner and when so taken may be used like other depositions, and

- Modify the procedures provided by the Indiana Rules of Trial Procedure for other methods of discovery. IN ST TRIAL P Rule 29.

- Admissions, stipulations and agreements concerning the proceedings in a case will not be enforced, unless submitted in writing or made of record. IN ST ALLEN SUPER AND CIR CT CIV Rule TR00-2.

ii. *Facsimile cover sheet.* Any document sent to the Clerk of the Circuit Court by electronic facsimile transmission shall be accompanied by a cover sheet which states the title of the document, case number, number of pages, identity and voice telephone number of the sending party and instructions for filing. The cover sheet shall contain the signature of the attorney or party, pro se, authorizing the filing. IN ST ADMIN Rule 12(D).

4. *Deposition pending appeal*

   a. *Required documents*

      i. *Motion for leave to take deposition and notice.* The requirement of notice is satisfied by service of the motion. IN ST TRIAL P Rule 7(B).

      ii. *Certificate of service.* An attorney or unrepresented party tendering a document to the Clerk for filing shall certify that service has been made, list the parties served, and specify the date and means of service. The certificate of service shall be placed at the end of the document and shall not be separately filed. The separate filing of a certificate of service, however, shall not be grounds for rejecting a document for filing. The Clerk may permit documents to be filed without a certificate of service but shall require prompt filing of a separate certificate of service. IN ST TRIAL P Rule 5(C).

   b. *Supplemental documents*

      i. *Stipulation regarding discovery procedure.* Unless the court orders otherwise, the parties may by written stipulation:

- Provide that depositions may be taken before any person, at any time or place, upon any notice, and in any manner and when so taken may be used like other depositions, and

- Modify the procedures provided by the Indiana Rules of Trial Procedure for other methods of discovery. IN ST TRIAL P Rule 29.

- Admissions, stipulations and agreements concerning the proceedings in a case will not be enforced, unless submitted in writing or made of record. IN ST ALLEN SUPER AND CIR CT CIV Rule TR00-2.

      ii. *Supporting evidence.* When a motion is based on facts not appearing of record the court may hear the matter on affidavits presented by the respective parties, but the court may direct that the matter be heard wholly or partly on oral testimony or depositions. IN ST TRIAL P Rule 43(B).

      iii. *Proposed order.* Unless local practice provides differently, a party should submit a proposed order with its written motion to be signed by the judge once the motion has been granted. 21 INPRAC § 13.8.

      iv. *Brief or memorandum.* If a party desires to file a brief or memorandum in support of any motion, such brief or memorandum shall be filed simultaneously with the motion, and a copy shall be promptly served upon the adverse party. IN ST ALLEN SUPER AND CIR CT CIV Rule 7-1(E).

      v. *Facsimile cover sheet.* Any document sent to the Clerk of the Circuit Court by electronic facsimile transmission shall be accompanied by a cover sheet which states the title of the document, case number, number of pages, identity and voice telephone number of the sending party and instructions for filing. The cover sheet shall contain the signature of the attorney or party, pro se, authorizing the filing. IN ST ADMIN Rule 12(D).

E. Format

1. *Form of notice.* The rules applicable to captions, and the signing and form of pleadings (IN ST TRIAL P Rule 8 through IN ST TRIAL P Rule 11), apply to all motions and other papers provided under the Indiana Rules of Trial Procedure. 22B INPRAC 7:2.

2. *Form of pleadings*

   a. *Caption; Names of parties.* Every pleading shall contain a caption setting forth the name of the court, the title of the action, the file number, and a designation as in IN ST TRIAL P Rule 7(A). In the complaint the title of the action shall include the names of all the parties, but in other pleadings it is sufficient to state the name of the first party on each side with an appropriate indication of other parties. IN ST TRIAL P Rule 10(A).

b. *Paragraphs; Separate statements.* All averments of a claim or defense shall be made in numbered paragraphs, the contents of each of which shall be limited as far as practicable to a statement of a single set of circumstances, and a paragraph may be referred to by number in all succeeding pleadings. Each claim founded upon a separate transaction or occurrence and each defense other than denials may be stated in a separate count or defense whenever a separation facilitates the clear presentation of the matters set forth. IN ST TRIAL P Rule 10(B).

c. *Adoption by reference; Exhibits.* Statements in a pleading may be adopted by reference in a different part of the same pleading or in another pleading or in any motion. A copy of any written instrument which is an exhibit to a pleading is a part thereof for all purposes. IN ST TRIAL P Rule 10(C).

d. *Citation.* Allen County Superior and Circuit court rules may be cited as L.R. _____. The Indiana Rules of Trial Procedure are hereinafter referred to as T.R. _____. IN ST ALLEN SUPER AND CIR CT CIV Rule AR00-1(B).

e. *Paper.* All pleadings must be printed on white paper. IN ST ALLEN SUPER AND CIR CT CIV Rule 8-1(A).

f. *Spacing.* The lines shall be double spaced except for quotations, which shall be indented and single-spaced. IN ST ALLEN SUPER AND CIR CT CIV Rule 8-1(A).

g. *Photocopies.* Photocopies are acceptable if legible. IN ST ALLEN SUPER AND CIR CT CIV Rule 8-1(A).

h. *Margins and binding.* Margins shall be one to one and one-half (1-1 1/2) inches on the left side and one-half (1/2) inch on the right. IN ST ALLEN SUPER AND CIR CT CIV Rule 8-1(B).

   i. Binding or stapling shall be at the top left and at no other place. IN ST ALLEN SUPER AND CIR CT CIV Rule 8-1(B).

   ii. Covers or backing shall not be used. IN ST ALLEN SUPER AND CIR CT CIV Rule 8-1(B).

i. *Flat filing.* The files of the Clerk of the Court shall be kept under the "flat filing" system. All pleadings presented for filing with the Clerk or Court shall be flat and unfolded. Only the original of any pleading shall be placed in the Court file. IN ST ALLEN SUPER AND CIR CT CIV Rule 77-1(A).

j. *Handwritten pleadings.* Handwritten pleadings may be accepted for filing in the discretion of the Court. IN ST ALLEN SUPER AND CIR CT CIV Rule 8-1(A).

3. *Size of papers for filing.* Effective January 1, 1992, all pleadings, copies, motions and documents filed with any trial court or appellate level court, typed or printed, with the exception of exhibits and existing wills, shall be prepared on eight and one-half by eleven inch (8 1/2" x 11") size paper. IN ST ADMIN Rule 11.

4. *Signature requirements*

   a. *Signature of attorney.* Every pleading or motion of a party represented by an attorney shall be signed by at least one (1) attorney of record in his individual name, whose address, telephone number, and attorney number shall be stated, except that this provision shall not apply to pleadings and motions made and transcribed at the trial or a hearing before the judge and received by him in such form. IN ST TRIAL P Rule 11(A). All pleadings to be signed by an attorney shall contain the written signature of the individual attorney, the attorney's printed name, Supreme Court Attorney Number, the name of the attorney's law firm, the attorney's address, telephone number, and a designation of the party for whom the attorney appears. IN ST ALLEN SUPER AND CIR CT CIV Rule 8-1(C). For the recommended signature format, refer to IN ST ALLEN SUPER AND CIR CT CIV Rule 8-1(C).

   i. The signature of an attorney constitutes a certificate by him that he has read the pleadings; that to the best of his knowledge, information, and belief, there is good ground to support it; and that it is not interposed for delay. IN ST TRIAL P Rule 11(A).

    ii. If a pleading or motion is not signed or is signed with intent to defeat the purpose of the rule, it may be stricken as sham and false and the action may proceed as though the pleading had not been served. IN ST TRIAL P Rule 11(A).

    iii. For a willful violation of IN ST TRIAL P Rule 11 an attorney may be subjected to appropriate disciplinary action. Similar action may be taken if scandalous or indecent matter is inserted. IN ST TRIAL P Rule 11(A).

    iv. Neither printed signatures, nor facsimile signatures shall be accepted on original documents. IN ST ALLEN SUPER AND CIR CT CIV Rule 8-1(C).

    v. Facsimile signatures are permitted on copies. IN ST ALLEN SUPER AND CIR CT CIV Rule 8-1(C).

  b. *Signature of unrepresented party.* A party who is not represented by an attorney shall sign his pleading and state his address. IN ST TRIAL P Rule 11(A).

  c. *Verification not generally required.* Except when specifically required by rule, pleadings or motions need not be verified or accompanied by affidavit. The rule in equity that the averments of an answer under oath must be overcome by the testimony of two (2) witnesses or of one (1) witness sustained by corroborating circumstances is abolished. IN ST TRIAL P Rule 11(A).

  d. *Verification by affirmation or representation.* When in connection with any civil or special statutory proceeding it is required that any pleading, motion, petition, supporting affidavit, or other document of any kind, be verified, or that an oath be taken, it shall be sufficient if the subscriber simply affirms the truth of the matter to be verified by an affirmation or representation. IN ST TRIAL P Rule 11(B). IN ST TRIAL P Rule 11(B) states that the affirmation or representation should be in substantially the following language: "I (we) affirm, under the penalties for perjury, that the foregoing representation(s) is (are) true. (Signed) _____."

    i. Any person who falsifies an affirmation or representation of fact shall be subject to the same penalties as are prescribed by law for the making of a false affidavit. IN ST TRIAL P Rule 11(B).

  e. *Verified pleadings, motions, and affidavits as evidence.* Pleadings, motions and affidavits accompanying or in support of such pleadings or motions when required to be verified or under oath shall be accepted as a representation that the signer had personal knowledge thereof or reasonable cause to believe the existence of the facts or matters stated or alleged therein; and, if otherwise competent or acceptable as evidence, may be admitted as evidence of the facts or matters stated or alleged therein when it is so provided in the Indiana Rules of Trial Procedure, by statute or other law, or to the extent the writing or signature expressly purports to be made upon the signer's personal knowledge. When such pleadings, motions and affidavits are verified or under oath they shall not require other or greater proof on the part of the adverse party than if not verified or not under oath unless expressly provided otherwise by the Indiana Rules of Trial Procedure, statute or other law. Affidavits upon motions for summary judgment under IN ST TRIAL P Rule 56 and in denial of execution under IN ST TRIAL P Rule 9.2 shall be made upon personal knowledge. IN ST TRIAL P Rule 11(C).

5. *Information excluded from public access.* Every document filed in a case shall separately identify information excluded from public access pursuant to IN ST ADMIN Rule 9(G)(1) as follows:

  a. Whole documents that are excluded from public access pursuant to IN ST ADMIN Rule 9(G)(1) shall be tendered on light green paper or have a light green coversheet attached to the document, marked "Not for Public Access" or "Confidential." IN ST TRIAL P Rule 5(G)(1).

  b. When only a portion of a document contains information excluded from public access pursuant to IN ST ADMIN Rule 9(G)(1), said information shall be omitted [or redacted] from the filed document, and set forth on a separate accompanying document on light green paper conspicuously marked "Not for Public Access" or "Confidential" and clearly designated [or identifying] the caption and number of the case and the document and location within the document to which the redacted material pertains. IN ST TRIAL P Rule 5(G)(2).

  c. With respect to documents filed in electronic format, the trial court, by local rule, may provide for compliance with IN ST TRIAL P Rule 5 in manner that separates and protects access to information excluded from public access. IN ST TRIAL P Rule 5(G)(3).

d. IN ST TRIAL P Rule 5(G) does not apply to a record sealed by the court pursuant to IN ST 5-14-3-5.5 or otherwise, nor to records, documents, or information filed in cases to which public access is prohibited pursuant to IN ST ADMIN Rule 9(G). IN ST TRIAL P Rule 5(G)(4).

e. The following information in case records is excluded from public access and is confidential:

   i. Information that is excluded from public access pursuant to federal law;

   ii. Information that is excluded from public access as declared confidential by Indiana statute or other court rule, including without limitation:

   - All adoption records created after July 8, 1941, as declared confidential by IN ST 31-19-19-1, et seq., except those specifically declared open by IN ST 31-19-13-2(2);

   - All records relating to chancroid, chlamydia, gonorrhea, hepatitis, human immunodeficiency virus (HIV), Lymphogranuloma venereum, syphilis, tuberculosis, as declared confidential by IN ST 16-41-8-1, et seq.;

   - All records relating to child abuse as declared confidential by IN ST 31-33-18-1, et seq.;

   - All records relating to drug tests as declared confidential by IN ST 5-14-3-4(a)(9);

   - Records of grand jury proceedings as declared confidential by IN ST 35-34-2-4;

   - Records of juvenile proceedings as declared confidential by IN ST 31-39-1-2, except those specifically open under statute;

   - All paternity records created after July 1, 1941 as declared confidential by IN ST 31-14-11-15, IN ST 31-19-5-23, IN ST 31-39-1-1 and IN ST 31-39-1-2 [Editor's note: IN ST 31-14-11-15 was repealed effective May 9, 2013];

   - All pre-sentence reports as declared confidential by IN ST 35-38-1-13;

   - Written petitions to permit marriages without consent and orders directing the Clerk of Court to issue a marriage license to underage persons, as declared confidential by IN ST 31-11-1-6;

   - Only those arrest warrants, search warrants, indictments and informations ordered confidential by the trial judge, prior to return of duly executed service as declared confidential by IN ST 5-14-3-4(b)(1);

   - All medical, mental health, or tax records unless determined by law or regulation of any governmental custodian not to be confidential, released by the subject of such records, or declared by a court of competent jurisdiction to be essential to the resolution of litigation as declared confidential by IN ST 16-39-3-10, IN ST 6-4.1-5-10, IN ST 6-4.1-12-12, and IN ST 6-8.1-7-1;

   - Personal information relating to jurors or prospective jurors, other than for the use of the parties and counsel, pursuant to IN ST JURY Rule 10;

   - Information relating to protection from abuse orders, no-contact orders and workplace violence restraining orders as declared confidential by IN ST 5-2-9-6, et seq.;

   - Mediation proceedings pursuant to IN ST ADR Rule 2.11, Mini-Trial proceedings pursuant to IN ST ADR Rule 4.4(C), and Summary Jury Trials pursuant to IN ST ADR Rule 5.6;

   - Information in probation files pursuant to the Probation Standards promulgated by the Judicial Conference of Indiana pursuant to IN ST 11-13-1-8(b);

   - Information deemed confidential pursuant to the Rules for Court Administered Alcohol and Drug Programs promulgated by the Judicial Conference of Indiana pursuant to IN ST 12-23-14-13;

   - Information deemed confidential pursuant to the Problem-Solving Court Rules promulgated by the Judicial Conference of Indiana pursuant to IN ST 33-23-16-16;

   - All records of the Department of workforce Development as declared confidential by IN ST 22-4-19-6;

- Information regarding interception of electronic communications that is sealed or deemed confidential as set forth in IN ST 35-33.5-2-1, et seq.

iii. Information excluded from public access by specific court order;

iv. Complete Social Security Numbers of living persons;

v. With the exception of names, information such as addresses, phone numbers, and dates of birth which explicitly identifies:

- Natural persons who are witnesses or victims (not including defendants) in criminal, domestic violence, stalking, sexual assault, juvenile, or civil protection order proceedings, provided that juveniles who are victims of sex crimes shall be identified by initials only;

- Places of residence of judicial officers, clerks and other employees of courts and clerks of court, unless the person or persons about whom the information pertains waives confidentiality;

vi. Complete account numbers of specific assets, loans, bank accounts, credit cards, and personal identification numbers (PINs);

vii. All orders of expungement entered in criminal or juvenile proceedings, orders to restrict access to criminal history information pursuant to IN ST 35-38-5-5.5 or IN ST 35-38-8-5 and records excluded from public access by such orders, and information related to infractions that is excluded from public access pursuant to IN ST 34-28-5-15 or IN ST 34-28-5-16 [Editor's note: IN ST 35-38-5-5.5, IN ST 35-38-8-5 and IN ST 34-28-5-16 were repealed effective July 1, 2013; for information on orders restricting access to criminal history, refer to IN ST 35-38-9-1, et seq.];

viii. All personal notes and e-mail, and deliberative material, of judges, jurors, court staff and judicial agencies, and information recorded in personal data assistants (PDA's) or organizers and personal calendars. IN ST ADMIN Rule 9(G)(1).

F. Filing and Service Requirements

1. *Filing requirements.* Except as otherwise provided in IN ST TRIAL P Rule 5(E)(2), all pleadings and papers subsequent to the complaint which are required to be served upon a party shall be filed with the Court either before service or within a reasonable period of time thereafter. IN ST TRIAL P Rule 5(E)(1).

   a. *Non-filing of discovery until necessary*

      i. *Non-filing of discovery; Exceptions.* No deposition or request for discovery or response thereto under IN ST TRIAL P Rule 27, IN ST TRIAL P Rule 30, IN ST TRIAL P Rule 31, IN ST TRIAL P Rule 33, IN ST TRIAL P Rule 34 or IN ST TRIAL P Rule 36 shall be filed with the Court unless:

         - A motion is filed pursuant to IN ST TRIAL P Rule 26(C) or IN ST TRIAL P Rule 37 and the original deposition or request for discovery or response thereto is necessary to enable the Court to rule; or

         - A party desires to use the deposition or request for discovery or response thereto for evidentiary purposes at trial or in connection with a motion, and the Court, either upon its own motion or that of any party, or as a part of any pre-trial order, orders the filing of the original. IN ST TRIAL P Rule 5(E)(2).

      ii. *Custody of original and period of retention*

         - The original of a deposition shall, subject to the provisions of IN ST TRIAL P Rule 30(E), be delivered by the reporter to the party taking it and shall be maintained by that party until filed with the Court pursuant to IN ST TRIAL P Rule 5(E)(2) or until the later of final judgment, agreed settlement of the litigation or all appellate rights have been exhausted. IN ST TRIAL P Rule 5(E)(3)(a).

         - The original or any request for discovery or response thereto under IN ST TRIAL P Rule 27, IN ST TRIAL P Rule 30, IN ST TRIAL P Rule 31, IN ST TRIAL P Rule 33, IN ST TRIAL P Rule 34 and IN ST TRIAL P Rule 36 shall be maintained by the party originating the request or response until filed with the Court pursuant to IN ST TRIAL P Rule 5(E)(2) or until the later of final judgment, agreed settlement or all appellate rights have been exhausted. IN ST TRIAL P Rule 5(E)(3)(b).

   iii. *Original unavailable; Copies.* In the event it is made to appear to the satisfaction of the Court that the original of a deposition or request for discovery or response thereto cannot be filed with the Court when required, the Court may allow use of a copy instead of the original. IN ST TRIAL P Rule 5(E)(4).

   iv. *Filing as publication.* The filing of any deposition shall constitute publication. IN ST TRIAL P Rule 5(E)(5).

b. *Filing with the court defined.* The filing of pleadings, motions, and other papers with the court as required by the Indiana Rules of Trial Procedure shall be made by one of the following methods:

   i. Delivery to the clerk of the court;

   ii. Sending by electronic transmission under the procedure adopted pursuant to IN ST ADMIN Rule 12;

   iii. Mailing to the clerk by registered, certified or express mail return receipt requested;

   iv. Depositing with any third-party commercial carrier for delivery to the clerk within three (3) calendar days, cost prepaid, properly addressed;

   v. If the court so permits, filing with the judge, in which event the judge shall note thereon the filing date and forthwith transmit them to the office of the clerk; or

   vi. Electronic filing, as approved by the Division of State Court Administration pursuant to IN ST ADMIN Rule 16. IN ST TRIAL P Rule 5(F).

   vii. Filing by registered or certified mail and by third-party commercial carrier shall be complete upon mailing or deposit. IN ST TRIAL P Rule 5(F).

c. *Facsimile filing*

   i. *Generally.* In counties where a majority of judges of the courts of record, by posted local rule, have authorized electronic facsimile filing and designated a telephone number to receive such transmissions, pleadings, motions, and other papers may be sent to the Clerk of Circuit Court by electronic facsimile transmission for filing in any case, provided:

- Such matter does not exceed ten (10) pages, including the cover sheet;
- Such matter does not require the payment of fees other than the electronic facsimile transcription fee set forth in IN ST ADMIN Rule 12(E);
- The sending party creates at the time of transmission a machine generated log for such transmission; and
- The original document and the transmission log are maintained by the sending party for the duration of the litigation. IN ST ADMIN Rule 12(B).

   ii. *Time of filing.* During normal, posted business hours, the time of filing shall be the time the duplicate document is produced in the office of the Clerk of the Circuit Court. Duplicate documents received at all other times shall be filed as of the next normal business day. IN ST ADMIN Rule 12(C).

- If the receiving fax machine endorses its own time and date stamp upon the transmitted documents and the receiving machine produces a delivery receipt which is electronically created and transmitted to the sending party, the time of filing shall be the date and time recorded on the transmitted document by the receiving fax machine. IN ST ADMIN Rule 12(C).

d. *Proof of filing.* Any party filing any paper by any method other than personal delivery to the clerk shall retain proof of filing. IN ST TRIAL P Rule 5(F).

2. *Service requirements.* Unless otherwise provided by the Indiana Rules of Trial Procedure or an order of the court, each party and special judge, if any, shall be served with: (1) every order required by its terms

to be served; (2) every pleading subsequent to the original complaint; (3) every written motion except one which may be heard ex parte; (4) every brief submitted to the trial court; (5) every paper relating to discovery required to be served upon a party; and (6) every written notice, appearance, demand, offer of judgment, designation of record on appeal, or similar paper. IN ST TRIAL P Rule 5(A).

a. *Methods of service*

    i. *Personal service.* Whenever a party is represented by an attorney of record, service shall be made upon such attorney unless service upon the party himself is ordered by the court. Service upon the attorney or party shall be made by delivering or mailing a copy of the papers to the last known address or where an attorney or party has consented to service by fax or e-mail, as provided in IN ST TRIAL P Rule 3.1(A)(4), by faxing or e-mailing a copy of the documents to the fax number or e-mail address set out in the appearance form or correction as required by IN ST TRIAL P Rule 3.1(E). IN ST TRIAL P Rule 5(B). Delivery of a copy within IN ST TRIAL P Rule 5 means:

- Offering or tendering it to the attorney or party and stating the nature of the papers being served. Refusal to accept an offered or tendered document is a waiver of any objection to the sufficiency or adequacy of service of that document;

- Leaving it at his office with a clerk or other person in charge thereof, or if there is no one in charge, leaving it in a conspicuous place therein; or

- If the office is closed, by leaving it at his dwelling house or usual place of abode with some person of suitable age and discretion then residing therein; or,

- Leaving it at some other suitable place, selected by the attorney upon whom service is being made, pursuant to duly promulgated local rule. IN ST TRIAL P Rule 5(B)(1).

    ii. *Service by mail.* If service is made by mail, the papers shall be deposited in the United States mail addressed to the person on whom they are being served, with postage prepaid. Service shall be deemed complete upon mailing. Proof of service of all papers permitted to be mailed may be made by written acknowledgment of service, by affidavit of the person who mailed the papers, or by certificate of an attorney. It shall be the duty of attorneys when entering their appearance in a cause or when filing pleadings or papers therein, to have noted in the Chronological Case Summary or said pleadings or papers so filed the address and telephone number of their office. Service by delivery or by mail at such address shall be deemed sufficient and complete. IN ST TRIAL P Rule 5(B)(2).

    iii. *Service by fax or e-mail.* A party who has consented to service by fax or e-mail may be served as follows:

- Service by e-mail shall be made by attaching the document being served in .pdf format. Discovery documents must also be served in accordance with IN ST TRIAL P Rule 26(A). IN ST TRIAL P Rule 5(B)(3)(a).

- Service by fax shall be deemed complete upon generation of a transmission record indicating the successful transmission of the entire document, except as provided in IN ST TRIAL P Rule 5(B)(3)(d). IN ST TRIAL P Rule 5(B)(3)(b).

- Service by e-mail shall be deemed complete upon transmission, except as provided in IN ST TRIAL P Rule 5(B)(3)(d). IN ST TRIAL P Rule 5(B)(3)(c).

- Service by fax or e-mail that occurs on a Saturday, Sunday, legal holiday, or day the court or agency in which the matter is pending is closed or after 5:00 PM local time of the recipient shall be deemed complete the next day that is not a Saturday, Sunday, legal holiday, or day that the court or agency in which the matter is pending is not closed. IN ST TRIAL P Rule 5(B)(3)(d).

    iv. *Additional service of electronic discovery.* In addition to service under Rule IN ST TRIAL P Rule 5(B) or a .pdf format electronic copy, a party propounding or responding to interrogatories, requests for production or requests for admission shall comply with IN ST TRIAL P Rule 26(A.1)(a) or IN ST TRIAL P Rule 26(A.1)(b). IN ST TRIAL P Rule 26(A.1).

- The party shall serve the discovery request or response in an electronic format (either on a disk or as an electronic document attachment) in any commercially available word processing software system. If transmitted on disk, each disk shall be labeled, identifying the caption of the case, the document, and the word processing version in which it is being submitted. If more than one (1) disk is used for the same document, each disk shall be labeled and also shall be sequentially numbered. If transmitted by electronic mail, the document must be accompanied by electronic memorandum providing the forgoing identifying information; or

- The party shall serve the opposing party with a verified statement that the attorney or party appealing pro se lacks the equipment and is unable to transmit the discovery as required by IN ST TRIAL P Rule 26(A.1). IN ST TRIAL P Rule 26(A.1).

    v. *Consent to alternate service.* Any Allen County Attorney or any Allen County law firm may, without charge, maintain an assigned Courthouse box in the library of the Allen County Courthouse for receipt of notices, pleadings, process orders, or other communications from the Court, the Clerk, and other attorneys or law firms. IN ST ALLEN SUPER AND CIR CT CIV Rule 5-1(A). For more information concerning the use of courthouse boxes, refer to IN ST ALLEN SUPER AND CIR CT CIV Rule 5-1.

  b. *Serving numerous defendants.* In any action in which there are unusually large numbers of defendants, the court, upon motion or of its own initiative, may order:

    i. That service of the pleadings of the defendants and replies thereto need not be made as between the defendants;

- That any cross-claim, counterclaim, or matter constituting an avoidance or affirmative defense contained therein shall be deemed to be denied or avoided by all other parties; and

- That the filing of any such pleading and service thereof upon the plaintiff constitutes due notice of it to the parties. IN ST TRIAL P Rule 5(D).

    ii. A copy of every such order shall be served upon the parties in such manner and form as the court directs. IN ST TRIAL P Rule 5(D).

  c. *Service on parties in default for failure to appear.* No service need be made on parties in default for failure to appear, except that pleadings asserting new or additional claims for relief against them shall be served upon them in the manner provided by service of summons in IN ST TRIAL P Rule 4. IN ST TRIAL P Rule 5(A).

G. Hearings

1. The Indiana rules do not contemplate a hearing related to the notice of deposition.

H. Forms

1. Notice of Deposition Forms for Indiana

  a. Notice of deposition; Individual. 5 INPRAC § 4:1.1.

  b. Notice of deposition; Deponent unknown. 5 INPRAC § 4:1.2.

  c. Notice of deposition; Corporation. 5 INPRAC § 4:1.3.

  d. Notice of deposition; With request for production of documents. 5 INPRAC § 4:1.4.

  e. Motion to limit scope of deposition. 5 INPRAC § 4:1.5.

  f. Motion to terminate deposition. 5 INPRAC § 4:1.6.

  g. Notice of hearing on petition for order to take deposition before action to perpetuate testimony. 5 INPRAC § 4:1.7.

  h. Petition to perpetuate testimony. 5 INPRAC § 4:1.7.30.

  i. Affidavit verifying petition to perpetuate testimony. 5 INPRAC § 4:1.7.70.

  j. Stipulation regarding deposition by remote electronic means. 5 INPRAC § 4:1.8.

  k. Petition to perpetuate testimony; Witness to automobile accident. 10 INPRAC § 59.3.

  l. Notice of hearing on petition to perpetuate testimony. 10 INPRAC § 59.6.

m. Petition to perpetuate testimony pending appeal. 10 INPRAC § 59.13.

n. Notice of deposition to perpetuate testimony pending appeal. 10 INPRAC § 59.15.

o. Notice of deposition upon oral examination; Individual. 10 INPRAC § 62.3.

p. Notice of deposition; Deponent unknown. 10 INPRAC § 62.4.

q. Notice of deposition; Corporation. 10 INPRAC § 62.5.

r. Notice of deposition; With request for production of documents. 10 INPRAC § 62.6.

s. Motion for leave to take deposition within twenty days of service. 10 INPRAC § 62.7.

t. Notice of deposition; Pursuant to order granting leave to take deposition. 10 INPRAC § 62.9.

u. Stipulation for deposition upon written questions. 10 INPRAC § 63.2.

v. Notice of deposition upon written questions. 10 INPRAC § 63.3.

w. Direct questions. 10 INPRAC § 63.4.

x. Cross questions. 10 INPRAC § 63.5.

y. Redirect questions. 10 INPRAC § 63.6.

z. Recross questions. 10 INPRAC § 63.7.

2. Official Notice of Deposition Forms for Allen County

a. Consent to alternate service. IN ST ALLEN SUPER AND CIR CT CIV App. A.

I. Checklist

(I) ❑ Matters to be considered by the party taking a deposition upon oral examination

  (a) ❑ Required documents

    (1) ❑ Notice of deposition

    (2) ❑ Certificate of service

  (b) ❑ Supplemental documents

    (1) ❑ Subpoena/subpoena duces tecum

    (2) ❑ Request for production

    (3) ❑ Stipulation regarding discovery procedure

    (4) ❑ Facsimile cover sheet

  (c) ❑ Timing

    (1) ❑ After commencement of the action, any party may take the testimony of any person, including a party, by deposition upon oral examination

(II) ❑ Matters to be considered by the party taking a deposition upon written questions

  (a) ❑ Required documents

    (1) ❑ Notice of deposition

    (2) ❑ Certificate of service

  (b) ❑ Supplemental documents

    (1) ❑ Subpoena

    (2) ❑ Stipulation regarding discovery procedure

    (3) ❑ Facsimile cover sheet

  (c) ❑ Timing

    (1) ❑ After commencement of the action, any party may take the testimony of any person, including a party, by deposition upon written questions

(III) ❑ Matters to be considered by the party taking a deposition before commencement of the action

    (a) ❑ Required documents

        (1) ❑ Notice of deposition

        (2) ❑ Petition

        (3) ❑ Certificate of service

    (b) ❑ Supplemental documents

        (1) ❑ Stipulation regarding discovery procedure

        (2) ❑ Facsimile cover sheet

    (c) ❑ Timing

        (1) ❑ At least twenty (20) days before the date of hearing the notice shall be served in the manner provided in IN ST TRIAL P Rule 4 for service of summons

(IV) ❑ Matters to be considered by the party taking a deposition pending appeal

    (a) ❑ Required documents

        (1) ❑ Motion for leave to take deposition and notice

        (2) ❑ Certificate of service

    (b) ❑ Supplemental documents

        (1) ❑ Stipulation regarding discovery procedure

        (2) ❑ Supporting evidence

        (3) ❑ Proposed order

        (4) ❑ Brief or memorandum

        (5) ❑ Facsimile cover sheet

    (c) ❑ Timing

        (1) ❑ The party who desires to perpetuate the testimony may make a motion in the court for leave to take the depositions, upon the same notice and service thereof as if the action was pending in the court

        (2) ❑ A written motion, other than one which may be heard ex parte, and notice of the hearing thereof shall be served not less than five (5) days before the time specified for the hearing, unless a different period is fixed by the Indiana Rules of Trial Procedure or by order of the court

        (3) ❑ All pleadings and papers subsequent to the complaint which are required to be served upon a party shall be filed with the Court either before service or within a reasonable period of time thereafter

Requests, Notices and Applications
Application for Temporary Restraining Order

Document Last Updated October 2013

A. Applicable Rules

  1. *State rules*

    a. Appearance. IN ST TRIAL P Rule 3.1.

    b. Process. IN ST TRIAL P Rule 4.

    c. Service and filing of pleadings and other papers. IN ST TRIAL P Rule 5.

    d. Time. IN ST TRIAL P Rule 6.

e. Pleadings. IN ST TRIAL P Rule 7; IN ST TRIAL P Rule 8; IN ST TRIAL P Rule 9.2; IN ST TRIAL P Rule 10.

f. Signing and verification of pleadings. IN ST TRIAL P Rule 11.

g. Evidence. IN ST TRIAL P Rule 43.

h. Judgment on the evidence (directed verdict). IN ST TRIAL P Rule 50.

i. Findings by the court. IN ST TRIAL P Rule 52.

j. Summary judgment. IN ST TRIAL P Rule 56.

k. Motion to correct error. IN ST TRIAL P Rule 59.

l. Relief from judgment or order. IN ST TRIAL P Rule 60.

m. Injunctions. IN ST TRIAL P Rule 65; IN ST 34-26-1-7; IN ST 34-26-1-8; IN ST 34-26-1-11.

n. Security; Proceedings against sureties. IN ST TRIAL P Rule 65.1.

o. Trial court and clerks. IN ST TRIAL P Rule 72.

p. Hearing of motions. IN ST TRIAL P Rule 73.

q. Access to court records. IN ST ADMIN Rule 9.

r. Paper size. IN ST ADMIN Rule 11.

s. Facsimile transmission. IN ST ADMIN Rule 12.

t. Electronic filing and electronic service pilot projects. IN ST ADMIN Rule 16.

u. Sealing of certain records by court; Hearing; Notice. IN ST 5-14-3-5.5.

v. Privacy and confidentiality. IN ST 5-2-9-6; IN ST 5-14-3-4; IN ST 6-4.1-5-10; IN ST 6-4.1-12-12; IN ST 6-8.1-7-1; IN ST 11-13-1-8; IN ST 12-23-14-13; IN ST 16-39-3-10; IN ST 16-41-8-1; IN ST 22-4-19-6; IN ST 31-11-1-6; IN ST 31-19-5-23; IN ST 31-19-13-2; IN ST 31-19-19-1; IN ST 31-33-18-1; IN ST 31-39-1-1; IN ST 31-39-1-2; IN ST 33-23-16-16; IN ST 35-34-2-4; IN ST 35-38-1-13; IN ST 35-38-9-1; IN ST ADR Rule 2.11; IN ST ADR Rule 4.4; IN ST ADR Rule 5.6; IN ST JURY Rule 10.

w. Civil protection orders. IN ST 34-26-5-1; IN ST 34-26-5-20.

2. *Local rules*

a. Applicability and citation of rules. IN ST ALLEN SUPER AND CIR CT CIV Rule AR00-1.

b. Proposed orders. IN ST ALLEN SUPER AND CIR CT CIV Rule TR00-1.

c. Appearances. IN ST ALLEN SUPER AND CIR CT CIV Rule 3.1-1.

d. Consent to alternate service. IN ST ALLEN SUPER AND CIR CT CIV Rule 5-1.

e. Preparation of pleadings. IN ST ALLEN SUPER AND CIR CT CIV Rule 8-1.

f. Filing. IN ST ALLEN SUPER AND CIR CT CIV Rule 77-1.

B. Timing

1. *Temporary restraining order without notice.* There are no specific timing requirements for submitting an application for a temporary restraining order without notice.

a. *Filing.* All pleadings and papers subsequent to the complaint which are required to be served upon a party shall be filed with the Court either before service or within a reasonable period of time thereafter. IN ST TRIAL P Rule 5(E)(1).

2. *Computation of time*

a. *Generally; Days excluded.* In computing any period of time prescribed or allowed by the Indiana Rules of Trial Procedure, by order of the court, or by any applicable statute, the day of the act, event, or default from which the designated period of time begins to run shall not be included. The last day of the period so computed is to be included unless it is:

   i. A Saturday,

      ii.   A Sunday,

      iii.   A legal holiday as defined by state statute, or

      iv.   A day the office in which the act is to be done is closed during regular business hours. IN ST TRIAL P Rule 6(A).

  b.   *Short periods.* In any event, the period runs until the end of the next day that is not a Saturday, a Sunday, a legal holiday, or a day on which the office is closed. When the period of time allowed is less than seven (7) days, intermediate Saturdays, Sundays, legal holidays, and days on which the office is closed shall be excluded from the computations. IN ST TRIAL P Rule 6(A).

  c.   *Additional time after service by United States mail.* Whenever a party has the right or is required to do some act or take some proceedings within a prescribed period after the service of a notice or other paper upon him and the notice or paper is served upon him by United States mail, three (3) days shall be added to the prescribed period. IN ST TRIAL P Rule 6(E).

  d.   *Enlargement of time.* When an act is required or allowed to be done at or within a specific time by the Indiana Rules of Trial Procedure, the court may at any time for cause shown:

      i.   Order the period enlarged, with or without motion or notice, if request therefor is made before the expiration of the period originally prescribed or extended by a previous order; or

      ii.   Upon motion made after the expiration of the specific period, permit the act to be done where the failure to act was the result of excusable neglect; but, the court may not extend the time for taking any action for judgment on the evidence under IN ST TRIAL P Rule 50(A), amendment of findings and judgment under IN ST TRIAL P Rule 52(B), to correct errors under IN ST TRIAL P Rule 59(C), statement in opposition to motion to correct error under IN ST TRIAL P Rule 59(E), or to obtain relief from final judgment under IN ST TRIAL P Rule 60(B), except to the extent and under the conditions stated in those rules. IN ST TRIAL P Rule 6(B).

C. General Requirements

1.   *Motions, generally.* Unless made during a hearing or trial, or otherwise ordered by the court, an application to the court for an order shall be made by written motion. The motion shall state the grounds therefor and the relief or order sought. IN ST TRIAL P Rule 7(B).

  a.   *Motions as distinct from pleadings.* Motions and responses to motions are not pleadings, and allegations contained in a motion are not admissions of a party. 22B INPRAC 7:2; Wachstetter v. County Properties, LLC, 832 N.E.2d 574 (Ind.Ct.App. 2005); Scott County Family YMCA, Inc. v. Hobbs, 817 N.E.2d 603 (Ind.Ct.App. 2004).

  b.   *Unopposed motions generally granted.* It is common for a trial court to grant procedural motions, such as motions for enlargement of time, discovery motions, or motions for continuance, unless an objection is filed. 21 INPRAC § 13.8.

2.   *Application for temporary restraining order.* Seeking a temporary restraining order should only be considered if there is a possibility that irreparable injury may occur before the hearing for a preliminary injunction can be held. 4 INPRAC R 65(65.4).

  a.   *Without notice*

      i.   *When notice not required.* A temporary restraining order may be granted without written or oral notice to the adverse party or his attorney only if:

- It clearly appears from specific facts shown by affidavit or by the verified complaint that immediate and irreparable injury, loss, or damage will result to the applicant before the adverse party or his attorney can be heard in opposition; and

- The applicant's attorney certifies to the court in writing the efforts, if any, which have been made to give notice and the reasons supporting his claim that notice should not be required. IN ST TRIAL P Rule 65(B).

      ii.   *Motion for dissolution or modification of temporary restraining order.* On two (2) days' notice to the party who obtained the temporary restraining order without notice or on such shorter notice to that party as the court may prescribe, the adverse party may appear and move its dissolution or modification and in that event the court shall proceed to hear and determine such motion as expeditiously as the ends of justice require. IN ST TRIAL P Rule 65(B).

b. *Temporary restraining orders with notice in Indiana.* IN ST TRIAL P Rule 65(B) in its entirety deals only with temporary restraining orders issued without notice. No mention is made of the issuance of temporary restraining orders with notice. 4 INPRAC R 65(65.4). Some Indiana cases have apparently held that there is no such thing as a temporary restraining order if the adverse party has notice and a hearing is held. 4 INPRAC R 65(65.4); Indiana State Dept. of Welfare v. Stagner, 410 N.E.2d 1348 (Ind.Ct.App. 1980); Szany v. City of Hammond, 170 Ind.App. 537, 352 N.E.2d 866 (Ind.Ct.App. 1976). Refer to the Indiana KeyRules Motion for Preliminary Injunction document for information on obtaining an injunction with notice to the opposing party.

c. *Application without notice as ex parte communication with judge.* The failure to follow the requirements of IN ST TRIAL P Rule 65(B) may constitute, in some circumstances, an improper ex parte communication between attorney and judge. 4 INPRAC R 65(65.4.1); Ace Bail Bonds v. Government Payment Service, Inc., 892 N.E.2d 702 (Ind.Ct.App. 2008), transfer denied (Ind. Jan. 15, 2009).

    i. When a party knows of the presence of another party's attorney in litigation, because each is present at hearings or at trial, then, even if an ex parte T.R.O. arguably meets the criteria in IN ST TRIAL P Rule 65(B), it is not valid unless it meets the standards in Smith v. Johnston, 711 N.E.2d 1259 (Ind.1999). 4 INPRAC R 65(65.4.1).

    ii. Smith v. Johnston, was an appeal to set a default judgment aside. The court granted relief because the party who obtained the default did not give notice to the defaulted party, even though IN ST TRIAL P Rule 4 and IN ST TRIAL P Rule 5 do not require that notice be served on the opposite party's attorney. 4 INPRAC R 65(65.4.1). Smith v. Johnston's rationale clearly states that if an attorney "has knowledge of his opponent's representation, then the Rules of Professional Conduct establish a duty to provide notice `before seeking any relief from the court.'" 4 INPRAC R 65(65.4.1); Smith v. Johnston, 711 N.E.2d 1259 (Ind.1999).

d. *Service of the temporary restraining order once issued.* Notice of the restraining order should be served upon the adverse party. The order may be served together with process in accordance with IN ST TRIAL P Rule 4, or, if obtained after service of process, then in accordance with IN ST TRIAL P Rule 5. 22 INPRAC § 29.2.

    i. IN ST 34-26-1-11 provides the "clerk shall issue a copy of the order of injunction, certified by the clerk, which shall be served promptly by delivering the order to the adverse party." 22 INPRAC § 29.2; IN ST 34-26-1-11.

    ii. However, service is not necessary to make the restraining order effective and binding, so long as the restrained party receives actual knowledge of the order. 22 INPRAC § 29.2; Reed Sign Service, Inc. v. Reid, 755 N.E.2d 690 (Ind.Ct.App. 2001).

e. *Form of order by judge*

    i. Every order granting temporary injunction and every restraining order shall include or be accompanied by findings as required by IN ST TRIAL P Rule 52; shall be specific in terms; shall describe in reasonable detail, and not by reference to the complaint or other document, the act or acts sought to be restrained; and is binding only upon the parties to the action, their officers, agents, servants, employees, and attorneys, and upon those persons in active concert or participation with them who receive actual notice of the order by personal service or otherwise. IN ST TRIAL P Rule 65(D).

    ii. Every temporary restraining order granted without notice shall be indorsed with the date and hour of issuance; shall be filed forthwith in the clerk's office and entered of record; shall define the injury and state why it is irreparable and why the order was granted without notice; and shall expire by its terms within such time after entry, not to exceed ten (10) days, as the court fixes, unless within the time so fixed the order, for good cause shown, is extended for a like period or unless the whereabouts of the party against whom the order is granted is unknown and cannot be determined by reasonable diligence or unless the party against whom the order is directed consents that it may be extended for a longer period. The reasons for the extension shall be entered of record. IN ST TRIAL P Rule 65(B).

 f. *Temporary restraining orders; Domestic relations cases.* Parties wishing protection from domestic or family violence in Domestic Relations cases shall petition the court pursuant to IN ST 34-26-5-1 through IN ST 34-26-5-20. IN ST TRIAL P Rule 65(E). For more information refer to IN ST TRIAL P Rule 65(E) and IN ST 34-26-5-1, et seq.

3. *Security*

 a. *Security requirement.* No restraining order or preliminary injunction shall issue except upon the giving of security by the applicant, in such sum as the court deems proper, for the payment of such costs and damages as may be incurred or suffered by any party who is found to have been wrongfully enjoined or restrained. No such security shall be required of a governmental organization, but such governmental organization shall be responsible for costs and damages as may be incurred or suffered by any party who is found to have been wrongfully enjoined or restrained. IN ST TRIAL P Rule 65(C).

  i. The provisions of IN ST TRIAL P Rule 65.1 apply to a surety upon a bond or undertaking under IN ST TRIAL P Rule 65. IN ST TRIAL P Rule 65(C).

 b. *Proceedings against sureties.* Whenever the Indiana Rules of Trial Procedure or other laws require or permit the giving of security by a party to a court action or proceeding, and security is given in the form of a bond or stipulation or other undertaking with one or more sureties, each surety submits himself to the jurisdiction of the court and irrevocably appoints the clerk of the court as his agent upon whom any papers affecting his liability on the bond or undertaking may be served. His liability may be enforced on motion without the necessity of an independent action. The motion and such notice of the motion as the court prescribes may be served on the clerk of the court, who shall forthwith mail copies to the sureties if their addresses are known. IN ST TRIAL P Rule 65.1 applies to bonds or security furnished on appeal, and enforcement shall be in the court to which the case is returned after appeal. IN ST TRIAL P Rule 65.1.

 c. *Bond generally used as security.* IN ST TRIAL P Rule 65(C) speaks only of the giving of security and does not expressly require a surety on a bond. In practice, however, the giving of a bond with an insurance company as surety in the amount set by the court is typically the device used to satisfy this section. 4 INPRAC R 65(65.6).

D. Documents

1. *Required documents*

 a. *Application for temporary restraining order.* Refer to the General Requirements section of this document for additional information on the contents of an application for a temporary restraining order.

 b. *Security.* No restraining order or preliminary injunction shall issue except upon the giving of security by the applicant, in such sum as the court deems proper, for the payment of such costs and damages as may be incurred or suffered by any party who is found to have been wrongfully enjoined or restrained. IN ST TRIAL P Rule 65(C). Refer to the General Requirements section of this document for more information.

 c. *Proposed order.* Unless local practice provides differently, a party should submit a proposed order with its written motion to be signed by the judge once the motion has been granted. 21 INPRAC § 13.8.

  i. *Copies of proposed orders.* All proposed orders shall be submitted in an original plus a number of copies equal to one (1) more than the number of pro se parties and attorneys of record contained in the prepared proof of notice under IN ST TRIAL P Rule 72(D). IN ST ALLEN SUPER AND CIR CT CIV Rule TR00-1(C).

  ii. *Proof of notice.* The proposed order shall also include a prepared proof of notice, under IN ST TRIAL P Rule 72(D). IN ST ALLEN SUPER AND CIR CT CIV Rule TR00-1(B).

  iii. Refer to the Format section of this document for information on the form and content of the proposed order and the proof of notice.

2. *Supplemental documents*

    a. *Supporting evidence.* When a motion is based on facts not appearing of record the court may hear the matter on affidavits presented by the respective parties, but the court may direct that the matter be heard wholly or partly on oral testimony or depositions. IN ST TRIAL P Rule 43(B).

    b. *Brief or memorandum.* If a party desires to file a brief or memorandum in support of any motion, such brief or memorandum shall be filed simultaneously with the motion, and a copy shall be promptly served upon the adverse party. IN ST ALLEN SUPER AND CIR CT CIV Rule 7-1(E).

    c. *Facsimile cover sheet.* Any document sent to the Clerk of the Circuit Court by electronic facsimile transmission shall be accompanied by a cover sheet which states the title of the document, case number, number of pages, identity and voice telephone number of the sending party and instructions for filing. The cover sheet shall contain the signature of the attorney or party, pro se, authorizing the filing. IN ST ADMIN Rule 12(D).

E. Format

1. *Form of motions.* The rules applicable to captions, and the signing and form of pleadings (IN ST TRIAL P Rule 8 through IN ST TRIAL P Rule 11), apply to all motions and other papers provided under the Indiana Rules of Trial Procedure. 22B INPRAC 7:2.

2. *Form of pleadings*

    a. *Caption; Names of parties.* Every pleading shall contain a caption setting forth the name of the court, the title of the action, the file number, and a designation as in IN ST TRIAL P Rule 7(A). In the complaint the title of the action shall include the names of all the parties, but in other pleadings it is sufficient to state the name of the first party on each side with an appropriate indication of other parties. IN ST TRIAL P Rule 10(A).

    b. *Paragraphs; Separate statements.* All averments of a claim or defense shall be made in numbered paragraphs, the contents of each of which shall be limited as far as practicable to a statement of a single set of circumstances, and a paragraph may be referred to by number in all succeeding pleadings. Each claim founded upon a separate transaction or occurrence and each defense other than denials may be stated in a separate count or defense whenever a separation facilitates the clear presentation of the matters set forth. IN ST TRIAL P Rule 10(B).

    c. *Adoption by reference; Exhibits.* Statements in a pleading may be adopted by reference in a different part of the same pleading or in another pleading or in any motion. A copy of any written instrument which is an exhibit to a pleading is a part thereof for all purposes. IN ST TRIAL P Rule 10(C).

    d. *Citation.* Allen County Superior and Circuit court rules may be cited as L.R. _____. The Indiana Rules of Trial Procedure are hereinafter referred to as T.R. _____. IN ST ALLEN SUPER AND CIR CT CIV Rule AR00-1(B).

    e. *Paper.* All pleadings must be printed on white paper. IN ST ALLEN SUPER AND CIR CT CIV Rule 8-1(A).

    f. *Spacing.* The lines shall be double spaced except for quotations, which shall be indented and single-spaced. IN ST ALLEN SUPER AND CIR CT CIV Rule 8-1(A).

    g. *Photocopies.* Photocopies are acceptable if legible. IN ST ALLEN SUPER AND CIR CT CIV Rule 8-1(A).

    h. *Margins and binding.* Margins shall be one to one and one-half (1-1 1/2) inches on the left side and one-half (1/2) inch on the right. IN ST ALLEN SUPER AND CIR CT CIV Rule 8-1(B).

       i. Binding or stapling shall be at the top left and at no other place. IN ST ALLEN SUPER AND CIR CT CIV Rule 8-1(B).

       ii. Covers or backing shall not be used. IN ST ALLEN SUPER AND CIR CT CIV Rule 8-1(B).

    i. *Flat filing.* The files of the Clerk of the Court shall be kept under the "flat filing" system. All pleadings presented for filing with the Clerk or Court shall be flat and unfolded. Only the original of any pleading shall be placed in the Court file. IN ST ALLEN SUPER AND CIR CT CIV Rule 77-1(A).

    j. *Handwritten pleadings.* Handwritten pleadings may be accepted for filing in the discretion of the Court. IN ST ALLEN SUPER AND CIR CT CIV Rule 8-1(A).

3. *Size of papers for filing.* Effective January 1, 1992, all pleadings, copies, motions and documents filed with any trial court or appellate level court, typed or printed, with the exception of exhibits and existing wills, shall be prepared on eight and one-half by eleven inch (8 1/2" x 11") size paper. IN ST ADMIN Rule 11.

4. *Form of proposed orders*

    a. *Form, caption, and title.* Any proposed order shall be a document that is separate and apart from the motion or application to which it relates and shall contain a caption showing the name of the court, the case number assigned to the case and the title of the case as shown by the complaint. IN ST ALLEN SUPER AND CIR CT CIV Rule TR00-1(B). If there are multiple parties, the title may be shortened to include only the first name plaintiff and defendant with appropriate indication that there are additional parties. IN ST ALLEN SUPER AND CIR CT CIV Rule TR00-1(B).

    b. *Paper.* The proposed order shall be on white paper, eight and one half by eleven inches (8 1/2" x 11") in size, and each page shall be numbered. IN ST ALLEN SUPER AND CIR CT CIV Rule TR00-1(B).

    c. *Signature line.* On the last page of the proposed order there shall be a line for the signature of the judge under which shall be typed "Judge, Allen Superior Court" or "Judge, Allen Circuit Court", whichever is applicable, to the left of which shall be the following: "Dated _____". IN ST ALLEN SUPER AND CIR CT CIV Rule TR00-1(B).

    d. *Allowance of space for clerk.* To allow space for the Clerk to make entries on the proposed order to show compliance with the notice requirements of IN ST TRIAL P Rule 72(D), the lower four (4) inches of the last page of the proposed order shall be left blank. IN ST ALLEN SUPER AND CIR CT CIV Rule TR00-1(B).

    e. *Proof of notice required.* The proposed order shall also include a prepared proof of notice, under IN ST TRIAL P Rule 72(D). The proof of notice shall conform to the format show in IN ST ALLEN SUPER AND CIR CT CIV Rule TR00-1(B). IN ST ALLEN SUPER AND CIR CT CIV Rule TR00-1(B).

5. *Signature requirements*

    a. *Signature of attorney.* Every pleading or motion of a party represented by an attorney shall be signed by at least one (1) attorney of record in his individual name, whose address, telephone number, and attorney number shall be stated, except that this provision shall not apply to pleadings and motions made and transcribed at the trial or a hearing before the judge and received by him in such form. IN ST TRIAL P Rule 11(A). All pleadings to be signed by an attorney shall contain the written signature of the individual attorney, the attorney's printed name, Supreme Court Attorney Number, the name of the attorney's law firm, the attorney's address, telephone number, and a designation of the party for whom the attorney appears. IN ST ALLEN SUPER AND CIR CT CIV Rule 8-1(C). For the recommended signature format, refer to IN ST ALLEN SUPER AND CIR CT CIV Rule 8-1(C).

       i. The signature of an attorney constitutes a certificate by him that he has read the pleadings; that to the best of his knowledge, information, and belief, there is good ground to support it; and that it is not interposed for delay. IN ST TRIAL P Rule 11(A).

      ii. If a pleading or motion is not signed or is signed with intent to defeat the purpose of the rule, it may be stricken as sham and false and the action may proceed as though the pleading had not been served. IN ST TRIAL P Rule 11(A).

     iii. For a willful violation of IN ST TRIAL P Rule 11 an attorney may be subjected to appropriate disciplinary action. Similar action may be taken if scandalous or indecent matter is inserted. IN ST TRIAL P Rule 11(A).

     iv. Neither printed signatures, nor facsimile signatures shall be accepted on original documents. IN ST ALLEN SUPER AND CIR CT CIV Rule 8-1(C).

      v. Facsimile signatures are permitted on copies. IN ST ALLEN SUPER AND CIR CT CIV Rule 8-1(C).

b. *Signature of unrepresented party.* A party who is not represented by an attorney shall sign his pleading and state his address. IN ST TRIAL P Rule 11(A).

c. *Verification not generally required.* Except when specifically required by rule, pleadings or motions need not be verified or accompanied by affidavit. The rule in equity that the averments of an answer under oath must be overcome by the testimony of two (2) witnesses or of one (1) witness sustained by corroborating circumstances is abolished. IN ST TRIAL P Rule 11(A).

d. *Verification by affirmation or representation.* When in connection with any civil or special statutory proceeding it is required that any pleading, motion, petition, supporting affidavit, or other document of any kind, be verified, or that an oath be taken, it shall be sufficient if the subscriber simply affirms the truth of the matter to be verified by an affirmation or representation. IN ST TRIAL P Rule 11(B). IN ST TRIAL P Rule 11(B) states that the affirmation or representation should be in substantially the following language: "I (we) affirm, under the penalties for perjury, that the foregoing representation(s) is (are) true. (Signed) _____ "

   i. Any person who falsifies an affirmation or representation of fact shall be subject to the same penalties as are prescribed by law for the making of a false affidavit. IN ST TRIAL P Rule 11(B).

e. *Verified pleadings, motions, and affidavits as evidence.* Pleadings, motions and affidavits accompanying or in support of such pleadings or motions when required to be verified or under oath shall be accepted as a representation that the signer had personal knowledge thereof or reasonable cause to believe the existence of the facts or matters stated or alleged therein; and, if otherwise competent or acceptable as evidence, may be admitted as evidence of the facts or matters stated or alleged therein when it is so provided in the Indiana Rules of Trial Procedure, by statute or other law, or to the extent the writing or signature expressly purports to be made upon the signer's personal knowledge. When such pleadings, motions and affidavits are verified or under oath they shall not require other or greater proof on the part of the adverse party than if not verified or not under oath unless expressly provided otherwise by the Indiana Rules of Trial Procedure, statute or other law. Affidavits upon motions for summary judgment under IN ST TRIAL P Rule 56 and in denial of execution under IN ST TRIAL P Rule 9.2 shall be made upon personal knowledge. IN ST TRIAL P Rule 11(C).

6. *Information excluded from public access.* Every document filed in a case shall separately identify information excluded from public access pursuant to IN ST ADMIN Rule 9(G)(1) as follows:

   a. Whole documents that are excluded from public access pursuant to IN ST ADMIN Rule 9(G)(1) shall be tendered on light green paper or have a light green coversheet attached to the document, marked "Not for Public Access" or "Confidential." IN ST TRIAL P Rule 5(G)(1).

   b. When only a portion of a document contains information excluded from public access pursuant to IN ST ADMIN Rule 9(G)(1), said information shall be omitted [or redacted] from the filed document, and set forth on a separate accompanying document on light green paper conspicuously marked "Not for Public Access" or "Confidential" and clearly designated [or identifying] the caption and number of the case and the document and location within the document to which the redacted material pertains. IN ST TRIAL P Rule 5(G)(2).

   c. With respect to documents filed in electronic format, the trial court, by local rule, may provide for compliance with IN ST TRIAL P Rule 5 in manner that separates and protects access to information excluded from public access. IN ST TRIAL P Rule 5(G)(3).

   d. IN ST TRIAL P Rule 5(G) does not apply to a record sealed by the court pursuant to IN ST 5-14-3-5.5 or otherwise, nor to records, documents, or information filed in cases to which public access is prohibited pursuant to IN ST ADMIN Rule 9(G). IN ST TRIAL P Rule 5(G)(4).

   e. The following information in case records is excluded from public access and is confidential:

      i. Information that is excluded from public access pursuant to federal law;

      ii. Information that is excluded from public access as declared confidential by Indiana statute or other court rule, including without limitation:

         • All adoption records created after July 8, 1941, as declared confidential by IN ST 31-19-19-1, et seq., except those specifically declared open by IN ST 31-19-13-2(2);

- All records relating to chancroid, chlamydia, gonorrhea, hepatitis, human immunodeficiency virus (HIV), Lymphogranuloma venereum, syphilis, tuberculosis, as declared confidential by IN ST 16-41-8-1, et seq.;

- All records relating to child abuse as declared confidential by IN ST 31-33-18-1, et seq.;

- All records relating to drug tests as declared confidential by IN ST 5-14-3-4(a)(9);

- Records of grand jury proceedings as declared confidential by IN ST 35-34-2-4;

- Records of juvenile proceedings as declared confidential by IN ST 31-39-1-2, except those specifically open under statute;

- All paternity records created after July 1, 1941 as declared confidential by IN ST 31-14-11-15, IN ST 31-19-5-23, IN ST 31-39-1-1 and IN ST 31-39-1-2 [Editor's note: IN ST 31-14-11-15 was repealed effective May 9, 2013];

- All pre-sentence reports as declared confidential by IN ST 35-38-1-13;

- Written petitions to permit marriages without consent and orders directing the Clerk of Court to issue a marriage license to underage persons, as declared confidential by IN ST 31-11-1-6;

- Only those arrest warrants, search warrants, indictments and informations ordered confidential by the trial judge, prior to return of duly executed service as declared confidential by IN ST 5-14-3-4(b)(1);

- All medical, mental health, or tax records unless determined by law or regulation of any governmental custodian not to be confidential, released by the subject of such records, or declared by a court of competent jurisdiction to be essential to the resolution of litigation as declared confidential by IN ST 16-39-3-10, IN ST 6-4.1-5-10, IN ST 6-4.1-12-12, and IN ST 6-8.1-7-1;

- Personal information relating to jurors or prospective jurors, other than for the use of the parties and counsel, pursuant to IN ST JURY Rule 10;

- Information relating to protection from abuse orders, no-contact orders and workplace violence restraining orders as declared confidential by IN ST 5-2-9-6, et seq.;

- Mediation proceedings pursuant to IN ST ADR Rule 2.11, Mini-Trial proceedings pursuant to IN ST ADR Rule 4.4(C), and Summary Jury Trials pursuant to IN ST ADR Rule 5.6;

- Information in probation files pursuant to the Probation Standards promulgated by the Judicial Conference of Indiana pursuant to IN ST 11-13-1-8(b);

- Information deemed confidential pursuant to the Rules for Court Administered Alcohol and Drug Programs promulgated by the Judicial Conference of Indiana pursuant to IN ST 12-23-14-13;

- Information deemed confidential pursuant to the Problem-Solving Court Rules promulgated by the Judicial Conference of Indiana pursuant to IN ST 33-23-16-16;

- All records of the Department of workforce Development as declared confidential by IN ST 22-4-19-6;

- Information regarding interception of electronic communications that is sealed or deemed confidential as set forth in IN ST 35-33.5-2-1, et seq.

iii.   Information excluded from public access by specific court order;

iv.   Complete Social Security Numbers of living persons;

v.   With the exception of names, information such as addresses, phone numbers, and dates of birth which explicitly identifies:

- Natural persons who are witnesses or victims (not including defendants) in criminal, domestic violence, stalking, sexual assault, juvenile, or civil protection order proceedings, provided that juveniles who are victims of sex crimes shall be identified by initials only;

- Places of residence of judicial officers, clerks and other employees of courts and clerks of court, unless the person or persons about whom the information pertains waives confidentiality;

vi. Complete account numbers of specific assets, loans, bank accounts, credit cards, and personal identification numbers (PINs);

vii. All orders of expungement entered in criminal or juvenile proceedings, orders to restrict access to criminal history information pursuant to IN ST 35-38-5-5.5 or IN ST 35-38-8-5 and records excluded from public access by such orders, and information related to infractions that is excluded from public access pursuant to IN ST 34-28-5-15 or IN ST 34-28-5-16 [Editor's note: IN ST 35-38-5-5.5, IN ST 35-38-8-5 and IN ST 34-28-5-16 were repealed effective July 1, 2013; for information on orders restricting access to criminal history, refer to IN ST 35-38-9-1, et seq.];

viii. All personal notes and e-mail, and deliberative material, of judges, jurors, court staff and judicial agencies, and information recorded in personal data assistants (PDA's) or organizers and personal calendars. IN ST ADMIN Rule 9(G)(1).

F. Filing and Service Requirements

1. *Filing requirements.* Except as otherwise provided in IN ST TRIAL P Rule 5(E)(2), all pleadings and papers subsequent to the complaint which are required to be served upon a party shall be filed with the Court either before service or within a reasonable period of time thereafter. IN ST TRIAL P Rule 5(E)(1).

   a. *Filing with the court defined.* The filing of pleadings, motions, and other papers with the court as required by the Indiana Rules of Trial Procedure shall be made by one of the following methods:

      i. Delivery to the clerk of the court;

      ii. Sending by electronic transmission under the procedure adopted pursuant to IN ST ADMIN Rule 12;

      iii. Mailing to the clerk by registered, certified or express mail return receipt requested;

      iv. Depositing with any third-party commercial carrier for delivery to the clerk within three (3) calendar days, cost prepaid, properly addressed;

      v. If the court so permits, filing with the judge, in which event the judge shall note thereon the filing date and forthwith transmit them to the office of the clerk; or

      vi. Electronic filing, as approved by the Division of State Court Administration pursuant to IN ST ADMIN Rule 16. IN ST TRIAL P Rule 5(F).

      vii. Filing by registered or certified mail and by third-party commercial carrier shall be complete upon mailing or deposit. IN ST TRIAL P Rule 5(F).

   b. *Facsimile filing*

      i. *Generally.* In counties where a majority of judges of the courts of record, by posted local rule, have authorized electronic facsimile filing and designated a telephone number to receive such transmissions, pleadings, motions, and other papers may be sent to the Clerk of Circuit Court by electronic facsimile transmission for filing in any case, provided:

         - Such matter does not exceed ten (10) pages, including the cover sheet;

         - Such matter does not require the payment of fees other than the electronic facsimile transcription fee set forth in IN ST ADMIN Rule 12(E);

         - The sending party creates at the time of transmission a machine generated log for such transmission; and

         - The original document and the transmission log are maintained by the sending party for the duration of the litigation. IN ST ADMIN Rule 12(B).

      ii. *Time of filing.* During normal, posted business hours, the time of filing shall be the time the duplicate document is produced in the office of the Clerk of the Circuit Court. Duplicate

documents received at all other times shall be filed as of the next normal business day. IN ST ADMIN Rule 12(C).

- If the receiving fax machine endorses its own time and date stamp upon the transmitted documents and the receiving machine produces a delivery receipt which is electronically created and transmitted to the sending party, the time of filing shall be the date and time recorded on the transmitted document by the receiving fax machine. IN ST ADMIN Rule 12(C).

c. *Proof of filing.* Any party filing any paper by any method other than personal delivery to the clerk shall retain proof of filing. IN ST TRIAL P Rule 5(F).

2. *Service requirements.* Unless otherwise provided by the Indiana Rules of Trial Procedure or an order of the court, each party and special judge, if any, shall be served with: (1) every order required by its terms to be served; (2) every pleading subsequent to the original complaint; (3) every written motion except one which may be heard ex parte; (4) every brief submitted to the trial court; (5) every paper relating to discovery required to be served upon a party; and (6) every written notice, appearance, demand, offer of judgment, designation of record on appeal, or similar paper. IN ST TRIAL P Rule 5(A).

a. *Methods of service*

i. *Personal service.* Whenever a party is represented by an attorney of record, service shall be made upon such attorney unless service upon the party himself is ordered by the court. Service upon the attorney or party shall be made by delivering or mailing a copy of the papers to the last known address or where an attorney or party has consented to service by fax or e-mail, as provided in IN ST TRIAL P Rule 3.1(A)(4), by faxing or e-mailing a copy of the documents to the fax number or e-mail address set out in the appearance form or correction as required by IN ST TRIAL P Rule 3.1(E). IN ST TRIAL P Rule 5(B). Delivery of a copy within IN ST TRIAL P Rule 5 means:

- Offering or tendering it to the attorney or party and stating the nature of the papers being served. Refusal to accept an offered or tendered document is a waiver of any objection to the sufficiency or adequacy of service of that document;

- Leaving it at his office with a clerk or other person in charge thereof, or if there is no one in charge, leaving it in a conspicuous place therein; or

- If the office is closed, by leaving it at his dwelling house or usual place of abode with some person of suitable age and discretion then residing therein; or,

- Leaving it at some other suitable place, selected by the attorney upon whom service is being made, pursuant to duly promulgated local rule. IN ST TRIAL P Rule 5(B)(1).

ii. *Service by mail.* If service is made by mail, the papers shall be deposited in the United States mail addressed to the person on whom they are being served, with postage prepaid. Service shall be deemed complete upon mailing. Proof of service of all papers permitted to be mailed may be made by written acknowledgment of service, by affidavit of the person who mailed the papers, or by certificate of an attorney. It shall be the duty of attorneys when entering their appearance in a cause or when filing pleadings or papers therein, to have noted in the Chronological Case Summary or said pleadings or papers so filed the address and telephone number of their office. Service by delivery or by mail at such address shall be deemed sufficient and complete. IN ST TRIAL P Rule 5(B)(2).

iii. *Service by fax or e-mail.* A party who has consented to service by fax or e-mail may be served as follows:

- Service by e-mail shall be made by attaching the document being served in .pdf format. Discovery documents must also be served in accordance with IN ST TRIAL P Rule 26(A). IN ST TRIAL P Rule 5(B)(3)(a).

- Service by fax shall be deemed complete upon generation of a transmission record indicating the successful transmission of the entire document, except as provided in IN ST TRIAL P Rule 5(B)(3)(d). IN ST TRIAL P Rule 5(B)(3)(b).

- Service by e-mail shall be deemed complete upon transmission, except as provided in IN ST TRIAL P Rule 5(B)(3)(d). IN ST TRIAL P Rule 5(B)(3)(c).

- Service by fax or e-mail that occurs on a Saturday, Sunday, legal holiday, or day the court or agency in which the matter is pending is closed or after 5:00 PM local time of the recipient shall be deemed complete the next day that is not a Saturday, Sunday, legal holiday, or day that the court or agency in which the matter is pending is not closed. IN ST TRIAL P Rule 5(B)(3)(d).

iv. *Consent to alternate service.* Any Allen County Attorney or any Allen County law firm may, without charge, maintain an assigned Courthouse box in the library of the Allen County Courthouse for receipt of notices, pleadings, process orders, or other communications from the Court, the Clerk, and other attorneys or law firms. IN ST ALLEN SUPER AND CIR CT CIV Rule 5-1(A). For more information concerning the use of courthouse boxes, refer to IN ST ALLEN SUPER AND CIR CT CIV Rule 5-1.

b. *Serving numerous defendants.* In any action in which there are unusually large numbers of defendants, the court, upon motion or of its own initiative, may order:

i. That service of the pleadings of the defendants and replies thereto need not be made as between the defendants;

- That any cross-claim, counterclaim, or matter constituting an avoidance or affirmative defense contained therein shall be deemed to be denied or avoided by all other parties; and

- That the filing of any such pleading and service thereof upon the plaintiff constitutes due notice of it to the parties. IN ST TRIAL P Rule 5(D).

ii. A copy of every such order shall be served upon the parties in such manner and form as the court directs. IN ST TRIAL P Rule 5(D).

c. *Service on parties in default for failure to appear.* No service need be made on parties in default for failure to appear, except that pleadings asserting new or additional claims for relief against them shall be served upon them in the manner provided by service of summons in IN ST TRIAL P Rule 4. IN ST TRIAL P Rule 5(A).

G. Hearings

1. *Hearing on motion.* Unless local conditions make it impracticable, each judge shall establish regular times and places, at intervals sufficiently frequent for the prompt dispatch of business, at which motions requiring notice and hearing may be heard and disposed of; but the judge at any time or place and on such notice, if any, as he considers reasonable may make order for the advancement, conduct, and hearing of actions. To expedite its business the court may direct the submission and determination of motions without oral hearing upon brief written statements of reasons in support and opposition, or direct or permit hearings by telephone conference call with all attorneys or other similar means of communication. IN ST TRIAL P Rule 73(A).

a. *Setting motions for hearing.* Except for the motions described in IN ST ALLEN SUPER AND CIR CT CIV Rule 7-1(E), all motions shall be set for hearing. IN ST ALLEN SUPER AND CIR CT CIV Rule 7-1(A). [Editor's note: While IN ST ALLEN SUPER AND CIR CT CIV Rule 7-1(A) refers to IN ST ALLEN SUPER AND CIR CT CIV Rule 7-1(E) as relating to hearings on motions, that reference is likely intended to be to IN ST ALLEN SUPER AND CIR CT CIV Rule 7-1(D).]

i. It shall be the responsibility of the moving party to request the date of such hearing from the Judicial Assistant, or if the case has already been assigned to a Judge, from the Judicial Law Clerk of the assigned Judge. IN ST ALLEN SUPER AND CIR CT CIV Rule 7-1(A).

b. *Responsibility for notice of hearing.* It shall be the responsibility of the moving party to give notice to all other parties of hearings scheduled on motions. IN ST ALLEN SUPER AND CIR CT CIV Rule 7-1(I).

2. *Presentation of evidence.* On the hearing of an application for a restraining order or temporary injunction, each party may read affidavits or documentary or record evidence. IN ST 34-26-1-8.

3. *Hearing for preliminary injunction.* In case a temporary restraining order is granted without notice, the

motion for a preliminary injunction shall be set down for hearing at the earliest possible time and takes precedence of all matters except older matters of the same character; and when the motion comes on for hearing the party who obtained the temporary restraining order shall proceed with the application for a preliminary injunction and, if he does not do so, the court shall dissolve the temporary restraining order. IN ST TRIAL P Rule 65(B). Refer to the Indiana KeyRules Motion for Preliminary Injunction document for more information.

H. Forms

1. Application for Temporary Restraining Order Forms for Indiana

a. Prayer in complaint for temporary restraining order. 5 INPRAC § 3:13.60.

b. Motion for temporary restraining order; With notice. 5 INPRAC § 3:13.80.

c. Notice of motion for temporary restraining order. 11 INPRAC § 97.2.

d. Motion for temporary restraining order; Without notice. 11 INPRAC § 97.3.

e. Affidavit in support of motion for temporary restraining order. 11 INPRAC § 97.4.

f. Certificate of efforts of attorney to give notice of application for temporary restraining order. 11 INPRAC § 97.5.

g. Temporary restraining order without notice and order to show cause why preliminary injunction should not issue; Real estate. 11 INPRAC § 97.6.

h. Motion to extend temporary restraining order. 11 INPRAC § 97.7.

i. Order granting motion to extend temporary restraining order. 11 INPRAC § 97.8.

j. Stipulation extending temporary restraining order. 11 INPRAC § 97.9.

k. Order granting extension of temporary restraining order pursuant to stipulation. 11 INPRAC § 97.10.

l. Motion for judge of adjourning circuit to rule upon motion for temporary restraining order. 11 INPRAC § 97.11.

m. Affidavit in support of motion for judge of adjoining county to rule on motion for temporary restraining order. 11 INPRAC § 97.12.

n. Motion to advance trial on merits for consolidation with hearing on preliminary injunction. 11 INPRAC § 97.13.

2. Official Application for Temporary Restraining Order Forms for Allen County

a. Consent to alternate service. IN ST ALLEN SUPER AND CIR CT CIV App. A.

I. Checklist

(I) ❑ Matters to be considered by the party filing the application without notice

  (a) ❑ Required documents

    (1) ❑ Application for temporary restraining order

    (2) ❑ Security

    (3) ❑ Proposed order

  (b) ❑ Supplemental documents

    (1) ❑ Supporting evidence

    (2) ❑ Brief or memorandum

    (3) ❑ Facsimile cover sheet

  (c) ❑ Timing

    (1) ❑ There are no specific timing requirements for submitting an application for a temporary restraining order without notice

Requests, Notices and Applications
Pretrial Conferences, Scheduling, Management

Document Last Updated October 2013

A. Applicable Rules

1. *State rules*

   a. Appearance. IN ST TRIAL P Rule 3.1.

   b. Process. IN ST TRIAL P Rule 4.

   c. Service and filing of pleadings and other papers. IN ST TRIAL P Rule 5.

   d. Time. IN ST TRIAL P Rule 6.

   e. Pleadings. IN ST TRIAL P Rule 7; IN ST TRIAL P Rule 8; IN ST TRIAL P Rule 9.2; IN ST TRIAL P Rule 10.

   f. Signing and verification of pleadings. IN ST TRIAL P Rule 11.

   g. Pre-trial procedure; Formulating issues. IN ST TRIAL P Rule 16.

   h. Evidence. IN ST TRIAL P Rule 43.

   i. Judgment on the evidence (directed verdict). IN ST TRIAL P Rule 50.

   j. Findings by the court. IN ST TRIAL P Rule 52.

   k. Summary judgment. IN ST TRIAL P Rule 56.

   l. Motion to correct error. IN ST TRIAL P Rule 59.

   m. Relief from judgment or order. IN ST TRIAL P Rule 60.

   n. Trial court and clerks. IN ST TRIAL P Rule 72.

   o. Access to court records. IN ST ADMIN Rule 9.

   p. Paper size. IN ST ADMIN Rule 11.

   q. Facsimile transmission. IN ST ADMIN Rule 12.

   r. Electronic filing and electronic service pilot projects. IN ST ADMIN Rule 16.

   s. Sealing of certain records by court; Hearing; Notice. IN ST 5-14-3-5.5.

   t. Privacy and confidentiality. IN ST 5-2-9-6; IN ST 5-14-3-4; IN ST 6-4.1-5-10; IN ST 6-4.1-12-12; IN ST 6-8.1-7-1; IN ST 11-13-1-8; IN ST 12-23-14-13; IN ST 16-39-3-10; IN ST 16-41-8-1; IN ST 22-4-19-6; IN ST 31-11-1-6; IN ST 31-19-5-23; IN ST 31-19-13-2; IN ST 31-19-19-1; IN ST 31-33-18-1; IN ST 31-39-1-1; IN ST 31-39-1-2; IN ST 33-23-16-16; IN ST 35-34-2-4; IN ST 35-38-1-13; IN ST 35-38-9-1; IN ST ADR Rule 2.11; IN ST ADR Rule 4.4; IN ST ADR Rule 5.6; IN ST JURY Rule 10.

2. *Local rules*

   a. Applicability and citation of rules. IN ST ALLEN SUPER AND CIR CT CIV Rule AR00-1.

   b. Proposed orders. IN ST ALLEN SUPER AND CIR CT CIV Rule TR00-1.

   c. Appearances. IN ST ALLEN SUPER AND CIR CT CIV Rule 3.1-1.

   d. Consent to alternate service. IN ST ALLEN SUPER AND CIR CT CIV Rule 5-1.

   e. Preparation of pleadings. IN ST ALLEN SUPER AND CIR CT CIV Rule 8-1.

   f. Filing. IN ST ALLEN SUPER AND CIR CT CIV Rule 77-1.

B. Timing

1. *Pretrial conference.* Unless otherwise ordered by the court the pretrial conference shall not be called until after reasonable opportunity for the completion of discovery. IN ST TRIAL P Rule 16(B). However, some Indiana courts will schedule a preliminary pretrial conference almost immediately after the case has

been filed in order to establish the ground rules for discovery, discovery cut-off dates, and the procedures for filing additional pleadings, motions, and the like. In addition, some courts will only schedule a trial date at the pretrial conference. 22 INPRAC § 28.2.

a. *Notice.* The clerks shall give at least thirty (30) days' notice of the pretrial conference unless otherwise directed by the court. IN ST TRIAL P Rule 16(B)(1).

b. *Pre-conference meeting.* Unless otherwise ordered by the court, at least ten (10) days prior to the pretrial conference, attorneys for each of the parties shall meet and confer. IN ST TRIAL P Rule 16(C). It shall be the duty of counsel for both plaintiff and defendant to arrange for the conference of attorneys at least ten (10) days in advance of the pretrial conference. IN ST TRIAL P Rule 16(E).

2. *Motion requesting pretrial conference*

a. *Timing of motion for pretrial conference.* There is no specific timing requirement for filing a motion requesting a pretrial conference.

    i. *Filing.* All pleadings and papers subsequent to the complaint which are required to be served upon a party shall be filed with the Court either before service or within a reasonable period of time thereafter. IN ST TRIAL P Rule 5(E)(1).

b. *Service*

    i. *Of motion.* A written motion, other than one which may be heard ex parte, and notice of the hearing thereof shall be served not less than five (5) days before the time specified for the hearing, unless a different period is fixed by the Indiana Rules of Trial Procedure or by order of the court. IN ST TRIAL P Rule 6(D).

    • *Of supporting affidavits.* When a motion is supported by affidavit, the affidavit shall be served with the motion. IN ST TRIAL P Rule 6(D).

    ii. *Of opposition.* Except as otherwise provided in IN ST TRIAL P Rule 59(D), opposing affidavits may be served not less than one (1) day before the hearing, unless the court permits them to be served at some other time. IN ST TRIAL P Rule 6(D).

3. *Computation of time*

a. *Generally; Days excluded.* In computing any period of time prescribed or allowed by the Indiana Rules of Trial Procedure, by order of the court, or by any applicable statute, the day of the act, event, or default from which the designated period of time begins to run shall not be included. The last day of the period so computed is to be included unless it is:

    i. A Saturday,

    ii. A Sunday,

    iii. A legal holiday as defined by state statute, or

    iv. A day the office in which the act is to be done is closed during regular business hours. IN ST TRIAL P Rule 6(A).

b. *Short periods.* In any event, the period runs until the end of the next day that is not a Saturday, a Sunday, a legal holiday, or a day on which the office is closed. When the period of time allowed is less than seven (7) days, intermediate Saturdays, Sundays, legal holidays, and days on which the office is closed shall be excluded from the computations. IN ST TRIAL P Rule 6(A).

c. *Additional time after service by United States mail.* Whenever a party has the right or is required to do some act or take some proceedings within a prescribed period after the service of a notice or other paper upon him and the notice or paper is served upon him by United States mail, three (3) days shall be added to the prescribed period. IN ST TRIAL P Rule 6(E).

d. *Enlargement of time.* When an act is required or allowed to be done at or within a specific time by the Indiana Rules of Trial Procedure, the court may at any time for cause shown:

    i. Order the period enlarged, with or without motion or notice, if request therefor is made before the expiration of the period originally prescribed or extended by a previous order; or

    ii. Upon motion made after the expiration of the specific period, permit the act to be done where

the failure to act was the result of excusable neglect; but, the court may not extend the time for taking any action for judgment on the evidence under IN ST TRIAL P Rule 50(A), amendment of findings and judgment under IN ST TRIAL P Rule 52(B), to correct errors under IN ST TRIAL P Rule 59(C), statement in opposition to motion to correct error under IN ST TRIAL P Rule 59(E), or to obtain relief from final judgment under IN ST TRIAL P Rule 60(B), except to the extent and under the conditions stated in those rules. IN ST TRIAL P Rule 6(B).

C. General Requirements

1. *Pretrial conference*

   a. *When required; Purpose.* In any action except criminal cases, the court may in its discretion and shall upon the motion of any party, direct the attorneys for the parties to appear before it for a conference to consider:

      i. The simplification of the issues;

      ii. The necessity or desirability of amendments to the pleadings;

      iii. The possibility of obtaining admissions of fact and of documents which will avoid unnecessary proof;

      iv. A limitation of the number of expert witnesses;

      v. An exchange of names of witnesses to be called during the trial and the general nature of their expected testimony;

      vi. The desirability of using one or more types of alternative dispute resolution under the rules therefor;

      vii. The desirability of setting deadlines for dispositive motions in light of the date set for trial; and

      viii. Such other matters as may aid in the disposition of the action. IN ST TRIAL P Rule 16(A).

   b. *Participants.* At least one (1) attorney planning to take part in the trial shall appear for each of the parties and participate in the pretrial conference. IN ST TRIAL P Rule 16(B)(2).

   c. *Conference of attorneys prior to pretrial conference*

      i. *Purpose of attorney conference.* In general, the purpose of the "pre-pretrial conference" is to ensure that the attorneys for both sides will be prepared to make maximum use of the pretrial conference itself. IN ST TRIAL P Rule 16 frees the pretrial conference itself from perfunctory matters; it is written to require that not only are attorneys very familiar with the case, but that routine matters are resolved before the pretrial conference so that it may be devoted to a determination of those issues and matters which will be litigated. 2 INPRAC R 16(16.3).

      ii. *Topics to be addressed at attorney conference.* Unless otherwise ordered by the court, at least ten (10) days prior to the pretrial conference, attorneys for each of the parties shall meet and confer for the following purposes:

      - *Exhibits.* Each attorney shall mark for identification and provide opposing counsel an opportunity to inspect and copy all exhibits which he expects to introduce at the trial. Numbers or marks placed on such exhibits shall be prefixed with the symbol "P/T", denoting its pretrial designation. When the exhibit is introduced at the trial of the case, the "P/T" designation will be stricken and the exhibits must also indicate the party identifying same. IN ST TRIAL P Rule 16(C)(1). Exhibits of the character which prohibit or make impracticable their production at conference shall be identified and notice given of their intended use. Necessary arrangements must be made to afford opposing counsel an opportunity to examine such exhibits. IN ST TRIAL P Rule 16(C)(1).

      - *Exhibit stipulations.* Written stipulations shall be prepared with reference to all exhibits exchanged or identified. The stipulations shall contain all agreements of the parties with reference to the exchanged and identified exhibits, and shall include, but not be limited to, the agreement of the parties with reference to the authenticity of the exhibits, their admissibility in evidence, their use in opening statements, and the provisions made for the inspection of identified exhibits. The original of the exhibit stipulations shall be presented to the court at the pretrial conference. IN ST TRIAL P Rule 16(C)(2).

- *Fact stipulation.* The attorneys shall stipulate in writing with reference to all facts and issues not in genuine dispute. The original of the stipulations shall be presented to the court at the time of the pretrial conference. IN ST TRIAL P Rule 16(C)(3).

- *Exchange list of witnesses.* Attorneys for each of the parties shall furnish opposing counsel with the written list of the names and addresses of all witnesses then known. The original of each witness list shall be presented to the court at the time of the pretrial conference. IN ST TRIAL P Rule 16(C)(4).

- *Discuss settlement.* The possibility of compromise settlement shall be fully discussed and explored. IN ST TRIAL P Rule 16(C)(5).

d. *Preparation for conference of attorneys and pretrial.* Each attorney shall completely familiarize himself with all aspects of the case in advance of the conference of attorneys and be prepared to enter into stipulations with reference to as many facts and issues and exhibits as possible. IN ST TRIAL P Rule 16(D).

e. *Refusal to stipulate.* If, following the conference of attorneys, either party determines that there are other facts or exhibits that should be stipulated and which opposing counsel refuses to stipulate upon, he shall compile a list of such facts or exhibits and furnish same to opposing counsel at least two (2) days in advance of the pretrial conference. The original of the list shall be presented to the court at the time of the pretrial conference. IN ST TRIAL P Rule 16(F).

f. *Witnesses or exhibits discovered subsequent to conference of attorneys and before a pretrial conference.* If, after the conference of the attorneys and before the pretrial conference, counsel discovers additional exhibits or names of additional witnesses, the same information required to be disclosed at the conference of the attorneys shall be immediately furnished opposing counsel. The original of any such disclosures shall be presented to the court at the time of the pretrial conference. IN ST TRIAL P Rule 16(G).

g. *More than one pretrial conference.* If necessary or advisable, the court may adjourn the pretrial conference from time to time or may order an additional pretrial conference. IN ST TRIAL P Rule 16(H).

h. *Witnesses or exhibits discovered subsequent to pretrial conference.* If, following the pretrial conference or during trial, counsel discovers additional exhibits or the names of additional witnesses, the same information required to be disclosed at the conference between attorneys shall be immediately furnished opposing counsel. The original of any such disclosure shall immediately be filed with the court and shall indicate the date it was furnished opposing counsel. IN ST TRIAL P Rule 16(I).

i. *Pretrial order.* The court shall make an order which recites the action taken at the conference, the amendments allowed to the pleading, and the agreements made by the parties as to any of the matters considered which limit the issues for trial to those not disposed of by admissions or agreement of counsel, and such order when entered shall control the subsequent course of action, unless modified thereafter to prevent manifest injustice. The court in its discretion may establish by rule a pretrial calendar on which actions may be placed for consideration as above provided, and may either confine the calendar to jury actions or non-jury actions or extend it to all actions. IN ST TRIAL P Rule 16(J).

    i. The pretrial order delineates the issues in the case and supplants allegations raised in the pleadings. All subsequent pleadings are then controlled by the order that the trial court enters in the case file, and court record. 2 INPRAC R 16(16.2); Dominguez v. Gallmeyer, 402 N.E.2d 1295, 1298 (Ind.Ct.App. 1980).

j. *Sanctions; Failure to appear.* If without just excuse or because of failure to give reasonable attention to the matter, no appearance is made on behalf of a party at a pre-trial conference, or if an attorney is grossly unprepared to participate in the conference, the court may order either one or both of the following:

    i. The payment by the delinquent attorney or party of the reasonable expenses, including attorney's fees, to the aggrieved party; or

305

  ii. Take such other action as may be appropriate. IN ST TRIAL P Rule 16(K).

  iii. Refer to the Indiana KeyRules Motion for Sanctions document for more information.

 2. *Motions, generally.* Unless made during a hearing or trial, or otherwise ordered by the court, an application to the court for an order shall be made by written motion. The motion shall state the grounds therefor and the relief or order sought. IN ST TRIAL P Rule 7(B).

  a. *Motions as distinct from pleadings.* Motions and responses to motions are not pleadings, and allegations contained in a motion are not admissions of a party. 22B INPRAC 7:2; Wachstetter v. County Properties, LLC, 832 N.E.2d 574 (Ind.Ct.App. 2005); Scott County Family YMCA, Inc. v. Hobbs, 817 N.E.2d 603 (Ind.Ct.App. 2004).

  b. *Unopposed motions generally granted.* It is common for a trial court to grant procedural motions, such as motions for enlargement of time, discovery motions, or motions for continuance, unless an objection is filed. 21 INPRAC § 13.8.

D. Documents

 1. *Pretrial conference*

  a. *Documents to consider*

   i. *Exhibits and stipulations.* Refer to the General Requirements section of this document for information on exhibits and stipulations.

 2. *Motion for pretrial conference*

  a. *Required documents*

   i. *Motion and notice.* The requirement of notice is satisfied by service of the motion. IN ST TRIAL P Rule 7(B). Refer to the General Requirements section of this document for information on the content of a motion for pretrial conference.

   ii. *Proposed order.* Unless local practice provides differently, a party should submit a proposed order with its written motion to be signed by the judge once the motion has been granted. 21 INPRAC § 13.8.

    • *Copies of proposed orders.* All proposed orders shall be submitted in an original plus a number of copies equal to one (1) more than the number of pro se parties and attorneys of record contained in the prepared proof of notice under IN ST TRIAL P Rule 72(D). IN ST ALLEN SUPER AND CIR CT CIV Rule TR00-1(C).

    • *Proof of notice.* The proposed order shall also include a prepared proof of notice, under IN ST TRIAL P Rule 72(D). IN ST ALLEN SUPER AND CIR CT CIV Rule TR00-1(B).

    • Refer to the Format section of this document for information on the form and content of the proposed order and the proof of notice.

   iii. *Certificate of service.* An attorney or unrepresented party tendering a document to the Clerk for filing shall certify that service has been made, list the parties served, and specify the date and means of service. The certificate of service shall be placed at the end of the document and shall not be separately filed. The separate filing of a certificate of service, however, shall not be grounds for rejecting a document for filing. The Clerk may permit documents to be filed without a certificate of service but shall require prompt filing of a separate certificate of service. IN ST TRIAL P Rule 5(C).

  b. *Supplemental documents*

   i. *Supporting evidence.* When a motion is based on facts not appearing of record the court may hear the matter on affidavits presented by the respective parties, but the court may direct that the matter be heard wholly or partly on oral testimony or depositions. IN ST TRIAL P Rule 43(B).

   ii. *Brief or memorandum.* If a party desires to file a brief or memorandum in support of any motion, such brief or memorandum shall be filed simultaneously with the motion, and a copy shall be promptly served upon the adverse party. IN ST ALLEN SUPER AND CIR CT CIV Rule 7-1(E).

iii. *Facsimile cover sheet.* Any document sent to the Clerk of the Circuit Court by electronic facsimile transmission shall be accompanied by a cover sheet which states the title of the document, case number, number of pages, identity and voice telephone number of the sending party and instructions for filing. The cover sheet shall contain the signature of the attorney or party, pro se, authorizing the filing. IN ST ADMIN Rule 12(D).

E. Format

1. *Form of papers.* The rules applicable to captions, and the signing and form of pleadings (IN ST TRIAL P Rule 8 through IN ST TRIAL P Rule 11), apply to all motions and other papers provided under the Indiana Rules of Trial Procedure. 22B INPRAC 7:2.

2. *Form of pleadings*

   a. *Caption; Names of parties.* Every pleading shall contain a caption setting forth the name of the court, the title of the action, the file number, and a designation as in IN ST TRIAL P Rule 7(A). In the complaint the title of the action shall include the names of all the parties, but in other pleadings it is sufficient to state the name of the first party on each side with an appropriate indication of other parties. IN ST TRIAL P Rule 10(A).

   b. *Paragraphs; Separate statements.* All averments of a claim or defense shall be made in numbered paragraphs, the contents of each of which shall be limited as far as practicable to a statement of a single set of circumstances, and a paragraph may be referred to by number in all succeeding pleadings. Each claim founded upon a separate transaction or occurrence and each defense other than denials may be stated in a separate count or defense whenever a separation facilitates the clear presentation of the matters set forth. IN ST TRIAL P Rule 10(B).

   c. *Adoption by reference; Exhibits.* Statements in a pleading may be adopted by reference in a different part of the same pleading or in another pleading or in any motion. A copy of any written instrument which is an exhibit to a pleading is a part thereof for all purposes. IN ST TRIAL P Rule 10(C).

   d. *Citation.* Allen County Superior and Circuit court rules may be cited as L.R. _____. The Indiana Rules of Trial Procedure are hereinafter referred to as T.R. _____. IN ST ALLEN SUPER AND CIR CT CIV Rule AR00-1(B).

   e. *Paper.* All pleadings must be printed on white paper. IN ST ALLEN SUPER AND CIR CT CIV Rule 8-1(A).

   f. *Spacing.* The lines shall be double spaced except for quotations, which shall be indented and single-spaced. IN ST ALLEN SUPER AND CIR CT CIV Rule 8-1(A).

   g. *Photocopies.* Photocopies are acceptable if legible. IN ST ALLEN SUPER AND CIR CT CIV Rule 8-1(A).

   h. *Margins and binding.* Margins shall be one to one and one-half (1-1 1/2) inches on the left side and one-half (1/2) inch on the right. IN ST ALLEN SUPER AND CIR CT CIV Rule 8-1(B).

      i. Binding or stapling shall be at the top left and at no other place. IN ST ALLEN SUPER AND CIR CT CIV Rule 8-1(B).

      ii. Covers or backing shall not be used. IN ST ALLEN SUPER AND CIR CT CIV Rule 8-1(B).

   i. *Flat filing.* The files of the Clerk of the Court shall be kept under the "flat filing" system. All pleadings presented for filing with the Clerk or Court shall be flat and unfolded. Only the original of any pleading shall be placed in the Court file. IN ST ALLEN SUPER AND CIR CT CIV Rule 77-1(A).

   j. *Handwritten pleadings.* Handwritten pleadings may be accepted for filing in the discretion of the Court. IN ST ALLEN SUPER AND CIR CT CIV Rule 8-1(A).

3. *Size of papers for filing.* Effective January 1, 1992, all pleadings, copies, motions and documents filed with any trial court or appellate level court, typed or printed, with the exception of exhibits and existing wills, shall be prepared on eight and one-half by eleven inch (8 1/2" x 11") size paper. IN ST ADMIN Rule 11.

4. *Form of proposed orders*

   a. *Form, caption, and title.* Any proposed order shall be a document that is separate and apart from the motion or application to which it relates and shall contain a caption showing the name of the court, the case number assigned to the case and the title of the case as shown by the complaint. IN ST ALLEN SUPER AND CIR CT CIV Rule TR00-1(B). If there are multiple parties, the title may be shortened to include only the first name plaintiff and defendant with appropriate indication that there are additional parties. IN ST ALLEN SUPER AND CIR CT CIV Rule TR00-1(B).

b. *Paper.* The proposed order shall be on white paper, eight and one half by eleven inches (8 1/2" x 11") in size, and each page shall be numbered. IN ST ALLEN SUPER AND CIR CT CIV Rule TR00-1(B).

c. *Signature line.* On the last page of the proposed order there shall be a line for the signature of the judge under which shall be typed "Judge, Allen Superior Court" or "Judge, Allen Circuit Court", whichever is applicable, to the left of which shall be the following: "Dated _____". IN ST ALLEN SUPER AND CIR CT CIV Rule TR00-1(B).

d. *Allowance of space for clerk.* To allow space for the Clerk to make entries on the proposed order to show compliance with the notice requirements of IN ST TRIAL P Rule 72(D), the lower four (4) inches of the last page of the proposed order shall be left blank. IN ST ALLEN SUPER AND CIR CT CIV Rule TR00-1(B).

e. *Proof of notice required.* The proposed order shall also include a prepared proof of notice, under IN ST TRIAL P Rule 72(D). The proof of notice shall conform to the format show in IN ST ALLEN SUPER AND CIR CT CIV Rule TR00-1(B). IN ST ALLEN SUPER AND CIR CT CIV Rule TR00-1(B).

5. *Signature requirements*

a. *Signature of attorney.* Every pleading or motion of a party represented by an attorney shall be signed by at least one (1) attorney of record in his individual name, whose address, telephone number, and attorney number shall be stated, except that this provision shall not apply to pleadings and motions made and transcribed at the trial or a hearing before the judge and received by him in such form. IN ST TRIAL P Rule 11(A). All pleadings to be signed by an attorney shall contain the written signature of the individual attorney, the attorney's printed name, Supreme Court Attorney Number, the name of the attorney's law firm, the attorney's address, telephone number, and a designation of the party for whom the attorney appears. IN ST ALLEN SUPER AND CIR CT CIV Rule 8-1(C). For the recommended signature format, refer to IN ST ALLEN SUPER AND CIR CT CIV Rule 8-1(C).

   i. The signature of an attorney constitutes a certificate by him that he has read the pleadings; that to the best of his knowledge, information, and belief, there is good ground to support it; and that it is not interposed for delay. IN ST TRIAL P Rule 11(A).

   ii. If a pleading or motion is not signed or is signed with intent to defeat the purpose of the rule, it may be stricken as sham and false and the action may proceed as though the pleading had not been served. IN ST TRIAL P Rule 11(A).

   iii. For a willful violation of IN ST TRIAL P Rule 11 an attorney may be subjected to appropriate disciplinary action. Similar action may be taken if scandalous or indecent matter is inserted. IN ST TRIAL P Rule 11(A).

   iv. Neither printed signatures, nor facsimile signatures shall be accepted on original documents. IN ST ALLEN SUPER AND CIR CT CIV Rule 8-1(C).

   v. Facsimile signatures are permitted on copies. IN ST ALLEN SUPER AND CIR CT CIV Rule 8-1(C).

b. *Signature of unrepresented party.* A party who is not represented by an attorney shall sign his pleading and state his address. IN ST TRIAL P Rule 11(A).

c. *Verification not generally required.* Except when specifically required by rule, pleadings or motions need not be verified or accompanied by affidavit. The rule in equity that the averments of an answer under oath must be overcome by the testimony of two (2) witnesses or of one (1) witness sustained by corroborating circumstances is abolished. IN ST TRIAL P Rule 11(A).

d. *Verification by affirmation or representation.* When in connection with any civil or special statutory

proceeding it is required that any pleading, motion, petition, supporting affidavit, or other document of any kind, be verified, or that an oath be taken, it shall be sufficient if the subscriber simply affirms the truth of the matter to be verified by an affirmation or representation. IN ST TRIAL P Rule 11(B). IN ST TRIAL P Rule 11(B) states that the affirmation or representation should be in substantially the following language: "I (we) affirm, under the penalties for perjury, that the foregoing representation(s) is (are) true. (Signed) _____."

    i.   Any person who falsifies an affirmation or representation of fact shall be subject to the same penalties as are prescribed by law for the making of a false affidavit. IN ST TRIAL P Rule 11(B).

    e.   *Verified pleadings, motions, and affidavits as evidence.* Pleadings, motions and affidavits accompanying or in support of such pleadings or motions when required to be verified or under oath shall be accepted as a representation that the signer had personal knowledge thereof or reasonable cause to believe the existence of the facts or matters stated or alleged therein; and, if otherwise competent or acceptable as evidence, may be admitted as evidence of the facts or matters stated or alleged therein when it is so provided in the Indiana Rules of Trial Procedure, by statute or other law, or to the extent the writing or signature expressly purports to be made upon the signer's personal knowledge. When such pleadings, motions and affidavits are verified or under oath they shall not require other or greater proof on the part of the adverse party than if not verified or not under oath unless expressly provided otherwise by the Indiana Rules of Trial Procedure, statute or other law. Affidavits upon motions for summary judgment under IN ST TRIAL P Rule 56 and in denial of execution under IN ST TRIAL P Rule 9.2 shall be made upon personal knowledge. IN ST TRIAL P Rule 11(C).

6.   *Information excluded from public access.* Every document filed in a case shall separately identify information excluded from public access pursuant to IN ST ADMIN Rule 9(G)(1) as follows:

    a.   Whole documents that are excluded from public access pursuant to IN ST ADMIN Rule 9(G)(1) shall be tendered on light green paper or have a light green coversheet attached to the document, marked "Not for Public Access" or "Confidential." IN ST TRIAL P Rule 5(G)(1).

    b.   When only a portion of a document contains information excluded from public access pursuant to IN ST ADMIN Rule 9(G)(1), said information shall be omitted [or redacted] from the filed document, and set forth on a separate accompanying document on light green paper conspicuously marked "Not for Public Access" or "Confidential" and clearly designated [or identifying] the caption and number of the case and the document and location within the document to which the redacted material pertains. IN ST TRIAL P Rule 5(G)(2).

    c.   With respect to documents filed in electronic format, the trial court, by local rule, may provide for compliance with IN ST TRIAL P Rule 5 in manner that separates and protects access to information excluded from public access. IN ST TRIAL P Rule 5(G)(3).

    d.   IN ST TRIAL P Rule 5(G) does not apply to a record sealed by the court pursuant to IN ST 5-14-3-5.5 or otherwise, nor to records, documents, or information filed in cases to which public access is prohibited pursuant to IN ST ADMIN Rule 9(G). IN ST TRIAL P Rule 5(G)(4).

    e.   The following information in case records is excluded from public access and is confidential:

       i.   Information that is excluded from public access pursuant to federal law;

      ii.   Information that is excluded from public access as declared confidential by Indiana statute or other court rule, including without limitation:

          • All adoption records created after July 8, 1941, as declared confidential by IN ST 31-19-19-1, et seq., except those specifically declared open by IN ST 31-19-13-2(2);

          • All records relating to chancroid, chlamydia, gonorrhea, hepatitis, human immunodeficiency virus (HIV), Lymphogranuloma venereum, syphilis, tuberculosis, as declared confidential by IN ST 16-41-8-1, et seq.;

          • All records relating to child abuse as declared confidential by IN ST 31-33-18-1, et seq.;

          • All records relating to drug tests as declared confidential by IN ST 5-14-3-4(a)(9);

          • Records of grand jury proceedings as declared confidential by IN ST 35-34-2-4;

- Records of juvenile proceedings as declared confidential by IN ST 31-39-1-2, except those specifically open under statute;

- All paternity records created after July 1, 1941 as declared confidential by IN ST 31-14-11-15, IN ST 31-19-5-23, IN ST 31-39-1-1 and IN ST 31-39-1-2 [Editor's note: IN ST 31-14-11-15 was repealed effective May 9, 2013];

- All pre-sentence reports as declared confidential by IN ST 35-38-1-13;

- Written petitions to permit marriages without consent and orders directing the Clerk of Court to issue a marriage license to underage persons, as declared confidential by IN ST 31-11-1-6;

- Only those arrest warrants, search warrants, indictments and informations ordered confidential by the trial judge, prior to return of duly executed service as declared confidential by IN ST 5-14-3-4(b)(1);

- All medical, mental health, or tax records unless determined by law or regulation of any governmental custodian not to be confidential, released by the subject of such records, or declared by a court of competent jurisdiction to be essential to the resolution of litigation as declared confidential by IN ST 16-39-3-10, IN ST 6-4.1-5-10, IN ST 6-4.1-12-12, and IN ST 6-8.1-7-1;

- Personal information relating to jurors or prospective jurors, other than for the use of the parties and counsel, pursuant to IN ST JURY Rule 10;

- Information relating to protection from abuse orders, no-contact orders and workplace violence restraining orders as declared confidential by IN ST 5-2-9-6, et seq.;

- Mediation proceedings pursuant to IN ST ADR Rule 2.11, Mini-Trial proceedings pursuant to IN ST ADR Rule 4.4(C), and Summary Jury Trials pursuant to IN ST ADR Rule 5.6;

- Information in probation files pursuant to the Probation Standards promulgated by the Judicial Conference of Indiana pursuant to IN ST 11-13-1-8(b);

- Information deemed confidential pursuant to the Rules for Court Administered Alcohol and Drug Programs promulgated by the Judicial Conference of Indiana pursuant to IN ST 12-23-14-13;

- Information deemed confidential pursuant to the Problem-Solving Court Rules promulgated by the Judicial Conference of Indiana pursuant to IN ST 33-23-16-16;

- All records of the Department of workforce Development as declared confidential by IN ST 22-4-19-6;

- Information regarding interception of electronic communications that is sealed or deemed confidential as set forth in IN ST 35-33.5-2-1, et seq.

iii. Information excluded from public access by specific court order;

iv. Complete Social Security Numbers of living persons;

v. With the exception of names, information such as addresses, phone numbers, and dates of birth which explicitly identifies:

- Natural persons who are witnesses or victims (not including defendants) in criminal, domestic violence, stalking, sexual assault, juvenile, or civil protection order proceedings, provided that juveniles who are victims of sex crimes shall be identified by initials only;

- Places of residence of judicial officers, clerks and other employees of courts and clerks of court, unless the person or persons about whom the information pertains waives confidentiality;

vi. Complete account numbers of specific assets, loans, bank accounts, credit cards, and personal identification numbers (PINs);

vii. All orders of expungement entered in criminal or juvenile proceedings, orders to restrict access

to criminal history information pursuant to IN ST 35-38-5-5.5 or IN ST 35-38-8-5 and records excluded from public access by such orders, and information related to infractions that is excluded from public access pursuant to IN ST 34-28-5-15 or IN ST 34-28-5-16 [Editor's note: IN ST 35-38-5-5.5, IN ST 35-38-8-5 and IN ST 34-28-5-16 were repealed effective July 1, 2013; for information on orders restricting access to criminal history, refer to IN ST 35-38-9-1, et seq.];

    viii. All personal notes and e-mail, and deliberative material, of judges, jurors, court staff and judicial agencies, and information recorded in personal data assistants (PDA's) or organizers and personal calendars. IN ST ADMIN Rule 9(G)(1).

F. Filing and Service Requirements

1. *Filing requirements.* Except as otherwise provided in IN ST TRIAL P Rule 5(E)(2), all pleadings and papers subsequent to the complaint which are required to be served upon a party shall be filed with the Court either before service or within a reasonable period of time thereafter. IN ST TRIAL P Rule 5(E)(1).

    a. *Filing with the court defined.* The filing of pleadings, motions, and other papers with the court as required by the Indiana Rules of Trial Procedure shall be made by one of the following methods:

        i. Delivery to the clerk of the court;

        ii. Sending by electronic transmission under the procedure adopted pursuant to IN ST ADMIN Rule 12;

        iii. Mailing to the clerk by registered, certified or express mail return receipt requested;

        iv. Depositing with any third-party commercial carrier for delivery to the clerk within three (3) calendar days, cost prepaid, properly addressed;

        v. If the court so permits, filing with the judge, in which event the judge shall note thereon the filing date and forthwith transmit them to the office of the clerk; or

        vi. Electronic filing, as approved by the Division of State Court Administration pursuant to IN ST ADMIN Rule 16. IN ST TRIAL P Rule 5(F).

        vii. Filing by registered or certified mail and by third-party commercial carrier shall be complete upon mailing or deposit. IN ST TRIAL P Rule 5(F).

    b. *Facsimile filing*

        i. *Generally.* In counties where a majority of judges of the courts of record, by posted local rule, have authorized electronic facsimile filing and designated a telephone number to receive such transmissions, pleadings, motions, and other papers may be sent to the Clerk of Circuit Court by electronic facsimile transmission for filing in any case, provided:

            • Such matter does not exceed ten (10) pages, including the cover sheet;

            • Such matter does not require the payment of fees other than the electronic facsimile transcription fee set forth in IN ST ADMIN Rule 12(E);

            • The sending party creates at the time of transmission a machine generated log for such transmission; and

            • The original document and the transmission log are maintained by the sending party for the duration of the litigation. IN ST ADMIN Rule 12(B).

        ii. *Time of filing.* During normal, posted business hours, the time of filing shall be the time the duplicate document is produced in the office of the Clerk of the Circuit Court. Duplicate documents received at all other times shall be filed as of the next normal business day. IN ST ADMIN Rule 12(C).

            • If the receiving fax machine endorses its own time and date stamp upon the transmitted documents and the receiving machine produces a delivery receipt which is electronically created and transmitted to the sending party, the time of filing shall be the date and time recorded on the transmitted document by the receiving fax machine. IN ST ADMIN Rule 12(C).

c. *Proof of filing.* Any party filing any paper by any method other than personal delivery to the clerk shall retain proof of filing. IN ST TRIAL P Rule 5(F).

2. *Service requirements.* Unless otherwise provided by the Indiana Rules of Trial Procedure or an order of the court, each party and special judge, if any, shall be served with: (1) every order required by its terms to be served; (2) every pleading subsequent to the original complaint; (3) every written motion except one which may be heard ex parte; (4) every brief submitted to the trial court; (5) every paper relating to discovery required to be served upon a party; and (6) every written notice, appearance, demand, offer of judgment, designation of record on appeal, or similar paper. IN ST TRIAL P Rule 5(A).

   a. *Methods of service*

      i. *Personal service.* Whenever a party is represented by an attorney of record, service shall be made upon such attorney unless service upon the party himself is ordered by the court. Service upon the attorney or party shall be made by delivering or mailing a copy of the papers to the last known address or where an attorney or party has consented to service by fax or e-mail, as provided in IN ST TRIAL P Rule 3.1(A)(4), by faxing or e-mailing a copy of the documents to the fax number or e-mail address set out in the appearance form or correction as required by IN ST TRIAL P Rule 3.1(E). IN ST TRIAL P Rule 5(B). Delivery of a copy within IN ST TRIAL P Rule 5 means:

         - Offering or tendering it to the attorney or party and stating the nature of the papers being served. Refusal to accept an offered or tendered document is a waiver of any objection to the sufficiency or adequacy of service of that document;

         - Leaving it at his office with a clerk or other person in charge thereof, or if there is no one in charge, leaving it in a conspicuous place therein; or

         - If the office is closed, by leaving it at his dwelling house or usual place of abode with some person of suitable age and discretion then residing therein; or,

         - Leaving it at some other suitable place, selected by the attorney upon whom service is being made, pursuant to duly promulgated local rule. IN ST TRIAL P Rule 5(B)(1).

      ii. *Service by mail.* If service is made by mail, the papers shall be deposited in the United States mail addressed to the person on whom they are being served, with postage prepaid. Service shall be deemed complete upon mailing. Proof of service of all papers permitted to be mailed may be made by written acknowledgment of service, by affidavit of the person who mailed the papers, or by certificate of an attorney. It shall be the duty of attorneys when entering their appearance in a cause or when filing pleadings or papers therein, to have noted in the Chronological Case Summary or said pleadings or papers so filed the address and telephone number of their office. Service by delivery or by mail at such address shall be deemed sufficient and complete. IN ST TRIAL P Rule 5(B)(2).

      iii. *Service by fax or e-mail.* A party who has consented to service by fax or e-mail may be served as follows:

         - Service by e-mail shall be made by attaching the document being served in .pdf format. Discovery documents must also be served in accordance with IN ST TRIAL P Rule 26(A). IN ST TRIAL P Rule 5(B)(3)(a).

         - Service by fax shall be deemed complete upon generation of a transmission record indicating the successful transmission of the entire document, except as provided in IN ST TRIAL P Rule 5(B)(3)(d). IN ST TRIAL P Rule 5(B)(3)(b).

         - Service by e-mail shall be deemed complete upon transmission, except as provided in IN ST TRIAL P Rule 5(B)(3)(d). IN ST TRIAL P Rule 5(B)(3)(c).

         - Service by fax or e-mail that occurs on a Saturday, Sunday, legal holiday, or day the court or agency in which the matter is pending is closed or after 5:00 PM local time of the recipient shall be deemed complete the next day that is not a Saturday, Sunday, legal holiday, or day that the court or agency in which the matter is pending is not closed. IN ST TRIAL P Rule 5(B)(3)(d).

    iv.   *Consent to alternate service.* Any Allen County Attorney or any Allen County law firm may, without charge, maintain an assigned Courthouse box in the library of the Allen County Courthouse for receipt of notices, pleadings, process orders, or other communications from the Court, the Clerk, and other attorneys or law firms. IN ST ALLEN SUPER AND CIR CT CIV Rule 5-1(A). For more information concerning the use of courthouse boxes, refer to IN ST ALLEN SUPER AND CIR CT CIV Rule 5-1.

  b. *Serving numerous defendants.* In any action in which there are unusually large numbers of defendants, the court, upon motion or of its own initiative, may order:

    i.   That service of the pleadings of the defendants and replies thereto need not be made as between the defendants;

- That any cross-claim, counterclaim, or matter constituting an avoidance or affirmative defense contained therein shall be deemed to be denied or avoided by all other parties; and

- That the filing of any such pleading and service thereof upon the plaintiff constitutes due notice of it to the parties. IN ST TRIAL P Rule 5(D).

    ii. A copy of every such order shall be served upon the parties in such manner and form as the court directs. IN ST TRIAL P Rule 5(D).

  c. *Service on parties in default for failure to appear.* No service need be made on parties in default for failure to appear, except that pleadings asserting new or additional claims for relief against them shall be served upon them in the manner provided by service of summons in IN ST TRIAL P Rule 4. IN ST TRIAL P Rule 5(A).

G. Hearings

1. The Indiana rules do not contemplate a hearing related to the pretrial conference.

H. Forms

1. Pretrial Conference, Scheduling, Management Forms for Indiana

  a. Motion for pretrial conference. 5 INPRAC § 5:1.1.

  b. Order for pretrial conference; Attorneys to hold preliminary conference. 5 INPRAC § 5:1.2.

  c. Letter; To arrange preliminary conference of attorneys. 5 INPRAC § 5:1.3.

  d. Letter; Documenting opposing counsel's failure to meet. 5 INPRAC § 5:1.4.

  e. Letter; Request to stipulate to facts and exhibits. 5 INPRAC § 5:1.5.

  f. Notice to court; Failure to stipulate. 5 INPRAC § 5:1.6.

  g. Agenda; Pretrial conference. 5 INPRAC § 5:1.7.

  h. Agenda for pretrial conference; Alternative. 5 INPRAC § 5:1.8.

  i. Preliminary pretrial order. 5 INPRAC § 5:1.9.

  j. Final pretrial order. 5 INPRAC § 5:1.10.

  k. Motion to amend pretrial order. 5 INPRAC § 5:1.11.

  l. Motion to extend discovery cutoff date. 5 INPRAC § 5:1.12.

  m. Motion for pretrial conference. 10 INPRAC § 70.2.

  n. Joint motion for pretrial conference. 10 INPRAC § 70.3.

  o. Order for pretrial conference; Attorneys to hold preliminary conference. 10 INPRAC § 70.4.

  p. Worksheet for preliminary conference of attorneys and pretrial conference. 10 INPRAC § 70.5.

  q. Joint motion for continuance of pretrial conference. 10 INPRAC § 70.6.

  r. Letter attempting to arrange preliminary conference of attorneys. 10 INPRAC § 70.7.

  s. Notice of conference of attorneys. 10 INPRAC § 70.8.

  t. Letter documenting opposing counsel's failure to meet for preliminary conference of attorneys. 10 INPRAC § 70.9.

u. Request that opposing party stipulate to facts and exhibits discovered after conference of attorneys. 10 INPRAC § 70.10.

v. Preliminary pretrial order. 10 INPRAC § 70.14.

w. Final pretrial order. 10 INPRAC § 70.15.

x. Motion to amend pretrial order; General form. 10 INPRAC § 70.16.

y. Motion to amend pretrial order; Party's contentions. 10 INPRAC § 70.17.

z. Motion for sanctions; Failure to attend pretrial conference. 10 INPRAC § 70.22.

2. Official Pretrial Conference, Scheduling, Management Forms for Allen County

a. Consent to alternate service. IN ST ALLEN SUPER AND CIR CT CIV App. A.

b. Final pre-trial order. IN ST ALLEN SUPER AND CIR CT CIV App. C.

I. Checklist

(I) ❑ Matters to be considered for the pretrial conference

    (a) ❑ Documents to consider

        (1) ❑ Exhibits and stipulations

    (b) ❑ Timing

        (1) ❑ Unless otherwise ordered by the court the pretrial conference shall not be called until after reasonable opportunity for the completion of discovery

        (2) ❑ The clerks shall give at least thirty (30) days' notice of the pretrial conference unless otherwise directed by the court

        (3) ❑ Unless otherwise ordered by the court, at least ten (10) days prior to the pretrial conference, attorneys for each of the parties shall meet and confer

(II) ❑ Matters to be considered by the party filing the motion for pretrial conference

    (a) ❑ Required documents

        (1) ❑ Motion and notice

        (2) ❑ Proposed order

        (3) ❑ Certificate of service

    (b) ❑ Supplemental documents

        (1) ❑ Supporting evidence

        (2) ❑ Brief or memorandum

        (3) ❑ Facsimile cover sheet

    (c) ❑ Timing

        (1) ❑ There is no specific timing requirement for filing a motion requesting a pretrial conference

        (2) ❑ A written motion, other than one which may be heard ex parte, and notice of the hearing thereof shall be served not less than five (5) days before the time specified for the hearing, unless a different period is fixed by the Indiana Rules of Trial Procedure or by order of the court

        (3) ❑ All pleadings and papers subsequent to the complaint which are required to be served upon a party shall be filed with the Court either before service or within a reasonable period of time thereafter

HAMILTON COUNTY

Pleadings
Complaint

Document Last Updated October 2013

A. Applicable Rules

1. *State rules*

   a. Commencement of an action. IN ST TRIAL P Rule 3.

   b. Appearance. IN ST TRIAL P Rule 3.1.

   c. Process. IN ST TRIAL P Rule 4.

   d. Service. IN ST TRIAL P Rule 4.1; IN ST TRIAL P Rule 4.2; IN ST TRIAL P Rule 4.3; IN ST TRIAL P Rule 4.4; IN ST TRIAL P Rule 4.5; IN ST TRIAL P Rule 4.6; IN ST TRIAL P Rule 4.7; IN ST TRIAL P Rule 4.8; IN ST TRIAL P Rule 4.9; IN ST TRIAL P Rule 4.10; IN ST TRIAL P Rule 4.11; IN ST TRIAL P Rule 4.12; IN ST TRIAL P Rule 4.13; IN ST TRIAL P Rule 4.14; IN ST TRIAL P Rule 4.15; IN ST TRIAL P Rule 5.

   e. Time. IN ST TRIAL P Rule 6.

   f. Pleadings allowed; Form of motion. IN ST TRIAL P Rule 7.

   g. Rules of pleading. IN ST TRIAL P Rule 8; IN ST TRIAL P Rule 9; IN ST TRIAL P Rule 9.1; IN ST TRIAL P Rule 9.2.

   h. Form of pleading. IN ST TRIAL P Rule 10.

   i. Signing and verification of pleadings. IN ST TRIAL P Rule 11.

   j. Joinder. IN ST TRIAL P Rule 18; IN ST TRIAL P Rule 19.

   k. Jury trial of right. IN ST TRIAL P Rule 38.

   l. Evidence. IN ST TRIAL P Rule 43.

   m. Determination of foreign law. IN ST TRIAL P Rule 44.1.

   n. Judgment on the evidence (directed verdict). IN ST TRIAL P Rule 50.

   o. Findings by the court. IN ST TRIAL P Rule 52.

   p. Summary judgment. IN ST TRIAL P Rule 56.

   q. Motion to correct error. IN ST TRIAL P Rule 59.

   r. Relief from judgment or order. IN ST TRIAL P Rule 60.

   s. Injunctions. IN ST TRIAL P Rule 65.

   t. Trial court and clerks. IN ST TRIAL P Rule 72.

   u. Uniform case numbering system; Access to court records. IN ST ADMIN Rule 8; IN ST ADMIN Rule 9.

   v. Paper size. IN ST ADMIN Rule 11.

   w. Facsimile and electronic transmission. IN ST ADMIN Rule 12; IN ST ADMIN Rule 16.

   x. Alternative dispute resolution. IN ST ADR Rule 1.1; IN ST ADR Rule 1.6; IN ST ADR Rule 8.8.

   y. Manner of service. IN ST 34-33-2-1.

   z. Sealing of certain records by court; Hearing; Notice; Privacy and confidentiality. IN ST 5-2-9-6; IN ST 5-14-3-4; IN ST 6-4.1-5-10; IN ST 5-14-3-5.5; IN ST 6-4.1-12-12; IN ST 6-8.1-7-1; IN ST 11-13-1-8; IN ST 12-23-14-13; IN ST 16-39-3-10; IN ST 16-41-8-1; IN ST 22-4-19-6; IN ST

31-11-1-6; IN ST 31-19-5-23; IN ST 31-19-13-2; IN ST 31-19-19-1; IN ST 31-33-18-1; IN ST 31-39-1-1; IN ST 31-39-1-2; IN ST 33-23-16-16; IN ST 35-34-2-4; IN ST 35-38-1-13; IN ST 35-38-9-1; IN ST ADR Rule 2.11; IN ST ADR Rule 4.4; IN ST ADR Rule 5.6; IN ST JURY Rule 10.

2. *Local rules*

a. Court hours. IN ST HAMILTON ADMIN Rule 101.

b. Facsimile transmissions. IN ST HAMILTON ADMIN Rule 103.

c. Filing of pleadings and entry of appearances. IN ST HAMILTON TRIAL Rule 201.

d. Proposed orders. IN ST HAMILTON TRIAL Rule 202.

e. Special judges. IN ST HAMILTON TRIAL Rule 204.

f. Continuances. IN ST HAMILTON TRIAL Rule 206.

B. Timing

1. *Filing.* A civil action is commenced by filing with the court a complaint or such equivalent pleading or document as may be specified by statute, by payment of the prescribed filing fee or filing an order waiving the filing fee, and, where service of process is required, by furnishing to the clerk as many copies of the complaint and summons as are necessary. IN ST TRIAL P Rule 3. The claimant typically bears the burden of commencing an action within the applicable statute of limitations. 22B INPRAC 3:1; Huff v. Huff, 892 N.E.2d 1241 (Ind.Ct.App. 2008).

2. *Service.* The trial rules require a party to exercise due diligence in securing service of process. 1 INPRAC R 4; Geiger and Peters, Inc. v. American Fletcher Nat. Bank & Trust Co., 428 N.E.2d 1279 (Ind.Ct.App. 1981). If person seeking service of process fails without cause for sixty (60) days or more to provide clerk with required summons for issuance or with other information necessary to effectuate service, person has failed to exercise due diligence in securing service of process. Geiger and Peters, Inc. v. American Fletcher Nat. Bank & Trust Co., 428 N.E.2d 1279, 1281 (Ind.Ct.App. 1981).

3. *Computation of time*

a. *Generally; Days excluded.* In computing any period of time prescribed or allowed by the Indiana Rules of Trial Procedure, by order of the court, or by any applicable statute, the day of the act, event, or default from which the designated period of time begins to run shall not be included. The last day of the period so computed is to be included unless it is:

i. A Saturday,

ii. A Sunday,

iii. A legal holiday as defined by state statute, or

iv. A day the office in which the act is to be done is closed during regular business hours. IN ST TRIAL P Rule 6(A).

b. *Short periods.* In any event, the period runs until the end of the next day that is not a Saturday, a Sunday, a legal holiday, or a day on which the office is closed. When the period of time allowed is less than seven (7) days, intermediate Saturdays, Sundays, legal holidays, and days on which the office is closed shall be excluded from the computations. IN ST TRIAL P Rule 6(A).

c. *Additional time after service by United States mail.* Whenever a party has the right or is required to do some act or take some proceedings within a prescribed period after the service of a notice or other paper upon him and the notice or paper is served upon him by United States mail, three (3) days shall be added to the prescribed period. IN ST TRIAL P Rule 6(E).

d. *Enlargement of time.* When an act is required or allowed to be done at or within a specific time by the Indiana Rules of Trial Procedure, the court may at any time for cause shown:

i. Order the period enlarged, with or without motion or notice, if request therefor is made before the expiration of the period originally prescribed or extended by a previous order; or

ii. Upon motion made after the expiration of the specific period, permit the act to be done where

the failure to act was the result of excusable neglect; but, the court may not extend the time for taking any action for judgment on the evidence under IN ST TRIAL P Rule 50(A), amendment of findings and judgment under IN ST TRIAL P Rule 52(B), to correct errors under IN ST TRIAL P Rule 59(C), statement in opposition to motion to correct error under IN ST TRIAL P Rule 59(E), or to obtain relief from final judgment under IN ST TRIAL P Rule 60(B), except to the extent and under the conditions stated in those rules. IN ST TRIAL P Rule 6(B).

    iii. For information on obtaining a continuance, refer to IN ST HAMILTON TRIAL Rule 206.

C. General Requirements

1. *Pleading, generally*

   a. *Pleadings to be concise.* Each averment of a pleading shall be simple, concise, and direct. No technical forms of pleading or motions are required. All fictions in pleading are abolished. IN ST TRIAL P Rule 8(E)(1).

   b. *Pleading in the alternative.* A pleading may set forth two (2) or more statements of a claim or defense alternatively or hypothetically, either in one (1) count or defense or in separate counts or defenses. When two (2) or more statements are made in the alternative and one (1) of them if made independently would be sufficient, the pleading is not made insufficient by the insufficiency of one or more of the alternative statements. A pleading may also state as many separate claims or defenses as the pleader has regardless of consistency and whether based on legal or equitable grounds. All statements shall be made subject to the obligations set forth in IN ST TRIAL P Rule 11. IN ST TRIAL P Rule 8(E)(2).

   c. *Motions and pleadings, joint and several.* All motions and pleadings of any kind addressed to two (2) or more paragraphs of any pleading, or filed by two (2) or more parties, shall be taken and construed as joint, separate, and several motions or pleadings to each of such paragraphs and by and against each of such parties. All motions or pleadings containing two (2) or more subject-matters shall be taken and construed as separate and several as to each subject-matter. All objections to rulings made by two (2) or more parties shall be taken and construed as the joint, separate, and several objections of each of such parties. IN ST TRIAL P Rule 8(E)(3).

       i. A complaint filed by or against two (2) or more plaintiffs shall be taken and construed as joint, separate, and several as to each of said plaintiffs. IN ST TRIAL P Rule 8(E).

   d. *Construction of pleadings.* All pleadings shall be so construed as to do substantial justice, lead to disposition on the merits, and avoid litigation of procedural points. IN ST TRIAL P Rule 8(F).

2. *Contents of the complaint*

   a. *Pleading for relief; Notice pleading.* Indiana is a "notice pleading" jurisdiction. 22B INPRAC 8:1; State v. American Family Voices, Inc., 898 N.E.2d 293 (Ind. 2008). Notice pleading replaces the technical and complex method of pleading which existed prior to 1970. Notice pleading is grounded in due process of law and must provide a defendant with reasonable notice of the plaintiff's claim or an opponent's defense. 22B INPRAC 8:1; Noblesville Redevelopment Com'n v. Noblesville Associates Ltd. Partnership, 674 N.E.2d 558 (Ind. 1996). Notice pleading does not require that the plaintiff state all elements or facts essential to a cause of action. 22B INPRAC 8:1; State v. American Family Voices, Inc., 898 N.E.2d 293 (Ind. 2008). Instead, the complaint must state "a short and plain statement of the claim" showing an entitlement to relief, and a demand for relief. 22B INPRAC 8:1; Trail v. Boys and Girls Clubs of Northwest Indiana, 845 N.E.2d 130 (Ind. 2006).

   b. *Claims for relief.* To state a claim for relief, whether an original claim, counterclaim, cross-claim, or third-party claim, a pleading must contain:

       i. A short and plain statement of the claim showing that the pleader is entitled to relief, and

       ii. A demand for relief to which the pleader deems entitled. Relief in the alternative or of several different types may be demanded. However, in any complaint seeking damages for personal injury or death, or seeking punitive damages, no dollar amount or figure shall be included in the demand. IN ST TRIAL P Rule 8(A).

   c. *Res ipsa loquitur.* Res ipsa loquitur or a similar doctrine may be pleaded by alleging generally that the facts connected with the action are unknown to the pleader and are within the knowledge of the opposing party. IN ST TRIAL P Rule 9.1(B).

d. *Bona fide purchaser.* When the rights of a person depend upon his status as a bona fide purchaser for value or upon similar requirements, such status must be pleaded and proved by the person asserting it, but it may be pleaded in general terms. Once it is established that the person has given any required value, unless such value is commercially unreasonable, and that he has met any requirements of recordation, filing, possession, or perfection, the trier of fact must find that such value was given or such perfection was made in accordance with any requirements of good faith, lack of knowledge, or lack of notice unless and until evidence is introduced which would support a finding of its non-existence. IN ST TRIAL P Rule 9.1(D).

e. *Presumption; Matters of judicial notice.* Neither presumptions of law nor matters of which judicial notice may be taken need be stated in a pleading. IN ST TRIAL P Rule 9.1(E).

   i. *Presumption of jurisdiction.* Jurisdiction is presumed in Indiana. 22B INPRAC 8:2. Consequently, there is no requirement to affirmatively plead the existence of jurisdiction in the complaint, unless the action involves a special proceeding requiring such an allegation. 22B INPRAC 8:2; Cardinal Industries, Inc. v. Schwartz, 483 N.E.2d 458 (Ind.Ct.App. 1985). The plaintiff bears no burden to prove jurisdiction unless and until it is challenged by the defendant. 22B INPRAC 8:2; Brokemond v. Marshall Field & Co., 612 N.E.2d 143 (Ind.Ct.App. 1993).

f. *Equitable and legal claims in multi-count actions.* In multi-count actions, the inclusion of an equitable claim, standing alone, will not automatically draw the entire action into equity. Something more than the presence of an equitable claim is required, and the court must examine the claims at issue. 22B INPRAC 38:1 COMMENT; Lucas v. U.S. Bank, N.A., 953 N.E.2d 457 (Ind. 2011). Factors the court may consider in evaluating the nature of the underlying substantive claims include: the substance and central character of the complaint, the rights and interests at issue, the relief demanded, and any issues arising out of discovery. 22B INPRAC 38:1 COMMENT; Songer v. Civitas Bank, 771 N.E.2d 61 (Ind. 2002).

3. *Pleading special matters*

   a. *Capacity.* It is not necessary to aver the capacity of a party to sue or be sued, the authority of a party to sue or be sued in a representative capacity, or the legal existence of an organization that is made a party. The burden of proving lack of such capacity, authority, or legal existence shall be upon the person asserting lack of it, and shall be pleaded as an affirmative defense. IN ST TRIAL P Rule 9(A).

   b. *Fraud, mistake, condition of the mind.* In all averments of fraud or mistake, the circumstances constituting fraud or mistake shall be specifically averred. Malice, intent, knowledge, and other conditions of mind may be averred generally. IN ST TRIAL P Rule 9(B).

   c. *Conditions precedent.* In pleading the performance or occurrence of promissory or non-promissory conditions precedent, it is sufficient to aver generally that all conditions precedent have been performed, have occurred, or have been excused. A denial of performance or occurrence shall be made specifically and with particularity, and a denial of excuse generally. IN ST TRIAL P Rule 9(C).

   d. *Official document or act.* In pleading an official document or official act it is sufficient to aver that the document was issued or the act done in compliance with law. IN ST TRIAL P Rule 9(D).

   e. *Judgment.* In pleading a judgment or decision of a domestic or foreign court, judicial or quasi-judicial tribunal, or of a board or officer, it is sufficient to aver the judgment or decision without setting forth matter showing jurisdiction to render it. IN ST TRIAL P Rule 9(E).

   f. *Time and place.* For the purpose of testing the sufficiency of a pleading, averments of time and place are material and shall be considered like all other averments of material matter. However, time and place need be stated only with such specificity as will enable the opposing party to prepare his defense. IN ST TRIAL P Rule 9(F).

   g. *Special damages; Damages where no answer.* When items of special damage are claimed, they shall be specifically stated. The relief granted to the plaintiff, if there be no answer, cannot exceed the relief demanded in his complaint; but, in any other case, the court may grant him any relief consistent with the facts or matters pleaded. IN ST TRIAL P Rule 9(G).

4. *Joinder*

    a. *Of claims.* A party asserting a claim for relief as an original claim, counterclaim, cross-claim, or third-party claim, may join, either as independent or as alternate claims, as many claims, whether legal, equitable, or statutory as he has against an opposing party. IN ST TRIAL P Rule 18(A).

    b. *Of remedies; Fraudulent conveyances.* Whenever a claim is one heretofore cognizable only after another claim has been prosecuted to a conclusion, the two (2) claims may be joined in a single action; but the court shall grant relief in that action only in accordance with the relative substantive rights of the parties. In particular, a plaintiff may state a claim for money and a claim to have set aside a conveyance fraudulent as to him, without first having obtained a judgment establishing the claim for money. IN ST TRIAL P Rule 18(B).

    c. *Of persons needed for just adjudication.* A person who is subject to service of process shall be joined as a party in the action if:

        i. In his absence complete relief cannot be accorded among those already parties; or

        ii. He claims an interest relating to the subject of the action and is so situated that the disposition of the action in his absence may:

            • As a practical matter impair or impede his ability to protect that interest, or

            • Leave any of the persons already parties subject to a substantial risk of incurring double, multiple, or otherwise inconsistent obligations by reason of his claimed interest. IN ST TRIAL P Rule 19(A).

        iii. If he has not been so joined, the court shall order that he be made a party. If he should join as a plaintiff but refuses to do so, he may be made a defendant. IN ST TRIAL P Rule 19(A).

5. *Trial by jury; Demand*

    a. *Causes triable by court and by jury.* Issues of law and issues of fact in causes that prior to the eighteenth day of June, 1852, were of exclusive equitable jurisdiction shall be tried by the court; issues of fact in all other causes shall be triable as the same are now triable. In case of the joinder of causes of action or defenses which, prior to said date, were of exclusive equitable jurisdiction with causes of action or defenses which, prior to said date, were designated as actions at law and triable by jury—the former shall be triable by the court, and the latter by a jury, unless waived; the trial of both may be at the same time or at different times, as the court may direct. IN ST TRIAL P Rule 38(A).

    b. *Demand.* Any party may demand a trial by jury of any issue triable of right by a jury by filing with the court and serving upon the other parties a demand therefor in writing at any time after the commencement of the action and not later than ten (10) days after the first responsive pleading to the complaint, or to a counterclaim, crossclaim or other claim if one properly is pleaded; and if no responsive pleading is filed or required, within ten (10) days after the time such pleading otherwise would have been required. Such demand is sufficient if indorsed upon a pleading of a party filed within such time. IN ST TRIAL P Rule 38(B).

    c. *Same; Specification of issues.* In his demand a party may specify the issues which he wishes so tried; otherwise he shall be deemed to have demanded trial by jury for all issues triable as of right by jury. Any other party must file a demand for jury trial to preserve his right to trial by jury:

        i. Of issues for which a right to trial by jury was not requested by another party; and

        ii. In case a request by another party was improper. But if a proper request for a trial by jury upon issues triable by jury as of right on his behalf is made by any party, such request shall be deemed to have been made on behalf of all parties entitled to a jury trial upon such issues. IN ST TRIAL P Rule 38(C).

    d. *Waiver.* The failure of a party to appear at the trial, and the failure of a party to serve a demand as required by IN ST TRIAL P Rule 38 and to file it as required by IN ST TRIAL P Rule 5(E) constitute waiver by him of trial by jury. A demand for trial by jury made as provided in IN ST TRIAL P Rule 38 may not be withdrawn without the consent of the other party or parties. IN ST TRIAL P Rule 38(D).

        i. The trial court shall not grant a demand for a trial by jury filed after the time fixed in IN ST

TRIAL P Rule 38(B) has elapsed except upon the written agreement of all of the parties to the action, which agreement shall be filed with the court and made a part of the record. If such agreement is filed then the court may, in its discretion, grant a trial by jury in which event the grant of a trial by jury may not be withdrawn except by the agreement of all of the parties. IN ST TRIAL P Rule 38(D).

e. *Arbitration.* Nothing in the Indiana Rules of Trial Procedure shall deny the parties the right by contract or agreement to submit or to agree to submit controversies to arbitration made before or after commencement of an action thereon or deny the courts power to specifically enforce such agreements. IN ST TRIAL P Rule 38(E).

f. *Equitable and legal claims in multi-count actions.* In multi-count actions, the inclusion of an equitable claim, standing alone, will not automatically draw the entire action into equity. Something more than the presence of an equitable claim is required, and the court must examine the claims at issue. 22B INPRAC 38:1 COMMENT; Lucas v. U.S. Bank, N.A., 953 N.E.2d 457 (Ind. 2011). Factors the court may consider in evaluating the nature of the underlying substantive claims include: the substance and central character of the complaint, the rights and interests at issue, the relief demanded, and any issues arising out of discovery. 22B INPRAC 38:1 COMMENT; Songer v. Civitas Bank, 771 N.E.2d 61 (Ind. 2002).

6. *Use of alternative dispute resolution.* Except as provided by the Indiana Rules for Alternative Dispute Resolution, a presiding judge may order any civil or domestic relations proceeding or selected issues in such proceedings referred to mediation, non-binding arbitration or mini-trial. The selection criteria which should be used by the court are defined under the Indiana Rules for Alternative Dispute Resolution. Binding arbitration and a summary jury trial may be ordered only upon the agreement of the parties as consistent with provisions in the Indiana Rules for Alternative Dispute Resolution which address each method. IN ST ADR Rule 1.6. For information on Indiana's ADR process refer to IN ST ADR Rule 1.1 through IN ST ADR Rule 8.8.

D. Documents

1. *Required documents*

   a. *Summons.* Contemporaneously with the filing of the complaint or equivalent pleading, the person seeking service or his attorney shall furnish to the clerk as many copies of the complaint and summons as are necessary. IN ST TRIAL P Rule 4(B).

   b. *Complaint.* Refer to the General Requirements section of this document for information on the contents of a complaint.

   c. *Appearance form.* At the time an action is commenced, the party initiating the proceeding shall file with the clerk of the court an appearance form setting forth the following information:

      i. Name, address and telephone number of the initiating party or parties filing the appearance form;

      ii. Name, address, attorney number, telephone number, FAX number, and e-mail address of any attorney representing the party, as applicable;

      iii. The case type of the proceeding [see IN ST ADMIN Rule 8];

      iv. A statement that the party will or will not accept service by fax or by e-mail from:
      - Other parties and/or
      - The court under IN ST TRIAL P Rule 72(D);

      v. In domestic relations, Uniform Reciprocal Enforcement of Support (URESA), paternity, delinquency, Child in Need of Services (CHINS), guardianship, and any other proceedings in which support may be an issue, the Social Security Identification Number of all family members;

      vi. The caption and case number of all related cases;

      vii. Such additional matters specified by state or local rule required to maintain the information management system employed by the court;

viii. In a proceeding involving a protection from abuse order, a workplace violence restraining order, or a no-contact order, the initiating party shall provide to the clerk a public mailing address for purposes of legal service. The initiating party may use the Attorney General Address Confidentiality program established by statute; and

ix. In a proceeding involving a mental health commitment, except seventy-two (72) hour emergency detentions, the initiating party shall provide the full name of the person with respect to whom commitment is sought and the person's state of residence. In addition, the initiating party shall provide at least one of the following identifiers for the person:

- Date of birth;
- Social Security Number;
- Driver's license number with state of issue and date of expiration;
- Department of Correction number;
- State ID number with state of issue and date of expiration; or
- FBI number. IN ST TRIAL P Rule 3.1; IN ST HAMILTON TRIAL Rule 201(201.30).

2. *Supplemental documents*

a. *Proof of written instrument.* When any pleading allowed by the Indiana Rules of Trial Procedure is founded on a written instrument, the original, or a copy thereof, must be included in or filed with the pleading. Such instrument, whether copied in the pleadings or not, shall be taken as part of the record. When any pleading allowed by the Indiana Rules of Trial Procedure is founded on an account, an Affidavit of Debt, in a form substantially similar to that which is provided in IN ST TRIAL P App. A-2, shall be attached. IN ST TRIAL P Rule 9.2(A).

b. *Notice of intent to use foreign law.* A party who intends to raise an issue concerning the law of a foreign country shall give notice in his pleadings or other reasonable written notice. The court, in determining foreign law, may consider any relevant material or source, including testimony, whether or not submitted by a party or admissible under IN ST TRIAL P Rule 43. The court's determination shall be treated as a ruling on a question of law. It shall be made by the court and not the jury and shall be reviewable. IN ST TRIAL P Rule 44.1(A).

c. *Praecipe.* Affidavits, requests, and any other information relating to the summons and its service as required or permitted by the Indiana Rules of Trial Procedure shall be included in a praecipe attached to or entered upon the summons. Such praecipe shall be deemed to be a part of the summons for purposes of the Indiana Rules of Trial Procedure. Separate or additional summons shall, as provided by the Indiana Rules of Trial Procedure, be issued by the clerk at any time upon proper request of the person seeking service or his attorney. IN ST TRIAL P Rule 4(B).

d. *Facsimile cover sheet.* Any document sent to the Clerk of the Circuit Court by electronic facsimile transmission shall be accompanied by a cover sheet which states the title of the document, case number, number of pages, identity and voice telephone number of the sending party and instructions for filing. The cover sheet shall contain the signature of the attorney or party, pro se, authorizing the filing. IN ST ADMIN Rule 12(D); IN ST HAMILTON ADMIN Rule 103(103.10)(a).

E. Format

1. *Form of pleadings*

a. *Caption; Names of parties.* Every pleading shall contain a caption setting forth the name of the court, the title of the action, the file number, and a designation as in IN ST TRIAL P Rule 7(A). In the complaint the title of the action shall include the names of all the parties, but in other pleadings it is sufficient to state the name of the first party on each side with an appropriate indication of other parties. IN ST TRIAL P Rule 10(A).

b. *Paragraphs; Separate statements.* All averments of a claim or defense shall be made in numbered paragraphs, the contents of each of which shall be limited as far as practicable to a statement of a single set of circumstances, and a paragraph may be referred to by number in all succeeding pleadings. Each claim founded upon a separate transaction or occurrence and each defense other

than denials may be stated in a separate count or defense whenever a separation facilitates the clear presentation of the matters set forth. IN ST TRIAL P Rule 10(B).

c. *Adoption by reference; Exhibits.* Statements in a pleading may be adopted by reference in a different part of the same pleading or in another pleading or in any motion. A copy of any written instrument which is an exhibit to a pleading is a part thereof for all purposes. IN ST TRIAL P Rule 10(C).

d. *Facsimile page limit.* Courts authorize the Hamilton County Clerk of Courts to accept pleadings, motions and other papers by electronic facsimile transmission for filing in any case pending before the Courts, subject to the requirement that The transmission may not exceed ten (10) pages in length including the cover sheet and proposed CCS entry. IN ST HAMILTON ADMIN Rule 103(103.10)(c).

e. *Emergency facsimile filings.* If the filing requires the immediate attention of the Judge, it shall so indicate in bold letters in an accompanying transmittal memorandum. IN ST HAMILTON ADMIN Rule 103(103.10)(f).

f. *Format rules strictly enforced.* All filings shall be in compliance with the Indiana Rules of Trial Procedure. If the documents received are not in proper form, such deficiencies will not be corrected by court personnel. IN ST HAMILTON TRIAL Rule 201(201.70). The Court shall not be required to act on any Motion, Petition or other request for relief unless filed in conformity with the Hamilton County Local Trial and Administrative rules. IN ST HAMILTON TRIAL Rule 202(202.20).

2. *Size of papers for filing.* Effective January 1, 1992, all pleadings, copies, motions and documents filed with any trial court or appellate level court, typed or printed, with the exception of exhibits and existing wills, shall be prepared on eight and one-half by eleven inch (8 1/2" x 11") size paper. IN ST ADMIN Rule 11.

a. *Form.* All documents filed in any Hamilton County Court, with the exception of exhibits and existing wills, shall be prepared on paper measuring eight and one-half by eleven inches (8 1/2" x 11"). IN ST HAMILTON TRIAL Rule 201(201.20).

3. *Signature requirements*

a. *Signature of attorney.* Every pleading or motion of a party represented by an attorney shall be signed by at least one (1) attorney of record in his individual name, whose address, telephone number, and attorney number shall be stated, except that this provision shall not apply to pleadings and motions made and transcribed at the trial or a hearing before the judge and received by him in such form. IN ST TRIAL P Rule 11(A).

    i. The signature of an attorney constitutes a certificate by him that he has read the pleadings; that to the best of his knowledge, information, and belief, there is good ground to support it; and that it is not interposed for delay. IN ST TRIAL P Rule 11(A).

    ii. If a pleading or motion is not signed or is signed with intent to defeat the purpose of the rule, it may be stricken as sham and false and the action may proceed as though the pleading had not been served. IN ST TRIAL P Rule 11(A).

    iii. For a willful violation of IN ST TRIAL P Rule 11 an attorney may be subjected to appropriate disciplinary action. Similar action may be taken if scandalous or indecent matter is inserted. IN ST TRIAL P Rule 11(A).

b. *Signature of unrepresented party.* A party who is not represented by an attorney shall sign his pleading and state his address. IN ST TRIAL P Rule 11(A).

c. *Verification not generally required.* Except when specifically required by rule, pleadings or motions need not be verified or accompanied by affidavit. The rule in equity that the averments of an answer under oath must be overcome by the testimony of two (2) witnesses or of one (1) witness sustained by corroborating circumstances is abolished. IN ST TRIAL P Rule 11(A).

d. *Verification by affirmation or representation.* When in connection with any civil or special statutory proceeding it is required that any pleading, motion, petition, supporting affidavit, or other document of any kind, be verified, or that an oath be taken, it shall be sufficient if the subscriber simply affirms the truth of the matter to be verified by an affirmation or representation. IN ST TRIAL P Rule 11(B).

IN ST TRIAL P Rule 11(B) states that the affirmation or representation should be in substantially the following language: "I (we) affirm, under the penalties for perjury, that the foregoing representation(s) is (are) true. (Signed) _____."

    i. Any person who falsifies an affirmation or representation of fact shall be subject to the same penalties as are prescribed by law for the making of a false affidavit. IN ST TRIAL P Rule 11(B).

e. *Verified pleadings, motions, and affidavits as evidence.* Pleadings, motions and affidavits accompanying or in support of such pleadings or motions when required to be verified or under oath shall be accepted as a representation that the signer had personal knowledge thereof or reasonable cause to believe the existence of the facts or matters stated or alleged therein; and, if otherwise competent or acceptable as evidence, may be admitted as evidence of the facts or matters stated or alleged therein when it is so provided in the Indiana Rules of Trial Procedure, by statute or other law, or to the extent the writing or signature expressly purports to be made upon the signer's personal knowledge. When such pleadings, motions and affidavits are verified or under oath they shall not require other or greater proof on the part of the adverse party than if not verified or not under oath unless expressly provided otherwise by the Indiana Rules of Trial Procedure, statute or other law. Affidavits upon motions for summary judgment under IN ST TRIAL P Rule 56 and in denial of execution under IN ST TRIAL P Rule 9.2 shall be made upon personal knowledge. IN ST TRIAL P Rule 11(C).

4. *Information excluded from public access.* Every document filed in a case shall separately identify information excluded from public access pursuant to IN ST ADMIN Rule 9(G)(1) as follows:

a. Whole documents that are excluded from public access pursuant to IN ST ADMIN Rule 9(G)(1) shall be tendered on light green paper or have a light green coversheet attached to the document, marked "Not for Public Access" or "Confidential." IN ST TRIAL P Rule 5(G)(1).

b. When only a portion of a document contains information excluded from public access pursuant to IN ST ADMIN Rule 9(G)(1), said information shall be omitted [or redacted] from the filed document, and set forth on a separate accompanying document on light green paper conspicuously marked "Not for Public Access" or "Confidential" and clearly designated [or identifying] the caption and number of the case and the document and location within the document to which the redacted material pertains. IN ST TRIAL P Rule 5(G)(2).

c. With respect to documents filed in electronic format, the trial court, by local rule, may provide for compliance with IN ST TRIAL P Rule 5 in manner that separates and protects access to information excluded from public access. IN ST TRIAL P Rule 5(G)(3).

d. IN ST TRIAL P Rule 5(G) does not apply to a record sealed by the court pursuant to IN ST 5-14-3-5.5 or otherwise, nor to records, documents, or information filed in cases to which public access is prohibited pursuant to IN ST ADMIN Rule 9(G). IN ST TRIAL P Rule 5(G)(4).

e. The following information in case records is excluded from public access and is confidential:

    i. Information that is excluded from public access pursuant to federal law;

    ii. Information that is excluded from public access as declared confidential by Indiana statute or other court rule, including without limitation:

- All adoption records created after July 8, 1941, as declared confidential by IN ST 31-19-19-1, et seq., except those specifically declared open by IN ST 31-19-13-2(2);

- All records relating to chancroid, chlamydia, gonorrhea, hepatitis, human immunodeficiency virus (HIV), Lymphogranuloma venereum, syphilis, tuberculosis, as declared confidential by IN ST 16-41-8-1, et seq.;

- All records relating to child abuse as declared confidential by IN ST 31-33-18-1, et seq.;

- All records relating to drug tests as declared confidential by IN ST 5-14-3-4(a)(9);

- Records of grand jury proceedings as declared confidential by IN ST 35-34-2-4;

- Records of juvenile proceedings as declared confidential by IN ST 31-39-1-2, except those specifically open under statute;

- All paternity records created after July 1, 1941 as declared confidential by IN ST 31-14-11-15, IN ST 31-19-5-23, IN ST 31-39-1-1 and IN ST 31-39-1-2 [Editor's note: IN ST 31-14-11-15 was repealed effective May 9, 2013];

- All pre-sentence reports as declared confidential by IN ST 35-38-1-13;

- Written petitions to permit marriages without consent and orders directing the Clerk of Court to issue a marriage license to underage persons, as declared confidential by IN ST 31-11-1-6;

- Only those arrest warrants, search warrants, indictments and informations ordered confidential by the trial judge, prior to return of duly executed service as declared confidential by IN ST 5-14-3-4(b)(1);

- All medical, mental health, or tax records unless determined by law or regulation of any governmental custodian not to be confidential, released by the subject of such records, or declared by a court of competent jurisdiction to be essential to the resolution of litigation as declared confidential by IN ST 16-39-3-10, IN ST 6-4.1-5-10, IN ST 6-4.1-12-12, and IN ST 6-8.1-7-1;

- Personal information relating to jurors or prospective jurors, other than for the use of the parties and counsel, pursuant to IN ST JURY Rule 10;

- Information relating to protection from abuse orders, no-contact orders and workplace violence restraining orders as declared confidential by IN ST 5-2-9-6, et seq.;

- Mediation proceedings pursuant to IN ST ADR Rule 2.11, Mini-Trial proceedings pursuant to IN ST ADR Rule 4.4(C), and Summary Jury Trials pursuant to IN ST ADR Rule 5.6;

- Information in probation files pursuant to the Probation Standards promulgated by the Judicial Conference of Indiana pursuant to IN ST 11-13-1-8(b);

- Information deemed confidential pursuant to the Rules for Court Administered Alcohol and Drug Programs promulgated by the Judicial Conference of Indiana pursuant to IN ST 12-23-14-13;

- Information deemed confidential pursuant to the Problem-Solving Court Rules promulgated by the Judicial Conference of Indiana pursuant to IN ST 33-23-16-16;

- All records of the Department of workforce Development as declared confidential by IN ST 22-4-19-6;

- Information regarding interception of electronic communications that is sealed or deemed confidential as set forth in IN ST 35-33.5-2-1, et seq.

iii. Information excluded from public access by specific court order;

iv. Complete Social Security Numbers of living persons;

v. With the exception of names, information such as addresses, phone numbers, and dates of birth which explicitly identifies:

- Natural persons who are witnesses or victims (not including defendants) in criminal, domestic violence, stalking, sexual assault, juvenile, or civil protection order proceedings, provided that juveniles who are victims of sex crimes shall be identified by initials only;

- Places of residence of judicial officers, clerks and other employees of courts and clerks of court, unless the person or persons about whom the information pertains waives confidentiality;

vi. Complete account numbers of specific assets, loans, bank accounts, credit cards, and personal identification numbers (PINs);

vii. All orders of expungement entered in criminal or juvenile proceedings, orders to restrict access to criminal history information pursuant to IN ST 35-38-5-5.5 or IN ST 35-38-8-5 and records excluded from public access by such orders, and information related to infractions that is excluded from public access pursuant to IN ST 34-28-5-15 or IN ST 34-28-5-16 [Editor's note: IN ST 35-38-5-5.5, IN ST 35-38-8-5 and IN ST 34-28-5-16 were repealed effective July 1, 2013; for information on orders restricting access to criminal history, refer to IN ST 35-38-9-1, et seq.];

viii. All personal notes and e-mail, and deliberative material, of judges, jurors, court staff and judicial agencies, and information recorded in personal data assistants (PDA's) or organizers and personal calendars. IN ST ADMIN Rule 9(G)(1).

5. *Form of the summons*

a. *Required contents of summons.* The summons shall contain:

i. The name and address of the person on whom the service is to be effected;

ii. The name, street address, and telephone number of the court and the cause number assigned to the case;

iii. The title of the case as shown by the complaint, but, if there are multiple parties, the title may be shortened to include only the first named plaintiff and defendant with an appropriate indication that there are additional parties;

iv. The name, address, and telephone number of the attorney for the person seeking service;

v. The time within which the Indiana Rules of Trial Procedure require the person being served to respond, and a clear statement that in case of his failure to do so, judgment by default may be rendered against him for the relief demanded in the complaint. IN ST TRIAL P Rule 4(C).

b. *Additional contents of summons.* The summons may also contain any additional information which will facilitate proper service. IN ST TRIAL P Rule 4(C).

F. Filing and Service Requirements

1. *Filing requirements.* A civil action is commenced by filing with the court a complaint or such equivalent pleading or document as may be specified by statute, by payment of the prescribed filing fee or filing an order waiving the filing fee, and, where service of process is required, by furnishing to the clerk as many copies of the complaint and summons as are necessary. IN ST TRIAL P Rule 3. An action may be commenced by E-filing only in a court which has adopted a pilot project plan approved by the Division of State Court Administration pursuant to IN ST ADMIN Rule 16. IN ST ADMIN Rule 16(F). All pleadings shall be filed with the Hamilton County Clerk with the exception of emergency orders under IN ST TRIAL P Rule 65. IN ST HAMILTON TRIAL Rule 201(201.10).

a. *Filing with the court defined.* The filing of pleadings, motions, and other papers with the court as required by the Indiana Rules of Trial Procedure shall be made by one of the following methods:

i. Delivery to the clerk of the court;

ii. Sending by electronic transmission under the procedure adopted pursuant to IN ST ADMIN Rule 12;

iii. Mailing to the clerk by registered, certified or express mail return receipt requested;

iv. Depositing with any third-party commercial carrier for delivery to the clerk within three (3) calendar days, cost prepaid, properly addressed;

v. If the court so permits, filing with the judge, in which event the judge shall note thereon the filing date and forthwith transmit them to the office of the clerk; or

vi. Electronic filing, as approved by the Division of State Court Administration pursuant to IN ST ADMIN Rule 16. IN ST TRIAL P Rule 5(F).

vii. Filing by registered or certified mail and by third-party commercial carrier shall be complete upon mailing or deposit. IN ST TRIAL P Rule 5(F).

b. *Facsimile filing.* As outlined in IN ST HAMILTON ADMIN Rule 103(103.10),facsimile filing is permitted in the Circuit and Superior Courts of Hamilton County. The Courts authorize the Hamilton County Clerk of Courts to accept pleadings, motions and other papers by electronic facsimile transmission for filing in any case pending before the Courts, subject to the requirements of IN ST

HAMILTON ADMIN Rule 103(103.10). IN ST HAMILTON ADMIN Rule 103(103.10); IN ST HAMILTON TRIAL Rule 201(201.80).

i.   *Generally.* In counties where a majority of judges of the courts of record, by posted local rule, have authorized electronic facsimile filing and designated a telephone number to receive such transmissions, pleadings, motions, and other papers may be sent to the Clerk of Circuit Court by electronic facsimile transmission for filing in any case, provided:

   - Such matter does not exceed ten (10) pages, including the cover sheet;

   - Such matter does not require the payment of fees other than the electronic facsimile transcription fee set forth in IN ST ADMIN Rule 12(E);

   - The sending party creates at the time of transmission a machine generated log for such transmission; and

   - The original document and the transmission log are maintained by the sending party for the duration of the litigation. IN ST ADMIN Rule 12(B); IN ST HAMILTON ADMIN Rule 103(103.10)(d).

   - Legibility of documents and timeliness of filing is the responsibility of the sender. IN ST HAMILTON ADMIN Rule 103(103.10)(g).

   - The Clerk shall accept electronic facsimile transmission filings only if received at the facsimile machine assigned by the Clerk. The telephone number designated to receive such transmission is available at IN ST HAMILTON ADMIN Rule 103(103.40). IN ST HAMILTON ADMIN Rule 103(103.40).

ii. *Time of filing.* During normal, posted business hours, the time of filing shall be the time the duplicate document is produced in the office of the Clerk of the Circuit Court. Duplicate documents received at all other times shall be filed as of the next normal business day. IN ST ADMIN Rule 12(C).

   - If the receiving fax machine endorses its own time and date stamp upon the transmitted documents and the receiving machine produces a delivery receipt which is electronically created and transmitted to the sending party, the time of filing shall be the date and time recorded on the transmitted document by the receiving fax machine. IN ST ADMIN Rule 12(C).

   - Electronic facsimile transmissions will be accepted for filing only during the regular business hours as set forth in IN ST HAMILTON ADMIN Rule 101. Transmissions received by the Hamilton County Clerk after close of business shall be filed effective the next regular business day. IN ST HAMILTON ADMIN Rule 103(103.30).

iii. *Filing fee.* The electronic facsimile transmission will not be accepted for filing if its filing requires the payment of any fee other than the electronic facsimile transcription fee set forth in IN ST HAMILTON ADMIN Rule 103(103.20). IN ST HAMILTON ADMIN Rule 103(103.10)(e).

   - Pursuant to Ordinance adopted by the Hamilton County Board of Commissioners, the Clerk shall collect an electronic facsimile transcription fee of One Dollar ($1.00) per page, to a maximum of Ten Dollars ($10.00) per transmission, for each electronic facsimile transmission accepted for filing with the Hamilton County Circuit and Superior Courts. IN ST HAMILTON ADMIN Rule 103(103.20).

   - The fee shall be assessed against the sending party and shall be paid upon receipt of invoice by that party and at the latest within thirty (30) days of the transmission. In the event the fee is not paid by the sending party within the time limits provided, the court may issue a show-cause order or enter a judgment in the matter. The Clerk may refuse an electronic facsimile transmission from any attorney or pro se litigant who has failed to pay these fees within thirty (30) days. IN ST HAMILTON ADMIN Rule 103(103.20).

iv. *No direct filing with court.* A party shall not send pleadings, motions and other papers by electronic facsimile transmission for filing directly to any Court without that Court's prior approval to do so. IN ST HAMILTON ADMIN Rule 103(103.50).

c. *Filing with special judge.* After a special judge has qualified, a copy of each pleading and Chronological Case Summary entries filed with the Court shall be mailed or delivered to the office of that Special judge by the counsel or pro se litigant with service indicated on the certificate of service. IN ST HAMILTON TRIAL Rule 204(204.20).

d. *Proof of filing.* Any party filing any paper by any method other than personal delivery to the clerk shall retain proof of filing. IN ST TRIAL P Rule 5(F).

2. *Service requirements.* The court acquires jurisdiction over a party or person who under the Indiana Rules of Trial Procedure commences or joins in the action, is served with summons or enters an appearance, or who is subjected to the power of the court under any other law. IN ST TRIAL P Rule 4(A).

a. *Designation of method of service of the summons.* The person seeking service or his attorney may designate the manner of service upon the summons. If not so designated, the clerk shall cause service to be made by mail or other public means provided the mailing address of the person to be served is indicated in the summons or can be determined. If a mailing address is not furnished or cannot be determined or if service by mail or other public means is returned without acceptance, the complaint and summons shall promptly be delivered to the sheriff or his deputy who, unless otherwise directed, shall serve the summons. IN ST TRIAL P Rule 4(D).

b. *Summons and complaint to be served together.* The summons and complaint shall be served together unless otherwise ordered by the court. When service of summons is made by publication, the complaint shall not be published. When jurisdiction over a party is dependent upon service of process by publication or by his appearance, summons and complaint shall be deemed to have been served at the end of the day of last required publication in the case of service by publication, and at the time of appearance in jurisdiction acquired by appearance. Whenever the summons and complaint are not served or published together, the summons shall contain the full, unabbreviated title of the case. IN ST TRIAL P Rule 4(E).

c. *Territorial limits and service under special order*

   i. *Territorial limits of effective service.* Process may be served anywhere within the territorial limits of this state and outside the state as provided in the Indiana Rules of Trial Procedure. IN ST TRIAL P Rule 4.14(A).

   ii. *Service under special order of court.* Upon application of any party the court in which any action is pending may make an appropriate order for service in a manner not provided by the Indiana Rules of Trial Procedure or statutes when such service is reasonably calculated to give the defendant actual knowledge of the proceedings and an opportunity to be heard. IN ST TRIAL P Rule 4.14(B).

d. *Return of service.* The person making service shall promptly make his return upon or attach it to a copy of the summons which shall be delivered to the clerk. The return shall be signed by the person making it, and shall include a statement:

   i. That service was made upon the person as required by law and the time, place, and manner thereof;

   ii. If service was not made, the particular manner in which it was thwarted in terms of fact or in terms of law;

   iii. Such other information as is expressly required by the Indiana Rules of Trial Procedure. IN ST TRIAL P Rule 4.15(A).

3. *Methods of service of the summons and complaint*

a. *In general*

   i. *Methods of service.* Service may be made upon an individual, or an individual acting in a representative capacity, by:

   - Sending a copy of the summons and complaint by registered or certified mail or other public means by which a written acknowledgment of receipt may be requested and obtained to his residence, place of business or employment with return receipt requested and returned showing receipt of the letter; or

- Delivering a copy of the summons and complaint to him personally; or

- Leaving a copy of the summons and complaint at his dwelling house or usual place of abode; or

- Serving his agent as provided by rule, statute or valid agreement. IN ST TRIAL P Rule 4.1(A).

ii. *Copy service to be followed with mail.* Whenever service is made under IN ST TRIAL P Rule 4.1(A)(3) [by leaving a copy at dwelling or usual place of abode] or IN ST TRIAL P Rule 4.1(A)(4) [by service of agent], the person making the service also shall send by first class mail, a copy of the summons without the complaint to the last known address of the person being served, and this fact shall be shown upon the return. IN ST TRIAL P Rule 4.1(B).

iii. *Service by fax or e-mail.* A party who has consented to service by fax or e-mail may be served as follows:

- Service by e-mail shall be made by attaching the document being served in PDF format. Discovery documents must also be served in accordance with IN ST TRIAL P Rule 26(A).

- Service by fax shall be deemed complete upon generation of a transmission record indicating the successful transmission of the entire document, except as provided in IN ST TRIAL P Rule 5(B)(3)(d).

- Service by e-mail shall be deemed complete upon transmission, except as provided in IN ST TRIAL P Rule 5(B)(3)(d).

- Service by fax or e-mail that occurs on a Saturday, Sunday, legal holiday, or day the court or agency in which the matter is pending is closed or after 5:00 PM local time of the recipient shall be deemed complete the next day that is not a Saturday, Sunday, legal holiday, or day that the court or agency in which the matter is pending is not closed. IN ST TRIAL P Rule 5(B)(3).

b. *Service upon infants or incompetents*

i. *Service upon infants.* Service upon an individual known to be an infant shall be made upon his next friend or guardian ad litem, if service is with respect to the same action in which the infant is so represented. If there is no next friend or guardian ad litem, service shall be made upon his court-appointed representative if one is known and can be served within this state. If there is no court-appointed representative, service shall be made upon either parent known to have custody of the infant, or if there is no parent, upon a person known to be standing in the position of custodian or parent. The infant shall also be served if he is fourteen (14) years of age or older. In the event that service, as provided above, is not possible, service shall be made on the infant. IN ST TRIAL P Rule 4.2(A).

ii. *Service upon incompetents.* Service upon an individual who has been adjudged to be of unsound mind, otherwise incompetent or who is believed to be such shall be made upon his next friend or guardian ad litem, if service is with respect to the same action in which the incompetent is so represented. If there is no next friend or guardian ad litem, service shall be made upon his court-appointed representative if one is known and can be served within this state. If there is no court-appointed representative, then upon the named party and also upon a person known to be standing in the position of custodian of his person. IN ST TRIAL P Rule 4.2(B).

iii. *Duty to inform court; Appearance.* Nothing herein is intended to affect the duty of a party to inform the court that a person is an infant or incompetent. An appearance by a court-appointed guardian, next friend or guardian ad litem or his attorney shall correct any defect in service under IN ST TRIAL P Rule 4.2 unless such defect be challenged. IN ST TRIAL P Rule 4.2(C).

c. *Service upon institutionalized persons.* Service of summons upon a person who is imprisoned or restrained in an institution shall be made by delivering or mailing a copy of the summons and complaint to the official in charge of the institution. It shall be the duty of said official to immediately deliver the summons and complaint to the person being served and allow him to make provisions for

COMPLAINT

adequate representation by counsel. The official shall indicate upon the return whether the person has received the summons and been allowed an opportunity to retain counsel. IN ST TRIAL P Rule 4.3.

d. *Service upon individuals whose acts serve as basis for jurisdiction.* A person subject to the jurisdiction of the courts of this state under IN ST TRIAL P Rule 4.4 may be served with summons:

   i. As provided by IN ST TRIAL P Rule 4.1 (service on individuals), IN ST TRIAL P Rule 4.5 (service upon resident who cannot be found or served within the state), IN ST TRIAL P Rule 4.6 (service upon organizations), IN ST TRIAL P Rule 4.9 (in rem actions); or

   ii. The person shall be deemed to have appointed the Secretary of State as his agent upon whom service of summons may be made as provided in IN ST TRIAL P Rule 4.10. IN ST TRIAL P Rule 4.4(B).

e. *Service upon resident who cannot be found or served within the state.* When the person to be served is a resident of this state who cannot be served personally or by agent in this state and either cannot be found, has concealed his whereabouts or has left the state, summons may be served in the manner provided by IN ST TRIAL P Rule 4.9 (summons in in rem actions). IN ST TRIAL P Rule 4.5.

f. *Service upon organizations*

   i. *Persons to be served.* Service upon an organization may be made as follows:

- In the case of a domestic or foreign organization upon an executive officer thereof, or if there is an agent appointed or deemed by law to have been appointed to receive service, then upon such agent. IN ST TRIAL P Rule 4.6(A)(1).

- In the case of a partnership, upon a general partner thereof. IN ST TRIAL P Rule 4.6(A)(2).

- In the case of a state governmental organization upon the executive officer thereof and also upon the Attorney General. IN ST TRIAL P Rule 4.6(A)(3).

- In the case of a local governmental organization, upon the executive thereof and upon the attorney for the local governmental organization. IN ST TRIAL P Rule 4.6(A)(4).

- When, in IN ST TRIAL P Rule 4.6(A)(3) and IN ST TRIAL P Rule 4.6(A)(4), a governmental representative is named as a party in his individual name or in such name along with his official title, then also upon such representative. IN ST TRIAL P Rule 4.6(A)(5).

   ii. *Manner of service.* Service under IN ST TRIAL P Rule 4.6(A) shall be made on the proper person in the manner provided by the Indiana Rules of Trial Procedure for service upon individuals, but a person seeking service or his attorney shall not knowingly direct service to be made at the person's dwelling house or place of abode, unless such is an address furnished under the requirements of a statute or valid agreement, or unless an affidavit on or attached to the summons states that service in another manner is impractical. IN ST TRIAL P Rule 4.6(B).

   iii. *Service at organization's office.* When shown upon an affidavit or in the return, that service upon an organization cannot be made as provided in IN ST TRIAL P Rule 4.6(A) or IN ST TRIAL P Rule 4.6(B), service may be made by leaving a copy of the summons and complaint at any office of such organization located within this state with the person in charge of such office. IN ST TRIAL P Rule 4.6(C).

g. *Summons; Service upon agent named by statute or agreement.* Whenever an agent (other than an agent appointed to receive service for a governmental organization of this state) has been designated by or pursuant to statute or valid agreement to receive service for the person being served, service may be made upon such agent as follows:

   i. If the agent is a governmental organization or officer designated by or pursuant to statute, service shall be made as provided in IN ST TRIAL P Rule 4.10. IN ST TRIAL P Rule 4.7(1).

   ii. If the agent is one other than that described in IN ST TRIAL P Rule 4.7(1), service shall be made upon him as provided in IN ST TRIAL P Rule 4.1 (service upon individuals) or IN ST TRIAL P Rule 4.6 (service upon organizations). If service cannot be made upon such agent, because

329

there is no address furnished as required by statute or valid agreement or his whereabouts in this state are unknown, then his principal shall be deemed to have appointed the Secretary of State as a replacement for the agent and service may be made upon the Secretary of State as provided in IN ST TRIAL P Rule 4.10. IN ST TRIAL P Rule 4.7(2).

h. *Summons; Service of pleadings or summons on Attorney General.* Service of a copy of the summons and complaint or any pleading upon the Attorney General under the Indiana Rules of Trial Procedure or any statute shall be made by personal service upon him, a deputy or clerk at his office, or by mail or other public means to him at such office in the manner provided by IN ST TRIAL P Rule 4.1(A)(1), and by IN ST TRIAL P Rule 4.11 to the extent applicable. IN ST TRIAL P Rule 4.8.

i. *Summons; In rem actions*

   i. *In general.* In any action involving a res situated within this state, service may be made as provided in IN ST TRIAL P Rule 4.9. The court may render a judgment or decree to the extent of its jurisdiction over the res. IN ST TRIAL P Rule 4.9(A).

   ii. *Manner of service.* Service under IN ST TRIAL P Rule 4.9 may be made as follows:

   • By service of summons upon a person or his agent pursuant to the Indiana Rules of Trial Procedure; or

   • By service of summons outside this state in a manner provided by IN ST TRIAL P Rule 4.1 (service upon individuals) or by publication outside this state in a manner provided by IN ST TRIAL P Rule 4.13 (service by publication) or outside this state in any other manner as provided by the Indiana Rules of Trial Procedure; or

   • By service by publication pursuant to IN ST TRIAL P Rule 4.13. IN ST TRIAL P Rule 4.9(A).

j. *Summons; Service upon Secretary of State or other governmental agent.* Whenever, under the Indiana Rules of Trial Procedure or any statute, service is made upon the Secretary of State or any other governmental organization or officer, as agent for the person being served, service may be made upon such agent as provided in IN ST TRIAL P Rule 4.10. IN ST TRIAL P Rule 4.10(A).

   i. The person seeking service or his attorney shall:

   • Submit his request for service upon the agent in the praecipe for summons, and state that the governmental organization or officer is the agent of the person being served;

   • State the address of the person being served as filed and recorded pursuant to a statute or valid agreement, or if no such address is known, then his last known mailing address, and, if no such address is known, then such shall be stated;

   • Pay any fee prescribed by statute to be forwarded together with sufficient copies of the summons, affidavit and complaint, to the agent by the clerk of the court. IN ST TRIAL P Rule 4.10(A)(1).

   ii. Upon receipt thereof the agent shall promptly:

   • Send to the person being served a copy of the summons and complaint by registered or certified mail or by other public means by which a written acknowledgment of receipt may be obtained;

   • Complete and deliver to the clerk an affidavit showing the date of the mailing, or if there was no mailing, the reason therefor;

   • Send to the clerk a copy of the return receipt along with a copy of the summons;

   • File and retain a copy of the return receipt. IN ST TRIAL P Rule 4.10(A)(2).

k. *Summons; Registered or certified mail.* Whenever service by registered or certified mail or other public means by which a return receipt may be requested is authorized, the clerk of the court or a governmental agent under IN ST TRIAL P Rule 4.10 shall send the summons and complaint to the person being served at the address supplied upon the summons, or furnished by the person seeking service. In his return the clerk of the court or the governmental agent shall show the date and place of mailing, a copy of the mailed or electronically-transmitted return receipt if and when received by him showing whether the mailing was accepted or returned, and, if accepted, by whom. The return along with the receipt shall be promptly filed by the clerk with the pleadings and become a part of the record. If a mailing by the clerk of the court is returned without acceptance, the clerk shall reissue the summons and complaint for service as requested, by the person seeking service. IN ST TRIAL P Rule 4.11.

l. *Summons; Service by sheriff or other officer*

    i. *In general.* Whenever service is made by delivering a copy to a person personally or by leaving a copy at his dwelling house or place of employment as provided by IN ST TRIAL P Rule 4.1, summons shall be issued to and served by the sheriff, his deputy, or some person specially or regularly appointed by the court for that purpose. Service shall be effective if made by a person not otherwise authorized by the Indiana Rules of Trial Procedure, but proof of service by such a person must be made by him as a witness or by deposition without allowance of expenses therefor as costs. The person to whom the summons is delivered for service must act promptly and exercise reasonable care to cause service to be made. IN ST TRIAL P Rule 4.12(A).

    ii. *Special service by police officers.* A sheriff, his deputy, or any full-time state or municipal police officer may serve summons in any county of this state if he agrees or has agreed to make the service. When specially requested in the praecipe for summons, the complaint and summons shall be delivered to such officer by the clerk or the attorney for the person seeking service. No agreement with the sheriff or his deputy for such service in the sheriff's own county shall be permitted. In no event shall any expenses agreed upon under this provision be assessed or recovered as costs or affect court costs otherwise imposed for regular service. IN ST TRIAL P Rule 4.12(B).

    iii. *Service in other counties.* A summons may be served in any county in this state. If service is to be made in another county, the summons may be issued by the clerk for service therein to the sheriff of such county or to a person authorized to make service by the Indiana Rules of Trial Procedure. IN ST TRIAL P Rule 4.12(C).

    iv. *Service outside the state.* Personal service, when permitted by the Indiana Rules of Trial Procedure to be made outside the state, may be made there by any disinterested person or by the attorney representing the person seeking such service. The expenses of such person may be assessed as costs only if they are reasonable and if service by mail or other public means cannot be made or is not successful. IN ST TRIAL P Rule 4.12(D).

m. *Summons; Service by publication*

    i. *Praecipe for summons by publication.* In any action where notice by publication is permitted by the Indiana Rules of Trial Procedure or by statute, service may be made by publication. Summons by publication may name all the persons to be served, and separate publications with respect to each party shall not be required. The person seeking such service, or his attorney, shall submit his request therefor upon the praecipe for summons along with supporting affidavits that diligent search has been made that the defendant cannot be found, has concealed his whereabouts, or has left the state, and shall prepare the contents of the summons to be published. The summons shall be signed by the clerk of the court or the sheriff in such manner as to indicate that it is made by his authority. IN ST TRIAL P Rule 4.13(A).

    ii. *Contents of summons by publication.* The summons shall contain the following information:

- The name of the person being sued, and the person to whom the notice is directed, and, if the person's whereabouts are unknown or some or all of the parties are unknown, a statement to that effect;

- The name of the court and cause number assigned to the case;

- The title of the case as shown by the complaint, but if there are multiple parties, the title may be shortened to include only the first named plaintiff and those defendants to be served by publication with an appropriate indication that there are additional parties;

- The name and address of the attorney representing the person seeking service;

- A brief statement of the nature of the suit, which need not contain the details and particulars of the claim. A description of any property, relationship, or other res involved in the action, and a statement that the person being sued claims some interest therein;

- A clear statement that the person being sued must respond within thirty (30) days after the last notice of the action is published, and in case he fails to do so, judgment by default may be entered against him for the relief demanded in the complaint. IN ST TRIAL P Rule 4.13(B).

iii. *Publication of summons.* The summons shall be published three (3) times by the clerk or person making it, the first publication promptly and each two (2) succeeding publications at least seven (7) and not more than fourteen (14) days after the prior publication, in a newspaper authorized by law to publish notices, and published in the county where the complaint or action is filed, where the res is located, or where the defendant resides or where he was known last to reside. If no newspaper is published in the county, then the summons shall be published in the county in this state nearest thereto in which any such paper may be printed, or in a place specially ordered by the court. The person seeking the service or his attorney may designate any qualified newspaper, and if he fails to do so, the selection may be made by the clerk. IN ST TRIAL P Rule 4.13(C).

iv. *By whom made or procured.* Service of summons by publication shall be made and procured by the clerk, by a person appointed by the court for that purpose, or by the clerk or sheriff of another county where publication is to be made. IN ST TRIAL P Rule 4.13(D).

v. *Return.* The clerk or person making the service shall prepare the return and include the following:

- Any supporting affidavits of the printer containing a copy of the summons which was published;

- An information or statement that the newspaper and the publication meet all legal requirements applicable to such publication;

- The dates of publication. IN ST TRIAL P Rule 4.13(E).

- The return and affidavits shall be filed with the pleadings and other papers in the case and shall become a part of the record as provided in the Indiana Rules of Trial Procedure. IN ST TRIAL P Rule 4.13(E).

n. *Service on agent of nonresident corporation.* In an action commenced in a court of general jurisdiction in Indiana by or against any corporation incorporated under the laws of Indiana, in which one (1) or more of the directors of the corporation is: (1) a necessary or proper party; and (2) a nonresident of Indiana; service of summons upon a director for the purpose of obtaining jurisdiction of the person of the director in the action is obtained by serving the summons on the resident agent of the corporation. IN ST 34-33-2-1.

o. *Mail box service.* Pursuant to IN ST TRIAL P Rule 5(B)(1)(d), the Circuit and Superior Courts of Hamilton County hereby designate the "mail boxes" located in the Clerk's order book office for service of pleadings upon attorneys who have such boxes. IN ST HAMILTON TRIAL Rule 201(201.50).

G. Hearings

1. The Indiana rules do not contemplate a hearing regarding the service of the summons and complaint.

H. Forms

1. Official Complaint Forms for Indiana

a. Affidavit of debt. IN ST TRIAL P App. A-2.

b. Appearance by attorney in civil case. IN ST TRIAL P App. B.

2. Complaint Forms for Indiana

a. Caption; Generally. 5 INPRAC § 3:1.1.

b. Caption; Multiple parties. 5 INPRAC § 3:1.2.

   c.   Single count. 5 INPRAC § 3:1.3.

   d.   Multiple counts; Single defendant. 5 INPRAC § 3:1.4.

   e.   Multiple counts; Multiple defendants. 5 INPRAC § 3:1.5.

   f.   Signature; By party. 5 INPRAC § 3:1.6.

   g.   Signature; By attorney. 5 INPRAC § 3:1.7.

   h.   Verification. 5 INPRAC § 3:1.8.

   i.   Individual defendant. 5 INPRAC § 3:2.1.

   j.   Resident agent of corporation. 5 INPRAC § 3:2.2.

   k.   Attorney general. 5 INPRAC § 3:2.3.

   l.   City attorney. 5 INPRAC § 3:2.4.

   m.   Certificate; Personal service. 5 INPRAC § 3:2.5.

   n.   Certificate; First class mail. 5 INPRAC § 3:2.6.

   o.   Certificate; Registered mail. 5 INPRAC § 3:2.7.

   p.   Certificate; Dwelling house. 5 INPRAC § 3:2.8.

   q.   Clerk's certificate of mailing. 5 INPRAC § 3:2.9.

   r.   Clerk's certificate of mailing; Acceptance by defendant. 5 INPRAC § 3:2.10.

   s.   Clerk's return on service of summons by mail; Not accepted by defendant. 5 INPRAC § 3:2.11.

   t.   Sheriff's return; Service of summons. 5 INPRAC § 3:2.12.

   u.   Motion to appoint person to serve process. 5 INPRAC § 3:2.13.

   v.   Published notice; Text. 5 INPRAC § 3:2.14.

   w.   Affidavit of publisher. 5 INPRAC § 3:2.15.

   x.   Clerk's return on service by publication. 5 INPRAC § 3:2.16.

   y.   Complaint; Single count. 9 INPRAC § 2.3.

   z.   Appearance by party initiating action; Form. 9 INPRAC § 6.3.

I. Checklist

  (I)   ❑ Matters to be considered by the plaintiff

    (a)   ❑ Required documents

      (1)   ❑ Summons

      (2)   ❑ Complaint

      (3)   ❑ Appearance form

    (b)   ❑ Supplemental documents

      (1)   ❑ Proof of written instrument

      (2)   ❑ Notice of intent to use foreign law

      (3)   ❑ Praecipe

      (4)   ❑ Facsimile cover sheet

    (c)   ❑ Timing

      (1)   ❑ The claimant typically bears the burden of commencing an action within the applicable statute of limitations

      (2)   ❑ If person seeking service of process fails without cause for sixty (60) days or more to provide clerk with required summons for issuance or with other information necessary to effectuate service, person has failed to exercise due diligence in securing service of process

(II) ❑ Matters to be considered by the defendant

    (a) ❑ Required documents

        (1) ❑ Answer

        (2) ❑ Appearance form

        (3) ❑ Certificate of service

    (b) ❑ Supplemental documents

        (1) ❑ Admission of service

        (2) ❑ Proof of written instrument

        (3) ❑ Notice of intent to use foreign law

        (4) ❑ Facsimile cover sheet

    (c) ❑ Timing

        (1) ❑ A responsive pleading required under the Indiana Rules of Trial Procedure, shall be served within twenty (20) days after service of the prior pleading

        (2) ❑ The service of a motion permitted under IN ST TRIAL P Rule 12 alters the time for service of responsive pleadings as follows, unless a different time is fixed by the court:

            (i) ❑ If the court does not grant the motion, the responsive pleading shall be served in ten (10) days after notice of the court's action;

            (ii) ❑ If the court grants the motion and the corrective action is allowed to be taken, it shall be taken within ten (10) days, and the responsive pleading shall be served within ten (10) days thereafter

        (3) ❑ All pleadings and papers subsequent to the complaint which are required to be served upon a party shall be filed with the Court either before service or within a reasonable period of time thereafter

Pleadings
Amended Complaint

Document Last Updated October 2013

A. Applicable Rules

1. *State rules*

    a. Appearance. IN ST TRIAL P Rule 3.1.

    b. Process. IN ST TRIAL P Rule 4.

    c. Service of the summons. IN ST TRIAL P Rule 4.1; IN ST TRIAL P Rule 4.2; IN ST TRIAL P Rule 4.3; IN ST TRIAL P Rule 4.4; IN ST TRIAL P Rule 4.5; IN ST TRIAL P Rule 4.6; IN ST TRIAL P Rule 4.7; IN ST TRIAL P Rule 4.8; IN ST TRIAL P Rule 4.9; IN ST TRIAL P Rule 4.10; IN ST TRIAL P Rule 4.11; IN ST TRIAL P Rule 4.12; IN ST TRIAL P Rule 4.13; IN ST TRIAL P Rule 4.14; IN ST TRIAL P Rule 4.15; IN ST 34-33-2-1.

    d. Service and filing of pleadings and other papers. IN ST TRIAL P Rule 5.

    e. Time. IN ST TRIAL P Rule 6.

    f. Pleadings. IN ST TRIAL P Rule 7; IN ST TRIAL P Rule 8; IN ST TRIAL P Rule 9; IN ST TRIAL P Rule 9.1; IN ST TRIAL P Rule 9.2; IN ST TRIAL P Rule 10.

    g. Signing and verification of pleadings. IN ST TRIAL P Rule 11.

    h. Amended and supplemental pleadings. IN ST TRIAL P Rule 15.

    i. Joinder. IN ST TRIAL P Rule 18; IN ST TRIAL P Rule 19.

    j. Evidence. IN ST TRIAL P Rule 43.

    k.   Determination of foreign law. IN ST TRIAL P Rule 44.1.

    l.   Judgment on the evidence (directed verdict). IN ST TRIAL P Rule 50.

    m.   Findings by the court. IN ST TRIAL P Rule 52.

    n.   Summary judgment. IN ST TRIAL P Rule 56.

    o.   Motion to correct error. IN ST TRIAL P Rule 59.

    p.   Relief from judgment or order. IN ST TRIAL P Rule 60.

    q.   Access to court records. IN ST ADMIN Rule 9.

    r.   Paper size. IN ST ADMIN Rule 11.

    s.   Facsimile transmission. IN ST ADMIN Rule 12.

    t.   Electronic filing and electronic service pilot projects. IN ST ADMIN Rule 16.

    u.   Sealing of certain records by court; Hearing; Notice. IN ST 5-14-3-5.5.

    v.   Privacy and confidentiality. IN ST 5-2-9-6; IN ST 5-14-3-4; IN ST 6-4.1-5-10; IN ST 6-4.1-12-12; IN ST 6-8.1-7-1; IN ST 11-13-1-8; IN ST 12-23-14-13; IN ST 16-39-3-10; IN ST 16-41-8-1; IN ST 22-4-19-6; IN ST 31-11-1-6; IN ST 31-19-5-23; IN ST 31-19-13-2; IN ST 31-19-19-1; IN ST 31-33-18-1; IN ST 31-39-1-1; IN ST 31-39-1-2; IN ST 33-23-16-16; IN ST 35-34-2-4; IN ST 35-38-1-13; IN ST 35-38-9-1; IN ST ADR Rule 2.11; IN ST ADR Rule 4.4; IN ST ADR Rule 5.6; IN ST JURY Rule 10.

2. *Local rules*

    a.   Court hours. IN ST HAMILTON ADMIN Rule 101.

    b.   Facsimile transmissions. IN ST HAMILTON ADMIN Rule 103.

    c.   Filing of pleadings and entry of appearances. IN ST HAMILTON TRIAL Rule 201.

    d.   Proposed orders. IN ST HAMILTON TRIAL Rule 202.

    e.   Special judges. IN ST HAMILTON TRIAL Rule 204.

    f.   Continuances. IN ST HAMILTON TRIAL Rule 206.

B. Timing

1. *Filing an amended pleading*

    a.   *As a matter of course.* A party may amend his pleading once as a matter of course at any time before a responsive pleading is served or, if the pleading is one to which no responsive pleading is permitted, and the action has not been placed upon the trial calendar, he may so amend it at any time within thirty (30) days after it is served. IN ST TRIAL P Rule 15(A).

    b.   *With leave of court.* Otherwise a party may amend his pleading only by leave of court or by written consent of the adverse party; and leave shall be given when justice so requires. IN ST TRIAL P Rule 15(A). Refer to the Indiana KeyRules Motion for Leave to Amend document for more information.

2. *Computation of time*

    a.   *Generally; Days excluded.* In computing any period of time prescribed or allowed by the Indiana Rules of Trial Procedure, by order of the court, or by any applicable statute, the day of the act, event, or default from which the designated period of time begins to run shall not be included. The last day of the period so computed is to be included unless it is:

        i.   A Saturday,

        ii.   A Sunday,

        iii.   A legal holiday as defined by state statute, or

        iv.   A day the office in which the act is to be done is closed during regular business hours. IN ST TRIAL P Rule 6(A).

    b.   *Short periods.* In any event, the period runs until the end of the next day that is not a Saturday, a Sunday, a legal holiday, or a day on which the office is closed. When the period of time allowed is

less than seven (7) days, intermediate Saturdays, Sundays, legal holidays, and days on which the office is closed shall be excluded from the computations. IN ST TRIAL P Rule 6(A).

c.   *Additional time after service by United States mail.* Whenever a party has the right or is required to do some act or take some proceedings within a prescribed period after the service of a notice or other paper upon him and the notice or paper is served upon him by United States mail, three (3) days shall be added to the prescribed period. IN ST TRIAL P Rule 6(E).

d.   *Enlargement of time.* When an act is required or allowed to be done at or within a specific time by the Indiana Rules of Trial Procedure, the court may at any time for cause shown:

    i.   Order the period enlarged, with or without motion or notice, if request therefor is made before the expiration of the period originally prescribed or extended by a previous order; or

    ii.   Upon motion made after the expiration of the specific period, permit the act to be done where the failure to act was the result of excusable neglect; but, the court may not extend the time for taking any action for judgment on the evidence under IN ST TRIAL P Rule 50(A), amendment of findings and judgment under IN ST TRIAL P Rule 52(B), to correct errors under IN ST TRIAL P Rule 59(C), statement in opposition to motion to correct error under IN ST TRIAL P Rule 59(E), or to obtain relief from final judgment under IN ST TRIAL P Rule 60(B), except to the extent and under the conditions stated in those rules. IN ST TRIAL P Rule 6(B).

    iii.   For information on obtaining a continuance, refer to IN ST HAMILTON TRIAL Rule 206.

C.   General Requirements

1.   *Amending pleadings.* The purpose of an amended pleading is to include matters that occurred before the filing of the original pleading but which were either overlooked by the pleader or unknown to him at the time. It is a substitute for the original and relates to the facts that existed when the original pleading was filed. An amended pleading supercedes the original as to those portions amended. 10 INPRAC § 46.1.

a.   *Amendments liberally allowed.* Amendments to pleadings are to be liberally allowed in order that all issues are presented in one action. 10 INPRAC § 46.1; Pinnacle Media, LLC v. Metropolitan Dev. Com'n of Marion County, 868 N.E.2d 894 (Ind.Ct.App. 2007).

b.   *Amendments to conform to the evidence.* When issues not raised by the pleadings are tried by express or implied consent of the parties, they shall be treated in all respects as if they had been raised in the pleadings. Such amendment of the pleadings as may be necessary to cause them to conform to the evidence and to raise these issues may be made upon motion of any party at any time, even after judgment, but failure so to amend does not affect the result of the trial of these issues. If evidence is objected to at the trial on the ground that it is not within the issues made by the pleadings, the court may allow the pleadings to be amended and shall do so freely when the presentation of the merits of the action will be subserved thereby and the objecting party fails to satisfy the court that the admission of such evidence would prejudice him in maintaining his action or defense upon the merits. The court may grant a continuance to enable the objecting party to meet such evidence. IN ST TRIAL P Rule 15(B).

c.   *Relation back of amendments*

    i.   Whenever the claim or defense asserted in the amended pleading arose out of the conduct, transaction, or occurrence set forth or attempted to be set forth in the original pleading, the amendment relates back to the date of the original pleading. An amendment changing the party against whom a claim is asserted relates back if the foregoing provision is satisfied and, within one hundred and twenty (120) days of commencement of the action, the party to be brought in by amendment:

      •   Has received such notice of the institution of the action that he will not be prejudiced in maintaining his defense on the merits; and

      •   Knew or should have known that but for a mistake concerning the identity of the proper party, the action would have been brought against him. IN ST TRIAL P Rule 15(C).

ii. The requirement of IN ST TRIAL P Rule 15(C)(1) and IN ST TRIAL P Rule 15(C)(2) with respect to a governmental organization to be brought into the action as defendant is satisfied:

- In the case of a state or governmental organization by delivery or mailing of process to the attorney general or to a governmental executive [IN ST TRIAL P Rule 4.6(A)(3)]; or

- In the case of a local governmental organization, by delivery or mailing of process to its attorney as provided by statute, to a governmental executive thereof [IN ST TRIAL P Rule 4.6(A)(4)], or to the officer holding the office if suit is against the officer or an office. IN ST TRIAL P Rule 15(C).

d. *Amendment by leave.* Amendments, other than an amendment by right, may be made only by leave of court or by written consent of the opposing party. 2 INPRAC R 15(15.2). Refer to the Indiana KeyRules Motion for Leave to Amend document for more information on amending with leave of court.

2. *Pleading, generally*

a. *Pleadings to be concise.* Each averment of a pleading shall be simple, concise, and direct. No technical forms of pleading or motions are required. All fictions in pleading are abolished. IN ST TRIAL P Rule 8(E)(1).

b. *Pleading in the alternative.* A pleading may set forth two (2) or more statements of a claim or defense alternatively or hypothetically, either in one (1) count or defense or in separate counts or defenses. When two (2) or more statements are made in the alternative and one (1) of them if made independently would be sufficient, the pleading is not made insufficient by the insufficiency of one or more of the alternative statements. A pleading may also state as many separate claims or defenses as the pleader has regardless of consistency and whether based on legal or equitable grounds. All statements shall be made subject to the obligations set forth in IN ST TRIAL P Rule 11. IN ST TRIAL P Rule 8(E)(2).

c. *Motions and pleadings, joint and several.* All motions and pleadings of any kind addressed to two (2) or more paragraphs of any pleading, or filed by two (2) or more parties, shall be taken and construed as joint, separate, and several motions or pleadings to each of such paragraphs and by and against each of such parties. All motions or pleadings containing two (2) or more subject-matters shall be taken and construed as separate and several as to each subject-matter. All objections to rulings made by two (2) or more parties shall be taken and construed as the joint, separate, and several objections of each of such parties. IN ST TRIAL P Rule 8(E)(3).

i. A complaint filed by or against two (2) or more plaintiffs shall be taken and construed as joint, separate, and several as to each of said plaintiffs. IN ST TRIAL P Rule 8(E).

d. *Construction of pleadings.* All pleadings shall be so construed as to do substantial justice, lead to disposition on the merits, and avoid litigation of procedural points. IN ST TRIAL P Rule 8(F).

3. *Contents of the complaint*

a. *Pleading for relief; Notice pleading.* Indiana is a "notice pleading" jurisdiction. 22B INPRAC 8:1; State v. American Family Voices, Inc., 898 N.E.2d 293 (Ind. 2008). Notice pleading replaces the technical and complex method of pleading which existed prior to 1970. Notice pleading is grounded in due process of law and must provide a defendant with reasonable notice of the plaintiff's claim or an opponent's defense. 22B INPRAC 8:1; Noblesville Redevelopment Com'n v. Noblesville Associates Ltd. Partnership, 674 N.E.2d 558 (Ind. 1996). Notice pleading does not require that the plaintiff state all elements or facts essential to a cause of action. 22B INPRAC 8:1; State v. American Family Voices, Inc., 898 N.E.2d 293 (Ind. 2008). Instead, the complaint must state "a short and plain statement of the claim" showing an entitlement to relief, and a demand for relief. 22B INPRAC 8:1; Trail v. Boys and Girls Clubs of Northwest Indiana, 845 N.E.2d 130 (Ind. 2006).

b. *Claims for relief.* To state a claim for relief, whether an original claim, counterclaim, cross-claim, or third-party claim, a pleading must contain:

i. A short and plain statement of the claim showing that the pleader is entitled to relief, and

ii. A demand for relief to which the pleader deems entitled. Relief in the alternative or of several different types may be demanded. However, in any complaint seeking damages for personal injury or death, or seeking punitive damages, no dollar amount or figure shall be included in the demand. IN ST TRIAL P Rule 8(A).

c. *Res ipsa loquitur.* Res ipsa loquitur or a similar doctrine may be pleaded by alleging generally that the facts connected with the action are unknown to the pleader and are within the knowledge of the opposing party. IN ST TRIAL P Rule 9.1(B).

d. *Bona fide purchaser.* When the rights of a person depend upon his status as a bona fide purchaser for value or upon similar requirements, such status must be pleaded and proved by the person asserting it, but it may be pleaded in general terms. Once it is established that the person has given any required value, unless such value is commercially unreasonable, and that he has met any requirements of recordation, filing, possession, or perfection, the trier of fact must find that such value was given or such perfection was made in accordance with any requirements of good faith, lack of knowledge, or lack of notice unless and until evidence is introduced which would support a finding of its non-existence. IN ST TRIAL P Rule 9.1(D).

e. *Presumption; Matters of judicial notice.* Neither presumptions of law nor matters of which judicial notice may be taken need be stated in a pleading. IN ST TRIAL P Rule 9.1(E).

   i. *Presumption of jurisdiction.* Jurisdiction is presumed in Indiana. 22B INPRAC 8:2. Consequently, there is no requirement to affirmatively plead the existence of jurisdiction in the complaint, unless the action involves a special proceeding requiring such an allegation. 22B INPRAC 8:2; Cardinal Industries, Inc. v. Schwartz, 483 N.E.2d 458 (Ind.Ct.App. 1985). The plaintiff bears no burden to prove jurisdiction unless and until it is challenged by the defendant. 22B INPRAC 8:2; Brokemond v. Marshall Field & Co., 612 N.E.2d 143 (Ind.Ct.App. 1993).

f. *Equitable and legal claims in multi-count actions.* In multi-count actions, the inclusion of an equitable claim, standing alone, will not automatically draw the entire action into equity. Something more than the presence of an equitable claim is required, and the court must examine the claims at issue. 22B INPRAC 38:1 COMMENT; Lucas v. U.S. Bank, N.A., 953 N.E.2d 457 (Ind. 2011). Factors the court may consider in evaluating the nature of the underlying substantive claims include: the substance and central character of the complaint, the rights and interests at issue, the relief demanded, and any issues arising out of discovery. 22B INPRAC 38:1 COMMENT; Songer v. Civitas Bank, 771 N.E.2d 61 (Ind. 2002).

4. *Pleading special matters*

   a. *Capacity.* It is not necessary to aver the capacity of a party to sue or be sued, the authority of a party to sue or be sued in a representative capacity, or the legal existence of an organization that is made a party. The burden of proving lack of such capacity, authority, or legal existence shall be upon the person asserting lack of it, and shall be pleaded as an affirmative defense. IN ST TRIAL P Rule 9(A).

   b. *Fraud, mistake, condition of the mind.* In all averments of fraud or mistake, the circumstances constituting fraud or mistake shall be specifically averred. Malice, intent, knowledge, and other conditions of mind may be averred generally. IN ST TRIAL P Rule 9(B).

   c. *Conditions precedent.* In pleading the performance or occurrence of promissory or non-promissory conditions precedent, it is sufficient to aver generally that all conditions precedent have been performed, have occurred, or have been excused. A denial of performance or occurrence shall be made specifically and with particularity, and a denial of excuse generally. IN ST TRIAL P Rule 9(C).

   d. *Official document or act.* In pleading an official document or official act it is sufficient to aver that the document was issued or the act done in compliance with law. IN ST TRIAL P Rule 9(D).

   e. *Judgment.* In pleading a judgment or decision of a domestic or foreign court, judicial or quasi-judicial tribunal, or of a board or officer, it is sufficient to aver the judgment or decision without setting forth matter showing jurisdiction to render it. IN ST TRIAL P Rule 9(E).

   f. *Time and place.* For the purpose of testing the sufficiency of a pleading, averments of time and place are material and shall be considered like all other averments of material matter. However, time and place need be stated only with such specificity as will enable the opposing party to prepare his defense. IN ST TRIAL P Rule 9(F).

g. *Special damages; Damages where no answer.* When items of special damage are claimed, they shall be specifically stated. The relief granted to the plaintiff, if there be no answer, cannot exceed the relief demanded in his complaint; but, in any other case, the court may grant him any relief consistent with the facts or matters pleaded. IN ST TRIAL P Rule 9(G).

5. *Joinder*

a. *Of claims.* A party asserting a claim for relief as an original claim, counterclaim, cross-claim, or third-party claim, may join, either as independent or as alternate claims, as many claims, whether legal, equitable, or statutory as he has against an opposing party. IN ST TRIAL P Rule 18(A).

b. *Of remedies; Fraudulent conveyances.* Whenever a claim is one heretofore cognizable only after another claim has been prosecuted to a conclusion, the two (2) claims may be joined in a single action; but the court shall grant relief in that action only in accordance with the relative substantive rights of the parties. In particular, a plaintiff may state a claim for money and a claim to have set aside a conveyance fraudulent as to him, without first having obtained a judgment establishing the claim for money. IN ST TRIAL P Rule 18(B).

c. *Of persons needed for just adjudication.* A person who is subject to service of process shall be joined as a party in the action if:

   i. In his absence complete relief cannot be accorded among those already parties; or

   ii. He claims an interest relating to the subject of the action and is so situated that the disposition of the action in his absence may:

   - As a practical matter impair or impede his ability to protect that interest, or

   - Leave any of the persons already parties subject to a substantial risk of incurring double, multiple, or otherwise inconsistent obligations by reason of his claimed interest. IN ST TRIAL P Rule 19(A).

   iii. If he has not been so joined, the court shall order that he be made a party. If he should join as a plaintiff but refuses to do so, he may be made a defendant. IN ST TRIAL P Rule 19(A).

6. *Trial by jury; Demand*

a. *Causes triable by court and by jury.* Issues of law and issues of fact in causes that prior to the eighteenth day of June, 1852, were of exclusive equitable jurisdiction shall be tried by the court; issues of fact in all other causes shall be triable as the same are now triable. In case of the joinder of causes of action or defenses which, prior to said date, were of exclusive equitable jurisdiction with causes of action or defenses which, prior to said date, were designated as actions at law and triable by jury—the former shall be triable by the court, and the latter by a jury, unless waived; the trial of both may be at the same time or at different times, as the court may direct. IN ST TRIAL P Rule 38(A).

b. *Demand.* Any party may demand a trial by jury of any issue triable of right by a jury by filing with the court and serving upon the other parties a demand therefor in writing at any time after the commencement of the action and not later than ten (10) days after the first responsive pleading to the complaint, or to a counterclaim, crossclaim or other claim if one properly is pleaded; and if no responsive pleading is filed or required, within ten (10) days after the time such pleading otherwise would have been required. Such demand is sufficient if indorsed upon a pleading of a party filed within such time. IN ST TRIAL P Rule 38(B).

c. *Same; Specification of issues.* In his demand a party may specify the issues which he wishes so tried; otherwise he shall be deemed to have demanded trial by jury for all issues triable as of right by jury. Any other party must file a demand for jury trial to preserve his right to trial by jury:

   i. Of issues for which a right to trial by jury was not requested by another party; and

   ii. In case a request by another party was improper. But if a proper request for a trial by jury upon issues triable by jury as of right on his behalf is made by any party, such request shall be deemed to have been made on behalf of all parties entitled to a jury trial upon such issues. IN ST TRIAL P Rule 38(C).

d. *Waiver.* The failure of a party to appear at the trial, and the failure of a party to serve a demand as required by IN ST TRIAL P Rule 38 and to file it as required by IN ST TRIAL P Rule 5(E) constitute waiver by him of trial by jury. A demand for trial by jury made as provided in IN ST TRIAL P Rule 38 may not be withdrawn without the consent of the other party or parties. IN ST TRIAL P Rule 38(D).

   i. The trial court shall not grant a demand for a trial by jury filed after the time fixed in IN ST TRIAL P Rule 38(B) has elapsed except upon the written agreement of all of the parties to the action, which agreement shall be filed with the court and made a part of the record. If such agreement is filed then the court may, in its discretion, grant a trial by jury in which event the grant of a trial by jury may not be withdrawn except by the agreement of all of the parties. IN ST TRIAL P Rule 38(D).

e. *Arbitration.* Nothing in the Indiana Rules of Trial Procedure shall deny the parties the right by contract or agreement to submit or to agree to submit controversies to arbitration made before or after commencement of an action thereon or deny the courts power to specifically enforce such agreements. IN ST TRIAL P Rule 38(E).

D. Documents

1. *Required documents*

a. *Amended complaint.* Refer to the General Requirements section of this document for information on the contents of an amended complaint.

b. *Certificate of service.* An attorney or unrepresented party tendering a document to the Clerk for filing shall certify that service has been made, list the parties served, and specify the date and means of service. The certificate of service shall be placed at the end of the document and shall not be separately filed. The separate filing of a certificate of service, however, shall not be grounds for rejecting a document for filing. The Clerk may permit documents to be filed without a certificate of service but shall require prompt filing of a separate certificate of service. IN ST TRIAL P Rule 5(C).

   i. All pleadings filed with the Court which require a certificate of service shall specifically name the individual party or attorney on whom service has been made, the address, the manner in which service was made and the date when service was made. IN ST HAMILTON TRIAL Rule 201(201.60).

2. *Supplemental documents*

a. *Proof of written instrument.* When any pleading allowed by the Indiana Rules of Trial Procedure is founded on a written instrument, the original, or a copy thereof, must be included in or filed with the pleading. Such instrument, whether copied in the pleadings or not, shall be taken as part of the record. When any pleading allowed by the Indiana Rules of Trial Procedure is founded on an account, an Affidavit of Debt, in a form substantially similar to that which is provided in IN ST TRIAL P App. A-2, shall be attached. IN ST TRIAL P Rule 9.2(A).

b. *Notice of intent to use foreign law.* A party who intends to raise an issue concerning the law of a foreign country shall give notice in his pleadings or other reasonable written notice. The court, in determining foreign law, may consider any relevant material or source, including testimony, whether or not submitted by a party or admissible under IN ST TRIAL P Rule 43. The court's determination shall be treated as a ruling on a question of law. It shall be made by the court and not the jury and shall be reviewable. IN ST TRIAL P Rule 44.1(A).

c. *Facsimile cover sheet.* Any document sent to the Clerk of the Circuit Court by electronic facsimile transmission shall be accompanied by a cover sheet which states the title of the document, case number, number of pages, identity and voice telephone number of the sending party and instructions for filing. The cover sheet shall contain the signature of the attorney or party, pro se, authorizing the filing. IN ST ADMIN Rule 12(D); IN ST HAMILTON ADMIN Rule 103(103.10)(a).

3. Refer to the Indiana KeyRules Complaint document for the required and supplemental documents for filing and serving an amended complaint against a new party.

E. Format

1. *Form of pleadings*

a. *Caption; Names of parties.* Every pleading shall contain a caption setting forth the name of the court, the title of the action, the file number, and a designation as in IN ST TRIAL P Rule 7(A). In the complaint the title of the action shall include the names of all the parties, but in other pleadings it is sufficient to state the name of the first party on each side with an appropriate indication of other parties. IN ST TRIAL P Rule 10(A).

b. *Paragraphs; Separate statements.* All averments of a claim or defense shall be made in numbered paragraphs, the contents of each of which shall be limited as far as practicable to a statement of a single set of circumstances, and a paragraph may be referred to by number in all succeeding pleadings. Each claim founded upon a separate transaction or occurrence and each defense other than denials may be stated in a separate count or defense whenever a separation facilitates the clear presentation of the matters set forth. IN ST TRIAL P Rule 10(B).

c. *Adoption by reference; Exhibits.* Statements in a pleading may be adopted by reference in a different part of the same pleading or in another pleading or in any motion. A copy of any written instrument which is an exhibit to a pleading is a part thereof for all purposes. IN ST TRIAL P Rule 10(C).

d. *Facsimile page limit.* Courts authorize the Hamilton County Clerk of Courts to accept pleadings, motions and other papers by electronic facsimile transmission for filing in any case pending before the Courts, subject to the requirement that The transmission may not exceed ten (10) pages in length including the cover sheet and proposed CCS entry. IN ST HAMILTON ADMIN Rule 103(103.10)(c).

e. *Emergency facsimile filings.* If the filing requires the immediate attention of the Judge, it shall so indicate in bold letters in an accompanying transmittal memorandum. IN ST HAMILTON ADMIN Rule 103(103.10)(f).

f. *Special judge heading.* After a special judge is selected, the attorneys or pro se litigants shall add to the caption of all pleadings to the right of the case title the following: "BEFORE SPECIAL JUDGE _____." IN ST HAMILTON TRIAL Rule 204(204.10).

g. *Format rules strictly enforced.* All filings shall be in compliance with the Indiana Rules of Trial Procedure. If the documents received are not in proper form, such deficiencies will not be corrected by court personnel. IN ST HAMILTON TRIAL Rule 201(201.70). The Court shall not be required to act on any Motion, Petition or other request for relief unless filed in conformity with the Hamilton County Local Trial and Administrative rules. IN ST HAMILTON TRIAL Rule 202(202.20).

2. *Size of papers for filing.* Effective January 1, 1992, all pleadings, copies, motions and documents filed with any trial court or appellate level court, typed or printed, with the exception of exhibits and existing wills, shall be prepared on eight and one-half by eleven inch (8 1/2" x 11") size paper. IN ST ADMIN Rule 11.

a. *Form.* All documents filed in any Hamilton County Court, with the exception of exhibits and existing wills, shall be prepared on paper measuring eight and one-half by eleven inches (8 1/2" x 11"). IN ST HAMILTON TRIAL Rule 201(201.20).

3. *Signature requirements*

a. *Signature of attorney.* Every pleading or motion of a party represented by an attorney shall be signed by at least one (1) attorney of record in his individual name, whose address, telephone number, and attorney number shall be stated, except that this provision shall not apply to pleadings and motions made and transcribed at the trial or a hearing before the judge and received by him in such form. IN ST TRIAL P Rule 11(A).

    i.   The signature of an attorney constitutes a certificate by him that he has read the pleadings; that to the best of his knowledge, information, and belief, there is good ground to support it; and that it is not interposed for delay. IN ST TRIAL P Rule 11(A).

    ii. If a pleading or motion is not signed or is signed with intent to defeat the purpose of the rule, it may be stricken as sham and false and the action may proceed as though the pleading had not been served. IN ST TRIAL P Rule 11(A).

    iii. For a willful violation of IN ST TRIAL P Rule 11 an attorney may be subjected to appropriate disciplinary action. Similar action may be taken if scandalous or indecent matter is inserted. IN ST TRIAL P Rule 11(A).

b. *Signature of unrepresented party.* A party who is not represented by an attorney shall sign his pleading and state his address. IN ST TRIAL P Rule 11(A).

c. *Verification not generally required.* Except when specifically required by rule, pleadings or motions need not be verified or accompanied by affidavit. The rule in equity that the averments of an answer under oath must be overcome by the testimony of two (2) witnesses or of one (1) witness sustained by corroborating circumstances is abolished. IN ST TRIAL P Rule 11(A).

d. *Verification by affirmation or representation.* When in connection with any civil or special statutory proceeding it is required that any pleading, motion, petition, supporting affidavit, or other document of any kind, be verified, or that an oath be taken, it shall be sufficient if the subscriber simply affirms the truth of the matter to be verified by an affirmation or representation. IN ST TRIAL P Rule 11(B). IN ST TRIAL P Rule 11(B) states that the affirmation or representation should be in substantially the following language: "I (we) affirm, under the penalties for perjury, that the foregoing representation(s) is (are) true. (Signed) _____."

   i. Any person who falsifies an affirmation or representation of fact shall be subject to the same penalties as are prescribed by law for the making of a false affidavit. IN ST TRIAL P Rule 11(B).

e. *Verified pleadings, motions, and affidavits as evidence.* Pleadings, motions and affidavits accompanying or in support of such pleadings or motions when required to be verified or under oath shall be accepted as a representation that the signer had personal knowledge thereof or reasonable cause to believe the existence of the facts or matters stated or alleged therein; and, if otherwise competent or acceptable as evidence, may be admitted as evidence of the facts or matters stated or alleged therein when it is so provided in the Indiana Rules of Trial Procedure, by statute or other law, or to the extent the writing or signature expressly purports to be made upon the signer's personal knowledge. When such pleadings, motions and affidavits are verified or under oath they shall not require other or greater proof on the part of the adverse party than if not verified or not under oath unless expressly provided otherwise by the Indiana Rules of Trial Procedure, statute or other law. Affidavits upon motions for summary judgment under IN ST TRIAL P Rule 56 and in denial of execution under IN ST TRIAL P Rule 9.2 shall be made upon personal knowledge. IN ST TRIAL P Rule 11(C).

4. *Information excluded from public access.* Every document filed in a case shall separately identify information excluded from public access pursuant to IN ST ADMIN Rule 9(G)(1) as follows:

   a. Whole documents that are excluded from public access pursuant to IN ST ADMIN Rule 9(G)(1) shall be tendered on light green paper or have a light green coversheet attached to the document, marked "Not for Public Access" or "Confidential." IN ST TRIAL P Rule 5(G)(1).

   b. When only a portion of a document contains information excluded from public access pursuant to IN ST ADMIN Rule 9(G)(1), said information shall be omitted [or redacted] from the filed document, and set forth on a separate accompanying document on light green paper conspicuously marked "Not for Public Access" or "Confidential" and clearly designated [or identifying] the caption and number of the case and the document and location within the document to which the redacted material pertains. IN ST TRIAL P Rule 5(G)(2).

   c. With respect to documents filed in electronic format, the trial court, by local rule, may provide for compliance with IN ST TRIAL P Rule 5 in manner that separates and protects access to information excluded from public access. IN ST TRIAL P Rule 5(G)(3).

   d. IN ST TRIAL P Rule 5(G) does not apply to a record sealed by the court pursuant to IN ST 5-14-3-5.5 or otherwise, nor to records, documents, or information filed in cases to which public access is prohibited pursuant to IN ST ADMIN Rule 9(G). IN ST TRIAL P Rule 5(G)(4).

   e. The following information in case records is excluded from public access and is confidential:

      i. Information that is excluded from public access pursuant to federal law;

      ii. Information that is excluded from public access as declared confidential by Indiana statute or other court rule, including without limitation:

         • All adoption records created after July 8, 1941, as declared confidential by IN ST 31-19-19-1, et seq., except those specifically declared open by IN ST 31-19-13-2(2);

- All records relating to chancroid, chlamydia, gonorrhea, hepatitis, human immunodeficiency virus (HIV), Lymphogranuloma venereum, syphilis, tuberculosis, as declared confidential by IN ST 16-41-8-1, et seq.;

- All records relating to child abuse as declared confidential by IN ST 31-33-18-1, et seq.;

- All records relating to drug tests as declared confidential by IN ST 5-14-3-4(a)(9);

- Records of grand jury proceedings as declared confidential by IN ST 35-34-2-4;

- Records of juvenile proceedings as declared confidential by IN ST 31-39-1-2, except those specifically open under statute;

- All paternity records created after July 1, 1941 as declared confidential by IN ST 31-14-11-15, IN ST 31-19-5-23, IN ST 31-39-1-1 and IN ST 31-39-1-2 [Editor's note: IN ST 31-14-11-15 was repealed effective May 9, 2013];

- All pre-sentence reports as declared confidential by IN ST 35-38-1-13;

- Written petitions to permit marriages without consent and orders directing the Clerk of Court to issue a marriage license to underage persons, as declared confidential by IN ST 31-11-1-6;

- Only those arrest warrants, search warrants, indictments and informations ordered confidential by the trial judge, prior to return of duly executed service as declared confidential by IN ST 5-14-3-4(b)(1);

- All medical, mental health, or tax records unless determined by law or regulation of any governmental custodian not to be confidential, released by the subject of such records, or declared by a court of competent jurisdiction to be essential to the resolution of litigation as declared confidential by IN ST 16-39-3-10, IN ST 6-4.1-5-10, IN ST 6-4.1-12-12, and IN ST 6-8.1-7-1;

- Personal information relating to jurors or prospective jurors, other than for the use of the parties and counsel, pursuant to IN ST JURY Rule 10;

- Information relating to protection from abuse orders, no-contact orders and workplace violence restraining orders as declared confidential by IN ST 5-2-9-6, et seq.;

- Mediation proceedings pursuant to IN ST ADR Rule 2.11, Mini-Trial proceedings pursuant to IN ST ADR Rule 4.4(C), and Summary Jury Trials pursuant to IN ST ADR Rule 5.6;

- Information in probation files pursuant to the Probation Standards promulgated by the Judicial Conference of Indiana pursuant to IN ST 11-13-1-8(b);

- Information deemed confidential pursuant to the Rules for Court Administered Alcohol and Drug Programs promulgated by the Judicial Conference of Indiana pursuant to IN ST 12-23-14-13;

- Information deemed confidential pursuant to the Problem-Solving Court Rules promulgated by the Judicial Conference of Indiana pursuant to IN ST 33-23-16-16;

- All records of the Department of workforce Development as declared confidential by IN ST 22-4-19-6;

- Information regarding interception of electronic communications that is sealed or deemed confidential as set forth in IN ST 35-33.5-2-1, et seq.

iii. Information excluded from public access by specific court order;

iv. Complete Social Security Numbers of living persons;

v. With the exception of names, information such as addresses, phone numbers, and dates of birth which explicitly identifies:

- Natural persons who are witnesses or victims (not including defendants) in criminal, domestic violence, stalking, sexual assault, juvenile, or civil protection order proceedings, provided that juveniles who are victims of sex crimes shall be identified by initials only;

- Places of residence of judicial officers, clerks and other employees of courts and clerks of court, unless the person or persons about whom the information pertains waives confidentiality;

vi. Complete account numbers of specific assets, loans, bank accounts, credit cards, and personal identification numbers (PINs);

vii. All orders of expungement entered in criminal or juvenile proceedings, orders to restrict access to criminal history information pursuant to IN ST 35-38-5-5.5 or IN ST 35-38-8-5 and records excluded from public access by such orders, and information related to infractions that is excluded from public access pursuant to IN ST 34-28-5-15 or IN ST 34-28-5-16 [Editor's note: IN ST 35-38-5-5.5, IN ST 35-38-8-5 and IN ST 34-28-5-16 were repealed effective July 1, 2013; for information on orders restricting access to criminal history, refer to IN ST 35-38-9-1, et seq.];

viii. All personal notes and e-mail, and deliberative material, of judges, jurors, court staff and judicial agencies, and information recorded in personal data assistants (PDA's) or organizers and personal calendars. IN ST ADMIN Rule 9(G)(1).

F. Filing and Service Requirements

1. *Filing requirements.* Except as otherwise provided in IN ST TRIAL P Rule 5(E)(2), all pleadings and papers subsequent to the complaint which are required to be served upon a party shall be filed with the Court either before service or within a reasonable period of time thereafter. IN ST TRIAL P Rule 5(E)(1). All pleadings shall be filed with the Hamilton County Clerk with the exception of emergency orders under IN ST TRIAL P Rule 65. IN ST HAMILTON TRIAL Rule 201(201.10).

   a. *Filing with the court defined.* The filing of pleadings, motions, and other papers with the court as required by the Indiana Rules of Trial Procedure shall be made by one of the following methods:

      i. Delivery to the clerk of the court;

      ii. Sending by electronic transmission under the procedure adopted pursuant to IN ST ADMIN Rule 12;

      iii. Mailing to the clerk by registered, certified or express mail return receipt requested;

      iv. Depositing with any third-party commercial carrier for delivery to the clerk within three (3) calendar days, cost prepaid, properly addressed;

      v. If the court so permits, filing with the judge, in which event the judge shall note thereon the filing date and forthwith transmit them to the office of the clerk; or

      vi. Electronic filing, as approved by the Division of State Court Administration pursuant to IN ST ADMIN Rule 16. IN ST TRIAL P Rule 5(F).

      vii. Filing by registered or certified mail and by third-party commercial carrier shall be complete upon mailing or deposit. IN ST TRIAL P Rule 5(F).

   b. *Facsimile filing.* As outlined in IN ST HAMILTON ADMIN Rule 103(103.10),facsimile filing is permitted in the Circuit and Superior Courts of Hamilton County. The Courts authorize the Hamilton County Clerk of Courts to accept pleadings, motions and other papers by electronic facsimile transmission for filing in any case pending before the Courts, subject to the requirements of IN ST HAMILTON ADMIN Rule 103(103.10). IN ST HAMILTON ADMIN Rule 103(103.10); IN ST HAMILTON TRIAL Rule 201(201.80).

      i. *Generally.* In counties where a majority of judges of the courts of record, by posted local rule, have authorized electronic facsimile filing and designated a telephone number to receive such transmissions, pleadings, motions, and other papers may be sent to the Clerk of Circuit Court by electronic facsimile transmission for filing in any case, provided:

         - Such matter does not exceed ten (10) pages, including the cover sheet;

         - Such matter does not require the payment of fees other than the electronic facsimile transcription fee set forth in IN ST ADMIN Rule 12(E);

         - The sending party creates at the time of transmission a machine generated log for such transmission; and

- The original document and the transmission log are maintained by the sending party for the duration of the litigation. IN ST ADMIN Rule 12(B); IN ST HAMILTON ADMIN Rule 103(103.10)(d).

- Legibility of documents and timeliness of filing is the responsibility of the sender. IN ST HAMILTON ADMIN Rule 103(103.10)(g).

- The Clerk shall accept electronic facsimile transmission filings only if received at the facsimile machine assigned by the Clerk. The telephone number designated to receive such transmission is available at IN ST HAMILTON ADMIN Rule 103(103.40). IN ST HAMILTON ADMIN Rule 103(103.40).

ii. *Time of filing.* During normal, posted business hours, the time of filing shall be the time the duplicate document is produced in the office of the Clerk of the Circuit Court. Duplicate documents received at all other times shall be filed as of the next normal business day. IN ST ADMIN Rule 12(C).

- If the receiving fax machine endorses its own time and date stamp upon the transmitted documents and the receiving machine produces a delivery receipt which is electronically created and transmitted to the sending party, the time of filing shall be the date and time recorded on the transmitted document by the receiving fax machine. IN ST ADMIN Rule 12(C).

- Electronic facsimile transmissions will be accepted for filing only during the regular business hours as set forth in IN ST HAMILTON ADMIN Rule 101. Transmissions received by the Hamilton County Clerk after close of business shall be filed effective the next regular business day. IN ST HAMILTON ADMIN Rule 103(103.30).

iii. *Filing fee.* The electronic facsimile transmission will not be accepted for filing if its filing requires the payment of any fee other than the electronic facsimile transcription fee set forth in IN ST HAMILTON ADMIN Rule 103(103.20). IN ST HAMILTON ADMIN Rule 103(103.10)(e).

- Pursuant to Ordinance adopted by the Hamilton County Board of Commissioners, the Clerk shall collect an electronic facsimile transcription fee of One Dollar ($1.00) per page, to a maximum of Ten Dollars ($10.00) per transmission, for each electronic facsimile transmission accepted for filing with the Hamilton County Circuit and Superior Courts. IN ST HAMILTON ADMIN Rule 103(103.20).

- The fee shall be assessed against the sending party and shall be paid upon receipt of invoice by that party and at the latest within thirty (30) days of the transmission. In the event the fee is not paid by the sending party within the time limits provided, the court may issue a show-cause order or enter a judgment in the matter. The Clerk may refuse an electronic facsimile transmission from any attorney or pro se litigant who has failed to pay these fees within thirty (30) days. IN ST HAMILTON ADMIN Rule 103(103.20).

iv. *No direct filing with court.* A party shall not send pleadings, motions and other papers by electronic facsimile transmission for filing directly to any Court without that Court's prior approval to do so. IN ST HAMILTON ADMIN Rule 103(103.50).

c. *Filing with special judge.* After a special judge has qualified, a copy of each pleading and Chronological Case Summary entries filed with the Court shall be mailed or delivered to the office of that Special judge by the counsel or pro se litigant with service indicated on the certificate of service. IN ST HAMILTON TRIAL Rule 204(204.20).

d. *Proof of filing.* Any party filing any paper by any method other than personal delivery to the clerk shall retain proof of filing. IN ST TRIAL P Rule 5(F).

2. *Service requirements.* Unless otherwise provided by the Indiana Rules of Trial Procedure or an order of the court, each party and special judge, if any, shall be served with: (1) every order required by its terms to be served; (2) every pleading subsequent to the original complaint; (3) every written motion except one which may be heard ex parte; (4) every brief submitted to the trial court; (5) every paper relating to

discovery required to be served upon a party; and (6) every written notice, appearance, demand, offer of judgment, designation of record on appeal, or similar paper. IN ST TRIAL P Rule 5(A).

a. *Methods of service*

   i. *Personal service.* Whenever a party is represented by an attorney of record, service shall be made upon such attorney unless service upon the party himself is ordered by the court. Service upon the attorney or party shall be made by delivering or mailing a copy of the papers to the last known address or where an attorney or party has consented to service by fax or e-mail, as provided in IN ST TRIAL P Rule 3.1(A)(4), by faxing or e-mailing a copy of the documents to the fax number or e-mail address set out in the appearance form or correction as required by IN ST TRIAL P Rule 3.1(E). IN ST TRIAL P Rule 5(B). Delivery of a copy within IN ST TRIAL P Rule 5 means:

   • Offering or tendering it to the attorney or party and stating the nature of the papers being served. Refusal to accept an offered or tendered document is a waiver of any objection to the sufficiency or adequacy of service of that document;

   • Leaving it at his office with a clerk or other person in charge thereof, or if there is no one in charge, leaving it in a conspicuous place therein; or

   • If the office is closed, by leaving it at his dwelling house or usual place of abode with some person of suitable age and discretion then residing therein; or,

   • Leaving it at some other suitable place, selected by the attorney upon whom service is being made, pursuant to duly promulgated local rule. IN ST TRIAL P Rule 5(B)(1).

   ii. *Service by mail.* If service is made by mail, the papers shall be deposited in the United States mail addressed to the person on whom they are being served, with postage prepaid. Service shall be deemed complete upon mailing. Proof of service of all papers permitted to be mailed may be made by written acknowledgment of service, by affidavit of the person who mailed the papers, or by certificate of an attorney. It shall be the duty of attorneys when entering their appearance in a cause or when filing pleadings or papers therein, to have noted in the Chronological Case Summary or said pleadings or papers so filed the address and telephone number of their office. Service by delivery or by mail at such address shall be deemed sufficient and complete. IN ST TRIAL P Rule 5(B)(2).

   iii. *Service by fax or e-mail.* A party who has consented to service by fax or e-mail may be served as follows:

   • Service by e-mail shall be made by attaching the document being served in .pdf format. Discovery documents must also be served in accordance with IN ST TRIAL P Rule 26(A). IN ST TRIAL P Rule 5(B)(3)(a).

   • Service by fax shall be deemed complete upon generation of a transmission record indicating the successful transmission of the entire document, except as provided in IN ST TRIAL P Rule 5(B)(3)(d). IN ST TRIAL P Rule 5(B)(3)(b).

   • Service by e-mail shall be deemed complete upon transmission, except as provided in IN ST TRIAL P Rule 5(B)(3)(d). IN ST TRIAL P Rule 5(B)(3)(c).

   • Service by fax or e-mail that occurs on a Saturday, Sunday, legal holiday, or day the court or agency in which the matter is pending is closed or after 5:00 PM local time of the recipient shall be deemed complete the next day that is not a Saturday, Sunday, legal holiday, or day that the court or agency in which the matter is pending is not closed. IN ST TRIAL P Rule 5(B)(3)(d).

   iv. *Mail box service.* Pursuant to IN ST TRIAL P Rule 5(B)(1)(d), the Circuit and Superior Courts of Hamilton County hereby designate the "mail boxes" located in the Clerk's order book office for service of pleadings upon attorneys who have such boxes. IN ST HAMILTON TRIAL Rule 201(201.50).

b. *Serving numerous defendants.* In any action in which there are unusually large numbers of defendants, the court, upon motion or of its own initiative, may order:

    i. That service of the pleadings of the defendants and replies thereto need not be made as between the defendants;

- That any cross-claim, counterclaim, or matter constituting an avoidance or affirmative defense contained therein shall be deemed to be denied or avoided by all other parties; and

- That the filing of any such pleading and service thereof upon the plaintiff constitutes due notice of it to the parties. IN ST TRIAL P Rule 5(D).

    ii. A copy of every such order shall be served upon the parties in such manner and form as the court directs. IN ST TRIAL P Rule 5(D).

c. *Service on parties in default for failure to appear.* No service need be made on parties in default for failure to appear, except that pleadings asserting new or additional claims for relief against them shall be served upon them in the manner provided by service of summons in IN ST TRIAL P Rule 4. IN ST TRIAL P Rule 5(A).

3. *Service requirements if adding a new party by amendment.* Refer to the Indiana KeyRules Complaint document for information on serving a new party added by amendment.

G. Hearings

1. The Indiana rules do not contemplate a hearing regarding the filing and service of an amended complaint.

H. Forms

1. Official Amended Complaint Forms for Indiana

a. Affidavit of debt. IN ST TRIAL P App. A-2.

2. Amended Complaint Forms for Indiana

a. Motion to file amended complaint. 5 INPRAC § 3:5.1.

b. Motion to file amended complaint; Another form. 5 INPRAC § 3:5.2.

c. Objections to motion to file amended complaint. 5 INPRAC § 3:5.3.

d. Motion to amend pleading to conform to evidence. 5 INPRAC § 3:5.4.

e. Amendment by stipulation. 10 INPRAC § 46.11.

f. Caption; Generally. 5 INPRAC § 3:1.1.

g. Caption; Multiple parties. 5 INPRAC § 3:1.2.

h. Single count. 5 INPRAC § 3:1.3.

i. Multiple counts; Single defendant. 5 INPRAC § 3:1.4.

j. Multiple counts; Multiple defendants. 5 INPRAC § 3:1.5.

k. Signature; By party. 5 INPRAC § 3:1.6.

l. Signature; By attorney. 5 INPRAC § 3:1.7.

m. Verification. 5 INPRAC § 3:1.8.

n. Individual defendant. 5 INPRAC § 3:2.1.

o. Resident agent of corporation. 5 INPRAC § 3:2.2.

p. Attorney general. 5 INPRAC § 3:2.3.

q. City attorney. 5 INPRAC § 3:2.4.

r. Certificate; Personal service. 5 INPRAC § 3:2.5.

s. Certificate; First class mail. 5 INPRAC § 3:2.6.

t. Certificate; Registered mail. 5 INPRAC § 3:2.7.

u. Certificate; Dwelling house. 5 INPRAC § 3:2.8.

v.   Clerk's certificate of mailing. 5 INPRAC § 3:2.9.

w. Clerk's certificate of mailing; Acceptance by defendant. 5 INPRAC § 3:2.10.

x.   Clerk's return on service of summons by mail; Not accepted by defendant. 5 INPRAC § 3:2.11.

y.   Sheriff's return; Service of summons. 5 INPRAC § 3:2.12.

z.   Motion to appoint person to serve process. 5 INPRAC § 3:2.13.

I. Checklist

(I) ❑ Matters to be considered by the party filing the amended complaint

  (a) ❑ Required documents if amending as matter of course

    (1) ❑ Amended complaint

    (2) ❑ Certificate of service

  (b) ❑ Supplemental documents

    (1) ❑ Proof of written instrument

    (2) ❑ Notice of intent to use foreign law

    (3) ❑ Facsimile cover sheet

  (c) ❑ Timing

    (1) ❑ A party may amend his pleading once as a matter of course at any time before a responsive pleading is served or, if the pleading is one to which no responsive pleading is permitted, and the action has not been placed upon the trial calendar, he may so amend it at any time within thirty (30) days after it is served

    (2) ❑ Otherwise a party may amend his pleading only by leave of court or by written consent of the adverse party

Pleadings
Answer

Document Last Updated October 2013

A. Applicable Rules

1. *State rules*

  a.   Appearance. IN ST TRIAL P Rule 3.1.

  b.   Process. IN ST TRIAL P Rule 4.

  c.   Service. IN ST TRIAL P Rule 4.15; IN ST TRIAL P Rule 4.16; IN ST TRIAL P Rule 5.

  d.   Time. IN ST TRIAL P Rule 6.

  e.   Pleadings. IN ST TRIAL P Rule 7; IN ST TRIAL P Rule 8; IN ST TRIAL P Rule 9; IN ST TRIAL P Rule 9.1; IN ST TRIAL P Rule 9.2; IN ST TRIAL P Rule 10.

  f.   Signing and verification of pleadings. IN ST TRIAL P Rule 11.

  g.   Defenses and objections; When and how presented; By pleading or motion; Motion for judgment on the pleadings. IN ST TRIAL P Rule 12.

  h.   Counterclaim and cross-claim. IN ST TRIAL P Rule 13.

  i.   Third-party practice. IN ST TRIAL P Rule 14.

  j.   Amended and supplemental pleadings. IN ST TRIAL P Rule 15.

  k.   Parties plaintiff and defendant; Capacity. IN ST TRIAL P Rule 17.

  l.   Joinder. IN ST TRIAL P Rule 19; IN ST TRIAL P Rule 20.

  m. Jury trial of right. IN ST TRIAL P Rule 38.

n.   Consolidation; Separate trials. IN ST TRIAL P Rule 42.

o.   Evidence. IN ST TRIAL P Rule 43.

p.   Determination of foreign law. IN ST TRIAL P Rule 44.1.

q.   Judgment. IN ST TRIAL P Rule 50; IN ST TRIAL P Rule 52; IN ST TRIAL P Rule 54; IN ST TRIAL P Rule 56; IN ST TRIAL P Rule 59; IN ST TRIAL P Rule 60.

r.   Venue requirements. IN ST TRIAL P Rule 75.

s.   Alternative dispute resolution. IN ST ADR Rule 1.1; IN ST ADR Rule 1.6; IN ST ADR Rule 8.8.

t.   Uniform case numbering system. IN ST ADMIN Rule 8.

u.   Access to court records. IN ST ADMIN Rule 9.

v.   Paper size. IN ST ADMIN Rule 11.

w.   Facsimile transmission. IN ST ADMIN Rule 12.

x.   Electronic filing and electronic service pilot projects. IN ST ADMIN Rule 16.

y.   Sealing of certain records by court; Hearing; Notice. IN ST 5-14-3-5.5.

z.   Privacy and confidentiality. IN ST 5-2-9-6; IN ST 5-14-3-4; IN ST 6-4.1-5-10; IN ST 6-4.1-12-12; IN ST 6-8.1-7-1; IN ST 11-13-1-8; IN ST 12-23-14-13; IN ST 16-39-3-10; IN ST 16-41-8-1; IN ST 22-4-19-6; IN ST 31-11-1-6; IN ST 31-19-5-23; IN ST 31-19-13-2; IN ST 31-19-19-1; IN ST 31-33-18-1; IN ST 31-39-1-1; IN ST 31-39-1-2; IN ST 33-23-16-16; IN ST 35-34-2-4; IN ST 35-38-1-13; IN ST 35-38-9-1; IN ST ADR Rule 2.11; IN ST ADR Rule 4.4; IN ST ADR Rule 5.6; IN ST JURY Rule 10.

2.   *Local rules*

a.   Court hours. IN ST HAMILTON ADMIN Rule 101.

b.   Facsimile transmissions. IN ST HAMILTON ADMIN Rule 103.

c.   Filing of pleadings and entry of appearances. IN ST HAMILTON TRIAL Rule 201.

d.   Proposed orders. IN ST HAMILTON TRIAL Rule 202.

e.   Special judges. IN ST HAMILTON TRIAL Rule 204.

f.   Continuances. IN ST HAMILTON TRIAL Rule 206.

B. Timing

1.   *Time to serve answer.* A responsive pleading required under the Indiana Rules of Trial Procedure, shall be served within twenty (20) days after service of the prior pleading. IN ST TRIAL P Rule 6(C).

a.   *Effect of IN ST TRIAL P Rule 12 motions.* The service of a motion permitted under IN ST TRIAL P Rule 12 alters the time for service of responsive pleadings as follows, unless a different time is fixed by the court:

i.   If the court does not grant the motion, the responsive pleading shall be served in ten (10) days after notice of the court's action;

ii. If the court grants the motion and the corrective action is allowed to be taken, it shall be taken within ten (10) days, and the responsive pleading shall be served within ten (10) days thereafter. IN ST TRIAL P Rule 6(C).

2.   *Responding to amended complaint.* A party shall plead in response to an amended pleading within the time remaining for response to the original pleading or within twenty (20) days after service of the amended pleading, whichever period may be the longer, unless the court otherwise orders. IN ST TRIAL P Rule 15(A).

3.   *Filing.* All pleadings and papers subsequent to the complaint which are required to be served upon a party shall be filed with the Court either before service or within a reasonable period of time thereafter. IN ST TRIAL P Rule 5(E)(1).

4.   *Filing of third-party complaint.* The third-party plaintiff must file the third-party complaint with his original answer or by leave of court thereafter with good cause shown. IN ST TRIAL P Rule 14(A).

5. *Computation of time*

    a. *Generally; Days excluded.* In computing any period of time prescribed or allowed by the Indiana Rules of Trial Procedure, by order of the court, or by any applicable statute, the day of the act, event, or default from which the designated period of time begins to run shall not be included. The last day of the period so computed is to be included unless it is:

        i. A Saturday,

        ii. A Sunday,

        iii. A legal holiday as defined by state statute, or

        iv. A day the office in which the act is to be done is closed during regular business hours. IN ST TRIAL P Rule 6(A).

    b. *Short periods.* In any event, the period runs until the end of the next day that is not a Saturday, a Sunday, a legal holiday, or a day on which the office is closed. When the period of time allowed is less than seven (7) days, intermediate Saturdays, Sundays, legal holidays, and days on which the office is closed shall be excluded from the computations. IN ST TRIAL P Rule 6(A).

    c. *Additional time after service by United States mail.* Whenever a party has the right or is required to do some act or take some proceedings within a prescribed period after the service of a notice or other paper upon him and the notice or paper is served upon him by United States mail, three (3) days shall be added to the prescribed period. IN ST TRIAL P Rule 6(E).

    d. *Enlargement of time.* When an act is required or allowed to be done at or within a specific time by the Indiana Rules of Trial Procedure, the court may at any time for cause shown:

        i. Order the period enlarged, with or without motion or notice, if request therefor is made before the expiration of the period originally prescribed or extended by a previous order; or

        ii. Upon motion made after the expiration of the specific period, permit the act to be done where the failure to act was the result of excusable neglect; but, the court may not extend the time for taking any action for judgment on the evidence under IN ST TRIAL P Rule 50(A), amendment of findings and judgment under IN ST TRIAL P Rule 52(B), to correct errors under IN ST TRIAL P Rule 59(C), statement in opposition to motion to correct error under IN ST TRIAL P Rule 59(E), or to obtain relief from final judgment under IN ST TRIAL P Rule 60(B), except to the extent and under the conditions stated in those rules. IN ST TRIAL P Rule 6(B).

        iii. For information on obtaining a continuance, refer to IN ST HAMILTON TRIAL Rule 206.

C. General Requirements

1. *Pleading, generally*

    a. *Pleadings to be concise.* Each averment of a pleading shall be simple, concise, and direct. No technical forms of pleading or motions are required. All fictions in pleading are abolished. IN ST TRIAL P Rule 8(E)(1).

    b. *Pleading in the alternative.* A pleading may set forth two (2) or more statements of a claim or defense alternatively or hypothetically, either in one (1) count or defense or in separate counts or defenses. When two (2) or more statements are made in the alternative and one (1) of them if made independently would be sufficient, the pleading is not made insufficient by the insufficiency of one or more of the alternative statements. A pleading may also state as many separate claims or defenses as the pleader has regardless of consistency and whether based on legal or equitable grounds. All statements shall be made subject to the obligations set forth in IN ST TRIAL P Rule 11. IN ST TRIAL P Rule 8(E)(2).

    c. *Motions and pleadings, joint and several.* All motions and pleadings of any kind addressed to two (2) or more paragraphs of any pleading, or filed by two (2) or more parties, shall be taken and construed as joint, separate, and several motions or pleadings to each of such paragraphs and by and against each of such parties. All motions or pleadings containing two (2) or more subject-matters shall be taken and construed as separate and several as to each subject-matter. All objections to rulings made

by two (2) or more parties shall be taken and construed as the joint, separate, and several objections of each of such parties. IN ST TRIAL P Rule 8(E)(3).

    i.   A complaint filed by or against two (2) or more plaintiffs shall be taken and construed as joint, separate, and several as to each of said plaintiffs. IN ST TRIAL P Rule 8(E).

  d. *Construction of pleadings.* All pleadings shall be so construed as to do substantial justice, lead to disposition on the merits, and avoid litigation of procedural points. IN ST TRIAL P Rule 8(F).

2. *Contents of the answer*

  a. *Defenses which may be raised by answer or motion.* Every defense, in law or fact, to a claim for relief in any pleading, whether a claim, counterclaim, cross-claim, or third-party claim, shall be asserted in the responsive pleading thereto if one is required; except that at the option of the pleader, the following defenses may be made by motion:

    i.   Lack of jurisdiction over the subject matter;

    ii. Lack of jurisdiction over the person;

    iii. Incorrect venue under IN ST TRIAL P Rule 75, or any statutory provision. The disposition of this motion shall be consistent with IN ST TRIAL P Rule 75;

    iv. Insufficiency of process;

    v. Insufficiency of service of process;

    vi. Failure to state a claim upon which relief can be granted, which shall include failure to name the real party in interest under IN ST TRIAL P Rule 17;

    vii. Failure to join a party needed for just adjudication under IN ST TRIAL P Rule 19;

    viii. The same action pending in another state court of this state. IN ST TRIAL P Rule 12(B).

    ix. A motion making any of these defenses shall be made before pleading if a further pleading is permitted or within twenty (20) days after service of the prior pleading if none is required. If a pleading sets forth a claim for relief to which the adverse party is not required to serve a responsive pleading, any of the defenses in section IN ST TRIAL P Rule 12(B)(2), IN ST TRIAL P Rule 12(B)(3), IN ST TRIAL P Rule 12(B)(4), IN ST TRIAL P Rule 12(B)(5) or IN ST TRIAL P Rule 12(B)(8) is waived to the extent constitutionally permissible unless made in a motion within twenty (20) days after service of the prior pleading. No defense or objection is waived by being joined with one (1) or more other defenses or objections in a responsive pleading or motion. IN ST TRIAL P Rule 12(B).

  b. *Waiver or preservation of certain defenses*

    i.   A defense of lack of jurisdiction over the person, improper venue, insufficiency of process, insufficiency of service of process, or the same action pending in another state court of this state is waived to the extent constitutionally permissible:

      • If omitted from a motion in the circumstances described in IN ST TRIAL P Rule 12(G),

      • If it is neither made by motion under IN ST TRIAL P Rule 12 nor included in a responsive pleading or an amendment thereof permitted by IN ST TRIAL P Rule 15(A) to be made as a matter of course. IN ST TRIAL P Rule 12(H)(1).

    ii. A defense of failure to state a claim upon which relief can be granted, a defense of failure to join an indispensable party under IN ST TRIAL P Rule 19(B), and an objection of failure to state a legal defense to a claim may be made in any pleading permitted or ordered under IN ST TRIAL P Rule 7(A) or by motion for judgment on the pleadings, or at the trial on the merits. IN ST TRIAL P Rule 12(H)(2).

  c. *Defenses; Form of denials*

    i.   A responsive pleading shall state in short and plain terms the pleader's defenses to each claim asserted and shall admit or controvert the averments set forth in the preceding pleading. If in good faith the pleader intends to deny all the averments in the preceding pleading, he may do so by general denial subject to the provisions of IN ST TRIAL P Rule 11. If he does not intend a general denial, he may:

- Specifically deny designated averments or paragraphs; or
- Generally deny all averments except such designated averments and paragraphs as he expressly admits. IN ST TRIAL P Rule 8(B).

    ii. If he lacks knowledge or information sufficient to form a belief as to the truth of an averment, he shall so state and his statement shall be considered a denial. If in good faith a pleader intends to deny only a part or a qualification of an averment, he shall specify so much of it as is true and material and deny the remainder. All denials shall fairly meet the substance of the averments denied. IN ST TRIAL P Rule 8 shall have no application to uncontested actions for divorce, or to answers required to be filed by clerks or guardians ad litem. IN ST TRIAL P Rule 8(B).

d. *Affirmative defenses.* A responsive pleading shall set forth affirmatively and carry the burden of proving: accord and satisfaction, arbitration and award, discharge in bankruptcy, duress, estoppel, failure of consideration, fraud, illegality, injury by fellow servant, laches, license, payment, release, res judicata, statute of frauds, statute of limitations, waiver, lack of jurisdiction over the subject-matter, lack of jurisdiction over the person, improper venue, insufficiency of process or service of process, the same action pending in another state court of this state, and any other matter constituting an avoidance, matter of abatement, or affirmative defense. A party required to affirmatively plead any matters, including matters formerly required to be pleaded affirmatively by reply, shall have the burden of proving such matters. The burden of proof imposed by this or any other provision of the Indiana Rules of Trial Procedure is subject to the rules of evidence or any statute fixing a different rule. If the pleading mistakenly designates a defense as a counterclaim or a counterclaim as a defense, the court shall treat the pleading as if there had been a proper designation. IN ST TRIAL P Rule 8(C).

    i. An affirmative defense, generally, must be affirmatively stated by the party who seeks its benefit. 1A INPRAC R 8(8.5); Rice v. Grant County Bd. of Com'rs, 472 N.E.2d 213 (Ind.Ct.App. 1984). If that party does not raise the affirmative defense, then it is waived. 1A INPRAC R 8(8.5); Piskorowski v. Shell Oil Co., 403 N.E.2d 838, 847 (Ind.Ct.App. 1980).

    ii. It is clear that the list of affirmative defenses found in IN ST TRIAL P Rule 8 is not exhaustive. The question comes: when is a defense to be treated as an affirmative defense, with all of the attending consequences? 1A INPRAC R 8(8.5). The "determination of whether a defense is affirmative depends on whether it controverts an element of the plaintiff's prima facie case or raises matter outside the scope of the prima facie case." 1A INPRAC R 8(8.5); Molargik v. West Enterprises, Inc., 605 N.E.2d 1197, 1198 (Ind.Ct.App. 1993).

e. *Defense of contributory negligence or assumed risk.* In all claims alleging negligence, the burden of pleading and proving contributory negligence, assumption of risk, or incurred risk shall be upon the defendant who may plead such by denial of the allegation. IN ST TRIAL P Rule 9.1(A).

f. *Res ipsa loquitur.* Res ipsa loquitur or a similar doctrine may be pleaded by alleging generally that the facts connected with the action are unknown to the pleader and are within the knowledge of the opposing party. IN ST TRIAL P Rule 9.1(B).

g. *Consideration.* When an action or defense is founded upon a written contract or release, lack of consideration for the promise or release is an affirmative defense, and the party asserting lack of it carries the burden of proof. IN ST TRIAL P Rule 9.1(C).

h. *Bona fide purchaser.* When the rights of a person depend upon his status as a bona fide purchaser for value or upon similar requirements, such status must be pleaded and proved by the person asserting it, but it may be pleaded in general terms. Once it is established that the person has given any required value, unless such value is commercially unreasonable, and that he has met any requirements of recordation, filing, possession, or perfection, the trier of fact must find that such value was given or such perfection was made in accordance with any requirements of good faith, lack of knowledge, or lack of notice unless and until evidence is introduced which would support a finding of its non-existence. IN ST TRIAL P Rule 9.1(D).

i. *Presumption; Matters of judicial notice.* Neither presumptions of law nor matters of which judicial notice may be taken need be stated in a pleading. IN ST TRIAL P Rule 9.1(E).

j. *Property distrained; Sufficient answer.* In an action to recover the possession of property distrained while doing damage, an answer that the defendant, or person by whose command he acted, was lawfully possessed of the real property upon which the distress was made, and that the property distrained was at the time doing damage thereon, shall be good without setting forth the title of such real property. IN ST TRIAL P Rule 9.1(F).

k. *Effect of failure to deny.* Averments in a pleading to which a responsive pleading is required, except those pertaining to amount of damages, are admitted when not denied in the responsive pleading. Averments in a pleading to which no responsive pleading is required or permitted shall be taken as denied or avoided. IN ST TRIAL P Rule 8(D).

l. *Effect of admission.* When a rhetorical paragraph or allegation is admitted, the effect in Indiana is to remove it from trial. Such an admission is a "judicial admission", and the claim or issue which is admitted cannot be denied later by the trier of the facts. Further, this admitted fact does not require evidence to "prove it"; it is established. It becomes, in short, controlling and indisputable in the litigation, unless the trial court permits an amendment to the pleading which might remove the controlling effect of the admission, and permit it to become another fact or item of evidence in the case. 1A INPRAC R 8(8.4); Aylesworth v. McKesson, 421 N.E.2d 422 (Ind.Ct.App. 1981).

3. *Pleading special matters*

a. *Capacity.* It is not necessary to aver the capacity of a party to sue or be sued, the authority of a party to sue or be sued in a representative capacity, or the legal existence of an organization that is made a party. The burden of proving lack of such capacity, authority, or legal existence shall be upon the person asserting lack of it, and shall be pleaded as an affirmative defense. IN ST TRIAL P Rule 9(A).

b. *Fraud, mistake, condition of the mind.* In all averments of fraud or mistake, the circumstances constituting fraud or mistake shall be specifically averred. Malice, intent, knowledge, and other conditions of mind may be averred generally. IN ST TRIAL P Rule 9(B).

c. *Conditions precedent.* In pleading the performance or occurrence of promissory or non-promissory conditions precedent, it is sufficient to aver generally that all conditions precedent have been performed, have occurred, or have been excused. A denial of performance or occurrence shall be made specifically and with particularity, and a denial of excuse generally. IN ST TRIAL P Rule 9(C).

d. *Official document or act.* In pleading an official document or official act it is sufficient to aver that the document was issued or the act done in compliance with law. IN ST TRIAL P Rule 9(D).

e. *Judgment.* In pleading a judgment or decision of a domestic or foreign court, judicial or quasi-judicial tribunal, or of a board or officer, it is sufficient to aver the judgment or decision without setting forth matter showing jurisdiction to render it. IN ST TRIAL P Rule 9(E).

f. *Time and place.* For the purpose of testing the sufficiency of a pleading, averments of time and place are material and shall be considered like all other averments of material matter. However, time and place need be stated only with such specificity as will enable the opposing party to prepare his defense. IN ST TRIAL P Rule 9(F).

g. *Special damages; Damages where no answer.* When items of special damage are claimed, they shall be specifically stated. The relief granted to the plaintiff, if there be no answer, cannot exceed the relief demanded in his complaint; but, in any other case, the court may grant him any relief consistent with the facts or matters pleaded. IN ST TRIAL P Rule 9(G).

4. *Counterclaim and cross-claim*

a. *Compulsory counterclaims.* A pleading shall state as a counterclaim any claim which at the time of serving the pleading the pleader has against any opposing party, if it arises out of the transaction or occurrence that is the subject-matter of the opposing party's claim and does not require for its adjudication the presence of third parties of whom the court cannot acquire jurisdiction. But the pleader need not state the claim if:

i. At the time the action was commenced the claim was the subject of another pending action; or

    ii.   The opposing party brought suit upon his claim by attachment or other process by which the court did not acquire jurisdiction to render a personal judgment on that claim, and the pleader is not stating any counterclaim under IN ST TRIAL P Rule 13. IN ST TRIAL P Rule 13(A).

b.   *Permissive counterclaims.* A pleading may state as a counterclaim any claim against an opposing party not arising out of the transaction or occurrence that is the subject-matter of the opposing party's claim. IN ST TRIAL P Rule 13(B).

c.   *Counterclaim exceeding opposing claim.* A counterclaim may or may not diminish or defeat the recovery sought by the opposing party. It may claim relief exceeding in amount or different in kind from that sought in the pleading of the opposing party. IN ST TRIAL P Rule 13(C).

d.   *Counterclaim against state.* IN ST TRIAL P Rule 13 shall not be construed to enlarge any right to assert a claim against the state. IN ST TRIAL P Rule 13(D).

e.   *Counterclaim maturing or acquired after pleading.* A claim which either matured or was acquired by the pleader after serving his pleading may, with the permission of the court, be presented as a counterclaim by supplemental pleading. A counterclaim or cross-claim which is not due may be asserted against a party who is insolvent or the representative of a party who has been subjected to insolvency proceedings, if recovery thereon will be impaired because of such party's insolvency. IN ST TRIAL P Rule 13(E).

f.   *Omitted counterclaim.* When a pleader fails to set up a counterclaim through oversight, inadvertence, or excusable neglect, or when justice requires, he may by leave of court set up the counterclaim by amendment. IN ST TRIAL P Rule 13(F).

g.   *Cross-claim against co-party.* A pleading may state as a cross-claim any claim by one party against a co-party. IN ST TRIAL P Rule 13(G).

h.   *Joinder of additional parties.* Persons other than those made parties to the original action may be made parties to a counterclaim or cross-claim in accordance with the provisions of IN ST TRIAL P Rule 14, IN ST TRIAL P Rule 19 and IN ST TRIAL P Rule 20. IN ST TRIAL P Rule 13(H).

i.   *Separate trials; Separate judgments*

    i.   If the court orders separate trials as provided in IN ST TRIAL P Rule 42(B), judgment on a counterclaim or cross-claim may be rendered in accordance with the terms of IN ST TRIAL P Rule 54(B) when the court has jurisdiction so to do, even if the claims of the opposing party have been dismissed or otherwise disposed of. In determining whether or not separate trial of a cross-claim shall be ordered, the court shall consider whether the cross-claim:

- Arises out of the transaction or occurrence or series of transactions or occurrences that is the subject-matter either of the original action or of a counterclaim therein;

- Relates to any property or contract that is the subject-matter of the original action; or

- Claims that the person against whom it is asserted is liable to the cross-claimant for all or part of plaintiff's claim against him. IN ST TRIAL P Rule 13(I).

    ii.   In addition, the court may consider any other relevant factors. IN ST TRIAL P Rule 13(I).

j.   *Effect of statute of limitations and other discharges at law.* The statute of limitations, a nonclaim statute or other discharge at law shall not bar a claim asserted as a counterclaim to the extent that:

    i.   It diminishes or defeats the opposing party's claim if it arises out of the transaction or occurrence that is the subject-matter of the opposing party's claim, or if it could have been asserted as a counterclaim to the opposing party's claim before it (the counterclaim) was barred; or

    ii.   It or the opposing party's claim relates to payment of or security for the other. IN ST TRIAL P Rule 13(J).

k.   *Counterclaim by and against transferees and successors.* A counterclaim may be asserted by or against the transferee or successor of a claim subject to the following provisions:

    i.   A successor who is a guardian, representative of a decedent's estate, receiver or assignee for the benefit of creditors, trustee or the like may interpose a claim to which he succeeds against claims or proceedings brought in or outside the court of administration. A claim owing by his predecessor may be interposed against any claim brought by such successor in or outside the court of administration without the necessity of filing such claim or cause of action in the administration proceedings. IN ST TRIAL P Rule 13(K)(1).

    ii.   A transferee or successor of a claim takes it subject to any defense or counterclaim that is the subject-matter of the opposing party's claim; or that is available to the obligor at the time of the assignment or before the obligor received notice of the assignment. IN ST TRIAL P Rule 13(K)(2).

    iii.   A surety or party with total or partial recourse upon a claim upon which he is being sued may interpose as a counterclaim:

- Any claim of his own; and

- Any claim owned by the person against whom he has recourse who either has notice of the suit, is a party to the suit, is insolvent, has assigned his claim to the surety or party asserting it, or cannot be found. IN ST TRIAL P Rule 13(K)(3).

- A counterclaim under IN ST TRIAL P Rule 13(K)(3)(b) must tend to diminish or defeat the opposing party's claim, or it or the opposing claim must relate to payment of or security for the other, unless the person against whom recourse may be had is a party to the suit or the counterclaim has been assigned to the party asserting it; and if recovery on the counterclaim exceeds the opposing party's claim, any excess recovered shall be held in trust for such person against whom there is a right of recourse. IN ST TRIAL P Rule 13(K)(3).

    iv.   IN ST TRIAL P Rule 13(K)(1), IN ST TRIAL P Rule 13(K)(2), and IN ST TRIAL P Rule 13(K)(3), are subject to subdivision IN ST TRIAL P Rule 13(L). IN ST TRIAL P Rule 13(K)(4).

  l.   *Counterclaim and cross-claim subject to substantive law principles.* Counterclaim and cross-claims are subject to restrictions imposed by other statutes and principles of substantive common law and equity, including rules of commercial law, agency, estoppel, contract and the like. In appropriate cases the court may impose terms or conditions upon its judgment or decree and may enter conditional or noncanceling cross judgments to satisfy such restrictions. This provision is intended to deny or limit counterclaims or cross-claims:

    i.   Where a creditor will receive an unfair priority because a claim is assigned after insolvency proceedings, or assigned before such proceedings if it results in an unlawful preference;

    ii.   Where an unfair priority will be allowed if a surety interposing a claim owned in his own right against the creditor suing on the principal's obligation when the principal is solvent and the creditor is not;

    iii.   Where a claim by or against a representative, such as a guardian, receiver, representative of a decedent's estate, assignee for the benefit of creditors, trustee or the like in his individual capacity is asserted against a claim owing or owed by the estate he represents;

    iv.   Where a claim by or against a partnership or two (2) or more obligors is opposed against or by a claim of an individual to the extent that the individual will be allowed unfairly to profit or if it will adversely affect the rights of creditors; or

    v.   Where a claim is cut off by a holder in due course or a transferee who is protected under principles of commercial law, estoppel, or contract. IN ST TRIAL P Rule 13(L).

  m.   *Satisfaction of judgment.* Satisfaction of a judgment or credits thereon may be ordered, for sufficient cause, upon notice and motion. "Credits" include any counterclaim which tends to diminish or defeat the judgment, or any counterclaim where it or the opposing claim relates to payment of or security for the other. IN ST TRIAL P Rule 13(M).

5.   *Third-party practice*

  a.   *When defendant may bring in third party.* A defending party, as a third-party plaintiff, may cause a summons and complaint to be served upon a person not a party to the action who is or may be liable to him for all or part of the plaintiff's claim against him. IN ST TRIAL P Rule 14(A). The person served with the summons and the third-party complaint, hereinafter called the third-party defendant, as provided in IN ST TRIAL P Rule 12 and IN ST TRIAL P Rule 13 may make:

    i.   His defenses, cross-claims and counterclaims to the third-party plaintiff's claims;

    ii.   His defenses, counterclaims and cross-claims against any other defendants or third-party defendants;

    iii.   Any defenses or claims which the third-party plaintiff has to the plaintiff's claim which are available to the third-party defendant against the plaintiff; and

    iv.   Any defenses or claims which the third-party defendant has as against the plaintiff. IN ST TRIAL P Rule 14(A).

    v.   The plaintiff may assert any claim against the third-party defendant who thereupon may assert his defenses, counterclaims and cross-claims, as provided in IN ST TRIAL P Rule 12 and IN ST TRIAL P Rule 13. A third-party defendant may proceed under IN ST TRIAL P Rule 14 against any person not a party to the action who is or may be liable to him for all or part of the claim made in the action against the third-party defendant. IN ST TRIAL P Rule 14(A).

  b. *When plaintiff may bring in third party.* When a counterclaim or other claim is asserted against a plaintiff, he may cause a third party to be brought in under circumstances, which, under IN ST TRIAL P Rule 14, would entitle a defendant to do so. IN ST TRIAL P Rule 14(B).

  c. *Severance; Parties improperly impleaded.* With his responsive pleading or by motion prior thereto, any party may move for severance of a third-party claim or ensuing claim as provided in IN ST TRIAL P Rule 14 or for a separate trial thereon. If the third-party defendant is a proper party to the proceedings under any other rule relating to parties, the action shall continue as in other cases where he is made a party. IN ST TRIAL P Rule 14(C).

6. *Trial by jury; Demand*

  a. *Causes triable by court and by jury.* Issues of law and issues of fact in causes that prior to the eighteenth day of June, 1852, were of exclusive equitable jurisdiction shall be tried by the court; issues of fact in all other causes shall be triable as the same are now triable. In case of the joinder of causes of action or defenses which, prior to said date, were of exclusive equitable jurisdiction with causes of action or defenses which, prior to said date, were designated as actions at law and triable by jury—the former shall be triable by the court, and the latter by a jury, unless waived; the trial of both may be at the same time or at different times, as the court may direct. IN ST TRIAL P Rule 38(A).

  b. *Demand.* Any party may demand a trial by jury of any issue triable of right by a jury by filing with the court and serving upon the other parties a demand therefor in writing at any time after the commencement of the action and not later than ten (10) days after the first responsive pleading to the complaint, or to a counterclaim, crossclaim or other claim if one properly is pleaded; and if no responsive pleading is filed or required, within ten (10) days after the time such pleading otherwise would have been required. Such demand is sufficient if indorsed upon a pleading of a party filed within such time. IN ST TRIAL P Rule 38(B).

  c. *Same; Specification of issues.* In his demand a party may specify the issues which he wishes so tried; otherwise he shall be deemed to have demanded trial by jury for all issues triable as of right by jury. Any other party must file a demand for jury trial to preserve his right to trial by jury:

    i.   Of issues for which a right to trial by jury was not requested by another party; and

    ii.   In case a request by another party was improper. But if a proper request for a trial by jury upon issues triable by jury as of right on his behalf is made by any party, such request shall be deemed to have been made on behalf of all parties entitled to a jury trial upon such issues. IN ST TRIAL P Rule 38(C).

  d. *Waiver.* The failure of a party to appear at the trial, and the failure of a party to serve a demand as required by IN ST TRIAL P Rule 38 and to file it as required by IN ST TRIAL P Rule 5(E) constitute waiver by him of trial by jury. A demand for trial by jury made as herein provided may not be withdrawn without the consent of the other party or parties. IN ST TRIAL P Rule 38(D).

    i. The trial court shall not grant a demand for a trial by jury filed after the time fixed in IN ST TRIAL P Rule 38(B) has elapsed except upon the written agreement of all of the parties to the action, which agreement shall be filed with the court and made a part of the record. If such agreement is filed then the court may, in its discretion, grant a trial by jury in which event the grant of a trial by jury may not be withdrawn except by the agreement of all of the parties. IN ST TRIAL P Rule 38(D).

e. *Arbitration.* Nothing in the Indiana Rules of Trial Procedure shall deny the parties the right by contract or agreement to submit or to agree to submit controversies to arbitration made before or after commencement of an action thereon or deny the courts power to specifically enforce such agreements. IN ST TRIAL P Rule 38(E).

f. *Equitable and legal claims in multi-count actions.* In multi-count actions, the inclusion of an equitable claim, standing alone, will not automatically draw the entire action into equity. Something more than the presence of an equitable claim is required, and the court must examine the claims at issue. 22B INPRAC 38:1 COMMENT; Lucas v. U.S. Bank, N.A., 953 N.E.2d 457 (Ind. 2011). Factors the court may consider in evaluating the nature of the underlying substantive claims include: the substance and central character of the complaint, the rights and interests at issue, the relief demanded, and any issues arising out of discovery. 22B INPRAC 38:1 COMMENT; Songer v. Civitas Bank, 771 N.E.2d 61 (Ind. 2002).

7. *Use of alternative dispute resolution.* Except as provided by the Indiana Rules for Alternative Dispute Resolution, a presiding judge may order any civil or domestic relations proceeding or selected issues in such proceedings referred to mediation, non-binding arbitration or mini-trial. The selection criteria which should be used by the court are defined under the Indiana Rules for Alternative Dispute Resolution. Binding arbitration and a summary jury trial may be ordered only upon the agreement of the parties as consistent with provisions in the Indiana Rules for Alternative Dispute Resolution which address each method. IN ST ADR Rule 1.6. For information on Indiana's ADR process refer to IN ST ADR Rule 1.1 through IN ST ADR Rule 8.8.

D. Documents

1. *Required documents*

a. *Answer.* Refer to the General Requirements section of this document for information on the contents of an answer.

b. *Appearance form.* At the time the responding party or parties first appears in a case, the attorney representing such party or parties or the party or parties, if not represented by an attorney, shall file an appearance form setting forth the information set out in IN ST TRIAL P Rule 3.1(A). IN ST TRIAL P Rule 3.1(B). The appearance form shall set forth the following information:

    i. Name, address and telephone number of the initiating party or parties filing the appearance form;

    ii. Name, address, attorney number, telephone number, FAX number, and e-mail address of any attorney representing the party, as applicable;

    iii. The case type of the proceeding [IN ST ADMIN Rule 8(B)(3)];

    iv. A statement that the party will or will not accept service by fax or by e-mail from:

- Other parties and/or
- The court under IN ST TRIAL P Rule 72(D);

    v. In domestic relations, Uniform Reciprocal Enforcement of Support (URESA), paternity, delinquency, Child in Need of Services (CHINS), guardianship, and any other proceedings in which support may be an issue, the Social Security Identification Number of all family members;

    vi. The caption and case number of all related cases;

vii.   Such additional matters specified by state or local rule required to maintain the information management system employed by the court;

viii.   In a proceeding involving a protection from abuse order, a workplace violence restraining order, or a no-contact order, the initiating party shall provide to the clerk a public mailing address for purposes of legal service. The initiating party may use the Attorney General Address Confidentiality program established by statute; and

ix.   In a proceeding involving a mental health commitment, except seventy-two (72) hour emergency detentions, the initiating party shall provide the full name of the person with respect to whom commitment is sought and the person's state of residence. In addition, the initiating party shall provide at least one of the following identifiers for the person:

- Date of birth;
- Social Security Number;
- Driver's license number with state of issue and date of expiration;
- Department of Correction number;
- State ID number with state of issue and date of expiration; or
- FBI number. IN ST TRIAL P Rule 3.1(A); IN ST HAMILTON TRIAL Rule 201(201.30).

c.   *Certificate of service.* An attorney or unrepresented party tendering a document to the Clerk for filing shall certify that service has been made, list the parties served, and specify the date and means of service. The certificate of service shall be placed at the end of the document and shall not be separately filed. The separate filing of a certificate of service, however, shall not be grounds for rejecting a document for filing. The Clerk may permit documents to be filed without a certificate of service but shall require prompt filing of a separate certificate of service. IN ST TRIAL P Rule 5(C).

i.   All pleadings filed with the Court which require a certificate of service shall specifically name the individual party or attorney on whom service has been made, the address, the manner in which service was made and the date when service was made. IN ST HAMILTON TRIAL Rule 201(201.60).

2. *Supplemental documents*

a.   *Admission of service.* A written admission stating the date and place of service, signed by the person being served, may be filed with the clerk who shall file it with the pleadings. Such admission shall become a part of the record, constitute evidence of proper service, and shall be allowed as evidence in any action or proceeding. IN ST TRIAL P Rule 4.15(D).

i.   It shall be the duty of every person being served under the Indiana Rules of Trial Procedure to cooperate, accept service, comply with the provisions of the Indiana Rules of Trial Procedure, and, when service is made upon him personally, acknowledge receipt of the papers in writing over his signature. IN ST TRIAL P Rule 4.16(A).

- Offering or tendering the papers to the person being served and advising the person that he or she is being served is adequate service. IN ST TRIAL P Rule 4.16(A)(1).
- A person who has refused to accept the offer or tender of the papers being served thereafter may not challenge the service of those papers. IN ST TRIAL P Rule 4.16(A)(2).

b.   *Proof of written instrument.* When any pleading allowed by the Indiana Rules of Trial Procedure is founded on a written instrument, the original, or a copy thereof, must be included in or filed with the pleading. Such instrument, whether copied in the pleadings or not, shall be taken as part of the record. When any pleading allowed by the Indiana Rules of Trial Procedure is founded on an account, an Affidavit of Debt, in a form substantially similar to that which is provided in IN ST TRIAL P App. A-2, shall be attached. IN ST TRIAL P Rule 9.2(A).

c.   *Notice of intent to use foreign law.* A party who intends to raise an issue concerning the law of a foreign country shall give notice in his pleadings or other reasonable written notice. The court, in determining foreign law, may consider any relevant material or source, including testimony, whether or not submitted by a party or admissible under IN ST TRIAL P Rule 43. The court's determination shall be treated as a ruling on a question of law. It shall be made by the court and not the jury and shall be reviewable. IN ST TRIAL P Rule 44.1(A).

    d. *Facsimile cover sheet.* Any document sent to the Clerk of the Circuit Court by electronic facsimile transmission shall be accompanied by a cover sheet which states the title of the document, case number, number of pages, identity and voice telephone number of the sending party and instructions for filing. The cover sheet shall contain the signature of the attorney or party, pro se, authorizing the filing. IN ST ADMIN Rule 12(D); IN ST HAMILTON ADMIN Rule 103(103.10)(a).

E. Format

1. *Form of pleadings*

    a. *Caption; Names of parties.* Every pleading shall contain a caption setting forth the name of the court, the title of the action, the file number, and a designation as in IN ST TRIAL P Rule 7(A). In the complaint the title of the action shall include the names of all the parties, but in other pleadings it is sufficient to state the name of the first party on each side with an appropriate indication of other parties. IN ST TRIAL P Rule 10(A).

    b. *Paragraphs; Separate statements.* All averments of a claim or defense shall be made in numbered paragraphs, the contents of each of which shall be limited as far as practicable to a statement of a single set of circumstances, and a paragraph may be referred to by number in all succeeding pleadings. Each claim founded upon a separate transaction or occurrence and each defense other than denials may be stated in a separate count or defense whenever a separation facilitates the clear presentation of the matters set forth. IN ST TRIAL P Rule 10(B).

    c. *Adoption by reference; Exhibits.* Statements in a pleading may be adopted by reference in a different part of the same pleading or in another pleading or in any motion. A copy of any written instrument which is an exhibit to a pleading is a part thereof for all purposes. IN ST TRIAL P Rule 10(C).

    d. *Facsimile page limit.* Courts authorize the Hamilton County Clerk of Courts to accept pleadings, motions and other papers by electronic facsimile transmission for filing in any case pending before the Courts, subject to the requirement that The transmission may not exceed ten (10) pages in length including the cover sheet and proposed CCS entry. IN ST HAMILTON ADMIN Rule 103(103.10)(c).

    e. *Emergency facsimile filings.* If the filing requires the immediate attention of the Judge, it shall so indicate in bold letters in an accompanying transmittal memorandum. IN ST HAMILTON ADMIN Rule 103(103.10)(f).

    f. *Special judge heading.* After a special judge is selected, the attorneys or pro se litigants shall add to the caption of all pleadings to the right of the case title the following: "BEFORE SPECIAL JUDGE _____." IN ST HAMILTON TRIAL Rule 204(204.10).

    g. *Format rules strictly enforced.* All filings shall be in compliance with the Indiana Rules of Trial Procedure. If the documents received are not in proper form, such deficiencies will not be corrected by court personnel. IN ST HAMILTON TRIAL Rule 201(201.70). The Court shall not be required to act on any Motion, Petition or other request for relief unless filed in conformity with the Hamilton County Local Trial and Administrative rules. IN ST HAMILTON TRIAL Rule 202(202.20).

2. *Size of papers for filing.* Effective January 1, 1992, all pleadings, copies, motions and documents filed with any trial court or appellate level court, typed or printed, with the exception of exhibits and existing wills, shall be prepared on eight and one-half by eleven inch (8 1/2" x 11") size paper. IN ST ADMIN Rule 11.

    a. *Form.* All documents filed in any Hamilton County Court, with the exception of exhibits and existing wills, shall be prepared on paper measuring eight and one-half by eleven inches (8 1/2" x 11"). IN ST HAMILTON TRIAL Rule 201(201.20).

3. *Signature requirements*

    a. *Signature of attorney.* Every pleading or motion of a party represented by an attorney shall be signed by at least one (1) attorney of record in his individual name, whose address, telephone number, and attorney number shall be stated, except that this provision shall not apply to pleadings and motions

made and transcribed at the trial or a hearing before the judge and received by him in such form. IN ST TRIAL P Rule 11(A).

    i.   The signature of an attorney constitutes a certificate by him that he has read the pleadings; that to the best of his knowledge, information, and belief, there is good ground to support it; and that it is not interposed for delay. IN ST TRIAL P Rule 11(A).

    ii.   If a pleading or motion is not signed or is signed with intent to defeat the purpose of the rule, it may be stricken as sham and false and the action may proceed as though the pleading had not been served. IN ST TRIAL P Rule 11(A).

    iii.   For a willful violation of IN ST TRIAL P Rule 11 an attorney may be subjected to appropriate disciplinary action. Similar action may be taken if scandalous or indecent matter is inserted. IN ST TRIAL P Rule 11(A).

b.   *Signature of unrepresented party.* A party who is not represented by an attorney shall sign his pleading and state his address. IN ST TRIAL P Rule 11(A).

c.   *Verification not generally required.* Except when specifically required by rule, pleadings or motions need not be verified or accompanied by affidavit. The rule in equity that the averments of an answer under oath must be overcome by the testimony of two (2) witnesses or of one (1) witness sustained by corroborating circumstances is abolished. IN ST TRIAL P Rule 11(A).

d.   *Verification by affirmation or representation.* When in connection with any civil or special statutory proceeding it is required that any pleading, motion, petition, supporting affidavit, or other document of any kind, be verified, or that an oath be taken, it shall be sufficient if the subscriber simply affirms the truth of the matter to be verified by an affirmation or representation. IN ST TRIAL P Rule 11(B). IN ST TRIAL P Rule 11(B) states that the affirmation or representation should be in substantially the following language: "I (we) affirm, under the penalties for perjury, that the foregoing representation(s) is (are) true. (Signed) _____."

    i.   Any person who falsifies an affirmation or representation of fact shall be subject to the same penalties as are prescribed by law for the making of a false affidavit. IN ST TRIAL P Rule 11(B).

e.   *Verified pleadings, motions, and affidavits as evidence.* Pleadings, motions and affidavits accompanying or in support of such pleadings or motions when required to be verified or under oath shall be accepted as a representation that the signer had personal knowledge thereof or reasonable cause to believe the existence of the facts or matters stated or alleged therein; and, if otherwise competent or acceptable as evidence, may be admitted as evidence of the facts or matters stated or alleged therein when it is so provided in the Indiana Rules of Trial Procedure, by statute or other law, or to the extent the writing or signature expressly purports to be made upon the signer's personal knowledge. When such pleadings, motions and affidavits are verified or under oath they shall not require other or greater proof on the part of the adverse party than if not verified or not under oath unless expressly provided otherwise by the Indiana Rules of Trial Procedure, statute or other law. Affidavits upon motions for summary judgment under IN ST TRIAL P Rule 56 and in denial of execution under IN ST TRIAL P Rule 9.2 shall be made upon personal knowledge. IN ST TRIAL P Rule 11(C).

4.   *Information excluded from public access.* Every document filed in a case shall separately identify information excluded from public access pursuant to IN ST ADMIN Rule 9(G)(1) as follows:

a.   Whole documents that are excluded from public access pursuant to IN ST ADMIN Rule 9(G)(1) shall be tendered on light green paper or have a light green coversheet attached to the document, marked "Not for Public Access" or "Confidential." IN ST TRIAL P Rule 5(G)(1).

b.   When only a portion of a document contains information excluded from public access pursuant to IN ST ADMIN Rule 9(G)(1), said information shall be omitted [or redacted] from the filed document, and set forth on a separate accompanying document on light green paper conspicuously marked "Not for Public Access" or "Confidential" and clearly designated [or identifying] the caption and number of the case and the document and location within the document to which the redacted material pertains. IN ST TRIAL P Rule 5(G)(2).

c.   With respect to documents filed in electronic format, the trial court, by local rule, may provide for

compliance with IN ST TRIAL P Rule 5 in manner that separates and protects access to information excluded from public access. IN ST TRIAL P Rule 5(G)(3).

d. IN ST TRIAL P Rule 5(G) does not apply to a record sealed by the court pursuant to IN ST 5-14-3-5.5 or otherwise, nor to records, documents, or information filed in cases to which public access is prohibited pursuant to IN ST ADMIN Rule 9(G). IN ST TRIAL P Rule 5(G)(4).

e. The following information in case records is excluded from public access and is confidential:

   i. Information that is excluded from public access pursuant to federal law;

   ii. Information that is excluded from public access as declared confidential by Indiana statute or other court rule, including without limitation:

- All adoption records created after July 8, 1941, as declared confidential by IN ST 31-19-19-1, et seq., except those specifically declared open by IN ST 31-19-13-2(2);

- All records relating to chancroid, chlamydia, gonorrhea, hepatitis, human immunodeficiency virus (HIV), Lymphogranuloma venereum, syphilis, tuberculosis, as declared confidential by IN ST 16-41-8-1, et seq.;

- All records relating to child abuse as declared confidential by IN ST 31-33-18-1, et seq.;

- All records relating to drug tests as declared confidential by IN ST 5-14-3-4(a)(9);

- Records of grand jury proceedings as declared confidential by IN ST 35-34-2-4;

- Records of juvenile proceedings as declared confidential by IN ST 31-39-1-2, except those specifically open under statute;

- All paternity records created after July 1, 1941 as declared confidential by IN ST 31-14-11-15, IN ST 31-19-5-23, IN ST 31-39-1-1 and IN ST 31-39-1-2 [Editor's note: IN ST 31-14-11-15 was repealed effective May 9, 2013];

- All pre-sentence reports as declared confidential by IN ST 35-38-1-13;

- Written petitions to permit marriages without consent and orders directing the Clerk of Court to issue a marriage license to underage persons, as declared confidential by IN ST 31-11-1-6;

- Only those arrest warrants, search warrants, indictments and informations ordered confidential by the trial judge, prior to return of duly executed service as declared confidential by IN ST 5-14-3-4(b)(1);

- All medical, mental health, or tax records unless determined by law or regulation of any governmental custodian not to be confidential, released by the subject of such records, or declared by a court of competent jurisdiction to be essential to the resolution of litigation as declared confidential by IN ST 16-39-3-10, IN ST 6-4.1-5-10, IN ST 6-4.1-12-12, and IN ST 6-8.1-7-1;

- Personal information relating to jurors or prospective jurors, other than for the use of the parties and counsel, pursuant to IN ST JURY Rule 10;

- Information relating to protection from abuse orders, no-contact orders and workplace violence restraining orders as declared confidential by IN ST 5-2-9-6, et seq.;

- Mediation proceedings pursuant to IN ST ADR Rule 2.11, Mini-Trial proceedings pursuant to IN ST ADR Rule 4.4(C), and Summary Jury Trials pursuant to IN ST ADR Rule 5.6;

- Information in probation files pursuant to the Probation Standards promulgated by the Judicial Conference of Indiana pursuant to IN ST 11-13-1-8(b);

- Information deemed confidential pursuant to the Rules for Court Administered Alcohol and Drug Programs promulgated by the Judicial Conference of Indiana pursuant to IN ST 12-23-14-13;

- Information deemed confidential pursuant to the Problem-Solving Court Rules promulgated by the Judicial Conference of Indiana pursuant to IN ST 33-23-16-16;

- All records of the Department of workforce Development as declared confidential by IN ST 22-4-19-6;
- Information regarding interception of electronic communications that is sealed or deemed confidential as set forth in IN ST 35-33.5-2-1, et seq.

iii. Information excluded from public access by specific court order;

iv. Complete Social Security Numbers of living persons;

v. With the exception of names, information such as addresses, phone numbers, and dates of birth which explicitly identifies:

- Natural persons who are witnesses or victims (not including defendants) in criminal, domestic violence, stalking, sexual assault, juvenile, or civil protection order proceedings, provided that juveniles who are victims of sex crimes shall be identified by initials only;
- Places of residence of judicial officers, clerks and other employees of courts and clerks of court, unless the person or persons about whom the information pertains waives confidentiality;

vi. Complete account numbers of specific assets, loans, bank accounts, credit cards, and personal identification numbers (PINs);

vii. All orders of expungement entered in criminal or juvenile proceedings, orders to restrict access to criminal history information pursuant to IN ST 35-38-5-5.5 or IN ST 35-38-8-5 and records excluded from public access by such orders, and information related to infractions that is excluded from public access pursuant to IN ST 34-28-5-15 or IN ST 34-28-5-16 [Editor's note: IN ST 35-38-5-5.5, IN ST 35-38-8-5 and IN ST 34-28-5-16 were repealed effective July 1, 2013; for information on orders restricting access to criminal history, refer to IN ST 35-38-9-1, et seq.];

viii. All personal notes and e-mail, and deliberative material, of judges, jurors, court staff and judicial agencies, and information recorded in personal data assistants (PDA's) or organizers and personal calendars. IN ST ADMIN Rule 9(G)(1).

F. Filing and Service Requirements

1. *Filing requirements.* Except as otherwise provided in IN ST TRIAL P Rule 5(E)(2), all pleadings and papers subsequent to the complaint which are required to be served upon a party shall be filed with the Court either before service or within a reasonable period of time thereafter. IN ST TRIAL P Rule 5(E)(1). All pleadings shall be filed with the Hamilton County Clerk with the exception of emergency orders under IN ST TRIAL P Rule 65. IN ST HAMILTON TRIAL Rule 201(201.10).

   a. *Filing with the court defined.* The filing of pleadings, motions, and other papers with the court as required by the Indiana Rules of Trial Procedure shall be made by one of the following methods:

      i. Delivery to the clerk of the court;

      ii. Sending by electronic transmission under the procedure adopted pursuant to IN ST ADMIN Rule 12;

      iii. Mailing to the clerk by registered, certified or express mail return receipt requested;

      iv. Depositing with any third-party commercial carrier for delivery to the clerk within three (3) calendar days, cost prepaid, properly addressed;

      v. If the court so permits, filing with the judge, in which event the judge shall note thereon the filing date and forthwith transmit them to the office of the clerk; or

      vi. Electronic filing, as approved by the Division of State Court Administration pursuant to IN ST ADMIN Rule 16. IN ST TRIAL P Rule 5(F).

      vii. Filing by registered or certified mail and by third-party commercial carrier shall be complete upon mailing or deposit. IN ST TRIAL P Rule 5(F).

   b. *Facsimile filing.* As outlined in IN ST HAMILTON ADMIN Rule 103(103.10),facsimile filing is permitted in the Circuit and Superior Courts of Hamilton County. The Courts authorize the Hamilton

County Clerk of Courts to accept pleadings, motions and other papers by electronic facsimile transmission for filing in any case pending before the Courts, subject to the requirements of IN ST HAMILTON ADMIN Rule 103(103.10). IN ST HAMILTON ADMIN Rule 103(103.10); IN ST HAMILTON TRIAL Rule 201(201.80).

i. *Generally.* In counties where a majority of judges of the courts of record, by posted local rule, have authorized electronic facsimile filing and designated a telephone number to receive such transmissions, pleadings, motions, and other papers may be sent to the Clerk of Circuit Court by electronic facsimile transmission for filing in any case, provided:

- Such matter does not exceed ten (10) pages, including the cover sheet;

- Such matter does not require the payment of fees other than the electronic facsimile transcription fee set forth in IN ST ADMIN Rule 12(E);

- The sending party creates at the time of transmission a machine generated log for such transmission; and

- The original document and the transmission log are maintained by the sending party for the duration of the litigation. IN ST ADMIN Rule 12(B); IN ST HAMILTON ADMIN Rule 103(103.10)(d).

- Legibility of documents and timeliness of filing is the responsibility of the sender. IN ST HAMILTON ADMIN Rule 103(103.10)(g).

- The Clerk shall accept electronic facsimile transmission filings only if received at the facsimile machine assigned by the Clerk. The telephone number designated to receive such transmission is available at IN ST HAMILTON ADMIN Rule 103(103.40). IN ST HAMILTON ADMIN Rule 103(103.40).

ii. *Time of filing.* During normal, posted business hours, the time of filing shall be the time the duplicate document is produced in the office of the Clerk of the Circuit Court. Duplicate documents received at all other times shall be filed as of the next normal business day. IN ST ADMIN Rule 12(C).

- If the receiving fax machine endorses its own time and date stamp upon the transmitted documents and the receiving machine produces a delivery receipt which is electronically created and transmitted to the sending party, the time of filing shall be the date and time recorded on the transmitted document by the receiving fax machine. IN ST ADMIN Rule 12(C).

- Electronic facsimile transmissions will be accepted for filing only during the regular business hours as set forth in IN ST HAMILTON ADMIN Rule 101. Transmissions received by the Hamilton County Clerk after close of business shall be filed effective the next regular business day. IN ST HAMILTON ADMIN Rule 103(103.30).

iii. *Filing fee.* The electronic facsimile transmission will not be accepted for filing if its filing requires the payment of any fee other than the electronic facsimile transcription fee set forth in IN ST HAMILTON ADMIN Rule 103(103.20). IN ST HAMILTON ADMIN Rule 103(103.10)(e).

- Pursuant to Ordinance adopted by the Hamilton County Board of Commissioners, the Clerk shall collect an electronic facsimile transcription fee of One Dollar ($1.00) per page, to a maximum of Ten Dollars ($10.00) per transmission, for each electronic facsimile transmission accepted for filing with the Hamilton County Circuit and Superior Courts. IN ST HAMILTON ADMIN Rule 103(103.20).

- The fee shall be assessed against the sending party and shall be paid upon receipt of invoice by that party and at the latest within thirty (30) days of the transmission. In the event the fee is not paid by the sending party within the time limits provided, the court may issue a show-cause order or enter a judgment in the matter. The Clerk may refuse an electronic facsimile transmission from any attorney or pro se litigant who has failed to pay these fees within thirty (30) days. IN ST HAMILTON ADMIN Rule 103(103.20).

iv. *No direct filing with court.* A party shall not send pleadings, motions and other papers by electronic facsimile transmission for filing directly to any Court without that Court's prior approval to do so. IN ST HAMILTON ADMIN Rule 103(103.50).

c. *Filing with special judge.* After a special judge has qualified, a copy of each pleading and Chronological Case Summary entries filed with the Court shall be mailed or delivered to the office of that Special judge by the counsel or pro se litigant with service indicated on the certificate of service. IN ST HAMILTON TRIAL Rule 204(204.20).

d. *Proof of filing.* Any party filing any paper by any method other than personal delivery to the clerk shall retain proof of filing. IN ST TRIAL P Rule 5(F).

2. *Service requirements.* Unless otherwise provided by the Indiana Rules of Trial Procedure or an order of the court, each party and special judge, if any, shall be served with: (1) every order required by its terms to be served; (2) every pleading subsequent to the original complaint; (3) every written motion except one which may be heard ex parte; (4) every brief submitted to the trial court; (5) every paper relating to discovery required to be served upon a party; and (6) every written notice, appearance, demand, offer of judgment, designation of record on appeal, or similar paper. IN ST TRIAL P Rule 5(A).

a. *Methods of service*

i. *Personal service.* Whenever a party is represented by an attorney of record, service shall be made upon such attorney unless service upon the party himself is ordered by the court. Service upon the attorney or party shall be made by delivering or mailing a copy of the papers to the last known address or where an attorney or party has consented to service by fax or e-mail, as provided in IN ST TRIAL P Rule 3.1(A)(4), by faxing or e-mailing a copy of the documents to the fax number or e-mail address set out in the appearance form or correction as required by IN ST TRIAL P Rule 3.1(E). IN ST TRIAL P Rule 5(B). Delivery of a copy within IN ST TRIAL P Rule 5 means:

- Offering or tendering it to the attorney or party and stating the nature of the papers being served. Refusal to accept an offered or tendered document is a waiver of any objection to the sufficiency or adequacy of service of that document;

- Leaving it at his office with a clerk or other person in charge thereof, or if there is no one in charge, leaving it in a conspicuous place therein; or

- If the office is closed, by leaving it at his dwelling house or usual place of abode with some person of suitable age and discretion then residing therein; or,

- Leaving it at some other suitable place, selected by the attorney upon whom service is being made, pursuant to duly promulgated local rule. IN ST TRIAL P Rule 5(B)(1).

ii. *Service by mail.* If service is made by mail, the papers shall be deposited in the United States mail addressed to the person on whom they are being served, with postage prepaid. Service shall be deemed complete upon mailing. Proof of service of all papers permitted to be mailed may be made by written acknowledgment of service, by affidavit of the person who mailed the papers, or by certificate of an attorney. It shall be the duty of attorneys when entering their appearance in a cause or when filing pleadings or papers therein, to have noted in the Chronological Case Summary or said pleadings or papers so filed the address and telephone number of their office. Service by delivery or by mail at such address shall be deemed sufficient and complete. IN ST TRIAL P Rule 5(B)(2).

iii. *Service by fax or e-mail.* A party who has consented to service by fax or e-mail may be served as follows:

- Service by e-mail shall be made by attaching the document being served in .pdf format. Discovery documents must also be served in accordance with IN ST TRIAL P Rule 26(A). IN ST TRIAL P Rule 5(B)(3)(a).

- Service by fax shall be deemed complete upon generation of a transmission record indicating the successful transmission of the entire document, except as provided in IN ST TRIAL P Rule 5(B)(3)(d). IN ST TRIAL P Rule 5(B)(3)(b).

- Service by e-mail shall be deemed complete upon transmission, except as provided in IN ST TRIAL P Rule 5(B)(3)(d). IN ST TRIAL P Rule 5(B)(3)(c).

- Service by fax or e-mail that occurs on a Saturday, Sunday, legal holiday, or day the court or agency in which the matter is pending is closed or after 5:00 PM local time of the recipient shall be deemed complete the next day that is not a Saturday, Sunday, legal holiday, or day that the court or agency in which the matter is pending is not closed. IN ST TRIAL P Rule 5(B)(3)(d).

    iv. *Mail box service.* Pursuant to IN ST TRIAL P Rule 5(B)(1)(d), the Circuit and Superior Courts of Hamilton County hereby designate the "mail boxes" located in the Clerk's order book office for service of pleadings upon attorneys who have such boxes. IN ST HAMILTON TRIAL Rule 201(201.50).

b. *Serving numerous defendants.* In any action in which there are unusually large numbers of defendants, the court, upon motion or of its own initiative, may order:

    i. That service of the pleadings of the defendants and replies thereto need not be made as between the defendants;

- That any cross-claim, counterclaim, or matter constituting an avoidance or affirmative defense contained therein shall be deemed to be denied or avoided by all other parties; and

- That the filing of any such pleading and service thereof upon the plaintiff constitutes due notice of it to the parties. IN ST TRIAL P Rule 5(D).

    ii. A copy of every such order shall be served upon the parties in such manner and form as the court directs. IN ST TRIAL P Rule 5(D).

c. *Service on parties in default for failure to appear.* No service need be made on parties in default for failure to appear, except that pleadings asserting new or additional claims for relief against them shall be served upon them in the manner provided by service of summons in IN ST TRIAL P Rule 4. IN ST TRIAL P Rule 5(A).

G. Hearings

1. The Indiana rules do not contemplate a hearing regarding the filing and service of an answer.

H. Forms

1. Official Answer Forms for Indiana

a. Affidavit of debt. IN ST TRIAL P App. A-2.

b. Appearance by attorney in civil case. IN ST TRIAL P App. B.

2. Answer Forms for Indiana

a. Appearance; By responding party. 9 INPRAC § 39.3.

b. Answer; Form and content. 9 INPRAC § 41.1.

c. Answer; General form. 9 INPRAC § 41.3.

d. Answer; Another form. 9 INPRAC § 41.4.

e. Answer; Another form. 9 INPRAC § 41.5.

f. General denial. 9 INPRAC § 41.6.

g. Specific denial of designated paragraph. 9 INPRAC § 41.7.

h. Specific admission of designated paragraph. 9 INPRAC § 41.8.

i. Denial of knowledge or information to form belief. 9 INPRAC § 41.9.

j. Denial of knowledge or information to form belief; Another form. 9 INPRAC § 41.10.

k. Partial denial and partial admission of designated paragraph. 9 INPRAC § 41.11.

l. Denial of designated paragraph for reason that document speaks for itself. 9 INPRAC § 41.12.

m. Adoption of admissions or denials by co-defendant's answer. 9 INPRAC § 41.13.

n. Denial of execution of instrument filed with pleading. 9 INPRAC § 41.14.

o. Answer to cross-claim. 9 INPRAC § 41.15.

p. Answer to third-party complaint. 9 INPRAC § 41.16.

q. Accord and satisfaction. 9 INPRAC § 41.21.

r. Answer. 5 INPRAC § 3:3.3.

s. Answer; Another form. 5 INPRAC § 3:3.4.

t. Certificate of service; Personal service. 9 INPRAC § 5.7.

u. Certificate of service; First class mail. 9 INPRAC § 5.8.

v. Signature; By party. 9 INPRAC § 4.5.

w. Signature; Attorney. 9 INPRAC § 4.6.

x. Signature; Attorney; Another form. 9 INPRAC § 4.7.

y. Signature; Attorney; Another form. 9 INPRAC § 4.8.

z. Verification; Official form. 9 INPRAC § 4.9.

I. Checklist

(I) ❑ Matters to be considered by the plaintiff

  (a) ❑ Required documents

    (1) ❑ Summons

    (2) ❑ Complaint

    (3) ❑ Appearance form

  (b) ❑ Supplemental documents

    (1) ❑ Proof of written instrument

    (2) ❑ Notice of intent to use foreign law

    (3) ❑ Praecipe

    (4) ❑ Facsimile cover sheet

  (c) ❑ Timing

    (1) ❑ The claimant typically bears the burden of commencing an action within the applicable statute of limitations

    (2) ❑ If person seeking service of process fails without cause for sixty (60) days or more to provide clerk with required summons for issuance or with other information necessary to effectuate service, person has failed to exercise due diligence in securing service of process

(II) ❑ Matters to be considered by the defendant

  (a) ❑ Required documents

    (1) ❑ Answer

    (2) ❑ Appearance form

    (3) ❑ Certificate of service

  (b) ❑ Supplemental documents

    (1) ❑ Admission of service

    (2) ❑ Proof of written instrument

    (3) ❑ Notice of intent to use foreign law

    (4) ❑ Facsimile cover sheet

(c) ❑ Timing

(1) ❑ A responsive pleading required under the Indiana Rules of Trial Procedure, shall be served within twenty (20) days after service of the prior pleading

(2) ❑ The service of a motion permitted under IN ST TRIAL P Rule 12 alters the time for service of responsive pleadings as follows, unless a different time is fixed by the court:

(i) ❑ If the court does not grant the motion, the responsive pleading shall be served in ten (10) days after notice of the court's action;

(ii) ❑ If the court grants the motion and the corrective action is allowed to be taken, it shall be taken within ten (10) days, and the responsive pleading shall be served within ten (10) days thereafter

(3) ❑ All pleadings and papers subsequent to the complaint which are required to be served upon a party shall be filed with the Court either before service or within a reasonable period of time thereafter

Pleadings
Amended Answer

Document Last Updated October 2013

A. Applicable Rules

1. *State rules*

   a. Appearance. IN ST TRIAL P Rule 3.1.

   b. Summons. IN ST TRIAL P Rule 4.

   c. Filing and service. IN ST TRIAL P Rule 4.6; IN ST TRIAL P Rule 5.

   d. Time. IN ST TRIAL P Rule 6.

   e. Pleadings. IN ST TRIAL P Rule 7; IN ST TRIAL P Rule 8; IN ST TRIAL P Rule 9; IN ST TRIAL P Rule 9.1; IN ST TRIAL P Rule 9.2; IN ST TRIAL P Rule 10.

   f. Signing and verification of pleadings. IN ST TRIAL P Rule 11.

   g. Defenses and objections; When and how presented; By pleading or motion; Motion for judgment on the pleadings. IN ST TRIAL P Rule 12.

   h. Counterclaim and cross-claim. IN ST TRIAL P Rule 13.

   i. Third-party practice. IN ST TRIAL P Rule 14.

   j. Amended and supplemental pleadings. IN ST TRIAL P Rule 15.

   k. Parties plaintiff and defendant; Capacity. IN ST TRIAL P Rule 17.

   l. Joinder. IN ST TRIAL P Rule 19; IN ST TRIAL P Rule 20.

   m. Consolidation; Separate trials. IN ST TRIAL P Rule 42.

   n. Evidence. IN ST TRIAL P Rule 43.

   o. Determination of foreign law. IN ST TRIAL P Rule 44.1.

   p. Judgment on the evidence (directed verdict). IN ST TRIAL P Rule 50.

   q. Findings by the court. IN ST TRIAL P Rule 52.

   r. Judgment; Costs. IN ST TRIAL P Rule 54.

   s. Summary judgment. IN ST TRIAL P Rule 56.

   t. Motion to correct error. IN ST TRIAL P Rule 59.

   u. Relief from judgment or order. IN ST TRIAL P Rule 60.

   v. Venue requirements. IN ST TRIAL P Rule 75.

w. Access to court records. IN ST ADMIN Rule 9.

x. Paper size. IN ST ADMIN Rule 11.

y. Facsimile and electronic transmission. IN ST ADMIN Rule 12; IN ST ADMIN Rule 16.

z. Sealing of certain records by court; Hearing; Notice; Privacy and confidentiality. IN ST 5-2-9-6; IN ST 5-14-3-4; IN ST 5-14-3-5.5; IN ST 6-4.1-5-10; IN ST 6-4.1-12-12; IN ST 6-8.1-7-1; IN ST 11-13-1-8; IN ST 12-23-14-13; IN ST 16-39-3-10; IN ST 16-41-8-1; IN ST 22-4-19-6; IN ST 31-11-1-6; IN ST 31-19-5-23; IN ST 31-19-13-2; IN ST 31-19-19-1; IN ST 31-33-18-1; IN ST 31-39-1-1; IN ST 31-39-1-2; IN ST 33-23-16-16; IN ST 35-34-2-4; IN ST 35-38-1-13; IN ST 35-38-9-1; IN ST ADR Rule 2.11; IN ST ADR Rule 4.4; IN ST ADR Rule 5.6; IN ST JURY Rule 10.

2. *Local rules*

a. Court hours. IN ST HAMILTON ADMIN Rule 101.

b. Facsimile transmissions. IN ST HAMILTON ADMIN Rule 103.

c. Filing of pleadings and entry of appearances. IN ST HAMILTON TRIAL Rule 201.

d. Proposed orders. IN ST HAMILTON TRIAL Rule 202.

e. Special judges. IN ST HAMILTON TRIAL Rule 204.

f. Continuances. IN ST HAMILTON TRIAL Rule 206.

B. Timing

1. *Filing an amended pleading*

a. *As a matter of course.* A party may amend his pleading once as a matter of course at any time before a responsive pleading is served or, if the pleading is one to which no responsive pleading is permitted, and the action has not been placed upon the trial calendar, he may so amend it at any time within thirty (30) days after it is served. IN ST TRIAL P Rule 15(A).

b. *With leave of court.* Otherwise a party may amend his pleading only by leave of court or by written consent of the adverse party; and leave shall be given when justice so requires. IN ST TRIAL P Rule 15(A). Refer to the Indiana KeyRules Motion for Leave to Amend document for more information.

2. *Computation of time*

a. *Generally; Days excluded.* In computing any period of time prescribed or allowed by the Indiana Rules of Trial Procedure, by order of the court, or by any applicable statute, the day of the act, event, or default from which the designated period of time begins to run shall not be included. The last day of the period so computed is to be included unless it is:

   i. A Saturday,

   ii. A Sunday,

   iii. A legal holiday as defined by state statute, or

   iv. A day the office in which the act is to be done is closed during regular business hours. IN ST TRIAL P Rule 6(A).

b. *Short periods.* In any event, the period runs until the end of the next day that is not a Saturday, a Sunday, a legal holiday, or a day on which the office is closed. When the period of time allowed is less than seven (7) days, intermediate Saturdays, Sundays, legal holidays, and days on which the office is closed shall be excluded from the computations. IN ST TRIAL P Rule 6(A).

c. *Additional time after service by United States mail.* Whenever a party has the right or is required to do some act or take some proceedings within a prescribed period after the service of a notice or other paper upon him and the notice or paper is served upon him by United States mail, three (3) days shall be added to the prescribed period. IN ST TRIAL P Rule 6(E).

d. *Enlargement of time.* When an act is required or allowed to be done at or within a specific time by the Indiana Rules of Trial Procedure, the court may at any time for cause shown:

   i. Order the period enlarged, with or without motion or notice, if request therefor is made before the expiration of the period originally prescribed or extended by a previous order; or

    ii.   Upon motion made after the expiration of the specific period, permit the act to be done where the failure to act was the result of excusable neglect; but, the court may not extend the time for taking any action for judgment on the evidence under IN ST TRIAL P Rule 50(A), amendment of findings and judgment under IN ST TRIAL P Rule 52(B), to correct errors under IN ST TRIAL P Rule 59(C), statement in opposition to motion to correct error under IN ST TRIAL P Rule 59(E), or to obtain relief from final judgment under IN ST TRIAL P Rule 60(B), except to the extent and under the conditions stated in those rules. IN ST TRIAL P Rule 6(B).

    iii.   For information on obtaining a continuance, refer to IN ST HAMILTON TRIAL Rule 206.

C. General Requirements

1. *Amending pleadings.* The purpose of an amended pleading is to include matters that occurred before the filing of the original pleading but which were either overlooked by the pleader or unknown to him at the time. It is a substitute for the original and relates to the facts that existed when the original pleading was filed. An amended pleading supercedes the original as to those portions amended. 10 INPRAC § 46.1.

  a. *Amendments liberally allowed.* Amendments to pleadings are to be liberally allowed in order that all issues are presented in one action. 10 INPRAC § 46.1; Pinnacle Media, LLC v. Metropolitan Dev. Com'n of Marion County, 868 N.E.2d 894 (Ind.Ct.App. 2007).

  b. *Amendments to conform to the evidence.* When issues not raised by the pleadings are tried by express or implied consent of the parties, they shall be treated in all respects as if they had been raised in the pleadings. Such amendment of the pleadings as may be necessary to cause them to conform to the evidence and to raise these issues may be made upon motion of any party at any time, even after judgment, but failure so to amend does not affect the result of the trial of these issues. If evidence is objected to at the trial on the ground that it is not within the issues made by the pleadings, the court may allow the pleadings to be amended and shall do so freely when the presentation of the merits of the action will be subserved thereby and the objecting party fails to satisfy the court that the admission of such evidence would prejudice him in maintaining his action or defense upon the merits. The court may grant a continuance to enable the objecting party to meet such evidence. IN ST TRIAL P Rule 15(B).

  c. *Relation back of amendments*

    i.   Whenever the claim or defense asserted in the amended pleading arose out of the conduct, transaction, or occurrence set forth or attempted to be set forth in the original pleading, the amendment relates back to the date of the original pleading. An amendment changing the party against whom a claim is asserted relates back if the foregoing provision is satisfied and, within one hundred and twenty (120) days of commencement of the action, the party to be brought in by amendment:

- Has received such notice of the institution of the action that he will not be prejudiced in maintaining his defense on the merits; and

- Knew or should have known that but for a mistake concerning the identity of the proper party, the action would have been brought against him. IN ST TRIAL P Rule 15(C).

    ii.   The requirement of subsections IN ST TRIAL P Rule 15(C)(1) and IN ST TRIAL P Rule 15(C)(2) with respect to a governmental organization to be brought into the action as defendant is satisfied:

- In the case of a state or governmental organization by delivery or mailing of process to the attorney general or to a governmental executive [IN ST TRIAL P Rule 4.6(A)(3)]; or

- In the case of a local governmental organization, by delivery or mailing of process to its attorney as provided by statute, to a governmental executive thereof [IN ST TRIAL P Rule 4.6(A)(4)], or to the officer holding the office if suit is against the officer or an office. IN ST TRIAL P Rule 15(C).

  d. *Amendment by leave.* Amendments, other than an amendment by right, may be made only by leave of court or by written consent of the opposing party. 2 INPRAC R 15(15.2). Refer to the Indiana KeyRules Motion for Leave to Amend document for more information on amending with leave of court.

2. *Pleading, generally*

   a. *Pleadings to be concise.* Each averment of a pleading shall be simple, concise, and direct. No technical forms of pleading or motions are required. All fictions in pleading are abolished. IN ST TRIAL P Rule 8(E)(1).

   b. *Pleading in the alternative.* A pleading may set forth two (2) or more statements of a claim or defense alternatively or hypothetically, either in one (1) count or defense or in separate counts or defenses. When two (2) or more statements are made in the alternative and one (1) of them if made independently would be sufficient, the pleading is not made insufficient by the insufficiency of one or more of the alternative statements. A pleading may also state as many separate claims or defenses as the pleader has regardless of consistency and whether based on legal or equitable grounds. All statements shall be made subject to the obligations set forth in IN ST TRIAL P Rule 11. IN ST TRIAL P Rule 8(E)(2).

   c. *Motions and pleadings, joint and several.* All motions and pleadings of any kind addressed to two (2) or more paragraphs of any pleading, or filed by two (2) or more parties, shall be taken and construed as joint, separate, and several motions or pleadings to each of such paragraphs and by and against each of such parties. All motions or pleadings containing two (2) or more subject-matters shall be taken and construed as separate and several as to each subject-matter. All objections to rulings made by two (2) or more parties shall be taken and construed as the joint, separate, and several objections of each of such parties. IN ST TRIAL P Rule 8(E)(3).

      i. A complaint filed by or against two (2) or more plaintiffs shall be taken and construed as joint, separate, and several as to each of said plaintiffs. IN ST TRIAL P Rule 8(E).

   d. *Construction of pleadings.* All pleadings shall be so construed as to do substantial justice, lead to disposition on the merits, and avoid litigation of procedural points. IN ST TRIAL P Rule 8(F).

3. *Contents of the answer*

   a. *Defenses which may be raised by answer or motion.* Every defense, in law or fact, to a claim for relief in any pleading, whether a claim, counterclaim, cross-claim, or third-party claim, shall be asserted in the responsive pleading thereto if one is required; except that at the option of the pleader, the following defenses may be made by motion:

      i. Lack of jurisdiction over the subject matter;

      ii. Lack of jurisdiction over the person;

      iii. Incorrect venue under IN ST TRIAL P Rule 75, or any statutory provision. The disposition of this motion shall be consistent with IN ST TRIAL P Rule 75;

      iv. Insufficiency of process;

      v. Insufficiency of service of process;

      vi. Failure to state a claim upon which relief can be granted, which shall include failure to name the real party in interest under IN ST TRIAL P Rule 17;

      vii. Failure to join a party needed for just adjudication under IN ST TRIAL P Rule 19;

      viii. The same action pending in another state court of this state. IN ST TRIAL P Rule 12(B).

      ix. A motion making any of these defenses shall be made before pleading if a further pleading is permitted or within twenty (20) days after service of the prior pleading if none is required. If a pleading sets forth a claim for relief to which the adverse party is not required to serve a responsive pleading, any of the defenses in section IN ST TRIAL P Rule 12(B)(2), IN ST TRIAL P Rule 12(B)(3), IN ST TRIAL P Rule 12(B)(4), IN ST TRIAL P Rule 12(B)(5) or IN ST TRIAL P Rule 12(B)(8) is waived to the extent constitutionally permissible unless made in a motion within twenty (20) days after service of the prior pleading. No defense or objection is waived by being joined with one (1) or more other defenses or objections in a responsive pleading or motion. IN ST TRIAL P Rule 12(B).

   b. *Waiver or preservation of certain defenses*

      i. A defense of lack of jurisdiction over the person, improper venue, insufficiency of process, insufficiency of service of process, or the same action pending in another state court of this state is waived to the extent constitutionally permissible:

- If omitted from a motion in the circumstances described in IN ST TRIAL P Rule 12(G),

- If it is neither made by motion under IN ST TRIAL P Rule 12 nor included in a responsive pleading or an amendment thereof permitted by IN ST TRIAL P Rule 15(A) to be made as a matter of course. IN ST TRIAL P Rule 12(H)(1).

    ii. A defense of failure to state a claim upon which relief can be granted, a defense of failure to join an indispensable party under IN ST TRIAL P Rule 19(B), and an objection of failure to state a legal defense to a claim may be made in any pleading permitted or ordered under IN ST TRIAL P Rule 7(A) or by motion for judgment on the pleadings, or at the trial on the merits. IN ST TRIAL P Rule 12(H)(2).

c. *Defenses; Form of denials*

    i. A responsive pleading shall state in short and plain terms the pleader's defenses to each claim asserted and shall admit or controvert the averments set forth in the preceding pleading. If in good faith the pleader intends to deny all the averments in the preceding pleading, he may do so by general denial subject to the provisions of IN ST TRIAL P Rule 11. If he does not intend a general denial, he may:

- Specifically deny designated averments or paragraphs; or

- Generally deny all averments except such designated averments and paragraphs as he expressly admits. IN ST TRIAL P Rule 8(B).

    ii. If he lacks knowledge or information sufficient to form a belief as to the truth of an averment, he shall so state and his statement shall be considered a denial. If in good faith a pleader intends to deny only a part or a qualification of an averment, he shall specify so much of it as is true and material and deny the remainder. All denials shall fairly meet the substance of the averments denied. IN ST TRIAL P Rule 8 shall have no application to uncontested actions for divorce, or to answers required to be filed by clerks or guardians ad litem. IN ST TRIAL P Rule 8(B).

d. *Affirmative defenses.* A responsive pleading shall set forth affirmatively and carry the burden of proving: accord and satisfaction, arbitration and award, discharge in bankruptcy, duress, estoppel, failure of consideration, fraud, illegality, injury by fellow servant, laches, license, payment, release, res judicata, statute of frauds, statute of limitations, waiver, lack of jurisdiction over the subject-matter, lack of jurisdiction over the person, improper venue, insufficiency of process or service of process, the same action pending in another state court of this state, and any other matter constituting an avoidance, matter of abatement, or affirmative defense. A party required to affirmatively plead any matters, including matters formerly required to be pleaded affirmatively by reply, shall have the burden of proving such matters. The burden of proof imposed by this or any other provision of the Indiana Rules of Trial Procedure is subject to the rules of evidence or any statute fixing a different rule. If the pleading mistakenly designates a defense as a counterclaim or a counterclaim as a defense, the court shall treat the pleading as if there had been a proper designation. IN ST TRIAL P Rule 8(C).

    i. An affirmative defense, generally, must be affirmatively stated by the party who seeks its benefit. 1A INPRAC R 8(8.5); Rice v. Grant County Bd. of Com'rs, 472 N.E.2d 213 (Ind.Ct.App. 1984). If that party does not raise the affirmative defense, then it is waived. 1A INPRAC R 8(8.5); Piskorowski v. Shell Oil Co., 403 N.E.2d 838, 847 (Ind.Ct.App. 1980).

    ii. It is clear that the list of affirmative defenses found in IN ST TRIAL P Rule 8 is not exhaustive. The question comes: when is a defense to be treated as an affirmative defense, with all of the attending consequences? 1A INPRAC R 8(8.5). The "determination of whether a defense is affirmative depends on whether it controverts an element of the plaintiff's prima facie case or raises matter outside the scope of the prima facie case." 1A INPRAC R 8(8.5); Molargik v. West Enterprises, Inc., 605 N.E.2d 1197, 1198 (Ind.Ct.App. 1993).

e. *Defense of contributory negligence or assumed risk.* In all claims alleging negligence, the burden of pleading and proving contributory negligence, assumption of risk, or incurred risk shall be upon the defendant who may plead such by denial of the allegation. IN ST TRIAL P Rule 9.1(A).

f. *Res ipsa loquitur.* Res ipsa loquitur or a similar doctrine may be pleaded by alleging generally that the facts connected with the action are unknown to the pleader and are within the knowledge of the opposing party. IN ST TRIAL P Rule 9.1(B).

g. *Consideration.* When an action or defense is founded upon a written contract or release, lack of consideration for the promise or release is an affirmative defense, and the party asserting lack of it carries the burden of proof. IN ST TRIAL P Rule 9.1(C).

h. *Bona fide purchaser.* When the rights of a person depend upon his status as a bona fide purchaser for value or upon similar requirements, such status must be pleaded and proved by the person asserting it, but it may be pleaded in general terms. Once it is established that the person has given any required value, unless such value is commercially unreasonable, and that he has met any requirements of recordation, filing, possession, or perfection, the trier of fact must find that such value was given or such perfection was made in accordance with any requirements of good faith, lack of knowledge, or lack of notice unless and until evidence is introduced which would support a finding of its non-existence. IN ST TRIAL P Rule 9.1(D).

i. *Presumption; Matters of judicial notice.* Neither presumptions of law nor matters of which judicial notice may be taken need be stated in a pleading. IN ST TRIAL P Rule 9.1(E).

j. *Property distrained; Sufficient answer.* In an action to recover the possession of property distrained while doing damage, an answer that the defendant, or person by whose command he acted, was lawfully possessed of the real property upon which the distress was made, and that the property distrained was at the time doing damage thereon, shall be good without setting forth the title of such real property. IN ST TRIAL P Rule 9.1(F).

k. *Effect of failure to deny.* Averments in a pleading to which a responsive pleading is required, except those pertaining to amount of damages, are admitted when not denied in the responsive pleading. Averments in a pleading to which no responsive pleading is required or permitted shall be taken as denied or avoided. IN ST TRIAL P Rule 8(D).

l. *Effect of admission.* When a rhetorical paragraph or allegation is admitted, the effect in Indiana is to remove it from trial. Such an admission is a "judicial admission", and the claim or issue which is admitted cannot be denied later by the trier of the facts. Further, this admitted fact does not require evidence to "prove it"; it is established. It becomes, in short, controlling and indisputable in the litigation, unless the trial court permits an amendment to the pleading which might remove the controlling effect of the admission, and permit it to become another fact or item of evidence in the case. 1A INPRAC R 8(8.4); Aylesworth v. McKesson, 421 N.E.2d 422 (Ind.Ct.App. 1981).

4. *Pleading special matters*

a. *Capacity.* It is not necessary to aver the capacity of a party to sue or be sued, the authority of a party to sue or be sued in a representative capacity, or the legal existence of an organization that is made a party. The burden of proving lack of such capacity, authority, or legal existence shall be upon the person asserting lack of it, and shall be pleaded as an affirmative defense. IN ST TRIAL P Rule 9(A).

b. *Fraud, mistake, condition of the mind.* In all averments of fraud or mistake, the circumstances constituting fraud or mistake shall be specifically averred. Malice, intent, knowledge, and other conditions of mind may be averred generally. IN ST TRIAL P Rule 9(B).

c. *Conditions precedent.* In pleading the performance or occurrence of promissory or non-promissory conditions precedent, it is sufficient to aver generally that all conditions precedent have been performed, have occurred, or have been excused. A denial of performance or occurrence shall be made specifically and with particularity, and a denial of excuse generally. IN ST TRIAL P Rule 9(C).

d. *Official document or act.* In pleading an official document or official act it is sufficient to aver that the document was issued or the act done in compliance with law. IN ST TRIAL P Rule 9(D).

e. *Judgment.* In pleading a judgment or decision of a domestic or foreign court, judicial or quasi-judicial tribunal, or of a board or officer, it is sufficient to aver the judgment or decision without setting forth matter showing jurisdiction to render it. IN ST TRIAL P Rule 9(E).

f. *Time and place.* For the purpose of testing the sufficiency of a pleading, averments of time and place are material and shall be considered like all other averments of material matter. However, time and place need be stated only with such specificity as will enable the opposing party to prepare his defense. IN ST TRIAL P Rule 9(F).

g. *Special damages; Damages where no answer.* When items of special damage are claimed, they shall be specifically stated. The relief granted to the plaintiff, if there be no answer, cannot exceed the relief demanded in his complaint; but, in any other case, the court may grant him any relief consistent with the facts or matters pleaded. IN ST TRIAL P Rule 9(G).

5. *Counterclaim and cross-claim*

a. *Compulsory counterclaims.* A pleading shall state as a counterclaim any claim which at the time of serving the pleading the pleader has against any opposing party, if it arises out of the transaction or occurrence that is the subject-matter of the opposing party's claim and does not require for its adjudication the presence of third parties of whom the court cannot acquire jurisdiction. But the pleader need not state the claim if:

   i. At the time the action was commenced the claim was the subject of another pending action; or

   ii. The opposing party brought suit upon his claim by attachment or other process by which the court did not acquire jurisdiction to render a personal judgment on that claim, and the pleader is not stating any counterclaim under IN ST TRIAL P Rule 13. IN ST TRIAL P Rule 13(A).

b. *Permissive counterclaims.* A pleading may state as a counterclaim any claim against an opposing party not arising out of the transaction or occurrence that is the subject-matter of the opposing party's claim. IN ST TRIAL P Rule 13(B).

c. *Counterclaim exceeding opposing claim.* A counterclaim may or may not diminish or defeat the recovery sought by the opposing party. It may claim relief exceeding in amount or different in kind from that sought in the pleading of the opposing party. IN ST TRIAL P Rule 13(C).

d. *Counterclaim against state.* IN ST TRIAL P Rule 13 shall not be construed to enlarge any right to assert a claim against the state. IN ST TRIAL P Rule 13(D).

e. *Counterclaim maturing or acquired after pleading.* A claim which either matured or was acquired by the pleader after serving his pleading may, with the permission of the court, be presented as a counterclaim by supplemental pleading. A counterclaim or cross-claim which is not due may be asserted against a party who is insolvent or the representative of a party who has been subjected to insolvency proceedings, if recovery thereon will be impaired because of such party's insolvency. IN ST TRIAL P Rule 13(E).

f. *Omitted counterclaim.* When a pleader fails to set up a counterclaim through oversight, inadvertence, or excusable neglect, or when justice requires, he may by leave of court set up the counterclaim by amendment. IN ST TRIAL P Rule 13(F).

g. *Cross-claim against co-party.* A pleading may state as a cross-claim any claim by one party against a co-party. IN ST TRIAL P Rule 13(G).

h. *Joinder of additional parties.* Persons other than those made parties to the original action may be made parties to a counterclaim or cross-claim in accordance with the provisions of IN ST TRIAL P Rule 14, IN ST TRIAL P Rule 19 and IN ST TRIAL P Rule 20. IN ST TRIAL P Rule 13(H).

i. *Separate trials; Separate judgments*

   i. If the court orders separate trials as provided in IN ST TRIAL P Rule 42(B), judgment on a counterclaim or cross-claim may be rendered in accordance with the terms of IN ST TRIAL P Rule 54(B) when the court has jurisdiction so to do, even if the claims of the opposing party have been dismissed or otherwise disposed of. In determining whether or not separate trial of a cross-claim shall be ordered, the court shall consider whether the cross-claim:

   - Arises out of the transaction or occurrence or series of transactions or occurrences that is the subject-matter either of the original action or of a counterclaim therein;

   - Relates to any property or contract that is the subject-matter of the original action; or

   - Claims that the person against whom it is asserted is liable to the cross-claimant for all or part of plaintiff's claim against him. IN ST TRIAL P Rule 13(I).

ii. In addition, the court may consider any other relevant factors. IN ST TRIAL P Rule 13(I).

j. *Effect of statute of limitations and other discharges at law.* The statute of limitations, a nonclaim statute or other discharge at law shall not bar a claim asserted as a counterclaim to the extent that:

    i. It diminishes or defeats the opposing party's claim if it arises out of the transaction or occurrence that is the subject-matter of the opposing party's claim, or if it could have been asserted as a counterclaim to the opposing party's claim before it (the counterclaim) was barred; or

    ii. It or the opposing party's claim relates to payment of or security for the other. IN ST TRIAL P Rule 13(J).

k. *Counterclaim by and against transferees and successors.* A counterclaim may be asserted by or against the transferee or successor of a claim subject to the following provisions:

    i. A successor who is a guardian, representative of a decedent's estate, receiver or assignee for the benefit of creditors, trustee or the like may interpose a claim to which he succeeds against claims or proceedings brought in or outside the court of administration. A claim owing by his predecessor may be interposed against any claim brought by such successor in or outside the court of administration without the necessity of filing such claim or cause of action in the administration proceedings. IN ST TRIAL P Rule 13(K)(1).

    ii. A transferee or successor of a claim takes it subject to any defense or counterclaim that is the subject-matter of the opposing party's claim; or that is available to the obligor at the time of the assignment or before the obligor received notice of the assignment. IN ST TRIAL P Rule 13(K)(2).

    iii. A surety or party with total or partial recourse upon a claim upon which he is being sued may interpose as a counterclaim:

        • Any claim of his own; and

        • Any claim owned by the person against whom he has recourse who either has notice of the suit, is a party to the suit, is insolvent, has assigned his claim to the surety or party asserting it, or cannot be found. IN ST TRIAL P Rule 13(K)(3).

        • A counterclaim under IN ST TRIAL P Rule 13(K)(3)(b) must tend to diminish or defeat the opposing party's claim, or it or the opposing claim must relate to payment of or security for the other, unless the person against whom recourse may be had is a party to the suit or the counterclaim has been assigned to the party asserting it; and if recovery on the counterclaim exceeds the opposing party's claim, any excess recovered shall be held in trust for such person against whom there is a right of recourse. IN ST TRIAL P Rule 13(K)(3).

    iv. IN ST TRIAL P Rule 13(K)(1), IN ST TRIAL P Rule 13(K)(2), and IN ST TRIAL P Rule 13(K)(3), are subject to subdivision IN ST TRIAL P Rule 13(L). IN ST TRIAL P Rule 13(K)(4).

l. *Counterclaim and cross-claim subject to substantive law principles.* Counterclaim and cross-claims are subject to restrictions imposed by other statutes and principles of substantive common law and equity, including rules of commercial law, agency, estoppel, contract and the like. In appropriate cases the court may impose terms or conditions upon its judgment or decree and may enter conditional or noncanceling cross judgments to satisfy such restrictions. This provision is intended to deny or limit counterclaims or cross-claims:

    i. Where a creditor will receive an unfair priority because a claim is assigned after insolvency proceedings, or assigned before such proceedings if it results in an unlawful preference;

    ii. Where an unfair priority will be allowed if a surety interposing a claim owned in his own right against the creditor suing on the principal's obligation when the principal is solvent and the creditor is not;

    iii. Where a claim by or against a representative, such as a guardian, receiver, representative of a decedent's estate, assignee for the benefit of creditors, trustee or the like in his individual capacity is asserted against a claim owing or owed by the estate he represents;

      iv.   Where a claim by or against a partnership or two (2) or more obligors is opposed against or by a claim of an individual to the extent that the individual will be allowed unfairly to profit or if it will adversely affect the rights of creditors; or

      v.   Where a claim is cut off by a holder in due course or a transferee who is protected under principles of commercial law, estoppel, or contract. IN ST TRIAL P Rule 13(L).

  m. *Satisfaction of judgment.* Satisfaction of a judgment or credits thereon may be ordered, for sufficient cause, upon notice and motion. "Credits" include any counterclaim which tends to diminish or defeat the judgment, or any counterclaim where it or the opposing claim relates to payment of or security for the other. IN ST TRIAL P Rule 13(M).

6. *Third-party practice*

  a. *When defendant may bring in third party.* A defending party, as a third-party plaintiff, may cause a summons and complaint to be served upon a person not a party to the action who is or may be liable to him for all or part of the plaintiff's claim against him. IN ST TRIAL P Rule 14(A). The person served with the summons and the third-party complaint, hereinafter called the third-party defendant, as provided in IN ST TRIAL P Rule 12 and IN ST TRIAL P Rule 13 may make:

      i.   His defenses, cross-claims and counterclaims to the third-party plaintiff's claims;

      ii. His defenses, counterclaims and cross-claims against any other defendants or third-party defendants;

      iii. Any defenses or claims which the third-party plaintiff has to the plaintiff's claim which are available to the third-party defendant against the plaintiff; and

      iv. Any defenses or claims which the third-party defendant has as against the plaintiff. IN ST TRIAL P Rule 14(A).

      v.   The plaintiff may assert any claim against the third-party defendant who thereupon may assert his defenses, counterclaims and cross-claims, as provided in IN ST TRIAL P Rule 12 and IN ST TRIAL P Rule 13. A third-party defendant may proceed under IN ST TRIAL P Rule 14 against any person not a party to the action who is or may be liable to him for all or part of the claim made in the action against the third-party defendant. IN ST TRIAL P Rule 14(A).

  b. *When plaintiff may bring in third party.* When a counterclaim or other claim is asserted against a plaintiff, he may cause a third party to be brought in under circumstances, which, under IN ST TRIAL P Rule 14, would entitle a defendant to do so. IN ST TRIAL P Rule 14(B).

  c. *Severance; Parties improperly impleaded.* With his responsive pleading or by motion prior thereto, any party may move for severance of a third-party claim or ensuing claim as provided in IN ST TRIAL P Rule 14 or for a separate trial thereon. If the third-party defendant is a proper party to the proceedings under any other rule relating to parties, the action shall continue as in other cases where he is made a party. IN ST TRIAL P Rule 14(C).

7. *Trial by jury; Demand*

  a. *Causes triable by court and by jury.* Issues of law and issues of fact in causes that prior to the eighteenth day of June, 1852, were of exclusive equitable jurisdiction shall be tried by the court; issues of fact in all other causes shall be triable as the same are now triable. In case of the joinder of causes of action or defenses which, prior to said date, were of exclusive equitable jurisdiction with causes of action or defenses which, prior to said date, were designated as actions at law and triable by jury—the former shall be triable by the court, and the latter by a jury, unless waived; the trial of both may be at the same time or at different times, as the court may direct. IN ST TRIAL P Rule 38(A).

  b. *Demand.* Any party may demand a trial by jury of any issue triable of right by a jury by filing with the court and serving upon the other parties a demand therefor in writing at any time after the commencement of the action and not later than ten (10) days after the first responsive pleading to the complaint, or to a counterclaim, crossclaim or other claim if one properly is pleaded; and if no responsive pleading is filed or required, within ten (10) days after the time such pleading otherwise would have been required. Such demand is sufficient if indorsed upon a pleading of a party filed within such time. IN ST TRIAL P Rule 38(B).

   c. *Same; Specification of issues.* In his demand a party may specify the issues which he wishes so tried; otherwise he shall be deemed to have demanded trial by jury for all issues triable as of right by jury. Any other party must file a demand for jury trial to preserve his right to trial by jury:

     i. Of issues for which a right to trial by jury was not requested by another party; and

     ii. In case a request by another party was improper. But if a proper request for a trial by jury upon issues triable by jury as of right on his behalf is made by any party, such request shall be deemed to have been made on behalf of all parties entitled to a jury trial upon such issues. IN ST TRIAL P Rule 38(C).

   d. *Waiver.* The failure of a party to appear at the trial, and the failure of a party to serve a demand as required by IN ST TRIAL P Rule 38 and to file it as required by IN ST TRIAL P Rule 5(E) constitute waiver by him of trial by jury. A demand for trial by jury made as provided in IN ST TRIAL P Rule 38 may not be withdrawn without the consent of the other party or parties. IN ST TRIAL P Rule 38(D).

     i. The trial court shall not grant a demand for a trial by jury filed after the time fixed in IN ST TRIAL P Rule 38(B) has elapsed except upon the written agreement of all of the parties to the action, which agreement shall be filed with the court and made a part of the record. If such agreement is filed then the court may, in its discretion, grant a trial by jury in which event the grant of a trial by jury may not be withdrawn except by the agreement of all of the parties. IN ST TRIAL P Rule 38(D).

   e. *Arbitration.* Nothing in the Indiana Rules of Trial Procedure shall deny the parties the right by contract or agreement to submit or to agree to submit controversies to arbitration made before or after commencement of an action thereon or deny the courts power to specifically enforce such agreements. IN ST TRIAL P Rule 38(E).

D. Documents

  1. *Required documents*

   a. *Amended answer.* Refer to the General Requirements section of this document for information on the contents of an amended answer.

   b. *Certificate of service.* An attorney or unrepresented party tendering a document to the Clerk for filing shall certify that service has been made, list the parties served, and specify the date and means of service. The certificate of service shall be placed at the end of the document and shall not be separately filed. The separate filing of a certificate of service, however, shall not be grounds for rejecting a document for filing. The Clerk may permit documents to be filed without a certificate of service but shall require prompt filing of a separate certificate of service. IN ST TRIAL P Rule 5(C).

     i. All pleadings filed with the Court which require a certificate of service shall specifically name the individual party or attorney on whom service has been made, the address, the manner in which service was made and the date when service was made. IN ST HAMILTON TRIAL Rule 201(201.60).

  2. *Supplemental documents*

   a. *Proof of written instrument.* When any pleading allowed by the Indiana Rules of Trial Procedure is founded on a written instrument, the original, or a copy thereof, must be included in or filed with the pleading. Such instrument, whether copied in the pleadings or not, shall be taken as part of the record. When any pleading allowed by the Indiana Rules of Trial Procedure is founded on an account, an Affidavit of Debt, in a form substantially similar to that which is provided in IN ST TRIAL P App. A-2, shall be attached. IN ST TRIAL P Rule 9.2(A).

   b. *Notice of intent to use foreign law.* A party who intends to raise an issue concerning the law of a foreign country shall give notice in his pleadings or other reasonable written notice. The court, in determining foreign law, may consider any relevant material or source, including testimony, whether or not submitted by a party or admissible under IN ST TRIAL P Rule 43. The court's determination shall be treated as a ruling on a question of law. It shall be made by the court and not the jury and shall be reviewable. IN ST TRIAL P Rule 44.1(A).

c. *Facsimile cover sheet.* Any document sent to the Clerk of the Circuit Court by electronic facsimile transmission shall be accompanied by a cover sheet which states the title of the document, case number, number of pages, identity and voice telephone number of the sending party and instructions for filing. The cover sheet shall contain the signature of the attorney or party, pro se, authorizing the filing. IN ST ADMIN Rule 12(D); IN ST HAMILTON ADMIN Rule 103(103.10)(a).

E. Format

1. *Form of pleadings*

   a. *Caption; Names of parties.* Every pleading shall contain a caption setting forth the name of the court, the title of the action, the file number, and a designation as in IN ST TRIAL P Rule 7(A). In the complaint the title of the action shall include the names of all the parties, but in other pleadings it is sufficient to state the name of the first party on each side with an appropriate indication of other parties. IN ST TRIAL P Rule 10(A).

   b. *Paragraphs; Separate statements.* All averments of a claim or defense shall be made in numbered paragraphs, the contents of each of which shall be limited as far as practicable to a statement of a single set of circumstances, and a paragraph may be referred to by number in all succeeding pleadings. Each claim founded upon a separate transaction or occurrence and each defense other than denials may be stated in a separate count or defense whenever a separation facilitates the clear presentation of the matters set forth. IN ST TRIAL P Rule 10(B).

   c. *Adoption by reference; Exhibits.* Statements in a pleading may be adopted by reference in a different part of the same pleading or in another pleading or in any motion. A copy of any written instrument which is an exhibit to a pleading is a part thereof for all purposes. IN ST TRIAL P Rule 10(C).

   d. *Facsimile page limit.* Courts authorize the Hamilton County Clerk of Courts to accept pleadings, motions and other papers by electronic facsimile transmission for filing in any case pending before the Courts, subject to the requirement that The transmission may not exceed ten (10) pages in length including the cover sheet and proposed CCS entry. IN ST HAMILTON ADMIN Rule 103(103.10)(c).

   e. *Emergency facsimile filings.* If the filing requires the immediate attention of the Judge, it shall so indicate in bold letters in an accompanying transmittal memorandum. IN ST HAMILTON ADMIN Rule 103(103.10)(f).

   f. *Special judge heading.* After a special judge is selected, the attorneys or pro se litigants shall add to the caption of all pleadings to the right of the case title the following: "BEFORE SPECIAL JUDGE _____." IN ST HAMILTON TRIAL Rule 204(204.10).

   g. *Format rules strictly enforced.* All filings shall be in compliance with the Indiana Rules of Trial Procedure. If the documents received are not in proper form, such deficiencies will not be corrected by court personnel. IN ST HAMILTON TRIAL Rule 201(201.70). The Court shall not be required to act on any Motion, Petition or other request for relief unless filed in conformity with the Hamilton County Local Trial and Administrative rules. IN ST HAMILTON TRIAL Rule 202(202.20).

2. *Size of papers for filing.* Effective January 1, 1992, all pleadings, copies, motions and documents filed with any trial court or appellate level court, typed or printed, with the exception of exhibits and existing wills, shall be prepared on eight and one-half by eleven inch (8 1/2" x 11") size paper. IN ST ADMIN Rule 11.

   a. *Form.* All documents filed in any Hamilton County Court, with the exception of exhibits and existing wills, shall be prepared on paper measuring eight and one-half by eleven inches (8 1/2" x 11"). IN ST HAMILTON TRIAL Rule 201(201.20).

3. *Signature requirements*

   a. *Signature of attorney.* Every pleading or motion of a party represented by an attorney shall be signed by at least one (1) attorney of record in his individual name, whose address, telephone number, and attorney number shall be stated, except that this provision shall not apply to pleadings and motions made and transcribed at the trial or a hearing before the judge and received by him in such form. IN ST TRIAL P Rule 11(A).

      i. The signature of an attorney constitutes a certificate by him that he has read the pleadings; that

to the best of his knowledge, information, and belief, there is good ground to support it; and that it is not interposed for delay. IN ST TRIAL P Rule 11(A).

ii.   If a pleading or motion is not signed or is signed with intent to defeat the purpose of the rule, it may be stricken as sham and false and the action may proceed as though the pleading had not been served. IN ST TRIAL P Rule 11(A).

iii. For a willful violation of IN ST TRIAL P Rule 11 an attorney may be subjected to appropriate disciplinary action. Similar action may be taken if scandalous or indecent matter is inserted. IN ST TRIAL P Rule 11(A).

b.   *Signature of unrepresented party.* A party who is not represented by an attorney shall sign his pleading and state his address. IN ST TRIAL P Rule 11(A).

c.   *Verification not generally required.* Except when specifically required by rule, pleadings or motions need not be verified or accompanied by affidavit. The rule in equity that the averments of an answer under oath must be overcome by the testimony of two (2) witnesses or of one (1) witness sustained by corroborating circumstances is abolished. IN ST TRIAL P Rule 11(A).

d.   *Verification by affirmation or representation.* When in connection with any civil or special statutory proceeding it is required that any pleading, motion, petition, supporting affidavit, or other document of any kind, be verified, or that an oath be taken, it shall be sufficient if the subscriber simply affirms the truth of the matter to be verified by an affirmation or representation. IN ST TRIAL P Rule 11(B). IN ST TRIAL P Rule 11(B) states that the affirmation or representation should be in substantially the following language: "I (we) affirm, under the penalties for perjury, that the foregoing representation(s) is (are) true. (Signed) _____."

i.   Any person who falsifies an affirmation or representation of fact shall be subject to the same penalties as are prescribed by law for the making of a false affidavit. IN ST TRIAL P Rule 11(B).

e.   *Verified pleadings, motions, and affidavits as evidence.* Pleadings, motions and affidavits accompanying or in support of such pleadings or motions when required to be verified or under oath shall be accepted as a representation that the signer had personal knowledge thereof or reasonable cause to believe the existence of the facts or matters stated or alleged therein; and, if otherwise competent or acceptable as evidence, may be admitted as evidence of the facts or matters stated or alleged therein when it is so provided in the Indiana Rules of Trial Procedure, by statute or other law, or to the extent the writing or signature expressly purports to be made upon the signer's personal knowledge. When such pleadings, motions and affidavits are verified or under oath they shall not require other or greater proof on the part of the adverse party than if not verified or not under oath unless expressly provided otherwise by the Indiana Rules of Trial Procedure, statute or other law. Affidavits upon motions for summary judgment under IN ST TRIAL P Rule 56 and in denial of execution under IN ST TRIAL P Rule 9.2 shall be made upon personal knowledge. IN ST TRIAL P Rule 11(C).

4.   *Information excluded from public access.* Every document filed in a case shall separately identify information excluded from public access pursuant to IN ST ADMIN Rule 9(G)(1) as follows:

a.   Whole documents that are excluded from public access pursuant to IN ST ADMIN Rule 9(G)(1) shall be tendered on light green paper or have a light green coversheet attached to the document, marked "Not for Public Access" or "Confidential." IN ST TRIAL P Rule 5(G)(1).

b.   When only a portion of a document contains information excluded from public access pursuant to IN ST ADMIN Rule 9(G)(1), said information shall be omitted [or redacted] from the filed document, and set forth on a separate accompanying document on light green paper conspicuously marked "Not for Public Access" or "Confidential" and clearly designated [or identifying] the caption and number of the case and the document and location within the document to which the redacted material pertains. IN ST TRIAL P Rule 5(G)(2).

c.   With respect to documents filed in electronic format, the trial court, by local rule, may provide for compliance with IN ST TRIAL P Rule 5 in manner that separates and protects access to information excluded from public access. IN ST TRIAL P Rule 5(G)(3).

d.   IN ST TRIAL P Rule 5(G) does not apply to a record sealed by the court pursuant to IN ST

5-14-3-5.5 or otherwise, nor to records, documents, or information filed in cases to which public access is prohibited pursuant to IN ST ADMIN Rule 9(G). IN ST TRIAL P Rule 5(G)(4).

e. The following information in case records is excluded from public access and is confidential:

   i. Information that is excluded from public access pursuant to federal law;

   ii. Information that is excluded from public access as declared confidential by Indiana statute or other court rule, including without limitation:

- All adoption records created after July 8, 1941, as declared confidential by IN ST 31-19-19-1, et seq., except those specifically declared open by IN ST 31-19-13-2(2);

- All records relating to chancroid, chlamydia, gonorrhea, hepatitis, human immunodeficiency virus (HIV), Lymphogranuloma venereum, syphilis, tuberculosis, as declared confidential by IN ST 16-41-8-1, et seq.;

- All records relating to child abuse as declared confidential by IN ST 31-33-18-1, et seq.;

- All records relating to drug tests as declared confidential by IN ST 5-14-3-4(a)(9);

- Records of grand jury proceedings as declared confidential by IN ST 35-34-2-4;

- Records of juvenile proceedings as declared confidential by IN ST 31-39-1-2, except those specifically open under statute;

- All paternity records created after July 1, 1941 as declared confidential by IN ST 31-14-11-15, IN ST 31-19-5-23, IN ST 31-39-1-1 and IN ST 31-39-1-2 [Editor's note: IN ST 31-14-11-15 was repealed effective May 9, 2013];

- All pre-sentence reports as declared confidential by IN ST 35-38-1-13;

- Written petitions to permit marriages without consent and orders directing the Clerk of Court to issue a marriage license to underage persons, as declared confidential by IN ST 31-11-1-6;

- Only those arrest warrants, search warrants, indictments and informations ordered confidential by the trial judge, prior to return of duly executed service as declared confidential by IN ST 5-14-3-4(b)(1);

- All medical, mental health, or tax records unless determined by law or regulation of any governmental custodian not to be confidential, released by the subject of such records, or declared by a court of competent jurisdiction to be essential to the resolution of litigation as declared confidential by IN ST 16-39-3-10, IN ST 6-4.1-5-10, IN ST 6-4.1-12-12, and IN ST 6-8.1-7-1;

- Personal information relating to jurors or prospective jurors, other than for the use of the parties and counsel, pursuant to IN ST JURY Rule 10;

- Information relating to protection from abuse orders, no-contact orders and workplace violence restraining orders as declared confidential by IN ST 5-2-9-6, et seq.;

- Mediation proceedings pursuant to IN ST ADR Rule 2.11, Mini-Trial proceedings pursuant to IN ST ADR Rule 4.4(C), and Summary Jury Trials pursuant to IN ST ADR Rule 5.6;

- Information in probation files pursuant to the Probation Standards promulgated by the Judicial Conference of Indiana pursuant to IN ST 11-13-1-8(b);

- Information deemed confidential pursuant to the Rules for Court Administered Alcohol and Drug Programs promulgated by the Judicial Conference of Indiana pursuant to IN ST 12-23-14-13;

- Information deemed confidential pursuant to the Problem-Solving Court Rules promulgated by the Judicial Conference of Indiana pursuant to IN ST 33-23-16-16;

- All records of the Department of workforce Development as declared confidential by IN ST 22-4-19-6;

- Information regarding interception of electronic communications that is sealed or deemed confidential as set forth in IN ST 35-33.5-2-1, et seq.

iii. Information excluded from public access by specific court order;

iv. Complete Social Security Numbers of living persons;

v. With the exception of names, information such as addresses, phone numbers, and dates of birth which explicitly identifies:

- Natural persons who are witnesses or victims (not including defendants) in criminal, domestic violence, stalking, sexual assault, juvenile, or civil protection order proceedings, provided that juveniles who are victims of sex crimes shall be identified by initials only;

- Places of residence of judicial officers, clerks and other employees of courts and clerks of court, unless the person or persons about whom the information pertains waives confidentiality;

vi. Complete account numbers of specific assets, loans, bank accounts, credit cards, and personal identification numbers (PINs);

vii. All orders of expungement entered in criminal or juvenile proceedings, orders to restrict access to criminal history information pursuant to IN ST 35-38-5-5.5 or IN ST 35-38-8-5 and records excluded from public access by such orders, and information related to infractions that is excluded from public access pursuant to IN ST 34-28-5-15 or IN ST 34-28-5-16 [Editor's note: IN ST 35-38-5-5.5, IN ST 35-38-8-5 and IN ST 34-28-5-16 were repealed effective July 1, 2013; for information on orders restricting access to criminal history, refer to IN ST 35-38-9-1, et seq.];

viii. All personal notes and e-mail, and deliberative material, of judges, jurors, court staff and judicial agencies, and information recorded in personal data assistants (PDA's) or organizers and personal calendars. IN ST ADMIN Rule 9(G)(1).

F. Filing and Service Requirements

1. *Filing requirements.* Except as otherwise provided in IN ST TRIAL P Rule 5(E)(2), all pleadings and papers subsequent to the complaint which are required to be served upon a party shall be filed with the Court either before service or within a reasonable period of time thereafter. IN ST TRIAL P Rule 5(E)(1). All pleadings shall be filed with the Hamilton County Clerk with the exception of emergency orders under IN ST TRIAL P Rule 65. IN ST HAMILTON TRIAL Rule 201(201.10).

   a. *Filing with the court defined.* The filing of pleadings, motions, and other papers with the court as required by the Indiana Rules of Trial Procedure shall be made by one of the following methods:

      i. Delivery to the clerk of the court;

      ii. Sending by electronic transmission under the procedure adopted pursuant to IN ST ADMIN Rule 12;

      iii. Mailing to the clerk by registered, certified or express mail return receipt requested;

      iv. Depositing with any third-party commercial carrier for delivery to the clerk within three (3) calendar days, cost prepaid, properly addressed;

      v. If the court so permits, filing with the judge, in which event the judge shall note thereon the filing date and forthwith transmit them to the office of the clerk; or

      vi. Electronic filing, as approved by the Division of State Court Administration pursuant to IN ST ADMIN Rule 16. IN ST TRIAL P Rule 5(F).

      vii. Filing by registered or certified mail and by third-party commercial carrier shall be complete upon mailing or deposit. IN ST TRIAL P Rule 5(F).

   b. *Facsimile filing.* As outlined in IN ST HAMILTON ADMIN Rule 103(103.10), facsimile filing is permitted in the Circuit and Superior Courts of Hamilton County. The Courts authorize the Hamilton County Clerk of Courts to accept pleadings, motions and other papers by electronic facsimile transmission for filing in any case pending before the Courts, subject to the requirements of IN ST

HAMILTON ADMIN Rule 103(103.10). IN ST HAMILTON ADMIN Rule 103(103.10); IN ST HAMILTON TRIAL Rule 201(201.80).

i. *Generally.* In counties where a majority of judges of the courts of record, by posted local rule, have authorized electronic facsimile filing and designated a telephone number to receive such transmissions, pleadings, motions, and other papers may be sent to the Clerk of Circuit Court by electronic facsimile transmission for filing in any case, provided:

- Such matter does not exceed ten (10) pages, including the cover sheet;

- Such matter does not require the payment of fees other than the electronic facsimile transcription fee set forth in IN ST ADMIN Rule 12(E);

- The sending party creates at the time of transmission a machine generated log for such transmission; and

- The original document and the transmission log are maintained by the sending party for the duration of the litigation. IN ST ADMIN Rule 12(B); IN ST HAMILTON ADMIN Rule 103(103.10)(d).

- Legibility of documents and timeliness of filing is the responsibility of the sender. IN ST HAMILTON ADMIN Rule 103(103.10)(g).

- The Clerk shall accept electronic facsimile transmission filings only if received at the facsimile machine assigned by the Clerk. The telephone number designated to receive such transmission is available at IN ST HAMILTON ADMIN Rule 103(103.40). IN ST HAMILTON ADMIN Rule 103(103.40).

ii. *Time of filing.* During normal, posted business hours, the time of filing shall be the time the duplicate document is produced in the office of the Clerk of the Circuit Court. Duplicate documents received at all other times shall be filed as of the next normal business day. IN ST ADMIN Rule 12(C).

- If the receiving fax machine endorses its own time and date stamp upon the transmitted documents and the receiving machine produces a delivery receipt which is electronically created and transmitted to the sending party, the time of filing shall be the date and time recorded on the transmitted document by the receiving fax machine. IN ST ADMIN Rule 12(C).

- Electronic facsimile transmissions will be accepted for filing only during the regular business hours as set forth in IN ST HAMILTON ADMIN Rule 101. Transmissions received by the Hamilton County Clerk after close of business shall be filed effective the next regular business day. IN ST HAMILTON ADMIN Rule 103(103.30).

iii. *Filing fee.* The electronic facsimile transmission will not be accepted for filing if its filing requires the payment of any fee other than the electronic facsimile transcription fee set forth in IN ST HAMILTON ADMIN Rule 103(103.20). IN ST HAMILTON ADMIN Rule 103(103.10)(e).

- Pursuant to Ordinance adopted by the Hamilton County Board of Commissioners, the Clerk shall collect an electronic facsimile transcription fee of One Dollar ($1.00) per page, to a maximum of Ten Dollars ($10.00) per transmission, for each electronic facsimile transmission accepted for filing with the Hamilton County Circuit and Superior Courts. IN ST HAMILTON ADMIN Rule 103(103.20).

- The fee shall be assessed against the sending party and shall be paid upon receipt of invoice by that party and at the latest within thirty (30) days of the transmission. In the event the fee is not paid by the sending party within the time limits provided, the court may issue a show-cause order or enter a judgment in the matter. The Clerk may refuse an electronic facsimile transmission from any attorney or pro se litigant who has failed to pay these fees within thirty (30) days. IN ST HAMILTON ADMIN Rule 103(103.20).

iv. *No direct filing with court.* A party shall not send pleadings, motions and other papers by electronic facsimile transmission for filing directly to any Court without that Court's prior approval to do so. IN ST HAMILTON ADMIN Rule 103(103.50).

c. *Filing with special judge.* After a special judge has qualified, a copy of each pleading and Chronological Case Summary entries filed with the Court shall be mailed or delivered to the office of that Special judge by the counsel or pro se litigant with service indicated on the certificate of service. IN ST HAMILTON TRIAL Rule 204(204.20).

d. *Proof of filing.* Any party filing any paper by any method other than personal delivery to the clerk shall retain proof of filing. IN ST TRIAL P Rule 5(F).

2. *Service requirements.* Unless otherwise provided by the Indiana Rules of Trial Procedure or an order of the court, each party and special judge, if any, shall be served with: (1) every order required by its terms to be served; (2) every pleading subsequent to the original complaint; (3) every written motion except one which may be heard ex parte; (4) every brief submitted to the trial court; (5) every paper relating to discovery required to be served upon a party; and (6) every written notice, appearance, demand, offer of judgment, designation of record on appeal, or similar paper. IN ST TRIAL P Rule 5(A).

a. *Methods of service*

   i. *Personal service.* Whenever a party is represented by an attorney of record, service shall be made upon such attorney unless service upon the party himself is ordered by the court. Service upon the attorney or party shall be made by delivering or mailing a copy of the papers to the last known address or where an attorney or party has consented to service by fax or e-mail, as provided in IN ST TRIAL P Rule 3.1(A)(4), by faxing or e-mailing a copy of the documents to the fax number or e-mail address set out in the appearance form or correction as required by IN ST TRIAL P Rule 3.1(E). IN ST TRIAL P Rule 5(B). Delivery of a copy within IN ST TRIAL P Rule 5 means:

   - Offering or tendering it to the attorney or party and stating the nature of the papers being served. Refusal to accept an offered or tendered document is a waiver of any objection to the sufficiency or adequacy of service of that document;

   - Leaving it at his office with a clerk or other person in charge thereof, or if there is no one in charge, leaving it in a conspicuous place therein; or

   - If the office is closed, by leaving it at his dwelling house or usual place of abode with some person of suitable age and discretion then residing therein; or,

   - Leaving it at some other suitable place, selected by the attorney upon whom service is being made, pursuant to duly promulgated local rule. IN ST TRIAL P Rule 5(B)(1).

   ii. *Service by mail.* If service is made by mail, the papers shall be deposited in the United States mail addressed to the person on whom they are being served, with postage prepaid. Service shall be deemed complete upon mailing. Proof of service of all papers permitted to be mailed may be made by written acknowledgment of service, by affidavit of the person who mailed the papers, or by certificate of an attorney. It shall be the duty of attorneys when entering their appearance in a cause or when filing pleadings or papers therein, to have noted in the Chronological Case Summary or said pleadings or papers so filed the address and telephone number of their office. Service by delivery or by mail at such address shall be deemed sufficient and complete. IN ST TRIAL P Rule 5(B)(2).

   iii. *Service by fax or e-mail.* A party who has consented to service by fax or e-mail may be served as follows:

   - Service by e-mail shall be made by attaching the document being served in .pdf format. Discovery documents must also be served in accordance with IN ST TRIAL P Rule 26(A). IN ST TRIAL P Rule 5(B)(3)(a).

   - Service by fax shall be deemed complete upon generation of a transmission record indicating the successful transmission of the entire document, except as provided in IN ST TRIAL P Rule 5(B)(3)(d). IN ST TRIAL P Rule 5(B)(3)(b).

   - Service by e-mail shall be deemed complete upon transmission, except as provided in IN ST TRIAL P Rule 5(B)(3)(d). IN ST TRIAL P Rule 5(B)(3)(c).

   - Service by fax or e-mail that occurs on a Saturday, Sunday, legal holiday, or day the court or agency in which the matter is pending is closed or after 5:00 PM local time of the recipient shall be deemed complete the next day that is not a Saturday, Sunday, legal holiday, or day that the court or agency in which the matter is pending is not closed. IN ST TRIAL P Rule 5(B)(3)(d).

 iv. *Mail box service.* Pursuant to IN ST TRIAL P Rule 5(B)(1)(d), the Circuit and Superior Courts of Hamilton County hereby designate the "mail boxes" located in the Clerk's order book office for service of pleadings upon attorneys who have such boxes. IN ST HAMILTON TRIAL Rule 201(201.50).

 b. *Serving numerous defendants.* In any action in which there are unusually large numbers of defendants, the court, upon motion or of its own initiative, may order:

  i. That service of the pleadings of the defendants and replies thereto need not be made as between the defendants;

   • That any cross-claim, counterclaim, or matter constituting an avoidance or affirmative defense contained therein shall be deemed to be denied or avoided by all other parties; and

   • That the filing of any such pleading and service thereof upon the plaintiff constitutes due notice of it to the parties. IN ST TRIAL P Rule 5(D).

  ii. A copy of every such order shall be served upon the parties in such manner and form as the court directs. IN ST TRIAL P Rule 5(D).

 c. *Service on parties in default for failure to appear.* No service need be made on parties in default for failure to appear, except that pleadings asserting new or additional claims for relief against them shall be served upon them in the manner provided by service of summons in IN ST TRIAL P Rule 4. IN ST TRIAL P Rule 5(A).

G. Hearings

1. The Indiana rules do not contemplate a hearing regarding the filing and service of an amended answer.

H. Forms

1. Official Amended Answer Forms for Indiana

 a. Affidavit of debt. IN ST TRIAL P App. A-2.

2. Amended Answer Forms for Indiana

 a. Amendment by stipulation. 10 INPRAC § 46.11.

 b. Amended answer by interlineations. 10 INPRAC § 46.12.

 c. Answer; Form and content. 9 INPRAC § 41.1.

 d. Answer; General form. 9 INPRAC § 41.3.

 e. Answer; Another form. 9 INPRAC § 41.4.

 f. Answer; Another form. 9 INPRAC § 41.5.

 g. General denial. 9 INPRAC § 41.6.

 h. Specific denial of designated paragraph. 9 INPRAC § 41.7.

 i. Specific admission of designated paragraph. 9 INPRAC § 41.8.

 j. Denial of knowledge or information to form belief. 9 INPRAC § 41.9.

 k. Denial of knowledge or information to form belief; Another form. 9 INPRAC § 41.10.

 l. Partial denial and partial admission of designated paragraph. 9 INPRAC § 41.11.

 m. Denial of designated paragraph for reason that document speaks for itself. 9 INPRAC § 41.12.

 n. Adoption of admissions or denials by co-defendant's answer. 9 INPRAC § 41.13.

 o. Denial of execution of instrument filed with pleading. 9 INPRAC § 41.14.

 p. Answer to cross-claim. 9 INPRAC § 41.15.

 q. Answer to third-party complaint. 9 INPRAC § 41.16.

    r.   Accord and satisfaction. 9 INPRAC § 41.21.

    s.   Answer. 5 INPRAC § 3:3.3.

    t.   Answer; Another form. 5 INPRAC § 3:3.4.

    u.   Certificate of service; Personal service. 9 INPRAC § 5.7.

    v.   Certificate of service; First class mail. 9 INPRAC § 5.8.

    w.   Signature; By party. 9 INPRAC § 4.5.

    x.   Signature; Attorney. 9 INPRAC § 4.6.

    y.   Signature; Attorney; Another form. 9 INPRAC § 4.7.

    z.   Signature; Attorney; Another form. 9 INPRAC § 4.8.

I. Checklist

(I) ❑ Matters to be considered by the party filing the amended answer

    (a) ❑ Required documents if amending as matter of course

        (1) ❑ Amended answer

        (2) ❑ Certificate of service

    (b) ❑ Supplemental documents

        (1) ❑ Proof of written instrument

        (2) ❑ Notice of intent to use foreign law

        (3) ❑ Facsimile cover sheet

    (c) ❑ Timing

        (1) ❑ A party may amend his pleading once as a matter of course at any time before a responsive pleading is served or, if the pleading is one to which no responsive pleading is permitted, and the action has not been placed upon the trial calendar, he may so amend it at any time within thirty (30) days after it is served

        (2) ❑ Otherwise a party may amend his pleading only by leave of court or by written consent of the adverse party

Motions, Oppositions and Replies
Motion to Strike

Document Last Updated October 2013

A. Applicable Rules

1. *State rules*

    a.   Appearance. IN ST TRIAL P Rule 3.1.

    b.   Process. IN ST TRIAL P Rule 4.

    c.   Service and filing of pleadings and other papers. IN ST TRIAL P Rule 5.

    d.   Time. IN ST TRIAL P Rule 6.

    e.   Pleadings. IN ST TRIAL P Rule 7; IN ST TRIAL P Rule 8; IN ST TRIAL P Rule 9.2; IN ST TRIAL P Rule 10; IN ST TRIAL P Rule 11.

    f.   Defenses and objections; When and how presented; By pleading or motion; Motion for judgment on the pleadings. IN ST TRIAL P Rule 12.

    g.   Amended and supplemental pleadings. IN ST TRIAL P Rule 15.

    h.   Joinder of person needed for just adjudication. IN ST TRIAL P Rule 19.

    i.   Evidence. IN ST TRIAL P Rule 43.

    j.   Judgment on the evidence (directed verdict). IN ST TRIAL P Rule 50.

    k.   Findings by the court. IN ST TRIAL P Rule 52.

    l.   Summary judgment. IN ST TRIAL P Rule 56.

    m.   Motion to correct error. IN ST TRIAL P Rule 59.

    n.   Relief from judgment or order. IN ST TRIAL P Rule 60.

    o.   Hearing of motions. IN ST TRIAL P Rule 73.

    p.   Access to court records. IN ST ADMIN Rule 9.

    q.   Paper size. IN ST ADMIN Rule 11.

    r.   Facsimile transmission. IN ST ADMIN Rule 12.

    s.   Electronic filing and electronic service pilot projects. IN ST ADMIN Rule 16.

    t.   Sealing of certain records by court; Hearing; Notice. IN ST 5-14-3-5.5.

    u.   Privacy and confidentiality. IN ST 5-2-9-6; IN ST 5-14-3-4; IN ST 6-4.1-5-10; IN ST 6-4.1-12-12; IN ST 6-8.1-7-1; IN ST 11-13-1-8; IN ST 12-23-14-13; IN ST 16-39-3-10; IN ST 16-41-8-1; IN ST 22-4-19-6; IN ST 31-11-1-6; IN ST 31-19-5-23; IN ST 31-19-13-2; IN ST 31-19-19-1; IN ST 31-33-18-1; IN ST 31-39-1-1; IN ST 31-39-1-2; IN ST 33-23-16-16; IN ST 35-34-2-4; IN ST 35-38-1-13; IN ST 35-38-9-1; IN ST ADR Rule 2.11; IN ST ADR Rule 4.4; IN ST ADR Rule 5.6; IN ST JURY Rule 10.

2.   *Local rules*

    a.   Court hours. IN ST HAMILTON ADMIN Rule 101.

    b.   Facsimile transmissions. IN ST HAMILTON ADMIN Rule 103.

    c.   Filing of pleadings and entry of appearances. IN ST HAMILTON TRIAL Rule 201.

    d.   Proposed orders. IN ST HAMILTON TRIAL Rule 202.

    e.   Briefs and memorandums. IN ST HAMILTON TRIAL Rule 203.

    f.   Special judges. IN ST HAMILTON TRIAL Rule 204.

    g.   Trial settings. IN ST HAMILTON TRIAL Rule 205.

    h.   Continuances. IN ST HAMILTON TRIAL Rule 206.

B. Timing

1.   *Motion to strike.* Upon motion made by a party before responding to a pleading, or, if no responsive pleading is permitted by Indiana Rules of Trial Procedure, upon motion made by a party within twenty (20) days after the service of the pleading upon him or at any time upon the court's own initiative, the court may order stricken from any pleading any insufficient claim or defense or any redundant, immaterial, impertinent, or scandalous matter. IN ST TRIAL P Rule 12(F).

    a.   *Time to file a responsive pleading.* A responsive pleading required under the Indiana Rules of Trial Procedure, shall be served within twenty (20) days after service of the prior pleading. IN ST TRIAL P Rule 6(C).

    b.   *Filing.* All pleadings and papers subsequent to the complaint which are required to be served upon a party shall be filed with the Court either before service or within a reasonable period of time thereafter. IN ST TRIAL P Rule 5(E)(1).

2.   *Service.* A written motion, other than one which may be heard ex parte, and notice of the hearing thereof shall be served not less than five (5) days before the time specified for the hearing, unless a different period is fixed by the Indiana Rules of Trial Procedure or by order of the court. IN ST TRIAL P Rule 6(D).

    a.   *Of supporting affidavits.* When a motion is supported by affidavit, the affidavit shall be served with the motion. IN ST TRIAL P Rule 6(D).

3.   *Service of opposition.* Except as otherwise provided in IN ST TRIAL P Rule 59(D), opposing affidavits may be served not less than one (1) day before the hearing, unless the court permits them to be served at some other time. IN ST TRIAL P Rule 6(D).

4. *Computation of time*

   a. *Generally; Days excluded.* In computing any period of time prescribed or allowed by the Indiana Rules of Trial Procedure, by order of the court, or by any applicable statute, the day of the act, event, or default from which the designated period of time begins to run shall not be included. The last day of the period so computed is to be included unless it is:

      i. A Saturday,

      ii. A Sunday,

      iii. A legal holiday as defined by state statute, or

      iv. A day the office in which the act is to be done is closed during regular business hours. IN ST TRIAL P Rule 6(A).

   b. *Short periods.* In any event, the period runs until the end of the next day that is not a Saturday, a Sunday, a legal holiday, or a day on which the office is closed. When the period of time allowed is less than seven (7) days, intermediate Saturdays, Sundays, legal holidays, and days on which the office is closed shall be excluded from the computations. IN ST TRIAL P Rule 6(A).

   c. *Additional time after service by United States mail.* Whenever a party has the right or is required to do some act or take some proceedings within a prescribed period after the service of a notice or other paper upon him and the notice or paper is served upon him by United States mail, three (3) days shall be added to the prescribed period. IN ST TRIAL P Rule 6(E).

   d. *Enlargement of time.* When an act is required or allowed to be done at or within a specific time by the Indiana Rules of Trial Procedure, the court may at any time for cause shown:

      i. Order the period enlarged, with or without motion or notice, if request therefor is made before the expiration of the period originally prescribed or extended by a previous order; or

      ii. Upon motion made after the expiration of the specific period, permit the act to be done where the failure to act was the result of excusable neglect; but, the court may not extend the time for taking any action for judgment on the evidence under IN ST TRIAL P Rule 50(A), amendment of findings and judgment under IN ST TRIAL P Rule 52(B), to correct errors under IN ST TRIAL P Rule 59(C), statement in opposition to motion to correct error under IN ST TRIAL P Rule 59(E), or to obtain relief from final judgment under IN ST TRIAL P Rule 60(B), except to the extent and under the conditions stated in those rules. IN ST TRIAL P Rule 6(B).

      iii. For information on obtaining a continuance, refer to IN ST HAMILTON TRIAL Rule 206.

C. General Requirements

1. *Motions, generally.* Unless made during a hearing or trial, or otherwise ordered by the court, an application to the court for an order shall be made by written motion. The motion shall state the grounds therefor and the relief or order sought. IN ST TRIAL P Rule 7(B).

   a. *Motions as distinct from pleadings.* Motions and responses to motions are not pleadings, and allegations contained in a motion are not admissions of a party. 22B INPRAC 7:2; Wachstetter v. County Properties, LLC, 832 N.E.2d 574 (Ind.Ct.App. 2005); Scott County Family YMCA, Inc. v. Hobbs, 817 N.E.2d 603 (Ind.Ct.App. 2004).

   b. *Unopposed motions generally granted.* It is common for a trial court to grant procedural motions, such as motions for enlargement of time, discovery motions, or motions for continuance, unless an objection is filed. 21 INPRAC § 13.8.

2. *Motion to strike*

   a. *Grounds generally.* Upon motion the court may order stricken from any pleading any insufficient claim or defense or any redundant, immaterial, impertinent, or scandalous matter. IN ST TRIAL P Rule 12(F).

      i. *Redundant.* Redundant matter refers to the needless repetition of immaterial factual allegations. 9 INPRAC § 42.20.

      ii. *Immaterial and impertinent.* Immaterial and impertinent matter consists of allegations that have no relevant or important relationship to plaintiff's claim. 9 INPRAC § 42.20.

      iii.   *Scandalous.* Scandalous matter includes unnecessary allegations that are derogatory to the party referred to in the pleading. 9 INPRAC § 42.20.

  b. *Availability and use of motion to strike.* A motion to strike redundant, immaterial, impertinent or scandalous matter is available to plaintiff and defendant alike, and may be employed against any pleading. 9 INPRAC § 42.20. Indiana's use of a motion to strike includes all of the uses which are found in federal practice plus the expanded use of the motion under Indiana's rule. Accordingly, a nonexclusive list of the uses of this motion will recognize that it is available:

      i.   To strike matter which is immaterial, impertinent or scandalous;

      ii.   To provide the plaintiff with a means by which to test the sufficiency of a defense;

      iii.   To strike any insufficient claim or defense;

      iv.   To strike a bad faith, or inadequate response to an order or rule; or

      v.   To strike a response to an order or rule which introduces new material or allegations not previously made and which are not introduced pursuant to a right to amend a pleading. 1A INPRAC R 12(12.18).

  c. *Trial court's discretion.* The trial court is given broad discretion to decide a motion to strike. 1A INPRAC R 12(12.18); City of Mishawaka v. Kvale, 810 N.E.2d 1129 (Ind.Ct.App. 2004).

  d. *Not a method to challenge timeliness.* Language in IN ST TRIAL P Rule 12(F) which permits the trial court to strike any "insufficient" claim or defense refers to the legal insufficiency of the content or substance of the claim or defense, not the untimeliness of a pleading. 1A INPRAC R 12(12.18); Dreyer & Reinbold v. AutoXchange.com., Inc., 771 N.E.2d 764, 765 (Ind.Ct.App. 2002). Rather, the proper mechanism for challenging the timeliness of a pleading is IN ST TRIAL P Rule 55, which governs default judgments. 1A INPRAC R 12(12.18).

3. *Consolidation and waiver*

  a. *Consolidation of defenses in motion.* A party who makes a motion under IN ST TRIAL P Rule 12 may join with it any other motions herein provided for and then available to him. If a party makes a motion under IN ST TRIAL P Rule 12 but omits therefrom any defense or objection then available to him which IN ST TRIAL P Rule 12 permits to be raised by motion, he shall not thereafter make a motion based on the defense or objection so omitted. He may, however, make such motions as are allowed under IN ST TRIAL P Rule 12(H)(2). IN ST TRIAL P Rule 12(G).

  b. *Waiver or preservation of certain defenses.* No defense or objection is waived by being joined with one or more other defenses or objections in a responsive pleading or motion. IN ST TRIAL P Rule 12(B).

D. Documents

1. *Required documents*

  a. *Motion and notice.* The requirement of notice is satisfied by service of the motion. IN ST TRIAL P Rule 7(B). Refer to the General Requirements section of this document for information on the content of a motion to strike.

  b. *Proposed order.* Unless local practice provides differently, a party should submit a proposed order with its written motion to be signed by the judge once the motion has been granted. 21 INPRAC § 13.8; IN ST HAMILTON ADMIN Rule 103(103.10)(b). Each Motion, Petition or other request for relief shall be accompanied by a proposed order. IN ST HAMILTON TRIAL Rule 202(202.10).

      i.   All proposed orders submitted by counsel pursuant to IN ST HAMILTON TRIAL Rule 202 shall meet the following requirements: (1) contain a complete distribution list of all attorneys and pro se litigants with full addresses; (2) stamped envelopes appropriately addressed for each attorney of record and/or pro se litigant on the distribution list. IN ST HAMILTON TRIAL Rule 202(202.30).

  c. *Certificate of service.* An attorney or unrepresented party tendering a document to the Clerk for filing shall certify that service has been made, list the parties served, and specify the date and means of service. The certificate of service shall be placed at the end of the document and shall not be separately filed. The separate filing of a certificate of service, however, shall not be grounds for rejecting a document for filing. The Clerk may permit documents to be filed without a certificate of service but shall require prompt filing of a separate certificate of service. IN ST TRIAL P Rule 5(C).

    i.   All pleadings filed with the Court which require a certificate of service shall specifically name the individual party or attorney on whom service has been made, the address, the manner in which service was made and the date when service was made. IN ST HAMILTON TRIAL Rule 201(201.60).

2. *Supplemental documents*

    a. *Supporting evidence.* When a motion is based on facts not appearing of record the court may hear the matter on affidavits presented by the respective parties, but the court may direct that the matter be heard wholly or partly on oral testimony or depositions. IN ST TRIAL P Rule 43(B).

    b. *Facsimile cover sheet.* Any document sent to the Clerk of the Circuit Court by electronic facsimile transmission shall be accompanied by a cover sheet which states the title of the document, case number, number of pages, identity and voice telephone number of the sending party and instructions for filing. The cover sheet shall contain the signature of the attorney or party, pro se, authorizing the filing. IN ST ADMIN Rule 12(D); IN ST HAMILTON ADMIN Rule 103(103.10)(a).

    c. *Request to schedule hearing.* All requests to schedule trials and hearings shall be in writing and shall contain the following information:

        i.   Type of trial or hearing (i.e., jury trial, court trial, final hearing in dissolution, etc.). IN ST HAMILTON TRIAL Rule 205(205.10).

        ii. A good-faith estimate of the total court time needed for the trial or hearing. IN ST HAMILTON TRIAL Rule 205(205.10).

        iii. Each request under IN ST HAMILTON TRIAL Rule 205(205.10) shall be accompanied by a proposed written order with appropriate blanks for date and time and shall further include reference to those items set forth in IN ST HAMILTON TRIAL Rule 205(205.10)(a) and IN ST HAMILTON TRIAL Rule 205(205.10)(b). IN ST HAMILTON TRIAL Rule 205(205.20).

    d. *Copies of unpublished opinions.* Authorities relied upon which are not cited in the Northeastern Reporter system shall be attached to counsel's brief. If the authority is cited for the first time in oral argument, a copy of the authority may be provided to the Court at the time of the argument. Sufficient copies shall be available to provide counsel for each party with a copy. IN ST HAMILTON TRIAL Rule 203(203.10).

E. Format

1. *Form of motions.* The rules applicable to captions, and the signing and form of pleadings (IN ST TRIAL P Rule 8 through IN ST TRIAL P Rule 11), apply to all motions and other papers provided under the Indiana Rules of Trial Procedure. 22B INPRAC 7:2.

2. *Form of pleadings*

    a. *Caption; Names of parties.* Every pleading shall contain a caption setting forth the name of the court, the title of the action, the file number, and a designation as in IN ST TRIAL P Rule 7(A). In the complaint the title of the action shall include the names of all the parties, but in other pleadings it is sufficient to state the name of the first party on each side with an appropriate indication of other parties. IN ST TRIAL P Rule 10(A).

    b. *Paragraphs; Separate statements.* All averments of a claim or defense shall be made in numbered paragraphs, the contents of each of which shall be limited as far as practicable to a statement of a single set of circumstances, and a paragraph may be referred to by number in all succeeding pleadings. Each claim founded upon a separate transaction or occurrence and each defense other than denials may be stated in a separate count or defense whenever a separation facilitates the clear presentation of the matters set forth. IN ST TRIAL P Rule 10(B).

    c. *Adoption by reference; Exhibits.* Statements in a pleading may be adopted by reference in a different part of the same pleading or in another pleading or in any motion. A copy of any written instrument which is an exhibit to a pleading is a part thereof for all purposes. IN ST TRIAL P Rule 10(C).

d. *Facsimile page limit.* Courts authorize the Hamilton County Clerk of Courts to accept pleadings, motions and other papers by electronic facsimile transmission for filing in any case pending before the Courts, subject to the requirement that The transmission may not exceed ten (10) pages in length including the cover sheet and proposed CCS entry. IN ST HAMILTON ADMIN Rule 103(103.10)(c).

e. *Emergency facsimile filings.* If the filing requires the immediate attention of the Judge, it shall so indicate in bold letters in an accompanying transmittal memorandum. IN ST HAMILTON ADMIN Rule 103(103.10)(f).

f. *Special judge heading.* After a special judge is selected, the attorneys or pro se litigants shall add to the caption of all pleadings to the right of the case title the following: "BEFORE SPECIAL JUDGE _____." IN ST HAMILTON TRIAL Rule 204(204.10).

g. *Format rules strictly enforced.* All filings shall be in compliance with the Indiana Rules of Trial Procedure. If the documents received are not in proper form, such deficiencies will not be corrected by court personnel. IN ST HAMILTON TRIAL Rule 201(201.70). The Court shall not be required to act on any Motion, Petition or other request for relief unless filed in conformity with the Hamilton County Local Trial and Administrative rules. IN ST HAMILTON TRIAL Rule 202(202.20).

3. *Size of papers for filing.* Effective January 1, 1992, all pleadings, copies, motions and documents filed with any trial court or appellate level court, typed or printed, with the exception of exhibits and existing wills, shall be prepared on eight and one-half by eleven inch (8 1/2" x 11") size paper. IN ST ADMIN Rule 11.

a. *Form.* All documents filed in any Hamilton County Court, with the exception of exhibits and existing wills, shall be prepared on paper measuring eight and one-half by eleven inches (8 1/2" x 11"). IN ST HAMILTON TRIAL Rule 201(201.20).

4. *Signature requirements*

a. *Signature of attorney.* Every pleading or motion of a party represented by an attorney shall be signed by at least one (1) attorney of record in his individual name, whose address, telephone number, and attorney number shall be stated, except that this provision shall not apply to pleadings and motions made and transcribed at the trial or a hearing before the judge and received by him in such form. IN ST TRIAL P Rule 11(A).

   i. The signature of an attorney constitutes a certificate by him that he has read the pleadings; that to the best of his knowledge, information, and belief, there is good ground to support it; and that it is not interposed for delay. IN ST TRIAL P Rule 11(A).

   ii. If a pleading or motion is not signed or is signed with intent to defeat the purpose of the rule, it may be stricken as sham and false and the action may proceed as though the pleading had not been served. IN ST TRIAL P Rule 11(A).

   iii. For a willful violation of IN ST TRIAL P Rule 11 an attorney may be subjected to appropriate disciplinary action. Similar action may be taken if scandalous or indecent matter is inserted. IN ST TRIAL P Rule 11(A).

b. *Signature of unrepresented party.* A party who is not represented by an attorney shall sign his pleading and state his address. IN ST TRIAL P Rule 11(A).

c. *Verification not generally required.* Except when specifically required by rule, pleadings or motions need not be verified or accompanied by affidavit. The rule in equity that the averments of an answer under oath must be overcome by the testimony of two (2) witnesses or of one (1) witness sustained by corroborating circumstances is abolished. IN ST TRIAL P Rule 11(A).

d. *Verification by affirmation or representation.* When in connection with any civil or special statutory proceeding it is required that any pleading, motion, petition, supporting affidavit, or other document of any kind, be verified, or that an oath be taken, it shall be sufficient if the subscriber simply affirms the truth of the matter to be verified by an affirmation or representation. IN ST TRIAL P Rule 11(B). IN ST TRIAL P Rule 11(B) states that the affirmation or representation should be in substantially the

following language: "I (we) affirm, under the penalties for perjury, that the foregoing representation(s) is (are) true. (Signed) _____."

    i.   Any person who falsifies an affirmation or representation of fact shall be subject to the same penalties as are prescribed by law for the making of a false affidavit. IN ST TRIAL P Rule 11(B).

  e. *Verified pleadings, motions, and affidavits as evidence.* Pleadings, motions and affidavits accompanying or in support of such pleadings or motions when required to be verified or under oath shall be accepted as a representation that the signer had personal knowledge thereof or reasonable cause to believe the existence of the facts or matters stated or alleged therein; and, if otherwise competent or acceptable as evidence, may be admitted as evidence of the facts or matters stated or alleged therein when it is so provided in the Indiana Rules of Trial Procedure, by statute or other law, or to the extent the writing or signature expressly purports to be made upon the signer's personal knowledge. When such pleadings, motions and affidavits are verified or under oath they shall not require other or greater proof on the part of the adverse party than if not verified or not under oath unless expressly provided otherwise by the Indiana Rules of Trial Procedure, statute or other law. Affidavits upon motions for summary judgment under IN ST TRIAL P Rule 56 and in denial of execution under IN ST TRIAL P Rule 9.2 shall be made upon personal knowledge. IN ST TRIAL P Rule 11(C).

5. *Information excluded from public access.* Every document filed in a case shall separately identify information excluded from public access pursuant to IN ST ADMIN Rule 9(G)(1) as follows:

  a. Whole documents that are excluded from public access pursuant to IN ST ADMIN Rule 9(G)(1) shall be tendered on light green paper or have a light green coversheet attached to the document, marked "Not for Public Access" or "Confidential." IN ST TRIAL P Rule 5(G)(1).

  b. When only a portion of a document contains information excluded from public access pursuant to IN ST ADMIN Rule 9(G)(1), said information shall be omitted [or redacted] from the filed document, and set forth on a separate accompanying document on light green paper conspicuously marked "Not for Public Access" or "Confidential" and clearly designated [or identifying] the caption and number of the case and the document and location within the document to which the redacted material pertains. IN ST TRIAL P Rule 5(G)(2).

  c. With respect to documents filed in electronic format, the trial court, by local rule, may provide for compliance with IN ST TRIAL P Rule 5 in manner that separates and protects access to information excluded from public access. IN ST TRIAL P Rule 5(G)(3).

  d. IN ST TRIAL P Rule 5(G) does not apply to a record sealed by the court pursuant to IN ST 5-14-3-5.5 or otherwise, nor to records, documents, or information filed in cases to which public access is prohibited pursuant to IN ST ADMIN Rule 9(G). IN ST TRIAL P Rule 5(G)(4).

  e. The following information in case records is excluded from public access and is confidential:

    i.   Information that is excluded from public access pursuant to federal law;

    ii. Information that is excluded from public access as declared confidential by Indiana statute or other court rule, including without limitation:

       • All adoption records created after July 8, 1941, as declared confidential by IN ST 31-19-19-1, et seq., except those specifically declared open by IN ST 31-19-13-2(2);

       • All records relating to chancroid, chlamydia, gonorrhea, hepatitis, human immunodeficiency virus (HIV), Lymphogranuloma venereum, syphilis, tuberculosis, as declared confidential by IN ST 16-41-8-1, et seq.;

       • All records relating to child abuse as declared confidential by IN ST 31-33-18-1, et seq.;

       • All records relating to drug tests as declared confidential by IN ST 5-14-3-4(a)(9);

       • Records of grand jury proceedings as declared confidential by IN ST 35-34-2-4;

       • Records of juvenile proceedings as declared confidential by IN ST 31-39-1-2, except those specifically open under statute;

       • All paternity records created after July 1, 1941 as declared confidential by IN ST

31-14-11-15, IN ST 31-19-5-23, IN ST 31-39-1-1 and IN ST 31-39-1-2 [Editor's note: IN ST 31-14-11-15 was repealed effective May 9, 2013];

- All pre-sentence reports as declared confidential by IN ST 35-38-1-13;

- Written petitions to permit marriages without consent and orders directing the Clerk of Court to issue a marriage license to underage persons, as declared confidential by IN ST 31-11-1-6;

- Only those arrest warrants, search warrants, indictments and informations ordered confidential by the trial judge, prior to return of duly executed service as declared confidential by IN ST 5-14-3-4(b)(1);

- All medical, mental health, or tax records unless determined by law or regulation of any governmental custodian not to be confidential, released by the subject of such records, or declared by a court of competent jurisdiction to be essential to the resolution of litigation as declared confidential by IN ST 16-39-3-10, IN ST 6-4.1-5-10, IN ST 6-4.1-12-12, and IN ST 6-8.1-7-1;

- Personal information relating to jurors or prospective jurors, other than for the use of the parties and counsel, pursuant to IN ST JURY Rule 10;

- Information relating to protection from abuse orders, no-contact orders and workplace violence restraining orders as declared confidential by IN ST 5-2-9-6, et seq.;

- Mediation proceedings pursuant to IN ST ADR Rule 2.11, Mini-Trial proceedings pursuant to IN ST ADR Rule 4.4(C), and Summary Jury Trials pursuant to IN ST ADR Rule 5.6;

- Information in probation files pursuant to the Probation Standards promulgated by the Judicial Conference of Indiana pursuant to IN ST 11-13-1-8(b);

- Information deemed confidential pursuant to the Rules for Court Administered Alcohol and Drug Programs promulgated by the Judicial Conference of Indiana pursuant to IN ST 12-23-14-13;

- Information deemed confidential pursuant to the Problem-Solving Court Rules promulgated by the Judicial Conference of Indiana pursuant to IN ST 33-23-16-16;

- All records of the Department of workforce Development as declared confidential by IN ST 22-4-19-6;

- Information regarding interception of electronic communications that is sealed or deemed confidential as set forth in IN ST 35-33.5-2-1, et seq.

iii. Information excluded from public access by specific court order;

iv. Complete Social Security Numbers of living persons;

v. With the exception of names, information such as addresses, phone numbers, and dates of birth which explicitly identifies:

- Natural persons who are witnesses or victims (not including defendants) in criminal, domestic violence, stalking, sexual assault, juvenile, or civil protection order proceedings, provided that juveniles who are victims of sex crimes shall be identified by initials only;

- Places of residence of judicial officers, clerks and other employees of courts and clerks of court, unless the person or persons about whom the information pertains waives confidentiality;

vi. Complete account numbers of specific assets, loans, bank accounts, credit cards, and personal identification numbers (PINs);

vii. All orders of expungement entered in criminal or juvenile proceedings, orders to restrict access to criminal history information pursuant to IN ST 35-38-5-5.5 or IN ST 35-38-8-5 and records excluded from public access by such orders, and information related to infractions that is excluded from public access pursuant to IN ST 34-28-5-15 or IN ST 34-28-5-16 [Editor's note:

IN ST 35-38-5-5.5, IN ST 35-38-8-5 and IN ST 34-28-5-16 were repealed effective July 1, 2013; for information on orders restricting access to criminal history, refer to IN ST 35-38-9-1, et seq.];

    viii. All personal notes and e-mail, and deliberative material, of judges, jurors, court staff and judicial agencies, and information recorded in personal data assistants (PDA's) or organizers and personal calendars. IN ST ADMIN Rule 9(G)(1).

F. Filing and Service Requirements

1. *Filing requirements.* Except as otherwise provided in IN ST TRIAL P Rule 5(E)(2), all pleadings and papers subsequent to the complaint which are required to be served upon a party shall be filed with the Court either before service or within a reasonable period of time thereafter. IN ST TRIAL P Rule 5(E)(1).

    a. *Filing with the court defined.* The filing of pleadings, motions, and other papers with the court as required by the Indiana Rules of Trial Procedure shall be made by one of the following methods:

        i. Delivery to the clerk of the court;

        ii. Sending by electronic transmission under the procedure adopted pursuant to IN ST ADMIN Rule 12;

        iii. Mailing to the clerk by registered, certified or express mail return receipt requested;

        iv. Depositing with any third-party commercial carrier for delivery to the clerk within three (3) calendar days, cost prepaid, properly addressed;

        v. If the court so permits, filing with the judge, in which event the judge shall note thereon the filing date and forthwith transmit them to the office of the clerk; or

        vi. Electronic filing, as approved by the Division of State Court Administration pursuant to IN ST ADMIN Rule 16. IN ST TRIAL P Rule 5(F).

        vii. Filing by registered or certified mail and by third-party commercial carrier shall be complete upon mailing or deposit. IN ST TRIAL P Rule 5(F).

    b. *Facsimile filing.* As outlined in IN ST HAMILTON ADMIN Rule 103(103.10),facsimile filing is permitted in the Circuit and Superior Courts of Hamilton County. The Courts authorize the Hamilton County Clerk of Courts to accept pleadings, motions and other papers by electronic facsimile transmission for filing in any case pending before the Courts, subject to the requirements of IN ST HAMILTON ADMIN Rule 103(103.10). IN ST HAMILTON ADMIN Rule 103(103.10); IN ST HAMILTON TRIAL Rule 201(201.80).

        i. *Generally.* In counties where a majority of judges of the courts of record, by posted local rule, have authorized electronic facsimile filing and designated a telephone number to receive such transmissions, pleadings, motions, and other papers may be sent to the Clerk of Circuit Court by electronic facsimile transmission for filing in any case, provided:

- Such matter does not exceed ten (10) pages, including the cover sheet;

- Such matter does not require the payment of fees other than the electronic facsimile transcription fee set forth in IN ST ADMIN Rule 12(E);

- The sending party creates at the time of transmission a machine generated log for such transmission; and

- The original document and the transmission log are maintained by the sending party for the duration of the litigation. IN ST ADMIN Rule 12(B); IN ST HAMILTON ADMIN Rule 103(103.10)(d).

- Legibility of documents and timeliness of filing is the responsibility of the sender. IN ST HAMILTON ADMIN Rule 103(103.10)(g).

- The Clerk shall accept electronic facsimile transmission filings only if received at the facsimile machine assigned by the Clerk. The telephone number designated to receive such transmission is available at IN ST HAMILTON ADMIN Rule 103(103.40). IN ST HAMILTON ADMIN Rule 103(103.40).

    ii. *Time of filing.* During normal, posted business hours, the time of filing shall be the time the duplicate document is produced in the office of the Clerk of the Circuit Court. Duplicate documents received at all other times shall be filed as of the next normal business day. IN ST ADMIN Rule 12(C).

- If the receiving fax machine endorses its own time and date stamp upon the transmitted documents and the receiving machine produces a delivery receipt which is electronically created and transmitted to the sending party, the time of filing shall be the date and time recorded on the transmitted document by the receiving fax machine. IN ST ADMIN Rule 12(C).

- Electronic facsimile transmissions will be accepted for filing only during the regular business hours as set forth in IN ST HAMILTON ADMIN Rule 101. Transmissions received by the Hamilton County Clerk after close of business shall be filed effective the next regular business day. IN ST HAMILTON ADMIN Rule 103(103.30).

    iii. *Filing fee.* The electronic facsimile transmission will not be accepted for filing if its filing requires the payment of any fee other than the electronic facsimile transcription fee set forth in IN ST HAMILTON ADMIN Rule 103(103.20). IN ST HAMILTON ADMIN Rule 103(103.10)(e).

- Pursuant to Ordinance adopted by the Hamilton County Board of Commissioners, the Clerk shall collect an electronic facsimile transcription fee of One Dollar ($1.00) per page, to a maximum of Ten Dollars ($10.00) per transmission, for each electronic facsimile transmission accepted for filing with the Hamilton County Circuit and Superior Courts. IN ST HAMILTON ADMIN Rule 103(103.20).

- The fee shall be assessed against the sending party and shall be paid upon receipt of invoice by that party and at the latest within thirty (30) days of the transmission. In the event the fee is not paid by the sending party within the time limits provided, the court may issue a show-cause order or enter a judgment in the matter. The Clerk may refuse an electronic facsimile transmission from any attorney or pro se litigant who has failed to pay these fees within thirty (30) days. IN ST HAMILTON ADMIN Rule 103(103.20).

    iv. *No direct filing with court.* A party shall not send pleadings, motions and other papers by electronic facsimile transmission for filing directly to any Court without that Court's prior approval to do so. IN ST HAMILTON ADMIN Rule 103(103.50).

  c. *Filing with special judge.* After a special judge has qualified, a copy of each pleading and Chronological Case Summary entries filed with the Court shall be mailed or delivered to the office of that Special judge by the counsel or pro se litigant with service indicated on the certificate of service. IN ST HAMILTON TRIAL Rule 204(204.20).

  d. *Proof of filing.* Any party filing any paper by any method other than personal delivery to the clerk shall retain proof of filing. IN ST TRIAL P Rule 5(F).

2. *Service requirements.* Unless otherwise provided by the Indiana Rules of Trial Procedure or an order of the court, each party and special judge, if any, shall be served with: (1) every order required by its terms to be served; (2) every pleading subsequent to the original complaint; (3) every written motion except one which may be heard ex parte; (4) every brief submitted to the trial court; (5) every paper relating to discovery required to be served upon a party; and (6) every written notice, appearance, demand, offer of judgment, designation of record on appeal, or similar paper. IN ST TRIAL P Rule 5(A).

  a. *Methods of service*

    i. *Personal service.* Whenever a party is represented by an attorney of record, service shall be made upon such attorney unless service upon the party himself is ordered by the court. Service upon the attorney or party shall be made by delivering or mailing a copy of the papers to the last known address or where an attorney or party has consented to service by fax or e-mail, as provided in IN ST TRIAL P Rule 3.1(A)(4), by faxing or e-mailing a copy of the documents to the fax number or e-mail address set out in the appearance form or correction as required by IN

ST TRIAL P Rule 3.1(E). IN ST TRIAL P Rule 5(B). Delivery of a copy within IN ST TRIAL P Rule 5 means:

- Offering or tendering it to the attorney or party and stating the nature of the papers being served. Refusal to accept an offered or tendered document is a waiver of any objection to the sufficiency or adequacy of service of that document;

- Leaving it at his office with a clerk or other person in charge thereof, or if there is no one in charge, leaving it in a conspicuous place therein; or

- If the office is closed, by leaving it at his dwelling house or usual place of abode with some person of suitable age and discretion then residing therein; or,

- Leaving it at some other suitable place, selected by the attorney upon whom service is being made, pursuant to duly promulgated local rule. IN ST TRIAL P Rule 5(B)(1).

ii. *Service by mail.* If service is made by mail, the papers shall be deposited in the United States mail addressed to the person on whom they are being served, with postage prepaid. Service shall be deemed complete upon mailing. Proof of service of all papers permitted to be mailed may be made by written acknowledgment of service, by affidavit of the person who mailed the papers, or by certificate of an attorney. It shall be the duty of attorneys when entering their appearance in a cause or when filing pleadings or papers therein, to have noted in the Chronological Case Summary or said pleadings or papers so filed the address and telephone number of their office. Service by delivery or by mail at such address shall be deemed sufficient and complete. IN ST TRIAL P Rule 5(B)(2).

iii. *Service by fax or e-mail.* A party who has consented to service by fax or e-mail may be served as follows:

- Service by e-mail shall be made by attaching the document being served in .pdf format. Discovery documents must also be served in accordance with IN ST TRIAL P Rule 26(A). IN ST TRIAL P Rule 5(B)(3)(a).

- Service by fax shall be deemed complete upon generation of a transmission record indicating the successful transmission of the entire document, except as provided in IN ST TRIAL P Rule 5(B)(3)(d). IN ST TRIAL P Rule 5(B)(3)(b).

- Service by e-mail shall be deemed complete upon transmission, except as provided in IN ST TRIAL P Rule 5(B)(3)(d). IN ST TRIAL P Rule 5(B)(3)(c).

- Service by fax or e-mail that occurs on a Saturday, Sunday, legal holiday, or day the court or agency in which the matter is pending is closed or after 5:00 PM local time of the recipient shall be deemed complete the next day that is not a Saturday, Sunday, legal holiday, or day that the court or agency in which the matter is pending is not closed. IN ST TRIAL P Rule 5(B)(3)(d).

iv. *Mail box service.* Pursuant to IN ST TRIAL P Rule 5(B)(1)(d), the Circuit and Superior Courts of Hamilton County hereby designate the "mail boxes" located in the Clerk's order book office for service of pleadings upon attorneys who have such boxes. IN ST HAMILTON TRIAL Rule 201(201.50).

b. *Serving numerous defendants.* In any action in which there are unusually large numbers of defendants, the court, upon motion or of its own initiative, may order:

i. That service of the pleadings of the defendants and replies thereto need not be made as between the defendants;

- That any cross-claim, counterclaim, or matter constituting an avoidance or affirmative defense contained therein shall be deemed to be denied or avoided by all other parties; and

- That the filing of any such pleading and service thereof upon the plaintiff constitutes due notice of it to the parties. IN ST TRIAL P Rule 5(D).

ii. A copy of every such order shall be served upon the parties in such manner and form as the court directs. IN ST TRIAL P Rule 5(D).

    c.   *Service on parties in default for failure to appear.* No service need be made on parties in default for failure to appear, except that pleadings asserting new or additional claims for relief against them shall be served upon them in the manner provided by service of summons in IN ST TRIAL P Rule 4. IN ST TRIAL P Rule 5(A).

G. Hearings

1.   *Hearing on motion.* Unless local conditions make it impracticable, each judge shall establish regular times and places, at intervals sufficiently frequent for the prompt dispatch of business, at which motions requiring notice and hearing may be heard and disposed of; but the judge at any time or place and on such notice, if any, as he considers reasonable may make order for the advancement, conduct, and hearing of actions. To expedite its business the court may direct the submission and determination of motions without oral hearing upon brief written statements of reasons in support and opposition, or direct or permit hearings by telephone conference call with all attorneys or other similar means of communication. IN ST TRIAL P Rule 73(A).

H. Forms

1. Motion to Strike Forms for Indiana

    a.   Motion to strike pleading not signed. 9 INPRAC § 4.18.

    b.   Motion to strike pleading as sham and false. 9 INPRAC § 4.19.

    c.   Motion to strike; Entire pleading. 9 INPRAC § 42.21.

    d.   Motion to strike; Portions of pleading. 9 INPRAC § 42.22.

    e.   Motion to strike; Insufficient defense in answer. 9 INPRAC § 42.23.

    f.   Motion to strike; Pleading that was not timely filed. 9 INPRAC § 42.24.

    g.   Motion to strike; Attorney fees claim. 9 INPRAC § 42.25.

    h.   Motion to strike; General denial in answer. 9 INPRAC § 42.26.

    i.   Motion to strike; Impertinent and scandalous material. 9 INPRAC § 42.27.

    j.   Motion to strike answer; Matter repleaded contrary to prior ruling. 9 INPRAC § 42.28.

    k.   Motion to strike; Failure to plead performance of conditions precedent. 9 INPRAC § 42.29.

    l.   Motion to strike; Appearance of defendant's attorney. 9 INPRAC § 42.30.

    m.   Certificate of service; Personal service. 9 INPRAC § 5.7.

    n.   Certificate of service; First class mail. 9 INPRAC § 5.8.

I. Checklist

(I) ❑ Matters to be considered by moving party

   (a) ❑ Required documents

      (1) ❑ Motion and notice

      (2) ❑ Proposed order

      (3) ❑ Certificate of service

   (b) ❑ Supplemental documents

      (1) ❑ Supporting evidence

      (2) ❑ Facsimile cover sheet

      (3) ❑ Request to schedule trial or hearing

      (4) ❑ Copies of unpublished opinions

   (c) ❑ Timing

      (1) ❑ Upon motion made by a party before responding to a pleading, or, if no responsive pleading is permitted by Indiana Rules of Trial Procedure, upon motion made by a party within twenty (20) days after the service of the pleading upon him or at any time upon the court's

own initiative, the court may order stricken from any pleading any insufficient claim or defense or any redundant, immaterial, impertinent, or scandalous matter

(2) ❑ A written motion, other than one which may be heard ex parte, and notice of the hearing thereof shall be served not less than five (5) days before the time specified for the hearing, unless a different period is fixed by the Indiana Rules of Trial Procedure or by order of the court

(3) ❑ All pleadings and papers subsequent to the complaint which are required to be served upon a party shall be filed with the Court either before service or within a reasonable period of time thereafter

(II) ❑ Matters to be considered by the responding party

   (a) ❑ Required documents

      (1) ❑ Opposition

      (2) ❑ Certificate of service

   (b) ❑ Supplemental documents

      (1) ❑ Supporting evidence

      (2) ❑ Alternative proposed order

      (3) ❑ Facsimile cover sheet

      (4) ❑ Request to schedule trial or hearing

      (5) ❑ Copies of unpublished opinions

   (c) ❑ Timing

      (1) ❑ Except as otherwise provided in IN ST TRIAL P Rule 59(D), opposing affidavits may be served not less than one (1) day before the hearing, unless the court permits them to be served at some other time

Motions, Oppositions and Replies
Motion to Dismiss for Improper Venue

Document Last Updated October 2013

A. Applicable Rules

1. *State rules*

   a. Appearance. IN ST TRIAL P Rule 3.1.

   b. Process. IN ST TRIAL P Rule 4.

   c. Service and filing of pleadings and other papers. IN ST TRIAL P Rule 5.

   d. Time. IN ST TRIAL P Rule 6.

   e. Pleadings. IN ST TRIAL P Rule 7; IN ST TRIAL P Rule 8; IN ST TRIAL P Rule 9.2; IN ST TRIAL P Rule 10.

   f. Signing and verification of pleadings. IN ST TRIAL P Rule 11.

   g. Defenses and objections; When and how presented; By pleading or motion; Motion for judgment on the pleadings. IN ST TRIAL P Rule 12.

   h. Amended and supplemental pleadings. IN ST TRIAL P Rule 15.

   i. Joinder of person needed for just adjudication. IN ST TRIAL P Rule 19.

   j. Misjoinder and non-joinder of parties; Venue and jurisdiction over the subject-matter. IN ST TRIAL P Rule 21.

   k. Evidence. IN ST TRIAL P Rule 43.

l.   Judgment on the evidence (directed verdict). IN ST TRIAL P Rule 50.

m. Findings by the court. IN ST TRIAL P Rule 52.

n.   Summary judgment. IN ST TRIAL P Rule 56.

o.   Motion to correct error. IN ST TRIAL P Rule 59.

p.   Relief from judgment or order. IN ST TRIAL P Rule 60.

q.   Hearing of motions. IN ST TRIAL P Rule 73.

r.   Venue requirements. IN ST TRIAL P Rule 75.

s.   Interlocutory appeals. IN ST RAP Rule 14.

t.   Access to court records. IN ST ADMIN Rule 9.

u.   Paper size. IN ST ADMIN Rule 11.

v.   Facsimile transmission. IN ST ADMIN Rule 12.

w. Electronic filing and electronic service pilot projects. IN ST ADMIN Rule 16.

x.   Sealing of certain records by court; Hearing; Notice. IN ST 5-14-3-5.5.

y.   Privacy and confidentiality. IN ST 5-2-9-6; IN ST 5-14-3-4; IN ST 6-4.1-5-10; IN ST 6-4.1-12-12; IN ST 6-8.1-7-1; IN ST 11-13-1-8; IN ST 12-23-14-13; IN ST 16-39-3-10; IN ST 16-41-8-1; IN ST 22-4-19-6; IN ST 31-11-1-6; IN ST 31-19-5-23; IN ST 31-19-13-2; IN ST 31-19-19-1; IN ST 31-33-18-1; IN ST 31-39-1-1; IN ST 31-39-1-2; IN ST 33-23-16-16; IN ST 35-34-2-4; IN ST 35-38-1-13; IN ST 35-38-9-1; IN ST ADR Rule 2.11; IN ST ADR Rule 4.4; IN ST ADR Rule 5.6; IN ST JURY Rule 10.

2. *Local rules*

a.   Court hours. IN ST HAMILTON ADMIN Rule 101.

b.   Facsimile transmissions. IN ST HAMILTON ADMIN Rule 103.

c.   Filing of pleadings and entry of appearances. IN ST HAMILTON TRIAL Rule 201.

d.   Proposed orders. IN ST HAMILTON TRIAL Rule 202.

e.   Briefs and memorandums. IN ST HAMILTON TRIAL Rule 203.

f.   Special judges. IN ST HAMILTON TRIAL Rule 204.

g.   Trial settings. IN ST HAMILTON TRIAL Rule 205.

h.   Continuances. IN ST HAMILTON TRIAL Rule 206.

B. Timing

1. *Motion to dismiss for improper venue.* A motion making the defense of incorrect venue under IN ST TRIAL P Rule 75, or any statutory provision, shall be made before pleading if a further pleading is permitted or within twenty (20) days after service of the prior pleading if none is required. IN ST TRIAL P Rule 12(B); IN ST TRIAL P Rule 75(A).

a.   *Time to file a responsive pleading.* A responsive pleading required under the Indiana Rules of Trial Procedure, shall be served within twenty (20) days after service of the prior pleading. IN ST TRIAL P Rule 6(C).

b.   *Waiver of certain IN ST TRIAL P Rule 12(B) defenses.* If a pleading sets forth a claim for relief to which the adverse party is not required to serve a responsive pleading, any of the defenses in IN ST TRIAL P Rule 12(B)(2), IN ST TRIAL P Rule 12(B)(3), IN ST TRIAL P Rule 12(B)(4), IN ST TRIAL P Rule 12(B)(5) or IN ST TRIAL P Rule 12(B)(8) is waived to the extent constitutionally permissible unless made in a motion within twenty (20) days after service of the prior pleading. IN ST TRIAL P Rule 12(B).

c.   *Filing.* All pleadings and papers subsequent to the complaint which are required to be served upon a party shall be filed with the Court either before service or within a reasonable period of time thereafter. IN ST TRIAL P Rule 5(E)(1).

2. *Service.* A written motion, other than one which may be heard ex parte, and notice of the hearing thereof shall be served not less than five (5) days before the time specified for the hearing, unless a different period is fixed by the Indiana Rules of Trial Procedure or by order of the court. IN ST TRIAL P Rule 6(D).

    a. *Of supporting affidavits.* When a motion is supported by affidavit, the affidavit shall be served with the motion; and,

3. *Service of opposition.* Except as otherwise provided in IN ST TRIAL P Rule 59(D), opposing affidavits may be served not less than one (1) day before the hearing, unless the court permits them to be served at some other time. IN ST TRIAL P Rule 6(D).

4. *Computation of time*

    a. *Generally; Days excluded.* In computing any period of time prescribed or allowed by the Indiana Rules of Trial Procedure, by order of the court, or by any applicable statute, the day of the act, event, or default from which the designated period of time begins to run shall not be included. The last day of the period so computed is to be included unless it is:

        i. A Saturday,

        ii. A Sunday,

        iii. A legal holiday as defined by state statute, or

        iv. A day the office in which the act is to be done is closed during regular business hours. IN ST TRIAL P Rule 6(A).

    b. *Short periods.* In any event, the period runs until the end of the next day that is not a Saturday, a Sunday, a legal holiday, or a day on which the office is closed. When the period of time allowed is less than seven (7) days, intermediate Saturdays, Sundays, legal holidays, and days on which the office is closed shall be excluded from the computations. IN ST TRIAL P Rule 6(A).

    c. *Additional time after service by United States mail.* Whenever a party has the right or is required to do some act or take some proceedings within a prescribed period after the service of a notice or other paper upon him and the notice or paper is served upon him by United States mail, three (3) days shall be added to the prescribed period. IN ST TRIAL P Rule 6(E).

    d. *Enlargement of time.* When an act is required or allowed to be done at or within a specific time by the Indiana Rules of Trial Procedure, the court may at any time for cause shown:

        i. Order the period enlarged, with or without motion or notice, if request therefor is made before the expiration of the period originally prescribed or extended by a previous order; or

        ii. Upon motion made after the expiration of the specific period, permit the act to be done where the failure to act was the result of excusable neglect; but, the court may not extend the time for taking any action for judgment on the evidence under IN ST TRIAL P Rule 50(A), amendment of findings and judgment under IN ST TRIAL P Rule 52(B), to correct errors under IN ST TRIAL P Rule 59(C), statement in opposition to motion to correct error under IN ST TRIAL P Rule 59(E), or to obtain relief from final judgment under IN ST TRIAL P Rule 60(B), except to the extent and under the conditions stated in those rules. IN ST TRIAL P Rule 6(B).

        iii. For information on obtaining a continuance, refer to IN ST HAMILTON TRIAL Rule 206.

C. General Requirements

1. *Motions, generally.* Unless made during a hearing or trial, or otherwise ordered by the court, an application to the court for an order shall be made by written motion. The motion shall state the grounds therefor and the relief or order sought. IN ST TRIAL P Rule 7(B).

    a. *Motions as distinct from pleadings.* Motions and responses to motions are not pleadings, and allegations contained in a motion are not admissions of a party. 22B INPRAC 7:2; Wachstetter v. County Properties, LLC, 832 N.E.2d 574 (Ind.Ct.App. 2005); Scott County Family YMCA, Inc. v. Hobbs, 817 N.E.2d 603 (Ind.Ct.App. 2004).

    b. *Unopposed motions generally granted.* It is common for a trial court to grant procedural motions, such as motions for enlargement of time, discovery motions, or motions for continuance, unless an objection is filed. 21 INPRAC § 13.8.

2. *Motion to dismiss for improper venue.* Every defense, in law or fact, to a claim for relief in any pleading, whether a claim, counterclaim, cross-claim, or third-party claim, shall be asserted in the responsive pleading thereto if one is required; except that at the option of the pleader, incorrect venue under IN ST TRIAL P Rule 75, or any statutory provision may be made by motion. IN ST TRIAL P Rule 12(B)(3). The disposition of this motion shall be consistent with IN ST TRIAL P Rule 75. IN ST TRIAL P Rule 12(B)(3). This means that, in almost every instance in which a motion is made under IN ST TRIAL P Rule 12(B)(3) or another statute, the action shall not be dismissed but transferred, consistent with IN ST TRIAL P Rule 75. 1A INPRAC R 12(12.7).

    a. *Venue.* Any case may be venued, commenced and decided in any court in any county, except, that upon the filing of a pleading or a motion to dismiss allowed by IN ST TRIAL P Rule 12(B)(3), the court, from allegations of the complaint or after hearing evidence thereon or considering affidavits or documentary evidence filed with the motion or in opposition to it, shall order the case transferred to a county or court selected by the party first properly filing such motion or pleading if the court determines that the county or court where the action was filed does not meet preferred venue requirements or is not authorized to decide the case and that the court or county selected has preferred venue and is authorized to decide the case. IN ST TRIAL P Rule 75(A).

    b. *Preferred venue.* Preferred venue lies in:

        i.   The county where the greater percentage of individual defendants included in the complaint resides, or, if there is no such greater percentage, the place where any individual defendant so named resides; or

        ii. The county where the land or some part thereof is located or the chattels or some part thereof are regularly located or kept, if the complaint includes a claim for injuries thereto or relating to such land or such chattels, including without limitation claims for recovery of possession or for injuries, to establish use or control, to quiet title or determine any interest, to avoid or set aside conveyances, to foreclose liens, to partition and to assert any matters for which in rem relief is or would be proper; or

        iii. The county where the accident or collision occurred, if the complaint includes a claim for injuries relating to the operation of a motor vehicle or a vehicle on railroad, street or interurban tracks; or

        iv. The county where either the principal office of a defendant organization is located or the office or agency of a defendant organization or individual to which the claim relates or out of which the claim arose is located, if one or more such organizations or individuals are included as defendants in the complaint; or

        v.   The county where either one or more individual plaintiffs reside, the principal office of a governmental organization is located, or the office of a governmental organization to which the claim relates or out of which the claim arose is located, if one or more governmental organizations are included as defendants in the complaint; or

        vi. The county or court fixed by written stipulations signed by all the parties named in the complaint or their attorneys and filed with the court before ruling on the motion to dismiss; or

        vii. The county where the individual is held in custody or is restrained, if the complaint seeks relief with respect to such individual's custody or restraint upon his freedom; or

        viii. The county where a claim in the plaintiff's complaint may be commenced under any statute recognizing or creating a special or general remedy or proceeding; or

        ix. The county where all or some of the property is located or can be found if the case seeks only judgment in rem against the property of a defendant being served by publication; or

        x.   The county where either one or more individual plaintiffs reside, the principal office of any plaintiff organization or governmental organization is located, or the office of any such plaintiff organization or governmental organization to which the claim relates or out of which the claim arose is located, if the case is not subject to the requirements of IN ST TRIAL P Rule 75(A)(1) through IN ST TRIAL P Rule 75(A)(9) or if all the defendants are nonresident individuals or nonresident organizations without a principal office in the state. IN ST TRIAL P Rule 75(A).

c. *Claim or proceeding filed in improper court*

    i. Whenever a claim or proceeding is filed which should properly have been filed in another court of this state, and proper objection is made, the court in which such action is filed shall not then dismiss the action, but shall order the action transferred to the court in which it should have been filed. IN ST TRIAL P Rule 75(B)(1).

    ii. The person filing the action shall, within twenty (20) days, pay such costs as are chargeable upon a change of venue and the papers and records shall be certified to the court of transfer in like manner as upon change of venue and the action shall be deemed commenced as of the date of filing the action in the original court. IN ST TRIAL P Rule 75(B)(2).

    iii. If the party filing the action does not pay the costs of transfer within twenty (20) days of the order transferring venue, the original court shall dismiss the action without prejudice and shall order payment of reasonable attorney fees to the party making proper objection. IN ST TRIAL P Rule 75(B)(3).

d. *Assessment of costs, traveling expenses and attorneys' fees in resisting venue.* When the case is ordered transferred under the provisions of IN ST TRIAL P Rule 75 or IN ST TRIAL P Rule 21(B) the court shall order the parties or persons filing the complaint to pay the filing costs of refiling the case in the proper court and pay mileage expenses reasonably incurred by the parties and their attorneys in resisting the venue; and if it appears that the case was commenced in the wrong county by sham pleading, in bad faith or without cause, the court shall order payment of reasonable attorneys' fees incurred by parties successfully resisting the venue. IN ST TRIAL P Rule 75(C).

e. *Other venue statutes superseded by IN ST TRIAL P Rule 75.* Any provision of the Indiana Rules of Trial Procedure and any special or general statute relating to venue, the place of trial or the authority of the court to hear the case shall be subject to IN ST TRIAL P Rule 75, and the provisions of any statute fixing more stringent rules thereon shall be ineffective. No statute or rule fixing the place of trial shall be deemed a requirement of jurisdiction. IN ST TRIAL P Rule 75(D).

f. *Appeal.* An order transferring or refusing to transfer a case under IN ST TRIAL P Rule 75 shall be an interlocutory order appealable pursuant to IN ST RAP Rule 14(A)(8); provided, however, that the appeal of an interlocutory order under IN ST TRIAL P Rule 75 shall not stay proceedings in the trial court unless the trial court or the Court of Appeals so orders. IN ST TRIAL P Rule 75(E).

3. *Consolidation and waiver*

a. *Consolidation of defenses in motion.* A party who makes a motion under IN ST TRIAL P Rule 12 may join with it any other motions herein provided for and then available to him. If a party makes a motion under IN ST TRIAL P Rule 12 but omits therefrom any defense or objection then available to him which IN ST TRIAL P Rule 12 permits to be raised by motion, he shall not thereafter make a motion based on the defense or objection so omitted. He may, however, make such motions as are allowed under IN ST TRIAL P Rule 12(H)(2). IN ST TRIAL P Rule 12(G).

b. *Waiver or preservation of certain defenses.* No defense or objection is waived by being joined with one or more other defenses or objections in a responsive pleading or motion. IN ST TRIAL P Rule 12(B).

D. Documents

1. *Required documents*

a. *Motion and notice.* The requirement of notice is satisfied by service of the motion. IN ST TRIAL P Rule 7(B). Refer to the General Requirements section of this document for information on the content of a motion to dismiss for improper venue.

b. *Proposed order.* Unless local practice provides differently, a party should submit a proposed order with its written motion to be signed by the judge once the motion has been granted. 21 INPRAC § 13.8; IN ST HAMILTON ADMIN Rule 103(103.10)(b). Each Motion, Petition or other request for relief shall be accompanied by a proposed order. IN ST HAMILTON TRIAL Rule 202(202.10).

    i. All proposed orders submitted by counsel pursuant to IN ST HAMILTON TRIAL Rule 202 shall meet the following requirements: (1) contain a complete distribution list of all attorneys

and pro se litigants with full addresses; (2) stamped envelopes appropriately addressed for each attorney of record and/or pro se litigant on the distribution list. IN ST HAMILTON TRIAL Rule 202(202.30).

c. *Certificate of service.* An attorney or unrepresented party tendering a document to the Clerk for filing shall certify that service has been made, list the parties served, and specify the date and means of service. The certificate of service shall be placed at the end of the document and shall not be separately filed. The separate filing of a certificate of service, however, shall not be grounds for rejecting a document for filing. The Clerk may permit documents to be filed without a certificate of service but shall require prompt filing of a separate certificate of service. IN ST TRIAL P Rule 5(C).

   i. All pleadings filed with the Court which require a certificate of service shall specifically name the individual party or attorney on whom service has been made, the address, the manner in which service was made and the date when service was made. IN ST HAMILTON TRIAL Rule 201(201.60).

2. *Supplemental documents*

a. *Supporting evidence.* When a motion is based on facts not appearing of record the court may hear the matter on affidavits presented by the respective parties, but the court may direct that the matter be heard wholly or partly on oral testimony or depositions. IN ST TRIAL P Rule 43(B).

b. *Facsimile cover sheet.* Any document sent to the Clerk of the Circuit Court by electronic facsimile transmission shall be accompanied by a cover sheet which states the title of the document, case number, number of pages, identity and voice telephone number of the sending party and instructions for filing. The cover sheet shall contain the signature of the attorney or party, pro se, authorizing the filing. IN ST ADMIN Rule 12(D); IN ST HAMILTON ADMIN Rule 103(103.10)(a).

c. *Request to schedule hearing.* All requests to schedule trials and hearings shall be in writing and shall contain the following information:

   i. Type of trial or hearing (i.e., jury trial, court trial, final hearing in dissolution, etc.). IN ST HAMILTON TRIAL Rule 205(205.10).

   ii. A good-faith estimate of the total court time needed for the trial or hearing. IN ST HAMILTON TRIAL Rule 205(205.10).

   iii. Each request under IN ST HAMILTON TRIAL Rule 205(205.10) shall be accompanied by a proposed written order with appropriate blanks for date and time and shall further include reference to those items set forth in IN ST HAMILTON TRIAL Rule 205(205.10)(a) and IN ST HAMILTON TRIAL Rule 205(205.10)(b). IN ST HAMILTON TRIAL Rule 205(205.20).

d. *Copies of unpublished opinions.* Authorities relied upon which are not cited in the Northeastern Reporter system shall be attached to counsel's brief. If the authority is cited for the first time in oral argument, a copy of the authority may be provided to the Court at the time of the argument. Sufficient copies shall be available to provide counsel for each party with a copy. IN ST HAMILTON TRIAL Rule 203(203.10).

E. Format

1. *Form of motions.* The rules applicable to captions, and the signing and form of pleadings (IN ST TRIAL P Rule 8 through IN ST TRIAL P Rule 11), apply to all motions and other papers provided under the Indiana Rules of Trial Procedure. 22B INPRAC 7:2.

2. *Form of pleadings*

a. *Caption; Names of parties.* Every pleading shall contain a caption setting forth the name of the court, the title of the action, the file number, and a designation as in IN ST TRIAL P Rule 7(A). In the complaint the title of the action shall include the names of all the parties, but in other pleadings it is sufficient to state the name of the first party on each side with an appropriate indication of other parties. IN ST TRIAL P Rule 10(A).

b. *Paragraphs; Separate statements.* All averments of a claim or defense shall be made in numbered paragraphs, the contents of each of which shall be limited as far as practicable to a statement of a single set of circumstances, and a paragraph may be referred to by number in all succeeding pleadings. Each claim founded upon a separate transaction or occurrence and each defense other than denials may be stated in a separate count or defense whenever a separation facilitates the clear presentation of the matters set forth. IN ST TRIAL P Rule 10(B).

c. *Adoption by reference; Exhibits.* Statements in a pleading may be adopted by reference in a different part of the same pleading or in another pleading or in any motion. A copy of any written instrument which is an exhibit to a pleading is a part thereof for all purposes. IN ST TRIAL P Rule 10(C).

d. *Facsimile page limit.* Courts authorize the Hamilton County Clerk of Courts to accept pleadings, motions and other papers by electronic facsimile transmission for filing in any case pending before the Courts, subject to the requirement that The transmission may not exceed ten (10) pages in length including the cover sheet and proposed CCS entry. IN ST HAMILTON ADMIN Rule 103(103.10)(c).

e. *Emergency facsimile filings.* If the filing requires the immediate attention of the Judge, it shall so indicate in bold letters in an accompanying transmittal memorandum. IN ST HAMILTON ADMIN Rule 103(103.10)(f).

f. *Special judge heading.* After a special judge is selected, the attorneys or pro se litigants shall add to the caption of all pleadings to the right of the case title the following: "BEFORE SPECIAL JUDGE _____." IN ST HAMILTON TRIAL Rule 204(204.10).

3. *Size of papers for filing.* Effective January 1, 1992, all pleadings, copies, motions and documents filed with any trial court or appellate level court, typed or printed, with the exception of exhibits and existing wills, shall be prepared on eight and one-half by eleven inch (8 1/2" x 11") size paper. IN ST ADMIN Rule 11.

a. *Form.* All documents filed in any Hamilton County Court, with the exception of exhibits and existing wills, shall be prepared on paper measuring eight and one-half by eleven inches (8 1/2" x 11"). IN ST HAMILTON TRIAL Rule 201(201.20).

4. *Signature requirements*

a. *Signature of attorney.* Every pleading or motion of a party represented by an attorney shall be signed by at least one (1) attorney of record in his individual name, whose address, telephone number, and attorney number shall be stated, except that this provision shall not apply to pleadings and motions made and transcribed at the trial or a hearing before the judge and received by him in such form. IN ST TRIAL P Rule 11(A).

  i. The signature of an attorney constitutes a certificate by him that he has read the pleadings; that to the best of his knowledge, information, and belief, there is good ground to support it; and that it is not interposed for delay. IN ST TRIAL P Rule 11(A).

  ii. If a pleading or motion is not signed or is signed with intent to defeat the purpose of the rule, it may be stricken as sham and false and the action may proceed as though the pleading had not been served. IN ST TRIAL P Rule 11(A).

  iii. For a willful violation of IN ST TRIAL P Rule 11 an attorney may be subjected to appropriate disciplinary action. Similar action may be taken if scandalous or indecent matter is inserted. IN ST TRIAL P Rule 11(A).

b. *Signature of unrepresented party.* A party who is not represented by an attorney shall sign his pleading and state his address. IN ST TRIAL P Rule 11(A).

c. *Verification not generally required.* Except when specifically required by rule, pleadings or motions need not be verified or accompanied by affidavit. The rule in equity that the averments of an answer under oath must be overcome by the testimony of two (2) witnesses or of one (1) witness sustained by corroborating circumstances is abolished. IN ST TRIAL P Rule 11(A).

d. *Verification by affirmation or representation.* When in connection with any civil or special statutory proceeding it is required that any pleading, motion, petition, supporting affidavit, or other document of any kind, be verified, or that an oath be taken, it shall be sufficient if the subscriber simply affirms the truth of the matter to be verified by an affirmation or representation. IN ST TRIAL P Rule 11(B). IN ST TRIAL P Rule 11(B) states that the affirmation or representation should be in substantially the

following language: "I (we) affirm, under the penalties for perjury, that the foregoing representation(s) is (are) true. (Signed) _____."

    i. Any person who falsifies an affirmation or representation of fact shall be subject to the same penalties as are prescribed by law for the making of a false affidavit. IN ST TRIAL P Rule 11(B).

e. *Verified pleadings, motions, and affidavits as evidence.* Pleadings, motions and affidavits accompanying or in support of such pleadings or motions when required to be verified or under oath shall be accepted as a representation that the signer had personal knowledge thereof or reasonable cause to believe the existence of the facts or matters stated or alleged therein; and, if otherwise competent or acceptable as evidence, may be admitted as evidence of the facts or matters stated or alleged therein when it is so provided in the Indiana Rules of Trial Procedure, by statute or other law, or to the extent the writing or signature expressly purports to be made upon the signer's personal knowledge. When such pleadings, motions and affidavits are verified or under oath they shall not require other or greater proof on the part of the adverse party than if not verified or not under oath unless expressly provided otherwise by the Indiana Rules of Trial Procedure, statute or other law. Affidavits upon motions for summary judgment under IN ST TRIAL P Rule 56 and in denial of execution under IN ST TRIAL P Rule 9.2 shall be made upon personal knowledge. IN ST TRIAL P Rule 11(C).

5. *Information excluded from public access.* Every document filed in a case shall separately identify information excluded from public access pursuant to IN ST ADMIN Rule 9(G)(1) as follows:

a. Whole documents that are excluded from public access pursuant to IN ST ADMIN Rule 9(G)(1) shall be tendered on light green paper or have a light green coversheet attached to the document, marked "Not for Public Access" or "Confidential." IN ST TRIAL P Rule 5(G)(1).

b. When only a portion of a document contains information excluded from public access pursuant to IN ST ADMIN Rule 9(G)(1), said information shall be omitted [or redacted] from the filed document, and set forth on a separate accompanying document on light green paper conspicuously marked "Not for Public Access" or "Confidential" and clearly designated [or identifying] the caption and number of the case and the document and location within the document to which the redacted material pertains. IN ST TRIAL P Rule 5(G)(2).

c. With respect to documents filed in electronic format, the trial court, by local rule, may provide for compliance with IN ST TRIAL P Rule 5 in manner that separates and protects access to information excluded from public access. IN ST TRIAL P Rule 5(G)(3).

d. IN ST TRIAL P Rule 5(G) does not apply to a record sealed by the court pursuant to IN ST 5-14-3-5.5 or otherwise, nor to records, documents, or information filed in cases to which public access is prohibited pursuant to IN ST ADMIN Rule 9(G). IN ST TRIAL P Rule 5(G)(4).

e. The following information in case records is excluded from public access and is confidential:

    i. Information that is excluded from public access pursuant to federal law;

    ii. Information that is excluded from public access as declared confidential by Indiana statute or other court rule, including without limitation:

- All adoption records created after July 8, 1941, as declared confidential by IN ST 31-19-19-1, et seq., except those specifically declared open by IN ST 31-19-13-2(2);

- All records relating to chancroid, chlamydia, gonorrhea, hepatitis, human immunodeficiency virus (HIV), Lymphogranuloma venereum, syphilis, tuberculosis, as declared confidential by IN ST 16-41-8-1, et seq.;

- All records relating to child abuse as declared confidential by IN ST 31-33-18-1, et seq.;

- All records relating to drug tests as declared confidential by IN ST 5-14-3-4(a)(9);

- Records of grand jury proceedings as declared confidential by IN ST 35-34-2-4;

- Records of juvenile proceedings as declared confidential by IN ST 31-39-1-2, except those specifically open under statute;

- All paternity records created after July 1, 1941 as declared confidential by IN ST

31-14-11-15, IN ST 31-19-5-23, IN ST 31-39-1-1 and IN ST 31-39-1-2 [Editor's note: IN ST 31-14-11-15 was repealed effective May 9, 2013];

- All pre-sentence reports as declared confidential by IN ST 35-38-1-13;

- Written petitions to permit marriages without consent and orders directing the Clerk of Court to issue a marriage license to underage persons, as declared confidential by IN ST 31-11-1-6;

- Only those arrest warrants, search warrants, indictments and informations ordered confidential by the trial judge, prior to return of duly executed service as declared confidential by IN ST 5-14-3-4(b)(1);

- All medical, mental health, or tax records unless determined by law or regulation of any governmental custodian not to be confidential, released by the subject of such records, or declared by a court of competent jurisdiction to be essential to the resolution of litigation as declared confidential by IN ST 16-39-3-10, IN ST 6-4.1-5-10, IN ST 6-4.1-12-12, and IN ST 6-8.1-7-1;

- Personal information relating to jurors or prospective jurors, other than for the use of the parties and counsel, pursuant to IN ST JURY Rule 10;

- Information relating to protection from abuse orders, no-contact orders and workplace violence restraining orders as declared confidential by IN ST 5-2-9-6, et seq.;

- Mediation proceedings pursuant to IN ST ADR Rule 2.11, Mini-Trial proceedings pursuant to IN ST ADR Rule 4.4(C), and Summary Jury Trials pursuant to IN ST ADR Rule 5.6;

- Information in probation files pursuant to the Probation Standards promulgated by the Judicial Conference of Indiana pursuant to IN ST 11-13-1-8(b);

- Information deemed confidential pursuant to the Rules for Court Administered Alcohol and Drug Programs promulgated by the Judicial Conference of Indiana pursuant to IN ST 12-23-14-13;

- Information deemed confidential pursuant to the Problem-Solving Court Rules promulgated by the Judicial Conference of Indiana pursuant to IN ST 33-23-16-16;

- All records of the Department of workforce Development as declared confidential by IN ST 22-4-19-6;

- Information regarding interception of electronic communications that is sealed or deemed confidential as set forth in IN ST 35-33.5-2-1, et seq.

iii. Information excluded from public access by specific court order;

iv. Complete Social Security Numbers of living persons;

v. With the exception of names, information such as addresses, phone numbers, and dates of birth which explicitly identifies:

- Natural persons who are witnesses or victims (not including defendants) in criminal, domestic violence, stalking, sexual assault, juvenile, or civil protection order proceedings, provided that juveniles who are victims of sex crimes shall be identified by initials only;

- Places of residence of judicial officers, clerks and other employees of courts and clerks of court, unless the person or persons about whom the information pertains waives confidentiality;

vi. Complete account numbers of specific assets, loans, bank accounts, credit cards, and personal identification numbers (PINs);

vii. All orders of expungement entered in criminal or juvenile proceedings, orders to restrict access to criminal history information pursuant to IN ST 35-38-5-5.5 or IN ST 35-38-8-5 and records excluded from public access by such orders, and information related to infractions that is excluded from public access pursuant to IN ST 34-28-5-15 or IN ST 34-28-5-16 [Editor's note:

IN ST 35-38-5-5.5, IN ST 35-38-8-5 and IN ST 34-28-5-16 were repealed effective July 1, 2013; for information on orders restricting access to criminal history, refer to IN ST 35-38-9-1, et seq.];

    viii.   All personal notes and e-mail, and deliberative material, of judges, jurors, court staff and judicial agencies, and information recorded in personal data assistants (PDA's) or organizers and personal calendars. IN ST ADMIN Rule 9(G)(1).

F. Filing and Service Requirements

1.   *Filing requirements.* Except as otherwise provided in IN ST TRIAL P Rule 5(E)(2), all pleadings and papers subsequent to the complaint which are required to be served upon a party shall be filed with the Court either before service or within a reasonable period of time thereafter. IN ST TRIAL P Rule 5(E)(1).

    a.   *Filing with the court defined.* The filing of pleadings, motions, and other papers with the court as required by the Indiana Rules of Trial Procedure shall be made by one of the following methods:

        i.   Delivery to the clerk of the court;

        ii.   Sending by electronic transmission under the procedure adopted pursuant to IN ST ADMIN Rule 12;

        iii.   Mailing to the clerk by registered, certified or express mail return receipt requested;

        iv.   Depositing with any third-party commercial carrier for delivery to the clerk within three (3) calendar days, cost prepaid, properly addressed;

        v.   If the court so permits, filing with the judge, in which event the judge shall note thereon the filing date and forthwith transmit them to the office of the clerk; or

        vi.   Electronic filing, as approved by the Division of State Court Administration pursuant to IN ST ADMIN Rule 16. IN ST TRIAL P Rule 5(F).

        vii.   Filing by registered or certified mail and by third-party commercial carrier shall be complete upon mailing or deposit. IN ST TRIAL P Rule 5(F).

    b.   *Facsimile filing.* As outlined in IN ST HAMILTON ADMIN Rule 103(103.10),facsimile filing is permitted in the Circuit and Superior Courts of Hamilton County. The Courts authorize the Hamilton County Clerk of Courts to accept pleadings, motions and other papers by electronic facsimile transmission for filing in any case pending before the Courts, subject to the requirements of IN ST HAMILTON ADMIN Rule 103(103.10). IN ST HAMILTON ADMIN Rule 103(103.10); IN ST HAMILTON TRIAL Rule 201(201.80).

        i.   *Generally.* In counties where a majority of judges of the courts of record, by posted local rule, have authorized electronic facsimile filing and designated a telephone number to receive such transmissions, pleadings, motions, and other papers may be sent to the Clerk of Circuit Court by electronic facsimile transmission for filing in any case, provided:

            • Such matter does not exceed ten (10) pages, including the cover sheet;

            • Such matter does not require the payment of fees other than the electronic facsimile transcription fee set forth in IN ST ADMIN Rule 12(E);

            • The sending party creates at the time of transmission a machine generated log for such transmission; and

            • The original document and the transmission log are maintained by the sending party for the duration of the litigation. IN ST ADMIN Rule 12(B); IN ST HAMILTON ADMIN Rule 103(103.10)(d).

            • Legibility of documents and timeliness of filing is the responsibility of the sender. IN ST HAMILTON ADMIN Rule 103(103.10)(g).

            • The Clerk shall accept electronic facsimile transmission filings only if received at the facsimile machine assigned by the Clerk. The telephone number designated to receive such transmission is available at IN ST HAMILTON ADMIN Rule 103(103.40). IN ST HAMILTON ADMIN Rule 103(103.40).

ii. *Time of filing.* During normal, posted business hours, the time of filing shall be the time the duplicate document is produced in the office of the Clerk of the Circuit Court. Duplicate documents received at all other times shall be filed as of the next normal business day. IN ST ADMIN Rule 12(C).

- If the receiving fax machine endorses its own time and date stamp upon the transmitted documents and the receiving machine produces a delivery receipt which is electronically created and transmitted to the sending party, the time of filing shall be the date and time recorded on the transmitted document by the receiving fax machine. IN ST ADMIN Rule 12(C).

- Electronic facsimile transmissions will be accepted for filing only during the regular business hours as set forth in IN ST HAMILTON ADMIN Rule 101. Transmissions received by the Hamilton County Clerk after close of business shall be filed effective the next regular business day. IN ST HAMILTON ADMIN Rule 103(103.30).

iii. *Filing fee.* The electronic facsimile transmission will not be accepted for filing if its filing requires the payment of any fee other than the electronic facsimile transcription fee set forth in IN ST HAMILTON ADMIN Rule 103(103.20). IN ST HAMILTON ADMIN Rule 103(103.10)(e).

- Pursuant to Ordinance adopted by the Hamilton County Board of Commissioners, the Clerk shall collect an electronic facsimile transcription fee of One Dollar ($1.00) per page, to a maximum of Ten Dollars ($10.00) per transmission, for each electronic facsimile transmission accepted for filing with the Hamilton County Circuit and Superior Courts. IN ST HAMILTON ADMIN Rule 103(103.20).

- The fee shall be assessed against the sending party and shall be paid upon receipt of invoice by that party and at the latest within thirty (30) days of the transmission. In the event the fee is not paid by the sending party within the time limits provided, the court may issue a show-cause order or enter a judgment in the matter. The Clerk may refuse an electronic facsimile transmission from any attorney or pro se litigant who has failed to pay these fees within thirty (30) days. IN ST HAMILTON ADMIN Rule 103(103.20).

iv. *No direct filing with court.* A party shall not send pleadings, motions and other papers by electronic facsimile transmission for filing directly to any Court without that Court's prior approval to do so. IN ST HAMILTON ADMIN Rule 103(103.50).

c. *Filing with special judge.* After a special judge has qualified, a copy of each pleading and Chronological Case Summary entries filed with the Court shall be mailed or delivered to the office of that Special judge by the counsel or pro se litigant with service indicated on the certificate of service. IN ST HAMILTON TRIAL Rule 204(204.20).

d. *Proof of filing.* Any party filing any paper by any method other than personal delivery to the clerk shall retain proof of filing. IN ST TRIAL P Rule 5(F).

2. *Service requirements.* Unless otherwise provided by the Indiana Rules of Trial Procedure or an order of the court, each party and special judge, if any, shall be served with: (1) every order required by its terms to be served; (2) every pleading subsequent to the original complaint; (3) every written motion except one which may be heard ex parte; (4) every brief submitted to the trial court; (5) every paper relating to discovery required to be served upon a party; and (6) every written notice, appearance, demand, offer of judgment, designation of record on appeal, or similar paper. IN ST TRIAL P Rule 5(A).

a. *Methods of service*

i. *Personal service.* Whenever a party is represented by an attorney of record, service shall be made upon such attorney unless service upon the party himself is ordered by the court. Service upon the attorney or party shall be made by delivering or mailing a copy of the papers to the last known address or where an attorney or party has consented to service by fax or e-mail, as provided in IN ST TRIAL P Rule 3.1(A)(4), by faxing or e-mailing a copy of the documents to the fax number or e-mail address set out in the appearance form or correction as required by IN

ST TRIAL P Rule 3.1(E). IN ST TRIAL P Rule 5(B). Delivery of a copy within IN ST TRIAL P Rule 5 means:

- Offering or tendering it to the attorney or party and stating the nature of the papers being served. Refusal to accept an offered or tendered document is a waiver of any objection to the sufficiency or adequacy of service of that document;

- Leaving it at his office with a clerk or other person in charge thereof, or if there is no one in charge, leaving it in a conspicuous place therein; or

- If the office is closed, by leaving it at his dwelling house or usual place of abode with some person of suitable age and discretion then residing therein; or,

- Leaving it at some other suitable place, selected by the attorney upon whom service is being made, pursuant to duly promulgated local rule. IN ST TRIAL P Rule 5(B)(1).

ii. *Service by mail.* If service is made by mail, the papers shall be deposited in the United States mail addressed to the person on whom they are being served, with postage prepaid. Service shall be deemed complete upon mailing. Proof of service of all papers permitted to be mailed may be made by written acknowledgment of service, by affidavit of the person who mailed the papers, or by certificate of an attorney. It shall be the duty of attorneys when entering their appearance in a cause or when filing pleadings or papers therein, to have noted in the Chronological Case Summary or said pleadings or papers so filed the address and telephone number of their office. Service by delivery or by mail at such address shall be deemed sufficient and complete. IN ST TRIAL P Rule 5(B)(2).

iii. *Service by fax or e-mail.* A party who has consented to service by fax or e-mail may be served as follows:

- Service by e-mail shall be made by attaching the document being served in .pdf format. Discovery documents must also be served in accordance with IN ST TRIAL P Rule 26(A). IN ST TRIAL P Rule 5(B)(3)(a).

- Service by fax shall be deemed complete upon generation of a transmission record indicating the successful transmission of the entire document, except as provided in IN ST TRIAL P Rule 5(B)(3)(d). IN ST TRIAL P Rule 5(B)(3)(b).

- Service by e-mail shall be deemed complete upon transmission, except as provided in IN ST TRIAL P Rule 5(B)(3)(d). IN ST TRIAL P Rule 5(B)(3)(c).

- Service by fax or e-mail that occurs on a Saturday, Sunday, legal holiday, or day the court or agency in which the matter is pending is closed or after 5:00 PM local time of the recipient shall be deemed complete the next day that is not a Saturday, Sunday, legal holiday, or day that the court or agency in which the matter is pending is not closed. IN ST TRIAL P Rule 5(B)(3)(d).

iv. *Mail box service.* Pursuant to IN ST TRIAL P Rule 5(B)(1)(d), the Circuit and Superior Courts of Hamilton County hereby designate the "mail boxes" located in the Clerk's order book office for service of pleadings upon attorneys who have such boxes. IN ST HAMILTON TRIAL Rule 201(201.50).

b. *Serving numerous defendants.* In any action in which there are unusually large numbers of defendants, the court, upon motion or of its own initiative, may order:

i. That service of the pleadings of the defendants and replies thereto need not be made as between the defendants;

- That any cross-claim, counterclaim, or matter constituting an avoidance or affirmative defense contained therein shall be deemed to be denied or avoided by all other parties; and

- That the filing of any such pleading and service thereof upon the plaintiff constitutes due notice of it to the parties. IN ST TRIAL P Rule 5(D).

ii. A copy of every such order shall be served upon the parties in such manner and form as the court directs. IN ST TRIAL P Rule 5(D).

    c. *Service on parties in default for failure to appear.* No service need be made on parties in default for failure to appear, except that pleadings asserting new or additional claims for relief against them shall be served upon them in the manner provided by service of summons in IN ST TRIAL P Rule 4. IN ST TRIAL P Rule 5(A).

G. Hearings

1. *Hearing on motion.* Unless local conditions make it impracticable, each judge shall establish regular times and places, at intervals sufficiently frequent for the prompt dispatch of business, at which motions requiring notice and hearing may be heard and disposed of; but the judge at any time or place and on such notice, if any, as he considers reasonable may make order for the advancement, conduct, and hearing of actions. To expedite its business the court may direct the submission and determination of motions without oral hearing upon brief written statements of reasons in support and opposition, or direct or permit hearings by telephone conference call with all attorneys or other similar means of communication. IN ST TRIAL P Rule 73(A).

H. Forms

1. Indiana Motion to Dismiss for Improper Venue Forms

    a. Incorrect venue. 9 INPRAC § 42.5.

    b. Motion to dismiss; Improper venue under contract. 9 INPRAC § 42.18.1.

    c. Motion to transfer from improper venue. 11 INPRAC § 111.2.

    d. Motion to transfer from improper venue. 5 INPRAC § 3:11.1.

    e. Motion for change of venue from county; For cause. 5 INPRAC § 3:11.2.

    f. Certificate of service; Personal service. 9 INPRAC § 5.7.

    g. Certificate of service; First class mail. 9 INPRAC § 5.8.

I. Checklist

(I) ❑ Matters to be considered by moving party

    (a) ❑ Required documents

        (1) ❑ Motion and notice

        (2) ❑ Proposed order

        (3) ❑ Certificate of service

    (b) ❑ Supplemental documents

        (1) ❑ Supporting evidence

        (2) ❑ Facsimile cover sheet

        (3) ❑ Request to schedule trial or hearing

        (4) ❑ Copies of unpublished opinions

    (c) ❑ Timing

        (1) ❑ A motion making the defense of incorrect venue under IN ST TRIAL P Rule 75, or any statutory provision, shall be made before pleading if a further pleading is permitted or within twenty (20) days after service of the prior pleading if none is required

        (2) ❑ A written motion, other than one which may be heard ex parte, and notice of the hearing thereof shall be served not less than five (5) days before the time specified for the hearing, unless a different period is fixed by the Indiana Rules of Trial Procedure or by order of the court

        (3) ❑ All pleadings and papers subsequent to the complaint which are required to be served upon a party shall be filed with the Court either before service or within a reasonable period of time thereafter

(II) ❏ Matters to be considered by the responding party

    (a) ❏ Required documents

        (1) ❏ Opposition

        (2) ❏ Certificate of service

    (b) ❏ Supplemental documents

        (1) ❏ Supporting evidence

        (2) ❏ Alternative proposed order

        (3) ❏ Facsimile cover sheet

        (4) ❏ Request to schedule trial or hearing

        (5) ❏ Copies of unpublished opinions

    (c) ❏ Timing

        (1) ❏ Except as otherwise provided in IN ST TRIAL P Rule 59(D), opposing affidavits may be served not less than one (1) day before the hearing, unless the court permits them to be served at some other time

Motions, Oppositions and Replies
Motion for Leave to Amend

Document Last Updated October 2013

A. Applicable Rules

  1. *State rules*

    a. Appearance. IN ST TRIAL P Rule 3.1.

    b. Summons. IN ST TRIAL P Rule 4; IN ST TRIAL P Rule 4.6.

    c. Service and filing of pleadings and other papers. IN ST TRIAL P Rule 5.

    d. Time. IN ST TRIAL P Rule 6.

    e. Pleadings and other papers. IN ST TRIAL P Rule 7; IN ST TRIAL P Rule 8; IN ST TRIAL P Rule 9.2; IN ST TRIAL P Rule 10.

    f. Signing and verification of pleadings. IN ST TRIAL P Rule 11.

    g. Amended and supplemental pleadings. IN ST TRIAL P Rule 15.

    h. Evidence. IN ST TRIAL P Rule 43.

    i. Judgment on the evidence (directed verdict). IN ST TRIAL P Rule 50.

    j. Findings by the court. IN ST TRIAL P Rule 52.

    k. Summary judgment. IN ST TRIAL P Rule 56.

    l. Motion to correct error. IN ST TRIAL P Rule 59.

    m. Relief from judgment or order. IN ST TRIAL P Rule 60.

    n. Hearing of motions. IN ST TRIAL P Rule 73.

    o. Access to court records. IN ST ADMIN Rule 9.

    p. Paper size. IN ST ADMIN Rule 11.

    q. Facsimile transmission. IN ST ADMIN Rule 12.

    r. Electronic filing and electronic service pilot projects. IN ST ADMIN Rule 16.

    s. Sealing of certain records by court; Hearing; Notice. IN ST 5-14-3-5.5.

    t. Privacy and confidentiality. IN ST 5-2-9-6; IN ST 5-14-3-4; IN ST 6-4.1-5-10; IN ST 6-4.1-12-12;

IN ST 6-8.1-7-1; IN ST 11-13-1-8; IN ST 12-23-14-13; IN ST 16-39-3-10; IN ST 16-41-8-1; IN ST 22-4-19-6; IN ST 31-11-1-6; IN ST 31-19-5-23; IN ST 31-19-13-2; IN ST 31-19-19-1; IN ST 31-33-18-1; IN ST 31-39-1-1; IN ST 31-39-1-2; IN ST 33-23-16-16; IN ST 35-34-2-4; IN ST 35-38-1-13; IN ST 35-38-9-1; IN ST ADR Rule 2.11; IN ST ADR Rule 4.4; IN ST ADR Rule 5.6; IN ST JURY Rule 10.

2. *Local rules*

   a. Court hours. IN ST HAMILTON ADMIN Rule 101.

   b. Facsimile transmissions. IN ST HAMILTON ADMIN Rule 103.

   c. Filing of pleadings and entry of appearances. IN ST HAMILTON TRIAL Rule 201.

   d. Proposed orders. IN ST HAMILTON TRIAL Rule 202.

   e. Briefs and memorandums. IN ST HAMILTON TRIAL Rule 203.

   f. Special judges. IN ST HAMILTON TRIAL Rule 204.

   g. Trial settings. IN ST HAMILTON TRIAL Rule 205.

   h. Continuances. IN ST HAMILTON TRIAL Rule 206.

B. Timing

1. *Time for amending pleadings*

   a. *As a matter of course.* A party may amend his pleading once as a matter of course at any time before a responsive pleading is served or, if the pleading is one to which no responsive pleading is permitted, and the action has not been placed upon the trial calendar, he may so amend it at any time within thirty (30) days after it is served. IN ST TRIAL P Rule 15(A). Refer to the Indiana KeyRules Amended Complaint and Amended Answer documents for additional information on amending pleadings as a matter of course.

   b. *With leave of court.* Otherwise a party may amend his pleading only by leave of court or by written consent of the adverse party; and leave shall be given when justice so requires. IN ST TRIAL P Rule 15(A).

   c. *Filing.* All pleadings and papers subsequent to the complaint which are required to be served upon a party shall be filed with the Court either before service or within a reasonable period of time thereafter. IN ST TRIAL P Rule 5(E)(1).

2. *Service.* A written motion, other than one which may be heard ex parte, and notice of the hearing thereof shall be served not less than five (5) days before the time specified for the hearing, unless a different period is fixed by the Indiana Rules of Trial Procedure or by order of the court. IN ST TRIAL P Rule 6(D).

   a. *Of supporting affidavits.* When a motion is supported by affidavit, the affidavit shall be served with the motion. IN ST TRIAL P Rule 6(D).

3. *Service of opposition.* Except as otherwise provided in IN ST TRIAL P Rule 59(D), opposing affidavits may be served not less than one (1) day before the hearing, unless the court permits them to be served at some other time. IN ST TRIAL P Rule 6(D).

4. *Computation of time*

   a. *Generally; Days excluded.* In computing any period of time prescribed or allowed by the Indiana Rules of Trial Procedure, by order of the court, or by any applicable statute, the day of the act, event, or default from which the designated period of time begins to run shall not be included. The last day of the period so computed is to be included unless it is:

      i. A Saturday,

      ii. A Sunday,

      iii. A legal holiday as defined by state statute, or

      iv. A day the office in which the act is to be done is closed during regular business hours. IN ST TRIAL P Rule 6(A).

   b. *Short periods.* In any event, the period runs until the end of the next day that is not a Saturday, a

Sunday, a legal holiday, or a day on which the office is closed. When the period of time allowed is less than seven (7) days, intermediate Saturdays, Sundays, legal holidays, and days on which the office is closed shall be excluded from the computations. IN ST TRIAL P Rule 6(A).

c. *Additional time after service by United States mail.* Whenever a party has the right or is required to do some act or take some proceedings within a prescribed period after the service of a notice or other paper upon him and the notice or paper is served upon him by United States mail, three (3) days shall be added to the prescribed period. IN ST TRIAL P Rule 6(E).

d. *Enlargement of time.* When an act is required or allowed to be done at or within a specific time by the Indiana Rules of Trial Procedure, the court may at any time for cause shown:

   i. Order the period enlarged, with or without motion or notice, if request therefor is made before the expiration of the period originally prescribed or extended by a previous order; or

   ii. Upon motion made after the expiration of the specific period, permit the act to be done where the failure to act was the result of excusable neglect; but, the court may not extend the time for taking any action for judgment on the evidence under IN ST TRIAL P Rule 50(A), amendment of findings and judgment under IN ST TRIAL P Rule 52(B), to correct errors under IN ST TRIAL P Rule 59(C), statement in opposition to motion to correct error under IN ST TRIAL P Rule 59(E), or to obtain relief from final judgment under IN ST TRIAL P Rule 60(B), except to the extent and under the conditions stated in those rules. IN ST TRIAL P Rule 6(B).

   iii. For information on obtaining a continuance, refer to IN ST HAMILTON TRIAL Rule 206.

C. General Requirements

1. *Motions, generally.* Unless made during a hearing or trial, or otherwise ordered by the court, an application to the court for an order shall be made by written motion. The motion shall state the grounds therefor and the relief or order sought. IN ST TRIAL P Rule 7(B).

   a. *Motions as distinct from pleadings.* Motions and responses to motions are not pleadings, and allegations contained in a motion are not admissions of a party. 22B INPRAC 7:2; Wachstetter v. County Properties, LLC, 832 N.E.2d 574 (Ind.Ct.App. 2005); Scott County Family YMCA, Inc. v. Hobbs, 817 N.E.2d 603 (Ind.Ct.App. 2004).

   b. *Unopposed motions generally granted.* It is common for a trial court to grant procedural motions, such as motions for enlargement of time, discovery motions, or motions for continuance, unless an objection is filed. 21 INPRAC § 13.8.

2. *Motion for leave to amend.* The purpose of an amended pleading is to include matters that occurred before the filing of the original pleading but which were either overlooked by the pleader or unknown to him at the time. It is a substitute for the original and relates to the facts that existed when the original pleading was filed. An amended pleading supercedes the original as to those portions amended. 10 INPRAC § 46.1.

   a. *Amendments liberally allowed.* Amendments to pleadings are to be liberally allowed in order that all issues are presented in one action. 10 INPRAC § 46.1; Pinnacle Media, LLC v. Metropolitan Dev. Com'n of Marion County, 868 N.E.2d 894 (Ind.Ct.App. 2007).

   b. *Amendments to conform to the evidence.* When issues not raised by the pleadings are tried by express or implied consent of the parties, they shall be treated in all respects as if they had been raised in the pleadings. Such amendment of the pleadings as may be necessary to cause them to conform to the evidence and to raise these issues may be made upon motion of any party at any time, even after judgment, but failure so to amend does not affect the result of the trial of these issues. If evidence is objected to at the trial on the ground that it is not within the issues made by the pleadings, the court may allow the pleadings to be amended and shall do so freely when the presentation of the merits of the action will be subserved thereby and the objecting party fails to satisfy the court that the admission of such evidence would prejudice him in maintaining his action or defense upon the merits. The court may grant a continuance to enable the objecting party to meet such evidence. IN ST TRIAL P Rule 15(B).

   c. *Relation back of amendments*

   i. Whenever the claim or defense asserted in the amended pleading arose out of the conduct,

411

transaction, or occurrence set forth or attempted to be set forth in the original pleading, the amendment relates back to the date of the original pleading. An amendment changing the party against whom a claim is asserted relates back if the foregoing provision is satisfied and, within one hundred and twenty (120) days of commencement of the action, the party to be brought in by amendment:

- Has received such notice of the institution of the action that he will not be prejudiced in maintaining his defense on the merits; and

- Knew or should have known that but for a mistake concerning the identity of the proper party, the action would have been brought against him. IN ST TRIAL P Rule 15(C).

    ii. The requirement of IN ST TRIAL P Rule 15(C)(1) and IN ST TRIAL P Rule 15(C)(2) with respect to a governmental organization to be brought into the action as defendant is satisfied:

- In the case of a state or governmental organization by delivery or mailing of process to the attorney general or to a governmental executive [IN ST TRIAL P Rule 4.6(A)(3)]; or

- In the case of a local governmental organization, by delivery or mailing of process to its attorney as provided by statute, to a governmental executive thereof [IN ST TRIAL P Rule 4.6(A)(4)], or to the officer holding the office if suit is against the officer or an office. IN ST TRIAL P Rule 15(C).

    d. *Amendment by leave.* Amendments, other than an amendment by right, may be made only by leave of court or by written consent of the opposing party. 2 INPRAC R 15(15.1).

    e. *Factors considered.* In deciding whether to permit a party to amend his pleading, the court must consider a number of factors: (1) undue delay, (2) bad faith or dilatory motive on the part of the movant, (3) repeated failure to cure deficiencies by amendments previously allowed, (4) undue prejudice to the opposing party by virtue of allowance of the amendment, and (5) the futility of the amendment. 10 INPRAC § 46.1; Crawford v. City of Muncie, 655 N.E.2d 614 (Ind.Ct.App. 1995); Selvia v. Reitmeyer, 156 Ind.App. 203, 295 N.E.2d 869 (Ind.Ct.App. 1973).

D. Documents

1. *Required documents*

    a. *Motion and notice.* The requirement of notice is satisfied by service of the motion. IN ST TRIAL P Rule 7(B). Refer to the General Requirements section of this document for information on the content of a motion for leave to amend.

    b. *Copy of amended pleading.* A copy of the proposed amendment should be attached to the motion for leave to amend, along with a proposed order by the court which permits the amendment. 2 INPRAC R 15.

    c. *Proposed order.* Unless local practice provides differently, a party should submit a proposed order with its written motion to be signed by the judge once the motion has been granted. 21 INPRAC § 13.8; IN ST HAMILTON ADMIN Rule 103(103.10)(b). Each Motion, Petition or other request for relief shall be accompanied by a proposed order. IN ST HAMILTON TRIAL Rule 202(202.10).

        i. All proposed orders submitted by counsel pursuant to IN ST HAMILTON TRIAL Rule 202 shall meet the following requirements: (1) contain a complete distribution list of all attorneys and pro se litigants with full addresses; (2) stamped envelopes appropriately addressed for each attorney of record and/or pro se litigant on the distribution list. IN ST HAMILTON TRIAL Rule 202(202.30).

    d. *Certificate of service.* An attorney or unrepresented party tendering a document to the Clerk for filing shall certify that service has been made, list the parties served, and specify the date and means of service. The certificate of service shall be placed at the end of the document and shall not be separately filed. The separate filing of a certificate of service, however, shall not be grounds for rejecting a document for filing. The Clerk may permit documents to be filed without a certificate of service but shall require prompt filing of a separate certificate of service. IN ST TRIAL P Rule 5(C).

        i. All pleadings filed with the Court which require a certificate of service shall specifically name the individual party or attorney on whom service has been made, the address, the manner in which service was made and the date when service was made. IN ST HAMILTON TRIAL Rule 201(201.60).

2. *Supplemental documents*

    a. *Supporting evidence.* When a motion is based on facts not appearing of record the court may hear the matter on affidavits presented by the respective parties, but the court may direct that the matter be heard wholly or partly on oral testimony or depositions. IN ST TRIAL P Rule 43(B).

    b. *Facsimile cover sheet.* Any document sent to the Clerk of the Circuit Court by electronic facsimile transmission shall be accompanied by a cover sheet which states the title of the document, case number, number of pages, identity and voice telephone number of the sending party and instructions for filing. The cover sheet shall contain the signature of the attorney or party, pro se, authorizing the filing. IN ST ADMIN Rule 12(D); IN ST HAMILTON ADMIN Rule 103(103.10)(a).

    c. *Request to schedule hearing.* All requests to schedule trials and hearings shall be in writing and shall contain the following information:

        i. Type of trial or hearing (i.e., jury trial, court trial, final hearing in dissolution, etc.). IN ST HAMILTON TRIAL Rule 205(205.10).

        ii. A good-faith estimate of the total court time needed for the trial or hearing. IN ST HAMILTON TRIAL Rule 205(205.10).

        iii. Each request under IN ST HAMILTON TRIAL Rule 205(205.10) shall be accompanied by a proposed written order with appropriate blanks for date and time and shall further include reference to those items set forth in IN ST HAMILTON TRIAL Rule 205(205.10)(a) and IN ST HAMILTON TRIAL Rule 205(205.10)(b). IN ST HAMILTON TRIAL Rule 205(205.20).

    d. *Copies of unpublished opinions.* Authorities relied upon which are not cited in the Northeastern Reporter system shall be attached to counsel's brief. If the authority is cited for the first time in oral argument, a copy of the authority may be provided to the Court at the time of the argument. Sufficient copies shall be available to provide counsel for each party with a copy. IN ST HAMILTON TRIAL Rule 203(203.10).

E. Format

1. *Form of motions.* The rules applicable to captions, and the signing and form of pleadings (IN ST TRIAL P Rule 8 through IN ST TRIAL P Rule 11), apply to all motions and other papers provided under the Indiana Rules of Trial Procedure. 22B INPRAC 7:2.

2. *Form of pleadings*

    a. *Caption; Names of parties.* Every pleading shall contain a caption setting forth the name of the court, the title of the action, the file number, and a designation as in IN ST TRIAL P Rule 7(A). In the complaint the title of the action shall include the names of all the parties, but in other pleadings it is sufficient to state the name of the first party on each side with an appropriate indication of other parties. IN ST TRIAL P Rule 10(A).

    b. *Paragraphs; Separate statements.* All averments of a claim or defense shall be made in numbered paragraphs, the contents of each of which shall be limited as far as practicable to a statement of a single set of circumstances, and a paragraph may be referred to by number in all succeeding pleadings. Each claim founded upon a separate transaction or occurrence and each defense other than denials may be stated in a separate count or defense whenever a separation facilitates the clear presentation of the matters set forth. IN ST TRIAL P Rule 10(B).

    c. *Adoption by reference; Exhibits.* Statements in a pleading may be adopted by reference in a different part of the same pleading or in another pleading or in any motion. A copy of any written instrument which is an exhibit to a pleading is a part thereof for all purposes. IN ST TRIAL P Rule 10(C).

    d. *Facsimile page limit.* Courts authorize the Hamilton County Clerk of Courts to accept pleadings, motions and other papers by electronic facsimile transmission for filing in any case pending before the Courts, subject to the requirement that The transmission may not exceed ten (10) pages in length including the cover sheet and proposed CCS entry. IN ST HAMILTON ADMIN Rule 103(103.10)(c).

e. *Emergency facsimile filings.* If the filing requires the immediate attention of the Judge, it shall so indicate in bold letters in an accompanying transmittal memorandum. IN ST HAMILTON ADMIN Rule 103(103.10)(f).

f. *Special judge heading.* After a special judge is selected, the attorneys or pro se litigants shall add to the caption of all pleadings to the right of the case title the following: "BEFORE SPECIAL JUDGE _____." IN ST HAMILTON TRIAL Rule 204(204.10).

g. *Format rules strictly enforced.* All filings shall be in compliance with the Indiana Rules of Trial Procedure. If the documents received are not in proper form, such deficiencies will not be corrected by court personnel. IN ST HAMILTON TRIAL Rule 201(201.70). The Court shall not be required to act on any Motion, Petition or other request for relief unless filed in conformity with the Hamilton County Local Trial and Administrative rules. IN ST HAMILTON TRIAL Rule 202(202.20).

3. *Size of papers for filing.* Effective January 1, 1992, all pleadings, copies, motions and documents filed with any trial court or appellate level court, typed or printed, with the exception of exhibits and existing wills, shall be prepared on eight and one-half by eleven inch (8 1/2" x 11") size paper. IN ST ADMIN Rule 11.

a. *Form.* All documents filed in any Hamilton County Court, with the exception of exhibits and existing wills, shall be prepared on paper measuring eight and one-half by eleven inches (8 1/2" x 11"). IN ST HAMILTON TRIAL Rule 201(201.20).

4. *Signature requirements*

a. *Signature of attorney.* Every pleading or motion of a party represented by an attorney shall be signed by at least one (1) attorney of record in his individual name, whose address, telephone number, and attorney number shall be stated, except that this provision shall not apply to pleadings and motions made and transcribed at the trial or a hearing before the judge and received by him in such form. IN ST TRIAL P Rule 11(A).

   i. The signature of an attorney constitutes a certificate by him that he has read the pleadings; that to the best of his knowledge, information, and belief, there is good ground to support it; and that it is not interposed for delay. IN ST TRIAL P Rule 11(A).

   ii. If a pleading or motion is not signed or is signed with intent to defeat the purpose of the rule, it may be stricken as sham and false and the action may proceed as though the pleading had not been served. IN ST TRIAL P Rule 11(A).

   iii. For a willful violation of IN ST TRIAL P Rule 11 an attorney may be subjected to appropriate disciplinary action. Similar action may be taken if scandalous or indecent matter is inserted. IN ST TRIAL P Rule 11(A).

b. *Signature of unrepresented party.* A party who is not represented by an attorney shall sign his pleading and state his address. IN ST TRIAL P Rule 11(A).

c. *Verification not generally required.* Except when specifically required by rule, pleadings or motions need not be verified or accompanied by affidavit. The rule in equity that the averments of an answer under oath must be overcome by the testimony of two (2) witnesses or of one (1) witness sustained by corroborating circumstances is abolished. IN ST TRIAL P Rule 11(A).

d. *Verification by affirmation or representation.* When in connection with any civil or special statutory proceeding it is required that any pleading, motion, petition, supporting affidavit, or other document of any kind, be verified, or that an oath be taken, it shall be sufficient if the subscriber simply affirms the truth of the matter to be verified by an affirmation or representation. IN ST TRIAL P Rule 11(B). IN ST TRIAL P Rule 11(B) states that the affirmation or representation should be in substantially the following language: "I (we) affirm, under the penalties for perjury, that the foregoing representation(s) is (are) true. (Signed) _____."

   i. Any person who falsifies an affirmation or representation of fact shall be subject to the same penalties as are prescribed by law for the making of a false affidavit. IN ST TRIAL P Rule 11(B).

e. *Verified pleadings, motions, and affidavits as evidence.* Pleadings, motions and affidavits accompa-

nying or in support of such pleadings or motions when required to be verified or under oath shall be accepted as a representation that the signer had personal knowledge thereof or reasonable cause to believe the existence of the facts or matters stated or alleged therein; and, if otherwise competent or acceptable as evidence, may be admitted as evidence of the facts or matters stated or alleged therein when it is so provided in the Indiana Rules of Trial Procedure, by statute or other law, or to the extent the writing or signature expressly purports to be made upon the signer's personal knowledge. When such pleadings, motions and affidavits are verified or under oath they shall not require other or greater proof on the part of the adverse party than if not verified or not under oath unless expressly provided otherwise by the Indiana Rules of Trial Procedure, statute or other law. Affidavits upon motions for summary judgment under IN ST TRIAL P Rule 56 and in denial of execution under IN ST TRIAL P Rule 9.2 shall be made upon personal knowledge. IN ST TRIAL P Rule 11(C).

5. *Information excluded from public access.* Every document filed in a case shall separately identify information excluded from public access pursuant to IN ST ADMIN Rule 9(G)(1) as follows:

a. Whole documents that are excluded from public access pursuant to IN ST ADMIN Rule 9(G)(1) shall be tendered on light green paper or have a light green coversheet attached to the document, marked "Not for Public Access" or "Confidential." IN ST TRIAL P Rule 5(G)(1).

b. When only a portion of a document contains information excluded from public access pursuant to IN ST ADMIN Rule 9(G)(1), said information shall be omitted [or redacted] from the filed document, and set forth on a separate accompanying document on light green paper conspicuously marked "Not for Public Access" or "Confidential" and clearly designated [or identifying] the caption and number of the case and the document and location within the document to which the redacted material pertains. IN ST TRIAL P Rule 5(G)(2).

c. With respect to documents filed in electronic format, the trial court, by local rule, may provide for compliance with IN ST TRIAL P Rule 5 in manner that separates and protects access to information excluded from public access. IN ST TRIAL P Rule 5(G)(3).

d. IN ST TRIAL P Rule 5(G) does not apply to a record sealed by the court pursuant to IN ST 5-14-3-5.5 or otherwise, nor to records, documents, or information filed in cases to which public access is prohibited pursuant to IN ST ADMIN Rule 9(G). IN ST TRIAL P Rule 5(G)(4).

e. The following information in case records is excluded from public access and is confidential:

i. Information that is excluded from public access pursuant to federal law;

ii. Information that is excluded from public access as declared confidential by Indiana statute or other court rule, including without limitation:

- All adoption records created after July 8, 1941, as declared confidential by IN ST 31-19-19-1, et seq., except those specifically declared open by IN ST 31-19-13-2(2);

- All records relating to chancroid, chlamydia, gonorrhea, hepatitis, human immunodeficiency virus (HIV), Lymphogranuloma venereum, syphilis, tuberculosis, as declared confidential by IN ST 16-41-8-1, et seq.;

- All records relating to child abuse as declared confidential by IN ST 31-33-18-1, et seq.;

- All records relating to drug tests as declared confidential by IN ST 5-14-3-4(a)(9);

- Records of grand jury proceedings as declared confidential by IN ST 35-34-2-4;

- Records of juvenile proceedings as declared confidential by IN ST 31-39-1-2, except those specifically open under statute;

- All paternity records created after July 1, 1941 as declared confidential by IN ST 31-14-11-15, IN ST 31-19-5-23, IN ST 31-39-1-1 and IN ST 31-39-1-2 [Editor's note: IN ST 31-14-11-15 was repealed effective May 9, 2013];

- All pre-sentence reports as declared confidential by IN ST 35-38-1-13;

- Written petitions to permit marriages without consent and orders directing the Clerk of Court to issue a marriage license to underage persons, as declared confidential by IN ST 31-11-1-6;

- Only those arrest warrants, search warrants, indictments and informations ordered confidential by the trial judge, prior to return of duly executed service as declared confidential by IN ST 5-14-3-4(b)(1);

- All medical, mental health, or tax records unless determined by law or regulation of any governmental custodian not to be confidential, released by the subject of such records, or declared by a court of competent jurisdiction to be essential to the resolution of litigation as declared confidential by IN ST 16-39-3-10, IN ST 6-4.1-5-10, IN ST 6-4.1-12-12, and IN ST 6-8.1-7-1;

- Personal information relating to jurors or prospective jurors, other than for the use of the parties and counsel, pursuant to IN ST JURY Rule 10;

- Information relating to protection from abuse orders, no-contact orders and workplace violence restraining orders as declared confidential by IN ST 5-2-9-6, et seq.;

- Mediation proceedings pursuant to IN ST ADR Rule 2.11, Mini-Trial proceedings pursuant to IN ST ADR Rule 4.4(C), and Summary Jury Trials pursuant to IN ST ADR Rule 5.6;

- Information in probation files pursuant to the Probation Standards promulgated by the Judicial Conference of Indiana pursuant to IN ST 11-13-1-8(b);

- Information deemed confidential pursuant to the Rules for Court Administered Alcohol and Drug Programs promulgated by the Judicial Conference of Indiana pursuant to IN ST 12-23-14-13;

- Information deemed confidential pursuant to the Problem-Solving Court Rules promulgated by the Judicial Conference of Indiana pursuant to IN ST 33-23-16-16;

- All records of the Department of workforce Development as declared confidential by IN ST 22-4-19-6;

- Information regarding interception of electronic communications that is sealed or deemed confidential as set forth in IN ST 35-33.5-2-1, et seq.

   iii.   Information excluded from public access by specific court order;

   iv.   Complete Social Security Numbers of living persons;

   v.   With the exception of names, information such as addresses, phone numbers, and dates of birth which explicitly identifies:

- Natural persons who are witnesses or victims (not including defendants) in criminal, domestic violence, stalking, sexual assault, juvenile, or civil protection order proceedings, provided that juveniles who are victims of sex crimes shall be identified by initials only;

- Places of residence of judicial officers, clerks and other employees of courts and clerks of court, unless the person or persons about whom the information pertains waives confidentiality;

   vi.   Complete account numbers of specific assets, loans, bank accounts, credit cards, and personal identification numbers (PINs);

   vii.   All orders of expungement entered in criminal or juvenile proceedings, orders to restrict access to criminal history information pursuant to IN ST 35-38-5-5.5 or IN ST 35-38-8-5 and records excluded from public access by such orders, and information related to infractions that is excluded from public access pursuant to IN ST 34-28-5-15 or IN ST 34-28-5-16 [Editor's note: IN ST 35-38-5-5.5, IN ST 35-38-8-5 and IN ST 34-28-5-16 were repealed effective July 1, 2013; for information on orders restricting access to criminal history, refer to IN ST 35-38-9-1, et seq.];

   viii.   All personal notes and e-mail, and deliberative material, of judges, jurors, court staff and judicial agencies, and information recorded in personal data assistants (PDA's) or organizers and personal calendars. IN ST ADMIN Rule 9(G)(1).

F. Filing and Service Requirements

   1. *Filing requirements.* Except as otherwise provided in IN ST TRIAL P Rule 5(E)(2), all pleadings and

papers subsequent to the complaint which are required to be served upon a party shall be filed with the Court either before service or within a reasonable period of time thereafter. IN ST TRIAL P Rule 5(E)(1).

a. *Filing with the court defined.* The filing of pleadings, motions, and other papers with the court as required by the Indiana Rules of Trial Procedure shall be made by one of the following methods:

   i. Delivery to the clerk of the court;

   ii. Sending by electronic transmission under the procedure adopted pursuant to IN ST ADMIN Rule 12;

   iii. Mailing to the clerk by registered, certified or express mail return receipt requested;

   iv. Depositing with any third-party commercial carrier for delivery to the clerk within three (3) calendar days, cost prepaid, properly addressed;

   v. If the court so permits, filing with the judge, in which event the judge shall note thereon the filing date and forthwith transmit them to the office of the clerk; or

   vi. Electronic filing, as approved by the Division of State Court Administration pursuant to IN ST ADMIN Rule 16. IN ST TRIAL P Rule 5(F).

   vii. Filing by registered or certified mail and by third-party commercial carrier shall be complete upon mailing or deposit. IN ST TRIAL P Rule 5(F).

b. *Facsimile filing.* As outlined in IN ST HAMILTON ADMIN Rule 103(103.10),facsimile filing is permitted in the Circuit and Superior Courts of Hamilton County. The Courts authorize the Hamilton County Clerk of Courts to accept pleadings, motions and other papers by electronic facsimile transmission for filing in any case pending before the Courts, subject to the requirements of IN ST HAMILTON ADMIN Rule 103(103.10). IN ST HAMILTON ADMIN Rule 103(103.10); IN ST HAMILTON TRIAL Rule 201(201.80).

   i. *Generally.* In counties where a majority of judges of the courts of record, by posted local rule, have authorized electronic facsimile filing and designated a telephone number to receive such transmissions, pleadings, motions, and other papers may be sent to the Clerk of Circuit Court by electronic facsimile transmission for filing in any case, provided:

   - Such matter does not exceed ten (10) pages, including the cover sheet;

   - Such matter does not require the payment of fees other than the electronic facsimile transcription fee set forth in IN ST ADMIN Rule 12(E);

   - The sending party creates at the time of transmission a machine generated log for such transmission; and

   - The original document and the transmission log are maintained by the sending party for the duration of the litigation. IN ST ADMIN Rule 12(B); IN ST HAMILTON ADMIN Rule 103(103.10)(d).

   - Legibility of documents and timeliness of filing is the responsibility of the sender. IN ST HAMILTON ADMIN Rule 103(103.10)(g).

   - The Clerk shall accept electronic facsimile transmission filings only if received at the facsimile machine assigned by the Clerk. The telephone number designated to receive such transmission is available at IN ST HAMILTON ADMIN Rule 103(103.40). IN ST HAMILTON ADMIN Rule 103(103.40).

   ii. *Time of filing.* During normal, posted business hours, the time of filing shall be the time the duplicate document is produced in the office of the Clerk of the Circuit Court. Duplicate documents received at all other times shall be filed as of the next normal business day. IN ST ADMIN Rule 12(C).

   - If the receiving fax machine endorses its own time and date stamp upon the transmitted documents and the receiving machine produces a delivery receipt which is electronically created and transmitted to the sending party, the time of filing shall be the date and time recorded on the transmitted document by the receiving fax machine. IN ST ADMIN Rule 12(C).

- Electronic facsimile transmissions will be accepted for filing only during the regular business hours as set forth in IN ST HAMILTON ADMIN Rule 101. Transmissions received by the Hamilton County Clerk after close of business shall be filed effective the next regular business day. IN ST HAMILTON ADMIN Rule 103(103.30).

    iii. *Filing fee.* The electronic facsimile transmission will not be accepted for filing if its filing requires the payment of any fee other than the electronic facsimile transcription fee set forth in IN ST HAMILTON ADMIN Rule 103(103.20). IN ST HAMILTON ADMIN Rule 103(103.10)(e).

- Pursuant to Ordinance adopted by the Hamilton County Board of Commissioners, the Clerk shall collect an electronic facsimile transcription fee of One Dollar ($1.00) per page, to a maximum of Ten Dollars ($10.00) per transmission, for each electronic facsimile transmission accepted for filing with the Hamilton County Circuit and Superior Courts. IN ST HAMILTON ADMIN Rule 103(103.20).

- The fee shall be assessed against the sending party and shall be paid upon receipt of invoice by that party and at the latest within thirty (30) days of the transmission. In the event the fee is not paid by the sending party within the time limits provided, the court may issue a show-cause order or enter a judgment in the matter. The Clerk may refuse an electronic facsimile transmission from any attorney or pro se litigant who has failed to pay these fees within thirty (30) days. IN ST HAMILTON ADMIN Rule 103(103.20).

    iv. *No direct filing with court.* A party shall not send pleadings, motions and other papers by electronic facsimile transmission for filing directly to any Court without that Court's prior approval to do so. IN ST HAMILTON ADMIN Rule 103(103.50).

  c. *Filing with special judge.* After a special judge has qualified, a copy of each pleading and Chronological Case Summary entries filed with the Court shall be mailed or delivered to the office of that Special judge by the counsel or pro se litigant with service indicated on the certificate of service. IN ST HAMILTON TRIAL Rule 204(204.20).

  d. *Proof of filing.* Any party filing any paper by any method other than personal delivery to the clerk shall retain proof of filing. IN ST TRIAL P Rule 5(F).

2. *Service requirements.* Unless otherwise provided by the Indiana Rules of Trial Procedure or an order of the court, each party and special judge, if any, shall be served with: (1) every order required by its terms to be served; (2) every pleading subsequent to the original complaint; (3) every written motion except one which may be heard ex parte; (4) every brief submitted to the trial court; (5) every paper relating to discovery required to be served upon a party; and (6) every written notice, appearance, demand, offer of judgment, designation of record on appeal, or similar paper. IN ST TRIAL P Rule 5(A).

  a. *Methods of service*

    i. *Personal service.* Whenever a party is represented by an attorney of record, service shall be made upon such attorney unless service upon the party himself is ordered by the court. Service upon the attorney or party shall be made by delivering or mailing a copy of the papers to the last known address or where an attorney or party has consented to service by fax or e-mail, as provided in IN ST TRIAL P Rule 3.1(A)(4), by faxing or e-mailing a copy of the documents to the fax number or e-mail address set out in the appearance form or correction as required by IN ST TRIAL P Rule 3.1(E). IN ST TRIAL P Rule 5(B). Delivery of a copy within IN ST TRIAL P Rule 5 means:

- Offering or tendering it to the attorney or party and stating the nature of the papers being served. Refusal to accept an offered or tendered document is a waiver of any objection to the sufficiency or adequacy of service of that document;

- Leaving it at his office with a clerk or other person in charge thereof, or if there is no one in charge, leaving it in a conspicuous place therein; or

- If the office is closed, by leaving it at his dwelling house or usual place of abode with some person of suitable age and discretion then residing therein; or,

- Leaving it at some other suitable place, selected by the attorney upon whom service is being made, pursuant to duly promulgated local rule. IN ST TRIAL P Rule 5(B)(1).

    ii. *Service by mail.* If service is made by mail, the papers shall be deposited in the United States mail addressed to the person on whom they are being served, with postage prepaid. Service shall be deemed complete upon mailing. Proof of service of all papers permitted to be mailed may be made by written acknowledgment of service, by affidavit of the person who mailed the papers, or by certificate of an attorney. It shall be the duty of attorneys when entering their appearance in a cause or when filing pleadings or papers therein, to have noted in the Chronological Case Summary or said pleadings or papers so filed the address and telephone number of their office. Service by delivery or by mail at such address shall be deemed sufficient and complete. IN ST TRIAL P Rule 5(B)(2).

    iii. *Service by fax or e-mail.* A party who has consented to service by fax or e-mail may be served as follows:

- Service by e-mail shall be made by attaching the document being served in .pdf format. Discovery documents must also be served in accordance with IN ST TRIAL P Rule 26(A). IN ST TRIAL P Rule 5(B)(3)(a).

- Service by fax shall be deemed complete upon generation of a transmission record indicating the successful transmission of the entire document, except as provided in IN ST TRIAL P Rule 5(B)(3)(d). IN ST TRIAL P Rule 5(B)(3)(b).

- Service by e-mail shall be deemed complete upon transmission, except as provided in IN ST TRIAL P Rule 5(B)(3)(d). IN ST TRIAL P Rule 5(B)(3)(c).

- Service by fax or e-mail that occurs on a Saturday, Sunday, legal holiday, or day the court or agency in which the matter is pending is closed or after 5:00 PM local time of the recipient shall be deemed complete the next day that is not a Saturday, Sunday, legal holiday, or day that the court or agency in which the matter is pending is not closed. IN ST TRIAL P Rule 5(B)(3)(d).

    iv. *Mail box service.* Pursuant to IN ST TRIAL P Rule 5(B)(1)(d), the Circuit and Superior Courts of Hamilton County hereby designate the "mail boxes" located in the Clerk's order book office for service of pleadings upon attorneys who have such boxes. IN ST HAMILTON TRIAL Rule 201(201.50).

  b. *Serving numerous defendants.* In any action in which there are unusually large numbers of defendants, the court, upon motion or of its own initiative, may order:

    i. That service of the pleadings of the defendants and replies thereto need not be made as between the defendants;

- That any cross-claim, counterclaim, or matter constituting an avoidance or affirmative defense contained therein shall be deemed to be denied or avoided by all other parties; and

- That the filing of any such pleading and service thereof upon the plaintiff constitutes due notice of it to the parties. IN ST TRIAL P Rule 5(D).

    ii. A copy of every such order shall be served upon the parties in such manner and form as the court directs. IN ST TRIAL P Rule 5(D).

  c. *Service on parties in default for failure to appear.* No service need be made on parties in default for failure to appear, except that pleadings asserting new or additional claims for relief against them shall be served upon them in the manner provided by service of summons in IN ST TRIAL P Rule 4. IN ST TRIAL P Rule 5(A).

G. Hearings

1. *Hearing on motion.* Unless local conditions make it impracticable, each judge shall establish regular times and places, at intervals sufficiently frequent for the prompt dispatch of business, at which motions requiring notice and hearing may be heard and disposed of; but the judge at any time or place and on such notice, if any, as he considers reasonable may make order for the advancement, conduct, and hearing of actions. To expedite its business the court may direct the submission and determination of motions without oral hearing upon brief written statements of reasons in support and opposition, or direct or permit hearings by telephone conference call with all attorneys or other similar means of communication. IN ST TRIAL P Rule 73(A).

H. Forms

1. Motion for Leave to Amend Forms for Indiana

a.   Motion to file amended complaint. 5 INPRAC § 3:5.1.

b.   Motion to file amended complaint; Another form. 5 INPRAC § 3:5.2.

c.   Motion to amend pleading to conform to evidence. 5 INPRAC § 3:5.4.

d.   Motion to amend complaint to compel joinder of defendant. 5 INPRAC § 3:7.2.

e.   Motion to amend caption. 9 INPRAC § 3.41.

f.   Affidavit in support of motion to amend caption. 9 INPRAC § 3.42.

g.   Motion for leave to amend complaint following dismissal. 9 INPRAC § 42.16.

h.   Motion for leave to file amended complaint against third party defendant. 10 INPRAC § 44.8.

i.   Motion to file amended complaint. 10 INPRAC § 46.7.

j.   Motion to amend complaint which has been dismissed; Filed more than 10 days after notice of dismissal. 10 INPRAC § 46.8.

k.   Motion to amend pleading; Another form. 10 INPRAC § 46.9.

l.   Order granting leave to amend complaint. 10 INPRAC § 46.10.

m.   Amendment by stipulation. 10 INPRAC § 46.11.

n.   Amended answer by interlineation. 10 INPRAC § 46.12.

o.   Objections to motion to amend complaint. 10 INPRAC § 46.13.

p.   Motion to amend pleading to conform to evidence. 10 INPRAC § 46.14.

q.   Motion for leave to change defendant after statute of limitations. 10 INPRAC § 46.16.

r.   Motion for leave to add party after statute of limitations. 10 INPRAC § 46.17.

s.   Motion to substitute real party in interest; Assignee of interest. 10 INPRAC § 47.10.

t.   Motion to amend complaint to compel joinder of defendant. 10 INPRAC § 49.3.

u.   Certificate of service; Personal service. 9 INPRAC § 5.7.

v.   Certificate of service; First class mail. 9 INPRAC § 5.8.

I. Checklist

(I)   ❑ Matters to be considered by moving party

  (a)   ❑ Required documents

    (1)   ❑ Motion and notice

    (2)   ❑ Copy of amended pleading

    (3)   ❑ Proposed order

    (4)   ❑ Certificate of service

  (b)   ❑ Supplemental documents

    (1)   ❑ Supporting evidence

    (2)   ❑ Facsimile cover sheet

    (3)   ❑ Request to schedule trial or hearing

    (4)   ❑ Copies of unpublished opinions

  (c)   ❑ Timing

    (1)   ❑ A party may amend his pleading once as a matter of course at any time before a responsive pleading is served or, if the pleading is one to which no responsive pleading is permitted, and the action has not been placed upon the trial calendar, he may so amend it at any time within thirty (30) days after it is served

(2) ❑ Otherwise a party may amend his pleading only by leave of court or by written consent of the adverse party

(3) ❑ A written motion, other than one which may be heard ex parte, and notice of the hearing thereof shall be served not less than five (5) days before the time specified for the hearing, unless a different period is fixed by the Indiana Rules of Trial Procedure or by order of the court

(4) ❑ All pleadings and papers subsequent to the complaint which are required to be served upon a party shall be filed with the Court either before service or within a reasonable period of time thereafter

(II) ❑ Matters to be considered by the responding party

    (a) ❑ Required documents

        (1) ❑ Opposition

        (2) ❑ Certificate of service

    (b) ❑ Supplemental documents

        (1) ❑ Supporting evidence

        (2) ❑ Alternative proposed order

        (3) ❑ Facsimile cover sheet

        (4) ❑ Request to schedule trial or hearing

        (5) ❑ Copies of unpublished opinions

    (c) ❑ Timing

        (1) ❑ Except as otherwise provided in IN ST TRIAL P Rule 59(D), opposing affidavits may be served not less than one (1) day before the hearing, unless the court permits them to be served at some other time

Motions, Oppositions and Replies
Motion for Summary Judgment

Document Last Updated October 2013

A. Applicable Rules

  1. *State rules*

    a. Appearance. IN ST TRIAL P Rule 3.1.

    b. Process. IN ST TRIAL P Rule 4.

    c. Service and filing of pleadings and other papers. IN ST TRIAL P Rule 5.

    d. Time. IN ST TRIAL P Rule 6.

    e. Pleadings. IN ST TRIAL P Rule 7; IN ST TRIAL P Rule 8; IN ST TRIAL P Rule 9.2; IN ST TRIAL P Rule 10.

    f. Signing and verification of pleadings. IN ST TRIAL P Rule 11.

    g. Evidence. IN ST TRIAL P Rule 43.

    h. Judgment on the evidence (directed verdict). IN ST TRIAL P Rule 50.

    i. Findings by the court. IN ST TRIAL P Rule 52.

    j. Summary judgment. IN ST TRIAL P Rule 56.

    k. Motion to correct error. IN ST TRIAL P Rule 59.

    l. Relief from judgment or order. IN ST TRIAL P Rule 60.

    m. Hearing of motions. IN ST TRIAL P Rule 73.

n. Access to court records. IN ST ADMIN Rule 9.

o. Paper size. IN ST ADMIN Rule 11.

p. Facsimile transmission. IN ST ADMIN Rule 12.

q. Electronic filing and electronic service pilot projects. IN ST ADMIN Rule 16.

r. Sealing of certain records by court; Hearing; Notice. IN ST 5-14-3-5.5.

s. Privacy and confidentiality. IN ST 5-2-9-6; IN ST 5-14-3-4; IN ST 6-4.1-5-10; IN ST 6-4.1-12-12; IN ST 6-8.1-7-1; IN ST 11-13-1-8; IN ST 12-23-14-13; IN ST 16-39-3-10; IN ST 16-41-8-1; IN ST 22-4-19-6; IN ST 31-11-1-6; IN ST 31-19-5-23; IN ST 31-19-13-2; IN ST 31-19-19-1; IN ST 31-33-18-1; IN ST 31-39-1-1; IN ST 31-39-1-2; IN ST 33-23-16-16; IN ST 35-34-2-4; IN ST 35-38-1-13; IN ST 35-38-9-1; IN ST ADR Rule 2.11; IN ST ADR Rule 4.4; IN ST ADR Rule 5.6; IN ST JURY Rule 10.

2. *Local rules*

a. Court hours. IN ST HAMILTON ADMIN Rule 101.

b. Facsimile transmissions. IN ST HAMILTON ADMIN Rule 103.

c. Filing of pleadings and entry of appearances. IN ST HAMILTON TRIAL Rule 201.

d. Proposed orders. IN ST HAMILTON TRIAL Rule 202.

e. Briefs and memorandums. IN ST HAMILTON TRIAL Rule 203.

f. Special judges. IN ST HAMILTON TRIAL Rule 204.

g. Trial settings. IN ST HAMILTON TRIAL Rule 205.

h. Continuances. IN ST HAMILTON TRIAL Rule 206.

B. Timing

1. *Time for moving for summary judgment*

a. *For claimant.* A party seeking to recover upon a claim, counterclaim, or cross-claim or to obtain a declaratory judgment may, at any time after the expiration of twenty (20) days from the commencement of the action or after service of a motion for summary judgment by the adverse party, move with or without supporting affidavits for a summary judgment in his favor upon all or any part thereof. IN ST TRIAL P Rule 56(A).

b. *For defending party.* A party against whom a claim, counterclaim, or cross-claim is asserted or a declaratory judgment is sought may, at any time, move with or without supporting affidavits for a summary judgment in his favor as to all or any part thereof. IN ST TRIAL P Rule 56(B).

c. *Filing.* All pleadings and papers subsequent to the complaint which are required to be served upon a party shall be filed with the Court either before service or within a reasonable period of time thereafter. IN ST TRIAL P Rule 5(E)(1).

2. *Service.* A written motion, other than one which may be heard ex parte, and notice of the hearing thereof shall be served not less than five (5) days before the time specified for the hearing, unless a different period is fixed by the Indiana Rules of Trial Procedure or by order of the court. IN ST TRIAL P Rule 6(D).

a. *Of supporting affidavits.* When a motion is supported by affidavit, the affidavit shall be served with the motion. IN ST TRIAL P Rule 6(D).

3. *Service of opposition.* An adverse party shall have thirty (30) days after service of the motion to serve a response and any opposing affidavits. IN ST TRIAL P Rule 56(C).

a. Except as otherwise provided in IN ST TRIAL P Rule 59(D), opposing affidavits may be served not less than one (1) day before the hearing, unless the court permits them to be served at some other time. IN ST TRIAL P Rule 6(D).

4. *Computation of time*

a. *Generally; Days excluded.* In computing any period of time prescribed or allowed by the Indiana Rules of Trial Procedure, by order of the court, or by any applicable statute, the day of the act, event,

or default from which the designated period of time begins to run shall not be included. The last day of the period so computed is to be included unless it is:

    i.   A Saturday,

    ii. A Sunday,

    iii. A legal holiday as defined by state statute, or

    iv. A day the office in which the act is to be done is closed during regular business hours. IN ST TRIAL P Rule 6(A).

b. *Short periods.* In any event, the period runs until the end of the next day that is not a Saturday, a Sunday, a legal holiday, or a day on which the office is closed. When the period of time allowed is less than seven (7) days, intermediate Saturdays, Sundays, legal holidays, and days on which the office is closed shall be excluded from the computations. IN ST TRIAL P Rule 6(A).

c. *Additional time after service by United States mail.* Whenever a party has the right or is required to do some act or take some proceedings within a prescribed period after the service of a notice or other paper upon him and the notice or paper is served upon him by United States mail, three (3) days shall be added to the prescribed period. IN ST TRIAL P Rule 6(E).

d. *Enlargement of time.* When an act is required or allowed to be done at or within a specific time by the Indiana Rules of Trial Procedure, the court may at any time for cause shown:

    i.   Order the period enlarged, with or without motion or notice, if request therefor is made before the expiration of the period originally prescribed or extended by a previous order; or

    ii. Upon motion made after the expiration of the specific period, permit the act to be done where the failure to act was the result of excusable neglect; but, the court may not extend the time for taking any action for judgment on the evidence under IN ST TRIAL P Rule 50(A), amendment of findings and judgment under IN ST TRIAL P Rule 52(B), to correct errors under IN ST TRIAL P Rule 59(C), statement in opposition to motion to correct error under IN ST TRIAL P Rule 59(E), or to obtain relief from final judgment under IN ST TRIAL P Rule 60(B), except to the extent and under the conditions stated in those rules. IN ST TRIAL P Rule 6(B).

    iii. For information on obtaining a continuance, refer to IN ST HAMILTON TRIAL Rule 206.

C. General Requirements

1. *Motions, generally.* Unless made during a hearing or trial, or otherwise ordered by the court, an application to the court for an order shall be made by written motion. The motion shall state the grounds therefor and the relief or order sought. IN ST TRIAL P Rule 7(B).

a. *Motions as distinct from pleadings.* Motions and responses to motions are not pleadings, and allegations contained in a motion are not admissions of a party. 22B INPRAC 7:2; Wachstetter v. County Properties, LLC, 832 N.E.2d 574 (Ind.Ct.App. 2005); Scott County Family YMCA, Inc. v. Hobbs, 817 N.E.2d 603 (Ind.Ct.App. 2004).

b. *Unopposed motions generally granted.* It is common for a trial court to grant procedural motions, such as motions for enlargement of time, discovery motions, or motions for continuance, unless an objection is filed. 21 INPRAC § 13.8.

2. *Motion for summary judgment.* Summary judgment is a procedure by which the trial court is asked to enter judgment when there are no genuine issues of material fact and the moving party is entitled to judgment as a matter of law. A summary judgment proceeding is not a trial, and is not intended to be a substitute for factual determinations where the facts are in dispute. Rather, summary judgment should be used to terminate litigation about which there is no factual dispute and which may be determined as a matter of law. 11 INPRAC § 90.1; LeBrun v. Conner, 702 N.E.2d 754 (Ind.Ct.App. 1998).

a. *Burden.* The judgment sought shall be rendered forthwith if the designated evidentiary matter shows that there is no genuine issue as to any material fact and that the moving party is entitled to a judgment as a matter of law. IN ST TRIAL P Rule 56(C).

    i. A "genuine" issue of material fact exists if the trier of fact must resolve the opposing party's differing version of the underlying facts or if the undisputed facts support conflicting reasonable inferences. A fact is "material" if it might affect the outcome of a case by helping to prove or disprove an essential element of a claim or defense, or it facilitates a resolution of an issue in the case. 22B INPRAC 56:1; Williams v. Tharp, 914 N.E.2d 756 (Ind. 2009).

   ii.   Summary judgment shall not be granted as of course because the opposing party fails to offer opposing affidavits or evidence, but the court shall make its determination from the evidentiary matter designated to the court. IN ST TRIAL P Rule 56(C).

   iii.   The trial court must evaluate the evidence in favor of the non-moving party. 22B INPRAC 56:1.

   iv.   Although Indiana courts are not consistent in describing the amount of proof required to sustain the moving party's initial burden, and IN ST TRIAL P Rule 56 is silent on the matter, a number of cases require "prima facie" proof. 22B INPRAC 56:5; DeHahn v. CSX Transp., Inc., 925 N.E.2d 442 (Ind.Ct.App. 2010). Once the moving party demonstrates the requirements for summary judgment, the burden shifts to the non-moving party to designate each material issue of fact which he asserts precludes entry of summary judgment and the evidence relevant to each designated fact. 22B INPRAC 56:5; Booth v. Wiley, 839 N.E.2d 1168 (Ind. 2005).

b.   *When motion not required.* When any party has moved for summary judgment, the court may grant summary judgment for any other party upon the issues raised by the motion although no motion for summary judgment is filed by such party. IN ST TRIAL P Rule 56(B).

c.   *Judgment on less than all issues or claims.* A summary judgment may be rendered upon less than all the issues or claims, including without limitation the issue of liability or damages alone although there is a genuine issue as to damages or liability as the case may be. IN ST TRIAL P Rule 56(C).

   i.   *Partial judgment not entered; Exceptions.* A summary judgment upon less than all the issues involved in a claim or with respect to less than all the claims or parties shall be interlocutory unless the court in writing expressly determines that there is no just reason for delay and in writing expressly directs entry of judgment as to less than all the issues, claims or parties. IN ST TRIAL P Rule 56(C).

   ii.   *Designation of specific findings.* The court shall designate the issues or claims upon which it finds no genuine issue as to any material facts. IN ST TRIAL P Rule 56(C).

   iii.   *Case not fully adjudicated on motion.* If on motion under IN ST TRIAL P Rule 56 judgment is not rendered upon the whole case or for all the relief asked and a trial is necessary, the court at the hearing of the motion, by examining the pleadings and the evidence before it and by interrogating counsel, shall if practicable ascertain what material facts exist without substantial controversy and what material facts are actually and in good faith controverted. It shall thereupon make an order specifying the facts that appear without substantial controversy, including the extent to which the amount of damages or other relief is not in controversy, and directing such further proceedings in the action as are just. Upon the trial of the action the facts so specified shall be deemed established, and the trial shall be conducted accordingly. IN ST TRIAL P Rule 56(D).

d.   *Form of affidavits; Further testimony; Defense required.* Supporting and opposing affidavits shall be made on personal knowledge, shall set forth such facts as would be admissible in evidence, and shall show affirmatively that the affiant is competent to testify to the matters stated therein. IN ST TRIAL P Rule 56(E).

   i.   Sworn or certified copies not previously self-authenticated of all papers or parts thereof referred to in an affidavit shall be attached thereto or served therewith. IN ST TRIAL P Rule 56(E).

   ii.   The court may permit affidavits to be supplemented or opposed by depositions, answers to interrogatories, or further affidavits. IN ST TRIAL P Rule 56(E).

   iii.   When a motion for summary judgment is made and supported as provided in IN ST TRIAL P Rule 56, an adverse party may not rest upon the mere allegations or denials of his pleading, but his response, by affidavits or as otherwise provided in IN ST TRIAL P Rule 56, must set forth specific facts showing that there is a genuine issue for trial. If he does not so respond, summary judgment, if appropriate, shall be entered against him. Denial of summary judgment may be challenged by a motion to correct errors after a final judgment or order is entered. IN ST TRIAL P Rule 56(E).

e. *When affidavits are unavailable.* Should it appear from the affidavits of a party opposing the motion that he cannot for reasons stated present by affidavit facts essential to justify his opposition, the court may refuse the application for judgment or may order a continuance to permit affidavits to be obtained or depositions to be taken or discovery to be had or may make such other order as is just. IN ST TRIAL P Rule 56(F).

f. *Affidavits made in bad faith.* Should it appear to the satisfaction of the court at any time that any of the affidavits presented pursuant to IN ST TRIAL P Rule 56 are presented in bad faith or solely for the purpose of delay, the court shall forthwith order the party employing them to pay to the other party the amount of the reasonable expenses which the filing of the affidavits caused him to incur, including reasonable attorney's fees, and any offending party or attorney may be adjudged guilty of contempt. IN ST TRIAL P Rule 56(G).

g. *Party opposing the motion.* A party opposing the motion shall also designate to the court each material issue of fact which that party asserts precludes entry of summary judgment and the evidence relevant thereto. IN ST TRIAL P Rule 56(C).

h. *Appeal; Reversal.* No judgment rendered on the motion shall be reversed on the ground that there is a genuine issue of material fact unless the material fact and the evidence relevant thereto shall have been specifically designated to the trial court. IN ST TRIAL P Rule 56(H).

D. Documents

1. *Required documents*

   a. *Motion and notice.* The requirement of notice is satisfied by service of the motion. IN ST TRIAL P Rule 7(B). Refer to the General Requirements section of this document for information on the content of a motion for summary judgment.

   b. *Supporting evidence.* At the time of filing the motion or response, a party shall designate to the court all parts of pleadings, depositions, answers to interrogatories, admissions, matters of judicial notice, and any other matters on which it relies for purposes of the motion. IN ST TRIAL P Rule 56(C).

      i. The party moving for judgment must designate sufficient evidence to establish that there is no genuine issue of material fact and that judgment is proper as a matter of law. 22B INPRAC 56:4; Jarboe v. Landmark Community Newspapers of Indiana, Inc., 644 N.E.2d 118 (Ind. 1994).

   c. *Proposed order.* Unless local practice provides differently, a party should submit a proposed order with its written motion to be signed by the judge once the motion has been granted. 21 INPRAC § 13.8; IN ST HAMILTON ADMIN Rule 103(103.10)(b). Each Motion, Petition or other request for relief shall be accompanied by a proposed order. IN ST HAMILTON TRIAL Rule 202(202.10).

      i. All proposed orders submitted by counsel pursuant to IN ST HAMILTON TRIAL Rule 202 shall meet the following requirements: (1) contain a complete distribution list of all attorneys and pro se litigants with full addresses; (2) stamped envelopes appropriately addressed for each attorney of record and/or pro se litigant on the distribution list. IN ST HAMILTON TRIAL Rule 202(202.30).

   d. *Certificate of service.* An attorney or unrepresented party tendering a document to the Clerk for filing shall certify that service has been made, list the parties served, and specify the date and means of service. The certificate of service shall be placed at the end of the document and shall not be separately filed. The separate filing of a certificate of service, however, shall not be grounds for rejecting a document for filing. The Clerk may permit documents to be filed without a certificate of service but shall require prompt filing of a separate certificate of service. IN ST TRIAL P Rule 5(C).

      i. All pleadings filed with the Court which require a certificate of service shall specifically name the individual party or attorney on whom service has been made, the address, the manner in which service was made and the date when service was made. IN ST HAMILTON TRIAL Rule 201(201.60).

2. *Supplemental documents*

   a. *Additional supporting evidence.* When a motion is based on facts not appearing of record the court may hear the matter on affidavits presented by the respective parties, but the court may direct that the matter be heard wholly or partly on oral testimony or depositions. IN ST TRIAL P Rule 43(B).

b. *Facsimile cover sheet.* Any document sent to the Clerk of the Circuit Court by electronic facsimile transmission shall be accompanied by a cover sheet which states the title of the document, case number, number of pages, identity and voice telephone number of the sending party and instructions for filing. The cover sheet shall contain the signature of the attorney or party, pro se, authorizing the filing. IN ST ADMIN Rule 12(D); IN ST HAMILTON ADMIN Rule 103(103.10)(a).

c. *Request to schedule hearing.* All requests to schedule trials and hearings shall be in writing and shall contain the following information:

    i. Type of trial or hearing (i.e., jury trial, court trial, final hearing in dissolution, etc.). IN ST HAMILTON TRIAL Rule 205(205.10).

    ii. A good-faith estimate of the total court time needed for the trial or hearing. IN ST HAMILTON TRIAL Rule 205(205.10).

    iii. Each request under IN ST HAMILTON TRIAL Rule 205(205.10) shall be accompanied by a proposed written order with appropriate blanks for date and time and shall further include reference to those items set forth in IN ST HAMILTON TRIAL Rule 205(205.10)(a) and IN ST HAMILTON TRIAL Rule 205(205.10)(b). IN ST HAMILTON TRIAL Rule 205(205.20).

d. *Copies of unpublished opinions.* Authorities relied upon which are not cited in the Northeastern Reporter system shall be attached to counsel's brief. If the authority is cited for the first time in oral argument, a copy of the authority may be provided to the Court at the time of the argument. Sufficient copies shall be available to provide counsel for each party with a copy. IN ST HAMILTON TRIAL Rule 203(203.10).

E. Format

1. *Form of motions.* The rules applicable to captions, and the signing and form of pleadings (IN ST TRIAL P Rule 8 through IN ST TRIAL P Rule 11), apply to all motions and other papers provided under the Indiana Rules of Trial Procedure. 22B INPRAC 7:2.

2. *Form of pleadings*

a. *Caption; Names of parties.* Every pleading shall contain a caption setting forth the name of the court, the title of the action, the file number, and a designation as in IN ST TRIAL P Rule 7(A). In the complaint the title of the action shall include the names of all the parties, but in other pleadings it is sufficient to state the name of the first party on each side with an appropriate indication of other parties. IN ST TRIAL P Rule 10(A).

b. *Paragraphs; Separate statements.* All averments of a claim or defense shall be made in numbered paragraphs, the contents of each of which shall be limited as far as practicable to a statement of a single set of circumstances, and a paragraph may be referred to by number in all succeeding pleadings. Each claim founded upon a separate transaction or occurrence and each defense other than denials may be stated in a separate count or defense whenever a separation facilitates the clear presentation of the matters set forth. IN ST TRIAL P Rule 10(B).

c. *Adoption by reference; Exhibits.* Statements in a pleading may be adopted by reference in a different part of the same pleading or in another pleading or in any motion. A copy of any written instrument which is an exhibit to a pleading is a part thereof for all purposes. IN ST TRIAL P Rule 10(C).

d. *Facsimile page limit.* Courts authorize the Hamilton County Clerk of Courts to accept pleadings, motions and other papers by electronic facsimile transmission for filing in any case pending before the Courts, subject to the requirement that The transmission may not exceed ten (10) pages in length including the cover sheet and proposed CCS entry. IN ST HAMILTON ADMIN Rule 103(103.10)(c).

e. *Emergency facsimile filings.* If the filing requires the immediate attention of the Judge, it shall so indicate in bold letters in an accompanying transmittal memorandum. IN ST HAMILTON ADMIN Rule 103(103.10)(f).

f. *Special judge heading.* After a special judge is selected, the attorneys or pro se litigants shall add to the caption of all pleadings to the right of the case title the following: "BEFORE SPECIAL JUDGE _____." IN ST HAMILTON TRIAL Rule 204(204.10).

g. *Format rules strictly enforced.* All filings shall be in compliance with the Indiana Rules of Trial Procedure. If the documents received are not in proper form, such deficiencies will not be corrected by court personnel. IN ST HAMILTON TRIAL Rule 201(201.70). The Court shall not be required to act on any Motion, Petition or other request for relief unless filed in conformity with the Hamilton County Local Trial and Administrative rules. IN ST HAMILTON TRIAL Rule 202(202.20).

3. *Size of papers for filing.* Effective January 1, 1992, all pleadings, copies, motions and documents filed with any trial court or appellate level court, typed or printed, with the exception of exhibits and existing wills, shall be prepared on eight and one-half by eleven inch (8 1/2" x 11") size paper. IN ST ADMIN Rule 11.

a. *Form.* All documents filed in any Hamilton County Court, with the exception of exhibits and existing wills, shall be prepared on paper measuring eight and one-half by eleven inches (8 1/2" x 11"). IN ST HAMILTON TRIAL Rule 201(201.20).

4. *Signature requirements*

a. *Signature of attorney.* Every pleading or motion of a party represented by an attorney shall be signed by at least one (1) attorney of record in his individual name, whose address, telephone number, and attorney number shall be stated, except that this provision shall not apply to pleadings and motions made and transcribed at the trial or a hearing before the judge and received by him in such form. IN ST TRIAL P Rule 11(A).

    i. The signature of an attorney constitutes a certificate by him that he has read the pleadings; that to the best of his knowledge, information, and belief, there is good ground to support it; and that it is not interposed for delay. IN ST TRIAL P Rule 11(A).

    ii. If a pleading or motion is not signed or is signed with intent to defeat the purpose of the rule, it may be stricken as sham and false and the action may proceed as though the pleading had not been served. IN ST TRIAL P Rule 11(A).

    iii. For a willful violation of IN ST TRIAL P Rule 11 an attorney may be subjected to appropriate disciplinary action. Similar action may be taken if scandalous or indecent matter is inserted. IN ST TRIAL P Rule 11(A).

b. *Signature of unrepresented party.* A party who is not represented by an attorney shall sign his pleading and state his address. IN ST TRIAL P Rule 11(A).

c. *Verification not generally required.* Except when specifically required by rule, pleadings or motions need not be verified or accompanied by affidavit. The rule in equity that the averments of an answer under oath must be overcome by the testimony of two (2) witnesses or of one (1) witness sustained by corroborating circumstances is abolished. IN ST TRIAL P Rule 11(A).

d. *Verification by affirmation or representation.* When in connection with any civil or special statutory proceeding it is required that any pleading, motion, petition, supporting affidavit, or other document of any kind, be verified, or that an oath be taken, it shall be sufficient if the subscriber simply affirms the truth of the matter to be verified by an affirmation or representation. IN ST TRIAL P Rule 11(B). IN ST TRIAL P Rule 11(B) states that the affirmation or representation should be in substantially the following language: "I (we) affirm, under the penalties for perjury, that the foregoing representation(s) is (are) true. (Signed) _____."

    i. Any person who falsifies an affirmation or representation of fact shall be subject to the same penalties as are prescribed by law for the making of a false affidavit. IN ST TRIAL P Rule 11(B).

e. *Verified pleadings, motions, and affidavits as evidence.* Pleadings, motions and affidavits accompanying or in support of such pleadings or motions when required to be verified or under oath shall be accepted as a representation that the signer had personal knowledge thereof or reasonable cause to believe the existence of the facts or matters stated or alleged therein; and, if otherwise competent or acceptable as evidence, may be admitted as evidence of the facts or matters stated or alleged therein when it is so provided in the Indiana Rules of Trial Procedure, by statute or other law, or to the extent the writing or signature expressly purports to be made upon the signer's personal knowledge. When such pleadings, motions and affidavits are verified or under oath they shall not require other or greater proof on the part of the adverse party than if not verified or not under oath unless expressly provided otherwise by the Indiana Rules of Trial Procedure, statute or other law. Affidavits upon motions for summary judgment under IN ST TRIAL P Rule 56 and in denial of execution under IN ST TRIAL P Rule 9.2 shall be made upon personal knowledge. IN ST TRIAL P Rule 11(C).

5. *Information excluded from public access.* Every document filed in a case shall separately identify information excluded from public access pursuant to IN ST ADMIN Rule 9(G)(1) as follows:

   a. Whole documents that are excluded from public access pursuant to IN ST ADMIN Rule 9(G)(1) shall be tendered on light green paper or have a light green coversheet attached to the document, marked "Not for Public Access" or "Confidential." IN ST TRIAL P Rule 5(G)(1).

   b. When only a portion of a document contains information excluded from public access pursuant to IN ST ADMIN Rule 9(G)(1), said information shall be omitted [or redacted] from the filed document, and set forth on a separate accompanying document on light green paper conspicuously marked "Not for Public Access" or "Confidential" and clearly designated [or identifying] the caption and number of the case and the document and location within the document to which the redacted material pertains. IN ST TRIAL P Rule 5(G)(2).

   c. With respect to documents filed in electronic format, the trial court, by local rule, may provide for compliance with IN ST TRIAL P Rule 5 in manner that separates and protects access to information excluded from public access. IN ST TRIAL P Rule 5(G)(3).

   d. IN ST TRIAL P Rule 5(G) does not apply to a record sealed by the court pursuant to IN ST 5-14-3-5.5 or otherwise, nor to records, documents, or information filed in cases to which public access is prohibited pursuant to IN ST ADMIN Rule 9(G). IN ST TRIAL P Rule 5(G)(4).

   e. The following information in case records is excluded from public access and is confidential:

      i. Information that is excluded from public access pursuant to federal law;

      ii. Information that is excluded from public access as declared confidential by Indiana statute or other court rule, including without limitation:

         • All adoption records created after July 8, 1941, as declared confidential by IN ST 31-19-19-1, et seq., except those specifically declared open by IN ST 31-19-13-2(2);

         • All records relating to chancroid, chlamydia, gonorrhea, hepatitis, human immunodeficiency virus (HIV), Lymphogranuloma venereum, syphilis, tuberculosis, as declared confidential by IN ST 16-41-8-1, et seq.;

         • All records relating to child abuse as declared confidential by IN ST 31-33-18-1, et seq.;

         • All records relating to drug tests as declared confidential by IN ST 5-14-3-4(a)(9);

         • Records of grand jury proceedings as declared confidential by IN ST 35-34-2-4;

         • Records of juvenile proceedings as declared confidential by IN ST 31-39-1-2, except those specifically open under statute;

         • All paternity records created after July 1, 1941 as declared confidential by IN ST 31-14-11-15, IN ST 31-19-5-23, IN ST 31-39-1-1 and IN ST 31-39-1-2 [Editor's note: IN ST 31-14-11-15 was repealed effective May 9, 2013];

         • All pre-sentence reports as declared confidential by IN ST 35-38-1-13;

         • Written petitions to permit marriages without consent and orders directing the Clerk of Court to issue a marriage license to underage persons, as declared confidential by IN ST 31-11-1-6;

         • Only those arrest warrants, search warrants, indictments and informations ordered confidential by the trial judge, prior to return of duly executed service as declared confidential by IN ST 5-14-3-4(b)(1);

         • All medical, mental health, or tax records unless determined by law or regulation of any governmental custodian not to be confidential, released by the subject of such records, or declared by a court of competent jurisdiction to be essential to the resolution of litigation as declared confidential by IN ST 16-39-3-10, IN ST 6-4.1-5-10, IN ST 6-4.1-12-12, and IN ST 6-8.1-7-1;

- Personal information relating to jurors or prospective jurors, other than for the use of the parties and counsel, pursuant to IN ST JURY Rule 10;

- Information relating to protection from abuse orders, no-contact orders and workplace violence restraining orders as declared confidential by IN ST 5-2-9-6, et seq.;

- Mediation proceedings pursuant to IN ST ADR Rule 2.11, Mini-Trial proceedings pursuant to IN ST ADR Rule 4.4(C), and Summary Jury Trials pursuant to IN ST ADR Rule 5.6;

- Information in probation files pursuant to the Probation Standards promulgated by the Judicial Conference of Indiana pursuant to IN ST 11-13-1-8(b);

- Information deemed confidential pursuant to the Rules for Court Administered Alcohol and Drug Programs promulgated by the Judicial Conference of Indiana pursuant to IN ST 12-23-14-13;

- Information deemed confidential pursuant to the Problem-Solving Court Rules promulgated by the Judicial Conference of Indiana pursuant to IN ST 33-23-16-16;

- All records of the Department of workforce Development as declared confidential by IN ST 22-4-19-6;

- Information regarding interception of electronic communications that is sealed or deemed confidential as set forth in IN ST 35-33.5-2-1, et seq.

iii. Information excluded from public access by specific court order;

iv. Complete Social Security Numbers of living persons;

v. With the exception of names, information such as addresses, phone numbers, and dates of birth which explicitly identifies:

- Natural persons who are witnesses or victims (not including defendants) in criminal, domestic violence, stalking, sexual assault, juvenile, or civil protection order proceedings, provided that juveniles who are victims of sex crimes shall be identified by initials only;

- Places of residence of judicial officers, clerks and other employees of courts and clerks of court, unless the person or persons about whom the information pertains waives confidentiality;

vi. Complete account numbers of specific assets, loans, bank accounts, credit cards, and personal identification numbers (PINs);

vii. All orders of expungement entered in criminal or juvenile proceedings, orders to restrict access to criminal history information pursuant to IN ST 35-38-5-5.5 or IN ST 35-38-8-5 and records excluded from public access by such orders, and information related to infractions that is excluded from public access pursuant to IN ST 34-28-5-15 or IN ST 34-28-5-16 [Editor's note: IN ST 35-38-5-5.5, IN ST 35-38-8-5 and IN ST 34-28-5-16 were repealed effective July 1, 2013; for information on orders restricting access to criminal history, refer to IN ST 35-38-9-1, et seq.];

viii. All personal notes and e-mail, and deliberative material, of judges, jurors, court staff and judicial agencies, and information recorded in personal data assistants (PDA's) or organizers and personal calendars. IN ST ADMIN Rule 9(G)(1).

F. Filing and Service Requirements

1. *Filing requirements.* Except as otherwise provided in IN ST TRIAL P Rule 5(E)(2), all pleadings and

papers subsequent to the complaint which are required to be served upon a party shall be filed with the Court either before service or within a reasonable period of time thereafter. IN ST TRIAL P Rule 5(E)(1).

a. *Filing with the court defined.* The filing of pleadings, motions, and other papers with the court as required by the Indiana Rules of Trial Procedure shall be made by one of the following methods:

    i. Delivery to the clerk of the court;

    ii. Sending by electronic transmission under the procedure adopted pursuant to IN ST ADMIN Rule 12;

    iii. Mailing to the clerk by registered, certified or express mail return receipt requested;

    iv. Depositing with any third-party commercial carrier for delivery to the clerk within three (3) calendar days, cost prepaid, properly addressed;

    v. If the court so permits, filing with the judge, in which event the judge shall note thereon the filing date and forthwith transmit them to the office of the clerk; or

    vi. Electronic filing, as approved by the Division of State Court Administration pursuant to IN ST ADMIN Rule 16. IN ST TRIAL P Rule 5(F).

    vii. Filing by registered or certified mail and by third-party commercial carrier shall be complete upon mailing or deposit. IN ST TRIAL P Rule 5(F).

b. *Facsimile filing.* As outlined in IN ST HAMILTON ADMIN Rule 103(103.10),facsimile filing is permitted in the Circuit and Superior Courts of Hamilton County. The Courts authorize the Hamilton County Clerk of Courts to accept pleadings, motions and other papers by electronic facsimile transmission for filing in any case pending before the Courts, subject to the requirements of IN ST HAMILTON ADMIN Rule 103(103.10). IN ST HAMILTON ADMIN Rule 103(103.10); IN ST HAMILTON TRIAL Rule 201(201.80).

    i. *Generally.* In counties where a majority of judges of the courts of record, by posted local rule, have authorized electronic facsimile filing and designated a telephone number to receive such transmissions, pleadings, motions, and other papers may be sent to the Clerk of Circuit Court by electronic facsimile transmission for filing in any case, provided:

- Such matter does not exceed ten (10) pages, including the cover sheet;
- Such matter does not require the payment of fees other than the electronic facsimile transcription fee set forth in IN ST ADMIN Rule 12(E);
- The sending party creates at the time of transmission a machine generated log for such transmission; and
- The original document and the transmission log are maintained by the sending party for the duration of the litigation. IN ST ADMIN Rule 12(B); IN ST HAMILTON ADMIN Rule 103(103.10)(d).
- Legibility of documents and timeliness of filing is the responsibility of the sender. IN ST HAMILTON ADMIN Rule 103(103.10)(g).
- The Clerk shall accept electronic facsimile transmission filings only if received at the facsimile machine assigned by the Clerk. The telephone number designated to receive such transmission is available at IN ST HAMILTON ADMIN Rule 103(103.40). IN ST HAMILTON ADMIN Rule 103(103.40).

    ii. *Time of filing.* During normal, posted business hours, the time of filing shall be the time the duplicate document is produced in the office of the Clerk of the Circuit Court. Duplicate documents received at all other times shall be filed as of the next normal business day. IN ST ADMIN Rule 12(C).

- If the receiving fax machine endorses its own time and date stamp upon the transmitted documents and the receiving machine produces a delivery receipt which is electronically created and transmitted to the sending party, the time of filing shall be the date and time recorded on the transmitted document by the receiving fax machine. IN ST ADMIN Rule 12(C).

- Electronic facsimile transmissions will be accepted for filing only during the regular business hours as set forth in IN ST HAMILTON ADMIN Rule 101. Transmissions received by the Hamilton County Clerk after close of business shall be filed effective the next regular business day. IN ST HAMILTON ADMIN Rule 103(103.30).

iii. *Filing fee.* The electronic facsimile transmission will not be accepted for filing if its filing requires the payment of any fee other than the electronic facsimile transcription fee set forth in IN ST HAMILTON ADMIN Rule 103(103.20). IN ST HAMILTON ADMIN Rule 103(103.10)(e).

- Pursuant to Ordinance adopted by the Hamilton County Board of Commissioners, the Clerk shall collect an electronic facsimile transcription fee of One Dollar ($1.00) per page, to a maximum of Ten Dollars ($10.00) per transmission, for each electronic facsimile transmission accepted for filing with the Hamilton County Circuit and Superior Courts. IN ST HAMILTON ADMIN Rule 103(103.20).

- The fee shall be assessed against the sending party and shall be paid upon receipt of invoice by that party and at the latest within thirty (30) days of the transmission. In the event the fee is not paid by the sending party within the time limits provided, the court may issue a show-cause order or enter a judgment in the matter. The Clerk may refuse an electronic facsimile transmission from any attorney or pro se litigant who has failed to pay these fees within thirty (30) days. IN ST HAMILTON ADMIN Rule 103(103.20).

iv. *No direct filing with court.* A party shall not send pleadings, motions and other papers by electronic facsimile transmission for filing directly to any Court without that Court's prior approval to do so. IN ST HAMILTON ADMIN Rule 103(103.50).

c. *Filing with special judge.* After a special judge has qualified, a copy of each pleading and Chronological Case Summary entries filed with the Court shall be mailed or delivered to the office of that Special judge by the counsel or pro se litigant with service indicated on the certificate of service. IN ST HAMILTON TRIAL Rule 204(204.20).

d. *Proof of filing.* Any party filing any paper by any method other than personal delivery to the clerk shall retain proof of filing. IN ST TRIAL P Rule 5(F).

2. *Service requirements.* Unless otherwise provided by the Indiana Rules of Trial Procedure or an order of the court, each party and special judge, if any, shall be served with: (1) every order required by its terms to be served; (2) every pleading subsequent to the original complaint; (3) every written motion except one which may be heard ex parte; (4) every brief submitted to the trial court; (5) every paper relating to discovery required to be served upon a party; and (6) every written notice, appearance, demand, offer of judgment, designation of record on appeal, or similar paper. IN ST TRIAL P Rule 5(A).

a. *Methods of service*

i. *Personal service.* Whenever a party is represented by an attorney of record, service shall be made upon such attorney unless service upon the party himself is ordered by the court. Service upon the attorney or party shall be made by delivering or mailing a copy of the papers to the last known address or where an attorney or party has consented to service by fax or e-mail, as provided in IN ST TRIAL P Rule 3.1(A)(4), by faxing or e-mailing a copy of the documents to the fax number or e-mail address set out in the appearance form or correction as required by IN ST TRIAL P Rule 3.1(E). IN ST TRIAL P Rule 5(B). Delivery of a copy within IN ST TRIAL P Rule 5 means:

- Offering or tendering it to the attorney or party and stating the nature of the papers being served. Refusal to accept an offered or tendered document is a waiver of any objection to the sufficiency or adequacy of service of that document;

- Leaving it at his office with a clerk or other person in charge thereof, or if there is no one in charge, leaving it in a conspicuous place therein; or

- If the office is closed, by leaving it at his dwelling house or usual place of abode with some person of suitable age and discretion then residing therein; or,

- Leaving it at some other suitable place, selected by the attorney upon whom service is being made, pursuant to duly promulgated local rule. IN ST TRIAL P Rule 5(B)(1).

ii. *Service by mail.* If service is made by mail, the papers shall be deposited in the United States mail addressed to the person on whom they are being served, with postage prepaid. Service shall be deemed complete upon mailing. Proof of service of all papers permitted to be mailed may be made by written acknowledgment of service, by affidavit of the person who mailed the papers, or by certificate of an attorney. It shall be the duty of attorneys when entering their appearance in a cause or when filing pleadings or papers therein, to have noted in the Chronological Case Summary or said pleadings or papers so filed the address and telephone number of their office. Service by delivery or by mail at such address shall be deemed sufficient and complete. IN ST TRIAL P Rule 5(B)(2).

iii. *Service by fax or e-mail.* A party who has consented to service by fax or e-mail may be served as follows:

- Service by e-mail shall be made by attaching the document being served in .pdf format. Discovery documents must also be served in accordance with IN ST TRIAL P Rule 26(A). IN ST TRIAL P Rule 5(B)(3)(a).

- Service by fax shall be deemed complete upon generation of a transmission record indicating the successful transmission of the entire document, except as provided in IN ST TRIAL P Rule 5(B)(3)(d). IN ST TRIAL P Rule 5(B)(3)(b).

- Service by e-mail shall be deemed complete upon transmission, except as provided in IN ST TRIAL P Rule 5(B)(3)(d). IN ST TRIAL P Rule 5(B)(3)(c).

- Service by fax or e-mail that occurs on a Saturday, Sunday, legal holiday, or day the court or agency in which the matter is pending is closed or after 5:00 PM local time of the recipient shall be deemed complete the next day that is not a Saturday, Sunday, legal holiday, or day that the court or agency in which the matter is pending is not closed. IN ST TRIAL P Rule 5(B)(3)(d).

iv. *Mail box service.* Pursuant to IN ST TRIAL P Rule 5(B)(1)(d), the Circuit and Superior Courts of Hamilton County hereby designate the "mail boxes" located in the Clerk's order book office for service of pleadings upon attorneys who have such boxes. IN ST HAMILTON TRIAL Rule 201(201.50).

b. *Serving numerous defendants.* In any action in which there are unusually large numbers of defendants, the court, upon motion or of its own initiative, may order:

i. That service of the pleadings of the defendants and replies thereto need not be made as between the defendants;

- That any cross-claim, counterclaim, or matter constituting an avoidance or affirmative defense contained therein shall be deemed to be denied or avoided by all other parties; and

- That the filing of any such pleading and service thereof upon the plaintiff constitutes due notice of it to the parties. IN ST TRIAL P Rule 5(D).

ii. A copy of every such order shall be served upon the parties in such manner and form as the court directs. IN ST TRIAL P Rule 5(D).

c. *Service on parties in default for failure to appear.* No service need be made on parties in default for failure to appear, except that pleadings asserting new or additional claims for relief against them shall be served upon them in the manner provided by service of summons in IN ST TRIAL P Rule 4. IN ST TRIAL P Rule 5(A).

G. Hearings

1. *Hearing on motion.* Unless local conditions make it impracticable, each judge shall establish regular times and places, at intervals sufficiently frequent for the prompt dispatch of business, at which motions requiring notice and hearing may be heard and disposed of; but the judge at any time or place and on such notice, if any, as he considers reasonable may make order for the advancement, conduct, and hearing of actions. To expedite its business the court may direct the submission and determination of motions without oral hearing upon brief written statements of reasons in support and opposition, or direct or permit hearings by telephone conference call with all attorneys or other similar means of communication. IN ST TRIAL P Rule 73(A).

2. *Hearing on summary judgment.* The court may conduct a hearing on the motion. However, upon motion of any party made no later than ten (10) days after the response was filed or was due, the court shall conduct a hearing on the motion which shall be held not less than ten (10) days after the time for filing the response. IN ST TRIAL P Rule 56(C).

H. Forms

1. Motion for Summary Judgment Forms for Indiana

    a. Notice of motion for summary judgment. 11 INPRAC § 90.2.

    b. Motion for summary judgment. 11 INPRAC § 90.3.

    c. Motion for summary judgment; Another form. 11 INPRAC § 90.4.

    d. Motion for summary judgment; Another form. 11 INPRAC § 90.5.

    e. Designation of materials relied upon in support of motion for summary judgment. 11 INPRAC § 90.6.

    f. Designation of material issues of fact that preclude entry of summary judgment. 11 INPRAC § 90.7.

    g. Response to statement of material issues of fact that preclude entry of summary judgment. 11 INPRAC § 90.8.

    h. Order granting motion for summary judgment. 11 INPRAC § 90.9.

    i. Order denying motion for summary judgment. 11 INPRAC § 90.10.

    j. Motion for partial summary judgment as to liability. 11 INPRAC § 90.11.

    k. Order for partial summary judgment as to liability. 11 INPRAC § 90.12.

    l. Order denying summary judgment and specifying issues. 11 INPRAC § 90.15.

    m. Affidavit in support of motion for summary judgment. 11 INPRAC § 90.16.

    n. Submission of proposed findings of fact, conclusions of law and proposed summary judgment. 11 INPRAC § 90.17.

    o. Findings of fact and conclusions of law in support of motion for summary judgment. 11 INPRAC § 90.18.

    p. Motion for hearing on motion for summary judgment. 11 INPRAC § 90.27.

    q. Certificate of service; Personal service. 9 INPRAC § 5.7.

    r. Certificate of service; First class mail. 9 INPRAC § 5.8.

I. Checklist

(I) ❑ Matters to be considered by moving party

    (a) ❑ Required documents

        (1) ❑ Motion and notice

        (2) ❑ Supporting evidence

        (3) ❑ Proposed order

        (4) ❑ Certificate of service

    (b) ❑ Supplemental documents

        (1) ❑ Additional supporting evidence

        (2) ❑ Facsimile cover sheet

        (3) ❑ Request to schedule trial or hearing

        (4) ❑ Copies of unpublished opinions

    (c) ❑ Timing

        (1) ❑ A party seeking to recover upon a claim, counterclaim, or cross-claim or to obtain a declaratory judgment may, at any time after the expiration of twenty (20) days from the

commencement of the action or after service of a motion for summary judgment by the adverse party, move with or without supporting affidavits for a summary judgment in his favor upon all or any part thereof

(2) ❏ A party against whom a claim, counterclaim, or cross-claim is asserted or a declaratory judgment is sought may, at any time, move with or without supporting affidavits for a summary judgment in his favor as to all or any part thereof

(3) ❏ A written motion, other than one which may be heard ex parte, and notice of the hearing thereof shall be served not less than five (5) days before the time specified for the hearing, unless a different period is fixed by the Indiana Rules of Trial Procedure or by order of the court

(4) ❏ All pleadings and papers subsequent to the complaint which are required to be served upon a party shall be filed with the Court either before service or within a reasonable period of time thereafter

(II) ❏ Matters to be considered by the responding party

    (a) ❏ Required documents

        (1) ❏ Opposition

        (2) ❏ Opposing evidence

        (3) ❏ Certificate of service

    (b) ❏ Supplemental documents

        (1) ❏ Additional evidence

        (2) ❏ Alternative proposed order

        (3) ❏ Facsimile cover sheet

        (4) ❏ Request to schedule trial or hearing

        (5) ❏ Copies of unpublished opinions

    (c) ❏ Timing

        (1) ❏ An adverse party shall have thirty (30) days after service of the motion to serve a response and any opposing affidavits

        (2) ❏ Except as otherwise provided in IN ST TRIAL P Rule 59(D), opposing affidavits may be served not less than one (1) day before the hearing, unless the court permits them to be served at some other time

Motions, Oppositions and Replies
Motion for Sanctions

Document Last Updated October 2013

A. Applicable Rules

1. *State rules*

    a. Appearance. IN ST TRIAL P Rule 3.1.

    b. Process. IN ST TRIAL P Rule 4.

    c. Service and filing of pleadings and other papers. IN ST TRIAL P Rule 5.

    d. Time. IN ST TRIAL P Rule 6.

    e. Pleadings. IN ST TRIAL P Rule 7; IN ST TRIAL P Rule 8; IN ST TRIAL P Rule 9.2; IN ST TRIAL P Rule 10.

    f. Signing and verification of pleadings. IN ST TRIAL P Rule 11.

    g. Evidence. IN ST TRIAL P Rule 43.

    h.   Judgment on the evidence (directed verdict). IN ST TRIAL P Rule 50.

    i.   Findings by the court. IN ST TRIAL P Rule 52.

    j.   Summary judgment. IN ST TRIAL P Rule 56.

    k.   Motion to correct error. IN ST TRIAL P Rule 59.

    l.   Relief from judgment or order. IN ST TRIAL P Rule 60.

    m.   Hearing of motions. IN ST TRIAL P Rule 73.

    n.   Access to court records. IN ST ADMIN Rule 9.

    o.   Paper size. IN ST ADMIN Rule 11.

    p.   Facsimile transmission. IN ST ADMIN Rule 12.

    q.   Electronic filing and electronic service pilot projects. IN ST ADMIN Rule 16.

    r.   Sealing of certain records by court; Hearing; Notice. IN ST 5-14-3-5.5.

    s.   Privacy and confidentiality. IN ST 5-2-9-6; IN ST 5-14-3-4; IN ST 6-4.1-5-10; IN ST 6-4.1-12-12; IN ST 6-8.1-7-1; IN ST 11-13-1-8; IN ST 12-23-14-13; IN ST 16-39-3-10; IN ST 16-41-8-1; IN ST 22-4-19-6; IN ST 31-11-1-6; IN ST 31-19-5-23; IN ST 31-19-13-2; IN ST 31-19-19-1; IN ST 31-33-18-1; IN ST 31-39-1-1; IN ST 31-39-1-2; IN ST 33-23-16-16; IN ST 35-34-2-4; IN ST 35-38-1-13; IN ST 35-38-9-1; IN ST ADR Rule 2.11; IN ST ADR Rule 4.4; IN ST ADR Rule 5.6; IN ST JURY Rule 10.

    t.   General recovery rule. IN ST 34-52-1-1.

2.   *Local rules*

    a.   Court hours. IN ST HAMILTON ADMIN Rule 101.

    b.   Facsimile transmissions. IN ST HAMILTON ADMIN Rule 103.

    c.   Filing of pleadings and entry of appearances. IN ST HAMILTON TRIAL Rule 201.

    d.   Proposed orders. IN ST HAMILTON TRIAL Rule 202.

    e.   Briefs and memorandums. IN ST HAMILTON TRIAL Rule 203.

    f.   Special judges. IN ST HAMILTON TRIAL Rule 204.

    g.   Trial settings. IN ST HAMILTON TRIAL Rule 205.

    h.   Continuances. IN ST HAMILTON TRIAL Rule 206.

B. Timing

1.   *Motion for sanctions.* There are no specific time requirements for when a party may file a motion for sanctions.

    a.   *Filing.* All pleadings and papers subsequent to the complaint which are required to be served upon a party shall be filed with the Court either before service or within a reasonable period of time thereafter. IN ST TRIAL P Rule 5(E)(1).

2.   *Service.* A written motion, other than one which may be heard ex parte, and notice of the hearing thereof shall be served not less than five (5) days before the time specified for the hearing, unless a different period is fixed by the Indiana Rules of Trial Procedure or by order of the court. IN ST TRIAL P Rule 6(D).

    a.   *Of supporting affidavits.* When a motion is supported by affidavit, the affidavit shall be served with the motion. IN ST TRIAL P Rule 6(D).

3.   *Service of opposition.* Except as otherwise provided in IN ST TRIAL P Rule 59(D), opposing affidavits may be served not less than one (1) day before the hearing, unless the court permits them to be served at some other time. IN ST TRIAL P Rule 6(D).

4.   *Computation of time*

    a.   *Generally; Days excluded.* In computing any period of time prescribed or allowed by the Indiana Rules of Trial Procedure, by order of the court, or by any applicable statute, the day of the act, event,

or default from which the designated period of time begins to run shall not be included. The last day of the period so computed is to be included unless it is:

    i.   A Saturday,

    ii. A Sunday,

    iii. A legal holiday as defined by state statute, or

    iv. A day the office in which the act is to be done is closed during regular business hours. IN ST TRIAL P Rule 6(A).

b. *Short periods.* In any event, the period runs until the end of the next day that is not a Saturday, a Sunday, a legal holiday, or a day on which the office is closed. When the period of time allowed is less than seven (7) days, intermediate Saturdays, Sundays, legal holidays, and days on which the office is closed shall be excluded from the computations. IN ST TRIAL P Rule 6(A).

c. *Additional time after service by United States mail.* Whenever a party has the right or is required to do some act or take some proceedings within a prescribed period after the service of a notice or other paper upon him and the notice or paper is served upon him by United States mail, three (3) days shall be added to the prescribed period. IN ST TRIAL P Rule 6(E).

d. *Enlargement of time.* When an act is required or allowed to be done at or within a specific time by the Indiana Rules of Trial Procedure, the court may at any time for cause shown:

    i.   Order the period enlarged, with or without motion or notice, if request therefor is made before the expiration of the period originally prescribed or extended by a previous order; or

    ii. Upon motion made after the expiration of the specific period, permit the act to be done where the failure to act was the result of excusable neglect; but, the court may not extend the time for taking any action for judgment on the evidence under IN ST TRIAL P Rule 50(A), amendment of findings and judgment under IN ST TRIAL P Rule 52(B), to correct errors under IN ST TRIAL P Rule 59(C), statement in opposition to motion to correct error under IN ST TRIAL P Rule 59(E), or to obtain relief from final judgment under IN ST TRIAL P Rule 60(B), except to the extent and under the conditions stated in those rules. IN ST TRIAL P Rule 6(B).

    iii. For information on obtaining a continuance, refer to IN ST HAMILTON TRIAL Rule 206.

C. General Requirements

1. *Motions, generally.* Unless made during a hearing or trial, or otherwise ordered by the court, an application to the court for an order shall be made by written motion. The motion shall state the grounds therefor and the relief or order sought. IN ST TRIAL P Rule 7(B).

  a. *Motions as distinct from pleadings.* Motions and responses to motions are not pleadings, and allegations contained in a motion are not admissions of a party. 22B INPRAC 7:2; Wachstetter v. County Properties, LLC, 832 N.E.2d 574 (Ind.Ct.App. 2005); Scott County Family YMCA, Inc. v. Hobbs, 817 N.E.2d 603 (Ind.Ct.App. 2004).

  b. *Unopposed motions generally granted.* It is common for a trial court to grant procedural motions, such as motions for enlargement of time, discovery motions, or motions for continuance, unless an objection is filed. 21 INPRAC § 13.8.

2. *Motion for sanctions*

  a. *Signature and certification.* Every pleading or motion of a party represented by an attorney shall be signed by at least one (1) attorney of record in his individual name, whose address, telephone number, and attorney number shall be stated, except that this provision shall not apply to pleadings and motions made and transcribed at the trial or a hearing before the judge and received by him in such form. A party who is not represented by an attorney shall sign his pleading and state his address. IN ST TRIAL P Rule 11(A).

    i. Refer to the General Requirements section of this document for information on sanctions.

  b. *Frivolous claims.* A claim or defense is "frivolous, unreasonable or groundless" if it has been asserted primarily for the purpose of harassment, if the attorney is unable to make a good faith and rational argument on the merits of the action, or if the lawyer is unable to support the action by good faith and a rational argument for extension, modification, or reversal of existing law. 9 INPRAC § 4.3; Garage Doors of Indianapolis, Inc. v. Morton, 682 N.E.2d 1296 (Ind.Ct.App. 1997).

    i. *Bad faith pleading.* For information on sanctions for bad faith pleading, refer to IN ST 34-52-1-1.

c. *Factors for determining reasonableness.* Five factors are relevant to determine whether a litigant's conduct is "unreasonable":

    i. The amount of time the attorney had to investigate facts, research the law and prepare documents;

    ii. The extent to which the attorney had to rely upon his client for the factual foundation;

    iii. The complexity of the facts and legal issues;

    iv. The ability to conduct a pre-filing investigation; and

    v. The plausibility of the arguments advanced by a party, including good faith efforts to extend or modify the law. 9 INPRAC § 4.3; General Collections, Inc. v. Decker, 545 N.E.2d 18 (Ind.Ct.App. 1989).

d. *Determination of sanction.* The determination of a reasonable attorney fee requires the consideration of all relevant matters including but not limited to the attorney's experience and reputation, the nature of the employment, and the responsibility involved and the results obtained. A contingency fee agreement should not be used as the basis for determining a reasonable fee to be paid by a nonparty to that agreement. 9 INPRAC § 4.3; Mason v. Mason, 561 N.E.2d 809 (Ind.Ct.App. 1990).

D. Documents

1. *Required documents*

a. *Motion and notice.* The requirement of notice is satisfied by service of the motion. IN ST TRIAL P Rule 7(B). Refer to the General Requirements section of this document for information on the content of a motion for sanctions.

b. *Proposed order.* Unless local practice provides differently, a party should submit a proposed order with its written motion to be signed by the judge once the motion has been granted. 21 INPRAC § 13.8; IN ST HAMILTON ADMIN Rule 103(103.10)(b). Each Motion, Petition or other request for relief shall be accompanied by a proposed order. IN ST HAMILTON TRIAL Rule 202(202.10).

    i. All proposed orders submitted by counsel pursuant to IN ST HAMILTON TRIAL Rule 202 shall meet the following requirements: (1) contain a complete distribution list of all attorneys and pro se litigants with full addresses; (2) stamped envelopes appropriately addressed for each attorney of record and/or pro se litigant on the distribution list. IN ST HAMILTON TRIAL Rule 202(202.30).

c. *Certificate of service.* An attorney or unrepresented party tendering a document to the Clerk for filing shall certify that service has been made, list the parties served, and specify the date and means of service. The certificate of service shall be placed at the end of the document and shall not be separately filed. The separate filing of a certificate of service, however, shall not be grounds for rejecting a document for filing. The Clerk may permit documents to be filed without a certificate of service but shall require prompt filing of a separate certificate of service. IN ST TRIAL P Rule 5(C).

    i. All pleadings filed with the Court which require a certificate of service shall specifically name the individual party or attorney on whom service has been made, the address, the manner in which service was made and the date when service was made. IN ST HAMILTON TRIAL Rule 201(201.60).

2. *Supplemental documents*

a. *Supporting evidence.* When a motion is based on facts not appearing of record the court may hear the matter on affidavits presented by the respective parties, but the court may direct that the matter be heard wholly or partly on oral testimony or depositions. IN ST TRIAL P Rule 43(B).

b. *Facsimile cover sheet.* Any document sent to the Clerk of the Circuit Court by electronic facsimile transmission shall be accompanied by a cover sheet which states the title of the document, case number, number of pages, identity and voice telephone number of the sending party and instructions for filing. The cover sheet shall contain the signature of the attorney or party, pro se, authorizing the filing. IN ST ADMIN Rule 12(D); IN ST HAMILTON ADMIN Rule 103(103.10)(a).

c. *Request to schedule hearing.* All requests to schedule trials and hearings shall be in writing and shall contain the following information:

   i. Type of trial or hearing (i.e., jury trial, court trial, final hearing in dissolution, etc.). IN ST HAMILTON TRIAL Rule 205(205.10).

   ii. A good-faith estimate of the total court time needed for the trial or hearing. IN ST HAMILTON TRIAL Rule 205(205.10).

   iii. Each request under IN ST HAMILTON TRIAL Rule 205(205.10) shall be accompanied by a proposed written order with appropriate blanks for date and time and shall further include reference to those items set forth in IN ST HAMILTON TRIAL Rule 205(205.10)(a) and IN ST HAMILTON TRIAL Rule 205(205.10)(b). IN ST HAMILTON TRIAL Rule 205(205.20).

d. *Copies of unpublished opinions.* Authorities relied upon which are not cited in the Northeastern Reporter system shall be attached to counsel's brief. If the authority is cited for the first time in oral argument, a copy of the authority may be provided to the Court at the time of the argument. Sufficient copies shall be available to provide counsel for each party with a copy. IN ST HAMILTON TRIAL Rule 203(203.10).

E. Format

1. *Form of motions.* The rules applicable to captions, and the signing and form of pleadings (IN ST TRIAL P Rule 8 through IN ST TRIAL P Rule 11), apply to all motions and other papers provided under the Indiana Rules of Trial Procedure. 22B INPRAC 7:2.

2. *Form of pleadings*

a. *Caption; Names of parties.* Every pleading shall contain a caption setting forth the name of the court, the title of the action, the file number, and a designation as in IN ST TRIAL P Rule 7(A). In the complaint the title of the action shall include the names of all the parties, but in other pleadings it is sufficient to state the name of the first party on each side with an appropriate indication of other parties. IN ST TRIAL P Rule 10(A).

b. *Paragraphs; Separate statements.* All averments of a claim or defense shall be made in numbered paragraphs, the contents of each of which shall be limited as far as practicable to a statement of a single set of circumstances, and a paragraph may be referred to by number in all succeeding pleadings. Each claim founded upon a separate transaction or occurrence and each defense other than denials may be stated in a separate count or defense whenever a separation facilitates the clear presentation of the matters set forth. IN ST TRIAL P Rule 10(B).

c. *Adoption by reference; Exhibits.* Statements in a pleading may be adopted by reference in a different part of the same pleading or in another pleading or in any motion. A copy of any written instrument which is an exhibit to a pleading is a part thereof for all purposes. IN ST TRIAL P Rule 10(C).

d. *Facsimile page limit.* Courts authorize the Hamilton County Clerk of Courts to accept pleadings, motions and other papers by electronic facsimile transmission for filing in any case pending before the Courts, subject to the requirement that The transmission may not exceed ten (10) pages in length including the cover sheet and proposed CCS entry. IN ST HAMILTON ADMIN Rule 103(103.10)(c).

e. *Emergency facsimile filings.* If the filing requires the immediate attention of the Judge, it shall so indicate in bold letters in an accompanying transmittal memorandum. IN ST HAMILTON ADMIN Rule 103(103.10)(f).

f. *Special judge heading.* After a special judge is selected, the attorneys or pro se litigants shall add to the caption of all pleadings to the right of the case title the following: "BEFORE SPECIAL JUDGE _____." IN ST HAMILTON TRIAL Rule 204(204.10).

g. *Format rules strictly enforced.* All filings shall be in compliance with the Indiana Rules of Trial Procedure. If the documents received are not in proper form, such deficiencies will not be corrected by court personnel. IN ST HAMILTON TRIAL Rule 201(201.70). The Court shall not be required to act on any Motion, Petition or other request for relief unless filed in conformity with the Hamilton County Local Trial and Administrative rules. IN ST HAMILTON TRIAL Rule 202(202.20).

3. *Size of papers for filing.* Effective January 1, 1992, all pleadings, copies, motions and documents filed with any trial court or appellate level court, typed or printed, with the exception of exhibits and existing wills, shall be prepared on eight and one-half by eleven inch (8 1/2" x 11") size paper. IN ST ADMIN Rule 11.

    a. *Form.* All documents filed in any Hamilton County Court, with the exception of exhibits and existing wills, shall be prepared on paper measuring eight and one-half by eleven inches (8 1/2" x 11"). IN ST HAMILTON TRIAL Rule 201(201.20).

4. *Signature requirements*

    a. *Signature of attorney.* Every pleading or motion of a party represented by an attorney shall be signed by at least one (1) attorney of record in his individual name, whose address, telephone number, and attorney number shall be stated, except that this provision shall not apply to pleadings and motions made and transcribed at the trial or a hearing before the judge and received by him in such form. IN ST TRIAL P Rule 11(A).

        i. The signature of an attorney constitutes a certificate by him that he has read the pleadings; that to the best of his knowledge, information, and belief, there is good ground to support it; and that it is not interposed for delay. IN ST TRIAL P Rule 11(A).

        ii. If a pleading or motion is not signed or is signed with intent to defeat the purpose of the rule, it may be stricken as sham and false and the action may proceed as though the pleading had not been served. IN ST TRIAL P Rule 11(A).

        iii. For a willful violation of IN ST TRIAL P Rule 11 an attorney may be subjected to appropriate disciplinary action. Similar action may be taken if scandalous or indecent matter is inserted. IN ST TRIAL P Rule 11(A).

    b. *Signature of unrepresented party.* A party who is not represented by an attorney shall sign his pleading and state his address. IN ST TRIAL P Rule 11(A).

    c. *Verification not generally required.* Except when specifically required by rule, pleadings or motions need not be verified or accompanied by affidavit. The rule in equity that the averments of an answer under oath must be overcome by the testimony of two (2) witnesses or of one (1) witness sustained by corroborating circumstances is abolished. IN ST TRIAL P Rule 11(A).

    d. *Verification by affirmation or representation.* When in connection with any civil or special statutory proceeding it is required that any pleading, motion, petition, supporting affidavit, or other document of any kind, be verified, or that an oath be taken, it shall be sufficient if the subscriber simply affirms the truth of the matter to be verified by an affirmation or representation. IN ST TRIAL P Rule 11(B). IN ST TRIAL P Rule 11(B) states that the affirmation or representation should be in substantially the following language: "I (we) affirm, under the penalties for perjury, that the foregoing representation(s) is (are) true. (Signed) _____."

        i. Any person who falsifies an affirmation or representation of fact shall be subject to the same penalties as are prescribed by law for the making of a false affidavit. IN ST TRIAL P Rule 11(B).

    e. *Verified pleadings, motions, and affidavits as evidence.* Pleadings, motions and affidavits accompanying or in support of such pleadings or motions when required to be verified or under oath shall be accepted as a representation that the signer had personal knowledge thereof or reasonable cause to believe the existence of the facts or matters stated or alleged therein; and, if otherwise competent or acceptable as evidence, may be admitted as evidence of the facts or matters stated or alleged therein when it is so provided in the Indiana Rules of Trial Procedure, by statute or other law, or to the extent the writing or signature expressly purports to be made upon the signer's personal knowledge. When such pleadings, motions and affidavits are verified or under oath they shall not require other or greater proof on the part of the adverse party than if not verified or not under oath unless expressly provided otherwise by the Indiana Rules of Trial Procedure, statute or other law. Affidavits upon motions for summary judgment under IN ST TRIAL P Rule 56 and in denial of execution under IN ST TRIAL P Rule 9.2 shall be made upon personal knowledge. IN ST TRIAL P Rule 11(C).

5. *Information excluded from public access.* Every document filed in a case shall separately identify information excluded from public access pursuant to IN ST ADMIN Rule 9(G)(1) as follows:

    a. Whole documents that are excluded from public access pursuant to IN ST ADMIN Rule 9(G)(1) shall be tendered on light green paper or have a light green coversheet attached to the document, marked "Not for Public Access" or "Confidential." IN ST TRIAL P Rule 5(G)(1).

    b. When only a portion of a document contains information excluded from public access pursuant to IN ST ADMIN Rule 9(G)(1), said information shall be omitted [or redacted] from the filed document, and set forth on a separate accompanying document on light green paper conspicuously marked "Not for Public Access" or "Confidential" and clearly designated [or identifying] the caption and number of the case and the document and location within the document to which the redacted material pertains. IN ST TRIAL P Rule 5(G)(2).

    c. With respect to documents filed in electronic format, the trial court, by local rule, may provide for compliance with IN ST TRIAL P Rule 5 in manner that separates and protects access to information excluded from public access. IN ST TRIAL P Rule 5(G)(3).

    d. IN ST TRIAL P Rule 5(G) does not apply to a record sealed by the court pursuant to IN ST 5-14-3-5.5 or otherwise, nor to records, documents, or information filed in cases to which public access is prohibited pursuant to IN ST ADMIN Rule 9(G). IN ST TRIAL P Rule 5(G)(4).

    e. The following information in case records is excluded from public access and is confidential:

        i. Information that is excluded from public access pursuant to federal law;

        ii. Information that is excluded from public access as declared confidential by Indiana statute or other court rule, including without limitation:

            •   All adoption records created after July 8, 1941, as declared confidential by IN ST 31-19-19-1, et seq., except those specifically declared open by IN ST 31-19-13-2(2);

            •   All records relating to chancroid, chlamydia, gonorrhea, hepatitis, human immunodeficiency virus (HIV), Lymphogranuloma venereum, syphilis, tuberculosis, as declared confidential by IN ST 16-41-8-1, et seq.;

            •   All records relating to child abuse as declared confidential by IN ST 31-33-18-1, et seq.;

            •   All records relating to drug tests as declared confidential by IN ST 5-14-3-4(a)(9);

            •   Records of grand jury proceedings as declared confidential by IN ST 35-34-2-4;

            •   Records of juvenile proceedings as declared confidential by IN ST 31-39-1-2, except those specifically open under statute;

            •   All paternity records created after July 1, 1941 as declared confidential by IN ST 31-14-11-15, IN ST 31-19-5-23, IN ST 31-39-1-1 and IN ST 31-39-1-2 [Editor's note: IN ST 31-14-11-15 was repealed effective May 9, 2013];

            •   All pre-sentence reports as declared confidential by IN ST 35-38-1-13;

            •   Written petitions to permit marriages without consent and orders directing the Clerk of Court to issue a marriage license to underage persons, as declared confidential by IN ST 31-11-1-6;

            •   Only those arrest warrants, search warrants, indictments and informations ordered confidential by the trial judge, prior to return of duly executed service as declared confidential by IN ST 5-14-3-4(b)(1);

            •   All medical, mental health, or tax records unless determined by law or regulation of any governmental custodian not to be confidential, released by the subject of such records, or declared by a court of competent jurisdiction to be essential to the resolution of litigation as declared confidential by IN ST 16-39-3-10, IN ST 6-4.1-5-10, IN ST 6-4.1-12-12, and IN ST 6-8.1-7-1;

- Personal information relating to jurors or prospective jurors, other than for the use of the parties and counsel, pursuant to IN ST JURY Rule 10;

- Information relating to protection from abuse orders, no-contact orders and workplace violence restraining orders as declared confidential by IN ST 5-2-9-6, et seq.;

- Mediation proceedings pursuant to IN ST ADR Rule 2.11, Mini-Trial proceedings pursuant to IN ST ADR Rule 4.4(C), and Summary Jury Trials pursuant to IN ST ADR Rule 5.6;

- Information in probation files pursuant to the Probation Standards promulgated by the Judicial Conference of Indiana pursuant to IN ST 11-13-1-8(b);

- Information deemed confidential pursuant to the Rules for Court Administered Alcohol and Drug Programs promulgated by the Judicial Conference of Indiana pursuant to IN ST 12-23-14-13;

- Information deemed confidential pursuant to the Problem-Solving Court Rules promulgated by the Judicial Conference of Indiana pursuant to IN ST 33-23-16-16;

- All records of the Department of workforce Development as declared confidential by IN ST 22-4-19-6;

- Information regarding interception of electronic communications that is sealed or deemed confidential as set forth in IN ST 35-33.5-2-1, et seq.

iii. Information excluded from public access by specific court order;

iv. Complete Social Security Numbers of living persons;

v. With the exception of names, information such as addresses, phone numbers, and dates of birth which explicitly identifies:

- Natural persons who are witnesses or victims (not including defendants) in criminal, domestic violence, stalking, sexual assault, juvenile, or civil protection order proceedings, provided that juveniles who are victims of sex crimes shall be identified by initials only;

- Places of residence of judicial officers, clerks and other employees of courts and clerks of court, unless the person or persons about whom the information pertains waives confidentiality;

vi. Complete account numbers of specific assets, loans, bank accounts, credit cards, and personal identification numbers (PINs);

vii. All orders of expungement entered in criminal or juvenile proceedings, orders to restrict access to criminal history information pursuant to IN ST 35-38-5-5.5 or IN ST 35-38-8-5 and records excluded from public access by such orders, and information related to infractions that is excluded from public access pursuant to IN ST 34-28-5-15 or IN ST 34-28-5-16 [Editor's note: IN ST 35-38-5-5.5, IN ST 35-38-8-5 and IN ST 34-28-5-16 were repealed effective July 1, 2013; for information on orders restricting access to criminal history, refer to IN ST 35-38-9-1, et seq.];

viii. All personal notes and e-mail, and deliberative material, of judges, jurors, court staff and judicial agencies, and information recorded in personal data assistants (PDA's) or organizers and personal calendars. IN ST ADMIN Rule 9(G)(1).

F. Filing and Service Requirements

1. *Filing requirements.* Except as otherwise provided in IN ST TRIAL P Rule 5(E)(2), all pleadings and papers subsequent to the complaint which are required to be served upon a party shall be filed with the Court either before service or within a reasonable period of time thereafter. IN ST TRIAL P Rule 5(E)(1).

  a. *Filing with the court defined.* The filing of pleadings, motions, and other papers with the court as required by the Indiana Rules of Trial Procedure shall be made by one of the following methods:

  i. Delivery to the clerk of the court;

  ii. Sending by electronic transmission under the procedure adopted pursuant to IN ST ADMIN Rule 12;

iii. Mailing to the clerk by registered, certified or express mail return receipt requested;

iv. Depositing with any third-party commercial carrier for delivery to the clerk within three (3) calendar days, cost prepaid, properly addressed;

v. If the court so permits, filing with the judge, in which event the judge shall note thereon the filing date and forthwith transmit them to the office of the clerk; or

vi. Electronic filing, as approved by the Division of State Court Administration pursuant to IN ST ADMIN Rule 16. IN ST TRIAL P Rule 5(F).

vii. Filing by registered or certified mail and by third-party commercial carrier shall be complete upon mailing or deposit. IN ST TRIAL P Rule 5(F).

b. *Facsimile filing.* As outlined in IN ST HAMILTON ADMIN Rule 103(103.10),facsimile filing is permitted in the Circuit and Superior Courts of Hamilton County. The Courts authorize the Hamilton County Clerk of Courts to accept pleadings, motions and other papers by electronic facsimile transmission for filing in any case pending before the Courts, subject to the requirements of IN ST HAMILTON ADMIN Rule 103(103.10). IN ST HAMILTON ADMIN Rule 103(103.10); IN ST HAMILTON TRIAL Rule 201(201.80).

i. *Generally.* In counties where a majority of judges of the courts of record, by posted local rule, have authorized electronic facsimile filing and designated a telephone number to receive such transmissions, pleadings, motions, and other papers may be sent to the Clerk of Circuit Court by electronic facsimile transmission for filing in any case, provided:

- Such matter does not exceed ten (10) pages, including the cover sheet;

- Such matter does not require the payment of fees other than the electronic facsimile transcription fee set forth in IN ST ADMIN Rule 12(E);

- The sending party creates at the time of transmission a machine generated log for such transmission; and

- The original document and the transmission log are maintained by the sending party for the duration of the litigation. IN ST ADMIN Rule 12(B); IN ST HAMILTON ADMIN Rule 103(103.10)(d).

- Legibility of documents and timeliness of filing is the responsibility of the sender. IN ST HAMILTON ADMIN Rule 103(103.10)(g).

- The Clerk shall accept electronic facsimile transmission filings only if received at the facsimile machine assigned by the Clerk. The telephone number designated to receive such transmission is available at IN ST HAMILTON ADMIN Rule 103(103.40). IN ST HAMILTON ADMIN Rule 103(103.40).

ii. *Time of filing.* During normal, posted business hours, the time of filing shall be the time the duplicate document is produced in the office of the Clerk of the Circuit Court. Duplicate documents received at all other times shall be filed as of the next normal business day. IN ST ADMIN Rule 12(C).

- If the receiving fax machine endorses its own time and date stamp upon the transmitted documents and the receiving machine produces a delivery receipt which is electronically created and transmitted to the sending party, the time of filing shall be the date and time recorded on the transmitted document by the receiving fax machine. IN ST ADMIN Rule 12(C).

- Electronic facsimile transmissions will be accepted for filing only during the regular business hours as set forth in IN ST HAMILTON ADMIN Rule 101. Transmissions received by the Hamilton County Clerk after close of business shall be filed effective the next regular business day. IN ST HAMILTON ADMIN Rule 103(103.30).

iii. *Filing fee.* The electronic facsimile transmission will not be accepted for filing if its filing requires the payment of any fee other than the electronic facsimile transcription fee set forth in

IN ST HAMILTON ADMIN Rule 103(103.20). IN ST HAMILTON ADMIN Rule 103(103.10)(e).

- Pursuant to Ordinance adopted by the Hamilton County Board of Commissioners, the Clerk shall collect an electronic facsimile transcription fee of One Dollar ($1.00) per page, to a maximum of Ten Dollars ($10.00) per transmission, for each electronic facsimile transmission accepted for filing with the Hamilton County Circuit and Superior Courts. IN ST HAMILTON ADMIN Rule 103(103.20).

- The fee shall be assessed against the sending party and shall be paid upon receipt of invoice by that party and at the latest within thirty (30) days of the transmission. In the event the fee is not paid by the sending party within the time limits provided, the court may issue a show-cause order or enter a judgment in the matter. The Clerk may refuse an electronic facsimile transmission from any attorney or pro se litigant who has failed to pay these fees within thirty (30) days. IN ST HAMILTON ADMIN Rule 103(103.20).

    iv. *No direct filing with court.* A party shall not send pleadings, motions and other papers by electronic facsimile transmission for filing directly to any Court without that Court's prior approval to do so. IN ST HAMILTON ADMIN Rule 103(103.50).

  c. *Filing with special judge.* After a special judge has qualified, a copy of each pleading and Chronological Case Summary entries filed with the Court shall be mailed or delivered to the office of that Special judge by the counsel or pro se litigant with service indicated on the certificate of service. IN ST HAMILTON TRIAL Rule 204(204.20).

  d. *Proof of filing.* Any party filing any paper by any method other than personal delivery to the clerk shall retain proof of filing. IN ST TRIAL P Rule 5(F).

2. *Service requirements.* Unless otherwise provided by the Indiana Rules of Trial Procedure or an order of the court, each party and special judge, if any, shall be served with: (1) every order required by its terms to be served; (2) every pleading subsequent to the original complaint; (3) every written motion except one which may be heard ex parte; (4) every brief submitted to the trial court; (5) every paper relating to discovery required to be served upon a party; and (6) every written notice, appearance, demand, offer of judgment, designation of record on appeal, or similar paper. IN ST TRIAL P Rule 5(A).

  a. *Methods of service*

    i. *Personal service.* Whenever a party is represented by an attorney of record, service shall be made upon such attorney unless service upon the party himself is ordered by the court. Service upon the attorney or party shall be made by delivering or mailing a copy of the papers to the last known address or where an attorney or party has consented to service by fax or e-mail, as provided in IN ST TRIAL P Rule 3.1(A)(4), by faxing or e-mailing a copy of the documents to the fax number or e-mail address set out in the appearance form or correction as required by IN ST TRIAL P Rule 3.1(E). IN ST TRIAL P Rule 5(B). Delivery of a copy within IN ST TRIAL P Rule 5 means:

- Offering or tendering it to the attorney or party and stating the nature of the papers being served. Refusal to accept an offered or tendered document is a waiver of any objection to the sufficiency or adequacy of service of that document;

- Leaving it at his office with a clerk or other person in charge thereof, or if there is no one in charge, leaving it in a conspicuous place therein; or

- If the office is closed, by leaving it at his dwelling house or usual place of abode with some person of suitable age and discretion then residing therein; or,

- Leaving it at some other suitable place, selected by the attorney upon whom service is being made, pursuant to duly promulgated local rule. IN ST TRIAL P Rule 5(B)(1).

    ii. *Service by mail.* If service is made by mail, the papers shall be deposited in the United States mail addressed to the person on whom they are being served, with postage prepaid. Service shall be deemed complete upon mailing. Proof of service of all papers permitted to be mailed may be made by written acknowledgment of service, by affidavit of the person who mailed the papers, or by certificate of an attorney. It shall be the duty of attorneys when entering their appearance in a cause or when filing pleadings or papers therein, to have noted in the Chronological Case Summary or said pleadings or papers so filed the address and telephone number of their office. Service by delivery or by mail at such address shall be deemed sufficient and complete. IN ST TRIAL P Rule 5(B)(2).

iii. *Service by fax or e-mail.* A party who has consented to service by fax or e-mail may be served as follows:

- Service by e-mail shall be made by attaching the document being served in .pdf format. Discovery documents must also be served in accordance with IN ST TRIAL P Rule 26(A). IN ST TRIAL P Rule 5(B)(3)(a).

- Service by fax shall be deemed complete upon generation of a transmission record indicating the successful transmission of the entire document, except as provided in IN ST TRIAL P Rule 5(B)(3)(d). IN ST TRIAL P Rule 5(B)(3)(b).

- Service by e-mail shall be deemed complete upon transmission, except as provided in IN ST TRIAL P Rule 5(B)(3)(d). IN ST TRIAL P Rule 5(B)(3)(c).

- Service by fax or e-mail that occurs on a Saturday, Sunday, legal holiday, or day the court or agency in which the matter is pending is closed or after 5:00 PM local time of the recipient shall be deemed complete the next day that is not a Saturday, Sunday, legal holiday, or day that the court or agency in which the matter is pending is not closed. IN ST TRIAL P Rule 5(B)(3)(d).

iv. *Mail box service.* Pursuant to IN ST TRIAL P Rule 5(B)(1)(d), the Circuit and Superior Courts of Hamilton County hereby designate the "mail boxes" located in the Clerk's order book office for service of pleadings upon attorneys who have such boxes. IN ST HAMILTON TRIAL Rule 201(201.50).

b. *Serving numerous defendants.* In any action in which there are unusually large numbers of defendants, the court, upon motion or of its own initiative, may order:

i. That service of the pleadings of the defendants and replies thereto need not be made as between the defendants;

- That any cross-claim, counterclaim, or matter constituting an avoidance or affirmative defense contained therein shall be deemed to be denied or avoided by all other parties; and

- That the filing of any such pleading and service thereof upon the plaintiff constitutes due notice of it to the parties. IN ST TRIAL P Rule 5(D).

ii. A copy of every such order shall be served upon the parties in such manner and form as the court directs. IN ST TRIAL P Rule 5(D).

c. *Service on parties in default for failure to appear.* No service need be made on parties in default for failure to appear, except that pleadings asserting new or additional claims for relief against them shall be served upon them in the manner provided by service of summons in IN ST TRIAL P Rule 4. IN ST TRIAL P Rule 5(A).

G. Hearings

1. *Hearing on motion.* Unless local conditions make it impracticable, each judge shall establish regular times and places, at intervals sufficiently frequent for the prompt dispatch of business, at which motions requiring notice and hearing may be heard and disposed of; but the judge at any time or place and on such notice, if any, as he considers reasonable may make order for the advancement, conduct, and hearing of actions. To expedite its business the court may direct the submission and determination of motions without oral hearing upon brief written statements of reasons in support and opposition, or direct or permit hearings by telephone conference call with all attorneys or other similar means of communication. IN ST TRIAL P Rule 73(A).

H. Forms

1. Motion for Sanctions Forms for Indiana

a. Signature; By party. 9 INPRAC § 4.5.

    b.   Signature; Attorney. 9 INPRAC § 4.6.

    c.   Signature; Attorney; Another form. 9 INPRAC § 4.7.

    d.   Signature; Attorney; Another form. 9 INPRAC § 4.8.

    e.   Motion to impose sanctions on defendant; Improper answer. 9 INPRAC § 4.20.

    f.   Certificate of service; Personal service. 9 INPRAC § 5.7.

    g.   Certificate of service; First class mail. 9 INPRAC § 5.8.

I. Checklist

(I)   ❑ Matters to be considered by moving party

    (a) ❑ Required documents

        (1) ❑ Motion and notice

        (2) ❑ Proposed order

        (3) ❑ Certificate of service

    (b) ❑ Supplemental documents

        (1) ❑ Supporting evidence

        (2) ❑ Facsimile cover sheet

        (3) ❑ Request to schedule trial or hearing

        (4) ❑ Copies of unpublished opinions

    (c) ❑ Timing

        (1) ❑ There are no specific time requirements for when a party may file a motion for sanctions

        (2) ❑ A written motion, other than one which may be heard ex parte, and notice of the hearing thereof shall be served not less than five (5) days before the time specified for the hearing, unless a different period is fixed by the Indiana Rules of Trial Procedure or by order of the court

        (3) ❑ All pleadings and papers subsequent to the complaint which are required to be served upon a party shall be filed with the Court either before service or within a reasonable period of time thereafter

(II) ❑ Matters to be considered by the responding party

    (a) ❑ Required documents

        (1) ❑ Opposition

        (2) ❑ Certificate of service

    (b) ❑ Supplemental documents

        (1) ❑ Supporting evidence

        (2) ❑ Alternative proposed order

        (3) ❑ Facsimile cover sheet

        (4) ❑ Request to schedule trial or hearing

        (5) ❑ Copies of unpublished opinions

    (c) ❑ Timing

        (1) ❑ Opposing affidavits may be served not less than one (1) day before the hearing

Motions, Oppositions and Replies
Motion to Compel Discovery

Document Last Updated October 2013

A. Applicable Rules

1. *State rules*

   a. Appearance. IN ST TRIAL P Rule 3.1.

   b. Summons. IN ST TRIAL P Rule 4.

   c. Service and filing of pleadings and other papers. IN ST TRIAL P Rule 5.

   d. Time. IN ST TRIAL P Rule 6.

   e. Pleadings. IN ST TRIAL P Rule 7; IN ST TRIAL P Rule 8; IN ST TRIAL P Rule 9.2; IN ST TRIAL P Rule 10.

   f. Signing and verification of pleadings. IN ST TRIAL P Rule 11.

   g. General provisions regarding discovery. IN ST TRIAL P Rule 26.

   h. Methods of discovery. IN ST TRIAL P Rule 27; IN ST TRIAL P Rule 30; IN ST TRIAL P Rule 31; IN ST TRIAL P Rule 33; IN ST TRIAL P Rule 34; IN ST TRIAL P Rule 36.

   i. Failure to make or cooperate in discovery; Sanctions. IN ST TRIAL P Rule 37.

   j. Evidence. IN ST TRIAL P Rule 43.

   k. Judgment on the evidence (directed verdict). IN ST TRIAL P Rule 50.

   l. Findings by the court. IN ST TRIAL P Rule 52.

   m. Summary judgment. IN ST TRIAL P Rule 56.

   n. Motion to correct error. IN ST TRIAL P Rule 59.

   o. Relief from judgment or order. IN ST TRIAL P Rule 60.

   p. Hearing of motions. IN ST TRIAL P Rule 73.

   q. Access to court records. IN ST ADMIN Rule 9.

   r. Paper size. IN ST ADMIN Rule 11.

   s. Facsimile transmission. IN ST ADMIN Rule 12.

   t. Electronic filing and electronic service pilot projects. IN ST ADMIN Rule 16.

   u. Sealing of certain records by court; Hearing; Notice. IN ST 5-14-3-5.5.

   v. Privacy and confidentiality. IN ST 5-2-9-6; IN ST 5-14-3-4; IN ST 6-4.1-5-10; IN ST 6-4.1-12-12; IN ST 6-8.1-7-1; IN ST 11-13-1-8; IN ST 12-23-14-13; IN ST 16-39-3-10; IN ST 16-41-8-1; IN ST 22-4-19-6; IN ST 31-11-1-6; IN ST 31-19-5-23; IN ST 31-19-13-2; IN ST 31-19-19-1; IN ST 31-33-18-1; IN ST 31-39-1-1; IN ST 31-39-1-2; IN ST 33-23-16-16; IN ST 35-34-2-4; IN ST 35-38-1-13; IN ST 35-38-9-1; IN ST ADR Rule 2.11; IN ST ADR Rule 4.4; IN ST ADR Rule 5.6; IN ST JURY Rule 10.

2. *Local rules*

   a. Court hours. IN ST HAMILTON ADMIN Rule 101.

   b. Facsimile transmissions. IN ST HAMILTON ADMIN Rule 103.

   c. Filing of pleadings and entry of appearances. IN ST HAMILTON TRIAL Rule 201.

   d. Proposed orders. IN ST HAMILTON TRIAL Rule 202.

   e. Briefs and memorandums. IN ST HAMILTON TRIAL Rule 203.

   f. Special judges. IN ST HAMILTON TRIAL Rule 204.

   g. Trial settings. IN ST HAMILTON TRIAL Rule 205.

    h.   Continuances. IN ST HAMILTON TRIAL Rule 206.

B. Timing

  1. *Motion to compel discovery.* There are no specific timing requirements for filing a motion to compel discovery. The moving party must provide reasonable notice of his intention to file a motion to compel with the other litigants and all affected persons. 10 INPRAC § 58.51.

    a.   *Filing.* All pleadings and papers subsequent to the complaint which are required to be served upon a party shall be filed with the Court either before service or within a reasonable period of time thereafter. IN ST TRIAL P Rule 5(E)(1).

  2. *Service.* A written motion, other than one which may be heard ex parte, and notice of the hearing thereof shall be served not less than five (5) days before the time specified for the hearing, unless a different period is fixed by the Indiana Rules of Trial Procedure or by order of the court. IN ST TRIAL P Rule 6(D).

    a.   *Of supporting affidavits.* When a motion is supported by affidavit, the affidavit shall be served with the motion. IN ST TRIAL P Rule 6(D).

  3. *Service of opposition.* Except as otherwise provided in IN ST TRIAL P Rule 59(D), opposing affidavits may be served not less than one (1) day before the hearing, unless the court permits them to be served at some other time. IN ST TRIAL P Rule 6(D).

  4. *Computation of time*

    a.   *Generally; Days excluded.* In computing any period of time prescribed or allowed by the Indiana Rules of Trial Procedure, by order of the court, or by any applicable statute, the day of the act, event, or default from which the designated period of time begins to run shall not be included. The last day of the period so computed is to be included unless it is:

      i.   A Saturday,

      ii.   A Sunday,

      iii.   A legal holiday as defined by state statute, or

      iv.   A day the office in which the act is to be done is closed during regular business hours. IN ST TRIAL P Rule 6(A).

    b.   *Short periods.* In any event, the period runs until the end of the next day that is not a Saturday, a Sunday, a legal holiday, or a day on which the office is closed. When the period of time allowed is less than seven (7) days, intermediate Saturdays, Sundays, legal holidays, and days on which the office is closed shall be excluded from the computations. IN ST TRIAL P Rule 6(A).

    c.   *Additional time after service by United States mail.* Whenever a party has the right or is required to do some act or take some proceedings within a prescribed period after the service of a notice or other paper upon him and the notice or paper is served upon him by United States mail, three (3) days shall be added to the prescribed period. IN ST TRIAL P Rule 6(E).

    d.   *Enlargement of time.* When an act is required or allowed to be done at or within a specific time by the Indiana Rules of Trial Procedure, the court may at any time for cause shown:

      i.   Order the period enlarged, with or without motion or notice, if request therefor is made before the expiration of the period originally prescribed or extended by a previous order; or

      ii.   Upon motion made after the expiration of the specific period, permit the act to be done where the failure to act was the result of excusable neglect; but, the court may not extend the time for taking any action for judgment on the evidence under IN ST TRIAL P Rule 50(A), amendment of findings and judgment under IN ST TRIAL P Rule 52(B), to correct errors under IN ST TRIAL P Rule 59(C), statement in opposition to motion to correct error under IN ST TRIAL P Rule 59(E), or to obtain relief from final judgment under IN ST TRIAL P Rule 60(B), except to the extent and under the conditions stated in those rules. IN ST TRIAL P Rule 6(B).

      iii.   For information on obtaining a continuance, refer to IN ST HAMILTON TRIAL Rule 206.

C. General Requirements

  1. *Motions, generally.* Unless made during a hearing or trial, or otherwise ordered by the court, an

application to the court for an order shall be made by written motion. The motion shall state the grounds therefor and the relief or order sought. IN ST TRIAL P Rule 7(B).

a. *Motions as distinct from pleadings.* Motions and responses to motions are not pleadings, and allegations contained in a motion are not admissions of a party. 22B INPRAC 7:2; Wachstetter v. County Properties, LLC, 832 N.E.2d 574 (Ind.Ct.App. 2005); Scott County Family YMCA, Inc. v. Hobbs, 817 N.E.2d 603 (Ind.Ct.App. 2004).

b. *Unopposed motions generally granted.* It is common for a trial court to grant procedural motions, such as motions for enlargement of time, discovery motions, or motions for continuance, unless an objection is filed. 21 INPRAC § 13.8.

2. *Motion to compel discovery.* Motions under IN ST TRIAL P Rule 37 are intended secure compliance with discovery requests and orders, ensure that one party will not profit from a failure to comply, and provide a general deterrence to discovery abuses. 22B INPRAC 37:1; Fifth Third Bank v. PNC Bank, 885 N.E.2d 52 (Ind.Ct.App. 2008).

a. *Appropriate court.* An application for an order to a party may be made to the court in which the action is pending, or alternately, on matters relating to a deposition or an order under IN ST TRIAL P Rule 34, to the court in the county where the deposition is being taken or where compliance is to be made under IN ST TRIAL P Rule 34. An application for an order to a deponent who is not a party shall be made to the court in the county where the deposition is being taken. IN ST TRIAL P Rule 37(A)(1).

b. *Motion.* If a party refuses to allow inspection under IN ST TRIAL P Rule 9.2(E), or if a deponent fails to answer a question propounded or submitted under IN ST TRIAL P Rule 30 or IN ST TRIAL P Rule 31, or an organization, including without limitation a governmental organization or a partnership, fails to make designation under IN ST TRIAL P Rule 30(B)(6) or IN ST TRIAL P Rule 31(A), or a party fails to answer an interrogatory submitted under IN ST TRIAL P Rule 33, or if a party or witness or other person, in response to a request submitted under IN ST TRIAL P Rule 34, fails to respond that inspection will be permitted as requested or fails to permit inspection as requested, the discovering party may move for an order compelling an answer, or a designation, or an order compelling inspection in accordance with the request. When taking a deposition on oral examination, the proponent of the question may complete or adjourn the examination before he applies for an order. IN ST TRIAL P Rule 37(A)(2).

   i. *Evasive or incomplete answer.* For purposes of IN ST TRIAL P Rule 37(A) an evasive or incomplete answer is to be treated as a failure to answer. IN ST TRIAL P Rule 37(A)(3).

c. *Content of motion.* A motion to compel discovery should state the history of the discovery dispute, evidence that the opposing party was properly served with the discovery request, the position taken by the parties, the grounds for the motion with supporting authority, and the relief sought. In addition, the motion should include a statement demonstrating compliance with the informal dispute resolution requirements of IN ST TRIAL P Rule 26(F). 10 INPRAC § 58.51.

d. *Request for relief.* A motion to compel, filed under IN ST TRIAL P Rule 37, may request the following relief:

   i. An order compelling a discovery response;

   ii. Sanctions under IN ST TRIAL P Rule 37(D) (this rule incorporates by reference the sanctions available to a trial court to punish a party who has refused to comply with a discovery order); and

   iii. An award of attorney fees and expenses incurred to obtain an order compelling discovery. 10 INPRAC § 58.51.

e. *Effect of granting or denial of the motion*

   i. *Denied in whole or in part.* If the court denies the motion in whole or in part, it may make such protective order as it would have been empowered to make on a motion made pursuant to IN ST TRIAL P Rule 26(C). IN ST TRIAL P Rule 37(A)(2).

   ii. *Granted in part and denied in part.* If the motion is granted in part and denied in part, the court may apportion the reasonable expenses incurred in relation to the motion among the parties and persons in a just manner. IN ST TRIAL P Rule 37(A)(4).

    iii. *Motion denied.* If the motion is denied, the court shall, after opportunity for hearing, require the moving party or the attorney advising the motion or both of them to pay to the party or deponent who opposed the motion the reasonable expenses incurred in opposing the motion, including attorney's fees, unless the court finds that the making of the motion was substantially justified or that other circumstances make an award of expenses unjust. IN ST TRIAL P Rule 37(A)(4).

    iv. *Motion granted.* If the motion is granted, the court shall, after opportunity for hearing, require the party or deponent whose conduct necessitated the motion or the party or attorney advising such conduct or both of them to pay to the moving party the reasonable expenses incurred in obtaining the order, including attorney's fees, unless the court finds that the opposition to the motion was substantially justified or that other circumstances make an award of expenses unjust. IN ST TRIAL P Rule 37(A)(4). Refer to the Indiana KeyRules Motion for Discovery Sanctions document for more information.

  f. *Expenses; Burden on non-prevailing party.* The non-prevailing party has the burden of proving that the reimbursement of expenses should not be awarded. 10 INPRAC § 58.51.

3. *Opposition to motion to compel; Information not reasonably accessible.* On motion to compel discovery or for a protective order, the party from whom discovery is sought must show that the information is not reasonably accessible because of undue burden or cost. If that showing is made, the court may nonetheless order discovery from such sources if the requesting party shows good cause. The court may specify conditions for the discovery. IN ST TRIAL P Rule 26(C)(9).

D. Documents

1. *Required documents*

  a. *Motion and notice.* The requirement of notice is satisfied by service of the motion. IN ST TRIAL P Rule 7(B). Refer to the General Requirements section of this document for information on the content of a motion to compel discovery.

  b. *Disputed discovery.* In addition, the motion should attach a copy of the disputed discovery in accordance with the requirements of IN ST TRIAL P Rule 5(D). 10 INPRAC § 58.51.

  c. *Attorney certification.* Before any party files any motion or request to compel discovery pursuant to IN ST TRIAL P Rule 37, or any motion for protection from discovery pursuant to IN ST TRIAL P Rule 26(C), or any other discovery motion which seeks to enforce, modify, or limit discovery, that party shall:

    i. Make a reasonable effort to reach agreement with the opposing party concerning the matter which is the subject of the motion or request; and

    ii. Include in the motion or request a statement showing that the attorney making the motion or request has made a reasonable effort to reach agreement with the opposing attorney(s) concerning the matter(s) set forth in the motion or request. This statement shall recite, in addition, the date, time and place of this effort to reach agreement, whether in person or by phone, and the names of all parties and attorneys participating therein. If an attorney for any party advises the court in writing that an opposing attorney has refused or delayed meeting and discussing the issues covered in IN ST TRIAL P Rule 26(F), the court may take such action as is appropriate. IN ST TRIAL P Rule 26(F).

    iii. The court may deny a discovery motion filed by a party who has failed to comply with the requirements of IN ST TRIAL P Rule 26(F). IN ST TRIAL P Rule 26(F).

  d. *Proposed order.* Unless local practice provides differently, a party should submit a proposed order with its written motion to be signed by the judge once the motion has been granted. 21 INPRAC § 13.8; IN ST HAMILTON ADMIN Rule 103(103.10)(b). Each Motion, Petition or other request for relief shall be accompanied by a proposed order. IN ST HAMILTON TRIAL Rule 202(202.10).

    i. All proposed orders submitted by counsel pursuant to IN ST HAMILTON TRIAL Rule 202 shall meet the following requirements: (1) contain a complete distribution list of all attorneys

and pro se litigants with full addresses; (2) stamped envelopes appropriately addressed for each attorney of record and/or pro se litigant on the distribution list. IN ST HAMILTON TRIAL Rule 202(202.30).

e. *Certificate of service.* An attorney or unrepresented party tendering a document to the Clerk for filing shall certify that service has been made, list the parties served, and specify the date and means of service. The certificate of service shall be placed at the end of the document and shall not be separately filed. The separate filing of a certificate of service, however, shall not be grounds for rejecting a document for filing. The Clerk may permit documents to be filed without a certificate of service but shall require prompt filing of a separate certificate of service. IN ST TRIAL P Rule 5(C).

   i. All pleadings filed with the Court which require a certificate of service shall specifically name the individual party or attorney on whom service has been made, the address, the manner in which service was made and the date when service was made. IN ST HAMILTON TRIAL Rule 201(201.60).

2. *Supplemental documents*

   a. *Supporting evidence.* When a motion is based on facts not appearing of record the court may hear the matter on affidavits presented by the respective parties, but the court may direct that the matter be heard wholly or partly on oral testimony or depositions. IN ST TRIAL P Rule 43(B).

   b. *Facsimile cover sheet.* Any document sent to the Clerk of the Circuit Court by electronic facsimile transmission shall be accompanied by a cover sheet which states the title of the document, case number, number of pages, identity and voice telephone number of the sending party and instructions for filing. The cover sheet shall contain the signature of the attorney or party, pro se, authorizing the filing. IN ST ADMIN Rule 12(D); IN ST HAMILTON ADMIN Rule 103(103.10)(a).

   c. *Request to schedule hearing.* All requests to schedule trials and hearings shall be in writing and shall contain the following information:

      i. Type of trial or hearing (i.e., jury trial, court trial, final hearing in dissolution, etc.). IN ST HAMILTON TRIAL Rule 205(205.10).

      ii. A good-faith estimate of the total court time needed for the trial or hearing. IN ST HAMILTON TRIAL Rule 205(205.10).

      iii. Each request under IN ST HAMILTON TRIAL Rule 205(205.10) shall be accompanied by a proposed written order with appropriate blanks for date and time and shall further include reference to those items set forth in IN ST HAMILTON TRIAL Rule 205(205.10)(a) and IN ST HAMILTON TRIAL Rule 205(205.10)(b). IN ST HAMILTON TRIAL Rule 205(205.20).

   d. *Copies of unpublished opinions.* Authorities relied upon which are not cited in the Northeastern Reporter system shall be attached to counsel's brief. If the authority is cited for the first time in oral argument, a copy of the authority may be provided to the Court at the time of the argument. Sufficient copies shall be available to provide counsel for each party with a copy. IN ST HAMILTON TRIAL Rule 203(203.10).

E. Format

1. *Form of motions.* The rules applicable to captions, and the signing and form of pleadings (IN ST TRIAL P Rule 8 through IN ST TRIAL P Rule 11), apply to all motions and other papers provided under the Indiana Rules of Trial Procedure. 22B INPRAC 7:2.

2. *Form of pleadings*

   a. *Caption; Names of parties.* Every pleading shall contain a caption setting forth the name of the court, the title of the action, the file number, and a designation as in IN ST TRIAL P Rule 7(A). In the complaint the title of the action shall include the names of all the parties, but in other pleadings it is sufficient to state the name of the first party on each side with an appropriate indication of other parties. IN ST TRIAL P Rule 10(A).

   b. *Paragraphs; Separate statements.* All averments of a claim or defense shall be made in numbered paragraphs, the contents of each of which shall be limited as far as practicable to a statement of a single set of circumstances, and a paragraph may be referred to by number in all succeeding pleadings. Each claim founded upon a separate transaction or occurrence and each defense other than denials may be stated in a separate count or defense whenever a separation facilitates the clear presentation of the matters set forth. IN ST TRIAL P Rule 10(B).

c. *Adoption by reference; Exhibits.* Statements in a pleading may be adopted by reference in a different part of the same pleading or in another pleading or in any motion. A copy of any written instrument which is an exhibit to a pleading is a part thereof for all purposes. IN ST TRIAL P Rule 10(C).

d. *Facsimile page limit.* Courts authorize the Hamilton County Clerk of Courts to accept pleadings, motions and other papers by electronic facsimile transmission for filing in any case pending before the Courts, subject to the requirement that The transmission may not exceed ten (10) pages in length including the cover sheet and proposed CCS entry. IN ST HAMILTON ADMIN Rule 103(103.10)(c).

e. *Emergency facsimile filings.* If the filing requires the immediate attention of the Judge, it shall so indicate in bold letters in an accompanying transmittal memorandum. IN ST HAMILTON ADMIN Rule 103(103.10)(f).

f. *Special judge heading.* After a special judge is selected, the attorneys or pro se litigants shall add to the caption of all pleadings to the right of the case title the following: "BEFORE SPECIAL JUDGE _____." IN ST HAMILTON TRIAL Rule 204(204.10).

g. *Format rules strictly enforced.* All filings shall be in compliance with the Indiana Rules of Trial Procedure. If the documents received are not in proper form, such deficiencies will not be corrected by court personnel. IN ST HAMILTON TRIAL Rule 201(201.70). The Court shall not be required to act on any Motion, Petition or other request for relief unless filed in conformity with the Hamilton County Local Trial and Administrative rules. IN ST HAMILTON TRIAL Rule 202(202.20).

3. *Size of papers for filing.* Effective January 1, 1992, all pleadings, copies, motions and documents filed with any trial court or appellate level court, typed or printed, with the exception of exhibits and existing wills, shall be prepared on eight and one-half by eleven inch (8 1/2" x 11") size paper. IN ST ADMIN Rule 11.

a. *Form.* All documents filed in any Hamilton County Court, with the exception of exhibits and existing wills, shall be prepared on paper measuring eight and one-half by eleven inches (8 1/2" x 11"). IN ST HAMILTON TRIAL Rule 201(201.20).

4. *Signature requirements*

a. *Signature of attorney.* Every pleading or motion of a party represented by an attorney shall be signed by at least one (1) attorney of record in his individual name, whose address, telephone number, and attorney number shall be stated, except that this provision shall not apply to pleadings and motions made and transcribed at the trial or a hearing before the judge and received by him in such form. IN ST TRIAL P Rule 11(A).

    i. The signature of an attorney constitutes a certificate by him that he has read the pleadings; that to the best of his knowledge, information, and belief, there is good ground to support it; and that it is not interposed for delay. IN ST TRIAL P Rule 11(A).

    ii. If a pleading or motion is not signed or is signed with intent to defeat the purpose of the rule, it may be stricken as sham and false and the action may proceed as though the pleading had not been served. IN ST TRIAL P Rule 11(A).

    iii. For a willful violation of IN ST TRIAL P Rule 11 an attorney may be subjected to appropriate disciplinary action. Similar action may be taken if scandalous or indecent matter is inserted. IN ST TRIAL P Rule 11(A).

b. *Signature of unrepresented party.* A party who is not represented by an attorney shall sign his pleading and state his address. IN ST TRIAL P Rule 11(A).

c. *Verification not generally required.* Except when specifically required by rule, pleadings or motions need not be verified or accompanied by affidavit. The rule in equity that the averments of an answer under oath must be overcome by the testimony of two (2) witnesses or of one (1) witness sustained by corroborating circumstances is abolished. IN ST TRIAL P Rule 11(A).

d. *Verification by affirmation or representation.* When in connection with any civil or special statutory proceeding it is required that any pleading, motion, petition, supporting affidavit, or other document of any kind, be verified, or that an oath be taken, it shall be sufficient if the subscriber simply affirms the truth of the matter to be verified by an affirmation or representation. IN ST TRIAL P Rule 11(B). IN ST TRIAL P Rule 11(B) states that the affirmation or representation should be in substantially the following language: "I (we) affirm, under the penalties for perjury, that the foregoing representation(s) is (are) true. (Signed) _____."

    i. Any person who falsifies an affirmation or representation of fact shall be subject to the same penalties as are prescribed by law for the making of a false affidavit. IN ST TRIAL P Rule 11(B).

e. *Verified pleadings, motions, and affidavits as evidence.* Pleadings, motions and affidavits accompanying or in support of such pleadings or motions when required to be verified or under oath shall be accepted as a representation that the signer had personal knowledge thereof or reasonable cause to believe the existence of the facts or matters stated or alleged therein; and, if otherwise competent or acceptable as evidence, may be admitted as evidence of the facts or matters stated or alleged therein when it is so provided in the Indiana Rules of Trial Procedure, by statute or other law, or to the extent the writing or signature expressly purports to be made upon the signer's personal knowledge. When such pleadings, motions and affidavits are verified or under oath they shall not require other or greater proof on the part of the adverse party than if not verified or not under oath unless expressly provided otherwise by the Indiana Rules of Trial Procedure, statute or other law. Affidavits upon motions for summary judgment under IN ST TRIAL P Rule 56 and in denial of execution under IN ST TRIAL P Rule 9.2 shall be made upon personal knowledge. IN ST TRIAL P Rule 11(C).

5. *Information excluded from public access.* Every document filed in a case shall separately identify information excluded from public access pursuant to IN ST ADMIN Rule 9(G)(1) as follows:

a. Whole documents that are excluded from public access pursuant to IN ST ADMIN Rule 9(G)(1) shall be tendered on light green paper or have a light green coversheet attached to the document, marked "Not for Public Access" or "Confidential." IN ST TRIAL P Rule 5(G)(1).

b. When only a portion of a document contains information excluded from public access pursuant to IN ST ADMIN Rule 9(G)(1), said information shall be omitted [or redacted] from the filed document, and set forth on a separate accompanying document on light green paper conspicuously marked "Not for Public Access" or "Confidential" and clearly designated [or identifying] the caption and number of the case and the document and location within the document to which the redacted material pertains. IN ST TRIAL P Rule 5(G)(2).

c. With respect to documents filed in electronic format, the trial court, by local rule, may provide for compliance with IN ST TRIAL P Rule 5 in manner that separates and protects access to information excluded from public access. IN ST TRIAL P Rule 5(G)(3).

d. IN ST TRIAL P Rule 5(G) does not apply to a record sealed by the court pursuant to IN ST 5-14-3-5.5 or otherwise, nor to records, documents, or information filed in cases to which public access is prohibited pursuant to IN ST ADMIN Rule 9(G). IN ST TRIAL P Rule 5(G)(4).

e. The following information in case records is excluded from public access and is confidential:

    i. Information that is excluded from public access pursuant to federal law;

    ii. Information that is excluded from public access as declared confidential by Indiana statute or other court rule, including without limitation:

- All adoption records created after July 8, 1941, as declared confidential by IN ST 31-19-19-1, et seq., except those specifically declared open by IN ST 31-19-13-2(2);

- All records relating to chancroid, chlamydia, gonorrhea, hepatitis, human immunodeficiency virus (HIV), Lymphogranuloma venereum, syphilis, tuberculosis, as declared confidential by IN ST 16-41-8-1, et seq.;

- All records relating to child abuse as declared confidential by IN ST 31-33-18-1, et seq.;

- All records relating to drug tests as declared confidential by IN ST 5-14-3-4(a)(9);

- Records of grand jury proceedings as declared confidential by IN ST 35-34-2-4;
- Records of juvenile proceedings as declared confidential by IN ST 31-39-1-2, except those specifically open under statute;
- All paternity records created after July 1, 1941 as declared confidential by IN ST 31-14-11-15, IN ST 31-19-5-23, IN ST 31-39-1-1 and IN ST 31-39-1-2 [Editor's note: IN ST 31-14-11-15 was repealed effective May 9, 2013];
- All pre-sentence reports as declared confidential by IN ST 35-38-1-13;
- Written petitions to permit marriages without consent and orders directing the Clerk of Court to issue a marriage license to underage persons, as declared confidential by IN ST 31-11-1-6;
- Only those arrest warrants, search warrants, indictments and informations ordered confidential by the trial judge, prior to return of duly executed service as declared confidential by IN ST 5-14-3-4(b)(1);
- All medical, mental health, or tax records unless determined by law or regulation of any governmental custodian not to be confidential, released by the subject of such records, or declared by a court of competent jurisdiction to be essential to the resolution of litigation as declared confidential by IN ST 16-39-3-10, IN ST 6-4.1-5-10, IN ST 6-4.1-12-12, and IN ST 6-8.1-7-1;
- Personal information relating to jurors or prospective jurors, other than for the use of the parties and counsel, pursuant to IN ST JURY Rule 10;
- Information relating to protection from abuse orders, no-contact orders and workplace violence restraining orders as declared confidential by IN ST 5-2-9-6, et seq.;
- Mediation proceedings pursuant to IN ST ADR Rule 2.11, Mini-Trial proceedings pursuant to IN ST ADR Rule 4.4(C), and Summary Jury Trials pursuant to IN ST ADR Rule 5.6;
- Information in probation files pursuant to the Probation Standards promulgated by the Judicial Conference of Indiana pursuant to IN ST 11-13-1-8(b);
- Information deemed confidential pursuant to the Rules for Court Administered Alcohol and Drug Programs promulgated by the Judicial Conference of Indiana pursuant to IN ST 12-23-14-13;
- Information deemed confidential pursuant to the Problem-Solving Court Rules promulgated by the Judicial Conference of Indiana pursuant to IN ST 33-23-16-16;
- All records of the Department of workforce Development as declared confidential by IN ST 22-4-19-6;
- Information regarding interception of electronic communications that is sealed or deemed confidential as set forth in IN ST 35-33.5-2-1, et seq.

iii. Information excluded from public access by specific court order;

iv. Complete Social Security Numbers of living persons;

v. With the exception of names, information such as addresses, phone numbers, and dates of birth which explicitly identifies:

- Natural persons who are witnesses or victims (not including defendants) in criminal, domestic violence, stalking, sexual assault, juvenile, or civil protection order proceedings, provided that juveniles who are victims of sex crimes shall be identified by initials only;
- Places of residence of judicial officers, clerks and other employees of courts and clerks of court, unless the person or persons about whom the information pertains waives confidentiality;

vi. Complete account numbers of specific assets, loans, bank accounts, credit cards, and personal identification numbers (PINs);

vii. All orders of expungement entered in criminal or juvenile proceedings, orders to restrict access to criminal history information pursuant to IN ST 35-38-5-5.5 or IN ST 35-38-8-5 and records excluded from public access by such orders, and information related to infractions that is excluded from public access pursuant to IN ST 34-28-5-15 or IN ST 34-28-5-16 [Editor's note: IN ST 35-38-5-5.5, IN ST 35-38-8-5 and IN ST 34-28-5-16 were repealed effective July 1, 2013; for information on orders restricting access to criminal history, refer to IN ST 35-38-9-1, et seq.];

viii. All personal notes and e-mail, and deliberative material, of judges, jurors, court staff and judicial agencies, and information recorded in personal data assistants (PDA's) or organizers and personal calendars. IN ST ADMIN Rule 9(G)(1).

F. Filing and Service Requirements

1. *Filing requirements.* Except as otherwise provided in IN ST TRIAL P Rule 5(E)(2), all pleadings and papers subsequent to the complaint which are required to be served upon a party shall be filed with the Court either before service or within a reasonable period of time thereafter. IN ST TRIAL P Rule 5(E)(1).

   a. *Filing with the court defined.* The filing of pleadings, motions, and other papers with the court as required by the Indiana Rules of Trial Procedure shall be made by one of the following methods:

      i. Delivery to the clerk of the court;

      ii. Sending by electronic transmission under the procedure adopted pursuant to IN ST ADMIN Rule 12;

      iii. Mailing to the clerk by registered, certified or express mail return receipt requested;

      iv. Depositing with any third-party commercial carrier for delivery to the clerk within three (3) calendar days, cost prepaid, properly addressed;

      v. If the court so permits, filing with the judge, in which event the judge shall note thereon the filing date and forthwith transmit them to the office of the clerk; or

      vi. Electronic filing, as approved by the Division of State Court Administration pursuant to IN ST ADMIN Rule 16. IN ST TRIAL P Rule 5(F).

      vii. Filing by registered or certified mail and by third-party commercial carrier shall be complete upon mailing or deposit. IN ST TRIAL P Rule 5(F).

   b. *Facsimile filing.* As outlined in IN ST HAMILTON ADMIN Rule 103(103.10),facsimile filing is permitted in the Circuit and Superior Courts of Hamilton County. The Courts authorize the Hamilton County Clerk of Courts to accept pleadings, motions and other papers by electronic facsimile transmission for filing in any case pending before the Courts, subject to the requirements of IN ST HAMILTON ADMIN Rule 103(103.10). IN ST HAMILTON ADMIN Rule 103(103.10); IN ST HAMILTON TRIAL Rule 201(201.80).

      i. *Generally.* In counties where a majority of judges of the courts of record, by posted local rule, have authorized electronic facsimile filing and designated a telephone number to receive such transmissions, pleadings, motions, and other papers may be sent to the Clerk of Circuit Court by electronic facsimile transmission for filing in any case, provided:

         • Such matter does not exceed ten (10) pages, including the cover sheet;

         • Such matter does not require the payment of fees other than the electronic facsimile transcription fee set forth in IN ST ADMIN Rule 12(E);

         • The sending party creates at the time of transmission a machine generated log for such transmission; and

         • The original document and the transmission log are maintained by the sending party for the duration of the litigation. IN ST ADMIN Rule 12(B); IN ST HAMILTON ADMIN Rule 103(103.10)(d).

         • Legibility of documents and timeliness of filing is the responsibility of the sender. IN ST HAMILTON ADMIN Rule 103(103.10)(g).

         • The Clerk shall accept electronic facsimile transmission filings only if received at the facsimile machine assigned by the Clerk. The telephone number designated to receive such transmission is available at IN ST HAMILTON ADMIN Rule 103(103.40). IN ST HAMILTON ADMIN Rule 103(103.40).

    ii. *Time of filing.* During normal, posted business hours, the time of filing shall be the time the duplicate document is produced in the office of the Clerk of the Circuit Court. Duplicate documents received at all other times shall be filed as of the next normal business day. IN ST ADMIN Rule 12(C).

- If the receiving fax machine endorses its own time and date stamp upon the transmitted documents and the receiving machine produces a delivery receipt which is electronically created and transmitted to the sending party, the time of filing shall be the date and time recorded on the transmitted document by the receiving fax machine. IN ST ADMIN Rule 12(C).

- Electronic facsimile transmissions will be accepted for filing only during the regular business hours as set forth in IN ST HAMILTON ADMIN Rule 101. Transmissions received by the Hamilton County Clerk after close of business shall be filed effective the next regular business day. IN ST HAMILTON ADMIN Rule 103(103.30).

    iii. *Filing fee.* The electronic facsimile transmission will not be accepted for filing if its filing requires the payment of any fee other than the electronic facsimile transcription fee set forth in IN ST HAMILTON ADMIN Rule 103(103.20). IN ST HAMILTON ADMIN Rule 103(103.10)(e).

- Pursuant to Ordinance adopted by the Hamilton County Board of Commissioners, the Clerk shall collect an electronic facsimile transcription fee of One Dollar ($1.00) per page, to a maximum of Ten Dollars ($10.00) per transmission, for each electronic facsimile transmission accepted for filing with the Hamilton County Circuit and Superior Courts. IN ST HAMILTON ADMIN Rule 103(103.20).

- The fee shall be assessed against the sending party and shall be paid upon receipt of invoice by that party and at the latest within thirty (30) days of the transmission. In the event the fee is not paid by the sending party within the time limits provided, the court may issue a show-cause order or enter a judgment in the matter. The Clerk may refuse an electronic facsimile transmission from any attorney or pro se litigant who has failed to pay these fees within thirty (30) days. IN ST HAMILTON ADMIN Rule 103(103.20).

    iv. *No direct filing with court.* A party shall not send pleadings, motions and other papers by electronic facsimile transmission for filing directly to any Court without that Court's prior approval to do so. IN ST HAMILTON ADMIN Rule 103(103.50).

  c. *Filing with special judge.* After a special judge has qualified, a copy of each pleading and Chronological Case Summary entries filed with the Court shall be mailed or delivered to the office of that Special judge by the counsel or pro se litigant with service indicated on the certificate of service. IN ST HAMILTON TRIAL Rule 204(204.20).

  d. *Proof of filing.* Any party filing any paper by any method other than personal delivery to the clerk shall retain proof of filing. IN ST TRIAL P Rule 5(F).

2. *Service requirements.* Unless otherwise provided by the Indiana Rules of Trial Procedure or an order of the court, each party and special judge, if any, shall be served with: (1) every order required by its terms to be served; (2) every pleading subsequent to the original complaint; (3) every written motion except one which may be heard ex parte; (4) every brief submitted to the trial court; (5) every paper relating to discovery required to be served upon a party; and (6) every written notice, appearance, demand, offer of judgment, designation of record on appeal, or similar paper. IN ST TRIAL P Rule 5(A).

  a. *Methods of service*

    i. *Personal service.* Whenever a party is represented by an attorney of record, service shall be made upon such attorney unless service upon the party himself is ordered by the court. Service upon the attorney or party shall be made by delivering or mailing a copy of the papers to the last known address or where an attorney or party has consented to service by fax or e-mail, as

provided in IN ST TRIAL P Rule 3.1(A)(4), by faxing or e-mailing a copy of the documents to the fax number or e-mail address set out in the appearance form or correction as required by IN ST TRIAL P Rule 3.1(E). IN ST TRIAL P Rule 5(B). Delivery of a copy within IN ST TRIAL P Rule 5 means:

- Offering or tendering it to the attorney or party and stating the nature of the papers being served. Refusal to accept an offered or tendered document is a waiver of any objection to the sufficiency or adequacy of service of that document;

- Leaving it at his office with a clerk or other person in charge thereof, or if there is no one in charge, leaving it in a conspicuous place therein; or

- If the office is closed, by leaving it at his dwelling house or usual place of abode with some person of suitable age and discretion then residing therein; or,

- Leaving it at some other suitable place, selected by the attorney upon whom service is being made, pursuant to duly promulgated local rule. IN ST TRIAL P Rule 5(B)(1).

ii. *Service by mail.* If service is made by mail, the papers shall be deposited in the United States mail addressed to the person on whom they are being served, with postage prepaid. Service shall be deemed complete upon mailing. Proof of service of all papers permitted to be mailed may be made by written acknowledgment of service, by affidavit of the person who mailed the papers, or by certificate of an attorney. It shall be the duty of attorneys when entering their appearance in a cause or when filing pleadings or papers therein, to have noted in the Chronological Case Summary or said pleadings or papers so filed the address and telephone number of their office. Service by delivery or by mail at such address shall be deemed sufficient and complete. IN ST TRIAL P Rule 5(B)(2).

iii. *Service by fax or e-mail.* A party who has consented to service by fax or e-mail may be served as follows:

- Service by e-mail shall be made by attaching the document being served in .pdf format. Discovery documents must also be served in accordance with IN ST TRIAL P Rule 26(A). IN ST TRIAL P Rule 5(B)(3)(a).

- Service by fax shall be deemed complete upon generation of a transmission record indicating the successful transmission of the entire document, except as provided in IN ST TRIAL P Rule 5(B)(3)(d). IN ST TRIAL P Rule 5(B)(3)(b).

- Service by e-mail shall be deemed complete upon transmission, except as provided in IN ST TRIAL P Rule 5(B)(3)(d). IN ST TRIAL P Rule 5(B)(3)(c).

- Service by fax or e-mail that occurs on a Saturday, Sunday, legal holiday, or day the court or agency in which the matter is pending is closed or after 5:00 PM local time of the recipient shall be deemed complete the next day that is not a Saturday, Sunday, legal holiday, or day that the court or agency in which the matter is pending is not closed. IN ST TRIAL P Rule 5(B)(3)(d).

iv. *Mail box service.* Pursuant to IN ST TRIAL P Rule 5(B)(1)(d), the Circuit and Superior Courts of Hamilton County hereby designate the "mail boxes" located in the Clerk's order book office for service of pleadings upon attorneys who have such boxes. IN ST HAMILTON TRIAL Rule 201(201.50).

b. *Serving numerous defendants.* In any action in which there are unusually large numbers of defendants, the court, upon motion or of its own initiative, may order:

i. That service of the pleadings of the defendants and replies thereto need not be made as between the defendants;

- That any cross-claim, counterclaim, or matter constituting an avoidance or affirmative defense contained therein shall be deemed to be denied or avoided by all other parties; and

- That the filing of any such pleading and service thereof upon the plaintiff constitutes due notice of it to the parties. IN ST TRIAL P Rule 5(D).

ii. A copy of every such order shall be served upon the parties in such manner and form as the court directs. IN ST TRIAL P Rule 5(D).

    c.   *Service on parties in default for failure to appear.* No service need be made on parties in default for failure to appear, except that pleadings asserting new or additional claims for relief against them shall be served upon them in the manner provided by service of summons in IN ST TRIAL P Rule 4. IN ST TRIAL P Rule 5(A).

G. Hearings

1.   *Hearing on motion.* Unless local conditions make it impracticable, each judge shall establish regular times and places, at intervals sufficiently frequent for the prompt dispatch of business, at which motions requiring notice and hearing may be heard and disposed of; but the judge at any time or place and on such notice, if any, as he considers reasonable may make order for the advancement, conduct, and hearing of actions. To expedite its business the court may direct the submission and determination of motions without oral hearing upon brief written statements of reasons in support and opposition, or direct or permit hearings by telephone conference call with all attorneys or other similar means of communication. IN ST TRIAL P Rule 73(A).

H. Forms

1. Motion to Compel Discovery Forms for Indiana

   a.   Notice. 5 INPRAC § 4:6.10.

   b.   Motion to compel. 5 INPRAC § 4:6.20.

   c.   Motion to compel; Failure to respond. 5 INPRAC § 4:6.30.

   d.   Motion to compel answers to interrogatories. 5 INPRAC § 4:6.40.

   e.   Motion to compel production of documents. 5 INPRAC § 4:6.50.

   f.   Motion to dismiss as sanction for failure to comply with court ordered discovery. 5 INPRAC § 4:6.60.

   g.   Notice of intention to file motion to compel discovery. 10 INPRAC § 58.54.

   h.   Motion to compel discovery; General form. 10 INPRAC § 58.55.

   i.   Order compelling requested discovery. 10 INPRAC § 58.56.

   j.   Order denying motion to compel discovery. 10 INPRAC § 58.57.

   k.   Motion to compel discovery; For failure to respond to discovery requests. 10 INPRAC § 58.58.

   l.   Motion to compel; Physician to release medical records. 10 INPRAC § 58.59.

   m.   Motion to compel plaintiff to execute medical records release. 10 INPRAC § 58.60.

   n.   Motion to compel; Production of surveillance videotape. 10 INPRAC § 58.61.

   o.   Motion for order that matters be taken as established. 10 INPRAC § 58.62.

   p.   Motion for order precluding litigation of issues. 10 INPRAC § 58.63.

   q.   Motion to compel; Failure to permit inspection of original documents. 10 INPRAC § 58.65.

   r.   Motion to compel; Answer to deposition questions. 10 INPRAC § 58.66.

   s.   Certificate of service; Personal service. 9 INPRAC § 5.7.

   t.   Certificate of service; First class mail. 9 INPRAC § 5.8.

I. Checklist

(I)   ❑ Matters to be considered by moving party

   (a) ❑ Required documents

      (1) ❑ Motion and notice

      (2) ❑ Disputed discovery

      (3) ❑ Attorney certification

      (4) ❑ Proposed order

      (5) ❑ Certificate of service

(b) ❑ Supplemental documents

   (1) ❑ Supporting evidence

   (2) ❑ Facsimile cover sheet

   (3) ❑ Request to schedule trial or hearing

   (4) ❑ Copies of unpublished opinions

(c) ❑ Timing

   (1) ❑ The moving party must provide reasonable notice of his intention to file a motion to compel with the other litigants and all affected persons

   (2) ❑ A written motion, other than one which may be heard ex parte, and notice of the hearing thereof shall be served not less than five (5) days before the time specified for the hearing, unless a different period is fixed by the Indiana Rules of Trial Procedure or by order of the court

   (3) ❑ All pleadings and papers subsequent to the complaint which are required to be served upon a party shall be filed with the Court either before service or within a reasonable period of time thereafter

(II) ❑ Matters to be considered by the responding party

(a) ❑ Required documents

   (1) ❑ Opposition

   (2) ❑ Certificate of service

(b) ❑ Supplemental documents

   (1) ❑ Supporting evidence

   (2) ❑ Alternative proposed order

   (3) ❑ Facsimile cover sheet

   (4) ❑ Request to schedule trial or hearing

   (5) ❑ Copies of unpublished opinions

(c) ❑ Timing

   (1) ❑ Except as otherwise provided in IN ST TRIAL P Rule 59(D), opposing affidavits may be served not less than one (1) day before the hearing, unless the court permits them to be served at some other time

Motions, Oppositions and Replies
Motion for Protective Order

Document Last Updated October 2013

A. Applicable Rules

1. *State rules*

   a. Appearance. IN ST TRIAL P Rule 3.1.

   b. Process. IN ST TRIAL P Rule 4.

   c. Service and filing of pleadings and other papers. IN ST TRIAL P Rule 5.

   d. Time. IN ST TRIAL P Rule 6.

   e. Pleadings. IN ST TRIAL P Rule 7; IN ST TRIAL P Rule 8; IN ST TRIAL P Rule 9.2; IN ST TRIAL P Rule 10.

   f. Signing and verification of pleadings. IN ST TRIAL P Rule 11.

   g. General provisions governing discovery. IN ST TRIAL P Rule 26.

h. Methods of discovery. IN ST TRIAL P Rule 27; IN ST TRIAL P Rule 30; IN ST TRIAL P Rule 31; IN ST TRIAL P Rule 33; IN ST TRIAL P Rule 34; IN ST TRIAL P Rule 36.

i. Failure to make or cooperate in discovery; Sanctions. IN ST TRIAL P Rule 37.

j. Evidence. IN ST TRIAL P Rule 43.

k. Judgment on the evidence (directed verdict). IN ST TRIAL P Rule 50.

l. Findings by the court. IN ST TRIAL P Rule 52.

m. Summary judgment. IN ST TRIAL P Rule 56.

n. Motion to correct error. IN ST TRIAL P Rule 59.

o. Relief from judgment or error. IN ST TRIAL P Rule 60.

p. Hearing of motions. IN ST TRIAL P Rule 73.

q. Access to court records. IN ST ADMIN Rule 9.

r. Paper size. IN ST ADMIN Rule 11.

s. Facsimile transmission. IN ST ADMIN Rule 12.

t. Electronic filing and electronic service pilot projects. IN ST ADMIN Rule 16.

u. Sealing of certain records by court; Hearing; Notice. IN ST 5-14-3-5.5.

v. Trade secrets. IN ST 24-2-3-1; IN ST 24-2-3-2.

w. Privacy and confidentiality. IN ST 5-2-9-6; IN ST 5-14-3-4; IN ST 6-4.1-5-10; IN ST 6-4.1-12-12; IN ST 6-8.1-7-1; IN ST 11-13-1-8; IN ST 12-23-14-13; IN ST 16-39-3-10; IN ST 16-41-8-1; IN ST 22-4-19-6; IN ST 31-11-1-6; IN ST 31-19-5-23; IN ST 31-19-13-2; IN ST 31-19-19-1; IN ST 31-33-18-1; IN ST 31-39-1-1; IN ST 31-39-1-2; IN ST 33-23-16-16; IN ST 35-34-2-4; IN ST 35-38-1-13; IN ST 35-38-9-1; IN ST ADR Rule 2.11; IN ST ADR Rule 4.4; IN ST ADR Rule 5.6; IN ST JURY Rule 10.

2. *Local rules*

a. Court hours. IN ST HAMILTON ADMIN Rule 101.

b. Facsimile transmissions. IN ST HAMILTON ADMIN Rule 103.

c. Filing of pleadings and entry of appearances. IN ST HAMILTON TRIAL Rule 201.

d. Proposed orders. IN ST HAMILTON TRIAL Rule 202.

e. Briefs and memorandums. IN ST HAMILTON TRIAL Rule 203.

f. Special judges. IN ST HAMILTON TRIAL Rule 204.

g. Trial settings. IN ST HAMILTON TRIAL Rule 205.

h. Continuances. IN ST HAMILTON TRIAL Rule 206.

B. Timing

1. *Motion for protective order.* There are no specific timing requirements for filing a motion for a protective order.

   a. *Filing.* All pleadings and papers subsequent to the complaint which are required to be served upon a party shall be filed with the Court either before service or within a reasonable period of time thereafter. IN ST TRIAL P Rule 5(E)(1).

2. *Service.* A written motion, other than one which may be heard ex parte, and notice of the hearing thereof shall be served not less than five (5) days before the time specified for the hearing, unless a different period is fixed by the Indiana Rules of Trial Procedure or by order of the court. IN ST TRIAL P Rule 6(D).

   a. *Of supporting affidavits.* When a motion is supported by affidavit, the affidavit shall be served with the motion. IN ST TRIAL P Rule 6(D).

3. *Service of opposition.* Except as otherwise provided in IN ST TRIAL P Rule 59(D), opposing affidavits may be served not less than one (1) day before the hearing, unless the court permits them to be served at some other time. IN ST TRIAL P Rule 6(D).

4. *Computation of time*

    a. *Generally; Days excluded.* In computing any period of time prescribed or allowed by the Indiana Rules of Trial Procedure, by order of the court, or by any applicable statute, the day of the act, event, or default from which the designated period of time begins to run shall not be included. The last day of the period so computed is to be included unless it is:

        i. A Saturday,

        ii. A Sunday,

        iii. A legal holiday as defined by state statute, or

        iv. A day the office in which the act is to be done is closed during regular business hours. IN ST TRIAL P Rule 6(A).

    b. *Short periods.* In any event, the period runs until the end of the next day that is not a Saturday, a Sunday, a legal holiday, or a day on which the office is closed. When the period of time allowed is less than seven (7) days, intermediate Saturdays, Sundays, legal holidays, and days on which the office is closed shall be excluded from the computations. IN ST TRIAL P Rule 6(A).

    c. *Additional time after service by United States mail.* Whenever a party has the right or is required to do some act or take some proceedings within a prescribed period after the service of a notice or other paper upon him and the notice or paper is served upon him by United States mail, three (3) days shall be added to the prescribed period. IN ST TRIAL P Rule 6(E).

    d. *Enlargement of time.* When an act is required or allowed to be done at or within a specific time by the Indiana Rules of Trial Procedure, the court may at any time for cause shown:

        i. Order the period enlarged, with or without motion or notice, if request therefor is made before the expiration of the period originally prescribed or extended by a previous order; or

        ii. Upon motion made after the expiration of the specific period, permit the act to be done where the failure to act was the result of excusable neglect; but, the court may not extend the time for taking any action for judgment on the evidence under IN ST TRIAL P Rule 50(A), amendment of findings and judgment under IN ST TRIAL P Rule 52(B), to correct errors under IN ST TRIAL P Rule 59(C), statement in opposition to motion to correct error under IN ST TRIAL P Rule 59(E), or to obtain relief from final judgment under IN ST TRIAL P Rule 60(B), except to the extent and under the conditions stated in those rules. IN ST TRIAL P Rule 6(B).

        iii. For information on obtaining a continuance, refer to IN ST HAMILTON TRIAL Rule 206.

C. General Requirements

1. *Motions, generally.* Unless made during a hearing or trial, or otherwise ordered by the court, an application to the court for an order shall be made by written motion. The motion shall state the grounds therefor and the relief or order sought. IN ST TRIAL P Rule 7(B).

    a. *Motions as distinct from pleadings.* Motions and responses to motions are not pleadings, and allegations contained in a motion are not admissions of a party. 22B INPRAC 7:2; Wachstetter v. County Properties, LLC, 832 N.E.2d 574 (Ind.Ct.App. 2005); Scott County Family YMCA, Inc. v. Hobbs, 817 N.E.2d 603 (Ind.Ct.App. 2004).

    b. *Unopposed motions generally granted.* It is common for a trial court to grant procedural motions, such as motions for enlargement of time, discovery motions, or motions for continuance, unless an objection is filed. 21 INPRAC § 13.8.

2. *Motion for protective order*

    a. *Forms of protective order.* Upon motion by any party or by the person from whom discovery is sought, and for good cause shown, the court in which the action is pending or alternatively, on matters relating to a deposition, the court in the county where the deposition is being taken, may make any order which justice requires to protect a party or person from annoyance, embarrassment, oppression, or undue burden or expense, including one or more of the following:

        i. That the discovery not be had;

        ii. That the discovery may be had only on specified terms and conditions, including a designation of the time or place;

    iii.   That the discovery may be had only by a method of discovery other than that selected by the party seeking discovery;

    iv.   That certain matters not be inquired into, or that the scope of the discovery be limited to certain matters;

    v.   That discovery be conducted with no one present except the parties and their attorneys and persons designated by the court;

    vi.   That a deposition after being sealed be opened only by order of the court;

    vii.   That a trade secret or other confidential research, development, or commercial information not be disclosed or be disclosed only in a designated way;

    viii.   That the parties simultaneously file specified documents or information enclosed in sealed envelopes to be opened as directed by the court;

    ix.   That a party need not provide discovery of electronically stored information from sources that the party identifies as not reasonably accessible because of undue burden or cost. IN ST TRIAL P Rule 26(C).

b.   *List in IN ST TRIAL P Rule 26(C) not exhaustive.* A court is not limited to the eight specified types of orders. A court may be as inventive as the case and the conditions require. A party or a nonparty may thus obtain any kind of protective order against any kind of discovery which is sought in the case, if "good cause" is shown. So also, however, if a protective order is sought and denied, the trial court may go further and issue an order to provide for or to permit the discovery. 2A INPRAC R 26(26.20).

c.   *Trade secrets.* A protectable trade secret has four characteristics: (1) information, (2) which derives independent economic value, (3) is not generally known, or readily ascertainable by proper means by other persons who can obtain economic value from its disclosure or use, and (4) the subject of efforts reasonable under the circumstances to maintain its secrecy. 2A INPRAC R 26(26.23.1).

    i.   *Nature of determination.* The determination of whether information is a trade secret is a fact sensitive determination. 2A INPRAC R 26(26.23.1).

    ii.   *Burden of proof.* The burden of proof is on the party asserting the trade secret to show that it is included in the categories of protectable trade secret information listed in the trade secrets statute. 2A INPRAC R 26(26.23.1); Northern Elec. Co., Inc. v. Torma, 819 N.E.2d 417 (Ind.Ct.App. 2004).

    iii.   *Uniform trade secrets act.* The application of IN ST TRIAL P Rule 26 to trade secrets should be informed by Indiana's enactment of the Uniform Trade Secrets Act (UTSA) (refer to IN ST 24-2-3-1, et seq.), which provides states with a common legal framework for protecting trade secrets from misappropriation. 2A INPRAC R 26(26.23.1(C)).

    iv.   *Trade secret defined.* "Trade secret" means information, including a formula, pattern, compilation, program, device, method, technique, or process, that:

- Derives independent economic value, actual or potential, from not being generally known to, and not being readily ascertainable by proper means by, other persons who can obtain economic value from its disclosure or use; and

- Is the subject of efforts that are reasonable under the circumstances to maintain its secrecy. IN ST 24-2-3-2.

d.   *Information not reasonably accessible.* On motion to compel discovery or for a protective order, the party from whom discovery is sought must show that the information is not reasonably accessible because of undue burden or cost. If that showing is made, the court may nonetheless order discovery from such sources if the requesting party shows good cause. The court may specify conditions for the discovery. IN ST TRIAL P Rule 26(C)(9).

    i.   When filing a motion for protective order under IN ST TRIAL P Rule 26(C), the movant, whether a party or non-party, must allege and prove good cause for his request for protective order. The court is empowered to make any order which "justice requires to protect a party or person from annoyance, embarrassment, oppression, or undue burden or expense." Typically, this protection means that discovery will be denied altogether, or limited in scope or to specific terms. 10 INPRAC § 58.20.

e. *Party justified in resisting discovery.* A litigant is substantially justified in seeking to compel or resist discovery if reasonable persons could conclude that genuine issue existed as to whether person was bound to comply with requested discovery. 10 INPRAC § 58.20; Munsell v. Hambright, 776 N.E.2d 1272 (Ind.Ct.App. 2002).

f. *Award of expenses of motion.* If the motion for a protective order is denied in whole or in part, the court may, on such terms and conditions as are just, order that any party or person provide or permit discovery. The provisions of IN ST TRIAL P Rule 37(A)(4) apply to the award of expenses incurred in relation to the motion. IN ST TRIAL P Rule 26(C).

D. Documents

1. *Required documents*

   a. *Motion and notice.* The requirement of notice is satisfied by service of the motion. IN ST TRIAL P Rule 7(B). Refer to the General Requirements section of this document for information on the content of a motion for a protective order.

   b. *Attorney certification.* Before any party files any motion or request to compel discovery pursuant to IN ST TRIAL P Rule 37, or any motion for protection from discovery pursuant to IN ST TRIAL P Rule 26(C), or any other discovery motion which seeks to enforce, modify, or limit discovery, that party shall:

      i. Make a reasonable effort to reach agreement with the opposing party concerning the matter which is the subject of the motion or request; and

      ii. Include in the motion or request a statement showing that the attorney making the motion or request has made a reasonable effort to reach agreement with the opposing attorney(s) concerning the matter(s) set forth in the motion or request. This statement shall recite, in addition, the date, time and place of this effort to reach agreement, whether in person or by phone, and the names of all parties and attorneys participating therein. If an attorney for any party advises the court in writing that an opposing attorney has refused or delayed meeting and discussing the issues covered in IN ST TRIAL P Rule 26(F), the court may take such action as is appropriate. IN ST TRIAL P Rule 26(F).

      iii. The court may deny a discovery motion filed by a party who has failed to comply with the requirements of IN ST TRIAL P Rule 26(F). IN ST TRIAL P Rule 26(F).

   c. *Proposed order.* Unless local practice provides differently, a party should submit a proposed order with its written motion to be signed by the judge once the motion has been granted. 21 INPRAC § 13.8; IN ST HAMILTON ADMIN Rule 103(103.10)(b). Each Motion, Petition or other request for relief shall be accompanied by a proposed order. IN ST HAMILTON TRIAL Rule 202(202.10).

      i. All proposed orders submitted by counsel pursuant to IN ST HAMILTON TRIAL Rule 202 shall meet the following requirements: (1) contain a complete distribution list of all attorneys and pro se litigants with full addresses; (2) stamped envelopes appropriately addressed for each attorney of record and/or pro se litigant on the distribution list. IN ST HAMILTON TRIAL Rule 202(202.30).

   d. *Certificate of service.* An attorney or unrepresented party tendering a document to the Clerk for filing shall certify that service has been made, list the parties served, and specify the date and means of service. The certificate of service shall be placed at the end of the document and shall not be separately filed. The separate filing of a certificate of service, however, shall not be grounds for rejecting a document for filing. The Clerk may permit documents to be filed without a certificate of service but shall require prompt filing of a separate certificate of service. IN ST TRIAL P Rule 5(C).

      i. All pleadings filed with the Court which require a certificate of service shall specifically name the individual party or attorney on whom service has been made, the address, the manner in which service was made and the date when service was made. IN ST HAMILTON TRIAL Rule 201(201.60).

2. *Supplemental documents*

  a. *Supporting evidence.* When a motion is based on facts not appearing of record the court may hear the matter on affidavits presented by the respective parties, but the court may direct that the matter be heard wholly or partly on oral testimony or depositions. IN ST TRIAL P Rule 43(B).

  b. *Facsimile cover sheet.* Any document sent to the Clerk of the Circuit Court by electronic facsimile transmission shall be accompanied by a cover sheet which states the title of the document, case number, number of pages, identity and voice telephone number of the sending party and instructions for filing. The cover sheet shall contain the signature of the attorney or party, pro se, authorizing the filing. IN ST ADMIN Rule 12(D); IN ST HAMILTON ADMIN Rule 103(103.10)(a).

  c. *Request to schedule hearing.* All requests to schedule trials and hearings shall be in writing and shall contain the following information:

    i. Type of trial or hearing (i.e., jury trial, court trial, final hearing in dissolution, etc.). IN ST HAMILTON TRIAL Rule 205(205.10).

    ii. A good-faith estimate of the total court time needed for the trial or hearing. IN ST HAMILTON TRIAL Rule 205(205.10).

    iii. Each request under IN ST HAMILTON TRIAL Rule 205(205.10) shall be accompanied by a proposed written order with appropriate blanks for date and time and shall further include reference to those items set forth in IN ST HAMILTON TRIAL Rule 205(205.10)(a) and IN ST HAMILTON TRIAL Rule 205(205.10)(b). IN ST HAMILTON TRIAL Rule 205(205.20).

  d. *Copies of unpublished opinions.* Authorities relied upon which are not cited in the Northeastern Reporter system shall be attached to counsel's brief. If the authority is cited for the first time in oral argument, a copy of the authority may be provided to the Court at the time of the argument. Sufficient copies shall be available to provide counsel for each party with a copy. IN ST HAMILTON TRIAL Rule 203(203.10).

E. Format

1. *Form of motions.* The rules applicable to captions, and the signing and form of pleadings (IN ST TRIAL P Rule 8 through IN ST TRIAL P Rule 11), apply to all motions and other papers provided under the Indiana Rules of Trial Procedure. 22B INPRAC 7:2.

2. *Form of pleadings*

  a. *Caption; Names of parties.* Every pleading shall contain a caption setting forth the name of the court, the title of the action, the file number, and a designation as in IN ST TRIAL P Rule 7(A). In the complaint the title of the action shall include the names of all the parties, but in other pleadings it is sufficient to state the name of the first party on each side with an appropriate indication of other parties. IN ST TRIAL P Rule 10(A).

  b. *Paragraphs; Separate statements.* All averments of a claim or defense shall be made in numbered paragraphs, the contents of each of which shall be limited as far as practicable to a statement of a single set of circumstances, and a paragraph may be referred to by number in all succeeding pleadings. Each claim founded upon a separate transaction or occurrence and each defense other than denials may be stated in a separate count or defense whenever a separation facilitates the clear presentation of the matters set forth. IN ST TRIAL P Rule 10(B).

  c. *Adoption by reference; Exhibits.* Statements in a pleading may be adopted by reference in a different part of the same pleading or in another pleading or in any motion. A copy of any written instrument which is an exhibit to a pleading is a part thereof for all purposes. IN ST TRIAL P Rule 10(C).

  d. *Facsimile page limit.* Courts authorize the Hamilton County Clerk of Courts to accept pleadings, motions and other papers by electronic facsimile transmission for filing in any case pending before the Courts, subject to the requirement that The transmission may not exceed ten (10) pages in length including the cover sheet and proposed CCS entry. IN ST HAMILTON ADMIN Rule 103(103.10)(c).

  e. *Emergency facsimile filings.* If the filing requires the immediate attention of the Judge, it shall so indicate in bold letters in an accompanying transmittal memorandum. IN ST HAMILTON ADMIN Rule 103(103.10)(f).

f. *Special judge heading.* After a special judge is selected, the attorneys or pro se litigants shall add to the caption of all pleadings to the right of the case title the following: "BEFORE SPECIAL JUDGE _____." IN ST HAMILTON TRIAL Rule 204(204.10).

g. *Format rules strictly enforced.* All filings shall be in compliance with the Indiana Rules of Trial Procedure. If the documents received are not in proper form, such deficiencies will not be corrected by court personnel. IN ST HAMILTON TRIAL Rule 201(201.70). The Court shall not be required to act on any Motion, Petition or other request for relief unless filed in conformity with the Hamilton County Local Trial and Administrative rules. IN ST HAMILTON TRIAL Rule 202(202.20).

3. *Size of papers for filing.* Effective January 1, 1992, all pleadings, copies, motions and documents filed with any trial court or appellate level court, typed or printed, with the exception of exhibits and existing wills, shall be prepared on eight and one-half by eleven inch (8 1/2" x 11") size paper. IN ST ADMIN Rule 11.

a. *Form.* All documents filed in any Hamilton County Court, with the exception of exhibits and existing wills, shall be prepared on paper measuring eight and one-half by eleven inches (8 1/2" x 11"). IN ST HAMILTON TRIAL Rule 201(201.20).

4. *Signature requirements*

a. *Signature of attorney.* Every pleading or motion of a party represented by an attorney shall be signed by at least one (1) attorney of record in his individual name, whose address, telephone number, and attorney number shall be stated, except that this provision shall not apply to pleadings and motions made and transcribed at the trial or a hearing before the judge and received by him in such form. IN ST TRIAL P Rule 11(A).

   i. The signature of an attorney constitutes a certificate by him that he has read the pleadings; that to the best of his knowledge, information, and belief, there is good ground to support it; and that it is not interposed for delay. IN ST TRIAL P Rule 11(A).

   ii. If a pleading or motion is not signed or is signed with intent to defeat the purpose of the rule, it may be stricken as sham and false and the action may proceed as though the pleading had not been served. IN ST TRIAL P Rule 11(A).

   iii. For a willful violation of IN ST TRIAL P Rule 11 an attorney may be subjected to appropriate disciplinary action. Similar action may be taken if scandalous or indecent matter is inserted. IN ST TRIAL P Rule 11(A).

b. *Signature of unrepresented party.* A party who is not represented by an attorney shall sign his pleading and state his address. IN ST TRIAL P Rule 11(A).

c. *Verification not generally required.* Except when specifically required by rule, pleadings or motions need not be verified or accompanied by affidavit. The rule in equity that the averments of an answer under oath must be overcome by the testimony of two (2) witnesses or of one (1) witness sustained by corroborating circumstances is abolished. IN ST TRIAL P Rule 11(A).

d. *Verification by affirmation or representation.* When in connection with any civil or special statutory proceeding it is required that any pleading, motion, petition, supporting affidavit, or other document of any kind, be verified, or that an oath be taken, it shall be sufficient if the subscriber simply affirms the truth of the matter to be verified by an affirmation or representation. IN ST TRIAL P Rule 11(B). IN ST TRIAL P Rule 11(B) states that the affirmation or representation should be in substantially the following language: "I (we) affirm, under the penalties for perjury, that the foregoing representation(s) is (are) true. (Signed) _____."

   i. Any person who falsifies an affirmation or representation of fact shall be subject to the same penalties as are prescribed by law for the making of a false affidavit. IN ST TRIAL P Rule 11(B).

e. *Verified pleadings, motions, and affidavits as evidence.* Pleadings, motions and affidavits accompanying or in support of such pleadings or motions when required to be verified or under oath shall be accepted as a representation that the signer had personal knowledge thereof or reasonable cause to believe the existence of the facts or matters stated or alleged therein; and, if otherwise competent or acceptable as evidence, may be admitted as evidence of the facts or matters stated or alleged therein when it is so provided in the Indiana Rules of Trial Procedure, by statute or other law, or to the extent the writing or signature expressly purports to be made upon the signer's personal knowledge. When such pleadings, motions and affidavits are verified or under oath they shall not require other or greater proof on the part of the adverse party than if not verified or not under oath unless expressly provided otherwise by the Indiana Rules of Trial Procedure, statute or other law. Affidavits upon motions for summary judgment under IN ST TRIAL P Rule 56 and in denial of execution under IN ST TRIAL P Rule 9.2 shall be made upon personal knowledge. IN ST TRIAL P Rule 11(C).

5. *Information excluded from public access.* Every document filed in a case shall separately identify information excluded from public access pursuant to IN ST ADMIN Rule 9(G)(1) as follows:

   a. Whole documents that are excluded from public access pursuant to IN ST ADMIN Rule 9(G)(1) shall be tendered on light green paper or have a light green coversheet attached to the document, marked "Not for Public Access" or "Confidential." IN ST TRIAL P Rule 5(G)(1).

   b. When only a portion of a document contains information excluded from public access pursuant to IN ST ADMIN Rule 9(G)(1), said information shall be omitted [or redacted] from the filed document, and set forth on a separate accompanying document on light green paper conspicuously marked "Not for Public Access" or "Confidential" and clearly designated [or identifying] the caption and number of the case and the document and location within the document to which the redacted material pertains. IN ST TRIAL P Rule 5(G)(2).

   c. With respect to documents filed in electronic format, the trial court, by local rule, may provide for compliance with IN ST TRIAL P Rule 5 in manner that separates and protects access to information excluded from public access. IN ST TRIAL P Rule 5(G)(3).

   d. IN ST TRIAL P Rule 5(G) does not apply to a record sealed by the court pursuant to IN ST 5-14-3-5.5 or otherwise, nor to records, documents, or information filed in cases to which public access is prohibited pursuant to IN ST ADMIN Rule 9(G). IN ST TRIAL P Rule 5(G)(4).

   e. The following information in case records is excluded from public access and is confidential:

      i. Information that is excluded from public access pursuant to federal law;

      ii. Information that is excluded from public access as declared confidential by Indiana statute or other court rule, including without limitation:

         • All adoption records created after July 8, 1941, as declared confidential by IN ST 31-19-19-1, et seq., except those specifically declared open by IN ST 31-19-13-2(2);

         • All records relating to chancroid, chlamydia, gonorrhea, hepatitis, human immunodeficiency virus (HIV), Lymphogranuloma venereum, syphilis, tuberculosis, as declared confidential by IN ST 16-41-8-1, et seq.;

         • All records relating to child abuse as declared confidential by IN ST 31-33-18-1, et seq.;

         • All records relating to drug tests as declared confidential by IN ST 5-14-3-4(a)(9);

         • Records of grand jury proceedings as declared confidential by IN ST 35-34-2-4;

         • Records of juvenile proceedings as declared confidential by IN ST 31-39-1-2, except those specifically open under statute;

         • All paternity records created after July 1, 1941 as declared confidential by IN ST 31-14-11-15, IN ST 31-19-5-23, IN ST 31-39-1-1 and IN ST 31-39-1-2 [Editor's note: IN ST 31-14-11-15 was repealed effective May 9, 2013];

         • All pre-sentence reports as declared confidential by IN ST 35-38-1-13;

         • Written petitions to permit marriages without consent and orders directing the Clerk of Court to issue a marriage license to underage persons, as declared confidential by IN ST 31-11-1-6;

         • Only those arrest warrants, search warrants, indictments and informations ordered confidential by the trial judge, prior to return of duly executed service as declared confidential by IN ST 5-14-3-4(b)(1);

- All medical, mental health, or tax records unless determined by law or regulation of any governmental custodian not to be confidential, released by the subject of such records, or declared by a court of competent jurisdiction to be essential to the resolution of litigation as declared confidential by IN ST 16-39-3-10, IN ST 6-4.1-5-10, IN ST 6-4.1-12-12, and IN ST 6-8.1-7-1;

- Personal information relating to jurors or prospective jurors, other than for the use of the parties and counsel, pursuant to IN ST JURY Rule 10;

- Information relating to protection from abuse orders, no-contact orders and workplace violence restraining orders as declared confidential by IN ST 5-2-9-6, et seq.;

- Mediation proceedings pursuant to IN ST ADR Rule 2.11, Mini-Trial proceedings pursuant to IN ST ADR Rule 4.4(C), and Summary Jury Trials pursuant to IN ST ADR Rule 5.6;

- Information in probation files pursuant to the Probation Standards promulgated by the Judicial Conference of Indiana pursuant to IN ST 11-13-1-8(b);

- Information deemed confidential pursuant to the Rules for Court Administered Alcohol and Drug Programs promulgated by the Judicial Conference of Indiana pursuant to IN ST 12-23-14-13;

- Information deemed confidential pursuant to the Problem-Solving Court Rules promulgated by the Judicial Conference of Indiana pursuant to IN ST 33-23-16-16;

- All records of the Department of workforce Development as declared confidential by IN ST 22-4-19-6;

- Information regarding interception of electronic communications that is sealed or deemed confidential as set forth in IN ST 35-33.5-2-1, et seq.

iii. Information excluded from public access by specific court order;

iv. Complete Social Security Numbers of living persons;

v. With the exception of names, information such as addresses, phone numbers, and dates of birth which explicitly identifies:

- Natural persons who are witnesses or victims (not including defendants) in criminal, domestic violence, stalking, sexual assault, juvenile, or civil protection order proceedings, provided that juveniles who are victims of sex crimes shall be identified by initials only;

- Places of residence of judicial officers, clerks and other employees of courts and clerks of court, unless the person or persons about whom the information pertains waives confidentiality;

vi. Complete account numbers of specific assets, loans, bank accounts, credit cards, and personal identification numbers (PINs);

vii. All orders of expungement entered in criminal or juvenile proceedings, orders to restrict access to criminal history information pursuant to IN ST 35-38-5-5.5 or IN ST 35-38-8-5 and records excluded from public access by such orders, and information related to infractions that is excluded from public access pursuant to IN ST 34-28-5-15 or IN ST 34-28-5-16 [Editor's note: IN ST 35-38-5-5.5, IN ST 35-38-8-5 and IN ST 34-28-5-16 were repealed effective July 1, 2013; for information on orders restricting access to criminal history, refer to IN ST 35-38-9-1, et seq.];

viii. All personal notes and e-mail, and deliberative material, of judges, jurors, court staff and judicial agencies, and information recorded in personal data assistants (PDA's) or organizers and personal calendars. IN ST ADMIN Rule 9(G)(1).

F. Filing and Service Requirements

1. *Filing requirements.* Except as otherwise provided in IN ST TRIAL P Rule 5(E)(2), all pleadings and

papers subsequent to the complaint which are required to be served upon a party shall be filed with the Court either before service or within a reasonable period of time thereafter. IN ST TRIAL P Rule 5(E)(1).

a. *Filing with the court defined.* The filing of pleadings, motions, and other papers with the court as required by the Indiana Rules of Trial Procedure shall be made by one of the following methods:

   i. Delivery to the clerk of the court;

   ii. Sending by electronic transmission under the procedure adopted pursuant to IN ST ADMIN Rule 12;

   iii. Mailing to the clerk by registered, certified or express mail return receipt requested;

   iv. Depositing with any third-party commercial carrier for delivery to the clerk within three (3) calendar days, cost prepaid, properly addressed;

   v. If the court so permits, filing with the judge, in which event the judge shall note thereon the filing date and forthwith transmit them to the office of the clerk; or

   vi. Electronic filing, as approved by the Division of State Court Administration pursuant to IN ST ADMIN Rule 16. IN ST TRIAL P Rule 5(F).

   vii. Filing by registered or certified mail and by third-party commercial carrier shall be complete upon mailing or deposit. IN ST TRIAL P Rule 5(F).

b. *Facsimile filing.* As outlined in IN ST HAMILTON ADMIN Rule 103(103.10),facsimile filing is permitted in the Circuit and Superior Courts of Hamilton County. The Courts authorize the Hamilton County Clerk of Courts to accept pleadings, motions and other papers by electronic facsimile transmission for filing in any case pending before the Courts, subject to the requirements of IN ST HAMILTON ADMIN Rule 103(103.10). IN ST HAMILTON ADMIN Rule 103(103.10); IN ST HAMILTON TRIAL Rule 201(201.80).

   i. *Generally.* In counties where a majority of judges of the courts of record, by posted local rule, have authorized electronic facsimile filing and designated a telephone number to receive such transmissions, pleadings, motions, and other papers may be sent to the Clerk of Circuit Court by electronic facsimile transmission for filing in any case, provided:

- Such matter does not exceed ten (10) pages, including the cover sheet;

- Such matter does not require the payment of fees other than the electronic facsimile transcription fee set forth in IN ST ADMIN Rule 12(E);

- The sending party creates at the time of transmission a machine generated log for such transmission; and

- The original document and the transmission log are maintained by the sending party for the duration of the litigation. IN ST ADMIN Rule 12(B); IN ST HAMILTON ADMIN Rule 103(103.10)(d).

- Legibility of documents and timeliness of filing is the responsibility of the sender. IN ST HAMILTON ADMIN Rule 103(103.10)(g).

- The Clerk shall accept electronic facsimile transmission filings only if received at the facsimile machine assigned by the Clerk. The telephone number designated to receive such transmission is available at IN ST HAMILTON ADMIN Rule 103(103.40). IN ST HAMILTON ADMIN Rule 103(103.40).

   ii. *Time of filing.* During normal, posted business hours, the time of filing shall be the time the duplicate document is produced in the office of the Clerk of the Circuit Court. Duplicate documents received at all other times shall be filed as of the next normal business day. IN ST ADMIN Rule 12(C).

- If the receiving fax machine endorses its own time and date stamp upon the transmitted documents and the receiving machine produces a delivery receipt which is electronically created and transmitted to the sending party, the time of filing shall be the date and time recorded on the transmitted document by the receiving fax machine. IN ST ADMIN Rule 12(C).

- Electronic facsimile transmissions will be accepted for filing only during the regular business hours as set forth in IN ST HAMILTON ADMIN Rule 101. Transmissions received by the Hamilton County Clerk after close of business shall be filed effective the next regular business day. IN ST HAMILTON ADMIN Rule 103(103.30).

    iii. *Filing fee.* The electronic facsimile transmission will not be accepted for filing if its filing requires the payment of any fee other than the electronic facsimile transcription fee set forth in IN ST HAMILTON ADMIN Rule 103(103.20). IN ST HAMILTON ADMIN Rule 103(103.10)(e).

- Pursuant to Ordinance adopted by the Hamilton County Board of Commissioners, the Clerk shall collect an electronic facsimile transcription fee of One Dollar ($1.00) per page, to a maximum of Ten Dollars ($10.00) per transmission, for each electronic facsimile transmission accepted for filing with the Hamilton County Circuit and Superior Courts. IN ST HAMILTON ADMIN Rule 103(103.20).

- The fee shall be assessed against the sending party and shall be paid upon receipt of invoice by that party and at the latest within thirty (30) days of the transmission. In the event the fee is not paid by the sending party within the time limits provided, the court may issue a show-cause order or enter a judgment in the matter. The Clerk may refuse an electronic facsimile transmission from any attorney or pro se litigant who has failed to pay these fees within thirty (30) days. IN ST HAMILTON ADMIN Rule 103(103.20).

    iv. *No direct filing with court.* A party shall not send pleadings, motions and other papers by electronic facsimile transmission for filing directly to any Court without that Court's prior approval to do so. IN ST HAMILTON ADMIN Rule 103(103.50).

  c. *Filing with special judge.* After a special judge has qualified, a copy of each pleading and Chronological Case Summary entries filed with the Court shall be mailed or delivered to the office of that Special judge by the counsel or pro se litigant with service indicated on the certificate of service. IN ST HAMILTON TRIAL Rule 204(204.20).

  d. *Proof of filing.* Any party filing any paper by any method other than personal delivery to the clerk shall retain proof of filing. IN ST TRIAL P Rule 5(F).

2. *Service requirements.* Unless otherwise provided by the Indiana Rules of Trial Procedure or an order of the court, each party and special judge, if any, shall be served with: (1) every order required by its terms to be served; (2) every pleading subsequent to the original complaint; (3) every written motion except one which may be heard ex parte; (4) every brief submitted to the trial court; (5) every paper relating to discovery required to be served upon a party; and (6) every written notice, appearance, demand, offer of judgment, designation of record on appeal, or similar paper. IN ST TRIAL P Rule 5(A).

  a. *Methods of service*

    i. *Personal service.* Whenever a party is represented by an attorney of record, service shall be made upon such attorney unless service upon the party himself is ordered by the court. Service upon the attorney or party shall be made by delivering or mailing a copy of the papers to the last known address or where an attorney or party has consented to service by fax or e-mail, as provided in IN ST TRIAL P Rule 3.1(A)(4), by faxing or e-mailing a copy of the documents to the fax number or e-mail address set out in the appearance form or correction as required by IN ST TRIAL P Rule 3.1(E). IN ST TRIAL P Rule 5(B). Delivery of a copy within IN ST TRIAL P Rule 5 means:

- Offering or tendering it to the attorney or party and stating the nature of the papers being served. Refusal to accept an offered or tendered document is a waiver of any objection to the sufficiency or adequacy of service of that document;

- Leaving it at his office with a clerk or other person in charge thereof, or if there is no one in charge, leaving it in a conspicuous place therein; or

- If the office is closed, by leaving it at his dwelling house or usual place of abode with some person of suitable age and discretion then residing therein; or,

- Leaving it at some other suitable place, selected by the attorney upon whom service is being made, pursuant to duly promulgated local rule. IN ST TRIAL P Rule 5(B)(1).

ii. *Service by mail.* If service is made by mail, the papers shall be deposited in the United States mail addressed to the person on whom they are being served, with postage prepaid. Service shall be deemed complete upon mailing. Proof of service of all papers permitted to be mailed may be made by written acknowledgment of service, by affidavit of the person who mailed the papers, or by certificate of an attorney. It shall be the duty of attorneys when entering their appearance in a cause or when filing pleadings or papers therein, to have noted in the Chronological Case Summary or said pleadings or papers so filed the address and telephone number of their office. Service by delivery or by mail at such address shall be deemed sufficient and complete. IN ST TRIAL P Rule 5(B)(2).

iii. *Service by fax or e-mail.* A party who has consented to service by fax or e-mail may be served as follows:

- Service by e-mail shall be made by attaching the document being served in .pdf format. Discovery documents must also be served in accordance with IN ST TRIAL P Rule 26(A). IN ST TRIAL P Rule 5(B)(3)(a).

- Service by fax shall be deemed complete upon generation of a transmission record indicating the successful transmission of the entire document, except as provided in IN ST TRIAL P Rule 5(B)(3)(d). IN ST TRIAL P Rule 5(B)(3)(b).

- Service by e-mail shall be deemed complete upon transmission, except as provided in IN ST TRIAL P Rule 5(B)(3)(d). IN ST TRIAL P Rule 5(B)(3)(c).

- Service by fax or e-mail that occurs on a Saturday, Sunday, legal holiday, or day the court or agency in which the matter is pending is closed or after 5:00 PM local time of the recipient shall be deemed complete the next day that is not a Saturday, Sunday, legal holiday, or day that the court or agency in which the matter is pending is not closed. IN ST TRIAL P Rule 5(B)(3)(d).

iv. *Mail box service.* Pursuant to IN ST TRIAL P Rule 5(B)(1)(d), the Circuit and Superior Courts of Hamilton County hereby designate the "mail boxes" located in the Clerk's order book office for service of pleadings upon attorneys who have such boxes. IN ST HAMILTON TRIAL Rule 201(201.50).

b. *Serving numerous defendants.* In any action in which there are unusually large numbers of defendants, the court, upon motion or of its own initiative, may order:

i. That service of the pleadings of the defendants and replies thereto need not be made as between the defendants;

- That any cross-claim, counterclaim, or matter constituting an avoidance or affirmative defense contained therein shall be deemed to be denied or avoided by all other parties; and

- That the filing of any such pleading and service thereof upon the plaintiff constitutes due notice of it to the parties. IN ST TRIAL P Rule 5(D).

ii. A copy of every such order shall be served upon the parties in such manner and form as the court directs. IN ST TRIAL P Rule 5(D).

c. *Service on parties in default for failure to appear.* No service need be made on parties in default for failure to appear, except that pleadings asserting new or additional claims for relief against them shall be served upon them in the manner provided by service of summons in IN ST TRIAL P Rule 4. IN ST TRIAL P Rule 5(A).

G. Hearings

1. *Hearing on motion.* Unless local conditions make it impracticable, each judge shall establish regular times and places, at intervals sufficiently frequent for the prompt dispatch of business, at which motions requiring notice and hearing may be heard and disposed of; but the judge at any time or place and on such notice, if any, as he considers reasonable may make order for the advancement, conduct, and hearing of actions. To expedite its business the court may direct the submission and determination of motions without oral hearing upon brief written statements of reasons in support and opposition, or direct or permit hearings by telephone conference call with all attorneys or other similar means of communication. IN ST TRIAL P Rule 73(A).

H. Forms

1. Motion for Protective Order Forms for Indiana

a. Pending motion. 5 INPRAC § 4:5.1.

b. Relevancy. 5 INPRAC § 4:5.2.

c. Unduly burdensome. 5 INPRAC § 4:5.3.

d. Privileged. 5 INPRAC § 4:5.4.

e. Mental impressions and legal conclusions. 5 INPRAC § 4:5.5.

f. Expert reports and papers. 5 INPRAC § 4:5.6.

g. Quash subpoena duces tecum. 5 INPRAC § 4:5.7.

h. Quash subpoena duces tecum; Non-party. 5 INPRAC § 4:5.8.

i. Trade secrets and confidential information. 5 INPRAC § 4:5.9.

j. Motion to lift protective order. 5 INPRAC § 4:5.10.

k. Motion for protective order; Discovery not be had; Protection against disclosure of expert report and papers. 10 INPRAC § 58.22.

l. Motion for protective order; Discovery not relevant to subject matter of action. 10 INPRAC § 58.23.

m. Motion for protective order; Discovery unduly burdensome; Alternative request for deposition. 10 INPRAC § 58.24.

n. Motion for protective order; Challenging date and time of deposition. 10 INPRAC § 58.25.

o. Motion for protective order; Challenging place of deposition. 10 INPRAC § 58.26.

p. Motion for protective order; To prevent the disclosure of trade secrets and confidential research and development. 10 INPRAC § 58.27.

q. Motion for protective order; To preclude further deposition of corporate officer. 10 INPRAC § 58.28.

r. Motion for protective order; To preclude taking expert deposition; Failure to obtain court order or to disclose expert opinions. 10 INPRAC § 58.30.

s. Motion for protective order; To preclude disclosure of privileged matters. 10 INPRAC § 58.31.

t. Motion for protective order; To have plaintiff's attorney and physician present during plaintiff's physical examination; Request to tape record physical examination. 10 INPRAC § 58.32.

u. Motion for protective order; To preclude defendant's attorney from conducting an informal interview of plaintiff's treating physician. 10 INPRAC § 58.33.

v. Motion for protective order; To produce documents at responding party's place of business. 10 INPRAC § 58.34.

w. Motion for protective order; Discovery limited to certain matter until court rules on pending motion. 10 INPRAC § 58.35.

x. Motion for protective order; Answers to discovery to be sealed to protect confidential commercial information. 10 INPRAC § 58.36.

y. Certificate of service; Personal service. 9 INPRAC § 5.7.

z. Certificate of service; First class mail. 9 INPRAC § 5.8.

I. Checklist

(I) ☐ Matters to be considered by moving party

  (a) ☐ Required documents

    (1) ☐ Motion and notice

    (2) ☐ Attorney certification

    (3) ☐ Proposed order

        (4)   ❑ Certificate of service

    (b)   ❑ Supplemental documents

        (1)   ❑ Supporting evidence

        (2)   ❑ Facsimile cover sheet

        (3)   ❑ Request to schedule trial or hearing

        (4)   ❑ Copies of unpublished opinions

    (c)   ❑ Timing

        (1)   ❑ There are no specific timing requirements for filing a motion for a protective order

        (2)   ❑ A written motion, other than one which may be heard ex parte, and notice of the hearing thereof shall be served not less than five (5) days before the time specified for the hearing, unless a different period is fixed by the Indiana Rules of Trial Procedure or by order of the court

        (3)   ❑ All pleadings and papers subsequent to the complaint which are required to be served upon a party shall be filed with the Court either before service or within a reasonable period of time thereafter

(II)   ❑ Matters to be considered by the responding party

    (a)   ❑ Required documents

        (1)   ❑ Opposition

        (2)   ❑ Certificate of service

    (b)   ❑ Supplemental documents

        (1)   ❑ Supporting evidence

        (2)   ❑ Alternative proposed order

        (3)   ❑ Facsimile cover sheet

        (4)   ❑ Request to schedule trial or hearing

        (5)   ❑ Copies of unpublished opinions

    (c)   ❑ Timing

        (1)   ❑ Except as otherwise provided in IN ST TRIAL P Rule 59(D), opposing affidavits may be served not less than one (1) day before the hearing, unless the court permits them to be served at some other time

Motions, Oppositions and Replies
Motion for Discovery Sanctions

Document Last Updated October 2013

A. Applicable Rules

1. *State rules*

    a.   Appearance. IN ST TRIAL P Rule 3.1.

    b.   Process. IN ST TRIAL P Rule 4.

    c.   Service and filing of pleadings and other papers. IN ST TRIAL P Rule 5.

    d.   Time. IN ST TRIAL P Rule 6.

    e.   Pleadings. IN ST TRIAL P Rule 7; IN ST TRIAL P Rule 8; IN ST TRIAL P Rule 9.2; IN ST TRIAL P Rule 10.

    f.   Signing and verification of pleadings. IN ST TRIAL P Rule 11.

    g.   General provisions governing discovery. IN ST TRIAL P Rule 26.

    h.   Methods of discovery. IN ST TRIAL P Rule 27; IN ST TRIAL P Rule 30; IN ST TRIAL P Rule 31; IN ST TRIAL P Rule 33; IN ST TRIAL P Rule 34; IN ST TRIAL P Rule 35; IN ST TRIAL P Rule 36.

    i.   Failure to make or cooperate in discovery; Sanctions. IN ST TRIAL P Rule 37.

    j.   Evidence. IN ST TRIAL P Rule 43.

    k.   Judgment on the evidence (directed verdict). IN ST TRIAL P Rule 50.

    l.   Findings by the court. IN ST TRIAL P Rule 52.

    m.   Summary judgment. IN ST TRIAL P Rule 56.

    n.   Motion to correct error. IN ST TRIAL P Rule 59.

    o.   Relief from judgment or order. IN ST TRIAL P Rule 60.

    p.   Hearing of motions. IN ST TRIAL P Rule 73.

    q.   Access to court records. IN ST ADMIN Rule 9.

    r.   Paper size. IN ST ADMIN Rule 11.

    s.   Facsimile transmission. IN ST ADMIN Rule 12.

    t.   Electronic filing and electronic service pilot projects. IN ST ADMIN Rule 16.

    u.   Sealing of certain records by court; Hearing; Notice. IN ST 5-14-3-5.5.

    v.   Privacy and confidentiality. IN ST 5-2-9-6; IN ST 5-14-3-4; IN ST 6-4.1-5-10; IN ST 6-4.1-12-12; IN ST 6-8.1-7-1; IN ST 11-13-1-8; IN ST 12-23-14-13; IN ST 16-39-3-10; IN ST 16-41-8-1; IN ST 22-4-19-6; IN ST 31-11-1-6; IN ST 31-19-5-23; IN ST 31-19-13-2; IN ST 31-19-19-1; IN ST 31-33-18-1; IN ST 31-39-1-1; IN ST 31-39-1-2; IN ST 33-23-16-16; IN ST 35-34-2-4; IN ST 35-38-1-13; IN ST 35-38-9-1; IN ST ADR Rule 2.11; IN ST ADR Rule 4.4; IN ST ADR Rule 5.6; IN ST JURY Rule 10.

2.   *Local rules*

    a.   Court hours. IN ST HAMILTON ADMIN Rule 101.

    b.   Facsimile transmissions. IN ST HAMILTON ADMIN Rule 103.

    c.   Filing of pleadings and entry of appearances. IN ST HAMILTON TRIAL Rule 201.

    d.   Proposed orders. IN ST HAMILTON TRIAL Rule 202.

    e.   Briefs and memorandums. IN ST HAMILTON TRIAL Rule 203.

    f.   Special judges. IN ST HAMILTON TRIAL Rule 204.

    g.   Trial settings. IN ST HAMILTON TRIAL Rule 205.

    h.   Continuances. IN ST HAMILTON TRIAL Rule 206.

B. Timing

1.   *Motion for discovery sanctions.* There are no specific timing requirements for filing a motion for discovery sanctions.

    a.   *Filing.* All pleadings and papers subsequent to the complaint which are required to be served upon a party shall be filed with the Court either before service or within a reasonable period of time thereafter. IN ST TRIAL P Rule 5(E)(1).

2.   *Service.* A written motion, other than one which may be heard ex parte, and notice of the hearing thereof shall be served not less than five (5) days before the time specified for the hearing, unless a different period is fixed by the Indiana Rules of Trial Procedure or by order of the court. IN ST TRIAL P Rule 6(D).

    a.   *Of supporting affidavits.* When a motion is supported by affidavit, the affidavit shall be served with the motion. IN ST TRIAL P Rule 6(D).

3.   *Service of opposition.* Except as otherwise provided in IN ST TRIAL P Rule 59(D), opposing affidavits

may be served not less than one (1) day before the hearing, unless the court permits them to be served at some other time. IN ST TRIAL P Rule 6(D).

4. *Computation of time*

   a. *Generally; Days excluded.* In computing any period of time prescribed or allowed by the Indiana Rules of Trial Procedure, by order of the court, or by any applicable statute, the day of the act, event, or default from which the designated period of time begins to run shall not be included. The last day of the period so computed is to be included unless it is:

      i. A Saturday,

      ii. A Sunday,

      iii. A legal holiday as defined by state statute, or

      iv. A day the office in which the act is to be done is closed during regular business hours. IN ST TRIAL P Rule 6(A).

   b. *Short periods.* In any event, the period runs until the end of the next day that is not a Saturday, a Sunday, a legal holiday, or a day on which the office is closed. When the period of time allowed is less than seven (7) days, intermediate Saturdays, Sundays, legal holidays, and days on which the office is closed shall be excluded from the computations. IN ST TRIAL P Rule 6(A).

   c. *Additional time after service by United States mail.* Whenever a party has the right or is required to do some act or take some proceedings within a prescribed period after the service of a notice or other paper upon him and the notice or paper is served upon him by United States mail, three (3) days shall be added to the prescribed period. IN ST TRIAL P Rule 6(E).

   d. *Enlargement of time.* When an act is required or allowed to be done at or within a specific time by the Indiana Rules of Trial Procedure, the court may at any time for cause shown:

      i. Order the period enlarged, with or without motion or notice, if request therefor is made before the expiration of the period originally prescribed or extended by a previous order; or

      ii. Upon motion made after the expiration of the specific period, permit the act to be done where the failure to act was the result of excusable neglect; but, the court may not extend the time for taking any action for judgment on the evidence under IN ST TRIAL P Rule 50(A), amendment of findings and judgment under IN ST TRIAL P Rule 52(B), to correct errors under IN ST TRIAL P Rule 59(C), statement in opposition to motion to correct error under IN ST TRIAL P Rule 59(E), or to obtain relief from final judgment under IN ST TRIAL P Rule 60(B), except to the extent and under the conditions stated in those rules. IN ST TRIAL P Rule 6(B).

      iii. For information on obtaining a continuance, refer to IN ST HAMILTON TRIAL Rule 206.

C. General Requirements

1. *Motions, generally.* Unless made during a hearing or trial, or otherwise ordered by the court, an application to the court for an order shall be made by written motion. The motion shall state the grounds therefor and the relief or order sought. IN ST TRIAL P Rule 7(B).

   a. *Motions as distinct from pleadings.* Motions and responses to motions are not pleadings, and allegations contained in a motion are not admissions of a party. 22B INPRAC 7:2; Wachstetter v. County Properties, LLC, 832 N.E.2d 574 (Ind.Ct.App. 2005); Scott County Family YMCA, Inc. v. Hobbs, 817 N.E.2d 603 (Ind.Ct.App. 2004).

   b. *Unopposed motions generally granted.* It is common for a trial court to grant procedural motions, such as motions for enlargement of time, discovery motions, or motions for continuance, unless an objection is filed. 21 INPRAC § 13.8.

2. *Motion for discovery sanctions*

   a. *Related to a motion to compel; Award of sanctions on motion*

      i. *Motion granted.* If the motion is granted, the court shall, after opportunity for hearing, require the party or deponent whose conduct necessitated the motion or the party or attorney advising such conduct or both of them to pay to the moving party the reasonable expenses incurred in obtaining the order, including attorney's fees, unless the court finds that the opposition to the motion was substantially justified or that other circumstances make an award of expenses unjust. IN ST TRIAL P Rule 37(A)(4).

ii. *Motion denied.* If the motion is denied, the court shall, after opportunity for hearing, require the moving party or the attorney advising the motion or both of them to pay to the party or deponent who opposed the motion the reasonable expenses incurred in opposing the motion, including attorney's fees, unless the court finds that the making of the motion was substantially justified or that other circumstances make an award of expenses unjust. IN ST TRIAL P Rule 37(A)(4).

iii. *Granted in part and denied in part.* If the motion is granted in part and denied in part, the court may apportion the reasonable expenses incurred in relation to the motion among the parties and persons in a just manner. IN ST TRIAL P Rule 37(A)(4).

iv. Refer to the Indiana KeyRules Motion to Compel Discovery document for more information.

b. *Failure to comply with order.* The trial court may impose sanctions upon a party who fails to obey an order regarding discovery. 22 INPRAC § 27.7. The first step to invoking sanctions under IN ST TRIAL P Rule 37(B) is to file a motion to compel discovery under IN ST TRIAL P Rule 37(A) and obtain an order from the court requiring the opposing party to take a specific action in discovery. If the opposing party then fails to take the action mandated by the trial court's discovery order, the second step is to return to the trial court and file a motion for sanctions under IN ST TRIAL P Rule 37(B). 22 INPRAC § 27.7.

i. *Sanctions by court in county where deposition is taken.* If a deponent fails to be sworn or to answer a question after being directed to do so by the court in the county in which the deposition is being taken, the failure may be considered a contempt of that court. IN ST TRIAL P Rule 37(B)(1).

ii. *Sanctions by court in which action is pending.* If a party or an officer, director, or managing agent of a party or an organization, including a governmental organization, or a person designated under IN ST TRIAL P Rule 30(B)(6) or IN ST TRIAL P Rule 31(A) to testify on behalf of a party or an organization, including a governmental organization, fails to obey an order to provide or permit discovery, including an order made under IN ST TRIAL P Rule 37(A) or IN ST TRIAL P Rule 35, the court in which the action is pending may make such orders in regard to the failure as are just, and among others the following:

- An order that the matters regarding which the order was made or any other designated facts shall be taken to be established for the purposes of the action in accordance with the claim of the party obtaining the order;

- An order refusing to allow the disobedient party to support or oppose designated claims or defenses, or prohibiting him from introducing designated matters in evidence;

- An order striking out pleadings or parts thereof, or staying further proceedings until the order is obeyed, or dismissing the action or proceeding or any part thereof, or rendering a judgment by default against the disobedient party;

- In lieu of any of the foregoing orders or in addition thereto, an order treating as a contempt of court the failure to obey any orders except an order to submit to a physical or mental examination under IN ST TRIAL P Rule 35;

- Where a party has failed to comply with an order under IN ST TRIAL P Rule 35(A) requiring him to produce another for examination, such orders as are listed in IN ST TRIAL P Rule 37(B)(2)(a), IN ST TRIAL P Rule 37(B)(2)(b), and IN ST TRIAL P Rule 37(B)(2)(c), unless the party failing to comply shows that he is unable to produce such person for examination. IN ST TRIAL P Rule 37(B)(2).

- In lieu of any of the foregoing orders or in addition thereto, the court shall require the party failing to obey the order or the attorney advising him or both to pay the reasonable expenses, including attorney's fees, caused by the failure, unless the court finds that the failure was substantially justified or that other circumstances make an award of expenses unjust. IN ST TRIAL P Rule 37(B)(2).

c. *Expenses on failure to admit.* If a party fails to admit the genuineness of any document or the truth of any matter as requested under IN ST TRIAL P Rule 36, and if the party requesting the admissions thereafter proves the genuineness of the document or the truth of the matter, he may apply to the court for an order requiring the other party to pay him the reasonable expenses incurred in making that proof, including reasonable attorney's fees. The court shall make the order unless it finds that:

   i. The request was held objectionable pursuant to IN ST TRIAL P Rule 36(A), or

   ii. The admission sought was of no substantial importance, or

   iii. The party failing to admit had reasonable ground to believe that he might prevail on the matter, or

   iv. There was other good reason for the failure to admit. IN ST TRIAL P Rule 37(C).

d. *Failure of party to attend at own deposition or serve answers to interrogatories or respond to requests for inspection*

   i. *Court order for failure to provide discovery.* If a party or an officer, director, or managing agent of a party or an organization, including without limitation a governmental organization, or a person designated under IN ST TRIAL P Rule 30(B)(6) or IN ST TRIAL P Rule 31(A) to testify on behalf of a party or an organization, including without limitation a governmental organiza-tion, fails (1) to appear before the officer who is to take his deposition, after being served with a proper notice, or (2) to serve answers or objections to interrogatories submitted under IN ST TRIAL P Rule 33, after proper service of the interrogatories, or (3) to serve a written response to a request for inspection submitted under IN ST TRIAL P Rule 34, after proper service of the request, the court in which the action is pending on motion may make such orders in regard to the failure as are just, and among others it may take any action authorized under IN ST TRIAL P Rule 37(B)(2)(a), IN ST TRIAL P Rule 37(B)(2)(b), and IN ST TRIAL P Rule 37(B)(2)(c). IN ST TRIAL P Rule 37(D).

   ii. *Attorney fees against party failing to provide discovery.* In lieu of any order or in addition thereto, the court shall require the party failing to act or the attorney advising him or both to pay the reasonable expenses, including attorney's fees, caused by the failure, unless the court finds that the failure was substantially justified or that other circumstances make an award of expenses unjust. IN ST TRIAL P Rule 37(D)

   iii. *Failure not excused for objectionable requests.* The failure to act described in IN ST TRIAL P Rule 37(D) may not be excused on the ground that the discovery sought is objectionable unless the party failing to act has applied for a protective order as provided by IN ST TRIAL P Rule 26(C). IN ST TRIAL P Rule 37(D). Refer to the Indiana KeyRules Motion for Protective Order document for more information.

   iv. *Showing required.* To invoke the sanctions under IN ST TRIAL P Rule 37(D), it is sufficient that notice of the deposition or other discovery request was properly served upon the non-responding party, but no response was provided. 22 INPRAC § 27.8.

e. *Sanctions for spoliation of evidence.* In some cases a duty arises imposing an affirmative obligation to avoid the destruction or loss of documents and materials that are relevant and discoverable to claims and defenses that either have been or may be asserted in an action. The destruction, mutilation, alteration or concealment of such materials is called "spoliation." 3 INPRAC R 37(37.2.2); Glotzbach v. Froman, 854 N.E.2d 337 (Ind. 2006).

   i. *Spoliation generally.* Spoliation typically presents itself in one of two ways:

   • A party to litigation destroys materials that are relevant and discoverable in an action; or

   • A non-party destroys materials that may be discoverable in an action to which that entity or individual will not be a party. 3 INPRAC R 37(37.2.2).

   ii. *Duty to maintain evidence must exist.* A key component of a spoliation claim is that the party who destroyed the materials must have had a duty not to do so. A duty may arise in a number of ways: imposed by statute or case law, imposed by contract or some third party beneficiary arrangement, or imposed by the actions of the parties by which one party assumes a duty in law or equity toward another. When duty arises from the conduct of the parties as opposed to one established by statute or contract, the Indiana courts have identified three primary factors to determine whether a duty exists:

- The relationship between the parties,
- The reasonable foreseeability of harm to the injured litigant, and
- The public policy promoted by recognizing an enforceable duty. 3 INPRAC R 37(37.2.2); Webb v. Jarvis, 575 N.E.2d 992 (Ind. 1991).
- This balancing test is particularly useful where the element of duty has not already been established between the parties. 3 INPRAC R 37(37.2.2); Northern Indiana Public Service Co. v. Sharp, 790 N.E.2d 462 (Ind. 2003).

   iii. *Factors to be considered by the court.* Even where the court finds an intentional spoliation, it is not mandatory that sanctions be imposed. Rather, the trial court should implement an approach by which it balances the nature of the offense against the harm suffered by the non-offending party because lost evidence is not available. 22 INPRAC § 27.9; Gribben v. Wal-Mart Stores, Inc., 824 N.E.2d 349 (Ind. 2005). Factors the court may consider include:

- The culpability of the spoliating party;
- The prejudice to the non-offending party;
- The degree of interference with the judicial process;
- Whether lesser sanctions are available to remedy any harm and deter future acts of spoliation;
- The amount of time lapsing from the date the spoliating party took possession of the evidence and the date of its loss or destruction;
- Protocols adopted, and followed, by the spoliating party to prevent the loss of evidence, such as a document retention policy;
- Whether evidence has been irretrievably lost and, if so, the circumstances of that loss;
- The existence of available alternatives that would allow the non-offending party to prove its case without the lost evidence;
- And whether sanctions will unfairly punish a party for the misconduct or mistake of his attorney or expert. 22 INPRAC § 27.9.

  f. *No sanctions for good-faith loss of electronically stored information.* Absent exceptional circumstances, a court may not impose sanctions under the Indiana Rules of Trial Procedure these rules on a party for failing to provide electronically stored information lost as a result of the routine, good faith operation of an electronic information system. IN ST TRIAL P Rule 37(E).

D. Documents

1. *Required documents*

  a. *Motion and notice.* The requirement of notice is satisfied by service of the motion. IN ST TRIAL P Rule 7(B). Refer to the General Requirements section of this document for information on the content of a motion for discovery sanctions.

  b. *Attorney certification.* Before any party files any motion or request to compel discovery pursuant to IN ST TRIAL P Rule 37, or any motion for protection from discovery pursuant to IN ST TRIAL P Rule 26(C), or any other discovery motion which seeks to enforce, modify, or limit discovery, that party shall:

   i. Make a reasonable effort to reach agreement with the opposing party concerning the matter which is the subject of the motion or request; and

   ii. Include in the motion or request a statement showing that the attorney making the motion or request has made a reasonable effort to reach agreement with the opposing attorney(s) concerning the matter(s) set forth in the motion or request. This statement shall recite, in addition, the date, time and place of this effort to reach agreement, whether in person or by phone, and the names of all parties and attorneys participating therein. If an attorney for any party advises the court in writing that an opposing attorney has refused or delayed meeting and discussing the issues covered in IN ST TRIAL P Rule 26(F), the court may take such action as is appropriate. IN ST TRIAL P Rule 26(F).

    iii. The court may deny a discovery motion filed by a party who has failed to comply with the requirements of IN ST TRIAL P Rule 26(F). IN ST TRIAL P Rule 26(F).

c. *Proposed order.* Unless local practice provides differently, a party should submit a proposed order with its written motion to be signed by the judge once the motion has been granted. 21 INPRAC § 13.8; IN ST HAMILTON ADMIN Rule 103(103.10)(b). Each Motion, Petition or other request for relief shall be accompanied by a proposed order. IN ST HAMILTON TRIAL Rule 202(202.10).

    i. All proposed orders submitted by counsel pursuant to IN ST HAMILTON TRIAL Rule 202 shall meet the following requirements: (1) contain a complete distribution list of all attorneys and pro se litigants with full addresses; (2) stamped envelopes appropriately addressed for each attorney of record and/or pro se litigant on the distribution list. IN ST HAMILTON TRIAL Rule 202(202.30).

d. *Certificate of service.* An attorney or unrepresented party tendering a document to the Clerk for filing shall certify that service has been made, list the parties served, and specify the date and means of service. The certificate of service shall be placed at the end of the document and shall not be separately filed. The separate filing of a certificate of service, however, shall not be grounds for rejecting a document for filing. The Clerk may permit documents to be filed without a certificate of service but shall require prompt filing of a separate certificate of service. IN ST TRIAL P Rule 5(C).

    i. All pleadings filed with the Court which require a certificate of service shall specifically name the individual party or attorney on whom service has been made, the address, the manner in which service was made and the date when service was made. IN ST HAMILTON TRIAL Rule 201(201.60).

2. *Supplemental documents*

a. *Supporting evidence.* When a motion is based on facts not appearing of record the court may hear the matter on affidavits presented by the respective parties, but the court may direct that the matter be heard wholly or partly on oral testimony or depositions. IN ST TRIAL P Rule 43(B).

b. *Facsimile cover sheet.* Any document sent to the Clerk of the Circuit Court by electronic facsimile transmission shall be accompanied by a cover sheet which states the title of the document, case number, number of pages, identity and voice telephone number of the sending party and instructions for filing. The cover sheet shall contain the signature of the attorney or party, pro se, authorizing the filing. IN ST ADMIN Rule 12(D); IN ST HAMILTON ADMIN Rule 103(103.10)(a).

c. *Request to schedule hearing.* All requests to schedule trials and hearings shall be in writing and shall contain the following information:

    i. Type of trial or hearing (i.e., jury trial, court trial, final hearing in dissolution, etc.). IN ST HAMILTON TRIAL Rule 205(205.10).

    ii. A good-faith estimate of the total court time needed for the trial or hearing. IN ST HAMILTON TRIAL Rule 205(205.10).

    iii. Each request under IN ST HAMILTON TRIAL Rule 205(205.10) shall be accompanied by a proposed written order with appropriate blanks for date and time and shall further include reference to those items set forth in IN ST HAMILTON TRIAL Rule 205(205.10)(a) and IN ST HAMILTON TRIAL Rule 205(205.10)(b). IN ST HAMILTON TRIAL Rule 205(205.20).

d. *Copies of unpublished opinions.* Authorities relied upon which are not cited in the Northeastern Reporter system shall be attached to counsel's brief. If the authority is cited for the first time in oral argument, a copy of the authority may be provided to the Court at the time of the argument. Sufficient copies shall be available to provide counsel for each party with a copy. IN ST HAMILTON TRIAL Rule 203(203.10).

E. Format

1. *Form of motions.* The rules applicable to captions, and the signing and form of pleadings (IN ST TRIAL P Rule 8 through IN ST TRIAL P Rule 11), apply to all motions and other papers provided under the Indiana Rules of Trial Procedure. 22B INPRAC 7:2.

2. *Form of pleadings*

   a. *Caption; Names of parties.* Every pleading shall contain a caption setting forth the name of the court, the title of the action, the file number, and a designation as in IN ST TRIAL P Rule 7(A). In the complaint the title of the action shall include the names of all the parties, but in other pleadings it is sufficient to state the name of the first party on each side with an appropriate indication of other parties. IN ST TRIAL P Rule 10(A).

   b. *Paragraphs; Separate statements.* All averments of a claim or defense shall be made in numbered paragraphs, the contents of each of which shall be limited as far as practicable to a statement of a single set of circumstances, and a paragraph may be referred to by number in all succeeding pleadings. Each claim founded upon a separate transaction or occurrence and each defense other than denials may be stated in a separate count or defense whenever a separation facilitates the clear presentation of the matters set forth. IN ST TRIAL P Rule 10(B).

   c. *Adoption by reference; Exhibits.* Statements in a pleading may be adopted by reference in a different part of the same pleading or in another pleading or in any motion. A copy of any written instrument which is an exhibit to a pleading is a part thereof for all purposes. IN ST TRIAL P Rule 10(C).

   d. *Facsimile page limit.* Courts authorize the Hamilton County Clerk of Courts to accept pleadings, motions and other papers by electronic facsimile transmission for filing in any case pending before the Courts, subject to the requirement that The transmission may not exceed ten (10) pages in length including the cover sheet and proposed CCS entry. IN ST HAMILTON ADMIN Rule 103(103.10)(c).

   e. *Emergency facsimile filings.* If the filing requires the immediate attention of the Judge, it shall so indicate in bold letters in an accompanying transmittal memorandum. IN ST HAMILTON ADMIN Rule 103(103.10)(f).

   f. *Special judge heading.* After a special judge is selected, the attorneys or pro se litigants shall add to the caption of all pleadings to the right of the case title the following: "BEFORE SPECIAL JUDGE _____." IN ST HAMILTON TRIAL Rule 204(204.10).

   g. *Format rules strictly enforced.* All filings shall be in compliance with the Indiana Rules of Trial Procedure. If the documents received are not in proper form, such deficiencies will not be corrected by court personnel. IN ST HAMILTON TRIAL Rule 201(201.70). The Court shall not be required to act on any Motion, Petition or other request for relief unless filed in conformity with the Hamilton County Local Trial and Administrative rules. IN ST HAMILTON TRIAL Rule 202(202.20).

3. *Size of papers for filing.* Effective January 1, 1992, all pleadings, copies, motions and documents filed with any trial court or appellate level court, typed or printed, with the exception of exhibits and existing wills, shall be prepared on eight and one-half by eleven inch (8 1/2" x 11") size paper. IN ST ADMIN Rule 11.

   a. *Form.* All documents filed in any Hamilton County Court, with the exception of exhibits and existing wills, shall be prepared on paper measuring eight and one-half by eleven inches (8 1/2" x 11"). IN ST HAMILTON TRIAL Rule 201(201.20).

4. *Signature requirements*

   a. *Signature of attorney.* Every pleading or motion of a party represented by an attorney shall be signed by at least one (1) attorney of record in his individual name, whose address, telephone number, and attorney number shall be stated, except that this provision shall not apply to pleadings and motions made and transcribed at the trial or a hearing before the judge and received by him in such form. IN ST TRIAL P Rule 11(A).

      i. The signature of an attorney constitutes a certificate by him that he has read the pleadings; that to the best of his knowledge, information, and belief, there is good ground to support it; and that it is not interposed for delay. IN ST TRIAL P Rule 11(A).

    ii.   If a pleading or motion is not signed or is signed with intent to defeat the purpose of the rule, it may be stricken as sham and false and the action may proceed as though the pleading had not been served. IN ST TRIAL P Rule 11(A).

    iii.   For a willful violation of IN ST TRIAL P Rule 11 an attorney may be subjected to appropriate disciplinary action. Similar action may be taken if scandalous or indecent matter is inserted. IN ST TRIAL P Rule 11(A).

b.   *Signature of unrepresented party.* A party who is not represented by an attorney shall sign his pleading and state his address. IN ST TRIAL P Rule 11(A).

c.   *Verification not generally required.* Except when specifically required by rule, pleadings or motions need not be verified or accompanied by affidavit. The rule in equity that the averments of an answer under oath must be overcome by the testimony of two (2) witnesses or of one (1) witness sustained by corroborating circumstances is abolished. IN ST TRIAL P Rule 11(A).

d.   *Verification by affirmation or representation.* When in connection with any civil or special statutory proceeding it is required that any pleading, motion, petition, supporting affidavit, or other document of any kind, be verified, or that an oath be taken, it shall be sufficient if the subscriber simply affirms the truth of the matter to be verified by an affirmation or representation. IN ST TRIAL P Rule 11(B). IN ST TRIAL P Rule 11(B) states that the affirmation or representation should be in substantially the following language: "I (we) affirm, under the penalties for perjury, that the foregoing representation(s) is (are) true. (Signed) _____."

    i.   Any person who falsifies an affirmation or representation of fact shall be subject to the same penalties as are prescribed by law for the making of a false affidavit. IN ST TRIAL P Rule 11(B).

e.   *Verified pleadings, motions, and affidavits as evidence.* Pleadings, motions and affidavits accompanying or in support of such pleadings or motions when required to be verified or under oath shall be accepted as a representation that the signer had personal knowledge thereof or reasonable cause to believe the existence of the facts or matters stated or alleged therein; and, if otherwise competent or acceptable as evidence, may be admitted as evidence of the facts or matters stated or alleged therein when it is so provided in the Indiana Rules of Trial Procedure, by statute or other law, or to the extent the writing or signature expressly purports to be made upon the signer's personal knowledge. When such pleadings, motions and affidavits are verified or under oath they shall not require other or greater proof on the part of the adverse party than if not verified or not under oath unless expressly provided otherwise by the Indiana Rules of Trial Procedure, statute or other law. Affidavits upon motions for summary judgment under IN ST TRIAL P Rule 56 and in denial of execution under IN ST TRIAL P Rule 9.2 shall be made upon personal knowledge. IN ST TRIAL P Rule 11(C).

5.   *Information excluded from public access.* Every document filed in a case shall separately identify information excluded from public access pursuant to IN ST ADMIN Rule 9(G)(1) as follows:

a.   Whole documents that are excluded from public access pursuant to IN ST ADMIN Rule 9(G)(1) shall be tendered on light green paper or have a light green coversheet attached to the document, marked "Not for Public Access" or "Confidential." IN ST TRIAL P Rule 5(G)(1).

b.   When only a portion of a document contains information excluded from public access pursuant to IN ST ADMIN Rule 9(G)(1), said information shall be omitted [or redacted] from the filed document, and set forth on a separate accompanying document on light green paper conspicuously marked "Not for Public Access" or "Confidential" and clearly designated [or identifying] the caption and number of the case and the document and location within the document to which the redacted material pertains. IN ST TRIAL P Rule 5(G)(2).

c.   With respect to documents filed in electronic format, the trial court, by local rule, may provide for compliance with IN ST TRIAL P Rule 5 in manner that separates and protects access to information excluded from public access. IN ST TRIAL P Rule 5(G)(3).

d.   IN ST TRIAL P Rule 5(G) does not apply to a record sealed by the court pursuant to IN ST 5-14-3-5.5 or otherwise, nor to records, documents, or information filed in cases to which public access is prohibited pursuant to IN ST ADMIN Rule 9(G). IN ST TRIAL P Rule 5(G)(4).

e. The following information in case records is excluded from public access and is confidential:

i. Information that is excluded from public access pursuant to federal law;

ii. Information that is excluded from public access as declared confidential by Indiana statute or other court rule, including without limitation:

- All adoption records created after July 8, 1941, as declared confidential by IN ST 31-19-19-1, et seq., except those specifically declared open by IN ST 31-19-13-2(2);

- All records relating to chancroid, chlamydia, gonorrhea, hepatitis, human immunodeficiency virus (HIV), Lymphogranuloma venereum, syphilis, tuberculosis, as declared confidential by IN ST 16-41-8-1, et seq.;

- All records relating to child abuse as declared confidential by IN ST 31-33-18-1, et seq.;

- All records relating to drug tests as declared confidential by IN ST 5-14-3-4(a)(9);

- Records of grand jury proceedings as declared confidential by IN ST 35-34-2-4;

- Records of juvenile proceedings as declared confidential by IN ST 31-39-1-2, except those specifically open under statute;

- All paternity records created after July 1, 1941 as declared confidential by IN ST 31-14-11-15, IN ST 31-19-5-23, IN ST 31-39-1-1 and IN ST 31-39-1-2 [Editor's note: IN ST 31-14-11-15 was repealed effective May 9, 2013];

- All pre-sentence reports as declared confidential by IN ST 35-38-1-13;

- Written petitions to permit marriages without consent and orders directing the Clerk of Court to issue a marriage license to underage persons, as declared confidential by IN ST 31-11-1-6;

- Only those arrest warrants, search warrants, indictments and informations ordered confidential by the trial judge, prior to return of duly executed service as declared confidential by IN ST 5-14-3-4(b)(1);

- All medical, mental health, or tax records unless determined by law or regulation of any governmental custodian not to be confidential, released by the subject of such records, or declared by a court of competent jurisdiction to be essential to the resolution of litigation as declared confidential by IN ST 16-39-3-10, IN ST 6-4.1-5-10, IN ST 6-4.1-12-12, and IN ST 6-8.1-7-1;

- Personal information relating to jurors or prospective jurors, other than for the use of the parties and counsel, pursuant to IN ST JURY Rule 10;

- Information relating to protection from abuse orders, no-contact orders and workplace violence restraining orders as declared confidential by IN ST 5-2-9-6, et seq.;

- Mediation proceedings pursuant to IN ST ADR Rule 2.11, Mini-Trial proceedings pursuant to IN ST ADR Rule 4.4(C), and Summary Jury Trials pursuant to IN ST ADR Rule 5.6;

- Information in probation files pursuant to the Probation Standards promulgated by the Judicial Conference of Indiana pursuant to IN ST 11-13-1-8(b);

- Information deemed confidential pursuant to the Rules for Court Administered Alcohol and Drug Programs promulgated by the Judicial Conference of Indiana pursuant to IN ST 12-23-14-13;

- Information deemed confidential pursuant to the Problem-Solving Court Rules promulgated by the Judicial Conference of Indiana pursuant to IN ST 33-23-16-16;

- All records of the Department of workforce Development as declared confidential by IN ST 22-4-19-6;

- Information regarding interception of electronic communications that is sealed or deemed confidential as set forth in IN ST 35-33.5-2-1, et seq.

480

    iii. Information excluded from public access by specific court order;

    iv. Complete Social Security Numbers of living persons;

    v. With the exception of names, information such as addresses, phone numbers, and dates of birth which explicitly identifies:

- Natural persons who are witnesses or victims (not including defendants) in criminal, domestic violence, stalking, sexual assault, juvenile, or civil protection order proceedings, provided that juveniles who are victims of sex crimes shall be identified by initials only;

- Places of residence of judicial officers, clerks and other employees of courts and clerks of court, unless the person or persons about whom the information pertains waives confidentiality;

    vi. Complete account numbers of specific assets, loans, bank accounts, credit cards, and personal identification numbers (PINs);

    vii. All orders of expungement entered in criminal or juvenile proceedings, orders to restrict access to criminal history information pursuant to IN ST 35-38-5-5.5 or IN ST 35-38-8-5 and records excluded from public access by such orders, and information related to infractions that is excluded from public access pursuant to IN ST 34-28-5-15 or IN ST 34-28-5-16 [Editor's note: IN ST 35-38-5-5.5, IN ST 35-38-8-5 and IN ST 34-28-5-16 were repealed effective July 1, 2013; for information on orders restricting access to criminal history, refer to IN ST 35-38-9-1, et seq.];

    viii. All personal notes and e-mail, and deliberative material, of judges, jurors, court staff and judicial agencies, and information recorded in personal data assistants (PDA's) or organizers and personal calendars. IN ST ADMIN Rule 9(G)(1).

F. Filing and Service Requirements

  1. *Filing requirements.* Except as otherwise provided in IN ST TRIAL P Rule 5(E)(2), all pleadings and papers subsequent to the complaint which are required to be served upon a party shall be filed with the Court either before service or within a reasonable period of time thereafter. IN ST TRIAL P Rule 5(E)(1).

    a. *Filing with the court defined.* The filing of pleadings, motions, and other papers with the court as required by the Indiana Rules of Trial Procedure shall be made by one of the following methods:

      i. Delivery to the clerk of the court;

      ii. Sending by electronic transmission under the procedure adopted pursuant to IN ST ADMIN Rule 12;

      iii. Mailing to the clerk by registered, certified or express mail return receipt requested;

      iv. Depositing with any third-party commercial carrier for delivery to the clerk within three (3) calendar days, cost prepaid, properly addressed;

      v. If the court so permits, filing with the judge, in which event the judge shall note thereon the filing date and forthwith transmit them to the office of the clerk; or

      vi. Electronic filing, as approved by the Division of State Court Administration pursuant to IN ST ADMIN Rule 16. IN ST TRIAL P Rule 5(F).

      vii. Filing by registered or certified mail and by third-party commercial carrier shall be complete upon mailing or deposit. IN ST TRIAL P Rule 5(F).

    b. *Facsimile filing.* As outlined in IN ST HAMILTON ADMIN Rule 103(103.10),facsimile filing is permitted in the Circuit and Superior Courts of Hamilton County. The Courts authorize the Hamilton County Clerk of Courts to accept pleadings, motions and other papers by electronic facsimile transmission for filing in any case pending before the Courts, subject to the requirements of IN ST HAMILTON ADMIN Rule 103(103.10). IN ST HAMILTON ADMIN Rule 103(103.10); IN ST HAMILTON TRIAL Rule 201(201.80).

      i. *Generally.* In counties where a majority of judges of the courts of record, by posted local rule, have authorized electronic facsimile filing and designated a telephone number to receive such

transmissions, pleadings, motions, and other papers may be sent to the Clerk of Circuit Court by electronic facsimile transmission for filing in any case, provided:

- Such matter does not exceed ten (10) pages, including the cover sheet;

- Such matter does not require the payment of fees other than the electronic facsimile transcription fee set forth in IN ST ADMIN Rule 12(E);

- The sending party creates at the time of transmission a machine generated log for such transmission; and

- The original document and the transmission log are maintained by the sending party for the duration of the litigation. IN ST ADMIN Rule 12(B); IN ST HAMILTON ADMIN Rule 103(103.10)(d).

- Legibility of documents and timeliness of filing is the responsibility of the sender. IN ST HAMILTON ADMIN Rule 103(103.10)(g).

- The Clerk shall accept electronic facsimile transmission filings only if received at the facsimile machine assigned by the Clerk. The telephone number designated to receive such transmission is available at IN ST HAMILTON ADMIN Rule 103(103.40). IN ST HAMILTON ADMIN Rule 103(103.40).

ii. *Time of filing.* During normal, posted business hours, the time of filing shall be the time the duplicate document is produced in the office of the Clerk of the Circuit Court. Duplicate documents received at all other times shall be filed as of the next normal business day. IN ST ADMIN Rule 12(C).

- If the receiving fax machine endorses its own time and date stamp upon the transmitted documents and the receiving machine produces a delivery receipt which is electronically created and transmitted to the sending party, the time of filing shall be the date and time recorded on the transmitted document by the receiving fax machine. IN ST ADMIN Rule 12(C).

- Electronic facsimile transmissions will be accepted for filing only during the regular business hours as set forth in IN ST HAMILTON ADMIN Rule 101. Transmissions received by the Hamilton County Clerk after close of business shall be filed effective the next regular business day. IN ST HAMILTON ADMIN Rule 103(103.30).

iii. *Filing fee.* The electronic facsimile transmission will not be accepted for filing if its filing requires the payment of any fee other than the electronic facsimile transcription fee set forth in IN ST HAMILTON ADMIN Rule 103(103.20). IN ST HAMILTON ADMIN Rule 103(103.10)(e).

- Pursuant to Ordinance adopted by the Hamilton County Board of Commissioners, the Clerk shall collect an electronic facsimile transcription fee of One Dollar ($1.00) per page, to a maximum of Ten Dollars ($10.00) per transmission, for each electronic facsimile transmission accepted for filing with the Hamilton County Circuit and Superior Courts. IN ST HAMILTON ADMIN Rule 103(103.20).

- The fee shall be assessed against the sending party and shall be paid upon receipt of invoice by that party and at the latest within thirty (30) days of the transmission. In the event the fee is not paid by the sending party within the time limits provided, the court may issue a show-cause order or enter a judgment in the matter. The Clerk may refuse an electronic facsimile transmission from any attorney or pro se litigant who has failed to pay these fees within thirty (30) days. IN ST HAMILTON ADMIN Rule 103(103.20).

iv. *No direct filing with court.* A party shall not send pleadings, motions and other papers by electronic facsimile transmission for filing directly to any Court without that Court's prior approval to do so. IN ST HAMILTON ADMIN Rule 103(103.50).

c. *Filing with special judge.* After a special judge has qualified, a copy of each pleading and Chronological Case Summary entries filed with the Court shall be mailed or delivered to the office of that Special judge by the counsel or pro se litigant with service indicated on the certificate of service. IN ST HAMILTON TRIAL Rule 204(204.20).

d. *Proof of filing.* Any party filing any paper by any method other than personal delivery to the clerk shall retain proof of filing. IN ST TRIAL P Rule 5(F).

2. *Service requirements.* Unless otherwise provided by the Indiana Rules of Trial Procedure or an order of the court, each party and special judge, if any, shall be served with: (1) every order required by its terms to be served; (2) every pleading subsequent to the original complaint; (3) every written motion except one which may be heard ex parte; (4) every brief submitted to the trial court; (5) every paper relating to discovery required to be served upon a party; and (6) every written notice, appearance, demand, offer of judgment, designation of record on appeal, or similar paper. IN ST TRIAL P Rule 5(A).

   a. *Methods of service*

      i. *Personal service.* Whenever a party is represented by an attorney of record, service shall be made upon such attorney unless service upon the party himself is ordered by the court. Service upon the attorney or party shall be made by delivering or mailing a copy of the papers to the last known address or where an attorney or party has consented to service by fax or e-mail, as provided in IN ST TRIAL P Rule 3.1(A)(4), by faxing or e-mailing a copy of the documents to the fax number or e-mail address set out in the appearance form or correction as required by IN ST TRIAL P Rule 3.1(E). IN ST TRIAL P Rule 5(B). Delivery of a copy within IN ST TRIAL P Rule 5 means:

         • Offering or tendering it to the attorney or party and stating the nature of the papers being served. Refusal to accept an offered or tendered document is a waiver of any objection to the sufficiency or adequacy of service of that document;

         • Leaving it at his office with a clerk or other person in charge thereof, or if there is no one in charge, leaving it in a conspicuous place therein; or

         • If the office is closed, by leaving it at his dwelling house or usual place of abode with some person of suitable age and discretion then residing therein; or,

         • Leaving it at some other suitable place, selected by the attorney upon whom service is being made, pursuant to duly promulgated local rule. IN ST TRIAL P Rule 5(B)(1).

      ii. *Service by mail.* If service is made by mail, the papers shall be deposited in the United States mail addressed to the person on whom they are being served, with postage prepaid. Service shall be deemed complete upon mailing. Proof of service of all papers permitted to be mailed may be made by written acknowledgment of service, by affidavit of the person who mailed the papers, or by certificate of an attorney. It shall be the duty of attorneys when entering their appearance in a cause or when filing pleadings or papers therein, to have noted in the Chronological Case Summary or said pleadings or papers so filed the address and telephone number of their office. Service by delivery or by mail at such address shall be deemed sufficient and complete. IN ST TRIAL P Rule 5(B)(2).

      iii. *Service by fax or e-mail.* A party who has consented to service by fax or e-mail may be served as follows:

         • Service by e-mail shall be made by attaching the document being served in .pdf format. Discovery documents must also be served in accordance with IN ST TRIAL P Rule 26(A). IN ST TRIAL P Rule 5(B)(3)(a).

         • Service by fax shall be deemed complete upon generation of a transmission record indicating the successful transmission of the entire document, except as provided in IN ST TRIAL P Rule 5(B)(3)(d). IN ST TRIAL P Rule 5(B)(3)(b).

         • Service by e-mail shall be deemed complete upon transmission, except as provided in IN ST TRIAL P Rule 5(B)(3)(d). IN ST TRIAL P Rule 5(B)(3)(c).

         • Service by fax or e-mail that occurs on a Saturday, Sunday, legal holiday, or day the court or agency in which the matter is pending is closed or after 5:00 PM local time of the recipient shall be deemed complete the next day that is not a Saturday, Sunday, legal holiday, or day that the court or agency in which the matter is pending is not closed. IN ST TRIAL P Rule 5(B)(3)(d).

iv. *Mail box service.* Pursuant to IN ST TRIAL P Rule 5(B)(1)(d), the Circuit and Superior Courts of Hamilton County hereby designate the "mail boxes" located in the Clerk's order book office for service of pleadings upon attorneys who have such boxes. IN ST HAMILTON TRIAL Rule 201(201.50).

b. *Serving numerous defendants.* In any action in which there are unusually large numbers of defendants, the court, upon motion or of its own initiative, may order:

    i. That service of the pleadings of the defendants and replies thereto need not be made as between the defendants;

- That any cross-claim, counterclaim, or matter constituting an avoidance or affirmative defense contained therein shall be deemed to be denied or avoided by all other parties; and

- That the filing of any such pleading and service thereof upon the plaintiff constitutes due notice of it to the parties. IN ST TRIAL P Rule 5(D).

    ii. A copy of every such order shall be served upon the parties in such manner and form as the court directs. IN ST TRIAL P Rule 5(D).

c. *Service on parties in default for failure to appear.* No service need be made on parties in default for failure to appear, except that pleadings asserting new or additional claims for relief against them shall be served upon them in the manner provided by service of summons in IN ST TRIAL P Rule 4. IN ST TRIAL P Rule 5(A).

G. Hearings

1. *Hearing on motion.* Unless local conditions make it impracticable, each judge shall establish regular times and places, at intervals sufficiently frequent for the prompt dispatch of business, at which motions requiring notice and hearing may be heard and disposed of; but the judge at any time or place and on such notice, if any, as he considers reasonable may make order for the advancement, conduct, and hearing of actions. To expedite its business the court may direct the submission and determination of motions without oral hearing upon brief written statements of reasons in support and opposition, or direct or permit hearings by telephone conference call with all attorneys or other similar means of communication. IN ST TRIAL P Rule 73(A).

2. *Hearings generally held before imposition of discovery sanctions.* As a general matter, most courts will conduct a hearing prior to imposing discovery sanctions, although IN ST TRIAL P Rule 37 and Indiana case law do not expressly require a court to do so. 22 INPRAC § 27.7.

H. Forms

1. Motion for Discovery Sanctions Forms for Indiana

a. Motion to dismiss as sanction for failure to comply with court ordered discovery. 5 INPRAC § 4:6.60.

b. Motion to dismiss action as sanction; For party's failure to comply with court ordered discovery. 10 INPRAC § 58.38.

c. Motion for order precluding litigation of issues. 10 INPRAC § 58.63.

d. Motion for judgment by default; As sanction for failure to comply with court order. 10 INPRAC § 58.64.

e. Motion to exclude expert witness at trial. 10 INPRAC § 70.24

f. Certificate of service; Personal service. 9 INPRAC § 5.7.

g. Certificate of service; First class mail. 9 INPRAC § 5.8.

I. Checklist

(I) ❏ Matters to be considered by moving party

    (a) ❏ Required documents

        (1) ❏ Motion and notice

        (2) ❏ Attorney certification

    (3) ❏ Proposed order

    (4) ❏ Certificate of service

 (b) ❏ Supplemental documents

    (1) ❏ Supporting evidence

    (2) ❏ Facsimile cover sheet

    (3) ❏ Request to schedule trial or hearing

    (4) ❏ Copies of unpublished opinions

 (c) ❏ Timing

    (1) ❏ There are no specific timing requirements for filing a motion for discovery sanctions

    (2) ❏ A written motion, other than one which may be heard ex parte, and notice of the hearing thereof shall be served not less than five (5) days before the time specified for the hearing, unless a different period is fixed by the Indiana Rules of Trial Procedure or by order of the court

    (3) ❏ All pleadings and papers subsequent to the complaint which are required to be served upon a party shall be filed with the Court either before service or within a reasonable period of time thereafter

(II) ❏ Matters to be considered by the responding party

 (a) ❏ Required documents

    (1) ❏ Opposition

    (2) ❏ Certificate of service

 (b) ❏ Supplemental documents

    (1) ❏ Supporting evidence

    (2) ❏ Alternative proposed order

    (3) ❏ Facsimile cover sheet

    (4) ❏ Request to schedule trial or hearing

    (5) ❏ Copies of unpublished opinions

 (c) ❏ Timing

    (1) ❏ Except as otherwise provided in IN ST TRIAL P Rule 59(D), opposing affidavits may be served not less than one (1) day before the hearing, unless the court permits them to be served at some other time

Motions, Oppositions and Replies
Motion for Preliminary Injunction

Document Last Updated October 2013

A. Applicable Rules

1. *State rules*

   a. Appearance. IN ST TRIAL P Rule 3.1.

   b. Process. IN ST TRIAL P Rule 4.

   c. Service and filing of pleadings and other papers. IN ST TRIAL P Rule 5.

   d. Time. IN ST TRIAL P Rule 6.

   e. Pleadings. IN ST TRIAL P Rule 7; IN ST TRIAL P Rule 8; IN ST TRIAL P Rule 9.2; IN ST TRIAL P Rule 10.

f. Signing and verification of pleadings. IN ST TRIAL P Rule 11.

g. Evidence. IN ST TRIAL P Rule 43.

h. Judgment on the evidence (directed verdict). IN ST TRIAL P Rule 50.

i. Findings by the court. IN ST TRIAL P Rule 52.

j. Summary judgment. IN ST TRIAL P Rule 56.

k. Motion to correct error. IN ST TRIAL P Rule 59.

l. Relief from judgment or order. IN ST TRIAL P Rule 60.

m. Injunctions. IN ST TRIAL P Rule 65; IN ST 34-26-1-7; IN ST 34-26-1-8.

n. Security; Proceedings against sureties. IN ST TRIAL P Rule 65.1.

o. Hearing of motions. IN ST TRIAL P Rule 73.

p. Access to court records. IN ST ADMIN Rule 9.

q. Paper size. IN ST ADMIN Rule 11.

r. Facsimile transmission. IN ST ADMIN Rule 12.

s. Electronic filing and electronic service pilot projects. IN ST ADMIN Rule 16.

t. Sealing of certain records by court; Hearing; Notice. IN ST 5-14-3-5.5.

u. Privacy and confidentiality. IN ST 5-2-9-6; IN ST 5-14-3-4; IN ST 6-4.1-5-10; IN ST 6-4.1-12-12; IN ST 6-8.1-7-1; IN ST 11-13-1-8; IN ST 12-23-14-13; IN ST 16-39-3-10; IN ST 16-41-8-1; IN ST 22-4-19-6; IN ST 31-11-1-6; IN ST 31-19-5-23; IN ST 31-19-13-2; IN ST 31-19-19-1; IN ST 31-33-18-1; IN ST 31-39-1-1; IN ST 31-39-1-2; IN ST 33-23-16-16; IN ST 35-34-2-4; IN ST 35-38-1-13; IN ST 35-38-9-1; IN ST ADR Rule 2.11; IN ST ADR Rule 4.4; IN ST ADR Rule 5.6; IN ST JURY Rule 10.

2. *Local rules*

a. Court hours. IN ST HAMILTON ADMIN Rule 101.

b. Facsimile transmissions. IN ST HAMILTON ADMIN Rule 103.

c. Filing of pleadings and entry of appearances. IN ST HAMILTON TRIAL Rule 201.

d. Proposed orders. IN ST HAMILTON TRIAL Rule 202.

e. Briefs and memorandums. IN ST HAMILTON TRIAL Rule 203.

f. Special judges. IN ST HAMILTON TRIAL Rule 204.

g. Trial settings. IN ST HAMILTON TRIAL Rule 205.

h. Continuances. IN ST HAMILTON TRIAL Rule 206.

B. Timing

1. *Motion for preliminary injunction.* The injunction may be granted at the time of commencing the action, or at any time afterwards before judgment is rendered in the proceeding. IN ST 34-26-1-7. IN ST TRIAL P Rule 65 does not state when notice must be given. 4 INPRAC R 65(65.2).

a. *Filing.* All pleadings and papers subsequent to the complaint which are required to be served upon a party shall be filed with the Court either before service or within a reasonable period of time thereafter. IN ST TRIAL P Rule 5(E)(1).

2. *Service.* A written motion, other than one which may be heard ex parte, and notice of the hearing thereof shall be served not less than five (5) days before the time specified for the hearing, unless a different period is fixed by the Indiana Rules of Trial Procedure or by order of the court. IN ST TRIAL P Rule 6(D).

a. *Of supporting affidavits.* When a motion is supported by affidavit, the affidavit shall be served with the motion. IN ST TRIAL P Rule 6(D).

3. *Service of opposition.* Except as otherwise provided in IN ST TRIAL P Rule 59(D), opposing affidavits may be served not less than one (1) day before the hearing, unless the court permits them to be served at some other time. IN ST TRIAL P Rule 6(D).

4. *Computation of time*

    a. *Generally; Days excluded.* In computing any period of time prescribed or allowed by the Indiana Rules of Trial Procedure, by order of the court, or by any applicable statute, the day of the act, event, or default from which the designated period of time begins to run shall not be included. The last day of the period so computed is to be included unless it is:

        i. A Saturday,

        ii. A Sunday,

        iii. A legal holiday as defined by state statute, or

        iv. A day the office in which the act is to be done is closed during regular business hours. IN ST TRIAL P Rule 6(A).

    b. *Short periods.* In any event, the period runs until the end of the next day that is not a Saturday, a Sunday, a legal holiday, or a day on which the office is closed. When the period of time allowed is less than seven (7) days, intermediate Saturdays, Sundays, legal holidays, and days on which the office is closed shall be excluded from the computations. IN ST TRIAL P Rule 6(A).

    c. *Additional time after service by United States mail.* Whenever a party has the right or is required to do some act or take some proceedings within a prescribed period after the service of a notice or other paper upon him and the notice or paper is served upon him by United States mail, three (3) days shall be added to the prescribed period. IN ST TRIAL P Rule 6(E).

    d. *Enlargement of time.* When an act is required or allowed to be done at or within a specific time by the Indiana Rules of Trial Procedure, the court may at any time for cause shown:

        i. Order the period enlarged, with or without motion or notice, if request therefor is made before the expiration of the period originally prescribed or extended by a previous order; or

        ii. Upon motion made after the expiration of the specific period, permit the act to be done where the failure to act was the result of excusable neglect; but, the court may not extend the time for taking any action for judgment on the evidence under IN ST TRIAL P Rule 50(A), amendment of findings and judgment under IN ST TRIAL P Rule 52(B), to correct errors under IN ST TRIAL P Rule 59(C), statement in opposition to motion to correct error under IN ST TRIAL P Rule 59(E), or to obtain relief from final judgment under IN ST TRIAL P Rule 60(B), except to the extent and under the conditions stated in those rules. IN ST TRIAL P Rule 6(B).

        iii. For information on obtaining a continuance, refer to IN ST HAMILTON TRIAL Rule 206.

C. General Requirements

1. *Motions, generally.* Unless made during a hearing or trial, or otherwise ordered by the court, an application to the court for an order shall be made by written motion. The motion shall state the grounds therefor and the relief or order sought. IN ST TRIAL P Rule 7(B).

    a. *Motions as distinct from pleadings.* Motions and responses to motions are not pleadings, and allegations contained in a motion are not admissions of a party. 22B INPRAC 7:2; Wachstetter v. County Properties, LLC, 832 N.E.2d 574 (Ind.Ct.App. 2005); Scott County Family YMCA, Inc. v. Hobbs, 817 N.E.2d 603 (Ind.Ct.App. 2004).

    b. *Unopposed motions generally granted.* It is common for a trial court to grant procedural motions, such as motions for enlargement of time, discovery motions, or motions for continuance, unless an objection is filed. 21 INPRAC § 13.8.

2. *Motion for preliminary injunction.* The general purpose of a temporary restraining order and a preliminary injunction is to maintain and preserve the status quo until the merits of the case can be heard. The status quo is the last actual, peaceful and noncontested status which preceded the pending controversy. 4 INPRAC R 65(65.1); Rees v. Panhandle Eastern Pipe Line Co., 176 Ind.App. 597, 377 N.E.2d 640 (Ind.Ct.App. 1978). An injunction does not create or enlarge the rights of a party, it merely protects existing rights and prevents harm to the aggrieved party that cannot be corrected by a final judgment. 22B INPRAC 65:1; Franke v. Honeywell, Inc., 516 N.E.2d 1090 (Ind.Ct.App. 1987); Indiana & Michigan Elec. Co. v. Whitley County Rural Elec. Membership Corp., 161 Ind.App. 492, 316 N.E.2d 584

(Ind.Ct.App. 1974); AGS Capital Corp., Inc. v. Product Action Intern., LLC, 884 N.E.2d 294 (Ind.Ct.App. 2008).

a.   *Injunctions in general.* Whether or not a preliminary injunction should issue rests in the sound discretion of the trial court. Discretion to grant or deny a preliminary injunction is measured by the following factors and the burden lies with the movant to prove each element by a preponderance of the evidence. 4 INPRAC R 65(65.1); Crossmann Communities, Inc. v. Dean, 767 N.E.2d 1035, 1040 (Ind.Ct.App. 2002); Mercho-Roushdi Corp. v. Blatchford, 742 N.E.2d 519, 524 (Ind.Ct.App. 2001).

   i.   If the movant fails to prove any of these requirements, the trial court's grant of an injunction is an abuse of discretion. 4 INPRAC R 65(65.1); Ind. Family and Soc. Servs. Admin. v. Walgreen Co., 769 N.E.2d 158, 161 (Ind. 2002):

   •   Whether the plaintiff's remedies at law are inadequate and the plaintiff will suffer irreparable harm pending the resolution of the substantive action if the injunction does not issue;

   •   Whether the plaintiff has demonstrated at least a reasonable likelihood of success at trial by establishing a prima facie case;

   •   Whether the threatened injury to the plaintiff outweighs the threatened harm the grant of the injunction may inflict on the defendant; and

   •   Whether the public interest would be disserved if the injunction is granted. 4 INPRAC R 65(65.1); Ind. Family and Soc. Servs. Admin. v. Walgreen Co., 769 N.E.2d 158, 161 (Ind. 2002); Daugherty v. Allen, 729 N.E.2d 228, 232 (Ind.Ct.App. 2000);

   ii.   Two (2) sweeping statements about the preliminary injunction often appear:

   •   Economic injury alone will not warrant the granting of a preliminary injunction. 4 INPRAC R 65(65.1); Wells v. Auberry, 429 N.E.2d 679 (Ind.Ct.App. 1982), and

   •   Injunctive relief is not appropriate if a remedy for damages is an adequate remedy and the defendant is solvent. 4 INPRAC R 65(65.1); Gaslight and Coke Company v. City of New Albany, 139 Ind. 660, 39 N.E. 462 (1894).

b.   *Consolidation of hearing with trial on merits.* Before or after the commencement of the hearing of an application for a preliminary injunction, the court may order the trial of the action on the merits to be advanced and consolidated with the hearing of the application. Even when this consolidation is not ordered, any evidence received upon an application for a preliminary injunction which would be admissible upon the trial on the merits becomes part of the record on the trial and need not be repeated upon the trial. IN ST TRIAL P Rule 65(A)(2).

   i.   The power of the court to order advancement and consolidation under IN ST TRIAL P Rule 65 is tempered by the due process requirements of fair notice and an opportunity to be heard. 4 INPRAC R 65(65.3); University of Texas v. Camenisch, 451 U.S. 390, 101 S.Ct. 1830, 68 L.Ed.2d 175 (1981). The court is required to give clear notice that consolidation of the trial on the merits with the hearing on the motion for preliminary injunction will be ordered, and the notice must be given at a time which will afford the parties a full opportunity to present their respective cases. 4 INPRAC R 65(65.3); Paris v. U.S. Department of Housing & Urban Dev., 713 F.2d 1341, 1345, (7th Cir. 1983).

c.   *Assignment of cases; Judge to act promptly.* Assignment of cases shall not be affected by the fact that a temporary restraining order or preliminary injunction is sought, but such case shall be assigned promptly and the judge regularly assigned to the case shall act upon and hear all matters relating to temporary restraining orders and preliminary injunctions. The judge shall make himself readily available to consider temporary restraining orders, conduct hearings, fix the manner of giving notice and the time and place for hearings under IN ST TRIAL P Rule 65, and shall act and require the parties to act promptly. IN ST TRIAL P Rule 65(A)(3).

   i.   If the party seeking relief or his attorney by affidavit establishes that the judge assigned to the case is not available or cannot be found to consider an application for a restraining order, to conduct a hearing, or to fix the manner of giving notice and the time and place for a hearing under IN ST TRIAL P Rule 65, he may apply to any other judge in the circuit who shall take all further action with respect to any temporary restraining order or preliminary injunction. If the affidavit establishes that no other judge in the circuit is available or to be found, he may apply to the judge of any adjoining circuit. Unless an order is entered within ten (10) days after the hearing upon the granting, modifying or dissolving of a temporary or preliminary injunction, the relief sought shall be subject to the provisions of IN ST TRIAL P Rule 53.1. IN ST TRIAL P Rule 65(A)(3).

d. *Modification of orders; Responsive pleadings.* Upon the court's own motion or the motion of any party, orders granting or denying temporary restraining orders or preliminary injunctions may be dissolved, modified, granted or reinstated. Responsive pleadings shall not be required in response to any pleadings or motions relating to temporary restraining orders or preliminary injunctions. IN ST TRIAL P Rule 65(A)(4).

e. *Form of order by judge.* Every order granting temporary injunction and every restraining order shall include or be accompanied by findings as required by IN ST TRIAL P Rule 52; shall be specific in terms; shall describe in reasonable detail, and not by reference to the complaint or other document, the act or acts sought to be restrained; and is binding only upon the parties to the action, their officers, agents, servants, employees, and attorneys, and upon those persons in active concert or participation with them who receive actual notice of the order by personal service or otherwise. IN ST TRIAL P Rule 65(D).

3. *Security*

a. *Security requirement.* No restraining order or preliminary injunction shall issue except upon the giving of security by the applicant, in such sum as the court deems proper, for the payment of such costs and damages as may be incurred or suffered by any party who is found to have been wrongfully enjoined or restrained. No such security shall be required of a governmental organization, but such governmental organization shall be responsible for costs and damages as may be incurred or suffered by any party who is found to have been wrongfully enjoined or restrained. IN ST TRIAL P Rule 65(C).

i. The provisions of IN ST TRIAL P Rule 65.1 apply to a surety upon a bond or undertaking under IN ST TRIAL P Rule 65. IN ST TRIAL P Rule 65(C).

b. *Proceedings against sureties.* Whenever the Indiana Rules of Trial Procedure or other laws require or permit the giving of security by a party to a court action or proceeding, and security is given in the form of a bond or stipulation or other undertaking with one or more sureties, each surety submits himself to the jurisdiction of the court and irrevocably appoints the clerk of the court as his agent upon whom any papers affecting his liability on the bond or undertaking may be served. His liability may be enforced on motion without the necessity of an independent action. The motion and such notice of the motion as the court prescribes may be served on the clerk of the court, who shall forthwith mail copies to the sureties if their addresses are known. IN ST TRIAL P Rule 65.1 applies to bonds or security furnished on appeal, and enforcement shall be in the court to which the case is returned after appeal. IN ST TRIAL P Rule 65.1.

c. *Bond generally used as security.* IN ST TRIAL P Rule 65(C) speaks only of the giving of security and does not expressly require a surety on a bond. In practice, however, the giving of a bond with an insurance company as surety in the amount set by the court is typically the device used to satisfy this section. 4 INPRAC R 65(65.6).

D. Documents

1. *Required documents*

a. *Motion and notice.* No preliminary injunction shall be issued without an opportunity for a hearing upon notice to the adverse party. IN ST TRIAL P Rule 65(A)(1). The requirement of notice is satisfied by service of the motion. IN ST TRIAL P Rule 7(B). Refer to the General Requirements section of this document for information on the content of a motion for preliminary injunction.

b. *Affidavit.* In all applications for an injunction, the complaint or as much of the complaint as pertains to the acts or proceedings to be enjoined, must be verified by affidavit. IN ST 34-26-1-7.

c. *Security.* No restraining order or preliminary injunction shall issue except upon the giving of security by the applicant, in such sum as the court deems proper, for the payment of such costs and damages as may be incurred or suffered by any party who is found to have been wrongfully enjoined or restrained. IN ST TRIAL P Rule 65(C). Refer to the General Requirements section of this document for more information.

d. *Proposed order.* Unless local practice provides differently, a party should submit a proposed order with its written motion to be signed by the judge once the motion has been granted. 21 INPRAC § 13.8; IN ST HAMILTON ADMIN Rule 103(103.10)(b). Each Motion, Petition or other request for relief shall be accompanied by a proposed order. IN ST HAMILTON TRIAL Rule 202(202.10).

  i. All proposed orders submitted by counsel pursuant to IN ST HAMILTON TRIAL Rule 202 shall meet the following requirements: (1) contain a complete distribution list of all attorneys and pro se litigants with full addresses; (2) stamped envelopes appropriately addressed for each attorney of record and/or pro se litigant on the distribution list. IN ST HAMILTON TRIAL Rule 202(202.30).

e. *Certificate of service.* An attorney or unrepresented party tendering a document to the Clerk for filing shall certify that service has been made, list the parties served, and specify the date and means of service. The certificate of service shall be placed at the end of the document and shall not be separately filed. The separate filing of a certificate of service, however, shall not be grounds for rejecting a document for filing. The Clerk may permit documents to be filed without a certificate of service but shall require prompt filing of a separate certificate of service. IN ST TRIAL P Rule 5(C).

  i. All pleadings filed with the Court which require a certificate of service shall specifically name the individual party or attorney on whom service has been made, the address, the manner in which service was made and the date when service was made. IN ST HAMILTON TRIAL Rule 201(201.60).

2. *Supplemental documents*

a. *Supporting evidence.* When a motion is based on facts not appearing of record the court may hear the matter on affidavits presented by the respective parties, but the court may direct that the matter be heard wholly or partly on oral testimony or depositions. IN ST TRIAL P Rule 43(B).

b. *Facsimile cover sheet.* Any document sent to the Clerk of the Circuit Court by electronic facsimile transmission shall be accompanied by a cover sheet which states the title of the document, case number, number of pages, identity and voice telephone number of the sending party and instructions for filing. The cover sheet shall contain the signature of the attorney or party, pro se, authorizing the filing. IN ST ADMIN Rule 12(D); IN ST HAMILTON ADMIN Rule 103(103.10)(a).

c. *Request to schedule hearing.* All requests to schedule trials and hearings shall be in writing and shall contain the following information:

  i. Type of trial or hearing (i.e., jury trial, court trial, final hearing in dissolution, etc.). IN ST HAMILTON TRIAL Rule 205(205.10).

  ii. A good-faith estimate of the total court time needed for the trial or hearing. IN ST HAMILTON TRIAL Rule 205(205.10).

  iii. Each request under IN ST HAMILTON TRIAL Rule 205(205.10) shall be accompanied by a proposed written order with appropriate blanks for date and time and shall further include reference to those items set forth in IN ST HAMILTON TRIAL Rule 205(205.10)(a) and IN ST HAMILTON TRIAL Rule 205(205.10)(b). IN ST HAMILTON TRIAL Rule 205(205.20).

d. *Copies of unpublished opinions.* Authorities relied upon which are not cited in the Northeastern Reporter system shall be attached to counsel's brief. If the authority is cited for the first time in oral argument, a copy of the authority may be provided to the Court at the time of the argument. Sufficient copies shall be available to provide counsel for each party with a copy. IN ST HAMILTON TRIAL Rule 203(203.10).

E. Format

1. *Form of motions.* The rules applicable to captions, and the signing and form of pleadings (IN ST TRIAL

P Rule 8 through IN ST TRIAL P Rule 11), apply to all motions and other papers provided under the Indiana Rules of Trial Procedure. 22B INPRAC 7:2.

2. *Form of pleadings*

   a. *Caption; Names of parties.* Every pleading shall contain a caption setting forth the name of the court, the title of the action, the file number, and a designation as in IN ST TRIAL P Rule 7(A). In the complaint the title of the action shall include the names of all the parties, but in other pleadings it is sufficient to state the name of the first party on each side with an appropriate indication of other parties. IN ST TRIAL P Rule 10(A).

   b. *Paragraphs; Separate statements.* All averments of a claim or defense shall be made in numbered paragraphs, the contents of each of which shall be limited as far as practicable to a statement of a single set of circumstances, and a paragraph may be referred to by number in all succeeding pleadings. Each claim founded upon a separate transaction or occurrence and each defense other than denials may be stated in a separate count or defense whenever a separation facilitates the clear presentation of the matters set forth. IN ST TRIAL P Rule 10(B).

   c. *Adoption by reference; Exhibits.* Statements in a pleading may be adopted by reference in a different part of the same pleading or in another pleading or in any motion. A copy of any written instrument which is an exhibit to a pleading is a part thereof for all purposes. IN ST TRIAL P Rule 10(C).

   d. *Facsimile page limit.* Courts authorize the Hamilton County Clerk of Courts to accept pleadings, motions and other papers by electronic facsimile transmission for filing in any case pending before the Courts, subject to the requirement that The transmission may not exceed ten (10) pages in length including the cover sheet and proposed CCS entry. IN ST HAMILTON ADMIN Rule 103(103.10)(c).

   e. *Emergency facsimile filings.* If the filing requires the immediate attention of the Judge, it shall so indicate in bold letters in an accompanying transmittal memorandum. IN ST HAMILTON ADMIN Rule 103(103.10)(f).

   f. *Special judge heading.* After a special judge is selected, the attorneys or pro se litigants shall add to the caption of all pleadings to the right of the case title the following: "BEFORE SPECIAL JUDGE _____." IN ST HAMILTON TRIAL Rule 204(204.10).

   g. *Format rules strictly enforced.* All filings shall be in compliance with the Indiana Rules of Trial Procedure. If the documents received are not in proper form, such deficiencies will not be corrected by court personnel. IN ST HAMILTON TRIAL Rule 201(201.70). The Court shall not be required to act on any Motion, Petition or other request for relief unless filed in conformity with the Hamilton County Local Trial and Administrative rules. IN ST HAMILTON TRIAL Rule 202(202.20).

3. *Size of papers for filing.* Effective January 1, 1992, all pleadings, copies, motions and documents filed with any trial court or appellate level court, typed or printed, with the exception of exhibits and existing wills, shall be prepared on eight and one-half by eleven inch (8 1/2" x 11") size paper. IN ST ADMIN Rule 11.

   a. *Form.* All documents filed in any Hamilton County Court, with the exception of exhibits and existing wills, shall be prepared on paper measuring eight and one-half by eleven inches (8 1/2" x 11"). IN ST HAMILTON TRIAL Rule 201(201.20).

4. *Signature requirements*

   a. *Signature of attorney.* Every pleading or motion of a party represented by an attorney shall be signed by at least one (1) attorney of record in his individual name, whose address, telephone number, and attorney number shall be stated, except that this provision shall not apply to pleadings and motions made and transcribed at the trial or a hearing before the judge and received by him in such form. IN ST TRIAL P Rule 11(A).

      i. The signature of an attorney constitutes a certificate by him that he has read the pleadings; that to the best of his knowledge, information, and belief, there is good ground to support it; and that it is not interposed for delay. IN ST TRIAL P Rule 11(A).

      ii. If a pleading or motion is not signed or is signed with intent to defeat the purpose of the rule, it

may be stricken as sham and false and the action may proceed as though the pleading had not been served. IN ST TRIAL P Rule 11(A).

   iii. For a willful violation of IN ST TRIAL P Rule 11 an attorney may be subjected to appropriate disciplinary action. Similar action may be taken if scandalous or indecent matter is inserted. IN ST TRIAL P Rule 11(A).

b. *Signature of unrepresented party.* A party who is not represented by an attorney shall sign his pleading and state his address. IN ST TRIAL P Rule 11(A).

c. *Verification not generally required.* Except when specifically required by rule, pleadings or motions need not be verified or accompanied by affidavit. The rule in equity that the averments of an answer under oath must be overcome by the testimony of two (2) witnesses or of one (1) witness sustained by corroborating circumstances is abolished. IN ST TRIAL P Rule 11(A).

d. *Verification by affirmation or representation.* When in connection with any civil or special statutory proceeding it is required that any pleading, motion, petition, supporting affidavit, or other document of any kind, be verified, or that an oath be taken, it shall be sufficient if the subscriber simply affirms the truth of the matter to be verified by an affirmation or representation. IN ST TRIAL P Rule 11(B). IN ST TRIAL P Rule 11(B) states that the affirmation or representation should be in substantially the following language: "I (we) affirm, under the penalties for perjury, that the foregoing representation(s) is (are) true. (Signed) _____."

   i. Any person who falsifies an affirmation or representation of fact shall be subject to the same penalties as are prescribed by law for the making of a false affidavit. IN ST TRIAL P Rule 11(B).

e. *Verified pleadings, motions, and affidavits as evidence.* Pleadings, motions and affidavits accompanying or in support of such pleadings or motions when required to be verified or under oath shall be accepted as a representation that the signer had personal knowledge thereof or reasonable cause to believe the existence of the facts or matters stated or alleged therein; and, if otherwise competent or acceptable as evidence, may be admitted as evidence of the facts or matters stated or alleged therein when it is so provided in the Indiana Rules of Trial Procedure, by statute or other law, or to the extent the writing or signature expressly purports to be made upon the signer's personal knowledge. When such pleadings, motions and affidavits are verified or under oath they shall not require other or greater proof on the part of the adverse party than if not verified or not under oath unless expressly provided otherwise by the Indiana Rules of Trial Procedure, statute or other law. Affidavits upon motions for summary judgment under IN ST TRIAL P Rule 56 and in denial of execution under IN ST TRIAL P Rule 9.2 shall be made upon personal knowledge. IN ST TRIAL P Rule 11(C).

5. *Information excluded from public access.* Every document filed in a case shall separately identify information excluded from public access pursuant to IN ST ADMIN Rule 9(G)(1) as follows:

a. Whole documents that are excluded from public access pursuant to IN ST ADMIN Rule 9(G)(1) shall be tendered on light green paper or have a light green coversheet attached to the document, marked "Not for Public Access" or "Confidential." IN ST TRIAL P Rule 5(G)(1).

b. When only a portion of a document contains information excluded from public access pursuant to IN ST ADMIN Rule 9(G)(1), said information shall be omitted [or redacted] from the filed document, and set forth on a separate accompanying document on light green paper conspicuously marked "Not for Public Access" or "Confidential" and clearly designated [or identifying] the caption and number of the case and the document and location within the document to which the redacted material pertains. IN ST TRIAL P Rule 5(G)(2).

c. With respect to documents filed in electronic format, the trial court, by local rule, may provide for compliance with IN ST TRIAL P Rule 5 in manner that separates and protects access to information excluded from public access. IN ST TRIAL P Rule 5(G)(3).

d. IN ST TRIAL P Rule 5(G) does not apply to a record sealed by the court pursuant to IN ST 5-14-3-5.5 or otherwise, nor to records, documents, or information filed in cases to which public access is prohibited pursuant to IN ST ADMIN Rule 9(G). IN ST TRIAL P Rule 5(G)(4).

e. The following information in case records is excluded from public access and is confidential:

   i. Information that is excluded from public access pursuant to federal law;

ii. Information that is excluded from public access as declared confidential by Indiana statute or other court rule, including without limitation:

- All adoption records created after July 8, 1941, as declared confidential by IN ST 31-19-19-1, et seq., except those specifically declared open by IN ST 31-19-13-2(2);

- All records relating to chancroid, chlamydia, gonorrhea, hepatitis, human immunodeficiency virus (HIV), Lymphogranuloma venereum, syphilis, tuberculosis, as declared confidential by IN ST 16-41-8-1, et seq.;

- All records relating to child abuse as declared confidential by IN ST 31-33-18-1, et seq.;

- All records relating to drug tests as declared confidential by IN ST 5-14-3-4(a)(9);

- Records of grand jury proceedings as declared confidential by IN ST 35-34-2-4;

- Records of juvenile proceedings as declared confidential by IN ST 31-39-1-2, except those specifically open under statute;

- All paternity records created after July 1, 1941 as declared confidential by IN ST 31-14-11-15, IN ST 31-19-5-23, IN ST 31-39-1-1 and IN ST 31-39-1-2 [Editor's note: IN ST 31-14-11-15 was repealed effective May 9, 2013];

- All pre-sentence reports as declared confidential by IN ST 35-38-1-13;

- Written petitions to permit marriages without consent and orders directing the Clerk of Court to issue a marriage license to underage persons, as declared confidential by IN ST 31-11-1-6;

- Only those arrest warrants, search warrants, indictments and informations ordered confidential by the trial judge, prior to return of duly executed service as declared confidential by IN ST 5-14-3-4(b)(1);

- All medical, mental health, or tax records unless determined by law or regulation of any governmental custodian not to be confidential, released by the subject of such records, or declared by a court of competent jurisdiction to be essential to the resolution of litigation as declared confidential by IN ST 16-39-3-10, IN ST 6-4.1-5-10, IN ST 6-4.1-12-12, and IN ST 6-8.1-7-1;

- Personal information relating to jurors or prospective jurors, other than for the use of the parties and counsel, pursuant to IN ST JURY Rule 10;

- Information relating to protection from abuse orders, no-contact orders and workplace violence restraining orders as declared confidential by IN ST 5-2-9-6, et seq.;

- Mediation proceedings pursuant to IN ST ADR Rule 2.11, Mini-Trial proceedings pursuant to IN ST ADR Rule 4.4(C), and Summary Jury Trials pursuant to IN ST ADR Rule 5.6;

- Information in probation files pursuant to the Probation Standards promulgated by the Judicial Conference of Indiana pursuant to IN ST 11-13-1-8(b);

- Information deemed confidential pursuant to the Rules for Court Administered Alcohol and Drug Programs promulgated by the Judicial Conference of Indiana pursuant to IN ST 12-23-14-13;

- Information deemed confidential pursuant to the Problem-Solving Court Rules promulgated by the Judicial Conference of Indiana pursuant to IN ST 33-23-16-16;

- All records of the Department of workforce Development as declared confidential by IN ST 22-4-19-6;

- Information regarding interception of electronic communications that is sealed or deemed confidential as set forth in IN ST 35-33.5-2-1, et seq.

iii. Information excluded from public access by specific court order;

iv. Complete Social Security Numbers of living persons;

v.   With the exception of names, information such as addresses, phone numbers, and dates of birth which explicitly identifies:

- Natural persons who are witnesses or victims (not including defendants) in criminal, domestic violence, stalking, sexual assault, juvenile, or civil protection order proceedings, provided that juveniles who are victims of sex crimes shall be identified by initials only;

- Places of residence of judicial officers, clerks and other employees of courts and clerks of court, unless the person or persons about whom the information pertains waives confidentiality;

vi.   Complete account numbers of specific assets, loans, bank accounts, credit cards, and personal identification numbers (PINs);

vii. All orders of expungement entered in criminal or juvenile proceedings, orders to restrict access to criminal history information pursuant to IN ST 35-38-5-5.5 or IN ST 35-38-8-5 and records excluded from public access by such orders, and information related to infractions that is excluded from public access pursuant to IN ST 34-28-5-15 or IN ST 34-28-5-16 [Editor's note: IN ST 35-38-5-5.5, IN ST 35-38-8-5 and IN ST 34-28-5-16 were repealed effective July 1, 2013; for information on orders restricting access to criminal history, refer to IN ST 35-38-9-1, et seq.];

viii. All personal notes and e-mail, and deliberative material, of judges, jurors, court staff and judicial agencies, and information recorded in personal data assistants (PDA's) or organizers and personal calendars. IN ST ADMIN Rule 9(G)(1).

F. Filing and Service Requirements

1. *Filing requirements.* Except as otherwise provided in IN ST TRIAL P Rule 5(E)(2), all pleadings and papers subsequent to the complaint which are required to be served upon a party shall be filed with the Court either before service or within a reasonable period of time thereafter. IN ST TRIAL P Rule 5(E)(1).

a. *Filing with the court defined.* The filing of pleadings, motions, and other papers with the court as required by the Indiana Rules of Trial Procedure shall be made by one of the following methods:

   i.   Delivery to the clerk of the court;

   ii.   Sending by electronic transmission under the procedure adopted pursuant to IN ST ADMIN Rule 12;

   iii. Mailing to the clerk by registered, certified or express mail return receipt requested;

   iv.   Depositing with any third-party commercial carrier for delivery to the clerk within three (3) calendar days, cost prepaid, properly addressed;

   v.   If the court so permits, filing with the judge, in which event the judge shall note thereon the filing date and forthwith transmit them to the office of the clerk; or

   vi.   Electronic filing, as approved by the Division of State Court Administration pursuant to IN ST ADMIN Rule 16. IN ST TRIAL P Rule 5(F).

   vii. Filing by registered or certified mail and by third-party commercial carrier shall be complete upon mailing or deposit. IN ST TRIAL P Rule 5(F).

b. *Facsimile filing.* As outlined in IN ST HAMILTON ADMIN Rule 103(103.10),facsimile filing is permitted in the Circuit and Superior Courts of Hamilton County. The Courts authorize the Hamilton County Clerk of Courts to accept pleadings, motions and other papers by electronic facsimile transmission for filing in any case pending before the Courts, subject to the requirements of IN ST HAMILTON ADMIN Rule 103(103.10). IN ST HAMILTON ADMIN Rule 103(103.10); IN ST HAMILTON TRIAL Rule 201(201.80).

   i.   *Generally.* In counties where a majority of judges of the courts of record, by posted local rule, have authorized electronic facsimile filing and designated a telephone number to receive such transmissions, pleadings, motions, and other papers may be sent to the Clerk of Circuit Court by electronic facsimile transmission for filing in any case, provided:

   - Such matter does not exceed ten (10) pages, including the cover sheet;

- Such matter does not require the payment of fees other than the electronic facsimile transcription fee set forth in IN ST ADMIN Rule 12(E);

- The sending party creates at the time of transmission a machine generated log for such transmission; and

- The original document and the transmission log are maintained by the sending party for the duration of the litigation. IN ST ADMIN Rule 12(B); IN ST HAMILTON ADMIN Rule 103(103.10)(d).

- Legibility of documents and timeliness of filing is the responsibility of the sender. IN ST HAMILTON ADMIN Rule 103(103.10)(g).

- The Clerk shall accept electronic facsimile transmission filings only if received at the facsimile machine assigned by the Clerk. The telephone number designated to receive such transmission is available at IN ST HAMILTON ADMIN Rule 103(103.40). IN ST HAMILTON ADMIN Rule 103(103.40).

ii. *Time of filing.* During normal, posted business hours, the time of filing shall be the time the duplicate document is produced in the office of the Clerk of the Circuit Court. Duplicate documents received at all other times shall be filed as of the next normal business day. IN ST ADMIN Rule 12(C).

- If the receiving fax machine endorses its own time and date stamp upon the transmitted documents and the receiving machine produces a delivery receipt which is electronically created and transmitted to the sending party, the time of filing shall be the date and time recorded on the transmitted document by the receiving fax machine. IN ST ADMIN Rule 12(C).

- Electronic facsimile transmissions will be accepted for filing only during the regular business hours as set forth in IN ST HAMILTON ADMIN Rule 101. Transmissions received by the Hamilton County Clerk after close of business shall be filed effective the next regular business day. IN ST HAMILTON ADMIN Rule 103(103.30).

iii. *Filing fee.* The electronic facsimile transmission will not be accepted for filing if its filing requires the payment of any fee other than the electronic facsimile transcription fee set forth in IN ST HAMILTON ADMIN Rule 103(103.20). IN ST HAMILTON ADMIN Rule 103(103.10)(e).

- Pursuant to Ordinance adopted by the Hamilton County Board of Commissioners, the Clerk shall collect an electronic facsimile transcription fee of One Dollar ($1.00) per page, to a maximum of Ten Dollars ($10.00) per transmission, for each electronic facsimile transmission accepted for filing with the Hamilton County Circuit and Superior Courts. IN ST HAMILTON ADMIN Rule 103(103.20).

- The fee shall be assessed against the sending party and shall be paid upon receipt of invoice by that party and at the latest within thirty (30) days of the transmission. In the event the fee is not paid by the sending party within the time limits provided, the court may issue a show-cause order or enter a judgment in the matter. The Clerk may refuse an electronic facsimile transmission from any attorney or pro se litigant who has failed to pay these fees within thirty (30) days. IN ST HAMILTON ADMIN Rule 103(103.20).

iv. *No direct filing with court.* A party shall not send pleadings, motions and other papers by electronic facsimile transmission for filing directly to any Court without that Court's prior approval to do so. IN ST HAMILTON ADMIN Rule 103(103.50).

c. *Filing with special judge.* After a special judge has qualified, a copy of each pleading and Chronological Case Summary entries filed with the Court shall be mailed or delivered to the office of that Special judge by the counsel or pro se litigant with service indicated on the certificate of service. IN ST HAMILTON TRIAL Rule 204(204.20).

d. *Proof of filing.* Any party filing any paper by any method other than personal delivery to the clerk shall retain proof of filing. IN ST TRIAL P Rule 5(F).

2. *Service requirements.* Unless otherwise provided by the Indiana Rules of Trial Procedure or an order of the court, each party and special judge, if any, shall be served with: (1) every order required by its terms to be served; (2) every pleading subsequent to the original complaint; (3) every written motion except one which may be heard ex parte; (4) every brief submitted to the trial court; (5) every paper relating to discovery required to be served upon a party; and (6) every written notice, appearance, demand, offer of judgment, designation of record on appeal, or similar paper. IN ST TRIAL P Rule 5(A).

a. *Methods of service*

i. *Personal service.* Whenever a party is represented by an attorney of record, service shall be made upon such attorney unless service upon the party himself is ordered by the court. Service upon the attorney or party shall be made by delivering or mailing a copy of the papers to the last known address or where an attorney or party has consented to service by fax or e-mail, as provided in IN ST TRIAL P Rule 3.1(A)(4), by faxing or e-mailing a copy of the documents to the fax number or e-mail address set out in the appearance form or correction as required by IN ST TRIAL P Rule 3.1(E). IN ST TRIAL P Rule 5(B). Delivery of a copy within IN ST TRIAL P Rule 5 means:

- Offering or tendering it to the attorney or party and stating the nature of the papers being served. Refusal to accept an offered or tendered document is a waiver of any objection to the sufficiency or adequacy of service of that document;

- Leaving it at his office with a clerk or other person in charge thereof, or if there is no one in charge, leaving it in a conspicuous place therein; or

- If the office is closed, by leaving it at his dwelling house or usual place of abode with some person of suitable age and discretion then residing therein; or,

- Leaving it at some other suitable place, selected by the attorney upon whom service is being made, pursuant to duly promulgated local rule. IN ST TRIAL P Rule 5(B)(1).

ii. *Service by mail.* If service is made by mail, the papers shall be deposited in the United States mail addressed to the person on whom they are being served, with postage prepaid. Service shall be deemed complete upon mailing. Proof of service of all papers permitted to be mailed may be made by written acknowledgment of service, by affidavit of the person who mailed the papers, or by certificate of an attorney. It shall be the duty of attorneys when entering their appearance in a cause or when filing pleadings or papers therein, to have noted in the Chronological Case Summary or said pleadings or papers so filed the address and telephone number of their office. Service by delivery or by mail at such address shall be deemed sufficient and complete. IN ST TRIAL P Rule 5(B)(2).

iii. *Service by fax or e-mail.* A party who has consented to service by fax or e-mail may be served as follows:

- Service by e-mail shall be made by attaching the document being served in .pdf format. Discovery documents must also be served in accordance with IN ST TRIAL P Rule 26(A). IN ST TRIAL P Rule 5(B)(3)(a).

- Service by fax shall be deemed complete upon generation of a transmission record indicating the successful transmission of the entire document, except as provided in IN ST TRIAL P Rule 5(B)(3)(d). IN ST TRIAL P Rule 5(B)(3)(b).

- Service by e-mail shall be deemed complete upon transmission, except as provided in IN ST TRIAL P Rule 5(B)(3)(d). IN ST TRIAL P Rule 5(B)(3)(c).

- Service by fax or e-mail that occurs on a Saturday, Sunday, legal holiday, or day the court or agency in which the matter is pending is closed or after 5:00 PM local time of the recipient shall be deemed complete the next day that is not a Saturday, Sunday, legal holiday, or day that the court or agency in which the matter is pending is not closed. IN ST TRIAL P Rule 5(B)(3)(d).

iv. *Mail box service.* Pursuant to IN ST TRIAL P Rule 5(B)(1)(d), the Circuit and Superior Courts of Hamilton County hereby designate the "mail boxes" located in the Clerk's order book office for service of pleadings upon attorneys who have such boxes. IN ST HAMILTON TRIAL Rule 201(201.50).

  b. *Serving numerous defendants.* In any action in which there are unusually large numbers of defendants, the court, upon motion or of its own initiative, may order:

    i. That service of the pleadings of the defendants and replies thereto need not be made as between the defendants;

- That any cross-claim, counterclaim, or matter constituting an avoidance or affirmative defense contained therein shall be deemed to be denied or avoided by all other parties; and

- That the filing of any such pleading and service thereof upon the plaintiff constitutes due notice of it to the parties. IN ST TRIAL P Rule 5(D).

    ii. A copy of every such order shall be served upon the parties in such manner and form as the court directs. IN ST TRIAL P Rule 5(D).

  c. *Service on parties in default for failure to appear.* No service need be made on parties in default for failure to appear, except that pleadings asserting new or additional claims for relief against them shall be served upon them in the manner provided by service of summons in IN ST TRIAL P Rule 4. IN ST TRIAL P Rule 5(A).

G. Hearings

1. *Hearing on motion.* Unless local conditions make it impracticable, each judge shall establish regular times and places, at intervals sufficiently frequent for the prompt dispatch of business, at which motions requiring notice and hearing may be heard and disposed of; but the judge at any time or place and on such notice, if any, as he considers reasonable may make order for the advancement, conduct, and hearing of actions. To expedite its business the court may direct the submission and determination of motions without oral hearing upon brief written statements of reasons in support and opposition, or direct or permit hearings by telephone conference call with all attorneys or other similar means of communication. IN ST TRIAL P Rule 73(A).

2. *Presentation of evidence.* On the hearing of an application for a restraining order or temporary injunction, each party may read affidavits or documentary or record evidence. IN ST 34-26-1-8.

H. Forms

1. Motion for Preliminary Injunction Forms for Indiana

  a. Prayer in complaint; For preliminary injunction. 5 INPRAC § 3:13.20.

  b. Motion for preliminary injunction. 5 INPRAC § 3:13.40.

  c. Notice of motion for preliminary injunction. 11 INPRAC § 97.14.

  d. Undertaking as security to support granting of injunction. 11 INPRAC § 97.14.1.

  e. Findings of fact in support of injunction. 11 INPRAC § 97.14.2.

  f. Motion to dissolve temporary restraining order. 11 INPRAC § 97.14.3.

  g. Motion for contempt for violation of injunction. 11 INPRAC § 97.14.4.

  h. Motion for preliminary injunction. 11 INPRAC § 97.15.

  i. Preliminary injunction. 11 INPRAC § 97.16.

  j. Motion to vacate preliminary injunction; Failure to post bond. 11 INPRAC § 97.17.

  k. Motion to vacate preliminary injunction; Another form. 11 INPRAC § 97.18.

  l. Certificate of service; Personal service. 9 INPRAC § 5.7.

  m. Certificate of service; First class mail. 9 INPRAC § 5.8.

I. Checklist

(I) ❑ Matters to be considered by moving party

  (a) ❑ Required documents

    (1) ❑ Motion and notice

(2) ❑ Affidavit

(3) ❑ Security

(4) ❑ Proposed order

(5) ❑ Certificate of service

(b) ❑ Supplemental documents

(1) ❑ Supporting evidence

(2) ❑ Facsimile cover sheet

(3) ❑ Request to schedule trial or hearing

(4) ❑ Copies of unpublished opinions

(c) ❑ Timing

(1) ❑ The injunction may be granted at the time of commencing the action, or at any time afterwards before judgment is rendered in the proceeding

(2) ❑ A written motion, other than one which may be heard ex parte, and notice of the hearing thereof shall be served not less than five (5) days before the time specified for the hearing, unless a different period is fixed by the Indiana Rules of Trial Procedure or by order of the court

(3) ❑ All pleadings and papers subsequent to the complaint which are required to be served upon a party shall be filed with the Court either before service or within a reasonable period of time thereafter

(II) ❑ Matters to be considered by the responding party

(a) ❑ Required documents

(1) ❑ Opposition

(2) ❑ Certificate of service

(b) ❑ Supplemental documents

(1) ❑ Supporting evidence

(2) ❑ Alternative proposed order

(3) ❑ Facsimile cover sheet

(4) ❑ Request to schedule trial or hearing

(5) ❑ Copies of unpublished opinions

(c) ❑ Timing

(1) ❑ Except as otherwise provided in IN ST TRIAL P Rule 59(D), opposing affidavits may be served not less than one (1) day before the hearing, unless the court permits them to be served at some other time

Motions, Oppositions and Replies
Motion to Dismiss for Failure to State a Claim

Document Last Updated October 2013

A. Applicable Rules

1. *State rules*

    a. Appearance. IN ST TRIAL P Rule 3.1.

    b. Process. IN ST TRIAL P Rule 4.

    c. Service and filing of pleadings and other papers. IN ST TRIAL P Rule 5.

d. Time. IN ST TRIAL P Rule 6.

e. Pleadings. IN ST TRIAL P Rule 7; IN ST TRIAL P Rule 8; IN ST TRIAL P Rule 9.2; IN ST TRIAL P Rule 10.

f. Signing and verification of pleadings. IN ST TRIAL P Rule 11.

g. Defenses and objections; When and how presented; By pleading or motion; Motion for judgment on the pleadings. IN ST TRIAL P Rule 12.

h. Parties plaintiff and defendant; Capacity. IN ST TRIAL P Rule 17.

i. Joinder of person needed for just adjudication. IN ST TRIAL P Rule 19.

j. Evidence. IN ST TRIAL P Rule 43.

k. Judgment on the evidence (directed verdict). IN ST TRIAL P Rule 50.

l. Findings by the court. IN ST TRIAL P Rule 52.

m. Summary judgment. IN ST TRIAL P Rule 56.

n. Motion to correct error. IN ST TRIAL P Rule 59.

o. Relief from judgment or order. IN ST TRIAL P Rule 60.

p. Hearing of motions. IN ST TRIAL P Rule 73.

q. Access to court records. IN ST ADMIN Rule 9.

r. Paper size. IN ST ADMIN Rule 11.

s. Facsimile transmission. IN ST ADMIN Rule 12.

t. Electronic filing and electronic service pilot projects. IN ST ADMIN Rule 16.

u. Sealing of certain records by court; Hearing; Notice. IN ST 5-14-3-5.5.

v. Privacy and confidentiality. IN ST 5-2-9-6; IN ST 5-14-3-4; IN ST 6-4.1-5-10; IN ST 6-4.1-12-12; IN ST 6-8.1-7-1; IN ST 11-13-1-8; IN ST 12-23-14-13; IN ST 16-39-3-10; IN ST 16-41-8-1; IN ST 22-4-19-6; IN ST 31-11-1-6; IN ST 31-19-5-23; IN ST 31-19-13-2; IN ST 31-19-19-1; IN ST 31-33-18-1; IN ST 31-39-1-1; IN ST 31-39-1-2; IN ST 33-23-16-16; IN ST 35-34-2-4; IN ST 35-38-1-13; IN ST 35-38-9-1; IN ST ADR Rule 2.11; IN ST ADR Rule 4.4; IN ST ADR Rule 5.6; IN ST JURY Rule 10.

2. *Local rules*

a. Court hours. IN ST HAMILTON ADMIN Rule 101.

b. Facsimile transmissions. IN ST HAMILTON ADMIN Rule 103.

c. Filing of pleadings and entry of appearances. IN ST HAMILTON TRIAL Rule 201.

d. Proposed orders. IN ST HAMILTON TRIAL Rule 202.

e. Briefs and memorandums. IN ST HAMILTON TRIAL Rule 203.

f. Special judges. IN ST HAMILTON TRIAL Rule 204.

g. Trial settings. IN ST HAMILTON TRIAL Rule 205.

h. Continuances. IN ST HAMILTON TRIAL Rule 206.

B. Timing

1. *Timing of motion to dismiss for failure to state a claim.* A motion making any of the defenses listed in IN ST TRIAL P Rule 12(B) shall be made before pleading if a further pleading is permitted or within twenty (20) days after service of the prior pleading if none is required. IN ST TRIAL P Rule 12(B).

a. *Time to file a responsive pleading.* A responsive pleading required under the Indiana Rules of Trial Procedure, shall be served within twenty (20) days after service of the prior pleading. IN ST TRIAL P Rule 6(C).

b. *Filing.* All pleadings and papers subsequent to the complaint which are required to be served upon a party shall be filed with the Court either before service or within a reasonable period of time thereafter. IN ST TRIAL P Rule 5(E)(1).

2. *Service.* A written motion, other than one which may be heard ex parte, and notice of the hearing thereof shall be served not less than five (5) days before the time specified for the hearing, unless a different period is fixed by the Indiana Rules of Trial Procedure or by order of the court. IN ST TRIAL P Rule 6(D).

    a. *Of supporting affidavits.* When a motion is supported by affidavit, the affidavit shall be served with the motion; and,

3. *Service of opposition.* Except as otherwise provided in IN ST TRIAL P Rule 59(D), opposing affidavits may be served not less than one (1) day before the hearing, unless the court permits them to be served at some other time. IN ST TRIAL P Rule 6(D).

4. *Computation of time*

    a. *Generally; Days excluded.* In computing any period of time prescribed or allowed by the Indiana Rules of Trial Procedure, by order of the court, or by any applicable statute, the day of the act, event, or default from which the designated period of time begins to run shall not be included. The last day of the period so computed is to be included unless it is:

        i. A Saturday,

        ii. A Sunday,

        iii. A legal holiday as defined by state statute, or

        iv. A day the office in which the act is to be done is closed during regular business hours. IN ST TRIAL P Rule 6(A).

    b. *Short periods.* In any event, the period runs until the end of the next day that is not a Saturday, a Sunday, a legal holiday, or a day on which the office is closed. When the period of time allowed is less than seven (7) days, intermediate Saturdays, Sundays, legal holidays, and days on which the office is closed shall be excluded from the computations. IN ST TRIAL P Rule 6(A).

    c. *Additional time after service by United States mail.* Whenever a party has the right or is required to do some act or take some proceedings within a prescribed period after the service of a notice or other paper upon him and the notice or paper is served upon him by United States mail, three (3) days shall be added to the prescribed period. IN ST TRIAL P Rule 6(E).

    d. *Enlargement of time.* When an act is required or allowed to be done at or within a specific time by the Indiana Rules of Trial Procedure, the court may at any time for cause shown:

        i. Order the period enlarged, with or without motion or notice, if request therefor is made before the expiration of the period originally prescribed or extended by a previous order; or

        ii. Upon motion made after the expiration of the specific period, permit the act to be done where the failure to act was the result of excusable neglect; but, the court may not extend the time for taking any action for judgment on the evidence under IN ST TRIAL P Rule 50(A), amendment of findings and judgment under IN ST TRIAL P Rule 52(B), to correct errors under IN ST TRIAL P Rule 59(C), statement in opposition to motion to correct error under IN ST TRIAL P Rule 59(E), or to obtain relief from final judgment under IN ST TRIAL P Rule 60(B), except to the extent and under the conditions stated in those rules. IN ST TRIAL P Rule 6(B).

        iii. For information on obtaining a continuance, refer to IN ST HAMILTON TRIAL Rule 206.

C. General Requirements

1. *Motions, generally.* Unless made during a hearing or trial, or otherwise ordered by the court, an application to the court for an order shall be made by written motion. The motion shall state the grounds therefor and the relief or order sought. IN ST TRIAL P Rule 7(B).

    a. *Motions as distinct from pleadings.* Motions and responses to motions are not pleadings, and allegations contained in a motion are not admissions of a party. 22B INPRAC 7:2; Wachstetter v. County Properties, LLC, 832 N.E.2d 574 (Ind.Ct.App. 2005); Scott County Family YMCA, Inc. v. Hobbs, 817 N.E.2d 603 (Ind.Ct.App. 2004).

    b. *Unopposed motions generally granted.* It is common for a trial court to grant procedural motions, such as motions for enlargement of time, discovery motions, or motions for continuance, unless an objection is filed. 21 INPRAC § 13.8.

2. *Motion to dismiss for failure to state a claim.* Every defense, in law or fact, to a claim for relief in any pleading, whether a claim, counterclaim, cross-claim, or third-party claim, shall be asserted in the responsive pleading thereto if one is required; except that at the option of the pleader, the defense of failure to state a claim upon which relief can be granted, which shall include failure to name the real party in interest under IN ST TRIAL P Rule 17, may be made by motion. IN ST TRIAL P Rule 12(B)(6). A motion under IN ST TRIAL P Rule 12(B)(6) is intended to test the legal sufficiency of a claim rather than the facts supporting that claim. 1A INPRAC R 12(12.9); Meyers v. Meyers, 861 N.E.2d 704 (Ind. 2007).

   a. *How motion made.* A defense of failure to state a claim upon which relief can be granted, a defense of failure to join an indispensable party under IN ST TRIAL P Rule 19(B), and an objection of failure to state a legal defense to a claim may be made in any pleading permitted or ordered under IN ST TRIAL P Rule 7(A) or by motion for judgment on the pleadings, or at the trial on the merits. IN ST TRIAL P Rule 12(H)(2).

   b. *Claim admitted for purpose of motion.* A motion to dismiss for failure to state a claim admits, for the purpose of the motion, the existence of the claim as stated in the complaint, but challenges the plaintiff's right to relief. 9 INPRAC § 42.10; Mills v. American Playground Device Co., 427 N.E.2d 1130 (Ind.Ct.App. 1981). Motions to dismiss under IN ST TRIAL P Rule 12 are disfavored because they undermine the policy that favors deciding cases on their merits. 22 INPRAC § 15.19; Droscha v. Shepherd, 931 N.E.2d 882 (Ind.Ct.App. 2010).

   c. *Motion decided on factual allegations of complaint.* The trial court should grant a motion to dismiss under IN ST TRIAL P Rule 12(B)(6) if the facts alleged in the complaint are incapable of supporting relief under any set of circumstances. 1A INPRAC R 12(12.9); McPeek v. McCardle, 888 N.E.2d 171 (Ind. 2008). In determining whether the facts alleged in the complaint are incapable of supporting relief, the court must look only to the complaint and may not resort to any other evidence in the record. When ruling on a motion to dismiss under IN ST TRIAL P Rule 12(B)(6), the court should consider all of the allegations in the complaint to be true and resolve all inferences in favor of the non-moving party. 1A INPRAC R 12(12.9); State v. American Family Voices, Inc., 898 N.E.2d 293 (Ind. 2008); Curtis v. Roob, 891 N.E.2d 577 (Ind.Ct.App. 2008).

   d. *Notice pleading and motions to dismiss.* Although notice pleading requirements under IN ST TRIAL P Rule 8(A) are fairly straightforward, and are well-grounded in Indiana jurisprudence, the mechanism for testing the legal sufficiency of the complaint, IN ST TRIAL P Rule 12(B)(6), has, over time, become somewhat limited because Indiana courts are instructed to dismiss an action under IN ST TRIAL P Rule 12(B)(6) only where the if the alleged facts do not support a claim for relief under any set of circumstances. 1A INPRAC R 12(12.9). Trial judges do not like to grant IN ST TRIAL P Rule 12(B)(6) motions where the claim is an inadequately pleaded complaint, which means a defendant's first meaningful opportunity to challenge a plaintiff's claim is the motion for summary judgment. 1A INPRAC R 12(12.9).

   e. *Conversion to motion for summary judgment.* A motion to dismiss under IN ST TRIAL P Rule 12(B)(6) for failure to state a claim upon which relief and Motion for Judgment on the Pleadings under IN ST TRIAL P Rule 12(C) will be converted into a motion for summary judgment under IN ST TRIAL P Rule 56 if the court considers matters outside the pleadings in deciding those motions. 11 INPRAC § 90.1; Duran v. Komyatte, 490 N.E.2d 388 (Ind.Ct.App. 1986). In such case, all parties shall be given reasonable opportunity to present all material made pertinent to such a motion by IN ST TRIAL P Rule 56. IN ST TRIAL P Rule 12(B).

   f. *Effect of granting of the motion.* When a motion to dismiss is sustained for failure to state a claim under IN ST TRIAL P Rule 12(B)(6) the pleading may be amended once as of right pursuant to IN ST TRIAL P Rule 15(A) within ten (10) days after service of notice of the court's order sustaining the motion and thereafter with permission of the court pursuant to such rule. IN ST TRIAL P Rule 12(B).

3. *Consolidation and waiver*

   a. *Consolidation of defenses in motion.* A party who makes a motion under IN ST TRIAL P Rule 12 may join with it any other motions herein provided for and then available to him. If a party makes a motion under IN ST TRIAL P Rule 12 but omits therefrom any defense or objection then available to him which IN ST TRIAL P Rule 12 permits to be raised by motion, he shall not thereafter make a motion based on the defense or objection so omitted. He may, however, make such motions as are allowed under IN ST TRIAL P Rule 12(H)(2). IN ST TRIAL P Rule 12(G).

b. *Waiver or preservation of certain defenses.* No defense or objection is waived by being joined with one or more other defenses or objections in a responsive pleading or motion. IN ST TRIAL P Rule 12(B).

D. Documents

1. *Required documents*

a. *Motion and notice.* The requirement of notice is satisfied by service of the motion. IN ST TRIAL P Rule 7(B). Refer to the General Requirements section of this document for information on the content of a motion to dismiss to dismiss for failure to state a claim.

b. *Proposed order.* Unless local practice provides differently, a party should submit a proposed order with its written motion to be signed by the judge once the motion has been granted. 21 INPRAC § 13.8; IN ST HAMILTON ADMIN Rule 103(103.10)(b). Each Motion, Petition or other request for relief shall be accompanied by a proposed order. IN ST HAMILTON TRIAL Rule 202(202.10).

i. All proposed orders submitted by counsel pursuant to IN ST HAMILTON TRIAL Rule 202 shall meet the following requirements: (1) contain a complete distribution list of all attorneys and pro se litigants with full addresses; (2) stamped envelopes appropriately addressed for each attorney of record and/or pro se litigant on the distribution list. IN ST HAMILTON TRIAL Rule 202(202.30).

c. *Certificate of service.* An attorney or unrepresented party tendering a document to the Clerk for filing shall certify that service has been made, list the parties served, and specify the date and means of service. The certificate of service shall be placed at the end of the document and shall not be separately filed. The separate filing of a certificate of service, however, shall not be grounds for rejecting a document for filing. The Clerk may permit documents to be filed without a certificate of service but shall require prompt filing of a separate certificate of service. IN ST TRIAL P Rule 5(C).

i. All pleadings filed with the Court which require a certificate of service shall specifically name the individual party or attorney on whom service has been made, the address, the manner in which service was made and the date when service was made. IN ST HAMILTON TRIAL Rule 201(201.60).

2. *Supplemental documents*

a. *Facsimile cover sheet.* Any document sent to the Clerk of the Circuit Court by electronic facsimile transmission shall be accompanied by a cover sheet which states the title of the document, case number, number of pages, identity and voice telephone number of the sending party and instructions for filing. The cover sheet shall contain the signature of the attorney or party, pro se, authorizing the filing. IN ST ADMIN Rule 12(D); IN ST HAMILTON ADMIN Rule 103(103.10)(a).

b. *Request to schedule hearing.* All requests to schedule trials and hearings shall be in writing and shall contain the following information:

i. Type of trial or hearing (i.e., jury trial, court trial, final hearing in dissolution, etc.). IN ST HAMILTON TRIAL Rule 205(205.10).

ii. A good-faith estimate of the total court time needed for the trial or hearing. IN ST HAMILTON TRIAL Rule 205(205.10).

iii. Each request under IN ST HAMILTON TRIAL Rule 205(205.10) shall be accompanied by a proposed written order with appropriate blanks for date and time and shall further include reference to those items set forth in IN ST HAMILTON TRIAL Rule 205(205.10)(a) and IN ST HAMILTON TRIAL Rule 205(205.10)(b). IN ST HAMILTON TRIAL Rule 205(205.20).

c. *Copies of unpublished opinions.* Authorities relied upon which are not cited in the Northeastern Reporter system shall be attached to counsel's brief. If the authority is cited for the first time in oral argument, a copy of the authority may be provided to the Court at the time of the argument. Sufficient copies shall be available to provide counsel for each party with a copy. IN ST HAMILTON TRIAL Rule 203(203.10).

E. Format

1. *Form of motions.* The rules applicable to captions, and the signing and form of pleadings (IN ST TRIAL P Rule 8 through IN ST TRIAL P Rule 11), apply to all motions and other papers provided under the Indiana Rules of Trial Procedure. 22B INPRAC 7:2.

2. *Form of pleadings*

   a. *Caption; Names of parties.* Every pleading shall contain a caption setting forth the name of the court, the title of the action, the file number, and a designation as in IN ST TRIAL P Rule 7(A). In the complaint the title of the action shall include the names of all the parties, but in other pleadings it is sufficient to state the name of the first party on each side with an appropriate indication of other parties. IN ST TRIAL P Rule 10(A).

   b. *Paragraphs; Separate statements.* All averments of a claim or defense shall be made in numbered paragraphs, the contents of each of which shall be limited as far as practicable to a statement of a single set of circumstances, and a paragraph may be referred to by number in all succeeding pleadings. Each claim founded upon a separate transaction or occurrence and each defense other than denials may be stated in a separate count or defense whenever a separation facilitates the clear presentation of the matters set forth. IN ST TRIAL P Rule 10(B).

   c. *Adoption by reference; Exhibits.* Statements in a pleading may be adopted by reference in a different part of the same pleading or in another pleading or in any motion. A copy of any written instrument which is an exhibit to a pleading is a part thereof for all purposes. IN ST TRIAL P Rule 10(C).

   d. *Facsimile page limit.* Courts authorize the Hamilton County Clerk of Courts to accept pleadings, motions and other papers by electronic facsimile transmission for filing in any case pending before the Courts, subject to the requirement that The transmission may not exceed ten (10) pages in length including the cover sheet and proposed CCS entry. IN ST HAMILTON ADMIN Rule 103(103.10)(c).

   e. *Emergency facsimile filings.* If the filing requires the immediate attention of the Judge, it shall so indicate in bold letters in an accompanying transmittal memorandum. IN ST HAMILTON ADMIN Rule 103(103.10)(f).

   f. *Special judge heading.* After a special judge is selected, the attorneys or pro se litigants shall add to the caption of all pleadings to the right of the case title the following: "BEFORE SPECIAL JUDGE _____." IN ST HAMILTON TRIAL Rule 204(204.10).

   g. *Format rules strictly enforced.* All filings shall be in compliance with the Indiana Rules of Trial Procedure. If the documents received are not in proper form, such deficiencies will not be corrected by court personnel. IN ST HAMILTON TRIAL Rule 201(201.70). The Court shall not be required to act on any Motion, Petition or other request for relief unless filed in conformity with the Hamilton County Local Trial and Administrative rules. IN ST HAMILTON TRIAL Rule 202(202.20).

3. *Size of papers for filing.* Effective January 1, 1992, all pleadings, copies, motions and documents filed with any trial court or appellate level court, typed or printed, with the exception of exhibits and existing wills, shall be prepared on eight and one-half by eleven inch (8 1/2" x 11") size paper. IN ST ADMIN Rule 11.

   a. *Form.* All documents filed in any Hamilton County Court, with the exception of exhibits and existing wills, shall be prepared on paper measuring eight and one-half by eleven inches (8 1/2" x 11"). IN ST HAMILTON TRIAL Rule 201(201.20).

4. *Signature requirements*

   a. *Signature of attorney.* Every pleading or motion of a party represented by an attorney shall be signed by at least one (1) attorney of record in his individual name, whose address, telephone number, and attorney number shall be stated, except that this provision shall not apply to pleadings and motions made and transcribed at the trial or a hearing before the judge and received by him in such form. IN ST TRIAL P Rule 11(A).

      i. The signature of an attorney constitutes a certificate by him that he has read the pleadings; that to the best of his knowledge, information, and belief, there is good ground to support it; and that it is not interposed for delay. IN ST TRIAL P Rule 11(A).

    ii.   If a pleading or motion is not signed or is signed with intent to defeat the purpose of the rule, it may be stricken as sham and false and the action may proceed as though the pleading had not been served. IN ST TRIAL P Rule 11(A).

    iii.   For a willful violation of IN ST TRIAL P Rule 11 an attorney may be subjected to appropriate disciplinary action. Similar action may be taken if scandalous or indecent matter is inserted. IN ST TRIAL P Rule 11(A).

  b. *Signature of unrepresented party.* A party who is not represented by an attorney shall sign his pleading and state his address. IN ST TRIAL P Rule 11(A).

  c. *Verification not generally required.* Except when specifically required by rule, pleadings or motions need not be verified or accompanied by affidavit. The rule in equity that the averments of an answer under oath must be overcome by the testimony of two (2) witnesses or of one (1) witness sustained by corroborating circumstances is abolished. IN ST TRIAL P Rule 11(A).

  d. *Verification by affirmation or representation.* When in connection with any civil or special statutory proceeding it is required that any pleading, motion, petition, supporting affidavit, or other document of any kind, be verified, or that an oath be taken, it shall be sufficient if the subscriber simply affirms the truth of the matter to be verified by an affirmation or representation. IN ST TRIAL P Rule 11(B). IN ST TRIAL P Rule 11(B) states that the affirmation or representation should be in substantially the following language: "I (we) affirm, under the penalties for perjury, that the foregoing representation(s) is (are) true. (Signed) _____."

    i.   Any person who falsifies an affirmation or representation of fact shall be subject to the same penalties as are prescribed by law for the making of a false affidavit. IN ST TRIAL P Rule 11(B).

  e. *Verified pleadings, motions, and affidavits as evidence.* Pleadings, motions and affidavits accompanying or in support of such pleadings or motions when required to be verified or under oath shall be accepted as a representation that the signer had personal knowledge thereof or reasonable cause to believe the existence of the facts or matters stated or alleged therein; and, if otherwise competent or acceptable as evidence, may be admitted as evidence of the facts or matters stated or alleged therein when it is so provided in the Indiana Rules of Trial Procedure, by statute or other law, or to the extent the writing or signature expressly purports to be made upon the signer's personal knowledge. When such pleadings, motions and affidavits are verified or under oath they shall not require other or greater proof on the part of the adverse party than if not verified or not under oath unless expressly provided otherwise by the Indiana Rules of Trial Procedure, statute or other law. Affidavits upon motions for summary judgment under IN ST TRIAL P Rule 56 and in denial of execution under IN ST TRIAL P Rule 9.2 shall be made upon personal knowledge. IN ST TRIAL P Rule 11(C).

5. *Information excluded from public access.* Every document filed in a case shall separately identify information excluded from public access pursuant to IN ST ADMIN Rule 9(G)(1) as follows:

  a. Whole documents that are excluded from public access pursuant to IN ST ADMIN Rule 9(G)(1) shall be tendered on light green paper or have a light green coversheet attached to the document, marked "Not for Public Access" or "Confidential." IN ST TRIAL P Rule 5(G)(1).

  b. When only a portion of a document contains information excluded from public access pursuant to IN ST ADMIN Rule 9(G)(1), said information shall be omitted [or redacted] from the filed document, and set forth on a separate accompanying document on light green paper conspicuously marked "Not for Public Access" or "Confidential" and clearly designated [or identifying] the caption and number of the case and the document and location within the document to which the redacted material pertains. IN ST TRIAL P Rule 5(G)(2).

  c. With respect to documents filed in electronic format, the trial court, by local rule, may provide for compliance with IN ST TRIAL P Rule 5 in manner that separates and protects access to information excluded from public access. IN ST TRIAL P Rule 5(G)(3).

  d. IN ST TRIAL P Rule 5(G) does not apply to a record sealed by the court pursuant to IN ST 5-14-3-5.5 or otherwise, nor to records, documents, or information filed in cases to which public access is prohibited pursuant to IN ST ADMIN Rule 9(G). IN ST TRIAL P Rule 5(G)(4).

e. The following information in case records is excluded from public access and is confidential:

   i. Information that is excluded from public access pursuant to federal law;

   ii. Information that is excluded from public access as declared confidential by Indiana statute or other court rule, including without limitation:

   - All adoption records created after July 8, 1941, as declared confidential by IN ST 31-19-19-1, et seq., except those specifically declared open by IN ST 31-19-13-2(2);

   - All records relating to chancroid, chlamydia, gonorrhea, hepatitis, human immunodeficiency virus (HIV), Lymphogranuloma venereum, syphilis, tuberculosis, as declared confidential by IN ST 16-41-8-1, et seq.;

   - All records relating to child abuse as declared confidential by IN ST 31-33-18-1, et seq.;

   - All records relating to drug tests as declared confidential by IN ST 5-14-3-4(a)(9);

   - Records of grand jury proceedings as declared confidential by IN ST 35-34-2-4;

   - Records of juvenile proceedings as declared confidential by IN ST 31-39-1-2, except those specifically open under statute;

   - All paternity records created after July 1, 1941 as declared confidential by IN ST 31-14-11-15, IN ST 31-19-5-23, IN ST 31-39-1-1 and IN ST 31-39-1-2 [Editor's note: IN ST 31-14-11-15 was repealed effective May 9, 2013];

   - All pre-sentence reports as declared confidential by IN ST 35-38-1-13;

   - Written petitions to permit marriages without consent and orders directing the Clerk of Court to issue a marriage license to underage persons, as declared confidential by IN ST 31-11-1-6;

   - Only those arrest warrants, search warrants, indictments and informations ordered confidential by the trial judge, prior to return of duly executed service as declared confidential by IN ST 5-14-3-4(b)(1);

   - All medical, mental health, or tax records unless determined by law or regulation of any governmental custodian not to be confidential, released by the subject of such records, or declared by a court of competent jurisdiction to be essential to the resolution of litigation as declared confidential by IN ST 16-39-3-10, IN ST 6-4.1-5-10, IN ST 6-4.1-12-12, and IN ST 6-8.1-7-1;

   - Personal information relating to jurors or prospective jurors, other than for the use of the parties and counsel, pursuant to IN ST JURY Rule 10;

   - Information relating to protection from abuse orders, no-contact orders and workplace violence restraining orders as declared confidential by IN ST 5-2-9-6, et seq.;

   - Mediation proceedings pursuant to IN ST ADR Rule 2.11, Mini-Trial proceedings pursuant to IN ST ADR Rule 4.4(C), and Summary Jury Trials pursuant to IN ST ADR Rule 5.6;

   - Information in probation files pursuant to the Probation Standards promulgated by the Judicial Conference of Indiana pursuant to IN ST 11-13-1-8(b);

   - Information deemed confidential pursuant to the Rules for Court Administered Alcohol and Drug Programs promulgated by the Judicial Conference of Indiana pursuant to IN ST 12-23-14-13;

   - Information deemed confidential pursuant to the Problem-Solving Court Rules promulgated by the Judicial Conference of Indiana pursuant to IN ST 33-23-16-16;

   - All records of the Department of workforce Development as declared confidential by IN ST 22-4-19-6;

   - Information regarding interception of electronic communications that is sealed or deemed confidential as set forth in IN ST 35-33.5-2-1, et seq.

iii. Information excluded from public access by specific court order;

iv. Complete Social Security Numbers of living persons;

v. With the exception of names, information such as addresses, phone numbers, and dates of birth which explicitly identifies:

- Natural persons who are witnesses or victims (not including defendants) in criminal, domestic violence, stalking, sexual assault, juvenile, or civil protection order proceedings, provided that juveniles who are victims of sex crimes shall be identified by initials only;

- Places of residence of judicial officers, clerks and other employees of courts and clerks of court, unless the person or persons about whom the information pertains waives confidentiality;

vi. Complete account numbers of specific assets, loans, bank accounts, credit cards, and personal identification numbers (PINs);

vii. All orders of expungement entered in criminal or juvenile proceedings, orders to restrict access to criminal history information pursuant to IN ST 35-38-5-5.5 or IN ST 35-38-8-5 and records excluded from public access by such orders, and information related to infractions that is excluded from public access pursuant to IN ST 34-28-5-15 or IN ST 34-28-5-16 [Editor's note: IN ST 35-38-5-5.5, IN ST 35-38-8-5 and IN ST 34-28-5-16 were repealed effective July 1, 2013; for information on orders restricting access to criminal history, refer to IN ST 35-38-9-1, et seq.];

viii. All personal notes and e-mail, and deliberative material, of judges, jurors, court staff and judicial agencies, and information recorded in personal data assistants (PDA's) or organizers and personal calendars. IN ST ADMIN Rule 9(G)(1).

F. Filing and Service Requirements

1. *Filing requirements.* Except as otherwise provided in IN ST TRIAL P Rule 5(E)(2), all pleadings and papers subsequent to the complaint which are required to be served upon a party shall be filed with the Court either before service or within a reasonable period of time thereafter. IN ST TRIAL P Rule 5(E)(1).

   a. *Filing with the court defined.* The filing of pleadings, motions, and other papers with the court as required by the Indiana Rules of Trial Procedure shall be made by one of the following methods:

      i. Delivery to the clerk of the court;

      ii. Sending by electronic transmission under the procedure adopted pursuant to IN ST ADMIN Rule 12;

      iii. Mailing to the clerk by registered, certified or express mail return receipt requested;

      iv. Depositing with any third-party commercial carrier for delivery to the clerk within three (3) calendar days, cost prepaid, properly addressed;

      v. If the court so permits, filing with the judge, in which event the judge shall note thereon the filing date and forthwith transmit them to the office of the clerk; or

      vi. Electronic filing, as approved by the Division of State Court Administration pursuant to IN ST ADMIN Rule 16. IN ST TRIAL P Rule 5(F).

      vii. Filing by registered or certified mail and by third-party commercial carrier shall be complete upon mailing or deposit. IN ST TRIAL P Rule 5(F).

   b. *Facsimile filing.* As outlined in IN ST HAMILTON ADMIN Rule 103(103.10),facsimile filing is permitted in the Circuit and Superior Courts of Hamilton County. The Courts authorize the Hamilton County Clerk of Courts to accept pleadings, motions and other papers by electronic facsimile transmission for filing in any case pending before the Courts, subject to the requirements of IN ST HAMILTON ADMIN Rule 103(103.10). IN ST HAMILTON ADMIN Rule 103(103.10); IN ST HAMILTON TRIAL Rule 201(201.80).

      i. *Generally.* In counties where a majority of judges of the courts of record, by posted local rule, have authorized electronic facsimile filing and designated a telephone number to receive such

transmissions, pleadings, motions, and other papers may be sent to the Clerk of Circuit Court by electronic facsimile transmission for filing in any case, provided:

- Such matter does not exceed ten (10) pages, including the cover sheet;

- Such matter does not require the payment of fees other than the electronic facsimile transcription fee set forth in IN ST ADMIN Rule 12(E);

- The sending party creates at the time of transmission a machine generated log for such transmission; and

- The original document and the transmission log are maintained by the sending party for the duration of the litigation. IN ST ADMIN Rule 12(B); IN ST HAMILTON ADMIN Rule 103(103.10)(d).

- Legibility of documents and timeliness of filing is the responsibility of the sender. IN ST HAMILTON ADMIN Rule 103(103.10)(g).

- The Clerk shall accept electronic facsimile transmission filings only if received at the facsimile machine assigned by the Clerk. The telephone number designated to receive such transmission is available at IN ST HAMILTON ADMIN Rule 103(103.40). IN ST HAMILTON ADMIN Rule 103(103.40).

ii. *Time of filing.* During normal, posted business hours, the time of filing shall be the time the duplicate document is produced in the office of the Clerk of the Circuit Court. Duplicate documents received at all other times shall be filed as of the next normal business day. IN ST ADMIN Rule 12(C).

- If the receiving fax machine endorses its own time and date stamp upon the transmitted documents and the receiving machine produces a delivery receipt which is electronically created and transmitted to the sending party, the time of filing shall be the date and time recorded on the transmitted document by the receiving fax machine. IN ST ADMIN Rule 12(C).

- Electronic facsimile transmissions will be accepted for filing only during the regular business hours as set forth in IN ST HAMILTON ADMIN Rule 101. Transmissions received by the Hamilton County Clerk after close of business shall be filed effective the next regular business day. IN ST HAMILTON ADMIN Rule 103(103.30).

iii. *Filing fee.* The electronic facsimile transmission will not be accepted for filing if its filing requires the payment of any fee other than the electronic facsimile transcription fee set forth in IN ST HAMILTON ADMIN Rule 103(103.20). IN ST HAMILTON ADMIN Rule 103(103.10)(e).

- Pursuant to Ordinance adopted by the Hamilton County Board of Commissioners, the Clerk shall collect an electronic facsimile transcription fee of One Dollar ($1.00) per page, to a maximum of Ten Dollars ($10.00) per transmission, for each electronic facsimile transmission accepted for filing with the Hamilton County Circuit and Superior Courts. IN ST HAMILTON ADMIN Rule 103(103.20).

- The fee shall be assessed against the sending party and shall be paid upon receipt of invoice by that party and at the latest within thirty (30) days of the transmission. In the event the fee is not paid by the sending party within the time limits provided, the court may issue a show-cause order or enter a judgment in the matter. The Clerk may refuse an electronic facsimile transmission from any attorney or pro se litigant who has failed to pay these fees within thirty (30) days. IN ST HAMILTON ADMIN Rule 103(103.20).

iv. *No direct filing with court.* A party shall not send pleadings, motions and other papers by electronic facsimile transmission for filing directly to any Court without that Court's prior approval to do so. IN ST HAMILTON ADMIN Rule 103(103.50).

c. *Filing with special judge.* After a special judge has qualified, a copy of each pleading and Chronological Case Summary entries filed with the Court shall be mailed or delivered to the office of that Special judge by the counsel or pro se litigant with service indicated on the certificate of service. IN ST HAMILTON TRIAL Rule 204(204.20).

    d. *Proof of filing.* Any party filing any paper by any method other than personal delivery to the clerk shall retain proof of filing. IN ST TRIAL P Rule 5(F).

2. *Service requirements.* Unless otherwise provided by the Indiana Rules of Trial Procedure or an order of the court, each party and special judge, if any, shall be served with: (1) every order required by its terms to be served; (2) every pleading subsequent to the original complaint; (3) every written motion except one which may be heard ex parte; (4) every brief submitted to the trial court; (5) every paper relating to discovery required to be served upon a party; and (6) every written notice, appearance, demand, offer of judgment, designation of record on appeal, or similar paper. IN ST TRIAL P Rule 5(A).

    a. *Methods of service*

        i. *Personal service.* Whenever a party is represented by an attorney of record, service shall be made upon such attorney unless service upon the party himself is ordered by the court. Service upon the attorney or party shall be made by delivering or mailing a copy of the papers to the last known address or where an attorney or party has consented to service by fax or e-mail, as provided in IN ST TRIAL P Rule 3.1(A)(4), by faxing or e-mailing a copy of the documents to the fax number or e-mail address set out in the appearance form or correction as required by IN ST TRIAL P Rule 3.1(E). IN ST TRIAL P Rule 5(B). Delivery of a copy within IN ST TRIAL P Rule 5 means:

- Offering or tendering it to the attorney or party and stating the nature of the papers being served. Refusal to accept an offered or tendered document is a waiver of any objection to the sufficiency or adequacy of service of that document;

- Leaving it at his office with a clerk or other person in charge thereof, or if there is no one in charge, leaving it in a conspicuous place therein; or

- If the office is closed, by leaving it at his dwelling house or usual place of abode with some person of suitable age and discretion then residing therein; or,

- Leaving it at some other suitable place, selected by the attorney upon whom service is being made, pursuant to duly promulgated local rule. IN ST TRIAL P Rule 5(B)(1).

        ii. *Service by mail.* If service is made by mail, the papers shall be deposited in the United States mail addressed to the person on whom they are being served, with postage prepaid. Service shall be deemed complete upon mailing. Proof of service of all papers permitted to be mailed may be made by written acknowledgment of service, by affidavit of the person who mailed the papers, or by certificate of an attorney. It shall be the duty of attorneys when entering their appearance in a cause or when filing pleadings or papers therein, to have noted in the Chronological Case Summary or said pleadings or papers so filed the address and telephone number of their office. Service by delivery or by mail at such address shall be deemed sufficient and complete. IN ST TRIAL P Rule 5(B)(2).

        iii. *Service by fax or e-mail.* A party who has consented to service by fax or e-mail may be served as follows:

- Service by e-mail shall be made by attaching the document being served in .pdf format. Discovery documents must also be served in accordance with IN ST TRIAL P Rule 26(A). IN ST TRIAL P Rule 5(B)(3)(a).

- Service by fax shall be deemed complete upon generation of a transmission record indicating the successful transmission of the entire document, except as provided in IN ST TRIAL P Rule 5(B)(3)(d). IN ST TRIAL P Rule 5(B)(3)(b).

- Service by e-mail shall be deemed complete upon transmission, except as provided in IN ST TRIAL P Rule 5(B)(3)(d). IN ST TRIAL P Rule 5(B)(3)(c).

- Service by fax or e-mail that occurs on a Saturday, Sunday, legal holiday, or day the court or agency in which the matter is pending is closed or after 5:00 PM local time of the recipient shall be deemed complete the next day that is not a Saturday, Sunday, legal holiday, or day that the court or agency in which the matter is pending is not closed. IN ST TRIAL P Rule 5(B)(3)(d).

      iv.   *Mail box service.* Pursuant to IN ST TRIAL P Rule 5(B)(1)(d), the Circuit and Superior Courts of Hamilton County hereby designate the "mail boxes" located in the Clerk's order book office for service of pleadings upon attorneys who have such boxes. IN ST HAMILTON TRIAL Rule 201(201.50).

   b.   *Serving numerous defendants.* In any action in which there are unusually large numbers of defendants, the court, upon motion or of its own initiative, may order:

      i.   That service of the pleadings of the defendants and replies thereto need not be made as between the defendants;

- That any cross-claim, counterclaim, or matter constituting an avoidance or affirmative defense contained therein shall be deemed to be denied or avoided by all other parties; and

- That the filing of any such pleading and service thereof upon the plaintiff constitutes due notice of it to the parties. IN ST TRIAL P Rule 5(D).

      ii.   A copy of every such order shall be served upon the parties in such manner and form as the court directs. IN ST TRIAL P Rule 5(D).

   c.   *Service on parties in default for failure to appear.* No service need be made on parties in default for failure to appear, except that pleadings asserting new or additional claims for relief against them shall be served upon them in the manner provided by service of summons in IN ST TRIAL P Rule 4. IN ST TRIAL P Rule 5(A).

G. Hearings

1.   *Hearing on motion.* Unless local conditions make it impracticable, each judge shall establish regular times and places, at intervals sufficiently frequent for the prompt dispatch of business, at which motions requiring notice and hearing may be heard and disposed of; but the judge at any time or place and on such notice, if any, as he considers reasonable may make order for the advancement, conduct, and hearing of actions. To expedite its business the court may direct the submission and determination of motions without oral hearing upon brief written statements of reasons in support and opposition, or direct or permit hearings by telephone conference call with all attorneys or other similar means of communication. IN ST TRIAL P Rule 73(A).

H. Forms

1. Motion to Dismiss for Failure to State a Claim Forms for Indiana

   a.   General form. 5 INPRAC § 3:4.1.

   b.   Failure to state a claim upon which relief can be granted. 5 INPRAC § 3:4.5.

   c.   Motion to dismiss plaintiff's complaint; General form. 9 INPRAC § 42.2.

   d.   Motion to dismiss; Failure to state a claim upon which relief can be granted. 9 INPRAC § 42.10.

   e.   Certificate of service; Personal service. 9 INPRAC § 5.7.

   f.   Certificate of service; First class mail. 9 INPRAC § 5.8.

   g.   Statute of limitations. 9 INPRAC § 42.12.

   h.   Application for hearing and preliminary determination of motion to dismiss. 9 INPRAC § 42.15.

I. Checklist

(I)   ❑ Matters to be considered by moving party

   (a)   ❑ Required documents

      (1)   ❑ Motion and notice

      (2)   ❑ Proposed order

      (3)   ❑ Certificate of service

   (b)   ❑ Supplemental documents

      (1)   ❑ Facsimile cover sheet

      (2)   ❑ Request to schedule trial or hearing

       (3) ❑ Copies of unpublished opinions

    (c) ❑ Timing

       (1) ❑ A motion to dismiss for failure to state a claim shall be made before pleading if a further pleading is permitted or within twenty (20) days after service of the prior pleading if none is required

       (2) ❑ A written motion, other than one which may be heard ex parte, and notice of the hearing thereof shall be served not less than five (5) days before the time specified for the hearing, unless a different period is fixed by the Indiana Rules of Trial Procedure or by order of the court

       (3) ❑ All pleadings and papers subsequent to the complaint which are required to be served upon a party shall be filed with the Court either before service or within a reasonable period of time thereafter

(II) ❑ Matters to be considered by the responding party

    (a) ❑ Required documents

       (1) ❑ Opposition

       (2) ❑ Certificate of service

    (b) ❑ Supplemental documents

       (1) ❑ Alternative proposed order

       (2) ❑ Facsimile cover sheet

       (3) ❑ Request to schedule trial or hearing

       (4) ❑ Copies of unpublished opinions

    (c) ❑ Timing

       (1) ❑ Except as otherwise provided in IN ST TRIAL P Rule 59(D), opposing affidavits may be served not less than one (1) day before the hearing, unless the court permits them to be served at some other time

Motions, Oppositions and Replies
Motion to Dismiss for Lack of Subject Matter Jurisdiction

Document Last Updated October 2013

A. Applicable Rules

1. *State rules*

    a. Appearance. IN ST TRIAL P Rule 3.1.

    b. Process. IN ST TRIAL P Rule 4.

    c. Service and filing of pleadings and other papers. IN ST TRIAL P Rule 5.

    d. Time. IN ST TRIAL P Rule 6.

    e. Pleadings. IN ST TRIAL P Rule 7; IN ST TRIAL P Rule 8; IN ST TRIAL P Rule 9.2; IN ST TRIAL P Rule 10.

    f. Signing and verification of pleadings. IN ST TRIAL P Rule 11.

    g. Defenses and objections; When and how presented; By pleading or motion; Motion for judgment on the pleadings. IN ST TRIAL P Rule 12.

    h. Amended and supplemental pleadings. IN ST TRIAL P Rule 15.

    i. Joinder of person needed for just adjudication. IN ST TRIAL P Rule 19.

    j. Evidence. IN ST TRIAL P Rule 43.

k. Judgment on the evidence (directed verdict). IN ST TRIAL P Rule 50.

l. Findings by the court. IN ST TRIAL P Rule 52.

m. Summary judgment. IN ST TRIAL P Rule 56.

n. Motion to correct error. IN ST TRIAL P Rule 59.

o. Relief from judgment or order. IN ST TRIAL P Rule 60.

p. Hearing of motions. IN ST TRIAL P Rule 73.

q. Access to court records. IN ST ADMIN Rule 9.

r. Paper size. IN ST ADMIN Rule 11.

s. Facsimile transmission. IN ST ADMIN Rule 12.

t. Electronic filing and electronic service pilot projects. IN ST ADMIN Rule 16.

u. Sealing of certain records by court; Hearing; Notice. IN ST 5-14-3-5.5.

v. Privacy and confidentiality. IN ST 5-2-9-6; IN ST 5-14-3-4; IN ST 6-4.1-5-10; IN ST 6-4.1-12-12; IN ST 6-8.1-7-1; IN ST 11-13-1-8; IN ST 12-23-14-13; IN ST 16-39-3-10; IN ST 16-41-8-1; IN ST 22-4-19-6; IN ST 31-11-1-6; IN ST 31-19-5-23; IN ST 31-19-13-2; IN ST 31-19-19-1; IN ST 31-33-18-1; IN ST 31-39-1-1; IN ST 31-39-1-2; IN ST 33-23-16-16; IN ST 35-34-2-4; IN ST 35-38-1-13; IN ST 35-38-9-1; IN ST ADR Rule 2.11; IN ST ADR Rule 4.4; IN ST ADR Rule 5.6; IN ST JURY Rule 10.

2. *Local rules*

a. Court hours. IN ST HAMILTON ADMIN Rule 101.

b. Facsimile transmissions. IN ST HAMILTON ADMIN Rule 103.

c. Filing of pleadings and entry of appearances. IN ST HAMILTON TRIAL Rule 201.

d. Proposed orders. IN ST HAMILTON TRIAL Rule 202.

e. Briefs and memorandums. IN ST HAMILTON TRIAL Rule 203.

f. Special judges. IN ST HAMILTON TRIAL Rule 204.

g. Trial settings. IN ST HAMILTON TRIAL Rule 205.

h. Continuances. IN ST HAMILTON TRIAL Rule 206.

B. Timing

1. *Timing of motion to dismiss for failure lack of subject matter jurisdiction.* A motion making any of the defenses listed in IN ST TRIAL P Rule 12(B) shall be made before pleading if a further pleading is permitted or within twenty (20) days after service of the prior pleading if none is required. IN ST TRIAL P Rule 12(B). Usually, the issue is raised in a motion that is filed before an Answer is filed; or the issue might be consolidated in the Answer. If it is not raised by the parties, it will be raised by the court, and an appellate court may raise the question sua sponte. 1A INPRAC R 12(12.5); Decatur County Rural Elec. Membership Corp. v. Public Serv. Co., 150 Ind.App. 193, 275 N.E.2d 857 (Ind.App. 1971).

a. *Time to file a responsive pleading.* A responsive pleading required under the Indiana Rules of Trial Procedure, shall be served within twenty (20) days after service of the prior pleading. IN ST TRIAL P Rule 6(C).

b. *Filing.* All pleadings and papers subsequent to the complaint which are required to be served upon a party shall be filed with the Court either before service or within a reasonable period of time thereafter. IN ST TRIAL P Rule 5(E)(1).

2. *Service.* A written motion, other than one which may be heard ex parte, and notice of the hearing thereof shall be served not less than five (5) days before the time specified for the hearing, unless a different period is fixed by the Indiana Rules of Trial Procedure or by order of the court. IN ST TRIAL P Rule 6(D).

a. *Of supporting affidavits.* When a motion is supported by affidavit, the affidavit shall be served with the motion. IN ST TRIAL P Rule 6(D).

3. *Service of opposition.* Except as otherwise provided in IN ST TRIAL P Rule 59(D), opposing affidavits

may be served not less than one (1) day before the hearing, unless the court permits them to be served at some other time. IN ST TRIAL P Rule 6(D).

4. *Computation of time*

   a. *Generally; Days excluded.* In computing any period of time prescribed or allowed by the Indiana Rules of Trial Procedure, by order of the court, or by any applicable statute, the day of the act, event, or default from which the designated period of time begins to run shall not be included. The last day of the period so computed is to be included unless it is:

      i. A Saturday,

      ii. A Sunday,

      iii. A legal holiday as defined by state statute, or

      iv. A day the office in which the act is to be done is closed during regular business hours. IN ST TRIAL P Rule 6(A).

   b. *Short periods.* In any event, the period runs until the end of the next day that is not a Saturday, a Sunday, a legal holiday, or a day on which the office is closed. When the period of time allowed is less than seven (7) days, intermediate Saturdays, Sundays, legal holidays, and days on which the office is closed shall be excluded from the computations. IN ST TRIAL P Rule 6(A).

   c. *Additional time after service by United States mail.* Whenever a party has the right or is required to do some act or take some proceedings within a prescribed period after the service of a notice or other paper upon him and the notice or paper is served upon him by United States mail, three (3) days shall be added to the prescribed period. IN ST TRIAL P Rule 6(E).

   d. *Enlargement of time.* When an act is required or allowed to be done at or within a specific time by the Indiana Rules of Trial Procedure, the court may at any time for cause shown:

      i. Order the period enlarged, with or without motion or notice, if request therefor is made before the expiration of the period originally prescribed or extended by a previous order; or

      ii. Upon motion made after the expiration of the specific period, permit the act to be done where the failure to act was the result of excusable neglect; but, the court may not extend the time for taking any action for judgment on the evidence under IN ST TRIAL P Rule 50(A), amendment of findings and judgment under IN ST TRIAL P Rule 52(B), to correct errors under IN ST TRIAL P Rule 59(C), statement in opposition to motion to correct error under IN ST TRIAL P Rule 59(E), or to obtain relief from final judgment under IN ST TRIAL P Rule 60(B), except to the extent and under the conditions stated in those rules. IN ST TRIAL P Rule 6(B).

      iii. For information on obtaining a continuance, refer to IN ST HAMILTON TRIAL Rule 206.

C. General Requirements

1. *Motions, generally.* Unless made during a hearing or trial, or otherwise ordered by the court, an application to the court for an order shall be made by written motion. The motion shall state the grounds therefor and the relief or order sought. IN ST TRIAL P Rule 7(B).

   a. *Motions as distinct from pleadings.* Motions and responses to motions are not pleadings, and allegations contained in a motion are not admissions of a party. 22B INPRAC 7:2; Wachstetter v. County Properties, LLC, 832 N.E.2d 574 (Ind.Ct.App. 2005); Scott County Family YMCA, Inc. v. Hobbs, 817 N.E.2d 603 (Ind.Ct.App. 2004).

   b. *Unopposed motions generally granted.* It is common for a trial court to grant procedural motions, such as motions for enlargement of time, discovery motions, or motions for continuance, unless an objection is filed. 21 INPRAC § 13.8.

2. *Motion to dismiss for lack of subject matter jurisdiction.* Every defense, in law or fact, to a claim for relief in any pleading, whether a claim, counterclaim, cross-claim, or third-party claim, shall be asserted in the responsive pleading thereto if one is required; except that at the option of the pleader, the defense of lack of jurisdiction over the subject matter may be made by motion. IN ST TRIAL P Rule 12(B)(1). Subject-matter jurisdiction refers to the power of the court or tribunal to entertain the general class of cases or disputes to which a pending case belongs. It means that the legislature or other authority, such as,

perhaps, a supreme court, has invested the court with judicial power with which to entertain a case or controversy, and to hear the litigation and dispute. 1A INPRAC R 12(12.5).

a. *Objection not waivable.* Subject-matter jurisdiction cannot be created by the parties to the litigation. Either it is there or it is not, quite independent of the conduct or the consent of the parties to the action. As such, the absence of subject-matter jurisdiction is never waivable and there is a positive duty on a court, whether trial or appellate, to raise the question of subject-matter jurisdiction whenever it might appear, if the parties have failed to present the question. 1A INPRAC R 12(12.5); Schoffstall v. Failey, 180 Ind.App. 528, 389 N.E. 361 (Ind.Ct.App. 1979).

b. *Motion not to be made as one for summary judgment.* A motion to dismiss under IN ST TRIAL P Rule 12(B)(1) may not be presented in the form of a motion for summary judgment. 9 INPRAC § 42.3.

c. *Precedence of subject matter jurisdiction.* Dismissal for lack of subject matter jurisdiction takes precedence over the determination of and action upon other substantive and procedural rights of the parties. 9 INPRAC § 42.3; Young v. Estate of Sweeney, 808 N.E.2d 1217 (Ind.Ct.App. 2004).

d. *Issues examined separately; Jurisdiction over one claim as jurisdiction over case.* In order to determine whether a case is properly before the trial court, the court should examine each issue presented. If at least one of the issues is within the jurisdiction of the trial court, the entire case falls within the court's jurisdiction. Where at least one issue or claim is a proper matter for judicial determination or resolution, a trial court is not ousted of subject matter jurisdiction by the presence in a case of one or more issues which arguably are within the jurisdiction of administrative or regulatory agency. 9 INPRAC § 42.3; Alexander v. Cottey, 801 N.E.2d 651 (Ind.Ct.App. 2004).

e. *Factual matters in determining subject matter jurisdiction.* The trial court considering a motion to dismiss for lack of subject matter jurisdiction has wide latitude to devise procedures to discover the facts relevant to jurisdiction and in weighing the evidence to resolve factual disputes affecting the jurisdictional challenge. 9 INPRAC § 42.3.

f. *Failure to exhaust administrative remedies.* The doctrine of exhaustion of administrative remedies provides that a trial court will not acquire subject matter jurisdiction until the aggrieved party has exhausted all available remedies before the administrative agency. 9 INPRAC § 41.44; Indiana Dept. of Environmental Management v. NJK Farms, Inc., 921 N.E.2d 834 (Ind.Ct.App. 2010).

   i. *Dismissal of workers' compensation cases.* A trial court must dismiss a matter for lack of subject matter jurisdiction pursuant to Indiana IN ST TRIAL P Rule 12(B)(1) where injuries claimed in the Plaintiff's complaint fall squarely within the Indiana Workers Compensation Act. 9 INPRAC § 42.3; ATFH Real Property, LLC v. Stewart, 879 N.E.2d 1184 (Ind.Ct.App. 2008).

g. *Leave to amend complaint if motion granted.* A dismissal for lack of subject matter jurisdiction is not an adjudication on the merits nor is it res judicata. If action is dismissed, plaintiff may file amended complaint as permitted by IN ST TRIAL P Rule 6(C). 9 INPRAC § 42.3; Hart v. Webster, 894 N.E.2d 1032 (Ind.Ct.App. 2008).

h. *Effect of judgment entered by court lacking subject matter jurisdiction.* A judgment entered by a court that lacks subject matter jurisdiction is void and may be attacked at any time. 9 INPRAC § 42.3; Roberson v. State, 903 N.E.2d 1009 (Ind.Ct.App. 2009).

3. *Consolidation and waiver*

a. *Consolidation of defenses in motion.* A party who makes a motion under IN ST TRIAL P Rule 12 may join with it any other motions herein provided for and then available to him. If a party makes a motion under IN ST TRIAL P Rule 12 but omits therefrom any defense or objection then available to him which IN ST TRIAL P Rule 12 permits to be raised by motion, he shall not thereafter make a motion based on the defense or objection so omitted. He may, however, make such motions as are allowed under IN ST TRIAL P Rule 12(H)(2). IN ST TRIAL P Rule 12(G).

b. *Waiver or preservation of certain defenses.* No defense or objection is waived by being joined with one or more other defenses or objections in a responsive pleading or motion. IN ST TRIAL P Rule 12(B).

D. Documents

1. *Required documents*

    a. *Motion and notice.* The requirement of notice is satisfied by service of the motion. IN ST TRIAL P Rule 7(B). Refer to the General Requirements section of this document for information on the content of a motion to dismiss for lack of subject matter jurisdiction.

    b. *Proposed order.* Unless local practice provides differently, a party should submit a proposed order with its written motion to be signed by the judge once the motion has been granted. 21 INPRAC § 13.8; IN ST HAMILTON ADMIN Rule 103(103.10)(b). Each Motion, Petition or other request for relief shall be accompanied by a proposed order. IN ST HAMILTON TRIAL Rule 202(202.10).

        i. All proposed orders submitted by counsel pursuant to IN ST HAMILTON TRIAL Rule 202 shall meet the following requirements: (1) contain a complete distribution list of all attorneys and pro se litigants with full addresses; (2) stamped envelopes appropriately addressed for each attorney of record and/or pro se litigant on the distribution list. IN ST HAMILTON TRIAL Rule 202(202.30).

    c. *Certificate of service.* An attorney or unrepresented party tendering a document to the Clerk for filing shall certify that service has been made, list the parties served, and specify the date and means of service. The certificate of service shall be placed at the end of the document and shall not be separately filed. The separate filing of a certificate of service, however, shall not be grounds for rejecting a document for filing. The Clerk may permit documents to be filed without a certificate of service but shall require prompt filing of a separate certificate of service. IN ST TRIAL P Rule 5(C).

        i. All pleadings filed with the Court which require a certificate of service shall specifically name the individual party or attorney on whom service has been made, the address, the manner in which service was made and the date when service was made. IN ST HAMILTON TRIAL Rule 201(201.60).

2. *Supplemental documents*

    a. *Supporting evidence.* When a motion is based on facts not appearing of record the court may hear the matter on affidavits presented by the respective parties, but the court may direct that the matter be heard wholly or partly on oral testimony or depositions. IN ST TRIAL P Rule 43(B).

    b. *Facsimile cover sheet.* Any document sent to the Clerk of the Circuit Court by electronic facsimile transmission shall be accompanied by a cover sheet which states the title of the document, case number, number of pages, identity and voice telephone number of the sending party and instructions for filing. The cover sheet shall contain the signature of the attorney or party, pro se, authorizing the filing. IN ST ADMIN Rule 12(D); IN ST HAMILTON ADMIN Rule 103(103.10)(a).

    c. *Request to schedule hearing.* All requests to schedule trials and hearings shall be in writing and shall contain the following information:

        i. Type of trial or hearing (i.e., jury trial, court trial, final hearing in dissolution, etc.). IN ST HAMILTON TRIAL Rule 205(205.10).

        ii. A good-faith estimate of the total court time needed for the trial or hearing. IN ST HAMILTON TRIAL Rule 205(205.10).

        iii. Each request under IN ST HAMILTON TRIAL Rule 205(205.10) shall be accompanied by a proposed written order with appropriate blanks for date and time and shall further include reference to those items set forth in IN ST HAMILTON TRIAL Rule 205(205.10)(a) and IN ST HAMILTON TRIAL Rule 205(205.10)(b). IN ST HAMILTON TRIAL Rule 205(205.20).

    d. *Copies of unpublished opinions.* Authorities relied upon which are not cited in the Northeastern Reporter system shall be attached to counsel's brief. If the authority is cited for the first time in oral argument, a copy of the authority may be provided to the Court at the time of the argument. Sufficient copies shall be available to provide counsel for each party with a copy. IN ST HAMILTON TRIAL Rule 203(203.10).

E. Format

1. *Form of motions.* The rules applicable to captions, and the signing and form of pleadings (IN ST TRIAL

P Rule 8 through IN ST TRIAL P Rule 11), apply to all motions and other papers provided under the Indiana Rules of Trial Procedure. 22B INPRAC 7:2.

2. *Form of pleadings*

   a. *Caption; Names of parties.* Every pleading shall contain a caption setting forth the name of the court, the title of the action, the file number, and a designation as in IN ST TRIAL P Rule 7(A). In the complaint the title of the action shall include the names of all the parties, but in other pleadings it is sufficient to state the name of the first party on each side with an appropriate indication of other parties. IN ST TRIAL P Rule 10(A).

   b. *Paragraphs; Separate statements.* All averments of a claim or defense shall be made in numbered paragraphs, the contents of each of which shall be limited as far as practicable to a statement of a single set of circumstances, and a paragraph may be referred to by number in all succeeding pleadings. Each claim founded upon a separate transaction or occurrence and each defense other than denials may be stated in a separate count or defense whenever a separation facilitates the clear presentation of the matters set forth. IN ST TRIAL P Rule 10(B).

   c. *Adoption by reference; Exhibits.* Statements in a pleading may be adopted by reference in a different part of the same pleading or in another pleading or in any motion. A copy of any written instrument which is an exhibit to a pleading is a part thereof for all purposes. IN ST TRIAL P Rule 10(C).

   d. *Facsimile page limit.* Courts authorize the Hamilton County Clerk of Courts to accept pleadings, motions and other papers by electronic facsimile transmission for filing in any case pending before the Courts, subject to the requirement that The transmission may not exceed ten (10) pages in length including the cover sheet and proposed CCS entry. IN ST HAMILTON ADMIN Rule 103(103.10)(c).

   e. *Emergency facsimile filings.* If the filing requires the immediate attention of the Judge, it shall so indicate in bold letters in an accompanying transmittal memorandum. IN ST HAMILTON ADMIN Rule 103(103.10)(f).

   f. *Special judge heading.* After a special judge is selected, the attorneys or pro se litigants shall add to the caption of all pleadings to the right of the case title the following: "BEFORE SPECIAL JUDGE _____." IN ST HAMILTON TRIAL Rule 204(204.10).

   g. *Format rules strictly enforced.* All filings shall be in compliance with the Indiana Rules of Trial Procedure. If the documents received are not in proper form, such deficiencies will not be corrected by court personnel. IN ST HAMILTON TRIAL Rule 201(201.70). The Court shall not be required to act on any Motion, Petition or other request for relief unless filed in conformity with the Hamilton County Local Trial and Administrative rules. IN ST HAMILTON TRIAL Rule 202(202.20).

3. *Size of papers for filing.* Effective January 1, 1992, all pleadings, copies, motions and documents filed with any trial court or appellate level court, typed or printed, with the exception of exhibits and existing wills, shall be prepared on eight and one-half by eleven inch (8 1/2" x 11") size paper. IN ST ADMIN Rule 11.

   a. *Form.* All documents filed in any Hamilton County Court, with the exception of exhibits and existing wills, shall be prepared on paper measuring eight and one-half by eleven inches (8 1/2" x 11"). IN ST HAMILTON TRIAL Rule 201(201.20).

4. *Signature requirements*

   a. *Signature of attorney.* Every pleading or motion of a party represented by an attorney shall be signed by at least one (1) attorney of record in his individual name, whose address, telephone number, and attorney number shall be stated, except that this provision shall not apply to pleadings and motions made and transcribed at the trial or a hearing before the judge and received by him in such form. IN ST TRIAL P Rule 11(A).

      i. The signature of an attorney constitutes a certificate by him that he has read the pleadings; that to the best of his knowledge, information, and belief, there is good ground to support it; and that it is not interposed for delay. IN ST TRIAL P Rule 11(A).

      ii. If a pleading or motion is not signed or is signed with intent to defeat the purpose of the rule, it

may be stricken as sham and false and the action may proceed as though the pleading had not been served. IN ST TRIAL P Rule 11(A).

    iii.   For a willful violation of IN ST TRIAL P Rule 11 an attorney may be subjected to appropriate disciplinary action. Similar action may be taken if scandalous or indecent matter is inserted. IN ST TRIAL P Rule 11(A).

  b.   *Signature of unrepresented party.* A party who is not represented by an attorney shall sign his pleading and state his address. IN ST TRIAL P Rule 11(A).

  c.   *Verification not generally required.* Except when specifically required by rule, pleadings or motions need not be verified or accompanied by affidavit. The rule in equity that the averments of an answer under oath must be overcome by the testimony of two (2) witnesses or of one (1) witness sustained by corroborating circumstances is abolished. IN ST TRIAL P Rule 11(A).

  d.   *Verification by affirmation or representation.* When in connection with any civil or special statutory proceeding it is required that any pleading, motion, petition, supporting affidavit, or other document of any kind, be verified, or that an oath be taken, it shall be sufficient if the subscriber simply affirms the truth of the matter to be verified by an affirmation or representation. IN ST TRIAL P Rule 11(B). IN ST TRIAL P Rule 11(B) states that the affirmation or representation should be in substantially the following language: "I (we) affirm, under the penalties for perjury, that the foregoing representation(s) is (are) true. (Signed) _____."

    i.   Any person who falsifies an affirmation or representation of fact shall be subject to the same penalties as are prescribed by law for the making of a false affidavit. IN ST TRIAL P Rule 11(B).

  e.   *Verified pleadings, motions, and affidavits as evidence.* Pleadings, motions and affidavits accompanying or in support of such pleadings or motions when required to be verified or under oath shall be accepted as a representation that the signer had personal knowledge thereof or reasonable cause to believe the existence of the facts or matters stated or alleged therein; and, if otherwise competent or acceptable as evidence, may be admitted as evidence of the facts or matters stated or alleged therein when it is so provided in the Indiana Rules of Trial Procedure, by statute or other law, or to the extent the writing or signature expressly purports to be made upon the signer's personal knowledge. When such pleadings, motions and affidavits are verified or under oath they shall not require other or greater proof on the part of the adverse party than if not verified or not under oath unless expressly provided otherwise by the Indiana Rules of Trial Procedure, statute or other law. Affidavits upon motions for summary judgment under IN ST TRIAL P Rule 56 and in denial of execution under IN ST TRIAL P Rule 9.2 shall be made upon personal knowledge. IN ST TRIAL P Rule 11(C).

5.   *Information excluded from public access.* Every document filed in a case shall separately identify information excluded from public access pursuant to IN ST ADMIN Rule 9(G)(1) as follows:

  a.   Whole documents that are excluded from public access pursuant to IN ST ADMIN Rule 9(G)(1) shall be tendered on light green paper or have a light green coversheet attached to the document, marked "Not for Public Access" or "Confidential." IN ST TRIAL P Rule 5(G)(1).

  b.   When only a portion of a document contains information excluded from public access pursuant to IN ST ADMIN Rule 9(G)(1), said information shall be omitted [or redacted] from the filed document, and set forth on a separate accompanying document on light green paper conspicuously marked "Not for Public Access" or "Confidential" and clearly designated [or identifying] the caption and number of the case and the document and location within the document to which the redacted material pertains. IN ST TRIAL P Rule 5(G)(2).

  c.   With respect to documents filed in electronic format, the trial court, by local rule, may provide for compliance with IN ST TRIAL P Rule 5 in manner that separates and protects access to information excluded from public access. IN ST TRIAL P Rule 5(G)(3).

  d.   IN ST TRIAL P Rule 5(G) does not apply to a record sealed by the court pursuant to IN ST 5-14-3-5.5 or otherwise, nor to records, documents, or information filed in cases to which public access is prohibited pursuant to IN ST ADMIN Rule 9(G). IN ST TRIAL P Rule 5(G)(4).

  e.   The following information in case records is excluded from public access and is confidential:

    i.   Information that is excluded from public access pursuant to federal law;

ii. Information that is excluded from public access as declared confidential by Indiana statute or other court rule, including without limitation:

- All adoption records created after July 8, 1941, as declared confidential by IN ST 31-19-19-1, et seq., except those specifically declared open by IN ST 31-19-13-2(2);

- All records relating to chancroid, chlamydia, gonorrhea, hepatitis, human immunodeficiency virus (HIV), Lymphogranuloma venereum, syphilis, tuberculosis, as declared confidential by IN ST 16-41-8-1, et seq.;

- All records relating to child abuse as declared confidential by IN ST 31-33-18-1, et seq.;

- All records relating to drug tests as declared confidential by IN ST 5-14-3-4(a)(9);

- Records of grand jury proceedings as declared confidential by IN ST 35-34-2-4;

- Records of juvenile proceedings as declared confidential by IN ST 31-39-1-2, except those specifically open under statute;

- All paternity records created after July 1, 1941 as declared confidential by IN ST 31-14-11-15, IN ST 31-19-5-23, IN ST 31-39-1-1 and IN ST 31-39-1-2 [Editor's note: IN ST 31-14-11-15 was repealed effective May 9, 2013];

- All pre-sentence reports as declared confidential by IN ST 35-38-1-13;

- Written petitions to permit marriages without consent and orders directing the Clerk of Court to issue a marriage license to underage persons, as declared confidential by IN ST 31-11-1-6;

- Only those arrest warrants, search warrants, indictments and informations ordered confidential by the trial judge, prior to return of duly executed service as declared confidential by IN ST 5-14-3-4(b)(1);

- All medical, mental health, or tax records unless determined by law or regulation of any governmental custodian not to be confidential, released by the subject of such records, or declared by a court of competent jurisdiction to be essential to the resolution of litigation as declared confidential by IN ST 16-39-3-10, IN ST 6-4.1-5-10, IN ST 6-4.1-12-12, and IN ST 6-8.1-7-1;

- Personal information relating to jurors or prospective jurors, other than for the use of the parties and counsel, pursuant to IN ST JURY Rule 10;

- Information relating to protection from abuse orders, no-contact orders and workplace violence restraining orders as declared confidential by IN ST 5-2-9-6, et seq.;

- Mediation proceedings pursuant to IN ST ADR Rule 2.11, Mini-Trial proceedings pursuant to IN ST ADR Rule 4.4(C), and Summary Jury Trials pursuant to IN ST ADR Rule 5.6;

- Information in probation files pursuant to the Probation Standards promulgated by the Judicial Conference of Indiana pursuant to IN ST 11-13-1-8(b);

- Information deemed confidential pursuant to the Rules for Court Administered Alcohol and Drug Programs promulgated by the Judicial Conference of Indiana pursuant to IN ST 12-23-14-13;

- Information deemed confidential pursuant to the Problem-Solving Court Rules promulgated by the Judicial Conference of Indiana pursuant to IN ST 33-23-16-16;

- All records of the Department of workforce Development as declared confidential by IN ST 22-4-19-6;

- Information regarding interception of electronic communications that is sealed or deemed confidential as set forth in IN ST 35-33.5-2-1, et seq.

iii. Information excluded from public access by specific court order;

iv. Complete Social Security Numbers of living persons;

v. With the exception of names, information such as addresses, phone numbers, and dates of birth which explicitly identifies:

- Natural persons who are witnesses or victims (not including defendants) in criminal, domestic violence, stalking, sexual assault, juvenile, or civil protection order proceedings, provided that juveniles who are victims of sex crimes shall be identified by initials only;

- Places of residence of judicial officers, clerks and other employees of courts and clerks of court, unless the person or persons about whom the information pertains waives confidentiality;

vi. Complete account numbers of specific assets, loans, bank accounts, credit cards, and personal identification numbers (PINs);

vii. All orders of expungement entered in criminal or juvenile proceedings, orders to restrict access to criminal history information pursuant to IN ST 35-38-5-5.5 or IN ST 35-38-8-5 and records excluded from public access by such orders, and information related to infractions that is excluded from public access pursuant to IN ST 34-28-5-15 or IN ST 34-28-5-16 [Editor's note: IN ST 35-38-5-5.5, IN ST 35-38-8-5 and IN ST 34-28-5-16 were repealed effective July 1, 2013; for information on orders restricting access to criminal history, refer to IN ST 35-38-9-1, et seq.];

viii. All personal notes and e-mail, and deliberative material, of judges, jurors, court staff and judicial agencies, and information recorded in personal data assistants (PDA's) or organizers and personal calendars. IN ST ADMIN Rule 9(G)(1).

F. Filing and Service Requirements

1. *Filing requirements.* Except as otherwise provided in IN ST TRIAL P Rule 5(E)(2), all pleadings and papers subsequent to the complaint which are required to be served upon a party shall be filed with the Court either before service or within a reasonable period of time thereafter. IN ST TRIAL P Rule 5(E)(1).

    a. *Filing with the court defined.* The filing of pleadings, motions, and other papers with the court as required by the Indiana Rules of Trial Procedure shall be made by one of the following methods:

        i. Delivery to the clerk of the court;

        ii. Sending by electronic transmission under the procedure adopted pursuant to IN ST ADMIN Rule 12;

        iii. Mailing to the clerk by registered, certified or express mail return receipt requested;

        iv. Depositing with any third-party commercial carrier for delivery to the clerk within three (3) calendar days, cost prepaid, properly addressed;

        v. If the court so permits, filing with the judge, in which event the judge shall note thereon the filing date and forthwith transmit them to the office of the clerk; or

        vi. Electronic filing, as approved by the Division of State Court Administration pursuant to IN ST ADMIN Rule 16. IN ST TRIAL P Rule 5(F).

        vii. Filing by registered or certified mail and by third-party commercial carrier shall be complete upon mailing or deposit. IN ST TRIAL P Rule 5(F).

    b. *Facsimile filing.* As outlined in IN ST HAMILTON ADMIN Rule 103(103.10), facsimile filing is permitted in the Circuit and Superior Courts of Hamilton County. The Courts authorize the Hamilton County Clerk of Courts to accept pleadings, motions and other papers by electronic facsimile transmission for filing in any case pending before the Courts, subject to the requirements of IN ST HAMILTON ADMIN Rule 103(103.10). IN ST HAMILTON ADMIN Rule 103(103.10); IN ST HAMILTON TRIAL Rule 201(201.80).

        i. *Generally.* In counties where a majority of judges of the courts of record, by posted local rule, have authorized electronic facsimile filing and designated a telephone number to receive such transmissions, pleadings, motions, and other papers may be sent to the Clerk of Circuit Court by electronic facsimile transmission for filing in any case, provided:

        - Such matter does not exceed ten (10) pages, including the cover sheet;

- Such matter does not require the payment of fees other than the electronic facsimile transcription fee set forth in IN ST ADMIN Rule 12(E);

- The sending party creates at the time of transmission a machine generated log for such transmission; and

- The original document and the transmission log are maintained by the sending party for the duration of the litigation. IN ST ADMIN Rule 12(B); IN ST HAMILTON ADMIN Rule 103(103.10)(d).

- Legibility of documents and timeliness of filing is the responsibility of the sender. IN ST HAMILTON ADMIN Rule 103(103.10)(g).

- The Clerk shall accept electronic facsimile transmission filings only if received at the facsimile machine assigned by the Clerk. The telephone number designated to receive such transmission is available at IN ST HAMILTON ADMIN Rule 103(103.40). IN ST HAMILTON ADMIN Rule 103(103.40).

ii.   *Time of filing.* During normal, posted business hours, the time of filing shall be the time the duplicate document is produced in the office of the Clerk of the Circuit Court. Duplicate documents received at all other times shall be filed as of the next normal business day. IN ST ADMIN Rule 12(C).

- If the receiving fax machine endorses its own time and date stamp upon the transmitted documents and the receiving machine produces a delivery receipt which is electronically created and transmitted to the sending party, the time of filing shall be the date and time recorded on the transmitted document by the receiving fax machine. IN ST ADMIN Rule 12(C).

- Electronic facsimile transmissions will be accepted for filing only during the regular business hours as set forth in IN ST HAMILTON ADMIN Rule 101. Transmissions received by the Hamilton County Clerk after close of business shall be filed effective the next regular business day. IN ST HAMILTON ADMIN Rule 103(103.30).

iii.   *Filing fee.* The electronic facsimile transmission will not be accepted for filing if its filing requires the payment of any fee other than the electronic facsimile transcription fee set forth in IN ST HAMILTON ADMIN Rule 103(103.20). IN ST HAMILTON ADMIN Rule 103(103.10)(e).

- Pursuant to Ordinance adopted by the Hamilton County Board of Commissioners, the Clerk shall collect an electronic facsimile transcription fee of One Dollar ($1.00) per page, to a maximum of Ten Dollars ($10.00) per transmission, for each electronic facsimile transmission accepted for filing with the Hamilton County Circuit and Superior Courts. IN ST HAMILTON ADMIN Rule 103(103.20).

- The fee shall be assessed against the sending party and shall be paid upon receipt of invoice by that party and at the latest within thirty (30) days of the transmission. In the event the fee is not paid by the sending party within the time limits provided, the court may issue a show-cause order or enter a judgment in the matter. The Clerk may refuse an electronic facsimile transmission from any attorney or pro se litigant who has failed to pay these fees within thirty (30) days. IN ST HAMILTON ADMIN Rule 103(103.20).

iv.   *No direct filing with court.* A party shall not send pleadings, motions and other papers by electronic facsimile transmission for filing directly to any Court without that Court's prior approval to do so. IN ST HAMILTON ADMIN Rule 103(103.50).

c.   *Filing with special judge.* After a special judge has qualified, a copy of each pleading and Chronological Case Summary entries filed with the Court shall be mailed or delivered to the office of that Special judge by the counsel or pro se litigant with service indicated on the certificate of service. IN ST HAMILTON TRIAL Rule 204(204.20).

d.   *Proof of filing.* Any party filing any paper by any method other than personal delivery to the clerk shall retain proof of filing. IN ST TRIAL P Rule 5(F).

2. *Service requirements.* Unless otherwise provided by the Indiana Rules of Trial Procedure or an order of the court, each party and special judge, if any, shall be served with: (1) every order required by its terms to be served; (2) every pleading subsequent to the original complaint; (3) every written motion except one which may be heard ex parte; (4) every brief submitted to the trial court; (5) every paper relating to discovery required to be served upon a party; and (6) every written notice, appearance, demand, offer of judgment, designation of record on appeal, or similar paper. IN ST TRIAL P Rule 5(A).

   a. *Methods of service*

      i. *Personal service.* Whenever a party is represented by an attorney of record, service shall be made upon such attorney unless service upon the party himself is ordered by the court. Service upon the attorney or party shall be made by delivering or mailing a copy of the papers to the last known address or where an attorney or party has consented to service by fax or e-mail, as provided in IN ST TRIAL P Rule 3.1(A)(4), by faxing or e-mailing a copy of the documents to the fax number or e-mail address set out in the appearance form or correction as required by IN ST TRIAL P Rule 3.1(E). IN ST TRIAL P Rule 5(B). Delivery of a copy within IN ST TRIAL P Rule 5 means:

- Offering or tendering it to the attorney or party and stating the nature of the papers being served. Refusal to accept an offered or tendered document is a waiver of any objection to the sufficiency or adequacy of service of that document;

- Leaving it at his office with a clerk or other person in charge thereof, or if there is no one in charge, leaving it in a conspicuous place therein; or

- If the office is closed, by leaving it at his dwelling house or usual place of abode with some person of suitable age and discretion then residing therein; or,

- Leaving it at some other suitable place, selected by the attorney upon whom service is being made, pursuant to duly promulgated local rule. IN ST TRIAL P Rule 5(B)(1).

      ii. *Service by mail.* If service is made by mail, the papers shall be deposited in the United States mail addressed to the person on whom they are being served, with postage prepaid. Service shall be deemed complete upon mailing. Proof of service of all papers permitted to be mailed may be made by written acknowledgment of service, by affidavit of the person who mailed the papers, or by certificate of an attorney. It shall be the duty of attorneys when entering their appearance in a cause or when filing pleadings or papers therein, to have noted in the Chronological Case Summary or said pleadings or papers so filed the address and telephone number of their office. Service by delivery or by mail at such address shall be deemed sufficient and complete. IN ST TRIAL P Rule 5(B)(2).

      iii. *Service by fax or e-mail.* A party who has consented to service by fax or e-mail may be served as follows:

- Service by e-mail shall be made by attaching the document being served in .pdf format. Discovery documents must also be served in accordance with IN ST TRIAL P Rule 26(A). IN ST TRIAL P Rule 5(B)(3)(a).

- Service by fax shall be deemed complete upon generation of a transmission record indicating the successful transmission of the entire document, except as provided in IN ST TRIAL P Rule 5(B)(3)(d). IN ST TRIAL P Rule 5(B)(3)(b).

- Service by e-mail shall be deemed complete upon transmission, except as provided in IN ST TRIAL P Rule 5(B)(3)(d). IN ST TRIAL P Rule 5(B)(3)(c).

- Service by fax or e-mail that occurs on a Saturday, Sunday, legal holiday, or day the court or agency in which the matter is pending is closed or after 5:00 PM local time of the recipient shall be deemed complete the next day that is not a Saturday, Sunday, legal holiday, or day that the court or agency in which the matter is pending is not closed. IN ST TRIAL P Rule 5(B)(3)(d).

      iv. *Mail box service.* Pursuant to IN ST TRIAL P Rule 5(B)(1)(d), the Circuit and Superior Courts of Hamilton County hereby designate the "mail boxes" located in the Clerk's order book office for service of pleadings upon attorneys who have such boxes. IN ST HAMILTON TRIAL Rule 201(201.50).

 b. *Serving numerous defendants.* In any action in which there are unusually large numbers of defendants, the court, upon motion or of its own initiative, may order:

  i. That service of the pleadings of the defendants and replies thereto need not be made as between the defendants;

   • That any cross-claim, counterclaim, or matter constituting an avoidance or affirmative defense contained therein shall be deemed to be denied or avoided by all other parties; and

   • That the filing of any such pleading and service thereof upon the plaintiff constitutes due notice of it to the parties. IN ST TRIAL P Rule 5(D).

  ii. A copy of every such order shall be served upon the parties in such manner and form as the court directs. IN ST TRIAL P Rule 5(D).

 c. *Service on parties in default for failure to appear.* No service need be made on parties in default for failure to appear, except that pleadings asserting new or additional claims for relief against them shall be served upon them in the manner provided by service of summons in IN ST TRIAL P Rule 4. IN ST TRIAL P Rule 5(A).

G. Hearings

 1. *Hearing on motion.* Unless local conditions make it impracticable, each judge shall establish regular times and places, at intervals sufficiently frequent for the prompt dispatch of business, at which motions requiring notice and hearing may be heard and disposed of; but the judge at any time or place and on such notice, if any, as he considers reasonable may make order for the advancement, conduct, and hearing of actions. To expedite its business the court may direct the submission and determination of motions without oral hearing upon brief written statements of reasons in support and opposition, or direct or permit hearings by telephone conference call with all attorneys or other similar means of communication. IN ST TRIAL P Rule 73(A).

H. Forms

 1. Motion to Dismiss for Lack of Subject Matter Jurisdiction Forms for Indiana

  a. General form. 5 INPRAC § 3:4.1.

  b. Lack of subject matter jurisdiction. 5 INPRAC § 3:4.2.

  c. Motion to dismiss plaintiff's complaint; General form. 9 INPRAC § 42.2.

  d. Lack of jurisdiction over the subject matter. 9 INPRAC § 42.3.

  e. Certificate of service; Personal service. 9 INPRAC § 5.7.

  f. Certificate of service; First class mail. 9 INPRAC § 5.8.

I. Checklist

 (I) ❑ Matters to be considered by moving party

  (a) ❑ Required documents

   (1) ❑ Motion and notice

   (2) ❑ Proposed order

   (3) ❑ Certificate of service

  (b) ❑ Supplemental documents

   (1) ❑ Supporting evidence

   (2) ❑ Facsimile cover sheet

   (3) ❑ Request to schedule trial or hearing

   (4) ❑ Copies of unpublished opinions

  (c) ❑ Timing

   (1) ❑ A motion to dismiss for lack of subject matter jurisdiction shall be made before pleading if

a further pleading is permitted or within twenty (20) days after service of the prior pleading if none is required

    (2) ❏ A written motion, other than one which may be heard ex parte, and notice of the hearing thereof shall be served not less than five (5) days before the time specified for the hearing, unless a different period is fixed by the Indiana Rules of Trial Procedure or by order of the court

    (3) ❏ All pleadings and papers subsequent to the complaint which are required to be served upon a party shall be filed with the Court either before service or within a reasonable period of time thereafter

(II) ❏ Matters to be considered by the responding party

    (a) ❏ Required documents

        (1) ❏ Opposition

        (2) ❏ Certificate of service

    (b) ❏ Supplemental documents

        (1) ❏ Supporting evidence

        (2) ❏ Alternative proposed order

        (3) ❏ Facsimile cover sheet

        (4) ❏ Request to schedule trial or hearing

        (5) ❏ Copies of unpublished opinions

    (c) ❏ Timing

        (1) ❏ Except as otherwise provided in IN ST TRIAL P Rule 59(D), opposing affidavits may be served not less than one (1) day before the hearing, unless the court permits them to be served at some other time

Motions, Oppositions and Replies
Motion to Dismiss for Lack of Personal Jurisdiction

Document Last Updated October 2013

A. Applicable Rules

1. *State rules*

    a. Appearance. IN ST TRIAL P Rule 3.1.

    b. Summons. IN ST TRIAL P Rule 4.

    c. Service and filing of pleadings and other papers. IN ST TRIAL P Rule 5.

    d. Time. IN ST TRIAL P Rule 6.

    e. Pleadings. IN ST TRIAL P Rule 7; IN ST TRIAL P Rule 8; IN ST TRIAL P Rule 9; IN ST TRIAL P Rule 9.2; IN ST TRIAL P Rule 10.

    f. Signing and verification of pleadings. IN ST TRIAL P Rule 11.

    g. Defenses and objections; When and how presented; By pleading or motion; Motion for judgment on the pleadings. IN ST TRIAL P Rule 12.

    h. Amended and supplemental pleadings. IN ST TRIAL P Rule 15.

    i. Joinder of person needed for just adjudication. IN ST TRIAL P Rule 19.

    j. Evidence. IN ST TRIAL P Rule 43.

    k. Judgment on the evidence (directed verdict). IN ST TRIAL P Rule 50.

    l. Findings by the court. IN ST TRIAL P Rule 52.

m. Summary judgment. IN ST TRIAL P Rule 56.

n. Motion to correct error. IN ST TRIAL P Rule 59.

o. Relief from judgment or order. IN ST TRIAL P Rule 60.

p. Hearing of motions. IN ST TRIAL P Rule 73.

q. Access to court records. IN ST ADMIN Rule 9.

r. Paper size. IN ST ADMIN Rule 11.

s. Facsimile transmission. IN ST ADMIN Rule 12.

t. Electronic filing and electronic service pilot projects. IN ST ADMIN Rule 16.

u. Sealing of certain records by court; Hearing; Notice. IN ST 5-14-3-5.5.

v. Privacy and confidentiality. IN ST 5-2-9-6; IN ST 5-14-3-4; IN ST 6-4.1-5-10; IN ST 6-4.1-12-12; IN ST 6-8.1-7-1; IN ST 11-13-1-8; IN ST 12-23-14-13; IN ST 16-39-3-10; IN ST 16-41-8-1; IN ST 22-4-19-6; IN ST 31-11-1-6; IN ST 31-19-5-23; IN ST 31-19-13-2; IN ST 31-19-19-1; IN ST 31-33-18-1; IN ST 31-39-1-1; IN ST 31-39-1-2; IN ST 33-23-16-16; IN ST 35-34-2-4; IN ST 35-38-1-13; IN ST 35-38-9-1; IN ST ADR Rule 2.11; IN ST ADR Rule 4.4; IN ST ADR Rule 5.6; IN ST JURY Rule 10.

2. *Local rules*

a. Court hours. IN ST HAMILTON ADMIN Rule 101.

b. Facsimile transmissions. IN ST HAMILTON ADMIN Rule 103.

c. Filing of pleadings and entry of appearances. IN ST HAMILTON TRIAL Rule 201.

d. Proposed orders. IN ST HAMILTON TRIAL Rule 202.

e. Briefs and memorandums. IN ST HAMILTON TRIAL Rule 203.

f. Special judges. IN ST HAMILTON TRIAL Rule 204.

g. Trial settings. IN ST HAMILTON TRIAL Rule 205.

h. Continuances. IN ST HAMILTON TRIAL Rule 206.

B. Timing

1. *Timing of motion to dismiss for failure lack of personal matter jurisdiction.* A motion making any of the defenses listed in IN ST TRIAL P Rule 12(B) shall be made before pleading if a further pleading is permitted or within twenty (20) days after service of the prior pleading if none is required. IN ST TRIAL P Rule 12(B).

a. *Time to file a responsive pleading.* A responsive pleading required under the Indiana Rules of Trial Procedure, shall be served within twenty (20) days after service of the prior pleading. IN ST TRIAL P Rule 6(C).

b. *Waiver of certain IN ST TRIAL P Rule 12(B) defenses.* If a pleading sets forth a claim for relief to which the adverse party is not required to serve a responsive pleading, any of the defenses in IN ST TRIAL P Rule 12(B)(2), IN ST TRIAL P Rule 12(B)(3), IN ST TRIAL P Rule 12(B)(4), IN ST TRIAL P Rule 12(B)(5) or IN ST TRIAL P Rule 12(B)(8) is waived to the extent constitutionally permissible unless made in a motion within twenty (20) days after service of the prior pleading. IN ST TRIAL P Rule 12(B).

c. *Filing.* All pleadings and papers subsequent to the complaint which are required to be served upon a party shall be filed with the Court either before service or within a reasonable period of time thereafter. IN ST TRIAL P Rule 5(E)(1).

2. *Service.* A written motion, other than one which may be heard ex parte, and notice of the hearing thereof shall be served not less than five (5) days before the time specified for the hearing, unless a different period is fixed by the Indiana Rules of Trial Procedure or by order of the court. IN ST TRIAL P Rule 6(D).

a. *Of supporting affidavits.* When a motion is supported by affidavit, the affidavit shall be served with the motion. IN ST TRIAL P Rule 6(D).

3. *Service of opposition.* Except as otherwise provided in IN ST TRIAL P Rule 59(D), opposing affidavits may be served not less than one (1) day before the hearing, unless the court permits them to be served at some other time. IN ST TRIAL P Rule 6(D).

4. *Computation of time*

   a. *Generally; Days excluded.* In computing any period of time prescribed or allowed by the Indiana Rules of Trial Procedure, by order of the court, or by any applicable statute, the day of the act, event, or default from which the designated period of time begins to run shall not be included. The last day of the period so computed is to be included unless it is:

      i. A Saturday,

      ii. A Sunday,

      iii. A legal holiday as defined by state statute, or

      iv. A day the office in which the act is to be done is closed during regular business hours. IN ST TRIAL P Rule 6(A).

   b. *Short periods.* In any event, the period runs until the end of the next day that is not a Saturday, a Sunday, a legal holiday, or a day on which the office is closed. When the period of time allowed is less than seven (7) days, intermediate Saturdays, Sundays, legal holidays, and days on which the office is closed shall be excluded from the computations. IN ST TRIAL P Rule 6(A).

   c. *Additional time after service by United States mail.* Whenever a party has the right or is required to do some act or take some proceedings within a prescribed period after the service of a notice or other paper upon him and the notice or paper is served upon him by United States mail, three (3) days shall be added to the prescribed period. IN ST TRIAL P Rule 6(E).

   d. *Enlargement of time.* When an act is required or allowed to be done at or within a specific time by the Indiana Rules of Trial Procedure, the court may at any time for cause shown:

      i. Order the period enlarged, with or without motion or notice, if request therefor is made before the expiration of the period originally prescribed or extended by a previous order; or

      ii. Upon motion made after the expiration of the specific period, permit the act to be done where the failure to act was the result of excusable neglect; but, the court may not extend the time for taking any action for judgment on the evidence under IN ST TRIAL P Rule 50(A), amendment of findings and judgment under IN ST TRIAL P Rule 52(B), to correct errors under IN ST TRIAL P Rule 59(C), statement in opposition to motion to correct error under IN ST TRIAL P Rule 59(E), or to obtain relief from final judgment under IN ST TRIAL P Rule 60(B), except to the extent and under the conditions stated in those rules. IN ST TRIAL P Rule 6(B).

      iii. For information on obtaining a continuance, refer to IN ST HAMILTON TRIAL Rule 206.

C. General Requirements

1. *Motions, generally.* Unless made during a hearing or trial, or otherwise ordered by the court, an application to the court for an order shall be made by written motion. The motion shall state the grounds therefor and the relief or order sought. IN ST TRIAL P Rule 7(B).

   a. *Motions as distinct from pleadings.* Motions and responses to motions are not pleadings, and allegations contained in a motion are not admissions of a party. 22B INPRAC 7:2; Wachstetter v. County Properties, LLC, 832 N.E.2d 574 (Ind.Ct.App. 2005); Scott County Family YMCA, Inc. v. Hobbs, 817 N.E.2d 603 (Ind.Ct.App. 2004).

   b. *Unopposed motions generally granted.* It is common for a trial court to grant procedural motions, such as motions for enlargement of time, discovery motions, or motions for continuance, unless an objection is filed. 21 INPRAC § 13.8.

2. *Motion to dismiss for lack of personal jurisdiction.* Every defense, in law or fact, to a claim for relief in any pleading, whether a claim, counterclaim, cross-claim, or third-party claim, shall be asserted in the responsive pleading thereto if one is required; except that at the option of the pleader, the defense of lack of jurisdiction over person may be made by motion. IN ST TRIAL P Rule 12(b)(2). If personal

jurisdiction is not present, then that party against whom jurisdiction is asserted must raise the question. 1A INPRAC R 12(12.6).

a. *Presumption of jurisdiction.* Jurisdiction is presumed and, therefore, the defense of lack of personal jurisdiction may be asserted by motion under IN ST TRIAL P Rule 12(B)(2), or in the defendant's answer as an affirmative defense. 22 INPRAC § 15.16; Adsit Co., Inc. v. Gustin, 874 N.E.2d 1018 (Ind.Ct.App. 2007); Keesling v. Winstead, 858 N.E.2d 996 (Ind.Ct.App. 2006). Refer to the Indiana KeyRules Answer document for more information.

b. *Personal jurisdiction.* The Due Process Clause of the Fourteenth Amendment requires that before a state may exercise jurisdiction over a defendant, the defendant must have certain minimum contacts with the state such that the maintenance of the suit does not offend traditional notions of fair play and substantial justice. 1A INPRAC R 12(12.6).

   i. *General jurisdiction.* If the defendant's contacts with the state are so continuous and systematic that the defendant should reasonably anticipate being haled into the courts of that state for any matter, then the defendant is subject to general jurisdiction, even in causes of action unrelated to the defendant's contacts with the forum state. 1A INPRAC R 12(12.6).

   ii. *Specific jurisdiction.* In cases where a defendant is not subject to general jurisdiction in a forum state, specific jurisdiction may be asserted if the controversy is related to or arises out of the defendant's contacts with the forum state. Specific jurisdiction requires that the defendant purposefully availed itself of the privilege of conducting activities within the forum state so that the defendant reasonably anticipates being haled into court there. A single contact with the forum state may be sufficient to establish specific jurisdiction over a defendant, if it creates a substantial connection with the forum state and the suit is related to that connection. 1A INPRAC R 12(12.6).

   iii. *Due process; Reasonableness.* A defendant cannot be haled into a jurisdiction solely as a result of random, fortuitous, or attenuated contacts or of the unilateral activity of another party or a third person. Once either general or specific jurisdiction has been established, due process requires that the assertion of personal jurisdiction over the defendant is reasonable. The assertion of personal jurisdiction will rarely be found unreasonable if minimum contacts are found. Five factors are used in determining reasonableness:

- The burden on the defendant;
- The forum State's interest in adjudicating the dispute;
- The plaintiff's interest in obtaining convenience and effective relief;
- The interstate judicial system's interest in obtaining the most efficient resolution of controversies; and
- The shared interest of the several States in furthering fundamental substantive social policies. 1A INPRAC R 12(12.6).

   iv. *Jurisdiction presumed.* Indiana state trial courts are courts of general jurisdiction and jurisdiction is presumed. The party contesting jurisdiction bears the burden of proving the lack of personal jurisdiction by a preponderance of the evidence, unless the lack of jurisdiction is apparent on the face of the complaint. A determination of the existence of personal jurisdiction is entitled to de novo review. 1A INPRAC R 12(12.6); Foley v. Schwartz, 943 N.E.2d 371 (Ind.Ct.App. 2011).

c. *Challenge to jurisdiction in first response to complaint.* The defendant may challenge the Indiana court's jurisdiction over him, without submitting to that jurisdiction, so long as the defense is asserted in the first response to the plaintiff's complaint and the defendant does not request affirmative relief from the court prior to asserting that defense. 22 INPRAC § 15.16.

d. *Burden shifting.* After the plaintiff establishes that there are minimum contacts between defendant and forum state to exercise personal jurisdiction without violating Due Process Clause, the defendant then carries the burden of proving that asserting jurisdiction is unfair and unreasonable. 1A INPRAC R 12(12.6); JPMorgan Chase Bank, N.A. v. Desert Palace, Inc., 882 N.E.2d 743 (Ind.Ct.App. 2008).

e. *Effect of granting of motion.* The dismissal of a complaint for lack of jurisdiction over the person is not an adjudication on the merits and does not prejudice the plaintiff's right to file another complaint if the court can obtain jurisdiction over the defendant. 9 INPRAC § 42.4.

3. *Consolidation and waiver*

a. *Consolidation of defenses in motion.* A party who makes a motion under IN ST TRIAL P Rule 12 may join with it any other motions herein provided for and then available to him. If a party makes a motion under IN ST TRIAL P Rule 12 but omits therefrom any defense or objection then available to him which IN ST TRIAL P Rule 12 permits to be raised by motion, he shall not thereafter make a motion based on the defense or objection so omitted. He may, however, make such motions as are allowed under IN ST TRIAL P Rule 12(H)(2). IN ST TRIAL P Rule 12(G).

b. *Waiver or preservation of certain defenses.* No defense or objection is waived by being joined with one or more other defenses or objections in a responsive pleading or motion. IN ST TRIAL P Rule 12(B).

D. Documents

1. *Required documents*

a. *Motion and notice.* The requirement of notice is satisfied by service of the motion. IN ST TRIAL P Rule 7(B). Refer to the General Requirements section of this document for information on the content of a motion to dismiss for lack of personal jurisdiction.

b. *Proposed order.* Unless local practice provides differently, a party should submit a proposed order with its written motion to be signed by the judge once the motion has been granted. 21 INPRAC § 13.8; IN ST HAMILTON ADMIN Rule 103(103.10)(b). Each Motion, Petition or other request for relief shall be accompanied by a proposed order. IN ST HAMILTON TRIAL Rule 202(202.10).

i. All proposed orders submitted by counsel pursuant to IN ST HAMILTON TRIAL Rule 202 shall meet the following requirements: (1) contain a complete distribution list of all attorneys and pro se litigants with full addresses; (2) stamped envelopes appropriately addressed for each attorney of record and/or pro se litigant on the distribution list. IN ST HAMILTON TRIAL Rule 202(202.30).

c. *Certificate of service.* An attorney or unrepresented party tendering a document to the Clerk for filing shall certify that service has been made, list the parties served, and specify the date and means of service. The certificate of service shall be placed at the end of the document and shall not be separately filed. The separate filing of a certificate of service, however, shall not be grounds for rejecting a document for filing. The Clerk may permit documents to be filed without a certificate of service but shall require prompt filing of a separate certificate of service. IN ST TRIAL P Rule 5(C).

i. All pleadings filed with the Court which require a certificate of service shall specifically name the individual party or attorney on whom service has been made, the address, the manner in which service was made and the date when service was made. IN ST HAMILTON TRIAL Rule 201(201.60).

2. *Supplemental documents*

a. *Supporting evidence.* When a motion is based on facts not appearing of record the court may hear the matter on affidavits presented by the respective parties, but the court may direct that the matter be heard wholly or partly on oral testimony or depositions. IN ST TRIAL P Rule 43(B).

b. *Facsimile cover sheet.* Any document sent to the Clerk of the Circuit Court by electronic facsimile transmission shall be accompanied by a cover sheet which states the title of the document, case number, number of pages, identity and voice telephone number of the sending party and instructions for filing. The cover sheet shall contain the signature of the attorney or party, pro se, authorizing the filing. IN ST ADMIN Rule 12(D); IN ST HAMILTON ADMIN Rule 103(103.10)(a).

c. *Request to schedule hearing.* All requests to schedule trials and hearings shall be in writing and shall contain the following information:

i. Type of trial or hearing (i.e., jury trial, court trial, final hearing in dissolution, etc.). IN ST HAMILTON TRIAL Rule 205(205.10).

      ii.   A good-faith estimate of the total court time needed for the trial or hearing. IN ST HAMILTON TRIAL Rule 205(205.10).

      iii. Each request under IN ST HAMILTON TRIAL Rule 205(205.10) shall be accompanied by a proposed written order with appropriate blanks for date and time and shall further include reference to those items set forth in IN ST HAMILTON TRIAL Rule 205(205.10)(a) and IN ST HAMILTON TRIAL Rule 205(205.10)(b). IN ST HAMILTON TRIAL Rule 205(205.20).

  d.   *Copies of unpublished opinions.* Authorities relied upon which are not cited in the Northeastern Reporter system shall be attached to counsel's brief. If the authority is cited for the first time in oral argument, a copy of the authority may be provided to the Court at the time of the argument. Sufficient copies shall be available to provide counsel for each party with a copy. IN ST HAMILTON TRIAL Rule 203(203.10).

E. Format

1. *Form of motions.* The rules applicable to captions, and the signing and form of pleadings (IN ST TRIAL P Rule 8 through IN ST TRIAL P Rule 11), apply to all motions and other papers provided under the Indiana Rules of Trial Procedure. 22B INPRAC 7:2.

2. *Form of pleadings*

  a.   *Caption; Names of parties.* Every pleading shall contain a caption setting forth the name of the court, the title of the action, the file number, and a designation as in IN ST TRIAL P Rule 7(A). In the complaint the title of the action shall include the names of all the parties, but in other pleadings it is sufficient to state the name of the first party on each side with an appropriate indication of other parties. IN ST TRIAL P Rule 10(A).

  b.   *Paragraphs; Separate statements.* All averments of a claim or defense shall be made in numbered paragraphs, the contents of each of which shall be limited as far as practicable to a statement of a single set of circumstances, and a paragraph may be referred to by number in all succeeding pleadings. Each claim founded upon a separate transaction or occurrence and each defense other than denials may be stated in a separate count or defense whenever a separation facilitates the clear presentation of the matters set forth. IN ST TRIAL P Rule 10(B).

  c.   *Adoption by reference; Exhibits.* Statements in a pleading may be adopted by reference in a different part of the same pleading or in another pleading or in any motion. A copy of any written instrument which is an exhibit to a pleading is a part thereof for all purposes. IN ST TRIAL P Rule 10(C).

  d.   *Facsimile page limit.* Courts authorize the Hamilton County Clerk of Courts to accept pleadings, motions and other papers by electronic facsimile transmission for filing in any case pending before the Courts, subject to the requirement that The transmission may not exceed ten (10) pages in length including the cover sheet and proposed CCS entry. IN ST HAMILTON ADMIN Rule 103(103.10)(c).

  e.   *Emergency facsimile filings.* If the filing requires the immediate attention of the Judge, it shall so indicate in bold letters in an accompanying transmittal memorandum. IN ST HAMILTON ADMIN Rule 103(103.10)(f).

  f.   *Special judge heading.* After a special judge is selected, the attorneys or pro se litigants shall add to the caption of all pleadings to the right of the case title the following: "BEFORE SPECIAL JUDGE _____." IN ST HAMILTON TRIAL Rule 204(204.10).

  g.   *Format rules strictly enforced.* All filings shall be in compliance with the Indiana Rules of Trial Procedure. If the documents received are not in proper form, such deficiencies will not be corrected by court personnel. IN ST HAMILTON TRIAL Rule 201(201.70). The Court shall not be required to act on any Motion, Petition or other request for relief unless filed in conformity with the Hamilton County Local Trial and Administrative rules. IN ST HAMILTON TRIAL Rule 202(202.20).

3. *Size of papers for filing.* Effective January 1, 1992, all pleadings, copies, motions and documents filed with any trial court or appellate level court, typed or printed, with the exception of exhibits and existing wills, shall be prepared on eight and one-half by eleven inch (8 1/2" x 11") size paper. IN ST ADMIN Rule 11.

  a.   *Form.* All documents filed in any Hamilton County Court, with the exception of exhibits and existing wills, shall be prepared on paper measuring eight and one-half by eleven inches (8 1/2" x 11"). IN ST HAMILTON TRIAL Rule 201(201.20).

4. *Signature requirements*

    a. *Signature of attorney.* Every pleading or motion of a party represented by an attorney shall be signed by at least one (1) attorney of record in his individual name, whose address, telephone number, and attorney number shall be stated, except that this provision shall not apply to pleadings and motions made and transcribed at the trial or a hearing before the judge and received by him in such form. IN ST TRIAL P Rule 11(A).

        i. The signature of an attorney constitutes a certificate by him that he has read the pleadings; that to the best of his knowledge, information, and belief, there is good ground to support it; and that it is not interposed for delay. IN ST TRIAL P Rule 11(A).

        ii. If a pleading or motion is not signed or is signed with intent to defeat the purpose of the rule, it may be stricken as sham and false and the action may proceed as though the pleading had not been served. IN ST TRIAL P Rule 11(A).

        iii. For a willful violation of IN ST TRIAL P Rule 11 an attorney may be subjected to appropriate disciplinary action. Similar action may be taken if scandalous or indecent matter is inserted. IN ST TRIAL P Rule 11(A).

    b. *Signature of unrepresented party.* A party who is not represented by an attorney shall sign his pleading and state his address. IN ST TRIAL P Rule 11(A).

    c. *Verification not generally required.* Except when specifically required by rule, pleadings or motions need not be verified or accompanied by affidavit. The rule in equity that the averments of an answer under oath must be overcome by the testimony of two (2) witnesses or of one (1) witness sustained by corroborating circumstances is abolished. IN ST TRIAL P Rule 11(A).

    d. *Verification by affirmation or representation.* When in connection with any civil or special statutory proceeding it is required that any pleading, motion, petition, supporting affidavit, or other document of any kind, be verified, or that an oath be taken, it shall be sufficient if the subscriber simply affirms the truth of the matter to be verified by an affirmation or representation. IN ST TRIAL P Rule 11(B). IN ST TRIAL P Rule 11(B) states that the affirmation or representation should be in substantially the following language: "I (we) affirm, under the penalties for perjury, that the foregoing representation(s) is (are) true. (Signed) _____."

        i. Any person who falsifies an affirmation or representation of fact shall be subject to the same penalties as are prescribed by law for the making of a false affidavit. IN ST TRIAL P Rule 11(B).

    e. *Verified pleadings, motions, and affidavits as evidence.* Pleadings, motions and affidavits accompanying or in support of such pleadings or motions when required to be verified or under oath shall be accepted as a representation that the signer had personal knowledge thereof or reasonable cause to believe the existence of the facts or matters stated or alleged therein; and, if otherwise competent or acceptable as evidence, may be admitted as evidence of the facts or matters stated or alleged therein when it is so provided in the Indiana Rules of Trial Procedure, by statute or other law, or to the extent the writing or signature expressly purports to be made upon the signer's personal knowledge. When such pleadings, motions and affidavits are verified or under oath they shall not require other or greater proof on the part of the adverse party than if not verified or not under oath unless expressly provided otherwise by the Indiana Rules of Trial Procedure, statute or other law. Affidavits upon motions for summary judgment under IN ST TRIAL P Rule 56 and in denial of execution under IN ST TRIAL P Rule 9.2 shall be made upon personal knowledge. IN ST TRIAL P Rule 11(C).

5. *Information excluded from public access.* Every document filed in a case shall separately identify information excluded from public access pursuant to IN ST ADMIN Rule 9(G)(1) as follows:

    a. Whole documents that are excluded from public access pursuant to IN ST ADMIN Rule 9(G)(1) shall be tendered on light green paper or have a light green coversheet attached to the document, marked "Not for Public Access" or "Confidential." IN ST TRIAL P Rule 5(G)(1).

    b. When only a portion of a document contains information excluded from public access pursuant to IN

ST ADMIN Rule 9(G)(1), said information shall be omitted [or redacted] from the filed document, and set forth on a separate accompanying document on light green paper conspicuously marked "Not for Public Access" or "Confidential" and clearly designated [or identifying] the caption and number of the case and the document and location within the document to which the redacted material pertains. IN ST TRIAL P Rule 5(G)(2).

c. With respect to documents filed in electronic format, the trial court, by local rule, may provide for compliance with IN ST TRIAL P Rule 5 in manner that separates and protects access to information excluded from public access. IN ST TRIAL P Rule 5(G)(3).

d. IN ST TRIAL P Rule 5(G) does not apply to a record sealed by the court pursuant to IN ST 5-14-3-5.5 or otherwise, nor to records, documents, or information filed in cases to which public access is prohibited pursuant to IN ST ADMIN Rule 9(G). IN ST TRIAL P Rule 5(G)(4).

e. The following information in case records is excluded from public access and is confidential:

i. Information that is excluded from public access pursuant to federal law;

ii. Information that is excluded from public access as declared confidential by Indiana statute or other court rule, including without limitation:

- All adoption records created after July 8, 1941, as declared confidential by IN ST 31-19-19-1, et seq., except those specifically declared open by IN ST 31-19-13-2(2);

- All records relating to chancroid, chlamydia, gonorrhea, hepatitis, human immunodeficiency virus (HIV), Lymphogranuloma venereum, syphilis, tuberculosis, as declared confidential by IN ST 16-41-8-1, et seq.;

- All records relating to child abuse as declared confidential by IN ST 31-33-18-1, et seq.;

- All records relating to drug tests as declared confidential by IN ST 5-14-3-4(a)(9);

- Records of grand jury proceedings as declared confidential by IN ST 35-34-2-4;

- Records of juvenile proceedings as declared confidential by IN ST 31-39-1-2, except those specifically open under statute;

- All paternity records created after July 1, 1941 as declared confidential by IN ST 31-14-11-15, IN ST 31-19-5-23, IN ST 31-39-1-1 and IN ST 31-39-1-2 [Editor's note: IN ST 31-14-11-15 was repealed effective May 9, 2013];

- All pre-sentence reports as declared confidential by IN ST 35-38-1-13;

- Written petitions to permit marriages without consent and orders directing the Clerk of Court to issue a marriage license to underage persons, as declared confidential by IN ST 31-11-1-6;

- Only those arrest warrants, search warrants, indictments and informations ordered confidential by the trial judge, prior to return of duly executed service as declared confidential by IN ST 5-14-3-4(b)(1);

- All medical, mental health, or tax records unless determined by law or regulation of any governmental custodian not to be confidential, released by the subject of such records, or declared by a court of competent jurisdiction to be essential to the resolution of litigation as declared confidential by IN ST 16-39-3-10, IN ST 6-4.1-5-10, IN ST 6-4.1-12-12, and IN ST 6-8.1-7-1;

- Personal information relating to jurors or prospective jurors, other than for the use of the parties and counsel, pursuant to IN ST JURY Rule 10;

- Information relating to protection from abuse orders, no-contact orders and workplace violence restraining orders as declared confidential by IN ST 5-2-9-6, et seq.;

- Mediation proceedings pursuant to IN ST ADR Rule 2.11, Mini-Trial proceedings pursuant to IN ST ADR Rule 4.4(C), and Summary Jury Trials pursuant to IN ST ADR Rule 5.6;

- Information in probation files pursuant to the Probation Standards promulgated by the Judicial Conference of Indiana pursuant to IN ST 11-13-1-8(b);

- Information deemed confidential pursuant to the Rules for Court Administered Alcohol and Drug Programs promulgated by the Judicial Conference of Indiana pursuant to IN ST 12-23-14-13;

- Information deemed confidential pursuant to the Problem-Solving Court Rules promulgated by the Judicial Conference of Indiana pursuant to IN ST 33-23-16-16;

- All records of the Department of workforce Development as declared confidential by IN ST 22-4-19-6;

- Information regarding interception of electronic communications that is sealed or deemed confidential as set forth in IN ST 35-33.5-2-1, et seq.

iii. Information excluded from public access by specific court order;

iv. Complete Social Security Numbers of living persons;

v. With the exception of names, information such as addresses, phone numbers, and dates of birth which explicitly identifies:

- Natural persons who are witnesses or victims (not including defendants) in criminal, domestic violence, stalking, sexual assault, juvenile, or civil protection order proceedings, provided that juveniles who are victims of sex crimes shall be identified by initials only;

- Places of residence of judicial officers, clerks and other employees of courts and clerks of court, unless the person or persons about whom the information pertains waives confidentiality;

vi. Complete account numbers of specific assets, loans, bank accounts, credit cards, and personal identification numbers (PINs);

vii. All orders of expungement entered in criminal or juvenile proceedings, orders to restrict access to criminal history information pursuant to IN ST 35-38-5-5.5 or IN ST 35-38-8-5 and records excluded from public access by such orders, and information related to infractions that is excluded from public access pursuant to IN ST 34-28-5-15 or IN ST 34-28-5-16 [Editor's note: IN ST 35-38-5-5.5, IN ST 35-38-8-5 and IN ST 34-28-5-16 were repealed effective July 1, 2013; for information on orders restricting access to criminal history, refer to IN ST 35-38-9-1, et seq.];

viii. All personal notes and e-mail, and deliberative material, of judges, jurors, court staff and judicial agencies, and information recorded in personal data assistants (PDA's) or organizers and personal calendars. IN ST ADMIN Rule 9(G)(1).

F. Filing and Service Requirements

1. *Filing requirements.* Except as otherwise provided in IN ST TRIAL P Rule 5(E)(2), all pleadings and papers subsequent to the complaint which are required to be served upon a party shall be filed with the Court either before service or within a reasonable period of time thereafter. IN ST TRIAL P Rule 5(E)(1).

   a. *Filing with the court defined.* The filing of pleadings, motions, and other papers with the court as required by the Indiana Rules of Trial Procedure shall be made by one of the following methods:

      i. Delivery to the clerk of the court;

      ii. Sending by electronic transmission under the procedure adopted pursuant to IN ST ADMIN Rule 12;

      iii. Mailing to the clerk by registered, certified or express mail return receipt requested;

      iv. Depositing with any third-party commercial carrier for delivery to the clerk within three (3) calendar days, cost prepaid, properly addressed;

      v. If the court so permits, filing with the judge, in which event the judge shall note thereon the filing date and forthwith transmit them to the office of the clerk; or

      vi. Electronic filing, as approved by the Division of State Court Administration pursuant to IN ST ADMIN Rule 16. IN ST TRIAL P Rule 5(F).

      vii. Filing by registered or certified mail and by third-party commercial carrier shall be complete upon mailing or deposit. IN ST TRIAL P Rule 5(F).

b. *Facsimile filing.* As outlined in IN ST HAMILTON ADMIN Rule 103(103.10),facsimile filing is permitted in the Circuit and Superior Courts of Hamilton County. The Courts authorize the Hamilton County Clerk of Courts to accept pleadings, motions and other papers by electronic facsimile transmission for filing in any case pending before the Courts, subject to the requirements of IN ST HAMILTON ADMIN Rule 103(103.10). IN ST HAMILTON ADMIN Rule 103(103.10); IN ST HAMILTON TRIAL Rule 201(201.80).

   i. *Generally.* In counties where a majority of judges of the courts of record, by posted local rule, have authorized electronic facsimile filing and designated a telephone number to receive such transmissions, pleadings, motions, and other papers may be sent to the Clerk of Circuit Court by electronic facsimile transmission for filing in any case, provided:

   - Such matter does not exceed ten (10) pages, including the cover sheet;
   - Such matter does not require the payment of fees other than the electronic facsimile transcription fee set forth in IN ST ADMIN Rule 12(E);
   - The sending party creates at the time of transmission a machine generated log for such transmission; and
   - The original document and the transmission log are maintained by the sending party for the duration of the litigation. IN ST ADMIN Rule 12(B); IN ST HAMILTON ADMIN Rule 103(103.10)(d).
   - Legibility of documents and timeliness of filing is the responsibility of the sender. IN ST HAMILTON ADMIN Rule 103(103.10)(g).
   - The Clerk shall accept electronic facsimile transmission filings only if received at the facsimile machine assigned by the Clerk. The telephone number designated to receive such transmission is available at IN ST HAMILTON ADMIN Rule 103(103.40). IN ST HAMILTON ADMIN Rule 103(103.40).

   ii. *Time of filing.* During normal, posted business hours, the time of filing shall be the time the duplicate document is produced in the office of the Clerk of the Circuit Court. Duplicate documents received at all other times shall be filed as of the next normal business day. IN ST ADMIN Rule 12(C).

   - If the receiving fax machine endorses its own time and date stamp upon the transmitted documents and the receiving machine produces a delivery receipt which is electronically created and transmitted to the sending party, the time of filing shall be the date and time recorded on the transmitted document by the receiving fax machine. IN ST ADMIN Rule 12(C).
   - Electronic facsimile transmissions will be accepted for filing only during the regular business hours as set forth in IN ST HAMILTON ADMIN Rule 101. Transmissions received by the Hamilton County Clerk after close of business shall be filed effective the next regular business day. IN ST HAMILTON ADMIN Rule 103(103.30).

   iii. *Filing fee.* The electronic facsimile transmission will not be accepted for filing if its filing requires the payment of any fee other than the electronic facsimile transcription fee set forth in IN ST HAMILTON ADMIN Rule 103(103.20). IN ST HAMILTON ADMIN Rule 103(103.10)(e).

   - Pursuant to Ordinance adopted by the Hamilton County Board of Commissioners, the Clerk shall collect an electronic facsimile transcription fee of One Dollar ($1.00) per page, to a maximum of Ten Dollars ($10.00) per transmission, for each electronic facsimile transmission accepted for filing with the Hamilton County Circuit and Superior Courts. IN ST HAMILTON ADMIN Rule 103(103.20).
   - The fee shall be assessed against the sending party and shall be paid upon receipt of invoice by that party and at the latest within thirty (30) days of the transmission. In the event the fee is not paid by the sending party within the time limits provided, the court may issue a show-cause order or enter a judgment in the matter. The Clerk may refuse an

electronic facsimile transmission from any attorney or pro se litigant who has failed to pay these fees within thirty (30) days. IN ST HAMILTON ADMIN Rule 103(103.20).

    iv. *No direct filing with court.* A party shall not send pleadings, motions and other papers by electronic facsimile transmission for filing directly to any Court without that Court's prior approval to do so. IN ST HAMILTON ADMIN Rule 103(103.50).

c. *Filing with special judge.* After a special judge has qualified, a copy of each pleading and Chronological Case Summary entries filed with the Court shall be mailed or delivered to the office of that Special judge by the counsel or pro se litigant with service indicated on the certificate of service. IN ST HAMILTON TRIAL Rule 204(204.20).

d. *Proof of filing.* Any party filing any paper by any method other than personal delivery to the clerk shall retain proof of filing. IN ST TRIAL P Rule 5(F).

2. *Service requirements.* Unless otherwise provided by the Indiana Rules of Trial Procedure or an order of the court, each party and special judge, if any, shall be served with: (1) every order required by its terms to be served; (2) every pleading subsequent to the original complaint; (3) every written motion except one which may be heard ex parte; (4) every brief submitted to the trial court; (5) every paper relating to discovery required to be served upon a party; and (6) every written notice, appearance, demand, offer of judgment, designation of record on appeal, or similar paper. IN ST TRIAL P Rule 5(A).

a. *Methods of service*

    i. *Personal service.* Whenever a party is represented by an attorney of record, service shall be made upon such attorney unless service upon the party himself is ordered by the court. Service upon the attorney or party shall be made by delivering or mailing a copy of the papers to the last known address or where an attorney or party has consented to service by fax or e-mail, as provided in IN ST TRIAL P Rule 3.1(A)(4), by faxing or e-mailing a copy of the documents to the fax number or e-mail address set out in the appearance form or correction as required by IN ST TRIAL P Rule 3.1(E). IN ST TRIAL P Rule 5(B). Delivery of a copy within IN ST TRIAL P Rule 5 means:

- Offering or tendering it to the attorney or party and stating the nature of the papers being served. Refusal to accept an offered or tendered document is a waiver of any objection to the sufficiency or adequacy of service of that document;

- Leaving it at his office with a clerk or other person in charge thereof, or if there is no one in charge, leaving it in a conspicuous place therein; or

- If the office is closed, by leaving it at his dwelling house or usual place of abode with some person of suitable age and discretion then residing therein; or,

- Leaving it at some other suitable place, selected by the attorney upon whom service is being made, pursuant to duly promulgated local rule. IN ST TRIAL P Rule 5(B)(1).

    ii. *Service by mail.* If service is made by mail, the papers shall be deposited in the United States mail addressed to the person on whom they are being served, with postage prepaid. Service shall be deemed complete upon mailing. Proof of service of all papers permitted to be mailed may be made by written acknowledgment of service, by affidavit of the person who mailed the papers, or by certificate of an attorney. It shall be the duty of attorneys when entering their appearance in a cause or when filing pleadings or papers therein, to have noted in the Chronological Case Summary or said pleadings or papers so filed the address and telephone number of their office. Service by delivery or by mail at such address shall be deemed sufficient and complete. IN ST TRIAL P Rule 5(B)(2).

    iii. *Service by fax or e-mail.* A party who has consented to service by fax or e-mail may be served as follows:

- Service by e-mail shall be made by attaching the document being served in .pdf format. Discovery documents must also be served in accordance with IN ST TRIAL P Rule 26(A). IN ST TRIAL P Rule 5(B)(3)(a).

- Service by fax shall be deemed complete upon generation of a transmission record indicating the successful transmission of the entire document, except as provided in IN ST TRIAL P Rule 5(B)(3)(d). IN ST TRIAL P Rule 5(B)(3)(b).

- Service by e-mail shall be deemed complete upon transmission, except as provided in IN ST TRIAL P Rule 5(B)(3)(d). IN ST TRIAL P Rule 5(B)(3)(c).

- Service by fax or e-mail that occurs on a Saturday, Sunday, legal holiday, or day the court or agency in which the matter is pending is closed or after 5:00 PM local time of the recipient shall be deemed complete the next day that is not a Saturday, Sunday, legal holiday, or day that the court or agency in which the matter is pending is not closed. IN ST TRIAL P Rule 5(B)(3)(d).

    iv. *Mail box service.* Pursuant to IN ST TRIAL P Rule 5(B)(1)(d), the Circuit and Superior Courts of Hamilton County hereby designate the "mail boxes" located in the Clerk's order book office for service of pleadings upon attorneys who have such boxes. IN ST HAMILTON TRIAL Rule 201(201.50).

  b. *Serving numerous defendants.* In any action in which there are unusually large numbers of defendants, the court, upon motion or of its own initiative, may order:

    i. That service of the pleadings of the defendants and replies thereto need not be made as between the defendants;

- That any cross-claim, counterclaim, or matter constituting an avoidance or affirmative defense contained therein shall be deemed to be denied or avoided by all other parties; and

- That the filing of any such pleading and service thereof upon the plaintiff constitutes due notice of it to the parties. IN ST TRIAL P Rule 5(D).

    ii. A copy of every such order shall be served upon the parties in such manner and form as the court directs. IN ST TRIAL P Rule 5(D).

  c. *Service on parties in default for failure to appear.* No service need be made on parties in default for failure to appear, except that pleadings asserting new or additional claims for relief against them shall be served upon them in the manner provided by service of summons in IN ST TRIAL P Rule 4. IN ST TRIAL P Rule 5(A).

G. Hearings

1. *Hearing on motion.* Unless local conditions make it impracticable, each judge shall establish regular times and places, at intervals sufficiently frequent for the prompt dispatch of business, at which motions requiring notice and hearing may be heard and disposed of; but the judge at any time or place and on such notice, if any, as he considers reasonable may make order for the advancement, conduct, and hearing of actions. To expedite its business the court may direct the submission and determination of motions without oral hearing upon brief written statements of reasons in support and opposition, or direct or permit hearings by telephone conference call with all attorneys or other similar means of communication. IN ST TRIAL P Rule 73(A).

H. Forms

1. Motion to Dismiss for Lack of Personal Jurisdiction Forms for Indiana

  a. General form. 5 INPRAC § 3:4.1.

  b. Lack of personal jurisdiction. 5 INPRAC § 3:4.3.

  c. Certificate of service; Personal service. 9 INPRAC § 5.7.

  d. Certificate of service; First class mail. 9 INPRAC § 5.8.

  e. Motion to dismiss plaintiff's complaint; General form. 9 INPRAC § 42.2.

  f. Lack of personal jurisdiction. 9 INPRAC § 42.4.

I. Checklist

  (I) ❏ Matters to be considered by moving party

    (a) ❏ Required documents

      (1) ❏ Motion and notice

    (2) ❑ Proposed order

    (3) ❑ Certificate of service

  (b) ❑ Supplemental documents

    (1) ❑ Supporting evidence

    (2) ❑ Facsimile cover sheet

    (3) ❑ Request to schedule trial or hearing

    (4) ❑ Copies of unpublished opinions

  (c) ❑ Timing

    (1) ❑ A motion to dismiss for lack of personal jurisdiction shall be made before pleading if a further pleading is permitted or within twenty (20) days after service of the prior pleading if none is required

    (2) ❑ A written motion, other than one which may be heard ex parte, and notice of the hearing thereof shall be served not less than five (5) days before the time specified for the hearing, unless a different period is fixed by the Indiana Rules of Trial Procedure or by order of the court

    (3) ❑ All pleadings and papers subsequent to the complaint which are required to be served upon a party shall be filed with the Court either before service or within a reasonable period of time thereafter

(II) ❑ Matters to be considered by the responding party

  (a) ❑ Required documents

    (1) ❑ Opposition

    (2) ❑ Certificate of service

  (b) ❑ Supplemental documents

    (1) ❑ Supporting evidence

    (2) ❑ Alternative proposed order

    (3) ❑ Facsimile cover sheet

    (4) ❑ Request to schedule trial or hearing

    (5) ❑ Copies of unpublished opinions

  (c) ❑ Timing

    (1) ❑ Except as otherwise provided in IN ST TRIAL P Rule 59(D), opposing affidavits may be served not less than one (1) day before the hearing, unless the court permits them to be served at some other time

Requests, Notices and Applications
Interrogatories

Document Last Updated October 2013

A. Applicable Rules

1. *State rules*

  a. Appearance. IN ST TRIAL P Rule 3.1.

  b. Process. IN ST TRIAL P Rule 4.

  c. Service and filing of pleadings and other papers. IN ST TRIAL P Rule 5.

  d. Time. IN ST TRIAL P Rule 6.

  e. Pleadings. IN ST TRIAL P Rule 7; IN ST TRIAL P Rule 9.2; IN ST TRIAL P Rule 10.

    f.   Signing and verification of pleadings. IN ST TRIAL P Rule 11.

    g.   General provisions governing discovery. IN ST TRIAL P Rule 26.

    h.   Methods of discovery. IN ST TRIAL P Rule 27; IN ST TRIAL P Rule 29; IN ST TRIAL P Rule 30; IN ST TRIAL P Rule 31; IN ST TRIAL P Rule 33; IN ST TRIAL P Rule 34; IN ST TRIAL P Rule 35; IN ST TRIAL P Rule 36.

    i.   Failure to make or cooperate in discovery; Sanctions. IN ST TRIAL P Rule 37.

    j.   Judgment on the evidence (directed verdict). IN ST TRIAL P Rule 50.

    k.   Findings by the court. IN ST TRIAL P Rule 52.

    l.   Summary judgment. IN ST TRIAL P Rule 56.

    m.   Motion to correct error. IN ST TRIAL P Rule 59.

    n.   Relief from judgment or order. IN ST TRIAL P Rule 60.

    o.   Access to court records. IN ST ADMIN Rule 9.

    p.   Paper size. IN ST ADMIN Rule 11.

    q.   Facsimile transmission. IN ST ADMIN Rule 12.

    r.   Electronic filing and electronic service pilot projects. IN ST ADMIN Rule 16.

    s.   Sealing of certain records by court; Hearing; Notice. IN ST 5-14-3-5.5.

    t.   Privacy and confidentiality. IN ST 5-2-9-6; IN ST 5-14-3-4; IN ST 6-4.1-5-10; IN ST 6-4.1-12-12; IN ST 6-8.1-7-1; IN ST 11-13-1-8; IN ST 12-23-14-13; IN ST 16-39-3-10; IN ST 16-41-8-1; IN ST 22-4-19-6; IN ST 31-11-1-6; IN ST 31-19-5-23; IN ST 31-19-13-2; IN ST 31-19-19-1; IN ST 31-33-18-1; IN ST 31-39-1-1; IN ST 31-39-1-2; IN ST 33-23-16-16; IN ST 35-34-2-4; IN ST 35-38-1-13; IN ST 35-38-9-1; IN ST ADR Rule 2.11; IN ST ADR Rule 4.4; IN ST ADR Rule 5.6; IN ST JURY Rule 10.

2. *Local rules*

    a.   Court hours. IN ST HAMILTON ADMIN Rule 101.

    b.   Facsimile transmissions. IN ST HAMILTON ADMIN Rule 103.

    c.   Filing of pleadings and entry of appearances. IN ST HAMILTON TRIAL Rule 201.

    d.   Proposed orders. IN ST HAMILTON TRIAL Rule 202.

    e.   Special judges. IN ST HAMILTON TRIAL Rule 204.

    f.   Continuances. IN ST HAMILTON TRIAL Rule 206.

B. Timing

1. *Service of interrogatories.* Interrogatories may, without leave of court, be served upon the plaintiff after commencement of the action and upon any other party with or after service of the summons and complaint upon that party. IN ST TRIAL P Rule 33(A).

2. *Service of responses to interrogatories.* The party upon whom the interrogatories have been served shall serve a copy of the answers and objections within a period designated by the party submitting the interrogatories, not less than thirty (30) days after the service thereof or within such shorter or longer time as the court may allow. IN ST TRIAL P Rule 33(C).

3. *Computation of time*

    a.   *Generally; Days excluded.* In computing any period of time prescribed or allowed by the Indiana Rules of Trial Procedure, by order of the court, or by any applicable statute, the day of the act, event, or default from which the designated period of time begins to run shall not be included. The last day of the period so computed is to be included unless it is:

        i.   A Saturday,

        ii.   A Sunday,

        iii.   A legal holiday as defined by state statute, or

    iv.   A day the office in which the act is to be done is closed during regular business hours. IN ST TRIAL P Rule 6(A).

  b. *Short periods.* In any event, the period runs until the end of the next day that is not a Saturday, a Sunday, a legal holiday, or a day on which the office is closed. When the period of time allowed is less than seven (7) days, intermediate Saturdays, Sundays, legal holidays, and days on which the office is closed shall be excluded from the computations. IN ST TRIAL P Rule 6(A).

  c. *Additional time after service by United States mail.* Whenever a party has the right or is required to do some act or take some proceedings within a prescribed period after the service of a notice or other paper upon him and the notice or paper is served upon him by United States mail, three (3) days shall be added to the prescribed period. IN ST TRIAL P Rule 6(E).

  d. *Enlargement of time.* When an act is required or allowed to be done at or within a specific time by the Indiana Rules of Trial Procedure, the court may at any time for cause shown:

    i.   Order the period enlarged, with or without motion or notice, if request therefor is made before the expiration of the period originally prescribed or extended by a previous order; or

    ii. Upon motion made after the expiration of the specific period, permit the act to be done where the failure to act was the result of excusable neglect; but, the court may not extend the time for taking any action for judgment on the evidence under IN ST TRIAL P Rule 50(A), amendment of findings and judgment under IN ST TRIAL P Rule 52(B), to correct errors under IN ST TRIAL P Rule 59(C), statement in opposition to motion to correct error under IN ST TRIAL P Rule 59(E), or to obtain relief from final judgment under IN ST TRIAL P Rule 60(B), except to the extent and under the conditions stated in those rules. IN ST TRIAL P Rule 6(B).

    iii. For information on obtaining a continuance, refer to IN ST HAMILTON TRIAL Rule 206.

C. General Requirements

  1. *Scope of discovery.* Unless otherwise limited by order of the court in accordance with the Indiana Rules of Trial Procedure, the scope of discovery is as follows:

  a. *In general.* Parties may obtain discovery regarding any matter, not privileged, which is relevant to the subject-matter involved in the pending action, whether it relates to the claim or defense of the party seeking discovery or the claim or defense of any other party, including the existence, description, nature, custody, condition and location of any books, documents, or other tangible things and the identity and location of persons having knowledge of any discoverable matter. It is not ground for objection that the information sought will be inadmissible at the trial if the information sought appears reasonably calculated to lead to the discovery of admissible evidence. IN ST TRIAL P Rule 26(B)(1).

    i.   *Limiting discovery upon court determination.* The frequency or extent of use of the discovery methods otherwise permitted under the Indiana Rules of Trial Procedure and by any local rule shall be limited by the court if it determines that:

      • The discovery sought is unreasonably cumulative or duplicative, or is obtainable from some other source that is more convenient, less burdensome, or less expensive;

      • The party seeking discovery has had ample opportunity by discovery in the action to obtain the information sought or;

      • The burden or expense of the proposed discovery outweighs its likely benefit, taking into account the needs of the case, the amount in controversy, the parties' resources, the importance of the issues at stake in the litigation, and the importance of the proposed discovery in resolving the issues. IN ST TRIAL P Rule 26(B)(1).

      • The court may act upon its own initiative after reasonable notice or pursuant to a motion under IN ST TRIAL P Rule 26(C). IN ST TRIAL P Rule 26(B)(1). Refer to the Indiana KeyRules Motion for Protective Order document for more information.

    ii. *Relevancy in the discovery context.* When the word "relevancy" is used in IN ST TRIAL P Rule 26(B), it does not mean "relevancy" as that word in used to determine the admissibility of evidence in a trial court. It is much broader. It means "relevancy" to the "subject matter" of the litigation or pending action and it may relate to the claim or defense of any party. Pretrial discovery is available as to any nonprivileged matter relevant to the subject matter of the lawsuit or to obtain information reasonably calculated to lead to admissible evidence. 2A INPRAC R 26(26.4); Kaufmann v. Credithrift Financial, Inc., 465 N.E.2d 207, 210 (Ind.Ct.App. 1984).

iii. *Tests for relevance.* Indiana case law has developed two (2) additional tests in this area. 2A INPRAC R 26(26.4).

- The first test determines when a document or a request for information is actually relevant to the subject matter in the pending action. A document [or discovery request] is relevant to discovery if there is the possibility the information sought may be relevant to the subject matter of the action. 2A INPRAC R 26(26.4); CIGNA-INA/Aetna v. Hagerman-Shambaugh, 473 N.E.2d 1033, 1036 (Ind.Ct.App. 1985).

- The second test speaks to appellate review of the trial court's determination that a document or discovery request is relevant to the subject matter of the pending action. The appellate court sees its review of the trial court's decision on relevancy to subject matter as being very limited. The court states: "Our review of the trial court's conclusion that the documents are relevant is limited. A trial court is vested with discretion in its rulings on discovery issues." 2A INPRAC R 26(26.4); Costanzi v. Ryan, 175 Ind.App. 257, 370 N.E.2d 1333 (Ind.Ct.App. 1978).

b. *Insurance agreements.* A party may obtain discovery of the existence and contents of any insurance agreement under which any person carrying on an insurance business may be liable to satisfy part or all of a judgment which may be entered in the action or to indemnify or reimburse for payments made to satisfy the judgment. Information concerning the insurance agreement is not by reason of disclosure admissible in evidence at trial. For purposes of IN ST TRIAL P Rule 26(B)(2), an application for insurance shall not be treated as part of an insurance agreement. IN ST TRIAL P Rule 26(B)(2).

c. *Trial preparation; Materials.* Subject to the provisions of IN ST TRIAL P Rule 26(B)(4), a party may obtain discovery of documents and tangible things otherwise discoverable under IN ST TRIAL P Rule 26(B)(1) and prepared in anticipation of litigation or for trial by or for another party or by or for that other party's representative (including his attorney, consultant, surety, indemnitor, insurer, or agent) only upon a showing that the party seeking discovery has substantial need of the materials in the preparation of his case and that he is unable without undue hardship to obtain the substantial equivalent of the materials by other means. In ordering discovery of such materials when the required showing has been made, the court shall protect against disclosure of the mental impressions, conclusions, opinions, or legal theories of an attorney or other representative of a party concerning the litigation. IN ST TRIAL P Rule 26(B)(3).

i. A party may obtain without the required showing a statement concerning the action or its subject matter previously made by that party. Upon request, a person not a party may obtain without the required showing a statement concerning the action or its subject matter previously made by that person. If the request is refused, the person may move for a court order. The provisions of IN ST TRIAL P Rule 37(A)(4) apply to the award of expenses incurred in relation to the motion. For purposes of IN ST TRIAL P Rule 26(B)(3), a statement previously made is:

- A written statement signed or otherwise adopted approved by the person making it, or

- A stenographic, mechanical, electrical, or other recording, or a transcription thereof, which is a substantially verbatim recital of an oral statement by the person making it and contemporaneously recorded. IN ST TRIAL P Rule 26(B)(3).

ii. The protection of IN ST TRIAL P Rule 26(B)(3) extends to material prepared or collected before litigation actually commences, but that some possibility of litigation must actually exist before the privilege and IN ST TRIAL P Rule 26(B)(3) become operative. 2A INPRAC R 26(26.9); CIGNA-INA/Aetna v. Hagerman-Shambaugh, 473 N.E.2d 1033, 1037 (Ind.Ct.App. 1985).

d. *Trial preparation; Experts.* Discovery of facts known and opinions held by experts, otherwise discoverable under the provisions of IN ST TRIAL P Rule 26(B)(1) and acquired or developed in anticipation of litigation or for trial, may be obtained as follows:

i. A party may through interrogatories require any other party to identify each person whom the other party expects to call as an expert witness at trial, to state the subject matter on which the expert is expected to testify, and to state the substance of the facts and opinions to which the expert is expected to testify and a summary of the grounds for each opinion. IN ST TRIAL P Rule 26(B)(4)(a)(i).

ii. Upon motion, the court may order further discovery by other means, subject to such restrictions as to scope and such provisions, pursuant to IN ST TRIAL P Rule 26(B)(4)(c), concerning fees and expenses as the court may deem appropriate. IN ST TRIAL P Rule 26(B)(4)(a)(ii).

iii. A party may discover facts known or opinions held by an expert who has been retained or specially employed by another party in anticipation of litigation or preparation for trial and who is not expected to be called as a witness at trial, only as provided in IN ST TRIAL P Rule 35(B) or upon a showing of exceptional circumstances under which it is impracticable for the party seeking discovery to obtain facts or opinions on the same subject by other means. IN ST TRIAL P Rule 26(B)(4)(b).

iv. Unless manifest injustice would result,

- The court shall require that the party seeking discovery pay the expert a reasonable fee for time spent in responding to discovery under IN ST TRIAL P Rule 26(B)(4)(a)(ii) and IN ST TRIAL P Rule 26(B)(4)(b); and

- With respect to discovery obtained under IN ST TRIAL P Rule 26(B)(4)(a)(ii) the court may require, and with respect to discovery obtained under IN ST TRIAL P Rule 26(B)(4)(b) the court shall require, the party seeking discovery to pay the other party a fair portion of the fees and expenses reasonably incurred by the latter party in obtaining facts and opinions from the expert. IN ST TRIAL P Rule 26(B)(4)(c).

e. *Claims of privilege or protection*

i. *Information withheld.* When a party withholds information otherwise discoverable under the Indiana Rules of Trial Procedure by claiming that it is privileged or subject to protection as trial preparation material, the party shall make the claim expressly and shall describe the nature of the documents, communications, or things not produced or disclosed in a manner that, without revealing information itself privileged or protected, will enable other parties to assess the applicability of the privilege or protection. IN ST TRIAL P Rule 26(B)(5)(a).

ii. *Information produced.* If information is produced in discovery that is subject to a claim of privilege or protection as trial-preparation material, the party making the claim may notify any party that received the information of the claim and the basis for it. After being notified, a party must promptly return, sequester, or destroy the specified information and any copies it has and may not use or disclose the information until the claim is resolved. A receiving party may promptly present the information to the court under seal for a determination of the claim. If the receiving party disclosed the information before being notified, it must take reasonable steps to retrieve it. The producing party must preserve the information until the claim is resolved. IN ST TRIAL P Rule 26(B)(5)(b).

iii. *Waiver.* The law of discovery has developed some holdings which indicate that "waiver" of a privileged communication in a discovery setting might be more exacting than "waiver" of a privileged communication when the only question at hand is an interpretation of the privilege itself. Thus, in litigation in which several documents are in issue, and some are released inadvertently, there is strong case law that holds that the "inadvertent production" of a privileged document does not constitute a waiver of the attorney-client privilege. 2A INPRAC R 26(26.5); Transamerica Computer Co. v. International Business Machines Corp., 573 F.2d 646 (9th Cir. 1978). Such a rule should be measured against the usual rule which suggests that a voluntary disclosure to a third person will generally suffice to show a waiver of the attorney-client privilege. 2A INPRAC R 26(26.5).

f. *Use not limited.* Unless the court orders otherwise under IN ST TRIAL P Rule 26(C), the frequency of use of the methods listed in IN ST TRIAL P Rule 26(A) is not limited. IN ST TRIAL P Rule 26(A).

g. *Sequence of discovery.* Unless the court upon motion, for the convenience of parties and witnesses and in the interests of justice, orders otherwise, methods of discovery may be used in any sequence and the fact that a party is conducting discovery, whether by deposition or otherwise, shall not operate to delay any other party's discovery. IN ST TRIAL P Rule 26(D).

2. *Interrogatories.* Parties may obtain discovery by written interrogatories. IN ST TRIAL P Rule 26(A)(2). An interrogatory is a written question served upon another party which requires a written response under oath. 22 INPRAC § 23.1. Any party may serve upon any other party written interrogatories to be answered by the party served or, if the party served is an organization including a governmental organization, or a partnership, by any officer or agent, who shall furnish such information as is available to the party. IN ST TRIAL P Rule 33(A).

a. *Subject of interrogatories.* Interrogatories may relate to any matters which can be inquired into under IN ST TRIAL P Rule 26(B), and the answers may be used to the extent permitted by the rules of evidence. IN ST TRIAL P Rule 33(D).

  i. This includes:

  - The existence, description, nature, custody, condition and location of books, documents, or other tangible things; and

  - The identity and location of persons having knowledge of relevant facts. 10 INPRAC § 65.1.

  ii. Interrogatories cannot be objected to on the ground that the information sought will be inadmissible at trial if the discovery appears reasonably calculated to lead to the discovery of admissible evidence. 10 INPRAC § 65.1.

b. *Available for parties only.* Interrogatories may not be served on non-parties. 10 INPRAC § 65.1. There is no requirement that the party served shall be an "adverse" party. 2A INPRAC R 33(33.2).

c. *Submission to personal jurisdiction.* Under the current trial rules, discovery is self-executing and interrogatories are not filed with the court, but retained by the originating party until a discovery dispute arises or the discovery is needed for proceedings before the court. As such, Indiana courts have had to revisit the issue of whether a party's mere service of interrogatories constitutes a waiver of an objection to the court's personal jurisdiction over that party. 22 INPRAC § 23.14.

  i. In Alberts v. Mack Trucks, Inc., the defendant served interrogatories before asserting a challenge to the court's personal jurisdiction. In ruling that serving interrogatories did not constitute a waiver of personal jurisdiction, the Indiana Court of Appeals noted the amendments to the Indiana Rules of Trial Procedure, which no longer require a party to file interrogatories with the court. Accordingly, the court held: By sending interrogatories to Alberts' counsel, NSC did not submit to the personal jurisdiction of the court. Jurisdiction will not be found to be waived until a party affirmatively uses the court's procedure, such as in a motion to compel answers to interrogatories. 22 INPRAC § 23.14; Alberts v. Mack Trucks, Inc., 540 N.E.2d 1268, 1271-72 (Ind.Ct.App. 1989).

  ii. Therefore, merely serving interrogatories upon an opposing party before challenging the court's personal jurisdiction over a defendant should not result in a waiver of the jurisdictional issue unless the party otherwise affirmatively uses the court's resources. 22 INPRAC § 23.14.

d. *Motion to compel discovery.* The party submitting the interrogatories may move for an order under IN ST TRIAL P Rule 37(A) with respect to any objection to or other failure to answer an interrogatory. IN ST TRIAL P Rule 33(C). Refer to the Indiana KeyRules Motion to Compel Discovery document for more information.

3. *Response to interrogatories*

a. *Form of objections.* Answers or objections to interrogatories shall include the interrogatory which is being answered or to which an objection is made. The interrogatory which is being answered or objected to shall be placed immediately preceding the answer or objection. IN ST TRIAL P Rule 33(B).

b. *Form of answer.* Each interrogatory shall be answered separately and fully in writing under oath, unless it is objected to, in which event the reasons for objections shall be stated in lieu of an answer. The answers are to be signed by the person making them, and the objections signed by the attorney making them. IN ST TRIAL P Rule 33(B).

c. *Objections.* In addition to the objection that the matter is privileged, interrogatories may be objected to on the ground that they are not within the scope of discovery which is defined in IN ST TRIAL P Rule 26(B) because they seek information that is not relevant to the subject matter in the pending litigation, or that the requisite showing under IN ST TRIAL P Rule 26(B) has not been made, or that the information is held by experts and it is not discoverable except as permitted under IN ST TRIAL P Rule 26(B)(4). 2A INPRAC R 33(33.4). Objections to interrogatories must be specific. Common objections include (1) relevancy; (2) vague and ambiguous; (3) unduly burdensome; and (4) excessive in number. 10 INPRAC § 65.2.

   i. *Objections to form.* The party upon whom the interrogatories have been served may object to the failure to follow the Format requirements in IN ST TRIAL P Rule 33(B) by returning the interrogatories to the party who caused them to be served. If this objection is to be made, the interrogatories shall be returned to the party who caused them to be served not later than the seventh (7th) day after they were received. If the interrogatories are not returned in that time, then this objection is waived. IN ST TRIAL P Rule 33(C).

   ii. *Information not available.* If the objecting party takes the position that the information is not available, it is that party's burden to show that it is not available. 2A INPRAC R 33(33.4).

   - As a general rule, a party may not refuse to answer an interrogatory on the ground that the information is not in his possession, in the sense that the party would have to consult books and records in order to answer. 2A INPRAC R 33(33.4); Flour Mills of America, Inc. v. Pace, 75 F.R.D. 676, 680 (E.D.Okl. 1977).

   - An interrogatory seeking information in the possession of the party's employee is not objectionable if the questions call for answers which could be readily obtained by the person answering the interrogatory. 2A INPRAC R 33(33.4); Ballard v. Allegheny Airlines, Inc., 54 F.R.D. 67 (E.D.Pa. 1972).

   iii. *Broad, burdensome, numerous.* An objection is permitted if the interrogatory is too broad, or too burdensome, or too many in the number and kinds of questions which are asked. 2A INPRAC R 33(33.4); Flour Mills of America, Inc. v. Pace, 75 F.R.D. 676, 680 (E.D.Okl. 1977); In re U.S. Financial Securities Litigation, 74 F.R.D. 497 (S.D.Cal. 1975).

   iv. *Other objections.* An interrogatory otherwise proper is not objectionable merely because an answer to the interrogatory involves an opinion, contention, or legal conclusion, but the court may order that such an interrogatory be answered at a later time, or after designated discovery has been completed, or at a pre-trial conference. IN ST TRIAL P Rule 33(D).

   - However, a party may not be forced to prepare his opponent's case for him. If the interrogatory would require a party to make extensive investigations, research, or compilation of data, it is an improper interrogatory, and it is burdensome and should be disallowed in a motion for a protective order. 2A INPRAC R 33(33.4); Halder v. International Telephone & Telegraph Co., 75 F.R.D. 657 (E.D.N.Y. 1977). Refer to the Indiana KeyRules Motion for Protective Order document for more information.

d. *Signature of responses.* The party served shall answer and sign the answer, and the attorney for the party served shall sign the objections. Both are then returned to the party taking the interrogatory. 2A INPRAC R 33(33.8).

   i. An unsigned and unverified response does not qualify as an answer to an interrogatory and generally may not be used as such. 22 INPRAC § 23.6; Cabales v. U.S., 51 F.R.D. 498 (S.D.N.Y. 1970).

e. *Option to produce business records.* Where the answer to an interrogatory may be derived or ascertained from the business records of the party upon whom the interrogatory has been served or from an examination, audit or inspection of such business records, including a compilation, abstract or summary thereof, and the burden of deriving or ascertaining the answer is substantially the same for the party serving the interrogatory as for the party served, it is a sufficient answer to such interrogatory to specify the records from which the answer may be derived or ascertained and to afford to the party serving the interrogatory reasonable opportunity to examine, audit or inspect such records and to make copies, compilations, abstracts or summaries. A specification shall be in sufficient detail to permit the interrogating party to locate and to identify, as readily as can the party served, the records from which the answer may be ascertained. IN ST TRIAL P Rule 33(E).

f. *Supplementation of responses.* A party who has responded to a request for discovery with a response that was complete when made is under no duty to supplement his response to include information thereafter acquired, except as follows:

    i. A party is under a duty seasonally to supplement his response with respect to any question directly addressed to:

- The identity and location of persons having knowledge of discoverable matters, and
- The identity of each person expected to be called as an expert witness at trial, the subject-matter on which he is expected to testify, and the substance of his testimony. IN ST TRIAL P Rule 26(E)(1).

    ii. A party is under a duty seasonally to amend a prior response if he obtains information upon the basis of which:

- He knows that the response was incorrect when made, or
- He knows that the response though correct when made is no longer true and the circumstances are such that a failure to amend the response is in substance a knowing concealment. IN ST TRIAL P Rule 26(E)(2).

    iii. A duty to supplement responses may be imposed by order of the court, agreement of the parties, or at any time prior to trial through new requests for supplementation of prior responses. IN ST TRIAL P Rule 26(E)(3).

    iv. The duty seasonally to supplement a discovery response is absolute and is not predicated on a court order. "It is a breach of a litigant's duty reasonably to supplement if the litigant postpones supplementing its response by not obtaining from its experts the information which is to be supplied in answer to interrogatories." 2A INPRAC R 26(26.27); Lucas v. Dorsey Corp., 609 N.E.2d 1191, 1196 (Ind.Ct.App. 1993).

D. Documents

1. *Required documents*

    a. *Interrogatories.* Refer to the General Requirements section of this document for information on the scope and content of interrogatories.

    b. *Certificate of service.* An attorney or unrepresented party tendering a document to the Clerk for filing shall certify that service has been made, list the parties served, and specify the date and means of service. The certificate of service shall be placed at the end of the document and shall not be separately filed. The separate filing of a certificate of service, however, shall not be grounds for rejecting a document for filing. The Clerk may permit documents to be filed without a certificate of service but shall require prompt filing of a separate certificate of service. IN ST TRIAL P Rule 5(C).

        i. All pleadings filed with the Court which require a certificate of service shall specifically name the individual party or attorney on whom service has been made, the address, the manner in which service was made and the date when service was made. IN ST HAMILTON TRIAL Rule 201(201.60).

2. *Supplemental documents*

    a. *Stipulation regarding discovery procedure.* Unless the court orders otherwise, the parties may by written stipulation:

        i. Provide that depositions may be taken before any person, at any time or place, upon any notice, and in any manner and when so taken may be used like other depositions, and

      ii.   Modify the procedures provided by the Indiana Rules of Trial Procedure for other methods of discovery. IN ST TRIAL P Rule 29.

   b.   *Facsimile cover sheet.* Any document sent to the Clerk of the Circuit Court by electronic facsimile transmission shall be accompanied by a cover sheet which states the title of the document, case number, number of pages, identity and voice telephone number of the sending party and instructions for filing. The cover sheet shall contain the signature of the attorney or party, pro se, authorizing the filing. IN ST ADMIN Rule 12(D); IN ST HAMILTON ADMIN Rule 103(103.10)(a).

E. Format

1.   *Format of interrogatories.* The rules applicable to captions, and the signing and form of pleadings (IN ST TRIAL P Rule 8 through IN ST TRIAL P Rule 11), apply to all motions and other papers provided under the Indiana Rules of Trial Procedure. 22B INPRAC 7:2. A party who serves written interrogatories under IN ST TRIAL P Rule 33 shall provide, after each interrogatory, a reasonable amount of space for a response or an objection. IN ST TRIAL P Rule 33(B).

   a.   An interrogatory should pose a single direct question phrased in a manner that will advise the responding party what information is requested of him. 22 INPRAC § 23.5.

   b.   An interrogatory may be divided into separate paragraphs and subparagraphs. The paragraphs should be identified as "1," "2," or "3"; or as "Interrogatory No. 1," "Interrogatory No. 2," etc. 22 INPRAC § 23.5.

2.   *Form of pleadings*

   a.   *Caption; Names of parties.* Every pleading shall contain a caption setting forth the name of the court, the title of the action, the file number, and a designation as in IN ST TRIAL P Rule 7(A). In the complaint the title of the action shall include the names of all the parties, but in other pleadings it is sufficient to state the name of the first party on each side with an appropriate indication of other parties. IN ST TRIAL P Rule 10(A).

   b.   *Paragraphs; Separate statements.* All averments of a claim or defense shall be made in numbered paragraphs, the contents of each of which shall be limited as far as practicable to a statement of a single set of circumstances, and a paragraph may be referred to by number in all succeeding pleadings. Each claim founded upon a separate transaction or occurrence and each defense other than denials may be stated in a separate count or defense whenever a separation facilitates the clear presentation of the matters set forth. IN ST TRIAL P Rule 10(B).

   c.   *Adoption by reference; Exhibits.* Statements in a pleading may be adopted by reference in a different part of the same pleading or in another pleading or in any motion. A copy of any written instrument which is an exhibit to a pleading is a part thereof for all purposes. IN ST TRIAL P Rule 10(C).

   d.   *Facsimile page limit.* Courts authorize the Hamilton County Clerk of Courts to accept pleadings, motions and other papers by electronic facsimile transmission for filing in any case pending before the Courts, subject to the requirement that The transmission may not exceed ten (10) pages in length including the cover sheet and proposed CCS entry. IN ST HAMILTON ADMIN Rule 103(103.10)(c).

   e.   *Emergency facsimile filings.* If the filing requires the immediate attention of the Judge, it shall so indicate in bold letters in an accompanying transmittal memorandum. IN ST HAMILTON ADMIN Rule 103(103.10)(f).

   f.   *Special judge heading.* After a special judge is selected, the attorneys or pro se litigants shall add to the caption of all pleadings to the right of the case title the following: "BEFORE SPECIAL JUDGE _____." IN ST HAMILTON TRIAL Rule 204(204.10).

   g.   *Format rules strictly enforced.* All filings shall be in compliance with the Indiana Rules of Trial Procedure. If the documents received are not in proper form, such deficiencies will not be corrected by court personnel. IN ST HAMILTON TRIAL Rule 201(201.70). The Court shall not be required to act on any Motion, Petition or other request for relief unless filed in conformity with the Hamilton County Local Trial and Administrative rules. IN ST HAMILTON TRIAL Rule 202(202.20).

3.   *Size of papers for filing.* Effective January 1, 1992, all pleadings, copies, motions and documents filed

with any trial court or appellate level court, typed or printed, with the exception of exhibits and existing wills, shall be prepared on eight and one-half by eleven inch (8 1/2" x 11") size paper. IN ST ADMIN Rule 11.

a. *Form.* All documents filed in any Hamilton County Court, with the exception of exhibits and existing wills, shall be prepared on paper measuring eight and one-half by eleven inches (8 1/2" x 11"). IN ST HAMILTON TRIAL Rule 201(201.20).

4. *Signature requirements*

a. *Signature of attorney.* Every pleading or motion of a party represented by an attorney shall be signed by at least one (1) attorney of record in his individual name, whose address, telephone number, and attorney number shall be stated, except that this provision shall not apply to pleadings and motions made and transcribed at the trial or a hearing before the judge and received by him in such form. IN ST TRIAL P Rule 11(A).

   i. The signature of an attorney constitutes a certificate by him that he has read the pleadings; that to the best of his knowledge, information, and belief, there is good ground to support it; and that it is not interposed for delay. IN ST TRIAL P Rule 11(A).

   ii. If a pleading or motion is not signed or is signed with intent to defeat the purpose of the rule, it may be stricken as sham and false and the action may proceed as though the pleading had not been served. IN ST TRIAL P Rule 11(A).

   iii. For a willful violation of IN ST TRIAL P Rule 11 an attorney may be subjected to appropriate disciplinary action. Similar action may be taken if scandalous or indecent matter is inserted. IN ST TRIAL P Rule 11(A).

b. *Signature of unrepresented party.* A party who is not represented by an attorney shall sign his pleading and state his address. IN ST TRIAL P Rule 11(A).

c. *Verification not generally required.* Except when specifically required by rule, pleadings or motions need not be verified or accompanied by affidavit. The rule in equity that the averments of an answer under oath must be overcome by the testimony of two (2) witnesses or of one (1) witness sustained by corroborating circumstances is abolished. IN ST TRIAL P Rule 11(A).

d. *Verification by affirmation or representation.* When in connection with any civil or special statutory proceeding it is required that any pleading, motion, petition, supporting affidavit, or other document of any kind, be verified, or that an oath be taken, it shall be sufficient if the subscriber simply affirms the truth of the matter to be verified by an affirmation or representation. IN ST TRIAL P Rule 11(B). IN ST TRIAL P Rule 11(B) states that the affirmation or representation should be in substantially the following language: "I (we) affirm, under the penalties for perjury, that the foregoing representation(s) is (are) true. (Signed) _____."

   i. Any person who falsifies an affirmation or representation of fact shall be subject to the same penalties as are prescribed by law for the making of a false affidavit. IN ST TRIAL P Rule 11(B).

e. *Verified pleadings, motions, and affidavits as evidence.* Pleadings, motions and affidavits accompanying or in support of such pleadings or motions when required to be verified or under oath shall be accepted as a representation that the signer had personal knowledge thereof or reasonable cause to believe the existence of the facts or matters stated or alleged therein; and, if otherwise competent or acceptable as evidence, may be admitted as evidence of the facts or matters stated or alleged therein when it is so provided in the Indiana Rules of Trial Procedure, by statute or other law, or to the extent the writing or signature expressly purports to be made upon the signer's personal knowledge. When such pleadings, motions and affidavits are verified or under oath they shall not require other or greater proof on the part of the adverse party than if not verified or not under oath unless expressly provided otherwise by the Indiana Rules of Trial Procedure, statute or other law. Affidavits upon motions for summary judgment under IN ST TRIAL P Rule 56 and in denial of execution under IN ST TRIAL P Rule 9.2 shall be made upon personal knowledge. IN ST TRIAL P Rule 11(C).

5. *Information excluded from public access.* Every document filed in a case shall separately identify information excluded from public access pursuant to IN ST ADMIN Rule 9(G)(1) as follows:

a. Whole documents that are excluded from public access pursuant to IN ST ADMIN Rule 9(G)(1) shall be tendered on light green paper or have a light green coversheet attached to the document, marked "Not for Public Access" or "Confidential." IN ST TRIAL P Rule 5(G)(1).

b. When only a portion of a document contains information excluded from public access pursuant to IN ST ADMIN Rule 9(G)(1), said information shall be omitted [or redacted] from the filed document, and set forth on a separate accompanying document on light green paper conspicuously marked "Not for Public Access" or "Confidential" and clearly designated [or identifying] the caption and number of the case and the document and location within the document to which the redacted material pertains. IN ST TRIAL P Rule 5(G)(2).

c. With respect to documents filed in electronic format, the trial court, by local rule, may provide for compliance with IN ST TRIAL P Rule 5 in manner that separates and protects access to information excluded from public access. IN ST TRIAL P Rule 5(G)(3).

d. IN ST TRIAL P Rule 5(G) does not apply to a record sealed by the court pursuant to IN ST 5-14-3-5.5 or otherwise, nor to records, documents, or information filed in cases to which public access is prohibited pursuant to IN ST ADMIN Rule 9(G). IN ST TRIAL P Rule 5(G)(4).

e. The following information in case records is excluded from public access and is confidential:

  i. Information that is excluded from public access pursuant to federal law;

  ii. Information that is excluded from public access as declared confidential by Indiana statute or other court rule, including without limitation:

- All adoption records created after July 8, 1941, as declared confidential by IN ST 31-19-19-1, et seq., except those specifically declared open by IN ST 31-19-13-2(2);
- All records relating to chancroid, chlamydia, gonorrhea, hepatitis, human immunodeficiency virus (HIV), Lymphogranuloma venereum, syphilis, tuberculosis, as declared confidential by IN ST 16-41-8-1, et seq.;
- All records relating to child abuse as declared confidential by IN ST 31-33-18-1, et seq.;
- All records relating to drug tests as declared confidential by IN ST 5-14-3-4(a)(9);
- Records of grand jury proceedings as declared confidential by IN ST 35-34-2-4;
- Records of juvenile proceedings as declared confidential by IN ST 31-39-1-2, except those specifically open under statute;
- All paternity records created after July 1, 1941 as declared confidential by IN ST 31-14-11-15, IN ST 31-19-5-23, IN ST 31-39-1-1 and IN ST 31-39-1-2 [Editor's note: IN ST 31-14-11-15 was repealed effective May 9, 2013];
- All pre-sentence reports as declared confidential by IN ST 35-38-1-13;
- Written petitions to permit marriages without consent and orders directing the Clerk of Court to issue a marriage license to underage persons, as declared confidential by IN ST 31-11-1-6;
- Only those arrest warrants, search warrants, indictments and informations ordered confidential by the trial judge, prior to return of duly executed service as declared confidential by IN ST 5-14-3-4(b)(1);
- All medical, mental health, or tax records unless determined by law or regulation of any governmental custodian not to be confidential, released by the subject of such records, or declared by a court of competent jurisdiction to be essential to the resolution of litigation as declared confidential by IN ST 16-39-3-10, IN ST 6-4.1-5-10, IN ST 6-4.1-12-12, and IN ST 6-8.1-7-1;
- Personal information relating to jurors or prospective jurors, other than for the use of the parties and counsel, pursuant to IN ST JURY Rule 10;
- Information relating to protection from abuse orders, no-contact orders and workplace violence restraining orders as declared confidential by IN ST 5-2-9-6, et seq.;
- Mediation proceedings pursuant to IN ST ADR Rule 2.11, Mini-Trial proceedings

pursuant to IN ST ADR Rule 4.4(C), and Summary Jury Trials pursuant to IN ST ADR Rule 5.6;

- Information in probation files pursuant to the Probation Standards promulgated by the Judicial Conference of Indiana pursuant to IN ST 11-13-1-8(b);

- Information deemed confidential pursuant to the Rules for Court Administered Alcohol and Drug Programs promulgated by the Judicial Conference of Indiana pursuant to IN ST 12-23-14-13;

- Information deemed confidential pursuant to the Problem-Solving Court Rules promulgated by the Judicial Conference of Indiana pursuant to IN ST 33-23-16-16;

- All records of the Department of workforce Development as declared confidential by IN ST 22-4-19-6;

- Information regarding interception of electronic communications that is sealed or deemed confidential as set forth in IN ST 35-33.5-2-1, et seq.

iii. Information excluded from public access by specific court order;

iv. Complete Social Security Numbers of living persons;

v. With the exception of names, information such as addresses, phone numbers, and dates of birth which explicitly identifies:

- Natural persons who are witnesses or victims (not including defendants) in criminal, domestic violence, stalking, sexual assault, juvenile, or civil protection order proceedings, provided that juveniles who are victims of sex crimes shall be identified by initials only;

- Places of residence of judicial officers, clerks and other employees of courts and clerks of court, unless the person or persons about whom the information pertains waives confidentiality;

vi. Complete account numbers of specific assets, loans, bank accounts, credit cards, and personal identification numbers (PINs);

vii. All orders of expungement entered in criminal or juvenile proceedings, orders to restrict access to criminal history information pursuant to IN ST 35-38-5-5.5 or IN ST 35-38-8-5 and records excluded from public access by such orders, and information related to infractions that is excluded from public access pursuant to IN ST 34-28-5-15 or IN ST 34-28-5-16 [Editor's note: IN ST 35-38-5-5.5, IN ST 35-38-8-5 and IN ST 34-28-5-16 were repealed effective July 1, 2013; for information on orders restricting access to criminal history, refer to IN ST 35-38-9-1, et seq.];

viii. All personal notes and e-mail, and deliberative material, of judges, jurors, court staff and judicial agencies, and information recorded in personal data assistants (PDA's) or organizers and personal calendars. IN ST ADMIN Rule 9(G)(1).

F. Filing and Service Requirements

1. *Filing requirements.* Except as otherwise provided in IN ST TRIAL P Rule 5(E)(2), all pleadings and papers subsequent to the complaint which are required to be served upon a party shall be filed with the Court either before service or within a reasonable period of time thereafter. IN ST TRIAL P Rule 5(E)(1).

   a. *Non-filing of discovery until necessary*

   i. *Non-filing of discovery; Exceptions.* No deposition or request for discovery or response thereto under IN ST TRIAL P Rule 27, IN ST TRIAL P Rule 30, IN ST TRIAL P Rule 31, IN ST TRIAL P Rule 33, IN ST TRIAL P Rule 34 or IN ST TRIAL P Rule 36 shall be filed with the Court unless:

   - A motion is filed pursuant to IN ST TRIAL P Rule 26(C) or IN ST TRIAL P Rule 37 and the original deposition or request for discovery or response thereto is necessary to enable the Court to rule; or

   - A party desires to use the deposition or request for discovery or response thereto for evidentiary purposes at trial or in connection with a motion, and the Court, either upon its own motion or that of any party, or as a part of any pre-trial order, orders the filing of the original. IN ST TRIAL P Rule 5(E)(2).

    ii. *Custody of original and period of retention*

- The original of a deposition shall, subject to the provisions of IN ST TRIAL P Rule 30(E), be delivered by the reporter to the party taking it and shall be maintained by that party until filed with the Court pursuant to IN ST TRIAL P Rule 5(E)(2) or until the later of final judgment, agreed settlement of the litigation or all appellate rights have been exhausted. IN ST TRIAL P Rule 5(E)(3)(a).

- The original or any request for discovery or response thereto under IN ST TRIAL P Rule 27, IN ST TRIAL P Rule 30, IN ST TRIAL P Rule 31, IN ST TRIAL P Rule 33, IN ST TRIAL P Rule 34 and IN ST TRIAL P Rule 36 shall be maintained by the party originating the request or response until filed with the Court pursuant to IN ST TRIAL P Rule 5(E)(2) or until the later of final judgment, agreed settlement or all appellate rights have been exhausted. IN ST TRIAL P Rule 5(E)(3)(b).

    iii. *Original unavailable; Copies.* In the event it is made to appear to the satisfaction of the Court that the original of a deposition or request for discovery or response thereto cannot be filed with the Court when required, the Court may allow use of a copy instead of the original. IN ST TRIAL P Rule 5(E)(4).

    iv. *Filing as publication.* The filing of any deposition shall constitute publication. IN ST TRIAL P Rule 5(E)(5).

b. *Filing with the court defined.* The filing of pleadings, motions, and other papers with the court as required by the Indiana Rules of Trial Procedure shall be made by one of the following methods:

    i. Delivery to the clerk of the court;

    ii. Sending by electronic transmission under the procedure adopted pursuant to IN ST ADMIN Rule 12;

    iii. Mailing to the clerk by registered, certified or express mail return receipt requested;

    iv. Depositing with any third-party commercial carrier for delivery to the clerk within three (3) calendar days, cost prepaid, properly addressed;

    v. If the court so permits, filing with the judge, in which event the judge shall note thereon the filing date and forthwith transmit them to the office of the clerk; or

    vi. Electronic filing, as approved by the Division of State Court Administration pursuant to IN ST ADMIN Rule 16. IN ST TRIAL P Rule 5(F).

    vii. Filing by registered or certified mail and by third-party commercial carrier shall be complete upon mailing or deposit. IN ST TRIAL P Rule 5(F).

c. *Facsimile filing.* As outlined in IN ST HAMILTON ADMIN Rule 103(103.10),facsimile filing is permitted in the Circuit and Superior Courts of Hamilton County. The Courts authorize the Hamilton County Clerk of Courts to accept pleadings, motions and other papers by electronic facsimile transmission for filing in any case pending before the Courts, subject to the requirements of IN ST HAMILTON ADMIN Rule 103(103.10). IN ST HAMILTON ADMIN Rule 103(103.10); IN ST HAMILTON TRIAL Rule 201(201.80).

    i. *Generally.* In counties where a majority of judges of the courts of record, by posted local rule, have authorized electronic facsimile filing and designated a telephone number to receive such transmissions, pleadings, motions, and other papers may be sent to the Clerk of Circuit Court by electronic facsimile transmission for filing in any case, provided:

- Such matter does not exceed ten (10) pages, including the cover sheet;

- Such matter does not require the payment of fees other than the electronic facsimile transcription fee set forth in IN ST ADMIN Rule 12(E);

- The sending party creates at the time of transmission a machine generated log for such transmission; and

- The original document and the transmission log are maintained by the sending party for the duration of the litigation. IN ST ADMIN Rule 12(B); IN ST HAMILTON ADMIN Rule 103(103.10)(d).

- Legibility of documents and timeliness of filing is the responsibility of the sender. IN ST HAMILTON ADMIN Rule 103(103.10)(g).

- The Clerk shall accept electronic facsimile transmission filings only if received at the facsimile machine assigned by the Clerk. The telephone number designated to receive such transmission is available at IN ST HAMILTON ADMIN Rule 103(103.40). IN ST HAMILTON ADMIN Rule 103(103.40).

ii. *Time of filing.* During normal, posted business hours, the time of filing shall be the time the duplicate document is produced in the office of the Clerk of the Circuit Court. Duplicate documents received at all other times shall be filed as of the next normal business day. IN ST ADMIN Rule 12(C).

- If the receiving fax machine endorses its own time and date stamp upon the transmitted documents and the receiving machine produces a delivery receipt which is electronically created and transmitted to the sending party, the time of filing shall be the date and time recorded on the transmitted document by the receiving fax machine. IN ST ADMIN Rule 12(C).

- Electronic facsimile transmissions will be accepted for filing only during the regular business hours as set forth in IN ST HAMILTON ADMIN Rule 101. Transmissions received by the Hamilton County Clerk after close of business shall be filed effective the next regular business day. IN ST HAMILTON ADMIN Rule 103(103.30).

iii. *Filing fee.* The electronic facsimile transmission will not be accepted for filing if its filing requires the payment of any fee other than the electronic facsimile transcription fee set forth in IN ST HAMILTON ADMIN Rule 103(103.20). IN ST HAMILTON ADMIN Rule 103(103.10)(e).

- Pursuant to Ordinance adopted by the Hamilton County Board of Commissioners, the Clerk shall collect an electronic facsimile transcription fee of One Dollar ($1.00) per page, to a maximum of Ten Dollars ($10.00) per transmission, for each electronic facsimile transmission accepted for filing with the Hamilton County Circuit and Superior Courts. IN ST HAMILTON ADMIN Rule 103(103.20).

- The fee shall be assessed against the sending party and shall be paid upon receipt of invoice by that party and at the latest within thirty (30) days of the transmission. In the event the fee is not paid by the sending party within the time limits provided, the court may issue a show-cause order or enter a judgment in the matter. The Clerk may refuse an electronic facsimile transmission from any attorney or pro se litigant who has failed to pay these fees within thirty (30) days. IN ST HAMILTON ADMIN Rule 103(103.20).

iv. *No direct filing with court.* A party shall not send pleadings, motions and other papers by electronic facsimile transmission for filing directly to any Court without that Court's prior approval to do so. IN ST HAMILTON ADMIN Rule 103(103.50).

d. *Filing with special judge.* After a special judge has qualified, a copy of each pleading and Chronological Case Summary entries filed with the Court shall be mailed or delivered to the office of that Special judge by the counsel or pro se litigant with service indicated on the certificate of service. IN ST HAMILTON TRIAL Rule 204(204.20).

e. *Proof of filing.* Any party filing any paper by any method other than personal delivery to the clerk shall retain proof of filing. IN ST TRIAL P Rule 5(F).

2. *Service requirements.* Unless otherwise provided by the Indiana Rules of Trial Procedure or an order of the court, each party and special judge, if any, shall be served with: (1) every order required by its terms to be served; (2) every pleading subsequent to the original complaint; (3) every written motion except one which may be heard ex parte; (4) every brief submitted to the trial court; (5) every paper relating to

discovery required to be served upon a party; and (6) every written notice, appearance, demand, offer of judgment, designation of record on appeal, or similar paper. IN ST TRIAL P Rule 5(A).

a. *Methods of service*

    i. *Personal service.* Whenever a party is represented by an attorney of record, service shall be made upon such attorney unless service upon the party himself is ordered by the court. Service upon the attorney or party shall be made by delivering or mailing a copy of the papers to the last known address or where an attorney or party has consented to service by fax or e-mail, as provided in IN ST TRIAL P Rule 3.1(A)(4), by faxing or e-mailing a copy of the documents to the fax number or e-mail address set out in the appearance form or correction as required by IN ST TRIAL P Rule 3.1(E). IN ST TRIAL P Rule 5(B). Delivery of a copy within IN ST TRIAL P Rule 5 means:

- Offering or tendering it to the attorney or party and stating the nature of the papers being served. Refusal to accept an offered or tendered document is a waiver of any objection to the sufficiency or adequacy of service of that document;

- Leaving it at his office with a clerk or other person in charge thereof, or if there is no one in charge, leaving it in a conspicuous place therein; or

- If the office is closed, by leaving it at his dwelling house or usual place of abode with some person of suitable age and discretion then residing therein; or,

- Leaving it at some other suitable place, selected by the attorney upon whom service is being made, pursuant to duly promulgated local rule. IN ST TRIAL P Rule 5(B)(1).

    ii. *Service by mail.* If service is made by mail, the papers shall be deposited in the United States mail addressed to the person on whom they are being served, with postage prepaid. Service shall be deemed complete upon mailing. Proof of service of all papers permitted to be mailed may be made by written acknowledgment of service, by affidavit of the person who mailed the papers, or by certificate of an attorney. It shall be the duty of attorneys when entering their appearance in a cause or when filing pleadings or papers therein, to have noted in the Chronological Case Summary or said pleadings or papers so filed the address and telephone number of their office. Service by delivery or by mail at such address shall be deemed sufficient and complete. IN ST TRIAL P Rule 5(B)(2).

    iii. *Service by fax or e-mail.* A party who has consented to service by fax or e-mail may be served as follows:

- Service by e-mail shall be made by attaching the document being served in .pdf format. Discovery documents must also be served in accordance with IN ST TRIAL P Rule 26(A). IN ST TRIAL P Rule 5(B)(3)(a).

- Service by fax shall be deemed complete upon generation of a transmission record indicating the successful transmission of the entire document, except as provided in IN ST TRIAL P Rule 5(B)(3)(d). IN ST TRIAL P Rule 5(B)(3)(b).

- Service by e-mail shall be deemed complete upon transmission, except as provided in IN ST TRIAL P Rule 5(B)(3)(d). IN ST TRIAL P Rule 5(B)(3)(c).

- Service by fax or e-mail that occurs on a Saturday, Sunday, legal holiday, or day the court or agency in which the matter is pending is closed or after 5:00 PM local time of the recipient shall be deemed complete the next day that is not a Saturday, Sunday, legal holiday, or day that the court or agency in which the matter is pending is not closed. IN ST TRIAL P Rule 5(B)(3)(d).

    iv. *Mail box service.* Pursuant to IN ST TRIAL P Rule 5(B)(1)(d), the Circuit and Superior Courts of Hamilton County hereby designate the "mail boxes" located in the Clerk's order book office for service of pleadings upon attorneys who have such boxes. IN ST HAMILTON TRIAL Rule 201(201.50).

    v. *Additional service of electronic discovery.* In addition to service under Rule IN ST TRIAL P Rule 5(B) or a .pdf format electronic copy, a party propounding or responding to interrogatories, requests for production or requests for admission shall comply with IN ST TRIAL P Rule 26(A.1)(a) or IN ST TRIAL P Rule 26(A.1)(b). IN ST TRIAL P Rule 26(A.1).

- The party shall serve the discovery request or response in an electronic format (either on a disk or as an electronic document attachment) in any commercially available word processing software system. If transmitted on disk, each disk shall be labeled, identifying the caption of the case, the document, and the word processing version in which it is being submitted. If more than one (1) disk is used for the same document, each disk shall be labeled and also shall be sequentially numbered. If transmitted by electronic mail, the document must be accompanied by electronic memorandum providing the forgoing identifying information; or

- The party shall serve the opposing party with a verified statement that the attorney or party appealing pro se lacks the equipment and is unable to transmit the discovery as required by IN ST TRIAL P Rule 26(A.1). IN ST TRIAL P Rule 26(A.1).

b. *Serving numerous defendants.* In any action in which there are unusually large numbers of defendants, the court, upon motion or of its own initiative, may order:

i. That service of the pleadings of the defendants and replies thereto need not be made as between the defendants;

- That any cross-claim, counterclaim, or matter constituting an avoidance or affirmative defense contained therein shall be deemed to be denied or avoided by all other parties; and

- That the filing of any such pleading and service thereof upon the plaintiff constitutes due notice of it to the parties. IN ST TRIAL P Rule 5(D).

ii. A copy of every such order shall be served upon the parties in such manner and form as the court directs. IN ST TRIAL P Rule 5(D).

c. *Service on parties in default for failure to appear.* No service need be made on parties in default for failure to appear, except that pleadings asserting new or additional claims for relief against them shall be served upon them in the manner provided by service of summons in IN ST TRIAL P Rule 4. IN ST TRIAL P Rule 5(A).

G. Hearings

1. The Indiana rules do not contemplate a hearing related to the filing and service of interrogatories.

H. Forms

1. Interrogatory Forms for Indiana

a. General form. 5 INPRAC § 4:2.10.

b. Motion to enlarge time to answer. 5 INPRAC § 4:2.20.

c. Answers and objections; General form. 5 INPRAC § 4:2.30.

d. Answer; General form with standard objections. 5 INPRAC § 4:2.40.

e. Answer; Offer to produce business records. 5 INPRAC § 4:2.50.

f. Sample interrogatories relating to electronically stored information. 5 INPRAC § 4:2.60.

g. Motion to seal answers to interrogatories. 10 INPRAC § 65.6.1.

h. Interrogatories; General form. 10 INPRAC § 65.7.

i. Interrogatories; Another form. 10 INPRAC § 65.8.

j. Interrogatory preliminary instructions; Comprehensive form. 10 INPRAC § 65.9.

k. Interrogatory preliminary instructions; Abbreviated form. 10 INPRAC § 65.10.

l. Interrogatory definitions. 10 INPRAC § 65.11.

m. Motion to enlarge time to answer interrogatories. 10 INPRAC § 65.12.

n. Motion for enlargement of time; Response due after discovery completed. 10 INPRAC § 65.13.

o. Motion to shorten time to respond to interrogatories. 10 INPRAC § 65.15.

p. Motion to strike interrogatories; Excessive number under local rules. 10 INPRAC § 65.16.

q. Interrogatories to determine minimum contacts with state. 10 INPRAC § 65.20.

r. Answers and objections to interrogatories; General form. 10 INPRAC § 65.30.

s. Answers and objections to interrogatories; Another form. 10 INPRAC § 65.31.

t. Standard objections to interrogatories; General form. 10 INPRAC § 65.32.

u. Standard objections to interrogatories. 10 INPRAC § 65.33.

v. Answer of interrogatory by offering to produce business records. 10 INPRAC § 65.34.

w. Motion to compel answers to interrogatories. 10 INPRAC § 65.35.

x. Attorney's signature as to objections; Alternate forms. 10 INPRAC § 65.36.

y. Conversion; Plaintiff's interrogatories. 10 INPRAC § 66.27.

z. Medical malpractice action. 10 INPRAC § 66.37.

I. Checklist

(I) ❑ Matters to be considered by the party serving the interrogatories

   (a) ❑ Required documents

      (1) ❑ Interrogatories

      (2) ❑ Certificate of service

   (b) ❑ Supplemental documents

      (1) ❑ Stipulation regarding discovery procedure

      (2) ❑ Facsimile cover sheet

   (c) ❑ Timing

      (1) ❑ Interrogatories may, without leave of court, be served upon the plaintiff after commencement of the action and upon any other party with or after service of the summons and complaint upon that party

(II) ❑ Matters to be considered by the responding party

   (a) ❑ Required documents

      (1) ❑ Response to interrogatories

      (2) ❑ Certificate of service

   (b) ❑ Supplemental documents

      (1) ❑ Business records

      (2) ❑ Stipulation regarding discovery procedure

      (3) ❑ Facsimile cover sheet

   (c) ❑ Timing

      (1) ❑ The party upon whom the interrogatories have been served shall serve a copy of the answers and objections within a period designated by the party submitting the interrogatories, not less than thirty (30) days after the service thereof or within such shorter or longer time as the court may allow

Requests, Notices and Applications
Request for Production of Documents

Document Last Updated October 2013

A. Applicable Rules

1. *State rules*

   a. Appearance. IN ST TRIAL P Rule 3.1.

   b. Process. IN ST TRIAL P Rule 4.

   c. Service and filing of pleadings and other papers. IN ST TRIAL P Rule 5.

   d. Time. IN ST TRIAL P Rule 6.

   e. Pleadings. IN ST TRIAL P Rule 7; IN ST TRIAL P Rule 9.2; IN ST TRIAL P Rule 10.

   f. Signing and verification of pleadings. IN ST TRIAL P Rule 11.

   g. General provisions governing discovery. IN ST TRIAL P Rule 26.

   h. Methods of discovery. IN ST TRIAL P Rule 27; IN ST TRIAL P Rule 29; IN ST TRIAL P Rule 30; IN ST TRIAL P Rule 31; IN ST TRIAL P Rule 33; IN ST TRIAL P Rule 34; IN ST TRIAL P Rule 35; IN ST TRIAL P Rule 36.

   i. Failure to make or cooperate in discovery; Sanctions. IN ST TRIAL P Rule 37.

   j. Subpoena. IN ST TRIAL P Rule 45.

   k. Judgment on the evidence (directed verdict). IN ST TRIAL P Rule 50.

   l. Findings by the court. IN ST TRIAL P Rule 52.

   m. Summary judgment. IN ST TRIAL P Rule 56.

   n. Motion to correct error. IN ST TRIAL P Rule 59.

   o. Relief from judgment or order. IN ST TRIAL P Rule 60.

   p. Access to court records. IN ST ADMIN Rule 9.

   q. Paper size. IN ST ADMIN Rule 11.

   r. Facsimile transmission. IN ST ADMIN Rule 12.

   s. Electronic filing and electronic service pilot projects. IN ST ADMIN Rule 16.

   t. Sealing of certain records by court; Hearing; Notice. IN ST 5-14-3-5.5.

   u. Privacy and confidentiality. IN ST 5-2-9-6; IN ST 5-14-3-4; IN ST 6-4.1-5-10; IN ST 6-4.1-12-12; IN ST 6-8.1-7-1; IN ST 11-13-1-8; IN ST 12-23-14-13; IN ST 16-39-3-10; IN ST 16-41-8-1; IN ST 22-4-19-6; IN ST 31-11-1-6; IN ST 31-19-5-23; IN ST 31-19-13-2; IN ST 31-19-19-1; IN ST 31-33-18-1; IN ST 31-39-1-1; IN ST 31-39-1-2; IN ST 33-23-16-16; IN ST 35-34-2-4; IN ST 35-38-1-13; IN ST 35-38-9-1; IN ST ADR Rule 2.11; IN ST ADR Rule 4.4; IN ST ADR Rule 5.6; IN ST JURY Rule 10.

2. *Local rules*

   a. Court hours. IN ST HAMILTON ADMIN Rule 101.

   b. Facsimile transmissions. IN ST HAMILTON ADMIN Rule 103.

   c. Filing of pleadings and entry of appearances. IN ST HAMILTON TRIAL Rule 201.

   d. Proposed orders. IN ST HAMILTON TRIAL Rule 202.

   e. Special judges. IN ST HAMILTON TRIAL Rule 204.

   f. Continuances. IN ST HAMILTON TRIAL Rule 206.

B. Timing

1. *Time for service of request for production of documents*

   a. *Service on parties.* The request may, without leave of court, be served upon the plaintiff after commencement of the action and upon any other party with or after service of the summons and complaint upon that party. IN ST TRIAL P Rule 34(B).

   b. *Service on non-parties.* Neither a request nor subpoena to produce or permit as permitted by IN ST TRIAL P Rule 34 shall be served upon a non-party until at least fifteen (15) days after the date on which the party intending to serve such request or subpoena serves a copy of the proposed request and subpoena on all other parties. Provided, however, that if such request or subpoena relates to a matter set for hearing within such fifteen (15) day period or arises out of a bona fide emergency, such request or subpoena may be served upon a non-party one (1) day after receipt of the proposed request or subpoena by all other parties. IN ST TRIAL P Rule 34(C)(2)

2. *Time for service of the response to the request for production of documents.* The party upon whom the request is served shall serve a written response within a period designated in the request, not less than thirty (30) days after the service thereof or within such shorter or longer time as the court may allow. IN ST TRIAL P Rule 34(B).

3. *Computation of time*

   a. *Generally; Days excluded.* In computing any period of time prescribed or allowed by the Indiana Rules of Trial Procedure, by order of the court, or by any applicable statute, the day of the act, event, or default from which the designated period of time begins to run shall not be included. The last day of the period so computed is to be included unless it is:

      i. A Saturday,

      ii. A Sunday,

      iii. A legal holiday as defined by state statute, or

      iv. A day the office in which the act is to be done is closed during regular business hours. IN ST TRIAL P Rule 6(A).

   b. *Short periods.* In any event, the period runs until the end of the next day that is not a Saturday, a Sunday, a legal holiday, or a day on which the office is closed. When the period of time allowed is less than seven (7) days, intermediate Saturdays, Sundays, legal holidays, and days on which the office is closed shall be excluded from the computations. IN ST TRIAL P Rule 6(A).

   c. *Additional time after service by United States mail.* Whenever a party has the right or is required to do some act or take some proceedings within a prescribed period after the service of a notice or other paper upon him and the notice or paper is served upon him by United States mail, three (3) days shall be added to the prescribed period. IN ST TRIAL P Rule 6(E).

   d. *Enlargement of time.* When an act is required or allowed to be done at or within a specific time by the Indiana Rules of Trial Procedure, the court may at any time for cause shown:

      i. Order the period enlarged, with or without motion or notice, if request therefor is made before the expiration of the period originally prescribed or extended by a previous order; or

      ii. Upon motion made after the expiration of the specific period, permit the act to be done where the failure to act was the result of excusable neglect; but, the court may not extend the time for taking any action for judgment on the evidence under IN ST TRIAL P Rule 50(A), amendment of findings and judgment under IN ST TRIAL P Rule 52(B), to correct errors under IN ST TRIAL P Rule 59(C), statement in opposition to motion to correct error under IN ST TRIAL P Rule 59(E), or to obtain relief from final judgment under IN ST TRIAL P Rule 60(B), except to the extent and under the conditions stated in those rules. IN ST TRIAL P Rule 6(B).

      iii. For information on obtaining a continuance, refer to IN ST HAMILTON TRIAL Rule 206.

C. General Requirements

1. *Scope of discovery.* Unless otherwise limited by order of the court in accordance with the Indiana Rules of Trial Procedure, the scope of discovery is as follows:

   a. *In general.* Parties may obtain discovery regarding any matter, not privileged, which is relevant to the subject-matter involved in the pending action, whether it relates to the claim or defense of the party seeking discovery or the claim or defense of any other party, including the existence, description, nature, custody, condition and location of any books, documents, or other tangible things and the identity and location of persons having knowledge of any discoverable matter. It is not ground for objection that the information sought will be inadmissible at the trial if the information sought appears reasonably calculated to lead to the discovery of admissible evidence. IN ST TRIAL P Rule 26(B)(1).

    i.   *Limiting discovery upon court determination.* The frequency or extent of use of the discovery methods otherwise permitted under the Indiana Rules of Trial Procedure and by any local rule shall be limited by the court if it determines that:

- The discovery sought is unreasonably cumulative or duplicative, or is obtainable from some other source that is more convenient, less burdensome, or less expensive;

- The party seeking discovery has had ample opportunity by discovery in the action to obtain the information sought or;

- The burden or expense of the proposed discovery outweighs its likely benefit, taking into account the needs of the case, the amount in controversy, the parties' resources, the importance of the issues at stake in the litigation, and the importance of the proposed discovery in resolving the issues. IN ST TRIAL P Rule 26(B)(1).

- The court may act upon its own initiative after reasonable notice or pursuant to a motion under IN ST TRIAL P Rule 26(C). IN ST TRIAL P Rule 26(B)(1). Refer to the Indiana KeyRules Motion for Protective Order document for more information.

    ii. *Relevancy in the discovery context.* When the word "relevancy" is used in IN ST TRIAL P Rule 26(B), it does not mean "relevancy" as that word in used to determine the admissibility of evidence in a trial court. It is much broader. It means "relevancy" to the "subject matter" of the litigation or pending action and it may relate to the claim or defense of any party. Pretrial discovery is available as to any nonprivileged matter relevant to the subject matter of the lawsuit or to obtain information reasonably calculated to lead to admissible evidence. 2A INPRAC R 26(26.4); Kaufmann v. Credithrift Financial, Inc., 465 N.E.2d 207, 210 (Ind.Ct.App. 1984).

    iii. *Tests for relevance.* Indiana case law has developed two (2) additional tests in this area. 2A INPRAC R 26(26.4).

- The first test determines when a document or a request for information is actually relevant to the subject matter in the pending action. A document [or discovery request] is relevant to discovery if there is the possibility the information sought may be relevant to the subject matter of the action. 2A INPRAC R 26(26.4); CIGNA-INA/Aetna v. Hagerman-Shambaugh, 473 N.E.2d 1033, 1036 (Ind.Ct.App. 1985).

- The second test speaks to appellate review of the trial court's determination that a document or discovery request is relevant to the subject matter of the pending action. The appellate court sees its review of the trial court's decision on relevancy to subject matter as being very limited. The court states: "Our review of the trial court's conclusion that the documents are relevant is limited. A trial court is vested with discretion in its rulings on discovery issues." 2A INPRAC R 26(26.4); Costanzi v. Ryan, 175 Ind.App. 257, 370 N.E.2d 1333 (Ind.Ct.App. 1978).

b. *Insurance agreements.* A party may obtain discovery of the existence and contents of any insurance agreement under which any person carrying on an insurance business may be liable to satisfy part or all of a judgment which may be entered in the action or to indemnify or reimburse for payments made to satisfy the judgment. Information concerning the insurance agreement is not by reason of disclosure admissible in evidence at trial. For purposes of IN ST TRIAL P Rule 26(B)(2), an application for insurance shall not be treated as part of an insurance agreement. IN ST TRIAL P Rule 26(B)(2).

c. *Trial preparation; Materials.* Subject to the provisions of IN ST TRIAL P Rule 26(B)(4), a party may obtain discovery of documents and tangible things otherwise discoverable under IN ST TRIAL P Rule 26(B)(1) and prepared in anticipation of litigation or for trial by or for another party or by or for that other party's representative (including his attorney, consultant, surety, indemnitor, insurer, or agent) only upon a showing that the party seeking discovery has substantial need of the materials in the preparation of his case and that he is unable without undue hardship to obtain the substantial equivalent of the materials by other means. In ordering discovery of such materials when the required showing has been made, the court shall protect against disclosure of the mental impressions, conclusions, opinions, or legal theories of an attorney or other representative of a party concerning the litigation. IN ST TRIAL P Rule 26(B)(3).

i. A party may obtain without the required showing a statement concerning the action or its subject matter previously made by that party. Upon request, a person not a party may obtain without the required showing a statement concerning the action or its subject matter previously made by that person. If the request is refused, the person may move for a court order. The provisions of IN ST TRIAL P Rule 37(A)(4) apply to the award of expenses incurred in relation to the motion. For purposes of IN ST TRIAL P Rule 26(B)(3), a statement previously made is:

- A written statement signed or otherwise adopted approved by the person making it, or

- A stenographic, mechanical, electrical, or other recording, or a transcription thereof, which is a substantially verbatim recital of an oral statement by the person making it and contemporaneously recorded. IN ST TRIAL P Rule 26(B)(3).

ii. The protection of IN ST TRIAL P Rule 26(B)(3) extends to material prepared or collected before litigation actually commences, but that some possibility of litigation must actually exist before the privilege and IN ST TRIAL P Rule 26(B)(3) become operative. 2A INPRAC R 26(26.9).

d. *Trial preparation; Experts.* Discovery of facts known and opinions held by experts, otherwise discoverable under the provisions of IN ST TRIAL P Rule 26(B)(1) and acquired or developed in anticipation of litigation or for trial, may be obtained as follows:

i. A party may through interrogatories require any other party to identify each person whom the other party expects to call as an expert witness at trial, to state the subject matter on which the expert is expected to testify, and to state the substance of the facts and opinions to which the expert is expected to testify and a summary of the grounds for each opinion. IN ST TRIAL P Rule 26(B)(4)(a)(i).

ii. Upon motion, the court may order further discovery by other means, subject to such restrictions as to scope and such provisions, pursuant to IN ST TRIAL P Rule 26(B)(4)(c), concerning fees and expenses as the court may deem appropriate. IN ST TRIAL P Rule 26(B)(4)(a)(ii).

iii. A party may discover facts known or opinions held by an expert who has been retained or specially employed by another party in anticipation of litigation or preparation for trial and who is not expected to be called as a witness at trial, only as provided in IN ST TRIAL P Rule 35(B) or upon a showing of exceptional circumstances under which it is impracticable for the party seeking discovery to obtain facts or opinions on the same subject by other means. IN ST TRIAL P Rule 26(B)(4)(b).

iv. Unless manifest injustice would result,

- The court shall require that the party seeking discovery pay the expert a reasonable fee for time spent in responding to discovery under IN ST TRIAL P Rule 26(B)(4)(a)(ii) and IN ST TRIAL P Rule 26(B)(4)(b); and

- With respect to discovery obtained under IN ST TRIAL P Rule 26(B)(4)(a)(ii) the court may require, and with respect to discovery obtained under IN ST TRIAL P Rule 26(B)(4)(b) the court shall require, the party seeking discovery to pay the other party a fair portion of the fees and expenses reasonably incurred by the latter party in obtaining facts and opinions from the expert. IN ST TRIAL P Rule 26(B)(4).

e. *Claims of privilege or protection*

i. *Information withheld.* When a party withholds information otherwise discoverable under the

Indiana Rules of Trial Procedure by claiming that it is privileged or subject to protection as trial preparation material, the party shall make the claim expressly and shall describe the nature of the documents, communications, or things not produced or disclosed in a manner that, without revealing information itself privileged or protected, will enable other parties to assess the applicability of the privilege or protection. IN ST TRIAL P Rule 26(B)(5)(a).

ii. *Information produced.* If information is produced in discovery that is subject to a claim of privilege or protection as trial-preparation material, the party making the claim may notify any party that received the information of the claim and the basis for it. After being notified, a party must promptly return, sequester, or destroy the specified information and any copies it has and may not use or disclose the information until the claim is resolved. A receiving party may promptly present the information to the court under seal for a determination of the claim. If the receiving party disclosed the information before being notified, it must take reasonable steps to retrieve it. The producing party must preserve the information until the claim is resolved. IN ST TRIAL P Rule 26(B)(5)(b).

iii. *Waiver.* The law of discovery has developed some holdings which indicate that "waiver" of a privileged communication in a discovery setting might be more exacting than "waiver" of a privileged communication when the only question at hand is an interpretation of the privilege itself. Thus, in litigation in which several documents are in issue, and some are released inadvertently, there is strong case law that holds that the "inadvertent production" of a privileged document does not constitute a waiver of the attorney-client privilege. 2A INPRAC R 26(26.5); Transamerica Computer Co. v. International Business Machines Corp., 573 F.2d 646 (9th Cir. 1978). Such a rule should be measured against the usual rule which suggests that a voluntary disclosure to a third person will generally suffice to show a waiver of the attorney-client privilege. 2A INPRAC R 26(26.5).

f. *Use not limited.* Unless the court orders otherwise under IN ST TRIAL P Rule 26(C), the frequency of use of the methods listed in IN ST TRIAL P Rule 26(A) is not limited. IN ST TRIAL P Rule 26(A).

g. *Sequence of discovery.* Unless the court upon motion, for the convenience of parties and witnesses and in the interests of justice, orders otherwise, methods of discovery may be used in any sequence and the fact that a party is conducting discovery, whether by deposition or otherwise, shall not operate to delay any other party's discovery. IN ST TRIAL P Rule 26.

2. *Request for production of documents*

a. *Content of the request.* The request shall set forth the items to be inspected either by individual item or by category, and describe each item and category with reasonable particularity. The request may specify the form or forms in which electronically stored information is to be produced. The request shall specify a reasonable time, place, and manner of making the inspection and performing the related acts. Service is dispensed with if the whereabouts of the parties is unknown. IN ST TRIAL P Rule 34(B).

i. *Reasonable particularity.* A recurring issue appears among cases. It is whether a request is adequate or describes the items sought with "reasonable particularity" as stated in IN ST TRIAL P Rule 34(B). The essence of this matter is found in these words: "When the party seeking discovery issues a 'shotgun' request that is unduly general, the court may avoid wading through documents by finding the items to be inspected not set forth with reasonable particularity, as required by IN ST TRIAL P Rule 34(B). 3 INPRAC R 34(34.1); Ray v. St. John's Health Care Corp., 582 N.E.2d 464, 474 (Ind.Ct.App. 1991); Richey v. Chappell, 572 N.E.2d 1338, 1339 (Ind.Ct.App. 1991).

b. *Requesting documents in specific form.* If a request for electronically stored information does not specify the form or forms of production, a responding party must produce the information in a form or forms in which it is ordinarily maintained or in a form or forms that are reasonably usable. IN ST TRIAL P Rule 34(B).

c. *Scope.* Any party may serve on any other party a request:

i. To produce and permit the party making the request, or someone acting on the requester's behalf, to inspect and copy, any designated documents or electronically stored information (including, without limitation, writings, drawings, graphs, charts, photographs, sound recordings, images and other data or data compilations from which information can be obtained or translated, if necessary, by the respondent into reasonably usable form) or to inspect and copy, test, or sample any designated tangible things which constitute or contain matters within the scope of IN ST TRIAL P Rule 26(B) and which are in the possession, custody or control of the party upon whom the request is served; or

ii. To permit entry upon designated land or other property in the possession or control of the party upon whom the request is served for the purpose of inspection and measuring, surveying, photographing, testing, or sampling the property or any designated object or operation thereon, within the scope of IN ST TRIAL P Rule 26(B). IN ST TRIAL P Rule 34(A).

d. *Application to non-parties.* A witness or person other than a party may be requested to produce or permit the matters allowed by IN ST TRIAL P Rule 34(A). Such request shall be served upon other parties and included in or with a subpoena served upon such witness or person. IN ST TRIAL P Rule 34(C)(1).

   i. *Content of request to non-parties*

   - The request shall contain the matter provided in IN ST TRIAL P Rule 34(B). IN ST TRIAL P Rule 34(C)(3).

   - It shall also state that the witness or person to whom it is directed is entitled to security against damages or payment of damages resulting from such request and may respond to such request by submitting to its terms, by proposing different terms, by objecting specifically or generally to the request by serving a written response to the party making the request within thirty (30) days, or by moving to quash as permitted by IN ST TRIAL P Rule 45(B). IN ST TRIAL P Rule 34(C)(3).

   ii. *Service of responses on other parties required.* A party receiving documents from a non-party pursuant to IN ST TRIAL P Rule 34(C) shall serve copies on all other parties within fifteen (15) days of receiving the documents. If the documents are voluminous and service of a complete set of copies is burdensome, the receiving party shall notify all parties within fifteen (15) days of receiving the documents that the documents are available for inspection at the location of their production by the non-party, or at another location agreed to by the parties. The parties shall agree to arrangements for copying, and any party desiring copies shall bear the cost of reproducing them. IN ST TRIAL P Rule 34(C)(4).

e. *Exception to best evidence rule.* When a party or witness in control of a writing or document subject to examination under IN ST TRIAL P Rule 34 or IN ST TRIAL P Rule 9.2(E) refuses or is unable to produce it, evidence thereof shall be allowed by other parties without compliance with the rule of evidence requiring production of the original document or writing as best evidence. IN ST TRIAL P Rule 34(D).

3. *Response to request for production of documents*

a. *Content of the response.* The response shall state, with respect to each item or category, that inspection and related activities will be permitted as requested, unless it is objected to, including an objection to the requested form or forms for producing electronically stored information, stating in which event the reasons for objection shall be stated. If objection is made to part of an item or category, the part shall be specified. IN ST TRIAL P Rule 34(B).

b. *Types of responses.* There are several responses that a party may make to a IN ST TRIAL P Rule 34 discovery request:

   i. Agree to produce the requested item or permit inspection at the time and place suggested by the discovering party. 10 INPRAC § 67.2.

   ii. Agree to production, but suggest another time and place. 10 INPRAC § 67.2.

   iii. Move for a protective order under IN ST TRIAL P Rule 26(C). 10 INPRAC § 67.2.

   iv. Object to the request. Common grounds for objection include:

   - The item sought does not exist. 10 INPRAC § 67.2.

- Respondent does not have possession, custody or control of the item requested. 10 INPRAC § 67.2.

- The request does not describe documents to be produced with reasonable particularity, or by individual item or category. 10 INPRAC § 67.2.

- The document requested fails to specify a reasonable time, place and manner of production. 10 INPRAC § 67.2.

- The discovery requested is privileged or constitutes work product (mental impressions, conclusions, opinions or legal theories of party or party's attorney). 10 INPRAC § 67.2.

- The discovery requested is not relevant to the subject matter of the litigation and not reasonably calculated to lead to the discovery of admissible evidence. 10 INPRAC § 67.2.

- The discovery requests documents prepared in anticipation of litigation when the requesting party does not have a substantial need of the materials in preparation of the case and is able to obtain the substantial equivalent of the materials without undue hardship and by other means. 10 INPRAC § 67.2.

- Nonparty's statement was prepared in anticipation of litigation and there has been no showing that the non-party's statement cannot be obtained without undue hardship by other means. 10 INPRAC § 67.2.

- The discovery requested contains opinions and facts of an expert who was retained and specially employed in anticipation of litigation or trial preparation and who is not expected to be called as a witness at trial and no exceptional circumstances exist which make it impracticable for the party seeking discovery to obtain the facts and opinions by other means. 10 INPRAC § 67.2.

- The requesting party refuses to pay a fair portion of costs incurred by responding party to produce documents. 10 INPRAC § 67.2.

- The testing procedure requested will destroy or materially alter the document or thing. 10 INPRAC § 67.2.

- The discovery requested is burdensome, oppressive or unduly expensive. 10 INPRAC § 67.2.

c. *Objection.* If objection is made to the requested form or forms for producing electronically stored information—or if no form was specified in the request—the responding party must state the form or forms it intends to use. The party submitting the request may move for an order under IN ST TRIAL P Rule 37(A) with respect to any objection to or other failure to respond to the request or any part thereof, or any failure to permit inspection as requested. IN ST TRIAL P Rule 34(B).

d. *Claims of privilege.* A blanket claim of privilege is not favored, and that the party who seeks to avoid discovery has the burden of establishing the essential elements of the privilege which is invoked. 3 INPRAC R 34(34.2); Ray v. St. John's Health Care Corp., 582 N.E.2d 464 (Ind.Ct.App. 1991).

e. *Electronically stored information; Production in multiple formats.* A party need not produce the same electronically stored information in more than one form. IN ST TRIAL P Rule 34(B).

f. *Response by a non-party.* Any party, or any witness or person upon whom the request properly is made may respond to the request as provided in IN ST TRIAL P Rule 34(B). If the response of the witness or person to whom it is directed is unfavorable, if he moves to quash, if he refuses to cooperate after responding or fails to respond, or if he objects, the party making the request may move for an order under IN ST TRIAL P Rule 37(A) with respect to any such response or objection. IN ST TRIAL P Rule 34(C)(3).

   i. In granting an order under IN ST TRIAL P Rule 34(C)(3) and IN ST TRIAL P Rule 37(A)(2) the court shall condition relief upon the prepayment of damages to be proximately incurred by the witness or person to whom the request is directed or require an adequate surety bond or other indemnity conditioned against such damages. Such damages shall include reasonable attorneys' fees incurred in reasonable resistance and in establishing such threatened damage or damages. IN ST TRIAL P Rule 34(C)(3).

ii.   Refer to the Indiana KeyRules Motion to Compel Discovery document more information.

g. *Supplementation of responses.* A party who has responded to a request for discovery with a response that was complete when made is under no duty to supplement his response to include information thereafter acquired, except as follows:

   i.   A party is under a duty seasonably to supplement his response with respect to any question directly addressed to:

   - The identity and location of persons having knowledge of discoverable matters, and
   - The identity of each person expected to be called as an expert witness at trial, the subject-matter on which he is expected to testify, and the substance of his testimony. IN ST TRIAL P Rule 26(E)(1).

   ii.   A party is under a duty seasonably to amend a prior response if he obtains information upon the basis of which:

   - He knows that the response was incorrect when made, or
   - He knows that the response though correct when made is no longer true and the circumstances are such that a failure to amend the response is in substance a knowing concealment. IN ST TRIAL P Rule 26(E)(2).

   iii. A duty to supplement responses may be imposed by order of the court, agreement of the parties, or at any time prior to trial through new requests for supplementation of prior responses. IN ST TRIAL P Rule 26(E)(3).

   iv.   The duty seasonably to supplement a discovery response is absolute and is not predicated on a court order. "It is a breach of a litigant's duty reasonably to supplement if the litigant postpones supplementing its response by not obtaining from its experts the information which is to be supplied in answer to interrogatories." 2A INPRAC R 26(26.27); Lucas v. Dorsey Corp., 609 N.E.2d 1191, 1196 (Ind.Ct.App. 1993).

D. Documents

1. *Required documents*

   a. *Request for production.* Refer to the General Requirements section of this document for information on the scope and content of a request for production of documents.

   b. *Certificate of service.* An attorney or unrepresented party tendering a document to the Clerk for filing shall certify that service has been made, list the parties served, and specify the date and means of service. The certificate of service shall be placed at the end of the document and shall not be separately filed. The separate filing of a certificate of service, however, shall not be grounds for rejecting a document for filing. The Clerk may permit documents to be filed without a certificate of service but shall require prompt filing of a separate certificate of service. IN ST TRIAL P Rule 5(C).

      i.   All pleadings filed with the Court which require a certificate of service shall specifically name the individual party or attorney on whom service has been made, the address, the manner in which service was made and the date when service was made. IN ST HAMILTON TRIAL Rule 201(201.60).

2. *Supplemental documents*

   a. *Stipulation regarding discovery procedure.* Unless the court orders otherwise, the parties may by written stipulation:

      i.   Provide that depositions may be taken before any person, at any time or place, upon any notice, and in any manner and when so taken may be used like other depositions, and

      ii.   Modify the procedures provided by the Indiana Rules of Trial Procedure for other methods of discovery. IN ST TRIAL P Rule 29.

   b. *Subpoena.* Requests upon non-parties shall be included in or with a subpoena served upon such witness or person. IN ST TRIAL P Rule 34(C)(1).

   c. *Facsimile cover sheet.* Any document sent to the Clerk of the Circuit Court by electronic facsimile transmission shall be accompanied by a cover sheet which states the title of the document, case number, number of pages, identity and voice telephone number of the sending party and instructions for filing. The cover sheet shall contain the signature of the attorney or party, pro se, authorizing the filing. IN ST ADMIN Rule 12(D); IN ST HAMILTON ADMIN Rule 103(103.10)(a).

E. Format

1. *Form of documents produced.* The rules applicable to captions, and the signing and form of pleadings (IN ST TRIAL P Rule 8 through IN ST TRIAL P Rule 11), apply to all motions and other papers provided under the Indiana Rules of Trial Procedure. 22B INPRAC 7:2. Unless the parties otherwise agree, or the court otherwise orders, a party who produces documents for inspection shall produce them as they are kept in the usual course of business or shall organize and label them to correspond with the categories in the request. IN ST TRIAL P Rule 34(B).

2. *Form of pleadings*

   a. *Caption; Names of parties.* Every pleading shall contain a caption setting forth the name of the court, the title of the action, the file number, and a designation as in IN ST TRIAL P Rule 7(A). In the complaint the title of the action shall include the names of all the parties, but in other pleadings it is sufficient to state the name of the first party on each side with an appropriate indication of other parties. IN ST TRIAL P Rule 10(A).

   b. *Paragraphs; Separate statements.* All averments of a claim or defense shall be made in numbered paragraphs, the contents of each of which shall be limited as far as practicable to a statement of a single set of circumstances, and a paragraph may be referred to by number in all succeeding pleadings. Each claim founded upon a separate transaction or occurrence and each defense other than denials may be stated in a separate count or defense whenever a separation facilitates the clear presentation of the matters set forth. IN ST TRIAL P Rule 10(B).

   c. *Adoption by reference; Exhibits.* Statements in a pleading may be adopted by reference in a different part of the same pleading or in another pleading or in any motion. A copy of any written instrument which is an exhibit to a pleading is a part thereof for all purposes. IN ST TRIAL P Rule 10(C).

   d. *Facsimile page limit.* Courts authorize the Hamilton County Clerk of Courts to accept pleadings, motions and other papers by electronic facsimile transmission for filing in any case pending before the Courts, subject to the requirement that The transmission may not exceed ten (10) pages in length including the cover sheet and proposed CCS entry. IN ST HAMILTON ADMIN Rule 103(103.10)(c).

   e. *Emergency facsimile filings.* If the filing requires the immediate attention of the Judge, it shall so indicate in bold letters in an accompanying transmittal memorandum. IN ST HAMILTON ADMIN Rule 103(103.10)(f).

   f. *Special judge heading.* After a special judge is selected, the attorneys or pro se litigants shall add to the caption of all pleadings to the right of the case title the following: "BEFORE SPECIAL JUDGE _____." IN ST HAMILTON TRIAL Rule 204(204.10).

   g. *Format rules strictly enforced.* All filings shall be in compliance with the Indiana Rules of Trial Procedure. If the documents received are not in proper form, such deficiencies will not be corrected by court personnel. IN ST HAMILTON TRIAL Rule 201(201.70). The Court shall not be required to act on any Motion, Petition or other request for relief unless filed in conformity with the Hamilton County Local Trial and Administrative rules. IN ST HAMILTON TRIAL Rule 202(202.20).

3. *Size of papers for filing.* Effective January 1, 1992, all pleadings, copies, motions and documents filed with any trial court or appellate level court, typed or printed, with the exception of exhibits and existing wills, shall be prepared on eight and one-half by eleven inch (8 1/2" x 11") size paper. IN ST ADMIN Rule 11.

   a. *Form.* All documents filed in any Hamilton County Court, with the exception of exhibits and existing wills, shall be prepared on paper measuring eight and one-half by eleven inches (8 1/2" x 11"). IN ST HAMILTON TRIAL Rule 201(201.20).

4. *Signature requirements*

   a. *Signature of attorney.* Every pleading or motion of a party represented by an attorney shall be signed

by at least one (1) attorney of record in his individual name, whose address, telephone number, and attorney number shall be stated, except that this provision shall not apply to pleadings and motions made and transcribed at the trial or a hearing before the judge and received by him in such form. IN ST TRIAL P Rule 11(A).

    i.   The signature of an attorney constitutes a certificate by him that he has read the pleadings; that to the best of his knowledge, information, and belief, there is good ground to support it; and that it is not interposed for delay. IN ST TRIAL P Rule 11(A).

    ii.   If a pleading or motion is not signed or is signed with intent to defeat the purpose of the rule, it may be stricken as sham and false and the action may proceed as though the pleading had not been served. IN ST TRIAL P Rule 11(A).

    iii.   For a willful violation of IN ST TRIAL P Rule 11 an attorney may be subjected to appropriate disciplinary action. Similar action may be taken if scandalous or indecent matter is inserted. IN ST TRIAL P Rule 11(A).

b.   *Signature of unrepresented party.* A party who is not represented by an attorney shall sign his pleading and state his address. IN ST TRIAL P Rule 11(A).

c.   *Verification not generally required.* Except when specifically required by rule, pleadings or motions need not be verified or accompanied by affidavit. The rule in equity that the averments of an answer under oath must be overcome by the testimony of two (2) witnesses or of one (1) witness sustained by corroborating circumstances is abolished. IN ST TRIAL P Rule 11(A).

d.   *Verification by affirmation or representation.* When in connection with any civil or special statutory proceeding it is required that any pleading, motion, petition, supporting affidavit, or other document of any kind, be verified, or that an oath be taken, it shall be sufficient if the subscriber simply affirms the truth of the matter to be verified by an affirmation or representation. IN ST TRIAL P Rule 11(B). IN ST TRIAL P Rule 11(B) states that the affirmation or representation should be in substantially the following language: "I (we) affirm, under the penalties for perjury, that the foregoing representation(s) is (are) true. (Signed) _____."

    i.   Any person who falsifies an affirmation or representation of fact shall be subject to the same penalties as are prescribed by law for the making of a false affidavit. IN ST TRIAL P Rule 11(B).

e.   *Verified pleadings, motions, and affidavits as evidence.* Pleadings, motions and affidavits accompanying or in support of such pleadings or motions when required to be verified or under oath shall be accepted as a representation that the signer had personal knowledge thereof or reasonable cause to believe the existence of the facts or matters stated or alleged therein; and, if otherwise competent or acceptable as evidence, may be admitted as evidence of the facts or matters stated or alleged therein when it is so provided in the Indiana Rules of Trial Procedure, by statute or other law, or to the extent the writing or signature expressly purports to be made upon the signer's personal knowledge. When such pleadings, motions and affidavits are verified or under oath they shall not require other or greater proof on the part of the adverse party than if not verified or not under oath unless expressly provided otherwise by the Indiana Rules of Trial Procedure, statute or other law. Affidavits upon motions for summary judgment under IN ST TRIAL P Rule 56 and in denial of execution under IN ST TRIAL P Rule 9.2 shall be made upon personal knowledge. IN ST TRIAL P Rule 11(C).

5.   *Information excluded from public access.* Every document filed in a case shall separately identify information excluded from public access pursuant to IN ST ADMIN Rule 9(G)(1) as follows:

a.   Whole documents that are excluded from public access pursuant to IN ST ADMIN Rule 9(G)(1) shall be tendered on light green paper or have a light green coversheet attached to the document, marked "Not for Public Access" or "Confidential." IN ST TRIAL P Rule 5(G)(1).

b.   When only a portion of a document contains information excluded from public access pursuant to IN ST ADMIN Rule 9(G)(1), said information shall be omitted [or redacted] from the filed document, and set forth on a separate accompanying document on light green paper conspicuously marked "Not for Public Access" or "Confidential" and clearly designated [or identifying] the caption and number of the case and the document and location within the document to which the redacted material pertains. IN ST TRIAL P Rule 5(G)(2).

c. With respect to documents filed in electronic format, the trial court, by local rule, may provide for compliance with IN ST TRIAL P Rule 5 in manner that separates and protects access to information excluded from public access. IN ST TRIAL P Rule 5(G)(3).

d. IN ST TRIAL P Rule 5(G) does not apply to a record sealed by the court pursuant to IN ST 5-14-3-5.5 or otherwise, nor to records, documents, or information filed in cases to which public access is prohibited pursuant to IN ST ADMIN Rule 9(G). IN ST TRIAL P Rule 5(G)(4).

e. The following information in case records is excluded from public access and is confidential:

   i. Information that is excluded from public access pursuant to federal law;

   ii. Information that is excluded from public access as declared confidential by Indiana statute or other court rule, including without limitation:

   - All adoption records created after July 8, 1941, as declared confidential by IN ST 31-19-19-1, et seq., except those specifically declared open by IN ST 31-19-13-2(2);

   - All records relating to chancroid, chlamydia, gonorrhea, hepatitis, human immunodeficiency virus (HIV), Lymphogranuloma venereum, syphilis, tuberculosis, as declared confidential by IN ST 16-41-8-1, et seq.;

   - All records relating to child abuse as declared confidential by IN ST 31-33-18-1, et seq.;

   - All records relating to drug tests as declared confidential by IN ST 5-14-3-4(a)(9);

   - Records of grand jury proceedings as declared confidential by IN ST 35-34-2-4;

   - Records of juvenile proceedings as declared confidential by IN ST 31-39-1-2, except those specifically open under statute;

   - All paternity records created after July 1, 1941 as declared confidential by IN ST 31-14-11-15, IN ST 31-19-5-23, IN ST 31-39-1-1 and IN ST 31-39-1-2 [Editor's note: IN ST 31-14-11-15 was repealed effective May 9, 2013];

   - All pre-sentence reports as declared confidential by IN ST 35-38-1-13;

   - Written petitions to permit marriages without consent and orders directing the Clerk of Court to issue a marriage license to underage persons, as declared confidential by IN ST 31-11-1-6;

   - Only those arrest warrants, search warrants, indictments and informations ordered confidential by the trial judge, prior to return of duly executed service as declared confidential by IN ST 5-14-3-4(b)(1);

   - All medical, mental health, or tax records unless determined by law or regulation of any governmental custodian not to be confidential, released by the subject of such records, or declared by a court of competent jurisdiction to be essential to the resolution of litigation as declared confidential by IN ST 16-39-3-10, IN ST 6-4.1-5-10, IN ST 6-4.1-12-12, and IN ST 6-8.1-7-1;

   - Personal information relating to jurors or prospective jurors, other than for the use of the parties and counsel, pursuant to IN ST JURY Rule 10;

   - Information relating to protection from abuse orders, no-contact orders and workplace violence restraining orders as declared confidential by IN ST 5-2-9-6, et seq.;

   - Mediation proceedings pursuant to IN ST ADR Rule 2.11, Mini-Trial proceedings pursuant to IN ST ADR Rule 4.4(C), and Summary Jury Trials pursuant to IN ST ADR Rule 5.6;

   - Information in probation files pursuant to the Probation Standards promulgated by the Judicial Conference of Indiana pursuant to IN ST 11-13-1-8(b);

   - Information deemed confidential pursuant to the Rules for Court Administered Alcohol and Drug Programs promulgated by the Judicial Conference of Indiana pursuant to IN ST 12-23-14-13;

   - Information deemed confidential pursuant to the Problem-Solving Court Rules promulgated by the Judicial Conference of Indiana pursuant to IN ST 33-23-16-16;

- All records of the Department of workforce Development as declared confidential by IN ST 22-4-19-6;
- Information regarding interception of electronic communications that is sealed or deemed confidential as set forth in IN ST 35-33.5-2-1, et seq.

iii. Information excluded from public access by specific court order;

iv. Complete Social Security Numbers of living persons;

v. With the exception of names, information such as addresses, phone numbers, and dates of birth which explicitly identifies:

- Natural persons who are witnesses or victims (not including defendants) in criminal, domestic violence, stalking, sexual assault, juvenile, or civil protection order proceedings, provided that juveniles who are victims of sex crimes shall be identified by initials only;
- Places of residence of judicial officers, clerks and other employees of courts and clerks of court, unless the person or persons about whom the information pertains waives confidentiality;

vi. Complete account numbers of specific assets, loans, bank accounts, credit cards, and personal identification numbers (PINs);

vii. All orders of expungement entered in criminal or juvenile proceedings, orders to restrict access to criminal history information pursuant to IN ST 35-38-5-5.5 or IN ST 35-38-8-5 and records excluded from public access by such orders, and information related to infractions that is excluded from public access pursuant to IN ST 34-28-5-15 or IN ST 34-28-5-16 [Editor's note: IN ST 35-38-5-5.5, IN ST 35-38-8-5 and IN ST 34-28-5-16 were repealed effective July 1, 2013; for information on orders restricting access to criminal history, refer to IN ST 35-38-9-1, et seq.];

viii. All personal notes and e-mail, and deliberative material, of judges, jurors, court staff and judicial agencies, and information recorded in personal data assistants (PDA's) or organizers and personal calendars. IN ST ADMIN Rule 9(G)(1).

F. Filing and Service Requirements

1. *Filing requirements.* Except as otherwise provided in IN ST TRIAL P Rule 5(E)(2), all pleadings and papers subsequent to the complaint which are required to be served upon a party shall be filed with the Court either before service or within a reasonable period of time thereafter. IN ST TRIAL P Rule 5(E)(1).

   a. *Non-filing of discovery until necessary*

      i. *Non-filing of discovery; Exceptions.* No deposition or request for discovery or response thereto under IN ST TRIAL P Rule 27, IN ST TRIAL P Rule 30, IN ST TRIAL P Rule 31, IN ST TRIAL P Rule 33, IN ST TRIAL P Rule 34 or IN ST TRIAL P Rule 36 shall be filed with the Court unless:

         - A motion is filed pursuant to IN ST TRIAL P Rule 26(C) or IN ST TRIAL P Rule 37 and the original deposition or request for discovery or response thereto is necessary to enable the Court to rule; or
         - A party desires to use the deposition or request for discovery or response thereto for evidentiary purposes at trial or in connection with a motion, and the Court, either upon its own motion or that of any party, or as a part of any pre-trial order, orders the filing of the original. IN ST TRIAL P Rule 5(E)(2).

      ii. *Custody of original and period of retention*

         - The original of a deposition shall, subject to the provisions of IN ST TRIAL P Rule 30(E), be delivered by the reporter to the party taking it and shall be maintained by that party until filed with the Court pursuant to IN ST TRIAL P Rule 5(E)(2) or until the later of final judgment, agreed settlement of the litigation or all appellate rights have been exhausted. IN ST TRIAL P Rule 5(E)(3)(a).
         - The original or any request for discovery or response thereto under IN ST TRIAL P Rule

27, IN ST TRIAL P Rule 30, IN ST TRIAL P Rule 31, IN ST TRIAL P Rule 33, IN ST TRIAL P Rule 34 and IN ST TRIAL P Rule 36 shall be maintained by the party originating the request or response until filed with the Court pursuant to IN ST TRIAL P Rule 5(E)(2) or until the later of final judgment, agreed settlement or all appellate rights have been exhausted. IN ST TRIAL P Rule 5(E)(3)(b).

iii. *Original unavailable; Copies.* In the event it is made to appear to the satisfaction of the Court that the original of a deposition or request for discovery or response thereto cannot be filed with the Court when required, the Court may allow use of a copy instead of the original. IN ST TRIAL P Rule 5(E)(4).

iv. *Filing as publication.* The filing of any deposition shall constitute publication. IN ST TRIAL P Rule 5(E)(5).

b. *Filing with the court defined.* The filing of pleadings, motions, and other papers with the court as required by the Indiana Rules of Trial Procedure shall be made by one of the following methods:

i. Delivery to the clerk of the court;

ii. Sending by electronic transmission under the procedure adopted pursuant to IN ST ADMIN Rule 12;

iii. Mailing to the clerk by registered, certified or express mail return receipt requested;

iv. Depositing with any third-party commercial carrier for delivery to the clerk within three (3) calendar days, cost prepaid, properly addressed;

v. If the court so permits, filing with the judge, in which event the judge shall note thereon the filing date and forthwith transmit them to the office of the clerk; or

vi. Electronic filing, as approved by the Division of State Court Administration pursuant to IN ST ADMIN Rule 16. IN ST TRIAL P Rule 5(F).

vii. Filing by registered or certified mail and by third-party commercial carrier shall be complete upon mailing or deposit. IN ST TRIAL P Rule 5(F).

c. *Facsimile filing.* As outlined in IN ST HAMILTON ADMIN Rule 103(103.10),facsimile filing is permitted in the Circuit and Superior Courts of Hamilton County. The Courts authorize the Hamilton County Clerk of Courts to accept pleadings, motions and other papers by electronic facsimile transmission for filing in any case pending before the Courts, subject to the requirements of IN ST HAMILTON ADMIN Rule 103(103.10). IN ST HAMILTON ADMIN Rule 103(103.10); IN ST HAMILTON TRIAL Rule 201(201.80).

i. *Generally.* In counties where a majority of judges of the courts of record, by posted local rule, have authorized electronic facsimile filing and designated a telephone number to receive such transmissions, pleadings, motions, and other papers may be sent to the Clerk of Circuit Court by electronic facsimile transmission for filing in any case, provided:

- Such matter does not exceed ten (10) pages, including the cover sheet;

- Such matter does not require the payment of fees other than the electronic facsimile transcription fee set forth in IN ST ADMIN Rule 12(E);

- The sending party creates at the time of transmission a machine generated log for such transmission; and

- The original document and the transmission log are maintained by the sending party for the duration of the litigation. IN ST ADMIN Rule 12(B); IN ST HAMILTON ADMIN Rule 103(103.10)(d).

- Legibility of documents and timeliness of filing is the responsibility of the sender. IN ST HAMILTON ADMIN Rule 103(103.10)(g).

- The Clerk shall accept electronic facsimile transmission filings only if received at the facsimile machine assigned by the Clerk. The telephone number designated to receive such transmission is available at IN ST HAMILTON ADMIN Rule 103(103.40). IN ST HAMILTON ADMIN Rule 103(103.40).

ii. *Time of filing.* During normal, posted business hours, the time of filing shall be the time the duplicate document is produced in the office of the Clerk of the Circuit Court. Duplicate documents received at all other times shall be filed as of the next normal business day. IN ST ADMIN Rule 12(C).

- If the receiving fax machine endorses its own time and date stamp upon the transmitted documents and the receiving machine produces a delivery receipt which is electronically created and transmitted to the sending party, the time of filing shall be the date and time recorded on the transmitted document by the receiving fax machine. IN ST ADMIN Rule 12(C).

- Electronic facsimile transmissions will be accepted for filing only during the regular business hours as set forth in IN ST HAMILTON ADMIN Rule 101. Transmissions received by the Hamilton County Clerk after close of business shall be filed effective the next regular business day. IN ST HAMILTON ADMIN Rule 103(103.30).

iii. *Filing fee.* The electronic facsimile transmission will not be accepted for filing if its filing requires the payment of any fee other than the electronic facsimile transcription fee set forth in IN ST HAMILTON ADMIN Rule 103(103.20). IN ST HAMILTON ADMIN Rule 103(103.10)(e).

- Pursuant to Ordinance adopted by the Hamilton County Board of Commissioners, the Clerk shall collect an electronic facsimile transcription fee of One Dollar ($1.00) per page, to a maximum of Ten Dollars ($10.00) per transmission, for each electronic facsimile transmission accepted for filing with the Hamilton County Circuit and Superior Courts. IN ST HAMILTON ADMIN Rule 103(103.20).

- The fee shall be assessed against the sending party and shall be paid upon receipt of invoice by that party and at the latest within thirty (30) days of the transmission. In the event the fee is not paid by the sending party within the time limits provided, the court may issue a show-cause order or enter a judgment in the matter. The Clerk may refuse an electronic facsimile transmission from any attorney or pro se litigant who has failed to pay these fees within thirty (30) days. IN ST HAMILTON ADMIN Rule 103(103.20).

iv. *No direct filing with court.* A party shall not send pleadings, motions and other papers by electronic facsimile transmission for filing directly to any Court without that Court's prior approval to do so. IN ST HAMILTON ADMIN Rule 103(103.50).

d. *Filing with special judge.* After a special judge has qualified, a copy of each pleading and Chronological Case Summary entries filed with the Court shall be mailed or delivered to the office of that Special judge by the counsel or pro se litigant with service indicated on the certificate of service. IN ST HAMILTON TRIAL Rule 204(204.20).

e. *Proof of filing.* Any party filing any paper by any method other than personal delivery to the clerk shall retain proof of filing. IN ST TRIAL P Rule 5(F).

2. *Service requirements.* Unless otherwise provided by the Indiana Rules of Trial Procedure or an order of the court, each party and special judge, if any, shall be served with: (1) every order required by its terms to be served; (2) every pleading subsequent to the original complaint; (3) every written motion except one which may be heard ex parte; (4) every brief submitted to the trial court; (5) every paper relating to discovery required to be served upon a party; and (6) every written notice, appearance, demand, offer of judgment, designation of record on appeal, or similar paper. IN ST TRIAL P Rule 5(A).

a. *Methods of service*

i. *Personal service.* Whenever a party is represented by an attorney of record, service shall be made upon such attorney unless service upon the party himself is ordered by the court. Service upon the attorney or party shall be made by delivering or mailing a copy of the papers to the last known address or where an attorney or party has consented to service by fax or e-mail, as provided in IN ST TRIAL P Rule 3.1(A)(4), by faxing or e-mailing a copy of the documents to the fax number or e-mail address set out in the appearance form or correction as required by IN

ST TRIAL P Rule 3.1(E). IN ST TRIAL P Rule 5(B). Delivery of a copy within IN ST TRIAL P Rule 5 means:

- Offering or tendering it to the attorney or party and stating the nature of the papers being served. Refusal to accept an offered or tendered document is a waiver of any objection to the sufficiency or adequacy of service of that document;

- Leaving it at his office with a clerk or other person in charge thereof, or if there is no one in charge, leaving it in a conspicuous place therein; or

- If the office is closed, by leaving it at his dwelling house or usual place of abode with some person of suitable age and discretion then residing therein; or,

- Leaving it at some other suitable place, selected by the attorney upon whom service is being made, pursuant to duly promulgated local rule. IN ST TRIAL P Rule 5(B)(1).

ii. *Service by mail.* If service is made by mail, the papers shall be deposited in the United States mail addressed to the person on whom they are being served, with postage prepaid. Service shall be deemed complete upon mailing. Proof of service of all papers permitted to be mailed may be made by written acknowledgment of service, by affidavit of the person who mailed the papers, or by certificate of an attorney. It shall be the duty of attorneys when entering their appearance in a cause or when filing pleadings or papers therein, to have noted in the Chronological Case Summary or said pleadings or papers so filed the address and telephone number of their office. Service by delivery or by mail at such address shall be deemed sufficient and complete. IN ST TRIAL P Rule 5(B)(2).

iii. *Service by fax or e-mail.* A party who has consented to service by fax or e-mail may be served as follows:

- Service by e-mail shall be made by attaching the document being served in .pdf format. Discovery documents must also be served in accordance with IN ST TRIAL P Rule 26(A). IN ST TRIAL P Rule 5(B)(3)(a).

- Service by fax shall be deemed complete upon generation of a transmission record indicating the successful transmission of the entire document, except as provided in IN ST TRIAL P Rule 5(B)(3)(d). IN ST TRIAL P Rule 5(B)(3)(b).

- Service by e-mail shall be deemed complete upon transmission, except as provided in IN ST TRIAL P Rule 5(B)(3)(d). IN ST TRIAL P Rule 5(B)(3)(c).

- Service by fax or e-mail that occurs on a Saturday, Sunday, legal holiday, or day the court or agency in which the matter is pending is closed or after 5:00 PM local time of the recipient shall be deemed complete the next day that is not a Saturday, Sunday, legal holiday, or day that the court or agency in which the matter is pending is not closed. IN ST TRIAL P Rule 5(B)(3)(d).

iv. *Mail box service.* Pursuant to IN ST TRIAL P Rule 5(B)(1)(d), the Circuit and Superior Courts of Hamilton County hereby designate the "mail boxes" located in the Clerk's order book office for service of pleadings upon attorneys who have such boxes. IN ST HAMILTON TRIAL Rule 201(201.50).

v. *Additional service of electronic discovery.* In addition to service under Rule IN ST TRIAL P Rule 5(B) or a .pdf format electronic copy, a party propounding or responding to interrogatories, requests for production or requests for admission shall comply with IN ST TRIAL P Rule 26(A.1)(a) or IN ST TRIAL P Rule 26(A.1)(b). IN ST TRIAL P Rule 26(A.1).

- The party shall serve the discovery request or response in an electronic format (either on a disk or as an electronic document attachment) in any commercially available word processing software system. If transmitted on disk, each disk shall be labeled, identifying the caption of the case, the document, and the word processing version in which it is being submitted. If more than one (1) disk is used for the same document, each disk shall be labeled and also shall be sequentially numbered. If transmitted by electronic mail, the document must be accompanied by electronic memorandum providing the forgoing identifying information; or

- The party shall serve the opposing party with a verified statement that the attorney or party appealing pro se lacks the equipment and is unable to transmit the discovery as required by IN ST TRIAL P Rule 26(A.1). IN ST TRIAL P Rule 26(A.1).

b. *Serving numerous defendants.* In any action in which there are unusually large numbers of defendants, the court, upon motion or of its own initiative, may order:

   i. That service of the pleadings of the defendants and replies thereto need not be made as between the defendants;

      - That any cross-claim, counterclaim, or matter constituting an avoidance or affirmative defense contained therein shall be deemed to be denied or avoided by all other parties; and

      - That the filing of any such pleading and service thereof upon the plaintiff constitutes due notice of it to the parties. IN ST TRIAL P Rule 5(D).

   ii. A copy of every such order shall be served upon the parties in such manner and form as the court directs. IN ST TRIAL P Rule 5(D).

c. *Service on parties in default for failure to appear.* No service need be made on parties in default for failure to appear, except that pleadings asserting new or additional claims for relief against them shall be served upon them in the manner provided by service of summons in IN ST TRIAL P Rule 4. IN ST TRIAL P Rule 5(A).

G. Hearings

1. The Indiana rules do not contemplate a hearing related to the filing and service of requests for production.

H. Forms

1. Request for Production of Documents Forms for Indiana

a. Request for production of documents. 5 INPRAC § 4:3.1.

b. Request for production of documents; Insurance company. 5 INPRAC § 4:3.2.

c. Request for production of documents; Medical records. 5 INPRAC § 4:3.3.

d. Request for production of documents; Non-party. 5 INPRAC § 4:3.4.

e. Motion to enlarge time to respond to request for production of documents. 5 INPRAC § 4:3.5.

f. Response to request for production of documents; General form with objections. 5 INPRAC § 4:3.6.

g. Request for production of documents; General form. 10 INPRAC § 67.6.

h. Request for entry upon land for inspection. 10 INPRAC § 67.7.

i. Request for production of documents; Products liability; Plaintiff to manufacturer. 10 INPRAC § 67.8.

j. Request for production of documents; Products liability; Property loss; Defendant. 10 INPRAC § 67.9.

k. Request for production of documents; Products liability; Vehicle; Plaintiff. 10 INPRAC § 67.10.

l. Products liability; Defendant to plaintiff regarding accident and injuries. 10 INPRAC § 67.11.

m. Request for production of documents; Action against insurance company. 10 INPRAC § 67.13.

n. Request for production of documents; Action against nursing home; Plaintiff. 10 INPRAC § 67.14.

o. Request for production of documents; Action against nursing home; Defendant. 10 INPRAC § 67.15.

p. Request for production of documents; Medical records. 10 INPRAC § 67.17.

q. Request for production of documents; To obtain corporate records. 10 INPRAC § 67.18.

r. Request for production of handwriting exemplars. 10 INPRAC § 67.19.

s. Response to request for production of documents; General form with objections. 10 INPRAC § 67.30.

t. Response to request for permission to enter upon land. 10 INPRAC § 67.31.

u. Motion to shorten time to respond to request for production. 10 INPRAC § 67.32.

v. Motion to enlarge time to respond to request for production. 10 INPRAC § 67.33.

w. Request for production of documents to nonparty; General form. 10 INPRAC § 67.40.

x. Request for production of documents to nonparty; Another form. 10 INPRAC § 67.41.

y. Request for production of documents to nonparty; Production of bank and financial records. 10 INPRAC § 67.42.

z. Request for production of documents to nonparty; Request that employer produce records relating to employee making personal injury claim. 10 INPRAC § 67.43.

I. Checklist

(I) ❑ Matters to be considered by the party serving the request for production

    (a) ❑ Required documents

        (1) ❑ Request for production of documents

        (2) ❑ Certificate of service

    (b) ❑ Supplemental documents

        (1) ❑ Stipulation regarding discovery procedure

        (2) ❑ Subpoena

        (3) ❑ Facsimile cover sheet

    (c) ❑ Timing

        (1) ❑ On parties: The request may, without leave of court, be served upon the plaintiff after commencement of the action and upon any other party with or after service of the summons and complaint upon that party

        (2) ❑ On non-parties: Neither a request nor subpoena to produce or permit as permitted by IN ST TRIAL P Rule 34 shall be served upon a non-party until at least fifteen (15) days after the date on which the party intending to serve such request or subpoena serves a copy of the proposed request and subpoena on all other parties

            (i) ❑ Provided, however, that if such request or subpoena relates to a matter set for hearing within such fifteen (15) day period or arises out of a bona fide emergency, such request or subpoena may be served upon a non-party one (1) day after receipt of the proposed request or subpoena by all other parties

(II) ❑ Matters to be considered by the responding party

    (a) ❑ Required documents

        (1) ❑ Response to request for production of documents

        (2) ❑ Certificate of service

    (b) ❑ Supplemental documents

        (1) ❑ Business records

        (2) ❑ Stipulation regarding discovery procedure

        (3) ❑ Facsimile cover sheet

    (c) ❑ Timing

        (1) ❑ The party upon whom the request is served shall serve a written response within a period designated in the request, not less than thirty (30) days after the service thereof or within such shorter for longer time as the court may allow

Requests, Notices and Applications
Request for Admissions

Document Last Updated October 2013

A. Applicable Rules

1. *State rules*

   a. Appearance. IN ST TRIAL P Rule 3.1.

   b. Process. IN ST TRIAL P Rule 4.

   c. Service and filing of pleadings and other papers. IN ST TRIAL P Rule 5.

   d. Time. IN ST TRIAL P Rule 6.

   e. Pleadings. IN ST TRIAL P Rule 7; IN ST TRIAL P Rule 9.2; IN ST TRIAL P Rule 10.

   f. Signing and verification of pleadings. IN ST TRIAL P Rule 11.

   g. Pre-trial procedure; Formulating issues. IN ST TRIAL P Rule 16.

   h. General provisions governing discovery. IN ST TRIAL P Rule 26.

   i. Methods of discovery. IN ST TRIAL P Rule 27; IN ST TRIAL P Rule 29; IN ST TRIAL P Rule 30; IN ST TRIAL P Rule 31; IN ST TRIAL P Rule 33; IN ST TRIAL P Rule 34; IN ST TRIAL P Rule 35; IN ST TRIAL P Rule 36.

   j. Failure to make or cooperate in discovery; Sanctions. IN ST TRIAL P Rule 37.

   k. Judgment on the evidence (directed verdict). IN ST TRIAL P Rule 50.

   l. Findings by the court. IN ST TRIAL P Rule 52.

   m. Summary judgment. IN ST TRIAL P Rule 56.

   n. Motion to correct error. IN ST TRIAL P Rule 59.

   o. Relief from judgment or order. IN ST TRIAL P Rule 60.

   p. Access to court records. IN ST ADMIN Rule 9.

   q. Paper size. IN ST ADMIN Rule 11.

   r. Facsimile transmission. IN ST ADMIN Rule 12.

   s. Electronic filing and electronic service pilot projects. IN ST ADMIN Rule 16.

   t. Sealing of certain records by court; Hearing; Notice. IN ST 5-14-3-5.5.

   u. Privacy and confidentiality. IN ST 5-2-9-6; IN ST 5-14-3-4; IN ST 6-4.1-5-10; IN ST 6-4.1-12-12; IN ST 6-8.1-7-1; IN ST 11-13-1-8; IN ST 12-23-14-13; IN ST 16-39-3-10; IN ST 16-41-8-1; IN ST 22-4-19-6; IN ST 31-11-1-6; IN ST 31-19-5-23; IN ST 31-19-13-2; IN ST 31-19-19-1; IN ST 31-33-18-1; IN ST 31-39-1-1; IN ST 31-39-1-2; IN ST 33-23-16-16; IN ST 35-34-2-4; IN ST 35-38-1-13; IN ST 35-38-9-1; IN ST ADR Rule 2.11; IN ST ADR Rule 4.4; IN ST ADR Rule 5.6; IN ST JURY Rule 10.

2. *Local rules*

   a. Court hours. IN ST HAMILTON ADMIN Rule 101.

   b. Facsimile transmissions. IN ST HAMILTON ADMIN Rule 103.

   c. Filing of pleadings and entry of appearances. IN ST HAMILTON TRIAL Rule 201.

   d. Proposed orders. IN ST HAMILTON TRIAL Rule 202.

   e. Special judges. IN ST HAMILTON TRIAL Rule 204.

   f. Continuances. IN ST HAMILTON TRIAL Rule 206.

B. Timing

1. *Time for service of request for admissions.* The request may, without leave of court, be served upon the

plaintiff after commencement of the action and upon any other party with or after service of the summons and complaint upon that party. IN ST TRIAL P Rule 36(A).

2. *Time for service of response.* The matter is admitted unless, within a period designated in the request, not less than thirty (30) days after service thereof or within such shorter or longer time as the court may allow, the party to whom the request is directed serves upon the party requesting the admission a written answer or objection addressed to the matter. IN ST TRIAL P Rule 36(A).

3. *Computation of time*

   a. *Generally; Days excluded.* In computing any period of time prescribed or allowed by the Indiana Rules of Trial Procedure, by order of the court, or by any applicable statute, the day of the act, event, or default from which the designated period of time begins to run shall not be included. The last day of the period so computed is to be included unless it is:

      i. A Saturday,

      ii. A Sunday,

      iii. A legal holiday as defined by state statute, or

      iv. A day the office in which the act is to be done is closed during regular business hours. IN ST TRIAL P Rule 6(A).

   b. *Short periods.* In any event, the period runs until the end of the next day that is not a Saturday, a Sunday, a legal holiday, or a day on which the office is closed. When the period of time allowed is less than seven (7) days, intermediate Saturdays, Sundays, legal holidays, and days on which the office is closed shall be excluded from the computations. IN ST TRIAL P Rule 6(A).

   c. *Additional time after service by United States mail.* Whenever a party has the right or is required to do some act or take some proceedings within a prescribed period after the service of a notice or other paper upon him and the notice or paper is served upon him by United States mail, three (3) days shall be added to the prescribed period. IN ST TRIAL P Rule 6(E).

   d. *Enlargement of time.* When an act is required or allowed to be done at or within a specific time by the Indiana Rules of Trial Procedure, the court may at any time for cause shown:

      i. Order the period enlarged, with or without motion or notice, if request therefor is made before the expiration of the period originally prescribed or extended by a previous order; or

      ii. Upon motion made after the expiration of the specific period, permit the act to be done where the failure to act was the result of excusable neglect; but, the court may not extend the time for taking any action for judgment on the evidence under IN ST TRIAL P Rule 50(A), amendment of findings and judgment under IN ST TRIAL P Rule 52(B), to correct errors under IN ST TRIAL P Rule 59(C), statement in opposition to motion to correct error under IN ST TRIAL P Rule 59(E), or to obtain relief from final judgment under IN ST TRIAL P Rule 60(B), except to the extent and under the conditions stated in those rules. IN ST TRIAL P Rule 6(B).

      iii. For information on obtaining a continuance, refer to IN ST HAMILTON TRIAL Rule 206.

C. General Requirements

1. *Scope of discovery.* Unless otherwise limited by order of the court in accordance with the Indiana Rules of Trial Procedure, the scope of discovery is as follows:

   a. *In general.* Parties may obtain discovery regarding any matter, not privileged, which is relevant to the subject-matter involved in the pending action, whether it relates to the claim or defense of the party seeking discovery or the claim or defense of any other party, including the existence, description, nature, custody, condition and location of any books, documents, or other tangible things and the identity and location of persons having knowledge of any discoverable matter. It is not ground for objection that the information sought will be inadmissible at the trial if the information sought appears reasonably calculated to lead to the discovery of admissible evidence. IN ST TRIAL P Rule 26(B)(1).

      i. *Limiting discovery upon court determination.* The frequency or extent of use of the discovery methods otherwise permitted under the Indiana Rules of Trial Procedure and by any local rule shall be limited by the court if it determines that:

- The discovery sought is unreasonably cumulative or duplicative, or is obtainable from some other source that is more convenient, less burdensome, or less expensive;

- The party seeking discovery has had ample opportunity by discovery in the action to obtain the information sought or;

- The burden or expense of the proposed discovery outweighs its likely benefit, taking into account the needs of the case, the amount in controversy, the parties' resources, the importance of the issues at stake in the litigation, and the importance of the proposed discovery in resolving the issues. IN ST TRIAL P Rule 26(B)(1).

- The court may act upon its own initiative after reasonable notice or pursuant to a motion under IN ST TRIAL P Rule 26(C). IN ST TRIAL P Rule 26(B)(1). Refer to the Indiana KeyRules Motion for Protective Order document for more information.

ii. *Relevancy in the discovery context.* When the word "relevancy" is used in IN ST TRIAL P Rule 26(B), it does not mean "relevancy" as that word in used to determine the admissibility of evidence in a trial court. It is much broader. It means "relevancy" to the "subject matter" of the litigation or pending action and it may relate to the claim or defense of any party. Pretrial discovery is available as to any nonprivileged matter relevant to the subject matter of the lawsuit or to obtain information reasonably calculated to lead to admissible evidence. 2A INPRAC R 26(26.4); Kaufmann v. Credithrift Financial, Inc., 465 N.E.2d 207, 210 (Ind.Ct.App. 1984).

iii. *Tests for relevance.* Indiana case law has developed two (2) additional tests in this area. 2A INPRAC R 26(26.4).

- The first test determines when a document or a request for information is actually relevant to the subject matter in the pending action. A document [or discovery request] is relevant to discovery if there is the possibility the information sought may be relevant to the subject matter of the action. 2A INPRAC R 26(26.4); CIGNA-INA/Aetna v. Hagerman-Shambaugh, 473 N.E.2d 1033, 1036 (Ind.Ct.App. 1985).

- The second test speaks to appellate review of the trial court's determination that a document or discovery request is relevant to the subject matter of the pending action. The appellate court sees its review of the trial court's decision on relevancy to subject matter as being very limited. The court states: "Our review of the trial court's conclusion that the documents are relevant is limited. A trial court is vested with discretion in its rulings on discovery issues." 2A INPRAC R 26(26.4); Costanzi v. Ryan, 175 Ind.App. 257, 370 N.E.2d 1333 (Ind.Ct.App. 1978).

b. *Insurance agreements.* A party may obtain discovery of the existence and contents of any insurance agreement under which any person carrying on an insurance business may be liable to satisfy part or all of a judgment which may be entered in the action or to indemnify or reimburse for payments made to satisfy the judgment. Information concerning the insurance agreement is not by reason of disclosure admissible in evidence at trial. For purposes of IN ST TRIAL P Rule 26(B)(2), an application for insurance shall not be treated as part of an insurance agreement. IN ST TRIAL P Rule 26(B)(2).

c. *Trial preparation; Materials.* Subject to the provisions of IN ST TRIAL P Rule 26(B)(4), a party may obtain discovery of documents and tangible things otherwise discoverable under IN ST TRIAL P Rule 26(B)(1) and prepared in anticipation of litigation or for trial by or for another party or by or for that other party's representative (including his attorney, consultant, surety, indemnitor, insurer, or agent) only upon a showing that the party seeking discovery has substantial need of the materials in the preparation of his case and that he is unable without undue hardship to obtain the substantial equivalent of the materials by other means. In ordering discovery of such materials when the required showing has been made, the court shall protect against disclosure of the mental impressions, conclusions, opinions, or legal theories of an attorney or other representative of a party concerning the litigation. IN ST TRIAL P Rule 26(B)(3).

i. A party may obtain without the required showing a statement concerning the action or its subject matter previously made by that party. Upon request, a person not a party may obtain without the required showing a statement concerning the action or its subject matter previously made by that person. If the request is refused, the person may move for a court order. The provisions of IN ST TRIAL P Rule 37(A)(4) apply to the award of expenses incurred in relation to the motion. For purposes of IN ST TRIAL P Rule 26(B)(3), a statement previously made is:

- A written statement signed or otherwise adopted approved by the person making it, or
- A stenographic, mechanical, electrical, or other recording, or a transcription thereof, which is a substantially verbatim recital of an oral statement by the person making it and contemporaneously recorded. IN ST TRIAL P Rule 26(B)(3).

ii. The protection of IN ST TRIAL P Rule 26(B)(3) extends to material prepared or collected before litigation actually commences, but that some possibility of litigation must actually exist before the privilege and IN ST TRIAL P Rule 26(B)(3) become operative. 2A INPRAC R 26(26.9); CIGNA-INA/Aetna v. Hagerman-Shambaugh, 473 N.E.2d 1033, 1037 (Ind.Ct.App. 1985).

d. *Trial preparation; Experts.* Discovery of facts known and opinions held by experts, otherwise discoverable under the provisions of IN ST TRIAL P Rule 26(B)(1) and acquired or developed in anticipation of litigation or for trial, may be obtained as follows:

i. A party may through interrogatories require any other party to identify each person whom the other party expects to call as an expert witness at trial, to state the subject matter on which the expert is expected to testify, and to state the substance of the facts and opinions to which the expert is expected to testify and a summary of the grounds for each opinion. IN ST TRIAL P Rule 26(B)(4)(a)(i).

ii. Upon motion, the court may order further discovery by other means, subject to such restrictions as to scope and such provisions, pursuant to IN ST TRIAL P Rule 26(B)(4)(c), concerning fees and expenses as the court may deem appropriate. IN ST TRIAL P Rule 26(B)(4)(a)(ii).

iii. A party may discover facts known or opinions held by an expert who has been retained or specially employed by another party in anticipation of litigation or preparation for trial and who is not expected to be called as a witness at trial, only as provided in IN ST TRIAL P Rule 35(B) or upon a showing of exceptional circumstances under which it is impracticable for the party seeking discovery to obtain facts or opinions on the same subject by other means. IN ST TRIAL P Rule 26(B)(4)(b).

iv. Unless manifest injustice would result,

- The court shall require that the party seeking discovery pay the expert a reasonable fee for time spent in responding to discovery under IN ST TRIAL P Rule 26(B)(4)(a)(ii) and IN ST TRIAL P Rule 26(B)(4)(b); and
- With respect to discovery obtained under IN ST TRIAL P Rule 26(B)(4)(a)(ii) the court may require, and with respect to discovery obtained under IN ST TRIAL P Rule 26(B)(4)(b) the court shall require, the party seeking discovery to pay the other party a fair portion of the fees and expenses reasonably incurred by the latter party in obtaining facts and opinions from the expert. IN ST TRIAL P Rule 26(B)(4)(c).

e. *Claims of privilege or protection*

i. *Information withheld.* When a party withholds information otherwise discoverable under the Indiana Rules of Trial Procedure by claiming that it is privileged or subject to protection as trial preparation material, the party shall make the claim expressly and shall describe the nature of the documents, communications, or things not produced or disclosed in a manner that, without revealing information itself privileged or protected, will enable other parties to assess the applicability of the privilege or protection. IN ST TRIAL P Rule 26(B)(5)(a).

ii. *Information produced.* If information is produced in discovery that is subject to a claim of privilege or protection as trial-preparation material, the party making the claim may notify any party that received the information of the claim and the basis for it. After being notified, a party must promptly return, sequester, or destroy the specified information and any copies it has and may not use or disclose the information until the claim is resolved. A receiving party may promptly present the information to the court under seal for a determination of the claim. If the receiving party disclosed the information before being notified, it must take reasonable steps to retrieve it. The producing party must preserve the information until the claim is resolved. IN ST TRIAL P Rule 26(B)(5)(b).

    iii. *Waiver.* The law of discovery has developed some holdings which indicate that "waiver" of a privileged communication in a discovery setting might be more exacting than "waiver" of a privileged communication when the only question at hand is an interpretation of the privilege itself. Thus, in litigation in which several documents are in issue, and some are released inadvertently, there is strong case law that holds that the "inadvertent production" of a privileged document does not constitute a waiver of the attorney-client privilege. 2A INPRAC R 26(26.5); Transamerica Computer Co. v. International Business Machines Corp., 573 F.2d 646 (9th Cir. 1978). Such a rule should be measured against the usual rule which suggests that a voluntary disclosure to a third person will generally suffice to show a waiver of the attorney-client privilege. 2A INPRAC R 26(26.5).

f. *Use not limited.* Unless the court orders otherwise under IN ST TRIAL P Rule 26(C), the frequency of use of the methods listed in IN ST TRIAL P Rule 26(A) is not limited. IN ST TRIAL P Rule 26(A).

g. *Sequence of discovery.* Unless the court upon motion, for the convenience of parties and witnesses and in the interests of justice, orders otherwise, methods of discovery may be used in any sequence and the fact that a party is conducting discovery, whether by deposition or otherwise, shall not operate to delay any other party's discovery. IN ST TRIAL P Rule 26(D).

2. *Request for admissions.* A request for admission is a method of discovery which allows a party to establish facts and information during the discovery stage of the action so that evidence on those matters will not be required at trial. 22 INPRAC § 26.1; Walker v. Employers Ins. of Wausau, 846 N.E.2d 1098 (Ind.Ct.App. 2006); Brown v. Dobbs, 691 N.E.2d 907 (Ind.Ct.App. 1998). Requests for admission under IN ST TRIAL P Rule 36 are designed to simplify and clarify the issues, to cut trial preparation time, and to encourage settlement. 10 INPRAC § 69.1.

a. *Request for admissions generally.* A party may serve upon any other party a written request for the admission, for purposes of the pending action only, of the truth of any matters within the scope of IN ST TRIAL P Rule 26(B) set forth in the request, including the genuineness of any documents described in the request. IN ST TRIAL P Rule 36(A).

b. *Mutually known matters.* Requests for admissions as to matters within the mutual knowledge of both parties are proper. The function of IN ST TRIAL P Rule 36 is to establish admissions that will obviate the necessity of proof and expedite the trial, or to transform "mutual knowledge" into the established facts of a case. 3 INPRAC R 36(36.5).

c. *Requests to be carefully drafted.* The burden on the requesting party is to carefully and artfully draft the statement of fact contained in the request for admission. The statement must be precise, unambiguous, and in no way mislead the answering party. 3 INPRAC R 36(36.2).

    i. Fairness demands that any error arising out of inartful drafting be borne by the requesting party. The burden imposed on the answering party is unfairly "increased when the request for admission propounds a statement of fact which lacks clarity, is ambiguous, or which otherwise might mislead the answering party." 3 INPRAC R 36(36.2); F.W. Means & Co. v. Carstens, 428 N.E.2d 251, 257 (Ind.Ct.App. 1981).

d. *Admissions by the requestor.* Propounding of requests for admissions admits nothing as to the requesting party. 3 INPRAC R 36(36.2); Indiana Construction Service v. Amoco Oil Company, 533 N.E.2d 1300 (Ind.Ct.App. 1989). This party in the action made an admission in the text of or during the request, to which the receiving party, of course, agreed. But it was not binding, as to the requesting party, the court held. Such a request is binding as to the party admitting the fact in response to a request. 3 INPRAC R 36(36.2); Indiana Construction Service v. Amoco Oil Company, 533 N.E.2d 1300 (Ind.Ct.App. 1989).

e. *Motion to compel.* The party who has requested the admissions may move for an order with respect to the answers or objections. Unless the court determines that an objection is justified, it shall order that an answer be served. If the court determines that an answer does not comply with the requirements of IN ST TRIAL P Rule 36, it may order either that the matter is admitted or that an amended answer be served. The court may, in lieu of these orders, determine that final disposition of the request be made at a pre-trial conference or at a designated time prior to trial. IN ST TRIAL P Rule 36(A).

    i.   The provisions of IN ST TRIAL P Rule 37(A)(4) apply to the award of expenses incurred in relation to the motion. IN ST TRIAL P Rule 36(A).

    ii. Refer to the Indiana KeyRules Motion to Compel Discovery document for more information.

3.   *Response to request for admissions.* The matter is admitted unless, within a period designated in the request, not less than thirty (30) days after service thereof or within such shorter or longer time as the court may allow, the party to whom the request is directed serves upon the party requesting the admission a written answer or objection addressed to the matter, signed by the party or by his attorney. IN ST TRIAL P Rule 36(A).

   a.   *Methods of response.* IN ST TRIAL P Rule 36 recognizes at least four (4) responses. The party:

    i.   May not respond, thereby admitting the request; or

    ii. Answer; or

    iii. Object to the request; or

    iv. File a qualified response. 3 INPRAC R 36(36.4).

   b.   *Effect of admission.* Any matter admitted under IN ST TRIAL P Rule 36 is conclusively established unless the court on motion permits withdrawal or amendment of the admission. IN ST TRIAL P Rule 36(B).

    i.   Any admission made by a party under IN ST TRIAL P Rule 36 is for the purpose of the pending action only and is not an admission by him for any other purpose nor may it be used against him in any other proceeding. IN ST TRIAL P Rule 36(B).

   c.   *Denials.* The answer shall specifically deny the matter or set forth in detail the reasons why the answering party cannot truthfully admit or deny the matter. A denial shall fairly meet the substance of the requested admission, and when good faith requires that a party qualify his answer or deny only a part of the matter of which an admission is requested, he shall specify so much of it as is true and qualify or deny the remainder. IN ST TRIAL P Rule 36(A).

   d.   *Lack of information or knowledge.* An answering party may not give lack of information or knowledge as a reason for failure to admit or deny unless he states that he has made reasonable inquiry and that the information known or readily obtainable by him is insufficient to enable him to admit or deny or that the inquiry would be unreasonably burdensome. IN ST TRIAL P Rule 36(A).

   e.   *Objections.* If objection is made, the reasons therefor shall be stated. IN ST TRIAL P Rule 36(A).

    i.   A party who considers that a matter of which an admission has been requested presents a genuine issue for trial may not, on that ground alone, object to the request; he may, subject to the provisions of IN ST TRIAL P Rule 37(C), deny the matter or set forth reasons why he cannot admit or deny it. IN ST TRIAL P Rule 36(A).

    ii. An objectionable request may not be properly attacked by a motion to strike, to dismiss, or to suppress. The party served must respond to the request and serve admissions or denials of all matters not deemed objectionable. 3 INPRAC R 36(36.4).

   f.   *Withdrawal or amendment of admissions.* Subject to the provisions of IN ST TRIAL P Rule 16 governing amendment of a pre-trial order, the court may permit withdrawal or amendment when the presentation of the merits of the action will be subserved thereby and the party who obtained the admission fails to satisfy the court that withdrawal or amendment will prejudice him in maintaining his action or defense on the merits. IN ST TRIAL P Rule 36(B).

    i.   It is within sound discretion of trial court to permit or deny amendment of pretrial order, but trial court should amend or modify pretrial order when requested if modification is necessary to prevent manifest injustice. 2 INPRAC R 16(7); Hacienda Mexican Restaurant of Kalamazoo Corp. v. Hacienda Franchise Group, Inc., 641 N.E.2d 1036 (Ind.Ct.App. 1994).

g. *Supplementation of responses.* A party who has responded to a request for discovery with a response that was complete when made is under no duty to supplement his response to include information thereafter acquired, except as follows:

    i. A party is under a duty seasonally to supplement his response with respect to any question directly addressed to:

- The identity and location of persons having knowledge of discoverable matters, and

- The identity of each person expected to be called as an expert witness at trial, the subject-matter on which he is expected to testify, and the substance of his testimony. IN ST TRIAL P Rule 26(E)(1).

    ii. A party is under a duty seasonally to amend a prior response if he obtains information upon the basis of which:

- He knows that the response was incorrect when made, or

- He knows that the response though correct when made is no longer true and the circumstances are such that a failure to amend the response is in substance a knowing concealment. IN ST TRIAL P Rule 26(E)(2).

    iii. A duty to supplement responses may be imposed by order of the court, agreement of the parties, or at any time prior to trial through new requests for supplementation of prior responses. IN ST TRIAL P Rule 26(E)(3).

    iv. The duty seasonally to supplement a discovery response is absolute and is not predicated on a court order. "It is a breach of a litigant's duty reasonably to supplement if the litigant postpones supplementing its response by not obtaining from its experts the information which is to be supplied in answer to interrogatories." 2A INPRAC R 26(26.27); Lucas v. Dorsey Corp., 609 N.E.2d 1191, 1196 (Ind.Ct.App. 1993).

D. Documents

1. *Required documents*

a. *Request for admissions.* Refer to the General Requirements section of this document for information on the scope and content of a request for admissions.

b. *Copies of documents.* Copies of documents shall be served with the request unless they have been or are otherwise furnished or made available for inspection and copying. IN ST TRIAL P Rule 36(A).

c. *Certificate of service.* An attorney or unrepresented party tendering a document to the Clerk for filing shall certify that service has been made, list the parties served, and specify the date and means of service. The certificate of service shall be placed at the end of the document and shall not be separately filed. The separate filing of a certificate of service, however, shall not be grounds for rejecting a document for filing. The Clerk may permit documents to be filed without a certificate of service but shall require prompt filing of a separate certificate of service. IN ST TRIAL P Rule 5(C).

    i. All pleadings filed with the Court which require a certificate of service shall specifically name the individual party or attorney on whom service has been made, the address, the manner in which service was made and the date when service was made. IN ST HAMILTON TRIAL Rule 201(201.60).

2. *Supplemental documents*

a. *Stipulation regarding discovery procedure.* Unless the court orders otherwise, the parties may by written stipulation:

    i. Provide that depositions may be taken before any person, at any time or place, upon any notice, and in any manner and when so taken may be used like other depositions, and

    ii. Modify the procedures provided by the Indiana Rules of Trial Procedure for other methods of discovery. IN ST TRIAL P Rule 29.

b. *Facsimile cover sheet.* Any document sent to the Clerk of the Circuit Court by electronic facsimile transmission shall be accompanied by a cover sheet which states the title of the document, case number, number of pages, identity and voice telephone number of the sending party and instructions for filing. The cover sheet shall contain the signature of the attorney or party, pro se, authorizing the filing. IN ST ADMIN Rule 12(D); IN ST HAMILTON ADMIN Rule 103(103.10)(a).

E. Format

1. *Form of requests for admissions.* The rules applicable to captions, and the signing and form of pleadings (IN ST TRIAL P Rule 8 through IN ST TRIAL P Rule 11), apply to all motions and other papers provided under the Indiana Rules of Trial Procedure. 22B INPRAC 7:2. Each matter of which an admission is requested shall be separately set forth. IN ST TRIAL P Rule 36(A).

2. *Form of pleadings*

   a. *Caption; Names of parties.* Every pleading shall contain a caption setting forth the name of the court, the title of the action, the file number, and a designation as in IN ST TRIAL P Rule 7(A). In the complaint the title of the action shall include the names of all the parties, but in other pleadings it is sufficient to state the name of the first party on each side with an appropriate indication of other parties. IN ST TRIAL P Rule 10(A).

   b. *Paragraphs; Separate statements.* All averments of a claim or defense shall be made in numbered paragraphs, the contents of each of which shall be limited as far as practicable to a statement of a single set of circumstances, and a paragraph may be referred to by number in all succeeding pleadings. Each claim founded upon a separate transaction or occurrence and each defense other than denials may be stated in a separate count or defense whenever a separation facilitates the clear presentation of the matters set forth. IN ST TRIAL P Rule 10(B).

   c. *Adoption by reference; Exhibits.* Statements in a pleading may be adopted by reference in a different part of the same pleading or in another pleading or in any motion. A copy of any written instrument which is an exhibit to a pleading is a part thereof for all purposes. IN ST TRIAL P Rule 10(C).

   d. *Facsimile page limit.* Courts authorize the Hamilton County Clerk of Courts to accept pleadings, motions and other papers by electronic facsimile transmission for filing in any case pending before the Courts, subject to the requirement that The transmission may not exceed ten (10) pages in length including the cover sheet and proposed CCS entry. IN ST HAMILTON ADMIN Rule 103(103.10)(c).

   e. *Emergency facsimile filings.* If the filing requires the immediate attention of the Judge, it shall so indicate in bold letters in an accompanying transmittal memorandum. IN ST HAMILTON ADMIN Rule 103(103.10)(f).

   f. *Special judge heading.* After a special judge is selected, the attorneys or pro se litigants shall add to the caption of all pleadings to the right of the case title the following: "BEFORE SPECIAL JUDGE _____." IN ST HAMILTON TRIAL Rule 204(204.10).

   g. *Format rules strictly enforced.* All filings shall be in compliance with the Indiana Rules of Trial Procedure. If the documents received are not in proper form, such deficiencies will not be corrected by court personnel. IN ST HAMILTON TRIAL Rule 201(201.70). The Court shall not be required to act on any Motion, Petition or other request for relief unless filed in conformity with the Hamilton County Local Trial and Administrative rules. IN ST HAMILTON TRIAL Rule 202(202.20).

3. *Size of papers for filing.* Effective January 1, 1992, all pleadings, copies, motions and documents filed with any trial court or appellate level court, typed or printed, with the exception of exhibits and existing wills, shall be prepared on eight and one-half by eleven inch (8 1/2" x 11") size paper. IN ST ADMIN Rule 11.

   a. *Form.* All documents filed in any Hamilton County Court, with the exception of exhibits and existing wills, shall be prepared on paper measuring eight and one-half by eleven inches (8 1/2" x 11"). IN ST HAMILTON TRIAL Rule 201(201.20).

4. *Signature requirements*

   a. *Signature of attorney.* Every pleading or motion of a party represented by an attorney shall be signed

by at least one (1) attorney of record in his individual name, whose address, telephone number, and attorney number shall be stated, except that this provision shall not apply to pleadings and motions made and transcribed at the trial or a hearing before the judge and received by him in such form. IN ST TRIAL P Rule 11(A).

    i. The signature of an attorney constitutes a certificate by him that he has read the pleadings; that to the best of his knowledge, information, and belief, there is good ground to support it; and that it is not interposed for delay. IN ST TRIAL P Rule 11(A).

    ii. If a pleading or motion is not signed or is signed with intent to defeat the purpose of the rule, it may be stricken as sham and false and the action may proceed as though the pleading had not been served. IN ST TRIAL P Rule 11(A).

    iii. For a willful violation of IN ST TRIAL P Rule 11 an attorney may be subjected to appropriate disciplinary action. Similar action may be taken if scandalous or indecent matter is inserted. IN ST TRIAL P Rule 11(A).

b. *Signature of unrepresented party.* A party who is not represented by an attorney shall sign his pleading and state his address. IN ST TRIAL P Rule 11(A).

c. *Verification not generally required.* Except when specifically required by rule, pleadings or motions need not be verified or accompanied by affidavit. The rule in equity that the averments of an answer under oath must be overcome by the testimony of two (2) witnesses or of one (1) witness sustained by corroborating circumstances is abolished. IN ST TRIAL P Rule 11(A).

d. *Verification by affirmation or representation.* When in connection with any civil or special statutory proceeding it is required that any pleading, motion, petition, supporting affidavit, or other document of any kind, be verified, or that an oath be taken, it shall be sufficient if the subscriber simply affirms the truth of the matter to be verified by an affirmation or representation. IN ST TRIAL P Rule 11(B). IN ST TRIAL P Rule 11(B) states that the affirmation or representation should be in substantially the following language: "I (we) affirm, under the penalties for perjury, that the foregoing representation(s) is (are) true. (Signed) _____ ."

    i. Any person who falsifies an affirmation or representation of fact shall be subject to the same penalties as are prescribed by law for the making of a false affidavit. IN ST TRIAL P Rule 11(B).

e. *Verified pleadings, motions, and affidavits as evidence.* Pleadings, motions and affidavits accompanying or in support of such pleadings or motions when required to be verified or under oath shall be accepted as a representation that the signer had personal knowledge thereof or reasonable cause to believe the existence of the facts or matters stated or alleged therein; and, if otherwise competent or acceptable as evidence, may be admitted as evidence of the facts or matters stated or alleged therein when it is so provided in the Indiana Rules of Trial Procedure, by statute or other law, or to the extent the writing or signature expressly purports to be made upon the signer's personal knowledge. When such pleadings, motions and affidavits are verified or under oath they shall not require other or greater proof on the part of the adverse party than if not verified or not under oath unless expressly provided otherwise by the Indiana Rules of Trial Procedure, statute or other law. Affidavits upon motions for summary judgment under IN ST TRIAL P Rule 56 and in denial of execution under IN ST TRIAL P Rule 9.2 shall be made upon personal knowledge. IN ST TRIAL P Rule 11(C).

5. *Information excluded from public access.* Every document filed in a case shall separately identify information excluded from public access pursuant to IN ST ADMIN Rule 9(G)(1) as follows:

a. Whole documents that are excluded from public access pursuant to IN ST ADMIN Rule 9(G)(1) shall be tendered on light green paper or have a light green coversheet attached to the document, marked "Not for Public Access" or "Confidential." IN ST TRIAL P Rule 5(G)(1).

b. When only a portion of a document contains information excluded from public access pursuant to IN ST ADMIN Rule 9(G)(1), said information shall be omitted [or redacted] from the filed document, and set forth on a separate accompanying document on light green paper conspicuously marked "Not for Public Access" or "Confidential" and clearly designated [or identifying] the caption and number of the case and the document and location within the document to which the redacted material pertains. IN ST TRIAL P Rule 5(G)(2).

c. With respect to documents filed in electronic format, the trial court, by local rule, may provide for compliance with IN ST TRIAL P Rule 5 in manner that separates and protects access to information excluded from public access. IN ST TRIAL P Rule 5(G)(3).

d. IN ST TRIAL P Rule 5(G) does not apply to a record sealed by the court pursuant to IN ST 5-14-3-5.5 or otherwise, nor to records, documents, or information filed in cases to which public access is prohibited pursuant to IN ST ADMIN Rule 9(G). IN ST TRIAL P Rule 5(G)(4).

e. The following information in case records is excluded from public access and is confidential:

   i.   Information that is excluded from public access pursuant to federal law;

   ii. Information that is excluded from public access as declared confidential by Indiana statute or other court rule, including without limitation:

   - All adoption records created after July 8, 1941, as declared confidential by IN ST 31-19-19-1, et seq., except those specifically declared open by IN ST 31-19-13-2(2);

   - All records relating to chancroid, chlamydia, gonorrhea, hepatitis, human immunodeficiency virus (HIV), Lymphogranuloma venereum, syphilis, tuberculosis, as declared confidential by IN ST 16-41-8-1, et seq.;

   - All records relating to child abuse as declared confidential by IN ST 31-33-18-1, et seq.;

   - All records relating to drug tests as declared confidential by IN ST 5-14-3-4(a)(9);

   - Records of grand jury proceedings as declared confidential by IN ST 35-34-2-4;

   - Records of juvenile proceedings as declared confidential by IN ST 31-39-1-2, except those specifically open under statute;

   - All paternity records created after July 1, 1941 as declared confidential by IN ST 31-14-11-15, IN ST 31-19-5-23, IN ST 31-39-1-1 and IN ST 31-39-1-2 [Editor's note: IN ST 31-14-11-15 was repealed effective May 9, 2013];

   - All pre-sentence reports as declared confidential by IN ST 35-38-1-13;

   - Written petitions to permit marriages without consent and orders directing the Clerk of Court to issue a marriage license to underage persons, as declared confidential by IN ST 31-11-1-6;

   - Only those arrest warrants, search warrants, indictments and informations ordered confidential by the trial judge, prior to return of duly executed service as declared confidential by IN ST 5-14-3-4(b)(1);

   - All medical, mental health, or tax records unless determined by law or regulation of any governmental custodian not to be confidential, released by the subject of such records, or declared by a court of competent jurisdiction to be essential to the resolution of litigation as declared confidential by IN ST 16-39-3-10, IN ST 6-4.1-5-10, IN ST 6-4.1-12-12, and IN ST 6-8.1-7-1;

   - Personal information relating to jurors or prospective jurors, other than for the use of the parties and counsel, pursuant to IN ST JURY Rule 10;

   - Information relating to protection from abuse orders, no-contact orders and workplace violence restraining orders as declared confidential by IN ST 5-2-9-6, et seq.;

   - Mediation proceedings pursuant to IN ST ADR Rule 2.11, Mini-Trial proceedings pursuant to IN ST ADR Rule 4.4(C), and Summary Jury Trials pursuant to IN ST ADR Rule 5.6;

   - Information in probation files pursuant to the Probation Standards promulgated by the Judicial Conference of Indiana pursuant to IN ST 11-13-1-8(b);

   - Information deemed confidential pursuant to the Rules for Court Administered Alcohol and Drug Programs promulgated by the Judicial Conference of Indiana pursuant to IN ST 12-23-14-13;

   - Information deemed confidential pursuant to the Problem-Solving Court Rules promulgated by the Judicial Conference of Indiana pursuant to IN ST 33-23-16-16;

- All records of the Department of workforce Development as declared confidential by IN ST 22-4-19-6;
- Information regarding interception of electronic communications that is sealed or deemed confidential as set forth in IN ST 35-33.5-2-1, et seq.

iii. Information excluded from public access by specific court order;

iv. Complete Social Security Numbers of living persons;

v. With the exception of names, information such as addresses, phone numbers, and dates of birth which explicitly identifies:

- Natural persons who are witnesses or victims (not including defendants) in criminal, domestic violence, stalking, sexual assault, juvenile, or civil protection order proceedings, provided that juveniles who are victims of sex crimes shall be identified by initials only;
- Places of residence of judicial officers, clerks and other employees of courts and clerks of court, unless the person or persons about whom the information pertains waives confidentiality;

vi. Complete account numbers of specific assets, loans, bank accounts, credit cards, and personal identification numbers (PINs);

vii. All orders of expungement entered in criminal or juvenile proceedings, orders to restrict access to criminal history information pursuant to IN ST 35-38-5-5.5 or IN ST 35-38-8-5 and records excluded from public access by such orders, and information related to infractions that is excluded from public access pursuant to IN ST 34-28-5-15 or IN ST 34-28-5-16 [Editor's note: IN ST 35-38-5-5.5, IN ST 35-38-8-5 and IN ST 34-28-5-16 were repealed effective July 1, 2013; for information on orders restricting access to criminal history, refer to IN ST 35-38-9-1, et seq.];

viii. All personal notes and e-mail, and deliberative material, of judges, jurors, court staff and judicial agencies, and information recorded in personal data assistants (PDA's) or organizers and personal calendars. IN ST ADMIN Rule 9(G)(1).

F. Filing and Service Requirements

1. *Filing requirements.* Except as otherwise provided in IN ST TRIAL P Rule 5(E)(2), all pleadings and papers subsequent to the complaint which are required to be served upon a party shall be filed with the Court either before service or within a reasonable period of time thereafter. IN ST TRIAL P Rule 5(E)(1).

   a. *Non-filing of discovery until necessary*

      i. *Non-filing of discovery; Exceptions.* No deposition or request for discovery or response thereto under IN ST TRIAL P Rule 27, IN ST TRIAL P Rule 30, IN ST TRIAL P Rule 31, IN ST TRIAL P Rule 33, IN ST TRIAL P Rule 34 or IN ST TRIAL P Rule 36 shall be filed with the Court unless:

         - A motion is filed pursuant to IN ST TRIAL P Rule 26(C) or IN ST TRIAL P Rule 37 and the original deposition or request for discovery or response thereto is necessary to enable the Court to rule; or
         - A party desires to use the deposition or request for discovery or response thereto for evidentiary purposes at trial or in connection with a motion, and the Court, either upon its own motion or that of any party, or as a part of any pre-trial order, orders the filing of the original. IN ST TRIAL P Rule 5(E)(2).

      ii. *Custody of original and period of retention*

         - The original of a deposition shall, subject to the provisions of IN ST TRIAL P Rule 30(E), be delivered by the reporter to the party taking it and shall be maintained by that party until filed with the Court pursuant to IN ST TRIAL P Rule 5(E)(2) or until the later of final judgment, agreed settlement of the litigation or all appellate rights have been exhausted. IN ST TRIAL P Rule 5(E)(3)(a).
         - The original or any request for discovery or response thereto under IN ST TRIAL P Rule

27, IN ST TRIAL P Rule 30, IN ST TRIAL P Rule 31, IN ST TRIAL P Rule 33, IN ST TRIAL P Rule 34 and IN ST TRIAL P Rule 36 shall be maintained by the party originating the request or response until filed with the Court pursuant to IN ST TRIAL P Rule 5(E)(2) or until the later of final judgment, agreed settlement or all appellate rights have been exhausted. IN ST TRIAL P Rule 5(E)(3)(b).

iii. *Original unavailable; Copies.* In the event it is made to appear to the satisfaction of the Court that the original of a deposition or request for discovery or response thereto cannot be filed with the Court when required, the Court may allow use of a copy instead of the original. IN ST TRIAL P Rule 5(E)(4).

iv. *Filing as publication.* The filing of any deposition shall constitute publication. IN ST TRIAL P Rule 5(E)(5).

b. *Filing with the court defined.* The filing of pleadings, motions, and other papers with the court as required by the Indiana Rules of Trial Procedure shall be made by one of the following methods:

i. Delivery to the clerk of the court;

ii. Sending by electronic transmission under the procedure adopted pursuant to IN ST ADMIN Rule 12;

iii. Mailing to the clerk by registered, certified or express mail return receipt requested;

iv. Depositing with any third-party commercial carrier for delivery to the clerk within three (3) calendar days, cost prepaid, properly addressed;

v. If the court so permits, filing with the judge, in which event the judge shall note thereon the filing date and forthwith transmit them to the office of the clerk; or

vi. Electronic filing, as approved by the Division of State Court Administration pursuant to IN ST ADMIN Rule 16. IN ST TRIAL P Rule 5(F).

vii. Filing by registered or certified mail and by third-party commercial carrier shall be complete upon mailing or deposit. IN ST TRIAL P Rule 5(F).

c. *Facsimile filing.* As outlined in IN ST HAMILTON ADMIN Rule 103(103.10),facsimile filing is permitted in the Circuit and Superior Courts of Hamilton County. The Courts authorize the Hamilton County Clerk of Courts to accept pleadings, motions and other papers by electronic facsimile transmission for filing in any case pending before the Courts, subject to the requirements of IN ST HAMILTON ADMIN Rule 103(103.10). IN ST HAMILTON ADMIN Rule 103(103.10); IN ST HAMILTON TRIAL Rule 201(201.80).

i. *Generally.* In counties where a majority of judges of the courts of record, by posted local rule, have authorized electronic facsimile filing and designated a telephone number to receive such transmissions, pleadings, motions, and other papers may be sent to the Clerk of Circuit Court by electronic facsimile transmission for filing in any case, provided:

- Such matter does not exceed ten (10) pages, including the cover sheet;

- Such matter does not require the payment of fees other than the electronic facsimile transcription fee set forth in IN ST ADMIN Rule 12(E);

- The sending party creates at the time of transmission a machine generated log for such transmission; and

- The original document and the transmission log are maintained by the sending party for the duration of the litigation. IN ST ADMIN Rule 12(B); IN ST HAMILTON ADMIN Rule 103(103.10)(d).

- Legibility of documents and timeliness of filing is the responsibility of the sender. IN ST HAMILTON ADMIN Rule 103(103.10)(g).

- The Clerk shall accept electronic facsimile transmission filings only if received at the facsimile machine assigned by the Clerk. The telephone number designated to receive such transmission is available at IN ST HAMILTON ADMIN Rule 103(103.40). IN ST HAMILTON ADMIN Rule 103(103.40).

ii. *Time of filing.* During normal, posted business hours, the time of filing shall be the time the duplicate document is produced in the office of the Clerk of the Circuit Court. Duplicate documents received at all other times shall be filed as of the next normal business day. IN ST ADMIN Rule 12(C).

- If the receiving fax machine endorses its own time and date stamp upon the transmitted documents and the receiving machine produces a delivery receipt which is electronically created and transmitted to the sending party, the time of filing shall be the date and time recorded on the transmitted document by the receiving fax machine. IN ST ADMIN Rule 12(C).

- Electronic facsimile transmissions will be accepted for filing only during the regular business hours as set forth in IN ST HAMILTON ADMIN Rule 101. Transmissions received by the Hamilton County Clerk after close of business shall be filed effective the next regular business day. IN ST HAMILTON ADMIN Rule 103(103.30).

iii. *Filing fee.* The electronic facsimile transmission will not be accepted for filing if its filing requires the payment of any fee other than the electronic facsimile transcription fee set forth in IN ST HAMILTON ADMIN Rule 103(103.20). IN ST HAMILTON ADMIN Rule 103(103.10)(e).

- Pursuant to Ordinance adopted by the Hamilton County Board of Commissioners, the Clerk shall collect an electronic facsimile transcription fee of One Dollar ($1.00) per page, to a maximum of Ten Dollars ($10.00) per transmission, for each electronic facsimile transmission accepted for filing with the Hamilton County Circuit and Superior Courts. IN ST HAMILTON ADMIN Rule 103(103.20).

- The fee shall be assessed against the sending party and shall be paid upon receipt of invoice by that party and at the latest within thirty (30) days of the transmission. In the event the fee is not paid by the sending party within the time limits provided, the court may issue a show-cause order or enter a judgment in the matter. The Clerk may refuse an electronic facsimile transmission from any attorney or pro se litigant who has failed to pay these fees within thirty (30) days. IN ST HAMILTON ADMIN Rule 103(103.20).

iv. *No direct filing with court.* A party shall not send pleadings, motions and other papers by electronic facsimile transmission for filing directly to any Court without that Court's prior approval to do so. IN ST HAMILTON ADMIN Rule 103(103.50).

d. *Filing with special judge.* After a special judge has qualified, a copy of each pleading and Chronological Case Summary entries filed with the Court shall be mailed or delivered to the office of that Special judge by the counsel or pro se litigant with service indicated on the certificate of service. IN ST HAMILTON TRIAL Rule 204(204.20).

e. *Proof of filing.* Any party filing any paper by any method other than personal delivery to the clerk shall retain proof of filing. IN ST TRIAL P Rule 5(F).

2. *Service requirements.* Unless otherwise provided by the Indiana Rules of Trial Procedure or an order of the court, each party and special judge, if any, shall be served with: (1) every order required by its terms to be served; (2) every pleading subsequent to the original complaint; (3) every written motion except one which may be heard ex parte; (4) every brief submitted to the trial court; (5) every paper relating to discovery required to be served upon a party; and (6) every written notice, appearance, demand, offer of judgment, designation of record on appeal, or similar paper. IN ST TRIAL P Rule 5(A).

a. *Methods of service*

i. *Personal service.* Whenever a party is represented by an attorney of record, service shall be made upon such attorney unless service upon the party himself is ordered by the court. Service upon the attorney or party shall be made by delivering or mailing a copy of the papers to the last known address or where an attorney or party has consented to service by fax or e-mail, as provided in IN ST TRIAL P Rule 3.1(A)(4), by faxing or e-mailing a copy of the documents to the fax number or e-mail address set out in the appearance form or correction as required by IN

ST TRIAL P Rule 3.1(E). IN ST TRIAL P Rule 5(B). Delivery of a copy within IN ST TRIAL P Rule 5 means:

- Offering or tendering it to the attorney or party and stating the nature of the papers being served. Refusal to accept an offered or tendered document is a waiver of any objection to the sufficiency or adequacy of service of that document;

- Leaving it at his office with a clerk or other person in charge thereof, or if there is no one in charge, leaving it in a conspicuous place therein; or

- If the office is closed, by leaving it at his dwelling house or usual place of abode with some person of suitable age and discretion then residing therein; or,

- Leaving it at some other suitable place, selected by the attorney upon whom service is being made, pursuant to duly promulgated local rule. IN ST TRIAL P Rule 5(B)(1).

ii. *Service by mail.* If service is made by mail, the papers shall be deposited in the United States mail addressed to the person on whom they are being served, with postage prepaid. Service shall be deemed complete upon mailing. Proof of service of all papers permitted to be mailed may be made by written acknowledgment of service, by affidavit of the person who mailed the papers, or by certificate of an attorney. It shall be the duty of attorneys when entering their appearance in a cause or when filing pleadings or papers therein, to have noted in the Chronological Case Summary or said pleadings or papers so filed the address and telephone number of their office. Service by delivery or by mail at such address shall be deemed sufficient and complete. IN ST TRIAL P Rule 5(B)(2).

iii. *Service by fax or e-mail.* A party who has consented to service by fax or e-mail may be served as follows:

- Service by e-mail shall be made by attaching the document being served in .pdf format. Discovery documents must also be served in accordance with IN ST TRIAL P Rule 26(A). IN ST TRIAL P Rule 5(B)(3)(a).

- Service by fax shall be deemed complete upon generation of a transmission record indicating the successful transmission of the entire document, except as provided in IN ST TRIAL P Rule 5(B)(3)(d). IN ST TRIAL P Rule 5(B)(3)(b).

- Service by e-mail shall be deemed complete upon transmission, except as provided in IN ST TRIAL P Rule 5(B)(3)(d). IN ST TRIAL P Rule 5(B)(3)(c).

- Service by fax or e-mail that occurs on a Saturday, Sunday, legal holiday, or day the court or agency in which the matter is pending is closed or after 5:00 PM local time of the recipient shall be deemed complete the next day that is not a Saturday, Sunday, legal holiday, or day that the court or agency in which the matter is pending is not closed. IN ST TRIAL P Rule 5(B)(3)(d).

iv. *Mail box service.* Pursuant to IN ST TRIAL P Rule 5(B)(1)(d), the Circuit and Superior Courts of Hamilton County hereby designate the "mail boxes" located in the Clerk's order book office for service of pleadings upon attorneys who have such boxes. IN ST HAMILTON TRIAL Rule 201(201.50).

v. *Additional service of electronic discovery.* In addition to service under Rule IN ST TRIAL P Rule 5(B) or a .pdf format electronic copy, a party propounding or responding to interrogatories, requests for production or requests for admission shall comply with IN ST TRIAL P Rule 26(A.1)(a) or IN ST TRIAL P Rule 26(A.1)(b). IN ST TRIAL P Rule 26(A.1).

- The party shall serve the discovery request or response in an electronic format (either on a disk or as an electronic document attachment) in any commercially available word processing software system. If transmitted on disk, each disk shall be labeled, identifying the caption of the case, the document, and the word processing version in which it is being submitted. If more than one (1) disk is used for the same document, each disk shall be labeled and also shall be sequentially numbered. If transmitted by electronic mail, the document must be accompanied by electronic memorandum providing the forgoing identifying information; or

- The party shall serve the opposing party with a verified statement that the attorney or party appealing pro se lacks the equipment and is unable to transmit the discovery as required by IN ST TRIAL P Rule 26(A.1). IN ST TRIAL P Rule 26(A.1).

b. *Serving numerous defendants.* In any action in which there are unusually large numbers of defendants, the court, upon motion or of its own initiative, may order:

  i. That service of the pleadings of the defendants and replies thereto need not be made as between the defendants;

- That any cross-claim, counterclaim, or matter constituting an avoidance or affirmative defense contained therein shall be deemed to be denied or avoided by all other parties; and

- That the filing of any such pleading and service thereof upon the plaintiff constitutes due notice of it to the parties. IN ST TRIAL P Rule 5(D).

  ii. A copy of every such order shall be served upon the parties in such manner and form as the court directs. IN ST TRIAL P Rule 5(D).

c. *Service on parties in default for failure to appear.* No service need be made on parties in default for failure to appear, except that pleadings asserting new or additional claims for relief against them shall be served upon them in the manner provided by service of summons in IN ST TRIAL P Rule 4. IN ST TRIAL P Rule 5(A).

G. Hearings

1. The Indiana rules do not contemplate a hearing related to the filing and service of requests for admissions.

H. Forms

1. Request for Admissions Forms for Indiana

a. Request for admission. 5 INPRAC § 4:4.1.

b. Response to request for admission. 5 INPRAC § 4:4.2.

c. Response to request for admission; Alternative form. 5 INPRAC § 4:4.3.

d. Motion for order that matter be deemed admitted. 5 INPRAC § 4:4.4.

e. Requests for admission; General form. 10 INPRAC § 69.6.

f. Requests for admission; Genuineness of document. 10 INPRAC § 69.7.

g. Requests for admission; Specific document and matters related thereto; Insurance contract. 10 INPRAC § 69.8.

h. Requests for admission; Action against bank. 10 INPRAC § 69.9.

i. Requests for admission; Automobile accident. 10 INPRAC § 69.10.

j. Requests for admission; Automobile accident; Respondeat superior. 10 INPRAC § 69.11.

k. Requests for admission; Action on account stated. 10 INPRAC § 69.12.

l. Requests for admission; Action to foreclose on mortgage. 10 INPRAC § 69.13.

m. Requests for admission; Action for attorney malpractice. 10 INPRAC § 69.14.

n. Requests for admission; Products liability action; Defective hair products; Defendants. 10 INPRAC § 69.15.

o. Response to requests for admission; General form. 10 INPRAC § 69.20.

p. Alternative responses to requests for admission. 10 INPRAC § 69.21.

q. Motion for enlargement of time to respond to requests for admission. 10 INPRAC § 69.22.

r. Motion to withdraw and amend response to requests for admission. 10 INPRAC § 69.23.

s. Order granting motion to withdraw and amend responses. 10 INPRAC § 69.24.

t. Motion for order that matter be deemed admitted. 10 INPRAC § 69.25.

u. Motion for order requiring party to pay expenses for refusal to admit matters. 10 INPRAC § 69.26.

I. Checklist

(I) ❑ Matters to be considered by the party serving the request

  (a) ❑ Required documents

    (1) ❑ Request for admissions

    (2) ❑ Copies of documents

    (3) ❑ Certificate of service

  (b) ❑ Supplemental documents

    (1) ❑ Stipulation regarding discovery procedure

    (2) ❑ Facsimile cover sheet

  (c) ❑ Timing

    (1) ❑ The request may, without leave of court, be served upon the plaintiff after commencement of the action and upon any other party with or after service of the summons and complaint upon that party

(II) ❑ Matters to be considered by the responding party

  (a) ❑ Required documents

    (1) ❑ Response to request for admissions

    (2) ❑ Certificate of service

  (b) ❑ Supplemental documents

    (1) ❑ Stipulation regarding discovery procedure

    (2) ❑ Facsimile cover sheet

  (c) ❑ Timing

    (1) ❑ The matter is admitted unless, within a period designated in the request, not less than thirty (30) days after service thereof or within such shorter or longer time as the court may allow, the party to whom the request is directed serves upon the party requesting the admission a written answer or objection addressed to the matter

Requests, Notices and Applications
Notice of Deposition

Document Last Updated October 2013

A. Applicable Rules

1. *State rules*

  a. Appearance. IN ST TRIAL P Rule 3.1.

  b. Process. IN ST TRIAL P Rule 4.

  c. Service and filing of pleadings and other papers. IN ST TRIAL P Rule 5.

  d. Time. IN ST TRIAL P Rule 6.

  e. Pleadings. IN ST TRIAL P Rule 7; IN ST TRIAL P Rule 9.2; IN ST TRIAL P Rule 10.

  f. Signing and verification of pleadings. IN ST TRIAL P Rule 11.

  g. Parties plaintiff and defendant; Capacity. IN ST TRIAL P Rule 17.

  h. General provisions governing discovery. IN ST TRIAL P Rule 26.

  i. Discovery methods. IN ST TRIAL P Rule 27; IN ST TRIAL P Rule 28; IN ST TRIAL P Rule 29; IN ST TRIAL P Rule 30; IN ST TRIAL P Rule 31; IN ST TRIAL P Rule 32; IN ST TRIAL P Rule 33; IN ST TRIAL P Rule 34; IN ST TRIAL P Rule 35; IN ST TRIAL P Rule 36.

j. Failure to make or cooperate in discovery; Sanctions. IN ST TRIAL P Rule 37.

k. Evidence. IN ST TRIAL P Rule 43.

l. Subpoena. IN ST TRIAL P Rule 45.

m. Judgment on the evidence (directed verdict). IN ST TRIAL P Rule 50.

n. Findings by the court. IN ST TRIAL P Rule 52.

o. Summary judgment. IN ST TRIAL P Rule 56.

p. Motion to correct error. IN ST TRIAL P Rule 59.

q. Relief from judgment or order. IN ST TRIAL P Rule 60.

r. Recording machines; Court reports; Stenographic report or transcript as evidence. IN ST TRIAL P Rule 74.

s. Access to court records. IN ST ADMIN Rule 9.

t. Paper size. IN ST ADMIN Rule 11.

u. Facsimile transmission. IN ST ADMIN Rule 12.

v. Electronic filing and electronic service pilot projects. IN ST ADMIN Rule 16.

w. Sealing of certain records by court; Hearing; Notice. IN ST 5-14-3-5.5.

x. Privacy and confidentiality. IN ST 5-2-9-6; IN ST 5-14-3-4; IN ST 6-4.1-5-10; IN ST 6-4.1-12-12; IN ST 6-8.1-7-1; IN ST 11-13-1-8; IN ST 12-23-14-13; IN ST 16-39-3-10; IN ST 16-41-8-1; IN ST 22-4-19-6; IN ST 31-11-1-6; IN ST 31-19-5-23; IN ST 31-19-13-2; IN ST 31-19-19-1; IN ST 31-33-18-1; IN ST 31-39-1-1; IN ST 31-39-1-2; IN ST 33-23-16-16; IN ST 35-34-2-4; IN ST 35-38-1-13; IN ST 35-38-9-1; IN ST ADR Rule 2.11; IN ST ADR Rule 4.4; IN ST ADR Rule 5.6; IN ST JURY Rule 10.

2. *Local rules*

a. Court hours. IN ST HAMILTON ADMIN Rule 101.

b. Facsimile transmissions. IN ST HAMILTON ADMIN Rule 103.

c. Filing of pleadings and entry of appearances. IN ST HAMILTON TRIAL Rule 201.

d. Proposed orders. IN ST HAMILTON TRIAL Rule 202.

e. Special judges. IN ST HAMILTON TRIAL Rule 204.

f. Trial settings. IN ST HAMILTON TRIAL Rule 205.

g. Continuances. IN ST HAMILTON TRIAL Rule 206.

B. Timing

1. *Time for notice of deposition*

a. *Depositions upon oral examination.* After commencement of the action, any party may take the testimony of any person, including a party, by deposition upon oral examination. IN ST TRIAL P Rule 30(A).

i. A party desiring to take the deposition of any person upon oral examination shall give reasonable notice in writing to every other party to the action. IN ST TRIAL P Rule 30(B)(1).

- The party who gives notice of taking a deposition must do so in a way which is sufficiently timely to permit the party who receives the notice to make arrangements to travel to the place where the deposition is to be taken, and the notice which is given must be in sufficient time to permit the party to seek a protective order under IN ST TRIAL P Rule 30(D) and IN ST TRIAL P Rule 26(C), if necessary. 2A INPRAC R 30(30.2).

ii. Leave of court, granted with or without notice, must be obtained only if the plaintiff seeks to take a deposition prior to the expiration of twenty (20) days after service of summons and complaint upon any defendant except that leave is not required:

- If a defendant has served a notice of taking deposition or otherwise sought discovery; or

- If special notice is given as provided in IN ST TRIAL P Rule 30(B)(2). IN ST TRIAL P Rule 30(A).

   iii. *Time to respond.* The court may for cause shown enlarge or shorten the time. IN ST TRIAL P Rule 31(A).

b. *Depositions upon written questions.* After commencement of the action, any party may take the testimony of any person, including a party, by deposition upon written questions. IN ST TRIAL P Rule 31(A).

   i. *Service of cross questions.* Within twenty (20) days after the notice and written questions are served, a party may serve cross questions upon all other parties. IN ST TRIAL P Rule 31(A).

   ii. *Service of redirect questions.* Within ten (10) days after being served with cross questions, a party may serve redirect questions upon all other parties. IN ST TRIAL P Rule 31(A).

   iii. *Service of recross questions.* Within ten (10) days after being served with redirect questions, a party may serve recross questions upon all other parties. IN ST TRIAL P Rule 31(A).

   iv. The court may for cause shown enlarge or shorten the time. IN ST TRIAL P Rule 31(A).

c. *For deposition before action.* At least twenty (20) days before the date of hearing the notice shall be served in the manner provided in IN ST TRIAL P Rule 4 for service of summons; but if such service cannot with due diligence be made upon any expected adverse party named in the petition, the court may make such order as is just for service by publication or otherwise, and shall appoint, for persons not served in the manner provided in IN ST TRIAL P Rule 4, an attorney who shall represent them, and, in case they are not otherwise represented, shall cross-examine the deponent. If any expected adverse party is a minor or incompetent the provisions of IN ST TRIAL P Rule 17(C) apply. IN ST TRIAL P Rule 27(A)(2).

   i. Refer to the Indiana KeyRules Complaint document for information regarding service under IN ST TRIAL P Rule 4.

d. *For deposition pending appeal.* The party who desires to perpetuate the testimony may make a motion in the court for leave to take the depositions, upon the same notice and service thereof as if the action was pending in the court. IN ST TRIAL P Rule 27(B).

   i. *Filing.* All pleadings and papers subsequent to the complaint which are required to be served upon a party shall be filed with the Court either before service or within a reasonable period of time thereafter. IN ST TRIAL P Rule 5(E)(1).

   ii. *Service.* A written motion, other than one which may be heard ex parte, and notice of the hearing thereof shall be served not less than five (5) days before the time specified for the hearing, unless a different period is fixed by the Indiana Rules of Trial Procedure or by order of the court. IN ST TRIAL P Rule 6(D).

- *Of supporting affidavits.* When a motion is supported by affidavit, the affidavit shall be served with the motion. IN ST TRIAL P Rule 6(D).

2. *Additional time after service by United States mail.* Whenever a party has the right or is required to do some act or take some proceedings within a prescribed period after the service of a notice or other paper upon him and the notice or paper is served upon him by United States mail, three (3) days shall be added to the prescribed period. IN ST TRIAL P Rule 6(E).

3. *Computation of time*

a. In computing any period of time prescribed or allowed by the Indiana Rules of Trial Procedure, by order of the court, or by any applicable statute, the day of the act, event, or default from which the designated period of time begins to run shall not be included. The last day of the period so computed is to be included unless it is:

   i. A Saturday,

   ii. A Sunday,

   iii. A legal holiday as defined by state statute, or

   iv. A day the office in which the act is to be done is closed during regular business hours. IN ST TRIAL P Rule 6(A).

b. In any event, the period runs until the end of the next day that is not a Saturday, a Sunday, a legal holiday, or a day on which the office is closed. When the period of time allowed is less than seven (7) days, intermediate Saturdays, Sundays, legal holidays, and days on which the office is closed shall be excluded from the computations. IN ST TRIAL P Rule 6(A).

4. *Enlargement of time.* When an act is required or allowed to be done at or within a specific time by the Indiana Rules of Trial Procedure, the court may at any time for cause shown:

a. Order the period enlarged, with or without motion or notice, if request therefor is made before the expiration of the period originally prescribed or extended by a previous order; or

b. Upon motion made after the expiration of the specific period, permit the act to be done where the failure to act was the result of excusable neglect; but, the court may not extend the time for taking any action for judgment on the evidence under IN ST TRIAL P Rule 50(A), amendment of findings and judgment under IN ST TRIAL P Rule 52(B), to correct errors under IN ST TRIAL P Rule 59(C), statement in opposition to motion to correct error under IN ST TRIAL P Rule 59(E), or to obtain relief from final judgment under IN ST TRIAL P Rule 60(B), except to the extent and under the conditions stated in those rules. IN ST TRIAL P Rule 6(B).

C. General Requirements

1. *Scope of discovery.* Unless otherwise limited by order of the court in accordance with the Indiana Rules of Trial Procedure, the scope of discovery is as follows:

a. *In general.* Parties may obtain discovery regarding any matter, not privileged, which is relevant to the subject-matter involved in the pending action, whether it relates to the claim or defense of the party seeking discovery or the claim or defense of any other party, including the existence, description, nature, custody, condition and location of any books, documents, or other tangible things and the identity and location of persons having knowledge of any discoverable matter. It is not ground for objection that the information sought will be inadmissible at the trial if the information sought appears reasonably calculated to lead to the discovery of admissible evidence. IN ST TRIAL P Rule 26(B)(1).

i. *Limiting discovery upon court determination.* The frequency or extent of use of the discovery methods otherwise permitted under the Indiana Rules of Trial Procedure and by any local rule shall be limited by the court if it determines that:

- The discovery sought is unreasonably cumulative or duplicative, or is obtainable from some other source that is more convenient, less burdensome, or less expensive;
- The party seeking discovery has had ample opportunity by discovery in the action to obtain the information sought or;
- The burden or expense of the proposed discovery outweighs its likely benefit, taking into account the needs of the case, the amount in controversy, the parties' resources, the importance of the issues at stake in the litigation, and the importance of the proposed discovery in resolving the issues. IN ST TRIAL P Rule 26(B)(1).
- The court may act upon its own initiative after reasonable notice or pursuant to a motion under IN ST TRIAL P Rule 26(C). IN ST TRIAL P Rule 26(B)(1). Refer to the Indiana KeyRules Motion for Protective Order document for more information.

ii. *Relevancy in the discovery context.* When the word "relevancy" is used in IN ST TRIAL P Rule 26(B), it does not mean "relevancy" as that word in used to determine the admissibility of evidence in a trial court. It is much broader. It means "relevancy" to the "subject matter" of the litigation or pending action and it may relate to the claim or defense of any party. Pretrial discovery is available as to any nonprivileged matter relevant to the subject matter of the lawsuit or to obtain information reasonably calculated to lead to admissible evidence. 2A INPRAC R 26(26.4); Kaufmann v. Credithrift Financial, Inc., 465 N.E.2d 207, 210 (Ind.Ct.App. 1984).

iii. *Tests for relevance.* Indiana case law has developed two (2) additional tests in this area. 2A INPRAC R 26(26.4).

- The first test determines when a document or a request for information is actually relevant to the subject matter in the pending action. A document [or discovery request] is relevant to discovery if there is the possibility the information sought may be relevant to the subject matter of the action. 2A INPRAC R 26(26.4); CIGNA-INA/Aetna v. Hagerman-Shambaugh, 473 N.E.2d 1033, 1036 (Ind.Ct.App. 1985).

- The second test speaks to appellate review of the trial court's determination that a document or discovery request is relevant to the subject matter of the pending action. The appellate court sees its review of the trial court's decision on relevancy to subject matter as being very limited. The court states: "Our review of the trial court's conclusion that the documents are relevant is limited. A trial court is vested with discretion in its rulings on discovery issues." 2A INPRAC R 26(26.4); Costanzi v. Ryan, 175 Ind.App. 257, 370 N.E.2d 1333 (Ind.Ct.App. 1978).

- The second test speaks to appellate review of the trial court's determination that a document or discovery request is relevant to the subject matter of the pending action. The appellate court sees its review of the trial court's decision on relevancy to subject matter as being very limited. The court states: "Our review of the trial court's conclusion that the documents are relevant is limited. A trial court is vested with discretion in its rulings on discovery issues. 2A INPRAC R 26(26.4); Costanzi v. Ryan, 175 Ind.App. 257, 370 N.E.2d 1333 (Ind.Ct.App. 1978).

b. *Insurance agreements.* A party may obtain discovery of the existence and contents of any insurance agreement under which any person carrying on an insurance business may be liable to satisfy part or all of a judgment which may be entered in the action or to indemnify or reimburse for payments made to satisfy the judgment. Information concerning the insurance agreement is not by reason of disclosure admissible in evidence at trial. For purposes of IN ST TRIAL P Rule 26(B)(2), an application for insurance shall not be treated as part of an insurance agreement. IN ST TRIAL P Rule 26(B)(2).

c. *Trial preparation; Materials.* Subject to the provisions of IN ST TRIAL P Rule 26(B)(4), a party may obtain discovery of documents and tangible things otherwise discoverable under IN ST TRIAL P Rule 26(B)(1) and prepared in anticipation of litigation or for trial by or for another party or by or for that other party's representative (including his attorney, consultant, surety, indemnitor, insurer, or agent) only upon a showing that the party seeking discovery has substantial need of the materials in the preparation of his case and that he is unable without undue hardship to obtain the substantial equivalent of the materials by other means. In ordering discovery of such materials when the required showing has been made, the court shall protect against disclosure of the mental impressions, conclusions, opinions, or legal theories of an attorney or other representative of a party concerning the litigation. IN ST TRIAL P Rule 26(B)(3).

  i. A party may obtain without the required showing a statement concerning the action or its subject matter previously made by that party. Upon request, a person not a party may obtain without the required showing a statement concerning the action or its subject matter previously made by that person. If the request is refused, the person may move for a court order. The provisions of IN ST TRIAL P Rule 37(A)(4) apply to the award of expenses incurred in relation to the motion. For purposes of IN ST TRIAL P Rule 26(B)(3), a statement previously made is:

    - A written statement signed or otherwise adopted approved by the person making it, or

    - A stenographic, mechanical, electrical, or other recording, or a transcription thereof, which is a substantially verbatim recital of an oral statement by the person making it and contemporaneously recorded. IN ST TRIAL P Rule 26(B)(3).

  ii. The protection of IN ST TRIAL P Rule 26(B)(3) extends to material prepared or collected before litigation actually commences, but that some possibility of litigation must actually exist before the privilege and IN ST TRIAL P Rule 26(B)(3) become operative. 2A INPRAC R 26(26.9).

d. *Trial preparation; Experts.* Discovery of facts known and opinions held by experts, otherwise discoverable under the provisions of IN ST TRIAL P Rule 26(B)(1) and acquired or developed in anticipation of litigation or for trial, may be obtained as follows:

  i. A party may through interrogatories require any other party to identify each person whom the

other party expects to call as an expert witness at trial, to state the subject matter on which the expert is expected to testify, and to state the substance of the facts and opinions to which the expert is expected to testify and a summary of the grounds for each opinion. IN ST TRIAL P Rule 26(B)(4)(a)(i).

ii. Upon motion, the court may order further discovery by other means, subject to such restrictions as to scope and such provisions, pursuant to IN ST TRIAL P Rule 26(B)(4)(c), concerning fees and expenses as the court may deem appropriate. IN ST TRIAL P Rule 26(B)(4)(a)(ii).

iii. A party may discover facts known or opinions held by an expert who has been retained or specially employed by another party in anticipation of litigation or preparation for trial and who is not expected to be called as a witness at trial, only as provided in IN ST TRIAL P Rule 35(B) or upon a showing of exceptional circumstances under which it is impracticable for the party seeking discovery to obtain facts or opinions on the same subject by other means. IN ST TRIAL P Rule 26(B)(4)(b).

iv. Unless manifest injustice would result,

- The court shall require that the party seeking discovery pay the expert a reasonable fee for time spent in responding to discovery under IN ST TRIAL P Rule 26(B)(4)(a)(ii) and IN ST TRIAL P Rule 26(B)(4)(b); and

- With respect to discovery obtained under IN ST TRIAL P Rule 26(B)(4)(a)(ii) the court may require, and with respect to discovery obtained under IN ST TRIAL P Rule 26(B)(4)(b) the court shall require, the party seeking discovery to pay the other party a fair portion of the fees and expenses reasonably incurred by the latter party in obtaining facts and opinions from the expert. IN ST TRIAL P Rule 26(B)(4).

e. *Claims of privilege or protection*

i. *Information withheld.* When a party withholds information otherwise discoverable under the Indiana Rules of Trial Procedure by claiming that it is privileged or subject to protection as trial preparation material, the party shall make the claim expressly and shall describe the nature of the documents, communications, or things not produced or disclosed in a manner that, without revealing information itself privileged or protected, will enable other parties to assess the applicability of the privilege or protection. IN ST TRIAL P Rule 26(B)(5)(a).

ii. *Information produced.* If information is produced in discovery that is subject to a claim of privilege or protection as trial-preparation material, the party making the claim may notify any party that received the information of the claim and the basis for it. After being notified, a party must promptly return, sequester, or destroy the specified information and any copies it has and may not use or disclose the information until the claim is resolved. A receiving party may promptly present the information to the court under seal for a determination of the claim. If the receiving party disclosed the information before being notified, it must take reasonable steps to retrieve it. The producing party must preserve the information until the claim is resolved. IN ST TRIAL P Rule 26(B)(5)(b).

iii. *Waiver.* The law of discovery has developed some holdings which indicate that "waiver" of a privileged communication in a discovery setting might be more exacting than "waiver" of a privileged communication when the only question at hand is an interpretation of the privilege itself. Thus, in litigation in which several documents are in issue, and some are released inadvertently, there is strong case law that holds that the "inadvertent production" of a privileged document does not constitute a waiver of the attorney-client privilege. 2A INPRAC R 26(26.5); Transamerica Computer Co. v. International Business Machines Corp., 573 F.2d 646 (9th Cir. 1978). Such a rule should be measured against the usual rule which suggests that a voluntary disclosure to a third person will generally suffice to show a waiver of the attorney-client privilege. 2A INPRAC R 26(26.5).

f. *Use not limited.* Unless the court orders otherwise under IN ST TRIAL P Rule 26(C), the frequency of use of the methods listed in IN ST TRIAL P Rule 26(A) is not limited. IN ST TRIAL P Rule 26(A).

g. *Sequence of discovery.* Unless the court upon motion, for the convenience of parties and witnesses

and in the interests of justice, orders otherwise, methods of discovery may be used in any sequence and the fact that a party is conducting discovery, whether by deposition or otherwise, shall not operate to delay any other party's discovery. IN ST TRIAL P Rule 26(D).

2. *Depositions upon oral examination.* IN ST TRIAL P Rule 30 provides for the pre-trial deposition on oral examination of a party, or a witness who is not a party. 2A INPRAC R 30(30.1).

   a. *Generally.* The deposition may be used to narrow issues, or to create and enlarge them. It will eliminate matters that are not disputed among the parties; it might introduce new issues and questions which become disputed. The range and purpose of the deposition's use is almost limitless, as long as it is taken consistent with IN ST TRIAL P Rule 26 and IN ST TRIAL P Rule 30 and the principles of IN ST TRIAL P Rule 32. The deposition may obtain evidence that is admissible at trial; it may go quite beyond admissibility at trial if the area of investigation is relevant to the subject matter of the case under IN ST TRIAL P Rule 26. It can disclose the existence and availability of facts that may lead to evidence which may be used at trial. 2A INPRAC R 30(30.1).

   b. *Notice*

      i. *Contents of notice.* The notice shall state the time and place for taking the deposition and the name and address of each person to be examined, if known, and if the name is not known, a general description sufficient to identify him or the particular class or group to which he belongs. If a subpoena duces tecum is to be served on the person to be examined, a designation of the materials to be produced thereunder shall be attached to or included in the notice. IN ST TRIAL P Rule 30(B)(1).

      ii. *Circumstances where leave of court required.* Leave of court, when required by IN ST TRIAL P Rule 30(A) is not required for the taking of a deposition by plaintiff if the notice:

         • States that the person to be examined is about to go out of the state or will be unavailable for examination unless his deposition is taken before expiration of the twenty (20) day period; and

         • Sets forth facts to support the statement. IN ST TRIAL P Rule 30(B)(2).

      iii. *Signature on notice.* The plaintiff's attorney shall sign the notice, and his signature constitutes a certification by him that to the best of his knowledge, information, and belief the statement and supporting facts are true. The sanctions provided by IN ST TRIAL P Rule 11 are applicable to the certification. IN ST TRIAL P Rule 30(B).

      iv. *Manner of recording.* If a party taking a deposition wishes to have the testimony recorded other than in a manner provided in IN ST TRIAL P Rule 74, the notice shall specify the manner of recording and preserving the deposition. The court may require stenographic taking or make any other order to assure that the recorded testimony will be accurate and trustworthy. IN ST TRIAL P Rule 30(B)(4).

      v. *Organization as deponent; Designation.* A party may in his notice name as the deponent an organization, including without limitation a governmental organization, or a partnership and designate with reasonable particularity the matters on which examination is requested. The organization so named shall designate one or more officers, directors, or managing agents, executive officers, or other persons duly authorized and consenting to testify on its behalf. The persons so designated shall testify as to matters known or available to the organization. IN ST TRIAL P Rule 30(B)(6) does not preclude taking a deposition by any other procedure authorized in the Indiana Rules of Trial Procedure. IN ST TRIAL P Rule 30(B)(6).

   c. *Improper service of notice.* If any party shows that when he was served with notice under IN ST TRIAL P Rule 30(B)(2) he was unable through the exercise of diligence to obtain counsel to represent him at the taking of the deposition, the deposition may not be used against him. IN ST TRIAL P Rule 30(B).

   d. *Examination and cross-examination; Record of examination; Oath; Objections.* Examination and cross-examination of witnesses may proceed as permitted at the trial under the provisions of IN ST TRIAL P Rule 43(B). The officer before whom the deposition is to be taken shall put the witness on oath and shall personally, or by someone acting under his direction and in his presence, record the

589

testimony of the witness. The testimony shall be taken stenographically or recorded by any other means designated in accordance with IN ST TRIAL P Rule 30(B)(4). If requested by one of the parties, the testimony shall be transcribed. IN ST TRIAL P Rule 30(C).

   i.   *Objections*

- All objections made at the time of the examination to the qualifications of the officer taking the deposition, or to the manner of taking it, or to the evidence presented, or to the conduct of any party, and any other objection to the proceedings, shall be noted by the officer upon the deposition. IN ST TRIAL P Rule 30(C).

- When there is an objection to a question, the objection and reason therefor shall be noted, and the question shall be answered unless the attorney instructs the deponent not to answer, or the deponent refuses to answer, in which case either party may have the question certified by the Reporter, and the question with the objection thereto when so certified shall be delivered to the party requesting the certification who may then proceed under IN ST TRIAL P Rule 37(A). IN ST TRIAL P Rule 30(C).

- In lieu of participating in the oral examination, parties may serve written questions on the party taking the deposition and require him to transmit them to the officer, who shall propound them to the witness and record the answers verbatim. IN ST TRIAL P Rule 30(C).

   e.   *Motion to terminate or limit examination.* At any time during the taking of the deposition, on motion of any party or of the deponent and upon a showing that the examination is being conducted in bad faith or in such manner as unreasonably to annoy, embarrass, or oppress the deponent or party, the court in which the action is pending or the court in the county where the deposition is being taken may order the officer conducting the examination to cease forthwith from taking the deposition, or may limit the scope and manner of the taking of the deposition as provided in IN ST TRIAL P Rule 26(C). IN ST TRIAL P Rule 30(D).

   i.   If the order made terminates the examination, it shall be resumed thereafter only upon the order of the court in which the action is pending. IN ST TRIAL P Rule 30(D).

   ii. Upon demand of the objecting party or deponent the taking of the deposition shall be suspended for the time necessary to make a motion for an order. The provisions of IN ST TRIAL P Rule 37(A)(4) apply to the award of expenses incurred in relation to the motion. IN ST TRIAL P Rule 30(D).

   iii. Refer to the Indiana KeyRules Motion for Protective Order and Motion for Discovery Sanctions documents for more information.

   f.   *Submission to witness; Changes; Signing*

   i.   When the testimony is fully transcribed, the deposition shall be submitted to the witness for reading and signing and shall be read to or by him, unless such reading and signing have been waived by the witness and by each party. "Submitted to the witness" as used in IN ST TRIAL P Rule 30(E)(1) shall mean:

- Mailing of written notification by registered or certified mail to the witness and each attorney attending the deposition that the deposition can be read and examined in the office of the officer before whom the deposition was taken, or

- Mailing the original deposition, by registered or certified mail, to the witness at an address designated by the witness or his attorney, if requested to do so by the witness, his attorney, or the party taking the deposition. IN ST TRIAL P Rule 30(E)(1).

   ii. If the witness desires to change any answer in the deposition submitted to him, each change, with a statement of the reason therefor, shall be made by the witness on a separate form provided by the officer, shall be signed by the witness and affixed to the original deposition by the officer. A copy of such changes shall be furnished by the officer to each party. IN ST TRIAL P Rule 30(E)(2).

   iii. If the reading and signing have not been waived by the witness and by each party the deposition shall be signed by the witness and returned by him to the officer within thirty (30) days after it is submitted to the witness. If the deposition has been returned to the officer and has not been signed by the witness, the officer shall execute a certificate of that fact, attach it to the original deposition and deliver it to the party taking it. In such event, the deposition may be used by any party with the same force and effect as though it had been signed by the witness. IN ST TRIAL P Rule 30(E)(3).

    iv.   In the event the deposition is not returned to the officer within thirty (30) days after it has been submitted to the witness, the reporter shall execute a certificate of that fact and cause the certificate to be delivered to the party taking it. In such event, any party may use a copy of the deposition with the same force and effect as though the original had been signed by the witness. IN ST TRIAL P Rule 30(E)(4).

  g. *Certification and filing; Exhibits; Copies*

    i.   The officer shall certify on the deposition that the witness was duly sworn by him and that the deposition is a true record of the testimony given by the witness. He shall then securely seal the deposition in an envelope endorsed with the title of the action and marked "Deposition of (here insert name of witness)" and shall promptly deliver it to the party taking the deposition. IN ST TRIAL P Rule 30(F)(1). Documents and things, unless objection is made to their production for inspection during the examination of the witness, shall be marked for identification and annexed to and returned with the deposition, and may be inspected and copied by any party, except that:

- The person producing the materials may substitute copies to be marked for identification, if he affords to all parties fair opportunity to verify the copies by comparison with the originals; and

- If the person producing the materials requests their return the officer shall mark them, give each party an opportunity to inspect and copy them, and return them to the person producing them, and the materials may then be used in the same manner as if annexed to and returned with the deposition. IN ST TRIAL P Rule 30(F)(1).

    ii.   Upon payment of reasonable charges therefor, the officer shall furnish a copy of the deposition to any party or the deponent. IN ST TRIAL P Rule 30(F)(2).

    iii.   The officer taking the deposition shall give prompt notice to all parties of its delivery to the party taking the deposition. IN ST TRIAL P Rule 30(F)(3).

    iv.   The filing of depositions shall be in accordance with the provisions of IN ST TRIAL P Rule 5(E). IN ST TRIAL P Rule 30(F)(4).

  h. *Failure to attend or to serve subpoena; Expenses*

    i.   If the party giving the notice of the taking of a deposition fails to attend and proceed therewith and another party attends in person or by attorney pursuant to the notice, the court may order the party giving the notice to pay to such other party the amount of the reasonable expenses incurred by him and his attorney in so attending, including reasonable attorney's fees. IN ST TRIAL P Rule 30(G)(1).

    ii.   If the party giving the notice of the taking of a deposition of a witness other than a party fails to serve a subpoena upon him and the witness because of such failure does not attend, and if another party attends in person or by attorney because he expects the deposition of that witness to be taken, the court may order the party giving the notice to pay to such other party the amount of the reasonable expenses incurred by him and his attorney in so attending, including reasonable attorney's fees. IN ST TRIAL P Rule 30(G)(2).

  i. *Depositions of prisoners.* The deposition of a person confined in prison may be taken only by leave of court on such terms as the court prescribes. IN ST TRIAL P Rule 30(A).

  j. *Cost of deposition.* In Indiana the rule is that the party who initiates a deposition pays for the cost necessarily incurred as a result of the deposition. Those costs are: (1) the stenographic reporter's fees, (2) the transcription and filing fees, and (3) transportation costs and perhaps other costs which might naturally arise in a particular situation. 2A INPRAC R 30(30.8); Briggs v. Clinton County Bank & Trust Co. of Frankfort, Ind., 452 N.E.2d 989, 1009 (Ind.Ct.App. 1983).

3.   *Deposition upon written questions.* The use of written questions under IN ST TRIAL P Rule 31 is often not as effective as taking a deposition on oral examination, and is generally, as a practical matter, not suitable for complicated cases or where cross-examination is necessary, as in the case of a reluctant or hostile witness. Written questions are, however, an inexpensive device where simple or formal facts are sought. 2A INPRAC R 31(31.1).

   a.   *Notice.* A party desiring to take a deposition upon written questions shall serve them upon every other party with a notice stating:

      i.   The name and address of the person who is to answer them, if known, and if the name is not known, a general description sufficient to identify him or the particular class or group to which he belongs; and

      ii.   The name or descriptive title and address of the officer before whom the deposition is to be taken. IN ST TRIAL P Rule 31(A).

   b.   *Depositions of specific persons*

      i.   *Prisoners.* The deposition of a person confined in prison may be taken only by leave of court on such terms as the court prescribes. IN ST TRIAL P Rule 31(A).

      ii.   *Organization.* A deposition upon written questions may be taken of an organization, including a governmental organization, or a partnership in accordance with the provisions of IN ST TRIAL P Rule 30(B)(6). IN ST TRIAL P Rule 31(A).

   c.   *Officer to take responses and prepare record.* A copy of the notice and copies of all questions served shall be delivered by the party taking the deposition to the officer designated in the notice, who shall proceed promptly, in the manner provided by IN ST TRIAL P Rule 30(C), IN ST TRIAL P Rule 30(E), and IN ST TRIAL P Rule 30(F), to take the testimony of the witness in response to the questions and to prepare, certify, and deliver the deposition, attaching thereto the copy of the notice and the questions received by him, in accordance with IN ST TRIAL P Rule 5(E). IN ST TRIAL P Rule 31(B).

   d.   *Notice of filing.* When the deposition is filed the party taking it shall promptly give notice thereof to all other parties. IN ST TRIAL P Rule 31(C).

4.   *Depositions before action or pending appeal*

   a.   *Use of deposition to perpetuate testimony.* IN ST TRIAL P Rule 27 does not exist to provide a method of discovery to determine whether a cause of action exists. Rather, the rule is intended to be used to "memorialize" evidence that is already known. Accordingly, a trial court should not grant a motion to perpetuate testimony by deposition on the mere possibility that witnesses may be transferred or leave current employment. 2A INPRAC R 27(27.2). IN ST TRIAL P Rule 27 is available for use "when a certain witness' testimony might become unavailable over time, and not to provide a method of discovery to determine whether a cause of action exits." 2A INPRAC R 27(27.2); Petition of Gary Construction, Inc., 96 F.R.D. 432 (D.C.Colo. 1983); Petition of Gurnsey, 223 F.Supp. 359 (D.D.C. 1963).

   b.   *Before action; Petition required*

      i.   *Petition.* A person who desires to perpetuate his own testimony or that of another person regarding any matter that may be cognizable in any court in which the action may be commenced, may file a verified petition in any such court of this state. IN ST TRIAL P Rule 27(A)(1). The petition shall be entitled in the name of the petitioner and shall state facts showing:

         •   That the petitioner expects to be a party to an action cognizable in a court of this or another state;

         •   The subject-matter of the expected action and his interest therein;

         •   The facts which he desires to establish by the proposed testimony and his reasons for desiring to perpetuate it;

- The names or a description of the persons he expects will be adverse parties and their addresses so far as known; and

- The names and addresses of the persons to be examined and the substance of the testimony which he expects to elicit from each, and shall ask for an order authorizing the petitioner to take the depositions of the persons to be examined named in the petition, for the purpose of perpetuating their testimony. IN ST TRIAL P Rule 27(A)(1).

    ii. *Notice and service.* The petitioner shall thereafter serve a notice upon each person named in the petition as an expected adverse party, together with a copy of the petition, stating that the petitioner will apply to the court, at a time and place named therein, for the order described in the petition. IN ST TRIAL P Rule 27(A)(2).

    iii. *Order and examination.* If the court is satisfied that the perpetuation of the testimony may prevent a failure or delay of justice, it shall make an order designating or describing the persons whose depositions may be taken and specifying the subject-matter of the examination or written interrogatories. The depositions may then be taken in accordance with the Indiana Rules of Trial Procedure; and the court may make orders of the character provided for by IN ST TRIAL P Rule 34 and IN ST TRIAL P Rule 35. For the purpose of applying the Indiana Rules of Trial Procedure to depositions for perpetuating testimony, each reference therein to the court in which the action is pending shall be deemed to refer to the court in which the petition for such deposition was filed. IN ST TRIAL P Rule 27(A)(3).

    iv. *Use of deposition.* If a deposition to perpetuate testimony is taken under the Indiana Rules of Trial Procedure or if, although not so taken, it would be admissible in evidence in the court of the state in which it is taken, it may be used in any action involving the same subject-matter subsequently brought in a court of this state in accordance with the provision of IN ST TRIAL P Rule 32. IN ST TRIAL P Rule 27(A)(3).

c. *Pending appeal.* If an appeal has been taken from a judgment of any court or before the taking of an appeal if the time therefor has not expired, the court in which the judgment was rendered may allow the taking of the depositions of witnesses to perpetuate their testimony for use in the event of further proceedings in such court. In such case the party who desires to perpetuate the testimony may make a motion in the court for leave to take the depositions, upon the same notice and service thereof as if the action was pending in the court. IN ST TRIAL P Rule 27(B).

    i. The motion shall show:

- The names and addresses of the persons to be examined and the substance of the testimony which he expects to elicit from each;

- The reasons for perpetuating their testimony. IN ST TRIAL P Rule 27(B).

    ii. If the court finds that the perpetuation of the testimony is proper to avoid a failure or delay of justice, it may make an order allowing the depositions to be taken and may make orders of the character provided for by IN ST TRIAL P Rule 34 and IN ST TRIAL P Rule 35, and thereupon the depositions may be taken and used in the same manner and under the same conditions as are prescribed in the Indiana Rules of Trial Procedure for depositions taken in actions pending in the court. IN ST TRIAL P Rule 27(B).

d. *Perpetuation by action.* IN ST TRIAL P Rule 27 does not limit the power of a court to entertain an action to perpetuate testimony. IN ST TRIAL P Rule 27(C).

e. *Filing deposition.* The filing or custody of any deposition or evidence obtained under IN ST TRIAL P Rule 27 shall be in accordance with IN ST TRIAL P Rule 5(E). IN ST TRIAL P Rule 27(D).

5. *Persons before whom depositions may be taken; Discovery across state lines; Before administrative agencies; And after judgment*

a. *Within the United States.* Within the United States or within a territory or insular possession subject to the dominion of the United States, depositions shall be taken before an officer authorized to administer oaths by the laws of the United States, or of the state of Indiana, or of the place where the examination is held, or before a person appointed by the court in which the action is pending. A person so appointed has power to administer oaths and take testimony. IN ST TRIAL P Rule 28(A).

b. *In foreign countries*

    i.   In a foreign country, depositions may be taken:

- On notice before a person authorized to administer oaths in the place in which the examination is held, either by the law thereof or by the law of the United States; or

- Before a person commissioned by the court, and a person so commissioned shall have the power by virtue of his commission to administer any necessary oath and take testimony; or

- Pursuant to a letter rogatory. IN ST TRIAL P Rule 28(B).

    ii. A commission or a letter rogatory shall be issued on application and notice and on terms that are just and appropriate. It is not requisite to the issuance of a commission or a letter rogatory that the taking of the deposition in any other manner is impracticable or inconvenient; and both a commission and a letter rogatory may be issued in proper cases. A notice or commission may designate the person before whom the deposition is to be taken either by name or descriptive title. A letter rogatory may be addressed "To the Appropriate Authority in (here name the country)." Evidence obtained in response to a letter rogatory need not be excluded merely for the reason that it is not a verbatim transcript or that the testimony was not taken under oath or for any similar departure from the requirements for depositions taken within the United States under the Indiana Rules of Trial Procedure. IN ST TRIAL P Rule 28(B).

c. *Disqualification for interest.* Unless otherwise permitted by the Indiana Rules of Trial Procedure, no deposition shall be taken before a person who is a relative or employee or attorney or counsel of any of the parties, or is a relative or employee of such attorney or counsel, or is financially interested in the action. IN ST TRIAL P Rule 28(C).

    i.   Disqualification of the person before whom the deposition is taken is one of the matters which is waived under IN ST TRIAL P Rule 32(D)(3) unless objection is made as soon as the disqualification is known or could have been known by reasonable diligence. 2A INPRAC R 28(28.3).

d. *Scope of discovery outside state; Protective and enforcement orders.* A deposition may be taken outside the state as provided in IN ST TRIAL P Rule 28(A) and IN ST TRIAL P Rule 28(B), and the deponent may be requested to produce documents and things, and may also be requested to allow inspections and copies as provided in IN ST TRIAL P Rule 34 to submit to examination under IN ST TRIAL P Rule 35. Protective orders may be granted by the court in which the action is pending and by the court where discovery is being made. Enforcement orders may be made by the court where the discovery is sought, and enforcement orders and sanctions may be made by the court where the action is pending as against parties and as against witnesses subject to the jurisdiction of the court. When no action is pending, a court of this state may authorize a deposition to be taken outside this state of any person and upon any matters allowed by IN ST TRIAL P Rule 27. IN ST TRIAL P Rule 28(D).

e. *Assistance to tribunals and litigants outside this state.* A court of this state may order a person who is domiciled or is found within this state to give his testimony or statement or to produce documents or other things, allow inspections and copies and permit physical and mental examinations for use in a proceeding in a tribunal outside this state. The order may be made upon the application of any interested person or in response to a letter rogatory and may prescribe the practice and procedure, which may be wholly or in part the practice and procedure of the tribunal outside this state, for taking the testimony or statement or producing the documents or other things. To the extent that the order does not prescribe otherwise, the practice and procedure shall be in accordance with that of the court of this state issuing the order. The order may direct that the testimony or statement be given, or document or other thing produced, before a person appointed by the court. The person appointed shall have power to administer any necessary oath. A person within this state may voluntarily give his testimony or statement or produce documents or other things allowing inspections and copies and permit physical and mental examinations for use in a proceeding before a tribunal outside this state. IN ST TRIAL P Rule 28(E).

f. *Discovery proceedings before administrative agencies.* Whenever an adjudicatory hearing, including any hearing in any proceeding subject to judicial review, is held by or before an administrative agency, any party to that adjudicatory hearing shall be entitled to use the discovery provisions of IN ST TRIAL P Rule 26 through IN ST TRIAL P Rule 37. Such discovery may include any relevant matter in the custody and control of the administrative agency. IN ST TRIAL P Rule 28(F).

    i. Protective and other orders shall be obtained first from the administrative agency, and if enforcement of such orders or right of discovery is necessary, it may be obtained in a court of general jurisdiction in the county where discovery is being made or sought, or where the hearing is being held. IN ST TRIAL P Rule 28(F).

  g. *Applicability of other laws.* IN ST TRIAL P Rule 28 does not repeal or modify any other law of this state permitting another procedure for obtaining discovery for use in this state or in a tribunal outside this state, except as expressly provided in the Indiana Rules of Trial Procedure. IN ST TRIAL P Rule 28(G).

  h. *Discovery after judgment.* Discovery after judgment may be had in proceedings to enforce or to challenge the judgment. IN ST TRIAL P Rule 28(H).

6. *Supplementation of responses.* A party who has responded to a request for discovery with a response that was complete when made is under no duty to supplement his response to include information thereafter acquired, except as follows:

  a. A party is under a duty seasonably to supplement his response with respect to any question directly addressed to:

    i. The identity and location of persons having knowledge of discoverable matters, and

    ii. The identity of each person expected to be called as an expert witness at trial, the subject-matter on which he is expected to testify, and the substance of his testimony. IN ST TRIAL P Rule 26(E)(1).

  b. A party is under a duty seasonably to amend a prior response if he obtains information upon the basis of which:

    i. He knows that the response was incorrect when made, or

    ii. He knows that the response though correct when made is no longer true and the circumstances are such that a failure to amend the response is in substance a knowing concealment. IN ST TRIAL P Rule 26(E)(2).

  c. A duty to supplement responses may be imposed by order of the court, agreement of the parties, or at any time prior to trial through new requests for supplementation of prior responses. IN ST TRIAL P Rule 26(E)(3).

  d. The duty seasonably to supplement a discovery response is absolute and is not predicated on a court order. "It is a breach of a litigant's duty reasonably to supplement if the litigant postpones supplementing its response by not obtaining from its experts the information which is to be supplied in answer to interrogatories." 2A INPRAC R 26(26.27); Lucas v. Dorsey Corp., 609 N.E.2d 1191, 1196 (Ind.Ct.App. 1993).

D. Documents

1. *Deposition upon oral examination*

  a. *Required documents*

    i. *Notice of deposition.* Refer to the General Requirements section of this document for information on the content of a notice of deposition.

    ii. *Certificate of service.* An attorney or unrepresented party tendering a document to the Clerk for filing shall certify that service has been made, list the parties served, and specify the date and means of service. The certificate of service shall be placed at the end of the document and shall not be separately filed. The separate filing of a certificate of service, however, shall not be grounds for rejecting a document for filing. The Clerk may permit documents to be filed without a certificate of service but shall require prompt filing of a separate certificate of service. IN ST TRIAL P Rule 5(C).

       • All pleadings filed with the Court which require a certificate of service shall specifically name the individual party or attorney on whom service has been made, the address, the manner in which service was made and the date when service was made. IN ST HAMIL-TON TRIAL Rule 201(201.60).

b. *Supplemental documents*

    i. *Subpoena/subpoena duces tecum.* The attendance of witnesses may be compelled by the use of subpoena as provided in IN ST TRIAL P Rule 45. IN ST TRIAL P Rule 30(A).

- Proof of service of a notice to take a deposition as provided in IN ST TRIAL P Rule 30(B) and IN ST TRIAL P Rule 31(A) constitutes a sufficient authorization for the issuance by the clerk of court for the county in which the deposition is to be taken of subpoenas for the persons named or described therein. The subpoena may command the person to whom it is directed to produce designated books, papers, documents, or tangible things which constitute or contain matters within the scope of the examination permitted by IN ST TRIAL P Rule 26(B), but in that event the subpoena will be subject to the provisions of IN ST TRIAL P Rule 26(C) and IN ST TRIAL P Rule 45(B). IN ST TRIAL P Rule 45(D)(1).

- An individual may be required to attend an examination only in the county wherein he resides or is employed or transacts his business in person, or at such other convenient place as is fixed by an order of court. A nonresident of the state may be required to attend only in the state and county wherein he is served with a subpoena, or within forty (40) miles from the place of service, or at such other convenient place as is fixed by an order of court. A non-resident plaintiff may be required to attend at his own expense an examination in the county of this state where the action is commenced or in a county fixed by the court. IN ST TRIAL P Rule 45(D)(2).

    ii. *Request for production.* The notice to a deponent may be accompanied by a request made in compliance with IN ST TRIAL P Rule 34 for the production of documents and tangible things at the taking of the deposition. IN ST TRIAL P Rule 30(B)(5).

    iii. *Stipulation regarding discovery procedure.* Unless the court orders otherwise, the parties may by written stipulation:

- Provide that depositions may be taken before any person, at any time or place, upon any notice, and in any manner and when so taken may be used like other depositions, and

- Modify the procedures provided by the Indiana Rules of Trial Procedure for other methods of discovery. IN ST TRIAL P Rule 29.

    iv. *Facsimile cover sheet.* Any document sent to the Clerk of the Circuit Court by electronic facsimile transmission shall be accompanied by a cover sheet which states the title of the document, case number, number of pages, identity and voice telephone number of the sending party and instructions for filing. The cover sheet shall contain the signature of the attorney or party, pro se, authorizing the filing. IN ST ADMIN Rule 12(D); IN ST HAMILTON ADMIN Rule 103(103.10)(a).

2. *Deposition upon written questions*

a. *Required documents*

    i. *Notice of deposition.* Refer to the General Requirements section of this document for information on the content of a notice of deposition.

    ii. *Certificate of service.* An attorney or unrepresented party tendering a document to the Clerk for filing shall certify that service has been made, list the parties served, and specify the date and means of service. The certificate of service shall be placed at the end of the document and shall not be separately filed. The separate filing of a certificate of service, however, shall not be grounds for rejecting a document for filing. The Clerk may permit documents to be filed without a certificate of service but shall require prompt filing of a separate certificate of service. IN ST TRIAL P Rule 5(C).

- All pleadings filed with the Court which require a certificate of service shall specifically name the individual party or attorney on whom service has been made, the address, the manner in which service was made and the date when service was made. IN ST HAMIL-TON TRIAL Rule 201(201.60).

b. *Supplemental documents*

    i. *Subpoena.* The attendance of witnesses may be compelled by the use of subpoena as provided in IN ST TRIAL P Rule 45. IN ST TRIAL P Rule 31(A).

- Proof of service of a notice to take a deposition as provided in IN ST TRIAL P Rule 30(B) and IN ST TRIAL P Rule 31(A) constitutes a sufficient authorization for the issuance by the clerk of court for the county in which the deposition is to be taken of subpoenas for the persons named or described therein. The subpoena may command the person to whom it is directed to produce designated books, papers, documents, or tangible things which constitute or contain matters within the scope of the examination permitted by IN ST TRIAL P Rule 26(B), but in that event the subpoena will be subject to the provisions of IN ST TRIAL P Rule 26(C) and IN ST TRIAL P Rule 45(B). IN ST TRIAL P Rule 45(D)(1).

- An individual may be required to attend an examination only in the county wherein he resides or is employed or transacts his business in person, or at such other convenient place as is fixed by an order of court. A nonresident of the state may be required to attend only in the state and county wherein he is served with a subpoena, or within forty (40) miles from the place of service, or at such other convenient place as is fixed by an order of court. A non-resident plaintiff may be required to attend at his own expense an examination in the county of this state where the action is commenced or in a county fixed by the court. IN ST TRIAL P Rule 45(D)(2).

    ii. *Stipulation regarding discovery procedure.* Unless the court orders otherwise, the parties may by written stipulation:

- Provide that depositions may be taken before any person, at any time or place, upon any notice, and in any manner and when so taken may be used like other depositions, and

- Modify the procedures provided by the Indiana Rules of Trial Procedure for other methods of discovery. IN ST TRIAL P Rule 29.

    iii. *Facsimile cover sheet.* Any document sent to the Clerk of the Circuit Court by electronic facsimile transmission shall be accompanied by a cover sheet which states the title of the document, case number, number of pages, identity and voice telephone number of the sending party and instructions for filing. The cover sheet shall contain the signature of the attorney or party, pro se, authorizing the filing. IN ST ADMIN Rule 12(D); IN ST HAMILTON ADMIN Rule 103(103.10)(a).

3. *Deposition before action*

a. *Required documents*

    i. *Notice of deposition.* Refer to the General Requirements section of this document for information on the contents of a notice of deposition.

    ii. *Petition.* Refer to the General Requirements section of this document for information on the content of a petition.

    iii. *Certificate of service.* An attorney or unrepresented party tendering a document to the Clerk for filing shall certify that service has been made, list the parties served, and specify the date and means of service. The certificate of service shall be placed at the end of the document and shall not be separately filed. The separate filing of a certificate of service, however, shall not be grounds for rejecting a document for filing. The Clerk may permit documents to be filed without a certificate of service but shall require prompt filing of a separate certificate of service. IN ST TRIAL P Rule 5(C).

- All pleadings filed with the Court which require a certificate of service shall specifically name the individual party or attorney on whom service has been made, the address, the manner in which service was made and the date when service was made. IN ST HAMIL-TON TRIAL Rule 201(201.60).

b. *Supplemental documents*

   i. *Stipulation regarding discovery procedure.* Unless the court orders otherwise, the parties may by written stipulation:

   - Provide that depositions may be taken before any person, at any time or place, upon any notice, and in any manner and when so taken may be used like other depositions, and

   - Modify the procedures provided by the Indiana Rules of Trial Procedure for other methods of discovery. IN ST TRIAL P Rule 29.

   ii. *Facsimile cover sheet.* Any document sent to the Clerk of the Circuit Court by electronic facsimile transmission shall be accompanied by a cover sheet which states the title of the document, case number, number of pages, identity and voice telephone number of the sending party and instructions for filing. The cover sheet shall contain the signature of the attorney or party, pro se, authorizing the filing. IN ST ADMIN Rule 12(D); IN ST HAMILTON ADMIN Rule 103(103.10)(a).

4. *Deposition pending appeal*

   a. *Required documents*

   i. *Motion for leave to take deposition and notice.* The requirement of notice is satisfied by service of the motion. IN ST TRIAL P Rule 7(B).

   ii. *Proposed order.* Unless local practice provides differently, a party should submit a proposed order with its written motion to be signed by the judge once the motion has been granted. 21 INPRAC § 13.8; IN ST HAMILTON ADMIN Rule 103(103.10)(b). Each Motion, Petition or other request for relief shall be accompanied by a proposed order. IN ST HAMILTON TRIAL Rule 202(202.10).

   - All proposed orders submitted by counsel pursuant to IN ST HAMILTON TRIAL Rule 202 shall meet the following requirements: (1) contain a complete distribution list of all attorneys and pro se litigants with full addresses; (2) stamped envelopes appropriately addressed for each attorney of record and/or pro se litigant on the distribution list. IN ST HAMILTON TRIAL Rule 202(202.30).

   iii. *Certificate of service.* An attorney or unrepresented party tendering a document to the Clerk for filing shall certify that service has been made, list the parties served, and specify the date and means of service. The certificate of service shall be placed at the end of the document and shall not be separately filed. The separate filing of a certificate of service, however, shall not be grounds for rejecting a document for filing. The Clerk may permit documents to be filed without a certificate of service but shall require prompt filing of a separate certificate of service. IN ST TRIAL P Rule 5(C).

   - All pleadings filed with the Court which require a certificate of service shall specifically name the individual party or attorney on whom service has been made, the address, the manner in which service was made and the date when service was made. IN ST HAMIL-TON TRIAL Rule 201(201.60).

   b. *Supplemental documents*

   i. *Stipulation regarding discovery procedure.* Unless the court orders otherwise, the parties may by written stipulation:

   - Provide that depositions may be taken before any person, at any time or place, upon any notice, and in any manner and when so taken may be used like other depositions, and

   - Modify the procedures provided by the Indiana Rules of Trial Procedure for other methods of discovery. IN ST TRIAL P Rule 29.

   ii. *Supporting evidence.* When a motion is based on facts not appearing of record the court may hear the matter on affidavits presented by the respective parties, but the court may direct that the matter be heard wholly or partly on oral testimony or depositions. IN ST TRIAL P Rule 43(B).

   iii. *Facsimile cover sheet.* Any document sent to the Clerk of the Circuit Court by electronic facsimile transmission shall be accompanied by a cover sheet which states the title of the document, case number, number of pages, identity and voice telephone number of the sending party and instructions for filing. The cover sheet shall contain the signature of the attorney or party, pro se, authorizing the filing. IN ST ADMIN Rule 12(D); IN ST HAMILTON ADMIN Rule 103(103.10)(a).

iv. *Request to schedule hearing.* All requests to schedule trials and hearings shall be in writing and shall contain the following information:

- Type of trial or hearing (i.e., jury trial, court trial, final hearing in dissolution, etc.). IN ST HAMILTON TRIAL Rule 205(205.10).

- A good-faith estimate of the total court time needed for the trial or hearing. IN ST HAMILTON TRIAL Rule 205(205.10).

- Each request under IN ST HAMILTON TRIAL Rule 205(205.10) shall be accompanied by a proposed written order with appropriate blanks for date and time and shall further include reference to those items set forth in IN ST HAMILTON TRIAL Rule 205(205.10)(a) and IN ST HAMILTON TRIAL Rule 205(205.10)(b). IN ST HAMILTON TRIAL Rule 205(205.20).

v. *Copies of unpublished opinions.* Authorities relied upon which are not cited in the Northeastern Reporter system shall be attached to counsel's brief. If the authority is cited for the first time in oral argument, a copy of the authority may be provided to the Court at the time of the argument. Sufficient copies shall be available to provide counsel for each party with a copy. IN ST HAMILTON TRIAL Rule 203(203.10).

E. Format

1. *Form of notice.* The rules applicable to captions, and the signing and form of pleadings (IN ST TRIAL P Rule 8 through IN ST TRIAL P Rule 11), apply to all motions and other papers provided under the Indiana Rules of Trial Procedure. 22B INPRAC 7:2.

2. *Form of pleadings*

a. *Caption; Names of parties.* Every pleading shall contain a caption setting forth the name of the court, the title of the action, the file number, and a designation as in IN ST TRIAL P Rule 7(A). In the complaint the title of the action shall include the names of all the parties, but in other pleadings it is sufficient to state the name of the first party on each side with an appropriate indication of other parties. IN ST TRIAL P Rule 10(A).

b. *Paragraphs; Separate statements.* All averments of a claim or defense shall be made in numbered paragraphs, the contents of each of which shall be limited as far as practicable to a statement of a single set of circumstances, and a paragraph may be referred to by number in all succeeding pleadings. Each claim founded upon a separate transaction or occurrence and each defense other than denials may be stated in a separate count or defense whenever a separation facilitates the clear presentation of the matters set forth. IN ST TRIAL P Rule 10(B).

c. *Adoption by reference; Exhibits.* Statements in a pleading may be adopted by reference in a different part of the same pleading or in another pleading or in any motion. A copy of any written instrument which is an exhibit to a pleading is a part thereof for all purposes. IN ST TRIAL P Rule 10(C).

d. *Facsimile page limit.* Courts authorize the Hamilton County Clerk of Courts to accept pleadings, motions and other papers by electronic facsimile transmission for filing in any case pending before the Courts, subject to the requirement that The transmission may not exceed ten (10) pages in length including the cover sheet and proposed CCS entry. IN ST HAMILTON ADMIN Rule 103(103.10)(c).

e. *Emergency facsimile filings.* If the filing requires the immediate attention of the Judge, it shall so indicate in bold letters in an accompanying transmittal memorandum. IN ST HAMILTON ADMIN Rule 103(103.10)(f).

f. *Special judge heading.* After a special judge is selected, the attorneys or pro se litigants shall add to the caption of all pleadings to the right of the case title the following: "BEFORE SPECIAL JUDGE _____." IN ST HAMILTON TRIAL Rule 204(204.10).

g. *Format rules strictly enforced.* All filings shall be in compliance with the Indiana Rules of Trial Procedure. If the documents received are not in proper form, such deficiencies will not be corrected by court personnel. IN ST HAMILTON TRIAL Rule 201(201.70). The Court shall not be required to act on any Motion, Petition or other request for relief unless filed in conformity with the Hamilton County Local Trial and Administrative rules. IN ST HAMILTON TRIAL Rule 202(202.20).

3. *Size of papers for filing.* Effective January 1, 1992, all pleadings, copies, motions and documents filed with any trial court or appellate level court, typed or printed, with the exception of exhibits and existing wills, shall be prepared on eight and one-half by eleven inch (8 1/2" x 11") size paper. IN ST ADMIN Rule 11.

a. *Form.* All documents filed in any Hamilton County Court, with the exception of exhibits and existing wills, shall be prepared on paper measuring eight and one-half by eleven inches (8 1/2" x 11"). IN ST HAMILTON TRIAL Rule 201(201.20).

4. *Signature requirements*

a. *Signature of attorney.* Every pleading or motion of a party represented by an attorney shall be signed by at least one (1) attorney of record in his individual name, whose address, telephone number, and attorney number shall be stated, except that this provision shall not apply to pleadings and motions made and transcribed at the trial or a hearing before the judge and received by him in such form. IN ST TRIAL P Rule 11(A).

   i. The signature of an attorney constitutes a certificate by him that he has read the pleadings; that to the best of his knowledge, information, and belief, there is good ground to support it; and that it is not interposed for delay. IN ST TRIAL P Rule 11(A).

   ii. If a pleading or motion is not signed or is signed with intent to defeat the purpose of the rule, it may be stricken as sham and false and the action may proceed as though the pleading had not been served. IN ST TRIAL P Rule 11(A).

   iii. For a willful violation of IN ST TRIAL P Rule 11 an attorney may be subjected to appropriate disciplinary action. Similar action may be taken if scandalous or indecent matter is inserted. IN ST TRIAL P Rule 11(A).

b. *Signature of unrepresented party.* A party who is not represented by an attorney shall sign his pleading and state his address. IN ST TRIAL P Rule 11(A).

c. *Verification not generally required.* Except when specifically required by rule, pleadings or motions need not be verified or accompanied by affidavit. The rule in equity that the averments of an answer under oath must be overcome by the testimony of two (2) witnesses or of one (1) witness sustained by corroborating circumstances is abolished. IN ST TRIAL P Rule 11(A).

d. *Verification by affirmation or representation.* When in connection with any civil or special statutory proceeding it is required that any pleading, motion, petition, supporting affidavit, or other document of any kind, be verified, or that an oath be taken, it shall be sufficient if the subscriber simply affirms the truth of the matter to be verified by an affirmation or representation. IN ST TRIAL P Rule 11(B). IN ST TRIAL P Rule 11(B) states that the affirmation or representation should be in substantially the following language: "I (we) affirm, under the penalties for perjury, that the foregoing representation(s) is (are) true. (Signed) _____."

   i. Any person who falsifies an affirmation or representation of fact shall be subject to the same penalties as are prescribed by law for the making of a false affidavit. IN ST TRIAL P Rule 11(B).

e. *Verified pleadings, motions, and affidavits as evidence.* Pleadings, motions and affidavits accompanying or in support of such pleadings or motions when required to be verified or under oath shall be accepted as a representation that the signer had personal knowledge thereof or reasonable cause to believe the existence of the facts or matters stated or alleged therein; and, if otherwise competent or acceptable as evidence, may be admitted as evidence of the facts or matters stated or alleged therein when it is so provided in the Indiana Rules of Trial Procedure, by statute or other law, or to the extent the writing or signature expressly purports to be made upon the signer's personal knowledge. When such pleadings, motions and affidavits are verified or under oath they shall not require other or greater proof on the part of the adverse party than if not verified or not under oath unless expressly provided otherwise by the Indiana Rules of Trial Procedure, statute or other law. Affidavits upon motions for summary judgment under IN ST TRIAL P Rule 56 and in denial of execution under IN ST TRIAL P Rule 9.2 shall be made upon personal knowledge. IN ST TRIAL P Rule 11(C).

5. *Information excluded from public access.* Every document filed in a case shall separately identify information excluded from public access pursuant to IN ST ADMIN Rule 9(G)(1) as follows:

   a. Whole documents that are excluded from public access pursuant to IN ST ADMIN Rule 9(G)(1) shall be tendered on light green paper or have a light green coversheet attached to the document, marked "Not for Public Access" or "Confidential." IN ST TRIAL P Rule 5(G)(1).

   b. When only a portion of a document contains information excluded from public access pursuant to IN ST ADMIN Rule 9(G)(1), said information shall be omitted [or redacted] from the filed document, and set forth on a separate accompanying document on light green paper conspicuously marked "Not for Public Access" or "Confidential" and clearly designated [or identifying] the caption and number of the case and the document and location within the document to which the redacted material pertains. IN ST TRIAL P Rule 5(G)(2).

   c. With respect to documents filed in electronic format, the trial court, by local rule, may provide for compliance with IN ST TRIAL P Rule 5 in manner that separates and protects access to information excluded from public access. IN ST TRIAL P Rule 5(G)(3).

   d. IN ST TRIAL P Rule 5(G) does not apply to a record sealed by the court pursuant to IN ST 5-14-3-5.5 or otherwise, nor to records, documents, or information filed in cases to which public access is prohibited pursuant to IN ST ADMIN Rule 9(G). IN ST TRIAL P Rule 5(G)(4).

   e. The following information in case records is excluded from public access and is confidential:

      i. Information that is excluded from public access pursuant to federal law;

      ii. Information that is excluded from public access as declared confidential by Indiana statute or other court rule, including without limitation:

      - All adoption records created after July 8, 1941, as declared confidential by IN ST 31-19-19-1, et seq., except those specifically declared open by IN ST 31-19-13-2(2);

      - All records relating to chancroid, chlamydia, gonorrhea, hepatitis, human immunodeficiency virus (HIV), Lymphogranuloma venereum, syphilis, tuberculosis, as declared confidential by IN ST 16-41-8-1, et seq.;

      - All records relating to child abuse as declared confidential by IN ST 31-33-18-1, et seq.;

      - All records relating to drug tests as declared confidential by IN ST 5-14-3-4(a)(9);

      - Records of grand jury proceedings as declared confidential by IN ST 35-34-2-4;

      - Records of juvenile proceedings as declared confidential by IN ST 31-39-1-2, except those specifically open under statute;

      - All paternity records created after July 1, 1941 as declared confidential by IN ST 31-14-11-15, IN ST 31-19-5-23, IN ST 31-39-1-1 and IN ST 31-39-1-2 [Editor's note: IN ST 31-14-11-15 was repealed effective May 9, 2013];

      - All pre-sentence reports as declared confidential by IN ST 35-38-1-13;

      - Written petitions to permit marriages without consent and orders directing the Clerk of Court to issue a marriage license to underage persons, as declared confidential by IN ST 31-11-1-6;

      - Only those arrest warrants, search warrants, indictments and informations ordered confidential by the trial judge, prior to return of duly executed service as declared confidential by IN ST 5-14-3-4(b)(1);

      - All medical, mental health, or tax records unless determined by law or regulation of any governmental custodian not to be confidential, released by the subject of such records, or declared by a court of competent jurisdiction to be essential to the resolution of litigation as declared confidential by IN ST 16-39-3-10, IN ST 6-4.1-5-10, IN ST 6-4.1-12-12, and IN ST 6-8.1-7-1;

- Personal information relating to jurors or prospective jurors, other than for the use of the parties and counsel, pursuant to IN ST JURY Rule 10;

- Information relating to protection from abuse orders, no-contact orders and workplace violence restraining orders as declared confidential by IN ST 5-2-9-6, et seq.;

- Mediation proceedings pursuant to IN ST ADR Rule 2.11, Mini-Trial proceedings pursuant to IN ST ADR Rule 4.4(C), and Summary Jury Trials pursuant to IN ST ADR Rule 5.6;

- Information in probation files pursuant to the Probation Standards promulgated by the Judicial Conference of Indiana pursuant to IN ST 11-13-1-8(b);

- Information deemed confidential pursuant to the Rules for Court Administered Alcohol and Drug Programs promulgated by the Judicial Conference of Indiana pursuant to IN ST 12-23-14-13;

- Information deemed confidential pursuant to the Problem-Solving Court Rules promulgated by the Judicial Conference of Indiana pursuant to IN ST 33-23-16-16;

- All records of the Department of workforce Development as declared confidential by IN ST 22-4-19-6;

- Information regarding interception of electronic communications that is sealed or deemed confidential as set forth in IN ST 35-33.5-2-1, et seq.

iii. Information excluded from public access by specific court order;

iv. Complete Social Security Numbers of living persons;

v. With the exception of names, information such as addresses, phone numbers, and dates of birth which explicitly identifies:

- Natural persons who are witnesses or victims (not including defendants) in criminal, domestic violence, stalking, sexual assault, juvenile, or civil protection order proceedings, provided that juveniles who are victims of sex crimes shall be identified by initials only;

- Places of residence of judicial officers, clerks and other employees of courts and clerks of court, unless the person or persons about whom the information pertains waives confidentiality;

vi. Complete account numbers of specific assets, loans, bank accounts, credit cards, and personal identification numbers (PINs);

vii. All orders of expungement entered in criminal or juvenile proceedings, orders to restrict access to criminal history information pursuant to IN ST 35-38-5-5.5 or IN ST 35-38-8-5 and records excluded from public access by such orders, and information related to infractions that is excluded from public access pursuant to IN ST 34-28-5-15 or IN ST 34-28-5-16 [Editor's note: IN ST 35-38-5-5.5, IN ST 35-38-8-5 and IN ST 34-28-5-16 were repealed effective July 1, 2013; for information on orders restricting access to criminal history, refer to IN ST 35-38-9-1, et seq.];

viii. All personal notes and e-mail, and deliberative material, of judges, jurors, court staff and judicial agencies, and information recorded in personal data assistants (PDA's) or organizers and personal calendars. IN ST ADMIN Rule 9(G)(1).

F. Filing and Service Requirements

1. *Filing requirements.* Except as otherwise provided in IN ST TRIAL P Rule 5(E)(2), all pleadings and papers subsequent to the complaint which are required to be served upon a party shall be filed with the Court either before service or within a reasonable period of time thereafter. IN ST TRIAL P Rule 5(E)(1).

   a. *Non-filing of discovery until necessary*

      i. *Non-filing of discovery; Exceptions.* No deposition or request for discovery or response thereto under IN ST TRIAL P Rule 27, IN ST TRIAL P Rule 30, IN ST TRIAL P Rule 31, IN ST TRIAL P Rule 33, IN ST TRIAL P Rule 34 or IN ST TRIAL P Rule 36 shall be filed with the Court unless:

- A motion is filed pursuant to IN ST TRIAL P Rule 26(C) or IN ST TRIAL P Rule 37 and the original deposition or request for discovery or response thereto is necessary to enable the Court to rule; or

- A party desires to use the deposition or request for discovery or response thereto for evidentiary purposes at trial or in connection with a motion, and the Court, either upon its own motion or that of any party, or as a part of any pre-trial order, orders the filing of the original. IN ST TRIAL P Rule 5(E)(2).

   ii. *Custody of original and period of retention*

- The original of a deposition shall, subject to the provisions of IN ST TRIAL P Rule 30(E), be delivered by the reporter to the party taking it and shall be maintained by that party until filed with the Court pursuant to IN ST TRIAL P Rule 5(E)(2) or until the later of final judgment, agreed settlement of the litigation or all appellate rights have been exhausted. IN ST TRIAL P Rule 5(E)(3)(a).

- The original or any request for discovery or response thereto under IN ST TRIAL P Rule 27, IN ST TRIAL P Rule 30, IN ST TRIAL P Rule 31, IN ST TRIAL P Rule 33, IN ST TRIAL P Rule 34 and IN ST TRIAL P Rule 36 shall be maintained by the party originating the request or response until filed with the Court pursuant to IN ST TRIAL P Rule 5(E)(2) or until the later of final judgment, agreed settlement or all appellate rights have been exhausted. IN ST TRIAL P Rule 5(E)(3)(b).

   iii. *Original unavailable; Copies.* In the event it is made to appear to the satisfaction of the Court that the original of a deposition or request for discovery or response thereto cannot be filed with the Court when required, the Court may allow use of a copy instead of the original. IN ST TRIAL P Rule 5(E)(4).

   iv. *Filing as publication.* The filing of any deposition shall constitute publication. IN ST TRIAL P Rule 5(E)(5).

b. *Filing with the court defined.* The filing of pleadings, motions, and other papers with the court as required by the Indiana Rules of Trial Procedure shall be made by one of the following methods:

   i. Delivery to the clerk of the court;

   ii. Sending by electronic transmission under the procedure adopted pursuant to IN ST ADMIN Rule 12;

   iii. Mailing to the clerk by registered, certified or express mail return receipt requested;

   iv. Depositing with any third-party commercial carrier for delivery to the clerk within three (3) calendar days, cost prepaid, properly addressed;

   v. If the court so permits, filing with the judge, in which event the judge shall note thereon the filing date and forthwith transmit them to the office of the clerk; or

   vi. Electronic filing, as approved by the Division of State Court Administration pursuant to IN ST ADMIN Rule 16. IN ST TRIAL P Rule 5(F).

   vii. Filing by registered or certified mail and by third-party commercial carrier shall be complete upon mailing or deposit. IN ST TRIAL P Rule 5(F).

c. *Facsimile filing.* As outlined in IN ST HAMILTON ADMIN Rule 103(103.10),facsimile filing is permitted in the Circuit and Superior Courts of Hamilton County. The Courts authorize the Hamilton County Clerk of Courts to accept pleadings, motions and other papers by electronic facsimile transmission for filing in any case pending before the Courts, subject to the requirements of IN ST HAMILTON ADMIN Rule 103(103.10). IN ST HAMILTON ADMIN Rule 103(103.10); IN ST HAMILTON TRIAL Rule 201(201.80).

   i. *Generally.* In counties where a majority of judges of the courts of record, by posted local rule,

have authorized electronic facsimile filing and designated a telephone number to receive such transmissions, pleadings, motions, and other papers may be sent to the Clerk of Circuit Court by electronic facsimile transmission for filing in any case, provided:

- Such matter does not exceed ten (10) pages, including the cover sheet;

- Such matter does not require the payment of fees other than the electronic facsimile transcription fee set forth in IN ST ADMIN Rule 12(E);

- The sending party creates at the time of transmission a machine generated log for such transmission; and

- The original document and the transmission log are maintained by the sending party for the duration of the litigation. IN ST ADMIN Rule 12(B); IN ST HAMILTON ADMIN Rule 103(103.10)(d).

- Legibility of documents and timeliness of filing is the responsibility of the sender. IN ST HAMILTON ADMIN Rule 103(103.10)(g).

- The Clerk shall accept electronic facsimile transmission filings only if received at the facsimile machine assigned by the Clerk. The telephone number designated to receive such transmission is available at IN ST HAMILTON ADMIN Rule 103(103.40). IN ST HAMILTON ADMIN Rule 103(103.40).

   ii. *Time of filing.* During normal, posted business hours, the time of filing shall be the time the duplicate document is produced in the office of the Clerk of the Circuit Court. Duplicate documents received at all other times shall be filed as of the next normal business day. IN ST ADMIN Rule 12(C).

- If the receiving fax machine endorses its own time and date stamp upon the transmitted documents and the receiving machine produces a delivery receipt which is electronically created and transmitted to the sending party, the time of filing shall be the date and time recorded on the transmitted document by the receiving fax machine. IN ST ADMIN Rule 12(C).

- Electronic facsimile transmissions will be accepted for filing only during the regular business hours as set forth in IN ST HAMILTON ADMIN Rule 101. Transmissions received by the Hamilton County Clerk after close of business shall be filed effective the next regular business day. IN ST HAMILTON ADMIN Rule 103(103.30).

   iii. *Filing fee.* The electronic facsimile transmission will not be accepted for filing if its filing requires the payment of any fee other than the electronic facsimile transcription fee set forth in IN ST HAMILTON ADMIN Rule 103(103.20). IN ST HAMILTON ADMIN Rule 103(103.10)(e).

- Pursuant to Ordinance adopted by the Hamilton County Board of Commissioners, the Clerk shall collect an electronic facsimile transcription fee of One Dollar ($1.00) per page, to a maximum of Ten Dollars ($10.00) per transmission, for each electronic facsimile transmission accepted for filing with the Hamilton County Circuit and Superior Courts. IN ST HAMILTON ADMIN Rule 103(103.20).

- The fee shall be assessed against the sending party and shall be paid upon receipt of invoice by that party and at the latest within thirty (30) days of the transmission. In the event the fee is not paid by the sending party within the time limits provided, the court may issue a show-cause order or enter a judgment in the matter. The Clerk may refuse an electronic facsimile transmission from any attorney or pro se litigant who has failed to pay these fees within thirty (30) days. IN ST HAMILTON ADMIN Rule 103(103.20).

   iv. *No direct filing with court.* A party shall not send pleadings, motions and other papers by electronic facsimile transmission for filing directly to any Court without that Court's prior approval to do so. IN ST HAMILTON ADMIN Rule 103(103.50).

  d. *Filing with special judge.* After a special judge has qualified, a copy of each pleading and Chronological Case Summary entries filed with the Court shall be mailed or delivered to the office of that Special judge by the counsel or pro se litigant with service indicated on the certificate of service. IN ST HAMILTON TRIAL Rule 204(204.20).

e. *Proof of filing*. Any party filing any paper by any method other than personal delivery to the clerk shall retain proof of filing. IN ST TRIAL P Rule 5(F).

2. *Service requirements*. Unless otherwise provided by the Indiana Rules of Trial Procedure or an order of the court, each party and special judge, if any, shall be served with: (1) every order required by its terms to be served; (2) every pleading subsequent to the original complaint; (3) every written motion except one which may be heard ex parte; (4) every brief submitted to the trial court; (5) every paper relating to discovery required to be served upon a party; and (6) every written notice, appearance, demand, offer of judgment, designation of record on appeal, or similar paper. IN ST TRIAL P Rule 5(A).

   a. *Methods of service*

      i. *Personal service*. Whenever a party is represented by an attorney of record, service shall be made upon such attorney unless service upon the party himself is ordered by the court. Service upon the attorney or party shall be made by delivering or mailing a copy of the papers to the last known address or where an attorney or party has consented to service by fax or e-mail, as provided in IN ST TRIAL P Rule 3.1(A)(4), by faxing or e-mailing a copy of the documents to the fax number or e-mail address set out in the appearance form or correction as required by IN ST TRIAL P Rule 3.1(E). IN ST TRIAL P Rule 5(B). Delivery of a copy within IN ST TRIAL P Rule 5 means:

      - Offering or tendering it to the attorney or party and stating the nature of the papers being served. Refusal to accept an offered or tendered document is a waiver of any objection to the sufficiency or adequacy of service of that document;

      - Leaving it at his office with a clerk or other person in charge thereof, or if there is no one in charge, leaving it in a conspicuous place therein; or

      - If the office is closed, by leaving it at his dwelling house or usual place of abode with some person of suitable age and discretion then residing therein; or,

      - Leaving it at some other suitable place, selected by the attorney upon whom service is being made, pursuant to duly promulgated local rule. IN ST TRIAL P Rule 5(B)(1).

      ii. *Service by mail*. If service is made by mail, the papers shall be deposited in the United States mail addressed to the person on whom they are being served, with postage prepaid. Service shall be deemed complete upon mailing. Proof of service of all papers permitted to be mailed may be made by written acknowledgment of service, by affidavit of the person who mailed the papers, or by certificate of an attorney. It shall be the duty of attorneys when entering their appearance in a cause or when filing pleadings or papers therein, to have noted in the Chronological Case Summary or said pleadings or papers so filed the address and telephone number of their office. Service by delivery or by mail at such address shall be deemed sufficient and complete. IN ST TRIAL P Rule 5(B)(2).

      iii. *Service by fax or e-mail*. A party who has consented to service by fax or e-mail may be served as follows:

      - Service by e-mail shall be made by attaching the document being served in .pdf format. Discovery documents must also be served in accordance with IN ST TRIAL P Rule 26(A). IN ST TRIAL P Rule 5(B)(3)(a).

      - Service by fax shall be deemed complete upon generation of a transmission record indicating the successful transmission of the entire document, except as provided in IN ST TRIAL P Rule 5(B)(3)(d). IN ST TRIAL P Rule 5(B)(3)(b).

      - Service by e-mail shall be deemed complete upon transmission, except as provided in IN ST TRIAL P Rule 5(B)(3)(d). IN ST TRIAL P Rule 5(B)(3)(c).

      - Service by fax or e-mail that occurs on a Saturday, Sunday, legal holiday, or day the court or agency in which the matter is pending is closed or after 5:00 PM local time of the recipient shall be deemed complete the next day that is not a Saturday, Sunday, legal holiday, or day that the court or agency in which the matter is pending is not closed. IN ST TRIAL P Rule 5(B)(3)(d).

    iv. *Mail box service.* Pursuant to IN ST TRIAL P Rule 5(B)(1)(d), the Circuit and Superior Courts of Hamilton County hereby designate the "mail boxes" located in the Clerk's order book office for service of pleadings upon attorneys who have such boxes. IN ST HAMILTON TRIAL Rule 201(201.50).

    v. *Additional service of electronic discovery.* In addition to service under Rule IN ST TRIAL P Rule 5(B) or a .pdf format electronic copy, a party propounding or responding to interrogatories, requests for production or requests for admission shall comply with IN ST TRIAL P Rule 26(A.1)(a) or IN ST TRIAL P Rule 26(A.1)(b). IN ST TRIAL P Rule 26(A.1).

- The party shall serve the discovery request or response in an electronic format (either on a disk or as an electronic document attachment) in any commercially available word processing software system. If transmitted on disk, each disk shall be labeled, identifying the caption of the case, the document, and the word processing version in which it is being submitted. If more than one (1) disk is used for the same document, each disk shall be labeled and also shall be sequentially numbered. If transmitted by electronic mail, the document must be accompanied by electronic memorandum providing the forgoing identifying information; or

- The party shall serve the opposing party with a verified statement that the attorney or party appealing pro se lacks the equipment and is unable to transmit the discovery as required by IN ST TRIAL P Rule 26(A.1). IN ST TRIAL P Rule 26(A.1).

  b. *Serving numerous defendants.* In any action in which there are unusually large numbers of defendants, the court, upon motion or of its own initiative, may order:

    i. That service of the pleadings of the defendants and replies thereto need not be made as between the defendants;

- That any cross-claim, counterclaim, or matter constituting an avoidance or affirmative defense contained therein shall be deemed to be denied or avoided by all other parties; and

- That the filing of any such pleading and service thereof upon the plaintiff constitutes due notice of it to the parties. IN ST TRIAL P Rule 5(D).

    ii. A copy of every such order shall be served upon the parties in such manner and form as the court directs. IN ST TRIAL P Rule 5(D).

  c. *Service on parties in default for failure to appear.* No service need be made on parties in default for failure to appear, except that pleadings asserting new or additional claims for relief against them shall be served upon them in the manner provided by service of summons in IN ST TRIAL P Rule 4. IN ST TRIAL P Rule 5(A).

G. Hearings

  1. The Indiana rules do not contemplate a hearing related to the notice of deposition.

H. Forms

1. Notice of Deposition Forms for Indiana

  a. Notice of deposition; Individual. 5 INPRAC § 4:1.1.

  b. Notice of deposition; Deponent unknown. 5 INPRAC § 4:1.2.

  c. Notice of deposition; Corporation. 5 INPRAC § 4:1.3.

  d. Notice of deposition; With request for production of documents. 5 INPRAC § 4:1.4.

  e. Motion to limit scope of deposition. 5 INPRAC § 4:1.5.

  f. Motion to terminate deposition. 5 INPRAC § 4:1.6.

  g. Notice of hearing on petition for order to take deposition before action to perpetuate testimony. 5 INPRAC § 4:1.7.

h.   Petition to perpetuate testimony. 5 INPRAC § 4:1.7.30.

i.   Affidavit verifying petition to perpetuate testimony. 5 INPRAC § 4:1.7.70.

j.   Stipulation regarding deposition by remote electronic means. 5 INPRAC § 4:1.8.

k.   Petition to perpetuate testimony; Witness to automobile accident. 10 INPRAC § 59.3.

l.   Notice of hearing on petition to perpetuate testimony. 10 INPRAC § 59.6.

m.   Petition to perpetuate testimony pending appeal. 10 INPRAC § 59.13.

n.   Notice of deposition to perpetuate testimony pending appeal. 10 INPRAC § 59.15.

o.   Notice of deposition upon oral examination; Individual. 10 INPRAC § 62.3.

p.   Notice of deposition; Deponent unknown. 10 INPRAC § 62.4.

q.   Notice of deposition; Corporation. 10 INPRAC § 62.5.

r.   Notice of deposition; With request for production of documents. 10 INPRAC § 62.6.

s.   Motion for leave to take deposition within twenty days of service. 10 INPRAC § 62.7.

t.   Notice of deposition; Pursuant to order granting leave to take deposition. 10 INPRAC § 62.9.

u.   Stipulation for deposition upon written questions. 10 INPRAC § 63.2.

v.   Notice of deposition upon written questions. 10 INPRAC § 63.3.

w.   Direct questions. 10 INPRAC § 63.4.

x.   Cross questions. 10 INPRAC § 63.5.

y.   Redirect questions. 10 INPRAC § 63.6.

z.   Recross questions. 10 INPRAC § 63.7.

I.   Checklist

(I)   ❑ Matters to be considered by the party taking a deposition upon oral examination

    (a)   ❑ Required documents

        (1)   ❑ Notice of deposition

        (2)   ❑ Certificate of service

    (b)   ❑ Supplemental documents

        (1)   ❑ Subpoena/subpoena duces tecum

        (2)   ❑ Request for production

        (3)   ❑ Stipulation regarding discovery procedure

        (4)   ❑ Facsimile cover sheet

    (c)   ❑ Timing

        (1)   ❑ After commencement of the action, any party may take the testimony of any person, including a party, by deposition upon oral examination

(II)   ❑ Matters to be considered by the party taking a deposition upon written questions

    (a)   ❑ Required documents

        (1)   ❑ Notice of deposition

        (2)   ❑ Certificate of service

    (b)   ❑ Supplemental documents

        (1)   ❑ Subpoena

        (2)   ❑ Stipulation regarding discovery procedure

        (3)   ❑ Facsimile cover sheet

(c) ❑ Timing

    (1) ❑ After commencement of the action, any party may take the testimony of any person, including a party, by deposition upon written questions

(III) ❑ Matters to be considered by the party taking a deposition before commencement of the action

    (a) ❑ Required documents

        (1) ❑ Notice of deposition

        (2) ❑ Petition

        (3) ❑ Certificate of service

    (b) ❑ Supplemental documents

        (1) ❑ Stipulation regarding discovery procedure

        (2) ❑ Facsimile cover sheet

    (c) ❑ Timing

        (1) ❑ At least twenty (20) days before the date of hearing the notice shall be served in the manner provided in IN ST TRIAL P Rule 4 for service of summons

(IV) ❑ Matters to be considered by the party taking a deposition pending appeal

    (a) ❑ Required documents

        (1) ❑ Motion for leave to take deposition and notice

        (2) ❑ Proposed order

        (3) ❑ Certificate of service

    (b) ❑ Supplemental documents

        (1) ❑ Stipulation regarding discovery procedure

        (2) ❑ Supporting evidence

        (3) ❑ Facsimile cover sheet

        (4) ❑ Request to schedule trial or hearing

        (5) ❑ Copies of unpublished opinions

    (c) ❑ Timing

        (1) ❑ The party who desires to perpetuate the testimony may make a motion in the court for leave to take the depositions, upon the same notice and service thereof as if the action was pending in the court

        (2) ❑ A written motion, other than one which may be heard ex parte, and notice of the hearing thereof shall be served not less than five (5) days before the time specified for the hearing, unless a different period is fixed by the Indiana Rules of Trial Procedure or by order of the court

        (3) ❑ All pleadings and papers subsequent to the complaint which are required to be served upon a party shall be filed with the Court either before service or within a reasonable period of time thereafter

Requests, Notices and Applications
Application for Temporary Restraining Order

Document Last Updated October 2013

A. **Applicable Rules**

    1. *State rules*

        a. Appearance. IN ST TRIAL P Rule 3.1.

    b.   Process. IN ST TRIAL P Rule 4.

    c.   Service and filing of pleadings and other papers. IN ST TRIAL P Rule 5.

    d.   Time. IN ST TRIAL P Rule 6.

    e.   Pleadings. IN ST TRIAL P Rule 7; IN ST TRIAL P Rule 8; IN ST TRIAL P Rule 9.2; IN ST TRIAL P Rule 10.

    f.   Signing and verification of pleadings. IN ST TRIAL P Rule 11.

    g.   Evidence. IN ST TRIAL P Rule 43.

    h.   Judgment on the evidence (directed verdict). IN ST TRIAL P Rule 50.

    i.   Findings by the court. IN ST TRIAL P Rule 52.

    j.   Summary judgment. IN ST TRIAL P Rule 56.

    k.   Motion to correct error. IN ST TRIAL P Rule 59.

    l.   Relief from judgment or order. IN ST TRIAL P Rule 60.

    m.   Injunctions. IN ST TRIAL P Rule 65; IN ST 34-26-1-7; IN ST 34-26-1-8; IN ST 34-26-1-11.

    n.   Security; Proceedings against sureties. IN ST TRIAL P Rule 65.1.

    o.   Hearing of motions. IN ST TRIAL P Rule 73.

    p.   Access to court records. IN ST ADMIN Rule 9.

    q.   Paper size. IN ST ADMIN Rule 11.

    r.   Facsimile transmission. IN ST ADMIN Rule 12.

    s.   Electronic filing and electronic service pilot projects. IN ST ADMIN Rule 16.

    t.   Sealing of certain records by court; Hearing; Notice. IN ST 5-14-3-5.5.

    u.   Civil protection orders. IN ST 34-26-5-1; IN ST 34-26-5-20.

    v.   Privacy and confidentiality. IN ST 5-2-9-6; IN ST 5-14-3-4; IN ST 6-4.1-5-10; IN ST 6-4.1-12-12; IN ST 6-8.1-7-1; IN ST 11-13-1-8; IN ST 12-23-14-13; IN ST 16-39-3-10; IN ST 16-41-8-1; IN ST 22-4-19-6; IN ST 31-11-1-6; IN ST 31-19-5-23; IN ST 31-19-13-2; IN ST 31-19-19-1; IN ST 31-33-18-1; IN ST 31-39-1-1; IN ST 31-39-1-2; IN ST 33-23-16-16; IN ST 35-34-2-4; IN ST 35-38-1-13; IN ST 35-38-9-1; IN ST ADR Rule 2.11; IN ST ADR Rule 4.4; IN ST ADR Rule 5.6; IN ST JURY Rule 10.

2. *Local rules*

    a.   Court hours. IN ST HAMILTON ADMIN Rule 101.

    b.   Facsimile transmissions. IN ST HAMILTON ADMIN Rule 103.

    c.   Filing of pleadings and entry of appearances. IN ST HAMILTON TRIAL Rule 201.

    d.   Proposed orders. IN ST HAMILTON TRIAL Rule 202.

    e.   Briefs and memorandums. IN ST HAMILTON TRIAL Rule 203.

    f.   Special judges. IN ST HAMILTON TRIAL Rule 204.

    g.   Trial settings. IN ST HAMILTON TRIAL Rule 205.

    h.   Continuances. IN ST HAMILTON TRIAL Rule 206.

B. Timing

1. *Temporary restraining order without notice.* There are no specific timing requirements for submitting an application for a temporary restraining order without notice.

    a.   *Filing.* All pleadings and papers subsequent to the complaint which are required to be served upon a party shall be filed with the Court either before service or within a reasonable period of time thereafter. IN ST TRIAL P Rule 5(E)(1).

2. *Computation of time*

    a.   *Generally; Days excluded.* In computing any period of time prescribed or allowed by the Indiana

Rules of Trial Procedure, by order of the court, or by any applicable statute, the day of the act, event, or default from which the designated period of time begins to run shall not be included. The last day of the period so computed is to be included unless it is:

    i.   A Saturday,

    ii. A Sunday,

    iii. A legal holiday as defined by state statute, or

    iv. A day the office in which the act is to be done is closed during regular business hours. IN ST TRIAL P Rule 6(A).

   b. *Short periods.* In any event, the period runs until the end of the next day that is not a Saturday, a Sunday, a legal holiday, or a day on which the office is closed. When the period of time allowed is less than seven (7) days, intermediate Saturdays, Sundays, legal holidays, and days on which the office is closed shall be excluded from the computations. IN ST TRIAL P Rule 6(A).

   c. *Additional time after service by United States mail.* Whenever a party has the right or is required to do some act or take some proceedings within a prescribed period after the service of a notice or other paper upon him and the notice or paper is served upon him by United States mail, three (3) days shall be added to the prescribed period. IN ST TRIAL P Rule 6(E).

   d. *Enlargement of time.* When an act is required or allowed to be done at or within a specific time by the Indiana Rules of Trial Procedure, the court may at any time for cause shown:

    i.   Order the period enlarged, with or without motion or notice, if request therefor is made before the expiration of the period originally prescribed or extended by a previous order; or

    ii. Upon motion made after the expiration of the specific period, permit the act to be done where the failure to act was the result of excusable neglect; but, the court may not extend the time for taking any action for judgment on the evidence under IN ST TRIAL P Rule 50(A), amendment of findings and judgment under IN ST TRIAL P Rule 52(B), to correct errors under IN ST TRIAL P Rule 59(C), statement in opposition to motion to correct error under IN ST TRIAL P Rule 59(E), or to obtain relief from final judgment under IN ST TRIAL P Rule 60(B), except to the extent and under the conditions stated in those rules. IN ST TRIAL P Rule 6(B).

    iii. For information on obtaining a continuance, refer to IN ST HAMILTON TRIAL Rule 206.

C. General Requirements

1. *Motions, generally.* Unless made during a hearing or trial, or otherwise ordered by the court, an application to the court for an order shall be made by written motion. The motion shall state the grounds therefor and the relief or order sought. IN ST TRIAL P Rule 7(B).

   a. *Motions as distinct from pleadings.* Motions and responses to motions are not pleadings, and allegations contained in a motion are not admissions of a party. 22B INPRAC 7:2; Wachstetter v. County Properties, LLC, 832 N.E.2d 574 (Ind.Ct.App. 2005); Scott County Family YMCA, Inc. v. Hobbs, 817 N.E.2d 603 (Ind.Ct.App. 2004).

   b. *Unopposed motions generally granted.* It is common for a trial court to grant procedural motions, such as motions for enlargement of time, discovery motions, or motions for continuance, unless an objection is filed. 21 INPRAC § 13.8.

2. *Application for temporary restraining order.* Seeking a temporary restraining order should only be considered if there is a possibility that irreparable injury may occur before the hearing for a preliminary injunction can be held. 4 INPRAC R 65(65.4).

   a. *Without notice*

    i.   *When notice not required.* A temporary restraining order may be granted without written or oral notice to the adverse party or his attorney only if:

      • It clearly appears from specific facts shown by affidavit or by the verified complaint that immediate and irreparable injury, loss, or damage will result to the applicant before the adverse party or his attorney can be heard in opposition; and

      • The applicant's attorney certifies to the court in writing the efforts, if any, which have been made to give notice and the reasons supporting his claim that notice should not be required. IN ST TRIAL P Rule 65(B).

    ii.   *Motion for dissolution or modification of temporary restraining order.* On two (2) days' notice to the party who obtained the temporary restraining order without notice or on such shorter notice to that party as the court may prescribe, the adverse party may appear and move its dissolution or modification and in that event the court shall proceed to hear and determine such motion as expeditiously as the ends of justice require. IN ST TRIAL P Rule 65(B).

b.   *Temporary restraining orders with notice in Indiana.* IN ST TRIAL P Rule 65(B) in its entirety deals only with temporary restraining orders issued without notice. No mention is made of the issuance of temporary restraining orders with notice. 4 INPRAC R 65(65.4). Some Indiana cases have apparently held that there is no such thing as a temporary restraining order if the adverse party has notice and a hearing is held. 4 INPRAC R 65(65.4); Indiana State Dept. of Welfare v. Stagner, 410 N.E.2d 1348 (Ind.Ct.App. 1980); Szany v. City of Hammond, 170 Ind.App. 537, 352 N.E.2d 866 (Ind.Ct.App. 1976). Refer to the Indiana KeyRules Motion for Preliminary Injunction document for information on obtaining an injunction with notice to the opposing party.

c.   *Application without notice as ex parte communication with judge.* The failure to follow the requirements of IN ST TRIAL P Rule 65(B) may constitute, in some circumstances, an improper ex parte communication between attorney and judge. 4 INPRAC R 65(65.4.1); Ace Bail Bonds v. Government Payment Service, Inc., 892 N.E.2d 702 (Ind.Ct.App. 2008), transfer denied (Ind. Jan. 15, 2009).

    i.   When a party knows of the presence of another party's attorney in litigation, because each is present at hearings or at trial, then, even if an ex parte T.R.O. arguably meets the criteria in IN ST TRIAL P Rule 65(B), it is not valid unless it meets the standards in Smith v. Johnston, 711 N.E.2d 1259 (Ind.1999). 4 INPRAC R 65(65.4.1).

    ii.   Smith v. Johnston, was an appeal to set a default judgment aside. The court granted relief because the party who obtained the default did not give notice to the defaulted party, even though IN ST TRIAL P Rule 4 and IN ST TRIAL P Rule 5 do not require that notice be served on the opposite party's attorney. 4 INPRAC R 65(65.4.1). Smith v. Johnston's rationale clearly states that if an attorney "has knowledge of his opponent's representation, then the Rules of Professional Conduct establish a duty to provide notice `before seeking any relief from the court.'" 4 INPRAC R 65(65.4.1); Smith v. Johnston, 711 N.E.2d 1259 (Ind.1999).

d.   *Service of the temporary restraining order once issued.* Notice of the restraining order should be served upon the adverse party. The order may be served together with process in accordance with IN ST TRIAL P Rule 4, or, if obtained after service of process, then in accordance with IN ST TRIAL P Rule 5. 22 INPRAC § 29.2.

    i.   IN ST 34-26-1-11 provides the "clerk shall issue a copy of the order of injunction, certified by the clerk, which shall be served promptly by delivering the order to the adverse party." 22 INPRAC § 29.2; IN ST 34-26-1-11.

    ii.   However, service is not necessary to make the restraining order effective and binding, so long as the restrained party receives actual knowledge of the order. 22 INPRAC § 29.2; Reed Sign Service, Inc. v. Reid, 755 N.E.2d 690 (Ind.Ct.App. 2001).

e.   *Form of order by judge*

    i.   Every order granting temporary injunction and every restraining order shall include or be accompanied by findings as required by IN ST TRIAL P Rule 52; shall be specific in terms; shall describe in reasonable detail, and not by reference to the complaint or other document, the act or acts sought to be restrained; and is binding only upon the parties to the action, their officers, agents, servants, employees, and attorneys, and upon those persons in active concert or participation with them who receive actual notice of the order by personal service or otherwise. IN ST TRIAL P Rule 65(D).

    ii.   Every temporary restraining order granted without notice shall be indorsed with the date and hour of issuance; shall be filed forthwith in the clerk's office and entered of record; shall define the injury and state why it is irreparable and why the order was granted without notice; and shall expire by its terms within such time after entry, not to exceed ten (10) days, as the court fixes, unless within the time so fixed the order, for good cause shown, is extended for a like period or unless the whereabouts of the party against whom the order is granted is unknown and cannot be determined by reasonable diligence or unless the party against whom the order is directed consents that it may be extended for a longer period. The reasons for the extension shall be entered of record. IN ST TRIAL P Rule 65(B).

    f.   *Temporary restraining orders; Domestic relations cases.* Parties wishing protection from domestic or family violence in Domestic Relations cases shall petition the court pursuant to IN ST 34-26-5-1 through IN ST 34-26-5-20. IN ST TRIAL P Rule 65(E). For more information refer to IN ST TRIAL P Rule 65(E) and IN ST 34-26-5-1, et seq.

3.   *Security*

    a.   *Security requirement.* No restraining order or preliminary injunction shall issue except upon the giving of security by the applicant, in such sum as the court deems proper, for the payment of such costs and damages as may be incurred or suffered by any party who is found to have been wrongfully enjoined or restrained. No such security shall be required of a governmental organization, but such governmental organization shall be responsible for costs and damages as may be incurred or suffered by any party who is found to have been wrongfully enjoined or restrained. IN ST TRIAL P Rule 65(C).

        i.   The provisions of IN ST TRIAL P Rule 65.1 apply to a surety upon a bond or undertaking under IN ST TRIAL P Rule 65. IN ST TRIAL P Rule 65(C).

    b.   *Proceedings against sureties.* Whenever the Indiana Rules of Trial Procedure or other laws require or permit the giving of security by a party to a court action or proceeding, and security is given in the form of a bond or stipulation or other undertaking with one or more sureties, each surety submits himself to the jurisdiction of the court and irrevocably appoints the clerk of the court as his agent upon whom any papers affecting his liability on the bond or undertaking may be served. His liability may be enforced on motion without the necessity of an independent action. The motion and such notice of the motion as the court prescribes may be served on the clerk of the court, who shall forthwith mail copies to the sureties if their addresses are known. IN ST TRIAL P Rule 65.1 applies to bonds or security furnished on appeal, and enforcement shall be in the court to which the case is returned after appeal. IN ST TRIAL P Rule 65.1.

    c.   *Bond generally used as security.* IN ST TRIAL P Rule 65(C) speaks only of the giving of security and does not expressly require a surety on a bond. In practice, however, the giving of a bond with an insurance company as surety in the amount set by the court is typically the device used to satisfy this section. 4 INPRAC R 65(65.6).

D. Documents

1.   *Required documents*

    a.   *Application for temporary restraining order.* Refer to the General Requirements section of this document for additional information on the contents of an application for a temporary restraining order.

    b.   *Security.* No restraining order or preliminary injunction shall issue except upon the giving of security by the applicant, in such sum as the court deems proper, for the payment of such costs and damages as may be incurred or suffered by any party who is found to have been wrongfully enjoined or restrained. IN ST TRIAL P Rule 65(C). Refer to the General Requirements section of this document for more information.

    c.   *Proposed order.* Unless local practice provides differently, a party should submit a proposed order with its written motion to be signed by the judge once the motion has been granted. 21 INPRAC § 13.8; IN ST HAMILTON ADMIN Rule 103(103.10)(b). Each Motion, Petition or other request for relief shall be accompanied by a proposed order. IN ST HAMILTON TRIAL Rule 202(202.10).

        i.   All proposed orders submitted by counsel pursuant to IN ST HAMILTON TRIAL Rule 202 shall meet the following requirements: (1) contain a complete distribution list of all attorneys

and pro se litigants with full addresses; (2) stamped envelopes appropriately addressed for each attorney of record and/or pro se litigant on the distribution list. IN ST HAMILTON TRIAL Rule 202(202.30).

2. *Supplemental documents*

    a. *Supporting evidence.* When a motion is based on facts not appearing of record the court may hear the matter on affidavits presented by the respective parties, but the court may direct that the matter be heard wholly or partly on oral testimony or depositions. IN ST TRIAL P Rule 43(B).

    b. *Facsimile cover sheet.* Any document sent to the Clerk of the Circuit Court by electronic facsimile transmission shall be accompanied by a cover sheet which states the title of the document, case number, number of pages, identity and voice telephone number of the sending party and instructions for filing. The cover sheet shall contain the signature of the attorney or party, pro se, authorizing the filing. IN ST ADMIN Rule 12(D); IN ST HAMILTON ADMIN Rule 103(103.10)(a).

    c. *Request to schedule hearing.* All requests to schedule trials and hearings shall be in writing and shall contain the following information:

        i. Type of trial or hearing (i.e., jury trial, court trial, final hearing in dissolution, etc.). IN ST HAMILTON TRIAL Rule 205(205.10).

        ii. A good-faith estimate of the total court time needed for the trial or hearing. IN ST HAMILTON TRIAL Rule 205(205.10).

        iii. Each request under IN ST HAMILTON TRIAL Rule 205(205.10) shall be accompanied by a proposed written order with appropriate blanks for date and time and shall further include reference to those items set forth in IN ST HAMILTON TRIAL Rule 205(205.10)(a) and IN ST HAMILTON TRIAL Rule 205(205.10)(b). IN ST HAMILTON TRIAL Rule 205(205.20).

    d. *Copies of unpublished opinions.* Authorities relied upon which are not cited in the Northeastern Reporter system shall be attached to counsel's brief. If the authority is cited for the first time in oral argument, a copy of the authority may be provided to the Court at the time of the argument. Sufficient copies shall be available to provide counsel for each party with a copy. IN ST HAMILTON TRIAL Rule 203(203.10).

E. Format

1. *Form of motions.* The rules applicable to captions, and the signing and form of pleadings (IN ST TRIAL P Rule 8 through IN ST TRIAL P Rule 11), apply to all motions and other papers provided under the Indiana Rules of Trial Procedure. 22B INPRAC 7:2.

2. *Form of pleadings*

    a. *Caption; Names of parties.* Every pleading shall contain a caption setting forth the name of the court, the title of the action, the file number, and a designation as in IN ST TRIAL P Rule 7(A). In the complaint the title of the action shall include the names of all the parties, but in other pleadings it is sufficient to state the name of the first party on each side with an appropriate indication of other parties. IN ST TRIAL P Rule 10(A).

    b. *Paragraphs; Separate statements.* All averments of a claim or defense shall be made in numbered paragraphs, the contents of each of which shall be limited as far as practicable to a statement of a single set of circumstances, and a paragraph may be referred to by number in all succeeding pleadings. Each claim founded upon a separate transaction or occurrence and each defense other than denials may be stated in a separate count or defense whenever a separation facilitates the clear presentation of the matters set forth. IN ST TRIAL P Rule 10(B).

    c. *Adoption by reference; Exhibits.* Statements in a pleading may be adopted by reference in a different part of the same pleading or in another pleading or in any motion. A copy of any written instrument which is an exhibit to a pleading is a part thereof for all purposes. IN ST TRIAL P Rule 10(C).

    d. *Facsimile page limit.* Courts authorize the Hamilton County Clerk of Courts to accept pleadings, motions and other papers by electronic facsimile transmission for filing in any case pending before the Courts, subject to the requirement that The transmission may not exceed ten (10) pages in length including the cover sheet and proposed CCS entry. IN ST HAMILTON ADMIN Rule 103(103.10)(c).

e. *Emergency facsimile filings.* If the filing requires the immediate attention of the Judge, it shall so indicate in bold letters in an accompanying transmittal memorandum. IN ST HAMILTON ADMIN Rule 103(103.10)(f).

f. *Special judge heading.* After a special judge is selected, the attorneys or pro se litigants shall add to the caption of all pleadings to the right of the case title the following: "BEFORE SPECIAL JUDGE _____." IN ST HAMILTON TRIAL Rule 204(204.10).

g. *Format rules strictly enforced.* All filings shall be in compliance with the Indiana Rules of Trial Procedure. If the documents received are not in proper form, such deficiencies will not be corrected by court personnel. IN ST HAMILTON TRIAL Rule 201(201.70). The Court shall not be required to act on any Motion, Petition or other request for relief unless filed in conformity with the Hamilton County Local Trial and Administrative rules. IN ST HAMILTON TRIAL Rule 202(202.20).

3. *Size of papers for filing.* Effective January 1, 1992, all pleadings, copies, motions and documents filed with any trial court or appellate level court, typed or printed, with the exception of exhibits and existing wills, shall be prepared on eight and one-half by eleven inch (8 1/2" x 11") size paper. IN ST ADMIN Rule 11.

a. *Form.* All documents filed in any Hamilton County Court, with the exception of exhibits and existing wills, shall be prepared on paper measuring eight and one-half by eleven inches (8 1/2" x 11"). IN ST HAMILTON TRIAL Rule 201(201.20).

4. *Signature requirements*

a. *Signature of attorney.* Every pleading or motion of a party represented by an attorney shall be signed by at least one (1) attorney of record in his individual name, whose address, telephone number, and attorney number shall be stated, except that this provision shall not apply to pleadings and motions made and transcribed at the trial or a hearing before the judge and received by him in such form. IN ST TRIAL P Rule 11(A).

    i. The signature of an attorney constitutes a certificate by him that he has read the pleadings; that to the best of his knowledge, information, and belief, there is good ground to support it; and that it is not interposed for delay. IN ST TRIAL P Rule 11(A).

    ii. If a pleading or motion is not signed or is signed with intent to defeat the purpose of the rule, it may be stricken as sham and false and the action may proceed as though the pleading had not been served. IN ST TRIAL P Rule 11(A).

    iii. For a willful violation of IN ST TRIAL P Rule 11 an attorney may be subjected to appropriate disciplinary action. Similar action may be taken if scandalous or indecent matter is inserted. IN ST TRIAL P Rule 11(A).

b. *Signature of unrepresented party.* A party who is not represented by an attorney shall sign his pleading and state his address. IN ST TRIAL P Rule 11(A).

c. *Verification not generally required.* Except when specifically required by rule, pleadings or motions need not be verified or accompanied by affidavit. The rule in equity that the averments of an answer under oath must be overcome by the testimony of two (2) witnesses or of one (1) witness sustained by corroborating circumstances is abolished. IN ST TRIAL P Rule 11(A).

d. *Verification by affirmation or representation.* When in connection with any civil or special statutory proceeding it is required that any pleading, motion, petition, supporting affidavit, or other document of any kind, be verified, or that an oath be taken, it shall be sufficient if the subscriber simply affirms the truth of the matter to be verified by an affirmation or representation. IN ST TRIAL P Rule 11(B). IN ST TRIAL P Rule 11(B) states that the affirmation or representation should be in substantially the following language: "I (we) affirm, under the penalties for perjury, that the foregoing representation(s) is (are) true. (Signed) _____."

    i. Any person who falsifies an affirmation or representation of fact shall be subject to the same penalties as are prescribed by law for the making of a false affidavit. IN ST TRIAL P Rule 11(B).

e. *Verified pleadings, motions, and affidavits as evidence.* Pleadings, motions and affidavits accompa-

nying or in support of such pleadings or motions when required to be verified or under oath shall be accepted as a representation that the signer had personal knowledge thereof or reasonable cause to believe the existence of the facts or matters stated or alleged therein; and, if otherwise competent or acceptable as evidence, may be admitted as evidence of the facts or matters stated or alleged therein when it is so provided in the Indiana Rules of Trial Procedure, by statute or other law, or to the extent the writing or signature expressly purports to be made upon the signer's personal knowledge. When such pleadings, motions and affidavits are verified or under oath they shall not require other or greater proof on the part of the adverse party than if not verified or not under oath unless expressly provided otherwise by the Indiana Rules of Trial Procedure, statute or other law. Affidavits upon motions for summary judgment under IN ST TRIAL P Rule 56 and in denial of execution under IN ST TRIAL P Rule 9.2 shall be made upon personal knowledge. IN ST TRIAL P Rule 11(C).

5. *Information excluded from public access.* Every document filed in a case shall separately identify information excluded from public access pursuant to IN ST ADMIN Rule 9(G)(1) as follows:

   a. Whole documents that are excluded from public access pursuant to IN ST ADMIN Rule 9(G)(1) shall be tendered on light green paper or have a light green coversheet attached to the document, marked "Not for Public Access" or "Confidential." IN ST TRIAL P Rule 5(G)(1).

   b. When only a portion of a document contains information excluded from public access pursuant to IN ST ADMIN Rule 9(G)(1), said information shall be omitted [or redacted] from the filed document, and set forth on a separate accompanying document on light green paper conspicuously marked "Not for Public Access" or "Confidential" and clearly designated [or identifying] the caption and number of the case and the document and location within the document to which the redacted material pertains. IN ST TRIAL P Rule 5(G)(2).

   c. With respect to documents filed in electronic format, the trial court, by local rule, may provide for compliance with IN ST TRIAL P Rule 5 in manner that separates and protects access to information excluded from public access. IN ST TRIAL P Rule 5(G)(3).

   d. IN ST TRIAL P Rule 5(G) does not apply to a record sealed by the court pursuant to IN ST 5-14-3-5.5 or otherwise, nor to records, documents, or information filed in cases to which public access is prohibited pursuant to IN ST ADMIN Rule 9(G). IN ST TRIAL P Rule 5(G)(4).

   e. The following information in case records is excluded from public access and is confidential:

      i. Information that is excluded from public access pursuant to federal law;

      ii. Information that is excluded from public access as declared confidential by Indiana statute or other court rule, including without limitation:

         • All adoption records created after July 8, 1941, as declared confidential by IN ST 31-19-19-1, et seq., except those specifically declared open by IN ST 31-19-13-2(2);

         • All records relating to chancroid, chlamydia, gonorrhea, hepatitis, human immunodeficiency virus (HIV), Lymphogranuloma venereum, syphilis, tuberculosis, as declared confidential by IN ST 16-41-8-1, et seq.;

         • All records relating to child abuse as declared confidential by IN ST 31-33-18-1, et seq.;

         • All records relating to drug tests as declared confidential by IN ST 5-14-3-4(a)(9);

         • Records of grand jury proceedings as declared confidential by IN ST 35-34-2-4;

         • Records of juvenile proceedings as declared confidential by IN ST 31-39-1-2, except those specifically open under statute;

         • All paternity records created after July 1, 1941 as declared confidential by IN ST 31-14-11-15, IN ST 31-19-5-23, IN ST 31-39-1-1 and IN ST 31-39-1-2 [Editor's note: IN ST 31-14-11-15 was repealed effective May 9, 2013];

         • All pre-sentence reports as declared confidential by IN ST 35-38-1-13;

         • Written petitions to permit marriages without consent and orders directing the Clerk of Court to issue a marriage license to underage persons, as declared confidential by IN ST 31-11-1-6;

- Only those arrest warrants, search warrants, indictments and informations ordered confidential by the trial judge, prior to return of duly executed service as declared confidential by IN ST 5-14-3-4(b)(1);

- All medical, mental health, or tax records unless determined by law or regulation of any governmental custodian not to be confidential, released by the subject of such records, or declared by a court of competent jurisdiction to be essential to the resolution of litigation as declared confidential by IN ST 16-39-3-10, IN ST 6-4.1-5-10, IN ST 6-4.1-12-12, and IN ST 6-8.1-7-1;

- Personal information relating to jurors or prospective jurors, other than for the use of the parties and counsel, pursuant to IN ST JURY Rule 10;

- Information relating to protection from abuse orders, no-contact orders and workplace violence restraining orders as declared confidential by IN ST 5-2-9-6, et seq.;

- Mediation proceedings pursuant to IN ST ADR Rule 2.11, Mini-Trial proceedings pursuant to IN ST ADR Rule 4.4(C), and Summary Jury Trials pursuant to IN ST ADR Rule 5.6;

- Information in probation files pursuant to the Probation Standards promulgated by the Judicial Conference of Indiana pursuant to IN ST 11-13-1-8(b);

- Information deemed confidential pursuant to the Rules for Court Administered Alcohol and Drug Programs promulgated by the Judicial Conference of Indiana pursuant to IN ST 12-23-14-13;

- Information deemed confidential pursuant to the Problem-Solving Court Rules promulgated by the Judicial Conference of Indiana pursuant to IN ST 33-23-16-16;

- All records of the Department of workforce Development as declared confidential by IN ST 22-4-19-6;

- Information regarding interception of electronic communications that is sealed or deemed confidential as set forth in IN ST 35-33.5-2-1, et seq.

iii. Information excluded from public access by specific court order;

iv. Complete Social Security Numbers of living persons;

v. With the exception of names, information such as addresses, phone numbers, and dates of birth which explicitly identifies:

- Natural persons who are witnesses or victims (not including defendants) in criminal, domestic violence, stalking, sexual assault, juvenile, or civil protection order proceedings, provided that juveniles who are victims of sex crimes shall be identified by initials only;

- Places of residence of judicial officers, clerks and other employees of courts and clerks of court, unless the person or persons about whom the information pertains waives confidentiality;

vi. Complete account numbers of specific assets, loans, bank accounts, credit cards, and personal identification numbers (PINs);

vii. All orders of expungement entered in criminal or juvenile proceedings, orders to restrict access to criminal history information pursuant to IN ST 35-38-5-5.5 or IN ST 35-38-8-5 and records excluded from public access by such orders, and information related to infractions that is excluded from public access pursuant to IN ST 34-28-5-15 or IN ST 34-28-5-16 [Editor's note: IN ST 35-38-5-5.5, IN ST 35-38-8-5 and IN ST 34-28-5-16 were repealed effective July 1, 2013; for information on orders restricting access to criminal history, refer to IN ST 35-38-9-1, et seq.];

viii. All personal notes and e-mail, and deliberative material, of judges, jurors, court staff and judicial agencies, and information recorded in personal data assistants (PDA's) or organizers and personal calendars. IN ST ADMIN Rule 9(G)(1).

F. Filing and Service Requirements

1. *Filing requirements.* Except as otherwise provided in IN ST TRIAL P Rule 5(E)(2), all pleadings and

papers subsequent to the complaint which are required to be served upon a party shall be filed with the Court either before service or within a reasonable period of time thereafter. IN ST TRIAL P Rule 5(E)(1).

a. *Filing with the court defined.* The filing of pleadings, motions, and other papers with the court as required by the Indiana Rules of Trial Procedure shall be made by one of the following methods:

    i. Delivery to the clerk of the court;

    ii. Sending by electronic transmission under the procedure adopted pursuant to IN ST ADMIN Rule 12;

    iii. Mailing to the clerk by registered, certified or express mail return receipt requested;

    iv. Depositing with any third-party commercial carrier for delivery to the clerk within three (3) calendar days, cost prepaid, properly addressed;

    v. If the court so permits, filing with the judge, in which event the judge shall note thereon the filing date and forthwith transmit them to the office of the clerk; or

    vi. Electronic filing, as approved by the Division of State Court Administration pursuant to IN ST ADMIN Rule 16. IN ST TRIAL P Rule 5(F).

    vii. Filing by registered or certified mail and by third-party commercial carrier shall be complete upon mailing or deposit. IN ST TRIAL P Rule 5(F).

b. *Facsimile filing.* As outlined in IN ST HAMILTON ADMIN Rule 103(103.10),facsimile filing is permitted in the Circuit and Superior Courts of Hamilton County. The Courts authorize the Hamilton County Clerk of Courts to accept pleadings, motions and other papers by electronic facsimile transmission for filing in any case pending before the Courts, subject to the requirements of IN ST HAMILTON ADMIN Rule 103(103.10). IN ST HAMILTON ADMIN Rule 103(103.10); IN ST HAMILTON TRIAL Rule 201(201.80).

    i. *Generally.* In counties where a majority of judges of the courts of record, by posted local rule, have authorized electronic facsimile filing and designated a telephone number to receive such transmissions, pleadings, motions, and other papers may be sent to the Clerk of Circuit Court by electronic facsimile transmission for filing in any case, provided:

        • Such matter does not exceed ten (10) pages, including the cover sheet;

        • Such matter does not require the payment of fees other than the electronic facsimile transcription fee set forth in IN ST ADMIN Rule 12(E);

        • The sending party creates at the time of transmission a machine generated log for such transmission; and

        • The original document and the transmission log are maintained by the sending party for the duration of the litigation. IN ST ADMIN Rule 12(B); IN ST HAMILTON ADMIN Rule 103(103.10)(d).

        • Legibility of documents and timeliness of filing is the responsibility of the sender. IN ST HAMILTON ADMIN Rule 103(103.10)(g).

        • The Clerk shall accept electronic facsimile transmission filings only if received at the facsimile machine assigned by the Clerk. The telephone number designated to receive such transmission is available at IN ST HAMILTON ADMIN Rule 103(103.40). IN ST HAMILTON ADMIN Rule 103(103.40).

    ii. *Time of filing.* During normal, posted business hours, the time of filing shall be the time the duplicate document is produced in the office of the Clerk of the Circuit Court. Duplicate documents received at all other times shall be filed as of the next normal business day. IN ST ADMIN Rule 12(C).

        • If the receiving fax machine endorses its own time and date stamp upon the transmitted documents and the receiving machine produces a delivery receipt which is electronically created and transmitted to the sending party, the time of filing shall be the date and time recorded on the transmitted document by the receiving fax machine. IN ST ADMIN Rule 12(C).

- Electronic facsimile transmissions will be accepted for filing only during the regular business hours as set forth in IN ST HAMILTON ADMIN Rule 101. Transmissions received by the Hamilton County Clerk after close of business shall be filed effective the next regular business day. IN ST HAMILTON ADMIN Rule 103(103.30).

iii. *Filing fee.* The electronic facsimile transmission will not be accepted for filing if its filing requires the payment of any fee other than the electronic facsimile transcription fee set forth in IN ST HAMILTON ADMIN Rule 103(103.20). IN ST HAMILTON ADMIN Rule 103(103.10)(e).

- Pursuant to Ordinance adopted by the Hamilton County Board of Commissioners, the Clerk shall collect an electronic facsimile transcription fee of One Dollar ($1.00) per page, to a maximum of Ten Dollars ($10.00) per transmission, for each electronic facsimile transmission accepted for filing with the Hamilton County Circuit and Superior Courts. IN ST HAMILTON ADMIN Rule 103(103.20).

- The fee shall be assessed against the sending party and shall be paid upon receipt of invoice by that party and at the latest within thirty (30) days of the transmission. In the event the fee is not paid by the sending party within the time limits provided, the court may issue a show-cause order or enter a judgment in the matter. The Clerk may refuse an electronic facsimile transmission from any attorney or pro se litigant who has failed to pay these fees within thirty (30) days. IN ST HAMILTON ADMIN Rule 103(103.20).

iv. *No direct filing with court.* A party shall not send pleadings, motions and other papers by electronic facsimile transmission for filing directly to any Court without that Court's prior approval to do so. IN ST HAMILTON ADMIN Rule 103(103.50).

c. *Filing with special judge.* After a special judge has qualified, a copy of each pleading and Chronological Case Summary entries filed with the Court shall be mailed or delivered to the office of that Special judge by the counsel or pro se litigant with service indicated on the certificate of service. IN ST HAMILTON TRIAL Rule 204(204.20).

d. *Proof of filing.* Any party filing any paper by any method other than personal delivery to the clerk shall retain proof of filing. IN ST TRIAL P Rule 5(F).

2. *Service requirements.* Unless otherwise provided by the Indiana Rules of Trial Procedure or an order of the court, each party and special judge, if any, shall be served with: (1) every order required by its terms to be served; (2) every pleading subsequent to the original complaint; (3) every written motion except one which may be heard ex parte; (4) every brief submitted to the trial court; (5) every paper relating to discovery required to be served upon a party; and (6) every written notice, appearance, demand, offer of judgment, designation of record on appeal, or similar paper. IN ST TRIAL P Rule 5(A).

a. *Methods of service*

i. *Personal service.* Whenever a party is represented by an attorney of record, service shall be made upon such attorney unless service upon the party himself is ordered by the court. Service upon the attorney or party shall be made by delivering or mailing a copy of the papers to the last known address or where an attorney or party has consented to service by fax or e-mail, as provided in IN ST TRIAL P Rule 3.1(A)(4), by faxing or e-mailing a copy of the documents to the fax number or e-mail address set out in the appearance form or correction as required by IN ST TRIAL P Rule 3.1(E). IN ST TRIAL P Rule 5(B). Delivery of a copy within IN ST TRIAL P Rule 5 means:

- Offering or tendering it to the attorney or party and stating the nature of the papers being served. Refusal to accept an offered or tendered document is a waiver of any objection to the sufficiency or adequacy of service of that document;

- Leaving it at his office with a clerk or other person in charge thereof, or if there is no one in charge, leaving it in a conspicuous place therein; or

- If the office is closed, by leaving it at his dwelling house or usual place of abode with some person of suitable age and discretion then residing therein; or,

- Leaving it at some other suitable place, selected by the attorney upon whom service is being made, pursuant to duly promulgated local rule. IN ST TRIAL P Rule 5(B)(1).

ii. *Service by mail.* If service is made by mail, the papers shall be deposited in the United States mail addressed to the person on whom they are being served, with postage prepaid. Service shall be deemed complete upon mailing. Proof of service of all papers permitted to be mailed may be made by written acknowledgment of service, by affidavit of the person who mailed the papers, or by certificate of an attorney. It shall be the duty of attorneys when entering their appearance in a cause or when filing pleadings or papers therein, to have noted in the Chronological Case Summary or said pleadings or papers so filed the address and telephone number of their office. Service by delivery or by mail at such address shall be deemed sufficient and complete. IN ST TRIAL P Rule 5(B)(2).

iii. *Service by fax or e-mail.* A party who has consented to service by fax or e-mail may be served as follows:

- Service by e-mail shall be made by attaching the document being served in .pdf format. Discovery documents must also be served in accordance with IN ST TRIAL P Rule 26(A). IN ST TRIAL P Rule 5(B)(3)(a).

- Service by fax shall be deemed complete upon generation of a transmission record indicating the successful transmission of the entire document, except as provided in IN ST TRIAL P Rule 5(B)(3)(d). IN ST TRIAL P Rule 5(B)(3)(b).

- Service by e-mail shall be deemed complete upon transmission, except as provided in IN ST TRIAL P Rule 5(B)(3)(d). IN ST TRIAL P Rule 5(B)(3)(c).

- Service by fax or e-mail that occurs on a Saturday, Sunday, legal holiday, or day the court or agency in which the matter is pending is closed or after 5:00 PM local time of the recipient shall be deemed complete the next day that is not a Saturday, Sunday, legal holiday, or day that the court or agency in which the matter is pending is not closed. IN ST TRIAL P Rule 5(B)(3)(d).

iv. *Mail box service.* Pursuant to IN ST TRIAL P Rule 5(B)(1)(d), the Circuit and Superior Courts of Hamilton County hereby designate the "mail boxes" located in the Clerk's order book office for service of pleadings upon attorneys who have such boxes. IN ST HAMILTON TRIAL Rule 201(201.50).

b. *Serving numerous defendants.* In any action in which there are unusually large numbers of defendants, the court, upon motion or of its own initiative, may order:

i. That service of the pleadings of the defendants and replies thereto need not be made as between the defendants;

- That any cross-claim, counterclaim, or matter constituting an avoidance or affirmative defense contained therein shall be deemed to be denied or avoided by all other parties; and

- That the filing of any such pleading and service thereof upon the plaintiff constitutes due notice of it to the parties. IN ST TRIAL P Rule 5(D).

ii. A copy of every such order shall be served upon the parties in such manner and form as the court directs. IN ST TRIAL P Rule 5(D).

c. *Service on parties in default for failure to appear.* No service need be made on parties in default for failure to appear, except that pleadings asserting new or additional claims for relief against them shall be served upon them in the manner provided by service of summons in IN ST TRIAL P Rule 4. IN ST TRIAL P Rule 5(A).

G. Hearings

1. *Hearing on motion.* Unless local conditions make it impracticable, each judge shall establish regular times and places, at intervals sufficiently frequent for the prompt dispatch of business, at which motions requiring notice and hearing may be heard and disposed of; but the judge at any time or place and on such notice, if any, as he considers reasonable may make order for the advancement, conduct, and hearing of actions. To expedite its business the court may direct the submission and determination of motions without oral hearing upon brief written statements of reasons in support and opposition, or direct or permit hearings by telephone conference call with all attorneys or other similar means of communication. IN ST TRIAL P Rule 73(A).

2. *Presentation of evidence.* On the hearing of an application for a restraining order or temporary injunction, each party may read affidavits or documentary or record evidence. IN ST 34-26-1-8.

3. *Hearing for preliminary injunction.* In case a temporary restraining order is granted without notice, the motion for a preliminary injunction shall be set down for hearing at the earliest possible time and takes precedence of all matters except older matters of the same character; and when the motion comes on for hearing the party who obtained the temporary restraining order shall proceed with the application for a preliminary injunction and, if he does not do so, the court shall dissolve the temporary restraining order. IN ST TRIAL P Rule 65(B). Refer to the Indiana KeyRules Motion for Preliminary Injunction document for more information.

H. Forms

1. Application for Temporary Restraining Order Forms for Indiana

a. Prayer in complaint for temporary restraining order. 5 INPRAC § 3:13.60.

b. Motion for temporary restraining order; With notice. 5 INPRAC § 3:13.80.

c. Notice of motion for temporary restraining order. 11 INPRAC § 97.2.

d. Motion for temporary restraining order; Without notice. 11 INPRAC § 97.3.

e. Affidavit in support of motion for temporary restraining order. 11 INPRAC § 97.4.

f. Certificate of efforts of attorney to give notice of application for temporary restraining order. 11 INPRAC § 97.5.

g. Temporary restraining order without notice and order to show cause why preliminary injunction should not issue; Real estate. 11 INPRAC § 97.6.

h. Motion to extend temporary restraining order. 11 INPRAC § 97.7.

i. Order granting motion to extend temporary restraining order. 11 INPRAC § 97.8.

j. Stipulation extending temporary restraining order. 11 INPRAC § 97.9.

k. Order granting extension of temporary restraining order pursuant to stipulation. 11 INPRAC § 97.10.

l. Motion for judge of adjourning circuit to rule upon motion for temporary restraining order. 11 INPRAC § 97.11.

m. Affidavit in support of motion for judge of adjoining county to rule on motion for temporary restraining order. 11 INPRAC § 97.12.

n. Motion to advance trial on merits for consolidation with hearing on preliminary injunction. 11 INPRAC § 97.13.

I. Checklist

(I) ❑ Matters to be considered by the party filing the application without notice

  (a) ❑ Required documents

    (1) ❑ Application for temporary restraining order

    (2) ❑ Security

    (3) ❑ Proposed order

  (b) ❑ Supplemental documents

    (1) ❑ Supporting evidence

    (2) ❑ Request to schedule trial or hearing

    (3) ❑ Facsimile cover sheet

    (4) ❑ Copies of unpublished opinions

  (c) ❑ Timing

    (1) ❑ There are no specific timing requirements for submitting an application for a temporary restraining order without notice

Requests, Notices and Applications
Pretrial Conferences, Scheduling, Management

Document Last Updated October 2013

A. Applicable Rules

1. *State rules*

   a. Appearance. IN ST TRIAL P Rule 3.1.

   b. Process. IN ST TRIAL P Rule 4.

   c. Service and filing of pleadings and other papers. IN ST TRIAL P Rule 5.

   d. Time. IN ST TRIAL P Rule 6.

   e. Pleadings. IN ST TRIAL P Rule 7; IN ST TRIAL P Rule 8; IN ST TRIAL P Rule 9.2; IN ST TRIAL P Rule 10.

   f. Signing and verification of pleadings. IN ST TRIAL P Rule 11.

   g. Pre-trial procedure; Formulating issues. IN ST TRIAL P Rule 16.

   h. Evidence. IN ST TRIAL P Rule 43.

   i. Judgment on the evidence (directed verdict). IN ST TRIAL P Rule 50.

   j. Findings by the court. IN ST TRIAL P Rule 52.

   k. Summary judgment. IN ST TRIAL P Rule 56.

   l. Motion to correct error. IN ST TRIAL P Rule 59.

   m. Relief from judgment or order. IN ST TRIAL P Rule 60.

   n. Access to court records. IN ST ADMIN Rule 9.

   o. Paper size. IN ST ADMIN Rule 11.

   p. Facsimile transmission. IN ST ADMIN Rule 12.

   q. Electronic filing and electronic service pilot projects. IN ST ADMIN Rule 16.

   r. Sealing of certain records by court; Hearing; Notice. IN ST 5-14-3-5.5.

   s. Privacy and confidentiality. IN ST 5-2-9-6; IN ST 5-14-3-4; IN ST 6-4.1-5-10; IN ST 6-4.1-12-12; IN ST 6-8.1-7-1; IN ST 11-13-1-8; IN ST 12-23-14-13; IN ST 16-39-3-10; IN ST 16-41-8-1; IN ST 22-4-19-6; IN ST 31-11-1-6; IN ST 31-19-5-23; IN ST 31-19-13-2; IN ST 31-19-19-1; IN ST 31-33-18-1; IN ST 31-39-1-1; IN ST 31-39-1-2; IN ST 33-23-16-16; IN ST 35-34-2-4; IN ST 35-38-1-13; IN ST 35-38-9-1; IN ST ADR Rule 2.11; IN ST ADR Rule 4.4; IN ST ADR Rule 5.6; IN ST JURY Rule 10.

2. *Local rules*

   a. Court hours. IN ST HAMILTON ADMIN Rule 101.

   b. Facsimile transmissions. IN ST HAMILTON ADMIN Rule 103.

   c. Filing of pleadings and entry of appearances. IN ST HAMILTON TRIAL Rule 201.

   d. Proposed orders. IN ST HAMILTON TRIAL Rule 202.

   e. Special judges. IN ST HAMILTON TRIAL Rule 204.

   f. Pretrial conferences. IN ST HAMILTON TRIAL Rule 207.

   g. Continuances. IN ST HAMILTON TRIAL Rule 206.

B. Timing

1. *Pretrial conference.* Unless otherwise ordered by the court the pretrial conference shall not be called until after reasonable opportunity for the completion of discovery. IN ST TRIAL P Rule 16(B). However, some Indiana courts will schedule a preliminary pretrial conference almost immediately after the case has

been filed in order to establish the ground rules for discovery, discovery cut-off dates, and the procedures for filing additional pleadings, motions, and the like. In addition, some courts will only schedule a trial date at the pretrial conference. 22 INPRAC § 28.2.

   a. *Notice.* The clerks shall give at least thirty (30) days' notice of the pretrial conference unless otherwise directed by the court. IN ST TRIAL P Rule 16(B)(1).

   b. *Pre-conference meeting.* Unless otherwise ordered by the court, at least ten (10) days prior to the pretrial conference, attorneys for each of the parties shall meet and confer. IN ST TRIAL P Rule 16(C). It shall be the duty of counsel for both plaintiff and defendant to arrange for the conference of attorneys at least ten (10) days in advance of the pretrial conference. IN ST TRIAL P Rule 16(E).

2. *Motion requesting pretrial conference*

   a. *Timing of motion for pretrial conference.* There is no specific timing requirement for filing a motion requesting a pretrial conference.

      i. *Filing.* All pleadings and papers subsequent to the complaint which are required to be served upon a party shall be filed with the Court either before service or within a reasonable period of time thereafter. IN ST TRIAL P Rule 5(E)(1).

   b. *Service*

      i. *Of motion.* A written motion, other than one which may be heard ex parte, and notice of the hearing thereof shall be served not less than five (5) days before the time specified for the hearing, unless a different period is fixed by the Indiana Rules of Trial Procedure or by order of the court. IN ST TRIAL P Rule 6(D).

         • *Of supporting affidavits.* When a motion is supported by affidavit, the affidavit shall be served with the motion. IN ST TRIAL P Rule 6(D).

      ii. *Of opposition.* Except as otherwise provided in IN ST TRIAL P Rule 59(D), opposing affidavits may be served not less than one (1) day before the hearing, unless the court permits them to be served at some other time. IN ST TRIAL P Rule 6(D).

3. *Computation of time*

   a. *Generally; Days excluded.* In computing any period of time prescribed or allowed by the Indiana Rules of Trial Procedure, by order of the court, or by any applicable statute, the day of the act, event, or default from which the designated period of time begins to run shall not be included. The last day of the period so computed is to be included unless it is:

      i. A Saturday,

      ii. A Sunday,

      iii. A legal holiday as defined by state statute, or

      iv. A day the office in which the act is to be done is closed during regular business hours. IN ST TRIAL P Rule 6(A).

   b. *Short periods.* In any event, the period runs until the end of the next day that is not a Saturday, a Sunday, a legal holiday, or a day on which the office is closed. When the period of time allowed is less than seven (7) days, intermediate Saturdays, Sundays, legal holidays, and days on which the office is closed shall be excluded from the computations. IN ST TRIAL P Rule 6(A).

   c. *Additional time after service by United States mail.* Whenever a party has the right or is required to do some act or take some proceedings within a prescribed period after the service of a notice or other paper upon him and the notice or paper is served upon him by United States mail, three (3) days shall be added to the prescribed period. IN ST TRIAL P Rule 6(E).

   d. *Enlargement of time.* When an act is required or allowed to be done at or within a specific time by the Indiana Rules of Trial Procedure, the court may at any time for cause shown:

      i. Order the period enlarged, with or without motion or notice, if request therefor is made before the expiration of the period originally prescribed or extended by a previous order; or

      ii. Upon motion made after the expiration of the specific period, permit the act to be done where

the failure to act was the result of excusable neglect; but, the court may not extend the time for taking any action for judgment on the evidence under IN ST TRIAL P Rule 50(A), amendment of findings and judgment under IN ST TRIAL P Rule 52(B), to correct errors under IN ST TRIAL P Rule 59(C), statement in opposition to motion to correct error under IN ST TRIAL P Rule 59(E), or to obtain relief from final judgment under IN ST TRIAL P Rule 60(B), except to the extent and under the conditions stated in those rules. IN ST TRIAL P Rule 6(B).

   iii.   For information on obtaining a continuance, refer to IN ST HAMILTON TRIAL Rule 206.

C. General Requirements

1. *Pretrial conference*

   a. *When required; Purpose.* In any action except criminal cases, the court may in its discretion and shall upon the motion of any party, direct the attorneys for the parties to appear before it for a conference to consider:

      i.   The simplification of the issues;

      ii.   The necessity or desirability of amendments to the pleadings;

      iii.   The possibility of obtaining admissions of fact and of documents which will avoid unnecessary proof;

      iv.   A limitation of the number of expert witnesses;

      v.   An exchange of names of witnesses to be called during the trial and the general nature of their expected testimony;

      vi.   The desirability of using one or more types of alternative dispute resolution under the rules therefor;

      vii.   The desirability of setting deadlines for dispositive motions in light of the date set for trial; and

      viii.   Such other matters as may aid in the disposition of the action. IN ST TRIAL P Rule 16(A).

   b. *Participants.* At least one (1) attorney planning to take part in the trial shall appear for each of the parties and participate in the pretrial conference. IN ST TRIAL P Rule 16(B)(2).

      i.   *Mandatory attendance.* An attorney who has the authority to stipulate to pre-trial matters shall attend the pre-trial conference. IN ST HAMILTON TRIAL Rule 207(207.10).

   c. *Conference of attorneys prior to pretrial conference*

      i.   *Purpose of attorney conference.* In general, the purpose of the "pre-pretrial conference" is to ensure that the attorneys for both sides will be prepared to make maximum use of the pretrial conference itself. IN ST TRIAL P Rule 16 frees the pretrial conference itself from perfunctory matters; it is written to require that not only are attorneys very familiar with the case, but that routine matters are resolved before the pretrial conference so that it may be devoted to a determination of those issues and matters which will be litigated. 2 INPRAC R 16(16.3).

      ii.   *Topics to be addressed at attorney conference.* Unless otherwise ordered by the court, at least ten (10) days prior to the pretrial conference, attorneys for each of the parties shall meet and confer for the following purposes:

      - *Exhibits.* Each attorney shall mark for identification and provide opposing counsel an opportunity to inspect and copy all exhibits which he expects to introduce at the trial. Numbers or marks placed on such exhibits shall be prefixed with the symbol "P/T", denoting its pretrial designation. When the exhibit is introduced at the trial of the case, the "P/T" designation will be stricken and the exhibits must also indicate the party identifying same. IN ST TRIAL P Rule 16(C)(1). Exhibits of the character which prohibit or make impracticable their production at conference shall be identified and notice given of their intended use. Necessary arrangements must be made to afford opposing counsel an opportunity to examine such exhibits. IN ST TRIAL P Rule 16(C)(1).

      - *Exhibit stipulations.* Written stipulations shall be prepared with reference to all exhibits exchanged or identified. The stipulations shall contain all agreements of the parties with reference to the exchanged and identified exhibits, and shall include, but not be limited to, the agreement of the parties with reference to the authenticity of the exhibits, their admissibility in evidence, their use in opening statements, and the provisions made for the inspection of identified exhibits. The original of the exhibit stipulations shall be presented to the court at the pretrial conference. IN ST TRIAL P Rule 16(C)(2).

- *Fact stipulation.* The attorneys shall stipulate in writing with reference to all facts and issues not in genuine dispute. The original of the stipulations shall be presented to the court at the time of the pretrial conference. IN ST TRIAL P Rule 16(C)(3).

- *Exchange list of witnesses.* Attorneys for each of the parties shall furnish opposing counsel with the written list of the names and addresses of all witnesses then known. The original of each witness list shall be presented to the court at the time of the pretrial conference. IN ST TRIAL P Rule 16(C)(4).

- *Discuss settlement.* The possibility of compromise settlement shall be fully discussed and explored. IN ST TRIAL P Rule 16(C)(5).

   iii.   *Written pre-trial entries.* The Court may order the parties to provide written pre-trial entries pursuant to IN ST TRIAL P Rule 16 at the pre-trial conference. IN ST HAMILTON TRIAL Rule 207(207.20).

d.   *Preparation for conference of attorneys and pretrial.* Each attorney shall completely familiarize himself with all aspects of the case in advance of the conference of attorneys and be prepared to enter into stipulations with reference to as many facts and issues and exhibits as possible. IN ST TRIAL P Rule 16(D).

e.   *Refusal to stipulate.* If, following the conference of attorneys, either party determines that there are other facts or exhibits that should be stipulated and which opposing counsel refuses to stipulate upon, he shall compile a list of such facts or exhibits and furnish same to opposing counsel at least two (2) days in advance of the pretrial conference. The original of the list shall be presented to the court at the time of the pretrial conference. IN ST TRIAL P Rule 16(F).

f.   *Witnesses or exhibits discovered subsequent to conference of attorneys and before a pretrial conference.* If, after the conference of the attorneys and before the pretrial conference, counsel discovers additional exhibits or names of additional witnesses, the same information required to be disclosed at the conference of the attorneys shall be immediately furnished opposing counsel. The original of any such disclosures shall be presented to the court at the time of the pretrial conference. IN ST TRIAL P Rule 16(G).

g.   *More than one pretrial conference.* If necessary or advisable, the court may adjourn the pretrial conference from time to time or may order an additional pretrial conference. IN ST TRIAL P Rule 16(H).

h.   *Witnesses or exhibits discovered subsequent to pretrial conference.* If, following the pretrial conference or during trial, counsel discovers additional exhibits or the names of additional witnesses, the same information required to be disclosed at the conference between attorneys shall be immediately furnished opposing counsel. The original of any such disclosure shall immediately be filed with the court and shall indicate the date it was furnished opposing counsel. IN ST TRIAL P Rule 16(I).

i.   *Pretrial order.* The court shall make an order which recites the action taken at the conference, the amendments allowed to the pleading, and the agreements made by the parties as to any of the matters considered which limit the issues for trial to those not disposed of by admissions or agreement of counsel, and such order when entered shall control the subsequent course of action, unless modified thereafter to prevent manifest injustice. The court in its discretion may establish by rule a pretrial calendar on which actions may be placed for consideration as above provided, and may either confine the calendar to jury actions or non-jury actions or extend it to all actions. IN ST TRIAL P Rule 16(J).

   i.   The pretrial order delineates the issues in the case and supplants allegations raised in the pleadings. All subsequent pleadings are then controlled by the order that the trial court enters in the case file, and court record. 2 INPRAC R 16(16.2); Dominguez v. Gallmeyer, 402 N.E.2d 1295, 1298 (Ind.Ct.App. 1980).

    j.   *Sanctions; Failure to appear.* If without just excuse or because of failure to give reasonable attention to the matter, no appearance is made on behalf of a party at a pre-trial conference, or if an attorney is grossly unprepared to participate in the conference, the court may order either one or both of the following:

        i.   The payment by the delinquent attorney or party of the reasonable expenses, including attorney's fees, to the aggrieved party; or

        ii.   Take such other action as may be appropriate. IN ST TRIAL P Rule 16(K).

        iii.   Refer to the Indiana KeyRules Motion for Sanctions document for more information.

2.   *Motions, generally.* Unless made during a hearing or trial, or otherwise ordered by the court, an application to the court for an order shall be made by written motion. The motion shall state the grounds therefor and the relief or order sought. IN ST TRIAL P Rule 7(B).

    a.   *Motions as distinct from pleadings.* Motions and responses to motions are not pleadings, and allegations contained in a motion are not admissions of a party. 22B INPRAC 7:2; Wachstetter v. County Properties, LLC, 832 N.E.2d 574 (Ind.Ct.App. 2005); Scott County Family YMCA, Inc. v. Hobbs, 817 N.E.2d 603 (Ind.Ct.App. 2004).

    b.   *Unopposed motions generally granted.* It is common for a trial court to grant procedural motions, such as motions for enlargement of time, discovery motions, or motions for continuance, unless an objection is filed. 21 INPRAC § 13.8.

D.   Documents

1.   *Pretrial conference*

    a.   *Documents to consider*

        i.   *Exhibits and stipulations.* Refer to the General Requirements section of this document for information on exhibits and stipulations.

2.   *Motion for pretrial conference*

    a.   *Required documents*

        i.   *Motion and notice.* The requirement of notice is satisfied by service of the motion. IN ST TRIAL P Rule 7(B). Refer to the General Requirements section of this document for information on the content of a motion for pretrial conference.

        ii.   *Proposed order.* Unless local practice provides differently, a party should submit a proposed order with its written motion to be signed by the judge once the motion has been granted. 21 INPRAC § 13.8; IN ST HAMILTON ADMIN Rule 103(103.10)(b). Each Motion, Petition or other request for relief shall be accompanied by a proposed order. IN ST HAMILTON TRIAL Rule 202(202.10).

          •   All proposed orders submitted by counsel pursuant to IN ST HAMILTON TRIAL Rule 202 shall meet the following requirements: (1) contain a complete distribution list of all attorneys and pro se litigants with full addresses; (2) stamped envelopes appropriately addressed for each attorney of record and/or pro se litigant on the distribution list. IN ST HAMILTON TRIAL Rule 202(202.30).

        iii.   *Certificate of service.* An attorney or unrepresented party tendering a document to the Clerk for filing shall certify that service has been made, list the parties served, and specify the date and means of service. The certificate of service shall be placed at the end of the document and shall not be separately filed. The separate filing of a certificate of service, however, shall not be grounds for rejecting a document for filing. The Clerk may permit documents to be filed without a certificate of service but shall require prompt filing of a separate certificate of service. IN ST TRIAL P Rule 5(C).

          •   All pleadings filed with the Court which require a certificate of service shall specifically name the individual party or attorney on whom service has been made, the address, the manner in which service was made and the date when service was made. IN ST HAMIL-TON TRIAL Rule 201(201.60).

b. *Supplemental documents*

    i. *Supporting evidence.* When a motion is based on facts not appearing of record the court may hear the matter on affidavits presented by the respective parties, but the court may direct that the matter be heard wholly or partly on oral testimony or depositions. IN ST TRIAL P Rule 43(B).

    ii. *Facsimile cover sheet.* Any document sent to the Clerk of the Circuit Court by electronic facsimile transmission shall be accompanied by a cover sheet which states the title of the document, case number, number of pages, identity and voice telephone number of the sending party and instructions for filing. The cover sheet shall contain the signature of the attorney or party, pro se, authorizing the filing. IN ST ADMIN Rule 12(D); IN ST HAMILTON ADMIN Rule 103(103.10)(a).

    iii. *Request to schedule hearing.* All requests to schedule trials and hearings shall be in writing and shall contain the following information:

- Type of trial or hearing (i.e., jury trial, court trial, final hearing in dissolution, etc.). IN ST HAMILTON TRIAL Rule 205(205.10).

- A good-faith estimate of the total court time needed for the trial or hearing. IN ST HAMILTON TRIAL Rule 205(205.10).

- Each request under IN ST HAMILTON TRIAL Rule 205(205.10) shall be accompanied by a proposed written order with appropriate blanks for date and time and shall further include reference to those items set forth in IN ST HAMILTON TRIAL Rule 205(205.10)(a) and IN ST HAMILTON TRIAL Rule 205(205.10)(b). IN ST HAMIL-TON TRIAL Rule 205(205.20).

    iv. *Copies of unpublished opinions.* Authorities relied upon which are not cited in the Northeastern Reporter system shall be attached to counsel's brief. If the authority is cited for the first time in oral argument, a copy of the authority may be provided to the Court at the time of the argument. Sufficient copies shall be available to provide counsel for each party with a copy. IN ST HAMILTON TRIAL Rule 203(203.10).

E. Format

1. *Form of papers.* The rules applicable to captions, and the signing and form of pleadings (IN ST TRIAL P Rule 8 through IN ST TRIAL P Rule 11), apply to all motions and other papers provided under the Indiana Rules of Trial Procedure. 22B INPRAC 7:2.

2. *Form of pleadings*

    a. *Caption; Names of parties.* Every pleading shall contain a caption setting forth the name of the court, the title of the action, the file number, and a designation as in IN ST TRIAL P Rule 7(A). In the complaint the title of the action shall include the names of all the parties, but in other pleadings it is sufficient to state the name of the first party on each side with an appropriate indication of other parties. IN ST TRIAL P Rule 10(A).

    b. *Paragraphs; Separate statements.* All averments of a claim or defense shall be made in numbered paragraphs, the contents of each of which shall be limited as far as practicable to a statement of a single set of circumstances, and a paragraph may be referred to by number in all succeeding pleadings. Each claim founded upon a separate transaction or occurrence and each defense other than denials may be stated in a separate count or defense whenever a separation facilitates the clear presentation of the matters set forth. IN ST TRIAL P Rule 10(B).

    c. *Adoption by reference; Exhibits.* Statements in a pleading may be adopted by reference in a different part of the same pleading or in another pleading or in any motion. A copy of any written instrument which is an exhibit to a pleading is a part thereof for all purposes. IN ST TRIAL P Rule 10(C).

    d. *Facsimile page limit.* Courts authorize the Hamilton County Clerk of Courts to accept pleadings, motions and other papers by electronic facsimile transmission for filing in any case pending before the Courts, subject to the requirement that The transmission may not exceed ten (10) pages in length including the cover sheet and proposed CCS entry. IN ST HAMILTON ADMIN Rule 103(103.10)(c).

e.   *Emergency facsimile filings.* If the filing requires the immediate attention of the Judge, it shall so indicate in bold letters in an accompanying transmittal memorandum. IN ST HAMILTON ADMIN Rule 103(103.10)(f).

f.   *Special judge heading.* After a special judge is selected, the attorneys or pro se litigants shall add to the caption of all pleadings to the right of the case title the following: "BEFORE SPECIAL JUDGE _____." IN ST HAMILTON TRIAL Rule 204(204.10).

g.   *Format rules strictly enforced.* All filings shall be in compliance with the Indiana Rules of Trial Procedure. If the documents received are not in proper form, such deficiencies will not be corrected by court personnel. IN ST HAMILTON TRIAL Rule 201(201.70). The Court shall not be required to act on any Motion, Petition or other request for relief unless filed in conformity with the Hamilton County Local Trial and Administrative rules. IN ST HAMILTON TRIAL Rule 202(202.20).

3.   *Size of papers for filing.* Effective January 1, 1992, all pleadings, copies, motions and documents filed with any trial court or appellate level court, typed or printed, with the exception of exhibits and existing wills, shall be prepared on eight and one-half by eleven inch (8 1/2" x 11") size paper. IN ST ADMIN Rule 11.

a.   *Form.* All documents filed in any Hamilton County Court, with the exception of exhibits and existing wills, shall be prepared on paper measuring eight and one-half by eleven inches (8 1/2" x 11"). IN ST HAMILTON TRIAL Rule 201(201.20).

4.   *Signature requirements*

a.   *Signature of attorney.* Every pleading or motion of a party represented by an attorney shall be signed by at least one (1) attorney of record in his individual name, whose address, telephone number, and attorney number shall be stated, except that this provision shall not apply to pleadings and motions made and transcribed at the trial or a hearing before the judge and received by him in such form. IN ST TRIAL P Rule 11(A).

   i.   The signature of an attorney constitutes a certificate by him that he has read the pleadings; that to the best of his knowledge, information, and belief, there is good ground to support it; and that it is not interposed for delay. IN ST TRIAL P Rule 11(A).

   ii.   If a pleading or motion is not signed or is signed with intent to defeat the purpose of the rule, it may be stricken as sham and false and the action may proceed as though the pleading had not been served. IN ST TRIAL P Rule 11(A).

   iii.   For a willful violation of IN ST TRIAL P Rule 11 an attorney may be subjected to appropriate disciplinary action. Similar action may be taken if scandalous or indecent matter is inserted. IN ST TRIAL P Rule 11(A).

b.   *Signature of unrepresented party.* A party who is not represented by an attorney shall sign his pleading and state his address. IN ST TRIAL P Rule 11(A).

c.   *Verification not generally required.* Except when specifically required by rule, pleadings or motions need not be verified or accompanied by affidavit. The rule in equity that the averments of an answer under oath must be overcome by the testimony of two (2) witnesses or of one (1) witness sustained by corroborating circumstances is abolished. IN ST TRIAL P Rule 11(A).

d.   *Verification by affirmation or representation.* When in connection with any civil or special statutory proceeding it is required that any pleading, motion, petition, supporting affidavit, or other document of any kind, be verified, or that an oath be taken, it shall be sufficient if the subscriber simply affirms the truth of the matter to be verified by an affirmation or representation. IN ST TRIAL P Rule 11(B). IN ST TRIAL P Rule 11(B) states that the affirmation or representation should be in substantially the following language: "I (we) affirm, under the penalties for perjury, that the foregoing representation(s) is (are) true. (Signed) _____."

   i.   Any person who falsifies an affirmation or representation of fact shall be subject to the same penalties as are prescribed by law for the making of a false affidavit. IN ST TRIAL P Rule 11(B).

e. *Verified pleadings, motions, and affidavits as evidence.* Pleadings, motions and affidavits accompanying or in support of such pleadings or motions when required to be verified or under oath shall be accepted as a representation that the signer had personal knowledge thereof or reasonable cause to believe the existence of the facts or matters stated or alleged therein; and, if otherwise competent or acceptable as evidence, may be admitted as evidence of the facts or matters stated or alleged therein when it is so provided in the Indiana Rules of Trial Procedure, by statute or other law, or to the extent the writing or signature expressly purports to be made upon the signer's personal knowledge. When such pleadings, motions and affidavits are verified or under oath they shall not require other or greater proof on the part of the adverse party than if not verified or not under oath unless expressly provided otherwise by the Indiana Rules of Trial Procedure, statute or other law. Affidavits upon motions for summary judgment under IN ST TRIAL P Rule 56 and in denial of execution under IN ST TRIAL P Rule 9.2 shall be made upon personal knowledge. IN ST TRIAL P Rule 11(C).

5. *Information excluded from public access.* Every document filed in a case shall separately identify information excluded from public access pursuant to IN ST ADMIN Rule 9(G)(1) as follows:

a. Whole documents that are excluded from public access pursuant to IN ST ADMIN Rule 9(G)(1) shall be tendered on light green paper or have a light green coversheet attached to the document, marked "Not for Public Access" or "Confidential." IN ST TRIAL P Rule 5(G)(1).

b. When only a portion of a document contains information excluded from public access pursuant to IN ST ADMIN Rule 9(G)(1), said information shall be omitted [or redacted] from the filed document, and set forth on a separate accompanying document on light green paper conspicuously marked "Not for Public Access" or "Confidential" and clearly designated [or identifying] the caption and number of the case and the document and location within the document to which the redacted material pertains. IN ST TRIAL P Rule 5(G)(2).

c. With respect to documents filed in electronic format, the trial court, by local rule, may provide for compliance with IN ST TRIAL P Rule 5 in manner that separates and protects access to information excluded from public access. IN ST TRIAL P Rule 5(G)(3).

d. IN ST TRIAL P Rule 5(G) does not apply to a record sealed by the court pursuant to IN ST 5-14-3-5.5 or otherwise, nor to records, documents, or information filed in cases to which public access is prohibited pursuant to IN ST ADMIN Rule 9(G). IN ST TRIAL P Rule 5(G)(4).

e. The following information in case records is excluded from public access and is confidential:

   i. Information that is excluded from public access pursuant to federal law;

   ii. Information that is excluded from public access as declared confidential by Indiana statute or other court rule, including without limitation:

   - All adoption records created after July 8, 1941, as declared confidential by IN ST 31-19-19-1, et seq., except those specifically declared open by IN ST 31-19-13-2(2);

   - All records relating to chancroid, chlamydia, gonorrhea, hepatitis, human immunodeficiency virus (HIV), Lymphogranuloma venereum, syphilis, tuberculosis, as declared confidential by IN ST 16-41-8-1, et seq.;

   - All records relating to child abuse as declared confidential by IN ST 31-33-18-1, et seq.;

   - All records relating to drug tests as declared confidential by IN ST 5-14-3-4(a)(9);

   - Records of grand jury proceedings as declared confidential by IN ST 35-34-2-4;

   - Records of juvenile proceedings as declared confidential by IN ST 31-39-1-2, except those specifically open under statute;

   - All paternity records created after July 1, 1941 as declared confidential by IN ST 31-14-11-15, IN ST 31-19-5-23, IN ST 31-39-1-1 and IN ST 31-39-1-2 [Editor's note: IN ST 31-14-11-15 was repealed effective May 9, 2013];

   - All pre-sentence reports as declared confidential by IN ST 35-38-1-13;

   - Written petitions to permit marriages without consent and orders directing the Clerk of Court to issue a marriage license to underage persons, as declared confidential by IN ST 31-11-1-6;

- Only those arrest warrants, search warrants, indictments and informations ordered confidential by the trial judge, prior to return of duly executed service as declared confidential by IN ST 5-14-3-4(b)(1);

- All medical, mental health, or tax records unless determined by law or regulation of any governmental custodian not to be confidential, released by the subject of such records, or declared by a court of competent jurisdiction to be essential to the resolution of litigation as declared confidential by IN ST 16-39-3-10, IN ST 6-4.1-5-10, IN ST 6-4.1-12-12, and IN ST 6-8.1-7-1;

- Personal information relating to jurors or prospective jurors, other than for the use of the parties and counsel, pursuant to IN ST JURY Rule 10;

- Information relating to protection from abuse orders, no-contact orders and workplace violence restraining orders as declared confidential by IN ST 5-2-9-6, et seq.;

- Mediation proceedings pursuant to IN ST ADR Rule 2.11, Mini-Trial proceedings pursuant to IN ST ADR Rule 4.4(C), and Summary Jury Trials pursuant to IN ST ADR Rule 5.6;

- Information in probation files pursuant to the Probation Standards promulgated by the Judicial Conference of Indiana pursuant to IN ST 11-13-1-8(b);

- Information deemed confidential pursuant to the Rules for Court Administered Alcohol and Drug Programs promulgated by the Judicial Conference of Indiana pursuant to IN ST 12-23-14-13;

- Information deemed confidential pursuant to the Problem-Solving Court Rules promulgated by the Judicial Conference of Indiana pursuant to IN ST 33-23-16-16;

- All records of the Department of workforce Development as declared confidential by IN ST 22-4-19-6;

- Information regarding interception of electronic communications that is sealed or deemed confidential as set forth in IN ST 35-33.5-2-1, et seq.

iii. Information excluded from public access by specific court order;

iv. Complete Social Security Numbers of living persons;

v. With the exception of names, information such as addresses, phone numbers, and dates of birth which explicitly identifies:

- Natural persons who are witnesses or victims (not including defendants) in criminal, domestic violence, stalking, sexual assault, juvenile, or civil protection order proceedings, provided that juveniles who are victims of sex crimes shall be identified by initials only;

- Places of residence of judicial officers, clerks and other employees of courts and clerks of court, unless the person or persons about whom the information pertains waives confidentiality;

vi. Complete account numbers of specific assets, loans, bank accounts, credit cards, and personal identification numbers (PINs);

vii. All orders of expungement entered in criminal or juvenile proceedings, orders to restrict access to criminal history information pursuant to IN ST 35-38-5-5.5 or IN ST 35-38-8-5 and records excluded from public access by such orders, and information related to infractions that is excluded from public access pursuant to IN ST 34-28-5-15 or IN ST 34-28-5-16 [Editor's note: IN ST 35-38-5-5.5, IN ST 35-38-8-5 and IN ST 34-28-5-16 were repealed effective July 1, 2013; for information on orders restricting access to criminal history, refer to IN ST 35-38-9-1, et seq.];

viii. All personal notes and e-mail, and deliberative material, of judges, jurors, court staff and judicial agencies, and information recorded in personal data assistants (PDA's) or organizers and personal calendars. IN ST ADMIN Rule 9(G)(1).

F. Filing and Service Requirements

1. *Filing requirements.* Except as otherwise provided in IN ST TRIAL P Rule 5(E)(2), all pleadings and

papers subsequent to the complaint which are required to be served upon a party shall be filed with the Court either before service or within a reasonable period of time thereafter. IN ST TRIAL P Rule 5(E)(1).

a. *Filing with the court defined.* The filing of pleadings, motions, and other papers with the court as required by the Indiana Rules of Trial Procedure shall be made by one of the following methods:

   i. Delivery to the clerk of the court;

   ii. Sending by electronic transmission under the procedure adopted pursuant to IN ST ADMIN Rule 12;

   iii. Mailing to the clerk by registered, certified or express mail return receipt requested;

   iv. Depositing with any third-party commercial carrier for delivery to the clerk within three (3) calendar days, cost prepaid, properly addressed;

   v. If the court so permits, filing with the judge, in which event the judge shall note thereon the filing date and forthwith transmit them to the office of the clerk; or

   vi. Electronic filing, as approved by the Division of State Court Administration pursuant to IN ST ADMIN Rule 16. IN ST TRIAL P Rule 5(F).

   vii. Filing by registered or certified mail and by third-party commercial carrier shall be complete upon mailing or deposit. IN ST TRIAL P Rule 5(F).

b. *Facsimile filing.* As outlined in IN ST HAMILTON ADMIN Rule 103(103.10),facsimile filing is permitted in the Circuit and Superior Courts of Hamilton County. The Courts authorize the Hamilton County Clerk of Courts to accept pleadings, motions and other papers by electronic facsimile transmission for filing in any case pending before the Courts, subject to the requirements of IN ST HAMILTON ADMIN Rule 103(103.10). IN ST HAMILTON ADMIN Rule 103(103.10); IN ST HAMILTON TRIAL Rule 201(201.80).

   i. *Generally.* In counties where a majority of judges of the courts of record, by posted local rule, have authorized electronic facsimile filing and designated a telephone number to receive such transmissions, pleadings, motions, and other papers may be sent to the Clerk of Circuit Court by electronic facsimile transmission for filing in any case, provided:

   • Such matter does not exceed ten (10) pages, including the cover sheet;

   • Such matter does not require the payment of fees other than the electronic facsimile transcription fee set forth in IN ST ADMIN Rule 12(E);

   • The sending party creates at the time of transmission a machine generated log for such transmission; and

   • The original document and the transmission log are maintained by the sending party for the duration of the litigation. IN ST ADMIN Rule 12(B); IN ST HAMILTON ADMIN Rule 103(103.10)(d).

   • Legibility of documents and timeliness of filing is the responsibility of the sender. IN ST HAMILTON ADMIN Rule 103(103.10)(g).

   • The Clerk shall accept electronic facsimile transmission filings only if received at the facsimile machine assigned by the Clerk. The telephone number designated to receive such transmission is available at IN ST HAMILTON ADMIN Rule 103(103.40). IN ST HAMILTON ADMIN Rule 103(103.40).

   ii. *Time of filing.* During normal, posted business hours, the time of filing shall be the time the duplicate document is produced in the office of the Clerk of the Circuit Court. Duplicate documents received at all other times shall be filed as of the next normal business day. IN ST ADMIN Rule 12(C).

   • If the receiving fax machine endorses its own time and date stamp upon the transmitted documents and the receiving machine produces a delivery receipt which is electronically created and transmitted to the sending party, the time of filing shall be the date and time recorded on the transmitted document by the receiving fax machine. IN ST ADMIN Rule 12(C).

- Electronic facsimile transmissions will be accepted for filing only during the regular business hours as set forth in IN ST HAMILTON ADMIN Rule 101. Transmissions received by the Hamilton County Clerk after close of business shall be filed effective the next regular business day. IN ST HAMILTON ADMIN Rule 103(103.30).

iii. *Filing fee.* The electronic facsimile transmission will not be accepted for filing if its filing requires the payment of any fee other than the electronic facsimile transcription fee set forth in IN ST HAMILTON ADMIN Rule 103(103.20). IN ST HAMILTON ADMIN Rule 103(103.10)(e).

- Pursuant to Ordinance adopted by the Hamilton County Board of Commissioners, the Clerk shall collect an electronic facsimile transcription fee of One Dollar ($1.00) per page, to a maximum of Ten Dollars ($10.00) per transmission, for each electronic facsimile transmission accepted for filing with the Hamilton County Circuit and Superior Courts. IN ST HAMILTON ADMIN Rule 103(103.20).

- The fee shall be assessed against the sending party and shall be paid upon receipt of invoice by that party and at the latest within thirty (30) days of the transmission. In the event the fee is not paid by the sending party within the time limits provided, the court may issue a show-cause order or enter a judgment in the matter. The Clerk may refuse an electronic facsimile transmission from any attorney or pro se litigant who has failed to pay these fees within thirty (30) days. IN ST HAMILTON ADMIN Rule 103(103.20).

iv. *No direct filing with court.* A party shall not send pleadings, motions and other papers by electronic facsimile transmission for filing directly to any Court without that Court's prior approval to do so. IN ST HAMILTON ADMIN Rule 103(103.50).

c. *Filing with special judge.* After a special judge has qualified, a copy of each pleading and Chronological Case Summary entries filed with the Court shall be mailed or delivered to the office of that Special judge by the counsel or pro se litigant with service indicated on the certificate of service. IN ST HAMILTON TRIAL Rule 204(204.20).

d. *Proof of filing.* Any party filing any paper by any method other than personal delivery to the clerk shall retain proof of filing. IN ST TRIAL P Rule 5(F).

2. *Service requirements.* Unless otherwise provided by the Indiana Rules of Trial Procedure or an order of the court, each party and special judge, if any, shall be served with: (1) every order required by its terms to be served; (2) every pleading subsequent to the original complaint; (3) every written motion except one which may be heard ex parte; (4) every brief submitted to the trial court; (5) every paper relating to discovery required to be served upon a party; and (6) every written notice, appearance, demand, offer of judgment, designation of record on appeal, or similar paper. IN ST TRIAL P Rule 5(A).

a. *Methods of service*

i. *Personal service.* Whenever a party is represented by an attorney of record, service shall be made upon such attorney unless service upon the party himself is ordered by the court. Service upon the attorney or party shall be made by delivering or mailing a copy of the papers to the last known address or where an attorney or party has consented to service by fax or e-mail, as provided in IN ST TRIAL P Rule 3.1(A)(4), by faxing or e-mailing a copy of the documents to the fax number or e-mail address set out in the appearance form or correction as required by IN ST TRIAL P Rule 3.1(E). IN ST TRIAL P Rule 5(B). Delivery of a copy within IN ST TRIAL P Rule 5 means:

- Offering or tendering it to the attorney or party and stating the nature of the papers being served. Refusal to accept an offered or tendered document is a waiver of any objection to the sufficiency or adequacy of service of that document;

- Leaving it at his office with a clerk or other person in charge thereof, or if there is no one in charge, leaving it in a conspicuous place therein; or

- If the office is closed, by leaving it at his dwelling house or usual place of abode with some person of suitable age and discretion then residing therein; or,

- Leaving it at some other suitable place, selected by the attorney upon whom service is being made, pursuant to duly promulgated local rule. IN ST TRIAL P Rule 5(B)(1).

    ii.   *Service by mail.* If service is made by mail, the papers shall be deposited in the United States mail addressed to the person on whom they are being served, with postage prepaid. Service shall be deemed complete upon mailing. Proof of service of all papers permitted to be mailed may be made by written acknowledgment of service, by affidavit of the person who mailed the papers, or by certificate of an attorney. It shall be the duty of attorneys when entering their appearance in a cause or when filing pleadings or papers therein, to have noted in the Chronological Case Summary or said pleadings or papers so filed the address and telephone number of their office. Service by delivery or by mail at such address shall be deemed sufficient and complete. IN ST TRIAL P Rule 5(B)(2).

    iii.   *Service by fax or e-mail.* A party who has consented to service by fax or e-mail may be served as follows:

- Service by e-mail shall be made by attaching the document being served in .pdf format. Discovery documents must also be served in accordance with IN ST TRIAL P Rule 26(A). IN ST TRIAL P Rule 5(B)(3)(a).

- Service by fax shall be deemed complete upon generation of a transmission record indicating the successful transmission of the entire document, except as provided in IN ST TRIAL P Rule 5(B)(3)(d). IN ST TRIAL P Rule 5(B)(3)(b).

- Service by e-mail shall be deemed complete upon transmission, except as provided in IN ST TRIAL P Rule 5(B)(3)(d). IN ST TRIAL P Rule 5(B)(3)(c).

- Service by fax or e-mail that occurs on a Saturday, Sunday, legal holiday, or day the court or agency in which the matter is pending is closed or after 5:00 PM local time of the recipient shall be deemed complete the next day that is not a Saturday, Sunday, legal holiday, or day that the court or agency in which the matter is pending is not closed. IN ST TRIAL P Rule 5(B)(3)(d).

    iv.   *Mail box service.* Pursuant to IN ST TRIAL P Rule 5(B)(1)(d), the Circuit and Superior Courts of Hamilton County hereby designate the "mail boxes" located in the Clerk's order book office for service of pleadings upon attorneys who have such boxes. IN ST HAMILTON TRIAL Rule 201(201.50).

  b. *Serving numerous defendants.* In any action in which there are unusually large numbers of defendants, the court, upon motion or of its own initiative, may order:

    i.   That service of the pleadings of the defendants and replies thereto need not be made as between the defendants;

- That any cross-claim, counterclaim, or matter constituting an avoidance or affirmative defense contained therein shall be deemed to be denied or avoided by all other parties; and

- That the filing of any such pleading and service thereof upon the plaintiff constitutes due notice of it to the parties. IN ST TRIAL P Rule 5(D).

    ii.   A copy of every such order shall be served upon the parties in such manner and form as the court directs. IN ST TRIAL P Rule 5(D).

  c. *Service on parties in default for failure to appear.* No service need be made on parties in default for failure to appear, except that pleadings asserting new or additional claims for relief against them shall be served upon them in the manner provided by service of summons in IN ST TRIAL P Rule 4. IN ST TRIAL P Rule 5(A).

G. Hearings

  1. The Indiana rules do not contemplate a hearing related to the pretrial conference.

H. Forms

  1. Pretrial Conference, Scheduling, Management Forms for Indiana

    a. Motion for pretrial conference. 5 INPRAC § 5:1.1.

    b. Order for pretrial conference; Attorneys to hold preliminary conference. 5 INPRAC § 5:1.2.

    c. Letter; To arrange preliminary conference of attorneys. 5 INPRAC § 5:1.3.

d. Letter; Documenting opposing counsel's failure to meet. 5 INPRAC § 5:1.4.

e. Letter; Request to stipulate to facts and exhibits. 5 INPRAC § 5:1.5.

f. Notice to court; Failure to stipulate. 5 INPRAC § 5:1.6.

g. Agenda; Pretrial conference. 5 INPRAC § 5:1.7.

h. Agenda for pretrial conference; Alternative. 5 INPRAC § 5:1.8.

i. Preliminary pretrial order. 5 INPRAC § 5:1.9.

j. Final pretrial order. 5 INPRAC § 5:1.10.

k. Motion to amend pretrial order. 5 INPRAC § 5:1.11.

l. Motion to extend discovery cutoff date. 5 INPRAC § 5:1.12.

m. Motion for pretrial conference. 10 INPRAC § 70.2.

n. Joint motion for pretrial conference. 10 INPRAC § 70.3.

o. Order for pretrial conference; Attorneys to hold preliminary conference. 10 INPRAC § 70.4.

p. Worksheet for preliminary conference of attorneys and pretrial conference. 10 INPRAC § 70.5.

q. Joint motion for continuance of pretrial conference. 10 INPRAC § 70.6.

r. Letter attempting to arrange preliminary conference of attorneys. 10 INPRAC § 70.7.

s. Notice of conference of attorneys. 10 INPRAC § 70.8.

t. Letter documenting opposing counsel's failure to meet for preliminary conference of attorneys. 10 INPRAC § 70.9.

u. Request that opposing party stipulate to facts and exhibits discovered after conference of attorneys. 10 INPRAC § 70.10.

v. Preliminary pretrial order. 10 INPRAC § 70.14.

w. Final pretrial order. 10 INPRAC § 70.15.

x. Motion to amend pretrial order; General form. 10 INPRAC § 70.16.

y. Motion to amend pretrial order; Party's contentions. 10 INPRAC § 70.17.

z. Motion for sanctions; Failure to attend pretrial conference. 10 INPRAC § 70.22.

I. Checklist

(I) ❑ Matters to be considered for the pretrial conference

    (a) ❑ Documents to consider

        (1) ❑ Exhibits and stipulations

    (b) ❑ Timing

        (1) ❑ Unless otherwise ordered by the court the pretrial conference shall not be called until after reasonable opportunity for the completion of discovery

        (2) ❑ The clerks shall give at least thirty (30) days' notice of the pretrial conference unless otherwise directed by the court

        (3) ❑ Unless otherwise ordered by the court, at least ten (10) days prior to the pretrial conference, attorneys for each of the parties shall meet and confer

(II) ❑ Matters to be considered by the party filing the motion for pretrial conference

    (a) ❑ Required documents

        (1) ❑ Motion and notice

        (2) ❑ Proposed order

        (3) ❑ Certificate of service

    (b) ❑ Supplemental documents

        (1) ❑ Supporting evidence

    (2) ❑ Facsimile cover sheet

    (3) ❑ Request to schedule trial or hearing

    (4) ❑ Copies of unpublished opinions

(c) ❑ Timing

    (1) ❑ There is no specific timing requirement for filing a motion requesting a pretrial conference

    (2) ❑ A written motion, other than one which may be heard ex parte, and notice of the hearing thereof shall be served not less than five (5) days before the time specified for the hearing, unless a different period is fixed by the Indiana Rules of Trial Procedure or by order of the court

    (3) ❑ All pleadings and papers subsequent to the complaint which are required to be served upon a party shall be filed with the Court either before service or within a reasonable period of time thereafter

LAKE COUNTY

Pleadings
Complaint

Document Last Updated October 2013

A. **Applicable Rules**

1. *State rules*

   a. Commencement of an action. IN ST TRIAL P Rule 3.

   b. Appearance. IN ST TRIAL P Rule 3.1.

   c. Process. IN ST TRIAL P Rule 4.

   d. Service. IN ST TRIAL P Rule 4.1; IN ST TRIAL P Rule 4.2; IN ST TRIAL P Rule 4.3; IN ST TRIAL P Rule 4.4; IN ST TRIAL P Rule 4.5; IN ST TRIAL P Rule 4.6; IN ST TRIAL P Rule 4.7; IN ST TRIAL P Rule 4.8; IN ST TRIAL P Rule 4.9; IN ST TRIAL P Rule 4.10; IN ST TRIAL P Rule 4.11; IN ST TRIAL P Rule 4.12; IN ST TRIAL P Rule 4.13; IN ST TRIAL P Rule 4.14; IN ST TRIAL P Rule 4.15; IN ST TRIAL P Rule 4.17; IN ST TRIAL P Rule 5.

   e. Time. IN ST TRIAL P Rule 6.

   f. Pleadings allowed; Form of motion. IN ST TRIAL P Rule 7.

   g. Rules of pleading. IN ST TRIAL P Rule 8; IN ST TRIAL P Rule 9; IN ST TRIAL P Rule 9.1; IN ST TRIAL P Rule 9.2.

   h. Form and signing of pleadings. IN ST TRIAL P Rule 10; IN ST TRIAL P Rule 11.

   i. Joinder. IN ST TRIAL P Rule 18; IN ST TRIAL P Rule 19.

   j. Jury trial of right. IN ST TRIAL P Rule 38.

   k. Evidence. IN ST TRIAL P Rule 43.

   l. Determination of foreign law. IN ST TRIAL P Rule 44.1.

   m. Judgment on the evidence (directed verdict). IN ST TRIAL P Rule 50.

   n. Findings by the court. IN ST TRIAL P Rule 52.

   o. Summary judgment. IN ST TRIAL P Rule 56.

   p. Motion to correct error. IN ST TRIAL P Rule 59.

   q. Relief from judgment or order. IN ST TRIAL P Rule 60.

   r. Trial court and clerks; Court records. IN ST TRIAL P Rule 72; IN ST TRIAL P Rule 77.

   s. Uniform case numbering system. IN ST ADMIN Rule 8.

   t. Access to court records. IN ST ADMIN Rule 9.

   u. Paper size. IN ST ADMIN Rule 11.

   v. Facsimile transmission. IN ST ADMIN Rule 12.

   w. Electronic filing and electronic service pilot projects. IN ST ADMIN Rule 16.

   x. Alternative dispute resolution. IN ST ADR Rule 1.1; IN ST ADR Rule 1.6; IN ST ADR Rule 8.8.

   y. Manner of service. IN ST 34-33-2-1.

   z. Privacy and confidentiality. IN ST 5-2-9-6; IN ST 5-14-3-4; IN ST 5-14-3-5.5; IN ST 6-4.1-5-10; IN ST 6-4.1-12-12; IN ST 6-8.1-7-1; IN ST 11-13-1-8; IN ST 12-23-14-13; IN ST 16-39-3-10; IN ST 16-41-8-1; IN ST 22-4-19-6; IN ST 31-11-1-6; IN ST 31-19-5-23; IN ST 31-19-13-2; IN ST 31-19-19-1; IN ST 31-33-18-1; IN ST 31-39-1-1; IN ST 31-39-1-2; IN ST 33-23-16-16; IN ST

35-34-2-4; IN ST 35-38-1-13; IN ST 35-38-9-1; IN ST ADR Rule 2.11; IN ST ADR Rule 4.4; IN ST ADR Rule 5.6; IN ST JURY Rule 10.

2. *Local rules*

   a. Scope and title. [IN ST LAKE RCP Rule 1, as amended by IN ORDER 13-0237, effective October 18, 2013].

   b. Preparation of pleadings, motions and other papers. IN ST LAKE RCP Rule 2.

   c. Filing. [IN ST LAKE RCP Rule 3, as amended by IN ORDER 13-0237, effective October 18, 2013].

   d. Appearance by attorney. IN ST LAKE RCP Rule 5.

   e. Confidential information and sealed documents. IN ST LAKE RCP Rule 16.

   f. Electronic filing and service. IN ST LAKE RCP Rule 17.

B. Timing

1. *Filing.* A civil action is commenced by filing with the court a complaint or such equivalent pleading or document as may be specified by statute, by payment of the prescribed filing fee or filing an order waiving the filing fee, and, where service of process is required, by furnishing to the clerk as many copies of the complaint and summons as are necessary. IN ST TRIAL P Rule 3. The claimant typically bears the burden of commencing an action within the applicable statute of limitations. 22B INPRAC 3:1; Huff v. Huff, 892 N.E.2d 1241 (Ind.Ct.App. 2008).

2. *Service.* The trial rules require a party to exercise due diligence in securing service of process. 1 INPRAC R 4; Geiger and Peters, Inc. v. American Fletcher Nat. Bank & Trust Co., 428 N.E.2d 1279 (Ind.Ct.App. 1981). If person seeking service of process fails without cause for sixty (60) days or more to provide clerk with required summons for issuance or with other information necessary to effectuate service, person has failed to exercise due diligence in securing service of process. Geiger and Peters, Inc. v. American Fletcher Nat. Bank & Trust Co., 428 N.E.2d 1279, 1281 (Ind.Ct.App. 1981).

3. *Computation of time*

   a. *Generally; Days excluded.* In computing any period of time prescribed or allowed by the Indiana Rules of Trial Procedure, by order of the court, or by any applicable statute, the day of the act, event, or default from which the designated period of time begins to run shall not be included. The last day of the period so computed is to be included unless it is:

      i. A Saturday,

      ii. A Sunday,

      iii. A legal holiday as defined by state statute, or

      iv. A day the office in which the act is to be done is closed during regular business hours. IN ST TRIAL P Rule 6(A).

   b. *Short periods.* In any event, the period runs until the end of the next day that is not a Saturday, a Sunday, a legal holiday, or a day on which the office is closed. When the period of time allowed is less than seven (7) days, intermediate Saturdays, Sundays, legal holidays, and days on which the office is closed shall be excluded from the computations. IN ST TRIAL P Rule 6(A).

   c. *Additional time after service by United States mail.* Whenever a party has the right or is required to do some act or take some proceedings within a prescribed period after the service of a notice or other paper upon him and the notice or paper is served upon him by United States mail, three (3) days shall be added to the prescribed period. IN ST TRIAL P Rule 6(E).

   d. *Electronic filing does not alter deadlines.* Filing electronically does not alter any filing deadlines or any time computation pursuant to state or federal statutes, any Rules of the Indiana Supreme Court, including without limitation the Rules of Trial Procedure, the Rules of Appellate Procedure or the Administrative Rules, or applicable Lake County Rules of Civil Procedure. The office of the Lake County Clerk is open for electronic filing under the Lake County Rules of Civil Procedure twenty-four (24) hours a day. A document is deemed filed at the date and time it is received by the LCOD server. Filing must be completed before midnight local time in order to be considered filed

COMPLAINT

that day. Lake County observes Central Time and electronic filers are strongly urged to file documents during hours when the Lake County Online Docket ("LCOD") help line is available, from 9:00 a.m. to 4:00 p.m. local time, although documents can be filed electronically twenty-four (24) hours a day. IN ST LAKE RCP Rule 17(I).

e. *Enlargement of time.* When an act is required or allowed to be done at or within a specific time by the Indiana Rules of Trial Procedure, the court may at any time for cause shown:

i. Order the period enlarged, with or without motion or notice, if request therefor is made before the expiration of the period originally prescribed or extended by a previous order; or

ii. Upon motion made after the expiration of the specific period, permit the act to be done where the failure to act was the result of excusable neglect; but, the court may not extend the time for taking any action for judgment on the evidence under IN ST TRIAL P Rule 50(A), amendment of findings and judgment under IN ST TRIAL P Rule 52(B), to correct errors under IN ST TRIAL P Rule 59(C), statement in opposition to motion to correct error under IN ST TRIAL P Rule 59(E), or to obtain relief from final judgment under IN ST TRIAL P Rule 60(B), except to the extent and under the conditions stated in those rules. IN ST TRIAL P Rule 6(B).

C. General Requirements

1. *Pleading, generally*

   a. *Pleadings to be concise.* Each averment of a pleading shall be simple, concise, and direct. No technical forms of pleading or motions are required. All fictions in pleading are abolished. IN ST TRIAL P Rule 8(E)(1).

   b. *Pleading in the alternative.* A pleading may set forth two (2) or more statements of a claim or defense alternatively or hypothetically, either in one (1) count or defense or in separate counts or defenses. When two (2) or more statements are made in the alternative and one (1) of them if made independently would be sufficient, the pleading is not made insufficient by the insufficiency of one or more of the alternative statements. A pleading may also state as many separate claims or defenses as the pleader has regardless of consistency and whether based on legal or equitable grounds. All statements shall be made subject to the obligations set forth in IN ST TRIAL P Rule 11. IN ST TRIAL P Rule 8(E)(2).

   c. *Motions and pleadings, joint and several.* All motions and pleadings of any kind addressed to two (2) or more paragraphs of any pleading, or filed by two (2) or more parties, shall be taken and construed as joint, separate, and several motions or pleadings to each of such paragraphs and by and against each of such parties. All motions or pleadings containing two (2) or more subject-matters shall be taken and construed as separate and several as to each subject-matter. All objections to rulings made by two (2) or more parties shall be taken and construed as the joint, separate, and several objections of each of such parties. IN ST TRIAL P Rule 8(E)(3).

      i. A complaint filed by or against two (2) or more plaintiffs shall be taken and construed as joint, separate, and several as to each of said plaintiffs. IN ST TRIAL P Rule 8(E).

   d. *Construction of pleadings.* All pleadings shall be so construed as to do substantial justice, lead to disposition on the merits, and avoid litigation of procedural points. IN ST TRIAL P Rule 8(F).

2. *Contents of the complaint*

   a. *Pleading for relief; Notice pleading.* Indiana is a "notice pleading" jurisdiction. 22B INPRAC 8:1; State v. American Family Voices, Inc., 898 N.E.2d 293 (Ind. 2008). Notice pleading replaces the technical and complex method of pleading which existed prior to 1970. Notice pleading is grounded in due process of law and must provide a defendant with reasonable notice of the plaintiff's claim or an opponent's defense. 22B INPRAC 8:1; Noblesville Redevelopment Com'n v. Noblesville Associates Ltd. Partnership, 674 N.E.2d 558 (Ind. 1996). Notice pleading does not require that the plaintiff state all elements or facts essential to a cause of action. 22B INPRAC 8:1; State v. American Family Voices, Inc., 898 N.E.2d 293 (Ind. 2008). Instead, the complaint must state "a short and plain statement of the claim" showing an entitlement to relief, and a demand for relief. 22B INPRAC 8:1; Trail v. Boys and Girls Clubs of Northwest Indiana, 845 N.E.2d 130 (Ind. 2006).

b. *Claims for relief.* To state a claim for relief, whether an original claim, counterclaim, cross-claim, or third-party claim, a pleading must contain:

    i.   A short and plain statement of the claim showing that the pleader is entitled to relief, and

    ii. A demand for relief to which the pleader deems entitled. Relief in the alternative or of several different types may be demanded. However, in any complaint seeking damages for personal injury or death, or seeking punitive damages, no dollar amount or figure shall be included in the demand. IN ST TRIAL P Rule 8(A).

c. *Res ipsa loquitur.* Res ipsa loquitur or a similar doctrine may be pleaded by alleging generally that the facts connected with the action are unknown to the pleader and are within the knowledge of the opposing party. IN ST TRIAL P Rule 9.1(B).

d. *Bona fide purchaser.* When the rights of a person depend upon his status as a bona fide purchaser for value or upon similar requirements, such status must be pleaded and proved by the person asserting it, but it may be pleaded in general terms. Once it is established that the person has given any required value, unless such value is commercially unreasonable, and that he has met any requirements of recordation, filing, possession, or perfection, the trier of fact must find that such value was given or such perfection was made in accordance with any requirements of good faith, lack of knowledge, or lack of notice unless and until evidence is introduced which would support a finding of its non-existence. IN ST TRIAL P Rule 9.1(D).

e. *Presumption; Matters of judicial notice.* Neither presumptions of law nor matters of which judicial notice may be taken need be stated in a pleading. IN ST TRIAL P Rule 9.1(E).

    i.   *Presumption of jurisdiction.* Jurisdiction is presumed in Indiana. 22B INPRAC 8:2. Consequently, there is no requirement to affirmatively plead the existence of jurisdiction in the complaint, unless the action involves a special proceeding requiring such an allegation. 22B INPRAC 8:2; Cardinal Industries, Inc. v. Schwartz, 483 N.E.2d 458 (Ind.Ct.App. 1985). The plaintiff bears no burden to prove jurisdiction unless and until it is challenged by the defendant. 22B INPRAC 8:2; Brokemond v. Marshall Field & Co., 612 N.E.2d 143 (Ind.Ct.App. 1993).

f. *Equitable and legal claims in multi-count actions.* In multi-count actions, the inclusion of an equitable claim, standing alone, will not automatically draw the entire action into equity. Something more than the presence of an equitable claim is required, and the court must examine the claims at issue. 22B INPRAC 38:1 COMMENT; Lucas v. U.S. Bank, N.A., 953 N.E.2d 457 (Ind. 2011). Factors the court may consider in evaluating the nature of the underlying substantive claims include: the substance and central character of the complaint, the rights and interests at issue, the relief demanded, and any issues arising out of discovery. 22B INPRAC 38:1 COMMENT; Songer v. Civitas Bank, 771 N.E.2d 61 (Ind. 2002).

3. *Pleading special matters*

a. *Capacity.* It is not necessary to aver the capacity of a party to sue or be sued, the authority of a party to sue or be sued in a representative capacity, or the legal existence of an organization that is made a party. The burden of proving lack of such capacity, authority, or legal existence shall be upon the person asserting lack of it, and shall be pleaded as an affirmative defense. IN ST TRIAL P Rule 9(A).

b. *Fraud, mistake, condition of the mind.* In all averments of fraud or mistake, the circumstances constituting fraud or mistake shall be specifically averred. Malice, intent, knowledge, and other conditions of mind may be averred generally. IN ST TRIAL P Rule 9(B).

c. *Conditions precedent.* In pleading the performance or occurrence of promissory or non-promissory conditions precedent, it is sufficient to aver generally that all conditions precedent have been performed, have occurred, or have been excused. A denial of performance or occurrence shall be made specifically and with particularity, and a denial of excuse generally. IN ST TRIAL P Rule 9(C).

d. *Official document or act.* In pleading an official document or official act it is sufficient to aver that the document was issued or the act done in compliance with law. IN ST TRIAL P Rule 9(D).

e. *Judgment.* In pleading a judgment or decision of a domestic or foreign court, judicial or quasi-judicial tribunal, or of a board or officer, it is sufficient to aver the judgment or decision without setting forth matter showing jurisdiction to render it. IN ST TRIAL P Rule 9(E).

f. *Time and place.* For the purpose of testing the sufficiency of a pleading, averments of time and place are material and shall be considered like all other averments of material matter. However, time and place need be stated only with such specificity as will enable the opposing party to prepare his defense. IN ST TRIAL P Rule 9(F).

g. *Special damages; Damages where no answer.* When items of special damage are claimed, they shall be specifically stated. The relief granted to the plaintiff, if there be no answer, cannot exceed the relief demanded in his complaint; but, in any other case, the court may grant him any relief consistent with the facts or matters pleaded. IN ST TRIAL P Rule 9(G).

4. *Joinder*

   a. *Of claims.* A party asserting a claim for relief as an original claim, counterclaim, cross-claim, or third-party claim, may join, either as independent or as alternate claims, as many claims, whether legal, equitable, or statutory as he has against an opposing party. IN ST TRIAL P Rule 18(A).

   b. *Of remedies; Fraudulent conveyances.* Whenever a claim is one heretofore cognizable only after another claim has been prosecuted to a conclusion, the two (2) claims may be joined in a single action; but the court shall grant relief in that action only in accordance with the relative substantive rights of the parties. In particular, a plaintiff may state a claim for money and a claim to have set aside a conveyance fraudulent as to him, without first having obtained a judgment establishing the claim for money. IN ST TRIAL P Rule 18(B).

   c. *Of persons needed for just adjudication.* A person who is subject to service of process shall be joined as a party in the action if:

      i. In his absence complete relief cannot be accorded among those already parties; or

      ii. He claims an interest relating to the subject of the action and is so situated that the disposition of the action in his absence may:

         • As a practical matter impair or impede his ability to protect that interest, or

         • Leave any of the persons already parties subject to a substantial risk of incurring double, multiple, or otherwise inconsistent obligations by reason of his claimed interest. IN ST TRIAL P Rule 19(A).

      iii. If he has not been so joined, the court shall order that he be made a party. If he should join as a plaintiff but refuses to do so, he may be made a defendant. IN ST TRIAL P Rule 19(A).

5. *Trial by jury; Demand*

   a. *Causes triable by court and by jury.* Issues of law and issues of fact in causes that prior to the eighteenth day of June, 1852, were of exclusive equitable jurisdiction shall be tried by the court; issues of fact in all other causes shall be triable as the same are now triable. In case of the joinder of causes of action or defenses which, prior to said date, were of exclusive equitable jurisdiction with causes of action or defenses which, prior to said date, were designated as actions at law and triable by jury—the former shall be triable by the court, and the latter by a jury, unless waived; the trial of both may be at the same time or at different times, as the court may direct. IN ST TRIAL P Rule 38(A).

   b. *Demand.* Any party may demand a trial by jury of any issue triable of right by a jury by filing with the court and serving upon the other parties a demand therefor in writing at any time after the commencement of the action and not later than ten (10) days after the first responsive pleading to the complaint, or to a counterclaim, crossclaim or other claim if one properly is pleaded; and if no responsive pleading is filed or required, within ten (10) days after the time such pleading otherwise would have been required. Such demand is sufficient if indorsed upon a pleading of a party filed within such time. IN ST TRIAL P Rule 38(B).

   c. *Same; Specification of issues.* In his demand a party may specify the issues which he wishes so tried; otherwise he shall be deemed to have demanded trial by jury for all issues triable as of right by jury. Any other party must file a demand for jury trial to preserve his right to trial by jury:

      i. Of issues for which a right to trial by jury was not requested by another party; and

      ii. In case a request by another party was improper. But if a proper request for a trial by jury upon issues triable by jury as of right on his behalf is made by any party, such request shall be deemed to have been made on behalf of all parties entitled to a jury trial upon such issues. IN ST TRIAL P Rule 38(C).

d. *Waiver.* The failure of a party to appear at the trial, and the failure of a party to serve a demand as required by IN ST TRIAL P Rule 38 and to file it as required by IN ST TRIAL P Rule 5(E) constitute waiver by him of trial by jury. A demand for trial by jury made as provided in IN ST TRIAL P Rule 38 may not be withdrawn without the consent of the other party or parties. IN ST TRIAL P Rule 38(D).

  i. The trial court shall not grant a demand for a trial by jury filed after the time fixed in IN ST TRIAL P Rule 38(B) has elapsed except upon the written agreement of all of the parties to the action, which agreement shall be filed with the court and made a part of the record. If such agreement is filed then the court may, in its discretion, grant a trial by jury in which event the grant of a trial by jury may not be withdrawn except by the agreement of all of the parties. IN ST TRIAL P Rule 38(D).

e. *Arbitration.* Nothing in the Indiana Rules of Trial Procedure shall deny the parties the right by contract or agreement to submit or to agree to submit controversies to arbitration made before or after commencement of an action thereon or deny the courts power to specifically enforce such agreements. IN ST TRIAL P Rule 38(E).

f. *Equitable and legal claims in multi-count actions.* In multi-count actions, the inclusion of an equitable claim, standing alone, will not automatically draw the entire action into equity. Something more than the presence of an equitable claim is required, and the court must examine the claims at issue. 22B INPRAC 38:1 COMMENT; Lucas v. U.S. Bank, N.A., 953 N.E.2d 457 (Ind. 2011). Factors the court may consider in evaluating the nature of the underlying substantive claims include: the substance and central character of the complaint, the rights and interests at issue, the relief demanded, and any issues arising out of discovery. 22B INPRAC 38:1 COMMENT; Songer v. Civitas Bank, 771 N.E.2d 61 (Ind. 2002).

6. *Use of alternative dispute resolution.* Except as provided by the Indiana Rules for Alternative Dispute Resolution, a presiding judge may order any civil or domestic relations proceeding or selected issues in such proceedings referred to mediation, non-binding arbitration or mini-trial. The selection criteria which should be used by the court are defined under the Indiana Rules for Alternative Dispute Resolution. Binding arbitration and a summary jury trial may be ordered only upon the agreement of the parties as consistent with provisions in the Indiana Rules for Alternative Dispute Resolution which address each method. IN ST ADR Rule 1.6. For information on Indiana's ADR process refer to IN ST ADR Rule 1.1 through IN ST ADR Rule 8.8.

D. Documents

1. *Required documents*

  a. *Summons.* Contemporaneously with the filing of the complaint or equivalent pleading, the person seeking service or his attorney shall furnish to the clerk as many copies of the complaint and summons as are necessary. IN ST TRIAL P Rule 4(B).

  b. *Complaint.* Refer to the General Requirements section of this document for information on the contents of a complaint.

  c. *Appearance form.* At the time an action is commenced, the party initiating the proceeding shall file with the clerk of the court an appearance form setting forth the following information:

   i. Name, address and telephone number of the initiating party or parties filing the appearance form;

   ii. Name, address, attorney number, telephone number, FAX number, and e-mail address of any attorney representing the party, as applicable;

   iii. The case type of the proceeding [see IN ST ADMIN Rule 8];

   iv. A statement that the party will or will not accept service by fax or by e-mail from:

    • Other parties and/or

- The court under IN ST TRIAL P Rule 72(D);

v. In domestic relations, Uniform Reciprocal Enforcement of Support (URESA), paternity, delinquency, Child in Need of Services (CHINS), guardianship, and any other proceedings in which support may be an issue, the Social Security Identification Number of all family members;

vi. The caption and case number of all related cases;

vii. Such additional matters specified by state or local rule required to maintain the information management system employed by the court;

viii. In a proceeding involving a protection from abuse order, a workplace violence restraining order, or a no-contact order, the initiating party shall provide to the clerk a public mailing address for purposes of legal service. The initiating party may use the Attorney General Address Confidentiality program established by statute; and

ix. In a proceeding involving a mental health commitment, except seventy-two (72) hour emergency detentions, the initiating party shall provide the full name of the person with respect to whom commitment is sought and the person's state of residence. In addition, the initiating party shall provide at least one of the following identifiers for the person:

- Date of birth;
- Social Security Number;
- Driver's license number with state of issue and date of expiration;
- Department of Correction number;
- State ID number with state of issue and date of expiration; or
- FBI number. IN ST TRIAL P Rule 3.1; IN ST LAKE RCP Rule 5(A)(2).

d. *Chronological case summary (CCS) entry forms.* All filings shall be accompanied by a Chronological Case Summary (CCS) Entry Form to define or identify the documents filed. The Form used should be substantially similar to IN ST LAKE RCP App. A. IN ST LAKE RCP Rule 3(C).

2. *Supplemental documents*

a. *Proof of written instrument.* When any pleading allowed by the Indiana Rules of Trial Procedure is founded on a written instrument, the original, or a copy thereof, must be included in or filed with the pleading. Such instrument, whether copied in the pleadings or not, shall be taken as part of the record. When any pleading allowed by the Indiana Rules of Trial Procedure is founded on an account, an Affidavit of Debt, in a form substantially similar to that which is provided in IN ST TRIAL P App. A-2, shall be attached. IN ST TRIAL P Rule 9.2(A).

b. *Notice of intent to use foreign law.* A party who intends to raise an issue concerning the law of a foreign country shall give notice in his pleadings or other reasonable written notice. The court, in determining foreign law, may consider any relevant material or source, including testimony, whether or not submitted by a party or admissible under IN ST TRIAL P Rule 43. The court's determination shall be treated as a ruling on a question of law. It shall be made by the court and not the jury and shall be reviewable. IN ST TRIAL P Rule 44.1(A).

c. *Praecipe.* Affidavits, requests, and any other information relating to the summons and its service as required or permitted by the Indiana Rules of Trial Procedure shall be included in a praecipe attached to or entered upon the summons. Such praecipe shall be deemed to be a part of the summons for purposes of the Indiana Rules of Trial Procedure. Separate or additional summons shall, as provided by the Indiana Rules of Trial Procedure, be issued by the clerk at any time upon proper request of the person seeking service or his attorney. IN ST TRIAL P Rule 4(B).

d. *Facsimile cover sheet.* Any document sent to the Clerk of the Circuit Court by electronic facsimile transmission shall be accompanied by a cover sheet which states the title of the document, case number, number of pages, identity and voice telephone number of the sending party and instructions for filing. The cover sheet shall contain the signature of the attorney or party, pro se, authorizing the filing. IN ST ADMIN Rule 12(D).

E. Format

1. *Form of pleadings.* For the purpose of uniformity, convenience, clarity and durability, requirements in IN ST LAKE RCP Rule 2 shall be observed in the preparation of all pleadings, motions and other papers. IN ST LAKE RCP Rule 2. Whenever materials submitted fail to meet the standards in IN ST LAKE RCP Rule 2, the Court may impose appropriate sanctions. IN ST LAKE RCP Rule 2(B).

   a. *Caption; Names of parties.* Every pleading shall contain a caption setting forth the name of the court, the title of the action, the file number, and a designation as in IN ST TRIAL P Rule 7(A). In the complaint the title of the action shall include the names of all the parties, but in other pleadings it is sufficient to state the name of the first party on each side with an appropriate indication of other parties. IN ST TRIAL P Rule 10(A).

      i. *Special judge matters.* The caption of all CCS Entry Forms, pleadings, motions, orders and other papers to be filed in a special judge case shall include in block text the words SPECIAL JUDGE and the name of the judge directly below the cause number on the caption. IN ST LAKE RCP Rule 2(D).

   b. *Paragraphs; Separate statements.* All averments of a claim or defense shall be made in numbered paragraphs, the contents of each of which shall be limited as far as practicable to a statement of a single set of circumstances, and a paragraph may be referred to by number in all succeeding pleadings. Each claim founded upon a separate transaction or occurrence and each defense other than denials may be stated in a separate count or defense whenever a separation facilitates the clear presentation of the matters set forth. IN ST TRIAL P Rule 10(B).

   c. *Adoption by reference; Exhibits.* Statements in a pleading may be adopted by reference in a different part of the same pleading or in another pleading or in any motion. A copy of any written instrument which is an exhibit to a pleading is a part thereof for all purposes. IN ST TRIAL P Rule 10(C).

   d. *Paper; Print, quality and binding*

      i. All pleadings, motions, chronological case summary entry forms, orders, process and other papers shall be neatly and legibly printed, typewritten or mechanically reproduced, on one (1) side only, on white opaque paper. To satisfy the recordkeeping requirements of IN ST TRIAL P Rule 77, the print shall be of sufficient density and clarity for preservation and reproduction of microfilming, optical disk or other secondary sources. For this reason, the use of non-letter-quality printers is discouraged. IN ST LAKE RCP Rule 2(A).

      ii. Paper and ink shall be of such quality as to withstand the test of time. All documents shall be produced on acid-free, non-thermal paper. It is recommended that a minimum of twenty (20) pound, twenty-five percent (25%) cotton paper product be used. Documents of multiple pages shall be submitted in bound or stapled fashion, and the binding or stapling shall be at the top only. Covers or backings shall not be used. IN ST LAKE RCP Rule 2(A).

   e. *Papers; Handwritten.* Handwritten papers may be filed only if approved by the Court and a typewritten or printed true rendition thereof is filed within three (3) days thereafter and approved by the Court. Upon such approval, they shall be deemed and filed as the original, while the handwritten papers shall be retained therewith for evidentiary purposes. IN ST LAKE RCP Rule 2(C).

   f. *Minute sheets; Motion blanks.* Minute sheets and motion blanks shall no longer be used. IN ST LAKE RCP Rule 2(D).

2. *Size of papers for filing.* Effective January 1, 1992, all pleadings, copies, motions and documents filed with any trial court or appellate level court, typed or printed, with the exception of exhibits and existing wills, shall be prepared on eight and one-half by eleven inch (8 1/2" x 11") size paper. IN ST ADMIN Rule 11.

3. *Signature requirements*

   a. *Signature of attorney.* Every pleading or motion of a party represented by an attorney shall be signed by at least one (1) attorney of record in his individual name, whose address, telephone number, and attorney number shall be stated, except that this provision shall not apply to pleadings and motions

made and transcribed at the trial or a hearing before the judge and received by him in such form. IN ST TRIAL P Rule 11(A).

   i. The signature of an attorney constitutes a certificate by him that he has read the pleadings; that to the best of his knowledge, information, and belief, there is good ground to support it; and that it is not interposed for delay. IN ST TRIAL P Rule 11(A).

   ii. If a pleading or motion is not signed or is signed with intent to defeat the purpose of the rule, it may be stricken as sham and false and the action may proceed as though the pleading had not been served. IN ST TRIAL P Rule 11(A).

   iii. For a willful violation of IN ST TRIAL P Rule 11 an attorney may be subjected to appropriate disciplinary action. Similar action may be taken if scandalous or indecent matter is inserted. IN ST TRIAL P Rule 11(A).

b. *Signature of unrepresented party.* A party who is not represented by an attorney shall sign his pleading and state his address. IN ST TRIAL P Rule 11(A).

c. *Verification not generally required.* Except when specifically required by rule, pleadings or motions need not be verified or accompanied by affidavit. The rule in equity that the averments of an answer under oath must be overcome by the testimony of two (2) witnesses or of one (1) witness sustained by corroborating circumstances is abolished. IN ST TRIAL P Rule 11(A).

d. *Verification by affirmation or representation.* When in connection with any civil or special statutory proceeding it is required that any pleading, motion, petition, supporting affidavit, or other document of any kind, be verified, or that an oath be taken, it shall be sufficient if the subscriber simply affirms the truth of the matter to be verified by an affirmation or representation. IN ST TRIAL P Rule 11(B). IN ST TRIAL P Rule 11(B) states that the affirmation or representation should be in substantially the following language: "I (we) affirm, under the penalties for perjury, that the foregoing representation(s) is (are) true. (Signed) _____."

   i. Any person who falsifies an affirmation or representation of fact shall be subject to the same penalties as are prescribed by law for the making of a false affidavit. IN ST TRIAL P Rule 11(B).

e. *Verified pleadings, motions, and affidavits as evidence.* Pleadings, motions and affidavits accompanying or in support of such pleadings or motions when required to be verified or under oath shall be accepted as a representation that the signer had personal knowledge thereof or reasonable cause to believe the existence of the facts or matters stated or alleged therein; and, if otherwise competent or acceptable as evidence, may be admitted as evidence of the facts or matters stated or alleged therein when it is so provided in the Indiana Rules of Trial Procedure, by statute or other law, or to the extent the writing or signature expressly purports to be made upon the signer's personal knowledge. When such pleadings, motions and affidavits are verified or under oath they shall not require other or greater proof on the part of the adverse party than if not verified or not under oath unless expressly provided otherwise by the Indiana Rules of Trial Procedure, statute or other law. Affidavits upon motions for summary judgment under IN ST TRIAL P Rule 56 and in denial of execution under IN ST TRIAL P Rule 9.2 shall be made upon personal knowledge. IN ST TRIAL P Rule 11(C).

f. *Electronic signature.* The filing of documents and information through the E-filing system by use of a valid username and password is presumed to have been authorized by the User to whom that username and password have been issued and documents filed through the E-filing system are presumed to have been signed by the same User. IN ST ADMIN Rule 16(E).

4. *Information excluded from public access.* Every document filed in a case shall separately identify information excluded from public access pursuant to IN ST ADMIN Rule 9(G)(1) as follows:

a. Whole documents that are excluded from public access pursuant to IN ST ADMIN Rule 9(G)(1) shall be tendered on light green paper or have a light green coversheet attached to the document, marked "Not for Public Access" or "Confidential." IN ST TRIAL P Rule 5(G)(1).

b. When only a portion of a document contains information excluded from public access pursuant to IN ST ADMIN Rule 9(G)(1), said information shall be omitted [or redacted] from the filed document, and set forth on a separate accompanying document on light green paper conspicuously marked "Not

for Public Access" or "Confidential" and clearly designated [or identifying] the caption and number of the case and the document and location within the document to which the redacted material pertains. IN ST TRIAL P Rule 5(G)(2).

c. With respect to documents filed in electronic format, the trial court, by local rule, may provide for compliance with IN ST TRIAL P Rule 5 in manner that separates and protects access to information excluded from public access. IN ST TRIAL P Rule 5(G)(3).

d. IN ST TRIAL P Rule 5(G) does not apply to a record sealed by the court pursuant to IN ST 5-14-3-5.5 or otherwise, nor to records, documents, or information filed in cases to which public access is prohibited pursuant to IN ST ADMIN Rule 9(G). IN ST TRIAL P Rule 5(G)(4).

e. The following information in case records is excluded from public access and is confidential:

    i. Information that is excluded from public access pursuant to federal law;

    ii. Information that is excluded from public access as declared confidential by Indiana statute or other court rule, including without limitation:

- All adoption records created after July 8, 1941, as declared confidential by IN ST 31-19-19-1, et seq., except those specifically declared open by IN ST 31-19-13-2(2);

- All records relating to chancroid, chlamydia, gonorrhea, hepatitis, human immunodeficiency virus (HIV), Lymphogranuloma venereum, syphilis, tuberculosis, as declared confidential by IN ST 16-41-8-1, et seq.;

- All records relating to child abuse as declared confidential by IN ST 31-33-18-1, et seq.;

- All records relating to drug tests as declared confidential by IN ST 5-14-3-4(a)(9);

- Records of grand jury proceedings as declared confidential by IN ST 35-34-2-4;

- Records of juvenile proceedings as declared confidential by IN ST 31-39-1-2, except those specifically open under statute;

- All paternity records created after July 1, 1941 as declared confidential by IN ST 31-14-11-15, IN ST 31-19-5-23, IN ST 31-39-1-1 and IN ST 31-39-1-2 [Editor's note: IN ST 31-14-11-15 was repealed effective May 9, 2013];

- All pre-sentence reports as declared confidential by IN ST 35-38-1-13;

- Written petitions to permit marriages without consent and orders directing the Clerk of Court to issue a marriage license to underage persons, as declared confidential by IN ST 31-11-1-6;

- Only those arrest warrants, search warrants, indictments and informations ordered confidential by the trial judge, prior to return of duly executed service as declared confidential by IN ST 5-14-3-4(b)(1);

- All medical, mental health, or tax records unless determined by law or regulation of any governmental custodian not to be confidential, released by the subject of such records, or declared by a court of competent jurisdiction to be essential to the resolution of litigation as declared confidential by IN ST 16-39-3-10, IN ST 6-4.1-5-10, IN ST 6-4.1-12-12, and IN ST 6-8.1-7-1;

- Personal information relating to jurors or prospective jurors, other than for the use of the parties and counsel, pursuant to IN ST JURY Rule 10;

- Information relating to protection from abuse orders, no-contact orders and workplace violence restraining orders as declared confidential by IN ST 5-2-9-6, et seq.;

- Mediation proceedings pursuant to IN ST ADR Rule 2.11, Mini-Trial proceedings pursuant to IN ST ADR Rule 4.4(C), and Summary Jury Trials pursuant to IN ST ADR Rule 5.6;

- Information in probation files pursuant to the Probation Standards promulgated by the Judicial Conference of Indiana pursuant to IN ST 11-13-1-8(b);

- Information deemed confidential pursuant to the Rules for Court Administered Alcohol

and Drug Programs promulgated by the Judicial Conference of Indiana pursuant to IN ST 12-23-14-13;

- Information deemed confidential pursuant to the Problem-Solving Court Rules promulgated by the Judicial Conference of Indiana pursuant to IN ST 33-23-16-16;

- All records of the Department of workforce Development as declared confidential by IN ST 22-4-19-6;

- Information regarding interception of electronic communications that is sealed or deemed confidential as set forth in IN ST 35-33.5-2-1, et seq.

iii. Information excluded from public access by specific court order;

iv. Complete Social Security Numbers of living persons;

v. With the exception of names, information such as addresses, phone numbers, and dates of birth which explicitly identifies:

- Natural persons who are witnesses or victims (not including defendants) in criminal, domestic violence, stalking, sexual assault, juvenile, or civil protection order proceedings, provided that juveniles who are victims of sex crimes shall be identified by initials only;

- Places of residence of judicial officers, clerks and other employees of courts and clerks of court, unless the person or persons about whom the information pertains waives confidentiality;

vi. Complete account numbers of specific assets, loans, bank accounts, credit cards, and personal identification numbers (PINs);

vii. All orders of expungement entered in criminal or juvenile proceedings, orders to restrict access to criminal history information pursuant to IN ST 35-38-5-5.5 or IN ST 35-38-8-5 and records excluded from public access by such orders, and information related to infractions that is excluded from public access pursuant to IN ST 34-28-5-15 or IN ST 34-28-5-16 [Editor's note: IN ST 35-38-5-5.5, IN ST 35-38-8-5 and IN ST 34-28-5-16 were repealed effective July 1, 2013; for information on orders restricting access to criminal history, refer to IN ST 35-38-9-1, et seq.];

viii. All personal notes and e-mail, and deliberative material, of judges, jurors, court staff and judicial agencies, and information recorded in personal data assistants (PDA's) or organizers and personal calendars. IN ST ADMIN Rule 9(G)(1).

5. *Form of the summons*

a. *Required contents of summons.* The summons shall contain:

i. The name and address of the person on whom the service is to be effected;

ii. The name, street address, and telephone number of the court and the cause number assigned to the case;

iii. The title of the case as shown by the complaint, but, if there are multiple parties, the title may be shortened to include only the first named plaintiff and defendant with an appropriate indication that there are additional parties;

iv. The name, address, and telephone number of the attorney for the person seeking service;

v. The time within which the Indiana Rules of Trial Procedure require the person being served to respond, and a clear statement that in case of his failure to do so, judgment by default may be rendered against him for the relief demanded in the complaint. IN ST TRIAL P Rule 4(C).

b. *Additional contents of summons.* The summons may also contain any additional information which will facilitate proper service. IN ST TRIAL P Rule 4(C).

6. *Format of electronically filed documents*

a. *Generally.* Electronically filed documents must meet the same requirements of format as documents conventionally filed pursuant to IN ST LAKE RCP Rule 2 or other applicable Lake County Rules of Civil Procedure. IN ST LAKE RCP Rule 17(D)(1).

b. *Titles of documents.* The person electronically filing a document will be responsible for designating a title for the document at the time it is filed. The LCOD will generate the appropriate entry onto the CCS to record the filing of the document. IN ST LAKE RCP Rule 17(D)(3).

c. *Citations and hyperlinks.* Electronically filed documents may contain hyperlink references to an external document as a convenient mechanism for accessing material cited in the document. Filers wishing to insert hyperlinks into documents shall continue to use the traditional method of citation to authority in addition to the hyperlink provided. The hyperlink is merely a convenience to the court and the material referenced is extraneous to the file and not a part of the court's record. IN ST LAKE RCP Rule 17(D)(5).

d. *Attachments and exhibits.* All documents which form part of a single submission and which are being filed at the same time and by the same filer may be electronically filed together under one document filing, e.g., the motion, supporting affidavits, memorandum in support, designation of evidence, exhibits. IN ST LAKE RCP Rule 17(D)(6).

    i. Large documents which do not exist in an electronic format shall be scanned into .pdf format and filed electronically as separate attachments. A scanner is available in each clerk's office for use by the public and the bar in scanning and saving image files if needed. IN ST LAKE RCP Rule 17(D)(6).

e. *Electronic signatures*

    i. *Electronic filing as signature.* The electronic filing of a document which is required to be signed shall constitute the filer's representation under IN ST TRIAL P Rule 11. Unless the electronically filed document has been scanned and shows the filer's original signature, the signature of the filer shall be indicated by As/Attorney's Name, or As/Party's Name as in the case of a pro se litigant, on the line where the signature would otherwise appear. IN ST LAKE RCP Rule 17(G)(1).

    ii. *Signatures on jointly signed or filed, verified or other documents.* In the case of a stipulation, agreed order, jointly signed motion or other document which needs to be signed by two (2) or more persons, or in the case of documents which must contain original signatures and which require verification or an unsworn declaration under rule or statute, the signatures may be indicated by either:

- Submitting a scanned copy of the originally signed document; or,
- Submitting the document with the use of As/Name in the signature block(s) where the original signature(s) appear(s) in the original document; provided, however, that the filer shall first obtain the physical signature of all persons necessary. IN ST LAKE RCP Rule 17(G)(2).

    iii. *Retention of original.* The filer shall retain the original executed document. IN ST LAKE RCP Rule 17(G).

7. *Citation of local rules.* The local rules for Lake County may be known as the Lake County Rules of Civil Procedure, and abbreviated as LR. IN ST LAKE RCP Rule 1(C).

F. Filing and Service Requirements

1. *Filing requirements.* A civil action is commenced by filing with the court a complaint or such equivalent pleading or document as may be specified by statute, by payment of the prescribed filing fee or filing an order waiving the filing fee, and, where service of process is required, by furnishing to the clerk as many copies of the complaint and summons as are necessary. IN ST TRIAL P Rule 3. An action may be commenced by E-filing only in a court which has adopted a pilot project plan approved by the Division of State Court Administration pursuant to IN ST ADMIN Rule 16. IN ST ADMIN Rule 16(F). All papers presented for filing shall be submitted to the Clerk and not to the court. IN ST LAKE RCP Rule 3(A).

    a. *Filing with the court defined.* The filing of pleadings, motions, and other papers with the court as required by the Indiana Rules of Trial Procedure shall be made by one of the following methods:

        i. Delivery to the clerk of the court;

        ii. Sending by electronic transmission under the procedure adopted pursuant to IN ST ADMIN Rule 12;

iii. Mailing to the clerk by registered, certified or express mail return receipt requested;

iv. Depositing with any third-party commercial carrier for delivery to the clerk within three (3) calendar days, cost prepaid, properly addressed;

v. If the court so permits, filing with the judge, in which event the judge shall note thereon the filing date and forthwith transmit them to the office of the clerk; or

vi. Electronic filing, as approved by the Division of State Court Administration pursuant to IN ST ADMIN Rule 16. IN ST TRIAL P Rule 5(F).

vii. Filing by registered or certified mail and by third-party commercial carrier shall be complete upon mailing or deposit. IN ST TRIAL P Rule 5(F).

b. *Mandatory electronic filing.* Unless otherwise permitted by the Lake County Rules of Civil Procedure or otherwise authorized by the judicial officer assigned to a particular case, all documents submitted for filing (including the original complaint, or equivalent pleading, and summons) shall be filed electronically with the clerk using the LCOD, no matter when the case was originally filed. IN ST LAKE RCP Rule 17(D).

i. *Of documents containing information excluded from public access pursuant to* IN ST ADMIN Rule 9. Documents containing information excluded from public access pursuant to IN ST ADMIN Rule 9, or documents which are ordered to be filed under seal shall be filed electronically, pursuant to IN ST LAKE RCP Rule 17(D)(9), whenever possible, along with a copy of the applicable order to seal the records, and the filer shall designate the documents as "Not for Public Access Pursuant to Administrative Rule 9(G)(1)" at the time of filing. IN ST LAKE RCP Rule 16(A)(1); IN ST LAKE RCP Rule 17(D)(9).

- *Conventional filing of documents containing information excluded from public access pursuant to* IN ST ADMIN Rule 9. Documents containing information excluded from public access pursuant to IN ST ADMIN Rule 9, or documents which are ordered to be filed under seal, which cannot be legibly scanned and filed electronically, shall be conventionally filed under seal and designated by the filer as "Not for Public Access Pursuant to Administrative Rule 9(G)(1)" at the time of filing. The unredacted version shall be filed on light green paper which is conspicuously marked "Not for Public Access"; and a redacted version, with confidential information deleted, shall be filed on white paper which shall be available for public access. The filer shall also electronically file a Notice of Manual Filing. IN ST LAKE RCP Rule 16(A)(2).

ii. *Technical failures.* If a registered user is unable to file a document in a timely manner due to technical difficulties in the LCOD, the registered user must file a document with the court as soon as possible notifying the court of the inability to file the document. A sample document titled Declaration that Party was Unable to File in a Timely Manner Due to Technical Difficulties can be found at IN ST LAKE RCP Form 4. Delayed filings shall be rejected unless accompanied by the declaration attesting to the filer's failed attempts to file electronically at least two (2) times, separated by at least one (1) hour, after noon on each day of delay due to such technical failure. IN ST LAKE RCP Rule 17(J).

iii. *Documents allowed to be filed conventionally.* Unless specifically authorized by the court, only the following documents may be filed conventionally and not electronically:

- Exhibits and other documents that cannot be converted to a legible electronic form, such as videotapes, x-rays, and similar materials
- Documents delivered to the clerk by pro se litigants
- Documents mailed to the clerk by pro se litigants
- Confidential documents
- Notice of manual filing
- Titles of documents
- Chronological case summary entry forms (CCS entry forms). IN ST LAKE RCP Rule 17(E).

- For more information on the documents which must be filed conventionally, refer to IN ST LAKE RCP Rule 17(E).

c. *Facsimile filing.* Only when necessary on an emergency basis (i.e., when certified mail or other means of filing will not bring the document to the Judge's attention prior to the scheduled hearing or ruling), pleadings, motions and other papers may be filed by electronic facsimile transmission, or when specifically authorized by the Court. IN ST LAKE RCP Rule 2(C).

    i. *Generally.* In counties where a majority of judges of the courts of record, by posted local rule, have authorized electronic facsimile filing and designated a telephone number to receive such transmissions, pleadings, motions, and other papers may be sent to the Clerk of Circuit Court by electronic facsimile transmission for filing in any case, provided:

- Such matter does not exceed ten (10) pages, including the cover sheet;
- Such matter does not require the payment of fees other than the electronic facsimile transcription fee set forth in IN ST ADMIN Rule 12(E);
- The sending party creates at the time of transmission a machine generated log for such transmission; and
- The original document and the transmission log are maintained by the sending party for the duration of the litigation. IN ST ADMIN Rule 12(B).

    ii. *Time of filing.* During normal, posted business hours, the time of filing shall be the time the duplicate document is produced in the office of the Clerk of the Circuit Court. Duplicate documents received at all other times shall be filed as of the next normal business day. IN ST ADMIN Rule 12(C).

- If the receiving fax machine endorses its own time and date stamp upon the transmitted documents and the receiving machine produces a delivery receipt which is electronically created and transmitted to the sending party, the time of filing shall be the date and time recorded on the transmitted document by the receiving fax machine. IN ST ADMIN Rule 12(C).

d. *Filing for special judges.* For special judge matters where the special judge is a full-time judge or magistrate serving within Lake County, all papers submitted for filing shall be delivered or mailed to the Clerk's office at the courthouse where the special judge regularly serves. IN ST LAKE RCP Rule 3(A).

e. *Proof of filing.* Any party filing any paper by any method other than personal delivery to the clerk shall retain proof of filing. IN ST TRIAL P Rule 5(F).

2. *Service requirements.* The court acquires jurisdiction over a party or person who under the Indiana Rules of Trial Procedure commences or joins in the action, is served with summons or enters an appearance, or who is subjected to the power of the court under any other law. IN ST TRIAL P Rule 4(A).

a. *Designation of method of service of the summons.* The person seeking service or his attorney may designate the manner of service upon the summons. If not so designated, the clerk shall cause service to be made by mail or other public means provided the mailing address of the person to be served is indicated in the summons or can be determined. If a mailing address is not furnished or cannot be determined or if service by mail or other public means is returned without acceptance, the complaint and summons shall promptly be delivered to the sheriff or his deputy who, unless otherwise directed, shall serve the summons. IN ST TRIAL P Rule 4(D).

b. *Summons and complaint to be served together.* The summons and complaint shall be served together unless otherwise ordered by the court. When service of summons is made by publication, the complaint shall not be published. When jurisdiction over a party is dependent upon service of process by publication or by his appearance, summons and complaint shall be deemed to have been served at the end of the day of last required publication in the case of service by publication, and at the time of appearance in jurisdiction acquired by appearance. Whenever the summons and complaint are not served or published together, the summons shall contain the full, unabbreviated title of the case. IN ST TRIAL P Rule 4(E).

c. *Territorial limits and service under special order*

    i. *Territorial limits of effective service.* Process may be served anywhere within the territorial limits of this state and outside the state as provided in the Indiana Rules of Trial Procedure. IN ST TRIAL P Rule 4.14(A).

    ii. *Service under special order of court.* Upon application of any party the court in which any action is pending may make an appropriate order for service in a manner not provided by the Indiana Rules of Trial Procedure or statutes when such service is reasonably calculated to give the defendant actual knowledge of the proceedings and an opportunity to be heard. IN ST TRIAL P Rule 4.14(B).

d. *Return of service.* The person making service shall promptly make his return upon or attach it to a copy of the summons which shall be delivered to the clerk. The return shall be signed by the person making it, and shall include a statement:

    i. That service was made upon the person as required by law and the time, place, and manner thereof;

    ii. If service was not made, the particular manner in which it was thwarted in terms of fact or in terms of law;

    iii. Such other information as is expressly required by the Indiana Rules of Trial Procedure. IN ST TRIAL P Rule 4.15(A).

3. *Methods of service of the summons and complaint*

a. *In general*

    i. *Methods of service.* Service may be made upon an individual, or an individual acting in a representative capacity, by:

- Sending a copy of the summons and complaint by registered or certified mail or other public means by which a written acknowledgment of receipt may be requested and obtained to his residence, place of business or employment with return receipt requested and returned showing receipt of the letter; or

- Delivering a copy of the summons and complaint to him personally; or

- Leaving a copy of the summons and complaint at his dwelling house or usual place of abode; or

- Serving his agent as provided by rule, statute or valid agreement. IN ST TRIAL P Rule 4.1(A).

    ii. *Service by sheriff.* The copies of the complaint or equivalent pleading and summons or other process, or any other documents such as an order to appear, necessary for service by sheriff shall be printed by the office of the clerk. The copies of the complaint and summons, or other documents, shall be forwarded to the sheriff for service and return. The clerk shall scan and electronically file the return of service and the paper original may then be discarded. IN ST LAKE RCP Rule 17(F)(1)(a).

    iii. *Copy service to be followed with mail.* Whenever service is made under IN ST TRIAL P Rule 4.1(A)(3) [by leaving a copy at dwelling or usual place of abode] or IN ST TRIAL P Rule 4.1(A)(4) [by service of agent], the person making the service also shall send by first class mail, a copy of the summons without the complaint to the last known address of the person being served, and this fact shall be shown upon the return. IN ST TRIAL P Rule 4.1(B).

- *Service by certified mail; Initial summons for a defendant.* If a plaintiff does not request service by sheriff, the clerk will upon request electronically issue a summons for service by certified mail, and the initial summons to be served upon a defendant will be printed and served by certified mail by the clerk. The clerk shall scan and electronically file the return receipt or notice of unsuccessful service when received by return mail, and the paper original may then be discarded. IN ST LAKE RCP Rule 17(F)(1)(b).

- *Service by certified mail; Additional summons or other process after initial service.* The clerk will electronically issue any additional summons or other process requested for service by certified mail or special process server, and the summons or other process will be printed and served by certified mail by the party or attorney requesting the documents to issue, or by the special process server appointed for that purpose. The party or attorney shall scan and electronically file the certificate of mailing and/or service, and the return receipt or notice of unsuccessful service when received by return mail, and retain the original documents. IN ST LAKE RCP Rule 17(F)(1)(c).

iv. *Service by fax or e-mail.* A party who has consented to service by fax or e-mail may be served as follows:

- Service by e-mail shall be made by attaching the document being served in PDF format. Discovery documents must also be served in accordance with IN ST TRIAL P Rule 26(A).

- Service by fax shall be deemed complete upon generation of a transmission record indicating the successful transmission of the entire document, except as provided in IN ST TRIAL P Rule 5(B)(3)(d).

- Service by e-mail shall be deemed complete upon transmission, except as provided in IN ST TRIAL P Rule 5(B)(3)(d).

- Service by fax or e-mail that occurs on a Saturday, Sunday, legal holiday, or day the court or agency in which the matter is pending is closed or after 5:00 PM local time of the recipient shall be deemed complete the next day that is not a Saturday, Sunday, legal holiday, or day that the court or agency in which the matter is pending is not closed. IN ST TRIAL P Rule 5(B)(3).

v. *Electronic service.* A party may not electronically serve a summons or other process and complaint or equivalent pleading, but instead must perfect service according to IN ST TRIAL P Rule 4, et seq. IN ST LAKE RCP Rule 17(F)(1).

b. *Service upon infants or incompetents*

i. *Service upon infants.* Service upon an individual known to be an infant shall be made upon his next friend or guardian ad litem, if service is with respect to the same action in which the infant is so represented. If there is no next friend or guardian ad litem, service shall be made upon his court-appointed representative if one is known and can be served within this state. If there is no court-appointed representative, service shall be made upon either parent known to have custody of the infant, or if there is no parent, upon a person known to be standing in the position of custodian or parent. The infant shall also be served if he is fourteen (14) years of age or older. In the event that service, as provided above, is not possible, service shall be made on the infant. IN ST TRIAL P Rule 4.2(A).

ii. *Service upon incompetents.* Service upon an individual who has been adjudged to be of unsound mind, otherwise incompetent or who is believed to be such shall be made upon his next friend or guardian ad litem, if service is with respect to the same action in which the incompetent is so represented. If there is no next friend or guardian ad litem, service shall be made upon his court-appointed representative if one is known and can be served within this state. If there is no court-appointed representative, then upon the named party and also upon a person known to be standing in the position of custodian of his person. IN ST TRIAL P Rule 4.2(B).

iii. *Duty to inform court; Appearance.* Nothing herein is intended to affect the duty of a party to inform the court that a person is an infant or incompetent. An appearance by a court-appointed guardian, next friend or guardian ad litem or his attorney shall correct any defect in service under IN ST TRIAL P Rule 4.2 unless such defect be challenged. IN ST TRIAL P Rule 4.2(C).

c. *Service upon institutionalized persons.* Service of summons upon a person who is imprisoned or restrained in an institution shall be made by delivering or mailing a copy of the summons and complaint to the official in charge of the institution. It shall be the duty of said official to immediately deliver the summons and complaint to the person being served and allow him to make provisions for adequate representation by counsel. The official shall indicate upon the return whether the person has received the summons and been allowed an opportunity to retain counsel. IN ST TRIAL P Rule 4.3.

d. *Service upon individuals whose acts serve as basis for jurisdiction.* A person subject to the jurisdiction of the courts of this state under IN ST TRIAL P Rule 4.4 may be served with summons:

    i. As provided by IN ST TRIAL P Rule 4.1 (service on individuals), IN ST TRIAL P Rule 4.5 (service upon resident who cannot be found or served within the state), IN ST TRIAL P Rule 4.6 (service upon organizations), IN ST TRIAL P Rule 4.9 (in rem actions); or

    ii. The person shall be deemed to have appointed the Secretary of State as his agent upon whom service of summons may be made as provided in IN ST TRIAL P Rule 4.10. IN ST TRIAL P Rule 4.4(B).

e. *Service upon resident who cannot be found or served within the state.* When the person to be served is a resident of this state who cannot be served personally or by agent in this state and either cannot be found, has concealed his whereabouts or has left the state, summons may be served in the manner provided by IN ST TRIAL P Rule 4.9 (summons in in rem actions). IN ST TRIAL P Rule 4.5.

f. *Service upon organizations*

    i. *Persons to be served.* Service upon an organization may be made as follows:

- In the case of a domestic or foreign organization upon an executive officer thereof, or if there is an agent appointed or deemed by law to have been appointed to receive service, then upon such agent. IN ST TRIAL P Rule 4.6(A)(1).

- In the case of a partnership, upon a general partner thereof. IN ST TRIAL P Rule 4.6(A)(2).

- In the case of a state governmental organization upon the executive officer thereof and also upon the Attorney General. IN ST TRIAL P Rule 4.6(A)(3).

- In the case of a local governmental organization, upon the executive thereof and upon the attorney for the local governmental organization. IN ST TRIAL P Rule 4.6(A)(4).

- When, in IN ST TRIAL P Rule 4.6(A)(3) and IN ST TRIAL P Rule 4.6(A)(4), a governmental representative is named as a party in his individual name or in such name along with his official title, then also upon such representative. IN ST TRIAL P Rule 4.6(A)(5).

    ii. *Manner of service.* Service under IN ST TRIAL P Rule 4.6(A) shall be made on the proper person in the manner provided by the Indiana Rules of Trial Procedure for service upon individuals, but a person seeking service or his attorney shall not knowingly direct service to be made at the person's dwelling house or place of abode, unless such is an address furnished under the requirements of a statute or valid agreement, or unless an affidavit on or attached to the summons states that service in another manner is impractical. IN ST TRIAL P Rule 4.6(B).

    iii. *Service at organization's office.* When shown upon an affidavit or in the return, that service upon an organization cannot be made as provided in IN ST TRIAL P Rule 4.6(A) or IN ST TRIAL P Rule 4.6(B), service may be made by leaving a copy of the summons and complaint at any office of such organization located within this state with the person in charge of such office. IN ST TRIAL P Rule 4.6(C).

g. *Summons; Service upon agent named by statute or agreement.* Whenever an agent (other than an agent appointed to receive service for a governmental organization of this state) has been designated by or pursuant to statute or valid agreement to receive service for the person being served, service may be made upon such agent as follows:

    i. If the agent is a governmental organization or officer designated by or pursuant to statute, service shall be made as provided in IN ST TRIAL P Rule 4.10. IN ST TRIAL P Rule 4.7(1).

    ii. If the agent is one other than that described in IN ST TRIAL P Rule 4.7(1), service shall be made upon him as provided in IN ST TRIAL P Rule 4.1 (service upon individuals) or IN ST TRIAL P Rule 4.6 (service upon organizations). If service cannot be made upon such agent, because there is no address furnished as required by statute or valid agreement or his whereabouts in this state are unknown, then his principal shall be deemed to have appointed the Secretary of State as a replacement for the agent and service may be made upon the Secretary of State as provided in IN ST TRIAL P Rule 4.10. IN ST TRIAL P Rule 4.7(2).

h. *Summons; Service of pleadings or summons on Attorney General.* Service of a copy of the summons and complaint or any pleading upon the Attorney General under the Indiana Rules of Trial Procedure or any statute shall be made by personal service upon him, a deputy or clerk at his office, or by mail or other public means to him at such office in the manner provided by IN ST TRIAL P Rule 4.1(A)(1), and by IN ST TRIAL P Rule 4.11 to the extent applicable. IN ST TRIAL P Rule 4.8.

i. *Summons; In rem actions*

   i. *In general.* In any action involving a res situated within this state, service may be made as provided in IN ST TRIAL P Rule 4.9. The court may render a judgment or decree to the extent of its jurisdiction over the res. IN ST TRIAL P Rule 4.9(A).

   ii. *Manner of service.* Service under IN ST TRIAL P Rule 4.9 may be made as follows:

   - By service of summons upon a person or his agent pursuant to the Indiana Rules of Trial Procedure; or

   - By service of summons outside this state in a manner provided by IN ST TRIAL P Rule 4.1 (service upon individuals) or by publication outside this state in a manner provided by IN ST TRIAL P Rule 4.13 (service by publication) or outside this state in any other manner as provided by the Indiana Rules of Trial Procedure; or

   - By service by publication pursuant to IN ST TRIAL P Rule 4.13. IN ST TRIAL P Rule 4.9(A).

j. *Summons; Service upon Secretary of State or other governmental agent.* Whenever, under the Indiana Rules of Trial Procedure or any statute, service is made upon the Secretary of State or any other governmental organization or officer, as agent for the person being served, service may be made upon such agent as provided in IN ST TRIAL P Rule 4.10. IN ST TRIAL P Rule 4.10(A).

   i. The person seeking service or his attorney shall:

   - Submit his request for service upon the agent in the praecipe for summons, and state that the governmental organization or officer is the agent of the person being served;

   - State the address of the person being served as filed and recorded pursuant to a statute or valid agreement, or if no such address is known, then his last known mailing address, and, if no such address is known, then such shall be stated;

   - Pay any fee prescribed by statute to be forwarded together with sufficient copies of the summons, affidavit and complaint, to the agent by the clerk of the court. IN ST TRIAL P Rule 4.10(A)(1).

   ii. Upon receipt thereof the agent shall promptly:

   - Send to the person being served a copy of the summons and complaint by registered or certified mail or by other public means by which a written acknowledgment of receipt may be obtained;

   - Complete and deliver to the clerk an affidavit showing the date of the mailing, or if there was no mailing, the reason therefor;

   - Send to the clerk a copy of the return receipt along with a copy of the summons;

   - File and retain a copy of the return receipt. IN ST TRIAL P Rule 4.10(A)(2).

k. *Summons; Registered or certified mail.* Whenever service by registered or certified mail or other public means by which a return receipt may be requested is authorized, the clerk of the court or a governmental agent under IN ST TRIAL P Rule 4.10 shall send the summons and complaint to the person being served at the address supplied upon the summons, or furnished by the person seeking service. In his return the clerk of the court or the governmental agent shall show the date and place of mailing, a copy of the mailed or electronically-transmitted return receipt if and when received by him showing whether the mailing was accepted or returned, and, if accepted, by whom. The return along with the receipt shall be promptly filed by the clerk with the pleadings and become a part of the record. If a mailing by the clerk of the court is returned without acceptance, the clerk shall reissue the summons and complaint for service as requested, by the person seeking service. IN ST TRIAL P Rule 4.11.

COMPLAINT

l. *Summons; Service by sheriff or other officer*

    i. *In general.* Whenever service is made by delivering a copy to a person personally or by leaving a copy at his dwelling house or place of employment as provided by IN ST TRIAL P Rule 4.1, summons shall be issued to and served by the sheriff, his deputy, or some person specially or regularly appointed by the court for that purpose. Service shall be effective if made by a person not otherwise authorized by the Indiana Rules of Trial Procedure, but proof of service by such a person must be made by him as a witness or by deposition without allowance of expenses therefor as costs. The person to whom the summons is delivered for service must act promptly and exercise reasonable care to cause service to be made. IN ST TRIAL P Rule 4.12(A).

    ii. *Special service by police officers.* A sheriff, his deputy, or any full-time state or municipal police officer may serve summons in any county of this state if he agrees or has agreed to make the service. When specially requested in the praecipe for summons, the complaint and summons shall be delivered to such officer by the clerk or the attorney for the person seeking service. No agreement with the sheriff or his deputy for such service in the sheriff's own county shall be permitted. In no event shall any expenses agreed upon under this provision be assessed or recovered as costs or affect court costs otherwise imposed for regular service. IN ST TRIAL P Rule 4.12(B).

    iii. *Service in other counties.* A summons may be served in any county in this state. If service is to be made in another county, the summons may be issued by the clerk for service therein to the sheriff of such county or to a person authorized to make service by the Indiana Rules of Trial Procedure. IN ST TRIAL P Rule 4.12(C).

    iv. *Service outside the state.* Personal service, when permitted by the Indiana Rules of Trial Procedure to be made outside the state, may be made there by any disinterested person or by the attorney representing the person seeking such service. The expenses of such person may be assessed as costs only if they are reasonable and if service by mail or other public means cannot be made or is not successful. IN ST TRIAL P Rule 4.12(D).

m. *Summons; Service by publication*

    i. *Praecipe for summons by publication.* In any action where notice by publication is permitted by the Indiana Rules of Trial Procedure or by statute, service may be made by publication. Summons by publication may name all the persons to be served, and separate publications with respect to each party shall not be required. The person seeking such service, or his attorney, shall submit his request therefor upon the praecipe for summons along with supporting affidavits that diligent search has been made that the defendant cannot be found, has concealed his whereabouts, or has left the state, and shall prepare the contents of the summons to be published. The summons shall be signed by the clerk of the court or the sheriff in such manner as to indicate that it is made by his authority. IN ST TRIAL P Rule 4.13(A).

    ii. *Contents of summons by publication.* The summons shall contain the following information:

- The name of the person being sued, and the person to whom the notice is directed, and, if the person's whereabouts are unknown or some or all of the parties are unknown, a statement to that effect;
- The name of the court and cause number assigned to the case;
- The title of the case as shown by the complaint, but if there are multiple parties, the title may be shortened to include only the first named plaintiff and those defendants to be served by publication with an appropriate indication that there are additional parties;
- The name and address of the attorney representing the person seeking service;
- A brief statement of the nature of the suit, which need not contain the details and particulars of the claim. A description of any property, relationship, or other res involved in the action, and a statement that the person being sued claims some interest therein;
- A clear statement that the person being sued must respond within thirty (30) days after the last notice of the action is published, and in case he fails to do so, judgment by default may

be entered against him for the relief demanded in the complaint. IN ST TRIAL P Rule 4.13(B).

iii. *Publication of summons.* The summons shall be published three (3) times by the clerk or person making it, the first publication promptly and each two (2) succeeding publications at least seven (7) and not more than fourteen (14) days after the prior publication, in a newspaper authorized by law to publish notices, and published in the county where the complaint or action is filed, where the res is located, or where the defendant resides or where he was known last to reside. If no newspaper is published in the county, then the summons shall be published in the county in this state nearest thereto in which any such paper may be printed, or in a place specially ordered by the court. The person seeking the service or his attorney may designate any qualified newspaper, and if he fails to do so, the selection may be made by the clerk. IN ST TRIAL P Rule 4.13(C).

iv. *By whom made or procured.* Service of summons by publication shall be made and procured by the clerk, by a person appointed by the court for that purpose, or by the clerk or sheriff of another county where publication is to be made. IN ST TRIAL P Rule 4.13(D).

v. *Return.* The clerk or person making the service shall prepare the return and include the following:

- Any supporting affidavits of the printer containing a copy of the summons which was published;

- An information or statement that the newspaper and the publication meet all legal requirements applicable to such publication;

- The dates of publication. IN ST TRIAL P Rule 4.13(E).

- The return and affidavits shall be filed with the pleadings and other papers in the case and shall become a part of the record as provided in the Indiana Rules of Trial Procedure. IN ST TRIAL P Rule 4.13(E).

n. *Service on agent of nonresident corporation.* In an action commenced in a court of general jurisdiction in Indiana by or against any corporation incorporated under the laws of Indiana, in which one (1) or more of the directors of the corporation is: (1) a necessary or proper party; and (2) a nonresident of Indiana; service of summons upon a director for the purpose of obtaining jurisdiction of the person of the director in the action is obtained by serving the summons on the resident agent of the corporation. IN ST 34-33-2-1.

G. Hearings

1. The Indiana rules do not contemplate a hearing regarding the service of the summons and complaint.

H. Forms

1. Official Complaint Forms for Indiana

a. Affidavit of debt. IN ST TRIAL P App. A-2.

b. Appearance by attorney in civil case. IN ST TRIAL P App. B.

2. Complaint Forms for Indiana

a. Caption; Generally. 5 INPRAC § 3:1.1.

b. Caption; Multiple parties. 5 INPRAC § 3:1.2.

c. Single count. 5 INPRAC § 3:1.3.

d. Multiple counts; Single defendant. 5 INPRAC § 3:1.4.

e. Multiple counts; Multiple defendants. 5 INPRAC § 3:1.5.

f. Signature; By party. 5 INPRAC § 3:1.6.

g. Signature; By attorney. 5 INPRAC § 3:1.7.

h. Verification. 5 INPRAC § 3:1.8.

i. Individual defendant. 5 INPRAC § 3:2.1.

j.   Resident agent of corporation. 5 INPRAC § 3:2.2.

k.   Attorney general. 5 INPRAC § 3:2.3.

l.   City attorney. 5 INPRAC § 3:2.4.

m.   Certificate; Personal service. 5 INPRAC § 3:2.5.

n.   Certificate; First class mail. 5 INPRAC § 3:2.6.

o.   Certificate; Registered mail. 5 INPRAC § 3:2.7.

p.   Certificate; Dwelling house. 5 INPRAC § 3:2.8.

q.   Clerk's certificate of mailing. 5 INPRAC § 3:2.9.

r.   Clerk's certificate of mailing; Acceptance by defendant. 5 INPRAC § 3:2.10.

s.   Clerk's return on service of summons by mail; Not accepted by defendant. 5 INPRAC § 3:2.11.

t.   Sheriff's return; Service of summons. 5 INPRAC § 3:2.12.

u.   Motion to appoint person to serve process. 5 INPRAC § 3:2.13.

v.   Published notice; Text. 5 INPRAC § 3:2.14.

w.   Affidavit of publisher. 5 INPRAC § 3:2.15.

x.   Clerk's return on service by publication. 5 INPRAC § 3:2.16.

y.   Complaint; Single count. 9 INPRAC § 2.3.

z.   Appearance by party initiating action; Form. 9 INPRAC § 6.3.

3. Official Complaint Forms for Lake County

a.   CCS entry form. IN ST LAKE RCP App. A.

b.   Notice of manual filing. IN ST LAKE RCP Form 2.

c.   Declaration that party was unable to file in a timely manner. IN ST LAKE RCP Form 4.

4. Complaint Forms for Lake County

a.   Notice of manual filing. EFORMST IN 5540.

I. Checklist

(I) ❑ Matters to be considered by the plaintiff

(a) ❑ Required documents

(1) ❑ Summons

(2) ❑ Complaint

(3) ❑ Appearance form

(4) ❑ Chronological case summary (CCS) entry forms

(b) ❑ Supplemental documents

(1) ❑ Proof of written instrument

(2) ❑ Notice of intent to use foreign law

(3) ❑ Praecipe

(4) ❑ Facsimile cover sheet

(c) ❑ Timing

(1) ❑ The claimant typically bears the burden of commencing an action within the applicable statute of limitations

(2) ❑ If person seeking service of process fails without cause for sixty (60) days or more to provide clerk with required summons for issuance or with other information necessary to effectuate service, person has failed to exercise due diligence in securing service of process

(II) ❑ Matters to be considered by the defendant

  (a) ❑ Required documents

    (1) ❑ Answer

    (2) ❑ Appearance form

    (3) ❑ Chronological case summary (CCS) entry forms

    (4) ❑ Certificate of service

  (b) ❑ Supplemental documents

    (1) ❑ Admission of service

    (2) ❑ Proof of written instrument

    (3) ❑ Notice of intent to use foreign law

    (4) ❑ Facsimile cover sheet

  (c) ❑ Timing

    (1) ❑ A responsive pleading required under the Indiana Rules of Trial Procedure, shall be served within twenty (20) days after service of the prior pleading

    (2) ❑ The service of a motion permitted under IN ST TRIAL P Rule 12 alters the time for service of responsive pleadings as follows, unless a different time is fixed by the court:

      (i) ❑ If the court does not grant the motion, the responsive pleading shall be served in ten (10) days after notice of the court's action;

      (ii) ❑ If the court grants the motion and the corrective action is allowed to be taken, it shall be taken within ten (10) days, and the responsive pleading shall be served within ten (10) days thereafter

    (3) ❑ All pleadings and papers subsequent to the complaint which are required to be served upon a party shall be filed with the Court either before service or within a reasonable period of time thereafter

    (4) ❑ Provided it is timely filed, the mere entry of appearance by a party or counsel in response to a summons in an action that requires an answer shall effect an extension of thirty (30) days from the filing thereof within which to respond

    (5) ❑ All pleadings, motions and other papers submitted for filing which are required to be served under IN ST TRIAL P Rule 5(A) shall be filed no later than three (3) days after service

    (6) ❑ If such papers are filed before service, proof of service thereof shall be filed no later than three (3) business days thereafter

Pleadings
Amended Complaint

Document Last Updated October 2013

A. Applicable Rules

1. *State rules*

  a. Appearance. IN ST TRIAL P Rule 3.1.

  b. Process. IN ST TRIAL P Rule 4.

  c. Service of the summons. IN ST TRIAL P Rule 4.1; IN ST TRIAL P Rule 4.2; IN ST TRIAL P Rule 4.3; IN ST TRIAL P Rule 4.4; IN ST TRIAL P Rule 4.5; IN ST TRIAL P Rule 4.6; IN ST TRIAL P Rule 4.7; IN ST TRIAL P Rule 4.8; IN ST TRIAL P Rule 4.9; IN ST TRIAL P Rule 4.10; IN ST TRIAL P Rule 4.11; IN ST TRIAL P Rule 4.12; IN ST TRIAL P Rule 4.13; IN ST TRIAL P Rule 4.14; IN ST TRIAL P Rule 4.15; IN ST 34-33-2-1.

    d.   Service and filing of pleadings and other papers. IN ST TRIAL P Rule 5.

    e.   Time. IN ST TRIAL P Rule 6.

    f.   Pleadings. IN ST TRIAL P Rule 7; IN ST TRIAL P Rule 8; IN ST TRIAL P Rule 9; IN ST TRIAL P Rule 9.1; IN ST TRIAL P Rule 9.2; IN ST TRIAL P Rule 10.

    g.   Signing and verification of pleadings. IN ST TRIAL P Rule 11.

    h.   Amended and supplemental pleadings. IN ST TRIAL P Rule 15.

    i.   Joinder. IN ST TRIAL P Rule 18; IN ST TRIAL P Rule 19.

    j.   Evidence. IN ST TRIAL P Rule 43.

    k.   Determination of foreign law. IN ST TRIAL P Rule 44.1.

    l.   Judgment on the evidence (directed verdict). IN ST TRIAL P Rule 50.

    m.   Findings by the court. IN ST TRIAL P Rule 52.

    n.   Summary judgment. IN ST TRIAL P Rule 56.

    o.   Motion to correct error. IN ST TRIAL P Rule 59.

    p.   Relief from judgment or order. IN ST TRIAL P Rule 60.

    q.   Court records. IN ST TRIAL P Rule 77.

    r.   Access to court records. IN ST ADMIN Rule 9.

    s.   Paper size. IN ST ADMIN Rule 11.

    t.   Facsimile transmission. IN ST ADMIN Rule 12.

    u.   Electronic filing and electronic service pilot projects. IN ST ADMIN Rule 16.

    v.   Privacy and confidentiality. IN ST 5-2-9-6; IN ST 5-14-3-4; IN ST 5-14-3-5.5; IN ST 6-4.1-5-10; IN ST 6-4.1-12-12; IN ST 6-8.1-7-1; IN ST 11-13-1-8; IN ST 12-23-14-13; IN ST 16-39-3-10; IN ST 16-41-8-1; IN ST 22-4-19-6; IN ST 31-11-1-6; IN ST 31-19-5-23; IN ST 31-19-13-2; IN ST 31-19-19-1; IN ST 31-33-18-1; IN ST 31-39-1-1; IN ST 31-39-1-2; IN ST 33-23-16-16; IN ST 35-34-2-4; IN ST 35-38-1-13; IN ST 35-38-9-1; IN ST ADR Rule 2.11; IN ST ADR Rule 4.4; IN ST ADR Rule 5.6; IN ST JURY Rule 10.

2. *Local rules*

    a.   Scope and title. [IN ST LAKE RCP Rule 1, as amended by IN ORDER 13-0237, effective October 18, 2013].

    b.   Preparation of pleadings, motions and other papers. IN ST LAKE RCP Rule 2.

    c.   Filing. [IN ST LAKE RCP Rule 3, as amended by IN ORDER 13-0237, effective October 18, 2013].

    d.   Confidential information and sealed documents. IN ST LAKE RCP Rule 16.

    e.   Electronic filing and service. IN ST LAKE RCP Rule 17.

B. Timing

1. *Filing an amended pleading*

    a.   *As a matter of course.* A party may amend his pleading once as a matter of course at any time before a responsive pleading is served or, if the pleading is one to which no responsive pleading is permitted, and the action has not been placed upon the trial calendar, he may so amend it at any time within thirty (30) days after it is served. IN ST TRIAL P Rule 15(A).

    b.   *With leave of court.* Otherwise a party may amend his pleading only by leave of court or by written consent of the adverse party; and leave shall be given when justice so requires. IN ST TRIAL P Rule 15(A). Refer to the Indiana KeyRules Motion for Leave to Amend document for more information.

    c.   *Time for filing.* All pleadings, motions and other papers submitted for filing which are required to be served under IN ST TRIAL P Rule 5(A) shall be filed no later than three (3) days after service. IN ST LAKE RCP Rule 3(A).

        i.   If such papers are filed before service, proof of service thereof shall be filed no later than three

(3) business days thereafter. Upon failure to comply with IN ST LAKE RCP Rule 3, the Court may, on motion of any party or on its own motion, impose appropriate sanctions. IN ST LAKE RCP Rule 3(A).

2. *Computation of time*

   a. *Generally; Days excluded.* In computing any period of time prescribed or allowed by the Indiana Rules of Trial Procedure, by order of the court, or by any applicable statute, the day of the act, event, or default from which the designated period of time begins to run shall not be included. The last day of the period so computed is to be included unless it is:

      i. A Saturday,

      ii. A Sunday,

      iii. A legal holiday as defined by state statute, or

      iv. A day the office in which the act is to be done is closed during regular business hours. IN ST TRIAL P Rule 6(A).

   b. *Short periods.* In any event, the period runs until the end of the next day that is not a Saturday, a Sunday, a legal holiday, or a day on which the office is closed. When the period of time allowed is less than seven (7) days, intermediate Saturdays, Sundays, legal holidays, and days on which the office is closed shall be excluded from the computations. IN ST TRIAL P Rule 6(A).

   c. *Additional time after service by United States mail.* Whenever a party has the right or is required to do some act or take some proceedings within a prescribed period after the service of a notice or other paper upon him and the notice or paper is served upon him by United States mail, three (3) days shall be added to the prescribed period. IN ST TRIAL P Rule 6(E).

   d. *Electronic filing does not alter deadlines.* Filing electronically does not alter any filing deadlines or any time computation pursuant to state or federal statutes, any Rules of the Indiana Supreme Court, including without limitation the Rules of Trial Procedure, the Rules of Appellate Procedure or the Administrative Rules, or applicable Lake County Rules of Civil Procedure. The office of the Lake County Clerk is open for electronic filing under the Lake County Rules of Civil Procedure twenty-four (24) hours a day. A document is deemed filed at the date and time it is received by the LCOD server. Filing must be completed before midnight local time in order to be considered filed that day. Lake County observes Central Time and electronic filers are strongly urged to file documents during hours when the Lake County Online Docket ("LCOD") help line is available, from 9:00 a.m. to 4:00 p.m. local time, although documents can be filed electronically twenty-four (24) hours a day. IN ST LAKE RCP Rule 17(I).

   e. *Enlargement of time.* When an act is required or allowed to be done at or within a specific time by the Indiana Rules of Trial Procedure, the court may at any time for cause shown:

      i. Order the period enlarged, with or without motion or notice, if request therefor is made before the expiration of the period originally prescribed or extended by a previous order; or

      ii. Upon motion made after the expiration of the specific period, permit the act to be done where the failure to act was the result of excusable neglect; but, the court may not extend the time for taking any action for judgment on the evidence under IN ST TRIAL P Rule 50(A), amendment of findings and judgment under IN ST TRIAL P Rule 52(B), to correct errors under IN ST TRIAL P Rule 59(C), statement in opposition to motion to correct error under IN ST TRIAL P Rule 59(E), or to obtain relief from final judgment under IN ST TRIAL P Rule 60(B), except to the extent and under the conditions stated in those rules. IN ST TRIAL P Rule 6(B).

C. General Requirements

1. *Amending pleadings.* The purpose of an amended pleading is to include matters that occurred before the filing of the original pleading but which were either overlooked by the pleader or unknown to him at the time. It is a substitute for the original and relates to the facts that existed when the original pleading was filed. An amended pleading supercedes the original as to those portions amended. 10 INPRAC § 46.1.

   a. *Amendments liberally allowed.* Amendments to pleadings are to be liberally allowed in order that all issues are presented in one action. 10 INPRAC § 46.1; Pinnacle Media, LLC v. Metropolitan Dev. Com'n of Marion County, 868 N.E.2d 894 (Ind.Ct.App. 2007).

b. *Amendments to conform to the evidence.* When issues not raised by the pleadings are tried by express or implied consent of the parties, they shall be treated in all respects as if they had been raised in the pleadings. Such amendment of the pleadings as may be necessary to cause them to conform to the evidence and to raise these issues may be made upon motion of any party at any time, even after judgment, but failure so to amend does not affect the result of the trial of these issues. If evidence is objected to at the trial on the ground that it is not within the issues made by the pleadings, the court may allow the pleadings to be amended and shall do so freely when the presentation of the merits of the action will be subserved thereby and the objecting party fails to satisfy the court that the admission of such evidence would prejudice him in maintaining his action or defense upon the merits. The court may grant a continuance to enable the objecting party to meet such evidence. IN ST TRIAL P Rule 15(B).

c. *Relation back of amendments*

    i. Whenever the claim or defense asserted in the amended pleading arose out of the conduct, transaction, or occurrence set forth or attempted to be set forth in the original pleading, the amendment relates back to the date of the original pleading. An amendment changing the party against whom a claim is asserted relates back if the foregoing provision is satisfied and, within one hundred and twenty (120) days of commencement of the action, the party to be brought in by amendment:

- Has received such notice of the institution of the action that he will not be prejudiced in maintaining his defense on the merits; and

- Knew or should have known that but for a mistake concerning the identity of the proper party, the action would have been brought against him. IN ST TRIAL P Rule 15(C).

    ii. The requirement of IN ST TRIAL P Rule 15(C)(1) and IN ST TRIAL P Rule 15(C)(2) with respect to a governmental organization to be brought into the action as defendant is satisfied:

- In the case of a state or governmental organization by delivery or mailing of process to the attorney general or to a governmental executive [IN ST TRIAL P Rule 4.6(A)(3)]; or

- In the case of a local governmental organization, by delivery or mailing of process to its attorney as provided by statute, to a governmental executive thereof [IN ST TRIAL P Rule 4.6(A)(4)], or to the officer holding the office if suit is against the officer or an office. IN ST TRIAL P Rule 15(C).

d. *Amendment by leave.* Amendments, other than an amendment by right, may be made only by leave of court or by written consent of the opposing party. 2 INPRAC R 15(15.2). Refer to the Indiana KeyRules Motion for Leave to Amend document for more information on amending with leave of court.

2. *Pleading, generally*

a. *Pleadings to be concise.* Each averment of a pleading shall be simple, concise, and direct. No technical forms of pleading or motions are required. All fictions in pleading are abolished. IN ST TRIAL P Rule 8(E)(1).

b. *Pleading in the alternative.* A pleading may set forth two (2) or more statements of a claim or defense alternatively or hypothetically, either in one (1) count or defense or in separate counts or defenses. When two (2) or more statements are made in the alternative and one (1) of them if made independently would be sufficient, the pleading is not made insufficient by the insufficiency of one or more of the alternative statements. A pleading may also state as many separate claims or defenses as the pleader has regardless of consistency and whether based on legal or equitable grounds. All statements shall be made subject to the obligations set forth in IN ST TRIAL P Rule 11. IN ST TRIAL P Rule 8(E)(2).

c. *Motions and pleadings, joint and several.* All motions and pleadings of any kind addressed to two (2) or more paragraphs of any pleading, or filed by two (2) or more parties, shall be taken and construed as joint, separate, and several motions or pleadings to each of such paragraphs and by and against each of such parties. All motions or pleadings containing two (2) or more subject-matters shall be taken and construed as separate and several as to each subject-matter. All objections to rulings made

by two (2) or more parties shall be taken and construed as the joint, separate, and several objections of each of such parties. IN ST TRIAL P Rule 8(E)(3).

 i. A complaint filed by or against two (2) or more plaintiffs shall be taken and construed as joint, separate, and several as to each of said plaintiffs. IN ST TRIAL P Rule 8(E).

 d. *Construction of pleadings.* All pleadings shall be so construed as to do substantial justice, lead to disposition on the merits, and avoid litigation of procedural points. IN ST TRIAL P Rule 8(F).

3. *Contents of the complaint*

 a. *Pleading for relief; Notice pleading.* Indiana is a "notice pleading" jurisdiction. 22B INPRAC 8:1; State v. American Family Voices, Inc., 898 N.E.2d 293 (Ind. 2008). Notice pleading replaces the technical and complex method of pleading which existed prior to 1970. Notice pleading is grounded in due process of law and must provide a defendant with reasonable notice of the plaintiff's claim or an opponent's defense. 22B INPRAC 8:1; Noblesville Redevelopment Com'n v. Noblesville Associates Ltd. Partnership, 674 N.E.2d 558 (Ind. 1996). Notice pleading does not require that the plaintiff state all elements or facts essential to a cause of action. 22B INPRAC 8:1; State v. American Family Voices, Inc., 898 N.E.2d 293 (Ind. 2008). Instead, the complaint must state "a short and plain statement of the claim" showing an entitlement to relief, and a demand for relief. 22B INPRAC 8:1; Trail v. Boys and Girls Clubs of Northwest Indiana, 845 N.E.2d 130 (Ind. 2006).

 b. *Claims for relief.* To state a claim for relief, whether an original claim, counterclaim, cross-claim, or third-party claim, a pleading must contain:

  i. A short and plain statement of the claim showing that the pleader is entitled to relief, and

  ii. A demand for relief to which the pleader deems entitled. Relief in the alternative or of several different types may be demanded. However, in any complaint seeking damages for personal injury or death, or seeking punitive damages, no dollar amount or figure shall be included in the demand. IN ST TRIAL P Rule 8(A).

 c. *Res ipsa loquitur.* Res ipsa loquitur or a similar doctrine may be pleaded by alleging generally that the facts connected with the action are unknown to the pleader and are within the knowledge of the opposing party. IN ST TRIAL P Rule 9.1(B).

 d. *Bona fide purchaser.* When the rights of a person depend upon his status as a bona fide purchaser for value or upon similar requirements, such status must be pleaded and proved by the person asserting it, but it may be pleaded in general terms. Once it is established that the person has given any required value, unless such value is commercially unreasonable, and that he has met any requirements of recordation, filing, possession, or perfection, the trier of fact must find that such value was given or such perfection was made in accordance with any requirements of good faith, lack of knowledge, or lack of notice unless and until evidence is introduced which would support a finding of its non-existence. IN ST TRIAL P Rule 9.1(D).

 e. *Presumption; Matters of judicial notice.* Neither presumptions of law nor matters of which judicial notice may be taken need be stated in a pleading. IN ST TRIAL P Rule 9.1(E).

  i. *Presumption of jurisdiction.* Jurisdiction is presumed in Indiana. 22B INPRAC 8:2. Consequently, there is no requirement to affirmatively plead the existence of jurisdiction in the complaint, unless the action involves a special proceeding requiring such an allegation. 22B INPRAC 8:2; Cardinal Industries, Inc. v. Schwartz, 483 N.E.2d 458 (Ind.Ct.App. 1985). The plaintiff bears no burden to prove jurisdiction unless and until it is challenged by the defendant. 22B INPRAC 8:2; Brokemond v. Marshall Field & Co., 612 N.E.2d 143 (Ind.Ct.App. 1993).

 f. *Equitable and legal claims in multi-count actions.* In multi-count actions, the inclusion of an equitable claim, standing alone, will not automatically draw the entire action into equity. Something more than the presence of an equitable claim is required, and the court must examine the claims at issue. 22B INPRAC 38:1 COMMENT; Lucas v. U.S. Bank, N.A., 953 N.E.2d 457 (Ind. 2011). Factors the court may consider in evaluating the nature of the underlying substantive claims include: the substance and central character of the complaint, the rights and interests at issue, the relief demanded, and any issues arising out of discovery. 22B INPRAC 38:1 COMMENT; Songer v. Civitas Bank, 771 N.E.2d 61 (Ind. 2002).

4. *Pleading special matters*

   a. *Capacity.* It is not necessary to aver the capacity of a party to sue or be sued, the authority of a party to sue or be sued in a representative capacity, or the legal existence of an organization that is made a party. The burden of proving lack of such capacity, authority, or legal existence shall be upon the person asserting lack of it, and shall be pleaded as an affirmative defense. IN ST TRIAL P Rule 9(A).

   b. *Fraud, mistake, condition of the mind.* In all averments of fraud or mistake, the circumstances constituting fraud or mistake shall be specifically averred. Malice, intent, knowledge, and other conditions of mind may be averred generally. IN ST TRIAL P Rule 9(B).

   c. *Conditions precedent.* In pleading the performance or occurrence of promissory or non-promissory conditions precedent, it is sufficient to aver generally that all conditions precedent have been performed, have occurred, or have been excused. A denial of performance or occurrence shall be made specifically and with particularity, and a denial of excuse generally. IN ST TRIAL P Rule 9(C).

   d. *Official document or act.* In pleading an official document or official act it is sufficient to aver that the document was issued or the act done in compliance with law. IN ST TRIAL P Rule 9(D).

   e. *Judgment.* In pleading a judgment or decision of a domestic or foreign court, judicial or quasi-judicial tribunal, or of a board or officer, it is sufficient to aver the judgment or decision without setting forth matter showing jurisdiction to render it. IN ST TRIAL P Rule 9(E).

   f. *Time and place.* For the purpose of testing the sufficiency of a pleading, averments of time and place are material and shall be considered like all other averments of material matter. However, time and place need be stated only with such specificity as will enable the opposing party to prepare his defense. IN ST TRIAL P Rule 9(F).

   g. *Special damages; Damages where no answer.* When items of special damage are claimed, they shall be specifically stated. The relief granted to the plaintiff, if there be no answer, cannot exceed the relief demanded in his complaint; but, in any other case, the court may grant him any relief consistent with the facts or matters pleaded. IN ST TRIAL P Rule 9(G).

5. *Joinder*

   a. *Of claims.* A party asserting a claim for relief as an original claim, counterclaim, cross-claim, or third-party claim, may join, either as independent or as alternate claims, as many claims, whether legal, equitable, or statutory as he has against an opposing party. IN ST TRIAL P Rule 18(A).

   b. *Of remedies; Fraudulent conveyances.* Whenever a claim is one heretofore cognizable only after another claim has been prosecuted to a conclusion, the two (2) claims may be joined in a single action; but the court shall grant relief in that action only in accordance with the relative substantive rights of the parties. In particular, a plaintiff may state a claim for money and a claim to have set aside a conveyance fraudulent as to him, without first having obtained a judgment establishing the claim for money. IN ST TRIAL P Rule 18(B).

   c. *Of persons needed for just adjudication.* A person who is subject to service of process shall be joined as a party in the action if:

      i. In his absence complete relief cannot be accorded among those already parties; or

      ii. He claims an interest relating to the subject of the action and is so situated that the disposition of the action in his absence may:

         • As a practical matter impair or impede his ability to protect that interest, or

         • Leave any of the persons already parties subject to a substantial risk of incurring double, multiple, or otherwise inconsistent obligations by reason of his claimed interest. IN ST TRIAL P Rule 19(A).

      iii. If he has not been so joined, the court shall order that he be made a party. If he should join as a plaintiff but refuses to do so, he may be made a defendant. IN ST TRIAL P Rule 19(A).

6. *Trial by jury; Demand*

   a. *Causes triable by court and by jury.* Issues of law and issues of fact in causes that prior to the eighteenth day of June, 1852, were of exclusive equitable jurisdiction shall be tried by the court;

LAKE COUNTY

issues of fact in all other causes shall be triable as the same are now triable. In case of the joinder of causes of action or defenses which, prior to said date, were of exclusive equitable jurisdiction with causes of action or defenses which, prior to said date, were designated as actions at law and triable by jury—the former shall be triable by the court, and the latter by a jury, unless waived; the trial of both may be at the same time or at different times, as the court may direct. IN ST TRIAL P Rule 38(A).

b. *Demand.* Any party may demand a trial by jury of any issue triable of right by a jury by filing with the court and serving upon the other parties a demand therefor in writing at any time after the commencement of the action and not later than ten (10) days after the first responsive pleading to the complaint, or to a counterclaim, crossclaim or other claim if one properly is pleaded; and if no responsive pleading is filed or required, within ten (10) days after the time such pleading otherwise would have been required. Such demand is sufficient if indorsed upon a pleading of a party filed within such time. IN ST TRIAL P Rule 38(B).

c. *Same; Specification of issues.* In his demand a party may specify the issues which he wishes so tried; otherwise he shall be deemed to have demanded trial by jury for all issues triable as of right by jury. Any other party must file a demand for jury trial to preserve his right to trial by jury:

   i. Of issues for which a right to trial by jury was not requested by another party; and

   ii. In case a request by another party was improper. But if a proper request for a trial by jury upon issues triable by jury as of right on his behalf is made by any party, such request shall be deemed to have been made on behalf of all parties entitled to a jury trial upon such issues. IN ST TRIAL P Rule 38(C).

d. *Waiver.* The failure of a party to appear at the trial, and the failure of a party to serve a demand as required by IN ST TRIAL P Rule 38 and to file it as required by IN ST TRIAL P Rule 5(E) constitute waiver by him of trial by jury. A demand for trial by jury made as provided in IN ST TRIAL P Rule 38 may not be withdrawn without the consent of the other party or parties. IN ST TRIAL P Rule 38(D).

   i. The trial court shall not grant a demand for a trial by jury filed after the time fixed in IN ST TRIAL P Rule 38(B) has elapsed except upon the written agreement of all of the parties to the action, which agreement shall be filed with the court and made a part of the record. If such agreement is filed then the court may, in its discretion, grant a trial by jury in which event the grant of a trial by jury may not be withdrawn except by the agreement of all of the parties. IN ST TRIAL P Rule 38(D).

e. *Arbitration.* Nothing in the Indiana Rules of Trial Procedure shall deny the parties the right by contract or agreement to submit or to agree to submit controversies to arbitration made before or after commencement of an action thereon or deny the courts power to specifically enforce such agreements. IN ST TRIAL P Rule 38(E).

D. Documents

1. *Required documents*

   a. *Amended complaint.* Refer to the General Requirements section of this document for information on the contents of an amended complaint.

   b. *Chronological case summary (CCS) entry forms.* All filings shall be accompanied by a Chronological Case Summary (CCS) Entry Form to define or identify the documents filed. The Form used should be substantially similar to IN ST LAKE RCP App. A. IN ST LAKE RCP Rule 3(C).

   c. *Certificate of service.* An attorney or unrepresented party tendering a document to the Clerk for filing shall certify that service has been made, list the parties served, and specify the date and means of service. The certificate of service shall be placed at the end of the document and shall not be separately filed. The separate filing of a certificate of service, however, shall not be grounds for rejecting a document for filing. The Clerk may permit documents to be filed without a certificate of service but shall require prompt filing of a separate certificate of service. IN ST TRIAL P Rule 5(C).

   i. All pleadings, motions and other papers submitted for filing which are required to be served under IN ST TRIAL P Rule 5(A) shall contain proof of service pursuant to IN ST TRIAL P Rule 5(B)(2). IN ST LAKE RCP Rule 3(A).

2. *Supplemental documents*

   a. *Proof of written instrument.* When any pleading allowed by the Indiana Rules of Trial Procedure is founded on a written instrument, the original, or a copy thereof, must be included in or filed with the pleading. Such instrument, whether copied in the pleadings or not, shall be taken as part of the record. When any pleading allowed by the Indiana Rules of Trial Procedure is founded on an account, an Affidavit of Debt, in a form substantially similar to that which is provided in IN ST TRIAL P App. A-2, shall be attached. IN ST TRIAL P Rule 9.2(A).

   b. *Notice of intent to use foreign law.* A party who intends to raise an issue concerning the law of a foreign country shall give notice in his pleadings or other reasonable written notice. The court, in determining foreign law, may consider any relevant material or source, including testimony, whether or not submitted by a party or admissible under IN ST TRIAL P Rule 43. The court's determination shall be treated as a ruling on a question of law. It shall be made by the court and not the jury and shall be reviewable. IN ST TRIAL P Rule 44.1(A).

   c. *Facsimile cover sheet.* Any document sent to the Clerk of the Circuit Court by electronic facsimile transmission shall be accompanied by a cover sheet which states the title of the document, case number, number of pages, identity and voice telephone number of the sending party and instructions for filing. The cover sheet shall contain the signature of the attorney or party, pro se, authorizing the filing. IN ST ADMIN Rule 12(D).

3. Refer to the Indiana KeyRules Complaint document for the required and supplemental documents for filing and serving an amended complaint against a new party.

E. Format

1. *Form of pleadings.* For the purpose of uniformity, convenience, clarity and durability, requirements in IN ST LAKE RCP Rule 2 shall be observed in the preparation of all pleadings, motions and other papers. IN ST LAKE RCP Rule 2. Whenever materials submitted fail to meet the standards in IN ST LAKE RCP Rule 2, the Court may impose appropriate sanctions. IN ST LAKE RCP Rule 2(B).

   a. *Caption; Names of parties.* Every pleading shall contain a caption setting forth the name of the court, the title of the action, the file number, and a designation as in IN ST TRIAL P Rule 7(A). In the complaint the title of the action shall include the names of all the parties, but in other pleadings it is sufficient to state the name of the first party on each side with an appropriate indication of other parties. IN ST TRIAL P Rule 10(A).

      i. *Special judge matters.* The caption of all CCS Entry Forms, pleadings, motions, orders and other papers to be filed in a special judge case shall include in block text the words SPECIAL JUDGE and the name of the judge directly below the cause number on the caption. IN ST LAKE RCP Rule 2(D).

   b. *Paragraphs; Separate statements.* All averments of a claim or defense shall be made in numbered paragraphs, the contents of each of which shall be limited as far as practicable to a statement of a single set of circumstances, and a paragraph may be referred to by number in all succeeding pleadings. Each claim founded upon a separate transaction or occurrence and each defense other than denials may be stated in a separate count or defense whenever a separation facilitates the clear presentation of the matters set forth. IN ST TRIAL P Rule 10(B).

   c. *Adoption by reference; Exhibits.* Statements in a pleading may be adopted by reference in a different part of the same pleading or in another pleading or in any motion. A copy of any written instrument which is an exhibit to a pleading is a part thereof for all purposes. IN ST TRIAL P Rule 10(C).

   d. *Paper; Print, quality and binding*

      i. All pleadings, motions, chronological case summary entry forms, orders, process and other papers shall be neatly and legibly printed, typewritten or mechanically reproduced, on one (1) side only, on white opaque paper. To satisfy the recordkeeping requirements of IN ST TRIAL P Rule 77, the print shall be of sufficient density and clarity for preservation and reproduction of microfilming, optical disk or other secondary sources. For this reason, the use of non-letter-quality printers is discouraged. IN ST LAKE RCP Rule 2(A).

ii. Paper and ink shall be of such quality as to withstand the test of time. All documents shall be produced on acid-free, non-thermal paper. It is recommended that a minimum of twenty (20) pound, twenty-five percent (25%) cotton paper product be used. Documents of multiple pages shall be submitted in bound or stapled fashion, and the binding or stapling shall be at the top only. Covers or backings shall not be used. IN ST LAKE RCP Rule 2(A).

e. *Papers; Handwritten.* Handwritten papers may be filed only if approved by the Court and a typewritten or printed true rendition thereof is filed within three (3) days thereafter and approved by the Court. Upon such approval, they shall be deemed and filed as the original, while the handwritten papers shall be retained therewith for evidentiary purposes. IN ST LAKE RCP Rule 2(C).

f. *Minute sheets; Motion blanks.* Minute sheets and motion blanks shall no longer be used. IN ST LAKE RCP Rule 2(D).

2. *Size of papers for filing.* Effective January 1, 1992, all pleadings, copies, motions and documents filed with any trial court or appellate level court, typed or printed, with the exception of exhibits and existing wills, shall be prepared on eight and one-half by eleven inch (8 1/2" x 11") size paper. IN ST ADMIN Rule 11.

3. *Signature requirements*

a. *Signature of attorney.* Every pleading or motion of a party represented by an attorney shall be signed by at least one (1) attorney of record in his individual name, whose address, telephone number, and attorney number shall be stated, except that this provision shall not apply to pleadings and motions made and transcribed at the trial or a hearing before the judge and received by him in such form. IN ST TRIAL P Rule 11(A).

i. The signature of an attorney constitutes a certificate by him that he has read the pleadings; that to the best of his knowledge, information, and belief, there is good ground to support it; and that it is not interposed for delay. IN ST TRIAL P Rule 11(A).

ii. If a pleading or motion is not signed or is signed with intent to defeat the purpose of the rule, it may be stricken as sham and false and the action may proceed as though the pleading had not been served. IN ST TRIAL P Rule 11(A).

iii. For a willful violation of IN ST TRIAL P Rule 11 an attorney may be subjected to appropriate disciplinary action. Similar action may be taken if scandalous or indecent matter is inserted. IN ST TRIAL P Rule 11(A).

b. *Signature of unrepresented party.* A party who is not represented by an attorney shall sign his pleading and state his address. IN ST TRIAL P Rule 11(A).

c. *Verification not generally required.* Except when specifically required by rule, pleadings or motions need not be verified or accompanied by affidavit. The rule in equity that the averments of an answer under oath must be overcome by the testimony of two (2) witnesses or of one (1) witness sustained by corroborating circumstances is abolished. IN ST TRIAL P Rule 11(A).

d. *Verification by affirmation or representation.* When in connection with any civil or special statutory proceeding it is required that any pleading, motion, petition, supporting affidavit, or other document of any kind, be verified, or that an oath be taken, it shall be sufficient if the subscriber simply affirms the truth of the matter to be verified by an affirmation or representation. IN ST TRIAL P Rule 11(B). IN ST TRIAL P Rule 11(B) states that the affirmation or representation should be in substantially the following language: "I (we) affirm, under the penalties for perjury, that the foregoing representation(s) is (are) true. (Signed) _____."

i. Any person who falsifies an affirmation or representation of fact shall be subject to the same penalties as are prescribed by law for the making of a false affidavit. IN ST TRIAL P Rule 11(B).

e. *Verified pleadings, motions, and affidavits as evidence.* Pleadings, motions and affidavits accompanying or in support of such pleadings or motions when required to be verified or under oath shall be

accepted as a representation that the signer had personal knowledge thereof or reasonable cause to believe the existence of the facts or matters stated or alleged therein; and, if otherwise competent or acceptable as evidence, may be admitted as evidence of the facts or matters stated or alleged therein when it is so provided in the Indiana Rules of Trial Procedure, by statute or other law, or to the extent the writing or signature expressly purports to be made upon the signer's personal knowledge. When such pleadings, motions and affidavits are verified or under oath they shall not require other or greater proof on the part of the adverse party than if not verified or not under oath unless expressly provided otherwise by the Indiana Rules of Trial Procedure, statute or other law. Affidavits upon motions for summary judgment under IN ST TRIAL P Rule 56 and in denial of execution under IN ST TRIAL P Rule 9.2 shall be made upon personal knowledge. IN ST TRIAL P Rule 11(C).

f. *Electronic signature.* The filing of documents and information through the E-filing system by use of a valid username and password is presumed to have been authorized by the User to whom that username and password have been issued and documents filed through the E-filing system are presumed to have been signed by the same User. IN ST ADMIN Rule 16(E).

4. *Information excluded from public access.* Every document filed in a case shall separately identify information excluded from public access pursuant to IN ST ADMIN Rule 9(G)(1) as follows:

a. Whole documents that are excluded from public access pursuant to IN ST ADMIN Rule 9(G)(1) shall be tendered on light green paper or have a light green coversheet attached to the document, marked "Not for Public Access" or "Confidential." IN ST TRIAL P Rule 5(G)(1).

b. When only a portion of a document contains information excluded from public access pursuant to IN ST ADMIN Rule 9(G)(1), said information shall be omitted [or redacted] from the filed document, and set forth on a separate accompanying document on light green paper conspicuously marked "Not for Public Access" or "Confidential" and clearly designated [or identifying] the caption and number of the case and the document and location within the document to which the redacted material pertains. IN ST TRIAL P Rule 5(G)(2).

c. With respect to documents filed in electronic format, the trial court, by local rule, may provide for compliance with IN ST TRIAL P Rule 5 in manner that separates and protects access to information excluded from public access. IN ST TRIAL P Rule 5(G)(3).

d. IN ST TRIAL P Rule 5(G) does not apply to a record sealed by the court pursuant to IN ST 5-14-3-5.5 or otherwise, nor to records, documents, or information filed in cases to which public access is prohibited pursuant to IN ST ADMIN Rule 9(G). IN ST TRIAL P Rule 5(G)(4).

e. The following information in case records is excluded from public access and is confidential:

i. Information that is excluded from public access pursuant to federal law;

ii. Information that is excluded from public access as declared confidential by Indiana statute or other court rule, including without limitation:

- All adoption records created after July 8, 1941, as declared confidential by IN ST 31-19-19-1, et seq., except those specifically declared open by IN ST 31-19-13-2(2);

- All records relating to chancroid, chlamydia, gonorrhea, hepatitis, human immunodeficiency virus (HIV), Lymphogranuloma venereum, syphilis, tuberculosis, as declared confidential by IN ST 16-41-8-1, et seq.;

- All records relating to child abuse as declared confidential by IN ST 31-33-18-1, et seq.;

- All records relating to drug tests as declared confidential by IN ST 5-14-3-4(a)(9);

- Records of grand jury proceedings as declared confidential by IN ST 35-34-2-4;

- Records of juvenile proceedings as declared confidential by IN ST 31-39-1-2, except those specifically open under statute;

- All paternity records created after July 1, 1941 as declared confidential by IN ST 31-14-11-15, IN ST 31-19-5-23, IN ST 31-39-1-1 and IN ST 31-39-1-2 [Editor's note: IN ST 31-14-11-15 was repealed effective May 9, 2013];

- All pre-sentence reports as declared confidential by IN ST 35-38-1-13;

- Written petitions to permit marriages without consent and orders directing the Clerk of Court to issue a marriage license to underage persons, as declared confidential by IN ST 31-11-1-6;

- Only those arrest warrants, search warrants, indictments and informations ordered confidential by the trial judge, prior to return of duly executed service as declared confidential by IN ST 5-14-3-4(b)(1);

- All medical, mental health, or tax records unless determined by law or regulation of any governmental custodian not to be confidential, released by the subject of such records, or declared by a court of competent jurisdiction to be essential to the resolution of litigation as declared confidential by IN ST 16-39-3-10, IN ST 6-4.1-5-10, IN ST 6-4.1-12-12, and IN ST 6-8.1-7-1;

- Personal information relating to jurors or prospective jurors, other than for the use of the parties and counsel, pursuant to IN ST JURY Rule 10;

- Information relating to protection from abuse orders, no-contact orders and workplace violence restraining orders as declared confidential by IN ST 5-2-9-6, et seq.;

- Mediation proceedings pursuant to IN ST ADR Rule 2.11, Mini-Trial proceedings pursuant to IN ST ADR Rule 4.4(C), and Summary Jury Trials pursuant to IN ST ADR Rule 5.6;

- Information in probation files pursuant to the Probation Standards promulgated by the Judicial Conference of Indiana pursuant to IN ST 11-13-1-8(b);

- Information deemed confidential pursuant to the Rules for Court Administered Alcohol and Drug Programs promulgated by the Judicial Conference of Indiana pursuant to IN ST 12-23-14-13;

- Information deemed confidential pursuant to the Problem-Solving Court Rules promulgated by the Judicial Conference of Indiana pursuant to IN ST 33-23-16-16;

- All records of the Department of workforce Development as declared confidential by IN ST 22-4-19-6;

- Information regarding interception of electronic communications that is sealed or deemed confidential as set forth in IN ST 35-33.5-2-1, et seq.

iii. Information excluded from public access by specific court order;

iv. Complete Social Security Numbers of living persons;

v. With the exception of names, information such as addresses, phone numbers, and dates of birth which explicitly identifies:

- Natural persons who are witnesses or victims (not including defendants) in criminal, domestic violence, stalking, sexual assault, juvenile, or civil protection order proceedings, provided that juveniles who are victims of sex crimes shall be identified by initials only;

- Places of residence of judicial officers, clerks and other employees of courts and clerks of court, unless the person or persons about whom the information pertains waives confidentiality;

vi. Complete account numbers of specific assets, loans, bank accounts, credit cards, and personal identification numbers (PINs);

vii. All orders of expungement entered in criminal or juvenile proceedings, orders to restrict access to criminal history information pursuant to IN ST 35-38-5-5.5 or IN ST 35-38-8-5 and records excluded from public access by such orders, and information related to infractions that is excluded from public access pursuant to IN ST 34-28-5-15 or IN ST 34-28-5-16 [Editor's note: IN ST 35-38-5-5.5, IN ST 35-38-8-5 and IN ST 34-28-5-16 were repealed effective July 1, 2013; for information on orders restricting access to criminal history, refer to IN ST 35-38-9-1, et seq.];

viii. All personal notes and e-mail, and deliberative material, of judges, jurors, court staff and

judicial agencies, and information recorded in personal data assistants (PDA's) or organizers and personal calendars. IN ST ADMIN Rule 9(G)(1).

5. *Format of electronically filed documents*

    a. *Generally.* Electronically filed documents must meet the same requirements of format as documents conventionally filed pursuant to IN ST LAKE RCP Rule 2 or other applicable Lake County Rules of Civil Procedure. IN ST LAKE RCP Rule 17(D)(1).

    b. *Titles of documents.* The person electronically filing a document will be responsible for designating a title for the document at the time it is filed. The LCOD will generate the appropriate entry onto the CCS to record the filing of the document. IN ST LAKE RCP Rule 17(D)(3).

    c. *Citations and hyperlinks.* Electronically filed documents may contain hyperlink references to an external document as a convenient mechanism for accessing material cited in the document. Filers wishing to insert hyperlinks into documents shall continue to use the traditional method of citation to authority in addition to the hyperlink provided. The hyperlink is merely a convenience to the court and the material referenced is extraneous to the file and not a part of the court's record. IN ST LAKE RCP Rule 17(D)(5).

    d. *Attachments and exhibits.* All documents which form part of a single submission and which are being filed at the same time and by the same filer may be electronically filed together under one document filing, e.g., the motion, supporting affidavits, memorandum in support, designation of evidence, exhibits. IN ST LAKE RCP Rule 17(D)(6).

       i. Large documents which do not exist in an electronic format shall be scanned into .pdf format and filed electronically as separate attachments. A scanner is available in each clerk's office for use by the public and the bar in scanning and saving image files if needed. IN ST LAKE RCP Rule 17(D)(6).

    e. *Electronic signatures*

       i. *Electronic filing as signature.* The electronic filing of a document which is required to be signed shall constitute the filer's representation under IN ST TRIAL P Rule 11. Unless the electronically filed document has been scanned and shows the filer's original signature, the signature of the filer shall be indicated by As/Attorney's Name, or As/Party's Name as in the case of a pro se litigant, on the line where the signature would otherwise appear. IN ST LAKE RCP Rule 17(G)(1).

       ii. *Signatures on jointly signed or filed, verified or other documents.* In the case of a stipulation, agreed order, jointly signed motion or other document which needs to be signed by two (2) or more persons, or in the case of documents which must contain original signatures and which require verification or an unsworn declaration under rule or statute, the signatures may be indicated by either:

         • Submitting a scanned copy of the originally signed document; or,

         • Submitting the document with the use of As/Name in the signature block(s) where the original signature(s) appear(s) in the original document; provided, however, that the filer shall first obtain the physical signature of all persons necessary. IN ST LAKE RCP Rule 17(G)(2).

       iii. *Retention of original.* The filer shall retain the original executed document. IN ST LAKE RCP Rule 17(G).

6. *Citation of local rules.* The local rules for Lake County may be known as the Lake County Rules of Civil Procedure, and abbreviated as LR. IN ST LAKE RCP Rule 1(C).

F. Filing and Service Requirements

1. *Filing requirements.* Except as otherwise provided in IN ST TRIAL P Rule 5(E)(2), all pleadings and papers subsequent to the complaint which are required to be served upon a party shall be filed with the Court either before service or within a reasonable period of time thereafter. IN ST TRIAL P Rule 5(E)(1). All papers presented for filing shall be submitted to the Clerk and not to the court. All papers submitted

for filing shall be mailed or delivered to the Clerk's office at the courthouse in which the case is pending. IN ST LAKE RCP Rule 3(A).

a. *Filing with the court defined.* The filing of pleadings, motions, and other papers with the court as required by the Indiana Rules of Trial Procedure shall be made by one of the following methods:

    i. Delivery to the clerk of the court;

    ii. Sending by electronic transmission under the procedure adopted pursuant to IN ST ADMIN Rule 12;

    iii. Mailing to the clerk by registered, certified or express mail return receipt requested;

    iv. Depositing with any third-party commercial carrier for delivery to the clerk within three (3) calendar days, cost prepaid, properly addressed;

    v. If the court so permits, filing with the judge, in which event the judge shall note thereon the filing date and forthwith transmit them to the office of the clerk; or

    vi. Electronic filing, as approved by the Division of State Court Administration pursuant to IN ST ADMIN Rule 16. IN ST TRIAL P Rule 5(F).

    vii. Filing by registered or certified mail and by third-party commercial carrier shall be complete upon mailing or deposit. IN ST TRIAL P Rule 5(F).

b. *Mandatory electronic filing.* Unless otherwise permitted by the Lake County Rules of Civil Procedure or otherwise authorized by the judicial officer assigned to a particular case, all documents submitted for filing (including the original complaint, or equivalent pleading, and summons) shall be filed electronically with the clerk using the LCOD, no matter when the case was originally filed. IN ST LAKE RCP Rule 17(D).

    i. *Of documents containing information excluded from public access pursuant to* IN ST ADMIN Rule 9. Documents containing information excluded from public access pursuant to IN ST ADMIN Rule 9, or documents which are ordered to be filed under seal shall be filed electronically, pursuant to IN ST LAKE RCP Rule 17(D)(9), whenever possible, along with a copy of the applicable order to seal the records, and the filer shall designate the documents as "Not for Public Access Pursuant to Administrative Rule 9(G)(1)" at the time of filing. IN ST LAKE RCP Rule 16(A)(1); IN ST LAKE RCP Rule 17(D)(9).

        • *Conventional filing of documents containing information excluded from public access pursuant to* IN ST ADMIN Rule 9. Documents containing information excluded from public access pursuant to IN ST ADMIN Rule 9, or documents which are ordered to be filed under seal, which cannot be legibly scanned and filed electronically, shall be conventionally filed under seal and designated by the filer as "Not for Public Access Pursuant to Administrative Rule 9(G)(1)" at the time of filing. The unredacted version shall be filed on light green paper which is conspicuously marked "Not for Public Access"; and a redacted version, with confidential information deleted, shall be filed on white paper which shall be available for public access. The filer shall also electronically file a Notice of Manual Filing. IN ST LAKE RCP Rule 16(A)(2).

    ii. *Technical failures.* If a registered user is unable to file a document in a timely manner due to technical difficulties in the LCOD, the registered user must file a document with the court as soon as possible notifying the court of the inability to file the document. A sample document titled Declaration that Party was Unable to File in a Timely Manner Due to Technical Difficulties can be found at IN ST LAKE RCP Form 4. Delayed filings shall be rejected unless accompanied by the declaration attesting to the filer's failed attempts to file electronically at least two (2) times, separated by at least one (1) hour, after noon on each day of delay due to such technical failure. IN ST LAKE RCP Rule 17(J).

    iii. *Documents allowed to be filed conventionally.* Unless specifically authorized by the court, only the following documents may be filed conventionally and not electronically:

        • Exhibits and other documents that cannot be converted to a legible electronic form, such as videotapes, x-rays, and similar materials

- Documents delivered to the clerk by pro se litigants
- Documents mailed to the clerk by pro se litigants
- Confidential documents
- Notice of manual filing
- Titles of documents
- Chronological case summary entry forms (CCS entry forms). IN ST LAKE RCP Rule 17(E).
- For more information on the documents which must be filed conventionally, refer to IN ST LAKE RCP Rule 17(E).

c. *Facsimile filing.* Only when necessary on an emergency basis (i.e., when certified mail or other means of filing will not bring the document to the Judge's attention prior to the scheduled hearing or ruling), pleadings, motions and other papers may be filed by electronic facsimile transmission, or when specifically authorized by the Court. IN ST LAKE RCP Rule 2(C).

   i. *Generally.* In counties where a majority of judges of the courts of record, by posted local rule, have authorized electronic facsimile filing and designated a telephone number to receive such transmissions, pleadings, motions, and other papers may be sent to the Clerk of Circuit Court by electronic facsimile transmission for filing in any case, provided:

   - Such matter does not exceed ten (10) pages, including the cover sheet;
   - Such matter does not require the payment of fees other than the electronic facsimile transcription fee set forth in IN ST ADMIN Rule 12(E);
   - The sending party creates at the time of transmission a machine generated log for such transmission; and
   - The original document and the transmission log are maintained by the sending party for the duration of the litigation. IN ST ADMIN Rule 12(B).

   ii. *Time of filing.* During normal, posted business hours, the time of filing shall be the time the duplicate document is produced in the office of the Clerk of the Circuit Court. Duplicate documents received at all other times shall be filed as of the next normal business day. IN ST ADMIN Rule 12(C).

   - If the receiving fax machine endorses its own time and date stamp upon the transmitted documents and the receiving machine produces a delivery receipt which is electronically created and transmitted to the sending party, the time of filing shall be the date and time recorded on the transmitted document by the receiving fax machine. IN ST ADMIN Rule 12(C).

d. *Filing for special judges.* For special judge matters where the special judge is a full-time judge or magistrate serving within Lake County, all papers submitted for filing shall be delivered or mailed to the Clerk's office at the courthouse where the special judge regularly serves. IN ST LAKE RCP Rule 3(A).

e. *Proof of filing.* Any party filing any paper by any method other than personal delivery to the clerk shall retain proof of filing. IN ST TRIAL P Rule 5(F).

2. *Service requirements.* Unless otherwise provided by the Indiana Rules of Trial Procedure or an order of the court, each party and special judge, if any, shall be served with: (1) every order required by its terms to be served; (2) every pleading subsequent to the original complaint; (3) every written motion except one which may be heard ex parte; (4) every brief submitted to the trial court; (5) every paper relating to discovery required to be served upon a party; and (6) every written notice, appearance, demand, offer of judgment, designation of record on appeal, or similar paper. IN ST TRIAL P Rule 5(A).

   a. *Methods of service*

   i. *Personal service.* Whenever a party is represented by an attorney of record, service shall be made upon such attorney unless service upon the party himself is ordered by the court. Service

upon the attorney or party shall be made by delivering or mailing a copy of the papers to the last known address or where an attorney or party has consented to service by fax or e-mail, as provided in IN ST TRIAL P Rule 3.1(A)(4), by faxing or e-mailing a copy of the documents to the fax number or e-mail address set out in the appearance form or correction as required by IN ST TRIAL P Rule 3.1(E). IN ST TRIAL P Rule 5(B). Delivery of a copy within IN ST TRIAL P Rule 5 means:

- Offering or tendering it to the attorney or party and stating the nature of the papers being served. Refusal to accept an offered or tendered document is a waiver of any objection to the sufficiency or adequacy of service of that document;

- Leaving it at his office with a clerk or other person in charge thereof, or if there is no one in charge, leaving it in a conspicuous place therein; or

- If the office is closed, by leaving it at his dwelling house or usual place of abode with some person of suitable age and discretion then residing therein; or,

- Leaving it at some other suitable place, selected by the attorney upon whom service is being made, pursuant to duly promulgated local rule. IN ST TRIAL P Rule 5(B)(1).

ii. *Service by mail.* If service is made by mail, the papers shall be deposited in the United States mail addressed to the person on whom they are being served, with postage prepaid. Service shall be deemed complete upon mailing. Proof of service of all papers permitted to be mailed may be made by written acknowledgment of service, by affidavit of the person who mailed the papers, or by certificate of an attorney. It shall be the duty of attorneys when entering their appearance in a cause or when filing pleadings or papers therein, to have noted in the Chronological Case Summary or said pleadings or papers so filed the address and telephone number of their office. Service by delivery or by mail at such address shall be deemed sufficient and complete. IN ST TRIAL P Rule 5(B)(2).

iii. *Service by fax or e-mail.* A party who has consented to service by fax or e-mail may be served as follows:

- Service by e-mail shall be made by attaching the document being served in .pdf format. Discovery documents must also be served in accordance with IN ST TRIAL P Rule 26(A). IN ST TRIAL P Rule 5(B)(3)(a).

- Service by fax shall be deemed complete upon generation of a transmission record indicating the successful transmission of the entire document, except as provided in IN ST TRIAL P Rule 5(B)(3)(d). IN ST TRIAL P Rule 5(B)(3)(b).

- Service by e-mail shall be deemed complete upon transmission, except as provided in IN ST TRIAL P Rule 5(B)(3)(d). IN ST TRIAL P Rule 5(B)(3)(c).

- Service by fax or e-mail that occurs on a Saturday, Sunday, legal holiday, or day the court or agency in which the matter is pending is closed or after 5:00 PM local time of the recipient shall be deemed complete the next day that is not a Saturday, Sunday, legal holiday, or day that the court or agency in which the matter is pending is not closed. IN ST TRIAL P Rule 5(B)(3)(d).

b. *Serving numerous defendants.* In any action in which there are unusually large numbers of defendants, the court, upon motion or of its own initiative, may order:

i. That service of the pleadings of the defendants and replies thereto need not be made as between the defendants;

- That any cross-claim, counterclaim, or matter constituting an avoidance or affirmative defense contained therein shall be deemed to be denied or avoided by all other parties; and

- That the filing of any such pleading and service thereof upon the plaintiff constitutes due notice of it to the parties. IN ST TRIAL P Rule 5(D).

ii. A copy of every such order shall be served upon the parties in such manner and form as the court directs. IN ST TRIAL P Rule 5(D).

c. *Service by electronic means.* The Lake County Online Docket will generate a Notice of Electronic

Filing and Service when any document is filed and served. This notice will be emailed to each registered user of record in a case, and an electronic service event will be added to the work queue of each registered user of record in the case. The party filing the document should retain a paper or electronic copy of the Notice of Electronic Filing and Service. This notice represents proof of filing and service of the document on registered users of record in that case. The filer shall not be required to conventionally serve any document on any party receiving electronic service. IN ST LAKE RCP Rule 17(F)(2).

    i. The filer shall also conventionally serve those parties not designated or able to receive electronic notice or service but who are nevertheless entitled to notice of said pleading or other document in accordance with the Indiana Rules of Civil Procedure and applicable Lake County Rules of Civil Procedure. In such cases, the filer shall also file a certificate of service, as appropriate. IN ST LAKE RCP Rule 17(F).

  d. *Service on parties in default for failure to appear.* No service need be made on parties in default for failure to appear, except that pleadings asserting new or additional claims for relief against them shall be served upon them in the manner provided by service of summons in IN ST TRIAL P Rule 4. IN ST TRIAL P Rule 5(A).

3. *Service requirements if adding a new party by amendment.* Refer to the Indiana KeyRules Complaint document for information on serving a new party added by amendment.

G. Hearings

1. The Indiana rules do not contemplate a hearing regarding the filing and service of an amended complaint.

H. Forms

1. Official Amended Complaint Forms for Indiana

  a. Affidavit of debt. IN ST TRIAL P App. A-2.

2. Amended Complaint Forms for Indiana

  a. Motion to file amended complaint. 5 INPRAC § 3:5.1.

  b. Motion to file amended complaint; Another form. 5 INPRAC § 3:5.2.

  c. Objections to motion to file amended complaint. 5 INPRAC § 3:5.3.

  d. Motion to amend pleading to conform to evidence. 5 INPRAC § 3:5.4.

  e. Amendment by stipulation. 10 INPRAC § 46.11.

  f. Caption; Generally. 5 INPRAC § 3:1.1.

  g. Caption; Multiple parties. 5 INPRAC § 3:1.2.

  h. Single count. 5 INPRAC § 3:1.3.

  i. Multiple counts; Single defendant. 5 INPRAC § 3:1.4.

  j. Multiple counts; Multiple defendants. 5 INPRAC § 3:1.5.

  k. Signature; By party. 5 INPRAC § 3:1.6.

  l. Signature; By attorney. 5 INPRAC § 3:1.7.

  m. Verification. 5 INPRAC § 3:1.8.

  n. Individual defendant. 5 INPRAC § 3:2.1.

  o. Resident agent of corporation. 5 INPRAC § 3:2.2.

  p. Attorney general. 5 INPRAC § 3:2.3.

  q. City attorney. 5 INPRAC § 3:2.4.

  r. Certificate; Personal service. 5 INPRAC § 3:2.5.

  s. Certificate; First class mail. 5 INPRAC § 3:2.6.

  t. Certificate; Registered mail. 5 INPRAC § 3:2.7.

  u. Certificate; Dwelling house. 5 INPRAC § 3:2.8.

    v.   Clerk's certificate of mailing. 5 INPRAC § 3:2.9.

    w. Clerk's certificate of mailing; Acceptance by defendant. 5 INPRAC § 3:2.10.

    x.   Clerk's return on service of summons by mail; Not accepted by defendant. 5 INPRAC § 3:2.11.

    y.   Sheriff's return; Service of summons. 5 INPRAC § 3:2.12.

    z.   Motion to appoint person to serve process. 5 INPRAC § 3:2.13.

3. Official Amended Complaint Forms for Lake County

    a.   CCS entry form. IN ST LAKE RCP App. A.

    b.   Notice of manual filing. IN ST LAKE RCP Form 2.

    c.   Certificate of service. IN ST LAKE RCP Form 3.

    d.   Declaration that party was unable to file in a timely manner. IN ST LAKE RCP Form 4.

4. Amended Complaint Forms for Lake County

    a.   Notice of manual filing. EFORMST IN 5540.

I. Checklist

(I) ❑ Matters to be considered by the party filing the amended complaint

    (a) ❑ Required documents if amending as matter of course

        (1) ❑ Amended complaint

        (2) ❑ Chronological case summary (CSS) entry forms

        (3) ❑ Certificate of service

    (b) ❑ Supplemental documents

        (1) ❑ Proof of written instrument

        (2) ❑ Notice of intent to use foreign law

        (3) ❑ Facsimile cover sheet

    (c) ❑ Timing

        (1) ❑ A party may amend his pleading once as a matter of course at any time before a responsive pleading is served or, if the pleading is one to which no responsive pleading is permitted, and the action has not been placed upon the trial calendar, he may so amend it at any time within thirty (30) days after it is served

        (2) ❑ Otherwise a party may amend his pleading only by leave of court or by written consent of the adverse party; and leave shall be given when justice so requires

        (3) ❑ All pleadings, motions and other papers submitted for filing which are required to be served under IN ST TRIAL P Rule 5(A) shall be filed no later than three (3) days after service

        (4) ❑ If such papers are filed before service, proof of service thereof shall be filed no later than three (3) business days thereafter

Pleadings
Answer

Document Last Updated October 2013

A. Applicable Rules

    1. *State rules*

        a.   Appearance. IN ST TRIAL P Rule 3.1.

        b.   Process. IN ST TRIAL P Rule 4.

        c.   Service. IN ST TRIAL P Rule 4.15; IN ST TRIAL P Rule 4.16; IN ST TRIAL P Rule 5.

d. Time. IN ST TRIAL P Rule 6.

e. Pleadings. IN ST TRIAL P Rule 7; IN ST TRIAL P Rule 8; IN ST TRIAL P Rule 9; IN ST TRIAL P Rule 9.1; IN ST TRIAL P Rule 9.2; IN ST TRIAL P Rule 10.

f. Signing and verification of pleadings. IN ST TRIAL P Rule 11.

g. Defenses and objections; When and how presented; By pleading or motion; Motion for judgment on the pleadings. IN ST TRIAL P Rule 12.

h. Counterclaim and cross-claim. IN ST TRIAL P Rule 13.

i. Third-party practice. IN ST TRIAL P Rule 14.

j. Amended and supplemental pleadings. IN ST TRIAL P Rule 15.

k. Parties plaintiff and defendant; Capacity. IN ST TRIAL P Rule 17.

l. Joinder. IN ST TRIAL P Rule 19; IN ST TRIAL P Rule 20.

m. Jury trial of right. IN ST TRIAL P Rule 38.

n. Consolidation; Separate trials. IN ST TRIAL P Rule 42.

o. Evidence. IN ST TRIAL P Rule 43.

p. Determination of foreign law. IN ST TRIAL P Rule 44.1.

q. Judgment. IN ST TRIAL P Rule 50; IN ST TRIAL P Rule 52; IN ST TRIAL P Rule 54; IN ST TRIAL P Rule 56; IN ST TRIAL P Rule 59; IN ST TRIAL P Rule 60.

r. Venue requirements. IN ST TRIAL P Rule 75.

s. Court records. IN ST TRIAL P Rule 77.

t. Alternative dispute resolution. IN ST ADR Rule 1.1; IN ST ADR Rule 1.6; IN ST ADR Rule 8.8.

u. Uniform case numbering system. IN ST ADMIN Rule 8.

v. Access to court records. IN ST ADMIN Rule 9.

w. Paper size. IN ST ADMIN Rule 11.

x. Facsimile transmission. IN ST ADMIN Rule 12.

y. Electronic filing and electronic service pilot projects. IN ST ADMIN Rule 16.

z. Privacy and confidentiality. IN ST 5-2-9-6; IN ST 5-14-3-4; IN ST 5-14-3-5.5; IN ST 6-4.1-5-10; IN ST 6-4.1-12-12; IN ST 6-8.1-7-1; IN ST 11-13-1-8; IN ST 12-23-14-13; IN ST 16-39-3-10; IN ST 16-41-8-1; IN ST 22-4-19-6; IN ST 31-11-1-6; IN ST 31-19-5-23; IN ST 31-19-13-2; IN ST 31-19-19-1; IN ST 31-33-18-1; IN ST 31-39-1-1; IN ST 31-39-1-2; IN ST 33-23-16-16; IN ST 35-34-2-4; IN ST 35-38-1-13; IN ST 35-38-9-1; IN ST ADR Rule 2.11; IN ST ADR Rule 4.4; IN ST ADR Rule 5.6; IN ST JURY Rule 10.

2. *Local rules*

a. Scope and title. [IN ST LAKE RCP Rule 1, as amended by IN ORDER 13-0237, effective October 18, 2013].

b. Preparation of pleadings, motions and other papers. IN ST LAKE RCP Rule 2.

c. Filing. [IN ST LAKE RCP Rule 3, as amended by IN ORDER 13-0237, effective October 18, 2013].

d. Appearance by attorney. IN ST LAKE RCP Rule 5.

e. Continuances; Extensions of time to answer. IN ST LAKE RCP Rule 7.

f. Confidential information and sealed documents. IN ST LAKE RCP Rule 16.

g. Electronic filing and service. IN ST LAKE RCP Rule 17.

B. Timing

1. *Time to serve answer.* A responsive pleading required under the Indiana Rules of Trial Procedure, shall be served within twenty (20) days after service of the prior pleading. IN ST TRIAL P Rule 6(C).

a. *Effect of IN ST TRIAL P Rule 12 motions.* The service of a motion permitted under IN ST TRIAL P

Rule 12 alters the time for service of responsive pleadings as follows, unless a different time is fixed by the court:

    i.   If the court does not grant the motion, the responsive pleading shall be served in ten (10) days after notice of the court's action;

    ii.   If the court grants the motion and the corrective action is allowed to be taken, it shall be taken within ten (10) days, and the responsive pleading shall be served within ten (10) days thereafter. IN ST TRIAL P Rule 6(C).

    b.   *Automatic extension of time for answer.* Provided it is timely filed, the mere entry of appearance by a party or counsel in response to a summons in an action that requires an answer shall effect an extension of thirty (30) days from the filing thereof within which to respond. IN ST LAKE RCP Rule 7(D) is inapplicable to actions in replevin and ejectment. IN ST LAKE RCP Rule 7(D).

2.   *Responding to amended complaint.* A party shall plead in response to an amended pleading within the time remaining for response to the original pleading or within twenty (20) days after service of the amended pleading, whichever period may be the longer, unless the court otherwise orders. IN ST TRIAL P Rule 15(A).

3.   *Filing.* All pleadings and papers subsequent to the complaint which are required to be served upon a party shall be filed with the Court either before service or within a reasonable period of time thereafter. IN ST TRIAL P Rule 5(E)(1).

    a.   *Time for filing.* All pleadings, motions and other papers submitted for filing which are required to be served under IN ST TRIAL P Rule 5(A) shall be filed no later than three (3) days after service. IN ST LAKE RCP Rule 3(A).

    i.   If such papers are filed before service, proof of service thereof shall be filed no later than three (3) business days thereafter. Upon failure to comply with IN ST LAKE RCP Rule 3, the Court may, on motion of any party or on its own motion, impose appropriate sanctions. IN ST LAKE RCP Rule 3(A).

4.   *Filing of third-party complaint.* The third-party plaintiff must file the third-party complaint with his original answer or by leave of court thereafter with good cause shown. IN ST TRIAL P Rule 14(A).

5.   *Computation of time*

    a.   *Generally; Days excluded.* In computing any period of time prescribed or allowed by the Indiana Rules of Trial Procedure, by order of the court, or by any applicable statute, the day of the act, event, or default from which the designated period of time begins to run shall not be included. The last day of the period so computed is to be included unless it is:

    i.   A Saturday,

    ii.   A Sunday,

    iii.   A legal holiday as defined by state statute, or

    iv.   A day the office in which the act is to be done is closed during regular business hours. IN ST TRIAL P Rule 6(A).

    b.   *Short periods.* In any event, the period runs until the end of the next day that is not a Saturday, a Sunday, a legal holiday, or a day on which the office is closed. When the period of time allowed is less than seven (7) days, intermediate Saturdays, Sundays, legal holidays, and days on which the office is closed shall be excluded from the computations. IN ST TRIAL P Rule 6(A).

    c.   *Additional time after service by United States mail.* Whenever a party has the right or is required to do some act or take some proceedings within a prescribed period after the service of a notice or other paper upon him and the notice or paper is served upon him by United States mail, three (3) days shall be added to the prescribed period. IN ST TRIAL P Rule 6(E).

    d.   *Electronic filing does not alter deadlines.* Filing electronically does not alter any filing deadlines or any time computation pursuant to state or federal statutes, any Rules of the Indiana Supreme Court, including without limitation the Rules of Trial Procedure, the Rules of Appellate Procedure or the Administrative Rules, or applicable Lake County Rules of Civil Procedure. The office of the Lake

County Clerk is open for electronic filing under the Lake County Rules of Civil Procedure twenty-four (24) hours a day. A document is deemed filed at the date and time it is received by the LCOD server. Filing must be completed before midnight local time in order to be considered filed that day. Lake County observes Central Time and electronic filers are strongly urged to file documents during hours when the Lake County Online Docket ("LCOD") help line is available, from 9:00 a.m. to 4:00 p.m. local time, although documents can be filed electronically twenty-four (24) hours a day. IN ST LAKE RCP Rule 17(I).

e. *Enlargement of time.* When an act is required or allowed to be done at or within a specific time by the Indiana Rules of Trial Procedure, the court may at any time for cause shown:

    i. Order the period enlarged, with or without motion or notice, if request therefor is made before the expiration of the period originally prescribed or extended by a previous order; or

    ii. Upon motion made after the expiration of the specific period, permit the act to be done where the failure to act was the result of excusable neglect; but, the court may not extend the time for taking any action for judgment on the evidence under IN ST TRIAL P Rule 50(A), amendment of findings and judgment under IN ST TRIAL P Rule 52(B), to correct errors under IN ST TRIAL P Rule 59(C), statement in opposition to motion to correct error under IN ST TRIAL P Rule 59(E), or to obtain relief from final judgment under IN ST TRIAL P Rule 60(B), except to the extent and under the conditions stated in those rules. IN ST TRIAL P Rule 6(B).

C. General Requirements

1. *Pleading, generally*

    a. *Pleadings to be concise.* Each averment of a pleading shall be simple, concise, and direct. No technical forms of pleading or motions are required. All fictions in pleading are abolished. IN ST TRIAL P Rule 8(E)(1).

    b. *Pleading in the alternative.* A pleading may set forth two (2) or more statements of a claim or defense alternatively or hypothetically, either in one (1) count or defense or in separate counts or defenses. When two (2) or more statements are made in the alternative and one (1) of them if made independently would be sufficient, the pleading is not made insufficient by the insufficiency of one or more of the alternative statements. A pleading may also state as many separate claims or defenses as the pleader has regardless of consistency and whether based on legal or equitable grounds. All statements shall be made subject to the obligations set forth in IN ST TRIAL P Rule 11. IN ST TRIAL P Rule 8(E)(2).

    c. *Motions and pleadings, joint and several.* All motions and pleadings of any kind addressed to two (2) or more paragraphs of any pleading, or filed by two (2) or more parties, shall be taken and construed as joint, separate, and several motions or pleadings to each of such paragraphs and by and against each of such parties. All motions or pleadings containing two (2) or more subject-matters shall be taken and construed as separate and several as to each subject-matter. All objections to rulings made by two (2) or more parties shall be taken and construed as the joint, separate, and several objections of each of such parties. IN ST TRIAL P Rule 8(E)(3).

      i. A complaint filed by or against two (2) or more plaintiffs shall be taken and construed as joint, separate, and several as to each of said plaintiffs. IN ST TRIAL P Rule 8(E).

    d. *Construction of pleadings.* All pleadings shall be so construed as to do substantial justice, lead to disposition on the merits, and avoid litigation of procedural points. IN ST TRIAL P Rule 8(F).

2. *Contents of the answer*

    a. *Defenses which may be raised by answer or motion.* Every defense, in law or fact, to a claim for relief in any pleading, whether a claim, counterclaim, cross-claim, or third-party claim, shall be asserted in the responsive pleading thereto if one is required; except that at the option of the pleader, the following defenses may be made by motion:

      i. Lack of jurisdiction over the subject matter;

      ii. Lack of jurisdiction over the person;

      iii. Incorrect venue under IN ST TRIAL P Rule 75, or any statutory provision. The disposition of this motion shall be consistent with IN ST TRIAL P Rule 75;

    iv.   Insufficiency of process;

    v.   Insufficiency of service of process;

    vi.   Failure to state a claim upon which relief can be granted, which shall include failure to name the real party in interest under IN ST TRIAL P Rule 17;

    vii.   Failure to join a party needed for just adjudication under IN ST TRIAL P Rule 19;

    viii.   The same action pending in another state court of this state. IN ST TRIAL P Rule 12(B).

    ix.   A motion making any of these defenses shall be made before pleading if a further pleading is permitted or within twenty (20) days after service of the prior pleading if none is required. If a pleading sets forth a claim for relief to which the adverse party is not required to serve a responsive pleading, any of the defenses in section IN ST TRIAL P Rule 12(B)(2), IN ST TRIAL P Rule 12(B)(3), IN ST TRIAL P Rule 12(B)(4), IN ST TRIAL P Rule 12(B)(5) or IN ST TRIAL P Rule 12(B)(8) is waived to the extent constitutionally permissible unless made in a motion within twenty (20) days after service of the prior pleading. No defense or objection is waived by being joined with one (1) or more other defenses or objections in a responsive pleading or motion. IN ST TRIAL P Rule 12(B).

b.   *Waiver or preservation of certain defenses*

    i.   A defense of lack of jurisdiction over the person, improper venue, insufficiency of process, insufficiency of service of process, or the same action pending in another state court of this state is waived to the extent constitutionally permissible:

- If omitted from a motion in the circumstances described in IN ST TRIAL P Rule 12(G),
- If it is neither made by motion under IN ST TRIAL P Rule 12 nor included in a responsive pleading or an amendment thereof permitted by IN ST TRIAL P Rule 15(A) to be made as a matter of course. IN ST TRIAL P Rule 12(H)(1).

    ii.   A defense of failure to state a claim upon which relief can be granted, a defense of failure to join an indispensable party under IN ST TRIAL P Rule 19(B), and an objection of failure to state a legal defense to a claim may be made in any pleading permitted or ordered under IN ST TRIAL P Rule 7(A) or by motion for judgment on the pleadings, or at the trial on the merits. IN ST TRIAL P Rule 12(H)(2).

c.   *Defenses; Form of denials*

    i.   A responsive pleading shall state in short and plain terms the pleader's defenses to each claim asserted and shall admit or controvert the averments set forth in the preceding pleading. If in good faith the pleader intends to deny all the averments in the preceding pleading, he may do so by general denial subject to the provisions of IN ST TRIAL P Rule 11. If he does not intend a general denial, he may:

- Specifically deny designated averments or paragraphs; or
- Generally deny all averments except such designated averments and paragraphs as he expressly admits. IN ST TRIAL P Rule 8(B).

    ii.   If he lacks knowledge or information sufficient to form a belief as to the truth of an averment, he shall so state and his statement shall be considered a denial. If in good faith a pleader intends to deny only a part or a qualification of an averment, he shall specify so much of it as is true and material and deny the remainder. All denials shall fairly meet the substance of the averments denied. IN ST TRIAL P Rule 8 shall have no application to uncontested actions for divorce, or to answers required to be filed by clerks or guardians ad litem. IN ST TRIAL P Rule 8(B).

d.   *Affirmative defenses.* A responsive pleading shall set forth affirmatively and carry the burden of proving: accord and satisfaction, arbitration and award, discharge in bankruptcy, duress, estoppel, failure of consideration, fraud, illegality, injury by fellow servant, laches, license, payment, release, res judicata, statute of frauds, statute of limitations, waiver, lack of jurisdiction over the subject-matter, lack of jurisdiction over the person, improper venue, insufficiency of process or service of process, the same action pending in another state court of this state, and any other matter constituting an avoidance, matter of abatement, or affirmative defense. A party required to affirmatively plead any matters, including matters formerly required to be pleaded affirmatively by reply, shall have the burden of proving such matters. The burden of proof imposed by this or any other provision of the Indiana Rules of Trial Procedure is subject to the rules of evidence or any statute fixing a different rule. If the pleading mistakenly designates a defense as a counterclaim or a counterclaim as a defense, the court shall treat the pleading as if there had been a proper designation. IN ST TRIAL P Rule 8(C).

    i. An affirmative defense, generally, must be affirmatively stated by the party who seeks its benefit. 1A INPRAC R 8(8.5); Rice v. Grant County Bd. of Com'rs, 472 N.E.2d 213 (Ind.Ct.App. 1984). If that party does not raise the affirmative defense, then it is waived. 1A INPRAC R 8(8.5); Piskorowski v. Shell Oil Co., 403 N.E.2d 838, 847 (Ind.Ct.App. 1980).

    ii. It is clear that the list of affirmative defenses found in IN ST TRIAL P Rule 8 is not exhaustive. The question comes: when is a defense to be treated as an affirmative defense, with all of the attending consequences? 1A INPRAC R 8(8.5). The "determination of whether a defense is affirmative depends on whether it controverts an element of the plaintiff's prima facie case or raises matter outside the scope of the prima facie case." 1A INPRAC R 8(8.5); Molargik v. West Enterprises, Inc., 605 N.E.2d 1197, 1198 (Ind.Ct.App. 1993).

e. *Defense of contributory negligence or assumed risk.* In all claims alleging negligence, the burden of pleading and proving contributory negligence, assumption of risk, or incurred risk shall be upon the defendant who may plead such by denial of the allegation. IN ST TRIAL P Rule 9.1(A).

f. *Res ipsa loquitur.* Res ipsa loquitur or a similar doctrine may be pleaded by alleging generally that the facts connected with the action are unknown to the pleader and are within the knowledge of the opposing party. IN ST TRIAL P Rule 9.1(B).

g. *Consideration.* When an action or defense is founded upon a written contract or release, lack of consideration for the promise or release is an affirmative defense, and the party asserting lack of it carries the burden of proof. IN ST TRIAL P Rule 9.1(C).

h. *Bona fide purchaser.* When the rights of a person depend upon his status as a bona fide purchaser for value or upon similar requirements, such status must be pleaded and proved by the person asserting it, but it may be pleaded in general terms. Once it is established that the person has given any required value, unless such value is commercially unreasonable, and that he has met any requirements of recordation, filing, possession, or perfection, the trier of fact must find that such value was given or such perfection was made in accordance with any requirements of good faith, lack of knowledge, or lack of notice unless and until evidence is introduced which would support a finding of its non-existence. IN ST TRIAL P Rule 9.1(D).

i. *Presumption; Matters of judicial notice.* Neither presumptions of law nor matters of which judicial notice may be taken need be stated in a pleading. IN ST TRIAL P Rule 9.1(E).

j. *Property distrained; Sufficient answer.* In an action to recover the possession of property distrained while doing damage, an answer that the defendant, or person by whose command he acted, was lawfully possessed of the real property upon which the distress was made, and that the property distrained was at the time doing damage thereon, shall be good without setting forth the title of such real property. IN ST TRIAL P Rule 9.1(F).

k. *Effect of failure to deny.* Averments in a pleading to which a responsive pleading is required, except those pertaining to amount of damages, are admitted when not denied in the responsive pleading. Averments in a pleading to which no responsive pleading is required or permitted shall be taken as denied or avoided. IN ST TRIAL P Rule 8(D).

l. *Effect of admission.* When a rhetorical paragraph or allegation is admitted, the effect in Indiana is to remove it from trial. Such an admission is a "judicial admission", and the claim or issue which is admitted cannot be denied later by the trier of the facts. Further, this admitted fact does not require evidence to "prove it"; it is established. It becomes, in short, controlling and indisputable in the litigation, unless the trial court permits an amendment to the pleading which might remove the controlling effect of the admission, and permit it to become another fact or item of evidence in the case. 1A INPRAC R 8(8.4); Aylesworth v. McKesson, 421 N.E.2d 422 (Ind.Ct.App. 1981).

3. *Pleading special matters*

    a.   *Capacity.* It is not necessary to aver the capacity of a party to sue or be sued, the authority of a party to sue or be sued in a representative capacity, or the legal existence of an organization that is made a party. The burden of proving lack of such capacity, authority, or legal existence shall be upon the person asserting lack of it, and shall be pleaded as an affirmative defense. IN ST TRIAL P Rule 9(A).

    b.   *Fraud, mistake, condition of the mind.* In all averments of fraud or mistake, the circumstances constituting fraud or mistake shall be specifically averred. Malice, intent, knowledge, and other conditions of mind may be averred generally. IN ST TRIAL P Rule 9(B).

    c.   *Conditions precedent.* In pleading the performance or occurrence of promissory or non-promissory conditions precedent, it is sufficient to aver generally that all conditions precedent have been performed, have occurred, or have been excused. A denial of performance or occurrence shall be made specifically and with particularity, and a denial of excuse generally. IN ST TRIAL P Rule 9(C).

    d.   *Official document or act.* In pleading an official document or official act it is sufficient to aver that the document was issued or the act done in compliance with law. IN ST TRIAL P Rule 9(D).

    e.   *Judgment.* In pleading a judgment or decision of a domestic or foreign court, judicial or quasi-judicial tribunal, or of a board or officer, it is sufficient to aver the judgment or decision without setting forth matter showing jurisdiction to render it. IN ST TRIAL P Rule 9(E).

    f.   *Time and place.* For the purpose of testing the sufficiency of a pleading, averments of time and place are material and shall be considered like all other averments of material matter. However, time and place need be stated only with such specificity as will enable the opposing party to prepare his defense. IN ST TRIAL P Rule 9(F).

    g.   *Special damages; Damages where no answer.* When items of special damage are claimed, they shall be specifically stated. The relief granted to the plaintiff, if there be no answer, cannot exceed the relief demanded in his complaint; but, in any other case, the court may grant him any relief consistent with the facts or matters pleaded. IN ST TRIAL P Rule 9(G).

4. *Counterclaim and cross-claim*

    a.   *Compulsory counterclaims.* A pleading shall state as a counterclaim any claim which at the time of serving the pleading the pleader has against any opposing party, if it arises out of the transaction or occurrence that is the subject-matter of the opposing party's claim and does not require for its adjudication the presence of third parties of whom the court cannot acquire jurisdiction. But the pleader need not state the claim if:

        i.   At the time the action was commenced the claim was the subject of another pending action; or

        ii.   The opposing party brought suit upon his claim by attachment or other process by which the court did not acquire jurisdiction to render a personal judgment on that claim, and the pleader is not stating any counterclaim under IN ST TRIAL P Rule 13. IN ST TRIAL P Rule 13(A).

    b.   *Permissive counterclaims.* A pleading may state as a counterclaim any claim against an opposing party not arising out of the transaction or occurrence that is the subject-matter of the opposing party's claim. IN ST TRIAL P Rule 13(B).

    c.   *Counterclaim exceeding opposing claim.* A counterclaim may or may not diminish or defeat the recovery sought by the opposing party. It may claim relief exceeding in amount or different in kind from that sought in the pleading of the opposing party. IN ST TRIAL P Rule 13(C).

    d.   *Counterclaim against state.* IN ST TRIAL P Rule 13 shall not be construed to enlarge any right to assert a claim against the state. IN ST TRIAL P Rule 13(D).

    e.   *Counterclaim maturing or acquired after pleading.* A claim which either matured or was acquired by the pleader after serving his pleading may, with the permission of the court, be presented as a counterclaim by supplemental pleading. A counterclaim or cross-claim which is not due may be asserted against a party who is insolvent or the representative of a party who has been subjected to insolvency proceedings, if recovery thereon will be impaired because of such party's insolvency. IN ST TRIAL P Rule 13(E).

    f.   *Omitted counterclaim.* When a pleader fails to set up a counterclaim through oversight, inadvertence, or excusable neglect, or when justice requires, he may by leave of court set up the counterclaim by amendment. IN ST TRIAL P Rule 13(F).

g. *Cross-claim against co-party.* A pleading may state as a cross-claim any claim by one party against a co-party. IN ST TRIAL P Rule 13(G).

h. *Joinder of additional parties.* Persons other than those made parties to the original action may be made parties to a counterclaim or cross-claim in accordance with the provisions of IN ST TRIAL P Rule 14, IN ST TRIAL P Rule 19 and IN ST TRIAL P Rule 20. IN ST TRIAL P Rule 13(H).

i. *Separate trials; Separate judgments*

   i. If the court orders separate trials as provided in IN ST TRIAL P Rule 42(B), judgment on a counterclaim or cross-claim may be rendered in accordance with the terms of IN ST TRIAL P Rule 54(B) when the court has jurisdiction so to do, even if the claims of the opposing party have been dismissed or otherwise disposed of. In determining whether or not separate trial of a cross-claim shall be ordered, the court shall consider whether the cross-claim:

   - Arises out of the transaction or occurrence or series of transactions or occurrences that is the subject-matter either of the original action or of a counterclaim therein;

   - Relates to any property or contract that is the subject-matter of the original action; or

   - Claims that the person against whom it is asserted is liable to the cross-claimant for all or part of plaintiff's claim against him. IN ST TRIAL P Rule 13(I).

   ii. In addition, the court may consider any other relevant factors. IN ST TRIAL P Rule 13(I).

j. *Effect of statute of limitations and other discharges at law.* The statute of limitations, a nonclaim statute or other discharge at law shall not bar a claim asserted as a counterclaim to the extent that:

   i. It diminishes or defeats the opposing party's claim if it arises out of the transaction or occurrence that is the subject-matter of the opposing party's claim, or if it could have been asserted as a counterclaim to the opposing party's claim before it (the counterclaim) was barred; or

   ii. It or the opposing party's claim relates to payment of or security for the other. IN ST TRIAL P Rule 13(J).

k. *Counterclaim by and against transferees and successors.* A counterclaim may be asserted by or against the transferee or successor of a claim subject to the following provisions:

   i. A successor who is a guardian, representative of a decedent's estate, receiver or assignee for the benefit of creditors, trustee or the like may interpose a claim to which he succeeds against claims or proceedings brought in or outside the court of administration. A claim owing by his predecessor may be interposed against any claim brought by such successor in or outside the court of administration without the necessity of filing such claim or cause of action in the administration proceedings. IN ST TRIAL P Rule 13(K)(1).

   ii. A transferee or successor of a claim takes it subject to any defense or counterclaim that is the subject-matter of the opposing party's claim; or that is available to the obligor at the time of the assignment or before the obligor received notice of the assignment. IN ST TRIAL P Rule 13(K)(2).

   iii. A surety or party with total or partial recourse upon a claim upon which he is being sued may interpose as a counterclaim:

   - Any claim of his own; and

   - Any claim owned by the person against whom he has recourse who either has notice of the suit, is a party to the suit, is insolvent, has assigned his claim to the surety or party asserting it, or cannot be found. IN ST TRIAL P Rule 13(K)(3).

   - A counterclaim under IN ST TRIAL P Rule 13(K)(3)(b) must tend to diminish or defeat the opposing party's claim, or it or the opposing claim must relate to payment of or security for the other, unless the person against whom recourse may be had is a party to the suit or the counterclaim has been assigned to the party asserting it; and if recovery on the counterclaim exceeds the opposing party's claim, any excess recovered shall be held in trust for such person against whom there is a right of recourse. IN ST TRIAL P Rule 13(K)(3).

iv. IN ST TRIAL P Rule 13(K)(1), IN ST TRIAL P Rule 13(K)(2), and IN ST TRIAL P Rule 13(K)(3), are subject to subdivision IN ST TRIAL P Rule 13(L). IN ST TRIAL P Rule 13(K)(4).

l. *Counterclaim and cross-claim subject to substantive law principles.* Counterclaim and cross-claims are subject to restrictions imposed by other statutes and principles of substantive common law and equity, including rules of commercial law, agency, estoppel, contract and the like. In appropriate cases the court may impose terms or conditions upon its judgment or decree and may enter conditional or noncanceling cross judgments to satisfy such restrictions. This provision is intended to deny or limit counterclaims or cross-claims:

i. Where a creditor will receive an unfair priority because a claim is assigned after insolvency proceedings, or assigned before such proceedings if it results in an unlawful preference;

ii. Where an unfair priority will be allowed if a surety interposing a claim owned in his own right against the creditor suing on the principal's obligation when the principal is solvent and the creditor is not;

iii. Where a claim by or against a representative, such as a guardian, receiver, representative of a decedent's estate, assignee for the benefit of creditors, trustee or the like in his individual capacity is asserted against a claim owing or owed by the estate he represents;

iv. Where a claim by or against a partnership or two (2) or more obligors is opposed against or by a claim of an individual to the extent that the individual will be allowed unfairly to profit or if it will adversely affect the rights of creditors; or

v. Where a claim is cut off by a holder in due course or a transferee who is protected under principles of commercial law, estoppel, or contract. IN ST TRIAL P Rule 13(L).

m. *Satisfaction of judgment.* Satisfaction of a judgment or credits thereon may be ordered, for sufficient cause, upon notice and motion. "Credits" include any counterclaim which tends to diminish or defeat the judgment, or any counterclaim where it or the opposing claim relates to payment of or security for the other. IN ST TRIAL P Rule 13(M).

5. *Third-party practice*

a. *When defendant may bring in third party.* A defending party, as a third-party plaintiff, may cause a summons and complaint to be served upon a person not a party to the action who is or may be liable to him for all or part of the plaintiff's claim against him. IN ST TRIAL P Rule 14(A). The person served with the summons and the third-party complaint, hereinafter called the third-party defendant, as provided in IN ST TRIAL P Rule 12 and IN ST TRIAL P Rule 13 may make:

i. His defenses, cross-claims and counterclaims to the third-party plaintiff's claims;

ii. His defenses, counterclaims and cross-claims against any other defendants or third-party defendants;

iii. Any defenses or claims which the third-party plaintiff has to the plaintiff's claim which are available to the third-party defendant against the plaintiff; and

iv. Any defenses or claims which the third-party defendant has as against the plaintiff. IN ST TRIAL P Rule 14(A).

v. The plaintiff may assert any claim against the third-party defendant who thereupon may assert his defenses, counterclaims and cross-claims, as provided in IN ST TRIAL P Rule 12 and IN ST TRIAL P Rule 13. A third-party defendant may proceed under IN ST TRIAL P Rule 14 against any person not a party to the action who is or may be liable to him for all or part of the claim made in the action against the third-party defendant. IN ST TRIAL P Rule 14(A).

b. *When plaintiff may bring in third party.* When a counterclaim or other claim is asserted against a plaintiff, he may cause a third party to be brought in under circumstances, which, under IN ST TRIAL P Rule 14, would entitle a defendant to do so. IN ST TRIAL P Rule 14(B).

    c.   *Severance; Parties improperly impleaded.* With his responsive pleading or by motion prior thereto, any party may move for severance of a third-party claim or ensuing claim as provided in IN ST TRIAL P Rule 14 or for a separate trial thereon. If the third-party defendant is a proper party to the proceedings under any other rule relating to parties, the action shall continue as in other cases where he is made a party. IN ST TRIAL P Rule 14(C).

6.   *Trial by jury; Demand*

    a.   *Causes triable by court and by jury.* Issues of law and issues of fact in causes that prior to the eighteenth day of June, 1852, were of exclusive equitable jurisdiction shall be tried by the court; issues of fact in all other causes shall be triable as the same are now triable. In case of the joinder of causes of action or defenses which, prior to said date, were of exclusive equitable jurisdiction with causes of action or defenses which, prior to said date, were designated as actions at law and triable by jury—the former shall be triable by the court, and the latter by a jury, unless waived; the trial of both may be at the same time or at different times, as the court may direct. IN ST TRIAL P Rule 38(A).

    b.   *Demand.* Any party may demand a trial by jury of any issue triable of right by a jury by filing with the court and serving upon the other parties a demand therefor in writing at any time after the commencement of the action and not later than ten (10) days after the first responsive pleading to the complaint, or to a counterclaim, crossclaim or other claim if one properly is pleaded; and if no responsive pleading is filed or required, within ten (10) days after the time such pleading otherwise would have been required. Such demand is sufficient if indorsed upon a pleading of a party filed within such time. IN ST TRIAL P Rule 38(B).

    c.   *Same; Specification of issues.* In his demand a party may specify the issues which he wishes so tried; otherwise he shall be deemed to have demanded trial by jury for all issues triable as of right by jury. Any other party must file a demand for jury trial to preserve his right to trial by jury:

       i.   Of issues for which a right to trial by jury was not requested by another party; and

      ii.   In case a request by another party was improper. But if a proper request for a trial by jury upon issues triable by jury as of right on his behalf is made by any party, such request shall be deemed to have been made on behalf of all parties entitled to a jury trial upon such issues. IN ST TRIAL P Rule 38(C).

    d.   *Waiver.* The failure of a party to appear at the trial, and the failure of a party to serve a demand as required by IN ST TRIAL P Rule 38 and to file it as required by IN ST TRIAL P Rule 5(E) constitute waiver by him of trial by jury. A demand for trial by jury made as herein provided may not be withdrawn without the consent of the other party or parties. IN ST TRIAL P Rule 38(D).

       i.   The trial court shall not grant a demand for a trial by jury filed after the time fixed in IN ST TRIAL P Rule 38(B) has elapsed except upon the written agreement of all of the parties to the action, which agreement shall be filed with the court and made a part of the record. If such agreement is filed then the court may, in its discretion, grant a trial by jury in which event the grant of a trial by jury may not be withdrawn except by the agreement of all of the parties. IN ST TRIAL P Rule 38(D).

    e.   *Arbitration.* Nothing in the Indiana Rules of Trial Procedure shall deny the parties the right by contract or agreement to submit or to agree to submit controversies to arbitration made before or after commencement of an action thereon or deny the courts power to specifically enforce such agreements. IN ST TRIAL P Rule 38(E).

    f.   *Equitable and legal claims in multi-count actions.* In multi-count actions, the inclusion of an equitable claim, standing alone, will not automatically draw the entire action into equity. Something more than the presence of an equitable claim is required, and the court must examine the claims at issue. 22B INPRAC 38:1 COMMENT; Lucas v. U.S. Bank, N.A., 953 N.E.2d 457 (Ind. 2011). Factors the court may consider in evaluating the nature of the underlying substantive claims include: the substance and central character of the complaint, the rights and interests at issue, the relief demanded, and any issues arising out of discovery. 22B INPRAC 38:1 COMMENT; Songer v. Civitas Bank, 771 N.E.2d 61 (Ind. 2002).

7. *Use of alternative dispute resolution.* Except as provided by the Indiana Rules for Alternative Dispute Resolution, a presiding judge may order any civil or domestic relations proceeding or selected issues in such proceedings referred to mediation, non-binding arbitration or mini-trial. The selection criteria which should be used by the court are defined under the Indiana Rules for Alternative Dispute Resolution. Binding arbitration and a summary jury trial may be ordered only upon the agreement of the parties as consistent with provisions in the Indiana Rules for Alternative Dispute Resolution which address each method. IN ST ADR Rule 1.6. For information on Indiana's ADR process refer to IN ST ADR Rule 1.1 through IN ST ADR Rule 8.8.

D. Documents

1. *Required documents*

   a. *Answer.* Refer to the General Requirements section of this document for information on the contents of an answer.

   b. *Appearance form.* At the time the responding party or parties first appears in a case, the attorney representing such party or parties or the party or parties, if not represented by an attorney, shall file an appearance form setting forth the information set out in IN ST TRIAL P Rule 3.1(A). IN ST TRIAL P Rule 3.1(B). The appearance form shall set forth the following information:

      i. Name, address and telephone number of the initiating party or parties filing the appearance form;

      ii. Name, address, attorney number, telephone number, FAX number, and e-mail address of any attorney representing the party, as applicable;

      iii. The case type of the proceeding [IN ST ADMIN Rule 8(B)(3)];

      iv. A statement that the party will or will not accept service by fax or by e-mail from:

         - Other parties and/or
         - The court under IN ST TRIAL P Rule 72(D);

      v. In domestic relations, Uniform Reciprocal Enforcement of Support (URESA), paternity, delinquency, Child in Need of Services (CHINS), guardianship, and any other proceedings in which support may be an issue, the Social Security Identification Number of all family members;

      vi. The caption and case number of all related cases;

      vii. Such additional matters specified by state or local rule required to maintain the information management system employed by the court;

      viii. In a proceeding involving a protection from abuse order, a workplace violence restraining order, or a no-contact order, the initiating party shall provide to the clerk a public mailing address for purposes of legal service. The initiating party may use the Attorney General Address Confidentiality program established by statute; and

      ix. In a proceeding involving a mental health commitment, except seventy-two (72) hour emergency detentions, the initiating party shall provide the full name of the person with respect to whom commitment is sought and the person's state of residence. In addition, the initiating party shall provide at least one of the following identifiers for the person:

         - Date of birth;
         - Social Security Number;
         - Driver's license number with state of issue and date of expiration;
         - Department of Correction number;
         - State ID number with state of issue and date of expiration; or
         - FBI number. IN ST TRIAL P Rule 3.1(A); IN ST LAKE RCP Rule 5(B)(2).

   c. *Chronological case summary (CCS) entry forms.* All filings shall be accompanied by a Chronological Case Summary (CCS) Entry Form to define or identify the documents filed. The Form used should be substantially similar to IN ST LAKE RCP App. A. IN ST LAKE RCP Rule 3(C).

d. *Certificate of service.* An attorney or unrepresented party tendering a document to the Clerk for filing shall certify that service has been made, list the parties served, and specify the date and means of service. The certificate of service shall be placed at the end of the document and shall not be separately filed. The separate filing of a certificate of service, however, shall not be grounds for rejecting a document for filing. The Clerk may permit documents to be filed without a certificate of service but shall require prompt filing of a separate certificate of service. IN ST TRIAL P Rule 5(C).

    i. All pleadings, motions and other papers submitted for filing which are required to be served under IN ST TRIAL P Rule 5(A) shall contain proof of service pursuant to IN ST TRIAL P Rule 5(B)(2). IN ST LAKE RCP Rule 3(A).

2. *Supplemental documents*

  a. *Admission of service.* A written admission stating the date and place of service, signed by the person being served, may be filed with the clerk who shall file it with the pleadings. Such admission shall become a part of the record, constitute evidence of proper service, and shall be allowed as evidence in any action or proceeding. IN ST TRIAL P Rule 4.15(D).

    i. It shall be the duty of every person being served under the Indiana Rules of Trial Procedure to cooperate, accept service, comply with the provisions of the Indiana Rules of Trial Procedure, and, when service is made upon him personally, acknowledge receipt of the papers in writing over his signature. IN ST TRIAL P Rule 4.16(A).

      • Offering or tendering the papers to the person being served and advising the person that he or she is being served is adequate service. IN ST TRIAL P Rule 4.16(A)(1).

      • A person who has refused to accept the offer or tender of the papers being served thereafter may not challenge the service of those papers. IN ST TRIAL P Rule 4.16(A)(2).

  b. *Proof of written instrument.* When any pleading allowed by the Indiana Rules of Trial Procedure is founded on a written instrument, the original, or a copy thereof, must be included in or filed with the pleading. Such instrument, whether copied in the pleadings or not, shall be taken as part of the record. When any pleading allowed by the Indiana Rules of Trial Procedure is founded on an account, an Affidavit of Debt, in a form substantially similar to that which is provided in IN ST TRIAL P App. A-2, shall be attached. IN ST TRIAL P Rule 9.2(A).

  c. *Notice of intent to use foreign law.* A party who intends to raise an issue concerning the law of a foreign country shall give notice in his pleadings or other reasonable written notice. The court, in determining foreign law, may consider any relevant material or source, including testimony, whether or not submitted by a party or admissible under IN ST TRIAL P Rule 43. The court's determination shall be treated as a ruling on a question of law. It shall be made by the court and not the jury and shall be reviewable. IN ST TRIAL P Rule 44.1(A).

  d. *Facsimile cover sheet.* Any document sent to the Clerk of the Circuit Court by electronic facsimile transmission shall be accompanied by a cover sheet which states the title of the document, case number, number of pages, identity and voice telephone number of the sending party and instructions for filing. The cover sheet shall contain the signature of the attorney or party, pro se, authorizing the filing. IN ST ADMIN Rule 12(D).

E. Format

1. *Form of pleadings.* For the purpose of uniformity, convenience, clarity and durability, requirements in IN ST LAKE RCP Rule 2 shall be observed in the preparation of all pleadings, motions and other papers. IN ST LAKE RCP Rule 2. Whenever materials submitted fail to meet the standards in IN ST LAKE RCP Rule 2, the Court may impose appropriate sanctions. IN ST LAKE RCP Rule 2(B).

  a. *Caption; Names of parties.* Every pleading shall contain a caption setting forth the name of the court, the title of the action, the file number, and a designation as in IN ST TRIAL P Rule 7(A). In the complaint the title of the action shall include the names of all the parties, but in other pleadings it is sufficient to state the name of the first party on each side with an appropriate indication of other parties. IN ST TRIAL P Rule 10(A).

    i. *Special judge matters.* The caption of all CCS Entry Forms, pleadings, motions, orders and other papers to be filed in a special judge case shall include in block text the words SPECIAL JUDGE and the name of the judge directly below the cause number on the caption. IN ST LAKE RCP Rule 2(D).

b. *Paragraphs; Separate statements.* All averments of a claim or defense shall be made in numbered paragraphs, the contents of each of which shall be limited as far as practicable to a statement of a single set of circumstances, and a paragraph may be referred to by number in all succeeding pleadings. Each claim founded upon a separate transaction or occurrence and each defense other than denials may be stated in a separate count or defense whenever a separation facilitates the clear presentation of the matters set forth. IN ST TRIAL P Rule 10(B).

c. *Adoption by reference; Exhibits.* Statements in a pleading may be adopted by reference in a different part of the same pleading or in another pleading or in any motion. A copy of any written instrument which is an exhibit to a pleading is a part thereof for all purposes. IN ST TRIAL P Rule 10(C).

d. *Paper; Print, quality and binding*

   i. All pleadings, motions, chronological case summary entry forms, orders, process and other papers shall be neatly and legibly printed, typewritten or mechanically reproduced, on one (1) side only, on white opaque paper. To satisfy the recordkeeping requirements of IN ST TRIAL P Rule 77, the print shall be of sufficient density and clarity for preservation and reproduction of microfilming, optical disk or other secondary sources. For this reason, the use of non-letter-quality printers is discouraged. IN ST LAKE RCP Rule 2(A).

   ii. Paper and ink shall be of such quality as to withstand the test of time. All documents shall be produced on acid-free, non-thermal paper. It is recommended that a minimum of twenty (20) pound, twenty-five percent (25%) cotton paper product be used. Documents of multiple pages shall be submitted in bound or stapled fashion, and the binding or stapling shall be at the top only. Covers or backings shall not be used. IN ST LAKE RCP Rule 2(A).

e. *Papers; Handwritten.* Handwritten papers may be filed only if approved by the Court and a typewritten or printed true rendition thereof is filed within three (3) days thereafter and approved by the Court. Upon such approval, they shall be deemed and filed as the original, while the handwritten papers shall be retained therewith for evidentiary purposes. IN ST LAKE RCP Rule 2(C).

f. *Minute sheets; Motion blanks.* Minute sheets and motion blanks shall no longer be used. IN ST LAKE RCP Rule 2(D).

2. *Size of papers for filing.* Effective January 1, 1992, all pleadings, copies, motions and documents filed with any trial court or appellate level court, typed or printed, with the exception of exhibits and existing wills, shall be prepared on eight and one-half by eleven inch (8 1/2" x 11") size paper. IN ST ADMIN Rule 11.

3. *Signature requirements*

a. *Signature of attorney.* Every pleading or motion of a party represented by an attorney shall be signed by at least one (1) attorney of record in his individual name, whose address, telephone number, and attorney number shall be stated, except that this provision shall not apply to pleadings and motions made and transcribed at the trial or a hearing before the judge and received by him in such form. IN ST TRIAL P Rule 11(A).

   i. The signature of an attorney constitutes a certificate by him that he has read the pleadings; that to the best of his knowledge, information, and belief, there is good ground to support it; and that it is not interposed for delay. IN ST TRIAL P Rule 11(A).

   ii. If a pleading or motion is not signed or is signed with intent to defeat the purpose of the rule, it may be stricken as sham and false and the action may proceed as though the pleading had not been served. IN ST TRIAL P Rule 11(A).

   iii. For a willful violation of IN ST TRIAL P Rule 11 an attorney may be subjected to appropriate disciplinary action. Similar action may be taken if scandalous or indecent matter is inserted. IN ST TRIAL P Rule 11(A).

b. *Signature of unrepresented party.* A party who is not represented by an attorney shall sign his pleading and state his address. IN ST TRIAL P Rule 11(A).

c. *Verification not generally required.* Except when specifically required by rule, pleadings or motions need not be verified or accompanied by affidavit. The rule in equity that the averments of an answer under oath must be overcome by the testimony of two (2) witnesses or of one (1) witness sustained by corroborating circumstances is abolished. IN ST TRIAL P Rule 11(A).

d. *Verification by affirmation or representation.* When in connection with any civil or special statutory proceeding it is required that any pleading, motion, petition, supporting affidavit, or other document of any kind, be verified, or that an oath be taken, it shall be sufficient if the subscriber simply affirms the truth of the matter to be verified by an affirmation or representation. IN ST TRIAL P Rule 11(B). IN ST TRIAL P Rule 11(B) states that the affirmation or representation should be in substantially the following language: "I (we) affirm, under the penalties for perjury, that the foregoing representation(s) is (are) true. (Signed) _____."

  i. Any person who falsifies an affirmation or representation of fact shall be subject to the same penalties as are prescribed by law for the making of a false affidavit. IN ST TRIAL P Rule 11(B).

e. *Verified pleadings, motions, and affidavits as evidence.* Pleadings, motions and affidavits accompanying or in support of such pleadings or motions when required to be verified or under oath shall be accepted as a representation that the signer had personal knowledge thereof or reasonable cause to believe the existence of the facts or matters stated or alleged therein; and, if otherwise competent or acceptable as evidence, may be admitted as evidence of the facts or matters stated or alleged therein when it is so provided in the Indiana Rules of Trial Procedure, by statute or other law, or to the extent the writing or signature expressly purports to be made upon the signer's personal knowledge. When such pleadings, motions and affidavits are verified or under oath they shall not require other or greater proof on the part of the adverse party than if not verified or not under oath unless expressly provided otherwise by the Indiana Rules of Trial Procedure, statute or other law. Affidavits upon motions for summary judgment under IN ST TRIAL P Rule 56 and in denial of execution under IN ST TRIAL P Rule 9.2 shall be made upon personal knowledge. IN ST TRIAL P Rule 11(C).

f. *Electronic signature.* The filing of documents and information through the E-filing system by use of a valid username and password is presumed to have been authorized by the User to whom that username and password have been issued and documents filed through the E-filing system are presumed to have been signed by the same User. IN ST ADMIN Rule 16(E).

4. *Information excluded from public access.* Every document filed in a case shall separately identify information excluded from public access pursuant to IN ST ADMIN Rule 9(G)(1) as follows:

  a. Whole documents that are excluded from public access pursuant to IN ST ADMIN Rule 9(G)(1) shall be tendered on light green paper or have a light green coversheet attached to the document, marked "Not for Public Access" or "Confidential." IN ST TRIAL P Rule 5(G)(1).

  b. When only a portion of a document contains information excluded from public access pursuant to IN ST ADMIN Rule 9(G)(1), said information shall be omitted [or redacted] from the filed document, and set forth on a separate accompanying document on light green paper conspicuously marked "Not for Public Access" or "Confidential" and clearly designated [or identifying] the caption and number of the case and the document and location within the document to which the redacted material pertains. IN ST TRIAL P Rule 5(G)(2).

  c. With respect to documents filed in electronic format, the trial court, by local rule, may provide for compliance with IN ST TRIAL P Rule 5 in manner that separates and protects access to information excluded from public access. IN ST TRIAL P Rule 5(G)(3).

  d. IN ST TRIAL P Rule 5(G) does not apply to a record sealed by the court pursuant to IN ST 5-14-3-5.5 or otherwise, nor to records, documents, or information filed in cases to which public access is prohibited pursuant to IN ST ADMIN Rule 9(G). IN ST TRIAL P Rule 5(G)(4).

  e. The following information in case records is excluded from public access and is confidential:

    i. Information that is excluded from public access pursuant to federal law;

ii. Information that is excluded from public access as declared confidential by Indiana statute or other court rule, including without limitation:

- All adoption records created after July 8, 1941, as declared confidential by IN ST 31-19-19-1, et seq., except those specifically declared open by IN ST 31-19-13-2(2);

- All records relating to chancroid, chlamydia, gonorrhea, hepatitis, human immunodeficiency virus (HIV), Lymphogranuloma venereum, syphilis, tuberculosis, as declared confidential by IN ST 16-41-8-1, et seq.;

- All records relating to child abuse as declared confidential by IN ST 31-33-18-1, et seq.;

- All records relating to drug tests as declared confidential by IN ST 5-14-3-4(a)(9);

- Records of grand jury proceedings as declared confidential by IN ST 35-34-2-4;

- Records of juvenile proceedings as declared confidential by IN ST 31-39-1-2, except those specifically open under statute;

- All paternity records created after July 1, 1941 as declared confidential by IN ST 31-14-11-15, IN ST 31-19-5-23, IN ST 31-39-1-1 and IN ST 31-39-1-2 [Editor's note: IN ST 31-14-11-15 was repealed effective May 9, 2013];

- All pre-sentence reports as declared confidential by IN ST 35-38-1-13;

- Written petitions to permit marriages without consent and orders directing the Clerk of Court to issue a marriage license to underage persons, as declared confidential by IN ST 31-11-1-6;

- Only those arrest warrants, search warrants, indictments and informations ordered confidential by the trial judge, prior to return of duly executed service as declared confidential by IN ST 5-14-3-4(b)(1);

- All medical, mental health, or tax records unless determined by law or regulation of any governmental custodian not to be confidential, released by the subject of such records, or declared by a court of competent jurisdiction to be essential to the resolution of litigation as declared confidential by IN ST 16-39-3-10, IN ST 6-4.1-5-10, IN ST 6-4.1-12-12, and IN ST 6-8.1-7-1;

- Personal information relating to jurors or prospective jurors, other than for the use of the parties and counsel, pursuant to IN ST JURY Rule 10;

- Information relating to protection from abuse orders, no-contact orders and workplace violence restraining orders as declared confidential by IN ST 5-2-9-6, et seq.;

- Mediation proceedings pursuant to IN ST ADR Rule 2.11, Mini-Trial proceedings pursuant to IN ST ADR Rule 4.4(C), and Summary Jury Trials pursuant to IN ST ADR Rule 5.6;

- Information in probation files pursuant to the Probation Standards promulgated by the Judicial Conference of Indiana pursuant to IN ST 11-13-1-8(b);

- Information deemed confidential pursuant to the Rules for Court Administered Alcohol and Drug Programs promulgated by the Judicial Conference of Indiana pursuant to IN ST 12-23-14-13;

- Information deemed confidential pursuant to the Problem-Solving Court Rules promulgated by the Judicial Conference of Indiana pursuant to IN ST 33-23-16-16;

- All records of the Department of workforce Development as declared confidential by IN ST 22-4-19-6;

- Information regarding interception of electronic communications that is sealed or deemed confidential as set forth in IN ST 35-33.5-2-1, et seq.

iii. Information excluded from public access by specific court order;

iv. Complete Social Security Numbers of living persons;

v. With the exception of names, information such as addresses, phone numbers, and dates of birth which explicitly identifies:

- Natural persons who are witnesses or victims (not including defendants) in criminal, domestic violence, stalking, sexual assault, juvenile, or civil protection order proceedings, provided that juveniles who are victims of sex crimes shall be identified by initials only;

- Places of residence of judicial officers, clerks and other employees of courts and clerks of court, unless the person or persons about whom the information pertains waives confidentiality;

vi. Complete account numbers of specific assets, loans, bank accounts, credit cards, and personal identification numbers (PINs);

vii. All orders of expungement entered in criminal or juvenile proceedings, orders to restrict access to criminal history information pursuant to IN ST 35-38-5-5.5 or IN ST 35-38-8-5 and records excluded from public access by such orders, and information related to infractions that is excluded from public access pursuant to IN ST 34-28-5-15 or IN ST 34-28-5-16 [Editor's note: IN ST 35-38-5-5.5, IN ST 35-38-8-5 and IN ST 34-28-5-16 were repealed effective July 1, 2013; for information on orders restricting access to criminal history, refer to IN ST 35-38-9-1, et seq.];

viii. All personal notes and e-mail, and deliberative material, of judges, jurors, court staff and judicial agencies, and information recorded in personal data assistants (PDA's) or organizers and personal calendars. IN ST ADMIN Rule 9(G)(1).

5. *Format of electronically filed documents*

a. *Generally.* Electronically filed documents must meet the same requirements of format as documents conventionally filed pursuant to IN ST LAKE RCP Rule 2 or other applicable Lake County Rules of Civil Procedure. IN ST LAKE RCP Rule 17(D)(1).

b. *Titles of documents.* The person electronically filing a document will be responsible for designating a title for the document at the time it is filed. The LCOD will generate the appropriate entry onto the CCS to record the filing of the document. IN ST LAKE RCP Rule 17(D)(3).

c. *Citations and hyperlinks.* Electronically filed documents may contain hyperlink references to an external document as a convenient mechanism for accessing material cited in the document. Filers wishing to insert hyperlinks into documents shall continue to use the traditional method of citation to authority in addition to the hyperlink provided. The hyperlink is merely a convenience to the court and the material referenced is extraneous to the file and not a part of the court's record. IN ST LAKE RCP Rule 17(D)(5).

d. *Attachments and exhibits.* All documents which form part of a single submission and which are being filed at the same time and by the same filer may be electronically filed together under one document filing, e.g., the motion, supporting affidavits, memorandum in support, designation of evidence, exhibits. IN ST LAKE RCP Rule 17(D)(6).

i. Large documents which do not exist in an electronic format shall be scanned into .pdf format and filed electronically as separate attachments. A scanner is available in each clerk's office for use by the public and the bar in scanning and saving image files if needed. IN ST LAKE RCP Rule 17(D)(6).

e. *Electronic signatures*

i. *Electronic filing as signature.* The electronic filing of a document which is required to be signed shall constitute the filer's representation under IN ST TRIAL P Rule 11. Unless the electronically filed document has been scanned and shows the filer's original signature, the signature of the filer shall be indicated by As/Attorney's Name, or As/Party's Name as in the case of a pro se litigant, on the line where the signature would otherwise appear. IN ST LAKE RCP Rule 17(G)(1).

ii. *Signatures on jointly signed or filed, verified or other documents.* In the case of a stipulation, agreed order, jointly signed motion or other document which needs to be signed by two (2) or more persons, or in the case of documents which must contain original signatures and which require verification or an unsworn declaration under rule or statute, the signatures may be indicated by either:

- Submitting a scanned copy of the originally signed document; or,

- Submitting the document with the use of As/Name in the signature block(s) where the original signature(s) appear(s) in the original document; provided, however, that the filer shall first obtain the physical signature of all persons necessary. IN ST LAKE RCP Rule 17(G)(2).

 iii. *Retention of original.* The filer shall retain the original executed document. IN ST LAKE RCP Rule 17(G).

6. *Citation of local rules.* The local rules for Lake County may be known as the Lake County Rules of Civil Procedure, and abbreviated as LR. IN ST LAKE RCP Rule 1(C).

F. Filing and Service Requirements

1. *Filing requirements.* Except as otherwise provided in IN ST TRIAL P Rule 5(E)(2), all pleadings and papers subsequent to the complaint which are required to be served upon a party shall be filed with the Court either before service or within a reasonable period of time thereafter. IN ST TRIAL P Rule 5(E)(1). All papers presented for filing shall be submitted to the Clerk and not to the court. All papers submitted for filing shall be mailed or delivered to the Clerk's office at the courthouse in which the case is pending. IN ST LAKE RCP Rule 3(A).

 a. *Filing with the court defined.* The filing of pleadings, motions, and other papers with the court as required by the Indiana Rules of Trial Procedure shall be made by one of the following methods:

  i. Delivery to the clerk of the court;

  ii. Sending by electronic transmission under the procedure adopted pursuant to IN ST ADMIN Rule 12;

  iii. Mailing to the clerk by registered, certified or express mail return receipt requested;

  iv. Depositing with any third-party commercial carrier for delivery to the clerk within three (3) calendar days, cost prepaid, properly addressed;

  v. If the court so permits, filing with the judge, in which event the judge shall note thereon the filing date and forthwith transmit them to the office of the clerk; or

  vi. Electronic filing, as approved by the Division of State Court Administration pursuant to IN ST ADMIN Rule 16. IN ST TRIAL P Rule 5(F).

  vii. Filing by registered or certified mail and by third-party commercial carrier shall be complete upon mailing or deposit. IN ST TRIAL P Rule 5(F).

 b. *Mandatory electronic filing.* Unless otherwise permitted by the Lake County Rules of Civil Procedure or otherwise authorized by the judicial officer assigned to a particular case, all documents submitted for filing (including the original complaint, or equivalent pleading, and summons) shall be filed electronically with the clerk using the LCOD, no matter when the case was originally filed. IN ST LAKE RCP Rule 17(D).

  i. *Of documents containing information excluded from public access pursuant to* IN ST ADMIN Rule 9. Documents containing information excluded from public access pursuant to IN ST ADMIN Rule 9, or documents which are ordered to be filed under seal shall be filed electronically, pursuant to IN ST LAKE RCP Rule 17(D)(9), whenever possible, along with a copy of the applicable order to seal the records, and the filer shall designate the documents as "Not for Public Access Pursuant to Administrative Rule 9(G)(1)" at the time of filing. IN ST LAKE RCP Rule 16(A)(1); IN ST LAKE RCP Rule 17(D)(9).

  - *Conventional filing of documents containing information excluded from public access pursuant to* IN ST ADMIN Rule 9. Documents containing information excluded from public access pursuant to IN ST ADMIN Rule 9, or documents which are ordered to be filed under seal, which cannot be legibly scanned and filed electronically, shall be conventionally filed under seal and designated by the filer as "Not for Public Access Pursuant to Administrative Rule 9(G)(1)" at the time of filing. The unredacted version shall be filed on light green paper which is conspicuously marked "Not for Public Access"; and a redacted version, with confidential information deleted, shall be filed on white paper which shall be available for public access. The filer shall also electronically file a Notice of Manual Filing. IN ST LAKE RCP Rule 16(A)(2).

ii. *Technical failures.* If a registered user is unable to file a document in a timely manner due to technical difficulties in the LCOD, the registered user must file a document with the court as soon as possible notifying the court of the inability to file the document. A sample document titled Declaration that Party was Unable to File in a Timely Manner Due to Technical Difficulties can be found at IN ST LAKE RCP Form 4. Delayed filings shall be rejected unless accompanied by the declaration attesting to the filer's failed attempts to file electronically at least two (2) times, separated by at least one (1) hour, after noon on each day of delay due to such technical failure. IN ST LAKE RCP Rule 17(J).

iii. *Documents allowed to be filed conventionally.* Unless specifically authorized by the court, only the following documents may be filed conventionally and not electronically:

- Exhibits and other documents that cannot be converted to a legible electronic form, such as videotapes, x-rays, and similar materials
- Documents delivered to the clerk by pro se litigants
- Documents mailed to the clerk by pro se litigants
- Confidential documents
- Notice of manual filing
- Titles of documents
- Chronological case summary entry forms (CCS entry forms). IN ST LAKE RCP Rule 17(E).
- For more information on the documents which must be filed conventionally, refer to IN ST LAKE RCP Rule 17(E).

c. *Facsimile filing.* Only when necessary on an emergency basis (i.e., when certified mail or other means of filing will not bring the document to the Judge's attention prior to the scheduled hearing or ruling), pleadings, motions and other papers may be filed by electronic facsimile transmission, or when specifically authorized by the Court. IN ST LAKE RCP Rule 2(C).

i. *Generally.* In counties where a majority of judges of the courts of record, by posted local rule, have authorized electronic facsimile filing and designated a telephone number to receive such transmissions, pleadings, motions, and other papers may be sent to the Clerk of Circuit Court by electronic facsimile transmission for filing in any case, provided:

- Such matter does not exceed ten (10) pages, including the cover sheet;
- Such matter does not require the payment of fees other than the electronic facsimile transcription fee set forth in IN ST ADMIN Rule 12(E);
- The sending party creates at the time of transmission a machine generated log for such transmission; and
- The original document and the transmission log are maintained by the sending party for the duration of the litigation. IN ST ADMIN Rule 12(B).

ii. *Time of filing.* During normal, posted business hours, the time of filing shall be the time the duplicate document is produced in the office of the Clerk of the Circuit Court. Duplicate documents received at all other times shall be filed as of the next normal business day. IN ST ADMIN Rule 12(C).

- If the receiving fax machine endorses its own time and date stamp upon the transmitted documents and the receiving machine produces a delivery receipt which is electronically created and transmitted to the sending party, the time of filing shall be the date and time recorded on the transmitted document by the receiving fax machine. IN ST ADMIN Rule 12(C).

d. *Filing for special judges.* For special judge matters where the special judge is a full-time judge or magistrate serving within Lake County, all papers submitted for filing shall be delivered or mailed to the Clerk's office at the courthouse where the special judge regularly serves. IN ST LAKE RCP Rule 3(A).

e. *Proof of filing.* Any party filing any paper by any method other than personal delivery to the clerk shall retain proof of filing. IN ST TRIAL P Rule 5(F).

2. *Service requirements.* Unless otherwise provided by the Indiana Rules of Trial Procedure or an order of the court, each party and special judge, if any, shall be served with: (1) every order required by its terms to be served; (2) every pleading subsequent to the original complaint; (3) every written motion except one which may be heard ex parte; (4) every brief submitted to the trial court; (5) every paper relating to discovery required to be served upon a party; and (6) every written notice, appearance, demand, offer of judgment, designation of record on appeal, or similar paper. IN ST TRIAL P Rule 5(A).

a. *Methods of service*

i. *Personal service.* Whenever a party is represented by an attorney of record, service shall be made upon such attorney unless service upon the party himself is ordered by the court. Service upon the attorney or party shall be made by delivering or mailing a copy of the papers to the last known address or where an attorney or party has consented to service by fax or e-mail, as provided in IN ST TRIAL P Rule 3.1(A)(4), by faxing or e-mailing a copy of the documents to the fax number or e-mail address set out in the appearance form or correction as required by IN ST TRIAL P Rule 3.1(E). IN ST TRIAL P Rule 5(B). Delivery of a copy within IN ST TRIAL P Rule 5 means:

- Offering or tendering it to the attorney or party and stating the nature of the papers being served. Refusal to accept an offered or tendered document is a waiver of any objection to the sufficiency or adequacy of service of that document;

- Leaving it at his office with a clerk or other person in charge thereof, or if there is no one in charge, leaving it in a conspicuous place therein; or

- If the office is closed, by leaving it at his dwelling house or usual place of abode with some person of suitable age and discretion then residing therein; or,

- Leaving it at some other suitable place, selected by the attorney upon whom service is being made, pursuant to duly promulgated local rule. IN ST TRIAL P Rule 5(B)(1).

ii. *Service by mail.* If service is made by mail, the papers shall be deposited in the United States mail addressed to the person on whom they are being served, with postage prepaid. Service shall be deemed complete upon mailing. Proof of service of all papers permitted to be mailed may be made by written acknowledgment of service, by affidavit of the person who mailed the papers, or by certificate of an attorney. It shall be the duty of attorneys when entering their appearance in a cause or when filing pleadings or papers therein, to have noted in the Chronological Case Summary or said pleadings or papers so filed the address and telephone number of their office. Service by delivery or by mail at such address shall be deemed sufficient and complete. IN ST TRIAL P Rule 5(B)(2).

iii. *Service by fax or e-mail.* A party who has consented to service by fax or e-mail may be served as follows:

- Service by e-mail shall be made by attaching the document being served in .pdf format. Discovery documents must also be served in accordance with IN ST TRIAL P Rule 26(A). IN ST TRIAL P Rule 5(B)(3)(a).

- Service by fax shall be deemed complete upon generation of a transmission record indicating the successful transmission of the entire document, except as provided in IN ST TRIAL P Rule 5(B)(3)(d). IN ST TRIAL P Rule 5(B)(3)(b).

- Service by e-mail shall be deemed complete upon transmission, except as provided in IN ST TRIAL P Rule 5(B)(3)(d). IN ST TRIAL P Rule 5(B)(3)(c).

- Service by fax or e-mail that occurs on a Saturday, Sunday, legal holiday, or day the court or agency in which the matter is pending is closed or after 5:00 PM local time of the recipient shall be deemed complete the next day that is not a Saturday, Sunday, legal holiday, or day that the court or agency in which the matter is pending is not closed. IN ST TRIAL P Rule 5(B)(3)(d).

b. *Serving numerous defendants.* In any action in which there are unusually large numbers of defendants, the court, upon motion or of its own initiative, may order:

    i. That service of the pleadings of the defendants and replies thereto need not be made as between the defendants;

- That any cross-claim, counterclaim, or matter constituting an avoidance or affirmative defense contained therein shall be deemed to be denied or avoided by all other parties; and

- That the filing of any such pleading and service thereof upon the plaintiff constitutes due notice of it to the parties. IN ST TRIAL P Rule 5(D).

    ii. A copy of every such order shall be served upon the parties in such manner and form as the court directs. IN ST TRIAL P Rule 5(D).

c. *Service by electronic means.* The Lake County Online Docket will generate a Notice of Electronic Filing and Service when any document is filed and served. This notice will be emailed to each registered user of record in a case, and an electronic service event will be added to the work queue of each registered user of record in the case. The party filing the document should retain a paper or electronic copy of the Notice of Electronic Filing and Service. This notice represents proof of filing and service of the document on registered users of record in that case. The filer shall not be required to conventionally serve any document on any party receiving electronic service. IN ST LAKE RCP Rule 17(F)(2).

    i. The filer shall also conventionally serve those parties not designated or able to receive electronic notice or service but who are nevertheless entitled to notice of said pleading or other document in accordance with the Indiana Rules of Civil Procedure and applicable Lake County Rules of Civil Procedure. In such cases, the filer shall also file a certificate of service, as appropriate. IN ST LAKE RCP Rule 17(F).

d. *Service on parties in default for failure to appear.* No service need be made on parties in default for failure to appear, except that pleadings asserting new or additional claims for relief against them shall be served upon them in the manner provided by service of summons in IN ST TRIAL P Rule 4. IN ST TRIAL P Rule 5(A).

G. Hearings

1. The Indiana rules do not contemplate a hearing regarding the filing and service of an answer.

H. Forms

1. Official Answer Forms for Indiana

    a. Affidavit of debt. IN ST TRIAL P App. A-2.

    b. Appearance by attorney in civil case. IN ST TRIAL P App. B.

2. Answer Forms for Indiana

    a. Appearance; By responding party. 9 INPRAC § 39.3.

    b. Answer; Form and content. 9 INPRAC § 41.1.

    c. Answer; General form. 9 INPRAC § 41.3.

    d. Answer; Another form. 9 INPRAC § 41.4.

    e. Answer; Another form. 9 INPRAC § 41.5.

    f. General denial. 9 INPRAC § 41.6.

    g. Specific denial of designated paragraph. 9 INPRAC § 41.7.

    h. Specific admission of designated paragraph. 9 INPRAC § 41.8.

    i.   Denial of knowledge or information to form belief. 9 INPRAC § 41.9.

    j.   Denial of knowledge or information to form belief; Another form. 9 INPRAC § 41.10.

    k.   Partial denial and partial admission of designated paragraph. 9 INPRAC § 41.11.

    l.   Denial of designated paragraph for reason that document speaks for itself. 9 INPRAC § 41.12.

    m.   Adoption of admissions or denials by co-defendant's answer. 9 INPRAC § 41.13.

    n.   Denial of execution of instrument filed with pleading. 9 INPRAC § 41.14.

    o.   Answer to cross-claim. 9 INPRAC § 41.15.

    p.   Answer to third-party complaint. 9 INPRAC § 41.16.

    q.   Accord and satisfaction. 9 INPRAC § 41.21.

    r.   Answer. 5 INPRAC § 3:3.3.

    s.   Answer; Another form. 5 INPRAC § 3:3.4.

    t.   Certificate of service; Personal service. 9 INPRAC § 5.7.

    u.   Certificate of service; First class mail. 9 INPRAC § 5.8.

    v.   Signature; By party. 9 INPRAC § 4.5.

    w.   Signature; Attorney. 9 INPRAC § 4.6.

    x.   Signature; Attorney; Another form. 9 INPRAC § 4.7.

    y.   Signature; Attorney; Another form. 9 INPRAC § 4.8.

    z.   Verification; Official form. 9 INPRAC § 4.9.

3.   Official Answer Forms for Lake County

    a.   CCS entry form. IN ST LAKE RCP App. A.

    b.   Notice of manual filing. IN ST LAKE RCP Form 2.

    c.   Certificate of service. IN ST LAKE RCP Form 3.

    d.   Declaration that party was unable to file in a timely manner. IN ST LAKE RCP Form 4.

4.   Answer Forms for Lake County

    a.   Notice of manual filing. EFORMST IN 5540.

I. Checklist

(I)   ❑ Matters to be considered by the plaintiff

    (a)   ❑ Required documents

        (1) ❑ Summons

        (2) ❑ Complaint

        (3) ❑ Appearance form

        (4) ❑ Chronological case summary (CCS) entry forms

    (b)   ❑ Supplemental documents

        (1) ❑ Proof of written instrument

        (2) ❑ Notice of intent to use foreign law

        (3) ❑ Praecipe

        (4) ❑ Facsimile cover sheet

    (c)   ❑ Timing

        (1) ❑ The claimant typically bears the burden of commencing an action within the applicable statute of limitations

        (2) ❑ If person seeking service of process fails without cause for sixty (60) days or more to provide

clerk with required summons for issuance or with other information necessary to effectuate service, person has failed to exercise due diligence in securing service of process

(II) ❑ Matters to be considered by the defendant

    (a) ❑ Required documents

        (1) ❑ Answer

        (2) ❑ Appearance form

        (3) ❑ Chronological case summary (CCS) entry forms

        (4) ❑ Certificate of service

    (b) ❑ Supplemental documents

        (1) ❑ Admission of service

        (2) ❑ Proof of written instrument

        (3) ❑ Notice of intent to use foreign law

        (4) ❑ Facsimile cover sheet

    (c) ❑ Timing

        (1) ❑ A responsive pleading required under the Indiana Rules of Trial Procedure, shall be served within twenty (20) days after service of the prior pleading

        (2) ❑ The service of a motion permitted under IN ST TRIAL P Rule 12 alters the time for service of responsive pleadings as follows, unless a different time is fixed by the court:

            (i) ❑ If the court does not grant the motion, the responsive pleading shall be served in ten (10) days after notice of the court's action;

            (ii) ❑ If the court grants the motion and the corrective action is allowed to be taken, it shall be taken within ten (10) days, and the responsive pleading shall be served within ten (10) days thereafter

        (3) ❑ All pleadings and papers subsequent to the complaint which are required to be served upon a party shall be filed with the Court either before service or within a reasonable period of time thereafter

        (4) ❑ Provided it is timely filed, the mere entry of appearance by a party or counsel in response to a summons in an action that requires an answer shall effect an extension of thirty (30) days from the filing thereof within which to respond

        (5) ❑ All pleadings, motions and other papers submitted for filing which are required to be served under IN ST TRIAL P Rule 5(A) shall be filed no later than three (3) days after service

        (6) ❑ If such papers are filed before service, proof of service thereof shall be filed no later than three (3) business days thereafter

Pleadings
Amended Answer

Document Last Updated October 2013

A. Applicable Rules

  1. *State rules*

    a. Appearance. IN ST TRIAL P Rule 3.1.

    b. Summons. IN ST TRIAL P Rule 4.

    c. Filing and service. IN ST TRIAL P Rule 4.6; IN ST TRIAL P Rule 5.

    d. Time. IN ST TRIAL P Rule 6.

e. Pleadings. IN ST TRIAL P Rule 7; IN ST TRIAL P Rule 8; IN ST TRIAL P Rule 9; IN ST TRIAL P Rule 9.1; IN ST TRIAL P Rule 9.2; IN ST TRIAL P Rule 10.

f. Signing and verification of pleadings. IN ST TRIAL P Rule 11.

g. Defenses and objections; When and how presented; By pleading or motion; Motion for judgment on the pleadings. IN ST TRIAL P Rule 12.

h. Counterclaim, cross-claim, and third-party practice. IN ST TRIAL P Rule 13; IN ST TRIAL P Rule 14.

i. Amended and supplemental pleadings. IN ST TRIAL P Rule 15.

j. Parties plaintiff and defendant; Capacity. IN ST TRIAL P Rule 17.

k. Joinder. IN ST TRIAL P Rule 19; IN ST TRIAL P Rule 20.

l. Consolidation; Separate trials. IN ST TRIAL P Rule 42.

m. Evidence. IN ST TRIAL P Rule 43.

n. Determination of foreign law. IN ST TRIAL P Rule 44.1.

o. Judgment on the evidence (directed verdict). IN ST TRIAL P Rule 50.

p. Findings by the court. IN ST TRIAL P Rule 52.

q. Judgment; Costs. IN ST TRIAL P Rule 54.

r. Summary judgment. IN ST TRIAL P Rule 56.

s. Motion to correct error. IN ST TRIAL P Rule 59.

t. Relief from judgment or order. IN ST TRIAL P Rule 60.

u. Venue requirements. IN ST TRIAL P Rule 75.

v. Court records. IN ST TRIAL P Rule 77.

w. Access to court records. IN ST ADMIN Rule 9.

x. Paper size. IN ST ADMIN Rule 11.

y. Facsimile transmission; Electronic filing and electronic service pilot projects. IN ST ADMIN Rule 12; IN ST ADMIN Rule 16.

z. Privacy and confidentiality. IN ST 5-2-9-6; IN ST 5-14-3-4; IN ST 5-14-3-5.5; IN ST 6-4.1-5-10; IN ST 6-4.1-12-12; IN ST 6-8.1-7-1; IN ST 11-13-1-8; IN ST 12-23-14-13; IN ST 16-39-3-10; IN ST 16-41-8-1; IN ST 22-4-19-6; IN ST 31-11-1-6; IN ST 31-19-5-23; IN ST 31-19-13-2; IN ST 31-19-19-1; IN ST 31-33-18-1; IN ST 31-39-1-1; IN ST 31-39-1-2; IN ST 33-23-16-16; IN ST 35-34-2-4; IN ST 35-38-1-13; IN ST 35-38-9-1; IN ST ADR Rule 2.11; IN ST ADR Rule 4.4; IN ST ADR Rule 5.6; IN ST JURY Rule 10.

2. *Local rules*

a. Scope and title. [IN ST LAKE RCP Rule 1, as amended by IN ORDER 13-0237, effective October 18, 2013].

b. Preparation of pleadings, motions and other papers. IN ST LAKE RCP Rule 2.

c. Filing. [IN ST LAKE RCP Rule 3, as amended by IN ORDER 13-0237, effective October 18, 2013].

d. Confidential information and sealed documents. IN ST LAKE RCP Rule 16.

e. Electronic filing and service. IN ST LAKE RCP Rule 17.

B. Timing

1. *Filing an amended pleading*

a. *As a matter of course.* A party may amend his pleading once as a matter of course at any time before a responsive pleading is served or, if the pleading is one to which no responsive pleading is permitted, and the action has not been placed upon the trial calendar, he may so amend it at any time within thirty (30) days after it is served. IN ST TRIAL P Rule 15(A).

b. *With leave of court.* Otherwise a party may amend his pleading only by leave of court or by written consent of the adverse party; and leave shall be given when justice so requires. IN ST TRIAL P Rule 15(A). Refer to the Indiana KeyRules Motion for Leave to Amend document for more information.

c. *Time for filing.* All pleadings, motions and other papers submitted for filing which are required to be served under IN ST TRIAL P Rule 5(A) shall be filed no later than three (3) days after service. IN ST LAKE RCP Rule 3(A).

    i. If such papers are filed before service, proof of service thereof shall be filed no later than three (3) business days thereafter. Upon failure to comply with IN ST LAKE RCP Rule 3, the Court may, on motion of any party or on its own motion, impose appropriate sanctions. IN ST LAKE RCP Rule 3(A).

2. *Computation of time*

a. *Generally; Days excluded.* In computing any period of time prescribed or allowed by the Indiana Rules of Trial Procedure, by order of the court, or by any applicable statute, the day of the act, event, or default from which the designated period of time begins to run shall not be included. The last day of the period so computed is to be included unless it is:

    i. A Saturday,

    ii. A Sunday,

    iii. A legal holiday as defined by state statute, or

    iv. A day the office in which the act is to be done is closed during regular business hours. IN ST TRIAL P Rule 6(A).

b. *Short periods.* In any event, the period runs until the end of the next day that is not a Saturday, a Sunday, a legal holiday, or a day on which the office is closed. When the period of time allowed is less than seven (7) days, intermediate Saturdays, Sundays, legal holidays, and days on which the office is closed shall be excluded from the computations. IN ST TRIAL P Rule 6(A).

c. *Additional time after service by United States mail.* Whenever a party has the right or is required to do some act or take some proceedings within a prescribed period after the service of a notice or other paper upon him and the notice or paper is served upon him by United States mail, three (3) days shall be added to the prescribed period. IN ST TRIAL P Rule 6(E).

d. *Electronic filing does not alter deadlines.* Filing electronically does not alter any filing deadlines or any time computation pursuant to state or federal statutes, any Rules of the Indiana Supreme Court, including without limitation the Rules of Trial Procedure, the Rules of Appellate Procedure or the Administrative Rules, or applicable Lake County Rules of Civil Procedure. The office of the Lake County Clerk is open for electronic filing under the Lake County Rules of Civil Procedure twenty-four (24) hours a day. A document is deemed filed at the date and time it is received by the LCOD server. Filing must be completed before midnight local time in order to be considered filed that day. Lake County observes Central Time and electronic filers are strongly urged to file documents during hours when the Lake County Online Docket ("LCOD") help line is available, from 9:00 a.m. to 4:00 p.m. local time, although documents can be filed electronically twenty-four (24) hours a day. IN ST LAKE RCP Rule 17(I).

e. *Enlargement of time.* When an act is required or allowed to be done at or within a specific time by the Indiana Rules of Trial Procedure, the court may at any time for cause shown:

    i. Order the period enlarged, with or without motion or notice, if request therefor is made before the expiration of the period originally prescribed or extended by a previous order; or

    ii. Upon motion made after the expiration of the specific period, permit the act to be done where the failure to act was the result of excusable neglect; but, the court may not extend the time for taking any action for judgment on the evidence under IN ST TRIAL P Rule 50(A), amendment of findings and judgment under IN ST TRIAL P Rule 52(B), to correct errors under IN ST TRIAL P Rule 59(C), statement in opposition to motion to correct error under IN ST TRIAL P Rule 59(E), or to obtain relief from final judgment under IN ST TRIAL P Rule 60(B), except to the extent and under the conditions stated in those rules. IN ST TRIAL P Rule 6(B).

C. General Requirements

1. *Pleading, generally*

   a. *Pleadings to be concise.* Each averment of a pleading shall be simple, concise, and direct. No technical forms of pleading or motions are required. All fictions in pleading are abolished. IN ST TRIAL P Rule 8(E)(1).

   b. *Pleading in the alternative.* A pleading may set forth two (2) or more statements of a claim or defense alternatively or hypothetically, either in one (1) count or defense or in separate counts or defenses. When two (2) or more statements are made in the alternative and one (1) of them if made independently would be sufficient, the pleading is not made insufficient by the insufficiency of one or more of the alternative statements. A pleading may also state as many separate claims or defenses as the pleader has regardless of consistency and whether based on legal or equitable grounds. All statements shall be made subject to the obligations set forth in IN ST TRIAL P Rule 11. IN ST TRIAL P Rule 8(E)(2).

   c. *Motions and pleadings, joint and several.* All motions and pleadings of any kind addressed to two (2) or more paragraphs of any pleading, or filed by two (2) or more parties, shall be taken and construed as joint, separate, and several motions or pleadings to each of such paragraphs and by and against each of such parties. All motions or pleadings containing two (2) or more subject-matters shall be taken and construed as separate and several as to each subject-matter. All objections to rulings made by two (2) or more parties shall be taken and construed as the joint, separate, and several objections of each of such parties. IN ST TRIAL P Rule 8(E)(3).

      i. A complaint filed by or against two (2) or more plaintiffs shall be taken and construed as joint, separate, and several as to each of said plaintiffs. IN ST TRIAL P Rule 8(E).

   d. *Construction of pleadings.* All pleadings shall be so construed as to do substantial justice, lead to disposition on the merits, and avoid litigation of procedural points. IN ST TRIAL P Rule 8(F).

2. *Amending pleadings.* The purpose of an amended pleading is to include matters that occurred before the filing of the original pleading but which were either overlooked by the pleader or unknown to him at the time. It is a substitute for the original and relates to the facts that existed when the original pleading was filed. An amended pleading supercedes the original as to those portions amended. 10 INPRAC § 46.1.

   a. *Amendments liberally allowed.* Amendments to pleadings are to be liberally allowed in order that all issues are presented in one action. 10 INPRAC § 46.1; Pinnacle Media, LLC v. Metropolitan Dev. Com'n of Marion County, 868 N.E.2d 894 (Ind.Ct.App. 2007).

   b. *Amendments to conform to the evidence.* When issues not raised by the pleadings are tried by express or implied consent of the parties, they shall be treated in all respects as if they had been raised in the pleadings. Such amendment of the pleadings as may be necessary to cause them to conform to the evidence and to raise these issues may be made upon motion of any party at any time, even after judgment, but failure so to amend does not affect the result of the trial of these issues. If evidence is objected to at the trial on the ground that it is not within the issues made by the pleadings, the court may allow the pleadings to be amended and shall do so freely when the presentation of the merits of the action will be subserved thereby and the objecting party fails to satisfy the court that the admission of such evidence would prejudice him in maintaining his action or defense upon the merits. The court may grant a continuance to enable the objecting party to meet such evidence. IN ST TRIAL P Rule 15(B).

   c. *Relation back of amendments*

      i. Whenever the claim or defense asserted in the amended pleading arose out of the conduct, transaction, or occurrence set forth or attempted to be set forth in the original pleading, the amendment relates back to the date of the original pleading. An amendment changing the party against whom a claim is asserted relates back if the foregoing provision is satisfied and, within one hundred and twenty (120) days of commencement of the action, the party to be brought in by amendment:

         • Has received such notice of the institution of the action that he will not be prejudiced in maintaining his defense on the merits; and

696

AMENDED ANSWER

- Knew or should have known that but for a mistake concerning the identity of the proper party, the action would have been brought against him. IN ST TRIAL P Rule 15(C).

    ii. The requirement of subsections IN ST TRIAL P Rule 15(C)(1) and IN ST TRIAL P Rule 15(C)(2) with respect to a governmental organization to be brought into the action as defendant is satisfied:

- In the case of a state or governmental organization by delivery or mailing of process to the attorney general or to a governmental executive [IN ST TRIAL P Rule 4.6(A)(3)]; or

- In the case of a local governmental organization, by delivery or mailing of process to its attorney as provided by statute, to a governmental executive thereof [IN ST TRIAL P Rule 4.6(A)(4)], or to the officer holding the office if suit is against the officer or an office. IN ST TRIAL P Rule 15(C).

  d. *Amendment by leave.* Amendments, other than an amendment by right, may be made only by leave of court or by written consent of the opposing party. 2 INPRAC R 15(15.2). Refer to the Indiana KeyRules Motion for Leave to Amend document for more information on amending with leave of court.

3. *Contents of the answer*

  a. *Defenses which may be raised by answer or motion.* Every defense, in law or fact, to a claim for relief in any pleading, whether a claim, counterclaim, cross-claim, or third-party claim, shall be asserted in the responsive pleading thereto if one is required; except that at the option of the pleader, the following defenses may be made by motion:

    i. Lack of jurisdiction over the subject matter;

    ii. Lack of jurisdiction over the person;

    iii. Incorrect venue under IN ST TRIAL P Rule 75, or any statutory provision. The disposition of this motion shall be consistent with IN ST TRIAL P Rule 75;

    iv. Insufficiency of process;

    v. Insufficiency of service of process;

    vi. Failure to state a claim upon which relief can be granted, which shall include failure to name the real party in interest under IN ST TRIAL P Rule 17;

    vii. Failure to join a party needed for just adjudication under IN ST TRIAL P Rule 19;

    viii. The same action pending in another state court of this state. IN ST TRIAL P Rule 12(B).

    ix. A motion making any of these defenses shall be made before pleading if a further pleading is permitted or within twenty (20) days after service of the prior pleading if none is required. If a pleading sets forth a claim for relief to which the adverse party is not required to serve a responsive pleading, any of the defenses in section IN ST TRIAL P Rule 12(B)(2), IN ST TRIAL P Rule 12(B)(3), IN ST TRIAL P Rule 12(B)(4), IN ST TRIAL P Rule 12(B)(5) or IN ST TRIAL P Rule 12(B)(8) is waived to the extent constitutionally permissible unless made in a motion within twenty (20) days after service of the prior pleading. No defense or objection is waived by being joined with one (1) or more other defenses or objections in a responsive pleading or motion. IN ST TRIAL P Rule 12(B).

  b. *Waiver or preservation of certain defenses*

    i. A defense of lack of jurisdiction over the person, improper venue, insufficiency of process, insufficiency of service of process, or the same action pending in another state court of this state is waived to the extent constitutionally permissible:

- If omitted from a motion in the circumstances described in IN ST TRIAL P Rule 12(G),

- If it is neither made by motion under IN ST TRIAL P Rule 12 nor included in a responsive pleading or an amendment thereof permitted by IN ST TRIAL P Rule 15(A) to be made as a matter of course. IN ST TRIAL P Rule 12(H)(1).

    ii. A defense of failure to state a claim upon which relief can be granted, a defense of failure to join

697

an indispensable party under IN ST TRIAL P Rule 19(B), and an objection of failure to state a legal defense to a claim may be made in any pleading permitted or ordered under IN ST TRIAL P Rule 7(A) or by motion for judgment on the pleadings, or at the trial on the merits. IN ST TRIAL P Rule 12(H)(2).

c. *Defenses; Form of denials*

   i. A responsive pleading shall state in short and plain terms the pleader's defenses to each claim asserted and shall admit or controvert the averments set forth in the preceding pleading. If in good faith the pleader intends to deny all the averments in the preceding pleading, he may do so by general denial subject to the provisions of IN ST TRIAL P Rule 11. If he does not intend a general denial, he may:

- Specifically deny designated averments or paragraphs; or
- Generally deny all averments except such designated averments and paragraphs as he expressly admits. IN ST TRIAL P Rule 8(B).

   ii. If he lacks knowledge or information sufficient to form a belief as to the truth of an averment, he shall so state and his statement shall be considered a denial. If in good faith a pleader intends to deny only a part or a qualification of an averment, he shall specify so much of it as is true and material and deny the remainder. All denials shall fairly meet the substance of the averments denied. IN ST TRIAL P Rule 8 shall have no application to uncontested actions for divorce, or to answers required to be filed by clerks or guardians ad litem. IN ST TRIAL P Rule 8(B).

d. *Affirmative defenses.* A responsive pleading shall set forth affirmatively and carry the burden of proving: accord and satisfaction, arbitration and award, discharge in bankruptcy, duress, estoppel, failure of consideration, fraud, illegality, injury by fellow servant, laches, license, payment, release, res judicata, statute of frauds, statute of limitations, waiver, lack of jurisdiction over the subject-matter, lack of jurisdiction over the person, improper venue, insufficiency of process or service of process, the same action pending in another state court of this state, and any other matter constituting an avoidance, matter of abatement, or affirmative defense. A party required to affirmatively plead any matters, including matters formerly required to be pleaded affirmatively by reply, shall have the burden of proving such matters. The burden of proof imposed by this or any other provision of the Indiana Rules of Trial Procedure is subject to the rules of evidence or any statute fixing a different rule. If the pleading mistakenly designates a defense as a counterclaim or a counterclaim as a defense, the court shall treat the pleading as if there had been a proper designation. IN ST TRIAL P Rule 8(C).

   i. An affirmative defense, generally, must be affirmatively stated by the party who seeks its benefit. 1A INPRAC R 8(8.5); Rice v. Grant County Bd. of Com'rs, 472 N.E.2d 213 (Ind.Ct.App. 1984). If that party does not raise the affirmative defense, then it is waived. 1A INPRAC R 8(8.5); Piskorowski v. Shell Oil Co., 403 N.E.2d 838, 847 (Ind.Ct.App. 1980).

   ii. It is clear that the list of affirmative defenses found in IN ST TRIAL P Rule 8 is not exhaustive. The question comes: when is a defense to be treated as an affirmative defense, with all of the attending consequences? 1A INPRAC R 8(8.5). The "determination of whether a defense is affirmative depends on whether it controverts an element of the plaintiff's prima facie case or raises matter outside the scope of the prima facie case." 1A INPRAC R 8(8.5); Molargik v. West Enterprises, Inc., 605 N.E.2d 1197, 1198 (Ind.Ct.App. 1993).

e. *Defense of contributory negligence or assumed risk.* In all claims alleging negligence, the burden of pleading and proving contributory negligence, assumption of risk, or incurred risk shall be upon the defendant who may plead such by denial of the allegation. IN ST TRIAL P Rule 9.1(A).

f. *Res ipsa loquitur.* Res ipsa loquitur or a similar doctrine may be pleaded by alleging generally that the facts connected with the action are unknown to the pleader and are within the knowledge of the opposing party. IN ST TRIAL P Rule 9.1(B).

g. *Consideration.* When an action or defense is founded upon a written contract or release, lack of consideration for the promise or release is an affirmative defense, and the party asserting lack of it carries the burden of proof. IN ST TRIAL P Rule 9.1(C).

h. *Bona fide purchaser.* When the rights of a person depend upon his status as a bona fide purchaser for value or upon similar requirements, such status must be pleaded and proved by the person asserting it, but it may be pleaded in general terms. Once it is established that the person has given any required value, unless such value is commercially unreasonable, and that he has met any requirements of recordation, filing, possession, or perfection, the trier of fact must find that such value was given or such perfection was made in accordance with any requirements of good faith, lack of knowledge, or lack of notice unless and until evidence is introduced which would support a finding of its non-existence. IN ST TRIAL P Rule 9.1(D).

i. *Presumption; Matters of judicial notice.* Neither presumptions of law nor matters of which judicial notice may be taken need be stated in a pleading. IN ST TRIAL P Rule 9.1(E).

j. *Property distrained; Sufficient answer.* In an action to recover the possession of property distrained while doing damage, an answer that the defendant, or person by whose command he acted, was lawfully possessed of the real property upon which the distress was made, and that the property distrained was at the time doing damage thereon, shall be good without setting forth the title of such real property. IN ST TRIAL P Rule 9.1(F).

k. *Effect of failure to deny.* Averments in a pleading to which a responsive pleading is required, except those pertaining to amount of damages, are admitted when not denied in the responsive pleading. Averments in a pleading to which no responsive pleading is required or permitted shall be taken as denied or avoided. IN ST TRIAL P Rule 8(D).

l. *Effect of admission.* When a rhetorical paragraph or allegation is admitted, the effect in Indiana is to remove it from trial. Such an admission is a "judicial admission", and the claim or issue which is admitted cannot be denied later by the trier of the facts. Further, this admitted fact does not require evidence to "prove it"; it is established. It becomes, in short, controlling and indisputable in the litigation, unless the trial court permits an amendment to the pleading which might remove the controlling effect of the admission, and permit it to become another fact or item of evidence in the case. 1A INPRAC R 8(8.4); Aylesworth v. McKesson, 421 N.E.2d 422 (Ind.Ct.App. 1981).

4. *Pleading special matters*

a. *Capacity.* It is not necessary to aver the capacity of a party to sue or be sued, the authority of a party to sue or be sued in a representative capacity, or the legal existence of an organization that is made a party. The burden of proving lack of such capacity, authority, or legal existence shall be upon the person asserting lack of it, and shall be pleaded as an affirmative defense. IN ST TRIAL P Rule 9(A).

b. *Fraud, mistake, condition of the mind.* In all averments of fraud or mistake, the circumstances constituting fraud or mistake shall be specifically averred. Malice, intent, knowledge, and other conditions of mind may be averred generally. IN ST TRIAL P Rule 9(B).

c. *Conditions precedent.* In pleading the performance or occurrence of promissory or non-promissory conditions precedent, it is sufficient to aver generally that all conditions precedent have been performed, have occurred, or have been excused. A denial of performance or occurrence shall be made specifically and with particularity, and a denial of excuse generally. IN ST TRIAL P Rule 9(C).

d. *Official document or act.* In pleading an official document or official act it is sufficient to aver that the document was issued or the act done in compliance with law. IN ST TRIAL P Rule 9(D).

e. *Judgment.* In pleading a judgment or decision of a domestic or foreign court, judicial or quasi-judicial tribunal, or of a board or officer, it is sufficient to aver the judgment or decision without setting forth matter showing jurisdiction to render it. IN ST TRIAL P Rule 9(E).

f. *Time and place.* For the purpose of testing the sufficiency of a pleading, averments of time and place are material and shall be considered like all other averments of material matter. However, time and place need be stated only with such specificity as will enable the opposing party to prepare his defense. IN ST TRIAL P Rule 9(F).

g. *Special damages; Damages where no answer.* When items of special damage are claimed, they shall be specifically stated. The relief granted to the plaintiff, if there be no answer, cannot exceed the relief demanded in his complaint; but, in any other case, the court may grant him any relief consistent with the facts or matters pleaded. IN ST TRIAL P Rule 9(G).

5. *Counterclaim and cross-claim*

    a. *Compulsory counterclaims.* A pleading shall state as a counterclaim any claim which at the time of serving the pleading the pleader has against any opposing party, if it arises out of the transaction or occurrence that is the subject-matter of the opposing party's claim and does not require for its adjudication the presence of third parties of whom the court cannot acquire jurisdiction. But the pleader need not state the claim if:

        i. At the time the action was commenced the claim was the subject of another pending action; or

        ii. The opposing party brought suit upon his claim by attachment or other process by which the court did not acquire jurisdiction to render a personal judgment on that claim, and the pleader is not stating any counterclaim under IN ST TRIAL P Rule 13. IN ST TRIAL P Rule 13(A).

    b. *Permissive counterclaims.* A pleading may state as a counterclaim any claim against an opposing party not arising out of the transaction or occurrence that is the subject-matter of the opposing party's claim. IN ST TRIAL P Rule 13(B).

    c. *Counterclaim exceeding opposing claim.* A counterclaim may or may not diminish or defeat the recovery sought by the opposing party. It may claim relief exceeding in amount or different in kind from that sought in the pleading of the opposing party. IN ST TRIAL P Rule 13(C).

    d. *Counterclaim against state.* IN ST TRIAL P Rule 13 shall not be construed to enlarge any right to assert a claim against the state. IN ST TRIAL P Rule 13(D).

    e. *Counterclaim maturing or acquired after pleading.* A claim which either matured or was acquired by the pleader after serving his pleading may, with the permission of the court, be presented as a counterclaim by supplemental pleading. A counterclaim or cross-claim which is not due may be asserted against a party who is insolvent or the representative of a party who has been subjected to insolvency proceedings, if recovery thereon will be impaired because of such party's insolvency. IN ST TRIAL P Rule 13(E).

    f. *Omitted counterclaim.* When a pleader fails to set up a counterclaim through oversight, inadvertence, or excusable neglect, or when justice requires, he may by leave of court set up the counterclaim by amendment. IN ST TRIAL P Rule 13(F).

    g. *Cross-claim against co-party.* A pleading may state as a cross-claim any claim by one party against a co-party. IN ST TRIAL P Rule 13(G).

    h. *Joinder of additional parties.* Persons other than those made parties to the original action may be made parties to a counterclaim or cross-claim in accordance with the provisions of IN ST TRIAL P Rule 14, IN ST TRIAL P Rule 19 and IN ST TRIAL P Rule 20. IN ST TRIAL P Rule 13(H).

    i. *Separate trials; Separate judgments*

        i. If the court orders separate trials as provided in IN ST TRIAL P Rule 42(B), judgment on a counterclaim or cross-claim may be rendered in accordance with the terms of IN ST TRIAL P Rule 54(B) when the court has jurisdiction so to do, even if the claims of the opposing party have been dismissed or otherwise disposed of. In determining whether or not separate trial of a cross-claim shall be ordered, the court shall consider whether the cross-claim:

            • Arises out of the transaction or occurrence or series of transactions or occurrences that is the subject-matter either of the original action or of a counterclaim therein;

            • Relates to any property or contract that is the subject-matter of the original action; or

            • Claims that the person against whom it is asserted is liable to the cross-claimant for all or part of plaintiff's claim against him. IN ST TRIAL P Rule 13(I).

        ii. In addition, the court may consider any other relevant factors. IN ST TRIAL P Rule 13(I).

    j. *Effect of statute of limitations and other discharges at law.* The statute of limitations, a nonclaim statute or other discharge at law shall not bar a claim asserted as a counterclaim to the extent that:

        i. It diminishes or defeats the opposing party's claim if it arises out of the transaction or occurrence that is the subject-matter of the opposing party's claim, or if it could have been asserted as a counterclaim to the opposing party's claim before it (the counterclaim) was barred; or

ii. It or the opposing party's claim relates to payment of or security for the other. IN ST TRIAL P Rule 13(J).

k. *Counterclaim by and against transferees and successors.* A counterclaim may be asserted by or against the transferee or successor of a claim subject to the following provisions:

    i. A successor who is a guardian, representative of a decedent's estate, receiver or assignee for the benefit of creditors, trustee or the like may interpose a claim to which he succeeds against claims or proceedings brought in or outside the court of administration. A claim owing by his predecessor may be interposed against any claim brought by such successor in or outside the court of administration without the necessity of filing such claim or cause of action in the administration proceedings. IN ST TRIAL P Rule 13(K)(1).

    ii. A transferee or successor of a claim takes it subject to any defense or counterclaim that is the subject-matter of the opposing party's claim; or that is available to the obligor at the time of the assignment or before the obligor received notice of the assignment. IN ST TRIAL P Rule 13(K)(2).

    iii. A surety or party with total or partial recourse upon a claim upon which he is being sued may interpose as a counterclaim:

- Any claim of his own; and

- Any claim owned by the person against whom he has recourse who either has notice of the suit, is a party to the suit, is insolvent, has assigned his claim to the surety or party asserting it, or cannot be found. IN ST TRIAL P Rule 13(K)(3).

- A counterclaim under IN ST TRIAL P Rule 13(K)(3)(b) must tend to diminish or defeat the opposing party's claim, or it or the opposing claim must relate to payment of or security for the other, unless the person against whom recourse may be had is a party to the suit or the counterclaim has been assigned to the party asserting it; and if recovery on the counterclaim exceeds the opposing party's claim, any excess recovered shall be held in trust for such person against whom there is a right of recourse. IN ST TRIAL P Rule 13(K)(3).

    iv. IN ST TRIAL P Rule 13(K)(1), IN ST TRIAL P Rule 13(K)(2), and IN ST TRIAL P Rule 13(K)(3), are subject to subdivision IN ST TRIAL P Rule 13(L). IN ST TRIAL P Rule 13(K)(4).

l. *Counterclaim and cross-claim subject to substantive law principles.* Counterclaim and cross-claims are subject to restrictions imposed by other statutes and principles of substantive common law and equity, including rules of commercial law, agency, estoppel, contract and the like. In appropriate cases the court may impose terms or conditions upon its judgment or decree and may enter conditional or noncanceling cross judgments to satisfy such restrictions. This provision is intended to deny or limit counterclaims or cross-claims:

    i. Where a creditor will receive an unfair priority because a claim is assigned after insolvency proceedings, or assigned before such proceedings if it results in an unlawful preference;

    ii. Where an unfair priority will be allowed if a surety interposing a claim owned in his own right against the creditor suing on the principal's obligation when the principal is solvent and the creditor is not;

    iii. Where a claim by or against a representative, such as a guardian, receiver, representative of a decedent's estate, assignee for the benefit of creditors, trustee or the like in his individual capacity is asserted against a claim owing or owed by the estate he represents;

    iv. Where a claim by or against a partnership or two (2) or more obligors is opposed against or by a claim of an individual to the extent that the individual will be allowed unfairly to profit or if it will adversely affect the rights of creditors; or

    v. Where a claim is cut off by a holder in due course or a transferee who is protected under principles of commercial law, estoppel, or contract. IN ST TRIAL P Rule 13(L).

m. *Satisfaction of judgment.* Satisfaction of a judgment or credits thereon may be ordered, for sufficient cause, upon notice and motion. "Credits" include any counterclaim which tends to diminish or defeat the judgment, or any counterclaim where it or the opposing claim relates to payment of or security for the other. IN ST TRIAL P Rule 13(M).

6. *Third-party practice*

   a. *When defendant may bring in third party.* A defending party, as a third-party plaintiff, may cause a summons and complaint to be served upon a person not a party to the action who is or may be liable to him for all or part of the plaintiff's claim against him. IN ST TRIAL P Rule 14(A). The person served with the summons and the third-party complaint, hereinafter called the third-party defendant, as provided in IN ST TRIAL P Rule 12 and IN ST TRIAL P Rule 13 may make:

      i. His defenses, cross-claims and counterclaims to the third-party plaintiff's claims;

      ii. His defenses, counterclaims and cross-claims against any other defendants or third-party defendants;

      iii. Any defenses or claims which the third-party plaintiff has to the plaintiff's claim which are available to the third-party defendant against the plaintiff; and

      iv. Any defenses or claims which the third-party defendant has as against the plaintiff. IN ST TRIAL P Rule 14(A).

      v. The plaintiff may assert any claim against the third-party defendant who thereupon may assert his defenses, counterclaims and cross-claims, as provided in IN ST TRIAL P Rule 12 and IN ST TRIAL P Rule 13. A third-party defendant may proceed under IN ST TRIAL P Rule 14 against any person not a party to the action who is or may be liable to him for all or part of the claim made in the action against the third-party defendant. IN ST TRIAL P Rule 14(A).

   b. *When plaintiff may bring in third party.* When a counterclaim or other claim is asserted against a plaintiff, he may cause a third party to be brought in under circumstances, which, under IN ST TRIAL P Rule 14, would entitle a defendant to do so. IN ST TRIAL P Rule 14(B).

   c. *Severance; Parties improperly impleaded.* With his responsive pleading or by motion prior thereto, any party may move for severance of a third-party claim or ensuing claim as provided in IN ST TRIAL P Rule 14 or for a separate trial thereon. If the third-party defendant is a proper party to the proceedings under any other rule relating to parties, the action shall continue as in other cases where he is made a party. IN ST TRIAL P Rule 14(C).

7. *Trial by jury; Demand*

   a. *Causes triable by court and by jury.* Issues of law and issues of fact in causes that prior to the eighteenth day of June, 1852, were of exclusive equitable jurisdiction shall be tried by the court; issues of fact in all other causes shall be triable as the same are now triable. In case of the joinder of causes of action or defenses which, prior to said date, were of exclusive equitable jurisdiction with causes of action or defenses which, prior to said date, were designated as actions at law and triable by jury—the former shall be triable by the court, and the latter by a jury, unless waived; the trial of both may be at the same time or at different times, as the court may direct. IN ST TRIAL P Rule 38(A).

   b. *Demand.* Any party may demand a trial by jury of any issue triable of right by a jury by filing with the court and serving upon the other parties a demand therefor in writing at any time after the commencement of the action and not later than ten (10) days after the first responsive pleading to the complaint, or to a counterclaim, crossclaim or other claim if one properly is pleaded; and if no responsive pleading is filed or required, within ten (10) days after the time such pleading otherwise would have been required. Such demand is sufficient if indorsed upon a pleading of a party filed within such time. IN ST TRIAL P Rule 38(B).

   c. *Same; Specification of issues.* In his demand a party may specify the issues which he wishes so tried; otherwise he shall be deemed to have demanded trial by jury for all issues triable as of right by jury. Any other party must file a demand for jury trial to preserve his right to trial by jury:

      i. Of issues for which a right to trial by jury was not requested by another party; and

      ii. In case a request by another party was improper. But if a proper request for a trial by jury upon issues triable by jury as of right on his behalf is made by any party, such request shall be deemed to have been made on behalf of all parties entitled to a jury trial upon such issues. IN ST TRIAL P Rule 38(C).

d. *Waiver.* The failure of a party to appear at the trial, and the failure of a party to serve a demand as required by IN ST TRIAL P Rule 38 and to file it as required by IN ST TRIAL P Rule 5(E) constitute waiver by him of trial by jury. A demand for trial by jury made as provided in IN ST TRIAL P Rule 38 may not be withdrawn without the consent of the other party or parties. IN ST TRIAL P Rule 38(D).

    i. The trial court shall not grant a demand for a trial by jury filed after the time fixed in IN ST TRIAL P Rule 38(B) has elapsed except upon the written agreement of all of the parties to the action, which agreement shall be filed with the court and made a part of the record. If such agreement is filed then the court may, in its discretion, grant a trial by jury in which event the grant of a trial by jury may not be withdrawn except by the agreement of all of the parties. IN ST TRIAL P Rule 38(D).

e. *Arbitration.* Nothing in the Indiana Rules of Trial Procedure shall deny the parties the right by contract or agreement to submit or to agree to submit controversies to arbitration made before or after commencement of an action thereon or deny the courts power to specifically enforce such agreements. IN ST TRIAL P Rule 38(E).

D. Documents

1. *Required documents*

   a. *Amended answer.* Refer to the General Requirements section of this document for information on the contents of an amended answer.

   b. *Chronological case summary (CCS) entry forms.* All filings shall be accompanied by a Chronological Case Summary (CCS) Entry Form to define or identify the documents filed. The Form used should be substantially similar to IN ST LAKE RCP App. A. IN ST LAKE RCP Rule 3(C).

   c. *Certificate of service.* An attorney or unrepresented party tendering a document to the Clerk for filing shall certify that service has been made, list the parties served, and specify the date and means of service. The certificate of service shall be placed at the end of the document and shall not be separately filed. The separate filing of a certificate of service, however, shall not be grounds for rejecting a document for filing. The Clerk may permit documents to be filed without a certificate of service but shall require prompt filing of a separate certificate of service. IN ST TRIAL P Rule 5(C).

       i. All pleadings, motions and other papers submitted for filing which are required to be served under IN ST TRIAL P Rule 5(A) shall contain proof of service pursuant to IN ST TRIAL P Rule 5(B)(2). IN ST LAKE RCP Rule 3(A).

2. *Supplemental documents*

   a. *Proof of written instrument.* When any pleading allowed by the Indiana Rules of Trial Procedure is founded on a written instrument, the original, or a copy thereof, must be included in or filed with the pleading. Such instrument, whether copied in the pleadings or not, shall be taken as part of the record. When any pleading allowed by the Indiana Rules of Trial Procedure is founded on an account, an Affidavit of Debt, in a form substantially similar to that which is provided in IN ST TRIAL P App. A-2, shall be attached. IN ST TRIAL P Rule 9.2(A).

   b. *Notice of intent to use foreign law.* A party who intends to raise an issue concerning the law of a foreign country shall give notice in his pleadings or other reasonable written notice. The court, in determining foreign law, may consider any relevant material or source, including testimony, whether or not submitted by a party or admissible under IN ST TRIAL P Rule 43. The court's determination shall be treated as a ruling on a question of law. It shall be made by the court and not the jury and shall be reviewable. IN ST TRIAL P Rule 44.1(A).

   c. *Facsimile cover sheet.* Any document sent to the Clerk of the Circuit Court by electronic facsimile transmission shall be accompanied by a cover sheet which states the title of the document, case number, number of pages, identity and voice telephone number of the sending party and instructions

for filing. The cover sheet shall contain the signature of the attorney or party, pro se, authorizing the filing. IN ST ADMIN Rule 12(D).

E. Format

1. *Form of pleadings.* For the purpose of uniformity, convenience, clarity and durability, requirements in IN ST LAKE RCP Rule 2 shall be observed in the preparation of all pleadings, motions and other papers. IN ST LAKE RCP Rule 2. Whenever materials submitted fail to meet the standards in IN ST LAKE RCP Rule 2, the Court may impose appropriate sanctions. IN ST LAKE RCP Rule 2(B).

   a. *Caption; Names of parties.* Every pleading shall contain a caption setting forth the name of the court, the title of the action, the file number, and a designation as in IN ST TRIAL P Rule 7(A). In the complaint the title of the action shall include the names of all the parties, but in other pleadings it is sufficient to state the name of the first party on each side with an appropriate indication of other parties. IN ST TRIAL P Rule 10(A).

      i. *Special judge matters.* The caption of all CCS Entry Forms, pleadings, motions, orders and other papers to be filed in a special judge case shall include in block text the words SPECIAL JUDGE and the name of the judge directly below the cause number on the caption. IN ST LAKE RCP Rule 2(D).

   b. *Paragraphs; Separate statements.* All averments of a claim or defense shall be made in numbered paragraphs, the contents of each of which shall be limited as far as practicable to a statement of a single set of circumstances, and a paragraph may be referred to by number in all succeeding pleadings. Each claim founded upon a separate transaction or occurrence and each defense other than denials may be stated in a separate count or defense whenever a separation facilitates the clear presentation of the matters set forth. IN ST TRIAL P Rule 10(B).

   c. *Adoption by reference; Exhibits.* Statements in a pleading may be adopted by reference in a different part of the same pleading or in another pleading or in any motion. A copy of any written instrument which is an exhibit to a pleading is a part thereof for all purposes. IN ST TRIAL P Rule 10(C).

   d. *Paper; Print, quality and binding*

      i. All pleadings, motions, chronological case summary entry forms, orders, process and other papers shall be neatly and legibly printed, typewritten or mechanically reproduced, on one (1) side only, on white opaque paper. To satisfy the recordkeeping requirements of IN ST TRIAL P Rule 77, the print shall be of sufficient density and clarity for preservation and reproduction of microfilming, optical disk or other secondary sources. For this reason, the use of non-letter-quality printers is discouraged. IN ST LAKE RCP Rule 2(A).

      ii. Paper and ink shall be of such quality as to withstand the test of time. All documents shall be produced on acid-free, non-thermal paper. It is recommended that a minimum of twenty (20) pound, twenty-five percent (25%) cotton paper product be used. Documents of multiple pages shall be submitted in bound or stapled fashion, and the binding or stapling shall be at the top only. Covers or backings shall not be used. IN ST LAKE RCP Rule 2(A).

   e. *Papers; Handwritten.* Handwritten papers may be filed only if approved by the Court and a typewritten or printed true rendition thereof is filed within three (3) days thereafter and approved by the Court. Upon such approval, they shall be deemed and filed as the original, while the handwritten papers shall be retained therewith for evidentiary purposes. IN ST LAKE RCP Rule 2(C).

   f. *Minute sheets; Motion blanks.* Minute sheets and motion blanks shall no longer be used. IN ST LAKE RCP Rule 2(D).

2. *Size of papers for filing.* Effective January 1, 1992, all pleadings, copies, motions and documents filed with any trial court or appellate level court, typed or printed, with the exception of exhibits and existing wills, shall be prepared on eight and one-half by eleven inch (8 1/2" x 11") size paper. IN ST ADMIN Rule 11.

3. *Signature requirements*

   a. *Signature of attorney.* Every pleading or motion of a party represented by an attorney shall be signed by at least one (1) attorney of record in his individual name, whose address, telephone number, and attorney number shall be stated, except that this provision shall not apply to pleadings and motions made and transcribed at the trial or a hearing before the judge and received by him in such form. IN ST TRIAL P Rule 11(A).

    i.   The signature of an attorney constitutes a certificate by him that he has read the pleadings; that to the best of his knowledge, information, and belief, there is good ground to support it; and that it is not interposed for delay. IN ST TRIAL P Rule 11(A).

    ii.   If a pleading or motion is not signed or is signed with intent to defeat the purpose of the rule, it may be stricken as sham and false and the action may proceed as though the pleading had not been served. IN ST TRIAL P Rule 11(A).

    iii.   For a willful violation of IN ST TRIAL P Rule 11 an attorney may be subjected to appropriate disciplinary action. Similar action may be taken if scandalous or indecent matter is inserted. IN ST TRIAL P Rule 11(A).

b.   *Signature of unrepresented party.* A party who is not represented by an attorney shall sign his pleading and state his address. IN ST TRIAL P Rule 11(A).

c.   *Verification not generally required.* Except when specifically required by rule, pleadings or motions need not be verified or accompanied by affidavit. The rule in equity that the averments of an answer under oath must be overcome by the testimony of two (2) witnesses or of one (1) witness sustained by corroborating circumstances is abolished. IN ST TRIAL P Rule 11(A).

d.   *Verification by affirmation or representation.* When in connection with any civil or special statutory proceeding it is required that any pleading, motion, petition, supporting affidavit, or other document of any kind, be verified, or that an oath be taken, it shall be sufficient if the subscriber simply affirms the truth of the matter to be verified by an affirmation or representation. IN ST TRIAL P Rule 11(B). IN ST TRIAL P Rule 11(B) states that the affirmation or representation should be in substantially the following language: "I (we) affirm, under the penalties for perjury, that the foregoing representation(s) is (are) true. (Signed) _____."

    i.   Any person who falsifies an affirmation or representation of fact shall be subject to the same penalties as are prescribed by law for the making of a false affidavit. IN ST TRIAL P Rule 11(B).

e.   *Verified pleadings, motions, and affidavits as evidence.* Pleadings, motions and affidavits accompanying or in support of such pleadings or motions when required to be verified or under oath shall be accepted as a representation that the signer had personal knowledge thereof or reasonable cause to believe the existence of the facts or matters stated or alleged therein; and, if otherwise competent or acceptable as evidence, may be admitted as evidence of the facts or matters stated or alleged therein when it is so provided in the Indiana Rules of Trial Procedure, by statute or other law, or to the extent the writing or signature expressly purports to be made upon the signer's personal knowledge. When such pleadings, motions and affidavits are verified or under oath they shall not require other or greater proof on the part of the adverse party than if not verified or not under oath unless expressly provided otherwise by the Indiana Rules of Trial Procedure, statute or other law. Affidavits upon motions for summary judgment under IN ST TRIAL P Rule 56 and in denial of execution under IN ST TRIAL P Rule 9.2 shall be made upon personal knowledge. IN ST TRIAL P Rule 11(C).

f.   *Electronic signature.* The filing of documents and information through the E-filing system by use of a valid username and password is presumed to have been authorized by the User to whom that username and password have been issued and documents filed through the E-filing system are presumed to have been signed by the same User. IN ST ADMIN Rule 16(E).

4.   *Information excluded from public access.* Every document filed in a case shall separately identify information excluded from public access pursuant to IN ST ADMIN Rule 9(G)(1) as follows:

a.   Whole documents that are excluded from public access pursuant to IN ST ADMIN Rule 9(G)(1) shall be tendered on light green paper or have a light green coversheet attached to the document, marked "Not for Public Access" or "Confidential." IN ST TRIAL P Rule 5(G)(1).

b.   When only a portion of a document contains information excluded from public access pursuant to IN ST ADMIN Rule 9(G)(1), said information shall be omitted [or redacted] from the filed document,

and set forth on a separate accompanying document on light green paper conspicuously marked "Not for Public Access" or "Confidential" and clearly designated [or identifying] the caption and number of the case and the document and location within the document to which the redacted material pertains. IN ST TRIAL P Rule 5(G)(2).

c. With respect to documents filed in electronic format, the trial court, by local rule, may provide for compliance with IN ST TRIAL P Rule 5 in manner that separates and protects access to information excluded from public access. IN ST TRIAL P Rule 5(G)(3).

d. IN ST TRIAL P Rule 5(G) does not apply to a record sealed by the court pursuant to IN ST 5-14-3-5.5 or otherwise, nor to records, documents, or information filed in cases to which public access is prohibited pursuant to IN ST ADMIN Rule 9(G). IN ST TRIAL P Rule 5(G)(4).

e. The following information in case records is excluded from public access and is confidential:

 i. Information that is excluded from public access pursuant to federal law;

 ii. Information that is excluded from public access as declared confidential by Indiana statute or other court rule, including without limitation:

 • All adoption records created after July 8, 1941, as declared confidential by IN ST 31-19-19-1, et seq., except those specifically declared open by IN ST 31-19-13-2(2);

 • All records relating to chancroid, chlamydia, gonorrhea, hepatitis, human immunodeficiency virus (HIV), Lymphogranuloma venereum, syphilis, tuberculosis, as declared confidential by IN ST 16-41-8-1, et seq.;

 • All records relating to child abuse as declared confidential by IN ST 31-33-18-1, et seq.;

 • All records relating to drug tests as declared confidential by IN ST 5-14-3-4(a)(9);

 • Records of grand jury proceedings as declared confidential by IN ST 35-34-2-4;

 • Records of juvenile proceedings as declared confidential by IN ST 31-39-1-2, except those specifically open under statute;

 • All paternity records created after July 1, 1941 as declared confidential by IN ST 31-14-11-15, IN ST 31-19-5-23, IN ST 31-39-1-1 and IN ST 31-39-1-2 [Editor's note: IN ST 31-14-11-15 was repealed effective May 9, 2013];

 • All pre-sentence reports as declared confidential by IN ST 35-38-1-13;

 • Written petitions to permit marriages without consent and orders directing the Clerk of Court to issue a marriage license to underage persons, as declared confidential by IN ST 31-11-1-6;

 • Only those arrest warrants, search warrants, indictments and informations ordered confidential by the trial judge, prior to return of duly executed service as declared confidential by IN ST 5-14-3-4(b)(1);

 • All medical, mental health, or tax records unless determined by law or regulation of any governmental custodian not to be confidential, released by the subject of such records, or declared by a court of competent jurisdiction to be essential to the resolution of litigation as declared confidential by IN ST 16-39-3-10, IN ST 6-4.1-5-10, IN ST 6-4.1-12-12, and IN ST 6-8.1-7-1;

 • Personal information relating to jurors or prospective jurors, other than for the use of the parties and counsel, pursuant to IN ST JURY Rule 10;

 • Information relating to protection from abuse orders, no-contact orders and workplace violence restraining orders as declared confidential by IN ST 5-2-9-6, et seq.;

 • Mediation proceedings pursuant to IN ST ADR Rule 2.11, Mini-Trial proceedings pursuant to IN ST ADR Rule 4.4(C), and Summary Jury Trials pursuant to IN ST ADR Rule 5.6;

 • Information in probation files pursuant to the Probation Standards promulgated by the Judicial Conference of Indiana pursuant to IN ST 11-13-1-8(b);

- Information deemed confidential pursuant to the Rules for Court Administered Alcohol and Drug Programs promulgated by the Judicial Conference of Indiana pursuant to IN ST 12-23-14-13;

- Information deemed confidential pursuant to the Problem-Solving Court Rules promulgated by the Judicial Conference of Indiana pursuant to IN ST 33-23-16-16;

- All records of the Department of workforce Development as declared confidential by IN ST 22-4-19-6;

- Information regarding interception of electronic communications that is sealed or deemed confidential as set forth in IN ST 35-33.5-2-1, et seq.

   iii. Information excluded from public access by specific court order;

   iv. Complete Social Security Numbers of living persons;

   v. With the exception of names, information such as addresses, phone numbers, and dates of birth which explicitly identifies:

- Natural persons who are witnesses or victims (not including defendants) in criminal, domestic violence, stalking, sexual assault, juvenile, or civil protection order proceedings, provided that juveniles who are victims of sex crimes shall be identified by initials only;

- Places of residence of judicial officers, clerks and other employees of courts and clerks of court, unless the person or persons about whom the information pertains waives confidentiality;

   vi. Complete account numbers of specific assets, loans, bank accounts, credit cards, and personal identification numbers (PINs);

   vii. All orders of expungement entered in criminal or juvenile proceedings, orders to restrict access to criminal history information pursuant to IN ST 35-38-5-5.5 or IN ST 35-38-8-5 and records excluded from public access by such orders, and information related to infractions that is excluded from public access pursuant to IN ST 34-28-5-15 or IN ST 34-28-5-16 [Editor's note: IN ST 35-38-5-5.5, IN ST 35-38-8-5 and IN ST 34-28-5-16 were repealed effective July 1, 2013; for information on orders restricting access to criminal history, refer to IN ST 35-38-9-1, et seq.];

   viii. All personal notes and e-mail, and deliberative material, of judges, jurors, court staff and judicial agencies, and information recorded in personal data assistants (PDA's) or organizers and personal calendars. IN ST ADMIN Rule 9(G)(1).

5. *Format of electronically filed documents*

   a. *Generally.* Electronically filed documents must meet the same requirements of format as documents conventionally filed pursuant to IN ST LAKE RCP Rule 2 or other applicable Lake County Rules of Civil Procedure. IN ST LAKE RCP Rule 17(D)(1).

   b. *Titles of documents.* The person electronically filing a document will be responsible for designating a title for the document at the time it is filed. The LCOD will generate the appropriate entry onto the CCS to record the filing of the document. IN ST LAKE RCP Rule 17(D)(3).

   c. *Citations and hyperlinks.* Electronically filed documents may contain hyperlink references to an external document as a convenient mechanism for accessing material cited in the document. Filers wishing to insert hyperlinks into documents shall continue to use the traditional method of citation to authority in addition to the hyperlink provided. The hyperlink is merely a convenience to the court and the material referenced is extraneous to the file and not a part of the court's record. IN ST LAKE RCP Rule 17(D)(5).

   d. *Attachments and exhibits.* All documents which form part of a single submission and which are being filed at the same time and by the same filer may be electronically filed together under one document filing, e.g., the motion, supporting affidavits, memorandum in support, designation of evidence, exhibits. IN ST LAKE RCP Rule 17(D)(6).

     i. Large documents which do not exist in an electronic format shall be scanned into .pdf format and filed electronically as separate attachments. A scanner is available in each clerk's office for use by the public and the bar in scanning and saving image files if needed. IN ST LAKE RCP Rule 17(D)(6).

    e. *Electronic signatures*

        i. *Electronic filing as signature.* The electronic filing of a document which is required to be signed shall constitute the filer's representation under IN ST TRIAL P Rule 11. Unless the electronically filed document has been scanned and shows the filer's original signature, the signature of the filer shall be indicated by As/Attorney's Name, or As/Party's Name as in the case of a pro se litigant, on the line where the signature would otherwise appear. IN ST LAKE RCP Rule 17(G)(1).

        ii. *Signatures on jointly signed or filed, verified or other documents.* In the case of a stipulation, agreed order, jointly signed motion or other document which needs to be signed by two (2) or more persons, or in the case of documents which must contain original signatures and which require verification or an unsworn declaration under rule or statute, the signatures may be indicated by either:

           • Submitting a scanned copy of the originally signed document; or,

           • Submitting the document with the use of As/Name in the signature block(s) where the original signature(s) appear(s) in the original document; provided, however, that the filer shall first obtain the physical signature of all persons necessary. IN ST LAKE RCP Rule 17(G)(2).

        iii. *Retention of original.* The filer shall retain the original executed document. IN ST LAKE RCP Rule 17(G).

  6. *Citation of local rules.* The local rules for Lake County may be known as the Lake County Rules of Civil Procedure, and abbreviated as LR. IN ST LAKE RCP Rule 1(C).

F. Filing and Service Requirements

  1. *Filing requirements.* Except as otherwise provided in IN ST TRIAL P Rule 5(E)(2), all pleadings and papers subsequent to the complaint which are required to be served upon a party shall be filed with the Court either before service or within a reasonable period of time thereafter. IN ST TRIAL P Rule 5(E)(1). All papers presented for filing shall be submitted to the Clerk and not to the court. All papers submitted for filing shall be mailed or delivered to the Clerk's office at the courthouse in which the case is pending. IN ST LAKE RCP Rule 3(A).

    a. *Filing with the court defined.* The filing of pleadings, motions, and other papers with the court as required by the Indiana Rules of Trial Procedure shall be made by one of the following methods:

        i. Delivery to the clerk of the court;

        ii. Sending by electronic transmission under the procedure adopted pursuant to IN ST ADMIN Rule 12;

        iii. Mailing to the clerk by registered, certified or express mail return receipt requested;

        iv. Depositing with any third-party commercial carrier for delivery to the clerk within three (3) calendar days, cost prepaid, properly addressed;

        v. If the court so permits, filing with the judge, in which event the judge shall note thereon the filing date and forthwith transmit them to the office of the clerk; or

        vi. Electronic filing, as approved by the Division of State Court Administration pursuant to IN ST ADMIN Rule 16. IN ST TRIAL P Rule 5(F).

        vii. Filing by registered or certified mail and by third-party commercial carrier shall be complete upon mailing or deposit. IN ST TRIAL P Rule 5(F).

    b. *Mandatory electronic filing.* Unless otherwise permitted by the Lake County Rules of Civil Procedure or otherwise authorized by the judicial officer assigned to a particular case, all documents submitted for filing (including the original complaint, or equivalent pleading, and summons) shall be filed electronically with the clerk using the LCOD, no matter when the case was originally filed. IN ST LAKE RCP Rule 17(D).

    i. *Of documents containing information excluded from public access pursuant to* IN ST ADMIN Rule 9. Documents containing information excluded from public access pursuant to IN ST ADMIN Rule 9, or documents which are ordered to be filed under seal shall be filed electronically, pursuant to IN ST LAKE RCP Rule 17(D)(9), whenever possible, along with a copy of the applicable order to seal the records, and the filer shall designate the documents as "Not for Public Access Pursuant to Administrative Rule 9(G)(1)" at the time of filing. IN ST LAKE RCP Rule 16(A)(1); IN ST LAKE RCP Rule 17(D)(9).

- *Conventional filing of documents containing information excluded from public access pursuant to* IN ST ADMIN Rule 9. Documents containing information excluded from public access pursuant to IN ST ADMIN Rule 9, or documents which are ordered to be filed under seal, which cannot be legibly scanned and filed electronically, shall be conventionally filed under seal and designated by the filer as "Not for Public Access Pursuant to Administrative Rule 9(G)(1)" at the time of filing. The unredacted version shall be filed on light green paper which is conspicuously marked "Not for Public Access"; and a redacted version, with confidential information deleted, shall be filed on white paper which shall be available for public access. The filer shall also electronically file a Notice of Manual Filing. IN ST LAKE RCP Rule 16(A)(2).

    ii. *Technical failures.* If a registered user is unable to file a document in a timely manner due to technical difficulties in the LCOD, the registered user must file a document with the court as soon as possible notifying the court of the inability to file the document. A sample document titled Declaration that Party was Unable to File in a Timely Manner Due to Technical Difficulties can be found at IN ST LAKE RCP Form 4. Delayed filings shall be rejected unless accompanied by the declaration attesting to the filer's failed attempts to file electronically at least two (2) times, separated by at least one (1) hour, after noon on each day of delay due to such technical failure. IN ST LAKE RCP Rule 17(J).

    iii. *Documents allowed to be filed conventionally.* Unless specifically authorized by the court, only the following documents may be filed conventionally and not electronically:

- Exhibits and other documents that cannot be converted to a legible electronic form, such as videotapes, x-rays, and similar materials
- Documents delivered to the clerk by pro se litigants
- Documents mailed to the clerk by pro se litigants
- Confidential documents
- Notice of manual filing
- Titles of documents
- Chronological case summary entry forms (CCS entry forms). IN ST LAKE RCP Rule 17(E).
- For more information on the documents which must be filed conventionally, refer to IN ST LAKE RCP Rule 17(E).

c. *Facsimile filing.* Only when necessary on an emergency basis (i.e., when certified mail or other means of filing will not bring the document to the Judge's attention prior to the scheduled hearing or ruling), pleadings, motions and other papers may be filed by electronic facsimile transmission, or when specifically authorized by the Court. IN ST LAKE RCP Rule 2(C).

    i. *Generally.* In counties where a majority of judges of the courts of record, by posted local rule, have authorized electronic facsimile filing and designated a telephone number to receive such transmissions, pleadings, motions, and other papers may be sent to the Clerk of Circuit Court by electronic facsimile transmission for filing in any case, provided:

- Such matter does not exceed ten (10) pages, including the cover sheet;
- Such matter does not require the payment of fees other than the electronic facsimile transcription fee set forth in IN ST ADMIN Rule 12(E);

- The sending party creates at the time of transmission a machine generated log for such transmission; and

- The original document and the transmission log are maintained by the sending party for the duration of the litigation. IN ST ADMIN Rule 12(B).

    ii. *Time of filing.* During normal, posted business hours, the time of filing shall be the time the duplicate document is produced in the office of the Clerk of the Circuit Court. Duplicate documents received at all other times shall be filed as of the next normal business day. IN ST ADMIN Rule 12(C).

- If the receiving fax machine endorses its own time and date stamp upon the transmitted documents and the receiving machine produces a delivery receipt which is electronically created and transmitted to the sending party, the time of filing shall be the date and time recorded on the transmitted document by the receiving fax machine. IN ST ADMIN Rule 12(C).

    d. *Filing for special judges.* For special judge matters where the special judge is a full-time judge or magistrate serving within Lake County, all papers submitted for filing shall be delivered or mailed to the Clerk's office at the courthouse where the special judge regularly serves. IN ST LAKE RCP Rule 3(A).

    e. *Proof of filing.* Any party filing any paper by any method other than personal delivery to the clerk shall retain proof of filing. IN ST TRIAL P Rule 5(F).

2. *Service requirements.* Unless otherwise provided by the Indiana Rules of Trial Procedure or an order of the court, each party and special judge, if any, shall be served with: (1) every order required by its terms to be served; (2) every pleading subsequent to the original complaint; (3) every written motion except one which may be heard ex parte; (4) every brief submitted to the trial court; (5) every paper relating to discovery required to be served upon a party; and (6) every written notice, appearance, demand, offer of judgment, designation of record on appeal, or similar paper. IN ST TRIAL P Rule 5(A).

    a. *Methods of service*

      i. *Personal service.* Whenever a party is represented by an attorney of record, service shall be made upon such attorney unless service upon the party himself is ordered by the court. Service upon the attorney or party shall be made by delivering or mailing a copy of the papers to the last known address or where an attorney or party has consented to service by fax or e-mail, as provided in IN ST TRIAL P Rule 3.1(A)(4), by faxing or e-mailing a copy of the documents to the fax number or e-mail address set out in the appearance form or correction as required by IN ST TRIAL P Rule 3.1(E). IN ST TRIAL P Rule 5(B). Delivery of a copy within IN ST TRIAL P Rule 5 means:

- Offering or tendering it to the attorney or party and stating the nature of the papers being served. Refusal to accept an offered or tendered document is a waiver of any objection to the sufficiency or adequacy of service of that document;

- Leaving it at his office with a clerk or other person in charge thereof, or if there is no one in charge, leaving it in a conspicuous place therein; or

- If the office is closed, by leaving it at his dwelling house or usual place of abode with some person of suitable age and discretion then residing therein; or,

- Leaving it at some other suitable place, selected by the attorney upon whom service is being made, pursuant to duly promulgated local rule. IN ST TRIAL P Rule 5(B)(1).

      ii. *Service by mail.* If service is made by mail, the papers shall be deposited in the United States mail addressed to the person on whom they are being served, with postage prepaid. Service shall be deemed complete upon mailing. Proof of service of all papers permitted to be mailed may be made by written acknowledgment of service, by affidavit of the person who mailed the papers, or by certificate of an attorney. It shall be the duty of attorneys when entering their appearance in a cause or when filing pleadings or papers therein, to have noted in the Chronological Case Summary or said pleadings or papers so filed the address and telephone number of their office. Service by delivery or by mail at such address shall be deemed sufficient and complete. IN ST TRIAL P Rule 5(B)(2).

    iii. *Service by fax or e-mail.* A party who has consented to service by fax or e-mail may be served as follows:

- Service by e-mail shall be made by attaching the document being served in .pdf format. Discovery documents must also be served in accordance with IN ST TRIAL P Rule 26(A). IN ST TRIAL P Rule 5(B)(3)(a).

- Service by fax shall be deemed complete upon generation of a transmission record indicating the successful transmission of the entire document, except as provided in IN ST TRIAL P Rule 5(B)(3)(d). IN ST TRIAL P Rule 5(B)(3)(b).

- Service by e-mail shall be deemed complete upon transmission, except as provided in IN ST TRIAL P Rule 5(B)(3)(d). IN ST TRIAL P Rule 5(B)(3)(c).

- Service by fax or e-mail that occurs on a Saturday, Sunday, legal holiday, or day the court or agency in which the matter is pending is closed or after 5:00 PM local time of the recipient shall be deemed complete the next day that is not a Saturday, Sunday, legal holiday, or day that the court or agency in which the matter is pending is not closed. IN ST TRIAL P Rule 5(B)(3)(d).

  b. *Serving numerous defendants.* In any action in which there are unusually large numbers of defendants, the court, upon motion or of its own initiative, may order:

    i. That service of the pleadings of the defendants and replies thereto need not be made as between the defendants;

- That any cross-claim, counterclaim, or matter constituting an avoidance or affirmative defense contained therein shall be deemed to be denied or avoided by all other parties; and

- That the filing of any such pleading and service thereof upon the plaintiff constitutes due notice of it to the parties. IN ST TRIAL P Rule 5(D).

    ii. A copy of every such order shall be served upon the parties in such manner and form as the court directs. IN ST TRIAL P Rule 5(D).

  c. *Service by electronic means.* The Lake County Online Docket will generate a Notice of Electronic Filing and Service when any document is filed and served. This notice will be emailed to each registered user of record in a case, and an electronic service event will be added to the work queue of each registered user of record in the case. The party filing the document should retain a paper or electronic copy of the Notice of Electronic Filing and Service. This notice represents proof of filing and service of the document on registered users of record in that case. The filer shall not be required to conventionally serve any document on any party receiving electronic service. IN ST LAKE RCP Rule 17(F)(2).

    i. The filer shall also conventionally serve those parties not designated or able to receive electronic notice or service but who are nevertheless entitled to notice of said pleading or other document in accordance with the Indiana Rules of Civil Procedure and applicable Lake County Rules of Civil Procedure. In such cases, the filer shall also file a certificate of service, as appropriate. IN ST LAKE RCP Rule 17(F).

  d. *Service on parties in default for failure to appear.* No service need be made on parties in default for failure to appear, except that pleadings asserting new or additional claims for relief against them shall be served upon them in the manner provided by service of summons in IN ST TRIAL P Rule 4. IN ST TRIAL P Rule 5(A).

G. Hearings

1. The Indiana rules do not contemplate a hearing regarding the filing and service of an amended answer.

H. Forms

1. Official Amended Answer Forms for Indiana

  a. Affidavit of debt. IN ST TRIAL P App. A-2.

2. **Amended Answer Forms for Indiana**

    a.   Amendment by stipulation. 10 INPRAC § 46.11.

    b.   Amended answer by interlineations. 10 INPRAC § 46.12.

    c.   Answer; Form and content. 9 INPRAC § 41.1.

    d.   Answer; General form. 9 INPRAC § 41.3.

    e.   Answer; Another form. 9 INPRAC § 41.4.

    f.   Answer; Another form. 9 INPRAC § 41.5.

    g.   General denial. 9 INPRAC § 41.6.

    h.   Specific denial of designated paragraph. 9 INPRAC § 41.7.

    i.   Specific admission of designated paragraph. 9 INPRAC § 41.8.

    j.   Denial of knowledge or information to form belief. 9 INPRAC § 41.9.

    k.   Denial of knowledge or information to form belief; Another form. 9 INPRAC § 41.10.

    l.   Partial denial and partial admission of designated paragraph. 9 INPRAC § 41.11.

    m.   Denial of designated paragraph for reason that document speaks for itself. 9 INPRAC § 41.12.

    n.   Adoption of admissions or denials by co-defendant's answer. 9 INPRAC § 41.13.

    o.   Denial of execution of instrument filed with pleading. 9 INPRAC § 41.14.

    p.   Answer to cross-claim. 9 INPRAC § 41.15.

    q.   Answer to third-party complaint. 9 INPRAC § 41.16.

    r.   Accord and satisfaction. 9 INPRAC § 41.21.

    s.   Answer. 5 INPRAC § 3:3.3.

    t.   Answer; Another form. 5 INPRAC § 3:3.4.

    u.   Certificate of service; Personal service. 9 INPRAC § 5.7.

    v.   Certificate of service; First class mail. 9 INPRAC § 5.8.

    w.   Signature; By party. 9 INPRAC § 4.5.

    x.   Signature; Attorney. 9 INPRAC § 4.6.

    y.   Signature; Attorney; Another form. 9 INPRAC § 4.7.

    z.   Signature; Attorney; Another form. 9 INPRAC § 4.8.

3. **Official Amended Answer Forms for Lake County**

    a.   CCS entry form. IN ST LAKE RCP App. A.

    b.   Notice of manual filing. IN ST LAKE RCP Form 2.

    c.   Certificate of service. IN ST LAKE RCP Form 3.

    d.   Declaration that party was unable to file in a timely manner. IN ST LAKE RCP Form 4.

4. **Amended Answer Forms for Lake County**

    a.   Notice of manual filing. EFORMST IN 5540.

I. Checklist

  (I) ❑ Matters to be considered by the party filing the amended answer

     (a) ❑ Required documents if amending as matter of course

        (1) ❑ Amended answer

        (2) ❑ Chronological case summary (CSS) entry forms

        (3) ❑ Certificate of service

(b) ❑ Supplemental documents

    (1) ❑ Proof of written instrument

    (2) ❑ Notice of intent to use foreign law

    (3) ❑ Facsimile cover sheet

(c) ❑ Timing

    (1) ❑ A party may amend his pleading once as a matter of course at any time before a responsive pleading is served or, if the pleading is one to which no responsive pleading is permitted, and the action has not been placed upon the trial calendar, he may so amend it at any time within thirty (30) days after it is served

    (2) ❑ Otherwise a party may amend his pleading only by leave of court or by written consent of the adverse party; and leave shall be given when justice so requires

    (3) ❑ All pleadings, motions and other papers submitted for filing which are required to be served under IN ST TRIAL P Rule 5(A) shall be filed no later than three (3) days after service

    (4) ❑ If such papers are filed before service, proof of service thereof shall be filed no later than three (3) business days thereafter

Motions, Oppositions and Replies
Motion to Strike

Document Last Updated October 2013

A. **Applicable Rules**

1. *State rules*

   a. Appearance. IN ST TRIAL P Rule 3.1.

   b. Process. IN ST TRIAL P Rule 4.

   c. Service and filing of pleadings and other papers. IN ST TRIAL P Rule 5.

   d. Time. IN ST TRIAL P Rule 6.

   e. Pleadings. IN ST TRIAL P Rule 7; IN ST TRIAL P Rule 8; IN ST TRIAL P Rule 9.2; IN ST TRIAL P Rule 10; IN ST TRIAL P Rule 11.

   f. Defenses and objections; When and how presented; By pleading or motion; Motion for judgment on the pleadings. IN ST TRIAL P Rule 12.

   g. Amended and supplemental pleadings. IN ST TRIAL P Rule 15.

   h. Joinder of person needed for just adjudication. IN ST TRIAL P Rule 19.

   i. Evidence. IN ST TRIAL P Rule 43.

   j. Judgment on the evidence (directed verdict). IN ST TRIAL P Rule 50.

   k. Findings by the court. IN ST TRIAL P Rule 52.

   l. Summary judgment. IN ST TRIAL P Rule 56.

   m. Motion to correct error. IN ST TRIAL P Rule 59.

   n. Relief from judgment or order. IN ST TRIAL P Rule 60.

   o. Hearing of motions. IN ST TRIAL P Rule 73.

   p. Court records. IN ST TRIAL P Rule 77.

   q. Access to court records. IN ST ADMIN Rule 9.

   r. Paper size. IN ST ADMIN Rule 11.

   s. Facsimile transmission. IN ST ADMIN Rule 12.

t.   Electronic filing and electronic service pilot projects. IN ST ADMIN Rule 16.

u.   Privacy and confidentiality. IN ST 5-2-9-6; IN ST 5-14-3-4; IN ST 5-14-3-5.5; IN ST 6-4.1-5-10; IN ST 6-4.1-12-12; IN ST 6-8.1-7-1; IN ST 11-13-1-8; IN ST 12-23-14-13; IN ST 16-39-3-10; IN ST 16-41-8-1; IN ST 22-4-19-6; IN ST 31-11-1-6; IN ST 31-19-5-23; IN ST 31-19-13-2; IN ST 31-19-19-1; IN ST 31-33-18-1; IN ST 31-39-1-1; IN ST 31-39-1-2; IN ST 33-23-16-16; IN ST 35-34-2-4; IN ST 35-38-1-13; IN ST 35-38-9-1; IN ST ADR Rule 2.11; IN ST ADR Rule 4.4; IN ST ADR Rule 5.6; IN ST JURY Rule 10.

2. *Local rules*

   a.   Scope and title. [IN ST LAKE RCP Rule 1, as amended by IN ORDER 13-0237, effective October 18, 2013].

   b.   Preparation of pleadings, motions and other papers. IN ST LAKE RCP Rule 2.

   c.   Filing. [IN ST LAKE RCP Rule 3, as amended by IN ORDER 13-0237, effective October 18, 2013].

   d.   Motions. IN ST LAKE RCP Rule 4.

   e.   Confidential information and sealed documents. IN ST LAKE RCP Rule 16.

   f.   Electronic filing and service. IN ST LAKE RCP Rule 17.

B. Timing

1. *Motion to strike.* Upon motion made by a party before responding to a pleading, or, if no responsive pleading is permitted by Indiana Rules of Trial Procedure, upon motion made by a party within twenty (20) days after the service of the pleading upon him or at any time upon the court's own initiative, the court may order stricken from any pleading any insufficient claim or defense or any redundant, immaterial, impertinent, or scandalous matter. IN ST TRIAL P Rule 12(F).

   a.   *Time to file a responsive pleading.* A responsive pleading required under the Indiana Rules of Trial Procedure, shall be served within twenty (20) days after service of the prior pleading. IN ST TRIAL P Rule 6(C).

   b.   *Filing.* All pleadings and papers subsequent to the complaint which are required to be served upon a party shall be filed with the Court either before service or within a reasonable period of time thereafter. IN ST TRIAL P Rule 5(E)(1). All pleadings, motions and other papers submitted for filing which are required to be served under IN ST TRIAL P Rule 5(A) shall be filed no later than three (3) days after service. IN ST LAKE RCP Rule 3(A).

      i.   If such papers are filed before service, proof of service thereof shall be filed no later than three (3) business days thereafter. Upon failure to comply with IN ST LAKE RCP Rule 3, the Court may, on motion of any party or on its own motion, impose appropriate sanctions. IN ST LAKE RCP Rule 3(A).

   c.   *Briefs.* Briefs, other than those addressed in IN ST LAKE RCP Rule 4 and IN ST LAKE RCP Rule 9, shall be filed no later than two (2) calendar days preceding the hearing or trial to which directed. IN ST LAKE RCP Rule 11.

2. *Service.* A written motion, other than one which may be heard ex parte, and notice of the hearing thereof shall be served not less than five (5) days before the time specified for the hearing, unless a different period is fixed by the Indiana Rules of Trial Procedure or by order of the court. IN ST TRIAL P Rule 6(D).

   a.   *Of supporting affidavits.* When a motion is supported by affidavit, the affidavit shall be served with the motion. IN ST TRIAL P Rule 6(D).

3. *Service of opposition.* Except as otherwise provided in IN ST TRIAL P Rule 59(D), opposing affidavits may be served not less than one (1) day before the hearing, unless the court permits them to be served at some other time. IN ST TRIAL P Rule 6(D).

   a.   An adverse party shall have thirty (30) days after service of the initial brief in which to serve and file an answer brief. IN ST LAKE RCP Rule 4(A).

4. *Reply.* The moving party shall have ten (10) days after service of the answer brief in which to serve and file a reply brief. IN ST LAKE RCP Rule 4(A).

5. *Computation of time*

   a. *Generally; Days excluded.* In computing any period of time prescribed or allowed by the Indiana Rules of Trial Procedure, by order of the court, or by any applicable statute, the day of the act, event, or default from which the designated period of time begins to run shall not be included. The last day of the period so computed is to be included unless it is:

      i. A Saturday,

      ii. A Sunday,

      iii. A legal holiday as defined by state statute, or

      iv. A day the office in which the act is to be done is closed during regular business hours. IN ST TRIAL P Rule 6(A).

   b. *Short periods.* In any event, the period runs until the end of the next day that is not a Saturday, a Sunday, a legal holiday, or a day on which the office is closed. When the period of time allowed is less than seven (7) days, intermediate Saturdays, Sundays, legal holidays, and days on which the office is closed shall be excluded from the computations. IN ST TRIAL P Rule 6(A).

   c. *Additional time after service by United States mail.* Whenever a party has the right or is required to do some act or take some proceedings within a prescribed period after the service of a notice or other paper upon him and the notice or paper is served upon him by United States mail, three (3) days shall be added to the prescribed period. IN ST TRIAL P Rule 6(E).

   d. *Electronic filing does not alter deadlines.* Filing electronically does not alter any filing deadlines or any time computation pursuant to state or federal statutes, any Rules of the Indiana Supreme Court, including without limitation the Rules of Trial Procedure, the Rules of Appellate Procedure or the Administrative Rules, or applicable Lake County Rules of Civil Procedure. The office of the Lake County Clerk is open for electronic filing under the Lake County Rules of Civil Procedure twenty-four (24) hours a day. A document is deemed filed at the date and time it is received by the LCOD server. Filing must be completed before midnight local time in order to be considered filed that day. Lake County observes Central Time and electronic filers are strongly urged to file documents during hours when the Lake County Online Docket ("LCOD") help line is available, from 9:00 a.m. to 4:00 p.m. local time, although documents can be filed electronically twenty-four (24) hours a day. IN ST LAKE RCP Rule 17(I).

   e. *Enlargement of time.* When an act is required or allowed to be done at or within a specific time by the Indiana Rules of Trial Procedure, the court may at any time for cause shown:

      i. Order the period enlarged, with or without motion or notice, if request therefor is made before the expiration of the period originally prescribed or extended by a previous order; or

      ii. Upon motion made after the expiration of the specific period, permit the act to be done where the failure to act was the result of excusable neglect; but, the court may not extend the time for taking any action for judgment on the evidence under IN ST TRIAL P Rule 50(A), amendment of findings and judgment under IN ST TRIAL P Rule 52(B), to correct errors under IN ST TRIAL P Rule 59(C), statement in opposition to motion to correct error under IN ST TRIAL P Rule 59(E), or to obtain relief from final judgment under IN ST TRIAL P Rule 60(B), except to the extent and under the conditions stated in those rules. IN ST TRIAL P Rule 6(B).

C. General Requirements

1. *Motions, generally.* Unless made during a hearing or trial, or otherwise ordered by the court, an application to the court for an order shall be made by written motion. The motion shall state the grounds therefor and the relief or order sought. IN ST TRIAL P Rule 7(B).

   a. *Motions as distinct from pleadings.* Motions and responses to motions are not pleadings, and allegations contained in a motion are not admissions of a party. 22B INPRAC 7:2; Wachstetter v. County Properties, LLC, 832 N.E.2d 574 (Ind.Ct.App. 2005); Scott County Family YMCA, Inc. v. Hobbs, 817 N.E.2d 603 (Ind.Ct.App. 2004).

   b. *Unopposed motions generally granted.* It is common for a trial court to grant procedural motions, such as motions for enlargement of time, discovery motions, or motions for continuance, unless an objection is filed. 21 INPRAC § 13.8.

    c. *Separate motions.* Each motion shall be separate, while alternative motions filed together shall each be identified on the caption. IN ST LAKE RCP Rule 4(A).

    d. *Answer and reply briefs.* Failure to file an answer brief or reply brief within the time prescribed shall be deemed a waiver of the right thereto and shall subject the motion to summary ruling. IN ST LAKE RCP Rule 4(A).

2. *Motion to strike*

    a. *Grounds generally.* Upon motion the court may order stricken from any pleading any insufficient claim or defense or any redundant, immaterial, impertinent, or scandalous matter. IN ST TRIAL P Rule 12(F).

       i. *Redundant.* Redundant matter refers to the needless repetition of immaterial factual allegations. 9 INPRAC § 42.20.

      ii. *Immaterial and impertinent.* Immaterial and impertinent matter consists of allegations that have no relevant or important relationship to plaintiff's claim. 9 INPRAC § 42.20.

     iii. *Scandalous.* Scandalous matter includes unnecessary allegations that are derogatory to the party referred to in the pleading. 9 INPRAC § 42.20.

    b. *Availability and use of motion to strike.* A motion to strike redundant, immaterial, impertinent or scandalous matter is available to plaintiff and defendant alike, and may be employed against any pleading. 9 INPRAC § 42.20. Indiana's use of a motion to strike includes all of the uses which are found in federal practice plus the expanded use of the motion under Indiana's rule. Accordingly, a nonexclusive list of the uses of this motion will recognize that it is available:

       i. To strike matter which is immaterial, impertinent or scandalous;

      ii. To provide the plaintiff with a means by which to test the sufficiency of a defense;

     iii. To strike any insufficient claim or defense;

     iv. To strike a bad faith, or inadequate response to an order or rule; or

      v. To strike a response to an order or rule which introduces new material or allegations not previously made and which are not introduced pursuant to a right to amend a pleading. 1A INPRAC R 12(12.18).

    c. *Trial court's discretion.* The trial court is given broad discretion to decide a motion to strike. 1A INPRAC R 12(12.18); City of Mishawaka v. Kvale, 810 N.E.2d 1129 (Ind.Ct.App. 2004).

    d. *Not a method to challenge timeliness.* Language in IN ST TRIAL P Rule 12(F) which permits the trial court to strike any "insufficient" claim or defense refers to the legal insufficiency of the content or substance of the claim or defense, not the untimeliness of a pleading. 1A INPRAC R 12(12.18); Dreyer & Reinbold v. AutoXchange.com., Inc., 771 N.E.2d 764, 765 (Ind.Ct.App. 2002). Rather, the proper mechanism for challenging the timeliness of a pleading is IN ST TRIAL P Rule 55, which governs default judgments. 1A INPRAC R 12(12.18).

3. *Consolidation and waiver*

    a. *Consolidation of defenses in motion.* A party who makes a motion under IN ST TRIAL P Rule 12 may join with it any other motions herein provided for and then available to him. If a party makes a motion under IN ST TRIAL P Rule 12 but omits therefrom any defense or objection then available to him which IN ST TRIAL P Rule 12 permits to be raised by motion, he shall not thereafter make a motion based on the defense or objection so omitted. He may, however, make such motions as are allowed under IN ST TRIAL P Rule 12(H)(2). IN ST TRIAL P Rule 12(G).

    b. *Waiver or preservation of certain defenses.* No defense or objection is waived by being joined with one or more other defenses or objections in a responsive pleading or motion. IN ST TRIAL P Rule 12(B).

D. Documents

1. *Required documents*

    a. *Motion and notice.* The requirement of notice is satisfied by service of the motion. IN ST TRIAL P

Rule 7(B). Refer to the General Requirements section of this document for information on the content of a motion to strike.

    b. *Brief.* All motions filed pursuant to IN ST TRIAL P Rule 12 and IN ST TRIAL P Rule 56 shall be accompanied by a separate supporting brief. IN ST LAKE RCP Rule 4(A).

    c. *Proposed order.* Unless local practice provides differently, a party should submit a proposed order with its written motion to be signed by the judge once the motion has been granted. 21 INPRAC § 13.8.

       i. Proposed orders, which are submitted for the court's convenience under IN ST LAKE RCP Rule 3 or other applicable Lake County Rules of Civil Procedure, shall be submitted as attachments to motions. IN ST LAKE RCP Rule 17(D)(8). Proposed orders shall be prepared and filed separately from the pleadings, petitions, motions or other papers to which they have reference. IN ST LAKE RCP Rule 3(B).

      ii. Orders, either routine in nature or uncontested including, for example, those setting or continuing a hearing, shall be effected by the chronological case summary entry only, which shall contain the concise substance of the order. IN ST LAKE RCP Rule 3(B).

      iii. All orders shall be accompanied with sufficient copies and stamped, pre-addressed envelopes, so that copies may be mailed to all parties. IN ST LAKE RCP Rule 3(B).

    d. *Chronological case summary (CCS) entry forms.* All filings shall be accompanied by a Chronological Case Summary (CCS) Entry Form to define or identify the documents filed. The Form used should be substantially similar to IN ST LAKE RCP App. A. IN ST LAKE RCP Rule 3(C).

    e. *Certificate of service.* An attorney or unrepresented party tendering a document to the Clerk for filing shall certify that service has been made, list the parties served, and specify the date and means of service. The certificate of service shall be placed at the end of the document and shall not be separately filed. The separate filing of a certificate of service, however, shall not be grounds for rejecting a document for filing. The Clerk may permit documents to be filed without a certificate of service but shall require prompt filing of a separate certificate of service. IN ST TRIAL P Rule 5(C).

      i. All pleadings, motions and other papers submitted for filing which are required to be served under IN ST TRIAL P Rule 5(A) shall contain proof of service pursuant to IN ST TRIAL P Rule 5(B)(2). IN ST LAKE RCP Rule 3(A).

2. *Supplemental documents*

    a. *Supporting evidence.* When a motion is based on facts not appearing of record the court may hear the matter on affidavits presented by the respective parties, but the court may direct that the matter be heard wholly or partly on oral testimony or depositions. IN ST TRIAL P Rule 43(B).

    b. *Facsimile cover sheet.* Any document sent to the Clerk of the Circuit Court by electronic facsimile transmission shall be accompanied by a cover sheet which states the title of the document, case number, number of pages, identity and voice telephone number of the sending party and instructions for filing. The cover sheet shall contain the signature of the attorney or party, pro se, authorizing the filing. IN ST ADMIN Rule 12(D).

E. Format

1. *Form of motions.* The rules applicable to captions, and the signing and form of pleadings (IN ST TRIAL P Rule 8 through IN ST TRIAL P Rule 11), apply to all motions and other papers provided under the Indiana Rules of Trial Procedure. 22B INPRAC 7:2.

2. *Form of pleadings.* For the purpose of uniformity, convenience, clarity and durability, requirements in IN ST LAKE RCP Rule 2 shall be observed in the preparation of all pleadings, motions and other papers. IN ST LAKE RCP Rule 2. Whenever materials submitted fail to meet the standards in IN ST LAKE RCP Rule 2, the Court may impose appropriate sanctions. IN ST LAKE RCP Rule 2(B).

    a. *Caption; Names of parties.* Every pleading shall contain a caption setting forth the name of the court, the title of the action, the file number, and a designation as in IN ST TRIAL P Rule 7(A). In the complaint the title of the action shall include the names of all the parties, but in other pleadings it is sufficient to state the name of the first party on each side with an appropriate indication of other parties. IN ST TRIAL P Rule 10(A).

    i. *Special judge matters.* The caption of all CCS Entry Forms, pleadings, motions, orders and other papers to be filed in a special judge case shall include in block text the words SPECIAL JUDGE and the name of the judge directly below the cause number on the caption. IN ST LAKE RCP Rule 2(D).

b. *Paragraphs; Separate statements.* All averments of a claim or defense shall be made in numbered paragraphs, the contents of each of which shall be limited as far as practicable to a statement of a single set of circumstances, and a paragraph may be referred to by number in all succeeding pleadings. Each claim founded upon a separate transaction or occurrence and each defense other than denials may be stated in a separate count or defense whenever a separation facilitates the clear presentation of the matters set forth. IN ST TRIAL P Rule 10(B).

c. *Adoption by reference; Exhibits.* Statements in a pleading may be adopted by reference in a different part of the same pleading or in another pleading or in any motion. A copy of any written instrument which is an exhibit to a pleading is a part thereof for all purposes. IN ST TRIAL P Rule 10(C).

d. *Paper; Print, quality and binding*

    i. All pleadings, motions, chronological case summary entry forms, orders, process and other papers shall be neatly and legibly printed, typewritten or mechanically reproduced, on one (1) side only, on white opaque paper. To satisfy the recordkeeping requirements of IN ST TRIAL P Rule 77, the print shall be of sufficient density and clarity for preservation and reproduction of microfilming, optical disk or other secondary sources. For this reason, the use of non-letter-quality printers is discouraged. IN ST LAKE RCP Rule 2(A).

    ii. Paper and ink shall be of such quality as to withstand the test of time. All documents shall be produced on acid-free, non-thermal paper. It is recommended that a minimum of twenty (20) pound, twenty-five percent (25%) cotton paper product be used. Documents of multiple pages shall be submitted in bound or stapled fashion, and the binding or stapling shall be at the top only. Covers or backings shall not be used. IN ST LAKE RCP Rule 2(A).

e. *Papers; Handwritten.* Handwritten papers may be filed only if approved by the Court and a typewritten or printed true rendition thereof is filed within three (3) days thereafter and approved by the Court. Upon such approval, they shall be deemed and filed as the original, while the handwritten papers shall be retained therewith for evidentiary purposes. IN ST LAKE RCP Rule 2(C).

f. *Minute sheets; Motion blanks.* Minute sheets and motion blanks shall no longer be used. IN ST LAKE RCP Rule 2(D).

3. *Size of papers for filing.* Effective January 1, 1992, all pleadings, copies, motions and documents filed with any trial court or appellate level court, typed or printed, with the exception of exhibits and existing wills, shall be prepared on eight and one-half by eleven inch (8 1/2" x 11") size paper. IN ST ADMIN Rule 11.

4. *Signature requirements*

a. *Signature of attorney.* Every pleading or motion of a party represented by an attorney shall be signed by at least one (1) attorney of record in his individual name, whose address, telephone number, and attorney number shall be stated, except that this provision shall not apply to pleadings and motions made and transcribed at the trial or a hearing before the judge and received by him in such form. IN ST TRIAL P Rule 11(A).

    i. The signature of an attorney constitutes a certificate by him that he has read the pleadings; that to the best of his knowledge, information, and belief, there is good ground to support it; and that it is not interposed for delay. IN ST TRIAL P Rule 11(A).

    ii. If a pleading or motion is not signed or is signed with intent to defeat the purpose of the rule, it may be stricken as sham and false and the action may proceed as though the pleading had not been served. IN ST TRIAL P Rule 11(A).

    iii. For a willful violation of IN ST TRIAL P Rule 11 an attorney may be subjected to appropriate

disciplinary action. Similar action may be taken if scandalous or indecent matter is inserted. IN ST TRIAL P Rule 11(A).

b. *Signature of unrepresented party.* A party who is not represented by an attorney shall sign his pleading and state his address. IN ST TRIAL P Rule 11(A).

c. *Verification not generally required.* Except when specifically required by rule, pleadings or motions need not be verified or accompanied by affidavit. The rule in equity that the averments of an answer under oath must be overcome by the testimony of two (2) witnesses or of one (1) witness sustained by corroborating circumstances is abolished. IN ST TRIAL P Rule 11(A).

d. *Verification by affirmation or representation.* When in connection with any civil or special statutory proceeding it is required that any pleading, motion, petition, supporting affidavit, or other document of any kind, be verified, or that an oath be taken, it shall be sufficient if the subscriber simply affirms the truth of the matter to be verified by an affirmation or representation. IN ST TRIAL P Rule 11(B). IN ST TRIAL P Rule 11(B) states that the affirmation or representation should be in substantially the following language: "I (we) affirm, under the penalties for perjury, that the foregoing representation(s) is (are) true. (Signed) _____."

    i. Any person who falsifies an affirmation or representation of fact shall be subject to the same penalties as are prescribed by law for the making of a false affidavit. IN ST TRIAL P Rule 11(B).

e. *Verified pleadings, motions, and affidavits as evidence.* Pleadings, motions and affidavits accompanying or in support of such pleadings or motions when required to be verified or under oath shall be accepted as a representation that the signer had personal knowledge thereof or reasonable cause to believe the existence of the facts or matters stated or alleged therein; and, if otherwise competent or acceptable as evidence, may be admitted as evidence of the facts or matters stated or alleged therein when it is so provided in the Indiana Rules of Trial Procedure, by statute or other law, or to the extent the writing or signature expressly purports to be made upon the signer's personal knowledge. When such pleadings, motions and affidavits are verified or under oath they shall not require other or greater proof on the part of the adverse party than if not verified or not under oath unless expressly provided otherwise by the Indiana Rules of Trial Procedure, statute or other law. Affidavits upon motions for summary judgment under IN ST TRIAL P Rule 56 and in denial of execution under IN ST TRIAL P Rule 9.2 shall be made upon personal knowledge. IN ST TRIAL P Rule 11(C).

f. *Electronic signature.* The filing of documents and information through the E-filing system by use of a valid username and password is presumed to have been authorized by the User to whom that username and password have been issued and documents filed through the E-filing system are presumed to have been signed by the same User. IN ST ADMIN Rule 16(E).

5. *Information excluded from public access.* Every document filed in a case shall separately identify information excluded from public access pursuant to IN ST ADMIN Rule 9(G)(1) as follows:

a. Whole documents that are excluded from public access pursuant to IN ST ADMIN Rule 9(G)(1) shall be tendered on light green paper or have a light green coversheet attached to the document, marked "Not for Public Access" or "Confidential." IN ST TRIAL P Rule 5(G)(1).

b. When only a portion of a document contains information excluded from public access pursuant to IN ST ADMIN Rule 9(G)(1), said information shall be omitted [or redacted] from the filed document, and set forth on a separate accompanying document on light green paper conspicuously marked "Not for Public Access" or "Confidential" and clearly designated [or identifying] the caption and number of the case and the document and location within the document to which the redacted material pertains. IN ST TRIAL P Rule 5(G)(2).

c. With respect to documents filed in electronic format, the trial court, by local rule, may provide for compliance with IN ST TRIAL P Rule 5 in manner that separates and protects access to information excluded from public access. IN ST TRIAL P Rule 5(G)(3).

d. IN ST TRIAL P Rule 5(G) does not apply to a record sealed by the court pursuant to IN ST 5-14-3-5.5 or otherwise, nor to records, documents, or information filed in cases to which public access is prohibited pursuant to IN ST ADMIN Rule 9(G). IN ST TRIAL P Rule 5(G)(4).

e. The following information in case records is excluded from public access and is confidential:

    i. Information that is excluded from public access pursuant to federal law;

    ii. Information that is excluded from public access as declared confidential by Indiana statute or other court rule, including without limitation:

- All adoption records created after July 8, 1941, as declared confidential by IN ST 31-19-19-1, et seq., except those specifically declared open by IN ST 31-19-13-2(2);

- All records relating to chancroid, chlamydia, gonorrhea, hepatitis, human immunodeficiency virus (HIV), Lymphogranuloma venereum, syphilis, tuberculosis, as declared confidential by IN ST 16-41-8-1, et seq.;

- All records relating to child abuse as declared confidential by IN ST 31-33-18-1, et seq.;

- All records relating to drug tests as declared confidential by IN ST 5-14-3-4(a)(9);

- Records of grand jury proceedings as declared confidential by IN ST 35-34-2-4;

- Records of juvenile proceedings as declared confidential by IN ST 31-39-1-2, except those specifically open under statute;

- All paternity records created after July 1, 1941 as declared confidential by IN ST 31-14-11-15, IN ST 31-19-5-23, IN ST 31-39-1-1 and IN ST 31-39-1-2 [Editor's note: IN ST 31-14-11-15 was repealed effective May 9, 2013];

- All pre-sentence reports as declared confidential by IN ST 35-38-1-13;

- Written petitions to permit marriages without consent and orders directing the Clerk of Court to issue a marriage license to underage persons, as declared confidential by IN ST 31-11-1-6;

- Only those arrest warrants, search warrants, indictments and informations ordered confidential by the trial judge, prior to return of duly executed service as declared confidential by IN ST 5-14-3-4(b)(1);

- All medical, mental health, or tax records unless determined by law or regulation of any governmental custodian not to be confidential, released by the subject of such records, or declared by a court of competent jurisdiction to be essential to the resolution of litigation as declared confidential by IN ST 16-39-3-10, IN ST 6-4.1-5-10, IN ST 6-4.1-12-12, and IN ST 6-8.1-7-1;

- Personal information relating to jurors or prospective jurors, other than for the use of the parties and counsel, pursuant to IN ST JURY Rule 10;

- Information relating to protection from abuse orders, no-contact orders and workplace violence restraining orders as declared confidential by IN ST 5-2-9-6, et seq.;

- Mediation proceedings pursuant to IN ST ADR Rule 2.11, Mini-Trial proceedings pursuant to IN ST ADR Rule 4.4(C), and Summary Jury Trials pursuant to IN ST ADR Rule 5.6;

- Information in probation files pursuant to the Probation Standards promulgated by the Judicial Conference of Indiana pursuant to IN ST 11-13-1-8(b);

- Information deemed confidential pursuant to the Rules for Court Administered Alcohol and Drug Programs promulgated by the Judicial Conference of Indiana pursuant to IN ST 12-23-14-13;

- Information deemed confidential pursuant to the Problem-Solving Court Rules promulgated by the Judicial Conference of Indiana pursuant to IN ST 33-23-16-16;

- All records of the Department of workforce Development as declared confidential by IN ST 22-4-19-6;

- Information regarding interception of electronic communications that is sealed or deemed confidential as set forth in IN ST 35-33.5-2-1, et seq.

   iii. Information excluded from public access by specific court order;

   iv. Complete Social Security Numbers of living persons;

   v. With the exception of names, information such as addresses, phone numbers, and dates of birth which explicitly identifies:

- Natural persons who are witnesses or victims (not including defendants) in criminal, domestic violence, stalking, sexual assault, juvenile, or civil protection order proceedings, provided that juveniles who are victims of sex crimes shall be identified by initials only;

- Places of residence of judicial officers, clerks and other employees of courts and clerks of court, unless the person or persons about whom the information pertains waives confidentiality;

   vi. Complete account numbers of specific assets, loans, bank accounts, credit cards, and personal identification numbers (PINs);

   vii. All orders of expungement entered in criminal or juvenile proceedings, orders to restrict access to criminal history information pursuant to IN ST 35-38-5-5.5 or IN ST 35-38-8-5 and records excluded from public access by such orders, and information related to infractions that is excluded from public access pursuant to IN ST 34-28-5-15 or IN ST 34-28-5-16 [Editor's note: IN ST 35-38-5-5.5, IN ST 35-38-8-5 and IN ST 34-28-5-16 were repealed effective July 1, 2013; for information on orders restricting access to criminal history, refer to IN ST 35-38-9-1, et seq.];

   viii. All personal notes and e-mail, and deliberative material, of judges, jurors, court staff and judicial agencies, and information recorded in personal data assistants (PDA's) or organizers and personal calendars. IN ST ADMIN Rule 9(G)(1).

6. *Format of electronically filed documents*

  a. *Generally.* Electronically filed documents must meet the same requirements of format as documents conventionally filed pursuant to IN ST LAKE RCP Rule 2 or other applicable Lake County Rules of Civil Procedure. IN ST LAKE RCP Rule 17(D)(1).

  b. *Titles of documents.* The person electronically filing a document will be responsible for designating a title for the document at the time it is filed. The LCOD will generate the appropriate entry onto the CCS to record the filing of the document. IN ST LAKE RCP Rule 17(D)(3).

  c. *Citations and hyperlinks.* Electronically filed documents may contain hyperlink references to an external document as a convenient mechanism for accessing material cited in the document. Filers wishing to insert hyperlinks into documents shall continue to use the traditional method of citation to authority in addition to the hyperlink provided. The hyperlink is merely a convenience to the court and the material referenced is extraneous to the file and not a part of the court's record. IN ST LAKE RCP Rule 17(D)(5).

  d. *Attachments and exhibits.* All documents which form part of a single submission and which are being filed at the same time and by the same filer may be electronically filed together under one document filing, e.g., the motion, supporting affidavits, memorandum in support, designation of evidence, exhibits. IN ST LAKE RCP Rule 17(D)(6).

   i. Large documents which do not exist in an electronic format shall be scanned into .pdf format and filed electronically as separate attachments. A scanner is available in each clerk's office for use by the public and the bar in scanning and saving image files if needed. IN ST LAKE RCP Rule 17(D)(6).

  e. *Electronic signatures*

   i. *Electronic filing as signature.* The electronic filing of a document which is required to be signed shall constitute the filer's representation under IN ST TRIAL P Rule 11. Unless the electronically filed document has been scanned and shows the filer's original signature, the signature of the filer shall be indicated by As/Attorney's Name, or As/Party's Name as in the case of a pro se litigant, on the line where the signature would otherwise appear. IN ST LAKE RCP Rule 17(G)(1).

ii. *Signatures on jointly signed or filed, verified or other documents.* In the case of a stipulation, agreed order, jointly signed motion or other document which needs to be signed by two (2) or more persons, or in the case of documents which must contain original signatures and which require verification or an unsworn declaration under rule or statute, the signatures may be indicated by either:

- Submitting a scanned copy of the originally signed document; or,
- Submitting the document with the use of As/Name in the signature block(s) where the original signature(s) appear(s) in the original document; provided, however, that the filer shall first obtain the physical signature of all persons necessary. IN ST LAKE RCP Rule 17(G)(2).

iii. *Retention of original.* The filer shall retain the original executed document. IN ST LAKE RCP Rule 17(G).

7. *Citation of local rules.* The local rules for Lake County may be known as the Lake County Rules of Civil Procedure, and abbreviated as LR. IN ST LAKE RCP Rule 1(C).

F. Filing and Service Requirements

1. *Filing requirements.* Except as otherwise provided in IN ST TRIAL P Rule 5(E)(2), all pleadings and papers subsequent to the complaint which are required to be served upon a party shall be filed with the Court either before service or within a reasonable period of time thereafter. IN ST TRIAL P Rule 5(E)(1). All papers presented for filing shall be submitted to the Clerk and not to the court. All papers submitted for filing shall be mailed or delivered to the Clerk's office at the courthouse in which the case is pending. IN ST LAKE RCP Rule 3(A).

   a. *Filing with the court defined.* The filing of pleadings, motions, and other papers with the court as required by the Indiana Rules of Trial Procedure shall be made by one of the following methods:

      i. Delivery to the clerk of the court;

      ii. Sending by electronic transmission under the procedure adopted pursuant to IN ST ADMIN Rule 12;

      iii. Mailing to the clerk by registered, certified or express mail return receipt requested;

      iv. Depositing with any third-party commercial carrier for delivery to the clerk within three (3) calendar days, cost prepaid, properly addressed;

      v. If the court so permits, filing with the judge, in which event the judge shall note thereon the filing date and forthwith transmit them to the office of the clerk; or

      vi. Electronic filing, as approved by the Division of State Court Administration pursuant to IN ST ADMIN Rule 16. IN ST TRIAL P Rule 5(F).

      vii. Filing by registered or certified mail and by third-party commercial carrier shall be complete upon mailing or deposit. IN ST TRIAL P Rule 5(F).

   b. *Mandatory electronic filing.* Unless otherwise permitted by the Lake County Rules of Civil Procedure or otherwise authorized by the judicial officer assigned to a particular case, all documents submitted for filing (including the original complaint, or equivalent pleading, and summons) shall be filed electronically with the clerk using the LCOD, no matter when the case was originally filed. IN ST LAKE RCP Rule 17(D).

      i. *Of documents containing information excluded from public access pursuant to* IN ST ADMIN Rule 9. Documents containing information excluded from public access pursuant to IN ST ADMIN Rule 9, or documents which are ordered to be filed under seal shall be filed electronically, pursuant to IN ST LAKE RCP Rule 17(D)(9), whenever possible, along with a copy of the applicable order to seal the records, and the filer shall designate the documents as "Not for Public Access Pursuant to Administrative Rule 9(G)(1)" at the time of filing. IN ST LAKE RCP Rule 16(A)(1); IN ST LAKE RCP Rule 17(D)(9).

      - *Conventional filing of documents containing information excluded from public access pursuant to* IN ST ADMIN Rule 9. Documents containing information excluded from public access pursuant to IN ST ADMIN Rule 9, or documents which are ordered to be filed under seal, which cannot be legibly scanned and filed electronically, shall be conventionally filed under seal and designated by the filer as "Not for Public Access Pursuant to Administrative Rule 9(G)(1)" at the time of filing. The unredacted version shall be filed on light green paper which is conspicuously marked "Not for Public Access"; and a redacted version, with confidential information deleted, shall be filed on white paper which shall be available for public access. The filer shall also electronically file a Notice of Manual Filing. IN ST LAKE RCP Rule 16(A)(2).

ii. *Technical failures.* If a registered user is unable to file a document in a timely manner due to technical difficulties in the LCOD, the registered user must file a document with the court as soon as possible notifying the court of the inability to file the document. A sample document titled Declaration that Party was Unable to File in a Timely Manner Due to Technical Difficulties can be found at IN ST LAKE RCP Form 4. Delayed filings shall be rejected unless accompanied by the declaration attesting to the filer's failed attempts to file electronically at least two (2) times, separated by at least one (1) hour, after noon on each day of delay due to such technical failure. IN ST LAKE RCP Rule 17(J).

iii. *Documents allowed to be filed conventionally.* Unless specifically authorized by the court, only the following documents may be filed conventionally and not electronically:

- Exhibits and other documents that cannot be converted to a legible electronic form, such as videotapes, x-rays, and similar materials
- Documents delivered to the clerk by pro se litigants
- Documents mailed to the clerk by pro se litigants
- Confidential documents
- Notice of manual filing
- Titles of documents
- Chronological case summary entry forms (CCS entry forms). IN ST LAKE RCP Rule 17(E).
- For more information on the documents which must be filed conventionally, refer to IN ST LAKE RCP Rule 17(E).

c. *Facsimile filing.* Only when necessary on an emergency basis (i.e., when certified mail or other means of filing will not bring the document to the Judge's attention prior to the scheduled hearing or ruling), pleadings, motions and other papers may be filed by electronic facsimile transmission, or when specifically authorized by the Court. IN ST LAKE RCP Rule 2(C).

i. *Generally.* In counties where a majority of judges of the courts of record, by posted local rule, have authorized electronic facsimile filing and designated a telephone number to receive such transmissions, pleadings, motions, and other papers may be sent to the Clerk of Circuit Court by electronic facsimile transmission for filing in any case, provided:

- Such matter does not exceed ten (10) pages, including the cover sheet;
- Such matter does not require the payment of fees other than the electronic facsimile transcription fee set forth in IN ST ADMIN Rule 12(E);
- The sending party creates at the time of transmission a machine generated log for such transmission; and
- The original document and the transmission log are maintained by the sending party for the duration of the litigation. IN ST ADMIN Rule 12(B).

ii. *Time of filing.* During normal, posted business hours, the time of filing shall be the time the duplicate document is produced in the office of the Clerk of the Circuit Court. Duplicate documents received at all other times shall be filed as of the next normal business day. IN ST ADMIN Rule 12(C).

- If the receiving fax machine endorses its own time and date stamp upon the transmitted

documents and the receiving machine produces a delivery receipt which is electronically created and transmitted to the sending party, the time of filing shall be the date and time recorded on the transmitted document by the receiving fax machine. IN ST ADMIN Rule 12(C).

d. *Filing for special judges.* For special judge matters where the special judge is a full-time judge or magistrate serving within Lake County, all papers submitted for filing shall be delivered or mailed to the Clerk's office at the courthouse where the special judge regularly serves. IN ST LAKE RCP Rule 3(A).

e. *Proof of filing.* Any party filing any paper by any method other than personal delivery to the clerk shall retain proof of filing. IN ST TRIAL P Rule 5(F).

2. *Service requirements.* Unless otherwise provided by the Indiana Rules of Trial Procedure or an order of the court, each party and special judge, if any, shall be served with: (1) every order required by its terms to be served; (2) every pleading subsequent to the original complaint; (3) every written motion except one which may be heard ex parte; (4) every brief submitted to the trial court; (5) every paper relating to discovery required to be served upon a party; and (6) every written notice, appearance, demand, offer of judgment, designation of record on appeal, or similar paper. IN ST TRIAL P Rule 5(A).

a. *Methods of service*

i. *Personal service.* Whenever a party is represented by an attorney of record, service shall be made upon such attorney unless service upon the party himself is ordered by the court. Service upon the attorney or party shall be made by delivering or mailing a copy of the papers to the last known address or where an attorney or party has consented to service by fax or e-mail, as provided in IN ST TRIAL P Rule 3.1(A)(4), by faxing or e-mailing a copy of the documents to the fax number or e-mail address set out in the appearance form or correction as required by IN ST TRIAL P Rule 3.1(E). IN ST TRIAL P Rule 5(B). Delivery of a copy within IN ST TRIAL P Rule 5 means:

- Offering or tendering it to the attorney or party and stating the nature of the papers being served. Refusal to accept an offered or tendered document is a waiver of any objection to the sufficiency or adequacy of service of that document;

- Leaving it at his office with a clerk or other person in charge thereof, or if there is no one in charge, leaving it in a conspicuous place therein; or

- If the office is closed, by leaving it at his dwelling house or usual place of abode with some person of suitable age and discretion then residing therein; or,

- Leaving it at some other suitable place, selected by the attorney upon whom service is being made, pursuant to duly promulgated local rule. IN ST TRIAL P Rule 5(B)(1).

ii. *Service by mail.* If service is made by mail, the papers shall be deposited in the United States mail addressed to the person on whom they are being served, with postage prepaid. Service shall be deemed complete upon mailing. Proof of service of all papers permitted to be mailed may be made by written acknowledgment of service, by affidavit of the person who mailed the papers, or by certificate of an attorney. It shall be the duty of attorneys when entering their appearance in a cause or when filing pleadings or papers therein, to have noted in the Chronological Case Summary or said pleadings or papers so filed the address and telephone number of their office. Service by delivery or by mail at such address shall be deemed sufficient and complete. IN ST TRIAL P Rule 5(B)(2).

iii. *Service by fax or e-mail.* A party who has consented to service by fax or e-mail may be served as follows:

- Service by e-mail shall be made by attaching the document being served in .pdf format. Discovery documents must also be served in accordance with IN ST TRIAL P Rule 26(A). IN ST TRIAL P Rule 5(B)(3)(a).

- Service by fax shall be deemed complete upon generation of a transmission record indicating the successful transmission of the entire document, except as provided in IN ST TRIAL P Rule 5(B)(3)(d). IN ST TRIAL P Rule 5(B)(3)(b).

- Service by e-mail shall be deemed complete upon transmission, except as provided in IN ST TRIAL P Rule 5(B)(3)(d). IN ST TRIAL P Rule 5(B)(3)(c).

- Service by fax or e-mail that occurs on a Saturday, Sunday, legal holiday, or day the court or agency in which the matter is pending is closed or after 5:00 PM local time of the recipient shall be deemed complete the next day that is not a Saturday, Sunday, legal holiday, or day that the court or agency in which the matter is pending is not closed. IN ST TRIAL P Rule 5(B)(3)(d).

b. *Serving numerous defendants.* In any action in which there are unusually large numbers of defendants, the court, upon motion or of its own initiative, may order:

    i. That service of the pleadings of the defendants and replies thereto need not be made as between the defendants;

- That any cross-claim, counterclaim, or matter constituting an avoidance or affirmative defense contained therein shall be deemed to be denied or avoided by all other parties; and

- That the filing of any such pleading and service thereof upon the plaintiff constitutes due notice of it to the parties. IN ST TRIAL P Rule 5(D).

    ii. A copy of every such order shall be served upon the parties in such manner and form as the court directs. IN ST TRIAL P Rule 5(D).

c. *Service by electronic means.* The Lake County Online Docket will generate a Notice of Electronic Filing and Service when any document is filed and served. This notice will be emailed to each registered user of record in a case, and an electronic service event will be added to the work queue of each registered user of record in the case. The party filing the document should retain a paper or electronic copy of the Notice of Electronic Filing and Service. This notice represents proof of filing and service of the document on registered users of record in that case. The filer shall not be required to conventionally serve any document on any party receiving electronic service. IN ST LAKE RCP Rule 17(F)(2).

    i. The filer shall also conventionally serve those parties not designated or able to receive electronic notice or service but who are nevertheless entitled to notice of said pleading or other document in accordance with the Indiana Rules of Civil Procedure and applicable Lake County Rules of Civil Procedure. In such cases, the filer shall also file a certificate of service, as appropriate. IN ST LAKE RCP Rule 17(F).

d. *Service on parties in default for failure to appear.* No service need be made on parties in default for failure to appear, except that pleadings asserting new or additional claims for relief against them shall be served upon them in the manner provided by service of summons in IN ST TRIAL P Rule 4. IN ST TRIAL P Rule 5(A).

G. Hearings

1. *Hearing on motion.* Unless local conditions make it impracticable, each judge shall establish regular times and places, at intervals sufficiently frequent for the prompt dispatch of business, at which motions requiring notice and hearing may be heard and disposed of; but the judge at any time or place and on such notice, if any, as he considers reasonable may make order for the advancement, conduct, and hearing of actions. To expedite its business the court may direct the submission and determination of motions without oral hearing upon brief written statements of reasons in support and opposition, or direct or permit hearings by telephone conference call with all attorneys or other similar means of communication. IN ST TRIAL P Rule 73(A).

2. *Oral argument discretionary.* The granting of a motion for oral argument, unless required by the Indiana Rules of Trial Procedure, shall be wholly discretionary with the court. IN ST LAKE RCP Rule 4(B).

H. Forms

1. Motion to Strike Forms for Indiana

    a. Motion to strike pleading not signed. 9 INPRAC § 4.18.

    b. Motion to strike pleading as sham and false. 9 INPRAC § 4.19.

    c.   Motion to strike; Entire pleading. 9 INPRAC § 42.21.

    d.   Motion to strike; Portions of pleading. 9 INPRAC § 42.22.

    e.   Motion to strike; Insufficient defense in answer. 9 INPRAC § 42.23.

    f.   Motion to strike; Pleading that was not timely filed. 9 INPRAC § 42.24.

    g.   Motion to strike; Attorney fees claim. 9 INPRAC § 42.25.

    h.   Motion to strike; General denial in answer. 9 INPRAC § 42.26.

    i.   Motion to strike; Impertinent and scandalous material. 9 INPRAC § 42.27.

    j.   Motion to strike answer; Matter repleaded contrary to prior ruling. 9 INPRAC § 42.28.

    k.   Motion to strike; Failure to plead performance of conditions precedent. 9 INPRAC § 42.29.

    l.   Motion to strike; Appearance of defendant's attorney. 9 INPRAC § 42.30.

    m.   Certificate of service; Personal service. 9 INPRAC § 5.7.

    n.   Certificate of service; First class mail. 9 INPRAC § 5.8.

2. Official Motion to Strike Forms for Lake County

    a.   CCS entry form. IN ST LAKE RCP App. A.

    b.   Notice of manual filing. IN ST LAKE RCP Form 2.

    c.   Certificate of service. IN ST LAKE RCP Form 3.

    d.   Declaration that party was unable to file in a timely manner. IN ST LAKE RCP Form 4.

3. Motion to Strike Forms for Lake County

    a.   Notice of manual filing. EFORMST IN 5540.

I. Checklist

(I) ❑ Matters to be considered by moving party

    (a) ❑ Required documents

        (1) ❑ Motion and notice

        (2) ❑ Brief

        (3) ❑ Proposed order

        (4) ❑ Chronological case summary (CSS) entry forms

        (5) ❑ Certificate of service

    (b) ❑ Supplemental documents

        (1) ❑ Supporting evidence

        (2) ❑ Facsimile cover sheet

    (c) ❑ Timing

        (1) ❑ Upon motion made by a party before responding to a pleading, or, if no responsive pleading is permitted by Indiana Rules of Trial Procedure, upon motion made by a party within twenty (20) days after the service of the pleading upon him or at any time upon the court's own initiative, the court may order stricken from any pleading any insufficient claim or defense or any redundant, immaterial, impertinent, or scandalous matter

        (2) ❑ A written motion, other than one which may be heard ex parte, and notice of the hearing thereof shall be served not less than five (5) days before the time specified for the hearing, unless a different period is fixed by the Indiana Rules of Trial Procedure or by order of the court

        (3) ❑ All pleadings and papers subsequent to the complaint which are required to be served upon a party shall be filed with the Court either before service or within a reasonable period of time thereafter

      (4) ❑ All pleadings, motions and other papers submitted for filing which are required to be served under IN ST TRIAL P Rule 5(A) shall be filed no later than three (3) days after service

      (5) ❑ If such papers are filed before service, proof of service thereof shall be filed no later than three (3) business days thereafter

(II) ❑ Matters to be considered by the responding party

  (a) ❑ Required documents

      (1) ❑ Opposition

      (2) ❑ Chronological case summary (CSS) entry forms

      (3) ❑ Certificate of service

  (b) ❑ Supplemental documents

      (1) ❑ Supporting evidence

      (2) ❑ Proposed order

      (3) ❑ Facsimile cover sheet

  (c) ❑ Timing

      (1) ❑ An adverse party shall have thirty (30) days after service of the initial brief in which to serve and file an answer brief

      (2) ❑ Except as otherwise provided in IN ST TRIAL P Rule 59(D), opposing affidavits may be served not less than one (1) day before the hearing, unless the court permits them to be served at some other time

Motions, Oppositions and Replies
Motion to Dismiss for Improper Venue

Document Last Updated October 2013

A. Applicable Rules

1. *State rules*

  a. Appearance. IN ST TRIAL P Rule 3.1.

  b. Process. IN ST TRIAL P Rule 4.

  c. Service and filing of pleadings and other papers. IN ST TRIAL P Rule 5.

  d. Time. IN ST TRIAL P Rule 6.

  e. Pleadings. IN ST TRIAL P Rule 7; IN ST TRIAL P Rule 8; IN ST TRIAL P Rule 9.2; IN ST TRIAL P Rule 10.

  f. Signing and verification of pleadings. IN ST TRIAL P Rule 11.

  g. Defenses and objections; When and how presented; By pleading or motion; Motion for judgment on the pleadings. IN ST TRIAL P Rule 12.

  h. Amended and supplemental pleadings. IN ST TRIAL P Rule 15.

  i. Joinder of person needed for just adjudication. IN ST TRIAL P Rule 19.

  j. Misjoinder and non-joinder of parties; Venue and jurisdiction over the subject-matter. IN ST TRIAL P Rule 21.

  k. Evidence. IN ST TRIAL P Rule 43.

  l. Judgment on the evidence (directed verdict). IN ST TRIAL P Rule 50.

  m. Findings by the court. IN ST TRIAL P Rule 52.

  n. Summary judgment. IN ST TRIAL P Rule 56.

o. Motion to correct error. IN ST TRIAL P Rule 59.

p. Relief from judgment or order. IN ST TRIAL P Rule 60.

q. Hearing of motions. IN ST TRIAL P Rule 73.

r. Venue requirements. IN ST TRIAL P Rule 75.

s. Court records. IN ST TRIAL P Rule 77.

t. Interlocutory appeals. IN ST RAP Rule 14.

u. Access to court records. IN ST ADMIN Rule 9.

v. Paper size. IN ST ADMIN Rule 11.

w. Facsimile transmission. IN ST ADMIN Rule 12.

x. Electronic filing and electronic service pilot projects. IN ST ADMIN Rule 16.

y. Privacy and confidentiality. IN ST 5-2-9-6; IN ST 5-14-3-4; IN ST 5-14-3-5.5; IN ST 6-4.1-5-10; IN ST 6-4.1-12-12; IN ST 6-8.1-7-1; IN ST 11-13-1-8; IN ST 12-23-14-13; IN ST 16-39-3-10; IN ST 16-41-8-1; IN ST 22-4-19-6; IN ST 31-11-1-6; IN ST 31-19-5-23; IN ST 31-19-13-2; IN ST 31-19-19-1; IN ST 31-33-18-1; IN ST 31-39-1-1; IN ST 31-39-1-2; IN ST 33-23-16-16; IN ST 35-34-2-4; IN ST 35-38-1-13; IN ST 35-38-9-1; IN ST ADR Rule 2.11; IN ST ADR Rule 4.4; IN ST ADR Rule 5.6; IN ST JURY Rule 10.

2. *Local rules*

a. Scope and title. [IN ST LAKE RCP Rule 1, as amended by IN ORDER 13-0237, effective October 18, 2013].

b. Preparation of pleadings, motions and other papers. IN ST LAKE RCP Rule 2.

c. Filing. [IN ST LAKE RCP Rule 3, as amended by IN ORDER 13-0237, effective October 18, 2013].

d. Motions. IN ST LAKE RCP Rule 4.

e. Confidential information and sealed documents. IN ST LAKE RCP Rule 16.

f. Electronic filing and service. IN ST LAKE RCP Rule 17.

B. Timing

1. *Motion to dismiss for improper venue.* A motion making the defense of incorrect venue under IN ST TRIAL P Rule 75, or any statutory provision, shall be made before pleading if a further pleading is permitted or within twenty (20) days after service of the prior pleading if none is required. IN ST TRIAL P Rule 12(B); IN ST TRIAL P Rule 75(A).

a. *Time to file a responsive pleading.* A responsive pleading required under the Indiana Rules of Trial Procedure, shall be served within twenty (20) days after service of the prior pleading. IN ST TRIAL P Rule 6(C).

b. *Waiver of certain IN ST TRIAL P Rule 12(B) defenses.* If a pleading sets forth a claim for relief to which the adverse party is not required to serve a responsive pleading, any of the defenses in IN ST TRIAL P Rule 12(B)(2), IN ST TRIAL P Rule 12(B)(3), IN ST TRIAL P Rule 12(B)(4), IN ST TRIAL P Rule 12(B)(5) or IN ST TRIAL P Rule 12(B)(8) is waived to the extent constitutionally permissible unless made in a motion within twenty (20) days after service of the prior pleading. IN ST TRIAL P Rule 12(B).

c. *Filing.* All pleadings and papers subsequent to the complaint which are required to be served upon a party shall be filed with the Court either before service or within a reasonable period of time thereafter. IN ST TRIAL P Rule 5(E)(1). All pleadings, motions and other papers submitted for filing which are required to be served under IN ST TRIAL P Rule 5(A) shall be filed no later than three (3) days after service. IN ST LAKE RCP Rule 3(A).

i. If such papers are filed before service, proof of service thereof shall be filed no later than three (3) business days thereafter. Upon failure to comply with IN ST LAKE RCP Rule 3, the Court may, on motion of any party or on its own motion, impose appropriate sanctions. IN ST LAKE RCP Rule 3(A).

    d.   *Briefs.* Briefs, other than those addressed in IN ST LAKE RCP Rule 4 and IN ST LAKE RCP Rule 9, shall be filed no later than two (2) calendar days preceding the hearing or trial to which directed. IN ST LAKE RCP Rule 11. •

2.   *Service.* A written motion, other than one which may be heard ex parte, and notice of the hearing thereof shall be served not less than five (5) days before the time specified for the hearing, unless a different period is fixed by the Indiana Rules of Trial Procedure or by order of the court. IN ST TRIAL P Rule 6(D).

    a.   *Of supporting affidavits.* When a motion is supported by affidavit, the affidavit shall be served with the motion; and,

3.   *Service of opposition.* Except as otherwise provided in IN ST TRIAL P Rule 59(D), opposing affidavits may be served not less than one (1) day before the hearing, unless the court permits them to be served at some other time. IN ST TRIAL P Rule 6(D).

    a.   An adverse party shall have thirty (30) days after service of the initial brief in which to serve and file an answer brief. IN ST LAKE RCP Rule 4(A).

4.   *Reply.* The moving party shall have ten (10) days after service of the answer brief in which to serve and file a reply brief. IN ST LAKE RCP Rule 4(A).

5.   *Computation of time*

    a.   *Generally; Days excluded.* In computing any period of time prescribed or allowed by the Indiana Rules of Trial Procedure, by order of the court, or by any applicable statute, the day of the act, event, or default from which the designated period of time begins to run shall not be included. The last day of the period so computed is to be included unless it is:

        i.   A Saturday,

        ii.   A Sunday,

        iii.   A legal holiday as defined by state statute, or

        iv.   A day the office in which the act is to be done is closed during regular business hours. IN ST TRIAL P Rule 6(A).

    b.   *Short periods.* In any event, the period runs until the end of the next day that is not a Saturday, a Sunday, a legal holiday, or a day on which the office is closed. When the period of time allowed is less than seven (7) days, intermediate Saturdays, Sundays, legal holidays, and days on which the office is closed shall be excluded from the computations. IN ST TRIAL P Rule 6(A).

    c.   *Additional time after service by United States mail.* Whenever a party has the right or is required to do some act or take some proceedings within a prescribed period after the service of a notice or other paper upon him and the notice or paper is served upon him by United States mail, three (3) days shall be added to the prescribed period. IN ST TRIAL P Rule 6(E).

    d.   *Electronic filing does not alter deadlines.* Filing electronically does not alter any filing deadlines or any time computation pursuant to state or federal statutes, any Rules of the Indiana Supreme Court, including without limitation the Rules of Trial Procedure, the Rules of Appellate Procedure or the Administrative Rules, or applicable Lake County Rules of Civil Procedure. The office of the Lake County Clerk is open for electronic filing under the Lake County Rules of Civil Procedure twenty-four (24) hours a day. A document is deemed filed at the date and time it is received by the LCOD server. Filing must be completed before midnight local time in order to be considered filed that day. Lake County observes Central Time and electronic filers are strongly urged to file documents during hours when the Lake County Online Docket ("LCOD") help line is available, from 9:00 a.m. to 4:00 p.m. local time, although documents can be filed electronically twenty-four (24) hours a day. IN ST LAKE RCP Rule 17(I).

    e.   *Enlargement of time.* When an act is required or allowed to be done at or within a specific time by the Indiana Rules of Trial Procedure, the court may at any time for cause shown:

        i.   Order the period enlarged, with or without motion or notice, if request therefor is made before the expiration of the period originally prescribed or extended by a previous order; or

        ii.   Upon motion made after the expiration of the specific period, permit the act to be done where

the failure to act was the result of excusable neglect; but, the court may not extend the time for taking any action for judgment on the evidence under IN ST TRIAL P Rule 50(A), amendment of findings and judgment under IN ST TRIAL P Rule 52(B), to correct errors under IN ST TRIAL P Rule 59(C), statement in opposition to motion to correct error under IN ST TRIAL P Rule 59(E), or to obtain relief from final judgment under IN ST TRIAL P Rule 60(B), except to the extent and under the conditions stated in those rules. IN ST TRIAL P Rule 6(B).

C. General Requirements

1. *Motions, generally.* Unless made during a hearing or trial, or otherwise ordered by the court, an application to the court for an order shall be made by written motion. The motion shall state the grounds therefor and the relief or order sought. IN ST TRIAL P Rule 7(B).

    a. *Motions as distinct from pleadings.* Motions and responses to motions are not pleadings, and allegations contained in a motion are not admissions of a party. 22B INPRAC 7:2; Wachstetter v. County Properties, LLC, 832 N.E.2d 574 (Ind.Ct.App. 2005); Scott County Family YMCA, Inc. v. Hobbs, 817 N.E.2d 603 (Ind.Ct.App. 2004).

    b. *Unopposed motions generally granted.* It is common for a trial court to grant procedural motions, such as motions for enlargement of time, discovery motions, or motions for continuance, unless an objection is filed. 21 INPRAC § 13.8.

    c. *Separate motions.* Each motion shall be separate, while alternative motions filed together shall each be identified on the caption. IN ST LAKE RCP Rule 4(A).

    d. *Answer and reply briefs.* Failure to file an answer brief or reply brief within the time prescribed shall be deemed a waiver of the right thereto and shall subject the motion to summary ruling. IN ST LAKE RCP Rule 4(A).

2. *Motion to dismiss for improper venue.* Every defense, in law or fact, to a claim for relief in any pleading, whether a claim, counterclaim, cross-claim, or third-party claim, shall be asserted in the responsive pleading thereto if one is required; except that at the option of the pleader, incorrect venue under IN ST TRIAL P Rule 75, or any statutory provision may be made by motion. IN ST TRIAL P Rule 12(B)(3). The disposition of this motion shall be consistent with IN ST TRIAL P Rule 75. IN ST TRIAL P Rule 12(B)(3). This means that, in almost every instance in which a motion is made under IN ST TRIAL P Rule 12(B)(3) or another statute, the action shall not be dismissed but transferred, consistent with IN ST TRIAL P Rule 75. 1A INPRAC R 12(12.7).

    a. *Venue.* Any case may be venued, commenced and decided in any court in any county, except, that upon the filing of a pleading or a motion to dismiss allowed by IN ST TRIAL P Rule 12(B)(3), the court, from allegations of the complaint or after hearing evidence thereon or considering affidavits or documentary evidence filed with the motion or in opposition to it, shall order the case transferred to a county or court selected by the party first properly filing such motion or pleading if the court determines that the county or court where the action was filed does not meet preferred venue requirements or is not authorized to decide the case and that the court or county selected has preferred venue and is authorized to decide the case. IN ST TRIAL P Rule 75(A).

    b. *Preferred venue.* Preferred venue lies in:

        i. The county where the greater percentage of individual defendants included in the complaint resides, or, if there is no such greater percentage, the place where any individual defendant so named resides; or

        ii. The county where the land or some part thereof is located or the chattels or some part thereof are regularly located or kept, if the complaint includes a claim for injuries thereto or relating to such land or such chattels, including without limitation claims for recovery of possession or for injuries, to establish use or control, to quiet title or determine any interest, to avoid or set aside conveyances, to foreclose liens, to partition and to assert any matters for which in rem relief is or would be proper; or

        iii. The county where the accident or collision occurred, if the complaint includes a claim for injuries relating to the operation of a motor vehicle or a vehicle on railroad, street or interurban tracks; or

    iv. The county where either the principal office of a defendant organization is located or the office or agency of a defendant organization or individual to which the claim relates or out of which the claim arose is located, if one or more such organizations or individuals are included as defendants in the complaint; or

    v. The county where either one or more individual plaintiffs reside, the principal office of a governmental organization is located, or the office of a governmental organization to which the claim relates or out of which the claim arose is located, if one or more governmental organizations are included as defendants in the complaint; or

    vi. The county or court fixed by written stipulations signed by all the parties named in the complaint or their attorneys and filed with the court before ruling on the motion to dismiss; or

    vii. The county where the individual is held in custody or is restrained, if the complaint seeks relief with respect to such individual's custody or restraint upon his freedom; or

    viii. The county where a claim in the plaintiff's complaint may be commenced under any statute recognizing or creating a special or general remedy or proceeding; or

    ix. The county where all or some of the property is located or can be found if the case seeks only judgment in rem against the property of a defendant being served by publication; or

    x. The county where either one or more individual plaintiffs reside, the principal office of any plaintiff organization or governmental organization is located, or the office of any such plaintiff organization or governmental organization to which the claim relates or out of which the claim arose is located, if the case is not subject to the requirements of IN ST TRIAL P Rule 75(A)(1) through IN ST TRIAL P Rule 75(A)(9) or if all the defendants are nonresident individuals or nonresident organizations without a principal office in the state. IN ST TRIAL P Rule 75(A).

  c. *Claim or proceeding filed in improper court*

    i. Whenever a claim or proceeding is filed which should properly have been filed in another court of this state, and proper objection is made, the court in which such action is filed shall not then dismiss the action, but shall order the action transferred to the court in which it should have been filed. IN ST TRIAL P Rule 75(B)(1).

    ii. The person filing the action shall, within twenty (20) days, pay such costs as are chargeable upon a change of venue and the papers and records shall be certified to the court of transfer in like manner as upon change of venue and the action shall be deemed commenced as of the date of filing the action in the original court. IN ST TRIAL P Rule 75(B)(2).

    iii. If the party filing the action does not pay the costs of transfer within twenty (20) days of the order transferring venue, the original court shall dismiss the action without prejudice and shall order payment of reasonable attorney fees to the party making proper objection. IN ST TRIAL P Rule 75(B)(3).

  d. *Assessment of costs, traveling expenses and attorneys' fees in resisting venue.* When the case is ordered transferred under the provisions of IN ST TRIAL P Rule 75 or IN ST TRIAL P Rule 21(B) the court shall order the parties or persons filing the complaint to pay the filing costs of refiling the case in the proper court and pay mileage expenses reasonably incurred by the parties and their attorneys in resisting the venue; and if it appears that the case was commenced in the wrong county by sham pleading, in bad faith or without cause, the court shall order payment of reasonable attorneys' fees incurred by parties successfully resisting the venue. IN ST TRIAL P Rule 75(C).

  e. *Other venue statutes superseded by IN ST TRIAL P Rule 75.* Any provision of the Indiana Rules of Trial Procedure and any special or general statute relating to venue, the place of trial or the authority of the court to hear the case shall be subject to IN ST TRIAL P Rule 75, and the provisions of any statute fixing more stringent rules thereon shall be ineffective. No statute or rule fixing the place of trial shall be deemed a requirement of jurisdiction. IN ST TRIAL P Rule 75(D).

  f. *Appeal.* An order transferring or refusing to transfer a case under IN ST TRIAL P Rule 75 shall be an interlocutory order appealable pursuant to IN ST RAP Rule 14(A)(8); provided, however, that the appeal of an interlocutory order under IN ST TRIAL P Rule 75 shall not stay proceedings in the trial court unless the trial court or the Court of Appeals so orders. IN ST TRIAL P Rule 75(E).

3. *Consolidation and waiver*

    a. *Consolidation of defenses in motion.* A party who makes a motion under IN ST TRIAL P Rule 12 may join with it any other motions herein provided for and then available to him. If a party makes a motion under IN ST TRIAL P Rule 12 but omits therefrom any defense or objection then available to him which IN ST TRIAL P Rule 12 permits to be raised by motion, he shall not thereafter make a motion based on the defense or objection so omitted. He may, however, make such motions as are allowed under IN ST TRIAL P Rule 12(H)(2). IN ST TRIAL P Rule 12(G).

    b. *Waiver or preservation of certain defenses.* No defense or objection is waived by being joined with one or more other defenses or objections in a responsive pleading or motion. IN ST TRIAL P Rule 12(B).

D. Documents

1. *Required documents*

    a. *Motion and notice.* The requirement of notice is satisfied by service of the motion. IN ST TRIAL P Rule 7(B). Refer to the General Requirements section of this document for information on the content of a motion to dismiss for improper venue.

    b. *Brief.* All motions filed pursuant to IN ST TRIAL P Rule 12 and IN ST TRIAL P Rule 56 shall be accompanied by a separate supporting brief. IN ST LAKE RCP Rule 4(A).

    c. *Proposed order.* Unless local practice provides differently, a party should submit a proposed order with its written motion to be signed by the judge once the motion has been granted. 21 INPRAC § 13.8.

        i. Proposed orders, which are submitted for the court's convenience under IN ST LAKE RCP Rule 3 or other applicable Lake County Rules of Civil Procedure, shall be submitted as attachments to motions. IN ST LAKE RCP Rule 17(D)(8). Proposed orders shall be prepared and filed separately from the pleadings, petitions, motions or other papers to which they have reference. IN ST LAKE RCP Rule 3(B).

        ii. Orders, either routine in nature or uncontested including, for example, those setting or continuing a hearing, shall be effected by the chronological case summary entry only, which shall contain the concise substance of the order. IN ST LAKE RCP Rule 3(B).

        iii. All orders shall be accompanied with sufficient copies and stamped, pre-addressed envelopes, so that copies may be mailed to all parties. IN ST LAKE RCP Rule 3(B).

    d. *Chronological case summary (CCS) entry forms.* All filings shall be accompanied by a Chronological Case Summary (CCS) Entry Form to define or identify the documents filed. The Form used should be substantially similar to IN ST LAKE RCP App. A. IN ST LAKE RCP Rule 3(C).

    e. *Certificate of service.* An attorney or unrepresented party tendering a document to the Clerk for filing shall certify that service has been made, list the parties served, and specify the date and means of service. The certificate of service shall be placed at the end of the document and shall not be separately filed. The separate filing of a certificate of service, however, shall not be grounds for rejecting a document for filing. The Clerk may permit documents to be filed without a certificate of service but shall require prompt filing of a separate certificate of service. IN ST TRIAL P Rule 5(C).

        i. All pleadings, motions and other papers submitted for filing which are required to be served under IN ST TRIAL P Rule 5(A) shall contain proof of service pursuant to IN ST TRIAL P Rule 5(B)(2). IN ST LAKE RCP Rule 3(A).

2. *Supplemental documents*

    a. *Supporting evidence.* When a motion is based on facts not appearing of record the court may hear the matter on affidavits presented by the respective parties, but the court may direct that the matter be heard wholly or partly on oral testimony or depositions. IN ST TRIAL P Rule 43(B).

    b. *Facsimile cover sheet.* Any document sent to the Clerk of the Circuit Court by electronic facsimile transmission shall be accompanied by a cover sheet which states the title of the document, case number, number of pages, identity and voice telephone number of the sending party and instructions

for filing. The cover sheet shall contain the signature of the attorney or party, pro se, authorizing the filing. IN ST ADMIN Rule 12(D).

E. Format

1. *Form of motions.* The rules applicable to captions, and the signing and form of pleadings (IN ST TRIAL P Rule 8 through IN ST TRIAL P Rule 11), apply to all motions and other papers provided under the Indiana Rules of Trial Procedure. 22B INPRAC 7:2.

2. *Form of pleadings.* For the purpose of uniformity, convenience, clarity and durability, requirements in IN ST LAKE RCP Rule 2 shall be observed in the preparation of all pleadings, motions and other papers. IN ST LAKE RCP Rule 2. Whenever materials submitted fail to meet the standards in IN ST LAKE RCP Rule 2, the Court may impose appropriate sanctions. IN ST LAKE RCP Rule 2(B).

    a. *Caption; Names of parties.* Every pleading shall contain a caption setting forth the name of the court, the title of the action, the file number, and a designation as in IN ST TRIAL P Rule 7(A). In the complaint the title of the action shall include the names of all the parties, but in other pleadings it is sufficient to state the name of the first party on each side with an appropriate indication of other parties. IN ST TRIAL P Rule 10(A).

        i. *Special judge matters.* The caption of all CCS Entry Forms, pleadings, motions, orders and other papers to be filed in a special judge case shall include in block text the words SPECIAL JUDGE and the name of the judge directly below the cause number on the caption. IN ST LAKE RCP Rule 2(D).

    b. *Paragraphs; Separate statements.* All averments of a claim or defense shall be made in numbered paragraphs, the contents of each of which shall be limited as far as practicable to a statement of a single set of circumstances, and a paragraph may be referred to by number in all succeeding pleadings. Each claim founded upon a separate transaction or occurrence and each defense other than denials may be stated in a separate count or defense whenever a separation facilitates the clear presentation of the matters set forth. IN ST TRIAL P Rule 10(B).

    c. *Adoption by reference; Exhibits.* Statements in a pleading may be adopted by reference in a different part of the same pleading or in another pleading or in any motion. A copy of any written instrument which is an exhibit to a pleading is a part thereof for all purposes. IN ST TRIAL P Rule 10(C).

    d. *Paper; Print, quality and binding*

        i. All pleadings, motions, chronological case summary entry forms, orders, process and other papers shall be neatly and legibly printed, typewritten or mechanically reproduced, on one (1) side only, on white opaque paper. To satisfy the recordkeeping requirements of IN ST TRIAL P Rule 77, the print shall be of sufficient density and clarity for preservation and reproduction of microfilming, optical disk or other secondary sources. For this reason, the use of non-letter-quality printers is discouraged. IN ST LAKE RCP Rule 2(A).

        ii. Paper and ink shall be of such quality as to withstand the test of time. All documents shall be produced on acid-free, non-thermal paper. It is recommended that a minimum of twenty (20) pound, twenty-five percent (25%) cotton paper product be used. Documents of multiple pages shall be submitted in bound or stapled fashion, and the binding or stapling shall be at the top only. Covers or backings shall not be used. IN ST LAKE RCP Rule 2(A).

    e. *Papers; Handwritten.* Handwritten papers may be filed only if approved by the Court and a typewritten or printed true rendition thereof is filed within three (3) days thereafter and approved by the Court. Upon such approval, they shall be deemed and filed as the original, while the handwritten papers shall be retained therewith for evidentiary purposes. IN ST LAKE RCP Rule 2(C).

    f. *Minute sheets; Motion blanks.* Minute sheets and motion blanks shall no longer be used. IN ST LAKE RCP Rule 2(D).

3. *Size of papers for filing.* Effective January 1, 1992, all pleadings, copies, motions and documents filed with any trial court or appellate level court, typed or printed, with the exception of exhibits and existing wills, shall be prepared on eight and one-half by eleven inch (8 1/2" x 11") size paper. IN ST ADMIN Rule 11.

4. *Signature requirements*

a. *Signature of attorney.* Every pleading or motion of a party represented by an attorney shall be signed by at least one (1) attorney of record in his individual name, whose address, telephone number, and attorney number shall be stated, except that this provision shall not apply to pleadings and motions made and transcribed at the trial or a hearing before the judge and received by him in such form. IN ST TRIAL P Rule 11(A).

    i. The signature of an attorney constitutes a certificate by him that he has read the pleadings; that to the best of his knowledge, information, and belief, there is good ground to support it; and that it is not interposed for delay. IN ST TRIAL P Rule 11(A).

    ii. If a pleading or motion is not signed or is signed with intent to defeat the purpose of the rule, it may be stricken as sham and false and the action may proceed as though the pleading had not been served. IN ST TRIAL P Rule 11(A).

    iii. For a willful violation of IN ST TRIAL P Rule 11 an attorney may be subjected to appropriate disciplinary action. Similar action may be taken if scandalous or indecent matter is inserted. IN ST TRIAL P Rule 11(A).

b. *Signature of unrepresented party.* A party who is not represented by an attorney shall sign his pleading and state his address. IN ST TRIAL P Rule 11(A).

c. *Verification not generally required.* Except when specifically required by rule, pleadings or motions need not be verified or accompanied by affidavit. The rule in equity that the averments of an answer under oath must be overcome by the testimony of two (2) witnesses or of one (1) witness sustained by corroborating circumstances is abolished. IN ST TRIAL P Rule 11(A).

d. *Verification by affirmation or representation.* When in connection with any civil or special statutory proceeding it is required that any pleading, motion, petition, supporting affidavit, or other document of any kind, be verified, or that an oath be taken, it shall be sufficient if the subscriber simply affirms the truth of the matter to be verified by an affirmation or representation. IN ST TRIAL P Rule 11(B). IN ST TRIAL P Rule 11(B) states that the affirmation or representation should be in substantially the following language: "I (we) affirm, under the penalties for perjury, that the foregoing representation(s) is (are) true. (Signed) _____."

    i. Any person who falsifies an affirmation or representation of fact shall be subject to the same penalties as are prescribed by law for the making of a false affidavit. IN ST TRIAL P Rule 11(B).

e. *Verified pleadings, motions, and affidavits as evidence.* Pleadings, motions and affidavits accompanying or in support of such pleadings or motions when required to be verified or under oath shall be accepted as a representation that the signer had personal knowledge thereof or reasonable cause to believe the existence of the facts or matters stated or alleged therein; and, if otherwise competent or acceptable as evidence, may be admitted as evidence of the facts or matters stated or alleged therein when it is so provided in the Indiana Rules of Trial Procedure, by statute or other law, or to the extent the writing or signature expressly purports to be made upon the signer's personal knowledge. When such pleadings, motions and affidavits are verified or under oath they shall not require other or greater proof on the part of the adverse party than if not verified or not under oath unless expressly provided otherwise by the Indiana Rules of Trial Procedure, statute or other law. Affidavits upon motions for summary judgment under IN ST TRIAL P Rule 56 and in denial of execution under IN ST TRIAL P Rule 9.2 shall be made upon personal knowledge. IN ST TRIAL P Rule 11(C).

f. *Electronic signature.* The filing of documents and information through the E-filing system by use of a valid username and password is presumed to have been authorized by the User to whom that username and password have been issued and documents filed through the E-filing system are presumed to have been signed by the same User. IN ST ADMIN Rule 16(E).

5. *Information excluded from public access.* Every document filed in a case shall separately identify information excluded from public access pursuant to IN ST ADMIN Rule 9(G)(1) as follows:

a. Whole documents that are excluded from public access pursuant to IN ST ADMIN Rule 9(G)(1) shall be tendered on light green paper or have a light green coversheet attached to the document, marked "Not for Public Access" or "Confidential." IN ST TRIAL P Rule 5(G)(1).

b. When only a portion of a document contains information excluded from public access pursuant to IN ST ADMIN Rule 9(G)(1), said information shall be omitted [or redacted] from the filed document, and set forth on a separate accompanying document on light green paper conspicuously marked "Not for Public Access" or "Confidential" and clearly designated [or identifying] the caption and number of the case and the document and location within the document to which the redacted material pertains. IN ST TRIAL P Rule 5(G)(2).

c. With respect to documents filed in electronic format, the trial court, by local rule, may provide for compliance with IN ST TRIAL P Rule 5 in manner that separates and protects access to information excluded from public access. IN ST TRIAL P Rule 5(G)(3).

d. IN ST TRIAL P Rule 5(G) does not apply to a record sealed by the court pursuant to IN ST 5-14-3-5.5 or otherwise, nor to records, documents, or information filed in cases to which public access is prohibited pursuant to IN ST ADMIN Rule 9(G). IN ST TRIAL P Rule 5(G)(4).

e. The following information in case records is excluded from public access and is confidential:

  i. Information that is excluded from public access pursuant to federal law;

  ii. Information that is excluded from public access as declared confidential by Indiana statute or other court rule, including without limitation:

  - All adoption records created after July 8, 1941, as declared confidential by IN ST 31-19-19-1, et seq., except those specifically declared open by IN ST 31-19-13-2(2);

  - All records relating to chancroid, chlamydia, gonorrhea, hepatitis, human immunodeficiency virus (HIV), Lymphogranuloma venereum, syphilis, tuberculosis, as declared confidential by IN ST 16-41-8-1, et seq.;

  - All records relating to child abuse as declared confidential by IN ST 31-33-18-1, et seq.;

  - All records relating to drug tests as declared confidential by IN ST 5-14-3-4(a)(9);

  - Records of grand jury proceedings as declared confidential by IN ST 35-34-2-4;

  - Records of juvenile proceedings as declared confidential by IN ST 31-39-1-2, except those specifically open under statute;

  - All paternity records created after July 1, 1941 as declared confidential by IN ST 31-14-11-15, IN ST 31-19-5-23, IN ST 31-39-1-1 and IN ST 31-39-1-2 [Editor's note: IN ST 31-14-11-15 was repealed effective May 9, 2013];

  - All pre-sentence reports as declared confidential by IN ST 35-38-1-13;

  - Written petitions to permit marriages without consent and orders directing the Clerk of Court to issue a marriage license to underage persons, as declared confidential by IN ST 31-11-1-6;

  - Only those arrest warrants, search warrants, indictments and informations ordered confidential by the trial judge, prior to return of duly executed service as declared confidential by IN ST 5-14-3-4(b)(1);

  - All medical, mental health, or tax records unless determined by law or regulation of any governmental custodian not to be confidential, released by the subject of such records, or declared by a court of competent jurisdiction to be essential to the resolution of litigation as declared confidential by IN ST 16-39-3-10, IN ST 6-4.1-5-10, IN ST 6-4.1-12-12, and IN ST 6-8.1-7-1;

  - Personal information relating to jurors or prospective jurors, other than for the use of the parties and counsel, pursuant to IN ST JURY Rule 10;

  - Information relating to protection from abuse orders, no-contact orders and workplace violence restraining orders as declared confidential by IN ST 5-2-9-6, et seq.;

  - Mediation proceedings pursuant to IN ST ADR Rule 2.11, Mini-Trial proceedings pursuant to IN ST ADR Rule 4.4(C), and Summary Jury Trials pursuant to IN ST ADR Rule 5.6;

- Information in probation files pursuant to the Probation Standards promulgated by the Judicial Conference of Indiana pursuant to IN ST 11-13-1-8(b);

- Information deemed confidential pursuant to the Rules for Court Administered Alcohol and Drug Programs promulgated by the Judicial Conference of Indiana pursuant to IN ST 12-23-14-13;

- Information deemed confidential pursuant to the Problem-Solving Court Rules promulgated by the Judicial Conference of Indiana pursuant to IN ST 33-23-16-16;

- All records of the Department of workforce Development as declared confidential by IN ST 22-4-19-6;

- Information regarding interception of electronic communications that is sealed or deemed confidential as set forth in IN ST 35-33.5-2-1, et seq.

 iii. Information excluded from public access by specific court order;

 iv. Complete Social Security Numbers of living persons;

 v. With the exception of names, information such as addresses, phone numbers, and dates of birth which explicitly identifies:

- Natural persons who are witnesses or victims (not including defendants) in criminal, domestic violence, stalking, sexual assault, juvenile, or civil protection order proceedings, provided that juveniles who are victims of sex crimes shall be identified by initials only;

- Places of residence of judicial officers, clerks and other employees of courts and clerks of court, unless the person or persons about whom the information pertains waives confidentiality;

 vi. Complete account numbers of specific assets, loans, bank accounts, credit cards, and personal identification numbers (PINs);

 vii. All orders of expungement entered in criminal or juvenile proceedings, orders to restrict access to criminal history information pursuant to IN ST 35-38-5-5.5 or IN ST 35-38-8-5 and records excluded from public access by such orders, and information related to infractions that is excluded from public access pursuant to IN ST 34-28-5-15 or IN ST 34-28-5-16 [Editor's note: IN ST 35-38-5-5.5, IN ST 35-38-8-5 and IN ST 34-28-5-16 were repealed effective July 1, 2013; for information on orders restricting access to criminal history, refer to IN ST 35-38-9-1, et seq.];

 viii. All personal notes and e-mail, and deliberative material, of judges, jurors, court staff and judicial agencies, and information recorded in personal data assistants (PDA's) or organizers and personal calendars. IN ST ADMIN Rule 9(G)(1).

6. *Format of electronically filed documents*

 a. *Generally.* Electronically filed documents must meet the same requirements of format as documents conventionally filed pursuant to IN ST LAKE RCP Rule 2 or other applicable Lake County Rules of Civil Procedure. IN ST LAKE RCP Rule 17(D)(1).

 b. *Titles of documents.* The person electronically filing a document will be responsible for designating a title for the document at the time it is filed. The LCOD will generate the appropriate entry onto the CCS to record the filing of the document. IN ST LAKE RCP Rule 17(D)(3).

 c. *Citations and hyperlinks.* Electronically filed documents may contain hyperlink references to an external document as a convenient mechanism for accessing material cited in the document. Filers wishing to insert hyperlinks into documents shall continue to use the traditional method of citation to authority in addition to the hyperlink provided. The hyperlink is merely a convenience to the court and the material referenced is extraneous to the file and not a part of the court's record. IN ST LAKE RCP Rule 17(D)(5).

 d. *Attachments and exhibits.* All documents which form part of a single submission and which are being filed at the same time and by the same filer may be electronically filed together under one document filing, e.g., the motion, supporting affidavits, memorandum in support, designation of evidence, exhibits. IN ST LAKE RCP Rule 17(D)(6).

    i. Large documents which do not exist in an electronic format shall be scanned into .pdf format and filed electronically as separate attachments. A scanner is available in each clerk's office for use by the public and the bar in scanning and saving image files if needed. IN ST LAKE RCP Rule 17(D)(6).

  e. *Electronic signatures*

    i. *Electronic filing as signature.* The electronic filing of a document which is required to be signed shall constitute the filer's representation under IN ST TRIAL P Rule 11. Unless the electronically filed document has been scanned and shows the filer's original signature, the signature of the filer shall be indicated by As/Attorney's Name, or As/Party's Name as in the case of a pro se litigant, on the line where the signature would otherwise appear. IN ST LAKE RCP Rule 17(G)(1).

    ii. *Signatures on jointly signed or filed, verified or other documents.* In the case of a stipulation, agreed order, jointly signed motion or other document which needs to be signed by two (2) or more persons, or in the case of documents which must contain original signatures and which require verification or an unsworn declaration under rule or statute, the signatures may be indicated by either:

      ● Submitting a scanned copy of the originally signed document; or,

      ● Submitting the document with the use of As/Name in the signature block(s) where the original signature(s) appear(s) in the original document; provided, however, that the filer shall first obtain the physical signature of all persons necessary. IN ST LAKE RCP Rule 17(G)(2).

    iii. *Retention of original.* The filer shall retain the original executed document. IN ST LAKE RCP Rule 17(G).

  7. *Citation of local rules.* The local rules for Lake County may be known as the Lake County Rules of Civil Procedure, and abbreviated as LR. IN ST LAKE RCP Rule 1(C).

F. Filing and Service Requirements

  1. *Filing requirements.* Except as otherwise provided in IN ST TRIAL P Rule 5(E)(2), all pleadings and papers subsequent to the complaint which are required to be served upon a party shall be filed with the Court either before service or within a reasonable period of time thereafter. IN ST TRIAL P Rule 5(E)(1). All papers presented for filing shall be submitted to the Clerk and not to the court. All papers submitted for filing shall be mailed or delivered to the Clerk's office at the courthouse in which the case is pending. IN ST LAKE RCP Rule 3(A).

  a. *Filing with the court defined.* The filing of pleadings, motions, and other papers with the court as required by the Indiana Rules of Trial Procedure shall be made by one of the following methods:

    i. Delivery to the clerk of the court;

    ii. Sending by electronic transmission under the procedure adopted pursuant to IN ST ADMIN Rule 12;

    iii. Mailing to the clerk by registered, certified or express mail return receipt requested;

    iv. Depositing with any third-party commercial carrier for delivery to the clerk within three (3) calendar days, cost prepaid, properly addressed;

    v. If the court so permits, filing with the judge, in which event the judge shall note thereon the filing date and forthwith transmit them to the office of the clerk; or

    vi. Electronic filing, as approved by the Division of State Court Administration pursuant to IN ST ADMIN Rule 16. IN ST TRIAL P Rule 5(F).

    vii. Filing by registered or certified mail and by third-party commercial carrier shall be complete upon mailing or deposit. IN ST TRIAL P Rule 5(F).

  b. *Mandatory electronic filing.* Unless otherwise permitted by the Lake County Rules of Civil

Procedure or otherwise authorized by the judicial officer assigned to a particular case, all documents submitted for filing (including the original complaint, or equivalent pleading, and summons) shall be filed electronically with the clerk using the LCOD, no matter when the case was originally filed. IN ST LAKE RCP Rule 17(D).

i. *Of documents containing information excluded from public access pursuant to* IN ST ADMIN Rule 9. Documents containing information excluded from public access pursuant to IN ST ADMIN Rule 9, or documents which are ordered to be filed under seal shall be filed electronically, pursuant to IN ST LAKE RCP Rule 17(D)(9), whenever possible, along with a copy of the applicable order to seal the records, and the filer shall designate the documents as "Not for Public Access Pursuant to Administrative Rule 9(G)(1)" at the time of filing. IN ST LAKE RCP Rule 16(A)(1); IN ST LAKE RCP Rule 17(D)(9).

   - *Conventional filing of documents containing information excluded from public access pursuant to* IN ST ADMIN Rule 9. Documents containing information excluded from public access pursuant to IN ST ADMIN Rule 9, or documents which are ordered to be filed under seal, which cannot be legibly scanned and filed electronically, shall be conventionally filed under seal and designated by the filer as "Not for Public Access Pursuant to Administrative Rule 9(G)(1)" at the time of filing. The unredacted version shall be filed on light green paper which is conspicuously marked "Not for Public Access"; and a redacted version, with confidential information deleted, shall be filed on white paper which shall be available for public access. The filer shall also electronically file a Notice of Manual Filing. IN ST LAKE RCP Rule 16(A)(2).

ii. *Technical failures.* If a registered user is unable to file a document in a timely manner due to technical difficulties in the LCOD, the registered user must file a document with the court as soon as possible notifying the court of the inability to file the document. A sample document titled Declaration that Party was Unable to File in a Timely Manner Due to Technical Difficulties can be found at IN ST LAKE RCP Form 4. Delayed filings shall be rejected unless accompanied by the declaration attesting to the filer's failed attempts to file electronically at least two (2) times, separated by at least one (1) hour, after noon on each day of delay due to such technical failure. IN ST LAKE RCP Rule 17(J).

iii. *Documents allowed to be filed conventionally.* Unless specifically authorized by the court, only the following documents may be filed conventionally and not electronically:

   - Exhibits and other documents that cannot be converted to a legible electronic form, such as videotapes, x-rays, and similar materials
   - Documents delivered to the clerk by pro se litigants
   - Documents mailed to the clerk by pro se litigants
   - Confidential documents
   - Notice of manual filing
   - Titles of documents
   - Chronological case summary entry forms (CCS entry forms). IN ST LAKE RCP Rule 17(E).
   - For more information on the documents which must be filed conventionally, refer to IN ST LAKE RCP Rule 17(E).

c. *Facsimile filing.* Only when necessary on an emergency basis (i.e., when certified mail or other means of filing will not bring the document to the Judge's attention prior to the scheduled hearing or ruling), pleadings, motions and other papers may be filed by electronic facsimile transmission, or when specifically authorized by the Court. IN ST LAKE RCP Rule 2(C).

   i. *Generally.* In counties where a majority of judges of the courts of record, by posted local rule, have authorized electronic facsimile filing and designated a telephone number to receive such transmissions, pleadings, motions, and other papers may be sent to the Clerk of Circuit Court by electronic facsimile transmission for filing in any case, provided:

   - Such matter does not exceed ten (10) pages, including the cover sheet;

- Such matter does not require the payment of fees other than the electronic facsimile transcription fee set forth in IN ST ADMIN Rule 12(E);

- The sending party creates at the time of transmission a machine generated log for such transmission; and

- The original document and the transmission log are maintained by the sending party for the duration of the litigation. IN ST ADMIN Rule 12(B).

    ii. *Time of filing.* During normal, posted business hours, the time of filing shall be the time the duplicate document is produced in the office of the Clerk of the Circuit Court. Duplicate documents received at all other times shall be filed as of the next normal business day. IN ST ADMIN Rule 12(C).

- If the receiving fax machine endorses its own time and date stamp upon the transmitted documents and the receiving machine produces a delivery receipt which is electronically created and transmitted to the sending party, the time of filing shall be the date and time recorded on the transmitted document by the receiving fax machine. IN ST ADMIN Rule 12(C).

  d. *Filing for special judges.* For special judge matters where the special judge is a full-time judge or magistrate serving within Lake County, all papers submitted for filing shall be delivered or mailed to the Clerk's office at the courthouse where the special judge regularly serves. IN ST LAKE RCP Rule 3(A).

  e. *Proof of filing.* Any party filing any paper by any method other than personal delivery to the clerk shall retain proof of filing. IN ST TRIAL P Rule 5(F).

2. *Service requirements.* Unless otherwise provided by the Indiana Rules of Trial Procedure or an order of the court, each party and special judge, if any, shall be served with: (1) every order required by its terms to be served; (2) every pleading subsequent to the original complaint; (3) every written motion except one which may be heard ex parte; (4) every brief submitted to the trial court; (5) every paper relating to discovery required to be served upon a party; and (6) every written notice, appearance, demand, offer of judgment, designation of record on appeal, or similar paper. IN ST TRIAL P Rule 5(A).

  a. *Methods of service*

    i. *Personal service.* Whenever a party is represented by an attorney of record, service shall be made upon such attorney unless service upon the party himself is ordered by the court. Service upon the attorney or party shall be made by delivering or mailing a copy of the papers to the last known address or where an attorney or party has consented to service by fax or e-mail, as provided in IN ST TRIAL P Rule 3.1(A)(4), by faxing or e-mailing a copy of the documents to the fax number or e-mail address set out in the appearance form or correction as required by IN ST TRIAL P Rule 3.1(E). IN ST TRIAL P Rule 5(B). Delivery of a copy within IN ST TRIAL P Rule 5 means:

- Offering or tendering it to the attorney or party and stating the nature of the papers being served. Refusal to accept an offered or tendered document is a waiver of any objection to the sufficiency or adequacy of service of that document;

- Leaving it at his office with a clerk or other person in charge thereof, or if there is no one in charge, leaving it in a conspicuous place therein; or

- If the office is closed, by leaving it at his dwelling house or usual place of abode with some person of suitable age and discretion then residing therein; or,

- Leaving it at some other suitable place, selected by the attorney upon whom service is being made, pursuant to duly promulgated local rule. IN ST TRIAL P Rule 5(B)(1).

    ii. *Service by mail.* If service is made by mail, the papers shall be deposited in the United States mail addressed to the person on whom they are being served, with postage prepaid. Service shall be deemed complete upon mailing. Proof of service of all papers permitted to be mailed may be made by written acknowledgment of service, by affidavit of the person who mailed the papers, or by certificate of an attorney. It shall be the duty of attorneys when entering their appearance in a cause or when filing pleadings or papers therein, to have noted in the Chronological Case Summary or said pleadings or papers so filed the address and telephone number of their office. Service by delivery or by mail at such address shall be deemed sufficient and complete. IN ST TRIAL P Rule 5(B)(2).

   iii. *Service by fax or e-mail.* A party who has consented to service by fax or e-mail may be served as follows:

- Service by e-mail shall be made by attaching the document being served in .pdf format. Discovery documents must also be served in accordance with IN ST TRIAL P Rule 26(A). IN ST TRIAL P Rule 5(B)(3)(a).

- Service by fax shall be deemed complete upon generation of a transmission record indicating the successful transmission of the entire document, except as provided in IN ST TRIAL P Rule 5(B)(3)(d). IN ST TRIAL P Rule 5(B)(3)(b).

- Service by e-mail shall be deemed complete upon transmission, except as provided in IN ST TRIAL P Rule 5(B)(3)(d). IN ST TRIAL P Rule 5(B)(3)(c).

- Service by fax or e-mail that occurs on a Saturday, Sunday, legal holiday, or day the court or agency in which the matter is pending is closed or after 5:00 PM local time of the recipient shall be deemed complete the next day that is not a Saturday, Sunday, legal holiday, or day that the court or agency in which the matter is pending is not closed. IN ST TRIAL P Rule 5(B)(3)(d).

b. *Serving numerous defendants.* In any action in which there are unusually large numbers of defendants, the court, upon motion or of its own initiative, may order:

   i. That service of the pleadings of the defendants and replies thereto need not be made as between the defendants;

- That any cross-claim, counterclaim, or matter constituting an avoidance or affirmative defense contained therein shall be deemed to be denied or avoided by all other parties; and

- That the filing of any such pleading and service thereof upon the plaintiff constitutes due notice of it to the parties. IN ST TRIAL P Rule 5(D).

   ii. A copy of every such order shall be served upon the parties in such manner and form as the court directs. IN ST TRIAL P Rule 5(D).

c. *Service by electronic means.* The Lake County Online Docket will generate a Notice of Electronic Filing and Service when any document is filed and served. This notice will be emailed to each registered user of record in a case, and an electronic service event will be added to the work queue of each registered user of record in the case. The party filing the document should retain a paper or electronic copy of the Notice of Electronic Filing and Service. This notice represents proof of filing and service of the document on registered users of record in that case. The filer shall not be required to conventionally serve any document on any party receiving electronic service. IN ST LAKE RCP Rule 17(F)(2).

   i. The filer shall also conventionally serve those parties not designated or able to receive electronic notice or service but who are nevertheless entitled to notice of said pleading or other document in accordance with the Indiana Rules of Civil Procedure and applicable Lake County Rules of Civil Procedure. In such cases, the filer shall also file a certificate of service, as appropriate. IN ST LAKE RCP Rule 17(F).

d. *Service on parties in default for failure to appear.* No service need be made on parties in default for failure to appear, except that pleadings asserting new or additional claims for relief against them shall be served upon them in the manner provided by service of summons in IN ST TRIAL P Rule 4. IN ST TRIAL P Rule 5(A).

G. Hearings

1. *Hearing on motion.* Unless local conditions make it impracticable, each judge shall establish regular times and places, at intervals sufficiently frequent for the prompt dispatch of business, at which motions requiring notice and hearing may be heard and disposed of; but the judge at any time or place and on such

notice, if any, as he considers reasonable may make order for the advancement, conduct, and hearing of actions. To expedite its business the court may direct the submission and determination of motions without oral hearing upon brief written statements of reasons in support and opposition, or direct or permit hearings by telephone conference call with all attorneys or other similar means of communication. IN ST TRIAL P Rule 73(A).

2. *Oral argument discretionary.* The granting of a motion for oral argument, unless required by the Indiana Rules of Trial Procedure, shall be wholly discretionary with the court. IN ST LAKE RCP Rule 4(B).

H. Forms

1. Indiana Motion to Dismiss for Improper Venue Forms

a. Incorrect venue. 9 INPRAC § 42.5.

b. Motion to dismiss; Improper venue under contract. 9 INPRAC § 42.18.1.

c. Motion to transfer from improper venue. 11 INPRAC § 111.2.

d. Motion to transfer from improper venue. 5 INPRAC § 3:11.1.

e. Motion for change of venue from county; For cause. 5 INPRAC § 3:11.2.

f. Certificate of service; Personal service. 9 INPRAC § 5.7.

g. Certificate of service; First class mail. 9 INPRAC § 5.8.

2. Official Motion to Dismiss for Improper Venue Forms for Lake County

a. CCS entry form. IN ST LAKE RCP App. A.

b. Notice of manual filing. IN ST LAKE RCP Form 2.

c. Certificate of service. IN ST LAKE RCP Form 3.

d. Declaration that party was unable to file in a timely manner. IN ST LAKE RCP Form 4.

3. Motion to Dismiss for Improper Venue Forms for Lake County

a. Notice of manual filing. EFORMST IN 5540.

I. Checklist

(I) ❑ Matters to be considered by moving party

   (a) ❑ Required documents

      (1) ❑ Motion and notice

      (2) ❑ Brief

      (3) ❑ Proposed order

      (4) ❑ Chronological case summary (CSS) entry forms

      (5) ❑ Certificate of service

   (b) ❑ Supplemental documents

      (1) ❑ Supporting evidence

      (2) ❑ Facsimile cover sheet

   (c) ❑ Timing

      (1) ❑ A motion making the defense of incorrect venue under IN ST TRIAL P Rule 75, or any statutory provision, shall be made before pleading if a further pleading is permitted or within twenty (20) days after service of the prior pleading if none is required

      (2) ❑ A written motion, other than one which may be heard ex parte, and notice of the hearing thereof shall be served not less than five (5) days before the time specified for the hearing, unless a different period is fixed by the Indiana Rules of Trial Procedure or by order of the court

      (3) ❑ All pleadings and papers subsequent to the complaint which are required to be served upon

a party shall be filed with the Court either before service or within a reasonable period of time thereafter

    (4) ❑ All pleadings, motions and other papers submitted for filing which are required to be served under IN ST TRIAL P Rule 5(A) shall be filed no later than three (3) days after service

    (5) ❑ If such papers are filed before service, proof of service thereof shall be filed no later than three (3) business days thereafter

(II) ❑ Matters to be considered by the responding party

  (a) ❑ Required documents

    (1) ❑ Opposition

    (2) ❑ Chronological case summary (CSS) entry forms

    (3) ❑ Certificate of service

  (b) ❑ Supplemental documents

    (1) ❑ Supporting evidence

    (2) ❑ Proposed order

    (3) ❑ Facsimile cover sheet

  (c) ❑ Timing

    (1) ❑ An adverse party shall have thirty (30) days after service of the initial brief in which to serve and file an answer brief

    (2) ❑ Except as otherwise provided in IN ST TRIAL P Rule 59(D), opposing affidavits may be served not less than one (1) day before the hearing, unless the court permits them to be served at some other time

Motions, Oppositions and Replies
Motion for Leave to Amend

Document Last Updated October 2013

A. Applicable Rules

1. *State rules*

  a. Appearance. IN ST TRIAL P Rule 3.1.

  b. Summons. IN ST TRIAL P Rule 4; IN ST TRIAL P Rule 4.6.

  c. Service and filing of pleadings and other papers. IN ST TRIAL P Rule 5.

  d. Time. IN ST TRIAL P Rule 6.

  e. Pleadings and other papers. IN ST TRIAL P Rule 7; IN ST TRIAL P Rule 8; IN ST TRIAL P Rule 9.2; IN ST TRIAL P Rule 10.

  f. Signing and verification of pleadings. IN ST TRIAL P Rule 11.

  g. Amended and supplemental pleadings. IN ST TRIAL P Rule 15.

  h. Evidence. IN ST TRIAL P Rule 43.

  i. Judgment on the evidence (directed verdict). IN ST TRIAL P Rule 50.

  j. Findings by the court. IN ST TRIAL P Rule 52.

  k. Summary judgment. IN ST TRIAL P Rule 56.

  l. Motion to correct error. IN ST TRIAL P Rule 59.

  m. Relief from judgment or order. IN ST TRIAL P Rule 60.

  n. Hearing of motions. IN ST TRIAL P Rule 73.

    o.   Court records. IN ST TRIAL P Rule 77.

    p.   Access to court records. IN ST ADMIN Rule 9.

    q.   Paper size. IN ST ADMIN Rule 11.

    r.   Facsimile transmission. IN ST ADMIN Rule 12.

    s.   Electronic filing and electronic service pilot projects. IN ST ADMIN Rule 16.

    t.   Privacy and confidentiality. IN ST 5-2-9-6; IN ST 5-14-3-4; IN ST 5-14-3-5.5; IN ST 6-4.1-5-10; IN ST 6-4.1-12-12; IN ST 6-8.1-7-1; IN ST 11-13-1-8; IN ST 12-23-14-13; IN ST 16-39-3-10; IN ST 16-41-8-1; IN ST 22-4-19-6; IN ST 31-11-1-6; IN ST 31-19-5-23; IN ST 31-19-13-2; IN ST 31-19-19-1; IN ST 31-33-18-1; IN ST 31-39-1-1; IN ST 31-39-1-2; IN ST 33-23-16-16; IN ST 35-34-2-4; IN ST 35-38-1-13; IN ST 35-38-9-1; IN ST ADR Rule 2.11; IN ST ADR Rule 4.4; IN ST ADR Rule 5.6; IN ST JURY Rule 10.

2.   *Local rules*

    a.   Scope and title. [IN ST LAKE RCP Rule 1, as amended by IN ORDER 13-0237, effective October 18, 2013].

    b.   Preparation of pleadings, motions and other papers. IN ST LAKE RCP Rule 2.

    c.   Filing. [IN ST LAKE RCP Rule 3, as amended by IN ORDER 13-0237, effective October 18, 2013].

    d.   Motions. IN ST LAKE RCP Rule 4.

    e.   Pretrial procedure. IN ST LAKE RCP Rule 9.

    f.   Briefs. IN ST LAKE RCP Rule 11.

    g.   Confidential information and sealed documents. IN ST LAKE RCP Rule 16.

    h.   Electronic filing and service. IN ST LAKE RCP Rule 17.

B. Timing

1.   *Time for amending pleadings*

    a.   *As a matter of course.* A party may amend his pleading once as a matter of course at any time before a responsive pleading is served or, if the pleading is one to which no responsive pleading is permitted, and the action has not been placed upon the trial calendar, he may so amend it at any time within thirty (30) days after it is served. IN ST TRIAL P Rule 15(A). Refer to the Indiana KeyRules Amended Complaint and Amended Answer documents for additional information on amending pleadings as a matter of course.

    b.   *With leave of court.* Otherwise a party may amend his pleading only by leave of court or by written consent of the adverse party; and leave shall be given when justice so requires. IN ST TRIAL P Rule 15(A).

    c.   *Filing.* All pleadings and papers subsequent to the complaint which are required to be served upon a party shall be filed with the Court either before service or within a reasonable period of time thereafter. IN ST TRIAL P Rule 5(E)(1). All pleadings, motions and other papers submitted for filing which are required to be served under IN ST TRIAL P Rule 5(A) shall be filed no later than three (3) days after service. IN ST LAKE RCP Rule 3(A).

        i.   If such papers are filed before service, proof of service thereof shall be filed no later than three (3) business days thereafter. Upon failure to comply with IN ST LAKE RCP Rule 3, the Court may, on motion of any party or on its own motion, impose appropriate sanctions. IN ST LAKE RCP Rule 3(A).

    d.   *Briefs.* Briefs, other than those addressed in IN ST LAKE RCP Rule 4 and IN ST LAKE RCP Rule 9, shall be filed no later than two (2) calendar days preceding the hearing or trial to which directed. IN ST LAKE RCP Rule 11.

2.   *Service.* A written motion, other than one which may be heard ex parte, and notice of the hearing thereof

shall be served not less than five (5) days before the time specified for the hearing, unless a different period is fixed by the Indiana Rules of Trial Procedure or by order of the court. IN ST TRIAL P Rule 6(D).

    a.   *Of supporting affidavits.* When a motion is supported by affidavit, the affidavit shall be served with the motion. IN ST TRIAL P Rule 6(D).

3.   *Service of opposition.* Except as otherwise provided in IN ST TRIAL P Rule 59(D), opposing affidavits may be served not less than one (1) day before the hearing, unless the court permits them to be served at some other time. IN ST TRIAL P Rule 6(D).

    a.   So long as consistent with the Indiana Rules of Trial Procedure, an adverse party wishing to respond shall do so within fifteen (15) days of service. IN ST LAKE RCP Rule 4(A).

4.   *Reply.* The moving party shall have ten (10) days after service of the response within which to reply. IN ST LAKE RCP Rule 4(A).

5.   *Computation of time*

    a.   *Generally; Days excluded.* In computing any period of time prescribed or allowed by the Indiana Rules of Trial Procedure, by order of the court, or by any applicable statute, the day of the act, event, or default from which the designated period of time begins to run shall not be included. The last day of the period so computed is to be included unless it is:

        i.   A Saturday,

        ii.   A Sunday,

        iii.   A legal holiday as defined by state statute, or

        iv.   A day the office in which the act is to be done is closed during regular business hours. IN ST TRIAL P Rule 6(A).

    b.   *Short periods.* In any event, the period runs until the end of the next day that is not a Saturday, a Sunday, a legal holiday, or a day on which the office is closed. When the period of time allowed is less than seven (7) days, intermediate Saturdays, Sundays, legal holidays, and days on which the office is closed shall be excluded from the computations. IN ST TRIAL P Rule 6(A).

    c.   *Additional time after service by United States mail.* Whenever a party has the right or is required to do some act or take some proceedings within a prescribed period after the service of a notice or other paper upon him and the notice or paper is served upon him by United States mail, three (3) days shall be added to the prescribed period. IN ST TRIAL P Rule 6(E).

    d.   *Electronic filing does not alter deadlines.* Filing electronically does not alter any filing deadlines or any time computation pursuant to state or federal statutes, any Rules of the Indiana Supreme Court, including without limitation the Rules of Trial Procedure, the Rules of Appellate Procedure or the Administrative Rules, or applicable Lake County Rules of Civil Procedure. The office of the Lake County Clerk is open for electronic filing under the Lake County Rules of Civil Procedure twenty-four (24) hours a day. A document is deemed filed at the date and time it is received by the LCOD server. Filing must be completed before midnight local time in order to be considered filed that day. Lake County observes Central Time and electronic filers are strongly urged to file documents during hours when the Lake County Online Docket ("LCOD") help line is available, from 9:00 a.m. to 4:00 p.m. local time, although documents can be filed electronically twenty-four (24) hours a day. IN ST LAKE RCP Rule 17(I).

    e.   *Enlargement of time.* When an act is required or allowed to be done at or within a specific time by the Indiana Rules of Trial Procedure, the court may at any time for cause shown:

        i.   Order the period enlarged, with or without motion or notice, if request therefor is made before the expiration of the period originally prescribed or extended by a previous order; or

        ii.   Upon motion made after the expiration of the specific period, permit the act to be done where the failure to act was the result of excusable neglect; but, the court may not extend the time for taking any action for judgment on the evidence under IN ST TRIAL P Rule 50(A), amendment of findings and judgment under IN ST TRIAL P Rule 52(B), to correct errors under IN ST TRIAL P Rule 59(C), statement in opposition to motion to correct error under IN ST TRIAL P

Rule 59(E), or to obtain relief from final judgment under IN ST TRIAL P Rule 60(B), except to the extent and under the conditions stated in those rules. IN ST TRIAL P Rule 6(B).

C. General Requirements

1. *Motions, generally.* Unless made during a hearing or trial, or otherwise ordered by the court, an application to the court for an order shall be made by written motion. The motion shall state the grounds therefor and the relief or order sought. IN ST TRIAL P Rule 7(B).

   a. *Motions as distinct from pleadings.* Motions and responses to motions are not pleadings, and allegations contained in a motion are not admissions of a party. 22B INPRAC 7:2; Wachstetter v. County Properties, LLC, 832 N.E.2d 574 (Ind.Ct.App. 2005); Scott County Family YMCA, Inc. v. Hobbs, 817 N.E.2d 603 (Ind.Ct.App. 2004).

   b. *Unopposed motions generally granted.* It is common for a trial court to grant procedural motions, such as motions for enlargement of time, discovery motions, or motions for continuance, unless an objection is filed. 21 INPRAC § 13.8.

   c. *Separate motions.* Each motion shall be separate, while alternative motions filed together shall each be identified on the caption. IN ST LAKE RCP Rule 4(A).

   d. *Answer and reply briefs.* Failure to file an answer brief or reply brief within the time prescribed shall be deemed a waiver of the right thereto and shall subject the motion to summary ruling. IN ST LAKE RCP Rule 4(A).

2. *Motion for leave to amend.* The purpose of an amended pleading is to include matters that occurred before the filing of the original pleading but which were either overlooked by the pleader or unknown to him at the time. It is a substitute for the original and relates to the facts that existed when the original pleading was filed. An amended pleading supercedes the original as to those portions amended. 10 INPRAC § 46.1.

   a. *Amendments liberally allowed.* Amendments to pleadings are to be liberally allowed in order that all issues are presented in one action. 10 INPRAC § 46.1; Pinnacle Media, LLC v. Metropolitan Dev. Com'n of Marion County, 868 N.E.2d 894 (Ind.Ct.App. 2007).

   b. *Amendments to conform to the evidence.* When issues not raised by the pleadings are tried by express or implied consent of the parties, they shall be treated in all respects as if they had been raised in the pleadings. Such amendment of the pleadings as may be necessary to cause them to conform to the evidence and to raise these issues may be made upon motion of any party at any time, even after judgment, but failure so to amend does not affect the result of the trial of these issues. If evidence is objected to at the trial on the ground that it is not within the issues made by the pleadings, the court may allow the pleadings to be amended and shall do so freely when the presentation of the merits of the action will be subserved thereby and the objecting party fails to satisfy the court that the admission of such evidence would prejudice him in maintaining his action or defense upon the merits. The court may grant a continuance to enable the objecting party to meet such evidence. IN ST TRIAL P Rule 15(B).

   c. *Relation back of amendments*

      i. Whenever the claim or defense asserted in the amended pleading arose out of the conduct, transaction, or occurrence set forth or attempted to be set forth in the original pleading, the amendment relates back to the date of the original pleading. An amendment changing the party against whom a claim is asserted relates back if the foregoing provision is satisfied and, within one hundred and twenty (120) days of commencement of the action, the party to be brought in by amendment:

         • Has received such notice of the institution of the action that he will not be prejudiced in maintaining his defense on the merits; and

         • Knew or should have known that but for a mistake concerning the identity of the proper party, the action would have been brought against him. IN ST TRIAL P Rule 15(C).

      ii. The requirement of IN ST TRIAL P Rule 15(C)(1) and IN ST TRIAL P Rule 15(C)(2) with respect to a governmental organization to be brought into the action as defendant is satisfied:

         • In the case of a state or governmental organization by delivery or mailing of process to the attorney general or to a governmental executive [IN ST TRIAL P Rule 4.6(A)(3)]; or

- In the case of a local governmental organization, by delivery or mailing of process to its attorney as provided by statute, to a governmental executive thereof [IN ST TRIAL P Rule 4.6(A)(4)], or to the officer holding the office if suit is against the officer or an office. IN ST TRIAL P Rule 15(C).

d. *Amendment by leave.* Amendments, other than an amendment by right, may be made only by leave of court or by written consent of the opposing party. 2 INPRAC R 15(15.1).

e. *Factors considered.* In deciding whether to permit a party to amend his pleading, the court must consider a number of factors: (1) undue delay, (2) bad faith or dilatory motive on the part of the movant, (3) repeated failure to cure deficiencies by amendments previously allowed, (4) undue prejudice to the opposing party by virtue of allowance of the amendment, and (5) the futility of the amendment. 10 INPRAC § 46.1; Crawford v. City of Muncie, 655 N.E.2d 614 (Ind.Ct.App. 1995); Selvia v. Reitmeyer, 156 Ind.App. 203, 295 N.E.2d 869 (Ind.Ct.App. 1973).

D. Documents

1. *Required documents*

   a. *Motion and notice.* The requirement of notice is satisfied by service of the motion. IN ST TRIAL P Rule 7(B). Refer to the General Requirements section of this document for information on the content of a motion for leave to amend.

   b. *Brief.* Briefs, other than those addressed in IN ST LAKE RCP Rule 4 and IN ST LAKE RCP Rule 9, shall be filed no later than two (2) calendar days preceding the hearing or trial to which directed. IN ST LAKE RCP Rule 11.

   c. *Proposed pleadings.* A copy of the proposed amendment should be attached to the motion for leave to amend, along with a proposed order by the court which permits the amendment. 2 INPRAC R 15. In order to file a document which requires leave of court, such as an amended pleading or a document to be filed late, the proposed document shall be attached as an exhibit to a motion. IN ST LAKE RCP Rule 17(D)(7).

   d. *Proposed order.* Unless local practice provides differently, a party should submit a proposed order with its written motion to be signed by the judge once the motion has been granted. 21 INPRAC § 13.8.

      i. Proposed orders, which are submitted for the court's convenience under IN ST LAKE RCP Rule 3 or other applicable Lake County Rules of Civil Procedure, shall be submitted as attachments to motions. IN ST LAKE RCP Rule 17(D)(8). Proposed orders shall be prepared and filed separately from the pleadings, petitions, motions or other papers to which they have reference. IN ST LAKE RCP Rule 3(B).

      ii. Orders, either routine in nature or uncontested including, for example, those setting or continuing a hearing, shall be effected by the chronological case summary entry only, which shall contain the concise substance of the order. IN ST LAKE RCP Rule 3(B).

      iii. All orders shall be accompanied with sufficient copies and stamped, pre-addressed envelopes, so that copies may be mailed to all parties. IN ST LAKE RCP Rule 3(B).

   e. *Chronological case summary (CCS) entry forms.* All filings shall be accompanied by a Chronological Case Summary (CCS) Entry Form to define or identify the documents filed. The Form used should be substantially similar to IN ST LAKE RCP App. A. IN ST LAKE RCP Rule 3(C).

   f. *Certificate of service.* An attorney or unrepresented party tendering a document to the Clerk for filing shall certify that service has been made, list the parties served, and specify the date and means of service. The certificate of service shall be placed at the end of the document and shall not be separately filed. The separate filing of a certificate of service, however, shall not be grounds for rejecting a document for filing. The Clerk may permit documents to be filed without a certificate of service but shall require prompt filing of a separate certificate of service. IN ST TRIAL P Rule 5(C).

      i. All pleadings, motions and other papers submitted for filing which are required to be served under IN ST TRIAL P Rule 5(A) shall contain proof of service pursuant to IN ST TRIAL P Rule 5(B)(2). IN ST LAKE RCP Rule 3(A).

2. *Supplemental documents*

    a. *Supporting evidence.* When a motion is based on facts not appearing of record the court may hear the matter on affidavits presented by the respective parties, but the court may direct that the matter be heard wholly or partly on oral testimony or depositions. IN ST TRIAL P Rule 43(B).

    b. *Facsimile cover sheet.* Any document sent to the Clerk of the Circuit Court by electronic facsimile transmission shall be accompanied by a cover sheet which states the title of the document, case number, number of pages, identity and voice telephone number of the sending party and instructions for filing. The cover sheet shall contain the signature of the attorney or party, pro se, authorizing the filing. IN ST ADMIN Rule 12(D).

E. Format

1. *Form of motions.* The rules applicable to captions, and the signing and form of pleadings (IN ST TRIAL P Rule 8 through IN ST TRIAL P Rule 11), apply to all motions and other papers provided under the Indiana Rules of Trial Procedure. 22B INPRAC 7:2.

2. *Form of pleadings.* For the purpose of uniformity, convenience, clarity and durability, requirements in IN ST LAKE RCP Rule 2 shall be observed in the preparation of all pleadings, motions and other papers. IN ST LAKE RCP Rule 2. Whenever materials submitted fail to meet the standards in IN ST LAKE RCP Rule 2, the Court may impose appropriate sanctions. IN ST LAKE RCP Rule 2(B).

    a. *Caption; Names of parties.* Every pleading shall contain a caption setting forth the name of the court, the title of the action, the file number, and a designation as in IN ST TRIAL P Rule 7(A). In the complaint the title of the action shall include the names of all the parties, but in other pleadings it is sufficient to state the name of the first party on each side with an appropriate indication of other parties. IN ST TRIAL P Rule 10(A).

        i. *Special judge matters.* The caption of all CCS Entry Forms, pleadings, motions, orders and other papers to be filed in a special judge case shall include in block text the words SPECIAL JUDGE and the name of the judge directly below the cause number on the caption. IN ST LAKE RCP Rule 2(D).

    b. *Paragraphs; Separate statements.* All averments of a claim or defense shall be made in numbered paragraphs, the contents of each of which shall be limited as far as practicable to a statement of a single set of circumstances, and a paragraph may be referred to by number in all succeeding pleadings. Each claim founded upon a separate transaction or occurrence and each defense other than denials may be stated in a separate count or defense whenever a separation facilitates the clear presentation of the matters set forth. IN ST TRIAL P Rule 10(B).

    c. *Adoption by reference; Exhibits.* Statements in a pleading may be adopted by reference in a different part of the same pleading or in another pleading or in any motion. A copy of any written instrument which is an exhibit to a pleading is a part thereof for all purposes. IN ST TRIAL P Rule 10(C).

    d. *Paper; Print, quality and binding*

        i. All pleadings, motions, chronological case summary entry forms, orders, process and other papers shall be neatly and legibly printed, typewritten or mechanically reproduced, on one (1) side only, on white opaque paper. To satisfy the recordkeeping requirements of IN ST TRIAL P Rule 77, the print shall be of sufficient density and clarity for preservation and reproduction of microfilming, optical disk or other secondary sources. For this reason, the use of non-letter-quality printers is discouraged. IN ST LAKE RCP Rule 2(A).

        ii. Paper and ink shall be of such quality as to withstand the test of time. All documents shall be produced on acid-free, non-thermal paper. It is recommended that a minimum of twenty (20) pound, twenty-five percent (25%) cotton paper product be used. Documents of multiple pages shall be submitted in bound or stapled fashion, and the binding or stapling shall be at the top only. Covers or backings shall not be used. IN ST LAKE RCP Rule 2(A).

    e. *Papers; Handwritten.* Handwritten papers may be filed only if approved by the Court and a typewritten or printed true rendition thereof is filed within three (3) days thereafter and approved by the Court. Upon such approval, they shall be deemed and filed as the original, while the handwritten papers shall be retained therewith for evidentiary purposes. IN ST LAKE RCP Rule 2(C).

    f.   *Minute sheets; Motion blanks.* Minute sheets and motion blanks shall no longer be used. IN ST LAKE RCP Rule 2(D).

3.   *Size of papers for filing.* Effective January 1, 1992, all pleadings, copies, motions and documents filed with any trial court or appellate level court, typed or printed, with the exception of exhibits and existing wills, shall be prepared on eight and one-half by eleven inch (8 1/2" x 11") size paper. IN ST ADMIN Rule 11.

4.   *Signature requirements*

    a.   *Signature of attorney.* Every pleading or motion of a party represented by an attorney shall be signed by at least one (1) attorney of record in his individual name, whose address, telephone number, and attorney number shall be stated, except that this provision shall not apply to pleadings and motions made and transcribed at the trial or a hearing before the judge and received by him in such form. IN ST TRIAL P Rule 11(A).

        i.   The signature of an attorney constitutes a certificate by him that he has read the pleadings; that to the best of his knowledge, information, and belief, there is good ground to support it; and that it is not interposed for delay. IN ST TRIAL P Rule 11(A).

        ii.   If a pleading or motion is not signed or is signed with intent to defeat the purpose of the rule, it may be stricken as sham and false and the action may proceed as though the pleading had not been served. IN ST TRIAL P Rule 11(A).

        iii.   For a willful violation of IN ST TRIAL P Rule 11 an attorney may be subjected to appropriate disciplinary action. Similar action may be taken if scandalous or indecent matter is inserted. IN ST TRIAL P Rule 11(A).

    b.   *Signature of unrepresented party.* A party who is not represented by an attorney shall sign his pleading and state his address. IN ST TRIAL P Rule 11(A).

    c.   *Verification not generally required.* Except when specifically required by rule, pleadings or motions need not be verified or accompanied by affidavit. The rule in equity that the averments of an answer under oath must be overcome by the testimony of two (2) witnesses or of one (1) witness sustained by corroborating circumstances is abolished. IN ST TRIAL P Rule 11(A).

    d.   *Verification by affirmation or representation.* When in connection with any civil or special statutory proceeding it is required that any pleading, motion, petition, supporting affidavit, or other document of any kind, be verified, or that an oath be taken, it shall be sufficient if the subscriber simply affirms the truth of the matter to be verified by an affirmation or representation. IN ST TRIAL P Rule 11(B). IN ST TRIAL P Rule 11(B) states that the affirmation or representation should be in substantially the following language: "I (we) affirm, under the penalties for perjury, that the foregoing representation(s) is (are) true. (Signed) _____ "

        i.   Any person who falsifies an affirmation or representation of fact shall be subject to the same penalties as are prescribed by law for the making of a false affidavit. IN ST TRIAL P Rule 11(B).

    e.   *Verified pleadings, motions, and affidavits as evidence.* Pleadings, motions and affidavits accompanying or in support of such pleadings or motions when required to be verified or under oath shall be accepted as a representation that the signer had personal knowledge thereof or reasonable cause to believe the existence of the facts or matters stated or alleged therein; and, if otherwise competent or acceptable as evidence, may be admitted as evidence of the facts or matters stated or alleged therein when it is so provided in the Indiana Rules of Trial Procedure, by statute or other law, or to the extent the writing or signature expressly purports to be made upon the signer's personal knowledge. When such pleadings, motions and affidavits are verified or under oath they shall not require other or greater proof on the part of the adverse party than if not verified or not under oath unless expressly provided otherwise by the Indiana Rules of Trial Procedure, statute or other law. Affidavits upon motions for summary judgment under IN ST TRIAL P Rule 56 and in denial of execution under IN ST TRIAL P Rule 9.2 shall be made upon personal knowledge. IN ST TRIAL P Rule 11(C).

    f.   *Electronic signature.* The filing of documents and information through the E-filing system by use of a valid username and password is presumed to have been authorized by the User to whom that username and password have been issued and documents filed through the E-filing system are presumed to have been signed by the same User. IN ST ADMIN Rule 16(E).

5. *Information excluded from public access.* Every document filed in a case shall separately identify information excluded from public access pursuant to IN ST ADMIN Rule 9(G)(1) as follows:

   a. Whole documents that are excluded from public access pursuant to IN ST ADMIN Rule 9(G)(1) shall be tendered on light green paper or have a light green coversheet attached to the document, marked "Not for Public Access" or "Confidential." IN ST TRIAL P Rule 5(G)(1).

   b. When only a portion of a document contains information excluded from public access pursuant to IN ST ADMIN Rule 9(G)(1), said information shall be omitted [or redacted] from the filed document, and set forth on a separate accompanying document on light green paper conspicuously marked "Not for Public Access" or "Confidential" and clearly designated [or identifying] the caption and number of the case and the document and location within the document to which the redacted material pertains. IN ST TRIAL P Rule 5(G)(2).

   c. With respect to documents filed in electronic format, the trial court, by local rule, may provide for compliance with IN ST TRIAL P Rule 5 in manner that separates and protects access to information excluded from public access. IN ST TRIAL P Rule 5(G)(3).

   d. IN ST TRIAL P Rule 5(G) does not apply to a record sealed by the court pursuant to IN ST 5-14-3-5.5 or otherwise, nor to records, documents, or information filed in cases to which public access is prohibited pursuant to IN ST ADMIN Rule 9(G). IN ST TRIAL P Rule 5(G)(4).

   e. The following information in case records is excluded from public access and is confidential:

      i. Information that is excluded from public access pursuant to federal law;

      ii. Information that is excluded from public access as declared confidential by Indiana statute or other court rule, including without limitation:

         • All adoption records created after July 8, 1941, as declared confidential by IN ST 31-19-19-1, et seq., except those specifically declared open by IN ST 31-19-13-2(2);

         • All records relating to chancroid, chlamydia, gonorrhea, hepatitis, human immunodeficiency virus (HIV), Lymphogranuloma venereum, syphilis, tuberculosis, as declared confidential by IN ST 16-41-8-1, et seq.;

         • All records relating to child abuse as declared confidential by IN ST 31-33-18-1, et seq.;

         • All records relating to drug tests as declared confidential by IN ST 5-14-3-4(a)(9);

         • Records of grand jury proceedings as declared confidential by IN ST 35-34-2-4;

         • Records of juvenile proceedings as declared confidential by IN ST 31-39-1-2, except those specifically open under statute;

         • All paternity records created after July 1, 1941 as declared confidential by IN ST 31-14-11-15, IN ST 31-19-5-23, IN ST 31-39-1-1 and IN ST 31-39-1-2 [Editor's note: IN ST 31-14-11-15 was repealed effective May 9, 2013];

         • All pre-sentence reports as declared confidential by IN ST 35-38-1-13;

         • Written petitions to permit marriages without consent and orders directing the Clerk of Court to issue a marriage license to underage persons, as declared confidential by IN ST 31-11-1-6;

         • Only those arrest warrants, search warrants, indictments and informations ordered confidential by the trial judge, prior to return of duly executed service as declared confidential by IN ST 5-14-3-4(b)(1);

         • All medical, mental health, or tax records unless determined by law or regulation of any governmental custodian not to be confidential, released by the subject of such records, or declared by a court of competent jurisdiction to be essential to the resolution of litigation as declared confidential by IN ST 16-39-3-10, IN ST 6-4.1-5-10, IN ST 6-4.1-12-12, and IN ST 6-8.1-7-1;

749

- Personal information relating to jurors or prospective jurors, other than for the use of the parties and counsel, pursuant to IN ST JURY Rule 10;

- Information relating to protection from abuse orders, no-contact orders and workplace violence restraining orders as declared confidential by IN ST 5-2-9-6, et seq.;

- Mediation proceedings pursuant to IN ST ADR Rule 2.11, Mini-Trial proceedings pursuant to IN ST ADR Rule 4.4(C), and Summary Jury Trials pursuant to IN ST ADR Rule 5.6;

- Information in probation files pursuant to the Probation Standards promulgated by the Judicial Conference of Indiana pursuant to IN ST 11-13-1-8(b);

- Information deemed confidential pursuant to the Rules for Court Administered Alcohol and Drug Programs promulgated by the Judicial Conference of Indiana pursuant to IN ST 12-23-14-13;

- Information deemed confidential pursuant to the Problem-Solving Court Rules promulgated by the Judicial Conference of Indiana pursuant to IN ST 33-23-16-16;

- All records of the Department of workforce Development as declared confidential by IN ST 22-4-19-6;

- Information regarding interception of electronic communications that is sealed or deemed confidential as set forth in IN ST 35-33.5-2-1, et seq.

  iii. Information excluded from public access by specific court order;

  iv. Complete Social Security Numbers of living persons;

  v. With the exception of names, information such as addresses, phone numbers, and dates of birth which explicitly identifies:

  - Natural persons who are witnesses or victims (not including defendants) in criminal, domestic violence, stalking, sexual assault, juvenile, or civil protection order proceedings, provided that juveniles who are victims of sex crimes shall be identified by initials only;

  - Places of residence of judicial officers, clerks and other employees of courts and clerks of court, unless the person or persons about whom the information pertains waives confidentiality;

  vi. Complete account numbers of specific assets, loans, bank accounts, credit cards, and personal identification numbers (PINs);

  vii. All orders of expungement entered in criminal or juvenile proceedings, orders to restrict access to criminal history information pursuant to IN ST 35-38-5-5.5 or IN ST 35-38-8-5 and records excluded from public access by such orders, and information related to infractions that is excluded from public access pursuant to IN ST 34-28-5-15 or IN ST 34-28-5-16 [Editor's note: IN ST 35-38-5-5.5, IN ST 35-38-8-5 and IN ST 34-28-5-16 were repealed effective July 1, 2013; for information on orders restricting access to criminal history, refer to IN ST 35-38-9-1, et seq.];

  viii. All personal notes and e-mail, and deliberative material, of judges, jurors, court staff and judicial agencies, and information recorded in personal data assistants (PDA's) or organizers and personal calendars. IN ST ADMIN Rule 9(G)(1).

6. *Format of electronically filed documents*

   a. *Generally.* Electronically filed documents must meet the same requirements of format as documents conventionally filed pursuant to IN ST LAKE RCP Rule 2 or other applicable Lake County Rules of Civil Procedure. IN ST LAKE RCP Rule 17(D)(1).

   b. *Titles of documents.* The person electronically filing a document will be responsible for designating a title for the document at the time it is filed. The LCOD will generate the appropriate entry onto the CCS to record the filing of the document. IN ST LAKE RCP Rule 17(D)(3).

   c. *Citations and hyperlinks.* Electronically filed documents may contain hyperlink references to an external document as a convenient mechanism for accessing material cited in the document. Filers wishing to insert hyperlinks into documents shall continue to use the traditional method of citation to authority in addition to the hyperlink provided. The hyperlink is merely a convenience to the court and the material referenced is extraneous to the file and not a part of the court's record. IN ST LAKE RCP Rule 17(D)(5).

d. *Attachments and exhibits.* All documents which form part of a single submission and which are being filed at the same time and by the same filer may be electronically filed together under one document filing, e.g., the motion, supporting affidavits, memorandum in support, designation of evidence, exhibits. IN ST LAKE RCP Rule 17(D)(6).

   i. Large documents which do not exist in an electronic format shall be scanned into .pdf format and filed electronically as separate attachments. A scanner is available in each clerk's office for use by the public and the bar in scanning and saving image files if needed. IN ST LAKE RCP Rule 17(D)(6).

e. *Electronic signatures*

   i. *Electronic filing as signature.* The electronic filing of a document which is required to be signed shall constitute the filer's representation under IN ST TRIAL P Rule 11. Unless the electronically filed document has been scanned and shows the filer's original signature, the signature of the filer shall be indicated by As/Attorney's Name, or As/Party's Name as in the case of a pro se litigant, on the line where the signature would otherwise appear. IN ST LAKE RCP Rule 17(G)(1).

   ii. *Signatures on jointly signed or filed, verified or other documents.* In the case of a stipulation, agreed order, jointly signed motion or other document which needs to be signed by two (2) or more persons, or in the case of documents which must contain original signatures and which require verification or an unsworn declaration under rule or statute, the signatures may be indicated by either:

   - Submitting a scanned copy of the originally signed document; or,

   - Submitting the document with the use of As/Name in the signature block(s) where the original signature(s) appear(s) in the original document; provided, however, that the filer shall first obtain the physical signature of all persons necessary. IN ST LAKE RCP Rule 17(G)(2).

   iii. *Retention of original.* The filer shall retain the original executed document. IN ST LAKE RCP Rule 17(G).

7. *Citation of local rules.* The local rules for Lake County may be known as the Lake County Rules of Civil Procedure, and abbreviated as LR. IN ST LAKE RCP Rule 1(C).

F. Filing and Service Requirements

1. *Filing requirements.* Except as otherwise provided in IN ST TRIAL P Rule 5(E)(2), all pleadings and papers subsequent to the complaint which are required to be served upon a party shall be filed with the Court either before service or within a reasonable period of time thereafter. IN ST TRIAL P Rule 5(E)(1). All papers presented for filing shall be submitted to the Clerk and not to the court. All papers submitted for filing shall be mailed or delivered to the Clerk's office at the courthouse in which the case is pending. IN ST LAKE RCP Rule 3(A).

   a. *Filing with the court defined.* The filing of pleadings, motions, and other papers with the court as required by the Indiana Rules of Trial Procedure shall be made by one of the following methods:

      i. Delivery to the clerk of the court;

      ii. Sending by electronic transmission under the procedure adopted pursuant to IN ST ADMIN Rule 12;

      iii. Mailing to the clerk by registered, certified or express mail return receipt requested;

      iv. Depositing with any third-party commercial carrier for delivery to the clerk within three (3) calendar days, cost prepaid, properly addressed;

v. If the court so permits, filing with the judge, in which event the judge shall note thereon the filing date and forthwith transmit them to the office of the clerk; or

vi. Electronic filing, as approved by the Division of State Court Administration pursuant to IN ST ADMIN Rule 16. IN ST TRIAL P Rule 5(F).

vii. Filing by registered or certified mail and by third-party commercial carrier shall be complete upon mailing or deposit. IN ST TRIAL P Rule 5(F).

b. *Mandatory electronic filing.* Unless otherwise permitted by the Lake County Rules of Civil Procedure or otherwise authorized by the judicial officer assigned to a particular case, all documents submitted for filing (including the original complaint, or equivalent pleading, and summons) shall be filed electronically with the clerk using the LCOD, no matter when the case was originally filed. IN ST LAKE RCP Rule 17(D).

   i. *Of documents containing information excluded from public access pursuant to* IN ST ADMIN Rule 9. Documents containing information excluded from public access pursuant to IN ST ADMIN Rule 9, or documents which are ordered to be filed under seal shall be filed electronically, pursuant to IN ST LAKE RCP Rule 17(D)(9), whenever possible, along with a copy of the applicable order to seal the records, and the filer shall designate the documents as "Not for Public Access Pursuant to Administrative Rule 9(G)(1)" at the time of filing. IN ST LAKE RCP Rule 16(A)(1); IN ST LAKE RCP Rule 17(D)(9).

   - *Conventional filing of documents containing information excluded from public access pursuant to* IN ST ADMIN Rule 9. Documents containing information excluded from public access pursuant to IN ST ADMIN Rule 9, or documents which are ordered to be filed under seal, which cannot be legibly scanned and filed electronically, shall be conventionally filed under seal and designated by the filer as "Not for Public Access Pursuant to Administrative Rule 9(G)(1)" at the time of filing. The unredacted version shall be filed on light green paper which is conspicuously marked "Not for Public Access"; and a redacted version, with confidential information deleted, shall be filed on white paper which shall be available for public access. The filer shall also electronically file a Notice of Manual Filing. IN ST LAKE RCP Rule 16(A)(2).

   ii. *Technical failures.* If a registered user is unable to file a document in a timely manner due to technical difficulties in the LCOD, the registered user must file a document with the court as soon as possible notifying the court of the inability to file the document. A sample document titled Declaration that Party was Unable to File in a Timely Manner Due to Technical Difficulties can be found at IN ST LAKE RCP Form 4. Delayed filings shall be rejected unless accompanied by the declaration attesting to the filer's failed attempts to file electronically at least two (2) times, separated by at least one (1) hour, after noon on each day of delay due to such technical failure. IN ST LAKE RCP Rule 17(J).

   iii. *Documents allowed to be filed conventionally.* Unless specifically authorized by the court, only the following documents may be filed conventionally and not electronically:

   - Exhibits and other documents that cannot be converted to a legible electronic form, such as videotapes, x-rays, and similar materials

   - Documents delivered to the clerk by pro se litigants

   - Documents mailed to the clerk by pro se litigants

   - Confidential documents

   - Notice of manual filing

   - Titles of documents

   - Chronological case summary entry forms (CCS entry forms). IN ST LAKE RCP Rule 17(E).

   - For more information on the documents which must be filed conventionally, refer to IN ST LAKE RCP Rule 17(E).

c. *Facsimile filing.* Only when necessary on an emergency basis (i.e., when certified mail or other means of filing will not bring the document to the Judge's attention prior to the scheduled hearing or ruling), pleadings, motions and other papers may be filed by electronic facsimile transmission, or when specifically authorized by the Court. IN ST LAKE RCP Rule 2(C).

    i. *Generally.* In counties where a majority of judges of the courts of record, by posted local rule, have authorized electronic facsimile filing and designated a telephone number to receive such transmissions, pleadings, motions, and other papers may be sent to the Clerk of Circuit Court by electronic facsimile transmission for filing in any case, provided:

- Such matter does not exceed ten (10) pages, including the cover sheet;
- Such matter does not require the payment of fees other than the electronic facsimile transcription fee set forth in IN ST ADMIN Rule 12(E);
- The sending party creates at the time of transmission a machine generated log for such transmission; and
- The original document and the transmission log are maintained by the sending party for the duration of the litigation. IN ST ADMIN Rule 12(B).

    ii. *Time of filing.* During normal, posted business hours, the time of filing shall be the time the duplicate document is produced in the office of the Clerk of the Circuit Court. Duplicate documents received at all other times shall be filed as of the next normal business day. IN ST ADMIN Rule 12(C).

- If the receiving fax machine endorses its own time and date stamp upon the transmitted documents and the receiving machine produces a delivery receipt which is electronically created and transmitted to the sending party, the time of filing shall be the date and time recorded on the transmitted document by the receiving fax machine. IN ST ADMIN Rule 12(C).

  d. *Filing for special judges.* For special judge matters where the special judge is a full-time judge or magistrate serving within Lake County, all papers submitted for filing shall be delivered or mailed to the Clerk's office at the courthouse where the special judge regularly serves. IN ST LAKE RCP Rule 3(A).

  e. *Proof of filing.* Any party filing any paper by any method other than personal delivery to the clerk shall retain proof of filing. IN ST TRIAL P Rule 5(F).

2. *Service requirements.* Unless otherwise provided by the Indiana Rules of Trial Procedure or an order of the court, each party and special judge, if any, shall be served with: (1) every order required by its terms to be served; (2) every pleading subsequent to the original complaint; (3) every written motion except one which may be heard ex parte; (4) every brief submitted to the trial court; (5) every paper relating to discovery required to be served upon a party; and (6) every written notice, appearance, demand, offer of judgment, designation of record on appeal, or similar paper. IN ST TRIAL P Rule 5(A).

  a. *Methods of service*

    i. *Personal service.* Whenever a party is represented by an attorney of record, service shall be made upon such attorney unless service upon the party himself is ordered by the court. Service upon the attorney or party shall be made by delivering or mailing a copy of the papers to the last known address or where an attorney or party has consented to service by fax or e-mail, as provided in IN ST TRIAL P Rule 3.1(A)(4), by faxing or e-mailing a copy of the documents to the fax number or e-mail address set out in the appearance form or correction as required by IN ST TRIAL P Rule 3.1(E). IN ST TRIAL P Rule 5(B). Delivery of a copy within IN ST TRIAL P Rule 5 means:

- Offering or tendering it to the attorney or party and stating the nature of the papers being served. Refusal to accept an offered or tendered document is a waiver of any objection to the sufficiency or adequacy of service of that document;
- Leaving it at his office with a clerk or other person in charge thereof, or if there is no one in charge, leaving it in a conspicuous place therein; or
- If the office is closed, by leaving it at his dwelling house or usual place of abode with some person of suitable age and discretion then residing therein; or,

- Leaving it at some other suitable place, selected by the attorney upon whom service is being made, pursuant to duly promulgated local rule. IN ST TRIAL P Rule 5(B)(1).

ii. *Service by mail.* If service is made by mail, the papers shall be deposited in the United States mail addressed to the person on whom they are being served, with postage prepaid. Service shall be deemed complete upon mailing. Proof of service of all papers permitted to be mailed may be made by written acknowledgment of service, by affidavit of the person who mailed the papers, or by certificate of an attorney. It shall be the duty of attorneys when entering their appearance in a cause or when filing pleadings or papers therein, to have noted in the Chronological Case Summary or said pleadings or papers so filed the address and telephone number of their office. Service by delivery or by mail at such address shall be deemed sufficient and complete. IN ST TRIAL P Rule 5(B)(2).

b. *Serving numerous defendants.* In any action in which there are unusually large numbers of defendants, the court, upon motion or of its own initiative, may order:

i. That service of the pleadings of the defendants and replies thereto need not be made as between the defendants;

- That any cross-claim, counterclaim, or matter constituting an avoidance or affirmative defense contained therein shall be deemed to be denied or avoided by all other parties; and

- That the filing of any such pleading and service thereof upon the plaintiff constitutes due notice of it to the parties. IN ST TRIAL P Rule 5(D).

ii. A copy of every such order shall be served upon the parties in such manner and form as the court directs. IN ST TRIAL P Rule 5(D).

iii. *Service by fax or e-mail.* A party who has consented to service by fax or e-mail may be served as follows:

- Service by e-mail shall be made by attaching the document being served in .pdf format. Discovery documents must also be served in accordance with IN ST TRIAL P Rule 26(A). IN ST TRIAL P Rule 5(B)(3)(a).

- Service by fax shall be deemed complete upon generation of a transmission record indicating the successful transmission of the entire document, except as provided in IN ST TRIAL P Rule 5(B)(3)(d). IN ST TRIAL P Rule 5(B)(3)(b).

- Service by e-mail shall be deemed complete upon transmission, except as provided in IN ST TRIAL P Rule 5(B)(3)(d). IN ST TRIAL P Rule 5(B)(3)(c).

- Service by fax or e-mail that occurs on a Saturday, Sunday, legal holiday, or day the court or agency in which the matter is pending is closed or after 5:00 PM local time of the recipient shall be deemed complete the next day that is not a Saturday, Sunday, legal holiday, or day that the court or agency in which the matter is pending is not closed. IN ST TRIAL P Rule 5(B)(3)(d).

c. *Service by electronic means.* The Lake County Online Docket will generate a Notice of Electronic Filing and Service when any document is filed and served. This notice will be emailed to each registered user of record in a case, and an electronic service event will be added to the work queue of each registered user of record in the case. The party filing the document should retain a paper or electronic copy of the Notice of Electronic Filing and Service. This notice represents proof of filing and service of the document on registered users of record in that case. The filer shall not be required to conventionally serve any document on any party receiving electronic service. IN ST LAKE RCP Rule 17(F)(2).

i. The filer shall also conventionally serve those parties not designated or able to receive electronic notice or service but who are nevertheless entitled to notice of said pleading or other document in accordance with the Indiana Rules of Civil Procedure and applicable Lake County Rules of Civil Procedure. In such cases, the filer shall also file a certificate of service, as appropriate. IN ST LAKE RCP Rule 17(F).

d. *Service on parties in default for failure to appear.* No service need be made on parties in default for failure to appear, except that pleadings asserting new or additional claims for relief against them shall be served upon them in the manner provided by service of summons in IN ST TRIAL P Rule 4. IN ST TRIAL P Rule 5(A).

G. Hearings

1. *Hearing on motion.* Unless local conditions make it impracticable, each judge shall establish regular times and places, at intervals sufficiently frequent for the prompt dispatch of business, at which motions requiring notice and hearing may be heard and disposed of; but the judge at any time or place and on such notice, if any, as he considers reasonable may make order for the advancement, conduct, and hearing of actions. To expedite its business the court may direct the submission and determination of motions without oral hearing upon brief written statements of reasons in support and opposition, or direct or permit hearings by telephone conference call with all attorneys or other similar means of communication. IN ST TRIAL P Rule 73(A).

2. *Oral argument discretionary.* The granting of a motion for oral argument, unless required by the Indiana Rules of Trial Procedure, shall be wholly discretionary with the court. IN ST LAKE RCP Rule 4(B).

H. Forms

1. Motion for Leave to Amend Forms for Indiana

a. Motion to file amended complaint. 5 INPRAC § 3:5.1.

b. Motion to file amended complaint; Another form. 5 INPRAC § 3:5.2.

c. Motion to amend pleading to conform to evidence. 5 INPRAC § 3:5.4.

d. Motion to amend complaint to compel joinder of defendant. 5 INPRAC § 3:7.2.

e. Motion to amend caption. 9 INPRAC § 3.41.

f. Affidavit in support of motion to amend caption. 9 INPRAC § 3.42.

g. Motion for leave to amend complaint following dismissal. 9 INPRAC § 42.16.

h. Motion for leave to file amended complaint against third party defendant. 10 INPRAC § 44.8.

i. Motion to file amended complaint. 10 INPRAC § 46.7.

j. Motion to amend complaint which has been dismissed; Filed more than 10 days after notice of dismissal. 10 INPRAC § 46.8.

k. Motion to amend pleading; Another form. 10 INPRAC § 46.9.

l. Order granting leave to amend complaint. 10 INPRAC § 46.10.

m. Amendment by stipulation. 10 INPRAC § 46.11.

n. Amended answer by interlineation. 10 INPRAC § 46.12.

o. Objections to motion to amend complaint. 10 INPRAC § 46.13.

p. Motion to amend pleading to conform to evidence. 10 INPRAC § 46.14.

q. Motion for leave to change defendant after statute of limitations. 10 INPRAC § 46.16.

r. Motion for leave to add party after statute of limitations. 10 INPRAC § 46.17.

s. Motion to substitute real party in interest; Assignee of interest. 10 INPRAC § 47.10.

t. Motion to amend complaint to compel joinder of defendant. 10 INPRAC § 49.3.

u. Certificate of service; Personal service. 9 INPRAC § 5.7.

v. Certificate of service; First class mail. 9 INPRAC § 5.8.

2. Official Motion for Leave to Amend Forms for Lake County

a. CCS entry form. IN ST LAKE RCP App. A.

b. Notice of manual filing. IN ST LAKE RCP Form 2.

c. Certificate of service. IN ST LAKE RCP Form 3.

d. Declaration that party was unable to file in a timely manner. IN ST LAKE RCP Form 4.

3. **Motion for Leave to Amend Forms for Lake County**

    a. Notice of manual filing. EFORMST IN 5540.

I. Checklist

(I) ❏ Matters to be considered by moving party

    (a) ❏ Required documents

        (1) ❏ Motion and notice

        (2) ❏ Brief

        (3) ❏ Proposed pleading

        (4) ❏ Proposed order

        (5) ❏ Chronological case summary (CSS) entry forms

        (6) ❏ Certificate of service

    (b) ❏ Supplemental documents

        (1) ❏ Supporting evidence

        (2) ❏ Facsimile cover sheet

    (c) ❏ Timing

        (1) ❏ A party may amend his pleading once as a matter of course at any time before a responsive pleading is served or, if the pleading is one to which no responsive pleading is permitted, and the action has not been placed upon the trial calendar, he may so amend it at any time within thirty (30) days after it is served

        (2) ❏ Otherwise a party may amend his pleading only by leave of court or by written consent of the adverse party; and leave shall be given when justice so requires

        (3) ❏ A written motion, other than one which may be heard ex parte, and notice of the hearing thereof shall be served not less than five (5) days before the time specified for the hearing, unless a different period is fixed by the Indiana Rules of Trial Procedure or by order of the court

        (4) ❏ All pleadings and papers subsequent to the complaint which are required to be served upon a party shall be filed with the Court either before service or within a reasonable period of time thereafter

        (5) ❏ All pleadings, motions and other papers submitted for filing which are required to be served under IN ST TRIAL P Rule 5(A) shall be filed no later than three (3) days after service

        (6) ❏ If such papers are filed before service, proof of service thereof shall be filed no later than three (3) business days thereafter

(II) ❏ Matters to be considered by the responding party

    (a) ❏ Required documents

        (1) ❏ Opposition

        (2) ❏ Chronological case summary (CSS) entry forms

        (3) ❏ Certificate of service

    (b) ❏ Supplemental documents

        (1) ❏ Supporting evidence

        (2) ❏ Proposed order

        (3) ❏ Facsimile cover sheet

    (c) ❏ Timing

        (1) ❏ So long as consistent with the Indiana Rules of Trial Procedure, an adverse party wishing to respond shall do so within fifteen (15) days of service

(2) ❏ Except as otherwise provided in IN ST TRIAL P Rule 59(D), opposing affidavits may be served not less than one (1) day before the hearing, unless the court permits them to be served at some other time

Motions, Oppositions and Replies
Motion for Summary Judgment

Document Last Updated October 2013

A. Applicable Rules

1. *State rules*

    a. Appearance. IN ST TRIAL P Rule 3.1.

    b. Process. IN ST TRIAL P Rule 4.

    c. Service and filing of pleadings and other papers. IN ST TRIAL P Rule 5.

    d. Time. IN ST TRIAL P Rule 6.

    e. Pleadings. IN ST TRIAL P Rule 7; IN ST TRIAL P Rule 8; IN ST TRIAL P Rule 9.2; IN ST TRIAL P Rule 10.

    f. Signing and verification of pleadings. IN ST TRIAL P Rule 11.

    g. Defenses and objections; When and how presented; By pleading or motion; Motion for judgment on the pleadings. IN ST TRIAL P Rule 12.

    h. Evidence. IN ST TRIAL P Rule 43.

    i. Judgment on the evidence (directed verdict). IN ST TRIAL P Rule 50.

    j. Findings by the court. IN ST TRIAL P Rule 52.

    k. Summary judgment. IN ST TRIAL P Rule 56.

    l. Motion to correct error. IN ST TRIAL P Rule 59.

    m. Relief from judgment or order. IN ST TRIAL P Rule 60.

    n. Hearing of motions. IN ST TRIAL P Rule 73.

    o. Court records. IN ST TRIAL P Rule 77.

    p. Access to court records. IN ST ADMIN Rule 9.

    q. Paper size. IN ST ADMIN Rule 11.

    r. Facsimile transmission. IN ST ADMIN Rule 12.

    s. Electronic filing and electronic service pilot projects. IN ST ADMIN Rule 16.

    t. Privacy and confidentiality. IN ST 5-2-9-6; IN ST 5-14-3-4; IN ST 5-14-3-5.5; IN ST 6-4.1-5-10; IN ST 6-4.1-12-12; IN ST 6-8.1-7-1; IN ST 11-13-1-8; IN ST 12-23-14-13; IN ST 16-39-3-10; IN ST 16-41-8-1; IN ST 22-4-19-6; IN ST 31-11-1-6; IN ST 31-19-5-23; IN ST 31-19-13-2; IN ST 31-19-19-1; IN ST 31-33-18-1; IN ST 31-39-1-1; IN ST 31-39-1-2; IN ST 33-23-16-16; IN ST 35-34-2-4; IN ST 35-38-1-13; IN ST 35-38-9-1; IN ST ADR Rule 2.11; IN ST ADR Rule 4.4; IN ST ADR Rule 5.6; IN ST JURY Rule 10.

2. *Local rules*

    a. Scope and title. [IN ST LAKE RCP Rule 1, as amended by IN ORDER 13-0237, effective October 18, 2013].

    b. Preparation of pleadings, motions and other papers. IN ST LAKE RCP Rule 2.

    c. Filing. [IN ST LAKE RCP Rule 3, as amended by IN ORDER 13-0237, effective October 18, 2013].

    d. Motions. IN ST LAKE RCP Rule 4.

    e. Confidential information and sealed documents. IN ST LAKE RCP Rule 16.

    f. Electronic filing and service. IN ST LAKE RCP Rule 17.

B. Timing

1. *Time for moving for summary judgment*

    a. *For claimant.* A party seeking to recover upon a claim, counterclaim, or cross-claim or to obtain a declaratory judgment may, at any time after the expiration of twenty (20) days from the commencement of the action or after service of a motion for summary judgment by the adverse party, move with or without supporting affidavits for a summary judgment in his favor upon all or any part thereof. IN ST TRIAL P Rule 56(A).

    b. *For defending party.* A party against whom a claim, counterclaim, or cross-claim is asserted or a declaratory judgment is sought may, at any time, move with or without supporting affidavits for a summary judgment in his favor as to all or any part thereof. IN ST TRIAL P Rule 56(B).

    c. *Filing.* All pleadings and papers subsequent to the complaint which are required to be served upon a party shall be filed with the Court either before service or within a reasonable period of time thereafter. IN ST TRIAL P Rule 5(E)(1). All pleadings, motions and other papers submitted for filing which are required to be served under IN ST TRIAL P Rule 5(A) shall be filed no later than three (3) days after service. IN ST LAKE RCP Rule 3(A).

        i. If such papers are filed before service, proof of service thereof shall be filed no later than three (3) business days thereafter. Upon failure to comply with IN ST LAKE RCP Rule 3, the Court may, on motion of any party or on its own motion, impose appropriate sanctions. IN ST LAKE RCP Rule 3(A).

    d. *Briefs.* Briefs, other than those addressed in IN ST LAKE RCP Rule 4 and IN ST LAKE RCP Rule 9, shall be filed no later than two (2) calendar days preceding the hearing or trial to which directed. IN ST LAKE RCP Rule 11.

2. *Service.* A written motion, other than one which may be heard ex parte, and notice of the hearing thereof shall be served not less than five (5) days before the time specified for the hearing, unless a different period is fixed by the Indiana Rules of Trial Procedure or by order of the court. IN ST TRIAL P Rule 6(D).

    a. *Of supporting affidavits.* When a motion is supported by affidavit, the affidavit shall be served with the motion. IN ST TRIAL P Rule 6(D).

3. *Service of opposition.* An adverse party shall have thirty (30) days after service of the motion to serve a response and any opposing affidavits. IN ST TRIAL P Rule 56(C). Except as otherwise provided in IN ST TRIAL P Rule 59(D), opposing affidavits may be served not less than one (1) day before the hearing, unless the court permits them to be served at some other time. IN ST TRIAL P Rule 6(D).

    a. An adverse party shall have thirty (30) days after service of the initial brief in which to serve and file an answer brief. IN ST LAKE RCP Rule 4(A).

4. *Reply.* The moving party shall have ten (10) days after service of the answer brief in which to serve and file a reply brief. IN ST LAKE RCP Rule 4(A).

5. *Computation of time*

    a. *Generally; Days excluded.* In computing any period of time prescribed or allowed by the Indiana Rules of Trial Procedure, by order of the court, or by any applicable statute, the day of the act, event, or default from which the designated period of time begins to run shall not be included. The last day of the period so computed is to be included unless it is:

        i. A Saturday,

        ii. A Sunday,

        iii. A legal holiday as defined by state statute, or

        iv. A day the office in which the act is to be done is closed during regular business hours. IN ST TRIAL P Rule 6(A).

    b. *Short periods.* In any event, the period runs until the end of the next day that is not a Saturday, a Sunday, a legal holiday, or a day on which the office is closed. When the period of time allowed is

less than seven (7) days, intermediate Saturdays, Sundays, legal holidays, and days on which the office is closed shall be excluded from the computations. IN ST TRIAL P Rule 6(A).

c. *Additional time after service by United States mail.* Whenever a party has the right or is required to do some act or take some proceedings within a prescribed period after the service of a notice or other paper upon him and the notice or paper is served upon him by United States mail, three (3) days shall be added to the prescribed period. IN ST TRIAL P Rule 6(E).

d. *Electronic filing does not alter deadlines.* Filing electronically does not alter any filing deadlines or any time computation pursuant to state or federal statutes, any Rules of the Indiana Supreme Court, including without limitation the Rules of Trial Procedure, the Rules of Appellate Procedure or the Administrative Rules, or applicable Lake County Rules of Civil Procedure. The office of the Lake County Clerk is open for electronic filing under the Lake County Rules of Civil Procedure twenty-four (24) hours a day. A document is deemed filed at the date and time it is received by the LCOD server. Filing must be completed before midnight local time in order to be considered filed that day. Lake County observes Central Time and electronic filers are strongly urged to file documents during hours when the Lake County Online Docket ("LCOD") help line is available, from 9:00 a.m. to 4:00 p.m. local time, although documents can be filed electronically twenty-four (24) hours a day. IN ST LAKE RCP Rule 17(I).

e. *Enlargement of time.* When an act is required or allowed to be done at or within a specific time by the Indiana Rules of Trial Procedure, the court may at any time for cause shown:

   i. Order the period enlarged, with or without motion or notice, if request therefor is made before the expiration of the period originally prescribed or extended by a previous order; or

   ii. Upon motion made after the expiration of the specific period, permit the act to be done where the failure to act was the result of excusable neglect; but, the court may not extend the time for taking any action for judgment on the evidence under IN ST TRIAL P Rule 50(A), amendment of findings and judgment under IN ST TRIAL P Rule 52(B), to correct errors under IN ST TRIAL P Rule 59(C), statement in opposition to motion to correct error under IN ST TRIAL P Rule 59(E), or to obtain relief from final judgment under IN ST TRIAL P Rule 60(B), except to the extent and under the conditions stated in those rules. IN ST TRIAL P Rule 6(B).

C. General Requirements

1. *Motions, generally.* Unless made during a hearing or trial, or otherwise ordered by the court, an application to the court for an order shall be made by written motion. The motion shall state the grounds therefor and the relief or order sought. IN ST TRIAL P Rule 7(B).

   a. *Motions as distinct from pleadings.* Motions and responses to motions are not pleadings, and allegations contained in a motion are not admissions of a party. 22B INPRAC 7:2; Wachstetter v. County Properties, LLC, 832 N.E.2d 574 (Ind.Ct.App. 2005); Scott County Family YMCA, Inc. v. Hobbs, 817 N.E.2d 603 (Ind.Ct.App. 2004).

   b. *Unopposed motions generally granted.* It is common for a trial court to grant procedural motions, such as motions for enlargement of time, discovery motions, or motions for continuance, unless an objection is filed. 21 INPRAC § 13.8.

   c. *Separate motions.* Each motion shall be separate, while alternative motions filed together shall each be identified on the caption. IN ST LAKE RCP Rule 4(A).

   d. *Answer and reply briefs.* Failure to file an answer brief or reply brief within the time prescribed shall be deemed a waiver of the right thereto and shall subject the motion to summary ruling. IN ST LAKE RCP Rule 4(A).

2. *Motion for summary judgment.* Summary judgment is a procedure by which the trial court is asked to enter judgment when there are no genuine issues of material fact and the moving party is entitled to judgment as a matter of law. A summary judgment proceeding is not a trial, and is not intended to be a substitute for factual determinations where the facts are in dispute. Rather, summary judgment should be used to terminate litigation about which there is no factual dispute and which may be determined as a matter of law. 11 INPRAC § 90.1; LeBrun v. Conner, 702 N.E.2d 754 (Ind.Ct.App. 1998).

   a. *Burden.* The judgment sought shall be rendered forthwith if the designated evidentiary matter shows that there is no genuine issue as to any material fact and that the moving party is entitled to a judgment as a matter of law. IN ST TRIAL P Rule 56(C).

    i.   A "genuine" issue of material fact exists if the trier of fact must resolve the opposing party's differing version of the underlying facts or if the undisputed facts support conflicting reasonable inferences. A fact is "material" if it might affect the outcome of a case by helping to prove or disprove an essential element of a claim or defense, or it facilitates a resolution of an issue in the case. 22B INPRAC 56:1; Williams v. Tharp, 914 N.E.2d 756 (Ind. 2009).

    ii.   Summary judgment shall not be granted as of course because the opposing party fails to offer opposing affidavits or evidence, but the court shall make its determination from the evidentiary matter designated to the court. IN ST TRIAL P Rule 56(C).

    iii.   The trial court must evaluate the evidence in favor of the non-moving party. 22B INPRAC 56:1.

    iv.   Although Indiana courts are not consistent in describing the amount of proof required to sustain the moving party's initial burden, and IN ST TRIAL P Rule 56 is silent on the matter, a number of cases require "prima facie" proof. 22B INPRAC 56:5; DeHahn v. CSX Transp., Inc., 925 N.E.2d 442 (Ind.Ct.App. 2010). Once the moving party demonstrates the requirements for summary judgment, the burden shifts to the non-moving party to designate each material issue of fact which he asserts precludes entry of summary judgment and the evidence relevant to each designated fact. 22B INPRAC 56:5; Booth v. Wiley, 839 N.E.2d 1168 (Ind. 2005).

b.   *When motion not required.* When any party has moved for summary judgment, the court may grant summary judgment for any other party upon the issues raised by the motion although no motion for summary judgment is filed by such party. IN ST TRIAL P Rule 56(B).

c.   *Judgment on less than all issues or claims.* A summary judgment may be rendered upon less than all the issues or claims, including without limitation the issue of liability or damages alone although there is a genuine issue as to damages or liability as the case may be. IN ST TRIAL P Rule 56(C).

    i.   *Partial judgment not entered; Exceptions.* A summary judgment upon less than all the issues involved in a claim or with respect to less than all the claims or parties shall be interlocutory unless the court in writing expressly determines that there is no just reason for delay and in writing expressly directs entry of judgment as to less than all the issues, claims or parties. IN ST TRIAL P Rule 56(C).

    ii.   *Designation of specific findings.* The court shall designate the issues or claims upon which it finds no genuine issue as to any material facts. IN ST TRIAL P Rule 56(C).

    iii.   *Case not fully adjudicated on motion.* If on motion under IN ST TRIAL P Rule 56 judgment is not rendered upon the whole case or for all the relief asked and a trial is necessary, the court at the hearing of the motion, by examining the pleadings and the evidence before it and by interrogating counsel, shall if practicable ascertain what material facts exist without substantial controversy and what material facts are actually and in good faith controverted. It shall thereupon make an order specifying the facts that appear without substantial controversy, including the extent to which the amount of damages or other relief is not in controversy, and directing such further proceedings in the action as are just. Upon the trial of the action the facts so specified shall be deemed established, and the trial shall be conducted accordingly. IN ST TRIAL P Rule 56(D).

d.   *Form of affidavits; Further testimony; Defense required.* Supporting and opposing affidavits shall be made on personal knowledge, shall set forth such facts as would be admissible in evidence, and shall show affirmatively that the affiant is competent to testify to the matters stated therein. IN ST TRIAL P Rule 56(E).

    i.   Sworn or certified copies not previously self-authenticated of all papers or parts thereof referred to in an affidavit shall be attached thereto or served therewith. IN ST TRIAL P Rule 56(E).

    ii.   The court may permit affidavits to be supplemented or opposed by depositions, answers to interrogatories, or further affidavits. IN ST TRIAL P Rule 56(E).

    iii.   When a motion for summary judgment is made and supported as provided in IN ST TRIAL P

Rule 56, an adverse party may not rest upon the mere allegations or denials of his pleading, but his response, by affidavits or as otherwise provided in IN ST TRIAL P Rule 56, must set forth specific facts showing that there is a genuine issue for trial. If he does not so respond, summary judgment, if appropriate, shall be entered against him. Denial of summary judgment may be challenged by a motion to correct errors after a final judgment or order is entered. IN ST TRIAL P Rule 56(E).

e. *When affidavits are unavailable.* Should it appear from the affidavits of a party opposing the motion that he cannot for reasons stated present by affidavit facts essential to justify his opposition, the court may refuse the application for judgment or may order a continuance to permit affidavits to be obtained or depositions to be taken or discovery to be had or may make such other order as is just. IN ST TRIAL P Rule 56(F).

f. *Affidavits made in bad faith.* Should it appear to the satisfaction of the court at any time that any of the affidavits presented pursuant to IN ST TRIAL P Rule 56 are presented in bad faith or solely for the purpose of delay, the court shall forthwith order the party employing them to pay to the other party the amount of the reasonable expenses which the filing of the affidavits caused him to incur, including reasonable attorney's fees, and any offending party or attorney may be adjudged guilty of contempt. IN ST TRIAL P Rule 56(G).

g. *Party opposing the motion.* A party opposing the motion shall also designate to the court each material issue of fact which that party asserts precludes entry of summary judgment and the evidence relevant thereto. IN ST TRIAL P Rule 56(C).

h. *Appeal; Reversal.* No judgment rendered on the motion shall be reversed on the ground that there is a genuine issue of material fact unless the material fact and the evidence relevant thereto shall have been specifically designated to the trial court. IN ST TRIAL P Rule 56(H).

D. Documents

1. *Required documents*

    a. *Motion and notice.* The requirement of notice is satisfied by service of the motion. IN ST TRIAL P Rule 7(B). Refer to the General Requirements section of this document for information on the content of a motion for summary judgment.

    b. *Brief.* All motions filed pursuant to IN ST TRIAL P Rule 12 and IN ST TRIAL P Rule 56 shall be accompanied by a separate supporting brief. IN ST LAKE RCP Rule 4(A).

    c. *Supporting evidence.* At the time of filing the motion or response, a party shall designate to the court all parts of pleadings, depositions, answers to interrogatories, admissions, matters of judicial notice, and any other matters on which it relies for purposes of the motion. IN ST TRIAL P Rule 56(C).

        i. The party moving for judgment must designate sufficient evidence to establish that there is no genuine issue of material fact and that judgment is proper as a matter of law. 22B INPRAC 56:4; Jarboe v. Landmark Community Newspapers of Indiana, Inc., 644 N.E.2d 118 (Ind. 1994).

    d. *Proposed order.* Unless local practice provides differently, a party should submit a proposed order with its written motion to be signed by the judge once the motion has been granted. 21 INPRAC § 13.8.

        i. Proposed orders, which are submitted for the court's convenience under IN ST LAKE RCP Rule 3 or other applicable Lake County Rules of Civil Procedure, shall be submitted as attachments to motions. IN ST LAKE RCP Rule 17(D)(8). Proposed orders shall be prepared and filed separately from the pleadings, petitions, motions or other papers to which they have reference. IN ST LAKE RCP Rule 3(B).

        ii. Orders, either routine in nature or uncontested including, for example, those setting or continuing a hearing, shall be effected by the chronological case summary entry only, which shall contain the concise substance of the order. IN ST LAKE RCP Rule 3(B).

        iii. All orders shall be accompanied with sufficient copies and stamped, pre-addressed envelopes, so that copies may be mailed to all parties. IN ST LAKE RCP Rule 3(B).

e. *Chronological case summary (CCS) entry forms.* All filings shall be accompanied by a Chronological Case Summary (CCS) Entry Form to define or identify the documents filed. The Form used should be substantially similar to IN ST LAKE RCP App. A. IN ST LAKE RCP Rule 3(C).

f. *Certificate of service.* An attorney or unrepresented party tendering a document to the Clerk for filing shall certify that service has been made, list the parties served, and specify the date and means of service. The certificate of service shall be placed at the end of the document and shall not be separately filed. The separate filing of a certificate of service, however, shall not be grounds for rejecting a document for filing. The Clerk may permit documents to be filed without a certificate of service but shall require prompt filing of a separate certificate of service. IN ST TRIAL P Rule 5(C).

  i. All pleadings, motions and other papers submitted for filing which are required to be served under IN ST TRIAL P Rule 5(A) shall contain proof of service pursuant to IN ST TRIAL P Rule 5(B)(2). IN ST LAKE RCP Rule 3(A).

2. *Supplemental documents*

a. *Additional supporting evidence.* When a motion is based on facts not appearing of record the court may hear the matter on affidavits presented by the respective parties, but the court may direct that the matter be heard wholly or partly on oral testimony or depositions. IN ST TRIAL P Rule 43(B).

b. *Facsimile cover sheet.* Any document sent to the Clerk of the Circuit Court by electronic facsimile transmission shall be accompanied by a cover sheet which states the title of the document, case number, number of pages, identity and voice telephone number of the sending party and instructions for filing. The cover sheet shall contain the signature of the attorney or party, pro se, authorizing the filing. IN ST ADMIN Rule 12(D).

E. Format

1. *Form of motions.* The rules applicable to captions, and the signing and form of pleadings (IN ST TRIAL P Rule 8 through IN ST TRIAL P Rule 11), apply to all motions and other papers provided under the Indiana Rules of Trial Procedure. 22B INPRAC 7:2.

2. *Form of pleadings.* For the purpose of uniformity, convenience, clarity and durability, requirements in IN ST LAKE RCP Rule 2 shall be observed in the preparation of all pleadings, motions and other papers. IN ST LAKE RCP Rule 2. Whenever materials submitted fail to meet the standards in IN ST LAKE RCP Rule 2, the Court may impose appropriate sanctions. IN ST LAKE RCP Rule 2(B).

a. *Caption; Names of parties.* Every pleading shall contain a caption setting forth the name of the court, the title of the action, the file number, and a designation as in IN ST TRIAL P Rule 7(A). In the complaint the title of the action shall include the names of all the parties, but in other pleadings it is sufficient to state the name of the first party on each side with an appropriate indication of other parties. IN ST TRIAL P Rule 10(A).

  i. *Special judge matters.* The caption of all CCS Entry Forms, pleadings, motions, orders and other papers to be filed in a special judge case shall include in block text the words SPECIAL JUDGE and the name of the judge directly below the cause number on the caption. IN ST LAKE RCP Rule 2(D).

b. *Paragraphs; Separate statements.* All averments of a claim or defense shall be made in numbered paragraphs, the contents of each of which shall be limited as far as practicable to a statement of a single set of circumstances, and a paragraph may be referred to by number in all succeeding pleadings. Each claim founded upon a separate transaction or occurrence and each defense other than denials may be stated in a separate count or defense whenever a separation facilitates the clear presentation of the matters set forth. IN ST TRIAL P Rule 10(B).

c. *Adoption by reference; Exhibits.* Statements in a pleading may be adopted by reference in a different part of the same pleading or in another pleading or in any motion. A copy of any written instrument which is an exhibit to a pleading is a part thereof for all purposes. IN ST TRIAL P Rule 10(C).

d. *Paper; Print, quality and binding*

  i. All pleadings, motions, chronological case summary entry forms, orders, process and other papers shall be neatly and legibly printed, typewritten or mechanically reproduced, on one (1) side only, on white opaque paper. To satisfy the recordkeeping requirements of IN ST TRIAL P Rule 77, the print shall be of sufficient density and clarity for preservation and reproduction of microfilming, optical disk or other secondary sources. For this reason, the use of non-letter-quality printers is discouraged. IN ST LAKE RCP Rule 2(A).

    ii.   Paper and ink shall be of such quality as to withstand the test of time. All documents shall be produced on acid-free, non-thermal paper. It is recommended that a minimum of twenty (20) pound, twenty-five percent (25%) cotton paper product be used. Documents of multiple pages shall be submitted in bound or stapled fashion, and the binding or stapling shall be at the top only. Covers or backings shall not be used. IN ST LAKE RCP Rule 2(A).

  e. *Papers; Handwritten.* Handwritten papers may be filed only if approved by the Court and a typewritten or printed true rendition thereof is filed within three (3) days thereafter and approved by the Court. Upon such approval, they shall be deemed and filed as the original, while the handwritten papers shall be retained therewith for evidentiary purposes. IN ST LAKE RCP Rule 2(C).

  f. *Minute sheets; Motion blanks.* Minute sheets and motion blanks shall no longer be used. IN ST LAKE RCP Rule 2(D).

3. *Size of papers for filing.* Effective January 1, 1992, all pleadings, copies, motions and documents filed with any trial court or appellate level court, typed or printed, with the exception of exhibits and existing wills, shall be prepared on eight and one-half by eleven inch (8 1/2" x 11") size paper. IN ST ADMIN Rule 11.

4. *Signature requirements*

  a. *Signature of attorney.* Every pleading or motion of a party represented by an attorney shall be signed by at least one (1) attorney of record in his individual name, whose address, telephone number, and attorney number shall be stated, except that this provision shall not apply to pleadings and motions made and transcribed at the trial or a hearing before the judge and received by him in such form. IN ST TRIAL P Rule 11(A).

    i.   The signature of an attorney constitutes a certificate by him that he has read the pleadings; that to the best of his knowledge, information, and belief, there is good ground to support it; and that it is not interposed for delay. IN ST TRIAL P Rule 11(A).

    ii. If a pleading or motion is not signed or is signed with intent to defeat the purpose of the rule, it may be stricken as sham and false and the action may proceed as though the pleading had not been served. IN ST TRIAL P Rule 11(A).

    iii. For a willful violation of IN ST TRIAL P Rule 11 an attorney may be subjected to appropriate disciplinary action. Similar action may be taken if scandalous or indecent matter is inserted. IN ST TRIAL P Rule 11(A).

  b. *Signature of unrepresented party.* A party who is not represented by an attorney shall sign his pleading and state his address. IN ST TRIAL P Rule 11(A).

  c. *Verification not generally required.* Except when specifically required by rule, pleadings or motions need not be verified or accompanied by affidavit. The rule in equity that the averments of an answer under oath must be overcome by the testimony of two (2) witnesses or of one (1) witness sustained by corroborating circumstances is abolished. IN ST TRIAL P Rule 11(A).

  d. *Verification by affirmation or representation.* When in connection with any civil or special statutory proceeding it is required that any pleading, motion, petition, supporting affidavit, or other document of any kind, be verified, or that an oath be taken, it shall be sufficient if the subscriber simply affirms the truth of the matter to be verified by an affirmation or representation. IN ST TRIAL P Rule 11(B). IN ST TRIAL P Rule 11(B) states that the affirmation or representation should be in substantially the following language: "I (we) affirm, under the penalties for perjury, that the foregoing representation(s) is (are) true. (Signed) _____."

    i.   Any person who falsifies an affirmation or representation of fact shall be subject to the same penalties as are prescribed by law for the making of a false affidavit. IN ST TRIAL P Rule 11(B).

e. *Verified pleadings, motions, and affidavits as evidence.* Pleadings, motions and affidavits accompanying or in support of such pleadings or motions when required to be verified or under oath shall be accepted as a representation that the signer had personal knowledge thereof or reasonable cause to believe the existence of the facts or matters stated or alleged therein; and, if otherwise competent or acceptable as evidence, may be admitted as evidence of the facts or matters stated or alleged therein when it is so provided in the Indiana Rules of Trial Procedure, by statute or other law, or to the extent the writing or signature expressly purports to be made upon the signer's personal knowledge. When such pleadings, motions and affidavits are verified or under oath they shall not require other or greater proof on the part of the adverse party than if not verified or not under oath unless expressly provided otherwise by the Indiana Rules of Trial Procedure, statute or other law. Affidavits upon motions for summary judgment under IN ST TRIAL P Rule 56 and in denial of execution under IN ST TRIAL P Rule 9.2 shall be made upon personal knowledge. IN ST TRIAL P Rule 11(C).

f. *Electronic signature.* The filing of documents and information through the E-filing system by use of a valid username and password is presumed to have been authorized by the User to whom that username and password have been issued and documents filed through the E-filing system are presumed to have been signed by the same User. IN ST ADMIN Rule 16(E).

5. *Information excluded from public access.* Every document filed in a case shall separately identify information excluded from public access pursuant to IN ST ADMIN Rule 9(G)(1) as follows:

a. Whole documents that are excluded from public access pursuant to IN ST ADMIN Rule 9(G)(1) shall be tendered on light green paper or have a light green coversheet attached to the document, marked "Not for Public Access" or "Confidential." IN ST TRIAL P Rule 5(G)(1).

b. When only a portion of a document contains information excluded from public access pursuant to IN ST ADMIN Rule 9(G)(1), said information shall be omitted [or redacted] from the filed document, and set forth on a separate accompanying document on light green paper conspicuously marked "Not for Public Access" or "Confidential" and clearly designated [or identifying] the caption and number of the case and the document and location within the document to which the redacted material pertains. IN ST TRIAL P Rule 5(G)(2).

c. With respect to documents filed in electronic format, the trial court, by local rule, may provide for compliance with IN ST TRIAL P Rule 5 in manner that separates and protects access to information excluded from public access. IN ST TRIAL P Rule 5(G)(3).

d. IN ST TRIAL P Rule 5(G) does not apply to a record sealed by the court pursuant to IN ST 5-14-3-5.5 or otherwise, nor to records, documents, or information filed in cases to which public access is prohibited pursuant to IN ST ADMIN Rule 9(G). IN ST TRIAL P Rule 5(G)(4).

e. The following information in case records is excluded from public access and is confidential:

i. Information that is excluded from public access pursuant to federal law;

ii. Information that is excluded from public access as declared confidential by Indiana statute or other court rule, including without limitation:

- All adoption records created after July 8, 1941, as declared confidential by IN ST 31-19-19-1, et seq., except those specifically declared open by IN ST 31-19-13-2(2);

- All records relating to chancroid, chlamydia, gonorrhea, hepatitis, human immunodeficiency virus (HIV), Lymphogranuloma venereum, syphilis, tuberculosis, as declared confidential by IN ST 16-41-8-1, et seq.;

- All records relating to child abuse as declared confidential by IN ST 31-33-18-1, et seq.;

- All records relating to drug tests as declared confidential by IN ST 5-14-3-4(a)(9);

- Records of grand jury proceedings as declared confidential by IN ST 35-34-2-4;

- Records of juvenile proceedings as declared confidential by IN ST 31-39-1-2, except those specifically open under statute;

- All paternity records created after July 1, 1941 as declared confidential by IN ST 31-14-11-15, IN ST 31-19-5-23, IN ST 31-39-1-1 and IN ST 31-39-1-2 [Editor's note: IN ST 31-14-11-15 was repealed effective May 9, 2013];

- All pre-sentence reports as declared confidential by IN ST 35-38-1-13;
- Written petitions to permit marriages without consent and orders directing the Clerk of Court to issue a marriage license to underage persons, as declared confidential by IN ST 31-11-1-6;
- Only those arrest warrants, search warrants, indictments and informations ordered confidential by the trial judge, prior to return of duly executed service as declared confidential by IN ST 5-14-3-4(b)(1);
- All medical, mental health, or tax records unless determined by law or regulation of any governmental custodian not to be confidential, released by the subject of such records, or declared by a court of competent jurisdiction to be essential to the resolution of litigation as declared confidential by IN ST 16-39-3-10, IN ST 6-4.1-5-10, IN ST 6-4.1-12-12, and IN ST 6-8.1-7-1;
- Personal information relating to jurors or prospective jurors, other than for the use of the parties and counsel, pursuant to IN ST JURY Rule 10;
- Information relating to protection from abuse orders, no-contact orders and workplace violence restraining orders as declared confidential by IN ST 5-2-9-6, et seq.;
- Mediation proceedings pursuant to IN ST ADR Rule 2.11, Mini-Trial proceedings pursuant to IN ST ADR Rule 4.4(C), and Summary Jury Trials pursuant to IN ST ADR Rule 5.6;
- Information in probation files pursuant to the Probation Standards promulgated by the Judicial Conference of Indiana pursuant to IN ST 11-13-1-8(b);
- Information deemed confidential pursuant to the Rules for Court Administered Alcohol and Drug Programs promulgated by the Judicial Conference of Indiana pursuant to IN ST 12-23-14-13;
- Information deemed confidential pursuant to the Problem-Solving Court Rules promulgated by the Judicial Conference of Indiana pursuant to IN ST 33-23-16-16;
- All records of the Department of workforce Development as declared confidential by IN ST 22-4-19-6;
- Information regarding interception of electronic communications that is sealed or deemed confidential as set forth in IN ST 35-33.5-2-1, et seq.

iii. Information excluded from public access by specific court order;

iv. Complete Social Security Numbers of living persons;

v. With the exception of names, information such as addresses, phone numbers, and dates of birth which explicitly identifies:

- Natural persons who are witnesses or victims (not including defendants) in criminal, domestic violence, stalking, sexual assault, juvenile, or civil protection order proceedings, provided that juveniles who are victims of sex crimes shall be identified by initials only;
- Places of residence of judicial officers, clerks and other employees of courts and clerks of court, unless the person or persons about whom the information pertains waives confidentiality;

vi. Complete account numbers of specific assets, loans, bank accounts, credit cards, and personal identification numbers (PINs);

vii. All orders of expungement entered in criminal or juvenile proceedings, orders to restrict access to criminal history information pursuant to IN ST 35-38-5-5.5 or IN ST 35-38-8-5 and records excluded from public access by such orders, and information related to infractions that is excluded from public access pursuant to IN ST 34-28-5-15 or IN ST 34-28-5-16 [Editor's note: IN ST 35-38-5-5.5, IN ST 35-38-8-5 and IN ST 34-28-5-16 were repealed effective July 1, 2013; for information on orders restricting access to criminal history, refer to IN ST 35-38-9-1, et seq.];

viii. All personal notes and e-mail, and deliberative material, of judges, jurors, court staff and judicial agencies, and information recorded in personal data assistants (PDA's) or organizers and personal calendars. IN ST ADMIN Rule 9(G)(1).

6. *Format of electronically filed documents*

   a. *Generally.* Electronically filed documents must meet the same requirements of format as documents conventionally filed pursuant to IN ST LAKE RCP Rule 2 or other applicable Lake County Rules of Civil Procedure. IN ST LAKE RCP Rule 17(D)(1).

   b. *Titles of documents.* The person electronically filing a document will be responsible for designating a title for the document at the time it is filed. The LCOD will generate the appropriate entry onto the CCS to record the filing of the document. IN ST LAKE RCP Rule 17(D)(3).

   c. *Citations and hyperlinks.* Electronically filed documents may contain hyperlink references to an external document as a convenient mechanism for accessing material cited in the document. Filers wishing to insert hyperlinks into documents shall continue to use the traditional method of citation to authority in addition to the hyperlink provided. The hyperlink is merely a convenience to the court and the material referenced is extraneous to the file and not a part of the court's record. IN ST LAKE RCP Rule 17(D)(5).

   d. *Attachments and exhibits.* All documents which form part of a single submission and which are being filed at the same time and by the same filer may be electronically filed together under one document filing, e.g., the motion, supporting affidavits, memorandum in support, designation of evidence, exhibits. IN ST LAKE RCP Rule 17(D)(6).

      i. Large documents which do not exist in an electronic format shall be scanned into .pdf format and filed electronically as separate attachments. A scanner is available in each clerk's office for use by the public and the bar in scanning and saving image files if needed. IN ST LAKE RCP Rule 17(D)(6).

   e. *Electronic signatures*

      i. *Electronic filing as signature.* The electronic filing of a document which is required to be signed shall constitute the filer's representation under IN ST TRIAL P Rule 11. Unless the electronically filed document has been scanned and shows the filer's original signature, the signature of the filer shall be indicated by As/Attorney's Name, or As/Party's Name as in the case of a pro se litigant, on the line where the signature would otherwise appear. IN ST LAKE RCP Rule 17(G)(1).

      ii. *Signatures on jointly signed or filed, verified or other documents.* In the case of a stipulation, agreed order, jointly signed motion or other document which needs to be signed by two (2) or more persons, or in the case of documents which must contain original signatures and which require verification or an unsworn declaration under rule or statute, the signatures may be indicated by either:

         • Submitting a scanned copy of the originally signed document; or,

         • Submitting the document with the use of As/Name in the signature block(s) where the original signature(s) appear(s) in the original document; provided, however, that the filer shall first obtain the physical signature of all persons necessary. IN ST LAKE RCP Rule 17(G)(2).

      iii. *Retention of original.* The filer shall retain the original executed document. IN ST LAKE RCP Rule 17(G).

7. *Citation of local rules.* The local rules for Lake County may be known as the Lake County Rules of Civil Procedure, and abbreviated as LR. IN ST LAKE RCP Rule 1(C).

F. Filing and Service Requirements

1. *Filing requirements.* Except as otherwise provided in IN ST TRIAL P Rule 5(E)(2), all pleadings and papers subsequent to the complaint which are required to be served upon a party shall be filed with the Court either before service or within a reasonable period of time thereafter. IN ST TRIAL P Rule 5(E)(1). All papers presented for filing shall be submitted to the Clerk and not to the court. All papers submitted

for filing shall be mailed or delivered to the Clerk's office at the courthouse in which the case is pending. IN ST LAKE RCP Rule 3(A).

a. *Filing with the court defined.* The filing of pleadings, motions, and other papers with the court as required by the Indiana Rules of Trial Procedure shall be made by one of the following methods:

   i. Delivery to the clerk of the court;

   ii. Sending by electronic transmission under the procedure adopted pursuant to IN ST ADMIN Rule 12;

   iii. Mailing to the clerk by registered, certified or express mail return receipt requested;

   iv. Depositing with any third-party commercial carrier for delivery to the clerk within three (3) calendar days, cost prepaid, properly addressed;

   v. If the court so permits, filing with the judge, in which event the judge shall note thereon the filing date and forthwith transmit them to the office of the clerk; or

   vi. Electronic filing, as approved by the Division of State Court Administration pursuant to IN ST ADMIN Rule 16. IN ST TRIAL P Rule 5(F).

   vii. Filing by registered or certified mail and by third-party commercial carrier shall be complete upon mailing or deposit. IN ST TRIAL P Rule 5(F).

b. *Mandatory electronic filing.* Unless otherwise permitted by the Lake County Rules of Civil Procedure or otherwise authorized by the judicial officer assigned to a particular case, all documents submitted for filing (including the original complaint, or equivalent pleading, and summons) shall be filed electronically with the clerk using the LCOD, no matter when the case was originally filed. IN ST LAKE RCP Rule 17(D).

   i. *Of documents containing information excluded from public access pursuant to* IN ST ADMIN Rule 9. Documents containing information excluded from public access pursuant to IN ST ADMIN Rule 9, or documents which are ordered to be filed under seal shall be filed electronically, pursuant to IN ST LAKE RCP Rule 17(D)(9), whenever possible, along with a copy of the applicable order to seal the records, and the filer shall designate the documents as "Not for Public Access Pursuant to Administrative Rule 9(G)(1)" at the time of filing. IN ST LAKE RCP Rule 16(A)(1); IN ST LAKE RCP Rule 17(D)(9).

      • *Conventional filing of documents containing information excluded from public access pursuant to* IN ST ADMIN Rule 9. Documents containing information excluded from public access pursuant to IN ST ADMIN Rule 9, or documents which are ordered to be filed under seal, which cannot be legibly scanned and filed electronically, shall be conventionally filed under seal and designated by the filer as "Not for Public Access Pursuant to Administrative Rule 9(G)(1)" at the time of filing. The unredacted version shall be filed on light green paper which is conspicuously marked "Not for Public Access"; and a redacted version, with confidential information deleted, shall be filed on white paper which shall be available for public access. The filer shall also electronically file a Notice of Manual Filing. IN ST LAKE RCP Rule 16(A)(2).

   ii. *Technical failures.* If a registered user is unable to file a document in a timely manner due to technical difficulties in the LCOD, the registered user must file a document with the court as soon as possible notifying the court of the inability to file the document. A sample document titled Declaration that Party was Unable to File in a Timely Manner Due to Technical Difficulties can be found at IN ST LAKE RCP Form 4. Delayed filings shall be rejected unless accompanied by the declaration attesting to the filer's failed attempts to file electronically at least two (2) times, separated by at least one (1) hour, after noon on each day of delay due to such technical failure. IN ST LAKE RCP Rule 17(J).

   iii. *Documents allowed to be filed conventionally.* Unless specifically authorized by the court, only the following documents may be filed conventionally and not electronically:

      • Exhibits and other documents that cannot be converted to a legible electronic form, such as videotapes, x-rays, and similar materials

- Documents delivered to the clerk by pro se litigants
- Documents mailed to the clerk by pro se litigants
- Confidential documents
- Notice of manual filing
- Titles of documents
- Chronological case summary entry forms (CCS entry forms). IN ST LAKE RCP Rule 17(E).
- For more information on the documents which must be filed conventionally, refer to IN ST LAKE RCP Rule 17(E).

c. *Facsimile filing.* Only when necessary on an emergency basis (i.e., when certified mail or other means of filing will not bring the document to the Judge's attention prior to the scheduled hearing or ruling), pleadings, motions and other papers may be filed by electronic facsimile transmission, or when specifically authorized by the Court. IN ST LAKE RCP Rule 2(C).

    i. *Generally.* In counties where a majority of judges of the courts of record, by posted local rule, have authorized electronic facsimile filing and designated a telephone number to receive such transmissions, pleadings, motions, and other papers may be sent to the Clerk of Circuit Court by electronic facsimile transmission for filing in any case, provided:

- Such matter does not exceed ten (10) pages, including the cover sheet;
- Such matter does not require the payment of fees other than the electronic facsimile transcription fee set forth in IN ST ADMIN Rule 12(E);
- The sending party creates at the time of transmission a machine generated log for such transmission; and
- The original document and the transmission log are maintained by the sending party for the duration of the litigation. IN ST ADMIN Rule 12(B).

    ii. *Time of filing.* During normal, posted business hours, the time of filing shall be the time the duplicate document is produced in the office of the Clerk of the Circuit Court. Duplicate documents received at all other times shall be filed as of the next normal business day. IN ST ADMIN Rule 12(C).

- If the receiving fax machine endorses its own time and date stamp upon the transmitted documents and the receiving machine produces a delivery receipt which is electronically created and transmitted to the sending party, the time of filing shall be the date and time recorded on the transmitted document by the receiving fax machine. IN ST ADMIN Rule 12(C).

d. *Filing for special judges.* For special judge matters where the special judge is a full-time judge or magistrate serving within Lake County, all papers submitted for filing shall be delivered or mailed to the Clerk's office at the courthouse where the special judge regularly serves. IN ST LAKE RCP Rule 3(A).

e. *Proof of filing.* Any party filing any paper by any method other than personal delivery to the clerk shall retain proof of filing. IN ST TRIAL P Rule 5(F).

2. *Service requirements.* Unless otherwise provided by the Indiana Rules of Trial Procedure or an order of the court, each party and special judge, if any, shall be served with: (1) every order required by its terms to be served; (2) every pleading subsequent to the original complaint; (3) every written motion except one which may be heard ex parte; (4) every brief submitted to the trial court; (5) every paper relating to discovery required to be served upon a party; and (6) every written notice, appearance, demand, offer of judgment, designation of record on appeal, or similar paper. IN ST TRIAL P Rule 5(A).

a. *Methods of service*

    i. *Personal service.* Whenever a party is represented by an attorney of record, service shall be made upon such attorney unless service upon the party himself is ordered by the court. Service

upon the attorney or party shall be made by delivering or mailing a copy of the papers to the last known address or where an attorney or party has consented to service by fax or e-mail, as provided in IN ST TRIAL P Rule 3.1(A)(4), by faxing or e-mailing a copy of the documents to the fax number or e-mail address set out in the appearance form or correction as required by IN ST TRIAL P Rule 3.1(E). IN ST TRIAL P Rule 5(B). Delivery of a copy within IN ST TRIAL P Rule 5 means:

- Offering or tendering it to the attorney or party and stating the nature of the papers being served. Refusal to accept an offered or tendered document is a waiver of any objection to the sufficiency or adequacy of service of that document;

- Leaving it at his office with a clerk or other person in charge thereof, or if there is no one in charge, leaving it in a conspicuous place therein; or

- If the office is closed, by leaving it at his dwelling house or usual place of abode with some person of suitable age and discretion then residing therein; or,

- Leaving it at some other suitable place, selected by the attorney upon whom service is being made, pursuant to duly promulgated local rule. IN ST TRIAL P Rule 5(B)(1).

ii. *Service by mail.* If service is made by mail, the papers shall be deposited in the United States mail addressed to the person on whom they are being served, with postage prepaid. Service shall be deemed complete upon mailing. Proof of service of all papers permitted to be mailed may be made by written acknowledgment of service, by affidavit of the person who mailed the papers, or by certificate of an attorney. It shall be the duty of attorneys when entering their appearance in a cause or when filing pleadings or papers therein, to have noted in the Chronological Case Summary or said pleadings or papers so filed the address and telephone number of their office. Service by delivery or by mail at such address shall be deemed sufficient and complete. IN ST TRIAL P Rule 5(B)(2).

iii. *Service by fax or e-mail.* A party who has consented to service by fax or e-mail may be served as follows:

- Service by e-mail shall be made by attaching the document being served in .pdf format. Discovery documents must also be served in accordance with IN ST TRIAL P Rule 26(A). IN ST TRIAL P Rule 5(B)(3)(a).

- Service by fax shall be deemed complete upon generation of a transmission record indicating the successful transmission of the entire document, except as provided in IN ST TRIAL P Rule 5(B)(3)(d). IN ST TRIAL P Rule 5(B)(3)(b).

- Service by e-mail shall be deemed complete upon transmission, except as provided in IN ST TRIAL P Rule 5(B)(3)(d). IN ST TRIAL P Rule 5(B)(3)(c).

- Service by fax or e-mail that occurs on a Saturday, Sunday, legal holiday, or day the court or agency in which the matter is pending is closed or after 5:00 PM local time of the recipient shall be deemed complete the next day that is not a Saturday, Sunday, legal holiday, or day that the court or agency in which the matter is pending is not closed. IN ST TRIAL P Rule 5(B)(3)(d).

b. *Serving numerous defendants.* In any action in which there are unusually large numbers of defendants, the court, upon motion or of its own initiative, may order:

i. That service of the pleadings of the defendants and replies thereto need not be made as between the defendants;

- That any cross-claim, counterclaim, or matter constituting an avoidance or affirmative defense contained therein shall be deemed to be denied or avoided by all other parties; and

- That the filing of any such pleading and service thereof upon the plaintiff constitutes due notice of it to the parties. IN ST TRIAL P Rule 5(D).

ii. A copy of every such order shall be served upon the parties in such manner and form as the court directs. IN ST TRIAL P Rule 5(D).

c. *Service by electronic means.* The Lake County Online Docket will generate a Notice of Electronic

Filing and Service when any document is filed and served. This notice will be emailed to each registered user of record in a case, and an electronic service event will be added to the work queue of each registered user of record in the case. The party filing the document should retain a paper or electronic copy of the Notice of Electronic Filing and Service. This notice represents proof of filing and service of the document on registered users of record in that case. The filer shall not be required to conventionally serve any document on any party receiving electronic service. IN ST LAKE RCP Rule 17(F)(2).

    i.   The filer shall also conventionally serve those parties not designated or able to receive electronic notice or service but who are nevertheless entitled to notice of said pleading or other document in accordance with the Indiana Rules of Civil Procedure and applicable Lake County Rules of Civil Procedure. In such cases, the filer shall also file a certificate of service, as appropriate. IN ST LAKE RCP Rule 17(F).

d.   *Service on parties in default for failure to appear.* No service need be made on parties in default for failure to appear, except that pleadings asserting new or additional claims for relief against them shall be served upon them in the manner provided by service of summons in IN ST TRIAL P Rule 4. IN ST TRIAL P Rule 5(A).

G. Hearings

1.   *Hearing on motion.* Unless local conditions make it impracticable, each judge shall establish regular times and places, at intervals sufficiently frequent for the prompt dispatch of business, at which motions requiring notice and hearing may be heard and disposed of; but the judge at any time or place and on such notice, if any, as he considers reasonable may make order for the advancement, conduct, and hearing of actions. To expedite its business the court may direct the submission and determination of motions without oral hearing upon brief written statements of reasons in support and opposition, or direct or permit hearings by telephone conference call with all attorneys or other similar means of communication. IN ST TRIAL P Rule 73(A).

2.   *Hearing on summary judgment.* The court may conduct a hearing on the motion. However, upon motion of any party made no later than ten (10) days after the response was filed or was due, the court shall conduct a hearing on the motion which shall be held not less than ten (10) days after the time for filing the response. IN ST TRIAL P Rule 56(C).

3.   *Oral argument discretionary.* The granting of a motion for oral argument, unless required by the Indiana Rules of Trial Procedure, shall be wholly discretionary with the court. IN ST LAKE RCP Rule 4(B).

H. Forms

1. Motion for Summary Judgment Forms for Indiana

a.   Notice of motion for summary judgment. 11 INPRAC § 90.2.

b.   Motion for summary judgment. 11 INPRAC § 90.3.

c.   Motion for summary judgment; Another form. 11 INPRAC § 90.4.

d.   Motion for summary judgment; Another form. 11 INPRAC § 90.5.

e.   Designation of materials relied upon in support of motion for summary judgment. 11 INPRAC § 90.6.

f.   Designation of material issues of fact that preclude entry of summary judgment. 11 INPRAC § 90.7.

g.   Response to statement of material issues of fact that preclude entry of summary judgment. 11 INPRAC § 90.8.

h.   Order granting motion for summary judgment. 11 INPRAC § 90.9.

i.   Order denying motion for summary judgment. 11 INPRAC § 90.10.

j.   Motion for partial summary judgment as to liability. 11 INPRAC § 90.11.

k.   Order for partial summary judgment as to liability. 11 INPRAC § 90.12.

l.   Order denying summary judgment and specifying issues. 11 INPRAC § 90.15.

m.   Affidavit in support of motion for summary judgment. 11 INPRAC § 90.16.

n. Submission of proposed findings of fact, conclusions of law and proposed summary judgment. 11 INPRAC § 90.17.

o. Findings of fact and conclusions of law in support of motion for summary judgment. 11 INPRAC § 90.18.

p. Motion for hearing on motion for summary judgment. 11 INPRAC § 90.27.

q. Certificate of service; Personal service. 9 INPRAC § 5.7.

r. Certificate of service; First class mail. 9 INPRAC § 5.8.

2. **Official Motion for Summary Judgment Forms for Lake County**

a. CCS entry form. IN ST LAKE RCP App. A.

b. Notice of manual filing. IN ST LAKE RCP Form 2.

c. Certificate of service. IN ST LAKE RCP Form 3.

d. Declaration that party was unable to file in a timely manner. IN ST LAKE RCP Form 4.

3. **Motion for Summary Judgment Forms for Lake County**

a. Notice of manual filing. EFORMST IN 5540.

I. Checklist

(I) ❑ Matters to be considered by moving party

   (a) ❑ Required documents

      (1) ❑ Motion and notice

      (2) ❑ Brief

      (3) ❑ Supporting evidence

      (4) ❑ Proposed order

      (5) ❑ Chronological case summary (CSS) entry forms

      (6) ❑ Certificate of service

   (b) ❑ Supplemental documents

      (1) ❑ Additional supporting evidence

      (2) ❑ Facsimile cover sheet

   (c) ❑ Timing

      (1) ❑ A party seeking to recover upon a claim, counterclaim, or cross-claim or to obtain a declaratory judgment may, at any time after the expiration of twenty (20) days from the commencement of the action or after service of a motion for summary judgment by the adverse party, move with or without supporting affidavits for a summary judgment in his favor upon all or any part thereof

      (2) ❑ A party against whom a claim, counterclaim, or cross-claim is asserted or a declaratory judgment is sought may, at any time, move with or without supporting affidavits for a summary judgment in his favor as to all or any part thereof

      (3) ❑ A written motion, other than one which may be heard ex parte, and notice of the hearing thereof shall be served not less than five (5) days before the time specified for the hearing, unless a different period is fixed by the Indiana Rules of Trial Procedure or by order of the court

      (4) ❑ All pleadings and papers subsequent to the complaint which are required to be served upon a party shall be filed with the Court either before service or within a reasonable period of time thereafter

      (5) ❑ All pleadings, motions and other papers submitted for filing which are required to be served under IN ST TRIAL P Rule 5(A) shall be filed no later than three (3) days after service

(6) ❑ If such papers are filed before service, proof of service thereof shall be filed no later than three (3) business days thereafter

(II) ❑ Matters to be considered by the responding party

   (a) ❑ Required documents

      (1) ❑ Opposition

      (2) ❑ Opposing evidence

      (3) ❑ Chronological case summary (CSS) entry forms

      (4) ❑ Certificate of service

   (b) ❑ Supplemental documents

      (1) ❑ Additional evidence

      (2) ❑ Proposed order

      (3) ❑ Facsimile cover sheet

   (c) ❑ Timing

      (1) ❑ An adverse party shall have thirty (30) days after service of the motion to serve a response and any opposing affidavits

      (2) ❑ An adverse party shall have thirty (30) days after service of the initial brief in which to serve and file an answer brief

      (3) ❑ Except as otherwise provided in IN ST TRIAL P Rule 59(D), opposing affidavits may be served not less than one (1) day before the hearing, unless the court permits them to be served at some other time

Motions, Oppositions and Replies
Motion for Sanctions

Document Last Updated October 2013

A. Applicable Rules

1. *State rules*

   a. Appearance. IN ST TRIAL P Rule 3.1.

   b. Process. IN ST TRIAL P Rule 4.

   c. Service and filing of pleadings and other papers. IN ST TRIAL P Rule 5.

   d. Time. IN ST TRIAL P Rule 6.

   e. Pleadings. IN ST TRIAL P Rule 7; IN ST TRIAL P Rule 8; IN ST TRIAL P Rule 9.2; IN ST TRIAL P Rule 10.

   f. Signing and verification of pleadings. IN ST TRIAL P Rule 11.

   g. Evidence. IN ST TRIAL P Rule 43.

   h. Judgment on the evidence (directed verdict). IN ST TRIAL P Rule 50.

   i. Findings by the court. IN ST TRIAL P Rule 52.

   j. Summary judgment. IN ST TRIAL P Rule 56.

   k. Motion to correct error. IN ST TRIAL P Rule 59.

   l. Relief from judgment or order. IN ST TRIAL P Rule 60.

   m. Hearing of motions. IN ST TRIAL P Rule 73.

   n. Access to court records. IN ST ADMIN Rule 9.

   o. Paper size. IN ST ADMIN Rule 11.

p. Facsimile transmission. IN ST ADMIN Rule 12.

q. Electronic filing and electronic service pilot projects. IN ST ADMIN Rule 16.

r. Privacy and confidentiality. IN ST 5-2-9-6; IN ST 5-14-3-4; IN ST 5-14-3-5.5; IN ST 6-4.1-5-10; IN ST 6-4.1-12-12; IN ST 6-8.1-7-1; IN ST 11-13-1-8; IN ST 12-23-14-13; IN ST 16-39-3-10; IN ST 16-41-8-1; IN ST 22-4-19-6; IN ST 31-11-1-6; IN ST 31-19-5-23; IN ST 31-19-13-2; IN ST 31-19-19-1; IN ST 31-33-18-1; IN ST 31-39-1-1; IN ST 31-39-1-2; IN ST 33-23-16-16; IN ST 35-34-2-4; IN ST 35-38-1-13; IN ST 35-38-9-1; IN ST ADR Rule 2.11; IN ST ADR Rule 4.4; IN ST ADR Rule 5.6; IN ST JURY Rule 10.

s. General recovery rule. IN ST 34-52-1-1.

2. *Local rules*

a. Scope and title. [IN ST LAKE RCP Rule 1, as amended by IN ORDER 13-0237, effective October 18, 2013].

b. Preparation of pleadings, motions and other papers. IN ST LAKE RCP Rule 2.

c. Filing. [IN ST LAKE RCP Rule 3, as amended by IN ORDER 13-0237, effective October 18, 2013].

d. Motions. IN ST LAKE RCP Rule 4.

e. Pretrial procedure. IN ST LAKE RCP Rule 9.

f. Briefs. IN ST LAKE RCP Rule 11.

g. Confidential information and sealed documents. IN ST LAKE RCP Rule 16.

h. Electronic filing and service. IN ST LAKE RCP Rule 17.

B. Timing

1. *Motion for sanctions.* There are no specific time requirements for when a party may file a motion for sanctions.

    a. *Filing.* All pleadings and papers subsequent to the complaint which are required to be served upon a party shall be filed with the Court either before service or within a reasonable period of time thereafter. IN ST TRIAL P Rule 5(E)(1). All pleadings, motions and other papers submitted for filing which are required to be served under IN ST TRIAL P Rule 5(A) shall be filed no later than three (3) days after service. IN ST LAKE RCP Rule 3(A).

        i. If such papers are filed before service, proof of service thereof shall be filed no later than three (3) business days thereafter. Upon failure to comply with IN ST LAKE RCP Rule 3, the Court may, on motion of any party or on its own motion, impose appropriate sanctions. IN ST LAKE RCP Rule 3(A).

    b. *Briefs.* Briefs, other than those addressed in IN ST LAKE RCP Rule 4 and IN ST LAKE RCP Rule 9, shall be filed no later than two (2) calendar days preceding the hearing or trial to which directed. IN ST LAKE RCP Rule 11.

2. *Service.* A written motion, other than one which may be heard ex parte, and notice of the hearing thereof shall be served not less than five (5) days before the time specified for the hearing, unless a different period is fixed by the Indiana Rules of Trial Procedure or by order of the court. IN ST TRIAL P Rule 6(D).

    a. *Of supporting affidavits.* When a motion is supported by affidavit, the affidavit shall be served with the motion. IN ST TRIAL P Rule 6(D).

3. *Service of opposition.* Except as otherwise provided in IN ST TRIAL P Rule 59(D), opposing affidavits may be served not less than one (1) day before the hearing, unless the court permits them to be served at some other time. IN ST TRIAL P Rule 6(D).

    a. So long as consistent with the Indiana Rules of Trial Procedure, an adverse party wishing to respond shall do so within fifteen (15) days of service. IN ST LAKE RCP Rule 4(A).

4. *Reply.* The moving party shall have ten (10) days after service of the response within which to reply. IN ST LAKE RCP Rule 4(A).

5. *Computation of time*

    a. *Generally; Days excluded.* In computing any period of time prescribed or allowed by the Indiana

Rules of Trial Procedure, by order of the court, or by any applicable statute, the day of the act, event, or default from which the designated period of time begins to run shall not be included. The last day of the period so computed is to be included unless it is:

    i.   A Saturday,

    ii.   A Sunday,

    iii.   A legal holiday as defined by state statute, or

    iv.   A day the office in which the act is to be done is closed during regular business hours. IN ST TRIAL P Rule 6(A).

   b.   *Short periods.* In any event, the period runs until the end of the next day that is not a Saturday, a Sunday, a legal holiday, or a day on which the office is closed. When the period of time allowed is less than seven (7) days, intermediate Saturdays, Sundays, legal holidays, and days on which the office is closed shall be excluded from the computations. IN ST TRIAL P Rule 6(A).

   c.   *Additional time after service by United States mail.* Whenever a party has the right or is required to do some act or take some proceedings within a prescribed period after the service of a notice or other paper upon him and the notice or paper is served upon him by United States mail, three (3) days shall be added to the prescribed period. IN ST TRIAL P Rule 6(E).

   d.   *Electronic filing does not alter deadlines.* Filing electronically does not alter any filing deadlines or any time computation pursuant to state or federal statutes, any Rules of the Indiana Supreme Court, including without limitation the Rules of Trial Procedure, the Rules of Appellate Procedure or the Administrative Rules, or applicable Lake County Rules of Civil Procedure. The office of the Lake County Clerk is open for electronic filing under the Lake County Rules of Civil Procedure twenty-four (24) hours a day. A document is deemed filed at the date and time it is received by the LCOD server. Filing must be completed before midnight local time in order to be considered filed that day. Lake County observes Central Time and electronic filers are strongly urged to file documents during hours when the Lake County Online Docket ("LCOD") help line is available, from 9:00 a.m. to 4:00 p.m. local time, although documents can be filed electronically twenty-four (24) hours a day. IN ST LAKE RCP Rule 17(I).

   e.   *Enlargement of time.* When an act is required or allowed to be done at or within a specific time by the Indiana Rules of Trial Procedure, the court may at any time for cause shown:

      i.   Order the period enlarged, with or without motion or notice, if request therefor is made before the expiration of the period originally prescribed or extended by a previous order; or

      ii.   Upon motion made after the expiration of the specific period, permit the act to be done where the failure to act was the result of excusable neglect; but, the court may not extend the time for taking any action for judgment on the evidence under IN ST TRIAL P Rule 50(A), amendment of findings and judgment under IN ST TRIAL P Rule 52(B), to correct errors under IN ST TRIAL P Rule 59(C), statement in opposition to motion to correct error under IN ST TRIAL P Rule 59(E), or to obtain relief from final judgment under IN ST TRIAL P Rule 60(B), except to the extent and under the conditions stated in those rules. IN ST TRIAL P Rule 6(B).

C. General Requirements

1.   *Motions, generally.* Unless made during a hearing or trial, or otherwise ordered by the court, an application to the court for an order shall be made by written motion. The motion shall state the grounds therefor and the relief or order sought. IN ST TRIAL P Rule 7(B).

   a.   *Motions as distinct from pleadings.* Motions and responses to motions are not pleadings, and allegations contained in a motion are not admissions of a party. 22B INPRAC 7:2; Wachstetter v. County Properties, LLC, 832 N.E.2d 574 (Ind.Ct.App. 2005); Scott County Family YMCA, Inc. v. Hobbs, 817 N.E.2d 603 (Ind.Ct.App. 2004).

   b.   *Unopposed motions generally granted.* It is common for a trial court to grant procedural motions, such as motions for enlargement of time, discovery motions, or motions for continuance, unless an objection is filed. 21 INPRAC § 13.8.

   c.   *Separate motions.* Each motion shall be separate, while alternative motions filed together shall each be identified on the caption. IN ST LAKE RCP Rule 4(A).

    d. *Answer and reply briefs.* Failure to file an answer brief or reply brief within the time prescribed shall be deemed a waiver of the right thereto and shall subject the motion to summary ruling. IN ST LAKE RCP Rule 4(A).

2. *Motion for sanctions*

    a. *Signature and certification.* Every pleading or motion of a party represented by an attorney shall be signed by at least one (1) attorney of record in his individual name, whose address, telephone number, and attorney number shall be stated, except that this provision shall not apply to pleadings and motions made and transcribed at the trial or a hearing before the judge and received by him in such form. A party who is not represented by an attorney shall sign his pleading and state his address. IN ST TRIAL P Rule 11(A).

        i. The signature of an attorney constitutes a certificate by him that he has read the pleadings; that to the best of his knowledge, information, and belief, there is good ground to support it; and that it is not interposed for delay. IN ST TRIAL P Rule 11(A).

        ii. If a pleading or motion is not signed or is signed with intent to defeat the purpose of the rule, it may be stricken as sham and false and the action may proceed as though the pleading had not been served. IN ST TRIAL P Rule 11(A).

        iii. For a willful violation of IN ST TRIAL P Rule 11 an attorney may be subjected to appropriate disciplinary action. Similar action may be taken if scandalous or indecent matter is inserted. IN ST TRIAL P Rule 11(A).

    b. *Frivolous claims.* A claim or defense is "frivolous, unreasonable or groundless" if it has been asserted primarily for the purpose of harassment, if the attorney is unable to make a good faith and rational argument on the merits of the action, or if the lawyer is unable to support the action by good faith and a rational argument for extension, modification, or reversal of existing law. 9 INPRAC § 4.3; Garage Doors of Indianapolis, Inc. v. Morton, 682 N.E.2d 1296 (Ind.Ct.App. 1997).

        i. *Bad faith pleading.* For information on sanctions for bad faith pleading, refer to IN ST 34-52-1-1.

    c. *Factors for determining reasonableness.* Five factors are relevant to determine whether a litigant's conduct is "unreasonable":

        i. The amount of time the attorney had to investigate facts, research the law and prepare documents;

        ii. The extent to which the attorney had to rely upon his client for the factual foundation;

        iii. The complexity of the facts and legal issues;

        iv. The ability to conduct a pre-filing investigation; and

        v. The plausibility of the arguments advanced by a party, including good faith efforts to extend or modify the law. 9 INPRAC § 4.3; General Collections, Inc. v. Decker, 545 N.E.2d 18 (Ind.Ct.App. 1989).

    d. *Determination of sanction.* The determination of a reasonable attorney fee requires the consideration of all relevant matters including but not limited to the attorney's experience and reputation, the nature of the employment, and the responsibility involved and the results obtained. A contingency fee agreement should not be used as the basis for determining a reasonable fee to be paid by a nonparty to that agreement. 9 INPRAC § 4.3; Mason v. Mason, 561 N.E.2d 809 (Ind.Ct.App. 1990).

D. Documents

1. *Required documents*

    a. *Motion and notice.* The requirement of notice is satisfied by service of the motion. IN ST TRIAL P Rule 7(B). Refer to the General Requirements section of this document for information on the content of a motion for sanctions.

    b. *Brief.* Briefs, other than those addressed in IN ST LAKE RCP Rule 4 and IN ST LAKE RCP Rule 9, shall be filed no later than two (2) calendar days preceding the hearing or trial to which directed. IN ST LAKE RCP Rule 11.

    c. *Proposed order.* Unless local practice provides differently, a party should submit a proposed order with its written motion to be signed by the judge once the motion has been granted. 21 INPRAC § 13.8.

        i. Proposed orders, which are submitted for the court's convenience under IN ST LAKE RCP Rule 3 or other applicable Lake County Rules of Civil Procedure, shall be submitted as attachments to motions. IN ST LAKE RCP Rule 17(D)(8). Proposed orders shall be prepared and filed separately from the pleadings, petitions, motions or other papers to which they have reference. IN ST LAKE RCP Rule 3(B).

        ii. Orders, either routine in nature or uncontested including, for example, those setting or continuing a hearing, shall be effected by the chronological case summary entry only, which shall contain the concise substance of the order. IN ST LAKE RCP Rule 3(B).

        iii. All orders shall be accompanied with sufficient copies and stamped, pre-addressed envelopes, so that copies may be mailed to all parties. IN ST LAKE RCP Rule 3(B).

    d. *Chronological case summary (CCS) entry forms.* All filings shall be accompanied by a Chronological Case Summary (CCS) Entry Form to define or identify the documents filed. The Form used should be substantially similar to IN ST LAKE RCP App. A. IN ST LAKE RCP Rule 3(C).

    e. *Certificate of service.* An attorney or unrepresented party tendering a document to the Clerk for filing shall certify that service has been made, list the parties served, and specify the date and means of service. The certificate of service shall be placed at the end of the document and shall not be separately filed. The separate filing of a certificate of service, however, shall not be grounds for rejecting a document for filing. The Clerk may permit documents to be filed without a certificate of service but shall require prompt filing of a separate certificate of service. IN ST TRIAL P Rule 5(C).

        i. All pleadings, motions and other papers submitted for filing which are required to be served under IN ST TRIAL P Rule 5(A) shall contain proof of service pursuant to IN ST TRIAL P Rule 5(B)(2). IN ST LAKE RCP Rule 3(A).

2. *Supplemental documents*

    a. *Supporting evidence.* When a motion is based on facts not appearing of record the court may hear the matter on affidavits presented by the respective parties, but the court may direct that the matter be heard wholly or partly on oral testimony or depositions. IN ST TRIAL P Rule 43(B).

    b. *Facsimile cover sheet.* Any document sent to the Clerk of the Circuit Court by electronic facsimile transmission shall be accompanied by a cover sheet which states the title of the document, case number, number of pages, identity and voice telephone number of the sending party and instructions for filing. The cover sheet shall contain the signature of the attorney or party, pro se, authorizing the filing. IN ST ADMIN Rule 12(D).

E. Format

1. *Form of motions.* The rules applicable to captions, and the signing and form of pleadings (IN ST TRIAL P Rule 8 through IN ST TRIAL P Rule 11), apply to all motions and other papers provided under the Indiana Rules of Trial Procedure. 22B INPRAC 7:2.

2. *Form of pleadings.* For the purpose of uniformity, convenience, clarity and durability, requirements in IN ST LAKE RCP Rule 2 shall be observed in the preparation of all pleadings, motions and other papers. IN ST LAKE RCP Rule 2. Whenever materials submitted fail to meet the standards in IN ST LAKE RCP Rule 2, the Court may impose appropriate sanctions. IN ST LAKE RCP Rule 2(B).

    a. *Caption; Names of parties.* Every pleading shall contain a caption setting forth the name of the court, the title of the action, the file number, and a designation as in IN ST TRIAL P Rule 7(A). In the complaint the title of the action shall include the names of all the parties, but in other pleadings it is sufficient to state the name of the first party on each side with an appropriate indication of other parties. IN ST TRIAL P Rule 10(A).

        i. *Special judge matters.* The caption of all CCS Entry Forms, pleadings, motions, orders and other papers to be filed in a special judge case shall include in block text the words SPECIAL JUDGE and the name of the judge directly below the cause number on the caption. IN ST LAKE RCP Rule 2(D).

b. *Paragraphs; Separate statements.* All averments of a claim or defense shall be made in numbered paragraphs, the contents of each of which shall be limited as far as practicable to a statement of a single set of circumstances, and a paragraph may be referred to by number in all succeeding pleadings. Each claim founded upon a separate transaction or occurrence and each defense other than denials may be stated in a separate count or defense whenever a separation facilitates the clear presentation of the matters set forth. IN ST TRIAL P Rule 10(B).

c. *Adoption by reference; Exhibits.* Statements in a pleading may be adopted by reference in a different part of the same pleading or in another pleading or in any motion. A copy of any written instrument which is an exhibit to a pleading is a part thereof for all purposes. IN ST TRIAL P Rule 10(C).

d. *Paper; Print, quality and binding*

   i. All pleadings, motions, chronological case summary entry forms, orders, process and other papers shall be neatly and legibly printed, typewritten or mechanically reproduced, on one (1) side only, on white opaque paper. To satisfy the recordkeeping requirements of IN ST TRIAL P Rule 77, the print shall be of sufficient density and clarity for preservation and reproduction of microfilming, optical disk or other secondary sources. For this reason, the use of non-letter-quality printers is discouraged. IN ST LAKE RCP Rule 2(A).

   ii. Paper and ink shall be of such quality as to withstand the test of time. All documents shall be produced on acid-free, non-thermal paper. It is recommended that a minimum of twenty (20) pound, twenty-five percent (25%) cotton paper product be used. Documents of multiple pages shall be submitted in bound or stapled fashion, and the binding or stapling shall be at the top only. Covers or backings shall not be used. IN ST LAKE RCP Rule 2(A).

e. *Papers; Handwritten.* Handwritten papers may be filed only if approved by the Court and a typewritten or printed true rendition thereof is filed within three (3) days thereafter and approved by the Court. Upon such approval, they shall be deemed and filed as the original, while the handwritten papers shall be retained therewith for evidentiary purposes. IN ST LAKE RCP Rule 2(C).

f. *Minute sheets; Motion blanks.* Minute sheets and motion blanks shall no longer be used. IN ST LAKE RCP Rule 2(D).

3. *Size of papers for filing.* Effective January 1, 1992, all pleadings, copies, motions and documents filed with any trial court or appellate level court, typed or printed, with the exception of exhibits and existing wills, shall be prepared on eight and one-half by eleven inch (8 1/2" x 11") size paper. IN ST ADMIN Rule 11.

4. *Signature requirements*

a. *Signature of attorney.* Every pleading or motion of a party represented by an attorney shall be signed by at least one (1) attorney of record in his individual name, whose address, telephone number, and attorney number shall be stated, except that this provision shall not apply to pleadings and motions made and transcribed at the trial or a hearing before the judge and received by him in such form. IN ST TRIAL P Rule 11(A).

   i. Refer to the General Requirements section of this document for information on sanctions.

b. *Signature of unrepresented party.* A party who is not represented by an attorney shall sign his pleading and state his address. IN ST TRIAL P Rule 11(A).

c. *Verification not generally required.* Except when specifically required by rule, pleadings or motions need not be verified or accompanied by affidavit. The rule in equity that the averments of an answer under oath must be overcome by the testimony of two (2) witnesses or of one (1) witness sustained by corroborating circumstances is abolished. IN ST TRIAL P Rule 11(A).

d. *Verification by affirmation or representation.* When in connection with any civil or special statutory proceeding it is required that any pleading, motion, petition, supporting affidavit, or other document of any kind, be verified, or that an oath be taken, it shall be sufficient if the subscriber simply affirms the truth of the matter to be verified by an affirmation or representation. IN ST TRIAL P Rule 11(B). IN ST TRIAL P Rule 11(B) states that the affirmation or representation should be in substantially the

following language: "I (we) affirm, under the penalties for perjury, that the foregoing representation(s) is (are) true. (Signed) _____."

    i.   Any person who falsifies an affirmation or representation of fact shall be subject to the same penalties as are prescribed by law for the making of a false affidavit. IN ST TRIAL P Rule 11(B).

e.   *Verified pleadings, motions, and affidavits as evidence.* Pleadings, motions and affidavits accompanying or in support of such pleadings or motions when required to be verified or under oath shall be accepted as a representation that the signer had personal knowledge thereof or reasonable cause to believe the existence of the facts or matters stated or alleged therein; and, if otherwise competent or acceptable as evidence, may be admitted as evidence of the facts or matters stated or alleged therein when it is so provided in the Indiana Rules of Trial Procedure, by statute or other law, or to the extent the writing or signature expressly purports to be made upon the signer's personal knowledge. When such pleadings, motions and affidavits are verified or under oath they shall not require other or greater proof on the part of the adverse party than if not verified or not under oath unless expressly provided otherwise by the Indiana Rules of Trial Procedure, statute or other law. Affidavits upon motions for summary judgment under IN ST TRIAL P Rule 56 and in denial of execution under IN ST TRIAL P Rule 9.2 shall be made upon personal knowledge. IN ST TRIAL P Rule 11(C).

f.   *Electronic signature.* The filing of documents and information through the E-filing system by use of a valid username and password is presumed to have been authorized by the User to whom that username and password have been issued and documents filed through the E-filing system are presumed to have been signed by the same User. IN ST ADMIN Rule 16(E).

5.   *Information excluded from public access.* Every document filed in a case shall separately identify information excluded from public access pursuant to IN ST ADMIN Rule 9(G)(1) as follows:

a.   Whole documents that are excluded from public access pursuant to IN ST ADMIN Rule 9(G)(1) shall be tendered on light green paper or have a light green coversheet attached to the document, marked "Not for Public Access" or "Confidential." IN ST TRIAL P Rule 5(G)(1).

b.   When only a portion of a document contains information excluded from public access pursuant to IN ST ADMIN Rule 9(G)(1), said information shall be omitted [or redacted] from the filed document, and set forth on a separate accompanying document on light green paper conspicuously marked "Not for Public Access" or "Confidential" and clearly designated [or identifying] the caption and number of the case and the document and location within the document to which the redacted material pertains. IN ST TRIAL P Rule 5(G)(2).

c.   With respect to documents filed in electronic format, the trial court, by local rule, may provide for compliance with IN ST TRIAL P Rule 5 in manner that separates and protects access to information excluded from public access. IN ST TRIAL P Rule 5(G)(3).

d.   IN ST TRIAL P Rule 5(G) does not apply to a record sealed by the court pursuant to IN ST 5-14-3-5.5 or otherwise, nor to records, documents, or information filed in cases to which public access is prohibited pursuant to IN ST ADMIN Rule 9(G). IN ST TRIAL P Rule 5(G)(4).

e.   The following information in case records is excluded from public access and is confidential:

    i.   Information that is excluded from public access pursuant to federal law;

    ii.   Information that is excluded from public access as declared confidential by Indiana statute or other court rule, including without limitation:

        • All adoption records created after July 8, 1941, as declared confidential by IN ST 31-19-19-1, et seq., except those specifically declared open by IN ST 31-19-13-2(2);

        • All records relating to chancroid, chlamydia, gonorrhea, hepatitis, human immunodeficiency virus (HIV), Lymphogranuloma venereum, syphilis, tuberculosis, as declared confidential by IN ST 16-41-8-1, et seq.;

        • All records relating to child abuse as declared confidential by IN ST 31-33-18-1, et seq.;

        • All records relating to drug tests as declared confidential by IN ST 5-14-3-4(a)(9);

        • Records of grand jury proceedings as declared confidential by IN ST 35-34-2-4;

- Records of juvenile proceedings as declared confidential by IN ST 31-39-1-2, except those specifically open under statute;
- All paternity records created after July 1, 1941 as declared confidential by IN ST 31-14-11-15, IN ST 31-19-5-23, IN ST 31-39-1-1 and IN ST 31-39-1-2 [Editor's note: IN ST 31-14-11-15 was repealed effective May 9, 2013];
- All pre-sentence reports as declared confidential by IN ST 35-38-1-13;
- Written petitions to permit marriages without consent and orders directing the Clerk of Court to issue a marriage license to underage persons, as declared confidential by IN ST 31-11-1-6;
- Only those arrest warrants, search warrants, indictments and informations ordered confidential by the trial judge, prior to return of duly executed service as declared confidential by IN ST 5-14-3-4(b)(1);
- All medical, mental health, or tax records unless determined by law or regulation of any governmental custodian not to be confidential, released by the subject of such records, or declared by a court of competent jurisdiction to be essential to the resolution of litigation as declared confidential by IN ST 16-39-3-10, IN ST 6-4.1-5-10, IN ST 6-4.1-12-12, and IN ST 6-8.1-7-1;
- Personal information relating to jurors or prospective jurors, other than for the use of the parties and counsel, pursuant to IN ST JURY Rule 10;
- Information relating to protection from abuse orders, no-contact orders and workplace violence restraining orders as declared confidential by IN ST 5-2-9-6, et seq.;
- Mediation proceedings pursuant to IN ST ADR Rule 2.11, Mini-Trial proceedings pursuant to IN ST ADR Rule 4.4(C), and Summary Jury Trials pursuant to IN ST ADR Rule 5.6;
- Information in probation files pursuant to the Probation Standards promulgated by the Judicial Conference of Indiana pursuant to IN ST 11-13-1-8(b);
- Information deemed confidential pursuant to the Rules for Court Administered Alcohol and Drug Programs promulgated by the Judicial Conference of Indiana pursuant to IN ST 12-23-14-13;
- Information deemed confidential pursuant to the Problem-Solving Court Rules promulgated by the Judicial Conference of Indiana pursuant to IN ST 33-23-16-16;
- All records of the Department of workforce Development as declared confidential by IN ST 22-4-19-6;
- Information regarding interception of electronic communications that is sealed or deemed confidential as set forth in IN ST 35-33.5-2-1, et seq.

iii. Information excluded from public access by specific court order;

iv. Complete Social Security Numbers of living persons;

v. With the exception of names, information such as addresses, phone numbers, and dates of birth which explicitly identifies:

- Natural persons who are witnesses or victims (not including defendants) in criminal, domestic violence, stalking, sexual assault, juvenile, or civil protection order proceedings, provided that juveniles who are victims of sex crimes shall be identified by initials only;
- Places of residence of judicial officers, clerks and other employees of courts and clerks of court, unless the person or persons about whom the information pertains waives confidentiality;

vi. Complete account numbers of specific assets, loans, bank accounts, credit cards, and personal identification numbers (PINs);

vii. All orders of expungement entered in criminal or juvenile proceedings, orders to restrict access

to criminal history information pursuant to IN ST 35-38-5-5.5 or IN ST 35-38-8-5 and records excluded from public access by such orders, and information related to infractions that is excluded from public access pursuant to IN ST 34-28-5-15 or IN ST 34-28-5-16 [Editor's note: IN ST 35-38-5-5.5, IN ST 35-38-8-5 and IN ST 34-28-5-16 were repealed effective July 1, 2013; for information on orders restricting access to criminal history, refer to IN ST 35-38-9-1, et seq.];

    viii. All personal notes and e-mail, and deliberative material, of judges, jurors, court staff and judicial agencies, and information recorded in personal data assistants (PDA's) or organizers and personal calendars. IN ST ADMIN Rule 9(G)(1).

6. *Format of electronically filed documents*

  a. *Generally.* Electronically filed documents must meet the same requirements of format as documents conventionally filed pursuant to IN ST LAKE RCP Rule 2 or other applicable Lake County Rules of Civil Procedure. IN ST LAKE RCP Rule 17(D)(1).

  b. *Titles of documents.* The person electronically filing a document will be responsible for designating a title for the document at the time it is filed. The LCOD will generate the appropriate entry onto the CCS to record the filing of the document. IN ST LAKE RCP Rule 17(D)(3).

  c. *Citations and hyperlinks.* Electronically filed documents may contain hyperlink references to an external document as a convenient mechanism for accessing material cited in the document. Filers wishing to insert hyperlinks into documents shall continue to use the traditional method of citation to authority in addition to the hyperlink provided. The hyperlink is merely a convenience to the court and the material referenced is extraneous to the file and not a part of the court's record. IN ST LAKE RCP Rule 17(D)(5).

  d. *Attachments and exhibits.* All documents which form part of a single submission and which are being filed at the same time and by the same filer may be electronically filed together under one document filing, e.g., the motion, supporting affidavits, memorandum in support, designation of evidence, exhibits. IN ST LAKE RCP Rule 17(D)(6).

    i. Large documents which do not exist in an electronic format shall be scanned into .pdf format and filed electronically as separate attachments. A scanner is available in each clerk's office for use by the public and the bar in scanning and saving image files if needed. IN ST LAKE RCP Rule 17(D)(6).

  e. *Electronic signatures*

    i. *Electronic filing as signature.* The electronic filing of a document which is required to be signed shall constitute the filer's representation under IN ST TRIAL P Rule 11. Unless the electronically filed document has been scanned and shows the filer's original signature, the signature of the filer shall be indicated by As/Attorney's Name, or As/Party's Name as in the case of a pro se litigant, on the line where the signature would otherwise appear. IN ST LAKE RCP Rule 17(G)(1).

    ii. *Signatures on jointly signed or filed, verified or other documents.* In the case of a stipulation, agreed order, jointly signed motion or other document which needs to be signed by two (2) or more persons, or in the case of documents which must contain original signatures and which require verification or an unsworn declaration under rule or statute, the signatures may be indicated by either:

- Submitting a scanned copy of the originally signed document; or,
- Submitting the document with the use of As/Name in the signature block(s) where the original signature(s) appear(s) in the original document; provided, however, that the filer shall first obtain the physical signature of all persons necessary. IN ST LAKE RCP Rule 17(G)(2).

    iii. *Retention of original.* The filer shall retain the original executed document. IN ST LAKE RCP Rule 17(G).

7. *Citation of local rules.* The local rules for Lake County may be known as the Lake County Rules of Civil Procedure, and abbreviated as LR. IN ST LAKE RCP Rule 1(C).

F. Filing and Service Requirements

1. *Filing requirements.* Except as otherwise provided in IN ST TRIAL P Rule 5(E)(2), all pleadings and papers subsequent to the complaint which are required to be served upon a party shall be filed with the Court either before service or within a reasonable period of time thereafter. IN ST TRIAL P Rule 5(E)(1). All papers presented for filing shall be submitted to the Clerk and not to the court. All papers submitted for filing shall be mailed or delivered to the Clerk's office at the courthouse in which the case is pending. IN ST LAKE RCP Rule 3(A).

    a. *Filing with the court defined.* The filing of pleadings, motions, and other papers with the court as required by the Indiana Rules of Trial Procedure shall be made by one of the following methods:

        i.   Delivery to the clerk of the court;

        ii. Sending by electronic transmission under the procedure adopted pursuant to IN ST ADMIN Rule 12;

        iii. Mailing to the clerk by registered, certified or express mail return receipt requested;

        iv. Depositing with any third-party commercial carrier for delivery to the clerk within three (3) calendar days, cost prepaid, properly addressed;

        v.   If the court so permits, filing with the judge, in which event the judge shall note thereon the filing date and forthwith transmit them to the office of the clerk; or

        vi. Electronic filing, as approved by the Division of State Court Administration pursuant to IN ST ADMIN Rule 16. IN ST TRIAL P Rule 5(F).

        vii. Filing by registered or certified mail and by third-party commercial carrier shall be complete upon mailing or deposit. IN ST TRIAL P Rule 5(F).

    b. *Mandatory electronic filing.* Unless otherwise permitted by the Lake County Rules of Civil Procedure or otherwise authorized by the judicial officer assigned to a particular case, all documents submitted for filing (including the original complaint, or equivalent pleading, and summons) shall be filed electronically with the clerk using the LCOD, no matter when the case was originally filed. IN ST LAKE RCP Rule 17(D).

        i.   *Of documents containing information excluded from public access pursuant to* IN ST ADMIN Rule 9. Documents containing information excluded from public access pursuant to IN ST ADMIN Rule 9, or documents which are ordered to be filed under seal shall be filed electronically, pursuant to IN ST LAKE RCP Rule 17(D)(9), whenever possible, along with a copy of the applicable order to seal the records, and the filer shall designate the documents as "Not for Public Access Pursuant to Administrative Rule 9(G)(1)" at the time of filing. IN ST LAKE RCP Rule 16(A)(1); IN ST LAKE RCP Rule 17(D)(9).

            *   *Conventional filing of documents containing information excluded from public access pursuant to* IN ST ADMIN Rule 9. Documents containing information excluded from public access pursuant to IN ST ADMIN Rule 9, or documents which are ordered to be filed under seal, which cannot be legibly scanned and filed electronically, shall be conventionally filed under seal and designated by the filer as "Not for Public Access Pursuant to Administrative Rule 9(G)(1)" at the time of filing. The unredacted version shall be filed on light green paper which is conspicuously marked "Not for Public Access"; and a redacted version, with confidential information deleted, shall be filed on white paper which shall be available for public access. The filer shall also electronically file a Notice of Manual Filing. IN ST LAKE RCP Rule 16(A)(2).

        ii. *Technical failures.* If a registered user is unable to file a document in a timely manner due to technical difficulties in the LCOD, the registered user must file a document with the court as soon as possible notifying the court of the inability to file the document. A sample document titled Declaration that Party was Unable to File in a Timely Manner Due to Technical Difficulties can be found at IN ST LAKE RCP Form 4. Delayed filings shall be rejected unless accompanied by the declaration attesting to the filer's failed attempts to file electronically at least two (2) times, separated by at least one (1) hour, after noon on each day of delay due to such technical failure. IN ST LAKE RCP Rule 17(J).

    iii. *Documents allowed to be filed conventionally.* Unless specifically authorized by the court, only the following documents may be filed conventionally and not electronically:

- Exhibits and other documents that cannot be converted to a legible electronic form, such as videotapes, x-rays, and similar materials
- Documents delivered to the clerk by pro se litigants
- Documents mailed to the clerk by pro se litigants
- Confidential documents
- Notice of manual filing
- Titles of documents
- Chronological case summary entry forms (CCS entry forms). IN ST LAKE RCP Rule 17(E).
- For more information on the documents which must be filed conventionally, refer to IN ST LAKE RCP Rule 17(E).

  c. *Facsimile filing.* Only when necessary on an emergency basis (i.e., when certified mail or other means of filing will not bring the document to the Judge's attention prior to the scheduled hearing or ruling), pleadings, motions and other papers may be filed by electronic facsimile transmission, or when specifically authorized by the Court. IN ST LAKE RCP Rule 2(C).

    i. *Generally.* In counties where a majority of judges of the courts of record, by posted local rule, have authorized electronic facsimile filing and designated a telephone number to receive such transmissions, pleadings, motions, and other papers may be sent to the Clerk of Circuit Court by electronic facsimile transmission for filing in any case, provided:

- Such matter does not exceed ten (10) pages, including the cover sheet;
- Such matter does not require the payment of fees other than the electronic facsimile transcription fee set forth in IN ST ADMIN Rule 12(E);
- The sending party creates at the time of transmission a machine generated log for such transmission; and
- The original document and the transmission log are maintained by the sending party for the duration of the litigation. IN ST ADMIN Rule 12(B).

    ii. *Time of filing.* During normal, posted business hours, the time of filing shall be the time the duplicate document is produced in the office of the Clerk of the Circuit Court. Duplicate documents received at all other times shall be filed as of the next normal business day. IN ST ADMIN Rule 12(C).

- If the receiving fax machine endorses its own time and date stamp upon the transmitted documents and the receiving machine produces a delivery receipt which is electronically created and transmitted to the sending party, the time of filing shall be the date and time recorded on the transmitted document by the receiving fax machine. IN ST ADMIN Rule 12(C).

  d. *Filing for special judges.* For special judge matters where the special judge is a full-time judge or magistrate serving within Lake County, all papers submitted for filing shall be delivered or mailed to the Clerk's office at the courthouse where the special judge regularly serves. IN ST LAKE RCP Rule 3(A).

  e. *Proof of filing.* Any party filing any paper by any method other than personal delivery to the clerk shall retain proof of filing. IN ST TRIAL P Rule 5(F).

2. *Service requirements.* Unless otherwise provided by the Indiana Rules of Trial Procedure or an order of the court, each party and special judge, if any, shall be served with: (1) every order required by its terms to be served; (2) every pleading subsequent to the original complaint; (3) every written motion except one which may be heard ex parte; (4) every brief submitted to the trial court; (5) every paper relating to

discovery required to be served upon a party; and (6) every written notice, appearance, demand, offer of judgment, designation of record on appeal, or similar paper. IN ST TRIAL P Rule 5(A).

  a. *Methods of service*

      i. *Personal service.* Whenever a party is represented by an attorney of record, service shall be made upon such attorney unless service upon the party himself is ordered by the court. Service upon the attorney or party shall be made by delivering or mailing a copy of the papers to the last known address or where an attorney or party has consented to service by fax or e-mail, as provided in IN ST TRIAL P Rule 3.1(A)(4), by faxing or e-mailing a copy of the documents to the fax number or e-mail address set out in the appearance form or correction as required by IN ST TRIAL P Rule 3.1(E). IN ST TRIAL P Rule 5(B). Delivery of a copy within IN ST TRIAL P Rule 5 means:

- Offering or tendering it to the attorney or party and stating the nature of the papers being served. Refusal to accept an offered or tendered document is a waiver of any objection to the sufficiency or adequacy of service of that document;

- Leaving it at his office with a clerk or other person in charge thereof, or if there is no one in charge, leaving it in a conspicuous place therein; or

- If the office is closed, by leaving it at his dwelling house or usual place of abode with some person of suitable age and discretion then residing therein; or,

- Leaving it at some other suitable place, selected by the attorney upon whom service is being made, pursuant to duly promulgated local rule. IN ST TRIAL P Rule 5(B)(1).

     ii. *Service by mail.* If service is made by mail, the papers shall be deposited in the United States mail addressed to the person on whom they are being served, with postage prepaid. Service shall be deemed complete upon mailing. Proof of service of all papers permitted to be mailed may be made by written acknowledgment of service, by affidavit of the person who mailed the papers, or by certificate of an attorney. It shall be the duty of attorneys when entering their appearance in a cause or when filing pleadings or papers therein, to have noted in the Chronological Case Summary or said pleadings or papers so filed the address and telephone number of their office. Service by delivery or by mail at such address shall be deemed sufficient and complete. IN ST TRIAL P Rule 5(B)(2).

    iii. *Service by fax or e-mail.* A party who has consented to service by fax or e-mail may be served as follows:

- Service by e-mail shall be made by attaching the document being served in .pdf format. Discovery documents must also be served in accordance with IN ST TRIAL P Rule 26(A). IN ST TRIAL P Rule 5(B)(3)(a).

- Service by fax shall be deemed complete upon generation of a transmission record indicating the successful transmission of the entire document, except as provided in IN ST TRIAL P Rule 5(B)(3)(d). IN ST TRIAL P Rule 5(B)(3)(b).

- Service by e-mail shall be deemed complete upon transmission, except as provided in IN ST TRIAL P Rule 5(B)(3)(d). IN ST TRIAL P Rule 5(B)(3)(c).

- Service by fax or e-mail that occurs on a Saturday, Sunday, legal holiday, or day the court or agency in which the matter is pending is closed or after 5:00 PM local time of the recipient shall be deemed complete the next day that is not a Saturday, Sunday, legal holiday, or day that the court or agency in which the matter is pending is not closed. IN ST TRIAL P Rule 5(B)(3)(d).

  b. *Serving numerous defendants.* In any action in which there are unusually large numbers of defendants, the court, upon motion or of its own initiative, may order:

      i. That service of the pleadings of the defendants and replies thereto need not be made as between the defendants;

- That any cross-claim, counterclaim, or matter constituting an avoidance or affirmative defense contained therein shall be deemed to be denied or avoided by all other parties; and

- That the filing of any such pleading and service thereof upon the plaintiff constitutes due notice of it to the parties. IN ST TRIAL P Rule 5(D).

  ii. A copy of every such order shall be served upon the parties in such manner and form as the court directs. IN ST TRIAL P Rule 5(D).

c. *Service by electronic means.* The Lake County Online Docket will generate a Notice of Electronic Filing and Service when any document is filed and served. This notice will be emailed to each registered user of record in a case, and an electronic service event will be added to the work queue of each registered user of record in the case. The party filing the document should retain a paper or electronic copy of the Notice of Electronic Filing and Service. This notice represents proof of filing and service of the document on registered users of record in that case. The filer shall not be required to conventionally serve any document on any party receiving electronic service. IN ST LAKE RCP Rule 17(F)(2).

  i. The filer shall also conventionally serve those parties not designated or able to receive electronic notice or service but who are nevertheless entitled to notice of said pleading or other document in accordance with the Indiana Rules of Civil Procedure and applicable Lake County Rules of Civil Procedure. In such cases, the filer shall also file a certificate of service, as appropriate. IN ST LAKE RCP Rule 17(F).

d. *Service on parties in default for failure to appear.* No service need be made on parties in default for failure to appear, except that pleadings asserting new or additional claims for relief against them shall be served upon them in the manner provided by service of summons in IN ST TRIAL P Rule 4. IN ST TRIAL P Rule 5(A).

G. Hearings

1. *Hearing on motion.* Unless local conditions make it impracticable, each judge shall establish regular times and places, at intervals sufficiently frequent for the prompt dispatch of business, at which motions requiring notice and hearing may be heard and disposed of; but the judge at any time or place and on such notice, if any, as he considers reasonable may make order for the advancement, conduct, and hearing of actions. To expedite its business the court may direct the submission and determination of motions without oral hearing upon brief written statements of reasons in support and opposition, or direct or permit hearings by telephone conference call with all attorneys or other similar means of communication. IN ST TRIAL P Rule 73(A).

2. *Oral argument discretionary.* The granting of a motion for oral argument, unless required by the Indiana Rules of Trial Procedure, shall be wholly discretionary with the court. IN ST LAKE RCP Rule 4(B).

H. Forms

1. Motion for Sanctions Forms for Indiana

a. Signature; By party. 9 INPRAC § 4.5.

b. Signature; Attorney. 9 INPRAC § 4.6.

c. Signature; Attorney; Another form. 9 INPRAC § 4.7.

d. Signature; Attorney; Another form. 9 INPRAC § 4.8.

e. Motion to impose sanctions on defendant; Improper answer. 9 INPRAC § 4.20.

f. Certificate of service; Personal service. 9 INPRAC § 5.7.

g. Certificate of service; First class mail. 9 INPRAC § 5.8.

2. Official Motion for Sanctions Forms for Lake County

a. CCS entry form. IN ST LAKE RCP App. A.

b. Notice of manual filing. IN ST LAKE RCP Form 2.

c. Certificate of service. IN ST LAKE RCP Form 3.

d. Declaration that party was unable to file in a timely manner. IN ST LAKE RCP Form 4.

3. Motion for Sanctions Forms for Lake County

a. Notice of manual filing. EFORMST IN 5540.

I. Checklist

(I) ❑ Matters to be considered by moving party

    (a) ❑ Required documents

        (1) ❑ Motion and notice

        (2) ❑ Brief

        (3) ❑ Proposed order

        (4) ❑ Chronological case summary (CSS) entry forms

        (5) ❑ Certificate of service

    (b) ❑ Supplemental documents

        (1) ❑ Supporting evidence

        (2) ❑ Facsimile cover sheet

    (c) ❑ Timing

        (1) ❑ There are no specific time requirements for when a party may file a motion for sanctions

        (2) ❑ A written motion, other than one which may be heard ex parte, and notice of the hearing thereof shall be served not less than five (5) days before the time specified for the hearing, unless a different period is fixed by the Indiana Rules of Trial Procedure or by order of the court

        (3) ❑ All pleadings and papers subsequent to the complaint which are required to be served upon a party shall be filed with the Court either before service or within a reasonable period of time thereafter

        (4) ❑ All pleadings, motions and other papers submitted for filing which are required to be served under IN ST TRIAL P Rule 5(A) shall be filed no later than three (3) days after service

        (5) ❑ If such papers are filed before service, proof of service thereof shall be filed no later than three (3) business days thereafter

(II) ❑ Matters to be considered by the responding party

    (a) ❑ Required documents

        (1) ❑ Opposition

        (2) ❑ Chronological case summary (CSS) entry forms

        (3) ❑ Certificate of service

    (b) ❑ Supplemental documents

        (1) ❑ Supporting evidence

        (2) ❑ Proposed order

        (3) ❑ Facsimile cover sheet

    (c) ❑ Timing

        (1) ❑ So long as consistent with the Indiana Rules of Trial Procedure, an adverse party wishing to respond shall do so within fifteen (15) days of service

        (2) ❑ Except as otherwise provided in IN ST TRIAL P Rule 59(D), opposing affidavits may be served not less than one (1) day before the hearing, unless the court permits them to be served at some other time

Motions, Oppositions and Replies
Motion to Compel Discovery

Document Last Updated October 2013

A. Applicable Rules

1. *State rules*

   a. Appearance. IN ST TRIAL P Rule 3.1.

   b. Summons. IN ST TRIAL P Rule 4.

   c. Service and filing of pleadings and other papers. IN ST TRIAL P Rule 5.

   d. Time. IN ST TRIAL P Rule 6.

   e. Pleadings. IN ST TRIAL P Rule 7; IN ST TRIAL P Rule 8; IN ST TRIAL P Rule 9.2; IN ST TRIAL P Rule 10.

   f. Signing and verification of pleadings. IN ST TRIAL P Rule 11.

   g. General provisions regarding discovery. IN ST TRIAL P Rule 26.

   h. Methods of discovery. IN ST TRIAL P Rule 27; IN ST TRIAL P Rule 30; IN ST TRIAL P Rule 31; IN ST TRIAL P Rule 33; IN ST TRIAL P Rule 34; IN ST TRIAL P Rule 36.

   i. Failure to make or cooperate in discovery; Sanctions. IN ST TRIAL P Rule 37.

   j. Evidence. IN ST TRIAL P Rule 43.

   k. Judgment on the evidence (directed verdict). IN ST TRIAL P Rule 50.

   l. Findings by the court. IN ST TRIAL P Rule 52.

   m. Summary judgment. IN ST TRIAL P Rule 56.

   n. Motion to correct error. IN ST TRIAL P Rule 59.

   o. Relief from judgment or order. IN ST TRIAL P Rule 60.

   p. Hearing of motions. IN ST TRIAL P Rule 73.

   q. Court records. IN ST TRIAL P Rule 77.

   r. Access to court records. IN ST ADMIN Rule 9.

   s. Paper size. IN ST ADMIN Rule 11.

   t. Facsimile transmission. IN ST ADMIN Rule 12.

   u. Electronic filing and electronic service pilot projects. IN ST ADMIN Rule 16.

   v. Privacy and confidentiality. IN ST 5-2-9-6; IN ST 5-14-3-4; IN ST 5-14-3-5.5; IN ST 6-4.1-5-10; IN ST 6-4.1-12-12; IN ST 6-8.1-7-1; IN ST 11-13-1-8; IN ST 12-23-14-13; IN ST 16-39-3-10; IN ST 16-41-8-1; IN ST 22-4-19-6; IN ST 31-11-1-6; IN ST 31-19-5-23; IN ST 31-19-13-2; IN ST 31-19-19-1; IN ST 31-33-18-1; IN ST 31-39-1-1; IN ST 31-39-1-2; IN ST 33-23-16-16; IN ST 35-34-2-4; IN ST 35-38-1-13; IN ST 35-38-9-1; IN ST ADR Rule 2.11; IN ST ADR Rule 4.4; IN ST ADR Rule 5.6; IN ST JURY Rule 10.

2. *Local rules*

   a. Scope and title. [IN ST LAKE RCP Rule 1, as amended by IN ORDER 13-0237, effective October 18, 2013].

   b. Preparation of pleadings, motions and other papers. IN ST LAKE RCP Rule 2.

   c. Filing. [IN ST LAKE RCP Rule 3, as amended by IN ORDER 13-0237, effective October 18, 2013].

   d. Motions. IN ST LAKE RCP Rule 4.

   e. Discovery. IN ST LAKE RCP Rule 8.

   f. Pretrial procedure. IN ST LAKE RCP Rule 9.

    g.   Briefs. IN ST LAKE RCP Rule 11.

    h.   Confidential information and sealed documents. IN ST LAKE RCP Rule 16.

    i.   Electronic filing and service. IN ST LAKE RCP Rule 17.

B. Timing

1.   *Motion to compel discovery.* There are no specific timing requirements for filing a motion to compel discovery. The moving party must provide reasonable notice of his intention to file a motion to compel with the other litigants and all affected persons. 10 INPRAC § 58.51.

    a.   *Filing.* All pleadings and papers subsequent to the complaint which are required to be served upon a party shall be filed with the Court either before service or within a reasonable period of time thereafter. IN ST TRIAL P Rule 5(E)(1). All pleadings, motions and other papers submitted for filing which are required to be served under IN ST TRIAL P Rule 5(A) shall be filed no later than three (3) days after service. IN ST LAKE RCP Rule 3(A).

        i.   If such papers are filed before service, proof of service thereof shall be filed no later than three (3) business days thereafter. Upon failure to comply with IN ST LAKE RCP Rule 3, the Court may, on motion of any party or on its own motion, impose appropriate sanctions. IN ST LAKE RCP Rule 3(A).

    b.   *Briefs.* Briefs, other than those addressed in IN ST LAKE RCP Rule 4 and IN ST LAKE RCP Rule 9, shall be filed no later than two (2) calendar days preceding the hearing or trial to which directed. IN ST LAKE RCP Rule 11.

2.   *Service.* A written motion, other than one which may be heard ex parte, and notice of the hearing thereof shall be served not less than five (5) days before the time specified for the hearing, unless a different period is fixed by the Indiana Rules of Trial Procedure or by order of the court. IN ST TRIAL P Rule 6(D).

    a.   *Of supporting affidavits.* When a motion is supported by affidavit, the affidavit shall be served with the motion. IN ST TRIAL P Rule 6(D).

3.   *Service of opposition.* Except as otherwise provided in IN ST TRIAL P Rule 59(D), opposing affidavits may be served not less than one (1) day before the hearing, unless the court permits them to be served at some other time. IN ST TRIAL P Rule 6(D).

    a.   So long as consistent with the Indiana Rules of Trial Procedure, an adverse party wishing to respond shall do so within fifteen (15) days of service. IN ST LAKE RCP Rule 4(A).

4.   *Reply.* The moving party shall have ten (10) days after service of the response within which to reply. IN ST LAKE RCP Rule 4(A).

5.   *Computation of time*

    a.   *Generally; Days excluded.* In computing any period of time prescribed or allowed by the Indiana Rules of Trial Procedure, by order of the court, or by any applicable statute, the day of the act, event, or default from which the designated period of time begins to run shall not be included. The last day of the period so computed is to be included unless it is:

        i.   A Saturday,

        ii.   A Sunday,

        iii.   A legal holiday as defined by state statute, or

        iv.   A day the office in which the act is to be done is closed during regular business hours. IN ST TRIAL P Rule 6(A).

    b.   *Short periods.* In any event, the period runs until the end of the next day that is not a Saturday, a Sunday, a legal holiday, or a day on which the office is closed. When the period of time allowed is less than seven (7) days, intermediate Saturdays, Sundays, legal holidays, and days on which the office is closed shall be excluded from the computations. IN ST TRIAL P Rule 6(A).

    c.   *Additional time after service by United States mail.* Whenever a party has the right or is required to do some act or take some proceedings within a prescribed period after the service of a notice or other paper upon him and the notice or paper is served upon him by United States mail, three (3) days shall be added to the prescribed period. IN ST TRIAL P Rule 6(E).

d. *Electronic filing does not alter deadlines.* Filing electronically does not alter any filing deadlines or any time computation pursuant to state or federal statutes, any Rules of the Indiana Supreme Court, including without limitation the Rules of Trial Procedure, the Rules of Appellate Procedure or the Administrative Rules, or applicable Lake County Rules of Civil Procedure. The office of the Lake County Clerk is open for electronic filing under the Lake County Rules of Civil Procedure twenty-four (24) hours a day. A document is deemed filed at the date and time it is received by the LCOD server. Filing must be completed before midnight local time in order to be considered filed that day. Lake County observes Central Time and electronic filers are strongly urged to file documents during hours when the Lake County Online Docket ("LCOD") help line is available, from 9:00 a.m. to 4:00 p.m. local time, although documents can be filed electronically twenty-four (24) hours a day. IN ST LAKE RCP Rule 17(I).

e. *Enlargement of time.* When an act is required or allowed to be done at or within a specific time by the Indiana Rules of Trial Procedure, the court may at any time for cause shown:

   i. Order the period enlarged, with or without motion or notice, if request therefor is made before the expiration of the period originally prescribed or extended by a previous order; or

   ii. Upon motion made after the expiration of the specific period, permit the act to be done where the failure to act was the result of excusable neglect; but, the court may not extend the time for taking any action for judgment on the evidence under IN ST TRIAL P Rule 50(A), amendment of findings and judgment under IN ST TRIAL P Rule 52(B), to correct errors under IN ST TRIAL P Rule 59(C), statement in opposition to motion to correct error under IN ST TRIAL P Rule 59(E), or to obtain relief from final judgment under IN ST TRIAL P Rule 60(B), except to the extent and under the conditions stated in those rules. IN ST TRIAL P Rule 6(B).

C. General Requirements

1. *Motions, generally.* Unless made during a hearing or trial, or otherwise ordered by the court, an application to the court for an order shall be made by written motion. The motion shall state the grounds therefor and the relief or order sought. IN ST TRIAL P Rule 7(B).

   a. *Motions as distinct from pleadings.* Motions and responses to motions are not pleadings, and allegations contained in a motion are not admissions of a party. 22B INPRAC 7:2; Wachstetter v. County Properties, LLC, 832 N.E.2d 574 (Ind.Ct.App. 2005); Scott County Family YMCA, Inc. v. Hobbs, 817 N.E.2d 603 (Ind.Ct.App. 2004).

   b. *Unopposed motions generally granted.* It is common for a trial court to grant procedural motions, such as motions for enlargement of time, discovery motions, or motions for continuance, unless an objection is filed. 21 INPRAC § 13.8.

   c. *Separate motions.* Each motion shall be separate, while alternative motions filed together shall each be identified on the caption. IN ST LAKE RCP Rule 4(A).

   d. *Answer and reply briefs.* Failure to file an answer brief or reply brief within the time prescribed shall be deemed a waiver of the right thereto and shall subject the motion to summary ruling. IN ST LAKE RCP Rule 4(A).

2. *Motion to compel discovery.* Motions under IN ST TRIAL P Rule 37 are intended secure compliance with discovery requests and orders, ensure that one party will not profit from a failure to comply, and provide a general deterrence to discovery abuses. 22B INPRAC 37:1; Fifth Third Bank v. PNC Bank, 885 N.E.2d 52 (Ind.Ct.App. 2008).

   a. *Appropriate court.* An application for an order to a party may be made to the court in which the action is pending, or alternately, on matters relating to a deposition or an order under IN ST TRIAL P Rule 34, to the court in the county where the deposition is being taken or where compliance is to be made under IN ST TRIAL P Rule 34. An application for an order to a deponent who is not a party shall be made to the court in the county where the deposition is being taken. IN ST TRIAL P Rule 37(A)(1).

   b. *Motion.* If a party refuses to allow inspection under IN ST TRIAL P Rule 9.2(E), or if a deponent fails to answer a question propounded or submitted under IN ST TRIAL P Rule 30 or IN ST TRIAL P Rule 31, or an organization, including without limitation a governmental organization or a partnership, fails to make designation under IN ST TRIAL P Rule 30(B)(6) or IN ST TRIAL P Rule 31(A), or a party fails to answer an interrogatory submitted under IN ST TRIAL P Rule 33, or if a party or witness or other person, in response to a request submitted under IN ST TRIAL P Rule 34, fails to respond that inspection will be permitted as requested or fails to permit inspection as requested, the discovering party may move for an order compelling an answer, or a designation, or an order compelling inspection in accordance with the request. When taking a deposition on oral examination, the proponent of the question may complete or adjourn the examination before he applies for an order. IN ST TRIAL P Rule 37(A)(2).

    i. *Evasive or incomplete answer.* For purposes of IN ST TRIAL P Rule 37(A) an evasive or incomplete answer is to be treated as a failure to answer. IN ST TRIAL P Rule 37(A)(3).

c. *Content of motion.* A motion to compel discovery should state the history of the discovery dispute, evidence that the opposing party was properly served with the discovery request, the position taken by the parties, the grounds for the motion with supporting authority, and the relief sought. In addition, the motion should include a statement demonstrating compliance with the informal dispute resolution requirements of IN ST TRIAL P Rule 26(F). 10 INPRAC § 58.51.

d. *Request for relief.* A motion to compel, filed under IN ST TRIAL P Rule 37, may request the following relief:

    i. An order compelling a discovery response;

    ii. Sanctions under IN ST TRIAL P Rule 37(D) (this rule incorporates by reference the sanctions available to a trial court to punish a party who has refused to comply with a discovery order); and

    iii. An award of attorney fees and expenses incurred to obtain an order compelling discovery. 10 INPRAC § 58.51.

e. *Effect of granting or denial of the motion*

    i. *Denied in whole or in part.* If the court denies the motion in whole or in part, it may make such protective order as it would have been empowered to make on a motion made pursuant to IN ST TRIAL P Rule 26(C). IN ST TRIAL P Rule 37(A)(2).

    ii. *Granted in part and denied in part.* If the motion is granted in part and denied in part, the court may apportion the reasonable expenses incurred in relation to the motion among the parties and persons in a just manner. IN ST TRIAL P Rule 37(A)(4).

    iii. *Motion denied.* If the motion is denied, the court shall, after opportunity for hearing, require the moving party or the attorney advising the motion or both of them to pay to the party or deponent who opposed the motion the reasonable expenses incurred in opposing the motion, including attorney's fees, unless the court finds that the making of the motion was substantially justified or that other circumstances make an award of expenses unjust. IN ST TRIAL P Rule 37(A)(4).

    iv. *Motion granted.* If the motion is granted, the court shall, after opportunity for hearing, require the party or deponent whose conduct necessitated the motion or the party or attorney advising such conduct or both of them to pay to the moving party the reasonable expenses incurred in obtaining the order, including attorney's fees, unless the court finds that the opposition to the motion was substantially justified or that other circumstances make an award of expenses unjust. IN ST TRIAL P Rule 37(A)(4). Refer to the Indiana KeyRules Motion for Discovery Sanctions document for more information.

f. *Expenses; Burden on non-prevailing party.* The non-prevailing party has the burden of proving that the reimbursement of expenses should not be awarded. 10 INPRAC § 58.51.

g. *Attorney conference on discovery* issues. Strict compliance with IN ST TRIAL P Rule 26 through IN ST TRIAL P Rule 37 is required. The discovery process is intended to be largely self-actuating, with minimal court supervision. Therefore, the court will not rule on motions related to discovery disputes unless moving counsel represents that, after personal or telephonic conference in good faith effort to resolve differences, counsel are unable to reach accord. If counsel advises the court, by way of motion or response thereto, that opposing counsel has refused or delayed resolution of the discovery dispute, the court may, after hearing, impose appropriate sanctions. IN ST LAKE RCP Rule 8(C).

3. *Opposition to motion to compel; Information not reasonably accessible.* On motion to compel discovery or for a protective order, the party from whom discovery is sought must show that the information is not reasonably accessible because of undue burden or cost. If that showing is made, the court may nonetheless order discovery from such sources if the requesting party shows good cause. The court may specify conditions for the discovery. IN ST TRIAL P Rule 26(C)(9).

D. Documents

1. *Required documents*

   a. *Motion and notice.* The requirement of notice is satisfied by service of the motion. IN ST TRIAL P Rule 7(B). Refer to the General Requirements section of this document for information on the content of a motion to compel discovery.

   b. *Brief.* Briefs, other than those addressed in IN ST LAKE RCP Rule 4 and IN ST LAKE RCP Rule 9, shall be filed no later than two (2) calendar days preceding the hearing or trial to which directed. IN ST LAKE RCP Rule 11.

   c. *Disputed discovery.* In addition, the motion should attach a copy of the disputed discovery in accordance with the requirements of IN ST TRIAL P Rule 5(D). 10 INPRAC § 58.51.

   d. *Attorney certification.* Before any party files any motion or request to compel discovery pursuant to IN ST TRIAL P Rule 37, or any motion for protection from discovery pursuant to IN ST TRIAL P Rule 26(C), or any other discovery motion which seeks to enforce, modify, or limit discovery, that party shall:

      i. Make a reasonable effort to reach agreement with the opposing party concerning the matter which is the subject of the motion or request; and

      ii. Include in the motion or request a statement showing that the attorney making the motion or request has made a reasonable effort to reach agreement with the opposing attorney(s) concerning the matter(s) set forth in the motion or request. This statement shall recite, in addition, the date, time and place of this effort to reach agreement, whether in person or by phone, and the names of all parties and attorneys participating therein. If an attorney for any party advises the court in writing that an opposing attorney has refused or delayed meeting and discussing the issues covered in IN ST TRIAL P Rule 26(F), the court may take such action as is appropriate. IN ST TRIAL P Rule 26(F).

      iii. The court may deny a discovery motion filed by a party who has failed to comply with the requirements of IN ST TRIAL P Rule 26(F). IN ST TRIAL P Rule 26(F).

   e. *Proposed order.* Unless local practice provides differently, a party should submit a proposed order with its written motion to be signed by the judge once the motion has been granted. 21 INPRAC § 13.8.

      i. Proposed orders, which are submitted for the court's convenience under IN ST LAKE RCP Rule 3 or other applicable Lake County Rules of Civil Procedure, shall be submitted as attachments to motions. IN ST LAKE RCP Rule 17(D)(8). Proposed orders shall be prepared and filed separately from the pleadings, petitions, motions or other papers to which they have reference. IN ST LAKE RCP Rule 3(B).

      ii. Orders, either routine in nature or uncontested including, for example, those setting or continuing a hearing, shall be effected by the chronological case summary entry only, which shall contain the concise substance of the order. IN ST LAKE RCP Rule 3(B).

      iii. All orders shall be accompanied with sufficient copies and stamped, pre-addressed envelopes, so that copies may be mailed to all parties. IN ST LAKE RCP Rule 3(B).

   f. *Chronological case summary (CCS) entry forms.* All filings shall be accompanied by a Chronological Case Summary (CCS) Entry Form to define or identify the documents filed. The Form used should be substantially similar to IN ST LAKE RCP App. A. IN ST LAKE RCP Rule 3(C).

   g. *Certificate of service.* An attorney or unrepresented party tendering a document to the Clerk for filing shall certify that service has been made, list the parties served, and specify the date and means of service. The certificate of service shall be placed at the end of the document and shall not be separately filed. The separate filing of a certificate of service, however, shall not be grounds for rejecting a document for filing. The Clerk may permit documents to be filed without a certificate of service but shall require prompt filing of a separate certificate of service. IN ST TRIAL P Rule 5(C).

    i. All pleadings, motions and other papers submitted for filing which are required to be served under IN ST TRIAL P Rule 5(A) shall contain proof of service pursuant to IN ST TRIAL P Rule 5(B)(2). IN ST LAKE RCP Rule 3(A).

2. *Supplemental documents*

    a. *Supporting evidence.* When a motion is based on facts not appearing of record the court may hear the matter on affidavits presented by the respective parties, but the court may direct that the matter be heard wholly or partly on oral testimony or depositions. IN ST TRIAL P Rule 43(B).

    b. *Facsimile cover sheet.* Any document sent to the Clerk of the Circuit Court by electronic facsimile transmission shall be accompanied by a cover sheet which states the title of the document, case number, number of pages, identity and voice telephone number of the sending party and instructions for filing. The cover sheet shall contain the signature of the attorney or party, pro se, authorizing the filing. IN ST ADMIN Rule 12(D).

E. Format

1. *Form of motions.* The rules applicable to captions, and the signing and form of pleadings (IN ST TRIAL P Rule 8 through IN ST TRIAL P Rule 11), apply to all motions and other papers provided under the Indiana Rules of Trial Procedure. 22B INPRAC 7:2.

2. *Form of pleadings.* For the purpose of uniformity, convenience, clarity and durability, requirements in IN ST LAKE RCP Rule 2 shall be observed in the preparation of all pleadings, motions and other papers. IN ST LAKE RCP Rule 2. Whenever materials submitted fail to meet the standards in IN ST LAKE RCP Rule 2, the Court may impose appropriate sanctions. IN ST LAKE RCP Rule 2(B).

    a. *Caption; Names of parties.* Every pleading shall contain a caption setting forth the name of the court, the title of the action, the file number, and a designation as in IN ST TRIAL P Rule 7(A). In the complaint the title of the action shall include the names of all the parties, but in other pleadings it is sufficient to state the name of the first party on each side with an appropriate indication of other parties. IN ST TRIAL P Rule 10(A).

        i. *Special judge matters.* The caption of all CCS Entry Forms, pleadings, motions, orders and other papers to be filed in a special judge case shall include in block text the words SPECIAL JUDGE and the name of the judge directly below the cause number on the caption. IN ST LAKE RCP Rule 2(D).

    b. *Paragraphs; Separate statements.* All averments of a claim or defense shall be made in numbered paragraphs, the contents of each of which shall be limited as far as practicable to a statement of a single set of circumstances, and a paragraph may be referred to by number in all succeeding pleadings. Each claim founded upon a separate transaction or occurrence and each defense other than denials may be stated in a separate count or defense whenever a separation facilitates the clear presentation of the matters set forth. IN ST TRIAL P Rule 10(B).

    c. *Adoption by reference; Exhibits.* Statements in a pleading may be adopted by reference in a different part of the same pleading or in another pleading or in any motion. A copy of any written instrument which is an exhibit to a pleading is a part thereof for all purposes. IN ST TRIAL P Rule 10(C).

    d. *Paper; Print, quality and binding*

        i. All pleadings, motions, chronological case summary entry forms, orders, process and other papers shall be neatly and legibly printed, typewritten or mechanically reproduced, on one (1) side only, on white opaque paper. To satisfy the recordkeeping requirements of IN ST TRIAL P Rule 77, the print shall be of sufficient density and clarity for preservation and reproduction of microfilming, optical disk or other secondary sources. For this reason, the use of non-letter-quality printers is discouraged. IN ST LAKE RCP Rule 2(A).

        ii. Paper and ink shall be of such quality as to withstand the test of time. All documents shall be produced on acid-free, non-thermal paper. It is recommended that a minimum of twenty (20) pound, twenty-five percent (25%) cotton paper product be used. Documents of multiple pages shall be submitted in bound or stapled fashion, and the binding or stapling shall be at the top only. Covers or backings shall not be used. IN ST LAKE RCP Rule 2(A).

e. *Papers; Handwritten.* Handwritten papers may be filed only if approved by the Court and a typewritten or printed true rendition thereof is filed within three (3) days thereafter and approved by the Court. Upon such approval, they shall be deemed and filed as the original, while the handwritten papers shall be retained therewith for evidentiary purposes. IN ST LAKE RCP Rule 2(C).

f. *Minute sheets; Motion blanks.* Minute sheets and motion blanks shall no longer be used. IN ST LAKE RCP Rule 2(D).

3. *Size of papers for filing.* Effective January 1, 1992, all pleadings, copies, motions and documents filed with any trial court or appellate level court, typed or printed, with the exception of exhibits and existing wills, shall be prepared on eight and one-half by eleven inch (8 1/2" x 11") size paper. IN ST ADMIN Rule 11.

4. *Signature requirements*

a. *Signature of attorney.* Every pleading or motion of a party represented by an attorney shall be signed by at least one (1) attorney of record in his individual name, whose address, telephone number, and attorney number shall be stated, except that this provision shall not apply to pleadings and motions made and transcribed at the trial or a hearing before the judge and received by him in such form. IN ST TRIAL P Rule 11(A).

   i. The signature of an attorney constitutes a certificate by him that he has read the pleadings; that to the best of his knowledge, information, and belief, there is good ground to support it; and that it is not interposed for delay. IN ST TRIAL P Rule 11(A).

   ii. If a pleading or motion is not signed or is signed with intent to defeat the purpose of the rule, it may be stricken as sham and false and the action may proceed as though the pleading had not been served. IN ST TRIAL P Rule 11(A).

   iii. For a willful violation of IN ST TRIAL P Rule 11 an attorney may be subjected to appropriate disciplinary action. Similar action may be taken if scandalous or indecent matter is inserted. IN ST TRIAL P Rule 11(A).

b. *Signature of unrepresented party.* A party who is not represented by an attorney shall sign his pleading and state his address. IN ST TRIAL P Rule 11(A).

c. *Verification not generally required.* Except when specifically required by rule, pleadings or motions need not be verified or accompanied by affidavit. The rule in equity that the averments of an answer under oath must be overcome by the testimony of two (2) witnesses or of one (1) witness sustained by corroborating circumstances is abolished. IN ST TRIAL P Rule 11(A).

d. *Verification by affirmation or representation.* When in connection with any civil or special statutory proceeding it is required that any pleading, motion, petition, supporting affidavit, or other document of any kind, be verified, or that an oath be taken, it shall be sufficient if the subscriber simply affirms the truth of the matter to be verified by an affirmation or representation. IN ST TRIAL P Rule 11(B). IN ST TRIAL P Rule 11(B) states that the affirmation or representation should be in substantially the following language: "I (we) affirm, under the penalties for perjury, that the foregoing representation(s) is (are) true. (Signed) _____."

   i. Any person who falsifies an affirmation or representation of fact shall be subject to the same penalties as are prescribed by law for the making of a false affidavit. IN ST TRIAL P Rule 11(B).

e. *Verified pleadings, motions, and affidavits as evidence.* Pleadings, motions and affidavits accompanying or in support of such pleadings or motions when required to be verified or under oath shall be accepted as a representation that the signer had personal knowledge thereof or reasonable cause to believe the existence of the facts or matters stated or alleged therein; and, if otherwise competent or acceptable as evidence, may be admitted as evidence of the facts or matters stated or alleged therein when it is so provided in the Indiana Rules of Trial Procedure, by statute or other law, or to the extent the writing or signature expressly purports to be made upon the signer's personal knowledge. When such pleadings, motions and affidavits are verified or under oath they shall not require other or greater proof on the part of the adverse party than if not verified or not under oath unless expressly provided otherwise by the Indiana Rules of Trial Procedure, statute or other law. Affidavits upon motions for summary judgment under IN ST TRIAL P Rule 56 and in denial of execution under IN ST TRIAL P Rule 9.2 shall be made upon personal knowledge. IN ST TRIAL P Rule 11(C).

f. *Electronic signature.* The filing of documents and information through the E-filing system by use of a valid username and password is presumed to have been authorized by the User to whom that username and password have been issued and documents filed through the E-filing system are presumed to have been signed by the same User. IN ST ADMIN Rule 16(E).

5. *Information excluded from public access.* Every document filed in a case shall separately identify information excluded from public access pursuant to IN ST ADMIN Rule 9(G)(1) as follows:

a. Whole documents that are excluded from public access pursuant to IN ST ADMIN Rule 9(G)(1) shall be tendered on light green paper or have a light green coversheet attached to the document, marked "Not for Public Access" or "Confidential." IN ST TRIAL P Rule 5(G)(1).

b. When only a portion of a document contains information excluded from public access pursuant to IN ST ADMIN Rule 9(G)(1), said information shall be omitted [or redacted] from the filed document, and set forth on a separate accompanying document on light green paper conspicuously marked "Not for Public Access" or "Confidential" and clearly designated [or identifying] the caption and number of the case and the document and location within the document to which the redacted material pertains. IN ST TRIAL P Rule 5(G)(2).

c. With respect to documents filed in electronic format, the trial court, by local rule, may provide for compliance with IN ST TRIAL P Rule 5 in manner that separates and protects access to information excluded from public access. IN ST TRIAL P Rule 5(G)(3).

d. IN ST TRIAL P Rule 5(G) does not apply to a record sealed by the court pursuant to IN ST 5-14-3-5.5 or otherwise, nor to records, documents, or information filed in cases to which public access is prohibited pursuant to IN ST ADMIN Rule 9(G). IN ST TRIAL P Rule 5(G)(4).

e. The following information in case records is excluded from public access and is confidential:

i. Information that is excluded from public access pursuant to federal law;

ii. Information that is excluded from public access as declared confidential by Indiana statute or other court rule, including without limitation:

- All adoption records created after July 8, 1941, as declared confidential by IN ST 31-19-19-1, et seq., except those specifically declared open by IN ST 31-19-13-2(2);
- All records relating to chancroid, chlamydia, gonorrhea, hepatitis, human immunodeficiency virus (HIV), Lymphogranuloma venereum, syphilis, tuberculosis, as declared confidential by IN ST 16-41-8-1, et seq.;
- All records relating to child abuse as declared confidential by IN ST 31-33-18-1, et seq.;
- All records relating to drug tests as declared confidential by IN ST 5-14-3-4(a)(9);
- Records of grand jury proceedings as declared confidential by IN ST 35-34-2-4;
- Records of juvenile proceedings as declared confidential by IN ST 31-39-1-2, except those specifically open under statute;
- All paternity records created after July 1, 1941 as declared confidential by IN ST 31-14-11-15, IN ST 31-19-5-23, IN ST 31-39-1-1 and IN ST 31-39-1-2 [Editor's note: IN ST 31-14-11-15 was repealed effective May 9, 2013];
- All pre-sentence reports as declared confidential by IN ST 35-38-1-13;
- Written petitions to permit marriages without consent and orders directing the Clerk of Court to issue a marriage license to underage persons, as declared confidential by IN ST 31-11-1-6;
- Only those arrest warrants, search warrants, indictments and informations ordered confi-

dential by the trial judge, prior to return of duly executed service as declared confidential by IN ST 5-14-3-4(b)(1);

- All medical, mental health, or tax records unless determined by law or regulation of any governmental custodian not to be confidential, released by the subject of such records, or declared by a court of competent jurisdiction to be essential to the resolution of litigation as declared confidential by IN ST 16-39-3-10, IN ST 6-4.1-5-10, IN ST 6-4.1-12-12, and IN ST 6-8.1-7-1;

- Personal information relating to jurors or prospective jurors, other than for the use of the parties and counsel, pursuant to IN ST JURY Rule 10;

- Information relating to protection from abuse orders, no-contact orders and workplace violence restraining orders as declared confidential by IN ST 5-2-9-6, et seq.;

- Mediation proceedings pursuant to IN ST ADR Rule 2.11, Mini-Trial proceedings pursuant to IN ST ADR Rule 4.4(C), and Summary Jury Trials pursuant to IN ST ADR Rule 5.6;

- Information in probation files pursuant to the Probation Standards promulgated by the Judicial Conference of Indiana pursuant to IN ST 11-13-1-8(b);

- Information deemed confidential pursuant to the Rules for Court Administered Alcohol and Drug Programs promulgated by the Judicial Conference of Indiana pursuant to IN ST 12-23-14-13;

- Information deemed confidential pursuant to the Problem-Solving Court Rules promulgated by the Judicial Conference of Indiana pursuant to IN ST 33-23-16-16;

- All records of the Department of workforce Development as declared confidential by IN ST 22-4-19-6;

- Information regarding interception of electronic communications that is sealed or deemed confidential as set forth in IN ST 35-33.5-2-1, et seq.

   iii. Information excluded from public access by specific court order;

   iv. Complete Social Security Numbers of living persons;

   v. With the exception of names, information such as addresses, phone numbers, and dates of birth which explicitly identifies:

- Natural persons who are witnesses or victims (not including defendants) in criminal, domestic violence, stalking, sexual assault, juvenile, or civil protection order proceedings, provided that juveniles who are victims of sex crimes shall be identified by initials only;

- Places of residence of judicial officers, clerks and other employees of courts and clerks of court, unless the person or persons about whom the information pertains waives confidentiality;

   vi. Complete account numbers of specific assets, loans, bank accounts, credit cards, and personal identification numbers (PINs);

   vii. All orders of expungement entered in criminal or juvenile proceedings, orders to restrict access to criminal history information pursuant to IN ST 35-38-5-5.5 or IN ST 35-38-8-5 and records excluded from public access by such orders, and information related to infractions that is excluded from public access pursuant to IN ST 34-28-5-15 or IN ST 34-28-5-16 [Editor's note: IN ST 35-38-5-5.5, IN ST 35-38-8-5 and IN ST 34-28-5-16 were repealed effective July 1, 2013; for information on orders restricting access to criminal history, refer to IN ST 35-38-9-1, et seq.];

   viii. All personal notes and e-mail, and deliberative material, of judges, jurors, court staff and judicial agencies, and information recorded in personal data assistants (PDA's) or organizers and personal calendars. IN ST ADMIN Rule 9(G)(1).

6. *Format of electronically filed documents*

   a. *Generally.* Electronically filed documents must meet the same requirements of format as documents conventionally filed pursuant to IN ST LAKE RCP Rule 2 or other applicable Lake County Rules of Civil Procedure. IN ST LAKE RCP Rule 17(D)(1).

b. *Titles of documents.* The person electronically filing a document will be responsible for designating a title for the document at the time it is filed. The LCOD will generate the appropriate entry onto the CCS to record the filing of the document. IN ST LAKE RCP Rule 17(D)(3).

c. *Citations and hyperlinks.* Electronically filed documents may contain hyperlink references to an external document as a convenient mechanism for accessing material cited in the document. Filers wishing to insert hyperlinks into documents shall continue to use the traditional method of citation to authority in addition to the hyperlink provided. The hyperlink is merely a convenience to the court and the material referenced is extraneous to the file and not a part of the court's record. IN ST LAKE RCP Rule 17(D)(5).

d. *Attachments and exhibits.* All documents which form part of a single submission and which are being filed at the same time and by the same filer may be electronically filed together under one document filing, e.g., the motion, supporting affidavits, memorandum in support, designation of evidence, exhibits. IN ST LAKE RCP Rule 17(D)(6).

    i. Large documents which do not exist in an electronic format shall be scanned into .pdf format and filed electronically as separate attachments. A scanner is available in each clerk's office for use by the public and the bar in scanning and saving image files if needed. IN ST LAKE RCP Rule 17(D)(6).

e. *Electronic signatures*

    i. *Electronic filing as signature.* The electronic filing of a document which is required to be signed shall constitute the filer's representation under IN ST TRIAL P Rule 11. Unless the electronically filed document has been scanned and shows the filer's original signature, the signature of the filer shall be indicated by As/Attorney's Name, or As/Party's Name as in the case of a pro se litigant, on the line where the signature would otherwise appear. IN ST LAKE RCP Rule 17(G)(1).

    ii. *Signatures on jointly signed or filed, verified or other documents.* In the case of a stipulation, agreed order, jointly signed motion or other document which needs to be signed by two (2) or more persons, or in the case of documents which must contain original signatures and which require verification or an unsworn declaration under rule or statute, the signatures may be indicated by either:

- Submitting a scanned copy of the originally signed document; or,
- Submitting the document with the use of As/Name in the signature block(s) where the original signature(s) appear(s) in the original document; provided, however, that the filer shall first obtain the physical signature of all persons necessary. IN ST LAKE RCP Rule 17(G)(2).

    iii. *Retention of original.* The filer shall retain the original executed document. IN ST LAKE RCP Rule 17(G).

7. *Citation of local rules.* The local rules for Lake County may be known as the Lake County Rules of Civil Procedure, and abbreviated as LR. IN ST LAKE RCP Rule 1(C).

F. Filing and Service Requirements

1. *Filing requirements.* Except as otherwise provided in IN ST TRIAL P Rule 5(E)(2), all pleadings and papers subsequent to the complaint which are required to be served upon a party shall be filed with the Court either before service or within a reasonable period of time thereafter. IN ST TRIAL P Rule 5(E)(1). All papers presented for filing shall be submitted to the Clerk and not to the court. All papers submitted for filing shall be mailed or delivered to the Clerk's office at the courthouse in which the case is pending. IN ST LAKE RCP Rule 3(A).

a. *Filing with the court defined.* The filing of pleadings, motions, and other papers with the court as required by the Indiana Rules of Trial Procedure shall be made by one of the following methods:

    i. Delivery to the clerk of the court;

ii. Sending by electronic transmission under the procedure adopted pursuant to IN ST ADMIN Rule 12;

iii. Mailing to the clerk by registered, certified or express mail return receipt requested;

iv. Depositing with any third-party commercial carrier for delivery to the clerk within three (3) calendar days, cost prepaid, properly addressed;

v. If the court so permits, filing with the judge, in which event the judge shall note thereon the filing date and forthwith transmit them to the office of the clerk; or

vi. Electronic filing, as approved by the Division of State Court Administration pursuant to IN ST ADMIN Rule 16. IN ST TRIAL P Rule 5(F).

vii. Filing by registered or certified mail and by third-party commercial carrier shall be complete upon mailing or deposit. IN ST TRIAL P Rule 5(F).

b. *Mandatory electronic filing.* Unless otherwise permitted by the Lake County Rules of Civil Procedure or otherwise authorized by the judicial officer assigned to a particular case, all documents submitted for filing (including the original complaint, or equivalent pleading, and summons) shall be filed electronically with the clerk using the LCOD, no matter when the case was originally filed. IN ST LAKE RCP Rule 17(D).

i. *Of documents containing information excluded from public access pursuant to* IN ST ADMIN Rule 9. Documents containing information excluded from public access pursuant to IN ST ADMIN Rule 9, or documents which are ordered to be filed under seal shall be filed electronically, pursuant to IN ST LAKE RCP Rule 17(D)(9), whenever possible, along with a copy of the applicable order to seal the records, and the filer shall designate the documents as "Not for Public Access Pursuant to Administrative Rule 9(G)(1)" at the time of filing. IN ST LAKE RCP Rule 16(A)(1); IN ST LAKE RCP Rule 17(D)(9).

- *Conventional filing of documents containing information excluded from public access pursuant to* IN ST ADMIN Rule 9. Documents containing information excluded from public access pursuant to IN ST ADMIN Rule 9, or documents which are ordered to be filed under seal, which cannot be legibly scanned and filed electronically, shall be conventionally filed under seal and designated by the filer as "Not for Public Access Pursuant to Administrative Rule 9(G)(1)" at the time of filing. The unredacted version shall be filed on light green paper which is conspicuously marked "Not for Public Access"; and a redacted version, with confidential information deleted, shall be filed on white paper which shall be available for public access. The filer shall also electronically file a Notice of Manual Filing. IN ST LAKE RCP Rule 16(A)(2).

ii. *Technical failures.* If a registered user is unable to file a document in a timely manner due to technical difficulties in the LCOD, the registered user must file a document with the court as soon as possible notifying the court of the inability to file the document. A sample document titled Declaration that Party was Unable to File in a Timely Manner Due to Technical Difficulties can be found at IN ST LAKE RCP Form 4. Delayed filings shall be rejected unless accompanied by the declaration attesting to the filer's failed attempts to file electronically at least two (2) times, separated by at least one (1) hour, after noon on each day of delay due to such technical failure. IN ST LAKE RCP Rule 17(J).

iii. *Documents allowed to be filed conventionally.* Unless specifically authorized by the court, only the following documents may be filed conventionally and not electronically:

- Exhibits and other documents that cannot be converted to a legible electronic form, such as videotapes, x-rays, and similar materials

- Documents delivered to the clerk by pro se litigants

- Documents mailed to the clerk by pro se litigants

- Confidential documents

- Notice of manual filing

- Titles of documents

- Chronological case summary entry forms (CCS entry forms). IN ST LAKE RCP Rule 17(E).

- For more information on the documents which must be filed conventionally, refer to IN ST LAKE RCP Rule 17(E).

c. *Facsimile filing.* Only when necessary on an emergency basis (i.e., when certified mail or other means of filing will not bring the document to the Judge's attention prior to the scheduled hearing or ruling), pleadings, motions and other papers may be filed by electronic facsimile transmission, or when specifically authorized by the Court. IN ST LAKE RCP Rule 2(C).

    i. *Generally.* In counties where a majority of judges of the courts of record, by posted local rule, have authorized electronic facsimile filing and designated a telephone number to receive such transmissions, pleadings, motions, and other papers may be sent to the Clerk of Circuit Court by electronic facsimile transmission for filing in any case, provided:

- Such matter does not exceed ten (10) pages, including the cover sheet;

- Such matter does not require the payment of fees other than the electronic facsimile transcription fee set forth in IN ST ADMIN Rule 12(E);

- The sending party creates at the time of transmission a machine generated log for such transmission; and

- The original document and the transmission log are maintained by the sending party for the duration of the litigation. IN ST ADMIN Rule 12(B).

    ii. *Time of filing.* During normal, posted business hours, the time of filing shall be the time the duplicate document is produced in the office of the Clerk of the Circuit Court. Duplicate documents received at all other times shall be filed as of the next normal business day. IN ST ADMIN Rule 12(C).

- If the receiving fax machine endorses its own time and date stamp upon the transmitted documents and the receiving machine produces a delivery receipt which is electronically created and transmitted to the sending party, the time of filing shall be the date and time recorded on the transmitted document by the receiving fax machine. IN ST ADMIN Rule 12(C).

d. *Filing for special judges.* For special judge matters where the special judge is a full-time judge or magistrate serving within Lake County, all papers submitted for filing shall be delivered or mailed to the Clerk's office at the courthouse where the special judge regularly serves. IN ST LAKE RCP Rule 3(A).

e. *Proof of filing.* Any party filing any paper by any method other than personal delivery to the clerk shall retain proof of filing. IN ST TRIAL P Rule 5(F).

2. *Service requirements.* Unless otherwise provided by the Indiana Rules of Trial Procedure or an order of the court, each party and special judge, if any, shall be served with: (1) every order required by its terms to be served; (2) every pleading subsequent to the original complaint; (3) every written motion except one which may be heard ex parte; (4) every brief submitted to the trial court; (5) every paper relating to discovery required to be served upon a party; and (6) every written notice, appearance, demand, offer of judgment, designation of record on appeal, or similar paper. IN ST TRIAL P Rule 5(A).

a. *Methods of service*

    i. *Personal service.* Whenever a party is represented by an attorney of record, service shall be made upon such attorney unless service upon the party himself is ordered by the court. Service upon the attorney or party shall be made by delivering or mailing a copy of the papers to the last known address or where an attorney or party has consented to service by fax or e-mail, as provided in IN ST TRIAL P Rule 3.1(A)(4), by faxing or e-mailing a copy of the documents to the fax number or e-mail address set out in the appearance form or correction as required by IN ST TRIAL P Rule 3.1(E). IN ST TRIAL P Rule 5(B). Delivery of a copy within IN ST TRIAL P Rule 5 means:

- Offering or tendering it to the attorney or party and stating the nature of the papers being served. Refusal to accept an offered or tendered document is a waiver of any objection to the sufficiency or adequacy of service of that document;

- Leaving it at his office with a clerk or other person in charge thereof, or if there is no one in charge, leaving it in a conspicuous place therein; or

- If the office is closed, by leaving it at his dwelling house or usual place of abode with some person of suitable age and discretion then residing therein; or,

- Leaving it at some other suitable place, selected by the attorney upon whom service is being made, pursuant to duly promulgated local rule. IN ST TRIAL P Rule 5(B)(1).

ii. *Service by mail.* If service is made by mail, the papers shall be deposited in the United States mail addressed to the person on whom they are being served, with postage prepaid. Service shall be deemed complete upon mailing. Proof of service of all papers permitted to be mailed may be made by written acknowledgment of service, by affidavit of the person who mailed the papers, or by certificate of an attorney. It shall be the duty of attorneys when entering their appearance in a cause or when filing pleadings or papers therein, to have noted in the Chronological Case Summary or said pleadings or papers so filed the address and telephone number of their office. Service by delivery or by mail at such address shall be deemed sufficient and complete. IN ST TRIAL P Rule 5(B)(2).

iii. *Service by fax or e-mail.* A party who has consented to service by fax or e-mail may be served as follows:

- Service by e-mail shall be made by attaching the document being served in .pdf format. Discovery documents must also be served in accordance with IN ST TRIAL P Rule 26(A). IN ST TRIAL P Rule 5(B)(3)(a).

- Service by fax shall be deemed complete upon generation of a transmission record indicating the successful transmission of the entire document, except as provided in IN ST TRIAL P Rule 5(B)(3)(d). IN ST TRIAL P Rule 5(B)(3)(b).

- Service by e-mail shall be deemed complete upon transmission, except as provided in IN ST TRIAL P Rule 5(B)(3)(d). IN ST TRIAL P Rule 5(B)(3)(c).

- Service by fax or e-mail that occurs on a Saturday, Sunday, legal holiday, or day the court or agency in which the matter is pending is closed or after 5:00 PM local time of the recipient shall be deemed complete the next day that is not a Saturday, Sunday, legal holiday, or day that the court or agency in which the matter is pending is not closed. IN ST TRIAL P Rule 5(B)(3)(d).

b. *Serving numerous defendants.* In any action in which there are unusually large numbers of defendants, the court, upon motion or of its own initiative, may order:

i. That service of the pleadings of the defendants and replies thereto need not be made as between the defendants;

- That any cross-claim, counterclaim, or matter constituting an avoidance or affirmative defense contained therein shall be deemed to be denied or avoided by all other parties; and

- That the filing of any such pleading and service thereof upon the plaintiff constitutes due notice of it to the parties. IN ST TRIAL P Rule 5(D).

ii. A copy of every such order shall be served upon the parties in such manner and form as the court directs. IN ST TRIAL P Rule 5(D).

c. *Service by electronic means.* The Lake County Online Docket will generate a Notice of Electronic Filing and Service when any document is filed and served. This notice will be emailed to each registered user of record in a case, and an electronic service event will be added to the work queue of each registered user of record in the case. The party filing the document should retain a paper or electronic copy of the Notice of Electronic Filing and Service. This notice represents proof of filing and service of the document on registered users of record in that case. The filer shall not be required to conventionally serve any document on any party receiving electronic service. IN ST LAKE RCP Rule 17(F)(2).

i. The filer shall also conventionally serve those parties not designated or able to receive electronic notice or service but who are nevertheless entitled to notice of said pleading or other document in accordance with the Indiana Rules of Civil Procedure and applicable Lake County Rules of Civil Procedure. In such cases, the filer shall also file a certificate of service, as appropriate. IN ST LAKE RCP Rule 17(F).

d. *Service on parties in default for failure to appear.* No service need be made on parties in default for failure to appear, except that pleadings asserting new or additional claims for relief against them shall be served upon them in the manner provided by service of summons in IN ST TRIAL P Rule 4. IN ST TRIAL P Rule 5(A).

G. Hearings

1. *Hearing on motion.* Unless local conditions make it impracticable, each judge shall establish regular times and places, at intervals sufficiently frequent for the prompt dispatch of business, at which motions requiring notice and hearing may be heard and disposed of; but the judge at any time or place and on such notice, if any, as he considers reasonable may make order for the advancement, conduct, and hearing of actions. To expedite its business the court may direct the submission and determination of motions without oral hearing upon brief written statements of reasons in support and opposition, or direct or permit hearings by telephone conference call with all attorneys or other similar means of communication. IN ST TRIAL P Rule 73(A).

2. *Oral argument discretionary.* The granting of a motion for oral argument, unless required by the Indiana Rules of Trial Procedure, shall be wholly discretionary with the court. IN ST LAKE RCP Rule 4(B).

H. Forms

1. Motion to Compel Discovery Forms for Indiana

a. Notice. 5 INPRAC § 4:6.10.

b. Motion to compel. 5 INPRAC § 4:6.20.

c. Motion to compel; Failure to respond. 5 INPRAC § 4:6.30.

d. Motion to compel answers to interrogatories. 5 INPRAC § 4:6.40.

e. Motion to compel production of documents. 5 INPRAC § 4:6.50.

f. Motion to dismiss as sanction for failure to comply with court ordered discovery. 5 INPRAC § 4:6.60.

g. Notice of intention to file motion to compel discovery. 10 INPRAC § 58.54.

h. Motion to compel discovery; General form. 10 INPRAC § 58.55.

i. Order compelling requested discovery. 10 INPRAC § 58.56.

j. Order denying motion to compel discovery. 10 INPRAC § 58.57.

k. Motion to compel discovery; For failure to respond to discovery requests. 10 INPRAC § 58.58.

l. Motion to compel; Physician to release medical records. 10 INPRAC § 58.59.

m. Motion to compel plaintiff to execute medical records release. 10 INPRAC § 58.60.

n. Motion to compel; Production of surveillance videotape. 10 INPRAC § 58.61.

o. Motion for order that matters be taken as established. 10 INPRAC § 58.62.

p. Motion for order precluding litigation of issues. 10 INPRAC § 58.63.

q. Motion to compel; Failure to permit inspection of original documents. 10 INPRAC § 58.65.

r. Motion to compel; Answer to deposition questions. 10 INPRAC § 58.66.

s. Certificate of service; Personal service. 9 INPRAC § 5.7.

t. Certificate of service; First class mail. 9 INPRAC § 5.8.

2. Official Motion to Compel Discovery Forms for Lake County

a. CCS entry form. IN ST LAKE RCP App. A.

b. Notice of manual filing. IN ST LAKE RCP Form 2.

    c.   Certificate of service. IN ST LAKE RCP Form 3.

    d.   Declaration that party was unable to file in a timely manner. IN ST LAKE RCP Form 4.

3. Motion to Compel Discovery Forms for Lake County

    a.   Notice of manual filing. EFORMST IN 5540.

I. Checklist

(I) ❑ Matters to be considered by moving party

  (a) ❑ Required documents

    (1) ❑ Motion and notice

    (2) ❑ Brief

    (3) ❑ Disputed discovery

    (4) ❑ Attorney certification

    (5) ❑ Proposed order

    (6) ❑ Chronological case summary (CSS) entry forms

    (7) ❑ Certificate of service

  (b) ❑ Supplemental documents

    (1) ❑ Supporting evidence

    (2) ❑ Facsimile cover sheet

  (c) ❑ Timing

    (1) ❑ The moving party must provide reasonable notice of his intention to file a motion to compel with the other litigants and all affected persons

    (2) ❑ A written motion, other than one which may be heard ex parte, and notice of the hearing thereof shall be served not less than five (5) days before the time specified for the hearing, unless a different period is fixed by the Indiana Rules of Trial Procedure or by order of the court

    (3) ❑ All pleadings and papers subsequent to the complaint which are required to be served upon a party shall be filed with the Court either before service or within a reasonable period of time thereafter

    (4) ❑ All pleadings, motions and other papers submitted for filing which are required to be served under IN ST TRIAL P Rule 5(A) shall be filed no later than three (3) days after service

    (5) ❑ If such papers are filed before service, proof of service thereof shall be filed no later than three (3) business days thereafter

(II) ❑ Matters to be considered by the responding party

  (a) ❑ Required documents

    (1) ❑ Opposition

    (2) ❑ Chronological case summary (CSS) entry forms

    (3) ❑ Certificate of service

  (b) ❑ Supplemental documents

    (1) ❑ Supporting evidence

    (2) ❑ Proposed order

    (3) ❑ Facsimile cover sheet

  (c) ❑ Timing

    (1) ❑ So long as consistent with the Indiana Rules of Trial Procedure, an adverse party wishing to respond shall do so within fifteen (15) days of service

(2) ❏ Except as otherwise provided in IN ST TRIAL P Rule 59(D), opposing affidavits may be served not less than one (1) day before the hearing, unless the court permits them to be served at some other time

Motions, Oppositions and Replies
Motion for Protective Order

Document Last Updated October 2013

A. Applicable Rules

1. *State rules*

   a. Appearance. IN ST TRIAL P Rule 3.1.

   b. Process. IN ST TRIAL P Rule 4.

   c. Service and filing of pleadings and other papers. IN ST TRIAL P Rule 5.

   d. Time. IN ST TRIAL P Rule 6.

   e. Pleadings. IN ST TRIAL P Rule 7; IN ST TRIAL P Rule 8; IN ST TRIAL P Rule 9.2; IN ST TRIAL P Rule 10.

   f. Signing and verification of pleadings. IN ST TRIAL P Rule 11.

   g. General provisions governing discovery. IN ST TRIAL P Rule 26.

   h. Methods of discovery. IN ST TRIAL P Rule 27; IN ST TRIAL P Rule 30; IN ST TRIAL P Rule 31; IN ST TRIAL P Rule 33; IN ST TRIAL P Rule 34; IN ST TRIAL P Rule 36.

   i. Failure to make or cooperate in discovery; Sanctions. IN ST TRIAL P Rule 37.

   j. Evidence. IN ST TRIAL P Rule 43.

   k. Judgment on the evidence (directed verdict). IN ST TRIAL P Rule 50.

   l. Findings by the court. IN ST TRIAL P Rule 52.

   m. Summary judgment. IN ST TRIAL P Rule 56.

   n. Motion to correct error. IN ST TRIAL P Rule 59.

   o. Relief from judgment or error. IN ST TRIAL P Rule 60.

   p. Hearing of motions. IN ST TRIAL P Rule 73.

   q. Court records. IN ST TRIAL P Rule 77.

   r. Access to court records. IN ST ADMIN Rule 9.

   s. Paper size. IN ST ADMIN Rule 11.

   t. Facsimile transmission. IN ST ADMIN Rule 12.

   u. Electronic filing and electronic service pilot projects. IN ST ADMIN Rule 16.

   v. Privacy and confidentiality. IN ST 5-2-9-6; IN ST 5-14-3-4; IN ST 5-14-3-5.5; IN ST 6-4.1-5-10; IN ST 6-4.1-12-12; IN ST 6-8.1-7-1; IN ST 11-13-1-8; IN ST 12-23-14-13; IN ST 16-39-3-10; IN ST 16-41-8-1; IN ST 22-4-19-6; IN ST 31-11-1-6; IN ST 31-19-5-23; IN ST 31-19-13-2; IN ST 31-19-19-1; IN ST 31-33-18-1; IN ST 31-39-1-1; IN ST 31-39-1-2; IN ST 33-23-16-16; IN ST 35-34-2-4; IN ST 35-38-1-13; IN ST 35-38-9-1; IN ST ADR Rule 2.11; IN ST ADR Rule 4.4; IN ST ADR Rule 5.6; IN ST JURY Rule 10.

   w. Trade secrets. IN ST 24-2-3-1; IN ST 24-2-3-2.

2. *Local rules*

   a. Scope and title. [IN ST LAKE RCP Rule 1, as amended by IN ORDER 13-0237, effective October 18, 2013].

   b. Preparation of pleadings, motions and other papers. IN ST LAKE RCP Rule 2.

c. Filing. [IN ST LAKE RCP Rule 3, as amended by IN ORDER 13-0237, effective October 18, 2013].

d. Motions. IN ST LAKE RCP Rule 4.

e. Discovery. IN ST LAKE RCP Rule 8.

f. Pretrial procedure. IN ST LAKE RCP Rule 9.

g. Briefs. IN ST LAKE RCP Rule 11.

h. Confidential information and sealed documents. IN ST LAKE RCP Rule 16.

i. Electronic filing and service. IN ST LAKE RCP Rule 17.

B. Timing

1. *Motion for protective order.* There are no specific timing requirements for filing a motion for a protective order.

    a. *Filing.* All pleadings and papers subsequent to the complaint which are required to be served upon a party shall be filed with the Court either before service or within a reasonable period of time thereafter. IN ST TRIAL P Rule 5(E)(1). All pleadings, motions and other papers submitted for filing which are required to be served under IN ST TRIAL P Rule 5(A) shall be filed no later than three (3) days after service. IN ST LAKE RCP Rule 3(A).

        i. If such papers are filed before service, proof of service thereof shall be filed no later than three (3) business days thereafter. Upon failure to comply with IN ST LAKE RCP Rule 3, the Court may, on motion of any party or on its own motion, impose appropriate sanctions. IN ST LAKE RCP Rule 3(A).

    b. *Briefs.* Briefs, other than those addressed in IN ST LAKE RCP Rule 4 and IN ST LAKE RCP Rule 9, shall be filed no later than two (2) calendar days preceding the hearing or trial to which directed. IN ST LAKE RCP Rule 11.

2. *Service.* A written motion, other than one which may be heard ex parte, and notice of the hearing thereof shall be served not less than five (5) days before the time specified for the hearing, unless a different period is fixed by the Indiana Rules of Trial Procedure or by order of the court. IN ST TRIAL P Rule 6(D).

    a. *Of supporting affidavits.* When a motion is supported by affidavit, the affidavit shall be served with the motion. IN ST TRIAL P Rule 6(D).

3. *Service of opposition.* Except as otherwise provided in IN ST TRIAL P Rule 59(D), opposing affidavits may be served not less than one (1) day before the hearing, unless the court permits them to be served at some other time. IN ST TRIAL P Rule 6(D).

    a. So long as consistent with the Indiana Rules of Trial Procedure, an adverse party wishing to respond shall do so within fifteen (15) days of service. IN ST LAKE RCP Rule 4(A).

4. *Reply.* The moving party shall have ten (10) days after service of the response within which to reply. IN ST LAKE RCP Rule 4(A).

5. *Computation of time*

    a. *Generally; Days excluded.* In computing any period of time prescribed or allowed by the Indiana Rules of Trial Procedure, by order of the court, or by any applicable statute, the day of the act, event, or default from which the designated period of time begins to run shall not be included. The last day of the period so computed is to be included unless it is:

        i. A Saturday,

        ii. A Sunday,

        iii. A legal holiday as defined by state statute, or

        iv. A day the office in which the act is to be done is closed during regular business hours. IN ST TRIAL P Rule 6(A).

    b. *Short periods.* In any event, the period runs until the end of the next day that is not a Saturday, a Sunday, a legal holiday, or a day on which the office is closed. When the period of time allowed is less than seven (7) days, intermediate Saturdays, Sundays, legal holidays, and days on which the office is closed shall be excluded from the computations. IN ST TRIAL P Rule 6(A).

    c.   *Additional time after service by United States mail.* Whenever a party has the right or is required to do some act or take some proceedings within a prescribed period after the service of a notice or other paper upon him and the notice or paper is served upon him by United States mail, three (3) days shall be added to the prescribed period. IN ST TRIAL P Rule 6(E).

    d.   *Electronic filing does not alter deadlines.* Filing electronically does not alter any filing deadlines or any time computation pursuant to state or federal statutes, any Rules of the Indiana Supreme Court, including without limitation the Rules of Trial Procedure, the Rules of Appellate Procedure or the Administrative Rules, or applicable Lake County Rules of Civil Procedure. The office of the Lake County Clerk is open for electronic filing under the Lake County Rules of Civil Procedure twenty-four (24) hours a day. A document is deemed filed at the date and time it is received by the LCOD server. Filing must be completed before midnight local time in order to be considered filed that day. Lake County observes Central Time and electronic filers are strongly urged to file documents during hours when the Lake County Online Docket ("LCOD") help line is available, from 9:00 a.m. to 4:00 p.m. local time, although documents can be filed electronically twenty-four (24) hours a day. IN ST LAKE RCP Rule 17(I).

    e.   *Enlargement of time.* When an act is required or allowed to be done at or within a specific time by the Indiana Rules of Trial Procedure, the court may at any time for cause shown:

        i.   Order the period enlarged, with or without motion or notice, if request therefor is made before the expiration of the period originally prescribed or extended by a previous order; or

        ii.   Upon motion made after the expiration of the specific period, permit the act to be done where the failure to act was the result of excusable neglect; but, the court may not extend the time for taking any action for judgment on the evidence under IN ST TRIAL P Rule 50(A), amendment of findings and judgment under IN ST TRIAL P Rule 52(B), to correct errors under IN ST TRIAL P Rule 59(C), statement in opposition to motion to correct error under IN ST TRIAL P Rule 59(E), or to obtain relief from final judgment under IN ST TRIAL P Rule 60(B), except to the extent and under the conditions stated in those rules. IN ST TRIAL P Rule 6(B).

C. General Requirements

1.   *Motions, generally.* Unless made during a hearing or trial, or otherwise ordered by the court, an application to the court for an order shall be made by written motion. The motion shall state the grounds therefor and the relief or order sought. IN ST TRIAL P Rule 7(B).

    a.   *Motions as distinct from pleadings.* Motions and responses to motions are not pleadings, and allegations contained in a motion are not admissions of a party. 22B INPRAC 7:2; Wachstetter v. County Properties, LLC, 832 N.E.2d 574 (Ind.Ct.App. 2005); Scott County Family YMCA, Inc. v. Hobbs, 817 N.E.2d 603 (Ind.Ct.App. 2004).

    b.   *Unopposed motions generally granted.* It is common for a trial court to grant procedural motions, such as motions for enlargement of time, discovery motions, or motions for continuance, unless an objection is filed. 21 INPRAC § 13.8.

    c.   *Separate motions.* Each motion shall be separate, while alternative motions filed together shall each be identified on the caption. IN ST LAKE RCP Rule 4(A).

    d.   *Answer and reply briefs.* Failure to file an answer brief or reply brief within the time prescribed shall be deemed a waiver of the right thereto and shall subject the motion to summary ruling. IN ST LAKE RCP Rule 4(A).

2.   *Motion for protective order*

    a.   *Forms of protective order.* Upon motion by any party or by the person from whom discovery is sought, and for good cause shown, the court in which the action is pending or alternatively, on matters relating to a deposition, the court in the county where the deposition is being taken, may make any order which justice requires to protect a party or person from annoyance, embarrassment, oppression, or undue burden or expense, including one or more of the following:

        i.   That the discovery not be had;

        ii.   That the discovery may be had only on specified terms and conditions, including a designation of the time or place;

    iii.   That the discovery may be had only by a method of discovery other than that selected by the party seeking discovery;

    iv.   That certain matters not be inquired into, or that the scope of the discovery be limited to certain matters;

    v.   That discovery be conducted with no one present except the parties and their attorneys and persons designated by the court;

    vi.   That a deposition after being sealed be opened only by order of the court;

    vii.   That a trade secret or other confidential research, development, or commercial information not be disclosed or be disclosed only in a designated way;

    viii.   That the parties simultaneously file specified documents or information enclosed in sealed envelopes to be opened as directed by the court;

    ix.   That a party need not provide discovery of electronically stored information from sources that the party identifies as not reasonably accessible because of undue burden or cost. IN ST TRIAL P Rule 26(C).

b.   *List in IN ST TRIAL P Rule 26(C) not exhaustive.* A court is not limited to the eight specified types of orders. A court may be as inventive as the case and the conditions require. A party or a nonparty may thus obtain any kind of protective order against any kind of discovery which is sought in the case, if "good cause" is shown. So also, however, if a protective order is sought and denied, the trial court may go further and issue an order to provide for or to permit the discovery. 2A INPRAC R 26(26.20).

c.   *Trade secrets.* A protectable trade secret has four characteristics: (1) information, (2) which derives independent economic value, (3) is not generally known, or readily ascertainable by proper means by other persons who can obtain economic value from its disclosure or use, and (4) the subject of efforts reasonable under the circumstances to maintain its secrecy. 2A INPRAC R 26(26.23.1).

    i.   *Nature of determination.* The determination of whether information is a trade secret is a fact sensitive determination. 2A INPRAC R 26(26.23.1).

    ii.   *Burden of proof.* The burden of proof is on the party asserting the trade secret to show that it is included in the categories of protectable trade secret information listed in the trade secrets statute. 2A INPRAC R 26(26.23.1); Northern Elec. Co., Inc. v. Torma, 819 N.E.2d 417 (Ind.Ct.App. 2004).

    iii.   *Uniform trade secrets act.* The application of IN ST TRIAL P Rule 26 to trade secrets should be informed by Indiana's enactment of the Uniform Trade Secrets Act (UTSA) (refer to IN ST 24-2-3-1, et seq.), which provides states with a common legal framework for protecting trade secrets from misappropriation. 2A INPRAC R 26(26.23.1(C)).

    iv.   *Trade secret defined.* "Trade secret" means information, including a formula, pattern, compilation, program, device, method, technique, or process, that:

- Derives independent economic value, actual or potential, from not being generally known to, and not being readily ascertainable by proper means by, other persons who can obtain economic value from its disclosure or use; and

- Is the subject of efforts that are reasonable under the circumstances to maintain its secrecy. IN ST 24-2-3-2.

d.   *Information not reasonably accessible.* On motion to compel discovery or for a protective order, the party from whom discovery is sought must show that the information is not reasonably accessible because of undue burden or cost. If that showing is made, the court may nonetheless order discovery from such sources if the requesting party shows good cause. The court may specify conditions for the discovery. IN ST TRIAL P Rule 26(C)(9).

    i.   When filing a motion for protective order under IN ST TRIAL P Rule 26(C), the movant, whether a party or non-party, must allege and prove good cause for his request for protective order. The court is empowered to make any order which "justice requires to protect a party or person from annoyance, embarrassment, oppression, or undue burden or expense." Typically, this protection means that discovery will be denied altogether, or limited in scope or to specific terms. 10 INPRAC § 58.20.

e. *Party justified in resisting discovery.* A litigant is substantially justified in seeking to compel or resist discovery if reasonable persons could conclude that genuine issue existed as to whether person was bound to comply with requested discovery. 10 INPRAC § 58.20; Munsell v. Hambright, 776 N.E.2d 1272 (Ind.Ct.App. 2002).

f. *Award of expenses of motion.* If the motion for a protective order is denied in whole or in part, the court may, on such terms and conditions as are just, order that any party or person provide or permit discovery. The provisions of IN ST TRIAL P Rule 37(A)(4) apply to the award of expenses incurred in relation to the motion. IN ST TRIAL P Rule 26(C).

g. *Attorney conference on discovery* issues. Strict compliance with IN ST TRIAL P Rule 26 through IN ST TRIAL P Rule 37 is required. The discovery process is intended to be largely self-actuating, with minimal court supervision. Therefore, the court will not rule on motions related to discovery disputes unless moving counsel represents that, after personal or telephonic conference in good faith effort to resolve differences, counsel are unable to reach accord. If counsel advises the court, by way of motion or response thereto, that opposing counsel has refused or delayed resolution of the discovery dispute, the court may, after hearing, impose appropriate sanctions. IN ST LAKE RCP Rule 8(C).

D. Documents

1. *Required documents*

   a. *Motion and notice.* The requirement of notice is satisfied by service of the motion. IN ST TRIAL P Rule 7(B). Refer to the General Requirements section of this document for information on the content of a motion for a protective order.

   b. *Brief.* Briefs, other than those addressed in IN ST LAKE RCP Rule 4 and IN ST LAKE RCP Rule 9, shall be filed no later than two (2) calendar days preceding the hearing or trial to which directed. IN ST LAKE RCP Rule 11.

   c. *Attorney certification.* Before any party files any motion or request to compel discovery pursuant to IN ST TRIAL P Rule 37, or any motion for protection from discovery pursuant to IN ST TRIAL P Rule 26(C), or any other discovery motion which seeks to enforce, modify, or limit discovery, that party shall:

      i. Make a reasonable effort to reach agreement with the opposing party concerning the matter which is the subject of the motion or request; and

      ii. Include in the motion or request a statement showing that the attorney making the motion or request has made a reasonable effort to reach agreement with the opposing attorney(s) concerning the matter(s) set forth in the motion or request. This statement shall recite, in addition, the date, time and place of this effort to reach agreement, whether in person or by phone, and the names of all parties and attorneys participating therein. If an attorney for any party advises the court in writing that an opposing attorney has refused or delayed meeting and discussing the issues covered in IN ST TRIAL P Rule 26(F), the court may take such action as is appropriate. IN ST TRIAL P Rule 26(F).

      iii. The court may deny a discovery motion filed by a party who has failed to comply with the requirements of IN ST TRIAL P Rule 26(F). IN ST TRIAL P Rule 26(F).

   d. *Proposed order.* Unless local practice provides differently, a party should submit a proposed order with its written motion to be signed by the judge once the motion has been granted. 21 INPRAC § 13.8.

      i. Proposed orders, which are submitted for the court's convenience under IN ST LAKE RCP Rule 3 or other applicable Lake County Rules of Civil Procedure, shall be submitted as attachments to motions. IN ST LAKE RCP Rule 17(D)(8). Proposed orders shall be prepared and filed separately from the pleadings, petitions, motions or other papers to which they have reference. IN ST LAKE RCP Rule 3(B).

    ii.   Orders, either routine in nature or uncontested including, for example, those setting or continuing a hearing, shall be effected by the chronological case summary entry only, which shall contain the concise substance of the order. IN ST LAKE RCP Rule 3(B).

    iii.   All orders shall be accompanied with sufficient copies and stamped, pre-addressed envelopes, so that copies may be mailed to all parties. IN ST LAKE RCP Rule 3(B).

e.   *Chronological case summary (CCS) entry forms.* All filings shall be accompanied by a Chronological Case Summary (CCS) Entry Form to define or identify the documents filed. The Form used should be substantially similar to IN ST LAKE RCP App. A. IN ST LAKE RCP Rule 3(C).

f.   *Certificate of service.* An attorney or unrepresented party tendering a document to the Clerk for filing shall certify that service has been made, list the parties served, and specify the date and means of service. The certificate of service shall be placed at the end of the document and shall not be separately filed. The separate filing of a certificate of service, however, shall not be grounds for rejecting a document for filing. The Clerk may permit documents to be filed without a certificate of service but shall require prompt filing of a separate certificate of service. IN ST TRIAL P Rule 5(C).

    i.   All pleadings, motions and other papers submitted for filing which are required to be served under IN ST TRIAL P Rule 5(A) shall contain proof of service pursuant to IN ST TRIAL P Rule 5(B)(2). IN ST LAKE RCP Rule 3(A).

2.   *Supplemental documents*

a.   *Supporting evidence.* When a motion is based on facts not appearing of record the court may hear the matter on affidavits presented by the respective parties, but the court may direct that the matter be heard wholly or partly on oral testimony or depositions. IN ST TRIAL P Rule 43(B).

b.   *Facsimile cover sheet.* Any document sent to the Clerk of the Circuit Court by electronic facsimile transmission shall be accompanied by a cover sheet which states the title of the document, case number, number of pages, identity and voice telephone number of the sending party and instructions for filing. The cover sheet shall contain the signature of the attorney or party, pro se, authorizing the filing. IN ST ADMIN Rule 12(D).

E. Format

1.   *Form of motions.* The rules applicable to captions, and the signing and form of pleadings (IN ST TRIAL P Rule 8 through IN ST TRIAL P Rule 11), apply to all motions and other papers provided under the Indiana Rules of Trial Procedure. 22B INPRAC 7:2.

2.   *Form of pleadings.* For the purpose of uniformity, convenience, clarity and durability, requirements in IN ST LAKE RCP Rule 2 shall be observed in the preparation of all pleadings, motions and other papers. IN ST LAKE RCP Rule 2. Whenever materials submitted fail to meet the standards in IN ST LAKE RCP Rule 2, the Court may impose appropriate sanctions. IN ST LAKE RCP Rule 2(B).

a.   *Caption; Names of parties.* Every pleading shall contain a caption setting forth the name of the court, the title of the action, the file number, and a designation as in IN ST TRIAL P Rule 7(A). In the complaint the title of the action shall include the names of all the parties, but in other pleadings it is sufficient to state the name of the first party on each side with an appropriate indication of other parties. IN ST TRIAL P Rule 10(A).

    i.   *Special judge matters.* The caption of all CCS Entry Forms, pleadings, motions, orders and other papers to be filed in a special judge case shall include in block text the words SPECIAL JUDGE and the name of the judge directly below the cause number on the caption. IN ST LAKE RCP Rule 2(D).

b.   *Paragraphs; Separate statements.* All averments of a claim or defense shall be made in numbered paragraphs, the contents of each of which shall be limited as far as practicable to a statement of a single set of circumstances, and a paragraph may be referred to by number in all succeeding pleadings. Each claim founded upon a separate transaction or occurrence and each defense other than denials may be stated in a separate count or defense whenever a separation facilitates the clear presentation of the matters set forth. IN ST TRIAL P Rule 10(B).

c.   *Adoption by reference; Exhibits.* Statements in a pleading may be adopted by reference in a different part of the same pleading or in another pleading or in any motion. A copy of any written instrument which is an exhibit to a pleading is a part thereof for all purposes. IN ST TRIAL P Rule 10(C).

   d.   *Paper; Print, quality and binding*

      i.   All pleadings, motions, chronological case summary entry forms, orders, process and other papers shall be neatly and legibly printed, typewritten or mechanically reproduced, on one (1) side only, on white opaque paper. To satisfy the recordkeeping requirements of IN ST TRIAL P Rule 77, the print shall be of sufficient density and clarity for preservation and reproduction of microfilming, optical disk or other secondary sources. For this reason, the use of non-letter-quality printers is discouraged. IN ST LAKE RCP Rule 2(A).

      ii.   Paper and ink shall be of such quality as to withstand the test of time. All documents shall be produced on acid-free, non-thermal paper. It is recommended that a minimum of twenty (20) pound, twenty-five percent (25%) cotton paper product be used. Documents of multiple pages shall be submitted in bound or stapled fashion, and the binding or stapling shall be at the top only. Covers or backings shall not be used. IN ST LAKE RCP Rule 2(A).

   e.   *Papers; Handwritten.* Handwritten papers may be filed only if approved by the Court and a typewritten or printed true rendition thereof is filed within three (3) days thereafter and approved by the Court. Upon such approval, they shall be deemed and filed as the original, while the handwritten papers shall be retained therewith for evidentiary purposes. IN ST LAKE RCP Rule 2(C).

   f.   *Minute sheets; Motion blanks.* Minute sheets and motion blanks shall no longer be used. IN ST LAKE RCP Rule 2(D).

3.   *Size of papers for filing.* Effective January 1, 1992, all pleadings, copies, motions and documents filed with any trial court or appellate level court, typed or printed, with the exception of exhibits and existing wills, shall be prepared on eight and one-half by eleven inch (8 1/2" x 11") size paper. IN ST ADMIN Rule 11.

4.   *Signature requirements*

   a.   *Signature of attorney.* Every pleading or motion of a party represented by an attorney shall be signed by at least one (1) attorney of record in his individual name, whose address, telephone number, and attorney number shall be stated, except that this provision shall not apply to pleadings and motions made and transcribed at the trial or a hearing before the judge and received by him in such form. IN ST TRIAL P Rule 11(A).

      i.   The signature of an attorney constitutes a certificate by him that he has read the pleadings; that to the best of his knowledge, information, and belief, there is good ground to support it; and that it is not interposed for delay. IN ST TRIAL P Rule 11(A).

      ii.   If a pleading or motion is not signed or is signed with intent to defeat the purpose of the rule, it may be stricken as sham and false and the action may proceed as though the pleading had not been served. IN ST TRIAL P Rule 11(A).

      iii.   For a willful violation of IN ST TRIAL P Rule 11 an attorney may be subjected to appropriate disciplinary action. Similar action may be taken if scandalous or indecent matter is inserted. IN ST TRIAL P Rule 11(A).

   b.   *Signature of unrepresented party.* A party who is not represented by an attorney shall sign his pleading and state his address. IN ST TRIAL P Rule 11(A).

   c.   *Verification not generally required.* Except when specifically required by rule, pleadings or motions need not be verified or accompanied by affidavit. The rule in equity that the averments of an answer under oath must be overcome by the testimony of two (2) witnesses or of one (1) witness sustained by corroborating circumstances is abolished. IN ST TRIAL P Rule 11(A).

   d.   *Verification by affirmation or representation.* When in connection with any civil or special statutory proceeding it is required that any pleading, motion, petition, supporting affidavit, or other document of any kind, be verified, or that an oath be taken, it shall be sufficient if the subscriber simply affirms the truth of the matter to be verified by an affirmation or representation. IN ST TRIAL P Rule 11(B). IN ST TRIAL P Rule 11(B) states that the affirmation or representation should be in substantially the

following language: "I (we) affirm, under the penalties for perjury, that the foregoing representation(s) is (are) true. (Signed) _____."

    i.   Any person who falsifies an affirmation or representation of fact shall be subject to the same penalties as are prescribed by law for the making of a false affidavit. IN ST TRIAL P Rule 11(B).

e.   *Verified pleadings, motions, and affidavits as evidence.* Pleadings, motions and affidavits accompanying or in support of such pleadings or motions when required to be verified or under oath shall be accepted as a representation that the signer had personal knowledge thereof or reasonable cause to believe the existence of the facts or matters stated or alleged therein; and, if otherwise competent or acceptable as evidence, may be admitted as evidence of the facts or matters stated or alleged therein when it is so provided in the Indiana Rules of Trial Procedure, by statute or other law, or to the extent the writing or signature expressly purports to be made upon the signer's personal knowledge. When such pleadings, motions and affidavits are verified or under oath they shall not require other or greater proof on the part of the adverse party than if not verified or not under oath unless expressly provided otherwise by the Indiana Rules of Trial Procedure, statute or other law. Affidavits upon motions for summary judgment under IN ST TRIAL P Rule 56 and in denial of execution under IN ST TRIAL P Rule 9.2 shall be made upon personal knowledge. IN ST TRIAL P Rule 11(C).

f.   *Electronic signature.* The filing of documents and information through the E-filing system by use of a valid username and password is presumed to have been authorized by the User to whom that username and password have been issued and documents filed through the E-filing system are presumed to have been signed by the same User. IN ST ADMIN Rule 16(E).

5.   *Information excluded from public access.* Every document filed in a case shall separately identify information excluded from public access pursuant to IN ST ADMIN Rule 9(G)(1) as follows:

a.   Whole documents that are excluded from public access pursuant to IN ST ADMIN Rule 9(G)(1) shall be tendered on light green paper or have a light green coversheet attached to the document, marked "Not for Public Access" or "Confidential." IN ST TRIAL P Rule 5(G)(1).

b.   When only a portion of a document contains information excluded from public access pursuant to IN ST ADMIN Rule 9(G)(1), said information shall be omitted [or redacted] from the filed document, and set forth on a separate accompanying document on light green paper conspicuously marked "Not for Public Access" or "Confidential" and clearly designated [or identifying] the caption and number of the case and the document and location within the document to which the redacted material pertains. IN ST TRIAL P Rule 5(G)(2).

c.   With respect to documents filed in electronic format, the trial court, by local rule, may provide for compliance with IN ST TRIAL P Rule 5 in manner that separates and protects access to information excluded from public access. IN ST TRIAL P Rule 5(G)(3).

d.   IN ST TRIAL P Rule 5(G) does not apply to a record sealed by the court pursuant to IN ST 5-14-3-5.5 or otherwise, nor to records, documents, or information filed in cases to which public access is prohibited pursuant to IN ST ADMIN Rule 9(G). IN ST TRIAL P Rule 5(G)(4).

e.   The following information in case records is excluded from public access and is confidential:

    i.   Information that is excluded from public access pursuant to federal law;

    ii.   Information that is excluded from public access as declared confidential by Indiana statute or other court rule, including without limitation:

- All adoption records created after July 8, 1941, as declared confidential by IN ST 31-19-19-1, et seq., except those specifically declared open by IN ST 31-19-13-2(2);

- All records relating to chancroid, chlamydia, gonorrhea, hepatitis, human immunodeficiency virus (HIV), Lymphogranuloma venereum, syphilis, tuberculosis, as declared confidential by IN ST 16-41-8-1, et seq.;

- All records relating to child abuse as declared confidential by IN ST 31-33-18-1, et seq.;

- All records relating to drug tests as declared confidential by IN ST 5-14-3-4(a)(9);

- Records of grand jury proceedings as declared confidential by IN ST 35-34-2-4;

- Records of juvenile proceedings as declared confidential by IN ST 31-39-1-2, except those specifically open under statute;

- All paternity records created after July 1, 1941 as declared confidential by IN ST 31-14-11-15, IN ST 31-19-5-23, IN ST 31-39-1-1 and IN ST 31-39-1-2 [Editor's note: IN ST 31-14-11-15 was repealed effective May 9, 2013];

- All pre-sentence reports as declared confidential by IN ST 35-38-1-13;

- Written petitions to permit marriages without consent and orders directing the Clerk of Court to issue a marriage license to underage persons, as declared confidential by IN ST 31-11-1-6;

- Only those arrest warrants, search warrants, indictments and informations ordered confidential by the trial judge, prior to return of duly executed service as declared confidential by IN ST 5-14-3-4(b)(1);

- All medical, mental health, or tax records unless determined by law or regulation of any governmental custodian not to be confidential, released by the subject of such records, or declared by a court of competent jurisdiction to be essential to the resolution of litigation as declared confidential by IN ST 16-39-3-10, IN ST 6-4.1-5-10, IN ST 6-4.1-12-12, and IN ST 6-8.1-7-1;

- Personal information relating to jurors or prospective jurors, other than for the use of the parties and counsel, pursuant to IN ST JURY Rule 10;

- Information relating to protection from abuse orders, no-contact orders and workplace violence restraining orders as declared confidential by IN ST 5-2-9-6, et seq.;

- Mediation proceedings pursuant to IN ST ADR Rule 2.11, Mini-Trial proceedings pursuant to IN ST ADR Rule 4.4(C), and Summary Jury Trials pursuant to IN ST ADR Rule 5.6;

- Information in probation files pursuant to the Probation Standards promulgated by the Judicial Conference of Indiana pursuant to IN ST 11-13-1-8(b);

- Information deemed confidential pursuant to the Rules for Court Administered Alcohol and Drug Programs promulgated by the Judicial Conference of Indiana pursuant to IN ST 12-23-14-13;

- Information deemed confidential pursuant to the Problem-Solving Court Rules promulgated by the Judicial Conference of Indiana pursuant to IN ST 33-23-16-16;

- All records of the Department of workforce Development as declared confidential by IN ST 22-4-19-6;

- Information regarding interception of electronic communications that is sealed or deemed confidential as set forth in IN ST 35-33.5-2-1, et seq.

iii. Information excluded from public access by specific court order;

iv. Complete Social Security Numbers of living persons;

v. With the exception of names, information such as addresses, phone numbers, and dates of birth which explicitly identifies:

- Natural persons who are witnesses or victims (not including defendants) in criminal, domestic violence, stalking, sexual assault, juvenile, or civil protection order proceedings, provided that juveniles who are victims of sex crimes shall be identified by initials only;

- Places of residence of judicial officers, clerks and other employees of courts and clerks of court, unless the person or persons about whom the information pertains waives confidentiality;

vi. Complete account numbers of specific assets, loans, bank accounts, credit cards, and personal identification numbers (PINs);

vii. All orders of expungement entered in criminal or juvenile proceedings, orders to restrict access

to criminal history information pursuant to IN ST 35-38-5-5.5 or IN ST 35-38-8-5 and records excluded from public access by such orders, and information related to infractions that is excluded from public access pursuant to IN ST 34-28-5-15 or IN ST 34-28-5-16 [Editor's note: IN ST 35-38-5-5.5, IN ST 35-38-8-5 and IN ST 34-28-5-16 were repealed effective July 1, 2013; for information on orders restricting access to criminal history, refer to IN ST 35-38-9-1, et seq.];

    viii. All personal notes and e-mail, and deliberative material, of judges, jurors, court staff and judicial agencies, and information recorded in personal data assistants (PDA's) or organizers and personal calendars. IN ST ADMIN Rule 9(G)(1).

6. *Format of electronically filed documents*

    a. *Generally.* Electronically filed documents must meet the same requirements of format as documents conventionally filed pursuant to IN ST LAKE RCP Rule 2 or other applicable Lake County Rules of Civil Procedure. IN ST LAKE RCP Rule 17(D)(1).

    b. *Titles of documents.* The person electronically filing a document will be responsible for designating a title for the document at the time it is filed. The LCOD will generate the appropriate entry onto the CCS to record the filing of the document. IN ST LAKE RCP Rule 17(D)(3).

    c. *Citations and hyperlinks.* Electronically filed documents may contain hyperlink references to an external document as a convenient mechanism for accessing material cited in the document. Filers wishing to insert hyperlinks into documents shall continue to use the traditional method of citation to authority in addition to the hyperlink provided. The hyperlink is merely a convenience to the court and the material referenced is extraneous to the file and not a part of the court's record. IN ST LAKE RCP Rule 17(D)(5).

    d. *Attachments and exhibits.* All documents which form part of a single submission and which are being filed at the same time and by the same filer may be electronically filed together under one document filing, e.g., the motion, supporting affidavits, memorandum in support, designation of evidence, exhibits. IN ST LAKE RCP Rule 17(D)(6).

        i. Large documents which do not exist in an electronic format shall be scanned into .pdf format and filed electronically as separate attachments. A scanner is available in each clerk's office for use by the public and the bar in scanning and saving image files if needed. IN ST LAKE RCP Rule 17(D)(6).

    e. *Electronic signatures*

        i. *Electronic filing as signature.* The electronic filing of a document which is required to be signed shall constitute the filer's representation under IN ST TRIAL P Rule 11. Unless the electronically filed document has been scanned and shows the filer's original signature, the signature of the filer shall be indicated by As/Attorney's Name, or As/Party's Name as in the case of a pro se litigant, on the line where the signature would otherwise appear. IN ST LAKE RCP Rule 17(G)(1).

        ii. *Signatures on jointly signed or filed, verified or other documents.* In the case of a stipulation, agreed order, jointly signed motion or other document which needs to be signed by two (2) or more persons, or in the case of documents which must contain original signatures and which require verification or an unsworn declaration under rule or statute, the signatures may be indicated by either:

          • Submitting a scanned copy of the originally signed document; or,

          • Submitting the document with the use of As/Name in the signature block(s) where the original signature(s) appear(s) in the original document; provided, however, that the filer shall first obtain the physical signature of all persons necessary. IN ST LAKE RCP Rule 17(G)(2).

        iii. *Retention of original.* The filer shall retain the original executed document. IN ST LAKE RCP Rule 17(G).

7. *Citation of local rules.* The local rules for Lake County may be known as the Lake County Rules of Civil Procedure, and abbreviated as LR. IN ST LAKE RCP Rule 1(C).

F. Filing and Service Requirements

1. *Filing requirements.* Except as otherwise provided in IN ST TRIAL P Rule 5(E)(2), all pleadings and papers subsequent to the complaint which are required to be served upon a party shall be filed with the Court either before service or within a reasonable period of time thereafter. IN ST TRIAL P Rule 5(E)(1). All papers presented for filing shall be submitted to the Clerk and not to the court. All papers submitted for filing shall be mailed or delivered to the Clerk's office at the courthouse in which the case is pending. IN ST LAKE RCP Rule 3(A).

    a. *Filing with the court defined.* The filing of pleadings, motions, and other papers with the court as required by the Indiana Rules of Trial Procedure shall be made by one of the following methods:

        i.   Delivery to the clerk of the court;

        ii. Sending by electronic transmission under the procedure adopted pursuant to IN ST ADMIN Rule 12;

        iii. Mailing to the clerk by registered, certified or express mail return receipt requested;

        iv. Depositing with any third-party commercial carrier for delivery to the clerk within three (3) calendar days, cost prepaid, properly addressed;

        v.   If the court so permits, filing with the judge, in which event the judge shall note thereon the filing date and forthwith transmit them to the office of the clerk; or

        vi. Electronic filing, as approved by the Division of State Court Administration pursuant to IN ST ADMIN Rule 16. IN ST TRIAL P Rule 5(F).

        vii. Filing by registered or certified mail and by third-party commercial carrier shall be complete upon mailing or deposit. IN ST TRIAL P Rule 5(F).

    b. *Mandatory electronic filing.* Unless otherwise permitted by the Lake County Rules of Civil Procedure or otherwise authorized by the judicial officer assigned to a particular case, all documents submitted for filing (including the original complaint, or equivalent pleading, and summons) shall be filed electronically with the clerk using the LCOD, no matter when the case was originally filed. IN ST LAKE RCP Rule 17(D).

        i. *Of documents containing information excluded from public access pursuant to* IN ST ADMIN Rule 9. Documents containing information excluded from public access pursuant to IN ST ADMIN Rule 9, or documents which are ordered to be filed under seal shall be filed electronically, pursuant to IN ST LAKE RCP Rule 17(D)(9), whenever possible, along with a copy of the applicable order to seal the records, and the filer shall designate the documents as "Not for Public Access Pursuant to Administrative Rule 9(G)(1)" at the time of filing. IN ST LAKE RCP Rule 16(A)(1); IN ST LAKE RCP Rule 17(D)(9).

            *   *Conventional filing of documents containing information excluded from public access pursuant to* IN ST ADMIN Rule 9. Documents containing information excluded from public access pursuant to IN ST ADMIN Rule 9, or documents which are ordered to be filed under seal, which cannot be legibly scanned and filed electronically, shall be conventionally filed under seal and designated by the filer as "Not for Public Access Pursuant to Administrative Rule 9(G)(1)" at the time of filing. The unredacted version shall be filed on light green paper which is conspicuously marked "Not for Public Access"; and a redacted version, with confidential information deleted, shall be filed on white paper which shall be available for public access. The filer shall also electronically file a Notice of Manual Filing. IN ST LAKE RCP Rule 16(A)(2).

        ii. *Technical failures.* If a registered user is unable to file a document in a timely manner due to technical difficulties in the LCOD, the registered user must file a document with the court as soon as possible notifying the court of the inability to file the document. A sample document titled Declaration that Party was Unable to File in a Timely Manner Due to Technical Difficulties can be found at IN ST LAKE RCP Form 4. Delayed filings shall be rejected unless accompanied by the declaration attesting to the filer's failed attempts to file electronically at least two (2) times, separated by at least one (1) hour, after noon on each day of delay due to such technical failure. IN ST LAKE RCP Rule 17(J).

iii. *Documents allowed to be filed conventionally.* Unless specifically authorized by the court, only the following documents may be filed conventionally and not electronically:

- Exhibits and other documents that cannot be converted to a legible electronic form, such as videotapes, x-rays, and similar materials
- Documents delivered to the clerk by pro se litigants
- Documents mailed to the clerk by pro se litigants
- Confidential documents
- Notice of manual filing
- Titles of documents
- Chronological case summary entry forms (CCS entry forms). IN ST LAKE RCP Rule 17(E).
- For more information on the documents which must be filed conventionally, refer to IN ST LAKE RCP Rule 17(E).

c. *Facsimile filing.* Only when necessary on an emergency basis (i.e., when certified mail or other means of filing will not bring the document to the Judge's attention prior to the scheduled hearing or ruling), pleadings, motions and other papers may be filed by electronic facsimile transmission, or when specifically authorized by the Court. IN ST LAKE RCP Rule 2(C).

i. *Generally.* In counties where a majority of judges of the courts of record, by posted local rule, have authorized electronic facsimile filing and designated a telephone number to receive such transmissions, pleadings, motions, and other papers may be sent to the Clerk of Circuit Court by electronic facsimile transmission for filing in any case, provided:

- Such matter does not exceed ten (10) pages, including the cover sheet;
- Such matter does not require the payment of fees other than the electronic facsimile transcription fee set forth in IN ST ADMIN Rule 12(E);
- The sending party creates at the time of transmission a machine generated log for such transmission; and
- The original document and the transmission log are maintained by the sending party for the duration of the litigation. IN ST ADMIN Rule 12(B).

ii. *Time of filing.* During normal, posted business hours, the time of filing shall be the time the duplicate document is produced in the office of the Clerk of the Circuit Court. Duplicate documents received at all other times shall be filed as of the next normal business day. IN ST ADMIN Rule 12(C).

- If the receiving fax machine endorses its own time and date stamp upon the transmitted documents and the receiving machine produces a delivery receipt which is electronically created and transmitted to the sending party, the time of filing shall be the date and time recorded on the transmitted document by the receiving fax machine. IN ST ADMIN Rule 12(C).

d. *Filing for special judges.* For special judge matters where the special judge is a full-time judge or magistrate serving within Lake County, all papers submitted for filing shall be delivered or mailed to the Clerk's office at the courthouse where the special judge regularly serves. IN ST LAKE RCP Rule 3(A).

e. *Proof of filing.* Any party filing any paper by any method other than personal delivery to the clerk shall retain proof of filing. IN ST TRIAL P Rule 5(F).

2. *Service requirements.* Unless otherwise provided by the Indiana Rules of Trial Procedure or an order of the court, each party and special judge, if any, shall be served with: (1) every order required by its terms to be served; (2) every pleading subsequent to the original complaint; (3) every written motion except one which may be heard ex parte; (4) every brief submitted to the trial court; (5) every paper relating to

discovery required to be served upon a party; and (6) every written notice, appearance, demand, offer of judgment, designation of record on appeal, or similar paper. IN ST TRIAL P Rule 5(A).

a. *Methods of service*

   i. *Personal service.* Whenever a party is represented by an attorney of record, service shall be made upon such attorney unless service upon the party himself is ordered by the court. Service upon the attorney or party shall be made by delivering or mailing a copy of the papers to the last known address or where an attorney or party has consented to service by fax or e-mail, as provided in IN ST TRIAL P Rule 3.1(A)(4), by faxing or e-mailing a copy of the documents to the fax number or e-mail address set out in the appearance form or correction as required by IN ST TRIAL P Rule 3.1(E). IN ST TRIAL P Rule 5(B). Delivery of a copy within IN ST TRIAL P Rule 5 means:

   - Offering or tendering it to the attorney or party and stating the nature of the papers being served. Refusal to accept an offered or tendered document is a waiver of any objection to the sufficiency or adequacy of service of that document;

   - Leaving it at his office with a clerk or other person in charge thereof, or if there is no one in charge, leaving it in a conspicuous place therein; or

   - If the office is closed, by leaving it at his dwelling house or usual place of abode with some person of suitable age and discretion then residing therein; or,

   - Leaving it at some other suitable place, selected by the attorney upon whom service is being made, pursuant to duly promulgated local rule. IN ST TRIAL P Rule 5(B)(1).

   ii. *Service by mail.* If service is made by mail, the papers shall be deposited in the United States mail addressed to the person on whom they are being served, with postage prepaid. Service shall be deemed complete upon mailing. Proof of service of all papers permitted to be mailed may be made by written acknowledgment of service, by affidavit of the person who mailed the papers, or by certificate of an attorney. It shall be the duty of attorneys when entering their appearance in a cause or when filing pleadings or papers therein, to have noted in the Chronological Case Summary or said pleadings or papers so filed the address and telephone number of their office. Service by delivery or by mail at such address shall be deemed sufficient and complete. IN ST TRIAL P Rule 5(B)(2).

   iii. *Service by fax or e-mail.* A party who has consented to service by fax or e-mail may be served as follows:

   - Service by e-mail shall be made by attaching the document being served in .pdf format. Discovery documents must also be served in accordance with IN ST TRIAL P Rule 26(A). IN ST TRIAL P Rule 5(B)(3)(a).

   - Service by fax shall be deemed complete upon generation of a transmission record indicating the successful transmission of the entire document, except as provided in IN ST TRIAL P Rule 5(B)(3)(d). IN ST TRIAL P Rule 5(B)(3)(b).

   - Service by e-mail shall be deemed complete upon transmission, except as provided in IN ST TRIAL P Rule 5(B)(3)(d). IN ST TRIAL P Rule 5(B)(3)(c).

   - Service by fax or e-mail that occurs on a Saturday, Sunday, legal holiday, or day the court or agency in which the matter is pending is closed or after 5:00 PM local time of the recipient shall be deemed complete the next day that is not a Saturday, Sunday, legal holiday, or day that the court or agency in which the matter is pending is not closed. IN ST TRIAL P Rule 5(B)(3)(d).

b. *Serving numerous defendants.* In any action in which there are unusually large numbers of defendants, the court, upon motion or of its own initiative, may order:

   i. That service of the pleadings of the defendants and replies thereto need not be made as between the defendants;

   - That any cross-claim, counterclaim, or matter constituting an avoidance or affirmative defense contained therein shall be deemed to be denied or avoided by all other parties; and

- That the filing of any such pleading and service thereof upon the plaintiff constitutes due notice of it to the parties. IN ST TRIAL P Rule 5(D).

   ii. A copy of every such order shall be served upon the parties in such manner and form as the court directs. IN ST TRIAL P Rule 5(D).

c. *Service by electronic means.* The Lake County Online Docket will generate a Notice of Electronic Filing and Service when any document is filed and served. This notice will be emailed to each registered user of record in a case, and an electronic service event will be added to the work queue of each registered user of record in the case. The party filing the document should retain a paper or electronic copy of the Notice of Electronic Filing and Service. This notice represents proof of filing and service of the document on registered users of record in that case. The filer shall not be required to conventionally serve any document on any party receiving electronic service. IN ST LAKE RCP Rule 17(F)(2).

   i. The filer shall also conventionally serve those parties not designated or able to receive electronic notice or service but who are nevertheless entitled to notice of said pleading or other document in accordance with the Indiana Rules of Civil Procedure and applicable Lake County Rules of Civil Procedure. In such cases, the filer shall also file a certificate of service, as appropriate. IN ST LAKE RCP Rule 17(F).

d. *Service on parties in default for failure to appear.* No service need be made on parties in default for failure to appear, except that pleadings asserting new or additional claims for relief against them shall be served upon them in the manner provided by service of summons in IN ST TRIAL P Rule 4. IN ST TRIAL P Rule 5(A).

G. Hearings

1. *Hearing on motion.* Unless local conditions make it impracticable, each judge shall establish regular times and places, at intervals sufficiently frequent for the prompt dispatch of business, at which motions requiring notice and hearing may be heard and disposed of; but the judge at any time or place and on such notice, if any, as he considers reasonable may make order for the advancement, conduct, and hearing of actions. To expedite its business the court may direct the submission and determination of motions without oral hearing upon brief written statements of reasons in support and opposition, or direct or permit hearings by telephone conference call with all attorneys or other similar means of communication. IN ST TRIAL P Rule 73(A).

2. *Oral argument discretionary.* The granting of a motion for oral argument, unless required by the Indiana Rules of Trial Procedure, shall be wholly discretionary with the court. IN ST LAKE RCP Rule 4(B).

H. Forms

1. Motion for Protective Order Forms for Indiana

a. Pending motion. 5 INPRAC § 4:5.1.
b. Relevancy. 5 INPRAC § 4:5.2.
c. Unduly burdensome. 5 INPRAC § 4:5.3.
d. Privileged. 5 INPRAC § 4:5.4.
e. Mental impressions and legal conclusions. 5 INPRAC § 4:5.5.
f. Expert reports and papers. 5 INPRAC § 4:5.6.
g. Quash subpoena duces tecum. 5 INPRAC § 4:5.7.
h. Quash subpoena duces tecum; Non-party. 5 INPRAC § 4:5.8.
i. Trade secrets and confidential information. 5 INPRAC § 4:5.9.
j. Motion to lift protective order. 5 INPRAC § 4:5.10.
k. Motion for protective order; Discovery not be had; Protection against disclosure of expert report and papers. 10 INPRAC § 58.22.
l. Motion for protective order; Discovery not relevant to subject matter of action. 10 INPRAC § 58.23.

  m. Motion for protective order; Discovery unduly burdensome; Alternative request for deposition. 10 INPRAC § 58.24.

  n. Motion for protective order; Challenging date and time of deposition. 10 INPRAC § 58.25.

  o. Motion for protective order; Challenging place of deposition. 10 INPRAC § 58.26.

  p. Motion for protective order; To prevent the disclosure of trade secrets and confidential research and development. 10 INPRAC § 58.27.

  q. Motion for protective order; To preclude further deposition of corporate officer. 10 INPRAC § 58.28.

  r. Motion for protective order; To preclude taking expert deposition; Failure to obtain court order or to disclose expert opinions. 10 INPRAC § 58.30.

  s. Motion for protective order; To preclude disclosure of privileged matters. 10 INPRAC § 58.31.

  t. Motion for protective order; To have plaintiff's attorney and physician present during plaintiff's physical examination; Request to tape record physical examination. 10 INPRAC § 58.32.

  u. Motion for protective order; To preclude defendant's attorney from conducting an informal interview of plaintiff's treating physician. 10 INPRAC § 58.33.

  v. Motion for protective order; To produce documents at responding party's place of business. 10 INPRAC § 58.34.

  w. Motion for protective order; Discovery limited to certain matter until court rules on pending motion. 10 INPRAC § 58.35.

  x. Motion for protective order; Answers to discovery to be sealed to protect confidential commercial information. 10 INPRAC § 58.36.

  y. Certificate of service; Personal service. 9 INPRAC § 5.7.

  z. Certificate of service; First class mail. 9 INPRAC § 5.8.

2. Official Motion for Protective Order Forms for Lake County

  a. CCS entry form. IN ST LAKE RCP App. A.

  b. Notice of manual filing. IN ST LAKE RCP Form 2.

  c. Certificate of service. IN ST LAKE RCP Form 3.

  d. Declaration that party was unable to file in a timely manner. IN ST LAKE RCP Form 4.

3. Motion for Protective Order Forms for Lake County

  a. Notice of manual filing. EFORMST IN 5540.

I. Checklist

 (I) ❑ Matters to be considered by moving party

  (a) ❑ Required documents

   (1) ❑ Motion and notice

   (2) ❑ Brief

   (3) ❑ Attorney certification

   (4) ❑ Proposed order

   (5) ❑ Chronological case summary (CSS) entry forms

   (6) ❑ Certificate of service

  (b) ❑ Supplemental documents

   (1) ❑ Supporting evidence

   (2) ❑ Facsimile cover sheet

  (c) ❑ Timing

   (1) ❑ There are no specific timing requirements for filing a motion for a protective order

(2) ❑ A written motion, other than one which may be heard ex parte, and notice of the hearing thereof shall be served not less than five (5) days before the time specified for the hearing, unless a different period is fixed by the Indiana Rules of Trial Procedure or by order of the court

(3) ❑ All pleadings and papers subsequent to the complaint which are required to be served upon a party shall be filed with the Court either before service or within a reasonable period of time thereafter

(4) ❑ All pleadings, motions and other papers submitted for filing which are required to be served under IN ST TRIAL P Rule 5(A) shall be filed no later than three (3) days after service

(5) ❑ If such papers are filed before service, proof of service thereof shall be filed no later than three (3) business days thereafter

(II) ❑ Matters to be considered by the responding party

  (a) ❑ Required documents

    (1) ❑ Opposition

    (2) ❑ Chronological case summary (CSS) entry forms

    (3) ❑ Certificate of service

  (b) ❑ Supplemental documents

    (1) ❑ Supporting evidence

    (2) ❑ Proposed order

    (3) ❑ Facsimile cover sheet

  (c) ❑ Timing

    (1) ❑ So long as consistent with the Indiana Rules of Trial Procedure, an adverse party wishing to respond shall do so within fifteen (15) days of service

    (2) ❑ Except as otherwise provided in IN ST TRIAL P Rule 59(D), opposing affidavits may be served not less than one (1) day before the hearing, unless the court permits them to be served at some other time

Motions, Oppositions and Replies
Motion for Discovery Sanctions

Document Last Updated October 2013

A. Applicable Rules

1. *State rules*

  a. Appearance. IN ST TRIAL P Rule 3.1.

  b. Process. IN ST TRIAL P Rule 4.

  c. Service and filing of pleadings and other papers. IN ST TRIAL P Rule 5.

  d. Time. IN ST TRIAL P Rule 6.

  e. Pleadings. IN ST TRIAL P Rule 7; IN ST TRIAL P Rule 8; IN ST TRIAL P Rule 9.2; IN ST TRIAL P Rule 10.

  f. Signing and verification of pleadings. IN ST TRIAL P Rule 11.

  g. General provisions governing discovery. IN ST TRIAL P Rule 26.

  h. Methods of discovery. IN ST TRIAL P Rule 27; IN ST TRIAL P Rule 30; IN ST TRIAL P Rule 31; IN ST TRIAL P Rule 33; IN ST TRIAL P Rule 34; IN ST TRIAL P Rule 35; IN ST TRIAL P Rule 36.

  i. Failure to make or cooperate in discovery; Sanctions. IN ST TRIAL P Rule 37.

j. Evidence. IN ST TRIAL P Rule 43.

k. Judgment on the evidence (directed verdict). IN ST TRIAL P Rule 50.

l. Findings by the court. IN ST TRIAL P Rule 52.

m. Summary judgment. IN ST TRIAL P Rule 56.

n. Motion to correct error. IN ST TRIAL P Rule 59.

o. Relief from judgment or order. IN ST TRIAL P Rule 60.

p. Hearing of motions. IN ST TRIAL P Rule 73.

q. Court records. IN ST TRIAL P Rule 77.

r. Access to court records. IN ST ADMIN Rule 9.

s. Paper size. IN ST ADMIN Rule 11.

t. Facsimile transmission. IN ST ADMIN Rule 12.

u. Electronic filing and electronic service pilot projects. IN ST ADMIN Rule 16.

v. Privacy and confidentiality. IN ST 5-2-9-6; IN ST 5-14-3-4; IN ST 5-14-3-5.5; IN ST 6-4.1-5-10; IN ST 6-4.1-12-12; IN ST 6-8.1-7-1; IN ST 11-13-1-8; IN ST 12-23-14-13; IN ST 16-39-3-10; IN ST 16-41-8-1; IN ST 22-4-19-6; IN ST 31-11-1-6; IN ST 31-19-5-23; IN ST 31-19-13-2; IN ST 31-19-19-1; IN ST 31-33-18-1; IN ST 31-39-1-1; IN ST 31-39-1-2; IN ST 33-23-16-16; IN ST 35-34-2-4; IN ST 35-38-1-13; IN ST 35-38-9-1; IN ST ADR Rule 2.11; IN ST ADR Rule 4.4; IN ST ADR Rule 5.6; IN ST JURY Rule 10.

2. *Local rules*

a. Scope and title. [IN ST LAKE RCP Rule 1, as amended by IN ORDER 13-0237, effective October 18, 2013].

b. Preparation of pleadings, motions and other papers. IN ST LAKE RCP Rule 2.

c. Filing. [IN ST LAKE RCP Rule 3, as amended by IN ORDER 13-0237, effective October 18, 2013].

d. Motions. IN ST LAKE RCP Rule 4.

e. Discovery. IN ST LAKE RCP Rule 8.

f. Pretrial procedure. IN ST LAKE RCP Rule 9.

g. Briefs. IN ST LAKE RCP Rule 11.

h. Confidential information and sealed documents. IN ST LAKE RCP Rule 16.

i. Electronic filing and service. IN ST LAKE RCP Rule 17.

B. Timing

1. *Motion for discovery sanctions.* There are no specific timing requirements for filing a motion for discovery sanctions.

a. *Filing.* All pleadings and papers subsequent to the complaint which are required to be served upon a party shall be filed with the Court either before service or within a reasonable period of time thereafter. IN ST TRIAL P Rule 5(E)(1). All pleadings, motions and other papers submitted for filing which are required to be served under IN ST TRIAL P Rule 5(A) shall be filed no later than three (3) days after service. IN ST LAKE RCP Rule 3(A).

   i. If such papers are filed before service, proof of service thereof shall be filed no later than three (3) business days thereafter. Upon failure to comply with IN ST LAKE RCP Rule 3, the Court may, on motion of any party or on its own motion, impose appropriate sanctions. IN ST LAKE RCP Rule 3(A).

b. *Briefs.* Briefs, other than those addressed in IN ST LAKE RCP Rule 4 and IN ST LAKE RCP Rule 9, shall be filed no later than two (2) calendar days preceding the hearing or trial to which directed. IN ST LAKE RCP Rule 11.

2. *Service.* A written motion, other than one which may be heard ex parte, and notice of the hearing thereof

shall be served not less than five (5) days before the time specified for the hearing, unless a different period is fixed by the Indiana Rules of Trial Procedure or by order of the court. IN ST TRIAL P Rule 6(D).

    a.   *Of supporting affidavits.* When a motion is supported by affidavit, the affidavit shall be served with the motion. IN ST TRIAL P Rule 6(D).

3.   *Service of opposition.* Except as otherwise provided in IN ST TRIAL P Rule 59(D), opposing affidavits may be served not less than one (1) day before the hearing, unless the court permits them to be served at some other time. IN ST TRIAL P Rule 6(D).

    a.   So long as consistent with the Indiana Rules of Trial Procedure, an adverse party wishing to respond shall do so within fifteen (15) days of service. IN ST LAKE RCP Rule 4(A).

4.   *Reply.* The moving party shall have ten (10) days after service of the response within which to reply. IN ST LAKE RCP Rule 4(A).

5.   *Computation of time*

    a.   *Generally; Days excluded.* In computing any period of time prescribed or allowed by the Indiana Rules of Trial Procedure, by order of the court, or by any applicable statute, the day of the act, event, or default from which the designated period of time begins to run shall not be included. The last day of the period so computed is to be included unless it is:

        i.   A Saturday,

        ii.   A Sunday,

        iii.   A legal holiday as defined by state statute, or

        iv.   A day the office in which the act is to be done is closed during regular business hours. IN ST TRIAL P Rule 6(A).

    b.   *Short periods.* In any event, the period runs until the end of the next day that is not a Saturday, a Sunday, a legal holiday, or a day on which the office is closed. When the period of time allowed is less than seven (7) days, intermediate Saturdays, Sundays, legal holidays, and days on which the office is closed shall be excluded from the computations. IN ST TRIAL P Rule 6(A).

    c.   *Additional time after service by United States mail.* Whenever a party has the right or is required to do some act or take some proceedings within a prescribed period after the service of a notice or other paper upon him and the notice or paper is served upon him by United States mail, three (3) days shall be added to the prescribed period. IN ST TRIAL P Rule 6(E).

    d.   *Electronic filing does not alter deadlines.* Filing electronically does not alter any filing deadlines or any time computation pursuant to state or federal statutes, any Rules of the Indiana Supreme Court, including without limitation the Rules of Trial Procedure, the Rules of Appellate Procedure or the Administrative Rules, or applicable Lake County Rules of Civil Procedure. The office of the Lake County Clerk is open for electronic filing under the Lake County Rules of Civil Procedure twenty-four (24) hours a day. A document is deemed filed at the date and time it is received by the LCOD server. Filing must be completed before midnight local time in order to be considered filed that day. Lake County observes Central Time and electronic filers are strongly urged to file documents during hours when the Lake County Online Docket ("LCOD") help line is available, from 9:00 a.m. to 4:00 p.m. local time, although documents can be filed electronically twenty-four (24) hours a day. IN ST LAKE RCP Rule 17(I).

    e.   *Enlargement of time.* When an act is required or allowed to be done at or within a specific time by the Indiana Rules of Trial Procedure, the court may at any time for cause shown:

        i.   Order the period enlarged, with or without motion or notice, if request therefor is made before the expiration of the period originally prescribed or extended by a previous order; or

        ii.   Upon motion made after the expiration of the specific period, permit the act to be done where the failure to act was the result of excusable neglect; but, the court may not extend the time for taking any action for judgment on the evidence under IN ST TRIAL P Rule 50(A), amendment of findings and judgment under IN ST TRIAL P Rule 52(B), to correct errors under IN ST TRIAL P Rule 59(C), statement in opposition to motion to correct error under IN ST TRIAL P

Rule 59(E), or to obtain relief from final judgment under IN ST TRIAL P Rule 60(B), except to the extent and under the conditions stated in those rules. IN ST TRIAL P Rule 6(B).

C. General Requirements

1. *Motions, generally.* Unless made during a hearing or trial, or otherwise ordered by the court, an application to the court for an order shall be made by written motion. The motion shall state the grounds therefor and the relief or order sought. IN ST TRIAL P Rule 7(B).

   a. *Motions as distinct from pleadings.* Motions and responses to motions are not pleadings, and allegations contained in a motion are not admissions of a party. 22B INPRAC 7:2; Wachstetter v. County Properties, LLC, 832 N.E.2d 574 (Ind.Ct.App. 2005); Scott County Family YMCA, Inc. v. Hobbs, 817 N.E.2d 603 (Ind.Ct.App. 2004).

   b. *Unopposed motions generally granted.* It is common for a trial court to grant procedural motions, such as motions for enlargement of time, discovery motions, or motions for continuance, unless an objection is filed. 21 INPRAC § 13.8.

   c. *Separate motions.* Each motion shall be separate, while alternative motions filed together shall each be identified on the caption. IN ST LAKE RCP Rule 4(A).

   d. *Answer and reply briefs.* Failure to file an answer brief or reply brief within the time prescribed shall be deemed a waiver of the right thereto and shall subject the motion to summary ruling. IN ST LAKE RCP Rule 4(A).

2. *Motion for discovery sanctions*

   a. *Related to a motion to compel; Award of sanctions on motion*

      i. *Motion granted.* If the motion is granted, the court shall, after opportunity for hearing, require the party or deponent whose conduct necessitated the motion or the party or attorney advising such conduct or both of them to pay to the moving party the reasonable expenses incurred in obtaining the order, including attorney's fees, unless the court finds that the opposition to the motion was substantially justified or that other circumstances make an award of expenses unjust. IN ST TRIAL P Rule 37(A)(4).

      ii. *Motion denied.* If the motion is denied, the court shall, after opportunity for hearing, require the moving party or the attorney advising the motion or both of them to pay to the party or deponent who opposed the motion the reasonable expenses incurred in opposing the motion, including attorney's fees, unless the court finds that the making of the motion was substantially justified or that other circumstances make an award of expenses unjust. IN ST TRIAL P Rule 37(A)(4).

      iii. *Granted in part and denied in part.* If the motion is granted in part and denied in part, the court may apportion the reasonable expenses incurred in relation to the motion among the parties and persons in a just manner. IN ST TRIAL P Rule 37(A)(4).

      iv. Refer to the Indiana KeyRules Motion to Compel Discovery document for more information.

   b. *Failure to comply with order.* The trial court may impose sanctions upon a party who fails to obey an order regarding discovery. 22 INPRAC § 27.7. The first step to invoking sanctions under IN ST TRIAL P Rule 37(B) is to file a motion to compel discovery under IN ST TRIAL P Rule 37(A) and obtain an order from the court requiring the opposing party to take a specific action in discovery. If the opposing party then fails to take the action mandated by the trial court's discovery order, the second step is to return to the trial court and file a motion for sanctions under IN ST TRIAL P Rule 37(B). 22 INPRAC § 27.7.

      i. *Sanctions by court in county where deposition is taken.* If a deponent fails to be sworn or to answer a question after being directed to do so by the court in the county in which the deposition is being taken, the failure may be considered a contempt of that court. IN ST TRIAL P Rule 37(B)(1).

      ii. *Sanctions by court in which action is pending.* If a party or an officer, director, or managing agent of a party or an organization, including a governmental organization, or a person designated under IN ST TRIAL P Rule 30(B)(6) or IN ST TRIAL P Rule 31(A) to testify on behalf of a party or an organization, including a governmental organization, fails to obey an order to provide or permit discovery, including an order made under IN ST TRIAL P Rule 37(A) or IN ST TRIAL P Rule 35, the court in which the action is pending may make such orders in regard to the failure as are just, and among others the following:

- An order that the matters regarding which the order was made or any other designated facts shall be taken to be established for the purposes of the action in accordance with the claim of the party obtaining the order;

- An order refusing to allow the disobedient party to support or oppose designated claims or defenses, or prohibiting him from introducing designated matters in evidence;

- An order striking out pleadings or parts thereof, or staying further proceedings until the order is obeyed, or dismissing the action or proceeding or any part thereof, or rendering a judgment by default against the disobedient party;

- In lieu of any of the foregoing orders or in addition thereto, an order treating as a contempt of court the failure to obey any orders except an order to submit to a physical or mental examination under IN ST TRIAL P Rule 35;

- Where a party has failed to comply with an order under IN ST TRIAL P Rule 35(A) requiring him to produce another for examination, such orders as are listed in IN ST TRIAL P Rule 37(B)(2)(a), IN ST TRIAL P Rule 37(B)(2)(b), and IN ST TRIAL P Rule 37(B)(2)(c), unless the party failing to comply shows that he is unable to produce such person for examination. IN ST TRIAL P Rule 37(B)(2).

- In lieu of any of the foregoing orders or in addition thereto, the court shall require the party failing to obey the order or the attorney advising him or both to pay the reasonable expenses, including attorney's fees, caused by the failure, unless the court finds that the failure was substantially justified or that other circumstances make an award of expenses unjust. IN ST TRIAL P Rule 37(B)(2).

c. *Expenses on failure to admit.* If a party fails to admit the genuineness of any document or the truth of any matter as requested under IN ST TRIAL P Rule 36, and if the party requesting the admissions thereafter proves the genuineness of the document or the truth of the matter, he may apply to the court for an order requiring the other party to pay him the reasonable expenses incurred in making that proof, including reasonable attorney's fees. The court shall make the order unless it finds that:

i. The request was held objectionable pursuant to IN ST TRIAL P Rule 36(A), or

ii. The admission sought was of no substantial importance, or

iii. The party failing to admit had reasonable ground to believe that he might prevail on the matter, or

iv. There was other good reason for the failure to admit. IN ST TRIAL P Rule 37(C).

d. *Failure of party to attend at own deposition or serve answers to interrogatories or respond to requests for inspection*

i. *Court order for failure to provide discovery.* If a party or an officer, director, or managing agent of a party or an organization, including without limitation a governmental organization, or a person designated under IN ST TRIAL P Rule 30(B)(6) or IN ST TRIAL P Rule 31(A) to testify on behalf of a party or an organization, including without limitation a governmental organization, fails (1) to appear before the officer who is to take his deposition, after being served with a proper notice, or (2) to serve answers or objections to interrogatories submitted under IN ST TRIAL P Rule 33, after proper service of the interrogatories, or (3) to serve a written response to a request for inspection submitted under IN ST TRIAL P Rule 34, after proper service of the request, the court in which the action is pending on motion may make such orders in regard to the failure as are just, and among others it may take any action authorized under IN ST TRIAL P Rule 37(B)(2)(a), IN ST TRIAL P Rule 37(B)(2)(b), and IN ST TRIAL P Rule 37(B)(2)(c). IN ST TRIAL P Rule 37(D).

ii. *Attorney fees against party failing to provide discovery.* In lieu of any order or in addition thereto, the court shall require the party failing to act or the attorney advising him or both to pay

820

the reasonable expenses, including attorney's fees, caused by the failure, unless the court finds that the failure was substantially justified or that other circumstances make an award of expenses unjust. IN ST TRIAL P Rule 37(D)

iii. *Failure not excused for objectionable requests.* The failure to act described in IN ST TRIAL P Rule 37(D) may not be excused on the ground that the discovery sought is objectionable unless the party failing to act has applied for a protective order as provided by IN ST TRIAL P Rule 26(C). IN ST TRIAL P Rule 37(D). Refer to the Indiana KeyRules Motion for Protective Order document for more information.

iv. *Showing required.* To invoke the sanctions under IN ST TRIAL P Rule 37(D), it is sufficient that notice of the deposition or other discovery request was properly served upon the non-responding party, but no response was provided. 22 INPRAC § 27.8.

e. *Sanctions for spoliation of evidence.* In some cases a duty arises imposing an affirmative obligation to avoid the destruction or loss of documents and materials that are relevant and discoverable to claims and defenses that either have been or may be asserted in an action. The destruction, mutilation, alteration or concealment of such materials is called "spoliation." 3 INPRAC R 37(37.2.2); Glotzbach v. Froman, 854 N.E.2d 337 (Ind. 2006).

 i. *Spoliation generally.* Spoliation typically presents itself in one of two ways:

 - A party to litigation destroys materials that are relevant and discoverable in an action; or

 - A non-party destroys materials that may be discoverable in an action to which that entity or individual will not be a party. 3 INPRAC R 37(37.2.2).

 ii. *Duty to maintain evidence must exist.* A key component of a spoliation claim is that the party who destroyed the materials must have had a duty not to do so. A duty may arise in a number of ways: imposed by statute or case law, imposed by contract or some third party beneficiary arrangement, or imposed by the actions of the parties by which one party assumes a duty in law or equity toward another. When duty arises from the conduct of the parties as opposed to one established by statute or contract, the Indiana courts have identified three primary factors to determine whether a duty exists:

 - The relationship between the parties,

 - The reasonable foreseeability of harm to the injured litigant, and

 - The public policy promoted by recognizing an enforceable duty. 3 INPRAC R 37(37.2.2); Webb v. Jarvis, 575 N.E.2d 992 (Ind. 1991).

 - This balancing test is particularly useful where the element of duty has not already been established between the parties. 3 INPRAC R 37(37.2.2); Northern Indiana Public Service Co. v. Sharp, 790 N.E.2d 462 (Ind. 2003).

 iii. *Factors to be considered by the court.* Even where the court finds an intentional spoliation, it is not mandatory that sanctions be imposed. Rather, the trial court should implement an approach by which it balances the nature of the offense against the harm suffered by the non-offending party because lost evidence is not available. 22 INPRAC § 27.9; Gribben v. Wal-Mart Stores, Inc., 824 N.E.2d 349 (Ind. 2005). Factors the court may consider include:

 - The culpability of the spoliating party;

 - The prejudice to the non-offending party;

 - The degree of interference with the judicial process;

 - Whether lesser sanctions are available to remedy any harm and deter future acts of spoliation;

 - The amount of time lapsing from the date the spoliating party took possession of the evidence and the date of its loss or destruction;

 - Protocols adopted, and followed, by the spoliating party to prevent the loss of evidence, such as a document retention policy;

 - Whether evidence has been irretrievably lost and, if so, the circumstances of that loss;

- The existence of available alternatives that would allow the non-offending party to prove its case without the lost evidence;

- And whether sanctions will unfairly punish a party for the misconduct or mistake of his attorney or expert. 22 INPRAC § 27.9.

f. *No sanctions for good-faith loss of electronically stored information.* Absent exceptional circumstances, a court may not impose sanctions under the Indiana Rules of Trial Procedure these rules on a party for failing to provide electronically stored information lost as a result of the routine, good faith operation of an electronic information system. IN ST TRIAL P Rule 37(E).

g. *Attorney conference on discovery* issues. Strict compliance with IN ST TRIAL P Rule 26 through IN ST TRIAL P Rule 37 is required. The discovery process is intended to be largely self-actuating, with minimal court supervision. Therefore, the court will not rule on motions related to discovery disputes unless moving counsel represents that, after personal or telephonic conference in good faith effort to resolve differences, counsel are unable to reach accord. If counsel advises the court, by way of motion or response thereto, that opposing counsel has refused or delayed resolution of the discovery dispute, the court may, after hearing, impose appropriate sanctions. IN ST LAKE RCP Rule 8(C).

D. Documents

1. *Required documents*

   a. *Motion and notice.* The requirement of notice is satisfied by service of the motion. IN ST TRIAL P Rule 7(B). Refer to the General Requirements section of this document for information on the content of a motion for discovery sanctions.

   b. *Brief.* Briefs, other than those addressed in IN ST LAKE RCP Rule 4 and IN ST LAKE RCP Rule 9, shall be filed no later than two (2) calendar days preceding the hearing or trial to which directed. IN ST LAKE RCP Rule 11.

   c. *Attorney certification.* Before any party files any motion or request to compel discovery pursuant to IN ST TRIAL P Rule 37, or any motion for protection from discovery pursuant to IN ST TRIAL P Rule 26(C), or any other discovery motion which seeks to enforce, modify, or limit discovery, that party shall:

      i. Make a reasonable effort to reach agreement with the opposing party concerning the matter which is the subject of the motion or request; and

      ii. Include in the motion or request a statement showing that the attorney making the motion or request has made a reasonable effort to reach agreement with the opposing attorney(s) concerning the matter(s) set forth in the motion or request. This statement shall recite, in addition, the date, time and place of this effort to reach agreement, whether in person or by phone, and the names of all parties and attorneys participating therein. If an attorney for any party advises the court in writing that an opposing attorney has refused or delayed meeting and discussing the issues covered in IN ST TRIAL P Rule 26(F), the court may take such action as is appropriate. IN ST TRIAL P Rule 26(F).

      iii. The court may deny a discovery motion filed by a party who has failed to comply with the requirements of IN ST TRIAL P Rule 26(F). IN ST TRIAL P Rule 26(F).

   d. *Proposed order.* Unless local practice provides differently, a party should submit a proposed order with its written motion to be signed by the judge once the motion has been granted. 21 INPRAC § 13.8.

      i. Proposed orders, which are submitted for the court's convenience under IN ST LAKE RCP Rule 3 or other applicable Lake County Rules of Civil Procedure, shall be submitted as attachments to motions. IN ST LAKE RCP Rule 17(D)(8). Proposed orders shall be prepared and filed separately from the pleadings, petitions, motions or other papers to which they have reference. IN ST LAKE RCP Rule 3(B).

      ii. Orders, either routine in nature or uncontested including, for example, those setting or continuing a hearing, shall be effected by the chronological case summary entry only, which shall contain the concise substance of the order. IN ST LAKE RCP Rule 3(B).

      iii. All orders shall be accompanied with sufficient copies and stamped, pre-addressed envelopes, so that copies may be mailed to all parties. IN ST LAKE RCP Rule 3(B).

  e. *Chronological case summary (CCS) entry forms.* All filings shall be accompanied by a Chronological Case Summary (CCS) Entry Form to define or identify the documents filed. The Form used should be substantially similar to IN ST LAKE RCP App. A. IN ST LAKE RCP Rule 3(C).

  f. *Certificate of service.* An attorney or unrepresented party tendering a document to the Clerk for filing shall certify that service has been made, list the parties served, and specify the date and means of service. The certificate of service shall be placed at the end of the document and shall not be separately filed. The separate filing of a certificate of service, however, shall not be grounds for rejecting a document for filing. The Clerk may permit documents to be filed without a certificate of service but shall require prompt filing of a separate certificate of service. IN ST TRIAL P Rule 5(C).

      i. All pleadings, motions and other papers submitted for filing which are required to be served under IN ST TRIAL P Rule 5(A) shall contain proof of service pursuant to IN ST TRIAL P Rule 5(B)(2). IN ST LAKE RCP Rule 3(A).

2. *Supplemental documents*

  a. *Supporting evidence.* When a motion is based on facts not appearing of record the court may hear the matter on affidavits presented by the respective parties, but the court may direct that the matter be heard wholly or partly on oral testimony or depositions. IN ST TRIAL P Rule 43(B).

  b. *Facsimile cover sheet.* Any document sent to the Clerk of the Circuit Court by electronic facsimile transmission shall be accompanied by a cover sheet which states the title of the document, case number, number of pages, identity and voice telephone number of the sending party and instructions for filing. The cover sheet shall contain the signature of the attorney or party, pro se, authorizing the filing. IN ST ADMIN Rule 12(D).

E. Format

1. *Form of motions.* The rules applicable to captions, and the signing and form of pleadings (IN ST TRIAL P Rule 8 through IN ST TRIAL P Rule 11), apply to all motions and other papers provided under the Indiana Rules of Trial Procedure. 22B INPRAC 7:2.

2. *Form of pleadings.* For the purpose of uniformity, convenience, clarity and durability, requirements in IN ST LAKE RCP Rule 2 shall be observed in the preparation of all pleadings, motions and other papers. IN ST LAKE RCP Rule 2. Whenever materials submitted fail to meet the standards in IN ST LAKE RCP Rule 2, the Court may impose appropriate sanctions. IN ST LAKE RCP Rule 2(B).

  a. *Caption; Names of parties.* Every pleading shall contain a caption setting forth the name of the court, the title of the action, the file number, and a designation as in IN ST TRIAL P Rule 7(A). In the complaint the title of the action shall include the names of all the parties, but in other pleadings it is sufficient to state the name of the first party on each side with an appropriate indication of other parties. IN ST TRIAL P Rule 10(A).

      i. *Special judge matters.* The caption of all CCS Entry Forms, pleadings, motions, orders and other papers to be filed in a special judge case shall include in block text the words SPECIAL JUDGE and the name of the judge directly below the cause number on the caption. IN ST LAKE RCP Rule 2(D).

  b. *Paragraphs; Separate statements.* All averments of a claim or defense shall be made in numbered paragraphs, the contents of each of which shall be limited as far as practicable to a statement of a single set of circumstances, and a paragraph may be referred to by number in all succeeding pleadings. Each claim founded upon a separate transaction or occurrence and each defense other than denials may be stated in a separate count or defense whenever a separation facilitates the clear presentation of the matters set forth. IN ST TRIAL P Rule 10(B).

  c. *Adoption by reference; Exhibits.* Statements in a pleading may be adopted by reference in a different part of the same pleading or in another pleading or in any motion. A copy of any written instrument which is an exhibit to a pleading is a part thereof for all purposes. IN ST TRIAL P Rule 10(C).

  d. *Paper; Print, quality and binding*

      i. All pleadings, motions, chronological case summary entry forms, orders, process and other papers shall be neatly and legibly printed, typewritten or mechanically reproduced, on one (1) side only, on white opaque paper. To satisfy the recordkeeping requirements of IN ST TRIAL P Rule 77, the print shall be of sufficient density and clarity for preservation and reproduction of microfilming, optical disk or other secondary sources. For this reason, the use of non-letter-quality printers is discouraged. IN ST LAKE RCP Rule 2(A).

    ii.   Paper and ink shall be of such quality as to withstand the test of time. All documents shall be produced on acid-free, non-thermal paper. It is recommended that a minimum of twenty (20) pound, twenty-five percent (25%) cotton paper product be used. Documents of multiple pages shall be submitted in bound or stapled fashion, and the binding or stapling shall be at the top only. Covers or backings shall not be used. IN ST LAKE RCP Rule 2(A).

  e. *Papers; Handwritten.* Handwritten papers may be filed only if approved by the Court and a typewritten or printed true rendition thereof is filed within three (3) days thereafter and approved by the Court. Upon such approval, they shall be deemed and filed as the original, while the handwritten papers shall be retained therewith for evidentiary purposes. IN ST LAKE RCP Rule 2(C).

  f. *Minute sheets; Motion blanks.* Minute sheets and motion blanks shall no longer be used. IN ST LAKE RCP Rule 2(D).

3. *Size of papers for filing.* Effective January 1, 1992, all pleadings, copies, motions and documents filed with any trial court or appellate level court, typed or printed, with the exception of exhibits and existing wills, shall be prepared on eight and one-half by eleven inch (8 1/2" x 11") size paper. IN ST ADMIN Rule 11.

4. *Signature requirements*

  a. *Signature of attorney.* Every pleading or motion of a party represented by an attorney shall be signed by at least one (1) attorney of record in his individual name, whose address, telephone number, and attorney number shall be stated, except that this provision shall not apply to pleadings and motions made and transcribed at the trial or a hearing before the judge and received by him in such form. IN ST TRIAL P Rule 11(A).

    i.   The signature of an attorney constitutes a certificate by him that he has read the pleadings; that to the best of his knowledge, information, and belief, there is good ground to support it; and that it is not interposed for delay. IN ST TRIAL P Rule 11(A).

    ii.   If a pleading or motion is not signed or is signed with intent to defeat the purpose of the rule, it may be stricken as sham and false and the action may proceed as though the pleading had not been served. IN ST TRIAL P Rule 11(A).

    iii. For a willful violation of IN ST TRIAL P Rule 11 an attorney may be subjected to appropriate disciplinary action. Similar action may be taken if scandalous or indecent matter is inserted. IN ST TRIAL P Rule 11(A).

  b. *Signature of unrepresented party.* A party who is not represented by an attorney shall sign his pleading and state his address. IN ST TRIAL P Rule 11(A).

  c. *Verification not generally required.* Except when specifically required by rule, pleadings or motions need not be verified or accompanied by affidavit. The rule in equity that the averments of an answer under oath must be overcome by the testimony of two (2) witnesses or of one (1) witness sustained by corroborating circumstances is abolished. IN ST TRIAL P Rule 11(A).

  d. *Verification by affirmation or representation.* When in connection with any civil or special statutory proceeding it is required that any pleading, motion, petition, supporting affidavit, or other document of any kind, be verified, or that an oath be taken, it shall be sufficient if the subscriber simply affirms the truth of the matter to be verified by an affirmation or representation. IN ST TRIAL P Rule 11(B). IN ST TRIAL P Rule 11(B) states that the affirmation or representation should be in substantially the following language: "I (we) affirm, under the penalties for perjury, that the foregoing representation(s) is (are) true. (Signed) _____."

    i.   Any person who falsifies an affirmation or representation of fact shall be subject to the same penalties as are prescribed by law for the making of a false affidavit. IN ST TRIAL P Rule 11(B).

e. *Verified pleadings, motions, and affidavits as evidence.* Pleadings, motions and affidavits accompanying or in support of such pleadings or motions when required to be verified or under oath shall be accepted as a representation that the signer had personal knowledge thereof or reasonable cause to believe the existence of the facts or matters stated or alleged therein; and, if otherwise competent or acceptable as evidence, may be admitted as evidence of the facts or matters stated or alleged therein when it is so provided in the Indiana Rules of Trial Procedure, by statute or other law, or to the extent the writing or signature expressly purports to be made upon the signer's personal knowledge. When such pleadings, motions and affidavits are verified or under oath they shall not require other or greater proof on the part of the adverse party than if not verified or not under oath unless expressly provided otherwise by the Indiana Rules of Trial Procedure, statute or other law. Affidavits upon motions for summary judgment under IN ST TRIAL P Rule 56 and in denial of execution under IN ST TRIAL P Rule 9.2 shall be made upon personal knowledge. IN ST TRIAL P Rule 11(C).

f. *Electronic signature.* The filing of documents and information through the E-filing system by use of a valid username and password is presumed to have been authorized by the User to whom that username and password have been issued and documents filed through the E-filing system are presumed to have been signed by the same User. IN ST ADMIN Rule 16(E).

5. *Information excluded from public access.* Every document filed in a case shall separately identify information excluded from public access pursuant to IN ST ADMIN Rule 9(G)(1) as follows:

a. Whole documents that are excluded from public access pursuant to IN ST ADMIN Rule 9(G)(1) shall be tendered on light green paper or have a light green coversheet attached to the document, marked "Not for Public Access" or "Confidential." IN ST TRIAL P Rule 5(G)(1).

b. When only a portion of a document contains information excluded from public access pursuant to IN ST ADMIN Rule 9(G)(1), said information shall be omitted [or redacted] from the filed document, and set forth on a separate accompanying document on light green paper conspicuously marked "Not for Public Access" or "Confidential" and clearly designated [or identifying] the caption and number of the case and the document and location within the document to which the redacted material pertains. IN ST TRIAL P Rule 5(G)(2).

c. With respect to documents filed in electronic format, the trial court, by local rule, may provide for compliance with IN ST TRIAL P Rule 5 in manner that separates and protects access to information excluded from public access. IN ST TRIAL P Rule 5(G)(3).

d. IN ST TRIAL P Rule 5(G) does not apply to a record sealed by the court pursuant to IN ST 5-14-3-5.5 or otherwise, nor to records, documents, or information filed in cases to which public access is prohibited pursuant to IN ST ADMIN Rule 9(G). IN ST TRIAL P Rule 5(G)(4).

e. The following information in case records is excluded from public access and is confidential:

   i. Information that is excluded from public access pursuant to federal law;

   ii. Information that is excluded from public access as declared confidential by Indiana statute or other court rule, including without limitation:

   - All adoption records created after July 8, 1941, as declared confidential by IN ST 31-19-19-1, et seq., except those specifically declared open by IN ST 31-19-13-2(2);

   - All records relating to chancroid, chlamydia, gonorrhea, hepatitis, human immunodeficiency virus (HIV), Lymphogranuloma venereum, syphilis, tuberculosis, as declared confidential by IN ST 16-41-8-1, et seq.;

   - All records relating to child abuse as declared confidential by IN ST 31-33-18-1, et seq.;

   - All records relating to drug tests as declared confidential by IN ST 5-14-3-4(a)(9);

   - Records of grand jury proceedings as declared confidential by IN ST 35-34-2-4;

   - Records of juvenile proceedings as declared confidential by IN ST 31-39-1-2, except those specifically open under statute;

   - All paternity records created after July 1, 1941 as declared confidential by IN ST 31-14-11-15, IN ST 31-19-5-23, IN ST 31-39-1-1 and IN ST 31-39-1-2 [Editor's note: IN ST 31-14-11-15 was repealed effective May 9, 2013];

- All pre-sentence reports as declared confidential by IN ST 35-38-1-13;

- Written petitions to permit marriages without consent and orders directing the Clerk of Court to issue a marriage license to underage persons, as declared confidential by IN ST 31-11-1-6;

- Only those arrest warrants, search warrants, indictments and informations ordered confidential by the trial judge, prior to return of duly executed service as declared confidential by IN ST 5-14-3-4(b)(1);

- All medical, mental health, or tax records unless determined by law or regulation of any governmental custodian not to be confidential, released by the subject of such records, or declared by a court of competent jurisdiction to be essential to the resolution of litigation as declared confidential by IN ST 16-39-3-10, IN ST 6-4.1-5-10, IN ST 6-4.1-12-12, and IN ST 6-8.1-7-1;

- Personal information relating to jurors or prospective jurors, other than for the use of the parties and counsel, pursuant to IN ST JURY Rule 10;

- Information relating to protection from abuse orders, no-contact orders and workplace violence restraining orders as declared confidential by IN ST 5-2-9-6, et seq.;

- Mediation proceedings pursuant to IN ST ADR Rule 2.11, Mini-Trial proceedings pursuant to IN ST ADR Rule 4.4(C), and Summary Jury Trials pursuant to IN ST ADR Rule 5.6;

- Information in probation files pursuant to the Probation Standards promulgated by the Judicial Conference of Indiana pursuant to IN ST 11-13-1-8(b);

- Information deemed confidential pursuant to the Rules for Court Administered Alcohol and Drug Programs promulgated by the Judicial Conference of Indiana pursuant to IN ST 12-23-14-13;

- Information deemed confidential pursuant to the Problem-Solving Court Rules promulgated by the Judicial Conference of Indiana pursuant to IN ST 33-23-16-16;

- All records of the Department of workforce Development as declared confidential by IN ST 22-4-19-6;

- Information regarding interception of electronic communications that is sealed or deemed confidential as set forth in IN ST 35-33.5-2-1, et seq.

iii. Information excluded from public access by specific court order;

iv. Complete Social Security Numbers of living persons;

v. With the exception of names, information such as addresses, phone numbers, and dates of birth which explicitly identifies:

- Natural persons who are witnesses or victims (not including defendants) in criminal, domestic violence, stalking, sexual assault, juvenile, or civil protection order proceedings, provided that juveniles who are victims of sex crimes shall be identified by initials only;

- Places of residence of judicial officers, clerks and other employees of courts and clerks of court, unless the person or persons about whom the information pertains waives confidentiality;

vi. Complete account numbers of specific assets, loans, bank accounts, credit cards, and personal identification numbers (PINs);

vii. All orders of expungement entered in criminal or juvenile proceedings, orders to restrict access to criminal history information pursuant to IN ST 35-38-5-5.5 or IN ST 35-38-8-5 and records excluded from public access by such orders, and information related to infractions that is excluded from public access pursuant to IN ST 34-28-5-15 or IN ST 34-28-5-16 [Editor's note: IN ST 35-38-5-5.5, IN ST 35-38-8-5 and IN ST 34-28-5-16 were repealed effective July 1, 2013; for information on orders restricting access to criminal history, refer to IN ST 35-38-9-1, et seq.];

viii. All personal notes and e-mail, and deliberative material, of judges, jurors, court staff and judicial agencies, and information recorded in personal data assistants (PDA's) or organizers and personal calendars. IN ST ADMIN Rule 9(G)(1).

6. *Format of electronically filed documents*

   a. *Generally.* Electronically filed documents must meet the same requirements of format as documents conventionally filed pursuant to IN ST LAKE RCP Rule 2 or other applicable Lake County Rules of Civil Procedure. IN ST LAKE RCP Rule 17(D)(1).

   b. *Titles of documents.* The person electronically filing a document will be responsible for designating a title for the document at the time it is filed. The LCOD will generate the appropriate entry onto the CCS to record the filing of the document. IN ST LAKE RCP Rule 17(D)(3).

   c. *Citations and hyperlinks.* Electronically filed documents may contain hyperlink references to an external document as a convenient mechanism for accessing material cited in the document. Filers wishing to insert hyperlinks into documents shall continue to use the traditional method of citation to authority in addition to the hyperlink provided. The hyperlink is merely a convenience to the court and the material referenced is extraneous to the file and not a part of the court's record. IN ST LAKE RCP Rule 17(D)(5).

   d. *Attachments and exhibits.* All documents which form part of a single submission and which are being filed at the same time and by the same filer may be electronically filed together under one document filing, e.g., the motion, supporting affidavits, memorandum in support, designation of evidence, exhibits. IN ST LAKE RCP Rule 17(D)(6).

      i. Large documents which do not exist in an electronic format shall be scanned into .pdf format and filed electronically as separate attachments. A scanner is available in each clerk's office for use by the public and the bar in scanning and saving image files if needed. IN ST LAKE RCP Rule 17(D)(6).

   e. *Electronic signatures*

      i. *Electronic filing as signature.* The electronic filing of a document which is required to be signed shall constitute the filer's representation under IN ST TRIAL P Rule 11. Unless the electronically filed document has been scanned and shows the filer's original signature, the signature of the filer shall be indicated by As/Attorney's Name, or As/Party's Name as in the case of a pro se litigant, on the line where the signature would otherwise appear. IN ST LAKE RCP Rule 17(G)(1).

      ii. *Signatures on jointly signed or filed, verified or other documents.* In the case of a stipulation, agreed order, jointly signed motion or other document which needs to be signed by two (2) or more persons, or in the case of documents which must contain original signatures and which require verification or an unsworn declaration under rule or statute, the signatures may be indicated by either:

         • Submitting a scanned copy of the originally signed document; or,

         • Submitting the document with the use of As/Name in the signature block(s) where the original signature(s) appear(s) in the original document; provided, however, that the filer shall first obtain the physical signature of all persons necessary. IN ST LAKE RCP Rule 17(G)(2).

      iii. *Retention of original.* The filer shall retain the original executed document. IN ST LAKE RCP Rule 17(G).

7. *Citation of local rules.* The local rules for Lake County may be known as the Lake County Rules of Civil Procedure, and abbreviated as LR. IN ST LAKE RCP Rule 1(C).

F. Filing and Service Requirements

1. *Filing requirements.* Except as otherwise provided in IN ST TRIAL P Rule 5(E)(2), all pleadings and papers subsequent to the complaint which are required to be served upon a party shall be filed with the Court either before service or within a reasonable period of time thereafter. IN ST TRIAL P Rule 5(E)(1). All papers presented for filing shall be submitted to the Clerk and not to the court. All papers submitted

for filing shall be mailed or delivered to the Clerk's office at the courthouse in which the case is pending. IN ST LAKE RCP Rule 3(A).

a. *Filing with the court defined.* The filing of pleadings, motions, and other papers with the court as required by the Indiana Rules of Trial Procedure shall be made by one of the following methods:

   i. Delivery to the clerk of the court;

   ii. Sending by electronic transmission under the procedure adopted pursuant to IN ST ADMIN Rule 12;

   iii. Mailing to the clerk by registered, certified or express mail return receipt requested;

   iv. Depositing with any third-party commercial carrier for delivery to the clerk within three (3) calendar days, cost prepaid, properly addressed;

   v. If the court so permits, filing with the judge, in which event the judge shall note thereon the filing date and forthwith transmit them to the office of the clerk; or

   vi. Electronic filing, as approved by the Division of State Court Administration pursuant to IN ST ADMIN Rule 16. IN ST TRIAL P Rule 5(F).

   vii. Filing by registered or certified mail and by third-party commercial carrier shall be complete upon mailing or deposit. IN ST TRIAL P Rule 5(F).

b. *Mandatory electronic filing.* Unless otherwise permitted by the Lake County Rules of Civil Procedure or otherwise authorized by the judicial officer assigned to a particular case, all documents submitted for filing (including the original complaint, or equivalent pleading, and summons) shall be filed electronically with the clerk using the LCOD, no matter when the case was originally filed. IN ST LAKE RCP Rule 17(D).

   i. *Of documents containing information excluded from public access pursuant to* IN ST ADMIN Rule 9. Documents containing information excluded from public access pursuant to IN ST ADMIN Rule 9, or documents which are ordered to be filed under seal shall be filed electronically, pursuant to IN ST LAKE RCP Rule 17(D)(9), whenever possible, along with a copy of the applicable order to seal the records, and the filer shall designate the documents as "Not for Public Access Pursuant to Administrative Rule 9(G)(1)" at the time of filing. IN ST LAKE RCP Rule 16(A)(1); IN ST LAKE RCP Rule 17(D)(9).

   • *Conventional filing of documents containing information excluded from public access pursuant to* IN ST ADMIN Rule 9. Documents containing information excluded from public access pursuant to IN ST ADMIN Rule 9, or documents which are ordered to be filed under seal, which cannot be legibly scanned and filed electronically, shall be conventionally filed under seal and designated by the filer as "Not for Public Access Pursuant to Administrative Rule 9(G)(1)" at the time of filing. The unredacted version shall be filed on light green paper which is conspicuously marked "Not for Public Access"; and a redacted version, with confidential information deleted, shall be filed on white paper which shall be available for public access. The filer shall also electronically file a Notice of Manual Filing. IN ST LAKE RCP Rule 16(A)(2).

   ii. *Technical failures.* If a registered user is unable to file a document in a timely manner due to technical difficulties in the LCOD, the registered user must file a document with the court as soon as possible notifying the court of the inability to file the document. A sample document titled Declaration that Party was Unable to File in a Timely Manner Due to Technical Difficulties can be found at IN ST LAKE RCP Form 4. Delayed filings shall be rejected unless accompanied by the declaration attesting to the filer's failed attempts to file electronically at least two (2) times, separated by at least one (1) hour, after noon on each day of delay due to such technical failure. IN ST LAKE RCP Rule 17(J).

   iii. *Documents allowed to be filed conventionally.* Unless specifically authorized by the court, only the following documents may be filed conventionally and not electronically:

   • Exhibits and other documents that cannot be converted to a legible electronic form, such as videotapes, x-rays, and similar materials

- Documents delivered to the clerk by pro se litigants
- Documents mailed to the clerk by pro se litigants
- Confidential documents
- Notice of manual filing
- Titles of documents
- Chronological case summary entry forms (CCS entry forms). IN ST LAKE RCP Rule 17(E).
- For more information on the documents which must be filed conventionally, refer to IN ST LAKE RCP Rule 17(E).

c. *Facsimile filing.* Only when necessary on an emergency basis (i.e., when certified mail or other means of filing will not bring the document to the Judge's attention prior to the scheduled hearing or ruling), pleadings, motions and other papers may be filed by electronic facsimile transmission, or when specifically authorized by the Court. IN ST LAKE RCP Rule 2(C).

    i. *Generally.* In counties where a majority of judges of the courts of record, by posted local rule, have authorized electronic facsimile filing and designated a telephone number to receive such transmissions, pleadings, motions, and other papers may be sent to the Clerk of Circuit Court by electronic facsimile transmission for filing in any case, provided:

- Such matter does not exceed ten (10) pages, including the cover sheet;
- Such matter does not require the payment of fees other than the electronic facsimile transcription fee set forth in IN ST ADMIN Rule 12(E);
- The sending party creates at the time of transmission a machine generated log for such transmission; and
- The original document and the transmission log are maintained by the sending party for the duration of the litigation. IN ST ADMIN Rule 12(B).

    ii. *Time of filing.* During normal, posted business hours, the time of filing shall be the time the duplicate document is produced in the office of the Clerk of the Circuit Court. Duplicate documents received at all other times shall be filed as of the next normal business day. IN ST ADMIN Rule 12(C).

- If the receiving fax machine endorses its own time and date stamp upon the transmitted documents and the receiving machine produces a delivery receipt which is electronically created and transmitted to the sending party, the time of filing shall be the date and time recorded on the transmitted document by the receiving fax machine. IN ST ADMIN Rule 12(C).

d. *Filing for special judges.* For special judge matters where the special judge is a full-time judge or magistrate serving within Lake County, all papers submitted for filing shall be delivered or mailed to the Clerk's office at the courthouse where the special judge regularly serves. IN ST LAKE RCP Rule 3(A).

e. *Proof of filing.* Any party filing any paper by any method other than personal delivery to the clerk shall retain proof of filing. IN ST TRIAL P Rule 5(F).

2. *Service requirements.* Unless otherwise provided by the Indiana Rules of Trial Procedure or an order of the court, each party and special judge, if any, shall be served with: (1) every order required by its terms to be served; (2) every pleading subsequent to the original complaint; (3) every written motion except one which may be heard ex parte; (4) every brief submitted to the trial court; (5) every paper relating to discovery required to be served upon a party; and (6) every written notice, appearance, demand, offer of judgment, designation of record on appeal, or similar paper. IN ST TRIAL P Rule 5(A).

a. *Methods of service*

    i. *Personal service.* Whenever a party is represented by an attorney of record, service shall be made upon such attorney unless service upon the party himself is ordered by the court. Service

upon the attorney or party shall be made by delivering or mailing a copy of the papers to the last known address or where an attorney or party has consented to service by fax or e-mail, as provided in IN ST TRIAL P Rule 3.1(A)(4), by faxing or e-mailing a copy of the documents to the fax number or e-mail address set out in the appearance form or correction as required by IN ST TRIAL P Rule 3.1(E). IN ST TRIAL P Rule 5(B). Delivery of a copy within IN ST TRIAL P Rule 5 means:

- Offering or tendering it to the attorney or party and stating the nature of the papers being served. Refusal to accept an offered or tendered document is a waiver of any objection to the sufficiency or adequacy of service of that document;

- Leaving it at his office with a clerk or other person in charge thereof, or if there is no one in charge, leaving it in a conspicuous place therein; or

- If the office is closed, by leaving it at his dwelling house or usual place of abode with some person of suitable age and discretion then residing therein; or,

- Leaving it at some other suitable place, selected by the attorney upon whom service is being made, pursuant to duly promulgated local rule. IN ST TRIAL P Rule 5(B)(1).

ii. *Service by mail.* If service is made by mail, the papers shall be deposited in the United States mail addressed to the person on whom they are being served, with postage prepaid. Service shall be deemed complete upon mailing. Proof of service of all papers permitted to be mailed may be made by written acknowledgment of service, by affidavit of the person who mailed the papers, or by certificate of an attorney. It shall be the duty of attorneys when entering their appearance in a cause or when filing pleadings or papers therein, to have noted in the Chronological Case Summary or said pleadings or papers so filed the address and telephone number of their office. Service by delivery or by mail at such address shall be deemed sufficient and complete. IN ST TRIAL P Rule 5(B)(2).

iii. *Service by fax or e-mail.* A party who has consented to service by fax or e-mail may be served as follows:

- Service by e-mail shall be made by attaching the document being served in .pdf format. Discovery documents must also be served in accordance with IN ST TRIAL P Rule 26(A). IN ST TRIAL P Rule 5(B)(3)(a).

- Service by fax shall be deemed complete upon generation of a transmission record indicating the successful transmission of the entire document, except as provided in IN ST TRIAL P Rule 5(B)(3)(d). IN ST TRIAL P Rule 5(B)(3)(b).

- Service by e-mail shall be deemed complete upon transmission, except as provided in IN ST TRIAL P Rule 5(B)(3)(d). IN ST TRIAL P Rule 5(B)(3)(c).

- Service by fax or e-mail that occurs on a Saturday, Sunday, legal holiday, or day the court or agency in which the matter is pending is closed or after 5:00 PM local time of the recipient shall be deemed complete the next day that is not a Saturday, Sunday, legal holiday, or day that the court or agency in which the matter is pending is not closed. IN ST TRIAL P Rule 5(B)(3)(d).

b. *Serving numerous defendants.* In any action in which there are unusually large numbers of defendants, the court, upon motion or of its own initiative, may order:

i. That service of the pleadings of the defendants and replies thereto need not be made as between the defendants;

- That any cross-claim, counterclaim, or matter constituting an avoidance or affirmative defense contained therein shall be deemed to be denied or avoided by all other parties; and

- That the filing of any such pleading and service thereof upon the plaintiff constitutes due notice of it to the parties. IN ST TRIAL P Rule 5(D).

ii. A copy of every such order shall be served upon the parties in such manner and form as the court directs. IN ST TRIAL P Rule 5(D).

c. *Service by electronic means.* The Lake County Online Docket will generate a Notice of Electronic

Filing and Service when any document is filed and served. This notice will be emailed to each registered user of record in a case, and an electronic service event will be added to the work queue of each registered user of record in the case. The party filing the document should retain a paper or electronic copy of the Notice of Electronic Filing and Service. This notice represents proof of filing and service of the document on registered users of record in that case. The filer shall not be required to conventionally serve any document on any party receiving electronic service. IN ST LAKE RCP Rule 17(F)(2).

    i. The filer shall also conventionally serve those parties not designated or able to receive electronic notice or service but who are nevertheless entitled to notice of said pleading or other document in accordance with the Indiana Rules of Civil Procedure and applicable Lake County Rules of Civil Procedure. In such cases, the filer shall also file a certificate of service, as appropriate. IN ST LAKE RCP Rule 17(F).

  d. *Service on parties in default for failure to appear.* No service need be made on parties in default for failure to appear, except that pleadings asserting new or additional claims for relief against them shall be served upon them in the manner provided by service of summons in IN ST TRIAL P Rule 4. IN ST TRIAL P Rule 5(A).

G. Hearings

1. *Hearing on motion.* Unless local conditions make it impracticable, each judge shall establish regular times and places, at intervals sufficiently frequent for the prompt dispatch of business, at which motions requiring notice and hearing may be heard and disposed of; but the judge at any time or place and on such notice, if any, as he considers reasonable may make order for the advancement, conduct, and hearing of actions. To expedite its business the court may direct the submission and determination of motions without oral hearing upon brief written statements of reasons in support and opposition, or direct or permit hearings by telephone conference call with all attorneys or other similar means of communication. IN ST TRIAL P Rule 73(A).

2. *Hearings generally held before imposition of discovery sanctions.* As a general matter, most courts will conduct a hearing prior to imposing discovery sanctions, although IN ST TRIAL P Rule 37 and Indiana case law do not expressly require a court to do so. 22 INPRAC § 27.7.

3. *Oral argument discretionary.* The granting of a motion for oral argument, unless required by the Indiana Rules of Trial Procedure, shall be wholly discretionary with the court. IN ST LAKE RCP Rule 4(B).

H. Forms

1. Motion for Discovery Sanctions Forms for Indiana

  a. Motion to dismiss as sanction for failure to comply with court ordered discovery. 5 INPRAC § 4:6.60.

  b. Motion to dismiss action as sanction; For party's failure to comply with court ordered discovery. 10 INPRAC § 58.38.

  c. Motion for order precluding litigation of issues. 10 INPRAC § 58.63.

  d. Motion for judgment by default; As sanction for failure to comply with court order. 10 INPRAC § 58.64.

  e. Motion to exclude expert witness at trial. 10 INPRAC § 70.24

  f. Certificate of service; Personal service. 9 INPRAC § 5.7.

  g. Certificate of service; First class mail. 9 INPRAC § 5.8.

2. Official Motion Discovery Sanctions Forms for Lake County

  a. CCS entry form. IN ST LAKE RCP App. A.

  b. Notice of manual filing. IN ST LAKE RCP Form 2.

  c. Certificate of service. IN ST LAKE RCP Form 3.

  d. Declaration that party was unable to file in a timely manner. IN ST LAKE RCP Form 4.

3. Motion for Discovery Sanctions Forms for Lake County

    a. Notice of manual filing. EFORMST IN 5540.

I. Checklist

(I) ❑ Matters to be considered by moving party

    (a) ❑ Required documents

        (1) ❑ Motion and notice

        (2) ❑ Brief

        (3) ❑ Attorney certification

        (4) ❑ Proposed order

        (5) ❑ Chronological case summary (CSS) entry forms

        (6) ❑ Certificate of service

    (b) ❑ Supplemental documents

        (1) ❑ Supporting evidence

        (2) ❑ Facsimile cover sheet

    (c) ❑ Timing

        (1) ❑ There are no specific timing requirements for filing a motion for discovery sanctions

        (2) ❑ A written motion, other than one which may be heard ex parte, and notice of the hearing thereof shall be served not less than five (5) days before the time specified for the hearing, unless a different period is fixed by the Indiana Rules of Trial Procedure or by order of the court

        (3) ❑ All pleadings and papers subsequent to the complaint which are required to be served upon a party shall be filed with the Court either before service or within a reasonable period of time thereafter

        (4) ❑ All pleadings, motions and other papers submitted for filing which are required to be served under IN ST TRIAL P Rule 5(A) shall be filed no later than three (3) days after service

        (5) ❑ If such papers are filed before service, proof of service thereof shall be filed no later than three (3) business days thereafter

(II) ❑ Matters to be considered by the responding party

    (a) ❑ Required documents

        (1) ❑ Opposition

        (2) ❑ Chronological case summary (CSS) entry forms

        (3) ❑ Certificate of service

    (b) ❑ Supplemental documents

        (1) ❑ Supporting evidence

        (2) ❑ Proposed order

        (3) ❑ Facsimile cover sheet

    (c) ❑ Timing

        (1) ❑ So long as consistent with the Indiana Rules of Trial Procedure, an adverse party wishing to respond shall do so within fifteen (15) days of service

        (2) ❑ Except as otherwise provided in IN ST TRIAL P Rule 59(D), opposing affidavits may be served not less than one (1) day before the hearing, unless the court permits them to be served at some other time

Motions, Oppositions and Replies
Motion for Preliminary Injunction

Document Last Updated October 2013

A. Applicable Rules

1. *State rules*

   a. Appearance. IN ST TRIAL P Rule 3.1.

   b. Process. IN ST TRIAL P Rule 4.

   c. Service and filing of pleadings and other papers. IN ST TRIAL P Rule 5.

   d. Time. IN ST TRIAL P Rule 6.

   e. Pleadings. IN ST TRIAL P Rule 7; IN ST TRIAL P Rule 8; IN ST TRIAL P Rule 9.2; IN ST TRIAL P Rule 10.

   f. Signing and verification of pleadings. IN ST TRIAL P Rule 11.

   g. Evidence. IN ST TRIAL P Rule 43.

   h. Judgment on the evidence (directed verdict). IN ST TRIAL P Rule 50.

   i. Findings by the court. IN ST TRIAL P Rule 52.

   j. Summary judgment. IN ST TRIAL P Rule 56.

   k. Motion to correct error. IN ST TRIAL P Rule 59.

   l. Relief from judgment or order. IN ST TRIAL P Rule 60.

   m. Injunctions. IN ST TRIAL P Rule 65; IN ST 34-26-1-7; IN ST 34-26-1-8.

   n. Security; Proceedings against sureties. IN ST TRIAL P Rule 65.1.

   o. Hearing of motions. IN ST TRIAL P Rule 73.

   p. Court records. IN ST TRIAL P Rule 77.

   q. Access to court records. IN ST ADMIN Rule 9.

   r. Paper size. IN ST ADMIN Rule 11.

   s. Facsimile transmission. IN ST ADMIN Rule 12.

   t. Electronic filing and electronic service pilot projects. IN ST ADMIN Rule 16.

   u. Privacy and confidentiality. IN ST 5-2-9-6; IN ST 5-14-3-4; IN ST 5-14-3-5.5; IN ST 6-4.1-5-10; IN ST 6-4.1-12-12; IN ST 6-8.1-7-1; IN ST 11-13-1-8; IN ST 12-23-14-13; IN ST 16-39-3-10; IN ST 16-41-8-1; IN ST 22-4-19-6; IN ST 31-11-1-6; IN ST 31-19-5-23; IN ST 31-19-13-2; IN ST 31-19-19-1; IN ST 31-33-18-1; IN ST 31-39-1-1; IN ST 31-39-1-2; IN ST 33-23-16-16; IN ST 35-34-2-4; IN ST 35-38-1-13; IN ST 35-38-9-1; IN ST ADR Rule 2.11; IN ST ADR Rule 4.4; IN ST ADR Rule 5.6; IN ST JURY Rule 10.

2. *Local rules*

   a. Scope and title. [IN ST LAKE RCP Rule 1, as amended by IN ORDER 13-0237, effective October 18, 2013].

   b. Preparation of pleadings, motions and other papers. IN ST LAKE RCP Rule 2.

   c. Filing. [IN ST LAKE RCP Rule 3, as amended by IN ORDER 13-0237, effective October 18, 2013].

   d. Motions. IN ST LAKE RCP Rule 4.

   e. Pretrial procedure. IN ST LAKE RCP Rule 9.

   f. Briefs. IN ST LAKE RCP Rule 11.

   g. Confidential information and sealed documents. IN ST LAKE RCP Rule 16.

   h. Electronic filing and service. IN ST LAKE RCP Rule 17.

833

B. Timing

1. *Motion for preliminary injunction.* The injunction may be granted at the time of commencing the action, or at any time afterwards before judgment is rendered in the proceeding. IN ST 34-26-1-7. IN ST TRIAL P Rule 65 does not state when notice must be given. 4 INPRAC R 65(65.2).

    a. *Filing.* All pleadings and papers subsequent to the complaint which are required to be served upon a party shall be filed with the Court either before service or within a reasonable period of time thereafter. IN ST TRIAL P Rule 5(E)(1). All pleadings, motions and other papers submitted for filing which are required to be served under IN ST TRIAL P Rule 5(A) shall be filed no later than three (3) days after service. IN ST LAKE RCP Rule 3(A).

        i. If such papers are filed before service, proof of service thereof shall be filed no later than three (3) business days thereafter. Upon failure to comply with IN ST LAKE RCP Rule 3, the Court may, on motion of any party or on its own motion, impose appropriate sanctions. IN ST LAKE RCP Rule 3(A).

    b. *Briefs.* Briefs, other than those addressed in IN ST LAKE RCP Rule 4 and IN ST LAKE RCP Rule 9, shall be filed no later than two (2) calendar days preceding the hearing or trial to which directed. IN ST LAKE RCP Rule 11.

2. *Service.* A written motion, other than one which may be heard ex parte, and notice of the hearing thereof shall be served not less than five (5) days before the time specified for the hearing, unless a different period is fixed by the Indiana Rules of Trial Procedure or by order of the court. IN ST TRIAL P Rule 6(D).

    a. *Of supporting affidavits.* When a motion is supported by affidavit, the affidavit shall be served with the motion. IN ST TRIAL P Rule 6(D).

3. *Service of opposition.* Except as otherwise provided in IN ST TRIAL P Rule 59(D), opposing affidavits may be served not less than one (1) day before the hearing, unless the court permits them to be served at some other time. IN ST TRIAL P Rule 6(D).

    a. So long as consistent with the Indiana Rules of Trial Procedure, an adverse party wishing to respond shall do so within fifteen (15) days of service. IN ST LAKE RCP Rule 4(A).

4. *Reply.* The moving party shall have ten (10) days after service of the response within which to reply. IN ST LAKE RCP Rule 4(A).

5. *Computation of time*

    a. *Generally; Days excluded.* In computing any period of time prescribed or allowed by the Indiana Rules of Trial Procedure, by order of the court, or by any applicable statute, the day of the act, event, or default from which the designated period of time begins to run shall not be included. The last day of the period so computed is to be included unless it is:

        i. A Saturday,

        ii. A Sunday,

        iii. A legal holiday as defined by state statute, or

        iv. A day the office in which the act is to be done is closed during regular business hours. IN ST TRIAL P Rule 6(A).

    b. *Short periods.* In any event, the period runs until the end of the next day that is not a Saturday, a Sunday, a legal holiday, or a day on which the office is closed. When the period of time allowed is less than seven (7) days, intermediate Saturdays, Sundays, legal holidays, and days on which the office is closed shall be excluded from the computations. IN ST TRIAL P Rule 6(A).

    c. *Additional time after service by United States mail.* Whenever a party has the right or is required to do some act or take some proceedings within a prescribed period after the service of a notice or other paper upon him and the notice or paper is served upon him by United States mail, three (3) days shall be added to the prescribed period. IN ST TRIAL P Rule 6(E).

    d. *Electronic filing does not alter deadlines.* Filing electronically does not alter any filing deadlines or any time computation pursuant to state or federal statutes, any Rules of the Indiana Supreme Court, including without limitation the Rules of Trial Procedure, the Rules of Appellate Procedure or the

Administrative Rules, or applicable Lake County Rules of Civil Procedure. The office of the Lake County Clerk is open for electronic filing under the Lake County Rules of Civil Procedure twenty-four (24) hours a day. A document is deemed filed at the date and time it is received by the LCOD server. Filing must be completed before midnight local time in order to be considered filed that day. Lake County observes Central Time and electronic filers are strongly urged to file documents during hours when the Lake County Online Docket ("LCOD") help line is available, from 9:00 a.m. to 4:00 p.m. local time, although documents can be filed electronically twenty-four (24) hours a day. IN ST LAKE RCP Rule 17(I).

e. *Enlargement of time.* When an act is required or allowed to be done at or within a specific time by the Indiana Rules of Trial Procedure, the court may at any time for cause shown:

   i. Order the period enlarged, with or without motion or notice, if request therefor is made before the expiration of the period originally prescribed or extended by a previous order; or

   ii. Upon motion made after the expiration of the specific period, permit the act to be done where the failure to act was the result of excusable neglect; but, the court may not extend the time for taking any action for judgment on the evidence under IN ST TRIAL P Rule 50(A), amendment of findings and judgment under IN ST TRIAL P Rule 52(B), to correct errors under IN ST TRIAL P Rule 59(C), statement in opposition to motion to correct error under IN ST TRIAL P Rule 59(E), or to obtain relief from final judgment under IN ST TRIAL P Rule 60(B), except to the extent and under the conditions stated in those rules. IN ST TRIAL P Rule 6(B).

C. General Requirements

1. *Motions, generally.* Unless made during a hearing or trial, or otherwise ordered by the court, an application to the court for an order shall be made by written motion. The motion shall state the grounds therefor and the relief or order sought. IN ST TRIAL P Rule 7(B).

   a. *Motions as distinct from pleadings.* Motions and responses to motions are not pleadings, and allegations contained in a motion are not admissions of a party. 22B INPRAC 7:2; Wachstetter v. County Properties, LLC, 832 N.E.2d 574 (Ind.Ct.App. 2005); Scott County Family YMCA, Inc. v. Hobbs, 817 N.E.2d 603 (Ind.Ct.App. 2004).

   b. *Unopposed motions generally granted.* It is common for a trial court to grant procedural motions, such as motions for enlargement of time, discovery motions, or motions for continuance, unless an objection is filed. 21 INPRAC § 13.8.

   c. *Separate motions.* Each motion shall be separate, while alternative motions filed together shall each be identified on the caption. IN ST LAKE RCP Rule 4(A).

   d. *Answer and reply briefs.* Failure to file an answer brief or reply brief within the time prescribed shall be deemed a waiver of the right thereto and shall subject the motion to summary ruling. IN ST LAKE RCP Rule 4(A).

2. *Motion for preliminary injunction.* The general purpose of a temporary restraining order and a preliminary injunction is to maintain and preserve the status quo until the merits of the case can be heard. The status quo is the last actual, peaceful and noncontested status which preceded the pending controversy. 4 INPRAC R 65(65.1); Rees v. Panhandle Eastern Pipe Line Co., 176 Ind.App. 597, 377 N.E.2d 640 (Ind.Ct.App. 1978). An injunction does not create or enlarge the rights of a party, it merely protects existing rights and prevents harm to the aggrieved party that cannot be corrected by a final judgment. 22B INPRAC 65:1; Franke v. Honeywell, Inc., 516 N.E.2d 1090 (Ind.Ct.App. 1987); Indiana & Michigan Elec. Co. v. Whitley County Rural Elec. Membership Corp., 161 Ind.App. 492, 316 N.E.2d 584 (Ind.Ct.App. 1974); AGS Capital Corp., Inc. v. Product Action Intern., LLC, 884 N.E.2d 294 (Ind.Ct.App. 2008).

   a. *Injunctions in general.* Whether or not a preliminary injunction should issue rests in the sound discretion of the trial court. Discretion to grant or deny a preliminary injunction is measured by the following factors and the burden lies with the movant to prove each element by a preponderance of the evidence. 4 INPRAC R 65(65.1); Crossmann Communities, Inc. v. Dean, 767 N.E.2d 1035, 1040 (Ind.Ct.App. 2002); Mercho-Roushdi Corp. v. Blatchford, 742 N.E.2d 519, 524 (Ind.Ct.App. 2001).

      i. If the movant fails to prove any of these requirements, the trial court's grant of an injunction is an abuse of discretion. 4 INPRAC R 65(65.1); Ind. Family and Soc. Servs. Admin. v. Walgreen Co., 769 N.E.2d 158, 161 (Ind. 2002):

- Whether the plaintiff's remedies at law are inadequate and the plaintiff will suffer irreparable harm pending the resolution of the substantive action if the injunction does not issue;
- Whether the plaintiff has demonstrated at least a reasonable likelihood of success at trial by establishing a prima facie case;
- Whether the threatened injury to the plaintiff outweighs the threatened harm the grant of the injunction may inflict on the defendant; and
- Whether the public interest would be disserved if the injunction is granted. 4 INPRAC R 65(65.1); Ind. Family and Soc. Servs. Admin. v. Walgreen Co., 769 N.E.2d 158, 161 (Ind. 2002); Daugherty v. Allen, 729 N.E.2d 228, 232 (Ind.Ct.App. 2000);

ii. Two (2) sweeping statements about the preliminary injunction often appear:

- Economic injury alone will not warrant the granting of a preliminary injunction. 4 INPRAC R 65(65.1); Wells v. Auberry, 429 N.E.2d 679 (Ind.Ct.App. 1982), and
- Injunctive relief is not appropriate if a remedy for damages is an adequate remedy and the defendant is solvent. 4 INPRAC R 65(65.1); Gaslight and Coke Company v. City of New Albany, 139 Ind. 660, 39 N.E. 462 (1894).

b. *Consolidation of hearing with trial on merits.* Before or after the commencement of the hearing of an application for a preliminary injunction, the court may order the trial of the action on the merits to be advanced and consolidated with the hearing of the application. Even when this consolidation is not ordered, any evidence received upon an application for a preliminary injunction which would be admissible upon the trial on the merits becomes part of the record on the trial and need not be repeated upon the trial. IN ST TRIAL P Rule 65(A)(2).

i. The power of the court to order advancement and consolidation under IN ST TRIAL P Rule 65 is tempered by the due process requirements of fair notice and an opportunity to be heard. 4 INPRAC R 65(65.3); University of Texas v. Camenisch, 451 U.S. 390, 101 S.Ct. 1830, 68 L.Ed.2d 175 (1981). The court is required to give clear notice that consolidation of the trial on the merits with the hearing on the motion for preliminary injunction will be ordered, and the notice must be given at a time which will afford the parties a full opportunity to present their respective cases. 4 INPRAC R 65(65.3); Paris v. U.S. Department of Housing & Urban Dev., 713 F.2d 1341, 1345, (7th Cir. 1983).

c. *Assignment of cases; Judge to act promptly.* Assignment of cases shall not be affected by the fact that a temporary restraining order or preliminary injunction is sought, but such case shall be assigned promptly and the judge regularly assigned to the case shall act upon and hear all matters relating to temporary restraining orders and preliminary injunctions. The judge shall make himself readily available to consider temporary restraining orders, conduct hearings, fix the manner of giving notice and the time and place for hearings under IN ST TRIAL P Rule 65, and shall act and require the parties to act promptly. IN ST TRIAL P Rule 65(A)(3).

i. If the party seeking relief or his attorney by affidavit establishes that the judge assigned to the case is not available or cannot be found to consider an application for a restraining order, to conduct a hearing, or to fix the manner of giving notice and the time and place for a hearing under IN ST TRIAL P Rule 65, he may apply to any other judge in the circuit who shall take all further action with respect to any temporary restraining order or preliminary injunction. If the affidavit establishes that no other judge in the circuit is available or to be found, he may apply to the judge of any adjoining circuit. Unless an order is entered within ten (10) days after the hearing upon the granting, modifying or dissolving of a temporary or preliminary injunction, the relief sought shall be subject to the provisions of IN ST TRIAL P Rule 53.1. IN ST TRIAL P Rule 65(A)(3).

d. *Modification of orders; Responsive pleadings.* Upon the court's own motion or the motion of any party, orders granting or denying temporary restraining orders or preliminary injunctions may be dissolved, modified, granted or reinstated. Responsive pleadings shall not be required in response to any pleadings or motions relating to temporary restraining orders or preliminary injunctions. IN ST TRIAL P Rule 65(A)(4).

e. *Form of order by judge.* Every order granting temporary injunction and every restraining order shall include or be accompanied by findings as required by IN ST TRIAL P Rule 52; shall be specific in terms; shall describe in reasonable detail, and not by reference to the complaint or other document, the act or acts sought to be restrained; and is binding only upon the parties to the action, their officers, agents, servants, employees, and attorneys, and upon those persons in active concert or participation with them who receive actual notice of the order by personal service or otherwise. IN ST TRIAL P Rule 65(D).

3. *Security*

   a. *Security requirement.* No restraining order or preliminary injunction shall issue except upon the giving of security by the applicant, in such sum as the court deems proper, for the payment of such costs and damages as may be incurred or suffered by any party who is found to have been wrongfully enjoined or restrained. No such security shall be required of a governmental organization, but such governmental organization shall be responsible for costs and damages as may be incurred or suffered by any party who is found to have been wrongfully enjoined or restrained. IN ST TRIAL P Rule 65(C).

      i. The provisions of IN ST TRIAL P Rule 65.1 apply to a surety upon a bond or undertaking under IN ST TRIAL P Rule 65. IN ST TRIAL P Rule 65(C).

   b. *Proceedings against sureties.* Whenever the Indiana Rules of Trial Procedure or other laws require or permit the giving of security by a party to a court action or proceeding, and security is given in the form of a bond or stipulation or other undertaking with one or more sureties, each surety submits himself to the jurisdiction of the court and irrevocably appoints the clerk of the court as his agent upon whom any papers affecting his liability on the bond or undertaking may be served. His liability may be enforced on motion without the necessity of an independent action. The motion and such notice of the motion as the court prescribes may be served on the clerk of the court, who shall forthwith mail copies to the sureties if their addresses are known. IN ST TRIAL P Rule 65.1 applies to bonds or security furnished on appeal, and enforcement shall be in the court to which the case is returned after appeal. IN ST TRIAL P Rule 65.1.

   c. *Bond generally used as security.* IN ST TRIAL P Rule 65(C) speaks only of the giving of security and does not expressly require a surety on a bond. In practice, however, the giving of a bond with an insurance company as surety in the amount set by the court is typically the device used to satisfy this section. 4 INPRAC R 65(65.6).

D. Documents

1. *Required documents*

   a. *Motion and notice.* No preliminary injunction shall be issued without an opportunity for a hearing upon notice to the adverse party. IN ST TRIAL P Rule 65(A)(1). The requirement of notice is satisfied by service of the motion. IN ST TRIAL P Rule 7(B). Refer to the General Requirements section of this document for information on the content of a motion for preliminary injunction.

   b. *Brief.* Briefs, other than those addressed in IN ST LAKE RCP Rule 4 and IN ST LAKE RCP Rule 9, shall be filed no later than two (2) calendar days preceding the hearing or trial to which directed. IN ST LAKE RCP Rule 11.

   c. *Affidavit.* In all applications for an injunction, the complaint or as much of the complaint as pertains to the acts or proceedings to be enjoined, must be verified by affidavit. IN ST 34-26-1-7.

   d. *Security.* No restraining order or preliminary injunction shall issue except upon the giving of security by the applicant, in such sum as the court deems proper, for the payment of such costs and damages as may be incurred or suffered by any party who is found to have been wrongfully enjoined or restrained. IN ST TRIAL P Rule 65(C). Refer to the General Requirements section of this document for more information.

   e. *Proposed order.* Unless local practice provides differently, a party should submit a proposed order with its written motion to be signed by the judge once the motion has been granted. 21 INPRAC § 13.8.

    i. Proposed orders, which are submitted for the court's convenience under IN ST LAKE RCP Rule 3 or other applicable Lake County Rules of Civil Procedure, shall be submitted as attachments to motions. IN ST LAKE RCP Rule 17(D)(8). Proposed orders shall be prepared and filed separately from the pleadings, petitions, motions or other papers to which they have reference. IN ST LAKE RCP Rule 3(B).

    ii. Orders, either routine in nature or uncontested including, for example, those setting or continuing a hearing, shall be effected by the chronological case summary entry only, which shall contain the concise substance of the order. IN ST LAKE RCP Rule 3(B).

    iii. All orders shall be accompanied with sufficient copies and stamped, pre-addressed envelopes, so that copies may be mailed to all parties. IN ST LAKE RCP Rule 3(B).

f. *Chronological case summary (CCS) entry forms.* All filings shall be accompanied by a Chronological Case Summary (CCS) Entry Form to define or identify the documents filed. The Form used should be substantially similar to IN ST LAKE RCP App. A. IN ST LAKE RCP Rule 3(C).

g. *Certificate of service.* An attorney or unrepresented party tendering a document to the Clerk for filing shall certify that service has been made, list the parties served, and specify the date and means of service. The certificate of service shall be placed at the end of the document and shall not be separately filed. The separate filing of a certificate of service, however, shall not be grounds for rejecting a document for filing. The Clerk may permit documents to be filed without a certificate of service but shall require prompt filing of a separate certificate of service. IN ST TRIAL P Rule 5(C).

    i. All pleadings, motions and other papers submitted for filing which are required to be served under IN ST TRIAL P Rule 5(A) shall contain proof of service pursuant to IN ST TRIAL P Rule 5(B)(2). IN ST LAKE RCP Rule 3(A).

2. *Supplemental documents*

a. *Supporting evidence.* When a motion is based on facts not appearing of record the court may hear the matter on affidavits presented by the respective parties, but the court may direct that the matter be heard wholly or partly on oral testimony or depositions. IN ST TRIAL P Rule 43(B).

b. *Facsimile cover sheet.* Any document sent to the Clerk of the Circuit Court by electronic facsimile transmission shall be accompanied by a cover sheet which states the title of the document, case number, number of pages, identity and voice telephone number of the sending party and instructions for filing. The cover sheet shall contain the signature of the attorney or party, pro se, authorizing the filing. IN ST ADMIN Rule 12(D).

E. Format

1. *Form of motions.* The rules applicable to captions, and the signing and form of pleadings (IN ST TRIAL P Rule 8 through IN ST TRIAL P Rule 11), apply to all motions and other papers provided under the Indiana Rules of Trial Procedure. 22B INPRAC 7:2.

2. *Form of pleadings.* For the purpose of uniformity, convenience, clarity and durability, requirements in IN ST LAKE RCP Rule 2 shall be observed in the preparation of all pleadings, motions and other papers. IN ST LAKE RCP Rule 2. Whenever materials submitted fail to meet the standards in IN ST LAKE RCP Rule 2, the Court may impose appropriate sanctions. IN ST LAKE RCP Rule 2(B).

a. *Caption; Names of parties.* Every pleading shall contain a caption setting forth the name of the court, the title of the action, the file number, and a designation as in IN ST TRIAL P Rule 7(A). In the complaint the title of the action shall include the names of all the parties, but in other pleadings it is sufficient to state the name of the first party on each side with an appropriate indication of other parties. IN ST TRIAL P Rule 10(A).

    i. *Special judge matters.* The caption of all CCS Entry Forms, pleadings, motions, orders and other papers to be filed in a special judge case shall include in block text the words SPECIAL JUDGE and the name of the judge directly below the cause number on the caption. IN ST LAKE RCP Rule 2(D).

b. *Paragraphs; Separate statements.* All averments of a claim or defense shall be made in numbered paragraphs, the contents of each of which shall be limited as far as practicable to a statement of a single set of circumstances, and a paragraph may be referred to by number in all succeeding pleadings. Each claim founded upon a separate transaction or occurrence and each defense other than denials may be stated in a separate count or defense whenever a separation facilitates the clear presentation of the matters set forth. IN ST TRIAL P Rule 10(B).

c. *Adoption by reference; Exhibits.* Statements in a pleading may be adopted by reference in a different part of the same pleading or in another pleading or in any motion. A copy of any written instrument which is an exhibit to a pleading is a part thereof for all purposes. IN ST TRIAL P Rule 10(C).

d. *Paper; Print, quality and binding*

   i. All pleadings, motions, chronological case summary entry forms, orders, process and other papers shall be neatly and legibly printed, typewritten or mechanically reproduced, on one (1) side only, on white opaque paper. To satisfy the recordkeeping requirements of IN ST TRIAL P Rule 77, the print shall be of sufficient density and clarity for preservation and reproduction of microfilming, optical disk or other secondary sources. For this reason, the use of non-letter-quality printers is discouraged. IN ST LAKE RCP Rule 2(A).

   ii. Paper and ink shall be of such quality as to withstand the test of time. All documents shall be produced on acid-free, non-thermal paper. It is recommended that a minimum of twenty (20) pound, twenty-five percent (25%) cotton paper product be used. Documents of multiple pages shall be submitted in bound or stapled fashion, and the binding or stapling shall be at the top only. Covers or backings shall not be used. IN ST LAKE RCP Rule 2(A).

e. *Papers; Handwritten.* Handwritten papers may be filed only if approved by the Court and a typewritten or printed true rendition thereof is filed within three (3) days thereafter and approved by the Court. Upon such approval, they shall be deemed and filed as the original, while the handwritten papers shall be retained therewith for evidentiary purposes. IN ST LAKE RCP Rule 2(C).

f. *Minute sheets; Motion blanks.* Minute sheets and motion blanks shall no longer be used. IN ST LAKE RCP Rule 2(D).

3. *Size of papers for filing.* Effective January 1, 1992, all pleadings, copies, motions and documents filed with any trial court or appellate level court, typed or printed, with the exception of exhibits and existing wills, shall be prepared on eight and one-half by eleven inch (8 1/2" x 11") size paper. IN ST ADMIN Rule 11.

4. *Signature requirements*

a. *Signature of attorney.* Every pleading or motion of a party represented by an attorney shall be signed by at least one (1) attorney of record in his individual name, whose address, telephone number, and attorney number shall be stated, except that this provision shall not apply to pleadings and motions made and transcribed at the trial or a hearing before the judge and received by him in such form. IN ST TRIAL P Rule 11(A).

   i. The signature of an attorney constitutes a certificate by him that he has read the pleadings; that to the best of his knowledge, information, and belief, there is good ground to support it; and that it is not interposed for delay. IN ST TRIAL P Rule 11(A).

   ii. If a pleading or motion is not signed or is signed with intent to defeat the purpose of the rule, it may be stricken as sham and false and the action may proceed as though the pleading had not been served. IN ST TRIAL P Rule 11(A).

   iii. For a willful violation of IN ST TRIAL P Rule 11 an attorney may be subjected to appropriate disciplinary action. Similar action may be taken if scandalous or indecent matter is inserted. IN ST TRIAL P Rule 11(A).

b. *Signature of unrepresented party.* A party who is not represented by an attorney shall sign his pleading and state his address. IN ST TRIAL P Rule 11(A).

c. *Verification not generally required.* Except when specifically required by rule, pleadings or motions need not be verified or accompanied by affidavit. The rule in equity that the averments of an answer under oath must be overcome by the testimony of two (2) witnesses or of one (1) witness sustained by corroborating circumstances is abolished. IN ST TRIAL P Rule 11(A).

d. *Verification by affirmation or representation.* When in connection with any civil or special statutory proceeding it is required that any pleading, motion, petition, supporting affidavit, or other document of any kind, be verified, or that an oath be taken, it shall be sufficient if the subscriber simply affirms the truth of the matter to be verified by an affirmation or representation. IN ST TRIAL P Rule 11(B). IN ST TRIAL P Rule 11(B) states that the affirmation or representation should be in substantially the following language: "I (we) affirm, under the penalties for perjury, that the foregoing representation(s) is (are) true. (Signed) _____."

   i. Any person who falsifies an affirmation or representation of fact shall be subject to the same penalties as are prescribed by law for the making of a false affidavit. IN ST TRIAL P Rule 11(B).

e. *Verified pleadings, motions, and affidavits as evidence.* Pleadings, motions and affidavits accompanying or in support of such pleadings or motions when required to be verified or under oath shall be accepted as a representation that the signer had personal knowledge thereof or reasonable cause to believe the existence of the facts or matters stated or alleged therein; and, if otherwise competent or acceptable as evidence, may be admitted as evidence of the facts or matters stated or alleged therein when it is so provided in the Indiana Rules of Trial Procedure, by statute or other law, or to the extent the writing or signature expressly purports to be made upon the signer's personal knowledge. When such pleadings, motions and affidavits are verified or under oath they shall not require other or greater proof on the part of the adverse party than if not verified or not under oath unless expressly provided otherwise by the Indiana Rules of Trial Procedure, statute or other law. Affidavits upon motions for summary judgment under IN ST TRIAL P Rule 56 and in denial of execution under IN ST TRIAL P Rule 9.2 shall be made upon personal knowledge. IN ST TRIAL P Rule 11(C).

f. *Electronic signature.* The filing of documents and information through the E-filing system by use of a valid username and password is presumed to have been authorized by the User to whom that username and password have been issued and documents filed through the E-filing system are presumed to have been signed by the same User. IN ST ADMIN Rule 16(E).

5. *Information excluded from public access.* Every document filed in a case shall separately identify information excluded from public access pursuant to IN ST ADMIN Rule 9(G)(1) as follows:

   a. Whole documents that are excluded from public access pursuant to IN ST ADMIN Rule 9(G)(1) shall be tendered on light green paper or have a light green coversheet attached to the document, marked "Not for Public Access" or "Confidential." IN ST TRIAL P Rule 5(G)(1).

   b. When only a portion of a document contains information excluded from public access pursuant to IN ST ADMIN Rule 9(G)(1), said information shall be omitted [or redacted] from the filed document, and set forth on a separate accompanying document on light green paper conspicuously marked "Not for Public Access" or "Confidential" and clearly designated [or identifying] the caption and number of the case and the document and location within the document to which the redacted material pertains. IN ST TRIAL P Rule 5(G)(2).

   c. With respect to documents filed in electronic format, the trial court, by local rule, may provide for compliance with IN ST TRIAL P Rule 5 in manner that separates and protects access to information excluded from public access. IN ST TRIAL P Rule 5(G)(3).

   d. IN ST TRIAL P Rule 5(G) does not apply to a record sealed by the court pursuant to IN ST 5-14-3-5.5 or otherwise, nor to records, documents, or information filed in cases to which public access is prohibited pursuant to IN ST ADMIN Rule 9(G). IN ST TRIAL P Rule 5(G)(4).

   e. The following information in case records is excluded from public access and is confidential:

      i. Information that is excluded from public access pursuant to federal law;

      ii. Information that is excluded from public access as declared confidential by Indiana statute or other court rule, including without limitation:

         • All adoption records created after July 8, 1941, as declared confidential by IN ST 31-19-19-1, et seq., except those specifically declared open by IN ST 31-19-13-2(2);

- All records relating to chancroid, chlamydia, gonorrhea, hepatitis, human immunodeficiency virus (HIV), Lymphogranuloma venereum, syphilis, tuberculosis, as declared confidential by IN ST 16-41-8-1, et seq.;
- All records relating to child abuse as declared confidential by IN ST 31-33-18-1, et seq.;
- All records relating to drug tests as declared confidential by IN ST 5-14-3-4(a)(9);
- Records of grand jury proceedings as declared confidential by IN ST 35-34-2-4;
- Records of juvenile proceedings as declared confidential by IN ST 31-39-1-2, except those specifically open under statute;
- All paternity records created after July 1, 1941 as declared confidential by IN ST 31-14-11-15, IN ST 31-19-5-23, IN ST 31-39-1-1 and IN ST 31-39-1-2 [Editor's note: IN ST 31-14-11-15 was repealed effective May 9, 2013];
- All pre-sentence reports as declared confidential by IN ST 35-38-1-13;
- Written petitions to permit marriages without consent and orders directing the Clerk of Court to issue a marriage license to underage persons, as declared confidential by IN ST 31-11-1-6;
- Only those arrest warrants, search warrants, indictments and informations ordered confidential by the trial judge, prior to return of duly executed service as declared confidential by IN ST 5-14-3-4(b)(1);
- All medical, mental health, or tax records unless determined by law or regulation of any governmental custodian not to be confidential, released by the subject of such records, or declared by a court of competent jurisdiction to be essential to the resolution of litigation as declared confidential by IN ST 16-39-3-10, IN ST 6-4.1-5-10, IN ST 6-4.1-12-12, and IN ST 6-8.1-7-1;
- Personal information relating to jurors or prospective jurors, other than for the use of the parties and counsel, pursuant to IN ST JURY Rule 10;
- Information relating to protection from abuse orders, no-contact orders and workplace violence restraining orders as declared confidential by IN ST 5-2-9-6, et seq.;
- Mediation proceedings pursuant to IN ST ADR Rule 2.11, Mini-Trial proceedings pursuant to IN ST ADR Rule 4.4(C), and Summary Jury Trials pursuant to IN ST ADR Rule 5.6;
- Information in probation files pursuant to the Probation Standards promulgated by the Judicial Conference of Indiana pursuant to IN ST 11-13-1-8(b);
- Information deemed confidential pursuant to the Rules for Court Administered Alcohol and Drug Programs promulgated by the Judicial Conference of Indiana pursuant to IN ST 12-23-14-13;
- Information deemed confidential pursuant to the Problem-Solving Court Rules promulgated by the Judicial Conference of Indiana pursuant to IN ST 33-23-16-16;
- All records of the Department of workforce Development as declared confidential by IN ST 22-4-19-6;
- Information regarding interception of electronic communications that is sealed or deemed confidential as set forth in IN ST 35-33.5-2-1, et seq.

iii. Information excluded from public access by specific court order;

iv. Complete Social Security Numbers of living persons;

v. With the exception of names, information such as addresses, phone numbers, and dates of birth which explicitly identifies:

- Natural persons who are witnesses or victims (not including defendants) in criminal, domestic violence, stalking, sexual assault, juvenile, or civil protection order proceedings, provided that juveniles who are victims of sex crimes shall be identified by initials only;

- Places of residence of judicial officers, clerks and other employees of courts and clerks of court, unless the person or persons about whom the information pertains waives confidentiality;

vi. Complete account numbers of specific assets, loans, bank accounts, credit cards, and personal identification numbers (PINs);

vii. All orders of expungement entered in criminal or juvenile proceedings, orders to restrict access to criminal history information pursuant to IN ST 35-38-5-5.5 or IN ST 35-38-8-5 and records excluded from public access by such orders, and information related to infractions that is excluded from public access pursuant to IN ST 34-28-5-15 or IN ST 34-28-5-16 [Editor's note: IN ST 35-38-5-5.5, IN ST 35-38-8-5 and IN ST 34-28-5-16 were repealed effective July 1, 2013; for information on orders restricting access to criminal history, refer to IN ST 35-38-9-1, et seq.];

viii. All personal notes and e-mail, and deliberative material, of judges, jurors, court staff and judicial agencies, and information recorded in personal data assistants (PDA's) or organizers and personal calendars. IN ST ADMIN Rule 9(G)(1).

6. *Format of electronically filed documents*

a. *Generally.* Electronically filed documents must meet the same requirements of format as documents conventionally filed pursuant to IN ST LAKE RCP Rule 2 or other applicable Lake County Rules of Civil Procedure. IN ST LAKE RCP Rule 17(D)(1).

b. *Titles of documents.* The person electronically filing a document will be responsible for designating a title for the document at the time it is filed. The LCOD will generate the appropriate entry onto the CCS to record the filing of the document. IN ST LAKE RCP Rule 17(D)(3).

c. *Citations and hyperlinks.* Electronically filed documents may contain hyperlink references to an external document as a convenient mechanism for accessing material cited in the document. Filers wishing to insert hyperlinks into documents shall continue to use the traditional method of citation to authority in addition to the hyperlink provided. The hyperlink is merely a convenience to the court and the material referenced is extraneous to the file and not a part of the court's record. IN ST LAKE RCP Rule 17(D)(5).

d. *Attachments and exhibits.* All documents which form part of a single submission and which are being filed at the same time and by the same filer may be electronically filed together under one document filing, e.g., the motion, supporting affidavits, memorandum in support, designation of evidence, exhibits. IN ST LAKE RCP Rule 17(D)(6).

i. Large documents which do not exist in an electronic format shall be scanned into .pdf format and filed electronically as separate attachments. A scanner is available in each clerk's office for use by the public and the bar in scanning and saving image files if needed. IN ST LAKE RCP Rule 17(D)(6).

e. *Electronic signatures*

i. *Electronic filing as signature.* The electronic filing of a document which is required to be signed shall constitute the filer's representation under IN ST TRIAL P Rule 11. Unless the electronically filed document has been scanned and shows the filer's original signature, the signature of the filer shall be indicated by As/Attorney's Name, or As/Party's Name as in the case of a pro se litigant, on the line where the signature would otherwise appear. IN ST LAKE RCP Rule 17(G)(1).

ii. *Signatures on jointly signed or filed, verified or other documents.* In the case of a stipulation, agreed order, jointly signed motion or other document which needs to be signed by two (2) or more persons, or in the case of documents which must contain original signatures and which require verification or an unsworn declaration under rule or statute, the signatures may be indicated by either:

- Submitting a scanned copy of the originally signed document; or,
- Submitting the document with the use of As/Name in the signature block(s) where the

original signature(s) appear(s) in the original document; provided, however, that the filer shall first obtain the physical signature of all persons necessary. IN ST LAKE RCP Rule 17(G)(2).

   iii. *Retention of original.* The filer shall retain the original executed document. IN ST LAKE RCP Rule 17(G).

7. *Citation of local rules.* The local rules for Lake County may be known as the Lake County Rules of Civil Procedure, and abbreviated as LR. IN ST LAKE RCP Rule 1(C).

F. Filing and Service Requirements

1. *Filing requirements.* Except as otherwise provided in IN ST TRIAL P Rule 5(E)(2), all pleadings and papers subsequent to the complaint which are required to be served upon a party shall be filed with the Court either before service or within a reasonable period of time thereafter. IN ST TRIAL P Rule 5(E)(1). All papers presented for filing shall be submitted to the Clerk and not to the court. All papers submitted for filing shall be mailed or delivered to the Clerk's office at the courthouse in which the case is pending. IN ST LAKE RCP Rule 3(A).

  a. *Filing with the court defined.* The filing of pleadings, motions, and other papers with the court as required by the Indiana Rules of Trial Procedure shall be made by one of the following methods:

    i. Delivery to the clerk of the court;

    ii. Sending by electronic transmission under the procedure adopted pursuant to IN ST ADMIN Rule 12;

    iii. Mailing to the clerk by registered, certified or express mail return receipt requested;

    iv. Depositing with any third-party commercial carrier for delivery to the clerk within three (3) calendar days, cost prepaid, properly addressed;

    v. If the court so permits, filing with the judge, in which event the judge shall note thereon the filing date and forthwith transmit them to the office of the clerk; or

    vi. Electronic filing, as approved by the Division of State Court Administration pursuant to IN ST ADMIN Rule 16. IN ST TRIAL P Rule 5(F).

    vii. Filing by registered or certified mail and by third-party commercial carrier shall be complete upon mailing or deposit. IN ST TRIAL P Rule 5(F).

  b. *Mandatory electronic filing.* Unless otherwise permitted by the Lake County Rules of Civil Procedure or otherwise authorized by the judicial officer assigned to a particular case, all documents submitted for filing (including the original complaint, or equivalent pleading, and summons) shall be filed electronically with the clerk using the LCOD, no matter when the case was originally filed. IN ST LAKE RCP Rule 17(D).

    i. *Of documents containing information excluded from public access pursuant to* IN ST ADMIN Rule 9. Documents containing information excluded from public access pursuant to IN ST ADMIN Rule 9, or documents which are ordered to be filed under seal shall be filed electronically, pursuant to IN ST LAKE RCP Rule 17(D)(9), whenever possible, along with a copy of the applicable order to seal the records, and the filer shall designate the documents as "Not for Public Access Pursuant to Administrative Rule 9(G)(1)" at the time of filing. IN ST LAKE RCP Rule 16(A)(1); IN ST LAKE RCP Rule 17(D)(9).

      • *Conventional filing of documents containing information excluded from public access pursuant to* IN ST ADMIN Rule 9. Documents containing information excluded from public access pursuant to IN ST ADMIN Rule 9, or documents which are ordered to be filed under seal, which cannot be legibly scanned and filed electronically, shall be conventionally filed under seal and designated by the filer as "Not for Public Access Pursuant to Administrative Rule 9(G)(1)" at the time of filing. The unredacted version shall be filed on light green paper which is conspicuously marked "Not for Public Access"; and a redacted version, with confidential information deleted, shall be filed on white paper which shall be available for public access. The filer shall also electronically file a Notice of Manual Filing. IN ST LAKE RCP Rule 16(A)(2).

ii. *Technical failures.* If a registered user is unable to file a document in a timely manner due to technical difficulties in the LCOD, the registered user must file a document with the court as soon as possible notifying the court of the inability to file the document. A sample document titled Declaration that Party was Unable to File in a Timely Manner Due to Technical Difficulties can be found at IN ST LAKE RCP Form 4. Delayed filings shall be rejected unless accompanied by the declaration attesting to the filer's failed attempts to file electronically at least two (2) times, separated by at least one (1) hour, after noon on each day of delay due to such technical failure. IN ST LAKE RCP Rule 17(J).

iii. *Documents allowed to be filed conventionally.* Unless specifically authorized by the court, only the following documents may be filed conventionally and not electronically:

- Exhibits and other documents that cannot be converted to a legible electronic form, such as videotapes, x-rays, and similar materials
- Documents delivered to the clerk by pro se litigants
- Documents mailed to the clerk by pro se litigants
- Confidential documents
- Notice of manual filing
- Titles of documents
- Chronological case summary entry forms (CCS entry forms). IN ST LAKE RCP Rule 17(E).
- For more information on the documents which must be filed conventionally, refer to IN ST LAKE RCP Rule 17(E).

c. *Facsimile filing.* Only when necessary on an emergency basis (i.e., when certified mail or other means of filing will not bring the document to the Judge's attention prior to the scheduled hearing or ruling), pleadings, motions and other papers may be filed by electronic facsimile transmission, or when specifically authorized by the Court. IN ST LAKE RCP Rule 2(C).

i. *Generally.* In counties where a majority of judges of the courts of record, by posted local rule, have authorized electronic facsimile filing and designated a telephone number to receive such transmissions, pleadings, motions, and other papers may be sent to the Clerk of Circuit Court by electronic facsimile transmission for filing in any case, provided:

- Such matter does not exceed ten (10) pages, including the cover sheet;
- Such matter does not require the payment of fees other than the electronic facsimile transcription fee set forth in IN ST ADMIN Rule 12(E);
- The sending party creates at the time of transmission a machine generated log for such transmission; and
- The original document and the transmission log are maintained by the sending party for the duration of the litigation. IN ST ADMIN Rule 12(B).

ii. *Time of filing.* During normal, posted business hours, the time of filing shall be the time the duplicate document is produced in the office of the Clerk of the Circuit Court. Duplicate documents received at all other times shall be filed as of the next normal business day. IN ST ADMIN Rule 12(C).

- If the receiving fax machine endorses its own time and date stamp upon the transmitted documents and the receiving machine produces a delivery receipt which is electronically created and transmitted to the sending party, the time of filing shall be the date and time recorded on the transmitted document by the receiving fax machine. IN ST ADMIN Rule 12(C).

d. *Filing for special judges.* For special judge matters where the special judge is a full-time judge or magistrate serving within Lake County, all papers submitted for filing shall be delivered or mailed to the Clerk's office at the courthouse where the special judge regularly serves. IN ST LAKE RCP Rule 3(A).

e. *Proof of filing.* Any party filing any paper by any method other than personal delivery to the clerk shall retain proof of filing. IN ST TRIAL P Rule 5(F).

2. *Service requirements.* Unless otherwise provided by the Indiana Rules of Trial Procedure or an order of the court, each party and special judge, if any, shall be served with: (1) every order required by its terms to be served; (2) every pleading subsequent to the original complaint; (3) every written motion except one which may be heard ex parte; (4) every brief submitted to the trial court; (5) every paper relating to discovery required to be served upon a party; and (6) every written notice, appearance, demand, offer of judgment, designation of record on appeal, or similar paper. IN ST TRIAL P Rule 5(A).

   a. *Methods of service*

      i. *Personal service.* Whenever a party is represented by an attorney of record, service shall be made upon such attorney unless service upon the party himself is ordered by the court. Service upon the attorney or party shall be made by delivering or mailing a copy of the papers to the last known address or where an attorney or party has consented to service by fax or e-mail, as provided in IN ST TRIAL P Rule 3.1(A)(4), by faxing or e-mailing a copy of the documents to the fax number or e-mail address set out in the appearance form or correction as required by IN ST TRIAL P Rule 3.1(E). IN ST TRIAL P Rule 5(B). Delivery of a copy within IN ST TRIAL P Rule 5 means:

- Offering or tendering it to the attorney or party and stating the nature of the papers being served. Refusal to accept an offered or tendered document is a waiver of any objection to the sufficiency or adequacy of service of that document;

- Leaving it at his office with a clerk or other person in charge thereof, or if there is no one in charge, leaving it in a conspicuous place therein; or

- If the office is closed, by leaving it at his dwelling house or usual place of abode with some person of suitable age and discretion then residing therein; or,

- Leaving it at some other suitable place, selected by the attorney upon whom service is being made, pursuant to duly promulgated local rule. IN ST TRIAL P Rule 5(B)(1).

      ii. *Service by mail.* If service is made by mail, the papers shall be deposited in the United States mail addressed to the person on whom they are being served, with postage prepaid. Service shall be deemed complete upon mailing. Proof of service of all papers permitted to be mailed may be made by written acknowledgment of service, by affidavit of the person who mailed the papers, or by certificate of an attorney. It shall be the duty of attorneys when entering their appearance in a cause or when filing pleadings or papers therein, to have noted in the Chronological Case Summary or said pleadings or papers so filed the address and telephone number of their office. Service by delivery or by mail at such address shall be deemed sufficient and complete. IN ST TRIAL P Rule 5(B)(2).

      iii. *Service by fax or e-mail.* A party who has consented to service by fax or e-mail may be served as follows:

- Service by e-mail shall be made by attaching the document being served in .pdf format. Discovery documents must also be served in accordance with IN ST TRIAL P Rule 26(A). IN ST TRIAL P Rule 5(B)(3)(a).

- Service by fax shall be deemed complete upon generation of a transmission record indicating the successful transmission of the entire document, except as provided in IN ST TRIAL P Rule 5(B)(3)(d). IN ST TRIAL P Rule 5(B)(3)(b).

- Service by e-mail shall be deemed complete upon transmission, except as provided in IN ST TRIAL P Rule 5(B)(3)(d). IN ST TRIAL P Rule 5(B)(3)(c).

- Service by fax or e-mail that occurs on a Saturday, Sunday, legal holiday, or day the court or agency in which the matter is pending is closed or after 5:00 PM local time of the recipient shall be deemed complete the next day that is not a Saturday, Sunday, legal holiday, or day that the court or agency in which the matter is pending is not closed. IN ST TRIAL P Rule 5(B)(3)(d).

b. *Serving numerous defendants.* In any action in which there are unusually large numbers of defendants, the court, upon motion or of its own initiative, may order:

    i. That service of the pleadings of the defendants and replies thereto need not be made as between the defendants;

- That any cross-claim, counterclaim, or matter constituting an avoidance or affirmative defense contained therein shall be deemed to be denied or avoided by all other parties; and
- That the filing of any such pleading and service thereof upon the plaintiff constitutes due notice of it to the parties. IN ST TRIAL P Rule 5(D).

    ii. A copy of every such order shall be served upon the parties in such manner and form as the court directs. IN ST TRIAL P Rule 5(D).

c. *Service by electronic means.* The Lake County Online Docket will generate a Notice of Electronic Filing and Service when any document is filed and served. This notice will be emailed to each registered user of record in a case, and an electronic service event will be added to the work queue of each registered user of record in the case. The party filing the document should retain a paper or electronic copy of the Notice of Electronic Filing and Service. This notice represents proof of filing and service of the document on registered users of record in that case. The filer shall not be required to conventionally serve any document on any party receiving electronic service. IN ST LAKE RCP Rule 17(F)(2).

    i. The filer shall also conventionally serve those parties not designated or able to receive electronic notice or service but who are nevertheless entitled to notice of said pleading or other document in accordance with the Indiana Rules of Civil Procedure and applicable Lake County Rules of Civil Procedure. In such cases, the filer shall also file a certificate of service, as appropriate. IN ST LAKE RCP Rule 17(F).

d. *Service on parties in default for failure to appear.* No service need be made on parties in default for failure to appear, except that pleadings asserting new or additional claims for relief against them shall be served upon them in the manner provided by service of summons in IN ST TRIAL P Rule 4. IN ST TRIAL P Rule 5(A).

G. Hearings

1. *Hearing on motion.* Unless local conditions make it impracticable, each judge shall establish regular times and places, at intervals sufficiently frequent for the prompt dispatch of business, at which motions requiring notice and hearing may be heard and disposed of; but the judge at any time or place and on such notice, if any, as he considers reasonable may make order for the advancement, conduct, and hearing of actions. To expedite its business the court may direct the submission and determination of motions without oral hearing upon brief written statements of reasons in support and opposition, or direct or permit hearings by telephone conference call with all attorneys or other similar means of communication. IN ST TRIAL P Rule 73(A).

2. *Presentation of evidence.* On the hearing of an application for a restraining order or temporary injunction, each party may read affidavits or documentary or record evidence. IN ST 34-26-1-8.

3. *Oral argument discretionary.* The granting of a motion for oral argument, unless required by the Indiana Rules of Trial Procedure, shall be wholly discretionary with the court. IN ST LAKE RCP Rule 4(B).

H. Forms

1. Motion for Preliminary Injunction Forms for Indiana

a. Prayer in complaint; For preliminary injunction. 5 INPRAC § 3:13.20.

b. Motion for preliminary injunction. 5 INPRAC § 3:13.40.

c. Notice of motion for preliminary injunction. 11 INPRAC § 97.14.

d. Undertaking as security to support granting of injunction. 11 INPRAC § 97.14.1.

e. Findings of fact in support of injunction. 11 INPRAC § 97.14.2.

f. Motion to dissolve temporary restraining order. 11 INPRAC § 97.14.3.

g. Motion for contempt for violation of injunction. 11 INPRAC § 97.14.4.

h. Motion for preliminary injunction. 11 INPRAC § 97.15.

i. Preliminary injunction. 11 INPRAC § 97.16.

j. Motion to vacate preliminary injunction; Failure to post bond. 11 INPRAC § 97.17.

k. Motion to vacate preliminary injunction; Another form. 11 INPRAC § 97.18.

l. Certificate of service; Personal service. 9 INPRAC § 5.7.

m. Certificate of service; First class mail. 9 INPRAC § 5.8.

2. **Official Motion for Preliminary Injunction Forms for Lake County**

a. CCS entry form. IN ST LAKE RCP App. A.

b. Notice of manual filing. IN ST LAKE RCP Form 2.

c. Certificate of service. IN ST LAKE RCP Form 3.

d. Declaration that party was unable to file in a timely manner. IN ST LAKE RCP Form 4.

3. **Motion for Preliminary Injunction Forms for Lake County**

a. Notice of manual filing. EFORMST IN 5540.

I. Checklist

(I) ❑ Matters to be considered by moving party

   (a) ❑ Required documents

      (1) ❑ Motion and notice

      (2) ❑ Brief

      (3) ❑ Affidavit

      (4) ❑ Security

      (5) ❑ Proposed order

      (6) ❑ Chronological case summary (CSS) entry forms

      (7) ❑ Certificate of service

   (b) ❑ Supplemental documents

      (1) ❑ Supporting evidence

      (2) ❑ Facsimile cover sheet

   (c) ❑ Timing

      (1) ❑ The injunction may be granted at the time of commencing the action, or at any time afterwards before judgment is rendered in the proceeding

      (2) ❑ A written motion, other than one which may be heard ex parte, and notice of the hearing thereof shall be served not less than five (5) days before the time specified for the hearing, unless a different period is fixed by the Indiana Rules of Trial Procedure or by order of the court

      (3) ❑ All pleadings and papers subsequent to the complaint which are required to be served upon a party shall be filed with the Court either before service or within a reasonable period of time thereafter

      (4) ❑ All pleadings, motions and other papers submitted for filing which are required to be served under IN ST TRIAL P Rule 5(A) shall be filed no later than three (3) days after service

      (5) ❑ If such papers are filed before service, proof of service thereof shall be filed no later than three (3) business days thereafter

(II) ❑ Matters to be considered by the responding party

    (a) ❑ Required documents

        (1) ❑ Opposition

        (2) ❑ Chronological case summary (CSS) entry forms

        (3) ❑ Certificate of service

    (b) ❑ Supplemental documents

        (1) ❑ Supporting evidence

        (2) ❑ Proposed order

        (3) ❑ Facsimile cover sheet

    (c) ❑ Timing

        (1) ❑ So long as consistent with the Indiana Rules of Trial Procedure, an adverse party wishing to respond shall do so within fifteen (15) days of service

        (2) ❑ Except as otherwise provided in IN ST TRIAL P Rule 59(D), opposing affidavits may be served not less than one (1) day before the hearing, unless the court permits them to be served at some other time

Motions, Oppositions and Replies
Motion to Dismiss for Failure to State a Claim

Document Last Updated October 2013

A. Applicable Rules

1. *State rules*

    a. Appearance. IN ST TRIAL P Rule 3.1.

    b. Process. IN ST TRIAL P Rule 4.

    c. Service and filing of pleadings and other papers. IN ST TRIAL P Rule 5.

    d. Time. IN ST TRIAL P Rule 6.

    e. Pleadings. IN ST TRIAL P Rule 7; IN ST TRIAL P Rule 8; IN ST TRIAL P Rule 9.2; IN ST TRIAL P Rule 10.

    f. Signing and verification of pleadings. IN ST TRIAL P Rule 11.

    g. Defenses and objections; When and how presented; By pleading or motion; Motion for judgment on the pleadings. IN ST TRIAL P Rule 12.

    h. Parties plaintiff and defendant; Capacity. IN ST TRIAL P Rule 17.

    i. Joinder of person needed for just adjudication. IN ST TRIAL P Rule 19.

    j. Evidence. IN ST TRIAL P Rule 43.

    k. Judgment on the evidence (directed verdict). IN ST TRIAL P Rule 50.

    l. Findings by the court. IN ST TRIAL P Rule 52.

    m. Summary judgment. IN ST TRIAL P Rule 56.

    n. Motion to correct error. IN ST TRIAL P Rule 59.

    o. Relief from judgment or order. IN ST TRIAL P Rule 60.

    p. Hearing of motions. IN ST TRIAL P Rule 73.

    q. Court records. IN ST TRIAL P Rule 77.

    r. Access to court records. IN ST ADMIN Rule 9.

    s. Paper size. IN ST ADMIN Rule 11.

t. Facsimile transmission. IN ST ADMIN Rule 12.

u. Electronic filing and electronic service pilot projects. IN ST ADMIN Rule 16.

v. Privacy and confidentiality. IN ST 5-2-9-6; IN ST 5-14-3-4; IN ST 5-14-3-5.5; IN ST 6-4.1-5-10; IN ST 6-4.1-12-12; IN ST 6-8.1-7-1; IN ST 11-13-1-8; IN ST 12-23-14-13; IN ST 16-39-3-10; IN ST 16-41-8-1; IN ST 22-4-19-6; IN ST 31-11-1-6; IN ST 31-19-5-23; IN ST 31-19-13-2; IN ST 31-19-19-1; IN ST 31-33-18-1; IN ST 31-39-1-1; IN ST 31-39-1-2; IN ST 33-23-16-16; IN ST 35-34-2-4; IN ST 35-38-1-13; IN ST 35-38-9-1; IN ST ADR Rule 2.11; IN ST ADR Rule 4.4; IN ST ADR Rule 5.6; IN ST JURY Rule 10.

2. *Local rules*

a. Scope and title. [IN ST LAKE RCP Rule 1, as amended by IN ORDER 13-0237, effective October 18, 2013].

b. Preparation of pleadings, motions and other papers. IN ST LAKE RCP Rule 2.

c. Filing. [IN ST LAKE RCP Rule 3, as amended by IN ORDER 13-0237, effective October 18, 2013].

d. Motions. IN ST LAKE RCP Rule 4.

e. Confidential information and sealed documents. IN ST LAKE RCP Rule 16.

f. Electronic filing and service. IN ST LAKE RCP Rule 17.

B. Timing

1. *Timing of motion to dismiss for failure to state a claim.* A motion making any of the defenses listed in IN ST TRIAL P Rule 12(B) shall be made before pleading if a further pleading is permitted or within twenty (20) days after service of the prior pleading if none is required. IN ST TRIAL P Rule 12(B).

a. *Time to file a responsive pleading.* A responsive pleading required under the Indiana Rules of Trial Procedure, shall be served within twenty (20) days after service of the prior pleading. IN ST TRIAL P Rule 6(C).

b. *Filing.* All pleadings and papers subsequent to the complaint which are required to be served upon a party shall be filed with the Court either before service or within a reasonable period of time thereafter. IN ST TRIAL P Rule 5(E)(1). All pleadings, motions and other papers submitted for filing which are required to be served under IN ST TRIAL P Rule 5(A) shall be filed no later than three (3) days after service. IN ST LAKE RCP Rule 3(A).

    i. If such papers are filed before service, proof of service thereof shall be filed no later than three (3) business days thereafter. Upon failure to comply with IN ST LAKE RCP Rule 3, the Court may, on motion of any party or on its own motion, impose appropriate sanctions. IN ST LAKE RCP Rule 3(A).

c. *Briefs.* Briefs, other than those addressed in IN ST LAKE RCP Rule 4 and IN ST LAKE RCP Rule 9, shall be filed no later than two (2) calendar days preceding the hearing or trial to which directed. IN ST LAKE RCP Rule 11.

2. *Service.* A written motion, other than one which may be heard ex parte, and notice of the hearing thereof shall be served not less than five (5) days before the time specified for the hearing, unless a different period is fixed by the Indiana Rules of Trial Procedure or by order of the court. IN ST TRIAL P Rule 6(D).

a. *Of supporting affidavits.* When a motion is supported by affidavit, the affidavit shall be served with the motion; and,

3. *Service of opposition.* Except as otherwise provided in IN ST TRIAL P Rule 59(D), opposing affidavits may be served not less than one (1) day before the hearing, unless the court permits them to be served at some other time. IN ST TRIAL P Rule 6(D).

a. An adverse party shall have thirty (30) days after service of the initial brief in which to serve and file an answer brief. IN ST LAKE RCP Rule 4(A).

4. *Reply.* The moving party shall have ten (10) days after service of the answer brief in which to serve and file a reply brief. IN ST LAKE RCP Rule 4(A).

5. *Computation of time*

   a. *Generally; Days excluded.* In computing any period of time prescribed or allowed by the Indiana Rules of Trial Procedure, by order of the court, or by any applicable statute, the day of the act, event, or default from which the designated period of time begins to run shall not be included. The last day of the period so computed is to be included unless it is:

      i. A Saturday,

      ii. A Sunday,

      iii. A legal holiday as defined by state statute, or

      iv. A day the office in which the act is to be done is closed during regular business hours. IN ST TRIAL P Rule 6(A).

   b. *Short periods.* In any event, the period runs until the end of the next day that is not a Saturday, a Sunday, a legal holiday, or a day on which the office is closed. When the period of time allowed is less than seven (7) days, intermediate Saturdays, Sundays, legal holidays, and days on which the office is closed shall be excluded from the computations. IN ST TRIAL P Rule 6(A).

   c. *Additional time after service by United States mail.* Whenever a party has the right or is required to do some act or take some proceedings within a prescribed period after the service of a notice or other paper upon him and the notice or paper is served upon him by United States mail, three (3) days shall be added to the prescribed period. IN ST TRIAL P Rule 6(E).

   d. *Electronic filing does not alter deadlines.* Filing electronically does not alter any filing deadlines or any time computation pursuant to state or federal statutes, any Rules of the Indiana Supreme Court, including without limitation the Rules of Trial Procedure, the Rules of Appellate Procedure or the Administrative Rules, or applicable Lake County Rules of Civil Procedure. The office of the Lake County Clerk is open for electronic filing under the Lake County Rules of Civil Procedure twenty-four (24) hours a day. A document is deemed filed at the date and time it is received by the LCOD server. Filing must be completed before midnight local time in order to be considered filed that day. Lake County observes Central Time and electronic filers are strongly urged to file documents during hours when the Lake County Online Docket ("LCOD") help line is available, from 9:00 a.m. to 4:00 p.m. local time, although documents can be filed electronically twenty-four (24) hours a day. IN ST LAKE RCP Rule 17(I).

   e. *Enlargement of time.* When an act is required or allowed to be done at or within a specific time by the Indiana Rules of Trial Procedure, the court may at any time for cause shown:

      i. Order the period enlarged, with or without motion or notice, if request therefor is made before the expiration of the period originally prescribed or extended by a previous order; or

      ii. Upon motion made after the expiration of the specific period, permit the act to be done where the failure to act was the result of excusable neglect; but, the court may not extend the time for taking any action for judgment on the evidence under IN ST TRIAL P Rule 50(A), amendment of findings and judgment under IN ST TRIAL P Rule 52(B), to correct errors under IN ST TRIAL P Rule 59(C), statement in opposition to motion to correct error under IN ST TRIAL P Rule 59(E), or to obtain relief from final judgment under IN ST TRIAL P Rule 60(B), except to the extent and under the conditions stated in those rules. IN ST TRIAL P Rule 6(B).

C. General Requirements

1. *Motions, generally.* Unless made during a hearing or trial, or otherwise ordered by the court, an application to the court for an order shall be made by written motion. The motion shall state the grounds therefor and the relief or order sought. IN ST TRIAL P Rule 7(B).

   a. *Motions as distinct from pleadings.* Motions and responses to motions are not pleadings, and allegations contained in a motion are not admissions of a party. 22B INPRAC 7:2; Wachstetter v. County Properties, LLC, 832 N.E.2d 574 (Ind.Ct.App. 2005); Scott County Family YMCA, Inc. v. Hobbs, 817 N.E.2d 603 (Ind.Ct.App. 2004).

   b. *Unopposed motions generally granted.* It is common for a trial court to grant procedural motions, such as motions for enlargement of time, discovery motions, or motions for continuance, unless an objection is filed. 21 INPRAC § 13.8.

    c.   *Separate motions.* Each motion shall be separate, while alternative motions filed together shall each be identified on the caption. IN ST LAKE RCP Rule 4(A).

    d.   *Answer and reply briefs.* Failure to file an answer brief or reply brief within the time prescribed shall be deemed a waiver of the right thereto and shall subject the motion to summary ruling. IN ST LAKE RCP Rule 4(A).

2.   *Motion to dismiss for failure to state a claim.* Every defense, in law or fact, to a claim for relief in any pleading, whether a claim, counterclaim, cross-claim, or third-party claim, shall be asserted in the responsive pleading thereto if one is required; except that at the option of the pleader, the defense of failure to state a claim upon which relief can be granted, which shall include failure to name the real party in interest under IN ST TRIAL P Rule 17, may be made by motion. IN ST TRIAL P Rule 12(B)(6). A motion under IN ST TRIAL P Rule 12(B)(6) is intended to test the legal sufficiency of a claim rather than the facts supporting that claim. 1A INPRAC R 12(12.9); Meyers v. Meyers, 861 N.E.2d 704 (Ind. 2007).

    a.   *How motion made.* A defense of failure to state a claim upon which relief can be granted, a defense of failure to join an indispensable party under IN ST TRIAL P Rule 19(B), and an objection of failure to state a legal defense to a claim may be made in any pleading permitted or ordered under IN ST TRIAL P Rule 7(A) or by motion for judgment on the pleadings, or at the trial on the merits. IN ST TRIAL P Rule 12(H)(2).

    b.   *Claim admitted for purpose of motion.* A motion to dismiss for failure to state a claim admits, for the purpose of the motion, the existence of the claim as stated in the complaint, but challenges the plaintiff's right to relief. 9 INPRAC § 42.10; Mills v. American Playground Device Co., 427 N.E.2d 1130 (Ind.Ct.App. 1981). Motions to dismiss under IN ST TRIAL P Rule 12 are disfavored because they undermine the policy that favors deciding cases on their merits. 22 INPRAC § 15.19; Droscha v. Shepherd, 931 N.E.2d 882 (Ind.Ct.App. 2010).

    c.   *Motion decided on factual allegations of complaint.* The trial court should grant a motion to dismiss under IN ST TRIAL P Rule 12(B)(6) if the facts alleged in the complaint are incapable of supporting relief under any set of circumstances. 1A INPRAC R 12(12.9); McPeek v. McCardle, 888 N.E.2d 171 (Ind. 2008). In determining whether the facts alleged in the complaint are incapable of supporting relief, the court must look only to the complaint and may not resort to any other evidence in the record. When ruling on a motion to dismiss under IN ST TRIAL P Rule 12(B)(6), the court should consider all of the allegations in the complaint to be true and resolve all inferences in favor of the non-moving party. 1A INPRAC R 12(12.9); State v. American Family Voices, Inc., 898 N.E.2d 293 (Ind. 2008); Curtis v. Roob, 891 N.E.2d 577 (Ind.Ct.App. 2008).

    d.   *Notice pleading and motions to dismiss.* Although notice pleading requirements under IN ST TRIAL P Rule 8(A) are fairly straightforward, and are well-grounded in Indiana jurisprudence, the mechanism for testing the legal sufficiency of the complaint, IN ST TRIAL P Rule 12(B)(6), has, over time, become somewhat limited because Indiana courts are instructed to dismiss an action under IN ST TRIAL P Rule 12(B)(6) only where the if the alleged facts do not support a claim for relief under any set of circumstances. 1A INPRAC R 12(12.9). Trial judges do not like to grant IN ST TRIAL P Rule 12(B)(6) motions where the claim is an inadequately pleaded complaint, which means a defendant's first meaningful opportunity to challenge a plaintiff's claim is the motion for summary judgment. 1A INPRAC R 12(12.9).

    e.   *Conversion to motion for summary judgment.* A motion to dismiss under IN ST TRIAL P Rule 12(B)(6) for failure to state a claim upon which relief and Motion for Judgment on the Pleadings under IN ST TRIAL P Rule 12(C) will be converted into a motion for summary judgment under IN ST TRIAL P Rule 56 if the court considers matters outside the pleadings in deciding those motions. 11 INPRAC § 90.1; Duran v. Komyatte, 490 N.E.2d 388 (Ind.Ct.App. 1986). In such case, all parties shall be given reasonable opportunity to present all material made pertinent to such a motion by IN ST TRIAL P Rule 56. IN ST TRIAL P Rule 12(B).

    f.   *Effect of granting of the motion.* When a motion to dismiss is sustained for failure to state a claim under IN ST TRIAL P Rule 12(B)(6) the pleading may be amended once as of right pursuant to IN ST TRIAL P Rule 15(A) within ten (10) days after service of notice of the court's order sustaining the motion and thereafter with permission of the court pursuant to such rule. IN ST TRIAL P Rule 12(B).

3. *Consolidation and waiver*

   a. *Consolidation of defenses in motion.* A party who makes a motion under IN ST TRIAL P Rule 12 may join with it any other motions herein provided for and then available to him. If a party makes a motion under IN ST TRIAL P Rule 12 but omits therefrom any defense or objection then available to him which IN ST TRIAL P Rule 12 permits to be raised by motion, he shall not thereafter make a motion based on the defense or objection so omitted. He may, however, make such motions as are allowed under IN ST TRIAL P Rule 12(H)(2). IN ST TRIAL P Rule 12(G).

   b. *Waiver or preservation of certain defenses.* No defense or objection is waived by being joined with one or more other defenses or objections in a responsive pleading or motion. IN ST TRIAL P Rule 12(B).

D. Documents

1. *Required documents*

   a. *Motion and notice.* The requirement of notice is satisfied by service of the motion. IN ST TRIAL P Rule 7(B). Refer to the General Requirements section of this document for information on the content of a motion to dismiss to dismiss for failure to state a claim.

   b. *Brief.* All motions filed pursuant to IN ST TRIAL P Rule 12 and IN ST TRIAL P Rule 56 shall be accompanied by a separate supporting brief. IN ST LAKE RCP Rule 4(A).

   c. *Proposed order.* Unless local practice provides differently, a party should submit a proposed order with its written motion to be signed by the judge once the motion has been granted. 21 INPRAC § 13.8.

      i. Proposed orders, which are submitted for the court's convenience under IN ST LAKE RCP Rule 3 or other applicable Lake County Rules of Civil Procedure, shall be submitted as attachments to motions. IN ST LAKE RCP Rule 17(D)(8). Proposed orders shall be prepared and filed separately from the pleadings, petitions, motions or other papers to which they have reference. IN ST LAKE RCP Rule 3(B).

      ii. Orders, either routine in nature or uncontested including, for example, those setting or continuing a hearing, shall be effected by the chronological case summary entry only, which shall contain the concise substance of the order. IN ST LAKE RCP Rule 3(B).

      iii. All orders shall be accompanied with sufficient copies and stamped, pre-addressed envelopes, so that copies may be mailed to all parties. IN ST LAKE RCP Rule 3(B).

   d. *Chronological case summary (CCS) entry forms.* All filings shall be accompanied by a Chronological Case Summary (CCS) Entry Form to define or identify the documents filed. The Form used should be substantially similar to IN ST LAKE RCP App. A. IN ST LAKE RCP Rule 3(C).

   e. *Certificate of service.* An attorney or unrepresented party tendering a document to the Clerk for filing shall certify that service has been made, list the parties served, and specify the date and means of service. The certificate of service shall be placed at the end of the document and shall not be separately filed. The separate filing of a certificate of service, however, shall not be grounds for rejecting a document for filing. The Clerk may permit documents to be filed without a certificate of service but shall require prompt filing of a separate certificate of service. IN ST TRIAL P Rule 5(C).

      i. All pleadings, motions and other papers submitted for filing which are required to be served under IN ST TRIAL P Rule 5(A) shall contain proof of service pursuant to IN ST TRIAL P Rule 5(B)(2). IN ST LAKE RCP Rule 3(A).

2. *Supplemental documents*

   a. *Facsimile cover sheet.* Any document sent to the Clerk of the Circuit Court by electronic facsimile transmission shall be accompanied by a cover sheet which states the title of the document, case number, number of pages, identity and voice telephone number of the sending party and instructions for filing. The cover sheet shall contain the signature of the attorney or party, pro se, authorizing the filing. IN ST ADMIN Rule 12(D).

E. Format

1. *Form of motions.* The rules applicable to captions, and the signing and form of pleadings (IN ST TRIAL

P Rule 8 through IN ST TRIAL P Rule 11), apply to all motions and other papers provided under the Indiana Rules of Trial Procedure. 22B INPRAC 7:2.

2. *Form of pleadings.* For the purpose of uniformity, convenience, clarity and durability, requirements in IN ST LAKE RCP Rule 2 shall be observed in the preparation of all pleadings, motions and other papers. IN ST LAKE RCP Rule 2. Whenever materials submitted fail to meet the standards in IN ST LAKE RCP Rule 2, the Court may impose appropriate sanctions. IN ST LAKE RCP Rule 2(B).

   a. *Caption; Names of parties.* Every pleading shall contain a caption setting forth the name of the court, the title of the action, the file number, and a designation as in IN ST TRIAL P Rule 7(A). In the complaint the title of the action shall include the names of all the parties, but in other pleadings it is sufficient to state the name of the first party on each side with an appropriate indication of other parties. IN ST TRIAL P Rule 10(A).

      i. *Special judge matters.* The caption of all CCS Entry Forms, pleadings, motions, orders and other papers to be filed in a special judge case shall include in block text the words SPECIAL JUDGE and the name of the judge directly below the cause number on the caption. IN ST LAKE RCP Rule 2(D).

   b. *Paragraphs; Separate statements.* All averments of a claim or defense shall be made in numbered paragraphs, the contents of each of which shall be limited as far as practicable to a statement of a single set of circumstances, and a paragraph may be referred to by number in all succeeding pleadings. Each claim founded upon a separate transaction or occurrence and each defense other than denials may be stated in a separate count or defense whenever a separation facilitates the clear presentation of the matters set forth. IN ST TRIAL P Rule 10(B).

   c. *Adoption by reference; Exhibits.* Statements in a pleading may be adopted by reference in a different part of the same pleading or in another pleading or in any motion. A copy of any written instrument which is an exhibit to a pleading is a part thereof for all purposes. IN ST TRIAL P Rule 10(C).

   d. *Paper; Print, quality and binding*

      i. All pleadings, motions, chronological case summary entry forms, orders, process and other papers shall be neatly and legibly printed, typewritten or mechanically reproduced, on one (1) side only, on white opaque paper. To satisfy the recordkeeping requirements of IN ST TRIAL P Rule 77, the print shall be of sufficient density and clarity for preservation and reproduction of microfilming, optical disk or other secondary sources. For this reason, the use of non-letter-quality printers is discouraged. IN ST LAKE RCP Rule 2(A).

      ii. Paper and ink shall be of such quality as to withstand the test of time. All documents shall be produced on acid-free, non-thermal paper. It is recommended that a minimum of twenty (20) pound, twenty-five percent (25%) cotton paper product be used. Documents of multiple pages shall be submitted in bound or stapled fashion, and the binding or stapling shall be at the top only. Covers or backings shall not be used. IN ST LAKE RCP Rule 2(A).

   e. *Papers; Handwritten.* Handwritten papers may be filed only if approved by the Court and a typewritten or printed true rendition thereof is filed within three (3) days thereafter and approved by the Court. Upon such approval, they shall be deemed and filed as the original, while the handwritten papers shall be retained therewith for evidentiary purposes. IN ST LAKE RCP Rule 2(C).

   f. *Minute sheets; Motion blanks.* Minute sheets and motion blanks shall no longer be used. IN ST LAKE RCP Rule 2(D).

3. *Size of papers for filing.* Effective January 1, 1992, all pleadings, copies, motions and documents filed with any trial court or appellate level court, typed or printed, with the exception of exhibits and existing wills, shall be prepared on eight and one-half by eleven inch (8 1/2" x 11") size paper. IN ST ADMIN Rule 11.

4. *Signature requirements*

   a. *Signature of attorney.* Every pleading or motion of a party represented by an attorney shall be signed by at least one (1) attorney of record in his individual name, whose address, telephone number, and attorney number shall be stated, except that this provision shall not apply to pleadings and motions

made and transcribed at the trial or a hearing before the judge and received by him in such form. IN ST TRIAL P Rule 11(A).

    i.   The signature of an attorney constitutes a certificate by him that he has read the pleadings; that to the best of his knowledge, information, and belief, there is good ground to support it; and that it is not interposed for delay. IN ST TRIAL P Rule 11(A).

    ii. If a pleading or motion is not signed or is signed with intent to defeat the purpose of the rule, it may be stricken as sham and false and the action may proceed as though the pleading had not been served. IN ST TRIAL P Rule 11(A).

    iii. For a willful violation of IN ST TRIAL P Rule 11 an attorney may be subjected to appropriate disciplinary action. Similar action may be taken if scandalous or indecent matter is inserted. IN ST TRIAL P Rule 11(A).

b.   *Signature of unrepresented party.* A party who is not represented by an attorney shall sign his pleading and state his address. IN ST TRIAL P Rule 11(A).

c.   *Verification not generally required.* Except when specifically required by rule, pleadings or motions need not be verified or accompanied by affidavit. The rule in equity that the averments of an answer under oath must be overcome by the testimony of two (2) witnesses or of one (1) witness sustained by corroborating circumstances is abolished. IN ST TRIAL P Rule 11(A).

d.   *Verification by affirmation or representation.* When in connection with any civil or special statutory proceeding it is required that any pleading, motion, petition, supporting affidavit, or other document of any kind, be verified, or that an oath be taken, it shall be sufficient if the subscriber simply affirms the truth of the matter to be verified by an affirmation or representation. IN ST TRIAL P Rule 11(B). IN ST TRIAL P Rule 11(B) states that the affirmation or representation should be in substantially the following language: "I (we) affirm, under the penalties for perjury, that the foregoing representation(s) is (are) true. (Signed) _____"

    i.   Any person who falsifies an affirmation or representation of fact shall be subject to the same penalties as are prescribed by law for the making of a false affidavit. IN ST TRIAL P Rule 11(B).

e.   *Verified pleadings, motions, and affidavits as evidence.* Pleadings, motions and affidavits accompanying or in support of such pleadings or motions when required to be verified or under oath shall be accepted as a representation that the signer had personal knowledge thereof or reasonable cause to believe the existence of the facts or matters stated or alleged therein; and, if otherwise competent or acceptable as evidence, may be admitted as evidence of the facts or matters stated or alleged therein when it is so provided in the Indiana Rules of Trial Procedure, by statute or other law, or to the extent the writing or signature expressly purports to be made upon the signer's personal knowledge. When such pleadings, motions and affidavits are verified or under oath they shall not require other or greater proof on the part of the adverse party than if not verified or not under oath unless expressly provided otherwise by the Indiana Rules of Trial Procedure, statute or other law. Affidavits upon motions for summary judgment under IN ST TRIAL P Rule 56 and in denial of execution under IN ST TRIAL P Rule 9.2 shall be made upon personal knowledge. IN ST TRIAL P Rule 11(C).

f.   *Electronic signature.* The filing of documents and information through the E-filing system by use of a valid username and password is presumed to have been authorized by the User to whom that username and password have been issued and documents filed through the E-filing system are presumed to have been signed by the same User. IN ST ADMIN Rule 16(E).

5. *Information excluded from public access.* Every document filed in a case shall separately identify information excluded from public access pursuant to IN ST ADMIN Rule 9(G)(1) as follows:

a.   Whole documents that are excluded from public access pursuant to IN ST ADMIN Rule 9(G)(1) shall be tendered on light green paper or have a light green coversheet attached to the document, marked "Not for Public Access" or "Confidential." IN ST TRIAL P Rule 5(G)(1).

b.   When only a portion of a document contains information excluded from public access pursuant to IN ST ADMIN Rule 9(G)(1), said information shall be omitted [or redacted] from the filed document, and set forth on a separate accompanying document on light green paper conspicuously marked "Not

for Public Access" or "Confidential" and clearly designated [or identifying] the caption and number of the case and the document and location within the document to which the redacted material pertains. IN ST TRIAL P Rule 5(G)(2).

c. With respect to documents filed in electronic format, the trial court, by local rule, may provide for compliance with IN ST TRIAL P Rule 5 in manner that separates and protects access to information excluded from public access. IN ST TRIAL P Rule 5(G)(3).

d. IN ST TRIAL P Rule 5(G) does not apply to a record sealed by the court pursuant to IN ST 5-14-3-5.5 or otherwise, nor to records, documents, or information filed in cases to which public access is prohibited pursuant to IN ST ADMIN Rule 9(G). IN ST TRIAL P Rule 5(G)(4).

e. The following information in case records is excluded from public access and is confidential:

i.   Information that is excluded from public access pursuant to federal law;

ii. Information that is excluded from public access as declared confidential by Indiana statute or other court rule, including without limitation:

- All adoption records created after July 8, 1941, as declared confidential by IN ST 31-19-19-1, et seq., except those specifically declared open by IN ST 31-19-13-2(2);

- All records relating to chancroid, chlamydia, gonorrhea, hepatitis, human immunodeficiency virus (HIV), Lymphogranuloma venereum, syphilis, tuberculosis, as declared confidential by IN ST 16-41-8-1, et seq.;

- All records relating to child abuse as declared confidential by IN ST 31-33-18-1, et seq.;

- All records relating to drug tests as declared confidential by IN ST 5-14-3-4(a)(9);

- Records of grand jury proceedings as declared confidential by IN ST 35-34-2-4;

- Records of juvenile proceedings as declared confidential by IN ST 31-39-1-2, except those specifically open under statute;

- All paternity records created after July 1, 1941 as declared confidential by IN ST 31-14-11-15, IN ST 31-19-5-23, IN ST 31-39-1-1 and IN ST 31-39-1-2 [Editor's note: IN ST 31-14-11-15 was repealed effective May 9, 2013];

- All pre-sentence reports as declared confidential by IN ST 35-38-1-13;

- Written petitions to permit marriages without consent and orders directing the Clerk of Court to issue a marriage license to underage persons, as declared confidential by IN ST 31-11-1-6;

- Only those arrest warrants, search warrants, indictments and informations ordered confidential by the trial judge, prior to return of duly executed service as declared confidential by IN ST 5-14-3-4(b)(1);

- All medical, mental health, or tax records unless determined by law or regulation of any governmental custodian not to be confidential, released by the subject of such records, or declared by a court of competent jurisdiction to be essential to the resolution of litigation as declared confidential by IN ST 16-39-3-10, IN ST 6-4.1-5-10, IN ST 6-4.1-12-12, and IN ST 6-8.1-7-1;

- Personal information relating to jurors or prospective jurors, other than for the use of the parties and counsel, pursuant to IN ST JURY Rule 10;

- Information relating to protection from abuse orders, no-contact orders and workplace violence restraining orders as declared confidential by IN ST 5-2-9-6, et seq.;

- Mediation proceedings pursuant to IN ST ADR Rule 2.11, Mini-Trial proceedings pursuant to IN ST ADR Rule 4.4(C), and Summary Jury Trials pursuant to IN ST ADR Rule 5.6;

- Information in probation files pursuant to the Probation Standards promulgated by the Judicial Conference of Indiana pursuant to IN ST 11-13-1-8(b);

- Information deemed confidential pursuant to the Rules for Court Administered Alcohol

and Drug Programs promulgated by the Judicial Conference of Indiana pursuant to IN ST 12-23-14-13;

- Information deemed confidential pursuant to the Problem-Solving Court Rules promulgated by the Judicial Conference of Indiana pursuant to IN ST 33-23-16-16;

- All records of the Department of workforce Development as declared confidential by IN ST 22-4-19-6;

- Information regarding interception of electronic communications that is sealed or deemed confidential as set forth in IN ST 35-33.5-2-1, et seq.

   iii.   Information excluded from public access by specific court order;

   iv.   Complete Social Security Numbers of living persons;

   v.   With the exception of names, information such as addresses, phone numbers, and dates of birth which explicitly identifies:

- Natural persons who are witnesses or victims (not including defendants) in criminal, domestic violence, stalking, sexual assault, juvenile, or civil protection order proceedings, provided that juveniles who are victims of sex crimes shall be identified by initials only;

- Places of residence of judicial officers, clerks and other employees of courts and clerks of court, unless the person or persons about whom the information pertains waives confidentiality;

   vi.   Complete account numbers of specific assets, loans, bank accounts, credit cards, and personal identification numbers (PINs);

   vii.   All orders of expungement entered in criminal or juvenile proceedings, orders to restrict access to criminal history information pursuant to IN ST 35-38-5-5.5 or IN ST 35-38-8-5 and records excluded from public access by such orders, and information related to infractions that is excluded from public access pursuant to IN ST 34-28-5-15 or IN ST 34-28-5-16 [Editor's note: IN ST 35-38-5-5.5, IN ST 35-38-8-5 and IN ST 34-28-5-16 were repealed effective July 1, 2013; for information on orders restricting access to criminal history, refer to IN ST 35-38-9-1, et seq.];

   viii.   All personal notes and e-mail, and deliberative material, of judges, jurors, court staff and judicial agencies, and information recorded in personal data assistants (PDA's) or organizers and personal calendars. IN ST ADMIN Rule 9(G)(1).

6. *Format of electronically filed documents*

   a.   *Generally.* Electronically filed documents must meet the same requirements of format as documents conventionally filed pursuant to IN ST LAKE RCP Rule 2 or other applicable Lake County Rules of Civil Procedure. IN ST LAKE RCP Rule 17(D)(1).

   b.   *Titles of documents.* The person electronically filing a document will be responsible for designating a title for the document at the time it is filed. The LCOD will generate the appropriate entry onto the CCS to record the filing of the document. IN ST LAKE RCP Rule 17(D)(3).

   c.   *Citations and hyperlinks.* Electronically filed documents may contain hyperlink references to an external document as a convenient mechanism for accessing material cited in the document. Filers wishing to insert hyperlinks into documents shall continue to use the traditional method of citation to authority in addition to the hyperlink provided. The hyperlink is merely a convenience to the court and the material referenced is extraneous to the file and not a part of the court's record. IN ST LAKE RCP Rule 17(D)(5).

   d.   *Attachments and exhibits.* All documents which form part of a single submission and which are being filed at the same time and by the same filer may be electronically filed together under one document filing, e.g., the motion, supporting affidavits, memorandum in support, designation of evidence, exhibits. IN ST LAKE RCP Rule 17(D)(6).

      i.   Large documents which do not exist in an electronic format shall be scanned into .pdf format and filed electronically as separate attachments. A scanner is available in each clerk's office for use by the public and the bar in scanning and saving image files if needed. IN ST LAKE RCP Rule 17(D)(6).

   e. *Electronic signatures*

      i. *Electronic filing as signature.* The electronic filing of a document which is required to be signed shall constitute the filer's representation under IN ST TRIAL P Rule 11. Unless the electronically filed document has been scanned and shows the filer's original signature, the signature of the filer shall be indicated by As/Attorney's Name, or As/Party's Name as in the case of a pro se litigant, on the line where the signature would otherwise appear. IN ST LAKE RCP Rule 17(G)(1).

      ii. *Signatures on jointly signed or filed, verified or other documents.* In the case of a stipulation, agreed order, jointly signed motion or other document which needs to be signed by two (2) or more persons, or in the case of documents which must contain original signatures and which require verification or an unsworn declaration under rule or statute, the signatures may be indicated by either:

- Submitting a scanned copy of the originally signed document; or,
- Submitting the document with the use of As/Name in the signature block(s) where the original signature(s) appear(s) in the original document; provided, however, that the filer shall first obtain the physical signature of all persons necessary. IN ST LAKE RCP Rule 17(G)(2).

      iii. *Retention of original.* The filer shall retain the original executed document. IN ST LAKE RCP Rule 17(G).

  7. *Citation of local rules.* The local rules for Lake County may be known as the Lake County Rules of Civil Procedure, and abbreviated as LR. IN ST LAKE RCP Rule 1(C).

F. Filing and Service Requirements

  1. *Filing requirements.* Except as otherwise provided in IN ST TRIAL P Rule 5(E)(2), all pleadings and papers subsequent to the complaint which are required to be served upon a party shall be filed with the Court either before service or within a reasonable period of time thereafter. IN ST TRIAL P Rule 5(E)(1). All papers presented for filing shall be submitted to the Clerk and not to the court. All papers submitted for filing shall be mailed or delivered to the Clerk's office at the courthouse in which the case is pending. IN ST LAKE RCP Rule 3(A).

   a. *Filing with the court defined.* The filing of pleadings, motions, and other papers with the court as required by the Indiana Rules of Trial Procedure shall be made by one of the following methods:

      i. Delivery to the clerk of the court;

      ii. Sending by electronic transmission under the procedure adopted pursuant to IN ST ADMIN Rule 12;

      iii. Mailing to the clerk by registered, certified or express mail return receipt requested;

      iv. Depositing with any third-party commercial carrier for delivery to the clerk within three (3) calendar days, cost prepaid, properly addressed;

      v. If the court so permits, filing with the judge, in which event the judge shall note thereon the filing date and forthwith transmit them to the office of the clerk; or

      vi. Electronic filing, as approved by the Division of State Court Administration pursuant to IN ST ADMIN Rule 16. IN ST TRIAL P Rule 5(F).

      vii. Filing by registered or certified mail and by third-party commercial carrier shall be complete upon mailing or deposit. IN ST TRIAL P Rule 5(F).

   b. *Mandatory electronic filing.* Unless otherwise permitted by the Lake County Rules of Civil Procedure or otherwise authorized by the judicial officer assigned to a particular case, all documents submitted for filing (including the original complaint, or equivalent pleading, and summons) shall be filed electronically with the clerk using the LCOD, no matter when the case was originally filed. IN ST LAKE RCP Rule 17(D).

      i. *Of documents containing information excluded from public access pursuant to* IN ST ADMIN

Rule 9. Documents containing information excluded from public access pursuant to IN ST ADMIN Rule 9, or documents which are ordered to be filed under seal shall be filed electronically, pursuant to IN ST LAKE RCP Rule 17(D)(9), whenever possible, along with a copy of the applicable order to seal the records, and the filer shall designate the documents as "Not for Public Access Pursuant to Administrative Rule 9(G)(1)" at the time of filing. IN ST LAKE RCP Rule 16(A)(1); IN ST LAKE RCP Rule 17(D)(9).

- *Conventional filing of documents containing information excluded from public access pursuant to* IN ST ADMIN Rule 9. Documents containing information excluded from public access pursuant to IN ST ADMIN Rule 9, or documents which are ordered to be filed under seal, which cannot be legibly scanned and filed electronically, shall be conventionally filed under seal and designated by the filer as "Not for Public Access Pursuant to Administrative Rule 9(G)(1)" at the time of filing. The unredacted version shall be filed on light green paper which is conspicuously marked "Not for Public Access"; and a redacted version, with confidential information deleted, shall be filed on white paper which shall be available for public access. The filer shall also electronically file a Notice of Manual Filing. IN ST LAKE RCP Rule 16(A)(2).

   ii. *Technical failures.* If a registered user is unable to file a document in a timely manner due to technical difficulties in the LCOD, the registered user must file a document with the court as soon as possible notifying the court of the inability to file the document. A sample document titled Declaration that Party was Unable to File in a Timely Manner Due to Technical Difficulties can be found at IN ST LAKE RCP Form 4. Delayed filings shall be rejected unless accompanied by the declaration attesting to the filer's failed attempts to file electronically at least two (2) times, separated by at least one (1) hour, after noon on each day of delay due to such technical failure. IN ST LAKE RCP Rule 17(J).

   iii. *Documents allowed to be filed conventionally.* Unless specifically authorized by the court, only the following documents may be filed conventionally and not electronically:

- Exhibits and other documents that cannot be converted to a legible electronic form, such as videotapes, x-rays, and similar materials

- Documents delivered to the clerk by pro se litigants

- Documents mailed to the clerk by pro se litigants

- Confidential documents

- Notice of manual filing

- Titles of documents

- Chronological case summary entry forms (CCS entry forms). IN ST LAKE RCP Rule 17(E).

- For more information on the documents which must be filed conventionally, refer to IN ST LAKE RCP Rule 17(E).

c. *Facsimile filing.* Only when necessary on an emergency basis (i.e., when certified mail or other means of filing will not bring the document to the Judge's attention prior to the scheduled hearing or ruling), pleadings, motions and other papers may be filed by electronic facsimile transmission, or when specifically authorized by the Court. IN ST LAKE RCP Rule 2(C).

   i. *Generally.* In counties where a majority of judges of the courts of record, by posted local rule, have authorized electronic facsimile filing and designated a telephone number to receive such transmissions, pleadings, motions, and other papers may be sent to the Clerk of Circuit Court by electronic facsimile transmission for filing in any case, provided:

- Such matter does not exceed ten (10) pages, including the cover sheet;

- Such matter does not require the payment of fees other than the electronic facsimile transcription fee set forth in IN ST ADMIN Rule 12(E);

- The sending party creates at the time of transmission a machine generated log for such transmission; and

- The original document and the transmission log are maintained by the sending party for the duration of the litigation. IN ST ADMIN Rule 12(B).

  ii. *Time of filing.* During normal, posted business hours, the time of filing shall be the time the duplicate document is produced in the office of the Clerk of the Circuit Court. Duplicate documents received at all other times shall be filed as of the next normal business day. IN ST ADMIN Rule 12(C).

- If the receiving fax machine endorses its own time and date stamp upon the transmitted documents and the receiving machine produces a delivery receipt which is electronically created and transmitted to the sending party, the time of filing shall be the date and time recorded on the transmitted document by the receiving fax machine. IN ST ADMIN Rule 12(C).

 d. *Filing for special judges.* For special judge matters where the special judge is a full-time judge or magistrate serving within Lake County, all papers submitted for filing shall be delivered or mailed to the Clerk's office at the courthouse where the special judge regularly serves. IN ST LAKE RCP Rule 3(A).

 e. *Proof of filing.* Any party filing any paper by any method other than personal delivery to the clerk shall retain proof of filing. IN ST TRIAL P Rule 5(F).

2. *Service requirements.* Unless otherwise provided by the Indiana Rules of Trial Procedure or an order of the court, each party and special judge, if any, shall be served with: (1) every order required by its terms to be served; (2) every pleading subsequent to the original complaint; (3) every written motion except one which may be heard ex parte; (4) every brief submitted to the trial court; (5) every paper relating to discovery required to be served upon a party; and (6) every written notice, appearance, demand, offer of judgment, designation of record on appeal, or similar paper. IN ST TRIAL P Rule 5(A).

 a. *Methods of service*

  i. *Personal service.* Whenever a party is represented by an attorney of record, service shall be made upon such attorney unless service upon the party himself is ordered by the court. Service upon the attorney or party shall be made by delivering or mailing a copy of the papers to the last known address or where an attorney or party has consented to service by fax or e-mail, as provided in IN ST TRIAL P Rule 3.1(A)(4), by faxing or e-mailing a copy of the documents to the fax number or e-mail address set out in the appearance form or correction as required by IN ST TRIAL P Rule 3.1(E). IN ST TRIAL P Rule 5(B). Delivery of a copy within IN ST TRIAL P Rule 5 means:

- Offering or tendering it to the attorney or party and stating the nature of the papers being served. Refusal to accept an offered or tendered document is a waiver of any objection to the sufficiency or adequacy of service of that document;

- Leaving it at his office with a clerk or other person in charge thereof, or if there is no one in charge, leaving it in a conspicuous place therein; or

- If the office is closed, by leaving it at his dwelling house or usual place of abode with some person of suitable age and discretion then residing therein; or,

- Leaving it at some other suitable place, selected by the attorney upon whom service is being made, pursuant to duly promulgated local rule. IN ST TRIAL P Rule 5(B)(1).

  ii. *Service by mail.* If service is made by mail, the papers shall be deposited in the United States mail addressed to the person on whom they are being served, with postage prepaid. Service shall be deemed complete upon mailing. Proof of service of all papers permitted to be mailed may be made by written acknowledgment of service, by affidavit of the person who mailed the papers, or by certificate of an attorney. It shall be the duty of attorneys when entering their appearance in a cause or when filing pleadings or papers therein, to have noted in the Chronological Case Summary or said pleadings or papers so filed the address and telephone number of their office. Service by delivery or by mail at such address shall be deemed sufficient and complete. IN ST TRIAL P Rule 5(B)(2).

      iii. *Service by fax or e-mail.* A party who has consented to service by fax or e-mail may be served as follows:

- Service by e-mail shall be made by attaching the document being served in .pdf format. Discovery documents must also be served in accordance with IN ST TRIAL P Rule 26(A). IN ST TRIAL P Rule 5(B)(3)(a).

- Service by fax shall be deemed complete upon generation of a transmission record indicating the successful transmission of the entire document, except as provided in IN ST TRIAL P Rule 5(B)(3)(d). IN ST TRIAL P Rule 5(B)(3)(b).

- Service by e-mail shall be deemed complete upon transmission, except as provided in IN ST TRIAL P Rule 5(B)(3)(d). IN ST TRIAL P Rule 5(B)(3)(c).

- Service by fax or e-mail that occurs on a Saturday, Sunday, legal holiday, or day the court or agency in which the matter is pending is closed or after 5:00 PM local time of the recipient shall be deemed complete the next day that is not a Saturday, Sunday, legal holiday, or day that the court or agency in which the matter is pending is not closed. IN ST TRIAL P Rule 5(B)(3)(d).

    b. *Serving numerous defendants.* In any action in which there are unusually large numbers of defendants, the court, upon motion or of its own initiative, may order:

      i. That service of the pleadings of the defendants and replies thereto need not be made as between the defendants;

- That any cross-claim, counterclaim, or matter constituting an avoidance or affirmative defense contained therein shall be deemed to be denied or avoided by all other parties; and

- That the filing of any such pleading and service thereof upon the plaintiff constitutes due notice of it to the parties. IN ST TRIAL P Rule 5(D).

      ii. A copy of every such order shall be served upon the parties in such manner and form as the court directs. IN ST TRIAL P Rule 5(D).

    c. *Service by electronic means.* The Lake County Online Docket will generate a Notice of Electronic Filing and Service when any document is filed and served. This notice will be emailed to each registered user of record in a case, and an electronic service event will be added to the work queue of each registered user of record in the case. The party filing the document should retain a paper or electronic copy of the Notice of Electronic Filing and Service. This notice represents proof of filing and service of the document on registered users of record in that case. The filer shall not be required to conventionally serve any document on any party receiving electronic service. IN ST LAKE RCP Rule 17(F)(2).

      i. The filer shall also conventionally serve those parties not designated or able to receive electronic notice or service but who are nevertheless entitled to notice of said pleading or other document in accordance with the Indiana Rules of Civil Procedure and applicable Lake County Rules of Civil Procedure. In such cases, the filer shall also file a certificate of service, as appropriate. IN ST LAKE RCP Rule 17(F).

    d. *Service on parties in default for failure to appear.* No service need be made on parties in default for failure to appear, except that pleadings asserting new or additional claims for relief against them shall be served upon them in the manner provided by service of summons in IN ST TRIAL P Rule 4. IN ST TRIAL P Rule 5(A).

G. Hearings

1. *Hearing on motion.* Unless local conditions make it impracticable, each judge shall establish regular times and places, at intervals sufficiently frequent for the prompt dispatch of business, at which motions requiring notice and hearing may be heard and disposed of; but the judge at any time or place and on such notice, if any, as he considers reasonable may make order for the advancement, conduct, and hearing of actions. To expedite its business the court may direct the submission and determination of motions without oral hearing upon brief written statements of reasons in support and opposition, or direct or permit hearings by telephone conference call with all attorneys or other similar means of communication. IN ST TRIAL P Rule 73(A).

2. *Oral argument discretionary.* The granting of a motion for oral argument, unless required by the Indiana Rules of Trial Procedure, shall be wholly discretionary with the court. IN ST LAKE RCP Rule 4(B).

H. Forms

1. Motion to Dismiss for Failure to State a Claim Forms for Indiana

a. General form. 5 INPRAC § 3:4.1.

b. Failure to state a claim upon which relief can be granted. 5 INPRAC § 3:4.5.

c. Motion to dismiss plaintiff's complaint; General form. 9 INPRAC § 42.2.

d. Motion to dismiss; Failure to state a claim upon which relief can be granted. 9 INPRAC § 42.10.

e. Certificate of service; Personal service. 9 INPRAC § 5.7.

f. Certificate of service; First class mail. 9 INPRAC § 5.8.

g. Statute of limitations. 9 INPRAC § 42.12.

h. Application for hearing and preliminary determination of motion to dismiss. 9 INPRAC § 42.15.

2. Official Motion to Dismiss for Failure to State a Claim Forms for Lake County

a. CCS entry form. IN ST LAKE RCP App. A.

b. Notice of manual filing. IN ST LAKE RCP Form 2.

c. Certificate of service. IN ST LAKE RCP Form 3.

d. Declaration that party was unable to file in a timely manner. IN ST LAKE RCP Form 4.

3. Motion to Dismiss for Failure to State a Claim Forms for Lake County

a. Notice of manual filing. EFORMST IN 5540.

I. Checklist

(I) ❑ Matters to be considered by moving party

  (a) ❑ Required documents

    (1) ❑ Motion and notice

    (2) ❑ Brief

    (3) ❑ Proposed order

    (4) ❑ Chronological case summary (CSS) entry forms

    (5) ❑ Certificate of service

  (b) ❑ Supplemental documents

    (1) ❑ Facsimile cover sheet

  (c) ❑ Timing

    (1) ❑ A motion to dismiss for failure to state a claim shall be made before pleading if a further pleading is permitted or within twenty (20) days after service of the prior pleading if none is required

    (2) ❑ A written motion, other than one which may be heard ex parte, and notice of the hearing thereof shall be served not less than five (5) days before the time specified for the hearing, unless a different period is fixed by the Indiana Rules of Trial Procedure or by order of the court

    (3) ❑ All pleadings and papers subsequent to the complaint which are required to be served upon a party shall be filed with the Court either before service or within a reasonable period of time thereafter

    (4) ❑ All pleadings, motions and other papers submitted for filing which are required to be served under IN ST TRIAL P Rule 5(A) shall be filed no later than three (3) days after service

    (5) ❑ If such papers are filed before service, proof of service thereof shall be filed no later than three (3) business days thereafter

(II) ❑ Matters to be considered by the responding party

    (a) ❑ Required documents

        (1) ❑ Opposition

        (2) ❑ Chronological case summary (CSS) entry forms

        (3) ❑ Certificate of service

    (b) ❑ Supplemental documents

        (1) ❑ Supporting evidence

        (2) ❑ Proposed order

        (3) ❑ Facsimile cover sheet

    (c) ❑ Timing

        (1) ❑ So long as consistent with the Indiana Rules of Trial Procedure, an adverse party wishing to respond shall do so within fifteen (15) days of service

        (2) ❑ Except as otherwise provided in IN ST TRIAL P Rule 59(D), opposing affidavits may be served not less than one (1) day before the hearing, unless the court permits them to be served at some other time

Motions, Oppositions and Replies
Motion to Dismiss for Lack of Subject Matter Jurisdiction

Document Last Updated October 2013

A. Applicable Rules

1. *State rules*

    a. Appearance. IN ST TRIAL P Rule 3.1.

    b. Process. IN ST TRIAL P Rule 4.

    c. Service and filing of pleadings and other papers. IN ST TRIAL P Rule 5.

    d. Time. IN ST TRIAL P Rule 6.

    e. Pleadings. IN ST TRIAL P Rule 7; IN ST TRIAL P Rule 8; IN ST TRIAL P Rule 9.2; IN ST TRIAL P Rule 10.

    f. Signing and verification of pleadings. IN ST TRIAL P Rule 11.

    g. Defenses and objections; When and how presented; By pleading or motion; Motion for judgment on the pleadings. IN ST TRIAL P Rule 12.

    h. Amended and supplemental pleadings. IN ST TRIAL P Rule 15.

    i. Joinder of person needed for just adjudication. IN ST TRIAL P Rule 19.

    j. Evidence. IN ST TRIAL P Rule 43.

    k. Judgment on the evidence (directed verdict). IN ST TRIAL P Rule 50.

    l. Findings by the court. IN ST TRIAL P Rule 52.

    m. Summary judgment. IN ST TRIAL P Rule 56.

    n. Motion to correct error. IN ST TRIAL P Rule 59.

    o. Relief from judgment or order. IN ST TRIAL P Rule 60.

    p. Hearing of motions. IN ST TRIAL P Rule 73.

    q. Court records. IN ST TRIAL P Rule 77.

    r. Access to court records. IN ST ADMIN Rule 9.

    s. Paper size. IN ST ADMIN Rule 11.

t. Facsimile transmission. IN ST ADMIN Rule 12.

u. Electronic filing and electronic service pilot projects. IN ST ADMIN Rule 16.

v. Privacy and confidentiality. IN ST 5-2-9-6; IN ST 5-14-3-4; IN ST 5-14-3-5.5; IN ST 6-4.1-5-10; IN ST 6-4.1-12-12; IN ST 6-8.1-7-1; IN ST 11-13-1-8; IN ST 12-23-14-13; IN ST 16-39-3-10; IN ST 16-41-8-1; IN ST 22-4-19-6; IN ST 31-11-1-6; IN ST 31-19-5-23; IN ST 31-19-13-2; IN ST 31-19-19-1; IN ST 31-33-18-1; IN ST 31-39-1-1; IN ST 31-39-1-2; IN ST 33-23-16-16; IN ST 35-34-2-4; IN ST 35-38-1-13; IN ST 35-38-9-1; IN ST ADR Rule 2.11; IN ST ADR Rule 4.4; IN ST ADR Rule 5.6; IN ST JURY Rule 10.

2. *Local rules*

   a. Scope and title. [IN ST LAKE RCP Rule 1, as amended by IN ORDER 13-0237, effective October 18, 2013].

   b. Preparation of pleadings, motions and other papers. IN ST LAKE RCP Rule 2.

   c. Filing. [IN ST LAKE RCP Rule 3, as amended by IN ORDER 13-0237, effective October 18, 2013].

   d. Motions. IN ST LAKE RCP Rule 4.

   e. Confidential information and sealed documents. IN ST LAKE RCP Rule 16.

   f. Electronic filing and service. IN ST LAKE RCP Rule 17.

B. Timing

1. *Timing of motion to dismiss for failure lack of subject matter jurisdiction.* A motion making any of the defenses listed in IN ST TRIAL P Rule 12(B) shall be made before pleading if a further pleading is permitted or within twenty (20) days after service of the prior pleading if none is required. IN ST TRIAL P Rule 12(B). Usually, the issue is raised in a motion that is filed before an Answer is filed; or the issue might be consolidated in the Answer. If it is not raised by the parties, it will be raised by the court, and an appellate court may raise the question sua sponte. 1A INPRAC R 12(12.5); Decatur County Rural Elec. Membership Corp. v. Public Serv. Co., 150 Ind.App. 193, 275 N.E.2d 857 (Ind.App. 1971).

   a. *Time to file a responsive pleading.* A responsive pleading required under the Indiana Rules of Trial Procedure, shall be served within twenty (20) days after service of the prior pleading. IN ST TRIAL P Rule 6(C).

   b. *Filing.* All pleadings and papers subsequent to the complaint which are required to be served upon a party shall be filed with the Court either before service or within a reasonable period of time thereafter. IN ST TRIAL P Rule 5(E)(1). All pleadings, motions and other papers submitted for filing which are required to be served under IN ST TRIAL P Rule 5(A) shall be filed no later than three (3) days after service. IN ST LAKE RCP Rule 3(A).

      i. If such papers are filed before service, proof of service thereof shall be filed no later than three (3) business days thereafter. Upon failure to comply with IN ST LAKE RCP Rule 3, the Court may, on motion of any party or on its own motion, impose appropriate sanctions. IN ST LAKE RCP Rule 3(A).

   c. *Briefs.* Briefs, other than those addressed in IN ST LAKE RCP Rule 4 and IN ST LAKE RCP Rule 9, shall be filed no later than two (2) calendar days preceding the hearing or trial to which directed. IN ST LAKE RCP Rule 11.

2. *Service.* A written motion, other than one which may be heard ex parte, and notice of the hearing thereof shall be served not less than five (5) days before the time specified for the hearing, unless a different period is fixed by the Indiana Rules of Trial Procedure or by order of the court. IN ST TRIAL P Rule 6(D).

   a. *Of supporting affidavits.* When a motion is supported by affidavit, the affidavit shall be served with the motion. IN ST TRIAL P Rule 6(D).

3. *Service of opposition.* Except as otherwise provided in IN ST TRIAL P Rule 59(D), opposing affidavits may be served not less than one (1) day before the hearing, unless the court permits them to be served at some other time. IN ST TRIAL P Rule 6(D).

   a. An adverse party shall have thirty (30) days after service of the initial brief in which to serve and file an answer brief. IN ST LAKE RCP Rule 4(A).

4. *Reply.* The moving party shall have ten (10) days after service of the answer brief in which to serve and file a reply brief. IN ST LAKE RCP Rule 4(A).

5. *Computation of time*

   a. *Generally; Days excluded.* In computing any period of time prescribed or allowed by the Indiana Rules of Trial Procedure, by order of the court, or by any applicable statute, the day of the act, event, or default from which the designated period of time begins to run shall not be included. The last day of the period so computed is to be included unless it is:

      i. A Saturday,

      ii. A Sunday,

      iii. A legal holiday as defined by state statute, or

      iv. A day the office in which the act is to be done is closed during regular business hours. IN ST TRIAL P Rule 6(A).

   b. *Short periods.* In any event, the period runs until the end of the next day that is not a Saturday, a Sunday, a legal holiday, or a day on which the office is closed. When the period of time allowed is less than seven (7) days, intermediate Saturdays, Sundays, legal holidays, and days on which the office is closed shall be excluded from the computations. IN ST TRIAL P Rule 6(A).

   c. *Additional time after service by United States mail.* Whenever a party has the right or is required to do some act or take some proceedings within a prescribed period after the service of a notice or other paper upon him and the notice or paper is served upon him by United States mail, three (3) days shall be added to the prescribed period. IN ST TRIAL P Rule 6(E).

   d. *Electronic filing does not alter deadlines.* Filing electronically does not alter any filing deadlines or any time computation pursuant to state or federal statutes, any Rules of the Indiana Supreme Court, including without limitation the Rules of Trial Procedure, the Rules of Appellate Procedure or the Administrative Rules, or applicable Lake County Rules of Civil Procedure. The office of the Lake County Clerk is open for electronic filing under the Lake County Rules of Civil Procedure twenty-four (24) hours a day. A document is deemed filed at the date and time it is received by the LCOD server. Filing must be completed before midnight local time in order to be considered filed that day. Lake County observes Central Time and electronic filers are strongly urged to file documents during hours when the Lake County Online Docket ("LCOD") help line is available, from 9:00 a.m. to 4:00 p.m. local time, although documents can be filed electronically twenty-four (24) hours a day. IN ST LAKE RCP Rule 17(I).

   e. *Enlargement of time.* When an act is required or allowed to be done at or within a specific time by the Indiana Rules of Trial Procedure, the court may at any time for cause shown:

      i. Order the period enlarged, with or without motion or notice, if request therefor is made before the expiration of the period originally prescribed or extended by a previous order; or

      ii. Upon motion made after the expiration of the specific period, permit the act to be done where the failure to act was the result of excusable neglect; but, the court may not extend the time for taking any action for judgment on the evidence under IN ST TRIAL P Rule 50(A), amendment of findings and judgment under IN ST TRIAL P Rule 52(B), to correct errors under IN ST TRIAL P Rule 59(C), statement in opposition to motion to correct error under IN ST TRIAL P Rule 59(E), or to obtain relief from final judgment under IN ST TRIAL P Rule 60(B), except to the extent and under the conditions stated in those rules. IN ST TRIAL P Rule 6(B).

C. General Requirements

1. *Motions, generally.* Unless made during a hearing or trial, or otherwise ordered by the court, an application to the court for an order shall be made by written motion. The motion shall state the grounds therefor and the relief or order sought. IN ST TRIAL P Rule 7(B).

   a. *Motions as distinct from pleadings.* Motions and responses to motions are not pleadings, and allegations contained in a motion are not admissions of a party. 22B INPRAC 7:2; Wachstetter v. County Properties, LLC, 832 N.E.2d 574 (Ind.Ct.App. 2005); Scott County Family YMCA, Inc. v. Hobbs, 817 N.E.2d 603 (Ind.Ct.App. 2004).

    b. *Unopposed motions generally granted.* It is common for a trial court to grant procedural motions, such as motions for enlargement of time, discovery motions, or motions for continuance, unless an objection is filed. 21 INPRAC § 13.8.

    c. *Separate motions.* Each motion shall be separate, while alternative motions filed together shall each be identified on the caption. IN ST LAKE RCP Rule 4(A).

    d. *Answer and reply briefs.* Failure to file an answer brief or reply brief within the time prescribed shall be deemed a waiver of the right thereto and shall subject the motion to summary ruling. IN ST LAKE RCP Rule 4(A).

2. *Motion to dismiss for lack of subject matter jurisdiction.* Every defense, in law or fact, to a claim for relief in any pleading, whether a claim, counterclaim, cross-claim, or third-party claim, shall be asserted in the responsive pleading thereto if one is required; except that at the option of the pleader, the defense of lack of jurisdiction over the subject matter may be made by motion. IN ST TRIAL P Rule 12(B)(1). Subject-matter jurisdiction refers to the power of the court or tribunal to entertain the general class of cases or disputes to which a pending case belongs. It means that the legislature or other authority, such as, perhaps, a supreme court, has invested the court with judicial power with which to entertain a case or controversy, and to hear the litigation and dispute. 1A INPRAC R 12(12.5).

    a. *Objection not waivable.* Subject-matter jurisdiction cannot be created by the parties to the litigation. Either it is there or it is not, quite independent of the conduct or the consent of the parties to the action. As such, the absence of subject-matter jurisdiction is never waivable and there is a positive duty on a court, whether trial or appellate, to raise the question of subject-matter jurisdiction whenever it might appear, if the parties have failed to present the question. 1A INPRAC R 12(12.5); Schoffstall v. Failey, 180 Ind.App. 528, 389 N.E. 361 (Ind.Ct.App. 1979).

    b. *Motion not to be made as one for summary judgment.* A motion to dismiss under IN ST TRIAL P Rule 12(B)(1) may not be presented in the form of a motion for summary judgment. 9 INPRAC § 42.3.

    c. *Precedence of subject matter jurisdiction.* Dismissal for lack of subject matter jurisdiction takes precedence over the determination of and action upon other substantive and procedural rights of the parties. 9 INPRAC § 42.3; Young v. Estate of Sweeney, 808 N.E.2d 1217 (Ind.Ct.App. 2004).

    d. *Issues examined separately; Jurisdiction over one claim as jurisdiction over case.* In order to determine whether a case is properly before the trial court, the court should examine each issue presented. If at least one of the issues is within the jurisdiction of the trial court, the entire case falls within the court's jurisdiction. Where at least one issue or claim is a proper matter for judicial determination or resolution, a trial court is not ousted of subject matter jurisdiction by the presence in a case of one or more issues which arguably are within the jurisdiction of administrative or regulatory agency. 9 INPRAC § 42.3; Alexander v. Cottey, 801 N.E.2d 651 (Ind.Ct.App. 2004).

    e. *Factual matters in determining subject matter jurisdiction.* The trial court considering a motion to dismiss for lack of subject matter jurisdiction has wide latitude to devise procedures to discover the facts relevant to jurisdiction and in weighing the evidence to resolve factual disputes affecting the jurisdictional challenge. 9 INPRAC § 42.3.

    f. *Failure to exhaust administrative remedies.* The doctrine of exhaustion of administrative remedies provides that a trial court will not acquire subject matter jurisdiction until the aggrieved party has exhausted all available remedies before the administrative agency. 9 INPRAC § 41.44; Indiana Dept. of Environmental Management v. NJK Farms, Inc., 921 N.E.2d 834 (Ind.Ct.App. 2010).

        i. *Dismissal of workers' compensation cases.* A trial court must dismiss a matter for lack of subject matter jurisdiction pursuant to Indiana IN ST TRIAL P Rule 12(B)(1) where injuries claimed in the Plaintiff's complaint fall squarely within the Indiana Workers Compensation Act. 9 INPRAC § 42.3; ATFH Real Property, LLC v. Stewart, 879 N.E.2d 1184 (Ind.Ct.App. 2008).

    g. *Leave to amend complaint if motion granted.* A dismissal for lack of subject matter jurisdiction is not an adjudication on the merits nor is it res judicata. If action is dismissed, plaintiff may file amended complaint as permitted by IN ST TRIAL P Rule 6(C). 9 INPRAC § 42.3; Hart v. Webster, 894 N.E.2d 1032 (Ind.Ct.App. 2008).

h. *Effect of judgment entered by court lacking subject matter jurisdiction.* A judgment entered by a court that lacks subject matter jurisdiction is void and may be attacked at any time. 9 INPRAC § 42.3; Roberson v. State, 903 N.E.2d 1009 (Ind.Ct.App. 2009).

3. *Consolidation and waiver*

   a. *Consolidation of defenses in motion.* A party who makes a motion under IN ST TRIAL P Rule 12 may join with it any other motions herein provided for and then available to him. If a party makes a motion under IN ST TRIAL P Rule 12 but omits therefrom any defense or objection then available to him which IN ST TRIAL P Rule 12 permits to be raised by motion, he shall not thereafter make a motion based on the defense or objection so omitted. He may, however, make such motions as are allowed under IN ST TRIAL P Rule 12(H)(2). IN ST TRIAL P Rule 12(G).

   b. *Waiver or preservation of certain defenses.* No defense or objection is waived by being joined with one or more other defenses or objections in a responsive pleading or motion. IN ST TRIAL P Rule 12(B).

D. Documents

1. *Required documents*

   a. *Motion and notice.* The requirement of notice is satisfied by service of the motion. IN ST TRIAL P Rule 7(B). Refer to the General Requirements section of this document for information on the content of a motion to dismiss for lack of subject matter jurisdiction.

   b. *Brief.* All motions filed pursuant to IN ST TRIAL P Rule 12 and IN ST TRIAL P Rule 56 shall be accompanied by a separate supporting brief. IN ST LAKE RCP Rule 4(A).

   c. *Proposed order.* Unless local practice provides differently, a party should submit a proposed order with its written motion to be signed by the judge once the motion has been granted. 21 INPRAC § 13.8.

      i. Proposed orders, which are submitted for the court's convenience under IN ST LAKE RCP Rule 3 or other applicable Lake County Rules of Civil Procedure, shall be submitted as attachments to motions. IN ST LAKE RCP Rule 17(D)(8). Proposed orders shall be prepared and filed separately from the pleadings, petitions, motions or other papers to which they have reference. IN ST LAKE RCP Rule 3(B).

      ii. Orders, either routine in nature or uncontested including, for example, those setting or continuing a hearing, shall be effected by the chronological case summary entry only, which shall contain the concise substance of the order. IN ST LAKE RCP Rule 3(B).

      iii. All orders shall be accompanied with sufficient copies and stamped, pre-addressed envelopes, so that copies may be mailed to all parties. IN ST LAKE RCP Rule 3(B).

   d. *Chronological case summary (CCS) entry forms.* All filings shall be accompanied by a Chronological Case Summary (CCS) Entry Form to define or identify the documents filed. The Form used should be substantially similar to IN ST LAKE RCP App. A. IN ST LAKE RCP Rule 3(C).

   e. *Certificate of service.* An attorney or unrepresented party tendering a document to the Clerk for filing shall certify that service has been made, list the parties served, and specify the date and means of service. The certificate of service shall be placed at the end of the document and shall not be separately filed. The separate filing of a certificate of service, however, shall not be grounds for rejecting a document for filing. The Clerk may permit documents to be filed without a certificate of service but shall require prompt filing of a separate certificate of service. IN ST TRIAL P Rule 5(C).

      i. All pleadings, motions and other papers submitted for filing which are required to be served under IN ST TRIAL P Rule 5(A) shall contain proof of service pursuant to IN ST TRIAL P Rule 5(B)(2). IN ST LAKE RCP Rule 3(A).

2. *Supplemental documents*

   a. *Supporting evidence.* When a motion is based on facts not appearing of record the court may hear the matter on affidavits presented by the respective parties, but the court may direct that the matter be heard wholly or partly on oral testimony or depositions. IN ST TRIAL P Rule 43(B).

b. *Facsimile cover sheet.* Any document sent to the Clerk of the Circuit Court by electronic facsimile transmission shall be accompanied by a cover sheet which states the title of the document, case number, number of pages, identity and voice telephone number of the sending party and instructions for filing. The cover sheet shall contain the signature of the attorney or party, pro se, authorizing the filing. IN ST ADMIN Rule 12(D).

E. Format

1. *Form of motions.* The rules applicable to captions, and the signing and form of pleadings (IN ST TRIAL P Rule 8 through IN ST TRIAL P Rule 11), apply to all motions and other papers provided under the Indiana Rules of Trial Procedure. 22B INPRAC 7:2.

2. *Form of pleadings.* For the purpose of uniformity, convenience, clarity and durability, requirements in IN ST LAKE RCP Rule 2 shall be observed in the preparation of all pleadings, motions and other papers. IN ST LAKE RCP Rule 2. Whenever materials submitted fail to meet the standards in IN ST LAKE RCP Rule 2, the Court may impose appropriate sanctions. IN ST LAKE RCP Rule 2(B).

    a. *Caption; Names of parties.* Every pleading shall contain a caption setting forth the name of the court, the title of the action, the file number, and a designation as in IN ST TRIAL P Rule 7(A). In the complaint the title of the action shall include the names of all the parties, but in other pleadings it is sufficient to state the name of the first party on each side with an appropriate indication of other parties. IN ST TRIAL P Rule 10(A).

        i. *Special judge matters.* The caption of all CCS Entry Forms, pleadings, motions, orders and other papers to be filed in a special judge case shall include in block text the words SPECIAL JUDGE and the name of the judge directly below the cause number on the caption. IN ST LAKE RCP Rule 2(D).

    b. *Paragraphs; Separate statements.* All averments of a claim or defense shall be made in numbered paragraphs, the contents of each of which shall be limited as far as practicable to a statement of a single set of circumstances, and a paragraph may be referred to by number in all succeeding pleadings. Each claim founded upon a separate transaction or occurrence and each defense other than denials may be stated in a separate count or defense whenever a separation facilitates the clear presentation of the matters set forth. IN ST TRIAL P Rule 10(B).

    c. *Adoption by reference; Exhibits.* Statements in a pleading may be adopted by reference in a different part of the same pleading or in another pleading or in any motion. A copy of any written instrument which is an exhibit to a pleading is a part thereof for all purposes. IN ST TRIAL P Rule 10(C).

    d. *Paper; Print, quality and binding*

        i. All pleadings, motions, chronological case summary entry forms, orders, process and other papers shall be neatly and legibly printed, typewritten or mechanically reproduced, on one (1) side only, on white opaque paper. To satisfy the recordkeeping requirements of IN ST TRIAL P Rule 77, the print shall be of sufficient density and clarity for preservation and reproduction of microfilming, optical disk or other secondary sources. For this reason, the use of non-letter-quality printers is discouraged. IN ST LAKE RCP Rule 2(A).

        ii. Paper and ink shall be of such quality as to withstand the test of time. All documents shall be produced on acid-free, non-thermal paper. It is recommended that a minimum of twenty (20) pound, twenty-five percent (25%) cotton paper product be used. Documents of multiple pages shall be submitted in bound or stapled fashion, and the binding or stapling shall be at the top only. Covers or backings shall not be used. IN ST LAKE RCP Rule 2(A).

    e. *Papers; Handwritten.* Handwritten papers may be filed only if approved by the Court and a typewritten or printed true rendition thereof is filed within three (3) days thereafter and approved by the Court. Upon such approval, they shall be deemed and filed as the original, while the handwritten papers shall be retained therewith for evidentiary purposes. IN ST LAKE RCP Rule 2(C).

    f. *Minute sheets; Motion blanks.* Minute sheets and motion blanks shall no longer be used. IN ST LAKE RCP Rule 2(D).

3. *Size of papers for filing.* Effective January 1, 1992, all pleadings, copies, motions and documents filed

with any trial court or appellate level court, typed or printed, with the exception of exhibits and existing wills, shall be prepared on eight and one-half by eleven inch (8 1/2" x 11") size paper. IN ST ADMIN Rule 11.

4. *Signature requirements*

   a. *Signature of attorney.* Every pleading or motion of a party represented by an attorney shall be signed by at least one (1) attorney of record in his individual name, whose address, telephone number, and attorney number shall be stated, except that this provision shall not apply to pleadings and motions made and transcribed at the trial or a hearing before the judge and received by him in such form. IN ST TRIAL P Rule 11(A).

      i. The signature of an attorney constitutes a certificate by him that he has read the pleadings; that to the best of his knowledge, information, and belief, there is good ground to support it; and that it is not interposed for delay. IN ST TRIAL P Rule 11(A).

      ii. If a pleading or motion is not signed or is signed with intent to defeat the purpose of the rule, it may be stricken as sham and false and the action may proceed as though the pleading had not been served. IN ST TRIAL P Rule 11(A).

      iii. For a willful violation of IN ST TRIAL P Rule 11 an attorney may be subjected to appropriate disciplinary action. Similar action may be taken if scandalous or indecent matter is inserted. IN ST TRIAL P Rule 11(A).

   b. *Signature of unrepresented party.* A party who is not represented by an attorney shall sign his pleading and state his address. IN ST TRIAL P Rule 11(A).

   c. *Verification not generally required.* Except when specifically required by rule, pleadings or motions need not be verified or accompanied by affidavit. The rule in equity that the averments of an answer under oath must be overcome by the testimony of two (2) witnesses or of one (1) witness sustained by corroborating circumstances is abolished. IN ST TRIAL P Rule 11(A).

   d. *Verification by affirmation or representation.* When in connection with any civil or special statutory proceeding it is required that any pleading, motion, petition, supporting affidavit, or other document of any kind, be verified, or that an oath be taken, it shall be sufficient if the subscriber simply affirms the truth of the matter to be verified by an affirmation or representation. IN ST TRIAL P Rule 11(B). IN ST TRIAL P Rule 11(B) states that the affirmation or representation should be in substantially the following language: "I (we) affirm, under the penalties for perjury, that the foregoing representation(s) is (are) true. (Signed) _____."

      i. Any person who falsifies an affirmation or representation of fact shall be subject to the same penalties as are prescribed by law for the making of a false affidavit. IN ST TRIAL P Rule 11(B).

   e. *Verified pleadings, motions, and affidavits as evidence.* Pleadings, motions and affidavits accompanying or in support of such pleadings or motions when required to be verified or under oath shall be accepted as a representation that the signer had personal knowledge thereof or reasonable cause to believe the existence of the facts or matters stated or alleged therein; and, if otherwise competent or acceptable as evidence, may be admitted as evidence of the facts or matters stated or alleged therein when it is so provided in the Indiana Rules of Trial Procedure, by statute or other law, or to the extent the writing or signature expressly purports to be made upon the signer's personal knowledge. When such pleadings, motions and affidavits are verified or under oath they shall not require other or greater proof on the part of the adverse party than if not verified or not under oath unless expressly provided otherwise by the Indiana Rules of Trial Procedure, statute or other law. Affidavits upon motions for summary judgment under IN ST TRIAL P Rule 56 and in denial of execution under IN ST TRIAL P Rule 9.2 shall be made upon personal knowledge. IN ST TRIAL P Rule 11(C).

   f. *Electronic signature.* The filing of documents and information through the E-filing system by use of a valid username and password is presumed to have been authorized by the User to whom that username and password have been issued and documents filed through the E-filing system are presumed to have been signed by the same User. IN ST ADMIN Rule 16(E).

5. *Information excluded from public access.* Every document filed in a case shall separately identify information excluded from public access pursuant to IN ST ADMIN Rule 9(G)(1) as follows:

   a. Whole documents that are excluded from public access pursuant to IN ST ADMIN Rule 9(G)(1) shall be tendered on light green paper or have a light green coversheet attached to the document, marked "Not for Public Access" or "Confidential." IN ST TRIAL P Rule 5(G)(1).

   b. When only a portion of a document contains information excluded from public access pursuant to IN ST ADMIN Rule 9(G)(1), said information shall be omitted [or redacted] from the filed document, and set forth on a separate accompanying document on light green paper conspicuously marked "Not for Public Access" or "Confidential" and clearly designated [or identifying] the caption and number of the case and the document and location within the document to which the redacted material pertains. IN ST TRIAL P Rule 5(G)(2).

   c. With respect to documents filed in electronic format, the trial court, by local rule, may provide for compliance with IN ST TRIAL P Rule 5 in manner that separates and protects access to information excluded from public access. IN ST TRIAL P Rule 5(G)(3).

   d. IN ST TRIAL P Rule 5(G) does not apply to a record sealed by the court pursuant to IN ST 5-14-3-5.5 or otherwise, nor to records, documents, or information filed in cases to which public access is prohibited pursuant to IN ST ADMIN Rule 9(G). IN ST TRIAL P Rule 5(G)(4).

   e. The following information in case records is excluded from public access and is confidential:

      i. Information that is excluded from public access pursuant to federal law;

      ii. Information that is excluded from public access as declared confidential by Indiana statute or other court rule, including without limitation:

         - All adoption records created after July 8, 1941, as declared confidential by IN ST 31-19-19-1, et seq., except those specifically declared open by IN ST 31-19-13-2(2);

         - All records relating to chancroid, chlamydia, gonorrhea, hepatitis, human immunodeficiency virus (HIV), Lymphogranuloma venereum, syphilis, tuberculosis, as declared confidential by IN ST 16-41-8-1, et seq.;

         - All records relating to child abuse as declared confidential by IN ST 31-33-18-1, et seq.;

         - All records relating to drug tests as declared confidential by IN ST 5-14-3-4(a)(9);

         - Records of grand jury proceedings as declared confidential by IN ST 35-34-2-4;

         - Records of juvenile proceedings as declared confidential by IN ST 31-39-1-2, except those specifically open under statute;

         - All paternity records created after July 1, 1941 as declared confidential by IN ST 31-14-11-15, IN ST 31-19-5-23, IN ST 31-39-1-1 and IN ST 31-39-1-2 [Editor's note: IN ST 31-14-11-15 was repealed effective May 9, 2013];

         - All pre-sentence reports as declared confidential by IN ST 35-38-1-13;

         - Written petitions to permit marriages without consent and orders directing the Clerk of Court to issue a marriage license to underage persons, as declared confidential by IN ST 31-11-1-6;

         - Only those arrest warrants, search warrants, indictments and informations ordered confidential by the trial judge, prior to return of duly executed service as declared confidential by IN ST 5-14-3-4(b)(1);

         - All medical, mental health, or tax records unless determined by law or regulation of any governmental custodian not to be confidential, released by the subject of such records, or declared by a court of competent jurisdiction to be essential to the resolution of litigation as declared confidential by IN ST 16-39-3-10, IN ST 6-4.1-5-10, IN ST 6-4.1-12-12, and IN ST 6-8.1-7-1;

         - Personal information relating to jurors or prospective jurors, other than for the use of the parties and counsel, pursuant to IN ST JURY Rule 10;

- Information relating to protection from abuse orders, no-contact orders and workplace violence restraining orders as declared confidential by IN ST 5-2-9-6, et seq.;

- Mediation proceedings pursuant to IN ST ADR Rule 2.11, Mini-Trial proceedings pursuant to IN ST ADR Rule 4.4(C), and Summary Jury Trials pursuant to IN ST ADR Rule 5.6;

- Information in probation files pursuant to the Probation Standards promulgated by the Judicial Conference of Indiana pursuant to IN ST 11-13-1-8(b);

- Information deemed confidential pursuant to the Rules for Court Administered Alcohol and Drug Programs promulgated by the Judicial Conference of Indiana pursuant to IN ST 12-23-14-13;

- Information deemed confidential pursuant to the Problem-Solving Court Rules promulgated by the Judicial Conference of Indiana pursuant to IN ST 33-23-16-16;

- All records of the Department of workforce Development as declared confidential by IN ST 22-4-19-6;

- Information regarding interception of electronic communications that is sealed or deemed confidential as set forth in IN ST 35-33.5-2-1, et seq.

iii. Information excluded from public access by specific court order;

iv. Complete Social Security Numbers of living persons;

v. With the exception of names, information such as addresses, phone numbers, and dates of birth which explicitly identifies:

- Natural persons who are witnesses or victims (not including defendants) in criminal, domestic violence, stalking, sexual assault, juvenile, or civil protection order proceedings, provided that juveniles who are victims of sex crimes shall be identified by initials only;

- Places of residence of judicial officers, clerks and other employees of courts and clerks of court, unless the person or persons about whom the information pertains waives confidentiality;

vi. Complete account numbers of specific assets, loans, bank accounts, credit cards, and personal identification numbers (PINs);

vii. All orders of expungement entered in criminal or juvenile proceedings, orders to restrict access to criminal history information pursuant to IN ST 35-38-5-5.5 or IN ST 35-38-8-5 and records excluded from public access by such orders, and information related to infractions that is excluded from public access pursuant to IN ST 34-28-5-15 or IN ST 34-28-5-16 [Editor's note: IN ST 35-38-5-5.5, IN ST 35-38-8-5 and IN ST 34-28-5-16 were repealed effective July 1, 2013; for information on orders restricting access to criminal history, refer to IN ST 35-38-9-1, et seq.];

viii. All personal notes and e-mail, and deliberative material, of judges, jurors, court staff and judicial agencies, and information recorded in personal data assistants (PDA's) or organizers and personal calendars. IN ST ADMIN Rule 9(G)(1).

6. *Format of electronically filed documents*

a. *Generally.* Electronically filed documents must meet the same requirements of format as documents conventionally filed pursuant to IN ST LAKE RCP Rule 2 or other applicable Lake County Rules of Civil Procedure. IN ST LAKE RCP Rule 17(D)(1).

b. *Titles of documents.* The person electronically filing a document will be responsible for designating a title for the document at the time it is filed. The LCOD will generate the appropriate entry onto the CCS to record the filing of the document. IN ST LAKE RCP Rule 17(D)(3).

c. *Citations and hyperlinks.* Electronically filed documents may contain hyperlink references to an external document as a convenient mechanism for accessing material cited in the document. Filers wishing to insert hyperlinks into documents shall continue to use the traditional method of citation to authority in addition to the hyperlink provided. The hyperlink is merely a convenience to the court and the material referenced is extraneous to the file and not a part of the court's record. IN ST LAKE RCP Rule 17(D)(5).

    d.   *Attachments and exhibits.* All documents which form part of a single submission and which are being filed at the same time and by the same filer may be electronically filed together under one document filing, e.g., the motion, supporting affidavits, memorandum in support, designation of evidence, exhibits. IN ST LAKE RCP Rule 17(D)(6).

        i.   Large documents which do not exist in an electronic format shall be scanned into .pdf format and filed electronically as separate attachments. A scanner is available in each clerk's office for use by the public and the bar in scanning and saving image files if needed. IN ST LAKE RCP Rule 17(D)(6).

    e.   *Electronic signatures*

        i.   *Electronic filing as signature.* The electronic filing of a document which is required to be signed shall constitute the filer's representation under IN ST TRIAL P Rule 11. Unless the electronically filed document has been scanned and shows the filer's original signature, the signature of the filer shall be indicated by As/Attorney's Name, or As/Party's Name as in the case of a pro se litigant, on the line where the signature would otherwise appear. IN ST LAKE RCP Rule 17(G)(1).

        ii.   *Signatures on jointly signed or filed, verified or other documents.* In the case of a stipulation, agreed order, jointly signed motion or other document which needs to be signed by two (2) or more persons, or in the case of documents which must contain original signatures and which require verification or an unsworn declaration under rule or statute, the signatures may be indicated by either:

           •   Submitting a scanned copy of the originally signed document; or,

           •   Submitting the document with the use of As/Name in the signature block(s) where the original signature(s) appear(s) in the original document; provided, however, that the filer shall first obtain the physical signature of all persons necessary. IN ST LAKE RCP Rule 17(G)(2).

        iii.   *Retention of original.* The filer shall retain the original executed document. IN ST LAKE RCP Rule 17(G).

    7.   *Citation of local rules.* The local rules for Lake County may be known as the Lake County Rules of Civil Procedure, and abbreviated as LR. IN ST LAKE RCP Rule 1(C).

F. Filing and Service Requirements

    1.   *Filing requirements.* Except as otherwise provided in IN ST TRIAL P Rule 5(E)(2), all pleadings and papers subsequent to the complaint which are required to be served upon a party shall be filed with the Court either before service or within a reasonable period of time thereafter. IN ST TRIAL P Rule 5(E)(1). All papers presented for filing shall be submitted to the Clerk and not to the court. All papers submitted for filing shall be mailed or delivered to the Clerk's office at the courthouse in which the case is pending. IN ST LAKE RCP Rule 3(A).

    a.   *Filing with the court defined.* The filing of pleadings, motions, and other papers with the court as required by the Indiana Rules of Trial Procedure shall be made by one of the following methods:

        i.   Delivery to the clerk of the court;

        ii.   Sending by electronic transmission under the procedure adopted pursuant to IN ST ADMIN Rule 12;

        iii.   Mailing to the clerk by registered, certified or express mail return receipt requested;

        iv.   Depositing with any third-party commercial carrier for delivery to the clerk within three (3) calendar days, cost prepaid, properly addressed;

        v.   If the court so permits, filing with the judge, in which event the judge shall note thereon the filing date and forthwith transmit them to the office of the clerk; or

        vi.   Electronic filing, as approved by the Division of State Court Administration pursuant to IN ST ADMIN Rule 16. IN ST TRIAL P Rule 5(F).

vii. Filing by registered or certified mail and by third-party commercial carrier shall be complete upon mailing or deposit. IN ST TRIAL P Rule 5(F).

b. *Mandatory electronic filing.* Unless otherwise permitted by the Lake County Rules of Civil Procedure or otherwise authorized by the judicial officer assigned to a particular case, all documents submitted for filing (including the original complaint, or equivalent pleading, and summons) shall be filed electronically with the clerk using the LCOD, no matter when the case was originally filed. IN ST LAKE RCP Rule 17(D).

   i. *Of documents containing information excluded from public access pursuant to* IN ST ADMIN Rule 9. Documents containing information excluded from public access pursuant to IN ST ADMIN Rule 9, or documents which are ordered to be filed under seal shall be filed electronically, pursuant to IN ST LAKE RCP Rule 17(D)(9), whenever possible, along with a copy of the applicable order to seal the records, and the filer shall designate the documents as "Not for Public Access Pursuant to Administrative Rule 9(G)(1)" at the time of filing. IN ST LAKE RCP Rule 16(A)(1); IN ST LAKE RCP Rule 17(D)(9).

   - *Conventional filing of documents containing information excluded from public access pursuant to* IN ST ADMIN Rule 9. Documents containing information excluded from public access pursuant to IN ST ADMIN Rule 9, or documents which are ordered to be filed under seal, which cannot be legibly scanned and filed electronically, shall be conventionally filed under seal and designated by the filer as "Not for Public Access Pursuant to Administrative Rule 9(G)(1)" at the time of filing. The unredacted version shall be filed on light green paper which is conspicuously marked "Not for Public Access"; and a redacted version, with confidential information deleted, shall be filed on white paper which shall be available for public access. The filer shall also electronically file a Notice of Manual Filing. IN ST LAKE RCP Rule 16(A)(2).

   ii. *Technical failures.* If a registered user is unable to file a document in a timely manner due to technical difficulties in the LCOD, the registered user must file a document with the court as soon as possible notifying the court of the inability to file the document. A sample document titled Declaration that Party was Unable to File in a Timely Manner Due to Technical Difficulties can be found at IN ST LAKE RCP Form 4. Delayed filings shall be rejected unless accompanied by the declaration attesting to the filer's failed attempts to file electronically at least two (2) times, separated by at least one (1) hour, after noon on each day of delay due to such technical failure. IN ST LAKE RCP Rule 17(J).

   iii. *Documents allowed to be filed conventionally.* Unless specifically authorized by the court, only the following documents may be filed conventionally and not electronically:

   - Exhibits and other documents that cannot be converted to a legible electronic form, such as videotapes, x-rays, and similar materials
   - Documents delivered to the clerk by pro se litigants
   - Documents mailed to the clerk by pro se litigants
   - Confidential documents
   - Notice of manual filing
   - Titles of documents
   - Chronological case summary entry forms (CCS entry forms). IN ST LAKE RCP Rule 17(E).
   - For more information on the documents which must be filed conventionally, refer to IN ST LAKE RCP Rule 17(E).

c. *Facsimile filing.* Only when necessary on an emergency basis (i.e., when certified mail or other means of filing will not bring the document to the Judge's attention prior to the scheduled hearing or ruling), pleadings, motions and other papers may be filed by electronic facsimile transmission, or when specifically authorized by the Court. IN ST LAKE RCP Rule 2(C).

   i. *Generally.* In counties where a majority of judges of the courts of record, by posted local rule,

have authorized electronic facsimile filing and designated a telephone number to receive such transmissions, pleadings, motions, and other papers may be sent to the Clerk of Circuit Court by electronic facsimile transmission for filing in any case, provided:

- Such matter does not exceed ten (10) pages, including the cover sheet;
- Such matter does not require the payment of fees other than the electronic facsimile transcription fee set forth in IN ST ADMIN Rule 12(E);
- The sending party creates at the time of transmission a machine generated log for such transmission; and
- The original document and the transmission log are maintained by the sending party for the duration of the litigation. IN ST ADMIN Rule 12(B).

ii. *Time of filing.* During normal, posted business hours, the time of filing shall be the time the duplicate document is produced in the office of the Clerk of the Circuit Court. Duplicate documents received at all other times shall be filed as of the next normal business day. IN ST ADMIN Rule 12(C).

- If the receiving fax machine endorses its own time and date stamp upon the transmitted documents and the receiving machine produces a delivery receipt which is electronically created and transmitted to the sending party, the time of filing shall be the date and time recorded on the transmitted document by the receiving fax machine. IN ST ADMIN Rule 12(C).

d. *Filing for special judges.* For special judge matters where the special judge is a full-time judge or magistrate serving within Lake County, all papers submitted for filing shall be delivered or mailed to the Clerk's office at the courthouse where the special judge regularly serves. IN ST LAKE RCP Rule 3(A).

e. *Proof of filing.* Any party filing any paper by any method other than personal delivery to the clerk shall retain proof of filing. IN ST TRIAL P Rule 5(F).

2. *Service requirements.* Unless otherwise provided by the Indiana Rules of Trial Procedure or an order of the court, each party and special judge, if any, shall be served with: (1) every order required by its terms to be served; (2) every pleading subsequent to the original complaint; (3) every written motion except one which may be heard ex parte; (4) every brief submitted to the trial court; (5) every paper relating to discovery required to be served upon a party; and (6) every written notice, appearance, demand, offer of judgment, designation of record on appeal, or similar paper. IN ST TRIAL P Rule 5(A).

a. *Methods of service*

i. *Personal service.* Whenever a party is represented by an attorney of record, service shall be made upon such attorney unless service upon the party himself is ordered by the court. Service upon the attorney or party shall be made by delivering or mailing a copy of the papers to the last known address or where an attorney or party has consented to service by fax or e-mail, as provided in IN ST TRIAL P Rule 3.1(A)(4), by faxing or e-mailing a copy of the documents to the fax number or e-mail address set out in the appearance form or correction as required by IN ST TRIAL P Rule 3.1(E). IN ST TRIAL P Rule 5(B). Delivery of a copy within IN ST TRIAL P Rule 5 means:

- Offering or tendering it to the attorney or party and stating the nature of the papers being served. Refusal to accept an offered or tendered document is a waiver of any objection to the sufficiency or adequacy of service of that document;
- Leaving it at his office with a clerk or other person in charge thereof, or if there is no one in charge, leaving it in a conspicuous place therein; or
- If the office is closed, by leaving it at his dwelling house or usual place of abode with some person of suitable age and discretion then residing therein; or,
- Leaving it at some other suitable place, selected by the attorney upon whom service is being made, pursuant to duly promulgated local rule. IN ST TRIAL P Rule 5(B)(1).

ii. *Service by mail.* If service is made by mail, the papers shall be deposited in the United States mail addressed to the person on whom they are being served, with postage prepaid. Service shall be deemed complete upon mailing. Proof of service of all papers permitted to be mailed may be made by written acknowledgment of service, by affidavit of the person who mailed the papers, or by certificate of an attorney. It shall be the duty of attorneys when entering their appearance in a cause or when filing pleadings or papers therein, to have noted in the Chronological Case Summary or said pleadings or papers so filed the address and telephone number of their office. Service by delivery or by mail at such address shall be deemed sufficient and complete. IN ST TRIAL P Rule 5(B)(2).

iii. *Service by fax or e-mail.* A party who has consented to service by fax or e-mail may be served as follows:

- Service by e-mail shall be made by attaching the document being served in .pdf format. Discovery documents must also be served in accordance with IN ST TRIAL P Rule 26(A). IN ST TRIAL P Rule 5(B)(3)(a).

- Service by fax shall be deemed complete upon generation of a transmission record indicating the successful transmission of the entire document, except as provided in IN ST TRIAL P Rule 5(B)(3)(d). IN ST TRIAL P Rule 5(B)(3)(b).

- Service by e-mail shall be deemed complete upon transmission, except as provided in IN ST TRIAL P Rule 5(B)(3)(d). IN ST TRIAL P Rule 5(B)(3)(c).

- Service by fax or e-mail that occurs on a Saturday, Sunday, legal holiday, or day the court or agency in which the matter is pending is closed or after 5:00 PM local time of the recipient shall be deemed complete the next day that is not a Saturday, Sunday, legal holiday, or day that the court or agency in which the matter is pending is not closed. IN ST TRIAL P Rule 5(B)(3)(d).

b. *Serving numerous defendants.* In any action in which there are unusually large numbers of defendants, the court, upon motion or of its own initiative, may order:

i. That service of the pleadings of the defendants and replies thereto need not be made as between the defendants;

- That any cross-claim, counterclaim, or matter constituting an avoidance or affirmative defense contained therein shall be deemed to be denied or avoided by all other parties; and

- That the filing of any such pleading and service thereof upon the plaintiff constitutes due notice of it to the parties. IN ST TRIAL P Rule 5(D).

ii. A copy of every such order shall be served upon the parties in such manner and form as the court directs. IN ST TRIAL P Rule 5(D).

c. *Service by electronic means.* The Lake County Online Docket will generate a Notice of Electronic Filing and Service when any document is filed and served. This notice will be emailed to each registered user of record in a case, and an electronic service event will be added to the work queue of each registered user of record in the case. The party filing the document should retain a paper or electronic copy of the Notice of Electronic Filing and Service. This notice represents proof of filing and service of the document on registered users of record in that case. The filer shall not be required to conventionally serve any document on any party receiving electronic service. IN ST LAKE RCP Rule 17(F)(2).

i. The filer shall also conventionally serve those parties not designated or able to receive electronic notice or service but who are nevertheless entitled to notice of said pleading or other document in accordance with the Indiana Rules of Civil Procedure and applicable Lake County Rules of Civil Procedure. In such cases, the filer shall also file a certificate of service, as appropriate. IN ST LAKE RCP Rule 17(F).

d. *Service on parties in default for failure to appear.* No service need be made on parties in default for failure to appear, except that pleadings asserting new or additional claims for relief against them shall be served upon them in the manner provided by service of summons in IN ST TRIAL P Rule 4. IN ST TRIAL P Rule 5(A).

G. Hearings

1. *Hearing on motion.* Unless local conditions make it impracticable, each judge shall establish regular times and places, at intervals sufficiently frequent for the prompt dispatch of business, at which motions requiring notice and hearing may be heard and disposed of; but the judge at any time or place and on such notice, if any, as he considers reasonable may make order for the advancement, conduct, and hearing of actions. To expedite its business the court may direct the submission and determination of motions without oral hearing upon brief written statements of reasons in support and opposition, or direct or permit hearings by telephone conference call with all attorneys or other similar means of communication. IN ST TRIAL P Rule 73(A).

2. *Oral argument discretionary.* The granting of a motion for oral argument, unless required by the Indiana Rules of Trial Procedure, shall be wholly discretionary with the court. IN ST LAKE RCP Rule 4(B).

H. Forms

1. Motion to Dismiss for Lack of Subject Matter Jurisdiction Forms for Indiana

   a. General form. 5 INPRAC § 3:4.1.

   b. Lack of subject matter jurisdiction. 5 INPRAC § 3:4.2.

   c. Motion to dismiss plaintiff's complaint; General form. 9 INPRAC § 42.2.

   d. Lack of jurisdiction over the subject matter. 9 INPRAC § 42.3.

   e. Certificate of service; Personal service. 9 INPRAC § 5.7.

   f. Certificate of service; First class mail. 9 INPRAC § 5.8.

2. Official Motion to Dismiss for Lack of Subject Matter Jurisdiction Forms for Lake County

   a. CCS entry form. IN ST LAKE RCP App. A.

   b. Notice of manual filing. IN ST LAKE RCP Form 2.

   c. Certificate of service. IN ST LAKE RCP Form 3.

   d. Declaration that party was unable to file in a timely manner. IN ST LAKE RCP Form 4.

3. Motion to Dismiss for Lack of Subject Matter Jurisdiction Forms for Lake County

   a. Notice of manual filing. EFORMST IN 5540.

I. Checklist

(I) ❑ Matters to be considered by moving party

   (a) ❑ Required documents

      (1) ❑ Motion and notice

      (2) ❑ Brief

      (3) ❑ Proposed order

      (4) ❑ Chronological case summary (CSS) entry sheets

      (5) ❑ Certificate of service

   (b) ❑ Supplemental documents

      (1) ❑ Supporting evidence

      (2) ❑ Facsimile cover sheet

   (c) ❑ Timing

      (1) ❑ A motion to dismiss for lack of subject matter jurisdiction shall be made before pleading if a further pleading is permitted or within twenty (20) days after service of the prior pleading if none is required

      (2) ❑ A written motion, other than one which may be heard ex parte, and notice of the hearing thereof shall be served not less than five (5) days before the time specified for the hearing, unless a different period is fixed by the Indiana Rules of Trial Procedure or by order of the court

(3) ❑ All pleadings and papers subsequent to the complaint which are required to be served upon a party shall be filed with the Court either before service or within a reasonable period of time thereafter

(4) ❑ All pleadings, motions and other papers submitted for filing which are required to be served under IN ST TRIAL P Rule 5(A) shall be filed no later than three (3) days after service

(5) ❑ If such papers are filed before service, proof of service thereof shall be filed no later than three (3) business days thereafter

(II) ❑ Matters to be considered by the responding party

    (a) ❑ Required documents

        (1) ❑ Opposition

        (2) ❑ Chronological case summary (CSS) entry sheets

        (3) ❑ Certificate of service

    (b) ❑ Supplemental documents

        (1) ❑ Supporting evidence

        (2) ❑ Proposed order

        (3) ❑ Facsimile cover sheet

    (c) ❑ Timing

        (1) ❑ So long as consistent with the Indiana Rules of Trial Procedure, an adverse party wishing to respond shall do so within fifteen (15) days of service

        (2) ❑ Except as otherwise provided in IN ST TRIAL P Rule 59(D), opposing affidavits may be served not less than one (1) day before the hearing, unless the court permits them to be served at some other time

Motions, Oppositions and Replies
Motion to Dismiss for Lack of Personal Jurisdiction

Document Last Updated October 2013

A. Applicable Rules

1. *State rules*

    a. Appearance. IN ST TRIAL P Rule 3.1.

    b. Summons. IN ST TRIAL P Rule 4.

    c. Service and filing of pleadings and other papers. IN ST TRIAL P Rule 5.

    d. Time. IN ST TRIAL P Rule 6.

    e. Pleadings. IN ST TRIAL P Rule 7; IN ST TRIAL P Rule 8; IN ST TRIAL P Rule 9; IN ST TRIAL P Rule 9.2; IN ST TRIAL P Rule 10.

    f. Signing and verification of pleadings. IN ST TRIAL P Rule 11.

    g. Defenses and objections; When and how presented; By pleading or motion; Motion for judgment on the pleadings. IN ST TRIAL P Rule 12.

    h. Amended and supplemental pleadings. IN ST TRIAL P Rule 15.

    i. Joinder of person needed for just adjudication. IN ST TRIAL P Rule 19.

    j. Evidence. IN ST TRIAL P Rule 43.

    k. Judgment on the evidence (directed verdict). IN ST TRIAL P Rule 50.

    l. Findings by the court. IN ST TRIAL P Rule 52.

    m. Summary judgment. IN ST TRIAL P Rule 56.

n. Motion to correct error. IN ST TRIAL P Rule 59.

o. Relief from judgment or order. IN ST TRIAL P Rule 60.

p. Hearing of motions. IN ST TRIAL P Rule 73.

q. Access to court records. IN ST ADMIN Rule 9.

r. Paper size. IN ST ADMIN Rule 11.

s. Facsimile transmission. IN ST ADMIN Rule 12.

t. Electronic filing and electronic service pilot projects. IN ST ADMIN Rule 16.

u. Privacy and confidentiality. IN ST 5-2-9-6; IN ST 5-14-3-4; IN ST 5-14-3-5.5; IN ST 6-4.1-5-10; IN ST 6-4.1-12-12; IN ST 6-8.1-7-1; IN ST 11-13-1-8; IN ST 12-23-14-13; IN ST 16-39-3-10; IN ST 16-41-8-1; IN ST 22-4-19-6; IN ST 31-11-1-6; IN ST 31-19-5-23; IN ST 31-19-13-2; IN ST 31-19-19-1; IN ST 31-33-18-1; IN ST 31-39-1-1; IN ST 31-39-1-2; IN ST 33-23-16-16; IN ST 35-34-2-4; IN ST 35-38-1-13; IN ST 35-38-9-1; IN ST ADR Rule 2.11; IN ST ADR Rule 4.4; IN ST ADR Rule 5.6; IN ST JURY Rule 10.

2. *Local rules*

a. Scope and title. [IN ST LAKE RCP Rule 1, as amended by IN ORDER 13-0237, effective October 18, 2013].

b. Preparation of pleadings, motions and other papers. IN ST LAKE RCP Rule 2.

c. Filing. [IN ST LAKE RCP Rule 3, as amended by IN ORDER 13-0237, effective October 18, 2013].

d. Motions. IN ST LAKE RCP Rule 4.

e. Confidential information and sealed documents. IN ST LAKE RCP Rule 16.

f. Electronic filing and service. IN ST LAKE RCP Rule 17.

B. Timing

1. *Timing of motion to dismiss for failure lack of personal matter jurisdiction.* A motion making any of the defenses listed in IN ST TRIAL P Rule 12(B) shall be made before pleading if a further pleading is permitted or within twenty (20) days after service of the prior pleading if none is required. IN ST TRIAL P Rule 12(B).

a. *Time to file a responsive pleading.* A responsive pleading required under the Indiana Rules of Trial Procedure, shall be served within twenty (20) days after service of the prior pleading. IN ST TRIAL P Rule 6(C).

b. *Waiver of certain IN ST TRIAL P Rule 12(B) defenses.* If a pleading sets forth a claim for relief to which the adverse party is not required to serve a responsive pleading, any of the defenses in IN ST TRIAL P Rule 12(B)(2), IN ST TRIAL P Rule 12(B)(3), IN ST TRIAL P Rule 12(B)(4), IN ST TRIAL P Rule 12(B)(5) or IN ST TRIAL P Rule 12(B)(8) is waived to the extent constitutionally permissible unless made in a motion within twenty (20) days after service of the prior pleading. IN ST TRIAL P Rule 12(B).

c. *Filing.* All pleadings and papers subsequent to the complaint which are required to be served upon a party shall be filed with the Court either before service or within a reasonable period of time thereafter. IN ST TRIAL P Rule 5(E)(1). All pleadings, motions and other papers submitted for filing which are required to be served under IN ST TRIAL P Rule 5(A) shall be filed no later than three (3) days after service. IN ST LAKE RCP Rule 3(A).

i. If such papers are filed before service, proof of service thereof shall be filed no later than three (3) business days thereafter. Upon failure to comply with IN ST LAKE RCP Rule 3, the Court may, on motion of any party or on its own motion, impose appropriate sanctions. IN ST LAKE RCP Rule 3(A).

d. *Briefs.* Briefs, other than those addressed in IN ST LAKE RCP Rule 4 and IN ST LAKE RCP Rule 9, shall be filed no later than two (2) calendar days preceding the hearing or trial to which directed. IN ST LAKE RCP Rule 11.

2. *Service.* A written motion, other than one which may be heard ex parte, and notice of the hearing thereof shall be served not less than five (5) days before the time specified for the hearing, unless a different period is fixed by the Indiana Rules of Trial Procedure or by order of the court. IN ST TRIAL P Rule 6(D).

   a. *Of supporting affidavits.* When a motion is supported by affidavit, the affidavit shall be served with the motion. IN ST TRIAL P Rule 6(D).

3. *Service of opposition.* Except as otherwise provided in IN ST TRIAL P Rule 59(D), opposing affidavits may be served not less than one (1) day before the hearing, unless the court permits them to be served at some other time. IN ST TRIAL P Rule 6(D).

   a. An adverse party shall have thirty (30) days after service of the initial brief in which to serve and file an answer brief. IN ST LAKE RCP Rule 4(A).

4. *Reply.* The moving party shall have ten (10) days after service of the answer brief in which to serve and file a reply brief. IN ST LAKE RCP Rule 4(A).

5. *Computation of time*

   a. *Generally; Days excluded.* In computing any period of time prescribed or allowed by the Indiana Rules of Trial Procedure, by order of the court, or by any applicable statute, the day of the act, event, or default from which the designated period of time begins to run shall not be included. The last day of the period so computed is to be included unless it is:

      i. A Saturday,

      ii. A Sunday,

      iii. A legal holiday as defined by state statute, or

      iv. A day the office in which the act is to be done is closed during regular business hours. IN ST TRIAL P Rule 6(A).

   b. *Short periods.* In any event, the period runs until the end of the next day that is not a Saturday, a Sunday, a legal holiday, or a day on which the office is closed. When the period of time allowed is less than seven (7) days, intermediate Saturdays, Sundays, legal holidays, and days on which the office is closed shall be excluded from the computations. IN ST TRIAL P Rule 6(A).

   c. *Additional time after service by United States mail.* Whenever a party has the right or is required to do some act or take some proceedings within a prescribed period after the service of a notice or other paper upon him and the notice or paper is served upon him by United States mail, three (3) days shall be added to the prescribed period. IN ST TRIAL P Rule 6(E).

   d. *Electronic filing does not alter deadlines.* Filing electronically does not alter any filing deadlines or any time computation pursuant to state or federal statutes, any Rules of the Indiana Supreme Court, including without limitation the Rules of Trial Procedure, the Rules of Appellate Procedure or the Administrative Rules, or applicable Lake County Rules of Civil Procedure. The office of the Lake County Clerk is open for electronic filing under the Lake County Rules of Civil Procedure twenty-four (24) hours a day. A document is deemed filed at the date and time it is received by the LCOD server. Filing must be completed before midnight local time in order to be considered filed that day. Lake County observes Central Time and electronic filers are strongly urged to file documents during hours when the Lake County Online Docket ("LCOD") help line is available, from 9:00 a.m. to 4:00 p.m. local time, although documents can be filed electronically twenty-four (24) hours a day. IN ST LAKE RCP Rule 17(I).

   e. *Enlargement of time.* When an act is required or allowed to be done at or within a specific time by the Indiana Rules of Trial Procedure, the court may at any time for cause shown:

      i. Order the period enlarged, with or without motion or notice, if request therefor is made before the expiration of the period originally prescribed or extended by a previous order; or

      ii. Upon motion made after the expiration of the specific period, permit the act to be done where the failure to act was the result of excusable neglect; but, the court may not extend the time for taking any action for judgment on the evidence under IN ST TRIAL P Rule 50(A), amendment of findings and judgment under IN ST TRIAL P Rule 52(B), to correct errors under IN ST

TRIAL P Rule 59(C), statement in opposition to motion to correct error under IN ST TRIAL P Rule 59(E), or to obtain relief from final judgment under IN ST TRIAL P Rule 60(B), except to the extent and under the conditions stated in those rules. IN ST TRIAL P Rule 6(B).

C. General Requirements

1. *Motions, generally.* Unless made during a hearing or trial, or otherwise ordered by the court, an application to the court for an order shall be made by written motion. The motion shall state the grounds therefor and the relief or order sought. IN ST TRIAL P Rule 7(B).

    a. *Motions as distinct from pleadings.* Motions and responses to motions are not pleadings, and allegations contained in a motion are not admissions of a party. 22B INPRAC 7:2; Wachstetter v. County Properties, LLC, 832 N.E.2d 574 (Ind.Ct.App. 2005); Scott County Family YMCA, Inc. v. Hobbs, 817 N.E.2d 603 (Ind.Ct.App. 2004).

    b. *Unopposed motions generally granted.* It is common for a trial court to grant procedural motions, such as motions for enlargement of time, discovery motions, or motions for continuance, unless an objection is filed. 21 INPRAC § 13.8.

    c. *Separate motions.* Each motion shall be separate, while alternative motions filed together shall each be identified on the caption. IN ST LAKE RCP Rule 4(A).

    d. *Answer and reply briefs.* Failure to file an answer brief or reply brief within the time prescribed shall be deemed a waiver of the right thereto and shall subject the motion to summary ruling. IN ST LAKE RCP Rule 4(A).

2. *Motion to dismiss for lack of personal jurisdiction.* Every defense, in law or fact, to a claim for relief in any pleading, whether a claim, counterclaim, cross-claim, or third-party claim, shall be asserted in the responsive pleading thereto if one is required; except that at the option of the pleader, the defense of lack of jurisdiction over person may be made by motion. IN ST TRIAL P Rule 12(b)(2). If personal jurisdiction is not present, then that party against whom jurisdiction is asserted must raise the question. 1A INPRAC R 12(12.6).

    a. *Presumption of jurisdiction.* Jurisdiction is presumed and, therefore, the defense of lack of personal jurisdiction may be asserted by motion under IN ST TRIAL P Rule 12(B)(2), or in the defendant's answer as an affirmative defense. 22 INPRAC § 15.16; Adsit Co., Inc. v. Gustin, 874 N.E.2d 1018 (Ind.Ct.App. 2007); Keesling v. Winstead, 858 N.E.2d 996 (Ind.Ct.App. 2006). Refer to the Indiana KeyRules Answer document for more information.

    b. *Personal jurisdiction.* The Due Process Clause of the Fourteenth Amendment requires that before a state may exercise jurisdiction over a defendant, the defendant must have certain minimum contacts with the state such that the maintenance of the suit does not offend traditional notions of fair play and substantial justice. 1A INPRAC R 12(12.6).

        i. *General jurisdiction.* If the defendant's contacts with the state are so continuous and systematic that the defendant should reasonably anticipate being haled into the courts of that state for any matter, then the defendant is subject to general jurisdiction, even in causes of action unrelated to the defendant's contacts with the forum state. 1A INPRAC R 12(12.6).

        ii. *Specific jurisdiction.* In cases where a defendant is not subject to general jurisdiction in a forum state, specific jurisdiction may be asserted if the controversy is related to or arises out of the defendant's contacts with the forum state. Specific jurisdiction requires that the defendant purposefully availed itself of the privilege of conducting activities within the forum state so that the defendant reasonably anticipates being haled into court there. A single contact with the forum state may be sufficient to establish specific jurisdiction over a defendant, if it creates a substantial connection with the forum state and the suit is related to that connection. 1A INPRAC R 12(12.6).

        iii. *Due process; Reasonableness.* A defendant cannot be haled into a jurisdiction solely as a result of random, fortuitous, or attenuated contacts or of the unilateral activity of another party or a third person. Once either general or specific jurisdiction has been established, due process requires that the assertion of personal jurisdiction over the defendant is reasonable. The assertion of personal jurisdiction will rarely be found unreasonable if minimum contacts are found. Five factors are used in determining reasonableness:

- The burden on the defendant;
- The forum State's interest in adjudicating the dispute;
- The plaintiff's interest in obtaining convenience and effective relief;
- The interstate judicial system's interest in obtaining the most efficient resolution of controversies; and
- The shared interest of the several States in furthering fundamental substantive social policies. 1A INPRAC R 12(12.6).

    iv. *Jurisdiction presumed.* Indiana state trial courts are courts of general jurisdiction and jurisdiction is presumed. The party contesting jurisdiction bears the burden of proving the lack of personal jurisdiction by a preponderance of the evidence, unless the lack of jurisdiction is apparent on the face of the complaint. A determination of the existence of personal jurisdiction is entitled to de novo review. 1A INPRAC R 12(12.6); Foley v. Schwartz, 943 N.E.2d 371 (Ind.Ct.App. 2011).

  c. *Challenge to jurisdiction in first response to complaint.* The defendant may challenge the Indiana court's jurisdiction over him, without submitting to that jurisdiction, so long as the defense is asserted in the first response to the plaintiff's complaint and the defendant does not request affirmative relief from the court prior to asserting that defense. 22 INPRAC § 15.16.

  d. *Burden shifting.* After the plaintiff establishes that there are minimum contacts between defendant and forum state to exercise personal jurisdiction without violating Due Process Clause, the defendant then carries the burden of proving that asserting jurisdiction is unfair and unreasonable. 1A INPRAC R 12(12.6); JPMorgan Chase Bank, N.A. v. Desert Palace, Inc., 882 N.E.2d 743 (Ind.Ct.App. 2008).

  e. *Effect of granting of motion.* The dismissal of a complaint for lack of jurisdiction over the person is not an adjudication on the merits and does not prejudice the plaintiff's right to file another complaint if the court can obtain jurisdiction over the defendant. 9 INPRAC § 42.4.

3. *Consolidation and waiver*

  a. *Consolidation of defenses in motion.* A party who makes a motion under IN ST TRIAL P Rule 12 may join with it any other motions herein provided for and then available to him. If a party makes a motion under IN ST TRIAL P Rule 12 but omits therefrom any defense or objection then available to him which IN ST TRIAL P Rule 12 permits to be raised by motion, he shall not thereafter make a motion based on the defense or objection so omitted. He may, however, make such motions as are allowed under IN ST TRIAL P Rule 12(H)(2). IN ST TRIAL P Rule 12(G).

  b. *Waiver or preservation of certain defenses.* No defense or objection is waived by being joined with one or more other defenses or objections in a responsive pleading or motion. IN ST TRIAL P Rule 12(B).

D. Documents

1. *Required documents*

  a. *Motion and notice.* The requirement of notice is satisfied by service of the motion. IN ST TRIAL P Rule 7(B). Refer to the General Requirements section of this document for information on the content of a motion to dismiss for lack of personal jurisdiction.

  b. *Brief.* All motions filed pursuant to IN ST TRIAL P Rule 12 and IN ST TRIAL P Rule 56 shall be accompanied by a separate supporting brief. IN ST LAKE RCP Rule 4(A).

  c. *Proposed order.* Unless local practice provides differently, a party should submit a proposed order with its written motion to be signed by the judge once the motion has been granted. 21 INPRAC § 13.8.

    i. Proposed orders, which are submitted for the court's convenience under IN ST LAKE RCP Rule 3 or other applicable Lake County Rules of Civil Procedure, shall be submitted as attachments to motions. IN ST LAKE RCP Rule 17(D)(8). Proposed orders shall be prepared and filed separately from the pleadings, petitions, motions or other papers to which they have reference. IN ST LAKE RCP Rule 3(B).

    ii. Orders, either routine in nature or uncontested including, for example, those setting or continuing a hearing, shall be effected by the chronological case summary entry only, which shall contain the concise substance of the order. IN ST LAKE RCP Rule 3(B).

    iii. All orders shall be accompanied with sufficient copies and stamped, pre-addressed envelopes, so that copies may be mailed to all parties. IN ST LAKE RCP Rule 3(B).

  d. *Chronological case summary (CCS) entry forms.* All filings shall be accompanied by a Chronological Case Summary (CCS) Entry Form to define or identify the documents filed. The Form used should be substantially similar to IN ST LAKE RCP App. A. IN ST LAKE RCP Rule 3(C).

  e. *Certificate of service.* An attorney or unrepresented party tendering a document to the Clerk for filing shall certify that service has been made, list the parties served, and specify the date and means of service. The certificate of service shall be placed at the end of the document and shall not be separately filed. The separate filing of a certificate of service, however, shall not be grounds for rejecting a document for filing. The Clerk may permit documents to be filed without a certificate of service but shall require prompt filing of a separate certificate of service. IN ST TRIAL P Rule 5(C).

    i. All pleadings, motions and other papers submitted for filing which are required to be served under IN ST TRIAL P Rule 5(A) shall contain proof of service pursuant to IN ST TRIAL P Rule 5(B)(2). IN ST LAKE RCP Rule 3(A).

2. *Supplemental documents*

  a. *Supporting evidence.* When a motion is based on facts not appearing of record the court may hear the matter on affidavits presented by the respective parties, but the court may direct that the matter be heard wholly or partly on oral testimony or depositions. IN ST TRIAL P Rule 43(B).

  b. *Facsimile cover sheet.* Any document sent to the Clerk of the Circuit Court by electronic facsimile transmission shall be accompanied by a cover sheet which states the title of the document, case number, number of pages, identity and voice telephone number of the sending party and instructions for filing. The cover sheet shall contain the signature of the attorney or party, pro se, authorizing the filing. IN ST ADMIN Rule 12(D).

E. Format

1. *Form of motions.* The rules applicable to captions, and the signing and form of pleadings (IN ST TRIAL P Rule 8 through IN ST TRIAL P Rule 11), apply to all motions and other papers provided under the Indiana Rules of Trial Procedure. 22B INPRAC 7:2.

2. *Form of pleadings.* For the purpose of uniformity, convenience, clarity and durability, requirements in IN ST LAKE RCP Rule 2 shall be observed in the preparation of all pleadings, motions and other papers. IN ST LAKE RCP Rule 2. Whenever materials submitted fail to meet the standards in IN ST LAKE RCP Rule 2, the Court may impose appropriate sanctions. IN ST LAKE RCP Rule 2(B).

  a. *Caption; Names of parties.* Every pleading shall contain a caption setting forth the name of the court, the title of the action, the file number, and a designation as in IN ST TRIAL P Rule 7(A). In the complaint the title of the action shall include the names of all the parties, but in other pleadings it is sufficient to state the name of the first party on each side with an appropriate indication of other parties. IN ST TRIAL P Rule 10(A).

    i. *Special judge matters.* The caption of all CCS Entry Forms, pleadings, motions, orders and other papers to be filed in a special judge case shall include in block text the words SPECIAL JUDGE and the name of the judge directly below the cause number on the caption. IN ST LAKE RCP Rule 2(D).

  b. *Paragraphs; Separate statements.* All averments of a claim or defense shall be made in numbered paragraphs, the contents of each of which shall be limited as far as practicable to a statement of a single set of circumstances, and a paragraph may be referred to by number in all succeeding pleadings. Each claim founded upon a separate transaction or occurrence and each defense other

than denials may be stated in a separate count or defense whenever a separation facilitates the clear presentation of the matters set forth. IN ST TRIAL P Rule 10(B).

c. *Adoption by reference; Exhibits.* Statements in a pleading may be adopted by reference in a different part of the same pleading or in another pleading or in any motion. A copy of any written instrument which is an exhibit to a pleading is a part thereof for all purposes. IN ST TRIAL P Rule 10(C).

d. *Paper; Print, quality and binding*

   i. All pleadings, motions, chronological case summary entry forms, orders, process and other papers shall be neatly and legibly printed, typewritten or mechanically reproduced, on one (1) side only, on white opaque paper. To satisfy the recordkeeping requirements of IN ST TRIAL P Rule 77, the print shall be of sufficient density and clarity for preservation and reproduction of microfilming, optical disk or other secondary sources. For this reason, the use of non-letter-quality printers is discouraged. IN ST LAKE RCP Rule 2(A).

   ii. Paper and ink shall be of such quality as to withstand the test of time. All documents shall be produced on acid-free, non-thermal paper. It is recommended that a minimum of twenty (20) pound, twenty-five percent (25%) cotton paper product be used. Documents of multiple pages shall be submitted in bound or stapled fashion, and the binding or stapling shall be at the top only. Covers or backings shall not be used. IN ST LAKE RCP Rule 2(A).

e. *Papers; Handwritten.* Handwritten papers may be filed only if approved by the Court and a typewritten or printed true rendition thereof is filed within three (3) days thereafter and approved by the Court. Upon such approval, they shall be deemed and filed as the original, while the handwritten papers shall be retained therewith for evidentiary purposes. IN ST LAKE RCP Rule 2(C).

f. *Minute sheets; Motion blanks.* Minute sheets and motion blanks shall no longer be used. IN ST LAKE RCP Rule 2(D).

3. *Size of papers for filing.* Effective January 1, 1992, all pleadings, copies, motions and documents filed with any trial court or appellate level court, typed or printed, with the exception of exhibits and existing wills, shall be prepared on eight and one-half by eleven inch (8 1/2" x 11") size paper. IN ST ADMIN Rule 11.

4. *Signature requirements*

a. *Signature of attorney.* Every pleading or motion of a party represented by an attorney shall be signed by at least one (1) attorney of record in his individual name, whose address, telephone number, and attorney number shall be stated, except that this provision shall not apply to pleadings and motions made and transcribed at the trial or a hearing before the judge and received by him in such form. IN ST TRIAL P Rule 11(A).

   i. The signature of an attorney constitutes a certificate by him that he has read the pleadings; that to the best of his knowledge, information, and belief, there is good ground to support it; and that it is not interposed for delay. IN ST TRIAL P Rule 11(A).

   ii. If a pleading or motion is not signed or is signed with intent to defeat the purpose of the rule, it may be stricken as sham and false and the action may proceed as though the pleading had not been served. IN ST TRIAL P Rule 11(A).

   iii. For a willful violation of IN ST TRIAL P Rule 11 an attorney may be subjected to appropriate disciplinary action. Similar action may be taken if scandalous or indecent matter is inserted. IN ST TRIAL P Rule 11(A).

b. *Signature of unrepresented party.* A party who is not represented by an attorney shall sign his pleading and state his address. IN ST TRIAL P Rule 11(A).

c. *Verification not generally required.* Except when specifically required by rule, pleadings or motions need not be verified or accompanied by affidavit. The rule in equity that the averments of an answer under oath must be overcome by the testimony of two (2) witnesses or of one (1) witness sustained by corroborating circumstances is abolished. IN ST TRIAL P Rule 11(A).

d. *Verification by affirmation or representation.* When in connection with any civil or special statutory proceeding it is required that any pleading, motion, petition, supporting affidavit, or other document

of any kind, be verified, or that an oath be taken, it shall be sufficient if the subscriber simply affirms the truth of the matter to be verified by an affirmation or representation. IN ST TRIAL P Rule 11(B). IN ST TRIAL P Rule 11(B) states that the affirmation or representation should be in substantially the following language: "I (we) affirm, under the penalties for perjury, that the foregoing representation(s) is (are) true. (Signed) _____."

    i. Any person who falsifies an affirmation or representation of fact shall be subject to the same penalties as are prescribed by law for the making of a false affidavit. IN ST TRIAL P Rule 11(B).

  e. *Verified pleadings, motions, and affidavits as evidence.* Pleadings, motions and affidavits accompanying or in support of such pleadings or motions when required to be verified or under oath shall be accepted as a representation that the signer had personal knowledge thereof or reasonable cause to believe the existence of the facts or matters stated or alleged therein; and, if otherwise competent or acceptable as evidence, may be admitted as evidence of the facts or matters stated or alleged therein when it is so provided in the Indiana Rules of Trial Procedure, by statute or other law, or to the extent the writing or signature expressly purports to be made upon the signer's personal knowledge. When such pleadings, motions and affidavits are verified or under oath they shall not require other or greater proof on the part of the adverse party than if not verified or not under oath unless expressly provided otherwise by the Indiana Rules of Trial Procedure, statute or other law. Affidavits upon motions for summary judgment under IN ST TRIAL P Rule 56 and in denial of execution under IN ST TRIAL P Rule 9.2 shall be made upon personal knowledge. IN ST TRIAL P Rule 11(C).

  f. *Electronic signature.* The filing of documents and information through the E-filing system by use of a valid username and password is presumed to have been authorized by the User to whom that username and password have been issued and documents filed through the E-filing system are presumed to have been signed by the same User. IN ST ADMIN Rule 16(E).

5. *Information excluded from public access.* Every document filed in a case shall separately identify information excluded from public access pursuant to IN ST ADMIN Rule 9(G)(1) as follows:

  a. Whole documents that are excluded from public access pursuant to IN ST ADMIN Rule 9(G)(1) shall be tendered on light green paper or have a light green coversheet attached to the document, marked "Not for Public Access" or "Confidential." IN ST TRIAL P Rule 5(G)(1).

  b. When only a portion of a document contains information excluded from public access pursuant to IN ST ADMIN Rule 9(G)(1), said information shall be omitted [or redacted] from the filed document, and set forth on a separate accompanying document on light green paper conspicuously marked "Not for Public Access" or "Confidential" and clearly designated [or identifying] the caption and number of the case and the document and location within the document to which the redacted material pertains. IN ST TRIAL P Rule 5(G)(2).

  c. With respect to documents filed in electronic format, the trial court, by local rule, may provide for compliance with IN ST TRIAL P Rule 5 in manner that separates and protects access to information excluded from public access. IN ST TRIAL P Rule 5(G)(3).

  d. IN ST TRIAL P Rule 5(G) does not apply to a record sealed by the court pursuant to IN ST 5-14-3-5.5 or otherwise, nor to records, documents, or information filed in cases to which public access is prohibited pursuant to IN ST ADMIN Rule 9(G). IN ST TRIAL P Rule 5(G)(4).

  e. The following information in case records is excluded from public access and is confidential:

    i. Information that is excluded from public access pursuant to federal law;

    ii. Information that is excluded from public access as declared confidential by Indiana statute or other court rule, including without limitation:

      • All adoption records created after July 8, 1941, as declared confidential by IN ST 31-19-19-1, et seq., except those specifically declared open by IN ST 31-19-13-2(2);

      • All records relating to chancroid, chlamydia, gonorrhea, hepatitis, human immunodeficiency virus (HIV), Lymphogranuloma venereum, syphilis, tuberculosis, as declared confidential by IN ST 16-41-8-1, et seq.;

- All records relating to child abuse as declared confidential by IN ST 31-33-18-1, et seq.;

- All records relating to drug tests as declared confidential by IN ST 5-14-3-4(a)(9);

- Records of grand jury proceedings as declared confidential by IN ST 35-34-2-4;

- Records of juvenile proceedings as declared confidential by IN ST 31-39-1-2, except those specifically open under statute;

- All paternity records created after July 1, 1941 as declared confidential by IN ST 31-14-11-15, IN ST 31-19-5-23, IN ST 31-39-1-1 and IN ST 31-39-1-2 [Editor's note: IN ST 31-14-11-15 was repealed effective May 9, 2013];

- All pre-sentence reports as declared confidential by IN ST 35-38-1-13;

- Written petitions to permit marriages without consent and orders directing the Clerk of Court to issue a marriage license to underage persons, as declared confidential by IN ST 31-11-1-6;

- Only those arrest warrants, search warrants, indictments and informations ordered confidential by the trial judge, prior to return of duly executed service as declared confidential by IN ST 5-14-3-4(b)(1);

- All medical, mental health, or tax records unless determined by law or regulation of any governmental custodian not to be confidential, released by the subject of such records, or declared by a court of competent jurisdiction to be essential to the resolution of litigation as declared confidential by IN ST 16-39-3-10, IN ST 6-4.1-5-10, IN ST 6-4.1-12-12, and IN ST 6-8.1-7-1;

- Personal information relating to jurors or prospective jurors, other than for the use of the parties and counsel, pursuant to IN ST JURY Rule 10;

- Information relating to protection from abuse orders, no-contact orders and workplace violence restraining orders as declared confidential by IN ST 5-2-9-6, et seq.;

- Mediation proceedings pursuant to IN ST ADR Rule 2.11, Mini-Trial proceedings pursuant to IN ST ADR Rule 4.4(C), and Summary Jury Trials pursuant to IN ST ADR Rule 5.6;

- Information in probation files pursuant to the Probation Standards promulgated by the Judicial Conference of Indiana pursuant to IN ST 11-13-1-8(b);

- Information deemed confidential pursuant to the Rules for Court Administered Alcohol and Drug Programs promulgated by the Judicial Conference of Indiana pursuant to IN ST 12-23-14-13;

- Information deemed confidential pursuant to the Problem-Solving Court Rules promulgated by the Judicial Conference of Indiana pursuant to IN ST 33-23-16-16;

- All records of the Department of workforce Development as declared confidential by IN ST 22-4-19-6;

- Information regarding interception of electronic communications that is sealed or deemed confidential as set forth in IN ST 35-33.5-2-1, et seq.

iii. Information excluded from public access by specific court order;

iv. Complete Social Security Numbers of living persons;

v. With the exception of names, information such as addresses, phone numbers, and dates of birth which explicitly identifies:

- Natural persons who are witnesses or victims (not including defendants) in criminal, domestic violence, stalking, sexual assault, juvenile, or civil protection order proceedings, provided that juveniles who are victims of sex crimes shall be identified by initials only;

- Places of residence of judicial officers, clerks and other employees of courts and clerks of court, unless the person or persons about whom the information pertains waives confidentiality;

     vi.   Complete account numbers of specific assets, loans, bank accounts, credit cards, and personal identification numbers (PINs);

    vii.   All orders of expungement entered in criminal or juvenile proceedings, orders to restrict access to criminal history information pursuant to IN ST 35-38-5-5.5 or IN ST 35-38-8-5 and records excluded from public access by such orders, and information related to infractions that is excluded from public access pursuant to IN ST 34-28-5-15 or IN ST 34-28-5-16 [Editor's note: IN ST 35-38-5-5.5, IN ST 35-38-8-5 and IN ST 34-28-5-16 were repealed effective July 1, 2013; for information on orders restricting access to criminal history, refer to IN ST 35-38-9-1, et seq.];

    viii.   All personal notes and e-mail, and deliberative material, of judges, jurors, court staff and judicial agencies, and information recorded in personal data assistants (PDA's) or organizers and personal calendars. IN ST ADMIN Rule 9(G)(1).

6.   *Format of electronically filed documents*

   a.   *Generally.* Electronically filed documents must meet the same requirements of format as documents conventionally filed pursuant to IN ST LAKE RCP Rule 2 or other applicable Lake County Rules of Civil Procedure. IN ST LAKE RCP Rule 17(D)(1).

   b.   *Titles of documents.* The person electronically filing a document will be responsible for designating a title for the document at the time it is filed. The LCOD will generate the appropriate entry onto the CCS to record the filing of the document. IN ST LAKE RCP Rule 17(D)(3).

   c.   *Citations and hyperlinks.* Electronically filed documents may contain hyperlink references to an external document as a convenient mechanism for accessing material cited in the document. Filers wishing to insert hyperlinks into documents shall continue to use the traditional method of citation to authority in addition to the hyperlink provided. The hyperlink is merely a convenience to the court and the material referenced is extraneous to the file and not a part of the court's record. IN ST LAKE RCP Rule 17(D)(5).

   d.   *Attachments and exhibits.* All documents which form part of a single submission and which are being filed at the same time and by the same filer may be electronically filed together under one document filing, e.g., the motion, supporting affidavits, memorandum in support, designation of evidence, exhibits. IN ST LAKE RCP Rule 17(D)(6).

     i.   Large documents which do not exist in an electronic format shall be scanned into .pdf format and filed electronically as separate attachments. A scanner is available in each clerk's office for use by the public and the bar in scanning and saving image files if needed. IN ST LAKE RCP Rule 17(D)(6).

   e.   *Electronic signatures*

     i.   *Electronic filing as signature.* The electronic filing of a document which is required to be signed shall constitute the filer's representation under IN ST TRIAL P Rule 11. Unless the electronically filed document has been scanned and shows the filer's original signature, the signature of the filer shall be indicated by As/Attorney's Name, or As/Party's Name as in the case of a pro se litigant, on the line where the signature would otherwise appear. IN ST LAKE RCP Rule 17(G)(1).

     ii.   *Signatures on jointly signed or filed, verified or other documents.* In the case of a stipulation, agreed order, jointly signed motion or other document which needs to be signed by two (2) or more persons, or in the case of documents which must contain original signatures and which require verification or an unsworn declaration under rule or statute, the signatures may be indicated by either:

       •   Submitting a scanned copy of the originally signed document; or,

       •   Submitting the document with the use of As/Name in the signature block(s) where the original signature(s) appear(s) in the original document; provided, however, that the filer shall first obtain the physical signature of all persons necessary. IN ST LAKE RCP Rule 17(G)(2).

iii. *Retention of original.* The filer shall retain the original executed document. IN ST LAKE RCP Rule 17(G).

7. *Citation of local rules.* The local rules for Lake County may be known as the Lake County Rules of Civil Procedure, and abbreviated as LR. IN ST LAKE RCP Rule 1(C).

F. Filing and Service Requirements

1. *Filing requirements.* Except as otherwise provided in IN ST TRIAL P Rule 5(E)(2), all pleadings and papers subsequent to the complaint which are required to be served upon a party shall be filed with the Court either before service or within a reasonable period of time thereafter. IN ST TRIAL P Rule 5(E)(1). All papers presented for filing shall be submitted to the Clerk and not to the court. All papers submitted for filing shall be mailed or delivered to the Clerk's office at the courthouse in which the case is pending. IN ST LAKE RCP Rule 3(A).

   a. *Filing with the court defined.* The filing of pleadings, motions, and other papers with the court as required by the Indiana Rules of Trial Procedure shall be made by one of the following methods:

      i. Delivery to the clerk of the court;

      ii. Sending by electronic transmission under the procedure adopted pursuant to IN ST ADMIN Rule 12;

      iii. Mailing to the clerk by registered, certified or express mail return receipt requested;

      iv. Depositing with any third-party commercial carrier for delivery to the clerk within three (3) calendar days, cost prepaid, properly addressed;

      v. If the court so permits, filing with the judge, in which event the judge shall note thereon the filing date and forthwith transmit them to the office of the clerk; or

      vi. Electronic filing, as approved by the Division of State Court Administration pursuant to IN ST ADMIN Rule 16. IN ST TRIAL P Rule 5(F).

      vii. Filing by registered or certified mail and by third-party commercial carrier shall be complete upon mailing or deposit. IN ST TRIAL P Rule 5(F).

   b. *Mandatory electronic filing.* Unless otherwise permitted by the Lake County Rules of Civil Procedure or otherwise authorized by the judicial officer assigned to a particular case, all documents submitted for filing (including the original complaint, or equivalent pleading, and summons) shall be filed electronically with the clerk using the LCOD, no matter when the case was originally filed. IN ST LAKE RCP Rule 17(D).

      i. *Of documents containing information excluded from public access pursuant to* IN ST ADMIN Rule 9. Documents containing information excluded from public access pursuant to IN ST ADMIN Rule 9, or documents which are ordered to be filed under seal shall be filed electronically, pursuant to IN ST LAKE RCP Rule 17(D)(9), whenever possible, along with a copy of the applicable order to seal the records, and the filer shall designate the documents as "Not for Public Access Pursuant to Administrative Rule 9(G)(1)" at the time of filing. IN ST LAKE RCP Rule 16(A)(1); IN ST LAKE RCP Rule 17(D)(9).

         • *Conventional filing of documents containing information excluded from public access pursuant to* IN ST ADMIN Rule 9. Documents containing information excluded from public access pursuant to IN ST ADMIN Rule 9, or documents which are ordered to be filed under seal, which cannot be legibly scanned and filed electronically, shall be conventionally filed under seal and designated by the filer as "Not for Public Access Pursuant to Administrative Rule 9(G)(1)" at the time of filing. The unredacted version shall be filed on light green paper which is conspicuously marked "Not for Public Access"; and a redacted version, with confidential information deleted, shall be filed on white paper which shall be available for public access. The filer shall also electronically file a Notice of Manual Filing. IN ST LAKE RCP Rule 16(A)(2).

      ii. *Technical failures.* If a registered user is unable to file a document in a timely manner due to technical difficulties in the LCOD, the registered user must file a document with the court as soon as possible notifying the court of the inability to file the document. A sample document titled Declaration that Party was Unable to File in a Timely Manner Due to Technical Difficulties can be found at IN ST LAKE RCP Form 4. Delayed filings shall be rejected unless accompanied by the declaration attesting to the filer's failed attempts to file electronically at least two (2) times, separated by at least one (1) hour, after noon on each day of delay due to such technical failure. IN ST LAKE RCP Rule 17(J).

    iii. *Documents allowed to be filed conventionally.* Unless specifically authorized by the court, only the following documents may be filed conventionally and not electronically:

- Exhibits and other documents that cannot be converted to a legible electronic form, such as videotapes, x-rays, and similar materials
- Documents delivered to the clerk by pro se litigants
- Documents mailed to the clerk by pro se litigants
- Confidential documents
- Notice of manual filing
- Titles of documents
- Chronological case summary entry forms (CCS entry forms). IN ST LAKE RCP Rule 17(E).
- For more information on the documents which must be filed conventionally, refer to IN ST LAKE RCP Rule 17(E).

  c. *Facsimile filing.* Only when necessary on an emergency basis (i.e., when certified mail or other means of filing will not bring the document to the Judge's attention prior to the scheduled hearing or ruling), pleadings, motions and other papers may be filed by electronic facsimile transmission, or when specifically authorized by the Court. IN ST LAKE RCP Rule 2(C).

    i. *Generally.* In counties where a majority of judges of the courts of record, by posted local rule, have authorized electronic facsimile filing and designated a telephone number to receive such transmissions, pleadings, motions, and other papers may be sent to the Clerk of Circuit Court by electronic facsimile transmission for filing in any case, provided:

- Such matter does not exceed ten (10) pages, including the cover sheet;
- Such matter does not require the payment of fees other than the electronic facsimile transcription fee set forth in IN ST ADMIN Rule 12(E);
- The sending party creates at the time of transmission a machine generated log for such transmission; and
- The original document and the transmission log are maintained by the sending party for the duration of the litigation. IN ST ADMIN Rule 12(B).

    ii. *Time of filing.* During normal, posted business hours, the time of filing shall be the time the duplicate document is produced in the office of the Clerk of the Circuit Court. Duplicate documents received at all other times shall be filed as of the next normal business day. IN ST ADMIN Rule 12(C).

- If the receiving fax machine endorses its own time and date stamp upon the transmitted documents and the receiving machine produces a delivery receipt which is electronically created and transmitted to the sending party, the time of filing shall be the date and time recorded on the transmitted document by the receiving fax machine. IN ST ADMIN Rule 12(C).

  d. *Filing for special judges.* For special judge matters where the special judge is a full-time judge or magistrate serving within Lake County, all papers submitted for filing shall be delivered or mailed to the Clerk's office at the courthouse where the special judge regularly serves. IN ST LAKE RCP Rule 3(A).

  e. *Proof of filing.* Any party filing any paper by any method other than personal delivery to the clerk shall retain proof of filing. IN ST TRIAL P Rule 5(F).

2. *Service requirements.* Unless otherwise provided by the Indiana Rules of Trial Procedure or an order of the court, each party and special judge, if any, shall be served with: (1) every order required by its terms to be served; (2) every pleading subsequent to the original complaint; (3) every written motion except one which may be heard ex parte; (4) every brief submitted to the trial court; (5) every paper relating to discovery required to be served upon a party; and (6) every written notice, appearance, demand, offer of judgment, designation of record on appeal, or similar paper. IN ST TRIAL P Rule 5(A).

    a. *Methods of service*

        i. *Personal service.* Whenever a party is represented by an attorney of record, service shall be made upon such attorney unless service upon the party himself is ordered by the court. Service upon the attorney or party shall be made by delivering or mailing a copy of the papers to the last known address or where an attorney or party has consented to service by fax or e-mail, as provided in IN ST TRIAL P Rule 3.1(A)(4), by faxing or e-mailing a copy of the documents to the fax number or e-mail address set out in the appearance form or correction as required by IN ST TRIAL P Rule 3.1(E). IN ST TRIAL P Rule 5(B). Delivery of a copy within IN ST TRIAL P Rule 5 means:

            *   Offering or tendering it to the attorney or party and stating the nature of the papers being served. Refusal to accept an offered or tendered document is a waiver of any objection to the sufficiency or adequacy of service of that document;

            *   Leaving it at his office with a clerk or other person in charge thereof, or if there is no one in charge, leaving it in a conspicuous place therein; or

            *   If the office is closed, by leaving it at his dwelling house or usual place of abode with some person of suitable age and discretion then residing therein; or,

            *   Leaving it at some other suitable place, selected by the attorney upon whom service is being made, pursuant to duly promulgated local rule. IN ST TRIAL P Rule 5(B)(1).

        ii. *Service by mail.* If service is made by mail, the papers shall be deposited in the United States mail addressed to the person on whom they are being served, with postage prepaid. Service shall be deemed complete upon mailing. Proof of service of all papers permitted to be mailed may be made by written acknowledgment of service, by affidavit of the person who mailed the papers, or by certificate of an attorney. It shall be the duty of attorneys when entering their appearance in a cause or when filing pleadings or papers therein, to have noted in the Chronological Case Summary or said pleadings or papers so filed the address and telephone number of their office. Service by delivery or by mail at such address shall be deemed sufficient and complete. IN ST TRIAL P Rule 5(B)(2).

        iii. *Service by fax or e-mail.* A party who has consented to service by fax or e-mail may be served as follows:

            *   Service by e-mail shall be made by attaching the document being served in .pdf format. Discovery documents must also be served in accordance with IN ST TRIAL P Rule 26(A). IN ST TRIAL P Rule 5(B)(3)(a).

            *   Service by fax shall be deemed complete upon generation of a transmission record indicating the successful transmission of the entire document, except as provided in IN ST TRIAL P Rule 5(B)(3)(d). IN ST TRIAL P Rule 5(B)(3)(b).

            *   Service by e-mail shall be deemed complete upon transmission, except as provided in IN ST TRIAL P Rule 5(B)(3)(d). IN ST TRIAL P Rule 5(B)(3)(c).

            *   Service by fax or e-mail that occurs on a Saturday, Sunday, legal holiday, or day the court or agency in which the matter is pending is closed or after 5:00 PM local time of the recipient shall be deemed complete the next day that is not a Saturday, Sunday, legal holiday, or day that the court or agency in which the matter is pending is not closed. IN ST TRIAL P Rule 5(B)(3)(d).

b. *Serving numerous defendants.* In any action in which there are unusually large numbers of defendants, the court, upon motion or of its own initiative, may order:

    i. That service of the pleadings of the defendants and replies thereto need not be made as between the defendants;

- That any cross-claim, counterclaim, or matter constituting an avoidance or affirmative defense contained therein shall be deemed to be denied or avoided by all other parties; and

- That the filing of any such pleading and service thereof upon the plaintiff constitutes due notice of it to the parties. IN ST TRIAL P Rule 5(D).

    ii. A copy of every such order shall be served upon the parties in such manner and form as the court directs. IN ST TRIAL P Rule 5(D).

c. *Service by electronic means.* The Lake County Online Docket will generate a Notice of Electronic Filing and Service when any document is filed and served. This notice will be emailed to each registered user of record in a case, and an electronic service event will be added to the work queue of each registered user of record in the case. The party filing the document should retain a paper or electronic copy of the Notice of Electronic Filing and Service. This notice represents proof of filing and service of the document on registered users of record in that case. The filer shall not be required to conventionally serve any document on any party receiving electronic service. IN ST LAKE RCP Rule 17(F)(2).

    i. The filer shall also conventionally serve those parties not designated or able to receive electronic notice or service but who are nevertheless entitled to notice of said pleading or other document in accordance with the Indiana Rules of Civil Procedure and applicable Lake County Rules of Civil Procedure. In such cases, the filer shall also file a certificate of service, as appropriate. IN ST LAKE RCP Rule 17(F).

d. *Service on parties in default for failure to appear.* No service need be made on parties in default for failure to appear, except that pleadings asserting new or additional claims for relief against them shall be served upon them in the manner provided by service of summons in IN ST TRIAL P Rule 4. IN ST TRIAL P Rule 5(A).

G. Hearings

1. *Hearing on motion.* Unless local conditions make it impracticable, each judge shall establish regular times and places, at intervals sufficiently frequent for the prompt dispatch of business, at which motions requiring notice and hearing may be heard and disposed of; but the judge at any time or place and on such notice, if any, as he considers reasonable may make order for the advancement, conduct, and hearing of actions. To expedite its business the court may direct the submission and determination of motions without oral hearing upon brief written statements of reasons in support and opposition, or direct or permit hearings by telephone conference call with all attorneys or other similar means of communication. IN ST TRIAL P Rule 73(A).

2. *Oral argument discretionary.* The granting of a motion for oral argument, unless required by the Indiana Rules of Trial Procedure, shall be wholly discretionary with the court. IN ST LAKE RCP Rule 4(B).

H. Forms

1. Motion to Dismiss for Lack of Personal Jurisdiction Forms for Indiana

a. General form. 5 INPRAC § 3:4.1.

b. Lack of personal jurisdiction. 5 INPRAC § 3:4.3.

c. Certificate of service; Personal service. 9 INPRAC § 5.7.

d. Certificate of service; First class mail. 9 INPRAC § 5.8.

e. Motion to dismiss plaintiff's complaint; General form. 9 INPRAC § 42.2.

f. Lack of personal jurisdiction. 9 INPRAC § 42.4.

2. Official Motion to Dismiss for Lack of Personal Jurisdiction Forms for Lake County

a. CCS entry form. IN ST LAKE RCP App. A.

     b.   Notice of manual filing. IN ST LAKE RCP Form 2.

     c.   Certificate of service. IN ST LAKE RCP Form 3.

     d.   Declaration that party was unable to file in a timely manner. IN ST LAKE RCP Form 4.

3. Motion to Dismiss for Lack of Personal Jurisdiction Forms for Lake County

     a.   Notice of manual filing. EFORMST IN 5540.

I. Checklist

  (I)   ❑ Matters to be considered by moving party

     (a)   ❑ Required documents

        (1) ❑ Motion and notice

        (2) ❑ Brief

        (3) ❑ Proposed order

        (4) ❑ Chronological case summary (CSS) entry forms

        (5) ❑ Certificate of service

     (b)   ❑ Supplemental documents

        (1) ❑ Supporting evidence

        (2) ❑ Facsimile cover sheet

     (c)   ❑ Timing

        (1) ❑ A motion to dismiss for lack of personal jurisdiction shall be made before pleading if a further pleading is permitted or within twenty (20) days after service of the prior pleading if none is required

        (2) ❑ A written motion, other than one which may be heard ex parte, and notice of the hearing thereof shall be served not less than five (5) days before the time specified for the hearing, unless a different period is fixed by the Indiana Rules of Trial Procedure or by order of the court

        (3) ❑ All pleadings and papers subsequent to the complaint which are required to be served upon a party shall be filed with the Court either before service or within a reasonable period of time thereafter

        (4) ❑ All pleadings, motions and other papers submitted for filing which are required to be served under IN ST TRIAL P Rule 5(A) shall be filed no later than three (3) days after service

        (5) ❑ If such papers are filed before service, proof of service thereof shall be filed no later than three (3) business days thereafter

  (II) ❑ Matters to be considered by the responding party

     (a)   ❑ Required documents

        (1) ❑ Opposition

        (2) ❑ Chronological case summary (CSS) entry forms

        (3) ❑ Certificate of service

     (b)   ❑ Supplemental documents

        (1) ❑ Supporting evidence

        (2) ❑ Proposed order

        (3) ❑ Facsimile cover sheet

     (c)   ❑ Timing

        (1) ❑ So long as consistent with the Indiana Rules of Trial Procedure, an adverse party wishing to respond shall do so within fifteen (15) days of service

(2) ❏ Except as otherwise provided in IN ST TRIAL P Rule 59(D), opposing affidavits may be served not less than one (1) day before the hearing, unless the court permits them to be served at some other time

Requests, Notices and Applications
Interrogatories

Document Last Updated October 2013

A. Applicable Rules

1. *State rules*

   a. Appearance. IN ST TRIAL P Rule 3.1.

   b. Process. IN ST TRIAL P Rule 4.

   c. Service and filing of pleadings and other papers. IN ST TRIAL P Rule 5.

   d. Time. IN ST TRIAL P Rule 6.

   e. Pleadings. IN ST TRIAL P Rule 7; IN ST TRIAL P Rule 9.2; IN ST TRIAL P Rule 10.

   f. Signing and verification of pleadings. IN ST TRIAL P Rule 11.

   g. General provisions governing discovery. IN ST TRIAL P Rule 26.

   h. Methods of discovery. IN ST TRIAL P Rule 27; IN ST TRIAL P Rule 29; IN ST TRIAL P Rule 30; IN ST TRIAL P Rule 31; IN ST TRIAL P Rule 33; IN ST TRIAL P Rule 34; IN ST TRIAL P Rule 35; IN ST TRIAL P Rule 36.

   i. Failure to make or cooperate in discovery; Sanctions. IN ST TRIAL P Rule 37.

   j. Judgment on the evidence (directed verdict). IN ST TRIAL P Rule 50.

   k. Findings by the court. IN ST TRIAL P Rule 52.

   l. Summary judgment. IN ST TRIAL P Rule 56.

   m. Motion to correct error. IN ST TRIAL P Rule 59.

   n. Relief from judgment or order. IN ST TRIAL P Rule 60.

   o. Court records. IN ST TRIAL P Rule 77.

   p. Access to court records. IN ST ADMIN Rule 9.

   q. Paper size. IN ST ADMIN Rule 11.

   r. Facsimile transmission. IN ST ADMIN Rule 12.

   s. Electronic filing and electronic service pilot projects. IN ST ADMIN Rule 16.

   t. Privacy and confidentiality. IN ST 5-2-9-6; IN ST 5-14-3-4; IN ST 5-14-3-5.5; IN ST 6-4.1-5-10; IN ST 6-4.1-12-12; IN ST 6-8.1-7-1; IN ST 11-13-1-8; IN ST 12-23-14-13; IN ST 16-39-3-10; IN ST 16-41-8-1; IN ST 22-4-19-6; IN ST 31-11-1-6; IN ST 31-19-5-23; IN ST 31-19-13-2; IN ST 31-19-19-1; IN ST 31-33-18-1; IN ST 31-39-1-1; IN ST 31-39-1-2; IN ST 33-23-16-16; IN ST 35-34-2-4; IN ST 35-38-1-13; IN ST 35-38-9-1; IN ST ADR Rule 2.11; IN ST ADR Rule 4.4; IN ST ADR Rule 5.6; IN ST JURY Rule 10.

2. *Local rules*

   a. Scope and title. [IN ST LAKE RCP Rule 1, as amended by IN ORDER 13-0237, effective October 18, 2013].

   b. Preparation of pleadings, motions and other papers. IN ST LAKE RCP Rule 2.

   c. Filing. [IN ST LAKE RCP Rule 3, as amended by IN ORDER 13-0237, effective October 18, 2013].

   d. Discovery. IN ST LAKE RCP Rule 8.

   e. Confidential information and sealed documents. IN ST LAKE RCP Rule 16.

f. Electronic filing and service. IN ST LAKE RCP Rule 17.

B. Timing

1. *Service of interrogatories.* Interrogatories may, without leave of court, be served upon the plaintiff after commencement of the action and upon any other party with or after service of the summons and complaint upon that party. IN ST TRIAL P Rule 33(A).

2. *Service of responses to interrogatories.* The party upon whom the interrogatories have been served shall serve a copy of the answers and objections within a period designated by the party submitting the interrogatories, not less than thirty (30) days after the service thereof or within such shorter or longer time as the court may allow. IN ST TRIAL P Rule 33(C).

3. *Computation of time*

   a. *Generally; Days excluded.* In computing any period of time prescribed or allowed by the Indiana Rules of Trial Procedure, by order of the court, or by any applicable statute, the day of the act, event, or default from which the designated period of time begins to run shall not be included. The last day of the period so computed is to be included unless it is:

      i. A Saturday,

      ii. A Sunday,

      iii. A legal holiday as defined by state statute, or

      iv. A day the office in which the act is to be done is closed during regular business hours. IN ST TRIAL P Rule 6(A).

   b. *Short periods.* In any event, the period runs until the end of the next day that is not a Saturday, a Sunday, a legal holiday, or a day on which the office is closed. When the period of time allowed is less than seven (7) days, intermediate Saturdays, Sundays, legal holidays, and days on which the office is closed shall be excluded from the computations. IN ST TRIAL P Rule 6(A).

   c. *Additional time after service by United States mail.* Whenever a party has the right or is required to do some act or take some proceedings within a prescribed period after the service of a notice or other paper upon him and the notice or paper is served upon him by United States mail, three (3) days shall be added to the prescribed period. IN ST TRIAL P Rule 6(E).

   d. *Electronic filing does not alter deadlines.* Filing electronically does not alter any filing deadlines or any time computation pursuant to state or federal statutes, any Rules of the Indiana Supreme Court, including without limitation the Rules of Trial Procedure, the Rules of Appellate Procedure or the Administrative Rules, or applicable Lake County Rules of Civil Procedure. The office of the Lake County Clerk is open for electronic filing under the Lake County Rules of Civil Procedure twenty-four (24) hours a day. A document is deemed filed at the date and time it is received by the LCOD server. Filing must be completed before midnight local time in order to be considered filed that day. Lake County observes Central Time and electronic filers are strongly urged to file documents during hours when the Lake County Online Docket ("LCOD") help line is available, from 9:00 a.m. to 4:00 p.m. local time, although documents can be filed electronically twenty-four (24) hours a day. IN ST LAKE RCP Rule 17(I).

   e. *Enlargement of time.* When an act is required or allowed to be done at or within a specific time by the Indiana Rules of Trial Procedure, the court may at any time for cause shown:

      i. Order the period enlarged, with or without motion or notice, if request therefor is made before the expiration of the period originally prescribed or extended by a previous order; or

      ii. Upon motion made after the expiration of the specific period, permit the act to be done where the failure to act was the result of excusable neglect; but, the court may not extend the time for taking any action for judgment on the evidence under IN ST TRIAL P Rule 50(A), amendment of findings and judgment under IN ST TRIAL P Rule 52(B), to correct errors under IN ST TRIAL P Rule 59(C), statement in opposition to motion to correct error under IN ST TRIAL P Rule 59(E), or to obtain relief from final judgment under IN ST TRIAL P Rule 60(B), except to the extent and under the conditions stated in those rules. IN ST TRIAL P Rule 6(B).

C. General Requirements

1. *Scope of discovery.* Unless otherwise limited by order of the court in accordance with the Indiana Rules of Trial Procedure, the scope of discovery is as follows:

   a. *In general.* Parties may obtain discovery regarding any matter, not privileged, which is relevant to the subject-matter involved in the pending action, whether it relates to the claim or defense of the party seeking discovery or the claim or defense of any other party, including the existence, description, nature, custody, condition and location of any books, documents, or other tangible things and the identity and location of persons having knowledge of any discoverable matter. It is not ground for objection that the information sought will be inadmissible at the trial if the information sought appears reasonably calculated to lead to the discovery of admissible evidence. IN ST TRIAL P Rule 26(B)(1).

      i. *Limiting discovery upon court determination.* The frequency or extent of use of the discovery methods otherwise permitted under the Indiana Rules of Trial Procedure and by any local rule shall be limited by the court if it determines that:

         - The discovery sought is unreasonably cumulative or duplicative, or is obtainable from some other source that is more convenient, less burdensome, or less expensive;

         - The party seeking discovery has had ample opportunity by discovery in the action to obtain the information sought or;

         - The burden or expense of the proposed discovery outweighs its likely benefit, taking into account the needs of the case, the amount in controversy, the parties' resources, the importance of the issues at stake in the litigation, and the importance of the proposed discovery in resolving the issues. IN ST TRIAL P Rule 26(B)(1).

         - The court may act upon its own initiative after reasonable notice or pursuant to a motion under IN ST TRIAL P Rule 26(C). IN ST TRIAL P Rule 26(B)(1). Refer to the Indiana KeyRules Motion for Protective Order document for more information.

      ii. *Relevancy in the discovery context.* When the word "relevancy" is used in IN ST TRIAL P Rule 26(B), it does not mean "relevancy" as that word in used to determine the admissibility of evidence in a trial court. It is much broader. It means "relevancy" to the "subject matter" of the litigation or pending action and it may relate to the claim or defense of any party. Pretrial discovery is available as to any nonprivileged matter relevant to the subject matter of the lawsuit or to obtain information reasonably calculated to lead to admissible evidence. 2A INPRAC R 26(26.4); Kaufmann v. Credithrift Financial, Inc., 465 N.E.2d 207, 210 (Ind.Ct.App. 1984).

      iii. *Tests for relevance.* Indiana case law has developed two (2) additional tests in this area. 2A INPRAC R 26(26.4).

         - The first test determines when a document or a request for information is actually relevant to the subject matter in the pending action. A document [or discovery request] is relevant to discovery if there is the possibility the information sought may be relevant to the subject matter of the action. 2A INPRAC R 26(26.4); CIGNA-INA/Aetna v. Hagerman-Shambaugh, 473 N.E.2d 1033, 1036 (Ind.Ct.App. 1985).

         - The second test speaks to appellate review of the trial court's determination that a document or discovery request is relevant to the subject matter of the pending action. The appellate court sees its review of the trial court's decision on relevancy to subject matter as being very limited. The court states: "Our review of the trial court's conclusion that the documents are relevant is limited. A trial court is vested with discretion in its rulings on discovery issues." 2A INPRAC R 26(26.4); Costanzi v. Ryan, 175 Ind.App. 257, 370 N.E.2d 1333 (Ind.Ct.App. 1978).

   b. *Insurance agreements.* A party may obtain discovery of the existence and contents of any insurance agreement under which any person carrying on an insurance business may be liable to satisfy part or all of a judgment which may be entered in the action or to indemnify or reimburse for payments made to satisfy the judgment. Information concerning the insurance agreement is not by reason of

disclosure admissible in evidence at trial. For purposes of IN ST TRIAL P Rule 26(B)(2), an application for insurance shall not be treated as part of an insurance agreement. IN ST TRIAL P Rule 26(B)(2).

c. *Trial preparation; Materials.* Subject to the provisions of IN ST TRIAL P Rule 26(B)(4), a party may obtain discovery of documents and tangible things otherwise discoverable under IN ST TRIAL P Rule 26(B)(1) and prepared in anticipation of litigation or for trial by or for another party or by or for that other party's representative (including his attorney, consultant, surety, indemnitor, insurer, or agent) only upon a showing that the party seeking discovery has substantial need of the materials in the preparation of his case and that he is unable without undue hardship to obtain the substantial equivalent of the materials by other means. In ordering discovery of such materials when the required showing has been made, the court shall protect against disclosure of the mental impressions, conclusions, opinions, or legal theories of an attorney or other representative of a party concerning the litigation. IN ST TRIAL P Rule 26(B)(3).

   i.   A party may obtain without the required showing a statement concerning the action or its subject matter previously made by that party. Upon request, a person not a party may obtain without the required showing a statement concerning the action or its subject matter previously made by that person. If the request is refused, the person may move for a court order. The provisions of IN ST TRIAL P Rule 37(A)(4) apply to the award of expenses incurred in relation to the motion. For purposes of IN ST TRIAL P Rule 26(B)(3), a statement previously made is:

   - A written statement signed or otherwise adopted approved by the person making it, or

   - A stenographic, mechanical, electrical, or other recording, or a transcription thereof, which is a substantially verbatim recital of an oral statement by the person making it and contemporaneously recorded. IN ST TRIAL P Rule 26(B)(3).

   ii. The protection of IN ST TRIAL P Rule 26(B)(3) extends to material prepared or collected before litigation actually commences, but that some possibility of litigation must actually exist before the privilege and IN ST TRIAL P Rule 26(B)(3) become operative. 2A INPRAC R 26(26.9); CIGNA-INA/Aetna v. Hagerman-Shambaugh, 473 N.E.2d 1033, 1037 (Ind.Ct.App. 1985).

d. *Trial preparation; Experts.* Discovery of facts known and opinions held by experts, otherwise discoverable under the provisions of IN ST TRIAL P Rule 26(B)(1) and acquired or developed in anticipation of litigation or for trial, may be obtained as follows:

   i.   A party may through interrogatories require any other party to identify each person whom the other party expects to call as an expert witness at trial, to state the subject matter on which the expert is expected to testify, and to state the substance of the facts and opinions to which the expert is expected to testify and a summary of the grounds for each opinion. IN ST TRIAL P Rule 26(B)(4)(a)(i).

   ii. Upon motion, the court may order further discovery by other means, subject to such restrictions as to scope and such provisions, pursuant to IN ST TRIAL P Rule 26(B)(4)(c), concerning fees and expenses as the court may deem appropriate. IN ST TRIAL P Rule 26(B)(4)(a)(ii).

   iii. A party may discover facts known or opinions held by an expert who has been retained or specially employed by another party in anticipation of litigation or preparation for trial and who is not expected to be called as a witness at trial, only as provided in IN ST TRIAL P Rule 35(B) or upon a showing of exceptional circumstances under which it is impracticable for the party seeking discovery to obtain facts or opinions on the same subject by other means. IN ST TRIAL P Rule 26(B)(4)(b).

   iv. Unless manifest injustice would result,

   - The court shall require that the party seeking discovery pay the expert a reasonable fee for time spent in responding to discovery under IN ST TRIAL P Rule 26(B)(4)(a)(ii) and IN ST TRIAL P Rule 26(B)(4)(b); and

   - With respect to discovery obtained under IN ST TRIAL P Rule 26(B)(4)(a)(ii) the court may require, and with respect to discovery obtained under IN ST TRIAL P Rule

26(B)(4)(b) the court shall require, the party seeking discovery to pay the other party a fair portion of the fees and expenses reasonably incurred by the latter party in obtaining facts and opinions from the expert. IN ST TRIAL P Rule 26(B)(4)(c).

e. *Claims of privilege or protection*

    i. *Information withheld.* When a party withholds information otherwise discoverable under the Indiana Rules of Trial Procedure by claiming that it is privileged or subject to protection as trial preparation material, the party shall make the claim expressly and shall describe the nature of the documents, communications, or things not produced or disclosed in a manner that, without revealing information itself privileged or protected, will enable other parties to assess the applicability of the privilege or protection. IN ST TRIAL P Rule 26(B)(5)(a).

    ii. *Information produced.* If information is produced in discovery that is subject to a claim of privilege or protection as trial-preparation material, the party making the claim may notify any party that received the information of the claim and the basis for it. After being notified, a party must promptly return, sequester, or destroy the specified information and any copies it has and may not use or disclose the information until the claim is resolved. A receiving party may promptly present the information to the court under seal for a determination of the claim. If the receiving party disclosed the information before being notified, it must take reasonable steps to retrieve it. The producing party must preserve the information until the claim is resolved. IN ST TRIAL P Rule 26(B)(5)(b).

    iii. *Waiver.* The law of discovery has developed some holdings which indicate that "waiver" of a privileged communication in a discovery setting might be more exacting than "waiver" of a privileged communication when the only question at hand is an interpretation of the privilege itself. Thus, in litigation in which several documents are in issue, and some are released inadvertently, there is strong case law that holds that the "inadvertent production" of a privileged document does not constitute a waiver of the attorney-client privilege. 2A INPRAC R 26(26.5); Transamerica Computer Co. v. International Business Machines Corp., 573 F.2d 646 (9th Cir. 1978). Such a rule should be measured against the usual rule which suggests that a voluntary disclosure to a third person will generally suffice to show a waiver of the attorney-client privilege. 2A INPRAC R 26(26.5).

f. *Use not limited.* Unless the court orders otherwise under IN ST TRIAL P Rule 26(C), the frequency of use of the methods listed in IN ST TRIAL P Rule 26(A) is not limited. IN ST TRIAL P Rule 26(A).

g. *Sequence of discovery.* Unless the court upon motion, for the convenience of parties and witnesses and in the interests of justice, orders otherwise, methods of discovery may be used in any sequence and the fact that a party is conducting discovery, whether by deposition or otherwise, shall not operate to delay any other party's discovery. IN ST TRIAL P Rule 26(D).

2. *Interrogatories.* Parties may obtain discovery by written interrogatories. IN ST TRIAL P Rule 26(A)(2). An interrogatory is a written question served upon another party which requires a written response under oath. 22 INPRAC § 23.1. Any party may serve upon any other party written interrogatories to be answered by the party served or, if the party served is an organization including a governmental organization, or a partnership, by any officer or agent, who shall furnish such information as is available to the party. IN ST TRIAL P Rule 33(A).

a. *Subject of interrogatories.* Interrogatories shall be tailored specifically to the cause in which they are served and numbered consecutively to facilitate response. IN ST LAKE RCP Rule 8(B). Interrogatories may relate to any matters which can be inquired into under IN ST TRIAL P Rule 26(B), and the answers may be used to the extent permitted by the rules of evidence. IN ST TRIAL P Rule 33(D).

    i. This includes:

- The existence, description, nature, custody, condition and location of books, documents, or other tangible things; and
- The identity and location of persons having knowledge of relevant facts. 10 INPRAC § 65.1.

    ii.   Interrogatories cannot be objected to on the ground that the information sought will be inadmissible at trial if the discovery appears reasonably calculated to lead to the discovery of admissible evidence. 10 INPRAC § 65.1.

  b. *Available for parties only.* Interrogatories may not be served on non-parties. 10 INPRAC § 65.1. There is no requirement that the party served shall be an "adverse" party. 2A INPRAC R 33(33.2).

  c. *Submission to personal jurisdiction.* Under the current trial rules, discovery is self-executing and interrogatories are not filed with the court, but retained by the originating party until a discovery dispute arises or the discovery is needed for proceedings before the court. As such, Indiana courts have had to revisit the issue of whether a party's mere service of interrogatories constitutes a waiver of an objection to the court's personal jurisdiction over that party. 22 INPRAC § 23.14.

    i.   In Alberts v. Mack Trucks, Inc., the defendant served interrogatories before asserting a challenge to the court's personal jurisdiction. In ruling that serving interrogatories did not constitute a waiver of personal jurisdiction, the Indiana Court of Appeals noted the amendments to the Indiana Rules of Trial Procedure, which no longer require a party to file interrogatories with the court. Accordingly, the court held: By sending interrogatories to Alberts' counsel, NSC did not submit to the personal jurisdiction of the court. Jurisdiction will not be found to be waived until a party affirmatively uses the court's procedure, such as in a motion to compel answers to interrogatories. 22 INPRAC § 23.14; Alberts v. Mack Trucks, Inc., 540 N.E.2d 1268, 1271-72 (Ind.Ct.App. 1989).

    ii.   Therefore, merely serving interrogatories upon an opposing party before challenging the court's personal jurisdiction over a defendant should not result in a waiver of the jurisdictional issue unless the party otherwise affirmatively uses the court's resources. 22 INPRAC § 23.14.

  d. *Limit on interrogatories.* No party shall serve on any other party more than thirty (30) interrogatories or more than thirty (30) requests for admission (other than requests relating to the authenticity or genuineness of documents in the aggregate), including subparagraphs, without leave of court. Subparagraphs shall relate directly to the subject matter of the interrogatory or request for admission. IN ST LAKE RCP Rule 8(B).

    i.   *Request for additional interrogatories.* Any party desiring to serve additional interrogatories or requests for admission shall file a written motion setting forth those proposed and the necessity therefor. IN ST LAKE RCP Rule 8(B).

  e. *Motion to compel discovery.* The party submitting the interrogatories may move for an order under IN ST TRIAL P Rule 37(A) with respect to any objection to or other failure to answer an interrogatory. IN ST TRIAL P Rule 33(C). Refer to the Indiana KeyRules Motion to Compel Discovery document for more information.

3. *Response to interrogatories*

  a. *Form of objections.* Answers or objections to interrogatories shall include the interrogatory which is being answered or to which an objection is made. The interrogatory which is being answered or objected to shall be placed immediately preceding the answer or objection. IN ST TRIAL P Rule 33(B).

  b. *Form of answer.* Each interrogatory shall be answered separately and fully in writing under oath, unless it is objected to, in which event the reasons for objections shall be stated in lieu of an answer. The answers are to be signed by the person making them, and the objections signed by the attorney making them. IN ST TRIAL P Rule 33(B).

  c. *Objections.* In addition to the objection that the matter is privileged, interrogatories may be objected to on the ground that they are not within the scope of discovery which is defined in IN ST TRIAL P Rule 26(B) because they seek information that is not relevant to the subject matter in the pending litigation, or that the requisite showing under IN ST TRIAL P Rule 26(B) has not been made, or that the information is held by experts and it is not discoverable except as permitted under IN ST TRIAL P Rule 26(B)(4). 2A INPRAC R 33(33.4). Objections to interrogatories must be specific. Common objections include (1) relevancy; (2) vague and ambiguous; (3) unduly burdensome; and (4) excessive in number. 10 INPRAC § 65.2.

    i.   *Objections to form.* The party upon whom the interrogatories have been served may object to the failure to follow the Format requirements in IN ST TRIAL P Rule 33(B) by returning the interrogatories to the party who caused them to be served. If this objection is to be made, the interrogatories shall be returned to the party who caused them to be served not later than the seventh (7th) day after they were received. If the interrogatories are not returned in that time, then this objection is waived. IN ST TRIAL P Rule 33(C).

ii.   *Information not available.* If the objecting party takes the position that the information is not available, it is that party's burden to show that it is not available. 2A INPRAC R 33(33.4).

- As a general rule, a party may not refuse to answer an interrogatory on the ground that the information is not in his possession, in the sense that the party would have to consult books and records in order to answer. 2A INPRAC R 33(33.4); Flour Mills of America, Inc. v. Pace, 75 F.R.D. 676, 680 (E.D.Okl. 1977).

- An interrogatory seeking information in the possession of the party's employee is not objectionable if the questions call for answers which could be readily obtained by the person answering the interrogatory. 2A INPRAC R 33(33.4); Ballard v. Allegheny Airlines, Inc., 54 F.R.D. 67 (E.D.Pa. 1972).

iii. *Broad, burdensome, numerous.* An objection is permitted if the interrogatory is too broad, or too burdensome, or too many in the number and kinds of questions which are asked. 2A INPRAC R 33(33.4); Flour Mills of America, Inc. v. Pace, 75 F.R.D. 676, 680 (E.D.Okl. 1977); In re U.S. Financial Securities Litigation, 74 F.R.D. 497 (S.D.Cal. 1975).

iv.   *Other objections.* An interrogatory otherwise proper is not objectionable merely because an answer to the interrogatory involves an opinion, contention, or legal conclusion, but the court may order that such an interrogatory be answered at a later time, or after designated discovery has been completed, or at a pre-trial conference. IN ST TRIAL P Rule 33(D).

- However, a party may not be forced to prepare his opponent's case for him. If the interrogatory would require a party to make extensive investigations, research, or compilation of data, it is an improper interrogatory, and it is burdensome and should be disallowed in a motion for a protective order. 2A INPRAC R 33(33.4); Halder v. International Telephone & Telegraph Co., 75 F.R.D. 657 (E.D.N.Y. 1977). Refer to the Indiana KeyRules Motion for Protective Order document for more information.

d.   *Signature of responses.* The party served shall answer and sign the answer, and the attorney for the party served shall sign the objections. Both are then returned to the party taking the interrogatory. 2A INPRAC R 33(33.8).

i.   An unsigned and unverified response does not qualify as an answer to an interrogatory and generally may not be used as such. 22 INPRAC § 23.6; Cabales v. U.S., 51 F.R.D. 498 (S.D.N.Y. 1970).

e.   *Option to produce business records.* Where the answer to an interrogatory may be derived or ascertained from the business records of the party upon whom the interrogatory has been served or from an examination, audit or inspection of such business records, including a compilation, abstract or summary thereof, and the burden of deriving or ascertaining the answer is substantially the same for the party serving the interrogatory as for the party served, it is a sufficient answer to such interrogatory to specify the records from which the answer may be derived or ascertained and to afford to the party serving the interrogatory reasonable opportunity to examine, audit or inspect such records and to make copies, compilations, abstracts or summaries. A specification shall be in sufficient detail to permit the interrogating party to locate and to identify, as readily as can the party served, the records from which the answer may be ascertained. IN ST TRIAL P Rule 33(E).

f.   *Supplementation of responses.* A party who has responded to a request for discovery with a response that was complete when made is under no duty to supplement his response to include information thereafter acquired, except as follows:

i.   A party is under a duty seasonally to supplement his response with respect to any question directly addressed to:

- The identity and location of persons having knowledge of discoverable matters, and

- The identity of each person expected to be called as an expert witness at trial, the subject-matter on which he is expected to testify, and the substance of his testimony. IN ST TRIAL P Rule 26(E)(1).

ii. A party is under a duty seasonally to amend a prior response if he obtains information upon the basis of which:

- He knows that the response was incorrect when made, or

- He knows that the response though correct when made is no longer true and the circumstances are such that a failure to amend the response is in substance a knowing concealment. IN ST TRIAL P Rule 26(E)(2).

iii. A duty to supplement responses may be imposed by order of the court, agreement of the parties, or at any time prior to trial through new requests for supplementation of prior responses. IN ST TRIAL P Rule 26(E)(3).

iv. The duty seasonally to supplement a discovery response is absolute and is not predicated on a court order. "It is a breach of a litigant's duty reasonably to supplement if the litigant postpones supplementing its response by not obtaining from its experts the information which is to be supplied in answer to interrogatories." 2A INPRAC R 26(26.27); Lucas v. Dorsey Corp., 609 N.E.2d 1191, 1196 (Ind.Ct.App. 1993).

D. Documents

1. *Required documents*

   a. *Interrogatories.* Refer to the General Requirements section of this document for information on the scope and content of interrogatories.

   b. *Certificate of service.* An attorney or unrepresented party tendering a document to the Clerk for filing shall certify that service has been made, list the parties served, and specify the date and means of service. The certificate of service shall be placed at the end of the document and shall not be separately filed. The separate filing of a certificate of service, however, shall not be grounds for rejecting a document for filing. The Clerk may permit documents to be filed without a certificate of service but shall require prompt filing of a separate certificate of service. IN ST TRIAL P Rule 5(C).

      i. All pleadings, motions and other papers submitted for filing which are required to be served under IN ST TRIAL P Rule 5(A) shall contain proof of service pursuant to IN ST TRIAL P Rule 5(B)(2). IN ST LAKE RCP Rule 3(A).

2. *Supplemental documents*

   a. *Stipulation regarding discovery procedure.* Unless the court orders otherwise, the parties may by written stipulation:

      i. Provide that depositions may be taken before any person, at any time or place, upon any notice, and in any manner and when so taken may be used like other depositions, and

      ii. Modify the procedures provided by the Indiana Rules of Trial Procedure for other methods of discovery. IN ST TRIAL P Rule 29.

   b. *Facsimile cover sheet.* Any document sent to the Clerk of the Circuit Court by electronic facsimile transmission shall be accompanied by a cover sheet which states the title of the document, case number, number of pages, identity and voice telephone number of the sending party and instructions for filing. The cover sheet shall contain the signature of the attorney or party, pro se, authorizing the filing. IN ST ADMIN Rule 12(D).

E. Format

1. *Format of interrogatories.* The rules applicable to captions, and the signing and form of pleadings (IN ST TRIAL P Rule 8 through IN ST TRIAL P Rule 11), apply to all motions and other papers provided under the Indiana Rules of Trial Procedure. 22B INPRAC 7:2. A party who serves written interrogatories under IN ST TRIAL P Rule 33 shall provide, after each interrogatory, a reasonable amount of space for a response or an objection. IN ST TRIAL P Rule 33(B).

   a. An interrogatory should pose a single direct question phrased in a manner that will advise the responding party what information is requested of him. 22 INPRAC § 23.5.

b. An interrogatory may be divided into separate paragraphs and subparagraphs. The paragraphs should be identified as "1," "2," or "3"; or as "Interrogatory No. 1," "Interrogatory No. 2," etc. 22 INPRAC § 23.5.

2. *Form of pleadings.* For the purpose of uniformity, convenience, clarity and durability, requirements in IN ST LAKE RCP Rule 2 shall be observed in the preparation of all pleadings, motions and other papers. IN ST LAKE RCP Rule 2. Whenever materials submitted fail to meet the standards in IN ST LAKE RCP Rule 2, the Court may impose appropriate sanctions. IN ST LAKE RCP Rule 2(B).

   a. *Caption; Names of parties.* Every pleading shall contain a caption setting forth the name of the court, the title of the action, the file number, and a designation as in IN ST TRIAL P Rule 7(A). In the complaint the title of the action shall include the names of all the parties, but in other pleadings it is sufficient to state the name of the first party on each side with an appropriate indication of other parties. IN ST TRIAL P Rule 10(A).

      i. *Special judge matters.* The caption of all CCS Entry Forms, pleadings, motions, orders and other papers to be filed in a special judge case shall include in block text the words SPECIAL JUDGE and the name of the judge directly below the cause number on the caption. IN ST LAKE RCP Rule 2(D).

   b. *Paragraphs; Separate statements.* All averments of a claim or defense shall be made in numbered paragraphs, the contents of each of which shall be limited as far as practicable to a statement of a single set of circumstances, and a paragraph may be referred to by number in all succeeding pleadings. Each claim founded upon a separate transaction or occurrence and each defense other than denials may be stated in a separate count or defense whenever a separation facilitates the clear presentation of the matters set forth. IN ST TRIAL P Rule 10(B).

   c. *Adoption by reference; Exhibits.* Statements in a pleading may be adopted by reference in a different part of the same pleading or in another pleading or in any motion. A copy of any written instrument which is an exhibit to a pleading is a part thereof for all purposes. IN ST TRIAL P Rule 10(C).

   d. *Paper; Print, quality and binding*

      i. All pleadings, motions, chronological case summary entry forms, orders, process and other papers shall be neatly and legibly printed, typewritten or mechanically reproduced, on one (1) side only, on white opaque paper. To satisfy the recordkeeping requirements of IN ST TRIAL P Rule 77, the print shall be of sufficient density and clarity for preservation and reproduction of microfilming, optical disk or other secondary sources. For this reason, the use of non-letter-quality printers is discouraged. IN ST LAKE RCP Rule 2(A).

      ii. Paper and ink shall be of such quality as to withstand the test of time. All documents shall be produced on acid-free, non-thermal paper. It is recommended that a minimum of twenty (20) pound, twenty-five percent (25%) cotton paper product be used. Documents of multiple pages shall be submitted in bound or stapled fashion, and the binding or stapling shall be at the top only. Covers or backings shall not be used. IN ST LAKE RCP Rule 2(A).

   e. *Papers; Handwritten.* Handwritten papers may be filed only if approved by the Court and a typewritten or printed true rendition thereof is filed within three (3) days thereafter and approved by the Court. Upon such approval, they shall be deemed and filed as the original, while the handwritten papers shall be retained therewith for evidentiary purposes. IN ST LAKE RCP Rule 2(C).

   f. *Minute sheets; Motion blanks.* Minute sheets and motion blanks shall no longer be used. IN ST LAKE RCP Rule 2(D).

3. *Size of papers for filing.* Effective January 1, 1992, all pleadings, copies, motions and documents filed with any trial court or appellate level court, typed or printed, with the exception of exhibits and existing wills, shall be prepared on eight and one-half by eleven inch (8 1/2" x 11") size paper. IN ST ADMIN Rule 11.

4. *Signature requirements*

   a. *Signature of attorney.* Every pleading or motion of a party represented by an attorney shall be signed by at least one (1) attorney of record in his individual name, whose address, telephone number, and attorney number shall be stated, except that this provision shall not apply to pleadings and motions made and transcribed at the trial or a hearing before the judge and received by him in such form. IN ST TRIAL P Rule 11(A).

   i. The signature of an attorney constitutes a certificate by him that he has read the pleadings; that to the best of his knowledge, information, and belief, there is good ground to support it; and that it is not interposed for delay. IN ST TRIAL P Rule 11(A).

   ii. If a pleading or motion is not signed or is signed with intent to defeat the purpose of the rule, it may be stricken as sham and false and the action may proceed as though the pleading had not been served. IN ST TRIAL P Rule 11(A).

   iii. For a willful violation of IN ST TRIAL P Rule 11 an attorney may be subjected to appropriate disciplinary action. Similar action may be taken if scandalous or indecent matter is inserted. IN ST TRIAL P Rule 11(A).

b. *Signature of unrepresented party.* A party who is not represented by an attorney shall sign his pleading and state his address. IN ST TRIAL P Rule 11(A).

c. *Verification not generally required.* Except when specifically required by rule, pleadings or motions need not be verified or accompanied by affidavit. The rule in equity that the averments of an answer under oath must be overcome by the testimony of two (2) witnesses or of one (1) witness sustained by corroborating circumstances is abolished. IN ST TRIAL P Rule 11(A).

d. *Verification by affirmation or representation.* When in connection with any civil or special statutory proceeding it is required that any pleading, motion, petition, supporting affidavit, or other document of any kind, be verified, or that an oath be taken, it shall be sufficient if the subscriber simply affirms the truth of the matter to be verified by an affirmation or representation. IN ST TRIAL P Rule 11(B). IN ST TRIAL P Rule 11(B) states that the affirmation or representation should be in substantially the following language: "I (we) affirm, under the penalties for perjury, that the foregoing representation(s) is (are) true. (Signed) _____."

   i. Any person who falsifies an affirmation or representation of fact shall be subject to the same penalties as are prescribed by law for the making of a false affidavit. IN ST TRIAL P Rule 11(B).

e. *Verified pleadings, motions, and affidavits as evidence.* Pleadings, motions and affidavits accompanying or in support of such pleadings or motions when required to be verified or under oath shall be accepted as a representation that the signer had personal knowledge thereof or reasonable cause to believe the existence of the facts or matters stated or alleged therein; and, if otherwise competent or acceptable as evidence, may be admitted as evidence of the facts or matters stated or alleged therein when it is so provided in the Indiana Rules of Trial Procedure, by statute or other law, or to the extent the writing or signature expressly purports to be made upon the signer's personal knowledge. When such pleadings, motions and affidavits are verified or under oath they shall not require other or greater proof on the part of the adverse party than if not verified or not under oath unless expressly provided otherwise by the Indiana Rules of Trial Procedure, statute or other law. Affidavits upon motions for summary judgment under IN ST TRIAL P Rule 56 and in denial of execution under IN ST TRIAL P Rule 9.2 shall be made upon personal knowledge. IN ST TRIAL P Rule 11(C).

f. *Electronic signature.* The filing of documents and information through the E-filing system by use of a valid username and password is presumed to have been authorized by the User to whom that username and password have been issued and documents filed through the E-filing system are presumed to have been signed by the same User. IN ST ADMIN Rule 16(E).

5. *Information excluded from public access.* Every document filed in a case shall separately identify information excluded from public access pursuant to IN ST ADMIN Rule 9(G)(1) as follows:

a. Whole documents that are excluded from public access pursuant to IN ST ADMIN Rule 9(G)(1) shall be tendered on light green paper or have a light green coversheet attached to the document, marked "Not for Public Access" or "Confidential." IN ST TRIAL P Rule 5(G)(1).

b. When only a portion of a document contains information excluded from public access pursuant to IN ST ADMIN Rule 9(G)(1), said information shall be omitted [or redacted] from the filed document,

and set forth on a separate accompanying document on light green paper conspicuously marked "Not for Public Access" or "Confidential" and clearly designated [or identifying] the caption and number of the case and the document and location within the document to which the redacted material pertains. IN ST TRIAL P Rule 5(G)(2).

c. With respect to documents filed in electronic format, the trial court, by local rule, may provide for compliance with IN ST TRIAL P Rule 5 in manner that separates and protects access to information excluded from public access. IN ST TRIAL P Rule 5(G)(3).

d. IN ST TRIAL P Rule 5(G) does not apply to a record sealed by the court pursuant to IN ST 5-14-3-5.5 or otherwise, nor to records, documents, or information filed in cases to which public access is prohibited pursuant to IN ST ADMIN Rule 9(G). IN ST TRIAL P Rule 5(G)(4).

e. The following information in case records is excluded from public access and is confidential:

i. Information that is excluded from public access pursuant to federal law;

ii. Information that is excluded from public access as declared confidential by Indiana statute or other court rule, including without limitation:

- All adoption records created after July 8, 1941, as declared confidential by IN ST 31-19-19-1, et seq., except those specifically declared open by IN ST 31-19-13-2(2);

- All records relating to chancroid, chlamydia, gonorrhea, hepatitis, human immunodeficiency virus (HIV), Lymphogranuloma venereum, syphilis, tuberculosis, as declared confidential by IN ST 16-41-8-1, et seq.;

- All records relating to child abuse as declared confidential by IN ST 31-33-18-1, et seq.;

- All records relating to drug tests as declared confidential by IN ST 5-14-3-4(a)(9);

- Records of grand jury proceedings as declared confidential by IN ST 35-34-2-4;

- Records of juvenile proceedings as declared confidential by IN ST 31-39-1-2, except those specifically open under statute;

- All paternity records created after July 1, 1941 as declared confidential by IN ST 31-14-11-15, IN ST 31-19-5-23, IN ST 31-39-1-1 and IN ST 31-39-1-2 [Editor's note: IN ST 31-14-11-15 was repealed effective May 9, 2013];

- All pre-sentence reports as declared confidential by IN ST 35-38-1-13;

- Written petitions to permit marriages without consent and orders directing the Clerk of Court to issue a marriage license to underage persons, as declared confidential by IN ST 31-11-1-6;

- Only those arrest warrants, search warrants, indictments and informations ordered confidential by the trial judge, prior to return of duly executed service as declared confidential by IN ST 5-14-3-4(b)(1);

- All medical, mental health, or tax records unless determined by law or regulation of any governmental custodian not to be confidential, released by the subject of such records, or declared by a court of competent jurisdiction to be essential to the resolution of litigation as declared confidential by IN ST 16-39-3-10, IN ST 6-4.1-5-10, IN ST 6-4.1-12-12, and IN ST 6-8.1-7-1;

- Personal information relating to jurors or prospective jurors, other than for the use of the parties and counsel, pursuant to IN ST JURY Rule 10;

- Information relating to protection from abuse orders, no-contact orders and workplace violence restraining orders as declared confidential by IN ST 5-2-9-6, et seq.;

- Mediation proceedings pursuant to IN ST ADR Rule 2.11, Mini-Trial proceedings pursuant to IN ST ADR Rule 4.4(C), and Summary Jury Trials pursuant to IN ST ADR Rule 5.6;

- Information in probation files pursuant to the Probation Standards promulgated by the Judicial Conference of Indiana pursuant to IN ST 11-13-1-8(b);

- Information deemed confidential pursuant to the Rules for Court Administered Alcohol and Drug Programs promulgated by the Judicial Conference of Indiana pursuant to IN ST 12-23-14-13;

- Information deemed confidential pursuant to the Problem-Solving Court Rules promulgated by the Judicial Conference of Indiana pursuant to IN ST 33-23-16-16;

- All records of the Department of workforce Development as declared confidential by IN ST 22-4-19-6;

- Information regarding interception of electronic communications that is sealed or deemed confidential as set forth in IN ST 35-33.5-2-1, et seq.

   iii. Information excluded from public access by specific court order;

   iv. Complete Social Security Numbers of living persons;

   v. With the exception of names, information such as addresses, phone numbers, and dates of birth which explicitly identifies:

- Natural persons who are witnesses or victims (not including defendants) in criminal, domestic violence, stalking, sexual assault, juvenile, or civil protection order proceedings, provided that juveniles who are victims of sex crimes shall be identified by initials only;

- Places of residence of judicial officers, clerks and other employees of courts and clerks of court, unless the person or persons about whom the information pertains waives confidentiality;

   vi. Complete account numbers of specific assets, loans, bank accounts, credit cards, and personal identification numbers (PINs);

   vii. All orders of expungement entered in criminal or juvenile proceedings, orders to restrict access to criminal history information pursuant to IN ST 35-38-5-5.5 or IN ST 35-38-8-5 and records excluded from public access by such orders, and information related to infractions that is excluded from public access pursuant to IN ST 34-28-5-15 or IN ST 34-28-5-16 [Editor's note: IN ST 35-38-5-5.5, IN ST 35-38-8-5 and IN ST 34-28-5-16 were repealed effective July 1, 2013; for information on orders restricting access to criminal history, refer to IN ST 35-38-9-1, et seq.];

   viii. All personal notes and e-mail, and deliberative material, of judges, jurors, court staff and judicial agencies, and information recorded in personal data assistants (PDA's) or organizers and personal calendars. IN ST ADMIN Rule 9(G)(1).

6. *Format of electronically filed documents*

   a. *Generally.* Electronically filed documents must meet the same requirements of format as documents conventionally filed pursuant to IN ST LAKE RCP Rule 2 or other applicable Lake County Rules of Civil Procedure. IN ST LAKE RCP Rule 17(D)(1).

   b. *Titles of documents.* The person electronically filing a document will be responsible for designating a title for the document at the time it is filed. The LCOD will generate the appropriate entry onto the CCS to record the filing of the document. IN ST LAKE RCP Rule 17(D)(3).

   c. *Citations and hyperlinks.* Electronically filed documents may contain hyperlink references to an external document as a convenient mechanism for accessing material cited in the document. Filers wishing to insert hyperlinks into documents shall continue to use the traditional method of citation to authority in addition to the hyperlink provided. The hyperlink is merely a convenience to the court and the material referenced is extraneous to the file and not a part of the court's record. IN ST LAKE RCP Rule 17(D)(5).

   d. *Attachments and exhibits.* All documents which form part of a single submission and which are being filed at the same time and by the same filer may be electronically filed together under one document filing, e.g., the motion, supporting affidavits, memorandum in support, designation of evidence, exhibits. IN ST LAKE RCP Rule 17(D)(6).

     i. Large documents which do not exist in an electronic format shall be scanned into .pdf format and filed electronically as separate attachments. A scanner is available in each clerk's office for use by the public and the bar in scanning and saving image files if needed. IN ST LAKE RCP Rule 17(D)(6).

e. *Electronic signatures*

    i. *Electronic filing as signature.* The electronic filing of a document which is required to be signed shall constitute the filer's representation under IN ST TRIAL P Rule 11. Unless the electronically filed document has been scanned and shows the filer's original signature, the signature of the filer shall be indicated by As/Attorney's Name, or As/Party's Name as in the case of a pro se litigant, on the line where the signature would otherwise appear. IN ST LAKE RCP Rule 17(G)(1).

    ii. *Signatures on jointly signed or filed, verified or other documents.* In the case of a stipulation, agreed order, jointly signed motion or other document which needs to be signed by two (2) or more persons, or in the case of documents which must contain original signatures and which require verification or an unsworn declaration under rule or statute, the signatures may be indicated by either:

- Submitting a scanned copy of the originally signed document; or,
- Submitting the document with the use of As/Name in the signature block(s) where the original signature(s) appear(s) in the original document; provided, however, that the filer shall first obtain the physical signature of all persons necessary. IN ST LAKE RCP Rule 17(G)(2).

    iii. *Retention of original.* The filer shall retain the original executed document. IN ST LAKE RCP Rule 17(G).

7. *Citation of local rules.* The local rules for Lake County may be known as the Lake County Rules of Civil Procedure, and abbreviated as LR. IN ST LAKE RCP Rule 1(C).

F. Filing and Service Requirements

1. *Filing requirements.* Except as otherwise provided in IN ST TRIAL P Rule 5(E)(2), all pleadings and papers subsequent to the complaint which are required to be served upon a party shall be filed with the Court either before service or within a reasonable period of time thereafter. IN ST TRIAL P Rule 5(E)(1). All papers presented for filing shall be submitted to the Clerk and not to the court. All papers submitted for filing shall be mailed or delivered to the Clerk's office at the courthouse in which the case is pending. IN ST LAKE RCP Rule 3(A).

a. *Non-filing of discovery until necessary*

    i. *Non-filing of discovery; Exceptions.* No deposition or request for discovery or response thereto under IN ST TRIAL P Rule 27, IN ST TRIAL P Rule 30, IN ST TRIAL P Rule 31, IN ST TRIAL P Rule 33, IN ST TRIAL P Rule 34 or IN ST TRIAL P Rule 36 shall be filed with the Court unless:

- A motion is filed pursuant to IN ST TRIAL P Rule 26(C) or IN ST TRIAL P Rule 37 and the original deposition or request for discovery or response thereto is necessary to enable the Court to rule; or
- A party desires to use the deposition or request for discovery or response thereto for evidentiary purposes at trial or in connection with a motion, and the Court, either upon its own motion or that of any party, or as a part of any pre-trial order, orders the filing of the original. IN ST TRIAL P Rule 5(E)(2).

    ii. *Custody of original and period of retention*

- The original of a deposition shall, subject to the provisions of IN ST TRIAL P Rule 30(E), be delivered by the reporter to the party taking it and shall be maintained by that party until filed with the Court pursuant to IN ST TRIAL P Rule 5(E)(2) or until the later of final judgment, agreed settlement of the litigation or all appellate rights have been exhausted. IN ST TRIAL P Rule 5(E)(3)(a).
- The original or any request for discovery or response thereto under IN ST TRIAL P Rule

27, IN ST TRIAL P Rule 30, IN ST TRIAL P Rule 31, IN ST TRIAL P Rule 33, IN ST TRIAL P Rule 34 and IN ST TRIAL P Rule 36 shall be maintained by the party originating the request or response until filed with the Court pursuant to IN ST TRIAL P Rule 5(E)(2) or until the later of final judgment, agreed settlement or all appellate rights have been exhausted. IN ST TRIAL P Rule 5(E)(3)(b).

iii. *Original unavailable; Copies.* In the event it is made to appear to the satisfaction of the Court that the original of a deposition or request for discovery or response thereto cannot be filed with the Court when required, the Court may allow use of a copy instead of the original. IN ST TRIAL P Rule 5(E)(4).

iv. *Filing as publication.* The filing of any deposition shall constitute publication. IN ST TRIAL P Rule 5(E)(5).

b. *Filing with the court defined.* The filing of pleadings, motions, and other papers with the court as required by the Indiana Rules of Trial Procedure shall be made by one of the following methods:

i. Delivery to the clerk of the court;

ii. Sending by electronic transmission under the procedure adopted pursuant to IN ST ADMIN Rule 12;

iii. Mailing to the clerk by registered, certified or express mail return receipt requested;

iv. Depositing with any third-party commercial carrier for delivery to the clerk within three (3) calendar days, cost prepaid, properly addressed;

v. If the court so permits, filing with the judge, in which event the judge shall note thereon the filing date and forthwith transmit them to the office of the clerk; or

vi. Electronic filing, as approved by the Division of State Court Administration pursuant to IN ST ADMIN Rule 16. IN ST TRIAL P Rule 5(F).

vii. Filing by registered or certified mail and by third-party commercial carrier shall be complete upon mailing or deposit. IN ST TRIAL P Rule 5(F).

c. *Mandatory electronic filing.* Unless otherwise permitted by the Lake County Rules of Civil Procedure or otherwise authorized by the judicial officer assigned to a particular case, all documents submitted for filing (including the original complaint, or equivalent pleading, and summons) shall be filed electronically with the clerk using the LCOD, no matter when the case was originally filed. IN ST LAKE RCP Rule 17(D).

i. *Of documents containing information excluded from public access pursuant to* IN ST ADMIN Rule 9. Documents containing information excluded from public access pursuant to IN ST ADMIN Rule 9, or documents which are ordered to be filed under seal shall be filed electronically, pursuant to IN ST LAKE RCP Rule 17(D)(9), whenever possible, along with a copy of the applicable order to seal the records, and the filer shall designate the documents as "Not for Public Access Pursuant to Administrative Rule 9(G)(1)" at the time of filing. IN ST LAKE RCP Rule 16(A)(1); IN ST LAKE RCP Rule 17(D)(9).

- *Conventional filing of documents containing information excluded from public access pursuant to* IN ST ADMIN Rule 9. Documents containing information excluded from public access pursuant to IN ST ADMIN Rule 9, or documents which are ordered to be filed under seal, which cannot be legibly scanned and filed electronically, shall be conventionally filed under seal and designated by the filer as "Not for Public Access Pursuant to Administrative Rule 9(G)(1)" at the time of filing. The unredacted version shall be filed on light green paper which is conspicuously marked "Not for Public Access"; and a redacted version, with confidential information deleted, shall be filed on white paper which shall be available for public access. The filer shall also electronically file a Notice of Manual Filing. IN ST LAKE RCP Rule 16(A)(2).

ii. *Technical failures.* If a registered user is unable to file a document in a timely manner due to technical difficulties in the LCOD, the registered user must file a document with the court as soon as possible notifying the court of the inability to file the document. A sample document titled Declaration that Party was Unable to File in a Timely Manner Due to Technical Difficulties can be found at IN ST LAKE RCP Form 4. Delayed filings shall be rejected unless accompanied by the declaration attesting to the filer's failed attempts to file electronically at least two (2) times, separated by at least one (1) hour, after noon on each day of delay due to such technical failure. IN ST LAKE RCP Rule 17(J).

    iii. *Documents allowed to be filed conventionally.* Unless specifically authorized by the court, only the following documents may be filed conventionally and not electronically:

- Exhibits and other documents that cannot be converted to a legible electronic form, such as videotapes, x-rays, and similar materials
- Documents delivered to the clerk by pro se litigants
- Documents mailed to the clerk by pro se litigants
- Confidential documents
- Notice of manual filing
- Titles of documents
- Chronological case summary entry forms (CCS entry forms). IN ST LAKE RCP Rule 17(E).
- For more information on the documents which must be filed conventionally, refer to IN ST LAKE RCP Rule 17(E).

d. *Facsimile filing.* Only when necessary on an emergency basis (i.e., when certified mail or other means of filing will not bring the document to the Judge's attention prior to the scheduled hearing or ruling), pleadings, motions and other papers may be filed by electronic facsimile transmission, or when specifically authorized by the Court. IN ST LAKE RCP Rule 2(C).

    i. *Generally.* In counties where a majority of judges of the courts of record, by posted local rule, have authorized electronic facsimile filing and designated a telephone number to receive such transmissions, pleadings, motions, and other papers may be sent to the Clerk of Circuit Court by electronic facsimile transmission for filing in any case, provided:

- Such matter does not exceed ten (10) pages, including the cover sheet;
- Such matter does not require the payment of fees other than the electronic facsimile transcription fee set forth in IN ST ADMIN Rule 12(E);
- The sending party creates at the time of transmission a machine generated log for such transmission; and
- The original document and the transmission log are maintained by the sending party for the duration of the litigation. IN ST ADMIN Rule 12(B).

    ii. *Time of filing.* During normal, posted business hours, the time of filing shall be the time the duplicate document is produced in the office of the Clerk of the Circuit Court. Duplicate documents received at all other times shall be filed as of the next normal business day. IN ST ADMIN Rule 12(C).

- If the receiving fax machine endorses its own time and date stamp upon the transmitted documents and the receiving machine produces a delivery receipt which is electronically created and transmitted to the sending party, the time of filing shall be the date and time recorded on the transmitted document by the receiving fax machine. IN ST ADMIN Rule 12(C).

e. *Filing for special judges.* For special judge matters where the special judge is a full-time judge or magistrate serving within Lake County, all papers submitted for filing shall be delivered or mailed to the Clerk's office at the courthouse where the special judge regularly serves. IN ST LAKE RCP Rule 3(A).

f. *Proof of filing.* Any party filing any paper by any method other than personal delivery to the clerk shall retain proof of filing. IN ST TRIAL P Rule 5(F).

2. *Service requirements.* Unless otherwise provided by the Indiana Rules of Trial Procedure or an order of the court, each party and special judge, if any, shall be served with: (1) every order required by its terms to be served; (2) every pleading subsequent to the original complaint; (3) every written motion except one which may be heard ex parte; (4) every brief submitted to the trial court; (5) every paper relating to discovery required to be served upon a party; and (6) every written notice, appearance, demand, offer of judgment, designation of record on appeal, or similar paper. IN ST TRIAL P Rule 5(A).

   a. *Methods of service*

      i. *Personal service.* Whenever a party is represented by an attorney of record, service shall be made upon such attorney unless service upon the party himself is ordered by the court. Service upon the attorney or party shall be made by delivering or mailing a copy of the papers to the last known address or where an attorney or party has consented to service by fax or e-mail, as provided in IN ST TRIAL P Rule 3.1(A)(4), by faxing or e-mailing a copy of the documents to the fax number or e-mail address set out in the appearance form or correction as required by IN ST TRIAL P Rule 3.1(E). IN ST TRIAL P Rule 5(B). Delivery of a copy within IN ST TRIAL P Rule 5 means:

- Offering or tendering it to the attorney or party and stating the nature of the papers being served. Refusal to accept an offered or tendered document is a waiver of any objection to the sufficiency or adequacy of service of that document;

- Leaving it at his office with a clerk or other person in charge thereof, or if there is no one in charge, leaving it in a conspicuous place therein; or

- If the office is closed, by leaving it at his dwelling house or usual place of abode with some person of suitable age and discretion then residing therein; or,

- Leaving it at some other suitable place, selected by the attorney upon whom service is being made, pursuant to duly promulgated local rule. IN ST TRIAL P Rule 5(B)(1).

      ii. *Service by mail.* If service is made by mail, the papers shall be deposited in the United States mail addressed to the person on whom they are being served, with postage prepaid. Service shall be deemed complete upon mailing. Proof of service of all papers permitted to be mailed may be made by written acknowledgment of service, by affidavit of the person who mailed the papers, or by certificate of an attorney. It shall be the duty of attorneys when entering their appearance in a cause or when filing pleadings or papers therein, to have noted in the Chronological Case Summary or said pleadings or papers so filed the address and telephone number of their office. Service by delivery or by mail at such address shall be deemed sufficient and complete. IN ST TRIAL P Rule 5(B)(2).

      iii. *Service by fax or e-mail.* A party who has consented to service by fax or e-mail may be served as follows:

- Service by e-mail shall be made by attaching the document being served in .pdf format. Discovery documents must also be served in accordance with IN ST TRIAL P Rule 26(A). IN ST TRIAL P Rule 5(B)(3)(a).

- Service by fax shall be deemed complete upon generation of a transmission record indicating the successful transmission of the entire document, except as provided in IN ST TRIAL P Rule 5(B)(3)(d). IN ST TRIAL P Rule 5(B)(3)(b).

- Service by e-mail shall be deemed complete upon transmission, except as provided in IN ST TRIAL P Rule 5(B)(3)(d). IN ST TRIAL P Rule 5(B)(3)(c).

- Service by fax or e-mail that occurs on a Saturday, Sunday, legal holiday, or day the court or agency in which the matter is pending is closed or after 5:00 PM local time of the recipient shall be deemed complete the next day that is not a Saturday, Sunday, legal holiday, or day that the court or agency in which the matter is pending is not closed. IN ST TRIAL P Rule 5(B)(3)(d).

      iv. *Additional service of electronic discovery.* In addition to service under Rule IN ST TRIAL P Rule 5(B) or a .pdf format electronic copy, a party propounding or responding to interrogatories, requests for production or requests for admission shall comply with IN ST TRIAL P Rule 26(A.1)(a) or IN ST TRIAL P Rule 26(A.1)(b). IN ST TRIAL P Rule 26(A.1).

- The party shall serve the discovery request or response in an electronic format (either on a disk or as an electronic document attachment) in any commercially available word processing software system. If transmitted on disk, each disk shall be labeled, identifying the caption of the case, the document, and the word processing version in which it is being submitted. If more than one (1) disk is used for the same document, each disk shall be labeled and also shall be sequentially numbered. If transmitted by electronic mail, the document must be accompanied by electronic memorandum providing the forgoing identifying information; or

- The party shall serve the opposing party with a verified statement that the attorney or party appealing pro se lacks the equipment and is unable to transmit the discovery as required by IN ST TRIAL P Rule 26(A.1). IN ST TRIAL P Rule 26(A.1).

    b. *Serving numerous defendants.* In any action in which there are unusually large numbers of defendants, the court, upon motion or of its own initiative, may order:

      i. That service of the pleadings of the defendants and replies thereto need not be made as between the defendants;

- That any cross-claim, counterclaim, or matter constituting an avoidance or affirmative defense contained therein shall be deemed to be denied or avoided by all other parties; and

- That the filing of any such pleading and service thereof upon the plaintiff constitutes due notice of it to the parties. IN ST TRIAL P Rule 5(D).

      ii. A copy of every such order shall be served upon the parties in such manner and form as the court directs. IN ST TRIAL P Rule 5(D).

    c. *Service by electronic means.* The Lake County Online Docket will generate a Notice of Electronic Filing and Service when any document is filed and served. This notice will be emailed to each registered user of record in a case, and an electronic service event will be added to the work queue of each registered user of record in the case. The party filing the document should retain a paper or electronic copy of the Notice of Electronic Filing and Service. This notice represents proof of filing and service of the document on registered users of record in that case. The filer shall not be required to conventionally serve any document on any party receiving electronic service. IN ST LAKE RCP Rule 17(F)(2).

      i. The filer shall also conventionally serve those parties not designated or able to receive electronic notice or service but who are nevertheless entitled to notice of said pleading or other document in accordance with the Indiana Rules of Civil Procedure and applicable Lake County Rules of Civil Procedure. In such cases, the filer shall also file a certificate of service, as appropriate. IN ST LAKE RCP Rule 17(F).

    d. *Service on parties in default for failure to appear.* No service need be made on parties in default for failure to appear, except that pleadings asserting new or additional claims for relief against them shall be served upon them in the manner provided by service of summons in IN ST TRIAL P Rule 4. IN ST TRIAL P Rule 5(A).

G. Hearings

    1. The Indiana rules do not contemplate a hearing related to the filing and service of interrogatories.

H. Forms

1. Interrogatory Forms for Indiana

    a. General form. 5 INPRAC § 4:2.10.

    b. Motion to enlarge time to answer. 5 INPRAC § 4:2.20.

    c. Answers and objections; General form. 5 INPRAC § 4:2.30.

    d. Answer; General form with standard objections. 5 INPRAC § 4:2.40.

    e. Answer; Offer to produce business records. 5 INPRAC § 4:2.50.

f. Sample interrogatories relating to electronically stored information. 5 INPRAC § 4:2.60.

g. Motion to seal answers to interrogatories. 10 INPRAC § 65.6.1.

h. Interrogatories; General form. 10 INPRAC § 65.7.

i. Interrogatories; Another form. 10 INPRAC § 65.8.

j. Interrogatory preliminary instructions; Comprehensive form. 10 INPRAC § 65.9.

k. Interrogatory preliminary instructions; Abbreviated form. 10 INPRAC § 65.10.

l. Interrogatory definitions. 10 INPRAC § 65.11.

m. Motion to enlarge time to answer interrogatories. 10 INPRAC § 65.12.

n. Motion for enlargement of time; Response due after discovery completed. 10 INPRAC § 65.13.

o. Motion to shorten time to respond to interrogatories. 10 INPRAC § 65.15.

p. Motion to strike interrogatories; Excessive number under local rules. 10 INPRAC § 65.16.

q. Interrogatories to determine minimum contacts with state. 10 INPRAC § 65.20.

r. Answers and objections to interrogatories; General form. 10 INPRAC § 65.30.

s. Answers and objections to interrogatories; Another form. 10 INPRAC § 65.31.

t. Standard objections to interrogatories; General form. 10 INPRAC § 65.32.

u. Standard objections to interrogatories. 10 INPRAC § 65.33.

v. Answer of interrogatory by offering to produce business records. 10 INPRAC § 65.34.

w. Motion to compel answers to interrogatories. 10 INPRAC § 65.35.

x. Attorney's signature as to objections; Alternate forms. 10 INPRAC § 65.36.

y. Conversion; Plaintiff's interrogatories. 10 INPRAC § 66.27.

z. Medical malpractice action. 10 INPRAC § 66.37.

2. Official Interrogatories Forms for Lake County

a. CCS entry form. IN ST LAKE RCP App. A.

b. Notice of manual filing. IN ST LAKE RCP Form 2.

c. Certificate of service. IN ST LAKE RCP Form 3.

d. Declaration that party was unable to file in a timely manner. IN ST LAKE RCP Form 4.

3. Interrogatories Forms for Lake County

a. Notice of manual filing. EFORMST IN 5540.

I. Checklist

(I) ❑ Matters to be considered by the party serving the interrogatories

  (a) ❑ Required documents

    (1) ❑ Interrogatories

    (2) ❑ Certificate of service

  (b) ❑ Supplemental documents

    (1) ❑ Stipulation regarding discovery procedure

    (2) ❑ Facsimile cover sheet

  (c) ❑ Timing

    (1) ❑ Interrogatories may, without leave of court, be served upon the plaintiff after commencement of the action and upon any other party with or after service of the summons and complaint upon that party

(II) ❑ Matters to be considered by the responding party

    (a) ❑ Required documents

        (1) ❑ Response to interrogatories

        (2) ❑ Certificate of service

    (b) ❑ Supplemental documents

        (1) ❑ Business records

        (2) ❑ Stipulation regarding discovery procedure

        (3) ❑ Facsimile cover sheet

    (c) ❑ Timing

        (1) ❑ The party upon whom the interrogatories have been served shall serve a copy of the answers and objections within a period designated by the party submitting the interrogatories, not less than thirty (30) days after the service thereof or within such shorter or longer time as the court may allow

Requests, Notices and Applications
Request for Production of Documents

Document Last Updated October 2013

A. Applicable Rules

  1. *State rules*

    a. Appearance. IN ST TRIAL P Rule 3.1.

    b. Process. IN ST TRIAL P Rule 4.

    c. Service and filing of pleadings and other papers. IN ST TRIAL P Rule 5.

    d. Time. IN ST TRIAL P Rule 6.

    e. Pleadings. IN ST TRIAL P Rule 7; IN ST TRIAL P Rule 9.2; IN ST TRIAL P Rule 10.

    f. Signing and verification of pleadings. IN ST TRIAL P Rule 11.

    g. General provisions governing discovery. IN ST TRIAL P Rule 26.

    h. Methods of discovery. IN ST TRIAL P Rule 27; IN ST TRIAL P Rule 29; IN ST TRIAL P Rule 30; IN ST TRIAL P Rule 31; IN ST TRIAL P Rule 33; IN ST TRIAL P Rule 34; IN ST TRIAL P Rule 35; IN ST TRIAL P Rule 36.

    i. Failure to make or cooperate in discovery; Sanctions. IN ST TRIAL P Rule 37.

    j. Subpoena. IN ST TRIAL P Rule 45.

    k. Judgment on the evidence (directed verdict). IN ST TRIAL P Rule 50.

    l. Findings by the court. IN ST TRIAL P Rule 52.

    m. Summary judgment. IN ST TRIAL P Rule 56.

    n. Motion to correct error. IN ST TRIAL P Rule 59.

    o. Relief from judgment or order. IN ST TRIAL P Rule 60.

    p. Access to court records. IN ST ADMIN Rule 9.

    q. Paper size. IN ST ADMIN Rule 11.

    r. Facsimile transmission. IN ST ADMIN Rule 12.

    s. Electronic filing and electronic service pilot projects. IN ST ADMIN Rule 16.

    t. Privacy and confidentiality. IN ST 5-2-9-6; IN ST 5-14-3-4; IN ST 5-14-3-5.5; IN ST 6-4.1-5-10; IN ST 6-4.1-12-12; IN ST 6-8.1-7-1; IN ST 11-13-1-8; IN ST 12-23-14-13; IN ST 16-39-3-10; IN ST

16-41-8-1; IN ST 22-4-19-6; IN ST 31-11-1-6; IN ST 31-19-5-23; IN ST 31-19-13-2; IN ST 31-19-19-1; IN ST 31-33-18-1; IN ST 31-39-1-1; IN ST 31-39-1-2; IN ST 33-23-16-16; IN ST 35-34-2-4; IN ST 35-38-1-13; IN ST 35-38-9-1; IN ST ADR Rule 2.11; IN ST ADR Rule 4.4; IN ST ADR Rule 5.6; IN ST JURY Rule 10.

2. *Local rules*

   a. Scope and title. [IN ST LAKE RCP Rule 1, as amended by IN ORDER 13-0237, effective October 18, 2013].

   b. Preparation of pleadings, motions and other papers. IN ST LAKE RCP Rule 2.

   c. Filing. [IN ST LAKE RCP Rule 3, as amended by IN ORDER 13-0237, effective October 18, 2013].

   d. Discovery. IN ST LAKE RCP Rule 8.

   e. Confidential information and sealed documents. IN ST LAKE RCP Rule 16.

   f. Electronic filing and service. IN ST LAKE RCP Rule 17.

B. Timing

1. *Time for service of request for production of documents*

   a. *Service on parties.* The request may, without leave of court, be served upon the plaintiff after commencement of the action and upon any other party with or after service of the summons and complaint upon that party. IN ST TRIAL P Rule 34(B).

   b. *Service on non-parties.* Neither a request nor subpoena to produce or permit as permitted by IN ST TRIAL P Rule 34 shall be served upon a non-party until at least fifteen (15) days after the date on which the party intending to serve such request or subpoena serves a copy of the proposed request and subpoena on all other parties. Provided, however, that if such request or subpoena relates to a matter set for hearing within such fifteen (15) day period or arises out of a bona fide emergency, such request or subpoena may be served upon a non-party one (1) day after receipt of the proposed request or subpoena by all other parties. IN ST TRIAL P Rule 34(C)(2)

2. *Time for service of the response to the request for production of documents.* The party upon whom the request is served shall serve a written response within a period designated in the request, not less than thirty (30) days after the service thereof or within such shorter or longer time as the court may allow. IN ST TRIAL P Rule 34(B).

3. *Computation of time*

   a. *Generally; Days excluded.* In computing any period of time prescribed or allowed by the Indiana Rules of Trial Procedure, by order of the court, or by any applicable statute, the day of the act, event, or default from which the designated period of time begins to run shall not be included. The last day of the period so computed is to be included unless it is:

      i. A Saturday,

      ii. A Sunday,

      iii. A legal holiday as defined by state statute, or

      iv. A day the office in which the act is to be done is closed during regular business hours. IN ST TRIAL P Rule 6(A).

   b. *Short periods.* In any event, the period runs until the end of the next day that is not a Saturday, a Sunday, a legal holiday, or a day on which the office is closed. When the period of time allowed is less than seven (7) days, intermediate Saturdays, Sundays, legal holidays, and days on which the office is closed shall be excluded from the computations. IN ST TRIAL P Rule 6(A).

   c. *Additional time after service by United States mail.* Whenever a party has the right or is required to do some act or take some proceedings within a prescribed period after the service of a notice or other paper upon him and the notice or paper is served upon him by United States mail, three (3) days shall be added to the prescribed period. IN ST TRIAL P Rule 6(E).

   d. *Electronic filing does not alter deadlines.* Filing electronically does not alter any filing deadlines or any time computation pursuant to state or federal statutes, any Rules of the Indiana Supreme Court, including without limitation the Rules of Trial Procedure, the Rules of Appellate Procedure or the Administrative Rules, or applicable Lake County Rules of Civil Procedure. The office of the Lake County Clerk is open for electronic filing under the Lake County Rules of Civil Procedure twenty-four (24) hours a day. A document is deemed filed at the date and time it is received by the LCOD server. Filing must be completed before midnight local time in order to be considered filed that day. Lake County observes Central Time and electronic filers are strongly urged to file documents during hours when the Lake County Online Docket ("LCOD") help line is available, from 9:00 a.m. to 4:00 p.m. local time, although documents can be filed electronically twenty-four (24) hours a day. IN ST LAKE RCP Rule 17(I).

e. *Enlargement of time.* When an act is required or allowed to be done at or within a specific time by the Indiana Rules of Trial Procedure, the court may at any time for cause shown:

   i. Order the period enlarged, with or without motion or notice, if request therefor is made before the expiration of the period originally prescribed or extended by a previous order; or

   ii. Upon motion made after the expiration of the specific period, permit the act to be done where the failure to act was the result of excusable neglect; but, the court may not extend the time for taking any action for judgment on the evidence under IN ST TRIAL P Rule 50(A), amendment of findings and judgment under IN ST TRIAL P Rule 52(B), to correct errors under IN ST TRIAL P Rule 59(C), statement in opposition to motion to correct error under IN ST TRIAL P Rule 59(E), or to obtain relief from final judgment under IN ST TRIAL P Rule 60(B), except to the extent and under the conditions stated in those rules. IN ST TRIAL P Rule 6(B).

C. General Requirements

1. *Scope of discovery.* Unless otherwise limited by order of the court in accordance with the Indiana Rules of Trial Procedure, the scope of discovery is as follows:

   a. *In general.* Parties may obtain discovery regarding any matter, not privileged, which is relevant to the subject-matter involved in the pending action, whether it relates to the claim or defense of the party seeking discovery or the claim or defense of any other party, including the existence, description, nature, custody, condition and location of any books, documents, or other tangible things and the identity and location of persons having knowledge of any discoverable matter. It is not ground for objection that the information sought will be inadmissible at the trial if the information sought appears reasonably calculated to lead to the discovery of admissible evidence. IN ST TRIAL P Rule 26(B)(1).

      i. *Limiting discovery upon court determination.* The frequency or extent of use of the discovery methods otherwise permitted under the Indiana Rules of Trial Procedure and by any local rule shall be limited by the court if it determines that:

         • The discovery sought is unreasonably cumulative or duplicative, or is obtainable from some other source that is more convenient, less burdensome, or less expensive;

         • The party seeking discovery has had ample opportunity by discovery in the action to obtain the information sought or;

         • The burden or expense of the proposed discovery outweighs its likely benefit, taking into account the needs of the case, the amount in controversy, the parties' resources, the importance of the issues at stake in the litigation, and the importance of the proposed discovery in resolving the issues. IN ST TRIAL P Rule 26(B)(1).

         • The court may act upon its own initiative after reasonable notice or pursuant to a motion under IN ST TRIAL P Rule 26(C). IN ST TRIAL P Rule 26(B)(1). Refer to the Indiana KeyRules Motion for Protective Order document for more information.

      ii. *Relevancy in the discovery context.* When the word "relevancy" is used in IN ST TRIAL P Rule 26(B), it does not mean "relevancy" as that word in used to determine the admissibility of evidence in a trial court. It is much broader. It means "relevancy" to the "subject matter" of the litigation or pending action and it may relate to the claim or defense of any party. Pretrial discovery is available as to any nonprivileged matter relevant to the subject matter of the lawsuit or to obtain information reasonably calculated to lead to admissible evidence. 2A INPRAC R 26(26.4); Kaufmann v. Credithrift Financial, Inc., 465 N.E.2d 207, 210 (Ind.Ct.App. 1984).

   iii. *Tests for relevance.* Indiana case law has developed two (2) additional tests in this area. 2A INPRAC R 26(26.4).

- The first test determines when a document or a request for information is actually relevant to the subject matter in the pending action. A document [or discovery request] is relevant to discovery if there is the possibility the information sought may be relevant to the subject matter of the action. 2A INPRAC R 26(26.4); CIGNA-INA/Aetna v. Hagerman-Shambaugh, 473 N.E.2d 1033, 1036 (Ind.Ct.App. 1985).

- The second test speaks to appellate review of the trial court's determination that a document or discovery request is relevant to the subject matter of the pending action. The appellate court sees its review of the trial court's decision on relevancy to subject matter as being very limited. The court states: "Our review of the trial court's conclusion that the documents are relevant is limited. A trial court is vested with discretion in its rulings on discovery issues." 2A INPRAC R 26(26.4); Costanzi v. Ryan, 175 Ind.App. 257, 370 N.E.2d 1333 (Ind.Ct.App. 1978).

b. *Insurance agreements.* A party may obtain discovery of the existence and contents of any insurance agreement under which any person carrying on an insurance business may be liable to satisfy part or all of a judgment which may be entered in the action or to indemnify or reimburse for payments made to satisfy the judgment. Information concerning the insurance agreement is not by reason of disclosure admissible in evidence at trial. For purposes of IN ST TRIAL P Rule 26(B)(2), an application for insurance shall not be treated as part of an insurance agreement. IN ST TRIAL P Rule 26(B)(2).

c. *Trial preparation; Materials.* Subject to the provisions of IN ST TRIAL P Rule 26(B)(4), a party may obtain discovery of documents and tangible things otherwise discoverable under IN ST TRIAL P Rule 26(B)(1) and prepared in anticipation of litigation or for trial by or for another party or by or for that other party's representative (including his attorney, consultant, surety, indemnitor, insurer, or agent) only upon a showing that the party seeking discovery has substantial need of the materials in the preparation of his case and that he is unable without undue hardship to obtain the substantial equivalent of the materials by other means. In ordering discovery of such materials when the required showing has been made, the court shall protect against disclosure of the mental impressions, conclusions, opinions, or legal theories of an attorney or other representative of a party concerning the litigation. IN ST TRIAL P Rule 26(B)(3).

   i. A party may obtain without the required showing a statement concerning the action or its subject matter previously made by that party. Upon request, a person not a party may obtain without the required showing a statement concerning the action or its subject matter previously made by that person. If the request is refused, the person may move for a court order. The provisions of IN ST TRIAL P Rule 37(A)(4) apply to the award of expenses incurred in relation to the motion. For purposes of IN ST TRIAL P Rule 26(B)(3), a statement previously made is:

- A written statement signed or otherwise adopted approved by the person making it, or

- A stenographic, mechanical, electrical, or other recording, or a transcription thereof, which is a substantially verbatim recital of an oral statement by the person making it and contemporaneously recorded. IN ST TRIAL P Rule 26(B)(3).

   ii. The protection of IN ST TRIAL P Rule 26(B)(3) extends to material prepared or collected before litigation actually commences, but that some possibility of litigation must actually exist before the privilege and IN ST TRIAL P Rule 26(B)(3) become operative. 2A INPRAC R 26(26.9).

d. *Trial preparation; Experts.* Discovery of facts known and opinions held by experts, otherwise discoverable under the provisions of IN ST TRIAL P Rule 26(B)(1) and acquired or developed in anticipation of litigation or for trial, may be obtained as follows:

   i. A party may through interrogatories require any other party to identify each person whom the

other party expects to call as an expert witness at trial, to state the subject matter on which the expert is expected to testify, and to state the substance of the facts and opinions to which the expert is expected to testify and a summary of the grounds for each opinion. IN ST TRIAL P Rule 26(B)(4)(a)(i).

ii.   Upon motion, the court may order further discovery by other means, subject to such restrictions as to scope and such provisions, pursuant to IN ST TRIAL P Rule 26(B)(4)(c), concerning fees and expenses as the court may deem appropriate. IN ST TRIAL P Rule 26(B)(4)(a)(ii).

iii. A party may discover facts known or opinions held by an expert who has been retained or specially employed by another party in anticipation of litigation or preparation for trial and who is not expected to be called as a witness at trial, only as provided in IN ST TRIAL P Rule 35(B) or upon a showing of exceptional circumstances under which it is impracticable for the party seeking discovery to obtain facts or opinions on the same subject by other means. IN ST TRIAL P Rule 26(B)(4)(b).

iv.   Unless manifest injustice would result,

- The court shall require that the party seeking discovery pay the expert a reasonable fee for time spent in responding to discovery under IN ST TRIAL P Rule 26(B)(4)(a)(ii) and IN ST TRIAL P Rule 26(B)(4)(b); and

- With respect to discovery obtained under IN ST TRIAL P Rule 26(B)(4)(a)(ii) the court may require, and with respect to discovery obtained under IN ST TRIAL P Rule 26(B)(4)(b) the court shall require, the party seeking discovery to pay the other party a fair portion of the fees and expenses reasonably incurred by the latter party in obtaining facts and opinions from the expert. IN ST TRIAL P Rule 26(B)(4).

e.   *Claims of privilege or protection*

i.   *Information withheld.* When a party withholds information otherwise discoverable under the Indiana Rules of Trial Procedure by claiming that it is privileged or subject to protection as trial preparation material, the party shall make the claim expressly and shall describe the nature of the documents, communications, or things not produced or disclosed in a manner that, without revealing information itself privileged or protected, will enable other parties to assess the applicability of the privilege or protection. IN ST TRIAL P Rule 26(B)(5)(a).

ii.   *Information produced.* If information is produced in discovery that is subject to a claim of privilege or protection as trial-preparation material, the party making the claim may notify any party that received the information of the claim and the basis for it. After being notified, a party must promptly return, sequester, or destroy the specified information and any copies it has and may not use or disclose the information until the claim is resolved. A receiving party may promptly present the information to the court under seal for a determination of the claim. If the receiving party disclosed the information before being notified, it must take reasonable steps to retrieve it. The producing party must preserve the information until the claim is resolved. IN ST TRIAL P Rule 26(B)(5)(b).

iii. *Waiver.* The law of discovery has developed some holdings which indicate that "waiver" of a privileged communication in a discovery setting might be more exacting than "waiver" of a privileged communication when the only question at hand is an interpretation of the privilege itself. Thus, in litigation in which several documents are in issue, and some are released inadvertently, there is strong case law that holds that the "inadvertent production" of a privileged document does not constitute a waiver of the attorney-client privilege. 2A INPRAC R 26(26.5); Transamerica Computer Co. v. International Business Machines Corp., 573 F.2d 646 (9th Cir. 1978). Such a rule should be measured against the usual rule which suggests that a voluntary disclosure to a third person will generally suffice to show a waiver of the attorney-client privilege. 2A INPRAC R 26(26.5).

f.   *Use not limited.* Unless the court orders otherwise under IN ST TRIAL P Rule 26(C), the frequency of use of the methods listed in IN ST TRIAL P Rule 26(A) is not limited. IN ST TRIAL P Rule 26(A).

g.   *Sequence of discovery.* Unless the court upon motion, for the convenience of parties and witnesses

and in the interests of justice, orders otherwise, methods of discovery may be used in any sequence and the fact that a party is conducting discovery, whether by deposition or otherwise, shall not operate to delay any other party's discovery. IN ST TRIAL P Rule 26.

2. *Request for production of documents*

   a. *Content of the request.* The request shall set forth the items to be inspected either by individual item or by category, and describe each item and category with reasonable particularity. The request may specify the form or forms in which electronically stored information is to be produced. The request shall specify a reasonable time, place, and manner of making the inspection and performing the related acts. Service is dispensed with if the whereabouts of the parties is unknown. IN ST TRIAL P Rule 34(B).

      i. *Reasonable particularity.* A recurring issue appears among cases. It is whether a request is adequate or describes the items sought with "reasonable particularity" as stated in IN ST TRIAL P Rule 34(B). The essence of this matter is found in these words: "When the party seeking discovery issues a `shotgun' request that is unduly general, the court may avoid wading through documents by finding the items to be inspected not set forth with reasonable particularity, as required by IN ST TRIAL P Rule 34(B). 3 INPRAC R 34(34.1); Ray v. St. John's Health Care Corp., 582 N.E.2d 464, 474 (Ind.Ct.App. 1991); Richey v. Chappell, 572 N.E.2d 1338, 1339 (Ind.Ct.App. 1991).

   b. *Requesting documents in specific form.* If a request for electronically stored information does not specify the form or forms of production, a responding party must produce the information in a form or forms in which it is ordinarily maintained or in a form or forms that are reasonably usable. IN ST TRIAL P Rule 34(B).

   c. *Scope.* Any party may serve on any other party a request:

      i. To produce and permit the party making the request, or someone acting on the requester's behalf, to inspect and copy, any designated documents or electronically stored information (including, without limitation, writings, drawings, graphs, charts, photographs, sound recordings, images and other data or data compilations from which information can be obtained or translated, if necessary, by the respondent into reasonably usable form) or to inspect and copy, test, or sample any designated tangible things which constitute or contain matters within the scope of IN ST TRIAL P Rule 26(B) and which are in the possession, custody or control of the party upon whom the request is served; or

      ii. To permit entry upon designated land or other property in the possession or control of the party upon whom the request is served for the purpose of inspection and measuring, surveying, photographing, testing, or sampling the property or any designated object or operation thereon, within the scope of IN ST TRIAL P Rule 26(B). IN ST TRIAL P Rule 34(A).

   d. *Application to non-parties.* A witness or person other than a party may be requested to produce or permit the matters allowed by IN ST TRIAL P Rule 34(A). Such request shall be served upon other parties and included in or with a subpoena served upon such witness or person. IN ST TRIAL P Rule 34(C)(1).

      i. *Content of request to non-parties*

         • The request shall contain the matter provided in IN ST TRIAL P Rule 34(B). IN ST TRIAL P Rule 34(C)(3).

         • It shall also state that the witness or person to whom it is directed is entitled to security against damages or payment of damages resulting from such request and may respond to such request by submitting to its terms, by proposing different terms, by objecting specifically or generally to the request by serving a written response to the party making the request within thirty (30) days, or by moving to quash as permitted by IN ST TRIAL P Rule 45(B). IN ST TRIAL P Rule 34(C)(3).

      ii. *Service of responses on other parties required.* A party receiving documents from a non-party pursuant to IN ST TRIAL P Rule 34(C) shall serve copies on all other parties within fifteen (15) days of receiving the documents. If the documents are voluminous and service of a complete set of copies is burdensome, the receiving party shall notify all parties within fifteen (15) days of receiving the documents that the documents are available for inspection at the location of their production by the non-party, or at another location agreed to by the parties. The parties shall agree to arrangements for copying, and any party desiring copies shall bear the cost of reproducing them. IN ST TRIAL P Rule 34(C)(4).

e. *Exception to best evidence rule.* When a party or witness in control of a writing or document subject to examination under IN ST TRIAL P Rule 34 or IN ST TRIAL P Rule 9.2(E) refuses or is unable to produce it, evidence thereof shall be allowed by other parties without compliance with the rule of evidence requiring production of the original document or writing as best evidence. IN ST TRIAL P Rule 34(D).

3. *Response to request for production of documents*

a. *Content of the response.* The response shall state, with respect to each item or category, that inspection and related activities will be permitted as requested, unless it is objected to, including an objection to the requested form or forms for producing electronically stored information, stating in which event the reasons for objection shall be stated. If objection is made to part of an item or category, the part shall be specified. IN ST TRIAL P Rule 34(B).

b. *Types of responses.* There are several responses that a party may make to a IN ST TRIAL P Rule 34 discovery request:

    i. Agree to produce the requested item or permit inspection at the time and place suggested by the discovering party. 10 INPRAC § 67.2.

    ii. Agree to production, but suggest another time and place. 10 INPRAC § 67.2.

    iii. Move for a protective order under IN ST TRIAL P Rule 26(C). 10 INPRAC § 67.2.

    iv. Object to the request. Common grounds for objection include:

      • The item sought does not exist. 10 INPRAC § 67.2.

      • Respondent does not have possession, custody or control of the item requested. 10 INPRAC § 67.2.

      • The request does not describe documents to be produced with reasonable particularity, or by individual item or category. 10 INPRAC § 67.2.

      • The document requested fails to specify a reasonable time, place and manner of production. 10 INPRAC § 67.2.

      • The discovery requested is privileged or constitutes work product (mental impressions, conclusions, opinions or legal theories of party or party's attorney). 10 INPRAC § 67.2.

      • The discovery requested is not relevant to the subject matter of the litigation and not reasonably calculated to lead to the discovery of admissible evidence. 10 INPRAC § 67.2.

      • The discovery requests documents prepared in anticipation of litigation when the requesting party does not have a substantial need of the materials in preparation of the case and is able to obtain the substantial equivalent of the materials without undue hardship and by other means. 10 INPRAC § 67.2.

      • Nonparty's statement was prepared in anticipation of litigation and there has been no showing that the non-party's statement cannot be obtained without undue hardship by other means. 10 INPRAC § 67.2.

      • The discovery requested contains opinions and facts of an expert who was retained and specially employed in anticipation of litigation or trial preparation and who is not expected to be called as a witness at trial and no exceptional circumstances exist which make it impracticable for the party seeking discovery to obtain the facts and opinions by other means. 10 INPRAC § 67.2.

      • The requesting party refuses to pay a fair portion of costs incurred by responding party to produce documents. 10 INPRAC § 67.2.

      • The testing procedure requested will destroy or materially alter the document or thing. 10 INPRAC § 67.2.

- The discovery requested is burdensome, oppressive or unduly expensive. 10 INPRAC § 67.2.

c. *Objection.* If objection is made to the requested form or forms for producing electronically stored information—or if no form was specified in the request—the responding party must state the form or forms it intends to use. The party submitting the request may move for an order under IN ST TRIAL P Rule 37(A) with respect to any objection to or other failure to respond to the request or any part thereof, or any failure to permit inspection as requested. IN ST TRIAL P Rule 34(B).

d. *Claims of privilege.* A blanket claim of privilege is not favored, and that the party who seeks to avoid discovery has the burden of establishing the essential elements of the privilege which is invoked. 3 INPRAC R 34(34.2); Ray v. St. John's Health Care Corp., 582 N.E.2d 464 (Ind.Ct.App. 1991).

e. *Electronically stored information; Production in multiple formats.* A party need not produce the same electronically stored information in more than one form. IN ST TRIAL P Rule 34(B).

f. *Response by a non-party.* Any party, or any witness or person upon whom the request properly is made may respond to the request as provided in IN ST TRIAL P Rule 34(B). If the response of the witness or person to whom it is directed is unfavorable, if he moves to quash, if he refuses to cooperate after responding or fails to respond, or if he objects, the party making the request may move for an order under IN ST TRIAL P Rule 37(A) with respect to any such response or objection. IN ST TRIAL P Rule 34(C)(3).

   i. In granting an order under IN ST TRIAL P Rule 34(C)(3) and IN ST TRIAL P Rule 37(A)(2) the court shall condition relief upon the prepayment of damages to be proximately incurred by the witness or person to whom the request is directed or require an adequate surety bond or other indemnity conditioned against such damages. Such damages shall include reasonable attorneys' fees incurred in reasonable resistance and in establishing such threatened damage or damages. IN ST TRIAL P Rule 34(C)(3).

   ii. Refer to the Indiana KeyRules Motion to Compel Discovery document more information.

g. *Supplementation of responses.* A party who has responded to a request for discovery with a response that was complete when made is under no duty to supplement his response to include information thereafter acquired, except as follows:

   i. A party is under a duty seasonably to supplement his response with respect to any question directly addressed to:

      - The identity and location of persons having knowledge of discoverable matters, and

      - The identity of each person expected to be called as an expert witness at trial, the subject-matter on which he is expected to testify, and the substance of his testimony. IN ST TRIAL P Rule 26(E)(1).

   ii. A party is under a duty seasonably to amend a prior response if he obtains information upon the basis of which:

      - He knows that the response was incorrect when made, or

      - He knows that the response though correct when made is no longer true and the circumstances are such that a failure to amend the response is in substance a knowing concealment. IN ST TRIAL P Rule 26(E)(2).

   iii. A duty to supplement responses may be imposed by order of the court, agreement of the parties, or at any time prior to trial through new requests for supplementation of prior responses. IN ST TRIAL P Rule 26(E)(3).

   iv. The duty seasonably to supplement a discovery response is absolute and is not predicated on a court order. "It is a breach of a litigant's duty reasonably to supplement if the litigant postpones supplementing its response by not obtaining from its experts the information which is to be supplied in answer to interrogatories." 2A INPRAC R 26(26.27); Lucas v. Dorsey Corp., 609 N.E.2d 1191, 1196 (Ind.Ct.App. 1993).

D. Documents

1. *Required documents*

   a. *Request for production.* Refer to the General Requirements section of this document for information on the scope and content of a request for production of documents.

   b. *Certificate of service.* An attorney or unrepresented party tendering a document to the Clerk for filing shall certify that service has been made, list the parties served, and specify the date and means of service. The certificate of service shall be placed at the end of the document and shall not be separately filed. The separate filing of a certificate CCS of service, however, shall not be grounds for rejecting a document for filing. The Clerk may permit documents to be filed without a certificate of service but shall require prompt filing of a separate certificate of service. IN ST TRIAL P Rule 5(C).

      i. All pleadings, motions and other papers submitted for filing which are required to be served under IN ST TRIAL P Rule 5(A) shall contain proof of service pursuant to IN ST TRIAL P Rule 5(B)(2). IN ST LAKE RCP Rule 3(A).

2. *Supplemental documents*

   a. *Stipulation regarding discovery procedure.* Unless the court orders otherwise, the parties may by written stipulation:

      i. Provide that depositions may be taken before any person, at any time or place, upon any notice, and in any manner and when so taken may be used like other depositions, and

      ii. Modify the procedures provided by the Indiana Rules of Trial Procedure for other methods of discovery. IN ST TRIAL P Rule 29.

   b. *Subpoena.* Requests upon non-parties shall be included in or with a subpoena served upon such witness or person. IN ST TRIAL P Rule 34(C)(1).

   c. *Facsimile cover sheet.* Any document sent to the Clerk of the Circuit Court by electronic facsimile transmission shall be accompanied by a cover sheet which states the title of the document, case number, number of pages, identity and voice telephone number of the sending party and instructions for filing. The cover sheet shall contain the signature of the attorney or party, pro se, authorizing the filing. IN ST ADMIN Rule 12(D).

E. Format

1. *Form of documents produced.* The rules applicable to captions, and the signing and form of pleadings (IN ST TRIAL P Rule 8 through IN ST TRIAL P Rule 11), apply to all motions and other papers provided under the Indiana Rules of Trial Procedure. 22B INPRAC 7:2. Unless the parties otherwise agree, or the court otherwise orders, a party who produces documents for inspection shall produce them as they are kept in the usual course of business or shall organize and label them to correspond with the categories in the request. IN ST TRIAL P Rule 34(B).

2. *Form of pleadings.* For the purpose of uniformity, convenience, clarity and durability, requirements in IN ST LAKE RCP Rule 2 shall be observed in the preparation of all pleadings, motions and other papers. IN ST LAKE RCP Rule 2. Whenever materials submitted fail to meet the standards in IN ST LAKE RCP Rule 2, the Court may impose appropriate sanctions. IN ST LAKE RCP Rule 2(B).

   a. *Caption; Names of parties.* Every pleading shall contain a caption setting forth the name of the court, the title of the action, the file number, and a designation as in IN ST TRIAL P Rule 7(A). In the complaint the title of the action shall include the names of all the parties, but in other pleadings it is sufficient to state the name of the first party on each side with an appropriate indication of other parties. IN ST TRIAL P Rule 10(A).

      i. *Special judge matters.* The caption of all CCS Entry Forms, pleadings, motions, orders and other papers to be filed in a special judge case shall include in block text the words SPECIAL JUDGE and the name of the judge directly below the cause number on the caption. IN ST LAKE RCP Rule 2(D).

   b. *Paragraphs; Separate statements.* All averments of a claim or defense shall be made in numbered paragraphs, the contents of each of which shall be limited as far as practicable to a statement of a

single set of circumstances, and a paragraph may be referred to by number in all succeeding pleadings. Each claim founded upon a separate transaction or occurrence and each defense other than denials may be stated in a separate count or defense whenever a separation facilitates the clear presentation of the matters set forth. IN ST TRIAL P Rule 10(B).

c. *Adoption by reference; Exhibits.* Statements in a pleading may be adopted by reference in a different part of the same pleading or in another pleading or in any motion. A copy of any written instrument which is an exhibit to a pleading is a part thereof for all purposes. IN ST TRIAL P Rule 10(C).

d. *Paper; Print, quality and binding*

    i. All pleadings, motions, chronological case summary entry forms, orders, process and other papers shall be neatly and legibly printed, typewritten or mechanically reproduced, on one (1) side only, on white opaque paper. To satisfy the recordkeeping requirements of IN ST TRIAL P Rule 77, the print shall be of sufficient density and clarity for preservation and reproduction of microfilming, optical disk or other secondary sources. For this reason, the use of non-letter-quality printers is discouraged. IN ST LAKE RCP Rule 2(A).

    ii. Paper and ink shall be of such quality as to withstand the test of time. All documents shall be produced on acid-free, non-thermal paper. It is recommended that a minimum of twenty (20) pound, twenty-five percent (25%) cotton paper product be used. Documents of multiple pages shall be submitted in bound or stapled fashion, and the binding or stapling shall be at the top only. Covers or backings shall not be used. IN ST LAKE RCP Rule 2(A).

e. *Papers; Handwritten.* Handwritten papers may be filed only if approved by the Court and a typewritten or printed true rendition thereof is filed within three (3) days thereafter and approved by the Court. Upon such approval, they shall be deemed and filed as the original, while the handwritten papers shall be retained therewith for evidentiary purposes. IN ST LAKE RCP Rule 2(C).

f. *Minute sheets; Motion blanks.* Minute sheets and motion blanks shall no longer be used. IN ST LAKE RCP Rule 2(D).

3. *Size of papers for filing.* Effective January 1, 1992, all pleadings, copies, motions and documents filed with any trial court or appellate level court, typed or printed, with the exception of exhibits and existing wills, shall be prepared on eight and one-half by eleven inch (8 1/2" x 11") size paper. IN ST ADMIN Rule 11.

4. *Signature requirements*

a. *Signature of attorney.* Every pleading or motion of a party represented by an attorney shall be signed by at least one (1) attorney of record in his individual name, whose address, telephone number, and attorney number shall be stated, except that this provision shall not apply to pleadings and motions made and transcribed at the trial or a hearing before the judge and received by him in such form. IN ST TRIAL P Rule 11(A).

    i. The signature of an attorney constitutes a certificate by him that he has read the pleadings; that to the best of his knowledge, information, and belief, there is good ground to support it; and that it is not interposed for delay. IN ST TRIAL P Rule 11(A).

    ii. If a pleading or motion is not signed or is signed with intent to defeat the purpose of the rule, it may be stricken as sham and false and the action may proceed as though the pleading had not been served. IN ST TRIAL P Rule 11(A).

    iii. For a willful violation of IN ST TRIAL P Rule 11 an attorney may be subjected to appropriate disciplinary action. Similar action may be taken if scandalous or indecent matter is inserted. IN ST TRIAL P Rule 11(A).

b. *Signature of unrepresented party.* A party who is not represented by an attorney shall sign his pleading and state his address. IN ST TRIAL P Rule 11(A).

c. *Verification not generally required.* Except when specifically required by rule, pleadings or motions need not be verified or accompanied by affidavit. The rule in equity that the averments of an answer under oath must be overcome by the testimony of two (2) witnesses or of one (1) witness sustained by corroborating circumstances is abolished. IN ST TRIAL P Rule 11(A).

d. *Verification by affirmation or representation.* When in connection with any civil or special statutory proceeding it is required that any pleading, motion, petition, supporting affidavit, or other document of any kind, be verified, or that an oath be taken, it shall be sufficient if the subscriber simply affirms the truth of the matter to be verified by an affirmation or representation. IN ST TRIAL P Rule 11(B). IN ST TRIAL P Rule 11(B) states that the affirmation or representation should be in substantially the following language: "I (we) affirm, under the penalties for perjury, that the foregoing representation(s) is (are) true. (Signed) _____."

    i. Any person who falsifies an affirmation or representation of fact shall be subject to the same penalties as are prescribed by law for the making of a false affidavit. IN ST TRIAL P Rule 11(B).

e. *Verified pleadings, motions, and affidavits as evidence.* Pleadings, motions and affidavits accompanying or in support of such pleadings or motions when required to be verified or under oath shall be accepted as a representation that the signer had personal knowledge thereof or reasonable cause to believe the existence of the facts or matters stated or alleged therein; and, if otherwise competent or acceptable as evidence, may be admitted as evidence of the facts or matters stated or alleged therein when it is so provided in the Indiana Rules of Trial Procedure, by statute or other law, or to the extent the writing or signature expressly purports to be made upon the signer's personal knowledge. When such pleadings, motions and affidavits are verified or under oath they shall not require other or greater proof on the part of the adverse party than if not verified or not under oath unless expressly provided otherwise by the Indiana Rules of Trial Procedure, statute or other law. Affidavits upon motions for summary judgment under IN ST TRIAL P Rule 56 and in denial of execution under IN ST TRIAL P Rule 9.2 shall be made upon personal knowledge. IN ST TRIAL P Rule 11(C).

f. *Electronic signature.* The filing of documents and information through the E-filing system by use of a valid username and password is presumed to have been authorized by the User to whom that username and password have been issued and documents filed through the E-filing system are presumed to have been signed by the same User. IN ST ADMIN Rule 16(E).

5. *Information excluded from public access.* Every document filed in a case shall separately identify information excluded from public access pursuant to IN ST ADMIN Rule 9(G)(1) as follows:

a. Whole documents that are excluded from public access pursuant to IN ST ADMIN Rule 9(G)(1) shall be tendered on light green paper or have a light green coversheet attached to the document, marked "Not for Public Access" or "Confidential." IN ST TRIAL P Rule 5(G)(1).

b. When only a portion of a document contains information excluded from public access pursuant to IN ST ADMIN Rule 9(G)(1), said information shall be omitted [or redacted] from the filed document, and set forth on a separate accompanying document on light green paper conspicuously marked "Not for Public Access" or "Confidential" and clearly designated [or identifying] the caption and number of the case and the document and location within the document to which the redacted material pertains. IN ST TRIAL P Rule 5(G)(2).

c. With respect to documents filed in electronic format, the trial court, by local rule, may provide for compliance with IN ST TRIAL P Rule 5 in manner that separates and protects access to information excluded from public access. IN ST TRIAL P Rule 5(G)(3).

d. IN ST TRIAL P Rule 5(G) does not apply to a record sealed by the court pursuant to IN ST 5-14-3-5.5 or otherwise, nor to records, documents, or information filed in cases to which public access is prohibited pursuant to IN ST ADMIN Rule 9(G). IN ST TRIAL P Rule 5(G)(4).

e. The following information in case records is excluded from public access and is confidential:

    i. Information that is excluded from public access pursuant to federal law;

    ii. Information that is excluded from public access as declared confidential by Indiana statute or other court rule, including without limitation:

- All adoption records created after July 8, 1941, as declared confidential by IN ST 31-19-19-1, et seq., except those specifically declared open by IN ST 31-19-13-2(2);

- All records relating to chancroid, chlamydia, gonorrhea, hepatitis, human immunodefi-

ciency virus (HIV), Lymphogranuloma venereum, syphilis, tuberculosis, as declared confidential by IN ST 16-41-8-1, et seq.;

- All records relating to child abuse as declared confidential by IN ST 31-33-18-1, et seq.;
- All records relating to drug tests as declared confidential by IN ST 5-14-3-4(a)(9);
- Records of grand jury proceedings as declared confidential by IN ST 35-34-2-4;
- Records of juvenile proceedings as declared confidential by IN ST 31-39-1-2, except those specifically open under statute;
- All paternity records created after July 1, 1941 as declared confidential by IN ST 31-14-11-15, IN ST 31-19-5-23, IN ST 31-39-1-1 and IN ST 31-39-1-2 [Editor's note: IN ST 31-14-11-15 was repealed effective May 9, 2013];
- All pre-sentence reports as declared confidential by IN ST 35-38-1-13;
- Written petitions to permit marriages without consent and orders directing the Clerk of Court to issue a marriage license to underage persons, as declared confidential by IN ST 31-11-1-6;
- Only those arrest warrants, search warrants, indictments and informations ordered confidential by the trial judge, prior to return of duly executed service as declared confidential by IN ST 5-14-3-4(b)(1);
- All medical, mental health, or tax records unless determined by law or regulation of any governmental custodian not to be confidential, released by the subject of such records, or declared by a court of competent jurisdiction to be essential to the resolution of litigation as declared confidential by IN ST 16-39-3-10, IN ST 6-4.1-5-10, IN ST 6-4.1-12-12, and IN ST 6-8.1-7-1;
- Personal information relating to jurors or prospective jurors, other than for the use of the parties and counsel, pursuant to IN ST JURY Rule 10;
- Information relating to protection from abuse orders, no-contact orders and workplace violence restraining orders as declared confidential by IN ST 5-2-9-6, et seq.;
- Mediation proceedings pursuant to IN ST ADR Rule 2.11, Mini-Trial proceedings pursuant to IN ST ADR Rule 4.4(C), and Summary Jury Trials pursuant to IN ST ADR Rule 5.6;
- Information in probation files pursuant to the Probation Standards promulgated by the Judicial Conference of Indiana pursuant to IN ST 11-13-1-8(b);
- Information deemed confidential pursuant to the Rules for Court Administered Alcohol and Drug Programs promulgated by the Judicial Conference of Indiana pursuant to IN ST 12-23-14-13;
- Information deemed confidential pursuant to the Problem-Solving Court Rules promulgated by the Judicial Conference of Indiana pursuant to IN ST 33-23-16-16;
- All records of the Department of workforce Development as declared confidential by IN ST 22-4-19-6;
- Information regarding interception of electronic communications that is sealed or deemed confidential as set forth in IN ST 35-33.5-2-1, et seq.

iii. Information excluded from public access by specific court order;

iv. Complete Social Security Numbers of living persons;

v. With the exception of names, information such as addresses, phone numbers, and dates of birth which explicitly identifies:

- Natural persons who are witnesses or victims (not including defendants) in criminal, domestic violence, stalking, sexual assault, juvenile, or civil protection order proceedings, provided that juveniles who are victims of sex crimes shall be identified by initials only;

- Places of residence of judicial officers, clerks and other employees of courts and clerks of court, unless the person or persons about whom the information pertains waives confidentiality;

vi. Complete account numbers of specific assets, loans, bank accounts, credit cards, and personal identification numbers (PINs);

vii. All orders of expungement entered in criminal or juvenile proceedings, orders to restrict access to criminal history information pursuant to IN ST 35-38-5-5.5 or IN ST 35-38-8-5 and records excluded from public access by such orders, and information related to infractions that is excluded from public access pursuant to IN ST 34-28-5-15 or IN ST 34-28-5-16 [Editor's note: IN ST 35-38-5-5.5, IN ST 35-38-8-5 and IN ST 34-28-5-16 were repealed effective July 1, 2013; for information on orders restricting access to criminal history, refer to IN ST 35-38-9-1, et seq.];

viii. All personal notes and e-mail, and deliberative material, of judges, jurors, court staff and judicial agencies, and information recorded in personal data assistants (PDA's) or organizers and personal calendars. IN ST ADMIN Rule 9(G)(1).

6. *Format of electronically filed documents*

   a. *Generally.* Electronically filed documents must meet the same requirements of format as documents conventionally filed pursuant to IN ST LAKE RCP Rule 2 or other applicable Lake County Rules of Civil Procedure. IN ST LAKE RCP Rule 17(D)(1).

   b. *Titles of documents.* The person electronically filing a document will be responsible for designating a title for the document at the time it is filed. The LCOD will generate the appropriate entry onto the CCS to record the filing of the document. IN ST LAKE RCP Rule 17(D)(3).

   c. *Citations and hyperlinks.* Electronically filed documents may contain hyperlink references to an external document as a convenient mechanism for accessing material cited in the document. Filers wishing to insert hyperlinks into documents shall continue to use the traditional method of citation to authority in addition to the hyperlink provided. The hyperlink is merely a convenience to the court and the material referenced is extraneous to the file and not a part of the court's record. IN ST LAKE RCP Rule 17(D)(5).

   d. *Attachments and exhibits.* All documents which form part of a single submission and which are being filed at the same time and by the same filer may be electronically filed together under one document filing, e.g., the motion, supporting affidavits, memorandum in support, designation of evidence, exhibits. IN ST LAKE RCP Rule 17(D)(6).

      i. Large documents which do not exist in an electronic format shall be scanned into .pdf format and filed electronically as separate attachments. A scanner is available in each clerk's office for use by the public and the bar in scanning and saving image files if needed. IN ST LAKE RCP Rule 17(D)(6).

   e. *Electronic signatures*

      i. *Electronic filing as signature.* The electronic filing of a document which is required to be signed shall constitute the filer's representation under IN ST TRIAL P Rule 11. Unless the electronically filed document has been scanned and shows the filer's original signature, the signature of the filer shall be indicated by As/Attorney's Name, or As/Party's Name as in the case of a pro se litigant, on the line where the signature would otherwise appear. IN ST LAKE RCP Rule 17(G)(1).

      ii. *Signatures on jointly signed or filed, verified or other documents.* In the case of a stipulation, agreed order, jointly signed motion or other document which needs to be signed by two (2) or more persons, or in the case of documents which must contain original signatures and which require verification or an unsworn declaration under rule or statute, the signatures may be indicated by either:

         - Submitting a scanned copy of the originally signed document; or,
         - Submitting the document with the use of As/Name in the signature block(s) where the

original signature(s) appear(s) in the original document; provided, however, that the filer shall first obtain the physical signature of all persons necessary. IN ST LAKE RCP Rule 17(G)(2).

    iii. *Retention of original.* The filer shall retain the original executed document. IN ST LAKE RCP Rule 17(G).

7. *Citation of local rules.* The local rules for Lake County may be known as the Lake County Rules of Civil Procedure, and abbreviated as LR. IN ST LAKE RCP Rule 1(C).

F. Filing and Service Requirements

1. *Filing requirements.* Except as otherwise provided in IN ST TRIAL P Rule 5(E)(2), all pleadings and papers subsequent to the complaint which are required to be served upon a party shall be filed with the Court either before service or within a reasonable period of time thereafter. IN ST TRIAL P Rule 5(E)(1). All papers presented for filing shall be submitted to the Clerk and not to the court. All papers submitted for filing shall be mailed or delivered to the Clerk's office at the courthouse in which the case is pending. IN ST LAKE RCP Rule 3(A).

    a. *Non-filing of discovery until necessary*

        i. *Non-filing of discovery; Exceptions.* No deposition or request for discovery or response thereto under IN ST TRIAL P Rule 27, IN ST TRIAL P Rule 30, IN ST TRIAL P Rule 31, IN ST TRIAL P Rule 33, IN ST TRIAL P Rule 34 or IN ST TRIAL P Rule 36 shall be filed with the Court unless:

- A motion is filed pursuant to IN ST TRIAL P Rule 26(C) or IN ST TRIAL P Rule 37 and the original deposition or request for discovery or response thereto is necessary to enable the Court to rule; or

- A party desires to use the deposition or request for discovery or response thereto for evidentiary purposes at trial or in connection with a motion, and the Court, either upon its own motion or that of any party, or as a part of any pre-trial order, orders the filing of the original. IN ST TRIAL P Rule 5(E)(2).

        ii. *Custody of original and period of retention*

- The original of a deposition shall, subject to the provisions of IN ST TRIAL P Rule 30(E), be delivered by the reporter to the party taking it and shall be maintained by that party until filed with the Court pursuant to IN ST TRIAL P Rule 5(E)(2) or until the later of final judgment, agreed settlement of the litigation or all appellate rights have been exhausted. IN ST TRIAL P Rule 5(E)(3)(a).

- The original or any request for discovery or response thereto under IN ST TRIAL P Rule 27, IN ST TRIAL P Rule 30, IN ST TRIAL P Rule 31, IN ST TRIAL P Rule 33, IN ST TRIAL P Rule 34 and IN ST TRIAL P Rule 36 shall be maintained by the party originating the request or response until filed with the Court pursuant to IN ST TRIAL P Rule 5(E)(2) or until the later of final judgment, agreed settlement or all appellate rights have been exhausted. IN ST TRIAL P Rule 5(E)(3)(b).

        iii. *Original unavailable; Copies.* In the event it is made to appear to the satisfaction of the Court that the original of a deposition or request for discovery or response thereto cannot be filed with the Court when required, the Court may allow use of a copy instead of the original. IN ST TRIAL P Rule 5(E)(4).

        iv. *Filing as publication.* The filing of any deposition shall constitute publication. IN ST TRIAL P Rule 5(E)(5).

    b. *Filing with the court defined.* The filing of pleadings, motions, and other papers with the court as required by the Indiana Rules of Trial Procedure shall be made by one of the following methods:

        i. Delivery to the clerk of the court;

        ii. Sending by electronic transmission under the procedure adopted pursuant to IN ST ADMIN Rule 12;

iii. Mailing to the clerk by registered, certified or express mail return receipt requested;

iv. Depositing with any third-party commercial carrier for delivery to the clerk within three (3) calendar days, cost prepaid, properly addressed;

v. If the court so permits, filing with the judge, in which event the judge shall note thereon the filing date and forthwith transmit them to the office of the clerk; or

vi. Electronic filing, as approved by the Division of State Court Administration pursuant to IN ST ADMIN Rule 16. IN ST TRIAL P Rule 5(F).

vii. Filing by registered or certified mail and by third-party commercial carrier shall be complete upon mailing or deposit. IN ST TRIAL P Rule 5(F).

c. *Mandatory electronic filing.* Unless otherwise permitted by the Lake County Rules of Civil Procedure or otherwise authorized by the judicial officer assigned to a particular case, all documents submitted for filing (including the original complaint, or equivalent pleading, and summons) shall be filed electronically with the clerk using the LCOD, no matter when the case was originally filed. IN ST LAKE RCP Rule 17(D).

i. *Of documents containing information excluded from public access pursuant to* IN ST ADMIN Rule 9. Documents containing information excluded from public access pursuant to IN ST ADMIN Rule 9, or documents which are ordered to be filed under seal shall be filed electronically, pursuant to IN ST LAKE RCP Rule 17(D)(9), whenever possible, along with a copy of the applicable order to seal the records, and the filer shall designate the documents as "Not for Public Access Pursuant to Administrative Rule 9(G)(1)" at the time of filing. IN ST LAKE RCP Rule 16(A)(1); IN ST LAKE RCP Rule 17(D)(9).

- *Conventional filing of documents containing information excluded from public access pursuant to* IN ST ADMIN Rule 9. Documents containing information excluded from public access pursuant to IN ST ADMIN Rule 9, or documents which are ordered to be filed under seal, which cannot be legibly scanned and filed electronically, shall be conventionally filed under seal and designated by the filer as "Not for Public Access Pursuant to Administrative Rule 9(G)(1)" at the time of filing. The unredacted version shall be filed on light green paper which is conspicuously marked "Not for Public Access"; and a redacted version, with confidential information deleted, shall be filed on white paper which shall be available for public access. The filer shall also electronically file a Notice of Manual Filing. IN ST LAKE RCP Rule 16(A)(2).

ii. *Technical failures.* If a registered user is unable to file a document in a timely manner due to technical difficulties in the LCOD, the registered user must file a document with the court as soon as possible notifying the court of the inability to file the document. A sample document titled Declaration that Party was Unable to File in a Timely Manner Due to Technical Difficulties can be found at IN ST LAKE RCP Form 4. Delayed filings shall be rejected unless accompanied by the declaration attesting to the filer's failed attempts to file electronically at least two (2) times, separated by at least one (1) hour, after noon on each day of delay due to such technical failure. IN ST LAKE RCP Rule 17(J).

iii. *Documents allowed to be filed conventionally.* Unless specifically authorized by the court, only the following documents may be filed conventionally and not electronically:

- Exhibits and other documents that cannot be converted to a legible electronic form, such as videotapes, x-rays, and similar materials

- Documents delivered to the clerk by pro se litigants

- Documents mailed to the clerk by pro se litigants

- Confidential documents

- Notice of manual filing

- Titles of documents

- Chronological case summary entry forms (CCS entry forms). IN ST LAKE RCP Rule 17(E).

- For more information on the documents which must be filed conventionally, refer to IN ST LAKE RCP Rule 17(E).

d. *Facsimile filing.* Only when necessary on an emergency basis (i.e., when certified mail or other means of filing will not bring the document to the Judge's attention prior to the scheduled hearing or ruling), pleadings, motions and other papers may be filed by electronic facsimile transmission, or when specifically authorized by the Court. IN ST LAKE RCP Rule 2(C).

  i. *Generally.* In counties where a majority of judges of the courts of record, by posted local rule, have authorized electronic facsimile filing and designated a telephone number to receive such transmissions, pleadings, motions, and other papers may be sent to the Clerk of Circuit Court by electronic facsimile transmission for filing in any case, provided:

   - Such matter does not exceed ten (10) pages, including the cover sheet;
   - Such matter does not require the payment of fees other than the electronic facsimile transcription fee set forth in IN ST ADMIN Rule 12(E);
   - The sending party creates at the time of transmission a machine generated log for such transmission; and
   - The original document and the transmission log are maintained by the sending party for the duration of the litigation. IN ST ADMIN Rule 12(B).

  ii. *Time of filing.* During normal, posted business hours, the time of filing shall be the time the duplicate document is produced in the office of the Clerk of the Circuit Court. Duplicate documents received at all other times shall be filed as of the next normal business day. IN ST ADMIN Rule 12(C).

   - If the receiving fax machine endorses its own time and date stamp upon the transmitted documents and the receiving machine produces a delivery receipt which is electronically created and transmitted to the sending party, the time of filing shall be the date and time recorded on the transmitted document by the receiving fax machine. IN ST ADMIN Rule 12(C).

e. *Filing for special judges.* For special judge matters where the special judge is a full-time judge or magistrate serving within Lake County, all papers submitted for filing shall be delivered or mailed to the Clerk's office at the courthouse where the special judge regularly serves. IN ST LAKE RCP Rule 3(A).

f. *Proof of filing.* Any party filing any paper by any method other than personal delivery to the clerk shall retain proof of filing. IN ST TRIAL P Rule 5(F).

2. *Service requirements.* Unless otherwise provided by the Indiana Rules of Trial Procedure or an order of the court, each party and special judge, if any, shall be served with: (1) every order required by its terms to be served; (2) every pleading subsequent to the original complaint; (3) every written motion except one which may be heard ex parte; (4) every brief submitted to the trial court; (5) every paper relating to discovery required to be served upon a party; and (6) every written notice, appearance, demand, offer of judgment, designation of record on appeal, or similar paper. IN ST TRIAL P Rule 5(A).

a. *Methods of service*

  i. *Personal service.* Whenever a party is represented by an attorney of record, service shall be made upon such attorney unless service upon the party himself is ordered by the court. Service upon the attorney or party shall be made by delivering or mailing a copy of the papers to the last known address or where an attorney or party has consented to service by fax or e-mail, as provided in IN ST TRIAL P Rule 3.1(A)(4), by faxing or e-mailing a copy of the documents to the fax number or e-mail address set out in the appearance form or correction as required by IN ST TRIAL P Rule 3.1(E). IN ST TRIAL P Rule 5(B). Delivery of a copy within IN ST TRIAL P Rule 5 means:

   - Offering or tendering it to the attorney or party and stating the nature of the papers being served. Refusal to accept an offered or tendered document is a waiver of any objection to the sufficiency or adequacy of service of that document;

REQUEST FOR PRODUCTION OF DOCUMENTS

- Leaving it at his office with a clerk or other person in charge thereof, or if there is no one in charge, leaving it in a conspicuous place therein; or

- If the office is closed, by leaving it at his dwelling house or usual place of abode with some person of suitable age and discretion then residing therein; or,

- Leaving it at some other suitable place, selected by the attorney upon whom service is being made, pursuant to duly promulgated local rule. IN ST TRIAL P Rule 5(B)(1).

ii. *Service by mail.* If service is made by mail, the papers shall be deposited in the United States mail addressed to the person on whom they are being served, with postage prepaid. Service shall be deemed complete upon mailing. Proof of service of all papers permitted to be mailed may be made by written acknowledgment of service, by affidavit of the person who mailed the papers, or by certificate of an attorney. It shall be the duty of attorneys when entering their appearance in a cause or when filing pleadings or papers therein, to have noted in the Chronological Case Summary or said pleadings or papers so filed the address and telephone number of their office. Service by delivery or by mail at such address shall be deemed sufficient and complete. IN ST TRIAL P Rule 5(B)(2).

iii. *Service by fax or e-mail.* A party who has consented to service by fax or e-mail may be served as follows:

- Service by e-mail shall be made by attaching the document being served in .pdf format. Discovery documents must also be served in accordance with IN ST TRIAL P Rule 26(A). IN ST TRIAL P Rule 5(B)(3)(a).

- Service by fax shall be deemed complete upon generation of a transmission record indicating the successful transmission of the entire document, except as provided in IN ST TRIAL P Rule 5(B)(3)(d). IN ST TRIAL P Rule 5(B)(3)(b).

- Service by e-mail shall be deemed complete upon transmission, except as provided in IN ST TRIAL P Rule 5(B)(3)(d). IN ST TRIAL P Rule 5(B)(3)(c).

- Service by fax or e-mail that occurs on a Saturday, Sunday, legal holiday, or day the court or agency in which the matter is pending is closed or after 5:00 PM local time of the recipient shall be deemed complete the next day that is not a Saturday, Sunday, legal holiday, or day that the court or agency in which the matter is pending is not closed. IN ST TRIAL P Rule 5(B)(3)(d).

iv. *Additional service of electronic discovery.* In addition to service under Rule IN ST TRIAL P Rule 5(B) or a .pdf format electronic copy, a party propounding or responding to interrogatories, requests for production or requests for admission shall comply with IN ST TRIAL P Rule 26(A.1)(a) or IN ST TRIAL P Rule 26(A.1)(b). IN ST TRIAL P Rule 26(A.1).

- The party shall serve the discovery request or response in an electronic format (either on a disk or as an electronic document attachment) in any commercially available word processing software system. If transmitted on disk, each disk shall be labeled, identifying the caption of the case, the document, and the word processing version in which it is being submitted. If more than one (1) disk is used for the same document, each disk shall be labeled and also shall be sequentially numbered. If transmitted by electronic mail, the document must be accompanied by electronic memorandum providing the forgoing identifying information; or

- The party shall serve the opposing party with a verified statement that the attorney or party appearing pro se lacks the equipment and is unable to transmit the discovery as required by IN ST TRIAL P Rule 26(A.1). IN ST TRIAL P Rule 26(A.1).

b. *Serving numerous defendants.* In any action in which there are unusually large numbers of defendants, the court, upon motion or of its own initiative, may order:

i. That service of the pleadings of the defendants and replies thereto need not be made as between the defendants;

- That any cross-claim, counterclaim, or matter constituting an avoidance or affirmative defense contained therein shall be deemed to be denied or avoided by all other parties; and

- That the filing of any such pleading and service thereof upon the plaintiff constitutes due notice of it to the parties. IN ST TRIAL P Rule 5(D).

 ii. A copy of every such order shall be served upon the parties in such manner and form as the court directs. IN ST TRIAL P Rule 5(D).

 c. *Service by electronic means.* The Lake County Online Docket will generate a Notice of Electronic Filing and Service when any document is filed and served. This notice will be emailed to each registered user of record in a case, and an electronic service event will be added to the work queue of each registered user of record in the case. The party filing the document should retain a paper or electronic copy of the Notice of Electronic Filing and Service. This notice represents proof of filing and service of the document on registered users of record in that case. The filer shall not be required to conventionally serve any document on any party receiving electronic service. IN ST LAKE RCP Rule 17(F)(2).

  i. The filer shall also conventionally serve those parties not designated or able to receive electronic notice or service but who are nevertheless entitled to notice of said pleading or other document in accordance with the Indiana Rules of Civil Procedure and applicable Lake County Rules of Civil Procedure. In such cases, the filer shall also file a certificate of service, as appropriate. IN ST LAKE RCP Rule 17(F).

 d. *Service on parties in default for failure to appear.* No service need be made on parties in default for failure to appear, except that pleadings asserting new or additional claims for relief against them shall be served upon them in the manner provided by service of summons in IN ST TRIAL P Rule 4. IN ST TRIAL P Rule 5(A).

G. Hearings

 1. The Indiana rules do not contemplate a hearing related to the filing and service of requests for production.

H. Forms

 1. Request for Production of Documents Forms for Indiana

  a. Request for production of documents. 5 INPRAC § 4:3.1.

  b. Request for production of documents; Insurance company. 5 INPRAC § 4:3.2.

  c. Request for production of documents; Medical records. 5 INPRAC § 4:3.3.

  d. Request for production of documents; Non-party. 5 INPRAC § 4:3.4.

  e. Motion to enlarge time to respond to request for production of documents. 5 INPRAC § 4:3.5.

  f. Response to request for production of documents; General form with objections. 5 INPRAC § 4:3.6.

  g. Request for production of documents; General form. 10 INPRAC § 67.6.

  h. Request for entry upon land for inspection. 10 INPRAC § 67.7.

  i. Request for production of documents; Products liability; Plaintiff to manufacturer. 10 INPRAC § 67.8.

  j. Request for production of documents; Products liability; Property loss; Defendant. 10 INPRAC § 67.9.

  k. Request for production of documents; Products liability; Vehicle; Plaintiff. 10 INPRAC § 67.10.

  l. Products liability; Defendant to plaintiff regarding accident and injuries. 10 INPRAC § 67.11.

  m. Request for production of documents; Action against insurance company. 10 INPRAC § 67.13.

  n. Request for production of documents; Action against nursing home; Plaintiff. 10 INPRAC § 67.14.

  o. Request for production of documents; Action against nursing home; Defendant. 10 INPRAC § 67.15.

  p. Request for production of documents; Medical records. 10 INPRAC § 67.17.

  q. Request for production of documents; To obtain corporate records. 10 INPRAC § 67.18.

  r. Request for production of handwriting exemplars. 10 INPRAC § 67.19.

    s.   Response to request for production of documents; General form with objections. 10 INPRAC § 67.30.

    t.   Response to request for permission to enter upon land. 10 INPRAC § 67.31.

    u.   Motion to shorten time to respond to request for production. 10 INPRAC § 67.32.

    v.   Motion to enlarge time to respond to request for production. 10 INPRAC § 67.33.

    w.   Request for production of documents to nonparty; General form. 10 INPRAC § 67.40.

    x.   Request for production of documents to nonparty; Another form. 10 INPRAC § 67.41.

    y.   Request for production of documents to nonparty; Production of bank and financial records. 10 INPRAC § 67.42.

    z.   Request for production of documents to nonparty; Request that employer produce records relating to employee making personal injury claim. 10 INPRAC § 67.43.

2. Official Request for Production of Documents Forms for Lake County

    a.   CCS entry form. IN ST LAKE RCP App. A.

    b.   Notice of manual filing. IN ST LAKE RCP Form 2.

    c.   Certificate of service. IN ST LAKE RCP Form 3.

    d.   Declaration that party was unable to file in a timely manner. IN ST LAKE RCP Form 4.

3. Request for Production of Documents Forms for Lake County

    a.   Notice of manual filing. EFORMST IN 5540.

I. Checklist

(I) ❑ Matters to be considered by the party serving the request for production

    (a) ❑ Required documents

        (1) ❑ Request for production of documents

        (2) ❑ Certificate of service

    (b) ❑ Supplemental documents

        (1) ❑ Stipulation regarding discovery procedure

        (2) ❑ Subpoena

        (3) ❑ Facsimile cover sheet

    (c) ❑ Timing

        (1) ❑ On parties: The request may, without leave of court, be served upon the plaintiff after commencement of the action and upon any other party with or after service of the summons and complaint upon that party

        (2) ❑ On non-parties: Neither a request nor subpoena to produce or permit as permitted by IN ST TRIAL P Rule 34 shall be served upon a non-party until at least fifteen (15) days after the date on which the party intending to serve such request or subpoena serves a copy of the proposed request and subpoena on all other parties

            (i) ❑ Provided, however, that if such request or subpoena relates to a matter set for hearing within such fifteen (15) day period or arises out of a bona fide emergency, such request or subpoena may be served upon a non-party one (1) day after receipt of the proposed request or subpoena by all other parties

(II) ❑ Matters to be considered by the responding party

    (a) ❑ Required documents

        (1) ❑ Response to request for production of documents

        (2) ❑ Certificate of service

(b) ❏ Supplemental documents

   (1) ❏ Business records

   (2) ❏ Stipulation regarding discovery procedure

   (3) ❏ Facsimile cover sheet

(c) ❏ Timing

   (1) ❏ The party upon whom the request is served shall serve a written response within a period designated in the request, not less than thirty (30) days after the service thereof or within such shorter for longer time as the court may allow

Requests, Notices and Applications
Request for Admissions

Document Last Updated October 2013

A. Applicable Rules

1. *State rules*

   a. Appearance. IN ST TRIAL P Rule 3.1.

   b. Process. IN ST TRIAL P Rule 4.

   c. Service and filing of pleadings and other papers. IN ST TRIAL P Rule 5.

   d. Time. IN ST TRIAL P Rule 6.

   e. Pleadings. IN ST TRIAL P Rule 7; IN ST TRIAL P Rule 9.2; IN ST TRIAL P Rule 10.

   f. Signing and verification of pleadings. IN ST TRIAL P Rule 11.

   g. Pre-trial procedure; Formulating issues. IN ST TRIAL P Rule 16.

   h. General provisions governing discovery. IN ST TRIAL P Rule 26.

   i. Methods of discovery. IN ST TRIAL P Rule 27; IN ST TRIAL P Rule 29; IN ST TRIAL P Rule 30; IN ST TRIAL P Rule 31; IN ST TRIAL P Rule 33; IN ST TRIAL P Rule 34; IN ST TRIAL P Rule 35; IN ST TRIAL P Rule 36.

   j. Failure to make or cooperate in discovery; Sanctions. IN ST TRIAL P Rule 37.

   k. Judgment on the evidence (directed verdict). IN ST TRIAL P Rule 50.

   l. Findings by the court. IN ST TRIAL P Rule 52.

   m. Summary judgment. IN ST TRIAL P Rule 56.

   n. Motion to correct error. IN ST TRIAL P Rule 59.

   o. Relief from judgment or order. IN ST TRIAL P Rule 60.

   p. Court records. IN ST TRIAL P Rule 77.

   q. Access to court records. IN ST ADMIN Rule 9.

   r. Paper size. IN ST ADMIN Rule 11.

   s. Facsimile transmission. IN ST ADMIN Rule 12.

   t. Electronic filing and electronic service pilot projects. IN ST ADMIN Rule 16.

   u. Privacy and confidentiality. IN ST 5-2-9-6; IN ST 5-14-3-4; IN ST 5-14-3-5.5; IN ST 6-4.1-5-10; IN ST 6-4.1-12-12; IN ST 6-8.1-7-1; IN ST 11-13-1-8; IN ST 12-23-14-13; IN ST 16-39-3-10; IN ST 16-41-8-1; IN ST 22-4-19-6; IN ST 31-11-1-6; IN ST 31-19-5-23; IN ST 31-19-13-2; IN ST 31-19-19-1; IN ST 31-33-18-1; IN ST 31-39-1-1; IN ST 31-39-1-2; IN ST 33-23-16-16; IN ST 35-34-2-4; IN ST 35-38-1-13; IN ST 35-38-9-1; IN ST ADR Rule 2.11; IN ST ADR Rule 4.4; IN ST ADR Rule 5.6; IN ST JURY Rule 10.

2. *Local rules*

   a. Scope and title. [IN ST LAKE RCP Rule 1, as amended by IN ORDER 13-0237, effective October 18, 2013].

   b. Preparation of pleadings, motions and other papers. IN ST LAKE RCP Rule 2.

   c. Filing. [IN ST LAKE RCP Rule 3, as amended by IN ORDER 13-0237, effective October 18, 2013].

   d. Discovery. IN ST LAKE RCP Rule 8.

   e. Confidential information and sealed documents. IN ST LAKE RCP Rule 16.

   f. Electronic filing and service. IN ST LAKE RCP Rule 17.

B. Timing

1. *Time for service of request for admissions.* The request may, without leave of court, be served upon the plaintiff after commencement of the action and upon any other party with or after service of the summons and complaint upon that party. IN ST TRIAL P Rule 36(A).

2. *Time for service of response.* The matter is admitted unless, within a period designated in the request, not less than thirty (30) days after service thereof or within such shorter or longer time as the court may allow, the party to whom the request is directed serves upon the party requesting the admission a written answer or objection addressed to the matter. IN ST TRIAL P Rule 36(A).

3. *Computation of time*

   a. *Generally; Days excluded.* In computing any period of time prescribed or allowed by the Indiana Rules of Trial Procedure, by order of the court, or by any applicable statute, the day of the act, event, or default from which the designated period of time begins to run shall not be included. The last day of the period so computed is to be included unless it is:

      i. A Saturday,

      ii. A Sunday,

      iii. A legal holiday as defined by state statute, or

      iv. A day the office in which the act is to be done is closed during regular business hours. IN ST TRIAL P Rule 6(A).

   b. *Short periods.* In any event, the period runs until the end of the next day that is not a Saturday, a Sunday, a legal holiday, or a day on which the office is closed. When the period of time allowed is less than seven (7) days, intermediate Saturdays, Sundays, legal holidays, and days on which the office is closed shall be excluded from the computations. IN ST TRIAL P Rule 6(A).

   c. *Additional time after service by United States mail.* Whenever a party has the right or is required to do some act or take some proceedings within a prescribed period after the service of a notice or other paper upon him and the notice or paper is served upon him by United States mail, three (3) days shall be added to the prescribed period. IN ST TRIAL P Rule 6(E).

   d. *Electronic filing does not alter deadlines.* Filing electronically does not alter any filing deadlines or any time computation pursuant to state or federal statutes, any Rules of the Indiana Supreme Court, including without limitation the Rules of Trial Procedure, the Rules of Appellate Procedure or the Administrative Rules, or applicable Lake County Rules of Civil Procedure. The office of the Lake County Clerk is open for electronic filing under the Lake County Rules of Civil Procedure twenty-four (24) hours a day. A document is deemed filed at the date and time it is received by the LCOD server. Filing must be completed before midnight local time in order to be considered filed that day. Lake County observes Central Time and electronic filers are strongly urged to file documents during hours when the Lake County Online Docket ("LCOD") help line is available, from 9:00 a.m. to 4:00 p.m. local time, although documents can be filed electronically twenty-four (24) hours a day. IN ST LAKE RCP Rule 17(I).

   e. *Enlargement of time.* When an act is required or allowed to be done at or within a specific time by the Indiana Rules of Trial Procedure, the court may at any time for cause shown:

      i. Order the period enlarged, with or without motion or notice, if request therefor is made before the expiration of the period originally prescribed or extended by a previous order; or

ii. Upon motion made after the expiration of the specific period, permit the act to be done where the failure to act was the result of excusable neglect; but, the court may not extend the time for taking any action for judgment on the evidence under IN ST TRIAL P Rule 50(A), amendment of findings and judgment under IN ST TRIAL P Rule 52(B), to correct errors under IN ST TRIAL P Rule 59(C), statement in opposition to motion to correct error under IN ST TRIAL P Rule 59(E), or to obtain relief from final judgment under IN ST TRIAL P Rule 60(B), except to the extent and under the conditions stated in those rules. IN ST TRIAL P Rule 6(B).

C. General Requirements

1. *Scope of discovery.* Unless otherwise limited by order of the court in accordance with the Indiana Rules of Trial Procedure, the scope of discovery is as follows:

   a. *In general.* Parties may obtain discovery regarding any matter, not privileged, which is relevant to the subject-matter involved in the pending action, whether it relates to the claim or defense of the party seeking discovery or the claim or defense of any other party, including the existence, description, nature, custody, condition and location of any books, documents, or other tangible things and the identity and location of persons having knowledge of any discoverable matter. It is not ground for objection that the information sought will be inadmissible at the trial if the information sought appears reasonably calculated to lead to the discovery of admissible evidence. IN ST TRIAL P Rule 26(B)(1).

      i. *Limiting discovery upon court determination.* The frequency or extent of use of the discovery methods otherwise permitted under the Indiana Rules of Trial Procedure and by any local rule shall be limited by the court if it determines that:

         • The discovery sought is unreasonably cumulative or duplicative, or is obtainable from some other source that is more convenient, less burdensome, or less expensive;

         • The party seeking discovery has had ample opportunity by discovery in the action to obtain the information sought or;

         • The burden or expense of the proposed discovery outweighs its likely benefit, taking into account the needs of the case, the amount in controversy, the parties' resources, the importance of the issues at stake in the litigation, and the importance of the proposed discovery in resolving the issues. IN ST TRIAL P Rule 26(B)(1).

         • The court may act upon its own initiative after reasonable notice or pursuant to a motion under IN ST TRIAL P Rule 26(C). IN ST TRIAL P Rule 26(B)(1). Refer to the Indiana KeyRules Motion for Protective Order document for more information.

      ii. *Relevancy in the discovery context.* When the word "relevancy" is used in IN ST TRIAL P Rule 26(B), it does not mean "relevancy" as that word in used to determine the admissibility of evidence in a trial court. It is much broader. It means "relevancy" to the "subject matter" of the litigation or pending action and it may relate to the claim or defense of any party. Pretrial discovery is available as to any nonprivileged matter relevant to the subject matter of the lawsuit or to obtain information reasonably calculated to lead to admissible evidence. 2A INPRAC R 26(26.4); Kaufmann v. Credithrift Financial, Inc., 465 N.E.2d 207, 210 (Ind.Ct.App. 1984).

      iii. *Tests for relevance.* Indiana case law has developed two (2) additional tests in this area. 2A INPRAC R 26(26.4).

         • The first test determines when a document or a request for information is actually relevant to the subject matter in the pending action. A document [or discovery request] is relevant to discovery if there is the possibility the information sought may be relevant to the subject matter of the action. 2A INPRAC R 26(26.4); CIGNA-INA/Aetna v. Hagerman-Shambaugh, 473 N.E.2d 1033, 1036 (Ind.Ct.App. 1985).

         • The second test speaks to appellate review of the trial court's determination that a document or discovery request is relevant to the subject matter of the pending action. The appellate court sees its review of the trial court's decision on relevancy to subject matter as being very limited. The court states: "Our review of the trial court's conclusion that the documents are relevant is limited. A trial court is vested with discretion in its rulings on discovery issues." 2A INPRAC R 26(26.4); Costanzi v. Ryan, 175 Ind.App. 257, 370 N.E.2d 1333 (Ind.Ct.App. 1978).

b. *Insurance agreements.* A party may obtain discovery of the existence and contents of any insurance agreement under which any person carrying on an insurance business may be liable to satisfy part or all of a judgment which may be entered in the action or to indemnify or reimburse for payments made to satisfy the judgment. Information concerning the insurance agreement is not by reason of disclosure admissible in evidence at trial. For purposes of IN ST TRIAL P Rule 26(B)(2), an application for insurance shall not be treated as part of an insurance agreement. IN ST TRIAL P Rule 26(B)(2).

c. *Trial preparation; Materials.* Subject to the provisions of IN ST TRIAL P Rule 26(B)(4), a party may obtain discovery of documents and tangible things otherwise discoverable under IN ST TRIAL P Rule 26(B)(1) and prepared in anticipation of litigation or for trial by or for another party or by or for that other party's representative (including his attorney, consultant, surety, indemnitor, insurer, or agent) only upon a showing that the party seeking discovery has substantial need of the materials in the preparation of his case and that he is unable without undue hardship to obtain the substantial equivalent of the materials by other means. In ordering discovery of such materials when the required showing has been made, the court shall protect against disclosure of the mental impressions, conclusions, opinions, or legal theories of an attorney or other representative of a party concerning the litigation. IN ST TRIAL P Rule 26(B)(3).

   i. A party may obtain without the required showing a statement concerning the action or its subject matter previously made by that party. Upon request, a person not a party may obtain without the required showing a statement concerning the action or its subject matter previously made by that person. If the request is refused, the person may move for a court order. The provisions of IN ST TRIAL P Rule 37(A)(4) apply to the award of expenses incurred in relation to the motion. For purposes of IN ST TRIAL P Rule 26(B)(3), a statement previously made is:

      - A written statement signed or otherwise adopted approved by the person making it, or

      - A stenographic, mechanical, electrical, or other recording, or a transcription thereof, which is a substantially verbatim recital of an oral statement by the person making it and contemporaneously recorded. IN ST TRIAL P Rule 26(B)(3).

   ii. The protection of IN ST TRIAL P Rule 26(B)(3) extends to material prepared or collected before litigation actually commences, but that some possibility of litigation must actually exist before the privilege and IN ST TRIAL P Rule 26(B)(3) become operative. 2A INPRAC R 26(26.9); CIGNA-INA/Aetna v. Hagerman-Shambaugh, 473 N.E.2d 1033, 1037 (Ind.Ct.App. 1985).

d. *Trial preparation; Experts.* Discovery of facts known and opinions held by experts, otherwise discoverable under the provisions of IN ST TRIAL P Rule 26(B)(1) and acquired or developed in anticipation of litigation or for trial, may be obtained as follows:

   i. A party may through interrogatories require any other party to identify each person whom the other party expects to call as an expert witness at trial, to state the subject matter on which the expert is expected to testify, and to state the substance of the facts and opinions to which the expert is expected to testify and a summary of the grounds for each opinion. IN ST TRIAL P Rule 26(B)(4)(a)(i).

   ii. Upon motion, the court may order further discovery by other means, subject to such restrictions as to scope and such provisions, pursuant to IN ST TRIAL P Rule 26(B)(4)(c), concerning fees and expenses as the court may deem appropriate. IN ST TRIAL P Rule 26(B)(4)(a)(ii).

   iii. A party may discover facts known or opinions held by an expert who has been retained or specially employed by another party in anticipation of litigation or preparation for trial and who is not expected to be called as a witness at trial, only as provided in IN ST TRIAL P Rule 35(B) or upon a showing of exceptional circumstances under which it is impracticable for the party seeking discovery to obtain facts or opinions on the same subject by other means. IN ST TRIAL P Rule 26(B)(4)(b).

iv. Unless manifest injustice would result,

- The court shall require that the party seeking discovery pay the expert a reasonable fee for time spent in responding to discovery under IN ST TRIAL P Rule 26(B)(4)(a)(ii) and IN ST TRIAL P Rule 26(B)(4)(b); and

- With respect to discovery obtained under IN ST TRIAL P Rule 26(B)(4)(a)(ii) the court may require, and with respect to discovery obtained under IN ST TRIAL P Rule 26(B)(4)(b) the court shall require, the party seeking discovery to pay the other party a fair portion of the fees and expenses reasonably incurred by the latter party in obtaining facts and opinions from the expert. IN ST TRIAL P Rule 26(B)(4)(c).

e. *Claims of privilege or protection*

i. *Information withheld.* When a party withholds information otherwise discoverable under the Indiana Rules of Trial Procedure by claiming that it is privileged or subject to protection as trial preparation material, the party shall make the claim expressly and shall describe the nature of the documents, communications, or things not produced or disclosed in a manner that, without revealing information itself privileged or protected, will enable other parties to assess the applicability of the privilege or protection. IN ST TRIAL P Rule 26(B)(5)(a).

ii. *Information produced.* If information is produced in discovery that is subject to a claim of privilege or protection as trial-preparation material, the party making the claim may notify any party that received the information of the claim and the basis for it. After being notified, a party must promptly return, sequester, or destroy the specified information and any copies it has and may not use or disclose the information until the claim is resolved. A receiving party may promptly present the information to the court under seal for a determination of the claim. If the receiving party disclosed the information before being notified, it must take reasonable steps to retrieve it. The producing party must preserve the information until the claim is resolved. IN ST TRIAL P Rule 26(B)(5)(b).

iii. *Waiver.* The law of discovery has developed some holdings which indicate that "waiver" of a privileged communication in a discovery setting might be more exacting than "waiver" of a privileged communication when the only question at hand is an interpretation of the privilege itself. Thus, in litigation in which several documents are in issue, and some are released inadvertently, there is strong case law that holds that the "inadvertent production" of a privileged document does not constitute a waiver of the attorney-client privilege. 2A INPRAC R 26(26.5); Transamerica Computer Co. v. International Business Machines Corp., 573 F.2d 646 (9th Cir. 1978). Such a rule should be measured against the usual rule which suggests that a voluntary disclosure to a third person will generally suffice to show a waiver of the attorney-client privilege. 2A INPRAC R 26(26.5).

f. *Use not limited.* Unless the court orders otherwise under IN ST TRIAL P Rule 26(C), the frequency of use of the methods listed in IN ST TRIAL P Rule 26(A) is not limited. IN ST TRIAL P Rule 26(A).

g. *Sequence of discovery.* Unless the court upon motion, for the convenience of parties and witnesses and in the interests of justice, orders otherwise, methods of discovery may be used in any sequence and the fact that a party is conducting discovery, whether by deposition or otherwise, shall not operate to delay any other party's discovery. IN ST TRIAL P Rule 26(D).

2. *Request for admissions.* A request for admission is a method of discovery which allows a party to establish facts and information during the discovery stage of the action so that evidence on those matters will not be required at trial. 22 INPRAC § 26.1; Walker v. Employers Ins. of Wausau, 846 N.E.2d 1098 (Ind.Ct.App. 2006); Brown v. Dobbs, 691 N.E.2d 907 (Ind.Ct.App. 1998). Requests for admission under IN ST TRIAL P Rule 36 are designed to simplify and clarify the issues, to cut trial preparation time, and to encourage settlement. 10 INPRAC § 69.1.

a. *Request for admissions generally.* A party may serve upon any other party a written request for the admission, for purposes of the pending action only, of the truth of any matters within the scope of IN ST TRIAL P Rule 26(B) set forth in the request, including the genuineness of any documents described in the request. IN ST TRIAL P Rule 36(A).

b. *Limit on requests.* No party shall serve on any other party more than thirty (30) requests for admission (other than requests relating to the authenticity or genuineness of documents in the aggregate), including subparagraphs, without leave of court. Subparagraphs shall relate directly to the subject matter of the request for admission. IN ST LAKE RCP Rule 8(B).

    i. *Request to file additional requests for admission.* Any party desiring to serve additional requests for admission shall file a written motion setting forth those proposed and the necessity therefor. IN ST LAKE RCP Rule 8(B).

c. *Mutually known matters.* Requests for admissions as to matters within the mutual knowledge of both parties are proper. The function of IN ST TRIAL P Rule 36 is to establish admissions that will obviate the necessity of proof and expedite the trial, or to transform "mutual knowledge" into the established facts of a case. 3 INPRAC R 36(36.5).

d. *Requests to be carefully drafted.* The burden on the requesting party is to carefully and artfully draft the statement of fact contained in the request for admission. The statement must be precise, unambiguous, and in no way mislead the answering party. 3 INPRAC R 36(36.2).

    i. Fairness demands that any error arising out of inartful drafting be borne by the requesting party. The burden imposed on the answering party is unfairly "increased when the request for admission propounds a statement of fact which lacks clarity, is ambiguous, or which otherwise might mislead the answering party." 3 INPRAC R 36(36.2); F.W. Means & Co. v. Carstens, 428 N.E.2d 251, 257 (Ind.Ct.App. 1981).

e. *Admissions by the requestor.* Propounding of requests for admissions admits nothing as to the requesting party. 3 INPRAC R 36(36.2); Indiana Construction Service v. Amoco Oil Company, 533 N.E.2d 1300 (Ind.Ct.App. 1989). This party in the action made an admission in the text of or during the request, to which the receiving party, of course, agreed. But it was not binding, as to the requesting party, the court held. Such a request is binding as to the party admitting the fact in response to a request. 3 INPRAC R 36(36.2); Indiana Construction Service v. Amoco Oil Company, 533 N.E.2d 1300 (Ind.Ct.App. 1989).

f. *Motion to compel.* The party who has requested the admissions may move for an order with respect to the answers or objections. Unless the court determines that an objection is justified, it shall order that an answer be served. If the court determines that an answer does not comply with the requirements of IN ST TRIAL P Rule 36, it may order either that the matter is admitted or that an amended answer be served. The court may, in lieu of these orders, determine that final disposition of the request be made at a pre-trial conference or at a designated time prior to trial. IN ST TRIAL P Rule 36(A).

    i. The provisions of IN ST TRIAL P Rule 37(A)(4) apply to the award of expenses incurred in relation to the motion. IN ST TRIAL P Rule 36(A).

    ii. Refer to the Indiana KeyRules Motion to Compel Discovery document for more information.

3. *Response to request for admissions.* The matter is admitted unless, within a period designated in the request, not less than thirty (30) days after service thereof or within such shorter or longer time as the court may allow, the party to whom the request is directed serves upon the party requesting the admission a written answer or objection addressed to the matter, signed by the party or by his attorney. IN ST TRIAL P Rule 36(A).

a. *Methods of response.* IN ST TRIAL P Rule 36 recognizes at least four (4) responses. The party:

    i. May not respond, thereby admitting the request; or

    ii. Answer; or

    iii. Object to the request; or

    iv. File a qualified response. 3 INPRAC R 36(36.4).

b. *Effect of admission.* Any matter admitted under IN ST TRIAL P Rule 36 is conclusively established unless the court on motion permits withdrawal or amendment of the admission. IN ST TRIAL P Rule 36(B).

    i. Any admission made by a party under IN ST TRIAL P Rule 36 is for the purpose of the pending action only and is not an admission by him for any other purpose nor may it be used against him in any other proceeding. IN ST TRIAL P Rule 36(B).

c. *Denials.* The answer shall specifically deny the matter or set forth in detail the reasons why the answering party cannot truthfully admit or deny the matter. A denial shall fairly meet the substance of the requested admission, and when good faith requires that a party qualify his answer or deny only a part of the matter of which an admission is requested, he shall specify so much of it as is true and qualify or deny the remainder. IN ST TRIAL P Rule 36(A).

d. *Lack of information or knowledge.* An answering party may not give lack of information or knowledge as a reason for failure to admit or deny unless he states that he has made reasonable inquiry and that the information known or readily obtainable by him is insufficient to enable him to admit or deny or that the inquiry would be unreasonably burdensome. IN ST TRIAL P Rule 36(A).

e. *Objections.* If objection is made, the reasons therefor shall be stated. IN ST TRIAL P Rule 36(A).

   i.   A party who considers that a matter of which an admission has been requested presents a genuine issue for trial may not, on that ground alone, object to the request; he may, subject to the provisions of IN ST TRIAL P Rule 37(C), deny the matter or set forth reasons why he cannot admit or deny it. IN ST TRIAL P Rule 36(A).

   ii. An objectionable request may not be properly attacked by a motion to strike, to dismiss, or to suppress. The party served must respond to the request and serve admissions or denials of all matters not deemed objectionable. 3 INPRAC R 36(36.4).

f. *Withdrawal or amendment of admissions.* Subject to the provisions of IN ST TRIAL P Rule 16 governing amendment of a pre-trial order, the court may permit withdrawal or amendment when the presentation of the merits of the action will be subserved thereby and the party who obtained the admission fails to satisfy the court that withdrawal or amendment will prejudice him in maintaining his action or defense on the merits. IN ST TRIAL P Rule 36(B).

   i.   It is within sound discretion of trial court to permit or deny amendment of pretrial order, but trial court should amend or modify pretrial order when requested if modification is necessary to prevent manifest injustice. 2 INPRAC R 16(7); Hacienda Mexican Restaurant of Kalamazoo Corp. v. Hacienda Franchise Group, Inc., 641 N.E.2d 1036 (Ind.Ct.App. 1994).

g. *Supplementation of responses.* A party who has responded to a request for discovery with a response that was complete when made is under no duty to supplement his response to include information thereafter acquired, except as follows:

   i.   A party is under a duty seasonably to supplement his response with respect to any question directly addressed to:

   - The identity and location of persons having knowledge of discoverable matters, and

   - The identity of each person expected to be called as an expert witness at trial, the subject-matter on which he is expected to testify, and the substance of his testimony. IN ST TRIAL P Rule 26(E)(1).

   ii. A party is under a duty seasonably to amend a prior response if he obtains information upon the basis of which:

   - He knows that the response was incorrect when made, or

   - He knows that the response though correct when made is no longer true and the circumstances are such that a failure to amend the response is in substance a knowing concealment. IN ST TRIAL P Rule 26(E)(2).

   iii. A duty to supplement responses may be imposed by order of the court, agreement of the parties, or at any time prior to trial through new requests for supplementation of prior responses. IN ST TRIAL P Rule 26(E)(3).

   iv. The duty seasonably to supplement a discovery response is absolute and is not predicated on a court order. "It is a breach of a litigant's duty reasonably to supplement if the litigant postpones supplementing its response by not obtaining from its experts the information which is to be supplied in answer to interrogatories." 2A INPRAC R 26(26.27); Lucas v. Dorsey Corp., 609 N.E.2d 1191, 1196 (Ind.Ct.App. 1993).

D. Documents

1. *Required documents*

   a. *Request for admissions.* Refer to the General Requirements section of this document for information on the scope and content of a request for admissions.

   b. *Copies of documents.* Copies of documents shall be served with the request unless they have been or are otherwise furnished or made available for inspection and copying. IN ST TRIAL P Rule 36(A).

   c. *Certificate of service.* An attorney or unrepresented party tendering a document to the Clerk for filing shall certify that service has been made, list the parties served, and specify the date and means of service. The certificate of service shall be placed at the end of the document and shall not be separately filed. The separate filing of a certificate of service, however, shall not be grounds for rejecting a document for filing. The Clerk may permit documents to be filed without a certificate of service but shall require prompt filing of a separate certificate of service. IN ST TRIAL P Rule 5(C).

      i. All pleadings, motions and other papers submitted for filing which are required to be served under IN ST TRIAL P Rule 5(A) shall contain proof of service pursuant to IN ST TRIAL P Rule 5(B)(2). IN ST LAKE RCP Rule 3(A).

2. *Supplemental documents*

   a. *Stipulation regarding discovery procedure.* Unless the court orders otherwise, the parties may by written stipulation:

      i. Provide that depositions may be taken before any person, at any time or place, upon any notice, and in any manner and when so taken may be used like other depositions, and

      ii. Modify the procedures provided by the Indiana Rules of Trial Procedure for other methods of discovery. IN ST TRIAL P Rule 29.

   b. *Facsimile cover sheet.* Any document sent to the Clerk of the Circuit Court by electronic facsimile transmission shall be accompanied by a cover sheet which states the title of the document, case number, number of pages, identity and voice telephone number of the sending party and instructions for filing. The cover sheet shall contain the signature of the attorney or party, pro se, authorizing the filing. IN ST ADMIN Rule 12(D).

E. Format

1. *Form of requests for admissions.* The rules applicable to captions, and the signing and form of pleadings (IN ST TRIAL P Rule 8 through IN ST TRIAL P Rule 11), apply to all motions and other papers provided under the Indiana Rules of Trial Procedure. 22B INPRAC 7:2. Each matter of which an admission is requested shall be separately set forth. IN ST TRIAL P Rule 36(A).

2. *Form of pleadings.* For the purpose of uniformity, convenience, clarity and durability, requirements in IN ST LAKE RCP Rule 2 shall be observed in the preparation of all pleadings, motions and other papers. IN ST LAKE RCP Rule 2. Whenever materials submitted fail to meet the standards in IN ST LAKE RCP Rule 2, the Court may impose appropriate sanctions. IN ST LAKE RCP Rule 2(B).

   a. *Caption; Names of parties.* Every pleading shall contain a caption setting forth the name of the court, the title of the action, the file number, and a designation as in IN ST TRIAL P Rule 7(A). In the complaint the title of the action shall include the names of all the parties, but in other pleadings it is sufficient to state the name of the first party on each side with an appropriate indication of other parties. IN ST TRIAL P Rule 10(A).

      i. *Special judge matters.* The caption of all CCS Entry Forms, pleadings, motions, orders and other papers to be filed in a special judge case shall include in block text the words SPECIAL JUDGE and the name of the judge directly below the cause number on the caption. IN ST LAKE RCP Rule 2(D).

   b. *Paragraphs; Separate statements.* All averments of a claim or defense shall be made in numbered paragraphs, the contents of each of which shall be limited as far as practicable to a statement of a

single set of circumstances, and a paragraph may be referred to by number in all succeeding pleadings. Each claim founded upon a separate transaction or occurrence and each defense other than denials may be stated in a separate count or defense whenever a separation facilitates the clear presentation of the matters set forth. IN ST TRIAL P Rule 10(B).

c. *Adoption by reference; Exhibits.* Statements in a pleading may be adopted by reference in a different part of the same pleading or in another pleading or in any motion. A copy of any written instrument which is an exhibit to a pleading is a part thereof for all purposes. IN ST TRIAL P Rule 10(C).

d. *Paper; Print, quality and binding*

   i. All pleadings, motions, chronological case summary entry forms, orders, process and other papers shall be neatly and legibly printed, typewritten or mechanically reproduced, on one (1) side only, on white opaque paper. To satisfy the recordkeeping requirements of IN ST TRIAL P Rule 77, the print shall be of sufficient density and clarity for preservation and reproduction of microfilming, optical disk or other secondary sources. For this reason, the use of non-letter-quality printers is discouraged. IN ST LAKE RCP Rule 2(A).

   ii. Paper and ink shall be of such quality as to withstand the test of time. All documents shall be produced on acid-free, non-thermal paper. It is recommended that a minimum of twenty (20) pound, twenty-five percent (25%) cotton paper product be used. Documents of multiple pages shall be submitted in bound or stapled fashion, and the binding or stapling shall be at the top only. Covers or backings shall not be used. IN ST LAKE RCP Rule 2(A).

e. *Papers; Handwritten.* Handwritten papers may be filed only if approved by the Court and a typewritten or printed true rendition thereof is filed within three (3) days thereafter and approved by the Court. Upon such approval, they shall be deemed and filed as the original, while the handwritten papers shall be retained therewith for evidentiary purposes. IN ST LAKE RCP Rule 2(C).

f. *Minute sheets; Motion blanks.* Minute sheets and motion blanks shall no longer be used. IN ST LAKE RCP Rule 2(D).

3. *Size of papers for filing.* Effective January 1, 1992, all pleadings, copies, motions and documents filed with any trial court or appellate level court, typed or printed, with the exception of exhibits and existing wills, shall be prepared on eight and one-half by eleven inch (8 1/2" x 11") size paper. IN ST ADMIN Rule 11.

4. *Signature requirements*

a. *Signature of attorney.* Every pleading or motion of a party represented by an attorney shall be signed by at least one (1) attorney of record in his individual name, whose address, telephone number, and attorney number shall be stated, except that this provision shall not apply to pleadings and motions made and transcribed at the trial or a hearing before the judge and received by him in such form. IN ST TRIAL P Rule 11(A).

   i. The signature of an attorney constitutes a certificate by him that he has read the pleadings; that to the best of his knowledge, information, and belief, there is good ground to support it; and that it is not interposed for delay. IN ST TRIAL P Rule 11(A).

   ii. If a pleading or motion is not signed or is signed with intent to defeat the purpose of the rule, it may be stricken as sham and false and the action may proceed as though the pleading had not been served. IN ST TRIAL P Rule 11(A).

   iii. For a willful violation of IN ST TRIAL P Rule 11 an attorney may be subjected to appropriate disciplinary action. Similar action may be taken if scandalous or indecent matter is inserted. IN ST TRIAL P Rule 11(A).

b. *Signature of unrepresented party.* A party who is not represented by an attorney shall sign his pleading and state his address. IN ST TRIAL P Rule 11(A).

c. *Verification not generally required.* Except when specifically required by rule, pleadings or motions need not be verified or accompanied by affidavit. The rule in equity that the averments of an answer under oath must be overcome by the testimony of two (2) witnesses or of one (1) witness sustained by corroborating circumstances is abolished. IN ST TRIAL P Rule 11(A).

d. *Verification by affirmation or representation.* When in connection with any civil or special statutory proceeding it is required that any pleading, motion, petition, supporting affidavit, or other document of any kind, be verified, or that an oath be taken, it shall be sufficient if the subscriber simply affirms the truth of the matter to be verified by an affirmation or representation. IN ST TRIAL P Rule 11(B). IN ST TRIAL P Rule 11(B) states that the affirmation or representation should be in substantially the following language: "I (we) affirm, under the penalties for perjury, that the foregoing representation(s) is (are) true. (Signed) _____."

   i. Any person who falsifies an affirmation or representation of fact shall be subject to the same penalties as are prescribed by law for the making of a false affidavit. IN ST TRIAL P Rule 11(B).

e. *Verified pleadings, motions, and affidavits as evidence.* Pleadings, motions and affidavits accompanying or in support of such pleadings or motions when required to be verified or under oath shall be accepted as a representation that the signer had personal knowledge thereof or reasonable cause to believe the existence of the facts or matters stated or alleged therein; and, if otherwise competent or acceptable as evidence, may be admitted as evidence of the facts or matters stated or alleged therein when it is so provided in the Indiana Rules of Trial Procedure, by statute or other law, or to the extent the writing or signature expressly purports to be made upon the signer's personal knowledge. When such pleadings, motions and affidavits are verified or under oath they shall not require other or greater proof on the part of the adverse party than if not verified or not under oath unless expressly provided otherwise by the Indiana Rules of Trial Procedure, statute or other law. Affidavits upon motions for summary judgment under IN ST TRIAL P Rule 56 and in denial of execution under IN ST TRIAL P Rule 9.2 shall be made upon personal knowledge. IN ST TRIAL P Rule 11(C).

f. *Electronic signature.* The filing of documents and information through the E-filing system by use of a valid username and password is presumed to have been authorized by the User to whom that username and password have been issued and documents filed through the E-filing system are presumed to have been signed by the same User. IN ST ADMIN Rule 16(E).

5. *Information excluded from public access.* Every document filed in a case shall separately identify information excluded from public access pursuant to IN ST ADMIN Rule 9(G)(1) as follows:

   a. Whole documents that are excluded from public access pursuant to IN ST ADMIN Rule 9(G)(1) shall be tendered on light green paper or have a light green coversheet attached to the document, marked "Not for Public Access" or "Confidential." IN ST TRIAL P Rule 5(G)(1).

   b. When only a portion of a document contains information excluded from public access pursuant to IN ST ADMIN Rule 9(G)(1), said information shall be omitted [or redacted] from the filed document, and set forth on a separate accompanying document on light green paper conspicuously marked "Not for Public Access" or "Confidential" and clearly designated [or identifying] the caption and number of the case and the document and location within the document to which the redacted material pertains. IN ST TRIAL P Rule 5(G)(2).

   c. With respect to documents filed in electronic format, the trial court, by local rule, may provide for compliance with IN ST TRIAL P Rule 5 in manner that separates and protects access to information excluded from public access. IN ST TRIAL P Rule 5(G)(3).

   d. IN ST TRIAL P Rule 5(G) does not apply to a record sealed by the court pursuant to IN ST 5-14-3-5.5 or otherwise, nor to records, documents, or information filed in cases to which public access is prohibited pursuant to IN ST ADMIN Rule 9(G). IN ST TRIAL P Rule 5(G)(4).

   e. The following information in case records is excluded from public access and is confidential:

      i. Information that is excluded from public access pursuant to federal law;

      ii. Information that is excluded from public access as declared confidential by Indiana statute or other court rule, including without limitation:

         • All adoption records created after July 8, 1941, as declared confidential by IN ST 31-19-19-1, et seq., except those specifically declared open by IN ST 31-19-13-2(2);

         • All records relating to chancroid, chlamydia, gonorrhea, hepatitis, human immunodefi-

937

ciency virus (HIV), Lymphogranuloma venereum, syphilis, tuberculosis, as declared confidential by IN ST 16-41-8-1, et seq.;

- All records relating to child abuse as declared confidential by IN ST 31-33-18-1, et seq.;

- All records relating to drug tests as declared confidential by IN ST 5-14-3-4(a)(9);

- Records of grand jury proceedings as declared confidential by IN ST 35-34-2-4;

- Records of juvenile proceedings as declared confidential by IN ST 31-39-1-2, except those specifically open under statute;

- All paternity records created after July 1, 1941 as declared confidential by IN ST 31-14-11-15, IN ST 31-19-5-23, IN ST 31-39-1-1 and IN ST 31-39-1-2 [Editor's note: IN ST 31-14-11-15 was repealed effective May 9, 2013];

- All pre-sentence reports as declared confidential by IN ST 35-38-1-13;

- Written petitions to permit marriages without consent and orders directing the Clerk of Court to issue a marriage license to underage persons, as declared confidential by IN ST 31-11-1-6;

- Only those arrest warrants, search warrants, indictments and informations ordered confidential by the trial judge, prior to return of duly executed service as declared confidential by IN ST 5-14-3-4(b)(1);

- All medical, mental health, or tax records unless determined by law or regulation of any governmental custodian not to be confidential, released by the subject of such records, or declared by a court of competent jurisdiction to be essential to the resolution of litigation as declared confidential by IN ST 16-39-3-10, IN ST 6-4.1-5-10, IN ST 6-4.1-12-12, and IN ST 6-8.1-7-1;

- Personal information relating to jurors or prospective jurors, other than for the use of the parties and counsel, pursuant to IN ST JURY Rule 10;

- Information relating to protection from abuse orders, no-contact orders and workplace violence restraining orders as declared confidential by IN ST 5-2-9-6, et seq.;

- Mediation proceedings pursuant to IN ST ADR Rule 2.11, Mini-Trial proceedings pursuant to IN ST ADR Rule 4.4(C), and Summary Jury Trials pursuant to IN ST ADR Rule 5.6;

- Information in probation files pursuant to the Probation Standards promulgated by the Judicial Conference of Indiana pursuant to IN ST 11-13-1-8(b);

- Information deemed confidential pursuant to the Rules for Court Administered Alcohol and Drug Programs promulgated by the Judicial Conference of Indiana pursuant to IN ST 12-23-14-13;

- Information deemed confidential pursuant to the Problem-Solving Court Rules promulgated by the Judicial Conference of Indiana pursuant to IN ST 33-23-16-16;

- All records of the Department of workforce Development as declared confidential by IN ST 22-4-19-6;

- Information regarding interception of electronic communications that is sealed or deemed confidential as set forth in IN ST 35-33.5-2-1, et seq.

iii. Information excluded from public access by specific court order;

iv. Complete Social Security Numbers of living persons;

v. With the exception of names, information such as addresses, phone numbers, and dates of birth which explicitly identifies:

- Natural persons who are witnesses or victims (not including defendants) in criminal, domestic violence, stalking, sexual assault, juvenile, or civil protection order proceedings, provided that juveniles who are victims of sex crimes shall be identified by initials only;

- Places of residence of judicial officers, clerks and other employees of courts and clerks of court, unless the person or persons about whom the information pertains waives confidentiality;

vi. Complete account numbers of specific assets, loans, bank accounts, credit cards, and personal identification numbers (PINs);

vii. All orders of expungement entered in criminal or juvenile proceedings, orders to restrict access to criminal history information pursuant to IN ST 35-38-5-5.5 or IN ST 35-38-8-5 and records excluded from public access by such orders, and information related to infractions that is excluded from public access pursuant to IN ST 34-28-5-15 or IN ST 34-28-5-16 [Editor's note: IN ST 35-38-5-5.5, IN ST 35-38-8-5 and IN ST 34-28-5-16 were repealed effective July 1, 2013; for information on orders restricting access to criminal history, refer to IN ST 35-38-9-1, et seq.];

viii. All personal notes and e-mail, and deliberative material, of judges, jurors, court staff and judicial agencies, and information recorded in personal data assistants (PDA's) or organizers and personal calendars. IN ST ADMIN Rule 9(G)(1).

6. *Format of electronically filed documents*

   a. *Generally.* Electronically filed documents must meet the same requirements of format as documents conventionally filed pursuant to IN ST LAKE RCP Rule 2 or other applicable Lake County Rules of Civil Procedure. IN ST LAKE RCP Rule 17(D)(1).

   b. *Titles of documents.* The person electronically filing a document will be responsible for designating a title for the document at the time it is filed. The LCOD will generate the appropriate entry onto the CCS to record the filing of the document. IN ST LAKE RCP Rule 17(D)(3).

   c. *Citations and hyperlinks.* Electronically filed documents may contain hyperlink references to an external document as a convenient mechanism for accessing material cited in the document. Filers wishing to insert hyperlinks into documents shall continue to use the traditional method of citation to authority in addition to the hyperlink provided. The hyperlink is merely a convenience to the court and the material referenced is extraneous to the file and not a part of the court's record. IN ST LAKE RCP Rule 17(D)(5).

   d. *Attachments and exhibits.* All documents which form part of a single submission and which are being filed at the same time and by the same filer may be electronically filed together under one document filing, e.g., the motion, supporting affidavits, memorandum in support, designation of evidence, exhibits. IN ST LAKE RCP Rule 17(D)(6).

      i. Large documents which do not exist in an electronic format shall be scanned into .pdf format and filed electronically as separate attachments. A scanner is available in each clerk's office for use by the public and the bar in scanning and saving image files if needed. IN ST LAKE RCP Rule 17(D)(6).

   e. *Electronic signatures*

      i. *Electronic filing as signature.* The electronic filing of a document which is required to be signed shall constitute the filer's representation under IN ST TRIAL P Rule 11. Unless the electronically filed document has been scanned and shows the filer's original signature, the signature of the filer shall be indicated by As/Attorney's Name, or As/Party's Name as in the case of a pro se litigant, on the line where the signature would otherwise appear. IN ST LAKE RCP Rule 17(G)(1).

      ii. *Signatures on jointly signed or filed, verified or other documents.* In the case of a stipulation, agreed order, jointly signed motion or other document which needs to be signed by two (2) or more persons, or in the case of documents which must contain original signatures and which require verification or an unsworn declaration under rule or statute, the signatures may be indicated by either:

      - Submitting a scanned copy of the originally signed document; or,
      - Submitting the document with the use of As/Name in the signature block(s) where the

original signature(s) appear(s) in the original document; provided, however, that the filer shall first obtain the physical signature of all persons necessary. IN ST LAKE RCP Rule 17(G)(2).

    iii. *Retention of original.* The filer shall retain the original executed document. IN ST LAKE RCP Rule 17(G).

7. *Citation of local rules.* The local rules for Lake County may be known as the Lake County Rules of Civil Procedure, and abbreviated as LR. IN ST LAKE RCP Rule 1(C).

F. Filing and Service Requirements

1. *Filing requirements.* Except as otherwise provided in IN ST TRIAL P Rule 5(E)(2), all pleadings and papers subsequent to the complaint which are required to be served upon a party shall be filed with the Court either before service or within a reasonable period of time thereafter. IN ST TRIAL P Rule 5(E)(1). All papers presented for filing shall be submitted to the Clerk and not to the court. All papers submitted for filing shall be mailed or delivered to the Clerk's office at the courthouse in which the case is pending. IN ST LAKE RCP Rule 3(A).

    a. *Non-filing of discovery until necessary*

        i. *Non-filing of discovery; Exceptions.* No deposition or request for discovery or response thereto under IN ST TRIAL P Rule 27, IN ST TRIAL P Rule 30, IN ST TRIAL P Rule 31, IN ST TRIAL P Rule 33, IN ST TRIAL P Rule 34 or IN ST TRIAL P Rule 36 shall be filed with the Court unless:

- A motion is filed pursuant to IN ST TRIAL P Rule 26(C) or IN ST TRIAL P Rule 37 and the original deposition or request for discovery or response thereto is necessary to enable the Court to rule; or

- A party desires to use the deposition or request for discovery or response thereto for evidentiary purposes at trial or in connection with a motion, and the Court, either upon its own motion or that of any party, or as a part of any pre-trial order, orders the filing of the original. IN ST TRIAL P Rule 5(E)(2).

        ii. *Custody of original and period of retention*

- The original of a deposition shall, subject to the provisions of IN ST TRIAL P Rule 30(E), be delivered by the reporter to the party taking it and shall be maintained by that party until filed with the Court pursuant to IN ST TRIAL P Rule 5(E)(2) or until the later of final judgment, agreed settlement of the litigation or all appellate rights have been exhausted. IN ST TRIAL P Rule 5(E)(3)(a).

- The original or any request for discovery or response thereto under IN ST TRIAL P Rule 27, IN ST TRIAL P Rule 30, IN ST TRIAL P Rule 31, IN ST TRIAL P Rule 33, IN ST TRIAL P Rule 34 and IN ST TRIAL P Rule 36 shall be maintained by the party originating the request or response until filed with the Court pursuant to IN ST TRIAL P Rule 5(E)(2) or until the later of final judgment, agreed settlement or all appellate rights have been exhausted. IN ST TRIAL P Rule 5(E)(3)(b).

        iii. *Original unavailable; Copies.* In the event it is made to appear to the satisfaction of the Court that the original of a deposition or request for discovery or response thereto cannot be filed with the Court when required, the Court may allow use of a copy instead of the original. IN ST TRIAL P Rule 5(E)(4).

        iv. *Filing as publication.* The filing of any deposition shall constitute publication. IN ST TRIAL P Rule 5(E)(5).

    b. *Filing with the court defined.* The filing of pleadings, motions, and other papers with the court as required by the Indiana Rules of Trial Procedure shall be made by one of the following methods:

        i. Delivery to the clerk of the court;

        ii. Sending by electronic transmission under the procedure adopted pursuant to IN ST ADMIN Rule 12;

iii. Mailing to the clerk by registered, certified or express mail return receipt requested;

iv. Depositing with any third-party commercial carrier for delivery to the clerk within three (3) calendar days, cost prepaid, properly addressed;

v. If the court so permits, filing with the judge, in which event the judge shall note thereon the filing date and forthwith transmit them to the office of the clerk; or

vi. Electronic filing, as approved by the Division of State Court Administration pursuant to IN ST ADMIN Rule 16. IN ST TRIAL P Rule 5(F).

vii. Filing by registered or certified mail and by third-party commercial carrier shall be complete upon mailing or deposit. IN ST TRIAL P Rule 5(F).

c. *Mandatory electronic filing.* Unless otherwise permitted by the Lake County Rules of Civil Procedure or otherwise authorized by the judicial officer assigned to a particular case, all documents submitted for filing (including the original complaint, or equivalent pleading, and summons) shall be filed electronically with the clerk using the LCOD, no matter when the case was originally filed. IN ST LAKE RCP Rule 17(D).

i. *Of documents containing information excluded from public access pursuant to* IN ST ADMIN Rule 9. Documents containing information excluded from public access pursuant to IN ST ADMIN Rule 9, or documents which are ordered to be filed under seal shall be filed electronically, pursuant to IN ST LAKE RCP Rule 17(D)(9), whenever possible, along with a copy of the applicable order to seal the records, and the filer shall designate the documents as "Not for Public Access Pursuant to Administrative Rule 9(G)(1)" at the time of filing. IN ST LAKE RCP Rule 16(A)(1); IN ST LAKE RCP Rule 17(D)(9).

- *Conventional filing of documents containing information excluded from public access pursuant to* IN ST ADMIN Rule 9. Documents containing information excluded from public access pursuant to IN ST ADMIN Rule 9, or documents which are ordered to be filed under seal, which cannot be legibly scanned and filed electronically, shall be conventionally filed under seal and designated by the filer as "Not for Public Access Pursuant to Administrative Rule 9(G)(1)" at the time of filing. The unredacted version shall be filed on light green paper which is conspicuously marked "Not for Public Access"; and a redacted version, with confidential information deleted, shall be filed on white paper which shall be available for public access. The filer shall also electronically file a Notice of Manual Filing. IN ST LAKE RCP Rule 16(A)(2).

ii. *Technical failures.* If a registered user is unable to file a document in a timely manner due to technical difficulties in the LCOD, the registered user must file a document with the court as soon as possible notifying the court of the inability to file the document. A sample document titled Declaration that Party was Unable to File in a Timely Manner Due to Technical Difficulties can be found at IN ST LAKE RCP Form 4. Delayed filings shall be rejected unless accompanied by the declaration attesting to the filer's failed attempts to file electronically at least two (2) times, separated by at least one (1) hour, after noon on each day of delay due to such technical failure. IN ST LAKE RCP Rule 17(J).

iii. *Documents allowed to be filed conventionally.* Unless specifically authorized by the court, only the following documents may be filed conventionally and not electronically:

- Exhibits and other documents that cannot be converted to a legible electronic form, such as videotapes, x-rays, and similar materials

- Documents delivered to the clerk by pro se litigants

- Documents mailed to the clerk by pro se litigants

- Confidential documents

- Notice of manual filing

- Titles of documents

- Chronological case summary entry forms (CCS entry forms). IN ST LAKE RCP Rule 17(E).

- For more information on the documents which must be filed conventionally, refer to IN ST LAKE RCP Rule 17(E).

d. *Facsimile filing.* Only when necessary on an emergency basis (i.e., when certified mail or other means of filing will not bring the document to the Judge's attention prior to the scheduled hearing or ruling), pleadings, motions and other papers may be filed by electronic facsimile transmission, or when specifically authorized by the Court. IN ST LAKE RCP Rule 2(C).

   i. *Generally.* In counties where a majority of judges of the courts of record, by posted local rule, have authorized electronic facsimile filing and designated a telephone number to receive such transmissions, pleadings, motions, and other papers may be sent to the Clerk of Circuit Court by electronic facsimile transmission for filing in any case, provided:

   - Such matter does not exceed ten (10) pages, including the cover sheet;

   - Such matter does not require the payment of fees other than the electronic facsimile transcription fee set forth in IN ST ADMIN Rule 12(E);

   - The sending party creates at the time of transmission a machine generated log for such transmission; and

   - The original document and the transmission log are maintained by the sending party for the duration of the litigation. IN ST ADMIN Rule 12(B).

   ii. *Time of filing.* During normal, posted business hours, the time of filing shall be the time the duplicate document is produced in the office of the Clerk of the Circuit Court. Duplicate documents received at all other times shall be filed as of the next normal business day. IN ST ADMIN Rule 12(C).

   - If the receiving fax machine endorses its own time and date stamp upon the transmitted documents and the receiving machine produces a delivery receipt which is electronically created and transmitted to the sending party, the time of filing shall be the date and time recorded on the transmitted document by the receiving fax machine. IN ST ADMIN Rule 12(C).

e. *Filing for special judges.* For special judge matters where the special judge is a full-time judge or magistrate serving within Lake County, all papers submitted for filing shall be delivered or mailed to the Clerk's office at the courthouse where the special judge regularly serves. IN ST LAKE RCP Rule 3(A).

f. *Proof of filing.* Any party filing any paper by any method other than personal delivery to the clerk shall retain proof of filing. IN ST TRIAL P Rule 5(F).

2. *Service requirements.* Unless otherwise provided by the Indiana Rules of Trial Procedure or an order of the court, each party and special judge, if any, shall be served with: (1) every order required by its terms to be served; (2) every pleading subsequent to the original complaint; (3) every written motion except one which may be heard ex parte; (4) every brief submitted to the trial court; (5) every paper relating to discovery required to be served upon a party; and (6) every written notice, appearance, demand, offer of judgment, designation of record on appeal, or similar paper. IN ST TRIAL P Rule 5(A).

a. *Methods of service*

   i. *Personal service.* Whenever a party is represented by an attorney of record, service shall be made upon such attorney unless service upon the party himself is ordered by the court. Service upon the attorney or party shall be made by delivering or mailing a copy of the papers to the last known address or where an attorney or party has consented to service by fax or e-mail, as provided in IN ST TRIAL P Rule 3.1(A)(4), by faxing or e-mailing a copy of the documents to the fax number or e-mail address set out in the appearance form or correction as required by IN ST TRIAL P Rule 3.1(E). IN ST TRIAL P Rule 5(B). Delivery of a copy within IN ST TRIAL P Rule 5 means:

   - Offering or tendering it to the attorney or party and stating the nature of the papers being served. Refusal to accept an offered or tendered document is a waiver of any objection to the sufficiency or adequacy of service of that document;

- Leaving it at his office with a clerk or other person in charge thereof, or if there is no one in charge, leaving it in a conspicuous place therein; or

- If the office is closed, by leaving it at his dwelling house or usual place of abode with some person of suitable age and discretion then residing therein; or,

- Leaving it at some other suitable place, selected by the attorney upon whom service is being made, pursuant to duly promulgated local rule. IN ST TRIAL P Rule 5(B)(1).

ii. *Service by mail.* If service is made by mail, the papers shall be deposited in the United States mail addressed to the person on whom they are being served, with postage prepaid. Service shall be deemed complete upon mailing. Proof of service of all papers permitted to be mailed may be made by written acknowledgment of service, by affidavit of the person who mailed the papers, or by certificate of an attorney. It shall be the duty of attorneys when entering their appearance in a cause or when filing pleadings or papers therein, to have noted in the Chronological Case Summary or said pleadings or papers so filed the address and telephone number of their office. Service by delivery or by mail at such address shall be deemed sufficient and complete. IN ST TRIAL P Rule 5(B)(2).

iii. *Service by fax or e-mail.* A party who has consented to service by fax or e-mail may be served as follows:

- Service by e-mail shall be made by attaching the document being served in .pdf format. Discovery documents must also be served in accordance with IN ST TRIAL P Rule 26(A). IN ST TRIAL P Rule 5(B)(3)(a).

- Service by fax shall be deemed complete upon generation of a transmission record indicating the successful transmission of the entire document, except as provided in IN ST TRIAL P Rule 5(B)(3)(d). IN ST TRIAL P Rule 5(B)(3)(b).

- Service by e-mail shall be deemed complete upon transmission, except as provided in IN ST TRIAL P Rule 5(B)(3)(d). IN ST TRIAL P Rule 5(B)(3)(c).

- Service by fax or e-mail that occurs on a Saturday, Sunday, legal holiday, or day the court or agency in which the matter is pending is closed or after 5:00 PM local time of the recipient shall be deemed complete the next day that is not a Saturday, Sunday, legal holiday, or day that the court or agency in which the matter is pending is not closed. IN ST TRIAL P Rule 5(B)(3)(d).

iv. *Additional service of electronic discovery.* In addition to service under Rule IN ST TRIAL P Rule 5(B) or a .pdf format electronic copy, a party propounding or responding to interrogatories, requests for production or requests for admission shall comply with IN ST TRIAL P Rule 26(A.1)(a) or IN ST TRIAL P Rule 26(A.1)(b). IN ST TRIAL P Rule 26(A.1).

- The party shall serve the discovery request or response in an electronic format (either on a disk or as an electronic document attachment) in any commercially available word processing software system. If transmitted on disk, each disk shall be labeled, identifying the caption of the case, the document, and the word processing version in which it is being submitted. If more than one (1) disk is used for the same document, each disk shall be labeled and also shall be sequentially numbered. If transmitted by electronic mail, the document must be accompanied by electronic memorandum providing the forgoing identifying information; or

- The party shall serve the opposing party with a verified statement that the attorney or party appealing pro se lacks the equipment and is unable to transmit the discovery as required by IN ST TRIAL P Rule 26(A.1). IN ST TRIAL P Rule 26(A.1).

b. *Serving numerous defendants.* In any action in which there are unusually large numbers of defendants, the court, upon motion or of its own initiative, may order:

i. That service of the pleadings of the defendants and replies thereto need not be made as between the defendants;

- That any cross-claim, counterclaim, or matter constituting an avoidance or affirmative defense contained therein shall be deemed to be denied or avoided by all other parties; and

- That the filing of any such pleading and service thereof upon the plaintiff constitutes due notice of it to the parties. IN ST TRIAL P Rule 5(D).

   ii.   A copy of every such order shall be served upon the parties in such manner and form as the court directs. IN ST TRIAL P Rule 5(D).

   c.   *Service by electronic means.* The Lake County Online Docket will generate a Notice of Electronic Filing and Service when any document is filed and served. This notice will be emailed to each registered user of record in a case, and an electronic service event will be added to the work queue of each registered user of record in the case. The party filing the document should retain a paper or electronic copy of the Notice of Electronic Filing and Service. This notice represents proof of filing and service of the document on registered users of record in that case. The filer shall not be required to conventionally serve any document on any party receiving electronic service. IN ST LAKE RCP Rule 17(F)(2).

      i.   The filer shall also conventionally serve those parties not designated or able to receive electronic notice or service but who are nevertheless entitled to notice of said pleading or other document in accordance with the Indiana Rules of Civil Procedure and applicable Lake County Rules of Civil Procedure. In such cases, the filer shall also file a certificate of service, as appropriate. IN ST LAKE RCP Rule 17(F).

   d.   *Service on parties in default for failure to appear.* No service need be made on parties in default for failure to appear, except that pleadings asserting new or additional claims for relief against them shall be served upon them in the manner provided by service of summons in IN ST TRIAL P Rule 4. IN ST TRIAL P Rule 5(A).

G. Hearings

1. The Indiana rules do not contemplate a hearing related to the filing and service of requests for admissions.

H. Forms

1. Request for Admissions Forms for Indiana

   a.   Request for admission. 5 INPRAC § 4:4.1.

   b.   Response to request for admission. 5 INPRAC § 4:4.2.

   c.   Response to request for admission; Alternative form. 5 INPRAC § 4:4.3.

   d.   Motion for order that matter be deemed admitted. 5 INPRAC § 4:4.4.

   e.   Requests for admission; General form. 10 INPRAC § 69.6.

   f.   Requests for admission; Genuineness of document. 10 INPRAC § 69.7.

   g.   Requests for admission; Specific document and matters related thereto; Insurance contract. 10 INPRAC § 69.8.

   h.   Requests for admission; Action against bank. 10 INPRAC § 69.9.

   i.   Requests for admission; Automobile accident. 10 INPRAC § 69.10.

   j.   Requests for admission; Automobile accident; Respondeat superior. 10 INPRAC § 69.11.

   k.   Requests for admission; Action on account stated. 10 INPRAC § 69.12.

   l.   Requests for admission; Action to foreclose on mortgage. 10 INPRAC § 69.13.

   m.   Requests for admission; Action for attorney malpractice. 10 INPRAC § 69.14.

   n.   Requests for admission; Products liability action; Defective hair products; Defendants. 10 INPRAC § 69.15.

   o.   Response to requests for admission; General form. 10 INPRAC § 69.20.

   p.   Alternative responses to requests for admission. 10 INPRAC § 69.21.

   q.   Motion for enlargement of time to respond to requests for admission. 10 INPRAC § 69.22.

   r.   Motion to withdraw and amend response to requests for admission. 10 INPRAC § 69.23.

   s.   Order granting motion to withdraw and amend responses. 10 INPRAC § 69.24.

t. Motion for order that matter be deemed admitted. 10 INPRAC § 69.25.

u. Motion for order requiring party to pay expenses for refusal to admit matters. 10 INPRAC § 69.26.

2. Official Request for Admissions Forms for Lake County

a. CCS entry form. IN ST LAKE RCP App. A.

b. Notice of manual filing. IN ST LAKE RCP Form 2.

c. Certificate of service. IN ST LAKE RCP Form 3.

d. Declaration that party was unable to file in a timely manner. IN ST LAKE RCP Form 4.

3. Request for Admissions Forms for Lake County

a. Notice of manual filing. EFORMST IN 5540.

I. Checklist

(I) ❑ Matters to be considered by the party serving the request

(a) ❑ Required documents

(1) ❑ Request for admissions

(2) ❑ Copies of documents

(3) ❑ Certificate of service

(b) ❑ Supplemental documents

(1) ❑ Stipulation regarding discovery procedure

(2) ❑ Facsimile cover sheet

(c) ❑ Timing

(1) ❑ The request may, without leave of court, be served upon the plaintiff after commencement of the action and upon any other party with or after service of the summons and complaint upon that party

(II) ❑ Matters to be considered by the responding party

(a) ❑ Required documents

(1) ❑ Response to request for admissions

(2) ❑ Certificate of service

(b) ❑ Supplemental documents

(1) ❑ Stipulation regarding discovery procedure

(2) ❑ Facsimile cover sheet

(c) ❑ Timing

(1) ❑ The matter is admitted unless, within a period designated in the request, not less than thirty (30) days after service thereof or within such shorter or longer time as the court may allow, the party to whom the request is directed serves upon the party requesting the admission a written answer or objection addressed to the matter

Requests, Notices and Applications
Notice of Deposition

Document Last Updated October 2013

A. Applicable Rules

1. *State rules*

a. Appearance. IN ST TRIAL P Rule 3.1.

b. Process. IN ST TRIAL P Rule 4.

c. Service and filing of pleadings and other papers. IN ST TRIAL P Rule 5.

d. Time. IN ST TRIAL P Rule 6.

e. Pleadings. IN ST TRIAL P Rule 7; IN ST TRIAL P Rule 9.2; IN ST TRIAL P Rule 10.

f. Signing and verification of pleadings. IN ST TRIAL P Rule 11.

g. Parties plaintiff and defendant; Capacity. IN ST TRIAL P Rule 17.

h. General provisions governing discovery. IN ST TRIAL P Rule 26.

i. Discovery methods. IN ST TRIAL P Rule 27; IN ST TRIAL P Rule 28; IN ST TRIAL P Rule 29; IN ST TRIAL P Rule 30; IN ST TRIAL P Rule 31; IN ST TRIAL P Rule 32; IN ST TRIAL P Rule 33; IN ST TRIAL P Rule 34; IN ST TRIAL P Rule 35; IN ST TRIAL P Rule 36.

j. Failure to make or cooperate in discovery; Sanctions. IN ST TRIAL P Rule 37.

k. Evidence. IN ST TRIAL P Rule 43.

l. Subpoena. IN ST TRIAL P Rule 45.

m. Judgment on the evidence (directed verdict). IN ST TRIAL P Rule 50.

n. Findings by the court. IN ST TRIAL P Rule 52.

o. Summary judgment. IN ST TRIAL P Rule 56.

p. Motion to correct error. IN ST TRIAL P Rule 59.

q. Relief from judgment or order. IN ST TRIAL P Rule 60.

r. Recording machines; Court reports; Stenographic report or transcript as evidence. IN ST TRIAL P Rule 74.

s. Court records. IN ST TRIAL P Rule 77.

t. Access to court records. IN ST ADMIN Rule 9.

u. Paper size. IN ST ADMIN Rule 11.

v. Facsimile transmission. IN ST ADMIN Rule 12.

w. Electronic filing and electronic service pilot projects. IN ST ADMIN Rule 16.

x. Privacy and confidentiality. IN ST 5-2-9-6; IN ST 5-14-3-4; IN ST 5-14-3-5.5; IN ST 6-4.1-5-10; IN ST 6-4.1-12-12; IN ST 6-8.1-7-1; IN ST 11-13-1-8; IN ST 12-23-14-13; IN ST 16-39-3-10; IN ST 16-41-8-1; IN ST 22-4-19-6; IN ST 31-11-1-6; IN ST 31-19-5-23; IN ST 31-19-13-2; IN ST 31-19-19-1; IN ST 31-33-18-1; IN ST 31-39-1-1; IN ST 31-39-1-2; IN ST 33-23-16-16; IN ST 35-34-2-4; IN ST 35-38-1-13; IN ST 35-38-9-1; IN ST ADR Rule 2.11; IN ST ADR Rule 4.4; IN ST ADR Rule 5.6; IN ST JURY Rule 10.

2. *Local rules*

a. Scope and title. [IN ST LAKE RCP Rule 1, as amended by IN ORDER 13-0237, effective October 18, 2013].

b. Preparation of pleadings, motions and other papers. IN ST LAKE RCP Rule 2.

c. Filing. [IN ST LAKE RCP Rule 3, as amended by IN ORDER 13-0237, effective October 18, 2013].

d. Discovery. IN ST LAKE RCP Rule 8.

e. Briefs. IN ST LAKE RCP Rule 11.

f. Confidential information and sealed documents. IN ST LAKE RCP Rule 16.

g. Electronic filing and service. IN ST LAKE RCP Rule 17.

B. Timing

1. *Time for notice of deposition*

a. *Depositions upon oral examination.* After commencement of the action, any party may take the testimony of any person, including a party, by deposition upon oral examination. IN ST TRIAL P Rule 30(A).

i. A party desiring to take the deposition of any person upon oral examination shall give reasonable notice in writing to every other party to the action. IN ST TRIAL P Rule 30(B)(1).

- The party who gives notice of taking a deposition must do so in a way which is sufficiently timely to permit the party who receives the notice to make arrangements to travel to the place where the deposition is to be taken, and the notice which is given must be in sufficient time to permit the party to seek a protective order under IN ST TRIAL P Rule 30(D) and IN ST TRIAL P Rule 26(C), if necessary. 2A INPRAC R 30(30.2).

ii. Leave of court, granted with or without notice, must be obtained only if the plaintiff seeks to take a deposition prior to the expiration of twenty (20) days after service of summons and complaint upon any defendant except that leave is not required:

- If a defendant has served a notice of taking deposition or otherwise sought discovery; or
- If special notice is given as provided in IN ST TRIAL P Rule 30(B)(2). IN ST TRIAL P Rule 30(A).

iii. The court may for cause shown enlarge or shorten the time for taking the deposition. IN ST TRIAL P Rule 30(B)(3).

b. *Depositions upon written questions.* After commencement of the action, any party may take the testimony of any person, including a party, by deposition upon written questions. IN ST TRIAL P Rule 31(A).

i. *Service of cross questions.* Within twenty (20) days after the notice and written questions are served, a party may serve cross questions upon all other parties. IN ST TRIAL P Rule 31(A).

ii. *Service of redirect questions.* Within ten (10) days after being served with cross questions, a party may serve redirect questions upon all other parties. IN ST TRIAL P Rule 31(A).

iii. *Service of recross questions.* Within ten (10) days after being served with redirect questions, a party may serve recross questions upon all other parties. IN ST TRIAL P Rule 31(A).

iv. *Time to respond.* The court may for cause shown enlarge or shorten the time. IN ST TRIAL P Rule 31(A).

c. *For deposition before action.* At least twenty (20) days before the date of hearing the notice shall be served in the manner provided in IN ST TRIAL P Rule 4 for service of summons; but if such service cannot with due diligence be made upon any expected adverse party named in the petition, the court may make such order as is just for service by publication or otherwise, and shall appoint, for persons not served in the manner provided in IN ST TRIAL P Rule 4, an attorney who shall represent them, and, in case they are not otherwise represented, shall cross-examine the deponent. If any expected adverse party is a minor or incompetent the provisions of IN ST TRIAL P Rule 17(C) apply. IN ST TRIAL P Rule 27(A)(2).

i. Refer to the Indiana KeyRules Complaint document for information regarding service under IN ST TRIAL P Rule 4.

d. *For deposition pending appeal.* The party who desires to perpetuate the testimony may make a motion in the court for leave to take the depositions, upon the same notice and service thereof as if the action was pending in the court. IN ST TRIAL P Rule 27(B).

i. *Filing.* All pleadings and papers subsequent to the complaint which are required to be served upon a party shall be filed with the Court either before service or within a reasonable period of time thereafter. IN ST TRIAL P Rule 5(E)(1). All pleadings, motions and other papers submitted for filing which are required to be served under IN ST TRIAL P Rule 5(A) shall be filed no later than three (3) days after service. IN ST LAKE RCP Rule 3(A).

- If such papers are filed before service, proof of service thereof shall be filed no later than three (3) business days thereafter. Upon failure to comply with IN ST LAKE RCP Rule 3, the Court may, on motion of any party or on its own motion, impose appropriate sanctions. IN ST LAKE RCP Rule 3(A).

    ii.   *Briefs.* Briefs, other than those addressed in IN ST LAKE RCP Rule 4 and IN ST LAKE RCP Rule 9, shall be filed no later than two (2) calendar days preceding the hearing or trial to which directed. IN ST LAKE RCP Rule 11.

    iii.   *Service.* A written motion, other than one which may be heard ex parte, and notice of the hearing thereof shall be served not less than five (5) days before the time specified for the hearing, unless a different period is fixed by the Indiana Rules of Trial Procedure or by order of the court. IN ST TRIAL P Rule 6(D).

- *Of supporting affidavits.* When a motion is supported by affidavit, the affidavit shall be served with the motion. IN ST TRIAL P Rule 6(D).

2. *Computation of time*

    a.   *Generally; Days excluded.* In computing any period of time prescribed or allowed by the Indiana Rules of Trial Procedure, by order of the court, or by any applicable statute, the day of the act, event, or default from which the designated period of time begins to run shall not be included. The last day of the period so computed is to be included unless it is:

        i.   A Saturday,

        ii.   A Sunday,

        iii.   A legal holiday as defined by state statute, or

        iv.   A day the office in which the act is to be done is closed during regular business hours. IN ST TRIAL P Rule 6(A).

    b.   *Short periods.* In any event, the period runs until the end of the next day that is not a Saturday, a Sunday, a legal holiday, or a day on which the office is closed. When the period of time allowed is less than seven (7) days, intermediate Saturdays, Sundays, legal holidays, and days on which the office is closed shall be excluded from the computations. IN ST TRIAL P Rule 6(A).

    c.   *Additional time after service by United States mail.* Whenever a party has the right or is required to do some act or take some proceedings within a prescribed period after the service of a notice or other paper upon him and the notice or paper is served upon him by United States mail, three (3) days shall be added to the prescribed period. IN ST TRIAL P Rule 6(E).

    d.   *Electronic filing does not alter deadlines.* Filing electronically does not alter any filing deadlines or any time computation pursuant to state or federal statutes, any Rules of the Indiana Supreme Court, including without limitation the Rules of Trial Procedure, the Rules of Appellate Procedure or the Administrative Rules, or applicable Lake County Rules of Civil Procedure. The office of the Lake County Clerk is open for electronic filing under the Lake County Rules of Civil Procedure twenty-four (24) hours a day. A document is deemed filed at the date and time it is received by the LCOD server. Filing must be completed before midnight local time in order to be considered filed that day. Lake County observes Central Time and electronic filers are strongly urged to file documents during hours when the Lake County Online Docket ("LCOD") help line is available, from 9:00 a.m. to 4:00 p.m. local time, although documents can be filed electronically twenty-four (24) hours a day. IN ST LAKE RCP Rule 17(I).

    e.   *Enlargement of time.* When an act is required or allowed to be done at or within a specific time by the Indiana Rules of Trial Procedure, the court may at any time for cause shown:

        i.   Order the period enlarged, with or without motion or notice, if request therefor is made before the expiration of the period originally prescribed or extended by a previous order; or

        ii.   Upon motion made after the expiration of the specific period, permit the act to be done where the failure to act was the result of excusable neglect; but, the court may not extend the time for taking any action for judgment on the evidence under IN ST TRIAL P Rule 50(A), amendment of findings and judgment under IN ST TRIAL P Rule 52(B), to correct errors under IN ST TRIAL P Rule 59(C), statement in opposition to motion to correct error under IN ST TRIAL P Rule 59(E), or to obtain relief from final judgment under IN ST TRIAL P Rule 60(B), except to the extent and under the conditions stated in those rules. IN ST TRIAL P Rule 6(B).

C. General Requirements

1. *Scope of discovery.* Unless otherwise limited by order of the court in accordance with the Indiana Rules of Trial Procedure, the scope of discovery is as follows:

   a. *In general.* Parties may obtain discovery regarding any matter, not privileged, which is relevant to the subject-matter involved in the pending action, whether it relates to the claim or defense of the party seeking discovery or the claim or defense of any other party, including the existence, description, nature, custody, condition and location of any books, documents, or other tangible things and the identity and location of persons having knowledge of any discoverable matter. It is not ground for objection that the information sought will be inadmissible at the trial if the information sought appears reasonably calculated to lead to the discovery of admissible evidence. IN ST TRIAL P Rule 26(B)(1).

      i. *Limiting discovery upon court determination.* The frequency or extent of use of the discovery methods otherwise permitted under the Indiana Rules of Trial Procedure and by any local rule shall be limited by the court if it determines that:

         - The discovery sought is unreasonably cumulative or duplicative, or is obtainable from some other source that is more convenient, less burdensome, or less expensive;

         - The party seeking discovery has had ample opportunity by discovery in the action to obtain the information sought or;

         - The burden or expense of the proposed discovery outweighs its likely benefit, taking into account the needs of the case, the amount in controversy, the parties' resources, the importance of the issues at stake in the litigation, and the importance of the proposed discovery in resolving the issues. IN ST TRIAL P Rule 26(B)(1).

         - The court may act upon its own initiative after reasonable notice or pursuant to a motion under IN ST TRIAL P Rule 26(C). IN ST TRIAL P Rule 26(B)(1). Refer to the Indiana KeyRules Motion for Protective Order document for more information.

      ii. *Relevancy in the discovery context.* When the word "relevancy" is used in IN ST TRIAL P Rule 26(B), it does not mean "relevancy" as that word in used to determine the admissibility of evidence in a trial court. It is much broader. It means "relevancy" to the "subject matter" of the litigation or pending action and it may relate to the claim or defense of any party. Pretrial discovery is available as to any nonprivileged matter relevant to the subject matter of the lawsuit or to obtain information reasonably calculated to lead to admissible evidence. 2A INPRAC R 26(26.4); Kaufmann v. Credithrift Financial, Inc., 465 N.E.2d 207, 210 (Ind.Ct.App. 1984).

      iii. *Tests for relevance.* Indiana case law has developed two (2) additional tests in this area. 2A INPRAC R 26(26.4).

         - The first test determines when a document or a request for information is actually relevant to the subject matter in the pending action. A document [or discovery request] is relevant to discovery if there is the possibility the information sought may be relevant to the subject matter of the action. 2A INPRAC R 26(26.4); CIGNA-INA/Aetna v. Hagerman-Shambaugh, 473 N.E.2d 1033, 1036 (Ind.Ct.App. 1985).

         - The second test speaks to appellate review of the trial court's determination that a document or discovery request is relevant to the subject matter of the pending action. The appellate court sees its review of the trial court's decision on relevancy to subject matter as being very limited. The court states: "Our review of the trial court's conclusion that the documents are relevant is limited. A trial court is vested with discretion in its rulings on discovery issues." 2A INPRAC R 26(26.4); Costanzi v. Ryan, 175 Ind.App. 257, 370 N.E.2d 1333 (Ind.Ct.App. 1978).

   b. *Insurance agreements.* A party may obtain discovery of the existence and contents of any insurance agreement under which any person carrying on an insurance business may be liable to satisfy part or all of a judgment which may be entered in the action or to indemnify or reimburse for payments made to satisfy the judgment. Information concerning the insurance agreement is not by reason of

disclosure admissible in evidence at trial. For purposes of IN ST TRIAL P Rule 26(B)(2), an application for insurance shall not be treated as part of an insurance agreement. IN ST TRIAL P Rule 26(B)(2).

c. *Trial preparation; Materials.* Subject to the provisions of IN ST TRIAL P Rule 26(B)(4), a party may obtain discovery of documents and tangible things otherwise discoverable under IN ST TRIAL P Rule 26(B)(1) and prepared in anticipation of litigation or for trial by or for another party or by or for that other party's representative (including his attorney, consultant, surety, indemnitor, insurer, or agent) only upon a showing that the party seeking discovery has substantial need of the materials in the preparation of his case and that he is unable without undue hardship to obtain the substantial equivalent of the materials by other means. In ordering discovery of such materials when the required showing has been made, the court shall protect against disclosure of the mental impressions, conclusions, opinions, or legal theories of an attorney or other representative of a party concerning the litigation. IN ST TRIAL P Rule 26(B)(3).

i. A party may obtain without the required showing a statement concerning the action or its subject matter previously made by that party. Upon request, a person not a party may obtain without the required showing a statement concerning the action or its subject matter previously made by that person. If the request is refused, the person may move for a court order. The provisions of IN ST TRIAL P Rule 37(A)(4) apply to the award of expenses incurred in relation to the motion. For purposes of IN ST TRIAL P Rule 26(B)(3), a statement previously made is:

- A written statement signed or otherwise adopted approved by the person making it, or
- A stenographic, mechanical, electrical, or other recording, or a transcription thereof, which is a substantially verbatim recital of an oral statement by the person making it and contemporaneously recorded. IN ST TRIAL P Rule 26(B)(3).

ii. The protection of IN ST TRIAL P Rule 26(B)(3) extends to material prepared or collected before litigation actually commences, but that some possibility of litigation must actually exist before the privilege and IN ST TRIAL P Rule 26(B)(3) become operative. 2A INPRAC R 26(26.9).

d. *Trial preparation; Experts.* Discovery of facts known and opinions held by experts, otherwise discoverable under the provisions of IN ST TRIAL P Rule 26(B)(1) and acquired or developed in anticipation of litigation or for trial, may be obtained as follows:

i. A party may through interrogatories require any other party to identify each person whom the other party expects to call as an expert witness at trial, to state the subject matter on which the expert is expected to testify, and to state the substance of the facts and opinions to which the expert is expected to testify and a summary of the grounds for each opinion. IN ST TRIAL P Rule 26(B)(4)(a)(i).

ii. Upon motion, the court may order further discovery by other means, subject to such restrictions as to scope and such provisions, pursuant to IN ST TRIAL P Rule 26(B)(4)(c), concerning fees and expenses as the court may deem appropriate. IN ST TRIAL P Rule 26(B)(4)(a)(ii).

iii. A party may discover facts known or opinions held by an expert who has been retained or specially employed by another party in anticipation of litigation or preparation for trial and who is not expected to be called as a witness at trial, only as provided in IN ST TRIAL P Rule 35(B) or upon a showing of exceptional circumstances under which it is impracticable for the party seeking discovery to obtain facts or opinions on the same subject by other means. IN ST TRIAL P Rule 26(B)(4)(b).

iv. Unless manifest injustice would result,

- The court shall require that the party seeking discovery pay the expert a reasonable fee for time spent in responding to discovery under IN ST TRIAL P Rule 26(B)(4)(a)(ii) and IN ST TRIAL P Rule 26(B)(4)(b); and
- With respect to discovery obtained under IN ST TRIAL P Rule 26(B)(4)(a)(ii) the court may require, and with respect to discovery obtained under IN ST TRIAL P Rule 26(B)(4)(b) the court shall require, the party seeking discovery to pay the other party a fair

portion of the fees and expenses reasonably incurred by the latter party in obtaining facts and opinions from the expert. IN ST TRIAL P Rule 26(B)(4).

e. *Claims of privilege or protection*

  i. *Information withheld.* When a party withholds information otherwise discoverable under the Indiana Rules of Trial Procedure by claiming that it is privileged or subject to protection as trial preparation material, the party shall make the claim expressly and shall describe the nature of the documents, communications, or things not produced or disclosed in a manner that, without revealing information itself privileged or protected, will enable other parties to assess the applicability of the privilege or protection. IN ST TRIAL P Rule 26(B)(5)(a).

  ii. *Information produced.* If information is produced in discovery that is subject to a claim of privilege or protection as trial-preparation material, the party making the claim may notify any party that received the information of the claim and the basis for it. After being notified, a party must promptly return, sequester, or destroy the specified information and any copies it has and may not use or disclose the information until the claim is resolved. A receiving party may promptly present the information to the court under seal for a determination of the claim. If the receiving party disclosed the information before being notified, it must take reasonable steps to retrieve it. The producing party must preserve the information until the claim is resolved. IN ST TRIAL P Rule 26(B)(5)(b).

  iii. *Waiver.* The law of discovery has developed some holdings which indicate that "waiver" of a privileged communication in a discovery setting might be more exacting than "waiver" of a privileged communication when the only question at hand is an interpretation of the privilege itself. Thus, in litigation in which several documents are in issue, and some are released inadvertently, there is strong case law that holds that the "inadvertent production" of a privileged document does not constitute a waiver of the attorney-client privilege. 2A INPRAC R 26(26.5); Transamerica Computer Co. v. International Business Machines Corp., 573 F.2d 646 (9th Cir. 1978). Such a rule should be measured against the usual rule which suggests that a voluntary disclosure to a third person will generally suffice to show a waiver of the attorney-client privilege. 2A INPRAC R 26(26.5).

f. *Use not limited.* Unless the court orders otherwise under IN ST TRIAL P Rule 26(C), the frequency of use of the methods listed in IN ST TRIAL P Rule 26(A) is not limited. IN ST TRIAL P Rule 26(A).

g. *Sequence of discovery.* Unless the court upon motion, for the convenience of parties and witnesses and in the interests of justice, orders otherwise, methods of discovery may be used in any sequence and the fact that a party is conducting discovery, whether by deposition or otherwise, shall not operate to delay any other party's discovery. IN ST TRIAL P Rule 26(D).

2. *Depositions upon oral examination.* IN ST TRIAL P Rule 30 provides for the pre-trial deposition on oral examination of a party, or a witness who is not a party. 2A INPRAC R 30(30.1).

a. *Generally.* The deposition may be used to narrow issues, or to create and enlarge them. It will eliminate matters that are not disputed among the parties; it might introduce new issues and questions which become disputed. The range and purpose of the deposition's use is almost limitless, as long as it is taken consistent with IN ST TRIAL P Rule 26 and IN ST TRIAL P Rule 30 and the principles of IN ST TRIAL P Rule 32. The deposition may obtain evidence that is admissible at trial; it may go quite beyond admissibility at trial if the area of investigation is relevant to the subject matter of the case under IN ST TRIAL P Rule 26. It can disclose the existence and availability of facts that may lead to evidence which may be used at trial. 2A INPRAC R 30(30.1).

b. *Notice*

  i. *Contents of notice.* The notice shall state the time and place for taking the deposition and the name and address of each person to be examined, if known, and if the name is not known, a general description sufficient to identify him or the particular class or group to which he belongs. If a subpoena duces tecum is to be served on the person to be examined, a designation of the materials to be produced thereunder shall be attached to or included in the notice. IN ST TRIAL P Rule 30(B)(1).

ii. *Circumstances where leave of court required.* Leave of court, when required by IN ST TRIAL P Rule 30(A) is not required for the taking of a deposition by plaintiff if the notice:

- States that the person to be examined is about to go out of the state or will be unavailable for examination unless his deposition is taken before expiration of the twenty (20) day period; and

- Sets forth facts to support the statement. IN ST TRIAL P Rule 30(B)(2).

iii. *Signature on notice.* The plaintiff's attorney shall sign the notice, and his signature constitutes a certification by him that to the best of his knowledge, information, and belief the statement and supporting facts are true. The sanctions provided by IN ST TRIAL P Rule 11 are applicable to the certification. IN ST TRIAL P Rule 30(B).

iv. *Manner of recording.* If a party taking a deposition wishes to have the testimony recorded other than in a manner provided in IN ST TRIAL P Rule 74, the notice shall specify the manner of recording and preserving the deposition. The court may require stenographic taking or make any other order to assure that the recorded testimony will be accurate and trustworthy. IN ST TRIAL P Rule 30(B)(4).

v. *Organization as deponent; Designation.* A party may in his notice name as the deponent an organization, including without limitation a governmental organization, or a partnership and designate with reasonable particularity the matters on which examination is requested. The organization so named shall designate one or more officers, directors, or managing agents, executive officers, or other persons duly authorized and consenting to testify on its behalf. The persons so designated shall testify as to matters known or available to the organization. IN ST TRIAL P Rule 30(B)(6) does not preclude taking a deposition by any other procedure authorized in the Indiana Rules of Trial Procedure. IN ST TRIAL P Rule 30(B)(6).

c. *Improper service of notice.* If any party shows that when he was served with notice under IN ST TRIAL P Rule 30(B)(2) he was unable through the exercise of diligence to obtain counsel to represent him at the taking of the deposition, the deposition may not be used against him. IN ST TRIAL P Rule 30(B).

d. *Examination and cross-examination; Record of examination; Oath; Objections.* Examination and cross-examination of witnesses may proceed as permitted at the trial under the provisions of IN ST TRIAL P Rule 43(B). The officer before whom the deposition is to be taken shall put the witness on oath and shall personally, or by someone acting under his direction and in his presence, record the testimony of the witness. The testimony shall be taken stenographically or recorded by any other means designated in accordance with IN ST TRIAL P Rule 30(B)(4). If requested by one of the parties, the testimony shall be transcribed. IN ST TRIAL P Rule 30(C).

i. *Objections*

- All objections made at the time of the examination to the qualifications of the officer taking the deposition, or to the manner of taking it, or to the evidence presented, or to the conduct of any party, and any other objection to the proceedings, shall be noted by the officer upon the deposition. IN ST TRIAL P Rule 30(C).

- When there is an objection to a question, the objection and reason therefor shall be noted, and the question shall be answered unless the attorney instructs the deponent not to answer, or the deponent refuses to answer, in which case either party may have the question certified by the Reporter, and the question with the objection thereto when so certified shall be delivered to the party requesting the certification who may then proceed under IN ST TRIAL P Rule 37(A). IN ST TRIAL P Rule 30(C).

- In lieu of participating in the oral examination, parties may serve written questions on the party taking the deposition and require him to transmit them to the officer, who shall propound them to the witness and record the answers verbatim. IN ST TRIAL P Rule 30(C).

e. *Motion to terminate or limit examination.* At any time during the taking of the deposition, on motion of any party or of the deponent and upon a showing that the examination is being conducted in bad faith or in such manner as unreasonably to annoy, embarrass, or oppress the deponent or party, the court in which the action is pending or the court in the county where the deposition is being taken may order the officer conducting the examination to cease forthwith from taking the deposition, or may limit the scope and manner of the taking of the deposition as provided in IN ST TRIAL P Rule 26(C). IN ST TRIAL P Rule 30(D).

    i.   If the order made terminates the examination, it shall be resumed thereafter only upon the order of the court in which the action is pending. IN ST TRIAL P Rule 30(D).

    ii.   Upon demand of the objecting party or deponent the taking of the deposition shall be suspended for the time necessary to make a motion for an order. The provisions of IN ST TRIAL P Rule 37(A)(4) apply to the award of expenses incurred in relation to the motion. IN ST TRIAL P Rule 30(D).

    iii.   Refer to the Indiana KeyRules Motion for Protective Order and Motion for Discovery Sanctions documents for more information.

f.   *Submission to witness; Changes; Signing*

    i.   When the testimony is fully transcribed, the deposition shall be submitted to the witness for reading and signing and shall be read to or by him, unless such reading and signing have been waived by the witness and by each party. "Submitted to the witness" as used in IN ST TRIAL P Rule 30(E)(1) shall mean:

- Mailing of written notification by registered or certified mail to the witness and each attorney attending the deposition that the deposition can be read and examined in the office of the officer before whom the deposition was taken, or

- Mailing the original deposition, by registered or certified mail, to the witness at an address designated by the witness or his attorney, if requested to do so by the witness, his attorney, or the party taking the deposition. IN ST TRIAL P Rule 30(E)(1).

    ii.   If the witness desires to change any answer in the deposition submitted to him, each change, with a statement of the reason therefor, shall be made by the witness on a separate form provided by the officer, shall be signed by the witness and affixed to the original deposition by the officer. A copy of such changes shall be furnished by the officer to each party. IN ST TRIAL P Rule 30(E)(2).

    iii.   If the reading and signing have not been waived by the witness and by each party the deposition shall be signed by the witness and returned by him to the officer within thirty (30) days after it is submitted to the witness. If the deposition has been returned to the officer and has not been signed by the witness, the officer shall execute a certificate of that fact, attach it to the original deposition and deliver it to the party taking it. In such event, the deposition may be used by any party with the same force and effect as though it had been signed by the witness. IN ST TRIAL P Rule 30(E)(3).

    iv.   In the event the deposition is not returned to the officer within thirty (30) days after it has been submitted to the witness, the reporter shall execute a certificate of that fact and cause the certificate to be delivered to the party taking it. In such event, any party may use a copy of the deposition with the same force and effect as though the original had been signed by the witness. IN ST TRIAL P Rule 30(E)(4).

g.   *Certification and filing; Exhibits; Copies*

    i.   The officer shall certify on the deposition that the witness was duly sworn by him and that the deposition is a true record of the testimony given by the witness. He shall then securely seal the deposition in an envelope endorsed with the title of the action and marked "Deposition of (here insert name of witness)" and shall promptly deliver it to the party taking the deposition. IN ST TRIAL P Rule 30(F)(1). Documents and things, unless objection is made to their production for inspection during the examination of the witness, shall be marked for identification and annexed to and returned with the deposition, and may be inspected and copied by any party, except that:

- The person producing the materials may substitute copies to be marked for identification, if he affords to all parties fair opportunity to verify the copies by comparison with the originals; and

- If the person producing the materials requests their return the officer shall mark them, give each party an opportunity to inspect and copy them, and return them to the person producing them, and the materials may then be used in the same manner as if annexed to and returned with the deposition. IN ST TRIAL P Rule 30(F)(1).

 ii. Upon payment of reasonable charges therefor, the officer shall furnish a copy of the deposition to any party or the deponent. IN ST TRIAL P Rule 30(F)(2).

 iii. The officer taking the deposition shall give prompt notice to all parties of its delivery to the party taking the deposition. IN ST TRIAL P Rule 30(F)(3).

 iv. The filing of depositions shall be in accordance with the provisions of IN ST TRIAL P Rule 5(E). IN ST TRIAL P Rule 30(F)(4).

h. *Failure to attend or to serve subpoena; Expenses*

 i. If the party giving the notice of the taking of a deposition fails to attend and proceed therewith and another party attends in person or by attorney pursuant to the notice, the court may order the party giving the notice to pay to such other party the amount of the reasonable expenses incurred by him and his attorney in so attending, including reasonable attorney's fees. IN ST TRIAL P Rule 30(G)(1).

 ii. If the party giving the notice of the taking of a deposition of a witness other than a party fails to serve a subpoena upon him and the witness because of such failure does not attend, and if another party attends in person or by attorney because he expects the deposition of that witness to be taken, the court may order the party giving the notice to pay to such other party the amount of the reasonable expenses incurred by him and his attorney in so attending, including reasonable attorney's fees. IN ST TRIAL P Rule 30(G)(2).

i. *Depositions of prisoners.* The deposition of a person confined in prison may be taken only by leave of court on such terms as the court prescribes. IN ST TRIAL P Rule 30(A).

j. *Cost of deposition.* In Indiana the rule is that the party who initiates a deposition pays for the cost necessarily incurred as a result of the deposition. Those costs are: (1) the stenographic reporter's fees, (2) the transcription and filing fees, and (3) transportation costs and perhaps other costs which might naturally arise in a particular situation. 2A INPRAC R 30(30.8); Briggs v. Clinton County Bank & Trust Co. of Frankfort, Ind., 452 N.E.2d 989, 1009 (Ind.Ct.App. 1983).

3. *Deposition upon written questions.* The use of written questions under IN ST TRIAL P Rule 31 is often not as effective as taking a deposition on oral examination, and is generally, as a practical matter, not suitable for complicated cases or where cross-examination is necessary, as in the case of a reluctant or hostile witness. Written questions are, however, an inexpensive device where simple or formal facts are sought. 2A INPRAC R 31(31.1).

a. *Notice.* A party desiring to take a deposition upon written questions shall serve them upon every other party with a notice stating:

 i. The name and address of the person who is to answer them, if known, and if the name is not known, a general description sufficient to identify him or the particular class or group to which he belongs; and

 ii. The name or descriptive title and address of the officer before whom the deposition is to be taken. IN ST TRIAL P Rule 31(A).

b. *Depositions of specific persons*

 i. *Prisoners.* The deposition of a person confined in prison may be taken only by leave of court on such terms as the court prescribes. IN ST TRIAL P Rule 31(A).

 ii. *Organization.* A deposition upon written questions may be taken of an organization, including a governmental organization, or a partnership in accordance with the provisions of IN ST TRIAL P Rule 30(B)(6). IN ST TRIAL P Rule 31(A).

c. *Officer to take responses and prepare record.* A copy of the notice and copies of all questions served shall be delivered by the party taking the deposition to the officer designated in the notice, who shall proceed promptly, in the manner provided by IN ST TRIAL P Rule 30(C), IN ST TRIAL P Rule 30(E), and IN ST TRIAL P Rule 30(F), to take the testimony of the witness in response to the questions and to prepare, certify, and deliver the deposition, attaching thereto the copy of the notice and the questions received by him, in accordance with IN ST TRIAL P Rule 5(E). IN ST TRIAL P Rule 31(B).

d. *Notice of filing.* When the deposition is filed the party taking it shall promptly give notice thereof to all other parties. IN ST TRIAL P Rule 31(C).

4. *Depositions before action or pending appeal*

a. *Use of deposition to perpetuate testimony.* IN ST TRIAL P Rule 27 does not exist to provide a method of discovery to determine whether a cause of action exists. Rather, the rule is intended to be used to "memorialize" evidence that is already known. Accordingly, a trial court should not grant a motion to perpetuate testimony by deposition on the mere possibility that witnesses may be transferred or leave current employment. 2A INPRAC R 27(27.2). IN ST TRIAL P Rule 27 is available for use "when a certain witness' testimony might become unavailable over time, and not to provide a method of discovery to determine whether a cause of action exits." 2A INPRAC R 27(27.2); Petition of Gary Construction, Inc., 96 F.R.D. 432 (D.C.Colo. 1983); Petition of Gurnsey, 223 F.Supp. 359 (D.D.C. 1963).

b. *Before action; Petition required*

i. *Petition.* A person who desires to perpetuate his own testimony or that of another person regarding any matter that may be cognizable in any court in which the action may be commenced, may file a verified petition in any such court of this state. IN ST TRIAL P Rule 27(A)(1). The petition shall be entitled in the name of the petitioner and shall state facts showing:

- That the petitioner expects to be a party to an action cognizable in a court of this or another state;
- The subject-matter of the expected action and his interest therein;
- The facts which he desires to establish by the proposed testimony and his reasons for desiring to perpetuate it;
- The names or a description of the persons he expects will be adverse parties and their addresses so far as known; and
- The names and addresses of the persons to be examined and the substance of the testimony which he expects to elicit from each, and shall ask for an order authorizing the petitioner to take the depositions of the persons to be examined named in the petition, for the purpose of perpetuating their testimony. IN ST TRIAL P Rule 27(A)(1).

ii. *Notice and service.* The petitioner shall thereafter serve a notice upon each person named in the petition as an expected adverse party, together with a copy of the petition, stating that the petitioner will apply to the court, at a time and place named therein, for the order described in the petition. IN ST TRIAL P Rule 27(A)(2).

iii. *Order and examination.* If the court is satisfied that the perpetuation of the testimony may prevent a failure or delay of justice, it shall make an order designating or describing the persons whose depositions may be taken and specifying the subject-matter of the examination or written interrogatories. The depositions may then be taken in accordance with the Indiana Rules of Trial Procedure; and the court may make orders of the character provided for by IN ST TRIAL P Rule 34 and IN ST TRIAL P Rule 35. For the purpose of applying the Indiana Rules of Trial Procedure to depositions for perpetuating testimony, each reference therein to the court in which the action is pending shall be deemed to refer to the court in which the petition for such deposition was filed. IN ST TRIAL P Rule 27(A)(3).

iv. *Use of deposition.* If a deposition to perpetuate testimony is taken under the Indiana Rules of

Trial Procedure or if, although not so taken, it would be admissible in evidence in the court of the state in which it is taken, it may be used in any action involving the same subject-matter subsequently brought in a court of this state in accordance with the provision of IN ST TRIAL P Rule 32. IN ST TRIAL P Rule 27(A)(3).

c. *Pending appeal.* If an appeal has been taken from a judgment of any court or before the taking of an appeal if the time therefor has not expired, the court in which the judgment was rendered may allow the taking of the depositions of witnesses to perpetuate their testimony for use in the event of further proceedings in such court. In such case the party who desires to perpetuate the testimony may make a motion in the court for leave to take the depositions, upon the same notice and service thereof as if the action was pending in the court. IN ST TRIAL P Rule 27(B).

   i. The motion shall show:

   - The names and addresses of the persons to be examined and the substance of the testimony which he expects to elicit from each;

   - The reasons for perpetuating their testimony. IN ST TRIAL P Rule 27(B).

   ii. If the court finds that the perpetuation of the testimony is proper to avoid a failure or delay of justice, it may make an order allowing the depositions to be taken and may make orders of the character provided for by IN ST TRIAL P Rule 34 and IN ST TRIAL P Rule 35, and thereupon the depositions may be taken and used in the same manner and under the same conditions as are prescribed in the Indiana Rules of Trial Procedure for depositions taken in actions pending in the court. IN ST TRIAL P Rule 27(B).

d. *Perpetuation by action.* IN ST TRIAL P Rule 27 does not limit the power of a court to entertain an action to perpetuate testimony. IN ST TRIAL P Rule 27(C).

e. *Filing deposition.* The filing or custody of any deposition or evidence obtained under IN ST TRIAL P Rule 27 shall be in accordance with IN ST TRIAL P Rule 5(E). IN ST TRIAL P Rule 27(D).

5. *Persons before whom depositions may be taken; Discovery across state lines; Before administrative agencies; And after judgment*

   a. *Within the United States.* Within the United States or within a territory or insular possession subject to the dominion of the United States, depositions shall be taken before an officer authorized to administer oaths by the laws of the United States, or of the state of Indiana, or of the place where the examination is held, or before a person appointed by the court in which the action is pending. A person so appointed has power to administer oaths and take testimony. IN ST TRIAL P Rule 28(A).

   b. *In foreign countries*

   i. In a foreign country, depositions may be taken:

   - On notice before a person authorized to administer oaths in the place in which the examination is held, either by the law thereof or by the law of the United States; or

   - Before a person commissioned by the court, and a person so commissioned shall have the power by virtue of his commission to administer any necessary oath and take testimony; or

   - Pursuant to a letter rogatory. IN ST TRIAL P Rule 28(B).

   ii. A commission or a letter rogatory shall be issued on application and notice and on terms that are just and appropriate. It is not requisite to the issuance of a commission or a letter rogatory that the taking of the deposition in any other manner is impracticable or inconvenient; and both a commission and a letter rogatory may be issued in proper cases. A notice or commission may designate the person before whom the deposition is to be taken either by name or descriptive title. A letter rogatory may be addressed "To the Appropriate Authority in (here name the country)." Evidence obtained in response to a letter rogatory need not be excluded merely for the reason that it is not a verbatim transcript or that the testimony was not taken under oath or for any similar departure from the requirements for depositions taken within the United States under the Indiana Rules of Trial Procedure. IN ST TRIAL P Rule 28(B).

   c. *Disqualification for interest.* Unless otherwise permitted by the Indiana Rules of Trial Procedure, no deposition shall be taken before a person who is a relative or employee or attorney or counsel of any of the parties, or is a relative or employee of such attorney or counsel, or is financially interested in the action. IN ST TRIAL P Rule 28(C).

    i.   Disqualification of the person before whom the deposition is taken is one of the matters which is waived under IN ST TRIAL P Rule 32(D)(3) unless objection is made as soon as the disqualification is known or could have been known by reasonable diligence. 2A INPRAC R 28(28.3).

d.   *Scope of discovery outside state; Protective and enforcement orders.* A deposition may be taken outside the state as provided in IN ST TRIAL P Rule 28(A) and IN ST TRIAL P Rule 28(B), and the deponent may be requested to produce documents and things, and may also be requested to allow inspections and copies as provided in IN ST TRIAL P Rule 34 to submit to examination under IN ST TRIAL P Rule 35. Protective orders may be granted by the court in which the action is pending and by the court where discovery is being made. Enforcement orders may be made by the court where the discovery is sought, and enforcement orders and sanctions may be made by the court where the action is pending as against parties and as against witnesses subject to the jurisdiction of the court. When no action is pending, a court of this state may authorize a deposition to be taken outside this state of any person and upon any matters allowed by IN ST TRIAL P Rule 27. IN ST TRIAL P Rule 28(D).

e.   *Assistance to tribunals and litigants outside this state.* A court of this state may order a person who is domiciled or is found within this state to give his testimony or statement or to produce documents or other things, allow inspections and copies and permit physical and mental examinations for use in a proceeding in a tribunal outside this state. The order may be made upon the application of any interested person or in response to a letter rogatory and may prescribe the practice and procedure, which may be wholly or in part the practice and procedure of the tribunal outside this state, for taking the testimony or statement or producing the documents or other things. To the extent that the order does not prescribe otherwise, the practice and procedure shall be in accordance with that of the court of this state issuing the order. The order may direct that the testimony or statement be given, or document or other thing produced, before a person appointed by the court. The person appointed shall have power to administer any necessary oath. A person within this state may voluntarily give his testimony or statement or produce documents or other things allowing inspections and copies and permit physical and mental examinations for use in a proceeding before a tribunal outside this state. IN ST TRIAL P Rule 28(E).

f.   *Discovery proceedings before administrative agencies.* Whenever an adjudicatory hearing, including any hearing in any proceeding subject to judicial review, is held by or before an administrative agency, any party to that adjudicatory hearing shall be entitled to use the discovery provisions of IN ST TRIAL P Rule 26 through IN ST TRIAL P Rule 37. Such discovery may include any relevant matter in the custody and control of the administrative agency. IN ST TRIAL P Rule 28(F).

    i.   Protective and other orders shall be obtained first from the administrative agency, and if enforcement of such orders or right of discovery is necessary, it may be obtained in a court of general jurisdiction in the county where discovery is being made or sought, or where the hearing is being held. IN ST TRIAL P Rule 28(F).

g.   *Applicability of other laws.* IN ST TRIAL P Rule 28 does not repeal or modify any other law of this state permitting another procedure for obtaining discovery for use in this state or in a tribunal outside this state, except as expressly provided in the Indiana Rules of Trial Procedure. IN ST TRIAL P Rule 28(G).

h.   *Discovery after judgment.* Discovery after judgment may be had in proceedings to enforce or to challenge the judgment. IN ST TRIAL P Rule 28(H).

6.   *Supplementation of responses.* A party who has responded to a request for discovery with a response that was complete when made is under no duty to supplement his response to include information thereafter acquired, except as follows:

a.   A party is under a duty seasonably to supplement his response with respect to any question directly addressed to:

    i.   The identity and location of persons having knowledge of discoverable matters, and

ii. The identity of each person expected to be called as an expert witness at trial, the subject-matter on which he is expected to testify, and the substance of his testimony. IN ST TRIAL P Rule 26(E)(1).

b. A party is under a duty seasonably to amend a prior response if he obtains information upon the basis of which:

i. He knows that the response was incorrect when made, or

ii. He knows that the response though correct when made is no longer true and the circumstances are such that a failure to amend the response is in substance a knowing concealment. IN ST TRIAL P Rule 26(E)(2).

c. A duty to supplement responses may be imposed by order of the court, agreement of the parties, or at any time prior to trial through new requests for supplementation of prior responses. IN ST TRIAL P Rule 26(E)(3).

d. The duty seasonably to supplement a discovery response is absolute and is not predicated on a court order. "It is a breach of a litigant's duty reasonably to supplement if the litigant postpones supplementing its response by not obtaining from its experts the information which is to be supplied in answer to interrogatories." 2A INPRAC R 26(26.27); Lucas v. Dorsey Corp., 609 N.E.2d 1191, 1196 (Ind.Ct.App. 1993).

D. Documents

1. *Deposition upon oral examination*

   a. *Required documents*

      i. *Notice of deposition.* Refer to the General Requirements section of this document for information on the content of a notice of deposition.

      ii. *Certificate of service.* An attorney or unrepresented party tendering a document to the Clerk for filing shall certify that service has been made, list the parties served, and specify the date and means of service. The certificate of service shall be placed at the end of the document and shall not be separately filed. The separate filing of a certificate of service, however, shall not be grounds for rejecting a document for filing. The Clerk may permit documents to be filed without a certificate of service but shall require prompt filing of a separate certificate of service. IN ST TRIAL P Rule 5(C).

         • All pleadings, motions and other papers submitted for filing which are required to be served under IN ST TRIAL P Rule 5(A) shall contain proof of service pursuant to IN ST TRIAL P Rule 5(B)(2). IN ST LAKE RCP Rule 3(A).

   b. *Supplemental documents*

      i. *Subpoena/subpoena duces tecum.* The attendance of witnesses may be compelled by the use of subpoena as provided in IN ST TRIAL P Rule 45. IN ST TRIAL P Rule 30(A).

         • Proof of service of a notice to take a deposition as provided in IN ST TRIAL P Rule 30(B) and IN ST TRIAL P Rule 31(A) constitutes a sufficient authorization for the issuance by the clerk of court for the county in which the deposition is to be taken of subpoenas for the persons named or described therein. The subpoena may command the person to whom it is directed to produce designated books, papers, documents, or tangible things which constitute or contain matters within the scope of the examination permitted by IN ST TRIAL P Rule 26(B), but in that event the subpoena will be subject to the provisions of IN ST TRIAL P Rule 26(C) and IN ST TRIAL P Rule 45(B). IN ST TRIAL P Rule 45(D)(1).

         • An individual may be required to attend an examination only in the county wherein he resides or is employed or transacts his business in person, or at such other convenient place as is fixed by an order of court. A nonresident of the state may be required to attend only in the state and county wherein he is served with a subpoena, or within forty (40) miles from the place of service, or at such other convenient place as is fixed by an order of court. A non-resident plaintiff may be required to attend at his own expense an examination in the county of this state where the action is commenced or in a county fixed by the court. IN ST TRIAL P Rule 45(D)(2).

ii. *Request for production.* The notice to a deponent may be accompanied by a request made in compliance with IN ST TRIAL P Rule 34 for the production of documents and tangible things at the taking of the deposition. IN ST TRIAL P Rule 30(B)(5).

iii. *Stipulation regarding discovery procedure.* Unless the court orders otherwise, the parties may by written stipulation:

- Provide that depositions may be taken before any person, at any time or place, upon any notice, and in any manner and when so taken may be used like other depositions, and

- Modify the procedures provided by the Indiana Rules of Trial Procedure for other methods of discovery. IN ST TRIAL P Rule 29.

iv. *Facsimile cover sheet.* Any document sent to the Clerk of the Circuit Court by electronic facsimile transmission shall be accompanied by a cover sheet which states the title of the document, case number, number of pages, identity and voice telephone number of the sending party and instructions for filing. The cover sheet shall contain the signature of the attorney or party, pro se, authorizing the filing. IN ST ADMIN Rule 12(D).

2. *Deposition upon written questions*

 a. *Required documents*

  i. *Notice of deposition.* Refer to the General Requirements section of this document for information on the content of a notice of deposition.

  ii. *Certificate of service.* An attorney or unrepresented party tendering a document to the Clerk for filing shall certify that service has been made, list the parties served, and specify the date and means of service. The certificate of service shall be placed at the end of the document and shall not be separately filed. The separate filing of a certificate of service, however, shall not be grounds for rejecting a document for filing. The Clerk may permit documents to be filed without a certificate of service but shall require prompt filing of a separate certificate of service. IN ST TRIAL P Rule 5(C).

   - All pleadings, motions and other papers submitted for filing which are required to be served under IN ST TRIAL P Rule 5(A) shall contain proof of service pursuant to IN ST TRIAL P Rule 5(B)(2). IN ST LAKE RCP Rule 3(A).

 b. *Supplemental documents*

  i. *Subpoena.* The attendance of witnesses may be compelled by the use of subpoena as provided in IN ST TRIAL P Rule 45. IN ST TRIAL P Rule 31(A).

   - Proof of service of a notice to take a deposition as provided in IN ST TRIAL P Rule 30(B) and IN ST TRIAL P Rule 31(A) constitutes a sufficient authorization for the issuance by the clerk of court for the county in which the deposition is to be taken of subpoenas for the persons named or described therein. The subpoena may command the person to whom it is directed to produce designated books, papers, documents, or tangible things which constitute or contain matters within the scope of the examination permitted by IN ST TRIAL P Rule 26(B), but in that event the subpoena will be subject to the provisions of IN ST TRIAL P Rule 26(C) and IN ST TRIAL P Rule 45(B). IN ST TRIAL P Rule 45(D)(1).

   - An individual may be required to attend an examination only in the county wherein he resides or is employed or transacts his business in person, or at such other convenient place as is fixed by an order of court. A nonresident of the state may be required to attend only in the state and county wherein he is served with a subpoena, or within forty (40) miles from the place of service, or at such other convenient place as is fixed by an order of court. A non-resident plaintiff may be required to attend at his own expense an examination in the county of this state where the action is commenced or in a county fixed by the court. IN ST TRIAL P Rule 45(D)(2).

  ii. *Stipulation regarding discovery procedure.* Unless the court orders otherwise, the parties may by written stipulation:

   - Provide that depositions may be taken before any person, at any time or place, upon any notice, and in any manner and when so taken may be used like other depositions, and

- Modify the procedures provided by the Indiana Rules of Trial Procedure for other methods of discovery. IN ST TRIAL P Rule 29.

  iii. *Facsimile cover sheet.* Any document sent to the Clerk of the Circuit Court by electronic facsimile transmission shall be accompanied by a cover sheet which states the title of the document, case number, number of pages, identity and voice telephone number of the sending party and instructions for filing. The cover sheet shall contain the signature of the attorney or party, pro se, authorizing the filing. IN ST ADMIN Rule 12(D).

3. *Deposition before action*

   a. *Required documents*

      i. *Notice of deposition.* Refer to the General Requirements section of this document for information on the contents of a notice of deposition.

      ii. *Petition.* Refer to the General Requirements section of this document for information on the content of a petition.

      iii. *Chronological case summary (CCS) entry forms.* All filings shall be accompanied by a Chronological Case Summary (CCS) Entry Form to define or identify the documents filed. The Form used should be substantially similar to IN ST LAKE RCP App. A. IN ST LAKE RCP Rule 3(C).

      iv. *Certificate of service.* An attorney or unrepresented party tendering a document to the Clerk for filing shall certify that service has been made, list the parties served, and specify the date and means of service. The certificate of service shall be placed at the end of the document and shall not be separately filed. The separate filing of a certificate of service, however, shall not be grounds for rejecting a document for filing. The Clerk may permit documents to be filed without a certificate of service but shall require prompt filing of a separate certificate of service. IN ST TRIAL P Rule 5(C).

         - All pleadings, motions and other papers submitted for filing which are required to be served under IN ST TRIAL P Rule 5(A) shall contain proof of service pursuant to IN ST TRIAL P Rule 5(B)(2). IN ST LAKE RCP Rule 3(A).

   b. *Supplemental documents*

      i. *Stipulation regarding discovery procedure.* Unless the court orders otherwise, the parties may by written stipulation:

         - Provide that depositions may be taken before any person, at any time or place, upon any notice, and in any manner and when so taken may be used like other depositions, and

         - Modify the procedures provided by the Indiana Rules of Trial Procedure for other methods of discovery. IN ST TRIAL P Rule 29.

      ii. *Facsimile cover sheet.* Any document sent to the Clerk of the Circuit Court by electronic facsimile transmission shall be accompanied by a cover sheet which states the title of the document, case number, number of pages, identity and voice telephone number of the sending party and instructions for filing. The cover sheet shall contain the signature of the attorney or party, pro se, authorizing the filing. IN ST ADMIN Rule 12(D).

4. *Deposition pending appeal*

   a. *Required documents*

      i. *Motion for leave to take deposition and notice.* The requirement of notice is satisfied by service of the motion. IN ST TRIAL P Rule 7(B).

      ii. *Brief.* Briefs, other than those addressed in IN ST LAKE RCP Rule 4 and IN ST LAKE RCP Rule 9, shall be filed no later than two (2) calendar days preceding the hearing or trial to which directed. IN ST LAKE RCP Rule 11.

      iii. *Proposed order.* Proposed orders, which are submitted for the court's convenience under IN ST LAKE RCP Rule 3 or other applicable Lake County Rules of Civil Procedure, shall be submitted as attachments to motions. IN ST LAKE RCP Rule 17(D)(8). Proposed orders shall be prepared and filed separately from the pleadings, petitions, motions or other papers to which they have reference. IN ST LAKE RCP Rule 3(B).

- Orders, either routine in nature or uncontested including, for example, those setting or continuing a hearing, shall be effected by the chronological case summary entry only, which shall contain the concise substance of the order. IN ST LAKE RCP Rule 3(B).
- All orders shall be accompanied with sufficient copies and stamped, pre-addressed envelopes, so that copies may be mailed to all parties. IN ST LAKE RCP Rule 3(B).

iv. *Chronological case summary (CCS) entry forms.* All filings shall be accompanied by a Chronological Case Summary (CCS) Entry Form to define or identify the documents filed. The Form used should be substantially similar to IN ST LAKE RCP App. A. IN ST LAKE RCP Rule 3(C).

v. *Certificate of service.* An attorney or unrepresented party tendering a document to the Clerk for filing shall certify that service has been made, list the parties served, and specify the date and means of service. The certificate of service shall be placed at the end of the document and shall not be separately filed. The separate filing of a certificate of service, however, shall not be grounds for rejecting a document for filing. The Clerk may permit documents to be filed without a certificate of service but shall require prompt filing of a separate certificate of service. IN ST TRIAL P Rule 5(C).

- All pleadings, motions and other papers submitted for filing which are required to be served under IN ST TRIAL P Rule 5(A) shall contain proof of service pursuant to IN ST TRIAL P Rule 5(B)(2). IN ST LAKE RCP Rule 3(A).

b. *Supplemental documents*

i. *Stipulation regarding discovery procedure.* Unless the court orders otherwise, the parties may by written stipulation:

- Provide that depositions may be taken before any person, at any time or place, upon any notice, and in any manner and when so taken may be used like other depositions, and
- Modify the procedures provided by the Indiana Rules of Trial Procedure for other methods of discovery. IN ST TRIAL P Rule 29.

ii. *Supporting evidence.* When a motion is based on facts not appearing of record the court may hear the matter on affidavits presented by the respective parties, but the court may direct that the matter be heard wholly or partly on oral testimony or depositions. IN ST TRIAL P Rule 43(B).

iii. *Facsimile cover sheet.* Any document sent to the Clerk of the Circuit Court by electronic facsimile transmission shall be accompanied by a cover sheet which states the title of the document, case number, number of pages, identity and voice telephone number of the sending party and instructions for filing. The cover sheet shall contain the signature of the attorney or party, pro se, authorizing the filing. IN ST ADMIN Rule 12(D).

E. Format

1. *Form of notice.* The rules applicable to captions, and the signing and form of pleadings (IN ST TRIAL P Rule 8 through IN ST TRIAL P Rule 11), apply to all motions and other papers provided under the Indiana Rules of Trial Procedure. 22B INPRAC 7:2.

2. *Form of pleadings.* For the purpose of uniformity, convenience, clarity and durability, requirements in IN ST LAKE RCP Rule 2 shall be observed in the preparation of all pleadings, motions and other papers. IN ST LAKE RCP Rule 2. Whenever materials submitted fail to meet the standards in IN ST LAKE RCP Rule 2, the Court may impose appropriate sanctions. IN ST LAKE RCP Rule 2(B).

a. *Caption; Names of parties.* Every pleading shall contain a caption setting forth the name of the court, the title of the action, the file number, and a designation as in IN ST TRIAL P Rule 7(A). In the complaint the title of the action shall include the names of all the parties, but in other pleadings it is sufficient to state the name of the first party on each side with an appropriate indication of other parties. IN ST TRIAL P Rule 10(A).

i. *Special judge matters.* The caption of all CCS Entry Forms, pleadings, motions, orders and other papers to be filed in a special judge case shall include in block text the words SPECIAL JUDGE and the name of the judge directly below the cause number on the caption. IN ST LAKE RCP Rule 2(D).

b. *Paragraphs; Separate statements.* All averments of a claim or defense shall be made in numbered paragraphs, the contents of each of which shall be limited as far as practicable to a statement of a single set of circumstances, and a paragraph may be referred to by number in all succeeding pleadings. Each claim founded upon a separate transaction or occurrence and each defense other than denials may be stated in a separate count or defense whenever a separation facilitates the clear presentation of the matters set forth. IN ST TRIAL P Rule 10(B).

c. *Adoption by reference; Exhibits.* Statements in a pleading may be adopted by reference in a different part of the same pleading or in another pleading or in any motion. A copy of any written instrument which is an exhibit to a pleading is a part thereof for all purposes. IN ST TRIAL P Rule 10(C).

d. *Paper; Print, quality and binding*

   i. All pleadings, motions, chronological case summary entry forms, orders, process and other papers shall be neatly and legibly printed, typewritten or mechanically reproduced, on one (1) side only, on white opaque paper. To satisfy the recordkeeping requirements of IN ST TRIAL P Rule 77, the print shall be of sufficient density and clarity for preservation and reproduction of microfilming, optical disk or other secondary sources. For this reason, the use of non-letter-quality printers is discouraged. IN ST LAKE RCP Rule 2(A).

   ii. Paper and ink shall be of such quality as to withstand the test of time. All documents shall be produced on acid-free, non-thermal paper. It is recommended that a minimum of twenty (20) pound, twenty-five percent (25%) cotton paper product be used. Documents of multiple pages shall be submitted in bound or stapled fashion, and the binding or stapling shall be at the top only. Covers or backings shall not be used. IN ST LAKE RCP Rule 2(A).

e. *Papers; Handwritten.* Handwritten papers may be filed only if approved by the Court and a typewritten or printed true rendition thereof is filed within three (3) days thereafter and approved by the Court. Upon such approval, they shall be deemed and filed as the original, while the handwritten papers shall be retained therewith for evidentiary purposes. IN ST LAKE RCP Rule 2(C).

f. *Minute sheets; Motion blanks.* Minute sheets and motion blanks shall no longer be used. IN ST LAKE RCP Rule 2(D).

3. *Size of papers for filing.* Effective January 1, 1992, all pleadings, copies, motions and documents filed with any trial court or appellate level court, typed or printed, with the exception of exhibits and existing wills, shall be prepared on eight and one-half by eleven inch (8 1/2" x 11") size paper. IN ST ADMIN Rule 11.

4. *Signature requirements*

a. *Signature of attorney.* Every pleading or motion of a party represented by an attorney shall be signed by at least one (1) attorney of record in his individual name, whose address, telephone number, and attorney number shall be stated, except that this provision shall not apply to pleadings and motions made and transcribed at the trial or a hearing before the judge and received by him in such form. IN ST TRIAL P Rule 11(A).

   i. The signature of an attorney constitutes a certificate by him that he has read the pleadings; that to the best of his knowledge, information, and belief, there is good ground to support it; and that it is not interposed for delay. IN ST TRIAL P Rule 11(A).

   ii. If a pleading or motion is not signed or is signed with intent to defeat the purpose of the rule, it may be stricken as sham and false and the action may proceed as though the pleading had not been served. IN ST TRIAL P Rule 11(A).

   iii. For a willful violation of IN ST TRIAL P Rule 11 an attorney may be subjected to appropriate disciplinary action. Similar action may be taken if scandalous or indecent matter is inserted. IN ST TRIAL P Rule 11(A).

b. *Signature of unrepresented party.* A party who is not represented by an attorney shall sign his pleading and state his address. IN ST TRIAL P Rule 11(A).

c. *Verification not generally required.* Except when specifically required by rule, pleadings or motions need not be verified or accompanied by affidavit. The rule in equity that the averments of an answer under oath must be overcome by the testimony of two (2) witnesses or of one (1) witness sustained by corroborating circumstances is abolished. IN ST TRIAL P Rule 11(A).

d. *Verification by affirmation or representation.* When in connection with any civil or special statutory proceeding it is required that any pleading, motion, petition, supporting affidavit, or other document of any kind, be verified, or that an oath be taken, it shall be sufficient if the subscriber simply affirms the truth of the matter to be verified by an affirmation or representation. IN ST TRIAL P Rule 11(B). IN ST TRIAL P Rule 11(B) states that the affirmation or representation should be in substantially the following language: "I (we) affirm, under the penalties for perjury, that the foregoing representation(s) is (are) true. (Signed) _____."

  i. Any person who falsifies an affirmation or representation of fact shall be subject to the same penalties as are prescribed by law for the making of a false affidavit. IN ST TRIAL P Rule 11(B).

e. *Verified pleadings, motions, and affidavits as evidence.* Pleadings, motions and affidavits accompanying or in support of such pleadings or motions when required to be verified or under oath shall be accepted as a representation that the signer had personal knowledge thereof or reasonable cause to believe the existence of the facts or matters stated or alleged therein; and, if otherwise competent or acceptable as evidence, may be admitted as evidence of the facts or matters stated or alleged therein when it is so provided in the Indiana Rules of Trial Procedure, by statute or other law, or to the extent the writing or signature expressly purports to be made upon the signer's personal knowledge. When such pleadings, motions and affidavits are verified or under oath they shall not require other or greater proof on the part of the adverse party than if not verified or not under oath unless expressly provided otherwise by the Indiana Rules of Trial Procedure, statute or other law. Affidavits upon motions for summary judgment under IN ST TRIAL P Rule 56 and in denial of execution under IN ST TRIAL P Rule 9.2 shall be made upon personal knowledge. IN ST TRIAL P Rule 11(C).

f. *Electronic signature.* The filing of documents and information through the E-filing system by use of a valid username and password is presumed to have been authorized by the User to whom that username and password have been issued and documents filed through the E-filing system are presumed to have been signed by the same User. IN ST ADMIN Rule 16(E).

5. *Information excluded from public access.* Every document filed in a case shall separately identify information excluded from public access pursuant to IN ST ADMIN Rule 9(G)(1) as follows:

  a. Whole documents that are excluded from public access pursuant to IN ST ADMIN Rule 9(G)(1) shall be tendered on light green paper or have a light green coversheet attached to the document, marked "Not for Public Access" or "Confidential." IN ST TRIAL P Rule 5(G)(1).

  b. When only a portion of a document contains information excluded from public access pursuant to IN ST ADMIN Rule 9(G)(1), said information shall be omitted [or redacted] from the filed document, and set forth on a separate accompanying document on light green paper conspicuously marked "Not for Public Access" or "Confidential" and clearly designated [or identifying] the caption and number of the case and the document and location within the document to which the redacted material pertains. IN ST TRIAL P Rule 5(G)(2).

  c. With respect to documents filed in electronic format, the trial court, by local rule, may provide for compliance with IN ST TRIAL P Rule 5 in manner that separates and protects access to information excluded from public access. IN ST TRIAL P Rule 5(G)(3).

  d. IN ST TRIAL P Rule 5(G) does not apply to a record sealed by the court pursuant to IN ST 5-14-3-5.5 or otherwise, nor to records, documents, or information filed in cases to which public access is prohibited pursuant to IN ST ADMIN Rule 9(G). IN ST TRIAL P Rule 5(G)(4).

  e. The following information in case records is excluded from public access and is confidential:

    i. Information that is excluded from public access pursuant to federal law;

ii. Information that is excluded from public access as declared confidential by Indiana statute or other court rule, including without limitation:

- All adoption records created after July 8, 1941, as declared confidential by IN ST 31-19-19-1, et seq., except those specifically declared open by IN ST 31-19-13-2(2);

- All records relating to chancroid, chlamydia, gonorrhea, hepatitis, human immunodeficiency virus (HIV), Lymphogranuloma venereum, syphilis, tuberculosis, as declared confidential by IN ST 16-41-8-1, et seq.;

- All records relating to child abuse as declared confidential by IN ST 31-33-18-1, et seq.;

- All records relating to drug tests as declared confidential by IN ST 5-14-3-4(a)(9);

- Records of grand jury proceedings as declared confidential by IN ST 35-34-2-4;

- Records of juvenile proceedings as declared confidential by IN ST 31-39-1-2, except those specifically open under statute;

- All paternity records created after July 1, 1941 as declared confidential by IN ST 31-14-11-15, IN ST 31-19-5-23, IN ST 31-39-1-1 and IN ST 31-39-1-2 [Editor's note: IN ST 31-14-11-15 was repealed effective May 9, 2013];

- All pre-sentence reports as declared confidential by IN ST 35-38-1-13;

- Written petitions to permit marriages without consent and orders directing the Clerk of Court to issue a marriage license to underage persons, as declared confidential by IN ST 31-11-1-6;

- Only those arrest warrants, search warrants, indictments and informations ordered confidential by the trial judge, prior to return of duly executed service as declared confidential by IN ST 5-14-3-4(b)(1);

- All medical, mental health, or tax records unless determined by law or regulation of any governmental custodian not to be confidential, released by the subject of such records, or declared by a court of competent jurisdiction to be essential to the resolution of litigation as declared confidential by IN ST 16-39-3-10, IN ST 6-4.1-5-10, IN ST 6-4.1-12-12, and IN ST 6-8.1-7-1;

- Personal information relating to jurors or prospective jurors, other than for the use of the parties and counsel, pursuant to IN ST JURY Rule 10;

- Information relating to protection from abuse orders, no-contact orders and workplace violence restraining orders as declared confidential by IN ST 5-2-9-6, et seq.;

- Mediation proceedings pursuant to IN ST ADR Rule 2.11, Mini-Trial proceedings pursuant to IN ST ADR Rule 4.4(C), and Summary Jury Trials pursuant to IN ST ADR Rule 5.6;

- Information in probation files pursuant to the Probation Standards promulgated by the Judicial Conference of Indiana pursuant to IN ST 11-13-1-8(b);

- Information deemed confidential pursuant to the Rules for Court Administered Alcohol and Drug Programs promulgated by the Judicial Conference of Indiana pursuant to IN ST 12-23-14-13;

- Information deemed confidential pursuant to the Problem-Solving Court Rules promulgated by the Judicial Conference of Indiana pursuant to IN ST 33-23-16-16;

- All records of the Department of workforce Development as declared confidential by IN ST 22-4-19-6;

- Information regarding interception of electronic communications that is sealed or deemed confidential as set forth in IN ST 35-33.5-2-1, et seq.

iii. Information excluded from public access by specific court order;

iv. Complete Social Security Numbers of living persons;

v.   With the exception of names, information such as addresses, phone numbers, and dates of birth which explicitly identifies:

- Natural persons who are witnesses or victims (not including defendants) in criminal, domestic violence, stalking, sexual assault, juvenile, or civil protection order proceedings, provided that juveniles who are victims of sex crimes shall be identified by initials only;

- Places of residence of judicial officers, clerks and other employees of courts and clerks of court, unless the person or persons about whom the information pertains waives confidentiality;

vi.   Complete account numbers of specific assets, loans, bank accounts, credit cards, and personal identification numbers (PINs);

vii.   All orders of expungement entered in criminal or juvenile proceedings, orders to restrict access to criminal history information pursuant to IN ST 35-38-5-5.5 or IN ST 35-38-8-5 and records excluded from public access by such orders, and information related to infractions that is excluded from public access pursuant to IN ST 34-28-5-15 or IN ST 34-28-5-16 [Editor's note: IN ST 35-38-5-5.5, IN ST 35-38-8-5 and IN ST 34-28-5-16 were repealed effective July 1, 2013; for information on orders restricting access to criminal history, refer to IN ST 35-38-9-1, et seq.];

viii.   All personal notes and e-mail, and deliberative material, of judges, jurors, court staff and judicial agencies, and information recorded in personal data assistants (PDA's) or organizers and personal calendars. IN ST ADMIN Rule 9(G)(1).

6.   *Format of electronically filed documents*

a.   *Generally.* Electronically filed documents must meet the same requirements of format as documents conventionally filed pursuant to IN ST LAKE RCP Rule 2 or other applicable Lake County Rules of Civil Procedure. IN ST LAKE RCP Rule 17(D)(1).

b.   *Titles of documents.* The person electronically filing a document will be responsible for designating a title for the document at the time it is filed. The LCOD will generate the appropriate entry onto the CCS to record the filing of the document. IN ST LAKE RCP Rule 17(D)(3).

c.   *Citations and hyperlinks.* Electronically filed documents may contain hyperlink references to an external document as a convenient mechanism for accessing material cited in the document. Filers wishing to insert hyperlinks into documents shall continue to use the traditional method of citation to authority in addition to the hyperlink provided. The hyperlink is merely a convenience to the court and the material referenced is extraneous to the file and not a part of the court's record. IN ST LAKE RCP Rule 17(D)(5).

d.   *Attachments and exhibits.* All documents which form part of a single submission and which are being filed at the same time and by the same filer may be electronically filed together under one document filing, e.g., the motion, supporting affidavits, memorandum in support, designation of evidence, exhibits. IN ST LAKE RCP Rule 17(D)(6).

i.   Large documents which do not exist in an electronic format shall be scanned into .pdf format and filed electronically as separate attachments. A scanner is available in each clerk's office for use by the public and the bar in scanning and saving image files if needed. IN ST LAKE RCP Rule 17(D)(6).

e.   *Electronic signatures*

i.   *Electronic filing as signature.* The electronic filing of a document which is required to be signed shall constitute the filer's representation under IN ST TRIAL P Rule 11. Unless the electronically filed document has been scanned and shows the filer's original signature, the signature of the filer shall be indicated by As/Attorney's Name, or As/Party's Name as in the case of a pro se litigant, on the line where the signature would otherwise appear. IN ST LAKE RCP Rule 17(G)(1).

ii.   *Signatures on jointly signed or filed, verified or other documents.* In the case of a stipulation, agreed order, jointly signed motion or other document which needs to be signed by two (2) or more persons, or in the case of documents which must contain original signatures and which require verification or an unsworn declaration under rule or statute, the signatures may be indicated by either:

- Submitting a scanned copy of the originally signed document; or,

- Submitting the document with the use of As/Name in the signature block(s) where the original signature(s) appear(s) in the original document; provided, however, that the filer shall first obtain the physical signature of all persons necessary. IN ST LAKE RCP Rule 17(G)(2).

iii. *Retention of original.* The filer shall retain the original executed document. IN ST LAKE RCP Rule 17(G).

7. *Citation of local rules.* The local rules for Lake County may be known as the Lake County Rules of Civil Procedure, and abbreviated as LR. IN ST LAKE RCP Rule 1(C).

F. Filing and Service Requirements

1. *Filing requirements.* Except as otherwise provided in IN ST TRIAL P Rule 5(E)(2), all pleadings and papers subsequent to the complaint which are required to be served upon a party shall be filed with the Court either before service or within a reasonable period of time thereafter. IN ST TRIAL P Rule 5(E)(1). All papers presented for filing shall be submitted to the Clerk and not to the court. All papers submitted for filing shall be mailed or delivered to the Clerk's office at the courthouse in which the case is pending. IN ST LAKE RCP Rule 3(A).

   a. *Non-filing of discovery until necessary*

      i. *Non-filing of discovery; Exceptions.* No deposition or request for discovery or response thereto under IN ST TRIAL P Rule 27, IN ST TRIAL P Rule 30, IN ST TRIAL P Rule 31, IN ST TRIAL P Rule 33, IN ST TRIAL P Rule 34 or IN ST TRIAL P Rule 36 shall be filed with the Court unless:

         - A motion is filed pursuant to IN ST TRIAL P Rule 26(C) or IN ST TRIAL P Rule 37 and the original deposition or request for discovery or response thereto is necessary to enable the Court to rule; or

         - A party desires to use the deposition or request for discovery or response thereto for evidentiary purposes at trial or in connection with a motion, and the Court, either upon its own motion or that of any party, or as a part of any pre-trial order, orders the filing of the original. IN ST TRIAL P Rule 5(E)(2).

      ii. *Custody of original and period of retention*

         - The original of a deposition shall, subject to the provisions of IN ST TRIAL P Rule 30(E), be delivered by the reporter to the party taking it and shall be maintained by that party until filed with the Court pursuant to IN ST TRIAL P Rule 5(E)(2) or until the later of final judgment, agreed settlement of the litigation or all appellate rights have been exhausted. IN ST TRIAL P Rule 5(E)(3)(a).

         - The original or any request for discovery or response thereto under IN ST TRIAL P Rule 27, IN ST TRIAL P Rule 30, IN ST TRIAL P Rule 31, IN ST TRIAL P Rule 33, IN ST TRIAL P Rule 34 and IN ST TRIAL P Rule 36 shall be maintained by the party originating the request or response until filed with the Court pursuant to IN ST TRIAL P Rule 5(E)(2) or until the later of final judgment, agreed settlement or all appellate rights have been exhausted. IN ST TRIAL P Rule 5(E)(3)(b).

      iii. *Original unavailable; Copies.* In the event it is made to appear to the satisfaction of the Court that the original of a deposition or request for discovery or response thereto cannot be filed with the Court when required, the Court may allow use of a copy instead of the original. IN ST TRIAL P Rule 5(E)(4).

      iv. *Filing as publication.* The filing of any deposition shall constitute publication. IN ST TRIAL P Rule 5(E)(5).

b. *Filing with the court defined.* The filing of pleadings, motions, and other papers with the court as required by the Indiana Rules of Trial Procedure shall be made by one of the following methods:

    i.   Delivery to the clerk of the court;

    ii.   Sending by electronic transmission under the procedure adopted pursuant to IN ST ADMIN Rule 12;

    iii.   Mailing to the clerk by registered, certified or express mail return receipt requested;

    iv.   Depositing with any third-party commercial carrier for delivery to the clerk within three (3) calendar days, cost prepaid, properly addressed;

    v.   If the court so permits, filing with the judge, in which event the judge shall note thereon the filing date and forthwith transmit them to the office of the clerk; or

    vi.   Electronic filing, as approved by the Division of State Court Administration pursuant to IN ST ADMIN Rule 16. IN ST TRIAL P Rule 5(F).

    vii.   Filing by registered or certified mail and by third-party commercial carrier shall be complete upon mailing or deposit. IN ST TRIAL P Rule 5(F).

c. *Mandatory electronic filing.* Unless otherwise permitted by the Lake County Rules of Civil Procedure or otherwise authorized by the judicial officer assigned to a particular case, all documents submitted for filing (including the original complaint, or equivalent pleading, and summons) shall be filed electronically with the clerk using the LCOD, no matter when the case was originally filed. IN ST LAKE RCP Rule 17(D).

    i.   *Of documents containing information excluded from public access pursuant to* IN ST ADMIN Rule 9. Documents containing information excluded from public access pursuant to IN ST ADMIN Rule 9, or documents which are ordered to be filed under seal shall be filed electronically, pursuant to IN ST LAKE RCP Rule 17(D)(9), whenever possible, along with a copy of the applicable order to seal the records, and the filer shall designate the documents as "Not for Public Access Pursuant to Administrative Rule 9(G)(1)" at the time of filing. IN ST LAKE RCP Rule 16(A)(1); IN ST LAKE RCP Rule 17(D)(9).

        •   *Conventional filing of documents containing information excluded from public access pursuant to* IN ST ADMIN Rule 9. Documents containing information excluded from public access pursuant to IN ST ADMIN Rule 9, or documents which are ordered to be filed under seal, which cannot be legibly scanned and filed electronically, shall be conventionally filed under seal and designated by the filer as "Not for Public Access Pursuant to Administrative Rule 9(G)(1)" at the time of filing. The unredacted version shall be filed on light green paper which is conspicuously marked "Not for Public Access"; and a redacted version, with confidential information deleted, shall be filed on white paper which shall be available for public access. The filer shall also electronically file a Notice of Manual Filing. IN ST LAKE RCP Rule 16(A)(2).

    ii.   *Technical failures.* If a registered user is unable to file a document in a timely manner due to technical difficulties in the LCOD, the registered user must file a document with the court as soon as possible notifying the court of the inability to file the document. A sample document titled Declaration that Party was Unable to File in a Timely Manner Due to Technical Difficulties can be found at IN ST LAKE RCP Form 4. Delayed filings shall be rejected unless accompanied by the declaration attesting to the filer's failed attempts to file electronically at least two (2) times, separated by at least one (1) hour, after noon on each day of delay due to such technical failure. IN ST LAKE RCP Rule 17(J).

    iii.   *Documents allowed to be filed conventionally.* Unless specifically authorized by the court, only the following documents may be filed conventionally and not electronically:

        •   Exhibits and other documents that cannot be converted to a legible electronic form, such as videotapes, x-rays, and similar materials

        •   Documents delivered to the clerk by pro se litigants

        •   Documents mailed to the clerk by pro se litigants

- Confidential documents
- Notice of manual filing
- Titles of documents
- Chronological case summary entry forms (CCS entry forms). IN ST LAKE RCP Rule 17(E).
- For more information on the documents which must be filed conventionally, refer to IN ST LAKE RCP Rule 17(E).

d. *Facsimile filing.* Only when necessary on an emergency basis (i.e., when certified mail or other means of filing will not bring the document to the Judge's attention prior to the scheduled hearing or ruling), pleadings, motions and other papers may be filed by electronic facsimile transmission, or when specifically authorized by the Court. IN ST LAKE RCP Rule 2(C).

    i. *Generally.* In counties where a majority of judges of the courts of record, by posted local rule, have authorized electronic facsimile filing and designated a telephone number to receive such transmissions, pleadings, motions, and other papers may be sent to the Clerk of Circuit Court by electronic facsimile transmission for filing in any case, provided:

- Such matter does not exceed ten (10) pages, including the cover sheet;
- Such matter does not require the payment of fees other than the electronic facsimile transcription fee set forth in IN ST ADMIN Rule 12(E);
- The sending party creates at the time of transmission a machine generated log for such transmission; and
- The original document and the transmission log are maintained by the sending party for the duration of the litigation. IN ST ADMIN Rule 12(B).

    ii. *Time of filing.* During normal, posted business hours, the time of filing shall be the time the duplicate document is produced in the office of the Clerk of the Circuit Court. Duplicate documents received at all other times shall be filed as of the next normal business day. IN ST ADMIN Rule 12(C).

- If the receiving fax machine endorses its own time and date stamp upon the transmitted documents and the receiving machine produces a delivery receipt which is electronically created and transmitted to the sending party, the time of filing shall be the date and time recorded on the transmitted document by the receiving fax machine. IN ST ADMIN Rule 12(C).

e. *Filing for special judges.* For special judge matters where the special judge is a full-time judge or magistrate serving within Lake County, all papers submitted for filing shall be delivered or mailed to the Clerk's office at the courthouse where the special judge regularly serves. IN ST LAKE RCP Rule 3(A).

f. *Proof of filing.* Any party filing any paper by any method other than personal delivery to the clerk shall retain proof of filing. IN ST TRIAL P Rule 5(F).

2. *Service requirements.* Unless otherwise provided by the Indiana Rules of Trial Procedure or an order of the court, each party and special judge, if any, shall be served with: (1) every order required by its terms to be served; (2) every pleading subsequent to the original complaint; (3) every written motion except one which may be heard ex parte; (4) every brief submitted to the trial court; (5) every paper relating to discovery required to be served upon a party; and (6) every written notice, appearance, demand, offer of judgment, designation of record on appeal, or similar paper. IN ST TRIAL P Rule 5(A).

a. *Methods of service*

    i. *Personal service.* Whenever a party is represented by an attorney of record, service shall be made upon such attorney unless service upon the party himself is ordered by the court. Service upon the attorney or party shall be made by delivering or mailing a copy of the papers to the last known address or where an attorney or party has consented to service by fax or e-mail, as provided in IN ST TRIAL P Rule 3.1(A)(4), by faxing or e-mailing a copy of the documents to the fax number or e-mail address set out in the appearance form or correction as required by IN ST TRIAL P Rule 3.1(E). IN ST TRIAL P Rule 5(B). Delivery of a copy within IN ST TRIAL P Rule 5 means:

- Offering or tendering it to the attorney or party and stating the nature of the papers being served. Refusal to accept an offered or tendered document is a waiver of any objection to the sufficiency or adequacy of service of that document;

- Leaving it at his office with a clerk or other person in charge thereof, or if there is no one in charge, leaving it in a conspicuous place therein; or

- If the office is closed, by leaving it at his dwelling house or usual place of abode with some person of suitable age and discretion then residing therein; or,

- Leaving it at some other suitable place, selected by the attorney upon whom service is being made, pursuant to duly promulgated local rule. IN ST TRIAL P Rule 5(B)(1).

ii. *Service by mail.* If service is made by mail, the papers shall be deposited in the United States mail addressed to the person on whom they are being served, with postage prepaid. Service shall be deemed complete upon mailing. Proof of service of all papers permitted to be mailed may be made by written acknowledgment of service, by affidavit of the person who mailed the papers, or by certificate of an attorney. It shall be the duty of attorneys when entering their appearance in a cause or when filing pleadings or papers therein, to have noted in the Chronological Case Summary or said pleadings or papers so filed the address and telephone number of their office. Service by delivery or by mail at such address shall be deemed sufficient and complete. IN ST TRIAL P Rule 5(B)(2).

iii. *Service by fax or e-mail.* A party who has consented to service by fax or e-mail may be served as follows:

- Service by e-mail shall be made by attaching the document being served in .pdf format. Discovery documents must also be served in accordance with IN ST TRIAL P Rule 26(A). IN ST TRIAL P Rule 5(B)(3)(a).

- Service by fax shall be deemed complete upon generation of a transmission record indicating the successful transmission of the entire document, except as provided in IN ST TRIAL P Rule 5(B)(3)(d). IN ST TRIAL P Rule 5(B)(3)(b).

- Service by e-mail shall be deemed complete upon transmission, except as provided in IN ST TRIAL P Rule 5(B)(3)(d). IN ST TRIAL P Rule 5(B)(3)(c).

- Service by fax or e-mail that occurs on a Saturday, Sunday, legal holiday, or day the court or agency in which the matter is pending is closed or after 5:00 PM local time of the recipient shall be deemed complete the next day that is not a Saturday, Sunday, legal holiday, or day that the court or agency in which the matter is pending is not closed. IN ST TRIAL P Rule 5(B)(3)(d).

iv. *Additional service of electronic discovery.* In addition to service under Rule IN ST TRIAL P Rule 5(B) or a .pdf format electronic copy, a party propounding or responding to interrogatories, requests for production or requests for admission shall comply with IN ST TRIAL P Rule 26(A.1)(a) or IN ST TRIAL P Rule 26(A.1)(b). IN ST TRIAL P Rule 26(A.1).

- The party shall serve the discovery request or response in an electronic format (either on a disk or as an electronic document attachment) in any commercially available word processing software system. If transmitted on disk, each disk shall be labeled, identifying the caption of the case, the document, and the word processing version in which it is being submitted. If more than one (1) disk is used for the same document, each disk shall be labeled and also shall be sequentially numbered. If transmitted by electronic mail, the document must be accompanied by electronic memorandum providing the forgoing identifying information; or

- The party shall serve the opposing party with a verified statement that the attorney or party appealing pro se lacks the equipment and is unable to transmit the discovery as required by IN ST TRIAL P Rule 26(A.1). IN ST TRIAL P Rule 26(A.1).

b. *Serving numerous defendants.* In any action in which there are unusually large numbers of defendants, the court, upon motion or of its own initiative, may order:

   i. That service of the pleadings of the defendants and replies thereto need not be made as between the defendants;

   - That any cross-claim, counterclaim, or matter constituting an avoidance or affirmative defense contained therein shall be deemed to be denied or avoided by all other parties; and

   - That the filing of any such pleading and service thereof upon the plaintiff constitutes due notice of it to the parties. IN ST TRIAL P Rule 5(D).

   ii. A copy of every such order shall be served upon the parties in such manner and form as the court directs. IN ST TRIAL P Rule 5(D).

c. *Service by electronic means.* The Lake County Online Docket will generate a Notice of Electronic Filing and Service when any document is filed and served. This notice will be emailed to each registered user of record in a case, and an electronic service event will be added to the work queue of each registered user of record in the case. The party filing the document should retain a paper or electronic copy of the Notice of Electronic Filing and Service. This notice represents proof of filing and service of the document on registered users of record in that case. The filer shall not be required to conventionally serve any document on any party receiving electronic service. IN ST LAKE RCP Rule 17(F)(2).

   i. The filer shall also conventionally serve those parties not designated or able to receive electronic notice or service but who are nevertheless entitled to notice of said pleading or other document in accordance with the Indiana Rules of Civil Procedure and applicable Lake County Rules of Civil Procedure. In such cases, the filer shall also file a certificate of service, as appropriate. IN ST LAKE RCP Rule 17(F).

d. *Service on parties in default for failure to appear.* No service need be made on parties in default for failure to appear, except that pleadings asserting new or additional claims for relief against them shall be served upon them in the manner provided by service of summons in IN ST TRIAL P Rule 4. IN ST TRIAL P Rule 5(A).

G. Hearings

1. The Indiana rules do not contemplate a hearing related to the notice of deposition.

H. Forms

1. Notice of Deposition Forms for Indiana

a. Notice of deposition; Individual. 5 INPRAC § 4:1.1.

b. Notice of deposition; Deponent unknown. 5 INPRAC § 4:1.2.

c. Notice of deposition; Corporation. 5 INPRAC § 4:1.3.

d. Notice of deposition; With request for production of documents. 5 INPRAC § 4:1.4.

e. Motion to limit scope of deposition. 5 INPRAC § 4:1.5.

f. Motion to terminate deposition. 5 INPRAC § 4:1.6.

g. Notice of hearing on petition for order to take deposition before action to perpetuate testimony. 5 INPRAC § 4:1.7.

h. Petition to perpetuate testimony. 5 INPRAC § 4:1.7.30.

i. Affidavit verifying petition to perpetuate testimony. 5 INPRAC § 4:1.7.70.

j. Stipulation regarding deposition by remote electronic means. 5 INPRAC § 4:1.8.

k. Petition to perpetuate testimony; Witness to automobile accident. 10 INPRAC § 59.3.

l. Notice of hearing on petition to perpetuate testimony. 10 INPRAC § 59.6.

m. Petition to perpetuate testimony pending appeal. 10 INPRAC § 59.13.

n. Notice of deposition to perpetuate testimony pending appeal. 10 INPRAC § 59.15.

o. Notice of deposition upon oral examination; Individual. 10 INPRAC § 62.3.

p. Notice of deposition; Deponent unknown. 10 INPRAC § 62.4.

q. Notice of deposition; Corporation. 10 INPRAC § 62.5.

r. Notice of deposition; With request for production of documents. 10 INPRAC § 62.6.

s. Motion for leave to take deposition within twenty days of service. 10 INPRAC § 62.7.

t. Notice of deposition; Pursuant to order granting leave to take deposition. 10 INPRAC § 62.9.

u. Stipulation for deposition upon written questions. 10 INPRAC § 63.2.

v. Notice of deposition upon written questions. 10 INPRAC § 63.3.

w. Direct questions. 10 INPRAC § 63.4.

x. Cross questions. 10 INPRAC § 63.5.

y. Redirect questions. 10 INPRAC § 63.6.

z. Recross questions. 10 INPRAC § 63.7.

2. **Official Notice of Deposition Forms for Lake County**

a. CCS entry form. IN ST LAKE RCP App. A.

b. Notice of manual filing. IN ST LAKE RCP Form 2.

c. Certificate of service. IN ST LAKE RCP Form 3.

d. Declaration that party was unable to file in a timely manner. IN ST LAKE RCP Form 4.

3. **Notice of Deposition Forms for Lake County**

a. Notice of manual filing. EFORMST IN 5540.

I. Checklist

(I) ❑ Matters to be considered by the party taking a deposition upon oral examination

  (a) ❑ Required documents

    (1) ❑ Notice of deposition

    (2) ❑ Certificate of service

  (b) ❑ Supplemental documents

    (1) ❑ Subpoena/subpoena duces tecum

    (2) ❑ Request for production

    (3) ❑ Stipulation regarding discovery procedure

    (4) ❑ Facsimile cover sheet

  (c) ❑ Timing

    (1) ❑ After commencement of the action, any party may take the testimony of any person, including a party, by deposition upon oral examination

(II) ❑ Matters to be considered by the party taking a deposition upon written questions

  (a) ❑ Required documents

    (1) ❑ Notice of deposition

    (2) ❑ Certificate of service

  (b) ❑ Supplemental documents

    (1) ❑ Subpoena

    (2) ❑ Stipulation regarding discovery procedure

    (3) ❑ Facsimile cover sheet

(c) ❑ Timing

    (1) ❑ After commencement of the action, any party may take the testimony of any person, including a party, by deposition upon written questions

(III) ❑ Matters to be considered by the party taking a deposition before commencement of the action

  (a) ❑ Required documents

    (1) ❑ Notice of deposition

    (2) ❑ Petition

    (3) ❑ Chronological case summary (CSS) entry forms

    (4) ❑ Certificate of service

  (b) ❑ Supplemental documents

    (1) ❑ Stipulation regarding discovery procedure

    (2) ❑ Facsimile cover sheet

  (c) ❑ Timing

    (1) ❑ At least twenty (20) days before the date of hearing the notice shall be served in the manner provided in IN ST TRIAL P Rule 4 for service of summons

(IV) ❑ Matters to be considered by the party taking a deposition pending appeal

  (a) ❑ Required documents

    (1) ❑ Motion for leave to take deposition and notice

    (2) ❑ Brief

    (3) ❑ Proposed order

    (4) ❑ Chronological case summary (CSS) entry forms

    (5) ❑ Certificate of service

  (b) ❑ Supplemental documents

    (1) ❑ Stipulation regarding discovery procedure

    (2) ❑ Supporting evidence

    (3) ❑ Facsimile cover sheet

  (c) ❑ Timing

    (1) ❑ The party who desires to perpetuate the testimony may make a motion in the court for leave to take the depositions, upon the same notice and service thereof as if the action was pending in the court

    (2) ❑ A written motion, other than one which may be heard ex parte, and notice of the hearing thereof shall be served not less than five (5) days before the time specified for the hearing, unless a different period is fixed by the Indiana Rules of Trial Procedure or by order of the court

    (3) ❑ All pleadings and papers subsequent to the complaint which are required to be served upon a party shall be filed with the Court either before service or within a reasonable period of time thereafter

    (4) ❑ All pleadings, motions and other papers submitted for filing which are required to be served under IN ST TRIAL P Rule 5(A) shall be filed no later than three (3) days after service

    (5) ❑ If such papers are filed before service, proof of service thereof shall be filed no later than three (3) business days thereafter

Requests, Notices and Applications
Application for Temporary Restraining Order

Document Last Updated October 2013

A. Applicable Rules

1. *State rules*

   a. Appearance. IN ST TRIAL P Rule 3.1.

   b. Process. IN ST TRIAL P Rule 4.

   c. Service and filing of pleadings and other papers. IN ST TRIAL P Rule 5.

   d. Time. IN ST TRIAL P Rule 6.

   e. Pleadings. IN ST TRIAL P Rule 7; IN ST TRIAL P Rule 8; IN ST TRIAL P Rule 9.2; IN ST TRIAL P Rule 10.

   f. Signing and verification of pleadings. IN ST TRIAL P Rule 11.

   g. Evidence. IN ST TRIAL P Rule 43.

   h. Judgment on the evidence (directed verdict). IN ST TRIAL P Rule 50.

   i. Findings by the court. IN ST TRIAL P Rule 52.

   j. Summary judgment. IN ST TRIAL P Rule 56.

   k. Motion to correct error. IN ST TRIAL P Rule 59.

   l. Relief from judgment or order. IN ST TRIAL P Rule 60.

   m. Injunctions. IN ST TRIAL P Rule 65; IN ST 34-26-1-7; IN ST 34-26-1-8; IN ST 34-26-1-11.

   n. Security; Proceedings against sureties. IN ST TRIAL P Rule 65.1.

   o. Hearing of motions. IN ST TRIAL P Rule 73.

   p. Court records. IN ST TRIAL P Rule 77.

   q. Access to court records. IN ST ADMIN Rule 9.

   r. Paper size. IN ST ADMIN Rule 11.

   s. Facsimile transmission. IN ST ADMIN Rule 12.

   t. Electronic filing and electronic service pilot projects. IN ST ADMIN Rule 16.

   u. Privacy and confidentiality. IN ST 5-2-9-6; IN ST 5-14-3-4; IN ST 5-14-3-5.5; IN ST 6-4.1-5-10; IN ST 6-4.1-12-12; IN ST 6-8.1-7-1; IN ST 11-13-1-8; IN ST 12-23-14-13; IN ST 16-39-3-10; IN ST 16-41-8-1; IN ST 22-4-19-6; IN ST 31-11-1-6; IN ST 31-19-5-23; IN ST 31-19-13-2; IN ST 31-19-19-1; IN ST 31-33-18-1; IN ST 31-39-1-1; IN ST 31-39-1-2; IN ST 33-23-16-16; IN ST 35-34-2-4; IN ST 35-38-1-13; IN ST 35-38-9-1; IN ST ADR Rule 2.11; IN ST ADR Rule 4.4; IN ST ADR Rule 5.6; IN ST JURY Rule 10.

   v. Civil protection orders. IN ST 34-26-5-1; IN ST 34-26-5-20.

2. *Local rules*

   a. Scope and title. [IN ST LAKE RCP Rule 1, as amended by IN ORDER 13-0237, effective October 18, 2013].

   b. Preparation of pleadings, motions and other papers. IN ST LAKE RCP Rule 2.

   c. Filing. [IN ST LAKE RCP Rule 3, as amended by IN ORDER 13-0237, effective October 18, 2013].

   d. Motions. IN ST LAKE RCP Rule 4.

   e. Pretrial procedure. IN ST LAKE RCP Rule 9.

   f. Briefs. IN ST LAKE RCP Rule 11.

   g. Confidential information and sealed documents. IN ST LAKE RCP Rule 16.

h. Electronic filing and service. IN ST LAKE RCP Rule 17.

B. Timing

1. *Temporary restraining order without notice.* There are no specific timing requirements for submitting an application for a temporary restraining order without notice.

   a. *Filing.* All pleadings and papers subsequent to the complaint which are required to be served upon a party shall be filed with the Court either before service or within a reasonable period of time thereafter. IN ST TRIAL P Rule 5(E)(1).

   b. *Briefs.* Briefs, other than those addressed in IN ST LAKE RCP Rule 4 and IN ST LAKE RCP Rule 9, shall be filed no later than two (2) calendar days preceding the hearing or trial to which directed. IN ST LAKE RCP Rule 11.

2. *Computation of time*

   a. *Generally; Days excluded.* In computing any period of time prescribed or allowed by the Indiana Rules of Trial Procedure, by order of the court, or by any applicable statute, the day of the act, event, or default from which the designated period of time begins to run shall not be included. The last day of the period so computed is to be included unless it is:

      i. A Saturday,

      ii. A Sunday,

      iii. A legal holiday as defined by state statute, or

      iv. A day the office in which the act is to be done is closed during regular business hours. IN ST TRIAL P Rule 6(A).

   b. *Short periods.* In any event, the period runs until the end of the next day that is not a Saturday, a Sunday, a legal holiday, or a day on which the office is closed. When the period of time allowed is less than seven (7) days, intermediate Saturdays, Sundays, legal holidays, and days on which the office is closed shall be excluded from the computations. IN ST TRIAL P Rule 6(A).

   c. *Additional time after service by United States mail.* Whenever a party has the right or is required to do some act or take some proceedings within a prescribed period after the service of a notice or other paper upon him and the notice or paper is served upon him by United States mail, three (3) days shall be added to the prescribed period. IN ST TRIAL P Rule 6(E).

   d. *Electronic filing does not alter deadlines.* Filing electronically does not alter any filing deadlines or any time computation pursuant to state or federal statutes, any Rules of the Indiana Supreme Court, including without limitation the Rules of Trial Procedure, the Rules of Appellate Procedure or the Administrative Rules, or applicable Lake County Rules of Civil Procedure. The office of the Lake County Clerk is open for electronic filing under the Lake County Rules of Civil Procedure twenty-four (24) hours a day. A document is deemed filed at the date and time it is received by the LCOD server. Filing must be completed before midnight local time in order to be considered filed that day. Lake County observes Central Time and electronic filers are strongly urged to file documents during hours when the Lake County Online Docket ("LCOD") help line is available, from 9:00 a.m. to 4:00 p.m. local time, although documents can be filed electronically twenty-four (24) hours a day. IN ST LAKE RCP Rule 17(I).

   e. *Enlargement of time.* When an act is required or allowed to be done at or within a specific time by the Indiana Rules of Trial Procedure, the court may at any time for cause shown:

      i. Order the period enlarged, with or without motion or notice, if request therefor is made before the expiration of the period originally prescribed or extended by a previous order; or

      ii. Upon motion made after the expiration of the specific period, permit the act to be done where the failure to act was the result of excusable neglect; but, the court may not extend the time for taking any action for judgment on the evidence under IN ST TRIAL P Rule 50(A), amendment of findings and judgment under IN ST TRIAL P Rule 52(B), to correct errors under IN ST TRIAL P Rule 59(C), statement in opposition to motion to correct error under IN ST TRIAL P Rule 59(E), or to obtain relief from final judgment under IN ST TRIAL P Rule 60(B), except to the extent and under the conditions stated in those rules. IN ST TRIAL P Rule 6(B).

C. General Requirements

1. *Motions, generally.* Unless made during a hearing or trial, or otherwise ordered by the court, an application to the court for an order shall be made by written motion. The motion shall state the grounds therefor and the relief or order sought. IN ST TRIAL P Rule 7(B).

    a. *Motions as distinct from pleadings.* Motions and responses to motions are not pleadings, and allegations contained in a motion are not admissions of a party. 22B INPRAC 7:2; Wachstetter v. County Properties, LLC, 832 N.E.2d 574 (Ind.Ct.App. 2005); Scott County Family YMCA, Inc. v. Hobbs, 817 N.E.2d 603 (Ind.Ct.App. 2004).

    b. *Unopposed motions generally granted.* It is common for a trial court to grant procedural motions, such as motions for enlargement of time, discovery motions, or motions for continuance, unless an objection is filed. 21 INPRAC § 13.8.

    c. *Separate motions.* Each motion shall be separate, while alternative motions filed together shall each be identified on the caption. IN ST LAKE RCP Rule 4(A).

    d. *Answer and reply briefs.* Failure to file an answer brief or reply brief within the time prescribed shall be deemed a waiver of the right thereto and shall subject the motion to summary ruling. IN ST LAKE RCP Rule 4(A).

2. *Application for temporary restraining order.* Seeking a temporary restraining order should only be considered if there is a possibility that irreparable injury may occur before the hearing for a preliminary injunction can be held. 4 INPRAC R 65(65.4).

    a. *Without notice*

        i. *When notice not required.* A temporary restraining order may be granted without written or oral notice to the adverse party or his attorney only if:

        - It clearly appears from specific facts shown by affidavit or by the verified complaint that immediate and irreparable injury, loss, or damage will result to the applicant before the adverse party or his attorney can be heard in opposition; and

        - The applicant's attorney certifies to the court in writing the efforts, if any, which have been made to give notice and the reasons supporting his claim that notice should not be required. IN ST TRIAL P Rule 65(B).

        ii. *Motion for dissolution or modification of temporary restraining order.* On two (2) days' notice to the party who obtained the temporary restraining order without notice or on such shorter notice to that party as the court may prescribe, the adverse party may appear and move its dissolution or modification and in that event the court shall proceed to hear and determine such motion as expeditiously as the ends of justice require. IN ST TRIAL P Rule 65(B).

    b. *Temporary restraining orders with notice in Indiana.* IN ST TRIAL P Rule 65(B) in its entirety deals only with temporary restraining orders issued without notice. No mention is made of the issuance of temporary restraining orders with notice. 4 INPRAC R 65(65.4). Some Indiana cases have apparently held that there is no such thing as a temporary restraining order if the adverse party has notice and a hearing is held. 4 INPRAC R 65(65.4); Indiana State Dept. of Welfare v. Stagner, 410 N.E.2d 1348 (Ind.Ct.App. 1980); Szany v. City of Hammond, 170 Ind.App. 537, 352 N.E.2d 866 (Ind.Ct.App. 1976). Refer to the Indiana KeyRules Motion for Preliminary Injunction document for information on obtaining an injunction with notice to the opposing party.

    c. *Application without notice as ex parte communication with judge.* The failure to follow the requirements of IN ST TRIAL P Rule 65(B) may constitute, in some circumstances, an improper ex parte communication between attorney and judge. 4 INPRAC R 65(65.4.1); Ace Bail Bonds v. Government Payment Service, Inc., 892 N.E.2d 702 (Ind.Ct.App. 2008), transfer denied (Ind. Jan. 15, 2009).

        i. When a party knows of the presence of another party's attorney in litigation, because each is present at hearings or at trial, then, even if an ex parte T.R.O. arguably meets the criteria in IN ST TRIAL P Rule 65(B), it is not valid unless it meets the standards in Smith v. Johnston, 711 N.E.2d 1259 (Ind.1999). 4 INPRAC R 65(65.4.1).

    ii.   Smith v. Johnston, was an appeal to set a default judgment aside. The court granted relief because the party who obtained the default did not give notice to the defaulted party, even though IN ST TRIAL P Rule 4 and IN ST TRIAL P Rule 5 do not require that notice be served on the opposite party's attorney. 4 INPRAC R 65(65.4.1). Smith v. Johnston's rationale clearly states that if an attorney "has knowledge of his opponent's representation, then the Rules of Professional Conduct establish a duty to provide notice `before seeking any relief from the court.'" 4 INPRAC R 65(65.4.1); Smith v. Johnston, 711 N.E.2d 1259 (Ind.1999).

  d. *Service of the temporary restraining order once issued.* Notice of the restraining order should be served upon the adverse party. The order may be served together with process in accordance with IN ST TRIAL P Rule 4, or, if obtained after service of process, then in accordance with IN ST TRIAL P Rule 5. 22 INPRAC § 29.2.

    i.   IN ST 34-26-1-11 provides the "clerk shall issue a copy of the order of injunction, certified by the clerk, which shall be served promptly by delivering the order to the adverse party." 22 INPRAC § 29.2; IN ST 34-26-1-11.

    ii.   However, service is not necessary to make the restraining order effective and binding, so long as the restrained party receives actual knowledge of the order. 22 INPRAC § 29.2; Reed Sign Service, Inc. v. Reid, 755 N.E.2d 690 (Ind.Ct.App. 2001).

  e. *Form of order by judge*

    i.   Every order granting temporary injunction and every restraining order shall include or be accompanied by findings as required by IN ST TRIAL P Rule 52; shall be specific in terms; shall describe in reasonable detail, and not by reference to the complaint or other document, the act or acts sought to be restrained; and is binding only upon the parties to the action, their officers, agents, servants, employees, and attorneys, and upon those persons in active concert or participation with them who receive actual notice of the order by personal service or otherwise. IN ST TRIAL P Rule 65(D).

    ii.   Every temporary restraining order granted without notice shall be indorsed with the date and hour of issuance; shall be filed forthwith in the clerk's office and entered of record; shall define the injury and state why it is irreparable and why the order was granted without notice; and shall expire by its terms within such time after entry, not to exceed ten (10) days, as the court fixes, unless within the time so fixed the order, for good cause shown, is extended for a like period or unless the whereabouts of the party against whom the order is granted is unknown and cannot be determined by reasonable diligence or unless the party against whom the order is directed consents that it may be extended for a longer period. The reasons for the extension shall be entered of record. IN ST TRIAL P Rule 65(B).

  f. *Temporary restraining orders; Domestic relations cases.* Parties wishing protection from domestic or family violence in Domestic Relations cases shall petition the court pursuant to IN ST 34-26-5-1 through IN ST 34-26-5-20. IN ST TRIAL P Rule 65(E). For more information refer to IN ST TRIAL P Rule 65(E) and IN ST 34-26-5-1, et seq.

3. *Security*

  a. *Security requirement.* No restraining order or preliminary injunction shall issue except upon the giving of security by the applicant, in such sum as the court deems proper, for the payment of such costs and damages as may be incurred or suffered by any party who is found to have been wrongfully enjoined or restrained. No such security shall be required of a governmental organization, but such governmental organization shall be responsible for costs and damages as may be incurred or suffered by any party who is found to have been wrongfully enjoined or restrained. IN ST TRIAL P Rule 65(C).

    i.   The provisions of IN ST TRIAL P Rule 65.1 apply to a surety upon a bond or undertaking under IN ST TRIAL P Rule 65. IN ST TRIAL P Rule 65(C).

  b. *Proceedings against sureties.* Whenever the Indiana Rules of Trial Procedure or other laws require or permit the giving of security by a party to a court action or proceeding, and security is given in the form of a bond or stipulation or other undertaking with one or more sureties, each surety submits himself to the jurisdiction of the court and irrevocably appoints the clerk of the court as his agent upon whom any papers affecting his liability on the bond or undertaking may be served. His liability may be enforced on motion without the necessity of an independent action. The motion and such notice of the motion as the court prescribes may be served on the clerk of the court, who shall forthwith mail copies to the sureties if their addresses are known. IN ST TRIAL P Rule 65.1 applies to bonds or security furnished on appeal, and enforcement shall be in the court to which the case is returned after appeal. IN ST TRIAL P Rule 65.1.

    c. *Bond generally used as security.* IN ST TRIAL P Rule 65(C) speaks only of the giving of security and does not expressly require a surety on a bond. In practice, however, the giving of a bond with an insurance company as surety in the amount set by the court is typically the device used to satisfy this section. 4 INPRAC R 65(65.6).

D. Documents

  1. *Required documents*

    a. *Application for temporary restraining order.* Refer to the General Requirements section of this document for additional information on the contents of an application for a temporary restraining order.

    b. *Brief.* Briefs, other than those addressed in IN ST LAKE RCP Rule 4 and IN ST LAKE RCP Rule 9, shall be filed no later than two (2) calendar days preceding the hearing or trial to which directed. IN ST LAKE RCP Rule 11.

    c. *Proposed order.* Unless local practice provides differently, a party should submit a proposed order with its written motion to be signed by the judge once the motion has been granted. 21 INPRAC § 13.8.

      i. Proposed orders, which are submitted for the court's convenience under IN ST LAKE RCP Rule 3 or other applicable Lake County Rules of Civil Procedure, shall be submitted as attachments to motions. IN ST LAKE RCP Rule 17(D)(8). Proposed orders shall be prepared and filed separately from the pleadings, petitions, motions or other papers to which they have reference. IN ST LAKE RCP Rule 3(B).

      ii. Orders, either routine in nature or uncontested including, for example, those setting or continuing a hearing, shall be effected by the chronological case summary entry only, which shall contain the concise substance of the order. IN ST LAKE RCP Rule 3(B).

      iii. All orders shall be accompanied with sufficient copies and stamped, pre-addressed envelopes, so that copies may be mailed to all parties. IN ST LAKE RCP Rule 3(B).

    d. *Security.* No restraining order or preliminary injunction shall issue except upon the giving of security by the applicant, in such sum as the court deems proper, for the payment of such costs and damages as may be incurred or suffered by any party who is found to have been wrongfully enjoined or restrained. IN ST TRIAL P Rule 65(C). Refer to the General Requirements section of this document for more information.

    e. *Chronological case summary (CCS) entry forms.* All filings shall be accompanied by a Chronological Case Summary (CCS) Entry Form to define or identify the documents filed. The Form used should be substantially similar to IN ST LAKE RCP App. A. IN ST LAKE RCP Rule 3(C).

  2. *Supplemental documents*

    a. *Supporting evidence.* When a motion is based on facts not appearing of record the court may hear the matter on affidavits presented by the respective parties, but the court may direct that the matter be heard wholly or partly on oral testimony or depositions. IN ST TRIAL P Rule 43(B).

    b. *Facsimile cover sheet.* Any document sent to the Clerk of the Circuit Court by electronic facsimile transmission shall be accompanied by a cover sheet which states the title of the document, case number, number of pages, identity and voice telephone number of the sending party and instructions for filing. The cover sheet shall contain the signature of the attorney or party, pro se, authorizing the filing. IN ST ADMIN Rule 12(D).

E. Format

  1. *Form of motions.* The rules applicable to captions, and the signing and form of pleadings (IN ST TRIAL

P Rule 8 through IN ST TRIAL P Rule 11), apply to all motions and other papers provided under the Indiana Rules of Trial Procedure. 22B INPRAC 7:2.

2. *Form of pleadings.* For the purpose of uniformity, convenience, clarity and durability, requirements in IN ST LAKE RCP Rule 2 shall be observed in the preparation of all pleadings, motions and other papers. IN ST LAKE RCP Rule 2. Whenever materials submitted fail to meet the standards in IN ST LAKE RCP Rule 2, the Court may impose appropriate sanctions. IN ST LAKE RCP Rule 2(B).

   a. *Caption; Names of parties.* Every pleading shall contain a caption setting forth the name of the court, the title of the action, the file number, and a designation as in IN ST TRIAL P Rule 7(A). In the complaint the title of the action shall include the names of all the parties, but in other pleadings it is sufficient to state the name of the first party on each side with an appropriate indication of other parties. IN ST TRIAL P Rule 10(A).

      i. *Special judge matters.* The caption of all CCS Entry Forms, pleadings, motions, orders and other papers to be filed in a special judge case shall include in block text the words SPECIAL JUDGE and the name of the judge directly below the cause number on the caption. IN ST LAKE RCP Rule 2(D).

   b. *Paragraphs; Separate statements.* All averments of a claim or defense shall be made in numbered paragraphs, the contents of each of which shall be limited as far as practicable to a statement of a single set of circumstances, and a paragraph may be referred to by number in all succeeding pleadings. Each claim founded upon a separate transaction or occurrence and each defense other than denials may be stated in a separate count or defense whenever a separation facilitates the clear presentation of the matters set forth. IN ST TRIAL P Rule 10(B).

   c. *Adoption by reference; Exhibits.* Statements in a pleading may be adopted by reference in a different part of the same pleading or in another pleading or in any motion. A copy of any written instrument which is an exhibit to a pleading is a part thereof for all purposes. IN ST TRIAL P Rule 10(C).

   d. *Paper; Print, quality and binding*

      i. All pleadings, motions, chronological case summary entry forms, orders, process and other papers shall be neatly and legibly printed, typewritten or mechanically reproduced, on one (1) side only, on white opaque paper. To satisfy the recordkeeping requirements of IN ST TRIAL P Rule 77, the print shall be of sufficient density and clarity for preservation and reproduction of microfilming, optical disk or other secondary sources. For this reason, the use of non-letter-quality printers is discouraged. IN ST LAKE RCP Rule 2(A).

      ii. Paper and ink shall be of such quality as to withstand the test of time. All documents shall be produced on acid-free, non-thermal paper. It is recommended that a minimum of twenty (20) pound, twenty-five percent (25%) cotton paper product be used. Documents of multiple pages shall be submitted in bound or stapled fashion, and the binding or stapling shall be at the top only. Covers or backings shall not be used. IN ST LAKE RCP Rule 2(A).

   e. *Papers; Handwritten.* Handwritten papers may be filed only if approved by the Court and a typewritten or printed true rendition thereof is filed within three (3) days thereafter and approved by the Court. Upon such approval, they shall be deemed and filed as the original, while the handwritten papers shall be retained therewith for evidentiary purposes. IN ST LAKE RCP Rule 2(C).

   f. *Minute sheets; Motion blanks.* Minute sheets and motion blanks shall no longer be used. IN ST LAKE RCP Rule 2(D).

3. *Size of papers for filing.* Effective January 1, 1992, all pleadings, copies, motions and documents filed with any trial court or appellate level court, typed or printed, with the exception of exhibits and existing wills, shall be prepared on eight and one-half by eleven inch (8 1/2" x 11") size paper. IN ST ADMIN Rule 11.

4. *Signature requirements*

   a. *Signature of attorney.* Every pleading or motion of a party represented by an attorney shall be signed by at least one (1) attorney of record in his individual name, whose address, telephone number, and attorney number shall be stated, except that this provision shall not apply to pleadings and motions

made and transcribed at the trial or a hearing before the judge and received by him in such form. IN ST TRIAL P Rule 11(A).

    i.   The signature of an attorney constitutes a certificate by him that he has read the pleadings; that to the best of his knowledge, information, and belief, there is good ground to support it; and that it is not interposed for delay. IN ST TRIAL P Rule 11(A).

    ii.   If a pleading or motion is not signed or is signed with intent to defeat the purpose of the rule, it may be stricken as sham and false and the action may proceed as though the pleading had not been served. IN ST TRIAL P Rule 11(A).

    iii.   For a willful violation of IN ST TRIAL P Rule 11 an attorney may be subjected to appropriate disciplinary action. Similar action may be taken if scandalous or indecent matter is inserted. IN ST TRIAL P Rule 11(A).

b.   *Signature of unrepresented party.* A party who is not represented by an attorney shall sign his pleading and state his address. IN ST TRIAL P Rule 11(A).

c.   *Verification not generally required.* Except when specifically required by rule, pleadings or motions need not be verified or accompanied by affidavit. The rule in equity that the averments of an answer under oath must be overcome by the testimony of two (2) witnesses or of one (1) witness sustained by corroborating circumstances is abolished. IN ST TRIAL P Rule 11(A).

d.   *Verification by affirmation or representation.* When in connection with any civil or special statutory proceeding it is required that any pleading, motion, petition, supporting affidavit, or other document of any kind, be verified, or that an oath be taken, it shall be sufficient if the subscriber simply affirms the truth of the matter to be verified by an affirmation or representation. IN ST TRIAL P Rule 11(B). IN ST TRIAL P Rule 11(B) states that the affirmation or representation should be in substantially the following language: "I (we) affirm, under the penalties for perjury, that the foregoing representation(s) is (are) true. (Signed) _____."

    i.   Any person who falsifies an affirmation or representation of fact shall be subject to the same penalties as are prescribed by law for the making of a false affidavit. IN ST TRIAL P Rule 11(B).

e.   *Verified pleadings, motions, and affidavits as evidence.* Pleadings, motions and affidavits accompanying or in support of such pleadings or motions when required to be verified or under oath shall be accepted as a representation that the signer had personal knowledge thereof or reasonable cause to believe the existence of the facts or matters stated or alleged therein; and, if otherwise competent or acceptable as evidence, may be admitted as evidence of the facts or matters stated or alleged therein when it is so provided in the Indiana Rules of Trial Procedure, by statute or other law, or to the extent the writing or signature expressly purports to be made upon the signer's personal knowledge. When such pleadings, motions and affidavits are verified or under oath they shall not require other or greater proof on the part of the adverse party than if not verified or not under oath unless expressly provided otherwise by the Indiana Rules of Trial Procedure, statute or other law. Affidavits upon motions for summary judgment under IN ST TRIAL P Rule 56 and in denial of execution under IN ST TRIAL P Rule 9.2 shall be made upon personal knowledge. IN ST TRIAL P Rule 11(C).

f.   *Electronic signature.* The filing of documents and information through the E-filing system by use of a valid username and password is presumed to have been authorized by the User to whom that username and password have been issued and documents filed through the E-filing system are presumed to have been signed by the same User. IN ST ADMIN Rule 16(E).

5. *Information excluded from public access.* Every document filed in a case shall separately identify information excluded from public access pursuant to IN ST ADMIN Rule 9(G)(1) as follows:

a.   Whole documents that are excluded from public access pursuant to IN ST ADMIN Rule 9(G)(1) shall be tendered on light green paper or have a light green coversheet attached to the document, marked "Not for Public Access" or "Confidential." IN ST TRIAL P Rule 5(G)(1).

b.   When only a portion of a document contains information excluded from public access pursuant to IN ST ADMIN Rule 9(G)(1), said information shall be omitted [or redacted] from the filed document, and set forth on a separate accompanying document on light green paper conspicuously marked "Not

for Public Access" or "Confidential" and clearly designated [or identifying] the caption and number of the case and the document and location within the document to which the redacted material pertains. IN ST TRIAL P Rule 5(G)(2).

c. With respect to documents filed in electronic format, the trial court, by local rule, may provide for compliance with IN ST TRIAL P Rule 5 in manner that separates and protects access to information excluded from public access. IN ST TRIAL P Rule 5(G)(3).

d. IN ST TRIAL P Rule 5(G) does not apply to a record sealed by the court pursuant to IN ST 5-14-3-5.5 or otherwise, nor to records, documents, or information filed in cases to which public access is prohibited pursuant to IN ST ADMIN Rule 9(G). IN ST TRIAL P Rule 5(G)(4).

e. The following information in case records is excluded from public access and is confidential:

i. Information that is excluded from public access pursuant to federal law;

ii. Information that is excluded from public access as declared confidential by Indiana statute or other court rule, including without limitation:

- All adoption records created after July 8, 1941, as declared confidential by IN ST 31-19-19-1, et seq., except those specifically declared open by IN ST 31-19-13-2(2);

- All records relating to chancroid, chlamydia, gonorrhea, hepatitis, human immunodeficiency virus (HIV), Lymphogranuloma venereum, syphilis, tuberculosis, as declared confidential by IN ST 16-41-8-1, et seq.;

- All records relating to child abuse as declared confidential by IN ST 31-33-18-1, et seq.;

- All records relating to drug tests as declared confidential by IN ST 5-14-3-4(a)(9);

- Records of grand jury proceedings as declared confidential by IN ST 35-34-2-4;

- Records of juvenile proceedings as declared confidential by IN ST 31-39-1-2, except those specifically open under statute;

- All paternity records created after July 1, 1941 as declared confidential by IN ST 31-14-11-15, IN ST 31-19-5-23, IN ST 31-39-1-1 and IN ST 31-39-1-2 [Editor's note: IN ST 31-14-11-15 was repealed effective May 9, 2013];

- All pre-sentence reports as declared confidential by IN ST 35-38-1-13;

- Written petitions to permit marriages without consent and orders directing the Clerk of Court to issue a marriage license to underage persons, as declared confidential by IN ST 31-11-1-6;

- Only those arrest warrants, search warrants, indictments and informations ordered confidential by the trial judge, prior to return of duly executed service as declared confidential by IN ST 5-14-3-4(b)(1);

- All medical, mental health, or tax records unless determined by law or regulation of any governmental custodian not to be confidential, released by the subject of such records, or declared by a court of competent jurisdiction to be essential to the resolution of litigation as declared confidential by IN ST 16-39-3-10, IN ST 6-4.1-5-10, IN ST 6-4.1-12-12, and IN ST 6-8.1-7-1;

- Personal information relating to jurors or prospective jurors, other than for the use of the parties and counsel, pursuant to IN ST JURY Rule 10;

- Information relating to protection from abuse orders, no-contact orders and workplace violence restraining orders as declared confidential by IN ST 5-2-9-6, et seq.;

- Mediation proceedings pursuant to IN ST ADR Rule 2.11, Mini-Trial proceedings pursuant to IN ST ADR Rule 4.4(C), and Summary Jury Trials pursuant to IN ST ADR Rule 5.6;

- Information in probation files pursuant to the Probation Standards promulgated by the Judicial Conference of Indiana pursuant to IN ST 11-13-1-8(b);

- Information deemed confidential pursuant to the Rules for Court Administered Alcohol

and Drug Programs promulgated by the Judicial Conference of Indiana pursuant to IN ST 12-23-14-13;

- Information deemed confidential pursuant to the Problem-Solving Court Rules promulgated by the Judicial Conference of Indiana pursuant to IN ST 33-23-16-16;

- All records of the Department of workforce Development as declared confidential by IN ST 22-4-19-6;

- Information regarding interception of electronic communications that is sealed or deemed confidential as set forth in IN ST 35-33.5-2-1, et seq.

   iii. Information excluded from public access by specific court order;

   iv. Complete Social Security Numbers of living persons;

   v. With the exception of names, information such as addresses, phone numbers, and dates of birth which explicitly identifies:

- Natural persons who are witnesses or victims (not including defendants) in criminal, domestic violence, stalking, sexual assault, juvenile, or civil protection order proceedings, provided that juveniles who are victims of sex crimes shall be identified by initials only;

- Places of residence of judicial officers, clerks and other employees of courts and clerks of court, unless the person or persons about whom the information pertains waives confidentiality;

   vi. Complete account numbers of specific assets, loans, bank accounts, credit cards, and personal identification numbers (PINs);

   vii. All orders of expungement entered in criminal or juvenile proceedings, orders to restrict access to criminal history information pursuant to IN ST 35-38-5-5.5 or IN ST 35-38-8-5 and records excluded from public access by such orders, and information related to infractions that is excluded from public access pursuant to IN ST 34-28-5-15 or IN ST 34-28-5-16 [Editor's note: IN ST 35-38-5-5.5, IN ST 35-38-8-5 and IN ST 34-28-5-16 were repealed effective July 1, 2013; for information on orders restricting access to criminal history, refer to IN ST 35-38-9-1, et seq.];

   viii. All personal notes and e-mail, and deliberative material, of judges, jurors, court staff and judicial agencies, and information recorded in personal data assistants (PDA's) or organizers and personal calendars. IN ST ADMIN Rule 9(G)(1).

6. *Format of electronically filed documents*

   a. *Generally.* Electronically filed documents must meet the same requirements of format as documents conventionally filed pursuant to IN ST LAKE RCP Rule 2 or other applicable Lake County Rules of Civil Procedure. IN ST LAKE RCP Rule 17(D)(1).

   b. *Titles of documents.* The person electronically filing a document will be responsible for designating a title for the document at the time it is filed. The LCOD will generate the appropriate entry onto the CCS to record the filing of the document. IN ST LAKE RCP Rule 17(D)(3).

   c. *Citations and hyperlinks.* Electronically filed documents may contain hyperlink references to an external document as a convenient mechanism for accessing material cited in the document. Filers wishing to insert hyperlinks into documents shall continue to use the traditional method of citation to authority in addition to the hyperlink provided. The hyperlink is merely a convenience to the court and the material referenced is extraneous to the file and not a part of the court's record. IN ST LAKE RCP Rule 17(D)(5).

   d. *Attachments and exhibits.* All documents which form part of a single submission and which are being filed at the same time and by the same filer may be electronically filed together under one document filing, e.g., the motion, supporting affidavits, memorandum in support, designation of evidence, exhibits. IN ST LAKE RCP Rule 17(D)(6).

      i. Large documents which do not exist in an electronic format shall be scanned into .pdf format and filed electronically as separate attachments. A scanner is available in each clerk's office for use by the public and the bar in scanning and saving image files if needed. IN ST LAKE RCP Rule 17(D)(6).

e. *Electronic signatures*

i. *Electronic filing as signature.* The electronic filing of a document which is required to be signed shall constitute the filer's representation under IN ST TRIAL P Rule 11. Unless the electronically filed document has been scanned and shows the filer's original signature, the signature of the filer shall be indicated by As/Attorney's Name, or As/Party's Name as in the case of a pro se litigant, on the line where the signature would otherwise appear. IN ST LAKE RCP Rule 17(G)(1).

ii. *Signatures on jointly signed or filed, verified or other documents.* In the case of a stipulation, agreed order, jointly signed motion or other document which needs to be signed by two (2) or more persons, or in the case of documents which must contain original signatures and which require verification or an unsworn declaration under rule or statute, the signatures may be indicated by either:

- Submitting a scanned copy of the originally signed document; or,
- Submitting the document with the use of As/Name in the signature block(s) where the original signature(s) appear(s) in the original document; provided, however, that the filer shall first obtain the physical signature of all persons necessary. IN ST LAKE RCP Rule 17(G)(2).

iii. *Retention of original.* The filer shall retain the original executed document. IN ST LAKE RCP Rule 17(G).

7. *Citation of local rules.* The local rules for Lake County may be known as the Lake County Rules of Civil Procedure, and abbreviated as LR. IN ST LAKE RCP Rule 1(C).

F. Filing and Service Requirements

1. *Filing requirements.* Except as otherwise provided in IN ST TRIAL P Rule 5(E)(2), all pleadings and papers subsequent to the complaint which are required to be served upon a party shall be filed with the Court either before service or within a reasonable period of time thereafter. IN ST TRIAL P Rule 5(E)(1). All papers presented for filing shall be submitted to the Clerk and not to the court. All papers submitted for filing shall be mailed or delivered to the Clerk's office at the courthouse in which the case is pending. IN ST LAKE RCP Rule 3(A).

    a. *Filing with the court defined.* The filing of pleadings, motions, and other papers with the court as required by the Indiana Rules of Trial Procedure shall be made by one of the following methods:

    i. Delivery to the clerk of the court;

    ii. Sending by electronic transmission under the procedure adopted pursuant to IN ST ADMIN Rule 12;

    iii. Mailing to the clerk by registered, certified or express mail return receipt requested;

    iv. Depositing with any third-party commercial carrier for delivery to the clerk within three (3) calendar days, cost prepaid, properly addressed;

    v. If the court so permits, filing with the judge, in which event the judge shall note thereon the filing date and forthwith transmit them to the office of the clerk; or

    vi. Electronic filing, as approved by the Division of State Court Administration pursuant to IN ST ADMIN Rule 16. IN ST TRIAL P Rule 5(F).

    vii. Filing by registered or certified mail and by third-party commercial carrier shall be complete upon mailing or deposit. IN ST TRIAL P Rule 5(F).

    b. *Mandatory electronic filing.* Unless otherwise permitted by the Lake County Rules of Civil Procedure or otherwise authorized by the judicial officer assigned to a particular case, all documents submitted for filing (including the original complaint, or equivalent pleading, and summons) shall be filed electronically with the clerk using the LCOD, no matter when the case was originally filed. IN ST LAKE RCP Rule 17(D).

    i. *Of documents containing information excluded from public access pursuant to* IN ST ADMIN

Rule 9. Documents containing information excluded from public access pursuant to IN ST ADMIN Rule 9, or documents which are ordered to be filed under seal shall be filed electronically, pursuant to IN ST LAKE RCP Rule 17(D)(9), whenever possible, along with a copy of the applicable order to seal the records, and the filer shall designate the documents as "Not for Public Access Pursuant to Administrative Rule 9(G)(1)" at the time of filing. IN ST LAKE RCP Rule 16(A)(1); IN ST LAKE RCP Rule 17(D)(9).

- *Conventional filing of documents containing information excluded from public access pursuant to* IN ST ADMIN Rule 9. Documents containing information excluded from public access pursuant to IN ST ADMIN Rule 9, or documents which are ordered to be filed under seal, which cannot be legibly scanned and filed electronically, shall be conventionally filed under seal and designated by the filer as "Not for Public Access Pursuant to Administrative Rule 9(G)(1)" at the time of filing. The unredacted version shall be filed on light green paper which is conspicuously marked "Not for Public Access"; and a redacted version, with confidential information deleted, shall be filed on white paper which shall be available for public access. The filer shall also electronically file a Notice of Manual Filing. IN ST LAKE RCP Rule 16(A)(2).

ii. *Technical failures.* If a registered user is unable to file a document in a timely manner due to technical difficulties in the LCOD, the registered user must file a document with the court as soon as possible notifying the court of the inability to file the document. A sample document titled Declaration that Party was Unable to File in a Timely Manner Due to Technical Difficulties can be found at IN ST LAKE RCP Form 4. Delayed filings shall be rejected unless accompanied by the declaration attesting to the filer's failed attempts to file electronically at least two (2) times, separated by at least one (1) hour, after noon on each day of delay due to such technical failure. IN ST LAKE RCP Rule 17(J).

iii. *Documents allowed to be filed conventionally.* Unless specifically authorized by the court, only the following documents may be filed conventionally and not electronically:

- Exhibits and other documents that cannot be converted to a legible electronic form, such as videotapes, x-rays, and similar materials
- Documents delivered to the clerk by pro se litigants
- Documents mailed to the clerk by pro se litigants
- Confidential documents
- Notice of manual filing
- Titles of documents
- Chronological case summary entry forms (CCS entry forms). IN ST LAKE RCP Rule 17(E).
- For more information on the documents which must be filed conventionally, refer to IN ST LAKE RCP Rule 17(E).

c. *Facsimile filing.* Only when necessary on an emergency basis (i.e., when certified mail or other means of filing will not bring the document to the Judge's attention prior to the scheduled hearing or ruling), pleadings, motions and other papers may be filed by electronic facsimile transmission, or when specifically authorized by the Court. IN ST LAKE RCP Rule 2(C).

i. *Generally.* In counties where a majority of judges of the courts of record, by posted local rule, have authorized electronic facsimile filing and designated a telephone number to receive such transmissions, pleadings, motions, and other papers may be sent to the Clerk of Circuit Court by electronic facsimile transmission for filing in any case, provided:

- Such matter does not exceed ten (10) pages, including the cover sheet;
- Such matter does not require the payment of fees other than the electronic facsimile transcription fee set forth in IN ST ADMIN Rule 12(E);
- The sending party creates at the time of transmission a machine generated log for such transmission; and

- The original document and the transmission log are maintained by the sending party for the duration of the litigation. IN ST ADMIN Rule 12(B).

ii. *Time of filing.* During normal, posted business hours, the time of filing shall be the time the duplicate document is produced in the office of the Clerk of the Circuit Court. Duplicate documents received at all other times shall be filed as of the next normal business day. IN ST ADMIN Rule 12(C).

- If the receiving fax machine endorses its own time and date stamp upon the transmitted documents and the receiving machine produces a delivery receipt which is electronically created and transmitted to the sending party, the time of filing shall be the date and time recorded on the transmitted document by the receiving fax machine. IN ST ADMIN Rule 12(C).

d. *Filing for special judges.* For special judge matters where the special judge is a full-time judge or magistrate serving within Lake County, all papers submitted for filing shall be delivered or mailed to the Clerk's office at the courthouse where the special judge regularly serves. IN ST LAKE RCP Rule 3(A).

e. *Proof of filing.* Any party filing any paper by any method other than personal delivery to the clerk shall retain proof of filing. IN ST TRIAL P Rule 5(F).

2. *Service requirements.* Unless otherwise provided by the Indiana Rules of Trial Procedure or an order of the court, each party and special judge, if any, shall be served with: (1) every order required by its terms to be served; (2) every pleading subsequent to the original complaint; (3) every written motion except one which may be heard ex parte; (4) every brief submitted to the trial court; (5) every paper relating to discovery required to be served upon a party; and (6) every written notice, appearance, demand, offer of judgment, designation of record on appeal, or similar paper. IN ST TRIAL P Rule 5(A).

a. *Methods of service*

i. *Personal service.* Whenever a party is represented by an attorney of record, service shall be made upon such attorney unless service upon the party himself is ordered by the court. Service upon the attorney or party shall be made by delivering or mailing a copy of the papers to the last known address or where an attorney or party has consented to service by fax or e-mail, as provided in IN ST TRIAL P Rule 3.1(A)(4), by faxing or e-mailing a copy of the documents to the fax number or e-mail address set out in the appearance form or correction as required by IN ST TRIAL P Rule 3.1(E). IN ST TRIAL P Rule 5(B). Delivery of a copy within IN ST TRIAL P Rule 5 means:

- Offering or tendering it to the attorney or party and stating the nature of the papers being served. Refusal to accept an offered or tendered document is a waiver of any objection to the sufficiency or adequacy of service of that document;

- Leaving it at his office with a clerk or other person in charge thereof, or if there is no one in charge, leaving it in a conspicuous place therein; or

- If the office is closed, by leaving it at his dwelling house or usual place of abode with some person of suitable age and discretion then residing therein; or,

- Leaving it at some other suitable place, selected by the attorney upon whom service is being made, pursuant to duly promulgated local rule. IN ST TRIAL P Rule 5(B)(1).

ii. *Service by mail.* If service is made by mail, the papers shall be deposited in the United States mail addressed to the person on whom they are being served, with postage prepaid. Service shall be deemed complete upon mailing. Proof of service of all papers permitted to be mailed may be made by written acknowledgment of service, by affidavit of the person who mailed the papers, or by certificate of an attorney. It shall be the duty of attorneys when entering their appearance in a cause or when filing pleadings or papers therein, to have noted in the Chronological Case Summary or said pleadings or papers so filed the address and telephone number of their office. Service by delivery or by mail at such address shall be deemed sufficient and complete. IN ST TRIAL P Rule 5(B)(2).

    iii. *Service by fax or e-mail.* A party who has consented to service by fax or e-mail may be served as follows:

- Service by e-mail shall be made by attaching the document being served in .pdf format. Discovery documents must also be served in accordance with IN ST TRIAL P Rule 26(A). IN ST TRIAL P Rule 5(B)(3)(a).
- Service by fax shall be deemed complete upon generation of a transmission record indicating the successful transmission of the entire document, except as provided in IN ST TRIAL P Rule 5(B)(3)(d). IN ST TRIAL P Rule 5(B)(3)(b).
- Service by e-mail shall be deemed complete upon transmission, except as provided in IN ST TRIAL P Rule 5(B)(3)(d). IN ST TRIAL P Rule 5(B)(3)(c).
- Service by fax or e-mail that occurs on a Saturday, Sunday, legal holiday, or day the court or agency in which the matter is pending is closed or after 5:00 PM local time of the recipient shall be deemed complete the next day that is not a Saturday, Sunday, legal holiday, or day that the court or agency in which the matter is pending is not closed. IN ST TRIAL P Rule 5(B)(3)(d).

  b. *Serving numerous defendants.* In any action in which there are unusually large numbers of defendants, the court, upon motion or of its own initiative, may order:

    i. That service of the pleadings of the defendants and replies thereto need not be made as between the defendants;

- That any cross-claim, counterclaim, or matter constituting an avoidance or affirmative defense contained therein shall be deemed to be denied or avoided by all other parties; and
- That the filing of any such pleading and service thereof upon the plaintiff constitutes due notice of it to the parties. IN ST TRIAL P Rule 5(D).

    ii. A copy of every such order shall be served upon the parties in such manner and form as the court directs. IN ST TRIAL P Rule 5(D).

  c. *Service by electronic means.* The Lake County Online Docket will generate a Notice of Electronic Filing and Service when any document is filed and served. This notice will be emailed to each registered user of record in a case, and an electronic service event will be added to the work queue of each registered user of record in the case. The party filing the document should retain a paper or electronic copy of the Notice of Electronic Filing and Service. This notice represents proof of filing and service of the document on registered users of record in that case. The filer shall not be required to conventionally serve any document on any party receiving electronic service. IN ST LAKE RCP Rule 17(F)(2).

    i. The filer shall also conventionally serve those parties not designated or able to receive electronic notice or service but who are nevertheless entitled to notice of said pleading or other document in accordance with the Indiana Rules of Civil Procedure and applicable Lake County Rules of Civil Procedure. In such cases, the filer shall also file a certificate of service, as appropriate. IN ST LAKE RCP Rule 17(F).

  d. *Service on parties in default for failure to appear.* No service need be made on parties in default for failure to appear, except that pleadings asserting new or additional claims for relief against them shall be served upon them in the manner provided by service of summons in IN ST TRIAL P Rule 4. IN ST TRIAL P Rule 5(A).

G. Hearings

1. *Hearing on motion.* Unless local conditions make it impracticable, each judge shall establish regular times and places, at intervals sufficiently frequent for the prompt dispatch of business, at which motions requiring notice and hearing may be heard and disposed of; but the judge at any time or place and on such notice, if any, as he considers reasonable may make order for the advancement, conduct, and hearing of actions. To expedite its business the court may direct the submission and determination of motions without oral hearing upon brief written statements of reasons in support and opposition, or direct or permit hearings by telephone conference call with all attorneys or other similar means of communication. IN ST TRIAL P Rule 73(A).

2. *Presentation of evidence.* On the hearing of an application for a restraining order or temporary injunction, each party may read affidavits or documentary or record evidence. IN ST 34-26-1-8.

3. *Hearing for preliminary injunction.* In case a temporary restraining order is granted without notice, the motion for a preliminary injunction shall be set down for hearing at the earliest possible time and takes precedence of all matters except older matters of the same character; and when the motion comes on for hearing the party who obtained the temporary restraining order shall proceed with the application for a preliminary injunction and, if he does not do so, the court shall dissolve the temporary restraining order. IN ST TRIAL P Rule 65(B). Refer to the Indiana KeyRules Motion for Preliminary Injunction document for more information.

4. *Oral argument discretionary.* The granting of a motion for oral argument, unless required by the Indiana Rules of Trial Procedure, shall be wholly discretionary with the court. IN ST LAKE RCP Rule 4(B).

H. Forms

1. Application for Temporary Restraining Order Forms for Indiana

a. Prayer in complaint for temporary restraining order. 5 INPRAC § 3:13.60.

b. Motion for temporary restraining order; With notice. 5 INPRAC § 3:13.80.

c. Notice of motion for temporary restraining order. 11 INPRAC § 97.2.

d. Motion for temporary restraining order; Without notice. 11 INPRAC § 97.3.

e. Affidavit in support of motion for temporary restraining order. 11 INPRAC § 97.4.

f. Certificate of efforts of attorney to give notice of application for temporary restraining order. 11 INPRAC § 97.5.

g. Temporary restraining order without notice and order to show cause why preliminary injunction should not issue; Real estate. 11 INPRAC § 97.6.

h. Motion to extend temporary restraining order. 11 INPRAC § 97.7.

i. Order granting motion to extend temporary restraining order. 11 INPRAC § 97.8.

j. Stipulation extending temporary restraining order. 11 INPRAC § 97.9.

k. Order granting extension of temporary restraining order pursuant to stipulation. 11 INPRAC § 97.10.

l. Motion for judge of adjourning circuit to rule upon motion for temporary restraining order. 11 INPRAC § 97.11.

m. Affidavit in support of motion for judge of adjoining county to rule on motion for temporary restraining order. 11 INPRAC § 97.12.

n. Motion to advance trial on merits for consolidation with hearing on preliminary injunction. 11 INPRAC § 97.13.

2. Official Application for Temporary Restraining Order Forms for Lake County

a. CCS entry form. IN ST LAKE RCP App. A.

b. Notice of manual filing. IN ST LAKE RCP Form 2.

c. Certificate of service. IN ST LAKE RCP Form 3.

d. Declaration that party was unable to file in a timely manner. IN ST LAKE RCP Form 4.

3. Application for Temporary Restraining Order Forms for Lake County

a. Notice of manual filing. EFORMST IN 5540.

I. Checklist

(I) ❑ Matters to be considered by the party filing the application without notice

    (a) ❑ Required documents

        (1) ❑ Application for temporary restraining order

        (2) ❑ Brief

    (3) ❑ Proposed order

    (4) ❑ Security

    (5) ❑ Chronological case summary (CSS) entry forms

  (b) ❑ Supplemental documents

    (1) ❑ Supporting evidence

    (2) ❑ Facsimile cover sheet

  (c) ❑ Timing

    (1) ❑ There are no specific timing requirements for submitting an application for a temporary restraining order without notice

Requests, Notices and Applications
Pretrial Conferences, Scheduling, Management

Document Last Updated October 2013

A. Applicable Rules

1. *State rules*

  a. Appearance. IN ST TRIAL P Rule 3.1.

  b. Process. IN ST TRIAL P Rule 4.

  c. Service and filing of pleadings and other papers. IN ST TRIAL P Rule 5.

  d. Time. IN ST TRIAL P Rule 6.

  e. Pleadings. IN ST TRIAL P Rule 7; IN ST TRIAL P Rule 8; IN ST TRIAL P Rule 9.2; IN ST TRIAL P Rule 10.

  f. Signing and verification of pleadings. IN ST TRIAL P Rule 11.

  g. Pre-trial procedure; Formulating issues. IN ST TRIAL P Rule 16.

  h. Evidence. IN ST TRIAL P Rule 43.

  i. Judgment on the evidence (directed verdict). IN ST TRIAL P Rule 50.

  j. Findings by the court. IN ST TRIAL P Rule 52.

  k. Summary judgment. IN ST TRIAL P Rule 56.

  l. Motion to correct error. IN ST TRIAL P Rule 59.

  m. Relief from judgment or order. IN ST TRIAL P Rule 60.

  n. Court records. IN ST TRIAL P Rule 77.

  o. Access to court records. IN ST ADMIN Rule 9.

  p. Paper size. IN ST ADMIN Rule 11.

  q. Facsimile transmission. IN ST ADMIN Rule 12.

  r. Electronic filing and electronic service pilot projects. IN ST ADMIN Rule 16.

  s. Privacy and confidentiality. IN ST 5-2-9-6; IN ST 5-14-3-4; IN ST 5-14-3-5.5; IN ST 6-4.1-5-10; IN ST 6-4.1-12-12; IN ST 6-8.1-7-1; IN ST 11-13-1-8; IN ST 12-23-14-13; IN ST 16-39-3-10; IN ST 16-41-8-1; IN ST 22-4-19-6; IN ST 31-11-1-6; IN ST 31-19-5-23; IN ST 31-19-13-2; IN ST 31-19-19-1; IN ST 31-33-18-1; IN ST 31-39-1-1; IN ST 31-39-1-2; IN ST 33-23-16-16; IN ST 35-34-2-4; IN ST 35-38-1-13; IN ST 35-38-9-1; IN ST ADR Rule 2.11; IN ST ADR Rule 4.4; IN ST ADR Rule 5.6; IN ST JURY Rule 10.

2. *Local rules*

  a. Scope and title. [IN ST LAKE RCP Rule 1, as amended by IN ORDER 13-0237, effective October 18, 2013].

    b. Preparation of pleadings, motions and other papers. IN ST LAKE RCP Rule 2.

    c. Filing. [IN ST LAKE RCP Rule 3, as amended by IN ORDER 13-0237, effective October 18, 2013].

    d. Motions. IN ST LAKE RCP Rule 4.

    e. Pretrial procedure. IN ST LAKE RCP Rule 9.

    f. Briefs. IN ST LAKE RCP Rule 11.

    g. Confidential information and sealed documents. IN ST LAKE RCP Rule 16.

    h. Electronic filing and service. IN ST LAKE RCP Rule 17.

B. Timing

1. *Pretrial conference.* Unless otherwise ordered by the court the pretrial conference shall not be called until after reasonable opportunity for the completion of discovery. IN ST TRIAL P Rule 16(B). However, some Indiana courts will schedule a preliminary pretrial conference almost immediately after the case has been filed in order to establish the ground rules for discovery, discovery cut-off dates, and the procedures for filing additional pleadings, motions, and the like. In addition, some courts will only schedule a trial date at the pretrial conference. 22 INPRAC § 28.2.

    a. *Notice.* The clerks shall give at least thirty (30) days' notice of the pretrial conference unless otherwise directed by the court. IN ST TRIAL P Rule 16(B)(1).

    b. *Pre-conference meeting.* Unless otherwise ordered by the court, at least ten (10) days prior to the pretrial conference, attorneys for each of the parties shall meet and confer. IN ST TRIAL P Rule 16(C). It shall be the duty of counsel for both plaintiff and defendant to arrange for the conference of attorneys at least ten (10) days in advance of the pretrial conference. IN ST TRIAL P Rule 16(E).

    c. *Exchange of trial documents.* The parties shall exchange written lists of witnesses and photocopies of exhibits, together with contentions and statements of issues of fact and law, at least thirty (30) days prior to the pre-trial conference. IN ST LAKE RCP Rule 9(C).

    d. *Submission of pretrial order.* Counsel for the plaintiff shall prepare a proposed pre-trial order, which shall be executed by counsel for all parties and filed not later than five (5) days prior to the pre-trial conference. IN ST LAKE RCP Rule 9(C).

2. *Motion requesting pretrial conference*

    a. *Timing of motion for pretrial conference.* There is no specific timing requirement for filing a motion requesting a pretrial conference.

        i. *Filing.* All pleadings and papers subsequent to the complaint which are required to be served upon a party shall be filed with the Court either before service or within a reasonable period of time thereafter. IN ST TRIAL P Rule 5(E)(1). All pleadings, motions and other papers submitted for filing which are required to be served under IN ST TRIAL P Rule 5(A) shall be filed no later than three (3) days after service. IN ST LAKE RCP Rule 3(A).

           • If such papers are filed before service, proof of service thereof shall be filed no later than three (3) business days thereafter. Upon failure to comply with IN ST LAKE RCP Rule 3, the Court may, on motion of any party or on its own motion, impose appropriate sanctions. IN ST LAKE RCP Rule 3(A).

        ii. *Briefs.* Briefs, other than those addressed in IN ST LAKE RCP Rule 4 and IN ST LAKE RCP Rule 9, shall be filed no later than two (2) calendar days preceding the hearing or trial to which directed. IN ST LAKE RCP Rule 11.

    b. *Service*

        i. *Of motion.* A written motion, other than one which may be heard ex parte, and notice of the hearing thereof shall be served not less than five (5) days before the time specified for the hearing, unless a different period is fixed by the Indiana Rules of Trial Procedure or by order of the court. IN ST TRIAL P Rule 6(D).

           • *Of supporting affidavits.* When a motion is supported by affidavit, the affidavit shall be served with the motion. IN ST TRIAL P Rule 6(D).

ii. *Service of opposition.* Except as otherwise provided in IN ST TRIAL P Rule 59(D), opposing affidavits may be served not less than one (1) day before the hearing, unless the court permits them to be served at some other time. IN ST TRIAL P Rule 6(D).

- So long as consistent with the Indiana Rules of Trial Procedure, an adverse party wishing to respond shall do so within fifteen (15) days of service. IN ST LAKE RCP Rule 4(A).

3. *Computation of time*

   a. *Generally; Days excluded.* In computing any period of time prescribed or allowed by the Indiana Rules of Trial Procedure, by order of the court, or by any applicable statute, the day of the act, event, or default from which the designated period of time begins to run shall not be included. The last day of the period so computed is to be included unless it is:

      i. A Saturday,

      ii. A Sunday,

      iii. A legal holiday as defined by state statute, or

      iv. A day the office in which the act is to be done is closed during regular business hours. IN ST TRIAL P Rule 6(A).

   b. *Short periods.* In any event, the period runs until the end of the next day that is not a Saturday, a Sunday, a legal holiday, or a day on which the office is closed. When the period of time allowed is less than seven (7) days, intermediate Saturdays, Sundays, legal holidays, and days on which the office is closed shall be excluded from the computations. IN ST TRIAL P Rule 6(A).

   c. *Additional time after service by United States mail.* Whenever a party has the right or is required to do some act or take some proceedings within a prescribed period after the service of a notice or other paper upon him and the notice or paper is served upon him by United States mail, three (3) days shall be added to the prescribed period. IN ST TRIAL P Rule 6(E).

   d. *Electronic filing does not alter deadlines.* Filing electronically does not alter any filing deadlines or any time computation pursuant to state or federal statutes, any Rules of the Indiana Supreme Court, including without limitation the Rules of Trial Procedure, the Rules of Appellate Procedure or the Administrative Rules, or applicable Lake County Rules of Civil Procedure. The office of the Lake County Clerk is open for electronic filing under the Lake County Rules of Civil Procedure twenty-four (24) hours a day. A document is deemed filed at the date and time it is received by the LCOD server. Filing must be completed before midnight local time in order to be considered filed that day. Lake County observes Central Time and electronic filers are strongly urged to file documents during hours when the Lake County Online Docket ("LCOD") help line is available, from 9:00 a.m. to 4:00 p.m. local time, although documents can be filed electronically twenty-four (24) hours a day. IN ST LAKE RCP Rule 17(I).

   e. *Enlargement of time.* When an act is required or allowed to be done at or within a specific time by the Indiana Rules of Trial Procedure, the court may at any time for cause shown:

      i. Order the period enlarged, with or without motion or notice, if request therefor is made before the expiration of the period originally prescribed or extended by a previous order; or

      ii. Upon motion made after the expiration of the specific period, permit the act to be done where the failure to act was the result of excusable neglect; but, the court may not extend the time for taking any action for judgment on the evidence under IN ST TRIAL P Rule 50(A), amendment of findings and judgment under IN ST TRIAL P Rule 52(B), to correct errors under IN ST TRIAL P Rule 59(C), statement in opposition to motion to correct error under IN ST TRIAL P Rule 59(E), or to obtain relief from final judgment under IN ST TRIAL P Rule 60(B), except to the extent and under the conditions stated in those rules. IN ST TRIAL P Rule 6(B).

C. General Requirements

1. *Initial status conference.* Upon motion of any party or the court, an initial status conference shall be

scheduled and held within six (6) months of the filing of any Complaint in a civil plenary or civil tort case. IN ST LAKE RCP Rule 9(A).

a. *Topics for discussion at conference.* Each party shall be represented at this conference by an attorney familiar with the case, who shall be prepared to discuss and enter into stipulations concerning:

    i. The exchange of lists of witnesses known to have knowledge of the facts supporting the pleadings. The parties thereafter shall be under a continuing obligation to advise opposing parties of other witnesses as they become known;

    ii. The exchange of all documents, and any other evidence reasonably available, contemplated for use in support of the pleadings;

    iii. A discovery schedule;

    iv. The necessity for additional conferences in complex litigation; and

    v. The necessity for amendments to the pleadings and the filing or hearing of dispositive motions. Absent agreement, the court shall schedule the filing, briefing and hearing thereof. IN ST LAKE RCP Rule 9(A).

b. *Case management order.* At the conclusion of the initial status conference, the court shall enter a case management order setting forth:

    i. A time limit for completion of discovery;

    ii. A time limit for joinder of additional parties and amendment of pleadings;

    iii. A time limit for filing all pre-trial dispositive motions;

    iv. The scheduling of a pre-trial conference; and

    v. Any other matters which the parties or the court have seen fit to address. IN ST LAKE RCP Rule 9(B).

2. *Pretrial conference.* A pre-trial conference shall be held in every civil plenary and civil tort action, at which each party shall be represented by the attorney who will conduct the trial. IN ST LAKE RCP Rule 9(C).

a. *When required; Purpose.* In any action except criminal cases, the court may in its discretion and shall upon the motion of any party, direct the attorneys for the parties to appear before it for a conference to consider:

    i. The simplification of the issues;

    ii. The necessity or desirability of amendments to the pleadings;

    iii. The possibility of obtaining admissions of fact and of documents which will avoid unnecessary proof;

    iv. A limitation of the number of expert witnesses;

    v. An exchange of names of witnesses to be called during the trial and the general nature of their expected testimony;

    vi. The desirability of using one or more types of alternative dispute resolution under the rules therefor;

    vii. The desirability of setting deadlines for dispositive motions in light of the date set for trial; and

    viii. Such other matters as may aid in the disposition of the action. IN ST TRIAL P Rule 16(A).

b. *Participants.* At least one (1) attorney planning to take part in the trial shall appear for each of the parties and participate in the pretrial conference. IN ST TRIAL P Rule 16(B)(2).

c. *Conference of attorneys prior to pretrial conference*

    i. *Purpose of attorney conference.* In general, the purpose of the "pre-pretrial conference" is to ensure that the attorneys for both sides will be prepared to make maximum use of the pretrial conference itself. IN ST TRIAL P Rule 16 frees the pretrial conference itself from perfunctory matters; it is written to require that not only are attorneys very familiar with the case, but that

990

routine matters are resolved before the pretrial conference so that it may be devoted to a determination of those issues and matters which will be litigated. 2 INPRAC R 16(16.3).

ii. *Topics to be addressed at attorney conference.* Unless otherwise ordered by the court, at least ten (10) days prior to the pretrial conference, attorneys for each of the parties shall meet and confer for the following purposes:

- *Exhibits.* Each attorney shall mark for identification and provide opposing counsel an opportunity to inspect and copy all exhibits which he expects to introduce at the trial. Numbers or marks placed on such exhibits shall be prefixed with the symbol "P/T", denoting its pretrial designation. When the exhibit is introduced at the trial of the case, the "P/T" designation will be stricken and the exhibits must also indicate the party identifying same. IN ST TRIAL P Rule 16(C)(1). Exhibits of the character which prohibit or make impracticable their production at conference shall be identified and notice given of their intended use. Necessary arrangements must be made to afford opposing counsel an opportunity to examine such exhibits. IN ST TRIAL P Rule 16(C)(1).

- *Exhibit stipulations.* Written stipulations shall be prepared with reference to all exhibits exchanged or identified. The stipulations shall contain all agreements of the parties with reference to the exchanged and identified exhibits, and shall include, but not be limited to, the agreement of the parties with reference to the authenticity of the exhibits, their admissibility in evidence, their use in opening statements, and the provisions made for the inspection of identified exhibits. The original of the exhibit stipulations shall be presented to the court at the pretrial conference. IN ST TRIAL P Rule 16(C)(2).

- *Fact stipulation.* The attorneys shall stipulate in writing with reference to all facts and issues not in genuine dispute. The original of the stipulations shall be presented to the court at the time of the pretrial conference. IN ST TRIAL P Rule 16(C)(3).

- *Exchange list of witnesses.* Attorneys for each of the parties shall furnish opposing counsel with the written list of the names and addresses of all witnesses then known. The original of each witness list shall be presented to the court at the time of the pretrial conference. IN ST TRIAL P Rule 16(C)(4).

- *Discuss settlement.* The possibility of compromise settlement shall be fully discussed and explored. IN ST TRIAL P Rule 16(C)(5).

d. *Preparation for conference of attorneys and pretrial.* Each attorney shall completely familiarize himself with all aspects of the case in advance of the conference of attorneys and be prepared to enter into stipulations with reference to as many facts and issues and exhibits as possible. IN ST TRIAL P Rule 16(D).

e. *Refusal to stipulate.* If, following the conference of attorneys, either party determines that there are other facts or exhibits that should be stipulated and which opposing counsel refuses to stipulate upon, he shall compile a list of such facts or exhibits and furnish same to opposing counsel at least two (2) days in advance of the pretrial conference. The original of the list shall be presented to the court at the time of the pretrial conference. IN ST TRIAL P Rule 16(F).

f. *Witnesses or exhibits discovered subsequent to conference of attorneys and before a pretrial conference.* If, after the conference of the attorneys and before the pretrial conference, counsel discovers additional exhibits or names of additional witnesses, the same information required to be disclosed at the conference of the attorneys shall be immediately furnished opposing counsel. The original of any such disclosures shall be presented to the court at the time of the pretrial conference. IN ST TRIAL P Rule 16(G).

g. *More than one pretrial conference.* If necessary or advisable, the court may adjourn the pretrial conference from time to time or may order an additional pretrial conference. IN ST TRIAL P Rule 16(H).

h. *Witnesses or exhibits discovered subsequent to pretrial conference.* If, following the pretrial conference or during trial, counsel discovers additional exhibits or the names of additional witnesses, the same information required to be disclosed at the conference between attorneys shall be immediately furnished opposing counsel. The original of any such disclosure shall immediately be filed with the court and shall indicate the date it was furnished opposing counsel. IN ST TRIAL P Rule 16(I).

i. *Pretrial order.* The court shall make an order which recites the action taken at the conference, the amendments allowed to the pleading, and the agreements made by the parties as to any of the matters considered which limit the issues for trial to those not disposed of by admissions or agreement of counsel, and such order when entered shall control the subsequent course of action, unless modified thereafter to prevent manifest injustice. The court in its discretion may establish by rule a pretrial calendar on which actions may be placed for consideration as above provided, and may either confine the calendar to jury actions or non-jury actions or extend it to all actions. IN ST TRIAL P Rule 16(J).

   i. The pretrial order delineates the issues in the case and supplants allegations raised in the pleadings. All subsequent pleadings are then controlled by the order that the trial court enters in the case file, and court record. 2 INPRAC R 16(16.2); Dominguez v. Gallmeyer, 402 N.E.2d 1295, 1298 (Ind.Ct.App. 1980).

   ii. Counsel for the plaintiff shall prepare a proposed pre-trial order, which shall be executed by counsel for all parties and filed not later than five (5) days prior to the pre-trial conference. IN ST LAKE RCP Rule 9(C). The pre-trial stipulation shall set forth in the following sequence:

   - The jurisdiction of the court;
   - The pleadings raising the issues;
   - A list of motions or other matters requiring action by the court;
   - A concise statement of stipulated facts, with reservations, if any;
   - A concise statement of issues of fact which remain to be litigated;
   - A concise statement of issues of law which remain for determination by the court;
   - The plaintiff's contentions;
   - The defendant's contentions;
   - The plaintiff's numbered list of trial exhibits;
   - The defendant's numbered list of trial exhibits;
   - The plaintiff's numbered list of trial witnesses, with addresses. Expert witnesses shall be so designated;
   - The defendant's numbered list of trial witnesses, with addresses. Expert witnesses shall be so designated; and
   - The estimated length of trial. IN ST LAKE RCP Rule 9(C).

   iii. When, for any reason, the pre-trial stipulation is not executed by all counsel, each shall file not later than five (5) days prior to the pre-trial conference a written statement of the reason therefor accompanied with a proposed pre-trial stipulation. IN ST LAKE RCP Rule 9(C).

   iv. At the conclusion of the pre-trial conference, the court shall render a pre-trial order which, when entered, shall control the course of the trial and may not be amended except by order of the court to prevent manifest injustice. IN ST LAKE RCP Rule 9(D).

j. *Sanctions; Failure to appear.* If without just excuse or because of failure to give reasonable attention to the matter, no appearance is made on behalf of a party at a pre-trial conference, or if an attorney is grossly unprepared to participate in the conference, the court may order either one or both of the following:

   i. The payment by the delinquent attorney or party of the reasonable expenses, including attorney's fees, to the aggrieved party; or

   ii. Take such other action as may be appropriate. IN ST TRIAL P Rule 16(K).

   iii. A failure of the parties or their attorneys to be prepared for the initial status conference, for the pre-trial conference, or to otherwise comply with IN ST LAKE RCP Rule 9, shall subject them to sanctions under IN ST TRIAL P Rule 16(K). IN ST LAKE RCP Rule 9(G).

    iv.   Refer to the Indiana KeyRules Motion for Sanctions document for more information.

3. *Motions, generally.* Unless made during a hearing or trial, or otherwise ordered by the court, an application to the court for an order shall be made by written motion. The motion shall state the grounds therefor and the relief or order sought. IN ST TRIAL P Rule 7(B).

    a.   *Motions as distinct from pleadings.* Motions and responses to motions are not pleadings, and allegations contained in a motion are not admissions of a party. 22B INPRAC 7:2; Wachstetter v. County Properties, LLC, 832 N.E.2d 574 (Ind.Ct.App. 2005); Scott County Family YMCA, Inc. v. Hobbs, 817 N.E.2d 603 (Ind.Ct.App. 2004).

    b.   *Unopposed motions generally granted.* It is common for a trial court to grant procedural motions, such as motions for enlargement of time, discovery motions, or motions for continuance, unless an objection is filed. 21 INPRAC § 13.8.

    c.   *Separate motions.* Each motion shall be separate, while alternative motions filed together shall each be identified on the caption. IN ST LAKE RCP Rule 4(A).

    d.   *Answer and reply briefs.* Failure to file an answer brief or reply brief within the time prescribed shall be deemed a waiver of the right thereto and shall subject the motion to summary ruling. IN ST LAKE RCP Rule 4(A).

D. Documents

1. *Pretrial conference*

    a.   *Documents to consider*

        i.   *Exhibits and stipulations.* Refer to the General Requirements section of this document for information on exhibits and stipulations.

2. *Motion for pretrial conference or initial status conference*

    a.   *Required documents*

        i.   *Motion and notice.* The requirement of notice is satisfied by service of the motion. IN ST TRIAL P Rule 7(B). Refer to the General Requirements section of this document for information on the content of a motion for pretrial conference.

        ii.   *Brief.* Briefs, other than those addressed in IN ST LAKE RCP Rule 4 and IN ST LAKE RCP Rule 9, shall be filed no later than two (2) calendar days preceding the hearing or trial to which directed. IN ST LAKE RCP Rule 11.

        iii.   *Proposed order.* Unless local practice provides differently, a party should submit a proposed order with its written motion to be signed by the judge once the motion has been granted. 21 INPRAC § 13.8.

- Proposed orders, which are submitted for the court's convenience under IN ST LAKE RCP Rule 3 or other applicable Lake County Rules of Civil Procedure, shall be submitted as attachments to motions. IN ST LAKE RCP Rule 17(D)(8). Proposed orders shall be prepared and filed separately from the pleadings, petitions, motions or other papers to which they have reference. IN ST LAKE RCP Rule 3(B).

- Orders, either routine in nature or uncontested including, for example, those setting or continuing a hearing, shall be effected by the chronological case summary entry only, which shall contain the concise substance of the order. IN ST LAKE RCP Rule 3(B).

- All orders shall be accompanied with sufficient copies and stamped, pre-addressed envelopes, so that copies may be mailed to all parties. IN ST LAKE RCP Rule 3(B).

        iv.   *Chronological case summary (CCS) entry forms.* All filings shall be accompanied by a Chronological Case Summary (CCS) Entry Form to define or identify the documents filed. The Form used should be substantially similar to IN ST LAKE RCP App. A. IN ST LAKE RCP Rule 3(C).

v. *Certificate of service.* An attorney or unrepresented party tendering a document to the Clerk for filing shall certify that service has been made, list the parties served, and specify the date and means of service. The certificate of service shall be placed at the end of the document and shall not be separately filed. The separate filing of a certificate of service, however, shall not be grounds for rejecting a document for filing. The Clerk may permit documents to be filed without a certificate of service but shall require prompt filing of a separate certificate of service. IN ST TRIAL P Rule 5(C).

- All pleadings, motions and other papers submitted for filing which are required to be served under IN ST TRIAL P Rule 5(A) shall contain proof of service pursuant to IN ST TRIAL P Rule 5(B)(2). IN ST LAKE RCP Rule 3(A).

b. *Supplemental documents*

i. *Supporting evidence.* When a motion is based on facts not appearing of record the court may hear the matter on affidavits presented by the respective parties, but the court may direct that the matter be heard wholly or partly on oral testimony or depositions. IN ST TRIAL P Rule 43(B).

ii. *Facsimile cover sheet.* Any document sent to the Clerk of the Circuit Court by electronic facsimile transmission shall be accompanied by a cover sheet which states the title of the document, case number, number of pages, identity and voice telephone number of the sending party and instructions for filing. The cover sheet shall contain the signature of the attorney or party, pro se, authorizing the filing. IN ST ADMIN Rule 12(D).

E. Format

1. *Form of papers.* The rules applicable to captions, and the signing and form of pleadings (IN ST TRIAL P Rule 8 through IN ST TRIAL P Rule 11), apply to all motions and other papers provided under the Indiana Rules of Trial Procedure. 22B INPRAC 7:2.

2. *Form of pleadings.* For the purpose of uniformity, convenience, clarity and durability, requirements in IN ST LAKE RCP Rule 2 shall be observed in the preparation of all pleadings, motions and other papers. IN ST LAKE RCP Rule 2. Whenever materials submitted fail to meet the standards in IN ST LAKE RCP Rule 2, the Court may impose appropriate sanctions. IN ST LAKE RCP Rule 2(B).

a. *Caption; Names of parties.* Every pleading shall contain a caption setting forth the name of the court, the title of the action, the file number, and a designation as in IN ST TRIAL P Rule 7(A). In the complaint the title of the action shall include the names of all the parties, but in other pleadings it is sufficient to state the name of the first party on each side with an appropriate indication of other parties. IN ST TRIAL P Rule 10(A).

i. *Special judge matters.* The caption of all CCS Entry Forms, pleadings, motions, orders and other papers to be filed in a special judge case shall include in block text the words SPECIAL JUDGE and the name of the judge directly below the cause number on the caption. IN ST LAKE RCP Rule 2(D).

b. *Paragraphs; Separate statements.* All averments of a claim or defense shall be made in numbered paragraphs, the contents of each of which shall be limited as far as practicable to a statement of a single set of circumstances, and a paragraph may be referred to by number in all succeeding pleadings. Each claim founded upon a separate transaction or occurrence and each defense other than denials may be stated in a separate count or defense whenever a separation facilitates the clear presentation of the matters set forth. IN ST TRIAL P Rule 10(B).

c. *Adoption by reference; Exhibits.* Statements in a pleading may be adopted by reference in a different part of the same pleading or in another pleading or in any motion. A copy of any written instrument which is an exhibit to a pleading is a part thereof for all purposes. IN ST TRIAL P Rule 10(C).

d. *Paper; Print, quality and binding*

i. All pleadings, motions, chronological case summary entry forms, orders, process and other papers shall be neatly and legibly printed, typewritten or mechanically reproduced, on one (1) side only, on white opaque paper. To satisfy the recordkeeping requirements of IN ST TRIAL P Rule 77, the print shall be of sufficient density and clarity for preservation and reproduction of microfilming, optical disk or other secondary sources. For this reason, the use of non-letter-quality printers is discouraged. IN ST LAKE RCP Rule 2(A).

    ii.   Paper and ink shall be of such quality as to withstand the test of time. All documents shall be produced on acid-free, non-thermal paper. It is recommended that a minimum of twenty (20) pound, twenty-five percent (25%) cotton paper product be used. Documents of multiple pages shall be submitted in bound or stapled fashion, and the binding or stapling shall be at the top only. Covers or backings shall not be used. IN ST LAKE RCP Rule 2(A).

  e. *Papers; Handwritten.* Handwritten papers may be filed only if approved by the Court and a typewritten or printed true rendition thereof is filed within three (3) days thereafter and approved by the Court. Upon such approval, they shall be deemed and filed as the original, while the handwritten papers shall be retained therewith for evidentiary purposes. IN ST LAKE RCP Rule 2(C).

  f. *Minute sheets; Motion blanks.* Minute sheets and motion blanks shall no longer be used. IN ST LAKE RCP Rule 2(D).

3. *Size of papers for filing.* Effective January 1, 1992, all pleadings, copies, motions and documents filed with any trial court or appellate level court, typed or printed, with the exception of exhibits and existing wills, shall be prepared on eight and one-half by eleven inch (8 1/2" x 11") size paper. IN ST ADMIN Rule 11.

4. *Signature requirements*

  a. *Signature of attorney.* Every pleading or motion of a party represented by an attorney shall be signed by at least one (1) attorney of record in his individual name, whose address, telephone number, and attorney number shall be stated, except that this provision shall not apply to pleadings and motions made and transcribed at the trial or a hearing before the judge and received by him in such form. IN ST TRIAL P Rule 11(A).

    i.   The signature of an attorney constitutes a certificate by him that he has read the pleadings; that to the best of his knowledge, information, and belief, there is good ground to support it; and that it is not interposed for delay. IN ST TRIAL P Rule 11(A).

    ii.   If a pleading or motion is not signed or is signed with intent to defeat the purpose of the rule, it may be stricken as sham and false and the action may proceed as though the pleading had not been served. IN ST TRIAL P Rule 11(A).

    iii. For a willful violation of IN ST TRIAL P Rule 11 an attorney may be subjected to appropriate disciplinary action. Similar action may be taken if scandalous or indecent matter is inserted. IN ST TRIAL P Rule 11(A).

  b. *Signature of unrepresented party.* A party who is not represented by an attorney shall sign his pleading and state his address. IN ST TRIAL P Rule 11(A).

  c. *Verification not generally required.* Except when specifically required by rule, pleadings or motions need not be verified or accompanied by affidavit. The rule in equity that the averments of an answer under oath must be overcome by the testimony of two (2) witnesses or of one (1) witness sustained by corroborating circumstances is abolished. IN ST TRIAL P Rule 11(A).

  d. *Verification by affirmation or representation.* When in connection with any civil or special statutory proceeding it is required that any pleading, motion, petition, supporting affidavit, or other document of any kind, be verified, or that an oath be taken, it shall be sufficient if the subscriber simply affirms the truth of the matter to be verified by an affirmation or representation. IN ST TRIAL P Rule 11(B). IN ST TRIAL P Rule 11(B) states that the affirmation or representation should be in substantially the following language: "I (we) affirm, under the penalties for perjury, that the foregoing representation(s) is (are) true. (Signed) _____."

    i.   Any person who falsifies an affirmation or representation of fact shall be subject to the same penalties as are prescribed by law for the making of a false affidavit. IN ST TRIAL P Rule 11(B).

  e. *Verified pleadings, motions, and affidavits as evidence.* Pleadings, motions and affidavits accompanying or in support of such pleadings or motions when required to be verified or under oath shall be

accepted as a representation that the signer had personal knowledge thereof or reasonable cause to believe the existence of the facts or matters stated or alleged therein; and, if otherwise competent or acceptable as evidence, may be admitted as evidence of the facts or matters stated or alleged therein when it is so provided in the Indiana Rules of Trial Procedure, by statute or other law, or to the extent the writing or signature expressly purports to be made upon the signer's personal knowledge. When such pleadings, motions and affidavits are verified or under oath they shall not require other or greater proof on the part of the adverse party than if not verified or not under oath unless expressly provided otherwise by the Indiana Rules of Trial Procedure, statute or other law. Affidavits upon motions for summary judgment under IN ST TRIAL P Rule 56 and in denial of execution under IN ST TRIAL P Rule 9.2 shall be made upon personal knowledge. IN ST TRIAL P Rule 11(C).

f. *Electronic signature.* The filing of documents and information through the E-filing system by use of a valid username and password is presumed to have been authorized by the User to whom that username and password have been issued and documents filed through the E-filing system are presumed to have been signed by the same User. IN ST ADMIN Rule 16(E).

5. *Information excluded from public access.* Every document filed in a case shall separately identify information excluded from public access pursuant to IN ST ADMIN Rule 9(G)(1) as follows:

a. Whole documents that are excluded from public access pursuant to IN ST ADMIN Rule 9(G)(1) shall be tendered on light green paper or have a light green coversheet attached to the document, marked "Not for Public Access" or "Confidential." IN ST TRIAL P Rule 5(G)(1).

b. When only a portion of a document contains information excluded from public access pursuant to IN ST ADMIN Rule 9(G)(1), said information shall be omitted [or redacted] from the filed document, and set forth on a separate accompanying document on light green paper conspicuously marked "Not for Public Access" or "Confidential" and clearly designated [or identifying] the caption and number of the case and the document and location within the document to which the redacted material pertains. IN ST TRIAL P Rule 5(G)(2).

c. With respect to documents filed in electronic format, the trial court, by local rule, may provide for compliance with IN ST TRIAL P Rule 5 in manner that separates and protects access to information excluded from public access. IN ST TRIAL P Rule 5(G)(3).

d. IN ST TRIAL P Rule 5(G) does not apply to a record sealed by the court pursuant to IN ST 5-14-3-5.5 or otherwise, nor to records, documents, or information filed in cases to which public access is prohibited pursuant to IN ST ADMIN Rule 9(G). IN ST TRIAL P Rule 5(G)(4).

e. The following information in case records is excluded from public access and is confidential:

   i. Information that is excluded from public access pursuant to federal law;

   ii. Information that is excluded from public access as declared confidential by Indiana statute or other court rule, including without limitation:

   - All adoption records created after July 8, 1941, as declared confidential by IN ST 31-19-19-1, et seq., except those specifically declared open by IN ST 31-19-13-2(2);

   - All records relating to chancroid, chlamydia, gonorrhea, hepatitis, human immunodeficiency virus (HIV), Lymphogranuloma venereum, syphilis, tuberculosis, as declared confidential by IN ST 16-41-8-1, et seq.;

   - All records relating to child abuse as declared confidential by IN ST 31-33-18-1, et seq.;

   - All records relating to drug tests as declared confidential by IN ST 5-14-3-4(a)(9);

   - Records of grand jury proceedings as declared confidential by IN ST 35-34-2-4;

   - Records of juvenile proceedings as declared confidential by IN ST 31-39-1-2, except those specifically open under statute;

   - All paternity records created after July 1, 1941 as declared confidential by IN ST 31-14-11-15, IN ST 31-19-5-23, IN ST 31-39-1-1 and IN ST 31-39-1-2 [Editor's note: IN ST 31-14-11-15 was repealed effective May 9, 2013];

   - All pre-sentence reports as declared confidential by IN ST 35-38-1-13;

- Written petitions to permit marriages without consent and orders directing the Clerk of Court to issue a marriage license to underage persons, as declared confidential by IN ST 31-11-1-6;

- Only those arrest warrants, search warrants, indictments and informations ordered confidential by the trial judge, prior to return of duly executed service as declared confidential by IN ST 5-14-3-4(b)(1);

- All medical, mental health, or tax records unless determined by law or regulation of any governmental custodian not to be confidential, released by the subject of such records, or declared by a court of competent jurisdiction to be essential to the resolution of litigation as declared confidential by IN ST 16-39-3-10, IN ST 6-4.1-5-10, IN ST 6-4.1-12-12, and IN ST 6-8.1-7-1;

- Personal information relating to jurors or prospective jurors, other than for the use of the parties and counsel, pursuant to IN ST JURY Rule 10;

- Information relating to protection from abuse orders, no-contact orders and workplace violence restraining orders as declared confidential by IN ST 5-2-9-6, et seq.;

- Mediation proceedings pursuant to IN ST ADR Rule 2.11, Mini-Trial proceedings pursuant to IN ST ADR Rule 4.4(C), and Summary Jury Trials pursuant to IN ST ADR Rule 5.6;

- Information in probation files pursuant to the Probation Standards promulgated by the Judicial Conference of Indiana pursuant to IN ST 11-13-1-8(b);

- Information deemed confidential pursuant to the Rules for Court Administered Alcohol and Drug Programs promulgated by the Judicial Conference of Indiana pursuant to IN ST 12-23-14-13;

- Information deemed confidential pursuant to the Problem-Solving Court Rules promulgated by the Judicial Conference of Indiana pursuant to IN ST 33-23-16-16;

- All records of the Department of workforce Development as declared confidential by IN ST 22-4-19-6;

- Information regarding interception of electronic communications that is sealed or deemed confidential as set forth in IN ST 35-33.5-2-1, et seq.

iii. Information excluded from public access by specific court order;

iv. Complete Social Security Numbers of living persons;

v. With the exception of names, information such as addresses, phone numbers, and dates of birth which explicitly identifies:

- Natural persons who are witnesses or victims (not including defendants) in criminal, domestic violence, stalking, sexual assault, juvenile, or civil protection order proceedings, provided that juveniles who are victims of sex crimes shall be identified by initials only;

- Places of residence of judicial officers, clerks and other employees of courts and clerks of court, unless the person or persons about whom the information pertains waives confidentiality;

vi. Complete account numbers of specific assets, loans, bank accounts, credit cards, and personal identification numbers (PINs);

vii. All orders of expungement entered in criminal or juvenile proceedings, orders to restrict access to criminal history information pursuant to IN ST 35-38-5-5.5 or IN ST 35-38-8-5 and records excluded from public access by such orders, and information related to infractions that is excluded from public access pursuant to IN ST 34-28-5-15 or IN ST 34-28-5-16 [Editor's note: IN ST 35-38-5-5.5, IN ST 35-38-8-5 and IN ST 34-28-5-16 were repealed effective July 1, 2013; for information on orders restricting access to criminal history, refer to IN ST 35-38-9-1, et seq.];

viii. All personal notes and e-mail, and deliberative material, of judges, jurors, court staff and

judicial agencies, and information recorded in personal data assistants (PDA's) or organizers and personal calendars. IN ST ADMIN Rule 9(G)(1).

6. *Format of electronically filed documents*

    a. *Generally.* Electronically filed documents must meet the same requirements of format as documents conventionally filed pursuant to IN ST LAKE RCP Rule 2 or other applicable Lake County Rules of Civil Procedure. IN ST LAKE RCP Rule 17(D)(1).

    b. *Titles of documents.* The person electronically filing a document will be responsible for designating a title for the document at the time it is filed. The LCOD will generate the appropriate entry onto the CCS to record the filing of the document. IN ST LAKE RCP Rule 17(D)(3).

    c. *Citations and hyperlinks.* Electronically filed documents may contain hyperlink references to an external document as a convenient mechanism for accessing material cited in the document. Filers wishing to insert hyperlinks into documents shall continue to use the traditional method of citation to authority in addition to the hyperlink provided. The hyperlink is merely a convenience to the court and the material referenced is extraneous to the file and not a part of the court's record. IN ST LAKE RCP Rule 17(D)(5).

    d. *Attachments and exhibits.* All documents which form part of a single submission and which are being filed at the same time and by the same filer may be electronically filed together under one document filing, e.g., the motion, supporting affidavits, memorandum in support, designation of evidence, exhibits. IN ST LAKE RCP Rule 17(D)(6).

        i. Large documents which do not exist in an electronic format shall be scanned into .pdf format and filed electronically as separate attachments. A scanner is available in each clerk's office for use by the public and the bar in scanning and saving image files if needed. IN ST LAKE RCP Rule 17(D)(6).

    e. *Electronic signatures*

        i. *Electronic filing as signature.* The electronic filing of a document which is required to be signed shall constitute the filer's representation under IN ST TRIAL P Rule 11. Unless the electronically filed document has been scanned and shows the filer's original signature, the signature of the filer shall be indicated by As/Attorney's Name, or As/Party's Name as in the case of a pro se litigant, on the line where the signature would otherwise appear. IN ST LAKE RCP Rule 17(G)(1).

        ii. *Signatures on jointly signed or filed, verified or other documents.* In the case of a stipulation, agreed order, jointly signed motion or other document which needs to be signed by two (2) or more persons, or in the case of documents which must contain original signatures and which require verification or an unsworn declaration under rule or statute, the signatures may be indicated by either:

          • Submitting a scanned copy of the originally signed document; or,

          • Submitting the document with the use of As/Name in the signature block(s) where the original signature(s) appear(s) in the original document; provided, however, that the filer shall first obtain the physical signature of all persons necessary. IN ST LAKE RCP Rule 17(G)(2).

        iii. *Retention of original.* The filer shall retain the original executed document. IN ST LAKE RCP Rule 17(G).

7. *Citation of local rules.* The local rules for Lake County may be known as the Lake County Rules of Civil Procedure, and abbreviated as LR. IN ST LAKE RCP Rule 1(C).

F. Filing and Service Requirements

1. *Filing requirements.* Except as otherwise provided in IN ST TRIAL P Rule 5(E)(2), all pleadings and papers subsequent to the complaint which are required to be served upon a party shall be filed with the Court either before service or within a reasonable period of time thereafter. IN ST TRIAL P Rule 5(E)(1). All papers presented for filing shall be submitted to the Clerk and not to the court. All papers submitted

for filing shall be mailed or delivered to the Clerk's office at the courthouse in which the case is pending. IN ST LAKE RCP Rule 3(A).

a. *Filing with the court defined.* The filing of pleadings, motions, and other papers with the court as required by the Indiana Rules of Trial Procedure shall be made by one of the following methods:

 i. Delivery to the clerk of the court;

 ii. Sending by electronic transmission under the procedure adopted pursuant to IN ST ADMIN Rule 12;

 iii. Mailing to the clerk by registered, certified or express mail return receipt requested;

 iv. Depositing with any third-party commercial carrier for delivery to the clerk within three (3) calendar days, cost prepaid, properly addressed;

 v. If the court so permits, filing with the judge, in which event the judge shall note thereon the filing date and forthwith transmit them to the office of the clerk; or

 vi. Electronic filing, as approved by the Division of State Court Administration pursuant to IN ST ADMIN Rule 16. IN ST TRIAL P Rule 5(F).

 vii. Filing by registered or certified mail and by third-party commercial carrier shall be complete upon mailing or deposit. IN ST TRIAL P Rule 5(F).

b. *Mandatory electronic filing.* Unless otherwise permitted by the Lake County Rules of Civil Procedure or otherwise authorized by the judicial officer assigned to a particular case, all documents submitted for filing (including the original complaint, or equivalent pleading, and summons) shall be filed electronically with the clerk using the LCOD, no matter when the case was originally filed. IN ST LAKE RCP Rule 17(D).

 i. *Of documents containing information excluded from public access pursuant to* IN ST ADMIN Rule 9. Documents containing information excluded from public access pursuant to IN ST ADMIN Rule 9, or documents which are ordered to be filed under seal shall be filed electronically, pursuant to IN ST LAKE RCP Rule 17(D)(9), whenever possible, along with a copy of the applicable order to seal the records, and the filer shall designate the documents as "Not for Public Access Pursuant to Administrative Rule 9(G)(1)" at the time of filing. IN ST LAKE RCP Rule 16(A)(1); IN ST LAKE RCP Rule 17(D)(9).

 - *Conventional filing of documents containing information excluded from public access pursuant to* IN ST ADMIN Rule 9. Documents containing information excluded from public access pursuant to IN ST ADMIN Rule 9, or documents which are ordered to be filed under seal, which cannot be legibly scanned and filed electronically, shall be conventionally filed under seal and designated by the filer as "Not for Public Access Pursuant to Administrative Rule 9(G)(1)" at the time of filing. The unredacted version shall be filed on light green paper which is conspicuously marked "Not for Public Access"; and a redacted version, with confidential information deleted, shall be filed on white paper which shall be available for public access. The filer shall also electronically file a Notice of Manual Filing. IN ST LAKE RCP Rule 16(A)(2).

 ii. *Technical failures.* If a registered user is unable to file a document in a timely manner due to technical difficulties in the LCOD, the registered user must file a document with the court as soon as possible notifying the court of the inability to file the document. A sample document titled Declaration that Party was Unable to File in a Timely Manner Due to Technical Difficulties can be found at IN ST LAKE RCP Form 4. Delayed filings shall be rejected unless accompanied by the declaration attesting to the filer's failed attempts to file electronically at least two (2) times, separated by at least one (1) hour, after noon on each day of delay due to such technical failure. IN ST LAKE RCP Rule 17(J).

 iii. *Documents allowed to be filed conventionally.* Unless specifically authorized by the court, only the following documents may be filed conventionally and not electronically:

 - Exhibits and other documents that cannot be converted to a legible electronic form, such as videotapes, x-rays, and similar materials

- Documents delivered to the clerk by pro se litigants
- Documents mailed to the clerk by pro se litigants
- Confidential documents
- Notice of manual filing
- Titles of documents
- Chronological case summary entry forms (CCS entry forms). IN ST LAKE RCP Rule 17(E).
- For more information on the documents which must be filed conventionally, refer to IN ST LAKE RCP Rule 17(E).

c. *Facsimile filing.* Only when necessary on an emergency basis (i.e., when certified mail or other means of filing will not bring the document to the Judge's attention prior to the scheduled hearing or ruling), pleadings, motions and other papers may be filed by electronic facsimile transmission, or when specifically authorized by the Court. IN ST LAKE RCP Rule 2(C).

   i. *Generally.* In counties where a majority of judges of the courts of record, by posted local rule, have authorized electronic facsimile filing and designated a telephone number to receive such transmissions, pleadings, motions, and other papers may be sent to the Clerk of Circuit Court by electronic facsimile transmission for filing in any case, provided:

   - Such matter does not exceed ten (10) pages, including the cover sheet;
   - Such matter does not require the payment of fees other than the electronic facsimile transcription fee set forth in IN ST ADMIN Rule 12(E);
   - The sending party creates at the time of transmission a machine generated log for such transmission; and
   - The original document and the transmission log are maintained by the sending party for the duration of the litigation. IN ST ADMIN Rule 12(B).

   ii. *Time of filing.* During normal, posted business hours, the time of filing shall be the time the duplicate document is produced in the office of the Clerk of the Circuit Court. Duplicate documents received at all other times shall be filed as of the next normal business day. IN ST ADMIN Rule 12(C).

   - If the receiving fax machine endorses its own time and date stamp upon the transmitted documents and the receiving machine produces a delivery receipt which is electronically created and transmitted to the sending party, the time of filing shall be the date and time recorded on the transmitted document by the receiving fax machine. IN ST ADMIN Rule 12(C).

d. *Filing for special judges.* For special judge matters where the special judge is a full-time judge or magistrate serving within Lake County, all papers submitted for filing shall be delivered or mailed to the Clerk's office at the courthouse where the special judge regularly serves. IN ST LAKE RCP Rule 3(A).

e. *Proof of filing.* Any party filing any paper by any method other than personal delivery to the clerk shall retain proof of filing. IN ST TRIAL P Rule 5(F).

2. *Service requirements.* Unless otherwise provided by the Indiana Rules of Trial Procedure or an order of the court, each party and special judge, if any, shall be served with: (1) every order required by its terms to be served; (2) every pleading subsequent to the original complaint; (3) every written motion except one which may be heard ex parte; (4) every brief submitted to the trial court; (5) every paper relating to discovery required to be served upon a party; and (6) every written notice, appearance, demand, offer of judgment, designation of record on appeal, or similar paper. IN ST TRIAL P Rule 5(A).

a. *Methods of service*

   i. *Personal service.* Whenever a party is represented by an attorney of record, service shall be made upon such attorney unless service upon the party himself is ordered by the court. Service

upon the attorney or party shall be made by delivering or mailing a copy of the papers to the last known address or where an attorney or party has consented to service by fax or e-mail, as provided in IN ST TRIAL P Rule 3.1(A)(4), by faxing or e-mailing a copy of the documents to the fax number or e-mail address set out in the appearance form or correction as required by IN ST TRIAL P Rule 3.1(E). IN ST TRIAL P Rule 5(B). Delivery of a copy within IN ST TRIAL P Rule 5 means:

- Offering or tendering it to the attorney or party and stating the nature of the papers being served. Refusal to accept an offered or tendered document is a waiver of any objection to the sufficiency or adequacy of service of that document;

- Leaving it at his office with a clerk or other person in charge thereof, or if there is no one in charge, leaving it in a conspicuous place therein; or

- If the office is closed, by leaving it at his dwelling house or usual place of abode with some person of suitable age and discretion then residing therein; or,

- Leaving it at some other suitable place, selected by the attorney upon whom service is being made, pursuant to duly promulgated local rule. IN ST TRIAL P Rule 5(B)(1).

ii. *Service by mail.* If service is made by mail, the papers shall be deposited in the United States mail addressed to the person on whom they are being served, with postage prepaid. Service shall be deemed complete upon mailing. Proof of service of all papers permitted to be mailed may be made by written acknowledgment of service, by affidavit of the person who mailed the papers, or by certificate of an attorney. It shall be the duty of attorneys when entering their appearance in a cause or when filing pleadings or papers therein, to have noted in the Chronological Case Summary or said pleadings or papers so filed the address and telephone number of their office. Service by delivery or by mail at such address shall be deemed sufficient and complete. IN ST TRIAL P Rule 5(B)(2).

iii. *Service by fax or e-mail.* A party who has consented to service by fax or e-mail may be served as follows:

- Service by e-mail shall be made by attaching the document being served in .pdf format. Discovery documents must also be served in accordance with IN ST TRIAL P Rule 26(A). IN ST TRIAL P Rule 5(B)(3)(a).

- Service by fax shall be deemed complete upon generation of a transmission record indicating the successful transmission of the entire document, except as provided in IN ST TRIAL P Rule 5(B)(3)(d). IN ST TRIAL P Rule 5(B)(3)(b).

- Service by e-mail shall be deemed complete upon transmission, except as provided in IN ST TRIAL P Rule 5(B)(3)(d). IN ST TRIAL P Rule 5(B)(3)(c).

- Service by fax or e-mail that occurs on a Saturday, Sunday, legal holiday, or day the court or agency in which the matter is pending is closed or after 5:00 PM local time of the recipient shall be deemed complete the next day that is not a Saturday, Sunday, legal holiday, or day that the court or agency in which the matter is pending is not closed. IN ST TRIAL P Rule 5(B)(3)(d).

b. *Serving numerous defendants.* In any action in which there are unusually large numbers of defendants, the court, upon motion or of its own initiative, may order:

i. That service of the pleadings of the defendants and replies thereto need not be made as between the defendants;

- That any cross-claim, counterclaim, or matter constituting an avoidance or affirmative defense contained therein shall be deemed to be denied or avoided by all other parties; and

- That the filing of any such pleading and service thereof upon the plaintiff constitutes due notice of it to the parties. IN ST TRIAL P Rule 5(D).

ii. A copy of every such order shall be served upon the parties in such manner and form as the court directs. IN ST TRIAL P Rule 5(D).

c. *Service by electronic means.* The Lake County Online Docket will generate a Notice of Electronic

Filing and Service when any document is filed and served. This notice will be emailed to each registered user of record in a case, and an electronic service event will be added to the work queue of each registered user of record in the case. The party filing the document should retain a paper or electronic copy of the Notice of Electronic Filing and Service. This notice represents proof of filing and service of the document on registered users of record in that case. The filer shall not be required to conventionally serve any document on any party receiving electronic service. IN ST LAKE RCP Rule 17(F)(2).

    i. The filer shall also conventionally serve those parties not designated or able to receive electronic notice or service but who are nevertheless entitled to notice of said pleading or other document in accordance with the Indiana Rules of Civil Procedure and applicable Lake County Rules of Civil Procedure. In such cases, the filer shall also file a certificate of service, as appropriate. IN ST LAKE RCP Rule 17(F).

d. *Service on parties in default for failure to appear.* No service need be made on parties in default for failure to appear, except that pleadings asserting new or additional claims for relief against them shall be served upon them in the manner provided by service of summons in IN ST TRIAL P Rule 4. IN ST TRIAL P Rule 5(A).

G. Hearings

1. The Indiana rules do not contemplate a hearing related to the pretrial conference.

H. Forms

1. Pretrial Conference, Scheduling, Management Forms for Indiana

a. Motion for pretrial conference. 5 INPRAC § 5:1.1.
b. Order for pretrial conference; Attorneys to hold preliminary conference. 5 INPRAC § 5:1.2.
c. Letter; To arrange preliminary conference of attorneys. 5 INPRAC § 5:1.3.
d. Letter; Documenting opposing counsel's failure to meet. 5 INPRAC § 5:1.4.
e. Letter; Request to stipulate to facts and exhibits. 5 INPRAC § 5:1.5.
f. Notice to court; Failure to stipulate. 5 INPRAC § 5:1.6.
g. Agenda; Pretrial conference. 5 INPRAC § 5:1.7.
h. Agenda for pretrial conference; Alternative. 5 INPRAC § 5:1.8.
i. Preliminary pretrial order. 5 INPRAC § 5:1.9.
j. Final pretrial order. 5 INPRAC § 5:1.10.
k. Motion to amend pretrial order. 5 INPRAC § 5:1.11.
l. Motion to extend discovery cutoff date. 5 INPRAC § 5:1.12.
m. Motion for pretrial conference. 10 INPRAC § 70.2.
n. Joint motion for pretrial conference. 10 INPRAC § 70.3.
o. Order for pretrial conference; Attorneys to hold preliminary conference. 10 INPRAC § 70.4.
p. Worksheet for preliminary conference of attorneys and pretrial conference. 10 INPRAC § 70.5.
q. Joint motion for continuance of pretrial conference. 10 INPRAC § 70.6.
r. Letter attempting to arrange preliminary conference of attorneys. 10 INPRAC § 70.7.
s. Notice of conference of attorneys. 10 INPRAC § 70.8.
t. Letter documenting opposing counsel's failure to meet for preliminary conference of attorneys. 10 INPRAC § 70.9.
u. Request that opposing party stipulate to facts and exhibits discovered after conference of attorneys. 10 INPRAC § 70.10.
v. Preliminary pretrial order. 10 INPRAC § 70.14.
w. Final pretrial order. 10 INPRAC § 70.15.

  x. Motion to amend pretrial order; General form. 10 INPRAC § 70.16.

  y. Motion to amend pretrial order; Party's contentions. 10 INPRAC § 70.17.

  z. Motion for sanctions; Failure to attend pretrial conference. 10 INPRAC § 70.22.

2. Official Pretrial Conference, Scheduling, Management Forms for Lake County

  a. CCS entry form. IN ST LAKE RCP App. A.

  b. Notice of manual filing. IN ST LAKE RCP Form 2.

  c. Certificate of service. IN ST LAKE RCP Form 3.

  d. Declaration that party was unable to file in a timely manner. IN ST LAKE RCP Form 4.

3. Pretrial Conference, Scheduling, Management Forms for Lake County

  a. Notice of manual filing. EFORMST IN 5540.

I. Checklist

 (I) ❑ Matters to be considered for the pretrial conference

  (a) ❑ Documents to consider

   (1) ❑ Exhibits and stipulations

  (b) ❑ Timing

   (1) ❑ Unless otherwise ordered by the court the pretrial conference shall not be called until after reasonable opportunity for the completion of discovery

   (2) ❑ The clerks shall give at least thirty (30) days' notice of the pretrial conference unless otherwise directed by the court

   (3) ❑ Unless otherwise ordered by the court, at least ten (10) days prior to the pretrial conference, attorneys for each of the parties shall meet and confer

 (II) ❑ Matters to be considered by the party filing the motion for pretrial conference

  (a) ❑ Required documents

   (1) ❑ Motion and notice

   (2) ❑ Brief

   (3) ❑ Proposed order

   (4) ❑ Chronological case summary

   (5) ❑ Certificate of service

  (b) ❑ Supplemental documents

   (1) ❑ Supporting evidence

   (2) ❑ Facsimile cover sheet

  (c) ❑ Timing

   (1) ❑ There is no specific timing requirement for filing a motion requesting a pretrial conference

   (2) ❑ A written motion, other than one which may be heard ex parte, and notice of the hearing thereof shall be served not less than five (5) days before the time specified for the hearing, unless a different period is fixed by the Indiana Rules of Trial Procedure or by order of the court

   (3) ❑ All pleadings and papers subsequent to the complaint which are required to be served upon a party shall be filed with the Court either before service or within a reasonable period of time thereafter

   (4) ❑ All pleadings, motions and other papers submitted for filing which are required to be served under IN ST TRIAL P Rule 5(A) shall be filed no later than three (3) days after service

   (5) ❑ If such papers are filed before service, proof of service thereof shall be filed no later than three (3) business days thereafter

MARION COUNTY

Pleadings
Complaint

Document Last Updated October 2013

A. Applicable Rules

1. *State rules*

   a. Commencement of an action. IN ST TRIAL P Rule 3.

   b. Appearance. IN ST TRIAL P Rule 3.1.

   c. Process. IN ST TRIAL P Rule 4.

   d. Service. IN ST TRIAL P Rule 4.1; IN ST TRIAL P Rule 4.2; IN ST TRIAL P Rule 4.3; IN ST TRIAL P Rule 4.4; IN ST TRIAL P Rule 4.5; IN ST TRIAL P Rule 4.6; IN ST TRIAL P Rule 4.7; IN ST TRIAL P Rule 4.8; IN ST TRIAL P Rule 4.9; IN ST TRIAL P Rule 4.10; IN ST TRIAL P Rule 4.11; IN ST TRIAL P Rule 4.12; IN ST TRIAL P Rule 4.13; IN ST TRIAL P Rule 4.14; IN ST TRIAL P Rule 4.15; IN ST TRIAL P Rule 5.

   e. Time. IN ST TRIAL P Rule 6.

   f. Pleadings allowed; Form of motion. IN ST TRIAL P Rule 7.

   g. Rules of pleading. IN ST TRIAL P Rule 8; IN ST TRIAL P Rule 9; IN ST TRIAL P Rule 9.1; IN ST TRIAL P Rule 9.2.

   h. Form of pleading. IN ST TRIAL P Rule 10.

   i. Signing and verification of pleadings. IN ST TRIAL P Rule 11.

   j. Joinder. IN ST TRIAL P Rule 18; IN ST TRIAL P Rule 19.

   k. Jury trial of right. IN ST TRIAL P Rule 38.

   l. Evidence. IN ST TRIAL P Rule 43.

   m. Determination of foreign law. IN ST TRIAL P Rule 44.1.

   n. Judgment on the evidence (directed verdict). IN ST TRIAL P Rule 50.

   o. Findings by the court. IN ST TRIAL P Rule 52.

   p. Summary judgment. IN ST TRIAL P Rule 56.

   q. Motion to correct error. IN ST TRIAL P Rule 59.

   r. Relief from judgment or order. IN ST TRIAL P Rule 60.

   s. Trial court and clerks. IN ST TRIAL P Rule 72.

   t. Uniform case numbering system. IN ST ADMIN Rule 8.

   u. Access to court records. IN ST ADMIN Rule 9.

   v. Paper size. IN ST ADMIN Rule 11.

   w. Facsimile and electronic transmission. IN ST ADMIN Rule 12; IN ST ADMIN Rule 16.

   x. Alternative dispute resolution. IN ST ADR Rule 1.1; IN ST ADR Rule 1.6; IN ST ADR Rule 2.1; IN ST ADR Rule 2.11; IN ST ADR Rule 8.8.

   y. Manner of service. IN ST 34-33-2-1.

   z. Sealing of certain records by court; Hearing; Notice; Privacy and confidentiality. IN ST 5-2-9-6; IN ST 5-14-3-4; IN ST 5-14-3-5.5; IN ST 6-4.1-5-10; IN ST 6-4.1-12-12; IN ST 6-8.1-7-1; IN ST 11-13-1-8; IN ST 12-23-14-13; IN ST 16-39-3-10; IN ST 16-41-8-1; IN ST 22-4-19-6; IN ST

31-11-1-6; IN ST 31-19-5-23; IN ST 31-19-13-2; IN ST 31-19-19-1; IN ST 31-33-18-1; IN ST 31-39-1-1; IN ST 31-39-1-2; IN ST 33-23-16-16; IN ST 35-34-2-4; IN ST 35-38-1-13; IN ST 35-38-9-1; IN ST ADR Rule 2.11; IN ST ADR Rule 4.4; IN ST ADR Rule 5.6; IN ST JURY Rule 10.

2. *Local rules*

   a. Requirements for motions. IN ST MARION CIR AND SUPER CTS CIV Rule 203.

   b. Preparation of pleadings, motions and other papers. IN ST MARION CIR AND SUPER CTS CIV Rule 204.

   c. Filing of pleadings, motions and other papers. IN ST MARION CIR AND SUPER CTS CIV Rule 205.

   d. Alternative dispute resolution; Mediation procedure. IN ST MARION CIR AND SUPER CTS CIV Rule 209.

   e. Motions for continuance. IN ST MARION CIR AND SUPER CTS CIV Rule 215.

   f. Electronic filing. IN ST MARION SUPER CT ADMIN Rule 311.

B. Timing

1. *Filing.* A civil action is commenced by filing with the court a complaint or such equivalent pleading or document as may be specified by statute, by payment of the prescribed filing fee or filing an order waiving the filing fee, and, where service of process is required, by furnishing to the clerk as many copies of the complaint and summons as are necessary. IN ST TRIAL P Rule 3. The claimant typically bears the burden of commencing an action within the applicable statute of limitations. 22B INPRAC 3:1; Huff v. Huff, 892 N.E.2d 1241 (Ind.Ct.App. 2008).

2. *Service.* The trial rules require a party to exercise due diligence in securing service of process. 1 INPRAC R 4; Geiger and Peters, Inc. v. American Fletcher Nat. Bank & Trust Co., 428 N.E.2d 1279 (Ind.Ct.App. 1981). If person seeking service of process fails without cause for sixty (60) days or more to provide clerk with required summons for issuance or with other information necessary to effectuate service, person has failed to exercise due diligence in securing service of process. Geiger and Peters, Inc. v. American Fletcher Nat. Bank & Trust Co., 428 N.E.2d 1279, 1281 (Ind.Ct.App. 1981).

3. *Computation of time*

   a. *Generally; Days excluded.* In computing any period of time prescribed or allowed by the Indiana Rules of Trial Procedure, by order of the court, or by any applicable statute, the day of the act, event, or default from which the designated period of time begins to run shall not be included. The last day of the period so computed is to be included unless it is:

      i. A Saturday,

      ii. A Sunday,

      iii. A legal holiday as defined by state statute, or

      iv. A day the office in which the act is to be done is closed during regular business hours. IN ST TRIAL P Rule 6(A).

   b. *Short periods.* In any event, the period runs until the end of the next day that is not a Saturday, a Sunday, a legal holiday, or a day on which the office is closed. When the period of time allowed is less than seven (7) days, intermediate Saturdays, Sundays, legal holidays, and days on which the office is closed shall be excluded from the computations. IN ST TRIAL P Rule 6(A).

   c. *Additional time after service by United States mail.* Whenever a party has the right or is required to do some act or take some proceedings within a prescribed period after the service of a notice or other paper upon him and the notice or paper is served upon him by United States mail, three (3) days shall be added to the prescribed period. IN ST TRIAL P Rule 6(E).

   d. *Enlargement of time.* When an act is required or allowed to be done at or within a specific time by the Indiana Rules of Trial Procedure, the court may at any time for cause shown:

      i. Order the period enlarged, with or without motion or notice, if request therefor is made before the expiration of the period originally prescribed or extended by a previous order; or

ii. Upon motion made after the expiration of the specific period, permit the act to be done where the failure to act was the result of excusable neglect; but, the court may not extend the time for taking any action for judgment on the evidence under IN ST TRIAL P Rule 50(A), amendment of findings and judgment under IN ST TRIAL P Rule 52(B), to correct errors under IN ST TRIAL P Rule 59(C), statement in opposition to motion to correct error under IN ST TRIAL P Rule 59(E), or to obtain relief from final judgment under IN ST TRIAL P Rule 60(B), except to the extent and under the conditions stated in those rules. IN ST TRIAL P Rule 6(B).

iii. Initial written motion for enlargement of time pursuant to IN ST TRIAL P Rule 6(B)(1) to respond to a claim shall be automatically allowed for an additional thirty (30) days from the original due date without a written order of the Court. Any motion filed pursuant to IN ST MARION CIR AND SUPER CTS CIV Rule 203 shall state the date when such a response is due and the date to which time is enlarged. The motion must be filed on or before the original due date or IN ST MARION CIR AND SUPER CTS CIV Rule 203 shall be inapplicable. All subsequent Motions shall be so designated and will be granted only for good cause shown. IN ST MARION CIR AND SUPER CTS CIV Rule 203(D).

e. *Continuances disfavored.* Motions for Continuance are discouraged. Neither side is entitled to an automatic continuance as a matter of right. IN ST MARION CIR AND SUPER CTS CIV Rule 215. For information on obtaining a continuance, refer to IN ST MARION CIR AND SUPER CTS CIV Rule 215.

C. General Requirements

1. *Pleading, generally*

   a. *Pleadings to be concise.* Each averment of a pleading shall be simple, concise, and direct. No technical forms of pleading or motions are required. All fictions in pleading are abolished. IN ST TRIAL P Rule 8(E)(1).

   b. *Pleading in the alternative.* A pleading may set forth two (2) or more statements of a claim or defense alternatively or hypothetically, either in one (1) count or defense or in separate counts or defenses. When two (2) or more statements are made in the alternative and one (1) of them if made independently would be sufficient, the pleading is not made insufficient by the insufficiency of one or more of the alternative statements. A pleading may also state as many separate claims or defenses as the pleader has regardless of consistency and whether based on legal or equitable grounds. All statements shall be made subject to the obligations set forth in IN ST TRIAL P Rule 11. IN ST TRIAL P Rule 8(E)(2).

   c. *Motions and pleadings, joint and several.* All motions and pleadings of any kind addressed to two (2) or more paragraphs of any pleading, or filed by two (2) or more parties, shall be taken and construed as joint, separate, and several motions or pleadings to each of such paragraphs and by and against each of such parties. All motions or pleadings containing two (2) or more subject-matters shall be taken and construed as separate and several as to each subject-matter. All objections to rulings made by two (2) or more parties shall be taken and construed as the joint, separate, and several objections of each of such parties. IN ST TRIAL P Rule 8(E)(3).

      i. A complaint filed by or against two (2) or more plaintiffs shall be taken and construed as joint, separate, and several as to each of said plaintiffs. IN ST TRIAL P Rule 8(E).

   d. *Construction of pleadings.* All pleadings shall be so construed as to do substantial justice, lead to disposition on the merits, and avoid litigation of procedural points. IN ST TRIAL P Rule 8(F).

2. *Contents of the complaint*

   a. *Pleading for relief; Notice pleading.* Indiana is a "notice pleading" jurisdiction. 22B INPRAC 8:1; State v. American Family Voices, Inc., 898 N.E.2d 293 (Ind. 2008). Notice pleading replaces the technical and complex method of pleading which existed prior to 1970. Notice pleading is grounded in due process of law and must provide a defendant with reasonable notice of the plaintiff's claim or an opponent's defense. 22B INPRAC 8:1; Noblesville Redevelopment Com'n v. Noblesville Associates Ltd. Partnership, 674 N.E.2d 558 (Ind. 1996). Notice pleading does not require that the plaintiff state all elements or facts essential to a cause of action. 22B INPRAC 8:1; State v. American

Family Voices, Inc., 898 N.E.2d 293 (Ind. 2008). Instead, the complaint must state "a short and plain statement of the claim" showing an entitlement to relief, and a demand for relief. 22B INPRAC 8:1; Trail v. Boys and Girls Clubs of Northwest Indiana, 845 N.E.2d 130 (Ind. 2006).

b. *Claims for relief.* To state a claim for relief, whether an original claim, counterclaim, cross-claim, or third-party claim, a pleading must contain:

    i. A short and plain statement of the claim showing that the pleader is entitled to relief, and

    ii. A demand for relief to which the pleader deems entitled. Relief in the alternative or of several different types may be demanded. However, in any complaint seeking damages for personal injury or death, or seeking punitive damages, no dollar amount or figure shall be included in the demand. IN ST TRIAL P Rule 8(A).

c. *Res ipsa loquitur.* Res ipsa loquitur or a similar doctrine may be pleaded by alleging generally that the facts connected with the action are unknown to the pleader and are within the knowledge of the opposing party. IN ST TRIAL P Rule 9.1(B).

d. *Bona fide purchaser.* When the rights of a person depend upon his status as a bona fide purchaser for value or upon similar requirements, such status must be pleaded and proved by the person asserting it, but it may be pleaded in general terms. Once it is established that the person has given any required value, unless such value is commercially unreasonable, and that he has met any requirements of recordation, filing, possession, or perfection, the trier of fact must find that such value was given or such perfection was made in accordance with any requirements of good faith, lack of knowledge, or lack of notice unless and until evidence is introduced which would support a finding of its non-existence. IN ST TRIAL P Rule 9.1(D).

e. *Presumption; Matters of judicial notice.* Neither presumptions of law nor matters of which judicial notice may be taken need be stated in a pleading. IN ST TRIAL P Rule 9.1(E).

    i. *Presumption of jurisdiction.* Jurisdiction is presumed in Indiana. 22B INPRAC 8:2. Consequently, there is no requirement to affirmatively plead the existence of jurisdiction in the complaint, unless the action involves a special proceeding requiring such an allegation. 22B INPRAC 8:2; Cardinal Industries, Inc. v. Schwartz, 483 N.E.2d 458 (Ind.Ct.App. 1985). The plaintiff bears no burden to prove jurisdiction unless and until it is challenged by the defendant. 22B INPRAC 8:2; Brokemond v. Marshall Field & Co., 612 N.E.2d 143 (Ind.Ct.App. 1993).

f. *Equitable and legal claims in multi-count actions.* In multi-count actions, the inclusion of an equitable claim, standing alone, will not automatically draw the entire action into equity. Something more than the presence of an equitable claim is required, and the court must examine the claims at issue. 22B INPRAC 38:1 COMMENT; Lucas v. U.S. Bank, N.A., 953 N.E.2d 457 (Ind. 2011). Factors the court may consider in evaluating the nature of the underlying substantive claims include: the substance and central character of the complaint, the rights and interests at issue, the relief demanded, and any issues arising out of discovery. 22B INPRAC 38:1 COMMENT; Songer v. Civitas Bank, 771 N.E.2d 61 (Ind. 2002).

3. *Pleading special matters*

a. *Capacity.* It is not necessary to aver the capacity of a party to sue or be sued, the authority of a party to sue or be sued in a representative capacity, or the legal existence of an organization that is made a party. The burden of proving lack of such capacity, authority, or legal existence shall be upon the person asserting lack of it, and shall be pleaded as an affirmative defense. IN ST TRIAL P Rule 9(A).

b. *Fraud, mistake, condition of the mind.* In all averments of fraud or mistake, the circumstances constituting fraud or mistake shall be specifically averred. Malice, intent, knowledge, and other conditions of mind may be averred generally. IN ST TRIAL P Rule 9(B).

c. *Conditions precedent.* In pleading the performance or occurrence of promissory or non-promissory conditions precedent, it is sufficient to aver generally that all conditions precedent have been performed, have occurred, or have been excused. A denial of performance or occurrence shall be made specifically and with particularity, and a denial of excuse generally. IN ST TRIAL P Rule 9(C).

d. *Official document or act.* In pleading an official document or official act it is sufficient to aver that the document was issued or the act done in compliance with law. IN ST TRIAL P Rule 9(D).

e. *Judgment.* In pleading a judgment or decision of a domestic or foreign court, judicial or quasi-judicial tribunal, or of a board or officer, it is sufficient to aver the judgment or decision without setting forth matter showing jurisdiction to render it. IN ST TRIAL P Rule 9(E).

f. *Time and place.* For the purpose of testing the sufficiency of a pleading, averments of time and place are material and shall be considered like all other averments of material matter. However, time and place need be stated only with such specificity as will enable the opposing party to prepare his defense. IN ST TRIAL P Rule 9(F).

g. *Special damages; Damages where no answer.* When items of special damage are claimed, they shall be specifically stated. The relief granted to the plaintiff, if there be no answer, cannot exceed the relief demanded in his complaint; but, in any other case, the court may grant him any relief consistent with the facts or matters pleaded. IN ST TRIAL P Rule 9(G).

4. *Joinder*

   a. *Of claims.* A party asserting a claim for relief as an original claim, counterclaim, cross-claim, or third-party claim, may join, either as independent or as alternate claims, as many claims, whether legal, equitable, or statutory as he has against an opposing party. IN ST TRIAL P Rule 18(A).

   b. *Of remedies; Fraudulent conveyances.* Whenever a claim is one heretofore cognizable only after another claim has been prosecuted to a conclusion, the two (2) claims may be joined in a single action; but the court shall grant relief in that action only in accordance with the relative substantive rights of the parties. In particular, a plaintiff may state a claim for money and a claim to have set aside a conveyance fraudulent as to him, without first having obtained a judgment establishing the claim for money. IN ST TRIAL P Rule 18(B).

   c. *Of persons needed for just adjudication.* A person who is subject to service of process shall be joined as a party in the action if:

      i. In his absence complete relief cannot be accorded among those already parties; or

      ii. He claims an interest relating to the subject of the action and is so situated that the disposition of the action in his absence may:

         • As a practical matter impair or impede his ability to protect that interest, or

         • Leave any of the persons already parties subject to a substantial risk of incurring double, multiple, or otherwise inconsistent obligations by reason of his claimed interest. IN ST TRIAL P Rule 19(A).

      iii. If he has not been so joined, the court shall order that he be made a party. If he should join as a plaintiff but refuses to do so, he may be made a defendant. IN ST TRIAL P Rule 19(A).

5. *Trial by jury; Demand*

   a. *Causes triable by court and by jury.* Issues of law and issues of fact in causes that prior to the eighteenth day of June, 1852, were of exclusive equitable jurisdiction shall be tried by the court; issues of fact in all other causes shall be triable as the same are now triable. In case of the joinder of causes of action or defenses which, prior to said date, were of exclusive equitable jurisdiction with causes of action or defenses which, prior to said date, were designated as actions at law and triable by jury—the former shall be triable by the court, and the latter by a jury, unless waived; the trial of both may be at the same time or at different times, as the court may direct. IN ST TRIAL P Rule 38(A).

   b. *Demand.* Any party may demand a trial by jury of any issue triable of right by a jury by filing with the court and serving upon the other parties a demand therefor in writing at any time after the commencement of the action and not later than ten (10) days after the first responsive pleading to the complaint, or to a counterclaim, crossclaim or other claim if one properly is pleaded; and if no responsive pleading is filed or required, within ten (10) days after the time such pleading otherwise would have been required. Such demand is sufficient if indorsed upon a pleading of a party filed within such time. IN ST TRIAL P Rule 38(B).

   c. *Same; Specification of issues.* In his demand a party may specify the issues which he wishes so tried;

otherwise he shall be deemed to have demanded trial by jury for all issues triable as of right by jury. Any other party must file a demand for jury trial to preserve his right to trial by jury:

    i.   Of issues for which a right to trial by jury was not requested by another party; and

    ii. In case a request by another party was improper. But if a proper request for a trial by jury upon issues triable by jury as of right on his behalf is made by any party, such request shall be deemed to have been made on behalf of all parties entitled to a jury trial upon such issues. IN ST TRIAL P Rule 38(C).

d. *Waiver.* The failure of a party to appear at the trial, and the failure of a party to serve a demand as required by IN ST TRIAL P Rule 38 and to file it as required by IN ST TRIAL P Rule 5(E) constitute waiver by him of trial by jury. A demand for trial by jury made as provided in IN ST TRIAL P Rule 38 may not be withdrawn without the consent of the other party or parties. IN ST TRIAL P Rule 38(D).

    i.   The trial court shall not grant a demand for a trial by jury filed after the time fixed in IN ST TRIAL P Rule 38(B) has elapsed except upon the written agreement of all of the parties to the action, which agreement shall be filed with the court and made a part of the record. If such agreement is filed then the court may, in its discretion, grant a trial by jury in which event the grant of a trial by jury may not be withdrawn except by the agreement of all of the parties. IN ST TRIAL P Rule 38(D).

e. *Arbitration.* Nothing in the Indiana Rules of Trial Procedure shall deny the parties the right by contract or agreement to submit or to agree to submit controversies to arbitration made before or after commencement of an action thereon or deny the courts power to specifically enforce such agreements. IN ST TRIAL P Rule 38(E).

f. *Equitable and legal claims in multi-count actions.* In multi-count actions, the inclusion of an equitable claim, standing alone, will not automatically draw the entire action into equity. Something more than the presence of an equitable claim is required, and the court must examine the claims at issue. 22B INPRAC 38:1 COMMENT; Lucas v. U.S. Bank, N.A., 953 N.E.2d 457 (Ind. 2011). Factors the court may consider in evaluating the nature of the underlying substantive claims include: the substance and central character of the complaint, the rights and interests at issue, the relief demanded, and any issues arising out of discovery. 22B INPRAC 38:1 COMMENT; Songer v. Civitas Bank, 771 N.E.2d 61 (Ind. 2002).

6. *Use of alternative dispute resolution.* Except as provided by the Indiana Rules for Alternative Dispute Resolution, a presiding judge may order any civil or domestic relations proceeding or selected issues in such proceedings referred to mediation, non-binding arbitration or mini-trial. The selection criteria which should be used by the court are defined under the Indiana Rules for Alternative Dispute Resolution. Binding arbitration and a summary jury trial may be ordered only upon the agreement of the parties as consistent with provisions in the Indiana Rules for Alternative Dispute Resolution which address each method. IN ST ADR Rule 1.6. For information on Indiana's ADR process refer to IN ST ADR Rule 1.1 through IN ST ADR Rule 8.8.

a. *Mandatory alternative dispute resolution.* All cases where a timely demand for jury trial is made, mediation pursuant to A.D.R. Rule 2 (IN ST ADR Rule 2.1 through IN ST ADR Rule 2.11) and IN ST MARION CIR AND SUPER CTS CIV Rule 209(A) is mandatory. IN ST MARION CIR AND SUPER CTS CIV Rule 209. For more information on mandatory alternative dispute resolution, refer to IN ST ADR Rule 2.1 through IN ST ADR Rule 2.11 and IN ST MARION CIR AND SUPER CTS CIV Rule 209.

D. Documents

1. *Required documents*

a. *Summons.* Contemporaneously with the filing of the complaint or equivalent pleading, the person seeking service or his attorney shall furnish to the clerk as many copies of the complaint and summons as are necessary. IN ST TRIAL P Rule 4(B).

b. *Complaint.* Refer to the General Requirements section of this document for information on the contents of a complaint.

c. *Appearance form.* Pursuant to IN ST TRIAL P Rule 3.1(A), an appearance form shall be filed by the initiating party at the time an action commenced. If the action is appropriate for filing and disposition in Marion Superior Court, Environmental Division, per Order of the Executive Committee of the Marion Superior Court, then the initiating party shall indicate such on the appearance form. IN ST MARION CIR AND SUPER CTS CIV Rule 205(E). At the time an action is commenced, the party initiating the proceeding shall file with the clerk of the court an appearance form setting forth the following information:

   i. Name, address and telephone number of the initiating party or parties filing the appearance form;

   ii. Name, address, attorney number, telephone number, FAX number, and e-mail address of any attorney representing the party, as applicable;

   iii. The case type of the proceeding [see IN ST ADMIN Rule 8];

   iv. A statement that the party will or will not accept service by fax or by e-mail from:
   - Other parties and/or
   - The court under IN ST TRIAL P Rule 72(D);

   v. In domestic relations, Uniform Reciprocal Enforcement of Support (URESA), paternity, delinquency, Child in Need of Services (CHINS), guardianship, and any other proceedings in which support may be an issue, the Social Security Identification Number of all family members;

   vi. The caption and case number of all related cases;

   vii. Such additional matters specified by state or local rule required to maintain the information management system employed by the court;

   viii. In a proceeding involving a protection from abuse order, a workplace violence restraining order, or a no-contact order, the initiating party shall provide to the clerk a public mailing address for purposes of legal service. The initiating party may use the Attorney General Address Confidentiality program established by statute; and

   ix. In a proceeding involving a mental health commitment, except seventy-two (72) hour emergency detentions, the initiating party shall provide the full name of the person with respect to whom commitment is sought and the person's state of residence. In addition, the initiating party shall provide at least one of the following identifiers for the person:
   - Date of birth;
   - Social Security Number;
   - Driver's license number with state of issue and date of expiration;
   - Department of Correction number;
   - State ID number with state of issue and date of expiration; or
   - FBI number. IN ST TRIAL P Rule 3.1.

2. *Supplemental documents*

   a. *Proof of written instrument.* When any pleading allowed by the Indiana Rules of Trial Procedure is founded on a written instrument, the original, or a copy thereof, must be included in or filed with the pleading. Such instrument, whether copied in the pleadings or not, shall be taken as part of the record. When any pleading allowed by the Indiana Rules of Trial Procedure is founded on an account, an Affidavit of Debt, in a form substantially similar to that which is provided in IN ST TRIAL P App. A-2, shall be attached. IN ST TRIAL P Rule 9.2(A).

   b. *Notice of intent to use foreign law.* A party who intends to raise an issue concerning the law of a foreign country shall give notice in his pleadings or other reasonable written notice. The court, in determining foreign law, may consider any relevant material or source, including testimony, whether or not submitted by a party or admissible under IN ST TRIAL P Rule 43. The court's determination shall be treated as a ruling on a question of law. It shall be made by the court and not the jury and shall be reviewable. IN ST TRIAL P Rule 44.1(A).

c. *Praecipe.* Affidavits, requests, and any other information relating to the summons and its service as required or permitted by the Indiana Rules of Trial Procedure shall be included in a praecipe attached to or entered upon the summons. Such praecipe shall be deemed to be a part of the summons for purposes of the Indiana Rules of Trial Procedure. Separate or additional summons shall, as provided by the Indiana Rules of Trial Procedure, be issued by the clerk at any time upon proper request of the person seeking service or his attorney. IN ST TRIAL P Rule 4(B).

d. *Facsimile cover sheet.* Any document sent to the Clerk of the Circuit Court by electronic facsimile transmission shall be accompanied by a cover sheet which states the title of the document, case number, number of pages, identity and voice telephone number of the sending party and instructions for filing. The cover sheet shall contain the signature of the attorney or party, pro se, authorizing the filing. IN ST ADMIN Rule 12(D).

E. Format

1. *Form of pleadings*

   a. *Caption; Names of parties.* Every pleading shall contain a caption setting forth the name of the court, the title of the action, the file number, and a designation as in IN ST TRIAL P Rule 7(A). In the complaint the title of the action shall include the names of all the parties, but in other pleadings it is sufficient to state the name of the first party on each side with an appropriate indication of other parties. IN ST TRIAL P Rule 10(A).

      i. Every pleading shall contain a caption setting forth the name of the Court, the Division and Room Number, the title of the action and the file number. IN ST MARION CIR AND SUPER CTS CIV Rule 204(B).

   b. *Paragraphs; Separate statements.* All averments of a claim or defense shall be made in numbered paragraphs, the contents of each of which shall be limited as far as practicable to a statement of a single set of circumstances, and a paragraph may be referred to by number in all succeeding pleadings. Each claim founded upon a separate transaction or occurrence and each defense other than denials may be stated in a separate count or defense whenever a separation facilitates the clear presentation of the matters set forth. IN ST TRIAL P Rule 10(B).

   c. *Adoption by reference; Exhibits.* Statements in a pleading may be adopted by reference in a different part of the same pleading or in another pleading or in any motion. A copy of any written instrument which is an exhibit to a pleading is a part thereof for all purposes. IN ST TRIAL P Rule 10(C).

   d. *Paper.* Pleadings, motions and other papers may be either printed or typewritten on white opaque paper of at least sixteen (16) pound weight, eight and one-half (8-1/2) inches wide and eleven (11) inches in length. IN ST MARION CIR AND SUPER CTS CIV Rule 204(A).

   e. *Copies.* All copies shall likewise be on white paper of sufficient strength and durability to resist normal wear and tear. IN ST MARION CIR AND SUPER CTS CIV Rule 204(A).

   f. *Line spacing.* If typewritten, the lines shall be double spaced, except for quotations, which shall be indented and single spaced. IN ST MARION CIR AND SUPER CTS CIV Rule 204(A).

   g. *Script type.* Script type shall not be used. IN ST MARION CIR AND SUPER CTS CIV Rule 204(A).

   h. *Titles.* Titles on all pleadings shall delineate each topic included in the pleading e.g. where a pleading contains an Answer, a Motion to Strike or Dismiss, or a Jury Request each shall be set forth in the title. IN ST MARION CIR AND SUPER CTS CIV Rule 204(C).

   i. *Margins and binding.* Margins shall be one (1) inch. Binding or stapling shall be at the top and at no other place. Covers or backing shall not be used. IN ST MARION CIR AND SUPER CTS CIV Rule 204(D).

2. *Size of papers for filing.* Effective January 1, 1992, all pleadings, copies, motions and documents filed with any trial court or appellate level court, typed or printed, with the exception of exhibits and existing wills, shall be prepared on eight and one-half by eleven inch (8 1/2" x 11") size paper. IN ST ADMIN Rule 11.

3. *Form of electronically filed documents.* All electronically filed and served pleadings shall, to the extent

practicable, be formatted in accordance with the applicable rules governing formatting of paper pleadings. IN ST MARION SUPER CT ADMIN Rule 311(2-103)(1).

    a. *Electronic document title.* The electronic document title of each pleading or other document shall include:

        i. Party or parties filing/serving the document,

        ii. Nature of the document,

        iii. Party or parties against whom relief, if any, is sought, and

        iv. Nature of the relief sought (e.g., Defendant ABC Corporation's Motion for Summary Judgment). IN ST MARION SUPER CT ADMIN Rule 311(2-103)(2).

4. *Signature requirements*

    a. *Signature of attorney.* Every pleading or motion of a party represented by an attorney shall be signed by at least one (1) attorney of record in his individual name, whose address, telephone number, and attorney number shall be stated, except that this provision shall not apply to pleadings and motions made and transcribed at the trial or a hearing before the judge and received by him in such form. IN ST TRIAL P Rule 11(A).

        i. All pleadings and motions shall contain the original or authorized signature of the attorney, the name of the attorney in typed or printed form, the name of the law firm if a member of a firm, the attorney's address, identification number, e-mail address, telephone number, fax number, and the designation as to the party for whom he appears. IN ST MARION CIR AND SUPER CTS CIV Rule 204(E).

        ii. The signature of an attorney constitutes a certificate by him that he has read the pleadings; that to the best of his knowledge, information, and belief, there is good ground to support it; and that it is not interposed for delay. IN ST TRIAL P Rule 11(A).

        iii. If a pleading or motion is not signed or is signed with intent to defeat the purpose of the rule, it may be stricken as sham and false and the action may proceed as though the pleading had not been served. IN ST TRIAL P Rule 11(A).

        iv. For a willful violation of IN ST TRIAL P Rule 11 an attorney may be subjected to appropriate disciplinary action. Similar action may be taken if scandalous or indecent matter is inserted. IN ST TRIAL P Rule 11(A).

        v. Every pleading, document, and instrument electronically filed or served shall be deemed to have been signed by the judge, clerk, attorney or declarant and shall bear a facsimile or typographical signature of such person, along with the typed name, address, telephone number, and Bar number of a signing attorney. Typographical signatures shall be treated as personal signatures for all purposes under these rules. IN ST MARION SUPER CT ADMIN Rule 311(2-105).

            • Documents containing signatures of third-parties (i.e., unopposed motions, affidavits, stipulations, etc.) may also be filed electronically by indicating that the original signatures are maintained by the filing party in paper-format. IN ST MARION SUPER CT ADMIN Rule 311(2-105).

            • Unless otherwise ordered by the Court or Clerk, a printed copy of all documents filed or served electronically, including original signatures, shall be maintained by the party filing the document and shall be made available, upon reasonable notice, for inspection by other counsel, the Clerk or Court. Parties shall retain originals until two (2) years after all time periods for appeal have expired. From time to time, it may be necessary to provide the Clerk or Court with a hard copy of an electronically filed document. IN ST MARION SUPER CT ADMIN Rule 311(2-105).

        vi. For the recommended format of a signature block, refer to IN ST MARION CIR AND SUPER CTS CIV Rule 204(E).

    b. *Signature of unrepresented party.* A party who is not represented by an attorney shall sign his pleading and state his address. IN ST TRIAL P Rule 11(A).

c. *Verification not generally required.* Except when specifically required by rule, pleadings or motions need not be verified or accompanied by affidavit. The rule in equity that the averments of an answer under oath must be overcome by the testimony of two (2) witnesses or of one (1) witness sustained by corroborating circumstances is abolished. IN ST TRIAL P Rule 11(A).

d. *Verification by affirmation or representation.* When in connection with any civil or special statutory proceeding it is required that any pleading, motion, petition, supporting affidavit, or other document of any kind, be verified, or that an oath be taken, it shall be sufficient if the subscriber simply affirms the truth of the matter to be verified by an affirmation or representation. IN ST TRIAL P Rule 11(B). IN ST TRIAL P Rule 11(B) states that the affirmation or representation should be in substantially the following language: "I (we) affirm, under the penalties for perjury, that the foregoing representation(s) is (are) true. (Signed) _____."

  i. Any person who falsifies an affirmation or representation of fact shall be subject to the same penalties as are prescribed by law for the making of a false affidavit. IN ST TRIAL P Rule 11(B).

e. *Verified pleadings, motions, and affidavits as evidence.* Pleadings, motions and affidavits accompanying or in support of such pleadings or motions when required to be verified or under oath shall be accepted as a representation that the signer had personal knowledge thereof or reasonable cause to believe the existence of the facts or matters stated or alleged therein; and, if otherwise competent or acceptable as evidence, may be admitted as evidence of the facts or matters stated or alleged therein when it is so provided in the Indiana Rules of Trial Procedure, by statute or other law, or to the extent the writing or signature expressly purports to be made upon the signer's personal knowledge. When such pleadings, motions and affidavits are verified or under oath they shall not require other or greater proof on the part of the adverse party than if not verified or not under oath unless expressly provided otherwise by the Indiana Rules of Trial Procedure, statute or other law. Affidavits upon motions for summary judgment under IN ST TRIAL P Rule 56 and in denial of execution under IN ST TRIAL P Rule 9.2 shall be made upon personal knowledge. IN ST TRIAL P Rule 11(C).

5. *Information excluded from public access.* Every document filed in a case shall separately identify information excluded from public access pursuant to IN ST ADMIN Rule 9(G)(1) as follows:

  a. Whole documents that are excluded from public access pursuant to IN ST ADMIN Rule 9(G)(1) shall be tendered on light green paper or have a light green coversheet attached to the document, marked "Not for Public Access" or "Confidential." IN ST TRIAL P Rule 5(G)(1).

  b. When only a portion of a document contains information excluded from public access pursuant to IN ST ADMIN Rule 9(G)(1), said information shall be omitted [or redacted] from the filed document, and set forth on a separate accompanying document on light green paper conspicuously marked "Not for Public Access" or "Confidential" and clearly designated [or identifying] the caption and number of the case and the document and location within the document to which the redacted material pertains. IN ST TRIAL P Rule 5(G)(2).

  c. With respect to documents filed in electronic format, the trial court, by local rule, may provide for compliance with IN ST TRIAL P Rule 5 in manner that separates and protects access to information excluded from public access. IN ST TRIAL P Rule 5(G)(3).

  d. IN ST TRIAL P Rule 5(G) does not apply to a record sealed by the court pursuant to IN ST 5-14-3-5.5 or otherwise, nor to records, documents, or information filed in cases to which public access is prohibited pursuant to IN ST ADMIN Rule 9(G). IN ST TRIAL P Rule 5(G)(4).

  e. The following information in case records is excluded from public access and is confidential:

  i. Information that is excluded from public access pursuant to federal law;

  ii. Information that is excluded from public access as declared confidential by Indiana statute or other court rule, including without limitation:

  • All adoption records created after July 8, 1941, as declared confidential by IN ST 31-19-19-1, et seq., except those specifically declared open by IN ST 31-19-13-2(2);

  • All records relating to chancroid, chlamydia, gonorrhea, hepatitis, human immunodefi-

ciency virus (HIV), Lymphogranuloma venereum, syphilis, tuberculosis, as declared confidential by IN ST 16-41-8-1, et seq.;

- All records relating to child abuse as declared confidential by IN ST 31-33-18-1, et seq.;
- All records relating to drug tests as declared confidential by IN ST 5-14-3-4(a)(9);
- Records of grand jury proceedings as declared confidential by IN ST 35-34-2-4;
- Records of juvenile proceedings as declared confidential by IN ST 31-39-1-2, except those specifically open under statute;
- All paternity records created after July 1, 1941 as declared confidential by IN ST 31-14-11-15, IN ST 31-19-5-23, IN ST 31-39-1-1 and IN ST 31-39-1-2 [Editor's note: IN ST 31-14-11-15 was repealed effective May 9, 2013];
- All pre-sentence reports as declared confidential by IN ST 35-38-1-13;
- Written petitions to permit marriages without consent and orders directing the Clerk of Court to issue a marriage license to underage persons, as declared confidential by IN ST 31-11-1-6;
- Only those arrest warrants, search warrants, indictments and informations ordered confidential by the trial judge, prior to return of duly executed service as declared confidential by IN ST 5-14-3-4(b)(1);
- All medical, mental health, or tax records unless determined by law or regulation of any governmental custodian not to be confidential, released by the subject of such records, or declared by a court of competent jurisdiction to be essential to the resolution of litigation as declared confidential by IN ST 16-39-3-10, IN ST 6-4.1-5-10, IN ST 6-4.1-12-12, and IN ST 6-8.1-7-1;
- Personal information relating to jurors or prospective jurors, other than for the use of the parties and counsel, pursuant to IN ST JURY Rule 10;
- Information relating to protection from abuse orders, no-contact orders and workplace violence restraining orders as declared confidential by IN ST 5-2-9-6, et seq.;
- Mediation proceedings pursuant to IN ST ADR Rule 2.11, Mini-Trial proceedings pursuant to IN ST ADR Rule 4.4(C), and Summary Jury Trials pursuant to IN ST ADR Rule 5.6;
- Information in probation files pursuant to the Probation Standards promulgated by the Judicial Conference of Indiana pursuant to IN ST 11-13-1-8(b);
- Information deemed confidential pursuant to the Rules for Court Administered Alcohol and Drug Programs promulgated by the Judicial Conference of Indiana pursuant to IN ST 12-23-14-13;
- Information deemed confidential pursuant to the Problem-Solving Court Rules promulgated by the Judicial Conference of Indiana pursuant to IN ST 33-23-16-16;
- All records of the Department of workforce Development as declared confidential by IN ST 22-4-19-6;
- Information regarding interception of electronic communications that is sealed or deemed confidential as set forth in IN ST 35-33.5-2-1, et seq.

iii. Information excluded from public access by specific court order;

iv. Complete Social Security Numbers of living persons;

v. With the exception of names, information such as addresses, phone numbers, and dates of birth which explicitly identifies:

- Natural persons who are witnesses or victims (not including defendants) in criminal, domestic violence, stalking, sexual assault, juvenile, or civil protection order proceedings, provided that juveniles who are victims of sex crimes shall be identified by initials only;

- Places of residence of judicial officers, clerks and other employees of courts and clerks of court, unless the person or persons about whom the information pertains waives confidentiality;

vi. Complete account numbers of specific assets, loans, bank accounts, credit cards, and personal identification numbers (PINs);

vii. All orders of expungement entered in criminal or juvenile proceedings, orders to restrict access to criminal history information pursuant to IN ST 35-38-5-5.5 or IN ST 35-38-8-5 and records excluded from public access by such orders, and information related to infractions that is excluded from public access pursuant to IN ST 34-28-5-15 or IN ST 34-28-5-16 [Editor's note: IN ST 35-38-5-5.5, IN ST 35-38-8-5 and IN ST 34-28-5-16 were repealed effective July 1, 2013; for information on orders restricting access to criminal history, refer to IN ST 35-38-9-1, et seq.];

viii. All personal notes and e-mail, and deliberative material, of judges, jurors, court staff and judicial agencies, and information recorded in personal data assistants (PDA's) or organizers and personal calendars. IN ST ADMIN Rule 9(G)(1).

6. *Form of the summons*

    a. *Required contents of summons.* The summons shall contain:

        i. The name and address of the person on whom the service is to be effected;

        ii. The name, street address, and telephone number of the court and the cause number assigned to the case;

        iii. The title of the case as shown by the complaint, but, if there are multiple parties, the title may be shortened to include only the first named plaintiff and defendant with an appropriate indication that there are additional parties;

        iv. The name, address, and telephone number of the attorney for the person seeking service;

        v. The time within which the Indiana Rules of Trial Procedure require the person being served to respond, and a clear statement that in case of his failure to do so, judgment by default may be rendered against him for the relief demanded in the complaint. IN ST TRIAL P Rule 4(C).

    b. *Additional contents of summons.* The summons may also contain any additional information which will facilitate proper service. IN ST TRIAL P Rule 4(C).

F. Filing and Service Requirements

1. *Filing requirements.* A civil action is commenced by filing with the court a complaint or such equivalent pleading or document as may be specified by statute, by payment of the prescribed filing fee or filing an order waiving the filing fee, and, where service of process is required, by furnishing to the clerk as many copies of the complaint and summons as are necessary. IN ST TRIAL P Rule 3. An action may be commenced by E-filing only in a court which has adopted a pilot project plan approved by the Division of State Court Administration pursuant to IN ST ADMIN Rule 16. IN ST ADMIN Rule 16(F).

    a. *Filing generally.* All pleadings, petitions and motions are filed with the Clerk designated by the Court at any time during office hours established by the Clerk and the Court. All orders submitted to the Court shall be in sufficient number and shall be accompanied by postage paid envelopes addressed to each party or counsel of record. IN ST MARION CIR AND SUPER CTS CIV Rule 205(A)

    b. *Filing with the court defined.* The filing of pleadings, motions, and other papers with the court as required by the Indiana Rules of Trial Procedure shall be made by one of the following methods:

        i. Delivery to the clerk of the court;

        ii. Sending by electronic transmission under the procedure adopted pursuant to IN ST ADMIN Rule 12;

        iii. Mailing to the clerk by registered, certified or express mail return receipt requested;

        iv. Depositing with any third-party commercial carrier for delivery to the clerk within three (3) calendar days, cost prepaid, properly addressed;

v. If the court so permits, filing with the judge, in which event the judge shall note thereon the filing date and forthwith transmit them to the office of the clerk; or

vi. Electronic filing, as approved by the Division of State Court Administration pursuant to IN ST ADMIN Rule 16. IN ST TRIAL P Rule 5(F).

vii. Filing by registered or certified mail and by third-party commercial carrier shall be complete upon mailing or deposit. IN ST TRIAL P Rule 5(F).

c. *Facsimile filing.* Facsimile filing is discouraged, but permitted in the Marion Circuit and Marion Superior Court. All documents filed by facsimile shall also be filed in hard copy within seven (7) days of the facsimile filing, along with proposed orders and stamped addressed envelopes, as required by IN ST MARION CIR AND SUPER CTS CIV Rule 203(E). To avoid duplicate filings, the hard copies of the facsimile filing shall indicate in bold letters that the pleading was previously filed by facsimile transmission. Proof of transmission by facsimile, including certificate of service and manner of service, shall be the responsibility of the filing party. If the filing requires immediate attention of the Judge, it shall be so indicated in bold letters in an accompanying transmittal memorandum. Legibility of documents and timeliness of filing is the responsibility of the sender. IN ST MARION CIR AND SUPER CTS CIV Rule 205(B).

i. *Generally.* In counties where a majority of judges of the courts of record, by posted local rule, have authorized electronic facsimile filing and designated a telephone number to receive such transmissions, pleadings, motions, and other papers may be sent to the Clerk of Circuit Court by electronic facsimile transmission for filing in any case, provided:

- Such matter does not exceed ten (10) pages, including the cover sheet;

- Such matter does not require the payment of fees other than the electronic facsimile transcription fee set forth in IN ST ADMIN Rule 12(E);

- The sending party creates at the time of transmission a machine generated log for such transmission; and

- The original document and the transmission log are maintained by the sending party for the duration of the litigation. IN ST ADMIN Rule 12(B).

ii. *Time of filing.* During normal, posted business hours, the time of filing shall be the time the duplicate document is produced in the office of the Clerk of the Circuit Court. Duplicate documents received at all other times shall be filed as of the next normal business day. IN ST ADMIN Rule 12(C).

- If the receiving fax machine endorses its own time and date stamp upon the transmitted documents and the receiving machine produces a delivery receipt which is electronically created and transmitted to the sending party, the time of filing shall be the date and time recorded on the transmitted document by the receiving fax machine. IN ST ADMIN Rule 12(C).

d. *Electronic filing.* Electronic filing and electronic service pilot projects are authorized pursuant to IN ST ADMIN Rule 16 and approved by the Division of State Court Administration. IN ST MARION SUPER CT ADMIN Rule 311(1-103).

i. *Cases where electronic filing accepted.* All Marion County Circuit and Superior civil courts may accept electronic filing and service of pleadings and other documents designated in this rule in mortgage foreclosure (hereinafter referred to as "MF"), civil collection(hereinafter referred to as "CC"), and individual cases that have been approved for electronic filing and service. IN ST MARION SUPER CT ADMIN Rule 311(1-104)(1).

- The Marion County Circuit Court may, upon the motion of a party or its own motion, designate a case that will involve multiple litigants, legally intricate issues, and an extensive number of documents a mass tort or complex litigation case. Any case so designated shall be subject to electronic filing and service using the county's approved Electronic Service Provider. IN ST MARION SUPER CT ADMIN Rule 311(1-104)(3).

- The filing of electronic pleadings and other documents in MF and CC cases is entirely voluntary; however, once the case is initially filed electronically, all subsequent filings in the case shall remain in electronic format until the time for appeal is exhausted. IN ST MARION SUPER CT ADMIN Rule 311(1-104)(5).

ii.   *Documents eligible for electronic filing.* The following pleadings may be filed and served electronically:

- New case complaint and petitions. IN ST MARION SUPER CT ADMIN Rule 311(1-104)(8)(a).

- Original answers. IN ST MARION SUPER CT ADMIN Rule 311(1-104)(8)(a).

- Any other pleadings or document including but not limited to motions and appearance forms. IN ST MARION SUPER CT ADMIN Rule 311(1-104)(8)(a).

iii.   *Manner of electronic filing.* Parties shall E-file a document either:

- By registering to use the Electronic Filing Service Provider; or

- In person at the Marion County Clerk's office, by electronically filing through the Public Access Terminal. Parties filing in this manner shall be responsible for furnishing the document in an electronic format that will be compatible with the clerk's office-system to be uploaded in person. IN ST MARION SUPER CT ADMIN Rule 311(1-104)(9). For information on the Electronic Filing Service Provider and Public Access Terminal, refer to IN ST MARION SUPER CT ADMIN Rule 311(1-101).

- Registered users shall pay statutory filing fees for E-filed documents electronically to the Court through their EFSP. Filing fees are due and payable at the time of filing. IN ST MARION SUPER CT ADMIN Rule 311(2-104)(1). For more information on electronic filing fees, refer to IN ST MARION SUPER CT ADMIN Rule 311(2-104).

iv.   *Effect of electronic filing.* Any pleading filed electronically shall be considered as filed with the court when the transmission to the EFSP is complete. Any document E-filed by 11:59 p.m. local Indianapolis, Indiana time shall be deemed filed on that date. The EFSP is an agent of the Court for the purpose of electronic filing, receipt, service and retrieval of electronic documents. IN ST MARION SUPER CT ADMIN Rule 311(2-102).

- Upon completion of filing, the EFSP shall issue a confirmation receipt that includes the date and time of receipt. The confirmation receipt shall serve as proof of filing. IN ST MARION SUPER CT ADMIN Rule 311(2-102).

- In the event the Court rejects the submitted documents following review, the documents shall not become part of the official Court record and the filer will receive notification of the rejection. Users may be required to refile the instruments to meet necessary filing requirements. Documents may be filed through an E-filing system at any time that the Clerk's office is open to receive the filing or at such other times as may be designated by the clerk and posted publicly. IN ST MARION SUPER CT ADMIN Rule 311(2-102).

- Documents filed through the E-filing system are deemed filed when received by the Clerk's office, except that documents received at times that the Clerk's office is closed shall be deemed filed the next regular time when the Clerk's office is open for filing. The time stamp issued by the E-filing system shall be presumed to be the time the document is received by the Clerk. IN ST MARION SUPER CT ADMIN Rule 311(2-102).

v.   *Electronically filed documents.* All pleadings and other documents designated in IN ST MARION SUPER CT ADMIN Rule 311 shall be filed and served electronically in any individual case which has been approved for electronic filing and service. IN ST MARION SUPER CT ADMIN Rule 311(1-104)(6).

vi.   *System failures.* When filing by electronic means is hindered by a technical failure, a party may file with the Clerk of Marion County in hard copy. With the exception of deadlines that by law cannot be extended, the time for filing of any paper that is delayed due to technical failure of the site shall be extended for one (1) day for each day on which such failure occurs, unless otherwise ordered by the Court. IN ST MARION SUPER CT ADMIN Rule 311(2-108).

vii. *Compliance with rules.* All filing shall comply with the requirements of IN ST ADMIN Rule 9 and IN ST ADMIN Rule 16; and the Indiana Rules of Court and the Marion County Local Rules. IN ST MARION SUPER CT ADMIN Rule 311(1-104)(11).

e. *Filing for special judge.* When a Special Judge who is not a Marion County Judge is selected, all parties or attorneys shall furnish such Judge with copies of all filings prior to the qualification of such Special Judge. Thereafter, copies of all filings shall be delivered in person, by mail or by facsimile to the office of the Special Judge with certificate of forwarding same made a part of the filing. IN ST MARION CIR AND SUPER CTS CIV Rule 205(C).

f. *Proof of filing.* Any party filing any paper by any method other than personal delivery to the clerk shall retain proof of filing. IN ST TRIAL P Rule 5(F).

2. *Service requirements.* The court acquires jurisdiction over a party or person who under the Indiana Rules of Trial Procedure commences or joins in the action, is served with summons or enters an appearance, or who is subjected to the power of the court under any other law. IN ST TRIAL P Rule 4(A).

a. *Designation of method of service of the summons.* The person seeking service or his attorney may designate the manner of service upon the summons. If not so designated, the clerk shall cause service to be made by mail or other public means provided the mailing address of the person to be served is indicated in the summons or can be determined. If a mailing address is not furnished or cannot be determined or if service by mail or other public means is returned without acceptance, the complaint and summons shall promptly be delivered to the sheriff or his deputy who, unless otherwise directed, shall serve the summons. IN ST TRIAL P Rule 4(D).

b. *Summons and complaint to be served together.* The summons and complaint shall be served together unless otherwise ordered by the court. When service of summons is made by publication, the complaint shall not be published. When jurisdiction over a party is dependent upon service of process by publication or by his appearance, summons and complaint shall be deemed to have been served at the end of the day of last required publication in the case of service by publication, and at the time of appearance in jurisdiction acquired by appearance. Whenever the summons and complaint are not served or published together, the summons shall contain the full, unabbreviated title of the case. IN ST TRIAL P Rule 4(E).

c. *Territorial limits and service under special order*

   i. *Territorial limits of effective service.* Process may be served anywhere within the territorial limits of this state and outside the state as provided in the Indiana Rules of Trial Procedure. IN ST TRIAL P Rule 4.14(A).

   ii. *Service under special order of court.* Upon application of any party the court in which any action is pending may make an appropriate order for service in a manner not provided by the Indiana Rules of Trial Procedure or statutes when such service is reasonably calculated to give the defendant actual knowledge of the proceedings and an opportunity to be heard. IN ST TRIAL P Rule 4.14(B).

d. *Return of service.* The person making service shall promptly make his return upon or attach it to a copy of the summons which shall be delivered to the clerk. The return shall be signed by the person making it, and shall include a statement:

   i. That service was made upon the person as required by law and the time, place, and manner thereof;

   ii. If service was not made, the particular manner in which it was thwarted in terms of fact or in terms of law;

   iii. Such other information as is expressly required by the Indiana Rules of Trial Procedure. IN ST TRIAL P Rule 4.15(A).

3. *Methods of service of the summons and complaint*

a. *In general*

   i. *Methods of service.* Service may be made upon an individual, or an individual acting in a representative capacity, by:

      • Sending a copy of the summons and complaint by registered or certified mail or other public means by which a written acknowledgment of receipt may be requested and obtained to his residence, place of business or employment with return receipt requested and returned showing receipt of the letter; or

- Delivering a copy of the summons and complaint to him personally; or
- Leaving a copy of the summons and complaint at his dwelling house or usual place of abode; or
- Serving his agent as provided by rule, statute or valid agreement. IN ST TRIAL P Rule 4.1(A).

ii. *Copy service to be followed with mail.* Whenever service is made under IN ST TRIAL P Rule 4.1(A)(3) [by leaving a copy at dwelling or usual place of abode] or IN ST TRIAL P Rule 4.1(A)(4) [by service of agent], the person making the service also shall send by first class mail, a copy of the summons without the complaint to the last known address of the person being served, and this fact shall be shown upon the return. IN ST TRIAL P Rule 4.1(B).

iii. *Service by fax or e-mail.* A party who has consented to service by fax or e-mail may be served as follows:

- Service by e-mail shall be made by attaching the document being served in PDF format. Discovery documents must also be served in accordance with IN ST TRIAL P Rule 26(A).
- Service by fax shall be deemed complete upon generation of a transmission record indicating the successful transmission of the entire document, except as provided in IN ST TRIAL P Rule 5(B)(3)(d).
- Service by e-mail shall be deemed complete upon transmission, except as provided in IN ST TRIAL P Rule 5(B)(3)(d).
- Service by fax or e-mail that occurs on a Saturday, Sunday, legal holiday, or day the court or agency in which the matter is pending is closed or after 5:00 PM local time of the recipient shall be deemed complete the next day that is not a Saturday, Sunday, legal holiday, or day that the court or agency in which the matter is pending is not closed. IN ST TRIAL P Rule 5(B)(3).

b. *Service upon infants or incompetents*

i. *Service upon infants.* Service upon an individual known to be an infant shall be made upon his next friend or guardian ad litem, if service is with respect to the same action in which the infant is so represented. If there is no next friend or guardian ad litem, service shall be made upon his court-appointed representative if one is known and can be served within this state. If there is no court-appointed representative, service shall be made upon either parent known to have custody of the infant, or if there is no parent, upon a person known to be standing in the position of custodian or parent. The infant shall also be served if he is fourteen (14) years of age or older. In the event that service, as provided above, is not possible, service shall be made on the infant. IN ST TRIAL P Rule 4.2(A).

ii. *Service upon incompetents.* Service upon an individual who has been adjudged to be of unsound mind, otherwise incompetent or who is believed to be such shall be made upon his next friend or guardian ad litem, if service is with respect to the same action in which the incompetent is so represented. If there is no next friend or guardian ad litem, service shall be made upon his court-appointed representative if one is known and can be served within this state. If there is no court-appointed representative, then upon the named party and also upon a person known to be standing in the position of custodian of his person. IN ST TRIAL P Rule 4.2(B).

iii. *Duty to inform court; Appearance.* Nothing herein is intended to affect the duty of a party to inform the court that a person is an infant or incompetent. An appearance by a court-appointed guardian, next friend or guardian ad litem or his attorney shall correct any defect in service under IN ST TRIAL P Rule 4.2 unless such defect be challenged. IN ST TRIAL P Rule 4.2(C).

c. *Service upon institutionalized persons.* Service of summons upon a person who is imprisoned or restrained in an institution shall be made by delivering or mailing a copy of the summons and complaint to the official in charge of the institution. It shall be the duty of said official to immediately deliver the summons and complaint to the person being served and allow him to make provisions for adequate representation by counsel. The official shall indicate upon the return whether the person has received the summons and been allowed an opportunity to retain counsel. IN ST TRIAL P Rule 4.3.

d. *Service upon individuals whose acts serve as basis for jurisdiction.* A person subject to the jurisdiction of the courts of this state under IN ST TRIAL P Rule 4.4 may be served with summons:

   i. As provided by IN ST TRIAL P Rule 4.1 (service on individuals), IN ST TRIAL P Rule 4.5 (service upon resident who cannot be found or served within the state), IN ST TRIAL P Rule 4.6 (service upon organizations), IN ST TRIAL P Rule 4.9 (in rem actions); or

   ii. The person shall be deemed to have appointed the Secretary of State as his agent upon whom service of summons may be made as provided in IN ST TRIAL P Rule 4.10. IN ST TRIAL P Rule 4.4(B).

e. *Service upon resident who cannot be found or served within the state.* When the person to be served is a resident of this state who cannot be served personally or by agent in this state and either cannot be found, has concealed his whereabouts or has left the state, summons may be served in the manner provided by IN ST TRIAL P Rule 4.9 (summons in in rem actions). IN ST TRIAL P Rule 4.5.

f. *Service upon organizations*

   i. *Persons to be served.* Service upon an organization may be made as follows:

   - In the case of a domestic or foreign organization upon an executive officer thereof, or if there is an agent appointed or deemed by law to have been appointed to receive service, then upon such agent. IN ST TRIAL P Rule 4.6(A)(1).

   - In the case of a partnership, upon a general partner thereof. IN ST TRIAL P Rule 4.6(A)(2).

   - In the case of a state governmental organization upon the executive officer thereof and also upon the Attorney General. IN ST TRIAL P Rule 4.6(A)(3).

   - In the case of a local governmental organization, upon the executive thereof and upon the attorney for the local governmental organization. IN ST TRIAL P Rule 4.6(A)(4).

   - When, in IN ST TRIAL P Rule 4.6(A)(3) and IN ST TRIAL P Rule 4.6(A)(4), a governmental representative is named as a party in his individual name or in such name along with his official title, then also upon such representative. IN ST TRIAL P Rule 4.6(A)(5).

   ii. *Manner of service.* Service under IN ST TRIAL P Rule 4.6(A) shall be made on the proper person in the manner provided by the Indiana Rules of Trial Procedure for service upon individuals, but a person seeking service or his attorney shall not knowingly direct service to be made at the person's dwelling house or place of abode, unless such is an address furnished under the requirements of a statute or valid agreement, or unless an affidavit on or attached to the summons states that service in another manner is impractical. IN ST TRIAL P Rule 4.6(B).

   iii. *Service at organization's office.* When shown upon an affidavit or in the return, that service upon an organization cannot be made as provided in IN ST TRIAL P Rule 4.6(A) or IN ST TRIAL P Rule 4.6(B), service may be made by leaving a copy of the summons and complaint at any office of such organization located within this state with the person in charge of such office. IN ST TRIAL P Rule 4.6(C).

g. *Summons; Service upon agent named by statute or agreement.* Whenever an agent (other than an agent appointed to receive service for a governmental organization of this state) has been designated by or pursuant to statute or valid agreement to receive service for the person being served, service may be made upon such agent as follows:

   i. If the agent is a governmental organization or officer designated by or pursuant to statute, service shall be made as provided in IN ST TRIAL P Rule 4.10. IN ST TRIAL P Rule 4.7(1).

   ii. If the agent is one other than that described in IN ST TRIAL P Rule 4.7(1), service shall be made upon him as provided in IN ST TRIAL P Rule 4.1 (service upon individuals) or IN ST TRIAL P Rule 4.6 (service upon organizations). If service cannot be made upon such agent, because there is no address furnished as required by statute or valid agreement or his whereabouts in this state are unknown, then his principal shall be deemed to have appointed the Secretary of State as a replacement for the agent and service may be made upon the Secretary of State as provided in IN ST TRIAL P Rule 4.10. IN ST TRIAL P Rule 4.7(2).

h. *Summons; Service of pleadings or summons on Attorney General.* Service of a copy of the summons and complaint or any pleading upon the Attorney General under the Indiana Rules of Trial Procedure or any statute shall be made by personal service upon him, a deputy or clerk at his office, or by mail or other public means to him at such office in the manner provided by IN ST TRIAL P Rule 4.1(A)(1), and by IN ST TRIAL P Rule 4.11 to the extent applicable. IN ST TRIAL P Rule 4.8.

i. *Summons; In rem actions*

   i. *In general.* In any action involving a res situated within this state, service may be made as provided in IN ST TRIAL P Rule 4.9. The court may render a judgment or decree to the extent of its jurisdiction over the res. IN ST TRIAL P Rule 4.9(A).

   ii. *Manner of service.* Service under IN ST TRIAL P Rule 4.9 may be made as follows:

- By service of summons upon a person or his agent pursuant to the Indiana Rules of Trial Procedure; or
- By service of summons outside this state in a manner provided by IN ST TRIAL P Rule 4.1 (service upon individuals) or by publication outside this state in a manner provided by IN ST TRIAL P Rule 4.13 (service by publication) or outside this state in any other manner as provided by the Indiana Rules of Trial Procedure; or
- By service by publication pursuant to IN ST TRIAL P Rule 4.13. IN ST TRIAL P Rule 4.9(A).

j. *Summons; Service upon Secretary of State or other governmental agent.* Whenever, under the Indiana Rules of Trial Procedure or any statute, service is made upon the Secretary of State or any other governmental organization or officer, as agent for the person being served, service may be made upon such agent as provided in IN ST TRIAL P Rule 4.10. IN ST TRIAL P Rule 4.10(A).

   i. The person seeking service or his attorney shall:

- Submit his request for service upon the agent in the praecipe for summons, and state that the governmental organization or officer is the agent of the person being served;
- State the address of the person being served as filed and recorded pursuant to a statute or valid agreement, or if no such address is known, then his last known mailing address, and, if no such address is known, then such shall be stated;
- Pay any fee prescribed by statute to be forwarded together with sufficient copies of the summons, affidavit and complaint, to the agent by the clerk of the court. IN ST TRIAL P Rule 4.10(A)(1).

   ii. Upon receipt thereof the agent shall promptly:

- Send to the person being served a copy of the summons and complaint by registered or certified mail or by other public means by which a written acknowledgment of receipt may be obtained;
- Complete and deliver to the clerk an affidavit showing the date of the mailing, or if there was no mailing, the reason therefor;
- Send to the clerk a copy of the return receipt along with a copy of the summons;
- File and retain a copy of the return receipt. IN ST TRIAL P Rule 4.10(A)(2).

k. *Summons; Registered or certified mail.* Whenever service by registered or certified mail or other public means by which a return receipt may be requested is authorized, the clerk of the court or a governmental agent under IN ST TRIAL P Rule 4.10 shall send the summons and complaint to the person being served at the address supplied upon the summons, or furnished by the person seeking service. In his return the clerk of the court or the governmental agent shall show the date and place of mailing, a copy of the mailed or electronically-transmitted return receipt if and when received by him showing whether the mailing was accepted or returned, and, if accepted, by whom. The return along with the receipt shall be promptly filed by the clerk with the pleadings and become a part of the record. If a mailing by the clerk of the court is returned without acceptance, the clerk shall reissue the summons and complaint for service as requested, by the person seeking service. IN ST TRIAL P Rule 4.11.

l.   *Summons; Service by sheriff or other officer*

   i.   *In general.* Whenever service is made by delivering a copy to a person personally or by leaving a copy at his dwelling house or place of employment as provided by IN ST TRIAL P Rule 4.1, summons shall be issued to and served by the sheriff, his deputy, or some person specially or regularly appointed by the court for that purpose. Service shall be effective if made by a person not otherwise authorized by the Indiana Rules of Trial Procedure, but proof of service by such a person must be made by him as a witness or by deposition without allowance of expenses therefor as costs. The person to whom the summons is delivered for service must act promptly and exercise reasonable care to cause service to be made. IN ST TRIAL P Rule 4.12(A).

   ii. *Special service by police officers.* A sheriff, his deputy, or any full-time state or municipal police officer may serve summons in any county of this state if he agrees or has agreed to make the service. When specially requested in the praecipe for summons, the complaint and summons shall be delivered to such officer by the clerk or the attorney for the person seeking service. No agreement with the sheriff or his deputy for such service in the sheriff's own county shall be permitted. In no event shall any expenses agreed upon under this provision be assessed or recovered as costs or affect court costs otherwise imposed for regular service. IN ST TRIAL P Rule 4.12(B).

   iii. *Service in other counties.* A summons may be served in any county in this state. If service is to be made in another county, the summons may be issued by the clerk for service therein to the sheriff of such county or to a person authorized to make service by the Indiana Rules of Trial Procedure. IN ST TRIAL P Rule 4.12(C).

   iv. *Service outside the state.* Personal service, when permitted by the Indiana Rules of Trial Procedure to be made outside the state, may be made there by any disinterested person or by the attorney representing the person seeking such service. The expenses of such person may be assessed as costs only if they are reasonable and if service by mail or other public means cannot be made or is not successful. IN ST TRIAL P Rule 4.12(D).

m. *Summons; Service by publication*

   i.   *Praecipe for summons by publication.* In any action where notice by publication is permitted by the Indiana Rules of Trial Procedure or by statute, service may be made by publication. Summons by publication may name all the persons to be served, and separate publications with respect to each party shall not be required. The person seeking such service, or his attorney, shall submit his request therefor upon the praecipe for summons along with supporting affidavits that diligent search has been made that the defendant cannot be found, has concealed his whereabouts, or has left the state, and shall prepare the contents of the summons to be published. The summons shall be signed by the clerk of the court or the sheriff in such manner as to indicate that it is made by his authority. IN ST TRIAL P Rule 4.13(A).

   ii. *Contents of summons by publication.* The summons shall contain the following information:

   • The name of the person being sued, and the person to whom the notice is directed, and, if the person's whereabouts are unknown or some or all of the parties are unknown, a statement to that effect;

   • The name of the court and cause number assigned to the case;

   • The title of the case as shown by the complaint, but if there are multiple parties, the title may be shortened to include only the first named plaintiff and those defendants to be served by publication with an appropriate indication that there are additional parties;

- The name and address of the attorney representing the person seeking service;

- A brief statement of the nature of the suit, which need not contain the details and particulars of the claim. A description of any property, relationship, or other res involved in the action, and a statement that the person being sued claims some interest therein;

- A clear statement that the person being sued must respond within thirty (30) days after the last notice of the action is published, and in case he fails to do so, judgment by default may be entered against him for the relief demanded in the complaint. IN ST TRIAL P Rule 4.13(B).

    iii. *Publication of summons.* The summons shall be published three (3) times by the clerk or person making it, the first publication promptly and each two (2) succeeding publications at least seven (7) and not more than fourteen (14) days after the prior publication, in a newspaper authorized by law to publish notices, and published in the county where the complaint or action is filed, where the res is located, or where the defendant resides or where he was known last to reside. If no newspaper is published in the county, then the summons shall be published in the county in this state nearest thereto in which any such paper may be printed, or in a place specially ordered by the court. The person seeking the service or his attorney may designate any qualified newspaper, and if he fails to do so, the selection may be made by the clerk. IN ST TRIAL P Rule 4.13(C).

    iv. *By whom made or procured.* Service of summons by publication shall be made and procured by the clerk, by a person appointed by the court for that purpose, or by the clerk or sheriff of another county where publication is to be made. IN ST TRIAL P Rule 4.13(D).

    v. *Return.* The clerk or person making the service shall prepare the return and include the following:

- Any supporting affidavits of the printer containing a copy of the summons which was published;

- An information or statement that the newspaper and the publication meet all legal requirements applicable to such publication;

- The dates of publication. IN ST TRIAL P Rule 4.13(E).

- The return and affidavits shall be filed with the pleadings and other papers in the case and shall become a part of the record as provided in the Indiana Rules of Trial Procedure. IN ST TRIAL P Rule 4.13(E).

  n. *Service on agent of nonresident corporation.* In an action commenced in a court of general jurisdiction in Indiana by or against any corporation incorporated under the laws of Indiana, in which one (1) or more of the directors of the corporation is: (1) a necessary or proper party; and (2) a nonresident of Indiana; service of summons upon a director for the purpose of obtaining jurisdiction of the person of the director in the action is obtained by serving the summons on the resident agent of the corporation. IN ST 34-33-2-1.

G. Hearings

1. The Indiana rules do not contemplate a hearing regarding the service of the summons and complaint.

H. Forms

1. Official Complaint Forms for Indiana

  a. Affidavit of debt. IN ST TRIAL P App. A-2.

  b. Appearance by attorney in civil case. IN ST TRIAL P App. B.

2. Complaint Forms for Indiana

  a. Caption; Generally. 5 INPRAC § 3:1.1.

  b. Caption; Multiple parties. 5 INPRAC § 3:1.2.

  c. Single count. 5 INPRAC § 3:1.3.

  d. Multiple counts; Single defendant. 5 INPRAC § 3:1.4.

e.   Multiple counts; Multiple defendants. 5 INPRAC § 3:1.5.

f.   Signature; By party. 5 INPRAC § 3:1.6.

g.   Signature; By attorney. 5 INPRAC § 3:1.7.

h.   Verification. 5 INPRAC § 3:1.8.

i.   Individual defendant. 5 INPRAC § 3:2.1.

j.   Resident agent of corporation. 5 INPRAC § 3:2.2.

k.   Attorney general. 5 INPRAC § 3:2.3.

l.   City attorney. 5 INPRAC § 3:2.4.

m.   Certificate; Personal service. 5 INPRAC § 3:2.5.

n.   Certificate; First class mail. 5 INPRAC § 3:2.6.

o.   Certificate; Registered mail. 5 INPRAC § 3:2.7.

p.   Certificate; Dwelling house. 5 INPRAC § 3:2.8.

q.   Clerk's certificate of mailing. 5 INPRAC § 3:2.9.

r.   Clerk's certificate of mailing; Acceptance by defendant. 5 INPRAC § 3:2.10.

s.   Clerk's return on service of summons by mail; Not accepted by defendant. 5 INPRAC § 3:2.11.

t.   Sheriff's return; Service of summons. 5 INPRAC § 3:2.12.

u.   Motion to appoint person to serve process. 5 INPRAC § 3:2.13.

v.   Published notice; Text. 5 INPRAC § 3:2.14.

w.   Affidavit of publisher. 5 INPRAC § 3:2.15.

x.   Clerk's return on service by publication. 5 INPRAC § 3:2.16.

y.   Complaint; Single count. 9 INPRAC § 2.3.

z.   Appearance by party initiating action; Form. 9 INPRAC § 6.3.

3.   Official Complaint Forms for Marion County

a.   Appearance form. IN ST MARION CIR AND SUPER CTS CIV App. B.

4.   Complaint Forms for Marion County

a.   Appearance form initiating; Responding party; Intervening party. EFORMST IN 5600.

b.   Summons. EFORMST IN 5930.

I. Checklist

(I)   ❑ Matters to be considered by the plaintiff

   (a)   ❑ Required documents

      (1)   ❑ Summons

      (2)   ❑ Complaint

      (3)   ❑ Appearance form

   (b)   ❑ Supplemental documents

      (1)   ❑ Proof of written instrument

      (2)   ❑ Notice of intent to use foreign law

      (3)   ❑ Praecipe

      (4)   ❑ Facsimile cover sheet

   (c)   ❑ Timing

      (1)   ❑ The claimant typically bears the burden of commencing an action within the applicable statute of limitations

(2) ❑ If person seeking service of process fails without cause for sixty (60) days or more to provide clerk with required summons for issuance or with other information necessary to effectuate service, person has failed to exercise due diligence in securing service of process

(II) ❑ Matters to be considered by the defendant

(a) ❑ Required documents

(1) ❑ Answer

(2) ❑ Appearance form

(3) ❑ Certificate of service

(b) ❑ Supplemental documents

(1) ❑ Admission of service

(2) ❑ Proof of written instrument

(3) ❑ Notice of intent to use foreign law

(4) ❑ Facsimile cover sheet

(c) ❑ Timing

(1) ❑ A responsive pleading required under the Indiana Rules of Trial Procedure, shall be served within twenty (20) days after service of the prior pleading

(2) ❑ The service of a motion permitted under IN ST TRIAL P Rule 12 alters the time for service of responsive pleadings as follows, unless a different time is fixed by the court:

(i) ❑ If the court does not grant the motion, the responsive pleading shall be served in ten (10) days after notice of the court's action;

(ii) ❑ If the court grants the motion and the corrective action is allowed to be taken, it shall be taken within ten (10) days, and the responsive pleading shall be served within ten (10) days thereafter

(3) ❑ All pleadings and papers subsequent to the complaint which are required to be served upon a party shall be filed with the Court either before service or within a reasonable period of time thereafter

Pleadings
Amended Complaint

Document Last Updated October 2013

A. Applicable Rules

1. *State rules*

a. Appearance. IN ST TRIAL P Rule 3.1.

b. Process. IN ST TRIAL P Rule 4.

c. Service of the summons. IN ST TRIAL P Rule 4.1; IN ST TRIAL P Rule 4.2; IN ST TRIAL P Rule 4.3; IN ST TRIAL P Rule 4.4; IN ST TRIAL P Rule 4.5; IN ST TRIAL P Rule 4.6; IN ST TRIAL P Rule 4.7; IN ST TRIAL P Rule 4.8; IN ST TRIAL P Rule 4.9; IN ST TRIAL P Rule 4.10; IN ST TRIAL P Rule 4.11; IN ST TRIAL P Rule 4.12; IN ST TRIAL P Rule 4.13; IN ST TRIAL P Rule 4.14; IN ST TRIAL P Rule 4.15; IN ST 34-33-2-1.

d. Service and filing of pleadings and other papers. IN ST TRIAL P Rule 5.

e. Time. IN ST TRIAL P Rule 6.

f. Pleadings. IN ST TRIAL P Rule 7; IN ST TRIAL P Rule 8; IN ST TRIAL P Rule 9; IN ST TRIAL P Rule 9.1; IN ST TRIAL P Rule 9.2; IN ST TRIAL P Rule 10.

g. Signing and verification of pleadings. IN ST TRIAL P Rule 11.

h. Amended and supplemental pleadings. IN ST TRIAL P Rule 15.

i. Joinder. IN ST TRIAL P Rule 18; IN ST TRIAL P Rule 19.

j. Evidence. IN ST TRIAL P Rule 43.

k. Determination of foreign law. IN ST TRIAL P Rule 44.1.

l. Judgment on the evidence (directed verdict). IN ST TRIAL P Rule 50.

m. Findings by the court. IN ST TRIAL P Rule 52.

n. Summary judgment. IN ST TRIAL P Rule 56.

o. Motion to correct error. IN ST TRIAL P Rule 59.

p. Relief from judgment or order. IN ST TRIAL P Rule 60.

q. Access to court records. IN ST ADMIN Rule 9.

r. Paper size. IN ST ADMIN Rule 11.

s. Facsimile transmission. IN ST ADMIN Rule 12.

t. Electronic filing and electronic service pilot projects. IN ST ADMIN Rule 16.

u. Sealing of certain records by court; Hearing; Notice. IN ST 5-14-3-5.5.

v. Privacy and confidentiality. IN ST 5-2-9-6; IN ST 5-14-3-4; IN ST 6-4.1-5-10; IN ST 6-4.1-12-12; IN ST 6-8.1-7-1; IN ST 11-13-1-8; IN ST 12-23-14-13; IN ST 16-39-3-10; IN ST 16-41-8-1; IN ST 22-4-19-6; IN ST 31-11-1-6; IN ST 31-19-5-23; IN ST 31-19-13-2; IN ST 31-19-19-1; IN ST 31-33-18-1; IN ST 31-39-1-1; IN ST 31-39-1-2; IN ST 33-23-16-16; IN ST 35-34-2-4; IN ST 35-38-1-13; IN ST 35-38-9-1; IN ST ADR Rule 2.11; IN ST ADR Rule 4.4; IN ST ADR Rule 5.6; IN ST JURY Rule 10.

2. *Local rules*

a. Requirements for motions. IN ST MARION CIR AND SUPER CTS CIV Rule 203.

b. Preparation of pleadings, motions and other papers. IN ST MARION CIR AND SUPER CTS CIV Rule 204.

c. Filing of pleadings, motions and other papers. IN ST MARION CIR AND SUPER CTS CIV Rule 205.

d. Signing and verification of pleadings, motions and other papers; Service on opposing party. IN ST MARION CIR AND SUPER CTS CIV Rule 206.

e. Motions for continuance. IN ST MARION CIR AND SUPER CTS CIV Rule 215.

f. Electronic filing. IN ST MARION SUPER CT ADMIN Rule 311.

B. Timing

1. *Filing an amended pleading*

a. *As a matter of course.* A party may amend his pleading once as a matter of course at any time before a responsive pleading is served or, if the pleading is one to which no responsive pleading is permitted, and the action has not been placed upon the trial calendar, he may so amend it at any time within thirty (30) days after it is served. IN ST TRIAL P Rule 15(A).

b. *With leave of court.* Otherwise a party may amend his pleading only by leave of court or by written consent of the adverse party; and leave shall be given when justice so requires. IN ST TRIAL P Rule 15(A). Refer to the Indiana KeyRules Motion for Leave to Amend document for more information.

2. *Computation of time*

a. *Generally; Days excluded.* In computing any period of time prescribed or allowed by the Indiana Rules of Trial Procedure, by order of the court, or by any applicable statute, the day of the act, event, or default from which the designated period of time begins to run shall not be included. The last day of the period so computed is to be included unless it is:

   i. A Saturday,

    ii. A Sunday,

    iii. A legal holiday as defined by state statute, or

    iv. A day the office in which the act is to be done is closed during regular business hours. IN ST TRIAL P Rule 6(A).

  b. *Short periods.* In any event, the period runs until the end of the next day that is not a Saturday, a Sunday, a legal holiday, or a day on which the office is closed. When the period of time allowed is less than seven (7) days, intermediate Saturdays, Sundays, legal holidays, and days on which the office is closed shall be excluded from the computations. IN ST TRIAL P Rule 6(A).

  c. *Additional time after service by United States mail.* Whenever a party has the right or is required to do some act or take some proceedings within a prescribed period after the service of a notice or other paper upon him and the notice or paper is served upon him by United States mail, three (3) days shall be added to the prescribed period. IN ST TRIAL P Rule 6(E).

  d. *Enlargement of time.* When an act is required or allowed to be done at or within a specific time by the Indiana Rules of Trial Procedure, the court may at any time for cause shown:

    i. Order the period enlarged, with or without motion or notice, if request therefor is made before the expiration of the period originally prescribed or extended by a previous order; or

    ii. Upon motion made after the expiration of the specific period, permit the act to be done where the failure to act was the result of excusable neglect; but, the court may not extend the time for taking any action for judgment on the evidence under IN ST TRIAL P Rule 50(A), amendment of findings and judgment under IN ST TRIAL P Rule 52(B), to correct errors under IN ST TRIAL P Rule 59(C), statement in opposition to motion to correct error under IN ST TRIAL P Rule 59(E), or to obtain relief from final judgment under IN ST TRIAL P Rule 60(B), except to the extent and under the conditions stated in those rules. IN ST TRIAL P Rule 6(B).

    iii. Initial written motion for enlargement of time pursuant to IN ST TRIAL P Rule 6(B)(1) to respond to a claim shall be automatically allowed for an additional thirty (30) days from the original due date without a written order of the Court. Any motion filed pursuant to IN ST MARION CIR AND SUPER CTS CIV Rule 203 shall state the date when such a response is due and the date to which time is enlarged. The motion must be filed on or before the original due date or IN ST MARION CIR AND SUPER CTS CIV Rule 203 shall be inapplicable. All subsequent Motions shall be so designated and will be granted only for good cause shown. IN ST MARION CIR AND SUPER CTS CIV Rule 203(D).

  e. *Continuances disfavored.* Motions for Continuance are discouraged. Neither side is entitled to an automatic continuance as a matter of right. IN ST MARION CIR AND SUPER CTS CIV Rule 215. For information on obtaining a continuance, refer to IN ST MARION CIR AND SUPER CTS CIV Rule 215.

C. General Requirements

1. *Amending pleadings.* The purpose of an amended pleading is to include matters that occurred before the filing of the original pleading but which were either overlooked by the pleader or unknown to him at the time. It is a substitute for the original and relates to the facts that existed when the original pleading was filed. An amended pleading supercedes the original as to those portions amended. 10 INPRAC § 46.1.

  a. *Amendments liberally allowed.* Amendments to pleadings are to be liberally allowed in order that all issues are presented in one action. 10 INPRAC § 46.1; Pinnacle Media, LLC v. Metropolitan Dev. Com'n of Marion County, 868 N.E.2d 894 (Ind.Ct.App. 2007).

  b. *Amendments to conform to the evidence.* When issues not raised by the pleadings are tried by express or implied consent of the parties, they shall be treated in all respects as if they had been raised in the pleadings. Such amendment of the pleadings as may be necessary to cause them to conform to the evidence and to raise these issues may be made upon motion of any party at any time, even after judgment, but failure so to amend does not affect the result of the trial of these issues. If evidence is objected to at the trial on the ground that it is not within the issues made by the pleadings, the court may allow the pleadings to be amended and shall do so freely when the presentation of the merits of the action will be subserved thereby and the objecting party fails to satisfy the court that the admission of such evidence would prejudice him in maintaining his action or defense upon the merits. The court may grant a continuance to enable the objecting party to meet such evidence. IN ST TRIAL P Rule 15(B).

c. *Relation back of amendments*

   i. Whenever the claim or defense asserted in the amended pleading arose out of the conduct, transaction, or occurrence set forth or attempted to be set forth in the original pleading, the amendment relates back to the date of the original pleading. An amendment changing the party against whom a claim is asserted relates back if the foregoing provision is satisfied and, within one hundred and twenty (120) days of commencement of the action, the party to be brought in by amendment:

- Has received such notice of the institution of the action that he will not be prejudiced in maintaining his defense on the merits; and

- Knew or should have known that but for a mistake concerning the identity of the proper party, the action would have been brought against him. IN ST TRIAL P Rule 15(C).

   ii. The requirement of IN ST TRIAL P Rule 15(C)(1) and IN ST TRIAL P Rule 15(C)(2) with respect to a governmental organization to be brought into the action as defendant is satisfied:

- In the case of a state or governmental organization by delivery or mailing of process to the attorney general or to a governmental executive [IN ST TRIAL P Rule 4.6(A)(3)]; or

- In the case of a local governmental organization, by delivery or mailing of process to its attorney as provided by statute, to a governmental executive thereof [IN ST TRIAL P Rule 4.6(A)(4)], or to the officer holding the office if suit is against the officer or an office. IN ST TRIAL P Rule 15(C).

d. *Amendment by leave.* Amendments, other than an amendment by right, may be made only by leave of court or by written consent of the opposing party. 2 INPRAC R 15(15.2). Refer to the Indiana KeyRules Motion for Leave to Amend document for more information on amending with leave of court.

2. *Pleading, generally*

a. *Pleadings to be concise.* Each averment of a pleading shall be simple, concise, and direct. No technical forms of pleading or motions are required. All fictions in pleading are abolished. IN ST TRIAL P Rule 8(E)(1).

b. *Pleading in the alternative.* A pleading may set forth two (2) or more statements of a claim or defense alternatively or hypothetically, either in one (1) count or defense or in separate counts or defenses. When two (2) or more statements are made in the alternative and one (1) of them if made independently would be sufficient, the pleading is not made insufficient by the insufficiency of one or more of the alternative statements. A pleading may also state as many separate claims or defenses as the pleader has regardless of consistency and whether based on legal or equitable grounds. All statements shall be made subject to the obligations set forth in IN ST TRIAL P Rule 11. IN ST TRIAL P Rule 8(E)(2).

c. *Motions and pleadings, joint and several.* All motions and pleadings of any kind addressed to two (2) or more paragraphs of any pleading, or filed by two (2) or more parties, shall be taken and construed as joint, separate, and several motions or pleadings to each of such paragraphs and by and against each of such parties. All motions or pleadings containing two (2) or more subject-matters shall be taken and construed as separate and several as to each subject-matter. All objections to rulings made by two (2) or more parties shall be taken and construed as the joint, separate, and several objections of each of such parties. IN ST TRIAL P Rule 8(E)(3).

   i. A complaint filed by or against two (2) or more plaintiffs shall be taken and construed as joint, separate, and several as to each of said plaintiffs. IN ST TRIAL P Rule 8(E).

d. *Construction of pleadings.* All pleadings shall be so construed as to do substantial justice, lead to disposition on the merits, and avoid litigation of procedural points. IN ST TRIAL P Rule 8(F).

3. *Contents of the complaint*

    a. *Pleading for relief; Notice pleading.* Indiana is a "notice pleading" jurisdiction. 22B INPRAC 8:1; State v. American Family Voices, Inc., 898 N.E.2d 293 (Ind. 2008). Notice pleading replaces the technical and complex method of pleading which existed prior to 1970. Notice pleading is grounded in due process of law and must provide a defendant with reasonable notice of the plaintiff's claim or an opponent's defense. 22B INPRAC 8:1; Noblesville Redevelopment Com'n v. Noblesville Associates Ltd. Partnership, 674 N.E.2d 558 (Ind. 1996). Notice pleading does not require that the plaintiff state all elements or facts essential to a cause of action. 22B INPRAC 8:1; State v. American Family Voices, Inc., 898 N.E.2d 293 (Ind. 2008). Instead, the complaint must state "a short and plain statement of the claim" showing an entitlement to relief, and a demand for relief. 22B INPRAC 8:1; Trail v. Boys and Girls Clubs of Northwest Indiana, 845 N.E.2d 130 (Ind. 2006).

    b. *Claims for relief.* To state a claim for relief, whether an original claim, counterclaim, cross-claim, or third-party claim, a pleading must contain:

        i. A short and plain statement of the claim showing that the pleader is entitled to relief, and

        ii. A demand for relief to which the pleader deems entitled. Relief in the alternative or of several different types may be demanded. However, in any complaint seeking damages for personal injury or death, or seeking punitive damages, no dollar amount or figure shall be included in the demand. IN ST TRIAL P Rule 8(A).

    c. *Res ipsa loquitur.* Res ipsa loquitur or a similar doctrine may be pleaded by alleging generally that the facts connected with the action are unknown to the pleader and are within the knowledge of the opposing party. IN ST TRIAL P Rule 9.1(B).

    d. *Bona fide purchaser.* When the rights of a person depend upon his status as a bona fide purchaser for value or upon similar requirements, such status must be pleaded and proved by the person asserting it, but it may be pleaded in general terms. Once it is established that the person has given any required value, unless such value is commercially unreasonable, and that he has met any requirements of recordation, filing, possession, or perfection, the trier of fact must find that such value was given or such perfection was made in accordance with any requirements of good faith, lack of knowledge, or lack of notice unless and until evidence is introduced which would support a finding of its non-existence. IN ST TRIAL P Rule 9.1(D).

    e. *Presumption; Matters of judicial notice.* Neither presumptions of law nor matters of which judicial notice may be taken need be stated in a pleading. IN ST TRIAL P Rule 9.1(E).

        i. *Presumption of jurisdiction.* Jurisdiction is presumed in Indiana. 22B INPRAC 8:2. Consequently, there is no requirement to affirmatively plead the existence of jurisdiction in the complaint, unless the action involves a special proceeding requiring such an allegation. 22B INPRAC 8:2; Cardinal Industries, Inc. v. Schwartz, 483 N.E.2d 458 (Ind.Ct.App. 1985). The plaintiff bears no burden to prove jurisdiction unless and until it is challenged by the defendant. 22B INPRAC 8:2; Brokemond v. Marshall Field & Co., 612 N.E.2d 143 (Ind.Ct.App. 1993).

    f. *Equitable and legal claims in multi-count actions.* In multi-count actions, the inclusion of an equitable claim, standing alone, will not automatically draw the entire action into equity. Something more than the presence of an equitable claim is required, and the court must examine the claims at issue. 22B INPRAC 38:1 COMMENT; Lucas v. U.S. Bank, N.A., 953 N.E.2d 457 (Ind. 2011). Factors the court may consider in evaluating the nature of the underlying substantive claims include: the substance and central character of the complaint, the rights and interests at issue, the relief demanded, and any issues arising out of discovery. 22B INPRAC 38:1 COMMENT; Songer v. Civitas Bank, 771 N.E.2d 61 (Ind. 2002).

4. *Pleading special matters*

    a. *Capacity.* It is not necessary to aver the capacity of a party to sue or be sued, the authority of a party to sue or be sued in a representative capacity, or the legal existence of an organization that is made a party. The burden of proving lack of such capacity, authority, or legal existence shall be upon the person asserting lack of it, and shall be pleaded as an affirmative defense. IN ST TRIAL P Rule 9(A).

    b. *Fraud, mistake, condition of the mind.* In all averments of fraud or mistake, the circumstances constituting fraud or mistake shall be specifically averred. Malice, intent, knowledge, and other conditions of mind may be averred generally. IN ST TRIAL P Rule 9(B).

c.   *Conditions precedent.* In pleading the performance or occurrence of promissory or non-promissory conditions precedent, it is sufficient to aver generally that all conditions precedent have been performed, have occurred, or have been excused. A denial of performance or occurrence shall be made specifically and with particularity, and a denial of excuse generally. IN ST TRIAL P Rule 9(C).

d.   *Official document or act.* In pleading an official document or official act it is sufficient to aver that the document was issued or the act done in compliance with law. IN ST TRIAL P Rule 9(D).

e.   *Judgment.* In pleading a judgment or decision of a domestic or foreign court, judicial or quasi-judicial tribunal, or of a board or officer, it is sufficient to aver the judgment or decision without setting forth matter showing jurisdiction to render it. IN ST TRIAL P Rule 9(E).

f.   *Time and place.* For the purpose of testing the sufficiency of a pleading, averments of time and place are material and shall be considered like all other averments of material matter. However, time and place need be stated only with such specificity as will enable the opposing party to prepare his defense. IN ST TRIAL P Rule 9(F).

g.   *Special damages; Damages where no answer.* When items of special damage are claimed, they shall be specifically stated. The relief granted to the plaintiff, if there be no answer, cannot exceed the relief demanded in his complaint; but, in any other case, the court may grant him any relief consistent with the facts or matters pleaded. IN ST TRIAL P Rule 9(G).

5.   *Joinder*

a.   *Of claims.* A party asserting a claim for relief as an original claim, counterclaim, cross-claim, or third-party claim, may join, either as independent or as alternate claims, as many claims, whether legal, equitable, or statutory as he has against an opposing party. IN ST TRIAL P Rule 18(A).

b.   *Of remedies; Fraudulent conveyances.* Whenever a claim is one heretofore cognizable only after another claim has been prosecuted to a conclusion, the two (2) claims may be joined in a single action; but the court shall grant relief in that action only in accordance with the relative substantive rights of the parties. In particular, a plaintiff may state a claim for money and a claim to have set aside a conveyance fraudulent as to him, without first having obtained a judgment establishing the claim for money. IN ST TRIAL P Rule 18(B).

c.   *Of persons needed for just adjudication.* A person who is subject to service of process shall be joined as a party in the action if:

  i.   In his absence complete relief cannot be accorded among those already parties; or

  ii. He claims an interest relating to the subject of the action and is so situated that the disposition of the action in his absence may:

   •   As a practical matter impair or impede his ability to protect that interest, or

   •   Leave any of the persons already parties subject to a substantial risk of incurring double, multiple, or otherwise inconsistent obligations by reason of his claimed interest. IN ST TRIAL P Rule 19(A).

  iii. If he has not been so joined, the court shall order that he be made a party. If he should join as a plaintiff but refuses to do so, he may be made a defendant. IN ST TRIAL P Rule 19(A).

6.   *Trial by jury; Demand*

a.   *Causes triable by court and by jury.* Issues of law and issues of fact in causes that prior to the eighteenth day of June, 1852, were of exclusive equitable jurisdiction shall be tried by the court; issues of fact in all other causes shall be triable as the same are now triable. In case of the joinder of causes of action or defenses which, prior to said date, were of exclusive equitable jurisdiction with causes of action or defenses which, prior to said date, were designated as actions at law and triable by jury—the former shall be triable by the court, and the latter by a jury, unless waived; the trial of both may be at the same time or at different times, as the court may direct. IN ST TRIAL P Rule 38(A).

b. *Demand.* Any party may demand a trial by jury of any issue triable of right by a jury by filing with the court and serving upon the other parties a demand therefor in writing at any time after the commencement of the action and not later than ten (10) days after the first responsive pleading to the complaint, or to a counterclaim, crossclaim or other claim if one properly is pleaded; and if no responsive pleading is filed or required, within ten (10) days after the time such pleading otherwise would have been required. Such demand is sufficient if indorsed upon a pleading of a party filed within such time. IN ST TRIAL P Rule 38(B).

c. *Same; Specification of issues.* In his demand a party may specify the issues which he wishes so tried; otherwise he shall be deemed to have demanded trial by jury for all issues triable as of right by jury. Any other party must file a demand for jury trial to preserve his right to trial by jury:

    i.   Of issues for which a right to trial by jury was not requested by another party; and

    ii.   In case a request by another party was improper. But if a proper request for a trial by jury upon issues triable by jury as of right on his behalf is made by any party, such request shall be deemed to have been made on behalf of all parties entitled to a jury trial upon such issues. IN ST TRIAL P Rule 38(C).

d. *Waiver.* The failure of a party to appear at the trial, and the failure of a party to serve a demand as required by IN ST TRIAL P Rule 38 and to file it as required by IN ST TRIAL P Rule 5(E) constitute waiver by him of trial by jury. A demand for trial by jury made as provided in IN ST TRIAL P Rule 38 may not be withdrawn without the consent of the other party or parties. IN ST TRIAL P Rule 38(D).

    i.   The trial court shall not grant a demand for a trial by jury filed after the time fixed in IN ST TRIAL P Rule 38(B) has elapsed except upon the written agreement of all of the parties to the action, which agreement shall be filed with the court and made a part of the record. If such agreement is filed then the court may, in its discretion, grant a trial by jury in which event the grant of a trial by jury may not be withdrawn except by the agreement of all of the parties. IN ST TRIAL P Rule 38(D).

e. *Arbitration.* Nothing in the Indiana Rules of Trial Procedure shall deny the parties the right by contract or agreement to submit or to agree to submit controversies to arbitration made before or after commencement of an action thereon or deny the courts power to specifically enforce such agreements. IN ST TRIAL P Rule 38(E).

D. Documents

1. *Required documents*

a. *Amended complaint.* Refer to the General Requirements section of this document for information on the contents of an amended complaint.

b. *Certificate of service.* An attorney or unrepresented party tendering a document to the Clerk for filing shall certify that service has been made, list the parties served, and specify the date and means of service. The certificate of service shall be placed at the end of the document and shall not be separately filed. The separate filing of a certificate of service, however, shall not be grounds for rejecting a document for filing. The Clerk may permit documents to be filed without a certificate of service but shall require prompt filing of a separate certificate of service. IN ST TRIAL P Rule 5(C). In all cases where any pleading or other document is required to be served upon opposing counsel, proof of such service may be made either by:

    i.   A certificate of service signed by counsel of record for the serving party and the certificate shall specify by name and address all counsel upon whom the pleading or document was served; or

    ii.   An acknowledgment of service signed by the party served or counsel of record. IN ST MARION CIR AND SUPER CTS CIV Rule 206.

2. *Supplemental documents*

a. *Proof of written instrument.* When any pleading allowed by the Indiana Rules of Trial Procedure is founded on a written instrument, the original, or a copy thereof, must be included in or filed with the pleading. Such instrument, whether copied in the pleadings or not, shall be taken as part of the record. When any pleading allowed by the Indiana Rules of Trial Procedure is founded on an account, an Affidavit of Debt, in a form substantially similar to that which is provided in IN ST TRIAL P App. A-2, shall be attached. IN ST TRIAL P Rule 9.2(A).

b. *Notice of intent to use foreign law.* A party who intends to raise an issue concerning the law of a foreign country shall give notice in his pleadings or other reasonable written notice. The court, in determining foreign law, may consider any relevant material or source, including testimony, whether or not submitted by a party or admissible under IN ST TRIAL P Rule 43. The court's determination shall be treated as a ruling on a question of law. It shall be made by the court and not the jury and shall be reviewable. IN ST TRIAL P Rule 44.1(A).

c. *Facsimile cover sheet.* Any document sent to the Clerk of the Circuit Court by electronic facsimile transmission shall be accompanied by a cover sheet which states the title of the document, case number, number of pages, identity and voice telephone number of the sending party and instructions for filing. The cover sheet shall contain the signature of the attorney or party, pro se, authorizing the filing. IN ST ADMIN Rule 12(D).

3. Refer to the Indiana KeyRules Complaint document for the required and supplemental documents for filing and serving an amended complaint against a new party.

E. Format

1. *Form of pleadings*

   a. *Caption; Names of parties.* Every pleading shall contain a caption setting forth the name of the court, the title of the action, the file number, and a designation as in IN ST TRIAL P Rule 7(A). In the complaint the title of the action shall include the names of all the parties, but in other pleadings it is sufficient to state the name of the first party on each side with an appropriate indication of other parties. IN ST TRIAL P Rule 10(A).

      i. Every pleading shall contain a caption setting forth the name of the Court, the Division and Room Number, the title of the action and the file number. IN ST MARION CIR AND SUPER CTS CIV Rule 204(B).

   b. *Paragraphs; Separate statements.* All averments of a claim or defense shall be made in numbered paragraphs, the contents of each of which shall be limited as far as practicable to a statement of a single set of circumstances, and a paragraph may be referred to by number in all succeeding pleadings. Each claim founded upon a separate transaction or occurrence and each defense other than denials may be stated in a separate count or defense whenever a separation facilitates the clear presentation of the matters set forth. IN ST TRIAL P Rule 10(B).

   c. *Adoption by reference; Exhibits.* Statements in a pleading may be adopted by reference in a different part of the same pleading or in another pleading or in any motion. A copy of any written instrument which is an exhibit to a pleading is a part thereof for all purposes. IN ST TRIAL P Rule 10(C).

   d. *Paper.* Pleadings, motions and other papers may be either printed or typewritten on white opaque paper of at least sixteen (16) pound weight, eight and one-half (8-1/2) inches wide and eleven (11) inches in length. IN ST MARION CIR AND SUPER CTS CIV Rule 204(A).

   e. *Copies.* All copies shall likewise be on white paper of sufficient strength and durability to resist normal wear and tear. IN ST MARION CIR AND SUPER CTS CIV Rule 204(A).

   f. *Line spacing.* If typewritten, the lines shall be double spaced, except for quotations, which shall be indented and single spaced. IN ST MARION CIR AND SUPER CTS CIV Rule 204(A).

   g. *Script type.* Script type shall not be used. IN ST MARION CIR AND SUPER CTS CIV Rule 204(A).

   h. *Titles.* Titles on all pleadings shall delineate each topic included in the pleading e.g. where a pleading contains an Answer, a Motion to Strike or Dismiss, or a Jury Request each shall be set forth in the title. IN ST MARION CIR AND SUPER CTS CIV Rule 204(C).

   i. *Margins and binding.* Margins shall be one (1) inch. Binding or stapling shall be at the top and at no other place. Covers or backing shall not be used. IN ST MARION CIR AND SUPER CTS CIV Rule 204(D).

2. *Size of papers for filing.* Effective January 1, 1992, all pleadings, copies, motions and documents filed

with any·trial court or appellate level court, typed or printed, with the exception of exhibits and existing wills, shall be prepared on eight and one-half by eleven inch (8 1/2" x 11") size paper. IN ST ADMIN Rule 11.

3. *Form of electronically filed documents.* All electronically filed and served pleadings shall, to the extent practicable, be formatted in accordance with the applicable rules governing formatting of paper pleadings. IN ST MARION SUPER CT ADMIN Rule 311(2-103)(1).

    a. *Electronic document title.* The electronic document title of each pleading or other document shall include:

        i. Party or parties filing/serving the document,

        ii. Nature of the document,

        iii. Party or parties against whom relief, if any, is sought, and

        iv. Nature of the relief sought (e.g., Defendant ABC Corporation's Motion for Summary Judgment). IN ST MARION SUPER CT ADMIN Rule 311(2-103)(2).

4. *Signature requirements*

    a. *Signature of attorney.* Every pleading or motion of a party represented by an attorney shall be signed by at least one (1) attorney of record in his individual name, whose address, telephone number, and attorney number shall be stated, except that this provision shall not apply to pleadings and motions made and transcribed at the trial or a hearing before the judge and received by him in such form. IN ST TRIAL P Rule 11(A).

        i. All pleadings and motions shall contain the original or authorized signature of the attorney, the name of the attorney in typed or printed form, the name of the law firm if a member of a firm, the attorney's address, identification number, e-mail address, telephone number, fax number, and the designation as to the party for whom he appears. IN ST MARION CIR AND SUPER CTS CIV Rule 204(E).

        ii. The signature of an attorney constitutes a certificate by him that he has read the pleadings; that to the best of his knowledge, information, and belief, there is good ground to support it; and that it is not interposed for delay. IN ST TRIAL P Rule 11(A).

        iii. If a pleading or motion is not signed or is signed with intent to defeat the purpose of the rule, it may be stricken as sham and false and the action may proceed as though the pleading had not been served. IN ST TRIAL P Rule 11(A).

        iv. For a willful violation of IN ST TRIAL P Rule 11 an attorney may be subjected to appropriate disciplinary action. Similar action may be taken if scandalous or indecent matter is inserted. IN ST TRIAL P Rule 11(A).

        v. Every pleading, document, and instrument electronically filed or served shall be deemed to have been signed by the judge, clerk, attorney or declarant and shall bear a facsimile or typographical signature of such person, along with the typed name, address, telephone number, and Bar number of a signing attorney. Typographical signatures shall be treated as personal signatures for all purposes under these rules. IN ST MARION SUPER CT ADMIN Rule 311(2-105).

           • Documents containing signatures of third-parties (i.e., unopposed motions, affidavits, stipulations, etc.) may also be filed electronically by indicating that the original signatures are maintained by the filing party in paper-format. IN ST MARION SUPER CT ADMIN Rule 311(2-105).

           • Unless otherwise ordered by the Court or Clerk, a printed copy of all documents filed or served electronically, including original signatures, shall be maintained by the party filing the document and shall be made available, upon reasonable notice, for inspection by other counsel, the Clerk or Court. Parties shall retain originals until two (2) years after all time periods for appeal have expired. From time to time, it may be necessary to provide the Clerk or Court with a hard copy of an electronically filed document. IN ST MARION SUPER CT ADMIN Rule 311(2-105).

vi. For the recommended format of a signature block, refer to IN ST MARION CIR AND SUPER CTS CIV Rule 204(E).

b. *Signature of unrepresented party.* A party who is not represented by an attorney shall sign his pleading and state his address. IN ST TRIAL P Rule 11(A).

c. *Verification not generally required.* Except when specifically required by rule, pleadings or motions need not be verified or accompanied by affidavit. The rule in equity that the averments of an answer under oath must be overcome by the testimony of two (2) witnesses or of one (1) witness sustained by corroborating circumstances is abolished. IN ST TRIAL P Rule 11(A).

d. *Verification by affirmation or representation.* When in connection with any civil or special statutory proceeding it is required that any pleading, motion, petition, supporting affidavit, or other document of any kind, be verified, or that an oath be taken, it shall be sufficient if the subscriber simply affirms the truth of the matter to be verified by an affirmation or representation. IN ST TRIAL P Rule 11(B). IN ST TRIAL P Rule 11(B) states that the affirmation or representation should be in substantially the following language: "I (we) affirm, under the penalties for perjury, that the foregoing representation(s) is (are) true. (Signed) _____."

   i. Any person who falsifies an affirmation or representation of fact shall be subject to the same penalties as are prescribed by law for the making of a false affidavit. IN ST TRIAL P Rule 11(B).

e. *Verified pleadings, motions, and affidavits as evidence.* Pleadings, motions and affidavits accompanying or in support of such pleadings or motions when required to be verified or under oath shall be accepted as a representation that the signer had personal knowledge thereof or reasonable cause to believe the existence of the facts or matters stated or alleged therein; and, if otherwise competent or acceptable as evidence, may be admitted as evidence of the facts or matters stated or alleged therein when it is so provided in the Indiana Rules of Trial Procedure, by statute or other law, or to the extent the writing or signature expressly purports to be made upon the signer's personal knowledge. When such pleadings, motions and affidavits are verified or under oath they shall not require other or greater proof on the part of the adverse party than if not verified or not under oath unless expressly provided otherwise by the Indiana Rules of Trial Procedure, statute or other law. Affidavits upon motions for summary judgment under IN ST TRIAL P Rule 56 and in denial of execution under IN ST TRIAL P Rule 9.2 shall be made upon personal knowledge. IN ST TRIAL P Rule 11(C).

5. *Information excluded from public access.* Every document filed in a case shall separately identify information excluded from public access pursuant to IN ST ADMIN Rule 9(G)(1) as follows:

   a. Whole documents that are excluded from public access pursuant to IN ST ADMIN Rule 9(G)(1) shall be tendered on light green paper or have a light green coversheet attached to the document, marked "Not for Public Access" or "Confidential." IN ST TRIAL P Rule 5(G)(1).

   b. When only a portion of a document contains information excluded from public access pursuant to IN ST ADMIN Rule 9(G)(1), said information shall be omitted [or redacted] from the filed document, and set forth on a separate accompanying document on light green paper conspicuously marked "Not for Public Access" or "Confidential" and clearly designated [or identifying] the caption and number of the case and the document and location within the document to which the redacted material pertains. IN ST TRIAL P Rule 5(G)(2).

   c. With respect to documents filed in electronic format, the trial court, by local rule, may provide for compliance with IN ST TRIAL P Rule 5 in manner that separates and protects access to information excluded from public access. IN ST TRIAL P Rule 5(G)(3).

   d. IN ST TRIAL P Rule 5(G) does not apply to a record sealed by the court pursuant to IN ST 5-14-3-5.5 or otherwise, nor to records, documents, or information filed in cases to which public access is prohibited pursuant to IN ST ADMIN Rule 9(G). IN ST TRIAL P Rule 5(G)(4).

   e. The following information in case records is excluded from public access and is confidential:

      i. Information that is excluded from public access pursuant to federal law;

ii. Information that is excluded from public access as declared confidential by Indiana statute or other court rule, including without limitation:

- All adoption records created after July 8, 1941, as declared confidential by IN ST 31-19-19-1, et seq., except those specifically declared open by IN ST 31-19-13-2(2);

- All records relating to chancroid, chlamydia, gonorrhea, hepatitis, human immunodeficiency virus (HIV), Lymphogranuloma venereum, syphilis, tuberculosis, as declared confidential by IN ST 16-41-8-1, et seq.;

- All records relating to child abuse as declared confidential by IN ST 31-33-18-1, et seq.;

- All records relating to drug tests as declared confidential by IN ST 5-14-3-4(a)(9);

- Records of grand jury proceedings as declared confidential by IN ST 35-34-2-4;

- Records of juvenile proceedings as declared confidential by IN ST 31-39-1-2, except those specifically open under statute;

- All paternity records created after July 1, 1941 as declared confidential by IN ST 31-14-11-15, IN ST 31-19-5-23, IN ST 31-39-1-1 and IN ST 31-39-1-2 [Editor's note: IN ST 31-14-11-15 was repealed effective May 9, 2013];

- All pre-sentence reports as declared confidential by IN ST 35-38-1-13;

- Written petitions to permit marriages without consent and orders directing the Clerk of Court to issue a marriage license to underage persons, as declared confidential by IN ST 31-11-1-6;

- Only those arrest warrants, search warrants, indictments and informations ordered confidential by the trial judge, prior to return of duly executed service as declared confidential by IN ST 5-14-3-4(b)(1);

- All medical, mental health, or tax records unless determined by law or regulation of any governmental custodian not to be confidential, released by the subject of such records, or declared by a court of competent jurisdiction to be essential to the resolution of litigation as declared confidential by IN ST 16-39-3-10, IN ST 6-4.1-5-10, IN ST 6-4.1-12-12, and IN ST 6-8.1-7-1;

- Personal information relating to jurors or prospective jurors, other than for the use of the parties and counsel, pursuant to IN ST JURY Rule 10;

- Information relating to protection from abuse orders, no-contact orders and workplace violence restraining orders as declared confidential by IN ST 5-2-9-6, et seq.;

- Mediation proceedings pursuant to IN ST ADR Rule 2.11, Mini-Trial proceedings pursuant to IN ST ADR Rule 4.4(C), and Summary Jury Trials pursuant to IN ST ADR Rule 5.6;

- Information in probation files pursuant to the Probation Standards promulgated by the Judicial Conference of Indiana pursuant to IN ST 11-13-1-8(b);

- Information deemed confidential pursuant to the Rules for Court Administered Alcohol and Drug Programs promulgated by the Judicial Conference of Indiana pursuant to IN ST 12-23-14-13;

- Information deemed confidential pursuant to the Problem-Solving Court Rules promulgated by the Judicial Conference of Indiana pursuant to IN ST 33-23-16-16;

- All records of the Department of workforce Development as declared confidential by IN ST 22-4-19-6;

- Information regarding interception of electronic communications that is sealed or deemed confidential as set forth in IN ST 35-33.5-2-1, et seq.

iii. Information excluded from public access by specific court order;

iv. Complete Social Security Numbers of living persons;

v. With the exception of names, information such as addresses, phone numbers, and dates of birth which explicitly identifies:

- Natural persons who are witnesses or victims (not including defendants) in criminal, domestic violence, stalking, sexual assault, juvenile, or civil protection order proceedings, provided that juveniles who are victims of sex crimes shall be identified by initials only;

- Places of residence of judicial officers, clerks and other employees of courts and clerks of court, unless the person or persons about whom the information pertains waives confidentiality;

vi. Complete account numbers of specific assets, loans, bank accounts, credit cards, and personal identification numbers (PINs);

vii. All orders of expungement entered in criminal or juvenile proceedings, orders to restrict access to criminal history information pursuant to IN ST 35-38-5-5.5 or IN ST 35-38-8-5 and records excluded from public access by such orders, and information related to infractions that is excluded from public access pursuant to IN ST 34-28-5-15 or IN ST 34-28-5-16 [Editor's note: IN ST 35-38-5-5.5, IN ST 35-38-8-5 and IN ST 34-28-5-16 were repealed effective July 1, 2013; for information on orders restricting access to criminal history, refer to IN ST 35-38-9-1, et seq.];

viii. All personal notes and e-mail, and deliberative material, of judges, jurors, court staff and judicial agencies, and information recorded in personal data assistants (PDA's) or organizers and personal calendars. IN ST ADMIN Rule 9(G)(1).

F. Filing and Service Requirements

1. *Filing requirements.* Except as otherwise provided in IN ST TRIAL P Rule 5(E)(2), all pleadings and papers subsequent to the complaint which are required to be served upon a party shall be filed with the Court either before service or within a reasonable period of time thereafter. IN ST TRIAL P Rule 5(E)(1).

   a. *Filing generally.* All pleadings, petitions and motions are filed with the Clerk designated by the Court at any time during office hours established by the Clerk and the Court. All orders submitted to the Court shall be in sufficient number and shall be accompanied by postage paid envelopes addressed to each party or counsel of record. IN ST MARION CIR AND SUPER CTS CIV Rule 205(A)

   b. *Filing with the court defined.* The filing of pleadings, motions, and other papers with the court as required by the Indiana Rules of Trial Procedure shall be made by one of the following methods:

      i. Delivery to the clerk of the court;

      ii. Sending by electronic transmission under the procedure adopted pursuant to IN ST ADMIN Rule 12;

      iii. Mailing to the clerk by registered, certified or express mail return receipt requested;

      iv. Depositing with any third-party commercial carrier for delivery to the clerk within three (3) calendar days, cost prepaid, properly addressed;

      v. If the court so permits, filing with the judge, in which event the judge shall note thereon the filing date and forthwith transmit them to the office of the clerk; or

      vi. Electronic filing, as approved by the Division of State Court Administration pursuant to IN ST ADMIN Rule 16. IN ST TRIAL P Rule 5(F).

      vii. Filing by registered or certified mail and by third-party commercial carrier shall be complete upon mailing or deposit. IN ST TRIAL P Rule 5(F).

   c. *Facsimile filing.* Facsimile filing is discouraged, but permitted in the Marion Circuit and Marion Superior Court. All documents filed by facsimile shall also be filed in hard copy within seven (7) days of the facsimile filing, along with proposed orders and stamped addressed envelopes, as required by IN ST MARION CIR AND SUPER CTS CIV Rule 203(E). To avoid duplicate filings, the hard copies of the facsimile filing shall indicate in bold letters that the pleading was previously filed by facsimile transmission. Proof of transmission by facsimile, including certificate of service and manner of service, shall be the responsibility of the filing party. If the filing requires immediate attention of the Judge, it shall be so indicated in bold letters in an accompanying transmittal memorandum. Legibility of documents and timeliness of filing is the responsibility of the sender. IN ST MARION CIR AND SUPER CTS CIV Rule 205(B).

    i.   *Generally.* In counties where a majority of judges of the courts of record, by posted local rule, have authorized electronic facsimile filing and designated a telephone number to receive such transmissions, pleadings, motions, and other papers may be sent to the Clerk of Circuit Court by electronic facsimile transmission for filing in any case, provided:

- Such matter does not exceed ten (10) pages, including the cover sheet;

- Such matter does not require the payment of fees other than the electronic facsimile transcription fee set forth in IN ST ADMIN Rule 12(E);

- The sending party creates at the time of transmission a machine generated log for such transmission; and

- The original document and the transmission log are maintained by the sending party for the duration of the litigation. IN ST ADMIN Rule 12(B).

    ii.   *Time of filing.* During normal, posted business hours, the time of filing shall be the time the duplicate document is produced in the office of the Clerk of the Circuit Court. Duplicate documents received at all other times shall be filed as of the next normal business day. IN ST ADMIN Rule 12(C).

- If the receiving fax machine endorses its own time and date stamp upon the transmitted documents and the receiving machine produces a delivery receipt which is electronically created and transmitted to the sending party, the time of filing shall be the date and time recorded on the transmitted document by the receiving fax machine. IN ST ADMIN Rule 12(C).

  d. *Electronic filing.* Electronic filing and electronic service pilot projects are authorized pursuant to IN ST ADMIN Rule 16 and approved by the Division of State Court Administration. IN ST MARION SUPER CT ADMIN Rule 311(1-103).

    i.   *Cases where electronic filing accepted.* All Marion County Circuit and Superior civil courts may accept electronic filing and service of pleadings and other documents designated in this rule in mortgage foreclosure (hereinafter referred to as "MF"), civil collection(hereinafter referred to as "CC"), and individual cases that have been approved for electronic filing and service. IN ST MARION SUPER CT ADMIN Rule 311(1-104)(1).

- The Marion County Circuit Court may, upon the motion of a party or its own motion, designate a case that will involve multiple litigants, legally intricate issues, and an extensive number of documents a mass tort or complex litigation case. Any case so designated shall be subject to electronic filing and service using the county's approved Electronic Service Provider. IN ST MARION SUPER CT ADMIN Rule 311(1-104)(3).

- The filing of electronic pleadings and other documents in MF and CC cases is entirely voluntary; however, once the case is initially filed electronically, all subsequent filings in the case shall remain in electronic format until the time for appeal is exhausted. IN ST MARION SUPER CT ADMIN Rule 311(1-104)(5).

    ii.   *Documents eligible for electronic filing.* The following pleadings may be filed and served electronically:

- New case complaint and petitions. IN ST MARION SUPER CT ADMIN Rule 311(1-104)(8)(a).

- Original answers. IN ST MARION SUPER CT ADMIN Rule 311(1-104)(8)(a).

- Any other pleadings or document including but not limited to motions and appearance forms. IN ST MARION SUPER CT ADMIN Rule 311(1-104)(8)(a).

    iii.   *Manner of electronic filing.* Parties shall E-file a document either:

- By registering to use the Electronic Filing Service Provider; or

- In person at the Marion County Clerk's office, by electronically filing through the Public Access Terminal. Parties filing in this manner shall be responsible for furnishing the document in an electronic format that will be compatible with the clerk's office-system to be uploaded in person. IN ST MARION SUPER CT ADMIN Rule 311(1-104)(9). For information on the Electronic Filing Service Provider and Public Access Terminal, refer to IN ST MARION SUPER CT ADMIN Rule 311(1-101).

- Registered users shall pay statutory filing fees for E-filed documents electronically to the Court through their EFSP. Filing fees are due and payable at the time of filing. IN ST MARION SUPER CT ADMIN Rule 311(2-104)(1). For more information on electronic filing fees, refer to IN ST MARION SUPER CT ADMIN Rule 311(2-104).

iv. *Effect of electronic filing.* Any pleading filed electronically shall be considered as filed with the court when the transmission to the EFSP is complete. Any document E-filed by 11:59 p.m. local Indianapolis, Indiana time shall be deemed filed on that date. The EFSP is an agent of the Court for the purpose of electronic filing, receipt, service and retrieval of electronic documents. IN ST MARION SUPER CT ADMIN Rule 311(2-102).

- Upon completion of filing, the EFSP shall issue a confirmation receipt that includes the date and time of receipt. The confirmation receipt shall serve as proof of filing. IN ST MARION SUPER CT ADMIN Rule 311(2-102).

- In the event the Court rejects the submitted documents following review, the documents shall not become part of the official Court record and the filer will receive notification of the rejection. Users may be required to refile the instruments to meet necessary filing requirements. Documents may be filed through an E-filing system at any time that the Clerk's office is open to receive the filing or at such other times as may be designated by the clerk and posted publicly. IN ST MARION SUPER CT ADMIN Rule 311(2-102).

- Documents filed through the E-filing system are deemed filed when received by the Clerk's office, except that documents received at times that the Clerk's office is closed shall be deemed filed the next regular time when the Clerk's office is open for filing. The time stamp issued by the E-filing system shall be presumed to be the time the document is received by the Clerk. IN ST MARION SUPER CT ADMIN Rule 311(2-102).

v. *Electronically filed documents.* All pleadings and other documents designated in IN ST MARION SUPER CT ADMIN Rule 311 shall be filed and served electronically in any individual case which has been approved for electronic filing and service. IN ST MARION SUPER CT ADMIN Rule 311(1-104)(6).

vi. *System failures.* When filing by electronic means is hindered by a technical failure, a party may file with the Clerk of Marion County in hard copy. With the exception of deadlines that by law cannot be extended, the time for filing of any paper that is delayed due to technical failure of the site shall be extended for one (1) day for each day on which such failure occurs, unless otherwise ordered by the Court. IN ST MARION SUPER CT ADMIN Rule 311(2-108).

vii. *Compliance with rules.* All filing shall comply with the requirements of IN ST ADMIN Rule 9 and IN ST ADMIN Rule 16; and the Indiana Rules of Court and the Marion County Local Rules. IN ST MARION SUPER CT ADMIN Rule 311(1-104)(11).

e. *Filing for special judge.* When a Special Judge who is not a Marion County Judge is selected, all parties or attorneys shall furnish such Judge with copies of all filings prior to the qualification of such Special Judge. Thereafter, copies of all filings shall be delivered in person, by mail or by facsimile to the office of the Special Judge with certificate of forwarding same made a part of the filing. IN ST MARION CIR AND SUPER CTS CIV Rule 205(C).

f. *Proof of filing.* Any party filing any paper by any method other than personal delivery to the clerk shall retain proof of filing. IN ST TRIAL P Rule 5(F).

2. *Service requirements.* Unless otherwise provided by the Indiana Rules of Trial Procedure or an order of the court, each party and special judge, if any, shall be served with: (1) every order required by its terms to be served; (2) every pleading subsequent to the original complaint; (3) every written motion except one

which may be heard ex parte; (4) every brief submitted to the trial court; (5) every paper relating to discovery required to be served upon a party; and (6) every written notice, appearance, demand, offer of judgment, designation of record on appeal, or similar paper. IN ST TRIAL P Rule 5(A).

a.   *Methods of service*

    i.   *Personal service.* Whenever a party is represented by an attorney of record, service shall be made upon such attorney unless service upon the party himself is ordered by the court. Service upon the attorney or party shall be made by delivering or mailing a copy of the papers to the last known address or where an attorney or party has consented to service by fax or e-mail, as provided in IN ST TRIAL P Rule 3.1(A)(4), by faxing or e-mailing a copy of the documents to the fax number or e-mail address set out in the appearance form or correction as required by IN ST TRIAL P Rule 3.1(E). IN ST TRIAL P Rule 5(B). Delivery of a copy within IN ST TRIAL P Rule 5 means:

- Offering or tendering it to the attorney or party and stating the nature of the papers being served. Refusal to accept an offered or tendered document is a waiver of any objection to the sufficiency or adequacy of service of that document;

- Leaving it at his office with a clerk or other person in charge thereof, or if there is no one in charge, leaving it in a conspicuous place therein; or

- If the office is closed, by leaving it at his dwelling house or usual place of abode with some person of suitable age and discretion then residing therein; or,

- Leaving it at some other suitable place, selected by the attorney upon whom service is being made, pursuant to duly promulgated local rule. IN ST TRIAL P Rule 5(B)(1).

    ii.   *Service by mail.* If service is made by mail, the papers shall be deposited in the United States mail addressed to the person on whom they are being served, with postage prepaid. Service shall be deemed complete upon mailing. Proof of service of all papers permitted to be mailed may be made by written acknowledgment of service, by affidavit of the person who mailed the papers, or by certificate of an attorney. It shall be the duty of attorneys when entering their appearance in a cause or when filing pleadings or papers therein, to have noted in the Chronological Case Summary or said pleadings or papers so filed the address and telephone number of their office. Service by delivery or by mail at such address shall be deemed sufficient and complete. IN ST TRIAL P Rule 5(B)(2).

    iii.   *Service by fax or e-mail.* A party who has consented to service by fax or e-mail may be served as follows:

- Service by e-mail shall be made by attaching the document being served in .pdf format. Discovery documents must also be served in accordance with IN ST TRIAL P Rule 26(A). IN ST TRIAL P Rule 5(B)(3)(a).

- Service by fax shall be deemed complete upon generation of a transmission record indicating the successful transmission of the entire document, except as provided in IN ST TRIAL P Rule 5(B)(3)(d). IN ST TRIAL P Rule 5(B)(3)(b).

- Service by e-mail shall be deemed complete upon transmission, except as provided in IN ST TRIAL P Rule 5(B)(3)(d). IN ST TRIAL P Rule 5(B)(3)(c).

- Service by fax or e-mail that occurs on a Saturday, Sunday, legal holiday, or day the court or agency in which the matter is pending is closed or after 5:00 PM local time of the recipient shall be deemed complete the next day that is not a Saturday, Sunday, legal holiday, or day that the court or agency in which the matter is pending is not closed. IN ST TRIAL P Rule 5(B)(3)(d).

    iv.   *Electronic service.* Delivery of E-service documents through the EFSP to other registered users shall be considered as valid and effective service and shall have the same legal effect as an original paper document. Recipients of E-service documents shall access their documents through the EFSP. IN ST MARION SUPER CT ADMIN Rule 311(2-107)(1).

- E-service shall be deemed complete when the transmission to the EFSP is completed. IN ST MARION SUPER CT ADMIN Rule 311(2-107)(2).

- For the purpose of computing time to respond to documents received via E-service, any document served on a day or at a time when the Clerk's office is not open for business shall be deemed served at the time of next opening of the Clerk's office for business. IN ST MARION SUPER CT ADMIN Rule 311(2-107)(3).

b. *Serving numerous defendants.* In any action in which there are unusually large numbers of defendants, the court, upon motion or of its own initiative, may order:

    i. That service of the pleadings of the defendants and replies thereto need not be made as between the defendants;

- That any cross-claim, counterclaim, or matter constituting an avoidance or affirmative defense contained therein shall be deemed to be denied or avoided by all other parties; and
- That the filing of any such pleading and service thereof upon the plaintiff constitutes due notice of it to the parties. IN ST TRIAL P Rule 5(D).

    ii. A copy of every such order shall be served upon the parties in such manner and form as the court directs. IN ST TRIAL P Rule 5(D).

c. *Service on parties in default for failure to appear.* No service need be made on parties in default for failure to appear, except that pleadings asserting new or additional claims for relief against them shall be served upon them in the manner provided by service of summons in IN ST TRIAL P Rule 4. IN ST TRIAL P Rule 5(A).

3. *Service requirements if adding a new party by amendment.* Refer to the Indiana KeyRules Complaint document for information on serving a new party added by amendment.

G. Hearings

1. The Indiana rules do not contemplate a hearing regarding the filing and service of an amended complaint.

H. Forms

1. Official Amended Complaint Forms for Indiana

a. Affidavit of debt. IN ST TRIAL P App. A-2.

2. Amended Complaint Forms for Indiana

a. Motion to file amended complaint. 5 INPRAC § 3:5.1.

b. Motion to file amended complaint; Another form. 5 INPRAC § 3:5.2.

c. Objections to motion to file amended complaint. 5 INPRAC § 3:5.3.

d. Motion to amend pleading to conform to evidence. 5 INPRAC § 3:5.4.

e. Amendment by stipulation. 10 INPRAC § 46.11.

f. Caption; Generally. 5 INPRAC § 3:1.1.

g. Caption; Multiple parties. 5 INPRAC § 3:1.2.

h. Single count. 5 INPRAC § 3:1.3.

i. Multiple counts; Single defendant. 5 INPRAC § 3:1.4.

j. Multiple counts; Multiple defendants. 5 INPRAC § 3:1.5.

k. Signature; By party. 5 INPRAC § 3:1.6.

l. Signature; By attorney. 5 INPRAC § 3:1.7.

m. Verification. 5 INPRAC § 3:1.8.

n. Individual defendant. 5 INPRAC § 3:2.1.

o. Resident agent of corporation. 5 INPRAC § 3:2.2.

p. Attorney general. 5 INPRAC § 3:2.3.

q. City attorney. 5 INPRAC § 3:2.4.

r. Certificate; Personal service. 5 INPRAC § 3:2.5.

s.   Certificate; First class mail. 5 INPRAC § 3:2.6.

t.   Certificate; Registered mail. 5 INPRAC § 3:2.7.

u.   Certificate; Dwelling house. 5 INPRAC § 3:2.8.

v.   Clerk's certificate of mailing. 5 INPRAC § 3:2.9.

w.   Clerk's certificate of mailing; Acceptance by defendant. 5 INPRAC § 3:2.10.

x.   Clerk's return on service of summons by mail; Not accepted by defendant. 5 INPRAC § 3:2.11.

y.   Sheriff's return; Service of summons. 5 INPRAC § 3:2.12.

z.   Motion to appoint person to serve process. 5 INPRAC § 3:2.13.

I. Checklist

(I)   ❑ Matters to be considered by the party filing the amended complaint

    (a)   ❑ Required documents if amending as matter of course

        (1)   ❑ Amended complaint

        (2)   ❑ Certificate of service

    (b)   ❑ Supplemental documents

        (1)   ❑ Proof of written instrument

        (2)   ❑ Notice of intent to use foreign law

        (3)   ❑ Facsimile cover sheet

    (c)   ❑ Timing

        (1)   ❑ As a matter of course before a responsive pleading is served, or, if the pleading is one to which no responsive pleading is permitted, within thirty (30) days after it is served

        (2)   ❑ At any time with leave of court

Pleadings
Answer

Document Last Updated October 2013

A. Applicable Rules

1. *State rules*

    a.   Appearance. IN ST TRIAL P Rule 3.1.

    b.   Process. IN ST TRIAL P Rule 4.

    c.   Service. IN ST TRIAL P Rule 4.15; IN ST TRIAL P Rule 4.16; IN ST TRIAL P Rule 5.

    d.   Time. IN ST TRIAL P Rule 6.

    e.   Pleadings. IN ST TRIAL P Rule 7; IN ST TRIAL P Rule 8; IN ST TRIAL P Rule 9; IN ST TRIAL P Rule 9.1; IN ST TRIAL P Rule 9.2; IN ST TRIAL P Rule 10.

    f.   Signing and verification of pleadings. IN ST TRIAL P Rule 11.

    g.   Defenses and objections; When and how presented; By pleading or motion; Motion for judgment on the pleadings. IN ST TRIAL P Rule 12.

    h.   Counterclaim and cross-claim. IN ST TRIAL P Rule 13.

    i.   Third-party practice. IN ST TRIAL P Rule 14.

    j.   Amended and supplemental pleadings. IN ST TRIAL P Rule 15.

    k.   Parties plaintiff and defendant; Capacity. IN ST TRIAL P Rule 17.

    l.   Joinder. IN ST TRIAL P Rule 19; IN ST TRIAL P Rule 20.

    m.   Jury trial of right. IN ST TRIAL P Rule 38.

    n.   Consolidation; Separate trials. IN ST TRIAL P Rule 42.

    o.   Evidence. IN ST TRIAL P Rule 43.

    p.   Determination of foreign law. IN ST TRIAL P Rule 44.1.

    q.   Judgment. IN ST TRIAL P Rule 50; IN ST TRIAL P Rule 52; IN ST TRIAL P Rule 54; IN ST TRIAL P Rule 56; IN ST TRIAL P Rule 59; IN ST TRIAL P Rule 60.

    r.   Venue requirements. IN ST TRIAL P Rule 75.

    s.   Alternative dispute resolution. IN ST ADR Rule 1.1; IN ST ADR Rule 1.6; IN ST ADR Rule 8.8.

    t.   Uniform case numbering system. IN ST ADMIN Rule 8.

    u.   Access to court records. IN ST ADMIN Rule 9.

    v.   Paper size. IN ST ADMIN Rule 11.

    w.   Facsimile transmission. IN ST ADMIN Rule 12.

    x.   Electronic filing and electronic service pilot projects. IN ST ADMIN Rule 16.

    y.   Sealing of certain records by court; Hearing; Notice. IN ST 5-14-3-5.5.

    z.   Privacy and confidentiality. IN ST 5-2-9-6; IN ST 5-14-3-4; IN ST 6-4.1-5-10; IN ST 6-4.1-12-12; IN ST 6-8.1-7-1; IN ST 11-13-1-8; IN ST 12-23-14-13; IN ST 16-39-3-10; IN ST 16-41-8-1; IN ST 22-4-19-6; IN ST 31-11-1-6; IN ST 31-19-5-23; IN ST 31-19-13-2; IN ST 31-19-19-1; IN ST 31-33-18-1; IN ST 31-39-1-1; IN ST 31-39-1-2; IN ST 33-23-16-16; IN ST 35-34-2-4; IN ST 35-38-1-13; IN ST 35-38-9-1; IN ST ADR Rule 2.11; IN ST ADR Rule 4.4; IN ST ADR Rule 5.6; IN ST JURY Rule 10.

2. *Local rules*

    a.   Requirements for motions. IN ST MARION CIR AND SUPER CTS CIV Rule 203.

    b.   Preparation of pleadings, motions and other papers. IN ST MARION CIR AND SUPER CTS CIV Rule 204.

    c.   Filing of pleadings, motions and other papers. IN ST MARION CIR AND SUPER CTS CIV Rule 205.

    d.   Signing and verification of pleadings, motions and other papers; Service on opposing party. IN ST MARION CIR AND SUPER CTS CIV Rule 206.

    e.   Alternative dispute resolution; Mediation procedure. IN ST MARION CIR AND SUPER CTS CIV Rule 209.

    f.   Motions for continuance. IN ST MARION CIR AND SUPER CTS CIV Rule 215.

    g.   Electronic filing. IN ST MARION SUPER CT ADMIN Rule 311.

B. Timing

1. *Time to serve answer.* A responsive pleading required under the Indiana Rules of Trial Procedure, shall be served within twenty (20) days after service of the prior pleading. IN ST TRIAL P Rule 6(C).

    a.   *Effect of IN ST TRIAL P Rule 12 motions.* The service of a motion permitted under IN ST TRIAL P Rule 12 alters the time for service of responsive pleadings as follows, unless a different time is fixed by the court:

        i.   If the court does not grant the motion, the responsive pleading shall be served in ten (10) days after notice of the court's action;

        ii.   If the court grants the motion and the corrective action is allowed to be taken, it shall be taken within ten (10) days, and the responsive pleading shall be served within ten (10) days thereafter. IN ST TRIAL P Rule 6(C).

2. *Responding to amended complaint.* A party shall plead in response to an amended pleading within the time remaining for response to the original pleading or within twenty (20) days after service of the

amended pleading, whichever period may be the longer, unless the court otherwise orders. IN ST TRIAL P Rule 15(A).

3. *Filing.* All pleadings and papers subsequent to the complaint which are required to be served upon a party shall be filed with the Court either before service or within a reasonable period of time thereafter. IN ST TRIAL P Rule 5(E)(1).

4. *Filing of third-party complaint.* The third-party plaintiff must file the third-party complaint with his original answer or by leave of court thereafter with good cause shown. IN ST TRIAL P Rule 14(A).

5. *Computation of time*

   a. *Generally; Days excluded.* In computing any period of time prescribed or allowed by the Indiana Rules of Trial Procedure, by order of the court, or by any applicable statute, the day of the act, event, or default from which the designated period of time begins to run shall not be included. The last day of the period so computed is to be included unless it is:

      i. A Saturday,

      ii. A Sunday,

      iii. A legal holiday as defined by state statute, or

      iv. A day the office in which the act is to be done is closed during regular business hours. IN ST TRIAL P Rule 6(A).

   b. *Short periods.* In any event, the period runs until the end of the next day that is not a Saturday, a Sunday, a legal holiday, or a day on which the office is closed. When the period of time allowed is less than seven (7) days, intermediate Saturdays, Sundays, legal holidays, and days on which the office is closed shall be excluded from the computations. IN ST TRIAL P Rule 6(A).

   c. *Additional time after service by United States mail.* Whenever a party has the right or is required to do some act or take some proceedings within a prescribed period after the service of a notice or other paper upon him and the notice or paper is served upon him by United States mail, three (3) days shall be added to the prescribed period. IN ST TRIAL P Rule 6(E).

   d. *Enlargement of time.* When an act is required or allowed to be done at or within a specific time by the Indiana Rules of Trial Procedure, the court may at any time for cause shown:

      i. Order the period enlarged, with or without motion or notice, if request therefor is made before the expiration of the period originally prescribed or extended by a previous order; or

      ii. Upon motion made after the expiration of the specific period, permit the act to be done where the failure to act was the result of excusable neglect; but, the court may not extend the time for taking any action for judgment on the evidence under IN ST TRIAL P Rule 50(A), amendment of findings and judgment under IN ST TRIAL P Rule 52(B), to correct errors under IN ST TRIAL P Rule 59(C), statement in opposition to motion to correct error under IN ST TRIAL P Rule 59(E), or to obtain relief from final judgment under IN ST TRIAL P Rule 60(B), except to the extent and under the conditions stated in those rules. IN ST TRIAL P Rule 6(B).

      iii. Initial written motion for enlargement of time pursuant to IN ST TRIAL P Rule 6(B)(1) to respond to a claim shall be automatically allowed for an additional thirty (30) days from the original due date without a written order of the Court. Any motion filed pursuant to IN ST MARION CIR AND SUPER CTS CIV Rule 203 shall state the date when such a response is due and the date to which time is enlarged. The motion must be filed on or before the original due date or IN ST MARION CIR AND SUPER CTS CIV Rule 203 shall be inapplicable. All subsequent Motions shall be so designated and will be granted only for good cause shown. IN ST MARION CIR AND SUPER CTS CIV Rule 203(D).

   e. *Continuances disfavored.* Motions for Continuance are discouraged. Neither side is entitled to an automatic continuance as a matter of right. IN ST MARION CIR AND SUPER CTS CIV Rule 215. For information on obtaining a continuance, refer to IN ST MARION CIR AND SUPER CTS CIV Rule 215.

C. General Requirements

1. *Pleading, generally*

   a. *Pleadings to be concise.* Each averment of a pleading shall be simple, concise, and direct. No technical forms of pleading or motions are required. All fictions in pleading are abolished. IN ST TRIAL P Rule 8(E)(1).

   b. *Pleading in the alternative.* A pleading may set forth two (2) or more statements of a claim or defense alternatively or hypothetically, either in one (1) count or defense or in separate counts or defenses. When two (2) or more statements are made in the alternative and one (1) of them if made independently would be sufficient, the pleading is not made insufficient by the insufficiency of one or more of the alternative statements. A pleading may also state as many separate claims or defenses as the pleader has regardless of consistency and whether based on legal or equitable grounds. All statements shall be made subject to the obligations set forth in IN ST TRIAL P Rule 11. IN ST TRIAL P Rule 8(E)(2).

   c. *Motions and pleadings, joint and several.* All motions and pleadings of any kind addressed to two (2) or more paragraphs of any pleading, or filed by two (2) or more parties, shall be taken and construed as joint, separate, and several motions or pleadings to each of such paragraphs and by and against each of such parties. All motions or pleadings containing two (2) or more subject-matters shall be taken and construed as separate and several as to each subject-matter. All objections to rulings made by two (2) or more parties shall be taken and construed as the joint, separate, and several objections of each of such parties. IN ST TRIAL P Rule 8(E)(3).

      i. A complaint filed by or against two (2) or more plaintiffs shall be taken and construed as joint, separate, and several as to each of said plaintiffs. IN ST TRIAL P Rule 8(E).

   d. *Construction of pleadings.* All pleadings shall be so construed as to do substantial justice, lead to disposition on the merits, and avoid litigation of procedural points. IN ST TRIAL P Rule 8(F).

2. *Contents of the answer*

   a. *Defenses which may be raised by answer or motion.* Every defense, in law or fact, to a claim for relief in any pleading, whether a claim, counterclaim, cross-claim, or third-party claim, shall be asserted in the responsive pleading thereto if one is required; except that at the option of the pleader, the following defenses may be made by motion:

      i. Lack of jurisdiction over the subject matter;

      ii. Lack of jurisdiction over the person;

      iii. Incorrect venue under IN ST TRIAL P Rule 75, or any statutory provision. The disposition of this motion shall be consistent with IN ST TRIAL P Rule 75;

      iv. Insufficiency of process;

      v. Insufficiency of service of process;

      vi. Failure to state a claim upon which relief can be granted, which shall include failure to name the real party in interest under IN ST TRIAL P Rule 17;

      vii. Failure to join a party needed for just adjudication under IN ST TRIAL P Rule 19;

      viii. The same action pending in another state court of this state. IN ST TRIAL P Rule 12(B).

      ix. A motion making any of these defenses shall be made before pleading if a further pleading is permitted or within twenty (20) days after service of the prior pleading if none is required. If a pleading sets forth a claim for relief to which the adverse party is not required to serve a responsive pleading, any of the defenses in section IN ST TRIAL P Rule 12(B)(2), IN ST TRIAL P Rule 12(B)(3), IN ST TRIAL P Rule 12(B)(4), IN ST TRIAL P Rule 12(B)(5) or IN ST TRIAL P Rule 12(B)(8) is waived to the extent constitutionally permissible unless made in a motion within twenty (20) days after service of the prior pleading. No defense or objection is waived by being joined with one (1) or more other defenses or objections in a responsive pleading or motion. IN ST TRIAL P Rule 12(B).

   b. *Waiver or preservation of certain defenses*

      i. A defense of lack of jurisdiction over the person, improper venue, insufficiency of process, insufficiency of service of process, or the same action pending in another state court of this state is waived to the extent constitutionally permissible:

- If omitted from a motion in the circumstances described in IN ST TRIAL P Rule 12(G),

- If it is neither made by motion under IN ST TRIAL P Rule 12 nor included in a responsive pleading or an amendment thereof permitted by IN ST TRIAL P Rule 15(A) to be made as a matter of course. IN ST TRIAL P Rule 12(H)(1).

    ii.   A defense of failure to state a claim upon which relief can be granted, a defense of failure to join an indispensable party under IN ST TRIAL P Rule 19(B), and an objection of failure to state a legal defense to a claim may be made in any pleading permitted or ordered under IN ST TRIAL P Rule 7(A) or by motion for judgment on the pleadings, or at the trial on the merits. IN ST TRIAL P Rule 12(H)(2).

  c. *Defenses; Form of denials*

    i.   A responsive pleading shall state in short and plain terms the pleader's defenses to each claim asserted and shall admit or controvert the averments set forth in the preceding pleading. If in good faith the pleader intends to deny all the averments in the preceding pleading, he may do so by general denial subject to the provisions of IN ST TRIAL P Rule 11. If he does not intend a general denial, he may:

- Specifically deny designated averments or paragraphs; or

- Generally deny all averments except such designated averments and paragraphs as he expressly admits. IN ST TRIAL P Rule 8(B).

    ii.   If he lacks knowledge or information sufficient to form a belief as to the truth of an averment, he shall so state and his statement shall be considered a denial. If in good faith a pleader intends to deny only a part or a qualification of an averment, he shall specify so much of it as is true and material and deny the remainder. All denials shall fairly meet the substance of the averments denied. IN ST TRIAL P Rule 8 shall have no application to uncontested actions for divorce, or to answers required to be filed by clerks or guardians ad litem. IN ST TRIAL P Rule 8(B).

  d. *Affirmative defenses.* A responsive pleading shall set forth affirmatively and carry the burden of proving: accord and satisfaction, arbitration and award, discharge in bankruptcy, duress, estoppel, failure of consideration, fraud, illegality, injury by fellow servant, laches, license, payment, release, res judicata, statute of frauds, statute of limitations, waiver, lack of jurisdiction over the subject-matter, lack of jurisdiction over the person, improper venue, insufficiency of process or service of process, the same action pending in another state court of this state, and any other matter constituting an avoidance, matter of abatement, or affirmative defense. A party required to affirmatively plead any matters, including matters formerly required to be pleaded affirmatively by reply, shall have the burden of proving such matters. The burden of proof imposed by this or any other provision of the Indiana Rules of Trial Procedure is subject to the rules of evidence or any statute fixing a different rule. If the pleading mistakenly designates a defense as a counterclaim or a counterclaim as a defense, the court shall treat the pleading as if there had been a proper designation. IN ST TRIAL P Rule 8(C).

    i.   An affirmative defense, generally, must be affirmatively stated by the party who seeks its benefit. 1A INPRAC R 8(8.5); Rice v. Grant County Bd. of Com'rs, 472 N.E.2d 213 (Ind.Ct.App. 1984). If that party does not raise the affirmative defense, then it is waived. 1A INPRAC R 8(8.5); Piskorowski v. Shell Oil Co., 403 N.E.2d 838, 847 (Ind.Ct.App. 1980).

    ii.   It is clear that the list of affirmative defenses found in IN ST TRIAL P Rule 8 is not exhaustive. The question comes: when is a defense to be treated as an affirmative defense, with all of the attending consequences? 1A INPRAC R 8(8.5). The "determination of whether a defense is affirmative depends on whether it controverts an element of the plaintiff's prima facie case or raises matter outside the scope of the prima facie case." 1A INPRAC R 8(8.5); Molargik v. West Enterprises, Inc., 605 N.E.2d 1197, 1198 (Ind.Ct.App. 1993).

  e. *Defense of contributory negligence or assumed risk.* In all claims alleging negligence, the burden of pleading and proving contributory negligence, assumption of risk, or incurred risk shall be upon the defendant who may plead such by denial of the allegation. IN ST TRIAL P Rule 9.1(A).

f. *Consideration.* When an action or defense is founded upon a written contract or release, lack of consideration for the promise or release is an affirmative defense, and the party asserting lack of it carries the burden of proof. IN ST TRIAL P Rule 9.1(C).

g. *Res ipsa loquitur.* Res ipsa loquitur or a similar doctrine may be pleaded by alleging generally that the facts connected with the action are unknown to the pleader and are within the knowledge of the opposing party. IN ST TRIAL P Rule 9.1(B).

h. *Bona fide purchaser.* When the rights of a person depend upon his status as a bona fide purchaser for value or upon similar requirements, such status must be pleaded and proved by the person asserting it, but it may be pleaded in general terms. Once it is established that the person has given any required value, unless such value is commercially unreasonable, and that he has met any requirements of recordation, filing, possession, or perfection, the trier of fact must find that such value was given or such perfection was made in accordance with any requirements of good faith, lack of knowledge, or lack of notice unless and until evidence is introduced which would support a finding of its non-existence. IN ST TRIAL P Rule 9.1(D).

i. *Presumption; Matters of judicial notice.* Neither presumptions of law nor matters of which judicial notice may be taken need be stated in a pleading. IN ST TRIAL P Rule 9.1(E).

j. *Property distrained; Sufficient answer.* In an action to recover the possession of property distrained while doing damage, an answer that the defendant, or person by whose command he acted, was lawfully possessed of the real property upon which the distress was made, and that the property distrained was at the time doing damage thereon, shall be good without setting forth the title of such real property. IN ST TRIAL P Rule 9.1(F).

k. *Effect of failure to deny.* Averments in a pleading to which a responsive pleading is required, except those pertaining to amount of damages, are admitted when not denied in the responsive pleading. Averments in a pleading to which no responsive pleading is required or permitted shall be taken as denied or avoided. IN ST TRIAL P Rule 8(D).

l. *Effect of admission.* When a rhetorical paragraph or allegation is admitted, the effect in Indiana is to remove it from trial. Such an admission is a "judicial admission", and the claim or issue which is admitted cannot be denied later by the trier of the facts. Further, this admitted fact does not require evidence to "prove it"; it is established. It becomes, in short, controlling and indisputable in the litigation, unless the trial court permits an amendment to the pleading which might remove the controlling effect of the admission, and permit it to become another fact or item of evidence in the case. 1A INPRAC R 8(8.4); Aylesworth v. McKesson, 421 N.E.2d 422 (Ind.Ct.App. 1981).

3. *Pleading special matters*

a. *Capacity.* It is not necessary to aver the capacity of a party to sue or be sued, the authority of a party to sue or be sued in a representative capacity, or the legal existence of an organization that is made a party. The burden of proving lack of such capacity, authority, or legal existence shall be upon the person asserting lack of it, and shall be pleaded as an affirmative defense. IN ST TRIAL P Rule 9(A).

b. *Fraud, mistake, condition of the mind.* In all averments of fraud or mistake, the circumstances constituting fraud or mistake shall be specifically averred. Malice, intent, knowledge, and other conditions of mind may be averred generally. IN ST TRIAL P Rule 9(B).

c. *Conditions precedent.* In pleading the performance or occurrence of promissory or non-promissory conditions precedent, it is sufficient to aver generally that all conditions precedent have been performed, have occurred, or have been excused. A denial of performance or occurrence shall be made specifically and with particularity, and a denial of excuse generally. IN ST TRIAL P Rule 9(C).

d. *Official document or act.* In pleading an official document or official act it is sufficient to aver that the document was issued or the act done in compliance with law. IN ST TRIAL P Rule 9(D).

e. *Judgment.* In pleading a judgment or decision of a domestic or foreign court, judicial or quasi-judicial tribunal, or of a board or officer, it is sufficient to aver the judgment or decision without setting forth matter showing jurisdiction to render it. IN ST TRIAL P Rule 9(E).

f. *Time and place.* For the purpose of testing the sufficiency of a pleading, averments of time and place are material and shall be considered like all other averments of material matter. However, time and place need be stated only with such specificity as will enable the opposing party to prepare his defense. IN ST TRIAL P Rule 9(F).

g. *Special damages; Damages where no answer.* When items of special damage are claimed, they shall be specifically stated. The relief granted to the plaintiff, if there be no answer, cannot exceed the relief demanded in his complaint; but, in any other case, the court may grant him any relief consistent with the facts or matters pleaded. IN ST TRIAL P Rule 9(G).

4. *Counterclaim and cross-claim*

a. *Compulsory counterclaims.* A pleading shall state as a counterclaim any claim which at the time of serving the pleading the pleader has against any opposing party, if it arises out of the transaction or occurrence that is the subject-matter of the opposing party's claim and does not require for its adjudication the presence of third parties of whom the court cannot acquire jurisdiction. But the pleader need not state the claim if:

   i. At the time the action was commenced the claim was the subject of another pending action; or

   ii. The opposing party brought suit upon his claim by attachment or other process by which the court did not acquire jurisdiction to render a personal judgment on that claim, and the pleader is not stating any counterclaim under IN ST TRIAL P Rule 13. IN ST TRIAL P Rule 13(A).

b. *Permissive counterclaims.* A pleading may state as a counterclaim any claim against an opposing party not arising out of the transaction or occurrence that is the subject-matter of the opposing party's claim. IN ST TRIAL P Rule 13(B).

c. *Counterclaim exceeding opposing claim.* A counterclaim may or may not diminish or defeat the recovery sought by the opposing party. It may claim relief exceeding in amount or different in kind from that sought in the pleading of the opposing party. IN ST TRIAL P Rule 13(C).

d. *Counterclaim against state.* IN ST TRIAL P Rule 13 shall not be construed to enlarge any right to assert a claim against the state. IN ST TRIAL P Rule 13(D).

e. *Counterclaim maturing or acquired after pleading.* A claim which either matured or was acquired by the pleader after serving his pleading may, with the permission of the court, be presented as a counterclaim by supplemental pleading. A counterclaim or cross-claim which is not due may be asserted against a party who is insolvent or the representative of a party who has been subjected to insolvency proceedings, if recovery thereon will be impaired because of such party's insolvency. IN ST TRIAL P Rule 13(E).

f. *Omitted counterclaim.* When a pleader fails to set up a counterclaim through oversight, inadvertence, or excusable neglect, or when justice requires, he may by leave of court set up the counterclaim by amendment. IN ST TRIAL P Rule 13(F).

g. *Cross-claim against co-party.* A pleading may state as a cross-claim any claim by one party against a co-party. IN ST TRIAL P Rule 13(G).

h. *Joinder of additional parties.* Persons other than those made parties to the original action may be made parties to a counterclaim or cross-claim in accordance with the provisions of IN ST TRIAL P Rule 14, IN ST TRIAL P Rule 19 and IN ST TRIAL P Rule 20. IN ST TRIAL P Rule 13(H).

i. *Separate trials; Separate judgments*

   i. If the court orders separate trials as provided in IN ST TRIAL P Rule 42(B), judgment on a counterclaim or cross-claim may be rendered in accordance with the terms of IN ST TRIAL P Rule 54(B) when the court has jurisdiction so to do, even if the claims of the opposing party have been dismissed or otherwise disposed of. In determining whether or not separate trial of a cross-claim shall be ordered, the court shall consider whether the cross-claim:

   - Arises out of the transaction or occurrence or series of transactions or occurrences that is the subject-matter either of the original action or of a counterclaim therein;

   - Relates to any property or contract that is the subject-matter of the original action; or

   - Claims that the person against whom it is asserted is liable to the cross-claimant for all or part of plaintiff's claim against him. IN ST TRIAL P Rule 13(I).

  ii. In addition, the court may consider any other relevant factors. IN ST TRIAL P Rule 13(I).

 j. *Effect of statute of limitations and other discharges at law.* The statute of limitations, a nonclaim statute or other discharge at law shall not bar a claim asserted as a counterclaim to the extent that:

  i. It diminishes or defeats the opposing party's claim if it arises out of the transaction or occurrence that is the subject-matter of the opposing party's claim, or if it could have been asserted as a counterclaim to the opposing party's claim before it (the counterclaim) was barred; or

  ii. It or the opposing party's claim relates to payment of or security for the other. IN ST TRIAL P Rule 13(J).

 k. *Counterclaim by and against transferees and successors.* A counterclaim may be asserted by or against the transferee or successor of a claim subject to the following provisions:

  i. A successor who is a guardian, representative of a decedent's estate, receiver or assignee for the benefit of creditors, trustee or the like may interpose a claim to which he succeeds against claims or proceedings brought in or outside the court of administration. A claim owing by his predecessor may be interposed against any claim brought by such successor in or outside the court of administration without the necessity of filing such claim or cause of action in the administration proceedings. IN ST TRIAL P Rule 13(K)(1).

  ii. A transferee or successor of a claim takes it subject to any defense or counterclaim that is the subject-matter of the opposing party's claim; or that is available to the obligor at the time of the assignment or before the obligor received notice of the assignment. IN ST TRIAL P Rule 13(K)(2).

  iii. A surety or party with total or partial recourse upon a claim upon which he is being sued may interpose as a counterclaim:

   • Any claim of his own; and

   • Any claim owned by the person against whom he has recourse who either has notice of the suit, is a party to the suit, is insolvent, has assigned his claim to the surety or party asserting it, or cannot be found. IN ST TRIAL P Rule 13(K)(3).

   • A counterclaim under IN ST TRIAL P Rule 13(K)(3)(b) must tend to diminish or defeat the opposing party's claim, or it or the opposing claim must relate to payment of or security for the other, unless the person against whom recourse may be had is a party to the suit or the counterclaim has been assigned to the party asserting it; and if recovery on the counterclaim exceeds the opposing party's claim, any excess recovered shall be held in trust for such person against whom there is a right of recourse. IN ST TRIAL P Rule 13(K)(3).

  iv. IN ST TRIAL P Rule 13(K)(1), IN ST TRIAL P Rule 13(K)(2), and IN ST TRIAL P Rule 13(K)(3), are subject to subdivision IN ST TRIAL P Rule 13(L). IN ST TRIAL P Rule 13(K)(4).

 l. *Counterclaim and cross-claim subject to substantive law principles.* Counterclaim and cross-claims are subject to restrictions imposed by other statutes and principles of substantive common law and equity, including rules of commercial law, agency, estoppel, contract and the like. In appropriate cases the court may impose terms or conditions upon its judgment or decree and may enter conditional or noncanceling cross judgments to satisfy such restrictions. This provision is intended to deny or limit counterclaims or cross-claims:

  i. Where a creditor will receive an unfair priority because a claim is assigned after insolvency proceedings, or assigned before such proceedings if it results in an unlawful preference;

  ii. Where an unfair priority will be allowed if a surety interposing a claim owned in his own right against the creditor suing on the principal's obligation when the principal is solvent and the creditor is not;

  iii. Where a claim by or against a representative, such as a guardian, receiver, representative of a decedent's estate, assignee for the benefit of creditors, trustee or the like in his individual capacity is asserted against a claim owing or owed by the estate he represents;

    iv. Where a claim by or against a partnership or two (2) or more obligors is opposed against or by a claim of an individual to the extent that the individual will be allowed unfairly to profit or if it will adversely affect the rights of creditors; or

    v. Where a claim is cut off by a holder in due course or a transferee who is protected under principles of commercial law, estoppel, or contract. IN ST TRIAL P Rule 13(L).

m. *Satisfaction of judgment.* Satisfaction of a judgment or credits thereon may be ordered, for sufficient cause, upon notice and motion. "Credits" include any counterclaim which tends to diminish or defeat the judgment, or any counterclaim where it or the opposing claim relates to payment of or security for the other. IN ST TRIAL P Rule 13(M).

5. *Third-party practice*

a. *When defendant may bring in third party.* A defending party, as a third-party plaintiff, may cause a summons and complaint to be served upon a person not a party to the action who is or may be liable to him for all or part of the plaintiff's claim against him. IN ST TRIAL P Rule 14(A). The person served with the summons and the third-party complaint, hereinafter called the third-party defendant, as provided in IN ST TRIAL P Rule 12 and IN ST TRIAL P Rule 13 may make:

    i. His defenses, cross-claims and counterclaims to the third-party plaintiff's claims;

    ii. His defenses, counterclaims and cross-claims against any other defendants or third-party defendants;

    iii. Any defenses or claims which the third-party plaintiff has to the plaintiff's claim which are available to the third-party defendant against the plaintiff; and

    iv. Any defenses or claims which the third-party defendant has as against the plaintiff. IN ST TRIAL P Rule 14(A).

    v. The plaintiff may assert any claim against the third-party defendant who thereupon may assert his defenses, counterclaims and cross-claims, as provided in IN ST TRIAL P Rule 12 and IN ST TRIAL P Rule 13. A third-party defendant may proceed under IN ST TRIAL P Rule 14 against any person not a party to the action who is or may be liable to him for all or part of the claim made in the action against the third-party defendant. IN ST TRIAL P Rule 14(A).

b. *When plaintiff may bring in third party.* When a counterclaim or other claim is asserted against a plaintiff, he may cause a third party to be brought in under circumstances, which, under IN ST TRIAL P Rule 14, would entitle a defendant to do so. IN ST TRIAL P Rule 14(B).

c. *Severance; Parties improperly impleaded.* With his responsive pleading or by motion prior thereto, any party may move for severance of a third-party claim or ensuing claim as provided in IN ST TRIAL P Rule 14 or for a separate trial thereon. If the third-party defendant is a proper party to the proceedings under any other rule relating to parties, the action shall continue as in other cases where he is made a party. IN ST TRIAL P Rule 14(C).

6. *Trial by jury; Demand*

a. *Causes triable by court and by jury.* Issues of law and issues of fact in causes that prior to the eighteenth day of June, 1852, were of exclusive equitable jurisdiction shall be tried by the court; issues of fact in all other causes shall be triable as the same are now triable. In case of the joinder of causes of action or defenses which, prior to said date, were of exclusive equitable jurisdiction with causes of action or defenses which, prior to said date, were designated as actions at law and triable by jury—the former shall be triable by the court, and the latter by a jury, unless waived; the trial of both may be at the same time or at different times, as the court may direct. IN ST TRIAL P Rule 38(A).

b. *Demand.* Any party may demand a trial by jury of any issue triable of right by a jury by filing with the court and serving upon the other parties a demand therefor in writing at any time after the commencement of the action and not later than ten (10) days after the first responsive pleading to the complaint, or to a counterclaim, crossclaim or other claim if one properly is pleaded; and if no responsive pleading is filed or required, within ten (10) days after the time such pleading otherwise would have been required. Such demand is sufficient if indorsed upon a pleading of a party filed within such time. IN ST TRIAL P Rule 38(B).

    c.   *Same; Specification of issues.* In his demand a party may specify the issues which he wishes so tried; otherwise he shall be deemed to have demanded trial by jury for all issues triable as of right by jury. Any other party must file a demand for jury trial to preserve his right to trial by jury:

        i.   Of issues for which a right to trial by jury was not requested by another party; and

        ii.   In case a request by another party was improper. But if a proper request for a trial by jury upon issues triable by jury as of right on his behalf is made by any party, such request shall be deemed to have been made on behalf of all parties entitled to a jury trial upon such issues. IN ST TRIAL P Rule 38(C).

    d.   *Waiver.* The failure of a party to appear at the trial, and the failure of a party to serve a demand as required by IN ST TRIAL P Rule 38 and to file it as required by IN ST TRIAL P Rule 5(E) constitute waiver by him of trial by jury. A demand for trial by jury made as herein provided may not be withdrawn without the consent of the other party or parties. IN ST TRIAL P Rule 38(D).

        i.   The trial court shall not grant a demand for a trial by jury filed after the time fixed in IN ST TRIAL P Rule 38(B) has elapsed except upon the written agreement of all of the parties to the action, which agreement shall be filed with the court and made a part of the record. If such agreement is filed then the court may, in its discretion, grant a trial by jury in which event the grant of a trial by jury may not be withdrawn except by the agreement of all of the parties. IN ST TRIAL P Rule 38(D).

    e.   *Arbitration.* Nothing in the Indiana Rules of Trial Procedure shall deny the parties the right by contract or agreement to submit or to agree to submit controversies to arbitration made before or after commencement of an action thereon or deny the courts power to specifically enforce such agreements. IN ST TRIAL P Rule 38(E).

    f.   *Equitable and legal claims in multi-count actions.* In multi-count actions, the inclusion of an equitable claim, standing alone, will not automatically draw the entire action into equity. Something more than the presence of an equitable claim is required, and the court must examine the claims at issue. 22B INPRAC 38:1 COMMENT; Lucas v. U.S. Bank, N.A., 953 N.E.2d 457 (Ind. 2011). Factors the court may consider in evaluating the nature of the underlying substantive claims include: the substance and central character of the complaint, the rights and interests at issue, the relief demanded, and any issues arising out of discovery. 22B INPRAC 38:1 COMMENT; Songer v. Civitas Bank, 771 N.E.2d 61 (Ind. 2002).

7.   *Use of alternative dispute resolution.* Except as provided by the Indiana Rules for Alternative Dispute Resolution, a presiding judge may order any civil or domestic relations proceeding or selected issues in such proceedings referred to mediation, non-binding arbitration or mini-trial. The selection criteria which should be used by the court are defined under the Indiana Rules for Alternative Dispute Resolution. Binding arbitration and a summary jury trial may be ordered only upon the agreement of the parties as consistent with provisions in the Indiana Rules for Alternative Dispute Resolution which address each method. IN ST ADR Rule 1.6. For information on Indiana's ADR process refer to IN ST ADR Rule 1.1 through IN ST ADR Rule 8.8.

    a.   *Mandatory alternative dispute resolution.* All cases where a timely demand for jury trial is made, mediation pursuant to A.D.R. Rule 2 (IN ST ADR Rule 2.1 through IN ST ADR Rule 2.11) and IN ST MARION CIR AND SUPER CTS CIV Rule 209(A) is mandatory. IN ST MARION CIR AND SUPER CTS CIV Rule 209. For more information on mandatory alternative dispute resolution, refer to IN ST ADR Rule 2.1 through IN ST ADR Rule 2.11 and IN ST MARION CIR AND SUPER CTS CIV Rule 209.

D. Documents

1.   *Required documents*

    a.   *Answer.* Refer to the General Requirements section of this document for information on the contents of an answer.

    b.   *Appearance form.* Pursuant to IN ST TRIAL P Rule 3.1(A), an appearance form shall be filed by the initiating party at the time an action commenced. If the action is appropriate for filing and disposition in Marion Superior Court, Environmental Division, per Order of the Executive Committee of the

ANSWER

Marion Superior Court, then the initiating party shall indicate such on the appearance form. IN ST MARION CIR AND SUPER CTS CIV Rule 205(E). At the time the responding party or parties first appears in a case, the attorney representing such party or parties or the party or parties, if not represented by an attorney, shall file an appearance form setting forth the information set out in IN ST TRIAL P Rule 3.1(A). IN ST TRIAL P Rule 3.1(B). The appearance form shall set forth the following information:

    i.   Name, address and telephone number of the initiating party or parties filing the appearance form;

    ii.   Name, address, attorney number, telephone number, FAX number, and e-mail address of any attorney representing the party, as applicable;

    iii.   The case type of the proceeding [IN ST ADMIN Rule 8(B)(3)];

    iv.   A statement that the party will or will not accept service by fax or by e-mail from:

- Other parties and/or
- The court under IN ST TRIAL P Rule 72(D);

    v.   In domestic relations, Uniform Reciprocal Enforcement of Support (URESA), paternity, delinquency, Child in Need of Services (CHINS), guardianship, and any other proceedings in which support may be an issue, the Social Security Identification Number of all family members;

    vi.   The caption and case number of all related cases;

    vii.   Such additional matters specified by state or local rule required to maintain the information management system employed by the court;

    viii.   In a proceeding involving a protection from abuse order, a workplace violence restraining order, or a no-contact order, the initiating party shall provide to the clerk a public mailing address for purposes of legal service. The initiating party may use the Attorney General Address Confidentiality program established by statute; and

    ix.   In a proceeding involving a mental health commitment, except seventy-two (72) hour emergency detentions, the initiating party shall provide the full name of the person with respect to whom commitment is sought and the person's state of residence. In addition, the initiating party shall provide at least one of the following identifiers for the person:

- Date of birth;
- Social Security Number;
- Driver's license number with state of issue and date of expiration;
- Department of Correction number;
- State ID number with state of issue and date of expiration; or
- FBI number. IN ST TRIAL P Rule 3.1(A).

c.   *Certificate of service.* An attorney or unrepresented party tendering a document to the Clerk for filing shall certify that service has been made, list the parties served, and specify the date and means of service. The certificate of service shall be placed at the end of the document and shall not be separately filed. The separate filing of a certificate of service, however, shall not be grounds for rejecting a document for filing. The Clerk may permit documents to be filed without a certificate of service but shall require prompt filing of a separate certificate of service. IN ST TRIAL P Rule 5(C). In all cases where any pleading or other document is required to be served upon opposing counsel, proof of such service may be made either by:

    i.   A certificate of service signed by counsel of record for the serving party and the certificate shall specify by name and address all counsel upon whom the pleading or document was served; or

    ii.   An acknowledgment of service signed by the party served or counsel of record. IN ST MARION CIR AND SUPER CTS CIV Rule 206.

2. *Supplemental documents*

    a. *Admission of service.* A written admission stating the date and place of service, signed by the person being served, may be filed with the clerk who shall file it with the pleadings. Such admission shall become a part of the record, constitute evidence of proper service, and shall be allowed as evidence in any action or proceeding. IN ST TRIAL P Rule 4.15(D).

        i. It shall be the duty of every person being served under the Indiana Rules of Trial Procedure to cooperate, accept service, comply with the provisions of the Indiana Rules of Trial Procedure, and, when service is made upon him personally, acknowledge receipt of the papers in writing over his signature. IN ST TRIAL P Rule 4.16(A).

- Offering or tendering the papers to the person being served and advising the person that he or she is being served is adequate service. IN ST TRIAL P Rule 4.16(A)(1).

- A person who has refused to accept the offer or tender of the papers being served thereafter may not challenge the service of those papers. IN ST TRIAL P Rule 4.16(A)(2).

    b. *Proof of written instrument.* When any pleading allowed by the Indiana Rules of Trial Procedure is founded on a written instrument, the original, or a copy thereof, must be included in or filed with the pleading. Such instrument, whether copied in the pleadings or not, shall be taken as part of the record. When any pleading allowed by the Indiana Rules of Trial Procedure is founded on an account, an Affidavit of Debt, in a form substantially similar to that which is provided in IN ST TRIAL P App. A-2, shall be attached. IN ST TRIAL P Rule 9.2(A).

    c. *Notice of intent to use foreign law.* A party who intends to raise an issue concerning the law of a foreign country shall give notice in his pleadings or other reasonable written notice. The court, in determining foreign law, may consider any relevant material or source, including testimony, whether or not submitted by a party or admissible under IN ST TRIAL P Rule 43. The court's determination shall be treated as a ruling on a question of law. It shall be made by the court and not the jury and shall be reviewable. IN ST TRIAL P Rule 44.1(A).

    d. *Facsimile cover sheet.* Any document sent to the Clerk of the Circuit Court by electronic facsimile transmission shall be accompanied by a cover sheet which states the title of the document, case number, number of pages, identity and voice telephone number of the sending party and instructions for filing. The cover sheet shall contain the signature of the attorney or party, pro se, authorizing the filing. IN ST ADMIN Rule 12(D).

E. Format

1. *Form of pleadings*

    a. *Caption; Names of parties.* Every pleading shall contain a caption setting forth the name of the court, the title of the action, the file number, and a designation as in IN ST TRIAL P Rule 7(A). In the complaint the title of the action shall include the names of all the parties, but in other pleadings it is sufficient to state the name of the first party on each side with an appropriate indication of other parties. IN ST TRIAL P Rule 10(A).

        i. *Caption.* Every pleading shall contain a caption setting forth the name of the Court, the Division and Room Number, the title of the action and the file number. IN ST MARION CIR AND SUPER CTS CIV Rule 204(B).

    b. *Paragraphs; Separate statements.* All averments of a claim or defense shall be made in numbered paragraphs, the contents of each of which shall be limited as far as practicable to a statement of a single set of circumstances, and a paragraph may be referred to by number in all succeeding pleadings. Each claim founded upon a separate transaction or occurrence and each defense other than denials may be stated in a separate count or defense whenever a separation facilitates the clear presentation of the matters set forth. IN ST TRIAL P Rule 10(B).

    c. *Adoption by reference; Exhibits.* Statements in a pleading may be adopted by reference in a different part of the same pleading or in another pleading or in any motion. A copy of any written instrument which is an exhibit to a pleading is a part thereof for all purposes. IN ST TRIAL P Rule 10(C).

    d. *Paper.* Pleadings, motions and other papers may be either printed or typewritten on white opaque paper of at least sixteen (16) pound weight, eight and one-half (8-1/2) inches wide and eleven (11) inches in length. IN ST MARION CIR AND SUPER CTS CIV Rule 204(A).

e. *Copies.* All copies shall likewise be on white paper of sufficient strength and durability to resist normal wear and tear. IN ST MARION CIR AND SUPER CTS CIV Rule 204(A).

f. *Line spacing.* If typewritten, the lines shall be double spaced, except for quotations, which shall be indented and single spaced. IN ST MARION CIR AND SUPER CTS CIV Rule 204(A).

g. *Script type.* Script type shall not be used. IN ST MARION CIR AND SUPER CTS CIV Rule 204(A).

h. *Titles.* Titles on all pleadings shall delineate each topic included in the pleading e.g. where a pleading contains an Answer, a Motion to Strike or Dismiss, or a Jury Request each shall be set forth in the title. IN ST MARION CIR AND SUPER CTS CIV Rule 204(C).

i. *Margins and binding.* Margins shall be one (1) inch. Binding or stapling shall be at the top and at no other place. Covers or backing shall not be used. IN ST MARION CIR AND SUPER CTS CIV Rule 204(D).

2. *Size of papers for filing.* Effective January 1, 1992, all pleadings, copies, motions and documents filed with any trial court or appellate level court, typed or printed, with the exception of exhibits and existing wills, shall be prepared on eight and one-half by eleven inch (8 1/2" x 11") size paper. IN ST ADMIN Rule 11.

3. *Form of electronically filed documents.* All electronically filed and served pleadings shall, to the extent practicable, be formatted in accordance with the applicable rules governing formatting of paper pleadings. IN ST MARION SUPER CT ADMIN Rule 311(2-103)(1).

a. *Electronic document title.* The electronic document title of each pleading or other document shall include:

   i. Party or parties filing/serving the document,

   ii. Nature of the document,

   iii. Party or parties against whom relief, if any, is sought, and

   iv. Nature of the relief sought (e.g., Defendant ABC Corporation's Motion for Summary Judgment). IN ST MARION SUPER CT ADMIN Rule 311(2-103)(2).

4. *Signature requirements*

a. *Signature of attorney.* Every pleading or motion of a party represented by an attorney shall be signed by at least one (1) attorney of record in his individual name, whose address, telephone number, and attorney number shall be stated, except that this provision shall not apply to pleadings and motions made and transcribed at the trial or a hearing before the judge and received by him in such form. IN ST TRIAL P Rule 11(A).

   i. All pleadings and motions shall contain the original or authorized signature of the attorney, the name of the attorney in typed or printed form, the name of the law firm if a member of a firm, the attorney's address, identification number, e-mail address, telephone number, fax number, and the designation as to the party for whom he appears. IN ST MARION CIR AND SUPER CTS CIV Rule 204(E).

   ii. The signature of an attorney constitutes a certificate by him that he has read the pleadings; that to the best of his knowledge, information, and belief, there is good ground to support it; and that it is not interposed for delay. IN ST TRIAL P Rule 11(A).

   iii. If a pleading or motion is not signed or is signed with intent to defeat the purpose of the rule, it may be stricken as sham and false and the action may proceed as though the pleading had not been served. IN ST TRIAL P Rule 11(A).

   iv. For a willful violation of IN ST TRIAL P Rule 11 an attorney may be subjected to appropriate disciplinary action. Similar action may be taken if scandalous or indecent matter is inserted. IN ST TRIAL P Rule 11(A).

   v. Every pleading, document, and instrument electronically filed or served shall be deemed to

have been signed by the judge, clerk, attorney or declarant and shall bear a facsimile or typographical signature of such person, along with the typed name, address, telephone number, and Bar number of a signing attorney. Typographical signatures shall be treated as personal signatures for all purposes under these rules. IN ST MARION SUPER CT ADMIN Rule 311(2-105).

- Documents containing signatures of third-parties (i.e., unopposed motions, affidavits, stipulations, etc.) may also be filed electronically by indicating that the original signatures are maintained by the filing party in paper-format. IN ST MARION SUPER CT ADMIN Rule 311(2-105).

- Unless otherwise ordered by the Court or Clerk, a printed copy of all documents filed or served electronically, including original signatures, shall be maintained by the party filing the document and shall be made available, upon reasonable notice, for inspection by other counsel, the Clerk or Court. Parties shall retain originals until two (2) years after all time periods for appeal have expired. From time to time, it may be necessary to provide the Clerk or Court with a hard copy of an electronically filed document. IN ST MARION SUPER CT ADMIN Rule 311(2-105).

vi. For the recommended format of a signature block, refer to IN ST MARION CIR AND SUPER CTS CIV Rule 204(E).

b. *Signature of unrepresented party.* A party who is not represented by an attorney shall sign his pleading and state his address. IN ST TRIAL P Rule 11(A).

c. *Verification not generally required.* Except when specifically required by rule, pleadings or motions need not be verified or accompanied by affidavit. The rule in equity that the averments of an answer under oath must be overcome by the testimony of two (2) witnesses or of one (1) witness sustained by corroborating circumstances is abolished. IN ST TRIAL P Rule 11(A).

d. *Verification by affirmation or representation.* When in connection with any civil or special statutory proceeding it is required that any pleading, motion, petition, supporting affidavit, or other document of any kind, be verified, or that an oath be taken, it shall be sufficient if the subscriber simply affirms the truth of the matter to be verified by an affirmation or representation. IN ST TRIAL P Rule 11(B). IN ST TRIAL P Rule 11(B) states that the affirmation or representation should be in substantially the following language: "I (we) affirm, under the penalties for perjury, that the foregoing representation(s) is (are) true. (Signed) _____."

i. Any person who falsifies an affirmation or representation of fact shall be subject to the same penalties as are prescribed by law for the making of a false affidavit. IN ST TRIAL P Rule 11(B).

e. *Verified pleadings, motions, and affidavits as evidence.* Pleadings, motions and affidavits accompanying or in support of such pleadings or motions when required to be verified or under oath shall be accepted as a representation that the signer had personal knowledge thereof or reasonable cause to believe the existence of the facts or matters stated or alleged therein; and, if otherwise competent or acceptable as evidence, may be admitted as evidence of the facts or matters stated or alleged therein when it is so provided in the Indiana Rules of Trial Procedure, by statute or other law, or to the extent the writing or signature expressly purports to be made upon the signer's personal knowledge. When such pleadings, motions and affidavits are verified or under oath they shall not require other or greater proof on the part of the adverse party than if not verified or not under oath unless expressly provided otherwise by the Indiana Rules of Trial Procedure, statute or other law. Affidavits upon motions for summary judgment under IN ST TRIAL P Rule 56 and in denial of execution under IN ST TRIAL P Rule 9.2 shall be made upon personal knowledge. IN ST TRIAL P Rule 11(C).

5. *Information excluded from public access.* Every document filed in a case shall separately identify information excluded from public access pursuant to IN ST ADMIN Rule 9(G)(1) as follows:

a. Whole documents that are excluded from public access pursuant to IN ST ADMIN Rule 9(G)(1) shall be tendered on light green paper or have a light green coversheet attached to the document, marked "Not for Public Access" or "Confidential." IN ST TRIAL P Rule 5(G)(1).

b. When only a portion of a document contains information excluded from public access pursuant to IN ST ADMIN Rule 9(G)(1), said information shall be omitted [or redacted] from the filed document, and set forth on a separate accompanying document on light green paper conspicuously marked "Not for Public Access" or "Confidential" and clearly designated [or identifying] the caption and number of the case and the document and location within the document to which the redacted material pertains. IN ST TRIAL P Rule 5(G)(2).

c. With respect to documents filed in electronic format, the trial court, by local rule, may provide for compliance with IN ST TRIAL P Rule 5 in manner that separates and protects access to information excluded from public access. IN ST TRIAL P Rule 5(G)(3).

d. IN ST TRIAL P Rule 5(G) does not apply to a record sealed by the court pursuant to IN ST 5-14-3-5.5 or otherwise, nor to records, documents, or information filed in cases to which public access is prohibited pursuant to IN ST ADMIN Rule 9(G). IN ST TRIAL P Rule 5(G)(4).

e. The following information in case records is excluded from public access and is confidential:

   i. Information that is excluded from public access pursuant to federal law;

   ii. Information that is excluded from public access as declared confidential by Indiana statute or other court rule, including without limitation:

   - All adoption records created after July 8, 1941, as declared confidential by IN ST 31-19-19-1, et seq., except those specifically declared open by IN ST 31-19-13-2(2);

   - All records relating to chancroid, chlamydia, gonorrhea, hepatitis, human immunodeficiency virus (HIV), Lymphogranuloma venereum, syphilis, tuberculosis, as declared confidential by IN ST 16-41-8-1, et seq.;

   - All records relating to child abuse as declared confidential by IN ST 31-33-18-1, et seq.;

   - All records relating to drug tests as declared confidential by IN ST 5-14-3-4(a)(9);

   - Records of grand jury proceedings as declared confidential by IN ST 35-34-2-4;

   - Records of juvenile proceedings as declared confidential by IN ST 31-39-1-2, except those specifically open under statute;

   - All paternity records created after July 1, 1941 as declared confidential by IN ST 31-14-11-15, IN ST 31-19-5-23, IN ST 31-39-1-1 and IN ST 31-39-1-2 [Editor's note: IN ST 31-14-11-15 was repealed effective May 9, 2013];

   - All pre-sentence reports as declared confidential by IN ST 35-38-1-13;

   - Written petitions to permit marriages without consent and orders directing the Clerk of Court to issue a marriage license to underage persons, as declared confidential by IN ST 31-11-1-6;

   - Only those arrest warrants, search warrants, indictments and informations ordered confidential by the trial judge, prior to return of duly executed service as declared confidential by IN ST 5-14-3-4(b)(1);

   - All medical, mental health, or tax records unless determined by law or regulation of any governmental custodian not to be confidential, released by the subject of such records, or declared by a court of competent jurisdiction to be essential to the resolution of litigation as declared confidential by IN ST 16-39-3-10, IN ST 6-4.1-5-10, IN ST 6-4.1-12-12, and IN ST 6-8.1-7-1;

   - Personal information relating to jurors or prospective jurors, other than for the use of the parties and counsel, pursuant to IN ST JURY Rule 10;

   - Information relating to protection from abuse orders, no-contact orders and workplace violence restraining orders as declared confidential by IN ST 5-2-9-6, et seq.;

   - Mediation proceedings pursuant to IN ST ADR Rule 2.11, Mini-Trial proceedings pursuant to IN ST ADR Rule 4.4(C), and Summary Jury Trials pursuant to IN ST ADR Rule 5.6;

- Information in probation files pursuant to the Probation Standards promulgated by the Judicial Conference of Indiana pursuant to IN ST 11-13-1-8(b);
- Information deemed confidential pursuant to the Rules for Court Administered Alcohol and Drug Programs promulgated by the Judicial Conference of Indiana pursuant to IN ST 12-23-14-13;
- Information deemed confidential pursuant to the Problem-Solving Court Rules promulgated by the Judicial Conference of Indiana pursuant to IN ST 33-23-16-16;
- All records of the Department of workforce Development as declared confidential by IN ST 22-4-19-6;
- Information regarding interception of electronic communications that is sealed or deemed confidential as set forth in IN ST 35-33.5-2-1, et seq.

iii. Information excluded from public access by specific court order;

iv. Complete Social Security Numbers of living persons;

v. With the exception of names, information such as addresses, phone numbers, and dates of birth which explicitly identifies:

- Natural persons who are witnesses or victims (not including defendants) in criminal, domestic violence, stalking, sexual assault, juvenile, or civil protection order proceedings, provided that juveniles who are victims of sex crimes shall be identified by initials only;
- Places of residence of judicial officers, clerks and other employees of courts and clerks of court, unless the person or persons about whom the information pertains waives confidentiality;

vi. Complete account numbers of specific assets, loans, bank accounts, credit cards, and personal identification numbers (PINs);

vii. All orders of expungement entered in criminal or juvenile proceedings, orders to restrict access to criminal history information pursuant to IN ST 35-38-5-5.5 or IN ST 35-38-8-5 and records excluded from public access by such orders, and information related to infractions that is excluded from public access pursuant to IN ST 34-28-5-15 or IN ST 34-28-5-16 [Editor's note: IN ST 35-38-5-5.5, IN ST 35-38-8-5 and IN ST 34-28-5-16 were repealed effective July 1, 2013; for information on orders restricting access to criminal history, refer to IN ST 35-38-9-1, et seq.];

viii. All personal notes and e-mail, and deliberative material, of judges, jurors, court staff and judicial agencies, and information recorded in personal data assistants (PDA's) or organizers and personal calendars. IN ST ADMIN Rule 9(G)(1).

F. Filing and Service Requirements

1. *Filing requirements.* Except as otherwise provided in IN ST TRIAL P Rule 5(E)(2), all pleadings and papers subsequent to the complaint which are required to be served upon a party shall be filed with the Court either before service or within a reasonable period of time thereafter. IN ST TRIAL P Rule 5(E)(1).

   a. *Filing generally.* All pleadings, petitions and motions are filed with the Clerk designated by the Court at any time during office hours established by the Clerk and the Court. All orders submitted to the Court shall be in sufficient number and shall be accompanied by postage paid envelopes addressed to each party or counsel of record. IN ST MARION CIR AND SUPER CTS CIV Rule 205(A)

   b. *Filing with the court defined.* The filing of pleadings, motions, and other papers with the court as required by the Indiana Rules of Trial Procedure shall be made by one of the following methods:

      i. Delivery to the clerk of the court;

      ii. Sending by electronic transmission under the procedure adopted pursuant to IN ST ADMIN Rule 12;

      iii. Mailing to the clerk by registered, certified or express mail return receipt requested;

    iv.   Depositing with any third-party commercial carrier for delivery to the clerk within three (3) calendar days, cost prepaid, properly addressed;

    v.   If the court so permits, filing with the judge, in which event the judge shall note thereon the filing date and forthwith transmit them to the office of the clerk; or

    vi.   Electronic filing, as approved by the Division of State Court Administration pursuant to IN ST ADMIN Rule 16. IN ST TRIAL P Rule 5(F).

    vii.   Filing by registered or certified mail and by third-party commercial carrier shall be complete upon mailing or deposit. IN ST TRIAL P Rule 5(F).

c.   *Facsimile filing.* Facsimile filing is discouraged, but permitted in the Marion Circuit and Marion Superior Court. All documents filed by facsimile shall also be filed in hard copy within seven (7) days of the facsimile filing, along with proposed orders and stamped addressed envelopes, as required by IN ST MARION CIR AND SUPER CTS CIV Rule 203(E). To avoid duplicate filings, the hard copies of the facsimile filing shall indicate in bold letters that the pleading was previously filed by facsimile transmission. Proof of transmission by facsimile, including certificate of service and manner of service, shall be the responsibility of the filing party. If the filing requires immediate attention of the Judge, it shall be so indicated in bold letters in an accompanying transmittal memorandum. Legibility of documents and timeliness of filing is the responsibility of the sender. IN ST MARION CIR AND SUPER CTS CIV Rule 205(B).

    i.   *Generally.* In counties where a majority of judges of the courts of record, by posted local rule, have authorized electronic facsimile filing and designated a telephone number to receive such transmissions, pleadings, motions, and other papers may be sent to the Clerk of Circuit Court by electronic facsimile transmission for filing in any case, provided:

        • Such matter does not exceed ten (10) pages, including the cover sheet;

        • Such matter does not require the payment of fees other than the electronic facsimile transcription fee set forth in IN ST ADMIN Rule 12(E);

        • The sending party creates at the time of transmission a machine generated log for such transmission; and

        • The original document and the transmission log are maintained by the sending party for the duration of the litigation. IN ST ADMIN Rule 12(B).

    ii.   *Time of filing.* During normal, posted business hours, the time of filing shall be the time the duplicate document is produced in the office of the Clerk of the Circuit Court. Duplicate documents received at all other times shall be filed as of the next normal business day. IN ST ADMIN Rule 12(C).

        • If the receiving fax machine endorses its own time and date stamp upon the transmitted documents and the receiving machine produces a delivery receipt which is electronically created and transmitted to the sending party, the time of filing shall be the date and time recorded on the transmitted document by the receiving fax machine. IN ST ADMIN Rule 12(C).

d.   *Electronic filing.* Electronic filing and electronic service pilot projects are authorized pursuant to IN ST ADMIN Rule 16 and approved by the Division of State Court Administration. IN ST MARION SUPER CT ADMIN Rule 311(1-103).

    i.   *Cases where electronic filing accepted.* All Marion County Circuit and Superior civil courts may accept electronic filing and service of pleadings and other documents designated in this rule in mortgage foreclosure (hereinafter referred to as "MF"), civil collection(hereinafter referred to as "CC"), and individual cases that have been approved for electronic filing and service. IN ST MARION SUPER CT ADMIN Rule 311(1-104)(1).

        • The Marion County Circuit Court may, upon the motion of a party or its own motion, designate a case that will involve multiple litigants, legally intricate issues, and an extensive number of documents a mass tort or complex litigation case. Any case so designated shall be subject to electronic filing and service using the county's approved Electronic Service Provider. IN ST MARION SUPER CT ADMIN Rule 311(1-104)(3).

- The filing of electronic pleadings and other documents in MF and CC cases is entirely voluntary; however, once the case is initially filed electronically, all subsequent filings in the case shall remain in electronic format until the time for appeal is exhausted. IN ST MARION SUPER CT ADMIN Rule 311(1-104)(5).

ii. *Documents eligible for electronic filing.* The following pleadings may be filed and served electronically:

- New case complaint and petitions. IN ST MARION SUPER CT ADMIN Rule 311(1-104)(8)(a).

- Original answers. IN ST MARION SUPER CT ADMIN Rule 311(1-104)(8)(a).

- Any other pleadings or document including but not limited to motions and appearance forms. IN ST MARION SUPER CT ADMIN Rule 311(1-104)(8)(a).

iii. *Manner of electronic filing.* Parties shall E-file a document either:

- By registering to use the Electronic Filing Service Provider; or

- In person at the Marion County Clerk's office, by electronically filing through the Public Access Terminal. Parties filing in this manner shall be responsible for furnishing the document in an electronic format that will be compatible with the clerk's office-system to be uploaded in person. IN ST MARION SUPER CT ADMIN Rule 311(1-104)(9). For information on the Electronic Filing Service Provider and Public Access Terminal, refer to IN ST MARION SUPER CT ADMIN Rule 311(1-101).

- Registered users shall pay statutory filing fees for E-filed documents electronically to the Court through their EFSP. Filing fees are due and payable at the time of filing. IN ST MARION SUPER CT ADMIN Rule 311(2-104)(1). For more information on electronic filing fees, refer to IN ST MARION SUPER CT ADMIN Rule 311(2-104).

iv. *Effect of electronic filing.* Any pleading filed electronically shall be considered as filed with the court when the transmission to the EFSP is complete. Any document E-filed by 11:59 p.m. local Indianapolis, Indiana time shall be deemed filed on that date. The EFSP is an agent of the Court for the purpose of electronic filing, receipt, service and retrieval of electronic documents. IN ST MARION SUPER CT ADMIN Rule 311(2-102).

- Upon completion of filing, the EFSP shall issue a confirmation receipt that includes the date and time of receipt. The confirmation receipt shall serve as proof of filing. IN ST MARION SUPER CT ADMIN Rule 311(2-102).

- In the event the Court rejects the submitted documents following review, the documents shall not become part of the official Court record and the filer will receive notification of the rejection. Users may be required to refile the instruments to meet necessary filing requirements. Documents may be filed through an E-filing system at any time that the Clerk's office is open to receive the filing or at such other times as may be designated by the clerk and posted publicly. IN ST MARION SUPER CT ADMIN Rule 311(2-102).

- Documents filed through the E-filing system are deemed filed when received by the Clerk's office, except that documents received at times that the Clerk's office is closed shall be deemed filed the next regular time when the Clerk's office is open for filing. The time stamp issued by the E-filing system shall be presumed to be the time the document is received by the Clerk. IN ST MARION SUPER CT ADMIN Rule 311(2-102).

v. *Electronically filed documents.* All pleadings and other documents designated in IN ST MARION SUPER CT ADMIN Rule 311 shall be filed and served electronically in any individual case which has been approved for electronic filing and service. IN ST MARION SUPER CT ADMIN Rule 311(1-104)(6).

vi. *System failures.* When filing by electronic means is hindered by a technical failure, a party may file with the Clerk of Marion County in hard copy. With the exception of deadlines that by law cannot be extended, the time for filing of any paper that is delayed due to technical failure of the site shall be extended for one (1) day for each day on which such failure occurs, unless otherwise ordered by the Court. IN ST MARION SUPER CT ADMIN Rule 311(2-108).

      vii.   *Compliance with rules.* All filing shall comply with the requirements of IN ST ADMIN Rule 9 and IN ST ADMIN Rule 16; and the Indiana Rules of Court and the Marion County Local Rules. IN ST MARION SUPER CT ADMIN Rule 311(1-104)(11).

   e.   *Filing for special judge.* When a Special Judge who is not a Marion County Judge is selected, all parties or attorneys shall furnish such Judge with copies of all filings prior to the qualification of such Special Judge. Thereafter, copies of all filings shall be delivered in person, by mail or by facsimile to the office of the Special Judge with certificate of forwarding same made a part of the filing. IN ST MARION CIR AND SUPER CTS CIV Rule 205(C).

   f.   *Proof of filing.* Any party filing any paper by any method other than personal delivery to the clerk shall retain proof of filing. IN ST TRIAL P Rule 5(F).

2.   *Service requirements.* Unless otherwise provided by the Indiana Rules of Trial Procedure or an order of the court, each party and special judge, if any, shall be served with: (1) every order required by its terms to be served; (2) every pleading subsequent to the original complaint; (3) every written motion except one which may be heard ex parte; (4) every brief submitted to the trial court; (5) every paper relating to discovery required to be served upon a party; and (6) every written notice, appearance, demand, offer of judgment, designation of record on appeal, or similar paper. IN ST TRIAL P Rule 5(A).

   a.   *Methods of service*

      i.   *Personal service.* Whenever a party is represented by an attorney of record, service shall be made upon such attorney unless service upon the party himself is ordered by the court. Service upon the attorney or party shall be made by delivering or mailing a copy of the papers to the last known address or where an attorney or party has consented to service by fax or e-mail, as provided in IN ST TRIAL P Rule 3.1(A)(4), by faxing or e-mailing a copy of the documents to the fax number or e-mail address set out in the appearance form or correction as required by IN ST TRIAL P Rule 3.1(E). IN ST TRIAL P Rule 5(B). Delivery of a copy within IN ST TRIAL P Rule 5 means:

- Offering or tendering it to the attorney or party and stating the nature of the papers being served. Refusal to accept an offered or tendered document is a waiver of any objection to the sufficiency or adequacy of service of that document;

- Leaving it at his office with a clerk or other person in charge thereof, or if there is no one in charge, leaving it in a conspicuous place therein; or

- If the office is closed, by leaving it at his dwelling house or usual place of abode with some person of suitable age and discretion then residing therein; or,

- Leaving it at some other suitable place, selected by the attorney upon whom service is being made, pursuant to duly promulgated local rule. IN ST TRIAL P Rule 5(B)(1).

      ii.   *Service by mail.* If service is made by mail, the papers shall be deposited in the United States mail addressed to the person on whom they are being served, with postage prepaid. Service shall be deemed complete upon mailing. Proof of service of all papers permitted to be mailed may be made by written acknowledgment of service, by affidavit of the person who mailed the papers, or by certificate of an attorney. It shall be the duty of attorneys when entering their appearance in a cause or when filing pleadings or papers therein, to have noted in the Chronological Case Summary or said pleadings or papers so filed the address and telephone number of their office. Service by delivery or by mail at such address shall be deemed sufficient and complete. IN ST TRIAL P Rule 5(B)(2).

      iii.   *Service by fax or e-mail.* A party who has consented to service by fax or e-mail may be served as follows:

- Service by e-mail shall be made by attaching the document being served in .pdf format. Discovery documents must also be served in accordance with IN ST TRIAL P Rule 26(A). IN ST TRIAL P Rule 5(B)(3)(a).

- Service by fax shall be deemed complete upon generation of a transmission record indicating the successful transmission of the entire document, except as provided in IN ST TRIAL P Rule 5(B)(3)(d). IN ST TRIAL P Rule 5(B)(3)(b).

- Service by e-mail shall be deemed complete upon transmission, except as provided in IN ST TRIAL P Rule 5(B)(3)(d). IN ST TRIAL P Rule 5(B)(3)(c).

- Service by fax or e-mail that occurs on a Saturday, Sunday, legal holiday, or day the court or agency in which the matter is pending is closed or after 5:00 PM local time of the recipient shall be deemed complete the next day that is not a Saturday, Sunday, legal holiday, or day that the court or agency in which the matter is pending is not closed. IN ST TRIAL P Rule 5(B)(3)(d).

    iv. *Electronic service.* Delivery of E-service documents through the EFSP to other registered users shall be considered as valid and effective service and shall have the same legal effect as an original paper document. Recipients of E-service documents shall access their documents through the EFSP. IN ST MARION SUPER CT ADMIN Rule 311(2-107)(1).

- E-service shall be deemed complete when the transmission to the EFSP is completed. IN ST MARION SUPER CT ADMIN Rule 311(2-107)(2).

- For the purpose of computing time to respond to documents received via E-service, any document served on a day or at a time when the Clerk's office is not open for business shall be deemed served at the time of next opening of the Clerk's office for business. IN ST MARION SUPER CT ADMIN Rule 311(2-107)(3).

  b. *Serving numerous defendants.* In any action in which there are unusually large numbers of defendants, the court, upon motion or of its own initiative, may order:

    i. That service of the pleadings of the defendants and replies thereto need not be made as between the defendants;

- That any cross-claim, counterclaim, or matter constituting an avoidance or affirmative defense contained therein shall be deemed to be denied or avoided by all other parties; and

- That the filing of any such pleading and service thereof upon the plaintiff constitutes due notice of it to the parties. IN ST TRIAL P Rule 5(D).

    ii. A copy of every such order shall be served upon the parties in such manner and form as the court directs. IN ST TRIAL P Rule 5(D).

  c. *Service on parties in default for failure to appear.* No service need be made on parties in default for failure to appear, except that pleadings asserting new or additional claims for relief against them shall be served upon them in the manner provided by service of summons in IN ST TRIAL P Rule 4. IN ST TRIAL P Rule 5(A).

G. Hearings

1. The Indiana rules do not contemplate a hearing regarding the filing and service of an answer.

H. Forms

1. Official Answer Forms for Indiana

  a. Affidavit of debt. IN ST TRIAL P App. A-2.

  b. Appearance by attorney in civil case. IN ST TRIAL P App. B.

2. Answer Forms for Indiana

  a. Appearance; By responding party. 9 INPRAC § 39.3.

  b. Answer; Form and content. 9 INPRAC § 41.1.

  c. Answer; General form. 9 INPRAC § 41.3.

  d. Answer; Another form. 9 INPRAC § 41.4.

  e. Answer; Another form. 9 INPRAC § 41.5.

  f. General denial. 9 INPRAC § 41.6.

  g. Specific denial of designated paragraph. 9 INPRAC § 41.7.

  h. Specific admission of designated paragraph. 9 INPRAC § 41.8.

      i.   Denial of knowledge or information to form belief. 9 INPRAC § 41.9.

      j.   Denial of knowledge or information to form belief; Another form. 9 INPRAC § 41.10.

      k.   Partial denial and partial admission of designated paragraph. 9 INPRAC § 41.11.

      l.   Denial of designated paragraph for reason that document speaks for itself. 9 INPRAC § 41.12.

      m.   Adoption of admissions or denials by co-defendant's answer. 9 INPRAC § 41.13.

      n.   Denial of execution of instrument filed with pleading. 9 INPRAC § 41.14.

      o.   Answer to cross-claim. 9 INPRAC § 41.15.

      p.   Answer to third-party complaint. 9 INPRAC § 41.16.

      q.   Accord and satisfaction. 9 INPRAC § 41.21.

      r.   Answer. 5 INPRAC § 3:3.3.

      s.   Answer; Another form. 5 INPRAC § 3:3.4.

      t.   Certificate of service; Personal service. 9 INPRAC § 5.7.

      u.   Certificate of service; First class mail. 9 INPRAC § 5.8.

      v.   Signature; By party. 9 INPRAC § 4.5.

      w.   Signature; Attorney. 9 INPRAC § 4.6.

      x.   Signature; Attorney; Another form. 9 INPRAC § 4.7.

      y.   Signature; Attorney; Another form. 9 INPRAC § 4.8.

      z.   Verification; Official form. 9 INPRAC § 4.9.

  3. Official Answer Forms for Marion County

      a.   Appearance form. IN ST MARION CIR AND SUPER CTS CIV App. B.

I. Checklist

  (I) ❑ Matters to be considered by the plaintiff

    (a) ❑ Required documents

      (1) ❑ Summons

      (2) ❑ Complaint

      (3) ❑ Appearance form

    (b) ❑ Supplemental documents

      (1) ❑ Proof of written instrument

      (2) ❑ Notice of intent to use foreign law

      (3) ❑ Praecipe

      (4) ❑ Facsimile cover sheet

    (c) ❑ Timing

      (1) ❑ The claimant typically bears the burden of commencing an action within the applicable statute of limitations

      (2) ❑ If person seeking service of process fails without cause for sixty (60) days or more to provide clerk with required summons for issuance or with other information necessary to effectuate service, person has failed to exercise due diligence in securing service of process

  (II) ❑ Matters to be considered by the defendant

    (a) ❑ Required documents

      (1) ❑ Answer

      (2) ❑ Appearance form

      (3) ❑ Certificate of service

(b) ❑ Supplemental documents

    (1) ❑ Admission of service

    (2) ❑ Proof of written instrument

    (3) ❑ Notice of intent to use foreign law

    (4) ❑ Facsimile cover sheet

(c) ❑ Timing

    (1) ❑ A responsive pleading required under the Indiana Rules of Trial Procedure, shall be served within twenty (20) days after service of the prior pleading

    (2) ❑ The service of a motion permitted under IN ST TRIAL P Rule 12 alters the time for service of responsive pleadings as follows, unless a different time is fixed by the court:

        (i) ❑ If the court does not grant the motion, the responsive pleading shall be served in ten (10) days after notice of the court's action;

        (ii) ❑ If the court grants the motion and the corrective action is allowed to be taken, it shall be taken within ten (10) days, and the responsive pleading shall be served within ten (10) days thereafter

    (3) ❑ All pleadings and papers subsequent to the complaint which are required to be served upon a party shall be filed with the Court either before service or within a reasonable period of time thereafter

Pleadings
Amended Answer

Document Last Updated October 2013

A. Applicable Rules

1. *State rules*

    a. Appearance. IN ST TRIAL P Rule 3.1.

    b. Summons. IN ST TRIAL P Rule 4.

    c. Filing and service. IN ST TRIAL P Rule 4.6; IN ST TRIAL P Rule 5.

    d. Time. IN ST TRIAL P Rule 6.

    e. Pleadings. IN ST TRIAL P Rule 7; IN ST TRIAL P Rule 8; IN ST TRIAL P Rule 9; IN ST TRIAL P Rule 9.1; IN ST TRIAL P Rule 9.2; IN ST TRIAL P Rule 10.

    f. Signing and verification of pleadings. IN ST TRIAL P Rule 11.

    g. Defenses and objections; When and how presented; By pleading or motion; Motion for judgment on the pleadings. IN ST TRIAL P Rule 12.

    h. Counterclaim and cross-claim. IN ST TRIAL P Rule 13.

    i. Third-party practice. IN ST TRIAL P Rule 14.

    j. Amended and supplemental pleadings. IN ST TRIAL P Rule 15.

    k. Parties plaintiff and defendant; Capacity. IN ST TRIAL P Rule 17.

    l. Joinder. IN ST TRIAL P Rule 19; IN ST TRIAL P Rule 20.

    m. Consolidation; Separate trials. IN ST TRIAL P Rule 42.

    n. Evidence. IN ST TRIAL P Rule 43.

    o. Determination of foreign law. IN ST TRIAL P Rule 44.1.

    p. Judgment on the evidence (directed verdict). IN ST TRIAL P Rule 50.

    q. Findings by the court. IN ST TRIAL P Rule 52.

r. Judgment; Costs. IN ST TRIAL P Rule 54.

s. Summary judgment. IN ST TRIAL P Rule 56.

t. Motion to correct error. IN ST TRIAL P Rule 59.

u. Relief from judgment or order. IN ST TRIAL P Rule 60.

v. Venue requirements. IN ST TRIAL P Rule 75.

w. Access to court records. IN ST ADMIN Rule 9.

x. Paper size. IN ST ADMIN Rule 11.

y. Facsimile and electronic transmission. IN ST ADMIN Rule 12; IN ST ADMIN Rule 16.

z. Sealing of certain records by court; Hearing; Notice; Privacy and confidentiality. IN ST 5-2-9-6; IN ST 5-14-3-4; IN ST 5-14-3-5.5; IN ST 6-4.1-5-10; IN ST 6-4.1-12-12; IN ST 6-8.1-7-1; IN ST 11-13-1-8; IN ST 12-23-14-13; IN ST 16-39-3-10; IN ST 16-41-8-1; IN ST 22-4-19-6; IN ST 31-11-1-6; IN ST 31-19-5-23; IN ST 31-19-13-2; IN ST 31-19-19-1; IN ST 31-33-18-1; IN ST 31-39-1-1; IN ST 31-39-1-2; IN ST 33-23-16-16; IN ST 35-34-2-4; IN ST 35-38-1-13; IN ST 35-38-9-1; IN ST ADR Rule 2.11; IN ST ADR Rule 4.4; IN ST ADR Rule 5.6; IN ST JURY Rule 10.

2. *Local rules*

   a. Requirements for motions. IN ST MARION CIR AND SUPER CTS CIV Rule 203.

   b. Preparation of pleadings, motions and other papers. IN ST MARION CIR AND SUPER CTS CIV Rule 204.

   c. Filing of pleadings, motions and other papers. IN ST MARION CIR AND SUPER CTS CIV Rule 205.

   d. Signing and verification of pleadings, motions and other papers; Service on opposing party. IN ST MARION CIR AND SUPER CTS CIV Rule 206.

   e. Motions for continuance. IN ST MARION CIR AND SUPER CTS CIV Rule 215.

   f. Electronic filing. IN ST MARION SUPER CT ADMIN Rule 311.

B. Timing

1. *Filing an amended pleading*

   a. *As a matter of course.* A party may amend his pleading once as a matter of course at any time before a responsive pleading is served or, if the pleading is one to which no responsive pleading is permitted, and the action has not been placed upon the trial calendar, he may so amend it at any time within thirty (30) days after it is served. IN ST TRIAL P Rule 15(A).

   b. *With leave of court.* Otherwise a party may amend his pleading only by leave of court or by written consent of the adverse party; and leave shall be given when justice so requires. IN ST TRIAL P Rule 15(A). Refer to the Indiana KeyRules Motion for Leave to Amend document for more information.

2. *Computation of time*

   a. *Generally; Days excluded.* In computing any period of time prescribed or allowed by the Indiana Rules of Trial Procedure, by order of the court, or by any applicable statute, the day of the act, event, or default from which the designated period of time begins to run shall not be included. The last day of the period so computed is to be included unless it is:

      i. A Saturday,

      ii. A Sunday,

      iii. A legal holiday as defined by state statute, or

      iv. A day the office in which the act is to be done is closed during regular business hours. IN ST TRIAL P Rule 6(A).

   b. *Short periods.* In any event, the period runs until the end of the next day that is not a Saturday, a Sunday, a legal holiday, or a day on which the office is closed. When the period of time allowed is

less than seven (7) days, intermediate Saturdays, Sundays, legal holidays, and days on which the office is closed shall be excluded from the computations. IN ST TRIAL P Rule 6(A).

c. *Additional time after service by United States mail.* Whenever a party has the right or is required to do some act or take some proceedings within a prescribed period after the service of a notice or other paper upon him and the notice or paper is served upon him by United States mail, three (3) days shall be added to the prescribed period. IN ST TRIAL P Rule 6(E).

d. *Enlargement of time.* When an act is required or allowed to be done at or within a specific time by the Indiana Rules of Trial Procedure, the court may at any time for cause shown:

    i. Order the period enlarged, with or without motion or notice, if request therefor is made before the expiration of the period originally prescribed or extended by a previous order; or

    ii. Upon motion made after the expiration of the specific period, permit the act to be done where the failure to act was the result of excusable neglect; but, the court may not extend the time for taking any action for judgment on the evidence under IN ST TRIAL P Rule 50(A), amendment of findings and judgment under IN ST TRIAL P Rule 52(B), to correct errors under IN ST TRIAL P Rule 59(C), statement in opposition to motion to correct error under IN ST TRIAL P Rule 59(E), or to obtain relief from final judgment under IN ST TRIAL P Rule 60(B), except to the extent and under the conditions stated in those rules. IN ST TRIAL P Rule 6(B).

    iii. Initial written motion for enlargement of time pursuant to IN ST TRIAL P Rule 6(B)(1) to respond to a claim shall be automatically allowed for an additional thirty (30) days from the original due date without a written order of the Court. Any motion filed pursuant to IN ST MARION CIR AND SUPER CTS CIV Rule 203 shall state the date when such a response is due and the date to which time is enlarged. The motion must be filed on or before the original due date or IN ST MARION CIR AND SUPER CTS CIV Rule 203 shall be inapplicable. All subsequent Motions shall be so designated and will be granted only for good cause shown. IN ST MARION CIR AND SUPER CTS CIV Rule 203(D).

e. *Continuances disfavored.* Motions for Continuance are discouraged. Neither side is entitled to an automatic continuance as a matter of right. IN ST MARION CIR AND SUPER CTS CIV Rule 215. For information on obtaining a continuance, refer to IN ST MARION CIR AND SUPER CTS CIV Rule 215.

C. General Requirements

1. *Amending pleadings.* The purpose of an amended pleading is to include matters that occurred before the filing of the original pleading but which were either overlooked by the pleader or unknown to him at the time. It is a substitute for the original and relates to the facts that existed when the original pleading was filed. An amended pleading supercedes the original as to those portions amended. 10 INPRAC § 46.1.

a. *Amendments liberally allowed.* Amendments to pleadings are to be liberally allowed in order that all issues are presented in one action. 10 INPRAC § 46.1; Pinnacle Media, LLC v. Metropolitan Dev. Com'n of Marion County, 868 N.E.2d 894 (Ind.Ct.App. 2007).

b. *Amendments to conform to the evidence.* When issues not raised by the pleadings are tried by express or implied consent of the parties, they shall be treated in all respects as if they had been raised in the pleadings. Such amendment of the pleadings as may be necessary to cause them to conform to the evidence and to raise these issues may be made upon motion of any party at any time, even after judgment, but failure so to amend does not affect the result of the trial of these issues. If evidence is objected to at the trial on the ground that it is not within the issues made by the pleadings, the court may allow the pleadings to be amended and shall do so freely when the presentation of the merits of the action will be subserved thereby and the objecting party fails to satisfy the court that the admission of such evidence would prejudice him in maintaining his action or defense upon the merits. The court may grant a continuance to enable the objecting party to meet such evidence. IN ST TRIAL P Rule 15(B).

c. *Relation back of amendments*

    i. Whenever the claim or defense asserted in the amended pleading arose out of the conduct, transaction, or occurrence set forth or attempted to be set forth in the original pleading, the amendment relates back to the date of the original pleading. An amendment changing the party against whom a claim is asserted relates back if the foregoing provision is satisfied and, within one hundred and twenty (120) days of commencement of the action, the party to be brought in by amendment:

- Has received such notice of the institution of the action that he will not be prejudiced in maintaining his defense on the merits; and

- Knew or should have known that but for a mistake concerning the identity of the proper party, the action would have been brought against him. IN ST TRIAL P Rule 15(C).

    ii. The requirement of subsections IN ST TRIAL P Rule 15(C)(1) and IN ST TRIAL P Rule 15(C)(2) with respect to a governmental organization to be brought into the action as defendant is satisfied:

- In the case of a state or governmental organization by delivery or mailing of process to the attorney general or to a governmental executive [IN ST TRIAL P Rule 4.6(A)(3)]; or

- In the case of a local governmental organization, by delivery or mailing of process to its attorney as provided by statute, to a governmental executive thereof [IN ST TRIAL P Rule 4.6(A)(4)], or to the officer holding the office if suit is against the officer or an office. IN ST TRIAL P Rule 15(C).

  d. *Amendment by leave.* Amendments, other than an amendment by right, may be made only by leave of court or by written consent of the opposing party. 2 INPRAC R 15(15.2). Refer to the Indiana KeyRules Motion for Leave to Amend document for more information on amending with leave of court.

2. *Pleading, generally*

  a. *Pleadings to be concise.* Each averment of a pleading shall be simple, concise, and direct. No technical forms of pleading or motions are required. All fictions in pleading are abolished. IN ST TRIAL P Rule 8(E)(1).

  b. *Pleading in the alternative.* A pleading may set forth two (2) or more statements of a claim or defense alternatively or hypothetically, either in one (1) count or defense or in separate counts or defenses. When two (2) or more statements are made in the alternative and one (1) of them if made independently would be sufficient, the pleading is not made insufficient by the insufficiency of one or more of the alternative statements. A pleading may also state as many separate claims or defenses as the pleader has regardless of consistency and whether based on legal or equitable grounds. All statements shall be made subject to the obligations set forth in IN ST TRIAL P Rule 11. IN ST TRIAL P Rule 8(E)(2).

  c. *Motions and pleadings, joint and several.* All motions and pleadings of any kind addressed to two (2) or more paragraphs of any pleading, or filed by two (2) or more parties, shall be taken and construed as joint, separate, and several motions or pleadings to each of such paragraphs and by and against each of such parties. All motions or pleadings containing two (2) or more subject-matters shall be taken and construed as separate and several as to each subject-matter. All objections to rulings made by two (2) or more parties shall be taken and construed as the joint, separate, and several objections of each of such parties. IN ST TRIAL P Rule 8(E)(3).

    i. A complaint filed by or against two (2) or more plaintiffs shall be taken and construed as joint, separate, and several as to each of said plaintiffs. IN ST TRIAL P Rule 8(E).

  d. *Construction of pleadings.* All pleadings shall be so construed as to do substantial justice, lead to disposition on the merits, and avoid litigation of procedural points. IN ST TRIAL P Rule 8(F).

3. *Contents of the answer*

  a. *Defenses which may be raised by answer or motion.* Every defense, in law or fact, to a claim for relief in any pleading, whether a claim, counterclaim, cross-claim, or third-party claim, shall be asserted in the responsive pleading thereto if one is required; except that at the option of the pleader, the following defenses may be made by motion:

    i. Lack of jurisdiction over the subject matter;

ii.   Lack of jurisdiction over the person;

iii.   Incorrect venue under IN ST TRIAL P Rule 75, or any statutory provision. The disposition of this motion shall be consistent with IN ST TRIAL P Rule 75;

iv.   Insufficiency of process;

v.   Insufficiency of service of process;

vi.   Failure to state a claim upon which relief can be granted, which shall include failure to name the real party in interest under IN ST TRIAL P Rule 17;

vii.   Failure to join a party needed for just adjudication under IN ST TRIAL P Rule 19;

viii.   The same action pending in another state court of this state. IN ST TRIAL P Rule 12(B).

ix.   A motion making any of these defenses shall be made before pleading if a further pleading is permitted or within twenty (20) days after service of the prior pleading if none is required. If a pleading sets forth a claim for relief to which the adverse party is not required to serve a responsive pleading, any of the defenses in section IN ST TRIAL P Rule 12(B)(2), IN ST TRIAL P Rule 12(B)(3), IN ST TRIAL P Rule 12(B)(4), IN ST TRIAL P Rule 12(B)(5) or IN ST TRIAL P Rule 12(B)(8) is waived to the extent constitutionally permissible unless made in a motion within twenty (20) days after service of the prior pleading. No defense or objection is waived by being joined with one (1) or more other defenses or objections in a responsive pleading or motion. IN ST TRIAL P Rule 12(B).

b. *Waiver or preservation of certain defenses*

i.   A defense of lack of jurisdiction over the person, improper venue, insufficiency of process, insufficiency of service of process, or the same action pending in another state court of this state is waived to the extent constitutionally permissible:

- If omitted from a motion in the circumstances described in IN ST TRIAL P Rule 12(G),
- If it is neither made by motion under IN ST TRIAL P Rule 12 nor included in a responsive pleading or an amendment thereof permitted by IN ST TRIAL P Rule 15(A) to be made as a matter of course. IN ST TRIAL P Rule 12(H)(1).

ii.   A defense of failure to state a claim upon which relief can be granted, a defense of failure to join an indispensable party under IN ST TRIAL P Rule 19(B), and an objection of failure to state a legal defense to a claim may be made in any pleading permitted or ordered under IN ST TRIAL P Rule 7(A) or by motion for judgment on the pleadings, or at the trial on the merits. IN ST TRIAL P Rule 12(H)(2).

c. *Defenses; Form of denials*

i.   A responsive pleading shall state in short and plain terms the pleader's defenses to each claim asserted and shall admit or controvert the averments set forth in the preceding pleading. If in good faith the pleader intends to deny all the averments in the preceding pleading, he may do so by general denial subject to the provisions of IN ST TRIAL P Rule 11. If he does not intend a general denial, he may:

- Specifically deny designated averments or paragraphs; or
- Generally deny all averments except such designated averments and paragraphs as he expressly admits. IN ST TRIAL P Rule 8(B).

ii.   If he lacks knowledge or information sufficient to form a belief as to the truth of an averment, he shall so state and his statement shall be considered a denial. If in good faith a pleader intends to deny only a part or a qualification of an averment, he shall specify so much of it as is true and material and deny the remainder. All denials shall fairly meet the substance of the averments denied. IN ST TRIAL P Rule 8 shall have no application to uncontested actions for divorce, or to answers required to be filed by clerks or guardians ad litem. IN ST TRIAL P Rule 8(B).

d. *Affirmative defenses.* A responsive pleading shall set forth affirmatively and carry the burden of proving: accord and satisfaction, arbitration and award, discharge in bankruptcy, duress, estoppel, failure of consideration, fraud, illegality, injury by fellow servant, laches, license, payment, release, res judicata, statute of frauds, statute of limitations, waiver, lack of jurisdiction over the subject-matter, lack of jurisdiction over the person, improper venue, insufficiency of process or service of process, the same action pending in another state court of this state, and any other matter constituting an avoidance, matter of abatement, or affirmative defense. A party required to affirmatively plead any matters, including matters formerly required to be pleaded affirmatively by reply, shall have the burden of proving such matters. The burden of proof imposed by this or any other provision of the Indiana Rules of Trial Procedure is subject to the rules of evidence or any statute fixing a different rule. If the pleading mistakenly designates a defense as a counterclaim or a counterclaim as a defense, the court shall treat the pleading as if there had been a proper designation. IN ST TRIAL P Rule 8(C).

    i.   An affirmative defense, generally, must be affirmatively stated by the party who seeks its benefit. 1A INPRAC R 8(8.5); Rice v. Grant County Bd. of Com'rs, 472 N.E.2d 213 (Ind.Ct.App. 1984). If that party does not raise the affirmative defense, then it is waived. 1A INPRAC R 8(8.5); Piskorowski v. Shell Oil Co., 403 N.E.2d 838, 847 (Ind.Ct.App. 1980).

    ii.   It is clear that the list of affirmative defenses found in IN ST TRIAL P Rule 8 is not exhaustive. The question comes: when is a defense to be treated as an affirmative defense, with all of the attending consequences? 1A INPRAC R 8(8.5). The "determination of whether a defense is affirmative depends on whether it controverts an element of the plaintiff's prima facie case or raises matter outside the scope of the prima facie case." 1A INPRAC R 8(8.5); Molargik v. West Enterprises, Inc., 605 N.E.2d 1197, 1198 (Ind.Ct.App. 1993).

e.   *Defense of contributory negligence or assumed risk.* In all claims alleging negligence, the burden of pleading and proving contributory negligence, assumption of risk, or incurred risk shall be upon the defendant who may plead such by denial of the allegation. IN ST TRIAL P Rule 9.1(A).

f.   *Consideration.* When an action or defense is founded upon a written contract or release, lack of consideration for the promise or release is an affirmative defense, and the party asserting lack of it carries the burden of proof. IN ST TRIAL P Rule 9.1(C).

g.   *Res ipsa loquitur.* Res ipsa loquitur or a similar doctrine may be pleaded by alleging generally that the facts connected with the action are unknown to the pleader and are within the knowledge of the opposing party. IN ST TRIAL P Rule 9.1(B).

h.   *Bona fide purchaser.* When the rights of a person depend upon his status as a bona fide purchaser for value or upon similar requirements, such status must be pleaded and proved by the person asserting it, but it may be pleaded in general terms. Once it is established that the person has given any required value, unless such value is commercially unreasonable, and that he has met any requirements of recordation, filing, possession, or perfection, the trier of fact must find that such value was given or such perfection was made in accordance with any requirements of good faith, lack of knowledge, or lack of notice unless and until evidence is introduced which would support a finding of its non-existence. IN ST TRIAL P Rule 9.1(D).

i.   *Presumption; Matters of judicial notice.* Neither presumptions of law nor matters of which judicial notice may be taken need be stated in a pleading. IN ST TRIAL P Rule 9.1(E).

j.   *Property distrained; Sufficient answer.* In an action to recover the possession of property distrained while doing damage, an answer that the defendant, or person by whose command he acted, was lawfully possessed of the real property upon which the distress was made, and that the property distrained was at the time doing damage thereon, shall be good without setting forth the title of such real property. IN ST TRIAL P Rule 9.1(F).

k.   *Effect of failure to deny.* Averments in a pleading to which a responsive pleading is required, except those pertaining to amount of damages, are admitted when not denied in the responsive pleading. Averments in a pleading to which no responsive pleading is required or permitted shall be taken as denied or avoided. IN ST TRIAL P Rule 8(D).

l.   *Effect of admission.* When a rhetorical paragraph or allegation is admitted, the effect in Indiana is to remove it from trial. Such an admission is a "judicial admission", and the claim or issue which is admitted cannot be denied later by the trier of the facts. Further, this admitted fact does not require evidence to "prove it"; it is established. It becomes, in short, controlling and indisputable in the litigation, unless the trial court permits an amendment to the pleading which might remove the controlling effect of the admission, and permit it to become another fact or item of evidence in the case. 1A INPRAC R 8(8.4); Aylesworth v. McKesson, 421 N.E.2d 422 (Ind.Ct.App. 1981).

4. *Pleading special matters*

a. *Capacity.* It is not necessary to aver the capacity of a party to sue or be sued, the authority of a party to sue or be sued in a representative capacity, or the legal existence of an organization that is made a party. The burden of proving lack of such capacity, authority, or legal existence shall be upon the person asserting lack of it, and shall be pleaded as an affirmative defense. IN ST TRIAL P Rule 9(A).

b. *Fraud, mistake, condition of the mind.* In all averments of fraud or mistake, the circumstances constituting fraud or mistake shall be specifically averred. Malice, intent, knowledge, and other conditions of mind may be averred generally. IN ST TRIAL P Rule 9(B).

c. *Conditions precedent.* In pleading the performance or occurrence of promissory or non-promissory conditions precedent, it is sufficient to aver generally that all conditions precedent have been performed, have occurred, or have been excused. A denial of performance or occurrence shall be made specifically and with particularity, and a denial of excuse generally. IN ST TRIAL P Rule 9(C).

d. *Official document or act.* In pleading an official document or official act it is sufficient to aver that the document was issued or the act done in compliance with law. IN ST TRIAL P Rule 9(D).

e. *Judgment.* In pleading a judgment or decision of a domestic or foreign court, judicial or quasi-judicial tribunal, or of a board or officer, it is sufficient to aver the judgment or decision without setting forth matter showing jurisdiction to render it. IN ST TRIAL P Rule 9(E).

f. *Time and place.* For the purpose of testing the sufficiency of a pleading, averments of time and place are material and shall be considered like all other averments of material matter. However, time and place need be stated only with such specificity as will enable the opposing party to prepare his defense. IN ST TRIAL P Rule 9(F).

g. *Special damages; Damages where no answer.* When items of special damage are claimed, they shall be specifically stated. The relief granted to the plaintiff, if there be no answer, cannot exceed the relief demanded in his complaint; but, in any other case, the court may grant him any relief consistent with the facts or matters pleaded. IN ST TRIAL P Rule 9(G).

5. *Counterclaim and cross-claim*

a. *Compulsory counterclaims.* A pleading shall state as a counterclaim any claim which at the time of serving the pleading the pleader has against any opposing party, if it arises out of the transaction or occurrence that is the subject-matter of the opposing party's claim and does not require for its adjudication the presence of third parties of whom the court cannot acquire jurisdiction. But the pleader need not state the claim if:

  i. At the time the action was commenced the claim was the subject of another pending action; or

  ii. The opposing party brought suit upon his claim by attachment or other process by which the court did not acquire jurisdiction to render a personal judgment on that claim, and the pleader is not stating any counterclaim under IN ST TRIAL P Rule 13. IN ST TRIAL P Rule 13(A).

b. *Permissive counterclaims.* A pleading may state as a counterclaim any claim against an opposing party not arising out of the transaction or occurrence that is the subject-matter of the opposing party's claim. IN ST TRIAL P Rule 13(B).

c. *Counterclaim exceeding opposing claim.* A counterclaim may or may not diminish or defeat the recovery sought by the opposing party. It may claim relief exceeding in amount or different in kind from that sought in the pleading of the opposing party. IN ST TRIAL P Rule 13(C).

d. *Counterclaim against state.* IN ST TRIAL P Rule 13 shall not be construed to enlarge any right to assert a claim against the state. IN ST TRIAL P Rule 13(D).

e. *Counterclaim maturing or acquired after pleading.* A claim which either matured or was acquired by the pleader after serving his pleading may, with the permission of the court, be presented as a counterclaim by supplemental pleading. A counterclaim or cross-claim which is not due may be asserted against a party who is insolvent or the representative of a party who has been subjected to insolvency proceedings, if recovery thereon will be impaired because of such party's insolvency. IN ST TRIAL P Rule 13(E).

f. *Omitted counterclaim.* When a pleader fails to set up a counterclaim through oversight, inadvertence, or excusable neglect, or when justice requires, he may by leave of court set up the counterclaim by amendment. IN ST TRIAL P Rule 13(F).

g. *Cross-claim against co-party.* A pleading may state as a cross-claim any claim by one party against a co-party. IN ST TRIAL P Rule 13(G).

h. *Joinder of additional parties.* Persons other than those made parties to the original action may be made parties to a counterclaim or cross-claim in accordance with the provisions of IN ST TRIAL P Rule 14, IN ST TRIAL P Rule 19 and IN ST TRIAL P Rule 20. IN ST TRIAL P Rule 13(H).

i. *Separate trials; Separate judgments*

    i. If the court orders separate trials as provided in IN ST TRIAL P Rule 42(B), judgment on a counterclaim or cross-claim may be rendered in accordance with the terms of IN ST TRIAL P Rule 54(B) when the court has jurisdiction so to do, even if the claims of the opposing party have been dismissed or otherwise disposed of. In determining whether or not separate trial of a cross-claim shall be ordered, the court shall consider whether the cross-claim:

        • Arises out of the transaction or occurrence or series of transactions or occurrences that is the subject-matter either of the original action or of a counterclaim therein;

        • Relates to any property or contract that is the subject-matter of the original action; or

        • Claims that the person against whom it is asserted is liable to the cross-claimant for all or part of plaintiff's claim against him. IN ST TRIAL P Rule 13(I).

    ii. In addition, the court may consider any other relevant factors. IN ST TRIAL P Rule 13(I).

j. *Effect of statute of limitations and other discharges at law.* The statute of limitations, a nonclaim statute or other discharge at law shall not bar a claim asserted as a counterclaim to the extent that:

    i. It diminishes or defeats the opposing party's claim if it arises out of the transaction or occurrence that is the subject-matter of the opposing party's claim, or if it could have been asserted as a counterclaim to the opposing party's claim before it (the counterclaim) was barred; or

    ii. It or the opposing party's claim relates to payment of or security for the other. IN ST TRIAL P Rule 13(J).

k. *Counterclaim by and against transferees and successors.* A counterclaim may be asserted by or against the transferee or successor of a claim subject to the following provisions:

    i. A successor who is a guardian, representative of a decedent's estate, receiver or assignee for the benefit of creditors, trustee or the like may interpose a claim to which he succeeds against claims or proceedings brought in or outside the court of administration. A claim owing by his predecessor may be interposed against any claim brought by such successor in or outside the court of administration without the necessity of filing such claim or cause of action in the administration proceedings. IN ST TRIAL P Rule 13(K)(1).

    ii. A transferee or successor of a claim takes it subject to any defense or counterclaim that is the subject-matter of the opposing party's claim; or that is available to the obligor at the time of the assignment or before the obligor received notice of the assignment. IN ST TRIAL P Rule 13(K)(2).

    iii. A surety or party with total or partial recourse upon a claim upon which he is being sued may interpose as a counterclaim:

        • Any claim of his own; and

        • Any claim owned by the person against whom he has recourse who either has notice of the suit, is a party to the suit, is insolvent, has assigned his claim to the surety or party asserting it, or cannot be found. IN ST TRIAL P Rule 13(K)(3).

- A counterclaim under IN ST TRIAL P Rule 13(K)(3)(b) must tend to diminish or defeat the opposing party's claim, or it or the opposing claim must relate to payment of or security for the other, unless the person against whom recourse may be had is a party to the suit or the counterclaim has been assigned to the party asserting it; and if recovery on the counterclaim exceeds the opposing party's claim, any excess recovered shall be held in trust for such person against whom there is a right of recourse. IN ST TRIAL P Rule 13(K)(3).

iv. IN ST TRIAL P Rule 13(K)(1), IN ST TRIAL P Rule 13(K)(2), and IN ST TRIAL P Rule 13(K)(3), are subject to subdivision IN ST TRIAL P Rule 13(L). IN ST TRIAL P Rule 13(K)(4).

l. *Counterclaim and cross-claim subject to substantive law principles.* Counterclaim and cross-claims are subject to restrictions imposed by other statutes and principles of substantive common law and equity, including rules of commercial law, agency, estoppel, contract and the like. In appropriate cases the court may impose terms or conditions upon its judgment or decree and may enter conditional or noncanceling cross judgments to satisfy such restrictions. This provision is intended to deny or limit counterclaims or cross-claims:

i. Where a creditor will receive an unfair priority because a claim is assigned after insolvency proceedings, or assigned before such proceedings if it results in an unlawful preference;

ii. Where an unfair priority will be allowed if a surety interposing a claim owned in his own right against the creditor suing on the principal's obligation when the principal is solvent and the creditor is not;

iii. Where a claim by or against a representative, such as a guardian, receiver, representative of a decedent's estate, assignee for the benefit of creditors, trustee or the like in his individual capacity is asserted against a claim owing or owed by the estate he represents;

iv. Where a claim by or against a partnership or two (2) or more obligors is opposed against or by a claim of an individual to the extent that the individual will be allowed unfairly to profit or if it will adversely affect the rights of creditors; or

v. Where a claim is cut off by a holder in due course or a transferee who is protected under principles of commercial law, estoppel, or contract. IN ST TRIAL P Rule 13(L).

m. *Satisfaction of judgment.* Satisfaction of a judgment or credits thereon may be ordered, for sufficient cause, upon notice and motion. "Credits" include any counterclaim which tends to diminish or defeat the judgment, or any counterclaim where it or the opposing claim relates to payment of or security for the other. IN ST TRIAL P Rule 13(M).

6. *Third-party practice*

a. *When defendant may bring in third party.* A defending party, as a third-party plaintiff, may cause a summons and complaint to be served upon a person not a party to the action who is or may be liable to him for all or part of the plaintiff's claim against him. IN ST TRIAL P Rule 14(A). The person served with the summons and the third-party complaint, hereinafter called the third-party defendant, as provided in IN ST TRIAL P Rule 12 and IN ST TRIAL P Rule 13 may make:

i. His defenses, cross-claims and counterclaims to the third-party plaintiff's claims;

ii. His defenses, counterclaims and cross-claims against any other defendants or third-party defendants;

iii. Any defenses or claims which the third-party plaintiff has to the plaintiff's claim which are available to the third-party defendant against the plaintiff; and

iv. Any defenses or claims which the third-party defendant has as against the plaintiff. IN ST TRIAL P Rule 14(A).

v. The plaintiff may assert any claim against the third-party defendant who thereupon may assert his defenses, counterclaims and cross-claims, as provided in IN ST TRIAL P Rule 12 and IN ST TRIAL P Rule 13. A third-party defendant may proceed under IN ST TRIAL P Rule 14 against any person not a party to the action who is or may be liable to him for all or part of the claim made in the action against the third-party defendant. IN ST TRIAL P Rule 14(A).

b. *When plaintiff may bring in third party.* When a counterclaim or other claim is asserted against a plaintiff, he may cause a third party to be brought in under circumstances, which, under IN ST TRIAL P Rule 14, would entitle a defendant to do so. IN ST TRIAL P Rule 14(B).

c. *Severance; Parties improperly impleaded.* With his responsive pleading or by motion prior thereto, any party may move for severance of a third-party claim or ensuing claim as provided in IN ST TRIAL P Rule 14 or for a separate trial thereon. If the third-party defendant is a proper party to the proceedings under any other rule relating to parties, the action shall continue as in other cases where he is made a party. IN ST TRIAL P Rule 14(C).

7. *Trial by jury; Demand*

a. *Causes triable by court and by jury.* Issues of law and issues of fact in causes that prior to the eighteenth day of June, 1852, were of exclusive equitable jurisdiction shall be tried by the court; issues of fact in all other causes shall be triable as the same are now triable. In case of the joinder of causes of action or defenses which, prior to said date, were of exclusive equitable jurisdiction with causes of action or defenses which, prior to said date, were designated as actions at law and triable by jury—the former shall be triable by the court, and the latter by a jury, unless waived; the trial of both may be at the same time or at different times, as the court may direct. IN ST TRIAL P Rule 38(A).

b. *Demand.* Any party may demand a trial by jury of any issue triable of right by a jury by filing with the court and serving upon the other parties a demand therefor in writing at any time after the commencement of the action and not later than ten (10) days after the first responsive pleading to the complaint, or to a counterclaim, crossclaim or other claim if one properly is pleaded; and if no responsive pleading is filed or required, within ten (10) days after the time such pleading otherwise would have been required. Such demand is sufficient if indorsed upon a pleading of a party filed within such time. IN ST TRIAL P Rule 38(B).

c. *Same; Specification of issues.* In his demand a party may specify the issues which he wishes so tried; otherwise he shall be deemed to have demanded trial by jury for all issues triable as of right by jury. Any other party must file a demand for jury trial to preserve his right to trial by jury:

   i. Of issues for which a right to trial by jury was not requested by another party; and

   ii. In case a request by another party was improper. But if a proper request for a trial by jury upon issues triable by jury as of right on his behalf is made by any party, such request shall be deemed to have been made on behalf of all parties entitled to a jury trial upon such issues. IN ST TRIAL P Rule 38(C).

d. *Waiver.* The failure of a party to appear at the trial, and the failure of a party to serve a demand as required by IN ST TRIAL P Rule 38 and to file it as required by IN ST TRIAL P Rule 5(E) constitute waiver by him of trial by jury. A demand for trial by jury made as provided in IN ST TRIAL P Rule 38 may not be withdrawn without the consent of the other party or parties. IN ST TRIAL P Rule 38(D).

   i. The trial court shall not grant a demand for a trial by jury filed after the time fixed in IN ST TRIAL P Rule 38(B) has elapsed except upon the written agreement of all of the parties to the action, which agreement shall be filed with the court and made a part of the record. If such agreement is filed then the court may, in its discretion, grant a trial by jury in which event the grant of a trial by jury may not be withdrawn except by the agreement of all of the parties. IN ST TRIAL P Rule 38(D).

e. *Arbitration.* Nothing in the Indiana Rules of Trial Procedure shall deny the parties the right by contract or agreement to submit or to agree to submit controversies to arbitration made before or after commencement of an action thereon or deny the courts power to specifically enforce such agreements. IN ST TRIAL P Rule 38(E).

D. Documents

1. *Required documents*

a. *Amended answer.* Refer to the General Requirements section of this document for information on the contents of an amended answer.

b. *Certificate of service.* An attorney or unrepresented party tendering a document to the Clerk for filing shall certify that service has been made, list the parties served, and specify the date and means of service. The certificate of service shall be placed at the end of the document and shall not be separately filed. The separate filing of a certificate of service, however, shall not be grounds for rejecting a document for filing. The Clerk may permit documents to be filed without a certificate of service but shall require prompt filing of a separate certificate of service. IN ST TRIAL P Rule 5(C). In all cases where any pleading or other document is required to be served upon opposing counsel, proof of such service may be made either by:

   i. A certificate of service signed by counsel of record for the serving party and the certificate shall specify by name and address all counsel upon whom the pleading or document was served; or

   ii. An acknowledgment of service signed by the party served or counsel of record. IN ST MARION CIR AND SUPER CTS CIV Rule 206.

2. *Supplemental documents*

   a. *Proof of written instrument.* When any pleading allowed by the Indiana Rules of Trial Procedure is founded on a written instrument, the original, or a copy thereof, must be included in or filed with the pleading. Such instrument, whether copied in the pleadings or not, shall be taken as part of the record. When any pleading allowed by the Indiana Rules of Trial Procedure is founded on an account, an Affidavit of Debt, in a form substantially similar to that which is provided in IN ST TRIAL P App. A-2, shall be attached. IN ST TRIAL P Rule 9.2(A).

   b. *Notice of intent to use foreign law.* A party who intends to raise an issue concerning the law of a foreign country shall give notice in his pleadings or other reasonable written notice. The court, in determining foreign law, may consider any relevant material or source, including testimony, whether or not submitted by a party or admissible under IN ST TRIAL P Rule 43. The court's determination shall be treated as a ruling on a question of law. It shall be made by the court and not the jury and shall be reviewable. IN ST TRIAL P Rule 44.1(A).

   c. *Facsimile cover sheet.* Any document sent to the Clerk of the Circuit Court by electronic facsimile transmission shall be accompanied by a cover sheet which states the title of the document, case number, number of pages, identity and voice telephone number of the sending party and instructions for filing. The cover sheet shall contain the signature of the attorney or party, pro se, authorizing the filing. IN ST ADMIN Rule 12(D).

E. Format

1. *Form of pleadings*

   a. *Caption; Names of parties.* Every pleading shall contain a caption setting forth the name of the court, the title of the action, the file number, and a designation as in IN ST TRIAL P Rule 7(A). In the complaint the title of the action shall include the names of all the parties, but in other pleadings it is sufficient to state the name of the first party on each side with an appropriate indication of other parties. IN ST TRIAL P Rule 10(A).

      i. Every pleading shall contain a caption setting forth the name of the Court, the Division and Room Number, the title of the action and the file number. IN ST MARION CIR AND SUPER CTS CIV Rule 204(B).

   b. *Paragraphs; Separate statements.* All averments of a claim or defense shall be made in numbered paragraphs, the contents of each of which shall be limited as far as practicable to a statement of a single set of circumstances, and a paragraph may be referred to by number in all succeeding pleadings. Each claim founded upon a separate transaction or occurrence and each defense other than denials may be stated in a separate count or defense whenever a separation facilitates the clear presentation of the matters set forth. IN ST TRIAL P Rule 10(B).

   c. *Adoption by reference; Exhibits.* Statements in a pleading may be adopted by reference in a different part of the same pleading or in another pleading or in any motion. A copy of any written instrument which is an exhibit to a pleading is a part thereof for all purposes. IN ST TRIAL P Rule 10(C).

   d. *Paper.* Pleadings, motions and other papers may be either printed or typewritten on white opaque paper of at least sixteen (16) pound weight, eight and one-half (8-1/2) inches wide and eleven (11) inches in length. IN ST MARION CIR AND SUPER CTS CIV Rule 204(A).

e. *Copies.* All copies shall likewise be on white paper of sufficient strength and durability to resist normal wear and tear. IN ST MARION CIR AND SUPER CTS CIV Rule 204(A).

f. *Line spacing.* If typewritten, the lines shall be double spaced, except for quotations, which shall be indented and single spaced. IN ST MARION CIR AND SUPER CTS CIV Rule 204(A).

g. *Script type.* Script type shall not be used. IN ST MARION CIR AND SUPER CTS CIV Rule 204(A).

h. *Titles.* Titles on all pleadings shall delineate each topic included in the pleading e.g. where a pleading contains an Answer, a Motion to Strike or Dismiss, or a Jury Request each shall be set forth in the title. IN ST MARION CIR AND SUPER CTS CIV Rule 204(C).

i. *Margins and binding.* Margins shall be one (1) inch. Binding or stapling shall be at the top and at no other place. Covers or backing shall not be used. IN ST MARION CIR AND SUPER CTS CIV Rule 204(D).

2. *Size of papers for filing.* Effective January 1, 1992, all pleadings, copies, motions and documents filed with any trial court or appellate level court, typed or printed, with the exception of exhibits and existing wills, shall be prepared on eight and one-half by eleven inch (8 1/2" x 11") size paper. IN ST ADMIN Rule 11.

3. *Form of electronically filed documents.* All electronically filed and served pleadings shall, to the extent practicable, be formatted in accordance with the applicable rules governing formatting of paper pleadings. IN ST MARION SUPER CT ADMIN Rule 311(2-103)(1).

a. *Electronic document title.* The electronic document title of each pleading or other document shall include:

   i. Party or parties filing/serving the document,

   ii. Nature of the document,

   iii. Party or parties against whom relief, if any, is sought, and

   iv. Nature of the relief sought (e.g., Defendant ABC Corporation's Motion for Summary Judgment). IN ST MARION SUPER CT ADMIN Rule 311(2-103)(2).

4. *Signature requirements*

a. *Signature of attorney.* Every pleading or motion of a party represented by an attorney shall be signed by at least one (1) attorney of record in his individual name, whose address, telephone number, and attorney number shall be stated, except that this provision shall not apply to pleadings and motions made and transcribed at the trial or a hearing before the judge and received by him in such form. IN ST TRIAL P Rule 11(A).

   i. All pleadings and motions shall contain the original or authorized signature of the attorney, the name of the attorney in typed or printed form, the name of the law firm if a member of a firm, the attorney's address, identification number, e-mail address, telephone number, fax number, and the designation as to the party for whom he appears. IN ST MARION CIR AND SUPER CTS CIV Rule 204(E).

   ii. The signature of an attorney constitutes a certificate by him that he has read the pleadings; that to the best of his knowledge, information, and belief, there is good ground to support it; and that it is not interposed for delay. IN ST TRIAL P Rule 11(A).

   iii. If a pleading or motion is not signed or is signed with intent to defeat the purpose of the rule, it may be stricken as sham and false and the action may proceed as though the pleading had not been served. IN ST TRIAL P Rule 11(A).

   iv. For a willful violation of IN ST TRIAL P Rule 11 an attorney may be subjected to appropriate disciplinary action. Similar action may be taken if scandalous or indecent matter is inserted. IN ST TRIAL P Rule 11(A).

   v. Every pleading, document, and instrument electronically filed or served shall be deemed to

have been signed by the judge, clerk, attorney or declarant and shall bear a facsimile or typographical signature of such person, along with the typed name, address, telephone number, and Bar number of a signing attorney. Typographical signatures shall be treated as personal signatures for all purposes under these rules. IN ST MARION SUPER CT ADMIN Rule 311(2-105).

- Documents containing signatures of third-parties (i.e., unopposed motions, affidavits, stipulations, etc.) may also be filed electronically by indicating that the original signatures are maintained by the filing party in paper-format. IN ST MARION SUPER CT ADMIN Rule 311(2-105).

- Unless otherwise ordered by the Court or Clerk, a printed copy of all documents filed or served electronically, including original signatures, shall be maintained by the party filing the document and shall be made available, upon reasonable notice, for inspection by other counsel, the Clerk or Court. Parties shall retain originals until two (2) years after all time periods for appeal have expired. From time to time, it may be necessary to provide the Clerk or Court with a hard copy of an electronically filed document. IN ST MARION SUPER CT ADMIN Rule 311(2-105).

   vi. For the recommended format of a signature block, refer to IN ST MARION CIR AND SUPER CTS CIV Rule 204(E).

b. *Signature of unrepresented party.* A party who is not represented by an attorney shall sign his pleading and state his address. IN ST TRIAL P Rule 11(A).

c. *Verification not generally required.* Except when specifically required by rule, pleadings or motions need not be verified or accompanied by affidavit. The rule in equity that the averments of an answer under oath must be overcome by the testimony of two (2) witnesses or of one (1) witness sustained by corroborating circumstances is abolished. IN ST TRIAL P Rule 11(A).

d. *Verification by affirmation or representation.* When in connection with any civil or special statutory proceeding it is required that any pleading, motion, petition, supporting affidavit, or other document of any kind, be verified, or that an oath be taken, it shall be sufficient if the subscriber simply affirms the truth of the matter to be verified by an affirmation or representation. IN ST TRIAL P Rule 11(B). IN ST TRIAL P Rule 11(B) states that the affirmation or representation should be in substantially the following language: "I (we) affirm, under the penalties for perjury, that the foregoing representation(s) is (are) true. (Signed) _____."

   i. Any person who falsifies an affirmation or representation of fact shall be subject to the same penalties as are prescribed by law for the making of a false affidavit. IN ST TRIAL P Rule 11(B).

e. *Verified pleadings, motions, and affidavits as evidence.* Pleadings, motions and affidavits accompanying or in support of such pleadings or motions when required to be verified or under oath shall be accepted as a representation that the signer had personal knowledge thereof or reasonable cause to believe the existence of the facts or matters stated or alleged therein; and, if otherwise competent or acceptable as evidence, may be admitted as evidence of the facts or matters stated or alleged therein when it is so provided in the Indiana Rules of Trial Procedure, by statute or other law, or to the extent the writing or signature expressly purports to be made upon the signer's personal knowledge. When such pleadings, motions and affidavits are verified or under oath they shall not require other or greater proof on the part of the adverse party than if not verified or not under oath unless expressly provided otherwise by the Indiana Rules of Trial Procedure, statute or other law. Affidavits upon motions for summary judgment under IN ST TRIAL P Rule 56 and in denial of execution under IN ST TRIAL P Rule 9.2 shall be made upon personal knowledge. IN ST TRIAL P Rule 11(C).

5. *Information excluded from public access.* Every document filed in a case shall separately identify information excluded from public access pursuant to IN ST ADMIN Rule 9(G)(1) as follows:

a. Whole documents that are excluded from public access pursuant to IN ST ADMIN Rule 9(G)(1) shall be tendered on light green paper or have a light green coversheet attached to the document, marked "Not for Public Access" or "Confidential." IN ST TRIAL P Rule 5(G)(1).

b. When only a portion of a document contains information excluded from public access pursuant to IN ST ADMIN Rule 9(G)(1), said information shall be omitted [or redacted] from the filed document, and set forth on a separate accompanying document on light green paper conspicuously marked "Not for Public Access" or "Confidential" and clearly designated [or identifying] the caption and number of the case and the document and location within the document to which the redacted material pertains. IN ST TRIAL P Rule 5(G)(2).

c. With respect to documents filed in electronic format, the trial court, by local rule, may provide for compliance with IN ST TRIAL P Rule 5 in manner that separates and protects access to information excluded from public access. IN ST TRIAL P Rule 5(G)(3).

d. IN ST TRIAL P Rule 5(G) does not apply to a record sealed by the court pursuant to IN ST 5-14-3-5.5 or otherwise, nor to records, documents, or information filed in cases to which public access is prohibited pursuant to IN ST ADMIN Rule 9(G). IN ST TRIAL P Rule 5(G)(4).

e. The following information in case records is excluded from public access and is confidential:

   i.   Information that is excluded from public access pursuant to federal law;

   ii. Information that is excluded from public access as declared confidential by Indiana statute or other court rule, including without limitation:

   • All adoption records created after July 8, 1941, as declared confidential by IN ST 31-19-19-1, et seq., except those specifically declared open by IN ST 31-19-13-2(2);

   • All records relating to chancroid, chlamydia, gonorrhea, hepatitis, human immunodeficiency virus (HIV), Lymphogranuloma venereum, syphilis, tuberculosis, as declared confidential by IN ST 16-41-8-1, et seq.;

   • All records relating to child abuse as declared confidential by IN ST 31-33-18-1, et seq.;

   • All records relating to drug tests as declared confidential by IN ST 5-14-3-4(a)(9);

   • Records of grand jury proceedings as declared confidential by IN ST 35-34-2-4;

   • Records of juvenile proceedings as declared confidential by IN ST 31-39-1-2, except those specifically open under statute;

   • All paternity records created after July 1, 1941 as declared confidential by IN ST 31-14-11-15, IN ST 31-19-5-23, IN ST 31-39-1-1 and IN ST 31-39-1-2 [Editor's note: IN ST 31-14-11-15 was repealed effective May 9, 2013];

   • All pre-sentence reports as declared confidential by IN ST 35-38-1-13;

   • Written petitions to permit marriages without consent and orders directing the Clerk of Court to issue a marriage license to underage persons, as declared confidential by IN ST 31-11-1-6;

   • Only those arrest warrants, search warrants, indictments and informations ordered confidential by the trial judge, prior to return of duly executed service as declared confidential by IN ST 5-14-3-4(b)(1);

   • All medical, mental health, or tax records unless determined by law or regulation of any governmental custodian not to be confidential, released by the subject of such records, or declared by a court of competent jurisdiction to be essential to the resolution of litigation as declared confidential by IN ST 16-39-3-10, IN ST 6-4.1-5-10, IN ST 6-4.1-12-12, and IN ST 6-8.1-7-1;

   • Personal information relating to jurors or prospective jurors, other than for the use of the parties and counsel, pursuant to IN ST JURY Rule 10;

   • Information relating to protection from abuse orders, no-contact orders and workplace violence restraining orders as declared confidential by IN ST 5-2-9-6, et seq.;

   • Mediation proceedings pursuant to IN ST ADR Rule 2.11, Mini-Trial proceedings pursuant to IN ST ADR Rule 4.4(C), and Summary Jury Trials pursuant to IN ST ADR Rule 5.6;

- Information in probation files pursuant to the Probation Standards promulgated by the Judicial Conference of Indiana pursuant to IN ST 11-13-1-8(b);

- Information deemed confidential pursuant to the Rules for Court Administered Alcohol and Drug Programs promulgated by the Judicial Conference of Indiana pursuant to IN ST 12-23-14-13;

- Information deemed confidential pursuant to the Problem-Solving Court Rules promulgated by the Judicial Conference of Indiana pursuant to IN ST 33-23-16-16;

- All records of the Department of workforce Development as declared confidential by IN ST 22-4-19-6;

- Information regarding interception of electronic communications that is sealed or deemed confidential as set forth in IN ST 35-33.5-2-1, et seq.

iii. Information excluded from public access by specific court order;

iv. Complete Social Security Numbers of living persons;

v. With the exception of names, information such as addresses, phone numbers, and dates of birth which explicitly identifies:

- Natural persons who are witnesses or victims (not including defendants) in criminal, domestic violence, stalking, sexual assault, juvenile, or civil protection order proceedings, provided that juveniles who are victims of sex crimes shall be identified by initials only;

- Places of residence of judicial officers, clerks and other employees of courts and clerks of court, unless the person or persons about whom the information pertains waives confidentiality;

vi. Complete account numbers of specific assets, loans, bank accounts, credit cards, and personal identification numbers (PINs);

vii. All orders of expungement entered in criminal or juvenile proceedings, orders to restrict access to criminal history information pursuant to IN ST 35-38-5-5.5 or IN ST 35-38-8-5 and records excluded from public access by such orders, and information related to infractions that is excluded from public access pursuant to IN ST 34-28-5-15 or IN ST 34-28-5-16 [Editor's note: IN ST 35-38-5-5.5, IN ST 35-38-8-5 and IN ST 34-28-5-16 were repealed effective July 1, 2013; for information on orders restricting access to criminal history, refer to IN ST 35-38-9-1, et seq.];

viii. All personal notes and e-mail, and deliberative material, of judges, jurors, court staff and judicial agencies, and information recorded in personal data assistants (PDA's) or organizers and personal calendars. IN ST ADMIN Rule 9(G)(1).

F. Filing and Service Requirements

1. *Filing requirements.* Except as otherwise provided in IN ST TRIAL P Rule 5(E)(2), all pleadings and papers subsequent to the complaint which are required to be served upon a party shall be filed with the Court either before service or within a reasonable period of time thereafter. IN ST TRIAL P Rule 5(E)(1).

   a. *Filing generally.* All pleadings, petitions and motions are filed with the Clerk designated by the Court at any time during office hours established by the Clerk and the Court. All orders submitted to the Court shall be in sufficient number and shall be accompanied by postage paid envelopes addressed to each party or counsel of record. IN ST MARION CIR AND SUPER CTS CIV Rule 205(A)

   b. *Filing with the court defined.* The filing of pleadings, motions, and other papers with the court as required by the Indiana Rules of Trial Procedure shall be made by one of the following methods:

      i. Delivery to the clerk of the court;

      ii. Sending by electronic transmission under the procedure adopted pursuant to IN ST ADMIN Rule 12;

      iii. Mailing to the clerk by registered, certified or express mail return receipt requested;

iv. Depositing with any third-party commercial carrier for delivery to the clerk within three (3) calendar days, cost prepaid, properly addressed;

v. If the court so permits, filing with the judge, in which event the judge shall note thereon the filing date and forthwith transmit them to the office of the clerk; or

vi. Electronic filing, as approved by the Division of State Court Administration pursuant to IN ST ADMIN Rule 16. IN ST TRIAL P Rule 5(F).

vii. Filing by registered or certified mail and by third-party commercial carrier shall be complete upon mailing or deposit. IN ST TRIAL P Rule 5(F).

c. *Facsimile filing.* Facsimile filing is discouraged, but permitted in the Marion Circuit and Marion Superior Court. All documents filed by facsimile shall also be filed in hard copy within seven (7) days of the facsimile filing, along with proposed orders and stamped addressed envelopes, as required by IN ST MARION CIR AND SUPER CTS CIV Rule 203(E). To avoid duplicate filings, the hard copies of the facsimile filing shall indicate in bold letters that the pleading was previously filed by facsimile transmission. Proof of transmission by facsimile, including certificate of service and manner of service, shall be the responsibility of the filing party. If the filing requires immediate attention of the Judge, it shall be so indicated in bold letters in an accompanying transmittal memorandum. Legibility of documents and timeliness of filing is the responsibility of the sender. IN ST MARION CIR AND SUPER CTS CIV Rule 205(B).

i. *Generally.* In counties where a majority of judges of the courts of record, by posted local rule, have authorized electronic facsimile filing and designated a telephone number to receive such transmissions, pleadings, motions, and other papers may be sent to the Clerk of Circuit Court by electronic facsimile transmission for filing in any case, provided:

- Such matter does not exceed ten (10) pages, including the cover sheet;

- Such matter does not require the payment of fees other than the electronic facsimile transcription fee set forth in IN ST ADMIN Rule 12(E);

- The sending party creates at the time of transmission a machine generated log for such transmission; and

- The original document and the transmission log are maintained by the sending party for the duration of the litigation. IN ST ADMIN Rule 12(B).

ii. *Time of filing.* During normal, posted business hours, the time of filing shall be the time the duplicate document is produced in the office of the Clerk of the Circuit Court. Duplicate documents received at all other times shall be filed as of the next normal business day. IN ST ADMIN Rule 12(C).

- If the receiving fax machine endorses its own time and date stamp upon the transmitted documents and the receiving machine produces a delivery receipt which is electronically created and transmitted to the sending party, the time of filing shall be the date and time recorded on the transmitted document by the receiving fax machine. IN ST ADMIN Rule 12(C).

d. *Electronic filing.* Electronic filing and electronic service pilot projects are authorized pursuant to IN ST ADMIN Rule 16 and approved by the Division of State Court Administration. IN ST MARION SUPER CT ADMIN Rule 311(1-103).

i. *Cases where electronic filing accepted.* All Marion County Circuit and Superior civil courts may accept electronic filing and service of pleadings and other documents designated in this rule in mortgage foreclosure (hereinafter referred to as "MF"), civil collection(hereinafter referred to as "CC"), and individual cases that have been approved for electronic filing and service. IN ST MARION SUPER CT ADMIN Rule 311(1-104)(1).

- The Marion County Circuit Court may, upon the motion of a party or its own motion, designate a case that will involve multiple litigants, legally intricate issues, and an extensive number of documents a mass tort or complex litigation case. Any case so designated shall be subject to electronic filing and service using the county's approved Electronic Service Provider. IN ST MARION SUPER CT ADMIN Rule 311(1-104)(3).

- The filing of electronic pleadings and other documents in MF and CC cases is entirely voluntary; however, once the case is initially filed electronically, all subsequent filings in the case shall remain in electronic format until the time for appeal is exhausted. IN ST MARION SUPER CT ADMIN Rule 311(1-104)(5).

ii. *Documents eligible for electronic filing.* The following pleadings may be filed and served electronically:

- New case complaint and petitions. IN ST MARION SUPER CT ADMIN Rule 311(1-104)(8)(a).

- Original answers. IN ST MARION SUPER CT ADMIN Rule 311(1-104)(8)(a).

- Any other pleadings or document including but not limited to motions and appearance forms. IN ST MARION SUPER CT ADMIN Rule 311(1-104)(8)(a).

iii. *Manner of electronic filing.* Parties shall E-file a document either:

- By registering to use the Electronic Filing Service Provider; or

- In person at the Marion County Clerk's office, by electronically filing through the Public Access Terminal. Parties filing in this manner shall be responsible for furnishing the document in an electronic format that will be compatible with the clerk's office-system to be uploaded in person. IN ST MARION SUPER CT ADMIN Rule 311(1-104)(9). For information on the Electronic Filing Service Provider and Public Access Terminal, refer to IN ST MARION SUPER CT ADMIN Rule 311(1-101).

- Registered users shall pay statutory filing fees for E-filed documents electronically to the Court through their EFSP. Filing fees are due and payable at the time of filing. IN ST MARION SUPER CT ADMIN Rule 311(2-104)(1). For more information on electronic filing fees, refer to IN ST MARION SUPER CT ADMIN Rule 311(2-104).

iv. *Effect of electronic filing.* Any pleading filed electronically shall be considered as filed with the court when the transmission to the EFSP is complete. Any document E-filed by 11:59 p.m. local Indianapolis, Indiana time shall be deemed filed on that date. The EFSP is an agent of the Court for the purpose of electronic filing, receipt, service and retrieval of electronic documents. IN ST MARION SUPER CT ADMIN Rule 311(2-102).

- Upon completion of filing, the EFSP shall issue a confirmation receipt that includes the date and time of receipt. The confirmation receipt shall serve as proof of filing. IN ST MARION SUPER CT ADMIN Rule 311(2-102).

- In the event the Court rejects the submitted documents following review, the documents shall not become part of the official Court record and the filer will receive notification of the rejection. Users may be required to refile the instruments to meet necessary filing requirements. Documents may be filed through an E-filing system at any time that the Clerk's office is open to receive the filing or at such other times as may be designated by the clerk and posted publicly. IN ST MARION SUPER CT ADMIN Rule 311(2-102).

- Documents filed through the E-filing system are deemed filed when received by the Clerk's office, except that documents received at times that the Clerk's office is closed shall be deemed filed the next regular time when the Clerk's office is open for filing. The time stamp issued by the E-filing system shall be presumed to be the time the document is received by the Clerk. IN ST MARION SUPER CT ADMIN Rule 311(2-102).

v. *Electronically filed documents.* All pleadings and other documents designated in IN ST MARION SUPER CT ADMIN Rule 311 shall be filed and served electronically in any individual case which has been approved for electronic filing and service. IN ST MARION SUPER CT ADMIN Rule 311(1-104)(6).

vi. *System failures.* When filing by electronic means is hindered by a technical failure, a party may file with the Clerk of Marion County in hard copy. With the exception of deadlines that by law cannot be extended, the time for filing of any paper that is delayed due to technical failure of the site shall be extended for one (1) day for each day on which such failure occurs, unless otherwise ordered by the Court. IN ST MARION SUPER CT ADMIN Rule 311(2-108).

vii. *Compliance with rules.* All filing shall comply with the requirements of IN ST ADMIN Rule 9 and IN ST ADMIN Rule 16; and the Indiana Rules of Court and the Marion County Local Rules. IN ST MARION SUPER CT ADMIN Rule 311(1-104)(11).

e. *Filing for special judge.* When a Special Judge who is not a Marion County Judge is selected, all parties or attorneys shall furnish such Judge with copies of all filings prior to the qualification of such Special Judge. Thereafter, copies of all filings shall be delivered in person, by mail or by facsimile to the office of the Special Judge with certificate of forwarding same made a part of the filing. IN ST MARION CIR AND SUPER CTS CIV Rule 205(C).

f. *Proof of filing.* Any party filing any paper by any method other than personal delivery to the clerk shall retain proof of filing. IN ST TRIAL P Rule 5(F).

2. *Service requirements.* Unless otherwise provided by the Indiana Rules of Trial Procedure or an order of the court, each party and special judge, if any, shall be served with: (1) every order required by its terms to be served; (2) every pleading subsequent to the original complaint; (3) every written motion except one which may be heard ex parte; (4) every brief submitted to the trial court; (5) every paper relating to discovery required to be served upon a party; and (6) every written notice, appearance, demand, offer of judgment, designation of record on appeal, or similar paper. IN ST TRIAL P Rule 5(A).

a. *Methods of service*

i. *Personal service.* Whenever a party is represented by an attorney of record, service shall be made upon such attorney unless service upon the party himself is ordered by the court. Service upon the attorney or party shall be made by delivering or mailing a copy of the papers to the last known address or where an attorney or party has consented to service by fax or e-mail, as provided in IN ST TRIAL P Rule 3.1(A)(4), by faxing or e-mailing a copy of the documents to the fax number or e-mail address set out in the appearance form or correction as required by IN ST TRIAL P Rule 3.1(E). IN ST TRIAL P Rule 5(B). Delivery of a copy within IN ST TRIAL P Rule 5 means:

- Offering or tendering it to the attorney or party and stating the nature of the papers being served. Refusal to accept an offered or tendered document is a waiver of any objection to the sufficiency or adequacy of service of that document;

- Leaving it at his office with a clerk or other person in charge thereof, or if there is no one in charge, leaving it in a conspicuous place therein; or

- If the office is closed, by leaving it at his dwelling house or usual place of abode with some person of suitable age and discretion then residing therein; or,

- Leaving it at some other suitable place, selected by the attorney upon whom service is being made, pursuant to duly promulgated local rule. IN ST TRIAL P Rule 5(B)(1).

ii. *Service by mail.* If service is made by mail, the papers shall be deposited in the United States mail addressed to the person on whom they are being served, with postage prepaid. Service shall be deemed complete upon mailing. Proof of service of all papers permitted to be mailed may be made by written acknowledgment of service, by affidavit of the person who mailed the papers, or by certificate of an attorney. It shall be the duty of attorneys when entering their appearance in a cause or when filing pleadings or papers therein, to have noted in the Chronological Case Summary or said pleadings or papers so filed the address and telephone number of their office. Service by delivery or by mail at such address shall be deemed sufficient and complete. IN ST TRIAL P Rule 5(B)(2).

iii. *Service by fax or e-mail.* A party who has consented to service by fax or e-mail may be served as follows:

- Service by e-mail shall be made by attaching the document being served in .pdf format. Discovery documents must also be served in accordance with IN ST TRIAL P Rule 26(A). IN ST TRIAL P Rule 5(B)(3)(a).

- Service by fax shall be deemed complete upon generation of a transmission record indicating the successful transmission of the entire document, except as provided in IN ST TRIAL P Rule 5(B)(3)(d). IN ST TRIAL P Rule 5(B)(3)(b).

- Service by e-mail shall be deemed complete upon transmission, except as provided in IN ST TRIAL P Rule 5(B)(3)(d). IN ST TRIAL P Rule 5(B)(3)(c).

- Service by fax or e-mail that occurs on a Saturday, Sunday, legal holiday, or day the court or agency in which the matter is pending is closed or after 5:00 PM local time of the recipient shall be deemed complete the next day that is not a Saturday, Sunday, legal holiday, or day that the court or agency in which the matter is pending is not closed. IN ST TRIAL P Rule 5(B)(3)(d).

    iv. *Electronic service.* Delivery of E-service documents through the EFSP to other registered users shall be considered as valid and effective service and shall have the same legal effect as an original paper document. Recipients of E-service documents shall access their documents through the EFSP. IN ST MARION SUPER CT ADMIN Rule 311(2-107)(1).

- E-service shall be deemed complete when the transmission to the EFSP is completed. IN ST MARION SUPER CT ADMIN Rule 311(2-107)(2).

- For the purpose of computing time to respond to documents received via E-service, any document served on a day or at a time when the Clerk's office is not open for business shall be deemed served at the time of next opening of the Clerk's office for business. IN ST MARION SUPER CT ADMIN Rule 311(2-107)(3).

  b. *Serving numerous defendants.* In any action in which there are unusually large numbers of defendants, the court, upon motion or of its own initiative, may order:

    i. That service of the pleadings of the defendants and replies thereto need not be made as between the defendants;

- That any cross-claim, counterclaim, or matter constituting an avoidance or affirmative defense contained therein shall be deemed to be denied or avoided by all other parties; and

- That the filing of any such pleading and service thereof upon the plaintiff constitutes due notice of it to the parties. IN ST TRIAL P Rule 5(D).

    ii. A copy of every such order shall be served upon the parties in such manner and form as the court directs. IN ST TRIAL P Rule 5(D).

  c. *Service on parties in default for failure to appear.* No service need be made on parties in default for failure to appear, except that pleadings asserting new or additional claims for relief against them shall be served upon them in the manner provided by service of summons in IN ST TRIAL P Rule 4. IN ST TRIAL P Rule 5(A).

G. Hearings

1. The Indiana rules do not contemplate a hearing regarding the filing and service of an amended answer.

H. Forms

1. Official Amended Answer Forms for Indiana

  a. Affidavit of debt. IN ST TRIAL P App. A-2.

2. Amended Answer Forms for Indiana

  a. Amendment by stipulation. 10 INPRAC § 46.11.

  b. Amended answer by interlineations. 10 INPRAC § 46.12.

  c. Answer; Form and content. 9 INPRAC § 41.1.

  d. Answer; General form. 9 INPRAC § 41.3.

  e. Answer; Another form. 9 INPRAC § 41.4.

  f. Answer; Another form. 9 INPRAC § 41.5.

  g. General denial. 9 INPRAC § 41.6.

  h. Specific denial of designated paragraph. 9 INPRAC § 41.7.

  i. Specific admission of designated paragraph. 9 INPRAC § 41.8.

j.   Denial of knowledge or information to form belief. 9 INPRAC § 41.9.

k.   Denial of knowledge or information to form belief; Another form. 9 INPRAC § 41.10.

l.   Partial denial and partial admission of designated paragraph. 9 INPRAC § 41.11.

m.   Denial of designated paragraph for reason that document speaks for itself. 9 INPRAC § 41.12.

n.   Adoption of admissions or denials by co-defendant's answer. 9 INPRAC § 41.13.

o.   Denial of execution of instrument filed with pleading. 9 INPRAC § 41.14.

p.   Answer to cross-claim. 9 INPRAC § 41.15.

q.   Answer to third-party complaint. 9 INPRAC § 41.16.

r.   Accord and satisfaction. 9 INPRAC § 41.21.

s.   Answer. 5 INPRAC § 3:3.3.

t.   Answer; Another form. 5 INPRAC § 3:3.4.

u.   Certificate of service; Personal service. 9 INPRAC § 5.7.

v.   Certificate of service; First class mail. 9 INPRAC § 5.8.

w.   Signature; By party. 9 INPRAC § 4.5.

x.   Signature; Attorney. 9 INPRAC § 4.6.

y.   Signature; Attorney; Another form. 9 INPRAC § 4.7.

z.   Signature; Attorney; Another form. 9 INPRAC § 4.8.

I. Checklist

(I) ❏ Matters to be considered by the party filing the amended answer

    (a) ❏ Required documents if amending as matter of course

        (1) ❏ Amended answer

        (2) ❏ Certificate of service

    (b) ❏ Supplemental documents

        (1) ❏ Proof of written instrument

        (2) ❏ Notice of intent to use foreign law

        (3) ❏ Facsimile cover sheet

    (c) ❏ Timing

        (1) ❏ As a matter of course before a responsive pleading is served, or, if the pleading is one to which no responsive pleading is permitted, within thirty (30) days after it is served

        (2) ❏ At any time with leave of court

Motions, Oppositions and Replies
Motion to Strike

Document Last Updated October 2013

A. Applicable Rules

1. *State rules*

    a.   Appearance. IN ST TRIAL P Rule 3.1.

    b.   Process. IN ST TRIAL P Rule 4.

    c.   Service and filing of pleadings and other papers. IN ST TRIAL P Rule 5.

    d.   Time. IN ST TRIAL P Rule 6.

e. Pleadings. IN ST TRIAL P Rule 7; IN ST TRIAL P Rule 8; IN ST TRIAL P Rule 9.2; IN ST TRIAL P Rule 10; IN ST TRIAL P Rule 11.

f. Defenses and objections; When and how presented; By pleading or motion; Motion for judgment on the pleadings. IN ST TRIAL P Rule 12.

g. Amended and supplemental pleadings. IN ST TRIAL P Rule 15.

h. Joinder of person needed for just adjudication. IN ST TRIAL P Rule 19.

i. Evidence. IN ST TRIAL P Rule 43.

j. Judgment on the evidence (directed verdict). IN ST TRIAL P Rule 50.

k. Findings by the court. IN ST TRIAL P Rule 52.

l. Summary judgment. IN ST TRIAL P Rule 56.

m. Motion to correct error. IN ST TRIAL P Rule 59.

n. Relief from judgment or order. IN ST TRIAL P Rule 60.

o. Hearing of motions. IN ST TRIAL P Rule 73.

p. Access to court records. IN ST ADMIN Rule 9.

q. Paper size. IN ST ADMIN Rule 11.

r. Facsimile transmission. IN ST ADMIN Rule 12.

s. Electronic filing and electronic service pilot projects. IN ST ADMIN Rule 16.

t. Sealing of certain records by court; Hearing; Notice. IN ST 5-14-3-5.5.

u. Privacy and confidentiality. IN ST 5-2-9-6; IN ST 5-14-3-4; IN ST 6-4.1-5-10; IN ST 6-4.1-12-12; IN ST 6-8.1-7-1; IN ST 11-13-1-8; IN ST 12-23-14-13; IN ST 16-39-3-10; IN ST 16-41-8-1; IN ST 22-4-19-6; IN ST 31-11-1-6; IN ST 31-19-5-23; IN ST 31-19-13-2; IN ST 31-19-19-1; IN ST 31-33-18-1; IN ST 31-39-1-1; IN ST 31-39-1-2; IN ST 33-23-16-16; IN ST 35-34-2-4; IN ST 35-38-1-13; IN ST 35-38-9-1; IN ST ADR Rule 2.11; IN ST ADR Rule 4.4; IN ST ADR Rule 5.6; IN ST JURY Rule 10.

2. *Local rules*

a. Requirements for motions. IN ST MARION CIR AND SUPER CTS CIV Rule 203.

b. Preparation of pleadings, motions and other papers. IN ST MARION CIR AND SUPER CTS CIV Rule 204.

c. Filing of pleadings, motions and other papers. IN ST MARION CIR AND SUPER CTS CIV Rule 205.

d. Signing and verification of pleadings, motions and other papers; Service on opposing party. IN ST MARION CIR AND SUPER CTS CIV Rule 206.

e. Motions for continuance. IN ST MARION CIR AND SUPER CTS CIV Rule 215.

f. Electronic filing. IN ST MARION SUPER CT ADMIN Rule 311.

B. Timing

1. *Motion to strike.* Upon motion made by a party before responding to a pleading, or, if no responsive pleading is permitted by Indiana Rules of Trial Procedure, upon motion made by a party within twenty (20) days after the service of the pleading upon him or at any time upon the court's own initiative, the court may order stricken from any pleading any insufficient claim or defense or any redundant, immaterial, impertinent, or scandalous matter. IN ST TRIAL P Rule 12(F).

a. *Time to file a responsive pleading.* A responsive pleading required under the Indiana Rules of Trial Procedure, shall be served within twenty (20) days after service of the prior pleading. IN ST TRIAL P Rule 6(C).

b. *Filing.* All pleadings and papers subsequent to the complaint which are required to be served upon a party shall be filed with the Court either before service or within a reasonable period of time thereafter. IN ST TRIAL P Rule 5(E)(1).

2. *Service.* A written motion, other than one which may be heard ex parte, and notice of the hearing thereof shall be served not less than five (5) days before the time specified for the hearing, unless a different period is fixed by the Indiana Rules of Trial Procedure or by order of the court. IN ST TRIAL P Rule 6(D).

    a. *Of supporting affidavits.* When a motion is supported by affidavit, the affidavit shall be served with the motion. IN ST TRIAL P Rule 6(D).

3. *Opposition*

    a. *Filing.* If the statement regarding the position of the opposing party(ies) required under IN ST MARION CIR AND SUPER CTS CIV Rule 203(A) indicates that objection to the granting of said motion may ensue, said objecting a party shall have fifteen (15) days from the date of filing to file a response to said motion. IN ST MARION CIR AND SUPER CTS CIV Rule 203(B).

    b. *Service.* Except as otherwise provided in IN ST TRIAL P Rule 59(D), opposing affidavits may be served not less than one (1) day before the hearing, unless the court permits them to be served at some other time. IN ST TRIAL P Rule 6(D).

4. *Computation of time*

    a. *Generally; Days excluded.* In computing any period of time prescribed or allowed by the Indiana Rules of Trial Procedure, by order of the court, or by any applicable statute, the day of the act, event, or default from which the designated period of time begins to run shall not be included. The last day of the period so computed is to be included unless it is:

        i. A Saturday,

        ii. A Sunday,

        iii. A legal holiday as defined by state statute, or

        iv. A day the office in which the act is to be done is closed during regular business hours. IN ST TRIAL P Rule 6(A).

    b. *Short periods.* In any event, the period runs until the end of the next day that is not a Saturday, a Sunday, a legal holiday, or a day on which the office is closed. When the period of time allowed is less than seven (7) days, intermediate Saturdays, Sundays, legal holidays, and days on which the office is closed shall be excluded from the computations. IN ST TRIAL P Rule 6(A).

    c. *Additional time after service by United States mail.* Whenever a party has the right or is required to do some act or take some proceedings within a prescribed period after the service of a notice or other paper upon him and the notice or paper is served upon him by United States mail, three (3) days shall be added to the prescribed period. IN ST TRIAL P Rule 6(E).

    d. *Enlargement of time.* When an act is required or allowed to be done at or within a specific time by the Indiana Rules of Trial Procedure, the court may at any time for cause shown:

        i. Order the period enlarged, with or without motion or notice, if request therefor is made before the expiration of the period originally prescribed or extended by a previous order; or

        ii. Upon motion made after the expiration of the specific period, permit the act to be done where the failure to act was the result of excusable neglect; but, the court may not extend the time for taking any action for judgment on the evidence under IN ST TRIAL P Rule 50(A), amendment of findings and judgment under IN ST TRIAL P Rule 52(B), to correct errors under IN ST TRIAL P Rule 59(C), statement in opposition to motion to correct error under IN ST TRIAL P Rule 59(E), or to obtain relief from final judgment under IN ST TRIAL P Rule 60(B), except to the extent and under the conditions stated in those rules. IN ST TRIAL P Rule 6(B).

    e. *Continuances disfavored.* Motions for Continuance are discouraged. Neither side is entitled to an automatic continuance as a matter of right. IN ST MARION CIR AND SUPER CTS CIV Rule 215. For information on obtaining a continuance, refer to IN ST MARION CIR AND SUPER CTS CIV Rule 215.

C. General Requirements

1. *Motions, generally.* Unless made during a hearing or trial, or otherwise ordered by the court, an

application to the court for an order shall be made by written motion. The motion shall state the grounds therefor and the relief or order sought. IN ST TRIAL P Rule 7(B).

  a. *Motions as distinct from pleadings.* Motions and responses to motions are not pleadings, and allegations contained in a motion are not admissions of a party. 22B INPRAC 7:2; Wachstetter v. County Properties, LLC, 832 N.E.2d 574 (Ind.Ct.App. 2005); Scott County Family YMCA, Inc. v. Hobbs, 817 N.E.2d 603 (Ind.Ct.App. 2004).

  b. *Unopposed motions generally granted.* It is common for a trial court to grant procedural motions, such as motions for enlargement of time, discovery motions, or motions for continuance, unless an objection is filed. 21 INPRAC § 13.8.

2. *Motion to strike*

  a. *Grounds generally.* Upon motion the court may order stricken from any pleading any insufficient claim or defense or any redundant, immaterial, impertinent, or scandalous matter. IN ST TRIAL P Rule 12(F).

    i. *Redundant.* Redundant matter refers to the needless repetition of immaterial factual allegations. 9 INPRAC § 42.20.

    ii. *Immaterial and impertinent.* Immaterial and impertinent matter consists of allegations that have no relevant or important relationship to plaintiff's claim. 9 INPRAC § 42.20.

    iii. *Scandalous.* Scandalous matter includes unnecessary allegations that are derogatory to the party referred to in the pleading. 9 INPRAC § 42.20.

  b. *Availability and use of motion to strike.* A motion to strike redundant, immaterial, impertinent or scandalous matter is available to plaintiff and defendant alike, and may be employed against any pleading. 9 INPRAC § 42.20. Indiana's use of a motion to strike includes all of the uses which are found in federal practice plus the expanded use of the motion under Indiana's rule. Accordingly, a nonexclusive list of the uses of this motion will recognize that it is available:

    i. To strike matter which is immaterial, impertinent or scandalous;

    ii. To provide the plaintiff with a means by which to test the sufficiency of a defense;

    iii. To strike any insufficient claim or defense;

    iv. To strike a bad faith, or inadequate response to an order or rule; or

    v. To strike a response to an order or rule which introduces new material or allegations not previously made and which are not introduced pursuant to a right to amend a pleading. 1A INPRAC R 12(12.18).

  c. *Trial court's discretion.* The trial court is given broad discretion to decide a motion to strike. 1A INPRAC R 12(12.18); City of Mishawaka v. Kvale, 810 N.E.2d 1129 (Ind.Ct.App. 2004).

  d. *Not a method to challenge timeliness.* Language in IN ST TRIAL P Rule 12(F) which permits the trial court to strike any "insufficient" claim or defense refers to the legal insufficiency of the content or substance of the claim or defense, not the untimeliness of a pleading. 1A INPRAC R 12(12.18); Dreyer & Reinbold v. AutoXchange.com., Inc., 771 N.E.2d 764, 765 (Ind.Ct.App. 2002). Rather, the proper mechanism for challenging the timeliness of a pleading is IN ST TRIAL P Rule 55, which governs default judgments. 1A INPRAC R 12(12.18).

3. *Consolidation and waiver*

  a. *Consolidation of defenses in motion.* A party who makes a motion under IN ST TRIAL P Rule 12 may join with it any other motions herein provided for and then available to him. If a party makes a motion under IN ST TRIAL P Rule 12 but omits therefrom any defense or objection then available to him which IN ST TRIAL P Rule 12 permits to be raised by motion, he shall not thereafter make a motion based on the defense or objection so omitted. He may, however, make such motions as are allowed under IN ST TRIAL P Rule 12(H)(2). IN ST TRIAL P Rule 12(G).

  b. *Waiver or preservation of certain defenses.* No defense or objection is waived by being joined with one or more other defenses or objections in a responsive pleading or motion. IN ST TRIAL P Rule 12(B).

D. Documents

1. *Required documents*

   a. *Motion and notice.* The requirement of notice is satisfied by service of the motion. IN ST TRIAL P Rule 7(B); IN ST MARION CIR AND SUPER CTS CIV Rule 203(A). Refer to the General Requirements section of this document for information on the content of a motion to strike.

   b. *Statement of approval or disapproval.* Except for initial motions made pursuant to IN ST MARION CIR AND SUPER CTS CIV Rule 203(D), all motions filed with the court shall include a brief statement indicating whether opposing party(ies) object to or approve of the granting of said motion. IN ST MARION CIR AND SUPER CTS CIV Rule 203(A).

   c. *Proposed order.* Unless local practice provides differently, a party should submit a proposed order with its written motion to be signed by the judge once the motion has been granted. 21 INPRAC § 13.8. All motions seeking an order of the Court shall be accompanied by a sufficient number of orders to be executed by the Court in granting said motion. In addition to the orders, the notice shall be accompanied by stamped, addressed envelopes to all parties of record. IN ST MARION CIR AND SUPER CTS CIV Rule 203(E).

   d. *Certificate of service.* An attorney or unrepresented party tendering a document to the Clerk for filing shall certify that service has been made, list the parties served, and specify the date and means of service. The certificate of service shall be placed at the end of the document and shall not be separately filed. The separate filing of a certificate of service, however, shall not be grounds for rejecting a document for filing. The Clerk may permit documents to be filed without a certificate of service but shall require prompt filing of a separate certificate of service. IN ST TRIAL P Rule 5(C). In all cases where any pleading or other document is required to be served upon opposing counsel, proof of such service may be made either by:

      i. A certificate of service signed by counsel of record for the serving party and the certificate shall specify by name and address all counsel upon whom the pleading or document was served; or

      ii. An acknowledgment of service signed by the party served or counsel of record. IN ST MARION CIR AND SUPER CTS CIV Rule 206.

2. *Supplemental documents*

   a. *Supporting evidence.* When a motion is based on facts not appearing of record the court may hear the matter on affidavits presented by the respective parties, but the court may direct that the matter be heard wholly or partly on oral testimony or depositions. IN ST TRIAL P Rule 43(B).

   b. *Request for oral argument.* When an oral argument is requested, the request shall be by separate instrument and filed with the pleading to be argued. Any such oral argument requested may be heard at the discretion of the Court, except for motions for summary judgment which shall be set for hearing upon request of any party. IN ST MARION CIR AND SUPER CTS CIV Rule 203(C).

   c. *Facsimile cover sheet.* Any document sent to the Clerk of the Circuit Court by electronic facsimile transmission shall be accompanied by a cover sheet which states the title of the document, case number, number of pages, identity and voice telephone number of the sending party and instructions for filing. The cover sheet shall contain the signature of the attorney or party, pro se, authorizing the filing. IN ST ADMIN Rule 12(D).

E. Format

1. *Form of motions.* The rules applicable to captions, and the signing and form of pleadings (IN ST TRIAL P Rule 8 through IN ST TRIAL P Rule 11), apply to all motions and other papers provided under the Indiana Rules of Trial Procedure. 22B INPRAC 7:2.

2. *Form of pleadings*

   a. *Caption; Names of parties.* Every pleading shall contain a caption setting forth the name of the court, the title of the action, the file number, and a designation as in IN ST TRIAL P Rule 7(A). In the complaint the title of the action shall include the names of all the parties, but in other pleadings it is sufficient to state the name of the first party on each side with an appropriate indication of other parties. IN ST TRIAL P Rule 10(A).

      i. Every pleading shall contain a caption setting forth the name of the Court, the Division and

Room Number, the title of the action and the file number. IN ST MARION CIR AND SUPER CTS CIV Rule 204(B).

b. *Paragraphs; Separate statements.* All averments of a claim or defense shall be made in numbered paragraphs, the contents of each of which shall be limited as far as practicable to a statement of a single set of circumstances, and a paragraph may be referred to by number in all succeeding pleadings. Each claim founded upon a separate transaction or occurrence and each defense other than denials may be stated in a separate count or defense whenever a separation facilitates the clear presentation of the matters set forth. IN ST TRIAL P Rule 10(B).

c. *Adoption by reference; Exhibits.* Statements in a pleading may be adopted by reference in a different part of the same pleading or in another pleading or in any motion. A copy of any written instrument which is an exhibit to a pleading is a part thereof for all purposes. IN ST TRIAL P Rule 10(C).

d. *Paper.* Pleadings, motions and other papers may be either printed or typewritten on white opaque paper of at least sixteen (16) pound weight, eight and one-half (8-1/2) inches wide and eleven (11) inches in length. IN ST MARION CIR AND SUPER CTS CIV Rule 204(A).

e. *Copies.* All copies shall likewise be on white paper of sufficient strength and durability to resist normal wear and tear. IN ST MARION CIR AND SUPER CTS CIV Rule 204(A).

f. *Line spacing.* If typewritten, the lines shall be double spaced, except for quotations, which shall be indented and single spaced. IN ST MARION CIR AND SUPER CTS CIV Rule 204(A).

g. *Script type.* Script type shall not be used. IN ST MARION CIR AND SUPER CTS CIV Rule 204(A).

h. *Titles.* Titles on all pleadings shall delineate each topic included in the pleading e.g. where a pleading contains an Answer, a Motion to Strike or Dismiss, or a Jury Request each shall be set forth in the title. IN ST MARION CIR AND SUPER CTS CIV Rule 204(C).

i. *Margins and binding.* Margins shall be one (1) inch. Binding or stapling shall be at the top and at no other place. Covers or backing shall not be used. IN ST MARION CIR AND SUPER CTS CIV Rule 204(D).

3. *Size of papers for filing.* Effective January 1, 1992, all pleadings, copies, motions and documents filed with any trial court or appellate level court, typed or printed, with the exception of exhibits and existing wills, shall be prepared on eight and one-half by eleven inch (8 1/2" x 11") size paper. IN ST ADMIN Rule 11.

4. *Form of electronically filed documents.* All electronically filed and served pleadings shall, to the extent practicable, be formatted in accordance with the applicable rules governing formatting of paper pleadings. IN ST MARION SUPER CT ADMIN Rule 311(2-103)(1).

a. *Electronic document title.* The electronic document title of each pleading or other document shall include:
   i. Party or parties filing/serving the document,
   ii. Nature of the document,
   iii. Party or parties against whom relief, if any, is sought, and
   iv. Nature of the relief sought (e.g., Defendant ABC Corporation's Motion for Summary Judgment). IN ST MARION SUPER CT ADMIN Rule 311(2-103)(2).

5. *Signature requirements*

a. *Signature of attorney.* Every pleading or motion of a party represented by an attorney shall be signed by at least one (1) attorney of record in his individual name, whose address, telephone number, and attorney number shall be stated, except that this provision shall not apply to pleadings and motions made and transcribed at the trial or a hearing before the judge and received by him in such form. IN ST TRIAL P Rule 11(A).
   i. All pleadings and motions shall contain the original or authorized signature of the attorney, the name of the attorney in typed or printed form, the name of the law firm if a member of a firm, the attorney's address, identification number, e-mail address, telephone number, fax number, and the designation as to the party for whom he appears. IN ST MARION CIR AND SUPER CTS CIV Rule 204(E).

ii. The signature of an attorney constitutes a certificate by him that he has read the pleadings; that to the best of his knowledge, information, and belief, there is good ground to support it; and that it is not interposed for delay. IN ST TRIAL P Rule 11(A).

iii. If a pleading or motion is not signed or is signed with intent to defeat the purpose of the rule, it may be stricken as sham and false and the action may proceed as though the pleading had not been served. IN ST TRIAL P Rule 11(A).

iv. For a willful violation of IN ST TRIAL P Rule 11 an attorney may be subjected to appropriate disciplinary action. Similar action may be taken if scandalous or indecent matter is inserted. IN ST TRIAL P Rule 11(A).

v. Every pleading, document, and instrument electronically filed or served shall be deemed to have been signed by the judge, clerk, attorney or declarant and shall bear a facsimile or typographical signature of such person, along with the typed name, address, telephone number, and Bar number of a signing attorney. Typographical signatures shall be treated as personal signatures for all purposes under these rules. IN ST MARION SUPER CT ADMIN Rule 311(2-105).

- Documents containing signatures of third-parties (i.e., unopposed motions, affidavits, stipulations, etc.) may also be filed electronically by indicating that the original signatures are maintained by the filing party in paper-format. IN ST MARION SUPER CT ADMIN Rule 311(2-105).

- Unless otherwise ordered by the Court or Clerk, a printed copy of all documents filed or served electronically, including original signatures, shall be maintained by the party filing the document and shall be made available, upon reasonable notice, for inspection by other counsel, the Clerk or Court. Parties shall retain originals until two (2) years after all time periods for appeal have expired. From time to time, it may be necessary to provide the Clerk or Court with a hard copy of an electronically filed document. IN ST MARION SUPER CT ADMIN Rule 311(2-105).

vi. For the recommended format of a signature block, refer to IN ST MARION CIR AND SUPER CTS CIV Rule 204(E).

b. *Signature of unrepresented party.* A party who is not represented by an attorney shall sign his pleading and state his address. IN ST TRIAL P Rule 11(A).

c. *Verification not generally required.* Except when specifically required by rule, pleadings or motions need not be verified or accompanied by affidavit. The rule in equity that the averments of an answer under oath must be overcome by the testimony of two (2) witnesses or of one (1) witness sustained by corroborating circumstances is abolished. IN ST TRIAL P Rule 11(A).

d. *Verification by affirmation or representation.* When in connection with any civil or special statutory proceeding it is required that any pleading, motion, petition, supporting affidavit, or other document of any kind, be verified, or that an oath be taken, it shall be sufficient if the subscriber simply affirms the truth of the matter to be verified by an affirmation or representation. IN ST TRIAL P Rule 11(B). IN ST TRIAL P Rule 11(B) states that the affirmation or representation should be in substantially the following language: "I (we) affirm, under the penalties for perjury, that the foregoing representation(s) is (are) true. (Signed) _____."

i. Any person who falsifies an affirmation or representation of fact shall be subject to the same penalties as are prescribed by law for the making of a false affidavit. IN ST TRIAL P Rule 11(B).

e. *Verified pleadings, motions, and affidavits as evidence.* Pleadings, motions and affidavits accompanying or in support of such pleadings or motions when required to be verified or under oath shall be accepted as a representation that the signer had personal knowledge thereof or reasonable cause to believe the existence of the facts or matters stated or alleged therein; and, if otherwise competent or acceptable as evidence, may be admitted as evidence of the facts or matters stated or alleged therein when it is so provided in the Indiana Rules of Trial Procedure, by statute or other law, or to the extent the writing or signature expressly purports to be made upon the signer's personal knowledge. When such pleadings, motions and affidavits are verified or under oath they shall not require other or greater proof on the part of the adverse party than if not verified or not under oath unless expressly provided otherwise by the Indiana Rules of Trial Procedure, statute or other law. Affidavits upon motions for summary judgment under IN ST TRIAL P Rule 56 and in denial of execution under IN ST TRIAL P Rule 9.2 shall be made upon personal knowledge. IN ST TRIAL P Rule 11(C).

6. *Information excluded from public access.* Every document filed in a case shall separately identify information excluded from public access pursuant to IN ST ADMIN Rule 9(G)(1) as follows:

a. Whole documents that are excluded from public access pursuant to IN ST ADMIN Rule 9(G)(1) shall be tendered on light green paper or have a light green coversheet attached to the document, marked "Not for Public Access" or "Confidential." IN ST TRIAL P Rule 5(G)(1).

b. When only a portion of a document contains information excluded from public access pursuant to IN ST ADMIN Rule 9(G)(1), said information shall be omitted [or redacted] from the filed document, and set forth on a separate accompanying document on light green paper conspicuously marked "Not for Public Access" or "Confidential" and clearly designated [or identifying] the caption and number of the case and the document and location within the document to which the redacted material pertains. IN ST TRIAL P Rule 5(G)(2).

c. With respect to documents filed in electronic format, the trial court, by local rule, may provide for compliance with IN ST TRIAL P Rule 5 in manner that separates and protects access to information excluded from public access. IN ST TRIAL P Rule 5(G)(3).

d. IN ST TRIAL P Rule 5(G) does not apply to a record sealed by the court pursuant to IN ST 5-14-3-5.5 or otherwise, nor to records, documents, or information filed in cases to which public access is prohibited pursuant to IN ST ADMIN Rule 9(G). IN ST TRIAL P Rule 5(G)(4).

e. The following information in case records is excluded from public access and is confidential:

 i. Information that is excluded from public access pursuant to federal law;

 ii. Information that is excluded from public access as declared confidential by Indiana statute or other court rule, including without limitation:

- All adoption records created after July 8, 1941, as declared confidential by IN ST 31-19-19-1, et seq., except those specifically declared open by IN ST 31-19-13-2(2);

- All records relating to chancroid, chlamydia, gonorrhea, hepatitis, human immunodeficiency virus (HIV), Lymphogranuloma venereum, syphilis, tuberculosis, as declared confidential by IN ST 16-41-8-1, et seq.;

- All records relating to child abuse as declared confidential by IN ST 31-33-18-1, et seq.;

- All records relating to drug tests as declared confidential by IN ST 5-14-3-4(a)(9);

- Records of grand jury proceedings as declared confidential by IN ST 35-34-2-4;

- Records of juvenile proceedings as declared confidential by IN ST 31-39-1-2, except those specifically open under statute;

- All paternity records created after July 1, 1941 as declared confidential by IN ST 31-14-11-15, IN ST 31-19-5-23, IN ST 31-39-1-1 and IN ST 31-39-1-2 [Editor's note: IN ST 31-14-11-15 was repealed effective May 9, 2013];

- All pre-sentence reports as declared confidential by IN ST 35-38-1-13;

- Written petitions to permit marriages without consent and orders directing the Clerk of Court to issue a marriage license to underage persons, as declared confidential by IN ST 31-11-1-6;

- Only those arrest warrants, search warrants, indictments and informations ordered confidential by the trial judge, prior to return of duly executed service as declared confidential by IN ST 5-14-3-4(b)(1);

- All medical, mental health, or tax records unless determined by law or regulation of any governmental custodian not to be confidential, released by the subject of such records, or declared by a court of competent jurisdiction to be essential to the resolution of litigation as declared confidential by IN ST 16-39-3-10, IN ST 6-4.1-5-10, IN ST 6-4.1-12-12, and IN ST 6-8.1-7-1;

- Personal information relating to jurors or prospective jurors, other than for the use of the parties and counsel, pursuant to IN ST JURY Rule 10;

- Information relating to protection from abuse orders, no-contact orders and workplace violence restraining orders as declared confidential by IN ST 5-2-9-6, et seq.;

- Mediation proceedings pursuant to IN ST ADR Rule 2.11, Mini-Trial proceedings pursuant to IN ST ADR Rule 4.4(C), and Summary Jury Trials pursuant to IN ST ADR Rule 5.6;

- Information in probation files pursuant to the Probation Standards promulgated by the Judicial Conference of Indiana pursuant to IN ST 11-13-1-8(b);

- Information deemed confidential pursuant to the Rules for Court Administered Alcohol and Drug Programs promulgated by the Judicial Conference of Indiana pursuant to IN ST 12-23-14-13;

- Information deemed confidential pursuant to the Problem-Solving Court Rules promulgated by the Judicial Conference of Indiana pursuant to IN ST 33-23-16-16;

- All records of the Department of workforce Development as declared confidential by IN ST 22-4-19-6;

- Information regarding interception of electronic communications that is sealed or deemed confidential as set forth in IN ST 35-33.5-2-1, et seq.

iii. Information excluded from public access by specific court order;

iv. Complete Social Security Numbers of living persons;

v. With the exception of names, information such as addresses, phone numbers, and dates of birth which explicitly identifies:

- Natural persons who are witnesses or victims (not including defendants) in criminal, domestic violence, stalking, sexual assault, juvenile, or civil protection order proceedings, provided that juveniles who are victims of sex crimes shall be identified by initials only;

- Places of residence of judicial officers, clerks and other employees of courts and clerks of court, unless the person or persons about whom the information pertains waives confidentiality;

vi. Complete account numbers of specific assets, loans, bank accounts, credit cards, and personal identification numbers (PINs);

vii. All orders of expungement entered in criminal or juvenile proceedings, orders to restrict access to criminal history information pursuant to IN ST 35-38-5-5.5 or IN ST 35-38-8-5 and records excluded from public access by such orders, and information related to infractions that is excluded from public access pursuant to IN ST 34-28-5-15 or IN ST 34-28-5-16 [Editor's note: IN ST 35-38-5-5.5, IN ST 35-38-8-5 and IN ST 34-28-5-16 were repealed effective July 1, 2013; for information on orders restricting access to criminal history, refer to IN ST 35-38-9-1, et seq.];

viii. All personal notes and e-mail, and deliberative material, of judges, jurors, court staff and judicial agencies, and information recorded in personal data assistants (PDA's) or organizers and personal calendars. IN ST ADMIN Rule 9(G)(1).

F. Filing and Service Requirements

1. *Filing requirements.* Except as otherwise provided in IN ST TRIAL P Rule 5(E)(2), all pleadings and papers subsequent to the complaint which are required to be served upon a party shall be filed with the Court either before service or within a reasonable period of time thereafter. IN ST TRIAL P Rule 5(E)(1). Counsel shall file with the court an original and one (1) copy of all briefs, and memoranda of law filed in support of a motion. IN ST MARION CIR AND SUPER CTS CIV Rule 205(D).

a. *Filing generally.* All pleadings, petitions and motions are filed with the Clerk designated by the

Court at any time during office hours established by the Clerk and the Court. All orders submitted to the Court shall be in sufficient number and shall be accompanied by postage paid envelopes addressed to each party or counsel of record. IN ST MARION CIR AND SUPER CTS CIV Rule 205(A)

b. *Filing with the court defined.* The filing of pleadings, motions, and other papers with the court as required by the Indiana Rules of Trial Procedure shall be made by one of the following methods:

    i.   Delivery to the clerk of the court;

    ii. Sending by electronic transmission under the procedure adopted pursuant to IN ST ADMIN Rule 12;

    iii. Mailing to the clerk by registered, certified or express mail return receipt requested;

    iv. Depositing with any third-party commercial carrier for delivery to the clerk within three (3) calendar days, cost prepaid, properly addressed;

    v. If the court so permits, filing with the judge, in which event the judge shall note thereon the filing date and forthwith transmit them to the office of the clerk; or

    vi. Electronic filing, as approved by the Division of State Court Administration pursuant to IN ST ADMIN Rule 16. IN ST TRIAL P Rule 5(F).

    vii. Filing by registered or certified mail and by third-party commercial carrier shall be complete upon mailing or deposit. IN ST TRIAL P Rule 5(F).

c. *Facsimile filing.* Facsimile filing is discouraged, but permitted in the Marion Circuit and Marion Superior Court. All documents filed by facsimile shall also be filed in hard copy within seven (7) days of the facsimile filing, along with proposed orders and stamped addressed envelopes, as required by IN ST MARION CIR AND SUPER CTS CIV Rule 203(E). To avoid duplicate filings, the hard copies of the facsimile filing shall indicate in bold letters that the pleading was previously filed by facsimile transmission. Proof of transmission by facsimile, including certificate of service and manner of service, shall be the responsibility of the filing party. If the filing requires immediate attention of the Judge, it shall be so indicated in bold letters in an accompanying transmittal memorandum. Legibility of documents and timeliness of filing is the responsibility of the sender. IN ST MARION CIR AND SUPER CTS CIV Rule 205(B).

    i.   *Generally.* In counties where a majority of judges of the courts of record, by posted local rule, have authorized electronic facsimile filing and designated a telephone number to receive such transmissions, pleadings, motions, and other papers may be sent to the Clerk of Circuit Court by electronic facsimile transmission for filing in any case, provided:

        • Such matter does not exceed ten (10) pages, including the cover sheet;

        • Such matter does not require the payment of fees other than the electronic facsimile transcription fee set forth in IN ST ADMIN Rule 12(E);

        • The sending party creates at the time of transmission a machine generated log for such transmission; and

        • The original document and the transmission log are maintained by the sending party for the duration of the litigation. IN ST ADMIN Rule 12(B).

    ii. *Time of filing.* During normal, posted business hours, the time of filing shall be the time the duplicate document is produced in the office of the Clerk of the Circuit Court. Duplicate documents received at all other times shall be filed as of the next normal business day. IN ST ADMIN Rule 12(C).

        • If the receiving fax machine endorses its own time and date stamp upon the transmitted documents and the receiving machine produces a delivery receipt which is electronically created and transmitted to the sending party, the time of filing shall be the date and time recorded on the transmitted document by the receiving fax machine. IN ST ADMIN Rule 12(C).

d. *Electronic filing.* Electronic filing and electronic service pilot projects are authorized pursuant to IN

ST ADMIN Rule 16 and approved by the Division of State Court Administration. IN ST MARION SUPER CT ADMIN Rule 311(1-103).

i.   *Cases where electronic filing accepted.* All Marion County Circuit and Superior civil courts may accept electronic filing and service of pleadings and other documents designated in this rule in mortgage foreclosure (hereinafter referred to as "MF"), civil collection(hereinafter referred to as "CC"), and individual cases that have been approved for electronic filing and service. IN ST MARION SUPER CT ADMIN Rule 311(1-104)(1).

   - The Marion County Circuit Court may, upon the motion of a party or its own motion, designate a case that will involve multiple litigants, legally intricate issues, and an extensive number of documents a mass tort or complex litigation case. Any case so designated shall be subject to electronic filing and service using the county's approved Electronic Service Provider. IN ST MARION SUPER CT ADMIN Rule 311(1-104)(3).

   - The filing of electronic pleadings and other documents in MF and CC cases is entirely voluntary; however, once the case is initially filed electronically, all subsequent filings in the case shall remain in electronic format until the time for appeal is exhausted. IN ST MARION SUPER CT ADMIN Rule 311(1-104)(5).

ii. *Documents eligible for electronic filing.* The following pleadings may be filed and served electronically:

   - New case complaint and petitions. IN ST MARION SUPER CT ADMIN Rule 311(1-104)(8)(a).

   - Original answers. IN ST MARION SUPER CT ADMIN Rule 311(1-104)(8)(a).

   - Any other pleadings or document including but not limited to motions and appearance forms. IN ST MARION SUPER CT ADMIN Rule 311(1-104)(8)(a).

iii. *Manner of electronic filing.* Parties shall E-file a document either:

   - By registering to use the Electronic Filing Service Provider; or

   - In person at the Marion County Clerk's office, by electronically filing through the Public Access Terminal. Parties filing in this manner shall be responsible for furnishing the document in an electronic format that will be compatible with the clerk's office-system to be uploaded in person. IN ST MARION SUPER CT ADMIN Rule 311(1-104)(9). For information on the Electronic Filing Service Provider and Public Access Terminal, refer to IN ST MARION SUPER CT ADMIN Rule 311(1-101).

   - Registered users shall pay statutory filing fees for E-filed documents electronically to the Court through their EFSP. Filing fees are due and payable at the time of filing. IN ST MARION SUPER CT ADMIN Rule 311(2-104)(1). For more information on electronic filing fees, refer to IN ST MARION SUPER CT ADMIN Rule 311(2-104).

iv. *Effect of electronic filing.* Any pleading filed electronically shall be considered as filed with the court when the transmission to the EFSP is complete. Any document E-filed by 11:59 p.m. local Indianapolis, Indiana time shall be deemed filed on that date. The EFSP is an agent of the Court for the purpose of electronic filing, receipt, service and retrieval of electronic documents. IN ST MARION SUPER CT ADMIN Rule 311(2-102).

   - Upon completion of filing, the EFSP shall issue a confirmation receipt that includes the date and time of receipt. The confirmation receipt shall serve as proof of filing. IN ST MARION SUPER CT ADMIN Rule 311(2-102).

   - In the event the Court rejects the submitted documents following review, the documents shall not become part of the official Court record and the filer will receive notification of the rejection. Users may be required to refile the instruments to meet necessary filing requirements. Documents may be filed through an E-filing system at any time that the Clerk's office is open to receive the filing or at such other times as may be designated by the clerk and posted publicly. IN ST MARION SUPER CT ADMIN Rule 311(2-102).

   - Documents filed through the E-filing system are deemed filed when received by the

Clerk's office, except that documents received at times that the Clerk's office is closed shall be deemed filed the next regular time when the Clerk's office is open for filing. The time stamp issued by the E-filing system shall be presumed to be the time the document is received by the Clerk. IN ST MARION SUPER CT ADMIN Rule 311(2-102).

v. *Electronically filed documents.* All pleadings and other documents designated in IN ST MARION SUPER CT ADMIN Rule 311 shall be filed and served electronically in any individual case which has been approved for electronic filing and service. IN ST MARION SUPER CT ADMIN Rule 311(1-104)(6).

vi. *System failures.* When filing by electronic means is hindered by a technical failure, a party may file with the Clerk of Marion County in hard copy. With the exception of deadlines that by law cannot be extended, the time for filing of any paper that is delayed due to technical failure of the site shall be extended for one (1) day for each day on which such failure occurs, unless otherwise ordered by the Court. IN ST MARION SUPER CT ADMIN Rule 311(2-108).

vii. *Compliance with rules.* All filing shall comply with the requirements of IN ST ADMIN Rule 9 and IN ST ADMIN Rule 16; and the Indiana Rules of Court and the Marion County Local Rules. IN ST MARION SUPER CT ADMIN Rule 311(1-104)(11).

e. *Filing for special judge.* When a Special Judge who is not a Marion County Judge is selected, all parties or attorneys shall furnish such Judge with copies of all filings prior to the qualification of such Special Judge. Thereafter, copies of all filings shall be delivered in person, by mail or by facsimile to the office of the Special Judge with certificate of forwarding same made a part of the filing. IN ST MARION CIR AND SUPER CTS CIV Rule 205(C).

f. *Proof of filing.* Any party filing any paper by any method other than personal delivery to the clerk shall retain proof of filing. IN ST TRIAL P Rule 5(F).

2. *Service requirements.* Unless otherwise provided by the Indiana Rules of Trial Procedure or an order of the court, each party and special judge, if any, shall be served with: (1) every order required by its terms to be served; (2) every pleading subsequent to the original complaint; (3) every written motion except one which may be heard ex parte; (4) every brief submitted to the trial court; (5) every paper relating to discovery required to be served upon a party; and (6) every written notice, appearance, demand, offer of judgment, designation of record on appeal, or similar paper. IN ST TRIAL P Rule 5(A).

a. *Methods of service*

i. *Personal service.* Whenever a party is represented by an attorney of record, service shall be made upon such attorney unless service upon the party himself is ordered by the court. Service upon the attorney or party shall be made by delivering or mailing a copy of the papers to the last known address or where an attorney or party has consented to service by fax or e-mail, as provided in IN ST TRIAL P Rule 3.1(A)(4), by faxing or e-mailing a copy of the documents to the fax number or e-mail address set out in the appearance form or correction as required by IN ST TRIAL P Rule 3.1(E). IN ST TRIAL P Rule 5(B). Delivery of a copy within IN ST TRIAL P Rule 5 means:

- Offering or tendering it to the attorney or party and stating the nature of the papers being served. Refusal to accept an offered or tendered document is a waiver of any objection to the sufficiency or adequacy of service of that document;

- Leaving it at his office with a clerk or other person in charge thereof, or if there is no one in charge, leaving it in a conspicuous place therein; or

- If the office is closed, by leaving it at his dwelling house or usual place of abode with some person of suitable age and discretion then residing therein; or,

- Leaving it at some other suitable place, selected by the attorney upon whom service is being made, pursuant to duly promulgated local rule. IN ST TRIAL P Rule 5(B)(1).

ii. *Service by mail.* If service is made by mail, the papers shall be deposited in the United States mail addressed to the person on whom they are being served, with postage prepaid. Service shall be deemed complete upon mailing. Proof of service of all papers permitted to be mailed may be made by written acknowledgment of service, by affidavit of the person who mailed the papers, or by certificate of an attorney. It shall be the duty of attorneys when entering their appearance in a cause or when filing pleadings or papers therein, to have noted in the Chronological Case Summary or said pleadings or papers so filed the address and telephone number of their office. Service by delivery or by mail at such address shall be deemed sufficient and complete. IN ST TRIAL P Rule 5(B)(2).

iii. *Service by fax or e-mail.* A party who has consented to service by fax or e-mail may be served as follows:

- Service by e-mail shall be made by attaching the document being served in .pdf format. Discovery documents must also be served in accordance with IN ST TRIAL P Rule 26(A). IN ST TRIAL P Rule 5(B)(3)(a).

- Service by fax shall be deemed complete upon generation of a transmission record indicating the successful transmission of the entire document, except as provided in IN ST TRIAL P Rule 5(B)(3)(d). IN ST TRIAL P Rule 5(B)(3)(b).

- Service by e-mail shall be deemed complete upon transmission, except as provided in IN ST TRIAL P Rule 5(B)(3)(d). IN ST TRIAL P Rule 5(B)(3)(c).

- Service by fax or e-mail that occurs on a Saturday, Sunday, legal holiday, or day the court or agency in which the matter is pending is closed or after 5:00 PM local time of the recipient shall be deemed complete the next day that is not a Saturday, Sunday, legal holiday, or day that the court or agency in which the matter is pending is not closed. IN ST TRIAL P Rule 5(B)(3)(d).

iv. *Electronic service.* Delivery of E-service documents through the EFSP to other registered users shall be considered as valid and effective service and shall have the same legal effect as an original paper document. Recipients of E-service documents shall access their documents through the EFSP. IN ST MARION SUPER CT ADMIN Rule 311(2-107)(1).

- E-service shall be deemed complete when the transmission to the EFSP is completed. IN ST MARION SUPER CT ADMIN Rule 311(2-107)(2).

- For the purpose of computing time to respond to documents received via E-service, any document served on a day or at a time when the Clerk's office is not open for business shall be deemed served at the time of next opening of the Clerk's office for business. IN ST MARION SUPER CT ADMIN Rule 311(2-107)(3).

b. *Serving numerous defendants.* In any action in which there are unusually large numbers of defendants, the court, upon motion or of its own initiative, may order:

i. That service of the pleadings of the defendants and replies thereto need not be made as between the defendants;

- That any cross-claim, counterclaim, or matter constituting an avoidance or affirmative defense contained therein shall be deemed to be denied or avoided by all other parties; and

- That the filing of any such pleading and service thereof upon the plaintiff constitutes due notice of it to the parties. IN ST TRIAL P Rule 5(D).

ii. A copy of every such order shall be served upon the parties in such manner and form as the court directs. IN ST TRIAL P Rule 5(D).

c. *Service by electronic means.* Courts wishing to establish an electronic service pilot project pursuant to the Indiana Administrative Rules must submit a written request for approval and a plan to the Division of State Court Administration. IN ST ADMIN Rule 16(B).

d. *Service on parties in default for failure to appear.* No service need be made on parties in default for failure to appear, except that pleadings asserting new or additional claims for relief against them shall be served upon them in the manner provided by service of summons in IN ST TRIAL P Rule 4. IN ST TRIAL P Rule 5(A).

G. Hearings

1. *Hearing on motion.* Unless local conditions make it impracticable, each judge shall establish regular

times and places, at intervals sufficiently frequent for the prompt dispatch of business, at which motions requiring notice and hearing may be heard and disposed of; but the judge at any time or place and on such notice, if any, as he considers reasonable may make order for the advancement, conduct, and hearing of actions. To expedite its business the court may direct the submission and determination of motions without oral hearing upon brief written statements of reasons in support and opposition, or direct or permit hearings by telephone conference call with all attorneys or other similar means of communication. IN ST TRIAL P Rule 73(A).

2. *Time and place of hearing.* If the motion requires a hearing or oral argument, the Court shall set the time and place of hearing or argument on the motion. IN ST MARION CIR AND SUPER CTS CIV Rule 203(A).

H. Forms

1. Motion to Strike Forms for Indiana

    a.   Motion to strike pleading not signed. 9 INPRAC § 4.18.

    b.   Motion to strike pleading as sham and false. 9 INPRAC § 4.19.

    c.   Motion to strike; Entire pleading. 9 INPRAC § 42.21.

    d.   Motion to strike; Portions of pleading. 9 INPRAC § 42.22.

    e.   Motion to strike; Insufficient defense in answer. 9 INPRAC § 42.23.

    f.   Motion to strike; Pleading that was not timely filed. 9 INPRAC § 42.24.

    g.   Motion to strike; Attorney fees claim. 9 INPRAC § 42.25.

    h.   Motion to strike; General denial in answer. 9 INPRAC § 42.26.

    i.   Motion to strike; Impertinent and scandalous material. 9 INPRAC § 42.27.

    j.   Motion to strike answer; Matter repleaded contrary to prior ruling. 9 INPRAC § 42.28.

    k.   Motion to strike; Failure to plead performance of conditions precedent. 9 INPRAC § 42.29.

    l.   Motion to strike; Appearance of defendant's attorney. 9 INPRAC § 42.30.

    m.   Certificate of service; Personal service. 9 INPRAC § 5.7.

    n.   Certificate of service; First class mail. 9 INPRAC § 5.8.

I. Checklist

(I) ❑ Matters to be considered by moving party

  (a) ❑ Required documents

    (1) ❑ Motion and notice

    (2) ❑ Statement of approval or disapproval

    (3) ❑ Proposed order

    (4) ❑ Certificate of service

  (b) ❑ Supplemental documents

    (1) ❑ Supporting evidence

    (2) ❑ Request for oral argument

    (3) ❑ Facsimile cover sheet

  (c) ❑ Timing

    (1) ❑ Upon motion made by a party before responding to a pleading, or, if no responsive pleading is permitted by Indiana Rules of Trial Procedure, upon motion made by a party within twenty (20) days after the service of the pleading upon him or at any time upon the court's own initiative, the court may order stricken from any pleading any insufficient claim or defense or any redundant, immaterial, impertinent, or scandalous matter

    (2) ❑ A written motion, other than one which may be heard ex parte, and notice of the hearing

thereof shall be served not less than five (5) days before the time specified for the hearing, unless a different period is fixed by the Indiana Rules of Trial Procedure or by order of the court

    (3) ❑ All pleadings and papers subsequent to the complaint which are required to be served upon a party shall be filed with the Court either before service or within a reasonable period of time thereafter

(II) ❑ Matters to be considered by the responding party

    (a) ❑ Required documents

        (1) ❑ Opposition

        (2) ❑ Certificate of service

    (b) ❑ Supplemental documents

        (1) ❑ Supporting evidence

        (2) ❑ Proposed order

        (3) ❑ Facsimile cover sheet

    (c) ❑ Timing

        (1) ❑ If the statement regarding the position of the opposing party(ies) required under IN ST MARION CIR AND SUPER CTS CIV Rule 203(A) indicates that objection to the granting of said motion may ensue, said objecting a party shall have fifteen (15) days from the date of filing to file a response to said motion

        (2) ❑ Except as otherwise provided in IN ST TRIAL P Rule 59(D), opposing affidavits may be served not less than one (1) day before the hearing, unless the court permits them to be served at some other time

Motions, Oppositions and Replies
Motion to Dismiss for Improper Venue

Document Last Updated October 2013

A. Applicable Rules

  1. *State rules*

    a. Appearance. IN ST TRIAL P Rule 3.1.

    b. Process. IN ST TRIAL P Rule 4.

    c. Service and filing of pleadings and other papers. IN ST TRIAL P Rule 5.

    d. Time. IN ST TRIAL P Rule 6.

    e. Pleadings. IN ST TRIAL P Rule 7; IN ST TRIAL P Rule 8; IN ST TRIAL P Rule 9.2; IN ST TRIAL P Rule 10.

    f. Signing and verification of pleadings. IN ST TRIAL P Rule 11.

    g. Defenses and objections; When and how presented; By pleading or motion; Motion for judgment on the pleadings. IN ST TRIAL P Rule 12.

    h. Amended and supplemental pleadings. IN ST TRIAL P Rule 15.

    i. Joinder of person needed for just adjudication. IN ST TRIAL P Rule 19.

    j. Misjoinder and non-joinder of parties; Venue and jurisdiction over the subject-matter. IN ST TRIAL P Rule 21.

    k. Evidence. IN ST TRIAL P Rule 43.

    l. Judgment on the evidence (directed verdict). IN ST TRIAL P Rule 50.

    m. Findings by the court. IN ST TRIAL P Rule 52.

n.   Summary judgment. IN ST TRIAL P Rule 56.

o.   Motion to correct error. IN ST TRIAL P Rule 59.

p.   Relief from judgment or order. IN ST TRIAL P Rule 60.

q.   Hearing of motions. IN ST TRIAL P Rule 73.

r.   Venue requirements. IN ST TRIAL P Rule 75.

s.   Interlocutory appeals. IN ST RAP Rule 14.

t.   Access to court records. IN ST ADMIN Rule 9.

u.   Paper size. IN ST ADMIN Rule 11.

v.   Facsimile transmission. IN ST ADMIN Rule 12.

w.   Electronic filing and electronic service pilot projects. IN ST ADMIN Rule 16.

x.   Sealing of certain records by court; Hearing; Notice. IN ST 5-14-3-5.5.

y.   Privacy and confidentiality. IN ST 5-2-9-6; IN ST 5-14-3-4; IN ST 6-4.1-5-10; IN ST 6-4.1-12-12; IN ST 6-8.1-7-1; IN ST 11-13-1-8; IN ST 12-23-14-13; IN ST 16-39-3-10; IN ST 16-41-8-1; IN ST 22-4-19-6; IN ST 31-11-1-6; IN ST 31-19-5-23; IN ST 31-19-13-2; IN ST 31-19-19-1; IN ST 31-33-18-1; IN ST 31-39-1-1; IN ST 31-39-1-2; IN ST 33-23-16-16; IN ST 35-34-2-4; IN ST 35-38-1-13; IN ST 35-38-9-1; IN ST ADR Rule 2.11; IN ST ADR Rule 4.4; IN ST ADR Rule 5.6; IN ST JURY Rule 10.

2. *Local rules*

a.   Requirements for motions. IN ST MARION CIR AND SUPER CTS CIV Rule 203.

b.   Preparation of pleadings, motions and other papers. IN ST MARION CIR AND SUPER CTS CIV Rule 204.

c.   Filing of pleadings, motions and other papers. IN ST MARION CIR AND SUPER CTS CIV Rule 205.

d.   Signing and verification of pleadings, motions and other papers; Service on opposing party. IN ST MARION CIR AND SUPER CTS CIV Rule 206.

e.   Motions for continuance. IN ST MARION CIR AND SUPER CTS CIV Rule 215.

f.   Electronic filing. IN ST MARION SUPER CT ADMIN Rule 311.

B. Timing

1. *Motion to dismiss for improper venue.* A motion making the defense of incorrect venue under IN ST TRIAL P Rule 75, or any statutory provision, shall be made before pleading if a further pleading is permitted or within twenty (20) days after service of the prior pleading if none is required. IN ST TRIAL P Rule 12(B); IN ST TRIAL P Rule 75(A).

a.   *Time to file a responsive pleading.* A responsive pleading required under the Indiana Rules of Trial Procedure, shall be served within twenty (20) days after service of the prior pleading. IN ST TRIAL P Rule 6(C).

b.   *Waiver of certain IN ST TRIAL P Rule 12(B) defenses.* If a pleading sets forth a claim for relief to which the adverse party is not required to serve a responsive pleading, any of the defenses in IN ST TRIAL P Rule 12(B)(2), IN ST TRIAL P Rule 12(B)(3), IN ST TRIAL P Rule 12(B)(4), IN ST TRIAL P Rule 12(B)(5) or IN ST TRIAL P Rule 12(B)(8) is waived to the extent constitutionally permissible unless made in a motion within twenty (20) days after service of the prior pleading. IN ST TRIAL P Rule 12(B).

c.   *Filing.* All pleadings and papers subsequent to the complaint which are required to be served upon a party shall be filed with the Court either before service or within a reasonable period of time thereafter. IN ST TRIAL P Rule 5(E)(1).

2. *Service.* A written motion, other than one which may be heard ex parte, and notice of the hearing thereof

shall be served not less than five (5) days before the time specified for the hearing, unless a different period is fixed by the Indiana Rules of Trial Procedure or by order of the court. IN ST TRIAL P Rule 6(D).

    a. *Of supporting affidavits.* When a motion is supported by affidavit, the affidavit shall be served with the motion. IN ST TRIAL P Rule 6(D).

3. *Opposition*

    a. *Filing.* If the statement regarding the position of the opposing party(ies) required under IN ST MARION CIR AND SUPER CTS CIV Rule 203(A) indicates that objection to the granting of said motion may ensue, said objecting a party shall have fifteen (15) days from the date of filing to file a response to said motion. IN ST MARION CIR AND SUPER CTS CIV Rule 203(B).

    b. *Service.* Except as otherwise provided in IN ST TRIAL P Rule 59(D), opposing affidavits may be served not less than one (1) day before the hearing, unless the court permits them to be served at some other time. IN ST TRIAL P Rule 6(D).

4. *Computation of time*

    a. *Generally; Days excluded.* In computing any period of time prescribed or allowed by the Indiana Rules of Trial Procedure, by order of the court, or by any applicable statute, the day of the act, event, or default from which the designated period of time begins to run shall not be included. The last day of the period so computed is to be included unless it is:

        i. A Saturday,

        ii. A Sunday,

        iii. A legal holiday as defined by state statute, or

        iv. A day the office in which the act is to be done is closed during regular business hours. IN ST TRIAL P Rule 6(A).

    b. *Short periods.* In any event, the period runs until the end of the next day that is not a Saturday, a Sunday, a legal holiday, or a day on which the office is closed. When the period of time allowed is less than seven (7) days, intermediate Saturdays, Sundays, legal holidays, and days on which the office is closed shall be excluded from the computations. IN ST TRIAL P Rule 6(A).

    c. *Additional time after service by United States mail.* Whenever a party has the right or is required to do some act or take some proceedings within a prescribed period after the service of a notice or other paper upon him and the notice or paper is served upon him by United States mail, three (3) days shall be added to the prescribed period. IN ST TRIAL P Rule 6(E).

    d. *Enlargement of time.* When an act is required or allowed to be done at or within a specific time by the Indiana Rules of Trial Procedure, the court may at any time for cause shown:

        i. Order the period enlarged, with or without motion or notice, if request therefor is made before the expiration of the period originally prescribed or extended by a previous order; or

        ii. Upon motion made after the expiration of the specific period, permit the act to be done where the failure to act was the result of excusable neglect; but, the court may not extend the time for taking any action for judgment on the evidence under IN ST TRIAL P Rule 50(A), amendment of findings and judgment under IN ST TRIAL P Rule 52(B), to correct errors under IN ST TRIAL P Rule 59(C), statement in opposition to motion to correct error under IN ST TRIAL P Rule 59(E), or to obtain relief from final judgment under IN ST TRIAL P Rule 60(B), except to the extent and under the conditions stated in those rules. IN ST TRIAL P Rule 6(B).

    e. *Continuances disfavored.* Motions for Continuance are discouraged. Neither side is entitled to an automatic continuance as a matter of right. IN ST MARION CIR AND SUPER CTS CIV Rule 215. For information on obtaining a continuance, refer to IN ST MARION CIR AND SUPER CTS CIV Rule 215.

C. General Requirements

1. *Motions, generally.* Unless made during a hearing or trial, or otherwise ordered by the court, an application to the court for an order shall be made by written motion. The motion shall state the grounds therefor and the relief or order sought. IN ST TRIAL P Rule 7(B).

    a. *Motions as distinct from pleadings.* Motions and responses to motions are not pleadings, and

allegations contained in a motion are not admissions of a party. 22B INPRAC 7:2; Wachstetter v. County Properties, LLC, 832 N.E.2d 574 (Ind.Ct.App. 2005); Scott County Family YMCA, Inc. v. Hobbs, 817 N.E.2d 603 (Ind.Ct.App. 2004).

b. *Unopposed motions generally granted.* It is common for a trial court to grant procedural motions, such as motions for enlargement of time, discovery motions, or motions for continuance, unless an objection is filed. 21 INPRAC § 13.8.

2. *Motion to dismiss for improper venue.* Every defense, in law or fact, to a claim for relief in any pleading, whether a claim, counterclaim, cross-claim, or third-party claim, shall be asserted in the responsive pleading thereto if one is required; except that at the option of the pleader, incorrect venue under IN ST TRIAL P Rule 75, or any statutory provision may be made by motion. IN ST TRIAL P Rule 12(B)(3). The disposition of this motion shall be consistent with IN ST TRIAL P Rule 75. IN ST TRIAL P Rule 12(B)(3). This means that, in almost every instance in which a motion is made under IN ST TRIAL P Rule 12(B)(3) or another statute, the action shall not be dismissed but transferred, consistent with IN ST TRIAL P Rule 75. 1A INPRAC R 12(12.7).

a. *Venue.* Any case may be venued, commenced and decided in any court in any county, except, that upon the filing of a pleading or a motion to dismiss allowed by IN ST TRIAL P Rule 12(B)(3), the court, from allegations of the complaint or after hearing evidence thereon or considering affidavits or documentary evidence filed with the motion or in opposition to it, shall order the case transferred to a county or court selected by the party first properly filing such motion or pleading if the court determines that the county or court where the action was filed does not meet preferred venue requirements or is not authorized to decide the case and that the court or county selected has preferred venue and is authorized to decide the case. IN ST TRIAL P Rule 75(A).

b. *Preferred venue.* Preferred venue lies in:

i. The county where the greater percentage of individual defendants included in the complaint resides, or, if there is no such greater percentage, the place where any individual defendant so named resides; or

ii. The county where the land or some part thereof is located or the chattels or some part thereof are regularly located or kept, if the complaint includes a claim for injuries thereto or relating to such land or such chattels, including without limitation claims for recovery of possession or for injuries, to establish use or control, to quiet title or determine any interest, to avoid or set aside conveyances, to foreclose liens, to partition and to assert any matters for which in rem relief is or would be proper; or

iii. The county where the accident or collision occurred, if the complaint includes a claim for injuries relating to the operation of a motor vehicle or a vehicle on railroad, street or interurban tracks; or

iv. The county where either the principal office of a defendant organization is located or the office or agency of a defendant organization or individual to which the claim relates or out of which the claim arose is located, if one or more such organizations or individuals are included as defendants in the complaint; or

v. The county where either one or more individual plaintiffs reside, the principal office of a governmental organization is located, or the office of a governmental organization to which the claim relates or out of which the claim arose is located, if one or more governmental organizations are included as defendants in the complaint; or

vi. The county or court fixed by written stipulations signed by all the parties named in the complaint or their attorneys and filed with the court before ruling on the motion to dismiss; or

vii. The county where the individual is held in custody or is restrained, if the complaint seeks relief with respect to such individual's custody or restraint upon his freedom; or

viii. The county where a claim in the plaintiff's complaint may be commenced under any statute recognizing or creating a special or general remedy or proceeding; or

ix. The county where all or some of the property is located or can be found if the case seeks only judgment in rem against the property of a defendant being served by publication; or

x. The county where either one or more individual plaintiffs reside, the principal office of any plaintiff organization or governmental organization is located, or the office of any such plaintiff organization or governmental organization to which the claim relates or out of which the claim arose is located, if the case is not subject to the requirements of IN ST TRIAL P Rule 75(A)(1) through IN ST TRIAL P Rule 75(A)(9) or if all the defendants are nonresident individuals or nonresident organizations without a principal office in the state. IN ST TRIAL P Rule 75(A).

c. *Claim or proceeding filed in improper court*

   i. Whenever a claim or proceeding is filed which should properly have been filed in another court of this state, and proper objection is made, the court in which such action is filed shall not then dismiss the action, but shall order the action transferred to the court in which it should have been filed. IN ST TRIAL P Rule 75(B)(1).

   ii. The person filing the action shall, within twenty (20) days, pay such costs as are chargeable upon a change of venue and the papers and records shall be certified to the court of transfer in like manner as upon change of venue and the action shall be deemed commenced as of the date of filing the action in the original court. IN ST TRIAL P Rule 75(B)(2).

   iii. If the party filing the action does not pay the costs of transfer within twenty (20) days of the order transferring venue, the original court shall dismiss the action without prejudice and shall order payment of reasonable attorney fees to the party making proper objection. IN ST TRIAL P Rule 75(B)(3).

d. *Assessment of costs, traveling expenses and attorneys' fees in resisting venue.* When the case is ordered transferred under the provisions of IN ST TRIAL P Rule 75 or IN ST TRIAL P Rule 21(B) the court shall order the parties or persons filing the complaint to pay the filing costs of refiling the case in the proper court and pay mileage expenses reasonably incurred by the parties and their attorneys in resisting the venue; and if it appears that the case was commenced in the wrong county by sham pleading, in bad faith or without cause, the court shall order payment of reasonable attorneys' fees incurred by parties successfully resisting the venue. IN ST TRIAL P Rule 75(C).

e. *Other venue statutes superseded by IN ST TRIAL P Rule 75.* Any provision of the Indiana Rules of Trial Procedure and any special or general statute relating to venue, the place of trial or the authority of the court to hear the case shall be subject to IN ST TRIAL P Rule 75, and the provisions of any statute fixing more stringent rules thereon shall be ineffective. No statute or rule fixing the place of trial shall be deemed a requirement of jurisdiction. IN ST TRIAL P Rule 75(D).

f. *Appeal.* An order transferring or refusing to transfer a case under IN ST TRIAL P Rule 75 shall be an interlocutory order appealable pursuant to IN ST RAP Rule 14(A)(8); provided, however, that the appeal of an interlocutory order under IN ST TRIAL P Rule 75 shall not stay proceedings in the trial court unless the trial court or the Court of Appeals so orders. IN ST TRIAL P Rule 75(E).

3. *Consolidation and waiver*

a. *Consolidation of defenses in motion.* A party who makes a motion under IN ST TRIAL P Rule 12 may join with it any other motions herein provided for and then available to him. If a party makes a motion under IN ST TRIAL P Rule 12 but omits therefrom any defense or objection then available to him which IN ST TRIAL P Rule 12 permits to be raised by motion, he shall not thereafter make a motion based on the defense or objection so omitted. He may, however, make such motions as are allowed under IN ST TRIAL P Rule 12(H)(2). IN ST TRIAL P Rule 12(G).

b. *Waiver or preservation of certain defenses.* No defense or objection is waived by being joined with one or more other defenses or objections in a responsive pleading or motion. IN ST TRIAL P Rule 12(B).

D. Documents

1. *Required documents*

a. *Motion and notice.* The requirement of notice is satisfied by service of the motion. IN ST TRIAL P Rule 7(B); IN ST MARION CIR AND SUPER CTS CIV Rule 203(A). Refer to the General Requirements section of this document for information on the content of a motion to dismiss for improper venue.

b. *Statement of approval or disapproval.* Except for initial motions made pursuant to IN ST MARION CIR AND SUPER CTS CIV Rule 203(D), all motions filed with the court shall include a brief statement indicating whether opposing party(ies) object to or approve of the granting of said motion. IN ST MARION CIR AND SUPER CTS CIV Rule 203(A).

c. *Proposed order.* Unless local practice provides differently, a party should submit a proposed order with its written motion to be signed by the judge once the motion has been granted. 21 INPRAC § 13.8. All motions seeking an order of the Court shall be accompanied by a sufficient number of orders to be executed by the Court in granting said motion. In addition to the orders, the notice shall be accompanied by stamped, addressed envelopes to all parties of record. IN ST MARION CIR AND SUPER CTS CIV Rule 203(E).

d. *Certificate of service.* An attorney or unrepresented party tendering a document to the Clerk for filing shall certify that service has been made, list the parties served, and specify the date and means of service. The certificate of service shall be placed at the end of the document and shall not be separately filed. The separate filing of a certificate of service, however, shall not be grounds for rejecting a document for filing. The Clerk may permit documents to be filed without a certificate of service but shall require prompt filing of a separate certificate of service. IN ST TRIAL P Rule 5(C). In all cases where any pleading or other document is required to be served upon opposing counsel, proof of such service may be made either by:

   i. A certificate of service signed by counsel of record for the serving party and the certificate shall specify by name and address all counsel upon whom the pleading or document was served; or

   ii. An acknowledgment of service signed by the party served or counsel of record. IN ST MARION CIR AND SUPER CTS CIV Rule 206.

2. *Supplemental documents*

   a. *Supporting evidence.* When a motion is based on facts not appearing of record the court may hear the matter on affidavits presented by the respective parties, but the court may direct that the matter be heard wholly or partly on oral testimony or depositions. IN ST TRIAL P Rule 43(B).

   b. *Request for oral argument.* When an oral argument is requested, the request shall be by separate instrument and filed with the pleading to be argued. Any such oral argument requested may be heard at the discretion of the Court, except for motions for summary judgment which shall be set for hearing upon request of any party. IN ST MARION CIR AND SUPER CTS CIV Rule 203(C).

   c. *Facsimile cover sheet.* Any document sent to the Clerk of the Circuit Court by electronic facsimile transmission shall be accompanied by a cover sheet which states the title of the document, case number, number of pages, identity and voice telephone number of the sending party and instructions for filing. The cover sheet shall contain the signature of the attorney or party, pro se, authorizing the filing. IN ST ADMIN Rule 12(D).

E. Format

1. *Form of motions.* The rules applicable to captions, and the signing and form of pleadings (IN ST TRIAL P Rule 8 through IN ST TRIAL P Rule 11), apply to all motions and other papers provided under the Indiana Rules of Trial Procedure. 22B INPRAC 7:2.

2. *Form of pleadings*

   a. *Caption; Names of parties.* Every pleading shall contain a caption setting forth the name of the court, the title of the action, the file number, and a designation as in IN ST TRIAL P Rule 7(A). In the complaint the title of the action shall include the names of all the parties, but in other pleadings it is sufficient to state the name of the first party on each side with an appropriate indication of other parties. IN ST TRIAL P Rule 10(A).

      i. Every pleading shall contain a caption setting forth the name of the Court, the Division and Room Number, the title of the action and the file number. IN ST MARION CIR AND SUPER CTS CIV Rule 204(B).

   b. *Paragraphs; Separate statements.* All averments of a claim or defense shall be made in numbered paragraphs, the contents of each of which shall be limited as far as practicable to a statement of a

single set of circumstances, and a paragraph may be referred to by number in all succeeding pleadings. Each claim founded upon a separate transaction or occurrence and each defense other than denials may be stated in a separate count or defense whenever a separation facilitates the clear presentation of the matters set forth. IN ST TRIAL P Rule 10(B).

c. *Adoption by reference; Exhibits.* Statements in a pleading may be adopted by reference in a different part of the same pleading or in another pleading or in any motion. A copy of any written instrument which is an exhibit to a pleading is a part thereof for all purposes. IN ST TRIAL P Rule 10(C).

d. *Paper.* Pleadings, motions and other papers may be either printed or typewritten on white opaque paper of at least sixteen (16) pound weight, eight and one-half (8-1/2) inches wide and eleven (11) inches in length. IN ST MARION CIR AND SUPER CTS CIV Rule 204(A).

e. *Copies.* All copies shall likewise be on white paper of sufficient strength and durability to resist normal wear and tear. IN ST MARION CIR AND SUPER CTS CIV Rule 204(A).

f. *Line spacing.* If typewritten, the lines shall be double spaced, except for quotations, which shall be indented and single spaced. IN ST MARION CIR AND SUPER CTS CIV Rule 204(A).

g. *Script type.* Script type shall not be used. IN ST MARION CIR AND SUPER CTS CIV Rule 204(A).

h. *Titles.* Titles on all pleadings shall delineate each topic included in the pleading e.g. where a pleading contains an Answer, a Motion to Strike or Dismiss, or a Jury Request each shall be set forth in the title. IN ST MARION CIR AND SUPER CTS CIV Rule 204(C).

i. *Margins and binding.* Margins shall be one (1) inch. Binding or stapling shall be at the top and at no other place. Covers or backing shall not be used. IN ST MARION CIR AND SUPER CTS CIV Rule 204(D).

3. *Size of papers for filing.* Effective January 1, 1992, all pleadings, copies, motions and documents filed with any trial court or appellate level court, typed or printed, with the exception of exhibits and existing wills, shall be prepared on eight and one-half by eleven inch (8 1/2" x 11") size paper. IN ST ADMIN Rule 11.

4. *Form of electronically filed documents.* All electronically filed and served pleadings shall, to the extent practicable, be formatted in accordance with the applicable rules governing formatting of paper pleadings. IN ST MARION SUPER CT ADMIN Rule 311(2-103)(1).

a. *Electronic document title.* The electronic document title of each pleading or other document shall include:

i. Party or parties filing/serving the document,

ii. Nature of the document,

iii. Party or parties against whom relief, if any, is sought, and

iv. Nature of the relief sought (e.g., Defendant ABC Corporation's Motion for Summary Judgment). IN ST MARION SUPER CT ADMIN Rule 311(2-103)(2).

5. *Signature requirements*

a. *Signature of attorney.* Every pleading or motion of a party represented by an attorney shall be signed by at least one (1) attorney of record in his individual name, whose address, telephone number, and attorney number shall be stated, except that this provision shall not apply to pleadings and motions made and transcribed at the trial or a hearing before the judge and received by him in such form. IN ST TRIAL P Rule 11(A).

i. All pleadings and motions shall contain the original or authorized signature of the attorney, the name of the attorney in typed or printed form, the name of the law firm if a member of a firm, the attorney's address, identification number, e-mail address, telephone number, fax number, and the designation as to the party for whom he appears. IN ST MARION CIR AND SUPER CTS CIV Rule 204(E).

ii. The signature of an attorney constitutes a certificate by him that he has read the pleadings; that to the best of his knowledge, information, and belief, there is good ground to support it; and that it is not interposed for delay. IN ST TRIAL P Rule 11(A).

iii. If a pleading or motion is not signed or is signed with intent to defeat the purpose of the rule, it may be stricken as sham and false and the action may proceed as though the pleading had not been served. IN ST TRIAL P Rule 11(A).

iv. For a willful violation of IN ST TRIAL P Rule 11 an attorney may be subjected to appropriate disciplinary action. Similar action may be taken if scandalous or indecent matter is inserted. IN ST TRIAL P Rule 11(A).

v. Every pleading, document, and instrument electronically filed or served shall be deemed to have been signed by the judge, clerk, attorney or declarant and shall bear a facsimile or typographical signature of such person, along with the typed name, address, telephone number, and Bar number of a signing attorney. Typographical signatures shall be treated as personal signatures for all purposes under these rules. IN ST MARION SUPER CT ADMIN Rule 311(2-105).

- Documents containing signatures of third-parties (i.e., unopposed motions, affidavits, stipulations, etc.) may also be filed electronically by indicating that the original signatures are maintained by the filing party in paper-format. IN ST MARION SUPER CT ADMIN Rule 311(2-105).

- Unless otherwise ordered by the Court or Clerk, a printed copy of all documents filed or served electronically, including original signatures, shall be maintained by the party filing the document and shall be made available, upon reasonable notice, for inspection by other counsel, the Clerk or Court. Parties shall retain originals until two (2) years after all time periods for appeal have expired. From time to time, it may be necessary to provide the Clerk or Court with a hard copy of an electronically filed document. IN ST MARION SUPER CT ADMIN Rule 311(2-105).

vi. For the recommended format of a signature block, refer to IN ST MARION CIR AND SUPER CTS CIV Rule 204(E).

b. *Signature of unrepresented party.* A party who is not represented by an attorney shall sign his pleading and state his address. IN ST TRIAL P Rule 11(A).

c. *Verification not generally required.* Except when specifically required by rule, pleadings or motions need not be verified or accompanied by affidavit. The rule in equity that the averments of an answer under oath must be overcome by the testimony of two (2) witnesses or of one (1) witness sustained by corroborating circumstances is abolished. IN ST TRIAL P Rule 11(A).

d. *Verification by affirmation or representation.* When in connection with any civil or special statutory proceeding it is required that any pleading, motion, petition, supporting affidavit, or other document of any kind, be verified, or that an oath be taken, it shall be sufficient if the subscriber simply affirms the truth of the matter to be verified by an affirmation or representation. IN ST TRIAL P Rule 11(B). IN ST TRIAL P Rule 11(B) states that the affirmation or representation should be in substantially the following language: "I (we) affirm, under the penalties for perjury, that the foregoing representation(s) is (are) true. (Signed) _____."

i. Any person who falsifies an affirmation or representation of fact shall be subject to the same penalties as are prescribed by law for the making of a false affidavit. IN ST TRIAL P Rule 11(B).

e. *Verified pleadings, motions, and affidavits as evidence.* Pleadings, motions and affidavits accompanying or in support of such pleadings or motions when required to be verified or under oath shall be accepted as a representation that the signer had personal knowledge thereof or reasonable cause to believe the existence of the facts or matters stated or alleged therein; and, if otherwise competent or acceptable as evidence, may be admitted as evidence of the facts or matters stated or alleged therein when it is so provided in the Indiana Rules of Trial Procedure, by statute or other law, or to the extent the writing or signature expressly purports to be made upon the signer's personal knowledge. When such pleadings, motions and affidavits are verified or under oath they shall not require other or greater proof on the part of the adverse party than if not verified or not under oath unless expressly provided otherwise by the Indiana Rules of Trial Procedure, statute or other law. Affidavits upon motions for summary judgment under IN ST TRIAL P Rule 56 and in denial of execution under IN ST TRIAL P Rule 9.2 shall be made upon personal knowledge. IN ST TRIAL P Rule 11(C).

6. *Information excluded from public access.* Every document filed in a case shall separately identify information excluded from public access pursuant to IN ST ADMIN Rule 9(G)(1) as follows:

a. Whole documents that are excluded from public access pursuant to IN ST ADMIN Rule 9(G)(1) shall be tendered on light green paper or have a light green coversheet attached to the document, marked "Not for Public Access" or "Confidential." IN ST TRIAL P Rule 5(G)(1).

b. When only a portion of a document contains information excluded from public access pursuant to IN ST ADMIN Rule 9(G)(1), said information shall be omitted [or redacted] from the filed document, and set forth on a separate accompanying document on light green paper conspicuously marked "Not for Public Access" or "Confidential" and clearly designated [or identifying] the caption and number of the case and the document and location within the document to which the redacted material pertains. IN ST TRIAL P Rule 5(G)(2).

c. With respect to documents filed in electronic format, the trial court, by local rule, may provide for compliance with IN ST TRIAL P Rule 5 in manner that separates and protects access to information excluded from public access. IN ST TRIAL P Rule 5(G)(3).

d. IN ST TRIAL P Rule 5(G) does not apply to a record sealed by the court pursuant to IN ST 5-14-3-5.5 or otherwise, nor to records, documents, or information filed in cases to which public access is prohibited pursuant to IN ST ADMIN Rule 9(G). IN ST TRIAL P Rule 5(G)(4).

e. The following information in case records is excluded from public access and is confidential:

i. Information that is excluded from public access pursuant to federal law;

ii. Information that is excluded from public access as declared confidential by Indiana statute or other court rule, including without limitation:

- All adoption records created after July 8, 1941, as declared confidential by IN ST 31-19-19-1, et seq., except those specifically declared open by IN ST 31-19-13-2(2);

- All records relating to chancroid, chlamydia, gonorrhea, hepatitis, human immunodeficiency virus (HIV), Lymphogranuloma venereum, syphilis, tuberculosis, as declared confidential by IN ST 16-41-8-1, et seq.;

- All records relating to child abuse as declared confidential by IN ST 31-33-18-1, et seq.;

- All records relating to drug tests as declared confidential by IN ST 5-14-3-4(a)(9);

- Records of grand jury proceedings as declared confidential by IN ST 35-34-2-4;

- Records of juvenile proceedings as declared confidential by IN ST 31-39-1-2, except those specifically open under statute;

- All paternity records created after July 1, 1941 as declared confidential by IN ST 31-14-11-15, IN ST 31-19-5-23, IN ST 31-39-1-1 and IN ST 31-39-1-2 [Editor's note: IN ST 31-14-11-15 was repealed effective May 9, 2013];

- All pre-sentence reports as declared confidential by IN ST 35-38-1-13;

- Written petitions to permit marriages without consent and orders directing the Clerk of Court to issue a marriage license to underage persons, as declared confidential by IN ST 31-11-1-6;

- Only those arrest warrants, search warrants, indictments and informations ordered confidential by the trial judge, prior to return of duly executed service as declared confidential by IN ST 5-14-3-4(b)(1);

- All medical, mental health, or tax records unless determined by law or regulation of any governmental custodian not to be confidential, released by the subject of such records, or declared by a court of competent jurisdiction to be essential to the resolution of litigation as declared confidential by IN ST 16-39-3-10, IN ST 6-4.1-5-10, IN ST 6-4.1-12-12, and IN ST 6-8.1-7-1;

- Personal information relating to jurors or prospective jurors, other than for the use of the parties and counsel, pursuant to IN ST JURY Rule 10;

- Information relating to protection from abuse orders, no-contact orders and workplace violence restraining orders as declared confidential by IN ST 5-2-9-6, et seq.;

- Mediation proceedings pursuant to IN ST ADR Rule 2.11, Mini-Trial proceedings pursuant to IN ST ADR Rule 4.4(C), and Summary Jury Trials pursuant to IN ST ADR Rule 5.6;

- Information in probation files pursuant to the Probation Standards promulgated by the Judicial Conference of Indiana pursuant to IN ST 11-13-1-8(b);

- Information deemed confidential pursuant to the Rules for Court Administered Alcohol and Drug Programs promulgated by the Judicial Conference of Indiana pursuant to IN ST 12-23-14-13;

- Information deemed confidential pursuant to the Problem-Solving Court Rules promulgated by the Judicial Conference of Indiana pursuant to IN ST 33-23-16-16;

- All records of the Department of workforce Development as declared confidential by IN ST 22-4-19-6;

- Information regarding interception of electronic communications that is sealed or deemed confidential as set forth in IN ST 35-33.5-2-1, et seq.

iii. Information excluded from public access by specific court order;

iv. Complete Social Security Numbers of living persons;

v. With the exception of names, information such as addresses, phone numbers, and dates of birth which explicitly identifies:

- Natural persons who are witnesses or victims (not including defendants) in criminal, domestic violence, stalking, sexual assault, juvenile, or civil protection order proceedings, provided that juveniles who are victims of sex crimes shall be identified by initials only;

- Places of residence of judicial officers, clerks and other employees of courts and clerks of court, unless the person or persons about whom the information pertains waives confidentiality;

vi. Complete account numbers of specific assets, loans, bank accounts, credit cards, and personal identification numbers (PINs);

vii. All orders of expungement entered in criminal or juvenile proceedings, orders to restrict access to criminal history information pursuant to IN ST 35-38-5-5.5 or IN ST 35-38-8-5 and records excluded from public access by such orders, and information related to infractions that is excluded from public access pursuant to IN ST 34-28-5-15 or IN ST 34-28-5-16 [Editor's note: IN ST 35-38-5-5.5, IN ST 35-38-8-5 and IN ST 34-28-5-16 were repealed effective July 1, 2013; for information on orders restricting access to criminal history, refer to IN ST 35-38-9-1, et seq.];

viii. All personal notes and e-mail, and deliberative material, of judges, jurors, court staff and judicial agencies, and information recorded in personal data assistants (PDA's) or organizers and personal calendars. IN ST ADMIN Rule 9(G)(1).

F. Filing and Service Requirements

1. *Filing requirements.* Except as otherwise provided in IN ST TRIAL P Rule 5(E)(2), all pleadings and papers subsequent to the complaint which are required to be served upon a party shall be filed with the Court either before service or within a reasonable period of time thereafter. IN ST TRIAL P Rule 5(E)(1). Counsel shall file with the court an original and one (1) copy of all briefs, and memoranda of law filed in support of a motion. IN ST MARION CIR AND SUPER CTS CIV Rule 205(D).

   a. *Filing generally.* All pleadings, petitions and motions are filed with the Clerk designated by the Court at any time during office hours established by the Clerk and the Court. All orders submitted to the Court shall be in sufficient number and shall be accompanied by postage paid envelopes addressed to each party or counsel of record. IN ST MARION CIR AND SUPER CTS CIV Rule 205(A)

b. *Filing with the court defined.* The filing of pleadings, motions, and other papers with the court as required by the Indiana Rules of Trial Procedure shall be made by one of the following methods:

    i. Delivery to the clerk of the court;

    ii. Sending by electronic transmission under the procedure adopted pursuant to IN ST ADMIN Rule 12;

    iii. Mailing to the clerk by registered, certified or express mail return receipt requested;

    iv. Depositing with any third-party commercial carrier for delivery to the clerk within three (3) calendar days, cost prepaid, properly addressed;

    v. If the court so permits, filing with the judge, in which event the judge shall note thereon the filing date and forthwith transmit them to the office of the clerk; or

    vi. Electronic filing, as approved by the Division of State Court Administration pursuant to IN ST ADMIN Rule 16. IN ST TRIAL P Rule 5(F).

    vii. Filing by registered or certified mail and by third-party commercial carrier shall be complete upon mailing or deposit. IN ST TRIAL P Rule 5(F).

c. *Facsimile filing.* Facsimile filing is discouraged, but permitted in the Marion Circuit and Marion Superior Court. All documents filed by facsimile shall also be filed in hard copy within seven (7) days of the facsimile filing, along with proposed orders and stamped addressed envelopes, as required by IN ST MARION CIR AND SUPER CTS CIV Rule 203(E). To avoid duplicate filings, the hard copies of the facsimile filing shall indicate in bold letters that the pleading was previously filed by facsimile transmission. Proof of transmission by facsimile, including certificate of service and manner of service, shall be the responsibility of the filing party. If the filing requires immediate attention of the Judge, it shall be so indicated in bold letters in an accompanying transmittal memorandum. Legibility of documents and timeliness of filing is the responsibility of the sender. IN ST MARION CIR AND SUPER CTS CIV Rule 205(B).

    i. *Generally.* In counties where a majority of judges of the courts of record, by posted local rule, have authorized electronic facsimile filing and designated a telephone number to receive such transmissions, pleadings, motions, and other papers may be sent to the Clerk of Circuit Court by electronic facsimile transmission for filing in any case, provided:

        • Such matter does not exceed ten (10) pages, including the cover sheet;

        • Such matter does not require the payment of fees other than the electronic facsimile transcription fee set forth in IN ST ADMIN Rule 12(E);

        • The sending party creates at the time of transmission a machine generated log for such transmission; and

        • The original document and the transmission log are maintained by the sending party for the duration of the litigation. IN ST ADMIN Rule 12(B).

    ii. *Time of filing.* During normal, posted business hours, the time of filing shall be the time the duplicate document is produced in the office of the Clerk of the Circuit Court. Duplicate documents received at all other times shall be filed as of the next normal business day. IN ST ADMIN Rule 12(C).

        • If the receiving fax machine endorses its own time and date stamp upon the transmitted documents and the receiving machine produces a delivery receipt which is electronically created and transmitted to the sending party, the time of filing shall be the date and time recorded on the transmitted document by the receiving fax machine. IN ST ADMIN Rule 12(C).

d. *Electronic filing.* Electronic filing and electronic service pilot projects are authorized pursuant to IN ST ADMIN Rule 16 and approved by the Division of State Court Administration. IN ST MARION SUPER CT ADMIN Rule 311(1-103).

    i. *Cases where electronic filing accepted.* All Marion County Circuit and Superior civil courts may accept electronic filing and service of pleadings and other documents designated in this rule in mortgage foreclosure (hereinafter referred to as "MF"), civil collection(hereinafter referred to as "CC"), and individual cases that have been approved for electronic filing and service. IN ST MARION SUPER CT ADMIN Rule 311(1-104)(1).

- The Marion County Circuit Court may, upon the motion of a party or its own motion, designate a case that will involve multiple litigants, legally intricate issues, and an extensive number of documents a mass tort or complex litigation case. Any case so designated shall be subject to electronic filing and service using the county's approved Electronic Service Provider. IN ST MARION SUPER CT ADMIN Rule 311(1-104)(3).

- The filing of electronic pleadings and other documents in MF and CC cases is entirely voluntary; however, once the case is initially filed electronically, all subsequent filings in the case shall remain in electronic format until the time for appeal is exhausted. IN ST MARION SUPER CT ADMIN Rule 311(1-104)(5).

ii. *Documents eligible for electronic filing.* The following pleadings may be filed and served electronically:

- New case complaint and petitions. IN ST MARION SUPER CT ADMIN Rule 311(1-104)(8)(a).

- Original answers. IN ST MARION SUPER CT ADMIN Rule 311(1-104)(8)(a).

- Any other pleadings or document including but not limited to motions and appearance forms. IN ST MARION SUPER CT ADMIN Rule 311(1-104)(8)(a).

iii. *Manner of electronic filing.* Parties shall E-file a document either:

- By registering to use the Electronic Filing Service Provider; or

- In person at the Marion County Clerk's office, by electronically filing through the Public Access Terminal. Parties filing in this manner shall be responsible for furnishing the document in an electronic format that will be compatible with the clerk's office-system to be uploaded in person. IN ST MARION SUPER CT ADMIN Rule 311(1-104)(9). For information on the Electronic Filing Service Provider and Public Access Terminal, refer to IN ST MARION SUPER CT ADMIN Rule 311(1-101).

- Registered users shall pay statutory filing fees for E-filed documents electronically to the Court through their EFSP. Filing fees are due and payable at the time of filing. IN ST MARION SUPER CT ADMIN Rule 311(2-104)(1). For more information on electronic filing fees, refer to IN ST MARION SUPER CT ADMIN Rule 311(2-104).

iv. *Effect of electronic filing.* Any pleading filed electronically shall be considered as filed with the court when the transmission to the EFSP is complete. Any document E-filed by 11:59 p.m. local Indianapolis, Indiana time shall be deemed filed on that date. The EFSP is an agent of the Court for the purpose of electronic filing, receipt, service and retrieval of electronic documents. IN ST MARION SUPER CT ADMIN Rule 311(2-102).

- Upon completion of filing, the EFSP shall issue a confirmation receipt that includes the date and time of receipt. The confirmation receipt shall serve as proof of filing. IN ST MARION SUPER CT ADMIN Rule 311(2-102).

- In the event the Court rejects the submitted documents following review, the documents shall not become part of the official Court record and the filer will receive notification of the rejection. Users may be required to refile the instruments to meet necessary filing requirements. Documents may be filed through an E-filing system at any time that the Clerk's office is open to receive the filing or at such other times as may be designated by the clerk and posted publicly. IN ST MARION SUPER CT ADMIN Rule 311(2-102).

- Documents filed through the E-filing system are deemed filed when received by the Clerk's office, except that documents received at times that the Clerk's office is closed shall be deemed filed the next regular time when the Clerk's office is open for filing. The time stamp issued by the E-filing system shall be presumed to be the time the document is received by the Clerk. IN ST MARION SUPER CT ADMIN Rule 311(2-102).

     v. *Electronically filed documents.* All pleadings and other documents designated in IN ST MARION SUPER CT ADMIN Rule 311 shall be filed and served electronically in any individual case which has been approved for electronic filing and service. IN ST MARION SUPER CT ADMIN Rule 311(1-104)(6).

     vi. *System failures.* When filing by electronic means is hindered by a technical failure, a party may file with the Clerk of Marion County in hard copy. With the exception of deadlines that by law cannot be extended, the time for filing of any paper that is delayed due to technical failure of the site shall be extended for one (1) day for each day on which such failure occurs, unless otherwise ordered by the Court. IN ST MARION SUPER CT ADMIN Rule 311(2-108).

     vii. *Compliance with rules.* All filing shall comply with the requirements of IN ST ADMIN Rule 9 and IN ST ADMIN Rule 16; and the Indiana Rules of Court and the Marion County Local Rules. IN ST MARION SUPER CT ADMIN Rule 311(1-104)(11).

  e. *Filing for special judge.* When a Special Judge who is not a Marion County Judge is selected, all parties or attorneys shall furnish such Judge with copies of all filings prior to the qualification of such Special Judge. Thereafter, copies of all filings shall be delivered in person, by mail or by facsimile to the office of the Special Judge with certificate of forwarding same made a part of the filing. IN ST MARION CIR AND SUPER CTS CIV Rule 205(C).

  f. *Proof of filing.* Any party filing any paper by any method other than personal delivery to the clerk shall retain proof of filing. IN ST TRIAL P Rule 5(F).

2. *Service requirements.* Unless otherwise provided by the Indiana Rules of Trial Procedure or an order of the court, each party and special judge, if any, shall be served with: (1) every order required by its terms to be served; (2) every pleading subsequent to the original complaint; (3) every written motion except one which may be heard ex parte; (4) every brief submitted to the trial court; (5) every paper relating to discovery required to be served upon a party; and (6) every written notice, appearance, demand, offer of judgment, designation of record on appeal, or similar paper. IN ST TRIAL P Rule 5(A).

  a. *Methods of service*

     i. *Personal service.* Whenever a party is represented by an attorney of record, service shall be made upon such attorney unless service upon the party himself is ordered by the court. Service upon the attorney or party shall be made by delivering or mailing a copy of the papers to the last known address or where an attorney or party has consented to service by fax or e-mail, as provided in IN ST TRIAL P Rule 3.1(A)(4), by faxing or e-mailing a copy of the documents to the fax number or e-mail address set out in the appearance form or correction as required by IN ST TRIAL P Rule 3.1(E). IN ST TRIAL P Rule 5(B). Delivery of a copy within IN ST TRIAL P Rule 5 means:

- Offering or tendering it to the attorney or party and stating the nature of the papers being served. Refusal to accept an offered or tendered document is a waiver of any objection to the sufficiency or adequacy of service of that document;

- Leaving it at his office with a clerk or other person in charge thereof, or if there is no one in charge, leaving it in a conspicuous place therein; or

- If the office is closed, by leaving it at his dwelling house or usual place of abode with some person of suitable age and discretion then residing therein; or,

- Leaving it at some other suitable place, selected by the attorney upon whom service is being made, pursuant to duly promulgated local rule. IN ST TRIAL P Rule 5(B)(1).

     ii. *Service by mail.* If service is made by mail, the papers shall be deposited in the United States mail addressed to the person on whom they are being served, with postage prepaid. Service shall be deemed complete upon mailing. Proof of service of all papers permitted to be mailed may be made by written acknowledgment of service, by affidavit of the person who mailed the papers, or by certificate of an attorney. It shall be the duty of attorneys when entering their appearance in a cause or when filing pleadings or papers therein, to have noted in the Chronological Case Summary or said pleadings or papers so filed the address and telephone number of their office. Service by delivery or by mail at such address shall be deemed sufficient and complete. IN ST TRIAL P Rule 5(B)(2).

iii. *Service by fax or e-mail.* A party who has consented to service by fax or e-mail may be served as follows:

- Service by e-mail shall be made by attaching the document being served in .pdf format. Discovery documents must also be served in accordance with IN ST TRIAL P Rule 26(A). IN ST TRIAL P Rule 5(B)(3)(a).

- Service by fax shall be deemed complete upon generation of a transmission record indicating the successful transmission of the entire document, except as provided in IN ST TRIAL P Rule 5(B)(3)(d). IN ST TRIAL P Rule 5(B)(3)(b).

- Service by e-mail shall be deemed complete upon transmission, except as provided in IN ST TRIAL P Rule 5(B)(3)(d). IN ST TRIAL P Rule 5(B)(3)(c).

- Service by fax or e-mail that occurs on a Saturday, Sunday, legal holiday, or day the court or agency in which the matter is pending is closed or after 5:00 PM local time of the recipient shall be deemed complete the next day that is not a Saturday, Sunday, legal holiday, or day that the court or agency in which the matter is pending is not closed. IN ST TRIAL P Rule 5(B)(3)(d).

iv. *Electronic service.* Delivery of E-service documents through the EFSP to other registered users shall be considered as valid and effective service and shall have the same legal effect as an original paper document. Recipients of E-service documents shall access their documents through the EFSP. IN ST MARION SUPER CT ADMIN Rule 311(2-107)(1).

- E-service shall be deemed complete when the transmission to the EFSP is completed. IN ST MARION SUPER CT ADMIN Rule 311(2-107)(2).

- For the purpose of computing time to respond to documents received via E-service, any document served on a day or at a time when the Clerk's office is not open for business shall be deemed served at the time of next opening of the Clerk's office for business. IN ST MARION SUPER CT ADMIN Rule 311(2-107)(3).

b. *Serving numerous defendants.* In any action in which there are unusually large numbers of defendants, the court, upon motion or of its own initiative, may order:

i. That service of the pleadings of the defendants and replies thereto need not be made as between the defendants;

- That any cross-claim, counterclaim, or matter constituting an avoidance or affirmative defense contained therein shall be deemed to be denied or avoided by all other parties; and

- That the filing of any such pleading and service thereof upon the plaintiff constitutes due notice of it to the parties. IN ST TRIAL P Rule 5(D).

ii. A copy of every such order shall be served upon the parties in such manner and form as the court directs. IN ST TRIAL P Rule 5(D).

c. *Service on parties in default for failure to appear.* No service need be made on parties in default for failure to appear, except that pleadings asserting new or additional claims for relief against them shall be served upon them in the manner provided by service of summons in IN ST TRIAL P Rule 4. IN ST TRIAL P Rule 5(A).

G. Hearings

1. *Hearing on motion.* Unless local conditions make it impracticable, each judge shall establish regular times and places, at intervals sufficiently frequent for the prompt dispatch of business, at which motions requiring notice and hearing may be heard and disposed of; but the judge at any time or place and on such notice, if any, as he considers reasonable may make order for the advancement, conduct, and hearing of actions. To expedite its business the court may direct the submission and determination of motions without oral hearing upon brief written statements of reasons in support and opposition, or direct or permit hearings by telephone conference call with all attorneys or other similar means of communication. IN ST TRIAL P Rule 73(A).

2. *Time and place of hearing.* If the motion requires a hearing or oral argument, the Court shall set the time

and place of hearing or argument on the motion. IN ST MARION CIR AND SUPER CTS CIV Rule 203(A).

H. Forms

    1. Indiana Motion to Dismiss for Improper Venue Forms

        a. Incorrect venue. 9 INPRAC § 42.5.

        b. Motion to dismiss; Improper venue under contract. 9 INPRAC § 42.18.1.

        c. Motion to transfer from improper venue. 11 INPRAC § 111.2.

        d. Motion to transfer from improper venue. 5 INPRAC § 3:11.1.

        e. Motion for change of venue from county; For cause. 5 INPRAC § 3:11.2.

        f. Certificate of service; Personal service. 9 INPRAC § 5.7.

        g. Certificate of service; First class mail. 9 INPRAC § 5.8.

I. Checklist

    (I) ❑ Matters to be considered by moving party

        (a) ❑ Required documents

            (1) ❑ Motion and notice

            (2) ❑ Statement of approval or disapproval

            (3) ❑ Proposed order

            (4) ❑ Certificate of service

        (b) ❑ Supplemental documents

            (1) ❑ Supporting evidence

            (2) ❑ Request for oral argument

            (3) ❑ Facsimile cover sheet

        (c) ❑ Timing

            (1) ❑ A motion making the defense of incorrect venue under IN ST TRIAL P Rule 75, or any statutory provision, shall be made before pleading if a further pleading is permitted or within twenty (20) days after service of the prior pleading if none is required

            (2) ❑ A written motion, other than one which may be heard ex parte, and notice of the hearing thereof shall be served not less than five (5) days before the time specified for the hearing, unless a different period is fixed by the Indiana Rules of Trial Procedure or by order of the court

            (3) ❑ All pleadings and papers subsequent to the complaint which are required to be served upon a party shall be filed with the Court either before service or within a reasonable period of time thereafter

    (II) ❑ Matters to be considered by the responding party

        (a) ❑ Required documents

            (1) ❑ Opposition

            (2) ❑ Certificate of service

        (b) ❑ Supplemental documents

            (1) ❑ Supporting evidence

            (2) ❑ Proposed order

            (3) ❑ Facsimile cover sheet

        (c) ❑ Timing

            (1) ❑ If the statement regarding the position of the opposing party(ies) required under IN ST

MARION CIR AND SUPER CTS CIV Rule 203(A) indicates that objection to the granting of said motion may ensue, said objecting a party shall have fifteen (15) days from the date of filing to file a response to said motion

(2) ❏ Except as otherwise provided in IN ST TRIAL P Rule 59(D), opposing affidavits may be served not less than one (1) day before the hearing, unless the court permits them to be served at some other time

Motions, Oppositions and Replies
Motion for Leave to Amend

Document Last Updated October 2013

A. Applicable Rules

1. *State rules*

   a. Appearance. IN ST TRIAL P Rule 3.1.

   b. Summons. IN ST TRIAL P Rule 4; IN ST TRIAL P Rule 4.6.

   c. Service and filing of pleadings and other papers. IN ST TRIAL P Rule 5.

   d. Time. IN ST TRIAL P Rule 6.

   e. Pleadings and other papers. IN ST TRIAL P Rule 7; IN ST TRIAL P Rule 8; IN ST TRIAL P Rule 9.2; IN ST TRIAL P Rule 10.

   f. Signing and verification of pleadings. IN ST TRIAL P Rule 11.

   g. Amended and supplemental pleadings. IN ST TRIAL P Rule 15.

   h. Evidence. IN ST TRIAL P Rule 43.

   i. Judgment on the evidence (directed verdict). IN ST TRIAL P Rule 50.

   j. Findings by the court. IN ST TRIAL P Rule 52.

   k. Summary judgment. IN ST TRIAL P Rule 56.

   l. Motion to correct error. IN ST TRIAL P Rule 59.

   m. Relief from judgment or order. IN ST TRIAL P Rule 60.

   n. Hearing of motions. IN ST TRIAL P Rule 73.

   o. Access to court records. IN ST ADMIN Rule 9.

   p. Paper size. IN ST ADMIN Rule 11.

   q. Facsimile transmission. IN ST ADMIN Rule 12.

   r. Electronic filing and electronic service pilot projects. IN ST ADMIN Rule 16.

   s. Sealing of certain records by court; Hearing; Notice. IN ST 5-14-3-5.5.

   t. Privacy and confidentiality. IN ST 5-2-9-6; IN ST 5-14-3-4; IN ST 6-4.1-5-10; IN ST 6-4.1-12-12; IN ST 6-8.1-7-1; IN ST 11-13-1-8; IN ST 12-23-14-13; IN ST 16-39-3-10; IN ST 16-41-8-1; IN ST 22-4-19-6; IN ST 31-11-1-6; IN ST 31-19-5-23; IN ST 31-19-13-2; IN ST 31-19-19-1; IN ST 31-33-18-1; IN ST 31-39-1-1; IN ST 31-39-1-2; IN ST 33-23-16-16; IN ST 35-34-2-4; IN ST 35-38-1-13; IN ST 35-38-9-1; IN ST ADR Rule 2.11; IN ST ADR Rule 4.4; IN ST ADR Rule 5.6; IN ST JURY Rule 10.

2. *Local rules*

   a. Requirements for motions. IN ST MARION CIR AND SUPER CTS CIV Rule 203.

   b. Preparation of pleadings, motions and other papers. IN ST MARION CIR AND SUPER CTS CIV Rule 204.

   c. Filing of pleadings, motions and other papers. IN ST MARION CIR AND SUPER CTS CIV Rule 205.

d. Signing and verification of pleadings, motions and other papers; Service on opposing party. IN ST MARION CIR AND SUPER CTS CIV Rule 206.

e. Motions for continuance. IN ST MARION CIR AND SUPER CTS CIV Rule 215.

f. Electronic filing. IN ST MARION SUPER CT ADMIN Rule 311.

B. Timing

1. *Time for amending pleadings*

    a. *As a matter of course.* A party may amend his pleading once as a matter of course at any time before a responsive pleading is served or, if the pleading is one to which no responsive pleading is permitted, and the action has not been placed upon the trial calendar, he may so amend it at any time within thirty (30) days after it is served. IN ST TRIAL P Rule 15(A). Refer to the Indiana KeyRules Amended Complaint and Amended Answer documents for additional information on amending pleadings as a matter of course.

    b. *With leave of court.* Otherwise a party may amend his pleading only by leave of court or by written consent of the adverse party; and leave shall be given when justice so requires. IN ST TRIAL P Rule 15(A).

    c. *Filing.* All pleadings and papers subsequent to the complaint which are required to be served upon a party shall be filed with the Court either before service or within a reasonable period of time thereafter. IN ST TRIAL P Rule 5(E)(1).

2. *Service.* A written motion, other than one which may be heard ex parte, and notice of the hearing thereof shall be served not less than five (5) days before the time specified for the hearing, unless a different period is fixed by the Indiana Rules of Trial Procedure or by order of the court. IN ST TRIAL P Rule 6(D).

    a. *Of supporting affidavits.* When a motion is supported by affidavit, the affidavit shall be served with the motion. IN ST TRIAL P Rule 6(D).

3. *Opposition*

    a. *Filing.* If the statement regarding the position of the opposing party(ies) required under IN ST MARION CIR AND SUPER CTS CIV Rule 203(A) indicates that objection to the granting of said motion may ensue, said objecting a party shall have fifteen (15) days from the date of filing to file a response to said motion. IN ST MARION CIR AND SUPER CTS CIV Rule 203(B).

    b. *Service.* Except as otherwise provided in IN ST TRIAL P Rule 59(D), opposing affidavits may be served not less than one (1) day before the hearing, unless the court permits them to be served at some other time. IN ST TRIAL P Rule 6(D).

4. *Computation of time*

    a. *Generally; Days excluded.* In computing any period of time prescribed or allowed by the Indiana Rules of Trial Procedure, by order of the court, or by any applicable statute, the day of the act, event, or default from which the designated period of time begins to run shall not be included. The last day of the period so computed is to be included unless it is:

        i. A Saturday,

        ii. A Sunday,

        iii. A legal holiday as defined by state statute, or

        iv. A day the office in which the act is to be done is closed during regular business hours. IN ST TRIAL P Rule 6(A).

    b. *Short periods.* In any event, the period runs until the end of the next day that is not a Saturday, a Sunday, a legal holiday, or a day on which the office is closed. When the period of time allowed is less than seven (7) days, intermediate Saturdays, Sundays, legal holidays, and days on which the office is closed shall be excluded from the computations. IN ST TRIAL P Rule 6(A).

    c. *Additional time after service by United States mail.* Whenever a party has the right or is required to do some act or take some proceedings within a prescribed period after the service of a notice or other paper upon him and the notice or paper is served upon him by United States mail, three (3) days shall be added to the prescribed period. IN ST TRIAL P Rule 6(E).

d. *Enlargement of time.* When an act is required or allowed to be done at or within a specific time by the Indiana Rules of Trial Procedure, the court may at any time for cause shown:

    i. Order the period enlarged, with or without motion or notice, if request therefor is made before the expiration of the period originally prescribed or extended by a previous order; or

    ii. Upon motion made after the expiration of the specific period, permit the act to be done where the failure to act was the result of excusable neglect; but, the court may not extend the time for taking any action for judgment on the evidence under IN ST TRIAL P Rule 50(A), amendment of findings and judgment under IN ST TRIAL P Rule 52(B), to correct errors under IN ST TRIAL P Rule 59(C), statement in opposition to motion to correct error under IN ST TRIAL P Rule 59(E), or to obtain relief from final judgment under IN ST TRIAL P Rule 60(B), except to the extent and under the conditions stated in those rules. IN ST TRIAL P Rule 6(B).

e. *Continuances disfavored.* Motions for Continuance are discouraged. Neither side is entitled to an automatic continuance as a matter of right. IN ST MARION CIR AND SUPER·CTS CIV Rule 215. For information on obtaining a continuance, refer to IN ST MARION CIR AND SUPER CTS CIV Rule 215.

C. General Requirements

1. *Motions, generally.* Unless made during a hearing or trial, or otherwise ordered by the court, an application to the court for an order shall be made by written motion. The motion shall state the grounds therefor and the relief or order sought. IN ST TRIAL P Rule 7(B).

    a. *Motions as distinct from pleadings.* Motions and responses to motions are not pleadings, and allegations contained in a motion are not admissions of a party. 22B INPRAC 7:2; Wachstetter v. County Properties, LLC, 832 N.E.2d 574 (Ind.Ct.App. 2005); Scott County Family YMCA, Inc. v. Hobbs, 817 N.E.2d 603 (Ind.Ct.App. 2004).

    b. *Unopposed motions generally granted.* It is common for a trial court to grant procedural motions, such as motions for enlargement of time, discovery motions, or motions for continuance, unless an objection is filed. 21 INPRAC § 13.8.

2. *Motion for leave to amend.* The purpose of an amended pleading is to include matters that occurred before the filing of the original pleading but which were either overlooked by the pleader or unknown to him at the time. It is a substitute for the original and relates to the facts that existed when the original pleading was filed. An amended pleading supercedes the original as to those portions amended. 10 INPRAC § 46.1.

    a. *Amendments liberally allowed.* Amendments to pleadings are to be liberally allowed in order that all issues are presented in one action. 10 INPRAC § 46.1; Pinnacle Media, LLC v. Metropolitan Dev. Com'n of Marion County, 868 N.E.2d 894 (Ind.Ct.App. 2007).

    b. *Amendments to conform to the evidence.* When issues not raised by the pleadings are tried by express or implied consent of the parties, they shall be treated in all respects as if they had been raised in the pleadings. Such amendment of the pleadings as may be necessary to cause them to conform to the evidence and to raise these issues may be made upon motion of any party at any time, even after judgment, but failure so to amend does not affect the result of the trial of these issues. If evidence is objected to at the trial on the ground that it is not within the issues made by the pleadings, the court may allow the pleadings to be amended and shall do so freely when the presentation of the merits of the action will be subserved thereby and the objecting party fails to satisfy the court that the admission of such evidence would prejudice him in maintaining his action or defense upon the merits. The court may grant a continuance to enable the objecting party to meet such evidence. IN ST TRIAL P Rule 15(B).

    c. *Relation back of amendments*

        i. Whenever the claim or defense asserted in the amended pleading arose out of the conduct, transaction, or occurrence set forth or attempted to be set forth in the original pleading, the amendment relates back to the date of the original pleading. An amendment changing the party against whom a claim is asserted relates back if the foregoing provision is satisfied and, within one hundred and twenty (120) days of commencement of the action, the party to be brought in by amendment:

- Has received such notice of the institution of the action that he will not be prejudiced in maintaining his defense on the merits; and

- Knew or should have known that but for a mistake concerning the identity of the proper party, the action would have been brought against him. IN ST TRIAL P Rule 15(C).

ii. The requirement of IN ST TRIAL P Rule 15(C)(1) and IN ST TRIAL P Rule 15(C)(2) with respect to a governmental organization to be brought into the action as defendant is satisfied:

- In the case of a state or governmental organization by delivery or mailing of process to the attorney general or to a governmental executive [IN ST TRIAL P Rule 4.6(A)(3)]; or

- In the case of a local governmental organization, by delivery or mailing of process to its attorney as provided by statute, to a governmental executive thereof [IN ST TRIAL P Rule 4.6(A)(4)], or to the officer holding the office if suit is against the officer or an office. IN ST TRIAL P Rule 15(C).

d. *Amendment by leave.* Amendments, other than an amendment by right, may be made only by leave of court or by written consent of the opposing party. 2 INPRAC R 15(15.1).

e. *Factors considered.* In deciding whether to permit a party to amend his pleading, the court must consider a number of factors: (1) undue delay, (2) bad faith or dilatory motive on the part of the movant, (3) repeated failure to cure deficiencies by amendments previously allowed, (4) undue prejudice to the opposing party by virtue of allowance of the amendment, and (5) the futility of the amendment. 10 INPRAC § 46.1; Crawford v. City of Muncie, 655 N.E.2d 614 (Ind.Ct.App. 1995); Selvia v. Reitmeyer, 156 Ind.App. 203, 295 N.E.2d 869 (Ind.Ct.App. 1973).

D. Documents

1. *Required documents*

a. *Motion and notice.* The requirement of notice is satisfied by service of the motion. IN ST TRIAL P Rule 7(B); IN ST MARION CIR AND SUPER CTS CIV Rule 203(A). Refer to the General Requirements section of this document for information on the content of a motion for leave to amend.

b. *Statement of approval or disapproval.* Except for initial motions made pursuant to IN ST MARION CIR AND SUPER CTS CIV Rule 203(D), all motions filed with the court shall include a brief statement indicating whether opposing party(ies) object to or approve of the granting of said motion. IN ST MARION CIR AND SUPER CTS CIV Rule 203(A).

c. *Copy of amended pleading.* A copy of the proposed amendment should be attached to the motion for leave to amend, along with a proposed order by the court which permits the amendment. 2 INPRAC R 15.

d. *Proposed order.* Unless local practice provides differently, a party should submit a proposed order with its written motion to be signed by the judge once the motion has been granted. 21 INPRAC § 13.8. All motions seeking an order of the Court shall be accompanied by a sufficient number of orders to be executed by the Court in granting said motion. In addition to the orders, the notice shall be accompanied by stamped, addressed envelopes to all parties of record. IN ST MARION CIR AND SUPER CTS CIV Rule 203(E).

e. *Certificate of service.* An attorney or unrepresented party tendering a document to the Clerk for filing shall certify that service has been made, list the parties served, and specify the date and means of service. The certificate of service shall be placed at the end of the document and shall not be separately filed. The separate filing of a certificate of service, however, shall not be grounds for rejecting a document for filing. The Clerk may permit documents to be filed without a certificate of service but shall require prompt filing of a separate certificate of service. IN ST TRIAL P Rule 5(C). In all cases where any pleading or other document is required to be served upon opposing counsel, proof of such service may be made either by:

i. A certificate of service signed by counsel of record for the serving party and the certificate shall specify by name and address all counsel upon whom the pleading or document was served; or

ii. An acknowledgment of service signed by the party served or counsel of record. IN ST MARION CIR AND SUPER CTS CIV Rule 206.

2. *Supplemental documents*

a. *Supporting evidence.* When a motion is based on facts not appearing of record the court may hear the matter on affidavits presented by the respective parties, but the court may direct that the matter be heard wholly or partly on oral testimony or depositions. IN ST TRIAL P Rule 43(B).

b. *Request for oral argument.* When an oral argument is requested, the request shall be by separate instrument and filed with the pleading to be argued. Any such oral argument requested may be heard at the discretion of the Court, except for motions for summary judgment which shall be set for hearing upon request of any party. IN ST MARION CIR AND SUPER CTS CIV Rule 203(C).

c. *Facsimile cover sheet.* Any document sent to the Clerk of the Circuit Court by electronic facsimile transmission shall be accompanied by a cover sheet which states the title of the document, case number, number of pages, identity and voice telephone number of the sending party and instructions for filing. The cover sheet shall contain the signature of the attorney or party, pro se, authorizing the filing. IN ST ADMIN Rule 12(D).

E. Format

1. *Form of motions.* The rules applicable to captions, and the signing and form of pleadings (IN ST TRIAL P Rule 8 through IN ST TRIAL P Rule 11), apply to all motions and other papers provided under the Indiana Rules of Trial Procedure. 22B INPRAC 7:2.

2. *Form of pleadings*

a. *Caption; Names of parties.* Every pleading shall contain a caption setting forth the name of the court, the title of the action, the file number, and a designation as in IN ST TRIAL P Rule 7(A). In the complaint the title of the action shall include the names of all the parties, but in other pleadings it is sufficient to state the name of the first party on each side with an appropriate indication of other parties. IN ST TRIAL P Rule 10(A).

   i. Every pleading shall contain a caption setting forth the name of the Court, the Division and Room Number, the title of the action and the file number. IN ST MARION CIR AND SUPER CTS CIV Rule 204(B).

b. *Paragraphs; Separate statements.* All averments of a claim or defense shall be made in numbered paragraphs, the contents of each of which shall be limited as far as practicable to a statement of a single set of circumstances, and a paragraph may be referred to by number in all succeeding pleadings. Each claim founded upon a separate transaction or occurrence and each defense other than denials may be stated in a separate count or defense whenever a separation facilitates the clear presentation of the matters set forth. IN ST TRIAL P Rule 10(B).

c. *Adoption by reference; Exhibits.* Statements in a pleading may be adopted by reference in a different part of the same pleading or in another pleading or in any motion. A copy of any written instrument which is an exhibit to a pleading is a part thereof for all purposes. IN ST TRIAL P Rule 10(C).

d. *Paper.* Pleadings, motions and other papers may be either printed or typewritten on white opaque paper of at least sixteen (16) pound weight, eight and one-half (8-1/2) inches wide and eleven (11) inches in length. IN ST MARION CIR AND SUPER CTS CIV Rule 204(A).

e. *Copies.* All copies shall likewise be on white paper of sufficient strength and durability to resist normal wear and tear. IN ST MARION CIR AND SUPER CTS CIV Rule 204(A).

f. *Line spacing.* If typewritten, the lines shall be double spaced, except for quotations, which shall be indented and single spaced. IN ST MARION CIR AND SUPER CTS CIV Rule 204(A).

g. *Script type.* Script type shall not be used. IN ST MARION CIR AND SUPER CTS CIV Rule 204(A).

h. *Titles.* Titles on all pleadings shall delineate each topic included in the pleading e.g. where a pleading contains an Answer, a Motion to Strike or Dismiss, or a Jury Request each shall be set forth in the title. IN ST MARION CIR AND SUPER CTS CIV Rule 204(C).

i. *Margins and binding.* Margins shall be one (1) inch. Binding or stapling shall be at the top and at no

other place. Covers or backing shall not be used. IN ST MARION CIR AND SUPER CTS CIV Rule 204(D).

3. *Size of papers for filing.* Effective January 1, 1992, all pleadings, copies, motions and documents filed with any trial court or appellate level court, typed or printed, with the exception of exhibits and existing wills, shall be prepared on eight and one-half by eleven inch (8 1/2" x 11") size paper. IN ST ADMIN Rule 11.

4. *Form of electronically filed documents.* All electronically filed and served pleadings shall, to the extent practicable, be formatted in accordance with the applicable rules governing formatting of paper pleadings. IN ST MARION SUPER CT ADMIN Rule 311(2-103)(1).

    a. *Electronic document title.* The electronic document title of each pleading or other document shall include:

        i. Party or parties filing/serving the document,

        ii. Nature of the document,

        iii. Party or parties against whom relief, if any, is sought, and

        iv. Nature of the relief sought (e.g., Defendant ABC Corporation's Motion for Summary Judgment). IN ST MARION SUPER CT ADMIN Rule 311(2-103)(2).

5. *Signature requirements*

    a. *Signature of attorney.* Every pleading or motion of a party represented by an attorney shall be signed by at least one (1) attorney of record in his individual name, whose address, telephone number, and attorney number shall be stated, except that this provision shall not apply to pleadings and motions made and transcribed at the trial or a hearing before the judge and received by him in such form. IN ST TRIAL P Rule 11(A).

        i. All pleadings and motions shall contain the original or authorized signature of the attorney, the name of the attorney in typed or printed form, the name of the law firm if a member of a firm, the attorney's address, identification number, e-mail address, telephone number, fax number, and the designation as to the party for whom he appears. IN ST MARION CIR AND SUPER CTS CIV Rule 204(E).

        ii. The signature of an attorney constitutes a certificate by him that he has read the pleadings; that to the best of his knowledge, information, and belief, there is good ground to support it; and that it is not interposed for delay. IN ST TRIAL P Rule 11(A).

        iii. If a pleading or motion is not signed or is signed with intent to defeat the purpose of the rule, it may be stricken as sham and false and the action may proceed as though the pleading had not been served. IN ST TRIAL P Rule 11(A).

        iv. For a willful violation of IN ST TRIAL P Rule 11 an attorney may be subjected to appropriate disciplinary action. Similar action may be taken if scandalous or indecent matter is inserted. IN ST TRIAL P Rule 11(A).

        v. Every pleading, document, and instrument electronically filed or served shall be deemed to have been signed by the judge, clerk, attorney or declarant and shall bear a facsimile or typographical signature of such person, along with the typed name, address, telephone number, and Bar number of a signing attorney. Typographical signatures shall be treated as personal signatures for all purposes under these rules. IN ST MARION SUPER CT ADMIN Rule 311(2-105).

            •   Documents containing signatures of third-parties (i.e., unopposed motions, affidavits, stipulations, etc.) may also be filed electronically by indicating that the original signatures are maintained by the filing party in paper-format. IN ST MARION SUPER CT ADMIN Rule 311(2-105).

            •   Unless otherwise ordered by the Court or Clerk, a printed copy of all documents filed or served electronically, including original signatures, shall be maintained by the party filing the document and shall be made available, upon reasonable notice, for inspection by other

counsel, the Clerk or Court. Parties shall retain originals until two (2) years after all time periods for appeal have expired. From time to time, it may be necessary to provide the Clerk or Court with a hard copy of an electronically filed document. IN ST MARION SUPER CT ADMIN Rule 311(2-105).

    vi. For the recommended format of a signature block, refer to IN ST MARION CIR AND SUPER CTS CIV Rule 204(E).

b. *Signature of unrepresented party.* A party who is not represented by an attorney shall sign his pleading and state his address. IN ST TRIAL P Rule 11(A).

c. *Verification not generally required.* Except when specifically required by rule, pleadings or motions need not be verified or accompanied by affidavit. The rule in equity that the averments of an answer under oath must be overcome by the testimony of two (2) witnesses or of one (1) witness sustained by corroborating circumstances is abolished. IN ST TRIAL P Rule 11(A).

d. *Verification by affirmation or representation.* When in connection with any civil or special statutory proceeding it is required that any pleading, motion, petition, supporting affidavit, or other document of any kind, be verified, or that an oath be taken, it shall be sufficient if the subscriber simply affirms the truth of the matter to be verified by an affirmation or representation. IN ST TRIAL P Rule 11(B). IN ST TRIAL P Rule 11(B) states that the affirmation or representation should be in substantially the following language: "I (we) affirm, under the penalties for perjury, that the foregoing representation(s) is (are) true. (Signed) _____."

    i. Any person who falsifies an affirmation or representation of fact shall be subject to the same penalties as are prescribed by law for the making of a false affidavit. IN ST TRIAL P Rule 11(B).

e. *Verified pleadings, motions, and affidavits as evidence.* Pleadings, motions and affidavits accompanying or in support of such pleadings or motions when required to be verified or under oath shall be accepted as a representation that the signer had personal knowledge thereof or reasonable cause to believe the existence of the facts or matters stated or alleged therein; and, if otherwise competent or acceptable as evidence, may be admitted as evidence of the facts or matters stated or alleged therein when it is so provided in the Indiana Rules of Trial Procedure, by statute or other law, or to the extent the writing or signature expressly purports to be made upon the signer's personal knowledge. When such pleadings, motions and affidavits are verified or under oath they shall not require other or greater proof on the part of the adverse party than if not verified or not under oath unless expressly provided otherwise by the Indiana Rules of Trial Procedure, statute or other law. Affidavits upon motions for summary judgment under IN ST TRIAL P Rule 56 and in denial of execution under IN ST TRIAL P Rule 9.2 shall be made upon personal knowledge. IN ST TRIAL P Rule 11(C).

6. *Information excluded from public access.* Every document filed in a case shall separately identify information excluded from public access pursuant to IN ST ADMIN Rule 9(G)(1) as follows:

    a. Whole documents that are excluded from public access pursuant to IN ST ADMIN Rule 9(G)(1) shall be tendered on light green paper or have a light green coversheet attached to the document, marked "Not for Public Access" or "Confidential." IN ST TRIAL P Rule 5(G)(1).

    b. When only a portion of a document contains information excluded from public access pursuant to IN ST ADMIN Rule 9(G)(1), said information shall be omitted [or redacted] from the filed document, and set forth on a separate accompanying document on light green paper conspicuously marked "Not for Public Access" or "Confidential" and clearly designated [or identifying] the caption and number of the case and the document and location within the document to which the redacted material pertains. IN ST TRIAL P Rule 5(G)(2).

    c. With respect to documents filed in electronic format, the trial court, by local rule, may provide for compliance with IN ST TRIAL P Rule 5 in manner that separates and protects access to information excluded from public access. IN ST TRIAL P Rule 5(G)(3).

    d. IN ST TRIAL P Rule 5(G) does not apply to a record sealed by the court pursuant to IN ST 5-14-3-5.5 or otherwise, nor to records, documents, or information filed in cases to which public access is prohibited pursuant to IN ST ADMIN Rule 9(G). IN ST TRIAL P Rule 5(G)(4).

MOTION FOR LEAVE TO AMEND

e. The following information in case records is excluded from public access and is confidential:

i. Information that is excluded from public access pursuant to federal law;

ii. Information that is excluded from public access as declared confidential by Indiana statute or other court rule, including without limitation:

- All adoption records created after July 8, 1941, as declared confidential by IN ST 31-19-19-1, et seq., except those specifically declared open by IN ST 31-19-13-2(2);

- All records relating to chancroid, chlamydia, gonorrhea, hepatitis, human immunodeficiency virus (HIV), Lymphogranuloma venereum, syphilis, tuberculosis, as declared confidential by IN ST 16-41-8-1, et seq.;

- All records relating to child abuse as declared confidential by IN ST 31-33-18-1, et seq.;

- All records relating to drug tests as declared confidential by IN ST 5-14-3-4(a)(9);

- Records of grand jury proceedings as declared confidential by IN ST 35-34-2-4;

- Records of juvenile proceedings as declared confidential by IN ST 31-39-1-2, except those specifically open under statute;

- All paternity records created after July 1, 1941 as declared confidential by IN ST 31-14-11-15, IN ST 31-19-5-23, IN ST 31-39-1-1 and IN ST 31-39-1-2 [Editor's note: IN ST 31-14-11-15 was repealed effective May 9, 2013];

- All pre-sentence reports as declared confidential by IN ST 35-38-1-13;

- Written petitions to permit marriages without consent and orders directing the Clerk of Court to issue a marriage license to underage persons, as declared confidential by IN ST 31-11-1-6;

- Only those arrest warrants, search warrants, indictments and informations ordered confidential by the trial judge, prior to return of duly executed service as declared confidential by IN ST 5-14-3-4(b)(1);

- All medical, mental health, or tax records unless determined by law or regulation of any governmental custodian not to be confidential, released by the subject of such records, or declared by a court of competent jurisdiction to be essential to the resolution of litigation as declared confidential by IN ST 16-39-3-10, IN ST 6-4.1-5-10, IN ST 6-4.1-12-12, and IN ST 6-8.1-7-1;

- Personal information relating to jurors or prospective jurors, other than for the use of the parties and counsel, pursuant to IN ST JURY Rule 10;

- Information relating to protection from abuse orders, no-contact orders and workplace violence restraining orders as declared confidential by IN ST 5-2-9-6, et seq.;

- Mediation proceedings pursuant to IN ST ADR Rule 2.11, Mini-Trial proceedings pursuant to IN ST ADR Rule 4.4(C), and Summary Jury Trials pursuant to IN ST ADR Rule 5.6;

- Information in probation files pursuant to the Probation Standards promulgated by the Judicial Conference of Indiana pursuant to IN ST 11-13-1-8(b);

- Information deemed confidential pursuant to the Rules for Court Administered Alcohol and Drug Programs promulgated by the Judicial Conference of Indiana pursuant to IN ST 12-23-14-13;

- Information deemed confidential pursuant to the Problem-Solving Court Rules promulgated by the Judicial Conference of Indiana pursuant to IN ST 33-23-16-16;

- All records of the Department of workforce Development as declared confidential by IN ST 22-4-19-6;

- Information regarding interception of electronic communications that is sealed or deemed confidential as set forth in IN ST 35-33.5-2-1, et seq.

iii. Information excluded from public access by specific court order;

iv. Complete Social Security Numbers of living persons;

v. With the exception of names, information such as addresses, phone numbers, and dates of birth which explicitly identifies:

- Natural persons who are witnesses or victims (not including defendants) in criminal, domestic violence, stalking, sexual assault, juvenile, or civil protection order proceedings, provided that juveniles who are victims of sex crimes shall be identified by initials only;

- Places of residence of judicial officers, clerks and other employees of courts and clerks of court, unless the person or persons about whom the information pertains waives confidentiality;

vi. Complete account numbers of specific assets, loans, bank accounts, credit cards, and personal identification numbers (PINs);

vii. All orders of expungement entered in criminal or juvenile proceedings, orders to restrict access to criminal history information pursuant to IN ST 35-38-5-5.5 or IN ST 35-38-8-5 and records excluded from public access by such orders, and information related to infractions that is excluded from public access pursuant to IN ST 34-28-5-15 or IN ST 34-28-5-16 [Editor's note: IN ST 35-38-5-5.5, IN ST 35-38-8-5 and IN ST 34-28-5-16 were repealed effective July 1, 2013; for information on orders restricting access to criminal history, refer to IN ST 35-38-9-1, et seq.];

viii. All personal notes and e-mail, and deliberative material, of judges, jurors, court staff and judicial agencies, and information recorded in personal data assistants (PDA's) or organizers and personal calendars. IN ST ADMIN Rule 9(G)(1).

F. Filing and Service Requirements

1. *Filing requirements.* Except as otherwise provided in IN ST TRIAL P Rule 5(E)(2), all pleadings and papers subsequent to the complaint which are required to be served upon a party shall be filed with the Court either before service or within a reasonable period of time thereafter. IN ST TRIAL P Rule 5(E)(1). Counsel shall file with the court an original and one (1) copy of all briefs, and memoranda of law filed in support of a motion. IN ST MARION CIR AND SUPER CTS CIV Rule 205(D).

   a. *Filing generally.* All pleadings, petitions and motions are filed with the Clerk designated by the Court at any time during office hours established by the Clerk and the Court. All orders submitted to the Court shall be in sufficient number and shall be accompanied by postage paid envelopes addressed to each party or counsel of record. IN ST MARION CIR AND SUPER CTS CIV Rule 205(A)

   b. *Filing with the court defined.* The filing of pleadings, motions, and other papers with the court as required by the Indiana Rules of Trial Procedure shall be made by one of the following methods:

      i. Delivery to the clerk of the court;

      ii. Sending by electronic transmission under the procedure adopted pursuant to IN ST ADMIN Rule 12;

      iii. Mailing to the clerk by registered, certified or express mail return receipt requested;

      iv. Depositing with any third-party commercial carrier for delivery to the clerk within three (3) calendar days, cost prepaid, properly addressed;

      v. If the court so permits, filing with the judge, in which event the judge shall note thereon the filing date and forthwith transmit them to the office of the clerk; or

      vi. Electronic filing, as approved by the Division of State Court Administration pursuant to IN ST ADMIN Rule 16. IN ST TRIAL P Rule 5(F).

      vii. Filing by registered or certified mail and by third-party commercial carrier shall be complete upon mailing or deposit. IN ST TRIAL P Rule 5(F).

   c. *Facsimile filing.* Facsimile filing is discouraged, but permitted in the Marion Circuit and Marion

Superior Court. All documents filed by facsimile shall also be filed in hard copy within seven (7) days of the facsimile filing, along with proposed orders and stamped addressed envelopes, as required by IN ST MARION CIR AND SUPER CTS CIV Rule 203(E). To avoid duplicate filings, the hard copies of the facsimile filing shall indicate in bold letters that the pleading was previously filed by facsimile transmission. Proof of transmission by facsimile, including certificate of service and manner of service, shall be the responsibility of the filing party. If the filing requires immediate attention of the Judge, it shall be so indicated in bold letters in an accompanying transmittal memorandum. Legibility of documents and timeliness of filing is the responsibility of the sender. IN ST MARION CIR AND SUPER CTS CIV Rule 205(B).

    i. *Generally.* In counties where a majority of judges of the courts of record, by posted local rule, have authorized electronic facsimile filing and designated a telephone number to receive such transmissions, pleadings, motions, and other papers may be sent to the Clerk of Circuit Court by electronic facsimile transmission for filing in any case, provided:

- Such matter does not exceed ten (10) pages, including the cover sheet;
- Such matter does not require the payment of fees other than the electronic facsimile transcription fee set forth in IN ST ADMIN Rule 12(E);
- The sending party creates at the time of transmission a machine generated log for such transmission; and
- The original document and the transmission log are maintained by the sending party for the duration of the litigation. IN ST ADMIN Rule 12(B).

    ii. *Time of filing.* During normal, posted business hours, the time of filing shall be the time the duplicate document is produced in the office of the Clerk of the Circuit Court. Duplicate documents received at all other times shall be filed as of the next normal business day. IN ST ADMIN Rule 12(C).

- If the receiving fax machine endorses its own time and date stamp upon the transmitted documents and the receiving machine produces a delivery receipt which is electronically created and transmitted to the sending party, the time of filing shall be the date and time recorded on the transmitted document by the receiving fax machine. IN ST ADMIN Rule 12(C).

d. *Electronic filing.* Electronic filing and electronic service pilot projects are authorized pursuant to IN ST ADMIN Rule 16 and approved by the Division of State Court Administration. IN ST MARION SUPER CT ADMIN Rule 311(1-103).

    i. *Cases where electronic filing accepted.* All Marion County Circuit and Superior civil courts may accept electronic filing and service of pleadings and other documents designated in this rule in mortgage foreclosure (hereinafter referred to as "MF"), civil collection(hereinafter referred to as "CC"), and individual cases that have been approved for electronic filing and service. IN ST MARION SUPER CT ADMIN Rule 311(1-104)(1).

- The Marion County Circuit Court may, upon the motion of a party or its own motion, designate a case that will involve multiple litigants, legally intricate issues, and an extensive number of documents a mass tort or complex litigation case. Any case so designated shall be subject to electronic filing and service using the county's approved Electronic Service Provider. IN ST MARION SUPER CT ADMIN Rule 311(1-104)(3).
- The filing of electronic pleadings and other documents in MF and CC cases is entirely voluntary; however, once the case is initially filed electronically, all subsequent filings in the case shall remain in electronic format until the time for appeal is exhausted. IN ST MARION SUPER CT ADMIN Rule 311(1-104)(5).

    ii. *Documents eligible for electronic filing.* The following pleadings may be filed and served electronically:

- New case complaint and petitions. IN ST MARION SUPER CT ADMIN Rule 311(1-104)(8)(a).

- Original answers. IN ST MARION SUPER CT ADMIN Rule 311(1-104)(8)(a).

- Any other pleadings or document including but not limited to motions and appearance forms. IN ST MARION SUPER CT ADMIN Rule 311(1-104)(8)(a).

   iii. *Manner of electronic filing.* Parties shall E-file a document either:

- By registering to use the Electronic Filing Service Provider; or

- In person at the Marion County Clerk's office, by electronically filing through the Public Access Terminal. Parties filing in this manner shall be responsible for furnishing the document in an electronic format that will be compatible with the clerk's office-system to be uploaded in person. IN ST MARION SUPER CT ADMIN Rule 311(1-104)(9). For information on the Electronic Filing Service Provider and Public Access Terminal, refer to IN ST MARION SUPER CT ADMIN Rule 311(1-101).

- Registered users shall pay statutory filing fees for E-filed documents electronically to the Court through their EFSP. Filing fees are due and payable at the time of filing. IN ST MARION SUPER CT ADMIN Rule 311(2-104)(1). For more information on electronic filing fees, refer to IN ST MARION SUPER CT ADMIN Rule 311(2-104).

   iv. *Effect of electronic filing.* Any pleading filed electronically shall be considered as filed with the court when the transmission to the EFSP is complete. Any document E-filed by 11:59 p.m. local Indianapolis, Indiana time shall be deemed filed on that date. The EFSP is an agent of the Court for the purpose of electronic filing, receipt, service and retrieval of electronic documents. IN ST MARION SUPER CT ADMIN Rule 311(2-102).

- Upon completion of filing, the EFSP shall issue a confirmation receipt that includes the date and time of receipt. The confirmation receipt shall serve as proof of filing. IN ST MARION SUPER CT ADMIN Rule 311(2-102).

- In the event the Court rejects the submitted documents following review, the documents shall not become part of the official Court record and the filer will receive notification of the rejection. Users may be required to refile the instruments to meet necessary filing requirements. Documents may be filed through an E-filing system at any time that the Clerk's office is open to receive the filing or at such other times as may be designated by the clerk and posted publicly. IN ST MARION SUPER CT ADMIN Rule 311(2-102).

- Documents filed through the E-filing system are deemed filed when received by the Clerk's office, except that documents received at times that the Clerk's office is closed shall be deemed filed the next regular time when the Clerk's office is open for filing. The time stamp issued by the E-filing system shall be presumed to be the time the document is received by the Clerk. IN ST MARION SUPER CT ADMIN Rule 311(2-102).

   v. *Electronically filed documents.* All pleadings and other documents designated in IN ST MARION SUPER CT ADMIN Rule 311 shall be filed and served electronically in any individual case which has been approved for electronic filing and service. IN ST MARION SUPER CT ADMIN Rule 311(1-104)(6).

   vi. *System failures.* When filing by electronic means is hindered by a technical failure, a party may file with the Clerk of Marion County in hard copy. With the exception of deadlines that by law cannot be extended, the time for filing of any paper that is delayed due to technical failure of the site shall be extended for one (1) day for each day on which such failure occurs, unless otherwise ordered by the Court. IN ST MARION SUPER CT ADMIN Rule 311(2-108).

   vii. *Compliance with rules.* All filing shall comply with the requirements of IN ST ADMIN Rule 9 and IN ST ADMIN Rule 16; and the Indiana Rules of Court and the Marion County Local Rules. IN ST MARION SUPER CT ADMIN Rule 311(1-104)(11).

  e. *Filing for special judge.* When a Special Judge who is not a Marion County Judge is selected, all parties or attorneys shall furnish such Judge with copies of all filings prior to the qualification of such Special Judge. Thereafter, copies of all filings shall be delivered in person, by mail or by facsimile to the office of the Special Judge with certificate of forwarding same made a part of the filing. IN ST MARION CIR AND SUPER CTS CIV Rule 205(C).

f. *Proof of filing.* Any party filing any paper by any method other than personal delivery to the clerk shall retain proof of filing. IN ST TRIAL P Rule 5(F).

2. *Service requirements.* Unless otherwise provided by the Indiana Rules of Trial Procedure or an order of the court, each party and special judge, if any, shall be served with: (1) every order required by its terms to be served; (2) every pleading subsequent to the original complaint; (3) every written motion except one which may be heard ex parte; (4) every brief submitted to the trial court; (5) every paper relating to discovery required to be served upon a party; and (6) every written notice, appearance, demand, offer of judgment, designation of record on appeal, or similar paper. IN ST TRIAL P Rule 5(A).

a. *Methods of service*

i. *Personal service.* Whenever a party is represented by an attorney of record, service shall be made upon such attorney unless service upon the party himself is ordered by the court. Service upon the attorney or party shall be made by delivering or mailing a copy of the papers to the last known address or where an attorney or party has consented to service by fax or e-mail, as provided in IN ST TRIAL P Rule 3.1(A)(4), by faxing or e-mailing a copy of the documents to the fax number or e-mail address set out in the appearance form or correction as required by IN ST TRIAL P Rule 3.1(E). IN ST TRIAL P Rule 5(B). Delivery of a copy within IN ST TRIAL P Rule 5 means:

- Offering or tendering it to the attorney or party and stating the nature of the papers being served. Refusal to accept an offered or tendered document is a waiver of any objection to the sufficiency or adequacy of service of that document;

- Leaving it at his office with a clerk or other person in charge thereof, or if there is no one in charge, leaving it in a conspicuous place therein; or

- If the office is closed, by leaving it at his dwelling house or usual place of abode with some person of suitable age and discretion then residing therein; or,

- Leaving it at some other suitable place, selected by the attorney upon whom service is being made, pursuant to duly promulgated local rule. IN ST TRIAL P Rule 5(B)(1).

ii. *Service by mail.* If service is made by mail, the papers shall be deposited in the United States mail addressed to the person on whom they are being served, with postage prepaid. Service shall be deemed complete upon mailing. Proof of service of all papers permitted to be mailed may be made by written acknowledgment of service, by affidavit of the person who mailed the papers, or by certificate of an attorney. It shall be the duty of attorneys when entering their appearance in a cause or when filing pleadings or papers therein, to have noted in the Chronological Case Summary or said pleadings or papers so filed the address and telephone number of their office. Service by delivery or by mail at such address shall be deemed sufficient and complete. IN ST TRIAL P Rule 5(B)(2).

iii. *Service by fax or e-mail.* A party who has consented to service by fax or e-mail may be served as follows:

- Service by e-mail shall be made by attaching the document being served in .pdf format. Discovery documents must also be served in accordance with IN ST TRIAL P Rule 26(A). IN ST TRIAL P Rule 5(B)(3)(a).

- Service by fax shall be deemed complete upon generation of a transmission record indicating the successful transmission of the entire document, except as provided in IN ST TRIAL P Rule 5(B)(3)(d). IN ST TRIAL P Rule 5(B)(3)(b).

- Service by e-mail shall be deemed complete upon transmission, except as provided in IN ST TRIAL P Rule 5(B)(3)(d). IN ST TRIAL P Rule 5(B)(3)(c).

- Service by fax or e-mail that occurs on a Saturday, Sunday, legal holiday, or day the court or agency in which the matter is pending is closed or after 5:00 PM local time of the recipient shall be deemed complete the next day that is not a Saturday, Sunday, legal holiday, or day that the court or agency in which the matter is pending is not closed. IN ST TRIAL P Rule 5(B)(3)(d).

iv. *Electronic service.* Delivery of E-service documents through the EFSP to other registered users shall be considered as valid and effective service and shall have the same legal effect as an original paper document. Recipients of E-service documents shall access their documents through the EFSP. IN ST MARION SUPER CT ADMIN Rule 311(2-107)(1).

- E-service shall be deemed complete when the transmission to the EFSP is completed. IN ST MARION SUPER CT ADMIN Rule 311(2-107)(2).

- For the purpose of computing time to respond to documents received via E-service, any document served on a day or at a time when the Clerk's office is not open for business shall be deemed served at the time of next opening of the Clerk's office for business. IN ST MARION SUPER CT ADMIN Rule 311(2-107)(3).

b. *Serving numerous defendants.* In any action in which there are unusually large numbers of defendants, the court, upon motion or of its own initiative, may order:

i. That service of the pleadings of the defendants and replies thereto need not be made as between the defendants;

- That any cross-claim, counterclaim, or matter constituting an avoidance or affirmative defense contained therein shall be deemed to be denied or avoided by all other parties; and

- That the filing of any such pleading and service thereof upon the plaintiff constitutes due notice of it to the parties. IN ST TRIAL P Rule 5(D).

ii. A copy of every such order shall be served upon the parties in such manner and form as the court directs. IN ST TRIAL P Rule 5(D).

c. *Service by electronic means.* Courts wishing to establish an electronic service pilot project pursuant to the Indiana Administrative Rules must submit a written request for approval and a plan to the Division of State Court Administration. IN ST ADMIN Rule 16(B).

d. *Service on parties in default for failure to appear.* No service need be made on parties in default for failure to appear, except that pleadings asserting new or additional claims for relief against them shall be served upon them in the manner provided by service of summons in IN ST TRIAL P Rule 4. IN ST TRIAL P Rule 5(A).

G. Hearings

1. *Hearing on motion.* Unless local conditions make it impracticable, each judge shall establish regular times and places, at intervals sufficiently frequent for the prompt dispatch of business, at which motions requiring notice and hearing may be heard and disposed of; but the judge at any time or place and on such notice, if any, as he considers reasonable may make order for the advancement, conduct, and hearing of actions. To expedite its business the court may direct the submission and determination of motions without oral hearing upon brief written statements of reasons in support and opposition, or direct or permit hearings by telephone conference call with all attorneys or other similar means of communication. IN ST TRIAL P Rule 73(A).

2. *Time and place of hearing.* If the motion requires a hearing or oral argument, the Court shall set the time and place of hearing or argument on the motion. IN ST MARION CIR AND SUPER CTS CIV Rule 203(A).

H. Forms

1. Motion for Leave to Amend Forms for Indiana

a. Motion to file amended complaint. 5 INPRAC § 3:5.1.

b. Motion to file amended complaint; Another form. 5 INPRAC § 3:5.2.

c. Motion to amend pleading to conform to evidence. 5 INPRAC § 3:5.4.

d. Motion to amend complaint to compel joinder of defendant. 5 INPRAC § 3:7.2.

e. Motion to amend caption. 9 INPRAC § 3.41.

f. Affidavit in support of motion to amend caption. 9 INPRAC § 3.42.

g. Motion for leave to amend complaint following dismissal. 9 INPRAC § 42.16.

h.   Motion for leave to file amended complaint against third party defendant. 10 INPRAC § 44.8.

i.   Motion to file amended complaint. 10 INPRAC § 46.7.

j.   Motion to amend complaint which has been dismissed; Filed more than 10 days after notice of dismissal. 10 INPRAC § 46.8.

k.   Motion to amend pleading; Another form. 10 INPRAC § 46.9.

l.   Order granting leave to amend complaint. 10 INPRAC § 46.10.

m.   Amendment by stipulation. 10 INPRAC § 46.11.

n.   Amended answer by interlineation. 10 INPRAC § 46.12.

o.   Objections to motion to amend complaint. 10 INPRAC § 46:13.

p.   Motion to amend pleading to conform to evidence. 10 INPRAC § 46.14.

q.   Motion for leave to change defendant after statute of limitations. 10 INPRAC § 46.16.

r.   Motion for leave to add party after statute of limitations. 10 INPRAC § 46.17.

s.   Motion to substitute real party in interest; Assignee of interest. 10 INPRAC § 47.10.

t.   Motion to amend complaint to compel joinder of defendant. 10 INPRAC § 49.3.

u.   Certificate of service; Personal service. 9 INPRAC § 5.7.

v.   Certificate of service; First class mail. 9 INPRAC § 5.8.

I.   Checklist

(I)   ❏ Matters to be considered by moving party

  (a)   ❏ Required documents

    (1)   ❏ Motion and notice

    (2)   ❏ Statement of approval or disapproval

    (3)   ❏ Copy of amended pleading

    (4)   ❏ Proposed order

    (5)   ❏ Certificate of service

  (b)   ❏ Supplemental documents

    (1)   ❏ Supporting evidence

    (2)   ❏ Request for oral argument

    (3)   ❏ Facsimile cover sheet

  (c)   ❏ Timing

    (1)   ❏ A party may amend his pleading once as a matter of course at any time before a responsive pleading is served or, if the pleading is one to which no responsive pleading is permitted, and the action has not been placed upon the trial calendar, he may so amend it at any time within thirty (30) days after it is served

    (2)   ❏ Otherwise a party may amend his pleading only by leave of court or by written consent of the adverse party; and leave shall be given when justice so requires

    (3)   ❏ A written motion, other than one which may be heard ex parte, and notice of the hearing thereof shall be served not less than five (5) days before the time specified for the hearing, unless a different period is fixed by the Indiana Rules of Trial Procedure or by order of the court

    (4)   ❏ All pleadings and papers subsequent to the complaint which are required to be served upon a party shall be filed with the Court either before service or within a reasonable period of time thereafter

(II) ❑ Matters to be considered by the responding party

   (a) ❑ Required documents

      (1) ❑ Opposition

      (2) ❑ Certificate of service

   (b) ❑ Supplemental documents

      (1) ❑ Supporting evidence

      (2) ❑ Proposed order

      (3) ❑ Facsimile cover sheet

   (c) ❑ Timing

      (1) ❑ If the statement regarding the position of the opposing party(ies) required under IN ST MARION CIR AND SUPER CTS CIV Rule 203(A) indicates that objection to the granting of said motion may ensue, said objecting a party shall have fifteen (15) days from the date of filing to file a response to said motion

      (2) ❑ Except as otherwise provided in IN ST TRIAL P Rule 59(D), opposing affidavits may be served not less than one (1) day before the hearing, unless the court permits them to be served at some other time

Motions, Oppositions and Replies
Motion for Summary Judgment

Document Last Updated October 2013

A. Applicable Rules

1. *State rules*

   a. Appearance. IN ST TRIAL P Rule 3.1.

   b. Process. IN ST TRIAL P Rule 4.

   c. Service and filing of pleadings and other papers. IN ST TRIAL P Rule 5.

   d. Time. IN ST TRIAL P Rule 6.

   e. Pleadings. IN ST TRIAL P Rule 7; IN ST TRIAL P Rule 8; IN ST TRIAL P Rule 9.2; IN ST TRIAL P Rule 10.

   f. Signing and verification of pleadings. IN ST TRIAL P Rule 11.

   g. Evidence. IN ST TRIAL P Rule 43.

   h. Judgment on the evidence (directed verdict). IN ST TRIAL P Rule 50.

   i. Findings by the court. IN ST TRIAL P Rule 52.

   j. Summary judgment. IN ST TRIAL P Rule 56.

   k. Motion to correct error. IN ST TRIAL P Rule 59.

   l. Relief from judgment or order. IN ST TRIAL P Rule 60.

   m. Hearing of motions. IN ST TRIAL P Rule 73.

   n. Access to court records. IN ST ADMIN Rule 9.

   o. Paper size. IN ST ADMIN Rule 11.

   p. Facsimile transmission. IN ST ADMIN Rule 12.

   q. Electronic filing and electronic service pilot projects. IN ST ADMIN Rule 16.

   r. Sealing of certain records by court; Hearing; Notice. IN ST 5-14-3-5.5.

   s. Privacy and confidentiality. IN ST 5-2-9-6; IN ST 5-14-3-4; IN ST 6-4.1-5-10; IN ST 6-4.1-12-12;

IN ST 6-8.1-7-1; IN ST 11-13-1-8; IN ST 12-23-14-13; IN ST 16-39-3-10; IN ST 16-41-8-1; IN ST 22-4-19-6; IN ST 31-11-1-6; IN ST 31-19-5-23; IN ST 31-19-13-2; IN ST 31-19-19-1; IN ST 31-33-18-1; IN ST 31-39-1-1; IN ST 31-39-1-2; IN ST 33-23-16-16; IN ST 35-34-2-4; IN ST 35-38-1-13; IN ST 35-38-9-1; IN ST ADR Rule 2.11; IN ST ADR Rule 4.4; IN ST ADR Rule 5.6; IN ST JURY Rule 10.

2. *Local rules*

   a. Requirements for motions. IN ST MARION CIR AND SUPER CTS CIV Rule 203.

   b. Preparation of pleadings, motions and other papers. IN ST MARION CIR AND SUPER CTS CIV Rule 204.

   c. Filing of pleadings, motions and other papers. IN ST MARION CIR AND SUPER CTS CIV Rule 205.

   d. Signing and verification of pleadings, motions and other papers; Service on opposing party. IN ST MARION CIR AND SUPER CTS CIV Rule 206.

   e. Motions for continuance. IN ST MARION CIR AND SUPER CTS CIV Rule 215.

   f. Electronic filing. IN ST MARION SUPER CT ADMIN Rule 311.

B. Timing

1. *Time for moving for summary judgment*

   a. *For claimant.* A party seeking to recover upon a claim, counterclaim, or cross-claim or to obtain a declaratory judgment may, at any time after the expiration of twenty (20) days from the commencement of the action or after service of a motion for summary judgment by the adverse party, move with or without supporting affidavits for a summary judgment in his favor upon all or any part thereof. IN ST TRIAL P Rule 56(A).

   b. *For defending party.* A party against whom a claim, counterclaim, or cross-claim is asserted or a declaratory judgment is sought may, at any time, move with or without supporting affidavits for a summary judgment in his favor as to all or any part thereof. IN ST TRIAL P Rule 56(B).

   c. *Filing.* All pleadings and papers subsequent to the complaint which are required to be served upon a party shall be filed with the Court either before service or within a reasonable period of time thereafter. IN ST TRIAL P Rule 5(E)(1).

2. *Service.* A written motion, other than one which may be heard ex parte, and notice of the hearing thereof shall be served not less than five (5) days before the time specified for the hearing, unless a different period is fixed by the Indiana Rules of Trial Procedure or by order of the court. IN ST TRIAL P Rule 6(D).

   a. *Of supporting affidavits.* When a motion is supported by affidavit, the affidavit shall be served with the motion. IN ST TRIAL P Rule 6(D).

3. *Service of opposition*

   a. *Filing.* If the statement regarding the position of the opposing party(ies) required under IN ST MARION CIR AND SUPER CTS CIV Rule 203(A) indicates that objection to the granting of said motion may ensue, said objecting a party shall have fifteen (15) days from the date of filing to file a response to said motion. IN ST MARION CIR AND SUPER CTS CIV Rule 203(B).

   b. *Service.* An adverse party shall have thirty (30) days after service of the motion to serve a response and any opposing affidavits. IN ST TRIAL P Rule 56(C).

      i. Except as otherwise provided in IN ST TRIAL P Rule 59(D), opposing affidavits may be served not less than one (1) day before the hearing, unless the court permits them to be served at some other time. IN ST TRIAL P Rule 6(D).

4. *Computation of time*

   a. *Generally; Days excluded.* In computing any period of time prescribed or allowed by the Indiana Rules of Trial Procedure, by order of the court, or by any applicable statute, the day of the act, event, or default from which the designated period of time begins to run shall not be included. The last day of the period so computed is to be included unless it is:

      i. A Saturday,

    ii.   A Sunday,

    iii.   A legal holiday as defined by state statute, or

    iv.   A day the office in which the act is to be done is closed during regular business hours. IN ST TRIAL P Rule 6(A).

b.   *Short periods.* In any event, the period runs until the end of the next day that is not a Saturday, a Sunday, a legal holiday, or a day on which the office is closed. When the period of time allowed is less than seven (7) days, intermediate Saturdays, Sundays, legal holidays, and days on which the office is closed shall be excluded from the computations. IN ST TRIAL P Rule 6(A).

c.   *Additional time after service by United States mail.* Whenever a party has the right or is required to do some act or take some proceedings within a prescribed period after the service of a notice or other paper upon him and the notice or paper is served upon him by United States mail, three (3) days shall be added to the prescribed period. IN ST TRIAL P Rule 6(E).

d.   *Enlargement of time.* When an act is required or allowed to be done at or within a specific time by the Indiana Rules of Trial Procedure, the court may at any time for cause shown:

    i.   Order the period enlarged, with or without motion or notice, if request therefor is made before the expiration of the period originally prescribed or extended by a previous order; or

    ii.   Upon motion made after the expiration of the specific period, permit the act to be done where the failure to act was the result of excusable neglect; but, the court may not extend the time for taking any action for judgment on the evidence under IN ST TRIAL P Rule 50(A), amendment of findings and judgment under IN ST TRIAL P Rule 52(B), to correct errors under IN ST TRIAL P Rule 59(C), statement in opposition to motion to correct error under IN ST TRIAL P Rule 59(E), or to obtain relief from final judgment under IN ST TRIAL P Rule 60(B), except to the extent and under the conditions stated in those rules. IN ST TRIAL P Rule 6(B).

e.   *Continuances disfavored.* Motions for Continuance are discouraged. Neither side is entitled to an automatic continuance as a matter of right. IN ST MARION CIR AND SUPER CTS CIV Rule 215. For information on obtaining a continuance, refer to IN ST MARION CIR AND SUPER CTS CIV Rule 215.

C. General Requirements

1.   *Motions, generally.* Unless made during a hearing or trial, or otherwise ordered by the court, an application to the court for an order shall be made by written motion. The motion shall state the grounds therefor and the relief or order sought. IN ST TRIAL P Rule 7(B).

   a.   *Motions as distinct from pleadings.* Motions and responses to motions are not pleadings, and allegations contained in a motion are not admissions of a party. 22B INPRAC 7:2; Wachstetter v. County Properties, LLC, 832 N.E.2d 574 (Ind.Ct.App. 2005); Scott County Family YMCA, Inc. v. Hobbs, 817 N.E.2d 603 (Ind.Ct.App. 2004).

   b.   *Unopposed motions generally granted.* It is common for a trial court to grant procedural motions, such as motions for enlargement of time, discovery motions, or motions for continuance, unless an objection is filed. 21 INPRAC § 13.8.

2.   *Motion for summary judgment.* Summary judgment is a procedure by which the trial court is asked to enter judgment when there are no genuine issues of material fact and the moving party is entitled to judgment as a matter of law. A summary judgment proceeding is not a trial, and is not intended to be a substitute for factual determinations where the facts are in dispute. Rather, summary judgment should be used to terminate litigation about which there is no factual dispute and which may be determined as a matter of law. 11 INPRAC § 90.1; LeBrun v. Conner, 702 N.E.2d 754 (Ind.Ct.App. 1998).

   a.   *Burden.* The judgment sought shall be rendered forthwith if the designated evidentiary matter shows that there is no genuine issue as to any material fact and that the moving party is entitled to a judgment as a matter of law. IN ST TRIAL P Rule 56(C).

    i.   A "genuine" issue of material fact exists if the trier of fact must resolve the opposing party's differing version of the underlying facts or if the undisputed facts support conflicting reasonable inferences. A fact is "material" if it might affect the outcome of a case by helping to prove or disprove an essential element of a claim or defense, or it facilitates a resolution of an issue in the case. 22B INPRAC 56:1; Williams v. Tharp, 914 N.E.2d 756 (Ind. 2009).

ii. Summary judgment shall not be granted as of course because the opposing party fails to offer opposing affidavits or evidence, but the court shall make its determination from the evidentiary matter designated to the court. IN ST TRIAL P Rule 56(C).

iii. The trial court must evaluate the evidence in favor of the non-moving party. 22B INPRAC 56:1.

iv. Although Indiana courts are not consistent in describing the amount of proof required to sustain the moving party's initial burden, and IN ST TRIAL P Rule 56 is silent on the matter, a number of cases require "prima facie" proof. 22B INPRAC 56:5; DeHahn v. CSX Transp., Inc., 925 N.E.2d 442 (Ind.Ct.App. 2010). Once the moving party demonstrates the requirements for summary judgment, the burden shifts to the non-moving party to designate each material issue of fact which he asserts precludes entry of summary judgment and the evidence relevant to each designated fact. 22B INPRAC 56:5; Booth v. Wiley, 839 N.E.2d 1168 (Ind. 2005).

b. *When motion not required.* When any party has moved for summary judgment, the court may grant summary judgment for any other party upon the issues raised by the motion although no motion for summary judgment is filed by such party. IN ST TRIAL P Rule 56(B).

c. *Judgment on less than all issues or claims.* A summary judgment may be rendered upon less than all the issues or claims, including without limitation the issue of liability or damages alone although there is a genuine issue as to damages or liability as the case may be. IN ST TRIAL P Rule 56(C).

i. *Partial judgment not entered; Exceptions.* A summary judgment upon less than all the issues involved in a claim or with respect to less than all the claims or parties shall be interlocutory unless the court in writing expressly determines that there is no just reason for delay and in writing expressly directs entry of judgment as to less than all the issues, claims or parties. IN ST TRIAL P Rule 56(C).

ii. *Designation of specific findings.* The court shall designate the issues or claims upon which it finds no genuine issue as to any material facts. IN ST TRIAL P Rule 56(C).

iii. *Case not fully adjudicated on motion.* If on motion under IN ST TRIAL P Rule 56 judgment is not rendered upon the whole case or for all the relief asked and a trial is necessary, the court at the hearing of the motion, by examining the pleadings and the evidence before it and by interrogating counsel, shall if practicable ascertain what material facts exist without substantial controversy and what material facts are actually and in good faith controverted. It shall thereupon make an order specifying the facts that appear without substantial controversy, including the extent to which the amount of damages or other relief is not in controversy, and directing such further proceedings in the action as are just. Upon the trial of the action the facts so specified shall be deemed established, and the trial shall be conducted accordingly. IN ST TRIAL P Rule 56(D).

d. *Form of affidavits; Further testimony; Defense required.* Supporting and opposing affidavits shall be made on personal knowledge, shall set forth such facts as would be admissible in evidence, and shall show affirmatively that the affiant is competent to testify to the matters stated therein. IN ST TRIAL P Rule 56(E).

i. Sworn or certified copies not previously self-authenticated of all papers or parts thereof referred to in an affidavit shall be attached thereto or served therewith. IN ST TRIAL P Rule 56(E).

ii. The court may permit affidavits to be supplemented or opposed by depositions, answers to interrogatories, or further affidavits. IN ST TRIAL P Rule 56(E).

iii. When a motion for summary judgment is made and supported as provided in IN ST TRIAL P Rule 56, an adverse party may not rest upon the mere allegations or denials of his pleading, but his response, by affidavits or as otherwise provided in IN ST TRIAL P Rule 56, must set forth specific facts showing that there is a genuine issue for trial. If he does not so respond, summary judgment, if appropriate, shall be entered against him. Denial of summary judgment may be challenged by a motion to correct errors after a final judgment or order is entered. IN ST TRIAL P Rule 56(E).

e. *When affidavits are unavailable.* Should it appear from the affidavits of a party opposing the motion that he cannot for reasons stated present by affidavit facts essential to justify his opposition, the court may refuse the application for judgment or may order a continuance to permit affidavits to be obtained or depositions to be taken or discovery to be had or may make such other order as is just. IN ST TRIAL P Rule 56(F).

f. *Affidavits made in bad faith.* Should it appear to the satisfaction of the court at any time that any of the affidavits presented pursuant to IN ST TRIAL P Rule 56 are presented in bad faith or solely for the purpose of delay, the court shall forthwith order the party employing them to pay to the other party the amount of the reasonable expenses which the filing of the affidavits caused him to incur, including reasonable attorney's fees, and any offending party or attorney may be adjudged guilty of contempt. IN ST TRIAL P Rule 56(G).

g. *Party opposing the motion.* A party opposing the motion shall also designate to the court each material issue of fact which that party asserts precludes entry of summary judgment and the evidence relevant thereto. IN ST TRIAL P Rule 56(C).

h. *Appeal; Reversal.* No judgment rendered on the motion shall be reversed on the ground that there is a genuine issue of material fact unless the material fact and the evidence relevant thereto shall have been specifically designated to the trial court. IN ST TRIAL P Rule 56(H).

D. Documents

1. *Required documents*

    a. *Motion and notice.* The requirement of notice is satisfied by service of the motion. IN ST TRIAL P Rule 7(B); IN ST MARION CIR AND SUPER CTS CIV Rule 203(A). Refer to the General Requirements section of this document for information on the content of a motion for summary judgment.

    b. *Supporting evidence.* At the time of filing the motion or response, a party shall designate to the court all parts of pleadings, depositions, answers to interrogatories, admissions, matters of judicial notice, and any other matters on which it relies for purposes of the motion. IN ST TRIAL P Rule 56(C).

        i. The party moving for judgment must designate sufficient evidence to establish that there is no genuine issue of material fact and that judgment is proper as a matter of law. 22B INPRAC 56:4; Jarboe v. Landmark Community Newspapers of Indiana, Inc., 644 N.E.2d 118 (Ind. 1994).

    c. *Statement of approval or disapproval.* Except for initial motions made pursuant to IN ST MARION CIR AND SUPER CTS CIV Rule 203(D), all motions filed with the court shall include a brief statement indicating whether opposing party(ies) object to or approve of the granting of said motion. IN ST MARION CIR AND SUPER CTS CIV Rule 203(A).

    d. *Proposed order.* Unless local practice provides differently, a party should submit a proposed order with its written motion to be signed by the judge once the motion has been granted. 21 INPRAC § 13.8. All motions seeking an order of the Court shall be accompanied by a sufficient number of orders to be executed by the Court in granting said motion. In addition to the orders, the notice shall be accompanied by stamped, addressed envelopes to all parties of record. IN ST MARION CIR AND SUPER CTS CIV Rule 203(E).

    e. *Certificate of service.* An attorney or unrepresented party tendering a document to the Clerk for filing shall certify that service has been made, list the parties served, and specify the date and means of service. The certificate of service shall be placed at the end of the document and shall not be separately filed. The separate filing of a certificate of service, however, shall not be grounds for rejecting a document for filing. The Clerk may permit documents to be filed without a certificate of service but shall require prompt filing of a separate certificate of service. IN ST TRIAL P Rule 5(C). In all cases where any pleading or other document is required to be served upon opposing counsel, proof of such service may be made either by:

        i. A certificate of service signed by counsel of record for the serving party and the certificate shall specify by name and address all counsel upon whom the pleading or document was served; or

        ii. An acknowledgment of service signed by the party served or counsel of record. IN ST MARION CIR AND SUPER CTS CIV Rule 206.

2. *Supplemental documents*

   a. *Additional supporting evidence.* When a motion is based on facts not appearing of record the court may hear the matter on affidavits presented by the respective parties, but the court may direct that the matter be heard wholly or partly on oral testimony or depositions. IN ST TRIAL P Rule 43(B).

   b. *Request for oral argument.* When an oral argument is requested, the request shall be by separate instrument and filed with the pleading to be argued. Any such oral argument requested may be heard at the discretion of the Court, except for motions for summary judgment which shall be set for hearing upon request of any party. IN ST MARION CIR AND SUPER CTS CIV Rule 203(C).

   c. *Facsimile cover sheet.* Any document sent to the Clerk of the Circuit Court by electronic facsimile transmission shall be accompanied by a cover sheet which states the title of the document, case number, number of pages, identity and voice telephone number of the sending party and instructions for filing. The cover sheet shall contain the signature of the attorney or party, pro se, authorizing the filing. IN ST ADMIN Rule 12(D).

E. Format

1. *Form of motions.* The rules applicable to captions, and the signing and form of pleadings (IN ST TRIAL P Rule 8 through IN ST TRIAL P Rule 11), apply to all motions and other papers provided under the Indiana Rules of Trial Procedure. 22B INPRAC 7:2.

2. *Form of pleadings*

   a. *Caption; Names of parties.* Every pleading shall contain a caption setting forth the name of the court, the title of the action, the file number, and a designation as in IN ST TRIAL P Rule 7(A). In the complaint the title of the action shall include the names of all the parties, but in other pleadings it is sufficient to state the name of the first party on each side with an appropriate indication of other parties. IN ST TRIAL P Rule 10(A).

      i. Every pleading shall contain a caption setting forth the name of the Court, the Division and Room Number, the title of the action and the file number. IN ST MARION CIR AND SUPER CTS CIV Rule 204(B).

   b. *Paragraphs; Separate statements.* All averments of a claim or defense shall be made in numbered paragraphs, the contents of each of which shall be limited as far as practicable to a statement of a single set of circumstances, and a paragraph may be referred to by number in all succeeding pleadings. Each claim founded upon a separate transaction or occurrence and each defense other than denials may be stated in a separate count or defense whenever a separation facilitates the clear presentation of the matters set forth. IN ST TRIAL P Rule 10(B).

   c. *Adoption by reference; Exhibits.* Statements in a pleading may be adopted by reference in a different part of the same pleading or in another pleading or in any motion. A copy of any written instrument which is an exhibit to a pleading is a part thereof for all purposes. IN ST TRIAL P Rule 10(C).

   d. *Paper.* Pleadings, motions and other papers may be either printed or typewritten on white opaque paper of at least sixteen (16) pound weight, eight and one-half (8-1/2) inches wide and eleven (11) inches in length. IN ST MARION CIR AND SUPER CTS CIV Rule 204(A).

   e. *Copies.* All copies shall likewise be on white paper of sufficient strength and durability to resist normal wear and tear. IN ST MARION CIR AND SUPER CTS CIV Rule 204(A).

   f. *Line spacing.* If typewritten, the lines shall be double spaced, except for quotations, which shall be indented and single spaced. IN ST MARION CIR AND SUPER CTS CIV Rule 204(A).

   g. *Script type.* Script type shall not be used. IN ST MARION CIR AND SUPER CTS CIV Rule 204(A).

   h. *Titles.* Titles on all pleadings shall delineate each topic included in the pleading e.g. where a pleading contains an Answer, a Motion to Strike or Dismiss, or a Jury Request each shall be set forth in the title. IN ST MARION CIR AND SUPER CTS CIV Rule 204(C).

   i. *Margins and binding.* Margins shall be one (1) inch. Binding or stapling shall be at the top and at no other place. Covers or backing shall not be used. IN ST MARION CIR AND SUPER CTS CIV Rule 204(D).

3. *Size of papers for filing.* Effective January 1, 1992, all pleadings, copies, motions and documents filed with any trial court or appellate level court, typed or printed, with the exception of exhibits and existing wills, shall be prepared on eight and one-half by eleven inch (8 1/2" x 11") size paper. IN ST ADMIN Rule 11.

4. *Form of electronically filed documents.* All electronically filed and served pleadings shall, to the extent practicable, be formatted in accordance with the applicable rules governing formatting of paper pleadings. IN ST MARION SUPER CT ADMIN Rule 311(2-103)(1).

   a. *Electronic document title.* The electronic document title of each pleading or other document shall include:

      i. Party or parties filing/serving the document,

      ii. Nature of the document,

      iii. Party or parties against whom relief, if any, is sought, and

      iv. Nature of the relief sought (e.g., Defendant ABC Corporation's Motion for Summary Judgment). IN ST MARION SUPER CT ADMIN Rule 311(2-103)(2).

5. *Signature requirements*

   a. *Signature of attorney.* Every pleading or motion of a party represented by an attorney shall be signed by at least one (1) attorney of record in his individual name, whose address, telephone number, and attorney number shall be stated, except that this provision shall not apply to pleadings and motions made and transcribed at the trial or a hearing before the judge and received by him in such form. IN ST TRIAL P Rule 11(A).

      i. All pleadings and motions shall contain the original or authorized signature of the attorney, the name of the attorney in typed or printed form, the name of the law firm if a member of a firm, the attorney's address, identification number, e-mail address, telephone number, fax number, and the designation as to the party for whom he appears. IN ST MARION CIR AND SUPER CTS CIV Rule 204(E).

      ii. The signature of an attorney constitutes a certificate by him that he has read the pleadings; that to the best of his knowledge, information, and belief, there is good ground to support it; and that it is not interposed for delay. IN ST TRIAL P Rule 11(A).

      iii. If a pleading or motion is not signed or is signed with intent to defeat the purpose of the rule, it may be stricken as sham and false and the action may proceed as though the pleading had not been served. IN ST TRIAL P Rule 11(A).

      iv. For a willful violation of IN ST TRIAL P Rule 11 an attorney may be subjected to appropriate disciplinary action. Similar action may be taken if scandalous or indecent matter is inserted. IN ST TRIAL P Rule 11(A).

      v. Every pleading, document, and instrument electronically filed or served shall be deemed to have been signed by the judge, clerk, attorney or declarant and shall bear a facsimile or typographical signature of such person, along with the typed name, address, telephone number, and Bar number of a signing attorney. Typographical signatures shall be treated as personal signatures for all purposes under these rules. IN ST MARION SUPER CT ADMIN Rule 311(2-105).

         - Documents containing signatures of third-parties (i.e., unopposed motions, affidavits, stipulations, etc.) may also be filed electronically by indicating that the original signatures are maintained by the filing party in paper-format. IN ST MARION SUPER CT ADMIN Rule 311(2-105).

         - Unless otherwise ordered by the Court or Clerk, a printed copy of all documents filed or served electronically, including original signatures, shall be maintained by the party filing the document and shall be made available, upon reasonable notice, for inspection by other counsel, the Clerk or Court. Parties shall retain originals until two (2) years after all time periods for appeal have expired. From time to time, it may be necessary to provide the Clerk or Court with a hard copy of an electronically filed document. IN ST MARION SUPER CT ADMIN Rule 311(2-105).

    vi.   For the recommended format of a signature block, refer to IN ST MARION CIR AND SUPER CTS CIV Rule 204(E).

  b.   *Signature of unrepresented party.* A party who is not represented by an attorney shall sign his pleading and state his address. IN ST TRIAL P Rule 11(A).

  c.   *Verification not generally required.* Except when specifically required by rule, pleadings or motions need not be verified or accompanied by affidavit. The rule in equity that the averments of an answer under oath must be overcome by the testimony of two (2) witnesses or of one (1) witness sustained by corroborating circumstances is abolished. IN ST TRIAL P Rule 11(A).

  d.   *Verification by affirmation or representation.* When in connection with any civil or special statutory proceeding it is required that any pleading, motion, petition, supporting affidavit, or other document of any kind, be verified, or that an oath be taken, it shall be sufficient if the subscriber simply affirms the truth of the matter to be verified by an affirmation or representation. IN ST TRIAL P Rule 11(B). IN ST TRIAL P Rule 11(B) states that the affirmation or representation should be in substantially the following language: "I (we) affirm, under the penalties for perjury, that the foregoing representation(s) is (are) true. (Signed) _____."

    i.   Any person who falsifies an affirmation or representation of fact shall be subject to the same penalties as are prescribed by law for the making of a false affidavit. IN ST TRIAL P Rule 11(B).

  e.   *Verified pleadings, motions, and affidavits as evidence.* Pleadings, motions and affidavits accompanying or in support of such pleadings or motions when required to be verified or under oath shall be accepted as a representation that the signer had personal knowledge thereof or reasonable cause to believe the existence of the facts or matters stated or alleged therein; and, if otherwise competent or acceptable as evidence, may be admitted as evidence of the facts or matters stated or alleged therein when it is so provided in the Indiana Rules of Trial Procedure, by statute or other law, or to the extent the writing or signature expressly purports to be made upon the signer's personal knowledge. When such pleadings, motions and affidavits are verified or under oath they shall not require other or greater proof on the part of the adverse party than if not verified or not under oath unless expressly provided otherwise by the Indiana Rules of Trial Procedure, statute or other law. Affidavits upon motions for summary judgment under IN ST TRIAL P Rule 56 and in denial of execution under IN ST TRIAL P Rule 9.2 shall be made upon personal knowledge. IN ST TRIAL P Rule 11(C).

6. *Information excluded from public access.* Every document filed in a case shall separately identify information excluded from public access pursuant to IN ST ADMIN Rule 9(G)(1) as follows:

  a.   Whole documents that are excluded from public access pursuant to IN ST ADMIN Rule 9(G)(1) shall be tendered on light green paper or have a light green coversheet attached to the document, marked "Not for Public Access" or "Confidential." IN ST TRIAL P Rule 5(G)(1).

  b.   When only a portion of a document contains information excluded from public access pursuant to IN ST ADMIN Rule 9(G)(1), said information shall be omitted [or redacted] from the filed document, and set forth on a separate accompanying document on light green paper conspicuously marked "Not for Public Access" or "Confidential" and clearly designated [or identifying] the caption and number of the case and the document and location within the document to which the redacted material pertains. IN ST TRIAL P Rule 5(G)(2).

  c.   With respect to documents filed in electronic format, the trial court, by local rule, may provide for compliance with IN ST TRIAL P Rule 5 in manner that separates and protects access to information excluded from public access. IN ST TRIAL P Rule 5(G)(3).

  d.   IN ST TRIAL P Rule 5(G) does not apply to a record sealed by the court pursuant to IN ST 5-14-3-5.5 or otherwise, nor to records, documents, or information filed in cases to which public access is prohibited pursuant to IN ST ADMIN Rule 9(G). IN ST TRIAL P Rule 5(G)(4).

  e.   The following information in case records is excluded from public access and is confidential:

    i.   Information that is excluded from public access pursuant to federal law;

ii. Information that is excluded from public access as declared confidential by Indiana statute or other court rule, including without limitation:

- All adoption records created after July 8, 1941, as declared confidential by IN ST 31-19-19-1, et seq., except those specifically declared open by IN ST 31-19-13-2(2);

- All records relating to chancroid, chlamydia, gonorrhea, hepatitis, human immunodeficiency virus (HIV), Lymphogranuloma venereum, syphilis, tuberculosis, as declared confidential by IN ST 16-41-8-1, et seq.;

- All records relating to child abuse as declared confidential by IN ST 31-33-18-1, et seq.;

- All records relating to drug tests as declared confidential by IN ST 5-14-3-4(a)(9);

- Records of grand jury proceedings as declared confidential by IN ST 35-34-2-4;

- Records of juvenile proceedings as declared confidential by IN ST 31-39-1-2, except those specifically open under statute;

- All paternity records created after July 1, 1941 as declared confidential by IN ST 31-14-11-15, IN ST 31-19-5-23, IN ST 31-39-1-1 and IN ST 31-39-1-2 [Editor's note: IN ST 31-14-11-15 was repealed effective May 9, 2013];

- All pre-sentence reports as declared confidential by IN ST 35-38-1-13;

- Written petitions to permit marriages without consent and orders directing the Clerk of Court to issue a marriage license to underage persons, as declared confidential by IN ST 31-11-1-6;

- Only those arrest warrants, search warrants, indictments and informations ordered confidential by the trial judge, prior to return of duly executed service as declared confidential by IN ST 5-14-3-4(b)(1);

- All medical, mental health, or tax records unless determined by law or regulation of any governmental custodian not to be confidential, released by the subject of such records, or declared by a court of competent jurisdiction to be essential to the resolution of litigation as declared confidential by IN ST 16-39-3-10, IN ST 6-4.1-5-10, IN ST 6-4.1-12-12, and IN ST 6-8.1-7-1;

- Personal information relating to jurors or prospective jurors, other than for the use of the parties and counsel, pursuant to IN ST JURY Rule 10;

- Information relating to protection from abuse orders, no-contact orders and workplace violence restraining orders as declared confidential by IN ST 5-2-9-6, et seq.;

- Mediation proceedings pursuant to IN ST ADR Rule 2.11, Mini-Trial proceedings pursuant to IN ST ADR Rule 4.4(C), and Summary Jury Trials pursuant to IN ST ADR Rule 5.6;

- Information in probation files pursuant to the Probation Standards promulgated by the Judicial Conference of Indiana pursuant to IN ST 11-13-1-8(b);

- Information deemed confidential pursuant to the Rules for Court Administered Alcohol and Drug Programs promulgated by the Judicial Conference of Indiana pursuant to IN ST 12-23-14-13;

- Information deemed confidential pursuant to the Problem-Solving Court Rules promulgated by the Judicial Conference of Indiana pursuant to IN ST 33-23-16-16;

- All records of the Department of workforce Development as declared confidential by IN ST 22-4-19-6;

- Information regarding interception of electronic communications that is sealed or deemed confidential as set forth in IN ST 35-33.5-2-1, et seq.

iii. Information excluded from public access by specific court order;

iv. Complete Social Security Numbers of living persons;

    v.   With the exception of names, information such as addresses, phone numbers, and dates of birth which explicitly identifies:

- Natural persons who are witnesses or victims (not including defendants) in criminal, domestic violence, stalking, sexual assault, juvenile, or civil protection order proceedings, provided that juveniles who are victims of sex crimes shall be identified by initials only;

- Places of residence of judicial officers, clerks and other employees of courts and clerks of court, unless the person or persons about whom the information pertains waives confidentiality;

    vi.   Complete account numbers of specific assets, loans, bank accounts, credit cards, and personal identification numbers (PINs);

    vii.   All orders of expungement entered in criminal or juvenile proceedings, orders to restrict access to criminal history information pursuant to IN ST 35-38-5-5.5 or IN ST 35-38-8-5 and records excluded from public access by such orders, and information related to infractions that is excluded from public access pursuant to IN ST 34-28-5-15 or IN ST 34-28-5-16 [Editor's note: IN ST 35-38-5-5.5, IN ST 35-38-8-5 and IN ST 34-28-5-16 were repealed effective July 1, 2013; for information on orders restricting access to criminal history, refer to IN ST 35-38-9-1, et seq.];

    viii.   All personal notes and e-mail, and deliberative material, of judges, jurors, court staff and judicial agencies, and information recorded in personal data assistants (PDA's) or organizers and personal calendars. IN ST ADMIN Rule 9(G)(1).

F. Filing and Service Requirements

1. *Filing requirements.* Except as otherwise provided in IN ST TRIAL P Rule 5(E)(2), all pleadings and papers subsequent to the complaint which are required to be served upon a party shall be filed with the Court either before service or within a reasonable period of time thereafter. IN ST TRIAL P Rule 5(E)(1). Counsel shall file with the court an original and one (1) copy of all briefs, and memoranda of law filed in support of a motion. IN ST MARION CIR AND SUPER CTS CIV Rule 205(D).

    a.   *Filing generally.* All pleadings, petitions and motions are filed with the Clerk designated by the Court at any time during office hours established by the Clerk and the Court. All orders submitted to the Court shall be in sufficient number and shall be accompanied by postage paid envelopes addressed to each party or counsel of record. IN ST MARION CIR AND SUPER CTS CIV Rule 205(A)

    b.   *Filing with the court defined.* The filing of pleadings, motions, and other papers with the court as required by the Indiana Rules of Trial Procedure shall be made by one of the following methods:

        i.   Delivery to the clerk of the court;

        ii.   Sending by electronic transmission under the procedure adopted pursuant to IN ST ADMIN Rule 12;

        iii.   Mailing to the clerk by registered, certified or express mail return receipt requested;

        iv.   Depositing with any third-party commercial carrier for delivery to the clerk within three (3) calendar days, cost prepaid, properly addressed;

        v.   If the court so permits, filing with the judge, in which event the judge shall note thereon the filing date and forthwith transmit them to the office of the clerk; or

        vi.   Electronic filing, as approved by the Division of State Court Administration pursuant to IN ST ADMIN Rule 16. IN ST TRIAL P Rule 5(F).

        vii.   Filing by registered or certified mail and by third-party commercial carrier shall be complete upon mailing or deposit. IN ST TRIAL P Rule 5(F).

    c.   *Facsimile filing.* Facsimile filing is discouraged, but permitted in the Marion Circuit and Marion Superior Court. All documents filed by facsimile shall also be filed in hard copy within seven (7) days of the facsimile filing, along with proposed orders and stamped addressed envelopes, as required by IN ST MARION CIR AND SUPER CTS CIV Rule 203(E). To avoid duplicate filings, the hard copies of the facsimile filing shall indicate in bold letters that the pleading was previously filed by facsimile transmission. Proof of transmission by facsimile, including certificate of service and manner of service, shall be the responsibility of the filing party. If the filing requires immediate attention of the Judge, it shall be so indicated in bold letters in an accompanying transmittal memorandum. Legibility of documents and timeliness of filing is the responsibility of the sender. IN ST MARION CIR AND SUPER CTS CIV Rule 205(B).

    i.   *Generally.* In counties where a majority of judges of the courts of record, by posted local rule, have authorized electronic facsimile filing and designated a telephone number to receive such transmissions, pleadings, motions, and other papers may be sent to the Clerk of Circuit Court by electronic facsimile transmission for filing in any case, provided:

- Such matter does not exceed ten (10) pages, including the cover sheet;

- Such matter does not require the payment of fees other than the electronic facsimile transcription fee set forth in IN ST ADMIN Rule 12(E);

- The sending party creates at the time of transmission a machine generated log for such transmission; and

- The original document and the transmission log are maintained by the sending party for the duration of the litigation. IN ST ADMIN Rule 12(B).

    ii.   *Time of filing.* During normal, posted business hours, the time of filing shall be the time the duplicate document is produced in the office of the Clerk of the Circuit Court. Duplicate documents received at all other times shall be filed as of the next normal business day. IN ST ADMIN Rule 12(C).

- If the receiving fax machine endorses its own time and date stamp upon the transmitted documents and the receiving machine produces a delivery receipt which is electronically created and transmitted to the sending party, the time of filing shall be the date and time recorded on the transmitted document by the receiving fax machine. IN ST ADMIN Rule 12(C).

  d. *Electronic filing.* Electronic filing and electronic service pilot projects are authorized pursuant to IN ST ADMIN Rule 16 and approved by the Division of State Court Administration. IN ST MARION SUPER CT ADMIN Rule 311(1-103).

    i.   *Cases where electronic filing accepted.* All Marion County Circuit and Superior civil courts may accept electronic filing and service of pleadings and other documents designated in this rule in mortgage foreclosure (hereinafter referred to as "MF"), civil collection(hereinafter referred to as "CC"), and individual cases that have been approved for electronic filing and service. IN ST MARION SUPER CT ADMIN Rule 311(1-104)(1).

- The Marion County Circuit Court may, upon the motion of a party or its own motion, designate a case that will involve multiple litigants, legally intricate issues, and an extensive number of documents a mass tort or complex litigation case. Any case so designated shall be subject to electronic filing and service using the county's approved Electronic Service Provider. IN ST MARION SUPER CT ADMIN Rule 311(1-104)(3).

- The filing of electronic pleadings and other documents in MF and CC cases is entirely voluntary; however, once the case is initially filed electronically, all subsequent filings in the case shall remain in electronic format until the time for appeal is exhausted. IN ST MARION SUPER CT ADMIN Rule 311(1-104)(5).

    ii.   *Documents eligible for electronic filing.* The following pleadings may be filed and served electronically:

- New case complaint and petitions. IN ST MARION SUPER CT ADMIN Rule 311(1-104)(8)(a).

- Original answers. IN ST MARION SUPER CT ADMIN Rule 311(1-104)(8)(a).

- Any other pleadings or document including but not limited to motions and appearance forms. IN ST MARION SUPER CT ADMIN Rule 311(1-104)(8)(a).

iii. *Manner of electronic filing.* Parties shall E-file a document either:

- By registering to use the Electronic Filing Service Provider; or

- In person at the Marion County Clerk's office, by electronically filing through the Public Access Terminal. Parties filing in this manner shall be responsible for furnishing the document in an electronic format that will be compatible with the clerk's office-system to be uploaded in person. IN ST MARION SUPER CT ADMIN Rule 311(1-104)(9). For information on the Electronic Filing Service Provider and Public Access Terminal, refer to IN ST MARION SUPER CT ADMIN Rule 311(1-101).

- Registered users shall pay statutory filing fees for E-filed documents electronically to the Court through their EFSP. Filing fees are due and payable at the time of filing. IN ST MARION SUPER CT ADMIN Rule 311(2-104)(1). For more information on electronic filing fees, refer to IN ST MARION SUPER CT ADMIN Rule 311(2-104).

iv. *Effect of electronic filing.* Any pleading filed electronically shall be considered as filed with the court when the transmission to the EFSP is complete. Any document E-filed by 11:59 p.m. local Indianapolis, Indiana time shall be deemed filed on that date. The EFSP is an agent of the Court for the purpose of electronic filing, receipt, service and retrieval of electronic documents. IN ST MARION SUPER CT ADMIN Rule 311(2-102).

- Upon completion of filing, the EFSP shall issue a confirmation receipt that includes the date and time of receipt. The confirmation receipt shall serve as proof of filing. IN ST MARION SUPER CT ADMIN Rule 311(2-102).

- In the event the Court rejects the submitted documents following review, the documents shall not become part of the official Court record and the filer will receive notification of the rejection. Users may be required to refile the instruments to meet necessary filing requirements. Documents may be filed through an E-filing system at any time that the Clerk's office is open to receive the filing or at such other times as may be designated by the clerk and posted publicly. IN ST MARION SUPER CT ADMIN Rule 311(2-102).

- Documents filed through the E-filing system are deemed filed when received by the Clerk's office, except that documents received at times that the Clerk's office is closed shall be deemed filed the next regular time when the Clerk's office is open for filing. The time stamp issued by the E-filing system shall be presumed to be the time the document is received by the Clerk. IN ST MARION SUPER CT ADMIN Rule 311(2-102).

v. *Electronically filed documents.* All pleadings and other documents designated in IN ST MARION SUPER CT ADMIN Rule 311 shall be filed and served electronically in any individual case which has been approved for electronic filing and service. IN ST MARION SUPER CT ADMIN Rule 311(1-104)(6).

vi. *System failures.* When filing by electronic means is hindered by a technical failure, a party may file with the Clerk of Marion County in hard copy. With the exception of deadlines that by law cannot be extended, the time for filing of any paper that is delayed due to technical failure of the site shall be extended for one (1) day for each day on which such failure occurs, unless otherwise ordered by the Court. IN ST MARION SUPER CT ADMIN Rule 311(2-108).

vii. *Compliance with rules.* All filing shall comply with the requirements of IN ST ADMIN Rule 9 and IN ST ADMIN Rule 16; and the Indiana Rules of Court and the Marion County Local Rules. IN ST MARION SUPER CT ADMIN Rule 311(1-104)(11).

e. *Filing for special judge.* When a Special Judge who is not a Marion County Judge is selected, all parties or attorneys shall furnish such Judge with copies of all filings prior to the qualification of such Special Judge. Thereafter, copies of all filings shall be delivered in person, by mail or by facsimile to the office of the Special Judge with certificate of forwarding same made a part of the filing. IN ST MARION CIR AND SUPER CTS CIV Rule 205(C).

f. *Proof of filing.* Any party filing any paper by any method other than personal delivery to the clerk shall retain proof of filing. IN ST TRIAL P Rule 5(F).

2. *Service requirements.* Unless otherwise provided by the Indiana Rules of Trial Procedure or an order of

the court, each party and special judge, if any, shall be served with: (1) every order required by its terms to be served; (2) every pleading subsequent to the original complaint; (3) every written motion except one which may be heard ex parte; (4) every brief submitted to the trial court; (5) every paper relating to discovery required to be served upon a party; and (6) every written notice, appearance, demand, offer of judgment, designation of record on appeal, or similar paper. IN ST TRIAL P Rule 5(A).

a. *Methods of service*

    i. *Personal service.* Whenever a party is represented by an attorney of record, service shall be made upon such attorney unless service upon the party himself is ordered by the court. Service upon the attorney or party shall be made by delivering or mailing a copy of the papers to the last known address or where an attorney or party has consented to service by fax or e-mail, as provided in IN ST TRIAL P Rule 3.1(A)(4), by faxing or e-mailing a copy of the documents to the fax number or e-mail address set out in the appearance form or correction as required by IN ST TRIAL P Rule 3.1(E). IN ST TRIAL P Rule 5(B). Delivery of a copy within IN ST TRIAL P Rule 5 means:

- Offering or tendering it to the attorney or party and stating the nature of the papers being served. Refusal to accept an offered or tendered document is a waiver of any objection to the sufficiency or adequacy of service of that document;

- Leaving it at his office with a clerk or other person in charge thereof, or if there is no one in charge, leaving it in a conspicuous place therein; or

- If the office is closed, by leaving it at his dwelling house or usual place of abode with some person of suitable age and discretion then residing therein; or,

- Leaving it at some other suitable place, selected by the attorney upon whom service is being made, pursuant to duly promulgated local rule. IN ST TRIAL P Rule 5(B)(1).

    ii. *Service by mail.* If service is made by mail, the papers shall be deposited in the United States mail addressed to the person on whom they are being served, with postage prepaid. Service shall be deemed complete upon mailing. Proof of service of all papers permitted to be mailed may be made by written acknowledgment of service, by affidavit of the person who mailed the papers, or by certificate of an attorney. It shall be the duty of attorneys when entering their appearance in a cause or when filing pleadings or papers therein, to have noted in the Chronological Case Summary or said pleadings or papers so filed the address and telephone number of their office. Service by delivery or by mail at such address shall be deemed sufficient and complete. IN ST TRIAL P Rule 5(B)(2).

    iii. *Service by fax or e-mail.* A party who has consented to service by fax or e-mail may be served as follows:

- Service by e-mail shall be made by attaching the document being served in .pdf format. Discovery documents must also be served in accordance with IN ST TRIAL P Rule 26(A). IN ST TRIAL P Rule 5(B)(3)(a).

- Service by fax shall be deemed complete upon generation of a transmission record indicating the successful transmission of the entire document, except as provided in IN ST TRIAL P Rule 5(B)(3)(d). IN ST TRIAL P Rule 5(B)(3)(b).

- Service by e-mail shall be deemed complete upon transmission, except as provided in IN ST TRIAL P Rule 5(B)(3)(d). IN ST TRIAL P Rule 5(B)(3)(c).

- Service by fax or e-mail that occurs on a Saturday, Sunday, legal holiday, or day the court or agency in which the matter is pending is closed or after 5:00 PM local time of the recipient shall be deemed complete the next day that is not a Saturday, Sunday, legal holiday, or day that the court or agency in which the matter is pending is not closed. IN ST TRIAL P Rule 5(B)(3)(d).

    iv. *Electronic service.* Delivery of E-service documents through the EFSP to other registered users shall be considered as valid and effective service and shall have the same legal effect as an original paper document. Recipients of E-service documents shall access their documents through the EFSP. IN ST MARION SUPER CT ADMIN Rule 311(2-107)(1).

- E-service shall be deemed complete when the transmission to the EFSP is completed. IN ST MARION SUPER CT ADMIN Rule 311(2-107)(2).

- For the purpose of computing time to respond to documents received via E-service, any document served on a day or at a time when the Clerk's office is not open for business shall be deemed served at the time of next opening of the Clerk's office for business. IN ST MARION SUPER CT ADMIN Rule 311(2-107)(3).

b. *Serving numerous defendants.* In any action in which there are unusually large numbers of defendants, the court, upon motion or of its own initiative, may order:

   i. That service of the pleadings of the defendants and replies thereto need not be made as between the defendants;

- That any cross-claim, counterclaim, or matter constituting an avoidance or affirmative defense contained therein shall be deemed to be denied or avoided by all other parties; and

- That the filing of any such pleading and service thereof upon the plaintiff constitutes due notice of it to the parties. IN ST TRIAL P Rule 5(D).

   ii. A copy of every such order shall be served upon the parties in such manner and form as the court directs. IN ST TRIAL P Rule 5(D).

c. *Service by electronic means.* Courts wishing to establish an electronic service pilot project pursuant to the Indiana Administrative Rules must submit a written request for approval and a plan to the Division of State Court Administration. IN ST ADMIN Rule 16(B).

d. *Service on parties in default for failure to appear.* No service need be made on parties in default for failure to appear, except that pleadings asserting new or additional claims for relief against them shall be served upon them in the manner provided by service of summons in IN ST TRIAL P Rule 4. IN ST TRIAL P Rule 5(A).

G. Hearings

1. *Hearing on motion.* Unless local conditions make it impracticable, each judge shall establish regular times and places, at intervals sufficiently frequent for the prompt dispatch of business, at which motions requiring notice and hearing may be heard and disposed of; but the judge at any time or place and on such notice, if any, as he considers reasonable may make order for the advancement, conduct, and hearing of actions. To expedite its business the court may direct the submission and determination of motions without oral hearing upon brief written statements of reasons in support and opposition, or direct or permit hearings by telephone conference call with all attorneys or other similar means of communication. IN ST TRIAL P Rule 73(A).

2. *Hearing on summary judgment.* The court may conduct a hearing on the motion. However, upon motion of any party made no later than ten (10) days after the response was filed or was due, the court shall conduct a hearing on the motion which shall be held not less than ten (10) days after the time for filing the response. IN ST TRIAL P Rule 56(C).

3. *Time and place of hearing.* If the motion requires a hearing or oral argument, the Court shall set the time and place of hearing or argument on the motion. IN ST MARION CIR AND SUPER CTS CIV Rule 203(A).

H. Forms

1. Motion for Summary Judgment Forms for Indiana

a. Notice of motion for summary judgment. 11 INPRAC § 90.2.

b. Motion for summary judgment. 11 INPRAC § 90.3.

c. Motion for summary judgment; Another form. 11 INPRAC § 90.4.

d. Motion for summary judgment; Another form. 11 INPRAC § 90.5.

e. Designation of materials relied upon in support of motion for summary judgment. 11 INPRAC § 90.6.

    f.   Designation of material issues of fact that preclude entry of summary judgment. 11 INPRAC § 90.7.

    g.   Response to statement of material issues of fact that preclude entry of summary judgment. 11 INPRAC § 90.8.

    h.   Order granting motion for summary judgment. 11 INPRAC § 90.9.

    i.   Order denying motion for summary judgment. 11 INPRAC § 90.10.

    j.   Motion for partial summary judgment as to liability. 11 INPRAC § 90.11.

    k.   Order for partial summary judgment as to liability. 11 INPRAC § 90.12.

    l.   Order denying summary judgment and specifying issues. 11 INPRAC § 90.15.

    m.   Affidavit in support of motion for summary judgment. 11 INPRAC § 90.16.

    n.   Submission of proposed findings of fact, conclusions of law and proposed summary judgment. 11 INPRAC § 90.17.

    o.   Findings of fact and conclusions of law in support of motion for summary judgment. 11 INPRAC § 90.18.

    p.   Motion for hearing on motion for summary judgment. 11 INPRAC § 90.27.

    q.   Certificate of service; Personal service. 9 INPRAC § 5.7.

    r.   Certificate of service; First class mail. 9 INPRAC § 5.8.

I. Checklist

(I)   ❑ Matters to be considered by moving party

    (a) ❑ Required documents

        (1) ❑ Motion and notice

        (2) ❑ Supporting evidence

        (3) ❑ Statement of approval or disapproval

        (4) ❑ Proposed order

        (5) ❑ Certificate of service

    (b) ❑ Supplemental documents

        (1) ❑ Additional supporting evidence

        (2) ❑ Request for oral argument

        (3) ❑ Facsimile cover sheet

    (c) ❑ Timing

        (1) ❑ For claimant, at any time after the expiration of twenty (20) days from the commencement of the action or after service of a motion for summary judgment by the adverse party

        (2) ❑ For a party against whom a claim, counterclaim, or cross-claim is asserted or a declaratory judgment is sought, at any time

        (3) ❑ A written motion, other than one which may be heard ex parte, and notice of the hearing thereof shall be served not less than five (5) days before the time specified for the hearing, unless a different period is fixed by the Indiana Rules of Trial Procedure or by order of the court

        (4) ❑ All pleadings and papers subsequent to the complaint which are required to be served upon a party shall be filed with the Court either before service or within a reasonable period of time thereafter

(II) ❑ Matters to be considered by the responding party

    (a) ❑ Required documents

        (1) ❑ Opposition

    (2) ❑ Opposing evidence

    (3) ❑ Certificate of service

(b) ❑ Supplemental documents

    (1) ❑ Additional evidence

    (2) ❑ Proposed order

    (3) ❑ Facsimile cover sheet

(c) ❑ Timing

    (1) ❑ If the statement regarding the position of the opposing party(ies) required under IN ST MARION CIR AND SUPER CTS CIV Rule 203(A) indicates that objection to the granting of said motion may ensue, said objecting a party shall have fifteen (15) days from the date of filing to file a response to said motion

    (2) ❑ Except as otherwise provided in IN ST TRIAL P Rule 59(D), opposing affidavits may be served not less than one (1) day before the hearing, unless the court permits them to be served at some other time

    (3) ❑ An adverse party shall have thirty (30) days after service of the motion to serve a response and any opposing affidavits

Motions, Oppositions and Replies
Motion for Sanctions

Document Last Updated October 2013

A. Applicable Rules

1. *State rules*

    a. Appearance. IN ST TRIAL P Rule 3.1.

    b. Process. IN ST TRIAL P Rule 4.

    c. Service and filing of pleadings and other papers. IN ST TRIAL P Rule 5.

    d. Time. IN ST TRIAL P Rule 6.

    e. Pleadings. IN ST TRIAL P Rule 7; IN ST TRIAL P Rule 8; IN ST TRIAL P Rule 9.2; IN ST TRIAL P Rule 10.

    f. Signing and verification of pleadings. IN ST TRIAL P Rule 11.

    g. Evidence. IN ST TRIAL P Rule 43.

    h. Judgment on the evidence (directed verdict). IN ST TRIAL P Rule 50.

    i. Findings by the court. IN ST TRIAL P Rule 52.

    j. Summary judgment. IN ST TRIAL P Rule 56.

    k. Motion to correct error. IN ST TRIAL P Rule 59.

    l. Relief from judgment or order. IN ST TRIAL P Rule 60.

    m. Hearing of motions. IN ST TRIAL P Rule 73.

    n. Access to court records. IN ST ADMIN Rule 9.

    o. Paper size. IN ST ADMIN Rule 11.

    p. Facsimile transmission. IN ST ADMIN Rule 12.

    q. Electronic filing and electronic service pilot projects. IN ST ADMIN Rule 16.

    r. Sealing of certain records by court; Hearing; Notice. IN ST 5-14-3-5.5.

    s. Privacy and confidentiality. IN ST 5-2-9-6; IN ST 5-14-3-4; IN ST 6-4.1-5-10; IN ST 6-4.1-12-12;

IN ST 6-8.1-7-1; IN ST 11-13-1-8; IN ST 12-23-14-13; IN ST 16-39-3-10; IN ST 16-41-8-1; IN ST 22-4-19-6; IN ST 31-11-1-6; IN ST 31-19-5-23; IN ST 31-19-13-2; IN ST 31-19-19-1; IN ST 31-33-18-1; IN ST 31-39-1-1; IN ST 31-39-1-2; IN ST 33-23-16-16; IN ST 35-34-2-4; IN ST 35-38-1-13; IN ST 35-38-9-1; IN ST ADR Rule 2.11; IN ST ADR Rule 4.4; IN ST ADR Rule 5.6; IN ST JURY Rule 10.

    t.   General recovery rule. IN ST 34-52-1-1.

2. *Local rules*

    a.   Requirements for motions. IN ST MARION CIR AND SUPER CTS CIV Rule 203.

    b.   Preparation of pleadings, motions and other papers. IN ST MARION CIR AND SUPER CTS CIV Rule 204.

    c.   Filing of pleadings, motions and other papers. IN ST MARION CIR AND SUPER CTS CIV Rule 205.

    d.   Signing and verification of pleadings, motions and other papers; Service on opposing party. IN ST MARION CIR AND SUPER CTS CIV Rule 206.

    e.   Motions for continuance. IN ST MARION CIR AND SUPER CTS CIV Rule 215.

    f.   Electronic filing. IN ST MARION SUPER CT ADMIN Rule 311.

B. Timing

1. *Motion for sanctions.* There are no specific time requirements for when a party may file a motion for sanctions.

    a.   *Filing.* All pleadings and papers subsequent to the complaint which are required to be served upon a party shall be filed with the Court either before service or within a reasonable period of time thereafter. IN ST TRIAL P Rule 5(E)(1).

2. *Service.* A written motion, other than one which may be heard ex parte, and notice of the hearing thereof shall be served not less than five (5) days before the time specified for the hearing, unless a different period is fixed by the Indiana Rules of Trial Procedure or by order of the court. IN ST TRIAL P Rule 6(D).

    a.   *Of supporting affidavits.* When a motion is supported by affidavit, the affidavit shall be served with the motion. IN ST TRIAL P Rule 6(D).

3. *Opposition*

    a.   *Filing.* If the statement regarding the position of the opposing party(ies) required under IN ST MARION CIR AND SUPER CTS CIV Rule 203(A) indicates that objection to the granting of said motion may ensue, said objecting a party shall have fifteen (15) days from the date of filing to file a response to said motion. IN ST MARION CIR AND SUPER CTS CIV Rule 203(B).

    b.   *Service.* Except as otherwise provided in IN ST TRIAL P Rule 59(D), opposing affidavits may be served not less than one (1) day before the hearing, unless the court permits them to be served at some other time. IN ST TRIAL P Rule 6(D).

4. *Computation of time*

    a.   *Generally; Days excluded.* In computing any period of time prescribed or allowed by the Indiana Rules of Trial Procedure, by order of the court, or by any applicable statute, the day of the act, event, or default from which the designated period of time begins to run shall not be included. The last day of the period so computed is to be included unless it is:

        i.   A Saturday,

        ii.   A Sunday,

        iii.   A legal holiday as defined by state statute, or

        iv.   A day the office in which the act is to be done is closed during regular business hours. IN ST TRIAL P Rule 6(A).

    b.   *Short periods.* In any event, the period runs until the end of the next day that is not a Saturday, a Sunday, a legal holiday, or a day on which the office is closed. When the period of time allowed is

less than seven (7) days, intermediate Saturdays, Sundays, legal holidays, and days on which the office is closed shall be excluded from the computations. IN ST TRIAL P Rule 6(A).

c. *Additional time after service by United States mail.* Whenever a party has the right or is required to do some act or take some proceedings within a prescribed period after the service of a notice or other paper upon him and the notice or paper is served upon him by United States mail, three (3) days shall be added to the prescribed period. IN ST TRIAL P Rule 6(E).

d. *Enlargement of time.* When an act is required or allowed to be done at or within a specific time by the Indiana Rules of Trial Procedure, the court may at any time for cause shown:

    i. Order the period enlarged, with or without motion or notice, if request therefor is made before the expiration of the period originally prescribed or extended by a previous order; or

    ii. Upon motion made after the expiration of the specific period, permit the act to be done where the failure to act was the result of excusable neglect; but, the court may not extend the time for taking any action for judgment on the evidence under IN ST TRIAL P Rule 50(A), amendment of findings and judgment under IN ST TRIAL P Rule 52(B), to correct errors under IN ST TRIAL P Rule 59(C), statement in opposition to motion to correct error under IN ST TRIAL P Rule 59(E), or to obtain relief from final judgment under IN ST TRIAL P Rule 60(B), except to the extent and under the conditions stated in those rules. IN ST TRIAL P Rule 6(B).

e. *Continuances disfavored.* Motions for Continuance are discouraged. Neither side is entitled to an automatic continuance as a matter of right. IN ST MARION CIR AND SUPER CTS CIV Rule 215. For information on obtaining a continuance, refer to IN ST MARION CIR AND SUPER CTS CIV Rule 215.

C. General Requirements

1. *Motions, generally.* Unless made during a hearing or trial, or otherwise ordered by the court, an application to the court for an order shall be made by written motion. The motion shall state the grounds therefor and the relief or order sought. IN ST TRIAL P Rule 7(B).

    a. *Motions as distinct from pleadings.* Motions and responses to motions are not pleadings, and allegations contained in a motion are not admissions of a party. 22B INPRAC 7:2; Wachstetter v. County Properties, LLC, 832 N.E.2d 574 (Ind.Ct.App. 2005); Scott County Family YMCA, Inc. v. Hobbs, 817 N.E.2d 603 (Ind.Ct.App. 2004).

    b. *Unopposed motions generally granted.* It is common for a trial court to grant procedural motions, such as motions for enlargement of time, discovery motions, or motions for continuance, unless an objection is filed. 21 INPRAC § 13.8.

2. *Motion for sanctions*

    a. *Signature and certification.* Every pleading or motion of a party represented by an attorney shall be signed by at least one (1) attorney of record in his individual name, whose address, telephone number, and attorney number shall be stated, except that this provision shall not apply to pleadings and motions made and transcribed at the trial or a hearing before the judge and received by him in such form. A party who is not represented by an attorney shall sign his pleading and state his address. IN ST TRIAL P Rule 11(A).

        i. The signature of an attorney constitutes a certificate by him that he has read the pleadings; that to the best of his knowledge, information, and belief, there is good ground to support it; and that it is not interposed for delay. IN ST TRIAL P Rule 11(A).

        ii. If a pleading or motion is not signed or is signed with intent to defeat the purpose of the rule, it may be stricken as sham and false and the action may proceed as though the pleading had not been served. IN ST TRIAL P Rule 11(A).

        iii. For a willful violation of IN ST TRIAL P Rule 11 an attorney may be subjected to appropriate disciplinary action. Similar action may be taken if scandalous or indecent matter is inserted. IN ST TRIAL P Rule 11(A).

    b. *Frivolous claims.* A claim or defense is "frivolous, unreasonable or groundless" if it has been asserted primarily for the purpose of harassment, if the attorney is unable to make a good faith and rational argument on the merits of the action, or if the lawyer is unable to support the action by good faith and a rational argument for extension, modification, or reversal of existing law. 9 INPRAC § 4.3; Garage Doors of Indianapolis, Inc. v. Morton, 682 N.E.2d 1296 (Ind.Ct.App. 1997).

  i.   *Bad faith pleading.* For information on sanctions for bad faith pleading, refer to IN ST 34-52-1-1.

 c. *Factors for determining reasonableness.* Five factors are relevant to determine whether a litigant's conduct is "unreasonable":

  i.   The amount of time the attorney had to investigate facts, research the law and prepare documents;

  ii. The extent to which the attorney had to rely upon his client for the factual foundation;

  iii. The complexity of the facts and legal issues;

  iv. The ability to conduct a pre-filing investigation; and

  v.   The plausibility of the arguments advanced by a party, including good faith efforts to extend or modify the law. 9 INPRAC § 4.3; General Collections, Inc. v. Decker, 545 N.E.2d 18 (Ind.Ct.App. 1989).

 d. *Determination of sanction.* The determination of a reasonable attorney fee requires the consideration of all relevant matters including but not limited to the attorney's experience and reputation, the nature of the employment, and the responsibility involved and the results obtained. A contingency fee agreement should not be used as the basis for determining a reasonable fee to be paid by a nonparty to that agreement. 9 INPRAC § 4.3; Mason v. Mason, 561 N.E.2d 809 (Ind.Ct.App. 1990).

D. Documents

1. *Required documents*

 a. *Motion and notice.* The requirement of notice is satisfied by service of the motion. IN ST TRIAL P Rule 7(B); IN ST MARION CIR AND SUPER CTS CIV Rule 203(A). Refer to the General Requirements section of this document for information on the content of a motion for sanctions.

 b. *Statement of approval or disapproval.* Except for initial motions made pursuant to IN ST MARION CIR AND SUPER CTS CIV Rule 203(D), all motions filed with the court shall include a brief statement indicating whether opposing party(ies) object to or approve of the granting of said motion. IN ST MARION CIR AND SUPER CTS CIV Rule 203(A).

 c. *Proposed order.* Unless local practice provides differently, a party should submit a proposed order with its written motion to be signed by the judge once the motion has been granted. 21 INPRAC § 13.8. All motions seeking an order of the Court shall be accompanied by a sufficient number of orders to be executed by the Court in granting said motion. In addition to the orders, the notice shall be accompanied by stamped, addressed envelopes to all parties of record. IN ST MARION CIR AND SUPER CTS CIV Rule 203(E).

 d. *Certificate of service.* An attorney or unrepresented party tendering a document to the Clerk for filing shall certify that service has been made, list the parties served, and specify the date and means of service. The certificate of service shall be placed at the end of the document and shall not be separately filed. The separate filing of a certificate of service, however, shall not be grounds for rejecting a document for filing. The Clerk may permit documents to be filed without a certificate of service but shall require prompt filing of a separate certificate of service. IN ST TRIAL P Rule 5(C). In all cases where any pleading or other document is required to be served upon opposing counsel, proof of such service may be made either by:

  i.   A certificate of service signed by counsel of record for the serving party and the certificate shall specify by name and address all counsel upon whom the pleading or document was served; or

  ii. An acknowledgment of service signed by the party served or counsel of record. IN ST MARION CIR AND SUPER CTS CIV Rule 206.

2. *Supplemental documents*

 a. *Supporting evidence.* When a motion is based on facts not appearing of record the court may hear the matter on affidavits presented by the respective parties, but the court may direct that the matter be heard wholly or partly on oral testimony or depositions. IN ST TRIAL P Rule 43(B).

    b. *Request for oral argument.* When an oral argument is requested, the request shall be by separate instrument and filed with the pleading to be argued. Any such oral argument requested may be heard at the discretion of the Court, except for motions for summary judgment which shall be set for hearing upon request of any party. IN ST MARION CIR AND SUPER CTS CIV Rule 203(C).

    c. *Facsimile cover sheet.* Any document sent to the Clerk of the Circuit Court by electronic facsimile transmission shall be accompanied by a cover sheet which states the title of the document, case number, number of pages, identity and voice telephone number of the sending party and instructions for filing. The cover sheet shall contain the signature of the attorney or party, pro se, authorizing the filing. IN ST ADMIN Rule 12(D).

E. Format

1. *Form of motions.* The rules applicable to captions, and the signing and form of pleadings (IN ST TRIAL P Rule 8 through IN ST TRIAL P Rule 11), apply to all motions and other papers provided under the Indiana Rules of Trial Procedure. 22B INPRAC 7:2.

2. *Form of pleadings*

    a. *Caption; Names of parties.* Every pleading shall contain a caption setting forth the name of the court, the title of the action, the file number, and a designation as in IN ST TRIAL P Rule 7(A). In the complaint the title of the action shall include the names of all the parties, but in other pleadings it is sufficient to state the name of the first party on each side with an appropriate indication of other parties. IN ST TRIAL P Rule 10(A).

      i. Every pleading shall contain a caption setting forth the name of the Court, the Division and Room Number, the title of the action and the file number. IN ST MARION CIR AND SUPER CTS CIV Rule 204(B).

    b. *Paragraphs; Separate statements.* All averments of a claim or defense shall be made in numbered paragraphs, the contents of each of which shall be limited as far as practicable to a statement of a single set of circumstances, and a paragraph may be referred to by number in all succeeding pleadings. Each claim founded upon a separate transaction or occurrence and each defense other than denials may be stated in a separate count or defense whenever a separation facilitates the clear presentation of the matters set forth. IN ST TRIAL P Rule 10(B).

    c. *Adoption by reference; Exhibits.* Statements in a pleading may be adopted by reference in a different part of the same pleading or in another pleading or in any motion. A copy of any written instrument which is an exhibit to a pleading is a part thereof for all purposes. IN ST TRIAL P Rule 10(C).

    d. *Paper.* Pleadings, motions and other papers may be either printed or typewritten on white opaque paper of at least sixteen (16) pound weight, eight and one-half (8-1/2) inches wide and eleven (11) inches in length. IN ST MARION CIR AND SUPER CTS CIV Rule 204(A).

    e. *Copies.* All copies shall likewise be on white paper of sufficient strength and durability to resist normal wear and tear. IN ST MARION CIR AND SUPER CTS CIV Rule 204(A).

    f. *Line spacing.* If typewritten, the lines shall be double spaced, except for quotations, which shall be indented and single spaced. IN ST MARION CIR AND SUPER CTS CIV Rule 204(A).

    g. *Script type.* Script type shall not be used. IN ST MARION CIR AND SUPER CTS CIV Rule 204(A).

    h. *Titles.* Titles on all pleadings shall delineate each topic included in the pleading e.g. where a pleading contains an Answer, a Motion to Strike or Dismiss, or a Jury Request each shall be set forth in the title. IN ST MARION CIR AND SUPER CTS CIV Rule 204(C).

    i. *Margins and binding.* Margins shall be one (1) inch. Binding or stapling shall be at the top and at no other place. Covers or backing shall not be used. IN ST MARION CIR AND SUPER CTS CIV Rule 204(D).

3. *Size of papers for filing.* Effective January 1, 1992, all pleadings, copies, motions and documents filed with any trial court or appellate level court, typed or printed, with the exception of exhibits and existing

wills, shall be prepared on eight and one-half by eleven inch (8 1/2" x 11") size paper. IN ST ADMIN Rule 11.

4. *Form of electronically filed documents.* All electronically filed and served pleadings shall, to the extent practicable, be formatted in accordance with the applicable rules governing formatting of paper pleadings. IN ST MARION SUPER CT ADMIN Rule 311(2-103)(1).

    a. *Electronic document title.* The electronic document title of each pleading or other document shall include:

        i. Party or parties filing/serving the document,

        ii. Nature of the document,

        iii. Party or parties against whom relief, if any, is sought, and

        iv. Nature of the relief sought (e.g., Defendant ABC Corporation's Motion for Summary Judgment). IN ST MARION SUPER CT ADMIN Rule 311(2-103)(2).

5. *Signature requirements*

    a. *Signature of attorney.* Every pleading or motion of a party represented by an attorney shall be signed by at least one (1) attorney of record in his individual name, whose address, telephone number, and attorney number shall be stated, except that this provision shall not apply to pleadings and motions made and transcribed at the trial or a hearing before the judge and received by him in such form. IN ST TRIAL P Rule 11(A).

        i. All pleadings and motions shall contain the original or authorized signature of the attorney, the name of the attorney in typed or printed form, the name of the law firm if a member of a firm, the attorney's address, identification number, e-mail address, telephone number, fax number, and the designation as to the party for whom he appears. IN ST MARION CIR AND SUPER CTS CIV Rule 204(E).

        ii. The signature of an attorney constitutes a certificate by him that he has read the pleadings; that to the best of his knowledge, information, and belief, there is good ground to support it; and that it is not interposed for delay. IN ST TRIAL P Rule 11(A).

        iii. If a pleading or motion is not signed or is signed with intent to defeat the purpose of the rule, it may be stricken as sham and false and the action may proceed as though the pleading had not been served. IN ST TRIAL P Rule 11(A).

        iv. For a willful violation of IN ST TRIAL P Rule 11 an attorney may be subjected to appropriate disciplinary action. Similar action may be taken if scandalous or indecent matter is inserted. IN ST TRIAL P Rule 11(A).

        v. Every pleading, document, and instrument electronically filed or served shall be deemed to have been signed by the judge, clerk, attorney or declarant and shall bear a facsimile or typographical signature of such person, along with the typed name, address, telephone number, and Bar number of a signing attorney. Typographical signatures shall be treated as personal signatures for all purposes under these rules. IN ST MARION SUPER CT ADMIN Rule 311(2-105).

          • Documents containing signatures of third-parties (i.e., unopposed motions, affidavits, stipulations, etc.) may also be filed electronically by indicating that the original signatures are maintained by the filing party in paper-format. IN ST MARION SUPER CT ADMIN Rule 311(2-105).

          • Unless otherwise ordered by the Court or Clerk, a printed copy of all documents filed or served electronically, including original signatures, shall be maintained by the party filing the document and shall be made available, upon reasonable notice, for inspection by other counsel, the Clerk or Court. Parties shall retain originals until two (2) years after all time periods for appeal have expired. From time to time, it may be necessary to provide the Clerk or Court with a hard copy of an electronically filed document. IN ST MARION SUPER CT ADMIN Rule 311(2-105).

        vi. For the recommended format of a signature block, refer to IN ST MARION CIR AND SUPER CTS CIV Rule 204(E).

b. *Signature of unrepresented party.* A party who is not represented by an attorney shall sign his pleading and state his address. IN ST TRIAL P Rule 11(A).

c. *Verification not generally required.* Except when specifically required by rule, pleadings or motions need not be verified or accompanied by affidavit. The rule in equity that the averments of an answer under oath must be overcome by the testimony of two (2) witnesses or of one (1) witness sustained by corroborating circumstances is abolished. IN ST TRIAL P Rule 11(A).

d. *Verification by affirmation or representation.* When in connection with any civil or special statutory proceeding it is required that any pleading, motion, petition, supporting affidavit, or other document of any kind, be verified, or that an oath be taken, it shall be sufficient if the subscriber simply affirms the truth of the matter to be verified by an affirmation or representation. IN ST TRIAL P Rule 11(B). IN ST TRIAL P Rule 11(B) states that the affirmation or representation should be in substantially the following language: "I (we) affirm, under the penalties for perjury, that the foregoing representation(s) is (are) true. (Signed) _____."

    i. Any person who falsifies an affirmation or representation of fact shall be subject to the same penalties as are prescribed by law for the making of a false affidavit. IN ST TRIAL P Rule 11(B).

e. *Verified pleadings, motions, and affidavits as evidence.* Pleadings, motions and affidavits accompanying or in support of such pleadings or motions when required to be verified or under oath shall be accepted as a representation that the signer had personal knowledge thereof or reasonable cause to believe the existence of the facts or matters stated or alleged therein; and, if otherwise competent or acceptable as evidence, may be admitted as evidence of the facts or matters stated or alleged therein when it is so provided in the Indiana Rules of Trial Procedure, by statute or other law, or to the extent the writing or signature expressly purports to be made upon the signer's personal knowledge. When such pleadings, motions and affidavits are verified or under oath they shall not require other or greater proof on the part of the adverse party than if not verified or not under oath unless expressly provided otherwise by the Indiana Rules of Trial Procedure, statute or other law. Affidavits upon motions for summary judgment under IN ST TRIAL P Rule 56 and in denial of execution under IN ST TRIAL P Rule 9.2 shall be made upon personal knowledge. IN ST TRIAL P Rule 11(C).

6. *Information excluded from public access.* Every document filed in a case shall separately identify information excluded from public access pursuant to IN ST ADMIN Rule 9(G)(1) as follows:

a. Whole documents that are excluded from public access pursuant to IN ST ADMIN Rule 9(G)(1) shall be tendered on light green paper or have a light green coversheet attached to the document, marked "Not for Public Access" or "Confidential." IN ST TRIAL P Rule 5(G)(1).

b. When only a portion of a document contains information excluded from public access pursuant to IN ST ADMIN Rule 9(G)(1), said information shall be omitted [or redacted] from the filed document, and set forth on a separate accompanying document on light green paper conspicuously marked "Not for Public Access" or "Confidential" and clearly designated [or identifying] the caption and number of the case and the document and location within the document to which the redacted material pertains. IN ST TRIAL P Rule 5(G)(2).

c. With respect to documents filed in electronic format, the trial court, by local rule, may provide for compliance with IN ST TRIAL P Rule 5 in manner that separates and protects access to information excluded from public access. IN ST TRIAL P Rule 5(G)(3).

d. IN ST TRIAL P Rule 5(G) does not apply to a record sealed by the court pursuant to IN ST 5-14-3-5.5 or otherwise, nor to records, documents, or information filed in cases to which public access is prohibited pursuant to IN ST ADMIN Rule 9(G). IN ST TRIAL P Rule 5(G)(4).

e. The following information in case records is excluded from public access and is confidential:

    i. Information that is excluded from public access pursuant to federal law;

    ii. Information that is excluded from public access as declared confidential by Indiana statute or other court rule, including without limitation:

        • All adoption records created after July 8, 1941, as declared confidential by IN ST 31-19-19-1, et seq., except those specifically declared open by IN ST 31-19-13-2(2);

- All records relating to chancroid, chlamydia, gonorrhea, hepatitis, human immunodeficiency virus (HIV), Lymphogranuloma venereum, syphilis, tuberculosis, as declared confidential by IN ST 16-41-8-1, et seq.;
- All records relating to child abuse as declared confidential by IN ST 31-33-18-1, et seq.;
- All records relating to drug tests as declared confidential by IN ST 5-14-3-4(a)(9);
- Records of grand jury proceedings as declared confidential by IN ST 35-34-2-4;
- Records of juvenile proceedings as declared confidential by IN ST 31-39-1-2, except those specifically open under statute;
- All paternity records created after July 1, 1941 as declared confidential by IN ST 31-14-11-15, IN ST 31-19-5-23, IN ST 31-39-1-1 and IN ST 31-39-1-2 [Editor's note: IN ST 31-14-11-15 was repealed effective May 9, 2013];
- All pre-sentence reports as declared confidential by IN ST 35-38-1-13;
- Written petitions to permit marriages without consent and orders directing the Clerk of Court to issue a marriage license to underage persons, as declared confidential by IN ST 31-11-1-6;
- Only those arrest warrants, search warrants, indictments and informations ordered confidential by the trial judge, prior to return of duly executed service as declared confidential by IN ST 5-14-3-4(b)(1);
- All medical, mental health, or tax records unless determined by law or regulation of any governmental custodian not to be confidential, released by the subject of such records, or declared by a court of competent jurisdiction to be essential to the resolution of litigation as declared confidential by IN ST 16-39-3-10, IN ST 6-4.1-5-10, IN ST 6-4.1-12-12, and IN ST 6-8.1-7-1;
- Personal information relating to jurors or prospective jurors, other than for the use of the parties and counsel, pursuant to IN ST JURY Rule 10;
- Information relating to protection from abuse orders, no-contact orders and workplace violence restraining orders as declared confidential by IN ST 5-2-9-6, et seq.;
- Mediation proceedings pursuant to IN ST ADR Rule 2.11, Mini-Trial proceedings pursuant to IN ST ADR Rule 4.4(C), and Summary Jury Trials pursuant to IN ST ADR Rule 5.6;
- Information in probation files pursuant to the Probation Standards promulgated by the Judicial Conference of Indiana pursuant to IN ST 11-13-1-8(b);
- Information deemed confidential pursuant to the Rules for Court Administered Alcohol and Drug Programs promulgated by the Judicial Conference of Indiana pursuant to IN ST 12-23-14-13;
- Information deemed confidential pursuant to the Problem-Solving Court Rules promulgated by the Judicial Conference of Indiana pursuant to IN ST 33-23-16-16;
- All records of the Department of workforce Development as declared confidential by IN ST 22-4-19-6;
- Information regarding interception of electronic communications that is sealed or deemed confidential as set forth in IN ST 35-33.5-2-1, et seq.

iii. Information excluded from public access by specific court order;

iv. Complete Social Security Numbers of living persons;

v. With the exception of names, information such as addresses, phone numbers, and dates of birth which explicitly identifies:

- Natural persons who are witnesses or victims (not including defendants) in criminal, domestic violence, stalking, sexual assault, juvenile, or civil protection order proceedings, provided that juveniles who are victims of sex crimes shall be identified by initials only;

- Places of residence of judicial officers, clerks and other employees of courts and clerks of court, unless the person or persons about whom the information pertains waives confidentiality;

vi. Complete account numbers of specific assets, loans, bank accounts, credit cards, and personal identification numbers (PINs);

vii. All orders of expungement entered in criminal or juvenile proceedings, orders to restrict access to criminal history information pursuant to IN ST 35-38-5-5.5 or IN ST 35-38-8-5 and records excluded from public access by such orders, and information related to infractions that is excluded from public access pursuant to IN ST 34-28-5-15 or IN ST 34-28-5-16 [Editor's note: IN ST 35-38-5-5.5, IN ST 35-38-8-5 and IN ST 34-28-5-16 were repealed effective July 1, 2013; for information on orders restricting access to criminal history, refer to IN ST 35-38-9-1, et seq.];

viii. All personal notes and e-mail, and deliberative material, of judges, jurors, court staff and judicial agencies, and information recorded in personal data assistants (PDA's) or organizers and personal calendars. IN ST ADMIN Rule 9(G)(1).

F. Filing and Service Requirements

1. *Filing requirements.* Except as otherwise provided in IN ST TRIAL P Rule 5(E)(2), all pleadings and papers subsequent to the complaint which are required to be served upon a party shall be filed with the Court either before service or within a reasonable period of time thereafter. IN ST TRIAL P Rule 5(E)(1). Counsel shall file with the court an original and one (1) copy of all briefs, and memoranda of law filed in support of a motion. IN ST MARION CIR AND SUPER CTS CIV Rule 205(D).

   a. *Filing generally.* All pleadings, petitions and motions are filed with the Clerk designated by the Court at any time during office hours established by the Clerk and the Court. All orders submitted to the Court shall be in sufficient number and shall be accompanied by postage paid envelopes addressed to each party or counsel of record. IN ST MARION CIR AND SUPER CTS CIV Rule 205(A)

   b. *Filing with the court defined.* The filing of pleadings, motions, and other papers with the court as required by the Indiana Rules of Trial Procedure shall be made by one of the following methods:

      i. Delivery to the clerk of the court;

      ii. Sending by electronic transmission under the procedure adopted pursuant to IN ST ADMIN Rule 12;

      iii. Mailing to the clerk by registered, certified or express mail return receipt requested;

      iv. Depositing with any third-party commercial carrier for delivery to the clerk within three (3) calendar days, cost prepaid, properly addressed;

      v. If the court so permits, filing with the judge, in which event the judge shall note thereon the filing date and forthwith transmit them to the office of the clerk; or

      vi. Electronic filing, as approved by the Division of State Court Administration pursuant to IN ST ADMIN Rule 16. IN ST TRIAL P Rule 5(F).

      vii. Filing by registered or certified mail and by third-party commercial carrier shall be complete upon mailing or deposit. IN ST TRIAL P Rule 5(F).

   c. *Facsimile filing.* Facsimile filing is discouraged, but permitted in the Marion Circuit and Marion Superior Court. All documents filed by facsimile shall also be filed in hard copy within seven (7) days of the facsimile filing, along with proposed orders and stamped addressed envelopes, as required by IN ST MARION CIR AND SUPER CTS CIV Rule 203(E). To avoid duplicate filings, the hard copies of the facsimile filing shall indicate in bold letters that the pleading was previously filed by facsimile transmission. Proof of transmission by facsimile, including certificate of service and manner of service, shall be the responsibility of the filing party. If the filing requires immediate attention of the Judge, it shall be so indicated in bold letters in an accompanying transmittal memorandum. Legibility of documents and timeliness of filing is the responsibility of the sender. IN ST MARION CIR AND SUPER CTS CIV Rule 205(B).

      i. *Generally.* In counties where a majority of judges of the courts of record, by posted local rule,

have authorized electronic facsimile filing and designated a telephone number to receive such transmissions, pleadings, motions, and other papers may be sent to the Clerk of Circuit Court by electronic facsimile transmission for filing in any case, provided:

- Such matter does not exceed ten (10) pages, including the cover sheet;
- Such matter does not require the payment of fees other than the electronic facsimile transcription fee set forth in IN ST ADMIN Rule 12(E);
- The sending party creates at the time of transmission a machine generated log for such transmission; and
- The original document and the transmission log are maintained by the sending party for the duration of the litigation. IN ST ADMIN Rule 12(B).

ii. *Time of filing.* During normal, posted business hours, the time of filing shall be the time the duplicate document is produced in the office of the Clerk of the Circuit Court. Duplicate documents received at all other times shall be filed as of the next normal business day. IN ST ADMIN Rule 12(C).

- If the receiving fax machine endorses its own time and date stamp upon the transmitted documents and the receiving machine produces a delivery receipt which is electronically created and transmitted to the sending party, the time of filing shall be the date and time recorded on the transmitted document by the receiving fax machine. IN ST ADMIN Rule 12(C).

d. *Electronic filing.* Electronic filing and electronic service pilot projects are authorized pursuant to IN ST ADMIN Rule 16 and approved by the Division of State Court Administration. IN ST MARION SUPER CT ADMIN Rule 311(1-103).

i. *Cases where electronic filing accepted.* All Marion County Circuit and Superior civil courts may accept electronic filing and service of pleadings and other documents designated in this rule in mortgage foreclosure (hereinafter referred to as "MF"), civil collection(hereinafter referred to as "CC"), and individual cases that have been approved for electronic filing and service. IN ST MARION SUPER CT ADMIN Rule 311(1-104)(1).

- The Marion County Circuit Court may, upon the motion of a party or its own motion, designate a case that will involve multiple litigants, legally intricate issues, and an extensive number of documents a mass tort or complex litigation case. Any case so designated shall be subject to electronic filing and service using the county's approved Electronic Service Provider. IN ST MARION SUPER CT ADMIN Rule 311(1-104)(3).
- The filing of electronic pleadings and other documents in MF and CC cases is entirely voluntary; however, once the case is initially filed electronically, all subsequent filings in the case shall remain in electronic format until the time for appeal is exhausted. IN ST MARION SUPER CT ADMIN Rule 311(1-104)(5).

ii. *Documents eligible for electronic filing.* The following pleadings may be filed and served electronically:

- New case complaint and petitions. IN ST MARION SUPER CT ADMIN Rule 311(1-104)(8)(a).
- Original answers. IN ST MARION SUPER CT ADMIN Rule 311(1-104)(8)(a).
- Any other pleadings or document including but not limited to motions and appearance forms. IN ST MARION SUPER CT ADMIN Rule 311(1-104)(8)(a).

iii. *Manner of electronic filing.* Parties shall E-file a document either:

- By registering to use the Electronic Filing Service Provider; or
- In person at the Marion County Clerk's office, by electronically filing through the Public Access Terminal. Parties filing in this manner shall be responsible for furnishing the document in an electronic format that will be compatible with the clerk's office-system to be uploaded in person. IN ST MARION SUPER CT ADMIN Rule 311(1-104)(9). For

information on the Electronic Filing Service Provider and Public Access Terminal, refer to IN ST MARION SUPER CT ADMIN Rule 311(1-101).

- Registered users shall pay statutory filing fees for E-filed documents electronically to the Court through their EFSP. Filing fees are due and payable at the time of filing. IN ST MARION SUPER CT ADMIN Rule 311(2-104)(1). For more information on electronic filing fees, refer to IN ST MARION SUPER CT ADMIN Rule 311(2-104).

iv. *Effect of electronic filing.* Any pleading filed electronically shall be considered as filed with the court when the transmission to the EFSP is complete. Any document E-filed by 11:59 p.m. local Indianapolis, Indiana time shall be deemed filed on that date. The EFSP is an agent of the Court for the purpose of electronic filing, receipt, service and retrieval of electronic documents. IN ST MARION SUPER CT ADMIN Rule 311(2-102).

- Upon completion of filing, the EFSP shall issue a confirmation receipt that includes the date and time of receipt. The confirmation receipt shall serve as proof of filing. IN ST MARION SUPER CT ADMIN Rule 311(2-102).

- In the event the Court rejects the submitted documents following review, the documents shall not become part of the official Court record and the filer will receive notification of the rejection. Users may be required to refile the instruments to meet necessary filing requirements. Documents may be filed through an E-filing system at any time that the Clerk's office is open to receive the filing or at such other times as may be designated by the clerk and posted publicly. IN ST MARION SUPER CT ADMIN Rule 311(2-102).

- Documents filed through the E-filing system are deemed filed when received by the Clerk's office, except that documents received at times that the Clerk's office is closed shall be deemed filed the next regular time when the Clerk's office is open for filing. The time stamp issued by the E-filing system shall be presumed to be the time the document is received by the Clerk. IN ST MARION SUPER CT ADMIN Rule 311(2-102).

v. *Electronically filed documents.* All pleadings and other documents designated in IN ST MARION SUPER CT ADMIN Rule 311 shall be filed and served electronically in any individual case which has been approved for electronic filing and service. IN ST MARION SUPER CT ADMIN Rule 311(1-104)(6).

vi. *System failures.* When filing by electronic means is hindered by a technical failure, a party may file with the Clerk of Marion County in hard copy. With the exception of deadlines that by law cannot be extended, the time for filing of any paper that is delayed due to technical failure of the site shall be extended for one (1) day for each day on which such failure occurs, unless otherwise ordered by the Court. IN ST MARION SUPER CT ADMIN Rule 311(2-108).

vii. *Compliance with rules.* All filing shall comply with the requirements of IN ST ADMIN Rule 9 and IN ST ADMIN Rule 16; and the Indiana Rules of Court and the Marion County Local Rules. IN ST MARION SUPER CT ADMIN Rule 311(1-104)(11).

e. *Filing for special judge.* When a Special Judge who is not a Marion County Judge is selected, all parties or attorneys shall furnish such Judge with copies of all filings prior to the qualification of such Special Judge. Thereafter, copies of all filings shall be delivered in person, by mail or by facsimile to the office of the Special Judge with certificate of forwarding same made a part of the filing. IN ST MARION CIR AND SUPER CTS CIV Rule 205(C).

f. *Proof of filing.* Any party filing any paper by any method other than personal delivery to the clerk shall retain proof of filing. IN ST TRIAL P Rule 5(F).

2. *Service requirements.* Unless otherwise provided by the Indiana Rules of Trial Procedure or an order of the court, each party and special judge, if any, shall be served with: (1) every order required by its terms to be served; (2) every pleading subsequent to the original complaint; (3) every written motion except one which may be heard ex parte; (4) every brief submitted to the trial court; (5) every paper relating to discovery required to be served upon a party; and (6) every written notice, appearance, demand, offer of judgment, designation of record on appeal, or similar paper. IN ST TRIAL P Rule 5(A).

a. *Methods of service*

i. *Personal service.* Whenever a party is represented by an attorney of record, service shall be

made upon such attorney unless service upon the party himself is ordered by the court. Service upon the attorney or party shall be made by delivering or mailing a copy of the papers to the last known address or where an attorney or party has consented to service by fax or e-mail, as provided in IN ST TRIAL P Rule 3.1(A)(4), by faxing or e-mailing a copy of the documents to the fax number or e-mail address set out in the appearance form or correction as required by IN ST TRIAL P Rule 3.1(E). IN ST TRIAL P Rule 5(B). Delivery of a copy within IN ST TRIAL P Rule 5 means:

- Offering or tendering it to the attorney or party and stating the nature of the papers being served. Refusal to accept an offered or tendered document is a waiver of any objection to the sufficiency or adequacy of service of that document;

- Leaving it at his office with a clerk or other person in charge thereof, or if there is no one in charge, leaving it in a conspicuous place therein; or

- If the office is closed, by leaving it at his dwelling house or usual place of abode with some person of suitable age and discretion then residing therein; or,

- Leaving it at some other suitable place, selected by the attorney upon whom service is being made, pursuant to duly promulgated local rule. IN ST TRIAL P Rule 5(B)(1).

ii. *Service by mail.* If service is made by mail, the papers shall be deposited in the United States mail addressed to the person on whom they are being served, with postage prepaid. Service shall be deemed complete upon mailing. Proof of service of all papers permitted to be mailed may be made by written acknowledgment of service, by affidavit of the person who mailed the papers, or by certificate of an attorney. It shall be the duty of attorneys when entering their appearance in a cause or when filing pleadings or papers therein, to have noted in the Chronological Case Summary or said pleadings or papers so filed the address and telephone number of their office. Service by delivery or by mail at such address shall be deemed sufficient and complete. IN ST TRIAL P Rule 5(B)(2).

iii. *Service by fax or e-mail.* A party who has consented to service by fax or e-mail may be served as follows:

- Service by e-mail shall be made by attaching the document being served in .pdf format. Discovery documents must also be served in accordance with IN ST TRIAL P Rule 26(A). IN ST TRIAL P Rule 5(B)(3)(a).

- Service by fax shall be deemed complete upon generation of a transmission record indicating the successful transmission of the entire document, except as provided in IN ST TRIAL P Rule 5(B)(3)(d). IN ST TRIAL P Rule 5(B)(3)(b).

- Service by e-mail shall be deemed complete upon transmission, except as provided in IN ST TRIAL P Rule 5(B)(3)(d). IN ST TRIAL P Rule 5(B)(3)(c).

- Service by fax or e-mail that occurs on a Saturday, Sunday, legal holiday, or day the court or agency in which the matter is pending is closed or after 5:00 PM local time of the recipient shall be deemed complete the next day that is not a Saturday, Sunday, legal holiday, or day that the court or agency in which the matter is pending is not closed. IN ST TRIAL P Rule 5(B)(3)(d).

iv. *Electronic service.* Delivery of E-service documents through the EFSP to other registered users shall be considered as valid and effective service and shall have the same legal effect as an original paper document. Recipients of E-service documents shall access their documents through the EFSP. IN ST MARION SUPER CT ADMIN Rule 311(2-107)(1).

- E-service shall be deemed complete when the transmission to the EFSP is completed. IN ST MARION SUPER CT ADMIN Rule 311(2-107)(2).

- For the purpose of computing time to respond to documents received via E-service, any document served on a day or at a time when the Clerk's office is not open for business shall be deemed served at the time of next opening of the Clerk's office for business. IN ST MARION SUPER CT ADMIN Rule 311(2-107)(3).

    b. *Serving numerous defendants.* In any action in which there are unusually large numbers of defendants, the court, upon motion or of its own initiative, may order:

        i. That service of the pleadings of the defendants and replies thereto need not be made as between the defendants;

- That any cross-claim, counterclaim, or matter constituting an avoidance or affirmative defense contained therein shall be deemed to be denied or avoided by all other parties; and

- That the filing of any such pleading and service thereof upon the plaintiff constitutes due notice of it to the parties. IN ST TRIAL P Rule 5(D).

        ii. A copy of every such order shall be served upon the parties in such manner and form as the court directs. IN ST TRIAL P Rule 5(D).

    c. *Service on parties in default for failure to appear.* No service need be made on parties in default for failure to appear, except that pleadings asserting new or additional claims for relief against them shall be served upon them in the manner provided by service of summons in IN ST TRIAL P Rule 4. IN ST TRIAL P Rule 5(A).

G. Hearings

1. *Hearing on motion.* Unless local conditions make it impracticable, each judge shall establish regular times and places, at intervals sufficiently frequent for the prompt dispatch of business, at which motions requiring notice and hearing may be heard and disposed of; but the judge at any time or place and on such notice, if any, as he considers reasonable may make order for the advancement, conduct, and hearing of actions. To expedite its business the court may direct the submission and determination of motions without oral hearing upon brief written statements of reasons in support and opposition, or direct or permit hearings by telephone conference call with all attorneys or other similar means of communication. IN ST TRIAL P Rule 73(A).

2. *Time and place of hearing.* If the motion requires a hearing or oral argument, the Court shall set the time and place of hearing or argument on the motion. IN ST MARION CIR AND SUPER CTS CIV Rule 203(A).

H. Forms

1. Motion for Sanctions Forms for Indiana

    a. Signature; By party. 9 INPRAC § 4.5.

    b. Signature; Attorney. 9 INPRAC § 4.6.

    c. Signature; Attorney; Another form. 9 INPRAC § 4.7.

    d. Signature; Attorney; Another form. 9 INPRAC § 4.8.

    e. Motion to impose sanctions on defendant; Improper answer. 9 INPRAC § 4.20.

    f. Certificate of service; Personal service. 9 INPRAC § 5.7.

    g. Certificate of service; First class mail. 9 INPRAC § 5.8.

I. Checklist

(I) ❑ Matters to be considered by moving party

    (a) ❑ Required documents

        (1) ❑ Motion and notice

        (2) ❑ Statement of approval or disapproval

        (3) ❑ Proposed order

        (4) ❑ Certificate of service

    (b) ❑ Supplemental documents

        (1) ❑ Supporting evidence

        (2) ❑ Request for oral argument

      (3) ❑ Facsimile cover sheet

   (c) ❑ Timing

      (1) ❑ There are no specific time requirements for when a party may file a motion for sanctions

      (2) ❑ A written motion, other than one which may be heard ex parte, and notice of the hearing thereof shall be served not less than five (5) days before the time specified for the hearing, unless a different period is fixed by the Indiana Rules of Trial Procedure or by order of the court

      (3) ❑ All pleadings and papers subsequent to the complaint which are required to be served upon a party shall be filed with the Court either before service or within a reasonable period of time thereafter

(II) ❑ Matters to be considered by the responding party

   (a) ❑ Required documents

      (1) ❑ Opposition

      (2) ❑ Certificate of service

   (b) ❑ Supplemental documents

      (1) ❑ Supporting evidence

      (2) ❑ Proposed order

      (3) ❑ Facsimile cover sheet

   (c) ❑ Timing

      (1) ❑ If the statement regarding the position of the opposing party(ies) required under IN ST MARION CIR AND SUPER CTS CIV Rule 203(A) indicates that objection to the granting of said motion may ensue, said objecting a party shall have fifteen (15) days from the date of filing to file a response to said motion

      (2) ❑ Except as otherwise provided in IN ST TRIAL P Rule 59(D), opposing affidavits may be served not less than one (1) day before the hearing, unless the court permits them to be served at some other time

Motions, Oppositions and Replies
Motion to Compel Discovery

Document Last Updated October 2013

A. Applicable Rules

  1. *State rules*

    a. Appearance. IN ST TRIAL P Rule 3.1.

    b. Summons. IN ST TRIAL P Rule 4.

    c. Service and filing of pleadings and other papers. IN ST TRIAL P Rule 5.

    d. Time. IN ST TRIAL P Rule 6.

    e. Pleadings. IN ST TRIAL P Rule 7; IN ST TRIAL P Rule 8; IN ST TRIAL P Rule 9.2; IN ST TRIAL P Rule 10.

    f. Signing and verification of pleadings. IN ST TRIAL P Rule 11.

    g. General provisions regarding discovery. IN ST TRIAL P Rule 26.

    h. Methods of discovery. IN ST TRIAL P Rule 27; IN ST TRIAL P Rule 30; IN ST TRIAL P Rule 31; IN ST TRIAL P Rule 33; IN ST TRIAL P Rule 34; IN ST TRIAL P Rule 36.

    i. Failure to make or cooperate in discovery; Sanctions. IN ST TRIAL P Rule 37.

    j. Evidence. IN ST TRIAL P Rule 43.

k.   Judgment on the evidence (directed verdict). IN ST TRIAL P Rule 50.

l.   Findings by the court. IN ST TRIAL P Rule 52.

m. Summary judgment. IN ST TRIAL P Rule 56.

n.   Motion to correct error. IN ST TRIAL P Rule 59.

o.   Relief from judgment or order. IN ST TRIAL P Rule 60.

p.   Hearing of motions. IN ST TRIAL P Rule 73.

q.   Access to court records. IN ST ADMIN Rule 9.

r.   Paper size. IN ST ADMIN Rule 11.

s.   Facsimile transmission. IN ST ADMIN Rule 12.

t.   Electronic filing and electronic service pilot projects. IN ST ADMIN Rule 16.

u.   Sealing of certain records by court; Hearing; Notice. IN ST 5-14-3-5.5.

v.   Privacy and confidentiality. IN ST 5-2-9-6; IN ST 5-14-3-4; IN ST 6-4.1-5-10; IN ST 6-4.1-12-12; IN ST 6-8.1-7-1; IN ST 11-13-1-8; IN ST 12-23-14-13; IN ST 16-39-3-10; IN ST 16-41-8-1; IN ST 22-4-19-6; IN ST 31-11-1-6; IN ST 31-19-5-23; IN ST 31-19-13-2; IN ST 31-19-19-1; IN ST 31-33-18-1; IN ST 31-39-1-1; IN ST 31-39-1-2; IN ST 33-23-16-16; IN ST 35-34-2-4; IN ST 35-38-1-13; IN ST 35-38-9-1; IN ST ADR Rule 2.11; IN ST ADR Rule 4.4; IN ST ADR Rule 5.6; IN ST JURY Rule 10.

2. *Local rules*

    a.   Requirements for motions. IN ST MARION CIR AND SUPER CTS CIV Rule 203.

    b.   Preparation of pleadings, motions and other papers. IN ST MARION CIR AND SUPER CTS CIV Rule 204.

    c.   Filing of pleadings, motions and other papers. IN ST MARION CIR AND SUPER CTS CIV Rule 205.

    d.   Signing and verification of pleadings, motions and other papers; Service on opposing party. IN ST MARION CIR AND SUPER CTS CIV Rule 206.

    e.   Motions for continuance. IN ST MARION CIR AND SUPER CTS CIV Rule 215.

    f.   Electronic filing. IN ST MARION SUPER CT ADMIN Rule 311.

B. Timing

1. *Motion to compel discovery.* There are no specific timing requirements for filing a motion to compel discovery. The moving party must provide reasonable notice of his intention to file a motion to compel with the other litigants and all affected persons. 10 INPRAC § 58.51.

    a.   *Filing.* All pleadings and papers subsequent to the complaint which are required to be served upon a party shall be filed with the Court either before service or within a reasonable period of time thereafter. IN ST TRIAL P Rule 5(E)(1).

2. *Service.* A written motion, other than one which may be heard ex parte, and notice of the hearing thereof shall be served not less than five (5) days before the time specified for the hearing, unless a different period is fixed by the Indiana Rules of Trial Procedure or by order of the court. IN ST TRIAL P Rule 6(D).

    a.   *Of supporting affidavits.* When a motion is supported by affidavit, the affidavit shall be served with the motion. IN ST TRIAL P Rule 6(D).

3. *Opposition*

    a.   *Filing.* If the statement regarding the position of the opposing party(ies) required under IN ST MARION CIR AND SUPER CTS CIV Rule 203(A) indicates that objection to the granting of said motion may ensue, said objecting a party shall have fifteen (15) days from the date of filing to file a response to said motion. IN ST MARION CIR AND SUPER CTS CIV Rule 203(B).

    b.   *Service.* Except as otherwise provided in IN ST TRIAL P Rule 59(D), opposing affidavits may be served not less than one (1) day before the hearing, unless the court permits them to be served at some other time. IN ST TRIAL P Rule 6(D).

4. *Computation of time*

    a. *Generally; Days excluded.* In computing any period of time prescribed or allowed by the Indiana Rules of Trial Procedure, by order of the court, or by any applicable statute, the day of the act, event, or default from which the designated period of time begins to run shall not be included. The last day of the period so computed is to be included unless it is:

        i. A Saturday,

        ii. A Sunday,

        iii. A legal holiday as defined by state statute, or

        iv. A day the office in which the act is to be done is closed during regular business hours. IN ST TRIAL P Rule 6(A).

    b. *Short periods.* In any event, the period runs until the end of the next day that is not a Saturday, a Sunday, a legal holiday, or a day on which the office is closed. When the period of time allowed is less than seven (7) days, intermediate Saturdays, Sundays, legal holidays, and days on which the office is closed shall be excluded from the computations. IN ST TRIAL P Rule 6(A).

    c. *Additional time after service by United States mail.* Whenever a party has the right or is required to do some act or take some proceedings within a prescribed period after the service of a notice or other paper upon him and the notice or paper is served upon him by United States mail, three (3) days shall be added to the prescribed period. IN ST TRIAL P Rule 6(E).

    d. *Enlargement of time.* When an act is required or allowed to be done at or within a specific time by the Indiana Rules of Trial Procedure, the court may at any time for cause shown:

        i. Order the period enlarged, with or without motion or notice, if request therefor is made before the expiration of the period originally prescribed or extended by a previous order; or

        ii. Upon motion made after the expiration of the specific period, permit the act to be done where the failure to act was the result of excusable neglect; but, the court may not extend the time for taking any action for judgment on the evidence under IN ST TRIAL P Rule 50(A), amendment of findings and judgment under IN ST TRIAL P Rule 52(B), to correct errors under IN ST TRIAL P Rule 59(C), statement in opposition to motion to correct error under IN ST TRIAL P Rule 59(E), or to obtain relief from final judgment under IN ST TRIAL P Rule 60(B), except to the extent and under the conditions stated in those rules. IN ST TRIAL P Rule 6(B).

    e. *Continuances disfavored.* Motions for Continuance are discouraged. Neither side is entitled to an automatic continuance as a matter of right. IN ST MARION CIR AND SUPER CTS CIV Rule 215. For information on obtaining a continuance, refer to IN ST MARION CIR AND SUPER CTS CIV Rule 215.

C. General Requirements

1. *Motions, generally.* Unless made during a hearing or trial, or otherwise ordered by the court, an application to the court for an order shall be made by written motion. The motion shall state the grounds therefor and the relief or order sought. IN ST TRIAL P Rule 7(B).

    a. *Motions as distinct from pleadings.* Motions and responses to motions are not pleadings, and allegations contained in a motion are not admissions of a party. 22B INPRAC 7:2; Wachstetter v. County Properties, LLC, 832 N.E.2d 574 (Ind.Ct.App. 2005); Scott County Family YMCA, Inc. v. Hobbs, 817 N.E.2d 603 (Ind.Ct.App. 2004).

    b. *Unopposed motions generally granted.* It is common for a trial court to grant procedural motions, such as motions for enlargement of time, discovery motions, or motions for continuance, unless an objection is filed. 21 INPRAC § 13.8.

2. *Motion to compel discovery.* Motions under IN ST TRIAL P Rule 37 are intended secure compliance with discovery requests and orders, ensure that one party will not profit from a failure to comply, and provide a general deterrence to discovery abuses. 22B INPRAC 37:1; Fifth Third Bank v. PNC Bank, 885 N.E.2d 52 (Ind.Ct.App. 2008).

    a. *Appropriate court.* An application for an order to a party may be made to the court in which the action is pending, or alternately, on matters relating to a deposition or an order under IN ST TRIAL P Rule 34, to the court in the county where the deposition is being taken or where compliance is to be made under IN ST TRIAL P Rule 34. An application for an order to a deponent who is not a party shall be made to the court in the county where the deposition is being taken. IN ST TRIAL P Rule 37(A)(1).

b. *Motion.* If a party refuses to allow inspection under IN ST TRIAL P Rule 9.2(E), or if a deponent fails to answer a question propounded or submitted under IN ST TRIAL P Rule 30 or IN ST TRIAL P Rule 31, or an organization, including without limitation a governmental organization or a partnership, fails to make designation under IN ST TRIAL P Rule 30(B)(6) or IN ST TRIAL P Rule 31(A), or a party fails to answer an interrogatory submitted under IN ST TRIAL P Rule 33, or if a party or witness or other person, in response to a request submitted under IN ST TRIAL P Rule 34, fails to respond that inspection will be permitted as requested or fails to permit inspection as requested, the discovering party may move for an order compelling an answer, or a designation, or an order compelling inspection in accordance with the request. When taking a deposition on oral examination, the proponent of the question may complete or adjourn the examination before he applies for an order. IN ST TRIAL P Rule 37(A)(2).

   i. *Evasive or incomplete answer.* For purposes of IN ST TRIAL P Rule 37(A) an evasive or incomplete answer is to be treated as a failure to answer. IN ST TRIAL P Rule 37(A)(3).

c. *Content of motion.* A motion to compel discovery should state the history of the discovery dispute, evidence that the opposing party was properly served with the discovery request, the position taken by the parties, the grounds for the motion with supporting authority, and the relief sought. In addition, the motion should include a statement demonstrating compliance with the informal dispute resolution requirements of IN ST TRIAL P Rule 26(F). 10 INPRAC § 58.51.

d. *Request for relief.* A motion to compel, filed under IN ST TRIAL P Rule 37, may request the following relief:

   i. An order compelling a discovery response;

   ii. Sanctions under IN ST TRIAL P Rule 37(D) (this rule incorporates by reference the sanctions available to a trial court to punish a party who has refused to comply with a discovery order); and

   iii. An award of attorney fees and expenses incurred to obtain an order compelling discovery. 10 INPRAC § 58.51.

e. *Effect of granting or denial of the motion*

   i. *Denied in whole or in part.* If the court denies the motion in whole or in part, it may make such protective order as it would have been empowered to make on a motion made pursuant to IN ST TRIAL P Rule 26(C). IN ST TRIAL P Rule 37(A)(2).

   ii. *Granted in part and denied in part.* If the motion is granted in part and denied in part, the court may apportion the reasonable expenses incurred in relation to the motion among the parties and persons in a just manner. IN ST TRIAL P Rule 37(A)(4).

   iii. *Motion denied.* If the motion is denied, the court shall, after opportunity for hearing, require the moving party or the attorney advising the motion or both of them to pay to the party or deponent who opposed the motion the reasonable expenses incurred in opposing the motion, including attorney's fees, unless the court finds that the making of the motion was substantially justified or that other circumstances make an award of expenses unjust. IN ST TRIAL P Rule 37(A)(4).

   iv. *Motion granted.* If the motion is granted, the court shall, after opportunity for hearing, require the party or deponent whose conduct necessitated the motion or the party or attorney advising such conduct or both of them to pay to the moving party the reasonable expenses incurred in obtaining the order, including attorney's fees, unless the court finds that the opposition to the motion was substantially justified or that other circumstances make an award of expenses unjust. IN ST TRIAL P Rule 37(A)(4). Refer to the Indiana KeyRules Motion for Discovery Sanctions document for more information.

f. *Expenses; Burden on non-prevailing party.* The non-prevailing party has the burden of proving that the reimbursement of expenses should not be awarded. 10 INPRAC § 58.51.

3. *Opposition to motion to compel; Information not reasonably accessible.* On motion to compel discovery or for a protective order, the party from whom discovery is sought must show that the information is not reasonably accessible because of undue burden or cost. If that showing is made, the court may nonetheless order discovery from such sources if the requesting party shows good cause. The court may specify conditions for the discovery. IN ST TRIAL P Rule 26(C)(9).

D. Documents

1. *Required documents*

   a. *Motion and notice.* The requirement of notice is satisfied by service of the motion. IN ST TRIAL P Rule 7(B); IN ST MARION CIR AND SUPER CTS CIV Rule 203(A). Refer to the General Requirements section of this document for information on the content of a motion to compel discovery.

   b. *Disputed discovery.* In addition, the motion should attach a copy of the disputed discovery in accordance with the requirements of IN ST TRIAL P Rule 5(D). 10 INPRAC § 58.51.

   c. *Attorney certification.* Before any party files any motion or request to compel discovery pursuant to IN ST TRIAL P Rule 37, or any motion for protection from discovery pursuant to IN ST TRIAL P Rule 26(C), or any other discovery motion which seeks to enforce, modify, or limit discovery, that party shall:

      i. Make a reasonable effort to reach agreement with the opposing party concerning the matter which is the subject of the motion or request; and

      ii. Include in the motion or request a statement showing that the attorney making the motion or request has made a reasonable effort to reach agreement with the opposing attorney(s) concerning the matter(s) set forth in the motion or request. This statement shall recite, in addition, the date, time and place of this effort to reach agreement, whether in person or by phone, and the names of all parties and attorneys participating therein. If an attorney for any party advises the court in writing that an opposing attorney has refused or delayed meeting and discussing the issues covered in IN ST TRIAL P Rule 26(F), the court may take such action as is appropriate. IN ST TRIAL P Rule 26(F).

      iii. The court may deny a discovery motion filed by a party who has failed to comply with the requirements of IN ST TRIAL P Rule 26(F). IN ST TRIAL P Rule 26(F).

   d. *Statement of approval or disapproval.* Except for initial motions made pursuant to IN ST MARION CIR AND SUPER CTS CIV Rule 203(D), all motions filed with the court shall include a brief statement indicating whether opposing party(ies) object to or approve of the granting of said motion. IN ST MARION CIR AND SUPER CTS CIV Rule 203(A).

   e. *Proposed order.* Unless local practice provides differently, a party should submit a proposed order with its written motion to be signed by the judge once the motion has been granted. 21 INPRAC § 13.8. All motions seeking an order of the Court shall be accompanied by a sufficient number of orders to be executed by the Court in granting said motion. In addition to the orders, the notice shall be accompanied by stamped, addressed envelopes to all parties of record. IN ST MARION CIR AND SUPER CTS CIV Rule 203(E).

   f. *Certificate of service.* An attorney or unrepresented party tendering a document to the Clerk for filing shall certify that service has been made, list the parties served, and specify the date and means of service. The certificate of service shall be placed at the end of the document and shall not be separately filed. The separate filing of a certificate of service, however, shall not be grounds for rejecting a document for filing. The Clerk may permit documents to be filed without a certificate of service but shall require prompt filing of a separate certificate of service. IN ST TRIAL P Rule 5(C). In all cases where any pleading or other document is required to be served upon opposing counsel, proof of such service may be made either by:

      i. A certificate of service signed by counsel of record for the serving party and the certificate shall specify by name and address all counsel upon whom the pleading or document was served; or

      ii. An acknowledgment of service signed by the party served or counsel of record. IN ST MARION CIR AND SUPER CTS CIV Rule 206.

2. *Supplemental documents*

    a. *Supporting evidence.* When a motion is based on facts not appearing of record the court may hear the matter on affidavits presented by the respective parties, but the court may direct that the matter be heard wholly or partly on oral testimony or depositions. IN ST TRIAL P Rule 43(B).

    b. *Request for oral argument.* When an oral argument is requested, the request shall be by separate instrument and filed with the pleading to be argued. Any such oral argument requested may be heard at the discretion of the Court, except for motions for summary judgment which shall be set for hearing upon request of any party. IN ST MARION CIR AND SUPER CTS CIV Rule 203(C).

    c. *Facsimile cover sheet.* Any document sent to the Clerk of the Circuit Court by electronic facsimile transmission shall be accompanied by a cover sheet which states the title of the document, case number, number of pages, identity and voice telephone number of the sending party and instructions for filing. The cover sheet shall contain the signature of the attorney or party, pro se, authorizing the filing. IN ST ADMIN Rule 12(D).

E. Format

1. *Form of motions.* The rules applicable to captions, and the signing and form of pleadings (IN ST TRIAL P Rule 8 through IN ST TRIAL P Rule 11), apply to all motions and other papers provided under the Indiana Rules of Trial Procedure. 22B INPRAC 7:2.

2. *Form of pleadings*

    a. *Caption; Names of parties.* Every pleading shall contain a caption setting forth the name of the court, the title of the action, the file number, and a designation as in IN ST TRIAL P Rule 7(A). In the complaint the title of the action shall include the names of all the parties, but in other pleadings it is sufficient to state the name of the first party on each side with an appropriate indication of other parties. IN ST TRIAL P Rule 10(A).

        i. Every pleading shall contain a caption setting forth the name of the Court, the Division and Room Number, the title of the action and the file number. IN ST MARION CIR AND SUPER CTS CIV Rule 204(B).

    b. *Paragraphs; Separate statements.* All averments of a claim or defense shall be made in numbered paragraphs, the contents of each of which shall be limited as far as practicable to a statement of a single set of circumstances, and a paragraph may be referred to by number in all succeeding pleadings. Each claim founded upon a separate transaction or occurrence and each defense other than denials may be stated in a separate count or defense whenever a separation facilitates the clear presentation of the matters set forth. IN ST TRIAL P Rule 10(B).

    c. *Adoption by reference; Exhibits.* Statements in a pleading may be adopted by reference in a different part of the same pleading or in another pleading or in any motion. A copy of any written instrument which is an exhibit to a pleading is a part thereof for all purposes. IN ST TRIAL P Rule 10(C).

    d. *Paper.* Pleadings, motions and other papers may be either printed or typewritten on white opaque paper of at least sixteen (16) pound weight, eight and one-half (8-1/2) inches wide and eleven (11) inches in length. IN ST MARION CIR AND SUPER CTS CIV Rule 204(A).

    e. *Copies.* All copies shall likewise be on white paper of sufficient strength and durability to resist normal wear and tear. IN ST MARION CIR AND SUPER CTS CIV Rule 204(A).

    f. *Line spacing.* If typewritten, the lines shall be double spaced, except for quotations, which shall be indented and single spaced. IN ST MARION CIR AND SUPER CTS CIV Rule 204(A).

    g. *Script type.* Script type shall not be used. IN ST MARION CIR AND SUPER CTS CIV Rule 204(A).

    h. *Titles.* Titles on all pleadings shall delineate each topic included in the pleading e.g. where a pleading contains an Answer, a Motion to Strike or Dismiss, or a Jury Request each shall be set forth in the title. IN ST MARION CIR AND SUPER CTS CIV Rule 204(C).

    i. *Margins and binding.* Margins shall be one (1) inch. Binding or stapling shall be at the top and at no other place. Covers or backing shall not be used. IN ST MARION CIR AND SUPER CTS CIV Rule 204(D).

3. *Size of papers for filing.* Effective January 1, 1992, all pleadings, copies, motions and documents filed with any trial court or appellate level court, typed or printed, with the exception of exhibits and existing wills, shall be prepared on eight and one-half by eleven inch (8 1/2" x 11") size paper. IN ST ADMIN Rule 11.

4. *Form of electronically filed documents.* All electronically filed and served pleadings shall, to the extent practicable, be formatted in accordance with the applicable rules governing formatting of paper pleadings. IN ST MARION SUPER CT ADMIN Rule 311(2-103)(1).

   a. *Electronic document title.* The electronic document title of each pleading or other document shall include:

      i. Party or parties filing/serving the document,

      ii. Nature of the document,

      iii. Party or parties against whom relief, if any, is sought, and

      iv. Nature of the relief sought (e.g., Defendant ABC Corporation's Motion for Summary Judgment). IN ST MARION SUPER CT ADMIN Rule 311(2-103)(2).

5. *Signature requirements*

   a. *Signature of attorney.* Every pleading or motion of a party represented by an attorney shall be signed by at least one (1) attorney of record in his individual name, whose address, telephone number, and attorney number shall be stated, except that this provision shall not apply to pleadings and motions made and transcribed at the trial or a hearing before the judge and received by him in such form. IN ST TRIAL P Rule 11(A).

      i. All pleadings and motions shall contain the original or authorized signature of the attorney, the name of the attorney in typed or printed form, the name of the law firm if a member of a firm, the attorney's address, identification number, e-mail address, telephone number, fax number, and the designation as to the party for whom he appears. IN ST MARION CIR AND SUPER CTS CIV Rule 204(E).

      ii. The signature of an attorney constitutes a certificate by him that he has read the pleadings; that to the best of his knowledge, information, and belief, there is good ground to support it; and that it is not interposed for delay. IN ST TRIAL P Rule 11(A).

      iii. If a pleading or motion is not signed or is signed with intent to defeat the purpose of the rule, it may be stricken as sham and false and the action may proceed as though the pleading had not been served. IN ST TRIAL P Rule 11(A).

      iv. For a willful violation of IN ST TRIAL P Rule 11 an attorney may be subjected to appropriate disciplinary action. Similar action may be taken if scandalous or indecent matter is inserted. IN ST TRIAL P Rule 11(A).

      v. Every pleading, document, and instrument electronically filed or served shall be deemed to have been signed by the judge, clerk, attorney or declarant and shall bear a facsimile or typographical signature of such person, along with the typed name, address, telephone number, and Bar number of a signing attorney. Typographical signatures shall be treated as personal signatures for all purposes under these rules. IN ST MARION SUPER CT ADMIN Rule 311(2-105).

         • Documents containing signatures of third-parties (i.e., unopposed motions, affidavits, stipulations, etc.) may also be filed electronically by indicating that the original signatures are maintained by the filing party in paper-format. IN ST MARION SUPER CT ADMIN Rule 311(2-105).

         • Unless otherwise ordered by the Court or Clerk, a printed copy of all documents filed or served electronically, including original signatures, shall be maintained by the party filing the document and shall be made available, upon reasonable notice, for inspection by other counsel, the Clerk or Court. Parties shall retain originals until two (2) years after all time periods for appeal have expired. From time to time, it may be necessary to provide the Clerk or Court with a hard copy of an electronically filed document. IN ST MARION SUPER CT ADMIN Rule 311(2-105).

    vi. For the recommended format of a signature block, refer to IN ST MARION CIR AND SUPER CTS CIV Rule 204(E).

b. *Signature of unrepresented party.* A party who is not represented by an attorney shall sign his pleading and state his address. IN ST TRIAL P Rule 11(A).

c. *Verification not generally required.* Except when specifically required by rule, pleadings or motions need not be verified or accompanied by affidavit. The rule in equity that the averments of an answer under oath must be overcome by the testimony of two (2) witnesses or of one (1) witness sustained by corroborating circumstances is abolished. IN ST TRIAL P Rule 11(A).

d. *Verification by affirmation or representation.* When in connection with any civil or special statutory proceeding it is required that any pleading, motion, petition, supporting affidavit, or other document of any kind, be verified, or that an oath be taken, it shall be sufficient if the subscriber simply affirms the truth of the matter to be verified by an affirmation or representation. IN ST TRIAL P Rule 11(B). IN ST TRIAL P Rule 11(B) states that the affirmation or representation should be in substantially the following language: "I (we) affirm, under the penalties for perjury, that the foregoing representation(s) is (are) true. (Signed) _____"

    i. Any person who falsifies an affirmation or representation of fact shall be subject to the same penalties as are prescribed by law for the making of a false affidavit. IN ST TRIAL P Rule 11(B).

e. *Verified pleadings, motions, and affidavits as evidence.* Pleadings, motions and affidavits accompanying or in support of such pleadings or motions when required to be verified or under oath shall be accepted as a representation that the signer had personal knowledge thereof or reasonable cause to believe the existence of the facts or matters stated or alleged therein; and, if otherwise competent or acceptable as evidence, may be admitted as evidence of the facts or matters stated or alleged therein when it is so provided in the Indiana Rules of Trial Procedure, by statute or other law, or to the extent the writing or signature expressly purports to be made upon the signer's personal knowledge. When such pleadings, motions and affidavits are verified or under oath they shall not require other or greater proof on the part of the adverse party than if not verified or not under oath unless expressly provided otherwise by the Indiana Rules of Trial Procedure, statute or other law. Affidavits upon motions for summary judgment under IN ST TRIAL P Rule 56 and in denial of execution under IN ST TRIAL P Rule 9.2 shall be made upon personal knowledge. IN ST TRIAL P Rule 11(C).

6. *Information excluded from public access.* Every document filed in a case shall separately identify information excluded from public access pursuant to IN ST ADMIN Rule 9(G)(1) as follows:

a. Whole documents that are excluded from public access pursuant to IN ST ADMIN Rule 9(G)(1) shall be tendered on light green paper or have a light green coversheet attached to the document, marked "Not for Public Access" or "Confidential." IN ST TRIAL P Rule 5(G)(1).

b. When only a portion of a document contains information excluded from public access pursuant to IN ST ADMIN Rule 9(G)(1), said information shall be omitted [or redacted] from the filed document, and set forth on a separate accompanying document on light green paper conspicuously marked "Not for Public Access" or "Confidential" and clearly designated [or identifying] the caption and number of the case and the document and location within the document to which the redacted material pertains. IN ST TRIAL P Rule 5(G)(2).

c. With respect to documents filed in electronic format, the trial court, by local rule, may provide for compliance with IN ST TRIAL P Rule 5 in manner that separates and protects access to information excluded from public access. IN ST TRIAL P Rule 5(G)(3).

d. IN ST TRIAL P Rule 5(G) does not apply to a record sealed by the court pursuant to IN ST 5-14-3-5.5 or otherwise, nor to records, documents, or information filed in cases to which public access is prohibited pursuant to IN ST ADMIN Rule 9(G). IN ST TRIAL P Rule 5(G)(4).

e. The following information in case records is excluded from public access and is confidential:

    i. Information that is excluded from public access pursuant to federal law;

ii. Information that is excluded from public access as declared confidential by Indiana statute or other court rule, including without limitation:

- All adoption records created after July 8, 1941, as declared confidential by IN ST 31-19-19-1, et seq., except those specifically declared open by IN ST 31-19-13-2(2);

- All records relating to chancroid, chlamydia, gonorrhea, hepatitis, human immunodeficiency virus (HIV), Lymphogranuloma venereum, syphilis, tuberculosis, as declared confidential by IN ST 16-41-8-1, et seq.;

- All records relating to child abuse as declared confidential by IN ST 31-33-18-1, et seq.;

- All records relating to drug tests as declared confidential by IN ST 5-14-3-4(a)(9);

- Records of grand jury proceedings as declared confidential by IN ST 35-34-2-4;

- Records of juvenile proceedings as declared confidential by IN ST 31-39-1-2, except those specifically open under statute;

- All paternity records created after July 1, 1941 as declared confidential by IN ST 31-14-11-15, IN ST 31-19-5-23, IN ST 31-39-1-1 and IN ST 31-39-1-2 [Editor's note: IN ST 31-14-11-15 was repealed effective May 9, 2013];

- All pre-sentence reports as declared confidential by IN ST 35-38-1-13;

- Written petitions to permit marriages without consent and orders directing the Clerk of Court to issue a marriage license to underage persons, as declared confidential by IN ST 31-11-1-6;

- Only those arrest warrants, search warrants, indictments and informations ordered confidential by the trial judge, prior to return of duly executed service as declared confidential by IN ST 5-14-3-4(b)(1);

- All medical, mental health, or tax records unless determined by law or regulation of any governmental custodian not to be confidential, released by the subject of such records, or declared by a court of competent jurisdiction to be essential to the resolution of litigation as declared confidential by IN ST 16-39-3-10, IN ST 6-4.1-5-10, IN ST 6-4.1-12-12, and IN ST 6-8.1-7-1;

- Personal information relating to jurors or prospective jurors, other than for the use of the parties and counsel, pursuant to IN ST JURY Rule 10;

- Information relating to protection from abuse orders, no-contact orders and workplace violence restraining orders as declared confidential by IN ST 5-2-9-6, et seq.;

- Mediation proceedings pursuant to IN ST ADR Rule 2.11, Mini-Trial proceedings pursuant to IN ST ADR Rule 4.4(C), and Summary Jury Trials pursuant to IN ST ADR Rule 5.6;

- Information in probation files pursuant to the Probation Standards promulgated by the Judicial Conference of Indiana pursuant to IN ST 11-13-1-8(b);

- Information deemed confidential pursuant to the Rules for Court Administered Alcohol and Drug Programs promulgated by the Judicial Conference of Indiana pursuant to IN ST 12-23-14-13;

- Information deemed confidential pursuant to the Problem-Solving Court Rules promulgated by the Judicial Conference of Indiana pursuant to IN ST 33-23-16-16;

- All records of the Department of workforce Development as declared confidential by IN ST 22-4-19-6;

- Information regarding interception of electronic communications that is sealed or deemed confidential as set forth in IN ST 35-33.5-2-1, et seq.

iii. Information excluded from public access by specific court order;

iv. Complete Social Security Numbers of living persons;

    v. With the exception of names, information such as addresses, phone numbers, and dates of birth which explicitly identifies:

- Natural persons who are witnesses or victims (not including defendants) in criminal, domestic violence, stalking, sexual assault, juvenile, or civil protection order proceedings, provided that juveniles who are victims of sex crimes shall be identified by initials only;

- Places of residence of judicial officers, clerks and other employees of courts and clerks of court, unless the person or persons about whom the information pertains waives confidentiality;

    vi. Complete account numbers of specific assets, loans, bank accounts, credit cards, and personal identification numbers (PINs);

    vii. All orders of expungement entered in criminal or juvenile proceedings, orders to restrict access to criminal history information pursuant to IN ST 35-38-5-5.5 or IN ST 35-38-8-5 and records excluded from public access by such orders, and information related to infractions that is excluded from public access pursuant to IN ST 34-28-5-15 or IN ST 34-28-5-16 [Editor's note: IN ST 35-38-5-5.5, IN ST 35-38-8-5 and IN ST 34-28-5-16 were repealed effective July 1, 2013; for information on orders restricting access to criminal history, refer to IN ST 35-38-9-1, et seq.];

    viii. All personal notes and e-mail, and deliberative material, of judges, jurors, court staff and judicial agencies, and information recorded in personal data assistants (PDA's) or organizers and personal calendars. IN ST ADMIN Rule 9(G)(1).

F. Filing and Service Requirements

1. *Filing requirements.* Except as otherwise provided in IN ST TRIAL P Rule 5(E)(2), all pleadings and papers subsequent to the complaint which are required to be served upon a party shall be filed with the Court either before service or within a reasonable period of time thereafter. IN ST TRIAL P Rule 5(E)(1). Counsel shall file with the court an original and one (1) copy of all briefs, and memoranda of law filed in support of a motion. IN ST MARION CIR AND SUPER CTS CIV Rule 205(D).

  a. *Filing generally.* All pleadings, petitions and motions are filed with the Clerk designated by the Court at any time during office hours established by the Clerk and the Court. All orders submitted to the Court shall be in sufficient number and shall be accompanied by postage paid envelopes addressed to each party or counsel of record. IN ST MARION CIR AND SUPER CTS CIV Rule 205(A)

  b. *Filing with the court defined.* The filing of pleadings, motions, and other papers with the court as required by the Indiana Rules of Trial Procedure shall be made by one of the following methods:

    i. Delivery to the clerk of the court;

    ii. Sending by electronic transmission under the procedure adopted pursuant to IN ST ADMIN Rule 12;

    iii. Mailing to the clerk by registered, certified or express mail return receipt requested;

    iv. Depositing with any third-party commercial carrier for delivery to the clerk within three (3) calendar days, cost prepaid, properly addressed;

    v. If the court so permits, filing with the judge, in which event the judge shall note thereon the filing date and forthwith transmit them to the office of the clerk; or

    vi. Electronic filing, as approved by the Division of State Court Administration pursuant to IN ST ADMIN Rule 16. IN ST TRIAL P Rule 5(F).

    vii. Filing by registered or certified mail and by third-party commercial carrier shall be complete upon mailing or deposit. IN ST TRIAL P Rule 5(F).

  c. *Facsimile filing.* Facsimile filing is discouraged, but permitted in the Marion Circuit and Marion Superior Court. All documents filed by facsimile shall also be filed in hard copy within seven (7) days of the facsimile filing, along with proposed orders and stamped addressed envelopes, as required by IN ST MARION CIR AND SUPER CTS CIV Rule 203(E). To avoid duplicate filings, the hard copies of the facsimile filing shall indicate in bold letters that the pleading was previously filed by facsimile transmission. Proof of transmission by facsimile, including certificate of service and manner of service, shall be the responsibility of the filing party. If the filing requires immediate attention of the Judge, it shall be so indicated in bold letters in an accompanying transmittal memorandum. Legibility of documents and timeliness of filing is the responsibility of the sender. IN ST MARION CIR AND SUPER CTS CIV Rule 205(B).

i. *Generally.* In counties where a majority of judges of the courts of record, by posted local rule, have authorized electronic facsimile filing and designated a telephone number to receive such transmissions, pleadings, motions, and other papers may be sent to the Clerk of Circuit Court by electronic facsimile transmission for filing in any case, provided:

- Such matter does not exceed ten (10) pages, including the cover sheet;
- Such matter does not require the payment of fees other than the electronic facsimile transcription fee set forth in IN ST ADMIN Rule 12(E);
- The sending party creates at the time of transmission a machine generated log for such transmission; and
- The original document and the transmission log are maintained by the sending party for the duration of the litigation. IN ST ADMIN Rule 12(B).

ii. *Time of filing.* During normal, posted business hours, the time of filing shall be the time the duplicate document is produced in the office of the Clerk of the Circuit Court. Duplicate documents received at all other times shall be filed as of the next normal business day. IN ST ADMIN Rule 12(C).

- If the receiving fax machine endorses its own time and date stamp upon the transmitted documents and the receiving machine produces a delivery receipt which is electronically created and transmitted to the sending party, the time of filing shall be the date and time recorded on the transmitted document by the receiving fax machine. IN ST ADMIN Rule 12(C).

d. *Electronic filing.* Electronic filing and electronic service pilot projects are authorized pursuant to IN ST ADMIN Rule 16 and approved by the Division of State Court Administration. IN ST MARION SUPER CT ADMIN Rule 311(1-103).

i. *Cases where electronic filing accepted.* All Marion County Circuit and Superior civil courts may accept electronic filing and service of pleadings and other documents designated in this rule in mortgage foreclosure (hereinafter referred to as "MF"), civil collection(hereinafter referred to as "CC"), and individual cases that have been approved for electronic filing and service. IN ST MARION SUPER CT ADMIN Rule 311(1-104)(1).

- The Marion County Circuit Court may, upon the motion of a party or its own motion, designate a case that will involve multiple litigants, legally intricate issues, and an extensive number of documents a mass tort or complex litigation case. Any case so designated shall be subject to electronic filing and service using the county's approved Electronic Service Provider. IN ST MARION SUPER CT ADMIN Rule 311(1-104)(3).
- The filing of electronic pleadings and other documents in MF and CC cases is entirely voluntary; however, once the case is initially filed electronically, all subsequent filings in the case shall remain in electronic format until the time for appeal is exhausted. IN ST MARION SUPER CT ADMIN Rule 311(1-104)(5).

ii. *Documents eligible for electronic filing.* The following pleadings may be filed and served electronically:

- New case complaint and petitions. IN ST MARION SUPER CT ADMIN Rule 311(1-104)(8)(a).
- Original answers. IN ST MARION SUPER CT ADMIN Rule 311(1-104)(8)(a).
- Any other pleadings or document including but not limited to motions and appearance forms. IN ST MARION SUPER CT ADMIN Rule 311(1-104)(8)(a).

iii. *Manner of electronic filing.* Parties shall E-file a document either:

- By registering to use the Electronic Filing Service Provider; or

- In person at the Marion County Clerk's office, by electronically filing through the Public Access Terminal. Parties filing in this manner shall be responsible for furnishing the document in an electronic format that will be compatible with the clerk's office-system to be uploaded in person. IN ST MARION SUPER CT ADMIN Rule 311(1-104)(9). For information on the Electronic Filing Service Provider and Public Access Terminal, refer to IN ST MARION SUPER CT ADMIN Rule 311(1-101).

- Registered users shall pay statutory filing fees for E-filed documents electronically to the Court through their EFSP. Filing fees are due and payable at the time of filing. IN ST MARION SUPER CT ADMIN Rule 311(2-104)(1). For more information on electronic filing fees, refer to IN ST MARION SUPER CT ADMIN Rule 311(2-104).

iv. *Effect of electronic filing.* Any pleading filed electronically shall be considered as filed with the court when the transmission to the EFSP is complete. Any document E-filed by 11:59 p.m. local Indianapolis, Indiana time shall be deemed filed on that date. The EFSP is an agent of the Court for the purpose of electronic filing, receipt, service and retrieval of electronic documents. IN ST MARION SUPER CT ADMIN Rule 311(2-102).

- Upon completion of filing, the EFSP shall issue a confirmation receipt that includes the date and time of receipt. The confirmation receipt shall serve as proof of filing. IN ST MARION SUPER CT ADMIN Rule 311(2-102).

- In the event the Court rejects the submitted documents following review, the documents shall not become part of the official Court record and the filer will receive notification of the rejection. Users may be required to refile the instruments to meet necessary filing requirements. Documents may be filed through an E-filing system at any time that the Clerk's office is open to receive the filing or at such other times as may be designated by the clerk and posted publicly. IN ST MARION SUPER CT ADMIN Rule 311(2-102).

- Documents filed through the E-filing system are deemed filed when received by the Clerk's office, except that documents received at times that the Clerk's office is closed shall be deemed filed the next regular time when the Clerk's office is open for filing. The time stamp issued by the E-filing system shall be presumed to be the time the document is received by the Clerk. IN ST MARION SUPER CT ADMIN Rule 311(2-102).

v. *Electronically filed documents.* All pleadings and other documents designated in IN ST MARION SUPER CT ADMIN Rule 311 shall be filed and served electronically in any individual case which has been approved for electronic filing and service. IN ST MARION SUPER CT ADMIN Rule 311(1-104)(6).

vi. *System failures.* When filing by electronic means is hindered by a technical failure, a party may file with the Clerk of Marion County in hard copy. With the exception of deadlines that by law cannot be extended, the time for filing of any paper that is delayed due to technical failure of the site shall be extended for one (1) day for each day on which such failure occurs, unless otherwise ordered by the Court. IN ST MARION SUPER CT ADMIN Rule 311(2-108).

vii. *Compliance with rules.* All filing shall comply with the requirements of IN ST ADMIN Rule 9 and IN ST ADMIN Rule 16; and the Indiana Rules of Court and the Marion County Local Rules. IN ST MARION SUPER CT ADMIN Rule 311(1-104)(11).

e. *Filing for special judge.* When a Special Judge who is not a Marion County Judge is selected, all parties or attorneys shall furnish such Judge with copies of all filings prior to the qualification of such Special Judge. Thereafter, copies of all filings shall be delivered in person, by mail or by facsimile to the office of the Special Judge with certificate of forwarding same made a part of the filing. IN ST MARION CIR AND SUPER CTS CIV Rule 205(C).

f. *Proof of filing.* Any party filing any paper by any method other than personal delivery to the clerk shall retain proof of filing. IN ST TRIAL P Rule 5(F).

2. *Service requirements.* Unless otherwise provided by the Indiana Rules of Trial Procedure or an order of

the court, each party and special judge, if any, shall be served with: (1) every order required by its terms to be served; (2) every pleading subsequent to the original complaint; (3) every written motion except one which may be heard ex parte; (4) every brief submitted to the trial court; (5) every paper relating to discovery required to be served upon a party; and (6) every written notice, appearance, demand, offer of judgment, designation of record on appeal, or similar paper. IN ST TRIAL P Rule 5(A).

a. *Methods of service*

   i. *Personal service.* Whenever a party is represented by an attorney of record, service shall be made upon such attorney unless service upon the party himself is ordered by the court. Service upon the attorney or party shall be made by delivering or mailing a copy of the papers to the last known address or where an attorney or party has consented to service by fax or e-mail, as provided in IN ST TRIAL P Rule 3.1(A)(4), by faxing or e-mailing a copy of the documents to the fax number or e-mail address set out in the appearance form or correction as required by IN ST TRIAL P Rule 3.1(E). IN ST TRIAL P Rule 5(B). Delivery of a copy within IN ST TRIAL P Rule 5 means:

- Offering or tendering it to the attorney or party and stating the nature of the papers being served. Refusal to accept an offered or tendered document is a waiver of any objection to the sufficiency or adequacy of service of that document;

- Leaving it at his office with a clerk or other person in charge thereof, or if there is no one in charge, leaving it in a conspicuous place therein; or

- If the office is closed, by leaving it at his dwelling house or usual place of abode with some person of suitable age and discretion then residing therein; or,

- Leaving it at some other suitable place, selected by the attorney upon whom service is being made, pursuant to duly promulgated local rule. IN ST TRIAL P Rule 5(B)(1).

   ii. *Service by mail.* If service is made by mail, the papers shall be deposited in the United States mail addressed to the person on whom they are being served, with postage prepaid. Service shall be deemed complete upon mailing. Proof of service of all papers permitted to be mailed may be made by written acknowledgment of service, by affidavit of the person who mailed the papers, or by certificate of an attorney. It shall be the duty of attorneys when entering their appearance in a cause or when filing pleadings or papers therein, to have noted in the Chronological Case Summary or said pleadings or papers so filed the address and telephone number of their office. Service by delivery or by mail at such address shall be deemed sufficient and complete. IN ST TRIAL P Rule 5(B)(2).

   iii. *Service by fax or e-mail.* A party who has consented to service by fax or e-mail may be served as follows:

- Service by e-mail shall be made by attaching the document being served in .pdf format. Discovery documents must also be served in accordance with IN ST TRIAL P Rule 26(A). IN ST TRIAL P Rule 5(B)(3)(a).

- Service by fax shall be deemed complete upon generation of a transmission record indicating the successful transmission of the entire document, except as provided in IN ST TRIAL P Rule 5(B)(3)(d). IN ST TRIAL P Rule 5(B)(3)(b).

- Service by e-mail shall be deemed complete upon transmission, except as provided in IN ST TRIAL P Rule 5(B)(3)(d). IN ST TRIAL P Rule 5(B)(3)(c).

- Service by fax or e-mail that occurs on a Saturday, Sunday, legal holiday, or day the court or agency in which the matter is pending is closed or after 5:00 PM local time of the recipient shall be deemed complete the next day that is not a Saturday, Sunday, legal holiday, or day that the court or agency in which the matter is pending is not closed. IN ST TRIAL P Rule 5(B)(3)(d).

   iv. *Electronic service.* Delivery of E-service documents through the EFSP to other registered users shall be considered as valid and effective service and shall have the same legal effect as an original paper document. Recipients of E-service documents shall access their documents through the EFSP. IN ST MARION SUPER CT ADMIN Rule 311(2-107)(1).

- E-service shall be deemed complete when the transmission to the EFSP is completed. IN ST MARION SUPER CT ADMIN Rule 311(2-107)(2).
- For the purpose of computing time to respond to documents received via E-service, any document served on a day or at a time when the Clerk's office is not open for business shall be deemed served at the time of next opening of the Clerk's office for business. IN ST MARION SUPER CT ADMIN Rule 311(2-107)(3).

    b. *Serving numerous defendants.* In any action in which there are unusually large numbers of defendants, the court, upon motion or of its own initiative, may order:

      i. That service of the pleadings of the defendants and replies thereto need not be made as between the defendants;

- That any cross-claim, counterclaim, or matter constituting an avoidance or affirmative defense contained therein shall be deemed to be denied or avoided by all other parties; and
- That the filing of any such pleading and service thereof upon the plaintiff constitutes due notice of it to the parties. IN ST TRIAL P Rule 5(D).

      ii. A copy of every such order shall be served upon the parties in such manner and form as the court directs. IN ST TRIAL P Rule 5(D).

    c. *Service by electronic means.* Courts wishing to establish an electronic service pilot project pursuant to the Indiana Administrative Rules must submit a written request for approval and a plan to the Division of State Court Administration. IN ST ADMIN Rule 16(B).

    d. *Service on parties in default for failure to appear.* No service need be made on parties in default for failure to appear, except that pleadings asserting new or additional claims for relief against them shall be served upon them in the manner provided by service of summons in IN ST TRIAL P Rule 4. IN ST TRIAL P Rule 5(A).

G. Hearings

1. *Hearing on motion.* Unless local conditions make it impracticable, each judge shall establish regular times and places, at intervals sufficiently frequent for the prompt dispatch of business, at which motions requiring notice and hearing may be heard and disposed of; but the judge at any time or place and on such notice, if any, as he considers reasonable may make order for the advancement, conduct, and hearing of actions. To expedite its business the court may direct the submission and determination of motions without oral hearing upon brief written statements of reasons in support and opposition, or direct or permit hearings by telephone conference call with all attorneys or other similar means of communication. IN ST TRIAL P Rule 73(A).

2. *Time and place of hearing.* If the motion requires a hearing or oral argument, the Court shall set the time and place of hearing or argument on the motion. IN ST MARION CIR AND SUPER CTS CIV Rule 203(A).

H. Forms

1. Motion to Compel Discovery Forms for Indiana

    a. Notice. 5 INPRAC § 4:6.10.

    b. Motion to compel. 5 INPRAC § 4:6.20.

    c. Motion to compel; Failure to respond. 5 INPRAC § 4:6.30.

    d. Motion to compel answers to interrogatories. 5 INPRAC § 4:6.40.

    e. Motion to compel production of documents. 5 INPRAC § 4:6.50.

    f. Motion to dismiss as sanction for failure to comply with court ordered discovery. 5 INPRAC § 4:6.60.

    g. Notice of intention to file motion to compel discovery. 10 INPRAC § 58.54.

h.   Motion to compel discovery; General form. 10 INPRAC § 58.55.

i.   Order compelling requested discovery. 10 INPRAC § 58.56.

j.   Order denying motion to compel discovery. 10 INPRAC § 58.57.

k.   Motion to compel discovery; For failure to respond to discovery requests. 10 INPRAC § 58.58.

l.   Motion to compel; Physician to release medical records. 10 INPRAC § 58.59.

m.   Motion to compel plaintiff to execute medical records release. 10 INPRAC § 58.60.

n.   Motion to compel; Production of surveillance videotape. 10 INPRAC § 58.61.

o.   Motion for order that matters be taken as established. 10 INPRAC § 58.62.

p.   Motion for order precluding litigation of issues. 10 INPRAC § 58.63.

q.   Motion to compel; Failure to permit inspection of original documents. 10 INPRAC § 58.65.

r.   Motion to compel; Answer to deposition questions. 10 INPRAC § 58.66.

s.   Certificate of service; Personal service. 9 INPRAC § 5.7.

t.   Certificate of service; First class mail. 9 INPRAC § 5.8.

I. Checklist

(I) ❑ Matters to be considered by moving party

    (a) ❑ Required documents

        (1) ❑ Motion and notice

        (2) ❑ Disputed discovery

        (3) ❑ Attorney certification

        (4) ❑ Statement of approval or disapproval

        (5) ❑ Proposed order

        (6) ❑ Certificate of service

    (b) ❑ Supplemental documents

        (1) ❑ Supporting evidence

        (2) ❑ Request for oral argument

        (3) ❑ Facsimile cover sheet

    (c) ❑ Timing

        (1) ❑ The moving party must provide reasonable notice of his intention to file a motion to compel with the other litigants and all affected persons

        (2) ❑ A written motion, other than one which may be heard ex parte, and notice of the hearing thereof shall be served not less than five (5) days before the time specified for the hearing, unless a different period is fixed by the Indiana Rules of Trial Procedure or by order of the court

        (3) ❑ All pleadings and papers subsequent to the complaint which are required to be served upon a party shall be filed with the Court either before service or within a reasonable period of time thereafter

(II) ❑ Matters to be considered by the responding party

    (a) ❑ Required documents

        (1) ❑ Opposition

        (2) ❑ Certificate of service

    (b) ❑ Supplemental documents

        (1) ❑ Supporting evidence

    (2) ❑ Proposed order

    (3) ❑ Facsimile cover sheet

(c) ❑ Timing

    (1) ❑ If the statement regarding the position of the opposing party(ies) required under IN ST MARION CIR AND SUPER CTS CIV Rule 203(A) indicates that objection to the granting of said motion may ensue, said objecting a party shall have fifteen (15) days from the date of filing to file a response to said motion

    (2) ❑ Except as otherwise provided in IN ST TRIAL P Rule 59(D), opposing affidavits may be served not less than one (1) day before the hearing, unless the court permits them to be served at some other time

Motions, Oppositions and Replies
Motion for Protective Order

Document Last Updated October 2013

A. Applicable Rules

1. *State rules*

    a. Appearance. IN ST TRIAL P Rule 3.1.

    b. Process. IN ST TRIAL P Rule 4.

    c. Service and filing of pleadings and other papers. IN ST TRIAL P Rule 5.

    d. Time. IN ST TRIAL P Rule 6.

    e. Pleadings. IN ST TRIAL P Rule 7; IN ST TRIAL P Rule 8; IN ST TRIAL P Rule 9.2; IN ST TRIAL P Rule 10.

    f. Signing and verification of pleadings. IN ST TRIAL P Rule 11.

    g. General provisions governing discovery. IN ST TRIAL P Rule 26.

    h. Methods of discovery. IN ST TRIAL P Rule 27; IN ST TRIAL P Rule 30; IN ST TRIAL P Rule 31; IN ST TRIAL P Rule 33; IN ST TRIAL P Rule 34; IN ST TRIAL P Rule 36.

    i. Failure to make or cooperate in discovery; Sanctions. IN ST TRIAL P Rule 37.

    j. Evidence. IN ST TRIAL P Rule 43.

    k. Judgment on the evidence (directed verdict). IN ST TRIAL P Rule 50.

    l. Findings by the court. IN ST TRIAL P Rule 52.

    m. Summary judgment. IN ST TRIAL P Rule 56.

    n. Motion to correct error. IN ST TRIAL P Rule 59.

    o. Relief from judgment or error. IN ST TRIAL P Rule 60.

    p. Hearing of motions. IN ST TRIAL P Rule 73.

    q. Access to court records. IN ST ADMIN Rule 9.

    r. Paper size. IN ST ADMIN Rule 11.

    s. Facsimile transmission. IN ST ADMIN Rule 12.

    t. Electronic filing and electronic service pilot projects. IN ST ADMIN Rule 16.

    u. Sealing of certain records by court; Hearing; Notice. IN ST 5-14-3-5.5.

    v. Trade secrets. IN ST 24-2-3-1; IN ST 24-2-3-2.

    w. Privacy and confidentiality. IN ST 5-2-9-6; IN ST 5-14-3-4; IN ST 6-4.1-5-10; IN ST 6-4.1-12-12; IN ST 6-8.1-7-1; IN ST 11-13-1-8; IN ST 12-23-14-13; IN ST 16-39-3-10; IN ST 16-41-8-1; IN ST

22-4-19-6; IN ST 31-11-1-6; IN ST 31-19-5-23; IN ST 31-19-13-2; IN ST 31-19-19-1; IN ST 31-33-18-1; IN ST 31-39-1-1; IN ST 31-39-1-2; IN ST 33-23-16-16; IN ST 35-34-2-4; IN ST 35-38-1-13; IN ST 35-38-9-1; IN ST ADR Rule 2.11; IN ST ADR Rule 4.4; IN ST ADR Rule 5.6; IN ST JURY Rule 10.

2. *Local rules*

    a. Requirements for motions. IN ST MARION CIR AND SUPER CTS CIV Rule 203.

    b. Preparation of pleadings, motions and other papers. IN ST MARION CIR AND SUPER CTS CIV Rule 204.

    c. Filing of pleadings, motions and other papers. IN ST MARION CIR AND SUPER CTS CIV Rule 205.

    d. Signing and verification of pleadings, motions and other papers; Service on opposing party. IN ST MARION CIR AND SUPER CTS CIV Rule 206.

    e. Motions for continuance. IN ST MARION CIR AND SUPER CTS CIV Rule 215.

    f. Electronic filing. IN ST MARION SUPER CT ADMIN Rule 311.

B. Timing

1. *Motion for protective order.* There are no specific timing requirements for filing a motion for a protective order.

    a. *Filing.* All pleadings and papers subsequent to the complaint which are required to be served upon a party shall be filed with the Court either before service or within a reasonable period of time thereafter. IN ST TRIAL P Rule 5(E)(1).

2. *Service.* A written motion, other than one which may be heard ex parte, and notice of the hearing thereof shall be served not less than five (5) days before the time specified for the hearing, unless a different period is fixed by the Indiana Rules of Trial Procedure or by order of the court. IN ST TRIAL P Rule 6(D).

    a. *Of supporting affidavits.* When a motion is supported by affidavit, the affidavit shall be served with the motion. IN ST TRIAL P Rule 6(D).

3. *Opposition*

    a. *Filing.* If the statement regarding the position of the opposing party(ies) required under IN ST MARION CIR AND SUPER CTS CIV Rule 203(A) indicates that objection to the granting of said motion may ensue, said objecting a party shall have fifteen (15) days from the date of filing to file a response to said motion. IN ST MARION CIR AND SUPER CTS CIV Rule 203(B).

    b. *Service.* Except as otherwise provided in IN ST TRIAL P Rule 59(D), opposing affidavits may be served not less than one (1) day before the hearing, unless the court permits them to be served at some other time. IN ST TRIAL P Rule 6(D).

4. *Computation of time*

    a. *Generally; Days excluded.* In computing any period of time prescribed or allowed by the Indiana Rules of Trial Procedure, by order of the court, or by any applicable statute, the day of the act, event, or default from which the designated period of time begins to run shall not be included. The last day of the period so computed is to be included unless it is:

        i. A Saturday,

        ii. A Sunday,

        iii. A legal holiday as defined by state statute, or

        iv. A day the office in which the act is to be done is closed during regular business hours. IN ST TRIAL P Rule 6(A).

    b. *Short periods.* In any event, the period runs until the end of the next day that is not a Saturday, a Sunday, a legal holiday, or a day on which the office is closed. When the period of time allowed is less than seven (7) days, intermediate Saturdays, Sundays, legal holidays, and days on which the office is closed shall be excluded from the computations. IN ST TRIAL P Rule 6(A).

c. *Additional time after service by United States mail.* Whenever a party has the right or is required to do some act or take some proceedings within a prescribed period after the service of a notice or other paper upon him and the notice or paper is served upon him by United States mail, three (3) days shall be added to the prescribed period. IN ST TRIAL P Rule 6(E).

d. *Enlargement of time.* When an act is required or allowed to be done at or within a specific time by the Indiana Rules of Trial Procedure, the court may at any time for cause shown:

    i. Order the period enlarged, with or without motion or notice, if request therefor is made before the expiration of the period originally prescribed or extended by a previous order; or

    ii. Upon motion made after the expiration of the specific period, permit the act to be done where the failure to act was the result of excusable neglect; but, the court may not extend the time for taking any action for judgment on the evidence under IN ST TRIAL P Rule 50(A), amendment of findings and judgment under IN ST TRIAL P Rule 52(B), to correct errors under IN ST TRIAL P Rule 59(C), statement in opposition to motion to correct error under IN ST TRIAL P Rule 59(E), or to obtain relief from final judgment under IN ST TRIAL P Rule 60(B), except to the extent and under the conditions stated in those rules. IN ST TRIAL P Rule 6(B).

e. *Continuances disfavored.* Motions for Continuance are discouraged. Neither side is entitled to an automatic continuance as a matter of right. IN ST MARION CIR AND SUPER CTS CIV Rule 215. For information on obtaining a continuance, refer to IN ST MARION CIR AND SUPER CTS CIV Rule 215.

C. General Requirements

1. *Motions, generally.* Unless made during a hearing or trial, or otherwise ordered by the court, an application to the court for an order shall be made by written motion. The motion shall state the grounds therefor and the relief or order sought. IN ST TRIAL P Rule 7(B).

    a. *Motions as distinct from pleadings.* Motions and responses to motions are not pleadings, and allegations contained in a motion are not admissions of a party. 22B INPRAC 7:2; Wachstetter v. County Properties, LLC, 832 N.E.2d 574 (Ind.Ct.App. 2005); Scott County Family YMCA, Inc. v. Hobbs, 817 N.E.2d 603 (Ind.Ct.App. 2004).

    b. *Unopposed motions generally granted.* It is common for a trial court to grant procedural motions, such as motions for enlargement of time, discovery motions, or motions for continuance, unless an objection is filed. 21 INPRAC § 13.8.

2. *Motion for protective order*

    a. *Forms of protective order.* Upon motion by any party or by the person from whom discovery is sought, and for good cause shown, the court in which the action is pending or alternatively, on matters relating to a deposition, the court in the county where the deposition is being taken, may make any order which justice requires to protect a party or person from annoyance, embarrassment, oppression, or undue burden or expense, including one or more of the following:

        i. That the discovery not be had;

        ii. That the discovery may be had only on specified terms and conditions, including a designation of the time or place;

        iii. That the discovery may be had only by a method of discovery other than that selected by the party seeking discovery;

        iv. That certain matters not be inquired into, or that the scope of the discovery be limited to certain matters;

        v. That discovery be conducted with no one present except the parties and their attorneys and persons designated by the court;

        vi. That a deposition after being sealed be opened only by order of the court;

        vii. That a trade secret or other confidential research, development, or commercial information not be disclosed or be disclosed only in a designated way;

        viii. That the parties simultaneously file specified documents or information enclosed in sealed envelopes to be opened as directed by the court;

    ix.   That a party need not provide discovery of electronically stored information from sources that the party identifies as not reasonably accessible because of undue burden or cost. IN ST TRIAL P Rule 26(C).

b.   *List in IN ST TRIAL P Rule 26(C) not exhaustive.* A court is not limited to the eight specified types of orders. A court may be as inventive as the case and the conditions require. A party or a nonparty may thus obtain any kind of protective order against any kind of discovery which is sought in the case, if "good cause" is shown. So also, however, if a protective order is sought and denied, the trial court may go further and issue an order to provide for or to permit the discovery. 2A INPRAC R 26(26.20).

c.   *Trade secrets.* A protectable trade secret has four characteristics: (1) information, (2) which derives independent economic value, (3) is not generally known, or readily ascertainable by proper means by other persons who can obtain economic value from its disclosure or use, and (4) the subject of efforts reasonable under the circumstances to maintain its secrecy. 2A INPRAC R 26(26.23.1).

    i.   *Nature of determination.* The determination of whether information is a trade secret is a fact sensitive determination. 2A INPRAC R 26(26.23.1).

    ii.   *Burden of proof.* The burden of proof is on the party asserting the trade secret to show that it is included in the categories of protectable trade secret information listed in the trade secrets statute. 2A INPRAC R 26(26.23.1); Northern Elec. Co., Inc. v. Torma, 819 N.E.2d 417 (Ind.Ct.App. 2004).

    iii.   *Uniform trade secrets act.* The application of IN ST TRIAL P Rule 26 to trade secrets should be informed by Indiana's enactment of the Uniform Trade Secrets Act (UTSA) (refer to IN ST 24-2-3-1, et seq.), which provides states with a common legal framework for protecting trade secrets from misappropriation. 2A INPRAC R 26(26.23.1(C)).

    iv.   *Trade secret defined.* "Trade secret" means information, including a formula, pattern, compilation, program, device, method, technique, or process, that:

- Derives independent economic value, actual or potential, from not being generally known to, and not being readily ascertainable by proper means by, other persons who can obtain economic value from its disclosure or use; and

- Is the subject of efforts that are reasonable under the circumstances to maintain its secrecy. IN ST 24-2-3-2.

d.   *Information not reasonably accessible.* On motion to compel discovery or for a protective order, the party from whom discovery is sought must show that the information is not reasonably accessible because of undue burden or cost. If that showing is made, the court may nonetheless order discovery from such sources if the requesting party shows good cause. The court may specify conditions for the discovery. IN ST TRIAL P Rule 26(C)(9).

    i.   When filing a motion for protective order under IN ST TRIAL P Rule 26(C), the movant, whether a party or non-party, must allege and prove good cause for his request for protective order. The court is empowered to make any order which "justice requires to protect a party or person from annoyance, embarrassment, oppression, or undue burden or expense." Typically, this protection means that discovery will be denied altogether, or limited in scope or to specific terms. 10 INPRAC § 58.20.

e.   *Party justified in resisting discovery.* A litigant is substantially justified in seeking to compel or resist discovery if reasonable persons could conclude that genuine issue existed as to whether person was bound to comply with requested discovery. 10 INPRAC § 58.20; Munsell v. Hambright, 776 N.E.2d 1272 (Ind.Ct.App. 2002).

f.   *Award of expenses of motion.* If the motion for a protective order is denied in whole or in part, the court may, on such terms and conditions as are just, order that any party or person provide or permit discovery. The provisions of IN ST TRIAL P Rule 37(A)(4) apply to the award of expenses incurred in relation to the motion. IN ST TRIAL P Rule 26(C).

D. Documents

1. *Required documents*

   a. *Motion and notice.* The requirement of notice is satisfied by service of the motion. IN ST TRIAL P Rule 7(B); IN ST MARION CIR AND SUPER CTS CIV Rule 203(A). Refer to the General Requirements section of this document for information on the content of a motion for a protective order.

   b. *Attorney certification.* Before any party files any motion or request to compel discovery pursuant to IN ST TRIAL P Rule 37, or any motion for protection from discovery pursuant to IN ST TRIAL P Rule 26(C), or any other discovery motion which seeks to enforce, modify, or limit discovery, that party shall:

      i. Make a reasonable effort to reach agreement with the opposing party concerning the matter which is the subject of the motion or request; and

      ii. Include in the motion or request a statement showing that the attorney making the motion or request has made a reasonable effort to reach agreement with the opposing attorney(s) concerning the matter(s) set forth in the motion or request. This statement shall recite, in addition, the date, time and place of this effort to reach agreement, whether in person or by phone, and the names of all parties and attorneys participating therein. If an attorney for any party advises the court in writing that an opposing attorney has refused or delayed meeting and discussing the issues covered in IN ST TRIAL P Rule 26(F), the court may take such action as is appropriate. IN ST TRIAL P Rule 26(F).

      iii. The court may deny a discovery motion filed by a party who has failed to comply with the requirements of IN ST TRIAL P Rule 26(F). IN ST TRIAL P Rule 26(F).

   c. *Statement of approval or disapproval.* Except for initial motions made pursuant to IN ST MARION CIR AND SUPER CTS CIV Rule 203(D), all motions filed with the court shall include a brief statement indicating whether opposing party(ies) object to or approve of the granting of said motion. IN ST MARION CIR AND SUPER CTS CIV Rule 203(A).

   d. *Proposed order.* Unless local practice provides differently, a party should submit a proposed order with its written motion to be signed by the judge once the motion has been granted. 21 INPRAC § 13.8. All motions seeking an order of the Court shall be accompanied by a sufficient number of orders to be executed by the Court in granting said motion. In addition to the orders, the notice shall be accompanied by stamped, addressed envelopes to all parties of record. IN ST MARION CIR AND SUPER CTS CIV Rule 203(E).

   e. *Certificate of service.* An attorney or unrepresented party tendering a document to the Clerk for filing shall certify that service has been made, list the parties served, and specify the date and means of service. The certificate of service shall be placed at the end of the document and shall not be separately filed. The separate filing of a certificate of service, however, shall not be grounds for rejecting a document for filing. The Clerk may permit documents to be filed without a certificate of service but shall require prompt filing of a separate certificate of service. IN ST TRIAL P Rule 5(C). In all cases where any pleading or other document is required to be served upon opposing counsel, proof of such service may be made either by:

      i. A certificate of service signed by counsel of record for the serving party and the certificate shall specify by name and address all counsel upon whom the pleading or document was served; or

      ii. An acknowledgment of service signed by the party served or counsel of record. IN ST MARION CIR AND SUPER CTS CIV Rule 206.

2. *Supplemental documents*

   a. *Supporting evidence.* When a motion is based on facts not appearing of record the court may hear the matter on affidavits presented by the respective parties, but the court may direct that the matter be heard wholly or partly on oral testimony or depositions. IN ST TRIAL P Rule 43(B).

   b. *Request for oral argument.* When an oral argument is requested, the request shall be by separate instrument and filed with the pleading to be argued. Any such oral argument requested may be heard at the discretion of the Court, except for motions for summary judgment which shall be set for hearing upon request of any party. IN ST MARION CIR AND SUPER CTS CIV Rule 203(C).

c. *Facsimile cover sheet.* Any document sent to the Clerk of the Circuit Court by electronic facsimile transmission shall be accompanied by a cover sheet which states the title of the document, case number, number of pages, identity and voice telephone number of the sending party and instructions for filing. The cover sheet shall contain the signature of the attorney or party, pro se, authorizing the filing. IN ST ADMIN Rule 12(D).

E. Format

1. *Form of motions.* The rules applicable to captions, and the signing and form of pleadings (IN ST TRIAL P Rule 8 through IN ST TRIAL P Rule 11), apply to all motions and other papers provided under the Indiana Rules of Trial Procedure. 22B INPRAC 7:2.

2. *Form of pleadings*

   a. *Caption; Names of parties.* Every pleading shall contain a caption setting forth the name of the court, the title of the action, the file number, and a designation as in IN ST TRIAL P Rule 7(A). In the complaint the title of the action shall include the names of all the parties, but in other pleadings it is sufficient to state the name of the first party on each side with an appropriate indication of other parties. IN ST TRIAL P Rule 10(A).

      i. Every pleading shall contain a caption setting forth the name of the Court, the Division and Room Number, the title of the action and the file number. IN ST MARION CIR AND SUPER CTS CIV Rule 204(B).

   b. *Paragraphs; Separate statements.* All averments of a claim or defense shall be made in numbered paragraphs, the contents of each of which shall be limited as far as practicable to a statement of a single set of circumstances, and a paragraph may be referred to by number in all succeeding pleadings. Each claim founded upon a separate transaction or occurrence and each defense other than denials may be stated in a separate count or defense whenever a separation facilitates the clear presentation of the matters set forth. IN ST TRIAL P Rule 10(B).

   c. *Adoption by reference; Exhibits.* Statements in a pleading may be adopted by reference in a different part of the same pleading or in another pleading or in any motion. A copy of any written instrument which is an exhibit to a pleading is a part thereof for all purposes. IN ST TRIAL P Rule 10(C).

   d. *Paper.* Pleadings, motions and other papers may be either printed or typewritten on white opaque paper of at least sixteen (16) pound weight, eight and one-half (8-1/2) inches wide and eleven (11) inches in length. IN ST MARION CIR AND SUPER CTS CIV Rule 204(A).

   e. *Copies.* All copies shall likewise be on white paper of sufficient strength and durability to resist normal wear and tear. IN ST MARION CIR AND SUPER CTS CIV Rule 204(A).

   f. *Line spacing.* If typewritten, the lines shall be double spaced, except for quotations, which shall be indented and single spaced. IN ST MARION CIR AND SUPER CTS CIV Rule 204(A).

   g. *Script type.* Script type shall not be used. IN ST MARION CIR AND SUPER CTS CIV Rule 204(A).

   h. *Titles.* Titles on all pleadings shall delineate each topic included in the pleading e.g. where a pleading contains an Answer, a Motion to Strike or Dismiss, or a Jury Request each shall be set forth in the title. IN ST MARION CIR AND SUPER CTS CIV Rule 204(C).

   i. *Margins and binding.* Margins shall be one (1) inch. Binding or stapling shall be at the top and at no other place. Covers or backing shall not be used. IN ST MARION CIR AND SUPER CTS CIV Rule 204(D).

3. *Size of papers for filing.* Effective January 1, 1992, all pleadings, copies, motions and documents filed with any trial court or appellate level court, typed or printed, with the exception of exhibits and existing wills, shall be prepared on eight and one-half by eleven inch (8 1/2" x 11") size paper. IN ST ADMIN Rule 11.

4. *Form of electronically filed documents.* All electronically filed and served pleadings shall, to the extent

practicable, be formatted in accordance with the applicable rules governing formatting of paper pleadings. IN ST MARION SUPER CT ADMIN Rule 311(2-103)(1).

a. *Electronic document title.* The electronic document title of each pleading or other document shall include:

    i. Party or parties filing/serving the document,

    ii. Nature of the document,

    iii. Party or parties against whom relief, if any, is sought, and

    iv. Nature of the relief sought (e.g., Defendant ABC Corporation's Motion for Summary Judgment). IN ST MARION SUPER CT ADMIN Rule 311(2-103)(2).

5. *Signature requirements*

a. *Signature of attorney.* Every pleading or motion of a party represented by an attorney shall be signed by at least one (1) attorney of record in his individual name, whose address, telephone number, and attorney number shall be stated, except that this provision shall not apply to pleadings and motions made and transcribed at the trial or a hearing before the judge and received by him in such form. IN ST TRIAL P Rule 11(A).

    i. All pleadings and motions shall contain the original or authorized signature of the attorney, the name of the attorney in typed or printed form, the name of the law firm if a member of a firm, the attorney's address, identification number, e-mail address, telephone number, fax number, and the designation as to the party for whom he appears. IN ST MARION CIR AND SUPER CTS CIV Rule 204(E).

    ii. The signature of an attorney constitutes a certificate by him that he has read the pleadings; that to the best of his knowledge, information, and belief, there is good ground to support it; and that it is not interposed for delay. IN ST TRIAL P Rule 11(A).

    iii. If a pleading or motion is not signed or is signed with intent to defeat the purpose of the rule, it may be stricken as sham and false and the action may proceed as though the pleading had not been served. IN ST TRIAL P Rule 11(A).

    iv. For a willful violation of IN ST TRIAL P Rule 11 an attorney may be subjected to appropriate disciplinary action. Similar action may be taken if scandalous or indecent matter is inserted. IN ST TRIAL P Rule 11(A).

    v. Every pleading, document, and instrument electronically filed or served shall be deemed to have been signed by the judge, clerk, attorney or declarant and shall bear a facsimile or typographical signature of such person, along with the typed name, address, telephone number, and Bar number of a signing attorney. Typographical signatures shall be treated as personal signatures for all purposes under these rules. IN ST MARION SUPER CT ADMIN Rule 311(2-105).

- Documents containing signatures of third-parties (i.e., unopposed motions, affidavits, stipulations, etc.) may also be filed electronically by indicating that the original signatures are maintained by the filing party in paper-format. IN ST MARION SUPER CT ADMIN Rule 311(2-105).

- Unless otherwise ordered by the Court or Clerk, a printed copy of all documents filed or served electronically, including original signatures, shall be maintained by the party filing the document and shall be made available, upon reasonable notice, for inspection by other counsel, the Clerk or Court. Parties shall retain originals until two (2) years after all time periods for appeal have expired. From time to time, it may be necessary to provide the Clerk or Court with a hard copy of an electronically filed document. IN ST MARION SUPER CT ADMIN Rule 311(2-105).

    vi. For the recommended format of a signature block, refer to IN ST MARION CIR AND SUPER CTS CIV Rule 204(E).

b. *Signature of unrepresented party.* A party who is not represented by an attorney shall sign his pleading and state his address. IN ST TRIAL P Rule 11(A).

c. *Verification not generally required.* Except when specifically required by rule, pleadings or motions need not be verified or accompanied by affidavit. The rule in equity that the averments of an answer under oath must be overcome by the testimony of two (2) witnesses or of one (1) witness sustained by corroborating circumstances is abolished. IN ST TRIAL P Rule 11(A).

d. *Verification by affirmation or representation.* When in connection with any civil or special statutory proceeding it is required that any pleading, motion, petition, supporting affidavit, or other document of any kind, be verified, or that an oath be taken, it shall be sufficient if the subscriber simply affirms the truth of the matter to be verified by an affirmation or representation. IN ST TRIAL P Rule 11(B). IN ST TRIAL P Rule 11(B) states that the affirmation or representation should be in substantially the following language: "I (we) affirm, under the penalties for perjury, that the foregoing representation(s) is (are) true. (Signed) _____."

   i. Any person who falsifies an affirmation or representation of fact shall be subject to the same penalties as are prescribed by law for the making of a false affidavit. IN ST TRIAL P Rule 11(B).

e. *Verified pleadings, motions, and affidavits as evidence.* Pleadings, motions and affidavits accompanying or in support of such pleadings or motions when required to be verified or under oath shall be accepted as a representation that the signer had personal knowledge thereof or reasonable cause to believe the existence of the facts or matters stated or alleged therein; and, if otherwise competent or acceptable as evidence, may be admitted as evidence of the facts or matters stated or alleged therein when it is so provided in the Indiana Rules of Trial Procedure, by statute or other law, or to the extent the writing or signature expressly purports to be made upon the signer's personal knowledge. When such pleadings, motions and affidavits are verified or under oath they shall not require other or greater proof on the part of the adverse party than if not verified or not under oath unless expressly provided otherwise by the Indiana Rules of Trial Procedure, statute or other law. Affidavits upon motions for summary judgment under IN ST TRIAL P Rule 56 and in denial of execution under IN ST TRIAL P Rule 9.2 shall be made upon personal knowledge. IN ST TRIAL P Rule 11(C).

6. *Information excluded from public access.* Every document filed in a case shall separately identify information excluded from public access pursuant to IN ST ADMIN Rule 9(G)(1) as follows:

   a. Whole documents that are excluded from public access pursuant to IN ST ADMIN Rule 9(G)(1) shall be tendered on light green paper or have a light green coversheet attached to the document, marked "Not for Public Access" or "Confidential." IN ST TRIAL P Rule 5(G)(1).

   b. When only a portion of a document contains information excluded from public access pursuant to IN ST ADMIN Rule 9(G)(1), said information shall be omitted [or redacted] from the filed document, and set forth on a separate accompanying document on light green paper conspicuously marked "Not for Public Access" or "Confidential" and clearly designated [or identifying] the caption and number of the case and the document and location within the document to which the redacted material pertains. IN ST TRIAL P Rule 5(G)(2).

   c. With respect to documents filed in electronic format, the trial court, by local rule, may provide for compliance with IN ST TRIAL P Rule 5 in manner that separates and protects access to information excluded from public access. IN ST TRIAL P Rule 5(G)(3).

   d. IN ST TRIAL P Rule 5(G) does not apply to a record sealed by the court pursuant to IN ST 5-14-3-5.5 or otherwise, nor to records, documents, or information filed in cases to which public access is prohibited pursuant to IN ST ADMIN Rule 9(G). IN ST TRIAL P Rule 5(G)(4).

   e. The following information in case records is excluded from public access and is confidential:

      i. Information that is excluded from public access pursuant to federal law;

      ii. Information that is excluded from public access as declared confidential by Indiana statute or other court rule, including without limitation:

         • All adoption records created after July 8, 1941, as declared confidential by IN ST 31-19-19-1, et seq., except those specifically declared open by IN ST 31-19-13-2(2);

         • All records relating to chancroid, chlamydia, gonorrhea, hepatitis, human immunodefi-

ciency virus (HIV), Lymphogranuloma venereum, syphilis, tuberculosis, as declared confidential by IN ST 16-41-8-1, et seq.;

- All records relating to child abuse as declared confidential by IN ST 31-33-18-1, et seq.;
- All records relating to drug tests as declared confidential by IN ST 5-14-3-4(a)(9);
- Records of grand jury proceedings as declared confidential by IN ST 35-34-2-4;
- Records of juvenile proceedings as declared confidential by IN ST 31-39-1-2, except those specifically open under statute;
- All paternity records created after July 1, 1941 as declared confidential by IN ST 31-14-11-15, IN ST 31-19-5-23, IN ST 31-39-1-1 and IN ST 31-39-1-2 [Editor's note: IN ST 31-14-11-15 was repealed effective May 9, 2013];
- All pre-sentence reports as declared confidential by IN ST 35-38-1-13;
- Written petitions to permit marriages without consent and orders directing the Clerk of Court to issue a marriage license to underage persons, as declared confidential by IN ST 31-11-1-6;
- Only those arrest warrants, search warrants, indictments and informations ordered confidential by the trial judge, prior to return of duly executed service as declared confidential by IN ST 5-14-3-4(b)(1);
- All medical, mental health, or tax records unless determined by law or regulation of any governmental custodian not to be confidential, released by the subject of such records, or declared by a court of competent jurisdiction to be essential to the resolution of litigation as declared confidential by IN ST 16-39-3-10, IN ST 6-4.1-5-10, IN ST 6-4.1-12-12, and IN ST 6-8.1-7-1;
- Personal information relating to jurors or prospective jurors, other than for the use of the parties and counsel, pursuant to IN ST JURY Rule 10;
- Information relating to protection from abuse orders, no-contact orders and workplace violence restraining orders as declared confidential by IN ST 5-2-9-6, et seq.;
- Mediation proceedings pursuant to IN ST ADR Rule 2.11, Mini-Trial proceedings pursuant to IN ST ADR Rule 4.4(C), and Summary Jury Trials pursuant to IN ST ADR Rule 5.6;
- Information in probation files pursuant to the Probation Standards promulgated by the Judicial Conference of Indiana pursuant to IN ST 11-13-1-8(b);
- Information deemed confidential pursuant to the Rules for Court Administered Alcohol and Drug Programs promulgated by the Judicial Conference of Indiana pursuant to IN ST 12-23-14-13;
- Information deemed confidential pursuant to the Problem-Solving Court Rules promulgated by the Judicial Conference of Indiana pursuant to IN ST 33-23-16-16;
- All records of the Department of workforce Development as declared confidential by IN ST 22-4-19-6;
- Information regarding interception of electronic communications that is sealed or deemed confidential as set forth in IN ST 35-33.5-2-1, et seq.

iii. Information excluded from public access by specific court order;

iv. Complete Social Security Numbers of living persons;

v. With the exception of names, information such as addresses, phone numbers, and dates of birth which explicitly identifies:

- Natural persons who are witnesses or victims (not including defendants) in criminal, domestic violence, stalking, sexual assault, juvenile, or civil protection order proceedings, provided that juveniles who are victims of sex crimes shall be identified by initials only;

- Places of residence of judicial officers, clerks and other employees of courts and clerks of court, unless the person or persons about whom the information pertains waives confidentiality;

vi. Complete account numbers of specific assets, loans, bank accounts, credit cards, and personal identification numbers (PINs);

vii. All orders of expungement entered in criminal or juvenile proceedings, orders to restrict access to criminal history information pursuant to IN ST 35-38-5-5.5 or IN ST 35-38-8-5 and records excluded from public access by such orders, and information related to infractions that is excluded from public access pursuant to IN ST 34-28-5-15 or IN ST 34-28-5-16 [Editor's note: IN ST 35-38-5-5.5, IN ST 35-38-8-5 and IN ST 34-28-5-16 were repealed effective July 1, 2013; for information on orders restricting access to criminal history, refer to IN ST 35-38-9-1, et seq.];

viii. All personal notes and e-mail, and deliberative material, of judges, jurors, court staff and judicial agencies, and information recorded in personal data assistants (PDA's) or organizers and personal calendars. IN ST ADMIN Rule 9(G)(1).

F. Filing and Service Requirements

1. *Filing requirements.* Except as otherwise provided in IN ST TRIAL P Rule 5(E)(2), all pleadings and papers subsequent to the complaint which are required to be served upon a party shall be filed with the Court either before service or within a reasonable period of time thereafter. IN ST TRIAL P Rule 5(E)(1). Counsel shall file with the court an original and one (1) copy of all briefs, and memoranda of law filed in support of a motion. IN ST MARION CIR AND SUPER CTS CIV Rule 205(D).

   a. *Filing generally.* All pleadings, petitions and motions are filed with the Clerk designated by the Court at any time during office hours established by the Clerk and the Court. All orders submitted to the Court shall be in sufficient number and shall be accompanied by postage paid envelopes addressed to each party or counsel of record. IN ST MARION CIR AND SUPER CTS CIV Rule 205(A)

   b. *Filing with the court defined.* The filing of pleadings, motions, and other papers with the court as required by the Indiana Rules of Trial Procedure shall be made by one of the following methods:

      i. Delivery to the clerk of the court;

      ii. Sending by electronic transmission under the procedure adopted pursuant to IN ST ADMIN Rule 12;

      iii. Mailing to the clerk by registered, certified or express mail return receipt requested;

      iv. Depositing with any third-party commercial carrier for delivery to the clerk within three (3) calendar days, cost prepaid, properly addressed;

      v. If the court so permits, filing with the judge, in which event the judge shall note thereon the filing date and forthwith transmit them to the office of the clerk; or

      vi. Electronic filing, as approved by the Division of State Court Administration pursuant to IN ST ADMIN Rule 16. IN ST TRIAL P Rule 5(F).

      vii. Filing by registered or certified mail and by third-party commercial carrier shall be complete upon mailing or deposit. IN ST TRIAL P Rule 5(F).

   c. *Facsimile filing.* Facsimile filing is discouraged, but permitted in the Marion Circuit and Marion Superior Court. All documents filed by facsimile shall also be filed in hard copy within seven (7) days of the facsimile filing, along with proposed orders and stamped addressed envelopes, as required by IN ST MARION CIR AND SUPER CTS CIV Rule 203(E). To avoid duplicate filings, the hard copies of the facsimile filing shall indicate in bold letters that the pleading was previously filed by facsimile transmission. Proof of transmission by facsimile, including certificate of service and manner of service, shall be the responsibility of the filing party. If the filing requires immediate attention of the Judge, it shall be so indicated in bold letters in an accompanying transmittal memorandum. Legibility of documents and timeliness of filing is the responsibility of the sender. IN ST MARION CIR AND SUPER CTS CIV Rule 205(B).

      i. *Generally.* In counties where a majority of judges of the courts of record, by posted local rule,

have authorized electronic facsimile filing and designated a telephone number to receive such transmissions, pleadings, motions, and other papers may be sent to the Clerk of Circuit Court by electronic facsimile transmission for filing in any case, provided:

- Such matter does not exceed ten (10) pages, including the cover sheet;

- Such matter does not require the payment of fees other than the electronic facsimile transcription fee set forth in IN ST ADMIN Rule 12(E);

- The sending party creates at the time of transmission a machine generated log for such transmission; and

- The original document and the transmission log are maintained by the sending party for the duration of the litigation. IN ST ADMIN Rule 12(B).

ii. *Time of filing.* During normal, posted business hours, the time of filing shall be the time the duplicate document is produced in the office of the Clerk of the Circuit Court. Duplicate documents received at all other times shall be filed as of the next normal business day. IN ST ADMIN Rule 12(C).

- If the receiving fax machine endorses its own time and date stamp upon the transmitted documents and the receiving machine produces a delivery receipt which is electronically created and transmitted to the sending party, the time of filing shall be the date and time recorded on the transmitted document by the receiving fax machine. IN ST ADMIN Rule 12(C).

d. *Electronic filing.* Electronic filing and electronic service pilot projects are authorized pursuant to IN ST ADMIN Rule 16 and approved by the Division of State Court Administration. IN ST MARION SUPER CT ADMIN Rule 311(1-103).

i. *Cases where electronic filing accepted.* All Marion County Circuit and Superior civil courts may accept electronic filing and service of pleadings and other documents designated in this rule in mortgage foreclosure (hereinafter referred to as "MF"), civil collection(hereinafter referred to as "CC"), and individual cases that have been approved for electronic filing and service. IN ST MARION SUPER CT ADMIN Rule 311(1-104)(1).

- The Marion County Circuit Court may, upon the motion of a party or its own motion, designate a case that will involve multiple litigants, legally intricate issues, and an extensive number of documents a mass tort or complex litigation case. Any case so designated shall be subject to electronic filing and service using the county's approved Electronic Service Provider. IN ST MARION SUPER CT ADMIN Rule 311(1-104)(3).

- The filing of electronic pleadings and other documents in MF and CC cases is entirely voluntary; however, once the case is initially filed electronically, all subsequent filings in the case shall remain in electronic format until the time for appeal is exhausted. IN ST MARION SUPER CT ADMIN Rule 311(1-104)(5).

ii. *Documents eligible for electronic filing.* The following pleadings may be filed and served electronically:

- New case complaint and petitions. IN ST MARION SUPER CT ADMIN Rule 311(1-104)(8)(a).

- Original answers. IN ST MARION SUPER CT ADMIN Rule 311(1-104)(8)(a).

- Any other pleadings or document including but not limited to motions and appearance forms. IN ST MARION SUPER CT ADMIN Rule 311(1-104)(8)(a).

iii. *Manner of electronic filing.* Parties shall E-file a document either:

- By registering to use the Electronic Filing Service Provider; or

- In person at the Marion County Clerk's office, by electronically filing through the Public Access Terminal. Parties filing in this manner shall be responsible for furnishing the document in an electronic format that will be compatible with the clerk's office-system to be uploaded in person. IN ST MARION SUPER CT ADMIN Rule 311(1-104)(9). For

information on the Electronic Filing Service Provider and Public Access Terminal, refer to IN ST MARION SUPER CT ADMIN Rule 311(1-101).

- Registered users shall pay statutory filing fees for E-filed documents electronically to the Court through their EFSP. Filing fees are due and payable at the time of filing. IN ST MARION SUPER CT ADMIN Rule 311(2-104)(1). For more information on electronic filing fees, refer to IN ST MARION SUPER CT ADMIN Rule 311(2-104).

iv. *Effect of electronic filing.* Any pleading filed electronically shall be considered as filed with the court when the transmission to the EFSP is complete. Any document E-filed by 11:59 p.m. local Indianapolis, Indiana time shall be deemed filed on that date. The EFSP is an agent of the Court for the purpose of electronic filing, receipt, service and retrieval of electronic documents. IN ST MARION SUPER CT ADMIN Rule 311(2-102).

- Upon completion of filing, the EFSP shall issue a confirmation receipt that includes the date and time of receipt. The confirmation receipt shall serve as proof of filing. IN ST MARION SUPER CT ADMIN Rule 311(2-102).

- In the event the Court rejects the submitted documents following review, the documents shall not become part of the official Court record and the filer will receive notification of the rejection. Users may be required to refile the instruments to meet necessary filing requirements. Documents may be filed through an E-filing system at any time that the Clerk's office is open to receive the filing or at such other times as may be designated by the clerk and posted publicly. IN ST MARION SUPER CT ADMIN Rule 311(2-102).

- Documents filed through the E-filing system are deemed filed when received by the Clerk's office, except that documents received at times that the Clerk's office is closed shall be deemed filed the next regular time when the Clerk's office is open for filing. The time stamp issued by the E-filing system shall be presumed to be the time the document is received by the Clerk. IN ST MARION SUPER CT ADMIN Rule 311(2-102).

v. *Electronically filed documents.* All pleadings and other documents designated in IN ST MARION SUPER CT ADMIN Rule 311 shall be filed and served electronically in any individual case which has been approved for electronic filing and service. IN ST MARION SUPER CT ADMIN Rule 311(1-104)(6).

vi. *System failures.* When filing by electronic means is hindered by a technical failure, a party may file with the Clerk of Marion County in hard copy. With the exception of deadlines that by law cannot be extended, the time for filing of any paper that is delayed due to technical failure of the site shall be extended for one (1) day for each day on which such failure occurs, unless otherwise ordered by the Court. IN ST MARION SUPER CT ADMIN Rule 311(2-108).

vii. *Compliance with rules.* All filing shall comply with the requirements of IN ST ADMIN Rule 9 and IN ST ADMIN Rule 16; and the Indiana Rules of Court and the Marion County Local Rules. IN ST MARION SUPER CT ADMIN Rule 311(1-104)(11).

e. *Filing for special judge.* When a Special Judge who is not a Marion County Judge is selected, all parties or attorneys shall furnish such Judge with copies of all filings prior to the qualification of such Special Judge. Thereafter, copies of all filings shall be delivered in person, by mail or by facsimile to the office of the Special Judge with certificate of forwarding same made a part of the filing. IN ST MARION CIR AND SUPER CTS CIV Rule 205(C).

f. *Proof of filing.* Any party filing any paper by any method other than personal delivery to the clerk shall retain proof of filing. IN ST TRIAL P Rule 5(F).

2. *Service requirements.* Unless otherwise provided by the Indiana Rules of Trial Procedure or an order of the court, each party and special judge, if any, shall be served with: (1) every order required by its terms to be served; (2) every pleading subsequent to the original complaint; (3) every written motion except one which may be heard ex parte; (4) every brief submitted to the trial court; (5) every paper relating to discovery required to be served upon a party; and (6) every written notice, appearance, demand, offer of judgment, designation of record on appeal, or similar paper. IN ST TRIAL P Rule 5(A).

a. *Methods of service*

i. *Personal service.* Whenever a party is represented by an attorney of record, service shall be

made upon such attorney unless service upon the party himself is ordered by the court. Service upon the attorney or party shall be made by delivering or mailing a copy of the papers to the last known address or where an attorney or party has consented to service by fax or e-mail, as provided in IN ST TRIAL P Rule 3.1(A)(4), by faxing or e-mailing a copy of the documents to the fax number or e-mail address set out in the appearance form or correction as required by IN ST TRIAL P Rule 3.1(E). IN ST TRIAL P Rule 5(B). Delivery of a copy within IN ST TRIAL P Rule 5 means:

- Offering or tendering it to the attorney or party and stating the nature of the papers being served. Refusal to accept an offered or tendered document is a waiver of any objection to the sufficiency or adequacy of service of that document;

- Leaving it at his office with a clerk or other person in charge thereof, or if there is no one in charge, leaving it in a conspicuous place therein; or

- If the office is closed, by leaving it at his dwelling house or usual place of abode with some person of suitable age and discretion then residing therein; or,

- Leaving it at some other suitable place, selected by the attorney upon whom service is being made, pursuant to duly promulgated local rule. IN ST TRIAL P Rule 5(B)(1).

ii. *Service by mail.* If service is made by mail, the papers shall be deposited in the United States mail addressed to the person on whom they are being served, with postage prepaid. Service shall be deemed complete upon mailing. Proof of service of all papers permitted to be mailed may be made by written acknowledgment of service, by affidavit of the person who mailed the papers, or by certificate of an attorney. It shall be the duty of attorneys when entering their appearance in a cause or when filing pleadings or papers therein, to have noted in the Chronological Case Summary or said pleadings or papers so filed the address and telephone number of their office. Service by delivery or by mail at such address shall be deemed sufficient and complete. IN ST TRIAL P Rule 5(B)(2).

iii. *Service by fax or e-mail.* A party who has consented to service by fax or e-mail may be served as follows:

- Service by e-mail shall be made by attaching the document being served in .pdf format. Discovery documents must also be served in accordance with IN ST TRIAL P Rule 26(A). IN ST TRIAL P Rule 5(B)(3)(a).

- Service by fax shall be deemed complete upon generation of a transmission record indicating the successful transmission of the entire document, except as provided in IN ST TRIAL P Rule 5(B)(3)(d). IN ST TRIAL P Rule 5(B)(3)(b).

- Service by e-mail shall be deemed complete upon transmission, except as provided in IN ST TRIAL P Rule 5(B)(3)(d). IN ST TRIAL P Rule 5(B)(3)(c).

- Service by fax or e-mail that occurs on a Saturday, Sunday, legal holiday, or day the court or agency in which the matter is pending is closed or after 5:00 PM local time of the recipient shall be deemed complete the next day that is not a Saturday, Sunday, legal holiday, or day that the court or agency in which the matter is pending is not closed. IN ST TRIAL P Rule 5(B)(3)(d).

iv. *Electronic service.* Delivery of E-service documents through the EFSP to other registered users shall be considered as valid and effective service and shall have the same legal effect as an original paper document. Recipients of E-service documents shall access their documents through the EFSP. IN ST MARION SUPER CT ADMIN Rule 311(2-107)(1).

- E-service shall be deemed complete when the transmission to the EFSP is completed. IN ST MARION SUPER CT ADMIN Rule 311(2-107)(2).

- For the purpose of computing time to respond to documents received via E-service, any document served on a day or at a time when the Clerk's office is not open for business shall be deemed served at the time of next opening of the Clerk's office for business. IN ST MARION SUPER CT ADMIN Rule 311(2-107)(3).

   b. *Serving numerous defendants.* In any action in which there are unusually large numbers of defendants, the court, upon motion or of its own initiative, may order:

      i. That service of the pleadings of the defendants and replies thereto need not be made as between the defendants;

- That any cross-claim, counterclaim, or matter constituting an avoidance or affirmative defense contained therein shall be deemed to be denied or avoided by all other parties; and

- That the filing of any such pleading and service thereof upon the plaintiff constitutes due notice of it to the parties. IN ST TRIAL P Rule 5(D).

      ii. A copy of every such order shall be served upon the parties in such manner and form as the court directs. IN ST TRIAL P Rule 5(D).

   c. *Service on parties in default for failure to appear.* No service need be made on parties in default for failure to appear, except that pleadings asserting new or additional claims for relief against them shall be served upon them in the manner provided by service of summons in IN ST TRIAL P Rule 4. IN ST TRIAL P Rule 5(A).

G. Hearings

1. *Hearing on motion.* Unless local conditions make it impracticable, each judge shall establish regular times and places, at intervals sufficiently frequent for the prompt dispatch of business, at which motions requiring notice and hearing may be heard and disposed of; but the judge at any time or place and on such notice, if any, as he considers reasonable may make order for the advancement, conduct, and hearing of actions. To expedite its business the court may direct the submission and determination of motions without oral hearing upon brief written statements of reasons in support and opposition, or direct or permit hearings by telephone conference call with all attorneys or other similar means of communication. IN ST TRIAL P Rule 73(A).

2. *Time and place of hearing.* If the motion requires a hearing or oral argument, the Court shall set the time and place of hearing or argument on the motion. IN ST MARION CIR AND SUPER CTS CIV Rule 203(A).

H. Forms

1. Motion for Protective Order Forms for Indiana

   a. Pending motion. 5 INPRAC § 4:5.1.

   b. Relevancy. 5 INPRAC § 4:5.2.

   c. Unduly burdensome. 5 INPRAC § 4:5.3.

   d. Privileged. 5 INPRAC § 4:5.4.

   e. Mental impressions and legal conclusions. 5 INPRAC § 4:5.5.

   f. Expert reports and papers. 5 INPRAC § 4:5.6.

   g. Quash subpoena duces tecum. 5 INPRAC § 4:5.7.

   h. Quash subpoena duces tecum; Non-party. 5 INPRAC § 4:5.8.

   i. Trade secrets and confidential information. 5 INPRAC § 4:5.9.

   j. Motion to lift protective order. 5 INPRAC § 4:5.10.

   k. Motion for protective order; Discovery not be had; Protection against disclosure of expert report and papers. 10 INPRAC § 58.22.

   l. Motion for protective order; Discovery not relevant to subject matter of action. 10 INPRAC § 58.23.

   m. Motion for protective order; Discovery unduly burdensome; Alternative request for deposition. 10 INPRAC § 58.24.

   n. Motion for protective order; Challenging date and time of deposition. 10 INPRAC § 58.25.

   o. Motion for protective order; Challenging place of deposition. 10 INPRAC § 58.26.

   p. Motion for protective order; To prevent the disclosure of trade secrets and confidential research and development. 10 INPRAC § 58.27.

q. Motion for protective order; To preclude further deposition of corporate officer. 10 INPRAC § 58.28.

r. Motion for protective order; To preclude taking expert deposition; Failure to obtain court order or to disclose expert opinions. 10 INPRAC § 58.30.

s. Motion for protective order; To preclude disclosure of privileged matters. 10 INPRAC § 58.31.

t. Motion for protective order; To have plaintiff's attorney and physician present during plaintiff's physical examination; Request to tape record physical examination. 10 INPRAC § 58.32.

u. Motion for protective order; To preclude defendant's attorney from conducting an informal interview of plaintiff's treating physician. 10 INPRAC § 58.33.

v. Motion for protective order; To produce documents at responding party's place of business. 10 INPRAC § 58.34.

w. Motion for protective order; Discovery limited to certain matter until court rules on pending motion. 10 INPRAC § 58.35.

x. Motion for protective order; Answers to discovery to be sealed to protect confidential commercial information. 10 INPRAC § 58.36.

y. Certificate of service; Personal service. 9 INPRAC § 5.7.

z. Certificate of service; First class mail. 9 INPRAC § 5.8.

I. Checklist

(I) ❑ Matters to be considered by moving party

    (a) ❑ Required documents

        (1) ❑ Motion and notice

        (2) ❑ Attorney certification

        (3) ❑ Statement of approval or disapproval

        (4) ❑ Proposed order

        (5) ❑ Certificate of service

    (b) ❑ Supplemental documents

        (1) ❑ Supporting evidence

        (2) ❑ Request for oral argument

        (3) ❑ Facsimile cover sheet

    (c) ❑ Timing

        (1) ❑ There are no specific timing requirements for filing a motion for a protective order

        (2) ❑ A written motion, other than one which may be heard ex parte, and notice of the hearing thereof shall be served not less than five (5) days before the time specified for the hearing, unless a different period is fixed by the Indiana Rules of Trial Procedure or by order of the court

        (3) ❑ All pleadings and papers subsequent to the complaint which are required to be served upon a party shall be filed with the Court either before service or within a reasonable period of time thereafter

(II) ❑ Matters to be considered by the responding party

    (a) ❑ Required documents

        (1) ❑ Opposition

        (2) ❑ Certificate of service

    (b) ❑ Supplemental documents

        (1) ❑ Supporting evidence

        (2) ❑ Proposed order

(3) ❑ Facsimile cover sheet

(c) ❑ Timing

    (1) ❑ If the statement regarding the position of the opposing party(ies) required under IN ST MARION CIR AND SUPER CTS CIV Rule 203(A) indicates that objection to the granting of said motion may ensue, said objecting a party shall have fifteen (15) days from the date of filing to file a response to said motion

    (2) ❑ Except as otherwise provided in IN ST TRIAL P Rule 59(D), opposing affidavits may be served not less than one (1) day before the hearing, unless the court permits them to be served at some other time

Motions, Oppositions and Replies
Motion for Discovery Sanctions

Document Last Updated October 2013

A. Applicable Rules

1. *State rules*

    a. Appearance. IN ST TRIAL P Rule 3.1.

    b. Process. IN ST TRIAL P Rule 4.

    c. Service and filing of pleadings and other papers. IN ST TRIAL P Rule 5.

    d. Time. IN ST TRIAL P Rule 6.

    e. Pleadings. IN ST TRIAL P Rule 7; IN ST TRIAL P Rule 8; IN ST TRIAL P Rule 9.2; IN ST TRIAL P Rule 10.

    f. Signing and verification of pleadings. IN ST TRIAL P Rule 11.

    g. General provisions governing discovery. IN ST TRIAL P Rule 26.

    h. Methods of discovery. IN ST TRIAL P Rule 27; IN ST TRIAL P Rule 30; IN ST TRIAL P Rule 31; IN ST TRIAL P Rule 33; IN ST TRIAL P Rule 34; IN ST TRIAL P Rule 35; IN ST TRIAL P Rule 36.

    i. Failure to make or cooperate in discovery; Sanctions. IN ST TRIAL P Rule 37.

    j. Evidence. IN ST TRIAL P Rule 43.

    k. Judgment on the evidence (directed verdict). IN ST TRIAL P Rule 50.

    l. Findings by the court. IN ST TRIAL P Rule 52.

    m. Summary judgment. IN ST TRIAL P Rule 56.

    n. Motion to correct error. IN ST TRIAL P Rule 59.

    o. Relief from judgment or order. IN ST TRIAL P Rule 60.

    p. Hearing of motions. IN ST TRIAL P Rule 73.

    q. Access to court records. IN ST ADMIN Rule 9.

    r. Paper size. IN ST ADMIN Rule 11.

    s. Facsimile transmission. IN ST ADMIN Rule 12.

    t. Electronic filing and electronic service pilot projects. IN ST ADMIN Rule 16.

    u. Sealing of certain records by court; Hearing; Notice. IN ST 5-14-3-5.5.

    v. Privacy and confidentiality. IN ST 5-2-9-6; IN ST 5-14-3-4; IN ST 6-4.1-5-10; IN ST 6-4.1-12-12; IN ST 6-8.1-7-1; IN ST 11-13-1-8; IN ST 12-23-14-13; IN ST 16-39-3-10; IN ST 16-41-8-1; IN ST 22-4-19-6; IN ST 31-11-1-6; IN ST 31-19-5-23; IN ST 31-19-13-2; IN ST 31-19-19-1; IN ST 31-33-18-1; IN ST 31-39-1-1; IN ST 31-39-1-2; IN ST 33-23-16-16; IN ST 35-34-2-4; IN ST

35-38-1-13; IN ST 35-38-9-1; IN ST ADR Rule 2.11; IN ST ADR Rule 4.4; IN ST ADR Rule 5.6; IN ST JURY Rule 10.

2. *Local rules*

   a. Requirements for motions. IN ST MARION CIR AND SUPER CTS CIV Rule 203.

   b. Preparation of pleadings, motions and other papers. IN ST MARION CIR AND SUPER CTS CIV Rule 204.

   c. Filing of pleadings, motions and other papers. IN ST MARION CIR AND SUPER CTS CIV Rule 205.

   d. Signing and verification of pleadings, motions and other papers; Service on opposing party. IN ST MARION CIR AND SUPER CTS CIV Rule 206.

   e. Motions for continuance. IN ST MARION CIR AND SUPER CTS CIV Rule 215.

   f. Electronic filing. IN ST MARION SUPER CT ADMIN Rule 311.

B. Timing

1. *Motion for discovery sanctions.* There are no specific timing requirements for filing a motion for discovery sanctions.

   a. *Filing.* All pleadings and papers subsequent to the complaint which are required to be served upon a party shall be filed with the Court either before service or within a reasonable period of time thereafter. IN ST TRIAL P Rule 5(E)(1).

2. *Service.* A written motion, other than one which may be heard ex parte, and notice of the hearing thereof shall be served not less than five (5) days before the time specified for the hearing, unless a different period is fixed by the Indiana Rules of Trial Procedure or by order of the court. IN ST TRIAL P Rule 6(D).

   a. *Of supporting affidavits.* When a motion is supported by affidavit, the affidavit shall be served with the motion. IN ST TRIAL P Rule 6(D).

3. *Opposition*

   a. *Filing.* If the statement regarding the position of the opposing party(ies) required under IN ST MARION CIR AND SUPER CTS CIV Rule 203(A) indicates that objection to the granting of said motion may ensue, said objecting a party shall have fifteen (15) days from the date of filing to file a response to said motion. IN ST MARION CIR AND SUPER CTS CIV Rule 203(B).

   b. *Service.* Except as otherwise provided in IN ST TRIAL P Rule 59(D), opposing affidavits may be served not less than one (1) day before the hearing, unless the court permits them to be served at some other time. IN ST TRIAL P Rule 6(D).

4. *Computation of time*

   a. *Generally; Days excluded.* In computing any period of time prescribed or allowed by the Indiana Rules of Trial Procedure, by order of the court, or by any applicable statute, the day of the act, event, or default from which the designated period of time begins to run shall not be included. The last day of the period so computed is to be included unless it is:

      i. A Saturday,

      ii. A Sunday,

      iii. A legal holiday as defined by state statute, or

      iv. A day the office in which the act is to be done is closed during regular business hours. IN ST TRIAL P Rule 6(A).

   b. *Short periods.* In any event, the period runs until the end of the next day that is not a Saturday, a Sunday, a legal holiday, or a day on which the office is closed. When the period of time allowed is less than seven (7) days, intermediate Saturdays, Sundays, legal holidays, and days on which the office is closed shall be excluded from the computations. IN ST TRIAL P Rule 6(A).

   c. *Additional time after service by United States mail.* Whenever a party has the right or is required to do some act or take some proceedings within a prescribed period after the service of a notice or other paper upon him and the notice or paper is served upon him by United States mail, three (3) days shall be added to the prescribed period. IN ST TRIAL P Rule 6(E).

d. *Enlargement of time.* When an act is required or allowed to be done at or within a specific time by the Indiana Rules of Trial Procedure, the court may at any time for cause shown:

   i. Order the period enlarged, with or without motion or notice, if request therefor is made before the expiration of the period originally prescribed or extended by a previous order; or

   ii. Upon motion made after the expiration of the specific period, permit the act to be done where the failure to act was the result of excusable neglect; but, the court may not extend the time for taking any action for judgment on the evidence under IN ST TRIAL P Rule 50(A), amendment of findings and judgment under IN ST TRIAL P Rule 52(B), to correct errors under IN ST TRIAL P Rule 59(C), statement in opposition to motion to correct error under IN ST TRIAL P Rule 59(E), or to obtain relief from final judgment under IN ST TRIAL P Rule 60(B), except to the extent and under the conditions stated in those rules. IN ST TRIAL P Rule 6(B).

e. *Continuances disfavored.* Motions for Continuance are discouraged. Neither side is entitled to an automatic continuance as a matter of right. IN ST MARION CIR AND SUPER CTS CIV Rule 215. For information on obtaining a continuance, refer to IN ST MARION CIR AND SUPER CTS CIV Rule 215.

C. General Requirements

1. *Motions, generally.* Unless made during a hearing or trial, or otherwise ordered by the court, an application to the court for an order shall be made by written motion. The motion shall state the grounds therefor and the relief or order sought. IN ST TRIAL P Rule 7(B).

   a. *Motions as distinct from pleadings.* Motions and responses to motions are not pleadings, and allegations contained in a motion are not admissions of a party. 22B INPRAC 7:2; Wachstetter v. County Properties, LLC, 832 N.E.2d 574 (Ind.Ct.App. 2005); Scott County Family YMCA, Inc. v. Hobbs, 817 N.E.2d 603 (Ind.Ct.App. 2004).

   b. *Unopposed motions generally granted.* It is common for a trial court to grant procedural motions, such as motions for enlargement of time, discovery motions, or motions for continuance, unless an objection is filed. 21 INPRAC § 13.8.

2. *Motion for discovery sanctions*

   a. *Related to a motion to compel; Award of sanctions on motion*

      i. *Motion granted.* If the motion is granted, the court shall, after opportunity for hearing, require the party or deponent whose conduct necessitated the motion or the party or attorney advising such conduct or both of them to pay to the moving party the reasonable expenses incurred in obtaining the order, including attorney's fees, unless the court finds that the opposition to the motion was substantially justified or that other circumstances make an award of expenses unjust. IN ST TRIAL P Rule 37(A)(4).

      ii. *Motion denied.* If the motion is denied, the court shall, after opportunity for hearing, require the moving party or the attorney advising the motion or both of them to pay to the party or deponent who opposed the motion the reasonable expenses incurred in opposing the motion, including attorney's fees, unless the court finds that the making of the motion was substantially justified or that other circumstances make an award of expenses unjust. IN ST TRIAL P Rule 37(A)(4).

      iii. *Granted in part and denied in part.* If the motion is granted in part and denied in part, the court may apportion the reasonable expenses incurred in relation to the motion among the parties and persons in a just manner. IN ST TRIAL P Rule 37(A)(4).

      iv. Refer to the Indiana KeyRules Motion to Compel Discovery document for more information.

   b. *Failure to comply with order.* The trial court may impose sanctions upon a party who fails to obey an order regarding discovery. 22 INPRAC § 27.7. The first step to invoking sanctions under IN ST TRIAL P Rule 37(B) is to file a motion to compel discovery under IN ST TRIAL P Rule 37(A) and obtain an order from the court requiring the opposing party to take a specific action in discovery. If the opposing party then fails to take the action mandated by the trial court's discovery order, the second step is to return to the trial court and file a motion for sanctions under IN ST TRIAL P Rule 37(B). 22 INPRAC § 27.7.

    i.   *Sanctions by court in county where deposition is taken.* If a deponent fails to be sworn or to answer a question after being directed to do so by the court in the county in which the deposition is being taken, the failure may be considered a contempt of that court. IN ST TRIAL P Rule 37(B)(1).

    ii.   *Sanctions by court in which action is pending.* If a party or an officer, director, or managing agent of a party or an organization, including a governmental organization, or a person designated under IN ST TRIAL P Rule 30(B)(6) or IN ST TRIAL P Rule 31(A) to testify on behalf of a party or an organization, including a governmental organization, fails to obey an order to provide or permit discovery, including an order made under IN ST TRIAL P Rule 37(A) or IN ST TRIAL P Rule 35, the court in which the action is pending may make such orders in regard to the failure as are just, and among others the following:

- An order that the matters regarding which the order was made or any other designated facts shall be taken to be established for the purposes of the action in accordance with the claim of the party obtaining the order;

- An order refusing to allow the disobedient party to support or oppose designated claims or defenses, or prohibiting him from introducing designated matters in evidence;

- An order striking out pleadings or parts thereof, or staying further proceedings until the order is obeyed, or dismissing the action or proceeding or any part thereof, or rendering a judgment by default against the disobedient party;

- In lieu of any of the foregoing orders or in addition thereto, an order treating as a contempt of court the failure to obey any orders except an order to submit to a physical or mental examination under IN ST TRIAL P Rule 35;

- Where a party has failed to comply with an order under IN ST TRIAL P Rule 35(A) requiring him to produce another for examination, such orders as are listed in IN ST TRIAL P Rule 37(B)(2)(a), IN ST TRIAL P Rule 37(B)(2)(b), and IN ST TRIAL P Rule 37(B)(2)(c), unless the party failing to comply shows that he is unable to produce such person for examination. IN ST TRIAL P Rule 37(B)(2).

- In lieu of any of the foregoing orders or in addition thereto, the court shall require the party failing to obey the order or the attorney advising him or both to pay the reasonable expenses, including attorney's fees, caused by the failure, unless the court finds that the failure was substantially justified or that other circumstances make an award of expenses unjust. IN ST TRIAL P Rule 37(B)(2).

c.   *Expenses on failure to admit.* If a party fails to admit the genuineness of any document or the truth of any matter as requested under IN ST TRIAL P Rule 36, and if the party requesting the admissions thereafter proves the genuineness of the document or the truth of the matter, he may apply to the court for an order requiring the other party to pay him the reasonable expenses incurred in making that proof, including reasonable attorney's fees. The court shall make the order unless it finds that:

    i.   The request was held objectionable pursuant to IN ST TRIAL P Rule 36(A), or

    ii.   The admission sought was of no substantial importance, or

    iii.   The party failing to admit had reasonable ground to believe that he might prevail on the matter, or

    iv.   There was other good reason for the failure to admit. IN ST TRIAL P Rule 37(C).

d.   *Failure of party to attend at own deposition or serve answers to interrogatories or respond to requests for inspection*

    i.   *Court order for failure to provide discovery.* If a party or an officer, director, or managing agent of a party or an organization, including without limitation a governmental organization, or a person designated under IN ST TRIAL P Rule 30(B)(6) or IN ST TRIAL P Rule 31(A) to testify on behalf of a party or an organization, including without limitation a governmental organization, fails (1) to appear before the officer who is to take his deposition, after being served with a proper notice, or (2) to serve answers or objections to interrogatories submitted under IN ST TRIAL P Rule 33, after proper service of the interrogatories, or (3) to serve a written response to a request for inspection submitted under IN ST TRIAL P Rule 34, after proper service of the request, the court in which the action is pending on motion may make such orders in regard to the failure as are just, and among others it may take any action authorized under IN ST TRIAL P Rule 37(B)(2)(a), IN ST TRIAL P Rule 37(B)(2)(b), and IN ST TRIAL P Rule 37(B)(2)(c). IN ST TRIAL P Rule 37(D).

ii. *Attorney fees against party failing to provide discovery.* In lieu of any order or in addition thereto, the court shall require the party failing to act or the attorney advising him or both to pay the reasonable expenses, including attorney's fees, caused by the failure, unless the court finds that the failure was substantially justified or that other circumstances make an award of expenses unjust. IN ST TRIAL P Rule 37(D)

iii. *Failure not excused for objectionable requests.* The failure to act described in IN ST TRIAL P Rule 37(D) may not be excused on the ground that the discovery sought is objectionable unless the party failing to act has applied for a protective order as provided by IN ST TRIAL P Rule 26(C). IN ST TRIAL P Rule 37(D). Refer to the Indiana KeyRules Motion for Protective Order document for more information.

iv. *Showing required.* To invoke the sanctions under IN ST TRIAL P Rule 37(D), it is sufficient that notice of the deposition or other discovery request was properly served upon the non-responding party, but no response was provided. 22 INPRAC § 27.8.

e. *Sanctions for spoliation of evidence.* In some cases a duty arises imposing an affirmative obligation to avoid the destruction or loss of documents and materials that are relevant and discoverable to claims and defenses that either have been or may be asserted in an action. The destruction, mutilation, alteration or concealment of such materials is called "spoliation." 3 INPRAC R 37(37.2.2); Glotzbach v. Froman, 854 N.E.2d 337 (Ind. 2006).

i. *Spoliation generally.* Spoliation typically presents itself in one of two ways:

- A party to litigation destroys materials that are relevant and discoverable in an action; or
- A non-party destroys materials that may be discoverable in an action to which that entity or individual will not be a party. 3 INPRAC R 37(37.2.2).

ii. *Duty to maintain evidence must exist.* A key component of a spoliation claim is that the party who destroyed the materials must have had a duty not to do so. A duty may arise in a number of ways: imposed by statute or case law, imposed by contract or some third party beneficiary arrangement, or imposed by the actions of the parties by which one party assumes a duty in law or equity toward another. When duty arises from the conduct of the parties as opposed to one established by statute or contract, the Indiana courts have identified three primary factors to determine whether a duty exists:

- The relationship between the parties,
- The reasonable foreseeability of harm to the injured litigant, and
- The public policy promoted by recognizing an enforceable duty. 3 INPRAC R 37(37.2.2); Webb v. Jarvis, 575 N.E.2d 992 (Ind. 1991).
- This balancing test is particularly useful where the element of duty has not already been established between the parties. 3 INPRAC R 37(37.2.2); Northern Indiana Public Service Co. v. Sharp, 790 N.E.2d 462 (Ind. 2003).

iii. *Factors to be considered by the court.* Even where the court finds an intentional spoliation, it is not mandatory that sanctions be imposed. Rather, the trial court should implement an approach by which it balances the nature of the offense against the harm suffered by the non-offending party because lost evidence is not available. 22 INPRAC § 27.9; Gribben v. Wal-Mart Stores, Inc., 824 N.E.2d 349 (Ind. 2005). Factors the court may consider include:

- The culpability of the spoliating party;

- The prejudice to the non-offending party;
- The degree of interference with the judicial process;
- Whether lesser sanctions are available to remedy any harm and deter future acts of spoliation;
- The amount of time lapsing from the date the spoliating party took possession of the evidence and the date of its loss or destruction;
- Protocols adopted, and followed, by the spoliating party to prevent the loss of evidence, such as a document retention policy;
- Whether evidence has been irretrievably lost and, if so, the circumstances of that loss;
- The existence of available alternatives that would allow the non-offending party to prove its case without the lost evidence;
- And whether sanctions will unfairly punish a party for the misconduct or mistake of his attorney or expert. 22 INPRAC § 27.9.

f. *No sanctions for good-faith loss of electronically stored information.* Absent exceptional circumstances, a court may not impose sanctions under the Indiana Rules of Trial Procedure these rules on a party for failing to provide electronically stored information lost as a result of the routine, good faith operation of an electronic information system. IN ST TRIAL P Rule 37(E).

D. Documents

1. *Required documents*

   a. *Motion and notice.* The requirement of notice is satisfied by service of the motion. IN ST TRIAL P Rule 7(B); IN ST MARION CIR AND SUPER CTS CIV Rule 203(A). Refer to the General Requirements section of this document for information on the content of a motion for discovery sanctions.

   b. *Attorney certification.* Before any party files any motion or request to compel discovery pursuant to IN ST TRIAL P Rule 37, or any motion for protection from discovery pursuant to IN ST TRIAL P Rule 26(C), or any other discovery motion which seeks to enforce, modify, or limit discovery, that party shall:

      i. Make a reasonable effort to reach agreement with the opposing party concerning the matter which is the subject of the motion or request; and

      ii. Include in the motion or request a statement showing that the attorney making the motion or request has made a reasonable effort to reach agreement with the opposing attorney(s) concerning the matter(s) set forth in the motion or request. This statement shall recite, in addition, the date, time and place of this effort to reach agreement, whether in person or by phone, and the names of all parties and attorneys participating therein. If an attorney for any party advises the court in writing that an opposing attorney has refused or delayed meeting and discussing the issues covered in IN ST TRIAL P Rule 26(F), the court may take such action as is appropriate. IN ST TRIAL P Rule 26(F).

      iii. The court may deny a discovery motion filed by a party who has failed to comply with the requirements of IN ST TRIAL P Rule 26(F). IN ST TRIAL P Rule 26(F).

   c. *Statement of approval or disapproval.* Except for initial motions made pursuant to IN ST MARION CIR AND SUPER CTS CIV Rule 203(D), all motions filed with the court shall include a brief statement indicating whether opposing party(ies) object to or approve of the granting of said motion. IN ST MARION CIR AND SUPER CTS CIV Rule 203(A).

   d. *Proposed order.* Unless local practice provides differently, a party should submit a proposed order with its written motion to be signed by the judge once the motion has been granted. 21 INPRAC § 13.8. All motions seeking an order of the Court shall be accompanied by a sufficient number of orders to be executed by the Court in granting said motion. In addition to the orders, the notice shall be accompanied by stamped, addressed envelopes to all parties of record. IN ST MARION CIR AND SUPER CTS CIV Rule 203(E).

    e.   *Certificate of service.* An attorney or unrepresented party tendering a document to the Clerk for filing shall certify that service has been made, list the parties served, and specify the date and means of service. The certificate of service shall be placed at the end of the document and shall not be separately filed. The separate filing of a certificate of service, however, shall not be grounds for rejecting a document for filing. The Clerk may permit documents to be filed without a certificate of service but shall require prompt filing of a separate certificate of service. IN ST TRIAL P Rule 5(C). In all cases where any pleading or other document is required to be served upon opposing counsel, proof of such service may be made either by:

        i.   A certificate of service signed by counsel of record for the serving party and the certificate shall specify by name and address all counsel upon whom the pleading or document was served; or

        ii.   An acknowledgment of service signed by the party served or counsel of record. IN ST MARION CIR AND SUPER CTS CIV Rule 206.

2.   *Supplemental documents*

    a.   *Supporting evidence.* When a motion is based on facts not appearing of record the court may hear the matter on affidavits presented by the respective parties, but the court may direct that the matter be heard wholly or partly on oral testimony or depositions. IN ST TRIAL P Rule 43(B).

    b.   *Request for oral argument.* When an oral argument is requested, the request shall be by separate instrument and filed with the pleading to be argued. Any such oral argument requested may be heard at the discretion of the Court, except for motions for summary judgment which shall be set for hearing upon request of any party. IN ST MARION CIR AND SUPER CTS CIV Rule 203(C).

    c.   *Facsimile cover sheet.* Any document sent to the Clerk of the Circuit Court by electronic facsimile transmission shall be accompanied by a cover sheet which states the title of the document, case number, number of pages, identity and voice telephone number of the sending party and instructions for filing. The cover sheet shall contain the signature of the attorney or party, pro se, authorizing the filing. IN ST ADMIN Rule 12(D).

E.   Format

1.   *Form of motions.* The rules applicable to captions, and the signing and form of pleadings (IN ST TRIAL P Rule 8 through IN ST TRIAL P Rule 11), apply to all motions and other papers provided under the Indiana Rules of Trial Procedure. 22B INPRAC 7:2.

2.   *Form of pleadings*

    a.   *Caption; Names of parties.* Every pleading shall contain a caption setting forth the name of the court, the title of the action, the file number, and a designation as in IN ST TRIAL P Rule 7(A). In the complaint the title of the action shall include the names of all the parties, but in other pleadings it is sufficient to state the name of the first party on each side with an appropriate indication of other parties. IN ST TRIAL P Rule 10(A).

        i.   Every pleading shall contain a caption setting forth the name of the Court, the Division and Room Number, the title of the action and the file number. IN ST MARION CIR AND SUPER CTS CIV Rule 204(B).

    b.   *Paragraphs; Separate statements.* All averments of a claim or defense shall be made in numbered paragraphs, the contents of each of which shall be limited as far as practicable to a statement of a single set of circumstances, and a paragraph may be referred to by number in all succeeding pleadings. Each claim founded upon a separate transaction or occurrence and each defense other than denials may be stated in a separate count or defense whenever a separation facilitates the clear presentation of the matters set forth. IN ST TRIAL P Rule 10(B).

    c.   *Adoption by reference; Exhibits.* Statements in a pleading may be adopted by reference in a different part of the same pleading or in another pleading or in any motion. A copy of any written instrument which is an exhibit to a pleading is a part thereof for all purposes. IN ST TRIAL P Rule 10(C).

    d.   *Paper.* Pleadings, motions and other papers may be either printed or typewritten on white opaque paper of at least sixteen (16) pound weight, eight and one-half (8-1/2) inches wide and eleven (11) inches in length. IN ST MARION CIR AND SUPER CTS CIV Rule 204(A).

e. *Copies.* All copies shall likewise be on white paper of sufficient strength and durability to resist normal wear and tear. IN ST MARION CIR AND SUPER CTS CIV Rule 204(A).

f. *Line spacing.* If typewritten, the lines shall be double spaced, except for quotations, which shall be indented and single spaced. IN ST MARION CIR AND SUPER CTS CIV Rule 204(A).

g. *Script type.* Script type shall not be used. IN ST MARION CIR AND SUPER CTS CIV Rule 204(A).

h. *Titles.* Titles on all pleadings shall delineate each topic included in the pleading e.g. where a pleading contains an Answer, a Motion to Strike or Dismiss, or a Jury Request each shall be set forth in the title. IN ST MARION CIR AND SUPER CTS CIV Rule 204(C).

i. *Margins and binding.* Margins shall be one (1) inch. Binding or stapling shall be at the top and at no other place. Covers or backing shall not be used. IN ST MARION CIR AND SUPER CTS CIV Rule 204(D).

3. *Size of papers for filing.* Effective January 1, 1992, all pleadings, copies, motions and documents filed with any trial court or appellate level court, typed or printed, with the exception of exhibits and existing wills, shall be prepared on eight and one-half by eleven inch (8 1/2" x 11") size paper. IN ST ADMIN Rule 11.

4. *Form of electronically filed documents.* All electronically filed and served pleadings shall, to the extent practicable, be formatted in accordance with the applicable rules governing formatting of paper pleadings. IN ST MARION SUPER CT ADMIN Rule 311(2-103)(1).

a. *Electronic document title.* The electronic document title of each pleading or other document shall include:

i. Party or parties filing/serving the document,

ii. Nature of the document,

iii. Party or parties against whom relief, if any, is sought, and

iv. Nature of the relief sought (e.g., Defendant ABC Corporation's Motion for Summary Judgment). IN ST MARION SUPER CT ADMIN Rule 311(2-103)(2).

5. *Signature requirements*

a. *Signature of attorney.* Every pleading or motion of a party represented by an attorney shall be signed by at least one (1) attorney of record in his individual name, whose address, telephone number, and attorney number shall be stated, except that this provision shall not apply to pleadings and motions made and transcribed at the trial or a hearing before the judge and received by him in such form. IN ST TRIAL P Rule 11(A).

i. All pleadings and motions shall contain the original or authorized signature of the attorney, the name of the attorney in typed or printed form, the name of the law firm if a member of a firm, the attorney's address, identification number, e-mail address, telephone number, fax number, and the designation as to the party for whom he appears. IN ST MARION CIR AND SUPER CTS CIV Rule 204(E).

ii. The signature of an attorney constitutes a certificate by him that he has read the pleadings; that to the best of his knowledge, information, and belief, there is good ground to support it; and that it is not interposed for delay. IN ST TRIAL P Rule 11(A).

iii. If a pleading or motion is not signed or is signed with intent to defeat the purpose of the rule, it may be stricken as sham and false and the action may proceed as though the pleading had not been served. IN ST TRIAL P Rule 11(A).

iv. For a willful violation of IN ST TRIAL P Rule 11 an attorney may be subjected to appropriate disciplinary action. Similar action may be taken if scandalous or indecent matter is inserted. IN ST TRIAL P Rule 11(A).

v. Every pleading, document, and instrument electronically filed or served shall be deemed to have been signed by the judge, clerk, attorney or declarant and shall bear a facsimile or typographical signature of such person, along with the typed name, address, telephone number, and Bar number of a signing attorney. Typographical signatures shall be treated as personal signatures for all purposes under these rules. IN ST MARION SUPER CT ADMIN Rule 311(2-105).

- Documents containing signatures of third-parties (i.e., unopposed motions, affidavits, stipulations, etc.) may also be filed electronically by indicating that the original signatures are maintained by the filing party in paper-format. IN ST MARION SUPER CT ADMIN Rule 311(2-105).

- Unless otherwise ordered by the Court or Clerk, a printed copy of all documents filed or served electronically, including original signatures, shall be maintained by the party filing the document and shall be made available, upon reasonable notice, for inspection by other counsel, the Clerk or Court. Parties shall retain originals until two (2) years after all time periods for appeal have expired. From time to time, it may be necessary to provide the Clerk or Court with a hard copy of an electronically filed document. IN ST MARION SUPER CT ADMIN Rule 311(2-105).

   vi. For the recommended format of a signature block, refer to IN ST MARION CIR AND SUPER CTS CIV Rule 204(E).

b. *Signature of unrepresented party.* A party who is not represented by an attorney shall sign his pleading and state his address. IN ST TRIAL P Rule 11(A).

c. *Verification not generally required.* Except when specifically required by rule, pleadings or motions need not be verified or accompanied by affidavit. The rule in equity that the averments of an answer under oath must be overcome by the testimony of two (2) witnesses or of one (1) witness sustained by corroborating circumstances is abolished. IN ST TRIAL P Rule 11(A).

d. *Verification by affirmation or representation.* When in connection with any civil or special statutory proceeding it is required that any pleading, motion, petition, supporting affidavit, or other document of any kind, be verified, or that an oath be taken, it shall be sufficient if the subscriber simply affirms the truth of the matter to be verified by an affirmation or representation. IN ST TRIAL P Rule 11(B). IN ST TRIAL P Rule 11(B) states that the affirmation or representation should be in substantially the following language: "I (we) affirm, under the penalties for perjury, that the foregoing representation(s) is (are) true. (Signed) _____."

   i. Any person who falsifies an affirmation or representation of fact shall be subject to the same penalties as are prescribed by law for the making of a false affidavit. IN ST TRIAL P Rule 11(B).

e. *Verified pleadings, motions, and affidavits as evidence.* Pleadings, motions and affidavits accompanying or in support of such pleadings or motions when required to be verified or under oath shall be accepted as a representation that the signer had personal knowledge thereof or reasonable cause to believe the existence of the facts or matters stated or alleged therein; and, if otherwise competent or acceptable as evidence, may be admitted as evidence of the facts or matters stated or alleged therein when it is so provided in the Indiana Rules of Trial Procedure, by statute or other law, or to the extent the writing or signature expressly purports to be made upon the signer's personal knowledge. When such pleadings, motions and affidavits are verified or under oath they shall not require other or greater proof on the part of the adverse party than if not verified or not under oath unless expressly provided otherwise by the Indiana Rules of Trial Procedure, statute or other law. Affidavits upon motions for summary judgment under IN ST TRIAL P Rule 56 and in denial of execution under IN ST TRIAL P Rule 9.2 shall be made upon personal knowledge. IN ST TRIAL P Rule 11(C).

6. *Information excluded from public access.* Every document filed in a case shall separately identify information excluded from public access pursuant to IN ST ADMIN Rule 9(G)(1) as follows:

a. Whole documents that are excluded from public access pursuant to IN ST ADMIN Rule 9(G)(1) shall be tendered on light green paper or have a light green coversheet attached to the document, marked "Not for Public Access" or "Confidential." IN ST TRIAL P Rule 5(G)(1).

b. When only a portion of a document contains information excluded from public access pursuant to IN ST ADMIN Rule 9(G)(1), said information shall be omitted [or redacted] from the filed document, and set forth on a separate accompanying document on light green paper conspicuously marked "Not

for Public Access" or "Confidential" and clearly designated [or identifying] the caption and number of the case and the document and location within the document to which the redacted material pertains. IN ST TRIAL P Rule 5(G)(2).

c. With respect to documents filed in electronic format, the trial court, by local rule, may provide for compliance with IN ST TRIAL P Rule 5 in manner that separates and protects access to information excluded from public access. IN ST TRIAL P Rule 5(G)(3).

d. IN ST TRIAL P Rule 5(G) does not apply to a record sealed by the court pursuant to IN ST 5-14-3-5.5 or otherwise, nor to records, documents, or information filed in cases to which public access is prohibited pursuant to IN ST ADMIN Rule 9(G). IN ST TRIAL P Rule 5(G)(4).

e. The following information in case records is excluded from public access and is confidential:

   i.   Information that is excluded from public access pursuant to federal law;

   ii. Information that is excluded from public access as declared confidential by Indiana statute or other court rule, including without limitation:

   - All adoption records created after July 8, 1941, as declared confidential by IN ST 31-19-19-1, et seq., except those specifically declared open by IN ST 31-19-13-2(2);

   - All records relating to chancroid, chlamydia, gonorrhea, hepatitis, human immunodeficiency virus (HIV), Lymphogranuloma venereum, syphilis, tuberculosis, as declared confidential by IN ST 16-41-8-1, et seq.;

   - All records relating to child abuse as declared confidential by IN ST 31-33-18-1, et seq.;

   - All records relating to drug tests as declared confidential by IN ST 5-14-3-4(a)(9);

   - Records of grand jury proceedings as declared confidential by IN ST 35-34-2-4;

   - Records of juvenile proceedings as declared confidential by IN ST 31-39-1-2, except those specifically open under statute;

   - All paternity records created after July 1, 1941 as declared confidential by IN ST 31-14-11-15, IN ST 31-19-5-23, IN ST 31-39-1-1 and IN ST 31-39-1-2 [Editor's note: IN ST 31-14-11-15 was repealed effective May 9, 2013];

   - All pre-sentence reports as declared confidential by IN ST 35-38-1-13;

   - Written petitions to permit marriages without consent and orders directing the Clerk of Court to issue a marriage license to underage persons, as declared confidential by IN ST 31-11-1-6;

   - Only those arrest warrants, search warrants, indictments and informations ordered confidential by the trial judge, prior to return of duly executed service as declared confidential by IN ST 5-14-3-4(b)(1);

   - All medical, mental health, or tax records unless determined by law or regulation of any governmental custodian not to be confidential, released by the subject of such records, or declared by a court of competent jurisdiction to be essential to the resolution of litigation as declared confidential by IN ST 16-39-3-10, IN ST 6-4.1-5-10, IN ST 6-4.1-12-12, and IN ST 6-8.1-7-1;

   - Personal information relating to jurors or prospective jurors, other than for the use of the parties and counsel, pursuant to IN ST JURY Rule 10;

   - Information relating to protection from abuse orders, no-contact orders and workplace violence restraining orders as declared confidential by IN ST 5-2-9-6, et seq.;

   - Mediation proceedings pursuant to IN ST ADR Rule 2.11, Mini-Trial proceedings pursuant to IN ST ADR Rule 4.4(C), and Summary Jury Trials pursuant to IN ST ADR Rule 5.6;

   - Information in probation files pursuant to the Probation Standards promulgated by the Judicial Conference of Indiana pursuant to IN ST 11-13-1-8(b);

   - Information deemed confidential pursuant to the Rules for Court Administered Alcohol

and Drug Programs promulgated by the Judicial Conference of Indiana pursuant to IN ST 12-23-14-13;

- Information deemed confidential pursuant to the Problem-Solving Court Rules promulgated by the Judicial Conference of Indiana pursuant to IN ST 33-23-16-16;

- All records of the Department of workforce Development as declared confidential by IN ST 22-4-19-6;

- Information regarding interception of electronic communications that is sealed or deemed confidential as set forth in IN ST 35-33.5-2-1, et seq.

iii. Information excluded from public access by specific court order;

iv. Complete Social Security Numbers of living persons;

v. With the exception of names, information such as addresses, phone numbers, and dates of birth which explicitly identifies:

- Natural persons who are witnesses or victims (not including defendants) in criminal, domestic violence, stalking, sexual assault, juvenile, or civil protection order proceedings, provided that juveniles who are victims of sex crimes shall be identified by initials only;

- Places of residence of judicial officers, clerks and other employees of courts and clerks of court, unless the person or persons about whom the information pertains waives confidentiality;

vi. Complete account numbers of specific assets, loans, bank accounts, credit cards, and personal identification numbers (PINs);

vii. All orders of expungement entered in criminal or juvenile proceedings, orders to restrict access to criminal history information pursuant to IN ST 35-38-5-5.5 or IN ST 35-38-8-5 and records excluded from public access by such orders, and information related to infractions that is excluded from public access pursuant to IN ST 34-28-5-15 or IN ST 34-28-5-16 [Editor's note: IN ST 35-38-5-5.5, IN ST 35-38-8-5 and IN ST 34-28-5-16 were repealed effective July 1, 2013; for information on orders restricting access to criminal history, refer to IN ST 35-38-9-1, et seq.];

viii. All personal notes and e-mail, and deliberative material, of judges, jurors, court staff and judicial agencies, and information recorded in personal data assistants (PDA's) or organizers and personal calendars. IN ST ADMIN Rule 9(G)(1).

F. Filing and Service Requirements

1. *Filing requirements.* Except as otherwise provided in IN ST TRIAL P Rule 5(E)(2), all pleadings and papers subsequent to the complaint which are required to be served upon a party shall be filed with the Court either before service or within a reasonable period of time thereafter. IN ST TRIAL P Rule 5(E)(1). Counsel shall file with the court an original and one (1) copy of all briefs, and memoranda of law filed in support of a motion. IN ST MARION CIR AND SUPER CTS CIV Rule 205(D).

   a. *Filing generally.* All pleadings, petitions and motions are filed with the Clerk designated by the Court at any time during office hours established by the Clerk and the Court. All orders submitted to the Court shall be in sufficient number and shall be accompanied by postage paid envelopes addressed to each party or counsel of record. IN ST MARION CIR AND SUPER CTS CIV Rule 205(A)

   b. *Filing with the court defined.* The filing of pleadings, motions, and other papers with the court as required by the Indiana Rules of Trial Procedure shall be made by one of the following methods:

      i. Delivery to the clerk of the court;

      ii. Sending by electronic transmission under the procedure adopted pursuant to IN ST ADMIN Rule 12;

      iii. Mailing to the clerk by registered, certified or express mail return receipt requested;

      iv. Depositing with any third-party commercial carrier for delivery to the clerk within three (3) calendar days, cost prepaid, properly addressed;

    v.   If the court so permits, filing with the judge, in which event the judge shall note thereon the filing date and forthwith transmit them to the office of the clerk; or

    vi. Electronic filing, as approved by the Division of State Court Administration pursuant to IN ST ADMIN Rule 16. IN ST TRIAL P Rule 5(F).

    vii. Filing by registered or certified mail and by third-party commercial carrier shall be complete upon mailing or deposit. IN ST TRIAL P Rule 5(F).

c.   *Facsimile filing.* Facsimile filing is discouraged, but permitted in the Marion Circuit and Marion Superior Court. All documents filed by facsimile shall also be filed in hard copy within seven (7) days of the facsimile filing, along with proposed orders and stamped addressed envelopes, as required by IN ST MARION CIR AND SUPER CTS CIV Rule 203(E). To avoid duplicate filings, the hard copies of the facsimile filing shall indicate in bold letters that the pleading was previously filed by facsimile transmission. Proof of transmission by facsimile, including certificate of service and manner of service, shall be the responsibility of the filing party. If the filing requires immediate attention of the Judge, it shall be so indicated in bold letters in an accompanying transmittal memorandum. Legibility of documents and timeliness of filing is the responsibility of the sender. IN ST MARION CIR AND SUPER CTS CIV Rule 205(B).

    i. *Generally.* In counties where a majority of judges of the courts of record, by posted local rule, have authorized electronic facsimile filing and designated a telephone number to receive such transmissions, pleadings, motions, and other papers may be sent to the Clerk of Circuit Court by electronic facsimile transmission for filing in any case, provided:

- Such matter does not exceed ten (10) pages, including the cover sheet;

- Such matter does not require the payment of fees other than the electronic facsimile transcription fee set forth in IN ST ADMIN Rule 12(E);

- The sending party creates at the time of transmission a machine generated log for such transmission; and

- The original document and the transmission log are maintained by the sending party for the duration of the litigation. IN ST ADMIN Rule 12(B).

    ii. *Time of filing.* During normal, posted business hours, the time of filing shall be the time the duplicate document is produced in the office of the Clerk of the Circuit Court. Duplicate documents received at all other times shall be filed as of the next normal business day. IN ST ADMIN Rule 12(C).

- If the receiving fax machine endorses its own time and date stamp upon the transmitted documents and the receiving machine produces a delivery receipt which is electronically created and transmitted to the sending party, the time of filing shall be the date and time recorded on the transmitted document by the receiving fax machine. IN ST ADMIN Rule 12(C).

d.   *Electronic filing.* Electronic filing and electronic service pilot projects are authorized pursuant to IN ST ADMIN Rule 16 and approved by the Division of State Court Administration. IN ST MARION SUPER CT ADMIN Rule 311(1-103).

    i. *Cases where electronic filing accepted.* All Marion County Circuit and Superior civil courts may accept electronic filing and service of pleadings and other documents designated in this rule in mortgage foreclosure (hereinafter referred to as "MF"), civil collection(hereinafter referred to as "CC"), and individual cases that have been approved for electronic filing and service. IN ST MARION SUPER CT ADMIN Rule 311(1-104)(1).

- The Marion County Circuit Court may, upon the motion of a party or its own motion, designate a case that will involve multiple litigants, legally intricate issues, and an extensive number of documents a mass tort or complex litigation case. Any case so designated shall be subject to electronic filing and service using the county's approved Electronic Service Provider. IN ST MARION SUPER CT ADMIN Rule 311(1-104)(3).

- The filing of electronic pleadings and other documents in MF and CC cases is entirely voluntary; however, once the case is initially filed electronically, all subsequent filings in the case shall remain in electronic format until the time for appeal is exhausted. IN ST MARION SUPER CT ADMIN Rule 311(1-104)(5).

ii. *Documents eligible for electronic filing.* The following pleadings may be filed and served electronically:

- New case complaint and petitions. IN ST MARION SUPER CT ADMIN Rule 311(1-104)(8)(a).

- Original answers. IN ST MARION SUPER CT ADMIN Rule 311(1-104)(8)(a).

- Any other pleadings or document including but not limited to motions and appearance forms. IN ST MARION SUPER CT ADMIN Rule 311(1-104)(8)(a).

iii. *Manner of electronic filing.* Parties shall E-file a document either:

- By registering to use the Electronic Filing Service Provider; or

- In person at the Marion County Clerk's office, by electronically filing through the Public Access Terminal. Parties filing in this manner shall be responsible for furnishing the document in an electronic format that will be compatible with the clerk's office-system to be uploaded in person. IN ST MARION SUPER CT ADMIN Rule 311(1-104)(9). For information on the Electronic Filing Service Provider and Public Access Terminal, refer to IN ST MARION SUPER CT ADMIN Rule 311(1-101).

- Registered users shall pay statutory filing fees for E-filed documents electronically to the Court through their EFSP. Filing fees are due and payable at the time of filing. IN ST MARION SUPER CT ADMIN Rule 311(2-104)(1). For more information on electronic filing fees, refer to IN ST MARION SUPER CT ADMIN Rule 311(2-104).

iv. *Effect of electronic filing.* Any pleading filed electronically shall be considered as filed with the court when the transmission to the EFSP is complete. Any document E-filed by 11:59 p.m. local Indianapolis, Indiana time shall be deemed filed on that date. The EFSP is an agent of the Court for the purpose of electronic filing, receipt, service and retrieval of electronic documents. IN ST MARION SUPER CT ADMIN Rule 311(2-102).

- Upon completion of filing, the EFSP shall issue a confirmation receipt that includes the date and time of receipt. The confirmation receipt shall serve as proof of filing. IN ST MARION SUPER CT ADMIN Rule 311(2-102).

- In the event the Court rejects the submitted documents following review, the documents shall not become part of the official Court record and the filer will receive notification of the rejection. Users may be required to refile the instruments to meet necessary filing requirements. Documents may be filed through an E-filing system at any time that the Clerk's office is open to receive the filing or at such other times as may be designated by the clerk and posted publicly. IN ST MARION SUPER CT ADMIN Rule 311(2-102).

- Documents filed through the E-filing system are deemed filed when received by the Clerk's office, except that documents received at times that the Clerk's office is closed shall be deemed filed the next regular time when the Clerk's office is open for filing. The time stamp issued by the E-filing system shall be presumed to be the time the document is received by the Clerk. IN ST MARION SUPER CT ADMIN Rule 311(2-102).

v. *Electronically filed documents.* All pleadings and other documents designated in IN ST MARION SUPER CT ADMIN Rule 311 shall be filed and served electronically in any individual case which has been approved for electronic filing and service. IN ST MARION SUPER CT ADMIN Rule 311(1-104)(6).

vi. *System failures.* When filing by electronic means is hindered by a technical failure, a party may file with the Clerk of Marion County in hard copy. With the exception of deadlines that by law cannot be extended, the time for filing of any paper that is delayed due to technical failure of the site shall be extended for one (1) day for each day on which such failure occurs, unless otherwise ordered by the Court. IN ST MARION SUPER CT ADMIN Rule 311(2-108).

    vii.   *Compliance with rules.* All filing shall comply with the requirements of IN ST ADMIN Rule 9 and IN ST ADMIN Rule 16; and the Indiana Rules of Court and the Marion County Local Rules. IN ST MARION SUPER CT ADMIN Rule 311(1-104)(11).

  e.   *Filing for special judge.* When a Special Judge who is not a Marion County Judge is selected, all parties or attorneys shall furnish such Judge with copies of all filings prior to the qualification of such Special Judge. Thereafter, copies of all filings shall be delivered in person, by mail or by facsimile to the office of the Special Judge with certificate of forwarding same made a part of the filing. IN ST MARION CIR AND SUPER CTS CIV Rule 205(C).

  f.   *Proof of filing.* Any party filing any paper by any method other than personal delivery to the clerk shall retain proof of filing. IN ST TRIAL P Rule 5(F).

2.   *Service requirements.* Unless otherwise provided by the Indiana Rules of Trial Procedure or an order of the court, each party and special judge, if any, shall be served with: (1) every order required by its terms to be served; (2) every pleading subsequent to the original complaint; (3) every written motion except one which may be heard ex parte; (4) every brief submitted to the trial court; (5) every paper relating to discovery required to be served upon a party; and (6) every written notice, appearance, demand, offer of judgment, designation of record on appeal, or similar paper. IN ST TRIAL P Rule 5(A).

  a.   *Methods of service*

    i.   *Personal service.* Whenever a party is represented by an attorney of record, service shall be made upon such attorney unless service upon the party himself is ordered by the court. Service upon the attorney or party shall be made by delivering or mailing a copy of the papers to the last known address or where an attorney or party has consented to service by fax or e-mail, as provided in IN ST TRIAL P Rule 3.1(A)(4), by faxing or e-mailing a copy of the documents to the fax number or e-mail address set out in the appearance form or correction as required by IN ST TRIAL P Rule 3.1(E). IN ST TRIAL P Rule 5(B). Delivery of a copy within IN ST TRIAL P Rule 5 means:

- Offering or tendering it to the attorney or party and stating the nature of the papers being served. Refusal to accept an offered or tendered document is a waiver of any objection to the sufficiency or adequacy of service of that document;

- Leaving it at his office with a clerk or other person in charge thereof, or if there is no one in charge, leaving it in a conspicuous place therein; or

- If the office is closed, by leaving it at his dwelling house or usual place of abode with some person of suitable age and discretion then residing therein; or,

- Leaving it at some other suitable place, selected by the attorney upon whom service is being made, pursuant to duly promulgated local rule. IN ST TRIAL P Rule 5(B)(1).

    ii.   *Service by mail.* If service is made by mail, the papers shall be deposited in the United States mail addressed to the person on whom they are being served, with postage prepaid. Service shall be deemed complete upon mailing. Proof of service of all papers permitted to be mailed may be made by written acknowledgment of service, by affidavit of the person who mailed the papers, or by certificate of an attorney. It shall be the duty of attorneys when entering their appearance in a cause or when filing pleadings or papers therein, to have noted in the Chronological Case Summary or said pleadings or papers so filed the address and telephone number of their office. Service by delivery or by mail at such address shall be deemed sufficient and complete. IN ST TRIAL P Rule 5(B)(2).

    iii.   *Service by fax or e-mail.* A party who has consented to service by fax or e-mail may be served as follows:

- Service by e-mail shall be made by attaching the document being served in .pdf format. Discovery documents must also be served in accordance with IN ST TRIAL P Rule 26(A). IN ST TRIAL P Rule 5(B)(3)(a).

- Service by fax shall be deemed complete upon generation of a transmission record indicating the successful transmission of the entire document, except as provided in IN ST TRIAL P Rule 5(B)(3)(d). IN ST TRIAL P Rule 5(B)(3)(b).

- Service by e-mail shall be deemed complete upon transmission, except as provided in IN ST TRIAL P Rule 5(B)(3)(d). IN ST TRIAL P Rule 5(B)(3)(c).

- Service by fax or e-mail that occurs on a Saturday, Sunday, legal holiday, or day the court or agency in which the matter is pending is closed or after 5:00 PM local time of the recipient shall be deemed complete the next day that is not a Saturday, Sunday, legal holiday, or day that the court or agency in which the matter is pending is not closed. IN ST TRIAL P Rule 5(B)(3)(d).

iv. *Electronic service.* Delivery of E-service documents through the EFSP to other registered users shall be considered as valid and effective service and shall have the same legal effect as an original paper document. Recipients of E-service documents shall access their documents through the EFSP. IN ST MARION SUPER CT ADMIN Rule 311(2-107)(1).

- E-service shall be deemed complete when the transmission to the EFSP is completed. IN ST MARION SUPER CT ADMIN Rule 311(2-107)(2).

- For the purpose of computing time to respond to documents received via E-service, any document served on a day or at a time when the Clerk's office is not open for business shall be deemed served at the time of next opening of the Clerk's office for business. IN ST MARION SUPER CT ADMIN Rule 311(2-107)(3).

b. *Serving numerous defendants.* In any action in which there are unusually large numbers of defendants, the court, upon motion or of its own initiative, may order:

i. That service of the pleadings of the defendants and replies thereto need not be made as between the defendants;

- That any cross-claim, counterclaim, or matter constituting an avoidance or affirmative defense contained therein shall be deemed to be denied or avoided by all other parties; and

- That the filing of any such pleading and service thereof upon the plaintiff constitutes due notice of it to the parties. IN ST TRIAL P Rule 5(D).

ii. A copy of every such order shall be served upon the parties in such manner and form as the court directs. IN ST TRIAL P Rule 5(D).

c. *Service on parties in default for failure to appear.* No service need be made on parties in default for failure to appear, except that pleadings asserting new or additional claims for relief against them shall be served upon them in the manner provided by service of summons in IN ST TRIAL P Rule 4. IN ST TRIAL P Rule 5(A).

G. Hearings

1. *Hearing on motion.* Unless local conditions make it impracticable, each judge shall establish regular times and places, at intervals sufficiently frequent for the prompt dispatch of business, at which motions requiring notice and hearing may be heard and disposed of; but the judge at any time or place and on such notice, if any, as he considers reasonable may make order for the advancement, conduct, and hearing of actions. To expedite its business the court may direct the submission and determination of motions without oral hearing upon brief written statements of reasons in support and opposition, or direct or permit hearings by telephone conference call with all attorneys or other similar means of communication. IN ST TRIAL P Rule 73(A).

2. *Hearings generally held before imposition of discovery sanctions.* As a general matter, most courts will conduct a hearing prior to imposing discovery sanctions, although IN ST TRIAL P Rule 37 and Indiana case law do not expressly require a court to do so. 22 INPRAC § 27.7.

3. *Time and place of hearing.* If the motion requires a hearing or oral argument, the Court shall set the time and place of hearing or argument on the motion. IN ST MARION CIR AND SUPER CTS CIV Rule 203(A).

H. Forms

1. Motion for Discovery Sanctions Forms for Indiana

a. Motion to dismiss as sanction for failure to comply with court ordered discovery. 5 INPRAC § 4:6.60.

    b.   Motion to dismiss action as sanction; For party's failure to comply with court ordered discovery. 10 INPRAC § 58.38.

    c.   Motion for order precluding litigation of issues. 10 INPRAC § 58.63.

    d.   Motion for judgment by default; As sanction for failure to comply with court order. 10 INPRAC § 58.64.

    e.   Motion to exclude expert witness at trial. 10 INPRAC § 70.24

    f.   Certificate of service; Personal service. 9 INPRAC § 5.7.

    g.   Certificate of service; First class mail. 9 INPRAC § 5.8.

I. Checklist

  (I) ❑ Matters to be considered by moving party

    (a) ❑ Required documents

      (1) ❑ Motion and notice

      (2) ❑ Attorney certification

      (3) ❑ Statement or approval or disapproval

      (4) ❑ Proposed order

      (5) ❑ Certificate of service

    (b) ❑ Supplemental documents

      (1) ❑ Supporting evidence

      (2) ❑ Request for oral argument

      (3) ❑ Facsimile cover sheet

    (c) ❑ Timing

      (1) ❑ There are no specific timing requirements for filing a motion for discovery sanctions

      (2) ❑ A written motion, other than one which may be heard ex parte, and notice of the hearing thereof shall be served not less than five (5) days before the time specified for the hearing, unless a different period is fixed by the Indiana Rules of Trial Procedure or by order of the court

      (3) ❑ All pleadings and papers subsequent to the complaint which are required to be served upon a party shall be filed with the Court either before service or within a reasonable period of time thereafter

  (II) ❑ Matters to be considered by the responding party

    (a) ❑ Required documents

      (1) ❑ Opposition

      (2) ❑ Certificate of service

    (b) ❑ Supplemental documents

      (1) ❑ Supporting evidence

      (2) ❑ Proposed order

      (3) ❑ Facsimile cover sheet

    (c) ❑ Timing

      (1) ❑ If the statement regarding the position of the opposing party(ies) required under IN ST MARION CIR AND SUPER CTS CIV Rule 203(A) indicates that objection to the granting of said motion may ensue, said objecting a party shall have fifteen (15) days from the date of filing to file a response to said motion

      (2) ❑ Except as otherwise provided in IN ST TRIAL P Rule 59(D), opposing affidavits may be

served not less than one (1) day before the hearing, unless the court permits them to be served at some other time

Motions, Oppositions and Replies
Motion for Preliminary Injunction

Document Last Updated October 2013

A. Applicable Rules

1. *State rules*

   a. Appearance. IN ST TRIAL P Rule 3.1.

   b. Process. IN ST TRIAL P Rule 4.

   c. Service and filing of pleadings and other papers. IN ST TRIAL P Rule 5.

   d. Time. IN ST TRIAL P Rule 6.

   e. Pleadings. IN ST TRIAL P Rule 7; IN ST TRIAL P Rule 8; IN ST TRIAL P Rule 9.2; IN ST TRIAL P Rule 10.

   f. Signing and verification of pleadings. IN ST TRIAL P Rule 11.

   g. Evidence. IN ST TRIAL P Rule 43.

   h. Judgment on the evidence (directed verdict). IN ST TRIAL P Rule 50.

   i. Findings by the court. IN ST TRIAL P Rule 52.

   j. Summary judgment. IN ST TRIAL P Rule 56.

   k. Motion to correct error. IN ST TRIAL P Rule 59.

   l. Relief from judgment or order. IN ST TRIAL P Rule 60.

   m. Injunctions. IN ST TRIAL P Rule 65; IN ST 34-26-1-7; IN ST 34-26-1-8.

   n. Security; Proceedings against sureties. IN ST TRIAL P Rule 65.1.

   o. Hearing of motions. IN ST TRIAL P Rule 73.

   p. Access to court records. IN ST ADMIN Rule 9.

   q. Paper size. IN ST ADMIN Rule 11.

   r. Facsimile transmission. IN ST ADMIN Rule 12.

   s. Electronic filing and electronic service pilot projects. IN ST ADMIN Rule 16.

   t. Sealing of certain records by court; Hearing; Notice. IN ST 5-14-3-5.5.

   u. Privacy and confidentiality. IN ST 5-2-9-6; IN ST 5-14-3-4; IN ST 6-4.1-5-10; IN ST 6-4.1-12-12; IN ST 6-8.1-7-1; IN ST 11-13-1-8; IN ST 12-23-14-13; IN ST 16-39-3-10; IN ST 16-41-8-1; IN ST 22-4-19-6; IN ST 31-11-1-6; IN ST 31-19-5-23; IN ST 31-19-13-2; IN ST 31-19-19-1; IN ST 31-33-18-1; IN ST 31-39-1-1; IN ST 31-39-1-2; IN ST 33-23-16-16; IN ST 35-34-2-4; IN ST 35-38-1-13; IN ST 35-38-9-1; IN ST ADR Rule 2.11; IN ST ADR Rule 4.4; IN ST ADR Rule 5.6; IN ST JURY Rule 10.

2. *Local rules*

   a. Requirements for motions. IN ST MARION CIR AND SUPER CTS CIV Rule 203.

   b. Preparation of pleadings, motions and other papers. IN ST MARION CIR AND SUPER CTS CIV Rule 204.

   c. Filing of pleadings, motions and other papers. IN ST MARION CIR AND SUPER CTS CIV Rule 205.

   d. Signing and verification of pleadings, motions and other papers; Service on opposing party. IN ST MARION CIR AND SUPER CTS CIV Rule 206.

    e.   Motions for continuance. IN ST MARION CIR AND SUPER CTS CIV Rule 215.

    f.   Electronic filing. IN ST MARION SUPER CT ADMIN Rule 311.

B. Timing

1. *Motion for preliminary injunction.* The injunction may be granted at the time of commencing the action, or at any time afterwards before judgment is rendered in the proceeding. IN ST 34-26-1-7. IN ST TRIAL P Rule 65 does not state when notice must be given. 4 INPRAC R 65(65.2).

    a.   *Filing.* All pleadings and papers subsequent to the complaint which are required to be served upon a party shall be filed with the Court either before service or within a reasonable period of time thereafter. IN ST TRIAL P Rule 5(E)(1).

2. *Service.* A written motion, other than one which may be heard ex parte, and notice of the hearing thereof shall be served not less than five (5) days before the time specified for the hearing, unless a different period is fixed by the Indiana Rules of Trial Procedure or by order of the court. IN ST TRIAL P Rule 6(D).

    a.   *Of supporting affidavits.* When a motion is supported by affidavit, the affidavit shall be served with the motion. IN ST TRIAL P Rule 6(D).

3. *Opposition*

    a.   *Filing.* If the statement regarding the position of the opposing party(ies) required under IN ST MARION CIR AND SUPER CTS CIV Rule 203(A) indicates that objection to the granting of said motion may ensue, said objecting a party shall have fifteen (15) days from the date of filing to file a response to said motion. IN ST MARION CIR AND SUPER CTS CIV Rule 203(B).

    b.   *Service.* Except as otherwise provided in IN ST TRIAL P Rule 59(D), opposing affidavits may be served not less than one (1) day before the hearing, unless the court permits them to be served at some other time. IN ST TRIAL P Rule 6(D).

4. *Computation of time*

    a.   *Generally; Days excluded.* In computing any period of time prescribed or allowed by the Indiana Rules of Trial Procedure, by order of the court, or by any applicable statute, the day of the act, event, or default from which the designated period of time begins to run shall not be included. The last day of the period so computed is to be included unless it is:

        i.   A Saturday,

        ii.   A Sunday,

        iii.   A legal holiday as defined by state statute, or

        iv.   A day the office in which the act is to be done is closed during regular business hours. IN ST TRIAL P Rule 6(A).

    b.   *Short periods.* In any event, the period runs until the end of the next day that is not a Saturday, a Sunday, a legal holiday, or a day on which the office is closed. When the period of time allowed is less than seven (7) days, intermediate Saturdays, Sundays, legal holidays, and days on which the office is closed shall be excluded from the computations. IN ST TRIAL P Rule 6(A).

    c.   *Additional time after service by United States mail.* Whenever a party has the right or is required to do some act or take some proceedings within a prescribed period after the service of a notice or other paper upon him and the notice or paper is served upon him by United States mail, three (3) days shall be added to the prescribed period. IN ST TRIAL P Rule 6(E).

    d.   *Enlargement of time.* When an act is required or allowed to be done at or within a specific time by the Indiana Rules of Trial Procedure, the court may at any time for cause shown:

        i.   Order the period enlarged, with or without motion or notice, if request therefor is made before the expiration of the period originally prescribed or extended by a previous order; or

        ii.   Upon motion made after the expiration of the specific period, permit the act to be done where the failure to act was the result of excusable neglect; but, the court may not extend the time for taking any action for judgment on the evidence under IN ST TRIAL P Rule 50(A), amendment of findings and judgment under IN ST TRIAL P Rule 52(B), to correct errors under IN ST

TRIAL P Rule 59(C), statement in opposition to motion to correct error under IN ST TRIAL P Rule 59(E), or to obtain relief from final judgment under IN ST TRIAL P Rule 60(B), except to the extent and under the conditions stated in those rules. IN ST TRIAL P Rule 6(B).

e. *Continuances disfavored.* Motions for Continuance are discouraged. Neither side is entitled to an automatic continuance as a matter of right. IN ST MARION CIR AND SUPER CTS CIV Rule 215. For information on obtaining a continuance, refer to IN ST MARION CIR AND SUPER CTS CIV Rule 215.

C. General Requirements

1. *Motions, generally.* Unless made during a hearing or trial, or otherwise ordered by the court, an application to the court for an order shall be made by written motion. The motion shall state the grounds therefor and the relief or order sought. IN ST TRIAL P Rule 7(B).

   a. *Motions as distinct from pleadings.* Motions and responses to motions are not pleadings, and allegations contained in a motion are not admissions of a party. 22B INPRAC 7:2; Wachstetter v. County Properties, LLC, 832 N.E.2d 574 (Ind.Ct.App. 2005); Scott County Family YMCA, Inc. v. Hobbs, 817 N.E.2d 603 (Ind.Ct.App. 2004).

   b. *Unopposed motions generally granted.* It is common for a trial court to grant procedural motions, such as motions for enlargement of time, discovery motions, or motions for continuance, unless an objection is filed. 21 INPRAC § 13.8.

2. *Motion for preliminary injunction.* The general purpose of a temporary restraining order and a preliminary injunction is to maintain and preserve the status quo until the merits of the case can be heard. The status quo is the last actual, peaceful and noncontested status which preceded the pending controversy. 4 INPRAC R 65(65.1); Rees v. Panhandle Eastern Pipe Line Co., 176 Ind.App. 597, 377 N.E.2d 640 (Ind.Ct.App. 1978). An injunction does not create or enlarge the rights of a party, it merely protects existing rights and prevents harm to the aggrieved party that cannot be corrected by a final judgment. 22B INPRAC 65:1; Franke v. Honeywell, Inc., 516 N.E.2d 1090 (Ind.Ct.App. 1987); Indiana & Michigan Elec. Co. v. Whitley County Rural Elec. Membership Corp., 161 Ind.App. 492, 316 N.E.2d 584 (Ind.Ct.App. 1974); AGS Capital Corp., Inc. v. Product Action Intern., LLC, 884 N.E.2d 294 (Ind.Ct.App. 2008).

   a. *Injunctions in general.* Whether or not a preliminary injunction should issue rests in the sound discretion of the trial court. Discretion to grant or deny a preliminary injunction is measured by the following factors and the burden lies with the movant to prove each element by a preponderance of the evidence. 4 INPRAC R 65(65.1); Crossmann Communities, Inc. v. Dean, 767 N.E.2d 1035, 1040 (Ind.Ct.App. 2002); Mercho-Roushdi Corp. v. Blatchford, 742 N.E.2d 519, 524 (Ind.Ct.App. 2001).

      i. If the movant fails to prove any of these requirements, the trial court's grant of an injunction is an abuse of discretion. 4 INPRAC R 65(65.1); Ind. Family and Soc. Servs. Admin. v. Walgreen Co., 769 N.E.2d 158, 161 (Ind. 2002):

         - Whether the plaintiff's remedies at law are inadequate and the plaintiff will suffer irreparable harm pending the resolution of the substantive action if the injunction does not issue;

         - Whether the plaintiff has demonstrated at least a reasonable likelihood of success at trial by establishing a prima facie case;

         - Whether the threatened injury to the plaintiff outweighs the threatened harm the grant of the injunction may inflict on the defendant; and

         - Whether the public interest would be disserved if the injunction is granted. 4 INPRAC R 65(65.1); Ind. Family and Soc. Servs. Admin. v. Walgreen Co., 769 N.E.2d 158, 161 (Ind. 2002); Daugherty v. Allen, 729 N.E.2d 228, 232 (Ind.Ct.App. 2000);

      ii. Two (2) sweeping statements about the preliminary injunction often appear:

         - Economic injury alone will not warrant the granting of a preliminary injunction. 4 INPRAC R 65(65.1); Wells v. Auberry, 429 N.E.2d 679 (Ind.Ct.App. 1982) and

         - Injunctive relief is not appropriate if a remedy for damages is an adequate remedy and the defendant is solvent. 4 INPRAC R 65(65.1); Gaslight and Coke Company v. City of New Albany, 139 Ind. 660, 39 N.E. 462 (1894).

b. *Consolidation of hearing with trial on merits.* Before or after the commencement of the hearing of an application for a preliminary injunction, the court may order the trial of the action on the merits to be advanced and consolidated with the hearing of the application. Even when this consolidation is not ordered, any evidence received upon an application for a preliminary injunction which would be admissible upon the trial on the merits becomes part of the record on the trial and need not be repeated upon the trial. IN ST TRIAL P Rule 65(A)(2).

   i. The power of the court to order advancement and consolidation under IN ST TRIAL P Rule 65 is tempered by the due process requirements of fair notice and an opportunity to be heard. 4 INPRAC R 65(65.3); University of Texas v. Camenisch, 451 U.S. 390, 101 S.Ct. 1830, 68 L.Ed.2d 175 (1981). The court is required to give clear notice that consolidation of the trial on the merits with the hearing on the motion for preliminary injunction will be ordered, and the notice must be given at a time which will afford the parties a full opportunity to present their respective cases. 4 INPRAC R 65(65.3); Paris v. U.S. Department of Housing & Urban Dev., 713 F.2d 1341, 1345, (7th Cir. 1983).

c. *Assignment of cases; Judge to act promptly.* Assignment of cases shall not be affected by the fact that a temporary restraining order or preliminary injunction is sought, but such case shall be assigned promptly and the judge regularly assigned to the case shall act upon and hear all matters relating to temporary restraining orders and preliminary injunctions. The judge shall make himself readily available to consider temporary restraining orders, conduct hearings, fix the manner of giving notice and the time and place for hearings under IN ST TRIAL P Rule 65, and shall act and require the parties to act promptly. IN ST TRIAL P Rule 65(A)(3).

   i. If the party seeking relief or his attorney by affidavit establishes that the judge assigned to the case is not available or cannot be found to consider an application for a restraining order, to conduct a hearing, or to fix the manner of giving notice and the time and place for a hearing under IN ST TRIAL P Rule 65, he may apply to any other judge in the circuit who shall take all further action with respect to any temporary restraining order or preliminary injunction. If the affidavit establishes that no other judge in the circuit is available or to be found, he may apply to the judge of any adjoining circuit. Unless an order is entered within ten (10) days after the hearing upon the granting, modifying or dissolving of a temporary or preliminary injunction, the relief sought shall be subject to the provisions of IN ST TRIAL P Rule 53.1. IN ST TRIAL P Rule 65(A)(3).

d. *Modification of orders; Responsive pleadings.* Upon the court's own motion or the motion of any party, orders granting or denying temporary restraining orders or preliminary injunctions may be dissolved, modified, granted or reinstated. Responsive pleadings shall not be required in response to any pleadings or motions relating to temporary restraining orders or preliminary injunctions. IN ST TRIAL P Rule 65(A)(4).

e. *Form of order by judge.* Every order granting temporary injunction and every restraining order shall include or be accompanied by findings as required by IN ST TRIAL P Rule 52; shall be specific in terms; shall describe in reasonable detail, and not by reference to the complaint or other document, the act or acts sought to be restrained; and is binding only upon the parties to the action, their officers, agents, servants, employees, and attorneys, and upon those persons in active concert or participation with them who receive actual notice of the order by personal service or otherwise. IN ST TRIAL P Rule 65(D).

3. *Security*

a. *Security requirement.* No restraining order or preliminary injunction shall issue except upon the giving of security by the applicant, in such sum as the court deems proper, for the payment of such costs and damages as may be incurred or suffered by any party who is found to have been wrongfully enjoined or restrained. No such security shall be required of a governmental organization, but such governmental organization shall be responsible for costs and damages as may be incurred or suffered by any party who is found to have been wrongfully enjoined or restrained. IN ST TRIAL P Rule 65(C).

    i.   The provisions of IN ST TRIAL P Rule 65.1 apply to a surety upon a bond or undertaking under IN ST TRIAL P Rule 65. IN ST TRIAL P Rule 65(C).

b.   *Proceedings against sureties.* Whenever the Indiana Rules of Trial Procedure or other laws require or permit the giving of security by a party to a court action or proceeding, and security is given in the form of a bond or stipulation or other undertaking with one or more sureties, each surety submits himself to the jurisdiction of the court and irrevocably appoints the clerk of the court as his agent upon whom any papers affecting his liability on the bond or undertaking may be served. His liability may be enforced on motion without the necessity of an independent action. The motion and such notice of the motion as the court prescribes may be served on the clerk of the court, who shall forthwith mail copies to the sureties if their addresses are known. IN ST TRIAL P Rule 65.1 applies to bonds or security furnished on appeal, and enforcement shall be in the court to which the case is returned after appeal. IN ST TRIAL P Rule 65.1.

c.   *Bond generally used as security.* IN ST TRIAL P Rule 65(C) speaks only of the giving of security and does not expressly require a surety on a bond. In practice, however, the giving of a bond with an insurance company as surety in the amount set by the court is typically the device used to satisfy this section. 4 INPRAC R 65(65.6).

D. Documents

1.   *Required documents*

    a.   *Motion and notice.* No preliminary injunction shall be issued without an opportunity for a hearing upon notice to the adverse party. IN ST TRIAL P Rule 65(A)(1). The requirement of notice is satisfied by service of the motion. IN ST TRIAL P Rule 7(B); IN ST MARION CIR AND SUPER CTS CIV Rule 203(A). Refer to the General Requirements section of this document for information on the content of a motion for preliminary injunction.

    b.   *Affidavit.* In all applications for an injunction, the complaint or as much of the complaint as pertains to the acts or proceedings to be enjoined, must be verified by affidavit. IN ST 34-26-1-7.

    c.   *Security.* No restraining order or preliminary injunction shall issue except upon the giving of security by the applicant, in such sum as the court deems proper, for the payment of such costs and damages as may be incurred or suffered by any party who is found to have been wrongfully enjoined or restrained. IN ST TRIAL P Rule 65(C). Refer to the General Requirements section of this document for more information.

    d.   *Statement of approval or disapproval.* Except for initial motions made pursuant to IN ST MARION CIR AND SUPER CTS CIV Rule 203(D), all motions filed with the court shall include a brief statement indicating whether opposing party(ies) object to or approve of the granting of said motion. IN ST MARION CIR AND SUPER CTS CIV Rule 203(A).

    e.   *Proposed order.* Unless local practice provides differently, a party should submit a proposed order with its written motion to be signed by the judge once the motion has been granted. 21 INPRAC § 13.8. All motions seeking an order of the Court shall be accompanied by a sufficient number of orders to be executed by the Court in granting said motion. In addition to the orders, the notice shall be accompanied by stamped, addressed envelopes to all parties of record. IN ST MARION CIR AND SUPER CTS CIV Rule 203(E).

    f.   *Certificate of service.* An attorney or unrepresented party tendering a document to the Clerk for filing shall certify that service has been made, list the parties served, and specify the date and means of service. The certificate of service shall be placed at the end of the document and shall not be separately filed. The separate filing of a certificate of service, however, shall not be grounds for rejecting a document for filing. The Clerk may permit documents to be filed without a certificate of service but shall require prompt filing of a separate certificate of service. IN ST TRIAL P Rule 5(C). In all cases where any pleading or other document is required to be served upon opposing counsel, proof of such service may be made either by:

        i.   A certificate of service signed by counsel of record for the serving party and the certificate shall specify by name and address all counsel upon whom the pleading or document was served; or

    ii.   An acknowledgment of service signed by the party served or counsel of record. IN ST MARION CIR AND SUPER CTS CIV Rule 206.

2. *Supplemental documents*

    a.   *Supporting evidence.* When a motion is based on facts not appearing of record the court may hear the matter on affidavits presented by the respective parties, but the court may direct that the matter be heard wholly or partly on oral testimony or depositions. IN ST TRIAL P Rule 43(B).

    b.   *Request for oral argument.* When an oral argument is requested, the request shall be by separate instrument and filed with the pleading to be argued. Any such oral argument requested may be heard at the discretion of the Court, except for motions for summary judgment which shall be set for hearing upon request of any party. IN ST MARION CIR AND SUPER CTS CIV Rule 203(C).

    c.   *Facsimile cover sheet.* Any document sent to the Clerk of the Circuit Court by electronic facsimile transmission shall be accompanied by a cover sheet which states the title of the document, case number, number of pages, identity and voice telephone number of the sending party and instructions for filing. The cover sheet shall contain the signature of the attorney or party, pro se, authorizing the filing. IN ST ADMIN Rule 12(D).

E. Format

1. *Form of motions.* The rules applicable to captions, and the signing and form of pleadings (IN ST TRIAL P Rule 8 through IN ST TRIAL P Rule 11), apply to all motions and other papers provided under the Indiana Rules of Trial Procedure. 22B INPRAC 7:2.

2. *Form of pleadings*

    a.   *Caption; Names of parties.* Every pleading shall contain a caption setting forth the name of the court, the title of the action, the file number, and a designation as in IN ST TRIAL P Rule 7(A). In the complaint the title of the action shall include the names of all the parties, but in other pleadings it is sufficient to state the name of the first party on each side with an appropriate indication of other parties. IN ST TRIAL P Rule 10(A).

        i.   Every pleading shall contain a caption setting forth the name of the Court, the Division and Room Number, the title of the action and the file number. IN ST MARION CIR AND SUPER CTS CIV Rule 204(B).

    b.   *Paragraphs; Separate statements.* All averments of a claim or defense shall be made in numbered paragraphs, the contents of each of which shall be limited as far as practicable to a statement of a single set of circumstances, and a paragraph may be referred to by number in all succeeding pleadings. Each claim founded upon a separate transaction or occurrence and each defense other than denials may be stated in a separate count or defense whenever a separation facilitates the clear presentation of the matters set forth. IN ST TRIAL P Rule 10(B).

    c.   *Adoption by reference; Exhibits.* Statements in a pleading may be adopted by reference in a different part of the same pleading or in another pleading or in any motion. A copy of any written instrument which is an exhibit to a pleading is a part thereof for all purposes. IN ST TRIAL P Rule 10(C).

    d.   *Paper.* Pleadings, motions and other papers may be either printed or typewritten on white opaque paper of at least sixteen (16) pound weight, eight and one-half (8-1/2) inches wide and eleven (11) inches in length. IN ST MARION CIR AND SUPER CTS CIV Rule 204(A).

    e.   *Copies.* All copies shall likewise be on white paper of sufficient strength and durability to resist normal wear and tear. IN ST MARION CIR AND SUPER CTS CIV Rule 204(A).

    f.   *Line spacing.* If typewritten, the lines shall be double spaced, except for quotations, which shall be indented and single spaced. IN ST MARION CIR AND SUPER CTS CIV Rule 204(A).

    g.   *Script type.* Script type shall not be used. IN ST MARION CIR AND SUPER CTS CIV Rule 204(A).

    h.   *Titles.* Titles on all pleadings shall delineate each topic included in the pleading e.g. where a pleading contains an Answer, a Motion to Strike or Dismiss, or a Jury Request each shall be set forth in the title. IN ST MARION CIR AND SUPER CTS CIV Rule 204(C).

    i.   *Margins and binding.* Margins shall be one (1) inch. Binding or stapling shall be at the top and at no

other place. Covers or backing shall not be used. IN ST MARION CIR AND SUPER CTS CIV Rule 204(D).

3. *Size of papers for filing.* Effective January 1, 1992, all pleadings, copies, motions and documents filed with any trial court or appellate level court, typed or printed, with the exception of exhibits and existing wills, shall be prepared on eight and one-half by eleven inch (8 1/2" x 11") size paper. IN ST ADMIN Rule 11.

4. *Form of electronically filed documents.* All electronically filed and served pleadings shall, to the extent practicable, be formatted in accordance with the applicable rules governing formatting of paper pleadings. IN ST MARION SUPER CT ADMIN Rule 311(2-103)(1).

   a. *Electronic document title.* The electronic document title of each pleading or other document shall include:

      i. Party or parties filing/serving the document,

      ii. Nature of the document,

      iii. Party or parties against whom relief, if any, is sought, and

      iv. Nature of the relief sought (e.g., Defendant ABC Corporation's Motion for Summary Judgment). IN ST MARION SUPER CT ADMIN Rule 311(2-103)(2).

5. *Signature requirements*

   a. *Signature of attorney.* Every pleading or motion of a party represented by an attorney shall be signed by at least one (1) attorney of record in his individual name, whose address, telephone number, and attorney number shall be stated, except that this provision shall not apply to pleadings and motions made and transcribed at the trial or a hearing before the judge and received by him in such form. IN ST TRIAL P Rule 11(A).

      i. All pleadings and motions shall contain the original or authorized signature of the attorney, the name of the attorney in typed or printed form, the name of the law firm if a member of a firm, the attorney's address, identification number, e-mail address, telephone number, fax number, and the designation as to the party for whom he appears. IN ST MARION CIR AND SUPER CTS CIV Rule 204(E).

      ii. The signature of an attorney constitutes a certificate by him that he has read the pleadings; that to the best of his knowledge, information, and belief, there is good ground to support it; and that it is not interposed for delay. IN ST TRIAL P Rule 11(A).

      iii. If a pleading or motion is not signed or is signed with intent to defeat the purpose of the rule, it may be stricken as sham and false and the action may proceed as though the pleading had not been served. IN ST TRIAL P Rule 11(A).

      iv. For a willful violation of IN ST TRIAL P Rule 11 an attorney may be subjected to appropriate disciplinary action. Similar action may be taken if scandalous or indecent matter is inserted. IN ST TRIAL P Rule 11(A).

      v. Every pleading, document, and instrument electronically filed or served shall be deemed to have been signed by the judge, clerk, attorney or declarant and shall bear a facsimile or typographical signature of such person, along with the typed name, address, telephone number, and Bar number of a signing attorney. Typographical signatures shall be treated as personal signatures for all purposes under these rules. IN ST MARION SUPER CT ADMIN Rule 311(2-105).

         • Documents containing signatures of third-parties (i.e., unopposed motions, affidavits, stipulations, etc.) may also be filed electronically by indicating that the original signatures are maintained by the filing party in paper-format. IN ST MARION SUPER CT ADMIN Rule 311(2-105).

         • Unless otherwise ordered by the Court or Clerk, a printed copy of all documents filed or served electronically, including original signatures, shall be maintained by the party filing the document and shall be made available, upon reasonable notice, for inspection by other

counsel, the Clerk or Court. Parties shall retain originals until two (2) years after all time periods for appeal have expired. From time to time, it may be necessary to provide the Clerk or Court with a hard copy of an electronically filed document. IN ST MARION SUPER CT ADMIN Rule 311(2-105).

vi. For the recommended format of a signature block, refer to IN ST MARION CIR AND SUPER CTS CIV Rule 204(E).

b. *Signature of unrepresented party.* A party who is not represented by an attorney shall sign his pleading and state his address. IN ST TRIAL P Rule 11(A).

c. *Verification not generally required.* Except when specifically required by rule, pleadings or motions need not be verified or accompanied by affidavit. The rule in equity that the averments of an answer under oath must be overcome by the testimony of two (2) witnesses or of one (1) witness sustained by corroborating circumstances is abolished. IN ST TRIAL P Rule 11(A).

d. *Verification by affirmation or representation.* When in connection with any civil or special statutory proceeding it is required that any pleading, motion, petition, supporting affidavit, or other document of any kind, be verified, or that an oath be taken, it shall be sufficient if the subscriber simply affirms the truth of the matter to be verified by an affirmation or representation. IN ST TRIAL P Rule 11(B). IN ST TRIAL P Rule 11(B) states that the affirmation or representation should be in substantially the following language: "I (we) affirm, under the penalties for perjury, that the foregoing representation(s) is (are) true. (Signed) _____."

i. Any person who falsifies an affirmation or representation of fact shall be subject to the same penalties as are prescribed by law for the making of a false affidavit. IN ST TRIAL P Rule 11(B).

e. *Verified pleadings, motions, and affidavits as evidence.* Pleadings, motions and affidavits accompanying or in support of such pleadings or motions when required to be verified or under oath shall be accepted as a representation that the signer had personal knowledge thereof or reasonable cause to believe the existence of the facts or matters stated or alleged therein; and, if otherwise competent or acceptable as evidence, may be admitted as evidence of the facts or matters stated or alleged therein when it is so provided in the Indiana Rules of Trial Procedure, by statute or other law, or to the extent the writing or signature expressly purports to be made upon the signer's personal knowledge. When such pleadings, motions and affidavits are verified or under oath they shall not require other or greater proof on the part of the adverse party than if not verified or not under oath unless expressly provided otherwise by the Indiana Rules of Trial Procedure, statute or other law. Affidavits upon motions for summary judgment under IN ST TRIAL P Rule 56 and in denial of execution under IN ST TRIAL P Rule 9.2 shall be made upon personal knowledge. IN ST TRIAL P Rule 11(C).

6. *Information excluded from public access.* Every document filed in a case shall separately identify information excluded from public access pursuant to IN ST ADMIN Rule 9(G)(1) as follows:

a. Whole documents that are excluded from public access pursuant to IN ST ADMIN Rule 9(G)(1) shall be tendered on light green paper or have a light green coversheet attached to the document, marked "Not for Public Access" or "Confidential." IN ST TRIAL P Rule 5(G)(1).

b. When only a portion of a document contains information excluded from public access pursuant to IN ST ADMIN Rule 9(G)(1), said information shall be omitted [or redacted] from the filed document, and set forth on a separate accompanying document on light green paper conspicuously marked "Not for Public Access" or "Confidential" and clearly designated [or identifying] the caption and number of the case and the document and location within the document to which the redacted material pertains. IN ST TRIAL P Rule 5(G)(2).

c. With respect to documents filed in electronic format, the trial court, by local rule, may provide for compliance with IN ST TRIAL P Rule 5 in manner that separates and protects access to information excluded from public access. IN ST TRIAL P Rule 5(G)(3).

d. IN ST TRIAL P Rule 5(G) does not apply to a record sealed by the court pursuant to IN ST 5-14-3-5.5 or otherwise, nor to records, documents, or information filed in cases to which public access is prohibited pursuant to IN ST ADMIN Rule 9(G). IN ST TRIAL P Rule 5(G)(4).

e. The following information in case records is excluded from public access and is confidential:

   i. Information that is excluded from public access pursuant to federal law;

   ii. Information that is excluded from public access as declared confidential by Indiana statute or other court rule, including without limitation:

- All adoption records created after July 8, 1941, as declared confidential by IN ST 31-19-19-1, et seq., except those specifically declared open by IN ST 31-19-13-2(2);

- All records relating to chancroid, chlamydia, gonorrhea, hepatitis, human immunodeficiency virus (HIV), Lymphogranuloma venereum, syphilis, tuberculosis, as declared confidential by IN ST 16-41-8-1, et seq.;

- All records relating to child abuse as declared confidential by IN ST 31-33-18-1, et seq.;

- All records relating to drug tests as declared confidential by IN ST 5-14-3-4(a)(9);

- Records of grand jury proceedings as declared confidential by IN ST 35-34-2-4;

- Records of juvenile proceedings as declared confidential by IN ST 31-39-1-2, except those specifically open under statute;

- All paternity records created after July 1, 1941 as declared confidential by IN ST 31-14-11-15, IN ST 31-19-5-23, IN ST 31-39-1-1 and IN ST 31-39-1-2 [Editor's note: IN ST 31-14-11-15 was repealed effective May 9, 2013];

- All pre-sentence reports as declared confidential by IN ST 35-38-1-13;

- Written petitions to permit marriages without consent and orders directing the Clerk of Court to issue a marriage license to underage persons, as declared confidential by IN ST 31-11-1-6;

- Only those arrest warrants, search warrants, indictments and informations ordered confidential by the trial judge, prior to return of duly executed service as declared confidential by IN ST 5-14-3-4(b)(1);

- All medical, mental health, or tax records unless determined by law or regulation of any governmental custodian not to be confidential, released by the subject of such records, or declared by a court of competent jurisdiction to be essential to the resolution of litigation as declared confidential by IN ST 16-39-3-10, IN ST 6-4.1-5-10, IN ST 6-4.1-12-12, and IN ST 6-8.1-7-1;

- Personal information relating to jurors or prospective jurors, other than for the use of the parties and counsel, pursuant to IN ST JURY Rule 10;

- Information relating to protection from abuse orders, no-contact orders and workplace violence restraining orders as declared confidential by IN ST 5-2-9-6, et seq.;

- Mediation proceedings pursuant to IN ST ADR Rule 2.11, Mini-Trial proceedings pursuant to IN ST ADR Rule 4.4(C), and Summary Jury Trials pursuant to IN ST ADR Rule 5.6;

- Information in probation files pursuant to the Probation Standards promulgated by the Judicial Conference of Indiana pursuant to IN ST 11-13-1-8(b);

- Information deemed confidential pursuant to the Rules for Court Administered Alcohol and Drug Programs promulgated by the Judicial Conference of Indiana pursuant to IN ST 12-23-14-13;

- Information deemed confidential pursuant to the Problem-Solving Court Rules promulgated by the Judicial Conference of Indiana pursuant to IN ST 33-23-16-16;

- All records of the Department of workforce Development as declared confidential by IN ST 22-4-19-6;

- Information regarding interception of electronic communications that is sealed or deemed confidential as set forth in IN ST 35-33.5-2-1, et seq.

iii. Information excluded from public access by specific court order;

iv. Complete Social Security Numbers of living persons;

v. With the exception of names, information such as addresses, phone numbers, and dates of birth which explicitly identifies:

- Natural persons who are witnesses or victims (not including defendants) in criminal, domestic violence, stalking, sexual assault, juvenile, or civil protection order proceedings, provided that juveniles who are victims of sex crimes shall be identified by initials only;

- Places of residence of judicial officers, clerks and other employees of courts and clerks of court, unless the person or persons about whom the information pertains waives confidentiality;

vi. Complete account numbers of specific assets, loans, bank accounts, credit cards, and personal identification numbers (PINs);

vii. All orders of expungement entered in criminal or juvenile proceedings, orders to restrict access to criminal history information pursuant to IN ST 35-38-5-5.5 or IN ST 35-38-8-5 and records excluded from public access by such orders, and information related to infractions that is excluded from public access pursuant to IN ST 34-28-5-15 or IN ST 34-28-5-16 [Editor's note: IN ST 35-38-5-5.5, IN ST 35-38-8-5 and IN ST 34-28-5-16 were repealed effective July 1, 2013; for information on orders restricting access to criminal history, refer to IN ST 35-38-9-1, et seq.];

viii. All personal notes and e-mail, and deliberative material, of judges, jurors, court staff and judicial agencies, and information recorded in personal data assistants (PDA's) or organizers and personal calendars. IN ST ADMIN Rule 9(G)(1).

F. Filing and Service Requirements

1. *Filing requirements.* Except as otherwise provided in IN ST TRIAL P Rule 5(E)(2), all pleadings and papers subsequent to the complaint which are required to be served upon a party shall be filed with the Court either before service or within a reasonable period of time thereafter. IN ST TRIAL P Rule 5(E)(1). Counsel shall file with the court an original and one (1) copy of all briefs, and memoranda of law filed in support of a motion. IN ST MARION CIR AND SUPER CTS CIV Rule 205(D).

   a. *Filing generally.* All pleadings, petitions and motions are filed with the Clerk designated by the Court at any time during office hours established by the Clerk and the Court. All orders submitted to the Court shall be in sufficient number and shall be accompanied by postage paid envelopes addressed to each party or counsel of record. IN ST MARION CIR AND SUPER CTS CIV Rule 205(A)

   b. *Filing with the court defined.* The filing of pleadings, motions, and other papers with the court as required by the Indiana Rules of Trial Procedure shall be made by one of the following methods:

      i. Delivery to the clerk of the court;

      ii. Sending by electronic transmission under the procedure adopted pursuant to IN ST ADMIN Rule 12;

      iii. Mailing to the clerk by registered, certified or express mail return receipt requested;

      iv. Depositing with any third-party commercial carrier for delivery to the clerk within three (3) calendar days, cost prepaid, properly addressed;

      v. If the court so permits, filing with the judge, in which event the judge shall note thereon the filing date and forthwith transmit them to the office of the clerk; or

      vi. Electronic filing, as approved by the Division of State Court Administration pursuant to IN ST ADMIN Rule 16. IN ST TRIAL P Rule 5(F).

      vii. Filing by registered or certified mail and by third-party commercial carrier shall be complete upon mailing or deposit. IN ST TRIAL P Rule 5(F).

   c. *Facsimile filing.* Facsimile filing is discouraged, but permitted in the Marion Circuit and Marion

Superior Court. All documents filed by facsimile shall also be filed in hard copy within seven (7) days of the facsimile filing, along with proposed orders and stamped addressed envelopes, as required by IN ST MARION CIR AND SUPER CTS CIV Rule 203(E). To avoid duplicate filings, the hard copies of the facsimile filing shall indicate in bold letters that the pleading was previously filed by facsimile transmission. Proof of transmission by facsimile, including certificate of service and manner of service, shall be the responsibility of the filing party. If the filing requires immediate attention of the Judge, it shall be so indicated in bold letters in an accompanying transmittal memorandum. Legibility of documents and timeliness of filing is the responsibility of the sender. IN ST MARION CIR AND SUPER CTS CIV Rule 205(B).

   i. *Generally.* In counties where a majority of judges of the courts of record, by posted local rule, have authorized electronic facsimile filing and designated a telephone number to receive such transmissions, pleadings, motions, and other papers may be sent to the Clerk of Circuit Court by electronic facsimile transmission for filing in any case, provided:

- Such matter does not exceed ten (10) pages, including the cover sheet;
- Such matter does not require the payment of fees other than the electronic facsimile transcription fee set forth in IN ST ADMIN Rule 12(E);
- The sending party creates at the time of transmission a machine generated log for such transmission; and
- The original document and the transmission log are maintained by the sending party for the duration of the litigation. IN ST ADMIN Rule 12(B).

   ii. *Time of filing.* During normal, posted business hours, the time of filing shall be the time the duplicate document is produced in the office of the Clerk of the Circuit Court. Duplicate documents received at all other times shall be filed as of the next normal business day. IN ST ADMIN Rule 12(C).

- If the receiving fax machine endorses its own time and date stamp upon the transmitted documents and the receiving machine produces a delivery receipt which is electronically created and transmitted to the sending party, the time of filing shall be the date and time recorded on the transmitted document by the receiving fax machine. IN ST ADMIN Rule 12(C).

  d. *Electronic filing.* Electronic filing and electronic service pilot projects are authorized pursuant to IN ST ADMIN Rule 16 and approved by the Division of State Court Administration. IN ST MARION SUPER CT ADMIN Rule 311(1-103).

   i. *Cases where electronic filing accepted.* All Marion County Circuit and Superior civil courts may accept electronic filing and service of pleadings and other documents designated in this rule in mortgage foreclosure (hereinafter referred to as "MF"), civil collection(hereinafter referred to as "CC"), and individual cases that have been approved for electronic filing and service. IN ST MARION SUPER CT ADMIN Rule 311(1-104)(1).

- The Marion County Circuit Court may, upon the motion of a party or its own motion, designate a case that will involve multiple litigants, legally intricate issues, and an extensive number of documents a mass tort or complex litigation case. Any case so designated shall be subject to electronic filing and service using the county's approved Electronic Service Provider. IN ST MARION SUPER CT ADMIN Rule 311(1-104)(3).
- The filing of electronic pleadings and other documents in MF and CC cases is entirely voluntary; however, once the case is initially filed electronically, all subsequent filings in the case shall remain in electronic format until the time for appeal is exhausted. IN ST MARION SUPER CT ADMIN Rule 311(1-104)(5).

   ii. *Documents eligible for electronic filing.* The following pleadings may be filed and served electronically:

- New case complaint and petitions. IN ST MARION SUPER CT ADMIN Rule 311(1-104)(8)(a).

- Original answers. IN ST MARION SUPER CT ADMIN Rule 311(1-104)(8)(a).

- Any other pleadings or document including but not limited to motions and appearance forms. IN ST MARION SUPER CT ADMIN Rule 311(1-104)(8)(a).

iii. *Manner of electronic filing.* Parties shall E-file a document either:

- By registering to use the Electronic Filing Service Provider; or

- In person at the Marion County Clerk's office, by electronically filing through the Public Access Terminal. Parties filing in this manner shall be responsible for furnishing the document in an electronic format that will be compatible with the clerk's office-system to be uploaded in person. IN ST MARION SUPER CT ADMIN Rule 311(1-104)(9). For information on the Electronic Filing Service Provider and Public Access Terminal, refer to IN ST MARION SUPER CT ADMIN Rule 311(1-101).

- Registered users shall pay statutory filing fees for E-filed documents electronically to the Court through their EFSP. Filing fees are due and payable at the time of filing. IN ST MARION SUPER CT ADMIN Rule 311(2-104)(1). For more information on electronic filing fees, refer to IN ST MARION SUPER CT ADMIN Rule 311(2-104).

iv. *Effect of electronic filing.* Any pleading filed electronically shall be considered as filed with the court when the transmission to the EFSP is complete. Any document E-filed by 11:59 p.m. local Indianapolis, Indiana time shall be deemed filed on that date. The EFSP is an agent of the Court for the purpose of electronic filing, receipt, service and retrieval of electronic documents. IN ST MARION SUPER CT ADMIN Rule 311(2-102).

- Upon completion of filing, the EFSP shall issue a confirmation receipt that includes the date and time of receipt. The confirmation receipt shall serve as proof of filing. IN ST MARION SUPER CT ADMIN Rule 311(2-102).

- In the event the Court rejects the submitted documents following review, the documents shall not become part of the official Court record and the filer will receive notification of the rejection. Users may be required to refile the instruments to meet necessary filing requirements. Documents may be filed through an E-filing system at any time that the Clerk's office is open to receive the filing or at such other times as may be designated by the clerk and posted publicly. IN ST MARION SUPER CT ADMIN Rule 311(2-102).

- Documents filed through the E-filing system are deemed filed when received by the Clerk's office, except that documents received at times that the Clerk's office is closed shall be deemed filed the next regular time when the Clerk's office is open for filing. The time stamp issued by the E-filing system shall be presumed to be the time the document is received by the Clerk. IN ST MARION SUPER CT ADMIN Rule 311(2-102).

v. *Electronically filed documents.* All pleadings and other documents designated in IN ST MARION SUPER CT ADMIN Rule 311 shall be filed and served electronically in any individual case which has been approved for electronic filing and service. IN ST MARION SUPER CT ADMIN Rule 311(1-104)(6).

vi. *System failures.* When filing by electronic means is hindered by a technical failure, a party may file with the Clerk of Marion County in hard copy. With the exception of deadlines that by law cannot be extended, the time for filing of any paper that is delayed due to technical failure of the site shall be extended for one (1) day for each day on which such failure occurs, unless otherwise ordered by the Court. IN ST MARION SUPER CT ADMIN Rule 311(2-108).

vii. *Compliance with rules.* All filing shall comply with the requirements of IN ST ADMIN Rule 9 and IN ST ADMIN Rule 16; and the Indiana Rules of Court and the Marion County Local Rules. IN ST MARION SUPER CT ADMIN Rule 311(1-104)(11).

e. *Filing for special judge.* When a Special Judge who is not a Marion County Judge is selected, all parties or attorneys shall furnish such Judge with copies of all filings prior to the qualification of such Special Judge. Thereafter, copies of all filings shall be delivered in person, by mail or by facsimile to the office of the Special Judge with certificate of forwarding same made a part of the filing. IN ST MARION CIR AND SUPER CTS CIV Rule 205(C).

f. *Proof of filing.* Any party filing any paper by any method other than personal delivery to the clerk shall retain proof of filing. IN ST TRIAL P Rule 5(F).

2. *Service requirements.* Unless otherwise provided by the Indiana Rules of Trial Procedure or an order of the court, each party and special judge, if any, shall be served with: (1) every order required by its terms to be served; (2) every pleading subsequent to the original complaint; (3) every written motion except one which may be heard ex parte; (4) every brief submitted to the trial court; (5) every paper relating to discovery required to be served upon a party; and (6) every written notice, appearance, demand, offer of judgment, designation of record on appeal, or similar paper. IN ST TRIAL P Rule 5(A).

a. *Methods of service*

i. *Personal service.* Whenever a party is represented by an attorney of record, service shall be made upon such attorney unless service upon the party himself is ordered by the court. Service upon the attorney or party shall be made by delivering or mailing a copy of the papers to the last known address or where an attorney or party has consented to service by fax or e-mail, as provided in IN ST TRIAL P Rule 3.1(A)(4), by faxing or e-mailing a copy of the documents to the fax number or e-mail address set out in the appearance form or correction as required by IN ST TRIAL P Rule 3.1(E). IN ST TRIAL P Rule 5(B). Delivery of a copy within IN ST TRIAL P Rule 5 means:

- Offering or tendering it to the attorney or party and stating the nature of the papers being served. Refusal to accept an offered or tendered document is a waiver of any objection to the sufficiency or adequacy of service of that document;

- Leaving it at his office with a clerk or other person in charge thereof, or if there is no one in charge, leaving it in a conspicuous place therein; or

- If the office is closed, by leaving it at his dwelling house or usual place of abode with some person of suitable age and discretion then residing therein; or,

- Leaving it at some other suitable place, selected by the attorney upon whom service is being made, pursuant to duly promulgated local rule. IN ST TRIAL P Rule 5(B)(1).

ii. *Service by mail.* If service is made by mail, the papers shall be deposited in the United States mail addressed to the person on whom they are being served, with postage prepaid. Service shall be deemed complete upon mailing. Proof of service of all papers permitted to be mailed may be made by written acknowledgment of service, by affidavit of the person who mailed the papers, or by certificate of an attorney. It shall be the duty of attorneys when entering their appearance in a cause or when filing pleadings or papers therein, to have noted in the Chronological Case Summary or said pleadings or papers so filed the address and telephone number of their office. Service by delivery or by mail at such address shall be deemed sufficient and complete. IN ST TRIAL P Rule 5(B)(2).

iii. *Service by fax or e-mail.* A party who has consented to service by fax or e-mail may be served as follows:

- Service by e-mail shall be made by attaching the document being served in .pdf format. Discovery documents must also be served in accordance with IN ST TRIAL P Rule 26(A). IN ST TRIAL P Rule 5(B)(3)(a).

- Service by fax shall be deemed complete upon generation of a transmission record indicating the successful transmission of the entire document, except as provided in IN ST TRIAL P Rule 5(B)(3)(d). IN ST TRIAL P Rule 5(B)(3)(b).

- Service by e-mail shall be deemed complete upon transmission, except as provided in IN ST TRIAL P Rule 5(B)(3)(d). IN ST TRIAL P Rule 5(B)(3)(c).

- Service by fax or e-mail that occurs on a Saturday, Sunday, legal holiday, or day the court or agency in which the matter is pending is closed or after 5:00 PM local time of the recipient shall be deemed complete the next day that is not a Saturday, Sunday, legal holiday, or day that the court or agency in which the matter is pending is not closed. IN ST TRIAL P Rule 5(B)(3)(d).

    iv.   *Electronic service.* Delivery of E-service documents through the EFSP to other registered users shall be considered as valid and effective service and shall have the same legal effect as an original paper document. Recipients of E-service documents shall access their documents through the EFSP. IN ST MARION SUPER CT ADMIN Rule 311(2-107)(1).

- E-service shall be deemed complete when the transmission to the EFSP is completed. IN ST MARION SUPER CT ADMIN Rule 311(2-107)(2).

- For the purpose of computing time to respond to documents received via E-service, any document served on a day or at a time when the Clerk's office is not open for business shall be deemed served at the time of next opening of the Clerk's office for business. IN ST MARION SUPER CT ADMIN Rule 311(2-107)(3).

   b.   *Serving numerous defendants.* In any action in which there are unusually large numbers of defendants, the court, upon motion or of its own initiative, may order:

    i.   That service of the pleadings of the defendants and replies thereto need not be made as between the defendants;

- That any cross-claim, counterclaim, or matter constituting an avoidance or affirmative defense contained therein shall be deemed to be denied or avoided by all other parties; and

- That the filing of any such pleading and service thereof upon the plaintiff constitutes due notice of it to the parties. IN ST TRIAL P Rule 5(D).

    ii.   A copy of every such order shall be served upon the parties in such manner and form as the court directs. IN ST TRIAL P Rule 5(D).

   c.   *Service by electronic means.* Courts wishing to establish an electronic service pilot project pursuant to the Indiana Administrative Rules must submit a written request for approval and a plan to the Division of State Court Administration. IN ST ADMIN Rule 16(B).

   d.   *Service on parties in default for failure to appear.* No service need be made on parties in default for failure to appear, except that pleadings asserting new or additional claims for relief against them shall be served upon them in the manner provided by service of summons in IN ST TRIAL P Rule 4. IN ST TRIAL P Rule 5(A).

G. Hearings

1.   *Hearing on motion.* Unless local conditions make it impracticable, each judge shall establish regular times and places, at intervals sufficiently frequent for the prompt dispatch of business, at which motions requiring notice and hearing may be heard and disposed of; but the judge at any time or place and on such notice, if any, as he considers reasonable may make order for the advancement, conduct, and hearing of actions. To expedite its business the court may direct the submission and determination of motions without oral hearing upon brief written statements of reasons in support and opposition, or direct or permit hearings by telephone conference call with all attorneys or other similar means of communication. IN ST TRIAL P Rule 73(A).

2.   *Presentation of evidence.* On the hearing of an application for a restraining order or temporary injunction, each party may read affidavits or documentary or record evidence. IN ST 34-26-1-8.

3.   *Time and place of hearing.* If the motion requires a hearing or oral argument, the Court shall set the time and place of hearing or argument on the motion. IN ST MARION CIR AND SUPER CTS CIV Rule 203(A).

H. Forms

1. Motion for Preliminary Injunction Forms for Indiana

   a.   Prayer in complaint; For preliminary injunction. 5 INPRAC § 3:13.20.

   b.   Motion for preliminary injunction. 5 INPRAC § 3:13.40.

   c.   Notice of motion for preliminary injunction. 11 INPRAC § 97.14.

   d.   Undertaking as security to support granting of injunction. 11 INPRAC § 97.14.1.

   e.   Findings of fact in support of injunction. 11 INPRAC § 97.14.2.

f. Motion to dissolve temporary restraining order. 11 INPRAC § 97.14.3.

g. Motion for contempt for violation of injunction. 11 INPRAC § 97.14.4.

h. Motion for preliminary injunction. 11 INPRAC § 97.15.

i. Preliminary injunction. 11 INPRAC § 97.16.

j. Motion to vacate preliminary injunction; Failure to post bond. 11 INPRAC § 97.17.

k. Motion to vacate preliminary injunction; Another form. 11 INPRAC § 97.18.

l. Certificate of service; Personal service. 9 INPRAC § 5.7.

m. Certificate of service; First class mail. 9 INPRAC § 5.8.

I. Checklist

(I) ❑ Matters to be considered by moving party

    (a) ❑ Required documents

        (1) ❑ Motion and notice

        (2) ❑ Affidavit

        (3) ❑ Security

        (4) ❑ Statement of approval or disapproval

        (5) ❑ Proposed order

        (6) ❑ Certificate of service

    (b) ❑ Supplemental documents

        (1) ❑ Supporting evidence

        (2) ❑ Request for oral argument

        (3) ❑ Facsimile cover sheet

    (c) ❑ Timing

        (1) ❑ The injunction may be granted at the time of commencing the action, or at any time afterwards before judgment is rendered in the proceeding

        (2) ❑ A written motion, other than one which may be heard ex parte, and notice of the hearing thereof shall be served not less than five (5) days before the time specified for the hearing, unless a different period is fixed by the Indiana Rules of Trial Procedure or by order of the court

        (3) ❑ All pleadings and papers subsequent to the complaint which are required to be served upon a party shall be filed with the Court either before service or within a reasonable period of time thereafter

(II) ❑ Matters to be considered by the responding party

    (a) ❑ Required documents

        (1) ❑ Opposition

        (2) ❑ Certificate of service

    (b) ❑ Supplemental documents

        (1) ❑ Supporting evidence

        (2) ❑ Proposed order

        (3) ❑ Facsimile cover sheet

    (c) ❑ Timing

        (1) ❑ If the statement regarding the position of the opposing party(ies) required under IN ST MARION CIR AND SUPER CTS CIV Rule 203(A) indicates that objection to the granting of said motion may ensue, said objecting a party shall have fifteen (15) days from the date of filing to file a response to said motion

(2)   ❑   Except as otherwise provided in IN ST TRIAL P Rule 59(D), opposing affidavits may be served not less than one (1) day before the hearing, unless the court permits them to be served at some other time

Motions, Oppositions and Replies
Motion to Dismiss for Failure to State a Claim

Document Last Updated October 2013

A. Applicable Rules

1. *State rules*

   a.   Appearance. IN ST TRIAL P Rule 3.1.

   b.   Process. IN ST TRIAL P Rule 4.

   c.   Service and filing of pleadings and other papers. IN ST TRIAL P Rule 5.

   d.   Time. IN ST TRIAL P Rule 6.

   e.   Pleadings. IN ST TRIAL P Rule 7; IN ST TRIAL P Rule 8; IN ST TRIAL P Rule 9.2; IN ST TRIAL P Rule 10.

   f.   Signing and verification of pleadings. IN ST TRIAL P Rule 11.

   g.   Defenses and objections; When and how presented; By pleading or motion; Motion for judgment on the pleadings. IN ST TRIAL P Rule 12.

   h.   Parties plaintiff and defendant; Capacity. IN ST TRIAL P Rule 17.

   i.   Joinder of person needed for just adjudication. IN ST TRIAL P Rule 19.

   j.   Evidence. IN ST TRIAL P Rule 43.

   k.   Judgment on the evidence (directed verdict). IN ST TRIAL P Rule 50.

   l.   Findings by the court. IN ST TRIAL P Rule 52.

   m.   Summary judgment. IN ST TRIAL P Rule 56.

   n.   Motion to correct error. IN ST TRIAL P Rule 59.

   o.   Relief from judgment or order. IN ST TRIAL P Rule 60.

   p.   Hearing of motions. IN ST TRIAL P Rule 73.

   q.   Access to court records. IN ST ADMIN Rule 9.

   r.   Paper size. IN ST ADMIN Rule 11.

   s.   Facsimile transmission. IN ST ADMIN Rule 12.

   t.   Electronic filing and electronic service pilot projects. IN ST ADMIN Rule 16.

   u.   Sealing of certain records by court; Hearing; Notice. IN ST 5-14-3-5.5.

   v.   Privacy and confidentiality. IN ST 5-2-9-6; IN ST 5-14-3-4; IN ST 6-4.1-5-10; IN ST 6-4.1-12-12; IN ST 6-8.1-7-1; IN ST 11-13-1-8; IN ST 12-23-14-13; IN ST 16-39-3-10; IN ST 16-41-8-1; IN ST 22-4-19-6; IN ST 31-11-1-6; IN ST 31-19-5-23; IN ST 31-19-13-2; IN ST 31-19-19-1; IN ST 31-33-18-1; IN ST 31-39-1-1; IN ST 31-39-1-2; IN ST 33-23-16-16; IN ST 35-34-2-4; IN ST 35-38-1-13; IN ST 35-38-9-1; IN ST ADR Rule 2.11; IN ST ADR Rule 4.4; IN ST ADR Rule 5.6; IN ST JURY Rule 10.

2. *Local rules*

   a.   Requirements for motions. IN ST MARION CIR AND SUPER CTS CIV Rule 203.

   b.   Preparation of pleadings, motions and other papers. IN ST MARION CIR AND SUPER CTS CIV Rule 204.

   c.   Filing of pleadings, motions and other papers. IN ST MARION CIR AND SUPER CTS CIV Rule 205.

d. Signing and verification of pleadings, motions and other papers; Service on opposing party. IN ST MARION CIR AND SUPER CTS CIV Rule 206.

e. Motions for continuance. IN ST MARION CIR AND SUPER CTS CIV Rule 215.

f. Electronic filing. IN ST MARION SUPER CT ADMIN Rule 311.

B. Timing

1. *Timing of motion to dismiss for failure to state a claim.* A motion making any of the defenses listed in IN ST TRIAL P Rule 12(B) shall be made before pleading if a further pleading is permitted or within twenty (20) days after service of the prior pleading if none is required. IN ST TRIAL P Rule 12(B).

   a. *Time to file a responsive pleading.* A responsive pleading required under the Indiana Rules of Trial Procedure, shall be served within twenty (20) days after service of the prior pleading. IN ST TRIAL P Rule 6(C).

   b. *Filing.* All pleadings and papers subsequent to the complaint which are required to be served upon a party shall be filed with the Court either before service or within a reasonable period of time thereafter. IN ST TRIAL P Rule 5(E)(1).

2. *Service.* A written motion, other than one which may be heard ex parte, and notice of the hearing thereof shall be served not less than five (5) days before the time specified for the hearing, unless a different period is fixed by the Indiana Rules of Trial Procedure or by order of the court. IN ST TRIAL P Rule 6(D).

   a. *Of supporting affidavits.* When a motion is supported by affidavit, the affidavit shall be served with the motion. IN ST TRIAL P Rule 6(D).

3. *Opposition*

   a. *Filing.* If the statement regarding the position of the opposing party(ies) required under IN ST MARION CIR AND SUPER CTS CIV Rule 203(A) indicates that objection to the granting of said motion may ensue, said objecting a party shall have fifteen (15) days from the date of filing to file a response to said motion. IN ST MARION CIR AND SUPER CTS CIV Rule 203(B).

   b. *Service.* Except as otherwise provided in IN ST TRIAL P Rule 59(D), opposing affidavits may be served not less than one (1) day before the hearing, unless the court permits them to be served at some other time. IN ST TRIAL P Rule 6(D).

4. *Computation of time*

   a. *Generally; Days excluded.* In computing any period of time prescribed or allowed by the Indiana Rules of Trial Procedure, by order of the court, or by any applicable statute, the day of the act, event, or default from which the designated period of time begins to run shall not be included. The last day of the period so computed is to be included unless it is:

      i. A Saturday,

      ii. A Sunday,

      iii. A legal holiday as defined by state statute, or

      iv. A day the office in which the act is to be done is closed during regular business hours. IN ST TRIAL P Rule 6(A).

   b. *Short periods.* In any event, the period runs until the end of the next day that is not a Saturday, a Sunday, a legal holiday, or a day on which the office is closed. When the period of time allowed is less than seven (7) days, intermediate Saturdays, Sundays, legal holidays, and days on which the office is closed shall be excluded from the computations. IN ST TRIAL P Rule 6(A).

   c. *Additional time after service by United States mail.* Whenever a party has the right or is required to do some act or take some proceedings within a prescribed period after the service of a notice or other paper upon him and the notice or paper is served upon him by United States mail, three (3) days shall be added to the prescribed period. IN ST TRIAL P Rule 6(E).

   d. *Enlargement of time.* When an act is required or allowed to be done at or within a specific time by the Indiana Rules of Trial Procedure, the court may at any time for cause shown:

      i. Order the period enlarged, with or without motion or notice, if request therefor is made before the expiration of the period originally prescribed or extended by a previous order; or

       ii. Upon motion made after the expiration of the specific period, permit the act to be done where the failure to act was the result of excusable neglect; but, the court may not extend the time for taking any action for judgment on the evidence under IN ST TRIAL P Rule 50(A), amendment of findings and judgment under IN ST TRIAL P Rule 52(B), to correct errors under IN ST TRIAL P Rule 59(C), statement in opposition to motion to correct error under IN ST TRIAL P Rule 59(E), or to obtain relief from final judgment under IN ST TRIAL P Rule 60(B), except to the extent and under the conditions stated in those rules. IN ST TRIAL P Rule 6(B).

    e. *Continuances disfavored.* Motions for Continuance are discouraged. Neither side is entitled to an automatic continuance as a matter of right. IN ST MARION CIR AND SUPER CTS CIV Rule 215. For information on obtaining a continuance, refer to IN ST MARION CIR AND SUPER CTS CIV Rule 215.

C. General Requirements

1. *Motions, generally.* Unless made during a hearing or trial, or otherwise ordered by the court, an application to the court for an order shall be made by written motion. The motion shall state the grounds therefor and the relief or order sought. IN ST TRIAL P Rule 7(B).

    a. *Motions as distinct from pleadings.* Motions and responses to motions are not pleadings, and allegations contained in a motion are not admissions of a party. 22B INPRAC 7:2; Wachstetter v. County Properties, LLC, 832 N.E.2d 574 (Ind.Ct.App. 2005); Scott County Family YMCA, Inc. v. Hobbs, 817 N.E.2d 603 (Ind.Ct.App. 2004).

    b. *Unopposed motions generally granted.* It is common for a trial court to grant procedural motions, such as motions for enlargement of time, discovery motions, or motions for continuance, unless an objection is filed. 21 INPRAC § 13.8.

2. *Motion to dismiss for failure to state a claim.* Every defense, in law or fact, to a claim for relief in any pleading, whether a claim, counterclaim, cross-claim, or third-party claim, shall be asserted in the responsive pleading thereto if one is required; except that at the option of the pleader, the defense of failure to state a claim upon which relief can be granted, which shall include failure to name the real party in interest under IN ST TRIAL P Rule 17, may be made by motion. IN ST TRIAL P Rule 12(B)(6). A motion under IN ST TRIAL P Rule 12(B)(6) is intended to test the legal sufficiency of a claim rather than the facts supporting that claim. 1A INPRAC R 12(12.9); Meyers v. Meyers, 861 N.E.2d 704 (Ind. 2007).

    a. *How motion made.* A defense of failure to state a claim upon which relief can be granted, a defense of failure to join an indispensable party under IN ST TRIAL P Rule 19(B), and an objection of failure to state a legal defense to a claim may be made in any pleading permitted or ordered under IN ST TRIAL P Rule 7(A) or by motion for judgment on the pleadings, or at the trial on the merits. IN ST TRIAL P Rule 12(H)(2).

    b. *Claim admitted for purpose of motion.* A motion to dismiss for failure to state a claim admits, for the purpose of the motion, the existence of the claim as stated in the complaint, but challenges the plaintiff's right to relief. 9 INPRAC § 42.10; Mills v. American Playground Device Co., 427 N.E.2d 1130 (Ind.Ct.App. 1981). Motions to dismiss under IN ST TRIAL P Rule 12 are disfavored because they undermine the policy that favors deciding cases on their merits. 22 INPRAC § 15.19; Droscha v. Shepherd, 931 N.E.2d 882 (Ind.Ct.App. 2010).

    c. *Motion decided on factual allegations of complaint.* The trial court should grant a motion to dismiss under IN ST TRIAL P Rule 12(B)(6) if the facts alleged in the complaint are incapable of supporting relief under any set of circumstances. 1A INPRAC R 12(12.9); McPeek v. McCardle, 888 N.E.2d 171 (Ind. 2008). In determining whether the facts alleged in the complaint are incapable of supporting relief, the court must look only to the complaint and may not resort to any other evidence in the record. When ruling on a motion to dismiss under IN ST TRIAL P Rule 12(B)(6), the court should consider all of the allegations in the complaint to be true and resolve all inferences in favor of the non-moving party. 1A INPRAC R 12(12.9); State v. American Family Voices, Inc., 898 N.E.2d 293 (Ind. 2008); Curtis v. Roob, 891 N.E.2d 577 (Ind.Ct.App. 2008).

    d. *Notice pleading and motions to dismiss.* Although notice pleading requirements under IN ST TRIAL P Rule 8(A) are fairly straightforward, and are well-grounded in Indiana jurisprudence, the mechanism for testing the legal sufficiency of the complaint, IN ST TRIAL P Rule 12(B)(6), has, over time, become somewhat limited because Indiana courts are instructed to dismiss an action under IN ST TRIAL P Rule 12(B)(6) only where the if the alleged facts do not support a claim for relief under any set of circumstances. 1A INPRAC R 12(12.9). Trial judges do not like to grant IN ST TRIAL P Rule 12(B)(6) motions where the claim is an inadequately pleaded complaint, which means a defendant's first meaningful opportunity to challenge a plaintiff's claim is the motion for summary judgment. 1A INPRAC R 12(12.9).

e. *Conversion to motion for summary judgment.* A motion to dismiss under IN ST TRIAL P Rule 12(B)(6) for failure to state a claim upon which relief and Motion for Judgment on the Pleadings under IN ST TRIAL P Rule 12(C) will be converted into a motion for summary judgment under IN ST TRIAL P Rule 56 if the court considers matters outside the pleadings in deciding those motions. 11 INPRAC § 90.1; Duran v. Komyatte, 490 N.E.2d 388 (Ind.Ct.App. 1986). In such case, all parties shall be given reasonable opportunity to present all material made pertinent to such a motion by IN ST TRIAL P Rule 56. IN ST TRIAL P Rule 12(B).

f. *Effect of granting of the motion.* When a motion to dismiss is sustained for failure to state a claim under IN ST TRIAL P Rule 12(B)(6) the pleading may be amended once as of right pursuant to IN ST TRIAL P Rule 15(A) within ten (10) days after service of notice of the court's order sustaining the motion and thereafter with permission of the court pursuant to such rule. IN ST TRIAL P Rule 12(B).

3. *Consolidation and waiver*

a. *Consolidation of defenses in motion.* A party who makes a motion under IN ST TRIAL P Rule 12 may join with it any other motions herein provided for and then available to him. If a party makes a motion under IN ST TRIAL P Rule 12 but omits therefrom any defense or objection then available to him which IN ST TRIAL P Rule 12 permits to be raised by motion, he shall not thereafter make a motion based on the defense or objection so omitted. He may, however, make such motions as are allowed under IN ST TRIAL P Rule 12(H)(2). IN ST TRIAL P Rule 12(G).

b. *Waiver or preservation of certain defenses.* No defense or objection is waived by being joined with one or more other defenses or objections in a responsive pleading or motion. IN ST TRIAL P Rule 12(B).

D. Documents

1. *Required documents*

a. *Motion and notice.* The requirement of notice is satisfied by service of the motion. IN ST TRIAL P Rule 7(B); IN ST MARION CIR AND SUPER CTS CIV Rule 203(A). Refer to the General Requirements section of this document for information on the content of a motion to dismiss to dismiss for failure to state a claim.

b. *Statement of approval or disapproval.* Except for initial motions made pursuant to IN ST MARION CIR AND SUPER CTS CIV Rule 203(D), all motions filed with the court shall include a brief statement indicating whether opposing party(ies) object to or approve of the granting of said motion. IN ST MARION CIR AND SUPER CTS CIV Rule 203(A).

c. *Proposed order.* Unless local practice provides differently, a party should submit a proposed order with its written motion to be signed by the judge once the motion has been granted. 21 INPRAC § 13.8. All motions seeking an order of the Court shall be accompanied by a sufficient number of orders to be executed by the Court in granting said motion. In addition to the orders, the notice shall be accompanied by stamped, addressed envelopes to all parties of record. IN ST MARION CIR AND SUPER CTS CIV Rule 203(E).

d. *Certificate of service.* An attorney or unrepresented party tendering a document to the Clerk for filing shall certify that service has been made, list the parties served, and specify the date and means of service. The certificate of service shall be placed at the end of the document and shall not be separately filed. The separate filing of a certificate of service, however, shall not be grounds for rejecting a document for filing. The Clerk may permit documents to be filed without a certificate of service but shall require prompt filing of a separate certificate of service. IN ST TRIAL P Rule 5(C).

In all cases where any pleading or other document is required to be served upon opposing counsel, proof of such service may be made either by:

    i.   A certificate of service signed by counsel of record for the serving party and the certificate shall specify by name and address all counsel upon whom the pleading or document was served; or

    ii. An acknowledgment of service signed by the party served or counsel of record. IN ST MARION CIR AND SUPER CTS CIV Rule 206.

2. *Supplemental documents*

    a. *Request for oral argument.* When an oral argument is requested, the request shall be by separate instrument and filed with the pleading to be argued. Any such oral argument requested may be heard at the discretion of the Court, except for motions for summary judgment which shall be set for hearing upon request of any party. IN ST MARION CIR AND SUPER CTS CIV Rule 203(C).

    b. *Facsimile cover sheet.* Any document sent to the Clerk of the Circuit Court by electronic facsimile transmission shall be accompanied by a cover sheet which states the title of the document, case number, number of pages, identity and voice telephone number of the sending party and instructions for filing. The cover sheet shall contain the signature of the attorney or party, pro se, authorizing the filing. IN ST ADMIN Rule 12(D).

E. Format

1. *Form of motions.* The rules applicable to captions, and the signing and form of pleadings (IN ST TRIAL P Rule 8 through IN ST TRIAL P Rule 11), apply to all motions and other papers provided under the Indiana Rules of Trial Procedure. 22B INPRAC 7:2.

2. *Form of pleadings*

    a. *Caption; Names of parties.* Every pleading shall contain a caption setting forth the name of the court, the title of the action, the file number, and a designation as in IN ST TRIAL P Rule 7(A). In the complaint the title of the action shall include the names of all the parties, but in other pleadings it is sufficient to state the name of the first party on each side with an appropriate indication of other parties. IN ST TRIAL P Rule 10(A).

        i.   Every pleading shall contain a caption setting forth the name of the Court, the Division and Room Number, the title of the action and the file number. IN ST MARION CIR AND SUPER CTS CIV Rule 204(B).

    b. *Paragraphs; Separate statements.* All averments of a claim or defense shall be made in numbered paragraphs, the contents of each of which shall be limited as far as practicable to a statement of a single set of circumstances, and a paragraph may be referred to by number in all succeeding pleadings. Each claim founded upon a separate transaction or occurrence and each defense other than denials may be stated in a separate count or defense whenever a separation facilitates the clear presentation of the matters set forth. IN ST TRIAL P Rule 10(B).

    c. *Adoption by reference; Exhibits.* Statements in a pleading may be adopted by reference in a different part of the same pleading or in another pleading or in any motion. A copy of any written instrument which is an exhibit to a pleading is a part thereof for all purposes. IN ST TRIAL P Rule 10(C).

    d. *Paper.* Pleadings, motions and other papers may be either printed or typewritten on white opaque paper of at least sixteen (16) pound weight, eight and one-half (8-1/2) inches wide and eleven (11) inches in length. IN ST MARION CIR AND SUPER CTS CIV Rule 204(A).

    e. *Copies.* All copies shall likewise be on white paper of sufficient strength and durability to resist normal wear and tear. IN ST MARION CIR AND SUPER CTS CIV Rule 204(A).

    f. *Line spacing.* If typewritten, the lines shall be double spaced, except for quotations, which shall be indented and single spaced. IN ST MARION CIR AND SUPER CTS CIV Rule 204(A).

    g. *Script type.* Script type shall not be used. IN ST MARION CIR AND SUPER CTS CIV Rule 204(A).

    h. *Titles.* Titles on all pleadings shall delineate each topic included in the pleading e.g. where a pleading contains an Answer, a Motion to Strike or Dismiss, or a Jury Request each shall be set forth in the title. IN ST MARION CIR AND SUPER CTS CIV Rule 204(C).

i. *Margins and binding.* Margins shall be one (1) inch. Binding or stapling shall be at the top and at no other place. Covers or backing shall not be used. IN ST MARION CIR AND SUPER CTS CIV Rule 204(D).

3. *Size of papers for filing.* Effective January 1, 1992, all pleadings, copies, motions and documents filed with any trial court or appellate level court, typed or printed, with the exception of exhibits and existing wills, shall be prepared on eight and one-half by eleven inch (8 1/2" x 11") size paper. IN ST ADMIN Rule 11.

4. *Form of electronically filed documents.* All electronically filed and served pleadings shall, to the extent practicable, be formatted in accordance with the applicable rules governing formatting of paper pleadings. IN ST MARION SUPER CT ADMIN Rule 311(2-103)(1).

   a. *Electronic document title.* The electronic document title of each pleading or other document shall include:

      i. Party or parties filing/serving the document,

      ii. Nature of the document,

      iii. Party or parties against whom relief, if any, is sought, and

      iv. Nature of the relief sought (e.g., Defendant ABC Corporation's Motion for Summary Judgment). IN ST MARION SUPER CT ADMIN Rule 311(2-103)(2).

5. *Signature requirements*

   a. *Signature of attorney.* Every pleading or motion of a party represented by an attorney shall be signed by at least one (1) attorney of record in his individual name, whose address, telephone number, and attorney number shall be stated, except that this provision shall not apply to pleadings and motions made and transcribed at the trial or a hearing before the judge and received by him in such form. IN ST TRIAL P Rule 11(A).

      i. All pleadings and motions shall contain the original or authorized signature of the attorney, the name of the attorney in typed or printed form, the name of the law firm if a member of a firm, the attorney's address, identification number, e-mail address, telephone number, fax number, and the designation as to the party for whom he appears. IN ST MARION CIR AND SUPER CTS CIV Rule 204(E).

      ii. The signature of an attorney constitutes a certificate by him that he has read the pleadings; that to the best of his knowledge, information, and belief, there is good ground to support it; and that it is not interposed for delay. IN ST TRIAL P Rule 11(A).

      iii. If a pleading or motion is not signed or is signed with intent to defeat the purpose of the rule, it may be stricken as sham and false and the action may proceed as though the pleading had not been served. IN ST TRIAL P Rule 11(A).

      iv. For a willful violation of IN ST TRIAL P Rule 11 an attorney may be subjected to appropriate disciplinary action. Similar action may be taken if scandalous or indecent matter is inserted. IN ST TRIAL P Rule 11(A).

      v. Every pleading, document, and instrument electronically filed or served shall be deemed to have been signed by the judge, clerk, attorney or declarant and shall bear a facsimile or typographical signature of such person, along with the typed name, address, telephone number, and Bar number of a signing attorney. Typographical signatures shall be treated as personal signatures for all purposes under these rules. IN ST MARION SUPER CT ADMIN Rule 311(2-105).

         • Documents containing signatures of third-parties (i.e., unopposed motions, affidavits, stipulations, etc.) may also be filed electronically by indicating that the original signatures are maintained by the filing party in paper-format. IN ST MARION SUPER CT ADMIN Rule 311(2-105).

         • Unless otherwise ordered by the Court or Clerk, a printed copy of all documents filed or served electronically, including original signatures, shall be maintained by the party filing the document and shall be made available, upon reasonable notice, for inspection by other counsel, the Clerk or Court. Parties shall retain originals until two (2) years after all time periods for appeal have expired. From time to time, it may be necessary to provide the Clerk or Court with a hard copy of an electronically filed document. IN ST MARION SUPER CT ADMIN Rule 311(2-105).

   vi.   For the recommended format of a signature block, refer to IN ST MARION CIR AND SUPER CTS CIV Rule 204(E).

  b. *Signature of unrepresented party.* A party who is not represented by an attorney shall sign his pleading and state his address. IN ST TRIAL P Rule 11(A).

  c. *Verification not generally required.* Except when specifically required by rule, pleadings or motions need not be verified or accompanied by affidavit. The rule in equity that the averments of an answer under oath must be overcome by the testimony of two (2) witnesses or of one (1) witness sustained by corroborating circumstances is abolished. IN ST TRIAL P Rule 11(A).

  d. *Verification by affirmation or representation.* When in connection with any civil or special statutory proceeding it is required that any pleading, motion, petition, supporting affidavit, or other document of any kind, be verified, or that an oath be taken, it shall be sufficient if the subscriber simply affirms the truth of the matter to be verified by an affirmation or representation. IN ST TRIAL P Rule 11(B). IN ST TRIAL P Rule 11(B) states that the affirmation or representation should be in substantially the following language: "I (we) affirm, under the penalties for perjury, that the foregoing representation(s) is (are) true. (Signed) _____."

   i.   Any person who falsifies an affirmation or representation of fact shall be subject to the same penalties as are prescribed by law for the making of a false affidavit. IN ST TRIAL P Rule 11(B).

  e. *Verified pleadings, motions, and affidavits as evidence.* Pleadings, motions and affidavits accompanying or in support of such pleadings or motions when required to be verified or under oath shall be accepted as a representation that the signer had personal knowledge thereof or reasonable cause to believe the existence of the facts or matters stated or alleged therein; and, if otherwise competent or acceptable as evidence, may be admitted as evidence of the facts or matters stated or alleged therein when it is so provided in the Indiana Rules of Trial Procedure, by statute or other law, or to the extent the writing or signature expressly purports to be made upon the signer's personal knowledge. When such pleadings, motions and affidavits are verified or under oath they shall not require other or greater proof on the part of the adverse party than if not verified or not under oath unless expressly provided otherwise by the Indiana Rules of Trial Procedure, statute or other law. Affidavits upon motions for summary judgment under IN ST TRIAL P Rule 56 and in denial of execution under IN ST TRIAL P Rule 9.2 shall be made upon personal knowledge. IN ST TRIAL P Rule 11(C).

6. *Information excluded from public access.* Every document filed in a case shall separately identify information excluded from public access pursuant to IN ST ADMIN Rule 9(G)(1) as follows:

  a. Whole documents that are excluded from public access pursuant to IN ST ADMIN Rule 9(G)(1) shall be tendered on light green paper or have a light green coversheet attached to the document, marked "Not for Public Access" or "Confidential." IN ST TRIAL P Rule 5(G)(1).

  b. When only a portion of a document contains information excluded from public access pursuant to IN ST ADMIN Rule 9(G)(1), said information shall be omitted [or redacted] from the filed document, and set forth on a separate accompanying document on light green paper conspicuously marked "Not for Public Access" or "Confidential" and clearly designated [or identifying] the caption and number of the case and the document and location within the document to which the redacted material pertains. IN ST TRIAL P Rule 5(G)(2).

  c. With respect to documents filed in electronic format, the trial court, by local rule, may provide for compliance with IN ST TRIAL P Rule 5 in manner that separates and protects access to information excluded from public access. IN ST TRIAL P Rule 5(G)(3).

  d. IN ST TRIAL P Rule 5(G) does not apply to a record sealed by the court pursuant to IN ST 5-14-3-5.5 or otherwise, nor to records, documents, or information filed in cases to which public access is prohibited pursuant to IN ST ADMIN Rule 9(G). IN ST TRIAL P Rule 5(G)(4).

MARION COUNTY

e. The following information in case records is excluded from public access and is confidential:

   i. Information that is excluded from public access pursuant to federal law;

   ii. Information that is excluded from public access as declared confidential by Indiana statute or other court rule, including without limitation:

- All adoption records created after July 8, 1941, as declared confidential by IN ST 31-19-19-1, et seq., except those specifically declared open by IN ST 31-19-13-2(2);

- All records relating to chancroid, chlamydia, gonorrhea, hepatitis, human immunodeficiency virus (HIV), Lymphogranuloma venereum, syphilis, tuberculosis, as declared confidential by IN ST 16-41-8-1, et seq.;

- All records relating to child abuse as declared confidential by IN ST 31-33-18-1, et seq.;

- All records relating to drug tests as declared confidential by IN ST 5-14-3-4(a)(9);

- Records of grand jury proceedings as declared confidential by IN ST 35-34-2-4;

- Records of juvenile proceedings as declared confidential by IN ST 31-39-1-2, except those specifically open under statute;

- All paternity records created after July 1, 1941 as declared confidential by IN ST 31-14-11-15, IN ST 31-19-5-23, IN ST 31-39-1-1 and IN ST 31-39-1-2 [Editor's note: IN ST 31-14-11-15 was repealed effective May 9, 2013];

- All pre-sentence reports as declared confidential by IN ST 35-38-1-13;

- Written petitions to permit marriages without consent and orders directing the Clerk of Court to issue a marriage license to underage persons, as declared confidential by IN ST 31-11-1-6;

- Only those arrest warrants, search warrants, indictments and informations ordered confidential by the trial judge, prior to return of duly executed service as declared confidential by IN ST 5-14-3-4(b)(1);

- All medical, mental health, or tax records unless determined by law or regulation of any governmental custodian not to be confidential, released by the subject of such records, or declared by a court of competent jurisdiction to be essential to the resolution of litigation as declared confidential by IN ST 16-39-3-10, IN ST 6-4.1-5-10, IN ST 6-4.1-12-12, and IN ST 6-8.1-7-1;

- Personal information relating to jurors or prospective jurors, other than for the use of the parties and counsel, pursuant to IN ST JURY Rule 10;

- Information relating to protection from abuse orders, no-contact orders and workplace violence restraining orders as declared confidential by IN ST 5-2-9-6, et seq.;

- Mediation proceedings pursuant to IN ST ADR Rule 2.11, Mini-Trial proceedings pursuant to IN ST ADR Rule 4.4(C), and Summary Jury Trials pursuant to IN ST ADR Rule 5.6;

- Information in probation files pursuant to the Probation Standards promulgated by the Judicial Conference of Indiana pursuant to IN ST 11-13-1-8(b);

- Information deemed confidential pursuant to the Rules for Court Administered Alcohol and Drug Programs promulgated by the Judicial Conference of Indiana pursuant to IN ST 12-23-14-13;

- Information deemed confidential pursuant to the Problem-Solving Court Rules promulgated by the Judicial Conference of Indiana pursuant to IN ST 33-23-16-16;

- All records of the Department of workforce Development as declared confidential by IN ST 22-4-19-6;

- Information regarding interception of electronic communications that is sealed or deemed confidential as set forth in IN ST 35-33.5-2-1, et seq.

    iii.   Information excluded from public access by specific court order;

    iv.   Complete Social Security Numbers of living persons;

    v.   With the exception of names, information such as addresses, phone numbers, and dates of birth which explicitly identifies:

- Natural persons who are witnesses or victims (not including defendants) in criminal, domestic violence, stalking, sexual assault, juvenile, or civil protection order proceedings, provided that juveniles who are victims of sex crimes shall be identified by initials only;

- Places of residence of judicial officers, clerks and other employees of courts and clerks of court, unless the person or persons about whom the information pertains waives confidentiality;

    vi.   Complete account numbers of specific assets, loans, bank accounts, credit cards, and personal identification numbers (PINs);

    vii.   All orders of expungement entered in criminal or juvenile proceedings, orders to restrict access to criminal history information pursuant to IN ST 35-38-5-5.5 or IN ST 35-38-8-5 and records excluded from public access by such orders, and information related to infractions that is excluded from public access pursuant to IN ST 34-28-5-15 or IN ST 34-28-5-16 [Editor's note: IN ST 35-38-5-5.5, IN ST 35-38-8-5 and IN ST 34-28-5-16 were repealed effective July 1, 2013; for information on orders restricting access to criminal history, refer to IN ST 35-38-9-1, et seq.];

    viii.   All personal notes and e-mail, and deliberative material, of judges, jurors, court staff and judicial agencies, and information recorded in personal data assistants (PDA's) or organizers and personal calendars. IN ST ADMIN Rule 9(G)(1).

F. Filing and Service Requirements

1. *Filing requirements.* Except as otherwise provided in IN ST TRIAL P Rule 5(E)(2), all pleadings and papers subsequent to the complaint which are required to be served upon a party shall be filed with the Court either before service or within a reasonable period of time thereafter. IN ST TRIAL P Rule 5(E)(1). Counsel shall file with the court an original and one (1) copy of all briefs, and memoranda of law filed in support of a motion. IN ST MARION CIR AND SUPER CTS CIV Rule 205(D).

    a.   *Filing generally.* All pleadings, petitions and motions are filed with the Clerk designated by the Court at any time during office hours established by the Clerk and the Court. All orders submitted to the Court shall be in sufficient number and shall be accompanied by postage paid envelopes addressed to each party or counsel of record. IN ST MARION CIR AND SUPER CTS CIV Rule 205(A)

    b.   *Filing with the court defined.* The filing of pleadings, motions, and other papers with the court as required by the Indiana Rules of Trial Procedure shall be made by one of the following methods:

        i.   Delivery to the clerk of the court;

        ii.   Sending by electronic transmission under the procedure adopted pursuant to IN ST ADMIN Rule 12;

        iii.   Mailing to the clerk by registered, certified or express mail return receipt requested;

        iv.   Depositing with any third-party commercial carrier for delivery to the clerk within three (3) calendar days, cost prepaid, properly addressed;

        v.   If the court so permits, filing with the judge, in which event the judge shall note thereon the filing date and forthwith transmit them to the office of the clerk; or

        vi.   Electronic filing, as approved by the Division of State Court Administration pursuant to IN ST ADMIN Rule 16. IN ST TRIAL P Rule 5(F).

        vii.   Filing by registered or certified mail and by third-party commercial carrier shall be complete upon mailing or deposit. IN ST TRIAL P Rule 5(F).

    c.   *Facsimile filing.* Facsimile filing is discouraged, but permitted in the Marion Circuit and Marion

Superior Court. All documents filed by facsimile shall also be filed in hard copy within seven (7) days of the facsimile filing, along with proposed orders and stamped addressed envelopes, as required by IN ST MARION CIR AND SUPER CTS CIV Rule 203(E). To avoid duplicate filings, the hard copies of the facsimile filing shall indicate in bold letters that the pleading was previously filed by facsimile transmission. Proof of transmission by facsimile, including certificate of service and manner of service, shall be the responsibility of the filing party. If the filing requires immediate attention of the Judge, it shall be so indicated in bold letters in an accompanying transmittal memorandum. Legibility of documents and timeliness of filing is the responsibility of the sender. IN ST MARION CIR AND SUPER CTS CIV Rule 205(B).

i. *Generally.* In counties where a majority of judges of the courts of record, by posted local rule, have authorized electronic facsimile filing and designated a telephone number to receive such transmissions, pleadings, motions, and other papers may be sent to the Clerk of Circuit Court by electronic facsimile transmission for filing in any case, provided:

- Such matter does not exceed ten (10) pages, including the cover sheet;

- Such matter does not require the payment of fees other than the electronic facsimile transcription fee set forth in IN ST ADMIN Rule 12(E);

- The sending party creates at the time of transmission a machine generated log for such transmission; and

- The original document and the transmission log are maintained by the sending party for the duration of the litigation. IN ST ADMIN Rule 12(B).

ii. *Time of filing.* During normal, posted business hours, the time of filing shall be the time the duplicate document is produced in the office of the Clerk of the Circuit Court. Duplicate documents received at all other times shall be filed as of the next normal business day. IN ST ADMIN Rule 12(C).

- If the receiving fax machine endorses its own time and date stamp upon the transmitted documents and the receiving machine produces a delivery receipt which is electronically created and transmitted to the sending party, the time of filing shall be the date and time recorded on the transmitted document by the receiving fax machine. IN ST ADMIN Rule 12(C).

d. *Electronic filing.* Electronic filing and electronic service pilot projects are authorized pursuant to IN ST ADMIN Rule 16 and approved by the Division of State Court Administration. IN ST MARION SUPER CT ADMIN Rule 311(1-103).

i. *Cases where electronic filing accepted.* All Marion County Circuit and Superior civil courts may accept electronic filing and service of pleadings and other documents designated in this rule in mortgage foreclosure (hereinafter referred to as "MF"), civil collection(hereinafter referred to as "CC"), and individual cases that have been approved for electronic filing and service. IN ST MARION SUPER CT ADMIN Rule 311(1-104)(1).

- The Marion County Circuit Court may, upon the motion of a party or its own motion, designate a case that will involve multiple litigants, legally intricate issues, and an extensive number of documents a mass tort or complex litigation case. Any case so designated shall be subject to electronic filing and service using the county's approved Electronic Service Provider. IN ST MARION SUPER CT ADMIN Rule 311(1-104)(3).

- The filing of electronic pleadings and other documents in MF and CC cases is entirely voluntary; however, once the case is initially filed electronically, all subsequent filings in the case shall remain in electronic format until the time for appeal is exhausted. IN ST MARION SUPER CT ADMIN Rule 311(1-104)(5).

ii. *Documents eligible for electronic filing.* The following pleadings may be filed and served electronically:

- New case complaint and petitions. IN ST MARION SUPER CT ADMIN Rule 311(1-104)(8)(a).

- Original answers. IN ST MARION SUPER CT ADMIN Rule 311(1-104)(8)(a).

- Any other pleadings or document including but not limited to motions and appearance forms. IN ST MARION SUPER CT ADMIN Rule 311(1-104)(8)(a).

iii. *Manner of electronic filing.* Parties shall E-file a document either:

- By registering to use the Electronic Filing Service Provider; or

- In person at the Marion County Clerk's office, by electronically filing through the Public Access Terminal. Parties filing in this manner shall be responsible for furnishing the document in an electronic format that will be compatible with the clerk's office-system to be uploaded in person. IN ST MARION SUPER CT ADMIN Rule 311(1-104)(9). For information on the Electronic Filing Service Provider and Public Access Terminal, refer to IN ST MARION SUPER CT ADMIN Rule 311(1-101).

- Registered users shall pay statutory filing fees for E-filed documents electronically to the Court through their EFSP. Filing fees are due and payable at the time of filing. IN ST MARION SUPER CT ADMIN Rule 311(2-104)(1). For more information on electronic filing fees, refer to IN ST MARION SUPER CT ADMIN Rule 311(2-104).

iv. *Effect of electronic filing.* Any pleading filed electronically shall be considered as filed with the court when the transmission to the EFSP is complete. Any document E-filed by 11:59 p.m. local Indianapolis, Indiana time shall be deemed filed on that date. The EFSP is an agent of the Court for the purpose of electronic filing, receipt, service and retrieval of electronic documents. IN ST MARION SUPER CT ADMIN Rule 311(2-102).

- Upon completion of filing, the EFSP shall issue a confirmation receipt that includes the date and time of receipt. The confirmation receipt shall serve as proof of filing. IN ST MARION SUPER CT ADMIN Rule 311(2-102).

- In the event the Court rejects the submitted documents following review, the documents shall not become part of the official Court record and the filer will receive notification of the rejection. Users may be required to refile the instruments to meet necessary filing requirements. Documents may be filed through an E-filing system at any time that the Clerk's office is open to receive the filing or at such other times as may be designated by the clerk and posted publicly. IN ST MARION SUPER CT ADMIN Rule 311(2-102).

- Documents filed through the E-filing system are deemed filed when received by the Clerk's office, except that documents received at times that the Clerk's office is closed shall be deemed filed the next regular time when the Clerk's office is open for filing. The time stamp issued by the E-filing system shall be presumed to be the time the document is received by the Clerk. IN ST MARION SUPER CT ADMIN Rule 311(2-102).

v. *Electronically filed documents.* All pleadings and other documents designated in IN ST MARION SUPER CT ADMIN Rule 311 shall be filed and served electronically in any individual case which has been approved for electronic filing and service. IN ST MARION SUPER CT ADMIN Rule 311(1-104)(6).

vi. *System failures.* When filing by electronic means is hindered by a technical failure, a party may file with the Clerk of Marion County in hard copy. With the exception of deadlines that by law cannot be extended, the time for filing of any paper that is delayed due to technical failure of the site shall be extended for one (1) day for each day on which such failure occurs, unless otherwise ordered by the Court. IN ST MARION SUPER CT ADMIN Rule 311(2-108).

vii. *Compliance with rules.* All filing shall comply with the requirements of IN ST ADMIN Rule 9 and IN ST ADMIN Rule 16; and the Indiana Rules of Court and the Marion County Local Rules. IN ST MARION SUPER CT ADMIN Rule 311(1-104)(11).

e. *Filing for special judge.* When a Special Judge who is not a Marion County Judge is selected, all parties or attorneys shall furnish such Judge with copies of all filings prior to the qualification of such Special Judge. Thereafter, copies of all filings shall be delivered in person, by mail or by facsimile to the office of the Special Judge with certificate of forwarding same made a part of the filing. IN ST MARION CIR AND SUPER CTS CIV Rule 205(C).

f. *Proof of filing.* Any party filing any paper by any method other than personal delivery to the clerk shall retain proof of filing. IN ST TRIAL P Rule 5(F).

2. *Service requirements.* Unless otherwise provided by the Indiana Rules of Trial Procedure or an order of the court, each party and special judge, if any, shall be served with: (1) every order required by its terms to be served; (2) every pleading subsequent to the original complaint; (3) every written motion except one which may be heard ex parte; (4) every brief submitted to the trial court; (5) every paper relating to discovery required to be served upon a party; and (6) every written notice, appearance, demand, offer of judgment, designation of record on appeal, or similar paper. IN ST TRIAL P Rule 5(A).

a. *Methods of service*

   i. *Personal service.* Whenever a party is represented by an attorney of record, service shall be made upon such attorney unless service upon the party himself is ordered by the court. Service upon the attorney or party shall be made by delivering or mailing a copy of the papers to the last known address or where an attorney or party has consented to service by fax or e-mail, as provided in IN ST TRIAL P Rule 3.1(A)(4), by faxing or e-mailing a copy of the documents to the fax number or e-mail address set out in the appearance form or correction as required by IN ST TRIAL P Rule 3.1(E). IN ST TRIAL P Rule 5(B). Delivery of a copy within IN ST TRIAL P Rule 5 means:

   - Offering or tendering it to the attorney or party and stating the nature of the papers being served. Refusal to accept an offered or tendered document is a waiver of any objection to the sufficiency or adequacy of service of that document;

   - Leaving it at his office with a clerk or other person in charge thereof, or if there is no one in charge, leaving it in a conspicuous place therein; or

   - If the office is closed, by leaving it at his dwelling house or usual place of abode with some person of suitable age and discretion then residing therein; or,

   - Leaving it at some other suitable place, selected by the attorney upon whom service is being made, pursuant to duly promulgated local rule. IN ST TRIAL P Rule 5(B)(1).

   ii. *Service by mail.* If service is made by mail, the papers shall be deposited in the United States mail addressed to the person on whom they are being served, with postage prepaid. Service shall be deemed complete upon mailing. Proof of service of all papers permitted to be mailed may be made by written acknowledgment of service, by affidavit of the person who mailed the papers, or by certificate of an attorney. It shall be the duty of attorneys when entering their appearance in a cause or when filing pleadings or papers therein, to have noted in the Chronological Case Summary or said pleadings or papers so filed the address and telephone number of their office. Service by delivery or by mail at such address shall be deemed sufficient and complete. IN ST TRIAL P Rule 5(B)(2).

   iii. *Service by fax or e-mail.* A party who has consented to service by fax or e-mail may be served as follows:

   - Service by e-mail shall be made by attaching the document being served in .pdf format. Discovery documents must also be served in accordance with IN ST TRIAL P Rule 26(A). IN ST TRIAL P Rule 5(B)(3)(a).

   - Service by fax shall be deemed complete upon generation of a transmission record indicating the successful transmission of the entire document, except as provided in IN ST TRIAL P Rule 5(B)(3)(d). IN ST TRIAL P Rule 5(B)(3)(b).

   - Service by e-mail shall be deemed complete upon transmission, except as provided in IN ST TRIAL P Rule 5(B)(3)(d). IN ST TRIAL P Rule 5(B)(3)(c).

   - Service by fax or e-mail that occurs on a Saturday, Sunday, legal holiday, or day the court or agency in which the matter is pending is closed or after 5:00 PM local time of the recipient shall be deemed complete the next day that is not a Saturday, Sunday, legal holiday, or day that the court or agency in which the matter is pending is not closed. IN ST TRIAL P Rule 5(B)(3)(d).

    iv. *Electronic service.* Delivery of E-service documents through the EFSP to other registered users shall be considered as valid and effective service and shall have the same legal effect as an original paper document. Recipients of E-service documents shall access their documents through the EFSP. IN ST MARION SUPER CT ADMIN Rule 311(2-107)(1).

- E-service shall be deemed complete when the transmission to the EFSP is completed. IN ST MARION SUPER CT ADMIN Rule 311(2-107)(2).

- For the purpose of computing time to respond to documents received via E-service, any document served on a day or at a time when the Clerk's office is not open for business shall be deemed served at the time of next opening of the Clerk's office for business. IN ST MARION SUPER CT ADMIN Rule 311(2-107)(3).

  b. *Serving numerous defendants.* In any action in which there are unusually large numbers of defendants, the court, upon motion or of its own initiative, may order:

    i. That service of the pleadings of the defendants and replies thereto need not be made as between the defendants;

- That any cross-claim, counterclaim, or matter constituting an avoidance or affirmative defense contained therein shall be deemed to be denied or avoided by all other parties; and

- That the filing of any such pleading and service thereof upon the plaintiff constitutes due notice of it to the parties. IN ST TRIAL P Rule 5(D).

    ii. A copy of every such order shall be served upon the parties in such manner and form as the court directs. IN ST TRIAL P Rule 5(D).

  c. *Service on parties in default for failure to appear.* No service need be made on parties in default for failure to appear, except that pleadings asserting new or additional claims for relief against them shall be served upon them in the manner provided by service of summons in IN ST TRIAL P Rule 4. IN ST TRIAL P Rule 5(A).

G. Hearings

1. *Hearing on motion.* Unless local conditions make it impracticable, each judge shall establish regular times and places, at intervals sufficiently frequent for the prompt dispatch of business, at which motions requiring notice and hearing may be heard and disposed of; but the judge at any time or place and on such notice, if any, as he considers reasonable may make order for the advancement, conduct, and hearing of actions. To expedite its business the court may direct the submission and determination of motions without oral hearing upon brief written statements of reasons in support and opposition, or direct or permit hearings by telephone conference call with all attorneys or other similar means of communication. IN ST TRIAL P Rule 73(A).

2. *Time and place of hearing.* If the motion requires a hearing or oral argument, the Court shall set the time and place of hearing or argument on the motion. IN ST MARION CIR AND SUPER CTS CIV Rule 203(A).

H. Forms

1. Motion to Dismiss for Failure to State a Claim Forms for Indiana

  a. General form. 5 INPRAC § 3:4.1.

  b. Failure to state a claim upon which relief can be granted. 5 INPRAC § 3:4.5.

  c. Motion to dismiss plaintiff's complaint; General form. 9 INPRAC § 42.2.

  d. Motion to dismiss; Failure to state a claim upon which relief can be granted. 9 INPRAC § 42.10.

  e. Certificate of service; Personal service. 9 INPRAC § 5.7.

  f. Certificate of service; First class mail. 9 INPRAC § 5.8.

  g. Statute of limitations. 9 INPRAC § 42.12.

  h. Application for hearing and preliminary determination of motion to dismiss. 9 INPRAC § 42.15.

I. Checklist

(I) ❑ Matters to be considered by moving party

    (a) ❑ Required documents

        (1) ❑ Motion and notice

        (2) ❑ Statement of approval or disapproval

        (3) ❑ Proposed order

        (4) ❑ Certificate of service

    (b) ❑ Supplemental documents

        (1) ❑ Request for oral argument

        (2) ❑ Facsimile cover sheet

    (c) ❑ Timing

        (1) ❑ A motion to dismiss for failure to state a claim shall be made before pleading if a further pleading is permitted or within twenty (20) days after service of the prior pleading if none is required

        (2) ❑ A written motion, other than one which may be heard ex parte, and notice of the hearing thereof shall be served not less than five (5) days before the time specified for the hearing, unless a different period is fixed by the Indiana Rules of Trial Procedure or by order of the court

        (3) ❑ All pleadings and papers subsequent to the complaint which are required to be served upon a party shall be filed with the Court either before service or within a reasonable period of time thereafter

(II) ❑ Matters to be considered by the responding party

    (a) ❑ Required documents

        (1) ❑ Opposition

        (2) ❑ Certificate of service

    (b) ❑ Supplemental documents

        (1) ❑ Proposed order

        (2) ❑ Facsimile cover sheet

    (c) ❑ Timing

        (1) ❑ If the statement regarding the position of the opposing party(ies) required under IN ST MARION CIR AND SUPER CTS CIV Rule 203(A) indicates that objection to the granting of said motion may ensue, said objecting a party shall have fifteen (15) days from the date of filing to file a response to said motion

        (2) ❑ Except as otherwise provided in IN ST TRIAL P Rule 59(D), opposing affidavits may be served not less than one (1) day before the hearing, unless the court permits them to be served at some other time

Motions, Oppositions and Replies
Motion to Dismiss for Lack of Subject Matter Jurisdiction

Document Last Updated October 2013

A. Applicable Rules

1. *State rules*

    a. Appearance. IN ST TRIAL P Rule 3.1.

    b. Process. IN ST TRIAL P Rule 4.

c. Service and filing of pleadings and other papers. IN ST TRIAL P Rule 5.

d. Time. IN ST TRIAL P Rule 6.

e. Pleadings. IN ST TRIAL P Rule 7; IN ST TRIAL P Rule 8; IN ST TRIAL P Rule 9.2; IN ST TRIAL P Rule 10.

f. Signing and verification of pleadings. IN ST TRIAL P Rule 11.

g. Defenses and objections; When and how presented; By pleading or motion; Motion for judgment on the pleadings. IN ST TRIAL P Rule 12.

h. Amended and supplemental pleadings. IN ST TRIAL P Rule 15.

i. Joinder of person needed for just adjudication. IN ST TRIAL P Rule 19.

j. Evidence. IN ST TRIAL P Rule 43.

k. Judgment on the evidence (directed verdict). IN ST TRIAL P Rule 50.

l. Findings by the court. IN ST TRIAL P Rule 52.

m. Summary judgment. IN ST TRIAL P Rule 56.

n. Motion to correct error. IN ST TRIAL P Rule 59.

o. Relief from judgment or order. IN ST TRIAL P Rule 60.

p. Hearing of motions. IN ST TRIAL P Rule 73.

q. Access to court records. IN ST ADMIN Rule 9.

r. Paper size. IN ST ADMIN Rule 11.

s. Facsimile transmission. IN ST ADMIN Rule 12.

t. Electronic filing and electronic service pilot projects. IN ST ADMIN Rule 16.

u. Sealing of certain records by court; Hearing; Notice. IN ST 5-14-3-5.5.

v. Privacy and confidentiality. IN ST 5-2-9-6; IN ST 5-14-3-4; IN ST 6-4.1-5-10; IN ST 6-4.1-12-12; IN ST 6-8.1-7-1; IN ST 11-13-1-8; IN ST 12-23-14-13; IN ST 16-39-3-10; IN ST 16-41-8-1; IN ST 22-4-19-6; IN ST 31-11-1-6; IN ST 31-19-5-23; IN ST 31-19-13-2; IN ST 31-19-19-1; IN ST 31-33-18-1; IN ST 31-39-1-1; IN ST 31-39-1-2; IN ST 33-23-16-16; IN ST 35-34-2-4; IN ST 35-38-1-13; IN ST 35-38-9-1; IN ST ADR Rule 2.11; IN ST ADR Rule 4.4; IN ST ADR Rule 5.6; IN ST JURY Rule 10.

2. *Local rules*

a. Requirements for motions. IN ST MARION CIR AND SUPER CTS CIV Rule 203.

b. Preparation of pleadings, motions and other papers. IN ST MARION CIR AND SUPER CTS CIV Rule 204.

c. Filing of pleadings, motions and other papers. IN ST MARION CIR AND SUPER CTS CIV Rule 205.

d. Signing and verification of pleadings, motions and other papers; Service on opposing party. IN ST MARION CIR AND SUPER CTS CIV Rule 206.

e. Motions for continuance. IN ST MARION CIR AND SUPER CTS CIV Rule 215.

f. Electronic filing. IN ST MARION SUPER CT ADMIN Rule 311.

B. Timing

1. *Timing of motion to dismiss for failure lack of subject matter jurisdiction.* A motion making any of the defenses listed in IN ST TRIAL P Rule 12(B) shall be made before pleading if a further pleading is permitted or within twenty (20) days after service of the prior pleading if none is required. IN ST TRIAL P Rule 12(B). Usually, the issue is raised in a motion that is filed before an Answer is filed; or the issue might be consolidated in the Answer. If it is not raised by the parties, it will be raised by the court, and an appellate court may raise the question sua sponte. 1A INPRAC R 12(12.5); Decatur County Rural Elec. Membership Corp. v. Public Serv. Co., 150 Ind.App. 193, 275 N.E.2d 857 (Ind.App. 1971).

a. *Time to file a responsive pleading.* A responsive pleading required under the Indiana Rules of Trial

Procedure, shall be served within twenty (20) days after service of the prior pleading. IN ST TRIAL P Rule 6(C).

b. *Filing.* All pleadings and papers subsequent to the complaint which are required to be served upon a party shall be filed with the Court either before service or within a reasonable period of time thereafter. IN ST TRIAL P Rule 5(E)(1).

2. *Service.* A written motion, other than one which may be heard ex parte, and notice of the hearing thereof shall be served not less than five (5) days before the time specified for the hearing, unless a different period is fixed by the Indiana Rules of Trial Procedure or by order of the court. IN ST TRIAL P Rule 6(D).

a. *Of supporting affidavits.* When a motion is supported by affidavit, the affidavit shall be served with the motion. IN ST TRIAL P Rule 6(D).

3. *Opposition*

a. *Filing.* If the statement regarding the position of the opposing party(ies) required under IN ST MARION CIR AND SUPER CTS CIV Rule 203(A) indicates that objection to the granting of said motion may ensue, said objecting a party shall have fifteen (15) days from the date of filing to file a response to said motion. IN ST MARION CIR AND SUPER CTS CIV Rule 203(B).

b. *Service.* Except as otherwise provided in IN ST TRIAL P Rule 59(D), opposing affidavits may be served not less than one (1) day before the hearing, unless the court permits them to be served at some other time. IN ST TRIAL P Rule 6(D).

4. *Computation of time*

a. *Generally; Days excluded.* In computing any period of time prescribed or allowed by the Indiana Rules of Trial Procedure, by order of the court, or by any applicable statute, the day of the act, event, or default from which the designated period of time begins to run shall not be included. The last day of the period so computed is to be included unless it is:

   i. A Saturday,

   ii. A Sunday,

   iii. A legal holiday as defined by state statute, or

   iv. A day the office in which the act is to be done is closed during regular business hours. IN ST TRIAL P Rule 6(A).

b. *Short periods.* In any event, the period runs until the end of the next day that is not a Saturday, a Sunday, a legal holiday, or a day on which the office is closed. When the period of time allowed is less than seven (7) days, intermediate Saturdays, Sundays, legal holidays, and days on which the office is closed shall be excluded from the computations. IN ST TRIAL P Rule 6(A).

c. *Additional time after service by United States mail.* Whenever a party has the right or is required to do some act or take some proceedings within a prescribed period after the service of a notice or other paper upon him and the notice or paper is served upon him by United States mail, three (3) days shall be added to the prescribed period. IN ST TRIAL P Rule 6(E).

d. *Enlargement of time.* When an act is required or allowed to be done at or within a specific time by the Indiana Rules of Trial Procedure, the court may at any time for cause shown:

   i. Order the period enlarged, with or without motion or notice, if request therefor is made before the expiration of the period originally prescribed or extended by a previous order; or

   ii. Upon motion made after the expiration of the specific period, permit the act to be done where the failure to act was the result of excusable neglect; but, the court may not extend the time for taking any action for judgment on the evidence under IN ST TRIAL P Rule 50(A), amendment of findings and judgment under IN ST TRIAL P Rule 52(B), to correct errors under IN ST TRIAL P Rule 59(C), statement in opposition to motion to correct error under IN ST TRIAL P Rule 59(E), or to obtain relief from final judgment under IN ST TRIAL P Rule 60(B), except to the extent and under the conditions stated in those rules. IN ST TRIAL P Rule 6(B).

e. *Continuances disfavored.* Motions for Continuance are discouraged. Neither side is entitled to an automatic continuance as a matter of right. IN ST MARION CIR AND SUPER CTS CIV Rule 215.

For information on obtaining a continuance, refer to IN ST MARION CIR AND SUPER CTS CIV Rule 215.

C. General Requirements

1. *Motions, generally:* Unless made during a hearing or trial, or otherwise ordered by the court, an application to the court for an order shall be made by written motion. The motion shall state the grounds therefor and the relief or order sought. IN ST TRIAL P Rule 7(B).

   a. *Motions as distinct from pleadings.* Motions and responses to motions are not pleadings, and allegations contained in a motion are not admissions of a party. 22B INPRAC 7:2; Wachstetter v. County Properties, LLC, 832 N.E.2d 574 (Ind.Ct.App. 2005); Scott County Family YMCA, Inc. v. Hobbs, 817 N.E.2d 603 (Ind.Ct.App. 2004).

   b. *Unopposed motions generally granted.* It is common for a trial court to grant procedural motions, such as motions for enlargement of time, discovery motions, or motions for continuance, unless an objection is filed. 21 INPRAC § 13.8.

2. *Motion to dismiss for lack of subject matter jurisdiction.* Every defense, in law or fact, to a claim for relief in any pleading, whether a claim, counterclaim, cross-claim, or third-party claim, shall be asserted in the responsive pleading thereto if one is required; except that at the option of the pleader, the defense of lack of jurisdiction over the subject matter may be made by motion. IN ST TRIAL P Rule 12(B)(1). Subject-matter jurisdiction refers to the power of the court or tribunal to entertain the general class of cases or disputes to which a pending case belongs. It means that the legislature or other authority, such as, perhaps, a supreme court, has invested the court with judicial power with which to entertain a case or controversy, and to hear the litigation and dispute. 1A INPRAC R 12(12.5).

   a. *Objection not waivable.* Subject-matter jurisdiction cannot be created by the parties to the litigation. Either it is there or it is not, quite independent of the conduct or the consent of the parties to the action. As such, the absence of subject-matter jurisdiction is never waivable and there is a positive duty on a court, whether trial or appellate, to raise the question of subject-matter jurisdiction whenever it might appear, if the parties have failed to present the question. 1A INPRAC R 12(12.5); Schoffstall v. Failey, 180 Ind.App. 528, 389 N.E. 361 (Ind.Ct.App. 1979).

   b. *Motion not to be made as one for summary judgment.* A motion to dismiss under IN ST TRIAL P Rule 12(B)(1) may not be presented in the form of a motion for summary judgment. 9 INPRAC § 42.3.

   c. *Precedence of subject matter jurisdiction.* Dismissal for lack of subject matter jurisdiction takes precedence over the determination of and action upon other substantive and procedural rights of the parties. 9 INPRAC § 42.3; Young v. Estate of Sweeney, 808 N.E.2d 1217 (Ind.Ct.App. 2004).

   d. *Issues examined separately; Jurisdiction over one claim as jurisdiction over case.* In order to determine whether a case is properly before the trial court, the court should examine each issue presented. If at least one of the issues is within the jurisdiction of the trial court, the entire case falls within the court's jurisdiction. Where at least one issue or claim is a proper matter for judicial determination or resolution, a trial court is not ousted of subject matter jurisdiction by the presence in a case of one or more issues which arguably are within the jurisdiction of administrative or regulatory agency. 9 INPRAC § 42.3; Alexander v. Cottey, 801 N.E.2d 651 (Ind.Ct.App. 2004).

   e. *Factual matters in determining subject matter jurisdiction.* The trial court considering a motion to dismiss for lack of subject matter jurisdiction has wide latitude to devise procedures to discover the facts relevant to jurisdiction and in weighing the evidence to resolve factual disputes affecting the jurisdictional challenge. 9 INPRAC § 42.3.

   f. *Failure to exhaust administrative remedies.* The doctrine of exhaustion of administrative remedies provides that a trial court will not acquire subject matter jurisdiction until the aggrieved party has exhausted all available remedies before the administrative agency. 9 INPRAC § 41.44; Indiana Dept. of Environmental Management v. NJK Farms, Inc., 921 N.E.2d 834 (Ind.Ct.App. 2010).

      i. *Dismissal of workers' compensation cases.* A trial court must dismiss a matter for lack of subject matter jurisdiction pursuant to Indiana IN ST TRIAL P Rule 12(B)(1) where injuries claimed in the Plaintiff's complaint fall squarely within the Indiana Workers Compensation

Act. 9 INPRAC § 42.3; ATFH Real Property, LLC v. Stewart, 879 N.E.2d 1184 (Ind.Ct.App. 2008).

g. *Leave to amend complaint if motion granted.* A dismissal for lack of subject matter jurisdiction is not an adjudication on the merits nor is it res judicata. If action is dismissed, plaintiff may file amended complaint as permitted by IN ST TRIAL P Rule 6(C). 9 INPRAC § 42.3; Hart v. Webster, 894 N.E.2d 1032 (Ind.Ct.App. 2008).

h. *Effect of judgment entered by court lacking subject matter jurisdiction.* A judgment entered by a court that lacks subject matter jurisdiction is void and may be attacked at any time. 9 INPRAC § 42.3; Roberson v. State, 903 N.E.2d 1009 (Ind.Ct.App. 2009).

3. *Consolidation and waiver*

a. *Consolidation of defenses in motion.* A party who makes a motion under IN ST TRIAL P Rule 12 may join with it any other motions herein provided for and then available to him. If a party makes a motion under IN ST TRIAL P Rule 12 but omits therefrom any defense or objection then available to him which IN ST TRIAL P Rule 12 permits to be raised by motion, he shall not thereafter make a motion based on the defense or objection so omitted. He may, however, make such motions as are allowed under IN ST TRIAL P Rule 12(H)(2). IN ST TRIAL P Rule 12(G).

b. *Waiver or preservation of certain defenses.* No defense or objection is waived by being joined with one or more other defenses or objections in a responsive pleading or motion. IN ST TRIAL P Rule 12(B).

D. Documents

1. *Required documents*

a. *Motion and notice.* The requirement of notice is satisfied by service of the motion. IN ST TRIAL P Rule 7(B); IN ST MARION CIR AND SUPER CTS CIV Rule 203(A). Refer to the General Requirements section of this document for information on the content of a motion to dismiss for lack of subject matter jurisdiction.

b. *Statement of approval or disapproval.* Except for initial motions made pursuant to IN ST MARION CIR AND SUPER CTS CIV Rule 203(D), all motions filed with the court shall include a brief statement indicating whether opposing party(ies) object to or approve of the granting of said motion. IN ST MARION CIR AND SUPER CTS CIV Rule 203(A).

c. *Proposed order.* Unless local practice provides differently, a party should submit a proposed order with its written motion to be signed by the judge once the motion has been granted. 21 INPRAC § 13.8. All motions seeking an order of the Court shall be accompanied by a sufficient number of orders to be executed by the Court in granting said motion. In addition to the orders, the notice shall be accompanied by stamped, addressed envelopes to all parties of record. IN ST MARION CIR AND SUPER CTS CIV Rule 203(E).

d. *Certificate of service.* An attorney or unrepresented party tendering a document to the Clerk for filing shall certify that service has been made, list the parties served, and specify the date and means of service. The certificate of service shall be placed at the end of the document and shall not be separately filed. The separate filing of a certificate of service, however, shall not be grounds for rejecting a document for filing. The Clerk may permit documents to be filed without a certificate of service but shall require prompt filing of a separate certificate of service. IN ST TRIAL P Rule 5(C). In all cases where any pleading or other document is required to be served upon opposing counsel, proof of such service may be made either by:

   i. A certificate of service signed by counsel of record for the serving party and the certificate shall specify by name and address all counsel upon whom the pleading or document was served; or

   ii. An acknowledgment of service signed by the party served or counsel of record. IN ST MARION CIR AND SUPER CTS CIV Rule 206.

2. *Supplemental documents*

a. *Supporting evidence.* When a motion is based on facts not appearing of record the court may hear the matter on affidavits presented by the respective parties, but the court may direct that the matter be heard wholly or partly on oral testimony or depositions. IN ST TRIAL P Rule 43(B).

b. *Request for oral argument.* When an oral argument is requested, the request shall be by separate instrument and filed with the pleading to be argued. Any such oral argument requested may be heard at the discretion of the Court, except for motions for summary judgment which shall be set for hearing upon request of any party. IN ST MARION CIR AND SUPER CTS CIV Rule 203(C).

c. *Facsimile cover sheet.* Any document sent to the Clerk of the Circuit Court by electronic facsimile transmission shall be accompanied by a cover sheet which states the title of the document, case number, number of pages, identity and voice telephone number of the sending party and instructions for filing. The cover sheet shall contain the signature of the attorney or party, pro se, authorizing the filing. IN ST ADMIN Rule 12(D).

E. Format

1. *Form of motions.* The rules applicable to captions, and the signing and form of pleadings (IN ST TRIAL P Rule 8 through IN ST TRIAL P Rule 11), apply to all motions and other papers provided under the Indiana Rules of Trial Procedure. 22B INPRAC 7:2.

2. *Form of pleadings*

   a. *Caption; Names of parties.* Every pleading shall contain a caption setting forth the name of the court, the title of the action, the file number, and a designation as in IN ST TRIAL P Rule 7(A). In the complaint the title of the action shall include the names of all the parties, but in other pleadings it is sufficient to state the name of the first party on each side with an appropriate indication of other parties. IN ST TRIAL P Rule 10(A).

      i. Every pleading shall contain a caption setting forth the name of the Court, the Division and Room Number, the title of the action and the file number. IN ST MARION CIR AND SUPER CTS CIV Rule 204(B).

   b. *Paragraphs; Separate statements.* All averments of a claim or defense shall be made in numbered paragraphs, the contents of each of which shall be limited as far as practicable to a statement of a single set of circumstances, and a paragraph may be referred to by number in all succeeding pleadings. Each claim founded upon a separate transaction or occurrence and each defense other than denials may be stated in a separate count or defense whenever a separation facilitates the clear presentation of the matters set forth. IN ST TRIAL P Rule 10(B).

   c. *Adoption by reference; Exhibits.* Statements in a pleading may be adopted by reference in a different part of the same pleading or in another pleading or in any motion. A copy of any written instrument which is an exhibit to a pleading is a part thereof for all purposes. IN ST TRIAL P Rule 10(C).

   d. *Paper.* Pleadings, motions and other papers may be either printed or typewritten on white opaque paper of at least sixteen (16) pound weight, eight and one-half (8-1/2) inches wide and eleven (11) inches in length. IN ST MARION CIR AND SUPER CTS CIV Rule 204(A).

   e. *Copies.* All copies shall likewise be on white paper of sufficient strength and durability to resist normal wear and tear. IN ST MARION CIR AND SUPER CTS CIV Rule 204(A).

   f. *Line spacing.* If typewritten, the lines shall be double spaced, except for quotations, which shall be indented and single spaced. IN ST MARION CIR AND SUPER CTS CIV Rule 204(A).

   g. *Script type.* Script type shall not be used. IN ST MARION CIR AND SUPER CTS CIV Rule 204(A).

   h. *Titles.* Titles on all pleadings shall delineate each topic included in the pleading e.g. where a pleading contains an Answer, a Motion to Strike or Dismiss, or a Jury Request each shall be set forth in the title. IN ST MARION CIR AND SUPER CTS CIV Rule 204(C).

   i. *Margins and binding.* Margins shall be one (1) inch. Binding or stapling shall be at the top and at no other place. Covers or backing shall not be used. IN ST MARION CIR AND SUPER CTS CIV Rule 204(D).

3. *Size of papers for filing.* Effective January 1, 1992, all pleadings, copies, motions and documents filed with any trial court or appellate level court, typed or printed, with the exception of exhibits and existing wills, shall be prepared on eight and one-half by eleven inch (8 1/2" x 11") size paper. IN ST ADMIN Rule 11.

4. *Form of electronically filed documents.* All electronically filed and served pleadings shall, to the extent

practicable, be formatted in accordance with the applicable rules governing formatting of paper pleadings. IN ST MARION SUPER CT ADMIN Rule 311(2-103)(1).

    a.   *Electronic document title.* The electronic document title of each pleading or other document shall include:

        i.   Party or parties filing/serving the document,

        ii.   Nature of the document,

        iii.   Party or parties against whom relief, if any, is sought, and

        iv.   Nature of the relief sought (e.g., Defendant ABC Corporation's Motion for Summary Judgment). IN ST MARION SUPER CT ADMIN Rule 311(2-103)(2).

5.   *Signature requirements*

    a.   *Signature of attorney.* Every pleading or motion of a party represented by an attorney shall be signed by at least one (1) attorney of record in his individual name, whose address, telephone number, and attorney number shall be stated, except that this provision shall not apply to pleadings and motions made and transcribed at the trial or a hearing before the judge and received by him in such form. IN ST TRIAL P Rule 11(A).

        i.   All pleadings and motions shall contain the original or authorized signature of the attorney, the name of the attorney in typed or printed form, the name of the law firm if a member of a firm, the attorney's address, identification number, e-mail address, telephone number, fax number, and the designation as to the party for whom he appears. IN ST MARION CIR AND SUPER CTS CIV Rule 204(E).

        ii.   The signature of an attorney constitutes a certificate by him that he has read the pleadings; that to the best of his knowledge, information, and belief, there is good ground to support it; and that it is not interposed for delay. IN ST TRIAL P Rule 11(A).

        iii.   If a pleading or motion is not signed or is signed with intent to defeat the purpose of the rule, it may be stricken as sham and false and the action may proceed as though the pleading had not been served. IN ST TRIAL P Rule 11(A).

        iv.   For a willful violation of IN ST TRIAL P Rule 11 an attorney may be subjected to appropriate disciplinary action. Similar action may be taken if scandalous or indecent matter is inserted. IN ST TRIAL P Rule 11(A).

        v.   Every pleading, document, and instrument electronically filed or served shall be deemed to have been signed by the judge, clerk, attorney or declarant and shall bear a facsimile or typographical signature of such person, along with the typed name, address, telephone number, and Bar number of a signing attorney. Typographical signatures shall be treated as personal signatures for all purposes under these rules. IN ST MARION SUPER CT ADMIN Rule 311(2-105).

          •   Documents containing signatures of third-parties (i.e., unopposed motions, affidavits, stipulations, etc.) may also be filed electronically by indicating that the original signatures are maintained by the filing party in paper-format. IN ST MARION SUPER CT ADMIN Rule 311(2-105).

          •   Unless otherwise ordered by the Court or Clerk, a printed copy of all documents filed or served electronically, including original signatures, shall be maintained by the party filing the document and shall be made available, upon reasonable notice, for inspection by other counsel, the Clerk or Court. Parties shall retain originals until two (2) years after all time periods for appeal have expired. From time to time, it may be necessary to provide the Clerk or Court with a hard copy of an electronically filed document. IN ST MARION SUPER CT ADMIN Rule 311(2-105).

        vi.   For the recommended format of a signature block, refer to IN ST MARION CIR AND SUPER CTS CIV Rule 204(E).

    b.   *Signature of unrepresented party.* A party who is not represented by an attorney shall sign his pleading and state his address. IN ST TRIAL P Rule 11(A).

    c.   *Verification not generally required.* Except when specifically required by rule, pleadings or motions need not be verified or accompanied by affidavit. The rule in equity that the averments of an answer under oath must be overcome by the testimony of two (2) witnesses or of one (1) witness sustained by corroborating circumstances is abolished. IN ST TRIAL P Rule 11(A).

    d.   *Verification by affirmation or representation.* When in connection with any civil or special statutory proceeding it is required that any pleading, motion, petition, supporting affidavit, or other document of any kind, be verified, or that an oath be taken, it shall be sufficient if the subscriber simply affirms the truth of the matter to be verified by an affirmation or representation. IN ST TRIAL P Rule 11(B). IN ST TRIAL P Rule 11(B) states that the affirmation or representation should be in substantially the following language: "I (we) affirm, under the penalties for perjury, that the foregoing representation(s) is (are) true. (Signed) _____."

        i.   Any person who falsifies an affirmation or representation of fact shall be subject to the same penalties as are prescribed by law for the making of a false affidavit. IN ST TRIAL P Rule 11(B).

    e.   *Verified pleadings, motions, and affidavits as evidence.* Pleadings, motions and affidavits accompanying or in support of such pleadings or motions when required to be verified or under oath shall be accepted as a representation that the signer had personal knowledge thereof or reasonable cause to believe the existence of the facts or matters stated or alleged therein; and, if otherwise competent or acceptable as evidence, may be admitted as evidence of the facts or matters stated or alleged therein when it is so provided in the Indiana Rules of Trial Procedure, by statute or other law, or to the extent the writing or signature expressly purports to be made upon the signer's personal knowledge. When such pleadings, motions and affidavits are verified or under oath they shall not require other or greater proof on the part of the adverse party than if not verified or not under oath unless expressly provided otherwise by the Indiana Rules of Trial Procedure, statute or other law. Affidavits upon motions for summary judgment under IN ST TRIAL P Rule 56 and in denial of execution under IN ST TRIAL P Rule 9.2 shall be made upon personal knowledge. IN ST TRIAL P Rule 11(C).

6.   *Information excluded from public access.* Every document filed in a case shall separately identify information excluded from public access pursuant to IN ST ADMIN Rule 9(G)(1) as follows:

    a.   Whole documents that are excluded from public access pursuant to IN ST ADMIN Rule 9(G)(1) shall be tendered on light green paper or have a light green coversheet attached to the document, marked "Not for Public Access" or "Confidential." IN ST TRIAL P Rule 5(G)(1).

    b.   When only a portion of a document contains information excluded from public access pursuant to IN ST ADMIN Rule 9(G)(1), said information shall be omitted [or redacted] from the filed document, and set forth on a separate accompanying document on light green paper conspicuously marked "Not for Public Access" or "Confidential" and clearly designated [or identifying] the caption and number of the case and the document and location within the document to which the redacted material pertains. IN ST TRIAL P Rule 5(G)(2).

    c.   With respect to documents filed in electronic format, the trial court, by local rule, may provide for compliance with IN ST TRIAL P Rule 5 in manner that separates and protects access to information excluded from public access. IN ST TRIAL P Rule 5(G)(3).

    d.   IN ST TRIAL P Rule 5(G) does not apply to a record sealed by the court pursuant to IN ST 5-14-3-5.5 or otherwise, nor to records, documents, or information filed in cases to which public access is prohibited pursuant to IN ST ADMIN Rule 9(G). IN ST TRIAL P Rule 5(G)(4).

    e.   The following information in case records is excluded from public access and is confidential:

        i.   Information that is excluded from public access pursuant to federal law;

        ii.   Information that is excluded from public access as declared confidential by Indiana statute or other court rule, including without limitation:

          •   All adoption records created after July 8, 1941, as declared confidential by IN ST 31-19-19-1, et seq., except those specifically declared open by IN ST 31-19-13-2(2);

          •   All records relating to chancroid, chlamydia, gonorrhea, hepatitis, human immunodefi-

ciency virus (HIV), Lymphogranuloma venereum, syphilis, tuberculosis, as declared confidential by IN ST 16-41-8-1, et seq.;

- All records relating to child abuse as declared confidential by IN ST 31-33-18-1, et seq.;

- All records relating to drug tests as declared confidential by IN ST 5-14-3-4(a)(9);

- Records of grand jury proceedings as declared confidential by IN ST 35-34-2-4;

- Records of juvenile proceedings as declared confidential by IN ST 31-39-1-2, except those specifically open under statute;

- All paternity records created after July 1, 1941 as declared confidential by IN ST 31-14-11-15, IN ST 31-19-5-23, IN ST 31-39-1-1 and IN ST 31-39-1-2 [Editor's note: IN ST 31-14-11-15 was repealed effective May 9, 2013];

- All pre-sentence reports as declared confidential by IN ST 35-38-1-13;

- Written petitions to permit marriages without consent and orders directing the Clerk of Court to issue a marriage license to underage persons, as declared confidential by IN ST 31-11-1-6;

- Only those arrest warrants, search warrants, indictments and informations ordered confidential by the trial judge, prior to return of duly executed service as declared confidential by IN ST 5-14-3-4(b)(1);

- All medical, mental health, or tax records unless determined by law or regulation of any governmental custodian not to be confidential, released by the subject of such records, or declared by a court of competent jurisdiction to be essential to the resolution of litigation as declared confidential by IN ST 16-39-3-10, IN ST 6-4.1-5-10, IN ST 6-4.1-12-12, and IN ST 6-8.1-7-1;

- Personal information relating to jurors or prospective jurors, other than for the use of the parties and counsel, pursuant to IN ST JURY Rule 10;

- Information relating to protection from abuse orders, no-contact orders and workplace violence restraining orders as declared confidential by IN ST 5-2-9-6, et seq.;

- Mediation proceedings pursuant to IN ST ADR Rule 2.11, Mini-Trial proceedings pursuant to IN ST ADR Rule 4.4(C), and Summary Jury Trials pursuant to IN ST ADR Rule 5.6;

- Information in probation files pursuant to the Probation Standards promulgated by the Judicial Conference of Indiana pursuant to IN ST 11-13-1-8(b);

- Information deemed confidential pursuant to the Rules for Court Administered Alcohol and Drug Programs promulgated by the Judicial Conference of Indiana pursuant to IN ST 12-23-14-13;

- Information deemed confidential pursuant to the Problem-Solving Court Rules promulgated by the Judicial Conference of Indiana pursuant to IN ST 33-23-16-16;

- All records of the Department of workforce Development as declared confidential by IN ST 22-4-19-6;

- Information regarding interception of electronic communications that is sealed or deemed confidential as set forth in IN ST 35-33.5-2-1, et seq.

iii. Information excluded from public access by specific court order;

iv. Complete Social Security Numbers of living persons;

v. With the exception of names, information such as addresses, phone numbers, and dates of birth which explicitly identifies:

- Natural persons who are witnesses or victims (not including defendants) in criminal, domestic violence, stalking, sexual assault, juvenile, or civil protection order proceedings, provided that juveniles who are victims of sex crimes shall be identified by initials only;

- Places of residence of judicial officers, clerks and other employees of courts and clerks of court, unless the person or persons about whom the information pertains waives confidentiality;

vi. Complete account numbers of specific assets, loans, bank accounts, credit cards, and personal identification numbers (PINs);

vii. All orders of expungement entered in criminal or juvenile proceedings, orders to restrict access to criminal history information pursuant to IN ST 35-38-5-5.5 or IN ST 35-38-8-5 and records excluded from public access by such orders, and information related to infractions that is excluded from public access pursuant to IN ST 34-28-5-15 or IN ST 34-28-5-16 [Editor's note: IN ST 35-38-5-5.5, IN ST 35-38-8-5 and IN ST 34-28-5-16 were repealed effective July 1, 2013; for information on orders restricting access to criminal history, refer to IN ST 35-38-9-1, et seq.];

viii. All personal notes and e-mail, and deliberative material, of judges, jurors, court staff and judicial agencies, and information recorded in personal data assistants (PDA's) or organizers and personal calendars. IN ST ADMIN Rule 9(G)(1).

F. Filing and Service Requirements

1. *Filing requirements.* Except as otherwise provided in IN ST TRIAL P Rule 5(E)(2), all pleadings and papers subsequent to the complaint which are required to be served upon a party shall be filed with the Court either before service or within a reasonable period of time thereafter. IN ST TRIAL P Rule 5(E)(1). Counsel shall file with the court an original and one (1) copy of all briefs, and memoranda of law filed in support of a motion. IN ST MARION CIR AND SUPER CTS CIV Rule 205(D).

   a. *Filing generally.* All pleadings, petitions and motions are filed with the Clerk designated by the Court at any time during office hours established by the Clerk and the Court. All orders submitted to the Court shall be in sufficient number and shall be accompanied by postage paid envelopes addressed to each party or counsel of record. IN ST MARION CIR AND SUPER CTS CIV Rule 205(A)

   b. *Filing with the court defined.* The filing of pleadings, motions, and other papers with the court as required by the Indiana Rules of Trial Procedure shall be made by one of the following methods:

      i. Delivery to the clerk of the court;

      ii. Sending by electronic transmission under the procedure adopted pursuant to IN ST ADMIN Rule 12;

      iii. Mailing to the clerk by registered, certified or express mail return receipt requested;

      iv. Depositing with any third-party commercial carrier for delivery to the clerk within three (3) calendar days, cost prepaid, properly addressed;

      v. If the court so permits, filing with the judge, in which event the judge shall note thereon the filing date and forthwith transmit them to the office of the clerk; or

      vi. Electronic filing, as approved by the Division of State Court Administration pursuant to IN ST ADMIN Rule 16. IN ST TRIAL P Rule 5(F).

      vii. Filing by registered or certified mail and by third-party commercial carrier shall be complete upon mailing or deposit. IN ST TRIAL P Rule 5(F).

   c. *Facsimile filing.* Facsimile filing is discouraged, but permitted in the Marion Circuit and Marion Superior Court. All documents filed by facsimile shall also be filed in hard copy within seven (7) days of the facsimile filing, along with proposed orders and stamped addressed envelopes, as required by IN ST MARION CIR AND SUPER CTS CIV Rule 203(E). To avoid duplicate filings, the hard copies of the facsimile filing shall indicate in bold letters that the pleading was previously filed by facsimile transmission. Proof of transmission by facsimile, including certificate of service and manner of service, shall be the responsibility of the filing party. If the filing requires immediate attention of the Judge, it shall be so indicated in bold letters in an accompanying transmittal memorandum. Legibility of documents and timeliness of filing is the responsibility of the sender. IN ST MARION CIR AND SUPER CTS CIV Rule 205(B).

      i. *Generally.* In counties where a majority of judges of the courts of record, by posted local rule,

have authorized electronic facsimile filing and designated a telephone number to receive such transmissions, pleadings, motions, and other papers may be sent to the Clerk of Circuit Court by electronic facsimile transmission for filing in any case, provided:

- Such matter does not exceed ten (10) pages, including the cover sheet;
- Such matter does not require the payment of fees other than the electronic facsimile transcription fee set forth in IN ST ADMIN Rule 12(E);
- The sending party creates at the time of transmission a machine generated log for such transmission; and
- The original document and the transmission log are maintained by the sending party for the duration of the litigation. IN ST ADMIN Rule 12(B).

ii. *Time of filing.* During normal, posted business hours, the time of filing shall be the time the duplicate document is produced in the office of the Clerk of the Circuit Court. Duplicate documents received at all other times shall be filed as of the next normal business day. IN ST ADMIN Rule 12(C).

- If the receiving fax machine endorses its own time and date stamp upon the transmitted documents and the receiving machine produces a delivery receipt which is electronically created and transmitted to the sending party, the time of filing shall be the date and time recorded on the transmitted document by the receiving fax machine. IN ST ADMIN Rule 12(C).

d. *Electronic filing.* Electronic filing and electronic service pilot projects are authorized pursuant to IN ST ADMIN Rule 16 and approved by the Division of State Court Administration. IN ST MARION SUPER CT ADMIN Rule 311(1-103).

i. *Cases where electronic filing accepted.* All Marion County Circuit and Superior civil courts may accept electronic filing and service of pleadings and other documents designated in this rule in mortgage foreclosure (hereinafter referred to as "MF"), civil collection(hereinafter referred to as "CC"), and individual cases that have been approved for electronic filing and service. IN ST MARION SUPER CT ADMIN Rule 311(1-104)(1).

- The Marion County Circuit Court may, upon the motion of a party or its own motion, designate a case that will involve multiple litigants, legally intricate issues, and an extensive number of documents a mass tort or complex litigation case. Any case so designated shall be subject to electronic filing and service using the county's approved Electronic Service Provider. IN ST MARION SUPER CT ADMIN Rule 311(1-104)(3).
- The filing of electronic pleadings and other documents in MF and CC cases is entirely voluntary; however, once the case is initially filed electronically, all subsequent filings in the case shall remain in electronic format until the time for appeal is exhausted. IN ST MARION SUPER CT ADMIN Rule 311(1-104)(5).

ii. *Documents eligible for electronic filing.* The following pleadings may be filed and served electronically:

- New case complaint and petitions. IN ST MARION SUPER CT ADMIN Rule 311(1-104)(8)(a).
- Original answers. IN ST MARION SUPER CT ADMIN Rule 311(1-104)(8)(a).
- Any other pleadings or document including but not limited to motions and appearance forms. IN ST MARION SUPER CT ADMIN Rule 311(1-104)(8)(a).

iii. *Manner of electronic filing.* Parties shall E-file a document either:

- By registering to use the Electronic Filing Service Provider; or
- In person at the Marion County Clerk's office, by electronically filing through the Public Access Terminal. Parties filing in this manner shall be responsible for furnishing the document in an electronic format that will be compatible with the clerk's office-system to be uploaded in person. IN ST MARION SUPER CT ADMIN Rule 311(1-104)(9). For

information on the Electronic Filing Service Provider and Public Access Terminal, refer to IN ST MARION SUPER CT ADMIN Rule 311(1-101).

- Registered users shall pay statutory filing fees for E-filed documents electronically to the Court through their EFSP. Filing fees are due and payable at the time of filing. IN ST MARION SUPER CT ADMIN Rule 311(2-104)(1). For more information on electronic filing fees, refer to IN ST MARION SUPER CT ADMIN Rule 311(2-104).

iv. *Effect of electronic filing.* Any pleading filed electronically shall be considered as filed with the court when the transmission to the EFSP is complete. Any document E-filed by 11:59 p.m. local Indianapolis, Indiana time shall be deemed filed on that date. The EFSP is an agent of the Court for the purpose of electronic filing, receipt, service and retrieval of electronic documents. IN ST MARION SUPER CT ADMIN Rule 311(2-102).

- Upon completion of filing, the EFSP shall issue a confirmation receipt that includes the date and time of receipt. The confirmation receipt shall serve as proof of filing. IN ST MARION SUPER CT ADMIN Rule 311(2-102).

- In the event the Court rejects the submitted documents following review, the documents shall not become part of the official Court record and the filer will receive notification of the rejection. Users may be required to refile the instruments to meet necessary filing requirements. Documents may be filed through an E-filing system at any time that the Clerk's office is open to receive the filing or at such other times as may be designated by the clerk and posted publicly. IN ST MARION SUPER CT ADMIN Rule 311(2-102).

- Documents filed through the E-filing system are deemed filed when received by the Clerk's office, except that documents received at times that the Clerk's office is closed shall be deemed filed the next regular time when the Clerk's office is open for filing. The time stamp issued by the E-filing system shall be presumed to be the time the document is received by the Clerk. IN ST MARION SUPER CT ADMIN Rule 311(2-102).

v. *Electronically filed documents.* All pleadings and other documents designated in IN ST MARION SUPER CT ADMIN Rule 311 shall be filed and served electronically in any individual case which has been approved for electronic filing and service. IN ST MARION SUPER CT ADMIN Rule 311(1-104)(6).

vi. *System failures.* When filing by electronic means is hindered by a technical failure, a party may file with the Clerk of Marion County in hard copy. With the exception of deadlines that by law cannot be extended, the time for filing of any paper that is delayed due to technical failure of the site shall be extended for one (1) day for each day on which such failure occurs, unless otherwise ordered by the Court. IN ST MARION SUPER CT ADMIN Rule 311(2-108).

vii. *Compliance with rules.* All filing shall comply with the requirements of IN ST ADMIN Rule 9 and IN ST ADMIN Rule 16; and the Indiana Rules of Court and the Marion County Local Rules. IN ST MARION SUPER CT ADMIN Rule 311(1-104)(11).

e. *Filing for special judge.* When a Special Judge who is not a Marion County Judge is selected, all parties or attorneys shall furnish such Judge with copies of all filings prior to the qualification of such Special Judge. Thereafter, copies of all filings shall be delivered in person, by mail or by facsimile to the office of the Special Judge with certificate of forwarding same made a part of the filing. IN ST MARION CIR AND SUPER CTS CIV Rule 205(C).

f. *Proof of filing.* Any party filing any paper by any method other than personal delivery to the clerk shall retain proof of filing. IN ST TRIAL P Rule 5(F).

2. *Service requirements.* Unless otherwise provided by the Indiana Rules of Trial Procedure or an order of the court, each party and special judge, if any, shall be served with: (1) every order required by its terms to be served; (2) every pleading subsequent to the original complaint; (3) every written motion except one which may be heard ex parte; (4) every brief submitted to the trial court; (5) every paper relating to discovery required to be served upon a party; and (6) every written notice, appearance, demand, offer of judgment, designation of record on appeal, or similar paper. IN ST TRIAL P Rule 5(A).

a. *Methods of service*

i. *Personal service.* Whenever a party is represented by an attorney of record, service shall be

made upon such attorney unless service upon the party himself is ordered by the court. Service upon the attorney or party shall be made by delivering or mailing a copy of the papers to the last known address or where an attorney or party has consented to service by fax or e-mail, as provided in IN ST TRIAL P Rule 3.1(A)(4), by faxing or e-mailing a copy of the documents to the fax number or e-mail address set out in the appearance form or correction as required by IN ST TRIAL P Rule 3.1(E). IN ST TRIAL P Rule 5(B). Delivery of a copy within IN ST TRIAL P Rule 5 means:

- Offering or tendering it to the attorney or party and stating the nature of the papers being served. Refusal to accept an offered or tendered document is a waiver of any objection to the sufficiency or adequacy of service of that document;

- Leaving it at his office with a clerk or other person in charge thereof, or if there is no one in charge, leaving it in a conspicuous place therein; or

- If the office is closed, by leaving it at his dwelling house or usual place of abode with some person of suitable age and discretion then residing therein; or,

- Leaving it at some other suitable place, selected by the attorney upon whom service is being made, pursuant to duly promulgated local rule. IN ST TRIAL P Rule 5(B)(1).

ii. *Service by mail.* If service is made by mail, the papers shall be deposited in the United States mail addressed to the person on whom they are being served, with postage prepaid. Service shall be deemed complete upon mailing. Proof of service of all papers permitted to be mailed may be made by written acknowledgment of service, by affidavit of the person who mailed the papers, or by certificate of an attorney. It shall be the duty of attorneys when entering their appearance in a cause or when filing pleadings or papers therein, to have noted in the Chronological Case Summary or said pleadings or papers so filed the address and telephone number of their office. Service by delivery or by mail at such address shall be deemed sufficient and complete. IN ST TRIAL P Rule 5(B)(2).

iii. *Service by fax or e-mail.* A party who has consented to service by fax or e-mail may be served as follows:

- Service by e-mail shall be made by attaching the document being served in .pdf format. Discovery documents must also be served in accordance with IN ST TRIAL P Rule 26(A). IN ST TRIAL P Rule 5(B)(3)(a).

- Service by fax shall be deemed complete upon generation of a transmission record indicating the successful transmission of the entire document, except as provided in IN ST TRIAL P Rule 5(B)(3)(d). IN ST TRIAL P Rule 5(B)(3)(b).

- Service by e-mail shall be deemed complete upon transmission, except as provided in IN ST TRIAL P Rule 5(B)(3)(d). IN ST TRIAL P Rule 5(B)(3)(c).

- Service by fax or e-mail that occurs on a Saturday, Sunday, legal holiday, or day the court or agency in which the matter is pending is closed or after 5:00 PM local time of the recipient shall be deemed complete the next day that is not a Saturday, Sunday, legal holiday, or day that the court or agency in which the matter is pending is not closed. IN ST TRIAL P Rule 5(B)(3)(d).

iv. *Electronic service.* Delivery of E-service documents through the EFSP to other registered users shall be considered as valid and effective service and shall have the same legal effect as an original paper document. Recipients of E-service documents shall access their documents through the EFSP. IN ST MARION SUPER CT ADMIN Rule 311(2-107)(1).

- E-service shall be deemed complete when the transmission to the EFSP is completed. IN ST MARION SUPER CT ADMIN Rule 311(2-107)(2).

- For the purpose of computing time to respond to documents received via E-service, any document served on a day or at a time when the Clerk's office is not open for business shall be deemed served at the time of next opening of the Clerk's office for business. IN ST MARION SUPER CT ADMIN Rule 311(2-107)(3).

b. *Serving numerous defendants.* In any action in which there are unusually large numbers of defendants, the court, upon motion or of its own initiative, may order:

    i. That service of the pleadings of the defendants and replies thereto need not be made as between the defendants;

- That any cross-claim, counterclaim, or matter constituting an avoidance or affirmative defense contained therein shall be deemed to be denied or avoided by all other parties; and

- That the filing of any such pleading and service thereof upon the plaintiff constitutes due notice of it to the parties. IN ST TRIAL P Rule 5(D).

    ii. A copy of every such order shall be served upon the parties in such manner and form as the court directs. IN ST TRIAL P Rule 5(D).

c. *Service on parties in default for failure to appear.* No service need be made on parties in default for failure to appear, except that pleadings asserting new or additional claims for relief against them shall be served upon them in the manner provided by service of summons in IN ST TRIAL P Rule 4. IN ST TRIAL P Rule 5(A).

G. Hearings

1. *Hearing on motion.* Unless local conditions make it impracticable, each judge shall establish regular times and places, at intervals sufficiently frequent for the prompt dispatch of business, at which motions requiring notice and hearing may be heard and disposed of; but the judge at any time or place and on such notice, if any, as he considers reasonable may make order for the advancement, conduct, and hearing of actions. To expedite its business the court may direct the submission and determination of motions without oral hearing upon brief written statements of reasons in support and opposition, or direct or permit hearings by telephone conference call with all attorneys or other similar means of communication. IN ST TRIAL P Rule 73(A).

2. *Time and place of hearing.* If the motion requires a hearing or oral argument, the Court shall set the time and place of hearing or argument on the motion. IN ST MARION CIR AND SUPER CTS CIV Rule 203(A).

H. Forms

1. Motion to Dismiss for Lack of Subject Matter Jurisdiction Forms for Indiana

a. General form. 5 INPRAC § 3:4.1.

b. Lack of subject matter jurisdiction. 5 INPRAC § 3:4.2.

c. Motion to dismiss plaintiff's complaint; General form. 9 INPRAC § 42.2.

d. Lack of jurisdiction over the subject matter. 9 INPRAC § 42.3.

e. Certificate of service; Personal service. 9 INPRAC § 5.7.

f. Certificate of service; First class mail. 9 INPRAC § 5.8.

I. Checklist

(I) ❑ Matters to be considered by moving party

  (a) ❑ Required documents

    (1) ❑ Motion and notice

    (2) ❑ Statement of approval or disapproval

    (3) ❑ Proposed order

    (4) ❑ Certificate of service

  (b) ❑ Supplemental documents

    (1) ❑ Supporting evidence

    (2) ❑ Request for oral argument

    (3) ❑ Facsimile cover sheet

(c) ❏ Timing

    (1) ❏ A motion to dismiss for lack of subject matter jurisdiction shall be made before pleading if a further pleading is permitted or within twenty (20) days after service of the prior pleading if none is required

    (2) ❏ A written motion, other than one which may be heard ex parte, and notice of the hearing thereof shall be served not less than five (5) days before the time specified for the hearing, unless a different period is fixed by the Indiana Rules of Trial Procedure or by order of the court

    (3) ❏ All pleadings and papers subsequent to the complaint which are required to be served upon a party shall be filed with the Court either before service or within a reasonable period of time thereafter

(II) ❏ Matters to be considered by the responding party

  (a) ❏ Required documents

    (1) ❏ Opposition

    (2) ❏ Certificate of service

  (b) ❏ Supplemental documents

    (1) ❏ Supporting evidence

    (2) ❏ Proposed order

    (3) ❏ Facsimile cover sheet

  (c) ❏ Timing

    (1) ❏ If the statement regarding the position of the opposing party(ies) required under IN ST MARION CIR AND SUPER CTS CIV Rule 203(A) indicates that objection to the granting of said motion may ensue, said objecting a party shall have fifteen (15) days from the date of filing to file a response to said motion

    (2) ❏ Except as otherwise provided in IN ST TRIAL P Rule 59(D), opposing affidavits may be served not less than one (1) day before the hearing, unless the court permits them to be served at some other time

Motions, Oppositions and Replies
Motion to Dismiss for Lack of Personal Jurisdiction

Document Last Updated October 2013

A. Applicable Rules

1. *State rules*

  a. Appearance. IN ST TRIAL P Rule 3.1.

  b. Summons. IN ST TRIAL P Rule 4.

  c. Service and filing of pleadings and other papers. IN ST TRIAL P Rule 5.

  d. Time. IN ST TRIAL P Rule 6.

  e. Pleadings. IN ST TRIAL P Rule 7; IN ST TRIAL P Rule 8; IN ST TRIAL P Rule 9; IN ST TRIAL P Rule 9.2; IN ST TRIAL P Rule 10.

  f. Signing and verification of pleadings. IN ST TRIAL P Rule 11.

  g. Defenses and objections; When and how presented; By pleading or motion; Motion for judgment on the pleadings. IN ST TRIAL P Rule 12.

  h. Amended and supplemental pleadings. IN ST TRIAL P Rule 15.

  i. Joinder of person needed for just adjudication. IN ST TRIAL P Rule 19.

j.   Evidence. IN ST TRIAL P Rule 43.

k.   Judgment on the evidence (directed verdict). IN ST TRIAL P Rule 50.

l.   Findings by the court. IN ST TRIAL P Rule 52.

m.   Summary judgment. IN ST TRIAL P Rule 56.

n.   Motion to correct error. IN ST TRIAL P Rule 59.

o.   Relief from judgment or order. IN ST TRIAL P Rule 60.

p.   Hearing of motions. IN ST TRIAL P Rule 73.

q.   Access to court records. IN ST ADMIN Rule 9.

r.   Paper size. IN ST ADMIN Rule 11.

s.   Facsimile transmission. IN ST ADMIN Rule 12.

t.   Electronic filing and electronic service pilot projects. IN ST ADMIN Rule 16.

u.   Sealing of certain records by court; Hearing; Notice. IN ST 5-14-3-5.5.

v.   Privacy and confidentiality. IN ST 5-2-9-6; IN ST 5-14-3-4; IN ST 6-4.1-5-10; IN ST 6-4.1-12-12; IN ST 6-8.1-7-1; IN ST 11-13-1-8; IN ST 12-23-14-13; IN ST 16-39-3-10; IN ST 16-41-8-1; IN ST 22-4-19-6; IN ST 31-11-1-6; IN ST 31-19-5-23; IN ST 31-19-13-2; IN ST 31-19-19-1; IN ST 31-33-18-1; IN ST 31-39-1-1; IN ST 31-39-1-2; IN ST 33-23-16-16; IN ST 35-34-2-4; IN ST 35-38-1-13; IN ST 35-38-9-1; IN ST ADR Rule 2.11; IN ST ADR Rule 4.4; IN ST ADR Rule 5.6; IN ST JURY Rule 10.

2.   *Local rules*

a.   Requirements for motions. IN ST MARION CIR AND SUPER CTS CIV Rule 203.

b.   Preparation of pleadings, motions and other papers. IN ST MARION CIR AND SUPER CTS CIV Rule 204.

c.   Filing of pleadings, motions and other papers. IN ST MARION CIR AND SUPER CTS CIV Rule 205.

d.   Signing and verification of pleadings, motions and other papers; Service on opposing party. IN ST MARION CIR AND SUPER CTS CIV Rule 206.

e.   Motions for continuance. IN ST MARION CIR AND SUPER CTS CIV Rule 215.

f.   Electronic filing. IN ST MARION SUPER CT ADMIN Rule 311.

B.   Timing

1.   *Timing of motion to dismiss for failure lack of personal matter jurisdiction.* A motion making any of the defenses listed in IN ST TRIAL P Rule 12(B) shall be made before pleading if a further pleading is permitted or within twenty (20) days after service of the prior pleading if none is required. IN ST TRIAL P Rule 12(B).

a.   *Time to file a responsive pleading.* A responsive pleading required under the Indiana Rules of Trial Procedure, shall be served within twenty (20) days after service of the prior pleading. IN ST TRIAL P Rule 6(C).

b.   *Waiver of certain IN ST TRIAL P Rule 12(B) defenses.* If a pleading sets forth a claim for relief to which the adverse party is not required to serve a responsive pleading, any of the defenses in IN ST TRIAL P Rule 12(B)(2), IN ST TRIAL P Rule 12(B)(3), IN ST TRIAL P Rule 12(B)(4), IN ST TRIAL P Rule 12(B)(5) or IN ST TRIAL P Rule 12(B)(8) is waived to the extent constitutionally permissible unless made in a motion within twenty (20) days after service of the prior pleading. IN ST TRIAL P Rule 12(B).

c.   *Filing.* All pleadings and papers subsequent to the complaint which are required to be served upon a party shall be filed with the Court either before service or within a reasonable period of time thereafter. IN ST TRIAL P Rule 5(E)(1).

2.   *Service.* A written motion, other than one which may be heard ex parte, and notice of the hearing thereof

shall be served not less than five (5) days before the time specified for the hearing, unless a different period is fixed by the Indiana Rules of Trial Procedure or by order of the court. IN ST TRIAL P Rule 6(D).

    a. *Of supporting affidavits.* When a motion is supported by affidavit, the affidavit shall be served with the motion. IN ST TRIAL P Rule 6(D).

3. *Opposition*

    a. *Filing.* If the statement regarding the position of the opposing party(ies) required under IN ST MARION CIR AND SUPER CTS CIV Rule 203(A) indicates that objection to the granting of said motion may ensue, said objecting a party shall have fifteen (15) days from the date of filing to file a response to said motion. IN ST MARION CIR AND SUPER CTS CIV Rule 203(B).

    b. *Service.* Except as otherwise provided in IN ST TRIAL P Rule 59(D), opposing affidavits may be served not less than one (1) day before the hearing, unless the court permits them to be served at some other time. IN ST TRIAL P Rule 6(D).

4. *Computation of time*

    a. *Generally; Days excluded.* In computing any period of time prescribed or allowed by the Indiana Rules of Trial Procedure, by order of the court, or by any applicable statute, the day of the act, event, or default from which the designated period of time begins to run shall not be included. The last day of the period so computed is to be included unless it is:

        i. A Saturday,

        ii. A Sunday,

        iii. A legal holiday as defined by state statute, or

        iv. A day the office in which the act is to be done is closed during regular business hours. IN ST TRIAL P Rule 6(A).

    b. *Short periods.* In any event, the period runs until the end of the next day that is not a Saturday, a Sunday, a legal holiday, or a day on which the office is closed. When the period of time allowed is less than seven (7) days, intermediate Saturdays, Sundays, legal holidays, and days on which the office is closed shall be excluded from the computations. IN ST TRIAL P Rule 6(A).

    c. *Additional time after service by United States mail.* Whenever a party has the right or is required to do some act or take some proceedings within a prescribed period after the service of a notice or other paper upon him and the notice or paper is served upon him by United States mail, three (3) days shall be added to the prescribed period. IN ST TRIAL P Rule 6(E).

    d. *Enlargement of time.* When an act is required or allowed to be done at or within a specific time by the Indiana Rules of Trial Procedure, the court may at any time for cause shown:

        i. Order the period enlarged, with or without motion or notice, if request therefor is made before the expiration of the period originally prescribed or extended by a previous order; or

        ii. Upon motion made after the expiration of the specific period, permit the act to be done where the failure to act was the result of excusable neglect; but, the court may not extend the time for taking any action for judgment on the evidence under IN ST TRIAL P Rule 50(A), amendment of findings and judgment under IN ST TRIAL P Rule 52(B), to correct errors under IN ST TRIAL P Rule 59(C), statement in opposition to motion to correct error under IN ST TRIAL P Rule 59(E), or to obtain relief from final judgment under IN ST TRIAL P Rule 60(B), except to the extent and under the conditions stated in those rules. IN ST TRIAL P Rule 6(B).

    e. *Continuances disfavored.* Motions for Continuance are discouraged. Neither side is entitled to an automatic continuance as a matter of right. IN ST MARION CIR AND SUPER CTS CIV Rule 215. For information on obtaining a continuance, refer to IN ST MARION CIR AND SUPER CTS CIV Rule 215.

C. General Requirements

1. *Motions, generally.* Unless made during a hearing or trial, or otherwise ordered by the court, an application to the court for an order shall be made by written motion. The motion shall state the grounds therefor and the relief or order sought. IN ST TRIAL P Rule 7(B).

    a. *Motions as distinct from pleadings.* Motions and responses to motions are not pleadings, and

allegations contained in a motion are not admissions of a party. 22B INPRAC 7:2; Wachstetter v. County Properties, LLC, 832 N.E.2d 574 (Ind.Ct.App. 2005); Scott County Family YMCA, Inc. v. Hobbs, 817 N.E.2d 603 (Ind.Ct.App. 2004).

    b. *Unopposed motions generally granted.* It is common for a trial court to grant procedural motions, such as motions for enlargement of time, discovery motions, or motions for continuance, unless an objection is filed. 21 INPRAC § 13.8.

2. *Motion to dismiss for lack of personal jurisdiction.* Every defense, in law or fact, to a claim for relief in any pleading, whether a claim, counterclaim, cross-claim, or third-party claim, shall be asserted in the responsive pleading thereto if one is required; except that at the option of the pleader, the defense of lack of jurisdiction over person may be made by motion. IN ST TRIAL P Rule 12(b)(2). If personal jurisdiction is not present, then that party against whom jurisdiction is asserted must raise the question. 1A INPRAC R 12(12.6).

    a. *Presumption of jurisdiction.* Jurisdiction is presumed and, therefore, the defense of lack of personal jurisdiction may be asserted by motion under IN ST TRIAL P Rule 12(B)(2), or in the defendant's answer as an affirmative defense. 22 INPRAC § 15.16; Adsit Co., Inc. v. Gustin, 874 N.E.2d 1018 (Ind.Ct.App. 2007); Keesling v. Winstead, 858 N.E.2d 996 (Ind.Ct.App. 2006). Refer to the Indiana KeyRules Answer document for more information.

    b. *Personal jurisdiction.* The Due Process Clause of the Fourteenth Amendment requires that before a state may exercise jurisdiction over a defendant, the defendant must have certain minimum contacts with the state such that the maintenance of the suit does not offend traditional notions of fair play and substantial justice. 1A INPRAC R 12(12.6).

        i. *General jurisdiction.* If the defendant's contacts with the state are so continuous and systematic that the defendant should reasonably anticipate being haled into the courts of that state for any matter, then the defendant is subject to general jurisdiction, even in causes of action unrelated to the defendant's contacts with the forum state. 1A INPRAC R 12(12.6).

        ii. *Specific jurisdiction.* In cases where a defendant is not subject to general jurisdiction in a forum state, specific jurisdiction may be asserted if the controversy is related to or arises out of the defendant's contacts with the forum state. Specific jurisdiction requires that the defendant purposefully availed itself of the privilege of conducting activities within the forum state so that the defendant reasonably anticipates being haled into court there. A single contact with the forum state may be sufficient to establish specific jurisdiction over a defendant, if it creates a substantial connection with the forum state and the suit is related to that connection. 1A INPRAC R 12(12.6).

        iii. *Due process; Reasonableness.* A defendant cannot be haled into a jurisdiction solely as a result of random, fortuitous, or attenuated contacts or of the unilateral activity of another party or a third person. Once either general or specific jurisdiction has been established, due process requires that the assertion of personal jurisdiction over the defendant is reasonable. The assertion of personal jurisdiction will rarely be found unreasonable if minimum contacts are found. Five factors are used in determining reasonableness:

- The burden on the defendant;
- The forum State's interest in adjudicating the dispute;
- The plaintiff's interest in obtaining convenience and effective relief;
- The interstate judicial system's interest in obtaining the most efficient resolution of controversies; and
- The shared interest of the several States in furthering fundamental substantive social policies. 1A INPRAC R 12(12.6).

        iv. *Jurisdiction presumed.* Indiana state trial courts are courts of general jurisdiction and jurisdiction is presumed. The party contesting jurisdiction bears the burden of proving the lack of personal jurisdiction by a preponderance of the evidence, unless the lack of jurisdiction is apparent on the face of the complaint. A determination of the existence of personal jurisdiction is entitled to de novo review. 1A INPRAC R 12(12.6); Foley v. Schwartz, 943 N.E.2d 371 (Ind.Ct.App. 2011).

c. *Challenge to jurisdiction in first response to complaint.* The defendant may challenge the Indiana court's jurisdiction over him, without submitting to that jurisdiction, so long as the defense is asserted in the first response to the plaintiff's complaint and the defendant does not request affirmative relief from the court prior to asserting that defense. 22 INPRAC § 15.16.

d. *Burden shifting.* After the plaintiff establishes that there are minimum contacts between defendant and forum state to exercise personal jurisdiction without violating Due Process Clause, the defendant then carries the burden of proving that asserting jurisdiction is unfair and unreasonable. 1A INPRAC R 12(12.6); JPMorgan Chase Bank, N.A. v. Desert Palace, Inc., 882 N.E.2d 743 (Ind.Ct.App. 2008).

e. *Effect of granting of motion.* The dismissal of a complaint for lack of jurisdiction over the person is not an adjudication on the merits and does not prejudice the plaintiff's right to file another complaint if the court can obtain jurisdiction over the defendant. 9 INPRAC § 42.4.

3. *Consolidation and waiver*

a. *Consolidation of defenses in motion.* A party who makes a motion under IN ST TRIAL P Rule 12 may join with it any other motions herein provided for and then available to him. If a party makes a motion under IN ST TRIAL P Rule 12 but omits therefrom any defense or objection then available to him which IN ST TRIAL P Rule 12 permits to be raised by motion, he shall not thereafter make a motion based on the defense or objection so omitted. He may, however, make such motions as are allowed under IN ST TRIAL P Rule 12(H)(2). IN ST TRIAL P Rule 12(G).

b. *Waiver or preservation of certain defenses.* No defense or objection is waived by being joined with one or more other defenses or objections in a responsive pleading or motion. IN ST TRIAL P Rule 12(B).

D. Documents

1. *Required documents*

a. *Motion and notice.* The requirement of notice is satisfied by service of the motion. IN ST TRIAL P Rule 7(B); IN ST MARION CIR AND SUPER CTS CIV Rule 203(A). Refer to the General Requirements section of this document for information on the content of a motion to dismiss for lack of personal jurisdiction.

b. *Statement of approval or disapproval.* Except for initial motions made pursuant to IN ST MARION CIR AND SUPER CTS CIV Rule 203(D), all motions filed with the court shall include a brief statement indicating whether opposing party(ies) object to or approve of the granting of said motion. IN ST MARION CIR AND SUPER CTS CIV Rule 203(A).

c. *Proposed order.* Unless local practice provides differently, a party should submit a proposed order with its written motion to be signed by the judge once the motion has been granted. 21 INPRAC § 13.8. All motions seeking an order of the Court shall be accompanied by a sufficient number of orders to be executed by the Court in granting said motion. In addition to the orders, the notice shall be accompanied by stamped, addressed envelopes to all parties of record. IN ST MARION CIR AND SUPER CTS CIV Rule 203(E).

d. *Certificate of service.* An attorney or unrepresented party tendering a document to the Clerk for filing shall certify that service has been made, list the parties served, and specify the date and means of service. The certificate of service shall be placed at the end of the document and shall not be separately filed. The separate filing of a certificate of service, however, shall not be grounds for rejecting a document for filing. The Clerk may permit documents to be filed without a certificate of service but shall require prompt filing of a separate certificate of service. IN ST TRIAL P Rule 5(C). In all cases where any pleading or other document is required to be served upon opposing counsel, proof of such service may be made either by:

i. A certificate of service signed by counsel of record for the serving party and the certificate shall specify by name and address all counsel upon whom the pleading or document was served; or

      ii.   An acknowledgment of service signed by the party served or counsel of record. IN ST MARION CIR AND SUPER CTS CIV Rule 206.

2. *Supplemental documents*

    a. *Supporting evidence.* When a motion is based on facts not appearing of record the court may hear the matter on affidavits presented by the respective parties, but the court may direct that the matter be heard wholly or partly on oral testimony or depositions. IN ST TRIAL P Rule 43(B).

    b. *Request for oral argument.* When an oral argument is requested, the request shall be by separate instrument and filed with the pleading to be argued. Any such oral argument requested may be heard at the discretion of the Court, except for motions for summary judgment which shall be set for hearing upon request of any party. IN ST MARION CIR AND SUPER CTS CIV Rule 203(C).

    c. *Facsimile cover sheet.* Any document sent to the Clerk of the Circuit Court by electronic facsimile transmission shall be accompanied by a cover sheet which states the title of the document, case number, number of pages, identity and voice telephone number of the sending party and instructions for filing. The cover sheet shall contain the signature of the attorney or party, pro se, authorizing the filing. IN ST ADMIN Rule 12(D).

E. Format

1. *Form of motions.* The rules applicable to captions, and the signing and form of pleadings (IN ST TRIAL P Rule 8 through IN ST TRIAL P Rule 11), apply to all motions and other papers provided under the Indiana Rules of Trial Procedure. 22B INPRAC 7:2.

2. *Form of pleadings*

    a. *Caption; Names of parties.* Every pleading shall contain a caption setting forth the name of the court, the title of the action, the file number, and a designation as in IN ST TRIAL P Rule 7(A). In the complaint the title of the action shall include the names of all the parties, but in other pleadings it is sufficient to state the name of the first party on each side with an appropriate indication of other parties. IN ST TRIAL P Rule 10(A).

      i.   Every pleading shall contain a caption setting forth the name of the Court, the Division and Room Number, the title of the action and the file number. IN ST MARION CIR AND SUPER CTS CIV Rule 204(B).

    b. *Paragraphs; Separate statements.* All averments of a claim or defense shall be made in numbered paragraphs, the contents of each of which shall be limited as far as practicable to a statement of a single set of circumstances, and a paragraph may be referred to by number in all succeeding pleadings. Each claim founded upon a separate transaction or occurrence and each defense other than denials may be stated in a separate count or defense whenever a separation facilitates the clear presentation of the matters set forth. IN ST TRIAL P Rule 10(B).

    c. *Adoption by reference; Exhibits.* Statements in a pleading may be adopted by reference in a different part of the same pleading or in another pleading or in any motion. A copy of any written instrument which is an exhibit to a pleading is a part thereof for all purposes. IN ST TRIAL P Rule 10(C).

    d. *Paper.* Pleadings, motions and other papers may be either printed or typewritten on white opaque paper of at least sixteen (16) pound weight, eight and one-half (8-1/2) inches wide and eleven (11) inches in length. IN ST MARION CIR AND SUPER CTS CIV Rule 204(A).

    e. *Copies.* All copies shall likewise be on white paper of sufficient strength and durability to resist normal wear and tear. IN ST MARION CIR AND SUPER CTS CIV Rule 204(A).

    f. *Line spacing.* If typewritten, the lines shall be double spaced, except for quotations, which shall be indented and single spaced. IN ST MARION CIR AND SUPER CTS CIV Rule 204(A).

    g. *Script type.* Script type shall not be used. IN ST MARION CIR AND SUPER CTS CIV Rule 204(A).

    h. *Titles.* Titles on all pleadings shall delineate each topic included in the pleading e.g. where a pleading contains an Answer, a Motion to Strike or Dismiss, or a Jury Request each shall be set forth in the title. IN ST MARION CIR AND SUPER CTS CIV Rule 204(C).

    i. *Margins and binding.* Margins shall be one (1) inch. Binding or stapling shall be at the top and at no

other place. Covers or backing shall not be used. IN ST MARION CIR AND SUPER CTS CIV Rule 204(D).

3. *Size of papers for filing.* Effective January 1, 1992, all pleadings, copies, motions and documents filed with any trial court or appellate level court, typed or printed, with the exception of exhibits and existing wills, shall be prepared on eight and one-half by eleven inch (8 1/2" x 11") size paper. IN ST ADMIN Rule 11.

4. *Form of electronically filed documents.* All electronically filed and served pleadings shall, to the extent practicable, be formatted in accordance with the applicable rules governing formatting of paper pleadings. IN ST MARION SUPER CT ADMIN Rule 311(2-103)(1).

   a. *Electronic document title.* The electronic document title of each pleading or other document shall include:

      i. Party or parties filing/serving the document,

      ii. Nature of the document,

      iii. Party or parties against whom relief, if any, is sought, and

      iv. Nature of the relief sought (e.g., Defendant ABC Corporation's Motion for Summary Judgment). IN ST MARION SUPER CT ADMIN Rule 311(2-103)(2).

5. *Signature requirements*

   a. *Signature of attorney.* Every pleading or motion of a party represented by an attorney shall be signed by at least one (1) attorney of record in his individual name, whose address, telephone number, and attorney number shall be stated, except that this provision shall not apply to pleadings and motions made and transcribed at the trial or a hearing before the judge and received by him in such form. IN ST TRIAL P Rule 11(A).

      i. All pleadings and motions shall contain the original or authorized signature of the attorney, the name of the attorney in typed or printed form, the name of the law firm if a member of a firm, the attorney's address, identification number, e-mail address, telephone number, fax number, and the designation as to the party for whom he appears. IN ST MARION CIR AND SUPER CTS CIV Rule 204(E).

      ii. The signature of an attorney constitutes a certificate by him that he has read the pleadings; that to the best of his knowledge, information, and belief, there is good ground to support it; and that it is not interposed for delay. IN ST TRIAL P Rule 11(A).

      iii. If a pleading or motion is not signed or is signed with intent to defeat the purpose of the rule, it may be stricken as sham and false and the action may proceed as though the pleading had not been served. IN ST TRIAL P Rule 11(A).

      iv. For a willful violation of IN ST TRIAL P Rule 11 an attorney may be subjected to appropriate disciplinary action. Similar action may be taken if scandalous or indecent matter is inserted. IN ST TRIAL P Rule 11(A).

      v. Every pleading, document, and instrument electronically filed or served shall be deemed to have been signed by the judge, clerk, attorney or declarant and shall bear a facsimile or typographical signature of such person, along with the typed name, address, telephone number, and Bar number of a signing attorney. Typographical signatures shall be treated as personal signatures for all purposes under these rules. IN ST MARION SUPER CT ADMIN Rule 311(2-105).

        • Documents containing signatures of third-parties (i.e., unopposed motions, affidavits, stipulations, etc.) may also be filed electronically by indicating that the original signatures are maintained by the filing party in paper-format. IN ST MARION SUPER CT ADMIN Rule 311(2-105).

        • Unless otherwise ordered by the Court or Clerk, a printed copy of all documents filed or served electronically, including original signatures, shall be maintained by the party filing the document and shall be made available, upon reasonable notice, for inspection by other

counsel, the Clerk or Court. Parties shall retain originals until two (2) years after all time periods for appeal have expired. From time to time, it may be necessary to provide the Clerk or Court with a hard copy of an electronically filed document. IN ST MARION SUPER CT ADMIN Rule 311(2-105).

    vi.   For the recommended format of a signature block, refer to IN ST MARION CIR AND SUPER CTS CIV Rule 204(E).

b.   *Signature of unrepresented party.* A party who is not represented by an attorney shall sign his pleading and state his address. IN ST TRIAL P Rule 11(A).

c.   *Verification not generally required.* Except when specifically required by rule, pleadings or motions need not be verified or accompanied by affidavit. The rule in equity that the averments of an answer under oath must be overcome by the testimony of two (2) witnesses or of one (1) witness sustained by corroborating circumstances is abolished. IN ST TRIAL P Rule 11(A).

d.   *Verification by affirmation or representation.* When in connection with any civil or special statutory proceeding it is required that any pleading, motion, petition, supporting affidavit, or other document of any kind, be verified, or that an oath be taken, it shall be sufficient if the subscriber simply affirms the truth of the matter to be verified by an affirmation or representation. IN ST TRIAL P Rule 11(B). IN ST TRIAL P Rule 11(B) states that the affirmation or representation should be in substantially the following language: "I (we) affirm, under the penalties for perjury, that the foregoing representation(s) is (are) true. (Signed) _____."

    i.   Any person who falsifies an affirmation or representation of fact shall be subject to the same penalties as are prescribed by law for the making of a false affidavit. IN ST TRIAL P Rule 11(B).

e.   *Verified pleadings, motions, and affidavits as evidence.* Pleadings, motions and affidavits accompanying or in support of such pleadings or motions when required to be verified or under oath shall be accepted as a representation that the signer had personal knowledge thereof or reasonable cause to believe the existence of the facts or matters stated or alleged therein; and, if otherwise competent or acceptable as evidence, may be admitted as evidence of the facts or matters stated or alleged therein when it is so provided in the Indiana Rules of Trial Procedure, by statute or other law, or to the extent the writing or signature expressly purports to be made upon the signer's personal knowledge. When such pleadings, motions and affidavits are verified or under oath they shall not require other or greater proof on the part of the adverse party than if not verified or not under oath unless expressly provided otherwise by the Indiana Rules of Trial Procedure, statute or other law. Affidavits upon motions for summary judgment under IN ST TRIAL P Rule 56 and in denial of execution under IN ST TRIAL P Rule 9.2 shall be made upon personal knowledge. IN ST TRIAL P Rule 11(C).

6.   *Information excluded from public access.* Every document filed in a case shall separately identify information excluded from public access pursuant to IN ST ADMIN Rule 9(G)(1) as follows:

a.   Whole documents that are excluded from public access pursuant to IN ST ADMIN Rule 9(G)(1) shall be tendered on light green paper or have a light green coversheet attached to the document, marked "Not for Public Access" or "Confidential." IN ST TRIAL P Rule 5(G)(1).

b.   When only a portion of a document contains information excluded from public access pursuant to IN ST ADMIN Rule 9(G)(1), said information shall be omitted [or redacted] from the filed document, and set forth on a separate accompanying document on light green paper conspicuously marked "Not for Public Access" or "Confidential" and clearly designated [or identifying] the caption and number of the case and the document and location within the document to which the redacted material pertains. IN ST TRIAL P Rule 5(G)(2).

c.   With respect to documents filed in electronic format, the trial court, by local rule, may provide for compliance with IN ST TRIAL P Rule 5 in manner that separates and protects access to information excluded from public access. IN ST TRIAL P Rule 5(G)(3).

d.   IN ST TRIAL P Rule 5(G) does not apply to a record sealed by the court pursuant to IN ST 5-14-3-5.5 or otherwise, nor to records, documents, or information filed in cases to which public access is prohibited pursuant to IN ST ADMIN Rule 9(G). IN ST TRIAL P Rule 5(G)(4).

e. The following information in case records is excluded from public access and is confidential:

i. Information that is excluded from public access pursuant to federal law;

ii. Information that is excluded from public access as declared confidential by Indiana statute or other court rule, including without limitation:

- All adoption records created after July 8, 1941, as declared confidential by IN ST 31-19-19-1, et seq., except those specifically declared open by IN ST 31-19-13-2(2);

- All records relating to chancroid, chlamydia, gonorrhea, hepatitis, human immunodeficiency virus (HIV), Lymphogranuloma venereum, syphilis, tuberculosis, as declared confidential by IN ST 16-41-8-1, et seq.;

- All records relating to child abuse as declared confidential by IN ST 31-33-18-1, et seq.;

- All records relating to drug tests as declared confidential by IN ST 5-14-3-4(a)(9);

- Records of grand jury proceedings as declared confidential by IN ST 35-34-2-4;

- Records of juvenile proceedings as declared confidential by IN ST 31-39-1-2, except those specifically open under statute;

- All paternity records created after July 1, 1941 as declared confidential by IN ST 31-14-11-15, IN ST 31-19-5-23, IN ST 31-39-1-1 and IN ST 31-39-1-2 [Editor's note: IN ST 31-14-11-15 was repealed effective May 9, 2013];

- All pre-sentence reports as declared confidential by IN ST 35-38-1-13;

- Written petitions to permit marriages without consent and orders directing the Clerk of Court to issue a marriage license to underage persons, as declared confidential by IN ST 31-11-1-6;

- Only those arrest warrants, search warrants, indictments and informations ordered confidential by the trial judge, prior to return of duly executed service as declared confidential by IN ST 5-14-3-4(b)(1);

- All medical, mental health, or tax records unless determined by law or regulation of any governmental custodian not to be confidential, released by the subject of such records, or declared by a court of competent jurisdiction to be essential to the resolution of litigation as declared confidential by IN ST 16-39-3-10, IN ST 6-4.1-5-10, IN ST 6-4.1-12-12, and IN ST 6-8.1-7-1;

- Personal information relating to jurors or prospective jurors, other than for the use of the parties and counsel, pursuant to IN ST JURY Rule 10;

- Information relating to protection from abuse orders, no-contact orders and workplace violence restraining orders as declared confidential by IN ST 5-2-9-6, et seq.;

- Mediation proceedings pursuant to IN ST ADR Rule 2.11, Mini-Trial proceedings pursuant to IN ST ADR Rule 4.4(C), and Summary Jury Trials pursuant to IN ST ADR Rule 5.6;

- Information in probation files pursuant to the Probation Standards promulgated by the Judicial Conference of Indiana pursuant to IN ST 11-13-1-8(b);

- Information deemed confidential pursuant to the Rules for Court Administered Alcohol and Drug Programs promulgated by the Judicial Conference of Indiana pursuant to IN ST 12-23-14-13;

- Information deemed confidential pursuant to the Problem-Solving Court Rules promulgated by the Judicial Conference of Indiana pursuant to IN ST 33-23-16-16;

- All records of the Department of workforce Development as declared confidential by IN ST 22-4-19-6;

- Information regarding interception of electronic communications that is sealed or deemed confidential as set forth in IN ST 35-33.5-2-1, et seq.

iii. Information excluded from public access by specific court order;

iv. Complete Social Security Numbers of living persons;

v. With the exception of names, information such as addresses, phone numbers, and dates of birth which explicitly identifies:

- Natural persons who are witnesses or victims (not including defendants) in criminal, domestic violence, stalking, sexual assault, juvenile, or civil protection order proceedings, provided that juveniles who are victims of sex crimes shall be identified by initials only;

- Places of residence of judicial officers, clerks and other employees of courts and clerks of court, unless the person or persons about whom the information pertains waives confidentiality;

vi. Complete account numbers of specific assets, loans, bank accounts, credit cards, and personal identification numbers (PINs);

vii. All orders of expungement entered in criminal or juvenile proceedings, orders to restrict access to criminal history information pursuant to IN ST 35-38-5-5.5 or IN ST 35-38-8-5 and records excluded from public access by such orders, and information related to infractions that is excluded from public access pursuant to IN ST 34-28-5-15 or IN ST 34-28-5-16 [Editor's note: IN ST 35-38-5-5.5, IN ST 35-38-8-5 and IN ST 34-28-5-16 were repealed effective July 1, 2013; for information on orders restricting access to criminal history, refer to IN ST 35-38-9-1, et seq.];

viii. All personal notes and e-mail, and deliberative material, of judges, jurors, court staff and judicial agencies, and information recorded in personal data assistants (PDA's) or organizers and personal calendars. IN ST ADMIN Rule 9(G)(1).

F. Filing and Service Requirements

1. *Filing requirements.* Except as otherwise provided in IN ST TRIAL P Rule 5(E)(2), all pleadings and papers subsequent to the complaint which are required to be served upon a party shall be filed with the Court either before service or within a reasonable period of time thereafter. IN ST TRIAL P Rule 5(E)(1). Counsel shall file with the court an original and one (1) copy of all briefs, and memoranda of law filed in support of a motion. IN ST MARION CIR AND SUPER CTS CIV Rule 205(D).

   a. *Filing generally.* All pleadings, petitions and motions are filed with the Clerk designated by the Court at any time during office hours established by the Clerk and the Court. All orders submitted to the Court shall be in sufficient number and shall be accompanied by postage paid envelopes addressed to each party or counsel of record. IN ST MARION CIR AND SUPER CTS CIV Rule 205(A)

   b. *Filing with the court defined.* The filing of pleadings, motions, and other papers with the court as required by the Indiana Rules of Trial Procedure shall be made by one of the following methods:

      i. Delivery to the clerk of the court;

      ii. Sending by electronic transmission under the procedure adopted pursuant to IN ST ADMIN Rule 12;

      iii. Mailing to the clerk by registered, certified or express mail return receipt requested;

      iv. Depositing with any third-party commercial carrier for delivery to the clerk within three (3) calendar days, cost prepaid, properly addressed;

      v. If the court so permits, filing with the judge, in which event the judge shall note thereon the filing date and forthwith transmit them to the office of the clerk; or

      vi. Electronic filing, as approved by the Division of State Court Administration pursuant to IN ST ADMIN Rule 16. IN ST TRIAL P Rule 5(F).

      vii. Filing by registered or certified mail and by third-party commercial carrier shall be complete upon mailing or deposit. IN ST TRIAL P Rule 5(F).

   c. *Facsimile filing.* Facsimile filing is discouraged, but permitted in the Marion Circuit and Marion

Superior Court. All documents filed by facsimile shall also be filed in hard copy within seven (7) days of the facsimile filing, along with proposed orders and stamped addressed envelopes, as required by IN ST MARION CIR AND SUPER CTS CIV Rule 203(E). To avoid duplicate filings, the hard copies of the facsimile filing shall indicate in bold letters that the pleading was previously filed by facsimile transmission. Proof of transmission by facsimile, including certificate of service and manner of service, shall be the responsibility of the filing party. If the filing requires immediate attention of the Judge, it shall be so indicated in bold letters in an accompanying transmittal memorandum. Legibility of documents and timeliness of filing is the responsibility of the sender. IN ST MARION CIR AND SUPER CTS CIV Rule 205(B).

 i. *Generally.* In counties where a majority of judges of the courts of record, by posted local rule, have authorized electronic facsimile filing and designated a telephone number to receive such transmissions, pleadings, motions, and other papers may be sent to the Clerk of Circuit Court by electronic facsimile transmission for filing in any case, provided:

- Such matter does not exceed ten (10) pages, including the cover sheet;
- Such matter does not require the payment of fees other than the electronic facsimile transcription fee set forth in IN ST ADMIN Rule 12(E);
- The sending party creates at the time of transmission a machine generated log for such transmission; and
- The original document and the transmission log are maintained by the sending party for the duration of the litigation. IN ST ADMIN Rule 12(B).

 ii. *Time of filing.* During normal, posted business hours, the time of filing shall be the time the duplicate document is produced in the office of the Clerk of the Circuit Court. Duplicate documents received at all other times shall be filed as of the next normal business day. IN ST ADMIN Rule 12(C).

- If the receiving fax machine endorses its own time and date stamp upon the transmitted documents and the receiving machine produces a delivery receipt which is electronically created and transmitted to the sending party, the time of filing shall be the date and time recorded on the transmitted document by the receiving fax machine. IN ST ADMIN Rule 12(C).

d. *Electronic filing.* Electronic filing and electronic service pilot projects are authorized pursuant to IN ST ADMIN Rule 16 and approved by the Division of State Court Administration. IN ST MARION SUPER CT ADMIN Rule 311(1-103).

 i. *Cases where electronic filing accepted.* All Marion County Circuit and Superior civil courts may accept electronic filing and service of pleadings and other documents designated in this rule in mortgage foreclosure (hereinafter referred to as "MF"), civil collection(hereinafter referred to as "CC"), and individual cases that have been approved for electronic filing and service. IN ST MARION SUPER CT ADMIN Rule 311(1-104)(1).

- The Marion County Circuit Court may, upon the motion of a party or its own motion, designate a case that will involve multiple litigants, legally intricate issues, and an extensive number of documents a mass tort or complex litigation case. Any case so designated shall be subject to electronic filing and service using the county's approved Electronic Service Provider. IN ST MARION SUPER CT ADMIN Rule 311(1-104)(3).
- The filing of electronic pleadings and other documents in MF and CC cases is entirely voluntary; however, once the case is initially filed electronically, all subsequent filings in the case shall remain in electronic format until the time for appeal is exhausted. IN ST MARION SUPER CT ADMIN Rule 311(1-104)(5).

 ii. *Documents eligible for electronic filing.* The following pleadings may be filed and served electronically:

- New case complaint and petitions. IN ST MARION SUPER CT ADMIN Rule 311(1-104)(8)(a).

- Original answers. IN ST MARION SUPER CT ADMIN Rule 311(1-104)(8)(a).
- Any other pleadings or document including but not limited to motions and appearance forms. IN ST MARION SUPER CT ADMIN Rule 311(1-104)(8)(a).

iii. *Manner of electronic filing.* Parties shall E-file a document either:

- By registering to use the Electronic Filing Service Provider; or
- In person at the Marion County Clerk's office, by electronically filing through the Public Access Terminal. Parties filing in this manner shall be responsible for furnishing the document in an electronic format that will be compatible with the clerk's office-system to be uploaded in person. IN ST MARION SUPER CT ADMIN Rule 311(1-104)(9). For information on the Electronic Filing Service Provider and Public Access Terminal, refer to IN ST MARION SUPER CT ADMIN Rule 311(1-101).
- Registered users shall pay statutory filing fees for E-filed documents electronically to the Court through their EFSP. Filing fees are due and payable at the time of filing. IN ST MARION SUPER CT ADMIN Rule 311(2-104)(1). For more information on electronic filing fees, refer to IN ST MARION SUPER CT ADMIN Rule 311(2-104).

iv. *Effect of electronic filing.* Any pleading filed electronically shall be considered as filed with the court when the transmission to the EFSP is complete. Any document E-filed by 11:59 p.m. local Indianapolis, Indiana time shall be deemed filed on that date. The EFSP is an agent of the Court for the purpose of electronic filing, receipt, service and retrieval of electronic documents. IN ST MARION SUPER CT ADMIN Rule 311(2-102).

- Upon completion of filing, the EFSP shall issue a confirmation receipt that includes the date and time of receipt. The confirmation receipt shall serve as proof of filing. IN ST MARION SUPER CT ADMIN Rule 311(2-102).
- In the event the Court rejects the submitted documents following review, the documents shall not become part of the official Court record and the filer will receive notification of the rejection. Users may be required to refile the instruments to meet necessary filing requirements. Documents may be filed through an E-filing system at any time that the Clerk's office is open to receive the filing or at such other times as may be designated by the clerk and posted publicly. IN ST MARION SUPER CT ADMIN Rule 311(2-102).
- Documents filed through the E-filing system are deemed filed when received by the Clerk's office, except that documents received at times that the Clerk's office is closed shall be deemed filed the next regular time when the Clerk's office is open for filing. The time stamp issued by the E-filing system shall be presumed to be the time the document is received by the Clerk. IN ST MARION SUPER CT ADMIN Rule 311(2-102).

v. *Electronically filed documents.* All pleadings and other documents designated in IN ST MARION SUPER CT ADMIN Rule 311 shall be filed and served electronically in any individual case which has been approved for electronic filing and service. IN ST MARION SUPER CT ADMIN Rule 311(1-104)(6).

vi. *System failures.* When filing by electronic means is hindered by a technical failure, a party may file with the Clerk of Marion County in hard copy. With the exception of deadlines that by law cannot be extended, the time for filing of any paper that is delayed due to technical failure of the site shall be extended for one (1) day for each day on which such failure occurs, unless otherwise ordered by the Court. IN ST MARION SUPER CT ADMIN Rule 311(2-108).

vii. *Compliance with rules.* All filing shall comply with the requirements of IN ST ADMIN Rule 9 and IN ST ADMIN Rule 16; and the Indiana Rules of Court and the Marion County Local Rules. IN ST MARION SUPER CT ADMIN Rule 311(1-104)(11).

e. *Filing for special judge.* When a Special Judge who is not a Marion County Judge is selected, all parties or attorneys shall furnish such Judge with copies of all filings prior to the qualification of such Special Judge. Thereafter, copies of all filings shall be delivered in person, by mail or by facsimile to the office of the Special Judge with certificate of forwarding same made a part of the filing. IN ST MARION CIR AND SUPER CTS CIV Rule 205(C).

f. *Proof of filing.* Any party filing any paper by any method other than personal delivery to the clerk shall retain proof of filing. IN ST TRIAL P Rule 5(F).

2. *Service requirements.* Unless otherwise provided by the Indiana Rules of Trial Procedure or an order of the court, each party and special judge, if any, shall be served with: (1) every order required by its terms to be served; (2) every pleading subsequent to the original complaint; (3) every written motion except one which may be heard ex parte; (4) every brief submitted to the trial court; (5) every paper relating to discovery required to be served upon a party; and (6) every written notice, appearance, demand, offer of judgment, designation of record on appeal, or similar paper. IN ST TRIAL P Rule 5(A).

   a. *Methods of service*

      i. *Personal service.* Whenever a party is represented by an attorney of record, service shall be made upon such attorney unless service upon the party himself is ordered by the court. Service upon the attorney or party shall be made by delivering or mailing a copy of the papers to the last known address or where an attorney or party has consented to service by fax or e-mail, as provided in IN ST TRIAL P Rule 3.1(A)(4), by faxing or e-mailing a copy of the documents to the fax number or e-mail address set out in the appearance form or correction as required by IN ST TRIAL P Rule 3.1(E). IN ST TRIAL P Rule 5(B). Delivery of a copy within IN ST TRIAL P Rule 5 means:

         • Offering or tendering it to the attorney or party and stating the nature of the papers being served. Refusal to accept an offered or tendered document is a waiver of any objection to the sufficiency or adequacy of service of that document;

         • Leaving it at his office with a clerk or other person in charge thereof, or if there is no one in charge, leaving it in a conspicuous place therein; or

         • If the office is closed, by leaving it at his dwelling house or usual place of abode with some person of suitable age and discretion then residing therein; or,

         • Leaving it at some other suitable place, selected by the attorney upon whom service is being made, pursuant to duly promulgated local rule. IN ST TRIAL P Rule 5(B)(1).

      ii. *Service by mail.* If service is made by mail, the papers shall be deposited in the United States mail addressed to the person on whom they are being served, with postage prepaid. Service shall be deemed complete upon mailing. Proof of service of all papers permitted to be mailed may be made by written acknowledgment of service, by affidavit of the person who mailed the papers, or by certificate of an attorney. It shall be the duty of attorneys when entering their appearance in a cause or when filing pleadings or papers therein, to have noted in the Chronological Case Summary or said pleadings or papers so filed the address and telephone number of their office. Service by delivery or by mail at such address shall be deemed sufficient and complete. IN ST TRIAL P Rule 5(B)(2).

      iii. *Service by fax or e-mail.* A party who has consented to service by fax or e-mail may be served as follows:

         • Service by e-mail shall be made by attaching the document being served in .pdf format. Discovery documents must also be served in accordance with IN ST TRIAL P Rule 26(A). IN ST TRIAL P Rule 5(B)(3)(a).

         • Service by fax shall be deemed complete upon generation of a transmission record indicating the successful transmission of the entire document, except as provided in IN ST TRIAL P Rule 5(B)(3)(d). IN ST TRIAL P Rule 5(B)(3)(b).

         • Service by e-mail shall be deemed complete upon transmission, except as provided in IN ST TRIAL P Rule 5(B)(3)(d). IN ST TRIAL P Rule 5(B)(3)(c).

         • Service by fax or e-mail that occurs on a Saturday, Sunday, legal holiday, or day the court or agency in which the matter is pending is closed or after 5:00 PM local time of the recipient shall be deemed complete the next day that is not a Saturday, Sunday, legal holiday, or day that the court or agency in which the matter is pending is not closed. IN ST TRIAL P Rule 5(B)(3)(d).

    iv. *Electronic service.* Delivery of E-service documents through the EFSP to other registered users shall be considered as valid and effective service and shall have the same legal effect as an original paper document. Recipients of E-service documents shall access their documents through the EFSP. IN ST MARION SUPER CT ADMIN Rule 311(2-107)(1).

- E-service shall be deemed complete when the transmission to the EFSP is completed. IN ST MARION SUPER CT ADMIN Rule 311(2-107)(2).

- For the purpose of computing time to respond to documents received via E-service, any document served on a day or at a time when the Clerk's office is not open for business shall be deemed served at the time of next opening of the Clerk's office for business. IN ST MARION SUPER CT ADMIN Rule 311(2-107)(3).

  b. *Serving numerous defendants.* In any action in which there are unusually large numbers of defendants, the court, upon motion or of its own initiative, may order:

    i. That service of the pleadings of the defendants and replies thereto need not be made as between the defendants;

- That any cross-claim, counterclaim, or matter constituting an avoidance or affirmative defense contained therein shall be deemed to be denied or avoided by all other parties; and

- That the filing of any such pleading and service thereof upon the plaintiff constitutes due notice of it to the parties. IN ST TRIAL P Rule 5(D).

    ii. A copy of every such order shall be served upon the parties in such manner and form as the court directs. IN ST TRIAL P Rule 5(D).

  c. *Service on parties in default for failure to appear.* No service need be made on parties in default for failure to appear, except that pleadings asserting new or additional claims for relief against them shall be served upon them in the manner provided by service of summons in IN ST TRIAL P Rule 4. IN ST TRIAL P Rule 5(A).

G. Hearings

1. *Hearing on motion.* Unless local conditions make it impracticable, each judge shall establish regular times and places, at intervals sufficiently frequent for the prompt dispatch of business, at which motions requiring notice and hearing may be heard and disposed of; but the judge at any time or place and on such notice, if any, as he considers reasonable may make order for the advancement, conduct, and hearing of actions. To expedite its business the court may direct the submission and determination of motions without oral hearing upon brief written statements of reasons in support and opposition, or direct or permit hearings by telephone conference call with all attorneys or other similar means of communication. IN ST TRIAL P Rule 73(A).

2. *Time and place of hearing.* If the motion requires a hearing or oral argument, the Court shall set the time and place of hearing or argument on the motion. IN ST MARION CIR AND SUPER CTS CIV Rule 203(A).

H. Forms

1. Motion to Dismiss for Lack of Personal Jurisdiction Forms for Indiana

  a. General form. 5 INPRAC § 3:4.1.

  b. Lack of personal jurisdiction. 5 INPRAC § 3:4.3.

  c. Certificate of service; Personal service. 9 INPRAC § 5.7.

  d. Certificate of service; First class mail. 9 INPRAC § 5.8.

  e. Motion to dismiss plaintiff's complaint; General form. 9 INPRAC § 42.2.

  f. Lack of personal jurisdiction. 9 INPRAC § 42.4.

I. Checklist

(I) ❑ Matters to be considered by moving party

  (a) ❑ Required documents

    (1) ❑ Motion and notice

     (2) ❑ Statement of approval or disapproval

     (3) ❑ Proposed order

     (4) ❑ Certificate of service

 (b) ❑ Supplemental documents

     (1) ❑ Supporting evidence

     (2) ❑ Request for oral argument

     (3) ❑ Facsimile cover sheet

 (c) ❑ Timing

     (1) ❑ A motion to dismiss for lack of personal jurisdiction shall be made before pleading if a further pleading is permitted or within twenty (20) days after service of the prior pleading if none is required

     (2) ❑ A written motion, other than one which may be heard ex parte, and notice of the hearing thereof shall be served not less than five (5) days before the time specified for the hearing, unless a different period is fixed by the Indiana Rules of Trial Procedure or by order of the court

     (3) ❑ All pleadings and papers subsequent to the complaint which are required to be served upon a party shall be filed with the Court either before service or within a reasonable period of time thereafter

(II) ❑ Matters to be considered by the responding party

 (a) ❑ Required documents

     (1) ❑ Opposition

     (2) ❑ Certificate of service

 (b) ❑ Supplemental documents

     (1) ❑ Supporting evidence

     (2) ❑ Proposed order

     (3) ❑ Facsimile cover sheet

 (c) ❑ Timing

     (1) ❑ If the statement regarding the position of the opposing party(ies) required under IN ST MARION CIR AND SUPER CTS CIV Rule 203(A) indicates that objection to the granting of said motion may ensue, said objecting a party shall have fifteen (15) days from the date of filing to file a response to said motion

     (2) ❑ Except as otherwise provided in IN ST TRIAL P Rule 59(D), opposing affidavits may be served not less than one (1) day before the hearing, unless the court permits them to be served at some other time

Requests, Notices and Applications
Interrogatories

Document Last Updated October 2013

A. Applicable Rules

1. *State rules*

   a. Appearance. IN ST TRIAL P Rule 3.1.

   b. Process. IN ST TRIAL P Rule 4.

   c. Service and filing of pleadings and other papers. IN ST TRIAL P Rule 5.

   d. Time. IN ST TRIAL P Rule 6.

e. Pleadings. IN ST TRIAL P Rule 7; IN ST TRIAL P Rule 9.2; IN ST TRIAL P Rule 10.

f. Signing and verification of pleadings. IN ST TRIAL P Rule 11.

g. General provisions governing discovery. IN ST TRIAL P Rule 26.

h. Methods of discovery. IN ST TRIAL P Rule 27; IN ST TRIAL P Rule 29; IN ST TRIAL P Rule 30; IN ST TRIAL P Rule 31; IN ST TRIAL P Rule 33; IN ST TRIAL P Rule 34; IN ST TRIAL P Rule 35; IN ST TRIAL P Rule 36.

i. Failure to make or cooperate in discovery; Sanctions. IN ST TRIAL P Rule 37.

j. Judgment on the evidence (directed verdict). IN ST TRIAL P Rule 50.

k. Findings by the court. IN ST TRIAL P Rule 52.

l. Summary judgment. IN ST TRIAL P Rule 56.

m. Motion to correct error. IN ST TRIAL P Rule 59.

n. Relief from judgment or order. IN ST TRIAL P Rule 60.

o. Access to court records. IN ST ADMIN Rule 9.

p. Paper size. IN ST ADMIN Rule 11.

q. Facsimile transmission. IN ST ADMIN Rule 12.

r. Electronic filing and electronic service pilot projects. IN ST ADMIN Rule 16.

s. Sealing of certain records by court; Hearing; Notice. IN ST 5-14-3-5.5.

t. Privacy and confidentiality. IN ST 5-2-9-6; IN ST 5-14-3-4; IN ST 6-4.1-5-10; IN ST 6-4.1-12-12; IN ST 6-8.1-7-1; IN ST 11-13-1-8; IN ST 12-23-14-13; IN ST 16-39-3-10; IN ST 16-41-8-1; IN ST 22-4-19-6; IN ST 31-11-1-6; IN ST 31-19-5-23; IN ST 31-19-13-2; IN ST 31-19-19-1; IN ST 31-33-18-1; IN ST 31-39-1-1; IN ST 31-39-1-2; IN ST 33-23-16-16; IN ST 35-34-2-4; IN ST 35-38-1-13; IN ST 35-38-9-1; IN ST ADR Rule 2.11; IN ST ADR Rule 4.4; IN ST ADR Rule 5.6; IN ST JURY Rule 10.

2. *Local rules*

a. Requirements for motions. IN ST MARION CIR AND SUPER CTS CIV Rule 203.

b. Preparation of pleadings, motions and other papers. IN ST MARION CIR AND SUPER CTS CIV Rule 204.

c. Filing of pleadings, motions and other papers. IN ST MARION CIR AND SUPER CTS CIV Rule 205.

d. Signing and verification of pleadings, motions and other papers; Service on opposing party. IN ST MARION CIR AND SUPER CTS CIV Rule 206.

e. Interrogatories. IN ST MARION CIR AND SUPER CTS CIV Rule 213.

f. Motions for continuance. IN ST MARION CIR AND SUPER CTS CIV Rule 215.

g. Electronic filing. IN ST MARION SUPER CT ADMIN Rule 311.

B. Timing

1. *Service of interrogatories.* Interrogatories may, without leave of court, be served upon the plaintiff after commencement of the action and upon any other party with or after service of the summons and complaint upon that party. IN ST TRIAL P Rule 33(A).

2. *Service of responses to interrogatories.* The party upon whom the interrogatories have been served shall serve a copy of the answers and objections within a period designated by the party submitting the interrogatories, not less than thirty (30) days after the service thereof or within such shorter or longer time as the court may allow. IN ST TRIAL P Rule 33(C).

3. *Computation of time*

a. *Generally; Days excluded.* In computing any period of time prescribed or allowed by the Indiana Rules of Trial Procedure, by order of the court, or by any applicable statute, the day of the act, event,

or default from which the designated period of time begins to run shall not be included. The last day of the period so computed is to be included unless it is:

    i.   A Saturday,

    ii. A Sunday,

    iii. A legal holiday as defined by state statute, or

    iv. A day the office in which the act is to be done is closed during regular business hours. IN ST TRIAL P Rule 6(A).

b. *Short periods.* In any event, the period runs until the end of the next day that is not a Saturday, a Sunday, a legal holiday, or a day on which the office is closed. When the period of time allowed is less than seven (7) days, intermediate Saturdays, Sundays, legal holidays, and days on which the office is closed shall be excluded from the computations. IN ST TRIAL P Rule 6(A).

c. *Additional time after service by United States mail.* Whenever a party has the right or is required to do some act or take some proceedings within a prescribed period after the service of a notice or other paper upon him and the notice or paper is served upon him by United States mail, three (3) days shall be added to the prescribed period. IN ST TRIAL P Rule 6(E).

d. *Enlargement of time.* When an act is required or allowed to be done at or within a specific time by the Indiana Rules of Trial Procedure, the court may at any time for cause shown:

    i.   Order the period enlarged, with or without motion or notice, if request therefor is made before the expiration of the period originally prescribed or extended by a previous order; or

    ii. Upon motion made after the expiration of the specific period, permit the act to be done where the failure to act was the result of excusable neglect; but, the court may not extend the time for taking any action for judgment on the evidence under IN ST TRIAL P Rule 50(A), amendment of findings and judgment under IN ST TRIAL P Rule 52(B), to correct errors under IN ST TRIAL P Rule 59(C), statement in opposition to motion to correct error under IN ST TRIAL P Rule 59(E), or to obtain relief from final judgment under IN ST TRIAL P Rule 60(B), except to the extent and under the conditions stated in those rules. IN ST TRIAL P Rule 6(B).

e. *Continuances disfavored.* Motions for Continuance are discouraged. Neither side is entitled to an automatic continuance as a matter of right. IN ST MARION CIR AND SUPER CTS CIV Rule 215. For information on obtaining a continuance, refer to IN ST MARION CIR AND SUPER CTS CIV Rule 215.

C. General Requirements

1. *Scope of discovery.* Unless otherwise limited by order of the court in accordance with the Indiana Rules of Trial Procedure, the scope of discovery is as follows:

  a. *In general.* Parties may obtain discovery regarding any matter, not privileged, which is relevant to the subject-matter involved in the pending action, whether it relates to the claim or defense of the party seeking discovery or the claim or defense of any other party, including the existence, description, nature, custody, condition and location of any books, documents, or other tangible things and the identity and location of persons having knowledge of any discoverable matter. It is not ground for objection that the information sought will be inadmissible at the trial if the information sought appears reasonably calculated to lead to the discovery of admissible evidence. IN ST TRIAL P Rule 26(B)(1).

    i. *Limiting discovery upon court determination.* The frequency or extent of use of the discovery methods otherwise permitted under the Indiana Rules of Trial Procedure and by any local rule shall be limited by the court if it determines that:

- The discovery sought is unreasonably cumulative or duplicative, or is obtainable from some other source that is more convenient, less burdensome, or less expensive;

- The party seeking discovery has had ample opportunity by discovery in the action to obtain the information sought or;

- The burden or expense of the proposed discovery outweighs its likely benefit, taking into account the needs of the case, the amount in controversy, the parties' resources, the importance of the issues at stake in the litigation, and the importance of the proposed discovery in resolving the issues. IN ST TRIAL P Rule 26(B)(1).

- The court may act upon its own initiative after reasonable notice or pursuant to a motion under IN ST TRIAL P Rule 26(C). IN ST TRIAL P Rule 26(B)(1). Refer to the Indiana KeyRules Motion for Protective Order document for more information.

ii. *Relevancy in the discovery context.* When the word "relevancy" is used in IN ST TRIAL P Rule 26(B), it does not mean "relevancy" as that word in used to determine the admissibility of evidence in a trial court. It is much broader. It means "relevancy" to the "subject matter" of the litigation or pending action and it may relate to the claim or defense of any party. Pretrial discovery is available as to any nonprivileged matter relevant to the subject matter of the lawsuit or to obtain information reasonably calculated to lead to admissible evidence. 2A INPRAC R 26(26.4); Kaufmann v. Credithrift Financial, Inc., 465 N.E.2d 207, 210 (Ind.Ct.App. 1984).

iii. *Tests for relevance.* Indiana case law has developed two (2) additional tests in this area. 2A INPRAC R 26(26.4).

- The first test determines when a document or a request for information is actually relevant to the subject matter in the pending action. A document [or discovery request] is relevant to discovery if there is the possibility the information sought may be relevant to the subject matter of the action. 2A INPRAC R 26(26.4); CIGNA-INA/Aetna v. Hagerman-Shambaugh, 473 N.E.2d 1033, 1036 (Ind.Ct.App. 1985).

- The second test speaks to appellate review of the trial court's determination that a document or discovery request is relevant to the subject matter of the pending action. The appellate court sees its review of the trial court's decision on relevancy to subject matter as being very limited. The court states: "Our review of the trial court's conclusion that the documents are relevant is limited. A trial court is vested with discretion in its rulings on discovery issues." 2A INPRAC R 26(26.4); Costanzi v. Ryan, 175 Ind.App. 257, 370 N.E.2d 1333 (Ind.Ct.App. 1978).

b. *Insurance agreements.* A party may obtain discovery of the existence and contents of any insurance agreement under which any person carrying on an insurance business may be liable to satisfy part or all of a judgment which may be entered in the action or to indemnify or reimburse for payments made to satisfy the judgment. Information concerning the insurance agreement is not by reason of disclosure admissible in evidence at trial. For purposes of IN ST TRIAL P Rule 26(B)(2), an application for insurance shall not be treated as part of an insurance agreement. IN ST TRIAL P Rule 26(B)(2).

c. *Trial preparation; Materials.* Subject to the provisions of IN ST TRIAL P Rule 26(B)(4), a party may obtain discovery of documents and tangible things otherwise discoverable under IN ST TRIAL P Rule 26(B)(1) and prepared in anticipation of litigation or for trial by or for another party or by or for that other party's representative (including his attorney, consultant, surety, indemnitor, insurer, or agent) only upon a showing that the party seeking discovery has substantial need of the materials in the preparation of his case and that he is unable without undue hardship to obtain the substantial equivalent of the materials by other means. In ordering discovery of such materials when the required showing has been made, the court shall protect against disclosure of the mental impressions, conclusions, opinions, or legal theories of an attorney or other representative of a party concerning the litigation. IN ST TRIAL P Rule 26(B)(3).

i. A party may obtain without the required showing a statement concerning the action or its subject matter previously made by that party. Upon request, a person not a party may obtain without the required showing a statement concerning the action or its subject matter previously made by that person. If the request is refused, the person may move for a court order. The provisions of IN ST TRIAL P Rule 37(A)(4) apply to the award of expenses incurred in relation to the motion. For purposes of IN ST TRIAL P Rule 26(B)(3), a statement previously made is:

- A written statement signed or otherwise adopted approved by the person making it, or

- A stenographic, mechanical, electrical, or other recording, or a transcription thereof, which is a substantially verbatim recital of an oral statement by the person making it and contemporaneously recorded. IN ST TRIAL P Rule 26(B)(3).

ii. The protection of IN ST TRIAL P Rule 26(B)(3) extends to material prepared or collected before litigation actually commences, but that some possibility of litigation must actually exist before the privilege and IN ST TRIAL P Rule 26(B)(3) become operative. 2A INPRAC R 26(26.9); CIGNA-INA/Aetna v. Hagerman-Shambaugh, 473 N.E.2d 1033, 1037 (Ind.Ct.App. 1985).

d. *Trial preparation; Experts.* Discovery of facts known and opinions held by experts, otherwise discoverable under the provisions of IN ST TRIAL P Rule 26(B)(1) and acquired or developed in anticipation of litigation or for trial, may be obtained as follows:

  i. A party may through interrogatories require any other party to identify each person whom the other party expects to call as an expert witness at trial, to state the subject matter on which the expert is expected to testify, and to state the substance of the facts and opinions to which the expert is expected to testify and a summary of the grounds for each opinion. IN ST TRIAL P Rule 26(B)(4)(a)(i).

  ii. Upon motion, the court may order further discovery by other means, subject to such restrictions as to scope and such provisions, pursuant to IN ST TRIAL P Rule 26(B)(4)(c), concerning fees and expenses as the court may deem appropriate. IN ST TRIAL P Rule 26(B)(4)(a)(ii).

  iii. A party may discover facts known or opinions held by an expert who has been retained or specially employed by another party in anticipation of litigation or preparation for trial and who is not expected to be called as a witness at trial, only as provided in IN ST TRIAL P Rule 35(B) or upon a showing of exceptional circumstances under which it is impracticable for the party seeking discovery to obtain facts or opinions on the same subject by other means. IN ST TRIAL P Rule 26(B)(4)(b).

  iv. Unless manifest injustice would result,

    - The court shall require that the party seeking discovery pay the expert a reasonable fee for time spent in responding to discovery under IN ST TRIAL P Rule 26(B)(4)(a)(ii) and IN ST TRIAL P Rule 26(B)(4)(b); and

    - With respect to discovery obtained under IN ST TRIAL P Rule 26(B)(4)(a)(ii) the court may require, and with respect to discovery obtained under IN ST TRIAL P Rule 26(B)(4)(b) the court shall require, the party seeking discovery to pay the other party a fair portion of the fees and expenses reasonably incurred by the latter party in obtaining facts and opinions from the expert. IN ST TRIAL P Rule 26(B)(4)(c).

e. *Claims of privilege or protection*

  i. *Information withheld.* When a party withholds information otherwise discoverable under the Indiana Rules of Trial Procedure by claiming that it is privileged or subject to protection as trial preparation material, the party shall make the claim expressly and shall describe the nature of the documents, communications, or things not produced or disclosed in a manner that, without revealing information itself privileged or protected, will enable other parties to assess the applicability of the privilege or protection. IN ST TRIAL P Rule 26(B)(5)(a).

  ii. *Information produced.* If information is produced in discovery that is subject to a claim of privilege or protection as trial-preparation material, the party making the claim may notify any party that received the information of the claim and the basis for it. After being notified, a party must promptly return, sequester, or destroy the specified information and any copies it has and may not use or disclose the information until the claim is resolved. A receiving party may promptly present the information to the court under seal for a determination of the claim. If the receiving party disclosed the information before being notified, it must take reasonable steps to retrieve it. The producing party must preserve the information until the claim is resolved. IN ST TRIAL P Rule 26(B)(5)(b).

  iii. *Waiver.* The law of discovery has developed some holdings which indicate that "waiver" of a privileged communication in a discovery setting might be more exacting than "waiver" of a privileged communication when the only question at hand is an interpretation of the privilege itself. Thus, in litigation in which several documents are in issue, and some are released inadvertently, there is strong case law that holds that the "inadvertent production" of a privileged document does not constitute a waiver of the attorney-client privilege. 2A INPRAC R 26(26.5); Transamerica Computer Co. v. International Business Machines Corp., 573 F.2d 646 (9th Cir. 1978). Such a rule should be measured against the usual rule which suggests that a voluntary disclosure to a third person will generally suffice to show a waiver of the attorney-client privilege. 2A INPRAC R 26(26.5).

f. *Use not limited.* Unless the court orders otherwise under IN ST TRIAL P Rule 26(C), the frequency of use of the methods listed in IN ST TRIAL P Rule 26(A) is not limited. IN ST TRIAL P Rule 26(A).

g. *Sequence of discovery.* Unless the court upon motion, for the convenience of parties and witnesses and in the interests of justice, orders otherwise, methods of discovery may be used in any sequence and the fact that a party is conducting discovery, whether by deposition or otherwise, shall not operate to delay any other party's discovery. IN ST TRIAL P Rule 26(D).

2. *Interrogatories.* Parties may obtain discovery by written interrogatories. IN ST TRIAL P Rule 26(A)(2). An interrogatory is a written question served upon another party which requires a written response under oath. 22 INPRAC § 23.1. Any party may serve upon any other party written interrogatories to be answered by the party served or, if the party served is an organization including a governmental organization, or a partnership, by any officer or agent, who shall furnish such information as is available to the party. IN ST TRIAL P Rule 33(A).

a. *Number limited.* Interrogatories shall be limited to a total of twenty-five (25) including subparts and shall be used solely for the purpose of discovery and shall not be used as a substitute for the taking of a deposition. For good cause shown and upon leave of Court additional interrogatories may be propounded. IN ST MARION CIR AND SUPER CTS CIV Rule 213(A).

b. *Duplicate forms.* No duplicated forms containing interrogatories shall be filed or served upon a party unless all interrogatories on such forms are consecutively numbered and applicable to the cause in which the same are filed and served. IN ST MARION CIR AND SUPER CTS CIV Rule 213(C).

c. *Subject of interrogatories.* Interrogatories may relate to any matters which can be inquired into under IN ST TRIAL P Rule 26(B), and the answers may be used to the extent permitted by the rules of evidence. IN ST TRIAL P Rule 33(D).

   i. This includes:

- The existence, description, nature, custody, condition and location of books, documents, or other tangible things; and

- The identity and location of persons having knowledge of relevant facts. 10 INPRAC § 65.1.

   ii. Interrogatories cannot be objected to on the ground that the information sought will be inadmissible at trial if the discovery appears reasonably calculated to lead to the discovery of admissible evidence. 10 INPRAC § 65.1.

d. *Available for parties only.* Interrogatories may not be served on non-parties. 10 INPRAC § 65.1. There is no requirement that the party served shall be an "adverse" party. 2A INPRAC R 33(33.2).

e. *Submission to personal jurisdiction.* Under the current trial rules, discovery is self-executing and interrogatories are not filed with the court, but retained by the originating party until a discovery dispute arises or the discovery is needed for proceedings before the court. As such, Indiana courts have had to revisit the issue of whether a party's mere service of interrogatories constitutes a waiver of an objection to the court's personal jurisdiction over that party. 22 INPRAC § 23.14.

   i. In Alberts v. Mack Trucks, Inc., the defendant served interrogatories before asserting a challenge to the court's personal jurisdiction. In ruling that serving interrogatories did not constitute a waiver of personal jurisdiction, the Indiana Court of Appeals noted the amendments to the Indiana Rules of Trial Procedure, which no longer require a party to file interrogatories with the court. Accordingly, the court held: By sending interrogatories to Alberts' counsel, NSC did not submit to the personal jurisdiction of the court. Jurisdiction will not be found to be waived until a party affirmatively uses the court's procedure, such as in a motion to compel answers to interrogatories. 22 INPRAC § 23.14; Alberts v. Mack Trucks, Inc., 540 N.E.2d 1268, 1271-72 (Ind.Ct.App. 1989).

    ii. Therefore, merely serving interrogatories upon an opposing party before challenging the court's personal jurisdiction over a defendant should not result in a waiver of the jurisdictional issue unless the party otherwise affirmatively uses the court's resources. 22 INPRAC § 23.14.

  f. *Motion to compel discovery.* The party submitting the interrogatories may move for an order under IN ST TRIAL P Rule 37(A) with respect to any objection to or other failure to answer an interrogatory. IN ST TRIAL P Rule 33(C). Refer to the Indiana KeyRules Motion to Compel Discovery document for more information.

3. *Response to interrogatories*

  a. *Form of objections.* Answers or objections to interrogatories shall include the interrogatory which is being answered or to which an objection is made. The interrogatory which is being answered or objected to shall be placed immediately preceding the answer or objection. IN ST TRIAL P Rule 33(B); IN ST MARION CIR AND SUPER CTS CIV Rule 213(B).

  b. *Form of answer.* Each interrogatory shall be answered separately and fully in writing under oath, unless it is objected to, in which event the reasons for objections shall be stated in lieu of an answer. The answers are to be signed by the person making them, and the objections signed by the attorney making them. IN ST TRIAL P Rule 33(B).

  c. *Objections.* In addition to the objection that the matter is privileged, interrogatories may be objected to on the ground that they are not within the scope of discovery which is defined in IN ST TRIAL P Rule 26(B) because they seek information that is not relevant to the subject matter in the pending litigation, or that the requisite showing under IN ST TRIAL P Rule 26(B) has not been made, or that the information is held by experts and it is not discoverable except as permitted under IN ST TRIAL P Rule 26(B)(4). 2A INPRAC R 33(33.4). Objections to interrogatories must be specific. Common objections include (1) relevancy; (2) vague and ambiguous; (3) unduly burdensome; and (4) excessive in number. 10 INPRAC § 65.2.

    i. *Objections to form.* The party upon whom the interrogatories have been served may object to the failure to follow the Format requirements in IN ST TRIAL P Rule 33(B) by returning the interrogatories to the party who caused them to be served. If this objection is to be made, the interrogatories shall be returned to the party who caused them to be served not later than the seventh (7th) day after they were received. If the interrogatories are not returned in that time, then this objection is waived. IN ST TRIAL P Rule 33(C).

    ii. *Information not available.* If the objecting party takes the position that the information is not available, it is that party's burden to show that it is not available. 2A INPRAC R 33(33.4).

      • As a general rule, a party may not refuse to answer an interrogatory on the ground that the information is not in his possession, in the sense that the party would have to consult books and records in order to answer. 2A INPRAC R 33(33.4); Flour Mills of America, Inc. v. Pace, 75 F.R.D. 676, 680 (E.D.Okl. 1977).

      • An interrogatory seeking information in the possession of the party's employee is not objectionable if the questions call for answers which could be readily obtained by the person answering the interrogatory. 2A INPRAC R 33(33.4); Ballard v. Allegheny Airlines, Inc., 54 F.R.D. 67 (E.D.Pa. 1972).

    iii. *Broad, burdensome, numerous.* An objection is permitted if the interrogatory is too broad, or too burdensome, or too many in the number and kinds of questions which are asked. 2A INPRAC R 33(33.4); Flour Mills of America, Inc. v. Pace, 75 F.R.D. 676, 680 (E.D.Okl. 1977); In re U.S. Financial Securities Litigation, 74 F.R.D. 497 (S.D.Cal. 1975).

    iv. *Other objections.* An interrogatory otherwise proper is not objectionable merely because an answer to the interrogatory involves an opinion, contention, or legal conclusion, but the court may order that such an interrogatory be answered at a later time, or after designated discovery has been completed, or at a pre-trial conference. IN ST TRIAL P Rule 33(D).

- However, a party may not be forced to prepare his opponent's case for him. If the interrogatory would require a party to make extensive investigations, research, or compilation of data, it is an improper interrogatory, and it is burdensome and should be disallowed in a motion for a protective order. 2A INPRAC R 33(33.4); Halder v. International Telephone & Telegraph Co., 75 F.R.D. 657 (E.D.N.Y. 1977). Refer to the Indiana KeyRules Motion for Protective Order document for more information.

d. *Signature of responses.* The party served shall answer and sign the answer, and the attorney for the party served shall sign the objections. Both are then returned to the party taking the interrogatory. 2A INPRAC R 33(33.8).

   i. An unsigned and unverified response does not qualify as an answer to an interrogatory and generally may not be used as such. 22 INPRAC § 23.6; Cabales v. U.S., 51 F.R.D. 498 (S.D.N.Y. 1970).

e. *Option to produce business records.* Where the answer to an interrogatory may be derived or ascertained from the business records of the party upon whom the interrogatory has been served or from an examination, audit or inspection of such business records, including a compilation, abstract or summary thereof, and the burden of deriving or ascertaining the answer is substantially the same for the party serving the interrogatory as for the party served, it is a sufficient answer to such interrogatory to specify the records from which the answer may be derived or ascertained and to afford to the party serving the interrogatory reasonable opportunity to examine, audit or inspect such records and to make copies, compilations, abstracts or summaries. A specification shall be in sufficient detail to permit the interrogating party to locate and to identify, as readily as can the party served, the records from which the answer may be ascertained. IN ST TRIAL P Rule 33(E).

f. *Supplementation of responses.* A party who has responded to a request for discovery with a response that was complete when made is under no duty to supplement his response to include information thereafter acquired, except as follows:

   i. A party is under a duty seasonably to supplement his response with respect to any question directly addressed to:

      - The identity and location of persons having knowledge of discoverable matters, and

      - The identity of each person expected to be called as an expert witness at trial, the subject-matter on which he is expected to testify, and the substance of his testimony. IN ST TRIAL P Rule 26(E)(1).

   ii. A party is under a duty seasonably to amend a prior response if he obtains information upon the basis of which:

      - He knows that the response was incorrect when made, or

      - He knows that the response though correct when made is no longer true and the circumstances are such that a failure to amend the response is in substance a knowing concealment. IN ST TRIAL P Rule 26(E)(2).

   iii. A duty to supplement responses may be imposed by order of the court, agreement of the parties, or at any time prior to trial through new requests for supplementation of prior responses. IN ST TRIAL P Rule 26(E)(3).

   iv. The duty seasonably to supplement a discovery response is absolute and is not predicated on a court order. "It is a breach of a litigant's duty reasonably to supplement if the litigant postpones supplementing its response by not obtaining from its experts the information which is to be supplied in answer to interrogatories." 2A INPRAC R 26(26.27); Lucas v. Dorsey Corp., 609 N.E.2d 1191, 1196 (Ind.Ct.App. 1993).

D. Documents

1. *Required documents*

   a. *Interrogatories.* Refer to the General Requirements section of this document for information on the scope and content of interrogatories.

b. *Certificate of service.* An attorney or unrepresented party tendering a document to the Clerk for filing shall certify that service has been made, list the parties served, and specify the date and means of service. The certificate of service shall be placed at the end of the document and shall not be separately filed. The separate filing of a certificate of service, however, shall not be grounds for rejecting a document for filing. The Clerk may permit documents to be filed without a certificate of service but shall require prompt filing of a separate certificate of service. IN ST TRIAL P Rule 5(C). In all cases where any pleading or other document is required to be served upon opposing counsel, proof of such service may be made either by:

  i. A certificate of service signed by counsel of record for the serving party and the certificate shall specify by name and address all counsel upon whom the pleading or document was served; or

  ii. An acknowledgment of service signed by the party served or counsel of record. IN ST MARION CIR AND SUPER CTS CIV Rule 206.

2. *Supplemental documents*

  a. *Stipulation regarding discovery procedure.* Unless the court orders otherwise, the parties may by written stipulation:

    i. Provide that depositions may be taken before any person, at any time or place, upon any notice, and in any manner and when so taken may be used like other depositions, and

    ii. Modify the procedures provided by the Indiana Rules of Trial Procedure for other methods of discovery. IN ST TRIAL P Rule 29.

  b. *Facsimile cover sheet.* Any document sent to the Clerk of the Circuit Court by electronic facsimile transmission shall be accompanied by a cover sheet which states the title of the document, case number, number of pages, identity and voice telephone number of the sending party and instructions for filing. The cover sheet shall contain the signature of the attorney or party, pro se, authorizing the filing. IN ST ADMIN Rule 12(D).

E. Format

1. *Format of interrogatories.* The rules applicable to captions, and the signing and form of pleadings (IN ST TRIAL P Rule 8 through IN ST TRIAL P Rule 11), apply to all motions and other papers provided under the Indiana Rules of Trial Procedure. 22B INPRAC 7:2. A party who serves written interrogatories under IN ST TRIAL P Rule 33 shall provide, after each interrogatory, a reasonable amount of space for a response or an objection. IN ST TRIAL P Rule 33(B).

  a. An interrogatory should pose a single direct question phrased in a manner that will advise the responding party what information is requested of him. 22 INPRAC § 23.5.

  b. An interrogatory may be divided into separate paragraphs and subparagraphs. The paragraphs should be identified as "1," "2," or "3"; or as "Interrogatory No. 1," "Interrogatory No. 2," etc. 22 INPRAC § 23.5.

2. *Form of pleadings*

  a. *Caption; Names of parties.* Every pleading shall contain a caption setting forth the name of the court, the title of the action, the file number, and a designation as in IN ST TRIAL P Rule 7(A). In the complaint the title of the action shall include the names of all the parties, but in other pleadings it is sufficient to state the name of the first party on each side with an appropriate indication of other parties. IN ST TRIAL P Rule 10(A).

    i. Every pleading shall contain a caption setting forth the name of the Court, the Division and Room Number, the title of the action and the file number. IN ST MARION CIR AND SUPER CTS CIV Rule 204(B).

  b. *Paragraphs; Separate statements.* All averments of a claim or defense shall be made in numbered paragraphs, the contents of each of which shall be limited as far as practicable to a statement of a single set of circumstances, and a paragraph may be referred to by number in all succeeding pleadings. Each claim founded upon a separate transaction or occurrence and each defense other than denials may be stated in a separate count or defense whenever a separation facilitates the clear presentation of the matters set forth. IN ST TRIAL P Rule 10(B).

c. *Adoption by reference; Exhibits.* Statements in a pleading may be adopted by reference in a different part of the same pleading or in another pleading or in any motion. A copy of any written instrument which is an exhibit to a pleading is a part thereof for all purposes. IN ST TRIAL P Rule 10(C).

d. *Paper.* Pleadings, motions and other papers may be either printed or typewritten on white opaque paper of at least sixteen (16) pound weight, eight and one-half (8-1/2) inches wide and eleven (11) inches in length. IN ST MARION CIR AND SUPER CTS CIV Rule 204(A).

e. *Copies.* All copies shall likewise be on white paper of sufficient strength and durability to resist normal wear and tear. IN ST MARION CIR AND SUPER CTS CIV Rule 204(A).

f. *Line spacing.* If typewritten, the lines shall be double spaced, except for quotations, which shall be indented and single spaced. IN ST MARION CIR AND SUPER CTS CIV Rule 204(A).

g. *Script type.* Script type shall not be used. IN ST MARION CIR AND SUPER CTS CIV Rule 204(A).

h. *Titles.* Titles on all pleadings shall delineate each topic included in the pleading e.g. where a pleading contains an Answer, a Motion to Strike or Dismiss, or a Jury Request each shall be set forth in the title. IN ST MARION CIR AND SUPER CTS CIV Rule 204(C).

i. *Margins and binding.* Margins shall be one (1) inch. Binding or stapling shall be at the top and at no other place. Covers or backing shall not be used. IN ST MARION CIR AND SUPER CTS CIV Rule 204(D).

3. *Size of papers for filing.* Effective January 1, 1992, all pleadings, copies, motions and documents filed with any trial court or appellate level court, typed or printed, with the exception of exhibits and existing wills, shall be prepared on eight and one-half by eleven inch (8 1/2" x 11") size paper. IN ST ADMIN Rule 11.

4. *Form of electronically filed documents.* All electronically filed and served pleadings shall, to the extent practicable, be formatted in accordance with the applicable rules governing formatting of paper pleadings. IN ST MARION SUPER CT ADMIN Rule 311(2-103)(1).

   a. *Electronic document title.* The electronic document title of each pleading or other document shall include:

      i. Party or parties filing/serving the document,

      ii. Nature of the document,

      iii. Party or parties against whom relief, if any, is sought, and

      iv. Nature of the relief sought (e.g., Defendant ABC Corporation's Motion for Summary Judgment). IN ST MARION SUPER CT ADMIN Rule 311(2-103)(2).

5. *Signature requirements*

   a. *Signature of attorney.* Every pleading or motion of a party represented by an attorney shall be signed by at least one (1) attorney of record in his individual name, whose address, telephone number, and attorney number shall be stated, except that this provision shall not apply to pleadings and motions made and transcribed at the trial or a hearing before the judge and received by him in such form. IN ST TRIAL P Rule 11(A).

      i. All pleadings and motions shall contain the original or authorized signature of the attorney, the name of the attorney in typed or printed form, the name of the law firm if a member of a firm, the attorney's address, identification number, e-mail address, telephone number, fax number, and the designation as to the party for whom he appears. IN ST MARION CIR AND SUPER CTS CIV Rule 204(E).

      ii. The signature of an attorney constitutes a certificate by him that he has read the pleadings; that to the best of his knowledge, information, and belief, there is good ground to support it; and that it is not interposed for delay. IN ST TRIAL P Rule 11(A).

      iii. If a pleading or motion is not signed or is signed with intent to defeat the purpose of the rule, it may be stricken as sham and false and the action may proceed as though the pleading had not been served. IN ST TRIAL P Rule 11(A).

      iv. For a willful violation of IN ST TRIAL P Rule 11 an attorney may be subjected to appropriate

disciplinary action. Similar action may be taken if scandalous or indecent matter is inserted. IN ST TRIAL P Rule 11(A).

v. Every pleading, document, and instrument electronically filed or served shall be deemed to have been signed by the judge, clerk, attorney or declarant and shall bear a facsimile or typographical signature of such person, along with the typed name, address, telephone number, and Bar number of a signing attorney. Typographical signatures shall be treated as personal signatures for all purposes under these rules. IN ST MARION SUPER CT ADMIN Rule 311(2-105).

- Documents containing signatures of third-parties (i.e., unopposed motions, affidavits, stipulations, etc.) may also be filed electronically by indicating that the original signatures are maintained by the filing party in paper-format. IN ST MARION SUPER CT ADMIN Rule 311(2-105).

- Unless otherwise ordered by the Court or Clerk, a printed copy of all documents filed or served electronically, including original signatures, shall be maintained by the party filing the document and shall be made available, upon reasonable notice, for inspection by other counsel, the Clerk or Court. Parties shall retain originals until two (2) years after all time periods for appeal have expired. From time to time, it may be necessary to provide the Clerk or Court with a hard copy of an electronically filed document. IN ST MARION SUPER CT ADMIN Rule 311(2-105).

vi. For the recommended format of a signature block, refer to IN ST MARION CIR AND SUPER CTS CIV Rule 204(E).

b. *Signature of unrepresented party.* A party who is not represented by an attorney shall sign his pleading and state his address. IN ST TRIAL P Rule 11(A).

c. *Verification not generally required.* Except when specifically required by rule, pleadings or motions need not be verified or accompanied by affidavit. The rule in equity that the averments of an answer under oath must be overcome by the testimony of two (2) witnesses or of one (1) witness sustained by corroborating circumstances is abolished. IN ST TRIAL P Rule 11(A).

d. *Verification by affirmation or representation.* When in connection with any civil or special statutory proceeding it is required that any pleading, motion, petition, supporting affidavit, or other document of any kind, be verified, or that an oath be taken, it shall be sufficient if the subscriber simply affirms the truth of the matter to be verified by an affirmation or representation. IN ST TRIAL P Rule 11(B). IN ST TRIAL P Rule 11(B) states that the affirmation or representation should be in substantially the following language: "I (we) affirm, under the penalties for perjury, that the foregoing representation(s) is (are) true. (Signed) _____."

i. Any person who falsifies an affirmation or representation of fact shall be subject to the same penalties as are prescribed by law for the making of a false affidavit. IN ST TRIAL P Rule 11(B).

e. *Verified pleadings, motions, and affidavits as evidence.* Pleadings, motions and affidavits accompanying or in support of such pleadings or motions when required to be verified or under oath shall be accepted as a representation that the signer had personal knowledge thereof or reasonable cause to believe the existence of the facts or matters stated or alleged therein; and, if otherwise competent or acceptable as evidence, may be admitted as evidence of the facts or matters stated or alleged therein when it is so provided in the Indiana Rules of Trial Procedure, by statute or other law, or to the extent the writing or signature expressly purports to be made upon the signer's personal knowledge. When such pleadings, motions and affidavits are verified or under oath they shall not require other or greater proof on the part of the adverse party than if not verified or not under oath unless expressly provided otherwise by the Indiana Rules of Trial Procedure, statute or other law. Affidavits upon motions for summary judgment under IN ST TRIAL P Rule 56 and in denial of execution under IN ST TRIAL P Rule 9.2 shall be made upon personal knowledge. IN ST TRIAL P Rule 11(C).

6. *Information excluded from public access.* Every document filed in a case shall separately identify information excluded from public access pursuant to IN ST ADMIN Rule 9(G)(1) as follows:

a. Whole documents that are excluded from public access pursuant to IN ST ADMIN Rule 9(G)(1)

INTERROGATORIES

shall be tendered on light green paper or have a light green coversheet attached to the document, marked "Not for Public Access" or "Confidential." IN ST TRIAL P Rule 5(G)(1).

b. When only a portion of a document contains information excluded from public access pursuant to IN ST ADMIN Rule 9(G)(1), said information shall be omitted [or redacted] from the filed document, and set forth on a separate accompanying document on light green paper conspicuously marked "Not for Public Access" or "Confidential" and clearly designated [or identifying] the caption and number of the case and the document and location within the document to which the redacted material pertains. IN ST TRIAL P Rule 5(G)(2).

c. With respect to documents filed in electronic format, the trial court, by local rule, may provide for compliance with IN ST TRIAL P Rule 5 in manner that separates and protects access to information excluded from public access. IN ST TRIAL P Rule 5(G)(3).

d. IN ST TRIAL P Rule 5(G) does not apply to a record sealed by the court pursuant to IN ST 5-14-3-5.5 or otherwise, nor to records, documents, or information filed in cases to which public access is prohibited pursuant to IN ST ADMIN Rule 9(G). IN ST TRIAL P Rule 5(G)(4).

e. The following information in case records is excluded from public access and is confidential:

  i. Information that is excluded from public access pursuant to federal law;

  ii. Information that is excluded from public access as declared confidential by Indiana statute or other court rule, including without limitation:

  - All adoption records created after July 8, 1941, as declared confidential by IN ST 31-19-19-1, et seq., except those specifically declared open by IN ST 31-19-13-2(2);

  - All records relating to chancroid, chlamydia, gonorrhea, hepatitis, human immunodeficiency virus (HIV), Lymphogranuloma venereum, syphilis, tuberculosis, as declared confidential by IN ST 16-41-8-1, et seq.;

  - All records relating to child abuse as declared confidential by IN ST 31-33-18-1, et seq.;

  - All records relating to drug tests as declared confidential by IN ST 5-14-3-4(a)(9);

  - Records of grand jury proceedings as declared confidential by IN ST 35-34-2-4;

  - Records of juvenile proceedings as declared confidential by IN ST 31-39-1-2, except those specifically open under statute;

  - All paternity records created after July 1, 1941 as declared confidential by IN ST 31-14-11-15, IN ST 31-19-5-23, IN ST 31-39-1-1 and IN ST 31-39-1-2 [Editor's note: IN ST 31-14-11-15 was repealed effective May 9, 2013];

  - All pre-sentence reports as declared confidential by IN ST 35-38-1-13;

  - Written petitions to permit marriages without consent and orders directing the Clerk of Court to issue a marriage license to underage persons, as declared confidential by IN ST 31-11-1-6;

  - Only those arrest warrants, search warrants, indictments and informations ordered confidential by the trial judge, prior to return of duly executed service as declared confidential by IN ST 5-14-3-4(b)(1);

  - All medical, mental health, or tax records unless determined by law or regulation of any governmental custodian not to be confidential, released by the subject of such records, or declared by a court of competent jurisdiction to be essential to the resolution of litigation as declared confidential by IN ST 16-39-3-10, IN ST 6-4.1-5-10, IN ST 6-4.1-12-12, and IN ST 6-8.1-7-1;

  - Personal information relating to jurors or prospective jurors, other than for the use of the parties and counsel, pursuant to IN ST JURY Rule 10;

  - Information relating to protection from abuse orders, no-contact orders and workplace violence restraining orders as declared confidential by IN ST 5-2-9-6, et seq.;

  - Mediation proceedings pursuant to IN ST ADR Rule 2.11, Mini-Trial proceedings pursuant to IN ST ADR Rule 4.4(C), and Summary Jury Trials pursuant to IN ST ADR Rule 5.6;

- Information in probation files pursuant to the Probation Standards promulgated by the Judicial Conference of Indiana pursuant to IN ST 11-13-1-8(b);

- Information deemed confidential pursuant to the Rules for Court Administered Alcohol and Drug Programs promulgated by the Judicial Conference of Indiana pursuant to IN ST 12-23-14-13;

- Information deemed confidential pursuant to the Problem-Solving Court Rules promulgated by the Judicial Conference of Indiana pursuant to IN ST 33-23-16-16;

- All records of the Department of workforce Development as declared confidential by IN ST 22-4-19-6;

- Information regarding interception of electronic communications that is sealed or deemed confidential as set forth in IN ST 35-33.5-2-1, et seq.

iii. Information excluded from public access by specific court order;

iv. Complete Social Security Numbers of living persons;

v. With the exception of names, information such as addresses, phone numbers, and dates of birth which explicitly identifies:

- Natural persons who are witnesses or victims (not including defendants) in criminal, domestic violence, stalking, sexual assault, juvenile, or civil protection order proceedings, provided that juveniles who are victims of sex crimes shall be identified by initials only;

- Places of residence of judicial officers, clerks and other employees of courts and clerks of court, unless the person or persons about whom the information pertains waives confidentiality;

vi. Complete account numbers of specific assets, loans, bank accounts, credit cards, and personal identification numbers (PINs);

vii. All orders of expungement entered in criminal or juvenile proceedings, orders to restrict access to criminal history information pursuant to IN ST 35-38-5-5.5 or IN ST 35-38-8-5 and records excluded from public access by such orders, and information related to infractions that is excluded from public access pursuant to IN ST 34-28-5-15 or IN ST 34-28-5-16 [Editor's note: IN ST 35-38-5-5.5, IN ST 35-38-8-5 and IN ST 34-28-5-16 were repealed effective July 1, 2013; for information on orders restricting access to criminal history, refer to IN ST 35-38-9-1, et seq.];

viii. All personal notes and e-mail, and deliberative material, of judges, jurors, court staff and judicial agencies, and information recorded in personal data assistants (PDA's) or organizers and personal calendars. IN ST ADMIN Rule 9(G)(1).

F. Filing and Service Requirements

1. *Filing requirements.* Except as otherwise provided in IN ST TRIAL P Rule 5(E)(2), all pleadings and papers subsequent to the complaint which are required to be served upon a party shall be filed with the Court either before service or within a reasonable period of time thereafter. IN ST TRIAL P Rule 5(E)(1).

a. *Non-filing of discovery until necessary*

i. *Non-filing of discovery; Exceptions.* No deposition or request for discovery or response thereto under IN ST TRIAL P Rule 27, IN ST TRIAL P Rule 30, IN ST TRIAL P Rule 31, IN ST TRIAL P Rule 33, IN ST TRIAL P Rule 34 or IN ST TRIAL P Rule 36 shall be filed with the Court unless:

- A motion is filed pursuant to IN ST TRIAL P Rule 26(C) or IN ST TRIAL P Rule 37 and the original deposition or request for discovery or response thereto is necessary to enable the Court to rule; or

- A party desires to use the deposition or request for discovery or response thereto for evidentiary purposes at trial or in connection with a motion, and the Court, either upon its own motion or that of any party, or as a part of any pre-trial order, orders the filing of the original. IN ST TRIAL P Rule 5(E)(2).

ii. *Custody of original and period of retention*

- The original of a deposition shall, subject to the provisions of IN ST TRIAL P Rule 30(E), be delivered by the reporter to the party taking it and shall be maintained by that party until filed with the Court pursuant to IN ST TRIAL P Rule 5(E)(2) or until the later of final judgment, agreed settlement of the litigation or all appellate rights have been exhausted. IN ST TRIAL P Rule 5(E)(3)(a).

- The original or any request for discovery or response thereto under IN ST TRIAL P Rule 27, IN ST TRIAL P Rule 30, IN ST TRIAL P Rule 31, IN ST TRIAL P Rule 33, IN ST TRIAL P Rule 34 and IN ST TRIAL P Rule 36 shall be maintained by the party originating the request or response until filed with the Court pursuant to IN ST TRIAL P Rule 5(E)(2) or until the later of final judgment, agreed settlement or all appellate rights have been exhausted. IN ST TRIAL P Rule 5(E)(3)(b).

iii. *Original unavailable; Copies.* In the event it is made to appear to the satisfaction of the Court that the original of a deposition or request for discovery or response thereto cannot be filed with the Court when required, the Court may allow use of a copy instead of the original. IN ST TRIAL P Rule 5(E)(4).

iv. *Filing as publication.* The filing of any deposition shall constitute publication. IN ST TRIAL P Rule 5(E)(5).

b. *Filing generally.* All pleadings, petitions and motions are filed with the Clerk designated by the Court at any time during office hours established by the Clerk and the Court. All orders submitted to the Court shall be in sufficient number and shall be accompanied by postage paid envelopes addressed to each party or counsel of record. IN ST MARION CIR AND SUPER CTS CIV Rule 205(A)

c. *Filing with the court defined.* The filing of pleadings, motions, and other papers with the court as required by the Indiana Rules of Trial Procedure shall be made by one of the following methods:

i. Delivery to the clerk of the court;

ii. Sending by electronic transmission under the procedure adopted pursuant to IN ST ADMIN Rule 12;

iii. Mailing to the clerk by registered, certified or express mail return receipt requested;

iv. Depositing with any third-party commercial carrier for delivery to the clerk within three (3) calendar days, cost prepaid, properly addressed;

v. If the court so permits, filing with the judge, in which event the judge shall note thereon the filing date and forthwith transmit them to the office of the clerk; or

vi. Electronic filing, as approved by the Division of State Court Administration pursuant to IN ST ADMIN Rule 16. IN ST TRIAL P Rule 5(F).

vii. Filing by registered or certified mail and by third-party commercial carrier shall be complete upon mailing or deposit. IN ST TRIAL P Rule 5(F).

d. *Facsimile filing.* Facsimile filing is discouraged, but permitted in the Marion Circuit and Marion Superior Court. All documents filed by facsimile shall also be filed in hard copy within seven (7) days of the facsimile filing, along with proposed orders and stamped addressed envelopes, as required by IN ST MARION CIR AND SUPER CTS CIV Rule 203(E). To avoid duplicate filings, the hard copies of the facsimile filing shall indicate in bold letters that the pleading was previously filed by facsimile transmission. Proof of transmission by facsimile, including certificate of service and manner of service, shall be the responsibility of the filing party. If the filing requires immediate attention of the Judge, it shall be so indicated in bold letters in an accompanying transmittal memorandum. Legibility of documents and timeliness of filing is the responsibility of the sender. IN ST MARION CIR AND SUPER CTS CIV Rule 205(B).

i. *Generally.* In counties where a majority of judges of the courts of record, by posted local rule,

have authorized electronic facsimile filing and designated a telephone number to receive such transmissions, pleadings, motions, and other papers may be sent to the Clerk of Circuit Court by electronic facsimile transmission for filing in any case, provided:

- Such matter does not exceed ten (10) pages, including the cover sheet;
- Such matter does not require the payment of fees other than the electronic facsimile transcription fee set forth in IN ST ADMIN Rule 12(E);
- The sending party creates at the time of transmission a machine generated log for such transmission; and
- The original document and the transmission log are maintained by the sending party for the duration of the litigation. IN ST ADMIN Rule 12(B).

ii. *Time of filing.* During normal, posted business hours, the time of filing shall be the time the duplicate document is produced in the office of the Clerk of the Circuit Court. Duplicate documents received at all other times shall be filed as of the next normal business day. IN ST ADMIN Rule 12(C).

- If the receiving fax machine endorses its own time and date stamp upon the transmitted documents and the receiving machine produces a delivery receipt which is electronically created and transmitted to the sending party, the time of filing shall be the date and time recorded on the transmitted document by the receiving fax machine. IN ST ADMIN Rule 12(C).

e. *Electronic filing.* Electronic filing and electronic service pilot projects are authorized pursuant to IN ST ADMIN Rule 16 and approved by the Division of State Court Administration. IN ST MARION SUPER CT ADMIN Rule 311(1-103).

i. *Cases where electronic filing accepted.* All Marion County Circuit and Superior civil courts may accept electronic filing and service of pleadings and other documents designated in this rule in mortgage foreclosure (hereinafter referred to as "MF"), civil collection(hereinafter referred to as "CC"), and individual cases that have been approved for electronic filing and service. IN ST MARION SUPER CT ADMIN Rule 311(1-104)(1).

- The Marion County Circuit Court may, upon the motion of a party or its own motion, designate a case that will involve multiple litigants, legally intricate issues, and an extensive number of documents a mass tort or complex litigation case. Any case so designated shall be subject to electronic filing and service using the county's approved Electronic Service Provider. IN ST MARION SUPER CT ADMIN Rule 311(1-104)(3).
- The filing of electronic pleadings and other documents in MF and CC cases is entirely voluntary; however, once the case is initially filed electronically, all subsequent filings in the case shall remain in electronic format until the time for appeal is exhausted. IN ST MARION SUPER CT ADMIN Rule 311(1-104)(5).

ii. *Documents eligible for electronic filing.* The following pleadings may be filed and served electronically:

- New case complaint and petitions. IN ST MARION SUPER CT ADMIN Rule 311(1-104)(8)(a).
- Original answers. IN ST MARION SUPER CT ADMIN Rule 311(1-104)(8)(a).
- Any other pleadings or document including but not limited to motions and appearance forms. IN ST MARION SUPER CT ADMIN Rule 311(1-104)(8)(a).

iii. *Manner of electronic filing.* Parties shall E-file a document either:

- By registering to use the Electronic Filing Service Provider; or
- In person at the Marion County Clerk's office, by electronically filing through the Public Access Terminal. Parties filing in this manner shall be responsible for furnishing the document in an electronic format that will be compatible with the clerk's office-system to be uploaded in person. IN ST MARION SUPER CT ADMIN Rule 311(1-104)(9). For

information on the Electronic Filing Service Provider and Public Access Terminal, refer to IN ST MARION SUPER CT ADMIN Rule 311(1-101).

- Registered users shall pay statutory filing fees for E-filed documents electronically to the Court through their EFSP. Filing fees are due and payable at the time of filing. IN ST MARION SUPER CT ADMIN Rule 311(2-104)(1). For more information on electronic filing fees, refer to IN ST MARION SUPER CT ADMIN Rule 311(2-104).

iv. *Effect of electronic filing.* Any pleading filed electronically shall be considered as filed with the court when the transmission to the EFSP is complete. Any document E-filed by 11:59 p.m. local Indianapolis, Indiana time shall be deemed filed on that date. The EFSP is an agent of the Court for the purpose of electronic filing, receipt, service and retrieval of electronic documents. IN ST MARION SUPER CT ADMIN Rule 311(2-102).

- Upon completion of filing, the EFSP shall issue a confirmation receipt that includes the date and time of receipt. The confirmation receipt shall serve as proof of filing. IN ST MARION SUPER CT ADMIN Rule 311(2-102).

- In the event the Court rejects the submitted documents following review, the documents shall not become part of the official Court record and the filer will receive notification of the rejection. Users may be required to refile the instruments to meet necessary filing requirements. Documents may be filed through an E-filing system at any time that the Clerk's office is open to receive the filing or at such other times as may be designated by the clerk and posted publicly. IN ST MARION SUPER CT ADMIN Rule 311(2-102).

- Documents filed through the E-filing system are deemed filed when received by the Clerk's office, except that documents received at times that the Clerk's office is closed shall be deemed filed the next regular time when the Clerk's office is open for filing. The time stamp issued by the E-filing system shall be presumed to be the time the document is received by the Clerk. IN ST MARION SUPER CT ADMIN Rule 311(2-102).

v. *Electronically filed documents.* All pleadings and other documents designated in IN ST MARION SUPER CT ADMIN Rule 311 shall be filed and served electronically in any individual case which has been approved for electronic filing and service. IN ST MARION SUPER CT ADMIN Rule 311(1-104)(6).

vi. *System failures.* When filing by electronic means is hindered by a technical failure, a party may file with the Clerk of Marion County in hard copy. With the exception of deadlines that by law cannot be extended, the time for filing of any paper that is delayed due to technical failure of the site shall be extended for one (1) day for each day on which such failure occurs, unless otherwise ordered by the Court. IN ST MARION SUPER CT ADMIN Rule 311(2-108).

vii. *Compliance with rules.* All filing shall comply with the requirements of IN ST ADMIN Rule 9 and IN ST ADMIN Rule 16; and the Indiana Rules of Court and the Marion County Local Rules. IN ST MARION SUPER CT ADMIN Rule 311(1-104)(11).

f. *Filing for special judge.* When a Special Judge who is not a Marion County Judge is selected, all parties or attorneys shall furnish such Judge with copies of all filings prior to the qualification of such Special Judge. Thereafter, copies of all filings shall be delivered in person, by mail or by facsimile to the office of the Special Judge with certificate of forwarding same made a part of the filing. IN ST MARION CIR AND SUPER CTS CIV Rule 205(C).

g. *Proof of filing.* Any party filing any paper by any method other than personal delivery to the clerk shall retain proof of filing. IN ST TRIAL P Rule 5(F).

2. *Service requirements.* Unless otherwise provided by the Indiana Rules of Trial Procedure or an order of the court, each party and special judge, if any, shall be served with: (1) every order required by its terms to be served; (2) every pleading subsequent to the original complaint; (3) every written motion except one which may be heard ex parte; (4) every brief submitted to the trial court; (5) every paper relating to discovery required to be served upon a party; and (6) every written notice, appearance, demand, offer of judgment, designation of record on appeal, or similar paper. IN ST TRIAL P Rule 5(A).

a. *Methods of service*

i. *Personal service.* Whenever a party is represented by an attorney of record, service shall be

made upon such attorney unless service upon the party himself is ordered by the court. Service upon the attorney or party shall be made by delivering or mailing a copy of the papers to the last known address or where an attorney or party has consented to service by fax or e-mail, as provided in IN ST TRIAL P Rule 3.1(A)(4), by faxing or e-mailing a copy of the documents to the fax number or e-mail address set out in the appearance form or correction as required by IN ST TRIAL P Rule 3.1(E). IN ST TRIAL P Rule 5(B). Delivery of a copy within IN ST TRIAL P Rule 5 means:

- Offering or tendering it to the attorney or party and stating the nature of the papers being served. Refusal to accept an offered or tendered document is a waiver of any objection to the sufficiency or adequacy of service of that document;

- Leaving it at his office with a clerk or other person in charge thereof, or if there is no one in charge, leaving it in a conspicuous place therein; or

- If the office is closed, by leaving it at his dwelling house or usual place of abode with some person of suitable age and discretion then residing therein; or,

- Leaving it at some other suitable place, selected by the attorney upon whom service is being made, pursuant to duly promulgated local rule. IN ST TRIAL P Rule 5(B)(1).

ii. *Service by mail.* If service is made by mail, the papers shall be deposited in the United States mail addressed to the person on whom they are being served, with postage prepaid. Service shall be deemed complete upon mailing. Proof of service of all papers permitted to be mailed may be made by written acknowledgment of service, by affidavit of the person who mailed the papers, or by certificate of an attorney. It shall be the duty of attorneys when entering their appearance in a cause or when filing pleadings or papers therein, to have noted in the Chronological Case Summary or said pleadings or papers so filed the address and telephone number of their office. Service by delivery or by mail at such address shall be deemed sufficient and complete. IN ST TRIAL P Rule 5(B)(2).

iii. *Service by fax or e-mail.* A party who has consented to service by fax or e-mail may be served as follows:

- Service by e-mail shall be made by attaching the document being served in .pdf format. Discovery documents must also be served in accordance with IN ST TRIAL P Rule 26(A). IN ST TRIAL P Rule 5(B)(3)(a).

- Service by fax shall be deemed complete upon generation of a transmission record indicating the successful transmission of the entire document, except as provided in IN ST TRIAL P Rule 5(B)(3)(d). IN ST TRIAL P Rule 5(B)(3)(b).

- Service by e-mail shall be deemed complete upon transmission, except as provided in IN ST TRIAL P Rule 5(B)(3)(d). IN ST TRIAL P Rule 5(B)(3)(c).

- Service by fax or e-mail that occurs on a Saturday, Sunday, legal holiday, or day the court or agency in which the matter is pending is closed or after 5:00 PM local time of the recipient shall be deemed complete the next day that is not a Saturday, Sunday, legal holiday, or day that the court or agency in which the matter is pending is not closed. IN ST TRIAL P Rule 5(B)(3)(d).

iv. *Electronic service.* Delivery of E-service documents through the EFSP to other registered users shall be considered as valid and effective service and shall have the same legal effect as an original paper document. Recipients of E-service documents shall access their documents through the EFSP. IN ST MARION SUPER CT ADMIN Rule 311(2-107)(1).

- E-service shall be deemed complete when the transmission to the EFSP is completed. IN ST MARION SUPER CT ADMIN Rule 311(2-107)(2).

- For the purpose of computing time to respond to documents received via E-service, any document served on a day or at a time when the Clerk's office is not open for business shall be deemed served at the time of next opening of the Clerk's office for business. IN ST MARION SUPER CT ADMIN Rule 311(2-107)(3).

v. *Additional service of electronic discovery.* In addition to service under Rule IN ST TRIAL P Rule 5(B) or a .pdf format electronic copy, a party propounding or responding to interrogatories, requests for production or requests for admission shall comply with IN ST TRIAL P Rule 26(A.1)(a) or IN ST TRIAL P Rule 26(A.1)(b). IN ST TRIAL P Rule 26(A.1).

- The party shall serve the discovery request or response in an electronic format (either on a disk or as an electronic document attachment) in any commercially available word processing software system. If transmitted on disk, each disk shall be labeled, identifying the caption of the case, the document, and the word processing version in which it is being submitted. If more than one (1) disk is used for the same document, each disk shall be labeled and also shall be sequentially numbered. If transmitted by electronic mail, the document must be accompanied by electronic memorandum providing the forgoing identifying information; or

- The party shall serve the opposing party with a verified statement that the attorney or party appealing pro se lacks the equipment and is unable to transmit the discovery as required by IN ST TRIAL P Rule 26(A.1). IN ST TRIAL P Rule 26(A.1).

b. *Serving numerous defendants.* In any action in which there are unusually large numbers of defendants, the court, upon motion or of its own initiative, may order:

i. That service of the pleadings of the defendants and replies thereto need not be made as between the defendants;

- That any cross-claim, counterclaim, or matter constituting an avoidance or affirmative defense contained therein shall be deemed to be denied or avoided by all other parties; and

- That the filing of any such pleading and service thereof upon the plaintiff constitutes due notice of it to the parties. IN ST TRIAL P Rule 5(D).

ii. A copy of every such order shall be served upon the parties in such manner and form as the court directs. IN ST TRIAL P Rule 5(D).

c. *Service on parties in default for failure to appear.* No service need be made on parties in default for failure to appear, except that pleadings asserting new or additional claims for relief against them shall be served upon them in the manner provided by service of summons in IN ST TRIAL P Rule 4. IN ST TRIAL P Rule 5(A).

G. Hearings

1. The Indiana rules do not contemplate a hearing related to the filing and service of interrogatories.

H. Forms

1. Interrogatory Forms for Indiana

a. General form. 5 INPRAC § 4:2.10.

b. Motion to enlarge time to answer. 5 INPRAC § 4:2.20.

c. Answers and objections; General form. 5 INPRAC § 4:2.30.

d. Answer; General form with standard objections. 5 INPRAC § 4:2.40.

e. Answer; Offer to produce business records. 5 INPRAC § 4:2.50.

f. Sample interrogatories relating to electronically stored information. 5 INPRAC § 4:2.60.

g. Motion to seal answers to interrogatories. 10 INPRAC § 65.6.1.

h. Interrogatories; General form. 10 INPRAC § 65.7.

i. Interrogatories; Another form. 10 INPRAC § 65.8.

j. Interrogatory preliminary instructions; Comprehensive form. 10 INPRAC § 65.9.

k. Interrogatory preliminary instructions; Abbreviated form. 10 INPRAC § 65.10.

l. Interrogatory definitions. 10 INPRAC § 65.11.

m. Motion to enlarge time to answer interrogatories. 10 INPRAC § 65.12.

n. Motion for enlargement of time; Response due after discovery completed. 10 INPRAC § 65.13.

o. Motion to shorten time to respond to interrogatories. 10 INPRAC § 65.15.

p. Motion to strike interrogatories; Excessive number under local rules. 10 INPRAC § 65.16.

q. Interrogatories to determine minimum contacts with state. 10 INPRAC § 65.20.

r. Answers and objections to interrogatories; General form. 10 INPRAC § 65.30.

s. Answers and objections to interrogatories; Another form. 10 INPRAC § 65.31.

t. Standard objections to interrogatories; General form. 10 INPRAC § 65.32.

u. Standard objections to interrogatories. 10 INPRAC § 65.33.

v. Answer of interrogatory by offering to produce business records. 10 INPRAC § 65.34.

w. Motion to compel answers to interrogatories. 10 INPRAC § 65.35.

x. Attorney's signature as to objections; Alternate forms. 10 INPRAC § 65.36.

y. Conversion; Plaintiff's interrogatories. 10 INPRAC § 66.27.

z. Medical malpractice action. 10 INPRAC § 66.37.

I. Checklist

(I) ❑ Matters to be considered by the party serving the interrogatories

    (a) ❑ Required documents

        (1) ❑ Interrogatories

        (2) ❑ Certificate of service

    (b) ❑ Supplemental documents

        (1) ❑ Stipulation regarding discovery procedure

        (2) ❑ Facsimile cover sheet

    (c) ❑ Timing

        (1) ❑ Interrogatories may, without leave of court, be served upon the plaintiff after commencement of the action and upon any other party with or after service of the summons and complaint upon that party

(II) ❑ Matters to be considered by the responding party

    (a) ❑ Required documents

        (1) ❑ Response to interrogatories

        (2) ❑ Certificate of service

    (b) ❑ Supplemental documents

        (1) ❑ Business records

        (2) ❑ Stipulation regarding discovery procedure

        (3) ❑ Facsimile cover sheet

    (c) ❑ Timing

        (1) ❑ The party upon whom the interrogatories have been served shall serve a copy of the answers and objections within a period designated by the party submitting the interrogatories, not less than thirty (30) days after the service thereof or within such shorter or longer time as the court may allow

Requests, Notices and Applications
Request for Production of Documents

Document Last Updated October 2013

A. Applicable Rules

1. *State rules*

   a. Appearance. IN ST TRIAL P Rule 3.1.

   b. Process. IN ST TRIAL P Rule 4.

   c. Service and filing of pleadings and other papers. IN ST TRIAL P Rule 5.

   d. Time. IN ST TRIAL P Rule 6.

   e. Pleadings. IN ST TRIAL P Rule 7; IN ST TRIAL P Rule 9.2; IN ST TRIAL P Rule 10.

   f. Signing and verification of pleadings. IN ST TRIAL P Rule 11.

   g. General provisions governing discovery. IN ST TRIAL P Rule 26.

   h. Methods of discovery. IN ST TRIAL P Rule 27.

   i. Depositions and discovery. IN ST TRIAL P Rule 29; IN ST TRIAL P Rule 30; IN ST TRIAL P Rule 31; IN ST TRIAL P Rule 33; IN ST TRIAL P Rule 34; IN ST TRIAL P Rule 35; IN ST TRIAL P Rule 36.

   j. Failure to make or cooperate in discovery; Sanctions. IN ST TRIAL P Rule 37.

   k. Subpoena. IN ST TRIAL P Rule 45.

   l. Judgment on the evidence (directed verdict). IN ST TRIAL P Rule 50.

   m. Findings by the court. IN ST TRIAL P Rule 52.

   n. Summary judgment. IN ST TRIAL P Rule 56.

   o. Motion to correct error. IN ST TRIAL P Rule 59.

   p. Relief from judgment or order. IN ST TRIAL P Rule 60.

   q. Access to court records. IN ST ADMIN Rule 9.

   r. Paper size. IN ST ADMIN Rule 11.

   s. Facsimile transmission. IN ST ADMIN Rule 12.

   t. Electronic filing and electronic service pilot projects. IN ST ADMIN Rule 16.

   u. Sealing of certain records by court; Hearing; Notice. IN ST 5-14-3-5.5.

   v. Privacy and confidentiality. IN ST 5-2-9-6; IN ST 5-14-3-4; IN ST 6-4.1-5-10; IN ST 6-4.1-12-12; IN ST 6-8.1-7-1; IN ST 11-13-1-8; IN ST 12-23-14-13; IN ST 16-39-3-10; IN ST 16-41-8-1; IN ST 22-4-19-6; IN ST 31-11-1-6; IN ST 31-19-5-23; IN ST 31-19-13-2; IN ST 31-19-19-1; IN ST 31-33-18-1; IN ST 31-39-1-1; IN ST 31-39-1-2; IN ST 33-23-16-16; IN ST 35-34-2-4; IN ST 35-38-1-13; IN ST 35-38-9-1; IN ST ADR Rule 2.11; IN ST ADR Rule 4.4; IN ST ADR Rule 5.6; IN ST JURY Rule 10.

2. *Local rules*

   a. Requirements for motions. IN ST MARION CIR AND SUPER CTS CIV Rule 203.

   b. Preparation of pleadings, motions and other papers. IN ST MARION CIR AND SUPER CTS CIV Rule 204.

   c. Filing of pleadings, motions and other papers. IN ST MARION CIR AND SUPER CTS CIV Rule 205.

   d. Signing and verification of pleadings, motions and other papers; Service on opposing party. IN ST MARION CIR AND SUPER CTS CIV Rule 206.

   e. Motions for continuance. IN ST MARION CIR AND SUPER CTS CIV Rule 215.

    f.   Electronic filing. IN ST MARION SUPER CT ADMIN Rule 311.

B. Timing

1. *Time for service of request for production of documents*

    a. *Service on parties.* The request may, without leave of court, be served upon the plaintiff after commencement of the action and upon any other party with or after service of the summons and complaint upon that party. IN ST TRIAL P Rule 34(B).

    b. *Service on non-parties.* Neither a request nor subpoena to produce or permit as permitted by IN ST TRIAL P Rule 34 shall be served upon a non-party until at least fifteen (15) days after the date on which the party intending to serve such request or subpoena serves a copy of the proposed request and subpoena on all other parties. Provided, however, that if such request or subpoena relates to a matter set for hearing within such fifteen (15) day period or arises out of a bona fide emergency, such request or subpoena may be served upon a non-party one (1) day after receipt of the proposed request or subpoena by all other parties. IN ST TRIAL P Rule 34(C)(2)

2. *Time for service of the response to the request for production of documents.* The party upon whom the request is served shall serve a written response within a period designated in the request, not less than thirty (30) days after the service thereof or within such shorter or longer time as the court may allow. IN ST TRIAL P Rule 34(B).

3. *Computation of time*

    a. *Generally; Days excluded.* In computing any period of time prescribed or allowed by the Indiana Rules of Trial Procedure, by order of the court, or by any applicable statute, the day of the act, event, or default from which the designated period of time begins to run shall not be included. The last day of the period so computed is to be included unless it is:

        i.   A Saturday,

        ii. A Sunday,

        iii. A legal holiday as defined by state statute, or

        iv. A day the office in which the act is to be done is closed during regular business hours. IN ST TRIAL P Rule 6(A).

    b. *Short periods.* In any event, the period runs until the end of the next day that is not a Saturday, a Sunday, a legal holiday, or a day on which the office is closed. When the period of time allowed is less than seven (7) days, intermediate Saturdays, Sundays, legal holidays, and days on which the office is closed shall be excluded from the computations. IN ST TRIAL P Rule 6(A).

    c. *Additional time after service by United States mail.* Whenever a party has the right or is required to do some act or take some proceedings within a prescribed period after the service of a notice or other paper upon him and the notice or paper is served upon him by United States mail, three (3) days shall be added to the prescribed period. IN ST TRIAL P Rule 6(E).

    d. *Enlargement of time.* When an act is required or allowed to be done at or within a specific time by the Indiana Rules of Trial Procedure, the court may at any time for cause shown:

        i.   Order the period enlarged, with or without motion or notice, if request therefor is made before the expiration of the period originally prescribed or extended by a previous order; or

        ii. Upon motion made after the expiration of the specific period, permit the act to be done where the failure to act was the result of excusable neglect; but, the court may not extend the time for taking any action for judgment on the evidence under IN ST TRIAL P Rule 50(A), amendment of findings and judgment under IN ST TRIAL P Rule 52(B), to correct errors under IN ST TRIAL P Rule 59(C), statement in opposition to motion to correct error under IN ST TRIAL P Rule 59(E), or to obtain relief from final judgment under IN ST TRIAL P Rule 60(B), except to the extent and under the conditions stated in those rules. IN ST TRIAL P Rule 6(B).

    e. *Continuances disfavored.* Motions for Continuance are discouraged. Neither side is entitled to an automatic continuance as a matter of right. IN ST MARION CIR AND SUPER CTS CIV Rule 215. For information on obtaining a continuance, refer to IN ST MARION CIR AND SUPER CTS CIV Rule 215.

C. General Requirements

1. *Scope of discovery.* Unless otherwise limited by order of the court in accordance with the Indiana Rules of Trial Procedure, the scope of discovery is as follows:

    a. *In general.* Parties may obtain discovery regarding any matter, not privileged, which is relevant to the subject-matter involved in the pending action, whether it relates to the claim or defense of the party seeking discovery or the claim or defense of any other party, including the existence, description, nature, custody, condition and location of any books, documents, or other tangible things and the identity and location of persons having knowledge of any discoverable matter. It is not ground for objection that the information sought will be inadmissible at the trial if the information sought appears reasonably calculated to lead to the discovery of admissible evidence. IN ST TRIAL P Rule 26(B)(1).

        i. *Limiting discovery upon court determination.* The frequency or extent of use of the discovery methods otherwise permitted under the Indiana Rules of Trial Procedure and by any local rule shall be limited by the court if it determines that:

            - The discovery sought is unreasonably cumulative or duplicative, or is obtainable from some other source that is more convenient, less burdensome, or less expensive;

            - The party seeking discovery has had ample opportunity by discovery in the action to obtain the information sought or;

            - The burden or expense of the proposed discovery outweighs its likely benefit, taking into account the needs of the case, the amount in controversy, the parties' resources, the importance of the issues at stake in the litigation, and the importance of the proposed discovery in resolving the issues. IN ST TRIAL P Rule 26(B)(1).

            - The court may act upon its own initiative after reasonable notice or pursuant to a motion under IN ST TRIAL P Rule 26(C). IN ST TRIAL P Rule 26(B)(1). Refer to the Indiana KeyRules Motion for Protective Order document for more information.

        ii. *Relevancy in the discovery context.* When the word "relevancy" is used in IN ST TRIAL P Rule 26(B), it does not mean "relevancy" as that word in used to determine the admissibility of evidence in a trial court. It is much broader. It means "relevancy" to the "subject matter" of the litigation or pending action and it may relate to the claim or defense of any party. Pretrial discovery is available as to any nonprivileged matter relevant to the subject matter of the lawsuit or to obtain information reasonably calculated to lead to admissible evidence. 2A INPRAC R 26(26.4); Kaufmann v. Credithrift Financial, Inc., 465 N.E.2d 207, 210 (Ind.Ct.App. 1984).

        iii. *Tests for relevance.* Indiana case law has developed two (2) additional tests in this area. 2A INPRAC R 26(26.4).

            - The first test determines when a document or a request for information is actually relevant to the subject matter in the pending action. A document [or discovery request] is relevant to discovery if there is the possibility the information sought may be relevant to the subject matter of the action. 2A INPRAC R 26(26.4); CIGNA-INA/Aetna v. Hagerman-Shambaugh, 473 N.E.2d 1033, 1036 (Ind.Ct.App. 1985).

            - The second test speaks to appellate review of the trial court's determination that a document or discovery request is relevant to the subject matter of the pending action. The appellate court sees its review of the trial court's decision on relevancy to subject matter as being very limited. The court states: "Our review of the trial court's conclusion that the documents are relevant is limited. A trial court is vested with discretion in its rulings on discovery issues." 2A INPRAC R 26(26.4); Costanzi v. Ryan, 175 Ind.App. 257, 370 N.E.2d 1333 (Ind.Ct.App. 1978).

    b. *Insurance agreements.* A party may obtain discovery of the existence and contents of any insurance agreement under which any person carrying on an insurance business may be liable to satisfy part or all of a judgment which may be entered in the action or to indemnify or reimburse for payments made to satisfy the judgment. Information concerning the insurance agreement is not by reason of

disclosure admissible in evidence at trial. For purposes of IN ST TRIAL P Rule 26(B)(2), an application for insurance shall not be treated as part of an insurance agreement. IN ST TRIAL P Rule 26(B)(2).

c. *Trial preparation; Materials.* Subject to the provisions of IN ST TRIAL P Rule 26(B)(4), a party may obtain discovery of documents and tangible things otherwise discoverable under IN ST TRIAL P Rule 26(B)(1) and prepared in anticipation of litigation or for trial by or for another party or by or for that other party's representative (including his attorney, consultant, surety, indemnitor, insurer, or agent) only upon a showing that the party seeking discovery has substantial need of the materials in the preparation of his case and that he is unable without undue hardship to obtain the substantial equivalent of the materials by other means. In ordering discovery of such materials when the required showing has been made, the court shall protect against disclosure of the mental impressions, conclusions, opinions, or legal theories of an attorney or other representative of a party concerning the litigation. IN ST TRIAL P Rule 26(B)(3).

  i.   A party may obtain without the required showing a statement concerning the action or its subject matter previously made by that party. Upon request, a person not a party may obtain without the required showing a statement concerning the action or its subject matter previously made by that person. If the request is refused, the person may move for a court order. The provisions of IN ST TRIAL P Rule 37(A)(4) apply to the award of expenses incurred in relation to the motion. For purposes of IN ST TRIAL P Rule 26(B)(3), a statement previously made is:

  - A written statement signed or otherwise adopted approved by the person making it, or

  - A stenographic, mechanical, electrical, or other recording, or a transcription thereof, which is a substantially verbatim recital of an oral statement by the person making it and contemporaneously recorded. IN ST TRIAL P Rule 26(B)(3).

  ii. The protection of IN ST TRIAL P Rule 26(B)(3) extends to material prepared or collected before litigation actually commences, but that some possibility of litigation must actually exist before the privilege and IN ST TRIAL P Rule 26(B)(3) become operative. 2A INPRAC R 26(26.9).

d. *Trial preparation; Experts.* Discovery of facts known and opinions held by experts, otherwise discoverable under the provisions of IN ST TRIAL P Rule 26(B)(1) and acquired or developed in anticipation of litigation or for trial, may be obtained as follows:

  i.   A party may through interrogatories require any other party to identify each person whom the other party expects to call as an expert witness at trial, to state the subject matter on which the expert is expected to testify, and to state the substance of the facts and opinions to which the expert is expected to testify and a summary of the grounds for each opinion. IN ST TRIAL P Rule 26(B)(4)(a)(i).

  ii. Upon motion, the court may order further discovery by other means, subject to such restrictions as to scope and such provisions, pursuant to IN ST TRIAL P Rule 26(B)(4)(c), concerning fees and expenses as the court may deem appropriate. IN ST TRIAL P Rule 26(B)(4)(a)(ii).

  iii. A party may discover facts known or opinions held by an expert who has been retained or specially employed by another party in anticipation of litigation or preparation for trial and who is not expected to be called as a witness at trial, only as provided in IN ST TRIAL P Rule 35(B) or upon a showing of exceptional circumstances under which it is impracticable for the party seeking discovery to obtain facts or opinions on the same subject by other means. IN ST TRIAL P Rule 26(B)(4)(b).

  iv. Unless manifest injustice would result,

  - The court shall require that the party seeking discovery pay the expert a reasonable fee for time spent in responding to discovery under IN ST TRIAL P Rule 26(B)(4)(a)(ii) and IN ST TRIAL P Rule 26(B)(4)(b); and

  - With respect to discovery obtained under IN ST TRIAL P Rule 26(B)(4)(a)(ii) the court may require, and with respect to discovery obtained under IN ST TRIAL P Rule 26(B)(4)(b) the court shall require, the party seeking discovery to pay the other party a fair portion of the fees and expenses reasonably incurred by the latter party in obtaining facts and opinions from the expert. IN ST TRIAL P Rule 26(B)(4).

e. *Claims of privilege or protection*

    i. *Information withheld.* When a party withholds information otherwise discoverable under the Indiana Rules of Trial Procedure by claiming that it is privileged or subject to protection as trial preparation material, the party shall make the claim expressly and shall describe the nature of the documents, communications, or things not produced or disclosed in a manner that, without revealing information itself privileged or protected, will enable other parties to assess the applicability of the privilege or protection. IN ST TRIAL P Rule 26(B)(5)(a).

    ii. *Information produced.* If information is produced in discovery that is subject to a claim of privilege or protection as trial-preparation material, the party making the claim may notify any party that received the information of the claim and the basis for it. After being notified, a party must promptly return, sequester, or destroy the specified information and any copies it has and may not use or disclose the information until the claim is resolved. A receiving party may promptly present the information to the court under seal for a determination of the claim. If the receiving party disclosed the information before being notified, it must take reasonable steps to retrieve it. The producing party must preserve the information until the claim is resolved. IN ST TRIAL P Rule 26(B)(5)(b).

    iii. *Waiver.* The law of discovery has developed some holdings which indicate that "waiver" of a privileged communication in a discovery setting might be more exacting than "waiver" of a privileged communication when the only question at hand is an interpretation of the privilege itself. Thus, in litigation in which several documents are in issue, and some are released inadvertently, there is strong case law that holds that the "inadvertent production" of a privileged document does not constitute a waiver of the attorney-client privilege. 2A INPRAC R 26(26.5); Transamerica Computer Co. v. International Business Machines Corp., 573 F.2d 646 (9th Cir. 1978). Such a rule should be measured against the usual rule which suggests that a voluntary disclosure to a third person will generally suffice to show a waiver of the attorney-client privilege. 2A INPRAC R 26(26.5).

f. *Use not limited.* Unless the court orders otherwise under IN ST TRIAL P Rule 26(C), the frequency of use of the methods listed in IN ST TRIAL P Rule 26(A) is not limited. IN ST TRIAL P Rule 26(A).

g. *Sequence of discovery.* Unless the court upon motion, for the convenience of parties and witnesses and in the interests of justice, orders otherwise, methods of discovery may be used in any sequence and the fact that a party is conducting discovery, whether by deposition or otherwise, shall not operate to delay any other party's discovery. IN ST TRIAL P Rule 26.

2. *Request for production of documents*

a. *Content of the request.* The request shall set forth the items to be inspected either by individual item or by category, and describe each item and category with reasonable particularity. The request may specify the form or forms in which electronically stored information is to be produced. The request shall specify a reasonable time, place, and manner of making the inspection and performing the related acts. Service is dispensed with if the whereabouts of the parties is unknown. IN ST TRIAL P Rule 34(B).

    i. *Reasonable particularity.* A recurring issue appears among cases. It is whether a request is adequate or describes the items sought with "reasonable particularity" as stated in IN ST TRIAL P Rule 34(B). The essence of this matter is found in these words: "When the party seeking discovery issues a `shotgun' request that is unduly general, the court may avoid wading through documents by finding the items to be inspected not set forth with reasonable particularity, as required by IN ST TRIAL P Rule 34(B). 3 INPRAC R 34(34.1); Ray v. St. John's Health Care Corp., 582 N.E.2d 464, 474 (Ind.Ct.App. 1991); Richey v. Chappell, 572 N.E.2d 1338, 1339 (Ind.Ct.App. 1991).

b. *Requesting documents in specific form.* If a request for electronically stored information does not specify the form or forms of production, a responding party must produce the information in a form or forms in which it is ordinarily maintained or in a form or forms that are reasonably usable. IN ST TRIAL P Rule 34(B).

c. *Scope.* Any party may serve on any other party a request:

    i. To produce and permit the party making the request, or someone acting on the requester's behalf, to inspect and copy, any designated documents or electronically stored information (including, without limitation, writings, drawings, graphs, charts, photographs, sound recordings, images and other data or data compilations from which information can be obtained or translated, if necessary, by the respondent into reasonably usable form) or to inspect and copy, test, or sample any designated tangible things which constitute or contain matters within the scope of IN ST TRIAL P Rule 26(B) and which are in the possession, custody or control of the party upon whom the request is served; or

    ii. To permit entry upon designated land or other property in the possession or control of the party upon whom the request is served for the purpose of inspection and measuring, surveying, photographing, testing, or sampling the property or any designated object or operation thereon, within the scope of IN ST TRIAL P Rule 26(B). IN ST TRIAL P Rule 34(A).

d. *Application to non-parties.* A witness or person other than a party may be requested to produce or permit the matters allowed by IN ST TRIAL P Rule 34(A). Such request shall be served upon other parties and included in or with a subpoena served upon such witness or person. IN ST TRIAL P Rule 34(C)(1).

    i. *Content of request to non-parties*

- The request shall contain the matter provided in IN ST TRIAL P Rule 34(B). IN ST TRIAL P Rule 34(C)(3).

- It shall also state that the witness or person to whom it is directed is entitled to security against damages or payment of damages resulting from such request and may respond to such request by submitting to its terms, by proposing different terms, by objecting specifically or generally to the request by serving a written response to the party making the request within thirty (30) days, or by moving to quash as permitted by IN ST TRIAL P Rule 45(B). IN ST TRIAL P Rule 34(C)(3).

    ii. *Service of responses on other parties required.* A party receiving documents from a non-party pursuant to IN ST TRIAL P Rule 34(C) shall serve copies on all other parties within fifteen (15) days of receiving the documents. If the documents are voluminous and service of a complete set of copies is burdensome, the receiving party shall notify all parties within fifteen (15) days of receiving the documents that the documents are available for inspection at the location of their production by the non-party, or at another location agreed to by the parties. The parties shall agree to arrangements for copying, and any party desiring copies shall bear the cost of reproducing them. IN ST TRIAL P Rule 34(C)(4).

e. *Exception to best evidence rule.* When a party or witness in control of a writing or document subject to examination under IN ST TRIAL P Rule 34 or IN ST TRIAL P Rule 9.2(E) refuses or is unable to produce it, evidence thereof shall be allowed by other parties without compliance with the rule of evidence requiring production of the original document or writing as best evidence. IN ST TRIAL P Rule 34(D).

3. *Response to request for production of documents*

a. *Content of the response.* The response shall state, with respect to each item or category, that inspection and related activities will be permitted as requested, unless it is objected to, including an objection to the requested form or forms for producing electronically stored information, stating in which event the reasons for objection shall be stated. If objection is made to part of an item or category, the part shall be specified. IN ST TRIAL P Rule 34(B).

b. *Types of responses.* There are several responses that a party may make to a IN ST TRIAL P Rule 34 discovery request:

    i. Agree to produce the requested item or permit inspection at the time and place suggested by the discovering party. 10 INPRAC § 67.2.

ii. Agree to production, but suggest another time and place. 10 INPRAC § 67.2.

iii. Move for a protective order under IN ST TRIAL P Rule 26(C). 10 INPRAC § 67.2.

iv. Object to the request. Common grounds for objection include:

- The item sought does not exist. 10 INPRAC § 67.2.

- Respondent does not have possession, custody or control of the item requested. 10 INPRAC § 67.2.

- The request does not describe documents to be produced with reasonable particularity, or by individual item or category. 10 INPRAC § 67.2.

- The document requested fails to specify a reasonable time, place and manner of production. 10 INPRAC § 67.2.

- The discovery requested is privileged or constitutes work product (mental impressions, conclusions, opinions or legal theories of party or party's attorney). 10 INPRAC § 67.2.

- The discovery requested is not relevant to the subject matter of the litigation and not reasonably calculated to lead to the discovery of admissible evidence. 10 INPRAC § 67.2.

- The discovery requests documents prepared in anticipation of litigation when the requesting party does not have a substantial need of the materials in preparation of the case and is able to obtain the substantial equivalent of the materials without undue hardship and by other means. 10 INPRAC § 67.2.

- Nonparty's statement was prepared in anticipation of litigation and there has been no showing that the non-party's statement cannot be obtained without undue hardship by other means. 10 INPRAC § 67.2.

- The discovery requested contains opinions and facts of an expert who was retained and specially employed in anticipation of litigation or trial preparation and who is not expected to be called as a witness at trial and no exceptional circumstances exist which make it impracticable for the party seeking discovery to obtain the facts and opinions by other means. 10 INPRAC § 67.2.

- The requesting party refuses to pay a fair portion of costs incurred by responding party to produce documents. 10 INPRAC § 67.2.

- The testing procedure requested will destroy or materially alter the document or thing. 10 INPRAC § 67.2.

- The discovery requested is burdensome, oppressive or unduly expensive. 10 INPRAC § 67.2.

c. *Objection.* If objection is made to the requested form or forms for producing electronically stored information—or if no form was specified in the request—the responding party must state the form or forms it intends to use. The party submitting the request may move for an order under IN ST TRIAL P Rule 37(A) with respect to any objection to or other failure to respond to the request or any part thereof, or any failure to permit inspection as requested. IN ST TRIAL P Rule 34(B).

d. *Claims of privilege.* A blanket claim of privilege is not favored, and that the party who seeks to avoid discovery has the burden of establishing the essential elements of the privilege which is invoked. 3 INPRAC R 34(34.2); Ray v. St. John's Health Care Corp., 582 N.E.2d 464 (Ind.Ct.App. 1991).

e. *Electronically stored information; Production in multiple formats.* A party need not produce the same electronically stored information in more than one form. IN ST TRIAL P Rule 34(B).

f. *Response by a non-party.* Any party, or any witness or person upon whom the request properly is made may respond to the request as provided in IN ST TRIAL P Rule 34(B). If the response of the witness or person to whom it is directed is unfavorable, if he moves to quash, if he refuses to cooperate after responding or fails to respond, or if he objects, the party making the request may move for an order under IN ST TRIAL P Rule 37(A) with respect to any such response or objection. IN ST TRIAL P Rule 34(C)(3).

i. In granting an order under IN ST TRIAL P Rule 34(C)(3) and IN ST TRIAL P Rule 37(A)(2) the court shall condition relief upon the prepayment of damages to be proximately incurred by the witness or person to whom the request is directed or require an adequate surety bond or other indemnity conditioned against such damages. Such damages shall include reasonable attorneys' fees incurred in reasonable resistance and in establishing such threatened damage or damages. IN ST TRIAL P Rule 34(C)(3).

    ii. Refer to the Indiana KeyRules Motion to Compel Discovery document more information.

  g. *Supplementation of responses.* A party who has responded to a request for discovery with a response that was complete when made is under no duty to supplement his response to include information thereafter acquired, except as follows:

    i. A party is under a duty seasonably to supplement his response with respect to any question directly addressed to:

- The identity and location of persons having knowledge of discoverable matters, and
- The identity of each person expected to be called as an expert witness at trial, the subject-matter on which he is expected to testify, and the substance of his testimony. IN ST TRIAL P Rule 26(E)(1).

    ii. A party is under a duty seasonably to amend a prior response if he obtains information upon the basis of which:

- He knows that the response was incorrect when made, or
- He knows that the response though correct when made is no longer true and the circumstances are such that a failure to amend the response is in substance a knowing concealment. IN ST TRIAL P Rule 26(E)(2).

    iii. A duty to supplement responses may be imposed by order of the court, agreement of the parties, or at any time prior to trial through new requests for supplementation of prior responses. IN ST TRIAL P Rule 26(E)(3).

    iv. The duty seasonably to supplement a discovery response is absolute and is not predicated on a court order. "It is a breach of a litigant's duty reasonably to supplement if the litigant postpones supplementing its response by not obtaining from its experts the information which is to be supplied in answer to interrogatories." 2A INPRAC R 26(26.27); Lucas v. Dorsey Corp., 609 N.E.2d 1191, 1196 (Ind.Ct.App. 1993).

D. Documents

1. *Required documents*

  a. *Request for production.* Refer to the General Requirements section of this document for information on the scope and content of a request for production of documents.

  b. *Certificate of service.* An attorney or unrepresented party tendering a document to the Clerk for filing shall certify that service has been made, list the parties served, and specify the date and means of service. The certificate of service shall be placed at the end of the document and shall not be separately filed. The separate filing of a certificate of service, however, shall not be grounds for rejecting a document for filing. The Clerk may permit documents to be filed without a certificate of service but shall require prompt filing of a separate certificate of service. IN ST TRIAL P Rule 5(C). In all cases where any pleading or other document is required to be served upon opposing counsel, proof of such service may be made either by:

    i. A certificate of service signed by counsel of record for the serving party and the certificate shall specify by name and address all counsel upon whom the pleading or document was served; or

    ii. An acknowledgment of service signed by the party served or counsel of record. IN ST MARION CIR AND SUPER CTS CIV Rule 206.

2. *Supplemental documents*

  a. *Stipulation regarding discovery procedure.* Unless the court orders otherwise, the parties may by written stipulation:

    i. Provide that depositions may be taken before any person, at any time or place, upon any notice, and in any manner and when so taken may be used like other depositions, and

      ii.   Modify the procedures provided by the Indiana Rules of Trial Procedure for other methods of discovery. IN ST TRIAL P Rule 29.

   b.   *Subpoena.* Requests upon non-parties shall be included in or with a subpoena served upon such witness or person. IN ST TRIAL P Rule 34(C)(1).

   c.   *Facsimile cover sheet.* Any document sent to the Clerk of the Circuit Court by electronic facsimile transmission shall be accompanied by a cover sheet which states the title of the document, case number, number of pages, identity and voice telephone number of the sending party and instructions for filing. The cover sheet shall contain the signature of the attorney or party, pro se, authorizing the filing. IN ST ADMIN Rule 12(D).

E. Format

1.   *Form of documents produced.* The rules applicable to captions, and the signing and form of pleadings (IN ST TRIAL P Rule 8 through IN ST TRIAL P Rule 11), apply to all motions and other papers provided under the Indiana Rules of Trial Procedure. 22B INPRAC 7:2. Unless the parties otherwise agree, or the court otherwise orders, a party who produces documents for inspection shall produce them as they are kept in the usual course of business or shall organize and label them to correspond with the categories in the request. IN ST TRIAL P Rule 34(B).

2.   *Form of pleadings*

   a.   *Caption; Names of parties.* Every pleading shall contain a caption setting forth the name of the court, the title of the action, the file number, and a designation as in IN ST TRIAL P Rule 7(A). In the complaint the title of the action shall include the names of all the parties, but in other pleadings it is sufficient to state the name of the first party on each side with an appropriate indication of other parties. IN ST TRIAL P Rule 10(A).

      i.   Every pleading shall contain a caption setting forth the name of the Court, the Division and Room Number, the title of the action and the file number. IN ST MARION CIR AND SUPER CTS CIV Rule 204(B).

   b.   *Paragraphs; Separate statements.* All averments of a claim or defense shall be made in numbered paragraphs, the contents of each of which shall be limited as far as practicable to a statement of a single set of circumstances, and a paragraph may be referred to by number in all succeeding pleadings. Each claim founded upon a separate transaction or occurrence and each defense other than denials may be stated in a separate count or defense whenever a separation facilitates the clear presentation of the matters set forth. IN ST TRIAL P Rule 10(B).

   c.   *Adoption by reference; Exhibits.* Statements in a pleading may be adopted by reference in a different part of the same pleading or in another pleading or in any motion. A copy of any written instrument which is an exhibit to a pleading is a part thereof for all purposes. IN ST TRIAL P Rule 10(C).

   d.   *Paper.* Pleadings, motions and other papers may be either printed or typewritten on white opaque paper of at least sixteen (16) pound weight, eight and one-half (8-1/2) inches wide and eleven (11) inches in length. IN ST MARION CIR AND SUPER CTS CIV Rule 204(A).

   e.   *Copies.* All copies shall likewise be on white paper of sufficient strength and durability to resist normal wear and tear. IN ST MARION CIR AND SUPER CTS CIV Rule 204(A).

   f.   *Line spacing.* If typewritten, the lines shall be double spaced, except for quotations, which shall be indented and single spaced. IN ST MARION CIR AND SUPER CTS CIV Rule 204(A).

   g.   *Script type.* Script type shall not be used. IN ST MARION CIR AND SUPER CTS CIV Rule 204(A).

   h.   *Titles.* Titles on all pleadings shall delineate each topic included in the pleading e.g. where a pleading contains an Answer, a Motion to Strike or Dismiss, or a Jury Request each shall be set forth in the title. IN ST MARION CIR AND SUPER CTS CIV Rule 204(C).

   i.   *Margins and binding.* Margins shall be one (1) inch. Binding or stapling shall be at the top and at no other place. Covers or backing shall not be used. IN ST MARION CIR AND SUPER CTS CIV Rule 204(D).

3.   *Size of papers for filing.* Effective January 1, 1992, all pleadings, copies, motions and documents filed

with any trial court or appellate level court, typed or printed, with the exception of exhibits and existing wills, shall be prepared on eight and one-half by eleven inch (8 1/2" x 11") size paper. IN ST ADMIN Rule 11.

4. *Form of electronically filed documents.* All electronically filed and served pleadings shall, to the extent practicable, be formatted in accordance with the applicable rules governing formatting of paper pleadings. IN ST MARION SUPER CT ADMIN Rule 311(2-103)(1).

   a. *Electronic document title.* The electronic document title of each pleading or other document shall include:

      i. Party or parties filing/serving the document,

      ii. Nature of the document,

      iii. Party or parties against whom relief, if any, is sought, and

      iv. Nature of the relief sought (e.g., Defendant ABC Corporation's Motion for Summary Judgment). IN ST MARION SUPER CT ADMIN Rule 311(2-103)(2).

5. *Signature requirements*

   a. *Signature of attorney.* Every pleading or motion of a party represented by an attorney shall be signed by at least one (1) attorney of record in his individual name, whose address, telephone number, and attorney number shall be stated, except that this provision shall not apply to pleadings and motions made and transcribed at the trial or a hearing before the judge and received by him in such form. IN ST TRIAL P Rule 11(A).

      i. All pleadings and motions shall contain the original or authorized signature of the attorney, the name of the attorney in typed or printed form, the name of the law firm if a member of a firm, the attorney's address, identification number, e-mail address, telephone number, fax number, and the designation as to the party for whom he appears. IN ST MARION CIR AND SUPER CTS CIV Rule 204(E).

      ii. The signature of an attorney constitutes a certificate by him that he has read the pleadings; that to the best of his knowledge, information, and belief, there is good ground to support it; and that it is not interposed for delay. IN ST TRIAL P Rule 11(A).

      iii. If a pleading or motion is not signed or is signed with intent to defeat the purpose of the rule, it may be stricken as sham and false and the action may proceed as though the pleading had not been served. IN ST TRIAL P Rule 11(A).

      iv. For a willful violation of IN ST TRIAL P Rule 11 an attorney may be subjected to appropriate disciplinary action. Similar action may be taken if scandalous or indecent matter is inserted. IN ST TRIAL P Rule 11(A).

      v. Every pleading, document, and instrument electronically filed or served shall be deemed to have been signed by the judge, clerk, attorney or declarant and shall bear a facsimile or typographical signature of such person, along with the typed name, address, telephone number, and Bar number of a signing attorney. Typographical signatures shall be treated as personal signatures for all purposes under these rules. IN ST MARION SUPER CT ADMIN Rule 311(2-105).

         - Documents containing signatures of third-parties (i.e., unopposed motions, affidavits, stipulations, etc.) may also be filed electronically by indicating that the original signatures are maintained by the filing party in paper-format. IN ST MARION SUPER CT ADMIN Rule 311(2-105).

         - Unless otherwise ordered by the Court or Clerk, a printed copy of all documents filed or served electronically, including original signatures, shall be maintained by the party filing the document and shall be made available, upon reasonable notice, for inspection by other counsel, the Clerk or Court. Parties shall retain originals until two (2) years after all time periods for appeal have expired. From time to time, it may be necessary to provide the Clerk or Court with a hard copy of an electronically filed document. IN ST MARION SUPER CT ADMIN Rule 311(2-105).

    vi. For the recommended format of a signature block, refer to IN ST MARION CIR AND SUPER CTS CIV Rule 204(E).

b. *Signature of unrepresented party.* A party who is not represented by an attorney shall sign his pleading and state his address. IN ST TRIAL P Rule 11(A).

c. *Verification not generally required.* Except when specifically required by rule, pleadings or motions need not be verified or accompanied by affidavit. The rule in equity that the averments of an answer under oath must be overcome by the testimony of two (2) witnesses or of one (1) witness sustained by corroborating circumstances is abolished. IN ST TRIAL P Rule 11(A).

d. *Verification by affirmation or representation.* When in connection with any civil or special statutory proceeding it is required that any pleading, motion, petition, supporting affidavit, or other document of any kind, be verified, or that an oath be taken, it shall be sufficient if the subscriber simply affirms the truth of the matter to be verified by an affirmation or representation. IN ST TRIAL P Rule 11(B). IN ST TRIAL P Rule 11(B) states that the affirmation or representation should be in substantially the following language: "I (we) affirm, under the penalties for perjury, that the foregoing representation(s) is (are) true. (Signed) _____."

    i. Any person who falsifies an affirmation or representation of fact shall be subject to the same penalties as are prescribed by law for the making of a false affidavit. IN ST TRIAL P Rule 11(B).

e. *Verified pleadings, motions, and affidavits as evidence.* Pleadings, motions and affidavits accompanying or in support of such pleadings or motions when required to be verified or under oath shall be accepted as a representation that the signer had personal knowledge thereof or reasonable cause to believe the existence of the facts or matters stated or alleged therein; and, if otherwise competent or acceptable as evidence, may be admitted as evidence of the facts or matters stated or alleged therein when it is so provided in the Indiana Rules of Trial Procedure, by statute or other law, or to the extent the writing or signature expressly purports to be made upon the signer's personal knowledge. When such pleadings, motions and affidavits are verified or under oath they shall not require other or greater proof on the part of the adverse party than if not verified or not under oath unless expressly provided otherwise by the Indiana Rules of Trial Procedure, statute or other law. Affidavits upon motions for summary judgment under IN ST TRIAL P Rule 56 and in denial of execution under IN ST TRIAL P Rule 9.2 shall be made upon personal knowledge. IN ST TRIAL P Rule 11(C).

6. *Information excluded from public access.* Every document filed in a case shall separately identify information excluded from public access pursuant to IN ST ADMIN Rule 9(G)(1) as follows:

a. Whole documents that are excluded from public access pursuant to IN ST ADMIN Rule 9(G)(1) shall be tendered on light green paper or have a light green coversheet attached to the document, marked "Not for Public Access" or "Confidential." IN ST TRIAL P Rule 5(G)(1).

b. When only a portion of a document contains information excluded from public access pursuant to IN ST ADMIN Rule 9(G)(1), said information shall be omitted [or redacted] from the filed document, and set forth on a separate accompanying document on light green paper conspicuously marked "Not for Public Access" or "Confidential" and clearly designated [or identifying] the caption and number of the case and the document and location within the document to which the redacted material pertains. IN ST TRIAL P Rule 5(G)(2).

c. With respect to documents filed in electronic format, the trial court, by local rule, may provide for compliance with IN ST TRIAL P Rule 5 in manner that separates and protects access to information excluded from public access. IN ST TRIAL P Rule 5(G)(3).

d. IN ST TRIAL P Rule 5(G) does not apply to a record sealed by the court pursuant to IN ST 5-14-3-5.5 or otherwise, nor to records, documents, or information filed in cases to which public access is prohibited pursuant to IN ST ADMIN Rule 9(G). IN ST TRIAL P Rule 5(G)(4).

e. The following information in case records is excluded from public access and is confidential:

    i. Information that is excluded from public access pursuant to federal law;

ii. Information that is excluded from public access as declared confidential by Indiana statute or other court rule, including without limitation:

- All adoption records created after July 8, 1941, as declared confidential by IN ST 31-19-19-1, et seq., except those specifically declared open by IN ST 31-19-13-2(2);

- All records relating to chancroid, chlamydia, gonorrhea, hepatitis, human immunodeficiency virus (HIV), Lymphogranuloma venereum, syphilis, tuberculosis, as declared confidential by IN ST 16-41-8-1, et seq.;

- All records relating to child abuse as declared confidential by IN ST 31-33-18-1, et seq.;

- All records relating to drug tests as declared confidential by IN ST 5-14-3-4(a)(9);

- Records of grand jury proceedings as declared confidential by IN ST 35-34-2-4;

- Records of juvenile proceedings as declared confidential by IN ST 31-39-1-2, except those specifically open under statute;

- All paternity records created after July 1, 1941 as declared confidential by IN ST 31-14-11-15, IN ST 31-19-5-23, IN ST 31-39-1-1 and IN ST 31-39-1-2 [Editor's note: IN ST 31-14-11-15 was repealed effective May 9, 2013];

- All pre-sentence reports as declared confidential by IN ST 35-38-1-13;

- Written petitions to permit marriages without consent and orders directing the Clerk of Court to issue a marriage license to underage persons, as declared confidential by IN ST 31-11-1-6;

- Only those arrest warrants, search warrants, indictments and informations ordered confidential by the trial judge, prior to return of duly executed service as declared confidential by IN ST 5-14-3-4(b)(1);

- All medical, mental health, or tax records unless determined by law or regulation of any governmental custodian not to be confidential, released by the subject of such records, or declared by a court of competent jurisdiction to be essential to the resolution of litigation as declared confidential by IN ST 16-39-3-10, IN ST 6-4.1-5-10, IN ST 6-4.1-12-12, and IN ST 6-8.1-7-1;

- Personal information relating to jurors or prospective jurors, other than for the use of the parties and counsel, pursuant to IN ST JURY Rule 10;

- Information relating to protection from abuse orders, no-contact orders and workplace violence restraining orders as declared confidential by IN ST 5-2-9-6, et seq.;

- Mediation proceedings pursuant to IN ST ADR Rule 2.11, Mini-Trial proceedings pursuant to IN ST ADR Rule 4.4(C), and Summary Jury Trials pursuant to IN ST ADR Rule 5.6;

- Information in probation files pursuant to the Probation Standards promulgated by the Judicial Conference of Indiana pursuant to IN ST 11-13-1-8(b);

- Information deemed confidential pursuant to the Rules for Court Administered Alcohol and Drug Programs promulgated by the Judicial Conference of Indiana pursuant to IN ST 12-23-14-13;

- Information deemed confidential pursuant to the Problem-Solving Court Rules promulgated by the Judicial Conference of Indiana pursuant to IN ST 33-23-16-16;

- All records of the Department of workforce Development as declared confidential by IN ST 22-4-19-6;

- Information regarding interception of electronic communications that is sealed or deemed confidential as set forth in IN ST 35-33.5-2-1, et seq.

iii. Information excluded from public access by specific court order;

iv. Complete Social Security Numbers of living persons;

    v.   With the exception of names, information such as addresses, phone numbers, and dates of birth which explicitly identifies:

- Natural persons who are witnesses or victims (not including defendants) in criminal, domestic violence, stalking, sexual assault, juvenile, or civil protection order proceedings, provided that juveniles who are victims of sex crimes shall be identified by initials only;

- Places of residence of judicial officers, clerks and other employees of courts and clerks of court, unless the person or persons about whom the information pertains waives confidentiality;

    vi.   Complete account numbers of specific assets, loans, bank accounts, credit cards, and personal identification numbers (PINs);

    vii.   All orders of expungement entered in criminal or juvenile proceedings, orders to restrict access to criminal history information pursuant to IN ST 35-38-5-5.5 or IN ST 35-38-8-5 and records excluded from public access by such orders, and information related to infractions that is excluded from public access pursuant to IN ST 34-28-5-15 or IN ST 34-28-5-16 [Editor's note: IN ST 35-38-5-5.5, IN ST 35-38-8-5 and IN ST 34-28-5-16 were repealed effective July 1, 2013; for information on orders restricting access to criminal history, refer to IN ST 35-38-9-1, et seq.];

    viii.   All personal notes and e-mail, and deliberative material, of judges, jurors, court staff and judicial agencies, and information recorded in personal data assistants (PDA's) or organizers and personal calendars. IN ST ADMIN Rule 9(G)(1).

F. Filing and Service Requirements

1. *Filing requirements.* Except as otherwise provided in IN ST TRIAL P Rule 5(E)(2), all pleadings and papers subsequent to the complaint which are required to be served upon a party shall be filed with the Court either before service or within a reasonable period of time thereafter. IN ST TRIAL P Rule 5(E)(1).

    a. *Non-filing of discovery until necessary*

        i. *Non-filing of discovery; Exceptions.* No deposition or request for discovery or response thereto under IN ST TRIAL P Rule 27, IN ST TRIAL P Rule 30, IN ST TRIAL P Rule 31, IN ST TRIAL P Rule 33, IN ST TRIAL P Rule 34 or IN ST TRIAL P Rule 36 shall be filed with the Court unless:

- A motion is filed pursuant to IN ST TRIAL P Rule 26(C) or IN ST TRIAL P Rule 37 and the original deposition or request for discovery or response thereto is necessary to enable the Court to rule; or

- A party desires to use the deposition or request for discovery or response thereto for evidentiary purposes at trial or in connection with a motion, and the Court, either upon its own motion or that of any party, or as a part of any pre-trial order, orders the filing of the original. IN ST TRIAL P Rule 5(E)(2).

        ii. *Custody of original and period of retention*

- The original of a deposition shall, subject to the provisions of IN ST TRIAL P Rule 30(E), be delivered by the reporter to the party taking it and shall be maintained by that party until filed with the Court pursuant to IN ST TRIAL P Rule 5(E)(2) or until the later of final judgment, agreed settlement of the litigation or all appellate rights have been exhausted. IN ST TRIAL P Rule 5(E)(3)(a).

- The original or any request for discovery or response thereto under IN ST TRIAL P Rule 27, IN ST TRIAL P Rule 30, IN ST TRIAL P Rule 31, IN ST TRIAL P Rule 33, IN ST TRIAL P Rule 34 and IN ST TRIAL P Rule 36 shall be maintained by the party originating the request or response until filed with the Court pursuant to IN ST TRIAL P Rule 5(E)(2) or until the later of final judgment, agreed settlement or all appellate rights have been exhausted. IN ST TRIAL P Rule 5(E)(3)(b).

        iii. *Original unavailable; Copies.* In the event it is made to appear to the satisfaction of the Court that the original of a deposition or request for discovery or response thereto cannot be filed with

the Court when required, the Court may allow use of a copy instead of the original. IN ST TRIAL P Rule 5(E)(4).

    iv. *Filing as publication.* The filing of any deposition shall constitute publication. IN ST TRIAL P Rule 5(E)(5).

b. *Filing generally.* All pleadings, petitions and motions are filed with the Clerk designated by the Court at any time during office hours established by the Clerk and the Court. All orders submitted to the Court shall be in sufficient number and shall be accompanied by postage paid envelopes addressed to each party or counsel of record. IN ST MARION CIR AND SUPER CTS CIV Rule 205(A)

c. *Filing with the court defined.* The filing of pleadings, motions, and other papers with the court as required by the Indiana Rules of Trial Procedure shall be made by one of the following methods:

    i. Delivery to the clerk of the court;

    ii. Sending by electronic transmission under the procedure adopted pursuant to IN ST ADMIN Rule 12;

    iii. Mailing to the clerk by registered, certified or express mail return receipt requested;

    iv. Depositing with any third-party commercial carrier for delivery to the clerk within three (3) calendar days, cost prepaid, properly addressed;

    v. If the court so permits, filing with the judge, in which event the judge shall note thereon the filing date and forthwith transmit them to the office of the clerk; or

    vi. Electronic filing, as approved by the Division of State Court Administration pursuant to IN ST ADMIN Rule 16. IN ST TRIAL P Rule 5(F).

    vii. Filing by registered or certified mail and by third-party commercial carrier shall be complete upon mailing or deposit. IN ST TRIAL P Rule 5(F).

d. *Facsimile filing.* Facsimile filing is discouraged, but permitted in the Marion Circuit and Marion Superior Court. All documents filed by facsimile shall also be filed in hard copy within seven (7) days of the facsimile filing, along with proposed orders and stamped addressed envelopes, as required by IN ST MARION CIR AND SUPER CTS CIV Rule 203(E). To avoid duplicate filings, the hard copies of the facsimile filing shall indicate in bold letters that the pleading was previously filed by facsimile transmission. Proof of transmission by facsimile, including certificate of service and manner of service, shall be the responsibility of the filing party. If the filing requires immediate attention of the Judge, it shall be so indicated in bold letters in an accompanying transmittal memorandum. Legibility of documents and timeliness of filing is the responsibility of the sender. IN ST MARION CIR AND SUPER CTS CIV Rule 205(B).

    i. *Generally.* In counties where a majority of judges of the courts of record, by posted local rule, have authorized electronic facsimile filing and designated a telephone number to receive such transmissions, pleadings, motions, and other papers may be sent to the Clerk of Circuit Court by electronic facsimile transmission for filing in any case, provided:

       • Such matter does not exceed ten (10) pages, including the cover sheet;

       • Such matter does not require the payment of fees other than the electronic facsimile transcription fee set forth in IN ST ADMIN Rule 12(E);

       • The sending party creates at the time of transmission a machine generated log for such transmission; and

       • The original document and the transmission log are maintained by the sending party for the duration of the litigation. IN ST ADMIN Rule 12(B).

    ii. *Time of filing.* During normal, posted business hours, the time of filing shall be the time the duplicate document is produced in the office of the Clerk of the Circuit Court. Duplicate documents received at all other times shall be filed as of the next normal business day. IN ST ADMIN Rule 12(C).

       • If the receiving fax machine endorses its own time and date stamp upon the transmitted

documents and the receiving machine produces a delivery receipt which is electronically created and transmitted to the sending party, the time of filing shall be the date and time recorded on the transmitted document by the receiving fax machine. IN ST ADMIN Rule 12(C).

e. *Electronic filing.* Electronic filing and electronic service pilot projects are authorized pursuant to IN ST ADMIN Rule 16 and approved by the Division of State Court Administration. IN ST MARION SUPER CT ADMIN Rule 311(1-103).

  i. *Cases where electronic filing accepted.* All Marion County Circuit and Superior civil courts may accept electronic filing and service of pleadings and other documents designated in this rule in mortgage foreclosure (hereinafter referred to as "MF"), civil collection(hereinafter referred to as "CC"), and individual cases that have been approved for electronic filing and service. IN ST MARION SUPER CT ADMIN Rule 311(1-104)(1).

   • The Marion County Circuit Court may, upon the motion of a party or its own motion, designate a case that will involve multiple litigants, legally intricate issues, and an extensive number of documents a mass tort or complex litigation case. Any case so designated shall be subject to electronic filing and service using the county's approved Electronic Service Provider. IN ST MARION SUPER CT ADMIN Rule 311(1-104)(3).

   • The filing of electronic pleadings and other documents in MF and CC cases is entirely voluntary; however, once the case is initially filed electronically, all subsequent filings in the case shall remain in electronic format until the time for appeal is exhausted. IN ST MARION SUPER CT ADMIN Rule 311(1-104)(5).

  ii. *Documents eligible for electronic filing.* The following pleadings may be filed and served electronically:

   • New case complaint and petitions. IN ST MARION SUPER CT ADMIN Rule 311(1-104)(8)(a).

   • Original answers. IN ST MARION SUPER CT ADMIN Rule 311(1-104)(8)(a).

   • Any other pleadings or document including but not limited to motions and appearance forms. IN ST MARION SUPER CT ADMIN Rule 311(1-104)(8)(a).

  iii. *Manner of electronic filing.* Parties shall E-file a document either:

   • By registering to use the Electronic Filing Service Provider; or

   • In person at the Marion County Clerk's office, by electronically filing through the Public Access Terminal. Parties filing in this manner shall be responsible for furnishing the document in an electronic format that will be compatible with the clerk's office-system to be uploaded in person. IN ST MARION SUPER CT ADMIN Rule 311(1-104)(9). For information on the Electronic Filing Service Provider and Public Access Terminal, refer to IN ST MARION SUPER CT ADMIN Rule 311(1-101).

   • Registered users shall pay statutory filing fees for E-filed documents electronically to the Court through their EFSP. Filing fees are due and payable at the time of filing. IN ST MARION SUPER CT ADMIN Rule 311(2-104)(1). For more information on electronic filing fees, refer to IN ST MARION SUPER CT ADMIN Rule 311(2-104).

  iv. *Effect of electronic filing.* Any pleading filed electronically shall be considered as filed with the court when the transmission to the EFSP is complete. Any document E-filed by 11:59 p.m. local Indianapolis, Indiana time shall be deemed filed on that date. The EFSP is an agent of the Court for the purpose of electronic filing, receipt, service and retrieval of electronic documents. IN ST MARION SUPER CT ADMIN Rule 311(2-102).

   • Upon completion of filing, the EFSP shall issue a confirmation receipt that includes the date and time of receipt. The confirmation receipt shall serve as proof of filing. IN ST MARION SUPER CT ADMIN Rule 311(2-102).

   • In the event the Court rejects the submitted documents following review, the documents shall not become part of the official Court record and the filer will receive notification of the rejection. Users may be required to refile the instruments to meet necessary filing requirements. Documents may be filed through an E-filing system at any time that the Clerk's office is open to receive the filing or at such other times as may be designated by the clerk and posted publicly. IN ST MARION SUPER CT ADMIN Rule 311(2-102).

- Documents filed through the E-filing system are deemed filed when received by the Clerk's office, except that documents received at times that the Clerk's office is closed shall be deemed filed the next regular time when the Clerk's office is open for filing. The time stamp issued by the E-filing system shall be presumed to be the time the document is received by the Clerk. IN ST MARION SUPER CT ADMIN Rule 311(2-102).

v. *Electronically filed documents.* All pleadings and other documents designated in IN ST MARION SUPER CT ADMIN Rule 311 shall be filed and served electronically in any individual case which has been approved for electronic filing and service. IN ST MARION SUPER CT ADMIN Rule 311(1-104)(6).

vi. *System failures.* When filing by electronic means is hindered by a technical failure, a party may file with the Clerk of Marion County in hard copy. With the exception of deadlines that by law cannot be extended, the time for filing of any paper that is delayed due to technical failure of the site shall be extended for one (1) day for each day on which such failure occurs, unless otherwise ordered by the Court. IN ST MARION SUPER CT ADMIN Rule 311(2-108).

vii. *Compliance with rules.* All filing shall comply with the requirements of IN ST ADMIN Rule 9 and IN ST ADMIN Rule 16; and the Indiana Rules of Court and the Marion County Local Rules. IN ST MARION SUPER CT ADMIN Rule 311(1-104)(11).

f. *Filing for special judge.* When a Special Judge who is not a Marion County Judge is selected, all parties or attorneys shall furnish such Judge with copies of all filings prior to the qualification of such Special Judge. Thereafter, copies of all filings shall be delivered in person, by mail or by facsimile to the office of the Special Judge with certificate of forwarding same made a part of the filing. IN ST MARION CIR AND SUPER CTS CIV Rule 205(C).

g. *Proof of filing.* Any party filing any paper by any method other than personal delivery to the clerk shall retain proof of filing. IN ST TRIAL P Rule 5(F).

2. *Service requirements.* Unless otherwise provided by the Indiana Rules of Trial Procedure or an order of the court, each party and special judge, if any, shall be served with: (1) every order required by its terms to be served; (2) every pleading subsequent to the original complaint; (3) every written motion except one which may be heard ex parte; (4) every brief submitted to the trial court; (5) every paper relating to discovery required to be served upon a party; and (6) every written notice, appearance, demand, offer of judgment, designation of record on appeal, or similar paper. IN ST TRIAL P Rule 5(A).

a. *Methods of service*

i. *Personal service.* Whenever a party is represented by an attorney of record, service shall be made upon such attorney unless service upon the party himself is ordered by the court. Service upon the attorney or party shall be made by delivering or mailing a copy of the papers to the last known address or where an attorney or party has consented to service by fax or e-mail, as provided in IN ST TRIAL P Rule 3.1(A)(4), by faxing or e-mailing a copy of the documents to the fax number or e-mail address set out in the appearance form or correction as required by IN ST TRIAL P Rule 3.1(E). IN ST TRIAL P Rule 5(B). Delivery of a copy within IN ST TRIAL P Rule 5 means:

- Offering or tendering it to the attorney or party and stating the nature of the papers being served. Refusal to accept an offered or tendered document is a waiver of any objection to the sufficiency or adequacy of service of that document;

- Leaving it at his office with a clerk or other person in charge thereof, or if there is no one in charge, leaving it in a conspicuous place therein; or

- If the office is closed, by leaving it at his dwelling house or usual place of abode with some person of suitable age and discretion then residing therein; or,

- Leaving it at some other suitable place, selected by the attorney upon whom service is being made, pursuant to duly promulgated local rule. IN ST TRIAL P Rule 5(B)(1).

ii. *Service by mail.* If service is made by mail, the papers shall be deposited in the United States mail addressed to the person on whom they are being served, with postage prepaid. Service shall be deemed complete upon mailing. Proof of service of all papers permitted to be mailed may be made by written acknowledgment of service, by affidavit of the person who mailed the papers, or by certificate of an attorney. It shall be the duty of attorneys when entering their appearance in a cause or when filing pleadings or papers therein, to have noted in the Chronological Case Summary or said pleadings or papers so filed the address and telephone number of their office. Service by delivery or by mail at such address shall be deemed sufficient and complete. IN ST TRIAL P Rule 5(B)(2).

iii. *Service by fax or e-mail.* A party who has consented to service by fax or e-mail may be served as follows:

- Service by e-mail shall be made by attaching the document being served in .pdf format. Discovery documents must also be served in accordance with IN ST TRIAL P Rule 26(A). IN ST TRIAL P Rule 5(B)(3)(a).

- Service by fax shall be deemed complete upon generation of a transmission record indicating the successful transmission of the entire document, except as provided in IN ST TRIAL P Rule 5(B)(3)(d). IN ST TRIAL P Rule 5(B)(3)(b).

- Service by e-mail shall be deemed complete upon transmission, except as provided in IN ST TRIAL P Rule 5(B)(3)(d). IN ST TRIAL P Rule 5(B)(3)(c).

- Service by fax or e-mail that occurs on a Saturday, Sunday, legal holiday, or day the court or agency in which the matter is pending is closed or after 5:00 PM local time of the recipient shall be deemed complete the next day that is not a Saturday, Sunday, legal holiday, or day that the court or agency in which the matter is pending is not closed. IN ST TRIAL P Rule 5(B)(3)(d).

iv. *Electronic service.* Delivery of E-service documents through the EFSP to other registered users shall be considered as valid and effective service and shall have the same legal effect as an original paper document. Recipients of E-service documents shall access their documents through the EFSP. IN ST MARION SUPER CT ADMIN Rule 311(2-107)(1).

- E-service shall be deemed complete when the transmission to the EFSP is completed. IN ST MARION SUPER CT ADMIN Rule 311(2-107)(2).

- For the purpose of computing time to respond to documents received via E-service, any document served on a day or at a time when the Clerk's office is not open for business shall be deemed served at the time of next opening of the Clerk's office for business. IN ST MARION SUPER CT ADMIN Rule 311(2-107)(3).

v. *Additional service of electronic discovery.* In addition to service under Rule IN ST TRIAL P Rule 5(B) or a .pdf format electronic copy, a party propounding or responding to interrogatories, requests for production or requests for admission shall comply with IN ST TRIAL P Rule 26(A.1)(a) or IN ST TRIAL P Rule 26(A.1)(b). IN ST TRIAL P Rule 26(A.1).

- The party shall serve the discovery request or response in an electronic format (either on a disk or as an electronic document attachment) in any commercially available word processing software system. If transmitted on disk, each disk shall be labeled, identifying the caption of the case, the document, and the word processing version in which it is being submitted. If more than one (1) disk is used for the same document, each disk shall be labeled and also shall be sequentially numbered. If transmitted by electronic mail, the document must be accompanied by electronic memorandum providing the forgoing identifying information; or

- The party shall serve the opposing party with a verified statement that the attorney or party appealing pro se lacks the equipment and is unable to transmit the discovery as required by IN ST TRIAL P Rule 26(A.1). IN ST TRIAL P Rule 26(A.1).

b. *Serving numerous defendants.* In any action in which there are unusually large numbers of defendants, the court, upon motion or of its own initiative, may order:

    i. That service of the pleadings of the defendants and replies thereto need not be made as between the defendants;

- That any cross-claim, counterclaim, or matter constituting an avoidance or affirmative defense contained therein shall be deemed to be denied or avoided by all other parties; and

- That the filing of any such pleading and service thereof upon the plaintiff constitutes due notice of it to the parties. IN ST TRIAL P Rule 5(D).

    ii. A copy of every such order shall be served upon the parties in such manner and form as the court directs. IN ST TRIAL P Rule 5(D).

c. *Service on parties in default for failure to appear.* No service need be made on parties in default for failure to appear, except that pleadings asserting new or additional claims for relief against them shall be served upon them in the manner provided by service of summons in IN ST TRIAL P Rule 4. IN ST TRIAL P Rule 5(A).

G. Hearings

1. The Indiana rules do not contemplate a hearing related to the filing and service of requests for production.

H. Forms

1. Request for Production of Documents Forms for Indiana

a. Request for production of documents. 5 INPRAC § 4:3.1.

b. Request for production of documents; Insurance company. 5 INPRAC § 4:3.2.

c. Request for production of documents; Medical records. 5 INPRAC § 4:3.3.

d. Request for production of documents; Non-party. 5 INPRAC § 4:3.4.

e. Motion to enlarge time to respond to request for production of documents. 5 INPRAC § 4:3.5.

f. Response to request for production of documents; General form with objections. 5 INPRAC § 4:3.6.

g. Request for production of documents; General form. 10 INPRAC § 67.6.

h. Request for entry upon land for inspection. 10 INPRAC § 67.7.

i. Request for production of documents; Products liability; Plaintiff to manufacturer. 10 INPRAC § 67.8.

j. Request for production of documents; Products liability; Property loss; Defendant. 10 INPRAC § 67.9.

k. Request for production of documents; Products liability; Vehicle; Plaintiff. 10 INPRAC § 67.10.

l. Products liability; Defendant to plaintiff regarding accident and injuries. 10 INPRAC § 67.11.

m. Request for production of documents; Action against insurance company. 10 INPRAC § 67.13.

n. Request for production of documents; Action against nursing home; Plaintiff. 10 INPRAC § 67.14.

o. Request for production of documents; Action against nursing home; Defendant. 10 INPRAC § 67.15.

p. Request for production of documents; Medical records. 10 INPRAC § 67.17.

q. Request for production of documents; To obtain corporate records. 10 INPRAC § 67.18.

r. Request for production of handwriting exemplars. 10 INPRAC § 67.19.

s. Response to request for production of documents; General form with objections. 10 INPRAC § 67.30.

t. Response to request for permission to enter upon land. 10 INPRAC § 67.31.

u. Motion to shorten time to respond to request for production. 10 INPRAC § 67.32.

v. Motion to enlarge time to respond to request for production. 10 INPRAC § 67.33.

w. Request for production of documents to nonparty; General form. 10 INPRAC § 67.40.

x. Request for production of documents to nonparty; Another form. 10 INPRAC § 67.41.

y. Request for production of documents to nonparty; Production of bank and financial records. 10 INPRAC § 67.42.

z. Request for production of documents to nonparty; Request that employer produce records relating to employee making personal injury claim. 10 INPRAC § 67.43.

I. Checklist

(I) ❑ Matters to be considered by the party serving the request for production

  (a) ❑ Required documents

    (1) ❑ Request for production of documents

    (2) ❑ Certificate of service

  (b) ❑ Supplemental documents

    (1) ❑ Stipulation regarding discovery procedure

    (2) ❑ Subpoena

    (3) ❑ Facsimile cover sheet

  (c) ❑ Timing

    (1) ❑ On parties: The request may, without leave of court, be served upon the plaintiff after commencement of the action and upon any other party with or after service of the summons and complaint upon that party

    (2) ❑ On non-parties: Neither a request nor subpoena to produce or permit as permitted by IN ST TRIAL P Rule 34 shall be served upon a non-party until at least fifteen (15) days after the date on which the party intending to serve such request or subpoena serves a copy of the proposed request and subpoena on all other parties

      (i) ❑ Provided, however, that if such request or subpoena relates to a matter set for hearing within such fifteen (15) day period or arises out of a bona fide emergency, such request or subpoena may be served upon a non-party one (1) day after receipt of the proposed request or subpoena by all other parties

(II) ❑ Matters to be considered by the responding party

  (a) ❑ Required documents

    (1) ❑ Response to request for production of documents

    (2) ❑ Certificate of service

  (b) ❑ Supplemental documents

    (1) ❑ Business records

    (2) ❑ Stipulation regarding discovery procedure

    (3) ❑ Facsimile cover sheet

  (c) ❑ Timing

    (1) ❑ The party upon whom the request is served shall serve a written response within a period designated in the request, not less than thirty (30) days after the service thereof or within such shorter for longer time as the court may allow

Requests, Notices and Applications
Request for Admissions

Document Last Updated October 2013

A. Applicable Rules

1. *State rules*

   a. Appearance. IN ST TRIAL P Rule 3.1.

   b. Process. IN ST TRIAL P Rule 4.

   c. Service and filing of pleadings and other papers. IN ST TRIAL P Rule 5.

   d. Time. IN ST TRIAL P Rule 6.

   e. Pleadings. IN ST TRIAL P Rule 7; IN ST TRIAL P Rule 9.2; IN ST TRIAL P Rule 10.

   f. Signing and verification of pleadings. IN ST TRIAL P Rule 11.

   g. Pre-trial procedure; Formulating issues. IN ST TRIAL P Rule 16.

   h. General provisions governing discovery. IN ST TRIAL P Rule 26.

   i. Methods of discovery. IN ST TRIAL P Rule 27; IN ST TRIAL P Rule 29; IN ST TRIAL P Rule 30; IN ST TRIAL P Rule 31; IN ST TRIAL P Rule 33; IN ST TRIAL P Rule 34; IN ST TRIAL P Rule 35; IN ST TRIAL P Rule 36.

   j. Failure to make or cooperate in discovery; Sanctions. IN ST TRIAL P Rule 37.

   k. Judgment on the evidence (directed verdict). IN ST TRIAL P Rule 50.

   l. Findings by the court. IN ST TRIAL P Rule 52.

   m. Summary judgment. IN ST TRIAL P Rule 56.

   n. Motion to correct error. IN ST TRIAL P Rule 59.

   o. Relief from judgment or order. IN ST TRIAL P Rule 60.

   p. Access to court records. IN ST ADMIN Rule 9.

   q. Paper size. IN ST ADMIN Rule 11.

   r. Facsimile transmission. IN ST ADMIN Rule 12.

   s. Electronic filing and electronic service pilot projects. IN ST ADMIN Rule 16.

   t. Sealing of certain records by court; Hearing; Notice. IN ST 5-14-3-5.5.

   u. Privacy and confidentiality. IN ST 5-2-9-6; IN ST 5-14-3-4; IN ST 6-4.1-5-10; IN ST 6-4.1-12-12; IN ST 6-8.1-7-1; IN ST 11-13-1-8; IN ST 12-23-14-13; IN ST 16-39-3-10; IN ST 16-41-8-1; IN ST 22-4-19-6; IN ST 31-11-1-6; IN ST 31-19-5-23; IN ST 31-19-13-2; IN ST 31-19-19-1; IN ST 31-33-18-1; IN ST 31-39-1-1; IN ST 31-39-1-2; IN ST 33-23-16-16; IN ST 35-34-2-4; IN ST 35-38-1-13; IN ST 35-38-9-1; IN ST ADR Rule 2.11; IN ST ADR Rule 4.4; IN ST ADR Rule 5.6; IN ST JURY Rule 10.

2. *Local rules*

   a. Requirements for motions. IN ST MARION CIR AND SUPER CTS CIV Rule 203.

   b. Preparation of pleadings, motions and other papers. IN ST MARION CIR AND SUPER CTS CIV Rule 204.

   c. Filing of pleadings, motions and other papers. IN ST MARION CIR AND SUPER CTS CIV Rule 205.

   d. Motions for continuance. IN ST MARION CIR AND SUPER CTS CIV Rule 215.

   e. Electronic filing. IN ST MARION SUPER CT ADMIN Rule 311.

B. Timing

1. *Time for service of request for admissions.* The request may, without leave of court, be served upon the

plaintiff after commencement of the action and upon any other party with or after service of the summons and complaint upon that party. IN ST TRIAL P Rule 36(A).

2. *Time for service of response.* The matter is admitted unless, within a period designated in the request, not less than thirty (30) days after service thereof or within such shorter or longer time as the court may allow, the party to whom the request is directed serves upon the party requesting the admission a written answer or objection addressed to the matter. IN ST TRIAL P Rule 36(A).

3. *Computation of time*

    a. *Generally; Days excluded.* In computing any period of time prescribed or allowed by the Indiana Rules of Trial Procedure, by order of the court, or by any applicable statute, the day of the act, event, or default from which the designated period of time begins to run shall not be included. The last day of the period so computed is to be included unless it is:

        i. A Saturday,

        ii. A Sunday,

        iii. A legal holiday as defined by state statute, or

        iv. A day the office in which the act is to be done is closed during regular business hours. IN ST TRIAL P Rule 6(A).

    b. *Short periods.* In any event, the period runs until the end of the next day that is not a Saturday, a Sunday, a legal holiday, or a day on which the office is closed. When the period of time allowed is less than seven (7) days, intermediate Saturdays, Sundays, legal holidays, and days on which the office is closed shall be excluded from the computations. IN ST TRIAL P Rule 6(A).

    c. *Additional time after service by United States mail.* Whenever a party has the right or is required to do some act or take some proceedings within a prescribed period after the service of a notice or other paper upon him and the notice or paper is served upon him by United States mail, three (3) days shall be added to the prescribed period. IN ST TRIAL P Rule 6(E).

    d. *Enlargement of time.* When an act is required or allowed to be done at or within a specific time by the Indiana Rules of Trial Procedure, the court may at any time for cause shown:

        i. Order the period enlarged, with or without motion or notice, if request therefor is made before the expiration of the period originally prescribed or extended by a previous order; or

        ii. Upon motion made after the expiration of the specific period, permit the act to be done where the failure to act was the result of excusable neglect; but, the court may not extend the time for taking any action for judgment on the evidence under IN ST TRIAL P Rule 50(A), amendment of findings and judgment under IN ST TRIAL P Rule 52(B), to correct errors under IN ST TRIAL P Rule 59(C), statement in opposition to motion to correct error under IN ST TRIAL P Rule 59(E), or to obtain relief from final judgment under IN ST TRIAL P Rule 60(B), except to the extent and under the conditions stated in those rules. IN ST TRIAL P Rule 6(B).

    e. *Continuances disfavored.* Motions for Continuance are discouraged. Neither side is entitled to an automatic continuance as a matter of right. IN ST MARION CIR AND SUPER CTS CIV Rule 215. For information on obtaining a continuance, refer to IN ST MARION CIR AND SUPER CTS CIV Rule 215.

C. General Requirements

1. *Scope of discovery.* Unless otherwise limited by order of the court in accordance with the Indiana Rules of Trial Procedure, the scope of discovery is as follows:

    a. *In general.* Parties may obtain discovery regarding any matter, not privileged, which is relevant to the subject-matter involved in the pending action, whether it relates to the claim or defense of the party seeking discovery or the claim or defense of any other party, including the existence, description, nature, custody, condition and location of any books, documents, or other tangible things and the identity and location of persons having knowledge of any discoverable matter. It is not ground for objection that the information sought will be inadmissible at the trial if the information sought appears reasonably calculated to lead to the discovery of admissible evidence. IN ST TRIAL P Rule 26(B)(1).

    i.   *Limiting discovery upon court determination.* The frequency or extent of use of the discovery methods otherwise permitted under the Indiana Rules of Trial Procedure and by any local rule shall be limited by the court if it determines that:

- The discovery sought is unreasonably cumulative or duplicative, or is obtainable from some other source that is more convenient, less burdensome, or less expensive;

- The party seeking discovery has had ample opportunity by discovery in the action to obtain the information sought or;

- The burden or expense of the proposed discovery outweighs its likely benefit, taking into account the needs of the case, the amount in controversy, the parties' resources, the importance of the issues at stake in the litigation, and the importance of the proposed discovery in resolving the issues. IN ST TRIAL P Rule 26(B)(1).

- The court may act upon its own initiative after reasonable notice or pursuant to a motion under IN ST TRIAL P Rule 26(C). IN ST TRIAL P Rule 26(B)(1). Refer to the Indiana KeyRules Motion for Protective Order document for more information.

    ii.   *Relevancy in the discovery context.* When the word "relevancy" is used in IN ST TRIAL P Rule 26(B), it does not mean "relevancy" as that word in used to determine the admissibility of evidence in a trial court. It is much broader. It means "relevancy" to the "subject matter" of the litigation or pending action and it may relate to the claim or defense of any party. Pretrial discovery is available as to any nonprivileged matter relevant to the subject matter of the lawsuit or to obtain information reasonably calculated to lead to admissible evidence. 2A INPRAC R 26(26.4); Kaufmann v. Credithrift Financial, Inc., 465 N.E.2d 207, 210 (Ind.Ct.App. 1984).

    iii.   *Tests for relevance.* Indiana case law has developed two (2) additional tests in this area. 2A INPRAC R 26(26.4).

- The first test determines when a document or a request for information is actually relevant to the subject matter in the pending action. A document [or discovery request] is relevant to discovery if there is the possibility the information sought may be relevant to the subject matter of the action. 2A INPRAC R 26(26.4); CIGNA-INA/Aetna v. Hagerman-Shambaugh, 473 N.E.2d 1033, 1036 (Ind.Ct.App. 1985).

- The second test speaks to appellate review of the trial court's determination that a document or discovery request is relevant to the subject matter of the pending action. The appellate court sees its review of the trial court's decision on relevancy to subject matter as being very limited. The court states: "Our review of the trial court's conclusion that the documents are relevant is limited. A trial court is vested with discretion in its rulings on discovery issues." 2A INPRAC R 26(26.4); Costanzi v. Ryan, 175 Ind.App. 257, 370 N.E.2d 1333 (Ind.Ct.App. 1978).

b.   *Insurance agreements.* A party may obtain discovery of the existence and contents of any insurance agreement under which any person carrying on an insurance business may be liable to satisfy part or all of a judgment which may be entered in the action or to indemnify or reimburse for payments made to satisfy the judgment. Information concerning the insurance agreement is not by reason of disclosure admissible in evidence at trial. For purposes of IN ST TRIAL P Rule 26(B)(2), an application for insurance shall not be treated as part of an insurance agreement. IN ST TRIAL P Rule 26(B)(2).

c.   *Trial preparation; Materials.* Subject to the provisions of IN ST TRIAL P Rule 26(B)(4), a party may obtain discovery of documents and tangible things otherwise discoverable under IN ST TRIAL P Rule 26(B)(1) and prepared in anticipation of litigation or for trial by or for another party or by or for that other party's representative (including his attorney, consultant, surety, indemnitor, insurer, or agent) only upon a showing that the party seeking discovery has substantial need of the materials in the preparation of his case and that he is unable without undue hardship to obtain the substantial equivalent of the materials by other means. In ordering discovery of such materials when the required showing has been made, the court shall protect against disclosure of the mental impressions, conclusions, opinions, or legal theories of an attorney or other representative of a party concerning the litigation. IN ST TRIAL P Rule 26(B)(3).

    i.   A party may obtain without the required showing a statement concerning the action or its subject matter previously made by that party. Upon request, a person not a party may obtain without the required showing a statement concerning the action or its subject matter previously made by that person. If the request is refused, the person may move for a court order. The provisions of IN ST TRIAL P Rule 37(A)(4) apply to the award of expenses incurred in relation to the motion. For purposes of IN ST TRIAL P Rule 26(B)(3), a statement previously made is:

- A written statement signed or otherwise adopted approved by the person making it, or

- A stenographic, mechanical, electrical, or other recording, or a transcription thereof, which is a substantially verbatim recital of an oral statement by the person making it and contemporaneously recorded. IN ST TRIAL P Rule 26(B)(3).

    ii.   The protection of IN ST TRIAL P Rule 26(B)(3) extends to material prepared or collected before litigation actually commences, but that some possibility of litigation must actually exist before the privilege and IN ST TRIAL P Rule 26(B)(3) become operative. 2A INPRAC R 26(26.9); CIGNA-INA/Aetna v. Hagerman-Shambaugh, 473 N.E.2d 1033, 1037 (Ind.Ct.App. 1985).

d.   *Trial preparation; Experts.* Discovery of facts known and opinions held by experts, otherwise discoverable under the provisions of IN ST TRIAL P Rule 26(B)(1) and acquired or developed in anticipation of litigation or for trial, may be obtained as follows:

    i.   A party may through interrogatories require any other party to identify each person whom the other party expects to call as an expert witness at trial, to state the subject matter on which the expert is expected to testify, and to state the substance of the facts and opinions to which the expert is expected to testify and a summary of the grounds for each opinion. IN ST TRIAL P Rule 26(B)(4)(a)(i).

    ii.   Upon motion, the court may order further discovery by other means, subject to such restrictions as to scope and such provisions, pursuant to IN ST TRIAL P Rule 26(B)(4)(c), concerning fees and expenses as the court may deem appropriate. IN ST TRIAL P Rule 26(B)(4)(a)(ii).

    iii.   A party may discover facts known or opinions held by an expert who has been retained or specially employed by another party in anticipation of litigation or preparation for trial and who is not expected to be called as a witness at trial, only as provided in IN ST TRIAL P Rule 35(B) or upon a showing of exceptional circumstances under which it is impracticable for the party seeking discovery to obtain facts or opinions on the same subject by other means. IN ST TRIAL P Rule 26(B)(4)(b).

    iv.   Unless manifest injustice would result,

- The court shall require that the party seeking discovery pay the expert a reasonable fee for time spent in responding to discovery under IN ST TRIAL P Rule 26(B)(4)(a)(ii) and IN ST TRIAL P Rule 26(B)(4)(b); and

- With respect to discovery obtained under IN ST TRIAL P Rule 26(B)(4)(a)(ii) the court may require, and with respect to discovery obtained under IN ST TRIAL P Rule 26(B)(4)(b) the court shall require, the party seeking discovery to pay the other party a fair portion of the fees and expenses reasonably incurred by the latter party in obtaining facts and opinions from the expert. IN ST TRIAL P Rule 26(B)(4)(c).

e.   *Claims of privilege or protection*

    i.   *Information withheld.* When a party withholds information otherwise discoverable under the Indiana Rules of Trial Procedure by claiming that it is privileged or subject to protection as trial preparation material, the party shall make the claim expressly and shall describe the nature of the documents, communications, or things not produced or disclosed in a manner that, without revealing information itself privileged or protected, will enable other parties to assess the applicability of the privilege or protection. IN ST TRIAL P Rule 26(B)(5)(a).

ii. *Information produced.* If information is produced in discovery that is subject to a claim of privilege or protection as trial-preparation material, the party making the claim may notify any party that received the information of the claim and the basis for it. After being notified, a party must promptly return, sequester, or destroy the specified information and any copies it has and may not use or disclose the information until the claim is resolved. A receiving party may promptly present the information to the court under seal for a determination of the claim. If the receiving party disclosed the information before being notified, it must take reasonable steps to retrieve it. The producing party must preserve the information until the claim is resolved. IN ST TRIAL P Rule 26(B)(5)(b).

iii. *Waiver.* The law of discovery has developed some holdings which indicate that "waiver" of a privileged communication in a discovery setting might be more exacting than "waiver" of a privileged communication when the only question at hand is an interpretation of the privilege itself. Thus, in litigation in which several documents are in issue, and some are released inadvertently, there is strong case law that holds that the "inadvertent production" of a privileged document does not constitute a waiver of the attorney-client privilege. 2A INPRAC R 26(26.5); Transamerica Computer Co. v. International Business Machines Corp., 573 F.2d 646 (9th Cir. 1978). Such a rule should be measured against the usual rule which suggests that a voluntary disclosure to a third person will generally suffice to show a waiver of the attorney-client privilege. 2A INPRAC R 26(26.5).

f. *Use not limited.* Unless the court orders otherwise under IN ST TRIAL P Rule 26(C), the frequency of use of the methods listed in IN ST TRIAL P Rule 26(A) is not limited. IN ST TRIAL P Rule 26(A).

g. *Sequence of discovery.* Unless the court upon motion, for the convenience of parties and witnesses and in the interests of justice, orders otherwise, methods of discovery may be used in any sequence and the fact that a party is conducting discovery, whether by deposition or otherwise, shall not operate to delay any other party's discovery. IN ST TRIAL P Rule 26(D).

2. *Request for admissions.* A request for admission is a method of discovery which allows a party to establish facts and information during the discovery stage of the action so that evidence on those matters will not be required at trial. 22 INPRAC § 26.1; Walker v. Employers Ins. of Wausau, 846 N.E.2d 1098 (Ind.Ct.App. 2006); Brown v. Dobbs, 691 N.E.2d 907 (Ind.Ct.App. 1998). Requests for admission under IN ST TRIAL P Rule 36 are designed to simplify and clarify the issues, to cut trial preparation time, and to encourage settlement. 10 INPRAC § 69.1.

a. *Request for admissions generally.* A party may serve upon any other party a written request for the admission, for purposes of the pending action only, of the truth of any matters within the scope of IN ST TRIAL P Rule 26(B) set forth in the request, including the genuineness of any documents described in the request. IN ST TRIAL P Rule 36(A).

b. *Mutually known matters.* Requests for admissions as to matters within the mutual knowledge of both parties are proper. The function of IN ST TRIAL P Rule 36 is to establish admissions that will obviate the necessity of proof and expedite the trial, or to transform "mutual knowledge" into the established facts of a case. 3 INPRAC R 36(36.5).

c. *Requests to be carefully drafted.* The burden on the requesting party is to carefully and artfully draft the statement of fact contained in the request for admission. The statement must be precise, unambiguous, and in no way mislead the answering party. 3 INPRAC R 36(36.2).

d. *Requests to be carefully drafted.* The burden on the requesting party is to carefully and artfully draft the statement of fact contained in the request for admission. The statement must be precise, unambiguous, and in no way mislead the answering party. 3 INPRAC R 36(36.2).

i. Fairness demands that any error arising out of inartful drafting be borne by the requesting party. The burden imposed on the answering party is unfairly "increased when the request for admission propounds a statement of fact which lacks clarity, is ambiguous, or which otherwise might mislead the answering party." 3 INPRAC R 36(36.2); F.W. Means & Co. v. Carstens, 428 N.E.2d 251, 257 (Ind.Ct.App. 1981).

e. *Admissions by the requestor.* Propounding of requests for admissions admits nothing as to the requesting party. 3 INPRAC R 36(36.2); Indiana Construction Service v. Amoco Oil Company, 533 N.E.2d 1300 (Ind.Ct.App. 1989). This party in the action made an admission in the text of or during the request, to which the receiving party, of course, agreed. But it was not binding, as to the requesting party, the court held. Such a request is binding as to the party admitting the fact in response to a request. 3 INPRAC R 36(36.2); Indiana Construction Service v. Amoco Oil Company, 533 N.E.2d 1300 (Ind.Ct.App. 1989).

f. *Motion to compel.* The party who has requested the admissions may move for an order with respect to the answers or objections. Unless the court determines that an objection is justified, it shall order that an answer be served. If the court determines that an answer does not comply with the requirements of IN ST TRIAL P Rule 36, it may order either that the matter is admitted or that an amended answer be served. The court may, in lieu of these orders, determine that final disposition of the request be made at a pre-trial conference or at a designated time prior to trial. IN ST TRIAL P Rule 36(A).

    i. The provisions of IN ST TRIAL P Rule 37(A)(4) apply to the award of expenses incurred in relation to the motion. IN ST TRIAL P Rule 36(A).

    ii. Refer to the Indiana KeyRules Motion to Compel Discovery document for more information.

3. *Response to request for admissions.* The matter is admitted unless, within a period designated in the request, not less than thirty (30) days after service thereof or within such shorter or longer time as the court may allow, the party to whom the request is directed serves upon the party requesting the admission a written answer or objection addressed to the matter, signed by the party or by his attorney. IN ST TRIAL P Rule 36(A).

a. *Methods of response.* IN ST TRIAL P Rule 36 recognizes at least four (4) responses. The party:

    i. May not respond, thereby admitting the request; or

    ii. Answer; or

    iii. Object to the request; or

    iv. File a qualified response. 3 INPRAC R 36(36.4).

b. *Effect of admission.* Any matter admitted under IN ST TRIAL P Rule 36 is conclusively established unless the court on motion permits withdrawal or amendment of the admission. IN ST TRIAL P Rule 36(B).

    i. Any admission made by a party under IN ST TRIAL P Rule 36 is for the purpose of the pending action only and is not an admission by him for any other purpose nor may it be used against him in any other proceeding. IN ST TRIAL P Rule 36(B).

c. *Denials.* The answer shall specifically deny the matter or set forth in detail the reasons why the answering party cannot truthfully admit or deny the matter. A denial shall fairly meet the substance of the requested admission, and when good faith requires that a party qualify his answer or deny only a part of the matter of which an admission is requested, he shall specify so much of it as is true and qualify or deny the remainder. IN ST TRIAL P Rule 36(A).

d. *Lack of information or knowledge.* An answering party may not give lack of information or knowledge as a reason for failure to admit or deny unless he states that he has made reasonable inquiry and that the information known or readily obtainable by him is insufficient to enable him to admit or deny or that the inquiry would be unreasonably burdensome. IN ST TRIAL P Rule 36(A).

e. *Objections.* If objection is made, the reasons therefor shall be stated. IN ST TRIAL P Rule 36(A).

    i. A party who considers that a matter of which an admission has been requested presents a genuine issue for trial may not, on that ground alone, object to the request; he may, subject to the provisions of IN ST TRIAL P Rule 37(C), deny the matter or set forth reasons why he cannot admit or deny it. IN ST TRIAL P Rule 36(A).

    ii. An objectionable request may not be properly attacked by a motion to strike, to dismiss, or to suppress. The party served must respond to the request and serve admissions or denials of all matters not deemed objectionable. 3 INPRAC R 36(36.4).

f. *Withdrawal or amendment of admissions.* Subject to the provisions of IN ST TRIAL P Rule 16 governing amendment of a pre-trial order, the court may permit withdrawal or amendment when the presentation of the merits of the action will be subserved thereby and the party who obtained the admission fails to satisfy the court that withdrawal or amendment will prejudice him in maintaining his action or defense on the merits. IN ST TRIAL P Rule 36(B).

  i. It is within sound discretion of trial court to permit or deny amendment of pretrial order, but trial court should amend or modify pretrial order when requested if modification is necessary to prevent manifest injustice. 2 INPRAC R 16(7); Hacienda Mexican Restaurant of Kalamazoo Corp. v. Hacienda Franchise Group, Inc., 641 N.E.2d 1036 (Ind.Ct.App. 1994).

g. *Supplementation of responses.* A party who has responded to a request for discovery with a response that was complete when made is under no duty to supplement his response to include information thereafter acquired, except as follows:

  i. A party is under a duty seasonally to supplement his response with respect to any question directly addressed to:

  - The identity and location of persons having knowledge of discoverable matters, and

  - The identity of each person expected to be called as an expert witness at trial, the subject-matter on which he is expected to testify, and the substance of his testimony. IN ST TRIAL P Rule 26(E)(1).

  ii. A party is under a duty seasonally to amend a prior response if he obtains information upon the basis of which:

  - He knows that the response was incorrect when made, or

  - He knows that the response though correct when made is no longer true and the circumstances are such that a failure to amend the response is in substance a knowing concealment. IN ST TRIAL P Rule 26(E)(2).

  iii. A duty to supplement responses may be imposed by order of the court, agreement of the parties, or at any time prior to trial through new requests for supplementation of prior responses. IN ST TRIAL P Rule 26(E)(3).

  iv. The duty seasonally to supplement a discovery response is absolute and is not predicated on a court order. "It is a breach of a litigant's duty reasonably to supplement if the litigant postpones supplementing its response by not obtaining from its experts the information which is to be supplied in answer to interrogatories." 2A INPRAC R 26(26.27); Lucas v. Dorsey Corp., 609 N.E.2d 1191, 1196 (Ind.Ct.App. 1993).

D. Documents

1. *Required documents*

  a. *Request for admissions.* Refer to the General Requirements section of this document for information on the scope and content of a request for admissions.

  b. *Copies of documents.* Copies of documents shall be served with the request unless they have been or are otherwise furnished or made available for inspection and copying. IN ST TRIAL P Rule 36(A).

  c. *Certificate of service.* An attorney or unrepresented party tendering a document to the Clerk for filing shall certify that service has been made, list the parties served, and specify the date and means of service. The certificate of service shall be placed at the end of the document and shall not be separately filed. The separate filing of a certificate of service, however, shall not be grounds for rejecting a document for filing. The Clerk may permit documents to be filed without a certificate of service but shall require prompt filing of a separate certificate of service. IN ST TRIAL P Rule 5(C). In all cases where any pleading or other document is required to be served upon opposing counsel, proof of such service may be made either by:

  i. A certificate of service signed by counsel of record for the serving party and the certificate shall specify by name and address all counsel upon whom the pleading or document was served; or

  ii. An acknowledgment of service signed by the party served or counsel of record. IN ST MARION CIR AND SUPER CTS CIV Rule 206.

2. *Supplemental documents*

   a. *Stipulation regarding discovery procedure.* Unless the court orders otherwise, the parties may by written stipulation:

      i. Provide that depositions may be taken before any person, at any time or place, upon any notice, and in any manner and when so taken may be used like other depositions, and

      ii. Modify the procedures provided by the Indiana Rules of Trial Procedure for other methods of discovery. IN ST TRIAL P Rule 29.

   b. *Facsimile cover sheet.* Any document sent to the Clerk of the Circuit Court by electronic facsimile transmission shall be accompanied by a cover sheet which states the title of the document, case number, number of pages, identity and voice telephone number of the sending party and instructions for filing. The cover sheet shall contain the signature of the attorney or party, pro se, authorizing the filing. IN ST ADMIN Rule 12(D).

E. Format

1. *Form of requests for admissions.* The rules applicable to captions, and the signing and form of pleadings (IN ST TRIAL P Rule 8 through IN ST TRIAL P Rule 11), apply to all motions and other papers provided under the Indiana Rules of Trial Procedure. 22B INPRAC 7:2. Each matter of which an admission is requested shall be separately set forth. IN ST TRIAL P Rule 36(A).

2. *Form of pleadings*

   a. *Caption; Names of parties.* Every pleading shall contain a caption setting forth the name of the court, the title of the action, the file number, and a designation as in IN ST TRIAL P Rule 7(A). In the complaint the title of the action shall include the names of all the parties, but in other pleadings it is sufficient to state the name of the first party on each side with an appropriate indication of other parties. IN ST TRIAL P Rule 10(A).

      i. Every pleading shall contain a caption setting forth the name of the Court, the Division and Room Number, the title of the action and the file number. IN ST MARION CIR AND SUPER CTS CIV Rule 204(B).

   b. *Paragraphs; Separate statements.* All averments of a claim or defense shall be made in numbered paragraphs, the contents of each of which shall be limited as far as practicable to a statement of a single set of circumstances, and a paragraph may be referred to by number in all succeeding pleadings. Each claim founded upon a separate transaction or occurrence and each defense other than denials may be stated in a separate count or defense whenever a separation facilitates the clear presentation of the matters set forth. IN ST TRIAL P Rule 10(B).

   c. *Adoption by reference; Exhibits.* Statements in a pleading may be adopted by reference in a different part of the same pleading or in another pleading or in any motion. A copy of any written instrument which is an exhibit to a pleading is a part thereof for all purposes. IN ST TRIAL P Rule 10(C).

   d. *Paper.* Pleadings, motions and other papers may be either printed or typewritten on white opaque paper of at least sixteen (16) pound weight, eight and one-half (8-1/2) inches wide and eleven (11) inches in length. IN ST MARION CIR AND SUPER CTS CIV Rule 204(A).

   e. *Copies.* All copies shall likewise be on white paper of sufficient strength and durability to resist normal wear and tear. IN ST MARION CIR AND SUPER CTS CIV Rule 204(A).

   f. *Line spacing.* If typewritten, the lines shall be double spaced, except for quotations, which shall be indented and single spaced. IN ST MARION CIR AND SUPER CTS CIV Rule 204(A).

   g. *Script type.* Script type shall not be used. IN ST MARION CIR AND SUPER CTS CIV Rule 204(A).

   h. *Titles.* Titles on all pleadings shall delineate each topic included in the pleading e.g. where a pleading contains an Answer, a Motion to Strike or Dismiss, or a Jury Request each shall be set forth in the title. IN ST MARION CIR AND SUPER CTS CIV Rule 204(C).

   i. *Margins and binding.* Margins shall be one (1) inch. Binding or stapling shall be at the top and at no other place. Covers or backing shall not be used. IN ST MARION CIR AND SUPER CTS CIV Rule 204(D).

3. *Size of papers for filing.* Effective January 1, 1992, all pleadings, copies, motions and documents filed with any trial court or appellate level court, typed or printed, with the exception of exhibits and existing wills, shall be prepared on eight and one-half by eleven inch (8 1/2" x 11") size paper. IN ST ADMIN Rule 11.

4. *Form of electronically filed documents.* All electronically filed and served pleadings shall, to the extent practicable, be formatted in accordance with the applicable rules governing formatting of paper pleadings. IN ST MARION SUPER CT ADMIN Rule 311(2-103)(1).

   a. *Electronic document title.* The electronic document title of each pleading or other document shall include:

      i. Party or parties filing/serving the document,

      ii. Nature of the document,

      iii. Party or parties against whom relief, if any, is sought, and

      iv. Nature of the relief sought (e.g., Defendant ABC Corporation's Motion for Summary Judgment). IN ST MARION SUPER CT ADMIN Rule 311(2-103)(2).

5. *Signature requirements*

   a. *Signature of attorney.* Every pleading or motion of a party represented by an attorney shall be signed by at least one (1) attorney of record in his individual name, whose address, telephone number, and attorney number shall be stated, except that this provision shall not apply to pleadings and motions made and transcribed at the trial or a hearing before the judge and received by him in such form. IN ST TRIAL P Rule 11(A).

      i. All pleadings and motions shall contain the original or authorized signature of the attorney, the name of the attorney in typed or printed form, the name of the law firm if a member of a firm, the attorney's address, identification number, e-mail address, telephone number, fax number, and the designation as to the party for whom he appears. IN ST MARION CIR AND SUPER CTS CIV Rule 204(E).

      ii. The signature of an attorney constitutes a certificate by him that he has read the pleadings; that to the best of his knowledge, information, and belief, there is good ground to support it; and that it is not interposed for delay. IN ST TRIAL P Rule 11(A).

      iii. If a pleading or motion is not signed or is signed with intent to defeat the purpose of the rule, it may be stricken as sham and false and the action may proceed as though the pleading had not been served. IN ST TRIAL P Rule 11(A).

      iv. For a willful violation of IN ST TRIAL P Rule 11 an attorney may be subjected to appropriate disciplinary action. Similar action may be taken if scandalous or indecent matter is inserted. IN ST TRIAL P Rule 11(A).

      v. Every pleading, document, and instrument electronically filed or served shall be deemed to have been signed by the judge, clerk, attorney or declarant and shall bear a facsimile or typographical signature of such person, along with the typed name, address, telephone number, and Bar number of a signing attorney. Typographical signatures shall be treated as personal signatures for all purposes under these rules. IN ST MARION SUPER CT ADMIN Rule 311(2-105).

         • Documents containing signatures of third-parties (i.e., unopposed motions, affidavits, stipulations, etc.) may also be filed electronically by indicating that the original signatures are maintained by the filing party in paper-format. IN ST MARION SUPER CT ADMIN Rule 311(2-105).

         • Unless otherwise ordered by the Court or Clerk, a printed copy of all documents filed or served electronically, including original signatures, shall be maintained by the party filing the document and shall be made available, upon reasonable notice, for inspection by other counsel, the Clerk or Court. Parties shall retain originals until two (2) years after all time periods for appeal have expired. From time to time, it may be necessary to provide the Clerk or Court with a hard copy of an electronically filed document. IN ST MARION SUPER CT ADMIN Rule 311(2-105).

      vi.   For the recommended format of a signature block, refer to IN ST MARION CIR AND SUPER CTS CIV Rule 204(E).

b. *Signature of unrepresented party.* A party who is not represented by an attorney shall sign his pleading and state his address. IN ST TRIAL P Rule 11(A).

c. *Verification not generally required.* Except when specifically required by rule, pleadings or motions need not be verified or accompanied by affidavit. The rule in equity that the averments of an answer under oath must be overcome by the testimony of two (2) witnesses or of one (1) witness sustained by corroborating circumstances is abolished. IN ST TRIAL P Rule 11(A).

d. *Verification by affirmation or representation.* When in connection with any civil or special statutory proceeding it is required that any pleading, motion, petition, supporting affidavit, or other document of any kind, be verified, or that an oath be taken, it shall be sufficient if the subscriber simply affirms the truth of the matter to be verified by an affirmation or representation. IN ST TRIAL P Rule 11(B). IN ST TRIAL P Rule 11(B) states that the affirmation or representation should be in substantially the following language: "I (we) affirm, under the penalties for perjury, that the foregoing representation(s) is (are) true. (Signed) _____"

      i.   Any person who falsifies an affirmation or representation of fact shall be subject to the same penalties as are prescribed by law for the making of a false affidavit. IN ST TRIAL P Rule 11(B).

e. *Verified pleadings, motions, and affidavits as evidence.* Pleadings, motions and affidavits accompanying or in support of such pleadings or motions when required to be verified or under oath shall be accepted as a representation that the signer had personal knowledge thereof or reasonable cause to believe the existence of the facts or matters stated or alleged therein; and, if otherwise competent or acceptable as evidence, may be admitted as evidence of the facts or matters stated or alleged therein when it is so provided in the Indiana Rules of Trial Procedure, by statute or other law, or to the extent the writing or signature expressly purports to be made upon the signer's personal knowledge. When such pleadings, motions and affidavits are verified or under oath they shall not require other or greater proof on the part of the adverse party than if not verified or not under oath unless expressly provided otherwise by the Indiana Rules of Trial Procedure, statute or other law. Affidavits upon motions for summary judgment under IN ST TRIAL P Rule 56 and in denial of execution under IN ST TRIAL P Rule 9.2 shall be made upon personal knowledge. IN ST TRIAL P Rule 11(C).

6. *Information excluded from public access.* Every document filed in a case shall separately identify information excluded from public access pursuant to IN ST ADMIN Rule 9(G)(1) as follows:

a. Whole documents that are excluded from public access pursuant to IN ST ADMIN Rule 9(G)(1) shall be tendered on light green paper or have a light green coversheet attached to the document, marked "Not for Public Access" or "Confidential." IN ST TRIAL P Rule 5(G)(1).

b. When only a portion of a document contains information excluded from public access pursuant to IN ST ADMIN Rule 9(G)(1), said information shall be omitted [or redacted] from the filed document, and set forth on a separate accompanying document on light green paper conspicuously marked "Not for Public Access" or "Confidential" and clearly designated [or identifying] the caption and number of the case and the document and location within the document to which the redacted material pertains. IN ST TRIAL P Rule 5(G)(2).

c. With respect to documents filed in electronic format, the trial court, by local rule, may provide for compliance with IN ST TRIAL P Rule 5 in manner that separates and protects access to information excluded from public access. IN ST TRIAL P Rule 5(G)(3).

d. IN ST TRIAL P Rule 5(G) does not apply to a record sealed by the court pursuant to IN ST 5-14-3-5.5 or otherwise, nor to records, documents, or information filed in cases to which public access is prohibited pursuant to IN ST ADMIN Rule 9(G). IN ST TRIAL P Rule 5(G)(4).

e. The following information in case records is excluded from public access and is confidential:

      i.   Information that is excluded from public access pursuant to federal law;

ii. Information that is excluded from public access as declared confidential by Indiana statute or other court rule, including without limitation:

- All adoption records created after July 8, 1941, as declared confidential by IN ST 31-19-19-1, et seq., except those specifically declared open by IN ST 31-19-13-2(2);

- All records relating to chancroid, chlamydia, gonorrhea, hepatitis, human immunodeficiency virus (HIV), Lymphogranuloma venereum, syphilis, tuberculosis, as declared confidential by IN ST 16-41-8-1, et seq.;

- All records relating to child abuse as declared confidential by IN ST 31-33-18-1, et seq.;

- All records relating to drug tests as declared confidential by IN ST 5-14-3-4(a)(9);

- Records of grand jury proceedings as declared confidential by IN ST 35-34-2-4;

- Records of juvenile proceedings as declared confidential by IN ST 31-39-1-2, except those specifically open under statute;

- All paternity records created after July 1, 1941 as declared confidential by IN ST 31-14-11-15, IN ST 31-19-5-23, IN ST 31-39-1-1 and IN ST 31-39-1-2 [Editor's note: IN ST 31-14-11-15 was repealed effective May 9, 2013];

- All pre-sentence reports as declared confidential by IN ST 35-38-1-13;

- Written petitions to permit marriages without consent and orders directing the Clerk of Court to issue a marriage license to underage persons, as declared confidential by IN ST 31-11-1-6;

- Only those arrest warrants, search warrants, indictments and informations ordered confidential by the trial judge, prior to return of duly executed service as declared confidential by IN ST 5-14-3-4(b)(1);

- All medical, mental health, or tax records unless determined by law or regulation of any governmental custodian not to be confidential, released by the subject of such records, or declared by a court of competent jurisdiction to be essential to the resolution of litigation as declared confidential by IN ST 16-39-3-10, IN ST 6-4.1-5-10, IN ST 6-4.1-12-12, and IN ST 6-8.1-7-1;

- Personal information relating to jurors or prospective jurors, other than for the use of the parties and counsel, pursuant to IN ST JURY Rule 10;

- Information relating to protection from abuse orders, no-contact orders and workplace violence restraining orders as declared confidential by IN ST 5-2-9-6, et seq.;

- Mediation proceedings pursuant to IN ST ADR Rule 2.11, Mini-Trial proceedings pursuant to IN ST ADR Rule 4.4(C), and Summary Jury Trials pursuant to IN ST ADR Rule 5.6;

- Information in probation files pursuant to the Probation Standards promulgated by the Judicial Conference of Indiana pursuant to IN ST 11-13-1-8(b);

- Information deemed confidential pursuant to the Rules for Court Administered Alcohol and Drug Programs promulgated by the Judicial Conference of Indiana pursuant to IN ST 12-23-14-13;

- Information deemed confidential pursuant to the Problem-Solving Court Rules promulgated by the Judicial Conference of Indiana pursuant to IN ST 33-23-16-16;

- All records of the Department of workforce Development as declared confidential by IN ST 22-4-19-6;

- Information regarding interception of electronic communications that is sealed or deemed confidential as set forth in IN ST 35-33.5-2-1, et seq.

iii. Information excluded from public access by specific court order;

iv. Complete Social Security Numbers of living persons;

v. With the exception of names, information such as addresses, phone numbers, and dates of birth which explicitly identifies:

- Natural persons who are witnesses or victims (not including defendants) in criminal, domestic violence, stalking, sexual assault, juvenile, or civil protection order proceedings, provided that juveniles who are victims of sex crimes shall be identified by initials only;

- Places of residence of judicial officers, clerks and other employees of courts and clerks of court, unless the person or persons about whom the information pertains waives confidentiality;

vi. Complete account numbers of specific assets, loans, bank accounts, credit cards, and personal identification numbers (PINs);

vii. All orders of expungement entered in criminal or juvenile proceedings, orders to restrict access to criminal history information pursuant to IN ST 35-38-5-5.5 or IN ST 35-38-8-5 and records excluded from public access by such orders, and information related to infractions that is excluded from public access pursuant to IN ST 34-28-5-15 or IN ST 34-28-5-16 [Editor's note: IN ST 35-38-5-5.5, IN ST 35-38-8-5 and IN ST 34-28-5-16 were repealed effective July 1, 2013; for information on orders restricting access to criminal history, refer to IN ST 35-38-9-1, et seq.];

viii. All personal notes and e-mail, and deliberative material, of judges, jurors, court staff and judicial agencies, and information recorded in personal data assistants (PDA's) or organizers and personal calendars. IN ST ADMIN Rule 9(G)(1).

F. Filing and Service Requirements

1. *Filing requirements.* Except as otherwise provided in IN ST TRIAL P Rule 5(E)(2), all pleadings and papers subsequent to the complaint which are required to be served upon a party shall be filed with the Court either before service or within a reasonable period of time thereafter. IN ST TRIAL P Rule 5(E)(1).

a. *Non-filing of discovery until necessary*

i. *Non-filing of discovery; Exceptions.* No deposition or request for discovery or response thereto under IN ST TRIAL P Rule 27, IN ST TRIAL P Rule 30, IN ST TRIAL P Rule 31, IN ST TRIAL P Rule 33, IN ST TRIAL P Rule 34 or IN ST TRIAL P Rule 36 shall be filed with the Court unless:

- A motion is filed pursuant to IN ST TRIAL P Rule 26(C) or IN ST TRIAL P Rule 37 and the original deposition or request for discovery or response thereto is necessary to enable the Court to rule; or

- A party desires to use the deposition or request for discovery or response thereto for evidentiary purposes at trial or in connection with a motion, and the Court, either upon its own motion or that of any party, or as a part of any pre-trial order, orders the filing of the original. IN ST TRIAL P Rule 5(E)(2).

ii. *Custody of original and period of retention*

- The original of a deposition shall, subject to the provisions of IN ST TRIAL P Rule 30(E), be delivered by the reporter to the party taking it and shall be maintained by that party until filed with the Court pursuant to IN ST TRIAL P Rule 5(E)(2) or until the later of final judgment, agreed settlement of the litigation or all appellate rights have been exhausted. IN ST TRIAL P Rule 5(E)(3)(a).

- The original or any request for discovery or response thereto under IN ST TRIAL P Rule 27, IN ST TRIAL P Rule 30, IN ST TRIAL P Rule 31, IN ST TRIAL P Rule 33, IN ST TRIAL P Rule 34 and IN ST TRIAL P Rule 36 shall be maintained by the party originating the request or response until filed with the Court pursuant to IN ST TRIAL P Rule 5(E)(2) or until the later of final judgment, agreed settlement or all appellate rights have been exhausted. IN ST TRIAL P Rule 5(E)(3)(b).

iii. *Original unavailable; Copies.* In the event it is made to appear to the satisfaction of the Court that the original of a deposition or request for discovery or response thereto cannot be filed with

the Court when required, the Court may allow use of a copy instead of the original. IN ST TRIAL P Rule 5(E)(4).

    iv. *Filing as publication.* The filing of any deposition shall constitute publication. IN ST TRIAL P Rule 5(E)(5).

b. *Filing generally.* All pleadings, petitions and motions are filed with the Clerk designated by the Court at any time during office hours established by the Clerk and the Court. All orders submitted to the Court shall be in sufficient number and shall be accompanied by postage paid envelopes addressed to each party or counsel of record. IN ST MARION CIR AND SUPER CTS CIV Rule 205(A)

c. *Filing with the court defined.* The filing of pleadings, motions, and other papers with the court as required by the Indiana Rules of Trial Procedure shall be made by one of the following methods:

    i. Delivery to the clerk of the court;

    ii. Sending by electronic transmission under the procedure adopted pursuant to IN ST ADMIN Rule 12;

    iii. Mailing to the clerk by registered, certified or express mail return receipt requested;

    iv. Depositing with any third-party commercial carrier for delivery to the clerk within three (3) calendar days, cost prepaid, properly addressed;

    v. If the court so permits, filing with the judge, in which event the judge shall note thereon the filing date and forthwith transmit them to the office of the clerk; or

    vi. Electronic filing, as approved by the Division of State Court Administration pursuant to IN ST ADMIN Rule 16. IN ST TRIAL P Rule 5(F).

    vii. Filing by registered or certified mail and by third-party commercial carrier shall be complete upon mailing or deposit. IN ST TRIAL P Rule 5(F).

d. *Facsimile filing.* Facsimile filing is discouraged, but permitted in the Marion Circuit and Marion Superior Court. All documents filed by facsimile shall also be filed in hard copy within seven (7) days of the facsimile filing, along with proposed orders and stamped addressed envelopes, as required by IN ST MARION CIR AND SUPER CTS CIV Rule 203(E). To avoid duplicate filings, the hard copies of the facsimile filing shall indicate in bold letters that the pleading was previously filed by facsimile transmission. Proof of transmission by facsimile, including certificate of service and manner of service, shall be the responsibility of the filing party. If the filing requires immediate attention of the Judge, it shall be so indicated in bold letters in an accompanying transmittal memorandum. Legibility of documents and timeliness of filing is the responsibility of the sender. IN ST MARION CIR AND SUPER CTS CIV Rule 205(B).

    i. *Generally.* In counties where a majority of judges of the courts of record, by posted local rule, have authorized electronic facsimile filing and designated a telephone number to receive such transmissions, pleadings, motions, and other papers may be sent to the Clerk of Circuit Court by electronic facsimile transmission for filing in any case, provided:

- Such matter does not exceed ten (10) pages, including the cover sheet;
- Such matter does not require the payment of fees other than the electronic facsimile transcription fee set forth in IN ST ADMIN Rule 12(E);
- The sending party creates at the time of transmission a machine generated log for such transmission; and
- The original document and the transmission log are maintained by the sending party for the duration of the litigation. IN ST ADMIN Rule 12(B).

    ii. *Time of filing.* During normal, posted business hours, the time of filing shall be the time the duplicate document is produced in the office of the Clerk of the Circuit Court. Duplicate documents received at all other times shall be filed as of the next normal business day. IN ST ADMIN Rule 12(C).

- If the receiving fax machine endorses its own time and date stamp upon the transmitted

documents and the receiving machine produces a delivery receipt which is electronically created and transmitted to the sending party, the time of filing shall be the date and time recorded on the transmitted document by the receiving fax machine. IN ST ADMIN Rule 12(C).

e. *Electronic filing.* Electronic filing and electronic service pilot projects are authorized pursuant to IN ST ADMIN Rule 16 and approved by the Division of State Court Administration. IN ST MARION SUPER CT ADMIN Rule 311(1-103).

    i. *Cases where electronic filing accepted.* All Marion County Circuit and Superior civil courts may accept electronic filing and service of pleadings and other documents designated in this rule in mortgage foreclosure (hereinafter referred to as "MF"), civil collection(hereinafter referred to as "CC"), and individual cases that have been approved for electronic filing and service. IN ST MARION SUPER CT ADMIN Rule 311(1-104)(1).

- The Marion County Circuit Court may, upon the motion of a party or its own motion, designate a case that will involve multiple litigants, legally intricate issues, and an extensive number of documents a mass tort or complex litigation case. Any case so designated shall be subject to electronic filing and service using the county's approved Electronic Service Provider. IN ST MARION SUPER CT ADMIN Rule 311(1-104)(3).

- The filing of electronic pleadings and other documents in MF and CC cases is entirely voluntary; however, once the case is initially filed electronically, all subsequent filings in the case shall remain in electronic format until the time for appeal is exhausted. IN ST MARION SUPER CT ADMIN Rule 311(1-104)(5).

    ii. *Documents eligible for electronic filing.* The following pleadings may be filed and served electronically:

- New case complaint and petitions. IN ST MARION SUPER CT ADMIN Rule 311(1-104)(8)(a).

- Original answers. IN ST MARION SUPER CT ADMIN Rule 311(1-104)(8)(a).

- Any other pleadings or document including but not limited to motions and appearance forms. IN ST MARION SUPER CT ADMIN Rule 311(1-104)(8)(a).

    iii. *Manner of electronic filing.* Parties shall E-file a document either:

- By registering to use the Electronic Filing Service Provider; or

- In person at the Marion County Clerk's office, by electronically filing through the Public Access Terminal. Parties filing in this manner shall be responsible for furnishing the document in an electronic format that will be compatible with the clerk's office-system to be uploaded in person. IN ST MARION SUPER CT ADMIN Rule 311(1-104)(9). For information on the Electronic Filing Service Provider and Public Access Terminal, refer to IN ST MARION SUPER CT ADMIN Rule 311(1-101).

- Registered users shall pay statutory filing fees for E-filed documents electronically to the Court through their EFSP. Filing fees are due and payable at the time of filing. IN ST MARION SUPER CT ADMIN Rule 311(2-104)(1). For more information on electronic filing fees, refer to IN ST MARION SUPER CT ADMIN Rule 311(2-104).

    iv. *Effect of electronic filing.* Any pleading filed electronically shall be considered as filed with the court when the transmission to the EFSP is complete. Any document E-filed by 11:59 p.m. local Indianapolis, Indiana time shall be deemed filed on that date. The EFSP is an agent of the Court for the purpose of electronic filing, receipt, service and retrieval of electronic documents. IN ST MARION SUPER CT ADMIN Rule 311(2-102).

- Upon completion of filing, the EFSP shall issue a confirmation receipt that includes the date and time of receipt. The confirmation receipt shall serve as proof of filing. IN ST MARION SUPER CT ADMIN Rule 311(2-102).

- In the event the Court rejects the submitted documents following review, the documents shall not become part of the official Court record and the filer will receive notification of the rejection. Users may be required to refile the instruments to meet necessary filing requirements. Documents may be filed through an E-filing system at any time that the Clerk's office is open to receive the filing or at such other times as may be designated by the clerk and posted publicly. IN ST MARION SUPER CT ADMIN Rule 311(2-102).

- Documents filed through the E-filing system are deemed filed when received by the Clerk's office, except that documents received at times that the Clerk's office is closed shall be deemed filed the next regular time when the Clerk's office is open for filing. The time stamp issued by the E-filing system shall be presumed to be the time the document is received by the Clerk. IN ST MARION SUPER CT ADMIN Rule 311(2-102).

v. *Electronically filed documents.* All pleadings and other documents designated in IN ST MARION SUPER CT ADMIN Rule 311 shall be filed and served electronically in any individual case which has been approved for electronic filing and service. IN ST MARION SUPER CT ADMIN Rule 311(1-104)(6).

vi. *System failures.* When filing by electronic means is hindered by a technical failure, a party may file with the Clerk of Marion County in hard copy. With the exception of deadlines that by law cannot be extended, the time for filing of any paper that is delayed due to technical failure of the site shall be extended for one (1) day for each day on which such failure occurs, unless otherwise ordered by the Court. IN ST MARION SUPER CT ADMIN Rule 311(2-108).

vii. *Compliance with rules.* All filing shall comply with the requirements of IN ST ADMIN Rule 9 and IN ST ADMIN Rule 16; and the Indiana Rules of Court and the Marion County Local Rules. IN ST MARION SUPER CT ADMIN Rule 311(1-104)(11).

f. *Filing for special judge.* When a Special Judge who is not a Marion County Judge is selected, all parties or attorneys shall furnish such Judge with copies of all filings prior to the qualification of such Special Judge. Thereafter, copies of all filings shall be delivered in person, by mail or by facsimile to the office of the Special Judge with certificate of forwarding same made a part of the filing. IN ST MARION CIR AND SUPER CTS CIV Rule 205(C).

g. *Proof of filing.* Any party filing any paper by any method other than personal delivery to the clerk shall retain proof of filing. IN ST TRIAL P Rule 5(F).

2. *Service requirements.* Unless otherwise provided by the Indiana Rules of Trial Procedure or an order of the court, each party and special judge, if any, shall be served with: (1) every order required by its terms to be served; (2) every pleading subsequent to the original complaint; (3) every written motion except one which may be heard ex parte; (4) every brief submitted to the trial court; (5) every paper relating to discovery required to be served upon a party; and (6) every written notice, appearance, demand, offer of judgment, designation of record on appeal, or similar paper. IN ST TRIAL P Rule 5(A).

a. *Methods of service*

i. *Personal service.* Whenever a party is represented by an attorney of record, service shall be made upon such attorney unless service upon the party himself is ordered by the court. Service upon the attorney or party shall be made by delivering or mailing a copy of the papers to the last known address or where an attorney or party has consented to service by fax or e-mail, as provided in IN ST TRIAL P Rule 3.1(A)(4), by faxing or e-mailing a copy of the documents to the fax number or e-mail address set out in the appearance form or correction as required by IN ST TRIAL P Rule 3.1(E). IN ST TRIAL P Rule 5(B). Delivery of a copy within IN ST TRIAL P Rule 5 means:

- Offering or tendering it to the attorney or party and stating the nature of the papers being served. Refusal to accept an offered or tendered document is a waiver of any objection to the sufficiency or adequacy of service of that document;

- Leaving it at his office with a clerk or other person in charge thereof, or if there is no one in charge, leaving it in a conspicuous place therein; or

- If the office is closed, by leaving it at his dwelling house or usual place of abode with some person of suitable age and discretion then residing therein; or,

- Leaving it at some other suitable place, selected by the attorney upon whom service is being made, pursuant to duly promulgated local rule. IN ST TRIAL P Rule 5(B)(1).

ii. *Service by mail.* If service is made by mail, the papers shall be deposited in the United States mail addressed to the person on whom they are being served, with postage prepaid. Service shall be deemed complete upon mailing. Proof of service of all papers permitted to be mailed may be made by written acknowledgment of service, by affidavit of the person who mailed the papers, or by certificate of an attorney. It shall be the duty of attorneys when entering their appearance in a cause or when filing pleadings or papers therein, to have noted in the Chronological Case Summary or said pleadings or papers so filed the address and telephone number of their office. Service by delivery or by mail at such address shall be deemed sufficient and complete. IN ST TRIAL P Rule 5(B)(2).

iii. *Service by fax or e-mail.* A party who has consented to service by fax or e-mail may be served as follows:

- Service by e-mail shall be made by attaching the document being served in .pdf format. Discovery documents must also be served in accordance with IN ST TRIAL P Rule 26(A). IN ST TRIAL P Rule 5(B)(3)(a).

- Service by fax shall be deemed complete upon generation of a transmission record indicating the successful transmission of the entire document, except as provided in IN ST TRIAL P Rule 5(B)(3)(d). IN ST TRIAL P Rule 5(B)(3)(b).

- Service by e-mail shall be deemed complete upon transmission, except as provided in IN ST TRIAL P Rule 5(B)(3)(d). IN ST TRIAL P Rule 5(B)(3)(c).

- Service by fax or e-mail that occurs on a Saturday, Sunday, legal holiday, or day the court or agency in which the matter is pending is closed or after 5:00 PM local time of the recipient shall be deemed complete the next day that is not a Saturday, Sunday, legal holiday, or day that the court or agency in which the matter is pending is not closed. IN ST TRIAL P Rule 5(B)(3)(d).

iv. *Electronic service.* Delivery of E-service documents through the EFSP to other registered users shall be considered as valid and effective service and shall have the same legal effect as an original paper document. Recipients of E-service documents shall access their documents through the EFSP. IN ST MARION SUPER CT ADMIN Rule 311(2-107)(1).

- E-service shall be deemed complete when the transmission to the EFSP is completed. IN ST MARION SUPER CT ADMIN Rule 311(2-107)(2).

- For the purpose of computing time to respond to documents received via E-service, any document served on a day or at a time when the Clerk's office is not open for business shall be deemed served at the time of next opening of the Clerk's office for business. IN ST MARION SUPER CT ADMIN Rule 311(2-107)(3).

v. *Additional service of electronic discovery.* In addition to service under Rule IN ST TRIAL P Rule 5(B) or a .pdf format electronic copy, a party propounding or responding to interrogatories, requests for production or requests for admission shall comply with IN ST TRIAL P Rule 26(A.1)(a) or IN ST TRIAL P Rule 26(A.1)(b). IN ST TRIAL P Rule 26(A.1).

- The party shall serve the discovery request or response in an electronic format (either on a disk or as an electronic document attachment) in any commercially available word processing software system. If transmitted on disk, each disk shall be labeled, identifying the caption of the case, the document, and the word processing version in which it is being submitted. If more than one (1) disk is used for the same document, each disk shall be labeled and also shall be sequentially numbered. If transmitted by electronic mail, the document must be accompanied by electronic memorandum providing the forgoing identifying information; or

- The party shall serve the opposing party with a verified statement that the attorney or party appealing pro se lacks the equipment and is unable to transmit the discovery as required by IN ST TRIAL P Rule 26(A.1). IN ST TRIAL P Rule 26(A.1).

b. *Serving numerous defendants.* In any action in which there are unusually large numbers of defendants, the court, upon motion or of its own initiative, may order:

   i. That service of the pleadings of the defendants and replies thereto need not be made as between the defendants;

- That any cross-claim, counterclaim, or matter constituting an avoidance or affirmative defense contained therein shall be deemed to be denied or avoided by all other parties; and

- That the filing of any such pleading and service thereof upon the plaintiff constitutes due notice of it to the parties. IN ST TRIAL P Rule 5(D).

   ii. A copy of every such order shall be served upon the parties in such manner and form as the court directs. IN ST TRIAL P Rule 5(D).

c. *Service on parties in default for failure to appear.* No service need be made on parties in default for failure to appear, except that pleadings asserting new or additional claims for relief against them shall be served upon them in the manner provided by service of summons in IN ST TRIAL P Rule 4. IN ST TRIAL P Rule 5(A).

G. Hearings

1. The Indiana rules do not contemplate a hearing related to the filing and service of requests for admissions.

H. Forms

1. Request for Admissions Forms for Indiana

a. Request for admission. 5 INPRAC § 4:4.1.

b. Response to request for admission. 5 INPRAC § 4:4.2.

c. Response to request for admission; Alternative form. 5 INPRAC § 4:4.3.

d. Motion for order that matter be deemed admitted. 5 INPRAC § 4:4.4.

e. Requests for admission; General form. 10 INPRAC § 69.6.

f. Requests for admission; Genuineness of document. 10 INPRAC § 69.7.

g. Requests for admission; Specific document and matters related thereto; Insurance contract. 10 INPRAC § 69.8.

h. Requests for admission; Action against bank. 10 INPRAC § 69.9.

i. Requests for admission; Automobile accident. 10 INPRAC § 69.10.

j. Requests for admission; Automobile accident; Respondeat superior. 10 INPRAC § 69.11.

k. Requests for admission; Action on account stated. 10 INPRAC § 69.12.

l. Requests for admission; Action to foreclose on mortgage. 10 INPRAC § 69.13.

m. Requests for admission; Action for attorney malpractice. 10 INPRAC § 69.14.

n. Requests for admission; Products liability action; Defective hair products; Defendants. 10 INPRAC § 69.15.

o. Response to requests for admission; General form. 10 INPRAC § 69.20.

p. Alternative responses to requests for admission. 10 INPRAC § 69.21.

q. Motion for enlargement of time to respond to requests for admission. 10 INPRAC § 69.22.

r. Motion to withdraw and amend response to requests for admission. 10 INPRAC § 69.23.

s. Order granting motion to withdraw and amend responses. 10 INPRAC § 69.24.

t. Motion for order that matter be deemed admitted. 10 INPRAC § 69.25.

u. Motion for order requiring party to pay expenses for refusal to admit matters. 10 INPRAC § 69.26.

I. Checklist

(I) ❏ Matters to be considered by the party serving the request

    (a) ❏ Required documents

        (1) ❏ Request for admissions

        (2) ❏ Copies of documents

        (3) ❏ Certificate of service

    (b) ❏ Supplemental documents

        (1) ❏ Stipulation regarding discovery procedure

        (2) ❏ Facsimile cover sheet

    (c) ❏ Timing

        (1) ❏ The request may, without leave of court, be served upon the plaintiff after commencement of the action and upon any other party with or after service of the summons and complaint upon that party

(II) ❏ Matters to be considered by the responding party

    (a) ❏ Required documents

        (1) ❏ Response to request for admissions

        (2) ❏ Certificate of service

    (b) ❏ Supplemental documents

        (1) ❏ Stipulation regarding discovery procedure

        (2) ❏ Facsimile cover sheet

    (c) ❏ Timing

        (1) ❏ The matter is admitted unless, within a period designated in the request, not less than thirty (30) days after service thereof or within such shorter or longer time as the court may allow, the party to whom the request is directed serves upon the party requesting the admission a written answer or objection addressed to the matter

Requests, Notices and Applications
Notice of Deposition

Document Last Updated October 2013

A. Applicable Rules

1. *State rules*

    a. Appearance. IN ST TRIAL P Rule 3.1.

    b. Process. IN ST TRIAL P Rule 4.

    c. Service and filing of pleadings and other papers. IN ST TRIAL P Rule 5.

    d. Time. IN ST TRIAL P Rule 6.

    e. Pleadings. IN ST TRIAL P Rule 7; IN ST TRIAL P Rule 9.2; IN ST TRIAL P Rule 10.

    f. Signing and verification of pleadings. IN ST TRIAL P Rule 11.

    g. Parties plaintiff and defendant; Capacity. IN ST TRIAL P Rule 17.

    h. General provisions governing discovery. IN ST TRIAL P Rule 26.

    i. Discovery methods. IN ST TRIAL P Rule 27; IN ST TRIAL P Rule 28; IN ST TRIAL P Rule 29; IN ST TRIAL P Rule 30; IN ST TRIAL P Rule 31; IN ST TRIAL P Rule 32; IN ST TRIAL P Rule 33; IN ST TRIAL P Rule 34; IN ST TRIAL P Rule 35; IN ST TRIAL P Rule 36.

j. Failure to make or cooperate in discovery; Sanctions. IN ST TRIAL P Rule 37.

k. Evidence. IN ST TRIAL P Rule 43.

l. Subpoena. IN ST TRIAL P Rule 45.

m. Judgment on the evidence (directed verdict). IN ST TRIAL P Rule 50.

n. Findings by the court. IN ST TRIAL P Rule 52.

o. Summary judgment. IN ST TRIAL P Rule 56.

p. Motion to correct error. IN ST TRIAL P Rule 59.

q. Relief from judgment or order. IN ST TRIAL P Rule 60.

r. Recording machines; Court reports; Stenographic report or transcript as evidence. IN ST TRIAL P Rule 74.

s. Access to court records. IN ST ADMIN Rule 9.

t. Paper size. IN ST ADMIN Rule 11.

u. Facsimile transmission. IN ST ADMIN Rule 12.

v. Electronic filing and electronic service pilot projects. IN ST ADMIN Rule 16.

w. Sealing of certain records by court; Hearing; Notice. IN ST 5-14-3-5.5.

x. Privacy and confidentiality. IN ST 5-2-9-6; IN ST 5-14-3-4; IN ST 6-4.1-5-10; IN ST 6-4.1-12-12; IN ST 6-8.1-7-1; IN ST 11-13-1-8; IN ST 12-23-14-13; IN ST 16-39-3-10; IN ST 16-41-8-1; IN ST 22-4-19-6; IN ST 31-11-1-6; IN ST 31-19-5-23; IN ST 31-19-13-2; IN ST 31-19-19-1; IN ST 31-33-18-1; IN ST 31-39-1-1; IN ST 31-39-1-2; IN ST 33-23-16-16; IN ST 35-34-2-4; IN ST 35-38-1-13; IN ST 35-38-9-1; IN ST ADR Rule 2.11; IN ST ADR Rule 4.4; IN ST ADR Rule 5.6; IN ST JURY Rule 10.

2. *Local rules*

a. Requirements for motions. IN ST MARION CIR AND SUPER CTS CIV Rule 203.

b. Preparation of pleadings, motions and other papers. IN ST MARION CIR AND SUPER CTS CIV Rule 204.

c. Filing of pleadings, motions and other papers. IN ST MARION CIR AND SUPER CTS CIV Rule 205.

d. Signing and verification of pleadings, motions and other papers; Service on opposing party. IN ST MARION CIR AND SUPER CTS CIV Rule 206.

e. Video tape depositions. IN ST MARION CIR AND SUPER CTS CIV Rule 212.

f. Motions for continuance. IN ST MARION CIR AND SUPER CTS CIV Rule 215.

g. Electronic filing. IN ST MARION SUPER CT ADMIN Rule 311.

B. Timing

1. *Time for notice of deposition*

a. *Depositions upon oral examination.* After commencement of the action, any party may take the testimony of any person, including a party, by deposition upon oral examination. IN ST TRIAL P Rule 30(A).

i. A party desiring to take the deposition of any person upon oral examination shall give reasonable notice in writing to every other party to the action. IN ST TRIAL P Rule 30(B)(1).

- The party who gives notice of taking a deposition must do so in a way which is sufficiently timely to permit the party who receives the notice to make arrangements to travel to the place where the deposition is to be taken, and the notice which is given must be in sufficient time to permit the party to seek a protective order under IN ST TRIAL P Rule 30(D) and IN ST TRIAL P Rule 26(C), if necessary. 2A INPRAC R 30(30.2).

ii. Leave of court, granted with or without notice, must be obtained only if the plaintiff seeks to take a deposition prior to the expiration of twenty (20) days after service of summons and complaint upon any defendant except that leave is not required:

- If a defendant has served a notice of taking deposition or otherwise sought discovery; or
- If special notice is given as provided in IN ST TRIAL P Rule 30(B)(2). IN ST TRIAL P Rule 30(A).

   iii. The court may for cause shown enlarge or shorten the time for taking the deposition. IN ST TRIAL P Rule 30(B)(3).

b. *Depositions upon written questions.* After commencement of the action, any party may take the testimony of any person, including a party, by deposition upon written questions. IN ST TRIAL P Rule 31(A).

   i. *Service of cross questions.* Within twenty (20) days after the notice and written questions are served, a party may serve cross questions upon all other parties. IN ST TRIAL P Rule 31(A).

   ii. *Service of redirect questions.* Within ten (10) days after being served with cross questions, a party may serve redirect questions upon all other parties. IN ST TRIAL P Rule 31(A).

   iii. *Service of recross questions.* Within ten (10) days after being served with redirect questions, a party may serve recross questions upon all other parties. IN ST TRIAL P Rule 31(A).

   iv. *Time to respond.* The court may for cause shown enlarge or shorten the time. IN ST TRIAL P Rule 31(A).

c. *For deposition before action.* At least twenty (20) days before the date of hearing the notice shall be served in the manner provided in IN ST TRIAL P Rule 4 for service of summons; but if such service cannot with due diligence be made upon any expected adverse party named in the petition, the court may make such order as is just for service by publication or otherwise, and shall appoint, for persons not served in the manner provided in IN ST TRIAL P Rule 4, an attorney who shall represent them, and, in case they are not otherwise represented, shall cross-examine the deponent. If any expected adverse party is a minor or incompetent the provisions of IN ST TRIAL P Rule 17(C) apply. IN ST TRIAL P Rule 27(A)(2).

   i. Refer to the Indiana KeyRules Complaint document for information regarding service under IN ST TRIAL P Rule 4.

d. *For deposition pending appeal.* The party who desires to perpetuate the testimony may make a motion in the court for leave to take the depositions, upon the same notice and service thereof as if the action was pending in the court. IN ST TRIAL P Rule 27(B).

   i. *Filing.* All pleadings and papers subsequent to the complaint which are required to be served upon a party shall be filed with the Court either before service or within a reasonable period of time thereafter. IN ST TRIAL P Rule 5(E)(1).

   ii. *Service.* A written motion, other than one which may be heard ex parte, and notice of the hearing thereof shall be served not less than five (5) days before the time specified for the hearing, unless a different period is fixed by the Indiana Rules of Trial Procedure or by order of the court. IN ST TRIAL P Rule 6(D).

- *Of supporting affidavits.* When a motion is supported by affidavit, the affidavit shall be served with the motion. IN ST TRIAL P Rule 6(D).

2. *Computation of time*

a. *Generally; Days excluded.* In computing any period of time prescribed or allowed by the Indiana Rules of Trial Procedure, by order of the court, or by any applicable statute, the day of the act, event, or default from which the designated period of time begins to run shall not be included. The last day of the period so computed is to be included unless it is:

   i. A Saturday,

   ii. A Sunday,

   iii. A legal holiday as defined by state statute, or

    iv.   A day the office in which the act is to be done is closed during regular business hours. IN ST TRIAL P Rule 6(A).

b.   *Short periods.* In any event, the period runs until the end of the next day that is not a Saturday, a Sunday, a legal holiday, or a day on which the office is closed. When the period of time allowed is less than seven (7) days, intermediate Saturdays, Sundays, legal holidays, and days on which the office is closed shall be excluded from the computations. IN ST TRIAL P Rule 6(A).

c.   *Additional time after service by United States mail.* Whenever a party has the right or is required to do some act or take some proceedings within a prescribed period after the service of a notice or other paper upon him and the notice or paper is served upon him by United States mail, three (3) days shall be added to the prescribed period. IN ST TRIAL P Rule 6(E).

d.   *Enlargement of time.* When an act is required or allowed to be done at or within a specific time by the Indiana Rules of Trial Procedure, the court may at any time for cause shown:

    i.   Order the period enlarged, with or without motion or notice, if request therefor is made before the expiration of the period originally prescribed or extended by a previous order; or

    ii.   Upon motion made after the expiration of the specific period, permit the act to be done where the failure to act was the result of excusable neglect; but, the court may not extend the time for taking any action for judgment on the evidence under IN ST TRIAL P Rule 50(A), amendment of findings and judgment under IN ST TRIAL P Rule 52(B), to correct errors under IN ST TRIAL P Rule 59(C), statement in opposition to motion to correct error under IN ST TRIAL P Rule 59(E), or to obtain relief from final judgment under IN ST TRIAL P Rule 60(B), except to the extent and under the conditions stated in those rules. IN ST TRIAL P Rule 6(B).

e.   *Continuances disfavored.* Motions for Continuance are discouraged. Neither side is entitled to an automatic continuance as a matter of right. IN ST MARION CIR AND SUPER CTS CIV Rule 215. For information on obtaining a continuance, refer to IN ST MARION CIR AND SUPER CTS CIV Rule 215.

C. General Requirements

1.   *Scope of discovery.* Unless otherwise limited by order of the court in accordance with the Indiana Rules of Trial Procedure, the scope of discovery is as follows:

a.   *In general.* Parties may obtain discovery regarding any matter, not privileged, which is relevant to the subject-matter involved in the pending action, whether it relates to the claim or defense of the party seeking discovery or the claim or defense of any other party, including the existence, description, nature, custody, condition and location of any books, documents, or other tangible things and the identity and location of persons having knowledge of any discoverable matter. It is not ground for objection that the information sought will be inadmissible at the trial if the information sought appears reasonably calculated to lead to the discovery of admissible evidence. IN ST TRIAL P Rule 26(B)(1).

    i.   *Limiting discovery upon court determination.* The frequency or extent of use of the discovery methods otherwise permitted under the Indiana Rules of Trial Procedure and by any local rule shall be limited by the court if it determines that:

- The discovery sought is unreasonably cumulative or duplicative, or is obtainable from some other source that is more convenient, less burdensome, or less expensive;

- The party seeking discovery has had ample opportunity by discovery in the action to obtain the information sought or;

- The burden or expense of the proposed discovery outweighs its likely benefit, taking into account the needs of the case, the amount in controversy, the parties' resources, the importance of the issues at stake in the litigation, and the importance of the proposed discovery in resolving the issues. IN ST TRIAL P Rule 26(B)(1).

- The court may act upon its own initiative after reasonable notice or pursuant to a motion under IN ST TRIAL P Rule 26(C). IN ST TRIAL P Rule 26(B)(1). Refer to the Indiana KeyRules Motion for Protective Order document for more information.

ii. *Relevancy in the discovery context.* When the word "relevancy" is used in IN ST TRIAL P Rule 26(B), it does not mean "relevancy" as that word in used to determine the admissibility of evidence in a trial court. It is much broader. It means "relevancy" to the "subject matter" of the litigation or pending action and it may relate to the claim or defense of any party. Pretrial discovery is available as to any nonprivileged matter relevant to the subject matter of the lawsuit or to obtain information reasonably calculated to lead to admissible evidence. 2A INPRAC R 26(26.4); Kaufmann v. Creditthrift Financial, Inc., 465 N.E.2d 207, 210 (Ind.Ct.App. 1984).

iii. *Tests for relevance.* Indiana case law has developed two (2) additional tests in this area. 2A INPRAC R 26(26.4).

- The first test determines when a document or a request for information is actually relevant to the subject matter in the pending action. A document [or discovery request] is relevant to discovery if there is the possibility the information sought may be relevant to the subject matter of the action. 2A INPRAC R 26(26.4); CIGNA-INA/Aetna v. Hagerman-Shambaugh, 473 N.E.2d 1033, 1036 (Ind.Ct.App. 1985).

- The second test speaks to appellate review of the trial court's determination that a document or discovery request is relevant to the subject matter of the pending action. The appellate court sees its review of the trial court's decision on relevancy to subject matter as being very limited. The court states: "Our review of the trial court's conclusion that the documents are relevant is limited. A trial court is vested with discretion in its rulings on discovery issues." 2A INPRAC R 26(26.4); Costanzi v. Ryan, 175 Ind.App. 257, 370 N.E.2d 1333 (Ind.Ct.App. 1978).

b. *Insurance agreements.* A party may obtain discovery of the existence and contents of any insurance agreement under which any person carrying on an insurance business may be liable to satisfy part or all of a judgment which may be entered in the action or to indemnify or reimburse for payments made to satisfy the judgment. Information concerning the insurance agreement is not by reason of disclosure admissible in evidence at trial. For purposes of IN ST TRIAL P Rule 26(B)(2), an application for insurance shall not be treated as part of an insurance agreement. IN ST TRIAL P Rule 26(B)(2).

c. *Trial preparation; Materials.* Subject to the provisions of IN ST TRIAL P Rule 26(B)(4), a party may obtain discovery of documents and tangible things otherwise discoverable under IN ST TRIAL P Rule 26(B)(1) and prepared in anticipation of litigation or for trial by or for another party or by or for that other party's representative (including his attorney, consultant, surety, indemnitor, insurer, or agent) only upon a showing that the party seeking discovery has substantial need of the materials in the preparation of his case and that he is unable without undue hardship to obtain the substantial equivalent of the materials by other means. In ordering discovery of such materials when the required showing has been made, the court shall protect against disclosure of the mental impressions, conclusions, opinions, or legal theories of an attorney or other representative of a party concerning the litigation. IN ST TRIAL P Rule 26(B)(3).

i. A party may obtain without the required showing a statement concerning the action or its subject matter previously made by that party. Upon request, a person not a party may obtain without the required showing a statement concerning the action or its subject matter previously made by that person. If the request is refused, the person may move for a court order. The provisions of IN ST TRIAL P Rule 37(A)(4) apply to the award of expenses incurred in relation to the motion. For purposes of IN ST TRIAL P Rule 26(B)(3), a statement previously made is:

- A written statement signed or otherwise adopted approved by the person making it, or

- A stenographic, mechanical, electrical, or other recording, or a transcription thereof, which is a substantially verbatim recital of an oral statement by the person making it and contemporaneously recorded. IN ST TRIAL P Rule 26(B)(3).

ii. The protection of IN ST TRIAL P Rule 26(B)(3) extends to material prepared or collected before litigation actually commences, but that some possibility of litigation must actually exist before the privilege and IN ST TRIAL P Rule 26(B)(3) become operative. 2A INPRAC R 26(26.9).

d. *Trial preparation; Experts.* Discovery of facts known and opinions held by experts, otherwise discoverable under the provisions of IN ST TRIAL P Rule 26(B)(1) and acquired or developed in anticipation of litigation or for trial, may be obtained as follows:

   i. A party may through interrogatories require any other party to identify each person whom the other party expects to call as an expert witness at trial, to state the subject matter on which the expert is expected to testify, and to state the substance of the facts and opinions to which the expert is expected to testify and a summary of the grounds for each opinion. IN ST TRIAL P Rule 26(B)(4)(a)(i).

   ii. Upon motion, the court may order further discovery by other means, subject to such restrictions as to scope and such provisions, pursuant to IN ST TRIAL P Rule 26(B)(4)(c), concerning fees and expenses as the court may deem appropriate. IN ST TRIAL P Rule 26(B)(4)(a)(ii).

   iii. A party may discover facts known or opinions held by an expert who has been retained or specially employed by another party in anticipation of litigation or preparation for trial and who is not expected to be called as a witness at trial, only as provided in IN ST TRIAL P Rule 35(B) or upon a showing of exceptional circumstances under which it is impracticable for the party seeking discovery to obtain facts or opinions on the same subject by other means. IN ST TRIAL P Rule 26(B)(4)(b).

   iv. Unless manifest injustice would result,

   - The court shall require that the party seeking discovery pay the expert a reasonable fee for time spent in responding to discovery under IN ST TRIAL P Rule 26(B)(4)(a)(ii) and IN ST TRIAL P Rule 26(B)(4)(b); and

   - With respect to discovery obtained under IN ST TRIAL P Rule 26(B)(4)(a)(ii) the court may require, and with respect to discovery obtained under IN ST TRIAL P Rule 26(B)(4)(b) the court shall require, the party seeking discovery to pay the other party a fair portion of the fees and expenses reasonably incurred by the latter party in obtaining facts and opinions from the expert. IN ST TRIAL P Rule 26(B)(4).

e. *Claims of privilege or protection*

   i. *Information withheld.* When a party withholds information otherwise discoverable under the Indiana Rules of Trial Procedure by claiming that it is privileged or subject to protection as trial preparation material, the party shall make the claim expressly and shall describe the nature of the documents, communications, or things not produced or disclosed in a manner that, without revealing information itself privileged or protected, will enable other parties to assess the applicability of the privilege or protection. IN ST TRIAL P Rule 26(B)(5)(a).

   ii. *Information produced.* If information is produced in discovery that is subject to a claim of privilege or protection as trial-preparation material, the party making the claim may notify any party that received the information of the claim and the basis for it. After being notified, a party must promptly return, sequester, or destroy the specified information and any copies it has and may not use or disclose the information until the claim is resolved. A receiving party may promptly present the information to the court under seal for a determination of the claim. If the receiving party disclosed the information before being notified, it must take reasonable steps to retrieve it. The producing party must preserve the information until the claim is resolved. IN ST TRIAL P Rule 26(B)(5)(b).

   iii. *Waiver.* The law of discovery has developed some holdings which indicate that "waiver" of a privileged communication in a discovery setting might be more exacting than "waiver" of a privileged communication when the only question at hand is an interpretation of the privilege itself. Thus, in litigation in which several documents are in issue, and some are released inadvertently, there is strong case law that holds that the "inadvertent production" of a privileged document does not constitute a waiver of the attorney-client privilege. 2A INPRAC R 26(26.5); Transamerica Computer Co. v. International Business Machines Corp., 573 F.2d 646 (9th Cir. 1978). Such a rule should be measured against the usual rule which suggests that a voluntary disclosure to a third person will generally suffice to show a waiver of the attorney-client privilege. 2A INPRAC R 26(26.5).

    f.   *Use not limited.* Unless the court orders otherwise under IN ST TRIAL P Rule 26(C), the frequency of use of the methods listed in IN ST TRIAL P Rule 26(A) is not limited. IN ST TRIAL P Rule 26(A).

    g.   *Sequence of discovery.* Unless the court upon motion, for the convenience of parties and witnesses and in the interests of justice, orders otherwise, methods of discovery may be used in any sequence and the fact that a party is conducting discovery, whether by deposition or otherwise, shall not operate to delay any other party's discovery. IN ST TRIAL P Rule 26(D).

2. *Depositions upon oral examination.* IN ST TRIAL P Rule 30 provides for the pre-trial deposition on oral examination of a party, or a witness who is not a party. 2A INPRAC R 30(30.1).

    a.   *Generally.* The deposition may be used to narrow issues, or to create and enlarge them. It will eliminate matters that are not disputed among the parties; it might introduce new issues and questions which become disputed. The range and purpose of the deposition's use is almost limitless, as long as it is taken consistent with IN ST TRIAL P Rule 26 and IN ST TRIAL P Rule 30 and the principles of IN ST TRIAL P Rule 32. The deposition may obtain evidence that is admissible at trial; it may go quite beyond admissibility at trial if the area of investigation is relevant to the subject matter of the case under IN ST TRIAL P Rule 26. It can disclose the existence and availability of facts that may lead to evidence which may be used at trial. 2A INPRAC R 30(30.1).

    b.   *Notice*

        i.   *Contents of notice.* The notice shall state the time and place for taking the deposition and the name and address of each person to be examined, if known, and if the name is not known, a general description sufficient to identify him or the particular class or group to which he belongs. If a subpoena duces tecum is to be served on the person to be examined, a designation of the materials to be produced thereunder shall be attached to or included in the notice. IN ST TRIAL P Rule 30(B)(1).

        ii.   *Circumstances where leave of court required.* Leave of court, when required by IN ST TRIAL P Rule 30(A) is not required for the taking of a deposition by plaintiff if the notice:

- States that the person to be examined is about to go out of the state or will be unavailable for examination unless his deposition is taken before expiration of the twenty (20) day period; and

- Sets forth facts to support the statement. IN ST TRIAL P Rule 30(B)(2).

        iii.   *Signature on notice.* The plaintiff's attorney shall sign the notice, and his signature constitutes a certification by him that to the best of his knowledge, information, and belief the statement and supporting facts are true. The sanctions provided by IN ST TRIAL P Rule 11 are applicable to the certification. IN ST TRIAL P Rule 30(B).

        iv.   *Manner of recording.* If a party taking a deposition wishes to have the testimony recorded other than in a manner provided in IN ST TRIAL P Rule 74, the notice shall specify the manner of recording and preserving the deposition. The court may require stenographic taking or make any other order to assure that the recorded testimony will be accurate and trustworthy. IN ST TRIAL P Rule 30(B)(4).

        v.   *Organization as deponent; Designation.* A party may in his notice name as the deponent an organization, including without limitation a governmental organization, or a partnership and designate with reasonable particularity the matters on which examination is requested. The organization so named shall designate one or more officers, directors, or managing agents, executive officers, or other persons duly authorized and consenting to testify on its behalf. The persons so designated shall testify as to matters known or available to the organization. IN ST TRIAL P Rule 30(B)(6) does not preclude taking a deposition by any other procedure authorized in the Indiana Rules of Trial Procedure. IN ST TRIAL P Rule 30(B)(6).

    c.   *Improper service of notice.* If any party shows that when he was served with notice under IN ST TRIAL P Rule 30(B)(2) he was unable through the exercise of diligence to obtain counsel to represent him at the taking of the deposition, the deposition may not be used against him. IN ST TRIAL P Rule 30(B).

    d.   *Examination and cross-examination; Record of examination; Oath; Objections.* Examination and cross-examination of witnesses may proceed as permitted at the trial under the provisions of IN ST TRIAL P Rule 43(B). The officer before whom the deposition is to be taken shall put the witness on oath and shall personally, or by someone acting under his direction and in his presence, record the testimony of the witness. The testimony shall be taken stenographically or recorded by any other means designated in accordance with IN ST TRIAL P Rule 30(B)(4). If requested by one of the parties, the testimony shall be transcribed. IN ST TRIAL P Rule 30(C).

    i. *Objections*

- All objections made at the time of the examination to the qualifications of the officer taking the deposition, or to the manner of taking it, or to the evidence presented, or to the conduct of any party, and any other objection to the proceedings, shall be noted by the officer upon the deposition. IN ST TRIAL P Rule 30(C).

- When there is an objection to a question, the objection and reason therefor shall be noted, and the question shall be answered unless the attorney instructs the deponent not to answer, or the deponent refuses to answer, in which case either party may have the question certified by the Reporter, and the question with the objection thereto when so certified shall be delivered to the party requesting the certification who may then proceed under IN ST TRIAL P Rule 37(A). IN ST TRIAL P Rule 30(C).

- In lieu of participating in the oral examination, parties may serve written questions on the party taking the deposition and require him to transmit them to the officer, who shall propound them to the witness and record the answers verbatim. IN ST TRIAL P Rule 30(C).

e. *Motion to terminate or limit examination.* At any time during the taking of the deposition, on motion of any party or of the deponent and upon a showing that the examination is being conducted in bad faith or in such manner as unreasonably to annoy, embarrass, or oppress the deponent or party, the court in which the action is pending or the court in the county where the deposition is being taken may order the officer conducting the examination to cease forthwith from taking the deposition, or may limit the scope and manner of the taking of the deposition as provided in IN ST TRIAL P Rule 26(C). IN ST TRIAL P Rule 30(D).

    i. If the order made terminates the examination, it shall be resumed thereafter only upon the order of the court in which the action is pending. IN ST TRIAL P Rule 30(D).

    ii. Upon demand of the objecting party or deponent the taking of the deposition shall be suspended for the time necessary to make a motion for an order. The provisions of IN ST TRIAL P Rule 37(A)(4) apply to the award of expenses incurred in relation to the motion. IN ST TRIAL P Rule 30(D).

    iii. Refer to the Indiana KeyRules Motion for Protective Order and Motion for Discovery Sanctions documents for more information.

f. *Submission to witness; Changes; Signing*

    i. When the testimony is fully transcribed, the deposition shall be submitted to the witness for reading and signing and shall be read to or by him, unless such reading and signing have been waived by the witness and by each party. "Submitted to the witness" as used in IN ST TRIAL P Rule 30(E)(1) shall mean:

- Mailing of written notification by registered or certified mail to the witness and each attorney attending the deposition that the deposition can be read and examined in the office of the officer before whom the deposition was taken, or

- Mailing the original deposition, by registered or certified mail, to the witness at an address designated by the witness or his attorney, if requested to do so by the witness, his attorney, or the party taking the deposition. IN ST TRIAL P Rule 30(E)(1).

    ii. If the witness desires to change any answer in the deposition submitted to him, each change, with a statement of the reason therefor, shall be made by the witness on a separate form provided by the officer, shall be signed by the witness and affixed to the original deposition by the officer. A copy of such changes shall be furnished by the officer to each party. IN ST TRIAL P Rule 30(E)(2).

iii. If the reading and signing have not been waived by the witness and by each party the deposition shall be signed by the witness and returned by him to the officer within thirty (30) days after it is submitted to the witness. If the deposition has been returned to the officer and has not been signed by the witness, the officer shall execute a certificate of that fact, attach it to the original deposition and deliver it to the party taking it. In such event, the deposition may be used by any party with the same force and effect as though it had been signed by the witness. IN ST TRIAL P Rule 30(E)(3).

iv. In the event the deposition is not returned to the officer within thirty (30) days after it has been submitted to the witness, the reporter shall execute a certificate of that fact and cause the certificate to be delivered to the party taking it. In such event, any party may use a copy of the deposition with the same force and effect as though the original had been signed by the witness. IN ST TRIAL P Rule 30(E)(4).

g. *Certification and filing; Exhibits; Copies*

i. The officer shall certify on the deposition that the witness was duly sworn by him and that the deposition is a true record of the testimony given by the witness. He shall then securely seal the deposition in an envelope endorsed with the title of the action and marked "Deposition of (here insert name of witness)" and shall promptly deliver it to the party taking the deposition. IN ST TRIAL P Rule 30(F)(1). Documents and things, unless objection is made to their production for inspection during the examination of the witness, shall be marked for identification and annexed to and returned with the deposition, and may be inspected and copied by any party, except that:

- The person producing the materials may substitute copies to be marked for identification, if he affords to all parties fair opportunity to verify the copies by comparison with the originals; and

- If the person producing the materials requests their return the officer shall mark them, give each party an opportunity to inspect and copy them, and return them to the person producing them, and the materials may then be used in the same manner as if annexed to and returned with the deposition. IN ST TRIAL P Rule 30(F)(1).

ii. Upon payment of reasonable charges therefor, the officer shall furnish a copy of the deposition to any party or the deponent. IN ST TRIAL P Rule 30(F)(2).

iii. The officer taking the deposition shall give prompt notice to all parties of its delivery to the party taking the deposition. IN ST TRIAL P Rule 30(F)(3).

iv. The filing of depositions shall be in accordance with the provisions of IN ST TRIAL P Rule 5(E). IN ST TRIAL P Rule 30(F)(4).

v. All video tape depositions filed with the Court shall be accompanied by a transcript of the testimony. IN ST MARION CIR AND SUPER CTS CIV Rule 212.

h. *Failure to attend or to serve subpoena; Expenses*

i. If the party giving the notice of the taking of a deposition fails to attend and proceed therewith and another party attends in person or by attorney pursuant to the notice, the court may order the party giving the notice to pay to such other party the amount of the reasonable expenses incurred by him and his attorney in so attending, including reasonable attorney's fees. IN ST TRIAL P Rule 30(G)(1).

ii. If the party giving the notice of the taking of a deposition of a witness other than a party fails to serve a subpoena upon him and the witness because of such failure does not attend, and if another party attends in person or by attorney because he expects the deposition of that witness to be taken, the court may order the party giving the notice to pay to such other party the amount of the reasonable expenses incurred by him and his attorney in so attending, including reasonable attorney's fees. IN ST TRIAL P Rule 30(G)(2).

i. *Depositions of prisoners.* The deposition of a person confined in prison may be taken only by leave of court on such terms as the court prescribes. IN ST TRIAL P Rule 30(A).

j. *Cost of deposition.* In Indiana the rule is that the party who initiates a deposition pays for the cost necessarily incurred as a result of the deposition. Those costs are: (1) the stenographic reporter's fees, (2) the transcription and filing fees, and (3) transportation costs and perhaps other costs which might naturally arise in a particular situation. 2A INPRAC R 30(30.8); Briggs v. Clinton County Bank & Trust Co. of Frankfort, Ind., 452 N.E.2d 989, 1009 (Ind.Ct.App. 1983).

3. *Deposition upon written questions.* The use of written questions under IN ST TRIAL P Rule 31 is often not as effective as taking a deposition on oral examination, and is generally, as a practical matter, not suitable for complicated cases or where cross-examination is necessary, as in the case of a reluctant or hostile witness. Written questions are, however, an inexpensive device where simple or formal facts are sought. 2A INPRAC R 31(31.1).

a. *Notice.* A party desiring to take a deposition upon written questions shall serve them upon every other party with a notice stating:

i. The name and address of the person who is to answer them, if known, and if the name is not known, a general description sufficient to identify him or the particular class or group to which he belongs; and

ii. The name or descriptive title and address of the officer before whom the deposition is to be taken. IN ST TRIAL P Rule 31(A).

b. *Depositions of specific persons*

i. *Prisoners.* The deposition of a person confined in prison may be taken only by leave of court on such terms as the court prescribes. IN ST TRIAL P Rule 31(A).

ii. *Organization.* A deposition upon written questions may be taken of an organization, including a governmental organization, or a partnership in accordance with the provisions of IN ST TRIAL P Rule 30(B)(6). IN ST TRIAL P Rule 31(A).

c. *Officer to take responses and prepare record.* A copy of the notice and copies of all questions served shall be delivered by the party taking the deposition to the officer designated in the notice, who shall proceed promptly, in the manner provided by IN ST TRIAL P Rule 30(C), IN ST TRIAL P Rule 30(E), and IN ST TRIAL P Rule 30(F), to take the testimony of the witness in response to the questions and to prepare, certify, and deliver the deposition, attaching thereto the copy of the notice and the questions received by him, in accordance with IN ST TRIAL P Rule 5(E). IN ST TRIAL P Rule 31(B).

d. *Notice of filing.* When the deposition is filed the party taking it shall promptly give notice thereof to all other parties. IN ST TRIAL P Rule 31(C).

4. *Depositions before action or pending appeal*

a. *Use of deposition to perpetuate testimony.* IN ST TRIAL P Rule 27 does not exist to provide a method of discovery to determine whether a cause of action exists. Rather, the rule is intended to be used to "memorialize" evidence that is already known. Accordingly, a trial court should not grant a motion to perpetuate testimony by deposition on the mere possibility that witnesses may be transferred or leave current employment. 2A INPRAC R 27(27.2). IN ST TRIAL P Rule 27 is available for use "when a certain witness' testimony might become unavailable over time, and not to provide a method of discovery to determine whether a cause of action exits." 2A INPRAC R 27(27.2); Petition of Gary Construction, Inc., 96 F.R.D. 432 (D.C.Colo. 1983); Petition of Gurnsey, 223 F.Supp. 359 (D.D.C. 1963).

b. *Before action; Petition required*

i. *Petition.* A person who desires to perpetuate his own testimony or that of another person regarding any matter that may be cognizable in any court in which the action may be commenced, may file a verified petition in any such court of this state. IN ST TRIAL P Rule

27(A)(1). The petition shall be entitled in the name of the petitioner and shall state facts showing:

- That the petitioner expects to be a party to an action cognizable in a court of this or another state;
- The subject-matter of the expected action and his interest therein;
- The facts which he desires to establish by the proposed testimony and his reasons for desiring to perpetuate it;
- The names or a description of the persons he expects will be adverse parties and their addresses so far as known; and
- The names and addresses of the persons to be examined and the substance of the testimony which he expects to elicit from each, and shall ask for an order authorizing the petitioner to take the depositions of the persons to be examined named in the petition, for the purpose of perpetuating their testimony. IN ST TRIAL P Rule 27(A)(1).

ii. *Notice and service.* The petitioner shall thereafter serve a notice upon each person named in the petition as an expected adverse party, together with a copy of the petition, stating that the petitioner will apply to the court, at a time and place named therein, for the order described in the petition. IN ST TRIAL P Rule 27(A)(2).

iii. *Order and examination.* If the court is satisfied that the perpetuation of the testimony may prevent a failure or delay of justice, it shall make an order designating or describing the persons whose depositions may be taken and specifying the subject-matter of the examination or written interrogatories. The depositions may then be taken in accordance with the Indiana Rules of Trial Procedure; and the court may make orders of the character provided for by IN ST TRIAL P Rule 34 and IN ST TRIAL P Rule 35. For the purpose of applying the Indiana Rules of Trial Procedure to depositions for perpetuating testimony, each reference therein to the court in which the action is pending shall be deemed to refer to the court in which the petition for such deposition was filed. IN ST TRIAL P Rule 27(A)(3).

iv. *Use of deposition.* If a deposition to perpetuate testimony is taken under the Indiana Rules of Trial Procedure or if, although not so taken, it would be admissible in evidence in the court of the state in which it is taken, it may be used in any action involving the same subject-matter subsequently brought in a court of this state in accordance with the provision of IN ST TRIAL P Rule 32. IN ST TRIAL P Rule 27(A)(3).

c. *Pending appeal.* If an appeal has been taken from a judgment of any court or before the taking of an appeal if the time therefor has not expired, the court in which the judgment was rendered may allow the taking of the depositions of witnesses to perpetuate their testimony for use in the event of further proceedings in such court. In such case the party who desires to perpetuate the testimony may make a motion in the court for leave to take the depositions, upon the same notice and service thereof as if the action was pending in the court. IN ST TRIAL P Rule 27(B).

i. The motion shall show:

- The names and addresses of the persons to be examined and the substance of the testimony which he expects to elicit from each;
- The reasons for perpetuating their testimony. IN ST TRIAL P Rule 27(B).

ii. If the court finds that the perpetuation of the testimony is proper to avoid a failure or delay of justice, it may make an order allowing the depositions to be taken and may make orders of the character provided for by IN ST TRIAL P Rule 34 and IN ST TRIAL P Rule 35, and thereupon the depositions may be taken and used in the same manner and under the same conditions as are prescribed in the Indiana Rules of Trial Procedure for depositions taken in actions pending in the court. IN ST TRIAL P Rule 27(B).

d. *Perpetuation by action.* IN ST TRIAL P Rule 27 does not limit the power of a court to entertain an action to perpetuate testimony. IN ST TRIAL P Rule 27(C).

e. *Filing deposition.* The filing or custody of any deposition or evidence obtained under IN ST TRIAL P Rule 27 shall be in accordance with IN ST TRIAL P Rule 5(E). IN ST TRIAL P Rule 27(D).

5. *Persons before whom depositions may be taken; Discovery across state lines; Before administrative agencies; And after judgment*

    a. *Within the United States.* Within the United States or within a territory or insular possession subject to the dominion of the United States, depositions shall be taken before an officer authorized to administer oaths by the laws of the United States, or of the state of Indiana, or of the place where the examination is held, or before a person appointed by the court in which the action is pending. A person so appointed has power to administer oaths and take testimony. IN ST TRIAL P Rule 28(A).

    b. *In foreign countries*

        i. In a foreign country, depositions may be taken:

- On notice before a person authorized to administer oaths in the place in which the examination is held, either by the law thereof or by the law of the United States; or

- Before a person commissioned by the court, and a person so commissioned shall have the power by virtue of his commission to administer any necessary oath and take testimony; or

- Pursuant to a letter rogatory. IN ST TRIAL P Rule 28(B).

        ii. A commission or a letter rogatory shall be issued on application and notice and on terms that are just and appropriate. It is not requisite to the issuance of a commission or a letter rogatory that the taking of the deposition in any other manner is impracticable or inconvenient; and both a commission and a letter rogatory may be issued in proper cases. A notice or commission may designate the person before whom the deposition is to be taken either by name or descriptive title. A letter rogatory may be addressed "To the Appropriate Authority in (here name the country)." Evidence obtained in response to a letter rogatory need not be excluded merely for the reason that it is not a verbatim transcript or that the testimony was not taken under oath or for any similar departure from the requirements for depositions taken within the United States under the Indiana Rules of Trial Procedure. IN ST TRIAL P Rule 28(B).

    c. *Disqualification for interest.* Unless otherwise permitted by the Indiana Rules of Trial Procedure, no deposition shall be taken before a person who is a relative or employee or attorney or counsel of any of the parties, or is a relative or employee of such attorney or counsel, or is financially interested in the action. IN ST TRIAL P Rule 28(C).

        i. Disqualification of the person before whom the deposition is taken is one of the matters which is waived under IN ST TRIAL P Rule 32(D)(3) unless objection is made as soon as the disqualification is known or could have been known by reasonable diligence. 2A INPRAC R 28(28.3).

    d. *Scope of discovery outside state; Protective and enforcement orders.* A deposition may be taken outside the state as provided in IN ST TRIAL P Rule 28(A) and IN ST TRIAL P Rule 28(B), and the deponent may be requested to produce documents and things, and may also be requested to allow inspections and copies as provided in IN ST TRIAL P Rule 34 to submit to examination under IN ST TRIAL P Rule 35. Protective orders may be granted by the court in which the action is pending and by the court where discovery is being made. Enforcement orders may be made by the court where the discovery is sought, and enforcement orders and sanctions may be made by the court where the action is pending as against parties and as against witnesses subject to the jurisdiction of the court. When no action is pending, a court of this state may authorize a deposition to be taken outside this state of any person and upon any matters allowed by IN ST TRIAL P Rule 27. IN ST TRIAL P Rule 28(D).

    e. *Assistance to tribunals and litigants outside this state.* A court of this state may order a person who is domiciled or is found within this state to give his testimony or statement or to produce documents or other things, allow inspections and copies and permit physical and mental examinations for use in a proceeding in a tribunal outside this state. The order may be made upon the application of any interested person or in response to a letter rogatory and may prescribe the practice and procedure, which may be wholly or in part the practice and procedure of the tribunal outside this state, for taking the testimony or statement or producing the documents or other things. To the extent that the order does not prescribe otherwise, the practice and procedure shall be in accordance with that of the court of this state issuing the order. The order may direct that the testimony or statement be given, or document or other thing produced, before a person appointed by the court. The person appointed shall have power to administer any necessary oath. A person within this state may voluntarily give his testimony or statement or produce documents or other things allowing inspections and copies and permit physical and mental examinations for use in a proceeding before a tribunal outside this state. IN ST TRIAL P Rule 28(E).

f. *Discovery proceedings before administrative agencies.* Whenever an adjudicatory hearing, including any hearing in any proceeding subject to judicial review, is held by or before an administrative agency, any party to that adjudicatory hearing shall be entitled to use the discovery provisions of IN ST TRIAL P Rule 26 through IN ST TRIAL P Rule 37. Such discovery may include any relevant matter in the custody and control of the administrative agency. IN ST TRIAL P Rule 28(F).

    i. Protective and other orders shall be obtained first from the administrative agency, and if enforcement of such orders or right of discovery is necessary, it may be obtained in a court of general jurisdiction in the county where discovery is being made or sought, or where the hearing is being held. IN ST TRIAL P Rule 28(F).

g. *Applicability of other laws.* IN ST TRIAL P Rule 28 does not repeal or modify any other law of this state permitting another procedure for obtaining discovery for use in this state or in a tribunal outside this state, except as expressly provided in the Indiana Rules of Trial Procedure. IN ST TRIAL P Rule 28(G).

h. *Discovery after judgment.* Discovery after judgment may be had in proceedings to enforce or to challenge the judgment. IN ST TRIAL P Rule 28(H).

6. *Supplementation of responses.* A party who has responded to a request for discovery with a response that was complete when made is under no duty to supplement his response to include information thereafter acquired, except as follows:

a. A party is under a duty seasonably to supplement his response with respect to any question directly addressed to:

    i. The identity and location of persons having knowledge of discoverable matters, and

    ii. The identity of each person expected to be called as an expert witness at trial, the subject-matter on which he is expected to testify, and the substance of his testimony. IN ST TRIAL P Rule 26(E)(1).

b. A party is under a duty seasonably to amend a prior response if he obtains information upon the basis of which:

    i. He knows that the response was incorrect when made, or

    ii. He knows that the response though correct when made is no longer true and the circumstances are such that a failure to amend the response is in substance a knowing concealment. IN ST TRIAL P Rule 26(E)(2).

c. A duty to supplement responses may be imposed by order of the court, agreement of the parties, or at any time prior to trial through new requests for supplementation of prior responses. IN ST TRIAL P Rule 26(E)(3).

d. The duty seasonably to supplement a discovery response is absolute and is not predicated on a court order. "It is a breach of a litigant's duty reasonably to supplement if the litigant postpones supplementing its response by not obtaining from its experts the information which is to be supplied in answer to interrogatories." 2A INPRAC R 26(26.27); Lucas v. Dorsey Corp., 609 N.E.2d 1191, 1196 (Ind.Ct.App. 1993).

D. Documents

1. *Deposition upon oral examination*

a. *Required documents*

    i. *Notice of deposition.* Refer to the General Requirements section of this document for information on the content of a notice of deposition.

ii. *Certificate of service.* An attorney or unrepresented party tendering a document to the Clerk for filing shall certify that service has been made, list the parties served, and specify the date and means of service. The certificate of service shall be placed at the end of the document and shall not be separately filed. The separate filing of a certificate of service, however, shall not be grounds for rejecting a document for filing. The Clerk may permit documents to be filed without a certificate of service but shall require prompt filing of a separate certificate of service. IN ST TRIAL P Rule 5(C). In all cases where any pleading or other document is required to be served upon opposing counsel, proof of such service may be made either by:

- A certificate of service signed by counsel of record for the serving party and the certificate shall specify by name and address all counsel upon whom the pleading or document was served; or

- An acknowledgment of service signed by the party served or counsel of record. IN ST MARION CIR AND SUPER CTS CIV Rule 206.

b. *Supplemental documents*

i. *Subpoena/subpoena duces tecum.* The attendance of witnesses may be compelled by the use of subpoena as provided in IN ST TRIAL P Rule 45. IN ST TRIAL P Rule 30(A).

- Proof of service of a notice to take a deposition as provided in IN ST TRIAL P Rule 30(B) and IN ST TRIAL P Rule 31(A) constitutes a sufficient authorization for the issuance by the clerk of court for the county in which the deposition is to be taken of subpoenas for the persons named or described therein. The subpoena may command the person to whom it is directed to produce designated books, papers, documents, or tangible things which constitute or contain matters within the scope of the examination permitted by IN ST TRIAL P Rule 26(B), but in that event the subpoena will be subject to the provisions of IN ST TRIAL P Rule 26(C) and IN ST TRIAL P Rule 45(B). IN ST TRIAL P Rule 45(D)(1).

- An individual may be required to attend an examination only in the county wherein he resides or is employed or transacts his business in person, or at such other convenient place as is fixed by an order of court. A nonresident of the state may be required to attend only in the state and county wherein he is served with a subpoena, or within forty (40) miles from the place of service, or at such other convenient place as is fixed by an order of court. A non-resident plaintiff may be required to attend at his own expense an examination in the county of this state where the action is commenced or in a county fixed by the court. IN ST TRIAL P Rule 45(D)(2).

ii. *Request for production.* The notice to a deponent may be accompanied by a request made in compliance with IN ST TRIAL P Rule 34 for the production of documents and tangible things at the taking of the deposition. IN ST TRIAL P Rule 30(B)(5).

iii. *Stipulation regarding discovery procedure.* Unless the court orders otherwise, the parties may by written stipulation:

- Provide that depositions may be taken before any person, at any time or place, upon any notice, and in any manner and when so taken may be used like other depositions, and

- Modify the procedures provided by the Indiana Rules of Trial Procedure for other methods of discovery. IN ST TRIAL P Rule 29.

iv. *Facsimile cover sheet.* Any document sent to the Clerk of the Circuit Court by electronic facsimile transmission shall be accompanied by a cover sheet which states the title of the document, case number, number of pages, identity and voice telephone number of the sending party and instructions for filing. The cover sheet shall contain the signature of the attorney or party, pro se, authorizing the filing. IN ST ADMIN Rule 12(D).

2. *Deposition upon written questions*

a. *Required documents*

i. *Notice of deposition.* Refer to the General Requirements section of this document for information on the content of a notice of deposition.

    ii. *Certificate of service.* An attorney or unrepresented party tendering a document to the Clerk for filing shall certify that service has been made, list the parties served, and specify the date and means of service. The certificate of service shall be placed at the end of the document and shall not be separately filed. The separate filing of a certificate of service, however, shall not be grounds for rejecting a document for filing. The Clerk may permit documents to be filed without a certificate of service but shall require prompt filing of a separate certificate of service. IN ST TRIAL P Rule 5(C). In all cases where any pleading or other document is required to be served upon opposing counsel, proof of such service may be made either by:

- A certificate of service signed by counsel of record for the serving party and the certificate shall specify by name and address all counsel upon whom the pleading or document was served; or

- An acknowledgment of service signed by the party served or counsel of record. IN ST MARION CIR AND SUPER CTS CIV Rule 206.

  b. *Supplemental documents*

    i. *Subpoena.* The attendance of witnesses may be compelled by the use of subpoena as provided in IN ST TRIAL P Rule 45. IN ST TRIAL P Rule 31(A).

- Proof of service of a notice to take a deposition as provided in IN ST TRIAL P Rule 30(B) and IN ST TRIAL P Rule 31(A) constitutes a sufficient authorization for the issuance by the clerk of court for the county in which the deposition is to be taken of subpoenas for the persons named or described therein. The subpoena may command the person to whom it is directed to produce designated books, papers, documents, or tangible things which constitute or contain matters within the scope of the examination permitted by IN ST TRIAL P Rule 26(B), but in that event the subpoena will be subject to the provisions of IN ST TRIAL P Rule 26(C) and IN ST TRIAL P Rule 45(B). IN ST TRIAL P Rule 45(D)(1).

- An individual may be required to attend an examination only in the county wherein he resides or is employed or transacts his business in person, or at such other convenient place as is fixed by an order of court. A nonresident of the state may be required to attend only in the state and county wherein he is served with a subpoena, or within forty (40) miles from the place of service, or at such other convenient place as is fixed by an order of court. A non-resident plaintiff may be required to attend at his own expense an examination in the county of this state where the action is commenced or in a county fixed by the court. IN ST TRIAL P Rule 45(D)(2).

    ii. *Stipulation regarding discovery procedure.* Unless the court orders otherwise, the parties may by written stipulation:

- Provide that depositions may be taken before any person, at any time or place, upon any notice, and in any manner and when so taken may be used like other depositions, and

- Modify the procedures provided by the Indiana Rules of Trial Procedure for other methods of discovery. IN ST TRIAL P Rule 29.

    iii. *Facsimile cover sheet.* Any document sent to the Clerk of the Circuit Court by electronic facsimile transmission shall be accompanied by a cover sheet which states the title of the document, case number, number of pages, identity and voice telephone number of the sending party and instructions for filing. The cover sheet shall contain the signature of the attorney or party, pro se, authorizing the filing. IN ST ADMIN Rule 12(D).

3. *Deposition before action*

  a. *Required documents*

    i. *Notice of deposition.* Refer to the General Requirements section of this document for information on the contents of a notice of deposition.

    ii. *Petition.* Refer to the General Requirements section of this document for information on the content of a petition.

    iii. *Certificate of service.* An attorney or unrepresented party tendering a document to the Clerk for filing shall certify that service has been made, list the parties served, and specify the date and means of service. The certificate of service shall be placed at the end of the document and shall not be separately filed. The separate filing of a certificate of service, however, shall not be grounds for rejecting a document for filing. The Clerk may permit documents to be filed without a certificate of service but shall require prompt filing of a separate certificate of service. IN ST TRIAL P Rule 5(C). In all cases where any pleading or other document is required to be served upon opposing counsel, proof of such service may be made either by:

- A certificate of service signed by counsel of record for the serving party and the certificate shall specify by name and address all counsel upon whom the pleading or document was served; or

- An acknowledgment of service signed by the party served or counsel of record. IN ST MARION CIR AND SUPER CTS CIV Rule 206.

   b. *Supplemental documents*

      i. *Stipulation regarding discovery procedure.* Unless the court orders otherwise, the parties may by written stipulation:

- Provide that depositions may be taken before any person, at any time or place, upon any notice, and in any manner and when so taken may be used like other depositions, and

- Modify the procedures provided by the Indiana Rules of Trial Procedure for other methods of discovery. IN ST TRIAL P Rule 29.

      ii. *Facsimile cover sheet.* Any document sent to the Clerk of the Circuit Court by electronic facsimile transmission shall be accompanied by a cover sheet which states the title of the document, case number, number of pages, identity and voice telephone number of the sending party and instructions for filing. The cover sheet shall contain the signature of the attorney or party, pro se, authorizing the filing. IN ST ADMIN Rule 12(D).

4. *Deposition pending appeal*

   a. *Required documents*

      i. *Motion for leave to take deposition and notice.* The requirement of notice is satisfied by service of the motion. IN ST TRIAL P Rule 7(B); IN ST MARION CIR AND SUPER CTS CIV Rule 203(A).

      ii. *Statement of approval or disapproval.* Except for initial motions made pursuant to IN ST MARION CIR AND SUPER CTS CIV Rule 203(D), all motions filed with the court shall include a brief statement indicating whether opposing party(ies) object to or approve of the granting of said motion. IN ST MARION CIR AND SUPER CTS CIV Rule 203(A).

      iii. *Proposed order.* Unless local practice provides differently, a party should submit a proposed order with its written motion to be signed by the judge once the motion has been granted. 21 INPRAC § 13.8. All motions seeking an order of the Court shall be accompanied by a sufficient number of orders to be executed by the Court in granting said motion. In addition to the orders, the notice shall be accompanied by stamped, addressed envelopes to all parties of record. IN ST MARION CIR AND SUPER CTS CIV Rule 203(E).

      iv. *Certificate of service.* An attorney or unrepresented party tendering a document to the Clerk for filing shall certify that service has been made, list the parties served, and specify the date and means of service. The certificate of service shall be placed at the end of the document and shall not be separately filed. The separate filing of a certificate of service, however, shall not be grounds for rejecting a document for filing. The Clerk may permit documents to be filed without a certificate of service but shall require prompt filing of a separate certificate of service. IN ST TRIAL P Rule 5(C). In all cases where any pleading or other document is required to be served upon opposing counsel, proof of such service may be made either by:

- A certificate of service signed by counsel of record for the serving party and the certificate shall specify by name and address all counsel upon whom the pleading or document was served; or

- An acknowledgment of service signed by the party served or counsel of record. IN ST MARION CIR AND SUPER CTS CIV Rule 206.

b. *Supplemental documents*

    i. *Stipulation regarding discovery procedure.* Unless the court orders otherwise, the parties may by written stipulation:

- Provide that depositions may be taken before any person, at any time or place, upon any notice, and in any manner and when so taken may be used like other depositions, and

- Modify the procedures provided by the Indiana Rules of Trial Procedure for other methods of discovery. IN ST TRIAL P Rule 29.

    ii. *Supporting evidence.* When a motion is based on facts not appearing of record the court may hear the matter on affidavits presented by the respective parties, but the court may direct that the matter be heard wholly or partly on oral testimony or depositions. IN ST TRIAL P Rule 43(B).

    iii. *Request for oral argument.* When an oral argument is requested, the request shall be by separate instrument and filed with the pleading to be argued. Any such oral argument requested may be heard at the discretion of the Court, except for motions for summary judgment which shall be set for hearing upon request of any party. IN ST MARION CIR AND SUPER CTS CIV Rule 203(C).

    iv. *Facsimile cover sheet.* Any document sent to the Clerk of the Circuit Court by electronic facsimile transmission shall be accompanied by a cover sheet which states the title of the document, case number, number of pages, identity and voice telephone number of the sending party and instructions for filing. The cover sheet shall contain the signature of the attorney or party, pro se, authorizing the filing. IN ST ADMIN Rule 12(D).

E. Format

1. *Form of notice.* The rules applicable to captions, and the signing and form of pleadings (IN ST TRIAL P Rule 8 through IN ST TRIAL P Rule 11), apply to all motions and other papers provided under the Indiana Rules of Trial Procedure. 22B INPRAC 7:2.

2. *Form of pleadings*

a. *Caption; Names of parties.* Every pleading shall contain a caption setting forth the name of the court, the title of the action, the file number, and a designation as in IN ST TRIAL P Rule 7(A). In the complaint the title of the action shall include the names of all the parties, but in other pleadings it is sufficient to state the name of the first party on each side with an appropriate indication of other parties. IN ST TRIAL P Rule 10(A).

    i. Every pleading shall contain a caption setting forth the name of the Court, the Division and Room Number, the title of the action and the file number. IN ST MARION CIR AND SUPER CTS CIV Rule 204(B).

b. *Paragraphs; Separate statements.* All averments of a claim or defense shall be made in numbered paragraphs, the contents of each of which shall be limited as far as practicable to a statement of a single set of circumstances, and a paragraph may be referred to by number in all succeeding pleadings. Each claim founded upon a separate transaction or occurrence and each defense other than denials may be stated in a separate count or defense whenever a separation facilitates the clear presentation of the matters set forth. IN ST TRIAL P Rule 10(B).

c. *Adoption by reference; Exhibits.* Statements in a pleading may be adopted by reference in a different part of the same pleading or in another pleading or in any motion. A copy of any written instrument which is an exhibit to a pleading is a part thereof for all purposes. IN ST TRIAL P Rule 10(C).

d. *Paper.* Pleadings, motions and other papers may be either printed or typewritten on white opaque paper of at least sixteen (16) pound weight, eight and one-half (8-1/2) inches wide and eleven (11) inches in length. IN ST MARION CIR AND SUPER CTS CIV Rule 204(A).

e. *Copies.* All copies shall likewise be on white paper of sufficient strength and durability to resist normal wear and tear. IN ST MARION CIR AND SUPER CTS CIV Rule 204(A).

f. *Line spacing.* If typewritten, the lines shall be double spaced, except for quotations, which shall be indented and single spaced. IN ST MARION CIR AND SUPER CTS CIV Rule 204(A).

g. *Script type.* Script type shall not be used. IN ST MARION CIR AND SUPER CTS CIV Rule 204(A).

h. *Titles.* Titles on all pleadings shall delineate each topic included in the pleading e.g. where a pleading contains an Answer, a Motion to Strike or Dismiss, or a Jury Request each shall be set forth in the title. IN ST MARION CIR AND SUPER CTS CIV Rule 204(C).

i. *Margins and binding.* Margins shall be one (1) inch. Binding or stapling shall be at the top and at no other place. Covers or backing shall not be used. IN ST MARION CIR AND SUPER CTS CIV Rule 204(D).

3. *Size of papers for filing.* Effective January 1, 1992, all pleadings, copies, motions and documents filed with any trial court or appellate level court, typed or printed, with the exception of exhibits and existing wills, shall be prepared on eight and one-half by eleven inch (8 1/2" x 11") size paper. IN ST ADMIN Rule 11.

4. *Form of electronically filed documents.* All electronically filed and served pleadings shall, to the extent practicable, be formatted in accordance with the applicable rules governing formatting of paper pleadings. IN ST MARION SUPER CT ADMIN Rule 311(2-103)(1).

a. *Electronic document title.* The electronic document title of each pleading or other document shall include:

i. Party or parties filing/serving the document,

ii. Nature of the document,

iii. Party or parties against whom relief, if any, is sought, and

iv. Nature of the relief sought (e.g., Defendant ABC Corporation's Motion for Summary Judgment). IN ST MARION SUPER CT ADMIN Rule 311(2-103)(2).

5. *Signature requirements*

a. *Signature of attorney.* Every pleading or motion of a party represented by an attorney shall be signed by at least one (1) attorney of record in his individual name, whose address, telephone number, and attorney number shall be stated, except that this provision shall not apply to pleadings and motions made and transcribed at the trial or a hearing before the judge and received by him in such form. IN ST TRIAL P Rule 11(A).

i. All pleadings and motions shall contain the original or authorized signature of the attorney, the name of the attorney in typed or printed form, the name of the law firm if a member of a firm, the attorney's address, identification number, e-mail address, telephone number, fax number, and the designation as to the party for whom he appears. IN ST MARION CIR AND SUPER CTS CIV Rule 204(E).

ii. The signature of an attorney constitutes a certificate by him that he has read the pleadings; that to the best of his knowledge, information, and belief, there is good ground to support it; and that it is not interposed for delay. IN ST TRIAL P Rule 11(A).

iii. If a pleading or motion is not signed or is signed with intent to defeat the purpose of the rule, it may be stricken as sham and false and the action may proceed as though the pleading had not been served. IN ST TRIAL P Rule 11(A).

iv. For a willful violation of IN ST TRIAL P Rule 11 an attorney may be subjected to appropriate disciplinary action. Similar action may be taken if scandalous or indecent matter is inserted. IN ST TRIAL P Rule 11(A).

v. For the recommended format of a signature block, refer to IN ST MARION CIR AND SUPER CTS CIV Rule 204(E).

b. *Signature of unrepresented party.* A party who is not represented by an attorney shall sign his pleading and state his address. IN ST TRIAL P Rule 11(A).

c. *Verification not generally required.* Except when specifically required by rule, pleadings or motions need not be verified or accompanied by affidavit. The rule in equity that the averments of an answer under oath must be overcome by the testimony of two (2) witnesses or of one (1) witness sustained by corroborating circumstances is abolished. IN ST TRIAL P Rule 11(A).

d. *Verification by affirmation or representation.* When in connection with any civil or special statutory proceeding it is required that any pleading, motion, petition, supporting affidavit, or other document of any kind, be verified, or that an oath be taken, it shall be sufficient if the subscriber simply affirms the truth of the matter to be verified by an affirmation or representation. IN ST TRIAL P Rule 11(B). IN ST TRIAL P Rule 11(B) states that the affirmation or representation should be in substantially the following language: "I (we) affirm, under the penalties for perjury, that the foregoing representation(s) is (are) true. (Signed) _____."

    i. Any person who falsifies an affirmation or representation of fact shall be subject to the same penalties as are prescribed by law for the making of a false affidavit. IN ST TRIAL P Rule 11(B).

e. *Verified pleadings, motions, and affidavits as evidence.* Pleadings, motions and affidavits accompanying or in support of such pleadings or motions when required to be verified or under oath shall be accepted as a representation that the signer had personal knowledge thereof or reasonable cause to believe the existence of the facts or matters stated or alleged therein; and, if otherwise competent or acceptable as evidence, may be admitted as evidence of the facts or matters stated or alleged therein when it is so provided in the Indiana Rules of Trial Procedure, by statute or other law, or to the extent the writing or signature expressly purports to be made upon the signer's personal knowledge. When such pleadings, motions and affidavits are verified or under oath they shall not require other or greater proof on the part of the adverse party than if not verified or not under oath unless expressly provided otherwise by the Indiana Rules of Trial Procedure, statute or other law. Affidavits upon motions for summary judgment under IN ST TRIAL P Rule 56 and in denial of execution under IN ST TRIAL P Rule 9.2 shall be made upon personal knowledge. IN ST TRIAL P Rule 11(C).

6. *Information excluded from public access.* Every document filed in a case shall separately identify information excluded from public access pursuant to IN ST ADMIN Rule 9(G)(1) as follows:

a. Whole documents that are excluded from public access pursuant to IN ST ADMIN Rule 9(G)(1) shall be tendered on light green paper or have a light green coversheet attached to the document, marked "Not for Public Access" or "Confidential." IN ST TRIAL P Rule 5(G)(1).

b. When only a portion of a document contains information excluded from public access pursuant to IN ST ADMIN Rule 9(G)(1), said information shall be omitted [or redacted] from the filed document, and set forth on a separate accompanying document on light green paper conspicuously marked "Not for Public Access" or "Confidential" and clearly designated [or identifying] the caption and number of the case and the document and location within the document to which the redacted material pertains. IN ST TRIAL P Rule 5(G)(2).

c. With respect to documents filed in electronic format, the trial court, by local rule, may provide for compliance with IN ST TRIAL P Rule 5 in manner that separates and protects access to information excluded from public access. IN ST TRIAL P Rule 5(G)(3).

d. IN ST TRIAL P Rule 5(G) does not apply to a record sealed by the court pursuant to IN ST 5-14-3-5.5 or otherwise, nor to records, documents, or information filed in cases to which public access is prohibited pursuant to IN ST ADMIN Rule 9(G). IN ST TRIAL P Rule 5(G)(4).

e. The following information in case records is excluded from public access and is confidential:

    i. Information that is excluded from public access pursuant to federal law;

    ii. Information that is excluded from public access as declared confidential by Indiana statute or other court rule, including without limitation:

- All adoption records created after July 8, 1941, as declared confidential by IN ST 31-19-19-1, et seq., except those specifically declared open by IN ST 31-19-13-2(2);

- All records relating to chancroid, chlamydia, gonorrhea, hepatitis, human immunodeficiency virus (HIV), Lymphogranuloma venereum, syphilis, tuberculosis, as declared confidential by IN ST 16-41-8-1, et seq.;

- All records relating to child abuse as declared confidential by IN ST 31-33-18-1, et seq.;
- All records relating to drug tests as declared confidential by IN ST 5-14-3-4(a)(9);
- Records of grand jury proceedings as declared confidential by IN ST 35-34-2-4;
- Records of juvenile proceedings as declared confidential by IN ST 31-39-1-2, except those specifically open under statute;
- All paternity records created after July 1, 1941 as declared confidential by IN ST 31-14-11-15, IN ST 31-19-5-23, IN ST 31-39-1-1 and IN ST 31-39-1-2 [Editor's note: IN ST 31-14-11-15 was repealed effective May 9, 2013];
- All pre-sentence reports as declared confidential by IN ST 35-38-1-13;
- Written petitions to permit marriages without consent and orders directing the Clerk of Court to issue a marriage license to underage persons, as declared confidential by IN ST 31-11-1-6;
- Only those arrest warrants, search warrants, indictments and informations ordered confidential by the trial judge, prior to return of duly executed service as declared confidential by IN ST 5-14-3-4(b)(1);
- All medical, mental health, or tax records unless determined by law or regulation of any governmental custodian not to be confidential, released by the subject of such records, or declared by a court of competent jurisdiction to be essential to the resolution of litigation as declared confidential by IN ST 16-39-3-10, IN ST 6-4.1-5-10, IN ST 6-4.1-12-12, and IN ST 6-8.1-7-1;
- Personal information relating to jurors or prospective jurors, other than for the use of the parties and counsel, pursuant to IN ST JURY Rule 10;
- Information relating to protection from abuse orders, no-contact orders and workplace violence restraining orders as declared confidential by IN ST 5-2-9-6, et seq.;
- Mediation proceedings pursuant to IN ST ADR Rule 2.11, Mini-Trial proceedings pursuant to IN ST ADR Rule 4.4(C), and Summary Jury Trials pursuant to IN ST ADR Rule 5.6;
- Information in probation files pursuant to the Probation Standards promulgated by the Judicial Conference of Indiana pursuant to IN ST 11-13-1-8(b);
- Information deemed confidential pursuant to the Rules for Court Administered Alcohol and Drug Programs promulgated by the Judicial Conference of Indiana pursuant to IN ST 12-23-14-13;
- Information deemed confidential pursuant to the Problem-Solving Court Rules promulgated by the Judicial Conference of Indiana pursuant to IN ST 33-23-16-16;
- All records of the Department of workforce Development as declared confidential by IN ST 22-4-19-6;
- Information regarding interception of electronic communications that is sealed or deemed confidential as set forth in IN ST 35-33.5-2-1, et seq.

iii. Information excluded from public access by specific court order;

iv. Complete Social Security Numbers of living persons;

v. With the exception of names, information such as addresses, phone numbers, and dates of birth which explicitly identifies:

- Natural persons who are witnesses or victims (not including defendants) in criminal, domestic violence, stalking, sexual assault, juvenile, or civil protection order proceedings, provided that juveniles who are victims of sex crimes shall be identified by initials only;
- Places of residence of judicial officers, clerks and other employees of courts and clerks of court, unless the person or persons about whom the information pertains waives confidentiality;

vi. Complete account numbers of specific assets, loans, bank accounts, credit cards, and personal identification numbers (PINs);

vii. All orders of expungement entered in criminal or juvenile proceedings, orders to restrict access to criminal history information pursuant to IN ST 35-38-5-5.5 or IN ST 35-38-8-5 and records excluded from public access by such orders, and information related to infractions that is excluded from public access pursuant to IN ST 34-28-5-15 or IN ST 34-28-5-16 [Editor's note: IN ST 35-38-5-5.5, IN ST 35-38-8-5 and IN ST 34-28-5-16 were repealed effective July 1, 2013; for information on orders restricting access to criminal history, refer to IN ST 35-38-9-1, et seq.];

viii. All personal notes and e-mail, and deliberative material, of judges, jurors, court staff and judicial agencies, and information recorded in personal data assistants (PDA's) or organizers and personal calendars. IN ST ADMIN Rule 9(G)(1).

F. Filing and Service Requirements

1. *Filing requirements.* Except as otherwise provided in IN ST TRIAL P Rule 5(E)(2), all pleadings and papers subsequent to the complaint which are required to be served upon a party shall be filed with the Court either before service or within a reasonable period of time thereafter. IN ST TRIAL P Rule 5(E)(1).

    a. *Non-filing of discovery until necessary*

        i. *Non-filing of discovery; Exceptions.* No deposition or request for discovery or response thereto under IN ST TRIAL P Rule 27, IN ST TRIAL P Rule 30, IN ST TRIAL P Rule 31, IN ST TRIAL P Rule 33, IN ST TRIAL P Rule 34 or IN ST TRIAL P Rule 36 shall be filed with the Court unless:

            • A motion is filed pursuant to IN ST TRIAL P Rule 26(C) or IN ST TRIAL P Rule 37 and the original deposition or request for discovery or response thereto is necessary to enable the Court to rule; or

            • A party desires to use the deposition or request for discovery or response thereto for evidentiary purposes at trial or in connection with a motion, and the Court, either upon its own motion or that of any party, or as a part of any pre-trial order, orders the filing of the original. IN ST TRIAL P Rule 5(E)(2).

        ii. *Custody of original and period of retention*

            • The original of a deposition shall, subject to the provisions of IN ST TRIAL P Rule 30(E), be delivered by the reporter to the party taking it and shall be maintained by that party until filed with the Court pursuant to IN ST TRIAL P Rule 5(E)(2) or until the later of final judgment, agreed settlement of the litigation or all appellate rights have been exhausted. IN ST TRIAL P Rule 5(E)(3)(a).

            • The original or any request for discovery or response thereto under IN ST TRIAL P Rule 27, IN ST TRIAL P Rule 30, IN ST TRIAL P Rule 31, IN ST TRIAL P Rule 33, IN ST TRIAL P Rule 34 and IN ST TRIAL P Rule 36 shall be maintained by the party originating the request or response until filed with the Court pursuant to IN ST TRIAL P Rule 5(E)(2) or until the later of final judgment, agreed settlement or all appellate rights have been exhausted. IN ST TRIAL P Rule 5(E)(3)(b).

        iii. *Original unavailable; Copies.* In the event it is made to appear to the satisfaction of the Court that the original of a deposition or request for discovery or response thereto cannot be filed with the Court when required, the Court may allow use of a copy instead of the original. IN ST TRIAL P Rule 5(E)(4).

        iv. *Filing as publication.* The filing of any deposition shall constitute publication. IN ST TRIAL P Rule 5(E)(5).

    b. *Filing generally.* All pleadings, petitions and motions are filed with the Clerk designated by the Court at any time during office hours established by the Clerk and the Court. All orders submitted to the Court shall be in sufficient number and shall be accompanied by postage paid envelopes addressed to each party or counsel of record. IN ST MARION CIR AND SUPER CTS CIV Rule 205(A)

   c. *Filing with the court defined.* The filing of pleadings, motions, and other papers with the court as required by the Indiana Rules of Trial Procedure shall be made by one of the following methods:

      i. Delivery to the clerk of the court;

      ii. Sending by electronic transmission under the procedure adopted pursuant to IN ST ADMIN Rule 12;

      iii. Mailing to the clerk by registered, certified or express mail return receipt requested;

      iv. Depositing with any third-party commercial carrier for delivery to the clerk within three (3) calendar days, cost prepaid, properly addressed;

      v. If the court so permits, filing with the judge, in which event the judge shall note thereon the filing date and forthwith transmit them to the office of the clerk; or

      vi. Electronic filing, as approved by the Division of State Court Administration pursuant to IN ST ADMIN Rule 16. IN ST TRIAL P Rule 5(F).

      vii. Filing by registered or certified mail and by third-party commercial carrier shall be complete upon mailing or deposit. IN ST TRIAL P Rule 5(F).

   d. *Facsimile filing.* Facsimile filing is discouraged, but permitted in the Marion Circuit and Marion Superior Court. All documents filed by facsimile shall also be filed in hard copy within seven (7) days of the facsimile filing, along with proposed orders and stamped addressed envelopes, as required by IN ST MARION CIR AND SUPER CTS CIV Rule 203(E). To avoid duplicate filings, the hard copies of the facsimile filing shall indicate in bold letters that the pleading was previously filed by facsimile transmission. Proof of transmission by facsimile, including certificate of service and manner of service, shall be the responsibility of the filing party. If the filing requires immediate attention of the Judge, it shall be so indicated in bold letters in an accompanying transmittal memorandum. Legibility of documents and timeliness of filing is the responsibility of the sender. IN ST MARION CIR AND SUPER CTS CIV Rule 205(B).

      i. *Generally.* In counties where a majority of judges of the courts of record, by posted local rule, have authorized electronic facsimile filing and designated a telephone number to receive such transmissions, pleadings, motions, and other papers may be sent to the Clerk of Circuit Court by electronic facsimile transmission for filing in any case, provided:

        • Such matter does not exceed ten (10) pages, including the cover sheet;

        • Such matter does not require the payment of fees other than the electronic facsimile transcription fee set forth in IN ST ADMIN Rule 12(E);

        • The sending party creates at the time of transmission a machine generated log for such transmission; and

        • The original document and the transmission log are maintained by the sending party for the duration of the litigation. IN ST ADMIN Rule 12(B).

      ii. *Time of filing.* During normal, posted business hours, the time of filing shall be the time the duplicate document is produced in the office of the Clerk of the Circuit Court. Duplicate documents received at all other times shall be filed as of the next normal business day. IN ST ADMIN Rule 12(C).

        • If the receiving fax machine endorses its own time and date stamp upon the transmitted documents and the receiving machine produces a delivery receipt which is electronically created and transmitted to the sending party, the time of filing shall be the date and time recorded on the transmitted document by the receiving fax machine. IN ST ADMIN Rule 12(C).

   e. *Electronic filing.* Electronic filing and electronic service pilot projects are authorized pursuant to IN ST ADMIN Rule 16 and approved by the Division of State Court Administration. IN ST MARION SUPER CT ADMIN Rule 311(1-103).

      i. *Cases where electronic filing accepted.* All Marion County Circuit and Superior civil courts may accept electronic filing and service of pleadings and other documents designated in this rule in mortgage foreclosure (hereinafter referred to as "MF"), civil collection(hereinafter referred to as "CC"), and individual cases that have been approved for electronic filing and service. IN ST MARION SUPER CT ADMIN Rule 311(1-104)(1).

- The Marion County Circuit Court may, upon the motion of a party or its own motion, designate a case that will involve multiple litigants, legally intricate issues, and an extensive number of documents a mass tort or complex litigation case. Any case so designated shall be subject to electronic filing and service using the county's approved Electronic Service Provider. IN ST MARION SUPER CT ADMIN Rule 311(1-104)(3).

- The filing of electronic pleadings and other documents in MF and CC cases is entirely voluntary; however, once the case is initially filed electronically, all subsequent filings in the case shall remain in electronic format until the time for appeal is exhausted. IN ST MARION SUPER CT ADMIN Rule 311(1-104)(5).

ii. *Documents eligible for electronic filing.* The following pleadings may be filed and served electronically:

- New case complaint and petitions. IN ST MARION SUPER CT ADMIN Rule 311(1-104)(8)(a).

- Original answers. IN ST MARION SUPER CT ADMIN Rule 311(1-104)(8)(a).

- Any other pleadings or document including but not limited to motions and appearance forms. IN ST MARION SUPER CT ADMIN Rule 311(1-104)(8)(a).

iii. *Manner of electronic filing.* Parties shall E-file a document either:

- By registering to use the Electronic Filing Service Provider; or

- In person at the Marion County Clerk's office, by electronically filing through the Public Access Terminal. Parties filing in this manner shall be responsible for furnishing the document in an electronic format that will be compatible with the clerk's office-system to be uploaded in person. IN ST MARION SUPER CT ADMIN Rule 311(1-104)(9). For information on the Electronic Filing Service Provider and Public Access Terminal, refer to IN ST MARION SUPER CT ADMIN Rule 311(1-101).

- Registered users shall pay statutory filing fees for E-filed documents electronically to the Court through their EFSP. Filing fees are due and payable at the time of filing. IN ST MARION SUPER CT ADMIN Rule 311(2-104)(1). For more information on electronic filing fees, refer to IN ST MARION SUPER CT ADMIN Rule 311(2-104).

iv. *Effect of electronic filing.* Any pleading filed electronically shall be considered as filed with the court when the transmission to the EFSP is complete. Any document E-filed by 11:59 p.m. local Indianapolis, Indiana time shall be deemed filed on that date. The EFSP is an agent of the Court for the purpose of electronic filing, receipt, service and retrieval of electronic documents. IN ST MARION SUPER CT ADMIN Rule 311(2-102).

- Upon completion of filing, the EFSP shall issue a confirmation receipt that includes the date and time of receipt. The confirmation receipt shall serve as proof of filing. IN ST MARION SUPER CT ADMIN Rule 311(2-102).

- In the event the Court rejects the submitted documents following review, the documents shall not become part of the official Court record and the filer will receive notification of the rejection. Users may be required to refile the instruments to meet necessary filing requirements. Documents may be filed through an E-filing system at any time that the Clerk's office is open to receive the filing or at such other times as may be designated by the clerk and posted publicly. IN ST MARION SUPER CT ADMIN Rule 311(2-102).

- Documents filed through the E-filing system are deemed filed when received by the Clerk's office, except that documents received at times that the Clerk's office is closed shall be deemed filed the next regular time when the Clerk's office is open for filing. The time stamp issued by the E-filing system shall be presumed to be the time the document is received by the Clerk. IN ST MARION SUPER CT ADMIN Rule 311(2-102).

v. *Electronically filed documents.* All pleadings and other documents designated in IN ST MARION SUPER CT ADMIN Rule 311 shall be filed and served electronically in any individual case which has been approved for electronic filing and service. IN ST MARION SUPER CT ADMIN Rule 311(1-104)(6).

vi. *System failures.* When filing by electronic means is hindered by a technical failure, a party may file with the Clerk of Marion County in hard copy. With the exception of deadlines that by law cannot be extended, the time for filing of any paper that is delayed due to technical failure of the site shall be extended for one (1) day for each day on which such failure occurs, unless otherwise ordered by the Court. IN ST MARION SUPER CT ADMIN Rule 311(2-108).

vii. *Compliance with rules.* All filing shall comply with the requirements of IN ST ADMIN Rule 9 and IN ST ADMIN Rule 16; and the Indiana Rules of Court and the Marion County Local Rules. IN ST MARION SUPER CT ADMIN Rule 311(1-104)(11).

f. *Filing for special judge.* When a Special Judge who is not a Marion County Judge is selected, all parties or attorneys shall furnish such Judge with copies of all filings prior to the qualification of such Special Judge. Thereafter, copies of all filings shall be delivered in person, by mail or by facsimile to the office of the Special Judge with certificate of forwarding same made a part of the filing. IN ST MARION CIR AND SUPER CTS CIV Rule 205(C).

g. *Proof of filing.* Any party filing any paper by any method other than personal delivery to the clerk shall retain proof of filing. IN ST TRIAL P Rule 5(F).

2. *Service requirements.* Unless otherwise provided by the Indiana Rules of Trial Procedure or an order of the court, each party and special judge, if any, shall be served with: (1) every order required by its terms to be served; (2) every pleading subsequent to the original complaint; (3) every written motion except one which may be heard ex parte; (4) every brief submitted to the trial court; (5) every paper relating to discovery required to be served upon a party; and (6) every written notice, appearance, demand, offer of judgment, designation of record on appeal, or similar paper. IN ST TRIAL P Rule 5(A).

a. *Methods of service*

i. *Personal service.* Whenever a party is represented by an attorney of record, service shall be made upon such attorney unless service upon the party himself is ordered by the court. Service upon the attorney or party shall be made by delivering or mailing a copy of the papers to the last known address or where an attorney or party has consented to service by fax or e-mail, as provided in IN ST TRIAL P Rule 3.1(A)(4), by faxing or e-mailing a copy of the documents to the fax number or e-mail address set out in the appearance form or correction as required by IN ST TRIAL P Rule 3.1(E). IN ST TRIAL P Rule 5(B). Delivery of a copy within IN ST TRIAL P Rule 5 means:

- Offering or tendering it to the attorney or party and stating the nature of the papers being served. Refusal to accept an offered or tendered document is a waiver of any objection to the sufficiency or adequacy of service of that document;

- Leaving it at his office with a clerk or other person in charge thereof, or if there is no one in charge, leaving it in a conspicuous place therein; or

- If the office is closed, by leaving it at his dwelling house or usual place of abode with some person of suitable age and discretion then residing therein; or,

- Leaving it at some other suitable place, selected by the attorney upon whom service is being made, pursuant to duly promulgated local rule. IN ST TRIAL P Rule 5(B)(1).

ii. *Service by mail.* If service is made by mail, the papers shall be deposited in the United States mail addressed to the person on whom they are being served, with postage prepaid. Service shall be deemed complete upon mailing. Proof of service of all papers permitted to be mailed may be made by written acknowledgment of service, by affidavit of the person who mailed the papers, or by certificate of an attorney. It shall be the duty of attorneys when entering their appearance in a cause or when filing pleadings or papers therein, to have noted in the Chronological Case Summary or said pleadings or papers so filed the address and telephone number of their office. Service by delivery or by mail at such address shall be deemed sufficient and complete. IN ST TRIAL P Rule 5(B)(2).

iii. *Service by fax or e-mail.* A party who has consented to service by fax or e-mail may be served as follows:

- Service by e-mail shall be made by attaching the document being served in .pdf format. Discovery documents must also be served in accordance with IN ST TRIAL P Rule 26(A). IN ST TRIAL P Rule 5(B)(3)(a).

- Service by fax shall be deemed complete upon generation of a transmission record indicating the successful transmission of the entire document, except as provided in IN ST TRIAL P Rule 5(B)(3)(d). IN ST TRIAL P Rule 5(B)(3)(b).

- Service by e-mail shall be deemed complete upon transmission, except as provided in IN ST TRIAL P Rule 5(B)(3)(d). IN ST TRIAL P Rule 5(B)(3)(c).

- Service by fax or e-mail that occurs on a Saturday, Sunday, legal holiday, or day the court or agency in which the matter is pending is closed or after 5:00 PM local time of the recipient shall be deemed complete the next day that is not a Saturday, Sunday, legal holiday, or day that the court or agency in which the matter is pending is not closed. IN ST TRIAL P Rule 5(B)(3)(d).

iv. *Electronic service.* Delivery of E-service documents through the EFSP to other registered users shall be considered as valid and effective service and shall have the same legal effect as an original paper document. Recipients of E-service documents shall access their documents through the EFSP. IN ST MARION SUPER CT ADMIN Rule 311(2-107)(1).

- E-service shall be deemed complete when the transmission to the EFSP is completed. IN ST MARION SUPER CT ADMIN Rule 311(2-107)(2).

- For the purpose of computing time to respond to documents received via E-service, any document served on a day or at a time when the Clerk's office is not open for business shall be deemed served at the time of next opening of the Clerk's office for business. IN ST MARION SUPER CT ADMIN Rule 311(2-107)(3).

v. *Additional service of electronic discovery.* In addition to service under Rule IN ST TRIAL P Rule 5(B) or a .pdf format electronic copy, a party propounding or responding to interrogatories, requests for production or requests for admission shall comply with IN ST TRIAL P Rule 26(A.1)(a) or IN ST TRIAL P Rule 26(A.1)(b). IN ST TRIAL P Rule 26(A.1).

- The party shall serve the discovery request or response in an electronic format (either on a disk or as an electronic document attachment) in any commercially available word processing software system. If transmitted on disk, each disk shall be labeled, identifying the caption of the case, the document, and the word processing version in which it is being submitted. If more than one (1) disk is used for the same document, each disk shall be labeled and also shall be sequentially numbered. If transmitted by electronic mail, the document must be accompanied by electronic memorandum providing the forgoing identifying information; or

- The party shall serve the opposing party with a verified statement that the attorney or party appealing pro se lacks the equipment and is unable to transmit the discovery as required by IN ST TRIAL P Rule 26(A.1). IN ST TRIAL P Rule 26(A.1).

b. *Serving numerous defendants.* In any action in which there are unusually large numbers of defendants, the court, upon motion or of its own initiative, may order:

i. That service of the pleadings of the defendants and replies thereto need not be made as between the defendants;

- That any cross-claim, counterclaim, or matter constituting an avoidance or affirmative defense contained therein shall be deemed to be denied or avoided by all other parties; and

- That the filing of any such pleading and service thereof upon the plaintiff constitutes due notice of it to the parties. IN ST TRIAL P Rule 5(D).

ii. A copy of every such order shall be served upon the parties in such manner and form as the court directs. IN ST TRIAL P Rule 5(D).

c. *Service on parties in default for failure to appear.* No service need be made on parties in default for failure to appear, except that pleadings asserting new or additional claims for relief against them shall be served upon them in the manner provided by service of summons in IN ST TRIAL P Rule 4. IN ST TRIAL P Rule 5(A).

G. Hearings

1. The Indiana rules do not contemplate a hearing related to the notice of deposition.

H. Forms

1. Notice of Deposition Forms for Indiana

a. Notice of deposition; Individual. 5 INPRAC § 4:1.1.

b. Notice of deposition; Deponent unknown. 5 INPRAC § 4:1.2.

c. Notice of deposition; Corporation. 5 INPRAC § 4:1.3.

d. Notice of deposition; With request for production of documents. 5 INPRAC § 4:1.4.

e. Motion to limit scope of deposition. 5 INPRAC § 4:1.5.

f. Motion to terminate deposition. 5 INPRAC § 4:1.6.

g. Notice of hearing on petition for order to take deposition before action to perpetuate testimony. 5 INPRAC § 4:1.7.

h. Petition to perpetuate testimony. 5 INPRAC § 4:1.7.30.

i. Affidavit verifying petition to perpetuate testimony. 5 INPRAC § 4:1.7.70.

j. Stipulation regarding deposition by remote electronic means. 5 INPRAC § 4:1.8.

k. Petition to perpetuate testimony; Witness to automobile accident. 10 INPRAC § 59.3.

l. Notice of hearing on petition to perpetuate testimony. 10 INPRAC § 59.6.

m. Petition to perpetuate testimony pending appeal. 10 INPRAC § 59.13.

n. Notice of deposition to perpetuate testimony pending appeal. 10 INPRAC § 59.15.

o. Notice of deposition upon oral examination; Individual. 10 INPRAC § 62.3.

p. Notice of deposition; Deponent unknown. 10 INPRAC § 62.4.

q. Notice of deposition; Corporation. 10 INPRAC § 62.5.

r. Notice of deposition; With request for production of documents. 10 INPRAC § 62.6.

s. Motion for leave to take deposition within twenty days of service. 10 INPRAC § 62.7.

t. Notice of deposition; Pursuant to order granting leave to take deposition. 10 INPRAC § 62.9.

u. Stipulation for deposition upon written questions. 10 INPRAC § 63.2.

v. Notice of deposition upon written questions. 10 INPRAC § 63.3.

w. Direct questions. 10 INPRAC § 63.4.

x. Cross questions. 10 INPRAC § 63.5.

y. Redirect questions. 10 INPRAC § 63.6.

z. Recross questions. 10 INPRAC § 63.7.

I. Checklist

(I) ❑ Matters to be considered by the party taking a deposition upon oral examination

    (a) ❑ Required documents

        (1) ❑ Notice of deposition

        (2) ❑ Certificate of service

    (b) ❑ Supplemental documents

        (1) ❑ Subpoena/subpoena duces tecum

        (2) ❑ Request for production

        (3) ❑ Stipulation regarding discovery procedure

        (4) ❑ Facsimile cover sheet

    (c) ❑ Timing

        (1) ❑ After commencement of the action, any party may take the testimony of any person, including a party, by deposition upon oral examination

(II) ❑ Matters to be considered by the party taking a deposition upon written questions

    (a) ❑ Required documents

        (1) ❑ Notice of deposition

        (2) ❑ Certificate of service

    (b) ❑ Supplemental documents

        (1) ❑ Subpoena

        (2) ❑ Stipulation regarding discovery procedure

        (3) ❑ Facsimile cover sheet

    (c) ❑ Timing

        (1) ❑ After commencement of the action, any party may take the testimony of any person, including a party, by deposition upon written questions

(III) ❑ Matters to be considered by the party taking a deposition before commencement of the action

    (a) ❑ Required documents

        (1) ❑ Notice of deposition

        (2) ❑ Petition

        (3) ❑ Certificate of service

    (b) ❑ Supplemental documents

        (1) ❑ Stipulation regarding discovery procedure

        (2) ❑ Facsimile cover sheet

    (c) ❑ Timing

        (1) ❑ At least twenty (20) days before the date of hearing the notice shall be served in the manner provided in IN ST TRIAL P Rule 4 for service of summons

(IV) ❑ Matters to be considered by the party taking a deposition pending appeal

    (a) ❑ Required documents

        (1) ❑ Motion for leave to take deposition and notice

        (2) ❑ Statement of approval or disapproval

        (3) ❑ Proposed order

        (4) ❑ Certificate of service

    (b) ❑ Supplemental documents

        (1) ❑ Stipulation regarding discovery procedure

        (2) ❑ Supporting evidence

        (3) ❑ Request for oral argument

        (4) ❑ Facsimile cover sheet

    (c) ❑ Timing

        (1) ❑ The party who desires to perpetuate the testimony may make a motion in the court for leave to take the depositions, upon the same notice and service thereof as if the action was pending in the court

(2) ❑ A written motion, other than one which may be heard ex parte, and notice of the hearing thereof shall be served not less than five (5) days before the time specified for the hearing, unless a different period is fixed by the Indiana Rules of Trial Procedure or by order of the court

(3) ❑ All pleadings and papers subsequent to the complaint which are required to be served upon a party shall be filed with the Court either before service or within a reasonable period of time thereafter

Requests, Notices and Applications
Application for Temporary Restraining Order

Document Last Updated October 2013

A. Applicable Rules

1. *State rules*

   a. Appearance. IN ST TRIAL P Rule 3.1.

   b. Process. IN ST TRIAL P Rule 4.

   c. Service and filing of pleadings and other papers. IN ST TRIAL P Rule 5.

   d. Time. IN ST TRIAL P Rule 6.

   e. Pleadings. IN ST TRIAL P Rule 7; IN ST TRIAL P Rule 8; IN ST TRIAL P Rule 9.2; IN ST TRIAL P Rule 10.

   f. Signing and verification of pleadings. IN ST TRIAL P Rule 11.

   g. Evidence. IN ST TRIAL P Rule 43.

   h. Judgment on the evidence (directed verdict). IN ST TRIAL P Rule 50.

   i. Findings by the court. IN ST TRIAL P Rule 52.

   j. Summary judgment. IN ST TRIAL P Rule 56.

   k. Motion to correct error. IN ST TRIAL P Rule 59.

   l. Relief from judgment or order. IN ST TRIAL P Rule 60.

   m. Injunctions. IN ST TRIAL P Rule 65; IN ST 34-26-1-7; IN ST 34-26-1-8; IN ST 34-26-1-11.

   n. Security; Proceedings against sureties. IN ST TRIAL P Rule 65.1.

   o. Hearing of motions. IN ST TRIAL P Rule 73.

   p. Access to court records. IN ST ADMIN Rule 9.

   q. Paper size. IN ST ADMIN Rule 11.

   r. Facsimile transmission. IN ST ADMIN Rule 12.

   s. Electronic filing and electronic service pilot projects. IN ST ADMIN Rule 16.

   t. Sealing of certain records by court; Hearing; Notice. IN ST 5-14-3-5.5.

   u. Civil protection orders. IN ST 34-26-5-1; IN ST 34-26-5-20.

   v. Privacy and confidentiality. IN ST 5-2-9-6; IN ST 5-14-3-4; IN ST 6-4.1-5-10; IN ST 6-4.1-12-12; IN ST 6-8.1-7-1; IN ST 11-13-1-8; IN ST 12-23-14-13; IN ST 16-39-3-10; IN ST 16-41-8-1; IN ST 22-4-19-6; IN ST 31-11-1-6; IN ST 31-19-5-23; IN ST 31-19-13-2; IN ST 31-19-19-1; IN ST 31-33-18-1; IN ST 31-39-1-1; IN ST 31-39-1-2; IN ST 33-23-16-16; IN ST 35-34-2-4; IN ST 35-38-1-13; IN ST 35-38-9-1; IN ST ADR Rule 2.11; IN ST ADR Rule 4.4; IN ST ADR Rule 5.6; IN ST JURY Rule 10.

2. *Local rules*

   a. Requirements for motions. IN ST MARION CIR AND SUPER CTS CIV Rule 203.

    b.   Preparation of pleadings, motions and other papers. IN ST MARION CIR AND SUPER CTS CIV Rule 204.

    c.   Filing of pleadings, motions and other papers. IN ST MARION CIR AND SUPER CTS CIV Rule 205.

    d.   Signing and verification of pleadings, motions and other papers; Service on opposing party. IN ST MARION CIR AND SUPER CTS CIV Rule 206.

    e.   Motions for continuance. IN ST MARION CIR AND SUPER CTS CIV Rule 215.

    f.   Electronic filing. IN ST MARION SUPER CT ADMIN Rule 311.

B. Timing

1. *Temporary restraining order without notice.* There are no specific timing requirements for submitting an application for a temporary restraining order without notice.

    a.   *Filing.* All pleadings and papers subsequent to the complaint which are required to be served upon a party shall be filed with the Court either before service or within a reasonable period of time thereafter. IN ST TRIAL P Rule 5(E)(1).

2. *Computation of time*

    a.   *Generally; Days excluded.* In computing any period of time prescribed or allowed by the Indiana Rules of Trial Procedure, by order of the court, or by any applicable statute, the day of the act, event, or default from which the designated period of time begins to run shall not be included. The last day of the period so computed is to be included unless it is:

        i.   A Saturday,

        ii.   A Sunday,

        iii.   A legal holiday as defined by state statute, or

        iv.   A day the office in which the act is to be done is closed during regular business hours. IN ST TRIAL P Rule 6(A).

    b.   *Short periods.* In any event, the period runs until the end of the next day that is not a Saturday, a Sunday, a legal holiday, or a day on which the office is closed. When the period of time allowed is less than seven (7) days, intermediate Saturdays, Sundays, legal holidays, and days on which the office is closed shall be excluded from the computations. IN ST TRIAL P Rule 6(A).

    c.   *Additional time after service by United States mail.* Whenever a party has the right or is required to do some act or take some proceedings within a prescribed period after the service of a notice or other paper upon him and the notice or paper is served upon him by United States mail, three (3) days shall be added to the prescribed period. IN ST TRIAL P Rule 6(E).

    d.   *Enlargement of time.* When an act is required or allowed to be done at or within a specific time by the Indiana Rules of Trial Procedure, the court may at any time for cause shown:

        i.   Order the period enlarged, with or without motion or notice, if request therefor is made before the expiration of the period originally prescribed or extended by a previous order; or

        ii.   Upon motion made after the expiration of the specific period, permit the act to be done where the failure to act was the result of excusable neglect; but, the court may not extend the time for taking any action for judgment on the evidence under IN ST TRIAL P Rule 50(A), amendment of findings and judgment under IN ST TRIAL P Rule 52(B), to correct errors under IN ST TRIAL P Rule 59(C), statement in opposition to motion to correct error under IN ST TRIAL P Rule 59(E), or to obtain relief from final judgment under IN ST TRIAL P Rule 60(B), except to the extent and under the conditions stated in those rules. IN ST TRIAL P Rule 6(B).

    e.   *Continuances disfavored.* Motions for Continuance are discouraged. Neither side is entitled to an automatic continuance as a matter of right. IN ST MARION CIR AND SUPER CTS CIV Rule 215. For information on obtaining a continuance, refer to IN ST MARION CIR AND SUPER CTS CIV Rule 215.

C. General Requirements

1. *Motions, generally.* Unless made during a hearing or trial, or otherwise ordered by the court, an

application to the court for an order shall be made by written motion. The motion shall state the grounds therefor and the relief or order sought. IN ST TRIAL P Rule 7(B).

a. *Motions as distinct from pleadings.* Motions and responses to motions are not pleadings, and allegations contained in a motion are not admissions of a party. 22B INPRAC 7:2; Wachstetter v. County Properties, LLC, 832 N.E.2d 574 (Ind.Ct.App. 2005); Scott County Family YMCA, Inc. v. Hobbs, 817 N.E.2d 603 (Ind.Ct.App. 2004).

b. *Unopposed motions generally granted.* It is common for a trial court to grant procedural motions, such as motions for enlargement of time, discovery motions, or motions for continuance, unless an objection is filed. 21 INPRAC § 13.8.

2. *Application for temporary restraining order.* Seeking a temporary restraining order should only be considered if there is a possibility that irreparable injury may occur before the hearing for a preliminary injunction can be held. 4 INPRAC R 65(65.4).

   a. *Without notice*

      i. *When notice not required.* A temporary restraining order may be granted without written or oral notice to the adverse party or his attorney only if:

         • It clearly appears from specific facts shown by affidavit or by the verified complaint that immediate and irreparable injury, loss, or damage will result to the applicant before the adverse party or his attorney can be heard in opposition; and

         • The applicant's attorney certifies to the court in writing the efforts, if any, which have been made to give notice and the reasons supporting his claim that notice should not be required. IN ST TRIAL P Rule 65(B).

      ii. *Motion for dissolution or modification of temporary restraining order.* On two (2) days' notice to the party who obtained the temporary restraining order without notice or on such shorter notice to that party as the court may prescribe, the adverse party may appear and move its dissolution or modification and in that event the court shall proceed to hear and determine such motion as expeditiously as the ends of justice require. IN ST TRIAL P Rule 65(B).

   b. *Temporary restraining orders with notice in Indiana.* IN ST TRIAL P Rule 65(B) in its entirety deals only with temporary restraining orders issued without notice. No mention is made of the issuance of temporary restraining orders with notice. 4 INPRAC R 65(65.4). Some Indiana cases have apparently held that there is no such thing as a temporary restraining order if the adverse party has notice and a hearing is held. 4 INPRAC R 65(65.4); Indiana State Dept. of Welfare v. Stagner, 410 N.E.2d 1348 (Ind.Ct.App. 1980); Szany v. City of Hammond, 170 Ind.App. 537, 352 N.E.2d 866 (Ind.Ct.App. 1976). Refer to the Indiana KeyRules Motion for Preliminary Injunction document for information on obtaining an injunction with notice to the opposing party.

   c. *Application without notice as ex parte communication with judge.* The failure to follow the requirements of IN ST TRIAL P Rule 65(B) may constitute, in some circumstances, an improper ex parte communication between attorney and judge. 4 INPRAC R 65(65.4.1); Ace Bail Bonds v. Government Payment Service, Inc., 892 N.E.2d 702 (Ind.Ct.App. 2008), transfer denied (Ind. Jan. 15, 2009).

      i. When a party knows of the presence of another party's attorney in litigation, because each is present at hearings or at trial, then, even if an ex parte T.R.O. arguably meets the criteria in IN ST TRIAL P Rule 65(B), it is not valid unless it meets the standards in Smith v. Johnston, 711 N.E.2d 1259 (Ind.1999). 4 INPRAC R 65(65.4.1).

      ii. Smith v. Johnston, was an appeal to set a default judgment aside. The court granted relief because the party who obtained the default did not give notice to the defaulted party, even though IN ST TRIAL P Rule 4 and IN ST TRIAL P Rule 5 do not require that notice be served on the opposite party's attorney. 4 INPRAC R 65(65.4.1). Smith v. Johnston's rationale clearly states that if an attorney "has knowledge of his opponent's representation, then the Rules of Professional Conduct establish a duty to provide notice `before seeking any relief from the court.'" 4 INPRAC R 65(65.4.1); Smith v. Johnston, 711 N.E.2d 1259 (Ind.1999).

   d. *Service of the temporary restraining order once issued.* Notice of the restraining order should be served upon the adverse party. The order may be served together with process in accordance with IN ST TRIAL P Rule 4, or, if obtained after service of process, then in accordance with IN ST TRIAL P Rule 5. 22 INPRAC § 29.2.

    i.   IN ST 34-26-1-11 provides the "clerk shall issue a copy of the order of injunction, certified by the clerk, which shall be served promptly by delivering the order to the adverse party." 22 INPRAC § 29.2; IN ST 34-26-1-11.

    ii.   However, service is not necessary to make the restraining order effective and binding, so long as the restrained party receives actual knowledge of the order. 22 INPRAC § 29.2; Reed Sign Service, Inc. v. Reid, 755 N.E.2d 690 (Ind.Ct.App. 2001).

e.   *Form of order by judge*

    i.   Every order granting temporary injunction and every restraining order shall include or be accompanied by findings as required by IN ST TRIAL P Rule 52; shall be specific in terms; shall describe in reasonable detail, and not by reference to the complaint or other document, the act or acts sought to be restrained; and is binding only upon the parties to the action, their officers, agents, servants, employees, and attorneys, and upon those persons in active concert or participation with them who receive actual notice of the order by personal service or otherwise. IN ST TRIAL P Rule 65(D).

    ii.   Every temporary restraining order granted without notice shall be indorsed with the date and hour of issuance; shall be filed forthwith in the clerk's office and entered of record; shall define the injury and state why it is irreparable and why the order was granted without notice; and shall expire by its terms within such time after entry, not to exceed ten (10) days, as the court fixes, unless within the time so fixed the order, for good cause shown, is extended for a like period or unless the whereabouts of the party against whom the order is granted is unknown and cannot be determined by reasonable diligence or unless the party against whom the order is directed consents that it may be extended for a longer period. The reasons for the extension shall be entered of record. IN ST TRIAL P Rule 65(B).

f.   *Temporary restraining orders; Domestic relations cases.* Parties wishing protection from domestic or family violence in Domestic Relations cases shall petition the court pursuant to IN ST 34-26-5-1 through IN ST 34-26-5-20. IN ST TRIAL P Rule 65(E). For more information refer to IN ST TRIAL P Rule 65(E) and IN ST 34-26-5-1, et seq.

3.   *Security*

a.   *Security requirement.* No restraining order or preliminary injunction shall issue except upon the giving of security by the applicant, in such sum as the court deems proper, for the payment of such costs and damages as may be incurred or suffered by any party who is found to have been wrongfully enjoined or restrained. No such security shall be required of a governmental organization, but such governmental organization shall be responsible for costs and damages as may be incurred or suffered by any party who is found to have been wrongfully enjoined or restrained. IN ST TRIAL P Rule 65(C).

    i.   The provisions of IN ST TRIAL P Rule 65.1 apply to a surety upon a bond or undertaking under IN ST TRIAL P Rule 65. IN ST TRIAL P Rule 65(C).

b.   *Proceedings against sureties.* Whenever the Indiana Rules of Trial Procedure or other laws require or permit the giving of security by a party to a court action or proceeding, and security is given in the form of a bond or stipulation or other undertaking with one or more sureties, each surety submits himself to the jurisdiction of the court and irrevocably appoints the clerk of the court as his agent upon whom any papers affecting his liability on the bond or undertaking may be served. His liability may be enforced on motion without the necessity of an independent action. The motion and such notice of the motion as the court prescribes may be served on the clerk of the court, who shall forthwith mail copies to the sureties if their addresses are known. IN ST TRIAL P Rule 65.1 applies to bonds or security furnished on appeal, and enforcement shall be in the court to which the case is returned after appeal. IN ST TRIAL P Rule 65.1.

c.   *Bond generally used as security.* IN ST TRIAL P Rule 65(C) speaks only of the giving of security and does not expressly require a surety on a bond. In practice, however, the giving of a bond with an insurance company as surety in the amount set by the court is typically the device used to satisfy this section. 4 INPRAC R 65(65.6).

D. Documents

1. *Required documents*

   a. *Application for temporary restraining order.* Refer to the General Requirements section of this document for additional information on the contents of an application for a temporary restraining order.

   b. *Security.* No restraining order or preliminary injunction shall issue except upon the giving of security by the applicant, in such sum as the court deems proper, for the payment of such costs and damages as may be incurred or suffered by any party who is found to have been wrongfully enjoined or restrained. IN ST TRIAL P Rule 65(C). Refer to the General Requirements section of this document for more information.

   c. *Proposed order.* Unless local practice provides differently, a party should submit a proposed order with its written motion to be signed by the judge once the motion has been granted. 21 INPRAC § 13.8. All motions seeking an order of the Court shall be accompanied by a sufficient number of orders to be executed by the Court in granting said motion. In addition to the orders, the notice shall be accompanied by stamped, addressed envelopes to all parties of record. IN ST MARION CIR AND SUPER CTS CIV Rule 203(E).

2. *Supplemental documents*

   a. *Supporting evidence.* When a motion is based on facts not appearing of record the court may hear the matter on affidavits presented by the respective parties, but the court may direct that the matter be heard wholly or partly on oral testimony or depositions. IN ST TRIAL P Rule 43(B).

   b. *Facsimile cover sheet.* Any document sent to the Clerk of the Circuit Court by electronic facsimile transmission shall be accompanied by a cover sheet which states the title of the document, case number, number of pages, identity and voice telephone number of the sending party and instructions for filing. The cover sheet shall contain the signature of the attorney or party, pro se, authorizing the filing. IN ST ADMIN Rule 12(D).

E. Format

1. *Form of motions.* The rules applicable to captions, and the signing and form of pleadings (IN ST TRIAL P Rule 8 through IN ST TRIAL P Rule 11), apply to all motions and other papers provided under the Indiana Rules of Trial Procedure. 22B INPRAC 7:2.

2. *Form of pleadings*

   a. *Caption; Names of parties.* Every pleading shall contain a caption setting forth the name of the court, the title of the action, the file number, and a designation as in IN ST TRIAL P Rule 7(A). In the complaint the title of the action shall include the names of all the parties, but in other pleadings it is sufficient to state the name of the first party on each side with an appropriate indication of other parties. IN ST TRIAL P Rule 10(A).

      i. Every pleading shall contain a caption setting forth the name of the Court, the Division and Room Number, the title of the action and the file number. IN ST MARION CIR AND SUPER CTS CIV Rule 204(B).

   b. *Paragraphs; Separate statements.* All averments of a claim or defense shall be made in numbered paragraphs, the contents of each of which shall be limited as far as practicable to a statement of a single set of circumstances, and a paragraph may be referred to by number in all succeeding pleadings. Each claim founded upon a separate transaction or occurrence and each defense other than denials may be stated in a separate count or defense whenever a separation facilitates the clear presentation of the matters set forth. IN ST TRIAL P Rule 10(B).

   c. *Adoption by reference; Exhibits.* Statements in a pleading may be adopted by reference in a different part of the same pleading or in another pleading or in any motion. A copy of any written instrument which is an exhibit to a pleading is a part thereof for all purposes. IN ST TRIAL P Rule 10(C).

    d.   *Paper.* Pleadings, motions and other papers may be either printed or typewritten on white opaque paper of at least sixteen (16) pound weight, eight and one-half (8-1/2) inches wide and eleven (11) inches in length. IN ST MARION CIR AND SUPER CTS CIV Rule 204(A).

    e.   *Copies.* All copies shall likewise be on white paper of sufficient strength and durability to resist normal wear and tear. IN ST MARION CIR AND SUPER CTS CIV Rule 204(A).

    f.   *Line spacing.* If typewritten, the lines shall be double spaced, except for quotations, which shall be indented and single spaced. IN ST MARION CIR AND SUPER CTS CIV Rule 204(A).

    g.   *Script type.* Script type shall not be used. IN ST MARION CIR AND SUPER CTS CIV Rule 204(A).

    h.   *Titles.* Titles on all pleadings shall delineate each topic included in the pleading e.g. where a pleading contains an Answer, a Motion to Strike or Dismiss, or a Jury Request each shall be set forth in the title. IN ST MARION CIR AND SUPER CTS CIV Rule 204(C).

    i.   *Margins and binding.* Margins shall be one (1) inch. Binding or stapling shall be at the top and at no other place. Covers or backing shall not be used. IN ST MARION CIR AND SUPER CTS CIV Rule 204(D).

3.   *Size of papers for filing.* Effective January 1, 1992, all pleadings, copies, motions and documents filed with any trial court or appellate level court, typed or printed, with the exception of exhibits and existing wills, shall be prepared on eight and one-half by eleven inch (8 1/2" x 11") size paper. IN ST ADMIN Rule 11.

4.   *Form of electronically filed documents.* All electronically filed and served pleadings shall, to the extent practicable, be formatted in accordance with the applicable rules governing formatting of paper pleadings. IN ST MARION SUPER CT ADMIN Rule 311(2-103)(1).

    a.   *Electronic document title.* The electronic document title of each pleading or other document shall include:

       i.   Party or parties filing/serving the document,

       ii.   Nature of the document,

       iii.   Party or parties against whom relief, if any, is sought, and

       iv.   Nature of the relief sought (e.g., Defendant ABC Corporation's Motion for Summary Judgment). IN ST MARION SUPER CT ADMIN Rule 311(2-103)(2).

5.   *Signature requirements*

    a.   *Signature of attorney.* Every pleading or motion of a party represented by an attorney shall be signed by at least one (1) attorney of record in his individual name, whose address, telephone number, and attorney number shall be stated, except that this provision shall not apply to pleadings and motions made and transcribed at the trial or a hearing before the judge and received by him in such form. IN ST TRIAL P Rule 11(A).

       i.   All pleadings and motions shall contain the original or authorized signature of the attorney, the name of the attorney in typed or printed form, the name of the law firm if a member of a firm, the attorney's address, identification number, e-mail address, telephone number, fax number, and the designation as to the party for whom he appears. IN ST MARION CIR AND SUPER CTS CIV Rule 204(E).

       ii.   The signature of an attorney constitutes a certificate by him that he has read the pleadings; that to the best of his knowledge, information, and belief, there is good ground to support it; and that it is not interposed for delay. IN ST TRIAL P Rule 11(A).

       iii.   If a pleading or motion is not signed or is signed with intent to defeat the purpose of the rule, it may be stricken as sham and false and the action may proceed as though the pleading had not been served. IN ST TRIAL P Rule 11(A).

       iv.   For a willful violation of IN ST TRIAL P Rule 11 an attorney may be subjected to appropriate disciplinary action. Similar action may be taken if scandalous or indecent matter is inserted. IN ST TRIAL P Rule 11(A).

       v.   Every pleading, document, and instrument electronically filed or served shall be deemed to

have been signed by the judge, clerk, attorney or declarant and shall bear a facsimile or typographical signature of such person, along with the typed name, address, telephone number, and Bar number of a signing attorney. Typographical signatures shall be treated as personal signatures for all purposes under these rules. IN ST MARION SUPER CT ADMIN Rule 311(2-105).

- Documents containing signatures of third-parties (i.e., unopposed motions, affidavits, stipulations, etc.) may also be filed electronically by indicating that the original signatures are maintained by the filing party in paper-format. IN ST MARION SUPER CT ADMIN Rule 311(2-105).

- Unless otherwise ordered by the Court or Clerk, a printed copy of all documents filed or served electronically, including original signatures, shall be maintained by the party filing the document and shall be made available, upon reasonable notice, for inspection by other counsel, the Clerk or Court. Parties shall retain originals until two (2) years after all time periods for appeal have expired. From time to time, it may be necessary to provide the Clerk or Court with a hard copy of an electronically filed document. IN ST MARION SUPER CT ADMIN Rule 311(2-105).

    vi. For the recommended format of a signature block, refer to IN ST MARION CIR AND SUPER CTS CIV Rule 204(E).

b. *Signature of unrepresented party.* A party who is not represented by an attorney shall sign his pleading and state his address. IN ST TRIAL P Rule 11(A).

c. *Verification not generally required.* Except when specifically required by rule, pleadings or motions need not be verified or accompanied by affidavit. The rule in equity that the averments of an answer under oath must be overcome by the testimony of two (2) witnesses or of one (1) witness sustained by corroborating circumstances is abolished. IN ST TRIAL P Rule 11(A).

d. *Verification by affirmation or representation.* When in connection with any civil or special statutory proceeding it is required that any pleading, motion, petition, supporting affidavit, or other document of any kind, be verified, or that an oath be taken, it shall be sufficient if the subscriber simply affirms the truth of the matter to be verified by an affirmation or representation. IN ST TRIAL P Rule 11(B). IN ST TRIAL P Rule 11(B) states that the affirmation or representation should be in substantially the following language: "I (we) affirm, under the penalties for perjury, that the foregoing representation(s) is (are) true. (Signed) _____."

    i. Any person who falsifies an affirmation or representation of fact shall be subject to the same penalties as are prescribed by law for the making of a false affidavit. IN ST TRIAL P Rule 11(B).

e. *Verified pleadings, motions, and affidavits as evidence.* Pleadings, motions and affidavits accompanying or in support of such pleadings or motions when required to be verified or under oath shall be accepted as a representation that the signer had personal knowledge thereof or reasonable cause to believe the existence of the facts or matters stated or alleged therein; and, if otherwise competent or acceptable as evidence, may be admitted as evidence of the facts or matters stated or alleged therein when it is so provided in the Indiana Rules of Trial Procedure, by statute or other law, or to the extent the writing or signature expressly purports to be made upon the signer's personal knowledge. When such pleadings, motions and affidavits are verified or under oath they shall not require other or greater proof on the part of the adverse party than if not verified or not under oath unless expressly provided otherwise by the Indiana Rules of Trial Procedure, statute or other law. Affidavits upon motions for summary judgment under IN ST TRIAL P Rule 56 and in denial of execution under IN ST TRIAL P Rule 9.2 shall be made upon personal knowledge. IN ST TRIAL P Rule 11(C).

6. *Information excluded from public access.* Every document filed in a case shall separately identify information excluded from public access pursuant to IN ST ADMIN Rule 9(G)(1) as follows:

a. Whole documents that are excluded from public access pursuant to IN ST ADMIN Rule 9(G)(1) shall be tendered on light green paper or have a light green coversheet attached to the document, marked "Not for Public Access" or "Confidential." IN ST TRIAL P Rule 5(G)(1).

b. When only a portion of a document contains information excluded from public access pursuant to IN ST ADMIN Rule 9(G)(1), said information shall be omitted [or redacted] from the filed document, and set forth on a separate accompanying document on light green paper conspicuously marked "Not for Public Access" or "Confidential" and clearly designated [or identifying] the caption and number of the case and the document and location within the document to which the redacted material pertains. IN ST TRIAL P Rule 5(G)(2).

c. With respect to documents filed in electronic format, the trial court, by local rule, may provide for compliance with IN ST TRIAL P Rule 5 in manner that separates and protects access to information excluded from public access. IN ST TRIAL P Rule 5(G)(3).

d. IN ST TRIAL P Rule 5(G) does not apply to a record sealed by the court pursuant to IN ST 5-14-3-5.5 or otherwise, nor to records, documents, or information filed in cases to which public access is prohibited pursuant to IN ST ADMIN Rule 9(G). IN ST TRIAL P Rule 5(G)(4).

e. The following information in case records is excluded from public access and is confidential:

   i. Information that is excluded from public access pursuant to federal law;

   ii. Information that is excluded from public access as declared confidential by Indiana statute or other court rule, including without limitation:

   - All adoption records created after July 8, 1941, as declared confidential by IN ST 31-19-19-1, et seq., except those specifically declared open by IN ST 31-19-13-2(2);

   - All records relating to chancroid, chlamydia, gonorrhea, hepatitis, human immunodeficiency virus (HIV), Lymphogranuloma venereum, syphilis, tuberculosis, as declared confidential by IN ST 16-41-8-1, et seq.;

   - All records relating to child abuse as declared confidential by IN ST 31-33-18-1, et seq.;

   - All records relating to drug tests as declared confidential by IN ST 5-14-3-4(a)(9);

   - Records of grand jury proceedings as declared confidential by IN ST 35-34-2-4;

   - Records of juvenile proceedings as declared confidential by IN ST 31-39-1-2, except those specifically open under statute;

   - All paternity records created after July 1, 1941 as declared confidential by IN ST 31-14-11-15, IN ST 31-19-5-23, IN ST 31-39-1-1 and IN ST 31-39-1-2 [Editor's note: IN ST 31-14-11-15 was repealed effective May 9, 2013];

   - All pre-sentence reports as declared confidential by IN ST 35-38-1-13;

   - Written petitions to permit marriages without consent and orders directing the Clerk of Court to issue a marriage license to underage persons, as declared confidential by IN ST 31-11-1-6;

   - Only those arrest warrants, search warrants, indictments and informations ordered confidential by the trial judge, prior to return of duly executed service as declared confidential by IN ST 5-14-3-4(b)(1);

   - All medical, mental health, or tax records unless determined by law or regulation of any governmental custodian not to be confidential, released by the subject of such records, or declared by a court of competent jurisdiction to be essential to the resolution of litigation as declared confidential by IN ST 16-39-3-10, IN ST 6-4.1-5-10, IN ST 6-4.1-12-12, and IN ST 6-8.1-7-1;

   - Personal information relating to jurors or prospective jurors, other than for the use of the parties and counsel, pursuant to IN ST JURY Rule 10;

   - Information relating to protection from abuse orders, no-contact orders and workplace violence restraining orders as declared confidential by IN ST 5-2-9-6, et seq.;

   - Mediation proceedings pursuant to IN ST ADR Rule 2.11, Mini-Trial proceedings pursuant to IN ST ADR Rule 4.4(C), and Summary Jury Trials pursuant to IN ST ADR Rule 5.6;

- Information in probation files pursuant to the Probation Standards promulgated by the Judicial Conference of Indiana pursuant to IN ST 11-13-1-8(b);

- Information deemed confidential pursuant to the Rules for Court Administered Alcohol and Drug Programs promulgated by the Judicial Conference of Indiana pursuant to IN ST 12-23-14-13;

- Information deemed confidential pursuant to the Problem-Solving Court Rules promulgated by the Judicial Conference of Indiana pursuant to IN ST 33-23-16-16;

- All records of the Department of workforce Development as declared confidential by IN ST 22-4-19-6;

- Information regarding interception of electronic communications that is sealed or deemed confidential as set forth in IN ST 35-33.5-2-1, et seq.

   iii. Information excluded from public access by specific court order;

   iv. Complete Social Security Numbers of living persons;

   v. With the exception of names, information such as addresses, phone numbers, and dates of birth which explicitly identifies:

- Natural persons who are witnesses or victims (not including defendants) in criminal, domestic violence, stalking, sexual assault, juvenile, or civil protection order proceedings, provided that juveniles who are victims of sex crimes shall be identified by initials only;

- Places of residence of judicial officers, clerks and other employees of courts and clerks of court, unless the person or persons about whom the information pertains waives confidentiality;

   vi. Complete account numbers of specific assets, loans, bank accounts, credit cards, and personal identification numbers (PINs);

   vii. All orders of expungement entered in criminal or juvenile proceedings, orders to restrict access to criminal history information pursuant to IN ST 35-38-5-5.5 or IN ST 35-38-8-5 and records excluded from public access by such orders, and information related to infractions that is excluded from public access pursuant to IN ST 34-28-5-15 or IN ST 34-28-5-16 [Editor's note: IN ST 35-38-5-5.5, IN ST 35-38-8-5 and IN ST 34-28-5-16 were repealed effective July 1, 2013; for information on orders restricting access to criminal history, refer to IN ST 35-38-9-1, et seq.];

   viii. All personal notes and e-mail, and deliberative material, of judges, jurors, court staff and judicial agencies, and information recorded in personal data assistants (PDA's) or organizers and personal calendars. IN ST ADMIN Rule 9(G)(1).

F. Filing and Service Requirements

1. *Filing requirements.* Except as otherwise provided in IN ST TRIAL P Rule 5(E)(2), all pleadings and papers subsequent to the complaint which are required to be served upon a party shall be filed with the Court either before service or within a reasonable period of time thereafter. IN ST TRIAL P Rule 5(E)(1). Counsel shall file with the court an original and one (1) copy of all briefs, and memoranda of law filed in support of a motion. IN ST MARION CIR AND SUPER CTS CIV Rule 205(D).

  a. *Filing generally.* All pleadings, petitions and motions are filed with the Clerk designated by the Court at any time during office hours established by the Clerk and the Court. All orders submitted to the Court shall be in sufficient number and shall be accompanied by postage paid envelopes addressed to each party or counsel of record. IN ST MARION CIR AND SUPER CTS CIV Rule 205(A)

  b. *Filing with the court defined.* The filing of pleadings, motions, and other papers with the court as required by the Indiana Rules of Trial Procedure shall be made by one of the following methods:

   i. Delivery to the clerk of the court;

   ii. Sending by electronic transmission under the procedure adopted pursuant to IN ST ADMIN Rule 12;

    iii. Mailing to the clerk by registered, certified or express mail return receipt requested;

    iv. Depositing with any third-party commercial carrier for delivery to the clerk within three (3) calendar days, cost prepaid, properly addressed;

    v. If the court so permits, filing with the judge, in which event the judge shall note thereon the filing date and forthwith transmit them to the office of the clerk; or

    vi. Electronic filing, as approved by the Division of State Court Administration pursuant to IN ST ADMIN Rule 16. IN ST TRIAL P Rule 5(F).

    vii. Filing by registered or certified mail and by third-party commercial carrier shall be complete upon mailing or deposit. IN ST TRIAL P Rule 5(F).

  c. *Facsimile filing.* Facsimile filing is discouraged, but permitted in the Marion Circuit and Marion Superior Court. All documents filed by facsimile shall also be filed in hard copy within seven (7) days of the facsimile filing, along with proposed orders and stamped addressed envelopes, as required by IN ST MARION CIR AND SUPER CTS CIV Rule 203(E). To avoid duplicate filings, the hard copies of the facsimile filing shall indicate in bold letters that the pleading was previously filed by facsimile transmission. Proof of transmission by facsimile, including certificate of service and manner of service, shall be the responsibility of the filing party. If the filing requires immediate attention of the Judge, it shall be so indicated in bold letters in an accompanying transmittal memorandum. Legibility of documents and timeliness of filing is the responsibility of the sender. IN ST MARION CIR AND SUPER CTS CIV Rule 205(B).

    i. *Generally.* In counties where a majority of judges of the courts of record, by posted local rule, have authorized electronic facsimile filing and designated a telephone number to receive such transmissions, pleadings, motions, and other papers may be sent to the Clerk of Circuit Court by electronic facsimile transmission for filing in any case, provided:

- Such matter does not exceed ten (10) pages, including the cover sheet;
- Such matter does not require the payment of fees other than the electronic facsimile transcription fee set forth in IN ST ADMIN Rule 12(E);
- The sending party creates at the time of transmission a machine generated log for such transmission; and
- The original document and the transmission log are maintained by the sending party for the duration of the litigation. IN ST ADMIN Rule 12(B).

    ii. *Time of filing.* During normal, posted business hours, the time of filing shall be the time the duplicate document is produced in the office of the Clerk of the Circuit Court. Duplicate documents received at all other times shall be filed as of the next normal business day. IN ST ADMIN Rule 12(C).

- If the receiving fax machine endorses its own time and date stamp upon the transmitted documents and the receiving machine produces a delivery receipt which is electronically created and transmitted to the sending party, the time of filing shall be the date and time recorded on the transmitted document by the receiving fax machine. IN ST ADMIN Rule 12(C).

  d. *Electronic filing.* Electronic filing and electronic service pilot projects are authorized pursuant to IN ST ADMIN Rule 16 and approved by the Division of State Court Administration. IN ST MARION SUPER CT ADMIN Rule 311(1-103).

    i. *Cases where electronic filing accepted.* All Marion County Circuit and Superior civil courts may accept electronic filing and service of pleadings and other documents designated in this rule in mortgage foreclosure (hereinafter referred to as "MF"), civil collection(hereinafter referred to as "CC"), and individual cases that have been approved for electronic filing and service. IN ST MARION SUPER CT ADMIN Rule 311(1-104)(1).

- The Marion County Circuit Court may, upon the motion of a party or its own motion, designate a case that will involve multiple litigants, legally intricate issues, and an extensive number of documents a mass tort or complex litigation case. Any case so designated shall be subject to electronic filing and service using the county's approved Electronic Service Provider. IN ST MARION SUPER CT ADMIN Rule 311(1-104)(3).

- The filing of electronic pleadings and other documents in MF and CC cases is entirely voluntary; however, once the case is initially filed electronically, all subsequent filings in the case shall remain in electronic format until the time for appeal is exhausted. IN ST MARION SUPER CT ADMIN Rule 311(1-104)(5).

ii. *Documents eligible for electronic filing.* The following pleadings may be filed and served electronically:

- New case complaint and petitions. IN ST MARION SUPER CT ADMIN Rule 311(1-104)(8)(a).

- Original answers. IN ST MARION SUPER CT ADMIN Rule 311(1-104)(8)(a).

- Any other pleadings or document including but not limited to motions and appearance forms. IN ST MARION SUPER CT ADMIN Rule 311(1-104)(8)(a).

iii. *Manner of electronic filing.* Parties shall E-file a document either:

- By registering to use the Electronic Filing Service Provider; or

- In person at the Marion County Clerk's office, by electronically filing through the Public Access Terminal. Parties filing in this manner shall be responsible for furnishing the document in an electronic format that will be compatible with the clerk's office-system to be uploaded in person. IN ST MARION SUPER CT ADMIN Rule 311(1-104)(9). For information on the Electronic Filing Service Provider and Public Access Terminal, refer to IN ST MARION SUPER CT ADMIN Rule 311(1-101).

- Registered users shall pay statutory filing fees for E-filed documents electronically to the Court through their EFSP. Filing fees are due and payable at the time of filing. IN ST MARION SUPER CT ADMIN Rule 311(2-104)(1). For more information on electronic filing fees, refer to IN ST MARION SUPER CT ADMIN Rule 311(2-104).

iv. *Effect of electronic filing.* Any pleading filed electronically shall be considered as filed with the court when the transmission to the EFSP is complete. Any document E-filed by 11:59 p.m. local Indianapolis, Indiana time shall be deemed filed on that date. The EFSP is an agent of the Court for the purpose of electronic filing, receipt, service and retrieval of electronic documents. IN ST MARION SUPER CT ADMIN Rule 311(2-102).

- Upon completion of filing, the EFSP shall issue a confirmation receipt that includes the date and time of receipt. The confirmation receipt shall serve as proof of filing. IN ST MARION SUPER CT ADMIN Rule 311(2-102).

- In the event the Court rejects the submitted documents following review, the documents shall not become part of the official Court record and the filer will receive notification of the rejection. Users may be required to refile the instruments to meet necessary filing requirements. Documents may be filed through an E-filing system at any time that the Clerk's office is open to receive the filing or at such other times as may be designated by the clerk and posted publicly. IN ST MARION SUPER CT ADMIN Rule 311(2-102).

- Documents filed through the E-filing system are deemed filed when received by the Clerk's office, except that documents received at times that the Clerk's office is closed shall be deemed filed the next regular time when the Clerk's office is open for filing. The time stamp issued by the E-filing system shall be presumed to be the time the document is received by the Clerk. IN ST MARION SUPER CT ADMIN Rule 311(2-102).

v. *Electronically filed documents.* All pleadings and other documents designated in IN ST MARION SUPER CT ADMIN Rule 311 shall be filed and served electronically in any individual case which has been approved for electronic filing and service. IN ST MARION SUPER CT ADMIN Rule 311(1-104)(6).

vi. *System failures.* When filing by electronic means is hindered by a technical failure, a party may file with the Clerk of Marion County in hard copy. With the exception of deadlines that by law cannot be extended, the time for filing of any paper that is delayed due to technical failure of the site shall be extended for one (1) day for each day on which such failure occurs, unless otherwise ordered by the Court. IN ST MARION SUPER CT ADMIN Rule 311(2-108).

    vii. *Compliance with rules.* All filing shall comply with the requirements of IN ST ADMIN Rule 9 and IN ST ADMIN Rule 16; and the Indiana Rules of Court and the Marion County Local Rules. IN ST MARION SUPER CT ADMIN Rule 311(1-104)(11).

  e. *Filing for special judge.* When a Special Judge who is not a Marion County Judge is selected, all parties or attorneys shall furnish such Judge with copies of all filings prior to the qualification of such Special Judge. Thereafter, copies of all filings shall be delivered in person, by mail or by facsimile to the office of the Special Judge with certificate of forwarding same made a part of the filing. IN ST MARION CIR AND SUPER CTS CIV Rule 205(C).

  f. *Proof of filing.* Any party filing any paper by any method other than personal delivery to the clerk shall retain proof of filing. IN ST TRIAL P Rule 5(F).

2. *Service requirements.* Unless otherwise provided by the Indiana Rules of Trial Procedure or an order of the court, each party and special judge, if any, shall be served with: (1) every order required by its terms to be served; (2) every pleading subsequent to the original complaint; (3) every written motion except one which may be heard ex parte; (4) every brief submitted to the trial court; (5) every paper relating to discovery required to be served upon a party; and (6) every written notice, appearance, demand, offer of judgment, designation of record on appeal, or similar paper. IN ST TRIAL P Rule 5(A).

  a. *Methods of service*

    i. *Personal service.* Whenever a party is represented by an attorney of record, service shall be made upon such attorney unless service upon the party himself is ordered by the court. Service upon the attorney or party shall be made by delivering or mailing a copy of the papers to the last known address or where an attorney or party has consented to service by fax or e-mail, as provided in IN ST TRIAL P Rule 3.1(A)(4), by faxing or e-mailing a copy of the documents to the fax number or e-mail address set out in the appearance form or correction as required by IN ST TRIAL P Rule 3.1(E). IN ST TRIAL P Rule 5(B). Delivery of a copy within IN ST TRIAL P Rule 5 means:

- Offering or tendering it to the attorney or party and stating the nature of the papers being served. Refusal to accept an offered or tendered document is a waiver of any objection to the sufficiency or adequacy of service of that document;

- Leaving it at his office with a clerk or other person in charge thereof, or if there is no one in charge, leaving it in a conspicuous place therein; or

- If the office is closed, by leaving it at his dwelling house or usual place of abode with some person of suitable age and discretion then residing therein; or,

- Leaving it at some other suitable place, selected by the attorney upon whom service is being made, pursuant to duly promulgated local rule. IN ST TRIAL P Rule 5(B)(1).

    ii. *Service by mail.* If service is made by mail, the papers shall be deposited in the United States mail addressed to the person on whom they are being served, with postage prepaid. Service shall be deemed complete upon mailing. Proof of service of all papers permitted to be mailed may be made by written acknowledgment of service, by affidavit of the person who mailed the papers, or by certificate of an attorney. It shall be the duty of attorneys when entering their appearance in a cause or when filing pleadings or papers therein, to have noted in the Chronological Case Summary or said pleadings or papers so filed the address and telephone number of their office. Service by delivery or by mail at such address shall be deemed sufficient and complete. IN ST TRIAL P Rule 5(B)(2).

    iii. *Service by fax or e-mail.* A party who has consented to service by fax or e-mail may be served as follows:

- Service by e-mail shall be made by attaching the document being served in .pdf format. Discovery documents must also be served in accordance with IN ST TRIAL P Rule 26(A). IN ST TRIAL P Rule 5(B)(3)(a).

- Service by fax shall be deemed complete upon generation of a transmission record indicating the successful transmission of the entire document, except as provided in IN ST TRIAL P Rule 5(B)(3)(d). IN ST TRIAL P Rule 5(B)(3)(b).

- Service by e-mail shall be deemed complete upon transmission, except as provided in IN ST TRIAL P Rule 5(B)(3)(d). IN ST TRIAL P Rule 5(B)(3)(c).

- Service by fax or e-mail that occurs on a Saturday, Sunday, legal holiday, or day the court or agency in which the matter is pending is closed or after 5:00 PM local time of the recipient shall be deemed complete the next day that is not a Saturday, Sunday, legal holiday, or day that the court or agency in which the matter is pending is not closed. IN ST TRIAL P Rule 5(B)(3)(d).

iv. *Electronic service.* Delivery of E-service documents through the EFSP to other registered users shall be considered as valid and effective service and shall have the same legal effect as an original paper document. Recipients of E-service documents shall access their documents through the EFSP. IN ST MARION SUPER CT ADMIN Rule 311(2-107)(1).

- E-service shall be deemed complete when the transmission to the EFSP is completed. IN ST MARION SUPER CT ADMIN Rule 311(2-107)(2).

- For the purpose of computing time to respond to documents received via E-service, any document served on a day or at a time when the Clerk's office is not open for business shall be deemed served at the time of next opening of the Clerk's office for business. IN ST MARION SUPER CT ADMIN Rule 311(2-107)(3).

b. *Serving numerous defendants.* In any action in which there are unusually large numbers of defendants, the court, upon motion or of its own initiative, may order:

i. That service of the pleadings of the defendants and replies thereto need not be made as between the defendants;

- That any cross-claim, counterclaim, or matter constituting an avoidance or affirmative defense contained therein shall be deemed to be denied or avoided by all other parties; and

- That the filing of any such pleading and service thereof upon the plaintiff constitutes due notice of it to the parties. IN ST TRIAL P Rule 5(D).

ii. A copy of every such order shall be served upon the parties in such manner and form as the court directs. IN ST TRIAL P Rule 5(D).

c. *Service on parties in default for failure to appear.* No service need be made on parties in default for failure to appear, except that pleadings asserting new or additional claims for relief against them shall be served upon them in the manner provided by service of summons in IN ST TRIAL P Rule 4. IN ST TRIAL P Rule 5(A).

G. Hearings

1. *Hearing on motion.* Unless local conditions make it impracticable, each judge shall establish regular times and places, at intervals sufficiently frequent for the prompt dispatch of business, at which motions requiring notice and hearing may be heard and disposed of; but the judge at any time or place and on such notice, if any, as he considers reasonable may make order for the advancement, conduct, and hearing of actions. To expedite its business the court may direct the submission and determination of motions without oral hearing upon brief written statements of reasons in support and opposition, or direct or permit hearings by telephone conference call with all attorneys or other similar means of communication. IN ST TRIAL P Rule 73(A).

2. *Presentation of evidence.* On the hearing of an application for a restraining order or temporary injunction, each party may read affidavits or documentary or record evidence. IN ST 34-26-1-8.

3. *Hearing for preliminary injunction.* In case a temporary restraining order is granted without notice, the motion for a preliminary injunction shall be set down for hearing at the earliest possible time and takes precedence of all matters except older matters of the same character; and when the motion comes on for hearing the party who obtained the temporary restraining order shall proceed with the application for a preliminary injunction and, if he does not do so, the court shall dissolve the temporary restraining order.

IN ST TRIAL P Rule 65(B). Refer to the Indiana KeyRules Motion for Preliminary Injunction document for more information.

4. *Time and place of hearing.* If the motion requires a hearing or oral argument, the Court shall set the time and place of hearing or argument on the motion. IN ST MARION CIR AND SUPER CTS CIV Rule 203(A).

H. Forms

1. Application for Temporary Restraining Order Forms for Indiana

a. Prayer in complaint for temporary restraining order. 5 INPRAC § 3:13.60.

b. Motion for temporary restraining order; With notice. 5 INPRAC § 3:13.80.

c. Notice of motion for temporary restraining order. 11 INPRAC § 97.2.

d. Motion for temporary restraining order; Without notice. 11 INPRAC § 97.3.

e. Affidavit in support of motion for temporary restraining order. 11 INPRAC § 97.4.

f. Certificate of efforts of attorney to give notice of application for temporary restraining order. 11 INPRAC § 97.5.

g. Temporary restraining order without notice and order to show cause why preliminary injunction should not issue; Real estate. 11 INPRAC § 97.6.

h. Motion to extend temporary restraining order. 11 INPRAC § 97.7.

i. Order granting motion to extend temporary restraining order. 11 INPRAC § 97.8.

j. Stipulation extending temporary restraining order. 11 INPRAC § 97.9.

k. Order granting extension of temporary restraining order pursuant to stipulation. 11 INPRAC § 97.10.

l. Motion for judge of adjourning circuit to rule upon motion for temporary restraining order. 11 INPRAC § 97.11.

m. Affidavit in support of motion for judge of adjoining county to rule on motion for temporary restraining order. 11 INPRAC § 97.12.

n. Motion to advance trial on merits for consolidation with hearing on preliminary injunction. 11 INPRAC § 97.13.

I. Checklist

(I) ❑ Matters to be considered by the party filing the application without notice

  (a) ❑ Required documents

    (1) ❑ Application for temporary restraining order

    (2) ❑ Security

    (3) ❑ Proposed order

  (b) ❑ Supplemental documents

    (1) ❑ Supporting evidence

    (2) ❑ Facsimile cover sheet

  (c) ❑ Timing

    (1) ❑ There are no specific timing requirements for submitting an application for a temporary restraining order without notice

Requests, Notices and Applications
Pretrial Conferences, Scheduling, Management

Document Last Updated October 2013

A. Applicable Rules

1. *State rules*

    a. Appearance. IN ST TRIAL P Rule 3.1.

    b. Process. IN ST TRIAL P Rule 4.

    c. Service and filing of pleadings and other papers. IN ST TRIAL P Rule 5.

    d. Time. IN ST TRIAL P Rule 6.

    e. Pleadings. IN ST TRIAL P Rule 7; IN ST TRIAL P Rule 8; IN ST TRIAL P Rule 9.2; IN ST TRIAL P Rule 10.

    f. Signing and verification of pleadings. IN ST TRIAL P Rule 11.

    g. Pre-trial procedure; Formulating issues. IN ST TRIAL P Rule 16.

    h. Evidence. IN ST TRIAL P Rule 43.

    i. Judgment on the evidence (directed verdict). IN ST TRIAL P Rule 50.

    j. Findings by the court. IN ST TRIAL P Rule 52.

    k. Summary judgment. IN ST TRIAL P Rule 56.

    l. Motion to correct error. IN ST TRIAL P Rule 59.

    m. Relief from judgment or order. IN ST TRIAL P Rule 60.

    n. Access to court records. IN ST ADMIN Rule 9.

    o. Paper size. IN ST ADMIN Rule 11.

    p. Facsimile transmission. IN ST ADMIN Rule 12.

    q. Electronic filing and electronic service pilot projects. IN ST ADMIN Rule 16.

    r. Sealing of certain records by court; Hearing; Notice. IN ST 5-14-3-5.5.

    s. Privacy and confidentiality. IN ST 5-2-9-6; IN ST 5-14-3-4; IN ST 6-4.1-5-10; IN ST 6-4.1-12-12; IN ST 6-8.1-7-1; IN ST 11-13-1-8; IN ST 12-23-14-13; IN ST 16-39-3-10; IN ST 16-41-8-1; IN ST 22-4-19-6; IN ST 31-11-1-6; IN ST 31-19-5-23; IN ST 31-19-13-2; IN ST 31-19-19-1; IN ST 31-33-18-1; IN ST 31-39-1-1; IN ST 31-39-1-2; IN ST 33-23-16-16; IN ST 35-34-2-4; IN ST 35-38-1-13; IN ST 35-38-9-1; IN ST ADR Rule 2.11; IN ST ADR Rule 4.4; IN ST ADR Rule 5.6; IN ST JURY Rule 10.

2. *Local rules*

    a. Requirements for motions. IN ST MARION CIR AND SUPER CTS CIV Rule 203.

    b. Preparation of pleadings, motions and other papers. IN ST MARION CIR AND SUPER CTS CIV Rule 204.

    c. Filing of pleadings, motions and other papers. IN ST MARION CIR AND SUPER CTS CIV Rule 205.

    d. Signing and verification of pleadings, motions and other papers; Service on opposing party. IN ST MARION CIR AND SUPER CTS CIV Rule 206.

    e. Case management. IN ST MARION CIR AND SUPER CTS CIV Rule 207.

    f. Pretrial conference. IN ST MARION CIR AND SUPER CTS CIV Rule 208.

    g. Motions for continuance. IN ST MARION CIR AND SUPER CTS CIV Rule 215.

    h. Electronic filing. IN ST MARION SUPER CT ADMIN Rule 311.

B. Timing

1. *Pretrial conference.* Unless otherwise ordered by the court the pretrial conference shall not be called until after reasonable opportunity for the completion of discovery. IN ST TRIAL P Rule 16(B). However, some Indiana courts will schedule a preliminary pretrial conference almost immediately after the case has been filed in order to establish the ground rules for discovery, discovery cut-off dates, and the procedures for filing additional pleadings, motions, and the like. In addition, some courts will only schedule a trial date at the pretrial conference. 22 INPRAC § 28.2.

    a. *Notice.* The clerks shall give at least thirty (30) days' notice of the pretrial conference unless otherwise directed by the court. IN ST TRIAL P Rule 16(B)(1).

    b. *Pre-conference meeting.* Unless otherwise ordered by the court, at least ten (10) days prior to the pretrial conference, attorneys for each of the parties shall meet and confer. IN ST TRIAL P Rule 16(C). It shall be the duty of counsel for both plaintiff and defendant to arrange for the conference of attorneys at least ten (10) days in advance of the pretrial conference. IN ST TRIAL P Rule 16(E).

    c. *Memoranda of law.* Counsel shall file memoranda treating any unusual questions of law involved in the trial no later than five (5) days prior to the pre-trial conference. IN ST MARION CIR AND SUPER CTS CIV Rule 208(D).

    d. *Pre-trial stipulation.* Counsel for the plaintiff shall see that a pre-trial stipulation is prepared, executed by counsel for all parties, and filed with the Court no later than five (5) days prior to the pre-trial conference. IN ST MARION CIR AND SUPER CTS CIV Rule 208(B).

        i. *Unilateral filing of pretrial stipulation where counsel do not agree.* If for any reason the pre-trial stipulation is not executed by all counsel, each counsel shall file a proposed pre-trial stipulation not later than five (5) days prior to the pre-trial conference with a statement why no agreement was reached. IN ST MARION CIR AND SUPER CTS CIV Rule 208(C).

2. *Motion requesting pretrial conference*

    a. *Timing of motion for pretrial conference.* There is no specific timing requirement for filing a motion requesting a pretrial conference.

        i. *Filing.* All pleadings and papers subsequent to the complaint which are required to be served upon a party shall be filed with the Court either before service or within a reasonable period of time thereafter. IN ST TRIAL P Rule 5(E)(1).

    b. *Service*

        i. *Of motion.* A written motion, other than one which may be heard ex parte, and notice of the hearing thereof shall be served not less than five (5) days before the time specified for the hearing, unless a different period is fixed by the Indiana Rules of Trial Procedure or by order of the court. IN ST TRIAL P Rule 6(D).

            • *Of supporting affidavits.* When a motion is supported by affidavit, the affidavit shall be served with the motion. IN ST TRIAL P Rule 6(D).

    c. *Opposition*

        i. *Filing.* If the statement regarding the position of the opposing party(ies) required under IN ST MARION CIR AND SUPER CTS CIV Rule 203(A) indicates that objection to the granting of said motion may ensue, said objecting a party shall have fifteen (15) days from the date of filing to file a response to said motion. IN ST MARION CIR AND SUPER CTS CIV Rule 203(B).

        ii. *Service.* Except as otherwise provided in IN ST TRIAL P Rule 59(D), opposing affidavits may be served not less than one (1) day before the hearing, unless the court permits them to be served at some other time. IN ST TRIAL P Rule 6(D).

3. *Case management conference.* Plaintiff shall arrange a meeting of all parties within ninety (90) days after the filing of a complaint. IN ST MARION CIR AND SUPER CTS CIV Rule 207(A).

    a. *Case management order.* Within ten (10) days after meeting those attending are to file a joint Case Management Order IN ST MARION CIR AND SUPER CTS CIV Rule 207(B).

4. *Computation of time*

    a. *Generally; Days excluded.* In computing any period of time prescribed or allowed by the Indiana

Rules of Trial Procedure, by order of the court, or by any applicable statute, the day of the act, event, or default from which the designated period of time begins to run shall not be included. The last day of the period so computed is to be included unless it is:

    i.   A Saturday,

    ii.   A Sunday,

    iii.   A legal holiday as defined by state statute, or

    iv.   A day the office in which the act is to be done is closed during regular business hours. IN ST TRIAL P Rule 6(A).

b.   *Short periods.* In any event, the period runs until the end of the next day that is not a Saturday, a Sunday, a legal holiday, or a day on which the office is closed. When the period of time allowed is less than seven (7) days, intermediate Saturdays, Sundays, legal holidays, and days on which the office is closed shall be excluded from the computations. IN ST TRIAL P Rule 6(A).

c.   *Additional time after service by United States mail.* Whenever a party has the right or is required to do some act or take some proceedings within a prescribed period after the service of a notice or other paper upon him and the notice or paper is served upon him by United States mail, three (3) days shall be added to the prescribed period. IN ST TRIAL P Rule 6(E).

d.   *Enlargement of time.* When an act is required or allowed to be done at or within a specific time by the Indiana Rules of Trial Procedure, the court may at any time for cause shown:

    i.   Order the period enlarged, with or without motion or notice, if request therefor is made before the expiration of the period originally prescribed or extended by a previous order; or

    ii.   Upon motion made after the expiration of the specific period, permit the act to be done where the failure to act was the result of excusable neglect; but, the court may not extend the time for taking any action for judgment on the evidence under IN ST TRIAL P Rule 50(A), amendment of findings and judgment under IN ST TRIAL P Rule 52(B), to correct errors under IN ST TRIAL P Rule 59(C), statement in opposition to motion to correct error under IN ST TRIAL P Rule 59(E), or to obtain relief from final judgment under IN ST TRIAL P Rule 60(B), except to the extent and under the conditions stated in those rules. IN ST TRIAL P Rule 6(B).

e.   *Continuances disfavored.* Motions for Continuance are discouraged. Neither side is entitled to an automatic continuance as a matter of right. IN ST MARION CIR AND SUPER CTS CIV Rule 215. For information on obtaining a continuance, refer to IN ST MARION CIR AND SUPER CTS CIV Rule 215.

C. General Requirements

1.   *Pretrial conference.* A pre-trial conference shall be held in every civil jury action. Each party shall be represented at the pre-trial conference by the attorney who will conduct the trial. IN ST MARION CIR AND SUPER CTS CIV Rule 208(A).

a.   *When required; Purpose.* In any action except criminal cases, the court may in its discretion and shall upon the motion of any party, direct the attorneys for the parties to appear before it for a conference to consider:

    i.   The simplification of the issues;

    ii.   The necessity or desirability of amendments to the pleadings;

    iii.   The possibility of obtaining admissions of fact and of documents which will avoid unnecessary proof;

    iv.   A limitation of the number of expert witnesses;

    v.   An exchange of names of witnesses to be called during the trial and the general nature of their expected testimony;

    vi.   The desirability of using one or more types of alternative dispute resolution under the rules therefor;

    vii.   The desirability of setting deadlines for dispositive motions in light of the date set for trial; and

      viii.   Such other matters as may aid in the disposition of the action. IN ST TRIAL P Rule 16(A).

  b. *Participants.* At least one (1) attorney planning to take part in the trial shall appear for each of the parties and participate in the pretrial conference. IN ST TRIAL P Rule 16(B)(2).

  c. *Conference of attorneys prior to pretrial conference*

      i.   *Purpose of attorney conference.* In general, the purpose of the "pre-pretrial conference" is to ensure that the attorneys for both sides will be prepared to make maximum use of the pretrial conference itself. IN ST TRIAL P Rule 16 frees the pretrial conference itself from perfunctory matters; it is written to require that not only are attorneys very familiar with the case, but that routine matters are resolved before the pretrial conference so that it may be devoted to a determination of those issues and matters which will be litigated. 2 INPRAC R 16(16.3).

      ii. *Topics to be addressed at attorney conference.* Unless otherwise ordered by the court, at least ten (10) days prior to the pretrial conference, attorneys for each of the parties shall meet and confer for the following purposes:

- *Exhibits.* Each attorney shall mark for identification and provide opposing counsel an opportunity to inspect and copy all exhibits which he expects to introduce at the trial. Numbers or marks placed on such exhibits shall be prefixed with the symbol "P/T", denoting its pretrial designation. When the exhibit is introduced at the trial of the case, the "P/T" designation will be stricken and the exhibits must also indicate the party identifying same. IN ST TRIAL P Rule 16(C)(1). Exhibits of the character which prohibit or make impracticable their production at conference shall be identified and notice given of their intended use. Necessary arrangements must be made to afford opposing counsel an opportunity to examine such exhibits. IN ST TRIAL P Rule 16(C)(1).

- *Exhibit stipulations.* Written stipulations shall be prepared with reference to all exhibits exchanged or identified. The stipulations shall contain all agreements of the parties with reference to the exchanged and identified exhibits, and shall include, but not be limited to, the agreement of the parties with reference to the authenticity of the exhibits, their admissibility in evidence, their use in opening statements, and the provisions made for the inspection of identified exhibits. The original of the exhibit stipulations shall be presented to the court at the pretrial conference. IN ST TRIAL P Rule 16(C)(2).

- *Fact stipulation.* The attorneys shall stipulate in writing with reference to all facts and issues not in genuine dispute. The original of the stipulations shall be presented to the court at the time of the pretrial conference. IN ST TRIAL P Rule 16(C)(3).

- *Exchange list of witnesses.* Attorneys for each of the parties shall furnish opposing counsel with the written list of the names and addresses of all witnesses then known. The original of each witness list shall be presented to the court at the time of the pretrial conference. IN ST TRIAL P Rule 16(C)(4).

- *Discuss settlement.* The possibility of compromise settlement shall be fully discussed and explored. IN ST TRIAL P Rule 16(C)(5).

  d. *Preparation for conference of attorneys and pretrial.* Each attorney shall completely familiarize himself with all aspects of the case in advance of the conference of attorneys and be prepared to enter into stipulations with reference to as many facts and issues and exhibits as possible. IN ST TRIAL P Rule 16(D).

  e. *Refusal to stipulate.* If, following the conference of attorneys, either party determines that there are other facts or exhibits that should be stipulated and which opposing counsel refuses to stipulate upon, he shall compile a list of such facts or exhibits and furnish same to opposing counsel at least two (2) days in advance of the pretrial conference. The original of the list shall be presented to the court at the time of the pretrial conference. IN ST TRIAL P Rule 16(F).

  f. *Witnesses or exhibits discovered subsequent to conference of attorneys and before a pretrial conference.* If, after the conference of the attorneys and before the pretrial conference, counsel discovers additional exhibits or names of additional witnesses, the same information required to be disclosed at the conference of the attorneys shall be immediately furnished opposing counsel. The original of any such disclosures shall be presented to the court at the time of the pretrial conference. IN ST TRIAL P Rule 16(G).

g. *More than one pretrial conference.* If necessary or advisable, the court may adjourn the pretrial conference from time to time or may order an additional pretrial conference. IN ST TRIAL P Rule 16(H).

h. *Witnesses or exhibits discovered subsequent to pretrial conference.* If, following the pretrial conference or during trial, counsel discovers additional exhibits or the names of additional witnesses, the same information required to be disclosed at the conference between attorneys shall be immediately furnished opposing counsel. The original of any such disclosure shall immediately be filed with the court and shall indicate the date it was furnished opposing counsel. IN ST TRIAL P Rule 16(I).

i. *Pretrial order.* The court shall make an order which recites the action taken at the conference, the amendments allowed to the pleading, and the agreements made by the parties as to any of the matters considered which limit the issues for trial to those not disposed of by admissions or agreement of counsel, and such order when entered shall control the subsequent course of action, unless modified thereafter to prevent manifest injustice. The court in its discretion may establish by rule a pretrial calendar on which actions may be placed for consideration as above provided, and may either confine the calendar to jury actions or non-jury actions or extend it to all actions. IN ST TRIAL P Rule 16(J).

   i. The pretrial order delineates the issues in the case and supplants allegations raised in the pleadings. All subsequent pleadings are then controlled by the order that the trial court enters in the case file, and court record. 2 INPRAC R 16(16.2); Dominguez v. Gallmeyer, 402 N.E.2d 1295, 1298 (Ind.Ct.App. 1980).

j. *Sanctions; Failure to appear.* If without just excuse or because of failure to give reasonable attention to the matter, no appearance is made on behalf of a party at a pre-trial conference, or if an attorney is grossly unprepared to participate in the conference, the court may order either one or both of the following:

   i. The payment by the delinquent attorney or party of the reasonable expenses, including attorney's fees, to the aggrieved party; or

   ii. Take such other action as may be appropriate. IN ST TRIAL P Rule 16(K).

   iii. Refer to the Indiana KeyRules Motion for Sanctions document for more information.

2. *Motions, generally.* Unless made during a hearing or trial, or otherwise ordered by the court, an application to the court for an order shall be made by written motion. The motion shall state the grounds therefor and the relief or order sought. IN ST TRIAL P Rule 7(B).

   a. *Motions as distinct from pleadings.* Motions and responses to motions are not pleadings, and allegations contained in a motion are not admissions of a party. 22B INPRAC 7:2; Wachstetter v. County Properties, LLC, 832 N.E.2d 574 (Ind.Ct.App. 2005); Scott County Family YMCA, Inc. v. Hobbs, 817 N.E.2d 603 (Ind.Ct.App. 2004).

   b. *Unopposed motions generally granted.* It is common for a trial court to grant procedural motions, such as motions for enlargement of time, discovery motions, or motions for continuance, unless an objection is filed. 21 INPRAC § 13.8.

3. *Case management conference and order*

   a. *Conference.* Plaintiff shall arrange a meeting of all parties within ninety (90) days after the filing of a complaint for the following purposes:

      i. *List of witnesses.* Exchange lists of witnesses known to have knowledge of the facts supporting the pleadings. The parties shall thereafter be under a continuing obligation to advise opposing parties of other witnesses as they become known. IN ST MARION CIR AND SUPER CTS CIV Rule 207(A)(1).

      ii. *Documents.* Exchange all documents which are contemplated to be used in support of the pleadings. Documents later shown to have been reasonably available to a party and not exchanged may be subject to exclusion at time of trial. IN ST MARION CIR AND SUPER CTS CIV Rule 207(A)(2).

    iii. *Other evidence.* Exchange any other evidence reasonably available to obviate the filing of unnecessary discovery motions. IN ST MARION CIR AND SUPER CTS CIV Rule 207(A)(3).

    iv. *Settlement.* Discuss settlement of the action. IN ST MARION CIR AND SUPER CTS CIV Rule 207(A)(4).

    v. *Discovery schedule.* Agree upon a preliminary schedule for all discovery. IN ST MARION CIR AND SUPER CTS CIV Rule 207(A)(5).

    vi. *Complicated case.* Discuss whether the action is sufficiently complicated so that additional conferences may be required. IN ST MARION CIR AND SUPER CTS CIV Rule 207(A)(6).

  b. *Case management order.* Within ten (10) days after meeting those attending are to file a joint Case Management Order setting forth:

    i. The likelihood of mediation and settlement;

    ii. A detailed schedule of discovery for each party;

    iii. A limitation on the time to join additional parties and to amend the pleadings;

    iv. A limitation on the time to file all pre-trial motions;

    v. Any other matters which the parties want to address;

    vi. A preliminary estimate of the time required for trial; and

    vii. The date by which the parties expect the matter to be ready for trial. IN ST MARION CIR AND SUPER CTS CIV Rule 207(B).

D. Documents

  1. *Pretrial conference*

    a. *Required documents*

      i. *Pre-trial stipulation.* Counsel for the plaintiff shall see that a pre-trial stipulation is prepared, executed by counsel for all parties, and filed with the Court no later than five (5) days prior to the pre-trial conference. The pre-trial stipulation shall contain the following statements in separate numbered paragraphs as indicated:

        • The nature of the action. IN ST MARION CIR AND SUPER CTS CIV Rule 208(B)(1).

        • The basis of jurisdiction. IN ST MARION CIR AND SUPER CTS CIV Rule 208(B)(2).

        • The pleadings raising the issues. IN ST MARION CIR AND SUPER CTS CIV Rule 208(B)(3).

        • A list of all motions or other matters requiring action by the Court. IN ST MARION CIR AND SUPER CTS CIV Rule 208(B)(4).

        • A concise statement of stipulated facts, with reservations, if any. IN ST MARION CIR AND SUPER CTS CIV Rule 208(B)(5).

        • A statement of issues of fact which remain to be litigated at trial. IN ST MARION CIR AND SUPER CTS CIV Rule 208(B)(6).

        • A concise statement of issues of law on which there is agreement. IN ST MARION CIR AND SUPER CTS CIV Rule 208(B)(7).

        • A concise statement of issues of law which remain for determination by the Court. IN ST MARION CIR AND SUPER CTS CIV Rule 208(B)(8).

        • Each party's numbered list of trial exhibits, other than impeachment exhibits, with objections, if any, to each exhibit. The list of exhibits shall be on separate schedules attached to the stipulation. IN ST MARION CIR AND SUPER CTS CIV Rule 208(B)(9).

        • Each party's numbered list of trial witnesses, with their addresses. Impeachment witnesses need not be listed. Expert witnesses shall be so designated. IN ST MARION CIR AND SUPER CTS CIV Rule 208(B)(10).

- Estimated trial time. IN ST MARION CIR AND SUPER CTS CIV Rule 208(B)(11).

ii. *Memoranda of law.* Counsel shall file memoranda treating any unusual questions of law involved in the trial no later than five (5) days prior to the pre-trial conference. IN ST MARION CIR AND SUPER CTS CIV Rule 208(D).

b. *Supplemental documents*

i. *Exhibits and stipulations.* Refer to the General Requirements section of this document for information on exhibits and stipulations.

2. *Motion for pretrial conference*

a. *Required documents*

i. *Motion and notice.* The requirement of notice is satisfied by service of the motion. IN ST TRIAL P Rule 7(B); IN ST MARION CIR AND SUPER CTS CIV Rule 203(A). Refer to the General Requirements section of this document for information on the content of a motion for pretrial conference.

ii. *Statement of approval or disapproval.* Except for initial motions made pursuant to IN ST MARION CIR AND SUPER CTS CIV Rule 203(D), all motions filed with the court shall include a brief statement indicating whether opposing party(ies) object to or approve of the granting of said motion. IN ST MARION CIR AND SUPER CTS CIV Rule 203(A).

iii. *Proposed order.* Unless local practice provides differently, a party should submit a proposed order with its written motion to be signed by the judge once the motion has been granted. 21 INPRAC § 13.8. All motions seeking an order of the Court shall be accompanied by a sufficient number of orders to be executed by the Court in granting said motion. In addition to the orders, the notice shall be accompanied by stamped, addressed envelopes to all parties of record. IN ST MARION CIR AND SUPER CTS CIV Rule 203(E).

iv. *Certificate of service.* An attorney or unrepresented party tendering a document to the Clerk for filing shall certify that service has been made, list the parties served, and specify the date and means of service. The certificate of service shall be placed at the end of the document and shall not be separately filed. The separate filing of a certificate of service, however, shall not be grounds for rejecting a document for filing. The Clerk may permit documents to be filed without a certificate of service but shall require prompt filing of a separate certificate of service. IN ST TRIAL P Rule 5(C). In all cases where any pleading or other document is required to be served upon opposing counsel, proof of such service may be made either by:

- A certificate of service signed by counsel of record for the serving party and the certificate shall specify by name and address all counsel upon whom the pleading or document was served; or

- An acknowledgment of service signed by the party served or counsel of record. IN ST MARION CIR AND SUPER CTS CIV Rule 206.

b. *Supplemental documents*

i. *Supporting evidence.* When a motion is based on facts not appearing of record the court may hear the matter on affidavits presented by the respective parties, but the court may direct that the matter be heard wholly or partly on oral testimony or depositions. IN ST TRIAL P Rule 43(B).

ii. *Request for oral argument.* When an oral argument is requested, the request shall be by separate instrument and filed with the pleading to be argued. Any such oral argument requested may be heard at the discretion of the Court, except for motions for summary judgment which shall be set for hearing upon request of any party. IN ST MARION CIR AND SUPER CTS CIV Rule 203(C).

iii. *Facsimile cover sheet.* Any document sent to the Clerk of the Circuit Court by electronic facsimile transmission shall be accompanied by a cover sheet which states the title of the document, case number, number of pages, identity and voice telephone number of the sending party and instructions for filing. The cover sheet shall contain the signature of the attorney or party, pro se, authorizing the filing. IN ST ADMIN Rule 12(D).

E. Format

1. *Form of papers.* The rules applicable to captions, and the signing and form of pleadings (IN ST TRIAL P Rule 8 through IN ST TRIAL P Rule 11), apply to all motions and other papers provided under the Indiana Rules of Trial Procedure. 22B INPRAC 7:2.

2. *Form of pleadings*

   a. *Caption; Names of parties.* Every pleading shall contain a caption setting forth the name of the court, the title of the action, the file number, and a designation as in IN ST TRIAL P Rule 7(A). In the complaint the title of the action shall include the names of all the parties, but in other pleadings it is sufficient to state the name of the first party on each side with an appropriate indication of other parties. IN ST TRIAL P Rule 10(A).

      i. Every pleading shall contain a caption setting forth the name of the Court, the Division and Room Number, the title of the action and the file number. IN ST MARION CIR AND SUPER CTS CIV Rule 204(B).

   b. *Paragraphs; Separate statements.* All averments of a claim or defense shall be made in numbered paragraphs, the contents of each of which shall be limited as far as practicable to a statement of a single set of circumstances, and a paragraph may be referred to by number in all succeeding pleadings. Each claim founded upon a separate transaction or occurrence and each defense other than denials may be stated in a separate count or defense whenever a separation facilitates the clear presentation of the matters set forth. IN ST TRIAL P Rule 10(B).

   c. *Adoption by reference; Exhibits.* Statements in a pleading may be adopted by reference in a different part of the same pleading or in another pleading or in any motion. A copy of any written instrument which is an exhibit to a pleading is a part thereof for all purposes. IN ST TRIAL P Rule 10(C).

   d. *Paper.* Pleadings, motions and other papers may be either printed or typewritten on white opaque paper of at least sixteen (16) pound weight, eight and one-half (8-1/2) inches wide and eleven (11) inches in length. IN ST MARION CIR AND SUPER CTS CIV Rule 204(A).

   e. *Copies.* All copies shall likewise be on white paper of sufficient strength and durability to resist normal wear and tear. IN ST MARION CIR AND SUPER CTS CIV Rule 204(A).

   f. *Line spacing.* If typewritten, the lines shall be double spaced, except for quotations, which shall be indented and single spaced. IN ST MARION CIR AND SUPER CTS CIV Rule 204(A).

   g. *Script type.* Script type shall not be used. IN ST MARION CIR AND SUPER CTS CIV Rule 204(A).

   h. *Titles.* Titles on all pleadings shall delineate each topic included in the pleading e.g. where a pleading contains an Answer, a Motion to Strike or Dismiss, or a Jury Request each shall be set forth in the title. IN ST MARION CIR AND SUPER CTS CIV Rule 204(C).

   i. *Margins and binding.* Margins shall be one (1) inch. Binding or stapling shall be at the top and at no other place. Covers or backing shall not be used. IN ST MARION CIR AND SUPER CTS CIV Rule 204(D).

3. *Size of papers for filing.* Effective January 1, 1992, all pleadings, copies, motions and documents filed with any trial court or appellate level court, typed or printed, with the exception of exhibits and existing wills, shall be prepared on eight and one-half by eleven inch (8 1/2" x 11") size paper. IN ST ADMIN Rule 11.

4. *Form of electronically filed documents.* All electronically filed and served pleadings shall, to the extent practicable, be formatted in accordance with the applicable rules governing formatting of paper pleadings. IN ST MARION SUPER CT ADMIN Rule 311(2-103)(1).

   a. *Electronic document title.* The electronic document title of each pleading or other document shall include:

      i. Party or parties filing/serving the document,

      ii. Nature of the document,

      iii. Party or parties against whom relief, if any, is sought, and

      iv. Nature of the relief sought (e.g., Defendant ABC Corporation's Motion for Summary Judgment). IN ST MARION SUPER CT ADMIN Rule 311(2-103)(2).

5. *Signature requirements*

   a.   *Signature of attorney.* Every pleading or motion of a party represented by an attorney shall be signed by at least one (1) attorney of record in his individual name, whose address, telephone number, and attorney number shall be stated, except that this provision shall not apply to pleadings and motions made and transcribed at the trial or a hearing before the judge and received by him in such form. IN ST TRIAL P Rule 11(A).

      i.   All pleadings and motions shall contain the original or authorized signature of the attorney, the name of the attorney in typed or printed form, the name of the law firm if a member of a firm, the attorney's address, identification number, e-mail address, telephone number, fax number, and the designation as to the party for whom he appears. IN ST MARION CIR AND SUPER CTS CIV Rule 204(E).

      ii.   The signature of an attorney constitutes a certificate by him that he has read the pleadings; that to the best of his knowledge, information, and belief, there is good ground to support it; and that it is not interposed for delay. IN ST TRIAL P Rule 11(A).

      iii.   If a pleading or motion is not signed or is signed with intent to defeat the purpose of the rule, it may be stricken as sham and false and the action may proceed as though the pleading had not been served. IN ST TRIAL P Rule 11(A).

      iv.   For a willful violation of IN ST TRIAL P Rule 11 an attorney may be subjected to appropriate disciplinary action. Similar action may be taken if scandalous or indecent matter is inserted. IN ST TRIAL P Rule 11(A).

      v.   Every pleading, document, and instrument electronically filed or served shall be deemed to have been signed by the judge, clerk, attorney or declarant and shall bear a facsimile or typographical signature of such person, along with the typed name, address, telephone number, and Bar number of a signing attorney. Typographical signatures shall be treated as personal signatures for all purposes under these rules. IN ST MARION SUPER CT ADMIN Rule 311(2-105).

        •   Documents containing signatures of third-parties (i.e., unopposed motions, affidavits, stipulations, etc.) may also be filed electronically by indicating that the original signatures are maintained by the filing party in paper-format. IN ST MARION SUPER CT ADMIN Rule 311(2-105).

        •   Unless otherwise ordered by the Court or Clerk, a printed copy of all documents filed or served electronically, including original signatures, shall be maintained by the party filing the document and shall be made available, upon reasonable notice, for inspection by other counsel, the Clerk or Court. Parties shall retain originals until two (2) years after all time periods for appeal have expired. From time to time, it may be necessary to provide the Clerk or Court with a hard copy of an electronically filed document. IN ST MARION SUPER CT ADMIN Rule 311(2-105).

      vi.   For the recommended format of a signature block, refer to IN ST MARION CIR AND SUPER CTS CIV Rule 204(E).

   b.   *Signature of unrepresented party.* A party who is not represented by an attorney shall sign his pleading and state his address. IN ST TRIAL P Rule 11(A).

   c.   *Verification not generally required.* Except when specifically required by rule, pleadings or motions need not be verified or accompanied by affidavit. The rule in equity that the averments of an answer under oath must be overcome by the testimony of two (2) witnesses or of one (1) witness sustained by corroborating circumstances is abolished. IN ST TRIAL P Rule 11(A).

   d.   *Verification by affirmation or representation.* When in connection with any civil or special statutory proceeding it is required that any pleading, motion, petition, supporting affidavit, or other document of any kind, be verified, or that an oath be taken, it shall be sufficient if the subscriber simply affirms the truth of the matter to be verified by an affirmation or representation. IN ST TRIAL P Rule 11(B). IN ST TRIAL P Rule 11(B) states that the affirmation or representation should be in substantially the

following language: "I (we) affirm, under the penalties for perjury, that the foregoing representation(s) is (are) true. (Signed) _____."

    i. Any person who falsifies an affirmation or representation of fact shall be subject to the same penalties as are prescribed by law for the making of a false affidavit. IN ST TRIAL P Rule 11(B).

  e. *Verified pleadings, motions, and affidavits as evidence.* Pleadings, motions and affidavits accompanying or in support of such pleadings or motions when required to be verified or under oath shall be accepted as a representation that the signer had personal knowledge thereof or reasonable cause to believe the existence of the facts or matters stated or alleged therein; and, if otherwise competent or acceptable as evidence, may be admitted as evidence of the facts or matters stated or alleged therein when it is so provided in the Indiana Rules of Trial Procedure, by statute or other law, or to the extent the writing or signature expressly purports to be made upon the signer's personal knowledge. When such pleadings, motions and affidavits are verified or under oath they shall not require other or greater proof on the part of the adverse party than if not verified or not under oath unless expressly provided otherwise by the Indiana Rules of Trial Procedure, statute or other law. Affidavits upon motions for summary judgment under IN ST TRIAL P Rule 56 and in denial of execution under IN ST TRIAL P Rule 9.2 shall be made upon personal knowledge. IN ST TRIAL P Rule 11(C).

6. *Information excluded from public access.* Every document filed in a case shall separately identify information excluded from public access pursuant to IN ST ADMIN Rule 9(G)(1) as follows:

  a. Whole documents that are excluded from public access pursuant to IN ST ADMIN Rule 9(G)(1) shall be tendered on light green paper or have a light green coversheet attached to the document, marked "Not for Public Access" or "Confidential." IN ST TRIAL P Rule 5(G)(1).

  b. When only a portion of a document contains information excluded from public access pursuant to IN ST ADMIN Rule 9(G)(1), said information shall be omitted [or redacted] from the filed document, and set forth on a separate accompanying document on light green paper conspicuously marked "Not for Public Access" or "Confidential" and clearly designated [or identifying] the caption and number of the case and the document and location within the document to which the redacted material pertains. IN ST TRIAL P Rule 5(G)(2).

  c. With respect to documents filed in electronic format, the trial court, by local rule, may provide for compliance with IN ST TRIAL P Rule 5 in manner that separates and protects access to information excluded from public access. IN ST TRIAL P Rule 5(G)(3).

  d. IN ST TRIAL P Rule 5(G) does not apply to a record sealed by the court pursuant to IN ST 5-14-3-5.5 or otherwise, nor to records, documents, or information filed in cases to which public access is prohibited pursuant to IN ST ADMIN Rule 9(G). IN ST TRIAL P Rule 5(G)(4).

  e. The following information in case records is excluded from public access and is confidential:

    i. Information that is excluded from public access pursuant to federal law;

    ii. Information that is excluded from public access as declared confidential by Indiana statute or other court rule, including without limitation:

- All adoption records created after July 8, 1941, as declared confidential by IN ST 31-19-19-1, et seq., except those specifically declared open by IN ST 31-19-13-2(2);

- All records relating to chancroid, chlamydia, gonorrhea, hepatitis, human immunodeficiency virus (HIV), Lymphogranuloma venereum, syphilis, tuberculosis, as declared confidential by IN ST 16-41-8-1, et seq.;

- All records relating to child abuse as declared confidential by IN ST 31-33-18-1, et seq.;

- All records relating to drug tests as declared confidential by IN ST 5-14-3-4(a)(9);

- Records of grand jury proceedings as declared confidential by IN ST 35-34-2-4;

- Records of juvenile proceedings as declared confidential by IN ST 31-39-1-2, except those specifically open under statute;

- All paternity records created after July 1, 1941 as declared confidential by IN ST

31-14-11-15, IN ST 31-19-5-23, IN ST 31-39-1-1 and IN ST 31-39-1-2 [Editor's note: IN ST 31-14-11-15 was repealed effective May 9, 2013];

- All pre-sentence reports as declared confidential by IN ST 35-38-1-13;

- Written petitions to permit marriages without consent and orders directing the Clerk of Court to issue a marriage license to underage persons, as declared confidential by IN ST 31-11-1-6;

- Only those arrest warrants, search warrants, indictments and informations ordered confidential by the trial judge, prior to return of duly executed service as declared confidential by IN ST 5-14-3-4(b)(1);

- All medical, mental health, or tax records unless determined by law or regulation of any governmental custodian not to be confidential, released by the subject of such records, or declared by a court of competent jurisdiction to be essential to the resolution of litigation as declared confidential by IN ST 16-39-3-10, IN ST 6-4.1-5-10, IN ST 6-4.1-12-12, and IN ST 6-8.1-7-1;

- Personal information relating to jurors or prospective jurors, other than for the use of the parties and counsel, pursuant to IN ST JURY Rule 10;

- Information relating to protection from abuse orders, no-contact orders and workplace violence restraining orders as declared confidential by IN ST 5-2-9-6, et seq.;

- Mediation proceedings pursuant to IN ST ADR Rule 2.11, Mini-Trial proceedings pursuant to IN ST ADR Rule 4.4(C), and Summary Jury Trials pursuant to IN ST ADR Rule 5.6;

- Information in probation files pursuant to the Probation Standards promulgated by the Judicial Conference of Indiana pursuant to IN ST 11-13-1-8(b);

- Information deemed confidential pursuant to the Rules for Court Administered Alcohol and Drug Programs promulgated by the Judicial Conference of Indiana pursuant to IN ST 12-23-14-13;

- Information deemed confidential pursuant to the Problem-Solving Court Rules promulgated by the Judicial Conference of Indiana pursuant to IN ST 33-23-16-16;

- All records of the Department of workforce Development as declared confidential by IN ST 22-4-19-6;

- Information regarding interception of electronic communications that is sealed or deemed confidential as set forth in IN ST 35-33.5-2-1, et seq.

iii. Information excluded from public access by specific court order;

iv. Complete Social Security Numbers of living persons;

v. With the exception of names, information such as addresses, phone numbers, and dates of birth which explicitly identifies:

- Natural persons who are witnesses or victims (not including defendants) in criminal, domestic violence, stalking, sexual assault, juvenile, or civil protection order proceedings, provided that juveniles who are victims of sex crimes shall be identified by initials only;

- Places of residence of judicial officers, clerks and other employees of courts and clerks of court, unless the person or persons about whom the information pertains waives confidentiality;

vi. Complete account numbers of specific assets, loans, bank accounts, credit cards, and personal identification numbers (PINs);

vii. All orders of expungement entered in criminal or juvenile proceedings, orders to restrict access to criminal history information pursuant to IN ST 35-38-5-5.5 or IN ST 35-38-8-5 and records excluded from public access by such orders, and information related to infractions that is excluded from public access pursuant to IN ST 34-28-5-15 or IN ST 34-28-5-16 [Editor's note:

IN ST 35-38-5-5.5, IN ST 35-38-8-5 and IN ST 34-28-5-16 were repealed effective July 1, 2013; for information on orders restricting access to criminal history, refer to IN ST 35-38-9-1, et seq.];

    viii. All personal notes and e-mail, and deliberative material, of judges, jurors, court staff and judicial agencies, and information recorded in personal data assistants (PDA's) or organizers and personal calendars. IN ST ADMIN Rule 9(G)(1).

F. Filing and Service Requirements

1. *Filing requirements.* Except as otherwise provided in IN ST TRIAL P Rule 5(E)(2), all pleadings and papers subsequent to the complaint which are required to be served upon a party shall be filed with the Court either before service or within a reasonable period of time thereafter. IN ST TRIAL P Rule 5(E)(1). Counsel shall file with the court an original and one (1) copy of all briefs, and memoranda of law filed in support of a motion. IN ST MARION CIR AND SUPER CTS CIV Rule 205(D).

  a. *Filing generally.* All pleadings, petitions and motions are filed with the Clerk designated by the Court at any time during office hours established by the Clerk and the Court. All orders submitted to the Court shall be in sufficient number and shall be accompanied by postage paid envelopes addressed to each party or counsel of record. IN ST MARION CIR AND SUPER CTS CIV Rule 205(A)

  b. *Filing with the court defined.* The filing of pleadings, motions, and other papers with the court as required by the Indiana Rules of Trial Procedure shall be made by one of the following methods:

    i. Delivery to the clerk of the court;

    ii. Sending by electronic transmission under the procedure adopted pursuant to IN ST ADMIN Rule 12;

    iii. Mailing to the clerk by registered, certified or express mail return receipt requested;

    iv. Depositing with any third-party commercial carrier for delivery to the clerk within three (3) calendar days, cost prepaid, properly addressed;

    v. If the court so permits, filing with the judge, in which event the judge shall note thereon the filing date and forthwith transmit them to the office of the clerk; or

    vi. Electronic filing, as approved by the Division of State Court Administration pursuant to IN ST ADMIN Rule 16. IN ST TRIAL P Rule 5(F).

    vii. Filing by registered or certified mail and by third-party commercial carrier shall be complete upon mailing or deposit. IN ST TRIAL P Rule 5(F).

  c. *Facsimile filing.* Facsimile filing is discouraged, but permitted in the Marion Circuit and Marion Superior Court. All documents filed by facsimile shall also be filed in hard copy within seven (7) days of the facsimile filing, along with proposed orders and stamped addressed envelopes, as required by IN ST MARION CIR AND SUPER CTS CIV Rule 203(E). To avoid duplicate filings, the hard copies of the facsimile filing shall indicate in bold letters that the pleading was previously filed by facsimile transmission. Proof of transmission by facsimile, including certificate of service and manner of service, shall be the responsibility of the filing party. If the filing requires immediate attention of the Judge, it shall be so indicated in bold letters in an accompanying transmittal memorandum. Legibility of documents and timeliness of filing is the responsibility of the sender. IN ST MARION CIR AND SUPER CTS CIV Rule 205(B).

    i. *Generally.* In counties where a majority of judges of the courts of record, by posted local rule, have authorized electronic facsimile filing and designated a telephone number to receive such transmissions, pleadings, motions, and other papers may be sent to the Clerk of Circuit Court by electronic facsimile transmission for filing in any case, provided:

      • Such matter does not exceed ten (10) pages, including the cover sheet;

      • Such matter does not require the payment of fees other than the electronic facsimile transcription fee set forth in IN ST ADMIN Rule 12(E);

      • The sending party creates at the time of transmission a machine generated log for such transmission; and

- The original document and the transmission log are maintained by the sending party for the duration of the litigation. IN ST ADMIN Rule 12(B).

ii. *Time of filing.* During normal, posted business hours, the time of filing shall be the time the duplicate document is produced in the office of the Clerk of the Circuit Court. Duplicate documents received at all other times shall be filed as of the next normal business day. IN ST ADMIN Rule 12(C).

- If the receiving fax machine endorses its own time and date stamp upon the transmitted documents and the receiving machine produces a delivery receipt which is electronically created and transmitted to the sending party, the time of filing shall be the date and time recorded on the transmitted document by the receiving fax machine. IN ST ADMIN Rule 12(C).

d. *Electronic filing.* Electronic filing and electronic service pilot projects are authorized pursuant to IN ST ADMIN Rule 16 and approved by the Division of State Court Administration. IN ST MARION SUPER CT ADMIN Rule 311(1-103).

i. *Cases where electronic filing accepted.* All Marion County Circuit and Superior civil courts may accept electronic filing and service of pleadings and other documents designated in this rule in mortgage foreclosure (hereinafter referred to as "MF"), civil collection(hereinafter referred to as "CC"), and individual cases that have been approved for electronic filing and service. IN ST MARION SUPER CT ADMIN Rule 311(1-104)(1).

- The Marion County Circuit Court may, upon the motion of a party or its own motion, designate a case that will involve multiple litigants, legally intricate issues, and an extensive number of documents a mass tort or complex litigation case. Any case so designated shall be subject to electronic filing and service using the county's approved Electronic Service Provider. IN ST MARION SUPER CT ADMIN Rule 311(1-104)(3).

- The filing of electronic pleadings and other documents in MF and CC cases is entirely voluntary; however, once the case is initially filed electronically, all subsequent filings in the case shall remain in electronic format until the time for appeal is exhausted. IN ST MARION SUPER CT ADMIN Rule 311(1-104)(5).

ii. *Documents eligible for electronic filing.* The following pleadings may be filed and served electronically:

- New case complaint and petitions. IN ST MARION SUPER CT ADMIN Rule 311(1-104)(8)(a).

- Original answers. IN ST MARION SUPER CT ADMIN Rule 311(1-104)(8)(a).

- Any other pleadings or document including but not limited to motions and appearance forms. IN ST MARION SUPER CT ADMIN Rule 311(1-104)(8)(a).

iii. *Manner of electronic filing.* Parties shall E-file a document either:

- By registering to use the Electronic Filing Service Provider; or

- In person at the Marion County Clerk's office, by electronically filing through the Public Access Terminal. Parties filing in this manner shall be responsible for furnishing the document in an electronic format that will be compatible with the clerk's office-system to be uploaded in person. IN ST MARION SUPER CT ADMIN Rule 311(1-104)(9). For information on the Electronic Filing Service Provider and Public Access Terminal, refer to IN ST MARION SUPER CT ADMIN Rule 311(1-101).

- Registered users shall pay statutory filing fees for E-filed documents electronically to the Court through their EFSP. Filing fees are due and payable at the time of filing. IN ST MARION SUPER CT ADMIN Rule 311(2-104)(1). For more information on electronic filing fees, refer to IN ST MARION SUPER CT ADMIN Rule 311(2-104).

iv. *Effect of electronic filing.* Any pleading filed electronically shall be considered as filed with the court when the transmission to the EFSP is complete. Any document E-filed by 11:59 p.m. local Indianapolis, Indiana time shall be deemed filed on that date. The EFSP is an agent of the Court for the purpose of electronic filing, receipt, service and retrieval of electronic documents. IN ST MARION SUPER CT ADMIN Rule 311(2-102).

- Upon completion of filing, the EFSP shall issue a confirmation receipt that includes the date and time of receipt. The confirmation receipt shall serve as proof of filing. IN ST MARION SUPER CT ADMIN Rule 311(2-102).

- In the event the Court rejects the submitted documents following review, the documents shall not become part of the official Court record and the filer will receive notification of the rejection. Users may be required to refile the instruments to meet necessary filing requirements. Documents may be filed through an E-filing system at any time that the Clerk's office is open to receive the filing or at such other times as may be designated by the clerk and posted publicly. IN ST MARION SUPER CT ADMIN Rule 311(2-102).

- Documents filed through the E-filing system are deemed filed when received by the Clerk's office, except that documents received at times that the Clerk's office is closed shall be deemed filed the next regular time when the Clerk's office is open for filing. The time stamp issued by the E-filing system shall be presumed to be the time the document is received by the Clerk. IN ST MARION SUPER CT ADMIN Rule 311(2-102).

v. *Electronically filed documents.* All pleadings and other documents designated in IN ST MARION SUPER CT ADMIN Rule 311 shall be filed and served electronically in any individual case which has been approved for electronic filing and service. IN ST MARION SUPER CT ADMIN Rule 311(1-104)(6).

vi. *System failures.* When filing by electronic means is hindered by a technical failure, a party may file with the Clerk of Marion County in hard copy. With the exception of deadlines that by law cannot be extended, the time for filing of any paper that is delayed due to technical failure of the site shall be extended for one (1) day for each day on which such failure occurs, unless otherwise ordered by the Court. IN ST MARION SUPER CT ADMIN Rule 311(2-108).

vii. *Compliance with rules.* All filing shall comply with the requirements of IN ST ADMIN Rule 9 and IN ST ADMIN Rule 16; and the Indiana Rules of Court and the Marion County Local Rules. IN ST MARION SUPER CT ADMIN Rule 311(1-104)(11).

e. *Filing for special judge.* When a Special Judge who is not a Marion County Judge is selected, all parties or attorneys shall furnish such Judge with copies of all filings prior to the qualification of such Special Judge. Thereafter, copies of all filings shall be delivered in person, by mail or by facsimile to the office of the Special Judge with certificate of forwarding same made a part of the filing. IN ST MARION CIR AND SUPER CTS CIV Rule 205(C).

f. *Proof of filing.* Any party filing any paper by any method other than personal delivery to the clerk shall retain proof of filing. IN ST TRIAL P Rule 5(F).

2. *Service requirements.* Unless otherwise provided by the Indiana Rules of Trial Procedure or an order of the court, each party and special judge, if any, shall be served with: (1) every order required by its terms to be served; (2) every pleading subsequent to the original complaint; (3) every written motion except one which may be heard ex parte; (4) every brief submitted to the trial court; (5) every paper relating to discovery required to be served upon a party; and (6) every written notice, appearance, demand, offer of judgment, designation of record on appeal, or similar paper. IN ST TRIAL P Rule 5(A).

a. *Methods of service*

i. *Personal service.* Whenever a party is represented by an attorney of record, service shall be made upon such attorney unless service upon the party himself is ordered by the court. Service upon the attorney or party shall be made by delivering or mailing a copy of the papers to the last known address or where an attorney or party has consented to service by fax or e-mail, as provided in IN ST TRIAL P Rule 3.1(A)(4), by faxing or e-mailing a copy of the documents to the fax number or e-mail address set out in the appearance form or correction as required by IN ST TRIAL P Rule 3.1(E). IN ST TRIAL P Rule 5(B). Delivery of a copy within IN ST TRIAL P Rule 5 means:

- Offering or tendering it to the attorney or party and stating the nature of the papers being served. Refusal to accept an offered or tendered document is a waiver of any objection to the sufficiency or adequacy of service of that document;

- Leaving it at his office with a clerk or other person in charge thereof, or if there is no one in charge, leaving it in a conspicuous place therein; or

- If the office is closed, by leaving it at his dwelling house or usual place of abode with some person of suitable age and discretion then residing therein; or,

- Leaving it at some other suitable place, selected by the attorney upon whom service is being made, pursuant to duly promulgated local rule. IN ST TRIAL P Rule 5(B)(1).

ii. *Service by mail.* If service is made by mail, the papers shall be deposited in the United States mail addressed to the person on whom they are being served, with postage prepaid. Service shall be deemed complete upon mailing. Proof of service of all papers permitted to be mailed may be made by written acknowledgment of service, by affidavit of the person who mailed the papers, or by certificate of an attorney. It shall be the duty of attorneys when entering their appearance in a cause or when filing pleadings or papers therein, to have noted in the Chronological Case Summary or said pleadings or papers so filed the address and telephone number of their office. Service by delivery or by mail at such address shall be deemed sufficient and complete. IN ST TRIAL P Rule 5(B)(2).

iii. *Service by fax or e-mail.* A party who has consented to service by fax or e-mail may be served as follows:

- Service by e-mail shall be made by attaching the document being served in .pdf format. Discovery documents must also be served in accordance with IN ST TRIAL P Rule 26(A). IN ST TRIAL P Rule 5(B)(3)(a).

- Service by fax shall be deemed complete upon generation of a transmission record indicating the successful transmission of the entire document, except as provided in IN ST TRIAL P Rule 5(B)(3)(d). IN ST TRIAL P Rule 5(B)(3)(b).

- Service by e-mail shall be deemed complete upon transmission, except as provided in IN ST TRIAL P Rule 5(B)(3)(d). IN ST TRIAL P Rule 5(B)(3)(c).

- Service by fax or e-mail that occurs on a Saturday, Sunday, legal holiday, or day the court or agency in which the matter is pending is closed or after 5:00 PM local time of the recipient shall be deemed complete the next day that is not a Saturday, Sunday, legal holiday, or day that the court or agency in which the matter is pending is not closed. IN ST TRIAL P Rule 5(B)(3)(d).

iv. *Electronic service.* Delivery of E-service documents through the EFSP to other registered users shall be considered as valid and effective service and shall have the same legal effect as an original paper document. Recipients of E-service documents shall access their documents through the EFSP. IN ST MARION SUPER CT ADMIN Rule 311(2-107)(1).

- E-service shall be deemed complete when the transmission to the EFSP is completed. IN ST MARION SUPER CT ADMIN Rule 311(2-107)(2).

- For the purpose of computing time to respond to documents received via E-service, any document served on a day or at a time when the Clerk's office is not open for business shall be deemed served at the time of next opening of the Clerk's office for business. IN ST MARION SUPER CT ADMIN Rule 311(2-107)(3).

b. *Serving numerous defendants.* In any action in which there are unusually large numbers of defendants, the court, upon motion or of its own initiative, may order:

i. That service of the pleadings of the defendants and replies thereto need not be made as between the defendants;

- That any cross-claim, counterclaim, or matter constituting an avoidance or affirmative defense contained therein shall be deemed to be denied or avoided by all other parties; and

- That the filing of any such pleading and service thereof upon the plaintiff constitutes due notice of it to the parties. IN ST TRIAL P Rule 5(D).

      ii.   A copy of every such order shall be served upon the parties in such manner and form as the court directs. IN ST TRIAL P Rule 5(D).

   c.   *Service on parties in default for failure to appear.* No service need be made on parties in default for failure to appear, except that pleadings asserting new or additional claims for relief against them shall be served upon them in the manner provided by service of summons in IN ST TRIAL P Rule 4. IN ST TRIAL P Rule 5(A).

G. Hearings

1. The Indiana rules do not contemplate a hearing related to the pretrial conference.

H. Forms

1. Pretrial Conference, Scheduling, Management Forms for Indiana

   a.   Motion for pretrial conference. 5 INPRAC § 5:1.1.

   b.   Order for pretrial conference; Attorneys to hold preliminary conference. 5 INPRAC § 5:1.2.

   c.   Letter; To arrange preliminary conference of attorneys. 5 INPRAC § 5:1.3.

   d.   Letter; Documenting opposing counsel's failure to meet. 5 INPRAC § 5:1.4.

   e.   Letter; Request to stipulate to facts and exhibits. 5 INPRAC § 5:1.5.

   f.   Notice to court; Failure to stipulate. 5 INPRAC § 5:1.6.

   g.   Agenda; Pretrial conference. 5 INPRAC § 5:1.7.

   h.   Agenda for pretrial conference; Alternative. 5 INPRAC § 5:1.8.

   i.   Preliminary pretrial order. 5 INPRAC § 5:1.9.

   j.   Final pretrial order. 5 INPRAC § 5:1.10.

   k.   Motion to amend pretrial order. 5 INPRAC § 5:1.11.

   l.   Motion to extend discovery cutoff date. 5 INPRAC § 5:1.12.

   m.   Motion for pretrial conference. 10 INPRAC § 70.2.

   n.   Joint motion for pretrial conference. 10 INPRAC § 70.3.

   o.   Order for pretrial conference; Attorneys to hold preliminary conference. 10 INPRAC § 70.4.

   p.   Worksheet for preliminary conference of attorneys and pretrial conference. 10 INPRAC § 70.5.

   q.   Joint motion for continuance of pretrial conference. 10 INPRAC § 70.6.

   r.   Letter attempting to arrange preliminary conference of attorneys. 10 INPRAC § 70.7.

   s.   Notice of conference of attorneys. 10 INPRAC § 70.8.

   t.   Letter documenting opposing counsel's failure to meet for preliminary conference of attorneys. 10 INPRAC § 70.9.

   u.   Request that opposing party stipulate to facts and exhibits discovered after conference of attorneys. 10 INPRAC § 70.10.

   v.   Preliminary pretrial order. 10 INPRAC § 70.14.

   w.   Final pretrial order. 10 INPRAC § 70.15.

   x.   Motion to amend pretrial order; General form. 10 INPRAC § 70.16.

   y.   Motion to amend pretrial order; Party's contentions. 10 INPRAC § 70.17.

   z.   Motion for sanctions; Failure to attend pretrial conference. 10 INPRAC § 70.22.

2. Official Pretrial Conference, Scheduling, Management Forms for Marion County

   a.   Notice and order for settlement conference. IN ST MARION CIR AND SUPER CTS CIV App. C.

   b.   Defendant(s) confirmation of attendance at settlement conference. IN ST MARION CIR AND SUPER CTS CIV App. E.

I. Checklist

(I) ❑ Matters to be considered for the pretrial conference

    (a) ❑ Required documents

        (1) ❑ Pre-trial stipulation

        (2) ❑ Memoranda of law

    (b) ❑ Supplemental documents

        (1) ❑ Exhibits and stipulations

    (c) ❑ Timing

        (1) ❑ Unless otherwise ordered by the court the pretrial conference shall not be called until after reasonable opportunity for the completion of discovery

        (2) ❑ The clerks shall give at least thirty (30) days' notice of the pretrial conference unless otherwise directed by the court

        (3) ❑ Unless otherwise ordered by the court, at least ten (10) days prior to the pretrial conference, attorneys for each of the parties shall meet and confer

        (4) ❑ Counsel shall file memoranda treating any unusual questions of law involved in the trial no later than five (5) days prior to the pre-trial conference; Counsel for the plaintiff shall see that a pre-trial stipulation is prepared, executed by counsel for all parties, and filed with the Court no later than five (5) days prior to the pre-trial conference

(II) ❑ Matters to be considered by the party filing the motion for pretrial conference

    (a) ❑ Required documents

        (1) ❑ Motion and notice

        (2) ❑ Statement of approval or disapproval

        (3) ❑ Proposed order

        (4) ❑ Certificate of service

    (b) ❑ Supplemental documents

        (1) ❑ Supporting evidence

        (2) ❑ Request for oral argument

        (3) ❑ Facsimile cover sheet

    (c) ❑ Timing

        (1) ❑ There is no specific timing requirement for filing a motion requesting a pretrial conference

        (2) ❑ A written motion, other than one which may be heard ex parte, and notice of the hearing thereof shall be served not less than five (5) days before the time specified for the hearing, unless a different period is fixed by the Indiana Rules of Trial Procedure or by order of the court

        (3) ❑ All pleadings and papers subsequent to the complaint which are required to be served upon a party shall be filed with the Court either before service or within a reasonable period of time thereafter

ST. JOSEPH COUNTY

Pleadings
Complaint

Document Last Updated October 2013

A. **Applicable Rules**

 1. *State rules*

    a. Commencement of an action. IN ST TRIAL P Rule 3.

    b. Appearance. IN ST TRIAL P Rule 3.1.

    c. Process. IN ST TRIAL P Rule 4.

    d. Service. IN ST TRIAL P Rule 4.1; IN ST TRIAL P Rule 4.2; IN ST TRIAL P Rule 4.3; IN ST TRIAL P Rule 4.4; IN ST TRIAL P Rule 4.5; IN ST TRIAL P Rule 4.6; IN ST TRIAL P Rule 4.7; IN ST TRIAL P Rule 4.8; IN ST TRIAL P Rule 4.9; IN ST TRIAL P Rule 4.10; IN ST TRIAL P Rule 4.11; IN ST TRIAL P Rule 4.12; IN ST TRIAL P Rule 4.13; IN ST TRIAL P Rule 4.14; IN ST TRIAL P Rule 4.15; IN ST TRIAL P Rule 5.

    e. Time. IN ST TRIAL P Rule 6.

    f. Pleadings allowed; Form of motion. IN ST TRIAL P Rule 7.

    g. Rules of pleading. IN ST TRIAL P Rule 8; IN ST TRIAL P Rule 9; IN ST TRIAL P Rule 9.1; IN ST TRIAL P Rule 9.2.

    h. Form of pleading. IN ST TRIAL P Rule 10.

    i. Signing and verification of pleadings. IN ST TRIAL P Rule 11.

    j. Joinder. IN ST TRIAL P Rule 18; IN ST TRIAL P Rule 19.

    k. Jury trial of right. IN ST TRIAL P Rule 38.

    l. Evidence. IN ST TRIAL P Rule 43.

    m. Determination of foreign law. IN ST TRIAL P Rule 44.1.

    n. Judgment on the evidence (directed verdict). IN ST TRIAL P Rule 50.

    o. Findings by the court. IN ST TRIAL P Rule 52.

    p. Summary judgment. IN ST TRIAL P Rule 56.

    q. Motion to correct error. IN ST TRIAL P Rule 59.

    r. Relief from judgment or order. IN ST TRIAL P Rule 60.

    s. Uniform case numbering system. IN ST ADMIN Rule 8.

    t. Paper size. IN ST ADMIN Rule 11.

    u. Facsimile and electronic transmission. IN ST ADMIN Rule 9; IN ST ADMIN Rule 12; IN ST ADMIN Rule 16.

    v. Alternative dispute resolution. IN ST ADR Rule 1.1; IN ST ADR Rule 1.6; IN ST ADR Rule 8.8.

    w. Manner of service. IN ST 34-33-2-1.

    x. Sealing of certain records by court; Hearing; Notice. IN ST 5-14-3-5.5.

    y. Sixtieth judicial circuit. IN ST 33-33-71-2; IN ST TRIAL P Rule 72.

    z. Privacy and confidentiality. IN ST 5-2-9-6; IN ST 5-14-3-4; IN ST 6-4.1-5-10; IN ST 6-4.1-12-12; IN ST 6-8.1-7-1; IN ST 11-13-1-8; IN ST 12-23-14-13; IN ST 16-39-3-10; IN ST 16-41-8-1; IN ST 22-4-19-6; IN ST 31-11-1-6; IN ST 31-19-5-23; IN ST 31-19-13-2; IN ST 31-19-19-1; IN ST

31-33-18-1; IN ST 31-39-1-1; IN ST 31-39-1-2; IN ST 33-23-16-16; IN ST 35-34-2-4; IN ST 35-38-1-13; IN ST 35-38-9-1; IN ST ADR Rule 2.11; IN ST ADR Rule 4.4; IN ST ADR Rule 5.6; IN ST JURY Rule 10.

2. *Local rules*

    a. Filing, pleading, and motions. IN ST ST JOSEPH CIV Rule 201.

    b. Uniform court and case number designation. IN ST ST JOSEPH CIV Rule 202.

    c. Appearance and withdrawal of appearance of counsel. IN ST ST JOSEPH CIV Rule 204.

    d. Pre-trial procedures. IN ST ST JOSEPH CIV Rule 209.

    e. Electronic filing of cases in St. Joseph County. IN ST ST JOSEPH ELECTRONIC Rule 701.

B. Timing

1. *Filing.* A civil action is commenced by filing with the court a complaint or such equivalent pleading or document as may be specified by statute, by payment of the prescribed filing fee or filing an order waiving the filing fee, and, where service of process is required, by furnishing to the clerk as many copies of the complaint and summons as are necessary. IN ST TRIAL P Rule 3. The claimant typically bears the burden of commencing an action within the applicable statute of limitations. 22B INPRAC 3:1; Huff v. Huff, 892 N.E.2d 1241 (Ind.Ct.App. 2008).

2. *Service.* The trial rules require a party to exercise due diligence in securing service of process. 1 INPRAC R 4; Geiger and Peters, Inc. v. American Fletcher Nat. Bank & Trust Co., 428 N.E.2d 1279 (Ind.Ct.App. 1981). If person seeking service of process fails without cause for sixty (60) days or more to provide clerk with required summons for issuance or with other information necessary to effectuate service, person has failed to exercise due diligence in securing service of process. Geiger and Peters, Inc. v. American Fletcher Nat. Bank & Trust Co., 428 N.E.2d 1279, 1281 (Ind.Ct.App. 1981).

3. *Computation of time*

    a. *Generally; Days excluded.* In computing any period of time prescribed or allowed by the Indiana Rules of Trial Procedure, by order of the court, or by any applicable statute, the day of the act, event, or default from which the designated period of time begins to run shall not be included. The last day of the period so computed is to be included unless it is:

        i. A Saturday,

        ii. A Sunday,

        iii. A legal holiday as defined by state statute, or

        iv. A day the office in which the act is to be done is closed during regular business hours. IN ST TRIAL P Rule 6(A).

    b. *Short periods.* In any event, the period runs until the end of the next day that is not a Saturday, a Sunday, a legal holiday, or a day on which the office is closed. When the period of time allowed is less than seven (7) days, intermediate Saturdays, Sundays, legal holidays, and days on which the office is closed shall be excluded from the computations. IN ST TRIAL P Rule 6(A).

    c. *Additional time after service by United States mail.* Whenever a party has the right or is required to do some act or take some proceedings within a prescribed period after the service of a notice or other paper upon him and the notice or paper is served upon him by United States mail, three (3) days shall be added to the prescribed period. IN ST TRIAL P Rule 6(E).

    d. *Enlargement of time.* When an act is required or allowed to be done at or within a specific time by the Indiana Rules of Trial Procedure, the court may at any time for cause shown:

        i. Order the period enlarged, with or without motion or notice, if request therefor is made before the expiration of the period originally prescribed or extended by a previous order; or

        ii. Upon motion made after the expiration of the specific period, permit the act to be done where the failure to act was the result of excusable neglect; but, the court may not extend the time for taking any action for judgment on the evidence under IN ST TRIAL P Rule 50(A), amendment of findings and judgment under IN ST TRIAL P Rule 52(B), to correct errors under IN ST

TRIAL P Rule 59(C), statement in opposition to motion to correct error under IN ST TRIAL P Rule 59(E), or to obtain relief from final judgment under IN ST TRIAL P Rule 60(B), except to the extent and under the conditions stated in those rules. IN ST TRIAL P Rule 6(B).

iii. An initial written motion for enlargement of time pursuant to IN ST TRIAL P Rule 6(B)(1) to answer a claim shall be routinely granted for an additional thirty (30) days from the original due date or other period the assigned Judge deems reasonable by written order of the Court. The motion must be filed on or before the original due date or IN ST ST JOSEPH CIV Rule 201 shall be inapplicable. IN ST ST JOSEPH CIV Rule 201(201.9.5).

- Any motion for enlargement of time shall state the date when such response is due and the date to which time is requested to be enlarged. IN ST ST JOSEPH CIV Rule 201(201.9.5).

- All subsequent motions for enlargement of time shall be so designated and will only be granted for good cause shown or in the interest of justice. IN ST ST JOSEPH CIV Rule 201(201.9.5).

C. General Requirements

1. *Pleading, generally*

   a. *Pleadings to be concise.* Each averment of a pleading shall be simple, concise, and direct. No technical forms of pleading or motions are required. All fictions in pleading are abolished. IN ST TRIAL P Rule 8(E)(1).

   b. *Pleading in the alternative.* A pleading may set forth two (2) or more statements of a claim or defense alternatively or hypothetically, either in one (1) count or defense or in separate counts or defenses. When two (2) or more statements are made in the alternative and one (1) of them if made independently would be sufficient, the pleading is not made insufficient by the insufficiency of one or more of the alternative statements. A pleading may also state as many separate claims or defenses as the pleader has regardless of consistency and whether based on legal or equitable grounds. All statements shall be made subject to the obligations set forth in IN ST TRIAL P Rule 11. IN ST TRIAL P Rule 8(E)(2).

   c. *Motions and pleadings, joint and several.* All motions and pleadings of any kind addressed to two (2) or more paragraphs of any pleading, or filed by two (2) or more parties, shall be taken and construed as joint, separate, and several motions or pleadings to each of such paragraphs and by and against each of such parties. All motions or pleadings containing two (2) or more subject-matters shall be taken and construed as separate and several as to each subject-matter. All objections to rulings made by two (2) or more parties shall be taken and construed as the joint, separate, and several objections of each of such parties. IN ST TRIAL P Rule 8(E)(3).

      i. A complaint filed by or against two (2) or more plaintiffs shall be taken and construed as joint, separate, and several as to each of said plaintiffs. IN ST TRIAL P Rule 8(E).

   d. *Construction of pleadings.* All pleadings shall be so construed as to do substantial justice, lead to disposition on the merits, and avoid litigation of procedural points. IN ST TRIAL P Rule 8(F).

2. *Contents of the complaint*

   a. *Pleading for relief; Notice pleading.* Indiana is a "notice pleading" jurisdiction. 22B INPRAC 8:1; State v. American Family Voices, Inc., 898 N.E.2d 293 (Ind. 2008). Notice pleading replaces the technical and complex method of pleading which existed prior to 1970. Notice pleading is grounded in due process of law and must provide a defendant with reasonable notice of the plaintiff's claim or an opponent's defense. 22B INPRAC 8:1; Noblesville Redevelopment Com'n v. Noblesville Associates Ltd. Partnership, 674 N.E.2d 558 (Ind. 1996). Notice pleading does not require that the plaintiff state all elements or facts essential to a cause of action. 22B INPRAC 8:1; State v. American Family Voices, Inc., 898 N.E.2d 293 (Ind. 2008). Instead, the complaint must state "a short and plain statement of the claim" showing an entitlement to relief, and a demand for relief. 22B INPRAC 8:1; Trail v. Boys and Girls Clubs of Northwest Indiana, 845 N.E.2d 130 (Ind. 2006).

   b. *Claims for relief.* To state a claim for relief, whether an original claim, counterclaim, cross-claim, or third-party claim, a pleading must contain:

      i. A short and plain statement of the claim showing that the pleader is entitled to relief, and

       ii. A demand for relief to which the pleader deems entitled. Relief in the alternative or of several different types may be demanded. However, in any complaint seeking damages for personal injury or death, or seeking punitive damages, no dollar amount or figure shall be included in the demand. IN ST TRIAL P Rule 8(A).

  c. *Res ipsa loquitur.* Res ipsa loquitur or a similar doctrine may be pleaded by alleging generally that the facts connected with the action are unknown to the pleader and are within the knowledge of the opposing party. IN ST TRIAL P Rule 9.1(B).

  d. *Bona fide purchaser.* When the rights of a person depend upon his status as a bona fide purchaser for value or upon similar requirements, such status must be pleaded and proved by the person asserting it, but it may be pleaded in general terms. Once it is established that the person has given any required value, unless such value is commercially unreasonable, and that he has met any requirements of recordation, filing, possession, or perfection, the trier of fact must find that such value was given or such perfection was made in accordance with any requirements of good faith, lack of knowledge, or lack of notice unless and until evidence is introduced which would support a finding of its non-existence. IN ST TRIAL P Rule 9.1(D).

  e. *Presumption; Matters of judicial notice.* Neither presumptions of law nor matters of which judicial notice may be taken need be stated in a pleading. IN ST TRIAL P Rule 9.1(E).

       i. *Presumption of jurisdiction.* Jurisdiction is presumed in Indiana. 22B INPRAC 8:2. Consequently, there is no requirement to affirmatively plead the existence of jurisdiction in the complaint, unless the action involves a special proceeding requiring such an allegation. 22B INPRAC 8:2; Cardinal Industries, Inc. v. Schwartz, 483 N.E.2d 458 (Ind.Ct.App. 1985). The plaintiff bears no burden to prove jurisdiction unless and until it is challenged by the defendant. 22B INPRAC 8:2; Brokemond v. Marshall Field & Co., 612 N.E.2d 143 (Ind.Ct.App. 1993).

  f. *Equitable and legal claims in multi-count actions.* In multi-count actions, the inclusion of an equitable claim, standing alone, will not automatically draw the entire action into equity. Something more than the presence of an equitable claim is required, and the court must examine the claims at issue. 22B INPRAC 38:1 COMMENT; Lucas v. U.S. Bank, N.A., 953 N.E.2d 457 (Ind. 2011). Factors the court may consider in evaluating the nature of the underlying substantive claims include: the substance and central character of the complaint, the rights and interests at issue, the relief demanded, and any issues arising out of discovery. 22B INPRAC 38:1 COMMENT; Songer v. Civitas Bank, 771 N.E.2d 61 (Ind. 2002).

3. *Pleading special matters*

  a. *Capacity.* It is not necessary to aver the capacity of a party to sue or be sued, the authority of a party to sue or be sued in a representative capacity, or the legal existence of an organization that is made a party. The burden of proving lack of such capacity, authority, or legal existence shall be upon the person asserting lack of it, and shall be pleaded as an affirmative defense. IN ST TRIAL P Rule 9(A).

  b. *Fraud, mistake, condition of the mind.* In all averments of fraud or mistake, the circumstances constituting fraud or mistake shall be specifically averred. Malice, intent, knowledge, and other conditions of mind may be averred generally. IN ST TRIAL P Rule 9(B).

  c. *Conditions precedent.* In pleading the performance or occurrence of promissory or non-promissory conditions precedent, it is sufficient to aver generally that all conditions precedent have been performed, have occurred, or have been excused. A denial of performance or occurrence shall be made specifically and with particularity, and a denial of excuse generally. IN ST TRIAL P Rule 9(C).

  d. *Official document or act.* In pleading an official document or official act it is sufficient to aver that the document was issued or the act done in compliance with law. IN ST TRIAL P Rule 9(D).

  e. *Judgment.* In pleading a judgment or decision of a domestic or foreign court, judicial or quasi-judicial tribunal, or of a board or officer, it is sufficient to aver the judgment or decision without setting forth matter showing jurisdiction to render it. IN ST TRIAL P Rule 9(E).

  f. *Time and place.* For the purpose of testing the sufficiency of a pleading, averments of time and place are material and shall be considered like all other averments of material matter. However, time and place need be stated only with such specificity as will enable the opposing party to prepare his defense. IN ST TRIAL P Rule 9(F).

g. *Special damages; Damages where no answer.* When items of special damage are claimed, they shall be specifically stated. The relief granted to the plaintiff, if there be no answer, cannot exceed the relief demanded in his complaint; but, in any other case, the court may grant him any relief consistent with the facts or matters pleaded. IN ST TRIAL P Rule 9(G).

4. *Joinder*

   a. *Of claims.* A party asserting a claim for relief as an original claim, counterclaim, cross-claim, or third-party claim, may join, either as independent or as alternate claims, as many claims, whether legal, equitable, or statutory as he has against an opposing party. IN ST TRIAL P Rule 18(A).

   b. *Of remedies; Fraudulent conveyances.* Whenever a claim is one heretofore cognizable only after another claim has been prosecuted to a conclusion, the two (2) claims may be joined in a single action; but the court shall grant relief in that action only in accordance with the relative substantive rights of the parties. In particular, a plaintiff may state a claim for money and a claim to have set aside a conveyance fraudulent as to him, without first having obtained a judgment establishing the claim for money. IN ST TRIAL P Rule 18(B).

   c. *Of persons needed for just adjudication.* A person who is subject to service of process shall be joined as a party in the action if:

      i. In his absence complete relief cannot be accorded among those already parties; or

      ii. He claims an interest relating to the subject of the action and is so situated that the disposition of the action in his absence may:

         • As a practical matter impair or impede his ability to protect that interest, or

         • Leave any of the persons already parties subject to a substantial risk of incurring double, multiple, or otherwise inconsistent obligations by reason of his claimed interest. IN ST TRIAL P Rule 19(A).

      iii. If he has not been so joined, the court shall order that he be made a party. If he should join as a plaintiff but refuses to do so, he may be made a defendant. IN ST TRIAL P Rule 19(A).

5. *Trial by jury; Demand*

   a. *Causes triable by court and by jury.* Issues of law and issues of fact in causes that prior to the eighteenth day of June, 1852, were of exclusive equitable jurisdiction shall be tried by the court; issues of fact in all other causes shall be triable as the same are now triable. In case of the joinder of causes of action or defenses which, prior to said date, were of exclusive equitable jurisdiction with causes of action or defenses which, prior to said date, were designated as actions at law and triable by jury—the former shall be triable by the court, and the latter by a jury, unless waived; the trial of both may be at the same time or at different times, as the court may direct. IN ST TRIAL P Rule 38(A).

   b. *Demand.* Any party may demand a trial by jury of any issue triable of right by a jury by filing with the court and serving upon the other parties a demand therefor in writing at any time after the commencement of the action and not later than ten (10) days after the first responsive pleading to the complaint, or to a counterclaim, crossclaim or other claim if one properly is pleaded; and if no responsive pleading is filed or required, within ten (10) days after the time such pleading otherwise would have been required. Such demand is sufficient if indorsed upon a pleading of a party filed within such time. IN ST TRIAL P Rule 38(B).

   c. *Same; Specification of issues.* In his demand a party may specify the issues which he wishes so tried; otherwise he shall be deemed to have demanded trial by jury for all issues triable as of right by jury. Any other party must file a demand for jury trial to preserve his right to trial by jury:

      i. Of issues for which a right to trial by jury was not requested by another party; and

      ii. In case a request by another party was improper. But if a proper request for a trial by jury upon issues triable by jury as of right on his behalf is made by any party, such request shall be deemed to have been made on behalf of all parties entitled to a jury trial upon such issues. IN ST TRIAL P Rule 38(C).

   d. *Waiver.* The failure of a party to appear at the trial, and the failure of a party to serve a demand as required by IN ST TRIAL P Rule 38 and to file it as required by IN ST TRIAL P Rule 5(E) constitute waiver by him of trial by jury. A demand for trial by jury made as provided in IN ST TRIAL P Rule 38 may not be withdrawn without the consent of the other party or parties. IN ST TRIAL P Rule 38(D).

   i. The trial court shall not grant a demand for a trial by jury filed after the time fixed in IN ST TRIAL P Rule 38(B) has elapsed except upon the written agreement of all of the parties to the action, which agreement shall be filed with the court and made a part of the record. If such agreement is filed then the court may, in its discretion, grant a trial by jury in which event the grant of a trial by jury may not be withdrawn except by the agreement of all of the parties. IN ST TRIAL P Rule 38(D).

   e. *Arbitration.* Nothing in the Indiana Rules of Trial Procedure shall deny the parties the right by contract or agreement to submit or to agree to submit controversies to arbitration made before or after commencement of an action thereon or deny the courts power to specifically enforce such agreements. IN ST TRIAL P Rule 38(E).

   f. *Equitable and legal claims in multi-count actions.* In multi-count actions, the inclusion of an equitable claim, standing alone, will not automatically draw the entire action into equity. Something more than the presence of an equitable claim is required, and the court must examine the claims at issue. 22B INPRAC 38:1 COMMENT; Lucas v. U.S. Bank, N.A., 953 N.E.2d 457 (Ind. 2011). Factors the court may consider in evaluating the nature of the underlying substantive claims include: the substance and central character of the complaint, the rights and interests at issue, the relief demanded, and any issues arising out of discovery. 22B INPRAC 38:1 COMMENT; Songer v. Civitas Bank, 771 N.E.2d 61 (Ind. 2002).

6. *Use of alternative dispute resolution.* Except as provided by the Indiana Rules for Alternative Dispute Resolution, a presiding judge may order any civil or domestic relations proceeding or selected issues in such proceedings referred to mediation, non-binding arbitration or mini-trial. The selection criteria which should be used by the court are defined under the Indiana Rules for Alternative Dispute Resolution. Binding arbitration and a summary jury trial may be ordered only upon the agreement of the parties as consistent with provisions in the Indiana Rules for Alternative Dispute Resolution which address each method. IN ST ADR Rule 1.6. For information on Indiana's ADR process refer to IN ST ADR Rule 1.1 through IN ST ADR Rule 8.8.

   a. *Alternative dispute resolution.* On the Court's own motion or initiative, the parties may be required to attempt alternative dispute resolution (ADR). Such ADR efforts may include, at the Court's discretion, mediation and/or settlement conferences and may require one or more sessions or sessions lasting a specific amount of time. IN ST ST JOSEPH CIV Rule 209(209.3).

D. Documents

1. *Required documents*

   a. *Summons.* Contemporaneously with the filing of the complaint or equivalent pleading, the person seeking service or his attorney shall furnish to the clerk as many copies of the complaint and summons as are necessary. IN ST TRIAL P Rule 4(B).

   b. *Complaint.* Refer to the General Requirements section of this document for information on the contents of a complaint.

   c. *Appearance form.* At the time an action is commenced, the party initiating the proceeding shall file with the clerk of the court an appearance form setting forth the following information:

     i. Name, address and telephone number of the initiating party or parties filing the appearance form;

     ii. Name, address, attorney number, telephone number, FAX number, and e-mail address of any attorney representing the party, as applicable;

     iii. The case type of the proceeding [see IN ST ADMIN Rule 8];

     iv. A statement that the party will or will not accept service by fax or by e-mail from:

       • Other parties and/or

- The court under IN ST TRIAL P Rule 72(D);

v. In domestic relations, Uniform Reciprocal Enforcement of Support (URESA), paternity, delinquency, Child in Need of Services (CHINS), guardianship, and any other proceedings in which support may be an issue, the Social Security Identification Number of all family members;

vi. The caption and case number of all related cases;

vii. Such additional matters specified by state or local rule required to maintain the information management system employed by the court;

viii. In a proceeding involving a protection from abuse order, a workplace violence restraining order, or a no-contact order, the initiating party shall provide to the clerk a public mailing address for purposes of legal service. The initiating party may use the Attorney General Address Confidentiality program established by statute; and

ix. In a proceeding involving a mental health commitment, except seventy-two (72) hour emergency detentions, the initiating party shall provide the full name of the person with respect to whom commitment is sought and the person's state of residence. In addition, the initiating party shall provide at least one of the following identifiers for the person:

- Date of birth;
- Social Security Number;
- Driver's license number with state of issue and date of expiration;
- Department of Correction number;
- State ID number with state of issue and date of expiration; or
- FBI number. IN ST TRIAL P Rule 3.1.

x. Counsel and unrepresented parties appearing after the filing of the original complaint shall forthwith notify all other counsel of record and unrepresented parties of such appearance and file proof of such notice. Each counsel or party shall file an appearance form (or its equivalent) that includes a mailing address and telephone number. The notice may include a post office box, but must include a physical street address to allow for proper service of process or other notification by the Court. IN ST ST JOSEPH CIV Rule 204(204.1).

2. *Supplemental documents*

a. *Proof of written instrument.* When any pleading allowed by the Indiana Rules of Trial Procedure is founded on a written instrument, the original, or a copy thereof, must be included in or filed with the pleading. Such instrument, whether copied in the pleadings or not, shall be taken as part of the record. When any pleading allowed by the Indiana Rules of Trial Procedure is founded on an account, an Affidavit of Debt, in a form substantially similar to that which is provided in IN ST TRIAL P App. A-2, shall be attached. IN ST TRIAL P Rule 9.2(A).

b. *Notice of intent to use foreign law.* A party who intends to raise an issue concerning the law of a foreign country shall give notice in his pleadings or other reasonable written notice. The court, in determining foreign law, may consider any relevant material or source, including testimony, whether or not submitted by a party or admissible under IN ST TRIAL P Rule 43. The court's determination shall be treated as a ruling on a question of law. It shall be made by the court and not the jury and shall be reviewable. IN ST TRIAL P Rule 44.1(A).

c. *Praecipe.* Affidavits, requests, and any other information relating to the summons and its service as required or permitted by the Indiana Rules of Trial Procedure shall be included in a praecipe attached to or entered upon the summons. Such praecipe shall be deemed to be a part of the summons for purposes of the Indiana Rules of Trial Procedure. Separate or additional summons shall, as provided by the Indiana Rules of Trial Procedure, be issued by the clerk at any time upon proper request of the person seeking service or his attorney. IN ST TRIAL P Rule 4(B).

d. *Facsimile cover sheet.* Any document sent to the Clerk of the Circuit Court by electronic facsimile transmission shall be accompanied by a cover sheet which states the title of the document, case number, number of pages, identity and voice telephone number of the sending party and instructions for filing. The cover sheet shall contain the signature of the attorney or party, pro se, authorizing the filing. IN ST ADMIN Rule 12(D).

E. Format

1. *Form of pleadings*

   a. *Caption; Names of parties.* Every pleading shall contain a caption setting forth the name of the court, the title of the action, the file number, and a designation as in IN ST TRIAL P Rule 7(A). In the complaint the title of the action shall include the names of all the parties, but in other pleadings it is sufficient to state the name of the first party on each side with an appropriate indication of other parties. IN ST TRIAL P Rule 10(A); IN ST ST JOSEPH CIV Rule 201(201.3.3). If a special judge has been assigned to the case, the pleading should also identify the special judge. IN ST ST JOSEPH CIV Rule 201(201.3.3).

      i. *Title.* All pleadings or motions shall include a title, which shall delineate each topic included in the pleading. For example, where a pleading contains an answer, a motion to dismiss, and a jury request, each topic shall be set forth in the title. IN ST ST JOSEPH CIV Rule 201(201.3.4).

   b. *Paragraphs; Separate statements.* All averments of a claim or defense shall be made in numbered paragraphs, the contents of each of which shall be limited as far as practicable to a statement of a single set of circumstances, and a paragraph may be referred to by number in all succeeding pleadings. Each claim founded upon a separate transaction or occurrence and each defense other than denials may be stated in a separate count or defense whenever a separation facilitates the clear presentation of the matters set forth. IN ST TRIAL P Rule 10(B).

   c. *Adoption by reference; Exhibits.* Statements in a pleading may be adopted by reference in a different part of the same pleading or in another pleading or in any motion. A copy of any written instrument which is an exhibit to a pleading is a part thereof for all purposes. IN ST TRIAL P Rule 10(C).

   d. *Flat filing.* In order that the Clerk's files may be kept under the system commonly known as "flat filing," all papers presented to the Clerk for filing shall be flat and unfolded. Pleadings shall have no covers or backs and shall be fastened together at the top left-hand corner only. IN ST ST JOSEPH CIV Rule 201(201.1).

   e. *One side of page used.* Printing shall be on one (1) side of the paper. IN ST ST JOSEPH CIV Rule 201(201.3.2).

   f. *Copies.* All copies shall be on white paper of sufficient strength and durability to resist normal wear and tear. IN ST ST JOSEPH CIV Rule 201(201.3.1).

   g. *Margins.* Margins shall be at least one inch (1"). IN ST ST JOSEPH CIV Rule 201(201.3.2).

   h. *Double-spaced.* If typewritten, the lines shall be double spaced except for quotations, which shall be indented and single-spaced. IN ST ST JOSEPH CIV Rule 201(201.3.2).

   i. *Font size.* Type face shall be twelve (12) font size or larger within the body of the document and ten (10) font size or larger in the footnotes. IN ST ST JOSEPH CIV Rule 201(201.3.2).

   j. *Font type.* The font type must be legible and script type shall not be used. IN ST ST JOSEPH CIV Rule 201(201.3.2).

   k. *Italics.* Italicized type may be used for quotations, references, or case citations. IN ST ST JOSEPH CIV Rule 201(201.3.2).

   l. *Court and case designation.* All filings shall conform to the requirements for uniform court and case number designation set by IN ST ADMIN Rule 8. In addition, all filings shall contain the proper court and case designation as described below. IN ST ST JOSEPH CIV Rule 202.

      i. *Court designation.* Pursuant to IN ST 33-33-71-2, St. Joseph County, Indiana, constitutes the Sixtieth Judicial Circuit. The legal names of the courts within the 60th Judicial Circuit are the St. Joseph Circuit Court, the St. Joseph Superior Court, and the St. Joseph Probate Court. All filings shall properly reflect the legal name of the applicable court. Any filing may be amended, rejected, or stricken if it does not contain the proper case name and/or the legal name of the court. IN ST ST JOSEPH CIV Rule 202(202.1).

ii.   *Case designation.* At the time of filing, the party initiating the case should properly designate the case type. IN ST ST JOSEPH CIV Rule 202(202.2).

iii.   *Designation upon filing.* The filing party (or the attorney for the filing party) shall designate the correct case type in the cause number line of each summons and complaint before presenting a new filing to the Clerk. IN ST ST JOSEPH CIV Rule 202(202.2.1).

iv.   *Proper designations.* Case type designations must conform to the requirements of IN ST ADMIN Rule 8(B)(3). Since January 1, 2003, "CP" is no longer allowed as a designator for civil plenary cases; "PL" is now the proper designation for these types of cases. IN ST ST JOSEPH CIV Rule 202(202.2.2).

v.   *Failure to designate.* If a filing is presented without a case type designation on each summons and complaint, the entire filing may be rejected or stricken. Should a case be accepted with an incorrect designation, the court may order the matter to be re-docketed with the correct case type designation and may require that the filing party pay a re-docketing fee. IN ST ST JOSEPH CIV Rule 202(202.2.3).

vi.   *Advice and assistance.* The Clerk or her deputies may provide assistance to the filing party in this regard, but should not be required to make a legal judgment as to the correct case type designation. Any questions or doubts should be referred to a judge or a magistrate in the court receiving the filing. IN ST ST JOSEPH CIV Rule 202(202.2.4).

2.   *Size of papers for filing.* Effective January 1, 1992, all pleadings, copies, motions and documents filed with any trial court or appellate level court, typed or printed, with the exception of exhibits and existing wills, shall be prepared on eight and one-half by eleven inch (8 1/2" x 11") size paper. IN ST ADMIN Rule 11.

a.   *Paper.* Pleadings, motions, and other papers shall be either legibly printed or typewritten on white opaque paper of good quality at least sixteen (16) pound weight, eight and one-half inches (8 1/2 ") in width and eleven inches (11") in length as required by IN ST ADMIN Rule 11. IN ST ST JOSEPH CIV Rule 201(201.3.1).

3.   *Signature requirements*

a.   *Signature of attorney.* Every pleading or motion of a party represented by an attorney shall be signed by at least one (1) attorney of record in his individual name, whose address, telephone number, and attorney number shall be stated, except that this provision shall not apply to pleadings and motions made and transcribed at the trial or a hearing before the judge and received by him in such form. IN ST TRIAL P Rule 11(A).

   i.   The signature of an attorney constitutes a certificate by him that he has read the pleadings; that to the best of his knowledge, information, and belief, there is good ground to support it; and that it is not interposed for delay. IN ST TRIAL P Rule 11(A).

   ii.   If a pleading or motion is not signed or is signed with intent to defeat the purpose of the rule, it may be stricken as sham and false and the action may proceed as though the pleading had not been served. IN ST TRIAL P Rule 11(A).

   iii.   For a willful violation of IN ST TRIAL P Rule 11 an attorney may be subjected to appropriate disciplinary action. Similar action may be taken if scandalous or indecent matter is inserted. IN ST TRIAL P Rule 11(A).

b.   *Signature of unrepresented party.* A party who is not represented by an attorney shall sign his pleading and state his address. IN ST TRIAL P Rule 11(A).

c.   *Verification not generally required.* Except when specifically required by rule, pleadings or motions need not be verified or accompanied by affidavit. The rule in equity that the averments of an answer under oath must be overcome by the testimony of two (2) witnesses or of one (1) witness sustained by corroborating circumstances is abolished. IN ST TRIAL P Rule 11(A).

d.   *Verification by affirmation or representation.* When in connection with any civil or special statutory proceeding it is required that any pleading, motion, petition, supporting affidavit, or other document of any kind, be verified, or that an oath be taken, it shall be sufficient if the subscriber simply affirms the truth of the matter to be verified by an affirmation or representation. IN ST TRIAL P Rule 11(B). IN ST TRIAL P Rule 11(B) states that the affirmation or representation should be in substantially the following language: "I (we) affirm, under the penalties for perjury, that the foregoing representation(s) is (are) true. (Signed) _____."

    i.   Any person who falsifies an affirmation or representation of fact shall be subject to the same penalties as are prescribed by law for the making of a false affidavit. IN ST TRIAL P Rule 11(B).

e.   *Verified pleadings, motions, and affidavits as evidence.* Pleadings, motions and affidavits accompanying or in support of such pleadings or motions when required to be verified or under oath shall be accepted as a representation that the signer had personal knowledge thereof or reasonable cause to believe the existence of the facts or matters stated or alleged therein; and, if otherwise competent or acceptable as evidence, may be admitted as evidence of the facts or matters stated or alleged therein when it is so provided in the Indiana Rules of Trial Procedure, by statute or other law, or to the extent the writing or signature expressly purports to be made upon the signer's personal knowledge. When such pleadings, motions and affidavits are verified or under oath they shall not require other or greater proof on the part of the adverse party than if not verified or not under oath unless expressly provided otherwise by the Indiana Rules of Trial Procedure, statute or other law. Affidavits upon motions for summary judgment under IN ST TRIAL P Rule 56 and in denial of execution under IN ST TRIAL P Rule 9.2 shall be made upon personal knowledge. IN ST TRIAL P Rule 11(C).

f.   *Signature, verification and other requirements.* Parties and their counsel are enjoined to comply with the verification requirements of IN ST TRIAL P Rule 11, and either the moving party or the party's attorney of record shall sign all pleadings and motions before filing with the Clerk of the Court. Every motion, petition, or other pleading filed with the Clerk shall contain the name, organization, physical address, telephone number, and facsimile number of the filing party or an attorney for that party. IN ST ST JOSEPH CIV Rule 201(201.3.6).

    i.   The Clerk shall not accept any motion, petition, notice or other pleading or a CCS entry form for filing from an unrepresented litigant unless the unrepresented litigant's current address and phone number appear on the pleading, and an opposing party may service notices and responses on an unrepresented litigant at any address he or she has provided on a pleading. IN ST ST JOSEPH CIV Rule 201(201.3.6).

4.   *Information excluded from public access.* Every document filed in a case shall separately identify information excluded from public access pursuant to IN ST ADMIN Rule 9(G)(1) as follows:

a.   Whole documents that are excluded from public access pursuant to IN ST ADMIN Rule 9(G)(1) shall be tendered on light green paper or have a light green coversheet attached to the document, marked "Not for Public Access" or "Confidential." IN ST TRIAL P Rule 5(G)(1).

b.   When only a portion of a document contains information excluded from public access pursuant to IN ST ADMIN Rule 9(G)(1), said information shall be omitted [or redacted] from the filed document, and set forth on a separate accompanying document on light green paper conspicuously marked "Not for Public Access" or "Confidential" and clearly designated [or identifying] the caption and number of the case and the document and location within the document to which the redacted material pertains. IN ST TRIAL P Rule 5(G)(2).

c.   With respect to documents filed in electronic format, the trial court, by local rule, may provide for compliance with IN ST TRIAL P Rule 5 in manner that separates and protects access to information excluded from public access. IN ST TRIAL P Rule 5(G)(3).

d.   IN ST TRIAL P Rule 5(G) does not apply to a record sealed by the court pursuant to IN ST 5-14-3-5.5 or otherwise, nor to records, documents, or information filed in cases to which public access is prohibited pursuant to IN ST ADMIN Rule 9(G). IN ST TRIAL P Rule 5(G)(4).

e.   The following information in case records is excluded from public access and is confidential:

    i.   Information that is excluded from public access pursuant to federal law;

ii. Information that is excluded from public access as declared confidential by Indiana statute or other court rule, including without limitation:

- All adoption records created after July 8, 1941, as declared confidential by IN ST 31-19-19-1, et seq., except those specifically declared open by IN ST 31-19-13-2(2);

- All records relating to chancroid, chlamydia, gonorrhea, hepatitis, human immunodeficiency virus (HIV), Lymphogranuloma venereum, syphilis, tuberculosis, as declared confidential by IN ST 16-41-8-1, et seq.;

- All records relating to child abuse as declared confidential by IN ST 31-33-18-1, et seq.;

- All records relating to drug tests as declared confidential by IN ST 5-14-3-4(a)(9);

- Records of grand jury proceedings as declared confidential by IN ST 35-34-2-4;

- Records of juvenile proceedings as declared confidential by IN ST 31-39-1-2, except those specifically open under statute;

- All paternity records created after July 1, 1941 as declared confidential by IN ST 31-14-11-15, IN ST 31-19-5-23, IN ST 31-39-1-1 and IN ST 31-39-1-2 [Editor's note: IN ST 31-14-11-15 was repealed effective May 9, 2013];

- All pre-sentence reports as declared confidential by IN ST 35-38-1-13;

- Written petitions to permit marriages without consent and orders directing the Clerk of Court to issue a marriage license to underage persons, as declared confidential by IN ST 31-11-1-6;

- Only those arrest warrants, search warrants, indictments and informations ordered confidential by the trial judge, prior to return of duly executed service as declared confidential by IN ST 5-14-3-4(b)(1);

- All medical, mental health, or tax records unless determined by law or regulation of any governmental custodian not to be confidential, released by the subject of such records, or declared by a court of competent jurisdiction to be essential to the resolution of litigation as declared confidential by IN ST 16-39-3-10, IN ST 6-4.1-5-10, IN ST 6-4.1-12-12, and IN ST 6-8.1-7-1;

- Personal information relating to jurors or prospective jurors, other than for the use of the parties and counsel, pursuant to IN ST JURY Rule 10;

- Information relating to protection from abuse orders, no-contact orders and workplace violence restraining orders as declared confidential by IN ST 5-2-9-6, et seq.;

- Mediation proceedings pursuant to IN ST ADR Rule 2.11, Mini-Trial proceedings pursuant to IN ST ADR Rule 4.4(C), and Summary Jury Trials pursuant to IN ST ADR Rule 5.6;

- Information in probation files pursuant to the Probation Standards promulgated by the Judicial Conference of Indiana pursuant to IN ST 11-13-1-8(b);

- Information deemed confidential pursuant to the Rules for Court Administered Alcohol and Drug Programs promulgated by the Judicial Conference of Indiana pursuant to IN ST 12-23-14-13;

- Information deemed confidential pursuant to the Problem-Solving Court Rules promulgated by the Judicial Conference of Indiana pursuant to IN ST 33-23-16-16;

- All records of the Department of workforce Development as declared confidential by IN ST 22-4-19-6;

- Information regarding interception of electronic communications that is sealed or deemed confidential as set forth in IN ST 35-33.5-2-1, et seq.

iii. Information excluded from public access by specific court order;

iv. Complete Social Security Numbers of living persons;

1377

      v.   With the exception of names, information such as addresses, phone numbers, and dates of birth which explicitly identifies:

- Natural persons who are witnesses or victims (not including defendants) in criminal, domestic violence, stalking, sexual assault, juvenile, or civil protection order proceedings, provided that juveniles who are victims of sex crimes shall be identified by initials only;

- Places of residence of judicial officers, clerks and other employees of courts and clerks of court, unless the person or persons about whom the information pertains waives confidentiality;

      vi.   Complete account numbers of specific assets, loans, bank accounts, credit cards, and personal identification numbers (PINs);

      vii.   All orders of expungement entered in criminal or juvenile proceedings, orders to restrict access to criminal history information pursuant to IN ST 35-38-5-5.5 or IN ST 35-38-8-5 and records excluded from public access by such orders, and information related to infractions that is excluded from public access pursuant to IN ST 34-28-5-15 or IN ST 34-28-5-16 [Editor's note: IN ST 35-38-5-5.5, IN ST 35-38-8-5 and IN ST 34-28-5-16 were repealed effective July 1, 2013; for information on orders restricting access to criminal history, refer to IN ST 35-38-9-1, et seq.];

      viii.   All personal notes and e-mail, and deliberative material, of judges, jurors, court staff and judicial agencies, and information recorded in personal data assistants (PDA's) or organizers and personal calendars. IN ST ADMIN Rule 9(G)(1).

5. *Form of the summons*

   a. *Required contents of summons.* The summons shall contain:

      i.   The name and address of the person on whom the service is to be effected;

      ii.   The name, street address, and telephone number of the court and the cause number assigned to the case;

      iii.   The title of the case as shown by the complaint, but, if there are multiple parties, the title may be shortened to include only the first named plaintiff and defendant with an appropriate indication that there are additional parties;

      iv.   The name, address, and telephone number of the attorney for the person seeking service;

      v.   The time within which the Indiana Rules of Trial Procedure require the person being served to respond, and a clear statement that in case of his failure to do so, judgment by default may be rendered against him for the relief demanded in the complaint. IN ST TRIAL P Rule 4(C).

   b. *Additional contents of summons.* The summons may also contain any additional information which will facilitate proper service. IN ST TRIAL P Rule 4(C).

F. Filing and Service Requirements

1. *Filing requirements.* A civil action is commenced by filing with the court a complaint or such equivalent pleading or document as may be specified by statute, by payment of the prescribed filing fee or filing an order waiving the filing fee, and, where service of process is required, by furnishing to the clerk as many copies of the complaint and summons as are necessary. IN ST TRIAL P Rule 3. An action may be commenced by E-filing only in a court which has adopted a pilot project plan approved by the Division of State Court Administration pursuant to IN ST ADMIN Rule 16. IN ST ADMIN Rule 16(F).

   a. *Filing with the court defined.* The filing of pleadings, motions, and other papers with the court as required by the Indiana Rules of Trial Procedure shall be made by one of the following methods:

      i.   Delivery to the clerk of the court;

      ii.   Sending by electronic transmission under the procedure adopted pursuant to IN ST ADMIN Rule 12;

      iii.   Mailing to the clerk by registered, certified or express mail return receipt requested;

      iv.   Depositing with any third-party commercial carrier for delivery to the clerk within three (3) calendar days, cost prepaid, properly addressed;

v. If the court so permits, filing with the judge, in which event the judge shall note thereon the filing date and forthwith transmit them to the office of the clerk; or

vi. Electronic filing, as approved by the Division of State Court Administration pursuant to IN ST ADMIN Rule 16. IN ST TRIAL P Rule 5(F).

vii. Filing by registered or certified mail and by third-party commercial carrier shall be complete upon mailing or deposit. IN ST TRIAL P Rule 5(F).

viii. All pleadings shall be filed with the Clerk, not directly with the Court, unless otherwise required by the Indiana Rules of Court. The entry of appearances and the filing of pleadings or other matters not requiring immediate Court action shall be filed with the Clerk and not in open Court. A Judge may permit papers to be filed in chambers, in which event he or she shall note thereon the filing date and transmit the papers to the Clerk. IN ST ST JOSEPH CIV Rule 201(201.2).

b. *Facsimile filing.* Unless otherwise authorized by IN ST ST JOSEPH ELECTRONIC Rule 701, electronic filing of pleadings by computerized or facsimile transmission is not permitted. IN ST ST JOSEPH CIV Rule 201(201.2).

c. *Additional copies.* In cases in which a party or counsel supplies the proposed order or decree, a sufficient number shall be prepared and filed as to provide the Clerk to retain two (2) copies, which shall be filed in the flat file and the record of judgments and orders. Should the party or counsel desire additional copies, a sufficient number of copies should be filed to effectuate that purpose. IN ST ST JOSEPH CIV Rule 201(201.6).

d. *Proof of filing.* Any party filing any paper by any method other than personal delivery to the clerk shall retain proof of filing. IN ST TRIAL P Rule 5(F).

2. *Service requirements.* The court acquires jurisdiction over a party or person who under the Indiana Rules of Trial Procedure commences or joins in the action, is served with summons or enters an appearance, or who is subjected to the power of the court under any other law. IN ST TRIAL P Rule 4(A).

a. *Service generally.* Every motion, petition, notice, or other pleading required to be served by IN ST TRIAL P Rule 5 shall be served on all counsel of record or unrepresented parties either before it is filed or on the day it is filed with the Court, and the date of filing shall be indicated on the Certificate of Service. IN ST ST JOSEPH CIV Rule 201(201.5.1).

i. *Copy.* A copy of the Clerk's CCS entry form of the filing shall also be served on all counsel of record or unrepresented parties whenever it contains an appearance of counsel or contains a date for Court hearing on the matter. IN ST ST JOSEPH CIV Rule 201(201.5.1).

b. *Designation of method of service of the summons.* The person seeking service or his attorney may designate the manner of service upon the summons. If not so designated, the clerk shall cause service to be made by mail or other public means provided the mailing address of the person to be served is indicated in the summons or can be determined. If a mailing address is not furnished or cannot be determined or if service by mail or other public means is returned without acceptance, the complaint and summons shall promptly be delivered to the sheriff or his deputy who, unless otherwise directed, shall serve the summons. IN ST TRIAL P Rule 4(D).

c. *Summons and complaint to be served together.* The summons and complaint shall be served together unless otherwise ordered by the court. When service of summons is made by publication, the complaint shall not be published. When jurisdiction over a party is dependent upon service of process by publication or by his appearance, summons and complaint shall be deemed to have been served at the end of the day of last required publication in the case of service by publication, and at the time of appearance in jurisdiction acquired by appearance. Whenever the summons and complaint are not served or published together, the summons shall contain the full, unabbreviated title of the case. IN ST TRIAL P Rule 4(E).

d. *Territorial limits and service under special order*

i. *Territorial limits of effective service.* Process may be served anywhere within the territorial limits of this state and outside the state as provided in the Indiana Rules of Trial Procedure. IN ST TRIAL P Rule 4.14(A).

    ii. *Service under special order of court.* Upon application of any party the court in which any action is pending may make an appropriate order for service in a manner not provided by the Indiana Rules of Trial Procedure or statutes when such service is reasonably calculated to give the defendant actual knowledge of the proceedings and an opportunity to be heard. IN ST TRIAL P Rule 4.14(B).

e. *Return of service.* The person making service shall promptly make his return upon or attach it to a copy of the summons which shall be delivered to the clerk. The return shall be signed by the person making it, and shall include a statement:

    i. That service was made upon the person as required by law and the time, place, and manner thereof;

    ii. If service was not made, the particular manner in which it was thwarted in terms of fact or in terms of law;

    iii. Such other information as is expressly required by the Indiana Rules of Trial Procedure. IN ST TRIAL P Rule 4.15(A).

3. *Methods of service of the summons and complaint*

  a. *In general*

    i. *Methods of service.* Service may be made upon an individual, or an individual acting in a representative capacity, by:

- Sending a copy of the summons and complaint by registered or certified mail or other public means by which a written acknowledgment of receipt may be requested and obtained to his residence, place of business or employment with return receipt requested and returned showing receipt of the letter; or

- Delivering a copy of the summons and complaint to him personally; or

- Leaving a copy of the summons and complaint at his dwelling house or usual place of abode; or

- Serving his agent as provided by rule, statute or valid agreement. IN ST TRIAL P Rule 4.1(A).

    ii. *Copy service to be followed with mail.* Whenever service is made under IN ST TRIAL P Rule 4.1(A)(3) [by leaving a copy at dwelling or usual place of abode] or IN ST TRIAL P Rule 4.1(A)(4) [by service of agent], the person making the service also shall send by first class mail, a copy of the summons without the complaint to the last known address of the person being served, and this fact shall be shown upon the return. IN ST TRIAL P Rule 4.1(B).

    iii. *Service by fax or e-mail.* A party who has consented to service by fax or e-mail may be served as follows:

- Service by e-mail shall be made by attaching the document being served in PDF format. Discovery documents must also be served in accordance with IN ST TRIAL P Rule 26(A).

- Service by fax shall be deemed complete upon generation of a transmission record indicating the successful transmission of the entire document, except as provided in IN ST TRIAL P Rule 5(B)(3)(d).

- Service by e-mail shall be deemed complete upon transmission, except as provided in IN ST TRIAL P Rule 5(B)(3)(d).

- Service by fax or e-mail that occurs on a Saturday, Sunday, legal holiday, or day the court or agency in which the matter is pending is closed or after 5:00 PM local time of the recipient shall be deemed complete the next day that is not a Saturday, Sunday, legal holiday, or day that the court or agency in which the matter is pending is not closed. IN ST TRIAL P Rule 5(B)(3).

    iv. *Service by the clerk.* Whenever the Clerk is required by rule or statute to give notice, the party or parties requesting such notice shall furnish the Clerk with sufficient copies of the notice to be given, along with stamped, addressed envelopes with the names and the addresses of the parties or their counsel to whom such notice is to be given. IN ST ST JOSEPH CIV Rule 201(201.5.4).

v. *Service on the court.* Service on a Judge may be made by delivering a copy to the Judge's secretary or mailing a copy to the Judge at his or her chambers. Service on a Judge may not be accomplished by facsimile transmission; however, a courtesy copy may be sent to the Judge's chambers by electronic mail or facsimile transmission contemporaneously with service by mail or otherwise. IN ST ST JOSEPH CIV Rule 201(201.5.5).

b. *Service upon infants or incompetents*

    i. *Service upon infants.* Service upon an individual known to be an infant shall be made upon his next friend or guardian ad litem, if service is with respect to the same action in which the infant is so represented. If there is no next friend or guardian ad litem, service shall be made upon his court-appointed representative if one is known and can be served within this state. If there is no court-appointed representative, service shall be made upon either parent known to have custody of the infant, or if there is no parent, upon a person known to be standing in the position of custodian or parent. The infant shall also be served if he is fourteen (14) years of age or older. In the event that service, as provided above, is not possible, service shall be made on the infant. IN ST TRIAL P Rule 4.2(A).

    ii. *Service upon incompetents.* Service upon an individual who has been adjudged to be of unsound mind, otherwise incompetent or who is believed to be such shall be made upon his next friend or guardian ad litem, if service is with respect to the same action in which the incompetent is so represented. If there is no next friend or guardian ad litem, service shall be made upon his court-appointed representative if one is known and can be served within this state. If there is no court-appointed representative, then upon the named party and also upon a person known to be standing in the position of custodian of his person. IN ST TRIAL P Rule 4.2(B).

    iii. *Duty to inform court; Appearance.* Nothing herein is intended to affect the duty of a party to inform the court that a person is an infant or incompetent. An appearance by a court-appointed guardian, next friend or guardian ad litem or his attorney shall correct any defect in service under IN ST TRIAL P Rule 4.2 unless such defect be challenged. IN ST TRIAL P Rule 4.2(C).

c. *Service upon institutionalized persons.* Service of summons upon a person who is imprisoned or restrained in an institution shall be made by delivering or mailing a copy of the summons and complaint to the official in charge of the institution. It shall be the duty of said official to immediately deliver the summons and complaint to the person being served and allow him to make provisions for adequate representation by counsel. The official shall indicate upon the return whether the person has received the summons and been allowed an opportunity to retain counsel. IN ST TRIAL P Rule 4.3.

d. *Service upon individuals whose acts serve as basis for jurisdiction.* A person subject to the jurisdiction of the courts of this state under IN ST TRIAL P Rule 4.4 may be served with summons:

    i. As provided by IN ST TRIAL P Rule 4.1 (service on individuals), IN ST TRIAL P Rule 4.5 (service upon resident who cannot be found or served within the state), IN ST TRIAL P Rule 4.6 (service upon organizations), IN ST TRIAL P Rule 4.9 (in rem actions); or

    ii. The person shall be deemed to have appointed the Secretary of State as his agent upon whom service of summons may be made as provided in IN ST TRIAL P Rule 4.10. IN ST TRIAL P Rule 4.4(B).

e. *Service upon resident who cannot be found or served within the state.* When the person to be served is a resident of this state who cannot be served personally or by agent in this state and either cannot be found, has concealed his whereabouts or has left the state, summons may be served in the manner provided by IN ST TRIAL P Rule 4.9 (summons in in rem actions). IN ST TRIAL P Rule 4.5.

f. *Service upon organizations*

    i. *Persons to be served.* Service upon an organization may be made as follows:

        • In the case of a domestic or foreign organization upon an executive officer thereof, or if there is an agent appointed or deemed by law to have been appointed to receive service, then upon such agent. IN ST TRIAL P Rule 4.6(A)(1).

        • In the case of a partnership, upon a general partner thereof. IN ST TRIAL P Rule 4.6(A)(2).

- In the case of a state governmental organization upon the executive officer thereof and also upon the Attorney General. IN ST TRIAL P Rule 4.6(A)(3).

- In the case of a local governmental organization, upon the executive thereof and upon the attorney for the local governmental organization. IN ST TRIAL P Rule 4.6(A)(4).

- When, in IN ST TRIAL P Rule 4.6(A)(3) and IN ST TRIAL P Rule 4.6(A)(4), a governmental representative is named as a party in his individual name or in such name along with his official title, then also upon such representative. IN ST TRIAL P Rule 4.6(A)(5).

ii. *Manner of service.* Service under IN ST TRIAL P Rule 4.6(A) shall be made on the proper person in the manner provided by the Indiana Rules of Trial Procedure for service upon individuals, but a person seeking service or his attorney shall not knowingly direct service to be made at the person's dwelling house or place of abode, unless such is an address furnished under the requirements of a statute or valid agreement, or unless an affidavit on or attached to the summons states that service in another manner is impractical. IN ST TRIAL P Rule 4.6(B).

iii. *Service at organization's office.* When shown upon an affidavit or in the return, that service upon an organization cannot be made as provided in IN ST TRIAL P Rule 4.6(A) or IN ST TRIAL P Rule 4.6(B), service may be made by leaving a copy of the summons and complaint at any office of such organization located within this state with the person in charge of such office. IN ST TRIAL P Rule 4.6(C).

g. *Summons; Service upon agent named by statute or agreement.* Whenever an agent (other than an agent appointed to receive service for a governmental organization of this state) has been designated by or pursuant to statute or valid agreement to receive service for the person being served, service may be made upon such agent as follows:

i. If the agent is a governmental organization or officer designated by or pursuant to statute, service shall be made as provided in IN ST TRIAL P Rule 4.10. IN ST TRIAL P Rule 4.7(1).

ii. If the agent is one other than that described in IN ST TRIAL P Rule 4.7(1), service shall be made upon him as provided in IN ST TRIAL P Rule 4.1 (service upon individuals) or IN ST TRIAL P Rule 4.6 (service upon organizations). If service cannot be made upon such agent, because there is no address furnished as required by statute or valid agreement or his whereabouts in this state are unknown, then his principal shall be deemed to have appointed the Secretary of State as a replacement for the agent and service may be made upon the Secretary of State as provided in IN ST TRIAL P Rule 4.10. IN ST TRIAL P Rule 4.7(2).

h. *Summons; Service of pleadings or summons on Attorney General.* Service of a copy of the summons and complaint or any pleading upon the Attorney General under the Indiana Rules of Trial Procedure or any statute shall be made by personal service upon him, a deputy or clerk at his office, or by mail or other public means to him at such office in the manner provided by IN ST TRIAL P Rule 4.1(A)(1), and by IN ST TRIAL P Rule 4.11 to the extent applicable. IN ST TRIAL P Rule 4.8.

i. *Summons; In rem actions*

i. *In general.* In any action involving a res situated within this state, service may be made as provided in IN ST TRIAL P Rule 4.9. The court may render a judgment or decree to the extent of its jurisdiction over the res. IN ST TRIAL P Rule 4.9(A).

ii. *Manner of service.* Service under IN ST TRIAL P Rule 4.9 may be made as follows:

- By service of summons upon a person or his agent pursuant to the Indiana Rules of Trial Procedure; or

- By service of summons outside this state in a manner provided by IN ST TRIAL P Rule 4.1 (service upon individuals) or by publication outside this state in a manner provided by IN ST TRIAL P Rule 4.13 (service by publication) or outside this state in any other manner as provided by the Indiana Rules of Trial Procedure; or

- By service by publication pursuant to IN ST TRIAL P Rule 4.13. IN ST TRIAL P Rule 4.9(A).

j. *Summons; Service upon Secretary of State or other governmental agent.* Whenever, under the Indiana Rules of Trial Procedure or any statute, service is made upon the Secretary of State or any other governmental organization or officer, as agent for the person being served, service may be made upon such agent as provided in IN ST TRIAL P Rule 4.10. IN ST TRIAL P Rule 4.10(A).

  i. The person seeking service or his attorney shall:

   - Submit his request for service upon the agent in the praecipe for summons, and state that the governmental organization or officer is the agent of the person being served;

   - State the address of the person being served as filed and recorded pursuant to a statute or valid agreement, or if no such address is known, then his last known mailing address, and, if no such address is known, then such shall be stated;

   - Pay any fee prescribed by statute to be forwarded together with sufficient copies of the summons, affidavit and complaint, to the agent by the clerk of the court. IN ST TRIAL P Rule 4.10(A)(1).

  ii. Upon receipt thereof the agent shall promptly:

   - Send to the person being served a copy of the summons and complaint by registered or certified mail or by other public means by which a written acknowledgment of receipt may be obtained;

   - Complete and deliver to the clerk an affidavit showing the date of the mailing, or if there was no mailing, the reason therefor;

   - Send to the clerk a copy of the return receipt along with a copy of the summons;

   - File and retain a copy of the return receipt. IN ST TRIAL P Rule 4.10(A)(2).

k. *Summons; Registered or certified mail.* Whenever service by registered or certified mail or other public means by which a return receipt may be requested is authorized, the clerk of the court or a governmental agent under IN ST TRIAL P Rule 4.10 shall send the summons and complaint to the person being served at the address supplied upon the summons, or furnished by the person seeking service. In his return the clerk of the court or the governmental agent shall show the date and place of mailing, a copy of the mailed or electronically-transmitted return receipt if and when received by him showing whether the mailing was accepted or returned, and, if accepted, by whom. The return along with the receipt shall be promptly filed by the clerk with the pleadings and become a part of the record. If a mailing by the clerk of the court is returned without acceptance, the clerk shall reissue the summons and complaint for service as requested, by the person seeking service. IN ST TRIAL P Rule 4.11.

l. *Summons; Service by sheriff or other officer*

  i. *In general.* Whenever service is made by delivering a copy to a person personally or by leaving a copy at his dwelling house or place of employment as provided by IN ST TRIAL P Rule 4.1, summons shall be issued to and served by the sheriff, his deputy, or some person specially or regularly appointed by the court for that purpose. Service shall be effective if made by a person not otherwise authorized by the Indiana Rules of Trial Procedure, but proof of service by such a person must be made by him as a witness or by deposition without allowance of expenses therefor as costs. The person to whom the summons is delivered for service must act promptly and exercise reasonable care to cause service to be made. IN ST TRIAL P Rule 4.12(A).

  ii. *Special service by police officers.* A sheriff, his deputy, or any full-time state or municipal police officer may serve summons in any county of this state if he agrees or has agreed to make the service. When specially requested in the praecipe for summons, the complaint and summons shall be delivered to such officer by the clerk or the attorney for the person seeking service. No agreement with the sheriff or his deputy for such service in the sheriff's own county shall be permitted. In no event shall any expenses agreed upon under this provision be assessed or recovered as costs or affect court costs otherwise imposed for regular service. IN ST TRIAL P Rule 4.12(B).

  iii. *Service in other counties.* A summons may be served in any county in this state. If service is to be made in another county, the summons may be issued by the clerk for service therein to the sheriff of such county or to a person authorized to make service by the Indiana Rules of Trial Procedure. IN ST TRIAL P Rule 4.12(C).

    iv. *Service outside the state.* Personal service, when permitted by the Indiana Rules of Trial Procedure to be made outside the state, may be made there by any disinterested person or by the attorney representing the person seeking such service. The expenses of such person may be assessed as costs only if they are reasonable and if service by mail or other public means cannot be made or is not successful. IN ST TRIAL P Rule 4.12(D).

m. *Summons; Service by publication*

    i. *Praecipe for summons by publication.* In any action where notice by publication is permitted by the Indiana Rules of Trial Procedure or by statute, service may be made by publication. Summons by publication may name all the persons to be served, and separate publications with respect to each party shall not be required. The person seeking such service, or his attorney, shall submit his request therefor upon the praecipe for summons along with supporting affidavits that diligent search has been made that the defendant cannot be found, has concealed his whereabouts, or has left the state, and shall prepare the contents of the summons to be published. The summons shall be signed by the clerk of the court or the sheriff in such manner as to indicate that it is made by his authority. IN ST TRIAL P Rule 4.13(A).

    ii. *Contents of summons by publication.* The summons shall contain the following information:

- The name of the person being sued, and the person to whom the notice is directed, and, if the person's whereabouts are unknown or some or all of the parties are unknown, a statement to that effect;
- The name of the court and cause number assigned to the case;
- The title of the case as shown by the complaint, but if there are multiple parties, the title may be shortened to include only the first named plaintiff and those defendants to be served by publication with an appropriate indication that there are additional parties;
- The name and address of the attorney representing the person seeking service;
- A brief statement of the nature of the suit, which need not contain the details and particulars of the claim. A description of any property, relationship, or other res involved in the action, and a statement that the person being sued claims some interest therein;
- A clear statement that the person being sued must respond within thirty (30) days after the last notice of the action is published, and in case he fails to do so, judgment by default may be entered against him for the relief demanded in the complaint. IN ST TRIAL P Rule 4.13(B).

    iii. *Publication of summons.* The summons shall be published three (3) times by the clerk or person making it, the first publication promptly and each two (2) succeeding publications at least seven (7) and not more than fourteen (14) days after the prior publication, in a newspaper authorized by law to publish notices, and published in the county where the complaint or action is filed, where the res is located, or where the defendant resides or where he was known last to reside. If no newspaper is published in the county, then the summons shall be published in the county in this state nearest thereto in which any such paper may be printed, or in a place specially ordered by the court. The person seeking the service or his attorney may designate any qualified newspaper, and if he fails to do so, the selection may be made by the clerk. IN ST TRIAL P Rule 4.13(C).

    iv. *By whom made or procured.* Service of summons by publication shall be made and procured by the clerk, by a person appointed by the court for that purpose, or by the clerk or sheriff of another county where publication is to be made. IN ST TRIAL P Rule 4.13(D).

    v. *Return.* The clerk or person making the service shall prepare the return and include the following:

- Any supporting affidavits of the printer containing a copy of the summons which was published;

- An information or statement that the newspaper and the publication meet all legal requirements applicable to such publication;

- The dates of publication. IN ST TRIAL P Rule 4.13(E).

- The return and affidavits shall be filed with the pleadings and other papers in the case and shall become a part of the record as provided in the Indiana Rules of Trial Procedure. IN ST TRIAL P Rule 4.13(E).

n. *Service on agent of nonresident corporation.* In an action commenced in a court of general jurisdiction in Indiana by or against any corporation incorporated under the laws of Indiana, in which one (1) or more of the directors of the corporation is: (1) a necessary or proper party; and (2) a nonresident of Indiana; service of summons upon a director for the purpose of obtaining jurisdiction of the person of the director in the action is obtained by serving the summons on the resident agent of the corporation. IN ST 34-33-2-1.

o. *Distribution.* Counsel or an unrepresented party submitting a motion, petition, notice, pleading or proposed order shall indicate the method of distribution desired on the Clerk's CCS entry form. The Clerk will not return or distribute copies of motions, petitions, pleadings, notices or proposed orders, other than those originated by the Court, by mail unless the Clerk is provided with stamped, addressed envelopes. IN ST ST JOSEPH CIV Rule 201(201.5.3).

p. *Mailbox.* As a matter of convenience to attorneys, each court provides a mailbox for the distribution filings and orders generated by the Court, and it is the responsibility of each attorney to periodically check these mailboxes for service and distribution of court-generated filings and orders. IN ST ST JOSEPH CIV Rule 201(201.5.3).

G. Hearings

1. The Indiana rules do not contemplate a hearing regarding the service of the summons and complaint.

H. Forms

1. Official Complaint Forms for Indiana

a. Affidavit of debt. IN ST TRIAL P App. A-2.

b. Appearance by attorney in civil case. IN ST TRIAL P App. B.

2. Complaint Forms for Indiana

a. Caption; Generally. 5 INPRAC § 3:1.1.

b. Caption; Multiple parties. 5 INPRAC § 3:1.2.

c. Single count. 5 INPRAC § 3:1.3.

d. Multiple counts; Single defendant. 5 INPRAC § 3:1.4.

e. Multiple counts; Multiple defendants. 5 INPRAC § 3:1.5.

f. Signature; By party. 5 INPRAC § 3:1.6.

g. Signature; By attorney. 5 INPRAC § 3:1.7.

h. Verification. 5 INPRAC § 3:1.8.

i. Individual defendant. 5 INPRAC § 3:2.1.

j. Resident agent of corporation. 5 INPRAC § 3:2.2.

k. Attorney general. 5 INPRAC § 3:2.3.

l. City attorney. 5 INPRAC § 3:2.4.

m. Certificate; Personal service. 5 INPRAC § 3:2.5.

n. Certificate; First class mail. 5 INPRAC § 3:2.6.

o. Certificate; Registered mail. 5 INPRAC § 3:2.7.

p. Certificate; Dwelling house. 5 INPRAC § 3:2.8.

q. Clerk's certificate of mailing. 5 INPRAC § 3:2.9.

r. Clerk's certificate of mailing; Acceptance by defendant. 5 INPRAC § 3:2.10.

s. Clerk's return on service of summons by mail; Not accepted by defendant. 5 INPRAC § 3:2.11.

t. Sheriff's return; Service of summons. 5 INPRAC § 3:2.12.

u. Motion to appoint person to serve process. 5 INPRAC § 3:2.13.

v. Published notice; Text. 5 INPRAC § 3:2.14.

w. Affidavit of publisher. 5 INPRAC § 3:2.15.

x. Clerk's return on service by publication. 5 INPRAC § 3:2.16.

y. Complaint; Single count. 9 INPRAC § 2.3.

z. Appearance by party initiating action; Form. 9 INPRAC § 6.3.

I. Checklist

(I) ❏ Matters to be considered by the plaintiff

   (a) ❏ Required documents

      (1) ❏ Summons

      (2) ❏ Complaint

      (3) ❏ Appearance form

   (b) ❏ Supplemental documents

      (1) ❏ Proof of written instrument

      (2) ❏ Notice of intent to use foreign law

      (3) ❏ Praecipe

      (4) ❏ Facsimile cover sheet

   (c) ❏ Timing

      (1) ❏ The claimant typically bears the burden of commencing an action within the applicable statute of limitations

      (2) ❏ If person seeking service of process fails without cause for sixty (60) days or more to provide clerk with required summons for issuance or with other information necessary to effectuate service, person has failed to exercise due diligence in securing service of process

(II) ❏ Matters to be considered by the defendant

   (a) ❏ Required documents

      (1) ❏ Answer

      (2) ❏ Appearance form

      (3) ❏ Chronological Case Summary (CCS) entry form

      (4) ❏ Certificate of service

   (b) ❏ Supplemental documents

      (1) ❏ Admission of service

      (2) ❏ Proof of written instrument

      (3) ❏ Notice of intent to use foreign law

      (4) ❏ Facsimile cover sheet

   (c) ❏ Timing

      (1) ❏ A responsive pleading required under the Indiana Rules of Trial Procedure, shall be served within twenty (20) days after service of the prior pleading

(2) ❑ The service of a motion permitted under IN ST TRIAL P Rule 12 alters the time for service of responsive pleadings as follows, unless a different time is fixed by the court:

    (i) ❑ If the court does not grant the motion, the responsive pleading shall be served in ten (10) days after notice of the court's action;

    (ii) ❑ If the court grants the motion and the corrective action is allowed to be taken, it shall be taken within ten (10) days, and the responsive pleading shall be served within ten (10) days thereafter

(3) ❑ All pleadings and papers subsequent to the complaint which are required to be served upon a party shall be filed with the Court either before service or within a reasonable period of time thereafter

Pleadings
Amended Complaint

Document Last Updated October 2013

A. Applicable Rules

1. *State rules*

    a. Appearance. IN ST TRIAL P Rule 3.1.

    b. Process. IN ST TRIAL P Rule 4.

    c. Service of the summons. IN ST TRIAL P Rule 4.1; IN ST TRIAL P Rule 4.2; IN ST TRIAL P Rule 4.3; IN ST TRIAL P Rule 4.4; IN ST TRIAL P Rule 4.5; IN ST TRIAL P Rule 4.6; IN ST TRIAL P Rule 4.7; IN ST TRIAL P Rule 4.8; IN ST TRIAL P Rule 4.9; IN ST TRIAL P Rule 4.10; IN ST TRIAL P Rule 4.11; IN ST TRIAL P Rule 4.12; IN ST TRIAL P Rule 4.13; IN ST TRIAL P Rule 4.14; IN ST TRIAL P Rule 4.15; IN ST 34-33-2-1.

    d. Service and filing of pleadings and other papers. IN ST TRIAL P Rule 5.

    e. Time. IN ST TRIAL P Rule 6.

    f. Pleadings. IN ST TRIAL P Rule 7; IN ST TRIAL P Rule 8; IN ST TRIAL P Rule 9; IN ST TRIAL P Rule 9.1; IN ST TRIAL P Rule 9.2; IN ST TRIAL P Rule 10.

    g. Signing and verification of pleadings. IN ST TRIAL P Rule 11.

    h. Amended and supplemental pleadings. IN ST TRIAL P Rule 15.

    i. Joinder. IN ST TRIAL P Rule 18; IN ST TRIAL P Rule 19.

    j. Evidence. IN ST TRIAL P Rule 43.

    k. Determination of foreign law. IN ST TRIAL P Rule 44.1.

    l. Judgment on the evidence (directed verdict). IN ST TRIAL P Rule 50.

    m. Findings by the court. IN ST TRIAL P Rule 52.

    n. Summary judgment. IN ST TRIAL P Rule 56.

    o. Motion to correct error. IN ST TRIAL P Rule 59.

    p. Relief from judgment or order. IN ST TRIAL P Rule 60.

    q. Access to court records. IN ST ADMIN Rule 9.

    r. Paper size. IN ST ADMIN Rule 11.

    s. Facsimile transmission. IN ST ADMIN Rule 12.

    t. Electronic filing and electronic service pilot projects. IN ST ADMIN Rule 16.

    u. Sealing of certain records by court; Hearing; Notice. IN ST 5-14-3-5.5.

    v. Sixtieth judicial circuit. IN ST 33-33-71-2.

w. Privacy and confidentiality. IN ST 5-2-9-6; IN ST 5-14-3-4; IN ST 6-4.1-5-10; IN ST 6-4.1-12-12; IN ST 6-8.1-7-1; IN ST 11-13-1-8; IN ST 12-23-14-13; IN ST 16-39-3-10; IN ST 16-41-8-1; IN ST 22-4-19-6; IN ST 31-11-1-6; IN ST 31-19-5-23; IN ST 31-19-13-2; IN ST 31-19-19-1; IN ST 31-33-18-1; IN ST 31-39-1-1; IN ST 31-39-1-2; IN ST 33-23-16-16; IN ST 35-34-2-4; IN ST 35-38-1-13; IN ST 35-38-9-1; IN ST ADR Rule 2.11; IN ST ADR Rule 4.4; IN ST ADR Rule 5.6; IN ST JURY Rule 10.

2. *Local rules*

   a. Filing, pleading, and motions. IN ST ST JOSEPH CIV Rule 201.

   b. Uniform court and case number designation. IN ST ST JOSEPH CIV Rule 202.

   c. Electronic filing of cases in St. Joseph County. IN ST ST JOSEPH ELECTRONIC Rule 701.

B. Timing

1. *Filing an amended pleading*

   a. *As a matter of course.* A party may amend his pleading once as a matter of course at any time before a responsive pleading is served or, if the pleading is one to which no responsive pleading is permitted, and the action has not been placed upon the trial calendar, he may so amend it at any time within thirty (30) days after it is served. IN ST TRIAL P Rule 15(A).

   b. *With leave of court.* Otherwise a party may amend his pleading only by leave of court or by written consent of the adverse party; and leave shall be given when justice so requires. IN ST TRIAL P Rule 15(A). Refer to the Indiana KeyRules Motion for Leave to Amend document for more information.

2. *Computation of time*

   a. *Generally; Days excluded.* In computing any period of time prescribed or allowed by the Indiana Rules of Trial Procedure, by order of the court, or by any applicable statute, the day of the act, event, or default from which the designated period of time begins to run shall not be included. The last day of the period so computed is to be included unless it is:

      i. A Saturday,

      ii. A Sunday,

      iii. A legal holiday as defined by state statute, or

      iv. A day the office in which the act is to be done is closed during regular business hours. IN ST TRIAL P Rule 6(A).

   b. *Short periods.* In any event, the period runs until the end of the next day that is not a Saturday, a Sunday, a legal holiday, or a day on which the office is closed. When the period of time allowed is less than seven (7) days, intermediate Saturdays, Sundays, legal holidays, and days on which the office is closed shall be excluded from the computations. IN ST TRIAL P Rule 6(A).

   c. *Additional time after service by United States mail.* Whenever a party has the right or is required to do some act or take some proceedings within a prescribed period after the service of a notice or other paper upon him and the notice or paper is served upon him by United States mail, three (3) days shall be added to the prescribed period. IN ST TRIAL P Rule 6(E).

   d. *Enlargement of time.* When an act is required or allowed to be done at or within a specific time by the Indiana Rules of Trial Procedure, the court may at any time for cause shown:

      i. Order the period enlarged, with or without motion or notice, if request therefor is made before the expiration of the period originally prescribed or extended by a previous order; or

      ii. Upon motion made after the expiration of the specific period, permit the act to be done where the failure to act was the result of excusable neglect; but, the court may not extend the time for taking any action for judgment on the evidence under IN ST TRIAL P Rule 50(A), amendment of findings and judgment under IN ST TRIAL P Rule 52(B), to correct errors under IN ST TRIAL P Rule 59(C), statement in opposition to motion to correct error under IN ST TRIAL P Rule 59(E), or to obtain relief from final judgment under IN ST TRIAL P Rule 60(B), except to the extent and under the conditions stated in those rules. IN ST TRIAL P Rule 6(B).

iii. An initial written motion for enlargement of time pursuant to IN ST TRIAL P Rule 6(B)(1) to answer a claim shall be routinely granted for an additional thirty (30) days from the original due date or other period the assigned Judge deems reasonable by written order of the Court. The motion must be filed on or before the original due date or IN ST ST JOSEPH CIV Rule 201 shall be inapplicable. IN ST ST JOSEPH CIV Rule 201(201.9.5).

- Any motion for enlargement of time shall state the date when such response is due and the date to which time is requested to be enlarged. IN ST ST JOSEPH CIV Rule 201(201.9.5).

- All subsequent motions for enlargement of time shall be so designated and will only be granted for good cause shown or in the interest of justice. IN ST ST JOSEPH CIV Rule 201(201.9.5).

C. General Requirements

1. *Amending pleadings.* The purpose of an amended pleading is to include matters that occurred before the filing of the original pleading but which were either overlooked by the pleader or unknown to him at the time. It is a substitute for the original and relates to the facts that existed when the original pleading was filed. An amended pleading supercedes the original as to those portions amended. 10 INPRAC § 46.1.

   a. *Amendments liberally allowed.* Amendments to pleadings are to be liberally allowed in order that all issues are presented in one action. 10 INPRAC § 46.1; Pinnacle Media, LLC v. Metropolitan Dev. Com'n of Marion County, 868 N.E.2d 894 (Ind.Ct.App. 2007).

   b. *Amendments to conform to the evidence.* When issues not raised by the pleadings are tried by express or implied consent of the parties, they shall be treated in all respects as if they had been raised in the pleadings. Such amendment of the pleadings as may be necessary to cause them to conform to the evidence and to raise these issues may be made upon motion of any party at any time, even after judgment, but failure so to amend does not affect the result of the trial of these issues. If evidence is objected to at the trial on the ground that it is not within the issues made by the pleadings, the court may allow the pleadings to be amended and shall do so freely when the presentation of the merits of the action will be subserved thereby and the objecting party fails to satisfy the court that the admission of such evidence would prejudice him in maintaining his action or defense upon the merits. The court may grant a continuance to enable the objecting party to meet such evidence. IN ST TRIAL P Rule 15(B).

   c. *Relation back of amendments*

      i. Whenever the claim or defense asserted in the amended pleading arose out of the conduct, transaction, or occurrence set forth or attempted to be set forth in the original pleading, the amendment relates back to the date of the original pleading. An amendment changing the party against whom a claim is asserted relates back if the foregoing provision is satisfied and, within one hundred and twenty (120) days of commencement of the action, the party to be brought in by amendment:

         - Has received such notice of the institution of the action that he will not be prejudiced in maintaining his defense on the merits; and

         - Knew or should have known that but for a mistake concerning the identity of the proper party, the action would have been brought against him. IN ST TRIAL P Rule 15(C).

      ii. The requirement of IN ST TRIAL P Rule 15(C)(1) and IN ST TRIAL P Rule 15(C)(2) with respect to a governmental organization to be brought into the action as defendant is satisfied:

         - In the case of a state or governmental organization by delivery or mailing of process to the attorney general or to a governmental executive [IN ST TRIAL P Rule 4.6(A)(3)]; or

         - In the case of a local governmental organization, by delivery or mailing of process to its attorney as provided by statute, to a governmental executive thereof [IN ST TRIAL P Rule 4.6(A)(4)], or to the officer holding the office if suit is against the officer or an office. IN ST TRIAL P Rule 15(C).

   d. *Amendment by leave.* Amendments, other than an amendment by right, may be made only by leave of court or by written consent of the opposing party. 2 INPRAC R 15(15.2). Refer to the Indiana

KeyRules Motion for Leave to Amend document for more information on amending with leave of court.

2. *Pleading, generally*

   a. *Pleadings to be concise.* Each averment of a pleading shall be simple, concise, and direct. No technical forms of pleading or motions are required. All fictions in pleading are abolished. IN ST TRIAL P Rule 8(E)(1).

   b. *Pleading in the alternative.* A pleading may set forth two (2) or more statements of a claim or defense alternatively or hypothetically, either in one (1) count or defense or in separate counts or defenses. When two (2) or more statements are made in the alternative and one (1) of them if made independently would be sufficient, the pleading is not made insufficient by the insufficiency of one or more of the alternative statements. A pleading may also state as many separate claims or defenses as the pleader has regardless of consistency and whether based on legal or equitable grounds. All statements shall be made subject to the obligations set forth in IN ST TRIAL P Rule 11. IN ST TRIAL P Rule 8(E)(2).

   c. *Motions and pleadings, joint and several.* All motions and pleadings of any kind addressed to two (2) or more paragraphs of any pleading, or filed by two (2) or more parties, shall be taken and construed as joint, separate, and several motions or pleadings to each of such paragraphs and by and against each of such parties. All motions or pleadings containing two (2) or more subject-matters shall be taken and construed as separate and several as to each subject-matter. All objections to rulings made by two (2) or more parties shall be taken and construed as the joint, separate, and several objections of each of such parties. IN ST TRIAL P Rule 8(E)(3).

      i. A complaint filed by or against two (2) or more plaintiffs shall be taken and construed as joint, separate, and several as to each of said plaintiffs. IN ST TRIAL P Rule 8(E).

   d. *Construction of pleadings.* All pleadings shall be so construed as to do substantial justice, lead to disposition on the merits, and avoid litigation of procedural points. IN ST TRIAL P Rule 8(F).

3. *Contents of the complaint*

   a. *Pleading for relief; Notice pleading.* Indiana is a "notice pleading" jurisdiction. 22B INPRAC 8:1; State v. American Family Voices, Inc., 898 N.E.2d 293 (Ind. 2008). Notice pleading replaces the technical and complex method of pleading which existed prior to 1970. Notice pleading is grounded in due process of law and must provide a defendant with reasonable notice of the plaintiff's claim or an opponent's defense. 22B INPRAC 8:1; Noblesville Redevelopment Com'n v. Noblesville Associates Ltd. Partnership, 674 N.E.2d 558 (Ind. 1996). Notice pleading does not require that the plaintiff state all elements or facts essential to a cause of action. 22B INPRAC 8:1; State v. American Family Voices, Inc., 898 N.E.2d 293 (Ind. 2008). Instead, the complaint must state "a short and plain statement of the claim" showing an entitlement to relief, and a demand for relief. 22B INPRAC 8:1; Trail v. Boys and Girls Clubs of Northwest Indiana, 845 N.E.2d 130 (Ind. 2006).

   b. *Claims for relief.* To state a claim for relief, whether an original claim, counterclaim, cross-claim, or third-party claim, a pleading must contain:

      i. A short and plain statement of the claim showing that the pleader is entitled to relief, and

      ii. A demand for relief to which the pleader deems entitled. Relief in the alternative or of several different types may be demanded. However, in any complaint seeking damages for personal injury or death, or seeking punitive damages, no dollar amount or figure shall be included in the demand. IN ST TRIAL P Rule 8(A).

   c. *Res ipsa loquitur.* Res ipsa loquitur or a similar doctrine may be pleaded by alleging generally that the facts connected with the action are unknown to the pleader and are within the knowledge of the opposing party. IN ST TRIAL P Rule 9.1(B).

   d. *Bona fide purchaser.* When the rights of a person depend upon his status as a bona fide purchaser for value or upon similar requirements, such status must be pleaded and proved by the person asserting it, but it may be pleaded in general terms. Once it is established that the person has given any required value, unless such value is commercially unreasonable, and that he has met any requirements of recordation, filing, possession, or perfection, the trier of fact must find that such value was given or such perfection was made in accordance with any requirements of good faith, lack of knowledge, or lack of notice unless and until evidence is introduced which would support a finding of its non-existence. IN ST TRIAL P Rule 9.1(D).

e. *Presumption; Matters of judicial notice.* Neither presumptions of law nor matters of which judicial notice may be taken need be stated in a pleading. IN ST TRIAL P Rule 9.1(E).

   i. *Presumption of jurisdiction.* Jurisdiction is presumed in Indiana. 22B INPRAC 8:2. Consequently, there is no requirement to affirmatively plead the existence of jurisdiction in the complaint, unless the action involves a special proceeding requiring such an allegation. 22B INPRAC 8:2; Cardinal Industries, Inc. v. Schwartz, 483 N.E.2d 458 (Ind.Ct.App. 1985). The plaintiff bears no burden to prove jurisdiction unless and until it is challenged by the defendant. 22B INPRAC 8:2; Brokemond v. Marshall Field & Co., 612 N.E.2d 143 (Ind.Ct.App. 1993).

f. *Equitable and legal claims in multi-count actions.* In multi-count actions, the inclusion of an equitable claim, standing alone, will not automatically draw the entire action into equity. Something more than the presence of an equitable claim is required, and the court must examine the claims at issue. 22B INPRAC 38:1 COMMENT; Lucas v. U.S. Bank, N.A., 953 N.E.2d 457 (Ind. 2011). Factors the court may consider in evaluating the nature of the underlying substantive claims include: the substance and central character of the complaint, the rights and interests at issue, the relief demanded, and any issues arising out of discovery. 22B INPRAC 38:1 COMMENT; Songer v. Civitas Bank, 771 N.E.2d 61 (Ind. 2002).

4. *Pleading special matters*

a. *Capacity.* It is not necessary to aver the capacity of a party to sue or be sued, the authority of a party to sue or be sued in a representative capacity, or the legal existence of an organization that is made a party. The burden of proving lack of such capacity, authority, or legal existence shall be upon the person asserting lack of it, and shall be pleaded as an affirmative defense. IN ST TRIAL P Rule 9(A).

b. *Fraud, mistake, condition of the mind.* In all averments of fraud or mistake, the circumstances constituting fraud or mistake shall be specifically averred. Malice, intent, knowledge, and other conditions of mind may be averred generally. IN ST TRIAL P Rule 9(B).

c. *Conditions precedent.* In pleading the performance or occurrence of promissory or non-promissory conditions precedent, it is sufficient to aver generally that all conditions precedent have been performed, have occurred, or have been excused. A denial of performance or occurrence shall be made specifically and with particularity, and a denial of excuse generally. IN ST TRIAL P Rule 9(C).

d. *Official document or act.* In pleading an official document or official act it is sufficient to aver that the document was issued or the act done in compliance with law. IN ST TRIAL P Rule 9(D).

e. *Judgment.* In pleading a judgment or decision of a domestic or foreign court, judicial or quasi-judicial tribunal, or of a board or officer, it is sufficient to aver the judgment or decision without setting forth matter showing jurisdiction to render it. IN ST TRIAL P Rule 9(E).

f. *Time and place.* For the purpose of testing the sufficiency of a pleading, averments of time and place are material and shall be considered like all other averments of material matter. However, time and place need be stated only with such specificity as will enable the opposing party to prepare his defense. IN ST TRIAL P Rule 9(F).

g. *Special damages; Damages where no answer.* When items of special damage are claimed, they shall be specifically stated. The relief granted to the plaintiff, if there be no answer, cannot exceed the relief demanded in his complaint; but, in any other case, the court may grant him any relief consistent with the facts or matters pleaded. IN ST TRIAL P Rule 9(G).

5. *Joinder*

a. *Of claims.* A party asserting a claim for relief as an original claim, counterclaim, cross-claim, or third-party claim, may join, either as independent or as alternate claims, as many claims, whether legal, equitable, or statutory as he has against an opposing party. IN ST TRIAL P Rule 18(A).

b. *Of remedies; Fraudulent conveyances.* Whenever a claim is one heretofore cognizable only after another claim has been prosecuted to a conclusion, the two (2) claims may be joined in a single action; but the court shall grant relief in that action only in accordance with the relative substantive rights of the parties. In particular, a plaintiff may state a claim for money and a claim to have set aside a conveyance fraudulent as to him, without first having obtained a judgment establishing the claim for money. IN ST TRIAL P Rule 18(B).

c. *Of persons needed for just adjudication.* A person who is subject to service of process shall be joined as a party in the action if:

   i. In his absence complete relief cannot be accorded among those already parties; or

   ii. He claims an interest relating to the subject of the action and is so situated that the disposition of the action in his absence may:

- As a practical matter impair or impede his ability to protect that interest, or
- Leave any of the persons already parties subject to a substantial risk of incurring double, multiple, or otherwise inconsistent obligations by reason of his claimed interest. IN ST TRIAL P Rule 19(A).

   iii. If he has not been so joined, the court shall order that he be made a party. If he should join as a plaintiff but refuses to do so, he may be made a defendant. IN ST TRIAL P Rule 19(A).

6. *Trial by jury; Demand*

a. *Causes triable by court and by jury.* Issues of law and issues of fact in causes that prior to the eighteenth day of June, 1852, were of exclusive equitable jurisdiction shall be tried by the court; issues of fact in all other causes shall be triable as the same are now triable. In case of the joinder of causes of action or defenses which, prior to said date, were of exclusive equitable jurisdiction with causes of action or defenses which, prior to said date, were designated as actions at law and triable by jury—the former shall be triable by the court, and the latter by a jury, unless waived; the trial of both may be at the same time or at different times, as the court may direct. IN ST TRIAL P Rule 38(A).

b. *Demand.* Any party may demand a trial by jury of any issue triable of right by a jury by filing with the court and serving upon the other parties a demand therefor in writing at any time after the commencement of the action and not later than ten (10) days after the first responsive pleading to the complaint, or to a counterclaim, crossclaim or other claim if one properly is pleaded; and if no responsive pleading is filed or required, within ten (10) days after the time such pleading otherwise would have been required. Such demand is sufficient if indorsed upon a pleading of a party filed within such time. IN ST TRIAL P Rule 38(B).

c. *Same; Specification of issues.* In his demand a party may specify the issues which he wishes so tried; otherwise he shall be deemed to have demanded trial by jury for all issues triable as of right by jury. Any other party must file a demand for jury trial to preserve his right to trial by jury:

   i. Of issues for which a right to trial by jury was not requested by another party; and

   ii. In case a request by another party was improper. But if a proper request for a trial by jury upon issues triable by jury as of right on his behalf is made by any party, such request shall be deemed to have been made on behalf of all parties entitled to a jury trial upon such issues. IN ST TRIAL P Rule 38(C).

d. *Waiver.* The failure of a party to appear at the trial, and the failure of a party to serve a demand as required by IN ST TRIAL P Rule 38 and to file it as required by IN ST TRIAL P Rule 5(E) constitute waiver by him of trial by jury. A demand for trial by jury made as provided in IN ST TRIAL P Rule 38 may not be withdrawn without the consent of the other party or parties. IN ST TRIAL P Rule 38(D).

   i. The trial court shall not grant a demand for a trial by jury filed after the time fixed in IN ST TRIAL P Rule 38(B) has elapsed except upon the written agreement of all of the parties to the action, which agreement shall be filed with the court and made a part of the record. If such agreement is filed then the court may, in its discretion, grant a trial by jury in which event the grant of a trial by jury may not be withdrawn except by the agreement of all of the parties. IN ST TRIAL P Rule 38(D).

    e.   *Arbitration.* Nothing in the Indiana Rules of Trial Procedure shall deny the parties the right by contract or agreement to submit or to agree to submit controversies to arbitration made before or after commencement of an action thereon or deny the courts power to specifically enforce such agreements. IN ST TRIAL P Rule 38(E).

D. Documents

1. *Required documents*

    a.   *Amended complaint.* Refer to the General Requirements section of this document for information on the contents of an amended complaint.

    b.   *Chronological Case Summary (CCS) entry form.* Every written motion, petition, or other pleading subsequent to the original complaint presented to the Clerk for filing shall be accompanied by a Chronological Case Summary (CCS) entry form in duplicate. IN ST ST JOSEPH CIV Rule 201(201.4). Refer to the Format section of this document for details on the format and filing requirements for the CCS entry form.

    c.   *Certificate of service.* An attorney or unrepresented party tendering a document to the Clerk for filing shall certify that service has been made, list the parties served, and specify the date and means of service. The certificate of service shall be placed at the end of the document and shall not be separately filed. The separate filing of a certificate of service, however, shall not be grounds for rejecting a document for filing. The Clerk may permit documents to be filed without a certificate of service but shall require prompt filing of a separate certificate of service. IN ST TRIAL P Rule 5(C).

2. *Supplemental documents*

    a.   *Proof of written instrument.* When any pleading allowed by the Indiana Rules of Trial Procedure is founded on a written instrument, the original, or a copy thereof, must be included in or filed with the pleading. Such instrument, whether copied in the pleadings or not, shall be taken as part of the record. When any pleading allowed by the Indiana Rules of Trial Procedure is founded on an account, an Affidavit of Debt, in a form substantially similar to that which is provided in IN ST TRIAL P App. A-2, shall be attached. IN ST TRIAL P Rule 9.2(A).

    b.   *Notice of intent to use foreign law.* A party who intends to raise an issue concerning the law of a foreign country shall give notice in his pleadings or other reasonable written notice. The court, in determining foreign law, may consider any relevant material or source, including testimony, whether or not submitted by a party or admissible under IN ST TRIAL P Rule 43. The court's determination shall be treated as a ruling on a question of law. It shall be made by the court and not the jury and shall be reviewable. IN ST TRIAL P Rule 44.1(A).

    c.   *Facsimile cover sheet.* Any document sent to the Clerk of the Circuit Court by electronic facsimile transmission shall be accompanied by a cover sheet which states the title of the document, case number, number of pages, identity and voice telephone number of the sending party and instructions for filing. The cover sheet shall contain the signature of the attorney or party, pro se, authorizing the filing. IN ST ADMIN Rule 12(D).

3. Refer to the Indiana KeyRules Complaint document for the required and supplemental documents for filing and serving an amended complaint against a new party.

E. Format

1. *Form of pleadings*

    a.   *Caption; Names of parties.* Every pleading shall contain a caption setting forth the name of the court, the title of the action, the file number, and a designation as in IN ST TRIAL P Rule 7(A). In the complaint the title of the action shall include the names of all the parties, but in other pleadings it is sufficient to state the name of the first party on each side with an appropriate indication of other parties. IN ST TRIAL P Rule 10(A); IN ST ST JOSEPH CIV Rule 201(201.3.3). If a special judge has been assigned to the case, the pleading should also identify the special judge. IN ST ST JOSEPH CIV Rule 201(201.3.3).

        i.   *Title.* All pleadings or motions shall include a title, which shall delineate each topic included in the pleading. For example, where a pleading contains an answer, a motion to dismiss, and a jury request, each topic shall be set forth in the title. IN ST ST JOSEPH CIV Rule 201(201.3.4).

b. *Paragraphs; Separate statements.* All averments of a claim or defense shall be made in numbered paragraphs, the contents of each of which shall be limited as far as practicable to a statement of a single set of circumstances, and a paragraph may be referred to by number in all succeeding pleadings. Each claim founded upon a separate transaction or occurrence and each defense other than denials may be stated in a separate count or defense whenever a separation facilitates the clear presentation of the matters set forth. IN ST TRIAL P Rule 10(B).

c. *Adoption by reference; Exhibits.* Statements in a pleading may be adopted by reference in a different part of the same pleading or in another pleading or in any motion. A copy of any written instrument which is an exhibit to a pleading is a part thereof for all purposes. IN ST TRIAL P Rule 10(C).

d. *Flat filing.* In order that the Clerk's files may be kept under the system commonly known as "flat filing," all papers presented to the Clerk for filing shall be flat and unfolded. Pleadings shall have no covers or backs and shall be fastened together at the top left-hand corner only. IN ST ST JOSEPH CIV Rule 201(201.1).

e. *One side of page used.* Printing shall be on one (1) side of the paper. IN ST ST JOSEPH CIV Rule 201(201.3.2).

f. *Copies.* All copies shall be on white paper of sufficient strength and durability to resist normal wear and tear. IN ST ST JOSEPH CIV Rule 201(201.3.1).

g. *Margins.* Margins shall be at least one inch (1"). IN ST ST JOSEPH CIV Rule 201(201.3.2).

h. *Double-spaced.* If typewritten, the lines shall be double spaced except for quotations, which shall be indented and single-spaced. IN ST ST JOSEPH CIV Rule 201(201.3.2).

i. *Font size.* Type face shall be twelve (12) font size or larger within the body of the document and ten (10) font size or larger in the footnotes. IN ST ST JOSEPH CIV Rule 201(201.3.2).

j. *Font type.* The font type must be legible and script type shall not be used. IN ST ST JOSEPH CIV Rule 201(201.3.2).

k. *Italics.* Italicized type may be used for quotations, references, or case citations. IN ST ST JOSEPH CIV Rule 201(201.3.2).

l. *Court and case designation.* All filings shall conform to the requirements for uniform court and case number designation set by IN ST ADMIN Rule 8. In addition, all filings shall contain the proper court and case designation as described below. IN ST ST JOSEPH CIV Rule 202.

    i. *Court designation.* Pursuant to IN ST 33-33-71-2, St. Joseph County, Indiana, constitutes the Sixtieth Judicial Circuit. The legal names of the courts within the 60th Judicial Circuit are the St. Joseph Circuit Court, the St. Joseph Superior Court, and the St. Joseph Probate Court. All filings shall properly reflect the legal name of the applicable court. Any filing may be amended, rejected, or stricken if it does not contain the proper case name and/or the legal name of the court. IN ST ST JOSEPH CIV Rule 202(202.1).

m. *Form of CCS entry.* Every written motion, petition, or other pleading subsequent to the original complaint presented to the Clerk for filing shall be accompanied by a Chronological Case Summary (CCS) entry form in duplicate which shall contain the title and cause number of the action, the date, and the proposed entry to appear on the docket. IN ST ST JOSEPH CIV Rule 201(201.4).

    i. *Identification and signature.* The CCS entry form shall identify the party making the filing, designate each pleading being filed, and shall be signed by counsel of record or the unrepresented litigant. IN ST ST JOSEPH CIV Rule 201(201.4).

    ii. *Date stamp.* The form shall be date stamped and presented to the Court Clerk, who shall initial the form and return the duplicate to the filing party. IN ST ST JOSEPH CIV Rule 201(201.4).

2. *Size of papers for filing.* Effective January 1, 1992, all pleadings, copies, motions and documents filed with any trial court or appellate level court, typed or printed, with the exception of exhibits and existing wills, shall be prepared on eight and one-half by eleven inch (8 1/2" x 11") size paper. IN ST ADMIN Rule 11.

a. *Paper.* Pleadings, motions, and other papers shall be either legibly printed or typewritten on white

opaque paper of good quality at least sixteen (16) pound weight, eight and one-half inches (8 1/2 ")
in width and eleven inches (11") in length as required by IN ST ADMIN Rule 11. IN ST ST JOSEPH
CIV Rule 201(201.3.1).

3.   *Signature requirements*

   a.   *Signature of attorney.* Every pleading or motion of a party represented by an attorney shall be signed
        by at least one (1) attorney of record in his individual name, whose address, telephone number, and
        attorney number shall be stated, except that this provision shall not apply to pleadings and motions
        made and transcribed at the trial or a hearing before the judge and received by him in such form. IN
        ST TRIAL P Rule 11(A).

        i.   The signature of an attorney constitutes a certificate by him that he has read the pleadings; that
              to the best of his knowledge, information, and belief, there is good ground to support it; and that
              it is not interposed for delay. IN ST TRIAL P Rule 11(A).

        ii.   If a pleading or motion is not signed or is signed with intent to defeat the purpose of the rule, it
              may be stricken as sham and false and the action may proceed as though the pleading had not
              been served. IN ST TRIAL P Rule 11(A).

        iii. For a willful violation of IN ST TRIAL P Rule 11 an attorney may be subjected to appropriate
              disciplinary action. Similar action may be taken if scandalous or indecent matter is inserted. IN
              ST TRIAL P Rule 11(A).

   b.   *Signature of unrepresented party.* A party who is not represented by an attorney shall sign his
        pleading and state his address. IN ST TRIAL P Rule 11(A).

   c.   *Verification not generally required.* Except when specifically required by rule, pleadings or motions
        need not be verified or accompanied by affidavit. The rule in equity that the averments of an answer
        under oath must be overcome by the testimony of two (2) witnesses or of one (1) witness sustained
        by corroborating circumstances is abolished. IN ST TRIAL P Rule 11(A).

   d.   *Verification by affirmation or representation.* When in connection with any civil or special statutory
        proceeding it is required that any pleading, motion, petition, supporting affidavit, or other document
        of any kind, be verified, or that an oath be taken, it shall be sufficient if the subscriber simply affirms
        the truth of the matter to be verified by an affirmation or representation. IN ST TRIAL P Rule 11(B).
        IN ST TRIAL P Rule 11(B) states that the affirmation or representation should be in substantially the
        following language: "I (we) affirm, under the penalties for perjury, that the foregoing
        representation(s) is (are) true. (Signed) _____"

        i.   Any person who falsifies an affirmation or representation of fact shall be subject to the same
              penalties as are prescribed by law for the making of a false affidavit. IN ST TRIAL P Rule
              11(B).

   e.   *Verified pleadings, motions, and affidavits as evidence.* Pleadings, motions and affidavits accompa-
        nying or in support of such pleadings or motions when required to be verified or under oath shall be
        accepted as a representation that the signer had personal knowledge thereof or reasonable cause to
        believe the existence of the facts or matters stated or alleged therein; and, if otherwise competent or
        acceptable as evidence, may be admitted as evidence of the facts or matters stated or alleged therein
        when it is so provided in the Indiana Rules of Trial Procedure, by statute or other law, or to the extent
        the writing or signature expressly purports to be made upon the signer's personal knowledge. When
        such pleadings, motions and affidavits are verified or under oath they shall not require other or greater
        proof on the part of the adverse party than if not verified or not under oath unless expressly provided
        otherwise by the Indiana Rules of Trial Procedure, statute or other law. Affidavits upon motions for
        summary judgment under IN ST TRIAL P Rule 56 and in denial of execution under IN ST TRIAL
        P Rule 9.2 shall be made upon personal knowledge. IN ST TRIAL P Rule 11(C).

   f.   *Signature, verification and other requirements.* Parties and their counsel are enjoined to comply
        with the verification requirements of IN ST TRIAL P Rule 11, and either the moving party or the
        party's attorney of record shall sign all pleadings and motions before filing with the Clerk of the
        Court. Every motion, petition, or other pleading filed with the Clerk shall contain the name,

organization, physical address, telephone number, and facsimile number of the filing party or an attorney for that party. IN ST ST JOSEPH CIV Rule 201(201.3.6).

    i.   The Clerk shall not accept any motion, petition, notice or other pleading or a CCS entry form for filing from an unrepresented litigant unless the unrepresented litigant's current address and phone number appear on the pleading, and an opposing party may service notices and responses on an unrepresented litigant at any address he or she has provided on a pleading. IN ST ST JOSEPH CIV Rule 201(201.3.6).

4. *Information excluded from public access.* Every document filed in a case shall separately identify information excluded from public access pursuant to IN ST ADMIN Rule 9(G)(1) as follows:

    a. Whole documents that are excluded from public access pursuant to IN ST ADMIN Rule 9(G)(1) shall be tendered on light green paper or have a light green coversheet attached to the document, marked "Not for Public Access" or "Confidential." IN ST TRIAL P Rule 5(G)(1).

    b. When only a portion of a document contains information excluded from public access pursuant to IN ST ADMIN Rule 9(G)(1), said information shall be omitted [or redacted] from the filed document, and set forth on a separate accompanying document on light green paper conspicuously marked "Not for Public Access" or "Confidential" and clearly designated [or identifying] the caption and number of the case and the document and location within the document to which the redacted material pertains. IN ST TRIAL P Rule 5(G)(2).

    c. With respect to documents filed in electronic format, the trial court, by local rule, may provide for compliance with IN ST TRIAL P Rule 5 in manner that separates and protects access to information excluded from public access. IN ST TRIAL P Rule 5(G)(3).

    d. IN ST TRIAL P Rule 5(G) does not apply to a record sealed by the court pursuant to IN ST 5-14-3-5.5 or otherwise, nor to records, documents, or information filed in cases to which public access is prohibited pursuant to IN ST ADMIN Rule 9(G). IN ST TRIAL P Rule 5(G)(4).

    e. The following information in case records is excluded from public access and is confidential:

        i.   Information that is excluded from public access pursuant to federal law;

       ii. Information that is excluded from public access as declared confidential by Indiana statute or other court rule, including without limitation:

- All adoption records created after July 8, 1941, as declared confidential by IN ST 31-19-19-1, et seq., except those specifically declared open by IN ST 31-19-13-2(2);

- All records relating to chancroid, chlamydia, gonorrhea, hepatitis, human immunodeficiency virus (HIV), Lymphogranuloma venereum, syphilis, tuberculosis, as declared confidential by IN ST 16-41-8-1, et seq.;

- All records relating to child abuse as declared confidential by IN ST 31-33-18-1, et seq.;

- All records relating to drug tests as declared confidential by IN ST 5-14-3-4(a)(9);

- Records of grand jury proceedings as declared confidential by IN ST 35-34-2-4;

- Records of juvenile proceedings as declared confidential by IN ST 31-39-1-2, except those specifically open under statute;

- All paternity records created after July 1, 1941 as declared confidential by IN ST 31-14-11-15, IN ST 31-19-5-23, IN ST 31-39-1-1 and IN ST 31-39-1-2 [Editor's note: IN ST 31-14-11-15 was repealed effective May 9, 2013];

- All pre-sentence reports as declared confidential by IN ST 35-38-1-13;

- Written petitions to permit marriages without consent and orders directing the Clerk of Court to issue a marriage license to underage persons, as declared confidential by IN ST 31-11-1-6;

- Only those arrest warrants, search warrants, indictments and informations ordered confidential by the trial judge, prior to return of duly executed service as declared confidential by IN ST 5-14-3-4(b)(1);

- All medical, mental health, or tax records unless determined by law or regulation of any governmental custodian not to be confidential, released by the subject of such records, or declared by a court of competent jurisdiction to be essential to the resolution of litigation as declared confidential by IN ST 16-39-3-10, IN ST 6-4.1-5-10, IN ST 6-4.1-12-12, and IN ST 6-8.1-7-1;

- Personal information relating to jurors or prospective jurors, other than for the use of the parties and counsel, pursuant to IN ST JURY Rule 10;

- Information relating to protection from abuse orders, no-contact orders and workplace violence restraining orders as declared confidential by IN ST 5-2-9-6, et seq.;

- Mediation proceedings pursuant to IN ST ADR Rule 2.11, Mini-Trial proceedings pursuant to IN ST ADR Rule 4.4(C), and Summary Jury Trials pursuant to IN ST ADR Rule 5.6;

- Information in probation files pursuant to the Probation Standards promulgated by the Judicial Conference of Indiana pursuant to IN ST 11-13-1-8(b);

- Information deemed confidential pursuant to the Rules for Court Administered Alcohol and Drug Programs promulgated by the Judicial Conference of Indiana pursuant to IN ST 12-23-14-13;

- Information deemed confidential pursuant to the Problem-Solving Court Rules promulgated by the Judicial Conference of Indiana pursuant to IN ST 33-23-16-16;

- All records of the Department of workforce Development as declared confidential by IN ST 22-4-19-6;

- Information regarding interception of electronic communications that is sealed or deemed confidential as set forth in IN ST 35-33.5-2-1, et seq.

iii. Information excluded from public access by specific court order;

iv. Complete Social Security Numbers of living persons;

v. With the exception of names, information such as addresses, phone numbers, and dates of birth which explicitly identifies:

- Natural persons who are witnesses or victims (not including defendants) in criminal, domestic violence, stalking, sexual assault, juvenile, or civil protection order proceedings, provided that juveniles who are victims of sex crimes shall be identified by initials only;

- Places of residence of judicial officers, clerks and other employees of courts and clerks of court, unless the person or persons about whom the information pertains waives confidentiality;

vi. Complete account numbers of specific assets, loans, bank accounts, credit cards, and personal identification numbers (PINs);

vii. All orders of expungement entered in criminal or juvenile proceedings, orders to restrict access to criminal history information pursuant to IN ST 35-38-5-5.5 or IN ST 35-38-8-5 and records excluded from public access by such orders, and information related to infractions that is excluded from public access pursuant to IN ST 34-28-5-15 or IN ST 34-28-5-16 [Editor's note: IN ST 35-38-5-5.5, IN ST 35-38-8-5 and IN ST 34-28-5-16 were repealed effective July 1, 2013; for information on orders restricting access to criminal history, refer to IN ST 35-38-9-1, et seq.];

viii. All personal notes and e-mail, and deliberative material, of judges, jurors, court staff and judicial agencies, and information recorded in personal data assistants (PDA's) or organizers and personal calendars. IN ST ADMIN Rule 9(G)(1).

F. Filing and Service Requirements

1. *Filing requirements.* Except as otherwise provided in IN ST TRIAL P Rule 5(E)(2), all pleadings and

papers subsequent to the complaint which are required to be served upon a party shall be filed with the Court either before service or within a reasonable period of time thereafter. IN ST TRIAL P Rule 5(E)(1).

a. *Filing with the court defined.* The filing of pleadings, motions, and other papers with the court as required by the Indiana Rules of Trial Procedure shall be made by one of the following methods:

    i. Delivery to the clerk of the court;

    ii. Sending by electronic transmission under the procedure adopted pursuant to IN ST ADMIN Rule 12;

    iii. Mailing to the clerk by registered, certified or express mail return receipt requested;

    iv. Depositing with any third-party commercial carrier for delivery to the clerk within three (3) calendar days, cost prepaid, properly addressed;

    v. If the court so permits, filing with the judge, in which event the judge shall note thereon the filing date and forthwith transmit them to the office of the clerk; or

    vi. Electronic filing, as approved by the Division of State Court Administration pursuant to IN ST ADMIN Rule 16. IN ST TRIAL P Rule 5(F).

    vii. Filing by registered or certified mail and by third-party commercial carrier shall be complete upon mailing or deposit. IN ST TRIAL P Rule 5(F).

    viii. All pleadings shall be filed with the Clerk, not directly with the Court, unless otherwise required by the Indiana Rules of Court. The entry of appearances and the filing of pleadings or other matters not requiring immediate Court action shall be filed with the Clerk and not in open Court. A Judge may permit papers to be filed in chambers, in which event he or she shall note thereon the filing date and transmit the papers to the Clerk. IN ST ST JOSEPH CIV Rule 201(201.2).

b. *Facsimile filing.* Unless otherwise authorized by IN ST ST JOSEPH ELECTRONIC Rule 701, electronic filing of pleadings by computerized or facsimile transmission is not permitted. IN ST ST JOSEPH CIV Rule 201(201.2).

c. *Additional copies.* In cases in which a party or counsel supplies the proposed order or decree, a sufficient number shall be prepared and filed as to provide the Clerk to retain two (2) copies, which shall be filed in the flat file and the record of judgments and orders. Should the party or counsel desire additional copies, a sufficient number of copies should be filed to effectuate that purpose. IN ST ST JOSEPH CIV Rule 201(201.6).

d. *Proof of filing.* Any party filing any paper by any method other than personal delivery to the clerk shall retain proof of filing. IN ST TRIAL P Rule 5(F).

2. *Service requirements.* Unless otherwise provided by the Indiana Rules of Trial Procedure or an order of the court, each party and special judge, if any, shall be served with: (1) every order required by its terms to be served; (2) every pleading subsequent to the original complaint; (3) every written motion except one which may be heard ex parte; (4) every brief submitted to the trial court; (5) every paper relating to discovery required to be served upon a party; and (6) every written notice, appearance, demand, offer of judgment, designation of record on appeal, or similar paper. IN ST TRIAL P Rule 5(A).

a. *Service generally.* Every motion, petition, notice, or other pleading required to be served by IN ST TRIAL P Rule 5 shall be served on all counsel of record or unrepresented parties either before it is filed or on the day it is filed with the Court, and the date of filing shall be indicated on the Certificate of Service. IN ST ST JOSEPH CIV Rule 201(201.5.1).

    i. *Copy.* A copy of the Clerk's CCS entry form of the filing shall also be served on all counsel of record or unrepresented parties whenever it contains an appearance of counsel or contains a date for Court hearing on the matter. IN ST ST JOSEPH CIV Rule 201(201.5.1).

b. *Methods of service*

    i. *Personal service.* Whenever a party is represented by an attorney of record, service shall be made upon such attorney unless service upon the party himself is ordered by the court. Service upon the attorney or party shall be made by delivering or mailing a copy of the papers to the last known address or where an attorney or party has consented to service by fax or e-mail, as

provided in IN ST TRIAL P Rule 3.1(A)(4), by faxing or e-mailing a copy of the documents to the fax number or e-mail address set out in the appearance form or correction as required by IN ST TRIAL P Rule 3.1(E). IN ST TRIAL P Rule 5(B). Delivery of a copy within IN ST TRIAL P Rule 5 means:

- Offering or tendering it to the attorney or party and stating the nature of the papers being served. Refusal to accept an offered or tendered document is a waiver of any objection to the sufficiency or adequacy of service of that document;

- Leaving it at his office with a clerk or other person in charge thereof, or if there is no one in charge, leaving it in a conspicuous place therein; or

- If the office is closed, by leaving it at his dwelling house or usual place of abode with some person of suitable age and discretion then residing therein; or,

- Leaving it at some other suitable place, selected by the attorney upon whom service is being made, pursuant to duly promulgated local rule. IN ST TRIAL P Rule 5(B)(1).

ii. *Service by the clerk.* Whenever the Clerk is required by rule or statute to give notice, the party or parties requesting such notice shall furnish the Clerk with sufficient copies of the notice to be given, along with stamped, addressed envelopes with the names and the addresses of the parties or their counsel to whom such notice is to be given. IN ST ST JOSEPH CIV Rule 201(201.5.4).

iii. *Service on the court.* Service on a Judge may be made by delivering a copy to the Judge's secretary or mailing a copy to the Judge at his or her chambers. Service on a Judge may not be accomplished by facsimile transmission; however, a courtesy copy may be sent to the Judge's chambers by electronic mail or facsimile transmission contemporaneously with service by mail or otherwise. IN ST ST JOSEPH CIV Rule 201(201.5.5).

iv. *Service by mail.* If service is made by mail, the papers shall be deposited in the United States mail addressed to the person on whom they are being served, with postage prepaid. Service shall be deemed complete upon mailing. Proof of service of all papers permitted to be mailed may be made by written acknowledgment of service, by affidavit of the person who mailed the papers, or by certificate of an attorney. It shall be the duty of attorneys when entering their appearance in a cause or when filing pleadings or papers therein, to have noted in the Chronological Case Summary or said pleadings or papers so filed the address and telephone number of their office. Service by delivery or by mail at such address shall be deemed sufficient and complete. IN ST TRIAL P Rule 5(B)(2).

v. *Service by fax or e-mail.* A party who has consented to service by fax or e-mail may be served as follows:

- Service by e-mail shall be made by attaching the document being served in .pdf format. Discovery documents must also be served in accordance with IN ST TRIAL P Rule 26(A). IN ST TRIAL P Rule 5(B)(3)(a).

- Service by fax shall be deemed complete upon generation of a transmission record indicating the successful transmission of the entire document, except as provided in IN ST TRIAL P Rule 5(B)(3)(d). IN ST TRIAL P Rule 5(B)(3)(b).

- Service by e-mail shall be deemed complete upon transmission, except as provided in IN ST TRIAL P Rule 5(B)(3)(d). IN ST TRIAL P Rule 5(B)(3)(c).

- Service by fax or e-mail that occurs on a Saturday, Sunday, legal holiday, or day the court or agency in which the matter is pending is closed or after 5:00 PM local time of the recipient shall be deemed complete the next day that is not a Saturday, Sunday, legal holiday, or day that the court or agency in which the matter is pending is not closed. IN ST TRIAL P Rule 5(B)(3)(d).

c. *Serving numerous defendants.* In any action in which there are unusually large numbers of defendants, the court, upon motion or of its own initiative, may order:

    i. That service of the pleadings of the defendants and replies thereto need not be made as between the defendants;

- That any cross-claim, counterclaim, or matter constituting an avoidance or affirmative defense contained therein shall be deemed to be denied or avoided by all other parties; and
- That the filing of any such pleading and service thereof upon the plaintiff constitutes due notice of it to the parties. IN ST TRIAL P Rule 5(D).

    ii. A copy of every such order shall be served upon the parties in such manner and form as the court directs. IN ST TRIAL P Rule 5(D).

d. *Service on parties in default for failure to appear.* No service need be made on parties in default for failure to appear, except that pleadings asserting new or additional claims for relief against them shall be served upon them in the manner provided by service of summons in IN ST TRIAL P Rule 4. IN ST TRIAL P Rule 5(A).

e. *Distribution.* Counsel or an unrepresented party submitting a motion, petition, notice, pleading or proposed order shall indicate the method of distribution desired on the Clerk's CCS entry form. The Clerk will not return or distribute copies of motions, petitions, pleadings, notices or proposed orders, other than those originated by the Court, by mail unless the Clerk is provided with stamped, addressed envelopes. IN ST ST JOSEPH CIV Rule 201(201.5.3).

f. *Mailbox.* As a matter of convenience to attorneys, each court provides a mailbox for the distribution filings and orders generated by the Court, and it is the responsibility of each attorney to periodically check these mailboxes for service and distribution of court-generated filings and orders. IN ST ST JOSEPH CIV Rule 201(201.5.3).

3. *Service requirements if adding a new party by amendment.* Refer to the Indiana KeyRules Complaint document for information on serving a new party added by amendment.

G. Hearings

1. The Indiana rules do not contemplate a hearing regarding the filing and service of an amended complaint.

H. Forms

1. Official Amended Complaint Forms for Indiana

a. Affidavit of debt. IN ST TRIAL P App. A-2.

2. Amended Complaint Forms for Indiana

a. Motion to file amended complaint. 5 INPRAC § 3:5.1.

b. Motion to file amended complaint; Another form. 5 INPRAC § 3:5.2.

c. Objections to motion to file amended complaint. 5 INPRAC § 3:5.3.

d. Motion to amend pleading to conform to evidence. 5 INPRAC § 3:5.4.

e. Amendment by stipulation. 10 INPRAC § 46.11.

f. Caption; Generally. 5 INPRAC § 3:1.1.

g. Caption; Multiple parties. 5 INPRAC § 3:1.2.

h. Single count. 5 INPRAC § 3:1.3.

i. Multiple counts; Single defendant. 5 INPRAC § 3:1.4.

j. Multiple counts; Multiple defendants. 5 INPRAC § 3:1.5.

k. Signature; By party. 5 INPRAC § 3:1.6.

l. Signature; By attorney. 5 INPRAC § 3:1.7.

m. Verification. 5 INPRAC § 3:1.8.

n. Individual defendant. 5 INPRAC § 3:2.1.

o.   Resident agent of corporation. 5 INPRAC § 3:2.2.

p.   Attorney general. 5 INPRAC § 3:2.3.

q.   City attorney. 5 INPRAC § 3:2.4.

r.   Certificate; Personal service. 5 INPRAC § 3:2.5.

s.   Certificate; First class mail. 5 INPRAC § 3:2.6.

t.   Certificate; Registered mail. 5 INPRAC § 3:2.7.

u.   Certificate; Dwelling house. 5 INPRAC § 3:2.8.

v.   Clerk's certificate of mailing. 5 INPRAC § 3:2.9.

w.   Clerk's certificate of mailing; Acceptance by defendant. 5 INPRAC § 3:2.10.

x.   Clerk's return on service of summons by mail; Not accepted by defendant. 5 INPRAC § 3:2.11.

y.   Sheriff's return; Service of summons. 5 INPRAC § 3:2.12.

z.   Motion to appoint person to serve process. 5 INPRAC § 3:2.13.

I. **Checklist**

(I)   ❑ Matters to be considered by the party filing the amended complaint

(a)   ❑ Required documents if amending as matter of course

(1)   ❑ Amended complaint

(2)   ❑ Chronological Case Summary (CCS) entry form

(3)   ❑ Certificate of service

(b)   ❑ Supplemental documents

(1)   ❑ Proof of written instrument

(2)   ❑ Notice of intent to use foreign law

(3)   ❑ Facsimile cover sheet

(c)   ❑ Timing

(1)   ❑ A party may amend his pleading once as a matter of course at any time before a responsive pleading is served or, if the pleading is one to which no responsive pleading is permitted, and the action has not been placed upon the trial calendar, he may so amend it at any time within thirty (30) days after it is served

(2)   ❑ Otherwise a party may amend his pleading only by leave of court or by written consent of the adverse party; and leave shall be given when justice so requires

Pleadings
Answer

Document Last Updated October 2013

A. **Applicable Rules**

1.   *State rules*

a.   Appearance. IN ST TRIAL P Rule 3.1.

b.   Process. IN ST TRIAL P Rule 4.

c.   Service. IN ST TRIAL P Rule 4.15; IN ST TRIAL P Rule 4.16; IN ST TRIAL P Rule 5.

d.   Time. IN ST TRIAL P Rule 6.

e.   Pleadings. IN ST TRIAL P Rule 7; IN ST TRIAL P Rule 8; IN ST TRIAL P Rule 9; IN ST TRIAL P Rule 9.1; IN ST TRIAL P Rule 9.2; IN ST TRIAL P Rule 10.

f.   Signing and verification of pleadings. IN ST TRIAL P Rule 11.

g. Defenses and objections; When and how presented; By pleading or motion; Motion for judgment on the pleadings. IN ST TRIAL P Rule 12.

h. Counterclaim and cross-claim. IN ST TRIAL P Rule 13.

i. Third-party practice. IN ST TRIAL P Rule 14.

j. Amended and supplemental pleadings. IN ST TRIAL P Rule 15.

k. Parties plaintiff and defendant; Capacity. IN ST TRIAL P Rule 17.

l. Joinder. IN ST TRIAL P Rule 19; IN ST TRIAL P Rule 20.

m. Jury trial of right. IN ST TRIAL P Rule 38.

n. Consolidation; Separate trials. IN ST TRIAL P Rule 42.

o. Evidence. IN ST TRIAL P Rule 43.

p. Determination of foreign law. IN ST TRIAL P Rule 44.1.

q. Judgment. IN ST TRIAL P Rule 50; IN ST TRIAL P Rule 52; IN ST TRIAL P Rule 54; IN ST TRIAL P Rule 56; IN ST TRIAL P Rule 59; IN ST TRIAL P Rule 60.

r. Venue requirements. IN ST TRIAL P Rule 75.

s. Alternative dispute resolution. IN ST ADR Rule 1.1; IN ST ADR Rule 1.6; IN ST ADR Rule 8.8.

t. Uniform case numbering system. IN ST ADMIN Rule 8.

u. Paper size. IN ST ADMIN Rule 11.

v. Facsimile and electronic transmission. IN ST ADMIN Rule 9; IN ST ADMIN Rule 12; IN ST ADMIN Rule 16.

w. Sealing of certain records by court; Hearing; Notice. IN ST 5-14-3-5.5.

x. Sixtieth judicial circuit. IN ST 33-33-71-2.

y. Privacy and confidentiality. IN ST 5-2-9-6; IN ST 5-14-3-4; IN ST 6-4.1-5-10; IN ST 6-4.1-12-12; IN ST 6-8.1-7-1; IN ST 11-13-1-8; IN ST 12-23-14-13; IN ST 16-39-3-10; IN ST 16-41-8-1; IN ST 22-4-19-6; IN ST 31-11-1-6; IN ST 31-19-5-23; IN ST 31-19-13-2; IN ST 31-19-19-1; IN ST 31-33-18-1; IN ST 31-39-1-1; IN ST 31-39-1-2; IN ST 33-23-16-16; IN ST 35-34-2-4; IN ST 35-38-1-13; IN ST 35-38-9-1; IN ST ADR Rule 2.11; IN ST ADR Rule 4.4; IN ST ADR Rule 5.6; IN ST JURY Rule 10.

2. *Local rules*

a. Filing, pleading, and motions. IN ST ST JOSEPH CIV Rule 201.

b. Uniform court and case number designation. IN ST ST JOSEPH CIV Rule 202.

c. Appearance and withdrawal of appearance of counsel. IN ST ST JOSEPH CIV Rule 204.

d. Pre-trial procedures. IN ST ST JOSEPH CIV Rule 209.

e. Electronic filing of cases in St. Joseph County. IN ST ST JOSEPH ELECTRONIC Rule 701.

B. Timing

1. *Time to serve answer.* A responsive pleading required under the Indiana Rules of Trial Procedure, shall be served within twenty (20) days after service of the prior pleading. IN ST TRIAL P Rule 6(C).

a. *Effect of IN ST TRIAL P Rule 12 motions.* The service of a motion permitted under IN ST TRIAL P Rule 12 alters the time for service of responsive pleadings as follows, unless a different time is fixed by the court:

i. If the court does not grant the motion, the responsive pleading shall be served in ten (10) days after notice of the court's action;

ii. If the court grants the motion and the corrective action is allowed to be taken, it shall be taken within ten (10) days, and the responsive pleading shall be served within ten (10) days thereafter. IN ST TRIAL P Rule 6(C).

2. *Responding to amended complaint.* A party shall plead in response to an amended pleading within the

time remaining for response to the original pleading or within twenty (20) days after service of the amended pleading, whichever period may be the longer, unless the court otherwise orders. IN ST TRIAL P Rule 15(A).

3. *Filing.* All pleadings and papers subsequent to the complaint which are required to be served upon a party shall be filed with the Court either before service or within a reasonable period of time thereafter. IN ST TRIAL P Rule 5(E)(1).

4. *Filing of third-party complaint.* The third-party plaintiff must file the third-party complaint with his original answer or by leave of court thereafter with good cause shown. IN ST TRIAL P Rule 14(A).

5. *Computation of time*

   a. *Generally; Days excluded.* In computing any period of time prescribed or allowed by the Indiana Rules of Trial Procedure, by order of the court, or by any applicable statute, the day of the act, event, or default from which the designated period of time begins to run shall not be included. The last day of the period so computed is to be included unless it is:

      i. A Saturday,

      ii. A Sunday,

      iii. A legal holiday as defined by state statute, or

      iv. A day the office in which the act is to be done is closed during regular business hours. IN ST TRIAL P Rule 6(A).

   b. *Short periods.* In any event, the period runs until the end of the next day that is not a Saturday, a Sunday, a legal holiday, or a day on which the office is closed. When the period of time allowed is less than seven (7) days, intermediate Saturdays, Sundays, legal holidays, and days on which the office is closed shall be excluded from the computations. IN ST TRIAL P Rule 6(A).

   c. *Additional time after service by United States mail.* Whenever a party has the right or is required to do some act or take some proceedings within a prescribed period after the service of a notice or other paper upon him and the notice or paper is served upon him by United States mail, three (3) days shall be added to the prescribed period. IN ST TRIAL P Rule 6(E).

   d. *Enlargement of time.* When an act is required or allowed to be done at or within a specific time by the Indiana Rules of Trial Procedure, the court may at any time for cause shown:

      i. Order the period enlarged, with or without motion or notice, if request therefor is made before the expiration of the period originally prescribed or extended by a previous order; or

      ii. Upon motion made after the expiration of the specific period, permit the act to be done where the failure to act was the result of excusable neglect; but, the court may not extend the time for taking any action for judgment on the evidence under IN ST TRIAL P Rule 50(A), amendment of findings and judgment under IN ST TRIAL P Rule 52(B), to correct errors under IN ST TRIAL P Rule 59(C), statement in opposition to motion to correct error under IN ST TRIAL P Rule 59(E), or to obtain relief from final judgment under IN ST TRIAL P Rule 60(B), except to the extent and under the conditions stated in those rules. IN ST TRIAL P Rule 6(B).

      iii. An initial written motion for enlargement of time pursuant to IN ST TRIAL P Rule 6(B)(1) to answer a claim shall be routinely granted for an additional thirty (30) days from the original due date or other period the assigned Judge deems reasonable by written order of the Court. The motion must be filed on or before the original due date or IN ST ST JOSEPH CIV Rule 201 shall be inapplicable. IN ST ST JOSEPH CIV Rule 201(201.9.5).

         • Any motion for enlargement of time shall state the date when such response is due and the date to which time is requested to be enlarged. IN ST ST JOSEPH CIV Rule 201(201.9.5).

         • All subsequent motions for enlargement of time shall be so designated and will only be granted for good cause shown or in the interest of justice. IN ST ST JOSEPH CIV Rule 201(201.9.5).

C. General Requirements

1. *Pleading, generally*

   a. *Pleadings to be concise.* Each averment of a pleading shall be simple, concise, and direct. No technical forms of pleading or motions are required. All fictions in pleading are abolished. IN ST TRIAL P Rule 8(E)(1).

b. *Pleading in the alternative.* A pleading may set forth two (2) or more statements of a claim or defense alternatively or hypothetically, either in one (1) count or defense or in separate counts or defenses. When two (2) or more statements are made in the alternative and one (1) of them if made independently would be sufficient, the pleading is not made insufficient by the insufficiency of one or more of the alternative statements. A pleading may also state as many separate claims or defenses as the pleader has regardless of consistency and whether based on legal or equitable grounds. All statements shall be made subject to the obligations set forth in IN ST TRIAL P Rule 11. IN ST TRIAL P Rule 8(E)(2).

c. *Motions and pleadings, joint and several.* All motions and pleadings of any kind addressed to two (2) or more paragraphs of any pleading, or filed by two (2) or more parties, shall be taken and construed as joint, separate, and several motions or pleadings to each of such paragraphs and by and against each of such parties. All motions or pleadings containing two (2) or more subject-matters shall be taken and construed as separate and several as to each subject-matter. All objections to rulings made by two (2) or more parties shall be taken and construed as the joint, separate, and several objections of each of such parties. IN ST TRIAL P Rule 8(E)(3).

   i. A complaint filed by or against two (2) or more plaintiffs shall be taken and construed as joint, separate, and several as to each of said plaintiffs. IN ST TRIAL P Rule 8(E).

d. *Construction of pleadings.* All pleadings shall be so construed as to do substantial justice, lead to disposition on the merits, and avoid litigation of procedural points. IN ST TRIAL P Rule 8(F).

2. *Contents of the answer*

a. *Defenses which may be raised by answer or motion.* Every defense, in law or fact, to a claim for relief in any pleading, whether a claim, counterclaim, cross-claim, or third-party claim, shall be asserted in the responsive pleading thereto if one is required; except that at the option of the pleader, the following defenses may be made by motion:

   i. Lack of jurisdiction over the subject matter;

   ii. Lack of jurisdiction over the person;

   iii. Incorrect venue under IN ST TRIAL P Rule 75, or any statutory provision. The disposition of this motion shall be consistent with IN ST TRIAL P Rule 75;

   iv. Insufficiency of process;

   v. Insufficiency of service of process;

   vi. Failure to state a claim upon which relief can be granted, which shall include failure to name the real party in interest under IN ST TRIAL P Rule 17;

   vii. Failure to join a party needed for just adjudication under IN ST TRIAL P Rule 19;

   viii. The same action pending in another state court of this state. IN ST TRIAL P Rule 12(B).

   ix. A motion making any of these defenses shall be made before pleading if a further pleading is permitted or within twenty (20) days after service of the prior pleading if none is required. If a pleading sets forth a claim for relief to which the adverse party is not required to serve a responsive pleading, any of the defenses in section IN ST TRIAL P Rule 12(B)(2), IN ST TRIAL P Rule 12(B)(3), IN ST TRIAL P Rule 12(B)(4), IN ST TRIAL P Rule 12(B)(5) or IN ST TRIAL P Rule 12(B)(8) is waived to the extent constitutionally permissible unless made in a motion within twenty (20) days after service of the prior pleading. No defense or objection is waived by being joined with one (1) or more other defenses or objections in a responsive pleading or motion. IN ST TRIAL P Rule 12(B).

b. *Waiver or preservation of certain defenses*

   i. A defense of lack of jurisdiction over the person, improper venue, insufficiency of process, insufficiency of service of process, or the same action pending in another state court of this state is waived to the extent constitutionally permissible:

     • If omitted from a motion in the circumstances described in IN ST TRIAL P Rule 12(G),

- If it is neither made by motion under IN ST TRIAL P Rule 12 nor included in a responsive pleading or an amendment thereof permitted by IN ST TRIAL P Rule 15(A) to be made as a matter of course. IN ST TRIAL P Rule 12(H)(1).

ii. A defense of failure to state a claim upon which relief can be granted, a defense of failure to join an indispensable party under IN ST TRIAL P Rule 19(B), and an objection of failure to state a legal defense to a claim may be made in any pleading permitted or ordered under IN ST TRIAL P Rule 7(A) or by motion for judgment on the pleadings, or at the trial on the merits. IN ST TRIAL P Rule 12(H)(2).

c. *Defenses; Form of denials*

i. A responsive pleading shall state in short and plain terms the pleader's defenses to each claim asserted and shall admit or controvert the averments set forth in the preceding pleading. If in good faith the pleader intends to deny all the averments in the preceding pleading, he may do so by general denial subject to the provisions of IN ST TRIAL P Rule 11. If he does not intend a general denial, he may:

- Specifically deny designated averments or paragraphs; or
- Generally deny all averments except such designated averments and paragraphs as he expressly admits. IN ST TRIAL P Rule 8(B).

ii. If he lacks knowledge or information sufficient to form a belief as to the truth of an averment, he shall so state and his statement shall be considered a denial. If in good faith a pleader intends to deny only a part or a qualification of an averment, he shall specify so much of it as is true and material and deny the remainder. All denials shall fairly meet the substance of the averments denied. IN ST TRIAL P Rule 8 shall have no application to uncontested actions for divorce, or to answers required to be filed by clerks or guardians ad litem. IN ST TRIAL P Rule 8(B).

d. *Affirmative defenses.* A responsive pleading shall set forth affirmatively and carry the burden of proving: accord and satisfaction, arbitration and award, discharge in bankruptcy, duress, estoppel, failure of consideration, fraud, illegality, injury by fellow servant, laches, license, payment, release, res judicata, statute of frauds, statute of limitations, waiver, lack of jurisdiction over the subject-matter, lack of jurisdiction over the person, improper venue, insufficiency of process or service of process, the same action pending in another state court of this state, and any other matter constituting an avoidance, matter of abatement, or affirmative defense. A party required to affirmatively plead any matters, including matters formerly required to be pleaded affirmatively by reply, shall have the burden of proving such matters. The burden of proof imposed by this or any other provision of the Indiana Rules of Trial Procedure is subject to the rules of evidence or any statute fixing a different rule. If the pleading mistakenly designates a defense as a counterclaim or a counterclaim as a defense, the court shall treat the pleading as if there had been a proper designation. IN ST TRIAL P Rule 8(C).

i. An affirmative defense, generally, must be affirmatively stated by the party who seeks its benefit. 1A INPRAC R 8(8.5); Rice v. Grant County Bd. of Com'rs, 472 N.E.2d 213 (Ind.Ct.App. 1984). If that party does not raise the affirmative defense, then it is waived. 1A INPRAC R 8(8.5); Piskorowski v. Shell Oil Co., 403 N.E.2d 838, 847 (Ind.Ct.App. 1980).

ii. It is clear that the list of affirmative defenses found in IN ST TRIAL P Rule 8 is not exhaustive. The question comes: when is a defense to be treated as an affirmative defense, with all of the attending consequences? 1A INPRAC R 8(8.5). The "determination of whether a defense is affirmative depends on whether it controverts an element of the plaintiff's prima facie case or raises matter outside the scope of the prima facie case." 1A INPRAC R 8(8.5); Molargik v. West Enterprises, Inc., 605 N.E.2d 1197, 1198 (Ind.Ct.App. 1993).

e. *Defense of contributory negligence or assumed risk.* In all claims alleging negligence, the burden of pleading and proving contributory negligence, assumption of risk, or incurred risk shall be upon the defendant who may plead such by denial of the allegation. IN ST TRIAL P Rule 9.1(A).

f. *Res ipsa loquitur.* Res ipsa loquitur or a similar doctrine may be pleaded by alleging generally that the facts connected with the action are unknown to the pleader and are within the knowledge of the opposing party. IN ST TRIAL P Rule 9.1(B).

g. *Consideration.* When an action or defense is founded upon a written contract or release, lack of consideration for the promise or release is an affirmative defense, and the party asserting lack of it carries the burden of proof. IN ST TRIAL P Rule 9.1(C).

h. *Bona fide purchaser.* When the rights of a person depend upon his status as a bona fide purchaser for value or upon similar requirements, such status must be pleaded and proved by the person asserting it, but it may be pleaded in general terms. Once it is established that the person has given any required value, unless such value is commercially unreasonable, and that he has met any requirements of recordation, filing, possession, or perfection, the trier of fact must find that such value was given or such perfection was made in accordance with any requirements of good faith, lack of knowledge, or lack of notice unless and until evidence is introduced which would support a finding of its non-existence. IN ST TRIAL P Rule 9.1(D).

i. *Presumption; Matters of judicial notice.* Neither presumptions of law nor matters of which judicial notice may be taken need be stated in a pleading. IN ST TRIAL P Rule 9.1(E).

j. *Property distrained; Sufficient answer.* In an action to recover the possession of property distrained while doing damage, an answer that the defendant, or person by whose command he acted, was lawfully possessed of the real property upon which the distress was made, and that the property distrained was at the time doing damage thereon, shall be good without setting forth the title of such real property. IN ST TRIAL P Rule 9.1(F).

k. *Effect of failure to deny.* Averments in a pleading to which a responsive pleading is required, except those pertaining to amount of damages, are admitted when not denied in the responsive pleading. Averments in a pleading to which no responsive pleading is required or permitted shall be taken as denied or avoided. IN ST TRIAL P Rule 8(D).

l. *Effect of admission.* When a rhetorical paragraph or allegation is admitted, the effect in Indiana is to remove it from trial. Such an admission is a "judicial admission", and the claim or issue which is admitted cannot be denied later by the trier of the facts. Further, this admitted fact does not require evidence to "prove it"; it is established. It becomes, in short, controlling and indisputable in the litigation, unless the trial court permits an amendment to the pleading which might remove the controlling effect of the admission, and permit it to become another fact or item of evidence in the case. 1A INPRAC R 8(8.4); Aylesworth v. McKesson, 421 N.E.2d 422 (Ind.Ct.App. 1981).

3. *Pleading special matters*

a. *Capacity.* It is not necessary to aver the capacity of a party to sue or be sued, the authority of a party to sue or be sued in a representative capacity, or the legal existence of an organization that is made a party. The burden of proving lack of such capacity, authority, or legal existence shall be upon the person asserting lack of it, and shall be pleaded as an affirmative defense. IN ST TRIAL P Rule 9(A).

b. *Fraud, mistake, condition of the mind.* In all averments of fraud or mistake, the circumstances constituting fraud or mistake shall be specifically averred. Malice, intent, knowledge, and other conditions of mind may be averred generally. IN ST TRIAL P Rule 9(B).

c. *Conditions precedent.* In pleading the performance or occurrence of promissory or non-promissory conditions precedent, it is sufficient to aver generally that all conditions precedent have been performed, have occurred, or have been excused. A denial of performance or occurrence shall be made specifically and with particularity, and a denial of excuse generally. IN ST TRIAL P Rule 9(C).

d. *Official document or act.* In pleading an official document or official act it is sufficient to aver that the document was issued or the act done in compliance with law. IN ST TRIAL P Rule 9(D).

e. *Judgment.* In pleading a judgment or decision of a domestic or foreign court, judicial or quasi-judicial tribunal, or of a board or officer, it is sufficient to aver the judgment or decision without setting forth matter showing jurisdiction to render it. IN ST TRIAL P Rule 9(E).

f. *Time and place.* For the purpose of testing the sufficiency of a pleading, averments of time and place are material and shall be considered like all other averments of material matter. However, time and place need be stated only with such specificity as will enable the opposing party to prepare his defense. IN ST TRIAL P Rule 9(F).

g. *Special damages; Damages where no answer.* When items of special damage are claimed, they shall be specifically stated. The relief granted to the plaintiff, if there be no answer, cannot exceed the relief demanded in his complaint; but, in any other case, the court may grant him any relief consistent with the facts or matters pleaded. IN ST TRIAL P Rule 9(G).

4. *Counterclaim and cross-claim*

 a. *Compulsory counterclaims.* A pleading shall state as a counterclaim any claim which at the time of serving the pleading the pleader has against any opposing party, if it arises out of the transaction or occurrence that is the subject-matter of the opposing party's claim and does not require for its adjudication the presence of third parties of whom the court cannot acquire jurisdiction. But the pleader need not state the claim if:

  i. At the time the action was commenced the claim was the subject of another pending action; or

  ii. The opposing party brought suit upon his claim by attachment or other process by which the court did not acquire jurisdiction to render a personal judgment on that claim, and the pleader is not stating any counterclaim under IN ST TRIAL P Rule 13. IN ST TRIAL P Rule 13(A).

 b. *Permissive counterclaims.* A pleading may state as a counterclaim any claim against an opposing party not arising out of the transaction or occurrence that is the subject-matter of the opposing party's claim. IN ST TRIAL P Rule 13(B).

 c. *Counterclaim exceeding opposing claim.* A counterclaim may or may not diminish or defeat the recovery sought by the opposing party. It may claim relief exceeding in amount or different in kind from that sought in the pleading of the opposing party. IN ST TRIAL P Rule 13(C).

 d. *Counterclaim against state.* IN ST TRIAL P Rule 13 shall not be construed to enlarge any right to assert a claim against the state. IN ST TRIAL P Rule 13(D).

 e. *Counterclaim maturing or acquired after pleading.* A claim which either matured or was acquired by the pleader after serving his pleading may, with the permission of the court, be presented as a counterclaim by supplemental pleading. A counterclaim or cross-claim which is not due may be asserted against a party who is insolvent or the representative of a party who has been subjected to insolvency proceedings, if recovery thereon will be impaired because of such party's insolvency. IN ST TRIAL P Rule 13(E).

 f. *Omitted counterclaim.* When a pleader fails to set up a counterclaim through oversight, inadvertence, or excusable neglect, or when justice requires, he may by leave of court set up the counterclaim by amendment. IN ST TRIAL P Rule 13(F).

 g. *Cross-claim against co-party.* A pleading may state as a cross-claim any claim by one party against a co-party. IN ST TRIAL P Rule 13(G).

 h. *Joinder of additional parties.* Persons other than those made parties to the original action may be made parties to a counterclaim or cross-claim in accordance with the provisions of IN ST TRIAL P Rule 14, IN ST TRIAL P Rule 19 and IN ST TRIAL P Rule 20. IN ST TRIAL P Rule 13(H).

 i. *Separate trials; Separate judgments*

  i. If the court orders separate trials as provided in IN ST TRIAL P Rule 42(B), judgment on a counterclaim or cross-claim may be rendered in accordance with the terms of IN ST TRIAL P Rule 54(B) when the court has jurisdiction so to do, even if the claims of the opposing party have been dismissed or otherwise disposed of. In determining whether or not separate trial of a cross-claim shall be ordered, the court shall consider whether the cross-claim:

   • Arises out of the transaction or occurrence or series of transactions or occurrences that is the subject-matter either of the original action or of a counterclaim therein;

   • Relates to any property or contract that is the subject-matter of the original action; or

   • Claims that the person against whom it is asserted is liable to the cross-claimant for all or part of plaintiff's claim against him. IN ST TRIAL P Rule 13(I).

  ii. In addition, the court may consider any other relevant factors. IN ST TRIAL P Rule 13(I).

 j. *Effect of statute of limitations and other discharges at law.* The statute of limitations, a nonclaim statute or other discharge at law shall not bar a claim asserted as a counterclaim to the extent that:

  i. It diminishes or defeats the opposing party's claim if it arises out of the transaction or occurrence that is the subject-matter of the opposing party's claim, or if it could have been asserted as a counterclaim to the opposing party's claim before it (the counterclaim) was barred; or

    ii.   It or the opposing party's claim relates to payment of or security for the other. IN ST TRIAL P Rule 13(J).

k.   *Counterclaim by and against transferees and successors.* A counterclaim may be asserted by or against the transferee or successor of a claim subject to the following provisions:

    i.   A successor who is a guardian, representative of a decedent's estate, receiver or assignee for the benefit of creditors, trustee or the like may interpose a claim to which he succeeds against claims or proceedings brought in or outside the court of administration. A claim owing by his predecessor may be interposed against any claim brought by such successor in or outside the court of administration without the necessity of filing such claim or cause of action in the administration proceedings. IN ST TRIAL P Rule 13(K)(1).

    ii.   A transferee or successor of a claim takes it subject to any defense or counterclaim that is the subject-matter of the opposing party's claim; or that is available to the obligor at the time of the assignment or before the obligor received notice of the assignment. IN ST TRIAL P Rule 13(K)(2).

    iii.   A surety or party with total or partial recourse upon a claim upon which he is being sued may interpose as a counterclaim:

- Any claim of his own; and

- Any claim owned by the person against whom he has recourse who either has notice of the suit, is a party to the suit, is insolvent, has assigned his claim to the surety or party asserting it, or cannot be found. IN ST TRIAL P Rule 13(K)(3).

- A counterclaim under IN ST TRIAL P Rule 13(K)(3)(b) must tend to diminish or defeat the opposing party's claim, or it or the opposing claim must relate to payment of or security for the other, unless the person against whom recourse may be had is a party to the suit or the counterclaim has been assigned to the party asserting it; and if recovery on the counterclaim exceeds the opposing party's claim, any excess recovered shall be held in trust for such person against whom there is a right of recourse. IN ST TRIAL P Rule 13(K)(3).

    iv.   IN ST TRIAL P Rule 13(K)(1), IN ST TRIAL P Rule 13(K)(2), and IN ST TRIAL P Rule 13(K)(3), are subject to subdivision IN ST TRIAL P Rule 13(L). IN ST TRIAL P Rule 13(K)(4).

l.   *Counterclaim and cross-claim subject to substantive law principles.* Counterclaim and cross-claims are subject to restrictions imposed by other statutes and principles of substantive common law and equity, including rules of commercial law, agency, estoppel, contract and the like. In appropriate cases the court may impose terms or conditions upon its judgment or decree and may enter conditional or noncanceling cross judgments to satisfy such restrictions. This provision is intended to deny or limit counterclaims or cross-claims:

    i.   Where a creditor will receive an unfair priority because a claim is assigned after insolvency proceedings, or assigned before such proceedings if it results in an unlawful preference;

    ii.   Where an unfair priority will be allowed if a surety interposing a claim owned in his own right against the creditor suing on the principal's obligation when the principal is solvent and the creditor is not;

    iii.   Where a claim by or against a representative, such as a guardian, receiver, representative of a decedent's estate, assignee for the benefit of creditors, trustee or the like in his individual capacity is asserted against a claim owing or owed by the estate he represents;

    iv.   Where a claim by or against a partnership or two (2) or more obligors is opposed against or by a claim of an individual to the extent that the individual will be allowed unfairly to profit or if it will adversely affect the rights of creditors; or

    v.   Where a claim is cut off by a holder in due course or a transferee who is protected under principles of commercial law, estoppel, or contract. IN ST TRIAL P Rule 13(L).

   m. *Satisfaction of judgment.* Satisfaction of a judgment or credits thereon may be ordered, for sufficient cause, upon notice and motion. "Credits" include any counterclaim which tends to diminish or defeat the judgment, or any counterclaim where it or the opposing claim relates to payment of or security for the other. IN ST TRIAL P Rule 13(M).

5. *Third-party practice*

   a. *When defendant may bring in third party.* A defending party, as a third-party plaintiff, may cause a summons and complaint to be served upon a person not a party to the action who is or may be liable to him for all or part of the plaintiff's claim against him. IN ST TRIAL P Rule 14(A). The person served with the summons and the third-party complaint, hereinafter called the third-party defendant, as provided in IN ST TRIAL P Rule 12 and IN ST TRIAL P Rule 13 may make:

     i.   His defenses, cross-claims and counterclaims to the third-party plaintiff's claims;

    ii.   His defenses, counterclaims and cross-claims against any other defendants or third-party defendants;

   iii. Any defenses or claims which the third-party plaintiff has to the plaintiff's claim which are available to the third-party defendant against the plaintiff; and

   iv. Any defenses or claims which the third-party defendant has as against the plaintiff. IN ST TRIAL P Rule 14(A).

    v.   The plaintiff may assert any claim against the third-party defendant who thereupon may assert his defenses, counterclaims and cross-claims, as provided in IN ST TRIAL P Rule 12 and IN ST TRIAL P Rule 13. A third-party defendant may proceed under IN ST TRIAL P Rule 14 against any person not a party to the action who is or may be liable to him for all or part of the claim made in the action against the third-party defendant. IN ST TRIAL P Rule 14(A).

   b. *When plaintiff may bring in third party.* When a counterclaim or other claim is asserted against a plaintiff, he may cause a third party to be brought in under circumstances, which, under IN ST TRIAL P Rule 14, would entitle a defendant to do so. IN ST TRIAL P Rule 14(B).

   c. *Severance; Parties improperly impleaded.* With his responsive pleading or by motion prior thereto, any party may move for severance of a third-party claim or ensuing claim as provided in IN ST TRIAL P Rule 14 or for a separate trial thereon. If the third-party defendant is a proper party to the proceedings under any other rule relating to parties, the action shall continue as in other cases where he is made a party. IN ST TRIAL P Rule 14(C).

6. *Trial by jury; Demand*

   a. *Causes triable by court and by jury.* Issues of law and issues of fact in causes that prior to the eighteenth day of June, 1852, were of exclusive equitable jurisdiction shall be tried by the court; issues of fact in all other causes shall be triable as the same are now triable. In case of the joinder of causes of action or defenses which, prior to said date, were of exclusive equitable jurisdiction with causes of action or defenses which, prior to said date, were designated as actions at law and triable by jury—the former shall be triable by the court, and the latter by a jury, unless waived; the trial of both may be at the same time or at different times, as the court may direct. IN ST TRIAL P Rule 38(A).

   b. *Demand.* Any party may demand a trial by jury of any issue triable of right by a jury by filing with the court and serving upon the other parties a demand therefor in writing at any time after the commencement of the action and not later than ten (10) days after the first responsive pleading to the complaint, or to a counterclaim, crossclaim or other claim if one properly is pleaded; and if no responsive pleading is filed or required, within ten (10) days after the time such pleading otherwise would have been required. Such demand is sufficient if indorsed upon a pleading of a party filed within such time. IN ST TRIAL P Rule 38(B).

   c. *Same; Specification of issues.* In his demand a party may specify the issues which he wishes so tried;

otherwise he shall be deemed to have demanded trial by jury for all issues triable as of right by jury. Any other party must file a demand for jury trial to preserve his right to trial by jury:

    i.   Of issues for which a right to trial by jury was not requested by another party; and

    ii.   In case a request by another party was improper. But if a proper request for a trial by jury upon issues triable by jury as of right on his behalf is made by any party, such request shall be deemed to have been made on behalf of all parties entitled to a jury trial upon such issues. IN ST TRIAL P Rule 38(C).

d.   *Waiver.* The failure of a party to appear at the trial, and the failure of a party to serve a demand as required by IN ST TRIAL P Rule 38 and to file it as required by IN ST TRIAL P Rule 5(E) constitute waiver by him of trial by jury. A demand for trial by jury made as herein provided may not be withdrawn without the consent of the other party or parties. IN ST TRIAL P Rule 38(D).

    i.   The trial court shall not grant a demand for a trial by jury filed after the time fixed in IN ST TRIAL P Rule 38(B) has elapsed except upon the written agreement of all of the parties to the action, which agreement shall be filed with the court and made a part of the record. If such agreement is filed then the court may, in its discretion, grant a trial by jury in which event the grant of a trial by jury may not be withdrawn except by the agreement of all of the parties. IN ST TRIAL P Rule 38(D).

e.   *Arbitration.* Nothing in the Indiana Rules of Trial Procedure shall deny the parties the right by contract or agreement to submit or to agree to submit controversies to arbitration made before or after commencement of an action thereon or deny the courts power to specifically enforce such agreements. IN ST TRIAL P Rule 38(E).

f.   *Equitable and legal claims in multi-count actions.* In multi-count actions, the inclusion of an equitable claim, standing alone, will not automatically draw the entire action into equity. Something more than the presence of an equitable claim is required, and the court must examine the claims at issue. 22B INPRAC 38:1 COMMENT; Lucas v. U.S. Bank, N.A., 953 N.E.2d 457 (Ind. 2011). Factors the court may consider in evaluating the nature of the underlying substantive claims include: the substance and central character of the complaint, the rights and interests at issue, the relief demanded, and any issues arising out of discovery. 22B INPRAC 38:1 COMMENT; Songer v. Civitas Bank, 771 N.E.2d 61 (Ind. 2002).

7.   *Use of alternative dispute resolution.* Except as provided by the Indiana Rules for Alternative Dispute Resolution, a presiding judge may order any civil or domestic relations proceeding or selected issues in such proceedings referred to mediation, non-binding arbitration or mini-trial. The selection criteria which should be used by the court are defined under the Indiana Rules for Alternative Dispute Resolution. Binding arbitration and a summary jury trial may be ordered only upon the agreement of the parties as consistent with provisions in the Indiana Rules for Alternative Dispute Resolution which address each method. IN ST ADR Rule 1.6. For information on Indiana's ADR process refer to IN ST ADR Rule 1.1 through IN ST ADR Rule 8.8.

a.   *Alternative dispute resolution.* On the Court's own motion or initiative, the parties may be required to attempt alternative dispute resolution (ADR). Such ADR efforts may include, at the Court's discretion, mediation and/or settlement conferences and may require one or more sessions or sessions lasting a specific amount of time. IN ST ST JOSEPH CIV Rule 209(209.3).

D. Documents

1.   *Required documents*

a.   *Answer.* Refer to the General Requirements section of this document for information on the contents of an answer.

b.   *Appearance form.* At the time the responding party or parties first appears in a case, such party or parties shall file an appearance form setting forth the information set out in IN ST TRIAL P Rule 3.1(A). IN ST TRIAL P Rule 3.1(B). The appearance form shall set forth the following information:

    i.   Name, address and telephone number of the initiating party or parties filing the appearance form;

ii. Name, address, attorney number, telephone number, FAX number, and e-mail address of any attorney representing the party, as applicable;

iii. The case type of the proceeding [IN ST ADMIN Rule 8];

iv. A statement that the party will or will not accept service by fax or by e-mail from:

- Other parties and/or
- The court under IN ST TRIAL P Rule 72(D);

v. In domestic relations, Uniform Reciprocal Enforcement of Support (URESA), paternity, delinquency, Child in Need of Services (CHINS), guardianship, and any other proceedings in which support may be an issue, the Social Security Identification Number of all family members;

vi. The caption and case number of all related cases;

vii. Such additional matters specified by state or local rule required to maintain the information management system employed by the court;

viii. In a proceeding involving a protection from abuse order, a workplace violence restraining order, or a no-contact order, the initiating party shall provide to the clerk a public mailing address for purposes of legal service. The initiating party may use the Attorney General Address Confidentiality program established by statute; and

ix. In a proceeding involving a mental health commitment, except seventy-two (72) hour emergency detentions, the initiating party shall provide the full name of the person with respect to whom commitment is sought and the person's state of residence. In addition, the initiating party shall provide at least one of the following identifiers for the person:

- Date of birth;
- Social Security Number;
- Driver's license number with state of issue and date of expiration;
- Department of Correction number;
- State ID number with state of issue and date of expiration; or
- FBI number. IN ST TRIAL P Rule 3.1(A).

x. Counsel and unrepresented parties appearing after the filing of the original complaint shall forthwith notify all other counsel of record and unrepresented parties of such appearance and file proof of such notice. Each counsel or party shall file an appearance form (or its equivalent) that includes a mailing address and telephone number. The notice may include a post office box, but must include a physical street address to allow for proper service of process or other notification by the Court. IN ST ST JOSEPH CIV Rule 204(204.1).

c. *Chronological Case Summary (CCS) entry form.* Every written motion, petition, or other pleading subsequent to the original complaint presented to the Clerk for filing shall be accompanied by a Chronological Case Summary (CCS) entry form in duplicate. IN ST ST JOSEPH CIV Rule 201(201.4). Refer to the Format section of this document for details on the format and filing requirements for the CCS entry form.

d. *Certificate of service.* An attorney or unrepresented party tendering a document to the Clerk for filing shall certify that service has been made, list the parties served, and specify the date and means of service. The certificate of service shall be placed at the end of the document and shall not be separately filed. The separate filing of a certificate of service, however, shall not be grounds for rejecting a document for filing. The Clerk may permit documents to be filed without a certificate of service but shall require prompt filing of a separate certificate of service. IN ST TRIAL P Rule 5(C).

2. *Supplemental documents*

a. *Admission of service.* A written admission stating the date and place of service, signed by the person being served, may be filed with the clerk who shall file it with the pleadings. Such admission shall become a part of the record, constitute evidence of proper service, and shall be allowed as evidence in any action or proceeding. IN ST TRIAL P Rule 4.15(D).

   i.   It shall be the duty of every person being served under the Indiana Rules of Trial Procedure to cooperate, accept service, comply with the provisions of the Indiana Rules of Trial Procedure, and, when service is made upon him personally, acknowledge receipt of the papers in writing over his signature. IN ST TRIAL P Rule 4.16(A).

- Offering or tendering the papers to the person being served and advising the person that he or she is being served is adequate service. IN ST TRIAL P Rule 4.16(A)(1).

- A person who has refused to accept the offer or tender of the papers being served thereafter may not challenge the service of those papers. IN ST TRIAL P Rule 4.16(A)(2).

b.   *Proof of written instrument.* When any pleading allowed by the Indiana Rules of Trial Procedure is founded on a written instrument, the original, or a copy thereof, must be included in or filed with the pleading. Such instrument, whether copied in the pleadings or not, shall be taken as part of the record. When any pleading allowed by the Indiana Rules of Trial Procedure is founded on an account, an Affidavit of Debt, in a form substantially similar to that which is provided in IN ST TRIAL P App. A-2, shall be attached. IN ST TRIAL P Rule 9.2(A).

c.   *Notice of intent to use foreign law.* A party who intends to raise an issue concerning the law of a foreign country shall give notice in his pleadings or other reasonable written notice. The court, in determining foreign law, may consider any relevant material or source, including testimony, whether or not submitted by a party or admissible under IN ST TRIAL P Rule 43. The court's determination shall be treated as a ruling on a question of law. It shall be made by the court and not the jury and shall be reviewable. IN ST TRIAL P Rule 44.1(A).

d.   *Facsimile cover sheet.* Any document sent to the Clerk of the Circuit Court by electronic facsimile transmission shall be accompanied by a cover sheet which states the title of the document, case number, number of pages, identity and voice telephone number of the sending party and instructions for filing. The cover sheet shall contain the signature of the attorney or party, pro se, authorizing the filing. IN ST ADMIN Rule 12(D).

E. Format

  1. *Form of pleadings*

a.   *Caption; Names of parties.* Every pleading shall contain a caption setting forth the name of the court, the title of the action, the file number, and a designation as in IN ST TRIAL P Rule 7(A). In the complaint the title of the action shall include the names of all the parties, but in other pleadings it is sufficient to state the name of the first party on each side with an appropriate indication of other parties. IN ST TRIAL P Rule 10(A); IN ST ST JOSEPH CIV Rule 201(201.3.3). If a special judge has been assigned to the case, the pleading should also identify the special judge. IN ST ST JOSEPH CIV Rule 201(201.3.3).

   i.   *Title.* All pleadings or motions shall include a title, which shall delineate each topic included in the pleading. For example, where a pleading contains an answer, a motion to dismiss, and a jury request, each topic shall be set forth in the title. IN ST ST JOSEPH CIV Rule 201(201.3.4).

b.   *Paragraphs; Separate statements.* All averments of a claim or defense shall be made in numbered paragraphs, the contents of each of which shall be limited as far as practicable to a statement of a single set of circumstances, and a paragraph may be referred to by number in all succeeding pleadings. Each claim founded upon a separate transaction or occurrence and each defense other than denials may be stated in a separate count or defense whenever a separation facilitates the clear presentation of the matters set forth. IN ST TRIAL P Rule 10(B).

c.   *Adoption by reference; Exhibits.* Statements in a pleading may be adopted by reference in a different part of the same pleading or in another pleading or in any motion. A copy of any written instrument which is an exhibit to a pleading is a part thereof for all purposes. IN ST TRIAL P Rule 10(C).

d.   *Flat filing.* In order that the Clerk's files may be kept under the system commonly known as "flat filing," all papers presented to the Clerk for filing shall be flat and unfolded. Pleadings shall have no covers or backs and shall be fastened together at the top left-hand corner only. IN ST ST JOSEPH CIV Rule 201(201.1).

e. *One side of page used.* Printing shall be on one (1) side of the paper. IN ST ST JOSEPH CIV Rule 201(201.3.2).

f. *Copies.* All copies shall be on white paper of sufficient strength and durability to resist normal wear and tear. IN ST ST JOSEPH CIV Rule 201(201.3.1).

g. *Margins.* Margins shall be at least one inch (1"). IN ST ST JOSEPH CIV Rule 201(201.3.2).

h. *Double-spaced.* If typewritten, the lines shall be double spaced except for quotations, which shall be indented and single-spaced. IN ST ST JOSEPH CIV Rule 201(201.3.2).

i. *Font size.* Type face shall be twelve (12) font size or larger within the body of the document and ten (10) font size or larger in the footnotes. IN ST ST JOSEPH CIV Rule 201(201.3.2).

j. *Font type.* The font type must be legible and script type shall not be used. IN ST ST JOSEPH CIV Rule 201(201.3.2).

k. *Italics.* Italicized type may be used for quotations, references, or case citations. IN ST ST JOSEPH CIV Rule 201(201.3.2).

l. *Court and case designation.* All filings shall conform to the requirements for uniform court and case number designation set by IN ST ADMIN Rule 8. In addition, all filings shall contain the proper court and case designation as described below. IN ST ST JOSEPH CIV Rule 202.

    i. *Court designation.* Pursuant to IN ST 33-33-71-2, St. Joseph County, Indiana, constitutes the Sixtieth Judicial Circuit. The legal names of the courts within the 60th Judicial Circuit are the St. Joseph Circuit Court, the St. Joseph Superior Court, and the St. Joseph Probate Court. All filings shall properly reflect the legal name of the applicable court. Any filing may be amended, rejected, or stricken if it does not contain the proper case name and/or the legal name of the court. IN ST ST JOSEPH CIV Rule 202(202.1).

m. *Form of CCS entry.* Every written motion, petition, or other pleading subsequent to the original complaint presented to the Clerk for filing shall be accompanied by a Chronological Case Summary (CCS) entry form in duplicate which shall contain the title and cause number of the action, the date, and the proposed entry to appear on the docket. IN ST ST JOSEPH CIV Rule 201(201.4).

    i. *Identification and signature.* The CCS entry form shall identify the party making the filing, designate each pleading being filed, and shall be signed by counsel of record or the unrepresented litigant. IN ST ST JOSEPH CIV Rule 201(201.4).

    ii. *Date stamp.* The form shall be date stamped and presented to the Court Clerk, who shall initial the form and return the duplicate to the filing party. IN ST ST JOSEPH CIV Rule 201(201.4).

2. *Size of papers for filing.* Effective January 1, 1992, all pleadings, copies, motions and documents filed with any trial court or appellate level court, typed or printed, with the exception of exhibits and existing wills, shall be prepared on eight and one-half by eleven inch (8 1/2" x 11") size paper. IN ST ADMIN Rule 11.

a. *Paper.* Pleadings, motions, and other papers shall be either legibly printed or typewritten on white opaque paper of good quality at least sixteen (16) pound weight, eight and one-half inches (8 1/2") in width and eleven inches (11") in length as required by IN ST ADMIN Rule 11. IN ST ST JOSEPH CIV Rule 201(201.3.1).

3. *Signature requirements*

a. *Signature of attorney.* Every pleading or motion of a party represented by an attorney shall be signed by at least one (1) attorney of record in his individual name, whose address, telephone number, and attorney number shall be stated, except that this provision shall not apply to pleadings and motions made and transcribed at the trial or a hearing before the judge and received by him in such form. IN ST TRIAL P Rule 11(A).

    i. The signature of an attorney constitutes a certificate by him that he has read the pleadings; that to the best of his knowledge, information, and belief, there is good ground to support it; and that it is not interposed for delay. IN ST TRIAL P Rule 11(A).

ST. JOSEPH COUNTY

ii. If a pleading or motion is not signed or is signed with intent to defeat the purpose of the rule, it may be stricken as sham and false and the action may proceed as though the pleading had not been served. IN ST TRIAL P Rule 11(A).

iii. For a willful violation of IN ST TRIAL P Rule 11 an attorney may be subjected to appropriate disciplinary action. Similar action may be taken if scandalous or indecent matter is inserted. IN ST TRIAL P Rule 11(A).

b. *Signature of unrepresented party.* A party who is not represented by an attorney shall sign his pleading and state his address. IN ST TRIAL P Rule 11(A).

c. *Verification not generally required.* Except when specifically required by rule, pleadings or motions need not be verified or accompanied by affidavit. The rule in equity that the averments of an answer under oath must be overcome by the testimony of two (2) witnesses or of one (1) witness sustained by corroborating circumstances is abolished. IN ST TRIAL P Rule 11(A).

d. *Verification by affirmation or representation.* When in connection with any civil or special statutory proceeding it is required that any pleading, motion, petition, supporting affidavit, or other document of any kind, be verified, or that an oath be taken, it shall be sufficient if the subscriber simply affirms the truth of the matter to be verified by an affirmation or representation. IN ST TRIAL P Rule 11(B). IN ST TRIAL P Rule 11(B) states that the affirmation or representation should be in substantially the following language: "I (we) affirm, under the penalties for perjury, that the foregoing representation(s) is (are) true. (Signed) _____."

i. Any person who falsifies an affirmation or representation of fact shall be subject to the same penalties as are prescribed by law for the making of a false affidavit. IN ST TRIAL P Rule 11(B).

e. *Verified pleadings, motions, and affidavits as evidence.* Pleadings, motions and affidavits accompanying or in support of such pleadings or motions when required to be verified or under oath shall be accepted as a representation that the signer had personal knowledge thereof or reasonable cause to believe the existence of the facts or matters stated or alleged therein; and, if otherwise competent or acceptable as evidence, may be admitted as evidence of the facts or matters stated or alleged therein when it is so provided in the Indiana Rules of Trial Procedure, by statute or other law, or to the extent the writing or signature expressly purports to be made upon the signer's personal knowledge. When such pleadings, motions and affidavits are verified or under oath they shall not require other or greater proof on the part of the adverse party than if not verified or not under oath unless expressly provided otherwise by the Indiana Rules of Trial Procedure, statute or other law. Affidavits upon motions for summary judgment under IN ST TRIAL P Rule 56 and in denial of execution under IN ST TRIAL P Rule 9.2 shall be made upon personal knowledge. IN ST TRIAL P Rule 11(C).

f. *Signature, verification and other requirements.* Parties and their counsel are enjoined to comply with the verification requirements of IN ST TRIAL P Rule 11, and either the moving party or the party's attorney of record shall sign all pleadings and motions before filing with the Clerk of the Court. Every motion, petition, or other pleading filed with the Clerk shall contain the name, organization, physical address, telephone number, and facsimile number of the filing party or an attorney for that party. IN ST ST JOSEPH CIV Rule 201(201.3.6).

i. The Clerk shall not accept any motion, petition, notice or other pleading or a CCS entry form for filing from an unrepresented litigant unless the unrepresented litigant's current address and phone number appear on the pleading, and an opposing party may service notices and responses on an unrepresented litigant at any address he or she has provided on a pleading. IN ST ST JOSEPH CIV Rule 201(201.3.6).

4. *Information excluded from public access.* Every document filed in a case shall separately identify information excluded from public access pursuant to IN ST ADMIN Rule 9(G)(1) as follows:

a. Whole documents that are excluded from public access pursuant to IN ST ADMIN Rule 9(G)(1) shall be tendered on light green paper or have a light green coversheet attached to the document, marked "Not for Public Access" or "Confidential." IN ST TRIAL P Rule 5(G)(1).

b. When only a portion of a document contains information excluded from public access pursuant to IN

1414

ST ADMIN Rule 9(G)(1), said information shall be omitted [or redacted] from the filed document, and set forth on a separate accompanying document on light green paper conspicuously marked "Not for Public Access" or "Confidential" and clearly designated [or identifying] the caption and number of the case and the document and location within the document to which the redacted material pertains. IN ST TRIAL P Rule 5(G)(2).

c. With respect to documents filed in electronic format, the trial court, by local rule, may provide for compliance with IN ST TRIAL P Rule 5 in manner that separates and protects access to information excluded from public access. IN ST TRIAL P Rule 5(G)(3).

d. IN ST TRIAL P Rule 5(G) does not apply to a record sealed by the court pursuant to IN ST 5-14-3-5.5 or otherwise, nor to records, documents, or information filed in cases to which public access is prohibited pursuant to IN ST ADMIN Rule 9(G). IN ST TRIAL P Rule 5(G)(4).

e. The following information in case records is excluded from public access and is confidential:

   i. Information that is excluded from public access pursuant to federal law;

   ii. Information that is excluded from public access as declared confidential by Indiana statute or other court rule, including without limitation:

   - All adoption records created after July 8, 1941, as declared confidential by IN ST 31-19-19-1, et seq., except those specifically declared open by IN ST 31-19-13-2(2);

   - All records relating to chancroid, chlamydia, gonorrhea, hepatitis, human immunodeficiency virus (HIV), Lymphogranuloma venereum, syphilis, tuberculosis, as declared confidential by IN ST 16-41-8-1, et seq.;

   - All records relating to child abuse as declared confidential by IN ST 31-33-18-1, et seq.;

   - All records relating to drug tests as declared confidential by IN ST 5-14-3-4(a)(9);

   - Records of grand jury proceedings as declared confidential by IN ST 35-34-2-4;

   - Records of juvenile proceedings as declared confidential by IN ST 31-39-1-2, except those specifically open under statute;

   - All paternity records created after July 1, 1941 as declared confidential by IN ST 31-14-11-15, IN ST 31-19-5-23, IN ST 31-39-1-1 and IN ST 31-39-1-2 [Editor's note: IN ST 31-14-11-15 was repealed effective May 9, 2013];

   - All pre-sentence reports as declared confidential by IN ST 35-38-1-13;

   - Written petitions to permit marriages without consent and orders directing the Clerk of Court to issue a marriage license to underage persons, as declared confidential by IN ST 31-11-1-6;

   - Only those arrest warrants, search warrants, indictments and informations ordered confidential by the trial judge, prior to return of duly executed service as declared confidential by IN ST 5-14-3-4(b)(1);

   - All medical, mental health, or tax records unless determined by law or regulation of any governmental custodian not to be confidential, released by the subject of such records, or declared by a court of competent jurisdiction to be essential to the resolution of litigation as declared confidential by IN ST 16-39-3-10, IN ST 6-4.1-5-10, IN ST 6-4.1-12-12, and IN ST 6-8.1-7-1;

   - Personal information relating to jurors or prospective jurors, other than for the use of the parties and counsel, pursuant to IN ST JURY Rule 10;

   - Information relating to protection from abuse orders, no-contact orders and workplace violence restraining orders as declared confidential by IN ST 5-2-9-6, et seq.;

   - Mediation proceedings pursuant to IN ST ADR Rule 2.11, Mini-Trial proceedings pursuant to IN ST ADR Rule 4.4(C), and Summary Jury Trials pursuant to IN ST ADR Rule 5.6;

   - Information in probation files pursuant to the Probation Standards promulgated by the Judicial Conference of Indiana pursuant to IN ST 11-13-1-8(b);

- Information deemed confidential pursuant to the Rules for Court Administered Alcohol and Drug Programs promulgated by the Judicial Conference of Indiana pursuant to IN ST 12-23-14-13;

- Information deemed confidential pursuant to the Problem-Solving Court Rules promulgated by the Judicial Conference of Indiana pursuant to IN ST 33-23-16-16;

- All records of the Department of workforce Development as declared confidential by IN ST 22-4-19-6;

- Information regarding interception of electronic communications that is sealed or deemed confidential as set forth in IN ST 35-33.5-2-1, et seq.

iii. Information excluded from public access by specific court order;

iv. Complete Social Security Numbers of living persons;

v. With the exception of names, information such as addresses, phone numbers, and dates of birth which explicitly identifies:

- Natural persons who are witnesses or victims (not including defendants) in criminal, domestic violence, stalking, sexual assault, juvenile, or civil protection order proceedings, provided that juveniles who are victims of sex crimes shall be identified by initials only;

- Places of residence of judicial officers, clerks and other employees of courts and clerks of court, unless the person or persons about whom the information pertains waives confidentiality;

vi. Complete account numbers of specific assets, loans, bank accounts, credit cards, and personal identification numbers (PINs);

vii. All orders of expungement entered in criminal or juvenile proceedings, orders to restrict access to criminal history information pursuant to IN ST 35-38-5-5.5 or IN ST 35-38-8-5 and records excluded from public access by such orders, and information related to infractions that is excluded from public access pursuant to IN ST 34-28-5-15 or IN ST 34-28-5-16 [Editor's note: IN ST 35-38-5-5.5, IN ST 35-38-8-5 and IN ST 34-28-5-16 were repealed effective July 1, 2013; for information on orders restricting access to criminal history, refer to IN ST 35-38-9-1, et seq.];

viii. All personal notes and e-mail, and deliberative material, of judges, jurors, court staff and judicial agencies, and information recorded in personal data assistants (PDA's) or organizers and personal calendars. IN ST ADMIN Rule 9(G)(1).

F. Filing and Service Requirements

1. *Filing requirements.* Except as otherwise provided in IN ST TRIAL P Rule 5(E)(2), all pleadings and papers subsequent to the complaint which are required to be served upon a party shall be filed with the Court either before service or within a reasonable period of time thereafter. IN ST TRIAL P Rule 5(E)(1).

   a. *Filing with the court defined.* The filing of pleadings, motions, and other papers with the court as required by the Indiana Rules of Trial Procedure shall be made by one of the following methods:

      i. Delivery to the clerk of the court;

      ii. Sending by electronic transmission under the procedure adopted pursuant to IN ST ADMIN Rule 12;

      iii. Mailing to the clerk by registered, certified or express mail return receipt requested;

      iv. Depositing with any third-party commercial carrier for delivery to the clerk within three (3) calendar days, cost prepaid, properly addressed;

      v. If the court so permits, filing with the judge, in which event the judge shall note thereon the filing date and forthwith transmit them to the office of the clerk; or

      vi. Electronic filing, as approved by the Division of State Court Administration pursuant to IN ST ADMIN Rule 16. IN ST TRIAL P Rule 5(F).

      vii. Filing by registered or certified mail and by third-party commercial carrier shall be complete upon mailing or deposit. IN ST TRIAL P Rule 5(F).

viii. All pleadings shall be filed with the Clerk, not directly with the Court, unless otherwise required by the Indiana Rules of Court. The entry of appearances and the filing of pleadings or other matters not requiring immediate Court action shall be filed with the Clerk and not in open Court. A Judge may permit papers to be filed in chambers, in which event he or she shall note thereon the filing date and transmit the papers to the Clerk. IN ST ST JOSEPH CIV Rule 201(201.2).

b. *Facsimile filing.* Unless otherwise authorized by IN ST ST JOSEPH ELECTRONIC Rule 701, electronic filing of pleadings by computerized or facsimile transmission is not permitted. IN ST ST JOSEPH CIV Rule 201(201.2).

c. *Additional copies.* In cases in which a party or counsel supplies the proposed order or decree, a sufficient number shall be prepared and filed as to provide the Clerk to retain two (2) copies, which shall be filed in the flat file and the record of judgments and orders. Should the party or counsel desire additional copies, a sufficient number of copies should be filed to effectuate that purpose. IN ST ST JOSEPH CIV Rule 201(201.6).

d. *Proof of filing.* Any party filing any paper by any method other than personal delivery to the clerk shall retain proof of filing. IN ST TRIAL P Rule 5(F).

2. *Service requirements.* Unless otherwise provided by the Indiana Rules of Trial Procedure or an order of the court, each party and special judge, if any, shall be served with: (1) every order required by its terms to be served; (2) every pleading subsequent to the original complaint; (3) every written motion except one which may be heard ex parte; (4) every brief submitted to the trial court; (5) every paper relating to discovery required to be served upon a party; and (6) every written notice, appearance, demand, offer of judgment, designation of record on appeal, or similar paper. IN ST TRIAL P Rule 5(A).

a. *Service generally.* Every motion, petition, notice, or other pleading required to be served by IN ST TRIAL P Rule 5 shall be served on all counsel of record or unrepresented parties either before it is filed or on the day it is filed with the Court, and the date of filing shall be indicated on the Certificate of Service. IN ST ST JOSEPH CIV Rule 201(201.5.1).

i. *Copy.* A copy of the Clerk's CCS entry form of the filing shall also be served on all counsel of record or unrepresented parties whenever it contains an appearance of counsel or contains a date for Court hearing on the matter. IN ST ST JOSEPH CIV Rule 201(201.5.1).

b. *Methods of service*

i. *Personal service.* Whenever a party is represented by an attorney of record, service shall be made upon such attorney unless service upon the party himself is ordered by the court. Service upon the attorney or party shall be made by delivering or mailing a copy of the papers to the last known address or where an attorney or party has consented to service by fax or e-mail, as provided in IN ST TRIAL P Rule 3.1(A)(4), by faxing or e-mailing a copy of the documents to the fax number or e-mail address set out in the appearance form or correction as required by IN ST TRIAL P Rule 3.1(E). IN ST TRIAL P Rule 5(B). Delivery of a copy within IN ST TRIAL P Rule 5 means:

- Offering or tendering it to the attorney or party and stating the nature of the papers being served. Refusal to accept an offered or tendered document is a waiver of any objection to the sufficiency or adequacy of service of that document;

- Leaving it at his office with a clerk or other person in charge thereof, or if there is no one in charge, leaving it in a conspicuous place therein; or

- If the office is closed, by leaving it at his dwelling house or usual place of abode with some person of suitable age and discretion then residing therein; or,

- Leaving it at some other suitable place, selected by the attorney upon whom service is being made, pursuant to duly promulgated local rule. IN ST TRIAL P Rule 5(B)(1).

ii. *Service by the clerk.* Whenever the Clerk is required by rule or statute to give notice, the party or parties requesting such notice shall furnish the Clerk with sufficient copies of the notice to be given, along with stamped, addressed envelopes with the names and the addresses of the parties or their counsel to whom such notice is to be given. IN ST ST JOSEPH CIV Rule 201(201.5.4).

iii. *Service on the court.* Service on a Judge may be made by delivering a copy to the Judge's secretary or mailing a copy to the Judge at his or her chambers. Service on a Judge may not be accomplished by facsimile transmission; however, a courtesy copy may be sent to the Judge's chambers by electronic mail or facsimile transmission contemporaneously with service by mail or otherwise. IN ST ST JOSEPH CIV Rule 201(201.5.5).

iv. *Service by mail.* If service is made by mail, the papers shall be deposited in the United States mail addressed to the person on whom they are being served, with postage prepaid. Service shall be deemed complete upon mailing. Proof of service of all papers permitted to be mailed may be made by written acknowledgment of service, by affidavit of the person who mailed the papers, or by certificate of an attorney. It shall be the duty of attorneys when entering their appearance in a cause or when filing pleadings or papers therein, to have noted in the Chronological Case Summary or said pleadings or papers so filed the address and telephone number of their office. Service by delivery or by mail at such address shall be deemed sufficient and complete. IN ST TRIAL P Rule 5(B)(2).

v. *Service by fax or e-mail.* A party who has consented to service by fax or e-mail may be served as follows:

- Service by e-mail shall be made by attaching the document being served in .pdf format. Discovery documents must also be served in accordance with IN ST TRIAL P Rule 26(A). IN ST TRIAL P Rule 5(B)(3)(a).

- Service by fax shall be deemed complete upon generation of a transmission record indicating the successful transmission of the entire document, except as provided in IN ST TRIAL P Rule 5(B)(3)(d). IN ST TRIAL P Rule 5(B)(3)(b).

- Service by e-mail shall be deemed complete upon transmission, except as provided in IN ST TRIAL P Rule 5(B)(3)(d). IN ST TRIAL P Rule 5(B)(3)(c).

- Service by fax or e-mail that occurs on a Saturday, Sunday, legal holiday, or day the court or agency in which the matter is pending is closed or after 5:00 PM local time of the recipient shall be deemed complete the next day that is not a Saturday, Sunday, legal holiday, or day that the court or agency in which the matter is pending is not closed. IN ST TRIAL P Rule 5(B)(3)(d).

c. *Serving numerous defendants.* In any action in which there are unusually large numbers of defendants, the court, upon motion or of its own initiative, may order:

i. That service of the pleadings of the defendants and replies thereto need not be made as between the defendants;

- That any cross-claim, counterclaim, or matter constituting an avoidance or affirmative defense contained therein shall be deemed to be denied or avoided by all other parties; and

- That the filing of any such pleading and service thereof upon the plaintiff constitutes due notice of it to the parties. IN ST TRIAL P Rule 5(D).

ii. A copy of every such order shall be served upon the parties in such manner and form as the court directs. IN ST TRIAL P Rule 5(D).

d. *Service on parties in default for failure to appear.* No service need be made on parties in default for failure to appear, except that pleadings asserting new or additional claims for relief against them shall be served upon them in the manner provided by service of summons in IN ST TRIAL P Rule 4. IN ST TRIAL P Rule 5(A).

e. *Distribution.* Counsel or an unrepresented party submitting a motion, petition, notice, pleading or proposed order shall indicate the method of distribution desired on the Clerk's CCS entry form. The Clerk will not return or distribute copies of motions, petitions, pleadings, notices or proposed orders, other than those originated by the Court, by mail unless the Clerk is provided with stamped, addressed envelopes. IN ST ST JOSEPH CIV Rule 201(201.5.3).

f. *Mailbox.* As a matter of convenience to attorneys, each court provides a mailbox for the distribution filings and orders generated by the Court, and it is the responsibility of each attorney to periodically

check these mailboxes for service and distribution of court-generated filings and orders. IN ST ST JOSEPH CIV Rule 201(201.5.3).

G. Hearings

1. The Indiana rules do not contemplate a hearing regarding the filing and service of an answer.

H. Forms

1. Official Answer Forms for Indiana

    a. Affidavit of debt. IN ST TRIAL P App. A-2.

    b. Appearance by attorney in civil case. IN ST TRIAL P App. B.

2. Answer Forms for Indiana

    a. Appearance; By responding party. 9 INPRAC § 39.3.

    b. Answer; Form and content. 9 INPRAC § 41.1.

    c. Answer; General form. 9 INPRAC § 41.3.

    d. Answer; Another form. 9 INPRAC § 41.4.

    e. Answer; Another form. 9 INPRAC § 41.5.

    f. General denial. 9 INPRAC § 41.6.

    g. Specific denial of designated paragraph. 9 INPRAC § 41.7.

    h. Specific admission of designated paragraph. 9 INPRAC § 41.8.

    i. Denial of knowledge or information to form belief. 9 INPRAC § 41.9.

    j. Denial of knowledge or information to form belief; Another form. 9 INPRAC § 41.10.

    k. Partial denial and partial admission of designated paragraph. 9 INPRAC § 41.11.

    l. Denial of designated paragraph for reason that document speaks for itself. 9 INPRAC § 41.12.

    m. Adoption of admissions or denials by co-defendant's answer. 9 INPRAC § 41.13.

    n. Denial of execution of instrument filed with pleading. 9 INPRAC § 41.14.

    o. Answer to cross-claim. 9 INPRAC § 41.15.

    p. Answer to third-party complaint. 9 INPRAC § 41.16.

    q. Accord and satisfaction. 9 INPRAC § 41.21.

    r. Answer. 5 INPRAC § 3:3.3.

    s. Answer; Another form. 5 INPRAC § 3:3.4.

    t. Certificate of service; Personal service. 9 INPRAC § 5.7.

    u. Certificate of service; First class mail. 9 INPRAC § 5.8.

    v. Signature; By party. 9 INPRAC § 4.5.

    w. Signature; Attorney. 9 INPRAC § 4.6.

    x. Signature; Attorney; Another form. 9 INPRAC § 4.7.

    y. Signature; Attorney; Another form. 9 INPRAC § 4.8.

    z. Verification; Official form. 9 INPRAC § 4.9.

I. Checklist

(I) ❑ Matters to be considered by the plaintiff

    (a) ❑ Required documents

        (1) ❑ Summons

        (2) ❑ Complaint

        (3) ❑ Appearance form

(b) ❑ Supplemental documents

    (1) ❑ Proof of written instrument

    (2) ❑ Notice of intent to use foreign law

    (3) ❑ Praecipe

    (4) ❑ Facsimile cover sheet

(c) ❑ Timing

    (1) ❑ The claimant typically bears the burden of commencing an action within the applicable statute of limitations

    (2) ❑ If person seeking service of process fails without cause for sixty (60) days or more to provide clerk with required summons for issuance or with other information necessary to effectuate service, person has failed to exercise due diligence in securing service of process

(II) ❑ Matters to be considered by the defendant

(a) ❑ Required documents

    (1) ❑ Answer

    (2) ❑ Appearance form

    (3) ❑ Chronological Case Summary (CCS) entry form

    (4) ❑ Certificate of service

(b) ❑ Supplemental documents

    (1) ❑ Admission of service

    (2) ❑ Proof of written instrument

    (3) ❑ Notice of intent to use foreign law

    (4) ❑ Facsimile cover sheet

(c) ❑ Timing

    (1) ❑ A responsive pleading required under the Indiana Rules of Trial Procedure, shall be served within twenty (20) days after service of the prior pleading

    (2) ❑ The service of a motion permitted under IN ST TRIAL P Rule 12 alters the time for service of responsive pleadings as follows, unless a different time is fixed by the court:

        (i) ❑ If the court does not grant the motion, the responsive pleading shall be served in ten (10) days after notice of the court's action;

        (ii) ❑ If the court grants the motion and the corrective action is allowed to be taken, it shall be taken within ten (10) days, and the responsive pleading shall be served within ten (10) days thereafter

    (3) ❑ All pleadings and papers subsequent to the complaint which are required to be served upon a party shall be filed with the Court either before service or within a reasonable period of time thereafter

Pleadings
Amended Answer

Document Last Updated October 2013

A. Applicable Rules

1. *State rules*

    a. Appearance. IN ST TRIAL P Rule 3.1.

    b. Summons. IN ST TRIAL P Rule 4.

    c.   Filing and service. IN ST TRIAL P Rule 4.6; IN ST TRIAL P Rule 5.

    d.   Time. IN ST TRIAL P Rule 6.

    e.   Pleadings. IN ST TRIAL P Rule 7; IN ST TRIAL P Rule 8; IN ST TRIAL P Rule 9; IN ST TRIAL P Rule 9.1; IN ST TRIAL P Rule 9.2; IN ST TRIAL P Rule 10.

    f.   Signing and verification of pleadings. IN ST TRIAL P Rule 11.

    g.   Defenses and objections; When and how presented; By pleading or motion; Motion for judgment on the pleadings. IN ST TRIAL P Rule 12.

    h.   Counterclaim and cross-claim; Third-party practice. IN ST TRIAL P Rule 13; IN ST TRIAL P Rule 14.

    i.   Amended and supplemental pleadings. IN ST TRIAL P Rule 15.

    j.   Parties plaintiff and defendant; Capacity. IN ST TRIAL P Rule 17.

    k.   Joinder. IN ST TRIAL P Rule 19; IN ST TRIAL P Rule 20.

    l.   Consolidation; Separate trials. IN ST TRIAL P Rule 42.

    m.   Evidence. IN ST TRIAL P Rule 43.

    n.   Determination of foreign law. IN ST TRIAL P Rule 44.1.

    o.   Judgment on the evidence (directed verdict). IN ST TRIAL P Rule 50.

    p.   Findings by the court. IN ST TRIAL P Rule 52.

    q.   Judgment; Costs. IN ST TRIAL P Rule 54.

    r.   Summary judgment. IN ST TRIAL P Rule 56.

    s.   Motion to correct error. IN ST TRIAL P Rule 59.

    t.   Relief from judgment or order. IN ST TRIAL P Rule 60.

    u.   Venue requirements. IN ST TRIAL P Rule 75.

    v.   Access to court records. IN ST ADMIN Rule 9; IN ST 5-14-3-5.5.

    w.   Paper size. IN ST ADMIN Rule 11.

    x.   Facsimile and electronic transmission. IN ST ADMIN Rule 12; IN ST ADMIN Rule 16.

    y.   Sixtieth judicial circuit. IN ST 33-33-71-2.

    z.   Privacy and confidentiality. IN ST 5-2-9-6; IN ST 5-14-3-4; IN ST 6-4.1-5-10; IN ST 6-4.1-12-12; IN ST 6-8.1-7-1; IN ST 11-13-1-8; IN ST 12-23-14-13; IN ST 16-39-3-10; IN ST 16-41-8-1; IN ST 22-4-19-6; IN ST 31-11-1-6; IN ST 31-19-5-23; IN ST 31-19-13-2; IN ST 31-19-19-1; IN ST 31-33-18-1; IN ST 31-39-1-1; IN ST 31-39-1-2; IN ST 33-23-16-16; IN ST 35-34-2-4; IN ST 35-38-1-13; IN ST 35-38-9-1; IN ST ADR Rule 2.11; IN ST ADR Rule 4.4; IN ST ADR Rule 5.6; IN ST JURY Rule 10.

2.   *Local rules*

    a.   Filing, pleading, and motions. IN ST ST JOSEPH CIV Rule 201.

    b.   Uniform court and case number designation. IN ST ST JOSEPH CIV Rule 202.

    c.   Electronic filing of cases in St. Joseph County. IN ST ST JOSEPH ELECTRONIC Rule 701.

B. Timing

1.   *Filing an amended pleading*

    a.   *As a matter of course.* A party may amend his pleading once as a matter of course at any time before a responsive pleading is served or, if the pleading is one to which no responsive pleading is permitted, and the action has not been placed upon the trial calendar, he may so amend it at any time within thirty (30) days after it is served. IN ST TRIAL P Rule 15(A).

    b.   *With leave of court.* Otherwise a party may amend his pleading only by leave of court or by written consent of the adverse party; and leave shall be given when justice so requires. IN ST TRIAL P Rule 15(A). Refer to the Indiana KeyRules Motion for Leave to Amend document for more information.

2. *Computation of time*

    a. *Generally; Days excluded.* In computing any period of time prescribed or allowed by the Indiana Rules of Trial Procedure, by order of the court, or by any applicable statute, the day of the act, event, or default from which the designated period of time begins to run shall not be included. The last day of the period so computed is to be included unless it is:

        i. A Saturday,

        ii. A Sunday,

        iii. A legal holiday as defined by state statute, or

        iv. A day the office in which the act is to be done is closed during regular business hours. IN ST TRIAL P Rule 6(A).

    b. *Short periods.* In any event, the period runs until the end of the next day that is not a Saturday, a Sunday, a legal holiday, or a day on which the office is closed. When the period of time allowed is less than seven (7) days, intermediate Saturdays, Sundays, legal holidays, and days on which the office is closed shall be excluded from the computations. IN ST TRIAL P Rule 6(A).

    c. *Additional time after service by United States mail.* Whenever a party has the right or is required to do some act or take some proceedings within a prescribed period after the service of a notice or other paper upon him and the notice or paper is served upon him by United States mail, three (3) days shall be added to the prescribed period. IN ST TRIAL P Rule 6(E).

    d. *Enlargement of time.* When an act is required or allowed to be done at or within a specific time by the Indiana Rules of Trial Procedure, the court may at any time for cause shown:

        i. Order the period enlarged, with or without motion or notice, if request therefor is made before the expiration of the period originally prescribed or extended by a previous order; or

        ii. Upon motion made after the expiration of the specific period, permit the act to be done where the failure to act was the result of excusable neglect; but, the court may not extend the time for taking any action for judgment on the evidence under IN ST TRIAL P Rule 50(A), amendment of findings and judgment under IN ST TRIAL P Rule 52(B), to correct errors under IN ST TRIAL P Rule 59(C), statement in opposition to motion to correct error under IN ST TRIAL P Rule 59(E), or to obtain relief from final judgment under IN ST TRIAL P Rule 60(B), except to the extent and under the conditions stated in those rules. IN ST TRIAL P Rule 6(B).

        iii. An initial written motion for enlargement of time pursuant to IN ST TRIAL P Rule 6(B)(1) to answer a claim shall be routinely granted for an additional thirty (30) days from the original due date or other period the assigned Judge deems reasonable by written order of the Court. The motion must be filed on or before the original due date or IN ST ST JOSEPH CIV Rule 201 shall be inapplicable. IN ST ST JOSEPH CIV Rule 201(201.9.5).

           • Any motion for enlargement of time shall state the date when such response is due and the date to which time is requested to be enlarged. IN ST ST JOSEPH CIV Rule 201(201.9.5).

           • All subsequent motions for enlargement of time shall be so designated and will only be granted for good cause shown or in the interest of justice. IN ST ST JOSEPH CIV Rule 201(201.9.5).

C. General Requirements

1. *Amending pleadings.* The purpose of an amended pleading is to include matters that occurred before the filing of the original pleading but which were either overlooked by the pleader or unknown to him at the time. It is a substitute for the original and relates to the facts that existed when the original pleading was filed. An amended pleading supercedes the original as to those portions amended. 10 INPRAC § 46.1.

    a. *Amendments liberally allowed.* Amendments to pleadings are to be liberally allowed in order that all issues are presented in one action. 10 INPRAC § 46.1; Pinnacle Media, LLC v. Metropolitan Dev. Com'n of Marion County, 868 N.E.2d 894 (Ind.Ct.App. 2007).

    b. *Amendments to conform to the evidence.* When issues not raised by the pleadings are tried by express or implied consent of the parties, they shall be treated in all respects as if they had been raised in the pleadings. Such amendment of the pleadings as may be necessary to cause them to conform to the evidence and to raise these issues may be made upon motion of any party at any time, even after judgment, but failure so to amend does not affect the result of the trial of these issues. If evidence is objected to at the trial on the ground that it is not within the issues made by the pleadings, the court may allow the pleadings to be amended and shall do so freely when the presentation of the merits of the action will be subserved thereby and the objecting party fails to satisfy the court that the admission of such evidence would prejudice him in maintaining his action or defense upon the merits. The court may grant a continuance to enable the objecting party to meet such evidence. IN ST TRIAL P Rule 15(B).

c. *Relation back of amendments*

   i. Whenever the claim or defense asserted in the amended pleading arose out of the conduct, transaction, or occurrence set forth or attempted to be set forth in the original pleading, the amendment relates back to the date of the original pleading. An amendment changing the party against whom a claim is asserted relates back if the foregoing provision is satisfied and, within one hundred and twenty (120) days of commencement of the action, the party to be brought in by amendment:

      • Has received such notice of the institution of the action that he will not be prejudiced in maintaining his defense on the merits; and

      • Knew or should have known that but for a mistake concerning the identity of the proper party, the action would have been brought against him. IN ST TRIAL P Rule 15(C).

   ii. The requirement of subsections IN ST TRIAL P Rule 15(C)(1) and IN ST TRIAL P Rule 15(C)(2) with respect to a governmental organization to be brought into the action as defendant is satisfied:

      • In the case of a state or governmental organization by delivery or mailing of process to the attorney general or to a governmental executive [IN ST TRIAL P Rule 4.6(A)(3)]; or

      • In the case of a local governmental organization, by delivery or mailing of process to its attorney as provided by statute, to a governmental executive thereof [IN ST TRIAL P Rule 4.6(A)(4)], or to the officer holding the office if suit is against the officer or an office. IN ST TRIAL P Rule 15(C).

d. *Amendment by leave.* Amendments, other than an amendment by right, may be made only by leave of court or by written consent of the opposing party. 2 INPRAC R 15(15.2). Refer to the Indiana KeyRules Motion for Leave to Amend document for more information on amending with leave of court.

2. *Pleading, generally*

   a. *Pleadings to be concise.* Each averment of a pleading shall be simple, concise, and direct. No technical forms of pleading or motions are required. All fictions in pleading are abolished. IN ST TRIAL P Rule 8(E)(1).

   b. *Pleading in the alternative.* A pleading may set forth two (2) or more statements of a claim or defense alternatively or hypothetically, either in one (1) count or defense or in separate counts or defenses. When two (2) or more statements are made in the alternative and one (1) of them if made independently would be sufficient, the pleading is not made insufficient by the insufficiency of one or more of the alternative statements. A pleading may also state as many separate claims or defenses as the pleader has regardless of consistency and whether based on legal or equitable grounds. All statements shall be made subject to the obligations set forth in IN ST TRIAL P Rule 11. IN ST TRIAL P Rule 8(E)(2).

   c. *Motions and pleadings, joint and several.* All motions and pleadings of any kind addressed to two (2) or more paragraphs of any pleading, or filed by two (2) or more parties, shall be taken and construed as joint, separate, and several motions or pleadings to each of such paragraphs and by and against each of such parties. All motions or pleadings containing two (2) or more subject-matters shall be taken and construed as separate and several as to each subject-matter. All objections to rulings made

by two (2) or more parties shall be taken and construed as the joint, separate, and several objections of each of such parties. IN ST TRIAL P Rule 8(E)(3).

    i.   A complaint filed by or against two (2) or more plaintiffs shall be taken and construed as joint, separate, and several as to each of said plaintiffs. IN ST TRIAL P Rule 8(E).

d.   *Construction of pleadings.* All pleadings shall be so construed as to do substantial justice, lead to disposition on the merits, and avoid litigation of procedural points. IN ST TRIAL P Rule 8(F).

3.   *Contents of the answer*

a.   *Defenses which may be raised by answer or motion.* Every defense, in law or fact, to a claim for relief in any pleading, whether a claim, counterclaim, cross-claim, or third-party claim, shall be asserted in the responsive pleading thereto if one is required; except that at the option of the pleader, the following defenses may be made by motion:

    i.   Lack of jurisdiction over the subject matter;

    ii.   Lack of jurisdiction over the person;

    iii.   Incorrect venue under IN ST TRIAL P Rule 75, or any statutory provision. The disposition of this motion shall be consistent with IN ST TRIAL P Rule 75;

    iv.   Insufficiency of process;

    v.   Insufficiency of service of process;

    vi.   Failure to state a claim upon which relief can be granted, which shall include failure to name the real party in interest under IN ST TRIAL P Rule 17;

    vii.   Failure to join a party needed for just adjudication under IN ST TRIAL P Rule 19;

    viii.   The same action pending in another state court of this state. IN ST TRIAL P Rule 12(B).

    ix.   A motion making any of these defenses shall be made before pleading if a further pleading is permitted or within twenty (20) days after service of the prior pleading if none is required. If a pleading sets forth a claim for relief to which the adverse party is not required to serve a responsive pleading, any of the defenses in section IN ST TRIAL P Rule 12(B)(2), IN ST TRIAL P Rule 12(B)(3), IN ST TRIAL P Rule 12(B)(4), IN ST TRIAL P Rule 12(B)(5) or IN ST TRIAL P Rule 12(B)(8) is waived to the extent constitutionally permissible unless made in a motion within twenty (20) days after service of the prior pleading. No defense or objection is waived by being joined with one (1) or more other defenses or objections in a responsive pleading or motion. IN ST TRIAL P Rule 12(B).

b.   *Waiver or preservation of certain defenses*

    i.   A defense of lack of jurisdiction over the person, improper venue, insufficiency of process, insufficiency of service of process, or the same action pending in another state court of this state is waived to the extent constitutionally permissible:

       •   If omitted from a motion in the circumstances described in IN ST TRIAL P Rule 12(G),

       •   If it is neither made by motion under IN ST TRIAL P Rule 12 nor included in a responsive pleading or an amendment thereof permitted by IN ST TRIAL P Rule 15(A) to be made as a matter of course. IN ST TRIAL P Rule 12(H)(1).

    ii.   A defense of failure to state a claim upon which relief can be granted, a defense of failure to join an indispensable party under IN ST TRIAL P Rule 19(B), and an objection of failure to state a legal defense to a claim may be made in any pleading permitted or ordered under IN ST TRIAL P Rule 7(A) or by motion for judgment on the pleadings, or at the trial on the merits. IN ST TRIAL P Rule 12(H)(2).

c.   *Defenses; Form of denials*

    i.   A responsive pleading shall state in short and plain terms the pleader's defenses to each claim asserted and shall admit or controvert the averments set forth in the preceding pleading. If in good faith the pleader intends to deny all the averments in the preceding pleading, he may do so by general denial subject to the provisions of IN ST TRIAL P Rule 11. If he does not intend a general denial, he may:

- Specifically deny designated averments or paragraphs; or

- Generally deny all averments except such designated averments and paragraphs as he expressly admits. IN ST TRIAL P Rule 8(B).

    ii.   If he lacks knowledge or information sufficient to form a belief as to the truth of an averment, he shall so state and his statement shall be considered a denial. If in good faith a pleader intends to deny only a part or a qualification of an averment, he shall specify so much of it as is true and material and deny the remainder. All denials shall fairly meet the substance of the averments denied. IN ST TRIAL P Rule 8 shall have no application to uncontested actions for divorce, or to answers required to be filed by clerks or guardians ad litem. IN ST TRIAL P Rule 8(B).

d. *Affirmative defenses.* A responsive pleading shall set forth affirmatively and carry the burden of proving: accord and satisfaction, arbitration and award, discharge in bankruptcy, duress, estoppel, failure of consideration, fraud, illegality, injury by fellow servant, laches, license, payment, release, res judicata, statute of frauds, statute of limitations, waiver, lack of jurisdiction over the subject-matter, lack of jurisdiction over the person, improper venue, insufficiency of process or service of process, the same action pending in another state court of this state, and any other matter constituting an avoidance, matter of abatement, or affirmative defense. A party required to affirmatively plead any matters, including matters formerly required to be pleaded affirmatively by reply, shall have the burden of proving such matters. The burden of proof imposed by this or any other provision of the Indiana Rules of Trial Procedure is subject to the rules of evidence or any statute fixing a different rule. If the pleading mistakenly designates a defense as a counterclaim or a counterclaim as a defense, the court shall treat the pleading as if there had been a proper designation. IN ST TRIAL P Rule 8(C).

    i.   An affirmative defense, generally, must be affirmatively stated by the party who seeks its benefit. 1A INPRAC R 8(8.5); Rice v. Grant County Bd. of Com'rs, 472 N.E.2d 213 (Ind.Ct.App. 1984). If that party does not raise the affirmative defense, then it is waived. 1A INPRAC R 8(8.5); Piskorowski v. Shell Oil Co., 403 N.E.2d 838, 847 (Ind.Ct.App. 1980).

    ii.   It is clear that the list of affirmative defenses found in IN ST TRIAL P Rule 8 is not exhaustive. The question comes: when is a defense to be treated as an affirmative defense, with all of the attending consequences? 1A INPRAC R 8(8.5). The "determination of whether a defense is affirmative depends on whether it controverts an element of the plaintiff's prima facie case or raises matter outside the scope of the prima facie case." 1A INPRAC R 8(8.5); Molargik v. West Enterprises, Inc., 605 N.E.2d 1197, 1198 (Ind.Ct.App. 1993).

e. *Defense of contributory negligence or assumed risk.* In all claims alleging negligence, the burden of pleading and proving contributory negligence, assumption of risk, or incurred risk shall be upon the defendant who may plead such by denial of the allegation. IN ST TRIAL P Rule 9.1(A).

f. *Res ipsa loquitur.* Res ipsa loquitur or a similar doctrine may be pleaded by alleging generally that the facts connected with the action are unknown to the pleader and are within the knowledge of the opposing party. IN ST TRIAL P Rule 9.1(B).

g. *Consideration.* When an action or defense is founded upon a written contract or release, lack of consideration for the promise or release is an affirmative defense, and the party asserting lack of it carries the burden of proof. IN ST TRIAL P Rule 9.1(C).

h. *Bona fide purchaser.* When the rights of a person depend upon his status as a bona fide purchaser for value or upon similar requirements, such status must be pleaded and proved by the person asserting it, but it may be pleaded in general terms. Once it is established that the person has given any required value, unless such value is commercially unreasonable, and that he has met any requirements of recordation, filing, possession, or perfection, the trier of fact must find that such value was given or such perfection was made in accordance with any requirements of good faith, lack of knowledge, or lack of notice unless and until evidence is introduced which would support a finding of its non-existence. IN ST TRIAL P Rule 9.1(D).

i. *Presumption; Matters of judicial notice.* Neither presumptions of law nor matters of which judicial notice may be taken need be stated in a pleading. IN ST TRIAL P Rule 9.1(E).

j. *Property distrained; Sufficient answer.* In an action to recover the possession of property distrained while doing damage, an answer that the defendant, or person by whose command he acted, was lawfully possessed of the real property upon which the distress was made, and that the property distrained was at the time doing damage thereon, shall be good without setting forth the title of such real property. IN ST TRIAL P Rule 9.1(F).

k. *Effect of failure to deny.* Averments in a pleading to which a responsive pleading is required, except those pertaining to amount of damages, are admitted when not denied in the responsive pleading. Averments in a pleading to which no responsive pleading is required or permitted shall be taken as denied or avoided. IN ST TRIAL P Rule 8(D).

l. *Effect of admission.* When a rhetorical paragraph or allegation is admitted, the effect in Indiana is to remove it from trial. Such an admission is a "judicial admission", and the claim or issue which is admitted cannot be denied later by the trier of the facts. Further, this admitted fact does not require evidence to "prove it"; it is established. It becomes, in short, controlling and indisputable in the litigation, unless the trial court permits an amendment to the pleading which might remove the controlling effect of the admission, and permit it to become another fact or item of evidence in the case. 1A INPRAC R 8(8.4); Aylesworth v. McKesson, 421 N.E.2d 422 (Ind.Ct.App. 1981).

4. *Pleading special matters*

a. *Capacity.* It is not necessary to aver the capacity of a party to sue or be sued, the authority of a party to sue or be sued in a representative capacity, or the legal existence of an organization that is made a party. The burden of proving lack of such capacity, authority, or legal existence shall be upon the person asserting lack of it, and shall be pleaded as an affirmative defense. IN ST TRIAL P Rule 9(A).

b. *Fraud, mistake, condition of the mind.* In all averments of fraud or mistake, the circumstances constituting fraud or mistake shall be specifically averred. Malice, intent, knowledge, and other conditions of mind may be averred generally. IN ST TRIAL P Rule 9(B).

c. *Conditions precedent.* In pleading the performance or occurrence of promissory or non-promissory conditions precedent, it is sufficient to aver generally that all conditions precedent have been performed, have occurred, or have been excused. A denial of performance or occurrence shall be made specifically and with particularity, and a denial of excuse generally. IN ST TRIAL P Rule 9(C).

d. *Official document or act.* In pleading an official document or official act it is sufficient to aver that the document was issued or the act done in compliance with law. IN ST TRIAL P Rule 9(D).

e. *Judgment.* In pleading a judgment or decision of a domestic or foreign court, judicial or quasi-judicial tribunal, or of a board or officer, it is sufficient to aver the judgment or decision without setting forth matter showing jurisdiction to render it. IN ST TRIAL P Rule 9(E).

f. *Time and place.* For the purpose of testing the sufficiency of a pleading, averments of time and place are material and shall be considered like all other averments of material matter. However, time and place need be stated only with such specificity as will enable the opposing party to prepare his defense. IN ST TRIAL P Rule 9(F).

g. *Special damages; Damages where no answer.* When items of special damage are claimed, they shall be specifically stated. The relief granted to the plaintiff, if there be no answer, cannot exceed the relief demanded in his complaint; but, in any other case, the court may grant him any relief consistent with the facts or matters pleaded. IN ST TRIAL P Rule 9(G).

5. *Counterclaim and cross-claim*

a. *Compulsory counterclaims.* A pleading shall state as a counterclaim any claim which at the time of serving the pleading the pleader has against any opposing party, if it arises out of the transaction or occurrence that is the subject-matter of the opposing party's claim and does not require for its adjudication the presence of third parties of whom the court cannot acquire jurisdiction. But the pleader need not state the claim if:

i. At the time the action was commenced the claim was the subject of another pending action; or

    ii.   The opposing party brought suit upon his claim by attachment or other process by which the court did not acquire jurisdiction to render a personal judgment on that claim, and the pleader is not stating any counterclaim under IN ST TRIAL P Rule 13. IN ST TRIAL P Rule 13(A).

b.   *Permissive counterclaims.* A pleading may state as a counterclaim any claim against an opposing party not arising out of the transaction or occurrence that is the subject-matter of the opposing party's claim. IN ST TRIAL P Rule 13(B).

c.   *Counterclaim exceeding opposing claim.* A counterclaim may or may not diminish or defeat the recovery sought by the opposing party. It may claim relief exceeding in amount or different in kind from that sought in the pleading of the opposing party. IN ST TRIAL P Rule 13(C).

d.   *Counterclaim against state.* IN ST TRIAL P Rule 13 shall not be construed to enlarge any right to assert a claim against the state. IN ST TRIAL P Rule 13(D).

e.   *Counterclaim maturing or acquired after pleading.* A claim which either matured or was acquired by the pleader after serving his pleading may, with the permission of the court, be presented as a counterclaim by supplemental pleading. A counterclaim or cross-claim which is not due may be asserted against a party who is insolvent or the representative of a party who has been subjected to insolvency proceedings, if recovery thereon will be impaired because of such party's insolvency. IN ST TRIAL P Rule 13(E).

f.   *Omitted counterclaim.* When a pleader fails to set up a counterclaim through oversight, inadvertence, or excusable neglect, or when justice requires, he may by leave of court set up the counterclaim by amendment. IN ST TRIAL P Rule 13(F).

g.   *Cross-claim against co-party.* A pleading may state as a cross-claim any claim by one party against a co-party. IN ST TRIAL P Rule 13(G).

h.   *Joinder of additional parties.* Persons other than those made parties to the original action may be made parties to a counterclaim or cross-claim in accordance with the provisions of IN ST TRIAL P Rule 14, IN ST TRIAL P Rule 19 and IN ST TRIAL P Rule 20. IN ST TRIAL P Rule 13(H).

i.   *Separate trials; Separate judgments*

    i.   If the court orders separate trials as provided in IN ST TRIAL P Rule 42(B), judgment on a counterclaim or cross-claim may be rendered in accordance with the terms of IN ST TRIAL P Rule 54(B) when the court has jurisdiction so to do, even if the claims of the opposing party have been dismissed or otherwise disposed of. In determining whether or not separate trial of a cross-claim shall be ordered, the court shall consider whether the cross-claim:

- Arises out of the transaction or occurrence or series of transactions or occurrences that is the subject-matter either of the original action or of a counterclaim therein;

- Relates to any property or contract that is the subject-matter of the original action; or

- Claims that the person against whom it is asserted is liable to the cross-claimant for all or part of plaintiff's claim against him. IN ST TRIAL P Rule 13(I).

    ii.   In addition, the court may consider any other relevant factors. IN ST TRIAL P Rule 13(I).

j.   *Effect of statute of limitations and other discharges at law.* The statute of limitations, a nonclaim statute or other discharge at law shall not bar a claim asserted as a counterclaim to the extent that:

    i.   It diminishes or defeats the opposing party's claim if it arises out of the transaction or occurrence that is the subject-matter of the opposing party's claim, or if it could have been asserted as a counterclaim to the opposing party's claim before it (the counterclaim) was barred; or

    ii.   It or the opposing party's claim relates to payment of or security for the other. IN ST TRIAL P Rule 13(J).

k.   *Counterclaim by and against transferees and successors.* A counterclaim may be asserted by or against the transferee or successor of a claim subject to the following provisions:

    i.   A successor who is a guardian, representative of a decedent's estate, receiver or assignee for the benefit of creditors, trustee or the like may interpose a claim to which he succeeds against claims or proceedings brought in or outside the court of administration. A claim owing by his predecessor may be interposed against any claim brought by such successor in or outside the court of administration without the necessity of filing such claim or cause of action in the administration proceedings. IN ST TRIAL P Rule 13(K)(1).

    ii. A transferee or successor of a claim takes it subject to any defense or counterclaim that is the subject-matter of the opposing party's claim; or that is available to the obligor at the time of the assignment or before the obligor received notice of the assignment. IN ST TRIAL P Rule 13(K)(2).

    iii. A surety or party with total or partial recourse upon a claim upon which he is being sued may interpose as a counterclaim:

- Any claim of his own; and

- Any claim owned by the person against whom he has recourse who either has notice of the suit, is a party to the suit, is insolvent, has assigned his claim to the surety or party asserting it, or cannot be found. IN ST TRIAL P Rule 13(K)(3).

- A counterclaim under IN ST TRIAL P Rule 13(K)(3)(b) must tend to diminish or defeat the opposing party's claim, or it or the opposing claim must relate to payment of or security for the other, unless the person against whom recourse may be had is a party to the suit or the counterclaim has been assigned to the party asserting it; and if recovery on the counterclaim exceeds the opposing party's claim, any excess recovered shall be held in trust for such person against whom there is a right of recourse. IN ST TRIAL P Rule 13(K)(3).

    iv. IN ST TRIAL P Rule 13(K)(1), IN ST TRIAL P Rule 13(K)(2), and IN ST TRIAL P Rule 13(K)(3), are subject to subdivision IN ST TRIAL P Rule 13(L). IN ST TRIAL P Rule 13(K)(4).

  l. *Counterclaim and cross-claim subject to substantive law principles.* Counterclaim and cross-claims are subject to restrictions imposed by other statutes and principles of substantive common law and equity, including rules of commercial law, agency, estoppel, contract and the like. In appropriate cases the court may impose terms or conditions upon its judgment or decree and may enter conditional or noncanceling cross judgments to satisfy such restrictions. This provision is intended to deny or limit counterclaims or cross-claims:

    i. Where a creditor will receive an unfair priority because a claim is assigned after insolvency proceedings, or assigned before such proceedings if it results in an unlawful preference;

    ii. Where an unfair priority will be allowed if a surety interposing a claim owned in his own right against the creditor suing on the principal's obligation when the principal is solvent and the creditor is not;

    iii. Where a claim by or against a representative, such as a guardian, receiver, representative of a decedent's estate, assignee for the benefit of creditors, trustee or the like in his individual capacity is asserted against a claim owing or owed by the estate he represents;

    iv. Where a claim by or against a partnership or two (2) or more obligors is opposed against or by a claim of an individual to the extent that the individual will be allowed unfairly to profit or if it will adversely affect the rights of creditors; or

    v. Where a claim is cut off by a holder in due course or a transferee who is protected under principles of commercial law, estoppel, or contract. IN ST TRIAL P Rule 13(L).

  m. *Satisfaction of judgment.* Satisfaction of a judgment or credits thereon may be ordered, for sufficient cause, upon notice and motion. "Credits" include any counterclaim which tends to diminish or defeat the judgment, or any counterclaim where it or the opposing claim relates to payment of or security for the other. IN ST TRIAL P Rule 13(M).

6. *Third-party practice*

  a. *When defendant may bring in third party.* A defending party, as a third-party plaintiff, may cause a summons and complaint to be served upon a person not a party to the action who is or may be liable to him for all or part of the plaintiff's claim against him. IN ST TRIAL P Rule 14(A). The person served with the summons and the third-party complaint, hereinafter called the third-party defendant, as provided in IN ST TRIAL P Rule 12 and IN ST TRIAL P Rule 13 may make:

i. His defenses, cross-claims and counterclaims to the third-party plaintiff's claims;

ii. His defenses, counterclaims and cross-claims against any other defendants or third-party defendants;

iii. Any defenses or claims which the third-party plaintiff has to the plaintiff's claim which are available to the third-party defendant against the plaintiff; and

iv. Any defenses or claims which the third-party defendant has as against the plaintiff. IN ST TRIAL P Rule 14(A).

v. The plaintiff may assert any claim against the third-party defendant who thereupon may assert his defenses, counterclaims and cross-claims, as provided in IN ST TRIAL P Rule 12 and IN ST TRIAL P Rule 13. A third-party defendant may proceed under IN ST TRIAL P Rule 14 against any person not a party to the action who is or may be liable to him for all or part of the claim made in the action against the third-party defendant. IN ST TRIAL P Rule 14(A).

b. *When plaintiff may bring in third party.* When a counterclaim or other claim is asserted against a plaintiff, he may cause a third party to be brought in under circumstances, which, under IN ST TRIAL P Rule 14, would entitle a defendant to do so. IN ST TRIAL P Rule 14(B).

c. *Severance; Parties improperly impleaded.* With his responsive pleading or by motion prior thereto, any party may move for severance of a third-party claim or ensuing claim as provided in IN ST TRIAL P Rule 14 or for a separate trial thereon. If the third-party defendant is a proper party to the proceedings under any other rule relating to parties, the action shall continue as in other cases where he is made a party. IN ST TRIAL P Rule 14(C).

7. *Trial by jury; Demand*

a. *Causes triable by court and by jury.* Issues of law and issues of fact in causes that prior to the eighteenth day of June, 1852, were of exclusive equitable jurisdiction shall be tried by the court; issues of fact in all other causes shall be triable as the same are now triable. In case of the joinder of causes of action or defenses which, prior to said date, were of exclusive equitable jurisdiction with causes of action or defenses which, prior to said date, were designated as actions at law and triable by jury—the former shall be triable by the court, and the latter by a jury, unless waived; the trial of both may be at the same time or at different times, as the court may direct. IN ST TRIAL P Rule 38(A).

b. *Demand.* Any party may demand a trial by jury of any issue triable of right by a jury by filing with the court and serving upon the other parties a demand therefor in writing at any time after the commencement of the action and not later than ten (10) days after the first responsive pleading to the complaint, or to a counterclaim, crossclaim or other claim if one properly is pleaded; and if no responsive pleading is filed or required, within ten (10) days after the time such pleading otherwise would have been required. Such demand is sufficient if indorsed upon a pleading of a party filed within such time. IN ST TRIAL P Rule 38(B).

c. *Same; Specification of issues.* In his demand a party may specify the issues which he wishes so tried; otherwise he shall be deemed to have demanded trial by jury for all issues triable as of right by jury. Any other party must file a demand for jury trial to preserve his right to trial by jury:

i. Of issues for which a right to trial by jury was not requested by another party; and

ii. In case a request by another party was improper. But if a proper request for a trial by jury upon issues triable by jury as of right on his behalf is made by any party, such request shall be deemed to have been made on behalf of all parties entitled to a jury trial upon such issues. IN ST TRIAL P Rule 38(C).

d. *Waiver.* The failure of a party to appear at the trial, and the failure of a party to serve a demand as required by IN ST TRIAL P Rule 38 and to file it as required by IN ST TRIAL P Rule 5(E) constitute waiver by him of trial by jury. A demand for trial by jury made as provided in IN ST TRIAL P Rule

38 may not be withdrawn without the consent of the other party or parties. IN ST TRIAL P Rule 38(D).

    i.   The trial court shall not grant a demand for a trial by jury filed after the time fixed in IN ST TRIAL P Rule 38(B) has elapsed except upon the written agreement of all of the parties to the action, which agreement shall be filed with the court and made a part of the record. If such agreement is filed then the court may, in its discretion, grant a trial by jury in which event the grant of a trial by jury may not be withdrawn except by the agreement of all of the parties. IN ST TRIAL P Rule 38(D).

  e. *Arbitration.* Nothing in the Indiana Rules of Trial Procedure shall deny the parties the right by contract or agreement to submit or to agree to submit controversies to arbitration made before or after commencement of an action thereon or deny the courts power to specifically enforce such agreements. IN ST TRIAL P Rule 38(E).

D. Documents

1. *Required documents*

  a. *Amended answer.* Refer to the General Requirements section of this document for information on the contents of an amended answer.

  b. *Chronological Case Summary (CCS) entry form.* Every written motion, petition, or other pleading subsequent to the original complaint presented to the Clerk for filing shall be accompanied by a Chronological Case Summary (CCS) entry form in duplicate. IN ST ST JOSEPH CIV Rule 201(201.4). Refer to the Format section of this document for details on the format and filing requirements for the CCS entry form.

  c. *Certificate of service.* An attorney or unrepresented party tendering a document to the Clerk for filing shall certify that service has been made, list the parties served, and specify the date and means of service. The certificate of service shall be placed at the end of the document and shall not be separately filed. The separate filing of a certificate of service, however, shall not be grounds for rejecting a document for filing. The Clerk may permit documents to be filed without a certificate of service but shall require prompt filing of a separate certificate of service. IN ST TRIAL P Rule 5(C).

2. *Supplemental documents*

  a. *Proof of written instrument.* When any pleading allowed by the Indiana Rules of Trial Procedure is founded on a written instrument, the original, or a copy thereof, must be included in or filed with the pleading. Such instrument, whether copied in the pleadings or not, shall be taken as part of the record. When any pleading allowed by the Indiana Rules of Trial Procedure is founded on an account, an Affidavit of Debt, in a form substantially similar to that which is provided in IN ST TRIAL P App. A-2, shall be attached. IN ST TRIAL P Rule 9.2(A).

  b. *Notice of intent to use foreign law.* A party who intends to raise an issue concerning the law of a foreign country shall give notice in his pleadings or other reasonable written notice. The court, in determining foreign law, may consider any relevant material or source, including testimony, whether or not submitted by a party or admissible under IN ST TRIAL P Rule 43. The court's determination shall be treated as a ruling on a question of law. It shall be made by the court and not the jury and shall be reviewable. IN ST TRIAL P Rule 44.1(A).

  c. *Facsimile cover sheet.* Any document sent to the Clerk of the Circuit Court by electronic facsimile transmission shall be accompanied by a cover sheet which states the title of the document, case number, number of pages, identity and voice telephone number of the sending party and instructions for filing. The cover sheet shall contain the signature of the attorney or party, pro se, authorizing the filing. IN ST ADMIN Rule 12(D).

E. Format

1. *Form of pleadings*

  a. *Caption; Names of parties.* Every pleading shall contain a caption setting forth the name of the court, the title of the action, the file number, and a designation as in IN ST TRIAL P Rule 7(A). In the complaint the title of the action shall include the names of all the parties, but in other pleadings it is sufficient to state the name of the first party on each side with an appropriate indication of other parties. IN ST TRIAL P Rule 10(A); IN ST ST JOSEPH CIV Rule 201(201.3.3). If a special judge has been assigned to the case, the pleading should also identify the special judge. IN ST ST JOSEPH CIV Rule 201(201.3.3).

    i.   *Title.* All pleadings or motions shall include a title, which shall delineate each topic included in the pleading. For example, where a pleading contains an answer, a motion to dismiss, and a jury request, each topic shall be set forth in the title. IN ST ST JOSEPH CIV Rule 201(201.3.4).

b.   *Paragraphs; Separate statements.* All averments of a claim or defense shall be made in numbered paragraphs, the contents of each of which shall be limited as far as practicable to a statement of a single set of circumstances, and a paragraph may be referred to by number in all succeeding pleadings. Each claim founded upon a separate transaction or occurrence and each defense other than denials may be stated in a separate count or defense whenever a separation facilitates the clear presentation of the matters set forth. IN ST TRIAL P Rule 10(B).

c.   *Adoption by reference; Exhibits.* Statements in a pleading may be adopted by reference in a different part of the same pleading or in another pleading or in any motion. A copy of any written instrument which is an exhibit to a pleading is a part thereof for all purposes. IN ST TRIAL P Rule 10(C).

d.   *Flat filing.* In order that the Clerk's files may be kept under the system commonly known as "flat filing," all papers presented to the Clerk for filing shall be flat and unfolded. Pleadings shall have no covers or backs and shall be fastened together at the top left-hand corner only. IN ST ST JOSEPH CIV Rule 201(201.1).

e.   *One side of page used.* Printing shall be on one (1) side of the paper. IN ST ST JOSEPH CIV Rule 201(201.3.2).

f.   *Copies.* All copies shall be on white paper of sufficient strength and durability to resist normal wear and tear. IN ST ST JOSEPH CIV Rule 201(201.3.1).

g.   *Margins.* Margins shall be at least one inch (1"). IN ST ST JOSEPH CIV Rule 201(201.3.2).

h.   *Double-spaced.* If typewritten, the lines shall be double spaced except for quotations, which shall be indented and single-spaced. IN ST ST JOSEPH CIV Rule 201(201.3.2).

i.   *Font size.* Type face shall be twelve (12) font size or larger within the body of the document and ten (10) font size or larger in the footnotes. IN ST ST JOSEPH CIV Rule 201(201.3.2).

j.   *Font type.* The font type must be legible and script type shall not be used. IN ST ST JOSEPH CIV Rule 201(201.3.2).

k.   *Italics.* Italicized type may be used for quotations, references, or case citations. IN ST ST JOSEPH CIV Rule 201(201.3.2).

l.   *Court and case designation.* All filings shall conform to the requirements for uniform court and case number designation set by IN ST ADMIN Rule 8. In addition, all filings shall contain the proper court and case designation as described below. IN ST ST JOSEPH CIV Rule 202.

    i.   *Court designation.* Pursuant to IN ST 33-33-71-2, St. Joseph County, Indiana, constitutes the Sixtieth Judicial Circuit. The legal names of the courts within the 60th Judicial Circuit are the St. Joseph Circuit Court, the St. Joseph Superior Court, and the St. Joseph Probate Court. All filings shall properly reflect the legal name of the applicable court. Any filing may be amended, rejected, or stricken if it does not contain the proper case name and/or the legal name of the court. IN ST ST JOSEPH CIV Rule 202(202.1).

m.   *Form of CCS entry.* Every written motion, petition, or other pleading subsequent to the original complaint presented to the Clerk for filing shall be accompanied by a Chronological Case Summary (CCS) entry form in duplicate which shall contain the title and cause number of the action, the date, and the proposed entry to appear on the docket. IN ST ST JOSEPH CIV Rule 201(201.4).

    i.   *Identification and signature.* The CCS entry form shall identify the party making the filing, designate each pleading being filed, and shall be signed by counsel of record or the unrepresented litigant. IN ST ST JOSEPH CIV Rule 201(201.4).

    ii.   *Date stamp.* The form shall be date stamped and presented to the Court Clerk, who shall initial the form and return the duplicate to the filing party. IN ST ST JOSEPH CIV Rule 201(201.4).

2. *Size of papers for filing.* Effective January 1, 1992, all pleadings, copies, motions and documents filed with any trial court or appellate level court, typed or printed, with the exception of exhibits and existing wills, shall be prepared on eight and one-half by eleven inch (8 1/2" x 11") size paper. IN ST ADMIN Rule 11.

   a. *Paper.* Pleadings, motions, and other papers shall be either legibly printed or typewritten on white opaque paper of good quality at least sixteen (16) pound weight, eight and one-half inches (8 1/2 ") in width and eleven inches (11") in length as required by IN ST ADMIN Rule 11. IN ST ST JOSEPH CIV Rule 201(201.3.1).

3. *Signature requirements*

   a. *Signature of attorney.* Every pleading or motion of a party represented by an attorney shall be signed by at least one (1) attorney of record in his individual name, whose address, telephone number, and attorney number shall be stated, except that this provision shall not apply to pleadings and motions made and transcribed at the trial or a hearing before the judge and received by him in such form. IN ST TRIAL P Rule 11(A).

      i. The signature of an attorney constitutes a certificate by him that he has read the pleadings; that to the best of his knowledge, information, and belief, there is good ground to support it; and that it is not interposed for delay. IN ST TRIAL P Rule 11(A).

      ii. If a pleading or motion is not signed or is signed with intent to defeat the purpose of the rule, it may be stricken as sham and false and the action may proceed as though the pleading had not been served. IN ST TRIAL P Rule 11(A).

      iii. For a willful violation of IN ST TRIAL P Rule 11 an attorney may be subjected to appropriate disciplinary action. Similar action may be taken if scandalous or indecent matter is inserted. IN ST TRIAL P Rule 11(A).

   b. *Signature of unrepresented party.* A party who is not represented by an attorney shall sign his pleading and state his address. IN ST TRIAL P Rule 11(A).

   c. *Verification not generally required.* Except when specifically required by rule, pleadings or motions need not be verified or accompanied by affidavit. The rule in equity that the averments of an answer under oath must be overcome by the testimony of two (2) witnesses or of one (1) witness sustained by corroborating circumstances is abolished. IN ST TRIAL P Rule 11(A).

   d. *Verification by affirmation or representation.* When in connection with any civil or special statutory proceeding it is required that any pleading, motion, petition, supporting affidavit, or other document of any kind, be verified, or that an oath be taken, it shall be sufficient if the subscriber simply affirms the truth of the matter to be verified by an affirmation or representation. IN ST TRIAL P Rule 11(B). IN ST TRIAL P Rule 11(B) states that the affirmation or representation should be in substantially the following language: "I (we) affirm, under the penalties for perjury, that the foregoing representation(s) is (are) true. (Signed) _____."

      i. Any person who falsifies an affirmation or representation of fact shall be subject to the same penalties as are prescribed by law for the making of a false affidavit. IN ST TRIAL P Rule 11(B).

   e. *Verified pleadings, motions, and affidavits as evidence.* Pleadings, motions and affidavits accompanying or in support of such pleadings or motions when required to be verified or under oath shall be accepted as a representation that the signer had personal knowledge thereof or reasonable cause to believe the existence of the facts or matters stated or alleged therein; and, if otherwise competent or acceptable as evidence, may be admitted as evidence of the facts or matters stated or alleged therein when it is so provided in the Indiana Rules of Trial Procedure, by statute or other law, or to the extent the writing or signature expressly purports to be made upon the signer's personal knowledge. When such pleadings, motions and affidavits are verified or under oath they shall not require other or greater proof on the part of the adverse party than if not verified or not under oath unless expressly provided otherwise by the Indiana Rules of Trial Procedure, statute or other law. Affidavits upon motions for summary judgment under IN ST TRIAL P Rule 56 and in denial of execution under IN ST TRIAL P Rule 9.2 shall be made upon personal knowledge. IN ST TRIAL P Rule 11(C).

  f. *Signature, verification and other requirements.* Parties and their counsel are enjoined to comply with the verification requirements of IN ST TRIAL P Rule 11, and either the moving party or the party's attorney of record shall sign all pleadings and motions before filing with the Clerk of the Court. Every motion, petition, or other pleading filed with the Clerk shall contain the name, organization, physical address, telephone number, and facsimile number of the filing party or an attorney for that party. IN ST ST JOSEPH CIV Rule 201(201.3.6).

    i. The Clerk shall not accept any motion, petition, notice or other pleading or a CCS entry form for filing from an unrepresented litigant unless the unrepresented litigant's current address and phone number appear on the pleading, and an opposing party may service notices and responses on an unrepresented litigant at any address he or she has provided on a pleading. IN ST ST JOSEPH CIV Rule 201(201.3.6).

4. *Information excluded from public access.* Every document filed in a case shall separately identify information excluded from public access pursuant to IN ST ADMIN Rule 9(G)(1) as follows:

  a. Whole documents that are excluded from public access pursuant to IN ST ADMIN Rule 9(G)(1) shall be tendered on light green paper or have a light green coversheet attached to the document, marked "Not for Public Access" or "Confidential." IN ST TRIAL P Rule 5(G)(1).

  b. When only a portion of a document contains information excluded from public access pursuant to IN ST ADMIN Rule 9(G)(1), said information shall be omitted [or redacted] from the filed document, and set forth on a separate accompanying document on light green paper conspicuously marked "Not for Public Access" or "Confidential" and clearly designated [or identifying] the caption and number of the case and the document and location within the document to which the redacted material pertains. IN ST TRIAL P Rule 5(G)(2).

  c. With respect to documents filed in electronic format, the trial court, by local rule, may provide for compliance with IN ST TRIAL P Rule 5 in manner that separates and protects access to information excluded from public access. IN ST TRIAL P Rule 5(G)(3).

  d. IN ST TRIAL P Rule 5(G) does not apply to a record sealed by the court pursuant to IN ST 5-14-3-5.5 or otherwise, nor to records, documents, or information filed in cases to which public access is prohibited pursuant to IN ST ADMIN Rule 9(G). IN ST TRIAL P Rule 5(G)(4).

  e. The following information in case records is excluded from public access and is confidential:

    i. Information that is excluded from public access pursuant to federal law;

    ii. Information that is excluded from public access as declared confidential by Indiana statute or other court rule, including without limitation:

      • All adoption records created after July 8, 1941, as declared confidential by IN ST 31-19-19-1, et seq., except those specifically declared open by IN ST 31-19-13-2(2);

      • All records relating to chancroid, chlamydia, gonorrhea, hepatitis, human immunodeficiency virus (HIV), Lymphogranuloma venereum, syphilis, tuberculosis, as declared confidential by IN ST 16-41-8-1, et seq.;

      • All records relating to child abuse as declared confidential by IN ST 31-33-18-1, et seq.;

      • All records relating to drug tests as declared confidential by IN ST 5-14-3-4(a)(9);

      • Records of grand jury proceedings as declared confidential by IN ST 35-34-2-4;

      • Records of juvenile proceedings as declared confidential by IN ST 31-39-1-2, except those specifically open under statute;

      • All paternity records created after July 1, 1941 as declared confidential by IN ST 31-14-11-15, IN ST 31-19-5-23, IN ST 31-39-1-1 and IN ST 31-39-1-2 [Editor's note: IN ST 31-14-11-15 was repealed effective May 9, 2013];

      • All pre-sentence reports as declared confidential by IN ST 35-38-1-13;

      • Written petitions to permit marriages without consent and orders directing the Clerk of Court to issue a marriage license to underage persons, as declared confidential by IN ST 31-11-1-6;

- Only those arrest warrants, search warrants, indictments and informations ordered confidential by the trial judge, prior to return of duly executed service as declared confidential by IN ST 5-14-3-4(b)(1);

- All medical, mental health, or tax records unless determined by law or regulation of any governmental custodian not to be confidential, released by the subject of such records, or declared by a court of competent jurisdiction to be essential to the resolution of litigation as declared confidential by IN ST 16-39-3-10, IN ST 6-4.1-5-10, IN ST 6-4.1-12-12, and IN ST 6-8.1-7-1;

- Personal information relating to jurors or prospective jurors, other than for the use of the parties and counsel, pursuant to IN ST JURY Rule 10;

- Information relating to protection from abuse orders, no-contact orders and workplace violence restraining orders as declared confidential by IN ST 5-2-9-6, et seq.;

- Mediation proceedings pursuant to IN ST ADR Rule 2.11, Mini-Trial proceedings pursuant to IN ST ADR Rule 4.4(C), and Summary Jury Trials pursuant to IN ST ADR Rule 5.6;

- Information in probation files pursuant to the Probation Standards promulgated by the Judicial Conference of Indiana pursuant to IN ST 11-13-1-8(b);

- Information deemed confidential pursuant to the Rules for Court Administered Alcohol and Drug Programs promulgated by the Judicial Conference of Indiana pursuant to IN ST 12-23-14-13;

- Information deemed confidential pursuant to the Problem-Solving Court Rules promulgated by the Judicial Conference of Indiana pursuant to IN ST 33-23-16-16;

- All records of the Department of workforce Development as declared confidential by IN ST 22-4-19-6;

- Information regarding interception of electronic communications that is sealed or deemed confidential as set forth in IN ST 35-33.5-2-1, et seq.

iii. Information excluded from public access by specific court order;

iv. Complete Social Security Numbers of living persons;

v. With the exception of names, information such as addresses, phone numbers, and dates of birth which explicitly identifies:

- Natural persons who are witnesses or victims (not including defendants) in criminal, domestic violence, stalking, sexual assault, juvenile, or civil protection order proceedings, provided that juveniles who are victims of sex crimes shall be identified by initials only;

- Places of residence of judicial officers, clerks and other employees of courts and clerks of court, unless the person or persons about whom the information pertains waives confidentiality;

vi. Complete account numbers of specific assets, loans, bank accounts, credit cards, and personal identification numbers (PINs);

vii. All orders of expungement entered in criminal or juvenile proceedings, orders to restrict access to criminal history information pursuant to IN ST 35-38-5-5.5 or IN ST 35-38-8-5 and records excluded from public access by such orders, and information related to infractions that is excluded from public access pursuant to IN ST 34-28-5-15 or IN ST 34-28-5-16 [Editor's note: IN ST 35-38-5-5.5, IN ST 35-38-8-5 and IN ST 34-28-5-16 were repealed effective July 1, 2013; for information on orders restricting access to criminal history, refer to IN ST 35-38-9-1, et seq.];

viii. All personal notes and e-mail, and deliberative material, of judges, jurors, court staff and judicial agencies, and information recorded in personal data assistants (PDA's) or organizers and personal calendars. IN ST ADMIN Rule 9(G)(1).

F. Filing and Service Requirements

1. *Filing requirements.* Except as otherwise provided in IN ST TRIAL P Rule 5(E)(2), all pleadings and

papers subsequent to the complaint which are required to be served upon a party shall be filed with the Court either before service or within a reasonable period of time thereafter. IN ST TRIAL P Rule 5(E)(1).

a. *Filing with the court defined.* The filing of pleadings, motions, and other papers with the court as required by the Indiana Rules of Trial Procedure shall be made by one of the following methods:

   i. Delivery to the clerk of the court;

   ii. Sending by electronic transmission under the procedure adopted pursuant to IN ST ADMIN Rule 12;

   iii. Mailing to the clerk by registered, certified or express mail return receipt requested;

   iv. Depositing with any third-party commercial carrier for delivery to the clerk within three (3) calendar days, cost prepaid, properly addressed;

   v. If the court so permits, filing with the judge, in which event the judge shall note thereon the filing date and forthwith transmit them to the office of the clerk; or

   vi. Electronic filing, as approved by the Division of State Court Administration pursuant to IN ST ADMIN Rule 16. IN ST TRIAL P Rule 5(F).

   vii. Filing by registered or certified mail and by third-party commercial carrier shall be complete upon mailing or deposit. IN ST TRIAL P Rule 5(F).

   viii. All pleadings shall be filed with the Clerk, not directly with the Court, unless otherwise required by the Indiana Rules of Court. The entry of appearances and the filing of pleadings or other matters not requiring immediate Court action shall be filed with the Clerk and not in open Court. A Judge may permit papers to be filed in chambers, in which event he or she shall note thereon the filing date and transmit the papers to the Clerk. IN ST ST JOSEPH CIV Rule 201(201.2).

b. *Facsimile filing.* Unless otherwise authorized by IN ST ST JOSEPH ELECTRONIC Rule 701, electronic filing of pleadings by computerized or facsimile transmission is not permitted. IN ST ST JOSEPH CIV Rule 201(201.2).

c. *Additional copies.* In cases in which a party or counsel supplies the proposed order or decree, a sufficient number shall be prepared and filed as to provide the Clerk to retain two (2) copies, which shall be filed in the flat file and the record of judgments and orders. Should the party or counsel desire additional copies, a sufficient number of copies should be filed to effectuate that purpose. IN ST ST JOSEPH CIV Rule 201(201.6).

d. *Proof of filing.* Any party filing any paper by any method other than personal delivery to the clerk shall retain proof of filing. IN ST TRIAL P Rule 5(F).

2. *Service requirements.* Unless otherwise provided by the Indiana Rules of Trial Procedure or an order of the court, each party and special judge, if any, shall be served with: (1) every order required by its terms to be served; (2) every pleading subsequent to the original complaint; (3) every written motion except one which may be heard ex parte; (4) every brief submitted to the trial court; (5) every paper relating to discovery required to be served upon a party; and (6) every written notice, appearance, demand, offer of judgment, designation of record on appeal, or similar paper. IN ST TRIAL P Rule 5(A).

a. *Service generally.* Every motion, petition, notice, or other pleading required to be served by IN ST TRIAL P Rule 5 shall be served on all counsel of record or unrepresented parties either before it is filed or on the day it is filed with the Court, and the date of filing shall be indicated on the Certificate of Service. IN ST ST JOSEPH CIV Rule 201(201.5.1).

   i. *Copy.* A copy of the Clerk's CCS entry form of the filing shall also be served on all counsel of record or unrepresented parties whenever it contains an appearance of counsel or contains a date for Court hearing on the matter. IN ST ST JOSEPH CIV Rule 201(201.5.1).

b. *Methods of service*

   i. *Personal service.* Whenever a party is represented by an attorney of record, service shall be made upon such attorney unless service upon the party himself is ordered by the court. Service upon the attorney or party shall be made by delivering or mailing a copy of the papers to the last known address or where an attorney or party has consented to service by fax or e-mail, as

provided in IN ST TRIAL P Rule 3.1(A)(4), by faxing or e-mailing a copy of the documents to the fax number or e-mail address set out in the appearance form or correction as required by IN ST TRIAL P Rule 3.1(E). IN ST TRIAL P Rule 5(B). Delivery of a copy within IN ST TRIAL P Rule 5 means:

- Offering or tendering it to the attorney or party and stating the nature of the papers being served. Refusal to accept an offered or tendered document is a waiver of any objection to the sufficiency or adequacy of service of that document;

- Leaving it at his office with a clerk or other person in charge thereof, or if there is no one in charge, leaving it in a conspicuous place therein; or

- If the office is closed, by leaving it at his dwelling house or usual place of abode with some person of suitable age and discretion then residing therein; or,

- Leaving it at some other suitable place, selected by the attorney upon whom service is being made, pursuant to duly promulgated local rule. IN ST TRIAL P Rule 5(B)(1).

ii. *Service by the clerk.* Whenever the Clerk is required by rule or statute to give notice, the party or parties requesting such notice shall furnish the Clerk with sufficient copies of the notice to be given, along with stamped, addressed envelopes with the names and the addresses of the parties or their counsel to whom such notice is to be given. IN ST ST JOSEPH CIV Rule 201(201.5.4).

iii. *Service on the court.* Service on a Judge may be made by delivering a copy to the Judge's secretary or mailing a copy to the Judge at his or her chambers. Service on a Judge may not be accomplished by facsimile transmission; however, a courtesy copy may be sent to the Judge's chambers by electronic mail or facsimile transmission contemporaneously with service by mail or otherwise. IN ST ST JOSEPH CIV Rule 201(201.5.5).

iv. *Service by mail.* If service is made by mail, the papers shall be deposited in the United States mail addressed to the person on whom they are being served, with postage prepaid. Service shall be deemed complete upon mailing. Proof of service of all papers permitted to be mailed may be made by written acknowledgment of service, by affidavit of the person who mailed the papers, or by certificate of an attorney. It shall be the duty of attorneys when entering their appearance in a cause or when filing pleadings or papers therein, to have noted in the Chronological Case Summary or said pleadings or papers so filed the address and telephone number of their office. Service by delivery or by mail at such address shall be deemed sufficient and complete. IN ST TRIAL P Rule 5(B)(2).

v. *Service by fax or e-mail.* A party who has consented to service by fax or e-mail may be served as follows:

- Service by e-mail shall be made by attaching the document being served in .pdf format. Discovery documents must also be served in accordance with IN ST TRIAL P Rule 26(A). IN ST TRIAL P Rule 5(B)(3)(a).

- Service by fax shall be deemed complete upon generation of a transmission record indicating the successful transmission of the entire document, except as provided in IN ST TRIAL P Rule 5(B)(3)(d). IN ST TRIAL P Rule 5(B)(3)(b).

- Service by e-mail shall be deemed complete upon transmission, except as provided in IN ST TRIAL P Rule 5(B)(3)(d). IN ST TRIAL P Rule 5(B)(3)(c).

- Service by fax or e-mail that occurs on a Saturday, Sunday, legal holiday, or day the court or agency in which the matter is pending is closed or after 5:00 PM local time of the recipient shall be deemed complete the next day that is not a Saturday, Sunday, legal holiday, or day that the court or agency in which the matter is pending is not closed. IN ST TRIAL P Rule 5(B)(3)(d).

   c.   *Serving numerous defendants.* In any action in which there are unusually large numbers of defendants, the court, upon motion or of its own initiative, may order:

      i.   That service of the pleadings of the defendants and replies thereto need not be made as between the defendants;

- That any cross-claim, counterclaim, or matter constituting an avoidance or affirmative defense contained therein shall be deemed to be denied or avoided by all other parties; and
- That the filing of any such pleading and service thereof upon the plaintiff constitutes due notice of it to the parties. IN ST TRIAL P Rule 5(D).

      ii.   A copy of every such order shall be served upon the parties in such manner and form as the court directs. IN ST TRIAL P Rule 5(D).

   d.   *Service on parties in default for failure to appear.* No service need be made on parties in default for failure to appear, except that pleadings asserting new or additional claims for relief against them shall be served upon them in the manner provided by service of summons in IN ST TRIAL P Rule 4. IN ST TRIAL P Rule 5(A).

   e.   *Distribution.* Counsel or an unrepresented party submitting a motion, petition, notice, pleading or proposed order shall indicate the method of distribution desired on the Clerk's CCS entry form. The Clerk will not return or distribute copies of motions, petitions, pleadings, notices or proposed orders, other than those originated by the Court, by mail unless the Clerk is provided with stamped, addressed envelopes. IN ST ST JOSEPH CIV Rule 201(201.5.3).

   f.   *Mailbox.* As a matter of convenience to attorneys, each court provides a mailbox for the distribution filings and orders generated by the Court, and it is the responsibility of each attorney to periodically check these mailboxes for service and distribution of court-generated filings and orders. IN ST ST JOSEPH CIV Rule 201(201.5.3).

G. Hearings

1. The Indiana rules do not contemplate a hearing regarding the filing and service of an amended answer.

H. Forms

1. Official Amended Answer Forms for Indiana

   a.   Affidavit of debt. IN ST TRIAL P App. A-2.

2. Amended Answer Forms for Indiana

   a.   Amendment by stipulation. 10 INPRAC § 46.11.

   b.   Amended answer by interlineations. 10 INPRAC § 46.12.

   c.   Answer; Form and content. 9 INPRAC § 41.1.

   d.   Answer; General form. 9 INPRAC § 41.3.

   e.   Answer; Another form. 9 INPRAC § 41.4.

   f.   Answer; Another form. 9 INPRAC § 41.5.

   g.   General denial. 9 INPRAC § 41.6.

   h.   Specific denial of designated paragraph. 9 INPRAC § 41.7.

   i.   Specific admission of designated paragraph. 9 INPRAC § 41.8.

   j.   Denial of knowledge or information to form belief. 9 INPRAC § 41.9.

   k.   Denial of knowledge or information to form belief; Another form. 9 INPRAC § 41.10.

   l.   Partial denial and partial admission of designated paragraph. 9 INPRAC § 41.11.

   m.   Denial of designated paragraph for reason that document speaks for itself. 9 INPRAC § 41.12.

   n.   Adoption of admissions or denials by co-defendant's answer. 9 INPRAC § 41.13.

   o.   Denial of execution of instrument filed with pleading. 9 INPRAC § 41.14.

   p.   Answer to cross-claim. 9 INPRAC § 41.15.

q.   Answer to third-party complaint. 9 INPRAC § 41.16.

r.   Accord and satisfaction. 9 INPRAC § 41.21.

s.   Answer. 5 INPRAC § 3:3.3.

t.   Answer; Another form. 5 INPRAC § 3:3.4.

u.   Certificate of service; Personal service. 9 INPRAC § 5.7.

v.   Certificate of service; First class mail. 9 INPRAC § 5.8.

w.   Signature; By party. 9 INPRAC § 4.5.

x.   Signature; Attorney. 9 INPRAC § 4.6.

y.   Signature; Attorney; Another form. 9 INPRAC § 4.7.

z.   Signature; Attorney; Another form. 9 INPRAC § 4.8.

I. Checklist

(I)   ❑ Matters to be considered by the party filing the amended answer

   (a)   ❑ Required documents if amending as matter of course

      (1)   ❑ Amended answer

      (2)   ❑ Chronological Case Summary (CCS) entry form

      (3)   ❑ Certificate of service

   (b)   ❑ Supplemental documents

      (1)   ❑ Proof of written instrument

      (2)   ❑ Notice of intent to use foreign law

      (3)   ❑ Facsimile cover sheet

   (c)   ❑ Timing

      (1)   ❑ As a matter of course before a responsive pleading is served, or, if the pleading is one to which no responsive pleading is permitted, within thirty (30) days after it is served

      (2)   ❑ At any time with leave of court

Motions, Oppositions and Replies
Motion to Strike

Document Last Updated October 2013

A. Applicable Rules

1. *State rules*

   a.   Appearance. IN ST TRIAL P Rule 3.1.

   b.   Process. IN ST TRIAL P Rule 4.

   c.   Service and filing of pleadings and other papers. IN ST TRIAL P Rule 5.

   d.   Time. IN ST TRIAL P Rule 6.

   e.   Pleadings. IN ST TRIAL P Rule 7; IN ST TRIAL P Rule 8; IN ST TRIAL P Rule 9.2; IN ST TRIAL P Rule 10; IN ST TRIAL P Rule 11.

   f.   Defenses and objections; When and how presented; By pleading or motion; Motion for judgment on the pleadings. IN ST TRIAL P Rule 12.

   g.   Amended and supplemental pleadings. IN ST TRIAL P Rule 15.

   h.   Joinder of person needed for just adjudication. IN ST TRIAL P Rule 19.

   i.   Evidence. IN ST TRIAL P Rule 43.

j. Judgment on the evidence (directed verdict). IN ST TRIAL P Rule 50.

k. Findings by the court. IN ST TRIAL P Rule 52.

l. Summary judgment. IN ST TRIAL P Rule 56.

m. Motion to correct error. IN ST TRIAL P Rule 59.

n. Relief from judgment or order. IN ST TRIAL P Rule 60.

o. Hearing of motions. IN ST TRIAL P Rule 73.

p. Access to court records. IN ST ADMIN Rule 9.

q. Paper size. IN ST ADMIN Rule 11.

r. Facsimile transmission. IN ST ADMIN Rule 12.

s. Electronic filing and electronic service pilot projects. IN ST ADMIN Rule 16.

t. Sealing of certain records by court; Hearing; Notice. IN ST 5-14-3-5.5.

u. Sixtieth judicial circuit. IN ST 33-33-71-2.

v. Privacy and confidentiality. IN ST 5-2-9-6; IN ST 5-14-3-4; IN ST 6-4.1-5-10; IN ST 6-4.1-12-12; IN ST 6-8.1-7-1; IN ST 11-13-1-8; IN ST 12-23-14-13; IN ST 16-39-3-10; IN ST 16-41-8-1; IN ST 22-4-19-6; IN ST 31-11-1-6; IN ST 31-19-5-23; IN ST 31-19-13-2; IN ST 31-19-19-1; IN ST 31-33-18-1; IN ST 31-39-1-1; IN ST 31-39-1-2; IN ST 33-23-16-16; IN ST 35-34-2-4; IN ST 35-38-1-13; IN ST 35-38-9-1; IN ST ADR Rule 2.11; IN ST ADR Rule 4.4; IN ST ADR Rule 5.6; IN ST JURY Rule 10.

2. *Local rules*

a. Court hours and scheduling. IN ST ST JOSEPH GEN AND ADMIN Rule 104.

b. Filing, pleading, and motions. IN ST ST JOSEPH CIV Rule 201.

c. Uniform court and case number designation. IN ST ST JOSEPH CIV Rule 202.

d. Pleading and motions under IN ST TRIAL P Rule 12 and IN ST TRIAL P Rule 56. IN ST ST JOSEPH CIV Rule 206.

e. Proposed order. IN ST ST JOSEPH CIV Rule 213.

f. Electronic filing of cases in St. Joseph County. IN ST ST JOSEPH ELECTRONIC Rule 701.

B. Timing

1. *Motion to strike.* Upon motion made by a party before responding to a pleading, or, if no responsive pleading is permitted by Indiana Rules of Trial Procedure, upon motion made by a party within twenty (20) days after the service of the pleading upon him or at any time upon the court's own initiative, the court may order stricken from any pleading any insufficient claim or defense or any redundant, immaterial, impertinent, or scandalous matter. IN ST TRIAL P Rule 12(F).

a. *Time to file a responsive pleading.* A responsive pleading required under the Indiana Rules of Trial Procedure, shall be served within twenty (20) days after service of the prior pleading. IN ST TRIAL P Rule 6(C).

b. *Filing.* All pleadings and papers subsequent to the complaint which are required to be served upon a party shall be filed with the Court either before service or within a reasonable period of time thereafter. IN ST TRIAL P Rule 5(E)(1).

2. *Service.* A written motion, other than one which may be heard ex parte, and notice of the hearing thereof shall be served not less than five (5) days before the time specified for the hearing, unless a different period is fixed by the Indiana Rules of Trial Procedure or by order of the court. IN ST TRIAL P Rule 6(D).

a. *Of supporting affidavits.* When a motion is supported by affidavit, the affidavit shall be served with the motion. IN ST TRIAL P Rule 6(D).

3. *Service of opposition.* Except as otherwise provided in IN ST TRIAL P Rule 59(D), opposing affidavits

may be served not less than one (1) day before the hearing, unless the court permits them to be served at some other time. IN ST TRIAL P Rule 6(D).

    a.   An adverse party shall have thirty (30) days after service of the motion in which to serve and file an answer brief. IN ST ST JOSEPH CIV Rule 206(206.1).

4. *Filing proposed orders.* Unless otherwise directed or given leave of the Court, proposed orders in emergency matters shall be filed within forty-eight (48) hours after a hearing; proposed orders in other matters shall be filed within seven (7) days as computed by IN ST TRIAL P Rule 6. IN ST ST JOSEPH CIV Rule 213(213.5).

5. *Computation of time*

    a.   *Generally; Days excluded.* In computing any period of time prescribed or allowed by the Indiana Rules of Trial Procedure, by order of the court, or by any applicable statute, the day of the act, event, or default from which the designated period of time begins to run shall not be included. The last day of the period so computed is to be included unless it is:

        i.   A Saturday,

        ii.   A Sunday,

        iii.   A legal holiday as defined by state statute, or

        iv.   A day the office in which the act is to be done is closed during regular business hours. IN ST TRIAL P Rule 6(A).

    b.   *Short periods.* In any event, the period runs until the end of the next day that is not a Saturday, a Sunday, a legal holiday, or a day on which the office is closed. When the period of time allowed is less than seven (7) days, intermediate Saturdays, Sundays, legal holidays, and days on which the office is closed shall be excluded from the computations. IN ST TRIAL P Rule 6(A).

    c.   *Additional time after service by United States mail.* Whenever a party has the right or is required to do some act or take some proceedings within a prescribed period after the service of a notice or other paper upon him and the notice or paper is served upon him by United States mail, three (3) days shall be added to the prescribed period. IN ST TRIAL P Rule 6(E).

    d.   *Enlargement of time.* When an act is required or allowed to be done at or within a specific time by the Indiana Rules of Trial Procedure, the court may at any time for cause shown:

        i.   Order the period enlarged, with or without motion or notice, if request therefor is made before the expiration of the period originally prescribed or extended by a previous order; or

        ii.   Upon motion made after the expiration of the specific period, permit the act to be done where the failure to act was the result of excusable neglect; but, the court may not extend the time for taking any action for judgment on the evidence under IN ST TRIAL P Rule 50(A), amendment of findings and judgment under IN ST TRIAL P Rule 52(B), to correct errors under IN ST TRIAL P Rule 59(C), statement in opposition to motion to correct error under IN ST TRIAL P Rule 59(E), or to obtain relief from final judgment under IN ST TRIAL P Rule 60(B), except to the extent and under the conditions stated in those rules. IN ST TRIAL P Rule 6(B).

        iii.   An initial written motion for enlargement of time pursuant to IN ST TRIAL P Rule 6(B)(1) to answer a claim shall be routinely granted for an additional thirty (30) days from the original due date or other period the assigned Judge deems reasonable by written order of the Court. The motion must be filed on or before the original due date or IN ST ST JOSEPH CIV Rule 201 shall be inapplicable. IN ST ST JOSEPH CIV Rule 201(201.9.5).

            ●   Any motion for enlargement of time shall state the date when such response is due and the date to which time is requested to be enlarged. IN ST ST JOSEPH CIV Rule 201(201.9.5).

            ●   All subsequent motions for enlargement of time shall be so designated and will only be granted for good cause shown or in the interest of justice. IN ST ST JOSEPH CIV Rule 201(201.9.5).

C. General Requirements

1. *Motions, generally.* Unless made during a hearing or trial, or otherwise ordered by the court, an

application to the court for an order shall be made by written motion. The motion shall state the grounds therefor and the relief or order sought. IN ST TRIAL P Rule 7(B).

a. *Motions as distinct from pleadings.* Motions and responses to motions are not pleadings, and allegations contained in a motion are not admissions of a party. 22B INPRAC 7:2; Wachstetter v. County Properties, LLC, 832 N.E.2d 574 (Ind.Ct.App. 2005); Scott County Family YMCA, Inc. v. Hobbs, 817 N.E.2d 603 (Ind.Ct.App. 2004).

b. *Unopposed motions generally granted.* It is common for a trial court to grant procedural motions, such as motions for enlargement of time, discovery motions, or motions for continuance, unless an objection is filed. 21 INPRAC § 13.8.

c. *Proposed orders.* As directed by the Court, a party or an attorney for a party shall prepare a proposed order based on the decision rendered by the Court. The party so directed shall prepare the proposed order in a timely manner and, upon filing, shall advise the chambers of the applicable judge that the proposed order has been prepared and filed. IN ST ST JOSEPH CIV Rule 213(213.2).

d. *Reply brief.* Subject to Court approval, the moving party may file a reply brief. IN ST ST JOSEPH CIV Rule 206(206.1).

2. *Motion to strike*

   a. *Grounds generally.* Upon motion the court may order stricken from any pleading any insufficient claim or defense or any redundant, immaterial, impertinent, or scandalous matter. IN ST TRIAL P Rule 12(F).

      i. *Redundant.* Redundant matter refers to the needless repetition of immaterial factual allegations. 9 INPRAC § 42.20.

      ii. *Immaterial and impertinent.* Immaterial and impertinent matter consists of allegations that have no relevant or important relationship to plaintiff's claim. 9 INPRAC § 42.20.

      iii. *Scandalous.* Scandalous matter includes unnecessary allegations that are derogatory to the party referred to in the pleading. 9 INPRAC § 42.20.

   b. *Availability and use of motion to strike.* A motion to strike redundant, immaterial, impertinent or scandalous matter is available to plaintiff and defendant alike, and may be employed against any pleading. 9 INPRAC § 42.20. Indiana's use of a motion to strike includes all of the uses which are found in federal practice plus the expanded use of the motion under Indiana's rule. Accordingly, a nonexclusive list of the uses of this motion will recognize that it is available:

      i. To strike matter which is immaterial, impertinent or scandalous;

      ii. To provide the plaintiff with a means by which to test the sufficiency of a defense;

      iii. To strike any insufficient claim or defense;

      iv. To strike a bad faith, or inadequate response to an order or rule; or

      v. To strike a response to an order or rule which introduces new material or allegations not previously made and which are not introduced pursuant to a right to amend a pleading. 1A INPRAC R 12(12.18).

   c. *Trial court's discretion.* The trial court is given broad discretion to decide a motion to strike. 1A INPRAC R 12(12.18); City of Mishawaka v. Kvale, 810 N.E.2d 1129 (Ind.Ct.App. 2004).

   d. *Not a method to challenge timeliness.* Language in IN ST TRIAL P Rule 12(F) which permits the trial court to strike any "insufficient" claim or defense refers to the legal insufficiency of the content or substance of the claim or defense, not the untimeliness of a pleading. 1A INPRAC R 12(12.18); Dreyer & Reinbold v. AutoXchange.com., Inc., 771 N.E.2d 764, 765 (Ind.Ct.App. 2002). Rather, the proper mechanism for challenging the timeliness of a pleading is IN ST TRIAL P Rule 55, which governs default judgments. 1A INPRAC R 12(12.18).

3. *Consolidation and waiver*

   a. *Consolidation of defenses in motion.* A party who makes a motion under IN ST TRIAL P Rule 12 may join with it any other motions herein provided for and then available to him. If a party makes a motion under IN ST TRIAL P Rule 12 but omits therefrom any defense or objection then available to him which IN ST TRIAL P Rule 12 permits to be raised by motion, he shall not thereafter make a motion based on the defense or objection so omitted. He may, however, make such motions as are allowed under IN ST TRIAL P Rule 12(H)(2). IN ST TRIAL P Rule 12(G).

b. *Waiver or preservation of certain defenses.* No defense or objection is waived by being joined with one or more other defenses or objections in a responsive pleading or motion. IN ST TRIAL P Rule 12(B).

4. *Opposition to a motion to strike.* Failure to file an answer brief or reply brief within the time prescribed shall be deemed a waiver of the right thereto and shall subject the motion to summary ruling. IN ST ST JOSEPH CIV Rule 206(206.1).

D. Documents

1. *Required documents*

   a. *Motion and notice.* The requirement of notice is satisfied by service of the motion. IN ST TRIAL P Rule 7(B). Refer to the General Requirements section of this document for information on the content of a motion to strike.

   b. *Chronological Case Summary (CCS) entry form.* Every written motion, petition, or other pleading subsequent to the original complaint presented to the Clerk for filing shall be accompanied by a Chronological Case Summary (CCS) entry form in duplicate. IN ST ST JOSEPH CIV Rule 201(201.4). Refer to the Format section of this document for details on the format and filing requirements for the CCS entry form.

   c. *Supporting memorandum of law.* All pleadings and motions filed pursuant to IN ST TRIAL P Rule 12 and IN ST TRIAL P Rule 56 shall be accompanied by a separate supporting brief. IN ST ST JOSEPH CIV Rule 206(206.1).

   d. *Proposed order.* Unless local practice provides differently, a party should submit a proposed order with its written motion to be signed by the judge once the motion has been granted. 21 INPRAC § 13.8. All proposed orders shall be submitted in an original plus a number of copies equal to one more than the number of pro se parties and attorneys of record contained in the prepared proof of notice under IN ST TRIAL P Rule 72(D). IN ST ST JOSEPH CIV Rule 213(213.3); IN ST ST JOSEPH CIV Rule 201(201.5.2).

   e. *Certificate of service.* An attorney or unrepresented party tendering a document to the Clerk for filing shall certify that service has been made, list the parties served, and specify the date and means of service. The certificate of service shall be placed at the end of the document and shall not be separately filed. The separate filing of a certificate of service, however, shall not be grounds for rejecting a document for filing. The Clerk may permit documents to be filed without a certificate of service but shall require prompt filing of a separate certificate of service. IN ST TRIAL P Rule 5(C).

2. *Supplemental documents*

   a. *Supporting evidence.* When a motion is based on facts not appearing of record the court may hear the matter on affidavits presented by the respective parties, but the court may direct that the matter be heard wholly or partly on oral testimony or depositions. IN ST TRIAL P Rule 43(B).

   b. *Facsimile cover sheet.* Any document sent to the Clerk of the Circuit Court by electronic facsimile transmission shall be accompanied by a cover sheet which states the title of the document, case number, number of pages, identity and voice telephone number of the sending party and instructions for filing. The cover sheet shall contain the signature of the attorney or party, pro se, authorizing the filing. IN ST ADMIN Rule 12(D).

E. Format

1. *Form of motions.* The rules applicable to captions, and the signing and form of pleadings (IN ST TRIAL P Rule 8 through IN ST TRIAL P Rule 11), apply to all motions and other papers provided under the Indiana Rules of Trial Procedure. 22B INPRAC 7:2.

   a. *Separate motions; Alternative motions.* Each motion shall be separate, while alternative motions filed together shall each be identified on the caption. IN ST ST JOSEPH CIV Rule 206(206.1).

2. *Form of pleadings*

    a. *Caption; Names of parties.* Every pleading shall contain a caption setting forth the name of the court, the title of the action, the file number, and a designation as in IN ST TRIAL P Rule 7(A). In the complaint the title of the action shall include the names of all the parties, but in other pleadings it is sufficient to state the name of the first party on each side with an appropriate indication of other parties. IN ST TRIAL P Rule 10(A); IN ST ST JOSEPH CIV Rule 201(201.3.3). If a special judge has been assigned to the case, the pleading should also identify the special judge. IN ST ST JOSEPH CIV Rule 201(201.3.3).

        i. *Title.* All pleadings or motions shall include a title, which shall delineate each topic included in the pleading. For example, where a pleading contains an answer, a motion to dismiss, and a jury request, each topic shall be set forth in the title. IN ST ST JOSEPH CIV Rule 201(201.3.4).

    b. *Paragraphs; Separate statements.* All averments of a claim or defense shall be made in numbered paragraphs, the contents of each of which shall be limited as far as practicable to a statement of a single set of circumstances, and a paragraph may be referred to by number in all succeeding pleadings. Each claim founded upon a separate transaction or occurrence and each defense other than denials may be stated in a separate count or defense whenever a separation facilitates the clear presentation of the matters set forth. IN ST TRIAL P Rule 10(B).

    c. *Adoption by reference; Exhibits.* Statements in a pleading may be adopted by reference in a different part of the same pleading or in another pleading or in any motion. A copy of any written instrument which is an exhibit to a pleading is a part thereof for all purposes. IN ST TRIAL P Rule 10(C).

    d. *Flat filing.* In order that the Clerk's files may be kept under the system commonly known as "flat filing," all papers presented to the Clerk for filing shall be flat and unfolded. Pleadings shall have no covers or backs and shall be fastened together at the top left-hand corner only. IN ST ST JOSEPH CIV Rule 201(201.1).

    e. *One side of page used.* Printing shall be on one (1) side of the paper. IN ST ST JOSEPH CIV Rule 201(201.3.2).

    f. *Copies.* All copies shall be on white paper of sufficient strength and durability to resist normal wear and tear. IN ST ST JOSEPH CIV Rule 201(201.3.1).

    g. *Margins.* Margins shall be at least one inch (1"). IN ST ST JOSEPH CIV Rule 201(201.3.2).

    h. *Double-spaced.* If typewritten, the lines shall be double spaced except for quotations, which shall be indented and single-spaced. IN ST ST JOSEPH CIV Rule 201(201.3.2).

    i. *Font size.* Type face shall be twelve (12) font size or larger within the body of the document and ten (10) font size or larger in the footnotes. IN ST ST JOSEPH CIV Rule 201(201.3.2).

    j. *Font type.* The font type must be legible and script type shall not be used. IN ST ST JOSEPH CIV Rule 201(201.3.2).

    k. *Italics.* Italicized type may be used for quotations, references, or case citations. IN ST ST JOSEPH CIV Rule 201(201.3.2).

    l. *Court and case designation.* All filings shall conform to the requirements for uniform court and case number designation set by IN ST ADMIN Rule 8. In addition, all filings shall contain the proper court and case designation as described below. IN ST ST JOSEPH CIV Rule 202.

        i. *Court designation.* Pursuant to IN ST 33-33-71-2, St. Joseph County, Indiana, constitutes the Sixtieth Judicial Circuit. The legal names of the courts within the 60th Judicial Circuit are the St. Joseph Circuit Court, the St. Joseph Superior Court, and the St. Joseph Probate Court. All filings shall properly reflect the legal name of the applicable court. Any filing may be amended, rejected, or stricken if it does not contain the proper case name and/or the legal name of the court. IN ST ST JOSEPH CIV Rule 202(202.1).

    m. *Form of CCS entry.* Every written motion, petition, or other pleading subsequent to the original complaint presented to the Clerk for filing shall be accompanied by a Chronological Case Summary (CCS) entry form in duplicate which shall contain the title and cause number of the action, the date, and the proposed entry to appear on the docket. IN ST ST JOSEPH CIV Rule 201(201.4).

        i. *Identification and signature.* The CCS entry form shall identify the party making the filing,

designate each pleading being filed, and shall be signed by counsel of record or the unrepresented litigant. IN ST ST JOSEPH CIV Rule 201(201.4).

    ii. *Date stamp.* The form shall be date stamped and presented to the Court Clerk, who shall initial the form and return the duplicate to the filing party. IN ST ST JOSEPH CIV Rule 201(201.4).

n. *Form of proposed order.* Any proposed order shall be a document that is separate and apart from the motion or application to which it relates and shall contain a caption showing the name of the court, the case number assigned to the case, and the title of the case as shown by the complaint pursuant to IN ST ST JOSEPH CIV Rule 201. IN ST ST JOSEPH CIV Rule 213(213.2).

    i. If there are multiple parties, the title may be shortened to include only the first name plaintiff and defendant with appropriate indication that there are additional parties. IN ST ST JOSEPH CIV Rule 213(213.2).

    ii. The proposed order shall be on white paper, eight and one-half by eleven inches (8 1/2" x 11") in size, and each page shall be numbered. IN ST ST JOSEPH CIV Rule 213(213.2).

    iii. The last page of the proposed order shall contain a line for the date, either "Dated _____" or "Signed on the date filemarked hereon." IN ST ST JOSEPH CIV Rule 213(213.2).

    iv. On the last page there also shall be a line for the signature of the Judge under which shall be typed "Judge, St. Joseph [Circuit or Superior or Probate] Court." IN ST ST JOSEPH CIV Rule 213(213.2).

    v. If the proposed order contains a recommendation from a Magistrate, the last page shall have a line for the signature of the Magistrate under which shall be typed "Magistrate, St. Joseph [Circuit or Superior or Probate] Court," to the left of which shall be the following, "So Recommended:" and beneath and to the left of which shall be typed, "Approved. So Ordered." IN ST ST JOSEPH CIV Rule 213(213.2).

    vi. To allow compliance with the notice requirements of IN ST TRIAL P Rule 72(D), the lower four (4) inches of the last page of the proposed order shall be left blank. The proposed order shall also include a prepared proof of notice under IN ST TRIAL P Rule 72(D), and in preparing such a notice the filing party shall complete all portions of the prepared proof of notice. IN ST ST JOSEPH CIV Rule 213(213.2).

3. *Size of papers for filing.* Effective January 1, 1992, all pleadings, copies, motions and documents filed with any trial court or appellate level court, typed or printed, with the exception of exhibits and existing wills, shall be prepared on eight and one-half by eleven inch (8 1/2" x 11") size paper. IN ST ADMIN Rule 11.

a. *Paper.* Pleadings, motions, and other papers shall be either legibly printed or typewritten on white opaque paper of good quality at least sixteen (16) pound weight, eight and one-half inches (8 1/2 ") in width and eleven inches (11") in length as required by IN ST ADMIN Rule 11. IN ST ST JOSEPH CIV Rule 201(201.3.1).

4. *Form of proposed order.* Any proposed order shall be a document that is separate and apart from the motion or application to which it relates and shall contain a caption showing the name of the court, the case number assigned to the case, and the title of the case as shown by the complaint pursuant to IN ST ST JOSEPH CIV Rule 201. IN ST ST JOSEPH CIV Rule 213 (213.2).

a. *Multiple parties.* If there are multiple parties, the title may be shortened to include only the first name plaintiff and defendant with appropriate indication that there are additional parties. IN ST ST JOSEPH CIV Rule 213 (213.2).

b. *Paper size; Numbering.* The proposed order shall be on white paper, 8 1/2" x 11" in size, and each page shall be numbered. IN ST ST JOSEPH CIV Rule 213 (213.2).

c. *Last page.* The last page of the proposed order shall contain a line for the date, either "Dated _____" or "Signed on the date filemarked hereon." On the last page there also shall be a line for the signature of the Judge under which shall be typed "Judge, St. Joseph [Circuit or Superior or Probate] Court." If the proposed order contains a recommendation from a Magistrate Judge, the last page shall have a line for the signature of the Magistrate Judge under which shall be typed

"Magistrate Judge, St. Joseph [Circuit or Superior or Probate] Court," to the left of which shall be the following, "So Recommended:" and beneath and to the left of which shall be typed, "Approved. So Ordered." IN ST ST JOSEPH CIV Rule 213 (213.2).

    i. To allow compliance with the notice requirements of IN ST TRIAL P Rule 72(D), the lower four (4) inches of the last page of the proposed order shall be left blank. The proposed order shall also include a prepared proof of notice under IN ST TRIAL P Rule 72(D), and in preparing such a notice the filing party shall complete all portions of the prepared proof of notice. IN ST ST JOSEPH CIV Rule 213 (213.2).

  d. *Copies.* All proposed orders shall be submitted in an original plus a number of copies equal to one (1) more than the number of pro se parties and attorneys of record contained in the prepared proof of notice under IN ST TRIAL P Rule 72(D). IN ST ST JOSEPH CIV Rule 213 (213.3).

5. *Signature requirements*

  a. *Signature of attorney.* Every pleading or motion of a party represented by an attorney shall be signed by at least one (1) attorney of record in his individual name, whose address, telephone number, and attorney number shall be stated, except that this provision shall not apply to pleadings and motions made and transcribed at the trial or a hearing before the judge and received by him in such form. IN ST TRIAL P Rule 11(A).

    i. The signature of an attorney constitutes a certificate by him that he has read the pleadings; that to the best of his knowledge, information, and belief, there is good ground to support it; and that it is not interposed for delay. IN ST TRIAL P Rule 11(A).

    ii. If a pleading or motion is not signed or is signed with intent to defeat the purpose of the rule, it may be stricken as sham and false and the action may proceed as though the pleading had not been served. IN ST TRIAL P Rule 11(A).

    iii. For a willful violation of IN ST TRIAL P Rule 11 an attorney may be subjected to appropriate disciplinary action. Similar action may be taken if scandalous or indecent matter is inserted. IN ST TRIAL P Rule 11(A).

  b. *Signature of unrepresented party.* A party who is not represented by an attorney shall sign his pleading and state his address. IN ST TRIAL P Rule 11(A).

  c. *Verification not generally required.* Except when specifically required by rule, pleadings or motions need not be verified or accompanied by affidavit. The rule in equity that the averments of an answer under oath must be overcome by the testimony of two (2) witnesses or of one (1) witness sustained by corroborating circumstances is abolished. IN ST TRIAL P Rule 11(A).

  d. *Verification by affirmation or representation.* When in connection with any civil or special statutory proceeding it is required that any pleading, motion, petition, supporting affidavit, or other document of any kind, be verified, or that an oath be taken, it shall be sufficient if the subscriber simply affirms the truth of the matter to be verified by an affirmation or representation. IN ST TRIAL P Rule 11(B). IN ST TRIAL P Rule 11(B) states that the affirmation or representation should be in substantially the following language: "I (we) affirm, under the penalties for perjury, that the foregoing representation(s) is (are) true. (Signed) _____."

    i. Any person who falsifies an affirmation or representation of fact shall be subject to the same penalties as are prescribed by law for the making of a false affidavit. IN ST TRIAL P Rule 11(B).

  e. *Verified pleadings, motions, and affidavits as evidence.* Pleadings, motions and affidavits accompanying or in support of such pleadings or motions when required to be verified or under oath shall be accepted as a representation that the signer had personal knowledge thereof or reasonable cause to believe the existence of the facts or matters stated or alleged therein; and, if otherwise competent or acceptable as evidence, may be admitted as evidence of the facts or matters stated or alleged therein when it is so provided in the Indiana Rules of Trial Procedure, by statute or other law, or to the extent the writing or signature expressly purports to be made upon the signer's personal knowledge. When such pleadings, motions and affidavits are verified or under oath they shall not require other or greater proof on the part of the adverse party than if not verified or not under oath unless expressly provided otherwise by the Indiana Rules of Trial Procedure, statute or other law. Affidavits upon motions for summary judgment under IN ST TRIAL P Rule 56 and in denial of execution under IN ST TRIAL P Rule 9.2 shall be made upon personal knowledge. IN ST TRIAL P Rule 11(C).

f. *Signature, verification and other requirements.* Parties and their counsel are enjoined to comply with the verification requirements of IN ST TRIAL P Rule 11, and either the moving party or the party's attorney of record shall sign all pleadings and motions before filing with the Clerk of the Court. Every motion, petition, or other pleading filed with the Clerk shall contain the name, organization, physical address, telephone number, and facsimile number of the filing party or an attorney for that party. IN ST ST JOSEPH CIV Rule 201(201.3.6).

   i. The Clerk shall not accept any motion, petition, notice or other pleading or a CCS entry form for filing from an unrepresented litigant unless the unrepresented litigant's current address and phone number appear on the pleading, and an opposing party may service notices and responses on an unrepresented litigant at any address he or she has provided on a pleading. IN ST ST JOSEPH CIV Rule 201(201.3.6).

6. *Information excluded from public access.* Every document filed in a case shall separately identify information excluded from public access pursuant to IN ST ADMIN Rule 9(G)(1) as follows:

   a. Whole documents that are excluded from public access pursuant to IN ST ADMIN Rule 9(G)(1) shall be tendered on light green paper or have a light green coversheet attached to the document, marked "Not for Public Access" or "Confidential." IN ST TRIAL P Rule 5(G)(1).

   b. When only a portion of a document contains information excluded from public access pursuant to IN ST ADMIN Rule 9(G)(1), said information shall be omitted [or redacted] from the filed document, and set forth on a separate accompanying document on light green paper conspicuously marked "Not for Public Access" or "Confidential" and clearly designated [or identifying] the caption and number of the case and the document and location within the document to which the redacted material pertains. IN ST TRIAL P Rule 5(G)(2).

   c. With respect to documents filed in electronic format, the trial court, by local rule, may provide for compliance with IN ST TRIAL P Rule 5 in manner that separates and protects access to information excluded from public access. IN ST TRIAL P Rule 5(G)(3).

   d. IN ST TRIAL P Rule 5(G) does not apply to a record sealed by the court pursuant to IN ST 5-14-3-5.5 or otherwise, nor to records, documents, or information filed in cases to which public access is prohibited pursuant to IN ST ADMIN Rule 9(G). IN ST TRIAL P Rule 5(G)(4).

   e. The following information in case records is excluded from public access and is confidential:

      i. Information that is excluded from public access pursuant to federal law;

      ii. Information that is excluded from public access as declared confidential by Indiana statute or other court rule, including without limitation:

         • All adoption records created after July 8, 1941, as declared confidential by IN ST 31-19-19-1, et seq., except those specifically declared open by IN ST 31-19-13-2(2);

         • All records relating to chancroid, chlamydia, gonorrhea, hepatitis, human immunodeficiency virus (HIV), Lymphogranuloma venereum, syphilis, tuberculosis, as declared confidential by IN ST 16-41-8-1, et seq.;

         • All records relating to child abuse as declared confidential by IN ST 31-33-18-1, et seq.;

         • All records relating to drug tests as declared confidential by IN ST 5-14-3-4(a)(9);

         • Records of grand jury proceedings as declared confidential by IN ST 35-34-2-4;

         • Records of juvenile proceedings as declared confidential by IN ST 31-39-1-2, except those specifically open under statute;

         • All paternity records created after July 1, 1941 as declared confidential by IN ST 31-14-11-15, IN ST 31-19-5-23, IN ST 31-39-1-1 and IN ST 31-39-1-2 [Editor's note: IN ST 31-14-11-15 was repealed effective May 9, 2013];

         • All pre-sentence reports as declared confidential by IN ST 35-38-1-13;

- Written petitions to permit marriages without consent and orders directing the Clerk of Court to issue a marriage license to underage persons, as declared confidential by IN ST 31-11-1-6;
- Only those arrest warrants, search warrants, indictments and informations ordered confidential by the trial judge, prior to return of duly executed service as declared confidential by IN ST 5-14-3-4(b)(1);
- All medical, mental health, or tax records unless determined by law or regulation of any governmental custodian not to be confidential, released by the subject of such records, or declared by a court of competent jurisdiction to be essential to the resolution of litigation as declared confidential by IN ST 16-39-3-10, IN ST 6-4.1-5-10, IN ST 6-4.1-12-12, and IN ST 6-8.1-7-1;
- Personal information relating to jurors or prospective jurors, other than for the use of the parties and counsel, pursuant to IN ST JURY Rule 10;
- Information relating to protection from abuse orders, no-contact orders and workplace violence restraining orders as declared confidential by IN ST 5-2-9-6, et seq.;
- Mediation proceedings pursuant to IN ST ADR Rule 2.11, Mini-Trial proceedings pursuant to IN ST ADR Rule 4.4(C), and Summary Jury Trials pursuant to IN ST ADR Rule 5.6;
- Information in probation files pursuant to the Probation Standards promulgated by the Judicial Conference of Indiana pursuant to IN ST 11-13-1-8(b);
- Information deemed confidential pursuant to the Rules for Court Administered Alcohol and Drug Programs promulgated by the Judicial Conference of Indiana pursuant to IN ST 12-23-14-13;
- Information deemed confidential pursuant to the Problem-Solving Court Rules promulgated by the Judicial Conference of Indiana pursuant to IN ST 33-23-16-16;
- All records of the Department of workforce Development as declared confidential by IN ST 22-4-19-6;
- Information regarding interception of electronic communications that is sealed or deemed confidential as set forth in IN ST 35-33.5-2-1, et seq.

iii. Information excluded from public access by specific court order;

iv. Complete Social Security Numbers of living persons;

v. With the exception of names, information such as addresses, phone numbers, and dates of birth which explicitly identifies:

- Natural persons who are witnesses or victims (not including defendants) in criminal, domestic violence, stalking, sexual assault, juvenile, or civil protection order proceedings, provided that juveniles who are victims of sex crimes shall be identified by initials only;
- Places of residence of judicial officers, clerks and other employees of courts and clerks of court, unless the person or persons about whom the information pertains waives confidentiality;

vi. Complete account numbers of specific assets, loans, bank accounts, credit cards, and personal identification numbers (PINs);

vii. All orders of expungement entered in criminal or juvenile proceedings, orders to restrict access to criminal history information pursuant to IN ST 35-38-5-5.5 or IN ST 35-38-8-5 and records excluded from public access by such orders, and information related to infractions that is excluded from public access pursuant to IN ST 34-28-5-15 or IN ST 34-28-5-16 [Editor's note: IN ST 35-38-5-5.5, IN ST 35-38-8-5 and IN ST 34-28-5-16 were repealed effective July 1, 2013; for information on orders restricting access to criminal history, refer to IN ST 35-38-9-1, et seq.];

viii. All personal notes and e-mail, and deliberative material, of judges, jurors, court staff and

judicial agencies, and information recorded in personal data assistants (PDA's) or organizers and personal calendars. IN ST ADMIN Rule 9(G)(1).

F. Filing and Service Requirements

1. *Filing requirements.* Except as otherwise provided in IN ST TRIAL P Rule 5(E)(2), all pleadings and papers subsequent to the complaint which are required to be served upon a party shall be filed with the Court either before service or within a reasonable period of time thereafter. IN ST TRIAL P Rule 5(E)(1).

   a. *Filing with the court defined.* The filing of pleadings, motions, and other papers with the court as required by the Indiana Rules of Trial Procedure shall be made by one of the following methods:

      i. Delivery to the clerk of the court;

      ii. Sending by electronic transmission under the procedure adopted pursuant to IN ST ADMIN Rule 12;

      iii. Mailing to the clerk by registered, certified or express mail return receipt requested;

      iv. Depositing with any third-party commercial carrier for delivery to the clerk within three (3) calendar days, cost prepaid, properly addressed;

      v. If the court so permits, filing with the judge, in which event the judge shall note thereon the filing date and forthwith transmit them to the office of the clerk; or

      vi. Electronic filing, as approved by the Division of State Court Administration pursuant to IN ST ADMIN Rule 16. IN ST TRIAL P Rule 5(F).

      vii. Filing by registered or certified mail and by third-party commercial carrier shall be complete upon mailing or deposit. IN ST TRIAL P Rule 5(F).

      viii. All pleadings shall be filed with the Clerk, not directly with the Court, unless otherwise required by the Indiana Rules of Court. The entry of appearances and the filing of pleadings or other matters not requiring immediate Court action shall be filed with the Clerk and not in open Court. A Judge may permit papers to be filed in chambers, in which event he or she shall note thereon the filing date and transmit the papers to the Clerk. IN ST ST JOSEPH CIV Rule 201(201.2).

   b. *Facsimile filing.* Unless otherwise authorized by IN ST ST JOSEPH ELECTRONIC Rule 701, electronic filing of pleadings by computerized or facsimile transmission is not permitted. IN ST ST JOSEPH CIV Rule 201(201.2).

   c. *Additional copies.* In cases in which a party or counsel supplies the proposed order or decree, a sufficient number shall be prepared and filed as to provide the Clerk to retain two (2) copies, which shall be filed in the flat file and the record of judgments and orders. Should the party or counsel desire additional copies, a sufficient number of copies should be filed to effectuate that purpose. IN ST ST JOSEPH CIV Rule 201(201.6).

   d. *Proof of filing.* Any party filing any paper by any method other than personal delivery to the clerk shall retain proof of filing. IN ST TRIAL P Rule 5(F).

2. *Service requirements.* Unless otherwise provided by the Indiana Rules of Trial Procedure or an order of the court, each party and special judge, if any, shall be served with: (1) every order required by its terms to be served; (2) every pleading subsequent to the original complaint; (3) every written motion except one which may be heard ex parte; (4) every brief submitted to the trial court; (5) every paper relating to discovery required to be served upon a party; and (6) every written notice, appearance, demand, offer of judgment, designation of record on appeal, or similar paper. IN ST TRIAL P Rule 5(A).

   a. *Service generally.* Every motion, petition, notice, or other pleading required to be served by IN ST TRIAL P Rule 5 shall be served on all counsel of record or unrepresented parties either before it is filed or on the day it is filed with the Court, and the date of filing shall be indicated on the Certificate of Service. IN ST ST JOSEPH CIV Rule 201(201.5.1).

      i. *Copy.* A copy of the Clerk's CCS entry form of the filing shall also be served on all counsel of record or unrepresented parties whenever it contains an appearance of counsel or contains a date for Court hearing on the matter. IN ST ST JOSEPH CIV Rule 201(201.5.1).

   b. *Methods of service*

      i. *Personal service.* Whenever a party is represented by an attorney of record, service shall be

made upon such attorney unless service upon the party himself is ordered by the court. Service upon the attorney or party shall be made by delivering or mailing a copy of the papers to the last known address or where an attorney or party has consented to service by fax or e-mail, as provided in IN ST TRIAL P Rule 3.1(A)(4), by faxing or e-mailing a copy of the documents to the fax number or e-mail address set out in the appearance form or correction as required by IN ST TRIAL P Rule 3.1(E). IN ST TRIAL P Rule 5(B). Delivery of a copy within IN ST TRIAL P Rule 5 means:

- Offering or tendering it to the attorney or party and stating the nature of the papers being served. Refusal to accept an offered or tendered document is a waiver of any objection to the sufficiency or adequacy of service of that document;

- Leaving it at his office with a clerk or other person in charge thereof, or if there is no one in charge, leaving it in a conspicuous place therein; or

- If the office is closed, by leaving it at his dwelling house or usual place of abode with some person of suitable age and discretion then residing therein; or,

- Leaving it at some other suitable place, selected by the attorney upon whom service is being made, pursuant to duly promulgated local rule. IN ST TRIAL P Rule 5(B)(1).

ii. *Service by the clerk.* Whenever the Clerk is required by rule or statute to give notice, the party or parties requesting such notice shall furnish the Clerk with sufficient copies of the notice to be given, along with stamped, addressed envelopes with the names and the addresses of the parties or their counsel to whom such notice is to be given. IN ST ST JOSEPH CIV Rule 201(201.5.4).

iii. *Service on the court.* Service on a Judge may be made by delivering a copy to the Judge's secretary or mailing a copy to the Judge at his or her chambers. Service on a Judge may not be accomplished by facsimile transmission; however, a courtesy copy may be sent to the Judge's chambers by electronic mail or facsimile transmission contemporaneously with service by mail or otherwise. IN ST ST JOSEPH CIV Rule 201(201.5.5).

iv. *Service by mail.* If service is made by mail, the papers shall be deposited in the United States mail addressed to the person on whom they are being served, with postage prepaid. Service shall be deemed complete upon mailing. Proof of service of all papers permitted to be mailed may be made by written acknowledgment of service, by affidavit of the person who mailed the papers, or by certificate of an attorney. It shall be the duty of attorneys when entering their appearance in a cause or when filing pleadings or papers therein, to have noted in the Chronological Case Summary or said pleadings or papers so filed the address and telephone number of their office. Service by delivery or by mail at such address shall be deemed sufficient and complete. IN ST TRIAL P Rule 5(B)(2).

v. *Service by fax or e-mail.* A party who has consented to service by fax or e-mail may be served as follows:

- Service by e-mail shall be made by attaching the document being served in .pdf format. Discovery documents must also be served in accordance with IN ST TRIAL P Rule 26(A). IN ST TRIAL P Rule 5(B)(3)(a).

- Service by fax shall be deemed complete upon generation of a transmission record indicating the successful transmission of the entire document, except as provided in IN ST TRIAL P Rule 5(B)(3)(d). IN ST TRIAL P Rule 5(B)(3)(b).

- Service by e-mail shall be deemed complete upon transmission, except as provided in IN ST TRIAL P Rule 5(B)(3)(d). IN ST TRIAL P Rule 5(B)(3)(c).

- Service by fax or e-mail that occurs on a Saturday, Sunday, legal holiday, or day the court or agency in which the matter is pending is closed or after 5:00 PM local time of the recipient shall be deemed complete the next day that is not a Saturday, Sunday, legal holiday, or day that the court or agency in which the matter is pending is not closed. IN ST TRIAL P Rule 5(B)(3)(d).

c. *Serving numerous defendants.* In any action in which there are unusually large numbers of defendants, the court, upon motion or of its own initiative, may order:

    i. That service of the pleadings of the defendants and replies thereto need not be made as between the defendants;

- That any cross-claim, counterclaim, or matter constituting an avoidance or affirmative defense contained therein shall be deemed to be denied or avoided by all other parties; and

- That the filing of any such pleading and service thereof upon the plaintiff constitutes due notice of it to the parties. IN ST TRIAL P Rule 5(D).

    ii. A copy of every such order shall be served upon the parties in such manner and form as the court directs. IN ST TRIAL P Rule 5(D).

d. *Service on parties in default for failure to appear.* No service need be made on parties in default for failure to appear, except that pleadings asserting new or additional claims for relief against them shall be served upon them in the manner provided by service of summons in IN ST TRIAL P Rule 4. IN ST TRIAL P Rule 5(A).

e. *Distribution.* Counsel or an unrepresented party submitting a motion, petition, notice, pleading or proposed order shall indicate the method of distribution desired on the Clerk's CCS entry form. The Clerk will not return or distribute copies of motions, petitions, pleadings, notices or proposed orders, other than those originated by the Court, by mail unless the Clerk is provided with stamped, addressed envelopes. IN ST ST JOSEPH CIV Rule 201(201.5.3).

f. *Mailbox.* As a matter of convenience to attorneys, each court provides a mailbox for the distribution filings and orders generated by the Court, and it is the responsibility of each attorney to periodically check these mailboxes for service and distribution of court-generated filings and orders. IN ST ST JOSEPH CIV Rule 201(201.5.3).

G. Hearings

1. *Hearing on motion.* Unless local conditions make it impracticable, each judge shall establish regular times and places, at intervals sufficiently frequent for the prompt dispatch of business, at which motions requiring notice and hearing may be heard and disposed of; but the judge at any time or place and on such notice, if any, as he considers reasonable may make order for the advancement, conduct, and hearing of actions. To expedite its business the court may direct the submission and determination of motions without oral hearing upon brief written statements of reasons in support and opposition, or direct or permit hearings by telephone conference call with all attorneys or other similar means of communication. IN ST TRIAL P Rule 73(A).

2. *Hearing dates.* Hearing dates for filings requiring Court action shall be obtained from the Court Clerk and incorporated in the CCS entry at the time the motion or other pleading is filed. If no date is obtained prior to the filing, the fact of the hearing should be noted with the date and time left blank. IN ST ST JOSEPH CIV Rule 201(201.4).

3. *Hearing on matters other than trials.* Each Judge shall reserve periods of time for hearing matters other than contested trials, such as pre-trial and post-trial motions, rules to show cause, defaults, uncontested dissolutions of marriage, etc. As necessary to minimize conflicts in scheduling, the Judges shall set these schedules after consultation. Hearings shall be scheduled as follows:

a. *Scheduling uncontested or routine matters.* Routine matters, procedural motions, domestic relations applications for provisional relief and contempt proceedings, uncontested petitions for dissolution of marriage, and all other matters appropriate for summary consideration and disposition will be heard on the daily calendar. IN ST ST JOSEPH GEN AND ADMIN Rule 104(104.3.1).

b. *Scheduling contested or complicated matters.* Other matters that will require a hearing reasonably estimated to last in excess of twenty (20) minutes will be scheduled as the Court's calendar allows. Counsel or a party proceeding pro se should contact the chambers of the assigned judge to arrange for an appropriate hearing date and time. IN ST ST JOSEPH GEN AND ADMIN Rule 104(104.3.2).

c. *Scheduling motions for hearings.* Except for motions to correct error or not likely to require a hearing (as described in IN ST ST JOSEPH CIV Rule 201), all motions shall be scheduled for hearing at the time they are filed. It shall the responsibility of the moving party or counsel for the moving party to secure the date and time of the hearing from the Clerk or Court personnel who maintain the calendar for each Judge or Magistrate Judge. It shall also be the responsibility of the moving party or counsel for the moving party to coordinate the hearing date with all opposing counsel or unrepresented parties. IN ST ST JOSEPH CIV Rule 201(201.9.1).

    d. *Oral arguments on motions and other pleadings.* Unless otherwise required by St. Joseph County Civil or Indiana Trial Rules, it is within the sound discretion of the assigned Judge whether to allow oral argument; however, any party may file a request for oral argument by filing a written request by separate motion contemporaneously or at any time before the Court has ruled upon the motion or pleadings to be argued. IN ST ST JOSEPH CIV Rule 201(201.9.4).

4. *Motions for summary judgment and for dismissal.* Motions for summary judgment or motions to dismiss pursuant to IN ST TRIAL P Rule 12 or IN ST TRIAL P Rule 41 shall be scheduled for hearing, unless the Court issues a written scheduling order providing otherwise. (Refer to IN ST ST JOSEPH CIV Rule 206 for specific requirements for Pleadings and Motions under IN ST TRIAL P Rule 12 and IN ST TRIAL P Rule 56). IN ST ST JOSEPH CIV Rule 201(201.9.6).

    a. *Dispositive motions date.* Notwithstanding any other rule of court, all IN ST TRIAL P Rule 12 or IN ST TRIAL P Rule 56 motions shall be set for hearing by the moving party at the time of filing unless otherwise ordered by the Court. Unless otherwise authorized by the Court, the hearing shall be scheduled for a day not fewer than fourteen (14) days after the time period allowed for filing of briefs as specified in IN ST ST JOSEPH CIV Rule 206(206.1). IN ST ST JOSEPH CIV Rule 206(206.2).

    b. *Waiver of hearing; Stipulation of the parties.* Adverse parties may stipulate that a IN ST TRIAL P Rule 12 or IN ST TRIAL P Rule 56 motion may be ruled upon by the Court without a hearing thereon, in which event the motion and stipulation shall be brought to the personal attention of the Judge by counsel or by a party proceeding pro se. IN ST ST JOSEPH CIV Rule 206(206.3).

    c. *Appearance by counsel at scheduled hearings.* Whenever the Court schedules a hearing on a motion pursuant to IN ST TRIAL P Rule 12 and/or IN ST TRIAL P Rule 56, counsel for all represented parties shall appear in person or by local co-counsel at such hearing. IN ST ST JOSEPH CIV Rule 206(206.5).

H. Forms

1. Motion to Strike Forms for Indiana

    a. Motion to strike pleading not signed. 9 INPRAC § 4.18.

    b. Motion to strike pleading as sham and false. 9 INPRAC § 4.19.

    c. Motion to strike; Entire pleading. 9 INPRAC § 42.21.

    d. Motion to strike; Portions of pleading. 9 INPRAC § 42.22.

    e. Motion to strike; Insufficient defense in answer. 9 INPRAC § 42.23.

    f. Motion to strike; Pleading that was not timely filed. 9 INPRAC § 42.24.

    g. Motion to strike; Attorney fees claim. 9 INPRAC § 42.25.

    h. Motion to strike; General denial in answer. 9 INPRAC § 42.26.

    i. Motion to strike; Impertinent and scandalous material. 9 INPRAC § 42.27.

    j. Motion to strike answer; Matter repleaded contrary to prior ruling. 9 INPRAC § 42.28.

    k. Motion to strike; Failure to plead performance of conditions precedent. 9 INPRAC § 42.29.

    l. Motion to strike; Appearance of defendant's attorney. 9 INPRAC § 42.30.

    m. Certificate of service; Personal service. 9 INPRAC § 5.7.

    n. Certificate of service; First class mail. 9 INPRAC § 5.8.

I. Checklist

- (I) ❑ Matters to be considered by moving party
  - (a) ❑ Required documents
    - (1) ❑ Motion and notice
    - (2) ❑ Chronological Case Summary (CCS) entry form
    - (3) ❑ Supporting memorandum of law
    - (4) ❑ Proposed order
    - (5) ❑ Certificate of service
  - (b) ❑ Supplemental documents
    - (1) ❑ Supporting evidence
    - (2) ❑ Facsimile cover sheet
  - (c) ❑ Timing
    - (1) ❑ Upon motion made by a party before responding to a pleading, or, if no responsive pleading is permitted by Indiana Rules of Trial Procedure, upon motion made by a party within twenty (20) days after the service of the pleading upon him or at any time upon the court's own initiative, the court may order stricken from any pleading any insufficient claim or defense or any redundant, immaterial, impertinent, or scandalous matter
    - (2) ❑ A written motion, other than one which may be heard ex parte, and notice of the hearing thereof shall be served not less than five (5) days before the time specified for the hearing, unless a different period is fixed by the Indiana Rules of Trial Procedure or by order of the court
    - (3) ❑ All pleadings and papers subsequent to the complaint which are required to be served upon a party shall be filed with the Court either before service or within a reasonable period of time thereafter
- (II) ❑ Matters to be considered by the responding party
  - (a) ❑ Required documents
    - (1) ❑ Opposition
    - (2) ❑ Chronological Case Summary (CCS) entry form
    - (3) ❑ Supporting memorandum of law
    - (4) ❑ Certificate of service
  - (b) ❑ Supplemental documents
    - (1) ❑ Supporting evidence
    - (2) ❑ Proposed order
    - (3) ❑ Facsimile cover sheet
  - (c) ❑ Timing
    - (1) ❑ An adverse party shall have thirty (30) days after service of the motion in which to serve and file an answer brief
    - (2) ❑ Except as otherwise provided in IN ST TRIAL P Rule 59(D), opposing affidavits may be served not less than one (1) day before the hearing, unless the court permits them to be served at some other time

Motions, Oppositions and Replies
Motion to Dismiss for Improper Venue

Document Last Updated October 2013

A. Applicable Rules

1. *State rules*

   a. Appearance. IN ST TRIAL P Rule 3.1.

   b. Process. IN ST TRIAL P Rule 4.

   c. Service and filing of pleadings and other papers. IN ST TRIAL P Rule 5.

   d. Time. IN ST TRIAL P Rule 6.

   e. Pleadings. IN ST TRIAL P Rule 7; IN ST TRIAL P Rule 8; IN ST TRIAL P Rule 9.2; IN ST TRIAL P Rule 10.

   f. Signing and verification of pleadings. IN ST TRIAL P Rule 11.

   g. Defenses and objections; When and how presented; By pleading or motion; Motion for judgment on the pleadings. IN ST TRIAL P Rule 12.

   h. Amended and supplemental pleadings. IN ST TRIAL P Rule 15.

   i. Joinder of person needed for just adjudication. IN ST TRIAL P Rule 19.

   j. Misjoinder and non-joinder of parties; Venue and jurisdiction over the subject-matter. IN ST TRIAL P Rule 21.

   k. Evidence. IN ST TRIAL P Rule 43.

   l. Judgment on the evidence (directed verdict). IN ST TRIAL P Rule 50.

   m. Findings by the court. IN ST TRIAL P Rule 52.

   n. Summary judgment. IN ST TRIAL P Rule 56.

   o. Motion to correct error. IN ST TRIAL P Rule 59.

   p. Relief from judgment or order. IN ST TRIAL P Rule 60.

   q. Hearing of motions. IN ST TRIAL P Rule 73.

   r. Venue requirements. IN ST TRIAL P Rule 75.

   s. Change of venue. IN ST TRIAL P Rule 76.

   t. Interlocutory appeals. IN ST RAP Rule 14.

   u. Access to court records. IN ST ADMIN Rule 9.

   v. Paper size. IN ST ADMIN Rule 11.

   w. Facsimile and electronic transmission. IN ST ADMIN Rule 12; IN ST ADMIN Rule 16.

   x. Sealing of certain records by court; Hearing; Notice. IN ST 5-14-3-5.5.

   y. Sixtieth judicial circuit. IN ST 33-33-71-2.

   z. Privacy and confidentiality. IN ST 5-2-9-6; IN ST 5-14-3-4; IN ST 6-4.1-5-10; IN ST 6-4.1-12-12; IN ST 6-8.1-7-1; IN ST 11-13-1-8; IN ST 12-23-14-13; IN ST 16-39-3-10; IN ST 16-41-8-1; IN ST 22-4-19-6; IN ST 31-11-1-6; IN ST 31-19-5-23; IN ST 31-19-13-2; IN ST 31-19-19-1; IN ST 31-33-18-1; IN ST 31-39-1-1; IN ST 31-39-1-2; IN ST 33-23-16-16; IN ST 35-34-2-4; IN ST 35-38-1-13; IN ST 35-38-9-1; IN ST ADR Rule 2.11; IN ST ADR Rule 4.4; IN ST ADR Rule 5.6; IN ST JURY Rule 10.

2. *Local rules*

   a. Court hours and scheduling. IN ST ST JOSEPH GEN AND ADMIN Rule 104.

   b. Filing, pleading, and motions. IN ST ST JOSEPH CIV Rule 201.

    c.   Uniform court and case number designation. IN ST ST JOSEPH CIV Rule 202.

    d.   Pleading and motions under IN ST TRIAL P Rule 12 and IN ST TRIAL P Rule 56. IN ST ST JOSEPH CIV Rule 206.

    e.   Proposed order. IN ST ST JOSEPH CIV Rule 213.

    f.   Change of venue. IN ST ST JOSEPH CIV Rule 215.

    g.   Electronic filing of cases in St. Joseph County. IN ST ST JOSEPH ELECTRONIC Rule 701.

B. Timing

1.   *Motion to dismiss for improper venue.* A motion making the defense of incorrect venue under IN ST TRIAL P Rule 75, or any statutory provision, shall be made before pleading if a further pleading is permitted or within twenty (20) days after service of the prior pleading if none is required. IN ST TRIAL P Rule 12(B); IN ST TRIAL P Rule 75(A).

    a.   *Time to file a responsive pleading.* A responsive pleading required under the Indiana Rules of Trial Procedure, shall be served within twenty (20) days after service of the prior pleading. IN ST TRIAL P Rule 6(C).

    b.   *Waiver of certain IN ST TRIAL P Rule 12(B) defenses.* If a pleading sets forth a claim for relief to which the adverse party is not required to serve a responsive pleading, any of the defenses in IN ST TRIAL P Rule 12(B)(2), IN ST TRIAL P Rule 12(B)(3), IN ST TRIAL P Rule 12(B)(4), IN ST TRIAL P Rule 12(B)(5) or IN ST TRIAL P Rule 12(B)(8) is waived to the extent constitutionally permissible unless made in a motion within twenty (20) days after service of the prior pleading. IN ST TRIAL P Rule 12(B).

    c.   *Filing.* All pleadings and papers subsequent to the complaint which are required to be served upon a party shall be filed with the Court either before service or within a reasonable period of time thereafter. IN ST TRIAL P Rule 5(E)(1).

2.   *Service.* A written motion, other than one which may be heard ex parte, and notice of the hearing thereof shall be served not less than five (5) days before the time specified for the hearing, unless a different period is fixed by the Indiana Rules of Trial Procedure or by order of the court. IN ST TRIAL P Rule 6(D).

    a.   *Of supporting affidavits.* When a motion is supported by affidavit, the affidavit shall be served with the motion; and,

3.   *Service of opposition.* Except as otherwise provided in IN ST TRIAL P Rule 59(D), opposing affidavits may be served not less than one (1) day before the hearing, unless the court permits them to be served at some other time. IN ST TRIAL P Rule 6(D).

    a.   An adverse party shall have thirty (30) days after service of the motion in which to serve and file an answer brief. IN ST ST JOSEPH CIV Rule 206(206.1).

4.   *Filing proposed orders.* Unless otherwise directed or given leave of the Court, proposed orders in emergency matters shall be filed within forty-eight (48) hours after a hearing; proposed orders in other matters shall be filed within seven (7) days as computed by IN ST TRIAL P Rule 6. IN ST ST JOSEPH CIV Rule 213(213.5).

5.   *Computation of time*

    a.   *Generally; Days excluded.* In computing any period of time prescribed or allowed by the Indiana Rules of Trial Procedure, by order of the court, or by any applicable statute, the day of the act, event, or default from which the designated period of time begins to run shall not be included. The last day of the period so computed is to be included unless it is:

        i.   A Saturday,

        ii.   A Sunday,

        iii.   A legal holiday as defined by state statute, or

        iv.   A day the office in which the act is to be done is closed during regular business hours. IN ST TRIAL P Rule 6(A).

    b.   *Short periods.* In any event, the period runs until the end of the next day that is not a Saturday, a

Sunday, a legal holiday, or a day on which the office is closed. When the period of time allowed is less than seven (7) days, intermediate Saturdays, Sundays, legal holidays, and days on which the office is closed shall be excluded from the computations. IN ST TRIAL P Rule 6(A).

c. *Additional time after service by United States mail.* Whenever a party has the right or is required to do some act or take some proceedings within a prescribed period after the service of a notice or other paper upon him and the notice or paper is served upon him by United States mail, three (3) days shall be added to the prescribed period. IN ST TRIAL P Rule 6(E).

d. *Enlargement of time.* When an act is required or allowed to be done at or within a specific time by the Indiana Rules of Trial Procedure, the court may at any time for cause shown:

   i. Order the period enlarged, with or without motion or notice, if request therefor is made before the expiration of the period originally prescribed or extended by a previous order; or

   ii. Upon motion made after the expiration of the specific period, permit the act to be done where the failure to act was the result of excusable neglect; but, the court may not extend the time for taking any action for judgment on the evidence under IN ST TRIAL P Rule 50(A), amendment of findings and judgment under IN ST TRIAL P Rule 52(B), to correct errors under IN ST TRIAL P Rule 59(C), statement in opposition to motion to correct error under IN ST TRIAL P Rule 59(E), or to obtain relief from final judgment under IN ST TRIAL P Rule 60(B), except to the extent and under the conditions stated in those rules. IN ST TRIAL P Rule 6(B).

   iii. An initial written motion for enlargement of time pursuant to IN ST TRIAL P Rule 6(B)(1) to answer a claim shall be routinely granted for an additional thirty (30) days from the original due date or other period the assigned Judge deems reasonable by written order of the Court. The motion must be filed on or before the original due date or IN ST ST JOSEPH CIV Rule 201 shall be inapplicable. IN ST ST JOSEPH CIV Rule 201(201.9.5).

     • Any motion for enlargement of time shall state the date when such response is due and the date to which time is requested to be enlarged. IN ST ST JOSEPH CIV Rule 201(201.9.5).

     • All subsequent motions for enlargement of time shall be so designated and will only be granted for good cause shown or in the interest of justice. IN ST ST JOSEPH CIV Rule 201(201.9.5).

C. General Requirements

1. *Motions, generally.* Unless made during a hearing or trial, or otherwise ordered by the court, an application to the court for an order shall be made by written motion. The motion shall state the grounds therefor and the relief or order sought. IN ST TRIAL P Rule 7(B).

a. *Motions as distinct from pleadings.* Motions and responses to motions are not pleadings, and allegations contained in a motion are not admissions of a party. 22B INPRAC 7:2; Wachstetter v. County Properties, LLC, 832 N.E.2d 574 (Ind.Ct.App. 2005); Scott County Family YMCA, Inc. v. Hobbs, 817 N.E.2d 603 (Ind.Ct.App. 2004).

b. *Unopposed motions generally granted.* It is common for a trial court to grant procedural motions, such as motions for enlargement of time, discovery motions, or motions for continuance, unless an objection is filed. 21 INPRAC § 13.8.

c. *Proposed orders.* As directed by the Court, a party or an attorney for a party shall prepare a proposed order based on the decision rendered by the Court. The party so directed shall prepare the proposed order in a timely manner and, upon filing, shall advise the chambers of the applicable judge that the proposed order has been prepared and filed. IN ST ST JOSEPH CIV Rule 213(213.2).

   i. Prior to entry by the Court of orders granting motions or applications, the moving party or applicant (or his or her attorney) shall, unless the Court directs otherwise, furnish the Court with proposed orders in matters of dismissal. IN ST ST JOSEPH CIV Rule 213(213.1(5)).

d. *Reply brief.* Subject to Court approval, the moving party may file a reply brief. IN ST ST JOSEPH CIV Rule 206(206.1).

2. *Motion to dismiss for improper venue.* Every defense, in law or fact, to a claim for relief in any pleading, whether a claim, counterclaim, cross-claim, or third-party claim, shall be asserted in the responsive

pleading thereto if one is required; except that at the option of the pleader, incorrect venue under IN ST TRIAL P Rule 75, or any statutory provision may be made by motion. IN ST TRIAL P Rule 12(B)(3). The disposition of this motion shall be consistent with IN ST TRIAL P Rule 75. IN ST TRIAL P Rule 12(B)(3). This means that, in almost every instance in which a motion is made under IN ST TRIAL P Rule 12(B)(3) or another statute, the action shall not be dismissed but transferred, consistent with IN ST TRIAL P Rule 75. 1A INPRAC R 12(12.7).

a. *Venue.* Any case may be venued, commenced and decided in any court in any county, except, that upon the filing of a pleading or a motion to dismiss allowed by IN ST TRIAL P Rule 12(B)(3), the court, from allegations of the complaint or after hearing evidence thereon or considering affidavits or documentary evidence filed with the motion or in opposition to it, shall order the case transferred to a county or court selected by the party first properly filing such motion or pleading if the court determines that the county or court where the action was filed does not meet preferred venue requirements or is not authorized to decide the case and that the court or county selected has preferred venue and is authorized to decide the case. IN ST TRIAL P Rule 75(A).

b. *Payment of transfer fee if venue changed.* When a change of venue from the County is granted, all accrued costs and the fee for transfer must be paid to the Clerk by the moving party within ten (10) days after the transfer order is entered. IN ST ST JOSEPH CIV Rule 215(215.1).

    i. *Failure to pay fee.* In the absence of such payment, the movant will be deemed to have abandoned the motion so the Clerk will not perfect the change, the cause will be restored to the docket of this Court, and this Court shall resume general jurisdiction of the cause in accordance with IN ST TRIAL P Rule 76. IN ST ST JOSEPH CIV Rule 215(215.2).

c. *Preferred venue.* Preferred venue lies in:

    i. The county where the greater percentage of individual defendants included in the complaint resides, or, if there is no such greater percentage, the place where any individual defendant so named resides; or

    ii. The county where the land or some part thereof is located or the chattels or some part thereof are regularly located or kept, if the complaint includes a claim for injuries thereto or relating to such land or such chattels, including without limitation claims for recovery of possession or for injuries, to establish use or control, to quiet title or determine any interest, to avoid or set aside conveyances, to foreclose liens, to partition and to assert any matters for which in rem relief is or would be proper; or

    iii. The county where the accident or collision occurred, if the complaint includes a claim for injuries relating to the operation of a motor vehicle or a vehicle on railroad, street or interurban tracks; or

    iv. The county where either the principal office of a defendant organization is located or the office or agency of a defendant organization or individual to which the claim relates or out of which the claim arose is located, if one or more such organizations or individuals are included as defendants in the complaint; or

    v. The county where either one or more individual plaintiffs reside, the principal office of a governmental organization is located, or the office of a governmental organization to which the claim relates or out of which the claim arose is located, if one or more governmental organizations are included as defendants in the complaint; or

    vi. The county or court fixed by written stipulations signed by all the parties named in the complaint or their attorneys and filed with the court before ruling on the motion to dismiss; or

    vii. The county where the individual is held in custody or is restrained, if the complaint seeks relief with respect to such individual's custody or restraint upon his freedom; or

    viii. The county where a claim in the plaintiff's complaint may be commenced under any statute recognizing or creating a special or general remedy or proceeding; or

    ix. The county where all or some of the property is located or can be found if the case seeks only judgment in rem against the property of a defendant being served by publication; or

    x.   The county where either one or more individual plaintiffs reside, the principal office of any plaintiff organization or governmental organization is located, or the office of any such plaintiff organization or governmental organization to which the claim relates or out of which the claim arose is located, if the case is not subject to the requirements of IN ST TRIAL P Rule 75(A)(1) through IN ST TRIAL P Rule 75(A)(9) or if all the defendants are nonresident individuals or nonresident organizations without a principal office in the state. IN ST TRIAL P Rule 75(A).

  d. *Claim or proceeding filed in improper court*

    i.   Whenever a claim or proceeding is filed which should properly have been filed in another court of this state, and proper objection is made, the court in which such action is filed shall not then dismiss the action, but shall order the action transferred to the court in which it should have been filed. IN ST TRIAL P Rule 75(B)(1).

    ii. The person filing the action shall, within twenty (20) days, pay such costs as are chargeable upon a change of venue and the papers and records shall be certified to the court of transfer in like manner as upon change of venue and the action shall be deemed commenced as of the date of filing the action in the original court. IN ST TRIAL P Rule 75(B)(2).

    iii. If the party filing the action does not pay the costs of transfer within twenty (20) days of the order transferring venue, the original court shall dismiss the action without prejudice and shall order payment of reasonable attorney fees to the party making proper objection. IN ST TRIAL P Rule 75(B)(3).

  e. *Assessment of costs, traveling expenses and attorneys' fees in resisting venue.* When the case is ordered transferred under the provisions of IN ST TRIAL P Rule 75 or IN ST TRIAL P Rule 21(B) the court shall order the parties or persons filing the complaint to pay the filing costs of refiling the case in the proper court and pay mileage expenses reasonably incurred by the parties and their attorneys in resisting the venue; and if it appears that the case was commenced in the wrong county by sham pleading, in bad faith or without cause, the court shall order payment of reasonable attorneys' fees incurred by parties successfully resisting the venue. IN ST TRIAL P Rule 75(C).

  f. *Other venue statutes superseded by IN ST TRIAL P Rule 75.* Any provision of the Indiana Rules of Trial Procedure and any special or general statute relating to venue, the place of trial or the authority of the court to hear the case shall be subject to IN ST TRIAL P Rule 75, and the provisions of any statute fixing more stringent rules thereon shall be ineffective. No statute or rule fixing the place of trial shall be deemed a requirement of jurisdiction. IN ST TRIAL P Rule 75(D).

  g. *Appeal.* An order transferring or refusing to transfer a case under IN ST TRIAL P Rule 75 shall be an interlocutory order appealable pursuant to IN ST RAP Rule 14(A)(8); provided, however, that the appeal of an interlocutory order under IN ST TRIAL P Rule 75 shall not stay proceedings in the trial court unless the trial court or the Court of Appeals so orders. IN ST TRIAL P Rule 75(E).

3. *Consolidation and waiver*

  a. *Consolidation of defenses in motion.* A party who makes a motion under IN ST TRIAL P Rule 12 may join with it any other motions herein provided for and then available to him. If a party makes a motion under IN ST TRIAL P Rule 12 but omits therefrom any defense or objection then available to him which IN ST TRIAL P Rule 12 permits to be raised by motion, he shall not thereafter make a motion based on the defense or objection so omitted. He may, however, make such motions as are allowed under IN ST TRIAL P Rule 12(H)(2). IN ST TRIAL P Rule 12(G).

  b. *Waiver or preservation of certain defenses.* No defense or objection is waived by being joined with one or more other defenses or objections in a responsive pleading or motion. IN ST TRIAL P Rule 12(B).

4. *Opposition to a motion to dismiss for improper venue.* Failure to file an answer brief or reply brief within the time prescribed shall be deemed a waiver of the right thereto and shall subject the motion to summary ruling. IN ST ST JOSEPH CIV Rule 206(206.1).

D. Documents

1. *Required documents*

  a. *Motion and notice.* The requirement of notice is satisfied by service of the motion. IN ST TRIAL P

Rule 7(B). Refer to the General Requirements section of this document for information on the content of a motion to dismiss for improper venue.

b. *Chronological Case Summary (CCS) entry form.* Every written motion, petition, or other pleading subsequent to the original complaint presented to the Clerk for filing shall be accompanied by a Chronological Case Summary (CCS) entry form in duplicate. IN ST ST JOSEPH CIV Rule 201(201.4). Refer to the Format section of this document for details on the format and filing requirements for the CCS entry form.

c. *Supporting memorandum of law.* All pleadings and motions filed pursuant to IN ST TRIAL P Rule 12 and IN ST TRIAL P Rule 56 shall be accompanied by a separate supporting brief. IN ST ST JOSEPH CIV Rule 206(206.1).

d. *Proposed order.* Unless local practice provides differently, a party should submit a proposed order with its written motion to be signed by the judge once the motion has been granted. 21 INPRAC § 13.8. All proposed orders shall be submitted in an original plus a number of copies equal to one more than the number of pro se parties and attorneys of record contained in the prepared proof of notice under IN ST TRIAL P Rule 72(D). IN ST ST JOSEPH CIV Rule 213(213.3); IN ST ST JOSEPH CIV Rule 201(201.5.2).

e. *Certificate of service.* An attorney or unrepresented party tendering a document to the Clerk for filing shall certify that service has been made, list the parties served, and specify the date and means of service. The certificate of service shall be placed at the end of the document and shall not be separately filed. The separate filing of a certificate of service, however, shall not be grounds for rejecting a document for filing. The Clerk may permit documents to be filed without a certificate of service but shall require prompt filing of a separate certificate of service. IN ST TRIAL P Rule 5(C).

2. *Supplemental documents*

a. *Supporting evidence.* When a motion is based on facts not appearing of record the court may hear the matter on affidavits presented by the respective parties, but the court may direct that the matter be heard wholly or partly on oral testimony or depositions. IN ST TRIAL P Rule 43(B).

b. *Facsimile cover sheet.* Any document sent to the Clerk of the Circuit Court by electronic facsimile transmission shall be accompanied by a cover sheet which states the title of the document, case number, number of pages, identity and voice telephone number of the sending party and instructions for filing. The cover sheet shall contain the signature of the attorney or party, pro se, authorizing the filing. IN ST ADMIN Rule 12(D).

E. Format

1. *Form of motions.* The rules applicable to captions, and the signing and form of pleadings (IN ST TRIAL P Rule 8 through IN ST TRIAL P Rule 11), apply to all motions and other papers provided under the Indiana Rules of Trial Procedure. 22B INPRAC 7:2.

a. *Separate motions; Alternative motions.* Each motion shall be separate, while alternative motions filed together shall each be identified on the caption. IN ST ST JOSEPH CIV Rule 206(206.1).

2. *Form of pleadings*

a. *Caption; Names of parties.* Every pleading shall contain a caption setting forth the name of the court, the title of the action, the file number, and a designation as in IN ST TRIAL P Rule 7(A). In the complaint the title of the action shall include the names of all the parties, but in other pleadings it is sufficient to state the name of the first party on each side with an appropriate indication of other parties. IN ST TRIAL P Rule 10(A); IN ST ST JOSEPH CIV Rule 201(201.3.3). If a special judge has been assigned to the case, the pleading should also identify the special judge. IN ST ST JOSEPH CIV Rule 201(201.3.3).

    i. *Title.* All pleadings or motions shall include a title, which shall delineate each topic included in the pleading. For example, where a pleading contains an answer, a motion to dismiss, and a jury request, each topic shall be set forth in the title. IN ST ST JOSEPH CIV Rule 201(201.3.4).

b. *Paragraphs; Separate statements.* All averments of a claim or defense shall be made in numbered paragraphs, the contents of each of which shall be limited as far as practicable to a statement of a

single set of circumstances, and a paragraph may be referred to by number in all succeeding pleadings. Each claim founded upon a separate transaction or occurrence and each defense other than denials may be stated in a separate count or defense whenever a separation facilitates the clear presentation of the matters set forth. IN ST TRIAL P Rule 10(B).

c. *Adoption by reference; Exhibits.* Statements in a pleading may be adopted by reference in a different part of the same pleading or in another pleading or in any motion. A copy of any written instrument which is an exhibit to a pleading is a part thereof for all purposes. IN ST TRIAL P Rule 10(C).

d. *Flat filing.* In order that the Clerk's files may be kept under the system commonly known as "flat filing," all papers presented to the Clerk for filing shall be flat and unfolded. Pleadings shall have no covers or backs and shall be fastened together at the top left-hand corner only. IN ST ST JOSEPH CIV Rule 201(201.1).

e. *One side of page used.* Printing shall be on one (1) side of the paper. IN ST ST JOSEPH CIV Rule 201(201.3.2).

f. *Copies.* All copies shall be on white paper of sufficient strength and durability to resist normal wear and tear. IN ST ST JOSEPH CIV Rule 201(201.3.1).

g. *Margins.* Margins shall be at least one inch (1"). IN ST ST JOSEPH CIV Rule 201(201.3.2).

h. *Double-spaced.* If typewritten, the lines shall be double spaced except for quotations, which shall be indented and single-spaced. IN ST ST JOSEPH CIV Rule 201(201.3.2).

i. *Font size.* Type face shall be twelve (12) font size or larger within the body of the document and ten (10) font size or larger in the footnotes. IN ST ST JOSEPH CIV Rule 201(201.3.2).

j. *Font type.* The font type must be legible and script type shall not be used. IN ST ST JOSEPH CIV Rule 201(201.3.2).

k. *Italics.* Italicized type may be used for quotations, references, or case citations. IN ST ST JOSEPH CIV Rule 201(201.3.2).

l. *Court and case designation.* All filings shall conform to the requirements for uniform court and case number designation set by IN ST ADMIN Rule 8. In addition, all filings shall contain the proper court and case designation as described below. IN ST ST JOSEPH CIV Rule 202.

    i. *Court designation.* Pursuant to IN ST 33-33-71-2, St. Joseph County, Indiana, constitutes the Sixtieth Judicial Circuit. The legal names of the courts within the 60th Judicial Circuit are the St. Joseph Circuit Court, the St. Joseph Superior Court, and the St. Joseph Probate Court. All filings shall properly reflect the legal name of the applicable court. Any filing may be amended, rejected, or stricken if it does not contain the proper case name and/or the legal name of the court. IN ST ST JOSEPH CIV Rule 202(202.1).

m. *Form of CCS entry.* Every written motion, petition, or other pleading subsequent to the original complaint presented to the Clerk for filing shall be accompanied by a Chronological Case Summary (CCS) entry form in duplicate which shall contain the title and cause number of the action, the date, and the proposed entry to appear on the docket. IN ST ST JOSEPH CIV Rule 201(201.4).

    i. *Identification and signature.* The CCS entry form shall identify the party making the filing, designate each pleading being filed, and shall be signed by counsel of record or the unrepresented litigant. IN ST ST JOSEPH CIV Rule 201(201.4).

    ii. *Date stamp.* The form shall be date stamped and presented to the Court Clerk, who shall initial the form and return the duplicate to the filing party. IN ST ST JOSEPH CIV Rule 201(201.4).

n. *Form of proposed order.* Any proposed order shall be a document that is separate and apart from the motion or application to which it relates and shall contain a caption showing the name of the court, the case number assigned to the case, and the title of the case as shown by the complaint pursuant to IN ST ST JOSEPH CIV Rule 201. IN ST ST JOSEPH CIV Rule 213(213.2).

    i. If there are multiple parties, the title may be shortened to include only the first name plaintiff and defendant with appropriate indication that there are additional parties. IN ST ST JOSEPH CIV Rule 213(213.2).

ii. The proposed order shall be on white paper, eight and one-half by eleven inches (8 1/2" x 11") in size, and each page shall be numbered. IN ST ST JOSEPH CIV Rule 213(213.2).

iii. The last page of the proposed order shall contain a line for the date, either "Dated _____" or "Signed on the date filemarked hereon." IN ST ST JOSEPH CIV Rule 213(213.2).

iv. On the last page there also shall be a line for the signature of the Judge under which shall be typed "Judge, St. Joseph [Circuit or Superior or Probate] Court." IN ST ST JOSEPH CIV Rule 213(213.2).

v. If the proposed order contains a recommendation from a Magistrate, the last page shall have a line for the signature of the Magistrate under which shall be typed "Magistrate, St. Joseph [Circuit or Superior or Probate] Court," to the left of which shall be the following, "So Recommended:" and beneath and to the left of which shall be typed, "Approved. So Ordered." IN ST ST JOSEPH CIV Rule 213(213.2).

vi. To allow compliance with the notice requirements of IN ST TRIAL P Rule 72(D), the lower four (4) inches of the last page of the proposed order shall be left blank. The proposed order shall also include a prepared proof of notice under IN ST TRIAL P Rule 72(D), and in preparing such a notice the filing party shall complete all portions of the prepared proof of notice. IN ST ST JOSEPH CIV Rule 213(213.2).

3. *Size of papers for filing.* Effective January 1, 1992, all pleadings, copies, motions and documents filed with any trial court or appellate level court, typed or printed, with the exception of exhibits and existing wills, shall be prepared on eight and one-half by eleven inch (8 1/2" x 11") size paper. IN ST ADMIN Rule 11.

a. *Paper.* Pleadings, motions, and other papers shall be either legibly printed or typewritten on white opaque paper of good quality at least sixteen (16) pound weight, eight and one-half inches (8 1/2 ") in width and eleven inches (11") in length as required by IN ST ADMIN Rule 11. IN ST ST JOSEPH CIV Rule 201(201.3.1).

4. *Signature requirements*

a. *Signature of attorney.* Every pleading or motion of a party represented by an attorney shall be signed by at least one (1) attorney of record in his individual name, whose address, telephone number, and attorney number shall be stated, except that this provision shall not apply to pleadings and motions made and transcribed at the trial or a hearing before the judge and received by him in such form. IN ST TRIAL P Rule 11(A).

i. The signature of an attorney constitutes a certificate by him that he has read the pleadings; that to the best of his knowledge, information, and belief, there is good ground to support it; and that it is not interposed for delay. IN ST TRIAL P Rule 11(A).

ii. If a pleading or motion is not signed or is signed with intent to defeat the purpose of the rule, it may be stricken as sham and false and the action may proceed as though the pleading had not been served. IN ST TRIAL P Rule 11(A).

iii. For a willful violation of IN ST TRIAL P Rule 11 an attorney may be subjected to appropriate disciplinary action. Similar action may be taken if scandalous or indecent matter is inserted. IN ST TRIAL P Rule 11(A).

b. *Signature of unrepresented party.* A party who is not represented by an attorney shall sign his pleading and state his address. IN ST TRIAL P Rule 11(A).

c. *Verification not generally required.* Except when specifically required by rule, pleadings or motions need not be verified or accompanied by affidavit. The rule in equity that the averments of an answer under oath must be overcome by the testimony of two (2) witnesses or of one (1) witness sustained by corroborating circumstances is abolished. IN ST TRIAL P Rule 11(A).

d. *Verification by affirmation or representation.* When in connection with any civil or special statutory proceeding it is required that any pleading, motion, petition, supporting affidavit, or other document of any kind, be verified, or that an oath be taken, it shall be sufficient if the subscriber simply affirms the truth of the matter to be verified by an affirmation or representation. IN ST TRIAL P Rule 11(B).

IN ST TRIAL P Rule 11(B) states that the affirmation or representation should be in substantially the following language: "I (we) affirm, under the penalties for perjury, that the foregoing representation(s) is (are) true. (Signed) _____."

    i. Any person who falsifies an affirmation or representation of fact shall be subject to the same penalties as are prescribed by law for the making of a false affidavit. IN ST TRIAL P Rule 11(B).

e. *Verified pleadings, motions, and affidavits as evidence.* Pleadings, motions and affidavits accompanying or in support of such pleadings or motions when required to be verified or under oath shall be accepted as a representation that the signer had personal knowledge thereof or reasonable cause to believe the existence of the facts or matters stated or alleged therein; and, if otherwise competent or acceptable as evidence, may be admitted as evidence of the facts or matters stated or alleged therein when it is so provided in the Indiana Rules of Trial Procedure, by statute or other law, or to the extent the writing or signature expressly purports to be made upon the signer's personal knowledge. When such pleadings, motions and affidavits are verified or under oath they shall not require other or greater proof on the part of the adverse party than if not verified or not under oath unless expressly provided otherwise by the Indiana Rules of Trial Procedure, statute or other law. Affidavits upon motions for summary judgment under IN ST TRIAL P Rule 56 and in denial of execution under IN ST TRIAL P Rule 9.2 shall be made upon personal knowledge. IN ST TRIAL P Rule 11(C).

f. *Signature, verification and other requirements.* Parties and their counsel are enjoined to comply with the verification requirements of IN ST TRIAL P Rule 11, and either the moving party or the party's attorney of record shall sign all pleadings and motions before filing with the Clerk of the Court. Every motion, petition, or other pleading filed with the Clerk shall contain the name, organization, physical address, telephone number, and facsimile number of the filing party or an attorney for that party. IN ST ST JOSEPH CIV Rule 201(201.3.6).

    i. The Clerk shall not accept any motion, petition, notice or other pleading or a CCS entry form for filing from an unrepresented litigant unless the unrepresented litigant's current address and phone number appear on the pleading, and an opposing party may service notices and responses on an unrepresented litigant at any address he or she has provided on a pleading. IN ST ST JOSEPH CIV Rule 201(201.3.6).

5. *Information excluded from public access.* Every document filed in a case shall separately identify information excluded from public access pursuant to IN ST ADMIN Rule 9(G)(1) as follows:

a. Whole documents that are excluded from public access pursuant to IN ST ADMIN Rule 9(G)(1) shall be tendered on light green paper or have a light green coversheet attached to the document, marked "Not for Public Access" or "Confidential." IN ST TRIAL P Rule 5(G)(1).

b. When only a portion of a document contains information excluded from public access pursuant to IN ST ADMIN Rule 9(G)(1), said information shall be omitted [or redacted] from the filed document, and set forth on a separate accompanying document on light green paper conspicuously marked "Not for Public Access" or "Confidential" and clearly designated [or identifying] the caption and number of the case and the document and location within the document to which the redacted material pertains. IN ST TRIAL P Rule 5(G)(2).

c. With respect to documents filed in electronic format, the trial court, by local rule, may provide for compliance with IN ST TRIAL P Rule 5 in manner that separates and protects access to information excluded from public access. IN ST TRIAL P Rule 5(G)(3).

d. IN ST TRIAL P Rule 5(G) does not apply to a record sealed by the court pursuant to IN ST 5-14-3-5.5 or otherwise, nor to records, documents, or information filed in cases to which public access is prohibited pursuant to IN ST ADMIN Rule 9(G). IN ST TRIAL P Rule 5(G)(4).

e. The following information in case records is excluded from public access and is confidential:

    i. Information that is excluded from public access pursuant to federal law;

    ii. Information that is excluded from public access as declared confidential by Indiana statute or other court rule, including without limitation:

        • All adoption records created after July 8, 1941, as declared confidential by IN ST 31-19-19-1, et seq., except those specifically declared open by IN ST 31-19-13-2(2);

- All records relating to chancroid, chlamydia, gonorrhea, hepatitis, human immunodeficiency virus (HIV), Lymphogranuloma venereum, syphilis, tuberculosis, as declared confidential by IN ST 16-41-8-1, et seq.;

- All records relating to child abuse as declared confidential by IN ST 31-33-18-1, et seq.;

- All records relating to drug tests as declared confidential by IN ST 5-14-3-4(a)(9);

- Records of grand jury proceedings as declared confidential by IN ST 35-34-2-4;

- Records of juvenile proceedings as declared confidential by IN ST 31-39-1-2, except those specifically open under statute;

- All paternity records created after July 1, 1941 as declared confidential by IN ST 31-14-11-15, IN ST 31-19-5-23, IN ST 31-39-1-1 and IN ST 31-39-1-2 [Editor's note: IN ST 31-14-11-15 was repealed effective May 9, 2013];

- All pre-sentence reports as declared confidential by IN ST 35-38-1-13;

- Written petitions to permit marriages without consent and orders directing the Clerk of Court to issue a marriage license to underage persons, as declared confidential by IN ST 31-11-1-6;

- Only those arrest warrants, search warrants, indictments and informations ordered confidential by the trial judge, prior to return of duly executed service as declared confidential by IN ST 5-14-3-4(b)(1);

- All medical, mental health, or tax records unless determined by law or regulation of any governmental custodian not to be confidential, released by the subject of such records, or declared by a court of competent jurisdiction to be essential to the resolution of litigation as declared confidential by IN ST 16-39-3-10, IN ST 6-4.1-5-10, IN ST 6-4.1-12-12, and IN ST 6-8.1-7-1;

- Personal information relating to jurors or prospective jurors, other than for the use of the parties and counsel, pursuant to IN ST JURY Rule 10;

- Information relating to protection from abuse orders, no-contact orders and workplace violence restraining orders as declared confidential by IN ST 5-2-9-6, et seq.;

- Mediation proceedings pursuant to IN ST ADR Rule 2.11, Mini-Trial proceedings pursuant to IN ST ADR Rule 4.4(C), and Summary Jury Trials pursuant to IN ST ADR Rule 5.6;

- Information in probation files pursuant to the Probation Standards promulgated by the Judicial Conference of Indiana pursuant to IN ST 11-13-1-8(b);

- Information deemed confidential pursuant to the Rules for Court Administered Alcohol and Drug Programs promulgated by the Judicial Conference of Indiana pursuant to IN ST 12-23-14-13;

- Information deemed confidential pursuant to the Problem-Solving Court Rules promulgated by the Judicial Conference of Indiana pursuant to IN ST 33-23-16-16;

- All records of the Department of workforce Development as declared confidential by IN ST 22-4-19-6;

- Information regarding interception of electronic communications that is sealed or deemed confidential as set forth in IN ST 35-33.5-2-1, et seq.

iii. Information excluded from public access by specific court order;

iv. Complete Social Security Numbers of living persons;

v. With the exception of names, information such as addresses, phone numbers, and dates of birth which explicitly identifies:

- Natural persons who are witnesses or victims (not including defendants) in criminal, domestic violence, stalking, sexual assault, juvenile, or civil protection order proceedings, provided that juveniles who are victims of sex crimes shall be identified by initials only;

- Places of residence of judicial officers, clerks and other employees of courts and clerks of court, unless the person or persons about whom the information pertains waives confidentiality;

    vi.   Complete account numbers of specific assets, loans, bank accounts, credit cards, and personal identification numbers (PINs);

    vii.   All orders of expungement entered in criminal or juvenile proceedings, orders to restrict access to criminal history information pursuant to IN ST 35-38-5-5.5 or IN ST 35-38-8-5 and records excluded from public access by such orders, and information related to infractions that is excluded from public access pursuant to IN ST 34-28-5-15 or IN ST 34-28-5-16 [Editor's note: IN ST 35-38-5-5.5, IN ST 35-38-8-5 and IN ST 34-28-5-16 were repealed effective July 1, 2013; for information on orders restricting access to criminal history, refer to IN ST 35-38-9-1, et seq.];

    viii.   All personal notes and e-mail, and deliberative material, of judges, jurors, court staff and judicial agencies, and information recorded in personal data assistants (PDA's) or organizers and personal calendars. IN ST ADMIN Rule 9(G)(1).

F. Filing and Service Requirements

1. *Filing requirements.* Except as otherwise provided in IN ST TRIAL P Rule 5(E)(2), all pleadings and papers subsequent to the complaint which are required to be served upon a party shall be filed with the Court either before service or within a reasonable period of time thereafter. IN ST TRIAL P Rule 5(E)(1).

    a.   *Filing with the court defined.* The filing of pleadings, motions, and other papers with the court as required by the Indiana Rules of Trial Procedure shall be made by one of the following methods:

        i.   Delivery to the clerk of the court;

        ii.   Sending by electronic transmission under the procedure adopted pursuant to IN ST ADMIN Rule 12;

        iii.   Mailing to the clerk by registered, certified or express mail return receipt requested;

        iv.   Depositing with any third-party commercial carrier for delivery to the clerk within three (3) calendar days, cost prepaid, properly addressed;

        v.   If the court so permits, filing with the judge, in which event the judge shall note thereon the filing date and forthwith transmit them to the office of the clerk; or

        vi.   Electronic filing, as approved by the Division of State Court Administration pursuant to IN ST ADMIN Rule 16. IN ST TRIAL P Rule 5(F).

        vii.   Filing by registered or certified mail and by third-party commercial carrier shall be complete upon mailing or deposit. IN ST TRIAL P Rule 5(F).

        viii.   All pleadings shall be filed with the Clerk, not directly with the Court, unless otherwise required by the Indiana Rules of Court. The entry of appearances and the filing of pleadings or other matters not requiring immediate Court action shall be filed with the Clerk and not in open Court. A Judge may permit papers to be filed in chambers, in which event he or she shall note thereon the filing date and transmit the papers to the Clerk. IN ST ST JOSEPH CIV Rule 201(201.2).

    b.   *Facsimile filing.* Unless otherwise authorized by IN ST ST JOSEPH ELECTRONIC Rule 701, electronic filing of pleadings by computerized or facsimile transmission is not permitted. IN ST ST JOSEPH CIV Rule 201(201.2).

    c.   *Additional copies.* In cases in which a party or counsel supplies the proposed order or decree, a sufficient number shall be prepared and filed as to provide the Clerk to retain two (2) copies, which shall be filed in the flat file and the record of judgments and orders. Should the party or counsel desire additional copies, a sufficient number of copies should be filed to effectuate that purpose. IN ST ST JOSEPH CIV Rule 201(201.6).

    d.   *Proof of filing.* Any party filing any paper by any method other than personal delivery to the clerk shall retain proof of filing. IN ST TRIAL P Rule 5(F).

2. *Service requirements.* Unless otherwise provided by the Indiana Rules of Trial Procedure or an order of

the court, each party and special judge, if any, shall be served with: (1) every order required by its terms to be served; (2) every pleading subsequent to the original complaint; (3) every written motion except one which may be heard ex parte; (4) every brief submitted to the trial court; (5) every paper relating to discovery required to be served upon a party; and (6) every written notice, appearance, demand, offer of judgment, designation of record on appeal, or similar paper. IN ST TRIAL P Rule 5(A).

a. *Service generally.* Every motion, petition, notice, or other pleading required to be served by IN ST TRIAL P Rule 5 shall be served on all counsel of record or unrepresented parties either before it is filed or on the day it is filed with the Court, and the date of filing shall be indicated on the Certificate of Service. IN ST ST JOSEPH CIV Rule 201(201.5.1).

   i. *Copy.* A copy of the Clerk's CCS entry form of the filing shall also be served on all counsel of record or unrepresented parties whenever it contains an appearance of counsel or contains a date for Court hearing on the matter. IN ST ST JOSEPH CIV Rule 201(201.5.1).

b. *Methods of service*

   i. *Personal service.* Whenever a party is represented by an attorney of record, service shall be made upon such attorney unless service upon the party himself is ordered by the court. Service upon the attorney or party shall be made by delivering or mailing a copy of the papers to the last known address or where an attorney or party has consented to service by fax or e-mail, as provided in IN ST TRIAL P Rule 3.1(A)(4), by faxing or e-mailing a copy of the documents to the fax number or e-mail address set out in the appearance form or correction as required by IN ST TRIAL P Rule 3.1(E). IN ST TRIAL P Rule 5(B). Delivery of a copy within IN ST TRIAL P Rule 5 means:

      • Offering or tendering it to the attorney or party and stating the nature of the papers being served. Refusal to accept an offered or tendered document is a waiver of any objection to the sufficiency or adequacy of service of that document;

      • Leaving it at his office with a clerk or other person in charge thereof, or if there is no one in charge, leaving it in a conspicuous place therein; or

      • If the office is closed, by leaving it at his dwelling house or usual place of abode with some person of suitable age and discretion then residing therein; or,

      • Leaving it at some other suitable place, selected by the attorney upon whom service is being made, pursuant to duly promulgated local rule. IN ST TRIAL P Rule 5(B)(1).

   ii. *Service by the clerk.* Whenever the Clerk is required by rule or statute to give notice, the party or parties requesting such notice shall furnish the Clerk with sufficient copies of the notice to be given, along with stamped, addressed envelopes with the names and the addresses of the parties or their counsel to whom such notice is to be given. IN ST ST JOSEPH CIV Rule 201(201.5.4).

   iii. *Service on the court.* Service on a Judge may be made by delivering a copy to the Judge's secretary or mailing a copy to the Judge at his or her chambers. Service on a Judge may not be accomplished by facsimile transmission; however, a courtesy copy may be sent to the Judge's chambers by electronic mail or facsimile transmission contemporaneously with service by mail or otherwise. IN ST ST JOSEPH CIV Rule 201(201.5.5).

   iv. *Service by mail.* If service is made by mail, the papers shall be deposited in the United States mail addressed to the person on whom they are being served, with postage prepaid. Service shall be deemed complete upon mailing. Proof of service of all papers permitted to be mailed may be made by written acknowledgment of service, by affidavit of the person who mailed the papers, or by certificate of an attorney. It shall be the duty of attorneys when entering their appearance in a cause or when filing pleadings or papers therein, to have noted in the Chronological Case Summary or said pleadings or papers so filed the address and telephone number of their office. Service by delivery or by mail at such address shall be deemed sufficient and complete. IN ST TRIAL P Rule 5(B)(2).

   v. *Service by fax or e-mail.* A party who has consented to service by fax or e-mail may be served as follows:

      • Service by e-mail shall be made by attaching the document being served in .pdf format.

Discovery documents must also be served in accordance with IN ST TRIAL P Rule 26(A). IN ST TRIAL P Rule 5(B)(3)(a).

- Service by fax shall be deemed complete upon generation of a transmission record indicating the successful transmission of the entire document, except as provided in IN ST TRIAL P Rule 5(B)(3)(d). IN ST TRIAL P Rule 5(B)(3)(b).

- Service by e-mail shall be deemed complete upon transmission, except as provided in IN ST TRIAL P Rule 5(B)(3)(d). IN ST TRIAL P Rule 5(B)(3)(c).

- Service by fax or e-mail that occurs on a Saturday, Sunday, legal holiday, or day the court or agency in which the matter is pending is closed or after 5:00 PM local time of the recipient shall be deemed complete the next day that is not a Saturday, Sunday, legal holiday, or day that the court or agency in which the matter is pending is not closed. IN ST TRIAL P Rule 5(B)(3)(d).

c. *Serving numerous defendants.* In any action in which there are unusually large numbers of defendants, the court, upon motion or of its own initiative, may order:

    i. That service of the pleadings of the defendants and replies thereto need not be made as between the defendants;

- That any cross-claim, counterclaim, or matter constituting an avoidance or affirmative defense contained therein shall be deemed to be denied or avoided by all other parties; and

- That the filing of any such pleading and service thereof upon the plaintiff constitutes due notice of it to the parties. IN ST TRIAL P Rule 5(D).

    ii. A copy of every such order shall be served upon the parties in such manner and form as the court directs. IN ST TRIAL P Rule 5(D).

d. *Service on parties in default for failure to appear.* No service need be made on parties in default for failure to appear, except that pleadings asserting new or additional claims for relief against them shall be served upon them in the manner provided by service of summons in IN ST TRIAL P Rule 4. IN ST TRIAL P Rule 5(A).

e. *Distribution.* Counsel or an unrepresented party submitting a motion, petition, notice, pleading or proposed order shall indicate the method of distribution desired on the Clerk's CCS entry form. The Clerk will not return or distribute copies of motions, petitions, pleadings, notices or proposed orders, other than those originated by the Court, by mail unless the Clerk is provided with stamped, addressed envelopes. IN ST ST JOSEPH CIV Rule 201(201.5.3).

f. *Mailbox.* As a matter of convenience to attorneys, each court provides a mailbox for the distribution filings and orders generated by the Court, and it is the responsibility of each attorney to periodically check these mailboxes for service and distribution of court-generated filings and orders. IN ST ST JOSEPH CIV Rule 201(201.5.3).

G. Hearings

1. *Hearing on motion.* Unless local conditions make it impracticable, each judge shall establish regular times and places, at intervals sufficiently frequent for the prompt dispatch of business, at which motions requiring notice and hearing may be heard and disposed of; but the judge at any time or place and on such notice, if any, as he considers reasonable may make order for the advancement, conduct, and hearing of actions. To expedite its business the court may direct the submission and determination of motions without oral hearing upon brief written statements of reasons in support and opposition, or direct or permit hearings by telephone conference call with all attorneys or other similar means of communication. IN ST TRIAL P Rule 73(A).

2. *Hearing dates.* Hearing dates for filings requiring Court action shall be obtained from the Court Clerk and incorporated in the CCS entry at the time the motion or other pleading is filed. If no date is obtained prior to the filing, the fact of the hearing should be noted with the date and time left blank. IN ST ST JOSEPH CIV Rule 201(201.4).

3. *Hearing on matters other than trials.* Each Judge shall reserve periods of time for hearing matters other than contested trials, such as pre-trial and post-trial motions, rules to show cause, defaults, uncontested

dissolutions of marriage, etc. As necessary to minimize conflicts in scheduling, the Judges shall set these schedules after consultation. Hearings shall be scheduled as follows:

a. *Scheduling uncontested or routine matters.* Routine matters, procedural motions, domestic relations applications for provisional relief and contempt proceedings, uncontested petitions for dissolution of marriage, and all other matters appropriate for summary consideration and disposition will be heard on the daily calendar. IN ST ST JOSEPH GEN AND ADMIN Rule 104(104.3.1).

b. *Scheduling contested or complicated matters.* Other matters that will require a hearing reasonably estimated to last in excess of twenty (20) minutes will be scheduled as the Court's calendar allows. Counsel or a party proceeding pro se should contact the chambers of the assigned judge to arrange for an appropriate hearing date and time. IN ST ST JOSEPH GEN AND ADMIN Rule 104(104.3.2).

c. *Scheduling motions for hearings.* Except for motions to correct error or not likely to require a hearing (as described in IN ST ST JOSEPH CIV Rule 201), all motions shall be scheduled for hearing at the time they are filed. It shall the responsibility of the moving party or counsel for the moving party to secure the date and time of the hearing from the Clerk or Court personnel who maintain the calendar for each Judge or Magistrate Judge. It shall also be the responsibility of the moving party or counsel for the moving party to coordinate the hearing date with all opposing counsel or unrepresented parties. IN ST ST JOSEPH CIV Rule 201(201.9.1).

d. *Oral arguments on motions and other pleadings.* Unless otherwise required by St. Joseph County Civil or Indiana Trial Rules, it is within the sound discretion of the assigned Judge whether to allow oral argument; however, any party may file a request for oral argument by filing a written request by separate motion contemporaneously or at any time before the Court has ruled upon the motion or pleadings to be argued. IN ST ST JOSEPH CIV Rule 201(201.9.4).

4. *Motions for summary judgment and for dismissal.* Motions for summary judgment or motions to dismiss pursuant to IN ST TRIAL P Rule 12 or IN ST TRIAL P Rule 41 shall be scheduled for hearing, unless the Court issues a written scheduling order providing otherwise. (Refer to IN ST ST JOSEPH CIV Rule 206 for specific requirements for Pleadings and Motions under IN ST TRIAL P Rule 12 and IN ST TRIAL P Rule 56). IN ST ST JOSEPH CIV Rule 201(201.9.6).

a. *Dispositive motions date.* Notwithstanding any other rule of court, all IN ST TRIAL P Rule 12 or IN ST TRIAL P Rule 56 motions shall be set for hearing by the moving party at the time of filing unless otherwise ordered by the Court. Unless otherwise authorized by the Court, the hearing shall be scheduled for a day not fewer than fourteen (14) days after the time period allowed for filing of briefs as specified in IN ST ST JOSEPH CIV Rule 206(206.1). IN ST ST JOSEPH CIV Rule 206(206.2).

b. *Waiver of hearing; Stipulation of the parties.* Adverse parties may stipulate that a IN ST TRIAL P Rule 12 or IN ST TRIAL P Rule 56 motion may be ruled upon by the Court without a hearing thereon, in which event the motion and stipulation shall be brought to the personal attention of the Judge by counsel or by a party proceeding pro se. IN ST ST JOSEPH CIV Rule 206(206.3).

c. *Appearance by counsel at scheduled hearings.* Whenever the Court schedules a hearing on a motion pursuant to IN ST TRIAL P Rule 12 and/or IN ST TRIAL P Rule 56, counsel for all represented parties shall appear in person or by local co-counsel at such hearing. IN ST ST JOSEPH CIV Rule 206(206.5).

H. Forms

1. Indiana Motion to Dismiss for Improper Venue Forms

a. Incorrect venue. 9 INPRAC § 42.5.

b. Motion to dismiss; Improper venue under contract. 9 INPRAC § 42.18.1.

c. Motion to transfer from improper venue. 11 INPRAC § 111.2.

d. Motion to transfer from improper venue. 5 INPRAC § 3:11.1.

e. Motion for change of venue from county; For cause. 5 INPRAC § 3:11.2.

f. Certificate of service; Personal service. 9 INPRAC § 5.7.

g. Certificate of service; First class mail. 9 INPRAC § 5.8.

I. Checklist

(I) ❑ Matters to be considered by moving party

    (a) ❑ Required documents

        (1) ❑ Motion and notice

        (2) ❑ Chronological Case Summary (CCS) entry form

        (3) ❑ Supporting memorandum of law

        (4) ❑ Proposed order

        (5) ❑ Certificate of service

    (b) ❑ Supplemental documents

        (1) ❑ Supporting evidence

        (2) ❑ Facsimile cover sheet

    (c) ❑ Timing

        (1) ❑ A motion making the defense of incorrect venue under IN ST TRIAL P Rule 75, or any statutory provision, shall be made before pleading if a further pleading is permitted or within twenty (20) days after service of the prior pleading if none is required

        (2) ❑ A written motion, other than one which may be heard ex parte, and notice of the hearing thereof shall be served not less than five (5) days before the time specified for the hearing, unless a different period is fixed by the Indiana Rules of Trial Procedure or by order of the court

        (3) ❑ All pleadings and papers subsequent to the complaint which are required to be served upon a party shall be filed with the Court either before service or within a reasonable period of time thereafter

(II) ❑ Matters to be considered by the responding party

    (a) ❑ Required documents

        (1) ❑ Opposition

        (2) ❑ Chronological Case Summary (CCS) entry form

        (3) ❑ Supporting memorandum of law

        (4) ❑ Certificate of service

    (b) ❑ Supplemental documents

        (1) ❑ Supporting evidence

        (2) ❑ Proposed order

        (3) ❑ Facsimile cover sheet

    (c) ❑ Timing

        (1) ❑ An adverse party shall have thirty (30) days after service of the motion in which to serve and file an answer brief

        (2) ❑ Except as otherwise provided in IN ST TRIAL P Rule 59(D), opposing affidavits may be served not less than one (1) day before the hearing, unless the court permits them to be served at some other time

ST. JOSEPH COUNTY

Motions, Oppositions and Replies
Motion for Leave to Amend

Document Last Updated October 2013

A. Applicable Rules

1. *State rules*

   a. Appearance. IN ST TRIAL P Rule 3.1.

   b. Summons. IN ST TRIAL P Rule 4; IN ST TRIAL P Rule 4.6.

   c. Service and filing of pleadings and other papers. IN ST TRIAL P Rule 5.

   d. Time. IN ST TRIAL P Rule 6.

   e. Pleadings and other papers. IN ST TRIAL P Rule 7; IN ST TRIAL P Rule 8; IN ST TRIAL P Rule 9.2; IN ST TRIAL P Rule 10.

   f. Signing and verification of pleadings. IN ST TRIAL P Rule 11.

   g. Amended and supplemental pleadings. IN ST TRIAL P Rule 15.

   h. Evidence. IN ST TRIAL P Rule 43.

   i. Judgment on the evidence (directed verdict). IN ST TRIAL P Rule 50.

   j. Findings by the court. IN ST TRIAL P Rule 52.

   k. Summary judgment. IN ST TRIAL P Rule 56.

   l. Motion to correct error. IN ST TRIAL P Rule 59.

   m. Relief from judgment or order. IN ST TRIAL P Rule 60.

   n. Hearing of motions. IN ST TRIAL P Rule 73.

   o. Access to court records. IN ST ADMIN Rule 9.

   p. Paper size. IN ST ADMIN Rule 11.

   q. Facsimile transmission. IN ST ADMIN Rule 12.

   r. Electronic filing and electronic service pilot projects. IN ST ADMIN Rule 16.

   s. Sealing of certain records by court; Hearing; Notice. IN ST 5-14-3-5.5.

   t. Sixtieth judicial circuit. IN ST 33-33-71-2.

   u. Privacy and confidentiality. IN ST 5-2-9-6; IN ST 5-14-3-4; IN ST 6-4.1-5-10; IN ST 6-4.1-12-12; IN ST 6-8.1-7-1; IN ST 11-13-1-8; IN ST 12-23-14-13; IN ST 16-39-3-10; IN ST 16-41-8-1; IN ST 22-4-19-6; IN ST 31-11-1-6; IN ST 31-19-5-23; IN ST 31-19-13-2; IN ST 31-19-19-1; IN ST 31-33-18-1; IN ST 31-39-1-1; IN ST 31-39-1-2; IN ST 33-23-16-16; IN ST 35-34-2-4; IN ST 35-38-1-13; IN ST 35-38-9-1; IN ST ADR Rule 2.11; IN ST ADR Rule 4.4; IN ST ADR Rule 5.6; IN ST JURY Rule 10.

2. *Local rules*

   a. Court hours and scheduling. IN ST ST JOSEPH GEN AND ADMIN Rule 104.

   b. Filing, pleading, and motions. IN ST ST JOSEPH CIV Rule 201.

   c. Uniform court and case number designation. IN ST ST JOSEPH CIV Rule 202.

   d. Pleading and motions under IN ST TRIAL P Rule 12 and IN ST TRIAL P Rule 56. IN ST ST JOSEPH CIV Rule 206.

   e. Proposed order. IN ST ST JOSEPH CIV Rule 213.

   f. Electronic filing of cases in St. Joseph County. IN ST ST JOSEPH ELECTRONIC Rule 701.

B. Timing

1. *Time for amending pleadings*

   a. *As a matter of course.* A party may amend his pleading once as a matter of course at any time before a responsive pleading is served or, if the pleading is one to which no responsive pleading is permitted, and the action has not been placed upon the trial calendar, he may so amend it at any time within thirty (30) days after it is served. IN ST TRIAL P Rule 15(A). Refer to the Indiana KeyRules Amended Complaint and Amended Answer documents for additional information on amending pleadings as a matter of course.

   b. *With leave of court.* Otherwise a party may amend his pleading only by leave of court or by written consent of the adverse party; and leave shall be given when justice so requires. IN ST TRIAL P Rule 15(A).

   c. *Filing.* All pleadings and papers subsequent to the complaint which are required to be served upon a party shall be filed with the Court either before service or within a reasonable period of time thereafter. IN ST TRIAL P Rule 5(E)(1).

2. *Service.* A written motion, other than one which may be heard ex parte, and notice of the hearing thereof shall be served not less than five (5) days before the time specified for the hearing, unless a different period is fixed by the Indiana Rules of Trial Procedure or by order of the court. IN ST TRIAL P Rule 6(D).

   a. *Of supporting affidavits.* When a motion is supported by affidavit, the affidavit shall be served with the motion. IN ST TRIAL P Rule 6(D).

3. *Service of opposition.* Except as otherwise provided in IN ST TRIAL P Rule 59(D), opposing affidavits may be served not less than one (1) day before the hearing, unless the court permits them to be served at some other time. IN ST TRIAL P Rule 6(D).

   a. *Memorandum of law.* So long as consistent with Indiana Rules of Trial Procedure, an adverse party wishing to respond shall do so within fifteen (15) days of service. IN ST ST JOSEPH CIV Rule 206(206.1).

4. *Filing proposed orders.* Unless otherwise directed or given leave of the Court, proposed orders in emergency matters shall be filed within forty-eight (48) hours after a hearing; proposed orders in other matters shall be filed within seven (7) days as computed by IN ST TRIAL P Rule 6. IN ST ST JOSEPH CIV Rule 213(213.5).

5. *Computation of time*

   a. *Generally; Days excluded.* In computing any period of time prescribed or allowed by the Indiana Rules of Trial Procedure, by order of the court, or by any applicable statute, the day of the act, event, or default from which the designated period of time begins to run shall not be included. The last day of the period so computed is to be included unless it is:

      i. A Saturday,

      ii. A Sunday,

      iii. A legal holiday as defined by state statute, or

      iv. A day the office in which the act is to be done is closed during regular business hours. IN ST TRIAL P Rule 6(A).

   b. *Short periods.* In any event, the period runs until the end of the next day that is not a Saturday, a Sunday, a legal holiday, or a day on which the office is closed. When the period of time allowed is less than seven (7) days, intermediate Saturdays, Sundays, legal holidays, and days on which the office is closed shall be excluded from the computations. IN ST TRIAL P Rule 6(A).

   c. *Additional time after service by United States mail.* Whenever a party has the right or is required to do some act or take some proceedings within a prescribed period after the service of a notice or other paper upon him and the notice or paper is served upon him by United States mail, three (3) days shall be added to the prescribed period. IN ST TRIAL P Rule 6(E).

    d. *Enlargement of time.* When an act is required or allowed to be done at or within a specific time by the Indiana Rules of Trial Procedure, the court may at any time for cause shown:

        i. Order the period enlarged, with or without motion or notice, if request therefor is made before the expiration of the period originally prescribed or extended by a previous order; or

        ii. Upon motion made after the expiration of the specific period, permit the act to be done where the failure to act was the result of excusable neglect; but, the court may not extend the time for taking any action for judgment on the evidence under IN ST TRIAL P Rule 50(A), amendment of findings and judgment under IN ST TRIAL P Rule 52(B), to correct errors under IN ST TRIAL P Rule 59(C), statement in opposition to motion to correct error under IN ST TRIAL P Rule 59(E), or to obtain relief from final judgment under IN ST TRIAL P Rule 60(B), except to the extent and under the conditions stated in those rules. IN ST TRIAL P Rule 6(B).

        iii. An initial written motion for enlargement of time pursuant to IN ST TRIAL P Rule 6(B)(1) to answer a claim shall be routinely granted for an additional thirty (30) days from the original due date or other period the assigned Judge deems reasonable by written order of the Court. The motion must be filed on or before the original due date or IN ST ST JOSEPH CIV Rule 201 shall be inapplicable. IN ST ST JOSEPH CIV Rule 201(201.9.5).

- Any motion for enlargement of time shall state the date when such response is due and the date to which time is requested to be enlarged. IN ST ST JOSEPH CIV Rule 201(201.9.5).

- All subsequent motions for enlargement of time shall be so designated and will only be granted for good cause shown or in the interest of justice. IN ST ST JOSEPH CIV Rule 201(201.9.5).

C. General Requirements

1. *Motions, generally.* Unless made during a hearing or trial, or otherwise ordered by the court, an application to the court for an order shall be made by written motion. The motion shall state the grounds therefor and the relief or order sought. IN ST TRIAL P Rule 7(B).

    a. *Motions as distinct from pleadings.* Motions and responses to motions are not pleadings, and allegations contained in a motion are not admissions of a party. 22B INPRAC 7:2; Wachstetter v. County Properties, LLC, 832 N.E.2d 574 (Ind.Ct.App. 2005); Scott County Family YMCA, Inc. v. Hobbs, 817 N.E.2d 603 (Ind.Ct.App. 2004).

    b. *Unopposed motions generally granted.* It is common for a trial court to grant procedural motions, such as motions for enlargement of time, discovery motions, or motions for continuance, unless an objection is filed. 21 INPRAC § 13.8.

    c. *Proposed orders.* As directed by the Court, a party or an attorney for a party shall prepare a proposed order based on the decision rendered by the Court. The party so directed shall prepare the proposed order in a timely manner and, upon filing, shall advise the chambers of the applicable judge that the proposed order has been prepared and filed. IN ST ST JOSEPH CIV Rule 213(213.2).

2. *Motion for leave to amend.* The purpose of an amended pleading is to include matters that occurred before the filing of the original pleading but which were either overlooked by the pleader or unknown to him at the time. It is a substitute for the original and relates to the facts that existed when the original pleading was filed. An amended pleading supercedes the original as to those portions amended. 10 INPRAC § 46.1.

    a. *Amendments liberally allowed.* Amendments to pleadings are to be liberally allowed in order that all issues are presented in one action. 10 INPRAC § 46.1; Pinnacle Media, LLC v. Metropolitan Dev. Com'n of Marion County, 868 N.E.2d 894 (Ind.Ct.App. 2007).

    b. *Amendments to conform to the evidence.* When issues not raised by the pleadings are tried by express or implied consent of the parties, they shall be treated in all respects as if they had been raised in the pleadings. Such amendment of the pleadings as may be necessary to cause them to conform to the evidence and to raise these issues may be made upon motion of any party at any time, even after judgment, but failure so to amend does not affect the result of the trial of these issues. If evidence is objected to at the trial on the ground that it is not within the issues made by the pleadings, the court may allow the pleadings to be amended and shall do so freely when the presentation of the merits of the action will be subserved thereby and the objecting party fails to satisfy the court that the admission of such evidence would prejudice him in maintaining his action or defense upon the merits. The court may grant a continuance to enable the objecting party to meet such evidence. IN ST TRIAL P Rule 15(B).

   c. *Relation back of amendments*

      i. Whenever the claim or defense asserted in the amended pleading arose out of the conduct, transaction, or occurrence set forth or attempted to be set forth in the original pleading, the amendment relates back to the date of the original pleading. An amendment changing the party against whom a claim is asserted relates back if the foregoing provision is satisfied and, within one hundred and twenty (120) days of commencement of the action, the party to be brought in by amendment:

        • Has received such notice of the institution of the action that he will not be prejudiced in maintaining his defense on the merits; and

        • Knew or should have known that but for a mistake concerning the identity of the proper party, the action would have been brought against him. IN ST TRIAL P Rule 15(C).

      ii. The requirement of IN ST TRIAL P Rule 15(C)(1) and IN ST TRIAL P Rule 15(C)(2) with respect to a governmental organization to be brought into the action as defendant is satisfied:

        • In the case of a state or governmental organization by delivery or mailing of process to the attorney general or to a governmental executive [IN ST TRIAL P Rule 4.6(A)(3)]; or

        • In the case of a local governmental organization, by delivery or mailing of process to its attorney as provided by statute, to a governmental executive thereof [IN ST TRIAL P Rule 4.6(A)(4)], or to the officer holding the office if suit is against the officer or an office. IN ST TRIAL P Rule 15(C).

   d. *Amendment by leave.* Amendments, other than an amendment by right, may be made only by leave of court or by written consent of the opposing party. 2 INPRAC R 15(15.1).

   e. *Factors considered.* In deciding whether to permit a party to amend his pleading, the court must consider a number of factors: (1) undue delay, (2) bad faith or dilatory motive on the part of the movant, (3) repeated failure to cure deficiencies by amendments previously allowed, (4) undue prejudice to the opposing party by virtue of allowance of the amendment, and (5) the futility of the amendment. 10 INPRAC § 46.1; Crawford v. City of Muncie, 655 N.E.2d 614 (Ind.Ct.App. 1995); Selvia v. Reitmeyer, 156 Ind.App. 203, 295 N.E.2d 869 (Ind.Ct.App. 1973).

  3. *Opposition to a motion for leave to amend.* Failure to file an answer brief or reply brief within the time prescribed shall be deemed a waiver of the right thereto and shall subject the motion to summary ruling. IN ST ST JOSEPH CIV Rule 206(206.1).

D. Documents

  1. *Required documents*

   a. *Motion and notice.* The requirement of notice is satisfied by service of the motion. IN ST TRIAL P Rule 7(B). Refer to the General Requirements section of this document for information on the content of a motion for leave to amend.

   b. *Chronological Case Summary (CCS) entry form.* Every written motion, petition, or other pleading subsequent to the original complaint presented to the Clerk for filing shall be accompanied by a Chronological Case Summary (CCS) entry form in duplicate. IN ST ST JOSEPH CIV Rule 201(201.4). Refer to the Format section of this document for details on the format and filing requirements for the CCS entry form.

   c. *Copy of amended pleading.* A copy of the proposed amendment should be attached to the motion for leave to amend, along with a proposed order by the court which permits the amendment. 2 INPRAC R 15.

   d. *Proposed order.* Unless local practice provides differently, a party should submit a proposed order with its written motion to be signed by the judge once the motion has been granted. 21 INPRAC §

13.8. All proposed orders shall be submitted in an original plus a number of copies equal to one more than the number of pro se parties and attorneys of record contained in the prepared proof of notice under IN ST TRIAL P Rule 72(D). IN ST ST JOSEPH CIV Rule 213(213.3); IN ST ST JOSEPH CIV Rule 201(201.5.2).

e. *Certificate of service.* An attorney or unrepresented party tendering a document to the Clerk for filing shall certify that service has been made, list the parties served, and specify the date and means of service. The certificate of service shall be placed at the end of the document and shall not be separately filed. The separate filing of a certificate of service, however, shall not be grounds for rejecting a document for filing. The Clerk may permit documents to be filed without a certificate of service but shall require prompt filing of a separate certificate of service. IN ST TRIAL P Rule 5(C).

2. *Supplemental documents*

a. *Supporting evidence.* When a motion is based on facts not appearing of record the court may hear the matter on affidavits presented by the respective parties, but the court may direct that the matter be heard wholly or partly on oral testimony or depositions. IN ST TRIAL P Rule 43(B).

b. *Facsimile cover sheet.* Any document sent to the Clerk of the Circuit Court by electronic facsimile transmission shall be accompanied by a cover sheet which states the title of the document, case number, number of pages, identity and voice telephone number of the sending party and instructions for filing. The cover sheet shall contain the signature of the attorney or party, pro se, authorizing the filing. IN ST ADMIN Rule 12(D).

E. Format

1. *Form of motions.* The rules applicable to captions, and the signing and form of pleadings (IN ST TRIAL P Rule 8 through IN ST TRIAL P Rule 11), apply to all motions and other papers provided under the Indiana Rules of Trial Procedure. 22B INPRAC 7:2.

a. *Separate motions; Alternative motions.* Each motion shall be separate, while alternative motions filed together shall each be identified on the caption. IN ST ST JOSEPH CIV Rule 206(206.1).

2. *Form of pleadings*

a. *Caption; Names of parties.* Every pleading shall contain a caption setting forth the name of the court, the title of the action, the file number, and a designation as in IN ST TRIAL P Rule 7(A). In the complaint the title of the action shall include the names of all the parties, but in other pleadings it is sufficient to state the name of the first party on each side with an appropriate indication of other parties. IN ST TRIAL P Rule 10(A); IN ST ST JOSEPH CIV Rule 201(201.3.3). If a special judge has been assigned to the case, the pleading should also identify the special judge. IN ST ST JOSEPH CIV Rule 201(201.3.3).

   i. *Title.* All pleadings or motions shall include a title, which shall delineate each topic included in the pleading. For example, where a pleading contains an answer, a motion to dismiss, and a jury request, each topic shall be set forth in the title. IN ST ST JOSEPH CIV Rule 201(201.3.4).

b. *Paragraphs; Separate statements.* All averments of a claim or defense shall be made in numbered paragraphs, the contents of each of which shall be limited as far as practicable to a statement of a single set of circumstances, and a paragraph may be referred to by number in all succeeding pleadings. Each claim founded upon a separate transaction or occurrence and each defense other than denials may be stated in a separate count or defense whenever a separation facilitates the clear presentation of the matters set forth. IN ST TRIAL P Rule 10(B).

c. *Adoption by reference; Exhibits.* Statements in a pleading may be adopted by reference in a different part of the same pleading or in another pleading or in any motion. A copy of any written instrument which is an exhibit to a pleading is a part thereof for all purposes. IN ST TRIAL P Rule 10(C).

d. *Flat filing.* In order that the Clerk's files may be kept under the system commonly known as "flat filing," all papers presented to the Clerk for filing shall be flat and unfolded. Pleadings shall have no covers or backs and shall be fastened together at the top left-hand corner only. IN ST ST JOSEPH CIV Rule 201(201.1).

e. *One side of page used.* Printing shall be on one (1) side of the paper. IN ST ST JOSEPH CIV Rule 201(201.3.2).

f.   *Copies.* All copies shall be on white paper of sufficient strength and durability to resist normal wear and tear. IN ST ST JOSEPH CIV Rule 201(201.3.1).

g.   *Margins.* Margins shall be at least one inch (1"). IN ST ST JOSEPH CIV Rule 201(201.3.2).

h.   *Double-spaced.* If typewritten, the lines shall be double spaced except for quotations, which shall be indented and single-spaced. IN ST ST JOSEPH CIV Rule 201(201.3.2).

i.   *Font size.* Type face shall be twelve (12) font size or larger within the body of the document and ten (10) font size or larger in the footnotes. IN ST ST JOSEPH CIV Rule 201(201.3.2).

j.   *Font type.* The font type must be legible and script type shall not be used. IN ST ST JOSEPH CIV Rule 201(201.3.2).

k.   *Italics.* Italicized type may be used for quotations, references, or case citations. IN ST ST JOSEPH CIV Rule 201(201.3.2).

l.   *Court and case designation.* All filings shall conform to the requirements for uniform court and case number designation set by IN ST ADMIN Rule 8. In addition, all filings shall contain the proper court and case designation as described below. IN ST ST JOSEPH CIV Rule 202.

  i.   *Court designation.* Pursuant to IN ST 33-33-71-2, St. Joseph County, Indiana, constitutes the Sixtieth Judicial Circuit. The legal names of the courts within the 60th Judicial Circuit are the St. Joseph Circuit Court, the St. Joseph Superior Court, and the St. Joseph Probate Court. All filings shall properly reflect the legal name of the applicable court. Any filing may be amended, rejected, or stricken if it does not contain the proper case name and/or the legal name of the court. IN ST ST JOSEPH CIV Rule 202(202.1).

m.   *Form of CCS entry.* Every written motion, petition, or other pleading subsequent to the original complaint presented to the Clerk for filing shall be accompanied by a Chronological Case Summary (CCS) entry form in duplicate which shall contain the title and cause number of the action, the date, and the proposed entry to appear on the docket. IN ST ST JOSEPH CIV Rule 201(201.4).

  i.   *Identification and signature.* The CCS entry form shall identify the party making the filing, designate each pleading being filed, and shall be signed by counsel of record or the unrepresented litigant. IN ST ST JOSEPH CIV Rule 201(201.4).

  ii.   *Date stamp.* The form shall be date stamped and presented to the Court Clerk, who shall initial the form and return the duplicate to the filing party. IN ST ST JOSEPH CIV Rule 201(201.4).

n.   *Form of proposed order.* Any proposed order shall be a document that is separate and apart from the motion or application to which it relates and shall contain a caption showing the name of the court, the case number assigned to the case, and the title of the case as shown by the complaint pursuant to IN ST ST JOSEPH CIV Rule 201. IN ST ST JOSEPH CIV Rule 213(213.2).

  i.   If there are multiple parties, the title may be shortened to include only the first name plaintiff and defendant with appropriate indication that there are additional parties. IN ST ST JOSEPH CIV Rule 213(213.2).

  ii.   The proposed order shall be on white paper, eight and one-half by eleven inches (8 1/2" x 11") in size, and each page shall be numbered. IN ST ST JOSEPH CIV Rule 213(213.2).

  iii.   The last page of the proposed order shall contain a line for the date, either "Dated _____" or "Signed on the date filemarked hereon." IN ST ST JOSEPH CIV Rule 213(213.2).

  iv.   On the last page there also shall be a line for the signature of the Judge under which shall be typed "Judge, St. Joseph [Circuit or Superior or Probate] Court." IN ST ST JOSEPH CIV Rule 213(213.2).

  v.   If the proposed order contains a recommendation from a Magistrate, the last page shall have a line for the signature of the Magistrate under which shall be typed "Magistrate, St. Joseph [Circuit or Superior or Probate] Court," to the left of which shall be the following, "So Recommended:" and beneath and to the left of which shall be typed, "Approved. So Ordered." IN ST ST JOSEPH CIV Rule 213(213.2).

  vi.   To allow compliance with the notice requirements of IN ST TRIAL P Rule 72(D), the lower four (4) inches of the last page of the proposed order shall be left blank. The proposed order shall also include a prepared proof of notice under IN ST TRIAL P Rule 72(D), and in preparing such a notice the filing party shall complete all portions of the prepared proof of notice. IN ST ST JOSEPH CIV Rule 213(213.2).

3. *Size of papers for filing.* Effective January 1, 1992, all pleadings, copies, motions and documents filed with any trial court or appellate level court, typed or printed, with the exception of exhibits and existing wills, shall be prepared on eight and one-half by eleven inch (8 1/2" x 11") size paper. IN ST ADMIN Rule 11.

   a. *Paper.* Pleadings, motions, and other papers shall be either legibly printed or typewritten on white opaque paper of good quality at least sixteen (16) pound weight, eight and one-half inches (8 1/2 ") in width and eleven inches (11") in length as required by IN ST ADMIN Rule 11. IN ST ST JOSEPH CIV Rule 201(201.3.1).

4. *Signature requirements*

   a. *Signature of attorney.* Every pleading or motion of a party represented by an attorney shall be signed by at least one (1) attorney of record in his individual name, whose address, telephone number, and attorney number shall be stated, except that this provision shall not apply to pleadings and motions made and transcribed at the trial or a hearing before the judge and received by him in such form. IN ST TRIAL P Rule 11(A).

      i. The signature of an attorney constitutes a certificate by him that he has read the pleadings; that to the best of his knowledge, information, and belief, there is good ground to support it; and that it is not interposed for delay. IN ST TRIAL P Rule 11(A).

      ii. If a pleading or motion is not signed or is signed with intent to defeat the purpose of the rule, it may be stricken as sham and false and the action may proceed as though the pleading had not been served. IN ST TRIAL P Rule 11(A).

      iii. For a willful violation of IN ST TRIAL P Rule 11 an attorney may be subjected to appropriate disciplinary action. Similar action may be taken if scandalous or indecent matter is inserted. IN ST TRIAL P Rule 11(A).

   b. *Signature of unrepresented party.* A party who is not represented by an attorney shall sign his pleading and state his address. IN ST TRIAL P Rule 11(A).

   c. *Verification not generally required.* Except when specifically required by rule, pleadings or motions need not be verified or accompanied by affidavit. The rule in equity that the averments of an answer under oath must be overcome by the testimony of two (2) witnesses or of one (1) witness sustained by corroborating circumstances is abolished. IN ST TRIAL P Rule 11(A).

   d. *Verification by affirmation or representation.* When in connection with any civil or special statutory proceeding it is required that any pleading, motion, petition, supporting affidavit, or other document of any kind, be verified, or that an oath be taken, it shall be sufficient if the subscriber simply affirms the truth of the matter to be verified by an affirmation or representation. IN ST TRIAL P Rule 11(B). IN ST TRIAL P Rule 11(B) states that the affirmation or representation should be in substantially the following language: "I (we) affirm, under the penalties for perjury, that the foregoing representation(s) is (are) true. (Signed) _____."

      i. Any person who falsifies an affirmation or representation of fact shall be subject to the same penalties as are prescribed by law for the making of a false affidavit. IN ST TRIAL P Rule 11(B).

   e. *Verified pleadings, motions, and affidavits as evidence.* Pleadings, motions and affidavits accompanying or in support of such pleadings or motions when required to be verified or under oath shall be accepted as a representation that the signer had personal knowledge thereof or reasonable cause to believe the existence of the facts or matters stated or alleged therein; and, if otherwise competent or acceptable as evidence, may be admitted as evidence of the facts or matters stated or alleged therein when it is so provided in the Indiana Rules of Trial Procedure, by statute or other law, or to the extent the writing or signature expressly purports to be made upon the signer's personal knowledge. When such pleadings, motions and affidavits are verified or under oath they shall not require other or greater proof on the part of the adverse party than if not verified or not under oath unless expressly provided otherwise by the Indiana Rules of Trial Procedure, statute or other law. Affidavits upon motions for summary judgment under IN ST TRIAL P Rule 56 and in denial of execution under IN ST TRIAL P Rule 9.2 shall be made upon personal knowledge. IN ST TRIAL P Rule 11(C).

f. *Signature, verification and other requirements.* Parties and their counsel are enjoined to comply with the verification requirements of IN ST TRIAL P Rule 11, and either the moving party or the party's attorney of record shall sign all pleadings and motions before filing with the Clerk of the Court. Every motion, petition, or other pleading filed with the Clerk shall contain the name, organization, physical address, telephone number, and facsimile number of the filing party or an attorney for that party. IN ST ST JOSEPH CIV Rule 201(201.3.6).

    i. The Clerk shall not accept any motion, petition, notice or other pleading or a CCS entry form for filing from an unrepresented litigant unless the unrepresented litigant's current address and phone number appear on the pleading, and an opposing party may service notices and responses on an unrepresented litigant at any address he or she has provided on a pleading. IN ST ST JOSEPH CIV Rule 201(201.3.6).

5. *Information excluded from public access.* Every document filed in a case shall separately identify information excluded from public access pursuant to IN ST ADMIN Rule 9(G)(1) as follows:

a. Whole documents that are excluded from public access pursuant to IN ST ADMIN Rule 9(G)(1) shall be tendered on light green paper or have a light green coversheet attached to the document, marked "Not for Public Access" or "Confidential." IN ST TRIAL P Rule 5(G)(1).

b. When only a portion of a document contains information excluded from public access pursuant to IN ST ADMIN Rule 9(G)(1), said information shall be omitted [or redacted] from the filed document, and set forth on a separate accompanying document on light green paper conspicuously marked "Not for Public Access" or "Confidential" and clearly designated [or identifying] the caption and number of the case and the document and location within the document to which the redacted material pertains. IN ST TRIAL P Rule 5(G)(2).

c. With respect to documents filed in electronic format, the trial court, by local rule, may provide for compliance with IN ST TRIAL P Rule 5 in manner that separates and protects access to information excluded from public access. IN ST TRIAL P Rule 5(G)(3).

d. IN ST TRIAL P Rule 5(G) does not apply to a record sealed by the court pursuant to IN ST 5-14-3-5.5 or otherwise, nor to records, documents, or information filed in cases to which public access is prohibited pursuant to IN ST ADMIN Rule 9(G). IN ST TRIAL P Rule 5(G)(4).

e. The following information in case records is excluded from public access and is confidential:

    i. Information that is excluded from public access pursuant to federal law;

    ii. Information that is excluded from public access as declared confidential by Indiana statute or other court rule, including without limitation:

- All adoption records created after July 8, 1941, as declared confidential by IN ST 31-19-19-1, et seq., except those specifically declared open by IN ST 31-19-13-2(2);

- All records relating to chancroid, chlamydia, gonorrhea, hepatitis, human immunodeficiency virus (HIV), Lymphogranuloma venereum, syphilis, tuberculosis, as declared confidential by IN ST 16-41-8-1, et seq.;

- All records relating to child abuse as declared confidential by IN ST 31-33-18-1, et seq.;

- All records relating to drug tests as declared confidential by IN ST 5-14-3-4(a)(9);

- Records of grand jury proceedings as declared confidential by IN ST 35-34-2-4;

- Records of juvenile proceedings as declared confidential by IN ST 31-39-1-2, except those specifically open under statute;

- All paternity records created after July 1, 1941 as declared confidential by IN ST 31-14-11-15, IN ST 31-19-5-23, IN ST 31-39-1-1 and IN ST 31-39-1-2 [Editor's note: IN ST 31-14-11-15 was repealed effective May 9, 2013];

- All pre-sentence reports as declared confidential by IN ST 35-38-1-13;

- Written petitions to permit marriages without consent and orders directing the Clerk of Court to issue a marriage license to underage persons, as declared confidential by IN ST 31-11-1-6;

- Only those arrest warrants, search warrants, indictments and informations ordered confidential by the trial judge, prior to return of duly executed service as declared confidential by IN ST 5-14-3-4(b)(1);

- All medical, mental health, or tax records unless determined by law or regulation of any governmental custodian not to be confidential, released by the subject of such records, or declared by a court of competent jurisdiction to be essential to the resolution of litigation as declared confidential by IN ST 16-39-3-10, IN ST 6-4.1-5-10, IN ST 6-4.1-12-12, and IN ST 6-8.1-7-1;

- Personal information relating to jurors or prospective jurors, other than for the use of the parties and counsel, pursuant to IN ST JURY Rule 10;

- Information relating to protection from abuse orders, no-contact orders and workplace violence restraining orders as declared confidential by IN ST 5-2-9-6, et seq.;

- Mediation proceedings pursuant to IN ST ADR Rule 2.11, Mini-Trial proceedings pursuant to IN ST ADR Rule 4.4(C), and Summary Jury Trials pursuant to IN ST ADR Rule 5.6;

- Information in probation files pursuant to the Probation Standards promulgated by the Judicial Conference of Indiana pursuant to IN ST 11-13-1-8(b);

- Information deemed confidential pursuant to the Rules for Court Administered Alcohol and Drug Programs promulgated by the Judicial Conference of Indiana pursuant to IN ST 12-23-14-13;

- Information deemed confidential pursuant to the Problem-Solving Court Rules promulgated by the Judicial Conference of Indiana pursuant to IN ST 33-23-16-16;

- All records of the Department of workforce Development as declared confidential by IN ST 22-4-19-6;

- Information regarding interception of electronic communications that is sealed or deemed confidential as set forth in IN ST 35-33.5-2-1, et seq.

iii. Information excluded from public access by specific court order;

iv. Complete Social Security Numbers of living persons;

v. With the exception of names, information such as addresses, phone numbers, and dates of birth which explicitly identifies:

- Natural persons who are witnesses or victims (not including defendants) in criminal, domestic violence, stalking, sexual assault, juvenile, or civil protection order proceedings, provided that juveniles who are victims of sex crimes shall be identified by initials only;

- Places of residence of judicial officers, clerks and other employees of courts and clerks of court, unless the person or persons about whom the information pertains waives confidentiality;

vi. Complete account numbers of specific assets, loans, bank accounts, credit cards, and personal identification numbers (PINs);

vii. All orders of expungement entered in criminal or juvenile proceedings, orders to restrict access to criminal history information pursuant to IN ST 35-38-5-5.5 or IN ST 35-38-8-5 and records excluded from public access by such orders, and information related to infractions that is excluded from public access pursuant to IN ST 34-28-5-15 or IN ST 34-28-5-16 [Editor's note: IN ST 35-38-5-5.5, IN ST 35-38-8-5 and IN ST 34-28-5-16 were repealed effective July 1, 2013; for information on orders restricting access to criminal history, refer to IN ST 35-38-9-1, et seq.];

      viii. All personal notes and e-mail, and deliberative material, of judges, jurors, court staff and judicial agencies, and information recorded in personal data assistants (PDA's) or organizers and personal calendars. IN ST ADMIN Rule 9(G)(1).

F. Filing and Service Requirements

1. *Filing requirements.* Except as otherwise provided in IN ST TRIAL P Rule 5(E)(2), all pleadings and papers subsequent to the complaint which are required to be served upon a party shall be filed with the Court either before service or within a reasonable period of time thereafter. IN ST TRIAL P Rule 5(E)(1).

    a. *Filing with the court defined.* The filing of pleadings, motions, and other papers with the court as required by the Indiana Rules of Trial Procedure shall be made by one of the following methods:

      i. Delivery to the clerk of the court;

      ii. Sending by electronic transmission under the procedure adopted pursuant to IN ST ADMIN Rule 12;

      iii. Mailing to the clerk by registered, certified or express mail return receipt requested;

      iv. Depositing with any third-party commercial carrier for delivery to the clerk within three (3) calendar days, cost prepaid, properly addressed;

      v. If the court so permits, filing with the judge, in which event the judge shall note thereon the filing date and forthwith transmit them to the office of the clerk; or

      vi. Electronic filing, as approved by the Division of State Court Administration pursuant to IN ST ADMIN Rule 16. IN ST TRIAL P Rule 5(F).

      vii. Filing by registered or certified mail and by third-party commercial carrier shall be complete upon mailing or deposit. IN ST TRIAL P Rule 5(F).

      viii. All pleadings shall be filed with the Clerk, not directly with the Court, unless otherwise required by the Indiana Rules of Court. The entry of appearances and the filing of pleadings or other matters not requiring immediate Court action shall be filed with the Clerk and not in open Court. A Judge may permit papers to be filed in chambers, in which event he or she shall note thereon the filing date and transmit the papers to the Clerk. IN ST ST JOSEPH CIV Rule 201(201.2).

    b. *Facsimile filing.* Unless otherwise authorized by IN ST ST JOSEPH ELECTRONIC Rule 701, electronic filing of pleadings by computerized or facsimile transmission is not permitted. IN ST ST JOSEPH CIV Rule 201(201.2).

    c. *Additional copies.* In cases in which a party or counsel supplies the proposed order or decree, a sufficient number shall be prepared and filed as to provide the Clerk to retain two (2) copies, which shall be filed in the flat file and the record of judgments and orders. Should the party or counsel desire additional copies, a sufficient number of copies should be filed to effectuate that purpose. IN ST ST JOSEPH CIV Rule 201(201.6).

    d. *Proof of filing.* Any party filing any paper by any method other than personal delivery to the clerk shall retain proof of filing. IN ST TRIAL P Rule 5(F).

2. *Service requirements.* Unless otherwise provided by the Indiana Rules of Trial Procedure or an order of the court, each party and special judge, if any, shall be served with: (1) every order required by its terms to be served; (2) every pleading subsequent to the original complaint; (3) every written motion except one which may be heard ex parte; (4) every brief submitted to the trial court; (5) every paper relating to discovery required to be served upon a party; and (6) every written notice, appearance, demand, offer of judgment, designation of record on appeal, or similar paper. IN ST TRIAL P Rule 5(A).

    a. *Service generally.* Every motion, petition, notice, or other pleading required to be served by IN ST TRIAL P Rule 5 shall be served on all counsel of record or unrepresented parties either before it is filed or on the day it is filed with the Court, and the date of filing shall be indicated on the Certificate of Service. IN ST ST JOSEPH CIV Rule 201(201.5.1).

      i. *Copy.* A copy of the Clerk's CCS entry form of the filing shall also be served on all counsel of record or unrepresented parties whenever it contains an appearance of counsel or contains a date for Court hearing on the matter. IN ST ST JOSEPH CIV Rule 201(201.5.1).

b. *Methods of service*

    i. *Personal service.* Whenever a party is represented by an attorney of record, service shall be made upon such attorney unless service upon the party himself is ordered by the court. Service upon the attorney or party shall be made by delivering or mailing a copy of the papers to the last known address or where an attorney or party has consented to service by fax or e-mail, as provided in IN ST TRIAL P Rule 3.1(A)(4), by faxing or e-mailing a copy of the documents to the fax number or e-mail address set out in the appearance form or correction as required by IN ST TRIAL P Rule 3.1(E). IN ST TRIAL P Rule 5(B). Delivery of a copy within IN ST TRIAL P Rule 5 means:

- Offering or tendering it to the attorney or party and stating the nature of the papers being served. Refusal to accept an offered or tendered document is a waiver of any objection to the sufficiency or adequacy of service of that document;

- Leaving it at his office with a clerk or other person in charge thereof, or if there is no one in charge, leaving it in a conspicuous place therein; or

- If the office is closed, by leaving it at his dwelling house or usual place of abode with some person of suitable age and discretion then residing therein; or,

- Leaving it at some other suitable place, selected by the attorney upon whom service is being made, pursuant to duly promulgated local rule. IN ST TRIAL P Rule 5(B)(1).

    ii. *Service by the clerk.* Whenever the Clerk is required by rule or statute to give notice, the party or parties requesting such notice shall furnish the Clerk with sufficient copies of the notice to be given, along with stamped, addressed envelopes with the names and the addresses of the parties or their counsel to whom such notice is to be given. IN ST ST JOSEPH CIV Rule 201(201.5.4).

    iii. *Service on the court.* Service on a Judge may be made by delivering a copy to the Judge's secretary or mailing a copy to the Judge at his or her chambers. Service on a Judge may not be accomplished by facsimile transmission; however, a courtesy copy may be sent to the Judge's chambers by electronic mail or facsimile transmission contemporaneously with service by mail or otherwise. IN ST ST JOSEPH CIV Rule 201(201.5.5).

    iv. *Service by mail.* If service is made by mail, the papers shall be deposited in the United States mail addressed to the person on whom they are being served, with postage prepaid. Service shall be deemed complete upon mailing. Proof of service of all papers permitted to be mailed may be made by written acknowledgment of service, by affidavit of the person who mailed the papers, or by certificate of an attorney. It shall be the duty of attorneys when entering their appearance in a cause or when filing pleadings or papers therein, to have noted in the Chronological Case Summary or said pleadings or papers so filed the address and telephone number of their office. Service by delivery or by mail at such address shall be deemed sufficient and complete. IN ST TRIAL P Rule 5(B)(2).

    v. *Service by fax or e-mail.* A party who has consented to service by fax or e-mail may be served as follows:

- Service by e-mail shall be made by attaching the document being served in .pdf format. Discovery documents must also be served in accordance with IN ST TRIAL P Rule 26(A). IN ST TRIAL P Rule 5(B)(3)(a).

- Service by fax shall be deemed complete upon generation of a transmission record indicating the successful transmission of the entire document, except as provided in IN ST TRIAL P Rule 5(B)(3)(d). IN ST TRIAL P Rule 5(B)(3)(b).

- Service by e-mail shall be deemed complete upon transmission, except as provided in IN ST TRIAL P Rule 5(B)(3)(d). IN ST TRIAL P Rule 5(B)(3)(c).

- Service by fax or e-mail that occurs on a Saturday, Sunday, legal holiday, or day the court or agency in which the matter is pending is closed or after 5:00 PM local time of the recipient shall be deemed complete the next day that is not a Saturday, Sunday, legal holiday, or day that the court or agency in which the matter is pending is not closed. IN ST TRIAL P Rule 5(B)(3)(d).

c. *Serving numerous defendants.* In any action in which there are unusually large numbers of defendants, the court, upon motion or of its own initiative, may order:

   i. That service of the pleadings of the defendants and replies thereto need not be made as between the defendants;

     • That any cross-claim, counterclaim, or matter constituting an avoidance or affirmative defense contained therein shall be deemed to be denied or avoided by all other parties; and

     • That the filing of any such pleading and service thereof upon the plaintiff constitutes due notice of it to the parties. IN ST TRIAL P Rule 5(D).

   ii. A copy of every such order shall be served upon the parties in such manner and form as the court directs. IN ST TRIAL P Rule 5(D).

d. *Service on parties in default for failure to appear.* No service need be made on parties in default for failure to appear, except that pleadings asserting new or additional claims for relief against them shall be served upon them in the manner provided by service of summons in IN ST TRIAL P Rule 4. IN ST TRIAL P Rule 5(A).

e. *Distribution.* Counsel or an unrepresented party submitting a motion, petition, notice, pleading or proposed order shall indicate the method of distribution desired on the Clerk's CCS entry form. The Clerk will not return or distribute copies of motions, petitions, pleadings, notices or proposed orders, other than those originated by the Court, by mail unless the Clerk is provided with stamped, addressed envelopes. IN ST ST JOSEPH CIV Rule 201(201.5.3).

f. *Mailbox.* As a matter of convenience to attorneys, each court provides a mailbox for the distribution filings and orders generated by the Court, and it is the responsibility of each attorney to periodically check these mailboxes for service and distribution of court-generated filings and orders. IN ST ST JOSEPH CIV Rule 201(201.5.3).

G. Hearings

1. *Hearing on motion.* Unless local conditions make it impracticable, each judge shall establish regular times and places, at intervals sufficiently frequent for the prompt dispatch of business, at which motions requiring notice and hearing may be heard and disposed of; but the judge at any time or place and on such notice, if any, as he considers reasonable may make order for the advancement, conduct, and hearing of actions. To expedite its business the court may direct the submission and determination of motions without oral hearing upon brief written statements of reasons in support and opposition, or direct or permit hearings by telephone conference call with all attorneys or other similar means of communication. IN ST TRIAL P Rule 73(A).

2. *Hearing dates.* Hearing dates for filings requiring Court action shall be obtained from the Court Clerk and incorporated in the CCS entry at the time the motion or other pleading is filed. If no date is obtained prior to the filing, the fact of the hearing should be noted with the date and time left blank. IN ST ST JOSEPH CIV Rule 201(201.4).

3. *Hearing on matters other than trials.* Each Judge shall reserve periods of time for hearing matters other than contested trials, such as pre-trial and post-trial motions, rules to show cause, defaults, uncontested dissolutions of marriage, etc. As necessary to minimize conflicts in scheduling, the Judges shall set these schedules after consultation. Hearings shall be scheduled as follows:

a. *Scheduling uncontested or routine matters.* Routine matters, procedural motions, domestic relations applications for provisional relief and contempt proceedings, uncontested petitions for dissolution of marriage, and all other matters appropriate for summary consideration and disposition will be heard on the daily calendar. IN ST ST JOSEPH GEN AND ADMIN Rule 104(104.3.1).

b. *Scheduling contested or complicated matters.* Other matters that will require a hearing reasonably estimated to last in excess of twenty (20) minutes will be scheduled as the Court's calendar allows. Counsel or a party proceeding pro se should contact the chambers of the assigned judge to arrange for an appropriate hearing date and time. IN ST ST JOSEPH GEN AND ADMIN Rule 104(104.3.2).

c. *Scheduling motions for hearings.* Except for motions to correct error or not likely to require a hearing (as described in IN ST ST JOSEPH CIV Rule 201), all motions shall be scheduled for hearing at the time they are filed. It shall the responsibility of the moving party or counsel for the moving party to secure the date and time of the hearing from the Clerk or Court personnel who maintain the calendar for each Judge or Magistrate Judge. It shall also be the responsibility of the moving party or counsel for the moving party to coordinate the hearing date with all opposing counsel or unrepresented parties. IN ST ST JOSEPH CIV Rule 201(201.9.1).

    d. *Oral arguments on motions and other pleadings.* Unless otherwise required by St. Joseph County Civil or Indiana Trial Rules, it is within the sound discretion of the assigned Judge whether to allow oral argument; however, any party may file a request for oral argument by filing a written request by separate motion contemporaneously or at any time before the Court has ruled upon the motion or pleadings to be argued. IN ST ST JOSEPH CIV Rule 201(201.9.4).

H. Forms

1. Motion for Leave to Amend Forms for Indiana

    a. Motion to file amended complaint. 5 INPRAC § 3:5.1.

    b. Motion to file amended complaint; Another form. 5 INPRAC § 3:5.2.

    c. Motion to amend pleading to conform to evidence. 5 INPRAC § 3:5.4.

    d. Motion to amend complaint to compel joinder of defendant. 5 INPRAC § 3:7.2.

    e. Motion to amend caption. 9 INPRAC § 3.41.

    f. Affidavit in support of motion to amend caption. 9 INPRAC § 3.42.

    g. Motion for leave to amend complaint following dismissal. 9 INPRAC § 42.16.

    h. Motion for leave to file amended complaint against third party defendant. 10 INPRAC § 44.8.

    i. Motion to file amended complaint. 10 INPRAC § 46.7.

    j. Motion to amend complaint which has been dismissed; Filed more than 10 days after notice of dismissal. 10 INPRAC § 46.8.

    k. Motion to amend pleading; Another form. 10 INPRAC § 46.9.

    l. Order granting leave to amend complaint. 10 INPRAC § 46.10.

    m. Amendment by stipulation. 10 INPRAC § 46.11.

    n. Amended answer by interlineation. 10 INPRAC § 46.12.

    o. Objections to motion to amend complaint. 10 INPRAC § 46.13.

    p. Motion to amend pleading to conform to evidence. 10 INPRAC § 46.14.

    q. Motion for leave to change defendant after statute of limitations. 10 INPRAC § 46.16.

    r. Motion for leave to add party after statute of limitations. 10 INPRAC § 46.17.

    s. Motion to substitute real party in interest; Assignee of interest. 10 INPRAC § 47.10.

    t. Motion to amend complaint to compel joinder of defendant. 10 INPRAC § 49.3.

    u. Certificate of service; Personal service. 9 INPRAC § 5.7.

    v. Certificate of service; First class mail. 9 INPRAC § 5.8.

I. Checklist

  (I) ❏ Matters to be considered by moving party

    (a) ❏ Required documents

      (1) ❏ Motion and notice

      (2) ❏ Chronological Case Cummary (CCS) entry form

      (3) ❏ Copy of amended pleading

      (4) ❏ Proposed order

      (5) ❏ Certificate of service

(b) ❑ Supplemental documents

    (1) ❑ Supporting evidence

    (2) ❑ Facsimile cover sheet

(c) ❑ Timing

    (1) ❑ A party may amend his pleading once as a matter of course at any time before a responsive pleading is served or, if the pleading is one to which no responsive pleading is permitted, and the action has not been placed upon the trial calendar, he may so amend it at any time within thirty (30) days after it is served

        (i) ❑ Otherwise a party may amend his pleading only by leave of court or by written consent of the adverse party; and leave shall be given when justice so requires

    (2) ❑ A written motion, other than one which may be heard ex parte, and notice of the hearing thereof shall be served not less than five (5) days before the time specified for the hearing, unless a different period is fixed by the Indiana Rules of Trial Procedure or by order of the court

    (3) ❑ All pleadings and papers subsequent to the complaint which are required to be served upon a party shall be filed with the Court either before service or within a reasonable period of time thereafter

(II) ❑ Matters to be considered by the responding party

  (a) ❑ Required documents

    (1) ❑ Opposition

    (2) ❑ Chronological Case Cummary (CCS) entry form

    (3) ❑ Certificate of service

  (b) ❑ Supplemental documents

    (1) ❑ Supporting evidence

    (2) ❑ Proposed order

    (3) ❑ Facsimile cover sheet

  (c) ❑ Timing

    (1) ❑ So long as consistent with Indiana Rules of Trial Procedure, an adverse party wishing to respond shall do so within fifteen (15) days of service

    (2) ❑ Except as otherwise provided in IN ST TRIAL P Rule 59(D), opposing affidavits may be served not less than one (1) day before the hearing, unless the court permits them to be served at some other time

Motions, Oppositions and Replies
Motion for Summary Judgment

Document Last Updated October 2013

A. Applicable Rules

  1. *State rules*

    a. Appearance. IN ST TRIAL P Rule 3.1.

    b. Process. IN ST TRIAL P Rule 4.

    c. Service and filing of pleadings and other papers. IN ST TRIAL P Rule 5.

    d. Time. IN ST TRIAL P Rule 6.

    e. Pleadings. IN ST TRIAL P Rule 7; IN ST TRIAL P Rule 8; IN ST TRIAL P Rule 9.2; IN ST TRIAL P Rule 10.

f.   Signing and verification of pleadings. IN ST TRIAL P Rule 11.

g.   Evidence. IN ST TRIAL P Rule 43.

h.   Judgment on the evidence (directed verdict). IN ST TRIAL P Rule 50.

i.   Findings by the court. IN ST TRIAL P Rule 52.

j.   Summary judgment. IN ST TRIAL P Rule 56.

k.   Motion to correct error. IN ST TRIAL P Rule 59.

l.   Relief from judgment or order. IN ST TRIAL P Rule 60.

m.   Hearing of motions. IN ST TRIAL P Rule 73.

n.   Access to court records. IN ST ADMIN Rule 9.

o.   Paper size. IN ST ADMIN Rule 11.

p.   Facsimile transmission. IN ST ADMIN Rule 12.

q.   Electronic filing and electronic service pilot projects. IN ST ADMIN Rule 16.

r.   Sealing of certain records by court; Hearing; Notice. IN ST 5-14-3-5.5.

s.   Sixtieth judicial circuit. IN ST 33-33-71-2.

t.   Privacy and confidentiality. IN ST 5-2-9-6; IN ST 5-14-3-4; IN ST 6-4.1-5-10; IN ST 6-4.1-12-12; IN ST 6-8.1-7-1; IN ST 11-13-1-8; IN ST 12-23-14-13; IN ST 16-39-3-10; IN ST 16-41-8-1; IN ST 22-4-19-6; IN ST 31-11-1-6; IN ST 31-19-5-23; IN ST 31-19-13-2; IN ST 31-19-19-1; IN ST 31-33-18-1; IN ST 31-39-1-1; IN ST 31-39-1-2; IN ST 33-23-16-16; IN ST 35-34-2-4; IN ST 35-38-1-13; IN ST 35-38-9-1; IN ST ADR Rule 2.11; IN ST ADR Rule 4:4; IN ST ADR Rule 5.6; IN ST JURY Rule 10.

2. *Local rules*

a.   Court hours and scheduling. IN ST ST JOSEPH GEN AND ADMIN Rule 104.

b.   Filing, pleading, and motions. IN ST ST JOSEPH CIV Rule 201.

c.   Uniform court and case number designation. IN ST ST JOSEPH CIV Rule 202.

d.   Pleading and motions under IN ST TRIAL P Rule 12 and IN ST TRIAL P Rule 56. IN ST ST JOSEPH CIV Rule 206.

e.   Proposed order. IN ST ST JOSEPH CIV Rule 213.

f.   Electronic filing of cases in St. Joseph County. IN ST ST JOSEPH ELECTRONIC Rule 701.

B. Timing

1. *Time for moving for summary judgment*

a.   *For claimant.* A party seeking to recover upon a claim, counterclaim, or cross-claim or to obtain a declaratory judgment may, at any time after the expiration of twenty (20) days from the commencement of the action or after service of a motion for summary judgment by the adverse party, move with or without supporting affidavits for a summary judgment in his favor upon all or any part thereof. IN ST TRIAL P Rule 56(A).

b.   *For defending party.* A party against whom a claim, counterclaim, or cross-claim is asserted or a declaratory judgment is sought may, at any time, move with or without supporting affidavits for a summary judgment in his favor as to all or any part thereof. IN ST TRIAL P Rule 56(B).

c.   *Filing.* All pleadings and papers subsequent to the complaint which are required to be served upon a party shall be filed with the Court either before service or within a reasonable period of time thereafter. IN ST TRIAL P Rule 5(E)(1).

2. *Service.* A written motion, other than one which may be heard ex parte, and notice of the hearing thereof shall be served not less than five (5) days before the time specified for the hearing, unless a different period is fixed by the Indiana Rules of Trial Procedure or by order of the court. IN ST TRIAL P Rule 6(D).

a.   *Of supporting affidavits.* When a motion is supported by affidavit, the affidavit shall be served with the motion. IN ST TRIAL P Rule 6(D).

3. *Service of opposition.* An adverse party shall have thirty (30) days after service of the motion to serve a response and any opposing affidavits. IN ST TRIAL P Rule 56(C).

   a. Except as otherwise provided in IN ST TRIAL P Rule 59(D), opposing affidavits may be served not less than one (1) day before the hearing, unless the court permits them to be served at some other time. IN ST TRIAL P Rule 6(D).

   b. An adverse party shall have thirty (30) days after service of the motion in which to serve and file an answer brief. IN ST ST JOSEPH CIV Rule 206(206.1).

4. *Filing proposed orders.* Unless otherwise directed or given leave of the Court, proposed orders in emergency matters shall be filed within forty-eight (48) hours after a hearing; proposed orders in other matters shall be filed within seven (7) days as computed by IN ST TRIAL P Rule 6. IN ST ST JOSEPH CIV Rule 213(213.5).

5. *Computation of time*

   a. *Generally; Days excluded.* In computing any period of time prescribed or allowed by the Indiana Rules of Trial Procedure, by order of the court, or by any applicable statute, the day of the act, event, or default from which the designated period of time begins to run shall not be included. The last day of the period so computed is to be included unless it is:

      i. A Saturday,

      ii. A Sunday,

      iii. A legal holiday as defined by state statute, or

      iv. A day the office in which the act is to be done is closed during regular business hours. IN ST TRIAL P Rule 6(A).

   b. *Short periods.* In any event, the period runs until the end of the next day that is not a Saturday, a Sunday, a legal holiday, or a day on which the office is closed. When the period of time allowed is less than seven (7) days, intermediate Saturdays, Sundays, legal holidays, and days on which the office is closed shall be excluded from the computations. IN ST TRIAL P Rule 6(A).

   c. *Additional time after service by United States mail.* Whenever a party has the right or is required to do some act or take some proceedings within a prescribed period after the service of a notice or other paper upon him and the notice or paper is served upon him by United States mail, three (3) days shall be added to the prescribed period. IN ST TRIAL P Rule 6(E).

   d. *Enlargement of time.* When an act is required or allowed to be done at or within a specific time by the Indiana Rules of Trial Procedure, the court may at any time for cause shown:

      i. Order the period enlarged, with or without motion or notice, if request therefor is made before the expiration of the period originally prescribed or extended by a previous order; or

      ii. Upon motion made after the expiration of the specific period, permit the act to be done where the failure to act was the result of excusable neglect; but, the court may not extend the time for taking any action for judgment on the evidence under IN ST TRIAL P Rule 50(A), amendment of findings and judgment under IN ST TRIAL P Rule 52(B), to correct errors under IN ST TRIAL P Rule 59(C), statement in opposition to motion to correct error under IN ST TRIAL P Rule 59(E), or to obtain relief from final judgment under IN ST TRIAL P Rule 60(B), except to the extent and under the conditions stated in those rules. IN ST TRIAL P Rule 6(B).

      iii. An initial written motion for enlargement of time pursuant to IN ST TRIAL P Rule 6(B)(1) to answer a claim shall be routinely granted for an additional thirty (30) days from the original due date or other period the assigned Judge deems reasonable by written order of the Court. The motion must be filed on or before the original due date or IN ST ST JOSEPH CIV Rule 201 shall be inapplicable. IN ST ST JOSEPH CIV Rule 201(201.9.5).

         • Any motion for enlargement of time shall state the date when such response is due and the date to which time is requested to be enlarged. IN ST ST JOSEPH CIV Rule 201(201.9.5).

         • All subsequent motions for enlargement of time shall be so designated and will only be granted for good cause shown or in the interest of justice. IN ST ST JOSEPH CIV Rule 201(201.9.5).

C. General Requirements

1. *Motions, generally.* Unless made during a hearing or trial, or otherwise ordered by the court, an application to the court for an order shall be made by written motion. The motion shall state the grounds therefor and the relief or order sought. IN ST TRIAL P Rule 7(B).

   a. *Motions as distinct from pleadings.* Motions and responses to motions are not pleadings, and allegations contained in a motion are not admissions of a party. 22B INPRAC 7:2; Wachstetter v. County Properties, LLC, 832 N.E.2d 574 (Ind.Ct.App. 2005); Scott County Family YMCA, Inc. v. Hobbs, 817 N.E.2d 603 (Ind.Ct.App. 2004).

   b. *Unopposed motions generally granted.* It is common for a trial court to grant procedural motions, such as motions for enlargement of time, discovery motions, or motions for continuance, unless an objection is filed. 21 INPRAC § 13.8.

   c. *Proposed orders.* As directed by the Court, a party or an attorney for a party shall prepare a proposed order based on the decision rendered by the Court. The party so directed shall prepare the proposed order in a timely manner and, upon filing, shall advise the chambers of the applicable judge that the proposed order has been prepared and filed. IN ST ST JOSEPH CIV Rule 213(213.2).

   d. *Reply brief.* Subject to Court approval, the moving party may file a reply brief. IN ST ST JOSEPH CIV Rule 206(206.1).

2. *Motion for summary judgment.* Summary judgment is a procedure by which the trial court is asked to enter judgment when there are no genuine issues of material fact and the moving party is entitled to judgment as a matter of law. A summary judgment proceeding is not a trial, and is not intended to be a substitute for factual determinations where the facts are in dispute. Rather, summary judgment should be used to terminate litigation about which there is no factual dispute and which may be determined as a matter of law. 11 INPRAC § 90.1; LeBrun v. Conner, 702 N.E.2d 754 (Ind.Ct.App. 1998).

   a. *Burden.* The judgment sought shall be rendered forthwith if the designated evidentiary matter shows that there is no genuine issue as to any material fact and that the moving party is entitled to a judgment as a matter of law. IN ST TRIAL P Rule 56(C).

      i. A "genuine" issue of material fact exists if the trier of fact must resolve the opposing party's differing version of the underlying facts or if the undisputed facts support conflicting reasonable inferences. A fact is "material" if it might affect the outcome of a case by helping to prove or disprove an essential element of a claim or defense, or it facilitates a resolution of an issue in the case. 22B INPRAC 56:1; Williams v. Tharp, 914 N.E.2d 756 (Ind. 2009).

      ii. Summary judgment shall not be granted as of course because the opposing party fails to offer opposing affidavits or evidence, but the court shall make its determination from the evidentiary matter designated to the court. IN ST TRIAL P Rule 56(C).

      iii. The trial court must evaluate the evidence in favor of the non-moving party. 22B INPRAC 56:1.

      iv. Although Indiana courts are not consistent in describing the amount of proof required to sustain the moving party's initial burden, and IN ST TRIAL P Rule 56 is silent on the matter, a number of cases require "prima facie" proof. 22B INPRAC 56:5; DeHahn v. CSX Transp., Inc., 925 N.E.2d 442 (Ind.Ct.App. 2010). Once the moving party demonstrates the requirements for summary judgment, the burden shifts to the non-moving party to designate each material issue of fact which he asserts precludes entry of summary judgment and the evidence relevant to each designated fact. 22B INPRAC 56:5; Booth v. Wiley, 839 N.E.2d 1168 (Ind. 2005).

   b. *When motion not required.* When any party has moved for summary judgment, the court may grant summary judgment for any other party upon the issues raised by the motion although no motion for summary judgment is filed by such party. IN ST TRIAL P Rule 56(B).

   c. *Judgment on less than all issues or claims.* A summary judgment may be rendered upon less than all the issues or claims, including without limitation the issue of liability or damages alone although there is a genuine issue as to damages or liability as the case may be. IN ST TRIAL P Rule 56(C).

      i. *Partial judgment not entered; Exceptions.* A summary judgment upon less than all the issues involved in a claim or with respect to less than all the claims or parties shall be interlocutory unless the court in writing expressly determines that there is no just reason for delay and in writing expressly directs entry of judgment as to less than all the issues, claims or parties. IN ST TRIAL P Rule 56(C).

    ii. *Designation of specific findings.* The court shall designate the issues or claims upon which it finds no genuine issue as to any material facts. IN ST TRIAL P Rule 56(C).

    iii. *Case not fully adjudicated on motion.* If on motion under IN ST TRIAL P Rule 56 judgment is not rendered upon the whole case or for all the relief asked and a trial is necessary, the court at the hearing of the motion, by examining the pleadings and the evidence before it and by interrogating counsel, shall if practicable ascertain what material facts exist without substantial controversy and what material facts are actually and in good faith controverted. It shall thereupon make an order specifying the facts that appear without substantial controversy, including the extent to which the amount of damages or other relief is not in controversy, and directing such further proceedings in the action as are just. Upon the trial of the action the facts so specified shall be deemed established, and the trial shall be conducted accordingly. IN ST TRIAL P Rule 56(D).

  d. *Form of affidavits; Further testimony; Defense required.* Supporting and opposing affidavits shall be made on personal knowledge, shall set forth such facts as would be admissible in evidence, and shall show affirmatively that the affiant is competent to testify to the matters stated therein. IN ST TRIAL P Rule 56(E).

    i. Sworn or certified copies not previously self-authenticated of all papers or parts thereof referred to in an affidavit shall be attached thereto or served therewith. IN ST TRIAL P Rule 56(E).

    ii. The court may permit affidavits to be supplemented or opposed by depositions, answers to interrogatories, or further affidavits. IN ST TRIAL P Rule 56(E).

    iii. When a motion for summary judgment is made and supported as provided in IN ST TRIAL P Rule 56, an adverse party may not rest upon the mere allegations or denials of his pleading, but his response, by affidavits or as otherwise provided in IN ST TRIAL P Rule 56, must set forth specific facts showing that there is a genuine issue for trial. If he does not so respond, summary judgment, if appropriate, shall be entered against him. Denial of summary judgment may be challenged by a motion to correct errors after a final judgment or order is entered. IN ST TRIAL P Rule 56(E).

  e. *When affidavits are unavailable.* Should it appear from the affidavits of a party opposing the motion that he cannot for reasons stated present by affidavit facts essential to justify his opposition, the court may refuse the application for judgment or may order a continuance to permit affidavits to be obtained or depositions to be taken or discovery to be had or may make such other order as is just. IN ST TRIAL P Rule 56(F).

  f. *Affidavits made in bad faith.* Should it appear to the satisfaction of the court at any time that any of the affidavits presented pursuant to IN ST TRIAL P Rule 56 are presented in bad faith or solely for the purpose of delay, the court shall forthwith order the party employing them to pay to the other party the amount of the reasonable expenses which the filing of the affidavits caused him to incur, including reasonable attorney's fees, and any offending party or attorney may be adjudged guilty of contempt. IN ST TRIAL P Rule 56(G).

  g. *Party opposing the motion.* A party opposing the motion shall also designate to the court each material issue of fact which that party asserts precludes entry of summary judgment and the evidence relevant thereto. IN ST TRIAL P Rule 56(C).

  h. *Appeal; Reversal.* No judgment rendered on the motion shall be reversed on the ground that there is a genuine issue of material fact unless the material fact and the evidence relevant thereto shall have been specifically designated to the trial court. IN ST TRIAL P Rule 56(H).

3. *Opposition to a motion for summary judgment.* Failure to file an answer brief or reply brief within the time prescribed shall be deemed a waiver of the right thereto and shall subject the motion to summary ruling. IN ST ST JOSEPH CIV Rule 206(206.1).

D. Documents

1. *Required documents*

   a. *Motion and notice.* The requirement of notice is satisfied by service of the motion. IN ST TRIAL P Rule 7(B). Refer to the General Requirements section of this document for information on the content of a motion for summary judgment.

   b. *Chronological Case Summary (CCS) entry form.* Every written motion, petition, or other pleading subsequent to the original complaint presented to the Clerk for filing shall be accompanied by a Chronological Case Summary (CCS) entry form in duplicate. IN ST ST JOSEPH CIV Rule 201(201.4). Refer to the Format section of this document for details on the format and filing requirements for the CCS entry form.

   c. *Supporting memorandum of law.* All pleadings and motions filed pursuant to IN ST TRIAL P Rule 12 and IN ST TRIAL P Rule 56 shall be accompanied by a separate supporting brief. IN ST ST JOSEPH CIV Rule 206(206.1).

   d. *Supporting evidence.* At the time of filing the motion or response, a party shall designate to the court all parts of pleadings, depositions, answers to interrogatories, admissions, matters of judicial notice, and any other matters on which it relies for purposes of the motion. IN ST TRIAL P Rule 56(C).

      i. The party moving for judgment must designate sufficient evidence to establish that there is no genuine issue of material fact and that judgment is proper as a matter of law. 22B INPRAC 56:4; Jarboe v. Landmark Community Newspapers of Indiana, Inc., 644 N.E.2d 118 (Ind. 1994).

   e. *Proposed order.* Unless local practice provides differently, a party should submit a proposed order with its written motion to be signed by the judge once the motion has been granted. 21 INPRAC § 13.8. All proposed orders shall be submitted in an original plus a number of copies equal to one more than the number of pro se parties and attorneys of record contained in the prepared proof of notice under IN ST TRIAL P Rule 72(D). IN ST ST JOSEPH CIV Rule 213(213.3); IN ST ST JOSEPH CIV Rule 201(201.5.2).

   f. *Certificate of service.* An attorney or unrepresented party tendering a document to the Clerk for filing shall certify that service has been made, list the parties served, and specify the date and means of service. The certificate of service shall be placed at the end of the document and shall not be separately filed. The separate filing of a certificate of service, however, shall not be grounds for rejecting a document for filing. The Clerk may permit documents to be filed without a certificate of service but shall require prompt filing of a separate certificate of service. IN ST TRIAL P Rule 5(C).

2. *Supplemental documents*

   a. *Additional supporting evidence.* When a motion is based on facts not appearing of record the court may hear the matter on affidavits presented by the respective parties, but the court may direct that the matter be heard wholly or partly on oral testimony or depositions. IN ST TRIAL P Rule 43(B).

   b. *Notice to unrepresented parties regarding IN ST TRIAL P Rule 56 motions.* Notwithstanding any other rule of court, if a party is proceeding pro se and an opposing party files a motion for summary judgment, counsel for the moving party must serve a notice upon the unrepresented party as set forth in IN ST ST JOSEPH CIV App. B, and made a party hereof. IN ST ST JOSEPH CIV Rule 206(206.4.2).

   c. *Facsimile cover sheet.* Any document sent to the Clerk of the Circuit Court by electronic facsimile transmission shall be accompanied by a cover sheet which states the title of the document, case number, number of pages, identity and voice telephone number of the sending party and instructions for filing. The cover sheet shall contain the signature of the attorney or party, pro se, authorizing the filing. IN ST ADMIN Rule 12(D).

E. Format

1. *Form of motions.* The rules applicable to captions, and the signing and form of pleadings (IN ST TRIAL

P Rule 8 through IN ST TRIAL P Rule 11), apply to all motions and other papers provided under the Indiana Rules of Trial Procedure. 22B INPRAC 7:2.

    a.   *Separate motions; Alternative motions.* Each motion shall be separate, while alternative motions filed together shall each be identified on the caption. IN ST ST JOSEPH CIV Rule 206(206.1).

2.   *Form of pleadings*

    a.   *Caption; Names of parties.* Every pleading shall contain a caption setting forth the name of the court, the title of the action, the file number, and a designation as in IN ST TRIAL P Rule 7(A). In the complaint the title of the action shall include the names of all the parties, but in other pleadings it is sufficient to state the name of the first party on each side with an appropriate indication of other parties. IN ST TRIAL P Rule 10(A); IN ST ST JOSEPH CIV Rule 201(201.3.3). If a special judge has been assigned to the case, the pleading should also identify the special judge. IN ST ST JOSEPH CIV Rule 201(201.3.3).

        i.   *Title.* All pleadings or motions shall include a title, which shall delineate each topic included in the pleading. For example, where a pleading contains an answer, a motion to dismiss, and a jury request, each topic shall be set forth in the title. IN ST ST JOSEPH CIV Rule 201(201.3.4).

    b.   *Paragraphs; Separate statements.* All averments of a claim or defense shall be made in numbered paragraphs, the contents of each of which shall be limited as far as practicable to a statement of a single set of circumstances, and a paragraph may be referred to by number in all succeeding pleadings. Each claim founded upon a separate transaction or occurrence and each defense other than denials may be stated in a separate count or defense whenever a separation facilitates the clear presentation of the matters set forth. IN ST TRIAL P Rule 10(B).

    c.   *Adoption by reference; Exhibits.* Statements in a pleading may be adopted by reference in a different part of the same pleading or in another pleading or in any motion. A copy of any written instrument which is an exhibit to a pleading is a part thereof for all purposes. IN ST TRIAL P Rule 10(C).

    d.   *Flat filing.* In order that the Clerk's files may be kept under the system commonly known as "flat filing," all papers presented to the Clerk for filing shall be flat and unfolded. Pleadings shall have no covers or backs and shall be fastened together at the top left-hand corner only. IN ST ST JOSEPH CIV Rule 201(201.1).

    e.   *One side of page used.* Printing shall be on one (1) side of the paper. IN ST ST JOSEPH CIV Rule 201(201.3.2).

    f.   *Copies.* All copies shall be on white paper of sufficient strength and durability to resist normal wear and tear. IN ST ST JOSEPH CIV Rule 201(201.3.1).

    g.   *Margins.* Margins shall be at least one inch (1"). IN ST ST JOSEPH CIV Rule 201(201.3.2).

    h.   *Double-spaced.* If typewritten, the lines shall be double spaced except for quotations, which shall be indented and single-spaced. IN ST ST JOSEPH CIV Rule 201(201.3.2).

    i.   *Font size.* Type face shall be twelve (12) font size or larger within the body of the document and ten (10) font size or larger in the footnotes. IN ST ST JOSEPH CIV Rule 201(201.3.2).

    j.   *Font type.* The font type must be legible and script type shall not be used. IN ST ST JOSEPH CIV Rule 201(201.3.2).

    k.   *Italics.* Italicized type may be used for quotations, references, or case citations. IN ST ST JOSEPH CIV Rule 201(201.3.2).

    l.   *Court and case designation.* All filings shall conform to the requirements for uniform court and case number designation set by IN ST ADMIN Rule 8. In addition, all filings shall contain the proper court and case designation as described below. IN ST ST JOSEPH CIV Rule 202.

        i.   *Court designation.* Pursuant to IN ST 33-33-71-2, St. Joseph County, Indiana, constitutes the Sixtieth Judicial Circuit. The legal names of the courts within the 60th Judicial Circuit are the St. Joseph Circuit Court, the St. Joseph Superior Court, and the St. Joseph Probate Court. All filings shall properly reflect the legal name of the applicable court. Any filing may be amended, rejected, or stricken if it does not contain the proper case name and/or the legal name of the court. IN ST ST JOSEPH CIV Rule 202(202.1).

m. *Form of CCS entry.* Every written motion, petition, or other pleading subsequent to the original complaint presented to the Clerk for filing shall be accompanied by a Chronological Case Summary (CCS) entry form in duplicate which shall contain the title and cause number of the action, the date, and the proposed entry to appear on the docket. IN ST ST JOSEPH CIV Rule 201(201.4).

   i. *Identification and signature.* The CCS entry form shall identify the party making the filing, designate each pleading being filed, and shall be signed by counsel of record or the unrepresented litigant. IN ST ST JOSEPH CIV Rule 201(201.4).

   ii. *Date stamp.* The form shall be date stamped and presented to the Court Clerk, who shall initial the form and return the duplicate to the filing party. IN ST ST JOSEPH CIV Rule 201(201.4).

n. *Form of proposed order.* Any proposed order shall be a document that is separate and apart from the motion or application to which it relates and shall contain a caption showing the name of the court, the case number assigned to the case, and the title of the case as shown by the complaint pursuant to IN ST ST JOSEPH CIV Rule 201. IN ST ST JOSEPH CIV Rule 213(213.2).

   i. If there are multiple parties, the title may be shortened to include only the first name plaintiff and defendant with appropriate indication that there are additional parties. IN ST ST JOSEPH CIV Rule 213(213.2).

   ii. The proposed order shall be on white paper, eight and one-half by eleven inches (8 1/2" x 11") in size, and each page shall be numbered. IN ST ST JOSEPH CIV Rule 213(213.2).

   iii. The last page of the proposed order shall contain a line for the date, either "Dated _____" or "Signed on the date filemarked hereon." IN ST ST JOSEPH CIV Rule 213(213.2).

   iv. On the last page there also shall be a line for the signature of the Judge under which shall be typed "Judge, St. Joseph [Circuit or Superior or Probate] Court." IN ST ST JOSEPH CIV Rule 213(213.2).

   v. If the proposed order contains a recommendation from a Magistrate, the last page shall have a line for the signature of the Magistrate under which shall be typed "Magistrate, St. Joseph [Circuit or Superior or Probate] Court," to the left of which shall be the following, "So Recommended:" and beneath and to the left of which shall be typed, "Approved. So Ordered." IN ST ST JOSEPH CIV Rule 213(213.2).

   vi. To allow compliance with the notice requirements of IN ST TRIAL P Rule 72(D), the lower four (4) inches of the last page of the proposed order shall be left blank. The proposed order shall also include a prepared proof of notice under IN ST TRIAL P Rule 72(D), and in preparing such a notice the filing party shall complete all portions of the prepared proof of notice. IN ST ST JOSEPH CIV Rule 213(213.2).

3. *Size of papers for filing.* Effective January 1, 1992, all pleadings, copies, motions and documents filed with any trial court or appellate level court, typed or printed, with the exception of exhibits and existing wills, shall be prepared on eight and one-half by eleven inch (8 1/2" x 11") size paper. IN ST ADMIN Rule 11.

a. *Paper.* Pleadings, motions, and other papers shall be either legibly printed or typewritten on white opaque paper of good quality at least sixteen (16) pound weight, eight and one-half inches (8 1/2 ") in width and eleven inches (11") in length as required by IN ST ADMIN Rule 11. IN ST ST JOSEPH CIV Rule 201(201.3.1).

4. *Signature requirements*

a. *Signature of attorney.* Every pleading or motion of a party represented by an attorney shall be signed by at least one (1) attorney of record in his individual name, whose address, telephone number, and attorney number shall be stated, except that this provision shall not apply to pleadings and motions made and transcribed at the trial or a hearing before the judge and received by him in such form. IN ST TRIAL P Rule 11(A).

   i. The signature of an attorney constitutes a certificate by him that he has read the pleadings; that to the best of his knowledge, information, and belief, there is good ground to support it; and that it is not interposed for delay. IN ST TRIAL P Rule 11(A).

    ii.   If a pleading or motion is not signed or is signed with intent to defeat the purpose of the rule, it may be stricken as sham and false and the action may proceed as though the pleading had not been served. IN ST TRIAL P Rule 11(A).

    iii. For a willful violation of IN ST TRIAL P Rule 11 an attorney may be subjected to appropriate disciplinary action. Similar action may be taken if scandalous or indecent matter is inserted. IN ST TRIAL P Rule 11(A).

  b.   *Signature of unrepresented party.* A party who is not represented by an attorney shall sign his pleading and state his address. IN ST TRIAL P Rule 11(A).

  c.   *Verification not generally required.* Except when specifically required by rule, pleadings or motions need not be verified or accompanied by affidavit. The rule in equity that the averments of an answer under oath must be overcome by the testimony of two (2) witnesses or of one (1) witness sustained by corroborating circumstances is abolished. IN ST TRIAL P Rule 11(A).

  d.   *Verification by affirmation or representation.* When in connection with any civil or special statutory proceeding it is required that any pleading, motion, petition, supporting affidavit, or other document of any kind, be verified, or that an oath be taken, it shall be sufficient if the subscriber simply affirms the truth of the matter to be verified by an affirmation or representation. IN ST TRIAL P Rule 11(B). IN ST TRIAL P Rule 11(B) states that the affirmation or representation should be in substantially the following language: "I (we) affirm, under the penalties for perjury, that the foregoing representation(s) is (are) true. (Signed) _____."

    i.   Any person who falsifies an affirmation or representation of fact shall be subject to the same penalties as are prescribed by law for the making of a false affidavit. IN ST TRIAL P Rule 11(B).

  e.   *Verified pleadings, motions, and affidavits as evidence.* Pleadings, motions and affidavits accompanying or in support of such pleadings or motions when required to be verified or under oath shall be accepted as a representation that the signer had personal knowledge thereof or reasonable cause to believe the existence of the facts or matters stated or alleged therein; and, if otherwise competent or acceptable as evidence, may be admitted as evidence of the facts or matters stated or alleged therein when it is so provided in the Indiana Rules of Trial Procedure, by statute or other law, or to the extent the writing or signature expressly purports to be made upon the signer's personal knowledge. When such pleadings, motions and affidavits are verified or under oath they shall not require other or greater proof on the part of the adverse party than if not verified or not under oath unless expressly provided otherwise by the Indiana Rules of Trial Procedure, statute or other law. Affidavits upon motions for summary judgment under IN ST TRIAL P Rule 56 and in denial of execution under IN ST TRIAL P Rule 9.2 shall be made upon personal knowledge. IN ST TRIAL P Rule 11(C).

  f.   *Signature, verification and other requirements.* Parties and their counsel are enjoined to comply with the verification requirements of IN ST TRIAL P Rule 11, and either the moving party or the party's attorney of record shall sign all pleadings and motions before filing with the Clerk of the Court. Every motion, petition, or other pleading filed with the Clerk shall contain the name, organization, physical address, telephone number, and facsimile number of the filing party or an attorney for that party. IN ST ST JOSEPH CIV Rule 201(201.3.6).

    i.   The Clerk shall not accept any motion, petition, notice or other pleading or a CCS entry form for filing from an unrepresented litigant unless the unrepresented litigant's current address and phone number appear on the pleading, and an opposing party may service notices and responses on an unrepresented litigant at any address he or she has provided on a pleading. IN ST ST JOSEPH CIV Rule 201(201.3.6).

5.   *Information excluded from public access.* Every document filed in a case shall separately identify information excluded from public access pursuant to IN ST ADMIN Rule 9(G)(1) as follows:

  a.   Whole documents that are excluded from public access pursuant to IN ST ADMIN Rule 9(G)(1) shall be tendered on light green paper or have a light green coversheet attached to the document, marked "Not for Public Access" or "Confidential." IN ST TRIAL P Rule 5(G)(1).

  b.   When only a portion of a document contains information excluded from public access pursuant to IN

ST ADMIN Rule 9(G)(1), said information shall be omitted [or redacted] from the filed document, and set forth on a separate accompanying document on light green paper conspicuously marked "Not for Public Access" or "Confidential" and clearly designated [or identifying] the caption and number of the case and the document and location within the document to which the redacted material pertains. IN ST TRIAL P Rule 5(G)(2).

c. With respect to documents filed in electronic format, the trial court, by local rule, may provide for compliance with IN ST TRIAL P Rule 5 in manner that separates and protects access to information excluded from public access. IN ST TRIAL P Rule 5(G)(3).

d. IN ST TRIAL P Rule 5(G) does not apply to a record sealed by the court pursuant to IN ST 5-14-3-5.5 or otherwise, nor to records, documents, or information filed in cases to which public access is prohibited pursuant to IN ST ADMIN Rule 9(G). IN ST TRIAL P Rule 5(G)(4).

e. The following information in case records is excluded from public access and is confidential:

i. Information that is excluded from public access pursuant to federal law;

ii. Information that is excluded from public access as declared confidential by Indiana statute or other court rule, including without limitation:

- All adoption records created after July 8, 1941, as declared confidential by IN ST 31-19-19-1, et seq., except those specifically declared open by IN ST 31-19-13-2(2);

- All records relating to chancroid, chlamydia, gonorrhea, hepatitis, human immunodeficiency virus (HIV), Lymphogranuloma venereum, syphilis, tuberculosis, as declared confidential by IN ST 16-41-8-1, et seq.;

- All records relating to child abuse as declared confidential by IN ST 31-33-18-1, et seq.;

- All records relating to drug tests as declared confidential by IN ST 5-14-3-4(a)(9);

- Records of grand jury proceedings as declared confidential by IN ST 35-34-2-4;

- Records of juvenile proceedings as declared confidential by IN ST 31-39-1-2, except those specifically open under statute;

- All paternity records created after July 1, 1941 as declared confidential by IN ST 31-14-11-15, IN ST 31-19-5-23, IN ST 31-39-1-1 and IN ST 31-39-1-2 [Editor's note: IN ST 31-14-11-15 was repealed effective May 9, 2013];

- All pre-sentence reports as declared confidential by IN ST 35-38-1-13;

- Written petitions to permit marriages without consent and orders directing the Clerk of Court to issue a marriage license to underage persons, as declared confidential by IN ST 31-11-1-6;

- Only those arrest warrants, search warrants, indictments and informations ordered confidential by the trial judge, prior to return of duly executed service as declared confidential by IN ST 5-14-3-4(b)(1);

- All medical, mental health, or tax records unless determined by law or regulation of any governmental custodian not to be confidential, released by the subject of such records, or declared by a court of competent jurisdiction to be essential to the resolution of litigation as declared confidential by IN ST 16-39-3-10, IN ST 6-4.1-5-10, IN ST 6-4.1-12-12, and IN ST 6-8.1-7-1;

- Personal information relating to jurors or prospective jurors, other than for the use of the parties and counsel, pursuant to IN ST JURY Rule 10;

- Information relating to protection from abuse orders, no-contact orders and workplace violence restraining orders as declared confidential by IN ST 5-2-9-6, et seq.;

- Mediation proceedings pursuant to IN ST ADR Rule 2.11, Mini-Trial proceedings pursuant to IN ST ADR Rule 4.4(C), and Summary Jury Trials pursuant to IN ST ADR Rule 5.6;

- Information in probation files pursuant to the Probation Standards promulgated by the Judicial Conference of Indiana pursuant to IN ST 11-13-1-8(b);

- Information deemed confidential pursuant to the Rules for Court Administered Alcohol and Drug Programs promulgated by the Judicial Conference of Indiana pursuant to IN ST 12-23-14-13;
- Information deemed confidential pursuant to the Problem-Solving Court Rules promulgated by the Judicial Conference of Indiana pursuant to IN ST 33-23-16-16;
- All records of the Department of workforce Development as declared confidential by IN ST 22-4-19-6;
- Information regarding interception of electronic communications that is sealed or deemed confidential as set forth in IN ST 35-33.5-2-1, et seq.

iii. Information excluded from public access by specific court order;

iv. Complete Social Security Numbers of living persons;

v. With the exception of names, information such as addresses, phone numbers, and dates of birth which explicitly identifies:

- Natural persons who are witnesses or victims (not including defendants) in criminal, domestic violence, stalking, sexual assault, juvenile, or civil protection order proceedings, provided that juveniles who are victims of sex crimes shall be identified by initials only;
- Places of residence of judicial officers, clerks and other employees of courts and clerks of court, unless the person or persons about whom the information pertains waives confidentiality;

vi. Complete account numbers of specific assets, loans, bank accounts, credit cards, and personal identification numbers (PINs);

vii. All orders of expungement entered in criminal or juvenile proceedings, orders to restrict access to criminal history information pursuant to IN ST 35-38-5-5.5 or IN ST 35-38-8-5 and records excluded from public access by such orders, and information related to infractions that is excluded from public access pursuant to IN ST 34-28-5-15 or IN ST 34-28-5-16 [Editor's note: IN ST 35-38-5-5.5, IN ST 35-38-8-5 and IN ST 34-28-5-16 were repealed effective July 1, 2013; for information on orders restricting access to criminal history, refer to IN ST 35-38-9-1, et seq.];

viii. All personal notes and e-mail, and deliberative material, of judges, jurors, court staff and judicial agencies, and information recorded in personal data assistants (PDA's) or organizers and personal calendars. IN ST ADMIN Rule 9(G)(1).

F. Filing and Service Requirements

1. *Filing requirements.* Except as otherwise provided in IN ST TRIAL P Rule 5(E)(2), all pleadings and papers subsequent to the complaint which are required to be served upon a party shall be filed with the Court either before service or within a reasonable period of time thereafter. IN ST TRIAL P Rule 5(E)(1).

   a. *Filing with the court defined.* The filing of pleadings, motions, and other papers with the court as required by the Indiana Rules of Trial Procedure shall be made by one of the following methods:

   i. Delivery to the clerk of the court;

   ii. Sending by electronic transmission under the procedure adopted pursuant to IN ST ADMIN Rule 12;

   iii. Mailing to the clerk by registered, certified or express mail return receipt requested;

   iv. Depositing with any third-party commercial carrier for delivery to the clerk within three (3) calendar days, cost prepaid, properly addressed;

   v. If the court so permits, filing with the judge, in which event the judge shall note thereon the filing date and forthwith transmit them to the office of the clerk; or

   vi. Electronic filing, as approved by the Division of State Court Administration pursuant to IN ST ADMIN Rule 16. IN ST TRIAL P Rule 5(F).

   vii. Filing by registered or certified mail and by third-party commercial carrier shall be complete upon mailing or deposit. IN ST TRIAL P Rule 5(F).

viii. All pleadings shall be filed with the Clerk, not directly with the Court, unless otherwise required by the Indiana Rules of Court. The entry of appearances and the filing of pleadings or other matters not requiring immediate Court action shall be filed with the Clerk and not in open Court. A Judge may permit papers to be filed in chambers, in which event he or she shall note thereon the filing date and transmit the papers to the Clerk. IN ST ST JOSEPH CIV Rule 201(201.2).

b. *Facsimile filing.* Unless otherwise authorized by IN ST ST JOSEPH ELECTRONIC Rule 701, electronic filing of pleadings by computerized or facsimile transmission is not permitted. IN ST ST JOSEPH CIV Rule 201(201.2).

c. *Additional copies.* In cases in which a party or counsel supplies the proposed order or decree, a sufficient number shall be prepared and filed as to provide the Clerk to retain two (2) copies, which shall be filed in the flat file and the record of judgments and orders. Should the party or counsel desire additional copies, a sufficient number of copies should be filed to effectuate that purpose. IN ST ST JOSEPH CIV Rule 201(201.6).

d. *Proof of filing.* Any party filing any paper by any method other than personal delivery to the clerk shall retain proof of filing. IN ST TRIAL P Rule 5(F).

2. *Service requirements.* Unless otherwise provided by the Indiana Rules of Trial Procedure or an order of the court, each party and special judge, if any, shall be served with: (1) every order required by its terms to be served; (2) every pleading subsequent to the original complaint; (3) every written motion except one which may be heard ex parte; (4) every brief submitted to the trial court; (5) every paper relating to discovery required to be served upon a party; and (6) every written notice, appearance, demand, offer of judgment, designation of record on appeal, or similar paper. IN ST TRIAL P Rule 5(A).

a. *Service generally.* Every motion, petition, notice, or other pleading required to be served by IN ST TRIAL P Rule 5 shall be served on all counsel of record or unrepresented parties either before it is filed or on the day it is filed with the Court, and the date of filing shall be indicated on the Certificate of Service. IN ST ST JOSEPH CIV Rule 201(201.5.1).

   i. *Copy.* A copy of the Clerk's CCS entry form of the filing shall also be served on all counsel of record or unrepresented parties whenever it contains an appearance of counsel or contains a date for Court hearing on the matter. IN ST ST JOSEPH CIV Rule 201(201.5.1).

b. *Methods of service*

   i. *Personal service.* Whenever a party is represented by an attorney of record, service shall be made upon such attorney unless service upon the party himself is ordered by the court. Service upon the attorney or party shall be made by delivering or mailing a copy of the papers to the last known address or where an attorney or party has consented to service by fax or e-mail, as provided in IN ST TRIAL P Rule 3.1(A)(4), by faxing or e-mailing a copy of the documents to the fax number or e-mail address set out in the appearance form or correction as required by IN ST TRIAL P Rule 3.1(E). IN ST TRIAL P Rule 5(B). Delivery of a copy within IN ST TRIAL P Rule 5 means:

   - Offering or tendering it to the attorney or party and stating the nature of the papers being served. Refusal to accept an offered or tendered document is a waiver of any objection to the sufficiency or adequacy of service of that document;

   - Leaving it at his office with a clerk or other person in charge thereof, or if there is no one in charge, leaving it in a conspicuous place therein; or

   - If the office is closed, by leaving it at his dwelling house or usual place of abode with some person of suitable age and discretion then residing therein; or,

   - Leaving it at some other suitable place, selected by the attorney upon whom service is being made, pursuant to duly promulgated local rule. IN ST TRIAL P Rule 5(B)(1).

   ii. *Service by the clerk.* Whenever the Clerk is required by rule or statute to give notice, the party or parties requesting such notice shall furnish the Clerk with sufficient copies of the notice to be given, along with stamped, addressed envelopes with the names and the addresses of the parties or their counsel to whom such notice is to be given. IN ST ST JOSEPH CIV Rule 201(201.5.4).

    iii. *Service on the court.* Service on a Judge may be made by delivering a copy to the Judge's secretary or mailing a copy to the Judge at his or her chambers. Service on a Judge may not be accomplished by facsimile transmission; however, a courtesy copy may be sent to the Judge's chambers by electronic mail or facsimile transmission contemporaneously with service by mail or otherwise. IN ST ST JOSEPH CIV Rule 201(201.5.5).

    iv. *Service by mail.* If service is made by mail, the papers shall be deposited in the United States mail addressed to the person on whom they are being served, with postage prepaid. Service shall be deemed complete upon mailing. Proof of service of all papers permitted to be mailed may be made by written acknowledgment of service, by affidavit of the person who mailed the papers, or by certificate of an attorney. It shall be the duty of attorneys when entering their appearance in a cause or when filing pleadings or papers therein, to have noted in the Chronological Case Summary or said pleadings or papers so filed the address and telephone number of their office. Service by delivery or by mail at such address shall be deemed sufficient and complete. IN ST TRIAL P Rule 5(B)(2).

    v. *Service by fax or e-mail.* A party who has consented to service by fax or e-mail may be served as follows:

- Service by e-mail shall be made by attaching the document being served in .pdf format. Discovery documents must also be served in accordance with IN ST TRIAL P Rule 26(A). IN ST TRIAL P Rule 5(B)(3)(a).

- Service by fax shall be deemed complete upon generation of a transmission record indicating the successful transmission of the entire document, except as provided in IN ST TRIAL P Rule 5(B)(3)(d). IN ST TRIAL P Rule 5(B)(3)(b).

- Service by e-mail shall be deemed complete upon transmission, except as provided in IN ST TRIAL P Rule 5(B)(3)(d). IN ST TRIAL P Rule 5(B)(3)(c).

- Service by fax or e-mail that occurs on a Saturday, Sunday, legal holiday, or day the court or agency in which the matter is pending is closed or after 5:00 PM local time of the recipient shall be deemed complete the next day that is not a Saturday, Sunday, legal holiday, or day that the court or agency in which the matter is pending is not closed. IN ST TRIAL P Rule 5(B)(3)(d).

c. *Serving numerous defendants.* In any action in which there are unusually large numbers of defendants, the court, upon motion or of its own initiative, may order:

    i. That service of the pleadings of the defendants and replies thereto need not be made as between the defendants;

- That any cross-claim, counterclaim, or matter constituting an avoidance or affirmative defense contained therein shall be deemed to be denied or avoided by all other parties; and

- That the filing of any such pleading and service thereof upon the plaintiff constitutes due notice of it to the parties. IN ST TRIAL P Rule 5(D).

    ii. A copy of every such order shall be served upon the parties in such manner and form as the court directs. IN ST TRIAL P Rule 5(D).

d. *Service on parties in default for failure to appear.* No service need be made on parties in default for failure to appear, except that pleadings asserting new or additional claims for relief against them shall be served upon them in the manner provided by service of summons in IN ST TRIAL P Rule 4. IN ST TRIAL P Rule 5(A).

e. *Distribution.* Counsel or an unrepresented party submitting a motion, petition, notice, pleading or proposed order shall indicate the method of distribution desired on the Clerk's CCS entry form. The Clerk will not return or distribute copies of motions, petitions, pleadings, notices or proposed orders, other than those originated by the Court, by mail unless the Clerk is provided with stamped, addressed envelopes. IN ST ST JOSEPH CIV Rule 201(201.5.3).

f. *Mailbox.* As a matter of convenience to attorneys, each court provides a mailbox for the distribution filings and orders generated by the Court, and it is the responsibility of each attorney to periodically

check these mailboxes for service and distribution of court-generated filings and orders. IN ST ST JOSEPH CIV Rule 201(201.5.3).

G. Hearings

1. *Hearing on motion.* Unless local conditions make it impracticable, each judge shall establish regular times and places, at intervals sufficiently frequent for the prompt dispatch of business, at which motions requiring notice and hearing may be heard and disposed of; but the judge at any time or place and on such notice, if any, as he considers reasonable may make order for the advancement, conduct, and hearing of actions. To expedite its business the court may direct the submission and determination of motions without oral hearing upon brief written statements of reasons in support and opposition, or direct or permit hearings by telephone conference call with all attorneys or other similar means of communication. IN ST TRIAL P Rule 73(A).

2. *Hearing on summary judgment.* The court may conduct a hearing on the motion. However, upon motion of any party made no later than ten (10) days after the response was filed or was due, the court shall conduct a hearing on the motion which shall be held not less than ten (10) days after the time for filing the response. IN ST TRIAL P Rule 56(C).

3. *Hearing dates.* Hearing dates for filings requiring Court action shall be obtained from the Court Clerk and incorporated in the CCS entry at the time the motion or other pleading is filed. If no date is obtained prior to the filing, the fact of the hearing should be noted with the date and time left blank. IN ST ST JOSEPH CIV Rule 201(201.4).

4. *Hearing on matters other than trials.* Each Judge shall reserve periods of time for hearing matters other than contested trials, such as pre-trial and post-trial motions, rules to show cause, defaults, uncontested dissolutions of marriage, etc. As necessary to minimize conflicts in scheduling, the Judges shall set these schedules after consultation. Hearings shall be scheduled as follows:

   a. *Scheduling uncontested or routine matters.* Routine matters, procedural motions, domestic relations applications for provisional relief and contempt proceedings, uncontested petitions for dissolution of marriage, and all other matters appropriate for summary consideration and disposition will be heard on the daily calendar. IN ST ST JOSEPH GEN AND ADMIN Rule 104(104.3.1).

   b. *Scheduling contested or complicated matters.* Other matters that will require a hearing reasonably estimated to last in excess of twenty (20) minutes will be scheduled as the Court's calendar allows. Counsel or a party proceeding pro se should contact the chambers of the assigned judge to arrange for an appropriate hearing date and time. IN ST ST JOSEPH GEN AND ADMIN Rule 104(104.3.2).

   c. *Scheduling motions for hearings.* Except for motions to correct error or not likely to require a hearing (as described in IN ST ST JOSEPH CIV Rule 201), all motions shall be scheduled for hearing at the time they are filed. It shall the responsibility of the moving party or counsel for the moving party to secure the date and time of the hearing from the Clerk or Court personnel who maintain the calendar for each Judge or Magistrate Judge. It shall also be the responsibility of the moving party or counsel for the moving party to coordinate the hearing date with all opposing counsel or unrepresented parties. IN ST ST JOSEPH CIV Rule 201(201.9.1).

   d. *Oral arguments on motions and other pleadings.* Unless otherwise required by St. Joseph County Civil or Indiana Trial Rules, it is within the sound discretion of the assigned Judge whether to allow oral argument; however, any party may file a request for oral argument by filing a written request by separate motion contemporaneously or at any time before the Court has ruled upon the motion or pleadings to be argued. IN ST ST JOSEPH CIV Rule 201(201.9.4).

5. *Motions for summary judgment and for dismissal.* Motions for summary judgment or motions to dismiss pursuant to IN ST TRIAL P Rule 12 or IN ST TRIAL P Rule 41 shall be scheduled for hearing, unless the Court issues a written scheduling order providing otherwise. (Refer to IN ST ST JOSEPH CIV Rule 206 for specific requirements for Pleadings and Motions under IN ST TRIAL P Rule 12 and IN ST TRIAL P Rule 56). IN ST ST JOSEPH CIV Rule 201(201.9.6).

   a. *Dispositive motions date.* Notwithstanding any other rule of court, all IN ST TRIAL P Rule 12 or IN ST TRIAL P Rule 56 motions shall be set for hearing by the moving party at the time of filing unless otherwise ordered by the Court. Unless otherwise authorized by the Court, the hearing shall be scheduled for a day not fewer than fourteen (14) days after the time period allowed for filing of briefs as specified in IN ST ST JOSEPH CIV Rule 206(206.1). IN ST ST JOSEPH CIV Rule 206(206.2).

b. *Waiver of hearing; Stipulation of the parties.* Adverse parties may stipulate that a IN ST TRIAL P Rule 12 or IN ST TRIAL P Rule 56 motion may be ruled upon by the Court without a hearing thereon, in which event the motion and stipulation shall be brought to the personal attention of the Judge by counsel or by a party proceeding pro se. IN ST ST JOSEPH CIV Rule 206(206.3).

c. *Appearance by counsel at scheduled hearings.* Whenever the Court schedules a hearing on a motion pursuant to IN ST TRIAL P Rule 12 and/or IN ST TRIAL P Rule 56, counsel for all represented parties shall appear in person or by local co-counsel at such hearing. IN ST ST JOSEPH CIV Rule 206(206.5).

d. *Prevailing party; Proposed order.* The Court may require that the attorney for the prevailing party prepare a form of order on a motion for summary judgment in accordance with the provisions of IN ST TRIAL P Rule 56. A proposed order on a motion for summary judgment may contain the language called for in IN ST TRIAL P Rule 56(C) that there is not just reason for delay and directs entry of final judgment as to less than all the issues, claims, or parties. IN ST ST JOSEPH CIV Rule 213(213.4).

H. Forms

1. Motion for Summary Judgment Forms for Indiana

a. Notice of motion for summary judgment. 11 INPRAC § 90.2.

b. Motion for summary judgment. 11 INPRAC § 90.3.

c. Motion for summary judgment; Another form. 11 INPRAC § 90.4.

d. Motion for summary judgment; Another form. 11 INPRAC § 90.5.

e. Designation of materials relied upon in support of motion for summary judgment. 11 INPRAC § 90.6.

f. Designation of material issues of fact that preclude entry of summary judgment. 11 INPRAC § 90.7.

g. Response to statement of material issues of fact that preclude entry of summary judgment. 11 INPRAC § 90.8.

h. Order granting motion for summary judgment. 11 INPRAC § 90.9.

i. Order denying motion for summary judgment. 11 INPRAC § 90.10.

j. Motion for partial summary judgment as to liability. 11 INPRAC § 90.11.

k. Order for partial summary judgment as to liability. 11 INPRAC § 90.12.

l. Order denying summary judgment and specifying issues. 11 INPRAC § 90.15.

m. Affidavit in support of motion for summary judgment. 11 INPRAC § 90.16.

n. Submission of proposed findings of fact, conclusions of law and proposed summary judgment. 11 INPRAC § 90.17.

o. Findings of fact and conclusions of law in support of motion for summary judgment. 11 INPRAC § 90.18.

p. Motion for hearing on motion for summary judgment. 11 INPRAC § 90.27.

q. Certificate of service; Personal service. 9 INPRAC § 5.7.

r. Certificate of service; First class mail. 9 INPRAC § 5.8.

2. Official Motion for Summary Judgment Forms for St. Joseph County

a. Notice regarding summary judgment motion. IN ST ST JOSEPH CIV App. B.

I. Checklist

(I) ❑ Matters to be considered by moving party

(a) ❑ Required documents

(1) ❑ Motion and notice

    (2) ❏ Chronological Case Summary (CCS) entry form

    (3) ❏ Supporting memorandum of law

    (4) ❏ Supporting evidence

    (5) ❏ Proposed order

    (6) ❏ Certificate of service

 (b) ❏ Supplemental documents

    (1) ❏ Additional supporting evidence

    (2) ❏ Notice to unrepresented parties regarding IN ST TRIAL P Rule 56 motions

    (3) ❏ Facsimile cover sheet

 (c) ❏ Timing

    (1) ❏ A party seeking to recover upon a claim, counterclaim, or cross-claim or to obtain a declaratory judgment may, at any time after the expiration of twenty (20) days from the commencement of the action or after service of a motion for summary judgment by the adverse party, move with or without supporting affidavits for a summary judgment in his favor upon all or any part thereof

    (2) ❏ A party against whom a claim, counterclaim, or cross-claim is asserted or a declaratory judgment is sought may, at any time, move with or without supporting affidavits for a summary judgment in his favor as to all or any part thereof

    (3) ❏ A written motion, other than one which may be heard ex parte, and notice of the hearing thereof shall be served not less than five (5) days before the time specified for the hearing, unless a different period is fixed by the Indiana Rules of Trial Procedure or by order of the court

    (4) ❏ All pleadings and papers subsequent to the complaint which are required to be served upon a party shall be filed with the Court either before service or within a reasonable period of time thereafter

(II) ❏ Matters to be considered by the responding party

 (a) ❏ Required documents

    (1) ❏ Opposition

    (2) ❏ Chronological Case Summary (CCS) entry form

    (3) ❏ Supporting memorandum of law

    (4) ❏ Opposing evidence

    (5) ❏ Certificate of service

 (b) ❏ Supplemental documents

    (1) ❏ Additional evidence

    (2) ❏ Proposed order

    (3) ❏ Facsimile cover sheet

 (c) ❏ Timing

    (1) ❏ An adverse party shall have thirty (30) days after service of the motion to serve a response and any opposing affidavits

    (2) ❏ An adverse party shall have thirty (30) days after service of the motion in which to serve and file an answer brief

    (3) ❏ Except as otherwise provided in IN ST TRIAL P Rule 59(D), opposing affidavits may be served not less than one (1) day before the hearing, unless the court permits them to be served at some other time

Motions, Oppositions and Replies
Motion for Sanctions

Document Last Updated October 2013

A. Applicable Rules

1. *State rules*

   a. Appearance. IN ST TRIAL P Rule 3.1.

   b. Process. IN ST TRIAL P Rule 4.

   c. Service and filing of pleadings and other papers. IN ST TRIAL P Rule 5.

   d. Time. IN ST TRIAL P Rule 6.

   e. Pleadings. IN ST TRIAL P Rule 7; IN ST TRIAL P Rule 8; IN ST TRIAL P Rule 9.2; IN ST TRIAL P Rule 10.

   f. Signing and verification of pleadings. IN ST TRIAL P Rule 11.

   g. Evidence. IN ST TRIAL P Rule 43.

   h. Judgment on the evidence (directed verdict). IN ST TRIAL P Rule 50.

   i. Findings by the court. IN ST TRIAL P Rule 52.

   j. Summary judgment. IN ST TRIAL P Rule 56.

   k. Motion to correct error. IN ST TRIAL P Rule 59.

   l. Relief from judgment or order. IN ST TRIAL P Rule 60.

   m. Hearing of motions. IN ST TRIAL P Rule 73.

   n. Access to court records. IN ST ADMIN Rule 9.

   o. Paper size. IN ST ADMIN Rule 11.

   p. Facsimile transmission. IN ST ADMIN Rule 12.

   q. Electronic filing and electronic service pilot projects. IN ST ADMIN Rule 16.

   r. Sealing of certain records by court; Hearing; Notice. IN ST 5-14-3-5.5.

   s. Sixtieth judicial circuit. IN ST 33-33-71-2.

   t. Privacy and confidentiality. IN ST 5-2-9-6; IN ST 5-14-3-4; IN ST 6-4.1-5-10; IN ST 6-4.1-12-12; IN ST 6-8.1-7-1; IN ST 11-13-1-8; IN ST 12-23-14-13; IN ST 16-39-3-10; IN ST 16-41-8-1; IN ST 22-4-19-6; IN ST 31-11-1-6; IN ST 31-19-5-23; IN ST 31-19-13-2; IN ST 31-19-19-1; IN ST 31-33-18-1; IN ST 31-39-1-1; IN ST 31-39-1-2; IN ST 33-23-16-16; IN ST 35-34-2-4; IN ST 35-38-1-13; IN ST 35-38-9-1; IN ST ADR Rule 2.11; IN ST ADR Rule 4.4; IN ST ADR Rule 5.6; IN ST JURY Rule 10.

   u. General recovery rule. IN ST 34-52-1-1.

2. *Local rules*

   a. Court hours and scheduling. IN ST ST JOSEPH GEN AND ADMIN Rule 104.

   b. Filing, pleading, and motions. IN ST ST JOSEPH CIV Rule 201.

   c. Uniform court and case number designation. IN ST ST JOSEPH CIV Rule 202.

   d. Pleading and motions under IN ST TRIAL P Rule 12 and IN ST TRIAL P Rule 56. IN ST ST JOSEPH CIV Rule 206.

   e. Proposed order. IN ST ST JOSEPH CIV Rule 213.

   f. Electronic filing of cases in St. Joseph County. IN ST ST JOSEPH ELECTRONIC Rule 701.

B. Timing

1. *Motion for sanctions.* There are no specific time requirements for when a party may file a motion for sanctions.

   a. *Filing.* All pleadings and papers subsequent to the complaint which are required to be served upon a party shall be filed with the Court either before service or within a reasonable period of time thereafter. IN ST TRIAL P Rule 5(E)(1).

2. *Service.* A written motion, other than one which may be heard ex parte, and notice of the hearing thereof shall be served not less than five (5) days before the time specified for the hearing, unless a different period is fixed by the Indiana Rules of Trial Procedure or by order of the court. IN ST TRIAL P Rule 6(D).

   a. *Of supporting affidavits.* When a motion is supported by affidavit, the affidavit shall be served with the motion. IN ST TRIAL P Rule 6(D).

3. *Service of opposition.* Except as otherwise provided in IN ST TRIAL P Rule 59(D), opposing affidavits may be served not less than one (1) day before the hearing, unless the court permits them to be served at some other time. IN ST TRIAL P Rule 6(D).

   a. *Memorandum of law.* So long as consistent with Indiana Rules of Trial Procedure, an adverse party wishing to respond shall do so within fifteen (15) days of service. IN ST ST JOSEPH CIV Rule 206(206.1).

4. *Filing proposed orders.* Unless otherwise directed or given leave of the Court, proposed orders in emergency matters shall be filed within forty-eight (48) hours after a hearing; proposed orders in other matters shall be filed within seven (7) days as computed by IN ST TRIAL P Rule 6. IN ST ST JOSEPH CIV Rule 213(213.5).

5. *Computation of time*

   a. *Generally; Days excluded.* In computing any period of time prescribed or allowed by the Indiana Rules of Trial Procedure, by order of the court, or by any applicable statute, the day of the act, event, or default from which the designated period of time begins to run shall not be included. The last day of the period so computed is to be included unless it is:

      i. A Saturday,

      ii. A Sunday,

      iii. A legal holiday as defined by state statute, or

      iv. A day the office in which the act is to be done is closed during regular business hours. IN ST TRIAL P Rule 6(A).

   b. *Short periods.* In any event, the period runs until the end of the next day that is not a Saturday, a Sunday, a legal holiday, or a day on which the office is closed. When the period of time allowed is less than seven (7) days, intermediate Saturdays, Sundays, legal holidays, and days on which the office is closed shall be excluded from the computations. IN ST TRIAL P Rule 6(A).

   c. *Additional time after service by United States mail.* Whenever a party has the right or is required to do some act or take some proceedings within a prescribed period after the service of a notice or other paper upon him and the notice or paper is served upon him by United States mail, three (3) days shall be added to the prescribed period. IN ST TRIAL P Rule 6(E).

   d. *Enlargement of time.* When an act is required or allowed to be done at or within a specific time by the Indiana Rules of Trial Procedure, the court may at any time for cause shown:

      i. Order the period enlarged, with or without motion or notice, if request therefor is made before the expiration of the period originally prescribed or extended by a previous order; or

      ii. Upon motion made after the expiration of the specific period, permit the act to be done where the failure to act was the result of excusable neglect; but, the court may not extend the time for taking any action for judgment on the evidence under IN ST TRIAL P Rule 50(A), amendment of findings and judgment under IN ST TRIAL P Rule 52(B), to correct errors under IN ST TRIAL P Rule 59(C), statement in opposition to motion to correct error under IN ST TRIAL P Rule 59(E), or to obtain relief from final judgment under IN ST TRIAL P Rule 60(B), except to the extent and under the conditions stated in those rules. IN ST TRIAL P Rule 6(B).

iii. An initial written motion for enlargement of time pursuant to IN ST TRIAL P Rule 6(B)(1) to answer a claim shall be routinely granted for an additional thirty (30) days from the original due date or other period the assigned Judge deems reasonable by written order of the Court. The motion must be filed on or before the original due date or IN ST ST JOSEPH CIV Rule 201 shall be inapplicable. IN ST ST JOSEPH CIV Rule 201(201.9.5).

- Any motion for enlargement of time shall state the date when such response is due and the date to which time is requested to be enlarged. IN ST ST JOSEPH CIV Rule 201(201.9.5).

- All subsequent motions for enlargement of time shall be so designated and will only be granted for good cause shown or in the interest of justice. IN ST ST JOSEPH CIV Rule 201(201.9.5).

C. General Requirements

1. *Motions, generally.* Unless made during a hearing or trial, or otherwise ordered by the court, an application to the court for an order shall be made by written motion. The motion shall state the grounds therefor and the relief or order sought. IN ST TRIAL P Rule 7(B).

    a. *Motions as distinct from pleadings.* Motions and responses to motions are not pleadings, and allegations contained in a motion are not admissions of a party. 22B INPRAC 7:2; Wachstetter v. County Properties, LLC, 832 N.E.2d 574 (Ind.Ct.App. 2005); Scott County Family YMCA, Inc. v. Hobbs, 817 N.E.2d 603 (Ind.Ct.App. 2004).

    b. *Unopposed motions generally granted.* It is common for a trial court to grant procedural motions, such as motions for enlargement of time, discovery motions, or motions for continuance, unless an objection is filed. 21 INPRAC § 13.8.

    c. *Proposed orders.* As directed by the Court, a party or an attorney for a party shall prepare a proposed order based on the decision rendered by the Court. The party so directed shall prepare the proposed order in a timely manner and, upon filing, shall advise the chambers of the applicable judge that the proposed order has been prepared and filed. IN ST ST JOSEPH CIV Rule 213(213.2).

2. *Motion for sanctions*

    a. *Signature and certification.* Every pleading or motion of a party represented by an attorney shall be signed by at least one (1) attorney of record in his individual name, whose address, telephone number, and attorney number shall be stated, except that this provision shall not apply to pleadings and motions made and transcribed at the trial or a hearing before the judge and received by him in such form. A party who is not represented by an attorney shall sign his pleading and state his address. IN ST TRIAL P Rule 11(A).

        i. The signature of an attorney constitutes a certificate by him that he has read the pleadings; that to the best of his knowledge, information, and belief, there is good ground to support it; and that it is not interposed for delay. IN ST TRIAL P Rule 11(A).

        ii. If a pleading or motion is not signed or is signed with intent to defeat the purpose of the rule, it may be stricken as sham and false and the action may proceed as though the pleading had not been served. IN ST TRIAL P Rule 11(A).

        iii. For a willful violation of IN ST TRIAL P Rule 11 an attorney may be subjected to appropriate disciplinary action. Similar action may be taken if scandalous or indecent matter is inserted. IN ST TRIAL P Rule 11(A).

    b. *Frivolous claims.* A claim or defense is "frivolous, unreasonable or groundless" if it has been asserted primarily for the purpose of harassment, if the attorney is unable to make a good faith and rational argument on the merits of the action, or if the lawyer is unable to support the action by good faith and a rational argument for extension, modification, or reversal of existing law. 9 INPRAC § 4.3; Garage Doors of Indianapolis, Inc. v. Morton, 682 N.E.2d 1296 (Ind.Ct.App. 1997).

        i. *Bad faith pleading.* For information on sanctions for bad faith pleading, refer to IN ST 34-52-1-1.

   c. *Factors for determining reasonableness.* Five factors are relevant to determine whether a litigant's conduct is "unreasonable":

     i. The amount of time the attorney had to investigate facts, research the law and prepare documents;

     ii. The extent to which the attorney had to rely upon his client for the factual foundation;

     iii. The complexity of the facts and legal issues;

     iv. The ability to conduct a pre-filing investigation; and

     v. The plausibility of the arguments advanced by a party, including good faith efforts to extend or modify the law. 9 INPRAC § 4.3; General Collections, Inc. v. Decker, 545 N.E.2d 18 (Ind.Ct.App. 1989).

   d. *Determination of sanction.* The determination of a reasonable attorney fee requires the consideration of all relevant matters including but not limited to the attorney's experience and reputation, the nature of the employment, and the responsibility involved and the results obtained. A contingency fee agreement should not be used as the basis for determining a reasonable fee to be paid by a nonparty to that agreement. 9 INPRAC § 4.3; Mason v. Mason, 561 N.E.2d 809 (Ind.Ct.App. 1990).

3. *Opposition to a motion for sanctions.* Failure to file an answer brief or reply brief within the time prescribed shall be deemed a waiver of the right thereto and shall subject the motion to summary ruling. IN ST ST JOSEPH CIV Rule 206(206.1).

D. Documents

1. *Required documents*

   a. *Motion and notice.* The requirement of notice is satisfied by service of the motion. IN ST TRIAL P Rule 7(B). Refer to the General Requirements section of this document for information on the content of a motion for sanctions.

   b. *Chronological Case Summary (CCS) entry form.* Every written motion, petition, or other pleading subsequent to the original complaint presented to the Clerk for filing shall be accompanied by a Chronological Case Summary (CCS) entry form in duplicate. IN ST ST JOSEPH CIV Rule 201(201.4). Refer to the Format section of this document for details on the format and filing requirements for the CCS entry form.

   c. *Proposed order.* Unless local practice provides differently, a party should submit a proposed order with its written motion to be signed by the judge once the motion has been granted. 21 INPRAC § 13.8. All proposed orders shall be submitted in an original plus a number of copies equal to one more than the number of pro se parties and attorneys of record contained in the prepared proof of notice under IN ST TRIAL P Rule 72(D). IN ST ST JOSEPH CIV Rule 213(213.3); IN ST ST JOSEPH CIV Rule 201(201.5.2).

   d. *Certificate of service.* An attorney or unrepresented party tendering a document to the Clerk for filing shall certify that service has been made, list the parties served, and specify the date and means of service. The certificate of service shall be placed at the end of the document and shall not be separately filed. The separate filing of a certificate of service, however, shall not be grounds for rejecting a document for filing. The Clerk may permit documents to be filed without a certificate of service but shall require prompt filing of a separate certificate of service. IN ST TRIAL P Rule 5(C).

2. *Supplemental documents*

   a. *Supporting evidence.* When a motion is based on facts not appearing of record the court may hear the matter on affidavits presented by the respective parties, but the court may direct that the matter be heard wholly or partly on oral testimony or depositions. IN ST TRIAL P Rule 43(B).

   b. *Facsimile cover sheet.* Any document sent to the Clerk of the Circuit Court by electronic facsimile transmission shall be accompanied by a cover sheet which states the title of the document, case number, number of pages, identity and voice telephone number of the sending party and instructions for filing. The cover sheet shall contain the signature of the attorney or party, pro se, authorizing the filing. IN ST ADMIN Rule 12(D).

E. Format

1. *Form of motions.* The rules applicable to captions, and the signing and form of pleadings (IN ST TRIAL P Rule 8 through IN ST TRIAL P Rule 11), apply to all motions and other papers provided under the Indiana Rules of Trial Procedure. 22B INPRAC 7:2.

   a. *Separate motions; Alternative motions.* Each motion shall be separate, while alternative motions filed together shall each be identified on the caption. IN ST ST JOSEPH CIV Rule 206(206.1).

2. *Form of pleadings*

   a. *Caption; Names of parties.* Every pleading shall contain a caption setting forth the name of the court, the title of the action, the file number, and a designation as in IN ST TRIAL P Rule 7(A). In the complaint the title of the action shall include the names of all the parties, but in other pleadings it is sufficient to state the name of the first party on each side with an appropriate indication of other parties. IN ST TRIAL P Rule 10(A); IN ST ST JOSEPH CIV Rule 201(201.3.3). If a special judge has been assigned to the case, the pleading should also identify the special judge. IN ST ST JOSEPH CIV Rule 201(201.3.3).

      i. *Title.* All pleadings or motions shall include a title, which shall delineate each topic included in the pleading. For example, where a pleading contains an answer, a motion to dismiss, and a jury request, each topic shall be set forth in the title. IN ST ST JOSEPH CIV Rule 201(201.3.4).

   b. *Paragraphs; Separate statements.* All averments of a claim or defense shall be made in numbered paragraphs, the contents of each of which shall be limited as far as practicable to a statement of a single set of circumstances, and a paragraph may be referred to by number in all succeeding pleadings. Each claim founded upon a separate transaction or occurrence and each defense other than denials may be stated in a separate count or defense whenever a separation facilitates the clear presentation of the matters set forth. IN ST TRIAL P Rule 10(B).

   c. *Adoption by reference; Exhibits.* Statements in a pleading may be adopted by reference in a different part of the same pleading or in another pleading or in any motion. A copy of any written instrument which is an exhibit to a pleading is a part thereof for all purposes. IN ST TRIAL P Rule 10(C).

   d. *Flat filing.* In order that the Clerk's files may be kept under the system commonly known as "flat filing," all papers presented to the Clerk for filing shall be flat and unfolded. Pleadings shall have no covers or backs and shall be fastened together at the top left-hand corner only. IN ST ST JOSEPH CIV Rule 201(201.1).

   e. *One side of page used.* Printing shall be on one (1) side of the paper. IN ST ST JOSEPH CIV Rule 201(201.3.2).

   f. *Copies.* All copies shall be on white paper of sufficient strength and durability to resist normal wear and tear. IN ST ST JOSEPH CIV Rule 201(201.3.1).

   g. *Margins.* Margins shall be at least one inch (1"). IN ST ST JOSEPH CIV Rule 201(201.3.2).

   h. *Double-spaced.* If typewritten, the lines shall be double spaced except for quotations, which shall be indented and single-spaced. IN ST ST JOSEPH CIV Rule 201(201.3.2).

   i. *Font size.* Type face shall be twelve (12) font size or larger within the body of the document and ten (10) font size or larger in the footnotes. IN ST ST JOSEPH CIV Rule 201(201.3.2).

   j. *Font type.* The font type must be legible and script type shall not be used. IN ST ST JOSEPH CIV Rule 201(201.3.2).

   k. *Italics.* Italicized type may be used for quotations, references, or case citations. IN ST ST JOSEPH CIV Rule 201(201.3.2).

   l. *Court and case designation.* All filings shall conform to the requirements for uniform court and case number designation set by IN ST ADMIN Rule 8. In addition, all filings shall contain the proper court and case designation as described below. IN ST ST JOSEPH CIV Rule 202.

      i. *Court designation.* Pursuant to IN ST 33-33-71-2, St. Joseph County, Indiana, constitutes the Sixtieth Judicial Circuit. The legal names of the courts within the 60th Judicial Circuit are the St. Joseph Circuit Court, the St. Joseph Superior Court, and the St. Joseph Probate Court. All filings shall properly reflect the legal name of the applicable court. Any filing may be amended, rejected, or stricken if it does not contain the proper case name and/or the legal name of the court. IN ST ST JOSEPH CIV Rule 202(202.1).

m. *Form of CCS entry.* Every written motion, petition, or other pleading subsequent to the original complaint presented to the Clerk for filing shall be accompanied by a Chronological Case Summary (CCS) entry form in duplicate which shall contain the title and cause number of the action, the date, and the proposed entry to appear on the docket. IN ST ST JOSEPH CIV Rule 201(201.4).

    i. *Identification and signature.* The CCS entry form shall identify the party making the filing, designate each pleading being filed, and shall be signed by counsel of record or the unrepresented litigant. IN ST ST JOSEPH CIV Rule 201(201.4).

    ii. *Date stamp.* The form shall be date stamped and presented to the Court Clerk, who shall initial the form and return the duplicate to the filing party. IN ST ST JOSEPH CIV Rule 201(201.4).

n. *Form of proposed order.* Any proposed order shall be a document that is separate and apart from the motion or application to which it relates and shall contain a caption showing the name of the court, the case number assigned to the case, and the title of the case as shown by the complaint pursuant to IN ST ST JOSEPH CIV Rule 201. IN ST ST JOSEPH CIV Rule 213(213.2).

    i. If there are multiple parties, the title may be shortened to include only the first name plaintiff and defendant with appropriate indication that there are additional parties. IN ST ST JOSEPH CIV Rule 213(213.2).

    ii. The proposed order shall be on white paper, eight and one-half by eleven inches (8 1/2" x 11") in size, and each page shall be numbered. IN ST ST JOSEPH CIV Rule 213(213.2).

    iii. The last page of the proposed order shall contain a line for the date, either "Dated _____" or "Signed on the date filemarked hereon." IN ST ST JOSEPH CIV Rule 213(213.2).

    iv. On the last page there also shall be a line for the signature of the Judge under which shall be typed "Judge, St. Joseph [Circuit or Superior or Probate] Court." IN ST ST JOSEPH CIV Rule 213(213.2).

    v. If the proposed order contains a recommendation from a Magistrate, the last page shall have a line for the signature of the Magistrate under which shall be typed "Magistrate, St. Joseph [Circuit or Superior or Probate] Court," to the left of which shall be the following, "So Recommended:" and beneath and to the left of which shall be typed, "Approved. So Ordered." IN ST ST JOSEPH CIV Rule 213(213.2).

    vi. To allow compliance with the notice requirements of IN ST TRIAL P Rule 72(D), the lower four (4) inches of the last page of the proposed order shall be left blank. The proposed order shall also include a prepared proof of notice under IN ST TRIAL P Rule 72(D), and in preparing such a notice the filing party shall complete all portions of the prepared proof of notice. IN ST ST JOSEPH CIV Rule 213(213.2).

3. *Size of papers for filing.* Effective January 1, 1992, all pleadings, copies, motions and documents filed with any trial court or appellate level court, typed or printed, with the exception of exhibits and existing wills, shall be prepared on eight and one-half by eleven inch (8 1/2" x 11") size paper. IN ST ADMIN Rule 11.

a. *Paper.* Pleadings, motions, and other papers shall be either legibly printed or typewritten on white opaque paper of good quality at least sixteen (16) pound weight, eight and one-half inches (8 1/2 ") in width and eleven inches (11") in length as required by IN ST ADMIN Rule 11. IN ST ST JOSEPH CIV Rule 201(201.3.1).

4. *Signature requirements*

a. *Signature of attorney.* Every pleading or motion of a party represented by an attorney shall be signed by at least one (1) attorney of record in his individual name, whose address, telephone number, and attorney number shall be stated, except that this provision shall not apply to pleadings and motions made and transcribed at the trial or a hearing before the judge and received by him in such form. IN ST TRIAL P Rule 11(A).

    i. Refer to the General Requirements section of this document for information on sanctions.

b. *Signature of unrepresented party.* A party who is not represented by an attorney shall sign his pleading and state his address. IN ST TRIAL P Rule 11(A).

c. *Verification not generally required.* Except when specifically required by rule, pleadings or motions need not be verified or accompanied by affidavit. The rule in equity that the averments of an answer under oath must be overcome by the testimony of two (2) witnesses or of one (1) witness sustained by corroborating circumstances is abolished. IN ST TRIAL P Rule 11(A).

d. *Verification by affirmation or representation.* When in connection with any civil or special statutory proceeding it is required that any pleading, motion, petition, supporting affidavit, or other document of any kind, be verified, or that an oath be taken, it shall be sufficient if the subscriber simply affirms the truth of the matter to be verified by an affirmation or representation. IN ST TRIAL P Rule 11(B). IN ST TRIAL P Rule 11(B) states that the affirmation or representation should be in substantially the following language: "I (we) affirm, under the penalties for perjury, that the foregoing representation(s) is (are) true. (Signed) _____."

   i. Any person who falsifies an affirmation or representation of fact shall be subject to the same penalties as are prescribed by law for the making of a false affidavit. IN ST TRIAL P Rule 11(B).

e. *Verified pleadings, motions, and affidavits as evidence.* Pleadings, motions and affidavits accompanying or in support of such pleadings or motions when required to be verified or under oath shall be accepted as a representation that the signer had personal knowledge thereof or reasonable cause to believe the existence of the facts or matters stated or alleged therein; and, if otherwise competent or acceptable as evidence, may be admitted as evidence of the facts or matters stated or alleged therein when it is so provided in the Indiana Rules of Trial Procedure, by statute or other law, or to the extent the writing or signature expressly purports to be made upon the signer's personal knowledge. When such pleadings, motions and affidavits are verified or under oath they shall not require other or greater proof on the part of the adverse party than if not verified or not under oath unless expressly provided otherwise by the Indiana Rules of Trial Procedure, statute or other law. Affidavits upon motions for summary judgment under IN ST TRIAL P Rule 56 and in denial of execution under IN ST TRIAL P Rule 9.2 shall be made upon personal knowledge. IN ST TRIAL P Rule 11(C).

f. *Signature, verification and other requirements.* Parties and their counsel are enjoined to comply with the verification requirements of IN ST TRIAL P Rule 11, and either the moving party or the party's attorney of record shall sign all pleadings and motions before filing with the Clerk of the Court. Every motion, petition, or other pleading filed with the Clerk shall contain the name, organization, physical address, telephone number, and facsimile number of the filing party or an attorney for that party. IN ST ST JOSEPH CIV Rule 201(201.3.6).

   i. The Clerk shall not accept any motion, petition, notice or other pleading or a CCS entry form for filing from an unrepresented litigant unless the unrepresented litigant's current address and phone number appear on the pleading, and an opposing party may service notices and responses on an unrepresented litigant at any address he or she has provided on a pleading. IN ST ST JOSEPH CIV Rule 201(201.3.6).

5. *Information excluded from public access.* Every document filed in a case shall separately identify information excluded from public access pursuant to IN ST ADMIN Rule 9(G)(1) as follows:

   a. Whole documents that are excluded from public access pursuant to IN ST ADMIN Rule 9(G)(1) shall be tendered on light green paper or have a light green coversheet attached to the document, marked "Not for Public Access" or "Confidential." IN ST TRIAL P Rule 5(G)(1).

   b. When only a portion of a document contains information excluded from public access pursuant to IN ST ADMIN Rule 9(G)(1), said information shall be omitted [or redacted] from the filed document, and set forth on a separate accompanying document on light green paper conspicuously marked "Not for Public Access" or "Confidential" and clearly designated [or identifying] the caption and number of the case and the document and location within the document to which the redacted material pertains. IN ST TRIAL P Rule 5(G)(2).

   c. With respect to documents filed in electronic format, the trial court, by local rule, may provide for

compliance with IN ST TRIAL P Rule 5 in manner that separates and protects access to information excluded from public access. IN ST TRIAL P Rule 5(G)(3).

d. IN ST TRIAL P Rule 5(G) does not apply to a record sealed by the court pursuant to IN ST 5-14-3-5.5 or otherwise, nor to records, documents, or information filed in cases to which public access is prohibited pursuant to IN ST ADMIN Rule 9(G). IN ST TRIAL P Rule 5(G)(4).

e. The following information in case records is excluded from public access and is confidential:

   i. Information that is excluded from public access pursuant to federal law;

   ii. Information that is excluded from public access as declared confidential by Indiana statute or other court rule, including without limitation:

   - All adoption records created after July 8, 1941, as declared confidential by IN ST 31-19-19-1, et seq., except those specifically declared open by IN ST 31-19-13-2(2);

   - All records relating to chancroid, chlamydia, gonorrhea, hepatitis, human immunodeficiency virus (HIV), Lymphogranuloma venereum, syphilis, tuberculosis, as declared confidential by IN ST 16-41-8-1, et seq.;

   - All records relating to child abuse as declared confidential by IN ST 31-33-18-1, et seq.;

   - All records relating to drug tests as declared confidential by IN ST 5-14-3-4(a)(9);

   - Records of grand jury proceedings as declared confidential by IN ST 35-34-2-4;

   - Records of juvenile proceedings as declared confidential by IN ST 31-39-1-2, except those specifically open under statute;

   - All paternity records created after July 1, 1941 as declared confidential by IN ST 31-14-11-15, IN ST 31-19-5-23, IN ST 31-39-1-1 and IN ST 31-39-1-2 [Editor's note: IN ST 31-14-11-15 was repealed effective May 9, 2013];

   - All pre-sentence reports as declared confidential by IN ST 35-38-1-13;

   - Written petitions to permit marriages without consent and orders directing the Clerk of Court to issue a marriage license to underage persons, as declared confidential by IN ST 31-11-1-6;

   - Only those arrest warrants, search warrants, indictments and informations ordered confidential by the trial judge, prior to return of duly executed service as declared confidential by IN ST 5-14-3-4(b)(1);

   - All medical, mental health, or tax records unless determined by law or regulation of any governmental custodian not to be confidential, released by the subject of such records, or declared by a court of competent jurisdiction to be essential to the resolution of litigation as declared confidential by IN ST 16-39-3-10, IN ST 6-4.1-5-10, IN ST 6-4.1-12-12, and IN ST 6-8.1-7-1;

   - Personal information relating to jurors or prospective jurors, other than for the use of the parties and counsel, pursuant to IN ST JURY Rule 10;

   - Information relating to protection from abuse orders, no-contact orders and workplace violence restraining orders as declared confidential by IN ST 5-2-9-6, et seq.;

   - Mediation proceedings pursuant to IN ST ADR Rule 2.11, Mini-Trial proceedings pursuant to IN ST ADR Rule 4.4(C), and Summary Jury Trials pursuant to IN ST ADR Rule 5.6;

   - Information in probation files pursuant to the Probation Standards promulgated by the Judicial Conference of Indiana pursuant to IN ST 11-13-1-8(b);

   - Information deemed confidential pursuant to the Rules for Court Administered Alcohol and Drug Programs promulgated by the Judicial Conference of Indiana pursuant to IN ST 12-23-14-13;

   - Information deemed confidential pursuant to the Problem-Solving Court Rules promulgated by the Judicial Conference of Indiana pursuant to IN ST 33-23-16-16;

- All records of the Department of workforce Development as declared confidential by IN ST 22-4-19-6;
- Information regarding interception of electronic communications that is sealed or deemed confidential as set forth in IN ST 35-33.5-2-1, et seq.

iii. Information excluded from public access by specific court order;

iv. Complete Social Security Numbers of living persons;

v. With the exception of names, information such as addresses, phone numbers, and dates of birth which explicitly identifies:

- Natural persons who are witnesses or victims (not including defendants) in criminal, domestic violence, stalking, sexual assault, juvenile, or civil protection order proceedings, provided that juveniles who are victims of sex crimes shall be identified by initials only;
- Places of residence of judicial officers, clerks and other employees of courts and clerks of court, unless the person or persons about whom the information pertains waives confidentiality;

vi. Complete account numbers of specific assets, loans, bank accounts, credit cards, and personal identification numbers (PINs);

vii. All orders of expungement entered in criminal or juvenile proceedings, orders to restrict access to criminal history information pursuant to IN ST 35-38-5-5.5 or IN ST 35-38-8-5 and records excluded from public access by such orders, and information related to infractions that is excluded from public access pursuant to IN ST 34-28-5-15 or IN ST 34-28-5-16 [Editor's note: IN ST 35-38-5-5.5, IN ST 35-38-8-5 and IN ST 34-28-5-16 were repealed effective July 1, 2013; for information on orders restricting access to criminal history, refer to IN ST 35-38-9-1, et seq.];

viii. All personal notes and e-mail, and deliberative material, of judges, jurors, court staff and judicial agencies, and information recorded in personal data assistants (PDA's) or organizers and personal calendars. IN ST ADMIN Rule 9(G)(1).

F. Filing and Service Requirements

1. *Filing requirements.* Except as otherwise provided in IN ST TRIAL P Rule 5(E)(2), all pleadings and papers subsequent to the complaint which are required to be served upon a party shall be filed with the Court either before service or within a reasonable period of time thereafter. IN ST TRIAL P Rule 5(E)(1).

    a. *Filing with the court defined.* The filing of pleadings, motions, and other papers with the court as required by the Indiana Rules of Trial Procedure shall be made by one of the following methods:

    i. Delivery to the clerk of the court;

    ii. Sending by electronic transmission under the procedure adopted pursuant to IN ST ADMIN Rule 12;

    iii. Mailing to the clerk by registered, certified or express mail return receipt requested;

    iv. Depositing with any third-party commercial carrier for delivery to the clerk within three (3) calendar days, cost prepaid, properly addressed;

    v. If the court so permits, filing with the judge, in which event the judge shall note thereon the filing date and forthwith transmit them to the office of the clerk; or

    vi. Electronic filing, as approved by the Division of State Court Administration pursuant to IN ST ADMIN Rule 16. IN ST TRIAL P Rule 5(F).

    vii. Filing by registered or certified mail and by third-party commercial carrier shall be complete upon mailing or deposit. IN ST TRIAL P Rule 5(F).

    viii. All pleadings shall be filed with the Clerk, not directly with the Court, unless otherwise required by the Indiana Rules of Court. The entry of appearances and the filing of pleadings or other matters not requiring immediate Court action shall be filed with the Clerk and not in open Court. A Judge may permit papers to be filed in chambers, in which event he or she shall note thereon the filing date and transmit the papers to the Clerk. IN ST ST JOSEPH CIV Rule 201(201.2).

b. *Facsimile filing.* Unless otherwise authorized by IN ST ST JOSEPH ELECTRONIC Rule 701, electronic filing of pleadings by computerized or facsimile transmission is not permitted. IN ST ST JOSEPH CIV Rule 201(201.2).

c. *Additional copies.* In cases in which a party or counsel supplies the proposed order or decree, a sufficient number shall be prepared and filed as to provide the Clerk to retain two (2) copies, which shall be filed in the flat file and the record of judgments and orders. Should the party or counsel desire additional copies, a sufficient number of copies should be filed to effectuate that purpose. IN ST ST JOSEPH CIV Rule 201(201.6).

d. *Proof of filing.* Any party filing any paper by any method other than personal delivery to the clerk shall retain proof of filing. IN ST TRIAL P Rule 5(F).

2. *Service requirements.* Unless otherwise provided by the Indiana Rules of Trial Procedure or an order of the court, each party and special judge, if any, shall be served with: (1) every order required by its terms to be served; (2) every pleading subsequent to the original complaint; (3) every written motion except one which may be heard ex parte; (4) every brief submitted to the trial court; (5) every paper relating to discovery required to be served upon a party; and (6) every written notice, appearance, demand, offer of judgment, designation of record on appeal, or similar paper. IN ST TRIAL P Rule 5(A).

a. *Service generally.* Every motion, petition, notice, or other pleading required to be served by IN ST TRIAL P Rule 5 shall be served on all counsel of record or unrepresented parties either before it is filed or on the day it is filed with the Court, and the date of filing shall be indicated on the Certificate of Service. IN ST ST JOSEPH CIV Rule 201(201.5.1).

    i. *Copy.* A copy of the Clerk's CCS entry form of the filing shall also be served on all counsel of record or unrepresented parties whenever it contains an appearance of counsel or contains a date for Court hearing on the matter. IN ST ST JOSEPH CIV Rule 201(201.5.1).

b. *Methods of service*

    i. *Personal service.* Whenever a party is represented by an attorney of record, service shall be made upon such attorney unless service upon the party himself is ordered by the court. Service upon the attorney or party shall be made by delivering or mailing a copy of the papers to the last known address or where an attorney or party has consented to service by fax or e-mail, as provided in IN ST TRIAL P Rule 3.1(A)(4), by faxing or e-mailing a copy of the documents to the fax number or e-mail address set out in the appearance form or correction as required by IN ST TRIAL P Rule 3.1(E). IN ST TRIAL P Rule 5(B). Delivery of a copy within IN ST TRIAL P Rule 5 means:

- Offering or tendering it to the attorney or party and stating the nature of the papers being served. Refusal to accept an offered or tendered document is a waiver of any objection to the sufficiency or adequacy of service of that document;

- Leaving it at his office with a clerk or other person in charge thereof, or if there is no one in charge, leaving it in a conspicuous place therein; or

- If the office is closed, by leaving it at his dwelling house or usual place of abode with some person of suitable age and discretion then residing therein; or,

- Leaving it at some other suitable place, selected by the attorney upon whom service is being made, pursuant to duly promulgated local rule. IN ST TRIAL P Rule 5(B)(1).

    ii. *Service by the clerk.* Whenever the Clerk is required by rule or statute to give notice, the party or parties requesting such notice shall furnish the Clerk with sufficient copies of the notice to be given, along with stamped, addressed envelopes with the names and the addresses of the parties or their counsel to whom such notice is to be given. IN ST ST JOSEPH CIV Rule 201(201.5.4).

    iii. *Service on the court.* Service on a Judge may be made by delivering a copy to the Judge's secretary or mailing a copy to the Judge at his or her chambers. Service on a Judge may not be accomplished by facsimile transmission; however, a courtesy copy may be sent to the Judge's chambers by electronic mail or facsimile transmission contemporaneously with service by mail or otherwise. IN ST ST JOSEPH CIV Rule 201(201.5.5).

    iv. *Service by mail.* If service is made by mail, the papers shall be deposited in the United States mail addressed to the person on whom they are being served, with postage prepaid. Service shall be deemed complete upon mailing. Proof of service of all papers permitted to be mailed may be made by written acknowledgment of service, by affidavit of the person who mailed the papers, or by certificate of an attorney. It shall be the duty of attorneys when entering their appearance in a cause or when filing pleadings or papers therein, to have noted in the Chronological Case Summary or said pleadings or papers so filed the address and telephone number of their office. Service by delivery or by mail at such address shall be deemed sufficient and complete. IN ST TRIAL P Rule 5(B)(2).

    v. *Service by fax or e-mail.* A party who has consented to service by fax or e-mail may be served as follows:

- Service by e-mail shall be made by attaching the document being served in .pdf format. Discovery documents must also be served in accordance with IN ST TRIAL P Rule 26(A). IN ST TRIAL P Rule 5(B)(3)(a).

- Service by fax shall be deemed complete upon generation of a transmission record indicating the successful transmission of the entire document, except as provided in IN ST TRIAL P Rule 5(B)(3)(d). IN ST TRIAL P Rule 5(B)(3)(b).

- Service by e-mail shall be deemed complete upon transmission, except as provided in IN ST TRIAL P Rule 5(B)(3)(d). IN ST TRIAL P Rule 5(B)(3)(c).

- Service by fax or e-mail that occurs on a Saturday, Sunday, legal holiday, or day the court or agency in which the matter is pending is closed or after 5:00 PM local time of the recipient shall be deemed complete the next day that is not a Saturday, Sunday, legal holiday, or day that the court or agency in which the matter is pending is not closed. IN ST TRIAL P Rule 5(B)(3)(d).

c. *Serving numerous defendants.* In any action in which there are unusually large numbers of defendants, the court, upon motion or of its own initiative, may order:

    i. That service of the pleadings of the defendants and replies thereto need not be made as between the defendants;

- That any cross-claim, counterclaim, or matter constituting an avoidance or affirmative defense contained therein shall be deemed to be denied or avoided by all other parties; and

- That the filing of any such pleading and service thereof upon the plaintiff constitutes due notice of it to the parties. IN ST TRIAL P Rule 5(D).

    ii. A copy of every such order shall be served upon the parties in such manner and form as the court directs. IN ST TRIAL P Rule 5(D).

d. *Service on parties in default for failure to appear.* No service need be made on parties in default for failure to appear, except that pleadings asserting new or additional claims for relief against them shall be served upon them in the manner provided by service of summons in IN ST TRIAL P Rule 4. IN ST TRIAL P Rule 5(A).

e. *Distribution.* Counsel or an unrepresented party submitting a motion, petition, notice, pleading or proposed order shall indicate the method of distribution desired on the Clerk's CCS entry form. The Clerk will not return or distribute copies of motions, petitions, pleadings, notices or proposed orders, other than those originated by the Court, by mail unless the Clerk is provided with stamped, addressed envelopes. IN ST ST JOSEPH CIV Rule 201(201.5.3).

f. *Mailbox.* As a matter of convenience to attorneys, each court provides a mailbox for the distribution filings and orders generated by the Court, and it is the responsibility of each attorney to periodically check these mailboxes for service and distribution of court-generated filings and orders. IN ST ST JOSEPH CIV Rule 201(201.5.3).

G. Hearings

1. *Hearing on motion.* Unless local conditions make it impracticable, each judge shall establish regular times and places, at intervals sufficiently frequent for the prompt dispatch of business, at which motions

requiring notice and hearing may be heard and disposed of; but the judge at any time or place and on such notice, if any, as he considers reasonable may make order for the advancement, conduct, and hearing of actions. To expedite its business the court may direct the submission and determination of motions without oral hearing upon brief written statements of reasons in support and opposition, or direct or permit hearings by telephone conference call with all attorneys or other similar means of communication. IN ST TRIAL P Rule 73(A).

2. *Hearing dates.* Hearing dates for filings requiring Court action shall be obtained from the Court Clerk and incorporated in the CCS entry at the time the motion or other pleading is filed. If no date is obtained prior to the filing, the fact of the hearing should be noted with the date and time left blank. IN ST ST JOSEPH CIV Rule 201(201.4).

3. *Hearing on matters other than trials.* Each Judge shall reserve periods of time for hearing matters other than contested trials, such as pre-trial and post-trial motions, rules to show cause, defaults, uncontested dissolutions of marriage, etc. As necessary to minimize conflicts in scheduling, the Judges shall set these schedules after consultation. Hearings shall be scheduled as follows:

   a. *Scheduling uncontested or routine matters.* Routine matters, procedural motions, domestic relations applications for provisional relief and contempt proceedings, uncontested petitions for dissolution of marriage, and all other matters appropriate for summary consideration and disposition will be heard on the daily calendar. IN ST ST JOSEPH GEN AND ADMIN Rule 104(104.3.1).

   b. *Scheduling contested or complicated matters.* Other matters that will require a hearing reasonably estimated to last in excess of twenty (20) minutes will be scheduled as the Court's calendar allows. Counsel or a party proceeding pro se should contact the chambers of the assigned judge to arrange for an appropriate hearing date and time. IN ST ST JOSEPH GEN AND ADMIN Rule 104(104.3.2).

   c. *Scheduling motions for hearings.* Except for motions to correct error or not likely to require a hearing (as described in IN ST ST JOSEPH CIV Rule 201), all motions shall be scheduled for hearing at the time they are filed. It shall the responsibility of the moving party or counsel for the moving party to secure the date and time of the hearing from the Clerk or Court personnel who maintain the calendar for each Judge or Magistrate Judge. It shall also be the responsibility of the moving party or counsel for the moving party to coordinate the hearing date with all opposing counsel or unrepresented parties. IN ST ST JOSEPH CIV Rule 201(201.9.1).

   d. *Oral arguments on motions and other pleadings.* Unless otherwise required by St. Joseph County Civil or Indiana Trial Rules, it is within the sound discretion of the assigned Judge whether to allow oral argument; however, any party may file a request for oral argument by filing a written request by separate motion contemporaneously or at any time before the Court has ruled upon the motion or pleadings to be argued. IN ST ST JOSEPH CIV Rule 201(201.9.4).

H. Forms

1. Motion for Sanctions Forms for Indiana

   a. Signature; By party. 9 INPRAC § 4.5.

   b. Signature; Attorney. 9 INPRAC § 4.6.

   c. Signature; Attorney; Another form. 9 INPRAC § 4.7.

   d. Signature; Attorney; Another form. 9 INPRAC § 4.8.

   e. Motion to impose sanctions on defendant; Improper answer. 9 INPRAC § 4.20.

   f. Certificate of service; Personal service. 9 INPRAC § 5.7.

   g. Certificate of service; First class mail. 9 INPRAC § 5.8.

I. Checklist

   (I) ❑ Matters to be considered by moving party

       (a) ❑ Required documents

           (1) ❑ Motion and notice

           (2) ❑ Chronological Case Summary (CCS) entry form

      (3)   ❑ Proposed order

      (4)   ❑ Certificate of service

  (b) ❑ Supplemental documents

      (1)   ❑ Supporting evidence

      (2)   ❑ Facsimile cover sheet

  (c) ❑ Timing

      (1)   ❑ There are no specific time requirements for when a party may file a motion for sanctions

      (2)   ❑ A written motion, other than one which may be heard ex parte, and notice of the hearing thereof shall be served not less than five (5) days before the time specified for the hearing, unless a different period is fixed by the Indiana Rules of Trial Procedure or by order of the court

      (3)   ❑ All pleadings and papers subsequent to the complaint which are required to be served upon a party shall be filed with the Court either before service or within a reasonable period of time thereafter

(II) ❑ Matters to be considered by the responding party

  (a) ❑ Required documents

      (1)   ❑ Opposition

      (2)   ❑ Chronological Case Summary (CCS) entry form

      (3)   ❑ Certificate of service

  (b) ❑ Supplemental documents

      (1)   ❑ Supporting evidence

      (2)   ❑ Proposed order

      (3)   ❑ Facsimile cover sheet

  (c) ❑ Timing

      (1)   ❑ So long as consistent with Indiana Rules of Trial Procedure, an adverse party wishing to respond shall do so within fifteen (15) days of service

      (2)   ❑ Except as otherwise provided in IN ST TRIAL P Rule 59(D), opposing affidavits may be served not less than one (1) day before the hearing, unless the court permits them to be served at some other time

Motions, Oppositions and Replies
Motion to Compel Discovery

Document Last Updated October 2013

A. Applicable Rules

  1. *State rules*

    a. Appearance. IN ST TRIAL P Rule 3.1.

    b. Summons. IN ST TRIAL P Rule 4.

    c. Service and filing of pleadings and other papers. IN ST TRIAL P Rule 5.

    d. Time. IN ST TRIAL P Rule 6.

    e. Pleadings. IN ST TRIAL P Rule 7; IN ST TRIAL P Rule 8; IN ST TRIAL P Rule 9.2; IN ST TRIAL P Rule 10.

    f. Signing and verification of pleadings. IN ST TRIAL P Rule 11.

    g. General provisions regarding discovery. IN ST TRIAL P Rule 26

h. Methods of discovery. IN ST TRIAL P Rule 27; IN ST TRIAL P Rule 30; IN ST TRIAL P Rule 31; IN ST TRIAL P Rule 33; IN ST TRIAL P Rule 34; IN ST TRIAL P Rule 36.

i. Failure to make or cooperate in discovery; Sanctions. IN ST TRIAL P Rule 37.

j. Evidence. IN ST TRIAL P Rule 43.

k. Judgment on the evidence (directed verdict). IN ST TRIAL P Rule 50.

l. Findings by the court. IN ST TRIAL P Rule 52.

m. Summary judgment. IN ST TRIAL P Rule 56.

n. Motion to correct error. IN ST TRIAL P Rule 59.

o. Relief from judgment or order. IN ST TRIAL P Rule 60.

p. Hearing of motions. IN ST TRIAL P Rule 73.

q. Access to court records. IN ST ADMIN Rule 9.

r. Paper size. IN ST ADMIN Rule 11.

s. Facsimile transmission. IN ST ADMIN Rule 12.

t. Electronic filing and electronic service pilot projects. IN ST ADMIN Rule 16.

u. Sealing of certain records by court; Hearing; Notice. IN ST 5-14-3-5.5.

v. Sixtieth judicial circuit. IN ST 33-33-71-2.

w. Privacy and confidentiality. IN ST 5-2-9-6; IN ST 5-14-3-4; IN ST 6-4.1-5-10; IN ST 6-4.1-12-12; IN ST 6-8.1-7-1; IN ST 11-13-1-8; IN ST 12-23-14-13; IN ST 16-39-3-10; IN ST 16-41-8-1; IN ST 22-4-19-6; IN ST 31-11-1-6; IN ST 31-19-5-23; IN ST 31-19-13-2; IN ST 31-19-19-1; IN ST 31-33-18-1; IN ST 31-39-1-1; IN ST 31-39-1-2; IN ST 33-23-16-16; IN ST 35-34-2-4; IN ST 35-38-1-13; IN ST 35-38-9-1; IN ST ADR Rule 2.11; IN ST ADR Rule 4.4; IN ST ADR Rule 5.6; IN ST JURY Rule 10.

2. *Local rules*

a. Court hours and scheduling. IN ST ST JOSEPH GEN AND ADMIN Rule 104.

b. Filing, pleading, and motions. IN ST ST JOSEPH CIV Rule 201.

c. Uniform court and case number designation. IN ST ST JOSEPH CIV Rule 202.

d. Pleading and motions under IN ST TRIAL P Rule 12 and IN ST TRIAL P Rule 56. IN ST ST JOSEPH CIV Rule 206.

e. Discovery requests. IN ST ST JOSEPH CIV Rule 208.

f. Proposed order. IN ST ST JOSEPH CIV Rule 213.

g. Electronic filing of cases in St. Joseph County. IN ST ST JOSEPH ELECTRONIC Rule 701.

B. Timing

1. *Motion to compel discovery.* There are no specific timing requirements for filing a motion to compel discovery. The moving party must provide reasonable notice of his intention to file a motion to compel with the other litigants and all affected persons. 10 INPRAC § 58.51.

a. *Filing.* All pleadings and papers subsequent to the complaint which are required to be served upon a party shall be filed with the Court either before service or within a reasonable period of time thereafter. IN ST TRIAL P Rule 5(E)(1).

2. *Service.* A written motion, other than one which may be heard ex parte, and notice of the hearing thereof shall be served not less than five (5) days before the time specified for the hearing, unless a different period is fixed by the Indiana Rules of Trial Procedure or by order of the court. IN ST TRIAL P Rule 6(D).

a. *Of supporting affidavits.* When a motion is supported by affidavit, the affidavit shall be served with the motion. IN ST TRIAL P Rule 6(D).

3. *Service of opposition.* Except as otherwise provided in IN ST TRIAL P Rule 59(D), opposing affidavits

may be served not less than one (1) day before the hearing, unless the court permits them to be served at some other time. IN ST TRIAL P Rule 6(D).

    a. *Memorandum of law.* So long as consistent with Indiana Rules of Trial Procedure, an adverse party wishing to respond shall do so within fifteen (15) days of service. IN ST ST JOSEPH CIV Rule 206(206.1).

4. *Filing proposed orders.* Unless otherwise directed or given leave of the Court, proposed orders in emergency matters shall be filed within forty-eight (48) hours after a hearing; proposed orders in other matters shall be filed within seven (7) days as computed by IN ST TRIAL P Rule 6. IN ST ST JOSEPH CIV Rule 213(213.5).

5. *Computation of time*

    a. *Generally; Days excluded.* In computing any period of time prescribed or allowed by the Indiana Rules of Trial Procedure, by order of the court, or by any applicable statute, the day of the act, event, or default from which the designated period of time begins to run shall not be included. The last day of the period so computed is to be included unless it is:

        i. A Saturday,

        ii. A Sunday,

        iii. A legal holiday as defined by state statute, or

        iv. A day the office in which the act is to be done is closed during regular business hours. IN ST TRIAL P Rule 6(A).

    b. *Short periods.* In any event, the period runs until the end of the next day that is not a Saturday, a Sunday, a legal holiday, or a day on which the office is closed. When the period of time allowed is less than seven (7) days, intermediate Saturdays, Sundays, legal holidays, and days on which the office is closed shall be excluded from the computations. IN ST TRIAL P Rule 6(A).

    c. *Additional time after service by United States mail.* Whenever a party has the right or is required to do some act or take some proceedings within a prescribed period after the service of a notice or other paper upon him and the notice or paper is served upon him by United States mail, three (3) days shall be added to the prescribed period. IN ST TRIAL P Rule 6(E).

    d. *Enlargement of time.* When an act is required or allowed to be done at or within a specific time by the Indiana Rules of Trial Procedure, the court may at any time for cause shown:

        i. Order the period enlarged, with or without motion or notice, if request therefor is made before the expiration of the period originally prescribed or extended by a previous order; or

        ii. Upon motion made after the expiration of the specific period, permit the act to be done where the failure to act was the result of excusable neglect; but, the court may not extend the time for taking any action for judgment on the evidence under IN ST TRIAL P Rule 50(A), amendment of findings and judgment under IN ST TRIAL P Rule 52(B), to correct errors under IN ST TRIAL P Rule 59(C), statement in opposition to motion to correct error under IN ST TRIAL P Rule 59(E), or to obtain relief from final judgment under IN ST TRIAL P Rule 60(B), except to the extent and under the conditions stated in those rules. IN ST TRIAL P Rule 6(B).

        iii. An initial written motion for enlargement of time pursuant to IN ST TRIAL P Rule 6(B)(1) to answer a claim shall be routinely granted for an additional thirty (30) days from the original due date or other period the assigned Judge deems reasonable by written order of the Court. The motion must be filed on or before the original due date or IN ST ST JOSEPH CIV Rule 201 shall be inapplicable. IN ST ST JOSEPH CIV Rule 201(201.9.5).

          • Any motion for enlargement of time shall state the date when such response is due and the date to which time is requested to be enlarged. IN ST ST JOSEPH CIV Rule 201(201.9.5).

          • All subsequent motions for enlargement of time shall be so designated and will only be granted for good cause shown or in the interest of justice. IN ST ST JOSEPH CIV Rule 201(201.9.5).

C. General Requirements

1. *Motions, generally.* Unless made during a hearing or trial, or otherwise ordered by the court, an

application to the court for an order shall be made by written motion. The motion shall state the grounds therefor and the relief or order sought. IN ST TRIAL P Rule 7(B).

a. *Motions as distinct from pleadings.* Motions and responses to motions are not pleadings, and allegations contained in a motion are not admissions of a party. 22B INPRAC 7:2; Wachstetter v. County Properties, LLC, 832 N.E.2d 574 (Ind.Ct.App. 2005); Scott County Family YMCA, Inc. v. Hobbs, 817 N.E.2d 603 (Ind.Ct.App. 2004).

b. *Unopposed motions generally granted.* It is common for a trial court to grant procedural motions, such as motions for enlargement of time, discovery motions, or motions for continuance, unless an objection is filed. 21 INPRAC § 13.8.

c. *Proposed orders.* As directed by the Court, a party or an attorney for a party shall prepare a proposed order based on the decision rendered by the Court. The party so directed shall prepare the proposed order in a timely manner and, upon filing, shall advise the chambers of the applicable judge that the proposed order has been prepared and filed. IN ST ST JOSEPH CIV Rule 213(213.2).

   i. Prior to entry by the Court of orders granting motions or applications, the moving party or applicant (or his or her attorney) shall, unless the Court directs otherwise, furnish the Court with proposed orders in matters of compelling discovery. IN ST ST JOSEPH CIV Rule 213(213.1(4)).

d. *Attorney certification in discovery disputes.* Before any party files any motion or request to compel discovery pursuant to IN ST TRIAL P Rule 37, or any motion for protection from discovery pursuant to IN ST TRIAL P Rule 26(C), or any other discovery motion which seeks to enforce, modify, or limit discovery, that party shall:

   i. Make a reasonable effort to reach agreement with the opposing party concerning the matter which is the subject of the motion or request; and

   ii. Include in the motion or request a statement showing that the attorney making the motion or request has made a reasonable effort to reach agreement with the opposing attorney(s) concerning the matter(s) set forth in the motion or request. This statement shall recite, in addition, the date, time and place of this effort to reach agreement, whether in person or by phone, and the names of all parties and attorneys participating therein. If an attorney for any party advises the court in writing that an opposing attorney has refused or delayed meeting and discussing the issues covered in IN ST TRIAL P Rule 26(F), the court may take such action as is appropriate. IN ST TRIAL P Rule 26(F).

   iii. The court may deny a discovery motion filed by a party who has failed to comply with the requirements of IN ST TRIAL P Rule 26(F). IN ST TRIAL P Rule 26(F).

2. *Motion to compel discovery.* Motions under IN ST TRIAL P Rule 37 are intended secure compliance with discovery requests and orders, ensure that one party will not profit from a failure to comply, and provide a general deterrence to discovery abuses. 22B INPRAC 37:1; Fifth Third Bank v. PNC Bank, 885 N.E.2d 52 (Ind.Ct.App. 2008).

a. *Appropriate court.* An application for an order to a party may be made to the court in which the action is pending, or alternately, on matters relating to a deposition or an order under IN ST TRIAL P Rule 34, to the court in the county where the deposition is being taken or where compliance is to be made under IN ST TRIAL P Rule 34. An application for an order to a deponent who is not a party shall be made to the court in the county where the deposition is being taken. IN ST TRIAL P Rule 37(A)(1).

b. *Discovery disputes.* To promote the orderly and expeditious handling of cases to trial readiness, counsel shall attempt in good faith to resolve all disagreements between or among themselves concerning the necessity for and scope of discovery, the necessity to seek sanctions, and/or protection against discovery under IN ST TRIAL P Rule 26 through IN ST TRIAL P Rule 37. IN ST ST JOSEPH CIV Rule 208(208.5).

   i. After personal consultation and good faith attempts to resolve differences as to the foregoing matters, counsel for any or all parties may move to compel discovery, invoke sanctions, or seek protection against discovery as aforesaid. IN ST ST JOSEPH CIV Rule 208(208.5).

    ii. As a part of such motion, the party shall recite the date, time, and place of the personal consultations and the names of the participants. If counsel for any party advises the Court in writing that counsel for any other party has refused or delayed consultation hereby contemplated, the Court shall take such action as is appropriate to preclude, obviate, or avoid further delay. IN ST ST JOSEPH CIV Rule 208(208.5).

c. *Motion.* If a party refuses to allow inspection under IN ST TRIAL P Rule 9.2(E), or if a deponent fails to answer a question propounded or submitted under IN ST TRIAL P Rule 30 or IN ST TRIAL P Rule 31, or an organization, including without limitation a governmental organization or a partnership, fails to make designation under IN ST TRIAL P Rule 30(B)(6) or IN ST TRIAL P Rule 31(A), or a party fails to answer an interrogatory submitted under IN ST TRIAL P Rule 33, or if a party or witness or other person, in response to a request submitted under IN ST TRIAL P Rule 34, fails to respond that inspection will be permitted as requested or fails to permit inspection as requested, the discovering party may move for an order compelling an answer, or a designation, or an order compelling inspection in accordance with the request. When taking a deposition on oral examination, the proponent of the question may complete or adjourn the examination before he applies for an order. IN ST TRIAL P Rule 37(A)(2).

    i. *Evasive or incomplete answer.* For purposes of IN ST TRIAL P Rule 37(A) an evasive or incomplete answer is to be treated as a failure to answer. IN ST TRIAL P Rule 37(A)(3).

d. *Content of motion.* A motion to compel discovery should state the history of the discovery dispute, evidence that the opposing party was properly served with the discovery request, the position taken by the parties, the grounds for the motion with supporting authority, and the relief sought. In addition, the motion should include a statement demonstrating compliance with the informal dispute resolution requirements of IN ST TRIAL P Rule 26(F). 10 INPRAC § 58.51.

e. *Request for relief.* A motion to compel, filed under IN ST TRIAL P Rule 37, may request the following relief:

    i. An order compelling a discovery response;

    ii. Sanctions under IN ST TRIAL P Rule 37(D) (this rule incorporates by reference the sanctions available to a trial court to punish a party who has refused to comply with a discovery order); and

    iii. An award of attorney fees and expenses incurred to obtain an order compelling discovery. 10 INPRAC § 58.51.

f. *Effect of granting or denial of the motion*

    i. *Denied in whole or in part.* If the court denies the motion in whole or in part, it may make such protective order as it would have been empowered to make on a motion made pursuant to IN ST TRIAL P Rule 26(C). IN ST TRIAL P Rule 37(A)(2).

    ii. *Granted in part and denied in part.* If the motion is granted in part and denied in part, the court may apportion the reasonable expenses incurred in relation to the motion among the parties and persons in a just manner. IN ST TRIAL P Rule 37(A)(4).

    iii. *Motion denied.* If the motion is denied, the court shall, after opportunity for hearing, require the moving party or the attorney advising the motion or both of them to pay to the party or deponent who opposed the motion the reasonable expenses incurred in opposing the motion, including attorney's fees, unless the court finds that the making of the motion was substantially justified or that other circumstances make an award of expenses unjust. IN ST TRIAL P Rule 37(A)(4).

    iv. *Motion granted.* If the motion is granted, the court shall, after opportunity for hearing, require the party or deponent whose conduct necessitated the motion or the party or attorney advising such conduct or both of them to pay to the moving party the reasonable expenses incurred in obtaining the order, including attorney's fees, unless the court finds that the opposition to the motion was substantially justified or that other circumstances make an award of expenses unjust. IN ST TRIAL P Rule 37(A)(4). Refer to the Indiana KeyRules Motion for Discovery Sanctions document for more information.

g. *Expenses; Burden on non-prevailing party.* The non-prevailing party has the burden of proving that the reimbursement of expenses should not be awarded. 10 INPRAC § 58.51.

3. *Opposition to motion to compel; Information not reasonably accessible.* On motion to compel discovery or for a protective order, the party from whom discovery is sought must show that the information is not reasonably accessible because of undue burden or cost. If that showing is made, the court may nonetheless order discovery from such sources if the requesting party shows good cause. The court may specify conditions for the discovery. IN ST TRIAL P Rule 26(C)(9).

4. *Opposition to a motion to compel discovery.* Failure to file an answer brief or reply brief within the time prescribed shall be deemed a waiver of the right thereto and shall subject the motion to summary ruling. IN ST ST JOSEPH CIV Rule 206(206.1).

D. Documents

1. *Required documents*

   a. *Motion and notice.* The requirement of notice is satisfied by service of the motion. IN ST TRIAL P Rule 7(B). Refer to the General Requirements section of this document for information on the content of a motion to compel discovery.

   b. *Chronological Case Summary (CCS) entry form.* Every written motion, petition, or other pleading subsequent to the original complaint presented to the Clerk for filing shall be accompanied by a Chronological Case Summary (CCS) entry form in duplicate. IN ST ST JOSEPH CIV Rule 201(201.4). Refer to the Format section of this document for details on the format and filing requirements for the CCS entry form.

   c. *Disputed discovery.* In addition, the motion should attach a copy of the disputed discovery in accordance with the requirements of IN ST TRIAL P Rule 5(D). 10 INPRAC § 58.51.

   d. *Attorney certification.* Refer to the General Requirements section of this document for information on the attorney certification.

   e. *Proposed order.* Unless local practice provides differently, a party should submit a proposed order with its written motion to be signed by the judge once the motion has been granted. 21 INPRAC § 13.8. All proposed orders shall be submitted in an original plus a number of copies equal to one more than the number of pro se parties and attorneys of record contained in the prepared proof of notice under IN ST TRIAL P Rule 72(D). IN ST ST JOSEPH CIV Rule 213(213.3); IN ST ST JOSEPH CIV Rule 201(201.5.2).

   f. *Certificate of service.* An attorney or unrepresented party tendering a document to the Clerk for filing shall certify that service has been made, list the parties served, and specify the date and means of service. The certificate of service shall be placed at the end of the document and shall not be separately filed. The separate filing of a certificate of service, however, shall not be grounds for rejecting a document for filing. The Clerk may permit documents to be filed without a certificate of service but shall require prompt filing of a separate certificate of service. IN ST TRIAL P Rule 5(C).

2. *Supplemental documents*

   a. *Supporting evidence.* When a motion is based on facts not appearing of record the court may hear the matter on affidavits presented by the respective parties, but the court may direct that the matter be heard wholly or partly on oral testimony or depositions. IN ST TRIAL P Rule 43(B).

   b. *Facsimile cover sheet.* Any document sent to the Clerk of the Circuit Court by electronic facsimile transmission shall be accompanied by a cover sheet which states the title of the document, case number, number of pages, identity and voice telephone number of the sending party and instructions for filing. The cover sheet shall contain the signature of the attorney or party, pro se, authorizing the filing. IN ST ADMIN Rule 12(D).

E. Format

1. *Form of motions.* The rules applicable to captions, and the signing and form of pleadings (IN ST TRIAL P Rule 8 through IN ST TRIAL P Rule 11), apply to all motions and other papers provided under the Indiana Rules of Trial Procedure. 22B INPRAC 7:2.

   a. *Separate motions; Alternative motions.* Each motion shall be separate, while alternative motions filed together shall each be identified on the caption. IN ST ST JOSEPH CIV Rule 206(206.1).

2. *Form of pleadings*

    a. *Caption; Names of parties.* Every pleading shall contain a caption setting forth the name of the court, the title of the action, the file number, and a designation as in IN ST TRIAL P Rule 7(A). In the complaint the title of the action shall include the names of all the parties, but in other pleadings it is sufficient to state the name of the first party on each side with an appropriate indication of other parties. IN ST TRIAL P Rule 10(A); IN ST ST JOSEPH CIV Rule 201(201.3.3). If a special judge has been assigned to the case, the pleading should also identify the special judge. IN ST ST JOSEPH CIV Rule 201(201.3.3).

        i. *Title.* All pleadings or motions shall include a title, which shall delineate each topic included in the pleading. For example, where a pleading contains an answer, a motion to dismiss, and a jury request, each topic shall be set forth in the title. IN ST ST JOSEPH CIV Rule 201(201.3.4).

    b. *Paragraphs; Separate statements.* All averments of a claim or defense shall be made in numbered paragraphs, the contents of each of which shall be limited as far as practicable to a statement of a single set of circumstances, and a paragraph may be referred to by number in all succeeding pleadings. Each claim founded upon a separate transaction or occurrence and each defense other than denials may be stated in a separate count or defense whenever a separation facilitates the clear presentation of the matters set forth. IN ST TRIAL P Rule 10(B).

    c. *Adoption by reference; Exhibits.* Statements in a pleading may be adopted by reference in a different part of the same pleading or in another pleading or in any motion. A copy of any written instrument which is an exhibit to a pleading is a part thereof for all purposes. IN ST TRIAL P Rule 10(C).

    d. *Flat filing.* In order that the Clerk's files may be kept under the system commonly known as "flat filing," all papers presented to the Clerk for filing shall be flat and unfolded. Pleadings shall have no covers or backs and shall be fastened together at the top left-hand corner only. IN ST ST JOSEPH CIV Rule 201(201.1).

    e. *One side of page used.* Printing shall be on one (1) side of the paper. IN ST ST JOSEPH CIV Rule 201(201.3.2).

    f. *Copies.* All copies shall be on white paper of sufficient strength and durability to resist normal wear and tear. IN ST ST JOSEPH CIV Rule 201(201.3.1).

    g. *Margins.* Margins shall be at least one inch (1"). IN ST ST JOSEPH CIV Rule 201(201.3.2).

    h. *Double-spaced.* If typewritten, the lines shall be double spaced except for quotations, which shall be indented and single-spaced. IN ST ST JOSEPH CIV Rule 201(201.3.2).

    i. *Font size.* Type face shall be twelve (12) font size or larger within the body of the document and ten (10) font size or larger in the footnotes. IN ST ST JOSEPH CIV Rule 201(201.3.2).

    j. *Font type.* The font type must be legible and script type shall not be used. IN ST ST JOSEPH CIV Rule 201(201.3.2).

    k. *Italics.* Italicized type may be used for quotations, references, or case citations. IN ST ST JOSEPH CIV Rule 201(201.3.2).

    l. *Court and case designation.* All filings shall conform to the requirements for uniform court and case number designation set by IN ST ADMIN Rule 8. In addition, all filings shall contain the proper court and case designation as described below. IN ST ST JOSEPH CIV Rule 202.

        i. *Court designation.* Pursuant to IN ST 33-33-71-2, St. Joseph County, Indiana, constitutes the Sixtieth Judicial Circuit. The legal names of the courts within the 60th Judicial Circuit are the St. Joseph Circuit Court, the St. Joseph Superior Court, and the St. Joseph Probate Court. All filings shall properly reflect the legal name of the applicable court. Any filing may be amended, rejected, or stricken if it does not contain the proper case name and/or the legal name of the court. IN ST ST JOSEPH CIV Rule 202(202.1).

    m. *Form of CCS entry.* Every written motion, petition, or other pleading subsequent to the original complaint presented to the Clerk for filing shall be accompanied by a Chronological Case Summary (CCS) entry form in duplicate which shall contain the title and cause number of the action, the date, and the proposed entry to appear on the docket. IN ST ST JOSEPH CIV Rule 201(201.4).

        i. *Identification and signature.* The CCS entry form shall identify the party making the filing,

designate each pleading being filed, and shall be signed by counsel of record or the unrepresented litigant. IN ST ST JOSEPH CIV Rule 201(201.4).

    ii. *Date stamp.* The form shall be date stamped and presented to the Court Clerk, who shall initial the form and return the duplicate to the filing party. IN ST ST JOSEPH CIV Rule 201(201.4).

n. *Form of proposed order.* Any proposed order shall be a document that is separate and apart from the motion or application to which it relates and shall contain a caption showing the name of the court, the case number assigned to the case, and the title of the case as shown by the complaint pursuant to IN ST ST JOSEPH CIV Rule 201. IN ST ST JOSEPH CIV Rule 213(213.2).

    i. If there are multiple parties, the title may be shortened to include only the first name plaintiff and defendant with appropriate indication that there are additional parties. IN ST ST JOSEPH CIV Rule 213(213.2).

    ii. The proposed order shall be on white paper, eight and one-half by eleven inches (8 1/2" x 11") in size, and each page shall be numbered. IN ST ST JOSEPH CIV Rule 213(213.2).

    iii. The last page of the proposed order shall contain a line for the date, either "Dated _____" or "Signed on the date filemarked hereon." IN ST ST JOSEPH CIV Rule 213(213.2).

    iv. On the last page there also shall be a line for the signature of the Judge under which shall be typed "Judge, St. Joseph [Circuit or Superior or Probate] Court." IN ST ST JOSEPH CIV Rule 213(213.2).

    v. If the proposed order contains a recommendation from a Magistrate, the last page shall have a line for the signature of the Magistrate under which shall be typed "Magistrate, St. Joseph [Circuit or Superior or Probate] Court," to the left of which shall be the following, "So Recommended:" and beneath and to the left of which shall be typed, "Approved. So Ordered." IN ST ST JOSEPH CIV Rule 213(213.2).

    vi. To allow compliance with the notice requirements of IN ST TRIAL P Rule 72(D), the lower four (4) inches of the last page of the proposed order shall be left blank. The proposed order shall also include a prepared proof of notice under IN ST TRIAL P Rule 72(D), and in preparing such a notice the filing party shall complete all portions of the prepared proof of notice. IN ST ST JOSEPH CIV Rule 213(213.2).

3. *Size of papers for filing.* Effective January 1, 1992, all pleadings, copies, motions and documents filed with any trial court or appellate level court, typed or printed, with the exception of exhibits and existing wills, shall be prepared on eight and one-half by eleven inch (8 1/2" x 11") size paper. IN ST ADMIN Rule 11.

a. *Paper.* Pleadings, motions, and other papers shall be either legibly printed or typewritten on white opaque paper of good quality at least sixteen (16) pound weight, eight and one-half inches (8 1/2 ") in width and eleven inches (11") in length as required by IN ST ADMIN Rule 11. IN ST ST JOSEPH CIV Rule 201(201.3.1).

4. *Signature requirements*

a. *Signature of attorney.* Every pleading or motion of a party represented by an attorney shall be signed by at least one (1) attorney of record in his individual name, whose address, telephone number, and attorney number shall be stated, except that this provision shall not apply to pleadings and motions made and transcribed at the trial or a hearing before the judge and received by him in such form. IN ST TRIAL P Rule 11(A).

    i. The signature of an attorney constitutes a certificate by him that he has read the pleadings; that to the best of his knowledge, information, and belief, there is good ground to support it; and that it is not interposed for delay. IN ST TRIAL P Rule 11(A).

    ii. If a pleading or motion is not signed or is signed with intent to defeat the purpose of the rule, it may be stricken as sham and false and the action may proceed as though the pleading had not been served. IN ST TRIAL P Rule 11(A).

    iii. For a willful violation of IN ST TRIAL P Rule 11 an attorney may be subjected to appropriate disciplinary action. Similar action may be taken if scandalous or indecent matter is inserted. IN ST TRIAL P Rule 11(A).

b. *Signature of unrepresented party.* A party who is not represented by an attorney shall sign his pleading and state his address. IN ST TRIAL P Rule 11(A).

c. *Verification not generally required.* Except when specifically required by rule, pleadings or motions need not be verified or accompanied by affidavit. The rule in equity that the averments of an answer under oath must be overcome by the testimony of two (2) witnesses or of one (1) witness sustained by corroborating circumstances is abolished. IN ST TRIAL P Rule 11(A).

d. *Verification by affirmation or representation.* When in connection with any civil or special statutory proceeding it is required that any pleading, motion, petition, supporting affidavit, or other document of any kind, be verified, or that an oath be taken, it shall be sufficient if the subscriber simply affirms the truth of the matter to be verified by an affirmation or representation. IN ST TRIAL P Rule 11(B). IN ST TRIAL P Rule 11(B) states that the affirmation or representation should be in substantially the following language: "I (we) affirm, under the penalties for perjury, that the foregoing representation(s) is (are) true. (Signed) _____."

   i. Any person who falsifies an affirmation or representation of fact shall be subject to the same penalties as are prescribed by law for the making of a false affidavit. IN ST TRIAL P Rule 11(B).

e. *Verified pleadings, motions, and affidavits as evidence.* Pleadings, motions and affidavits accompanying or in support of such pleadings or motions when required to be verified or under oath shall be accepted as a representation that the signer had personal knowledge thereof or reasonable cause to believe the existence of the facts or matters stated or alleged therein; and, if otherwise competent or acceptable as evidence, may be admitted as evidence of the facts or matters stated or alleged therein when it is so provided in the Indiana Rules of Trial Procedure, by statute or other law, or to the extent the writing or signature expressly purports to be made upon the signer's personal knowledge. When such pleadings, motions and affidavits are verified or under oath they shall not require other or greater proof on the part of the adverse party than if not verified or not under oath unless expressly provided otherwise by the Indiana Rules of Trial Procedure, statute or other law. Affidavits upon motions for summary judgment under IN ST TRIAL P Rule 56 and in denial of execution under IN ST TRIAL P Rule 9.2 shall be made upon personal knowledge. IN ST TRIAL P Rule 11(C).

f. *Signature, verification and other requirements.* Parties and their counsel are enjoined to comply with the verification requirements of IN ST TRIAL P Rule 11, and either the moving party or the party's attorney of record shall sign all pleadings and motions before filing with the Clerk of the Court. Every motion, petition, or other pleading filed with the Clerk shall contain the name, organization, physical address, telephone number, and facsimile number of the filing party or an attorney for that party. IN ST ST JOSEPH CIV Rule 201(201.3.6).

   i. The Clerk shall not accept any motion, petition, notice or other pleading or a CCS entry form for filing from an unrepresented litigant unless the unrepresented litigant's current address and phone number appear on the pleading, and an opposing party may service notices and responses on an unrepresented litigant at any address he or she has provided on a pleading. IN ST ST JOSEPH CIV Rule 201(201.3.6).

5. *Information excluded from public access.* Every document filed in a case shall separately identify information excluded from public access pursuant to IN ST ADMIN Rule 9(G)(1) as follows:

a. Whole documents that are excluded from public access pursuant to IN ST ADMIN Rule 9(G)(1) shall be tendered on light green paper or have a light green coversheet attached to the document, marked "Not for Public Access" or "Confidential." IN ST TRIAL P Rule 5(G)(1).

b. When only a portion of a document contains information excluded from public access pursuant to IN ST ADMIN Rule 9(G)(1), said information shall be omitted [or redacted] from the filed document, and set forth on a separate accompanying document on light green paper conspicuously marked "Not for Public Access" or "Confidential" and clearly designated [or identifying] the caption and number of the case and the document and location within the document to which the redacted material pertains. IN ST TRIAL P Rule 5(G)(2).

c. With respect to documents filed in electronic format, the trial court, by local rule, may provide for

compliance with IN ST TRIAL P Rule 5 in manner that separates and protects access to information excluded from public access. IN ST TRIAL P Rule 5(G)(3).

d. IN ST TRIAL P Rule 5(G) does not apply to a record sealed by the court pursuant to IN ST 5-14-3-5.5 or otherwise, nor to records, documents, or information filed in cases to which public access is prohibited pursuant to IN ST ADMIN Rule 9(G). IN ST TRIAL P Rule 5(G)(4).

e. The following information in case records is excluded from public access and is confidential:

   i. Information that is excluded from public access pursuant to federal law;

   ii. Information that is excluded from public access as declared confidential by Indiana statute or other court rule, including without limitation:

   - All adoption records created after July 8, 1941, as declared confidential by IN ST 31-19-19-1, et seq., except those specifically declared open by IN ST 31-19-13-2(2);

   - All records relating to chancroid, chlamydia, gonorrhea, hepatitis, human immunodeficiency virus (HIV), Lymphogranuloma venereum, syphilis, tuberculosis, as declared confidential by IN ST 16-41-8-1, et seq.;

   - All records relating to child abuse as declared confidential by IN ST 31-33-18-1, et seq.;

   - All records relating to drug tests as declared confidential by IN ST 5-14-3-4(a)(9);

   - Records of grand jury proceedings as declared confidential by IN ST 35-34-2-4;

   - Records of juvenile proceedings as declared confidential by IN ST 31-39-1-2, except those specifically open under statute;

   - All paternity records created after July 1, 1941 as declared confidential by IN ST 31-14-11-15, IN ST 31-19-5-23, IN ST 31-39-1-1 and IN ST 31-39-1-2 [Editor's note: IN ST 31-14-11-15 was repealed effective May 9, 2013];

   - All pre-sentence reports as declared confidential by IN ST 35-38-1-13;

   - Written petitions to permit marriages without consent and orders directing the Clerk of Court to issue a marriage license to underage persons, as declared confidential by IN ST 31-11-1-6;

   - Only those arrest warrants, search warrants, indictments and informations ordered confidential by the trial judge, prior to return of duly executed service as declared confidential by IN ST 5-14-3-4(b)(1);

   - All medical, mental health, or tax records unless determined by law or regulation of any governmental custodian not to be confidential, released by the subject of such records, or declared by a court of competent jurisdiction to be essential to the resolution of litigation as declared confidential by IN ST 16-39-3-10, IN ST 6-4.1-5-10, IN ST 6-4.1-12-12, and IN ST 6-8.1-7-1;

   - Personal information relating to jurors or prospective jurors, other than for the use of the parties and counsel, pursuant to IN ST JURY Rule 10;

   - Information relating to protection from abuse orders, no-contact orders and workplace violence restraining orders as declared confidential by IN ST 5-2-9-6, et seq.;

   - Mediation proceedings pursuant to IN ST ADR Rule 2.11, Mini-Trial proceedings pursuant to IN ST ADR Rule 4.4(C), and Summary Jury Trials pursuant to IN ST ADR Rule 5.6;

   - Information in probation files pursuant to the Probation Standards promulgated by the Judicial Conference of Indiana pursuant to IN ST 11-13-1-8(b);

   - Information deemed confidential pursuant to the Rules for Court Administered Alcohol and Drug Programs promulgated by the Judicial Conference of Indiana pursuant to IN ST 12-23-14-13;

   - Information deemed confidential pursuant to the Problem-Solving Court Rules promulgated by the Judicial Conference of Indiana pursuant to IN ST 33-23-16-16;

- All records of the Department of workforce Development as declared confidential by IN ST 22-4-19-6;
- Information regarding interception of electronic communications that is sealed or deemed confidential as set forth in IN ST 35-33.5-2-1, et seq.

iii. Information excluded from public access by specific court order;

iv. Complete Social Security Numbers of living persons;

v. With the exception of names, information such as addresses, phone numbers, and dates of birth which explicitly identifies:

- Natural persons who are witnesses or victims (not including defendants) in criminal, domestic violence, stalking, sexual assault, juvenile, or civil protection order proceedings, provided that juveniles who are victims of sex crimes shall be identified by initials only;
- Places of residence of judicial officers, clerks and other employees of courts and clerks of court, unless the person or persons about whom the information pertains waives confidentiality;

vi. Complete account numbers of specific assets, loans, bank accounts, credit cards, and personal identification numbers (PINs);

vii. All orders of expungement entered in criminal or juvenile proceedings, orders to restrict access to criminal history information pursuant to IN ST 35-38-5-5.5 or IN ST 35-38-8-5 and records excluded from public access by such orders, and information related to infractions that is excluded from public access pursuant to IN ST 34-28-5-15 or IN ST 34-28-5-16 [Editor's note: IN ST 35-38-5-5.5, IN ST 35-38-8-5 and IN ST 34-28-5-16 were repealed effective July 1, 2013; for information on orders restricting access to criminal history, refer to IN ST 35-38-9-1, et seq.];

viii. All personal notes and e-mail, and deliberative material, of judges, jurors, court staff and judicial agencies, and information recorded in personal data assistants (PDA's) or organizers and personal calendars. IN ST ADMIN Rule 9(G)(1).

F. Filing and Service Requirements

1. *Filing requirements.* Except as otherwise provided in IN ST TRIAL P Rule 5(E)(2), all pleadings and papers subsequent to the complaint which are required to be served upon a party shall be filed with the Court either before service or within a reasonable period of time thereafter. IN ST TRIAL P Rule 5(E)(1).

    a. *Filing with the court defined.* The filing of pleadings, motions, and other papers with the court as required by the Indiana Rules of Trial Procedure shall be made by one of the following methods:

    i. Delivery to the clerk of the court;

    ii. Sending by electronic transmission under the procedure adopted pursuant to IN ST ADMIN Rule 12;

    iii. Mailing to the clerk by registered, certified or express mail return receipt requested;

    iv. Depositing with any third-party commercial carrier for delivery to the clerk within three (3) calendar days, cost prepaid, properly addressed;

    v. If the court so permits, filing with the judge, in which event the judge shall note thereon the filing date and forthwith transmit them to the office of the clerk; or

    vi. Electronic filing, as approved by the Division of State Court Administration pursuant to IN ST ADMIN Rule 16. IN ST TRIAL P Rule 5(F).

    vii. Filing by registered or certified mail and by third-party commercial carrier shall be complete upon mailing or deposit. IN ST TRIAL P Rule 5(F).

    viii. All pleadings shall be filed with the Clerk, not directly with the Court, unless otherwise required by the Indiana Rules of Court. The entry of appearances and the filing of pleadings or other matters not requiring immediate Court action shall be filed with the Clerk and not in open Court. A Judge may permit papers to be filed in chambers, in which event he or she shall note thereon the filing date and transmit the papers to the Clerk. IN ST ST JOSEPH CIV Rule 201(201.2).

b. *Facsimile filing.* Unless otherwise authorized by IN ST ST JOSEPH ELECTRONIC Rule 701, electronic filing of pleadings by computerized or facsimile transmission is not permitted. IN ST ST JOSEPH CIV Rule 201(201.2).

c. *Additional copies.* In cases in which a party or counsel supplies the proposed order or decree, a sufficient number shall be prepared and filed as to provide the Clerk to retain two (2) copies, which shall be filed in the flat file and the record of judgments and orders. Should the party or counsel desire additional copies, a sufficient number of copies should be filed to effectuate that purpose. IN ST ST JOSEPH CIV Rule 201(201.6).

d. *Proof of filing.* Any party filing any paper by any method other than personal delivery to the clerk shall retain proof of filing. IN ST TRIAL P Rule 5(F).

2. *Service requirements.* Unless otherwise provided by the Indiana Rules of Trial Procedure or an order of the court, each party and special judge, if any, shall be served with: (1) every order required by its terms to be served; (2) every pleading subsequent to the original complaint; (3) every written motion except one which may be heard ex parte; (4) every brief submitted to the trial court; (5) every paper relating to discovery required to be served upon a party; and (6) every written notice, appearance, demand, offer of judgment, designation of record on appeal, or similar paper. IN ST TRIAL P Rule 5(A).

a. *Service generally.* Every motion, petition, notice, or other pleading required to be served by IN ST TRIAL P Rule 5 shall be served on all counsel of record or unrepresented parties either before it is filed or on the day it is filed with the Court, and the date of filing shall be indicated on the Certificate of Service. IN ST ST JOSEPH CIV Rule 201(201.5.1).

   i. *Copy.* A copy of the Clerk's CCS entry form of the filing shall also be served on all counsel of record or unrepresented parties whenever it contains an appearance of counsel or contains a date for Court hearing on the matter. IN ST ST JOSEPH CIV Rule 201(201.5.1).

b. *Methods of service*

   i. *Personal service.* Whenever a party is represented by an attorney of record, service shall be made upon such attorney unless service upon the party himself is ordered by the court. Service upon the attorney or party shall be made by delivering or mailing a copy of the papers to the last known address or where an attorney or party has consented to service by fax or e-mail, as provided in IN ST TRIAL P Rule 3.1(A)(4), by faxing or e-mailing a copy of the documents to the fax number or e-mail address set out in the appearance form or correction as required by IN ST TRIAL P Rule 3.1(E). IN ST TRIAL P Rule 5(B). Delivery of a copy within IN ST TRIAL P Rule 5 means:

   - Offering or tendering it to the attorney or party and stating the nature of the papers being served. Refusal to accept an offered or tendered document is a waiver of any objection to the sufficiency or adequacy of service of that document;

   - Leaving it at his office with a clerk or other person in charge thereof, or if there is no one in charge, leaving it in a conspicuous place therein; or

   - If the office is closed, by leaving it at his dwelling house or usual place of abode with some person of suitable age and discretion then residing therein; or,

   - Leaving it at some other suitable place, selected by the attorney upon whom service is being made, pursuant to duly promulgated local rule. IN ST TRIAL P Rule 5(B)(1).

   ii. *Service by the clerk.* Whenever the Clerk is required by rule or statute to give notice, the party or parties requesting such notice shall furnish the Clerk with sufficient copies of the notice to be given, along with stamped, addressed envelopes with the names and the addresses of the parties or their counsel to whom such notice is to be given. IN ST ST JOSEPH CIV Rule 201(201.5.4).

   iii. *Service on the court.* Service on a Judge may be made by delivering a copy to the Judge's secretary or mailing a copy to the Judge at his or her chambers. Service on a Judge may not be accomplished by facsimile transmission; however, a courtesy copy may be sent to the Judge's chambers by electronic mail or facsimile transmission contemporaneously with service by mail or otherwise. IN ST ST JOSEPH CIV Rule 201(201.5.5).

iv. *Service by mail.* If service is made by mail, the papers shall be deposited in the United States mail addressed to the person on whom they are being served, with postage prepaid. Service shall be deemed complete upon mailing. Proof of service of all papers permitted to be mailed may be made by written acknowledgment of service, by affidavit of the person who mailed the papers, or by certificate of an attorney. It shall be the duty of attorneys when entering their appearance in a cause or when filing pleadings or papers therein, to have noted in the Chronological Case Summary or said pleadings or papers so filed the address and telephone number of their office. Service by delivery or by mail at such address shall be deemed sufficient and complete. IN ST TRIAL P Rule 5(B)(2).

v. *Service by fax or e-mail.* A party who has consented to service by fax or e-mail may be served as follows:

- Service by e-mail shall be made by attaching the document being served in .pdf format. Discovery documents must also be served in accordance with IN ST TRIAL P Rule 26(A). IN ST TRIAL P Rule 5(B)(3)(a).

- Service by fax shall be deemed complete upon generation of a transmission record indicating the successful transmission of the entire document, except as provided in IN ST TRIAL P Rule 5(B)(3)(d). IN ST TRIAL P Rule 5(B)(3)(b).

- Service by e-mail shall be deemed complete upon transmission, except as provided in IN ST TRIAL P Rule 5(B)(3)(d). IN ST TRIAL P Rule 5(B)(3)(c).

- Service by fax or e-mail that occurs on a Saturday, Sunday, legal holiday, or day the court or agency in which the matter is pending is closed or after 5:00 PM local time of the recipient shall be deemed complete the next day that is not a Saturday, Sunday, legal holiday, or day that the court or agency in which the matter is pending is not closed. IN ST TRIAL P Rule 5(B)(3)(d).

c. *Serving numerous defendants.* In any action in which there are unusually large numbers of defendants, the court, upon motion or of its own initiative, may order:

i. That service of the pleadings of the defendants and replies thereto need not be made as between the defendants;

- That any cross-claim, counterclaim, or matter constituting an avoidance or affirmative defense contained therein shall be deemed to be denied or avoided by all other parties; and

- That the filing of any such pleading and service thereof upon the plaintiff constitutes due notice of it to the parties. IN ST TRIAL P Rule 5(D).

ii. A copy of every such order shall be served upon the parties in such manner and form as the court directs. IN ST TRIAL P Rule 5(D).

d. *Service on parties in default for failure to appear.* No service need be made on parties in default for failure to appear, except that pleadings asserting new or additional claims for relief against them shall be served upon them in the manner provided by service of summons in IN ST TRIAL P Rule 4. IN ST TRIAL P Rule 5(A).

e. *Distribution.* Counsel or an unrepresented party submitting a motion, petition, notice, pleading or proposed order shall indicate the method of distribution desired on the Clerk's CCS entry form. The Clerk will not return or distribute copies of motions, petitions, pleadings, notices or proposed orders, other than those originated by the Court, by mail unless the Clerk is provided with stamped, addressed envelopes. IN ST ST JOSEPH CIV Rule 201(201.5.3).

f. *Mailbox.* As a matter of convenience to attorneys, each court provides a mailbox for the distribution filings and orders generated by the Court, and it is the responsibility of each attorney to periodically check these mailboxes for service and distribution of court-generated filings and orders. IN ST ST JOSEPH CIV Rule 201(201.5.3).

G. Hearings

1. *Hearing on motion.* Unless local conditions make it impracticable, each judge shall establish regular times and places, at intervals sufficiently frequent for the prompt dispatch of business, at which motions

requiring notice and hearing may be heard and disposed of; but the judge at any time or place and on such notice, if any, as he considers reasonable may make order for the advancement, conduct, and hearing of actions. To expedite its business the court may direct the submission and determination of motions without oral hearing upon brief written statements of reasons in support and opposition, or direct or permit hearings by telephone conference call with all attorneys or other similar means of communication. IN ST TRIAL P Rule 73(A).

2. *Hearing dates.* Hearing dates for filings requiring Court action shall be obtained from the Court Clerk and incorporated in the CCS entry at the time the motion or other pleading is filed. If no date is obtained prior to the filing, the fact of the hearing should be noted with the date and time left blank. IN ST ST JOSEPH CIV Rule 201(201.4).

3. *Hearing on matters other than trials.* Each Judge shall reserve periods of time for hearing matters other than contested trials, such as pre-trial and post-trial motions, rules to show cause, defaults, uncontested dissolutions of marriage, etc. As necessary to minimize conflicts in scheduling, the Judges shall set these schedules after consultation. Hearings shall be scheduled as follows:

   a. *Scheduling uncontested or routine matters.* Routine matters, procedural motions, domestic relations applications for provisional relief and contempt proceedings, uncontested petitions for dissolution of marriage, and all other matters appropriate for summary consideration and disposition will be heard on the daily calendar. IN ST ST JOSEPH GEN AND ADMIN Rule 104(104.3.1).

   b. *Scheduling contested or complicated matters.* Other matters that will require a hearing reasonably estimated to last in excess of twenty (20) minutes will be scheduled as the Court's calendar allows. Counsel or a party proceeding pro se should contact the chambers of the assigned judge to arrange for an appropriate hearing date and time. IN ST ST JOSEPH GEN AND ADMIN Rule 104(104.3.2).

   c. *Scheduling motions for hearings.* Except for motions to correct error or not likely to require a hearing (as described in IN ST ST JOSEPH CIV Rule 201), all motions shall be scheduled for hearing at the time they are filed. It shall the responsibility of the moving party or counsel for the moving party to secure the date and time of the hearing from the Clerk or Court personnel who maintain the calendar for each Judge or Magistrate Judge. It shall also be the responsibility of the moving party or counsel for the moving party to coordinate the hearing date with all opposing counsel or unrepresented parties. IN ST ST JOSEPH CIV Rule 201(201.9.1).

   d. *Oral arguments on motions and other pleadings.* Unless otherwise required by St. Joseph County Civil or Indiana Trial Rules, it is within the sound discretion of the assigned Judge whether to allow oral argument; however, any party may file a request for oral argument by filing a written request by separate motion contemporaneously or at any time before the Court has ruled upon the motion or pleadings to be argued. IN ST ST JOSEPH CIV Rule 201(201.9.4).

4. *Hearings not likely required on motion to compel.* At the time of the filing, a moving party shall bring the Motion to Compel Responses to Interrogatories or Requests for Production to the attention of the assigned judge. Such motions may be summarily granted or denied ex parte and without the necessity for hearing, unless the Judge, in his or her discretion, determines that a hearing should be scheduled on any such motion and schedules a hearing on the Court's own motion. IN ST ST JOSEPH CIV Rule 201(201.9.2(d)).

H. Forms

1. Motion to Compel Discovery Forms for Indiana

   a. Notice. 5 INPRAC § 4:6.10.

   b. Motion to compel. 5 INPRAC § 4:6.20.

   c. Motion to compel; Failure to respond. 5 INPRAC § 4:6.30.

   d. Motion to compel answers to interrogatories. 5 INPRAC § 4:6.40.

   e. Motion to compel production of documents. 5 INPRAC § 4:6.50.

   f. Motion to dismiss as sanction for failure to comply with court ordered discovery. 5 INPRAC § 4:6.60.

   g. Notice of intention to file motion to compel discovery. 10 INPRAC § 58.54.

h.   Motion to compel discovery; General form. 10 INPRAC § 58.55.

i.   Order compelling requested discovery. 10 INPRAC § 58.56.

j.   Order denying motion to compel discovery. 10 INPRAC § 58.57.

k.   Motion to compel discovery; For failure to respond to discovery requests. 10 INPRAC § 58.58.

l.   Motion to compel; Physician to release medical records. 10 INPRAC § 58.59.

m.   Motion to compel plaintiff to execute medical records release. 10 INPRAC § 58.60.

n.   Motion to compel; Production of surveillance videotape. 10 INPRAC § 58.61.

o.   Motion for order that matters be taken as established. 10 INPRAC § 58.62.

p.   Motion for order precluding litigation of issues. 10 INPRAC § 58.63.

q.   Motion to compel; Failure to permit inspection of original documents. 10 INPRAC § 58.65.

r.   Motion to compel; Answer to deposition questions. 10 INPRAC § 58.66.

s.   Certificate of service; Personal service. 9 INPRAC § 5.7.

t.   Certificate of service; First class mail. 9 INPRAC § 5.8.

I. Checklist

(I) ❑ Matters to be considered by moving party

    (a) ❑ Required documents

        (1) ❑ Motion and notice

        (2) ❑ Chronological Case Summary (CCS) entry form

        (3) ❑ Disputed discovery

        (4) ❑ Attorney certification

        (5) ❑ Proposed order

        (6) ❑ Certificate of service

    (b) ❑ Supplemental documents

        (1) ❑ Supporting evidence

        (2) ❑ Facsimile cover sheet

    (c) ❑ Timing

        (1) ❑ The moving party must provide reasonable notice of his intention to file a motion to compel with the other litigants and all affected persons

        (2) ❑ A written motion, other than one which may be heard ex parte, and notice of the hearing thereof shall be served not less than five (5) days before the time specified for the hearing, unless a different period is fixed by the Indiana Rules of Trial Procedure or by order of the court

        (3) ❑ All pleadings and papers subsequent to the complaint which are required to be served upon a party shall be filed with the Court either before service or within a reasonable period of time thereafter

(II) ❑ Matters to be considered by the responding party

    (a) ❑ Required documents

        (1) ❑ Opposition

        (2) ❑ Chronological Case Summary (CCS) entry form

        (3) ❑ Certificate of service

    (b) ❑ Supplemental documents

        (1) ❑ Supporting evidence

(2) ❑ Proposed order

(3) ❑ Facsimile cover sheet

(c) ❑ Timing

    (1) ❑ So long as consistent with Indiana Rules of Trial Procedure, an adverse party wishing to respond shall do so within fifteen (15) days of service

    (2) ❑ Except as otherwise provided in IN ST TRIAL P Rule 59(D), opposing affidavits may be served not less than one (1) day before the hearing, unless the court permits them to be served at some other time

Motions, Oppositions and Replies
Motion for Protective Order

Document Last Updated October 2013

A. Applicable Rules

1. *State rules*

    a. Appearance. IN ST TRIAL P Rule 3.1.

    b. Process. IN ST TRIAL P Rule 4.

    c. Service and filing of pleadings and other papers. IN ST TRIAL P Rule 5.

    d. Time. IN ST TRIAL P Rule 6.

    e. Pleadings. IN ST TRIAL P Rule 7; IN ST TRIAL P Rule 8; IN ST TRIAL P Rule 9.2; IN ST TRIAL P Rule 10.

    f. Signing and verification of pleadings. IN ST TRIAL P Rule 11.

    g. General provisions governing discovery. IN ST TRIAL P Rule 26

    h. Methods of discovery. IN ST TRIAL P Rule 27; IN ST TRIAL P Rule 30; IN ST TRIAL P Rule 31; IN ST TRIAL P Rule 33; IN ST TRIAL P Rule 34; IN ST TRIAL P Rule 36.

    i. Failure to make or cooperate in discovery; Sanctions. IN ST TRIAL P Rule 37.

    j. Evidence. IN ST TRIAL P Rule 43.

    k. Judgment on the evidence (directed verdict). IN ST TRIAL P Rule 50.

    l. Findings by the court. IN ST TRIAL P Rule 52.

    m. Summary judgment. IN ST TRIAL P Rule 56.

    n. Motion to correct error. IN ST TRIAL P Rule 59.

    o. Relief from judgment or error. IN ST TRIAL P Rule 60.

    p. Hearing of motions. IN ST TRIAL P Rule 73.

    q. Access to court records. IN ST ADMIN Rule 9.

    r. Paper size. IN ST ADMIN Rule 11.

    s. Facsimile transmission. IN ST ADMIN Rule 12.

    t. Electronic filing and electronic service pilot projects. IN ST ADMIN Rule 16.

    u. Sealing of certain records by court; Hearing; Notice. IN ST 5-14-3-5.5.

    v. Trade secrets. IN ST 24-2-3-1; IN ST 24-2-3-2.

    w. Sixtieth judicial circuit. IN ST 33-33-71-2.

    x. Privacy and confidentiality. IN ST 5-2-9-6; IN ST 5-14-3-4; IN ST 6-4.1-5-10; IN ST 6-4.1-12-12; IN ST 6-8.1-7-1; IN ST 11-13-1-8; IN ST 12-23-14-13; IN ST 16-39-3-10; IN ST 16-41-8-1; IN ST 22-4-19-6; IN ST 31-11-1-6; IN ST 31-19-5-23; IN ST 31-19-13-2; IN ST 31-19-19-1; IN ST

31-33-18-1; IN ST 31-39-1-1; IN ST 31-39-1-2; IN ST 33-23-16-16; IN ST 35-34-2-4; IN ST 35-38-1-13; IN ST 35-38-9-1; IN ST ADR Rule 2.11; IN ST ADR Rule 4.4; IN ST ADR Rule 5.6; IN ST JURY Rule 10.

2. *Local rules*

    a. Court hours and scheduling. IN ST ST JOSEPH GEN AND ADMIN Rule 104.

    b. Filing, pleading, and motions. IN ST ST JOSEPH CIV Rule 201.

    c. Uniform court and case number designation. IN ST ST JOSEPH CIV Rule 202.

    d. Pleading and motions under IN ST TRIAL P Rule 12 and IN ST TRIAL P Rule 56. IN ST ST JOSEPH CIV Rule 206.

    e. Discovery requests. IN ST ST JOSEPH CIV Rule 208.

    f. Proposed order. IN ST ST JOSEPH CIV Rule 213.

    g. Electronic filing of cases in St. Joseph County. IN ST ST JOSEPH ELECTRONIC Rule 701.

B. Timing

1. *Motion for protective order.* There are no specific timing requirements for filing a motion for a protective order.

    a. *Filing.* All pleadings and papers subsequent to the complaint which are required to be served upon a party shall be filed with the Court either before service or within a reasonable period of time thereafter. IN ST TRIAL P Rule 5(E)(1).

2. *Service.* A written motion, other than one which may be heard ex parte, and notice of the hearing thereof shall be served not less than five (5) days before the time specified for the hearing, unless a different period is fixed by the Indiana Rules of Trial Procedure or by order of the court. IN ST TRIAL P Rule 6(D).

    a. *Of supporting affidavits.* When a motion is supported by affidavit, the affidavit shall be served with the motion. IN ST TRIAL P Rule 6(D).

3. *Service of opposition.* Except as otherwise provided in IN ST TRIAL P Rule 59(D), opposing affidavits may be served not less than one (1) day before the hearing, unless the court permits them to be served at some other time. IN ST TRIAL P Rule 6(D).

    a. *Memorandum of law.* So long as consistent with Indiana Rules of Trial Procedure, an adverse party wishing to respond shall do so within fifteen (15) days of service. IN ST ST JOSEPH CIV Rule 206(206.1).

4. *Filing proposed orders.* Unless otherwise directed or given leave of the Court, proposed orders in emergency matters shall be filed within forty-eight (48) hours after a hearing; proposed orders in other matters shall be filed within seven (7) days as computed by IN ST TRIAL P Rule 6. IN ST ST JOSEPH CIV Rule 213(213.5).

5. *Computation of time*

    a. *Generally; Days excluded.* In computing any period of time prescribed or allowed by the Indiana Rules of Trial Procedure, by order of the court, or by any applicable statute, the day of the act, event, or default from which the designated period of time begins to run shall not be included. The last day of the period so computed is to be included unless it is:

        i. A Saturday,

        ii. A Sunday,

        iii. A legal holiday as defined by state statute, or

        iv. A day the office in which the act is to be done is closed during regular business hours. IN ST TRIAL P Rule 6(A).

    b. *Short periods.* In any event, the period runs until the end of the next day that is not a Saturday, a Sunday, a legal holiday, or a day on which the office is closed. When the period of time allowed is less than seven (7) days, intermediate Saturdays, Sundays, legal holidays, and days on which the office is closed shall be excluded from the computations. IN ST TRIAL P Rule 6(A).

    c. *Additional time after service by United States mail.* Whenever a party has the right or is required to do some act or take some proceedings within a prescribed period after the service of a notice or other paper upon him and the notice or paper is served upon him by United States mail, three (3) days shall be added to the prescribed period. IN ST TRIAL P Rule 6(E).

    d. *Enlargement of time.* When an act is required or allowed to be done at or within a specific time by the Indiana Rules of Trial Procedure, the court may at any time for cause shown:

        i. Order the period enlarged, with or without motion or notice, if request therefor is made before the expiration of the period originally prescribed or extended by a previous order; or

        ii. Upon motion made after the expiration of the specific period, permit the act to be done where the failure to act was the result of excusable neglect; but, the court may not extend the time for taking any action for judgment on the evidence under IN ST TRIAL P Rule 50(A), amendment of findings and judgment under IN ST TRIAL P Rule 52(B), to correct errors under IN ST TRIAL P Rule 59(C), statement in opposition to motion to correct error under IN ST TRIAL P Rule 59(E), or to obtain relief from final judgment under IN ST TRIAL P Rule 60(B), except to the extent and under the conditions stated in those rules. IN ST TRIAL P Rule 6(B).

        iii. An initial written motion for enlargement of time pursuant to IN ST TRIAL P Rule 6(B)(1) to answer a claim shall be routinely granted for an additional thirty (30) days from the original due date or other period the assigned Judge deems reasonable by written order of the Court. The motion must be filed on or before the original due date or IN ST ST JOSEPH CIV Rule 201 shall be inapplicable. IN ST ST JOSEPH CIV Rule 201(201.9.5).

           • Any motion for enlargement of time shall state the date when such response is due and the date to which time is requested to be enlarged. IN ST ST JOSEPH CIV Rule 201(201.9.5).

           • All subsequent motions for enlargement of time shall be so designated and will only be granted for good cause shown or in the interest of justice. IN ST ST JOSEPH CIV Rule 201(201.9.5).

C. General Requirements

1. *Motions, generally.* Unless made during a hearing or trial, or otherwise ordered by the court, an application to the court for an order shall be made by written motion. The motion shall state the grounds therefor and the relief or order sought. IN ST TRIAL P Rule 7(B).

    a. *Motions as distinct from pleadings.* Motions and responses to motions are not pleadings, and allegations contained in a motion are not admissions of a party. 22B INPRAC 7:2; Wachstetter v. County Properties, LLC, 832 N.E.2d 574 (Ind.Ct.App. 2005); Scott County Family YMCA, Inc. v. Hobbs, 817 N.E.2d 603 (Ind.Ct.App. 2004).

    b. *Unopposed motions generally granted.* It is common for a trial court to grant procedural motions, such as motions for enlargement of time, discovery motions, or motions for continuance, unless an objection is filed. 21 INPRAC § 13.8.

    c. *Proposed orders.* As directed by the Court, a party or an attorney for a party shall prepare a proposed order based on the decision rendered by the Court. The party so directed shall prepare the proposed order in a timely manner and, upon filing, shall advise the chambers of the applicable judge that the proposed order has been prepared and filed. IN ST ST JOSEPH CIV Rule 213(213.2).

    d. *Attorney certification in discovery disputes.* Before any party files any motion or request to compel discovery pursuant to IN ST TRIAL P Rule 37, or any motion for protection from discovery pursuant to IN ST TRIAL P Rule 26(C), or any other discovery motion which seeks to enforce, modify, or limit discovery, that party shall:

        i. Make a reasonable effort to reach agreement with the opposing party concerning the matter which is the subject of the motion or request; and

        ii. Include in the motion or request a statement showing that the attorney making the motion or request has made a reasonable effort to reach agreement with the opposing attorney(s) concerning the matter(s) set forth in the motion or request. This statement shall recite, in addition, the date, time and place of this effort to reach agreement, whether in person or by phone, and the names of all parties and attorneys participating therein. If an attorney for any party advises the court in writing that an opposing attorney has refused or delayed meeting and discussing the issues covered in IN ST TRIAL P Rule 26(F), the court may take such action as is appropriate. IN ST TRIAL P Rule 26(F).

   iii. The court may deny a discovery motion filed by a party who has failed to comply with the requirements of IN ST TRIAL P Rule 26(F). IN ST TRIAL P Rule 26(F).

2. *Motion for protective order*

   a. *Forms of protective order.* Upon motion by any party or by the person from whom discovery is sought, and for good cause shown, the court in which the action is pending or alternatively, on matters relating to a deposition, the court in the county where the deposition is being taken, may make any order which justice requires to protect a party or person from annoyance, embarrassment, oppression, or undue burden or expense, including one or more of the following:

     i. That the discovery not be had;

     ii. That the discovery may be had only on specified terms and conditions, including a designation of the time or place;

     iii. That the discovery may be had only by a method of discovery other than that selected by the party seeking discovery;

     iv. That certain matters not be inquired into, or that the scope of the discovery be limited to certain matters;

     v. That discovery be conducted with no one present except the parties and their attorneys and persons designated by the court;

     vi. That a deposition after being sealed be opened only by order of the court;

     vii. That a trade secret or other confidential research, development, or commercial information not be disclosed or be disclosed only in a designated way;

     viii. That the parties simultaneously file specified documents or information enclosed in sealed envelopes to be opened as directed by the court;

     ix. That a party need not provide discovery of electronically stored information from sources that the party identifies as not reasonably accessible because of undue burden or cost. IN ST TRIAL P Rule 26(C).

   b. *List in IN ST TRIAL P Rule 26(C) not exhaustive.* A court is not limited to the eight specified types of orders. A court may be as inventive as the case and the conditions require. A party or a nonparty may thus obtain any kind of protective order against any kind of discovery which is sought in the case, if "good cause" is shown. So also, however, if a protective order is sought and denied, the trial court may go further and issue an order to provide for or to permit the discovery. 2A INPRAC R 26(26.20).

   c. *Trade secrets.* A protectable trade secret has four characteristics: (1) information, (2) which derives independent economic value, (3) is not generally known, or readily ascertainable by proper means by other persons who can obtain economic value from its disclosure or use, and (4) the subject of efforts reasonable under the circumstances to maintain its secrecy. 2A INPRAC R 26(26.23.1).

     i. *Nature of determination.* The determination of whether information is a trade secret is a fact sensitive determination. 2A INPRAC R 26(26.23.1).

     ii. *Burden of proof.* The burden of proof is on the party asserting the trade secret to show that it is included in the categories of protectable trade secret information listed in the trade secrets statute. 2A INPRAC R 26(26.23.1); Northern Elec. Co., Inc. v. Torma, 819 N.E.2d 417 (Ind.Ct.App. 2004).

     iii. *Uniform trade secrets act.* The application of IN ST TRIAL P Rule 26 to trade secrets should be informed by Indiana's enactment of the Uniform Trade Secrets Act (UTSA) (refer to IN ST 24-2-3-1, et seq.), which provides states with a common legal framework for protecting trade secrets from misappropriation. 2A INPRAC R 26(26.23.1(C)).

iv. *Trade secret defined.* "Trade secret" means information, including a formula, pattern, compilation, program, device, method, technique, or process, that:

- Derives independent economic value, actual or potential, from not being generally known to, and not being readily ascertainable by proper means by, other persons who can obtain economic value from its disclosure or use; and

- Is the subject of efforts that are reasonable under the circumstances to maintain its secrecy. IN ST 24-2-3-2.

d. *Information not reasonably accessible.* On motion to compel discovery or for a protective order, the party from whom discovery is sought must show that the information is not reasonably accessible because of undue burden or cost. If that showing is made, the court may nonetheless order discovery from such sources if the requesting party shows good cause. The court may specify conditions for the discovery. IN ST TRIAL P Rule 26(C)(9).

   i. When filing a motion for protective order under IN ST TRIAL P Rule 26(C), the movant, whether a party or non-party, must allege and prove good cause for his request for protective order. The court is empowered to make any order which "justice requires to protect a party or person from annoyance, embarrassment, oppression, or undue burden or expense." Typically, this protection means that discovery will be denied altogether, or limited in scope or to specific terms. 10 INPRAC § 58.20.

e. *Party justified in resisting discovery.* A litigant is substantially justified in seeking to compel or resist discovery if reasonable persons could conclude that genuine issue existed as to whether person was bound to comply with requested discovery. 10 INPRAC § 58.20; Munsell v. Hambright, 776 N.E.2d 1272 (Ind.Ct.App. 2002).

f. *Discovery disputes.* To promote the orderly and expeditious handling of cases to trial readiness, counsel shall attempt in good faith to resolve all disagreements between or among themselves concerning the necessity for and scope of discovery, the necessity to seek sanctions, and/or protection against discovery under IN ST TRIAL P Rule 26 through IN ST TRIAL P Rule 37. IN ST ST JOSEPH CIV Rule 208(208.5).

   i. After personal consultation and good faith attempts to resolve differences as to the foregoing matters, counsel for any or all parties may move to compel discovery, invoke sanctions, or seek protection against discovery as aforesaid. IN ST ST JOSEPH CIV Rule 208(208.5).

   ii. As a part of such motion, the party shall recite the date, time, and place of the personal consultations and the names of the participants. If counsel for any party advises the Court in writing that counsel for any other party has refused or delayed consultation hereby contemplated, the Court shall take such action as is appropriate to preclude, obviate, or avoid further delay. IN ST ST JOSEPH CIV Rule 208(208.5).

g. *Award of expenses of motion.* If the motion for a protective order is denied in whole or in part, the court may, on such terms and conditions as are just, order that any party or person provide or permit discovery. The provisions of IN ST TRIAL P Rule 37(A)(4) apply to the award of expenses incurred in relation to the motion. IN ST TRIAL P Rule 26(C).

3. *Opposition to a motion for sanctions.* Failure to file an answer brief or reply brief within the time prescribed shall be deemed a waiver of the right thereto and shall subject the motion to summary ruling. IN ST ST JOSEPH CIV Rule 206(206.1).

D. Documents

1. *Required documents*

   a. *Motion and notice.* The requirement of notice is satisfied by service of the motion. IN ST TRIAL P Rule 7(B). Refer to the General Requirements section of this document for information on the content of a motion for a protective order.

   b. *Chronological Case Summary (CCS) entry form.* Every written motion, petition, or other pleading subsequent to the original complaint presented to the Clerk for filing shall be accompanied by a Chronological Case Summary (CCS) entry form in duplicate. IN ST ST JOSEPH CIV Rule

201(201.4). Refer to the Format section of this document for details on the format and filing requirements for the CCS entry form.

c. *Attorney certification.* Refer to the General Requirements section of this document for information on the attorney certification.

d. *Proposed order.* Unless local practice provides differently, a party should submit a proposed order with its written motion to be signed by the judge once the motion has been granted. 21 INPRAC § 13.8. All proposed orders shall be submitted in an original plus a number of copies equal to one more than the number of pro se parties and attorneys of record contained in the prepared proof of notice under IN ST TRIAL P Rule 72(D). IN ST ST JOSEPH CIV Rule 213(213.3); IN ST ST JOSEPH CIV Rule 201(201.5.2).

e. *Certificate of service.* An attorney or unrepresented party tendering a document to the Clerk for filing shall certify that service has been made, list the parties served, and specify the date and means of service. The certificate of service shall be placed at the end of the document and shall not be separately filed. The separate filing of a certificate of service, however, shall not be grounds for rejecting a document for filing. The Clerk may permit documents to be filed without a certificate of service but shall require prompt filing of a separate certificate of service. IN ST TRIAL P Rule 5(C).

2. *Supplemental documents*

a. *Supporting evidence.* When a motion is based on facts not appearing of record the court may hear the matter on affidavits presented by the respective parties, but the court may direct that the matter be heard wholly or partly on oral testimony or depositions. IN ST TRIAL P Rule 43(B).

b. *Facsimile cover sheet.* Any document sent to the Clerk of the Circuit Court by electronic facsimile transmission shall be accompanied by a cover sheet which states the title of the document, case number, number of pages, identity and voice telephone number of the sending party and instructions for filing. The cover sheet shall contain the signature of the attorney or party, pro se, authorizing the filing. IN ST ADMIN Rule 12(D).

E. Format

1. *Form of motions.* The rules applicable to captions, and the signing and form of pleadings (IN ST TRIAL P Rule 8 through IN ST TRIAL P Rule 11), apply to all motions and other papers provided under the Indiana Rules of Trial Procedure. 22B INPRAC 7:2.

a. *Separate motions; Alternative motions.* Each motion shall be separate, while alternative motions filed together shall each be identified on the caption. IN ST ST JOSEPH CIV Rule 206(206.1).

2. *Form of pleadings*

a. *Caption; Names of parties.* Every pleading shall contain a caption setting forth the name of the court, the title of the action, the file number, and a designation as in IN ST TRIAL P Rule 7(A). In the complaint the title of the action shall include the names of all the parties, but in other pleadings it is sufficient to state the name of the first party on each side with an appropriate indication of other parties. IN ST TRIAL P Rule 10(A); IN ST ST JOSEPH CIV Rule 201(201.3.3). If a special judge has been assigned to the case, the pleading should also identify the special judge. IN ST ST JOSEPH CIV Rule 201(201.3.3).

i. *Title.* All pleadings or motions shall include a title, which shall delineate each topic included in the pleading. For example, where a pleading contains an answer, a motion to dismiss, and a jury request, each topic shall be set forth in the title. IN ST ST JOSEPH CIV Rule 201(201.3.4).

b. *Paragraphs; Separate statements.* All averments of a claim or defense shall be made in numbered paragraphs, the contents of each of which shall be limited as far as practicable to a statement of a single set of circumstances, and a paragraph may be referred to by number in all succeeding pleadings. Each claim founded upon a separate transaction or occurrence and each defense other than denials may be stated in a separate count or defense whenever a separation facilitates the clear presentation of the matters set forth. IN ST TRIAL P Rule 10(B).

c. *Adoption by reference; Exhibits.* Statements in a pleading may be adopted by reference in a different part of the same pleading or in another pleading or in any motion. A copy of any written instrument which is an exhibit to a pleading is a part thereof for all purposes. IN ST TRIAL P Rule 10(C).

d. *Flat filing.* In order that the Clerk's files may be kept under the system commonly known as "flat filing," all papers presented to the Clerk for filing shall be flat and unfolded. Pleadings shall have no covers or backs and shall be fastened together at the top left-hand corner only. IN ST ST JOSEPH CIV Rule 201(201.1).

e. *One side of page used.* Printing shall be on one (1) side of the paper. IN ST ST JOSEPH CIV Rule 201(201.3.2).

f. *Copies.* All copies shall be on white paper of sufficient strength and durability to resist normal wear and tear. IN ST ST JOSEPH CIV Rule 201(201.3.1).

g. *Margins.* Margins shall be at least one inch (1"). IN ST ST JOSEPH CIV Rule 201(201.3.2).

h. *Double-spaced.* If typewritten, the lines shall be double spaced except for quotations, which shall be indented and single-spaced. IN ST ST JOSEPH CIV Rule 201(201.3.2).

i. *Font size.* Type face shall be twelve (12) font size or larger within the body of the document and ten (10) font size or larger in the footnotes. IN ST ST JOSEPH CIV Rule 201(201.3.2).

j. *Font type.* The font type must be legible and script type shall not be used. IN ST ST JOSEPH CIV Rule 201(201.3.2).

k. *Italics.* Italicized type may be used for quotations, references, or case citations. IN ST ST JOSEPH CIV Rule 201(201.3.2).

l. *Court and case designation.* All filings shall conform to the requirements for uniform court and case number designation set by IN ST ADMIN Rule 8. In addition, all filings shall contain the proper court and case designation as described below. IN ST ST JOSEPH CIV Rule 202.

    i. *Court designation.* Pursuant to IN ST 33-33-71-2, St. Joseph County, Indiana, constitutes the Sixtieth Judicial Circuit. The legal names of the courts within the 60th Judicial Circuit are the St. Joseph Circuit Court, the St. Joseph Superior Court, and the St. Joseph Probate Court. All filings shall properly reflect the legal name of the applicable court. Any filing may be amended, rejected, or stricken if it does not contain the proper case name and/or the legal name of the court. IN ST ST JOSEPH CIV Rule 202(202.1).

m. *Form of CCS entry.* Every written motion, petition, or other pleading subsequent to the original complaint presented to the Clerk for filing shall be accompanied by a Chronological Case Summary (CCS) entry form in duplicate which shall contain the title and cause number of the action, the date, and the proposed entry to appear on the docket. IN ST ST JOSEPH CIV Rule 201(201.4).

    i. *Identification and signature.* The CCS entry form shall identify the party making the filing, designate each pleading being filed, and shall be signed by counsel of record or the unrepresented litigant. IN ST ST JOSEPH CIV Rule 201(201.4).

    ii. *Date stamp.* The form shall be date stamped and presented to the Court Clerk, who shall initial the form and return the duplicate to the filing party. IN ST ST JOSEPH CIV Rule 201(201.4).

n. *Form of proposed order.* Any proposed order shall be a document that is separate and apart from the motion or application to which it relates and shall contain a caption showing the name of the court, the case number assigned to the case, and the title of the case as shown by the complaint pursuant to IN ST ST JOSEPH CIV Rule 201. IN ST ST JOSEPH CIV Rule 213(213.2).

    i. If there are multiple parties, the title may be shortened to include only the first name plaintiff and defendant with appropriate indication that there are additional parties. IN ST ST JOSEPH CIV Rule 213(213.2).

    ii. The proposed order shall be on white paper, eight and one-half by eleven inches (8 1/2" x 11") in size, and each page shall be numbered. IN ST ST JOSEPH CIV Rule 213(213.2).

    iii. The last page of the proposed order shall contain a line for the date, either "Dated _____" or "Signed on the date filemarked hereon." IN ST ST JOSEPH CIV Rule 213(213.2).

    iv. On the last page there also shall be a line for the signature of the Judge under which shall be typed "Judge, St. Joseph [Circuit or Superior or Probate] Court." IN ST ST JOSEPH CIV Rule 213(213.2).

    v.   If the proposed order contains a recommendation from a Magistrate, the last page shall have a line for the signature of the Magistrate under which shall be typed "Magistrate, St. Joseph [Circuit or Superior or Probate] Court," to the left of which shall be the following, "So Recommended:" and beneath and to the left of which shall be typed, "Approved. So Ordered." IN ST ST JOSEPH CIV Rule 213(213.2).

    vi.   To allow compliance with the notice requirements of IN ST TRIAL P Rule 72(D), the lower four (4) inches of the last page of the proposed order shall be left blank. The proposed order shall also include a prepared proof of notice under IN ST TRIAL P Rule 72(D), and in preparing such a notice the filing party shall complete all portions of the prepared proof of notice. IN ST ST JOSEPH CIV Rule 213(213.2).

3. *Size of papers for filing.* Effective January 1, 1992, all pleadings, copies, motions and documents filed with any trial court or appellate level court, typed or printed, with the exception of exhibits and existing wills, shall be prepared on eight and one-half by eleven inch (8 1/2" x 11") size paper. IN ST ADMIN Rule 11.

    a. *Paper.* Pleadings, motions, and other papers shall be either legibly printed or typewritten on white opaque paper of good quality at least sixteen (16) pound weight, eight and one-half inches (8 1/2 ") in width and eleven inches (11") in length as required by IN ST ADMIN Rule 11. IN ST ST JOSEPH CIV Rule 201(201.3.1).

4. *Signature requirements*

    a. *Signature of attorney.* Every pleading or motion of a party represented by an attorney shall be signed by at least one (1) attorney of record in his individual name, whose address, telephone number, and attorney number shall be stated, except that this provision shall not apply to pleadings and motions made and transcribed at the trial or a hearing before the judge and received by him in such form. IN ST TRIAL P Rule 11(A).

        i.   The signature of an attorney constitutes a certificate by him that he has read the pleadings; that to the best of his knowledge, information, and belief, there is good ground to support it; and that it is not interposed for delay. IN ST TRIAL P Rule 11(A).

        ii.   If a pleading or motion is not signed or is signed with intent to defeat the purpose of the rule, it may be stricken as sham and false and the action may proceed as though the pleading had not been served. IN ST TRIAL P Rule 11(A).

        iii.   For a willful violation of IN ST TRIAL P Rule 11 an attorney may be subjected to appropriate disciplinary action. Similar action may be taken if scandalous or indecent matter is inserted. IN ST TRIAL P Rule 11(A).

    b. *Signature of unrepresented party.* A party who is not represented by an attorney shall sign his pleading and state his address. IN ST TRIAL P Rule 11(A).

    c. *Verification not generally required.* Except when specifically required by rule, pleadings or motions need not be verified or accompanied by affidavit. The rule in equity that the averments of an answer under oath must be overcome by the testimony of two (2) witnesses or of one (1) witness sustained by corroborating circumstances is abolished. IN ST TRIAL P Rule 11(A).

    d. *Verification by affirmation or representation.* When in connection with any civil or special statutory proceeding it is required that any pleading, motion, petition, supporting affidavit, or other document of any kind, be verified, or that an oath be taken, it shall be sufficient if the subscriber simply affirms the truth of the matter to be verified by an affirmation or representation. IN ST TRIAL P Rule 11(B). IN ST TRIAL P Rule 11(B) states that the affirmation or representation should be in substantially the following language: "I (we) affirm, under the penalties for perjury, that the foregoing representation(s) is (are) true. (Signed) _____."

        i.   Any person who falsifies an affirmation or representation of fact shall be subject to the same penalties as are prescribed by law for the making of a false affidavit. IN ST TRIAL P Rule 11(B).

    e. *Verified pleadings, motions, and affidavits as evidence.* Pleadings, motions and affidavits accompa-

nying or in support of such pleadings or motions when required to be verified or under oath shall be accepted as a representation that the signer had personal knowledge thereof or reasonable cause to believe the existence of the facts or matters stated or alleged therein; and, if otherwise competent or acceptable as evidence, may be admitted as evidence of the facts or matters stated or alleged therein when it is so provided in the Indiana Rules of Trial Procedure, by statute or other law, or to the extent the writing or signature expressly purports to be made upon the signer's personal knowledge. When such pleadings, motions and affidavits are verified or under oath they shall not require other or greater proof on the part of the adverse party than if not verified or not under oath unless expressly provided otherwise by the Indiana Rules of Trial Procedure, statute or other law. Affidavits upon motions for summary judgment under IN ST TRIAL P Rule 56 and in denial of execution under IN ST TRIAL P Rule 9.2 shall be made upon personal knowledge. IN ST TRIAL P Rule 11(C).

f. *Signature, verification and other requirements.* Parties and their counsel are enjoined to comply with the verification requirements of IN ST TRIAL P Rule 11, and either the moving party or the party's attorney of record shall sign all pleadings and motions before filing with the Clerk of the Court. Every motion, petition, or other pleading filed with the Clerk shall contain the name, organization, physical address, telephone number, and facsimile number of the filing party or an attorney for that party. IN ST ST JOSEPH CIV Rule 201(201.3.6).

 i. The Clerk shall not accept any motion, petition, notice or other pleading or a CCS entry form for filing from an unrepresented litigant unless the unrepresented litigant's current address and phone number appear on the pleading, and an opposing party may service notices and responses on an unrepresented litigant at any address he or she has provided on a pleading. IN ST ST JOSEPH CIV Rule 201(201.3.6).

5. *Information excluded from public access.* Every document filed in a case shall separately identify information excluded from public access pursuant to IN ST ADMIN Rule 9(G)(1) as follows:

a. Whole documents that are excluded from public access pursuant to IN ST ADMIN Rule 9(G)(1) shall be tendered on light green paper or have a light green coversheet attached to the document, marked "Not for Public Access" or "Confidential." IN ST TRIAL P Rule 5(G)(1).

b. When only a portion of a document contains information excluded from public access pursuant to IN ST ADMIN Rule 9(G)(1), said information shall be omitted [or redacted] from the filed document, and set forth on a separate accompanying document on light green paper conspicuously marked "Not for Public Access" or "Confidential" and clearly designated [or identifying] the caption and number of the case and the document and location within the document to which the redacted material pertains. IN ST TRIAL P Rule 5(G)(2).

c. With respect to documents filed in electronic format, the trial court, by local rule, may provide for compliance with IN ST TRIAL P Rule 5 in manner that separates and protects access to information excluded from public access. IN ST TRIAL P Rule 5(G)(3).

d. IN ST TRIAL P Rule 5(G) does not apply to a record sealed by the court pursuant to IN ST 5-14-3-5.5 or otherwise, nor to records, documents, or information filed in cases to which public access is prohibited pursuant to IN ST ADMIN Rule 9(G). IN ST TRIAL P Rule 5(G)(4).

e. The following information in case records is excluded from public access and is confidential:

 i. Information that is excluded from public access pursuant to federal law;

 ii. Information that is excluded from public access as declared confidential by Indiana statute or other court rule, including without limitation:

- All adoption records created after July 8, 1941, as declared confidential by IN ST 31-19-19-1, et seq., except those specifically declared open by IN ST 31-19-13-2(2);
- All records relating to chancroid, chlamydia, gonorrhea, hepatitis, human immunodeficiency virus (HIV), Lymphogranuloma venereum, syphilis, tuberculosis, as declared confidential by IN ST 16-41-8-1, et seq.;
- All records relating to child abuse as declared confidential by IN ST 31-33-18-1, et seq.;
- All records relating to drug tests as declared confidential by IN ST 5-14-3-4(a)(9);

- Records of grand jury proceedings as declared confidential by IN ST 35-34-2-4;

- Records of juvenile proceedings as declared confidential by IN ST 31-39-1-2, except those specifically open under statute;

- All paternity records created after July 1, 1941 as declared confidential by IN ST 31-14-11-15, IN ST 31-19-5-23, IN ST 31-39-1-1 and IN ST 31-39-1-2 [Editor's note: IN ST 31-14-11-15 was repealed effective May 9, 2013];

- All pre-sentence reports as declared confidential by IN ST 35-38-1-13;

- Written petitions to permit marriages without consent and orders directing the Clerk of Court to issue a marriage license to underage persons, as declared confidential by IN ST 31-11-1-6;

- Only those arrest warrants, search warrants, indictments and informations ordered confidential by the trial judge, prior to return of duly executed service as declared confidential by IN ST 5-14-3-4(b)(1);

- All medical, mental health, or tax records unless determined by law or regulation of any governmental custodian not to be confidential, released by the subject of such records, or declared by a court of competent jurisdiction to be essential to the resolution of litigation as declared confidential by IN ST 16-39-3-10, IN ST 6-4.1-5-10, IN ST 6-4.1-12-12, and IN ST 6-8.1-7-1;

- Personal information relating to jurors or prospective jurors, other than for the use of the parties and counsel, pursuant to IN ST JURY Rule 10;

- Information relating to protection from abuse orders, no-contact orders and workplace violence restraining orders as declared confidential by IN ST 5-2-9-6, et seq.;

- Mediation proceedings pursuant to IN ST ADR Rule 2.11, Mini-Trial proceedings pursuant to IN ST ADR Rule 4.4(C), and Summary Jury Trials pursuant to IN ST ADR Rule 5.6;

- Information in probation files pursuant to the Probation Standards promulgated by the Judicial Conference of Indiana pursuant to IN ST 11-13-1-8(b);

- Information deemed confidential pursuant to the Rules for Court Administered Alcohol and Drug Programs promulgated by the Judicial Conference of Indiana pursuant to IN ST 12-23-14-13;

- Information deemed confidential pursuant to the Problem-Solving Court Rules promulgated by the Judicial Conference of Indiana pursuant to IN ST 33-23-16-16;

- All records of the Department of workforce Development as declared confidential by IN ST 22-4-19-6;

- Information regarding interception of electronic communications that is sealed or deemed confidential as set forth in IN ST 35-33.5-2-1, et seq.

iii. Information excluded from public access by specific court order;

iv. Complete Social Security Numbers of living persons;

v. With the exception of names, information such as addresses, phone numbers, and dates of birth which explicitly identifies:

- Natural persons who are witnesses or victims (not including defendants) in criminal, domestic violence, stalking, sexual assault, juvenile, or civil protection order proceedings, provided that juveniles who are victims of sex crimes shall be identified by initials only;

- Places of residence of judicial officers, clerks and other employees of courts and clerks of court, unless the person or persons about whom the information pertains waives confidentiality;

vi. Complete account numbers of specific assets, loans, bank accounts, credit cards, and personal identification numbers (PINs);

vii. All orders of expungement entered in criminal or juvenile proceedings, orders to restrict access to criminal history information pursuant to IN ST 35-38-5-5.5 or IN ST 35-38-8-5 and records excluded from public access by such orders, and information related to infractions that is excluded from public access pursuant to IN ST 34-28-5-15 or IN ST 34-28-5-16 [Editor's note: IN ST 35-38-5-5.5, IN ST 35-38-8-5 and IN ST 34-28-5-16 were repealed effective July 1, 2013; for information on orders restricting access to criminal history, refer to IN ST 35-38-9-1, et seq.];

viii. All personal notes and e-mail, and deliberative material, of judges, jurors, court staff and judicial agencies, and information recorded in personal data assistants (PDA's) or organizers and personal calendars. IN ST ADMIN Rule 9(G)(1).

F. Filing and Service Requirements

1. *Filing requirements.* Except as otherwise provided in IN ST TRIAL P Rule 5(E)(2), all pleadings and papers subsequent to the complaint which are required to be served upon a party shall be filed with the Court either before service or within a reasonable period of time thereafter. IN ST TRIAL P Rule 5(E)(1).

   a. *Filing with the court defined.* The filing of pleadings, motions, and other papers with the court as required by the Indiana Rules of Trial Procedure shall be made by one of the following methods:

      i. Delivery to the clerk of the court;

      ii. Sending by electronic transmission under the procedure adopted pursuant to IN ST ADMIN Rule 12;

      iii. Mailing to the clerk by registered, certified or express mail return receipt requested;

      iv. Depositing with any third-party commercial carrier for delivery to the clerk within three (3) calendar days, cost prepaid, properly addressed;

      v. If the court so permits, filing with the judge, in which event the judge shall note thereon the filing date and forthwith transmit them to the office of the clerk; or

      vi. Electronic filing, as approved by the Division of State Court Administration pursuant to IN ST ADMIN Rule 16. IN ST TRIAL P Rule 5(F).

      vii. Filing by registered or certified mail and by third-party commercial carrier shall be complete upon mailing or deposit. IN ST TRIAL P Rule 5(F).

      viii. All pleadings shall be filed with the Clerk, not directly with the Court, unless otherwise required by the Indiana Rules of Court. The entry of appearances and the filing of pleadings or other matters not requiring immediate Court action shall be filed with the Clerk and not in open Court. A Judge may permit papers to be filed in chambers, in which event he or she shall note thereon the filing date and transmit the papers to the Clerk. IN ST ST JOSEPH CIV Rule 201(201.2).

   b. *Facsimile filing.* Unless otherwise authorized by IN ST ST JOSEPH ELECTRONIC Rule 701, electronic filing of pleadings by computerized or facsimile transmission is not permitted. IN ST ST JOSEPH CIV Rule 201(201.2).

   c. *Additional copies.* In cases in which a party or counsel supplies the proposed order or decree, a sufficient number shall be prepared and filed as to provide the Clerk to retain two (2) copies, which shall be filed in the flat file and the record of judgments and orders. Should the party or counsel desire additional copies, a sufficient number of copies should be filed to effectuate that purpose. IN ST ST JOSEPH CIV Rule 201(201.6).

   d. *Proof of filing.* Any party filing any paper by any method other than personal delivery to the clerk shall retain proof of filing. IN ST TRIAL P Rule 5(F).

2. *Service requirements.* Unless otherwise provided by the Indiana Rules of Trial Procedure or an order of the court, each party and special judge, if any, shall be served with: (1) every order required by its terms to be served; (2) every pleading subsequent to the original complaint; (3) every written motion except one which may be heard ex parte; (4) every brief submitted to the trial court; (5) every paper relating to discovery required to be served upon a party; and (6) every written notice, appearance, demand, offer of judgment, designation of record on appeal, or similar paper. IN ST TRIAL P Rule 5(A).

   a. *Service generally.* Every motion, petition, notice, or other pleading required to be served by IN ST

TRIAL P Rule 5 shall be served on all counsel of record or unrepresented parties either before it is filed or on the day it is filed with the Court, and the date of filing shall be indicated on the Certificate of Service. IN ST ST JOSEPH CIV Rule 201(201.5.1).

    i. *Copy.* A copy of the Clerk's CCS entry form of the filing shall also be served on all counsel of record or unrepresented parties whenever it contains an appearance of counsel or contains a date for Court hearing on the matter. IN ST ST JOSEPH CIV Rule 201(201.5.1).

b. *Methods of service*

    i. *Personal service.* Whenever a party is represented by an attorney of record, service shall be made upon such attorney unless service upon the party himself is ordered by the court. Service upon the attorney or party shall be made by delivering or mailing a copy of the papers to the last known address or where an attorney or party has consented to service by fax or e-mail, as provided in IN ST TRIAL P Rule 3.1(A)(4), by faxing or e-mailing a copy of the documents to the fax number or e-mail address set out in the appearance form or correction as required by IN ST TRIAL P Rule 3.1(E). IN ST TRIAL P Rule 5(B). Delivery of a copy within IN ST TRIAL P Rule 5 means:

- Offering or tendering it to the attorney or party and stating the nature of the papers being served. Refusal to accept an offered or tendered document is a waiver of any objection to the sufficiency or adequacy of service of that document;

- Leaving it at his office with a clerk or other person in charge thereof, or if there is no one in charge, leaving it in a conspicuous place therein; or

- If the office is closed, by leaving it at his dwelling house or usual place of abode with some person of suitable age and discretion then residing therein; or,

- Leaving it at some other suitable place, selected by the attorney upon whom service is being made, pursuant to duly promulgated local rule. IN ST TRIAL P Rule 5(B)(1).

    ii. *Service by the clerk.* Whenever the Clerk is required by rule or statute to give notice, the party or parties requesting such notice shall furnish the Clerk with sufficient copies of the notice to be given, along with stamped, addressed envelopes with the names and the addresses of the parties or their counsel to whom such notice is to be given. IN ST ST JOSEPH CIV Rule 201(201.5.4).

    iii. *Service on the court.* Service on a Judge may be made by delivering a copy to the Judge's secretary or mailing a copy to the Judge at his or her chambers. Service on a Judge may not be accomplished by facsimile transmission; however, a courtesy copy may be sent to the Judge's chambers by electronic mail or facsimile transmission contemporaneously with service by mail or otherwise. IN ST ST JOSEPH CIV Rule 201(201.5.5).

    iv. *Service by mail.* If service is made by mail, the papers shall be deposited in the United States mail addressed to the person on whom they are being served, with postage prepaid. Service shall be deemed complete upon mailing. Proof of service of all papers permitted to be mailed may be made by written acknowledgment of service, by affidavit of the person who mailed the papers, or by certificate of an attorney. It shall be the duty of attorneys when entering their appearance in a cause or when filing pleadings or papers therein, to have noted in the Chronological Case Summary or said pleadings or papers so filed the address and telephone number of their office. Service by delivery or by mail at such address shall be deemed sufficient and complete. IN ST TRIAL P Rule 5(B)(2).

    v. *Service by fax or e-mail.* A party who has consented to service by fax or e-mail may be served as follows:

- Service by e-mail shall be made by attaching the document being served in .pdf format. Discovery documents must also be served in accordance with IN ST TRIAL P Rule 26(A). IN ST TRIAL P Rule 5(B)(3)(a).

- Service by fax shall be deemed complete upon generation of a transmission record indicating the successful transmission of the entire document, except as provided in IN ST TRIAL P Rule 5(B)(3)(d). IN ST TRIAL P Rule 5(B)(3)(b).

- Service by e-mail shall be deemed complete upon transmission, except as provided in IN ST TRIAL P Rule 5(B)(3)(d). IN ST TRIAL P Rule 5(B)(3)(c).

- Service by fax or e-mail that occurs on a Saturday, Sunday, legal holiday, or day the court or agency in which the matter is pending is closed or after 5:00 PM local time of the recipient shall be deemed complete the next day that is not a Saturday, Sunday, legal holiday, or day that the court or agency in which the matter is pending is not closed. IN ST TRIAL P Rule 5(B)(3)(d).

c. *Serving numerous defendants.* In any action in which there are unusually large numbers of defendants, the court, upon motion or of its own initiative, may order:

   i. That service of the pleadings of the defendants and replies thereto need not be made as between the defendants;

- That any cross-claim, counterclaim, or matter constituting an avoidance or affirmative defense contained therein shall be deemed to be denied or avoided by all other parties; and

- That the filing of any such pleading and service thereof upon the plaintiff constitutes due notice of it to the parties. IN ST TRIAL P Rule 5(D).

   ii. A copy of every such order shall be served upon the parties in such manner and form as the court directs. IN ST TRIAL P Rule 5(D).

d. *Service on parties in default for failure to appear.* No service need be made on parties in default for failure to appear, except that pleadings asserting new or additional claims for relief against them shall be served upon them in the manner provided by service of summons in IN ST TRIAL P Rule 4. IN ST TRIAL P Rule 5(A).

e. *Distribution.* Counsel or an unrepresented party submitting a motion, petition, notice, pleading or proposed order shall indicate the method of distribution desired on the Clerk's CCS entry form. The Clerk will not return or distribute copies of motions, petitions, pleadings, notices or proposed orders, other than those originated by the Court, by mail unless the Clerk is provided with stamped, addressed envelopes. IN ST ST JOSEPH CIV Rule 201(201.5.3).

f. *Mailbox.* As a matter of convenience to attorneys, each court provides a mailbox for the distribution filings and orders generated by the Court, and it is the responsibility of each attorney to periodically check these mailboxes for service and distribution of court-generated filings and orders. IN ST ST JOSEPH CIV Rule 201(201.5.3).

G. Hearings

1. *Hearing on motion.* Unless local conditions make it impracticable, each judge shall establish regular times and places, at intervals sufficiently frequent for the prompt dispatch of business, at which motions requiring notice and hearing may be heard and disposed of; but the judge at any time or place and on such notice, if any, as he considers reasonable may make order for the advancement, conduct, and hearing of actions. To expedite its business the court may direct the submission and determination of motions without oral hearing upon brief written statements of reasons in support and opposition, or direct or permit hearings by telephone conference call with all attorneys or other similar means of communication. IN ST TRIAL P Rule 73(A).

2. *Hearing dates.* Hearing dates for filings requiring Court action shall be obtained from the Court Clerk and incorporated in the CCS entry at the time the motion or other pleading is filed. If no date is obtained prior to the filing, the fact of the hearing should be noted with the date and time left blank. IN ST ST JOSEPH CIV Rule 201(201.4).

3. *Hearing on matters other than trials.* Each Judge shall reserve periods of time for hearing matters other than contested trials, such as pre-trial and post-trial motions, rules to show cause, defaults, uncontested dissolutions of marriage, etc. As necessary to minimize conflicts in scheduling, the Judges shall set these schedules after consultation. Hearings shall be scheduled as follows:

a. *Scheduling uncontested or routine matters.* Routine matters, procedural motions, domestic relations applications for provisional relief and contempt proceedings, uncontested petitions for dissolution of marriage, and all other matters appropriate for summary consideration and disposition will be heard on the daily calendar. IN ST ST JOSEPH GEN AND ADMIN Rule 104(104.3.1).

b. *Scheduling contested or complicated matters.* Other matters that will require a hearing reasonably estimated to last in excess of twenty (20) minutes will be scheduled as the Court's calendar allows. Counsel or a party proceeding pro se should contact the chambers of the assigned judge to arrange for an appropriate hearing date and time. IN ST ST JOSEPH GEN AND ADMIN Rule 104(104.3.2).

c. *Scheduling motions for hearings.* Except for motions to correct error or not likely to require a hearing (as described in IN ST ST JOSEPH CIV Rule 201), all motions shall be scheduled for hearing at the time they are filed. It shall the responsibility of the moving party or counsel for the moving party to secure the date and time of the hearing from the Clerk or Court personnel who maintain the calendar for each Judge or Magistrate Judge. It shall also be the responsibility of the moving party or counsel for the moving party to coordinate the hearing date with all opposing counsel or unrepresented parties. IN ST ST JOSEPH CIV Rule 201(201.9.1).

d. *Oral arguments on motions and other pleadings.* Unless otherwise required by St. Joseph County Civil or Indiana Trial Rules, it is within the sound discretion of the assigned Judge whether to allow oral argument; however, any party may file a request for oral argument by filing a written request by separate motion contemporaneously or at any time before the Court has ruled upon the motion or pleadings to be argued. IN ST ST JOSEPH CIV Rule 201(201.9.4).

H. Forms

1. Motion for Protective Order Forms for Indiana

a. Pending motion. 5 INPRAC § 4:5.1.

b. Relevancy. 5 INPRAC § 4:5.2.

c. Unduly burdensome. 5 INPRAC § 4:5.3.

d. Privileged. 5 INPRAC § 4:5.4.

e. Mental impressions and legal conclusions. 5 INPRAC § 4:5.5.

f. Expert reports and papers. 5 INPRAC § 4:5.6.

g. Quash subpoena duces tecum. 5 INPRAC § 4:5.7.

h. Quash subpoena duces tecum; Non-party. 5 INPRAC § 4:5.8.

i. Trade secrets and confidential information. 5 INPRAC § 4:5.9.

j. Motion to lift protective order. 5 INPRAC § 4:5.10.

k. Motion for protective order; Discovery not be had; Protection against disclosure of expert report and papers. 10 INPRAC § 58.22.

l. Motion for protective order; Discovery not relevant to subject matter of action. 10 INPRAC § 58.23.

m. Motion for protective order; Discovery unduly burdensome; Alternative request for deposition. 10 INPRAC § 58.24.

n. Motion for protective order; Challenging date and time of deposition. 10 INPRAC § 58.25.

o. Motion for protective order; Challenging place of deposition. 10 INPRAC § 58.26.

p. Motion for protective order; To prevent the disclosure of trade secrets and confidential research and development. 10 INPRAC § 58.27.

q. Motion for protective order; To preclude further deposition of corporate officer. 10 INPRAC § 58.28.

r. Motion for protective order; To preclude taking expert deposition; Failure to obtain court order or to disclose expert opinions. 10 INPRAC § 58.30.

s. Motion for protective order; To preclude disclosure of privileged matters. 10 INPRAC § 58.31.

t. Motion for protective order; To have plaintiff's attorney and physician present during plaintiff's physical examination; Request to tape record physical examination. 10 INPRAC § 58.32.

u. Motion for protective order; To preclude defendant's attorney from conducting an informal interview of plaintiff's treating physician. 10 INPRAC § 58.33.

v. Motion for protective order; To produce documents at responding party's place of business. 10 INPRAC § 58.34.

w. Motion for protective order; Discovery limited to certain matter until court rules on pending motion. 10 INPRAC § 58.35.

x. Motion for protective order; Answers to discovery to be sealed to protect confidential commercial information. 10 INPRAC § 58.36.

y. Certificate of service; Personal service. 9 INPRAC § 5.7.

z. Certificate of service; First class mail. 9 INPRAC § 5.8.

I. Checklist

(I) ❏ Matters to be considered by moving party

  (a) ❏ Required documents

    (1) ❏ Motion and notice

    (2) ❏ Chronological Case Summary (CCS) entry form

    (3) ❏ Attorney certification

    (4) ❏ Proposed order

    (5) ❏ Certificate of service

  (b) ❏ Supplemental documents

    (1) ❏ Supporting evidence

    (2) ❏ Facsimile cover sheet

  (c) ❏ Timing

    (1) ❏ There are no specific timing requirements for filing a motion for a protective order

    (2) ❏ A written motion, other than one which may be heard ex parte, and notice of the hearing thereof shall be served not less than five (5) days before the time specified for the hearing, unless a different period is fixed by the Indiana Rules of Trial Procedure or by order of the court

    (3) ❏ All pleadings and papers subsequent to the complaint which are required to be served upon a party shall be filed with the Court either before service or within a reasonable period of time thereafter

(II) ❏ Matters to be considered by the responding party

  (a) ❏ Required documents

    (1) ❏ Opposition

    (2) ❏ Chronological Case Summary (CCS) entry form

    (3) ❏ Certificate of service

  (b) ❏ Supplemental documents

    (1) ❏ Supporting evidence

    (2) ❏ Proposed order

    (3) ❏ Facsimile cover sheet

  (c) ❏ Timing

    (1) ❏ So long as consistent with Indiana Rules of Trial Procedure, an adverse party wishing to respond shall do so within fifteen (15) days of service

    (2) ❏ Except as otherwise provided in IN ST TRIAL P Rule 59(D), opposing affidavits may be served not less than one (1) day before the hearing, unless the court permits them to be served at some other time

Motions, Oppositions and Replies
Motion for Discovery Sanctions

Document Last Updated October 2013

A. Applicable Rules

1. *State rules*

    a. Appearance. IN ST TRIAL P Rule 3.1.

    b. Process. IN ST TRIAL P Rule 4.

    c. Service and filing of pleadings and other papers. IN ST TRIAL P Rule 5.

    d. Time. IN ST TRIAL P Rule 6.

    e. Pleadings. IN ST TRIAL P Rule 7; IN ST TRIAL P Rule 8; IN ST TRIAL P Rule 9.2; IN ST TRIAL P Rule 10.

    f. Signing and verification of pleadings. IN ST TRIAL P Rule 11.

    g. General provisions governing discovery. IN ST TRIAL P Rule 26

    h. Methods of discovery. IN ST TRIAL P Rule 27; IN ST TRIAL P Rule 30; IN ST TRIAL P Rule 31; IN ST TRIAL P Rule 33; IN ST TRIAL P Rule 34; IN ST TRIAL P Rule 35; IN ST TRIAL P Rule 36.

    i. Failure to make or cooperate in discovery; Sanctions. IN ST TRIAL P Rule 37.

    j. Evidence. IN ST TRIAL P Rule 43.

    k. Judgment on the evidence (directed verdict). IN ST TRIAL P Rule 50.

    l. Findings by the court. IN ST TRIAL P Rule 52.

    m. Summary judgment. IN ST TRIAL P Rule 56.

    n. Motion to correct error. IN ST TRIAL P Rule 59.

    o. Relief from judgment or order. IN ST TRIAL P Rule 60.

    p. Hearing of motions. IN ST TRIAL P Rule 73.

    q. Access to court records. IN ST ADMIN Rule 9.

    r. Paper size. IN ST ADMIN Rule 11.

    s. Facsimile transmission. IN ST ADMIN Rule 12.

    t. Electronic filing and electronic service pilot projects. IN ST ADMIN Rule 16.

    u. Sealing of certain records by court; Hearing; Notice. IN ST 5-14-3-5.5.

    v. Privacy and confidentiality. IN ST 5-2-9-6; IN ST 5-14-3-4; IN ST 6-4.1-5-10; IN ST 6-4.1-12-12; IN ST 6-8.1-7-1; IN ST 11-13-1-8; IN ST 12-23-14-13; IN ST 16-39-3-10; IN ST 16-41-8-1; IN ST 22-4-19-6; IN ST 31-11-1-6; IN ST 31-19-5-23; IN ST 31-19-13-2; IN ST 31-19-19-1; IN ST 31-33-18-1; IN ST 31-39-1-1; IN ST 31-39-1-2; IN ST 33-23-16-16; IN ST 35-34-2-4; IN ST 35-38-1-13; IN ST 35-38-9-1; IN ST ADR Rule 2.11; IN ST ADR Rule 4.4; IN ST ADR Rule 5.6; IN ST JURY Rule 10.

2. *Local rules*

    a. Court hours and scheduling. IN ST ST JOSEPH GEN AND ADMIN Rule 104.

    b. Filing, pleading, and motions. IN ST ST JOSEPH CIV Rule 201.

    c. Uniform court and case number designation. IN ST ST JOSEPH CIV Rule 202.

    d. Pleading and motions under IN ST TRIAL P Rule 12 and IN ST TRIAL P Rule 56. IN ST ST JOSEPH CIV Rule 206.

    e. Discovery requests. IN ST ST JOSEPH CIV Rule 208.

    f.   Proposed order. IN ST ST JOSEPH CIV Rule 213.

    g.   Electronic filing of cases in St. Joseph County. IN ST ST JOSEPH ELECTRONIC Rule 701.

B. Timing

1. *Motion for discovery sanctions.* There are no specific timing requirements for filing a motion for discovery sanctions.

    a.   *Filing.* All pleadings and papers subsequent to the complaint which are required to be served upon a party shall be filed with the Court either before service or within a reasonable period of time thereafter. IN ST TRIAL P Rule 5(E)(1).

2. *Service.* A written motion, other than one which may be heard ex parte, and notice of the hearing thereof shall be served not less than five (5) days before the time specified for the hearing, unless a different period is fixed by the Indiana Rules of Trial Procedure or by order of the court. IN ST TRIAL P Rule 6(D).

    a.   *Of supporting affidavits.* When a motion is supported by affidavit, the affidavit shall be served with the motion. IN ST TRIAL P Rule 6(D).

3. *Service of opposition.* Except as otherwise provided in IN ST TRIAL P Rule 59(D), opposing affidavits may be served not less than one (1) day before the hearing, unless the court permits them to be served at some other time. IN ST TRIAL P Rule 6(D).

    a.   *Memorandum of law.* So long as consistent with Indiana Rules of Trial Procedure, an adverse party wishing to respond shall do so within fifteen (15) days of service. IN ST ST JOSEPH CIV Rule 206(206.1).

4. *Filing proposed orders.* Unless otherwise directed or given leave of the Court, proposed orders in emergency matters shall be filed within forty-eight (48) hours after a hearing; proposed orders in other matters shall be filed within seven (7) days as computed by IN ST TRIAL P Rule 6. IN ST ST JOSEPH CIV Rule 213(213.5).

5. *Computation of time*

    a.   *Generally; Days excluded.* In computing any period of time prescribed or allowed by the Indiana Rules of Trial Procedure, by order of the court, or by any applicable statute, the day of the act, event, or default from which the designated period of time begins to run shall not be included. The last day of the period so computed is to be included unless it is:

        i.   A Saturday,

        ii.   A Sunday,

        iii.   A legal holiday as defined by state statute, or

        iv.   A day the office in which the act is to be done is closed during regular business hours. IN ST TRIAL P Rule 6(A).

    b.   *Short periods.* In any event, the period runs until the end of the next day that is not a Saturday, a Sunday, a legal holiday, or a day on which the office is closed. When the period of time allowed is less than seven (7) days, intermediate Saturdays, Sundays, legal holidays, and days on which the office is closed shall be excluded from the computations. IN ST TRIAL P Rule 6(A).

    c.   *Additional time after service by United States mail.* Whenever a party has the right or is required to do some act or take some proceedings within a prescribed period after the service of a notice or other paper upon him and the notice or paper is served upon him by United States mail, three (3) days shall be added to the prescribed period. IN ST TRIAL P Rule 6(E).

    d.   *Enlargement of time.* When an act is required or allowed to be done at or within a specific time by the Indiana Rules of Trial Procedure, the court may at any time for cause shown:

        i.   Order the period enlarged, with or without motion or notice, if request therefor is made before the expiration of the period originally prescribed or extended by a previous order; or

        ii.   Upon motion made after the expiration of the specific period, permit the act to be done where the failure to act was the result of excusable neglect; but, the court may not extend the time for taking any action for judgment on the evidence under IN ST TRIAL P Rule 50(A), amendment of findings and judgment under IN ST TRIAL P Rule 52(B), to correct errors under IN ST TRIAL P Rule 59(C), statement in opposition to motion to correct error under IN ST TRIAL P Rule 59(E), or to obtain relief from final judgment under IN ST TRIAL P Rule 60(B), except to the extent and under the conditions stated in those rules. IN ST TRIAL P Rule 6(B).

iii. An initial written motion for enlargement of time pursuant to IN ST TRIAL P Rule 6(B)(1) to answer a claim shall be routinely granted for an additional thirty (30) days from the original due date or other period the assigned Judge deems reasonable by written order of the Court. The motion must be filed on or before the original due date or IN ST ST JOSEPH CIV Rule 201 shall be inapplicable. IN ST ST JOSEPH CIV Rule 201(201.9.5).

- Any motion for enlargement of time shall state the date when such response is due and the date to which time is requested to be enlarged. IN ST ST JOSEPH CIV Rule 201(201.9.5).

- All subsequent motions for enlargement of time shall be so designated and will only be granted for good cause shown or in the interest of justice. IN ST ST JOSEPH CIV Rule 201(201.9.5).

C. General Requirements

1. *Motions, generally.* Unless made during a hearing or trial, or otherwise ordered by the court, an application to the court for an order shall be made by written motion. The motion shall state the grounds therefor and the relief or order sought. IN ST TRIAL P Rule 7(B).

   a. *Motions as distinct from pleadings.* Motions and responses to motions are not pleadings, and allegations contained in a motion are not admissions of a party. 22B INPRAC 7:2; Wachstetter v. County Properties, LLC, 832 N.E.2d 574 (Ind.Ct.App. 2005); Scott County Family YMCA, Inc. v. Hobbs, 817 N.E.2d 603 (Ind.Ct.App. 2004).

   b. *Unopposed motions generally granted.* It is common for a trial court to grant procedural motions, such as motions for enlargement of time, discovery motions, or motions for continuance, unless an objection is filed. 21 INPRAC § 13.8.

   c. *Proposed orders.* As directed by the Court, a party or an attorney for a party shall prepare a proposed order based on the decision rendered by the Court. The party so directed shall prepare the proposed order in a timely manner and, upon filing, shall advise the chambers of the applicable judge that the proposed order has been prepared and filed. IN ST ST JOSEPH CIV Rule 213(213.2).

   d. *Attorney certification in discovery disputes.* Before any party files any motion or request to compel discovery pursuant to IN ST TRIAL P Rule 37, or any motion for protection from discovery pursuant to IN ST TRIAL P Rule 26(C), or any other discovery motion which seeks to enforce, modify, or limit discovery, that party shall:

      i. Make a reasonable effort to reach agreement with the opposing party concerning the matter which is the subject of the motion or request; and

      ii. Include in the motion or request a statement showing that the attorney making the motion or request has made a reasonable effort to reach agreement with the opposing attorney(s) concerning the matter(s) set forth in the motion or request. This statement shall recite, in addition, the date, time and place of this effort to reach agreement, whether in person or by phone, and the names of all parties and attorneys participating therein. If an attorney for any party advises the court in writing that an opposing attorney has refused or delayed meeting and discussing the issues covered in IN ST TRIAL P Rule 26(F), the court may take such action as is appropriate. IN ST TRIAL P Rule 26(F).

      iii. The court may deny a discovery motion filed by a party who has failed to comply with the requirements of IN ST TRIAL P Rule 26(F). IN ST TRIAL P Rule 26(F).

2. *Motion for discovery sanctions*

   a. *Related to a motion to compel; Award of sanctions on motion*

      i. *Motion granted.* If the motion is granted, the court shall, after opportunity for hearing, require the party or deponent whose conduct necessitated the motion or the party or attorney advising such conduct or both of them to pay to the moving party the reasonable expenses incurred in obtaining the order, including attorney's fees, unless the court finds that the opposition to the motion was substantially justified or that other circumstances make an award of expenses unjust. IN ST TRIAL P Rule 37(A)(4).

ii. *Motion denied.* If the motion is denied, the court shall, after opportunity for hearing, require the moving party or the attorney advising the motion or both of them to pay to the party or deponent who opposed the motion the reasonable expenses incurred in opposing the motion, including attorney's fees, unless the court finds that the making of the motion was substantially justified or that other circumstances make an award of expenses unjust. IN ST TRIAL P Rule 37(A)(4).

iii. *Granted in part and denied in part.* If the motion is granted in part and denied in part, the court may apportion the reasonable expenses incurred in relation to the motion among the parties and persons in a just manner. IN ST TRIAL P Rule 37(A)(4).

iv. Refer to the Indiana KeyRules Motion to Compel Discovery document for more information.

b. *Failure to comply with order.* The trial court may impose sanctions upon a party who fails to obey an order regarding discovery. 22 INPRAC § 27.7. The first step to invoking sanctions under IN ST TRIAL P Rule 37(B) is to file a motion to compel discovery under IN ST TRIAL P Rule 37(A) and obtain an order from the court requiring the opposing party to take a specific action in discovery. If the opposing party then fails to take the action mandated by the trial court's discovery order, the second step is to return to the trial court and file a motion for sanctions under IN ST TRIAL P Rule 37(B). 22 INPRAC § 27.7.

i. *Sanctions by court in county where deposition is taken.* If a deponent fails to be sworn or to answer a question after being directed to do so by the court in the county in which the deposition is being taken, the failure may be considered a contempt of that court. IN ST TRIAL P Rule 37(B)(1).

ii. *Sanctions by court in which action is pending.* If a party or an officer, director, or managing agent of a party or an organization, including a governmental organization, or a person designated under IN ST TRIAL P Rule 30(B)(6) or IN ST TRIAL P Rule 31(A) to testify on behalf of a party or an organization, including a governmental organization, fails to obey an order to provide or permit discovery, including an order made under IN ST TRIAL P Rule 37(A) or IN ST TRIAL P Rule 35, the court in which the action is pending may make such orders in regard to the failure as are just, and among others the following:

- An order that the matters regarding which the order was made or any other designated facts shall be taken to be established for the purposes of the action in accordance with the claim of the party obtaining the order;

- An order refusing to allow the disobedient party to support or oppose designated claims or defenses, or prohibiting him from introducing designated matters in evidence;

- An order striking out pleadings or parts thereof, or staying further proceedings until the order is obeyed, or dismissing the action or proceeding or any part thereof, or rendering a judgment by default against the disobedient party;

- In lieu of any of the foregoing orders or in addition thereto, an order treating as a contempt of court the failure to obey any orders except an order to submit to a physical or mental examination under IN ST TRIAL P Rule 35;

- Where a party has failed to comply with an order under IN ST TRIAL P Rule 35(A) requiring him to produce another for examination, such orders as are listed in IN ST TRIAL P Rule 37(B)(2)(a), IN ST TRIAL P Rule 37(B)(2)(b), and IN ST TRIAL P Rule 37(B)(2)(c), unless the party failing to comply shows that he is unable to produce such person for examination. IN ST TRIAL P Rule 37(B)(2).

- In lieu of any of the foregoing orders or in addition thereto, the court shall require the party failing to obey the order or the attorney advising him or both to pay the reasonable expenses, including attorney's fees, caused by the failure, unless the court finds that the failure was substantially justified or that other circumstances make an award of expenses unjust. IN ST TRIAL P Rule 37(B)(2).

c. *Discovery disputes.* To promote the orderly and expeditious handling of cases to trial readiness, counsel shall attempt in good faith to resolve all disagreements between or among themselves concerning the necessity for and scope of discovery, the necessity to seek sanctions, and/or protection against discovery under IN ST TRIAL P Rule 26 through IN ST TRIAL P Rule 37. IN ST ST JOSEPH CIV Rule 208(208.5).

    i. After personal consultation and good faith attempts to resolve differences as to the foregoing matters, counsel for any or all parties may move to compel discovery, invoke sanctions, or seek protection against discovery as aforesaid. IN ST ST JOSEPH CIV Rule 208(208.5).

    ii. As a part of such motion, the party shall recite the date, time, and place of the personal consultations and the names of the participants. If counsel for any party advises the Court in writing that counsel for any other party has refused or delayed consultation hereby contemplated, the Court shall take such action as is appropriate to preclude, obviate, or avoid further delay. IN ST ST JOSEPH CIV Rule 208(208.5).

d. *Expenses on failure to admit.* If a party fails to admit the genuineness of any document or the truth of any matter as requested under IN ST TRIAL P Rule 36, and if the party requesting the admissions thereafter proves the genuineness of the document or the truth of the matter, he may apply to the court for an order requiring the other party to pay him the reasonable expenses incurred in making that proof, including reasonable attorney's fees. The court shall make the order unless it finds that:

    i. The request was held objectionable pursuant to IN ST TRIAL P Rule 36(A), or

    ii. The admission sought was of no substantial importance, or

    iii. The party failing to admit had reasonable ground to believe that he might prevail on the matter, or

    iv. There was other good reason for the failure to admit. IN ST TRIAL P Rule 37(C).

e. *Failure of party to attend at own deposition or serve answers to interrogatories or respond to requests for inspection*

    i. *Court order for failure to provide discovery.* If a party or an officer, director, or managing agent of a party or an organization, including without limitation a governmental organization, or a person designated under IN ST TRIAL P Rule 30(B)(6) or IN ST TRIAL P Rule 31(A) to testify on behalf of a party or an organization, including without limitation a governmental organization, fails (1) to appear before the officer who is to take his deposition, after being served with a proper notice, or (2) to serve answers or objections to interrogatories submitted under IN ST TRIAL P Rule 33, after proper service of the interrogatories, or (3) to serve a written response to a request for inspection submitted under IN ST TRIAL P Rule 34, after proper service of the request, the court in which the action is pending on motion may make such orders in regard to the failure as are just, and among others it may take any action authorized under IN ST TRIAL P Rule 37(B)(2)(a), IN ST TRIAL P Rule 37(B)(2)(b), and IN ST TRIAL P Rule 37(B)(2)(c). IN ST TRIAL P Rule 37(D).

    ii. *Attorney fees against party failing to provide discovery.* In lieu of any order or in addition thereto, the court shall require the party failing to act or the attorney advising him or both to pay the reasonable expenses, including attorney's fees, caused by the failure, unless the court finds that the failure was substantially justified or that other circumstances make an award of expenses unjust. IN ST TRIAL P Rule 37(D)

    iii. *Failure not excused for objectionable requests.* The failure to act described in IN ST TRIAL P Rule 37(D) may not be excused on the ground that the discovery sought is objectionable unless the party failing to act has applied for a protective order as provided by IN ST TRIAL P Rule 26(C). IN ST TRIAL P Rule 37(D). Refer to the Indiana KeyRules Motion for Protective Order document for more information.

    iv. *Showing required.* To invoke the sanctions under IN ST TRIAL P Rule 37(D), it is sufficient that notice of the deposition or other discovery request was properly served upon the non-responding party, but no response was provided. 22 INPRAC § 27.8.

f. *Sanctions for spoliation of evidence.* In some cases a duty arises imposing an affirmative obligation to avoid the destruction or loss of documents and materials that are relevant and discoverable to claims and defenses that either have been or may be asserted in an action. The destruction, mutilation, alteration or concealment of such materials is called "spoliation." 3 INPRAC R 37(37.2.2); Glotzbach v. Froman, 854 N.E.2d 337 (Ind. 2006).

    i. *Spoliation generally.* Spoliation typically presents itself in one of two ways:

- A party to litigation destroys materials that are relevant and discoverable in an action; or

- A non-party destroys materials that may be discoverable in an action to which that entity or individual will not be a party. 3 INPRAC R 37(37.2.2).

    ii. *Duty to maintain evidence must exist.* A key component of a spoliation claim is that the party who destroyed the materials must have had a duty not to do so. A duty may arise in a number of ways: imposed by statute or case law, imposed by contract or some third party beneficiary arrangement, or imposed by the actions of the parties by which one party assumes a duty in law or equity toward another. When duty arises from the conduct of the parties as opposed to one established by statute or contract, the Indiana courts have identified three primary factors to determine whether a duty exists:

- The relationship between the parties,

- The reasonable foreseeability of harm to the injured litigant, and

- The public policy promoted by recognizing an enforceable duty. 3 INPRAC R 37(37.2.2); Webb v. Jarvis, 575 N.E.2d 992 (Ind. 1991).

- This balancing test is particularly useful where the element of duty has not already been established between the parties. 3 INPRAC R 37(37.2.2); Northern Indiana Public Service Co. v. Sharp, 790 N.E.2d 462 (Ind. 2003).

    iii. *Factors to be considered by the court.* Even where the court finds an intentional spoliation, it is not mandatory that sanctions be imposed. Rather, the trial court should implement an approach by which it balances the nature of the offense against the harm suffered by the non-offending party because lost evidence is not available. 22 INPRAC § 27.9; Gribben v. Wal-Mart Stores, Inc., 824 N.E.2d 349 (Ind. 2005). Factors the court may consider include:

- The culpability of the spoliating party;

- The prejudice to the non-offending party;

- The degree of interference with the judicial process;

- Whether lesser sanctions are available to remedy any harm and deter future acts of spoliation;

- The amount of time lapsing from the date the spoliating party took possession of the evidence and the date of its loss or destruction;

- Protocols adopted, and followed, by the spoliating party to prevent the loss of evidence, such as a document retention policy;

- Whether evidence has been irretrievably lost and, if so, the circumstances of that loss;

- The existence of available alternatives that would allow the non-offending party to prove its case without the lost evidence;

- And whether sanctions will unfairly punish a party for the misconduct or mistake of his attorney or expert. 22 INPRAC § 27.9.

    g. *No sanctions for good-faith loss of electronically stored information.* Absent exceptional circumstances, a court may not impose sanctions under the Indiana Rules of Trial Procedure these rules on a party for failing to provide electronically stored information lost as a result of the routine, good faith operation of an electronic information system. IN ST TRIAL P Rule 37(E).

3. *Opposition to a motion for discovery sanctions.* Failure to file an answer brief or reply brief within the time prescribed shall be deemed a waiver of the right thereto and shall subject the motion to summary ruling. IN ST ST JOSEPH CIV Rule 206(206.1).

D. Documents

1. *Required documents*

   a. *Motion and notice.* The requirement of notice is satisfied by service of the motion. IN ST TRIAL P Rule 7(B). Refer to the General Requirements section of this document for information on the content of a motion for discovery sanctions.

   b. *Chronological Case Summary (CCS) entry form.* Every written motion, petition, or other pleading subsequent to the original complaint presented to the Clerk for filing shall be accompanied by a Chronological Case Summary (CCS) entry form in duplicate. IN ST ST JOSEPH CIV Rule 201(201.4). Refer to the Format section of this document for details on the format and filing requirements for the CCS entry form.

   c. *Attorney certification.* Refer to the General Requirements section of this document for information on the attorney certification.

   d. *Proposed order.* Unless local practice provides differently, a party should submit a proposed order with its written motion to be signed by the judge once the motion has been granted. 21 INPRAC § 13.8. All proposed orders shall be submitted in an original plus a number of copies equal to one more than the number of pro se parties and attorneys of record contained in the prepared proof of notice under IN ST TRIAL P Rule 72(D). IN ST ST JOSEPH CIV Rule 213(213.3); IN ST ST JOSEPH CIV Rule 201(201.5.2).

   e. *Certificate of service.* An attorney or unrepresented party tendering a document to the Clerk for filing shall certify that service has been made, list the parties served, and specify the date and means of service. The certificate of service shall be placed at the end of the document and shall not be separately filed. The separate filing of a certificate of service, however, shall not be grounds for rejecting a document for filing. The Clerk may permit documents to be filed without a certificate of service but shall require prompt filing of a separate certificate of service. IN ST TRIAL P Rule 5(C).

2. *Supplemental documents*

   a. *Supporting evidence.* When a motion is based on facts not appearing of record the court may hear the matter on affidavits presented by the respective parties, but the court may direct that the matter be heard wholly or partly on oral testimony or depositions. IN ST TRIAL P Rule 43(B).

   b. *Facsimile cover sheet.* Any document sent to the Clerk of the Circuit Court by electronic facsimile transmission shall be accompanied by a cover sheet which states the title of the document, case number, number of pages, identity and voice telephone number of the sending party and instructions for filing. The cover sheet shall contain the signature of the attorney or party, pro se, authorizing the filing. IN ST ADMIN Rule 12(D).

E. Format

1. *Form of motions.* The rules applicable to captions, and the signing and form of pleadings (IN ST TRIAL P Rule 8 through IN ST TRIAL P Rule 11), apply to all motions and other papers provided under the Indiana Rules of Trial Procedure. 22B INPRAC 7:2.

   a. *Separate motions; Alternative motions.* Each motion shall be separate, while alternative motions filed together shall each be identified on the caption. IN ST ST JOSEPH CIV Rule 206(206.1).

2. *Form of pleadings*

   a. *Caption; Names of parties.* Every pleading shall contain a caption setting forth the name of the court, the title of the action, the file number, and a designation as in IN ST TRIAL P Rule 7(A). In the complaint the title of the action shall include the names of all the parties, but in other pleadings it is sufficient to state the name of the first party on each side with an appropriate indication of other parties. IN ST TRIAL P Rule 10(A); IN ST ST JOSEPH CIV Rule 201(201.3.3). If a special judge has been assigned to the case, the pleading should also identify the special judge. IN ST ST JOSEPH CIV Rule 201(201.3.3).

      i. *Title.* All pleadings or motions shall include a title, which shall delineate each topic included in the pleading. For example, where a pleading contains an answer, a motion to dismiss, and a jury request, each topic shall be set forth in the title. IN ST ST JOSEPH CIV Rule 201(201.3.4).

b. *Paragraphs; Separate statements.* All averments of a claim or defense shall be made in numbered paragraphs, the contents of each of which shall be limited as far as practicable to a statement of a single set of circumstances, and a paragraph may be referred to by number in all succeeding pleadings. Each claim founded upon a separate transaction or occurrence and each defense other than denials may be stated in a separate count or defense whenever a separation facilitates the clear presentation of the matters set forth. IN ST TRIAL P Rule 10(B).

c. *Adoption by reference; Exhibits.* Statements in a pleading may be adopted by reference in a different part of the same pleading or in another pleading or in any motion. A copy of any written instrument which is an exhibit to a pleading is a part thereof for all purposes. IN ST TRIAL P Rule 10(C).

d. *Flat filing.* In order that the Clerk's files may be kept under the system commonly known as "flat filing," all papers presented to the Clerk for filing shall be flat and unfolded. Pleadings shall have no covers or backs and shall be fastened together at the top left-hand corner only. IN ST ST JOSEPH CIV Rule 201(201.1).

e. *One side of page used.* Printing shall be on one (1) side of the paper. IN ST ST JOSEPH CIV Rule 201(201.3.2).

f. *Copies.* All copies shall be on white paper of sufficient strength and durability to resist normal wear and tear. IN ST ST JOSEPH CIV Rule 201(201.3.1).

g. *Margins.* Margins shall be at least one inch (1"). IN ST ST JOSEPH CIV Rule 201(201.3.2).

h. *Double-spaced.* If typewritten, the lines shall be double spaced except for quotations, which shall be indented and single-spaced. IN ST ST JOSEPH CIV Rule 201(201.3.2).

i. *Font size.* Type face shall be twelve (12) font size or larger within the body of the document and ten (10) font size or larger in the footnotes. IN ST ST JOSEPH CIV Rule 201(201.3.2).

j. *Font type.* The font type must be legible and script type shall not be used. IN ST ST JOSEPH CIV Rule 201(201.3.2).

k. *Italics.* Italicized type may be used for quotations, references, or case-citations. IN ST ST JOSEPH CIV Rule 201(201.3.2).

l. *Court and case designation.* All filings shall conform to the requirements for uniform court and case number designation set by IN ST ADMIN Rule 8. In addition, all filings shall contain the proper court and case designation as described below. IN ST ST JOSEPH CIV Rule 202.

    i. *Court designation.* Pursuant to IN ST 33-33-71-2, St. Joseph County, Indiana, constitutes the Sixtieth Judicial Circuit. The legal names of the courts within the 60th Judicial Circuit are the St. Joseph Circuit Court, the St. Joseph Superior Court, and the St. Joseph Probate Court. All filings shall properly reflect the legal name of the applicable court. Any filing may be amended, rejected, or stricken if it does not contain the proper case name and/or the legal name of the court. IN ST ST JOSEPH CIV Rule 202(202.1).

m. *Form of CCS entry.* Every written motion, petition, or other pleading subsequent to the original complaint presented to the Clerk for filing shall be accompanied by a Chronological Case Summary (CCS) entry form in duplicate which shall contain the title and cause number of the action, the date, and the proposed entry to appear on the docket. IN ST ST JOSEPH CIV Rule 201(201.4).

    i. *Identification and signature.* The CCS entry form shall identify the party making the filing, designate each pleading being filed, and shall be signed by counsel of record or the unrepresented litigant. IN ST ST JOSEPH CIV Rule 201(201.4).

    ii. *Date stamp.* The form shall be date stamped and presented to the Court Clerk, who shall initial the form and return the duplicate to the filing party. IN ST ST JOSEPH CIV Rule 201(201.4).

n. *Form of proposed order.* Any proposed order shall be a document that is separate and apart from the motion or application to which it relates and shall contain a caption showing the name of the court, the case number assigned to the case, and the title of the case as shown by the complaint pursuant to IN ST ST JOSEPH CIV Rule 201. IN ST ST JOSEPH CIV Rule 213(213.2).

    i. If there are multiple parties, the title may be shortened to include only the first name plaintiff and

defendant with appropriate indication that there are additional parties. IN ST ST JOSEPH CIV Rule 213(213.2).

ii. The proposed order shall be on white paper, eight and one-half by eleven inches (8 1/2" x 11") in size, and each page shall be numbered. IN ST ST JOSEPH CIV Rule 213(213.2).

iii. The last page of the proposed order shall contain a line for the date, either "Dated _____" or "Signed on the date filemarked hereon." IN ST ST JOSEPH CIV Rule 213(213.2).

iv. On the last page there also shall be a line for the signature of the Judge under which shall be typed "Judge, St. Joseph [Circuit or Superior or Probate] Court." IN ST ST JOSEPH CIV Rule 213(213.2).

v. If the proposed order contains a recommendation from a Magistrate, the last page shall have a line for the signature of the Magistrate under which shall be typed "Magistrate, St. Joseph [Circuit or Superior or Probate] Court," to the left of which shall be the following, "So Recommended:" and beneath and to the left of which shall be typed, "Approved. So Ordered." IN ST ST JOSEPH CIV Rule 213(213.2).

vi. To allow compliance with the notice requirements of IN ST TRIAL P Rule 72(D), the lower four (4) inches of the last page of the proposed order shall be left blank. The proposed order shall also include a prepared proof of notice under IN ST TRIAL P Rule 72(D), and in preparing such a notice the filing party shall complete all portions of the prepared proof of notice. IN ST ST JOSEPH CIV Rule 213(213.2).

3. *Size of papers for filing.* Effective January 1, 1992, all pleadings, copies, motions and documents filed with any trial court or appellate level court, typed or printed, with the exception of exhibits and existing wills, shall be prepared on eight and one-half by eleven inch (8 1/2" x 11") size paper. IN ST ADMIN Rule 11.

a. *Paper.* Pleadings, motions, and other papers shall be either legibly printed or typewritten on white opaque paper of good quality at least sixteen (16) pound weight, eight and one-half inches (8 1/2 ") in width and eleven inches (11") in length as required by IN ST ADMIN Rule 11. IN ST ST JOSEPH CIV Rule 201(201.3.1).

4. *Signature requirements*

a. *Signature of attorney.* Every pleading or motion of a party represented by an attorney shall be signed by at least one (1) attorney of record in his individual name, whose address, telephone number, and attorney number shall be stated, except that this provision shall not apply to pleadings and motions made and transcribed at the trial or a hearing before the judge and received by him in such form. IN ST TRIAL P Rule 11(A).

i. The signature of an attorney constitutes a certificate by him that he has read the pleadings; that to the best of his knowledge, information, and belief, there is good ground to support it; and that it is not interposed for delay. IN ST TRIAL P Rule 11(A).

ii. If a pleading or motion is not signed or is signed with intent to defeat the purpose of the rule, it may be stricken as sham and false and the action may proceed as though the pleading had not been served. IN ST TRIAL P Rule 11(A).

iii. For a willful violation of IN ST TRIAL P Rule 11 an attorney may be subjected to appropriate disciplinary action. Similar action may be taken if scandalous or indecent matter is inserted. IN ST TRIAL P Rule 11(A).

b. *Signature of unrepresented party.* A party who is not represented by an attorney shall sign his pleading and state his address. IN ST TRIAL P Rule 11(A).

c. *Verification not generally required.* Except when specifically required by rule, pleadings or motions need not be verified or accompanied by affidavit. The rule in equity that the averments of an answer under oath must be overcome by the testimony of two (2) witnesses or of one (1) witness sustained by corroborating circumstances is abolished. IN ST TRIAL P Rule 11(A).

d. *Verification by affirmation or representation.* When in connection with any civil or special statutory proceeding it is required that any pleading, motion, petition, supporting affidavit, or other document

of any kind, be verified, or that an oath be taken, it shall be sufficient if the subscriber simply affirms the truth of the matter to be verified by an affirmation or representation. IN ST TRIAL P Rule 11(B). IN ST TRIAL P Rule 11(B) states that the affirmation or representation should be in substantially the following language: "I (we) affirm, under the penalties for perjury, that the foregoing representation(s) is (are) true. (Signed) _____."

    i.   Any person who falsifies an affirmation or representation of fact shall be subject to the same penalties as are prescribed by law for the making of a false affidavit. IN ST TRIAL P Rule 11(B).

e. *Verified pleadings, motions, and affidavits as evidence.* Pleadings, motions and affidavits accompanying or in support of such pleadings or motions when required to be verified or under oath shall be accepted as a representation that the signer had personal knowledge thereof or reasonable cause to believe the existence of the facts or matters stated or alleged therein; and, if otherwise competent or acceptable as evidence, may be admitted as evidence of the facts or matters stated or alleged therein when it is so provided in the Indiana Rules of Trial Procedure, by statute or other law, or to the extent the writing or signature expressly purports to be made upon the signer's personal knowledge. When such pleadings, motions and affidavits are verified or under oath they shall not require other or greater proof on the part of the adverse party than if not verified or not under oath unless expressly provided otherwise by the Indiana Rules of Trial Procedure, statute or other law. Affidavits upon motions for summary judgment under IN ST TRIAL P Rule 56 and in denial of execution under IN ST TRIAL P Rule 9.2 shall be made upon personal knowledge. IN ST TRIAL P Rule 11(C).

f. *Signature, verification and other requirements.* Parties and their counsel are enjoined to comply with the verification requirements of IN ST TRIAL P Rule 11, and either the moving party or the party's attorney of record shall sign all pleadings and motions before filing with the Clerk of the Court. Every motion, petition, or other pleading filed with the Clerk shall contain the name, organization, physical address, telephone number, and facsimile number of the filing party or an attorney for that party. IN ST ST JOSEPH CIV Rule 201(201.3.6).

    i.   The Clerk shall not accept any motion, petition, notice or other pleading or a CCS entry form for filing from an unrepresented litigant unless the unrepresented litigant's current address and phone number appear on the pleading, and an opposing party may service notices and responses on an unrepresented litigant at any address he or she has provided on a pleading. IN ST ST JOSEPH CIV Rule 201(201.3.6).

5. *Information excluded from public access.* Every document filed in a case shall separately identify information excluded from public access pursuant to IN ST ADMIN Rule 9(G)(1) as follows:

a. Whole documents that are excluded from public access pursuant to IN ST ADMIN Rule 9(G)(1) shall be tendered on light green paper or have a light green coversheet attached to the document, marked "Not for Public Access" or "Confidential." IN ST TRIAL P Rule 5(G)(1).

b. When only a portion of a document contains information excluded from public access pursuant to IN ST ADMIN Rule 9(G)(1), said information shall be omitted [or redacted] from the filed document, and set forth on a separate accompanying document on light green paper conspicuously marked "Not for Public Access" or "Confidential" and clearly designated [or identifying] the caption and number of the case and the document and location within the document to which the redacted material pertains. IN ST TRIAL P Rule 5(G)(2).

c. With respect to documents filed in electronic format, the trial court, by local rule, may provide for compliance with IN ST TRIAL P Rule 5 in manner that separates and protects access to information excluded from public access. IN ST TRIAL P Rule 5(G)(3).

d. IN ST TRIAL P Rule 5(G) does not apply to a record sealed by the court pursuant to IN ST 5-14-3-5.5 or otherwise, nor to records, documents, or information filed in cases to which public access is prohibited pursuant to IN ST ADMIN Rule 9(G). IN ST TRIAL P Rule 5(G)(4).

e. The following information in case records is excluded from public access and is confidential:

    i.   Information that is excluded from public access pursuant to federal law;

ii. Information that is excluded from public access as declared confidential by Indiana statute or other court rule, including without limitation:

- All adoption records created after July 8, 1941, as declared confidential by IN ST 31-19-19-1, et seq., except those specifically declared open by IN ST 31-19-13-2(2);

- All records relating to chancroid, chlamydia, gonorrhea, hepatitis, human immunodeficiency virus (HIV), Lymphogranuloma venereum, syphilis, tuberculosis, as declared confidential by IN ST 16-41-8-1, et seq.;

- All records relating to child abuse as declared confidential by IN ST 31-33-18-1, et seq.;

- All records relating to drug tests as declared confidential by IN ST 5-14-3-4(a)(9);

- Records of grand jury proceedings as declared confidential by IN ST 35-34-2-4;

- Records of juvenile proceedings as declared confidential by IN ST 31-39-1-2, except those specifically open under statute;

- All paternity records created after July 1, 1941 as declared confidential by IN ST 31-14-11-15, IN ST 31-19-5-23, IN ST 31-39-1-1 and IN ST 31-39-1-2 [Editor's note: IN ST 31-14-11-15 was repealed effective May 9, 2013];

- All pre-sentence reports as declared confidential by IN ST 35-38-1-13;

- Written petitions to permit marriages without consent and orders directing the Clerk of Court to issue a marriage license to underage persons, as declared confidential by IN ST 31-11-1-6;

- Only those arrest warrants, search warrants, indictments and informations ordered confidential by the trial judge, prior to return of duly executed service as declared confidential by IN ST 5-14-3-4(b)(1);

- All medical, mental health, or tax records unless determined by law or regulation of any governmental custodian not to be confidential, released by the subject of such records, or declared by a court of competent jurisdiction to be essential to the resolution of litigation as declared confidential by IN ST 16-39-3-10, IN ST 6-4.1-5-10, IN ST 6-4.1-12-12, and IN ST 6-8.1-7-1;

- Personal information relating to jurors or prospective jurors, other than for the use of the parties and counsel, pursuant to IN ST JURY Rule 10;

- Information relating to protection from abuse orders, no-contact orders and workplace violence restraining orders as declared confidential by IN ST 5-2-9-6, et seq.;

- Mediation proceedings pursuant to IN ST ADR Rule 2.11, Mini-Trial proceedings pursuant to IN ST ADR Rule 4.4(C), and Summary Jury Trials pursuant to IN ST ADR Rule 5.6;

- Information in probation files pursuant to the Probation Standards promulgated by the Judicial Conference of Indiana pursuant to IN ST 11-13-1-8(b);

- Information deemed confidential pursuant to the Rules for Court Administered Alcohol and Drug Programs promulgated by the Judicial Conference of Indiana pursuant to IN ST 12-23-14-13;

- Information deemed confidential pursuant to the Problem-Solving Court Rules promulgated by the Judicial Conference of Indiana pursuant to IN ST 33-23-16-16;

- All records of the Department of workforce Development as declared confidential by IN ST 22-4-19-6;

- Information regarding interception of electronic communications that is sealed or deemed confidential as set forth in IN ST 35-33.5-2-1, et seq.

iii. Information excluded from public access by specific court order;

iv. Complete Social Security Numbers of living persons;

     v.   With the exception of names, information such as addresses, phone numbers, and dates of birth which explicitly identifies:

- Natural persons who are witnesses or victims (not including defendants) in criminal, domestic violence, stalking, sexual assault, juvenile, or civil protection order proceedings, provided that juveniles who are victims of sex crimes shall be identified by initials only;

- Places of residence of judicial officers, clerks and other employees of courts and clerks of court, unless the person or persons about whom the information pertains waives confidentiality;

     vi.   Complete account numbers of specific assets, loans, bank accounts, credit cards, and personal identification numbers (PINs);

     vii.   All orders of expungement entered in criminal or juvenile proceedings, orders to restrict access to criminal history information pursuant to IN ST 35-38-5-5.5 or IN ST 35-38-8-5 and records excluded from public access by such orders, and information related to infractions that is excluded from public access pursuant to IN ST 34-28-5-15 or IN ST 34-28-5-16 [Editor's note: IN ST 35-38-5-5.5, IN ST 35-38-8-5 and IN ST 34-28-5-16 were repealed effective July 1, 2013; for information on orders restricting access to criminal history, refer to IN ST 35-38-9-1, et seq.];

     viii.   All personal notes and e-mail, and deliberative material, of judges, jurors, court staff and judicial agencies, and information recorded in personal data assistants (PDA's) or organizers and personal calendars. IN ST ADMIN Rule 9(G)(1).

F. Filing and Service Requirements

1. *Filing requirements.* Except as otherwise provided in IN ST TRIAL P Rule 5(E)(2), all pleadings and papers subsequent to the complaint which are required to be served upon a party shall be filed with the Court either before service or within a reasonable period of time thereafter. IN ST TRIAL P Rule 5(E)(1).

   a.   *Filing with the court defined.* The filing of pleadings, motions, and other papers with the court as required by the Indiana Rules of Trial Procedure shall be made by one of the following methods:

     i.   Delivery to the clerk of the court;

     ii.   Sending by electronic transmission under the procedure adopted pursuant to IN ST ADMIN Rule 12;

     iii.   Mailing to the clerk by registered, certified or express mail return receipt requested;

     iv.   Depositing with any third-party commercial carrier for delivery to the clerk within three (3) calendar days, cost prepaid, properly addressed;

     v.   If the court so permits, filing with the judge, in which event the judge shall note thereon the filing date and forthwith transmit them to the office of the clerk; or

     vi.   Electronic filing, as approved by the Division of State Court Administration pursuant to IN ST ADMIN Rule 16. IN ST TRIAL P Rule 5(F).

     vii.   Filing by registered or certified mail and by third-party commercial carrier shall be complete upon mailing or deposit. IN ST TRIAL P Rule 5(F).

     viii.   All pleadings shall be filed with the Clerk, not directly with the Court, unless otherwise required by the Indiana Rules of Court. The entry of appearances and the filing of pleadings or other matters not requiring immediate Court action shall be filed with the Clerk and not in open Court. A Judge may permit papers to be filed in chambers, in which event he or she shall note thereon the filing date and transmit the papers to the Clerk. IN ST ST JOSEPH CIV Rule 201(201.2).

   b.   *Facsimile filing.* Unless otherwise authorized by IN ST ST JOSEPH ELECTRONIC Rule 701, electronic filing of pleadings by computerized or facsimile transmission is not permitted. IN ST ST JOSEPH CIV Rule 201(201.2).

   c.   *Additional copies.* In cases in which a party or counsel supplies the proposed order or decree, a sufficient number shall be prepared and filed as to provide the Clerk to retain two (2) copies, which shall be filed in the flat file and the record of judgments and orders. Should the party or counsel desire

additional copies, a sufficient number of copies should be filed to effectuate that purpose. IN ST ST JOSEPH CIV Rule 201(201.6).

d. *Proof of filing.* Any party filing any paper by any method other than personal delivery to the clerk shall retain proof of filing. IN ST TRIAL P Rule 5(F).

2. *Service requirements.* Unless otherwise provided by the Indiana Rules of Trial Procedure or an order of the court, each party and special judge, if any, shall be served with: (1) every order required by its terms to be served; (2) every pleading subsequent to the original complaint; (3) every written motion except one which may be heard ex parte; (4) every brief submitted to the trial court; (5) every paper relating to discovery required to be served upon a party; and (6) every written notice, appearance, demand, offer of judgment, designation of record on appeal, or similar paper. IN ST TRIAL P Rule 5(A).

a. *Service generally.* Every motion, petition, notice, or other pleading required to be served by IN ST TRIAL P Rule 5 shall be served on all counsel of record or unrepresented parties either before it is filed or on the day it is filed with the Court, and the date of filing shall be indicated on the Certificate of Service. IN ST ST JOSEPH CIV Rule 201(201.5.1).

  i. *Copy.* A copy of the Clerk's CCS entry form of the filing shall also be served on all counsel of record or unrepresented parties whenever it contains an appearance of counsel or contains a date for Court hearing on the matter. IN ST ST JOSEPH CIV Rule 201(201.5.1).

b. *Methods of service*

  i. *Personal service.* Whenever a party is represented by an attorney of record, service shall be made upon such attorney unless service upon the party himself is ordered by the court. Service upon the attorney or party shall be made by delivering or mailing a copy of the papers to the last known address or where an attorney or party has consented to service by fax or e-mail, as provided in IN ST TRIAL P Rule 3.1(A)(4), by faxing or e-mailing a copy of the documents to the fax number or e-mail address set out in the appearance form or correction as required by IN ST TRIAL P Rule 3.1(E). IN ST TRIAL P Rule 5(B). Delivery of a copy within IN ST TRIAL P Rule 5 means:

    • Offering or tendering it to the attorney or party and stating the nature of the papers being served. Refusal to accept an offered or tendered document is a waiver of any objection to the sufficiency or adequacy of service of that document;

    • Leaving it at his office with a clerk or other person in charge thereof, or if there is no one in charge, leaving it in a conspicuous place therein; or

    • If the office is closed, by leaving it at his dwelling house or usual place of abode with some person of suitable age and discretion then residing therein; or,

    • Leaving it at some other suitable place, selected by the attorney upon whom service is being made, pursuant to duly promulgated local rule. IN ST TRIAL P Rule 5(B)(1).

  ii. *Service by the clerk.* Whenever the Clerk is required by rule or statute to give notice, the party or parties requesting such notice shall furnish the Clerk with sufficient copies of the notice to be given, along with stamped, addressed envelopes with the names and the addresses of the parties or their counsel to whom such notice is to be given. IN ST ST JOSEPH CIV Rule 201(201.5.4).

  iii. *Service on the court.* Service on a Judge may be made by delivering a copy to the Judge's secretary or mailing a copy to the Judge at his or her chambers. Service on a Judge may not be accomplished by facsimile transmission; however, a courtesy copy may be sent to the Judge's chambers by electronic mail or facsimile transmission contemporaneously with service by mail or otherwise. IN ST ST JOSEPH CIV Rule 201(201.5.5).

  iv. *Service by mail.* If service is made by mail, the papers shall be deposited in the United States mail addressed to the person on whom they are being served, with postage prepaid. Service shall be deemed complete upon mailing. Proof of service of all papers permitted to be mailed may be made by written acknowledgment of service, by affidavit of the person who mailed the papers, or by certificate of an attorney. It shall be the duty of attorneys when entering their appearance in a cause or when filing pleadings or papers therein, to have noted in the

Chronological Case Summary or said pleadings or papers so filed the address and telephone number of their office. Service by delivery or by mail at such address shall be deemed sufficient and complete. IN ST TRIAL P Rule 5(B)(2).

v. *Service by fax or e-mail.* A party who has consented to service by fax or e-mail may be served as follows:

- Service by e-mail shall be made by attaching the document being served in .pdf format. Discovery documents must also be served in accordance with IN ST TRIAL P Rule 26(A). IN ST TRIAL P Rule 5(B)(3)(a).

- Service by fax shall be deemed complete upon generation of a transmission record indicating the successful transmission of the entire document, except as provided in IN ST TRIAL P Rule 5(B)(3)(d). IN ST TRIAL P Rule 5(B)(3)(b).

- Service by e-mail shall be deemed complete upon transmission, except as provided in IN ST TRIAL P Rule 5(B)(3)(d). IN ST TRIAL P Rule 5(B)(3)(c).

- Service by fax or e-mail that occurs on a Saturday, Sunday, legal holiday, or day the court or agency in which the matter is pending is closed or after 5:00 PM local time of the recipient shall be deemed complete the next day that is not a Saturday, Sunday, legal holiday, or day that the court or agency in which the matter is pending is not closed. IN ST TRIAL P Rule 5(B)(3)(d).

c. *Serving numerous defendants.* In any action in which there are unusually large numbers of defendants, the court, upon motion or of its own initiative, may order:

i. That service of the pleadings of the defendants and replies thereto need not be made as between the defendants;

- That any cross-claim, counterclaim, or matter constituting an avoidance or affirmative defense contained therein shall be deemed to be denied or avoided by all other parties; and

- That the filing of any such pleading and service thereof upon the plaintiff constitutes due notice of it to the parties. IN ST TRIAL P Rule 5(D).

ii. A copy of every such order shall be served upon the parties in such manner and form as the court directs. IN ST TRIAL P Rule 5(D).

d. *Service on parties in default for failure to appear.* No service need be made on parties in default for failure to appear, except that pleadings asserting new or additional claims for relief against them shall be served upon them in the manner provided by service of summons in IN ST TRIAL P Rule 4. IN ST TRIAL P Rule 5(A).

e. *Distribution.* Counsel or an unrepresented party submitting a motion, petition, notice, pleading or proposed order shall indicate the method of distribution desired on the Clerk's CCS entry form. The Clerk will not return or distribute copies of motions, petitions, pleadings, notices or proposed orders, other than those originated by the Court, by mail unless the Clerk is provided with stamped, addressed envelopes. IN ST ST JOSEPH CIV Rule 201(201.5.3).

f. *Mailbox.* As a matter of convenience to attorneys, each court provides a mailbox for the distribution filings and orders generated by the Court, and it is the responsibility of each attorney to periodically check these mailboxes for service and distribution of court-generated filings and orders. IN ST ST JOSEPH CIV Rule 201(201.5.3).

G. Hearings

1. *Hearing on motion.* Unless local conditions make it impracticable, each judge shall establish regular times and places, at intervals sufficiently frequent for the prompt dispatch of business, at which motions requiring notice and hearing may be heard and disposed of; but the judge at any time or place and on such notice, if any, as he considers reasonable may make order for the advancement, conduct, and hearing of actions. To expedite its business the court may direct the submission and determination of motions without oral hearing upon brief written statements of reasons in support and opposition, or direct or permit hearings by telephone conference call with all attorneys or other similar means of communication. IN ST TRIAL P Rule 73(A).

2. *Hearings generally held before imposition of discovery sanctions.* As a general matter, most courts will conduct a hearing prior to imposing discovery sanctions, although IN ST TRIAL P Rule 37 and Indiana case law do not expressly require a court to do so. 22 INPRAC § 27.7.

3. *Hearing dates.* Hearing dates for filings requiring Court action shall be obtained from the Court Clerk and incorporated in the CCS entry at the time the motion or other pleading is filed. If no date is obtained prior to the filing, the fact of the hearing should be noted with the date and time left blank. IN ST ST JOSEPH CIV Rule 201(201.4).

4. *Hearing on matters other than trials.* Each Judge shall reserve periods of time for hearing matters other than contested trials, such as pre-trial and post-trial motions, rules to show cause, defaults, uncontested dissolutions of marriage, etc. As necessary to minimize conflicts in scheduling, the Judges shall set these schedules after consultation. Hearings shall be scheduled as follows:

    a. *Scheduling uncontested or routine matters.* Routine matters, procedural motions, domestic relations applications for provisional relief and contempt proceedings, uncontested petitions for dissolution of marriage, and all other matters appropriate for summary consideration and disposition will be heard on the daily calendar. IN ST ST JOSEPH GEN AND ADMIN Rule 104(104.3.1).

    b. *Scheduling contested or complicated matters.* Other matters that will require a hearing reasonably estimated to last in excess of twenty (20) minutes will be scheduled as the Court's calendar allows. Counsel or a party proceeding pro se should contact the chambers of the assigned judge to arrange for an appropriate hearing date and time. IN ST ST JOSEPH GEN AND ADMIN Rule 104(104.3.2).

    c. *Scheduling motions for hearings.* Except for motions to correct error or not likely to require a hearing (as described in IN ST ST JOSEPH CIV Rule 201), all motions shall be scheduled for hearing at the time they are filed. It shall the responsibility of the moving party or counsel for the moving party to secure the date and time of the hearing from the Clerk or Court personnel who maintain the calendar for each Judge or Magistrate Judge. It shall also be the responsibility of the moving party or counsel for the moving party to coordinate the hearing date with all opposing counsel or unrepresented parties. IN ST ST JOSEPH CIV Rule 201(201.9.1).

    d. *Oral arguments on motions and other pleadings.* Unless otherwise required by St. Joseph County Civil or Indiana Trial Rules, it is within the sound discretion of the assigned Judge whether to allow oral argument; however, any party may file a request for oral argument by filing a written request by separate motion contemporaneously or at any time before the Court has ruled upon the motion or pleadings to be argued. IN ST ST JOSEPH CIV Rule 201(201.9.4).

H. Forms

1. Motion for Discovery Sanctions Forms for Indiana

    a. Motion to dismiss as sanction for failure to comply with court ordered discovery. 5 INPRAC § 4:6.60.

    b. Motion to dismiss action as sanction; For party's failure to comply with court ordered discovery. 10 INPRAC § 58.38.

    c. Motion for order precluding litigation of issues. 10 INPRAC § 58.63.

    d. Motion for judgment by default; As sanction for failure to comply with court order. 10 INPRAC § 58.64.

    e. Motion to exclude expert witness at trial. 10 INPRAC § 70.24.

    f. Certificate of service; Personal service. 9 INPRAC § 5.7.

    g. Certificate of service; First class mail. 9 INPRAC § 5.8.

I. Checklist

    (I) ❑ Matters to be considered by moving party

        (a) ❑ Required documents

            (1) ❑ Motion and notice

            (2) ❑ Chronological Case Summary (CCS) entry form

    (3) ❑ Attorney certification

    (4) ❑ Proposed order

    (5) ❑ Certificate of service

(b) ❑ Supplemental documents

    (1) ❑ Supporting evidence

    (2) ❑ Facsimile cover sheet

(c) ❑ Timing

    (1) ❑ There are no specific timing requirements for filing a motion for discovery sanctions

    (2) ❑ A written motion, other than one which may be heard ex parte, and notice of the hearing thereof shall be served not less than five (5) days before the time specified for the hearing, unless a different period is fixed by the Indiana Rules of Trial Procedure or by order of the court

    (3) ❑ All pleadings and papers subsequent to the complaint which are required to be served upon a party shall be filed with the Court either before service or within a reasonable period of time thereafter

(II) ❑ Matters to be considered by the responding party

(a) ❑ Required documents

    (1) ❑ Opposition

    (2) ❑ Chronological Case Summary (CCS) entry form

    (3) ❑ Certificate of service

(b) ❑ Supplemental documents

    (1) ❑ Supporting evidence

    (2) ❑ Proposed order

(c) ❑ Timing

    (1) ❑ So long as consistent with Indiana Rules of Trial Procedure, an adverse party wishing to respond shall do so within fifteen (15) days of service

    (2) ❑ Except as otherwise provided in IN ST TRIAL P Rule 59(D), opposing affidavits may be served not less than one (1) day before the hearing, unless the court permits them to be served at some other time

Motions, Oppositions and Replies
Motion for Preliminary Injunction

Document Last Updated October 2013

A. Applicable Rules

  1. *State rules*

    a. Appearance. IN ST TRIAL P Rule 3.1.

    b. Process. IN ST TRIAL P Rule 4.

    c. Service and filing of pleadings and other papers. IN ST TRIAL P Rule 5.

    d. Time. IN ST TRIAL P Rule 6.

    e. Pleadings. IN ST TRIAL P Rule 7; IN ST TRIAL P Rule 8; IN ST TRIAL P Rule 9.2; IN ST TRIAL P Rule 10.

    f. Signing and verification of pleadings. IN ST TRIAL P Rule 11.

    g. Evidence. IN ST TRIAL P Rule 43.

    h.   Judgment on the evidence (directed verdict). IN ST TRIAL P Rule 50.

    i.   Findings by the court. IN ST TRIAL P Rule 52.

    j.   Summary judgment. IN ST TRIAL P Rule 56.

    k.   Motion to correct error. IN ST TRIAL P Rule 59.

    l.   Relief from judgment or order. IN ST TRIAL P Rule 60.

    m.   Injunctions. IN ST TRIAL P Rule 65; IN ST 34-26-1-7; IN ST 34-26-1-8.

    n.   Security; Proceedings against sureties. IN ST TRIAL P Rule 65.1.

    o.   Hearing of motions. IN ST TRIAL P Rule 73.

    p.   Access to court records. IN ST ADMIN Rule 9.

    q.   Paper size. IN ST ADMIN Rule 11.

    r.   Facsimile transmission. IN ST ADMIN Rule 12.

    s.   Electronic filing and electronic service pilot projects. IN ST ADMIN Rule 16.

    t.   Sealing of certain records by court; Hearing; Notice. IN ST 5-14-3-5.5.

    u.   Sixtieth judicial circuit. IN ST 33-33-71-2.

    v.   Privacy and confidentiality. IN ST 5-2-9-6; IN ST 5-14-3-4; IN ST 6-4.1-5-10; IN ST 6-4.1-12-12; IN ST 6-8.1-7-1; IN ST 11-13-1-8; IN ST 12-23-14-13; IN ST 16-39-3-10; IN ST 16-41-8-1; IN ST 22-4-19-6; IN ST 31-11-1-6; IN ST 31-19-5-23; IN ST 31-19-13-2; IN ST 31-19-19-1; IN ST 31-33-18-1; IN ST 31-39-1-1; IN ST 31-39-1-2; IN ST 33-23-16-16; IN ST 35-34-2-4; IN ST 35-38-1-13; IN ST 35-38-9-1; IN ST ADR Rule 2.11; IN ST ADR Rule 4.4; IN ST ADR Rule 5.6; IN ST JURY Rule 10.

2.   *Local rules*

    a.   Court hours and scheduling. IN ST ST JOSEPH GEN AND ADMIN Rule 104.

    b.   Filing, pleading, and motions. IN ST ST JOSEPH CIV Rule 201.

    c.   Uniform court and case number designation. IN ST ST JOSEPH CIV Rule 202.

    d.   Pleading and motions under IN ST TRIAL P Rule 12 and IN ST TRIAL P Rule 56. IN ST ST JOSEPH CIV Rule 206.

    e.   Proposed order. IN ST ST JOSEPH CIV Rule 213.

    f.   Electronic filing of cases in St. Joseph County. IN ST ST JOSEPH ELECTRONIC Rule 701.

B. Timing

1.   *Motion for preliminary injunction.* The injunction may be granted at the time of commencing the action, or at any time afterwards before judgment is rendered in the proceeding. IN ST 34-26-1-7. IN ST TRIAL P Rule 65 does not state when notice must be given. 4 INPRAC R 65(65.2).

    a.   *Filing.* All pleadings and papers subsequent to the complaint which are required to be served upon a party shall be filed with the Court either before service or within a reasonable period of time thereafter. IN ST TRIAL P Rule 5(E)(1).

2.   *Service.* A written motion, other than one which may be heard ex parte, and notice of the hearing thereof shall be served not less than five (5) days before the time specified for the hearing, unless a different period is fixed by the Indiana Rules of Trial Procedure or by order of the court. IN ST TRIAL P Rule 6(D).

    a.   *Of supporting affidavits.* When a motion is supported by affidavit, the affidavit shall be served with the motion. IN ST TRIAL P Rule 6(D).

3.   *Service of opposition.* Except as otherwise provided in IN ST TRIAL P Rule 59(D), opposing affidavits may be served not less than one (1) day before the hearing, unless the court permits them to be served at some other time. IN ST TRIAL P Rule 6(D).

    a.   *Memorandum of law.* So long as consistent with Indiana Rules of Trial Procedure, an adverse party wishing to respond shall do so within fifteen (15) days of service. IN ST ST JOSEPH CIV Rule 206(206.1).

4. *Filing proposed orders.* Unless otherwise directed or given leave of the Court, proposed orders in emergency matters shall be filed within forty-eight (48) hours after a hearing; proposed orders in other matters shall be filed within seven (7) days as computed by IN ST TRIAL P Rule 6. IN ST ST JOSEPH CIV Rule 213(213.5).

5. *Computation of time*

   a. *Generally; Days excluded.* In computing any period of time prescribed or allowed by the Indiana Rules of Trial Procedure, by order of the court, or by any applicable statute, the day of the act, event, or default from which the designated period of time begins to run shall not be included. The last day of the period so computed is to be included unless it is:

      i. A Saturday,

      ii. A Sunday,

      iii. A legal holiday as defined by state statute, or

      iv. A day the office in which the act is to be done is closed during regular business hours. IN ST TRIAL P Rule 6(A).

   b. *Short periods.* In any event, the period runs until the end of the next day that is not a Saturday, a Sunday, a legal holiday, or a day on which the office is closed. When the period of time allowed is less than seven (7) days, intermediate Saturdays, Sundays, legal holidays, and days on which the office is closed shall be excluded from the computations. IN ST TRIAL P Rule 6(A).

   c. *Additional time after service by United States mail.* Whenever a party has the right or is required to do some act or take some proceedings within a prescribed period after the service of a notice or other paper upon him and the notice or paper is served upon him by United States mail, three (3) days shall be added to the prescribed period. IN ST TRIAL P Rule 6(E).

   d. *Enlargement of time.* When an act is required or allowed to be done at or within a specific time by the Indiana Rules of Trial Procedure, the court may at any time for cause shown:

      i. Order the period enlarged, with or without motion or notice, if request therefor is made before the expiration of the period originally prescribed or extended by a previous order; or

      ii. Upon motion made after the expiration of the specific period, permit the act to be done where the failure to act was the result of excusable neglect; but, the court may not extend the time for taking any action for judgment on the evidence under IN ST TRIAL P Rule 50(A), amendment of findings and judgment under IN ST TRIAL P Rule 52(B), to correct errors under IN ST TRIAL P Rule 59(C), statement in opposition to motion to correct error under IN ST TRIAL P Rule 59(E), or to obtain relief from final judgment under IN ST TRIAL P Rule 60(B), except to the extent and under the conditions stated in those rules. IN ST TRIAL P Rule 6(B).

      iii. An initial written motion for enlargement of time pursuant to IN ST TRIAL P Rule 6(B)(1) to answer a claim shall be routinely granted for an additional thirty (30) days from the original due date or other period the assigned Judge deems reasonable by written order of the Court. The motion must be filed on or before the original due date or IN ST ST JOSEPH CIV Rule 201 shall be inapplicable. IN ST ST JOSEPH CIV Rule 201(201.9.5).

         • Any motion for enlargement of time shall state the date when such response is due and the date to which time is requested to be enlarged. IN ST ST JOSEPH CIV Rule 201(201.9.5).

         • All subsequent motions for enlargement of time shall be so designated and will only be granted for good cause shown or in the interest of justice. IN ST ST JOSEPH CIV Rule 201(201.9.5).

C. General Requirements

1. *Motions, generally.* Unless made during a hearing or trial, or otherwise ordered by the court, an application to the court for an order shall be made by written motion. The motion shall state the grounds therefor and the relief or order sought. IN ST TRIAL P Rule 7(B).

   a. *Motions as distinct from pleadings.* Motions and responses to motions are not pleadings, and allegations contained in a motion are not admissions of a party. 22B INPRAC 7:2; Wachstetter v.

County Properties, LLC, 832 N.E.2d 574 (Ind.Ct.App. 2005); Scott County Family YMCA, Inc. v. Hobbs, 817 N.E.2d 603 (Ind.Ct.App. 2004).

b. *Unopposed motions generally granted.* It is common for a trial court to grant procedural motions, such as motions for enlargement of time, discovery motions, or motions for continuance, unless an objection is filed. 21 INPRAC § 13.8.

c. *Proposed orders.* As directed by the Court, a party or an attorney for a party shall prepare a proposed order based on the decision rendered by the Court. The party so directed shall prepare the proposed order in a timely manner and, upon filing, shall advise the chambers of the applicable judge that the proposed order has been prepared and filed. IN ST ST JOSEPH CIV Rule 213(213.2).

   i. Prior to entry by the Court of orders granting motions or applications, the moving party or applicant (or his or her attorney) shall, unless the Court directs otherwise, furnish the Court with proposed orders in the matter of restraining orders, temporary, or permanent injunctions. IN ST ST JOSEPH CIV Rule 213(213.1(8)).

2. *Motion for preliminary injunction.* The general purpose of a temporary restraining order and a preliminary injunction is to maintain and preserve the status quo until the merits of the case can be heard. The status quo is the last actual, peaceful and noncontested status which preceded the pending controversy. 4 INPRAC R 65(65.1); Rees v. Panhandle Eastern Pipe Line Co., 176 Ind.App. 597, 377 N.E.2d 640 (Ind.Ct.App. 1978). An injunction does not create or enlarge the rights of a party, it merely protects existing rights and prevents harm to the aggrieved party that cannot be corrected by a final judgment. 22B INPRAC 65:1; Franke v. Honeywell, Inc., 516 N.E.2d 1090 (Ind.Ct.App. 1987); Indiana & Michigan Elec. Co. v. Whitley County Rural Elec. Membership Corp., 161 Ind.App. 492, 316 N.E.2d 584 (Ind.Ct.App. 1974); AGS Capital Corp., Inc. v. Product Action Intern., LLC, 884 N.E.2d 294 (Ind.Ct.App. 2008).

   a. *Injunctions in general.* Whether or not a preliminary injunction should issue rests in the sound discretion of the trial court. Discretion to grant or deny a preliminary injunction is measured by the following factors and the burden lies with the movant to prove each element by a preponderance of the evidence. 4 INPRAC R 65(65.1); Crossmann Communities, Inc. v. Dean, 767 N.E.2d 1035, 1040 (Ind.Ct.App. 2002); Mercho-Roushdi Corp. v. Blatchford, 742 N.E.2d 519, 524 (Ind.Ct.App. 2001).

      i. If the movant fails to prove any of these requirements, the trial court's grant of an injunction is an abuse of discretion. 4 INPRAC R 65(65.1); Ind. Family and Soc. Servs. Admin. v. Walgreen Co., 769 N.E.2d 158, 161 (Ind. 2002):

         • Whether the plaintiff's remedies at law are inadequate and the plaintiff will suffer irreparable harm pending the resolution of the substantive action if the injunction does not issue;

         • Whether the plaintiff has demonstrated at least a reasonable likelihood of success at trial by establishing a prima facie case;

         • Whether the threatened injury to the plaintiff outweighs the threatened harm the grant of the injunction may inflict on the defendant; and

         • Whether the public interest would be disserved if the injunction is granted. 4 INPRAC R 65(65.1); Ind. Family and Soc. Servs. Admin. v. Walgreen Co., 769 N.E.2d 158, 161 (Ind. 2002); Daugherty v. Allen, 729 N.E.2d 228, 232 (Ind.Ct.App. 2000);

      ii. Two (2) sweeping statements about the preliminary injunction often appear:

         • Economic injury alone will not warrant the granting of a preliminary injunction. 4 INPRAC R 65(65.1); Wells v. Auberry, 429 N.E.2d 679 (Ind.Ct.App. 1982), and

         • Injunctive relief is not appropriate if a remedy for damages is an adequate remedy and the defendant is solvent. 4 INPRAC R 65(65.1); Gaslight and Coke Company v. City of New Albany, 139 Ind. 660, 39 N.E. 462 (1894).

   b. *Consolidation of hearing with trial on merits.* Before or after the commencement of the hearing of an application for a preliminary injunction, the court may order the trial of the action on the merits to be advanced and consolidated with the hearing of the application. Even when this consolidation is not ordered, any evidence received upon an application for a preliminary injunction which would be admissible upon the trial on the merits becomes part of the record on the trial and need not be repeated upon the trial. IN ST TRIAL P Rule 65(A)(2).

 i. The power of the court to order advancement and consolidation under IN ST TRIAL P Rule 65 is tempered by the due process requirements of fair notice and an opportunity to be heard. 4 INPRAC R 65(65.3); University of Texas v. Camenisch, 451 U.S. 390, 101 S.Ct. 1830, 68 L.Ed.2d 175 (1981). The court is required to give clear notice that consolidation of the trial on the merits with the hearing on the motion for preliminary injunction will be ordered, and the notice must be given at a time which will afford the parties a full opportunity to present their respective cases. 4 INPRAC R 65(65.3); Paris v. U.S. Department of Housing & Urban Dev., 713 F.2d 1341, 1345, (7th Cir. 1983).

c. *Assignment of cases; Judge to act promptly.* Assignment of cases shall not be affected by the fact that a temporary restraining order or preliminary injunction is sought, but such case shall be assigned promptly and the judge regularly assigned to the case shall act upon and hear all matters relating to temporary restraining orders and preliminary injunctions. The judge shall make himself readily available to consider temporary restraining orders, conduct hearings, fix the manner of giving notice and the time and place for hearings under IN ST TRIAL P Rule 65, and shall act and require the parties to act promptly. IN ST TRIAL P Rule 65(A)(3).

 i. If the party seeking relief or his attorney by affidavit establishes that the judge assigned to the case is not available or cannot be found to consider an application for a restraining order, to conduct a hearing, or to fix the manner of giving notice and the time and place for a hearing under IN ST TRIAL P Rule 65, he may apply to any other judge in the circuit who shall take all further action with respect to any temporary restraining order or preliminary injunction. If the affidavit establishes that no other judge in the circuit is available or to be found, he may apply to the judge of any adjoining circuit. Unless an order is entered within ten (10) days after the hearing upon the granting, modifying or dissolving of a temporary or preliminary injunction, the relief sought shall be subject to the provisions of IN ST TRIAL P Rule 53.1. IN ST TRIAL P Rule 65(A)(3).

d. *Modification of orders; Responsive pleadings.* Upon the court's own motion or the motion of any party, orders granting or denying temporary restraining orders or preliminary injunctions may be dissolved, modified, granted or reinstated. Responsive pleadings shall not be required in response to any pleadings or motions relating to temporary restraining orders or preliminary injunctions. IN ST TRIAL P Rule 65(A)(4).

e. *Form of order by judge.* Every order granting temporary injunction and every restraining order shall include or be accompanied by findings as required by IN ST TRIAL P Rule 52; shall be specific in terms; shall describe in reasonable detail, and not by reference to the complaint or other document, the act or acts sought to be restrained; and is binding only upon the parties to the action, their officers, agents, servants, employees, and attorneys, and upon those persons in active concert or participation with them who receive actual notice of the order by personal service or otherwise. IN ST TRIAL P Rule 65(D).

3. *Security*

a. *Security requirement.* No restraining order or preliminary injunction shall issue except upon the giving of security by the applicant, in such sum as the court deems proper, for the payment of such costs and damages as may be incurred or suffered by any party who is found to have been wrongfully enjoined or restrained. No such security shall be required of a governmental organization, but such governmental organization shall be responsible for costs and damages as may be incurred or suffered by any party who is found to have been wrongfully enjoined or restrained. IN ST TRIAL P Rule 65(C).

 i. The provisions of IN ST TRIAL P Rule 65.1 apply to a surety upon a bond or undertaking under IN ST TRIAL P Rule 65. IN ST TRIAL P Rule 65(C).

b. *Proceedings against sureties.* Whenever the Indiana Rules of Trial Procedure or other laws require or permit the giving of security by a party to a court action or proceeding, and security is given in the form of a bond or stipulation or other undertaking with one or more sureties, each surety submits himself to the jurisdiction of the court and irrevocably appoints the clerk of the court as his agent upon whom any papers affecting his liability on the bond or undertaking may be served. His liability may be enforced on motion without the necessity of an independent action. The motion and such notice of the motion as the court prescribes may be served on the clerk of the court, who shall forthwith mail copies to the sureties if their addresses are known. IN ST TRIAL P Rule 65.1 applies to bonds or security furnished on appeal, and enforcement shall be in the court to which the case is returned after appeal. IN ST TRIAL P Rule 65.1.

    c. *Bond generally used as security.* IN ST TRIAL P Rule 65(C) speaks only of the giving of security and does not expressly require a surety on a bond. In practice, however, the giving of a bond with an insurance company as surety in the amount set by the court is typically the device used to satisfy this section. 4 INPRAC R 65(65.6).

4. *Opposition to a motion for preliminary injunction.* Failure to file an answer brief or reply brief within the time prescribed shall be deemed a waiver of the right thereto and shall subject the motion to summary ruling. IN ST ST JOSEPH CIV Rule 206(206.1).

D. Documents

1. *Required documents*

    a. *Motion and notice.* No preliminary injunction shall be issued without an opportunity for a hearing upon notice to the adverse party. IN ST TRIAL P Rule 65(A)(1). The requirement of notice is satisfied by service of the motion. IN ST TRIAL P Rule 7(B). Refer to the General Requirements section of this document for information on the content of a motion for preliminary injunction.

    b. *Chronological Case Summary (CCS) entry form.* Every written motion, petition, or other pleading subsequent to the original complaint presented to the Clerk for filing shall be accompanied by a Chronological Case Summary (CCS) entry form in duplicate. IN ST ST JOSEPH CIV Rule 201(201.4). Refer to the Format section of this document for details on the format and filing requirements for the CCS entry form.

    c. *Affidavit.* In all applications for an injunction, the complaint or as much of the complaint as pertains to the acts or proceedings to be enjoined, must be verified by affidavit. IN ST 34-26-1-7.

    d. *Security.* No restraining order or preliminary injunction shall issue except upon the giving of security by the applicant, in such sum as the court deems proper, for the payment of such costs and damages as may be incurred or suffered by any party who is found to have been wrongfully enjoined or restrained. IN ST TRIAL P Rule 65(C). Refer to the General Requirements section of this document for more information.

    e. *Proposed order.* Unless local practice provides differently, a party should submit a proposed order with its written motion to be signed by the judge once the motion has been granted. 21 INPRAC § 13.8. All proposed orders shall be submitted in an original plus a number of copies equal to one more than the number of pro se parties and attorneys of record contained in the prepared proof of notice under IN ST TRIAL P Rule 72(D). IN ST ST JOSEPH CIV Rule 213(213.3); IN ST ST JOSEPH CIV Rule 201(201.5.2).

    f. *Certificate of service.* An attorney or unrepresented party tendering a document to the Clerk for filing shall certify that service has been made, list the parties served, and specify the date and means of service. The certificate of service shall be placed at the end of the document and shall not be separately filed. The separate filing of a certificate of service, however, shall not be grounds for rejecting a document for filing. The Clerk may permit documents to be filed without a certificate of service but shall require prompt filing of a separate certificate of service. IN ST TRIAL P Rule 5(C).

2. *Supplemental documents*

    a. *Supporting evidence.* When a motion is based on facts not appearing of record the court may hear the matter on affidavits presented by the respective parties, but the court may direct that the matter be heard wholly or partly on oral testimony or depositions. IN ST TRIAL P Rule 43(B).

    b. *Facsimile cover sheet.* Any document sent to the Clerk of the Circuit Court by electronic facsimile transmission shall be accompanied by a cover sheet which states the title of the document, case number, number of pages, identity and voice telephone number of the sending party and instructions for filing. The cover sheet shall contain the signature of the attorney or party, pro se, authorizing the filing. IN ST ADMIN Rule 12(D).

E. Format

1. *Form of motions.* The rules applicable to captions, and the signing and form of pleadings (IN ST TRIAL P Rule 8 through IN ST TRIAL P Rule 11), apply to all motions and other papers provided under the Indiana Rules of Trial Procedure. 22B INPRAC 7:2.

   a. *Separate motions; Alternative motions.* Each motion shall be separate, while alternative motions filed together shall each be identified on the caption. IN ST ST JOSEPH CIV Rule 206(206.1).

2. *Form of pleadings*

   a. *Caption; Names of parties.* Every pleading shall contain a caption setting forth the name of the court, the title of the action, the file number, and a designation as in IN ST TRIAL P Rule 7(A). In the complaint the title of the action shall include the names of all the parties, but in other pleadings it is sufficient to state the name of the first party on each side with an appropriate indication of other parties. IN ST TRIAL P Rule 10(A); IN ST ST JOSEPH CIV Rule 201(201.3.3). If a special judge has been assigned to the case, the pleading should also identify the special judge. IN ST ST JOSEPH CIV Rule 201(201.3.3).

      i. *Title.* All pleadings or motions shall include a title, which shall delineate each topic included in the pleading. For example, where a pleading contains an answer, a motion to dismiss, and a jury request, each topic shall be set forth in the title. IN ST ST JOSEPH CIV Rule 201(201.3.4).

   b. *Paragraphs; Separate statements.* All averments of a claim or defense shall be made in numbered paragraphs, the contents of each of which shall be limited as far as practicable to a statement of a single set of circumstances, and a paragraph may be referred to by number in all succeeding pleadings. Each claim founded upon a separate transaction or occurrence and each defense other than denials may be stated in a separate count or defense whenever a separation facilitates the clear presentation of the matters set forth. IN ST TRIAL P Rule 10(B).

   c. *Adoption by reference; Exhibits.* Statements in a pleading may be adopted by reference in a different part of the same pleading or in another pleading or in any motion. A copy of any written instrument which is an exhibit to a pleading is a part thereof for all purposes. IN ST TRIAL P Rule 10(C).

   d. *Flat filing.* In order that the Clerk's files may be kept under the system commonly known as "flat filing," all papers presented to the Clerk for filing shall be flat and unfolded. Pleadings shall have no covers or backs and shall be fastened together at the top left-hand corner only. IN ST ST JOSEPH CIV Rule 201(201.1).

   e. *One side of page used.* Printing shall be on one (1) side of the paper. IN ST ST JOSEPH CIV Rule 201(201.3.2).

   f. *Copies.* All copies shall be on white paper of sufficient strength and durability to resist normal wear and tear. IN ST ST JOSEPH CIV Rule 201(201.3.1).

   g. *Margins.* Margins shall be at least one inch (1"). IN ST ST JOSEPH CIV Rule 201(201.3.2).

   h. *Double-spaced.* If typewritten, the lines shall be double spaced except for quotations, which shall be indented and single-spaced. IN ST ST JOSEPH CIV Rule 201(201.3.2).

   i. *Font size.* Type face shall be twelve (12) font size or larger within the body of the document and ten (10) font size or larger in the footnotes. IN ST ST JOSEPH CIV Rule 201(201.3.2).

   j. *Font type.* The font type must be legible and script type shall not be used. IN ST ST JOSEPH CIV Rule 201(201.3.2).

   k. *Italics.* Italicized type may be used for quotations, references, or case citations. IN ST ST JOSEPH CIV Rule 201(201.3.2).

   l. *Court and case designation.* All filings shall conform to the requirements for uniform court and case number designation set by IN ST ADMIN Rule 8. In addition, all filings shall contain the proper court and case designation as described below. IN ST ST JOSEPH CIV Rule 202.

    i.   *Court designation.* Pursuant to IN ST 33-33-71-2, St. Joseph County, Indiana, constitutes the Sixtieth Judicial Circuit. The legal names of the courts within the 60th Judicial Circuit are the St. Joseph Circuit Court, the St. Joseph Superior Court, and the St. Joseph Probate Court. All filings shall properly reflect the legal name of the applicable court. Any filing may be amended, rejected, or stricken if it does not contain the proper case name and/or the legal name of the court. IN ST ST JOSEPH CIV Rule 202(202.1).

m.   *Form of CCS entry.* Every written motion, petition, or other pleading subsequent to the original complaint presented to the Clerk for filing shall be accompanied by a Chronological Case Summary (CCS) entry form in duplicate which shall contain the title and cause number of the action, the date, and the proposed entry to appear on the docket. IN ST ST JOSEPH CIV Rule 201(201.4).

    i.   *Identification and signature.* The CCS entry form shall identify the party making the filing, designate each pleading being filed, and shall be signed by counsel of record or the unrepresented litigant. IN ST ST JOSEPH CIV Rule 201(201.4).

    ii.   *Date stamp.* The form shall be date stamped and presented to the Court Clerk, who shall initial the form and return the duplicate to the filing party. IN ST ST JOSEPH CIV Rule 201(201.4).

n.   *Form of proposed order.* Any proposed order shall be a document that is separate and apart from the motion or application to which it relates and shall contain a caption showing the name of the court, the case number assigned to the case, and the title of the case as shown by the complaint pursuant to IN ST ST JOSEPH CIV Rule 201. IN ST ST JOSEPH CIV Rule 213(213.2).

    i.   If there are multiple parties, the title may be shortened to include only the first name plaintiff and defendant with appropriate indication that there are additional parties. IN ST ST JOSEPH CIV Rule 213(213.2).

    ii.   The proposed order shall be on white paper, eight and one-half by eleven inches (8 1/2" x 11") in size, and each page shall be numbered. IN ST ST JOSEPH CIV Rule 213(213.2).

    iii.   The last page of the proposed order shall contain a line for the date, either "Dated _____" or "Signed on the date filemarked hereon." IN ST ST JOSEPH CIV Rule 213(213.2).

    iv.   On the last page there also shall be a line for the signature of the Judge under which shall be typed "Judge, St. Joseph [Circuit or Superior or Probate] Court." IN ST ST JOSEPH CIV Rule 213(213.2).

    v.   If the proposed order contains a recommendation from a Magistrate, the last page shall have a line for the signature of the Magistrate under which shall be typed "Magistrate, St. Joseph [Circuit or Superior or Probate] Court," to the left of which shall be the following, "So Recommended:" and beneath and to the left of which shall be typed, "Approved. So Ordered." IN ST ST JOSEPH CIV Rule 213(213.2).

    vi.   To allow compliance with the notice requirements of IN ST TRIAL P Rule 72(D), the lower four (4) inches of the last page of the proposed order shall be left blank. The proposed order shall also include a prepared proof of notice under IN ST TRIAL P Rule 72(D), and in preparing such a notice the filing party shall complete all portions of the prepared proof of notice. IN ST ST JOSEPH CIV Rule 213(213.2).

3.   *Size of papers for filing.* Effective January 1, 1992, all pleadings, copies, motions and documents filed with any trial court or appellate level court, typed or printed, with the exception of exhibits and existing wills, shall be prepared on eight and one-half by eleven inch (8 1/2" x 11") size paper. IN ST ADMIN Rule 11.

a.   *Paper.* Pleadings, motions, and other papers shall be either legibly printed or typewritten on white opaque paper of good quality at least sixteen (16) pound weight, eight and one-half inches (8 1/2 ") in width and eleven inches (11") in length as required by IN ST ADMIN Rule 11. IN ST ST JOSEPH CIV Rule 201(201.3.1).

4.   *Signature requirements*

a.   *Signature of attorney.* Every pleading or motion of a party represented by an attorney shall be signed

by at least one (1) attorney of record in his individual name, whose address, telephone number, and attorney number shall be stated, except that this provision shall not apply to pleadings and motions made and transcribed at the trial or a hearing before the judge and received by him in such form. IN ST TRIAL P Rule 11(A).

    i.   The signature of an attorney constitutes a certificate by him that he has read the pleadings; that to the best of his knowledge, information, and belief, there is good ground to support it; and that it is not interposed for delay. IN ST TRIAL P Rule 11(A).

    ii.   If a pleading or motion is not signed or is signed with intent to defeat the purpose of the rule, it may be stricken as sham and false and the action may proceed as though the pleading had not been served. IN ST TRIAL P Rule 11(A).

    iii.   For a willful violation of IN ST TRIAL P Rule 11 an attorney may be subjected to appropriate disciplinary action. Similar action may be taken if scandalous or indecent matter is inserted. IN ST TRIAL P Rule 11(A).

b.   *Signature of unrepresented party.* A party who is not represented by an attorney shall sign his pleading and state his address. IN ST TRIAL P Rule 11(A).

c.   *Verification not generally required.* Except when specifically required by rule, pleadings or motions need not be verified or accompanied by affidavit. The rule in equity that the averments of an answer under oath must be overcome by the testimony of two (2) witnesses or of one (1) witness sustained by corroborating circumstances is abolished. IN ST TRIAL P Rule 11(A).

d.   *Verification by affirmation or representation.* When in connection with any civil or special statutory proceeding it is required that any pleading, motion, petition, supporting affidavit, or other document of any kind, be verified, or that an oath be taken, it shall be sufficient if the subscriber simply affirms the truth of the matter to be verified by an affirmation or representation. IN ST TRIAL P Rule 11(B). IN ST TRIAL P Rule 11(B) states that the affirmation or representation should be in substantially the following language: "I (we) affirm, under the penalties for perjury, that the foregoing representation(s) is (are) true. (Signed) _____."

    i.   Any person who falsifies an affirmation or representation of fact shall be subject to the same penalties as are prescribed by law for the making of a false affidavit. IN ST TRIAL P Rule 11(B).

e.   *Verified pleadings, motions, and affidavits as evidence.* Pleadings, motions and affidavits accompanying or in support of such pleadings or motions when required to be verified or under oath shall be accepted as a representation that the signer had personal knowledge thereof or reasonable cause to believe the existence of the facts or matters stated or alleged therein; and, if otherwise competent or acceptable as evidence, may be admitted as evidence of the facts or matters stated or alleged therein when it is so provided in the Indiana Rules of Trial Procedure, by statute or other law, or to the extent the writing or signature expressly purports to be made upon the signer's personal knowledge. When such pleadings, motions and affidavits are verified or under oath they shall not require other or greater proof on the part of the adverse party than if not verified or not under oath unless expressly provided otherwise by the Indiana Rules of Trial Procedure, statute or other law. Affidavits upon motions for summary judgment under IN ST TRIAL P Rule 56 and in denial of execution under IN ST TRIAL P Rule 9.2 shall be made upon personal knowledge. IN ST TRIAL P Rule 11(C).

f.   *Signature, verification and other requirements.* Parties and their counsel are enjoined to comply with the verification requirements of IN ST TRIAL P Rule 11, and either the moving party or the party's attorney of record shall sign all pleadings and motions before filing with the Clerk of the Court. Every motion, petition, or other pleading filed with the Clerk shall contain the name, organization, physical address, telephone number, and facsimile number of the filing party or an attorney for that party. IN ST ST JOSEPH CIV Rule 201(201.3.6).

    i.   The Clerk shall not accept any motion, petition, notice or other pleading or a CCS entry form for filing from an unrepresented litigant unless the unrepresented litigant's current address and phone number appear on the pleading, and an opposing party may service notices and responses on an unrepresented litigant at any address he or she has provided on a pleading. IN ST ST JOSEPH CIV Rule 201(201.3.6).

5. *Information excluded from public access.* Every document filed in a case shall separately identify information excluded from public access pursuant to IN ST ADMIN Rule 9(G)(1) as follows:

   a. Whole documents that are excluded from public access pursuant to IN ST ADMIN Rule 9(G)(1) shall be tendered on light green paper or have a light green coversheet attached to the document, marked "Not for Public Access" or "Confidential." IN ST TRIAL P Rule 5(G)(1).

   b. When only a portion of a document contains information excluded from public access pursuant to IN ST ADMIN Rule 9(G)(1), said information shall be omitted [or redacted] from the filed document, and set forth on a separate accompanying document on light green paper conspicuously marked "Not for Public Access" or "Confidential" and clearly designated [or identifying] the caption and number of the case and the document and location within the document to which the redacted material pertains. IN ST TRIAL P Rule 5(G)(2).

   c. With respect to documents filed in electronic format, the trial court, by local rule, may provide for compliance with IN ST TRIAL P Rule 5 in manner that separates and protects access to information excluded from public access. IN ST TRIAL P Rule 5(G)(3).

   d. IN ST TRIAL P Rule 5(G) does not apply to a record sealed by the court pursuant to IN ST 5-14-3-5.5 or otherwise, nor to records, documents, or information filed in cases to which public access is prohibited pursuant to IN ST ADMIN Rule 9(G). IN ST TRIAL P Rule 5(G)(4).

   e. The following information in case records is excluded from public access and is confidential:

      i. Information that is excluded from public access pursuant to federal law;

      ii. Information that is excluded from public access as declared confidential by Indiana statute or other court rule, including without limitation:

         • All adoption records created after July 8, 1941, as declared confidential by IN ST 31-19-19-1, et seq., except those specifically declared open by IN ST 31-19-13-2(2);

         • All records relating to chancroid, chlamydia, gonorrhea, hepatitis, human immunodeficiency virus (HIV), Lymphogranuloma venereum, syphilis, tuberculosis, as declared confidential by IN ST 16-41-8-1, et seq.;

         • All records relating to child abuse as declared confidential by IN ST 31-33-18-1, et seq.;

         • All records relating to drug tests as declared confidential by IN ST 5-14-3-4(a)(9);

         • Records of grand jury proceedings as declared confidential by IN ST 35-34-2-4;

         • Records of juvenile proceedings as declared confidential by IN ST 31-39-1-2, except those specifically open under statute;

         • All paternity records created after July 1, 1941 as declared confidential by IN ST 31-14-11-15, IN ST 31-19-5-23, IN ST 31-39-1-1 and IN ST 31-39-1-2 [Editor's note: IN ST 31-14-11-15 was repealed effective May 9, 2013];

         • All pre-sentence reports as declared confidential by IN ST 35-38-1-13;

         • Written petitions to permit marriages without consent and orders directing the Clerk of Court to issue a marriage license to underage persons, as declared confidential by IN ST 31-11-1-6;

         • Only those arrest warrants, search warrants, indictments and informations ordered confidential by the trial judge, prior to return of duly executed service as declared confidential by IN ST 5-14-3-4(b)(1);

         • All medical, mental health, or tax records unless determined by law or regulation of any governmental custodian not to be confidential, released by the subject of such records, or declared by a court of competent jurisdiction to be essential to the resolution of litigation as declared confidential by IN ST 16-39-3-10, IN ST 6-4.1-5-10, IN ST 6-4.1-12-12, and IN ST 6-8.1-7-1;

         • Personal information relating to jurors or prospective jurors, other than for the use of the parties and counsel, pursuant to IN ST JURY Rule 10;

- Information relating to protection from abuse orders, no-contact orders and workplace violence restraining orders as declared confidential by IN ST 5-2-9-6, et seq.;

- Mediation proceedings pursuant to IN ST ADR Rule 2.11, Mini-Trial proceedings pursuant to IN ST ADR Rule 4.4(C), and Summary Jury Trials pursuant to IN ST ADR Rule 5.6;

- Information in probation files pursuant to the Probation Standards promulgated by the Judicial Conference of Indiana pursuant to IN ST 11-13-1-8(b);

- Information deemed confidential pursuant to the Rules for Court Administered Alcohol and Drug Programs promulgated by the Judicial Conference of Indiana pursuant to IN ST 12-23-14-13;

- Information deemed confidential pursuant to the Problem-Solving Court Rules promulgated by the Judicial Conference of Indiana pursuant to IN ST 33-23-16-16;

- All records of the Department of workforce Development as declared confidential by IN ST 22-4-19-6;

- Information regarding interception of electronic communications that is sealed or deemed confidential as set forth in IN ST 35-33.5-2-1, et seq.

   iii. Information excluded from public access by specific court order;

   iv. Complete Social Security Numbers of living persons;

   v. With the exception of names, information such as addresses, phone numbers, and dates of birth which explicitly identifies:

- Natural persons who are witnesses or victims (not including defendants) in criminal, domestic violence, stalking, sexual assault, juvenile, or civil protection order proceedings, provided that juveniles who are victims of sex crimes shall be identified by initials only;

- Places of residence of judicial officers, clerks and other employees of courts and clerks of court, unless the person or persons about whom the information pertains waives confidentiality;

   vi. Complete account numbers of specific assets, loans, bank accounts, credit cards, and personal identification numbers (PINs);

   vii. All orders of expungement entered in criminal or juvenile proceedings, orders to restrict access to criminal history information pursuant to IN ST 35-38-5-5.5 or IN ST 35-38-8-5 and records excluded from public access by such orders, and information related to infractions that is excluded from public access pursuant to IN ST 34-28-5-15 or IN ST 34-28-5-16 [Editor's note: IN ST 35-38-5-5.5, IN ST 35-38-8-5 and IN ST 34-28-5-16 were repealed effective July 1, 2013; for information on orders restricting access to criminal history, refer to IN ST 35-38-9-1, et seq.];

   viii. All personal notes and e-mail, and deliberative material, of judges, jurors, court staff and judicial agencies, and information recorded in personal data assistants (PDA's) or organizers and personal calendars. IN ST ADMIN Rule 9(G)(1).

F. Filing and Service Requirements

1. *Filing requirements.* Except as otherwise provided in IN ST TRIAL P Rule 5(E)(2), all pleadings and papers subsequent to the complaint which are required to be served upon a party shall be filed with the Court either before service or within a reasonable period of time thereafter. IN ST TRIAL P Rule 5(E)(1).

   a. *Filing with the court defined.* The filing of pleadings, motions, and other papers with the court as required by the Indiana Rules of Trial Procedure shall be made by one of the following methods:

      i. Delivery to the clerk of the court;

      ii. Sending by electronic transmission under the procedure adopted pursuant to IN ST ADMIN Rule 12;

      iii. Mailing to the clerk by registered, certified or express mail return receipt requested;

    iv. Depositing with any third-party commercial carrier for delivery to the clerk within three (3) calendar days, cost prepaid, properly addressed;

    v. If the court so permits, filing with the judge, in which event the judge shall note thereon the filing date and forthwith transmit them to the office of the clerk; or

    vi. Electronic filing, as approved by the Division of State Court Administration pursuant to IN ST ADMIN Rule 16. IN ST TRIAL P Rule 5(F).

    vii. Filing by registered or certified mail and by third-party commercial carrier shall be complete upon mailing or deposit. IN ST TRIAL P Rule 5(F).

    viii. All pleadings shall be filed with the Clerk, not directly with the Court, unless otherwise required by the Indiana Rules of Court. The entry of appearances and the filing of pleadings or other matters not requiring immediate Court action shall be filed with the Clerk and not in open Court. A Judge may permit papers to be filed in chambers, in which event he or she shall note thereon the filing date and transmit the papers to the Clerk. IN ST ST JOSEPH CIV Rule 201(201.2).

  b. *Facsimile filing.* Unless otherwise authorized by IN ST ST JOSEPH ELECTRONIC Rule 701, electronic filing of pleadings by computerized or facsimile transmission is not permitted. IN ST ST JOSEPH CIV Rule 201(201.2).

  c. *Additional copies.* In cases in which a party or counsel supplies the proposed order or decree, a sufficient number shall be prepared and filed as to provide the Clerk to retain two (2) copies, which shall be filed in the flat file and the record of judgments and orders. Should the party or counsel desire additional copies, a sufficient number of copies should be filed to effectuate that purpose. IN ST ST JOSEPH CIV Rule 201(201.6).

  d. *Proof of filing.* Any party filing any paper by any method other than personal delivery to the clerk shall retain proof of filing. IN ST TRIAL P Rule 5(F).

2. *Service requirements.* Unless otherwise provided by the Indiana Rules of Trial Procedure or an order of the court, each party and special judge, if any, shall be served with: (1) every order required by its terms to be served; (2) every pleading subsequent to the original complaint; (3) every written motion except one which may be heard ex parte; (4) every brief submitted to the trial court; (5) every paper relating to discovery required to be served upon a party; and (6) every written notice, appearance, demand, offer of judgment, designation of record on appeal, or similar paper. IN ST TRIAL P Rule 5(A).

  a. *Service generally.* Every motion, petition, notice, or other pleading required to be served by IN ST TRIAL P Rule 5 shall be served on all counsel of record or unrepresented parties either before it is filed or on the day it is filed with the Court, and the date of filing shall be indicated on the Certificate of Service. IN ST ST JOSEPH CIV Rule 201(201.5.1).

    i. *Copy.* A copy of the Clerk's CCS entry form of the filing shall also be served on all counsel of record or unrepresented parties whenever it contains an appearance of counsel or contains a date for Court hearing on the matter. IN ST ST JOSEPH CIV Rule 201(201.5.1).

  b. *Methods of service*

    i. *Personal service.* Whenever a party is represented by an attorney of record, service shall be made upon such attorney unless service upon the party himself is ordered by the court. Service upon the attorney or party shall be made by delivering or mailing a copy of the papers to the last known address or where an attorney or party has consented to service by fax or e-mail, as provided in IN ST TRIAL P Rule 3.1(A)(4), by faxing or e-mailing a copy of the documents to the fax number or e-mail address set out in the appearance form or correction as required by IN ST TRIAL P Rule 3.1(E). IN ST TRIAL P Rule 5(B). Delivery of a copy within IN ST TRIAL P Rule 5 means:

      • Offering or tendering it to the attorney or party and stating the nature of the papers being served. Refusal to accept an offered or tendered document is a waiver of any objection to the sufficiency or adequacy of service of that document;

      • Leaving it at his office with a clerk or other person in charge thereof, or if there is no one in charge, leaving it in a conspicuous place therein; or

- If the office is closed, by leaving it at his dwelling house or usual place of abode with some person of suitable age and discretion then residing therein; or,

- Leaving it at some other suitable place, selected by the attorney upon whom service is being made, pursuant to duly promulgated local rule. IN ST TRIAL P Rule 5(B)(1).

ii. *Service by the clerk.* Whenever the Clerk is required by rule or statute to give notice, the party or parties requesting such notice shall furnish the Clerk with sufficient copies of the notice to be given, along with stamped, addressed envelopes with the names and the addresses of the parties or their counsel to whom such notice is to be given. IN ST ST JOSEPH CIV Rule 201(201.5.4).

iii. *Service on the court.* Service on a Judge may be made by delivering a copy to the Judge's secretary or mailing a copy to the Judge at his or her chambers. Service on a Judge may not be accomplished by facsimile transmission; however, a courtesy copy may be sent to the Judge's chambers by electronic mail or facsimile transmission contemporaneously with service by mail or otherwise. IN ST ST JOSEPH CIV Rule 201(201.5.5).

iv. *Service by mail.* If service is made by mail, the papers shall be deposited in the United States mail addressed to the person on whom they are being served, with postage prepaid. Service shall be deemed complete upon mailing. Proof of service of all papers permitted to be mailed may be made by written acknowledgment of service, by affidavit of the person who mailed the papers, or by certificate of an attorney. It shall be the duty of attorneys when entering their appearance in a cause or when filing pleadings or papers therein, to have noted in the Chronological Case Summary or said pleadings or papers so filed the address and telephone number of their office. Service by delivery or by mail at such address shall be deemed sufficient and complete. IN ST TRIAL P Rule 5(B)(2).

v. *Service by fax or e-mail.* A party who has consented to service by fax or e-mail may be served as follows:

- Service by e-mail shall be made by attaching the document being served in .pdf format. Discovery documents must also be served in accordance with IN ST TRIAL P Rule 26(A). IN ST TRIAL P Rule 5(B)(3)(a).

- Service by fax shall be deemed complete upon generation of a transmission record indicating the successful transmission of the entire document, except as provided in IN ST TRIAL P Rule 5(B)(3)(d). IN ST TRIAL P Rule 5(B)(3)(b).

- Service by e-mail shall be deemed complete upon transmission, except as provided in IN ST TRIAL P Rule 5(B)(3)(d). IN ST TRIAL P Rule 5(B)(3)(c).

- Service by fax or e-mail that occurs on a Saturday, Sunday, legal holiday, or day the court or agency in which the matter is pending is closed or after 5:00 PM local time of the recipient shall be deemed complete the next day that is not a Saturday, Sunday, legal holiday, or day that the court or agency in which the matter is pending is not closed. IN ST TRIAL P Rule 5(B)(3)(d).

c. *Serving numerous defendants.* In any action in which there are unusually large numbers of defendants, the court, upon motion or of its own initiative, may order:

i. That service of the pleadings of the defendants and replies thereto need not be made as between the defendants;

- That any cross-claim, counterclaim, or matter constituting an avoidance or affirmative defense contained therein shall be deemed to be denied or avoided by all other parties; and

- That the filing of any such pleading and service thereof upon the plaintiff constitutes due notice of it to the parties. IN ST TRIAL P Rule 5(D).

ii. A copy of every such order shall be served upon the parties in such manner and form as the court directs. IN ST TRIAL P Rule 5(D).

d. *Service on parties in default for failure to appear.* No service need be made on parties in default for failure to appear, except that pleadings asserting new or additional claims for relief against them shall be served upon them in the manner provided by service of summons in IN ST TRIAL P Rule 4. IN ST TRIAL P Rule 5(A).

e. *Distribution.* Counsel or an unrepresented party submitting a motion, petition, notice, pleading or proposed order shall indicate the method of distribution desired on the Clerk's CCS entry form. The Clerk will not return or distribute copies of motions, petitions, pleadings, notices or proposed orders, other than those originated by the Court, by mail unless the Clerk is provided with stamped, addressed envelopes. IN ST ST JOSEPH CIV Rule 201(201.5.3).

f. *Mailbox.* As a matter of convenience to attorneys, each court provides a mailbox for the distribution filings and orders generated by the Court, and it is the responsibility of each attorney to periodically check these mailboxes for service and distribution of court-generated filings and orders. IN ST ST JOSEPH CIV Rule 201(201.5.3).

G. Hearings

1. *Hearing on motion.* Unless local conditions make it impracticable, each judge shall establish regular times and places, at intervals sufficiently frequent for the prompt dispatch of business, at which motions requiring notice and hearing may be heard and disposed of; but the judge at any time or place and on such notice, if any, as he considers reasonable may make order for the advancement, conduct, and hearing of actions. To expedite its business the court may direct the submission and determination of motions without oral hearing upon brief written statements of reasons in support and opposition, or direct or permit hearings by telephone conference call with all attorneys or other similar means of communication. IN ST TRIAL P Rule 73(A).

2. *Presentation of evidence.* On the hearing of an application for a restraining order or temporary injunction, each party may read affidavits or documentary or record evidence. IN ST 34-26-1-8.

3. *Hearing dates.* Hearing dates for filings requiring Court action shall be obtained from the Court Clerk and incorporated in the CCS entry at the time the motion or other pleading is filed. If no date is obtained prior to the filing, the fact of the hearing should be noted with the date and time left blank. IN ST ST JOSEPH CIV Rule 201(201.4).

4. *Hearing on matters other than trials.* Each Judge shall reserve periods of time for hearing matters other than contested trials, such as pre-trial and post-trial motions, rules to show cause, defaults, uncontested dissolutions of marriage, etc. As necessary to minimize conflicts in scheduling, the Judges shall set these schedules after consultation. Hearings shall be scheduled as follows:

   a. *Scheduling uncontested or routine matters.* Routine matters, procedural motions, domestic relations applications for provisional relief and contempt proceedings, uncontested petitions for dissolution of marriage, and all other matters appropriate for summary consideration and disposition will be heard on the daily calendar. IN ST ST JOSEPH GEN AND ADMIN Rule 104(104.3.1).

   b. *Scheduling contested or complicated matters.* Other matters that will require a hearing reasonably estimated to last in excess of twenty (20) minutes will be scheduled as the Court's calendar allows. Counsel or a party proceeding pro se should contact the chambers of the assigned judge to arrange for an appropriate hearing date and time. IN ST ST JOSEPH GEN AND ADMIN Rule 104(104.3.2).

   c. *Scheduling motions for hearings.* Except for motions to correct error or not likely to require a hearing (as described in IN ST ST JOSEPH CIV Rule 201), all motions shall be scheduled for hearing at the time they are filed. It shall the responsibility of the moving party or counsel for the moving party to secure the date and time of the hearing from the Clerk or Court personnel who maintain the calendar for each Judge or Magistrate Judge. It shall also be the responsibility of the moving party or counsel for the moving party to coordinate the hearing date with all opposing counsel or unrepresented parties. IN ST ST JOSEPH CIV Rule 201(201.9.1).

   d. *Oral arguments on motions and other pleadings.* Unless otherwise required by St. Joseph County Civil or Indiana Trial Rules, it is within the sound discretion of the assigned Judge whether to allow oral argument; however, any party may file a request for oral argument by filing a written request by separate motion contemporaneously or at any time before the Court has ruled upon the motion or pleadings to be argued. IN ST ST JOSEPH CIV Rule 201(201.9.4).

H. Forms

1. Motion for Preliminary Injunction Forms for Indiana

   a. Prayer in complaint; For preliminary injunction. 5 INPRAC § 3:13.20.

b. Motion for preliminary injunction. 5 INPRAC § 3:13.40.

c. Notice of motion for preliminary injunction. 11 INPRAC § 97.14.

d. Undertaking as security to support granting of injunction. 11 INPRAC § 97.14.1.

e. Findings of fact in support of injunction. 11 INPRAC § 97.14.2.

f. Motion to dissolve temporary restraining order. 11 INPRAC § 97.14.3.

g. Motion for contempt for violation of injunction. 11 INPRAC § 97.14.4.

h. Motion for preliminary injunction. 11 INPRAC § 97.15.

i. Preliminary injunction. 11 INPRAC § 97.16.

j. Motion to vacate preliminary injunction; Failure to post bond. 11 INPRAC § 97.17.

k. Motion to vacate preliminary injunction; Another form. 11 INPRAC § 97.18.

l. Certificate of service; Personal service. 9 INPRAC § 5.7.

m. Certificate of service; First class mail. 9 INPRAC § 5.8.

I. Checklist

(I) ❑ Matters to be considered by moving party

  (a) ❑ Required documents

    (1) ❑ Motion and notice

    (2) ❑ Chronological Case Summary (CCS) entry form

    (3) ❑ Affidavit

    (4) ❑ Security

    (5) ❑ Proposed order

    (6) ❑ Certificate of service

  (b) ❑ Supplemental documents

    (1) ❑ Supporting evidence

    (2) ❑ Facsimile cover sheet

  (c) ❑ Timing

    (1) ❑ The injunction may be granted at the time of commencing the action, or at any time afterwards before judgment is rendered in the proceeding

    (2) ❑ A written motion, other than one which may be heard ex parte, and notice of the hearing thereof shall be served not less than five (5) days before the time specified for the hearing, unless a different period is fixed by the Indiana Rules of Trial Procedure or by order of the court

    (3) ❑ All pleadings and papers subsequent to the complaint which are required to be served upon a party shall be filed with the Court either before service or within a reasonable period of time thereafter

(II) ❑ Matters to be considered by the responding party

  (a) ❑ Required documents

    (1) ❑ Opposition

    (2) ❑ Chronological Case Summary (CCS) entry form

    (3) ❑ Certificate of service

  (b) ❑ Supplemental documents

    (1) ❑ Supporting evidence

    (2) ❑ Proposed order

(3) ❏ Facsimile cover sheet

(c) ❏ Timing

(1) ❏ So long as consistent with Indiana Rules of Trial Procedure, an adverse party wishing to respond shall do so within fifteen (15) days of service

(2) ❏ Except as otherwise provided in IN ST TRIAL P Rule 59(D), opposing affidavits may be served not less than one (1) day before the hearing, unless the court permits them to be served at some other time

Motions, Oppositions and Replies
Motion to Dismiss for Failure to State a Claim

Document Last Updated October 2013

A. Applicable Rules

1. *State rules*

    a. Appearance. IN ST TRIAL P Rule 3.1.

    b. Process. IN ST TRIAL P Rule 4.

    c. Service and filing of pleadings and other papers. IN ST TRIAL P Rule 5.

    d. Time. IN ST TRIAL P Rule 6.

    e. Pleadings. IN ST TRIAL P Rule 7; IN ST TRIAL P Rule 8; IN ST TRIAL P Rule 9.2; IN ST TRIAL P Rule 10.

    f. Signing and verification of pleadings. IN ST TRIAL P Rule 11.

    g. Defenses and objections; When and how presented; By pleading or motion; Motion for judgment on the pleadings. IN ST TRIAL P Rule 12.

    h. Parties plaintiff and defendant; Capacity. IN ST TRIAL P Rule 17.

    i. Joinder of person needed for just adjudication. IN ST TRIAL P Rule 19.

    j. Evidence. IN ST TRIAL P Rule 43.

    k. Judgment on the evidence (directed verdict). IN ST TRIAL P Rule 50.

    l. Findings by the court. IN ST TRIAL P Rule 52.

    m. Summary judgment. IN ST TRIAL P Rule 56.

    n. Motion to correct error. IN ST TRIAL P Rule 59.

    o. Relief from judgment or order. IN ST TRIAL P Rule 60.

    p. Hearing of motions. IN ST TRIAL P Rule 73.

    q. Access to court records. IN ST ADMIN Rule 9.

    r. Paper size. IN ST ADMIN Rule 11.

    s. Facsimile transmission. IN ST ADMIN Rule 12.

    t. Electronic filing and electronic service pilot projects. IN ST ADMIN Rule 16.

    u. Sealing of certain records by court; Hearing; Notice. IN ST 5-14-3-5.5.

    v. Sixtieth judicial circuit. IN ST 33-33-71-2.

    w. Privacy and confidentiality. IN ST 5-2-9-6; IN ST 5-14-3-4; IN ST 6-4.1-5-10; IN ST 6-4.1-12-12; IN ST 6-8.1-7-1; IN ST 11-13-1-8; IN ST 12-23-14-13; IN ST 16-39-3-10; IN ST 16-41-8-1; IN ST 22-4-19-6; IN ST 31-11-1-6; IN ST 31-19-5-23; IN ST 31-19-13-2; IN ST 31-19-19-1; IN ST 31-33-18-1; IN ST 31-39-1-1; IN ST 31-39-1-2; IN ST 33-23-16-16; IN ST 35-34-2-4; IN ST 35-38-1-13; IN ST 35-38-9-1; IN ST ADR Rule 2.11; IN ST ADR Rule 4.4; IN ST ADR Rule 5.6; IN ST JURY Rule 10.

2. *Local rules*

    a. Court hours and scheduling. IN ST ST JOSEPH GEN AND ADMIN Rule 104.

    b. Filing, pleading, and motions. IN ST ST JOSEPH CIV Rule 201.

    c. Uniform court and case number designation. IN ST ST JOSEPH CIV Rule 202.

    d. Pleading and motions under IN ST TRIAL P Rule 12 and IN ST TRIAL P Rule 56. IN ST ST JOSEPH CIV Rule 206.

    e. Proposed order. IN ST ST JOSEPH CIV Rule 213.

    f. Electronic filing of cases in St. Joseph County. IN ST ST JOSEPH ELECTRONIC Rule 701.

B. Timing

1. *Timing of motion to dismiss for failure to state a claim.* A motion making any of the defenses listed in IN ST TRIAL P Rule 12(B) shall be made before pleading if a further pleading is permitted or within twenty (20) days after service of the prior pleading if none is required. IN ST TRIAL P Rule 12(B).

    a. *Time to file a responsive pleading.* A responsive pleading required under the Indiana Rules of Trial Procedure, shall be served within twenty (20) days after service of the prior pleading. IN ST TRIAL P Rule 6(C).

    b. *Filing.* All pleadings and papers subsequent to the complaint which are required to be served upon a party shall be filed with the Court either before service or within a reasonable period of time thereafter. IN ST TRIAL P Rule 5(E)(1).

2. *Service.* A written motion, other than one which may be heard ex parte, and notice of the hearing thereof shall be served not less than five (5) days before the time specified for the hearing, unless a different period is fixed by the Indiana Rules of Trial Procedure or by order of the court. IN ST TRIAL P Rule 6(D).

    a. *Of supporting affidavits.* When a motion is supported by affidavit, the affidavit shall be served with the motion; and,

3. *Service of opposition.* Except as otherwise provided in IN ST TRIAL P Rule 59(D), opposing affidavits may be served not less than one (1) day before the hearing, unless the court permits them to be served at some other time. IN ST TRIAL P Rule 6(D).

    a. An adverse party shall have thirty (30) days after service of the motion in which to serve and file an answer brief. IN ST ST JOSEPH CIV Rule 206(206.1).

4. *Filing proposed orders.* Unless otherwise directed or given leave of the Court, proposed orders in emergency matters shall be filed within forty-eight (48) hours after a hearing; proposed orders in other matters shall be filed within seven (7) days as computed by IN ST TRIAL P Rule 6. IN ST ST JOSEPH CIV Rule 213(213.5).

5. *Computation of time*

    a. *Generally; Days excluded.* In computing any period of time prescribed or allowed by the Indiana Rules of Trial Procedure, by order of the court, or by any applicable statute, the day of the act, event, or default from which the designated period of time begins to run shall not be included. The last day of the period so computed is to be included unless it is:

        i. A Saturday,

        ii. A Sunday,

        iii. A legal holiday as defined by state statute, or

        iv. A day the office in which the act is to be done is closed during regular business hours. IN ST TRIAL P Rule 6(A).

    b. *Short periods.* In any event, the period runs until the end of the next day that is not a Saturday, a Sunday, a legal holiday, or a day on which the office is closed. When the period of time allowed is less than seven (7) days, intermediate Saturdays, Sundays, legal holidays, and days on which the office is closed shall be excluded from the computations. IN ST TRIAL P Rule 6(A).

    c. *Additional time after service by United States mail.* Whenever a party has the right or is required to do some act or take some proceedings within a prescribed period after the service of a notice or other paper upon him and the notice or paper is served upon him by United States mail, three (3) days shall be added to the prescribed period. IN ST TRIAL P Rule 6(E).

d. *Enlargement of time.* When an act is required or allowed to be done at or within a specific time by the Indiana Rules of Trial Procedure, the court may at any time for cause shown:

    i. Order the period enlarged, with or without motion or notice, if request therefor is made before the expiration of the period originally prescribed or extended by a previous order; or

    ii. Upon motion made after the expiration of the specific period, permit the act to be done where the failure to act was the result of excusable neglect; but, the court may not extend the time for taking any action for judgment on the evidence under IN ST TRIAL P Rule 50(A), amendment of findings and judgment under IN ST TRIAL P Rule 52(B), to correct errors under IN ST TRIAL P Rule 59(C), statement in opposition to motion to correct error under IN ST TRIAL P Rule 59(E), or to obtain relief from final judgment under IN ST TRIAL P Rule 60(B), except to the extent and under the conditions stated in those rules. IN ST TRIAL P Rule 6(B).

    iii. An initial written motion for enlargement of time pursuant to IN ST TRIAL P Rule 6(B)(1) to answer a claim shall be routinely granted for an additional thirty (30) days from the original due date or other period the assigned Judge deems reasonable by written order of the Court. The motion must be filed on or before the original due date or IN ST ST JOSEPH CIV Rule 201 shall be inapplicable. IN ST ST JOSEPH CIV Rule 201(201.9.5).

       • Any motion for enlargement of time shall state the date when such response is due and the date to which time is requested to be enlarged. IN ST ST JOSEPH CIV Rule 201(201.9.5).

       • All subsequent motions for enlargement of time shall be so designated and will only be granted for good cause shown or in the interest of justice. IN ST ST JOSEPH CIV Rule 201(201.9.5).

C. General Requirements

1. *Motions, generally.* Unless made during a hearing or trial, or otherwise ordered by the court, an application to the court for an order shall be made by written motion. The motion shall state the grounds therefor and the relief or order sought. IN ST TRIAL P Rule 7(B).

    a. *Motions as distinct from pleadings.* Motions and responses to motions are not pleadings, and allegations contained in a motion are not admissions of a party. 22B INPRAC 7:2; Wachstetter v. County Properties, LLC, 832 N.E.2d 574 (Ind.Ct.App. 2005); Scott County Family YMCA, Inc. v. Hobbs, 817 N.E.2d 603 (Ind.Ct.App. 2004).

    b. *Unopposed motions generally granted.* It is common for a trial court to grant procedural motions, such as motions for enlargement of time, discovery motions, or motions for continuance, unless an objection is filed. 21 INPRAC § 13.8.

    c. *Proposed orders.* As directed by the Court, a party or an attorney for a party shall prepare a proposed order based on the decision rendered by the Court. The party so directed shall prepare the proposed order in a timely manner and, upon filing, shall advise the chambers of the applicable judge that the proposed order has been prepared and filed. IN ST ST JOSEPH CIV Rule 213(213.2).

       i. Prior to entry by the Court of orders granting motions or applications, the moving party or applicant (or his or her attorney) shall, unless the Court directs otherwise, furnish the Court with proposed orders in matters of dismissal. IN ST ST JOSEPH CIV Rule 213(213.1(5)).

    d. *Reply brief.* Subject to Court approval, the moving party may file a reply brief. IN ST ST JOSEPH CIV Rule 206(206.1).

2. *Motion to dismiss for failure to state a claim.* Every defense, in law or fact, to a claim for relief in any pleading, whether a claim, counterclaim, cross-claim, or third-party claim, shall be asserted in the responsive pleading thereto if one is required; except that at the option of the pleader, the defense of failure to state a claim upon which relief can be granted, which shall include failure to name the real party in interest under IN ST TRIAL P Rule 17, may be made by motion. IN ST TRIAL P Rule 12(B)(6). A

motion under IN ST TRIAL P Rule 12(B)(6) is intended to test the legal sufficiency of a claim rather than the facts supporting that claim. 1A INPRAC R 12(12.9); Meyers v. Meyers, 861 N.E.2d 704 (Ind. 2007).

a. *How motion made.* A defense of failure to state a claim upon which relief can be granted, a defense of failure to join an indispensable party under IN ST TRIAL P Rule 19(B), and an objection of failure to state a legal defense to a claim may be made in any pleading permitted or ordered under IN ST TRIAL P Rule 7(A) or by motion for judgment on the pleadings, or at the trial on the merits. IN ST TRIAL P Rule 12(H)(2).

b. *Claim admitted for purpose of motion.* A motion to dismiss for failure to state a claim admits, for the purpose of the motion, the existence of the claim as stated in the complaint, but challenges the plaintiff's right to relief. 9 INPRAC § 42.10; Mills v. American Playground Device Co., 427 N.E.2d 1130 (Ind.Ct.App. 1981). Motions to dismiss under IN ST TRIAL P Rule 12 are disfavored because they undermine the policy that favors deciding cases on their merits. 22 INPRAC § 15.19; Droscha v. Shepherd, 931 N.E.2d 882 (Ind.Ct.App. 2010).

c. *Motion decided on factual allegations of complaint.* The trial court should grant a motion to dismiss under IN ST TRIAL P Rule 12(B)(6) if the facts alleged in the complaint are incapable of supporting relief under any set of circumstances. 1A INPRAC R 12(12.9); McPeek v. McCardle, 888 N.E.2d 171 (Ind. 2008). In determining whether the facts alleged in the complaint are incapable of supporting relief, the court must look only to the complaint and may not resort to any other evidence in the record. When ruling on a motion to dismiss under IN ST TRIAL P Rule 12(B)(6), the court should consider all of the allegations in the complaint to be true and resolve all inferences in favor of the non-moving party. 1A INPRAC R 12(12.9); State v. American Family Voices, Inc., 898 N.E.2d 293 (Ind. 2008); Curtis v. Roob, 891 N.E.2d 577 (Ind.Ct.App. 2008).

d. *Notice pleading and motions to dismiss.* Although notice pleading requirements under IN ST TRIAL P Rule 8(A) are fairly straightforward, and are well-grounded in Indiana jurisprudence, the mechanism for testing the legal sufficiency of the complaint, IN ST TRIAL P Rule 12(B)(6), has, over time, become somewhat limited because Indiana courts are instructed to dismiss an action under IN ST TRIAL P Rule 12(B)(6) only where the if the alleged facts do not support a claim for relief under any set of circumstances. 1A INPRAC R 12(12.9). Trial judges do not like to grant IN ST TRIAL P Rule 12(B)(6) motions where the claim is an inadequately pleaded complaint, which means a defendant's first meaningful opportunity to challenge a plaintiff's claim is the motion for summary judgment. 1A INPRAC R 12(12.9).

e. *Conversion to motion for summary judgment.* A motion to dismiss under IN ST TRIAL P Rule 12(B)(6) for failure to state a claim upon which relief and Motion for Judgment on the Pleadings under IN ST TRIAL P Rule 12(C) will be converted into a motion for summary judgment under IN ST TRIAL P Rule 56 if the court considers matters outside the pleadings in deciding those motions. 11 INPRAC § 90.1; Duran v. Komyatte, 490 N.E.2d 388 (Ind.Ct.App. 1986). In such case, all parties shall be given reasonable opportunity to present all material made pertinent to such a motion by IN ST TRIAL P Rule 56. IN ST TRIAL P Rule 12(B).

f. *Effect of granting of the motion.* When a motion to dismiss is sustained for failure to state a claim under IN ST TRIAL P Rule 12(B)(6) the pleading may be amended once as of right pursuant to IN ST TRIAL P Rule 15(A) within ten (10) days after service of notice of the court's order sustaining the motion and thereafter with permission of the court pursuant to such rule. IN ST TRIAL P Rule 12(B).

3. *Consolidation and waiver*

a. *Consolidation of defenses in motion.* A party who makes a motion under IN ST TRIAL P Rule 12 may join with it any other motions herein provided for and then available to him. If a party makes a motion under IN ST TRIAL P Rule 12 but omits therefrom any defense or objection then available to him which IN ST TRIAL P Rule 12 permits to be raised by motion, he shall not thereafter make a motion based on the defense or objection so omitted. He may, however, make such motions as are allowed under IN ST TRIAL P Rule 12(H)(2). IN ST TRIAL P Rule 12(G).

b. *Waiver or preservation of certain defenses.* No defense or objection is waived by being joined with one or more other defenses or objections in a responsive pleading or motion. IN ST TRIAL P Rule 12(B).

4. *Opposition to a motion to dismiss for failure to state a claim.* Failure to file an answer brief or reply brief within the time prescribed shall be deemed a waiver of the right thereto and shall subject the motion to summary ruling. IN ST ST JOSEPH CIV Rule 206(206.1).

D. Documents

1. *Required documents*

   a. *Motion and notice.* The requirement of notice is satisfied by service of the motion. IN ST TRIAL P Rule 7(B). Refer to the General Requirements section of this document for information on the content of a motion to dismiss to dismiss for failure to state a claim.

   b. *Chronological Case Summary (CCS) entry form.* Every written motion, petition, or other pleading subsequent to the original complaint presented to the Clerk for filing shall be accompanied by a Chronological Case Summary (CCS) entry form in duplicate. IN ST ST JOSEPH CIV Rule 201(201.4). Refer to the Format section of this document for details on the format and filing requirements for the CCS entry form.

   c. *Supporting memorandum of law.* All pleadings and motions filed pursuant to IN ST TRIAL P Rule 12 and IN ST TRIAL P Rule 56 shall be accompanied by a separate supporting brief. IN ST ST JOSEPH CIV Rule 206(206.1).

   d. *Proposed order.* Unless local practice provides differently, a party should submit a proposed order with its written motion to be signed by the judge once the motion has been granted. 21 INPRAC § 13.8. All proposed orders shall be submitted in an original plus a number of copies equal to one more than the number of pro se parties and attorneys of record contained in the prepared proof of notice under IN ST TRIAL P Rule 72(D). IN ST ST JOSEPH CIV Rule 213(213.3); IN ST ST JOSEPH CIV Rule 201(201.5.2).

   e. *Certificate of service.* An attorney or unrepresented party tendering a document to the Clerk for filing shall certify that service has been made, list the parties served, and specify the date and means of service. The certificate of service shall be placed at the end of the document and shall not be separately filed. The separate filing of a certificate of service, however, shall not be grounds for rejecting a document for filing. The Clerk may permit documents to be filed without a certificate of service but shall require prompt filing of a separate certificate of service. IN ST TRIAL P Rule 5(C).

2. *Supplemental documents*

   a. *Facsimile cover sheet.* Any document sent to the Clerk of the Circuit Court by electronic facsimile transmission shall be accompanied by a cover sheet which states the title of the document, case number, number of pages, identity and voice telephone number of the sending party and instructions for filing. The cover sheet shall contain the signature of the attorney or party, pro se, authorizing the filing. IN ST ADMIN Rule 12(D).

E. Format

1. *Form of motions.* The rules applicable to captions, and the signing and form of pleadings (IN ST TRIAL P Rule 8 through IN ST TRIAL P Rule 11), apply to all motions and other papers provided under the Indiana Rules of Trial Procedure. 22B INPRAC 7:2.

   a. *Separate motions; Alternative motions.* Each motion shall be separate, while alternative motions filed together shall each be identified on the caption. IN ST ST JOSEPH CIV Rule 206(206.1).

2. *Form of pleadings*

   a. *Caption; Names of parties.* Every pleading shall contain a caption setting forth the name of the court, the title of the action, the file number, and a designation as in IN ST TRIAL P Rule 7(A). In the complaint the title of the action shall include the names of all the parties, but in other pleadings it is sufficient to state the name of the first party on each side with an appropriate indication of other parties. IN ST TRIAL P Rule 10(A); IN ST ST JOSEPH CIV Rule 201(201.3.3). If a special judge has been assigned to the case, the pleading should also identify the special judge. IN ST ST JOSEPH CIV Rule 201(201.3.3).

      i. *Title.* All pleadings or motions shall include a title, which shall delineate each topic included in the pleading. For example, where a pleading contains an answer, a motion to dismiss, and a jury request, each topic shall be set forth in the title. IN ST ST JOSEPH CIV Rule 201(201.3.4).

b. *Paragraphs; Separate statements.* All averments of a claim or defense shall be made in numbered paragraphs, the contents of each of which shall be limited as far as practicable to a statement of a single set of circumstances, and a paragraph may be referred to by number in all succeeding pleadings. Each claim founded upon a separate transaction or occurrence and each defense other than denials may be stated in a separate count or defense whenever a separation facilitates the clear presentation of the matters set forth. IN ST TRIAL P Rule 10(B).

c. *Adoption by reference; Exhibits.* Statements in a pleading may be adopted by reference in a different part of the same pleading or in another pleading or in any motion. A copy of any written instrument which is an exhibit to a pleading is a part thereof for all purposes. IN ST TRIAL P Rule 10(C).

d. *Flat filing.* In order that the Clerk's files may be kept under the system commonly known as "flat filing," all papers presented to the Clerk for filing shall be flat and unfolded. Pleadings shall have no covers or backs and shall be fastened together at the top left-hand corner only. IN ST ST JOSEPH CIV Rule 201(201.1).

e. *One side of page used.* Printing shall be on one (1) side of the paper. IN ST ST JOSEPH CIV Rule 201(201.3.2).

f. *Copies.* All copies shall be on white paper of sufficient strength and durability to resist normal wear and tear. IN ST ST JOSEPH CIV Rule 201(201.3.1).

g. *Margins.* Margins shall be at least one inch (1"). IN ST ST JOSEPH CIV Rule 201(201.3.2).

h. *Double-spaced.* If typewritten, the lines shall be double spaced except for quotations, which shall be indented and single-spaced. IN ST ST JOSEPH CIV Rule 201(201.3.2).

i. *Font size.* Type face shall be twelve (12) font size or larger within the body of the document and ten (10) font size or larger in the footnotes. IN ST ST JOSEPH CIV Rule 201(201.3.2).

j. *Font type.* The font type must be legible and script type shall not be used. IN ST ST JOSEPH CIV Rule 201(201.3.2).

k. *Italics.* Italicized type may be used for quotations, references, or case citations. IN ST ST JOSEPH CIV Rule 201(201.3.2).

l. *Court and case designation.* All filings shall conform to the requirements for uniform court and case number designation set by IN ST ADMIN Rule 8. In addition, all filings shall contain the proper court and case designation as described below. IN ST ST JOSEPH CIV Rule 202.

    i. *Court designation.* Pursuant to IN ST 33-33-71-2, St. Joseph County, Indiana, constitutes the Sixtieth Judicial Circuit. The legal names of the courts within the 60th Judicial Circuit are the St. Joseph Circuit Court, the St. Joseph Superior Court, and the St. Joseph Probate Court. All filings shall properly reflect the legal name of the applicable court. Any filing may be amended, rejected, or stricken if it does not contain the proper case name and/or the legal name of the court. IN ST ST JOSEPH CIV Rule 202(202.1).

m. *Form of CCS entry.* Every written motion, petition, or other pleading subsequent to the original complaint presented to the Clerk for filing shall be accompanied by a Chronological Case Summary (CCS) entry form in duplicate which shall contain the title and cause number of the action, the date, and the proposed entry to appear on the docket. IN ST ST JOSEPH CIV Rule 201(201.4).

    i. *Identification and signature.* The CCS entry form shall identify the party making the filing, designate each pleading being filed, and shall be signed by counsel of record or the unrepresented litigant. IN ST ST JOSEPH CIV Rule 201(201.4).

    ii. *Date stamp.* The form shall be date stamped and presented to the Court Clerk, who shall initial the form and return the duplicate to the filing party. IN ST ST JOSEPH CIV Rule 201(201.4).

n. *Form of proposed order.* Any proposed order shall be a document that is separate and apart from the motion or application to which it relates and shall contain a caption showing the name of the court, the case number assigned to the case, and the title of the case as shown by the complaint pursuant to IN ST ST JOSEPH CIV Rule 201. IN ST ST JOSEPH CIV Rule 213(213.2).

    i. If there are multiple parties, the title may be shortened to include only the first name plaintiff and

defendant with appropriate indication that there are additional parties. IN ST ST JOSEPH CIV Rule 213(213.2).

ii. The proposed order shall be on white paper, eight and one-half by eleven inches (8 1/2" x 11") in size, and each page shall be numbered. IN ST ST JOSEPH CIV Rule 213(213.2).

iii. The last page of the proposed order shall contain a line for the date, either "Dated _____" or "Signed on the date filemarked hereon." IN ST ST JOSEPH CIV Rule 213(213.2).

iv. On the last page there also shall be a line for the signature of the Judge under which shall be typed "Judge, St. Joseph [Circuit or Superior or Probate] Court." IN ST ST JOSEPH CIV Rule 213(213.2).

v. If the proposed order contains a recommendation from a Magistrate, the last page shall have a line for the signature of the Magistrate under which shall be typed "Magistrate, St. Joseph [Circuit or Superior or Probate] Court," to the left of which shall be the following, "So Recommended:" and beneath and to the left of which shall be typed, "Approved. So Ordered." IN ST ST JOSEPH CIV Rule 213(213.2).

vi. To allow compliance with the notice requirements of IN ST TRIAL P Rule 72(D), the lower four (4) inches of the last page of the proposed order shall be left blank. The proposed order shall also include a prepared proof of notice under IN ST TRIAL P Rule 72(D), and in preparing such a notice the filing party shall complete all portions of the prepared proof of notice. IN ST ST JOSEPH CIV Rule 213(213.2).

3. *Size of papers for filing.* Effective January 1, 1992, all pleadings, copies, motions and documents filed with any trial court or appellate level court, typed or printed, with the exception of exhibits and existing wills, shall be prepared on eight and one-half by eleven inch (8 1/2" x 11") size paper. IN ST ADMIN Rule 11.

a. *Paper.* Pleadings, motions, and other papers shall be either legibly printed or typewritten on white opaque paper of good quality at least sixteen (16) pound weight, eight and one-half inches (8 1/2 ") in width and eleven inches (11") in length as required by IN ST ADMIN Rule 11. IN ST ST JOSEPH CIV Rule 201(201.3.1).

4. *Signature requirements*

a. *Signature of attorney.* Every pleading or motion of a party represented by an attorney shall be signed by at least one (1) attorney of record in his individual name, whose address, telephone number, and attorney number shall be stated, except that this provision shall not apply to pleadings and motions made and transcribed at the trial or a hearing before the judge and received by him in such form. IN ST TRIAL P Rule 11(A).

i. The signature of an attorney constitutes a certificate by him that he has read the pleadings; that to the best of his knowledge, information, and belief, there is good ground to support it; and that it is not interposed for delay. IN ST TRIAL P Rule 11(A).

ii. If a pleading or motion is not signed or is signed with intent to defeat the purpose of the rule, it may be stricken as sham and false and the action may proceed as though the pleading had not been served. IN ST TRIAL P Rule 11(A).

iii. For a willful violation of IN ST TRIAL P Rule 11 an attorney may be subjected to appropriate disciplinary action. Similar action may be taken if scandalous or indecent matter is inserted. IN ST TRIAL P Rule 11(A).

b. *Signature of unrepresented party.* A party who is not represented by an attorney shall sign his pleading and state his address. IN ST TRIAL P Rule 11(A).

c. *Verification not generally required.* Except when specifically required by rule, pleadings or motions need not be verified or accompanied by affidavit. The rule in equity that the averments of an answer under oath must be overcome by the testimony of two (2) witnesses or of one (1) witness sustained by corroborating circumstances is abolished. IN ST TRIAL P Rule 11(A).

d. *Verification by affirmation or representation.* When in connection with any civil or special statutory proceeding it is required that any pleading, motion, petition, supporting affidavit, or other document

of any kind, be verified, or that an oath be taken, it shall be sufficient if the subscriber simply affirms the truth of the matter to be verified by an affirmation or representation. IN ST TRIAL P Rule 11(B). IN ST TRIAL P Rule 11(B) states that the affirmation or representation should be in substantially the following language: "I (we) affirm, under the penalties for perjury, that the foregoing representation(s) is (are) true. (Signed) _____."

    i. Any person who falsifies an affirmation or representation of fact shall be subject to the same penalties as are prescribed by law for the making of a false affidavit. IN ST TRIAL P Rule 11(B).

e. *Verified pleadings, motions, and affidavits as evidence.* Pleadings, motions and affidavits accompanying or in support of such pleadings or motions when required to be verified or under oath shall be accepted as a representation that the signer had personal knowledge thereof or reasonable cause to believe the existence of the facts or matters stated or alleged therein; and, if otherwise competent or acceptable as evidence, may be admitted as evidence of the facts or matters stated or alleged therein when it is so provided in the Indiana Rules of Trial Procedure, by statute or other law, or to the extent the writing or signature expressly purports to be made upon the signer's personal knowledge. When such pleadings, motions and affidavits are verified or under oath they shall not require other or greater proof on the part of the adverse party than if not verified or not under oath unless expressly provided otherwise by the Indiana Rules of Trial Procedure, statute or other law. Affidavits upon motions for summary judgment under IN ST TRIAL P Rule 56 and in denial of execution under IN ST TRIAL P Rule 9.2 shall be made upon personal knowledge. IN ST TRIAL P Rule 11(C).

f. *Signature, verification and other requirements.* Parties and their counsel are enjoined to comply with the verification requirements of IN ST TRIAL P Rule 11, and either the moving party or the party's attorney of record shall sign all pleadings and motions before filing with the Clerk of the Court. Every motion, petition, or other pleading filed with the Clerk shall contain the name, organization, physical address, telephone number, and facsimile number of the filing party or an attorney for that party. IN ST ST JOSEPH CIV Rule 201(201.3.6).

    i. The Clerk shall not accept any motion, petition, notice or other pleading or a CCS entry form for filing from an unrepresented litigant unless the unrepresented litigant's current address and phone number appear on the pleading, and an opposing party may service notices and responses on an unrepresented litigant at any address he or she has provided on a pleading. IN ST ST JOSEPH CIV Rule 201(201.3.6).

5. *Information excluded from public access.* Every document filed in a case shall separately identify information excluded from public access pursuant to IN ST ADMIN Rule 9(G)(1) as follows:

a. Whole documents that are excluded from public access pursuant to IN ST ADMIN Rule 9(G)(1) shall be tendered on light green paper or have a light green coversheet attached to the document, marked "Not for Public Access" or "Confidential." IN ST TRIAL P Rule 5(G)(1).

b. When only a portion of a document contains information excluded from public access pursuant to IN ST ADMIN Rule 9(G)(1), said information shall be omitted [or redacted] from the filed document, and set forth on a separate accompanying document on light green paper conspicuously marked "Not for Public Access" or "Confidential" and clearly designated [or identifying] the caption and number of the case and the document and location within the document to which the redacted material pertains. IN ST TRIAL P Rule 5(G)(2).

c. With respect to documents filed in electronic format, the trial court, by local rule, may provide for compliance with IN ST TRIAL P Rule 5 in manner that separates and protects access to information excluded from public access. IN ST TRIAL P Rule 5(G)(3).

d. IN ST TRIAL P Rule 5(G) does not apply to a record sealed by the court pursuant to IN ST 5-14-3-5.5 or otherwise, nor to records, documents, or information filed in cases to which public access is prohibited pursuant to IN ST ADMIN Rule 9(G). IN ST TRIAL P Rule 5(G)(4).

e. The following information in case records is excluded from public access and is confidential:

    i. Information that is excluded from public access pursuant to federal law;

ii. Information that is excluded from public access as declared confidential by Indiana statute or other court rule, including without limitation:

- All adoption records created after July 8, 1941, as declared confidential by IN ST 31-19-19-1, et seq., except those specifically declared open by IN ST 31-19-13-2(2);

- All records relating to chancroid, chlamydia, gonorrhea, hepatitis, human immunodeficiency virus (HIV), Lymphogranuloma venereum, syphilis, tuberculosis, as declared confidential by IN ST 16-41-8-1, et seq.;

- All records relating to child abuse as declared confidential by IN ST 31-33-18-1, et seq.;

- All records relating to drug tests as declared confidential by IN ST 5-14-3-4(a)(9);

- Records of grand jury proceedings as declared confidential by IN ST 35-34-2-4;

- Records of juvenile proceedings as declared confidential by IN ST 31-39-1-2, except those specifically open under statute;

- All paternity records created after July 1, 1941 as declared confidential by IN ST 31-14-11-15, IN ST 31-19-5-23, IN ST 31-39-1-1 and IN ST 31-39-1-2 [Editor's note: IN ST 31-14-11-15 was repealed effective May 9, 2013];

- All pre-sentence reports as declared confidential by IN ST 35-38-1-13;

- Written petitions to permit marriages without consent and orders directing the Clerk of Court to issue a marriage license to underage persons, as declared confidential by IN ST 31-11-1-6;

- Only those arrest warrants, search warrants, indictments and informations ordered confidential by the trial judge, prior to return of duly executed service as declared confidential by IN ST 5-14-3-4(b)(1);

- All medical, mental health, or tax records unless determined by law or regulation of any governmental custodian not to be confidential, released by the subject of such records, or declared by a court of competent jurisdiction to be essential to the resolution of litigation as declared confidential by IN ST 16-39-3-10, IN ST 6-4.1-5-10, IN ST 6-4.1-12-12, and IN ST 6-8.1-7-1;

- Personal information relating to jurors or prospective jurors, other than for the use of the parties and counsel, pursuant to IN ST JURY Rule 10;

- Information relating to protection from abuse orders, no-contact orders and workplace violence restraining orders as declared confidential by IN ST 5-2-9-6, et seq.;

- Mediation proceedings pursuant to IN ST ADR Rule 2.11, Mini-Trial proceedings pursuant to IN ST ADR Rule 4.4(C), and Summary Jury Trials pursuant to IN ST ADR Rule 5.6;

- Information in probation files pursuant to the Probation Standards promulgated by the Judicial Conference of Indiana pursuant to IN ST 11-13-1-8(b);

- Information deemed confidential pursuant to the Rules for Court Administered Alcohol and Drug Programs promulgated by the Judicial Conference of Indiana pursuant to IN ST 12-23-14-13;

- Information deemed confidential pursuant to the Problem-Solving Court Rules promulgated by the Judicial Conference of Indiana pursuant to IN ST 33-23-16-16;

- All records of the Department of workforce Development as declared confidential by IN ST 22-4-19-6;

- Information regarding interception of electronic communications that is sealed or deemed confidential as set forth in IN ST 35-33.5-2-1, et seq.

iii. Information excluded from public access by specific court order;

iv. Complete Social Security Numbers of living persons;

    v.   With the exception of names, information such as addresses, phone numbers, and dates of birth which explicitly identifies:

- Natural persons who are witnesses or victims (not including defendants) in criminal, domestic violence, stalking, sexual assault, juvenile, or civil protection order proceedings, provided that juveniles who are victims of sex crimes shall be identified by initials only;

- Places of residence of judicial officers, clerks and other employees of courts and clerks of court, unless the person or persons about whom the information pertains waives confidentiality;

    vi.   Complete account numbers of specific assets, loans, bank accounts, credit cards, and personal identification numbers (PINs);

    vii.   All orders of expungement entered in criminal or juvenile proceedings, orders to restrict access to criminal history information pursuant to IN ST 35-38-5-5.5 or IN ST 35-38-8-5 and records excluded from public access by such orders, and information related to infractions that is excluded from public access pursuant to IN ST 34-28-5-15 or IN ST 34-28-5-16 [Editor's note: IN ST 35-38-5-5.5, IN ST 35-38-8-5 and IN ST 34-28-5-16 were repealed effective July 1, 2013; for information on orders restricting access to criminal history, refer to IN ST 35-38-9-1, et seq.];

    viii.   All personal notes and e-mail, and deliberative material, of judges, jurors, court staff and judicial agencies, and information recorded in personal data assistants (PDA's) or organizers and personal calendars. IN ST ADMIN Rule 9(G)(1).

F. Filing and Service Requirements

1. *Filing requirements.* Except as otherwise provided in IN ST TRIAL P Rule 5(E)(2), all pleadings and papers subsequent to the complaint which are required to be served upon a party shall be filed with the Court either before service or within a reasonable period of time thereafter. IN ST TRIAL P Rule 5(E)(1).

    a.   *Filing with the court defined.* The filing of pleadings, motions, and other papers with the court as required by the Indiana Rules of Trial Procedure shall be made by one of the following methods:

       i.   Delivery to the clerk of the court;

       ii.   Sending by electronic transmission under the procedure adopted pursuant to IN ST ADMIN Rule 12;

       iii.   Mailing to the clerk by registered, certified or express mail return receipt requested;

       iv.   Depositing with any third-party commercial carrier for delivery to the clerk within three (3) calendar days, cost prepaid, properly addressed;

       v.   If the court so permits, filing with the judge, in which event the judge shall note thereon the filing date and forthwith transmit them to the office of the clerk; or

       vi.   Electronic filing, as approved by the Division of State Court Administration pursuant to IN ST ADMIN Rule 16. IN ST TRIAL P Rule 5(F).

       vii.   Filing by registered or certified mail and by third-party commercial carrier shall be complete upon mailing or deposit. IN ST TRIAL P Rule 5(F).

       viii.   All pleadings shall be filed with the Clerk, not directly with the Court, unless otherwise required by the Indiana Rules of Court. The entry of appearances and the filing of pleadings or other matters not requiring immediate Court action shall be filed with the Clerk and not in open Court. A Judge may permit papers to be filed in chambers, in which event he or she shall note thereon the filing date and transmit the papers to the Clerk. IN ST ST JOSEPH CIV Rule 201(201.2).

    b.   *Facsimile filing.* Unless otherwise authorized by IN ST ST JOSEPH ELECTRONIC Rule 701, electronic filing of pleadings by computerized or facsimile transmission is not permitted. IN ST ST JOSEPH CIV Rule 201(201.2).

    c.   *Additional copies.* In cases in which a party or counsel supplies the proposed order or decree, a sufficient number shall be prepared and filed as to provide the Clerk to retain two (2) copies, which shall be filed in the flat file and the record of judgments and orders. Should the party or counsel desire

additional copies, a sufficient number of copies should be filed to effectuate that purpose. IN ST ST JOSEPH CIV Rule 201(201.6).

    d. *Proof of filing.* Any party filing any paper by any method other than personal delivery to the clerk shall retain proof of filing. IN ST TRIAL P Rule 5(F).

2. *Service requirements.* Unless otherwise provided by the Indiana Rules of Trial Procedure or an order of the court, each party and special judge, if any, shall be served with: (1) every order required by its terms to be served; (2) every pleading subsequent to the original complaint; (3) every written motion except one which may be heard ex parte; (4) every brief submitted to the trial court; (5) every paper relating to discovery required to be served upon a party; and (6) every written notice, appearance, demand, offer of judgment, designation of record on appeal, or similar paper. IN ST TRIAL P Rule 5(A).

    a. *Service generally.* Every motion, petition, notice, or other pleading required to be served by IN ST TRIAL P Rule 5 shall be served on all counsel of record or unrepresented parties either before it is filed or on the day it is filed with the Court, and the date of filing shall be indicated on the Certificate of Service. IN ST ST JOSEPH CIV Rule 201(201.5.1).

        i. *Copy.* A copy of the Clerk's CCS entry form of the filing shall also be served on all counsel of record or unrepresented parties whenever it contains an appearance of counsel or contains a date for Court hearing on the matter. IN ST ST JOSEPH CIV Rule 201(201.5.1).

    b. *Methods of service*

        i. *Personal service.* Whenever a party is represented by an attorney of record, service shall be made upon such attorney unless service upon the party himself is ordered by the court. Service upon the attorney or party shall be made by delivering or mailing a copy of the papers to the last known address or where an attorney or party has consented to service by fax or e-mail, as provided in IN ST TRIAL P Rule 3.1(A)(4), by faxing or e-mailing a copy of the documents to the fax number or e-mail address set out in the appearance form or correction as required by IN ST TRIAL P Rule 3.1(E). IN ST TRIAL P Rule 5(B). Delivery of a copy within IN ST TRIAL P Rule 5 means:

- Offering or tendering it to the attorney or party and stating the nature of the papers being served. Refusal to accept an offered or tendered document is a waiver of any objection to the sufficiency or adequacy of service of that document;

- Leaving it at his office with a clerk or other person in charge thereof, or if there is no one in charge, leaving it in a conspicuous place therein; or

- If the office is closed, by leaving it at his dwelling house or usual place of abode with some person of suitable age and discretion then residing therein; or,

- Leaving it at some other suitable place, selected by the attorney upon whom service is being made, pursuant to duly promulgated local rule. IN ST TRIAL P Rule 5(B)(1).

        ii. *Service by the clerk.* Whenever the Clerk is required by rule or statute to give notice, the party or parties requesting such notice shall furnish the Clerk with sufficient copies of the notice to be given, along with stamped, addressed envelopes with the names and the addresses of the parties or their counsel to whom such notice is to be given. IN ST ST JOSEPH CIV Rule 201(201.5.4).

        iii. *Service on the court.* Service on a Judge may be made by delivering a copy to the Judge's secretary or mailing a copy to the Judge at his or her chambers. Service on a Judge may not be accomplished by facsimile transmission; however, a courtesy copy may be sent to the Judge's chambers by electronic mail or facsimile transmission contemporaneously with service by mail or otherwise. IN ST ST JOSEPH CIV Rule 201(201.5.5).

        iv. *Service by mail.* If service is made by mail, the papers shall be deposited in the United States mail addressed to the person on whom they are being served, with postage prepaid. Service shall be deemed complete upon mailing. Proof of service of all papers permitted to be mailed may be made by written acknowledgment of service, by affidavit of the person who mailed the papers, or by certificate of an attorney. It shall be the duty of attorneys when entering their appearance in a cause or when filing pleadings or papers therein, to have noted in the

Chronological Case Summary or said pleadings or papers so filed the address and telephone number of their office. Service by delivery or by mail at such address shall be deemed sufficient and complete. IN ST TRIAL P Rule 5(B)(2).

v. *Service by fax or e-mail.* A party who has consented to service by fax or e-mail may be served as follows:

- Service by e-mail shall be made by attaching the document being served in .pdf format. Discovery documents must also be served in accordance with IN ST TRIAL P Rule 26(A). IN ST TRIAL P Rule 5(B)(3)(a).

- Service by fax shall be deemed complete upon generation of a transmission record indicating the successful transmission of the entire document, except as provided in IN ST TRIAL P Rule 5(B)(3)(d). IN ST TRIAL P Rule 5(B)(3)(b).

- Service by e-mail shall be deemed complete upon transmission, except as provided in IN ST TRIAL P Rule 5(B)(3)(d). IN ST TRIAL P Rule 5(B)(3)(c).

- Service by fax or e-mail that occurs on a Saturday, Sunday, legal holiday, or day the court or agency in which the matter is pending is closed or after 5:00 PM local time of the recipient shall be deemed complete the next day that is not a Saturday, Sunday, legal holiday, or day that the court or agency in which the matter is pending is not closed. IN ST TRIAL P Rule 5(B)(3)(d).

c. *Serving numerous defendants.* In any action in which there are unusually large numbers of defendants, the court, upon motion or of its own initiative, may order:

i. That service of the pleadings of the defendants and replies thereto need not be made as between the defendants;

- That any cross-claim, counterclaim, or matter constituting an avoidance or affirmative defense contained therein shall be deemed to be denied or avoided by all other parties; and

- That the filing of any such pleading and service thereof upon the plaintiff constitutes due notice of it to the parties. IN ST TRIAL P Rule 5(D).

ii. A copy of every such order shall be served upon the parties in such manner and form as the court directs. IN ST TRIAL P Rule 5(D).

d. *Service on parties in default for failure to appear.* No service need be made on parties in default for failure to appear, except that pleadings asserting new or additional claims for relief against them shall be served upon them in the manner provided by service of summons in IN ST TRIAL P Rule 4. IN ST TRIAL P Rule 5(A).

e. *Distribution.* Counsel or an unrepresented party submitting a motion, petition, notice, pleading or proposed order shall indicate the method of distribution desired on the Clerk's CCS entry form. The Clerk will not return or distribute copies of motions, petitions, pleadings, notices or proposed orders, other than those originated by the Court, by mail unless the Clerk is provided with stamped, addressed envelopes. IN ST ST JOSEPH CIV Rule 201(201.5.3).

f. *Mailbox.* As a matter of convenience to attorneys, each court provides a mailbox for the distribution filings and orders generated by the Court, and it is the responsibility of each attorney to periodically check these mailboxes for service and distribution of court-generated filings and orders. IN ST ST JOSEPH CIV Rule 201(201.5.3).

G. Hearings

1. *Hearing on motion.* Unless local conditions make it impracticable, each judge shall establish regular times and places, at intervals sufficiently frequent for the prompt dispatch of business, at which motions requiring notice and hearing may be heard and disposed of; but the judge at any time or place and on such notice, if any, as he considers reasonable may make order for the advancement, conduct, and hearing of actions. To expedite its business the court may direct the submission and determination of motions without oral hearing upon brief written statements of reasons in support and opposition, or direct or permit hearings by telephone conference call with all attorneys or other similar means of communication. IN ST TRIAL P Rule 73(A).

2. *Hearing dates.* Hearing dates for filings requiring Court action shall be obtained from the Court Clerk and incorporated in the CCS entry at the time the motion or other pleading is filed. If no date is obtained prior to the filing, the fact of the hearing should be noted with the date and time left blank. IN ST ST JOSEPH CIV Rule 201(201.4).

3. *Hearing on matters other than trials.* Each Judge shall reserve periods of time for hearing matters other than contested trials, such as pre-trial and post-trial motions, rules to show cause, defaults, uncontested dissolutions of marriage, etc. As necessary to minimize conflicts in scheduling, the Judges shall set these schedules after consultation. Hearings shall be scheduled as follows:

   a. *Scheduling uncontested or routine matters.* Routine matters, procedural motions, domestic relations applications for provisional relief and contempt proceedings, uncontested petitions for dissolution of marriage, and all other matters appropriate for summary consideration and disposition will be heard on the daily calendar. IN ST ST JOSEPH GEN AND ADMIN Rule 104(104.3.1).

   b. *Scheduling contested or complicated matters.* Other matters that will require a hearing reasonably estimated to last in excess of twenty (20) minutes will be scheduled as the Court's calendar allows. Counsel or a party proceeding pro se should contact the chambers of the assigned judge to arrange for an appropriate hearing date and time. IN ST ST JOSEPH GEN AND ADMIN Rule 104(104.3.2).

   c. *Scheduling motions for hearings.* Except for motions to correct error or not likely to require a hearing (as described in IN ST ST JOSEPH CIV Rule 201), all motions shall be scheduled for hearing at the time they are filed. It shall the responsibility of the moving party or counsel for the moving party to secure the date and time of the hearing from the Clerk or Court personnel who maintain the calendar for each Judge or Magistrate Judge. It shall also be the responsibility of the moving party or counsel for the moving party to coordinate the hearing date with all opposing counsel or unrepresented parties. IN ST ST JOSEPH CIV Rule 201(201.9.1).

   d. *Oral arguments on motions and other pleadings.* Unless otherwise required by St. Joseph County Civil or Indiana Trial Rules, it is within the sound discretion of the assigned Judge whether to allow oral argument; however, any party may file a request for oral argument by filing a written request by separate motion contemporaneously or at any time before the Court has ruled upon the motion or pleadings to be argued. IN ST ST JOSEPH CIV Rule 201(201.9.4).

4. *Motions for summary judgment and for dismissal.* Motions for summary judgment or motions to dismiss pursuant to IN ST TRIAL P Rule 12 or IN ST TRIAL P Rule 41 shall be scheduled for hearing, unless the Court issues a written scheduling order providing otherwise. (Refer to IN ST ST JOSEPH CIV Rule 206 for specific requirements for Pleadings and Motions under IN ST TRIAL P Rule 12 and IN ST TRIAL P Rule 56). IN ST ST JOSEPH CIV Rule 201(201.9.6).

   a. *Dispositive motions date.* Notwithstanding any other rule of court, all IN ST TRIAL P Rule 12 or IN ST TRIAL P Rule 56 motions shall be set for hearing by the moving party at the time of filing unless otherwise ordered by the Court. Unless otherwise authorized by the Court, the hearing shall be scheduled for a day not fewer than fourteen (14) days after the time period allowed for filing of briefs as specified in IN ST ST JOSEPH CIV Rule 206(206.1). IN ST ST JOSEPH CIV Rule 206(206.2).

   b. *Waiver of hearing; Stipulation of the parties.* Adverse parties may stipulate that a IN ST TRIAL P Rule 12 or IN ST TRIAL P Rule 56 motion may be ruled upon by the Court without a hearing thereon, in which event the motion and stipulation shall be brought to the personal attention of the Judge by counsel or by a party proceeding pro se. IN ST ST JOSEPH CIV Rule 206(206.3).

   c. *Appearance by counsel at scheduled hearings.* Whenever the Court schedules a hearing on a motion pursuant to IN ST TRIAL P Rule 12 and/or IN ST TRIAL P Rule 56, counsel for all represented parties shall appear in person or by local co-counsel at such hearing. IN ST ST JOSEPH CIV Rule 206(206.5).

H. Forms

1. Motion to Dismiss for Failure to State a Claim Forms for Indiana

   a. General form. 5 INPRAC § 3:4.1.

   b. Failure to state a claim upon which relief can be granted. 5 INPRAC § 3:4.5.

c. Motion to dismiss plaintiff's complaint; General form. 9 INPRAC § 42.2.

d. Motion to dismiss; Failure to state a claim upon which relief can be granted. 9 INPRAC § 42.10.

e. Certificate of service; Personal service. 9 INPRAC § 5.7.

f. Certificate of service; First class mail. 9 INPRAC § 5.8.

g. Statute of limitations. 9 INPRAC § 42.12.

h. Application for hearing and preliminary determination of motion to dismiss. 9 INPRAC § 42.15.

I. Checklist

(I) ❑ Matters to be considered by moving party

  (a) ❑ Required documents

    (1) ❑ Motion and notice

    (2) ❑ Chronological Case Summary (CCS) entry form

    (3) ❑ Supporting memorandum of law

    (4) ❑ Proposed order

    (5) ❑ Certificate of service

  (b) ❑ Supplemental documents

    (1) ❑ Facsimile cover sheet

  (c) ❑ Timing

    (1) ❑ A motion to dismiss for failure to state a claim shall be made before pleading if a further pleading is permitted or within twenty (20) days after service of the prior pleading if none is required

    (2) ❑ A written motion, other than one which may be heard ex parte, and notice of the hearing thereof shall be served not less than five (5) days before the time specified for the hearing, unless a different period is fixed by the Indiana Rules of Trial Procedure or by order of the court

    (3) ❑ All pleadings and papers subsequent to the complaint which are required to be served upon a party shall be filed with the Court either before service or within a reasonable period of time thereafter

(II) ❑ Matters to be considered by the responding party

  (a) ❑ Required documents

    (1) ❑ Opposition

    (2) ❑ Chronological Case Summary (CCS) entry form

    (3) ❑ Supporting memorandum of law

    (4) ❑ Certificate of service

  (b) ❑ Supplemental documents

    (1) ❑ Proposed order

    (2) ❑ Facsimile cover sheet

  (c) ❑ Timing

    (1) ❑ An adverse party shall have thirty (30) days after service of the motion in which to serve and file an answer brief

    (2) ❑ Except as otherwise provided in IN ST TRIAL P Rule 59(D), opposing affidavits may be served not less than one (1) day before the hearing, unless the court permits them to be served at some other time

Motions, Oppositions and Replies
Motion to Dismiss for Lack of Subject Matter Jurisdiction

Document Last Updated October 2013

A. Applicable Rules

1. *State rules*

   a. Appearance. IN ST TRIAL P Rule 3.1.

   b. Process. IN ST TRIAL P Rule 4.

   c. Service and filing of pleadings and other papers. IN ST TRIAL P Rule 5.

   d. Time. IN ST TRIAL P Rule 6.

   e. Pleadings. IN ST TRIAL P Rule 7; IN ST TRIAL P Rule 8; IN ST TRIAL P Rule 9.2; IN ST TRIAL P Rule 10.

   f. Signing and verification of pleadings. IN ST TRIAL P Rule 11.

   g. Defenses and objections; When and how presented; By pleading or motion; Motion for judgment on the pleadings. IN ST TRIAL P Rule 12.

   h. Amended and supplemental pleadings. IN ST TRIAL P Rule 15.

   i. Joinder of person needed for just adjudication. IN ST TRIAL P Rule 19.

   j. Evidence. IN ST TRIAL P Rule 43.

   k. Judgment on the evidence (directed verdict). IN ST TRIAL P Rule 50.

   l. Findings by the court. IN ST TRIAL P Rule 52.

   m. Summary judgment. IN ST TRIAL P Rule 56.

   n. Motion to correct error. IN ST TRIAL P Rule 59.

   o. Relief from judgment or order. IN ST TRIAL P Rule 60.

   p. Hearing of motions. IN ST TRIAL P Rule 73.

   q. Access to court records. IN ST ADMIN Rule 9.

   r. Paper size. IN ST ADMIN Rule 11.

   s. Facsimile transmission. IN ST ADMIN Rule 12.

   t. Electronic filing and electronic service pilot projects. IN ST ADMIN Rule 16.

   u. Sealing of certain records by court; Hearing; Notice. IN ST 5-14-3-5.5.

   v. Sixtieth judicial circuit. IN ST 33-33-71-2.

   w. Privacy and confidentiality. IN ST 5-2-9-6; IN ST 5-14-3-4; IN ST 6-4.1-5-10; IN ST 6-4.1-12-12; IN ST 6-8.1-7-1; IN ST 11-13-1-8; IN ST 12-23-14-13; IN ST 16-39-3-10; IN ST 16-41-8-1; IN ST 22-4-19-6; IN ST 31-11-1-6; IN ST 31-19-5-23; IN ST 31-19-13-2; IN ST 31-19-19-1; IN ST 31-33-18-1; IN ST 31-39-1-1; IN ST 31-39-1-2; IN ST 33-23-16-16; IN ST 35-34-2-4; IN ST 35-38-1-13; IN ST 35-38-9-1; IN ST ADR Rule 2.11; IN ST ADR Rule 4.4; IN ST ADR Rule 5.6; IN ST JURY Rule 10.

2. *Local rules*

   a. Court hours and scheduling. IN ST ST JOSEPH GEN AND ADMIN Rule 104.

   b. Filing, pleading, and motions. IN ST ST JOSEPH CIV Rule 201.

   c. Uniform court and case number designation. IN ST ST JOSEPH CIV Rule 202.

   d. Pleading and motions under IN ST TRIAL P Rule 12 and IN ST TRIAL P Rule 56. IN ST ST JOSEPH CIV Rule 206.

   e. Proposed order. IN ST ST JOSEPH CIV Rule 213.

f. Electronic filing of cases in St. Joseph County. IN ST ST JOSEPH ELECTRONIC Rule 701.

B. Timing

1. *Timing of motion to dismiss for failure lack of subject matter jurisdiction.* A motion making any of the defenses listed in IN ST TRIAL P Rule 12(B) shall be made before pleading if a further pleading is permitted or within twenty (20) days after service of the prior pleading if none is required. IN ST TRIAL P Rule 12(B). Usually, the issue is raised in a motion that is filed before an Answer is filed; or the issue might be consolidated in the Answer. If it is not raised by the parties, it will be raised by the court, and an appellate court may raise the question sua sponte. 1A INPRAC R 12(12.5); Decatur County Rural Elec. Membership Corp. v. Public Serv. Co., 150 Ind.App. 193, 275 N.E.2d 857 (Ind.App. 1971).

   a. *Time to file a responsive pleading.* A responsive pleading required under the Indiana Rules of Trial Procedure, shall be served within twenty (20) days after service of the prior pleading. IN ST TRIAL P Rule 6(C).

   b. *Filing.* All pleadings and papers subsequent to the complaint which are required to be served upon a party shall be filed with the Court either before service or within a reasonable period of time thereafter. IN ST TRIAL P Rule 5(E)(1).

2. *Service.* A written motion, other than one which may be heard ex parte, and notice of the hearing thereof shall be served not less than five (5) days before the time specified for the hearing, unless a different period is fixed by the Indiana Rules of Trial Procedure or by order of the court. IN ST TRIAL P Rule 6(D).

   a. *Of supporting affidavits.* When a motion is supported by affidavit, the affidavit shall be served with the motion. IN ST TRIAL P Rule 6(D).

3. *Service of opposition.* Except as otherwise provided in IN ST TRIAL P Rule 59(D), opposing affidavits may be served not less than one (1) day before the hearing, unless the court permits them to be served at some other time. IN ST TRIAL P Rule 6(D).

   a. An adverse party shall have thirty (30) days after service of the motion in which to serve and file an answer brief. IN ST ST JOSEPH CIV Rule 206(206.1).

4. *Filing proposed orders.* Unless otherwise directed or given leave of the Court, proposed orders in emergency matters shall be filed within forty-eight (48) hours after a hearing; proposed orders in other matters shall be filed within seven (7) days as computed by IN ST TRIAL P Rule 6. IN ST ST JOSEPH CIV Rule 213(213.5).

5. *Computation of time*

   a. *Generally; Days excluded.* In computing any period of time prescribed or allowed by the Indiana Rules of Trial Procedure, by order of the court, or by any applicable statute, the day of the act, event, or default from which the designated period of time begins to run shall not be included. The last day of the period so computed is to be included unless it is:

      i. A Saturday,

      ii. A Sunday,

      iii. A legal holiday as defined by state statute, or

      iv. A day the office in which the act is to be done is closed during regular business hours. IN ST TRIAL P Rule 6(A).

   b. *Short periods.* In any event, the period runs until the end of the next day that is not a Saturday, a Sunday, a legal holiday, or a day on which the office is closed. When the period of time allowed is less than seven (7) days, intermediate Saturdays, Sundays, legal holidays, and days on which the office is closed shall be excluded from the computations. IN ST TRIAL P Rule 6(A).

   c. *Additional time after service by United States mail.* Whenever a party has the right or is required to do some act or take some proceedings within a prescribed period after the service of a notice or other paper upon him and the notice or paper is served upon him by United States mail, three (3) days shall be added to the prescribed period. IN ST TRIAL P Rule 6(E).

d. *Enlargement of time.* When an act is required or allowed to be done at or within a specific time by the Indiana Rules of Trial Procedure, the court may at any time for cause shown:

    i. Order the period enlarged, with or without motion or notice, if request therefor is made before the expiration of the period originally prescribed or extended by a previous order; or

    ii. Upon motion made after the expiration of the specific period, permit the act to be done where the failure to act was the result of excusable neglect; but, the court may not extend the time for taking any action for judgment on the evidence under IN ST TRIAL P Rule 50(A), amendment of findings and judgment under IN ST TRIAL P Rule 52(B), to correct errors under IN ST TRIAL P Rule 59(C), statement in opposition to motion to correct error under IN ST TRIAL P Rule 59(E), or to obtain relief from final judgment under IN ST TRIAL P Rule 60(B), except to the extent and under the conditions stated in those rules. IN ST TRIAL P Rule 6(B).

    iii. An initial written motion for enlargement of time pursuant to IN ST TRIAL P Rule 6(B)(1) to answer a claim shall be routinely granted for an additional thirty (30) days from the original due date or other period the assigned Judge deems reasonable by written order of the Court. The motion must be filed on or before the original due date or IN ST ST JOSEPH CIV Rule 201 shall be inapplicable. IN ST ST JOSEPH CIV Rule 201(201.9.5).

     • Any motion for enlargement of time shall state the date when such response is due and the date to which time is requested to be enlarged. IN ST ST JOSEPH CIV Rule 201(201.9.5).

     • All subsequent motions for enlargement of time shall be so designated and will only be granted for good cause shown or in the interest of justice. IN ST ST JOSEPH CIV Rule 201(201.9.5).

C. General Requirements

1. *Motions, generally.* Unless made during a hearing or trial, or otherwise ordered by the court, an application to the court for an order shall be made by written motion. The motion shall state the grounds therefor and the relief or order sought. IN ST TRIAL P Rule 7(B).

    a. *Motions as distinct from pleadings.* Motions and responses to motions are not pleadings, and allegations contained in a motion are not admissions of a party. 22B INPRAC 7:2; Wachstetter v. County Properties, LLC, 832 N.E.2d 574 (Ind.Ct.App. 2005); Scott County Family YMCA, Inc. v. Hobbs, 817 N.E.2d 603 (Ind.Ct.App. 2004).

    b. *Unopposed motions generally granted.* It is common for a trial court to grant procedural motions, such as motions for enlargement of time, discovery motions, or motions for continuance, unless an objection is filed. 21 INPRAC § 13.8.

    c. *Proposed orders.* As directed by the Court, a party or an attorney for a party shall prepare a proposed order based on the decision rendered by the Court. The party so directed shall prepare the proposed order in a timely manner and, upon filing, shall advise the chambers of the applicable judge that the proposed order has been prepared and filed. IN ST ST JOSEPH CIV Rule 213(213.2).

     i. Prior to entry by the Court of orders granting motions or applications, the moving party or applicant (or his or her attorney) shall, unless the Court directs otherwise, furnish the Court with proposed orders in matters of dismissal. IN ST ST JOSEPH CIV Rule 213(213.1(5)).

    d. *Reply brief.* Subject to Court approval, the moving party may file a reply brief. IN ST ST JOSEPH CIV Rule 206(206.1).

2. *Motion to dismiss for lack of subject matter jurisdiction.* Every defense, in law or fact, to a claim for relief in any pleading, whether a claim, counterclaim, cross-claim, or third-party claim, shall be asserted in the responsive pleading thereto if one is required; except that at the option of the pleader, the defense of lack of jurisdiction over the subject matter may be made by motion. IN ST TRIAL P Rule 12(B)(1). Subject-matter jurisdiction refers to the power of the court or tribunal to entertain the general class of cases or disputes to which a pending case belongs. It means that the legislature or other authority, such as, perhaps, a supreme court, has invested the court with judicial power with which to entertain a case or controversy, and to hear the litigation and dispute. 1A INPRAC R 12(12.5).

    a. *Objection not waivable.* Subject-matter jurisdiction cannot be created by the parties to the litigation.

Either it is there or it is not, quite independent of the conduct or the consent of the parties to the action. As such, the absence of subject-matter jurisdiction is never waivable and there is a positive duty on a court, whether trial or appellate, to raise the question of subject-matter jurisdiction whenever it might appear, if the parties have failed to present the question. 1A INPRAC R 12(12.5); Schoffstall v. Failey, 180 Ind.App. 528, 389 N.E. 361 (Ind.Ct.App. 1979).

b. *Motion not to be made as one for summary judgment.* A motion to dismiss under IN ST TRIAL P Rule 12(B)(1) may not be presented in the form of a motion for summary judgment. 9 INPRAC § 42.3.

c. *Precedence of subject matter jurisdiction.* Dismissal for lack of subject matter jurisdiction takes precedence over the determination of and action upon other substantive and procedural rights of the parties. 9 INPRAC § 42.3; Young v. Estate of Sweeney, 808 N.E.2d 1217 (Ind.Ct.App. 2004).

d. *Issues examined separately; Jurisdiction over one claim as jurisdiction over case.* In order to determine whether a case is properly before the trial court, the court should examine each issue presented. If at least one of the issues is within the jurisdiction of the trial court, the entire case falls within the court's jurisdiction. Where at least one issue or claim is a proper matter for judicial determination or resolution, a trial court is not ousted of subject matter jurisdiction by the presence in a case of one or more issues which arguably are within the jurisdiction of administrative or regulatory agency. 9 INPRAC § 42.3; Alexander v. Cottey, 801 N.E.2d 651 (Ind.Ct.App. 2004).

e. *Factual matters in determining subject matter jurisdiction.* The trial court considering a motion to dismiss for lack of subject matter jurisdiction has wide latitude to devise procedures to discover the facts relevant to jurisdiction and in weighing the evidence to resolve factual disputes affecting the jurisdictional challenge. 9 INPRAC § 42.3.

f. *Failure to exhaust administrative remedies.* The doctrine of exhaustion of administrative remedies provides that a trial court will not acquire subject matter jurisdiction until the aggrieved party has exhausted all available remedies before the administrative agency. 9 INPRAC § 41.44; Indiana Dept. of Environmental Management v. NJK Farms, Inc., 921 N.E.2d 834 (Ind.Ct.App. 2010).

    i. *Dismissal of workers' compensation cases.* A trial court must dismiss a matter for lack of subject matter jurisdiction pursuant to Indiana IN ST TRIAL P Rule 12(B)(1) where injuries claimed in the Plaintiff's complaint fall squarely within the Indiana Workers Compensation Act. 9 INPRAC § 42.3; ATFH Real Property, LLC v. Stewart, 879 N.E.2d 1184 (Ind.Ct.App. 2008).

g. *Leave to amend complaint if motion granted.* A dismissal for lack of subject matter jurisdiction is not an adjudication on the merits nor is it res judicata. If action is dismissed, plaintiff may file amended complaint as permitted by IN ST TRIAL P Rule 6(C). 9 INPRAC § 42.3; Hart v. Webster, 894 N.E.2d 1032 (Ind.Ct.App. 2008).

h. *Effect of judgment entered by court lacking subject matter jurisdiction.* A judgment entered by a court that lacks subject matter jurisdiction is void and may be attacked at any time. 9 INPRAC § 42.3; Roberson v. State, 903 N.E.2d 1009 (Ind.Ct.App. 2009).

3. *Consolidation and waiver*

a. *Consolidation of defenses in motion.* A party who makes a motion under IN ST TRIAL P Rule 12 may join with it any other motions herein provided for and then available to him. If a party makes a motion under IN ST TRIAL P Rule 12 but omits therefrom any defense or objection then available to him which IN ST TRIAL P Rule 12 permits to be raised by motion, he shall not thereafter make a motion based on the defense or objection so omitted. He may, however, make such motions as are allowed under IN ST TRIAL P Rule 12(H)(2). IN ST TRIAL P Rule 12(G).

b. *Waiver or preservation of certain defenses.* No defense or objection is waived by being joined with one or more other defenses or objections in a responsive pleading or motion. IN ST TRIAL P Rule 12(B).

4. *Opposition to a motion for lack of subject matter jurisdiction.* Failure to file an answer brief or reply brief within the time prescribed shall be deemed a waiver of the right thereto and shall subject the motion to summary ruling. IN ST ST JOSEPH CIV Rule 206(206.1).

D. Documents

1. *Required documents*

   a. *Motion and notice.* The requirement of notice is satisfied by service of the motion. IN ST TRIAL P Rule 7(B). Refer to the General Requirements section of this document for information on the content of a motion to dismiss for lack of subject matter jurisdiction.

   b. *Chronological Case Summary (CCS) entry form.* Every written motion, petition, or other pleading subsequent to the original complaint presented to the Clerk for filing shall be accompanied by a Chronological Case Summary (CCS) entry form in duplicate. IN ST ST JOSEPH CIV Rule 201(201.4). Refer to the Format section of this document for details on the format and filing requirements for the CCS entry form.

   c. *Supporting memorandum of law.* All pleadings and motions filed pursuant to IN ST TRIAL P Rule 12 and IN ST TRIAL P Rule 56 shall be accompanied by a separate supporting brief. IN ST ST JOSEPH CIV Rule 206(206.1).

   d. *Proposed order.* Unless local practice provides differently, a party should submit a proposed order with its written motion to be signed by the judge once the motion has been granted. 21 INPRAC § 13.8. All proposed orders shall be submitted in an original plus a number of copies equal to one more than the number of pro se parties and attorneys of record contained in the prepared proof of notice under IN ST TRIAL P Rule 72(D). IN ST ST JOSEPH CIV Rule 213(213.3); IN ST ST JOSEPH CIV Rule 201(201.5.2).

   e. *Certificate of service.* An attorney or unrepresented party tendering a document to the Clerk for filing shall certify that service has been made, list the parties served, and specify the date and means of service. The certificate of service shall be placed at the end of the document and shall not be separately filed. The separate filing of a certificate of service, however, shall not be grounds for rejecting a document for filing. The Clerk may permit documents to be filed without a certificate of service but shall require prompt filing of a separate certificate of service. IN ST TRIAL P Rule 5(C).

2. *Supplemental documents*

   a. *Supporting evidence.* When a motion is based on facts not appearing of record the court may hear the matter on affidavits presented by the respective parties, but the court may direct that the matter be heard wholly or partly on oral testimony or depositions. IN ST TRIAL P Rule 43(B).

   b. *Facsimile cover sheet.* Any document sent to the Clerk of the Circuit Court by electronic facsimile transmission shall be accompanied by a cover sheet which states the title of the document, case number, number of pages, identity and voice telephone number of the sending party and instructions for filing. The cover sheet shall contain the signature of the attorney or party, pro se, authorizing the filing. IN ST ADMIN Rule 12(D).

E. Format

1. *Form of motions.* The rules applicable to captions, and the signing and form of pleadings (IN ST TRIAL P Rule 8 through IN ST TRIAL P Rule 11), apply to all motions and other papers provided under the Indiana Rules of Trial Procedure. 22B INPRAC 7:2.

   a. *Separate motions; Alternative motions.* Each motion shall be separate, while alternative motions filed together shall each be identified on the caption. IN ST ST JOSEPH CIV Rule 206(206.1).

2. *Form of pleadings*

   a. *Caption; Names of parties.* Every pleading shall contain a caption setting forth the name of the court, the title of the action, the file number, and a designation as in IN ST TRIAL P Rule 7(A). In the complaint the title of the action shall include the names of all the parties, but in other pleadings it is sufficient to state the name of the first party on each side with an appropriate indication of other parties. IN ST TRIAL P Rule 10(A); IN ST ST JOSEPH CIV Rule 201(201.3.3). If a special judge has been assigned to the case, the pleading should also identify the special judge. IN ST ST JOSEPH CIV Rule 201(201.3.3).

      i. *Title.* All pleadings or motions shall include a title, which shall delineate each topic included in the pleading. For example, where a pleading contains an answer, a motion to dismiss, and a jury request, each topic shall be set forth in the title. IN ST ST JOSEPH CIV Rule 201(201.3.4).

b. *Paragraphs; Separate statements.* All averments of a claim or defense shall be made in numbered paragraphs, the contents of each of which shall be limited as far as practicable to a statement of a single set of circumstances, and a paragraph may be referred to by number in all succeeding pleadings. Each claim founded upon a separate transaction or occurrence and each defense other than denials may be stated in a separate count or defense whenever a separation facilitates the clear presentation of the matters set forth. IN ST TRIAL P Rule 10(B).

c. *Adoption by reference; Exhibits.* Statements in a pleading may be adopted by reference in a different part of the same pleading or in another pleading or in any motion. A copy of any written instrument which is an exhibit to a pleading is a part thereof for all purposes. IN ST TRIAL P Rule 10(C).

d. *Flat filing.* In order that the Clerk's files may be kept under the system commonly known as "flat filing," all papers presented to the Clerk for filing shall be flat and unfolded. Pleadings shall have no covers or backs and shall be fastened together at the top left-hand corner only. IN ST ST JOSEPH CIV Rule 201(201.1).

e. *One side of page used.* Printing shall be on one (1) side of the paper. IN ST ST JOSEPH CIV Rule 201(201.3.2).

f. *Copies.* All copies shall be on white paper of sufficient strength and durability to resist normal wear and tear. IN ST ST JOSEPH CIV Rule 201(201.3.1).

g. *Margins.* Margins shall be at least one inch (1"). IN ST ST JOSEPH CIV Rule 201(201.3.2).

h. *Double-spaced.* If typewritten, the lines shall be double spaced except for quotations, which shall be indented and single-spaced. IN ST ST JOSEPH CIV Rule 201(201.3.2).

i. *Font size.* Type face shall be twelve (12) font size or larger within the body of the document and ten (10) font size or larger in the footnotes. IN ST ST JOSEPH CIV Rule 201(201.3.2).

j. *Font type.* The font type must be legible and script type shall not be used. IN ST ST JOSEPH CIV Rule 201(201.3.2).

k. *Italics.* Italicized type may be used for quotations, references, or case citations. IN ST ST JOSEPH CIV Rule 201(201.3.2).

l. *Court and case designation.* All filings shall conform to the requirements for uniform court and case number designation set by IN ST ADMIN Rule 8. In addition, all filings shall contain the proper court and case designation as described below. IN ST ST JOSEPH CIV Rule 202.

   i. *Court designation.* Pursuant to IN ST 33-33-71-2, St. Joseph County, Indiana, constitutes the Sixtieth Judicial Circuit. The legal names of the courts within the 60th Judicial Circuit are the St. Joseph Circuit Court, the St. Joseph Superior Court, and the St. Joseph Probate Court. All filings shall properly reflect the legal name of the applicable court. Any filing may be amended, rejected, or stricken if it does not contain the proper case name and/or the legal name of the court. IN ST ST JOSEPH CIV Rule 202(202.1).

m. *Form of CCS entry.* Every written motion, petition, or other pleading subsequent to the original complaint presented to the Clerk for filing shall be accompanied by a Chronological Case Summary (CCS) entry form in duplicate which shall contain the title and cause number of the action, the date, and the proposed entry to appear on the docket. IN ST ST JOSEPH CIV Rule 201(201.4).

   i. *Identification and signature.* The CCS entry form shall identify the party making the filing, designate each pleading being filed, and shall be signed by counsel of record or the unrepresented litigant. IN ST ST JOSEPH CIV Rule 201(201.4).

   ii. *Date stamp.* The form shall be date stamped and presented to the Court Clerk, who shall initial the form and return the duplicate to the filing party. IN ST ST JOSEPH CIV Rule 201(201.4).

n. *Form of proposed order.* Any proposed order shall be a document that is separate and apart from the motion or application to which it relates and shall contain a caption showing the name of the court, the case number assigned to the case, and the title of the case as shown by the complaint pursuant to IN ST ST JOSEPH CIV Rule 201. IN ST ST JOSEPH CIV Rule 213(213.2).

   i. If there are multiple parties, the title may be shortened to include only the first name plaintiff and

       defendant with appropriate indication that there are additional parties. IN ST ST JOSEPH CIV Rule 213(213.2).

    ii.   The proposed order shall be on white paper, eight and one-half by eleven inches (8 1/2" x 11") in size, and each page shall be numbered. IN ST ST JOSEPH CIV Rule 213(213.2).

    iii. The last page of the proposed order shall contain a line for the date, either "Dated _____" or "Signed on the date filemarked hereon." IN ST ST JOSEPH CIV Rule 213(213.2).

    iv. On the last page there also shall be a line for the signature of the Judge under which shall be typed "Judge, St. Joseph [Circuit or Superior or Probate] Court." IN ST ST JOSEPH CIV Rule 213(213.2).

    v.   If the proposed order contains a recommendation from a Magistrate, the last page shall have a line for the signature of the Magistrate under which shall be typed "Magistrate, St. Joseph [Circuit or Superior or Probate] Court," to the left of which shall be the following, "So Recommended:" and beneath and to the left of which shall be typed, "Approved. So Ordered." IN ST ST JOSEPH CIV Rule 213(213.2).

    vi. To allow compliance with the notice requirements of IN ST TRIAL P Rule 72(D), the lower four (4) inches of the last page of the proposed order shall be left blank. The proposed order shall also include a prepared proof of notice under IN ST TRIAL P Rule 72(D), and in preparing such a notice the filing party shall complete all portions of the prepared proof of notice. IN ST ST JOSEPH CIV Rule 213(213.2).

3.   *Size of papers for filing.* Effective January 1, 1992, all pleadings, copies, motions and documents filed with any trial court or appellate level court, typed or printed, with the exception of exhibits and existing wills, shall be prepared on eight and one-half by eleven inch (8 1/2" x 11") size paper. IN ST ADMIN Rule 11.

    a.   *Paper.* Pleadings, motions, and other papers shall be either legibly printed or typewritten on white opaque paper of good quality at least sixteen (16) pound weight, eight and one-half inches (8 1/2 ") in width and eleven inches (11") in length as required by IN ST ADMIN Rule 11. IN ST ST JOSEPH CIV Rule 201(201.3.1).

4.   *Signature requirements*

    a.   *Signature of attorney.* Every pleading or motion of a party represented by an attorney shall be signed by at least one (1) attorney of record in his individual name, whose address, telephone number, and attorney number shall be stated, except that this provision shall not apply to pleadings and motions made and transcribed at the trial or a hearing before the judge and received by him in such form. IN ST TRIAL P Rule 11(A).

       i.   The signature of an attorney constitutes a certificate by him that he has read the pleadings; that to the best of his knowledge, information, and belief, there is good ground to support it; and that it is not interposed for delay. IN ST TRIAL P Rule 11(A).

       ii. If a pleading or motion is not signed or is signed with intent to defeat the purpose of the rule, it may be stricken as sham and false and the action may proceed as though the pleading had not been served. IN ST TRIAL P Rule 11(A).

       iii. For a willful violation of IN ST TRIAL P Rule 11 an attorney may be subjected to appropriate disciplinary action. Similar action may be taken if scandalous or indecent matter is inserted. IN ST TRIAL P Rule 11(A).

    b.   *Signature of unrepresented party.* A party who is not represented by an attorney shall sign his pleading and state his address. IN ST TRIAL P Rule 11(A).

    c.   *Verification not generally required.* Except when specifically required by rule, pleadings or motions need not be verified or accompanied by affidavit. The rule in equity that the averments of an answer under oath must be overcome by the testimony of two (2) witnesses or of one (1) witness sustained by corroborating circumstances is abolished. IN ST TRIAL P Rule 11(A).

    d.   *Verification by affirmation or representation.* When in connection with any civil or special statutory proceeding it is required that any pleading, motion, petition, supporting affidavit, or other document

of any kind, be verified, or that an oath be taken, it shall be sufficient if the subscriber simply affirms the truth of the matter to be verified by an affirmation or representation. IN ST TRIAL P Rule 11(B). IN ST TRIAL P Rule 11(B) states that the affirmation or representation should be in substantially the following language: "I (we) affirm, under the penalties for perjury, that the foregoing representation(s) is (are) true. (Signed) _____"

    i. Any person who falsifies an affirmation or representation of fact shall be subject to the same penalties as are prescribed by law for the making of a false affidavit. IN ST TRIAL P Rule 11(B).

e. *Verified pleadings, motions, and affidavits as evidence.* Pleadings, motions and affidavits accompanying or in support of such pleadings or motions when required to be verified or under oath shall be accepted as a representation that the signer had personal knowledge thereof or reasonable cause to believe the existence of the facts or matters stated or alleged therein; and, if otherwise competent or acceptable as evidence, may be admitted as evidence of the facts or matters stated or alleged therein when it is so provided in the Indiana Rules of Trial Procedure, by statute or other law, or to the extent the writing or signature expressly purports to be made upon the signer's personal knowledge. When such pleadings, motions and affidavits are verified or under oath they shall not require other or greater proof on the part of the adverse party than if not verified or not under oath unless expressly provided otherwise by the Indiana Rules of Trial Procedure, statute or other law. Affidavits upon motions for summary judgment under IN ST TRIAL P Rule 56 and in denial of execution under IN ST TRIAL P Rule 9.2 shall be made upon personal knowledge. IN ST TRIAL P Rule 11(C).

f. *Signature, verification and other requirements.* Parties and their counsel are enjoined to comply with the verification requirements of IN ST TRIAL P Rule 11, and either the moving party or the party's attorney of record shall sign all pleadings and motions before filing with the Clerk of the Court. Every motion, petition, or other pleading filed with the Clerk shall contain the name, organization, physical address, telephone number, and facsimile number of the filing party or an attorney for that party. IN ST ST JOSEPH CIV Rule 201(201.3.6).

    i. The Clerk shall not accept any motion, petition, notice or other pleading or a CCS entry form for filing from an unrepresented litigant unless the unrepresented litigant's current address and phone number appear on the pleading, and an opposing party may service notices and responses on an unrepresented litigant at any address he or she has provided on a pleading. IN ST ST JOSEPH CIV Rule 201(201.3.6).

5. *Information excluded from public access.* Every document filed in a case shall separately identify information excluded from public access pursuant to IN ST ADMIN Rule 9(G)(1) as follows:

a. Whole documents that are excluded from public access pursuant to IN ST ADMIN Rule 9(G)(1) shall be tendered on light green paper or have a light green coversheet attached to the document, marked "Not for Public Access" or "Confidential." IN ST TRIAL P Rule 5(G)(1).

b. When only a portion of a document contains information excluded from public access pursuant to IN ST ADMIN Rule 9(G)(1), said information shall be omitted [or redacted] from the filed document, and set forth on a separate accompanying document on light green paper conspicuously marked "Not for Public Access" or "Confidential" and clearly designated [or identifying] the caption and number of the case and the document and location within the document to which the redacted material pertains. IN ST TRIAL P Rule 5(G)(2).

c. With respect to documents filed in electronic format, the trial court, by local rule, may provide for compliance with IN ST TRIAL P Rule 5 in manner that separates and protects access to information excluded from public access. IN ST TRIAL P Rule 5(G)(3).

d. IN ST TRIAL P Rule 5(G) does not apply to a record sealed by the court pursuant to IN ST 5-14-3-5.5 or otherwise, nor to records, documents, or information filed in cases to which public access is prohibited pursuant to IN ST ADMIN Rule 9(G). IN ST TRIAL P Rule 5(G)(4).

e. The following information in case records is excluded from public access and is confidential:

    i. Information that is excluded from public access pursuant to federal law;

ii. Information that is excluded from public access as declared confidential by Indiana statute or other court rule, including without limitation:

- All adoption records created after July 8, 1941, as declared confidential by IN ST 31-19-19-1, et seq., except those specifically declared open by IN ST 31-19-13-2(2);

- All records relating to chancroid, chlamydia, gonorrhea, hepatitis, human immunodeficiency virus (HIV), Lymphogranuloma venereum, syphilis, tuberculosis, as declared confidential by IN ST 16-41-8-1, et seq.;

- All records relating to child abuse as declared confidential by IN ST 31-33-18-1, et seq.;

- All records relating to drug tests as declared confidential by IN ST 5-14-3-4(a)(9);

- Records of grand jury proceedings as declared confidential by IN ST 35-34-2-4;

- Records of juvenile proceedings as declared confidential by IN ST 31-39-1-2, except those specifically open under statute;

- All paternity records created after July 1, 1941 as declared confidential by IN ST 31-14-11-15, IN ST 31-19-5-23, IN ST 31-39-1-1 and IN ST 31-39-1-2 [Editor's note: IN ST 31-14-11-15 was repealed effective May 9, 2013];

- All pre-sentence reports as declared confidential by IN ST 35-38-1-13;

- Written petitions to permit marriages without consent and orders directing the Clerk of Court to issue a marriage license to underage persons, as declared confidential by IN ST 31-11-1-6;

- Only those arrest warrants, search warrants, indictments and informations ordered confidential by the trial judge, prior to return of duly executed service as declared confidential by IN ST 5-14-3-4(b)(1);

- All medical, mental health, or tax records unless determined by law or regulation of any governmental custodian not to be confidential, released by the subject of such records, or declared by a court of competent jurisdiction to be essential to the resolution of litigation as declared confidential by IN ST 16-39-3-10, IN ST 6-4.1-5-10, IN ST 6-4.1-12-12, and IN ST 6-8.1-7-1;

- Personal information relating to jurors or prospective jurors, other than for the use of the parties and counsel, pursuant to IN ST JURY Rule 10;

- Information relating to protection from abuse orders, no-contact orders and workplace violence restraining orders as declared confidential by IN ST 5-2-9-6, et seq.;

- Mediation proceedings pursuant to IN ST ADR Rule 2.11, Mini-Trial proceedings pursuant to IN ST ADR Rule 4.4(C), and Summary Jury Trials pursuant to IN ST ADR Rule 5.6;

- Information in probation files pursuant to the Probation Standards promulgated by the Judicial Conference of Indiana pursuant to IN ST 11-13-1-8(b);

- Information deemed confidential pursuant to the Rules for Court Administered Alcohol and Drug Programs promulgated by the Judicial Conference of Indiana pursuant to IN ST 12-23-14-13;

- Information deemed confidential pursuant to the Problem-Solving Court Rules promulgated by the Judicial Conference of Indiana pursuant to IN ST 33-23-16-16;

- All records of the Department of workforce Development as declared confidential by IN ST 22-4-19-6;

- Information regarding interception of electronic communications that is sealed or deemed confidential as set forth in IN ST 35-33.5-2-1, et seq.

iii. Information excluded from public access by specific court order;

iv. Complete Social Security Numbers of living persons;

v. With the exception of names, information such as addresses, phone numbers, and dates of birth which explicitly identifies:

- Natural persons who are witnesses or victims (not including defendants) in criminal, domestic violence, stalking, sexual assault, juvenile, or civil protection order proceedings, provided that juveniles who are victims of sex crimes shall be identified by initials only;

- Places of residence of judicial officers, clerks and other employees of courts and clerks of court, unless the person or persons about whom the information pertains waives confidentiality;

vi. Complete account numbers of specific assets, loans, bank accounts, credit cards, and personal identification numbers (PINs);

vii. All orders of expungement entered in criminal or juvenile proceedings, orders to restrict access to criminal history information pursuant to IN ST 35-38-5-5.5 or IN ST 35-38-8-5 and records excluded from public access by such orders, and information related to infractions that is excluded from public access pursuant to IN ST 34-28-5-15 or IN ST 34-28-5-16 [Editor's note: IN ST 35-38-5-5.5, IN ST 35-38-8-5 and IN ST 34-28-5-16 were repealed effective July 1, 2013; for information on orders restricting access to criminal history, refer to IN ST 35-38-9-1, et seq.];

viii. All personal notes and e-mail, and deliberative material, of judges, jurors, court staff and judicial agencies, and information recorded in personal data assistants (PDA's) or organizers and personal calendars. IN ST ADMIN Rule 9(G)(1).

F. Filing and Service Requirements

1. *Filing requirements.* Except as otherwise provided in IN ST TRIAL P Rule 5(E)(2), all pleadings and papers subsequent to the complaint which are required to be served upon a party shall be filed with the Court either before service or within a reasonable period of time thereafter. IN ST TRIAL P Rule 5(E)(1).

   a. *Filing with the court defined.* The filing of pleadings, motions, and other papers with the court as required by the Indiana Rules of Trial Procedure shall be made by one of the following methods:

      i. Delivery to the clerk of the court;

      ii. Sending by electronic transmission under the procedure adopted pursuant to IN ST ADMIN Rule 12;

      iii. Mailing to the clerk by registered, certified or express mail return receipt requested;

      iv. Depositing with any third-party commercial carrier for delivery to the clerk within three (3) calendar days, cost prepaid, properly addressed;

      v. If the court so permits, filing with the judge, in which event the judge shall note thereon the filing date and forthwith transmit them to the office of the clerk; or

      vi. Electronic filing, as approved by the Division of State Court Administration pursuant to IN ST ADMIN Rule 16. IN ST TRIAL P Rule 5(F).

      vii. Filing by registered or certified mail and by third-party commercial carrier shall be complete upon mailing or deposit. IN ST TRIAL P Rule 5(F).

      viii. All pleadings shall be filed with the Clerk, not directly with the Court, unless otherwise required by the Indiana Rules of Court. The entry of appearances and the filing of pleadings or other matters not requiring immediate Court action shall be filed with the Clerk and not in open Court. A Judge may permit papers to be filed in chambers, in which event he or she shall note thereon the filing date and transmit the papers to the Clerk. IN ST ST JOSEPH CIV Rule 201(201.2).

   b. *Facsimile filing.* Unless otherwise authorized by IN ST ST JOSEPH ELECTRONIC Rule 701, electronic filing of pleadings by computerized or facsimile transmission is not permitted. IN ST ST JOSEPH CIV Rule 201(201.2).

   c. *Additional copies.* In cases in which a party or counsel supplies the proposed order or decree, a sufficient number shall be prepared and filed as to provide the Clerk to retain two (2) copies, which shall be filed in the flat file and the record of judgments and orders. Should the party or counsel desire

additional copies, a sufficient number of copies should be filed to effectuate that purpose. IN ST ST JOSEPH CIV Rule 201(201.6).

   d.   *Proof of filing.* Any party filing any paper by any method other than personal delivery to the clerk shall retain proof of filing. IN ST TRIAL P Rule 5(F).

2.   *Service requirements.* Unless otherwise provided by the Indiana Rules of Trial Procedure or an order of the court, each party and special judge, if any, shall be served with: (1) every order required by its terms to be served; (2) every pleading subsequent to the original complaint; (3) every written motion except one which may be heard ex parte; (4) every brief submitted to the trial court; (5) every paper relating to discovery required to be served upon a party; and (6) every written notice, appearance, demand, offer of judgment, designation of record on appeal, or similar paper. IN ST TRIAL P Rule 5(A).

   a.   *Service generally.* Every motion, petition, notice, or other pleading required to be served by IN ST TRIAL P Rule 5 shall be served on all counsel of record or unrepresented parties either before it is filed or on the day it is filed with the Court, and the date of filing shall be indicated on the Certificate of Service. IN ST ST JOSEPH CIV Rule 201(201.5.1).

      i.   *Copy.* A copy of the Clerk's CCS entry form of the filing shall also be served on all counsel of record or unrepresented parties whenever it contains an appearance of counsel or contains a date for Court hearing on the matter. IN ST ST JOSEPH CIV Rule 201(201.5.1).

   b.   *Methods of service*

      i.   *Personal service.* Whenever a party is represented by an attorney of record, service shall be made upon such attorney unless service upon the party himself is ordered by the court. Service upon the attorney or party shall be made by delivering or mailing a copy of the papers to the last known address or where an attorney or party has consented to service by fax or e-mail, as provided in IN ST TRIAL P Rule 3.1(A)(4), by faxing or e-mailing a copy of the documents to the fax number or e-mail address set out in the appearance form or correction as required by IN ST TRIAL P Rule 3.1(E). IN ST TRIAL P Rule 5(B). Delivery of a copy within IN ST TRIAL P Rule 5 means:

         •   Offering or tendering it to the attorney or party and stating the nature of the papers being served. Refusal to accept an offered or tendered document is a waiver of any objection to the sufficiency or adequacy of service of that document;

         •   Leaving it at his office with a clerk or other person in charge thereof, or if there is no one in charge, leaving it in a conspicuous place therein; or

         •   If the office is closed, by leaving it at his dwelling house or usual place of abode with some person of suitable age and discretion then residing therein; or,

         •   Leaving it at some other suitable place, selected by the attorney upon whom service is being made, pursuant to duly promulgated local rule. IN ST TRIAL P Rule 5(B)(1).

      ii.   *Service by the clerk.* Whenever the Clerk is required by rule or statute to give notice, the party or parties requesting such notice shall furnish the Clerk with sufficient copies of the notice to be given, along with stamped, addressed envelopes with the names and the addresses of the parties or their counsel to whom such notice is to be given. IN ST ST JOSEPH CIV Rule 201(201.5.4).

      iii.   *Service on the court.* Service on a Judge may be made by delivering a copy to the Judge's secretary or mailing a copy to the Judge at his or her chambers. Service on a Judge may not be accomplished by facsimile transmission; however, a courtesy copy may be sent to the Judge's chambers by electronic mail or facsimile transmission contemporaneously with service by mail or otherwise. IN ST ST JOSEPH CIV Rule 201(201.5.5).

      iv.   *Service by mail.* If service is made by mail, the papers shall be deposited in the United States mail addressed to the person on whom they are being served, with postage prepaid. Service shall be deemed complete upon mailing. Proof of service of all papers permitted to be mailed may be made by written acknowledgment of service, by affidavit of the person who mailed the papers, or by certificate of an attorney. It shall be the duty of attorneys when entering their appearance in a cause or when filing pleadings or papers therein, to have noted in the

Chronological Case Summary or said pleadings or papers so filed the address and telephone number of their office. Service by delivery or by mail at such address shall be deemed sufficient and complete. IN ST TRIAL P Rule 5(B)(2).

    v. *Service by fax or e-mail.* A party who has consented to service by fax or e-mail may be served as follows:

- Service by e-mail shall be made by attaching the document being served in .pdf format. Discovery documents must also be served in accordance with IN ST TRIAL P Rule 26(A). IN ST TRIAL P Rule 5(B)(3)(a).

- Service by fax shall be deemed complete upon generation of a transmission record indicating the successful transmission of the entire document, except as provided in IN ST TRIAL P Rule 5(B)(3)(d). IN ST TRIAL P Rule 5(B)(3)(b).

- Service by e-mail shall be deemed complete upon transmission, except as provided in IN ST TRIAL P Rule 5(B)(3)(d). IN ST TRIAL P Rule 5(B)(3)(c).

- Service by fax or e-mail that occurs on a Saturday, Sunday, legal holiday, or day the court or agency in which the matter is pending is closed or after 5:00 PM local time of the recipient shall be deemed complete the next day that is not a Saturday, Sunday, legal holiday, or day that the court or agency in which the matter is pending is not closed. IN ST TRIAL P Rule 5(B)(3)(d).

c. *Serving numerous defendants.* In any action in which there are unusually large numbers of defendants, the court, upon motion or of its own initiative, may order:

    i. That service of the pleadings of the defendants and replies thereto need not be made as between the defendants;

- That any cross-claim, counterclaim, or matter constituting an avoidance or affirmative defense contained therein shall be deemed to be denied or avoided by all other parties; and

- That the filing of any such pleading and service thereof upon the plaintiff constitutes due notice of it to the parties. IN ST TRIAL P Rule 5(D).

    ii. A copy of every such order shall be served upon the parties in such manner and form as the court directs. IN ST TRIAL P Rule 5(D).

d. *Service on parties in default for failure to appear.* No service need be made on parties in default for failure to appear, except that pleadings asserting new or additional claims for relief against them shall be served upon them in the manner provided by service of summons in IN ST TRIAL P Rule 4. IN ST TRIAL P Rule 5(A).

e. *Distribution.* Counsel or an unrepresented party submitting a motion, petition, notice, pleading or proposed order shall indicate the method of distribution desired on the Clerk's CCS entry form. The Clerk will not return or distribute copies of motions, petitions, pleadings, notices or proposed orders, other than those originated by the Court, by mail unless the Clerk is provided with stamped, addressed envelopes. IN ST ST JOSEPH CIV Rule 201(201.5.3).

f. *Mailbox.* As a matter of convenience to attorneys, each court provides a mailbox for the distribution filings and orders generated by the Court, and it is the responsibility of each attorney to periodically check these mailboxes for service and distribution of court-generated filings and orders. IN ST ST JOSEPH CIV Rule 201(201.5.3).

G. Hearings

1. *Hearing on motion.* Unless local conditions make it impracticable, each judge shall establish regular times and places, at intervals sufficiently frequent for the prompt dispatch of business, at which motions requiring notice and hearing may be heard and disposed of; but the judge at any time or place and on such notice, if any, as he considers reasonable may make order for the advancement, conduct, and hearing of actions. To expedite its business the court may direct the submission and determination of motions without oral hearing upon brief written statements of reasons in support and opposition, or direct or permit hearings by telephone conference call with all attorneys or other similar means of communication. IN ST TRIAL P Rule 73(A).

2. *Hearing dates.* Hearing dates for filings requiring Court action shall be obtained from the Court Clerk and incorporated in the CCS entry at the time the motion or other pleading is filed. If no date is obtained prior to the filing, the fact of the hearing should be noted with the date and time left blank. IN ST ST JOSEPH CIV Rule 201(201.4).

3. *Hearing on matters other than trials.* Each Judge shall reserve periods of time for hearing matters other than contested trials, such as pre-trial and post-trial motions, rules to show cause, defaults, uncontested dissolutions of marriage, etc. As necessary to minimize conflicts in scheduling, the Judges shall set these schedules after consultation. Hearings shall be scheduled as follows:

   a. *Scheduling uncontested or routine matters.* Routine matters, procedural motions, domestic relations applications for provisional relief and contempt proceedings, uncontested petitions for dissolution of marriage, and all other matters appropriate for summary consideration and disposition will be heard on the daily calendar. IN ST ST JOSEPH GEN AND ADMIN Rule 104(104.3.1).

   b. *Scheduling contested or complicated matters.* Other matters that will require a hearing reasonably estimated to last in excess of twenty (20) minutes will be scheduled as the Court's calendar allows. Counsel or a party proceeding pro se should contact the chambers of the assigned judge to arrange for an appropriate hearing date and time. IN ST ST JOSEPH GEN AND ADMIN Rule 104(104.3.2).

   c. *Scheduling motions for hearings.* Except for motions to correct error or not likely to require a hearing (as described in IN ST ST JOSEPH CIV Rule 201), all motions shall be scheduled for hearing at the time they are filed. It shall the responsibility of the moving party or counsel for the moving party to secure the date and time of the hearing from the Clerk or Court personnel who maintain the calendar for each Judge or Magistrate Judge. It shall also be the responsibility of the moving party or counsel for the moving party to coordinate the hearing date with all opposing counsel or unrepresented parties. IN ST ST JOSEPH CIV Rule 201(201.9.1).

   d. *Oral arguments on motions and other pleadings.* Unless otherwise required by St. Joseph County Civil or Indiana Trial Rules, it is within the sound discretion of the assigned Judge whether to allow oral argument; however, any party may file a request for oral argument by filing a written request by separate motion contemporaneously or at any time before the Court has ruled upon the motion or pleadings to be argued. IN ST ST JOSEPH CIV Rule 201(201.9.4).

4. *Motions for summary judgment and for dismissal.* Motions for summary judgment or motions to dismiss pursuant to IN ST TRIAL P Rule 12 or IN ST TRIAL P Rule 41 shall be scheduled for hearing, unless the Court issues a written scheduling order providing otherwise. (Refer to IN ST ST JOSEPH CIV Rule 206 for specific requirements for Pleadings and Motions under IN ST TRIAL P Rule 12 and IN ST TRIAL P Rule 56). IN ST ST JOSEPH CIV Rule 201(201.9.6).

   a. *Dispositive motions date.* Notwithstanding any other rule of court, all IN ST TRIAL P Rule 12 or IN ST TRIAL P Rule 56 motions shall be set for hearing by the moving party at the time of filing unless otherwise ordered by the Court. Unless otherwise authorized by the Court, the hearing shall be scheduled for a day not fewer than fourteen (14) days after the time period allowed for filing of briefs as specified in IN ST ST JOSEPH CIV Rule 206(206.1). IN ST ST JOSEPH CIV Rule 206(206.2).

   b. *Waiver of hearing; Stipulation of the parties.* Adverse parties may stipulate that a IN ST TRIAL P Rule 12 or IN ST TRIAL P Rule 56 motion may be ruled upon by the Court without a hearing thereon, in which event the motion and stipulation shall be brought to the personal attention of the Judge by counsel or by a party proceeding pro se. IN ST ST JOSEPH CIV Rule 206(206.3).

   c. *Appearance by counsel at scheduled hearings.* Whenever the Court schedules a hearing on a motion pursuant to IN ST TRIAL P Rule 12 and/or IN ST TRIAL P Rule 56, counsel for all represented parties shall appear in person or by local co-counsel at such hearing. IN ST ST JOSEPH CIV Rule 206(206.5).

H. Forms

1. Motion to Dismiss for Lack of Subject Matter Jurisdiction Forms for Indiana

   a. General form. 5 INPRAC § 3:4.1.

   b. Lack of subject matter jurisdiction. 5 INPRAC § 3:4.2.

    c.   Motion to dismiss plaintiff's complaint; General form. 9 INPRAC § 42.2.

    d.   Lack of jurisdiction over the subject matter. 9 INPRAC § 42.3.

    e.   Certificate of service; Personal service. 9 INPRAC § 5.7.

    f.   Certificate of service; First class mail. 9 INPRAC § 5.8.

I. Checklist

(I) ❑ Matters to be considered by moving party

    (a) ❑ Required documents

        (1) ❑ Motion and notice

        (2) ❑ Chronological Case Summary (CCS) entry form

        (3) ❑ Supporting memorandum of law

        (4) ❑ Proposed order

        (5) ❑ Certificate of service

    (b) ❑ Supplemental documents

        (1) ❑ Supporting evidence

        (2) ❑ Facsimile cover sheet

    (c) ❑ Timing

        (1) ❑ A motion to dismiss for lack of subject matter jurisdiction shall be made before pleading if a further pleading is permitted or within twenty (20) days after service of the prior pleading if none is required

        (2) ❑ A written motion, other than one which may be heard ex parte, and notice of the hearing thereof shall be served not less than five (5) days before the time specified for the hearing, unless a different period is fixed by the Indiana Rules of Trial Procedure or by order of the court

        (3) ❑ All pleadings and papers subsequent to the complaint which are required to be served upon a party shall be filed with the Court either before service or within a reasonable period of time thereafter

(II) ❑ Matters to be considered by the responding party

    (a) ❑ Required documents

        (1) ❑ Opposition

        (2) ❑ Chronological Case Summary (CCS) entry form

        (3) ❑ Supporting memorandum of law

        (4) ❑ Certificate of service

    (b) ❑ Supplemental documents

        (1) ❑ Supporting evidence

        (2) ❑ Facsimile cover sheet

    (c) ❑ Timing

        (1) ❑ An adverse party shall have thirty (30) days after service of the motion in which to serve and file an answer brief

        (2) ❑ Except as otherwise provided in IN ST TRIAL P Rule 59(D), opposing affidavits may be served not less than one (1) day before the hearing, unless the court permits them to be served at some other time

Motions, Oppositions and Replies
Motion to Dismiss for Lack of Personal Jurisdiction

Document Last Updated October 2013

A. Applicable Rules

1. *State rules*

   a. Appearance. IN ST TRIAL P Rule 3.1.

   b. Summons. IN ST TRIAL P Rule 4.

   c. Service and filing of pleadings and other papers. IN ST TRIAL P Rule 5.

   d. Time. IN ST TRIAL P Rule 6.

   e. Pleadings. IN ST TRIAL P Rule 7; IN ST TRIAL P Rule 8; IN ST TRIAL P Rule 9; IN ST TRIAL P Rule 9.2; IN ST TRIAL P Rule 10.

   f. Signing and verification of pleadings. IN ST TRIAL P Rule 11.

   g. Defenses and objections; When and how presented; By pleading or motion; Motion for judgment on the pleadings. IN ST TRIAL P Rule 12.

   h. Amended and supplemental pleadings. IN ST TRIAL P Rule 15.

   i. Joinder of person needed for just adjudication. IN ST TRIAL P Rule 19.

   j. Evidence. IN ST TRIAL P Rule 43.

   k. Judgment on the evidence (directed verdict). IN ST TRIAL P Rule 50.

   l. Findings by the court. IN ST TRIAL P Rule 52.

   m. Summary judgment. IN ST TRIAL P Rule 56.

   n. Motion to correct error. IN ST TRIAL P Rule 59.

   o. Relief from judgment or order. IN ST TRIAL P Rule 60.

   p. Hearing of motions. IN ST TRIAL P Rule 73.

   q. Access to court records. IN ST ADMIN Rule 9.

   r. Paper size. IN ST ADMIN Rule 11.

   s. Facsimile transmission. IN ST ADMIN Rule 12.

   t. Electronic filing and electronic service pilot projects. IN ST ADMIN Rule 16.

   u. Sealing of certain records by court; Hearing; Notice. IN ST 5-14-3-5.5.

   v. Sixtieth judicial circuit. IN ST 33-33-71-2.

   w. Privacy and confidentiality. IN ST 5-2-9-6; IN ST 5-14-3-4; IN ST 6-4.1-5-10; IN ST 6-4.1-12-12; IN ST 6-8.1-7-1; IN ST 11-13-1-8; IN ST 12-23-14-13; IN ST 16-39-3-10; IN ST 16-41-8-1; IN ST 22-4-19-6; IN ST 31-11-1-6; IN ST 31-19-5-23; IN ST 31-19-13-2; IN ST 31-19-19-1; IN ST 31-33-18-1; IN ST 31-39-1-1; IN ST 31-39-1-2; IN ST 33-23-16-16; IN ST 35-34-2-4; IN ST 35-38-1-13; IN ST 35-38-9-1; IN ST ADR Rule 2.11; IN ST ADR Rule 4.4; IN ST ADR Rule 5.6; IN ST JURY Rule 10.

2. *Local rules*

   a. Court hours and scheduling. IN ST ST JOSEPH GEN AND ADMIN Rule 104.

   b. Filing, pleading, and motions. IN ST ST JOSEPH CIV Rule 201.

   c. Uniform court and case number designation. IN ST ST JOSEPH CIV Rule 202.

   d. Pleading and motions under IN ST TRIAL P Rule 12 and IN ST TRIAL P Rule 56. IN ST ST JOSEPH CIV Rule 206.

   e. Proposed order. IN ST ST JOSEPH CIV Rule 213.

f. Electronic filing of cases in St. Joseph County. IN ST ST JOSEPH ELECTRONIC Rule 701.

B. Timing

1. *Timing of motion to dismiss for failure lack of personal matter jurisdiction.* A motion making any of the defenses listed in IN ST TRIAL P Rule 12(B) shall be made before pleading if a further pleading is permitted or within twenty (20) days after service of the prior pleading if none is required. IN ST TRIAL P Rule 12(B).

   a. *Time to file a responsive pleading.* A responsive pleading required under the Indiana Rules of Trial Procedure, shall be served within twenty (20) days after service of the prior pleading. IN ST TRIAL P Rule 6(C).

   b. *Waiver of certain IN ST TRIAL P Rule 12(B) defenses.* If a pleading sets forth a claim for relief to which the adverse party is not required to serve a responsive pleading, any of the defenses in IN ST TRIAL P Rule 12(B)(2), IN ST TRIAL P Rule 12(B)(3), IN ST TRIAL P Rule 12(B)(4), IN ST TRIAL P Rule 12(B)(5) or IN ST TRIAL P Rule 12(B)(8) is waived to the extent constitutionally permissible unless made in a motion within twenty (20) days after service of the prior pleading. IN ST TRIAL P Rule 12(B).

   c. *Filing.* All pleadings and papers subsequent to the complaint which are required to be served upon a party shall be filed with the Court either before service or within a reasonable period of time thereafter. IN ST TRIAL P Rule 5(E)(1).

2. *Service.* A written motion, other than one which may be heard ex parte, and notice of the hearing thereof shall be served not less than five (5) days before the time specified for the hearing, unless a different period is fixed by the Indiana Rules of Trial Procedure or by order of the court. IN ST TRIAL P Rule 6(D).

   a. *Of supporting affidavits.* When a motion is supported by affidavit, the affidavit shall be served with the motion. IN ST TRIAL P Rule 6(D).

3. *Service of opposition.* Except as otherwise provided in IN ST TRIAL P Rule 59(D), opposing affidavits may be served not less than one (1) day before the hearing, unless the court permits them to be served at some other time. IN ST TRIAL P Rule 6(D).

   a. An adverse party shall have thirty (30) days after service of the motion in which to serve and file an answer brief. IN ST ST JOSEPH CIV Rule 206(206.1).

4. *Filing proposed orders.* Unless otherwise directed or given leave of the Court, proposed orders in emergency matters shall be filed within forty-eight (48) hours after a hearing; proposed orders in other matters shall be filed within seven (7) days as computed by IN ST TRIAL P Rule 6. IN ST ST JOSEPH CIV Rule 213(213.5).

5. *Computation of time*

   a. *Generally; Days excluded.* In computing any period of time prescribed or allowed by the Indiana Rules of Trial Procedure, by order of the court, or by any applicable statute, the day of the act, event, or default from which the designated period of time begins to run shall not be included. The last day of the period so computed is to be included unless it is:

      i. A Saturday,

      ii. A Sunday,

      iii. A legal holiday as defined by state statute, or

      iv. A day the office in which the act is to be done is closed during regular business hours. IN ST TRIAL P Rule 6(A).

   b. *Short periods.* In any event, the period runs until the end of the next day that is not a Saturday, a Sunday, a legal holiday, or a day on which the office is closed. When the period of time allowed is less than seven (7) days, intermediate Saturdays, Sundays, legal holidays, and days on which the office is closed shall be excluded from the computations. IN ST TRIAL P Rule 6(A).

   c. *Additional time after service by United States mail.* Whenever a party has the right or is required to do some act or take some proceedings within a prescribed period after the service of a notice or other paper upon him and the notice or paper is served upon him by United States mail, three (3) days shall be added to the prescribed period. IN ST TRIAL P Rule 6(E).

    d. *Enlargement of time.* When an act is required or allowed to be done at or within a specific time by the Indiana Rules of Trial Procedure, the court may at any time for cause shown:

        i. Order the period enlarged, with or without motion or notice, if request therefor is made before the expiration of the period originally prescribed or extended by a previous order; or

        ii. Upon motion made after the expiration of the specific period, permit the act to be done where the failure to act was the result of excusable neglect; but, the court may not extend the time for taking any action for judgment on the evidence under IN ST TRIAL P Rule 50(A), amendment of findings and judgment under IN ST TRIAL P Rule 52(B), to correct errors under IN ST TRIAL P Rule 59(C), statement in opposition to motion to correct error under IN ST TRIAL P Rule 59(E), or to obtain relief from final judgment under IN ST TRIAL P Rule 60(B), except to the extent and under the conditions stated in those rules. IN ST TRIAL P Rule 6(B).

        iii. An initial written motion for enlargement of time pursuant to IN ST TRIAL P Rule 6(B)(1) to answer a claim shall be routinely granted for an additional thirty (30) days from the original due date or other period the assigned Judge deems reasonable by written order of the Court. The motion must be filed on or before the original due date or IN ST ST JOSEPH CIV Rule 201 shall be inapplicable. IN ST ST JOSEPH CIV Rule 201(201.9.5).

- Any motion for enlargement of time shall state the date when such response is due and the date to which time is requested to be enlarged. IN ST ST JOSEPH CIV Rule 201(201.9.5).

- All subsequent motions for enlargement of time shall be so designated and will only be granted for good cause shown or in the interest of justice. IN ST ST JOSEPH CIV Rule 201(201.9.5).

C. General Requirements

1. *Motions, generally.* Unless made during a hearing or trial, or otherwise ordered by the court, an application to the court for an order shall be made by written motion. The motion shall state the grounds therefor and the relief or order sought. IN ST TRIAL P Rule 7(B).

    a. *Motions as distinct from pleadings.* Motions and responses to motions are not pleadings, and allegations contained in a motion are not admissions of a party. 22B INPRAC 7:2; Wachstetter v. County Properties, LLC, 832 N.E.2d 574 (Ind.Ct.App. 2005); Scott County Family YMCA, Inc. v. Hobbs, 817 N.E.2d 603 (Ind.Ct.App. 2004).

    b. *Unopposed motions generally granted.* It is common for a trial court to grant procedural motions, such as motions for enlargement of time, discovery motions, or motions for continuance, unless an objection is filed. 21 INPRAC § 13.8.

    c. *Proposed orders.* As directed by the Court, a party or an attorney for a party shall prepare a proposed order based on the decision rendered by the Court. The party so directed shall prepare the proposed order in a timely manner and, upon filing, shall advise the chambers of the applicable judge that the proposed order has been prepared and filed. IN ST ST JOSEPH CIV Rule 213(213.2).

        i. Prior to entry by the Court of orders granting motions or applications, the moving party or applicant (or his or her attorney) shall, unless the Court directs otherwise, furnish the Court with proposed orders in matters of dismissal. IN ST ST JOSEPH CIV Rule 213(213.1(5)).

    d. *Reply brief.* Subject to Court approval, the moving party may file a reply brief. IN ST ST JOSEPH CIV Rule 206(206.1).

2. *Motion to dismiss for lack of personal jurisdiction.* Every defense, in law or fact, to a claim for relief in any pleading, whether a claim, counterclaim, cross-claim, or third-party claim, shall be asserted in the responsive pleading thereto if one is required; except that at the option of the pleader, the defense of lack of jurisdiction over person may be made by motion. IN ST TRIAL P Rule 12(b)(2). If personal jurisdiction is not present, then that party against whom jurisdiction is asserted must raise the question. 1A INPRAC R 12(12.6).

    a. *Presumption of jurisdiction.* Jurisdiction is presumed and, therefore, the defense of lack of personal jurisdiction may be asserted by motion under IN ST TRIAL P Rule 12(B)(2), or in the defendant's answer as an affirmative defense. 22 INPRAC § 15.16; Adsit Co., Inc. v. Gustin, 874 N.E.2d 1018

(Ind.Ct.App. 2007); Keesling v. Winstead, 858 N.E.2d 996 (Ind.Ct.App. 2006). Refer to the Indiana KeyRules Answer document for more information.

b. *Personal jurisdiction.* The Due Process Clause of the Fourteenth Amendment requires that before a state may exercise jurisdiction over a defendant, the defendant must have certain minimum contacts with the state such that the maintenance of the suit does not offend traditional notions of fair play and substantial justice. 1A INPRAC R 12(12.6).

    i. *General jurisdiction.* If the defendant's contacts with the state are so continuous and systematic that the defendant should reasonably anticipate being haled into the courts of that state for any matter, then the defendant is subject to general jurisdiction, even in causes of action unrelated to the defendant's contacts with the forum state. 1A INPRAC R 12(12.6).

    ii. *Specific jurisdiction.* In cases where a defendant is not subject to general jurisdiction in a forum state, specific jurisdiction may be asserted if the controversy is related to or arises out of the defendant's contacts with the forum state. Specific jurisdiction requires that the defendant purposefully availed itself of the privilege of conducting activities within the forum state so that the defendant reasonably anticipates being haled into court there. A single contact with the forum state may be sufficient to establish specific jurisdiction over a defendant, if it creates a substantial connection with the forum state and the suit is related to that connection. 1A INPRAC R 12(12.6).

    iii. *Due process; Reasonableness.* A defendant cannot be haled into a jurisdiction solely as a result of random, fortuitous, or attenuated contacts or of the unilateral activity of another party or a third person. Once either general or specific jurisdiction has been established, due process requires that the assertion of personal jurisdiction over the defendant is reasonable. The assertion of personal jurisdiction will rarely be found unreasonable if minimum contacts are found. Five factors are used in determining reasonableness:

- The burden on the defendant;
- The forum State's interest in adjudicating the dispute;
- The plaintiff's interest in obtaining convenience and effective relief;
- The interstate judicial system's interest in obtaining the most efficient resolution of controversies; and
- The shared interest of the several States in furthering fundamental substantive social policies. 1A INPRAC R 12(12.6).

    iv. *Jurisdiction presumed.* Indiana state trial courts are courts of general jurisdiction and jurisdiction is presumed. The party contesting jurisdiction bears the burden of proving the lack of personal jurisdiction by a preponderance of the evidence, unless the lack of jurisdiction is apparent on the face of the complaint. A determination of the existence of personal jurisdiction is entitled to de novo review. 1A INPRAC R 12(12.6); Foley v. Schwartz, 943 N.E.2d 371 (Ind.Ct.App. 2011).

c. *Challenge to jurisdiction in first response to complaint.* The defendant may challenge the Indiana court's jurisdiction over him, without submitting to that jurisdiction, so long as the defense is asserted in the first response to the plaintiff's complaint and the defendant does not request affirmative relief from the court prior to asserting that defense. 22 INPRAC § 15.16.

d. *Burden shifting.* After the plaintiff establishes that there are minimum contacts between defendant and forum state to exercise personal jurisdiction without violating Due Process Clause, the defendant then carries the burden of proving that asserting jurisdiction is unfair and unreasonable. 1A INPRAC R 12(12.6); JPMorgan Chase Bank, N.A. v. Desert Palace, Inc., 882 N.E.2d 743 (Ind.Ct.App. 2008).

e. *Effect of granting of motion.* The dismissal of a complaint for lack of jurisdiction over the person is not an adjudication on the merits and does not prejudice the plaintiff's right to file another complaint if the court can obtain jurisdiction over the defendant. 9 INPRAC § 42.4.

3. *Consolidation and waiver*

    a. *Consolidation of defenses in motion.* A party who makes a motion under IN ST TRIAL P Rule 12 may join with it any other motions herein provided for and then available to him. If a party makes a motion under IN ST TRIAL P Rule 12 but omits therefrom any defense or objection then available to him which IN ST TRIAL P Rule 12 permits to be raised by motion, he shall not thereafter make a motion based on the defense or objection so omitted. He may, however, make such motions as are allowed under IN ST TRIAL P Rule 12(H)(2). IN ST TRIAL P Rule 12(G).

    b. *Waiver or preservation of certain defenses.* No defense or objection is waived by being joined with one or more other defenses or objections in a responsive pleading or motion. IN ST TRIAL P Rule 12(B).

4. *Opposition to a motion to dismiss for lack of personal jurisdiction.* Failure to file an answer brief or reply brief within the time prescribed shall be deemed a waiver of the right thereto and shall subject the motion to summary ruling. IN ST ST JOSEPH CIV Rule 206(206.1).

D. Documents

1. *Required documents*

    a. *Motion and notice.* The requirement of notice is satisfied by service of the motion. IN ST TRIAL P Rule 7(B). Refer to the General Requirements section of this document for information on the content of a motion to dismiss for lack of personal jurisdiction.

    b. *Chronological Case Summary (CCS) entry form.* Every written motion, petition, or other pleading subsequent to the original complaint presented to the Clerk for filing shall be accompanied by a Chronological Case Summary (CCS) entry form in duplicate. IN ST ST JOSEPH CIV Rule 201(201.4). Refer to the Format section of this document for details on the format and filing requirements for the CCS entry form.

    c. *Supporting memorandum of law.* All pleadings and motions filed pursuant to IN ST TRIAL P Rule 12 and IN ST TRIAL P Rule 56 shall be accompanied by a separate supporting brief. IN ST ST JOSEPH CIV Rule 206(206.1).

    d. *Proposed order.* Unless local practice provides differently, a party should submit a proposed order with its written motion to be signed by the judge once the motion has been granted. 21 INPRAC § 13.8. All proposed orders shall be submitted in an original plus a number of copies equal to one more than the number of pro se parties and attorneys of record contained in the prepared proof of notice under IN ST TRIAL P Rule 72(D). IN ST ST JOSEPH CIV Rule 213(213.3); IN ST ST JOSEPH CIV Rule 201(201.5.2).

    e. *Certificate of service.* An attorney or unrepresented party tendering a document to the Clerk for filing shall certify that service has been made, list the parties served, and specify the date and means of service. The certificate of service shall be placed at the end of the document and shall not be separately filed. The separate filing of a certificate of service, however, shall not be grounds for rejecting a document for filing. The Clerk may permit documents to be filed without a certificate of service but shall require prompt filing of a separate certificate of service. IN ST TRIAL P Rule 5(C).

2. *Supplemental documents*

    a. *Supporting evidence.* When a motion is based on facts not appearing of record the court may hear the matter on affidavits presented by the respective parties, but the court may direct that the matter be heard wholly or partly on oral testimony or depositions. IN ST TRIAL P Rule 43(B).

    b. *Facsimile cover sheet.* Any document sent to the Clerk of the Circuit Court by electronic facsimile transmission shall be accompanied by a cover sheet which states the title of the document, case number, number of pages, identity and voice telephone number of the sending party and instructions for filing. The cover sheet shall contain the signature of the attorney or party, pro se, authorizing the filing. IN ST ADMIN Rule 12(D).

E. Format

1. *Form of motions.* The rules applicable to captions, and the signing and form of pleadings (IN ST TRIAL P Rule 8 through IN ST TRIAL P Rule 11), apply to all motions and other papers provided under the Indiana Rules of Trial Procedure. 22B INPRAC 7:2.

    a. *Separate motions; Alternative motions.* Each motion shall be separate, while alternative motions filed together shall each be identified on the caption. IN ST ST JOSEPH CIV Rule 206(206.1).

2. *Form of pleadings*

   a. *Caption; Names of parties.* Every pleading shall contain a caption setting forth the name of the court, the title of the action, the file number, and a designation as in IN ST TRIAL P Rule 7(A). In the complaint the title of the action shall include the names of all the parties, but in other pleadings it is sufficient to state the name of the first party on each side with an appropriate indication of other parties. IN ST TRIAL P Rule 10(A); IN ST ST JOSEPH CIV Rule 201(201.3.3). If a special judge has been assigned to the case, the pleading should also identify the special judge. IN ST ST JOSEPH CIV Rule 201(201.3.3).

      i. *Title.* All pleadings or motions shall include a title, which shall delineate each topic included in the pleading. For example, where a pleading contains an answer, a motion to dismiss, and a jury request, each topic shall be set forth in the title. IN ST ST JOSEPH CIV Rule 201(201.3.4).

   b. *Paragraphs; Separate statements.* All averments of a claim or defense shall be made in numbered paragraphs, the contents of each of which shall be limited as far as practicable to a statement of a single set of circumstances, and a paragraph may be referred to by number in all succeeding pleadings. Each claim founded upon a separate transaction or occurrence and each defense other than denials may be stated in a separate count or defense whenever a separation facilitates the clear presentation of the matters set forth. IN ST TRIAL P Rule 10(B).

   c. *Adoption by reference; Exhibits.* Statements in a pleading may be adopted by reference in a different part of the same pleading or in another pleading or in any motion. A copy of any written instrument which is an exhibit to a pleading is a part thereof for all purposes. IN ST TRIAL P Rule 10(C).

   d. *Flat filing.* In order that the Clerk's files may be kept under the system commonly known as "flat filing," all papers presented to the Clerk for filing shall be flat and unfolded. Pleadings shall have no covers or backs and shall be fastened together at the top left-hand corner only. IN ST ST JOSEPH CIV Rule 201(201.1).

   e. *One side of page used.* Printing shall be on one (1) side of the paper. IN ST ST JOSEPH CIV Rule 201(201.3.2).

   f. *Copies.* All copies shall be on white paper of sufficient strength and durability to resist normal wear and tear. IN ST ST JOSEPH CIV Rule 201(201.3.1).

   g. *Margins.* Margins shall be at least one inch (1"). IN ST ST JOSEPH CIV Rule 201(201.3.2).

   h. *Double-spaced.* If typewritten, the lines shall be double spaced except for quotations, which shall be indented and single-spaced. IN ST ST JOSEPH CIV Rule 201(201.3.2).

   i. *Font size.* Type face shall be twelve (12) font size or larger within the body of the document and ten (10) font size or larger in the footnotes. IN ST ST JOSEPH CIV Rule 201(201.3.2).

   j. *Font type.* The font type must be legible and script type shall not be used. IN ST ST JOSEPH CIV Rule 201(201.3.2).

   k. *Italics.* Italicized type may be used for quotations, references, or case citations. IN ST ST JOSEPH CIV Rule 201(201.3.2).

   l. *Court and case designation.* All filings shall conform to the requirements for uniform court and case number designation set by IN ST ADMIN Rule 8. In addition, all filings shall contain the proper court and case designation as described below. IN ST ST JOSEPH CIV Rule 202.

      i. *Court designation.* Pursuant to IN ST 33-33-71-2, St. Joseph County, Indiana, constitutes the Sixtieth Judicial Circuit. The legal names of the courts within the 60th Judicial Circuit are the St. Joseph Circuit Court, the St. Joseph Superior Court, and the St. Joseph Probate Court. All filings shall properly reflect the legal name of the applicable court. Any filing may be amended, rejected, or stricken if it does not contain the proper case name and/or the legal name of the court. IN ST ST JOSEPH CIV Rule 202(202.1).

   m. *Form of CCS entry.* Every written motion, petition, or other pleading subsequent to the original complaint presented to the Clerk for filing shall be accompanied by a Chronological Case Summary (CCS) entry form in duplicate which shall contain the title and cause number of the action, the date, and the proposed entry to appear on the docket. IN ST ST JOSEPH CIV Rule 201(201.4).

      i. *Identification and signature.* The CCS entry form shall identify the party making the filing,

designate each pleading being filed, and shall be signed by counsel of record or the unrepresented litigant. IN ST ST JOSEPH CIV Rule 201(201.4).

    ii. *Date stamp.* The form shall be date stamped and presented to the Court Clerk, who shall initial the form and return the duplicate to the filing party. IN ST ST JOSEPH CIV Rule 201(201.4).

n. *Form of proposed order.* Any proposed order shall be a document that is separate and apart from the motion or application to which it relates and shall contain a caption showing the name of the court, the case number assigned to the case, and the title of the case as shown by the complaint pursuant to IN ST ST JOSEPH CIV Rule 201. IN ST ST JOSEPH CIV Rule 213(213.2).

    i. If there are multiple parties, the title may be shortened to include only the first name plaintiff and defendant with appropriate indication that there are additional parties. IN ST ST JOSEPH CIV Rule 213(213.2).

    ii. The proposed order shall be on white paper, eight and one-half by eleven inches (8 1/2" x 11") in size, and each page shall be numbered. IN ST ST JOSEPH CIV Rule 213(213.2).

    iii. The last page of the proposed order shall contain a line for the date, either "Dated _____" or "Signed on the date filemarked hereon." IN ST ST JOSEPH CIV Rule 213(213.2).

    iv. On the last page there also shall be a line for the signature of the Judge under which shall be typed "Judge, St. Joseph [Circuit or Superior or Probate] Court." IN ST ST JOSEPH CIV Rule 213(213.2).

    v. If the proposed order contains a recommendation from a Magistrate, the last page shall have a line for the signature of the Magistrate under which shall be typed "Magistrate, St. Joseph [Circuit or Superior or Probate] Court," to the left of which shall be the following, "So Recommended:" and beneath and to the left of which shall be typed, "Approved. So Ordered." IN ST ST JOSEPH CIV Rule 213(213.2).

    vi. To allow compliance with the notice requirements of IN ST TRIAL P Rule 72(D), the lower four (4) inches of the last page of the proposed order shall be left blank. The proposed order shall also include a prepared proof of notice under IN ST TRIAL P Rule 72(D), and in preparing such a notice the filing party shall complete all portions of the prepared proof of notice. IN ST ST JOSEPH CIV Rule 213(213.2).

3. *Size of papers for filing.* Effective January 1, 1992, all pleadings, copies, motions and documents filed with any trial court or appellate level court, typed or printed, with the exception of exhibits and existing wills, shall be prepared on eight and one-half by eleven inch (8 1/2" x 11") size paper. IN ST ADMIN Rule 11.

a. *Paper.* Pleadings, motions, and other papers shall be either legibly printed or typewritten on white opaque paper of good quality at least sixteen (16) pound weight, eight and one-half inches (8 1/2") in width and eleven inches (11") in length as required by IN ST ADMIN Rule 11. IN ST ST JOSEPH CIV Rule 201(201.3.1).

4. *Signature requirements*

a. *Signature of attorney.* Every pleading or motion of a party represented by an attorney shall be signed by at least one (1) attorney of record in his individual name, whose address, telephone number, and attorney number shall be stated, except that this provision shall not apply to pleadings and motions made and transcribed at the trial or a hearing before the judge and received by him in such form. IN ST TRIAL P Rule 11(A).

    i. The signature of an attorney constitutes a certificate by him that he has read the pleadings; that to the best of his knowledge, information, and belief, there is good ground to support it; and that it is not interposed for delay. IN ST TRIAL P Rule 11(A).

    ii. If a pleading or motion is not signed or is signed with intent to defeat the purpose of the rule, it may be stricken as sham and false and the action may proceed as though the pleading had not been served. IN ST TRIAL P Rule 11(A).

    iii. For a willful violation of IN ST TRIAL P Rule 11 an attorney may be subjected to appropriate disciplinary action. Similar action may be taken if scandalous or indecent matter is inserted. IN ST TRIAL P Rule 11(A).

b. *Signature of unrepresented party.* A party who is not represented by an attorney shall sign his pleading and state his address. IN ST TRIAL P Rule 11(A).

c. *Verification not generally required.* Except when specifically required by rule, pleadings or motions need not be verified or accompanied by affidavit. The rule in equity that the averments of an answer under oath must be overcome by the testimony of two (2) witnesses or of one (1) witness sustained by corroborating circumstances is abolished. IN ST TRIAL P Rule 11(A).

d. *Verification by affirmation or representation.* When in connection with any civil or special statutory proceeding it is required that any pleading, motion, petition, supporting affidavit, or other document of any kind, be verified, or that an oath be taken, it shall be sufficient if the subscriber simply affirms the truth of the matter to be verified by an affirmation or representation. IN ST TRIAL P Rule 11(B). IN ST TRIAL P Rule 11(B) states that the affirmation or representation should be in substantially the following language: "I (we) affirm, under the penalties for perjury, that the foregoing representation(s) is (are) true. (Signed) _____."

 i. Any person who falsifies an affirmation or representation of fact shall be subject to the same penalties as are prescribed by law for the making of a false affidavit. IN ST TRIAL P Rule 11(B).

e. *Verified pleadings, motions, and affidavits as evidence.* Pleadings, motions and affidavits accompanying or in support of such pleadings or motions when required to be verified or under oath shall be accepted as a representation that the signer had personal knowledge thereof or reasonable cause to believe the existence of the facts or matters stated or alleged therein; and, if otherwise competent or acceptable as evidence, may be admitted as evidence of the facts or matters stated or alleged therein when it is so provided in the Indiana Rules of Trial Procedure, by statute or other law, or to the extent the writing or signature expressly purports to be made upon the signer's personal knowledge. When such pleadings, motions and affidavits are verified or under oath they shall not require other or greater proof on the part of the adverse party than if not verified or not under oath unless expressly provided otherwise by the Indiana Rules of Trial Procedure, statute or other law. Affidavits upon motions for summary judgment under IN ST TRIAL P Rule 56 and in denial of execution under IN ST TRIAL P Rule 9.2 shall be made upon personal knowledge. IN ST TRIAL P Rule 11(C).

f. *Signature, verification and other requirements.* Parties and their counsel are enjoined to comply with the verification requirements of IN ST TRIAL P Rule 11, and either the moving party or the party's attorney of record shall sign all pleadings and motions before filing with the Clerk of the Court. Every motion, petition, or other pleading filed with the Clerk shall contain the name, organization, physical address, telephone number, and facsimile number of the filing party or an attorney for that party. IN ST ST JOSEPH CIV Rule 201(201.3.6).

 i. The Clerk shall not accept any motion, petition, notice or other pleading or a CCS entry form for filing from an unrepresented litigant unless the unrepresented litigant's current address and phone number appear on the pleading, and an opposing party may service notices and responses on an unrepresented litigant at any address he or she has provided on a pleading. IN ST ST JOSEPH CIV Rule 201(201.3.6).

5. *Information excluded from public access.* Every document filed in a case shall separately identify information excluded from public access pursuant to IN ST ADMIN Rule 9(G)(1) as follows:

a. Whole documents that are excluded from public access pursuant to IN ST ADMIN Rule 9(G)(1) shall be tendered on light green paper or have a light green coversheet attached to the document, marked "Not for Public Access" or "Confidential." IN ST TRIAL P Rule 5(G)(1).

b. When only a portion of a document contains information excluded from public access pursuant to IN ST ADMIN Rule 9(G)(1), said information shall be omitted [or redacted] from the filed document, and set forth on a separate accompanying document on light green paper conspicuously marked "Not for Public Access" or "Confidential" and clearly designated [or identifying] the caption and number of the case and the document and location within the document to which the redacted material pertains. IN ST TRIAL P Rule 5(G)(2).

c. With respect to documents filed in electronic format, the trial court, by local rule, may provide for

compliance with IN ST TRIAL P Rule 5 in manner that separates and protects access to information excluded from public access. IN ST TRIAL P Rule 5(G)(3).

d.   IN ST TRIAL P Rule 5(G) does not apply to a record sealed by the court pursuant to IN ST 5-14-3-5.5 or otherwise, nor to records, documents, or information filed in cases to which public access is prohibited pursuant to IN ST ADMIN Rule 9(G). IN ST TRIAL P Rule 5(G)(4).

e.   The following information in case records is excluded from public access and is confidential:

   i.   Information that is excluded from public access pursuant to federal law;

   ii.   Information that is excluded from public access as declared confidential by Indiana statute or other court rule, including without limitation:

   •   All adoption records created after July 8, 1941, as declared confidential by IN ST 31-19-19-1, et seq., except those specifically declared open by IN ST 31-19-13-2(2);

   •   All records relating to chancroid, chlamydia, gonorrhea, hepatitis, human immunodeficiency virus (HIV), Lymphogranuloma venereum, syphilis, tuberculosis, as declared confidential by IN ST 16-41-8-1, et seq.;

   •   All records relating to child abuse as declared confidential by IN ST 31-33-18-1, et seq.;

   •   All records relating to drug tests as declared confidential by IN ST 5-14-3-4(a)(9);

   •   Records of grand jury proceedings as declared confidential by IN ST 35-34-2-4;

   •   Records of juvenile proceedings as declared confidential by IN ST 31-39-1-2, except those specifically open under statute;

   •   All paternity records created after July 1, 1941 as declared confidential by IN ST 31-14-11-15, IN ST 31-19-5-23, IN ST 31-39-1-1 and IN ST 31-39-1-2 [Editor's note: IN ST 31-14-11-15 was repealed effective May 9, 2013];

   •   All pre-sentence reports as declared confidential by IN ST 35-38-1-13;

   •   Written petitions to permit marriages without consent and orders directing the Clerk of Court to issue a marriage license to underage persons, as declared confidential by IN ST 31-11-1-6;

   •   Only those arrest warrants, search warrants, indictments and informations ordered confidential by the trial judge, prior to return of duly executed service as declared confidential by IN ST 5-14-3-4(b)(1);

   •   All medical, mental health, or tax records unless determined by law or regulation of any governmental custodian not to be confidential, released by the subject of such records, or declared by a court of competent jurisdiction to be essential to the resolution of litigation as declared confidential by IN ST 16-39-3-10, IN ST 6-4.1-5-10, IN ST 6-4.1-12-12, and IN ST 6-8.1-7-1;

   •   Personal information relating to jurors or prospective jurors, other than for the use of the parties and counsel, pursuant to IN ST JURY Rule 10;

   •   Information relating to protection from abuse orders, no-contact orders and workplace violence restraining orders as declared confidential by IN ST 5-2-9-6, et seq.;

   •   Mediation proceedings pursuant to IN ST ADR Rule 2.11, Mini-Trial proceedings pursuant to IN ST ADR Rule 4.4(C), and Summary Jury Trials pursuant to IN ST ADR Rule 5.6;

   •   Information in probation files pursuant to the Probation Standards promulgated by the Judicial Conference of Indiana pursuant to IN ST 11-13-1-8(b);

   •   Information deemed confidential pursuant to the Rules for Court Administered Alcohol and Drug Programs promulgated by the Judicial Conference of Indiana pursuant to IN ST 12-23-14-13;

   •   Information deemed confidential pursuant to the Problem-Solving Court Rules promulgated by the Judicial Conference of Indiana pursuant to IN ST 33-23-16-16;

- All records of the Department of workforce Development as declared confidential by IN ST 22-4-19-6;
- Information regarding interception of electronic communications that is sealed or deemed confidential as set forth in IN ST 35-33.5-2-1, et seq.

iii. Information excluded from public access by specific court order;

iv. Complete Social Security Numbers of living persons;

v. With the exception of names, information such as addresses, phone numbers, and dates of birth which explicitly identifies:

- Natural persons who are witnesses or victims (not including defendants) in criminal, domestic violence, stalking, sexual assault, juvenile, or civil protection order proceedings, provided that juveniles who are victims of sex crimes shall be identified by initials only;
- Places of residence of judicial officers, clerks and other employees of courts and clerks of court, unless the person or persons about whom the information pertains waives confidentiality;

vi. Complete account numbers of specific assets, loans, bank accounts, credit cards, and personal identification numbers (PINs);

vii. All orders of expungement entered in criminal or juvenile proceedings, orders to restrict access to criminal history information pursuant to IN ST 35-38-5-5.5 or IN ST 35-38-8-5 and records excluded from public access by such orders, and information related to infractions that is excluded from public access pursuant to IN ST 34-28-5-15 or IN ST 34-28-5-16 [Editor's note: IN ST 35-38-5-5.5, IN ST 35-38-8-5 and IN ST 34-28-5-16 were repealed effective July 1, 2013; for information on orders restricting access to criminal history, refer to IN ST 35-38-9-1, et seq.];

viii. All personal notes and e-mail, and deliberative material, of judges, jurors, court staff and judicial agencies, and information recorded in personal data assistants (PDA's) or organizers and personal calendars. IN ST ADMIN Rule 9(G)(1).

F. Filing and Service Requirements

1. *Filing requirements.* Except as otherwise provided in IN ST TRIAL P Rule 5(E)(2), all pleadings and papers subsequent to the complaint which are required to be served upon a party shall be filed with the Court either before service or within a reasonable period of time thereafter. IN ST TRIAL P Rule 5(E)(1).

   a. *Filing with the court defined.* The filing of pleadings, motions, and other papers with the court as required by the Indiana Rules of Trial Procedure shall be made by one of the following methods:

   i. Delivery to the clerk of the court;

   ii. Sending by electronic transmission under the procedure adopted pursuant to IN ST ADMIN Rule 12;

   iii. Mailing to the clerk by registered, certified or express mail return receipt requested;

   iv. Depositing with any third-party commercial carrier for delivery to the clerk within three (3) calendar days, cost prepaid, properly addressed;

   v. If the court so permits, filing with the judge, in which event the judge shall note thereon the filing date and forthwith transmit them to the office of the clerk; or

   vi. Electronic filing, as approved by the Division of State Court Administration pursuant to IN ST ADMIN Rule 16. IN ST TRIAL P Rule 5(F).

   vii. Filing by registered or certified mail and by third-party commercial carrier shall be complete upon mailing or deposit. IN ST TRIAL P Rule 5(F).

   viii. All pleadings shall be filed with the Clerk, not directly with the Court, unless otherwise required by the Indiana Rules of Court. The entry of appearances and the filing of pleadings or other matters not requiring immediate Court action shall be filed with the Clerk and not in open Court. A Judge may permit papers to be filed in chambers, in which event he or she shall note thereon the filing date and transmit the papers to the Clerk. IN ST ST JOSEPH CIV Rule 201(201.2).

b. *Facsimile filing.* Unless otherwise authorized by IN ST ST JOSEPH ELECTRONIC Rule 701, electronic filing of pleadings by computerized or facsimile transmission is not permitted. IN ST ST JOSEPH CIV Rule 201(201.2).

c. *Additional copies.* In cases in which a party or counsel supplies the proposed order or decree, a sufficient number shall be prepared and filed as to provide the Clerk to retain two (2) copies, which shall be filed in the flat file and the record of judgments and orders. Should the party or counsel desire additional copies, a sufficient number of copies should be filed to effectuate that purpose. IN ST ST JOSEPH CIV Rule 201(201.6).

d. *Proof of filing.* Any party filing any paper by any method other than personal delivery to the clerk shall retain proof of filing. IN ST TRIAL P Rule 5(F).

2. *Service requirements.* Unless otherwise provided by the Indiana Rules of Trial Procedure or an order of the court, each party and special judge, if any, shall be served with: (1) every order required by its terms to be served; (2) every pleading subsequent to the original complaint; (3) every written motion except one which may be heard ex parte; (4) every brief submitted to the trial court; (5) every paper relating to discovery required to be served upon a party; and (6) every written notice, appearance, demand, offer of judgment, designation of record on appeal, or similar paper. IN ST TRIAL P Rule 5(A).

a. *Service generally.* Every motion, petition, notice, or other pleading required to be served by IN ST TRIAL P Rule 5 shall be served on all counsel of record or unrepresented parties either before it is filed or on the day it is filed with the Court, and the date of filing shall be indicated on the Certificate of Service. IN ST ST JOSEPH CIV Rule 201(201.5.1).

   i. *Copy.* A copy of the Clerk's CCS entry form of the filing shall also be served on all counsel of record or unrepresented parties whenever it contains an appearance of counsel or contains a date for Court hearing on the matter. IN ST ST JOSEPH CIV Rule 201(201.5.1).

b. *Methods of service*

   i. *Personal service.* Whenever a party is represented by an attorney of record, service shall be made upon such attorney unless service upon the party himself is ordered by the court. Service upon the attorney or party shall be made by delivering or mailing a copy of the papers to the last known address or where an attorney or party has consented to service by fax or e-mail, as provided in IN ST TRIAL P Rule 3.1(A)(4), by faxing or e-mailing a copy of the documents to the fax number or e-mail address set out in the appearance form or correction as required by IN ST TRIAL P Rule 3.1(E). IN ST TRIAL P Rule 5(B). Delivery of a copy within IN ST TRIAL P Rule 5 means:

      • Offering or tendering it to the attorney or party and stating the nature of the papers being served. Refusal to accept an offered or tendered document is a waiver of any objection to the sufficiency or adequacy of service of that document;

      • Leaving it at his office with a clerk or other person in charge thereof, or if there is no one in charge, leaving it in a conspicuous place therein; or

      • If the office is closed, by leaving it at his dwelling house or usual place of abode with some person of suitable age and discretion then residing therein; or,

      • Leaving it at some other suitable place, selected by the attorney upon whom service is being made, pursuant to duly promulgated local rule. IN ST TRIAL P Rule 5(B)(1).

   ii. *Service by the clerk.* Whenever the Clerk is required by rule or statute to give notice, the party or parties requesting such notice shall furnish the Clerk with sufficient copies of the notice to be given, along with stamped, addressed envelopes with the names and the addresses of the parties or their counsel to whom such notice is to be given. IN ST ST JOSEPH CIV Rule 201(201.5.4).

   iii. *Service on the court.* Service on a Judge may be made by delivering a copy to the Judge's secretary or mailing a copy to the Judge at his or her chambers. Service on a Judge may not be accomplished by facsimile transmission; however, a courtesy copy may be sent to the Judge's chambers by electronic mail or facsimile transmission contemporaneously with service by mail or otherwise. IN ST ST JOSEPH CIV Rule 201(201.5.5).

    iv. *Service by mail.* If service is made by mail, the papers shall be deposited in the United States mail addressed to the person on whom they are being served, with postage prepaid. Service shall be deemed complete upon mailing. Proof of service of all papers permitted to be mailed may be made by written acknowledgment of service, by affidavit of the person who mailed the papers, or by certificate of an attorney. It shall be the duty of attorneys when entering their appearance in a cause or when filing pleadings or papers therein, to have noted in the Chronological Case Summary or said pleadings or papers so filed the address and telephone number of their office. Service by delivery or by mail at such address shall be deemed sufficient and complete. IN ST TRIAL P Rule 5(B)(2).

    v. *Service by fax or e-mail.* A party who has consented to service by fax or e-mail may be served as follows:

- Service by e-mail shall be made by attaching the document being served in .pdf format. Discovery documents must also be served in accordance with IN ST TRIAL P Rule 26(A). IN ST TRIAL P Rule 5(B)(3)(a).

- Service by fax shall be deemed complete upon generation of a transmission record indicating the successful transmission of the entire document, except as provided in IN ST TRIAL P Rule 5(B)(3)(d). IN ST TRIAL P Rule 5(B)(3)(b).

- Service by e-mail shall be deemed complete upon transmission, except as provided in IN ST TRIAL P Rule 5(B)(3)(d). IN ST TRIAL P Rule 5(B)(3)(c).

- Service by fax or e-mail that occurs on a Saturday, Sunday, legal holiday, or day the court or agency in which the matter is pending is closed or after 5:00 PM local time of the recipient shall be deemed complete the next day that is not a Saturday, Sunday, legal holiday, or day that the court or agency in which the matter is pending is not closed. IN ST TRIAL P Rule 5(B)(3)(d).

c. *Serving numerous defendants.* In any action in which there are unusually large numbers of defendants, the court, upon motion or of its own initiative, may order:

    i. That service of the pleadings of the defendants and replies thereto need not be made as between the defendants;

- That any cross-claim, counterclaim, or matter constituting an avoidance or affirmative defense contained therein shall be deemed to be denied or avoided by all other parties; and

- That the filing of any such pleading and service thereof upon the plaintiff constitutes due notice of it to the parties. IN ST TRIAL P Rule 5(D).

    ii. A copy of every such order shall be served upon the parties in such manner and form as the court directs. IN ST TRIAL P Rule 5(D).

d. *Service on parties in default for failure to appear.* No service need be made on parties in default for failure to appear, except that pleadings asserting new or additional claims for relief against them shall be served upon them in the manner provided by service of summons in IN ST TRIAL P Rule 4. IN ST TRIAL P Rule 5(A).

e. *Distribution.* Counsel or an unrepresented party submitting a motion, petition, notice, pleading or proposed order shall indicate the method of distribution desired on the Clerk's CCS entry form. The Clerk will not return or distribute copies of motions, petitions, pleadings, notices or proposed orders, other than those originated by the Court, by mail unless the Clerk is provided with stamped, addressed envelopes. IN ST ST JOSEPH CIV Rule 201(201.5.3).

f. *Mailbox.* As a matter of convenience to attorneys, each court provides a mailbox for the distribution filings and orders generated by the Court, and it is the responsibility of each attorney to periodically check these mailboxes for service and distribution of court-generated filings and orders. IN ST ST JOSEPH CIV Rule 201(201.5.3).

G. Hearings

1. *Hearing on motion.* Unless local conditions make it impracticable, each judge shall establish regular times and places, at intervals sufficiently frequent for the prompt dispatch of business, at which motions

requiring notice and hearing may be heard and disposed of; but the judge at any time or place and on such notice, if any, as he considers reasonable may make order for the advancement, conduct, and hearing of actions. To expedite its business the court may direct the submission and determination of motions without oral hearing upon brief written statements of reasons in support and opposition, or direct or permit hearings by telephone conference call with all attorneys or other similar means of communication. IN ST TRIAL P Rule 73(A).

2. *Hearing dates.* Hearing dates for filings requiring Court action shall be obtained from the Court Clerk and incorporated in the CCS entry at the time the motion or other pleading is filed. If no date is obtained prior to the filing, the fact of the hearing should be noted with the date and time left blank. IN ST ST JOSEPH CIV Rule 201(201.4).

3. *Hearing on matters other than trials.* Each Judge shall reserve periods of time for hearing matters other than contested trials, such as pre-trial and post-trial motions, rules to show cause, defaults, uncontested dissolutions of marriage, etc. As necessary to minimize conflicts in scheduling, the Judges shall set these schedules after consultation. Hearings shall be scheduled as follows:

    a. *Scheduling uncontested or routine matters.* Routine matters, procedural motions, domestic relations applications for provisional relief and contempt proceedings, uncontested petitions for dissolution of marriage, and all other matters appropriate for summary consideration and disposition will be heard on the daily calendar. IN ST ST JOSEPH GEN AND ADMIN Rule 104(104.3.1).

    b. *Scheduling contested or complicated matters.* Other matters that will require a hearing reasonably estimated to last in excess of twenty (20) minutes will be scheduled as the Court's calendar allows. Counsel or a party proceeding pro se should contact the chambers of the assigned judge to arrange for an appropriate hearing date and time. IN ST ST JOSEPH GEN AND ADMIN Rule 104(104.3.2).

    c. *Scheduling motions for hearings.* Except for motions to correct error or not likely to require a hearing (as described in IN ST ST JOSEPH CIV Rule 201), all motions shall be scheduled for hearing at the time they are filed. It shall be the responsibility of the moving party or counsel for the moving party to secure the date and time of the hearing from the Clerk or Court personnel who maintain the calendar for each Judge or Magistrate Judge. It shall also be the responsibility of the moving party or counsel for the moving party to coordinate the hearing date with all opposing counsel or unrepresented parties. IN ST ST JOSEPH CIV Rule 201(201.9.1).

    d. *Oral arguments on motions and other pleadings.* Unless otherwise required by St. Joseph County Civil or Indiana Trial Rules, it is within the sound discretion of the assigned Judge whether to allow oral argument; however, any party may file a request for oral argument by filing a written request by separate motion contemporaneously or at any time before the Court has ruled upon the motion or pleadings to be argued. IN ST ST JOSEPH CIV Rule 201(201.9.4).

4. *Motions for summary judgment and for dismissal.* Motions for summary judgment or motions to dismiss pursuant to IN ST TRIAL P Rule 12 or IN ST TRIAL P Rule 41 shall be scheduled for hearing, unless the Court issues a written scheduling order providing otherwise. (Refer to IN ST ST JOSEPH CIV Rule 206 for specific requirements for Pleadings and Motions under IN ST TRIAL P Rule 12 and IN ST TRIAL P Rule 56). IN ST ST JOSEPH CIV Rule 201(201.9.6).

    a. *Dispositive motions date.* Notwithstanding any other rule of court, all IN ST TRIAL P Rule 12 or IN ST TRIAL P Rule 56 motions shall be set for hearing by the moving party at the time of filing unless otherwise ordered by the Court. Unless otherwise authorized by the Court, the hearing shall be scheduled for a day not fewer than fourteen (14) days after the time period allowed for filing of briefs as specified in IN ST ST JOSEPH CIV Rule 206(206.1). IN ST ST JOSEPH CIV Rule 206(206.2).

    b. *Waiver of hearing; Stipulation of the parties.* Adverse parties may stipulate that a IN ST TRIAL P Rule 12 or IN ST TRIAL P Rule 56 motion may be ruled upon by the Court without a hearing thereon, in which event the motion and stipulation shall be brought to the personal attention of the Judge by counsel or by a party proceeding pro se. IN ST ST JOSEPH CIV Rule 206(206.3).

    c. *Appearance by counsel at scheduled hearings.* Whenever the Court schedules a hearing on a motion pursuant to IN ST TRIAL P Rule 12 and/or IN ST TRIAL P Rule 56, counsel for all represented parties shall appear in person or by local co-counsel at such hearing. IN ST ST JOSEPH CIV Rule 206(206.5).

H. Forms

1. Motion to Dismiss for Lack of Personal Jurisdiction Forms for Indiana

   a.   General form. 5 INPRAC § 3:4.1.

   b.   Lack of personal jurisdiction. 5 INPRAC § 3:4.3.

   c.   Certificate of service; Personal service. 9 INPRAC § 5.7.

   d.   Certificate of service; First class mail. 9 INPRAC § 5.8.

   e.   Motion to dismiss plaintiff's complaint; General form. 9 INPRAC § 42.2.

   f.   Lack of personal jurisdiction. 9 INPRAC § 42.4.

I. Checklist

   (I)   ❑ Matters to be considered by moving party

   (a)   ❑ Required documents

   (1)   ❑ Motion and notice

   (2)   ❑ Chronological Case Summary (CCS) entry form

   (3)   ❑ Supporting memorandum of law

   (4)   ❑ Proposed order

   (5)   ❑ Certificate of service

   (b)   ❑ Supplemental documents

   (1)   ❑ Supporting evidence

   (2)   ❑ Facsimile cover sheet

   (c)   ❑ Timing

   (1)   ❑ A motion to dismiss for lack of personal jurisdiction shall be made before pleading if a further pleading is permitted or within twenty (20) days after service of the prior pleading if none is required

   (2)   ❑ A written motion, other than one which may be heard ex parte, and notice of the hearing thereof shall be served not less than five (5) days before the time specified for the hearing, unless a different period is fixed by the Indiana Rules of Trial Procedure or by order of the court

   (3)   ❑ All pleadings and papers subsequent to the complaint which are required to be served upon a party shall be filed with the Court either before service or within a reasonable period of time thereafter

   (II)   ❑ Matters to be considered by the responding party

   (a)   ❑ Required documents

   (1)   ❑ Opposition

   (2)   ❑ Chronological Case Summary (CCS) entry form

   (3)   ❑ Supporting memorandum of law

   (4)   ❑ Certificate of service

   (b)   ❑ Supplemental documents

   (1)   ❑ Supporting evidence

   (2)   ❑ Proposed order

   (3)   ❑ Facsimile cover sheet

   (c)   ❑ Timing

   (1)   ❑ An adverse party shall have thirty (30) days after service of the motion in which to serve and file an answer brief

(2)   ❏ Except as otherwise provided in IN ST TRIAL P Rule 59(D), opposing affidavits may be served not less than one (1) day before the hearing, unless the court permits them to be served at some other time

Requests, Notices and Applications
Interrogatories

Document Last Updated October 2013

A. Applicable Rules

1. *State rules*

   a. Appearance. IN ST TRIAL P Rule 3.1.

   b. Process. IN ST TRIAL P Rule 4.

   c. Service and filing of pleadings and other papers. IN ST TRIAL P Rule 5.

   d. Time. IN ST TRIAL P Rule 6.

   e. Pleadings. IN ST TRIAL P Rule 7; IN ST TRIAL P Rule 9.2; IN ST TRIAL P Rule 10.

   f. Signing and verification of pleadings. IN ST TRIAL P Rule 11.

   g. General provisions governing discovery. IN ST TRIAL P Rule 26

   h. Methods of discovery. IN ST TRIAL P Rule 27; IN ST TRIAL P Rule 29; IN ST TRIAL P Rule 30; IN ST TRIAL P Rule 31; IN ST TRIAL P Rule 33; IN ST TRIAL P Rule 34; IN ST TRIAL P Rule 35; IN ST TRIAL P Rule 36.

   i. Failure to make or cooperate in discovery; Sanctions. IN ST TRIAL P Rule 37.

   j. Judgment on the evidence (directed verdict). IN ST TRIAL P Rule 50.

   k. Findings by the court. IN ST TRIAL P Rule 52.

   l. Summary judgment. IN ST TRIAL P Rule 56.

   m. Motion to correct error. IN ST TRIAL P Rule 59.

   n. Relief from judgment or order. IN ST TRIAL P Rule 60.

   o. Access to court records. IN ST ADMIN Rule 9.

   p. Paper size. IN ST ADMIN Rule 11.

   q. Facsimile transmission. IN ST ADMIN Rule 12.

   r. Electronic filing and electronic service pilot projects. IN ST ADMIN Rule 16.

   s. Sealing of certain records by court; Hearing; Notice. IN ST 5-14-3-5.5.

   t. Sixtieth judicial circuit. IN ST 33-33-71-2.

   u. Privacy and confidentiality. IN ST 5-2-9-6; IN ST 5-14-3-4; IN ST 6-4.1-5-10; IN ST 6-4.1-12-12; IN ST 6-8.1-7-1; IN ST 11-13-1-8; IN ST 12-23-14-13; IN ST 16-39-3-10; IN ST 16-41-8-1; IN ST 22-4-19-6; IN ST 31-11-1-6; IN ST 31-19-5-23; IN ST 31-19-13-2; IN ST 31-19-19-1; IN ST 31-33-18-1; IN ST 31-39-1-1; IN ST 31-39-1-2; IN ST 33-23-16-16; IN ST 35-34-2-4; IN ST 35-38-1-13; IN ST 35-38-9-1; IN ST ADR Rule 2.11; IN ST ADR Rule 4.4; IN ST ADR Rule 5.6; IN ST JURY Rule 10.

2. *Local rules*

   a. Filing, pleading, and motions. IN ST ST JOSEPH CIV Rule 201.

   b. Uniform court and case number designation. IN ST ST JOSEPH CIV Rule 202.

   c. Discovery requests. IN ST ST JOSEPH CIV Rule 208.

   d. Pre-trial procedures. IN ST ST JOSEPH CIV Rule 209.

   e. Electronic filing of cases in St. Joseph County. IN ST ST JOSEPH ELECTRONIC Rule 701.

B. Timing

1. *Service of interrogatories.* Interrogatories may, without leave of court, be served upon the plaintiff after commencement of the action and upon any other party with or after service of the summons and complaint upon that party. IN ST TRIAL P Rule 33(A).

2. *Service of responses to interrogatories.* The party upon whom the interrogatories have been served shall serve a copy of the answers and objections within a period designated by the party submitting the interrogatories, not less than thirty (30) days after the service thereof or within such shorter or longer time as the court may allow. IN ST TRIAL P Rule 33(C).

3. *Completion of discovery pursuant to pretrial scheduling order.* In cases in which a preliminary pre-trial conference has been held under Rule 12(B) [Editor's note: this is likely supposed to be a reference to IN ST TRIAL P Rule 16(B)], discovery shall be made in accordance with the scheduling thereof then ordered. In cases in which no preliminary pre-trial conference has been held, all discovery shall be completed prior to the pre-trial conference and no discovery shall be conducted thereafter unless, upon motion or stipulation showing good cause therefore, an order is entered permitting further discovery within time to be prescribed by the Court. IN ST ST JOSEPH CIV Rule 209(209.5).

4. *Computation of time*

   a. *Generally; Days excluded.* In computing any period of time prescribed or allowed by the Indiana Rules of Trial Procedure, by order of the court, or by any applicable statute, the day of the act, event, or default from which the designated period of time begins to run shall not be included. The last day of the period so computed is to be included unless it is:

      i. A Saturday,

      ii. A Sunday,

      iii. A legal holiday as defined by state statute, or

      iv. A day the office in which the act is to be done is closed during regular business hours. IN ST TRIAL P Rule 6(A).

   b. *Short periods.* In any event, the period runs until the end of the next day that is not a Saturday, a Sunday, a legal holiday, or a day on which the office is closed. When the period of time allowed is less than seven (7) days, intermediate Saturdays, Sundays, legal holidays, and days on which the office is closed shall be excluded from the computations. IN ST TRIAL P Rule 6(A).

   c. *Additional time after service by United States mail.* Whenever a party has the right or is required to do some act or take some proceedings within a prescribed period after the service of a notice or other paper upon him and the notice or paper is served upon him by United States mail, three (3) days shall be added to the prescribed period. IN ST TRIAL P Rule 6(E).

   d. *Enlargement of time.* When an act is required or allowed to be done at or within a specific time by the Indiana Rules of Trial Procedure, the court may at any time for cause shown:

      i. Order the period enlarged, with or without motion or notice, if request therefor is made before the expiration of the period originally prescribed or extended by a previous order; or

      ii. Upon motion made after the expiration of the specific period, permit the act to be done where the failure to act was the result of excusable neglect; but, the court may not extend the time for taking any action for judgment on the evidence under IN ST TRIAL P Rule 50(A), amendment of findings and judgment under IN ST TRIAL P Rule 52(B), to correct errors under IN ST TRIAL P Rule 59(C), statement in opposition to motion to correct error under IN ST TRIAL P Rule 59(E), or to obtain relief from final judgment under IN ST TRIAL P Rule 60(B), except to the extent and under the conditions stated in those rules. IN ST TRIAL P Rule 6(B).

      iii. An initial written motion for enlargement of time pursuant to IN ST TRIAL P Rule 6(B)(1) to answer a claim shall be routinely granted for an additional thirty (30) days from the original due date or other period the assigned Judge deems reasonable by written order of the Court. The motion must be filed on or before the original due date or IN ST ST JOSEPH CIV Rule 201 shall be inapplicable. IN ST ST JOSEPH CIV Rule 201(201.9.5).

         • Any motion for enlargement of time shall state the date when such response is due and the date to which time is requested to be enlarged. IN ST ST JOSEPH CIV Rule 201(201.9.5).

- All subsequent motions for enlargement of time shall be so designated and will only be granted for good cause shown or in the interest of justice. IN ST ST JOSEPH CIV Rule 201(201.9.5).

C. General Requirements

1. *Scope of discovery.* Unless otherwise limited by order of the court in accordance with the Indiana Rules of Trial Procedure, the scope of discovery is as follows:

    a. *In general.* Parties may obtain discovery regarding any matter, not privileged, which is relevant to the subject-matter involved in the pending action, whether it relates to the claim or defense of the party seeking discovery or the claim or defense of any other party, including the existence, description, nature, custody, condition and location of any books, documents, or other tangible things and the identity and location of persons having knowledge of any discoverable matter. It is not ground for objection that the information sought will be inadmissible at the trial if the information sought appears reasonably calculated to lead to the discovery of admissible evidence. IN ST TRIAL P Rule 26(B)(1).

        i. *Limiting discovery upon court determination.* The frequency or extent of use of the discovery methods otherwise permitted under the Indiana Rules of Trial Procedure and by any local rule shall be limited by the court if it determines that:

        - The discovery sought is unreasonably cumulative or duplicative, or is obtainable from some other source that is more convenient, less burdensome, or less expensive;

        - The party seeking discovery has had ample opportunity by discovery in the action to obtain the information sought or;

        - The burden or expense of the proposed discovery outweighs its likely benefit, taking into account the needs of the case, the amount in controversy, the parties' resources, the importance of the issues at stake in the litigation, and the importance of the proposed discovery in resolving the issues. IN ST TRIAL P Rule 26(B)(1).

        - The court may act upon its own initiative after reasonable notice or pursuant to a motion under IN ST TRIAL P Rule 26(C). IN ST TRIAL P Rule 26(B)(1). Refer to the Indiana KeyRules Motion for Protective Order document for more information.

        ii. *Relevancy in the discovery context.* When the word "relevancy" is used in IN ST TRIAL P Rule 26(B), it does not mean "relevancy" as that word in used to determine the admissibility of evidence in a trial court. It is much broader. It means "relevancy" to the "subject matter" of the litigation or pending action and it may relate to the claim or defense of any party. Pretrial discovery is available as to any nonprivileged matter relevant to the subject matter of the lawsuit or to obtain information reasonably calculated to lead to admissible evidence. 2A INPRAC R 26(26.4); Kaufmann v. Credithrift Financial, Inc., 465 N.E.2d 207, 210 (Ind.Ct.App. 1984).

        iii. *Tests for relevance.* Indiana case law has developed two (2) additional tests in this area. 2A INPRAC R 26(26.4).

        - The first test determines when a document or a request for information is actually relevant to the subject matter in the pending action. A document [or discovery request] is relevant to discovery if there is the possibility the information sought may be relevant to the subject matter of the action. 2A INPRAC R 26(26.4); CIGNA-INA/Aetna v. Hagerman-Shambaugh, 473 N.E.2d 1033, 1036 (Ind.Ct.App. 1985).

        - The second test speaks to appellate review of the trial court's determination that a document or discovery request is relevant to the subject matter of the pending action. The appellate court sees its review of the trial court's decision on relevancy to subject matter as being very limited. The court states: "Our review of the trial court's conclusion that the documents are relevant is limited. A trial court is vested with discretion in its rulings on discovery issues." 2A INPRAC R 26(26.4); Costanzi v. Ryan, 175 Ind.App. 257, 370 N.E.2d 1333 (Ind.Ct.App. 1978).

    b. *Insurance agreements.* A party may obtain discovery of the existence and contents of any insurance agreement under which any person carrying on an insurance business may be liable to satisfy part or all of a judgment which may be entered in the action or to indemnify or reimburse for payments made to satisfy the judgment. Information concerning the insurance agreement is not by reason of disclosure admissible in evidence at trial. For purposes of IN ST TRIAL P Rule 26(B)(2), an application for insurance shall not be treated as part of an insurance agreement. IN ST TRIAL P Rule 26(B)(2).

c. *Trial preparation; Materials.* Subject to the provisions of IN ST TRIAL P Rule 26(B)(4), a party may obtain discovery of documents and tangible things otherwise discoverable under IN ST TRIAL P Rule 26(B)(1) and prepared in anticipation of litigation or for trial by or for another party or by or for that other party's representative (including his attorney, consultant, surety, indemnitor, insurer, or agent) only upon a showing that the party seeking discovery has substantial need of the materials in the preparation of his case and that he is unable without undue hardship to obtain the substantial equivalent of the materials by other means. In ordering discovery of such materials when the required showing has been made, the court shall protect against disclosure of the mental impressions, conclusions, opinions, or legal theories of an attorney or other representative of a party concerning the litigation. IN ST TRIAL P Rule 26(B)(3).

i. A party may obtain without the required showing a statement concerning the action or its subject matter previously made by that party. Upon request, a person not a party may obtain without the required showing a statement concerning the action or its subject matter previously made by that person. If the request is refused, the person may move for a court order. The provisions of IN ST TRIAL P Rule 37(A)(4) apply to the award of expenses incurred in relation to the motion. For purposes of IN ST TRIAL P Rule 26(B)(3), a statement previously made is:

- A written statement signed or otherwise adopted approved by the person making it, or

- A stenographic, mechanical, electrical, or other recording, or a transcription thereof, which is a substantially verbatim recital of an oral statement by the person making it and contemporaneously recorded. IN ST TRIAL P Rule 26(B)(3).

ii. The protection of IN ST TRIAL P Rule 26(B)(3) extends to material prepared or collected before litigation actually commences, but that some possibility of litigation must actually exist before the privilege and IN ST TRIAL P Rule 26(B)(3) become operative. 2A INPRAC R 26(26.9); CIGNA-INA/Aetna v. Hagerman-Shambaugh, 473 N.E.2d 1033, 1037 (Ind.Ct.App. 1985).

d. *Trial preparation; Experts.* Discovery of facts known and opinions held by experts, otherwise discoverable under the provisions of IN ST TRIAL P Rule 26(B)(1) and acquired or developed in anticipation of litigation or for trial, may be obtained as follows:

i. A party may through interrogatories require any other party to identify each person whom the other party expects to call as an expert witness at trial, to state the subject matter on which the expert is expected to testify, and to state the substance of the facts and opinions to which the expert is expected to testify and a summary of the grounds for each opinion. IN ST TRIAL P Rule 26(B)(4)(a)(i).

ii. Upon motion, the court may order further discovery by other means, subject to such restrictions as to scope and such provisions, pursuant to IN ST TRIAL P Rule 26(B)(4)(c), concerning fees and expenses as the court may deem appropriate. IN ST TRIAL P Rule 26(B)(4)(a)(ii).

iii. A party may discover facts known or opinions held by an expert who has been retained or specially employed by another party in anticipation of litigation or preparation for trial and who is not expected to be called as a witness at trial, only as provided in IN ST TRIAL P Rule 35(B) or upon a showing of exceptional circumstances under which it is impracticable for the party seeking discovery to obtain facts or opinions on the same subject by other means. IN ST TRIAL P Rule 26(B)(4)(b).

iv. Unless manifest injustice would result,

- The court shall require that the party seeking discovery pay the expert a reasonable fee for time spent in responding to discovery under IN ST TRIAL P Rule 26(B)(4)(a)(ii) and IN ST TRIAL P Rule 26(B)(4)(b); and

- With respect to discovery obtained under IN ST TRIAL P Rule 26(B)(4)(a)(ii) the court may require, and with respect to discovery obtained under IN ST TRIAL P Rule 26(B)(4)(b) the court shall require, the party seeking discovery to pay the other party a fair portion of the fees and expenses reasonably incurred by the latter party in obtaining facts and opinions from the expert. IN ST TRIAL P Rule 26(B)(4)(c).

e. *Claims of privilege or protection*

   i. *Information withheld.* When a party withholds information otherwise discoverable under the Indiana Rules of Trial Procedure by claiming that it is privileged or subject to protection as trial preparation material, the party shall make the claim expressly and shall describe the nature of the documents, communications, or things not produced or disclosed in a manner that, without revealing information itself privileged or protected, will enable other parties to assess the applicability of the privilege or protection. IN ST TRIAL P Rule 26(B)(5)(a).

   ii. *Information produced.* If information is produced in discovery that is subject to a claim of privilege or protection as trial-preparation material, the party making the claim may notify any party that received the information of the claim and the basis for it. After being notified, a party must promptly return, sequester, or destroy the specified information and any copies it has and may not use or disclose the information until the claim is resolved. A receiving party may promptly present the information to the court under seal for a determination of the claim. If the receiving party disclosed the information before being notified, it must take reasonable steps to retrieve it. The producing party must preserve the information until the claim is resolved. IN ST TRIAL P Rule 26(B)(5)(b).

   iii. *Waiver.* The law of discovery has developed some holdings which indicate that "waiver" of a privileged communication in a discovery setting might be more exacting than "waiver" of a privileged communication when the only question at hand is an interpretation of the privilege itself. Thus, in litigation in which several documents are in issue, and some are released inadvertently, there is strong case law that holds that the "inadvertent production" of a privileged document does not constitute a waiver of the attorney-client privilege. 2A INPRAC R 26(26.5); Transamerica Computer Co. v. International Business Machines Corp., 573 F.2d 646 (9th Cir. 1978). Such a rule should be measured against the usual rule which suggests that a voluntary disclosure to a third person will generally suffice to show a waiver of the attorney-client privilege. 2A INPRAC R 26(26.5).

f. *Use not limited.* Unless the court orders otherwise under IN ST TRIAL P Rule 26(C), the frequency of use of the methods listed in IN ST TRIAL P Rule 26(A) is not limited. IN ST TRIAL P Rule 26(A).

g. *Sequence of discovery.* Unless the court upon motion, for the convenience of parties and witnesses and in the interests of justice, orders otherwise, methods of discovery may be used in any sequence and the fact that a party is conducting discovery, whether by deposition or otherwise, shall not operate to delay any other party's discovery. IN ST TRIAL P Rule 26(D).

h. *Discovery disputes.* To promote the orderly and expeditious handling of cases to trial readiness, counsel shall attempt in good faith to resolve all disagreements between or among themselves concerning the necessity for and scope of discovery, the necessity to seek sanctions, and/or protection against discovery under IN ST TRIAL P Rule 26 through IN ST TRIAL P Rule 37. IN ST ST JOSEPH CIV Rule 208(208.5).

   i. After personal consultation and good faith attempts to resolve differences as to the foregoing matters, counsel for any or all parties may move to compel discovery, invoke sanctions, or seek protection against discovery as aforesaid. IN ST ST JOSEPH CIV Rule 208(208.5).

   ii. As a part of such motion, the party shall recite the date, time, and place of the personal consultations and the names of the participants. If counsel for any party advises the Court in writing that counsel for any other party has refused or delayed consultation hereby contemplated, the Court shall take such action as is appropriate to preclude, obviate, or avoid further delay. IN ST ST JOSEPH CIV Rule 208(208.5).

2. *Interrogatories.* Parties may obtain discovery by written interrogatories. IN ST TRIAL P Rule 26(A)(2).

An interrogatory is a written question served upon another party which requires a written response under oath. 22 INPRAC § 23.1. Any party may serve upon any other party written interrogatories to be answered by the party served or, if the party served is an organization including a governmental organization, or a partnership, by any officer or agent, who shall furnish such information as is available to the party. IN ST TRIAL P Rule 33(A).

a. *Subject of interrogatories.* Interrogatories may relate to any matters which can be inquired into under IN ST TRIAL P Rule 26(B), and the answers may be used to the extent permitted by the rules of evidence. IN ST TRIAL P Rule 33(D).

    i. This includes:

- The existence, description, nature, custody, condition and location of books, documents, or other tangible things; and

- The identity and location of persons having knowledge of relevant facts. 10 INPRAC § 65.1.

    ii. Interrogatories cannot be objected to on the ground that the information sought will be inadmissible at trial if the discovery appears reasonably calculated to lead to the discovery of admissible evidence. 10 INPRAC § 65.1.

b. *Available for parties only.* Interrogatories may not be served on non-parties. 10 INPRAC § 65.1. There is no requirement that the party served shall be an "adverse" party. 2A INPRAC R 33(33.2).

c. *Submission to personal jurisdiction.* Under the current trial rules, discovery is self-executing and interrogatories are not filed with the court, but retained by the originating party until a discovery dispute arises or the discovery is needed for proceedings before the court. As such, Indiana courts have had to revisit the issue of whether a party's mere service of interrogatories constitutes a waiver of an objection to the court's personal jurisdiction over that party. 22 INPRAC § 23.14.

    i. In Alberts v. Mack Trucks, Inc., the defendant served interrogatories before asserting a challenge to the court's personal jurisdiction. In ruling that serving interrogatories did not constitute a waiver of personal jurisdiction, the Indiana Court of Appeals noted the amendments to the Indiana Rules of Trial Procedure, which no longer require a party to file interrogatories with the court. Accordingly, the court held: By sending interrogatories to Alberts' counsel, NSC did not submit to the personal jurisdiction of the court. Jurisdiction will not be found to be waived until a party affirmatively uses the court's procedure, such as in a motion to compel answers to interrogatories. 22 INPRAC § 23.14; Alberts v. Mack Trucks, Inc., 540 N.E.2d 1268, 1271-72 (Ind.Ct.App. 1989).

    ii. Therefore, merely serving interrogatories upon an opposing party before challenging the court's personal jurisdiction over a defendant should not result in a waiver of the jurisdictional issue unless the party otherwise affirmatively uses the court's resources. 22 INPRAC § 23.14.

d. *Motion to compel discovery.* The party submitting the interrogatories may move for an order under IN ST TRIAL P Rule 37(A) with respect to any objection to or other failure to answer an interrogatory. IN ST TRIAL P Rule 33(C). Refer to the Indiana KeyRules Motion to Compel Discovery document for more information.

3. *Response to interrogatories*

a. *Form of objections.* Answers or objections to interrogatories shall include the interrogatory which is being answered or to which an objection is made. The interrogatory which is being answered or objected to shall be placed immediately preceding the answer or objection. IN ST TRIAL P Rule 33(B).

b. *Form of answer.* Each interrogatory shall be answered separately and fully in writing under oath, unless it is objected to, in which event the reasons for objections shall be stated in lieu of an answer. The answers are to be signed by the person making them, and the objections signed by the attorney making them. IN ST TRIAL P Rule 33(B).

c. *Objections.* In addition to the objection that the matter is privileged, interrogatories may be objected to on the ground that they are not within the scope of discovery which is defined in IN ST TRIAL P

Rule 26(B) because they seek information that is not relevant to the subject matter in the pending litigation, or that the requisite showing under IN ST TRIAL P Rule 26(B) has not been made, or that the information is held by experts and it is not discoverable except as permitted under IN ST TRIAL P Rule 26(B)(4). 2A INPRAC R 33(33.4). Objections to interrogatories must be specific. Common objections include (1) relevancy; (2) vague and ambiguous; (3) unduly burdensome; and (4) excessive in number. 10 INPRAC § 65.2.

   i.   *Objections to form.* The party upon whom the interrogatories have been served may object to the failure to follow the Format requirements in IN ST TRIAL P Rule 33(B) by returning the interrogatories to the party who caused them to be served. If this objection is to be made, the interrogatories shall be returned to the party who caused them to be served not later than the seventh (7th) day after they were received. If the interrogatories are not returned in that time, then this objection is waived. IN ST TRIAL P Rule 33(C).

   ii. *Information not available.* If the objecting party takes the position that the information is not available, it is that party's burden to show that it is not available. 2A INPRAC R 33(33.4).

   - As a general rule, a party may not refuse to answer an interrogatory on the ground that the information is not in his possession, in the sense that the party would have to consult books and records in order to answer. 2A INPRAC R 33(33.4); Flour Mills of America, Inc. v. Pace, 75 F.R.D. 676, 680 (E.D.Okl. 1977).

   - An interrogatory seeking information in the possession of the party's employee is not objectionable if the questions call for answers which could be readily obtained by the person answering the interrogatory. 2A INPRAC R 33(33.4); Ballard v. Allegheny Airlines, Inc., 54 F.R.D. 67 (E.D.Pa. 1972).

   iii. *Broad, burdensome, numerous.* An objection is permitted if the interrogatory is too broad, or too burdensome, or too many in the number and kinds of questions which are asked. 2A INPRAC R 33(33.4); Flour Mills of America, Inc. v. Pace, 75 F.R.D. 676, 680 (E.D.Okl. 1977); In re U.S. Financial Securities Litigation, 74 F.R.D. 497 (S.D.Cal. 1975).

   iv. *Other objections.* An interrogatory otherwise proper is not objectionable merely because an answer to the interrogatory involves an opinion, contention, or legal conclusion, but the court may order that such an interrogatory be answered at a later time, or after designated discovery has been completed, or at a pre-trial conference. IN ST TRIAL P Rule 33(D).

   - However, a party may not be forced to prepare his opponent's case for him. If the interrogatory would require a party to make extensive investigations, research, or compilation of data, it is an improper interrogatory, and it is burdensome and should be disallowed in a motion for a protective order. 2A INPRAC R 33(33.4); Halder v. International Telephone & Telegraph Co., 75 F.R.D. 657 (E.D.N.Y. 1977). Refer to the Indiana KeyRules Motion for Protective Order document for more information.

d. *Signature of responses.* The party served shall answer and sign the answer, and the attorney for the party served shall sign the objections. Both are then returned to the party taking the interrogatory. 2A INPRAC R 33(33.8).

   i.   An unsigned and unverified response does not qualify as an answer to an interrogatory and generally may not be used as such. 22 INPRAC § 23.6; Cabales v. U.S., 51 F.R.D. 498 (S.D.N.Y. 1970).

e. *Option to produce business records.* Where the answer to an interrogatory may be derived or ascertained from the business records of the party upon whom the interrogatory has been served or from an examination, audit or inspection of such business records, including a compilation, abstract or summary thereof, and the burden of deriving or ascertaining the answer is substantially the same for the party serving the interrogatory as for the party served, it is a sufficient answer to such interrogatory to specify the records from which the answer may be derived or ascertained and to afford to the party serving the interrogatory reasonable opportunity to examine, audit or inspect such records and to make copies, compilations, abstracts or summaries. A specification shall be in sufficient detail to permit the interrogating party to locate and to identify, as readily as can the party served, the records from which the answer may be ascertained. IN ST TRIAL P Rule 33(E).

f. *Supplementation of responses.* A party who has responded to a request for discovery with a response that was complete when made is under no duty to supplement his response to include information thereafter acquired, except as follows:

    i. A party is under a duty seasonably to supplement his response with respect to any question directly addressed to:

- The identity and location of persons having knowledge of discoverable matters, and
- The identity of each person expected to be called as an expert witness at trial, the subject-matter on which he is expected to testify, and the substance of his testimony. IN ST TRIAL P Rule 26(E)(1).

    ii. A party is under a duty seasonably to amend a prior response if he obtains information upon the basis of which:

- He knows that the response was incorrect when made, or
- He knows that the response though correct when made is no longer true and the circumstances are such that a failure to amend the response is in substance a knowing concealment. IN ST TRIAL P Rule 26(E)(2).

    iii. A duty to supplement responses may be imposed by order of the court, agreement of the parties, or at any time prior to trial through new requests for supplementation of prior responses. IN ST TRIAL P Rule 26(E)(3).

    iv. The duty seasonably to supplement a discovery response is absolute and is not predicated on a court order. "It is a breach of a litigant's duty reasonably to supplement if the litigant postpones supplementing its response by not obtaining from its experts the information which is to be supplied in answer to interrogatories." 2A INPRAC R 26(26.27); Lucas v. Dorsey Corp., 609 N.E.2d 1191, 1196 (Ind.Ct.App. 1993).

g. *Additional pages for answer.* If additional space is required for an answer, the responder shall attach supplemental pages, incorporated by reference, to comply with the spirit of IN ST TRIAL P Rule 33. IN ST ST JOSEPH CIV Rule 208(208.3)(2).

    i. The responding party shall type the requested answers, supply the jurat, and serve the original and one duplicate on propounding counsel. IN ST ST JOSEPH CIV Rule 208(208.3)(4).

D. Documents

1. *Required documents*

a. *Interrogatories.* Refer to the General Requirements section of this document for information on the scope and content of interrogatories.

b. *Certificate of service.* An attorney or unrepresented party tendering a document to the Clerk for filing shall certify that service has been made, list the parties served, and specify the date and means of service. The certificate of service shall be placed at the end of the document and shall not be separately filed. The separate filing of a certificate of service, however, shall not be grounds for rejecting a document for filing. The Clerk may permit documents to be filed without a certificate of service but shall require prompt filing of a separate certificate of service. IN ST TRIAL P Rule 5(C).

2. *Supplemental documents*

a. *Stipulation regarding discovery procedure.* Unless the court orders otherwise, the parties may by written stipulation:

    i. Provide that depositions may be taken before any person, at any time or place, upon any notice, and in any manner and when so taken may be used like other depositions, and

    ii. Modify the procedures provided by the Indiana Rules of Trial Procedure for other methods of discovery. IN ST TRIAL P Rule 29.

b. *Facsimile cover sheet.* Any document sent to the Clerk of the Circuit Court by electronic facsimile transmission shall be accompanied by a cover sheet which states the title of the document, case number, number of pages, identity and voice telephone number of the sending party and instructions

for filing. The cover sheet shall contain the signature of the attorney or party, pro se, authorizing the filing. IN ST ADMIN Rule 12(D).

E. Format

1. *Format of interrogatories.* The rules applicable to captions, and the signing and form of pleadings (IN ST TRIAL P Rule 8 through IN ST TRIAL P Rule 11), apply to all motions and other papers provided under the Indiana Rules of Trial Procedure. 22B INPRAC 7:2. A party who serves written interrogatories under IN ST TRIAL P Rule 33 shall provide, after each interrogatory, a reasonable amount of space for a response or an objection. IN ST TRIAL P Rule 33(B).

   a. An interrogatory should pose a single direct question phrased in a manner that will advise the responding party what information is requested of him. 22 INPRAC § 23.5.

   b. An interrogatory may be divided into separate paragraphs and subparagraphs. The paragraphs should be identified as "1," "2," or "3"; or as "Interrogatory No. 1," "Interrogatory No. 2," etc. 22 INPRAC § 23.5.

   c. Whenever agreed by the parties or otherwise ordered by the Court, a party shall forward simultaneously with the hard copy discovery request (interrogatories, requests for production, requests for admissions, or other requests for discovery) either a floppy disk or an electronic mail message with a copy of the request attached in digital format. Otherwise, an original and two (2) duplicate copies shall be prepared and served on the party required to answer. IN ST ST JOSEPH CIV Rule 208(208.2).

   d. All interrogatories to parties propounded pursuant to IN ST TRIAL P Rule 33 shall be prepared as follows:

      i. The propounding party or the attorney of record for the propounding party shall sign and date the interrogatories as of the date of service. IN ST ST JOSEPH CIV Rule 208(208.3)(1).

      ii. After each interrogatory, sufficient blank space shall be left by the propounding party as is reasonably anticipated may be required for the responder's typewritten answer. IN ST ST JOSEPH CIV Rule 208(208.3)(2).

      iii. Additional space shall be left by the propounding party at the close of the interrogatories for the signature and appropriate typed oath or affirmation to be supplied by the responder. IN ST ST JOSEPH CIV Rule 208(208.3)(3).

2. *Form of pleadings*

   a. *Caption; Names of parties.* Every pleading shall contain a caption setting forth the name of the court, the title of the action, the file number, and a designation as in IN ST TRIAL P Rule 7(A). In the complaint the title of the action shall include the names of all the parties, but in other pleadings it is sufficient to state the name of the first party on each side with an appropriate indication of other parties. IN ST TRIAL P Rule 10(A); IN ST ST JOSEPH CIV Rule 201(201.3.3). If a special judge has been assigned to the case, the pleading should also identify the special judge. IN ST ST JOSEPH CIV Rule 201(201.3.3).

      i. *Title.* All pleadings or motions shall include a title, which shall delineate each topic included in the pleading. For example, where a pleading contains an answer, a motion to dismiss, and a jury request, each topic shall be set forth in the title. IN ST ST JOSEPH CIV Rule 201(201.3.4).

   b. *Paragraphs; Separate statements.* All averments of a claim or defense shall be made in numbered paragraphs, the contents of each of which shall be limited as far as practicable to a statement of a single set of circumstances, and a paragraph may be referred to by number in all succeeding pleadings. Each claim founded upon a separate transaction or occurrence and each defense other than denials may be stated in a separate count or defense whenever a separation facilitates the clear presentation of the matters set forth. IN ST TRIAL P Rule 10(B).

   c. *Adoption by reference; Exhibits.* Statements in a pleading may be adopted by reference in a different part of the same pleading or in another pleading or in any motion. A copy of any written instrument which is an exhibit to a pleading is a part thereof for all purposes. IN ST TRIAL P Rule 10(C).

   d. *Flat filing.* In order that the Clerk's files may be kept under the system commonly known as "flat filing," all papers presented to the Clerk for filing shall be flat and unfolded. Pleadings shall have no covers or backs and shall be fastened together at the top left-hand corner only. IN ST ST JOSEPH CIV Rule 201(201.1).

e. *One side of page used.* Printing shall be on one (1) side of the paper. IN ST ST JOSEPH CIV Rule 201(201.3.2).

f. *Copies.* All copies shall be on white paper of sufficient strength and durability to resist normal wear and tear. IN ST ST JOSEPH CIV Rule 201(201.3.1).

g. *Margins.* Margins shall be at least one inch (1"). IN ST ST JOSEPH CIV Rule 201(201.3.2).

h. *Double-spaced.* If typewritten, the lines shall be double spaced except for quotations, which shall be indented and single-spaced. IN ST ST JOSEPH CIV Rule 201(201.3.2).

i. *Font size.* Type face shall be twelve (12) font size or larger within the body of the document and ten (10) font size or larger in the footnotes. IN ST ST JOSEPH CIV Rule 201(201.3.2).

j. *Font type.* The font type must be legible and script type shall not be used. IN ST ST JOSEPH CIV Rule 201(201.3.2).

k. *Italics.* Italicized type may be used for quotations, references, or case citations. IN ST ST JOSEPH CIV Rule 201(201.3.2).

l. *Court and case designation.* All filings shall conform to the requirements for uniform court and case number designation set by IN ST ADMIN Rule 8. In addition, all filings shall contain the proper court and case designation as described below. IN ST ST JOSEPH CIV Rule 202.

   i. *Court designation.* Pursuant to IN ST 33-33-71-2, St. Joseph County, Indiana, constitutes the Sixtieth Judicial Circuit. The legal names of the courts within the 60th Judicial Circuit are the St. Joseph Circuit Court, the St. Joseph Superior Court, and the St. Joseph Probate Court. All filings shall properly reflect the legal name of the applicable court. Any filing may be amended, rejected, or stricken if it does not contain the proper case name and/or the legal name of the court. IN ST ST JOSEPH CIV Rule 202(202.1).

m. *Form of CCS entry.* Every written motion, petition, or other pleading subsequent to the original complaint presented to the Clerk for filing shall be accompanied by a Chronological Case Summary (CCS) entry form in duplicate which shall contain the title and cause number of the action, the date, and the proposed entry to appear on the docket. IN ST ST JOSEPH CIV Rule 201(201.4).

   i. *Identification and signature.* The CCS entry form shall identify the party making the filing, designate each pleading being filed, and shall be signed by counsel of record or the unrepresented litigant. IN ST ST JOSEPH CIV Rule 201(201.4).

   ii. *Date stamp.* The form shall be date stamped and presented to the Court Clerk, who shall initial the form and return the duplicate to the filing party. IN ST ST JOSEPH CIV Rule 201(201.4).

3. *Size of papers for filing.* Effective January 1, 1992, all pleadings, copies, motions and documents filed with any trial court or appellate level court, typed or printed, with the exception of exhibits and existing wills, shall be prepared on eight and one-half by eleven inch (8 1/2" x 11") size paper. IN ST ADMIN Rule 11.

   a. *Paper.* Pleadings, motions, and other papers shall be either legibly printed or typewritten on white opaque paper of good quality at least sixteen (16) pound weight, eight and one-half inches (8 1/2") in width and eleven inches (11") in length as required by IN ST ADMIN Rule 11. IN ST ST JOSEPH CIV Rule 201(201.3.1).

4. *Signature requirements*

   a. *Signature of attorney.* Every pleading or motion of a party represented by an attorney shall be signed by at least one (1) attorney of record in his individual name, whose address, telephone number, and attorney number shall be stated, except that this provision shall not apply to pleadings and motions made and transcribed at the trial or a hearing before the judge and received by him in such form. IN ST TRIAL P Rule 11(A).

      i. The signature of an attorney constitutes a certificate by him that he has read the pleadings; that

to the best of his knowledge, information, and belief, there is good ground to support it; and that it is not interposed for delay. IN ST TRIAL P Rule 11(A).

ii. If a pleading or motion is not signed or is signed with intent to defeat the purpose of the rule, it may be stricken as sham and false and the action may proceed as though the pleading had not been served. IN ST TRIAL P Rule 11(A).

iii. For a willful violation of IN ST TRIAL P Rule 11 an attorney may be subjected to appropriate disciplinary action. Similar action may be taken if scandalous or indecent matter is inserted. IN ST TRIAL P Rule 11(A).

b. *Signature of unrepresented party.* A party who is not represented by an attorney shall sign his pleading and state his address. IN ST TRIAL P Rule 11(A).

c. *Verification not generally required.* Except when specifically required by rule, pleadings or motions need not be verified or accompanied by affidavit. The rule in equity that the averments of an answer under oath must be overcome by the testimony of two (2) witnesses or of one (1) witness sustained by corroborating circumstances is abolished. IN ST TRIAL P Rule 11(A).

d. *Verification by affirmation or representation.* When in connection with any civil or special statutory proceeding it is required that any pleading, motion, petition, supporting affidavit, or other document of any kind, be verified, or that an oath be taken, it shall be sufficient if the subscriber simply affirms the truth of the matter to be verified by an affirmation or representation. IN ST TRIAL P Rule 11(B). IN ST TRIAL P Rule 11(B) states that the affirmation or representation should be in substantially the following language: "I (we) affirm, under the penalties for perjury, that the foregoing representation(s) is (are) true. (Signed) _____."

i. Any person who falsifies an affirmation or representation of fact shall be subject to the same penalties as are prescribed by law for the making of a false affidavit. IN ST TRIAL P Rule 11(B).

e. *Verified pleadings, motions, and affidavits as evidence.* Pleadings, motions and affidavits accompanying or in support of such pleadings or motions when required to be verified or under oath shall be accepted as a representation that the signer had personal knowledge thereof or reasonable cause to believe the existence of the facts or matters stated or alleged therein; and, if otherwise competent or acceptable as evidence, may be admitted as evidence of the facts or matters stated or alleged therein when it is so provided in the Indiana Rules of Trial Procedure, by statute or other law, or to the extent the writing or signature expressly purports to be made upon the signer's personal knowledge. When such pleadings, motions and affidavits are verified or under oath they shall not require other or greater proof on the part of the adverse party than if not verified or not under oath unless expressly provided otherwise by the Indiana Rules of Trial Procedure, statute or other law. Affidavits upon motions for summary judgment under IN ST TRIAL P Rule 56 and in denial of execution under IN ST TRIAL P Rule 9.2 shall be made upon personal knowledge. IN ST TRIAL P Rule 11(C).

f. *Signature, verification and other requirements.* Parties and their counsel are enjoined to comply with the verification requirements of IN ST TRIAL P Rule 11, and either the moving party or the party's attorney of record shall sign all pleadings and motions before filing with the Clerk of the Court. Every motion, petition, or other pleading filed with the Clerk shall contain the name, organization, physical address, telephone number, and facsimile number of the filing party or an attorney for that party. IN ST ST JOSEPH CIV Rule 201(201.3.6).

i. The Clerk shall not accept any motion, petition, notice or other pleading or a CCS entry form for filing from an unrepresented litigant unless the unrepresented litigant's current address and phone number appear on the pleading, and an opposing party may service notices and responses on an unrepresented litigant at any address he or she has provided on a pleading. IN ST ST JOSEPH CIV Rule 201(201.3.6).

5. *Information excluded from public access.* Every document filed in a case shall separately identify information excluded from public access pursuant to IN ST ADMIN Rule 9(G)(1) as follows:

a. Whole documents that are excluded from public access pursuant to IN ST ADMIN Rule 9(G)(1) shall be tendered on light green paper or have a light green coversheet attached to the document, marked "Not for Public Access" or "Confidential." IN ST TRIAL P Rule 5(G)(1).

b. When only a portion of a document contains information excluded from public access pursuant to IN ST ADMIN Rule 9(G)(1), said information shall be omitted [or redacted] from the filed document, and set forth on a separate accompanying document on light green paper conspicuously marked "Not for Public Access" or "Confidential" and clearly designated [or identifying] the caption and number of the case and the document and location within the document to which the redacted material pertains. IN ST TRIAL P Rule 5(G)(2).

c. With respect to documents filed in electronic format, the trial court, by local rule, may provide for compliance with IN ST TRIAL P Rule 5 in manner that separates and protects access to information excluded from public access. IN ST TRIAL P Rule 5(G)(3).

d. IN ST TRIAL P Rule 5(G) does not apply to a record sealed by the court pursuant to IN ST 5-14-3-5.5 or otherwise, nor to records, documents, or information filed in cases to which public access is prohibited pursuant to IN ST ADMIN Rule 9(G). IN ST TRIAL P Rule 5(G)(4).

e. The following information in case records is excluded from public access and is confidential:

   i. Information that is excluded from public access pursuant to federal law;

   ii. Information that is excluded from public access as declared confidential by Indiana statute or other court rule, including without limitation:

   - All adoption records created after July 8, 1941, as declared confidential by IN ST 31-19-19-1, et seq., except those specifically declared open by IN ST 31-19-13-2(2);

   - All records relating to chancroid, chlamydia, gonorrhea, hepatitis, human immunodeficiency virus (HIV), Lymphogranuloma venereum, syphilis, tuberculosis, as declared confidential by IN ST 16-41-8-1, et seq.;

   - All records relating to child abuse as declared confidential by IN ST 31-33-18-1, et seq.;

   - All records relating to drug tests as declared confidential by IN ST 5-14-3-4(a)(9);

   - Records of grand jury proceedings as declared confidential by IN ST 35-34-2-4;

   - Records of juvenile proceedings as declared confidential by IN ST 31-39-1-2, except those specifically open under statute;

   - All paternity records created after July 1, 1941 as declared confidential by IN ST 31-14-11-15, IN ST 31-19-5-23, IN ST 31-39-1-1 and IN ST 31-39-1-2 [Editor's note: IN ST 31-14-11-15 was repealed effective May 9, 2013];

   - All pre-sentence reports as declared confidential by IN ST 35-38-1-13;

   - Written petitions to permit marriages without consent and orders directing the Clerk of Court to issue a marriage license to underage persons, as declared confidential by IN ST 31-11-1-6;

   - Only those arrest warrants, search warrants, indictments and informations ordered confidential by the trial judge, prior to return of duly executed service as declared confidential by IN ST 5-14-3-4(b)(1);

   - All medical, mental health, or tax records unless determined by law or regulation of any governmental custodian not to be confidential, released by the subject of such records, or declared by a court of competent jurisdiction to be essential to the resolution of litigation as declared confidential by IN ST 16-39-3-10, IN ST 6-4.1-5-10, IN ST 6-4.1-12-12, and IN ST 6-8.1-7-1;

   - Personal information relating to jurors or prospective jurors, other than for the use of the parties and counsel, pursuant to IN ST JURY Rule 10;

   - Information relating to protection from abuse orders, no-contact orders and workplace violence restraining orders as declared confidential by IN ST 5-2-9-6, et seq.;

   - Mediation proceedings pursuant to IN ST ADR Rule 2.11, Mini-Trial proceedings pursuant to IN ST ADR Rule 4.4(C), and Summary Jury Trials pursuant to IN ST ADR Rule 5.6;

- Information in probation files pursuant to the Probation Standards promulgated by the Judicial Conference of Indiana pursuant to IN ST 11-13-1-8(b);

- Information deemed confidential pursuant to the Rules for Court Administered Alcohol and Drug Programs promulgated by the Judicial Conference of Indiana pursuant to IN ST 12-23-14-13;

- Information deemed confidential pursuant to the Problem-Solving Court Rules promulgated by the Judicial Conference of Indiana pursuant to IN ST 33-23-16-16;

- All records of the Department of workforce Development as declared confidential by IN ST 22-4-19-6;

- Information regarding interception of electronic communications that is sealed or deemed confidential as set forth in IN ST 35-33.5-2-1, et seq.

iii. Information excluded from public access by specific court order;

iv. Complete Social Security Numbers of living persons;

v. With the exception of names, information such as addresses, phone numbers, and dates of birth which explicitly identifies:

- Natural persons who are witnesses or victims (not including defendants) in criminal, domestic violence, stalking, sexual assault, juvenile, or civil protection order proceedings, provided that juveniles who are victims of sex crimes shall be identified by initials only;

- Places of residence of judicial officers, clerks and other employees of courts and clerks of court, unless the person or persons about whom the information pertains waives confidentiality;

vi. Complete account numbers of specific assets, loans, bank accounts, credit cards, and personal identification numbers (PINs);

vii. All orders of expungement entered in criminal or juvenile proceedings, orders to restrict access to criminal history information pursuant to IN ST 35-38-5-5.5 or IN ST 35-38-8-5 and records excluded from public access by such orders, and information related to infractions that is excluded from public access pursuant to IN ST 34-28-5-15 or IN ST 34-28-5-16 [Editor's note: IN ST 35-38-5-5.5, IN ST 35-38-8-5 and IN ST 34-28-5-16 were repealed effective July 1, 2013; for information on orders restricting access to criminal history, refer to IN ST 35-38-9-1, et seq.];

viii. All personal notes and e-mail, and deliberative material, of judges, jurors, court staff and judicial agencies, and information recorded in personal data assistants (PDA's) or organizers and personal calendars. IN ST ADMIN Rule 9(G)(1).

F. Filing and Service Requirements

1. *Filing requirements.* Except as otherwise provided in IN ST TRIAL P Rule 5(E)(2), all pleadings and papers subsequent to the complaint which are required to be served upon a party shall be filed with the Court either before service or within a reasonable period of time thereafter. IN ST TRIAL P Rule 5(E)(1).

   a. *Non-filing of discovery until necessary*

      i. *Non-filing of discovery; Exceptions.* No deposition or request for discovery or response thereto under IN ST TRIAL P Rule 27, IN ST TRIAL P Rule 30, IN ST TRIAL P Rule 31, IN ST TRIAL P Rule 33, IN ST TRIAL P Rule 34 or IN ST TRIAL P Rule 36 shall be filed with the Court unless:

      - A motion is filed pursuant to IN ST TRIAL P Rule 26(C) or IN ST TRIAL P Rule 37 and the original deposition or request for discovery or response thereto is necessary to enable the Court to rule; or

      - A party desires to use the deposition or request for discovery or response thereto for evidentiary purposes at trial or in connection with a motion, and the Court, either upon its own motion or that of any party, or as a part of any pre-trial order, orders the filing of the original. IN ST TRIAL P Rule 5(E)(2).

    ii.   *Custody of original and period of retention*

- The original of a deposition shall, subject to the provisions of IN ST TRIAL P Rule 30(E), be delivered by the reporter to the party taking it and shall be maintained by that party until filed with the Court pursuant to IN ST TRIAL P Rule 5(E)(2) or until the later of final judgment, agreed settlement of the litigation or all appellate rights have been exhausted. IN ST TRIAL P Rule 5(E)(3)(a).

- The original or any request for discovery or response thereto under IN ST TRIAL P Rule 27, IN ST TRIAL P Rule 30, IN ST TRIAL P Rule 31, IN ST TRIAL P Rule 33, IN ST TRIAL P Rule 34 and IN ST TRIAL P Rule 36 shall be maintained by the party originating the request or response until filed with the Court pursuant to IN ST TRIAL P Rule 5(E)(2) or until the later of final judgment, agreed settlement or all appellate rights have been exhausted. IN ST TRIAL P Rule 5(E)(3)(b).

    iii. *Original unavailable; Copies.* In the event it is made to appear to the satisfaction of the Court that the original of a deposition or request for discovery or response thereto cannot be filed with the Court when required, the Court may allow use of a copy instead of the original. IN ST TRIAL P Rule 5(E)(4).

    iv. *Filing as publication.* The filing of any deposition shall constitute publication. IN ST TRIAL P Rule 5(E)(5).

  b. *Filing with the court defined.* The filing of pleadings, motions, and other papers with the court as required by the Indiana Rules of Trial Procedure shall be made by one of the following methods:

    i.   Delivery to the clerk of the court;

    ii. Sending by electronic transmission under the procedure adopted pursuant to IN ST ADMIN Rule 12;

    iii. Mailing to the clerk by registered, certified or express mail return receipt requested;

    iv. Depositing with any third-party commercial carrier for delivery to the clerk within three (3) calendar days, cost prepaid, properly addressed;

    v. If the court so permits, filing with the judge, in which event the judge shall note thereon the filing date and forthwith transmit them to the office of the clerk; or

    vi. Electronic filing, as approved by the Division of State Court Administration pursuant to IN ST ADMIN Rule 16. IN ST TRIAL P Rule 5(F).

    vii. Filing by registered or certified mail and by third-party commercial carrier shall be complete upon mailing or deposit. IN ST TRIAL P Rule 5(F).

    viii. All pleadings shall be filed with the Clerk, not directly with the Court, unless otherwise required by the Indiana Rules of Court. The entry of appearances and the filing of pleadings or other matters not requiring immediate Court action shall be filed with the Clerk and not in open Court. A Judge may permit papers to be filed in chambers, in which event he or she shall note thereon the filing date and transmit the papers to the Clerk. IN ST ST JOSEPH CIV Rule 201(201.2).

  c. *Facsimile filing.* Unless otherwise authorized by IN ST ST JOSEPH ELECTRONIC Rule 701, electronic filing of pleadings by computerized or facsimile transmission is not permitted. IN ST ST JOSEPH CIV Rule 201(201.2).

  d. *Additional copies.* In cases in which a party or counsel supplies the proposed order or decree, a sufficient number shall be prepared and filed as to provide the Clerk to retain two (2) copies, which shall be filed in the flat file and the record of judgments and orders. Should the party or counsel desire additional copies, a sufficient number of copies should be filed to effectuate that purpose. IN ST ST JOSEPH CIV Rule 201(201.6).

  e. *Proof of filing.* Any party filing any paper by any method other than personal delivery to the clerk shall retain proof of filing. IN ST TRIAL P Rule 5(F).

2. *Service requirements.* Unless otherwise provided by the Indiana Rules of Trial Procedure or an order of the court, each party and special judge, if any, shall be served with: (1) every order required by its terms

to be served; (2) every pleading subsequent to the original complaint; (3) every written motion except one which may be heard ex parte; (4) every brief submitted to the trial court; (5) every paper relating to discovery required to be served upon a party; and (6) every written notice, appearance, demand, offer of judgment, designation of record on appeal, or similar paper. IN ST TRIAL P Rule 5(A).

a. *Service generally.* Every motion, petition, notice, or other pleading required to be served by IN ST TRIAL P Rule 5 shall be served on all counsel of record or unrepresented parties either before it is filed or on the day it is filed with the Court, and the date of filing shall be indicated on the Certificate of Service. IN ST ST JOSEPH CIV Rule 201(201.5.1).

   i. *Copy.* A copy of the Clerk's CCS entry form of the filing shall also be served on all counsel of record or unrepresented parties whenever it contains an appearance of counsel or contains a date for Court hearing on the matter. IN ST ST JOSEPH CIV Rule 201(201.5.1).

b. *Methods of service*

   i. *Personal service.* Whenever a party is represented by an attorney of record, service shall be made upon such attorney unless service upon the party himself is ordered by the court. Service upon the attorney or party shall be made by delivering or mailing a copy of the papers to the last known address or where an attorney or party has consented to service by fax or e-mail, as provided in IN ST TRIAL P Rule 3.1(A)(4), by faxing or e-mailing a copy of the documents to the fax number or e-mail address set out in the appearance form or correction as required by IN ST TRIAL P Rule 3.1(E). IN ST TRIAL P Rule 5(B). Delivery of a copy within IN ST TRIAL P Rule 5 means:

      • Offering or tendering it to the attorney or party and stating the nature of the papers being served. Refusal to accept an offered or tendered document is a waiver of any objection to the sufficiency or adequacy of service of that document;

      • Leaving it at his office with a clerk or other person in charge thereof, or if there is no one in charge, leaving it in a conspicuous place therein; or

      • If the office is closed, by leaving it at his dwelling house or usual place of abode with some person of suitable age and discretion then residing therein; or,

      • Leaving it at some other suitable place, selected by the attorney upon whom service is being made, pursuant to duly promulgated local rule. IN ST TRIAL P Rule 5(B)(1).

   ii. *Service by the clerk.* Whenever the Clerk is required by rule or statute to give notice, the party or parties requesting such notice shall furnish the Clerk with sufficient copies of the notice to be given, along with stamped, addressed envelopes with the names and the addresses of the parties or their counsel to whom such notice is to be given. IN ST ST JOSEPH CIV Rule 201(201.5.4).

   iii. *Service on the court.* Service on a Judge may be made by delivering a copy to the Judge's secretary or mailing a copy to the Judge at his or her chambers. Service on a Judge may not be accomplished by facsimile transmission; however, a courtesy copy may be sent to the Judge's chambers by electronic mail or facsimile transmission contemporaneously with service by mail or otherwise. IN ST ST JOSEPH CIV Rule 201(201.5.5).

   iv. *Service by mail.* If service is made by mail, the papers shall be deposited in the United States mail addressed to the person on whom they are being served, with postage prepaid. Service shall be deemed complete upon mailing. Proof of service of all papers permitted to be mailed may be made by written acknowledgment of service, by affidavit of the person who mailed the papers, or by certificate of an attorney. It shall be the duty of attorneys when entering their appearance in a cause or when filing pleadings or papers therein, to have noted in the Chronological Case Summary or said pleadings or papers so filed the address and telephone number of their office. Service by delivery or by mail at such address shall be deemed sufficient and complete. IN ST TRIAL P Rule 5(B)(2).

   v. *Service by fax or e-mail.* A party who has consented to service by fax or e-mail may be served as follows:

      • Service by e-mail shall be made by attaching the document being served in .pdf format.

Discovery documents must also be served in accordance with IN ST TRIAL P Rule 26(A). IN ST TRIAL P Rule 5(B)(3)(a).

- Service by fax shall be deemed complete upon generation of a transmission record indicating the successful transmission of the entire document, except as provided in IN ST TRIAL P Rule 5(B)(3)(d). IN ST TRIAL P Rule 5(B)(3)(b).

- Service by e-mail shall be deemed complete upon transmission, except as provided in IN ST TRIAL P Rule 5(B)(3)(d). IN ST TRIAL P Rule 5(B)(3)(c).

- Service by fax or e-mail that occurs on a Saturday, Sunday, legal holiday, or day the court or agency in which the matter is pending is closed or after 5:00 PM local time of the recipient shall be deemed complete the next day that is not a Saturday, Sunday, legal holiday, or day that the court or agency in which the matter is pending is not closed. IN ST TRIAL P Rule 5(B)(3)(d).

vi. *Additional service of electronic discovery.* In addition to service under Rule IN ST TRIAL P Rule 5(B) or a .pdf format electronic copy, a party propounding or responding to interrogatories, requests for production or requests for admission shall comply with IN ST TRIAL P Rule 26(A.1)(a) or IN ST TRIAL P Rule 26(A.1)(b). IN ST TRIAL P Rule 26(A.1).

- The party shall serve the discovery request or response in an electronic format (either on a disk or as an electronic document attachment) in any commercially available word processing software system. If transmitted on disk, each disk shall be labeled, identifying the caption of the case, the document, and the word processing version in which it is being submitted. If more than one (1) disk is used for the same document, each disk shall be labeled and also shall be sequentially numbered. If transmitted by electronic mail, the document must be accompanied by electronic memorandum providing the forgoing identifying information; or

- The party shall serve the opposing party with a verified statement that the attorney or party appealing pro se lacks the equipment and is unable to transmit the discovery as required by IN ST TRIAL P Rule 26(A.1). IN ST TRIAL P Rule 26(A.1).

c. *Serving numerous defendants.* In any action in which there are unusually large numbers of defendants, the court, upon motion or of its own initiative, may order:

i. That service of the pleadings of the defendants and replies thereto need not be made as between the defendants;

- That any cross-claim, counterclaim, or matter constituting an avoidance or affirmative defense contained therein shall be deemed to be denied or avoided by all other parties; and

- That the filing of any such pleading and service thereof upon the plaintiff constitutes due notice of it to the parties. IN ST TRIAL P Rule 5(D).

ii. A copy of every such order shall be served upon the parties in such manner and form as the court directs. IN ST TRIAL P Rule 5(D).

d. *Service on parties in default for failure to appear.* No service need be made on parties in default for failure to appear, except that pleadings asserting new or additional claims for relief against them shall be served upon them in the manner provided by service of summons in IN ST TRIAL P Rule 4. IN ST TRIAL P Rule 5(A).

e. *Distribution.* Counsel or an unrepresented party submitting a motion, petition, notice, pleading or proposed order shall indicate the method of distribution desired on the Clerk's CCS entry form. The Clerk will not return or distribute copies of motions, petitions, pleadings, notices or proposed orders, other than those originated by the Court, by mail unless the Clerk is provided with stamped, addressed envelopes. IN ST ST JOSEPH CIV Rule 201(201.5.3).

f. *Mailbox.* As a matter of convenience to attorneys, each court provides a mailbox for the distribution filings and orders generated by the Court, and it is the responsibility of each attorney to periodically check these mailboxes for service and distribution of court-generated filings and orders. IN ST ST JOSEPH CIV Rule 201(201.5.3).

G. Hearings

1. The Indiana rules do not contemplate a hearing related to the filing and service of interrogatories.

H. Forms

1. Interrogatory Forms for Indiana

a. General form. 5 INPRAC § 4:2.10.

b. Motion to enlarge time to answer. 5 INPRAC § 4:2.20.

c. Answers and objections; General form. 5 INPRAC § 4:2.30.

d. Answer; General form with standard objections. 5 INPRAC § 4:2.40.

e. Answer; Offer to produce business records. 5 INPRAC § 4:2.50.

f. Sample interrogatories relating to electronically stored information. 5 INPRAC § 4:2.60.

g. Motion to seal answers to interrogatories. 10 INPRAC § 65.6.1.

h. Interrogatories; General form. 10 INPRAC § 65.7.

i. Interrogatories; Another form. 10 INPRAC § 65.8.

j. Interrogatory preliminary instructions; Comprehensive form. 10 INPRAC § 65.9.

k. Interrogatory preliminary instructions; Abbreviated form. 10 INPRAC § 65.10.

l. Interrogatory definitions. 10 INPRAC § 65.11.

m. Motion to enlarge time to answer interrogatories. 10 INPRAC § 65.12.

n. Motion for enlargement of time; Response due after discovery completed. 10 INPRAC § 65.13.

o. Motion to shorten time to respond to interrogatories. 10 INPRAC § 65.15.

p. Motion to strike interrogatories; Excessive number under local rules. 10 INPRAC § 65.16.

q. Interrogatories to determine minimum contacts with state. 10 INPRAC § 65.20.

r. Answers and objections to interrogatories; General form. 10 INPRAC § 65.30.

s. Answers and objections to interrogatories; Another form. 10 INPRAC § 65.31.

t. Standard objections to interrogatories; General form. 10 INPRAC § 65.32.

u. Standard objections to interrogatories. 10 INPRAC § 65.33.

v. Answer of interrogatory by offering to produce business records. 10 INPRAC § 65.34.

w. Motion to compel answers to interrogatories. 10 INPRAC § 65.35.

x. Attorney's signature as to objections; Alternate forms. 10 INPRAC § 65.36.

y. Conversion; Plaintiff's interrogatories. 10 INPRAC § 66.27.

z. Medical malpractice action. 10 INPRAC § 66.37.

I. Checklist

(I) ❑ Matters to be considered by the party serving the interrogatories

    (a) ❑ Required documents

        (1) ❑ Interrogatories

        (2) ❑ Certificate of service

    (b) ❑ Supplemental documents

        (1) ❑ Stipulation regarding discovery procedure

        (2) ❑ Facsimile cover sheet

    (c) ❑ Timing

        (1) ❑ Interrogatories may, without leave of court, be served upon the plaintiff after commencement of the action and upon any other party with or after service of the summons and complaint upon that party

(II) ❏ Matters to be considered by the responding party
   (a) ❏ Required documents
      (1) ❏ Response to interrogatories
      (2) ❏ Certificate of service
   (b) ❏ Supplemental documents
      (1) ❏ Business records
      (2) ❏ Stipulation regarding discovery procedure
      (3) ❏ Facsimile cover sheet
   (c) ❏ Timing
      (1) ❏ The party upon whom the interrogatories have been served shall serve a copy of the answers and objections within a period designated by the party submitting the interrogatories, not less than thirty (30) days after the service thereof or within such shorter or longer time as the court may allow

Requests, Notices and Applications
Request for Production of Documents

Document Last Updated October 2013

A. Applicable Rules

1. *State rules*
  a. Appearance. IN ST TRIAL P Rule 3.1.
  b. Process. IN ST TRIAL P Rule 4.
  c. Service and filing of pleadings and other papers. IN ST TRIAL P Rule 5.
  d. Time. IN ST TRIAL P Rule 6.
  e. Pleadings. IN ST TRIAL P Rule 7; IN ST TRIAL P Rule 9.2; IN ST TRIAL P Rule 10.
  f. Signing and verification of pleadings. IN ST TRIAL P Rule 11.
  g. General provisions governing discovery. IN ST TRIAL P Rule 26
  h. Methods of discovery. IN ST TRIAL P Rule 27.
  i. Discovery. IN ST TRIAL P Rule 29; IN ST TRIAL P Rule 30; IN ST TRIAL P Rule 31; IN ST TRIAL P Rule 33; IN ST TRIAL P Rule 34; IN ST TRIAL P Rule 35; IN ST TRIAL P Rule 36.
  j. Failure to make or cooperate in discovery; Sanctions. IN ST TRIAL P Rule 37.
  k. Subpoena. IN ST TRIAL P Rule 45.
  l. Judgment on the evidence (directed verdict). IN ST TRIAL P Rule 50.
  m. Findings by the court. IN ST TRIAL P Rule 52.
  n. Summary judgment. IN ST TRIAL P Rule 56.
  o. Motion to correct error. IN ST TRIAL P Rule 59.
  p. Relief from judgment or order. IN ST TRIAL P Rule 60.
  q. Access to court records. IN ST ADMIN Rule 9.
  r. Paper size. IN ST ADMIN Rule 11.
  s. Facsimile transmission. IN ST ADMIN Rule 12.
  t. Electronic filing and electronic service pilot projects. IN ST ADMIN Rule 16.
  u. Sealing of certain records by court; Hearing; Notice. IN ST 5-14-3-5.5.

v. Sixtieth judicial circuit. IN ST 33-33-71-2.

w. Privacy and confidentiality. IN ST 5-2-9-6; IN ST 5-14-3-4; IN ST 6-4.1-5-10; IN ST 6-4.1-12-12; IN ST 6-8.1-7-1; IN ST 11-13-1-8; IN ST 12-23-14-13; IN ST 16-39-3-10; IN ST 16-41-8-1; IN ST 22-4-19-6; IN ST 31-11-1-6; IN ST 31-19-5-23; IN ST 31-19-13-2; IN ST 31-19-19-1; IN ST 31-33-18-1; IN ST 31-39-1-1; IN ST 31-39-1-2; IN ST 33-23-16-16; IN ST 35-34-2-4; IN ST 35-38-1-13; IN ST 35-38-9-1; IN ST ADR Rule 2.11; IN ST ADR Rule 4.4; IN ST ADR Rule 5.6; IN ST JURY Rule 10.

2. *Local rules*

a. Filing, pleading, and motions. IN ST ST JOSEPH CIV Rule 201.

b. Uniform court and case number designation. IN ST ST JOSEPH CIV Rule 202.

c. Discovery requests. IN ST ST JOSEPH CIV Rule 208.

d. Pre-trial procedures. IN ST ST JOSEPH CIV Rule 209.

e. Electronic filing of cases in St. Joseph County. IN ST ST JOSEPH ELECTRONIC Rule 701.

B. Timing

1. *Time for service of request for production of documents*

a. *Service on parties.* The request may, without leave of court, be served upon the plaintiff after commencement of the action and upon any other party with or after service of the summons and complaint upon that party. IN ST TRIAL P Rule 34(B).

b. *Service on non-parties.* Neither a request nor subpoena to produce or permit as permitted by IN ST TRIAL P Rule 34 shall be served upon a non-party until at least fifteen (15) days after the date on which the party intending to serve such request or subpoena serves a copy of the proposed request and subpoena on all other parties. Provided, however, that if such request or subpoena relates to a matter set for hearing within such fifteen (15) day period or arises out of a bona fide emergency, such request or subpoena may be served upon a non-party one (1) day after receipt of the proposed request or subpoena by all other parties. IN ST TRIAL P Rule 34(C)(2)

2. *Time for service of the response to the request for production of documents.* The party upon whom the request is served shall serve a written response within a period designated in the request, not less than thirty (30) days after the service thereof or within such shorter or longer time as the court may allow. IN ST TRIAL P Rule 34(B).

3. *Completion of discovery pursuant to pretrial scheduling order.* In cases in which a preliminary pre-trial conference has been held under Rule 12(B) [Editor's note: this is likely supposed to be a reference to IN ST TRIAL P Rule 16(B)], discovery shall be made in accordance with the scheduling thereof then ordered. In cases in which no preliminary pre-trial conference has been held, all discovery shall be completed prior to the pre-trial conference and no discovery shall be conducted thereafter unless, upon motion or stipulation showing good cause therefore, an order is entered permitting further discovery within time to be prescribed by the Court. IN ST ST JOSEPH CIV Rule 209(209.5).

4. *Computation of time*

a. *Generally; Days excluded.* In computing any period of time prescribed or allowed by the Indiana Rules of Trial Procedure, by order of the court, or by any applicable statute, the day of the act, event, or default from which the designated period of time begins to run shall not be included. The last day of the period so computed is to be included unless it is:

i. A Saturday,

ii. A Sunday,

iii. A legal holiday as defined by state statute, or

iv. A day the office in which the act is to be done is closed during regular business hours. IN ST TRIAL P Rule 6(A).

b. *Short periods.* In any event, the period runs until the end of the next day that is not a Saturday, a Sunday, a legal holiday, or a day on which the office is closed. When the period of time allowed is

less than seven (7) days, intermediate Saturdays, Sundays, legal holidays, and days on which the office is closed shall be excluded from the computations. IN ST TRIAL P Rule 6(A).

c. *Additional time after service by United States mail.* Whenever a party has the right or is required to do some act or take some proceedings within a prescribed period after the service of a notice or other paper upon him and the notice or paper is served upon him by United States mail, three (3) days shall be added to the prescribed period. IN ST TRIAL P Rule 6(E).

d. *Enlargement of time.* When an act is required or allowed to be done at or within a specific time by the Indiana Rules of Trial Procedure, the court may at any time for cause shown:

   i.   Order the period enlarged, with or without motion or notice, if request therefor is made before the expiration of the period originally prescribed or extended by a previous order; or

   ii. Upon motion made after the expiration of the specific period, permit the act to be done where the failure to act was the result of excusable neglect; but, the court may not extend the time for taking any action for judgment on the evidence under IN ST TRIAL P Rule 50(A), amendment of findings and judgment under IN ST TRIAL P Rule 52(B), to correct errors under IN ST TRIAL P Rule 59(C), statement in opposition to motion to correct error under IN ST TRIAL P Rule 59(E), or to obtain relief from final judgment under IN ST TRIAL P Rule 60(B), except to the extent and under the conditions stated in those rules. IN ST TRIAL P Rule 6(B).

   iii. An initial written motion for enlargement of time pursuant to IN ST TRIAL P Rule 6(B)(1) to answer a claim shall be routinely granted for an additional thirty (30) days from the original due date or other period the assigned Judge deems reasonable by written order of the Court. The motion must be filed on or before the original due date or IN ST ST JOSEPH CIV Rule 201 shall be inapplicable. IN ST ST JOSEPH CIV Rule 201(201.9.5).

   - Any motion for enlargement of time shall state the date when such response is due and the date to which time is requested to be enlarged. IN ST ST JOSEPH CIV Rule 201(201.9.5).

   - All subsequent motions for enlargement of time shall be so designated and will only be granted for good cause shown or in the interest of justice. IN ST ST JOSEPH CIV Rule 201(201.9.5).

C. General Requirements

1. *Scope of discovery.* Unless otherwise limited by order of the court in accordance with the Indiana Rules of Trial Procedure, the scope of discovery is as follows:

   a. *In general.* Parties may obtain discovery regarding any matter, not privileged, which is relevant to the subject-matter involved in the pending action, whether it relates to the claim or defense of the party seeking discovery or the claim or defense of any other party, including the existence, description, nature, custody, condition and location of any books, documents, or other tangible things and the identity and location of persons having knowledge of any discoverable matter. It is not ground for objection that the information sought will be inadmissible at the trial if the information sought appears reasonably calculated to lead to the discovery of admissible evidence. IN ST TRIAL P Rule 26(B)(1).

      i. *Limiting discovery upon court determination.* The frequency or extent of use of the discovery methods otherwise permitted under the Indiana Rules of Trial Procedure and by any local rule shall be limited by the court if it determines that:

         - The discovery sought is unreasonably cumulative or duplicative, or is obtainable from some other source that is more convenient, less burdensome, or less expensive;

         - The party seeking discovery has had ample opportunity by discovery in the action to obtain the information sought or;

         - The burden or expense of the proposed discovery outweighs its likely benefit, taking into account the needs of the case, the amount in controversy, the parties' resources, the importance of the issues at stake in the litigation, and the importance of the proposed discovery in resolving the issues. IN ST TRIAL P Rule 26(B)(1).

         - The court may act upon its own initiative after reasonable notice or pursuant to a motion under IN ST TRIAL P Rule 26(C). IN ST TRIAL P Rule 26(B)(1). Refer to the Indiana KeyRules Motion for Protective Order document for more information.

ii. *Relevancy in the discovery context.* When the word "relevancy" is used in IN ST TRIAL P Rule 26(B), it does not mean "relevancy" as that word in used to determine the admissibility of evidence in a trial court. It is much broader. It means "relevancy" to the "subject matter" of the litigation or pending action and it may relate to the claim or defense of any party. Pretrial discovery is available as to any nonprivileged matter relevant to the subject matter of the lawsuit or to obtain information reasonably calculated to lead to admissible evidence. 2A INPRAC R 26(26.4); Kaufmann v. Credithrift Financial, Inc., 465 N.E.2d 207, 210 (Ind.Ct.App. 1984).

iii. *Tests for relevance.* Indiana case law has developed two (2) additional tests in this area. 2A INPRAC R 26(26.4).

- The first test determines when a document or a request for information is actually relevant to the subject matter in the pending action. A document [or discovery request] is relevant to discovery if there is the possibility the information sought may be relevant to the subject matter of the action. 2A INPRAC R 26(26.4); CIGNA-INA/Aetna v. Hagerman-Shambaugh, 473 N.E.2d 1033, 1036 (Ind.Ct.App. 1985).

- The second test speaks to appellate review of the trial court's determination that a document or discovery request is relevant to the subject matter of the pending action. The appellate court sees its review of the trial court's decision on relevancy to subject matter as being very limited. The court states: "Our review of the trial court's conclusion that the documents are relevant is limited. A trial court is vested with discretion in its rulings on discovery issues." 2A INPRAC R 26(26.4); Costanzi v. Ryan, 175 Ind.App. 257, 370 N.E.2d 1333 (Ind.Ct.App. 1978).

b. *Insurance agreements.* A party may obtain discovery of the existence and contents of any insurance agreement under which any person carrying on an insurance business may be liable to satisfy part or all of a judgment which may be entered in the action or to indemnify or reimburse for payments made to satisfy the judgment. Information concerning the insurance agreement is not by reason of disclosure admissible in evidence at trial. For purposes of IN ST TRIAL P Rule 26(B)(2), an application for insurance shall not be treated as part of an insurance agreement. IN ST TRIAL P Rule 26(B)(2).

c. *Trial preparation; Materials.* Subject to the provisions of IN ST TRIAL P Rule 26(B)(4), a party may obtain discovery of documents and tangible things otherwise discoverable under IN ST TRIAL P Rule 26(B)(1) and prepared in anticipation of litigation or for trial by or for another party or by or for that other party's representative (including his attorney, consultant, surety, indemnitor, insurer, or agent) only upon a showing that the party seeking discovery has substantial need of the materials in the preparation of his case and that he is unable without undue hardship to obtain the substantial equivalent of the materials by other means. In ordering discovery of such materials when the required showing has been made, the court shall protect against disclosure of the mental impressions, conclusions, opinions, or legal theories of an attorney or other representative of a party concerning the litigation. IN ST TRIAL P Rule 26(B)(3).

i. A party may obtain without the required showing a statement concerning the action or its subject matter previously made by that party. Upon request, a person not a party may obtain without the required showing a statement concerning the action or its subject matter previously made by that person. If the request is refused, the person may move for a court order. The provisions of IN ST TRIAL P Rule 37(A)(4) apply to the award of expenses incurred in relation to the motion. For purposes of IN ST TRIAL P Rule 26(B)(3), a statement previously made is:

- A written statement signed or otherwise adopted approved by the person making it, or

- A stenographic, mechanical, electrical, or other recording, or a transcription thereof, which is a substantially verbatim recital of an oral statement by the person making it and contemporaneously recorded. IN ST TRIAL P Rule 26(B)(3).

ii. The protection of IN ST TRIAL P Rule 26(B)(3) extends to material prepared or collected before litigation actually commences, but that some possibility of litigation must actually exist before the privilege and IN ST TRIAL P Rule 26(B)(3) become operative. 2A INPRAC R 26(26.9).

d. *Trial preparation; Experts.* Discovery of facts known and opinions held by experts, otherwise discoverable under the provisions of IN ST TRIAL P Rule 26(B)(1) and acquired or developed in anticipation of litigation or for trial, may be obtained as follows:

  i. A party may through interrogatories require any other party to identify each person whom the other party expects to call as an expert witness at trial, to state the subject matter on which the expert is expected to testify, and to state the substance of the facts and opinions to which the expert is expected to testify and a summary of the grounds for each opinion. IN ST TRIAL P Rule 26(B)(4)(a)(i).

  ii. Upon motion, the court may order further discovery by other means, subject to such restrictions as to scope and such provisions, pursuant to IN ST TRIAL P Rule 26(B)(4)(c), concerning fees and expenses as the court may deem appropriate. IN ST TRIAL P Rule 26(B)(4)(a)(ii).

  iii. A party may discover facts known or opinions held by an expert who has been retained or specially employed by another party in anticipation of litigation or preparation for trial and who is not expected to be called as a witness at trial, only as provided in IN ST TRIAL P Rule 35(B) or upon a showing of exceptional circumstances under which it is impracticable for the party seeking discovery to obtain facts or opinions on the same subject by other means. IN ST TRIAL P Rule 26(B)(4)(b).

  iv. Unless manifest injustice would result,

  - The court shall require that the party seeking discovery pay the expert a reasonable fee for time spent in responding to discovery under IN ST TRIAL P Rule 26(B)(4)(a)(ii) and IN ST TRIAL P Rule 26(B)(4)(b); and

  - With respect to discovery obtained under IN ST TRIAL P Rule 26(B)(4)(a)(ii) the court may require, and with respect to discovery obtained under IN ST TRIAL P Rule 26(B)(4)(b) the court shall require, the party seeking discovery to pay the other party a fair portion of the fees and expenses reasonably incurred by the latter party in obtaining facts and opinions from the expert. IN ST TRIAL P Rule 26(B)(4).

e. *Claims of privilege or protection*

  i. *Information withheld.* When a party withholds information otherwise discoverable under the Indiana Rules of Trial Procedure by claiming that it is privileged or subject to protection as trial preparation material, the party shall make the claim expressly and shall describe the nature of the documents, communications, or things not produced or disclosed in a manner that, without revealing information itself privileged or protected, will enable other parties to assess the applicability of the privilege or protection. IN ST TRIAL P Rule 26(B)(5)(a).

  ii. *Information produced.* If information is produced in discovery that is subject to a claim of privilege or protection as trial-preparation material, the party making the claim may notify any party that received the information of the claim and the basis for it. After being notified, a party must promptly return, sequester, or destroy the specified information and any copies it has and may not use or disclose the information until the claim is resolved. A receiving party may promptly present the information to the court under seal for a determination of the claim. If the receiving party disclosed the information before being notified, it must take reasonable steps to retrieve it. The producing party must preserve the information until the claim is resolved. IN ST TRIAL P Rule 26(B)(5)(b).

  iii. *Waiver.* The law of discovery has developed some holdings which indicate that "waiver" of a privileged communication in a discovery setting might be more exacting than "waiver" of a privileged communication when the only question at hand is an interpretation of the privilege itself. Thus, in litigation in which several documents are in issue, and some are released inadvertently, there is strong case law that holds that the "inadvertent production" of a privileged document does not constitute a waiver of the attorney-client privilege. 2A INPRAC

R 26(26.5); Transamerica Computer Co. v. International Business Machines Corp., 573 F.2d 646 (9th Cir. 1978). Such a rule should be measured against the usual rule which suggests that a voluntary disclosure to a third person will generally suffice to show a waiver of the attorney-client privilege. 2A INPRAC R 26(26.5).

f. *Use not limited.* Unless the court orders otherwise under IN ST TRIAL P Rule 26(C), the frequency of use of the methods listed in IN ST TRIAL P Rule 26(A) is not limited. IN ST TRIAL P Rule 26(A).

g. *Sequence of discovery.* Unless the court upon motion, for the convenience of parties and witnesses and in the interests of justice, orders otherwise, methods of discovery may be used in any sequence and the fact that a party is conducting discovery, whether by deposition or otherwise, shall not operate to delay any other party's discovery. IN ST TRIAL P Rule 26.

h. *Discovery disputes.* To promote the orderly and expeditious handling of cases to trial readiness, counsel shall attempt in good faith to resolve all disagreements between or among themselves concerning the necessity for and scope of discovery, the necessity to seek sanctions, and/or protection against discovery under IN ST TRIAL P Rule 26 through IN ST TRIAL P Rule 37. IN ST ST JOSEPH CIV Rule 208(208.5).

   i. After personal consultation and good faith attempts to resolve differences as to the foregoing matters, counsel for any or all parties may move to compel discovery, invoke sanctions, or seek protection against discovery as aforesaid. IN ST ST JOSEPH CIV Rule 208(208.5).

   ii. As a part of such motion, the party shall recite the date, time, and place of the personal consultations and the names of the participants. If counsel for any party advises the Court in writing that counsel for any other party has refused or delayed consultation hereby contemplated, the Court shall take such action as is appropriate to preclude, obviate, or avoid further delay. IN ST ST JOSEPH CIV Rule 208(208.5).

2. *Request for production of documents*

a. *Content of the request.* The request shall set forth the items to be inspected either by individual item or by category, and describe each item and category with reasonable particularity. The request may specify the form or forms in which electronically stored information is to be produced. The request shall specify a reasonable time, place, and manner of making the inspection and performing the related acts. Service is dispensed with if the whereabouts of the parties is unknown. IN ST TRIAL P Rule 34(B).

   i. *Reasonable particularity.* A recurring issue appears among cases. It is whether a request is adequate or describes the items sought with "reasonable particularity" as stated in IN ST TRIAL P Rule 34(B). The essence of this matter is found in these words: "When the party seeking discovery issues a `shotgun' request that is unduly general, the court may avoid wading through documents by finding the items to be inspected not set forth with reasonable particularity, as required by IN ST TRIAL P Rule 34(B). 3 INPRAC R 34(34.1); Ray v. St. John's Health Care Corp., 582 N.E.2d 464, 474 (Ind.Ct.App. 1991); Richey v. Chappell, 572 N.E.2d 1338, 1339 (Ind.Ct.App. 1991).

b. *Requesting documents in specific form.* If a request for electronically stored information does not specify the form or forms of production, a responding party must produce the information in a form or forms in which it is ordinarily maintained or in a form or forms that are reasonably usable. IN ST TRIAL P Rule 34(B).

c. *Scope.* Any party may serve on any other party a request:

   i. To produce and permit the party making the request, or someone acting on the requester's behalf, to inspect and copy, any designated documents or electronically stored information (including, without limitation, writings, drawings, graphs, charts, photographs, sound recordings, images and other data or data compilations from which information can be obtained or translated, if necessary, by the respondent into reasonably usable form) or to inspect and copy, test, or sample any designated tangible things which constitute or contain matters within the scope of IN ST TRIAL P Rule 26(B) and which are in the possession, custody or control of the party upon whom the request is served; or

ii. To permit entry upon designated land or other property in the possession or control of the party upon whom the request is served for the purpose of inspection and measuring, surveying, photographing, testing, or sampling the property or any designated object or operation thereon, within the scope of IN ST TRIAL P Rule 26(B). IN ST TRIAL P Rule 34(A).

d. *Application to non-parties.* A witness or person other than a party may be requested to produce or permit the matters allowed by IN ST TRIAL P Rule 34(A). Such request shall be served upon other parties and included in or with a subpoena served upon such witness or person. IN ST TRIAL P Rule 34(C)(1).

   i. *Content of request to non-parties*

- The request shall contain the matter provided in IN ST TRIAL P Rule 34(B). IN ST TRIAL P Rule 34(C)(3).

- It shall also state that the witness or person to whom it is directed is entitled to security against damages or payment of damages resulting from such request and may respond to such request by submitting to its terms, by proposing different terms, by objecting specifically or generally to the request by serving a written response to the party making the request within thirty (30) days, or by moving to quash as permitted by IN ST TRIAL P Rule 45(B). IN ST TRIAL P Rule 34(C)(3).

   ii. *Service of responses on other parties required.* A party receiving documents from a non-party pursuant to IN ST TRIAL P Rule 34(C) shall serve copies on all other parties within fifteen (15) days of receiving the documents. If the documents are voluminous and service of a complete set of copies is burdensome, the receiving party shall notify all parties within fifteen (15) days of receiving the documents that the documents are available for inspection at the location of their production by the non-party, or at another location agreed to by the parties. The parties shall agree to arrangements for copying, and any party desiring copies shall bear the cost of reproducing them. IN ST TRIAL P Rule 34(C)(4).

e. *Exception to best evidence rule.* When a party or witness in control of a writing or document subject to examination under IN ST TRIAL P Rule 34 or IN ST TRIAL P Rule 9.2(E) refuses or is unable to produce it, evidence thereof shall be allowed by other parties without compliance with the rule of evidence requiring production of the original document or writing as best evidence. IN ST TRIAL P Rule 34(D).

3. *Response to request for production of documents*

a. *Content of the response.* The response shall state, with respect to each item or category, that inspection and related activities will be permitted as requested, unless it is objected to, including an objection to the requested form or forms for producing electronically stored information, stating in which event the reasons for objection shall be stated. If objection is made to part of an item or category, the part shall be specified. IN ST TRIAL P Rule 34(B).

b. *Types of responses.* There are several responses that a party may make to a IN ST TRIAL P Rule 34 discovery request:

   i. Agree to produce the requested item or permit inspection at the time and place suggested by the discovering party. 10 INPRAC § 67.2.

   ii. Agree to production, but suggest another time and place. 10 INPRAC § 67.2.

   iii. Move for a protective order under IN ST TRIAL P Rule 26(C). 10 INPRAC § 67.2.

   iv. Object to the request. Common grounds for objection include:

- The item sought does not exist. 10 INPRAC § 67.2.

- Respondent does not have possession, custody or control of the item requested. 10 INPRAC § 67.2.

- The request does not describe documents to be produced with reasonable particularity, or by individual item or category. 10 INPRAC § 67.2.

- The document requested fails to specify a reasonable time, place and manner of production. 10 INPRAC § 67.2.

- The discovery requested is privileged or constitutes work product (mental impressions, conclusions, opinions or legal theories of party or party's attorney). 10 INPRAC § 67.2.

- The discovery requested is not relevant to the subject matter of the litigation and not reasonably calculated to lead to the discovery of admissible evidence. 10 INPRAC § 67.2.

- The discovery requests documents prepared in anticipation of litigation when the requesting party does not have a substantial need of the materials in preparation of the case and is able to obtain the substantial equivalent of the materials without undue hardship and by other means. 10 INPRAC § 67.2.

- Nonparty's statement was prepared in anticipation of litigation and there has been no showing that the non-party's statement cannot be obtained without undue hardship by other means. 10 INPRAC § 67.2.

- The discovery requested contains opinions and facts of an expert who was retained and specially employed in anticipation of litigation or trial preparation and who is not expected to be called as a witness at trial and no exceptional circumstances exist which make it impracticable for the party seeking discovery to obtain the facts and opinions by other means. 10 INPRAC § 67.2.

- The requesting party refuses to pay a fair portion of costs incurred by responding party to produce documents. 10 INPRAC § 67.2.

- The testing procedure requested will destroy or materially alter the document or thing. 10 INPRAC § 67.2.

- The discovery requested is burdensome, oppressive or unduly expensive. 10 INPRAC § 67.2.

c. *Objection.* If objection is made to the requested form or forms for producing electronically stored information—or if no form was specified in the request—the responding party must state the form or forms it intends to use. The party submitting the request may move for an order under IN ST TRIAL P Rule 37(A) with respect to any objection to or other failure to respond to the request or any part thereof, or any failure to permit inspection as requested. IN ST TRIAL P Rule 34(B).

d. *Claims of privilege.* A blanket claim of privilege is not favored, and that the party who seeks to avoid discovery has the burden of establishing the essential elements of the privilege which is invoked. 3 INPRAC R 34(34.2); Ray v. St. John's Health Care Corp., 582 N.E.2d 464 (Ind.Ct.App. 1991).

e. *Electronically stored information; Production in multiple formats.* A party need not produce the same electronically stored information in more than one form. IN ST TRIAL P Rule 34(B).

f. *Response by a non-party.* Any party, or any witness or person upon whom the request properly is made may respond to the request as provided in IN ST TRIAL P Rule 34(B). If the response of the witness or person to whom it is directed is unfavorable, if he moves to quash, if he refuses to cooperate after responding or fails to respond, or if he objects, the party making the request may move for an order under IN ST TRIAL P Rule 37(A) with respect to any such response or objection. IN ST TRIAL P Rule 34(C)(3).

  i. In granting an order under IN ST TRIAL P Rule 34(C)(3) and IN ST TRIAL P Rule 37(A)(2) the court shall condition relief upon the prepayment of damages to be proximately incurred by the witness or person to whom the request is directed or require an adequate surety bond or other indemnity conditioned against such damages. Such damages shall include reasonable attorneys' fees incurred in reasonable resistance and in establishing such threatened damage or damages. IN ST TRIAL P Rule 34(C)(3).

  ii. Refer to the Indiana KeyRules Motion to Compel Discovery document more information.

g. *Supplementation of responses.* A party who has responded to a request for discovery with a response that was complete when made is under no duty to supplement his response to include information thereafter acquired, except as follows:

  i. A party is under a duty seasonally to supplement his response with respect to any question directly addressed to:

  - The identity and location of persons having knowledge of discoverable matters, and

- The identity of each person expected to be called as an expert witness at trial, the subject-matter on which he is expected to testify, and the substance of his testimony. IN ST TRIAL P Rule 26(E)(1).

    ii. A party is under a duty seasonally to amend a prior response if he obtains information upon the basis of which:

- He knows that the response was incorrect when made, or

- He knows that the response though correct when made is no longer true and the circumstances are such that a failure to amend the response is in substance a knowing concealment. IN ST TRIAL P Rule 26(E)(2).

    iii. A duty to supplement responses may be imposed by order of the court, agreement of the parties, or at any time prior to trial through new requests for supplementation of prior responses. IN ST TRIAL P Rule 26(E)(3).

    iv. The duty seasonably to supplement a discovery response is absolute and is not predicated on a court order. "It is a breach of a litigant's duty reasonably to supplement if the litigant postpones supplementing its response by not obtaining from its experts the information which is to be supplied in answer to interrogatories." 2A INPRAC R 26(26.27); Lucas v. Dorsey Corp., 609 N.E.2d 1191, 1196 (Ind.Ct.App. 1993).

D. Documents

1. *Required documents*

    a. *Request for production.* Refer to the General Requirements section of this document for information on the scope and content of a request for production of documents.

    b. *Certificate of service.* An attorney or unrepresented party tendering a document to the Clerk for filing shall certify that service has been made, list the parties served, and specify the date and means of service. The certificate of service shall be placed at the end of the document and shall not be separately filed. The separate filing of a certificate of service, however, shall not be grounds for rejecting a document for filing. The Clerk may permit documents to be filed without a certificate of service but shall require prompt filing of a separate certificate of service. IN ST TRIAL P Rule 5(C).

2. *Supplemental documents*

    a. *Stipulation regarding discovery procedure.* Unless the court orders otherwise, the parties may by written stipulation:

      i. Provide that depositions may be taken before any person, at any time or place, upon any notice, and in any manner and when so taken may be used like other depositions, and

      ii. Modify the procedures provided by the Indiana Rules of Trial Procedure for other methods of discovery. IN ST TRIAL P Rule 29.

    b. *Subpoena.* Requests upon non-parties shall be included in or with a subpoena served upon such witness or person. IN ST TRIAL P Rule 34(C)(1).

    c. *Facsimile cover sheet.* Any document sent to the Clerk of the Circuit Court by electronic facsimile transmission shall be accompanied by a cover sheet which states the title of the document, case number, number of pages, identity and voice telephone number of the sending party and instructions for filing. The cover sheet shall contain the signature of the attorney or party, pro se, authorizing the filing. IN ST ADMIN Rule 12(D).

E. Format

1. *Form of documents produced.* The rules applicable to captions, and the signing and form of pleadings (IN ST TRIAL P Rule 8 through IN ST TRIAL P Rule 11), apply to all motions and other papers provided under the Indiana Rules of Trial Procedure. 22B INPRAC 7:2. Unless the parties otherwise agree, or the court otherwise orders, a party who produces documents for inspection shall produce them as they are kept in the usual course of business or shall organize and label them to correspond with the categories in the request. IN ST TRIAL P Rule 34(B).

    a. *Format of discovery requests.* Whenever agreed by the parties or otherwise ordered by the Court, a party shall forward simultaneously with the hard copy discovery request (interrogatories, requests for production, requests for admissions, or other requests for discovery) either a floppy disk or an electronic mail message with a copy of the request attached in digital format. Otherwise, an original and two (2) duplicate copies shall be prepared and served on the party required to answer. IN ST ST JOSEPH CIV Rule 208(208.2).

2. *Form of pleadings*

   a. *Caption; Names of parties.* Every pleading shall contain a caption setting forth the name of the court, the title of the action, the file number, and a designation as in IN ST TRIAL P Rule 7(A). In the complaint the title of the action shall include the names of all the parties, but in other pleadings it is sufficient to state the name of the first party on each side with an appropriate indication of other parties. IN ST TRIAL P Rule 10(A); IN ST ST JOSEPH CIV Rule 201(201.3.3). If a special judge has been assigned to the case, the pleading should also identify the special judge. IN ST ST JOSEPH CIV Rule 201(201.3.3).

      i. *Title.* All pleadings or motions shall include a title, which shall delineate each topic included in the pleading. For example, where a pleading contains an answer, a motion to dismiss, and a jury request, each topic shall be set forth in the title. IN ST ST JOSEPH CIV Rule 201(201.3.4).

   b. *Paragraphs; Separate statements.* All averments of a claim or defense shall be made in numbered paragraphs, the contents of each of which shall be limited as far as practicable to a statement of a single set of circumstances, and a paragraph may be referred to by number in all succeeding pleadings. Each claim founded upon a separate transaction or occurrence and each defense other than denials may be stated in a separate count or defense whenever a separation facilitates the clear presentation of the matters set forth. IN ST TRIAL P Rule 10(B).

   c. *Adoption by reference; Exhibits.* Statements in a pleading may be adopted by reference in a different part of the same pleading or in another pleading or in any motion. A copy of any written instrument which is an exhibit to a pleading is a part thereof for all purposes. IN ST TRIAL P Rule 10(C).

   d. *Flat filing.* In order that the Clerk's files may be kept under the system commonly known as "flat filing," all papers presented to the Clerk for filing shall be flat and unfolded. Pleadings shall have no covers or backs and shall be fastened together at the top left-hand corner only. IN ST ST JOSEPH CIV Rule 201(201.1).

   e. *One side of page used.* Printing shall be on one (1) side of the paper. IN ST ST JOSEPH CIV Rule 201(201.3.2).

   f. *Copies.* All copies shall be on white paper of sufficient strength and durability to resist normal wear and tear. IN ST ST JOSEPH CIV Rule 201(201.3.1).

   g. *Margins.* Margins shall be at least one inch (1"). IN ST ST JOSEPH CIV Rule 201(201.3.2).

   h. *Double-spaced.* If typewritten, the lines shall be double spaced except for quotations, which shall be indented and single-spaced. IN ST ST JOSEPH CIV Rule 201(201.3.2).

   i. *Font size.* Type face shall be twelve (12) font size or larger within the body of the document and ten (10) font size or larger in the footnotes. IN ST ST JOSEPH CIV Rule 201(201.3.2).

   j. *Font type.* The font type must be legible and script type shall not be used. IN ST ST JOSEPH CIV Rule 201(201.3.2).

   k. *Italics.* Italicized type may be used for quotations, references, or case citations. IN ST ST JOSEPH CIV Rule 201(201.3.2).

   l. *Court and case designation.* All filings shall conform to the requirements for uniform court and case number designation set by IN ST ADMIN Rule 8. In addition, all filings shall contain the proper court and case designation as described below. IN ST ST JOSEPH CIV Rule 202.

      i. *Court designation.* Pursuant to IN ST 33-33-71-2, St. Joseph County, Indiana, constitutes the Sixtieth Judicial Circuit. The legal names of the courts within the 60th Judicial Circuit are the St. Joseph Circuit Court, the St. Joseph Superior Court, and the St. Joseph Probate Court. All filings shall properly reflect the legal name of the applicable court. Any filing may be amended, rejected, or stricken if it does not contain the proper case name and/or the legal name of the court. IN ST ST JOSEPH CIV Rule 202(202.1).

m. *Form of CCS entry.* Every written motion, petition, or other pleading subsequent to the original complaint presented to the Clerk for filing shall be accompanied by a Chronological Case Summary (CCS) entry form in duplicate which shall contain the title and cause number of the action, the date, and the proposed entry to appear on the docket. IN ST ST JOSEPH CIV Rule 201(201.4).

    i. *Identification and signature.* The CCS entry form shall identify the party making the filing, designate each pleading being filed, and shall be signed by counsel of record or the unrepresented litigant. IN ST ST JOSEPH CIV Rule 201(201.4).

    ii. *Date stamp.* The form shall be date stamped and presented to the Court Clerk, who shall initial the form and return the duplicate to the filing party. IN ST ST JOSEPH CIV Rule 201(201.4).

3. *Size of papers for filing.* Effective January 1, 1992, all pleadings, copies, motions and documents filed with any trial court or appellate level court, typed or printed, with the exception of exhibits and existing wills, shall be prepared on eight and one-half by eleven inch (8 1/2" x 11") size paper. IN ST ADMIN Rule 11.

  a. *Paper.* Pleadings, motions, and other papers shall be either legibly printed or typewritten on white opaque paper of good quality at least sixteen (16) pound weight, eight and one-half inches (8 1/2 ") in width and eleven inches (11") in length as required by IN ST ADMIN Rule 11. IN ST ST JOSEPH CIV Rule 201(201.3.1).

4. *Signature requirements*

  a. *Signature of attorney.* Every pleading or motion of a party represented by an attorney shall be signed by at least one (1) attorney of record in his individual name, whose address, telephone number, and attorney number shall be stated, except that this provision shall not apply to pleadings and motions made and transcribed at the trial or a hearing before the judge and received by him in such form. IN ST TRIAL P Rule 11(A).

    i. The signature of an attorney constitutes a certificate by him that he has read the pleadings; that to the best of his knowledge, information, and belief, there is good ground to support it; and that it is not interposed for delay. IN ST TRIAL P Rule 11(A).

    ii. If a pleading or motion is not signed or is signed with intent to defeat the purpose of the rule, it may be stricken as sham and false and the action may proceed as though the pleading had not been served. IN ST TRIAL P Rule 11(A).

    iii. For a willful violation of IN ST TRIAL P Rule 11 an attorney may be subjected to appropriate disciplinary action. Similar action may be taken if scandalous or indecent matter is inserted. IN ST TRIAL P Rule 11(A).

  b. *Signature of unrepresented party.* A party who is not represented by an attorney shall sign his pleading and state his address. IN ST TRIAL P Rule 11(A).

  c. *Verification not generally required.* Except when specifically required by rule, pleadings or motions need not be verified or accompanied by affidavit. The rule in equity that the averments of an answer under oath must be overcome by the testimony of two (2) witnesses or of one (1) witness sustained by corroborating circumstances is abolished. IN ST TRIAL P Rule 11(A).

  d. *Verification by affirmation or representation.* When in connection with any civil or special statutory proceeding it is required that any pleading, motion, petition, supporting affidavit, or other document of any kind, be verified, or that an oath be taken, it shall be sufficient if the subscriber simply affirms the truth of the matter to be verified by an affirmation or representation. IN ST TRIAL P Rule 11(B). IN ST TRIAL P Rule 11(B) states that the affirmation or representation should be in substantially the following language: "I (we) affirm, under the penalties for perjury, that the foregoing representation(s) is (are) true. (Signed) _____."

    i. Any person who falsifies an affirmation or representation of fact shall be subject to the same penalties as are prescribed by law for the making of a false affidavit. IN ST TRIAL P Rule 11(B).

  e. *Verified pleadings, motions, and affidavits as evidence.* Pleadings, motions and affidavits accompanying or in support of such pleadings or motions when required to be verified or under oath shall be

accepted as a representation that the signer had personal knowledge thereof or reasonable cause to believe the existence of the facts or matters stated or alleged therein; and, if otherwise competent or acceptable as evidence, may be admitted as evidence of the facts or matters stated or alleged therein when it is so provided in the Indiana Rules of Trial Procedure, by statute or other law, or to the extent the writing or signature expressly purports to be made upon the signer's personal knowledge. When such pleadings, motions and affidavits are verified or under oath they shall not require other or greater proof on the part of the adverse party than if not verified or not under oath unless expressly provided otherwise by the Indiana Rules of Trial Procedure, statute or other law. Affidavits upon motions for summary judgment under IN ST TRIAL P Rule 56 and in denial of execution under IN ST TRIAL P Rule 9.2 shall be made upon personal knowledge. IN ST TRIAL P Rule 11(C).

    f.   *Signature, verification and other requirements.* Parties and their counsel are enjoined to comply with the verification requirements of IN ST TRIAL P Rule 11, and either the moving party or the party's attorney of record shall sign all pleadings and motions before filing with the Clerk of the Court. Every motion, petition, or other pleading filed with the Clerk shall contain the name, organization, physical address, telephone number, and facsimile number of the filing party or an attorney for that party. IN ST ST JOSEPH CIV Rule 201(201.3.6).

        i.   The Clerk shall not accept any motion, petition, notice or other pleading or a CCS entry form for filing from an unrepresented litigant unless the unrepresented litigant's current address and phone number appear on the pleading, and an opposing party may service notices and responses on an unrepresented litigant at any address he or she has provided on a pleading. IN ST ST JOSEPH CIV Rule 201(201.3.6).

5. *Information excluded from public access.* Every document filed in a case shall separately identify information excluded from public access pursuant to IN ST ADMIN Rule 9(G)(1) as follows:

    a.   Whole documents that are excluded from public access pursuant to IN ST ADMIN Rule 9(G)(1) shall be tendered on light green paper or have a light green coversheet attached to the document, marked "Not for Public Access" or "Confidential." IN ST TRIAL P Rule 5(G)(1).

    b.   When only a portion of a document contains information excluded from public access pursuant to IN ST ADMIN Rule 9(G)(1), said information shall be omitted [or redacted] from the filed document, and set forth on a separate accompanying document on light green paper conspicuously marked "Not for Public Access" or "Confidential" and clearly designated [or identifying] the caption and number of the case and the document and location within the document to which the redacted material pertains. IN ST TRIAL P Rule 5(G)(2).

    c.   With respect to documents filed in electronic format, the trial court, by local rule, may provide for compliance with IN ST TRIAL P Rule 5 in manner that separates and protects access to information excluded from public access. IN ST TRIAL P Rule 5(G)(3).

    d.   IN ST TRIAL P Rule 5(G) does not apply to a record sealed by the court pursuant to IN ST 5-14-3-5.5 or otherwise, nor to records, documents, or information filed in cases to which public access is prohibited pursuant to IN ST ADMIN Rule 9(G). IN ST TRIAL P Rule 5(G)(4).

    e.   The following information in case records is excluded from public access and is confidential:

        i.   Information that is excluded from public access pursuant to federal law;

        ii.   Information that is excluded from public access as declared confidential by Indiana statute or other court rule, including without limitation:

- All adoption records created after July 8, 1941, as declared confidential by IN ST 31-19-19-1, et seq., except those specifically declared open by IN ST 31-19-13-2(2);
- All records relating to chancroid, chlamydia, gonorrhea, hepatitis, human immunodeficiency virus (HIV), Lymphogranuloma venereum, syphilis, tuberculosis, as declared confidential by IN ST 16-41-8-1, et seq.;
- All records relating to child abuse as declared confidential by IN ST 31-33-18-1, et seq.;
- All records relating to drug tests as declared confidential by IN ST 5-14-3-4(a)(9);
- Records of grand jury proceedings as declared confidential by IN ST 35-34-2-4;

- Records of juvenile proceedings as declared confidential by IN ST 31-39-1-2, except those specifically open under statute;
- All paternity records created after July 1, 1941 as declared confidential by IN ST 31-14-11-15, IN ST 31-19-5-23, IN ST 31-39-1-1 and IN ST 31-39-1-2 [Editor's note: IN ST 31-14-11-15 was repealed effective May 9, 2013];
- All pre-sentence reports as declared confidential by IN ST 35-38-1-13;
- Written petitions to permit marriages without consent and orders directing the Clerk of Court to issue a marriage license to underage persons, as declared confidential by IN ST 31-11-1-6;
- Only those arrest warrants, search warrants, indictments and informations ordered confidential by the trial judge, prior to return of duly executed service as declared confidential by IN ST 5-14-3-4(b)(1);
- All medical, mental health, or tax records unless determined by law or regulation of any governmental custodian not to be confidential, released by the subject of such records, or declared by a court of competent jurisdiction to be essential to the resolution of litigation as declared confidential by IN ST 16-39-3-10, IN ST 6-4.1-5-10, IN ST 6-4.1-12-12, and IN ST 6-8.1-7-1;
- Personal information relating to jurors or prospective jurors, other than for the use of the parties and counsel, pursuant to IN ST JURY Rule 10;
- Information relating to protection from abuse orders, no-contact orders and workplace violence restraining orders as declared confidential by IN ST 5-2-9-6, et seq.;
- Mediation proceedings pursuant to IN ST ADR Rule 2.11, Mini-Trial proceedings pursuant to IN ST ADR Rule 4.4(C), and Summary Jury Trials pursuant to IN ST ADR Rule 5.6;
- Information in probation files pursuant to the Probation Standards promulgated by the Judicial Conference of Indiana pursuant to IN ST 11-13-1-8(b);
- Information deemed confidential pursuant to the Rules for Court Administered Alcohol and Drug Programs promulgated by the Judicial Conference of Indiana pursuant to IN ST 12-23-14-13;
- Information deemed confidential pursuant to the Problem-Solving Court Rules promulgated by the Judicial Conference of Indiana pursuant to IN ST 33-23-16-16;
- All records of the Department of workforce Development as declared confidential by IN ST 22-4-19-6;
- Information regarding interception of electronic communications that is sealed or deemed confidential as set forth in IN ST 35-33.5-2-1, et seq.

iii. Information excluded from public access by specific court order;

iv. Complete Social Security Numbers of living persons;

v. With the exception of names, information such as addresses, phone numbers, and dates of birth which explicitly identifies:

- Natural persons who are witnesses or victims (not including defendants) in criminal, domestic violence, stalking, sexual assault, juvenile, or civil protection order proceedings, provided that juveniles who are victims of sex crimes shall be identified by initials only;
- Places of residence of judicial officers, clerks and other employees of courts and clerks of court, unless the person or persons about whom the information pertains waives confidentiality;

vi. Complete account numbers of specific assets, loans, bank accounts, credit cards, and personal identification numbers (PINs);

vii. All orders of expungement entered in criminal or juvenile proceedings, orders to restrict access

to criminal history information pursuant to IN ST 35-38-5-5.5 or IN ST 35-38-8-5 and records excluded from public access by such orders, and information related to infractions that is excluded from public access pursuant to IN ST 34-28-5-15 or IN ST 34-28-5-16 [Editor's note: IN ST 35-38-5-5.5, IN ST 35-38-8-5 and IN ST 34-28-5-16 were repealed effective July 1, 2013; for information on orders restricting access to criminal history, refer to IN ST 35-38-9-1, et seq.];

  viii. All personal notes and e-mail, and deliberative material, of judges, jurors, court staff and judicial agencies, and information recorded in personal data assistants (PDA's) or organizers and personal calendars. IN ST ADMIN Rule 9(G)(1).

F. Filing and Service Requirements

1. *Filing requirements.* Except as otherwise provided in IN ST TRIAL P Rule 5(E)(2), all pleadings and papers subsequent to the complaint which are required to be served upon a party shall be filed with the Court either before service or within a reasonable period of time thereafter. IN ST TRIAL P Rule 5(E)(1).

   a. *Non-filing of discovery until necessary*

      i. *Non-filing of discovery; Exceptions.* No deposition or request for discovery or response thereto under IN ST TRIAL P Rule 27, IN ST TRIAL P Rule 30, IN ST TRIAL P Rule 31, IN ST TRIAL P Rule 33, IN ST TRIAL P Rule 34 or IN ST TRIAL P Rule 36 shall be filed with the Court unless:

         • A motion is filed pursuant to IN ST TRIAL P Rule 26(C) or IN ST TRIAL P Rule 37 and the original deposition or request for discovery or response thereto is necessary to enable the Court to rule; or

         • A party desires to use the deposition or request for discovery or response thereto for evidentiary purposes at trial or in connection with a motion, and the Court, either upon its own motion or that of any party, or as a part of any pre-trial order, orders the filing of the original. IN ST TRIAL P Rule 5(E)(2).

      ii. *Custody of original and period of retention*

         • The original of a deposition shall, subject to the provisions of IN ST TRIAL P Rule 30(E), be delivered by the reporter to the party taking it and shall be maintained by that party until filed with the Court pursuant to IN ST TRIAL P Rule 5(E)(2) or until the later of final judgment, agreed settlement of the litigation or all appellate rights have been exhausted. IN ST TRIAL P Rule 5(E)(3)(a).

         • The original or any request for discovery or response thereto under IN ST TRIAL P Rule 27, IN ST TRIAL P Rule 30, IN ST TRIAL P Rule 31, IN ST TRIAL P Rule 33, IN ST TRIAL P Rule 34 and IN ST TRIAL P Rule 36 shall be maintained by the party originating the request or response until filed with the Court pursuant to IN ST TRIAL P Rule 5(E)(2) or until the later of final judgment, agreed settlement or all appellate rights have been exhausted. IN ST TRIAL P Rule 5(E)(3)(b).

      iii. *Original unavailable; Copies.* In the event it is made to appear to the satisfaction of the Court that the original of a deposition or request for discovery or response thereto cannot be filed with the Court when required, the Court may allow use of a copy instead of the original. IN ST TRIAL P Rule 5(E)(4).

      iv. *Filing as publication.* The filing of any deposition shall constitute publication. IN ST TRIAL P Rule 5(E)(5).

   b. *Filing with the court defined.* The filing of pleadings, motions, and other papers with the court as required by the Indiana Rules of Trial Procedure shall be made by one of the following methods:

      i. Delivery to the clerk of the court;

      ii. Sending by electronic transmission under the procedure adopted pursuant to IN ST ADMIN Rule 12;

      iii. Mailing to the clerk by registered, certified or express mail return receipt requested;

iv. Depositing with any third-party commercial carrier for delivery to the clerk within three (3) calendar days, cost prepaid, properly addressed;

v. If the court so permits, filing with the judge, in which event the judge shall note thereon the filing date and forthwith transmit them to the office of the clerk; or

vi. Electronic filing, as approved by the Division of State Court Administration pursuant to IN ST ADMIN Rule 16. IN ST TRIAL P Rule 5(F).

vii. Filing by registered or certified mail and by third-party commercial carrier shall be complete upon mailing or deposit. IN ST TRIAL P Rule 5(F).

viii. All pleadings shall be filed with the Clerk, not directly with the Court, unless otherwise required by the Indiana Rules of Court. The entry of appearances and the filing of pleadings or other matters not requiring immediate Court action shall be filed with the Clerk and not in open Court. A Judge may permit papers to be filed in chambers, in which event he or she shall note thereon the filing date and transmit the papers to the Clerk. IN ST ST JOSEPH CIV Rule 201(201.2).

c. *Facsimile filing.* Unless otherwise authorized by IN ST ST JOSEPH ELECTRONIC Rule 701, electronic filing of pleadings by computerized or facsimile transmission is not permitted. IN ST ST JOSEPH CIV Rule 201(201.2).

d. *Additional copies.* In cases in which a party or counsel supplies the proposed order or decree, a sufficient number shall be prepared and filed as to provide the Clerk to retain two (2) copies, which shall be filed in the flat file and the record of judgments and orders. Should the party or counsel desire additional copies, a sufficient number of copies should be filed to effectuate that purpose. IN ST ST JOSEPH CIV Rule 201(201.6).

e. *Proof of filing.* Any party filing any paper by any method other than personal delivery to the clerk shall retain proof of filing. IN ST TRIAL P Rule 5(F).

2. *Service requirements.* Unless otherwise provided by the Indiana Rules of Trial Procedure or an order of the court, each party and special judge, if any, shall be served with: (1) every order required by its terms to be served; (2) every pleading subsequent to the original complaint; (3) every written motion except one which may be heard ex parte; (4) every brief submitted to the trial court; (5) every paper relating to discovery required to be served upon a party; and (6) every written notice, appearance, demand, offer of judgment, designation of record on appeal, or similar paper. IN ST TRIAL P Rule 5(A).

a. *Service generally.* Every motion, petition, notice, or other pleading required to be served by IN ST TRIAL P Rule 5 shall be served on all counsel of record or unrepresented parties either before it is filed or on the day it is filed with the Court, and the date of filing shall be indicated on the Certificate of Service. IN ST ST JOSEPH CIV Rule 201(201.5.1).

i. *Copy.* A copy of the Clerk's CCS entry form of the filing shall also be served on all counsel of record or unrepresented parties whenever it contains an appearance of counsel or contains a date for Court hearing on the matter. IN ST ST JOSEPH CIV Rule 201(201.5.1).

b. *Methods of service*

i. *Personal service.* Whenever a party is represented by an attorney of record, service shall be made upon such attorney unless service upon the party himself is ordered by the court. Service upon the attorney or party shall be made by delivering or mailing a copy of the papers to the last known address or where an attorney or party has consented to service by fax or e-mail, as provided in IN ST TRIAL P Rule 3.1(A)(4), by faxing or e-mailing a copy of the documents to the fax number or e-mail address set out in the appearance form or correction as required by IN ST TRIAL P Rule 3.1(E). IN ST TRIAL P Rule 5(B). Delivery of a copy within IN ST TRIAL P Rule 5 means:

- Offering or tendering it to the attorney or party and stating the nature of the papers being served. Refusal to accept an offered or tendered document is a waiver of any objection to the sufficiency or adequacy of service of that document;

- Leaving it at his office with a clerk or other person in charge thereof, or if there is no one in charge, leaving it in a conspicuous place therein; or

1642

- If the office is closed, by leaving it at his dwelling house or usual place of abode with some person of suitable age and discretion then residing therein; or,

- Leaving it at some other suitable place, selected by the attorney upon whom service is being made, pursuant to duly promulgated local rule. IN ST TRIAL P Rule 5(B)(1).

ii. *Service by the clerk.* Whenever the Clerk is required by rule or statute to give notice, the party or parties requesting such notice shall furnish the Clerk with sufficient copies of the notice to be given, along with stamped, addressed envelopes with the names and the addresses of the parties or their counsel to whom such notice is to be given. IN ST ST JOSEPH CIV Rule 201(201.5.4).

iii. *Service on the court.* Service on a Judge may be made by delivering a copy to the Judge's secretary or mailing a copy to the Judge at his or her chambers. Service on a Judge may not be accomplished by facsimile transmission; however, a courtesy copy may be sent to the Judge's chambers by electronic mail or facsimile transmission contemporaneously with service by mail or otherwise. IN ST ST JOSEPH CIV Rule 201(201.5.5).

iv. *Service by mail.* If service is made by mail, the papers shall be deposited in the United States mail addressed to the person on whom they are being served, with postage prepaid. Service shall be deemed complete upon mailing. Proof of service of all papers permitted to be mailed may be made by written acknowledgment of service, by affidavit of the person who mailed the papers, or by certificate of an attorney. It shall be the duty of attorneys when entering their appearance in a cause or when filing pleadings or papers therein, to have noted in the Chronological Case Summary or said pleadings or papers so filed the address and telephone number of their office. Service by delivery or by mail at such address shall be deemed sufficient and complete. IN ST TRIAL P Rule 5(B)(2).

v. *Service by fax or e-mail.* A party who has consented to service by fax or e-mail may be served as follows:

- Service by e-mail shall be made by attaching the document being served in .pdf format. Discovery documents must also be served in accordance with IN ST TRIAL P Rule 26(A). IN ST TRIAL P Rule 5(B)(3)(a).

- Service by fax shall be deemed complete upon generation of a transmission record indicating the successful transmission of the entire document, except as provided in IN ST TRIAL P Rule 5(B)(3)(d). IN ST TRIAL P Rule 5(B)(3)(b).

- Service by e-mail shall be deemed complete upon transmission, except as provided in IN ST TRIAL P Rule 5(B)(3)(d). IN ST TRIAL P Rule 5(B)(3)(c).

- Service by fax or e-mail that occurs on a Saturday, Sunday, legal holiday, or day the court or agency in which the matter is pending is closed or after 5:00 PM local time of the recipient shall be deemed complete the next day that is not a Saturday, Sunday, legal holiday, or day that the court or agency in which the matter is pending is not closed. IN ST TRIAL P Rule 5(B)(3)(d).

vi. *Additional service of electronic discovery.* In addition to service under Rule IN ST TRIAL P Rule 5(B) or a .pdf format electronic copy, a party propounding or responding to interrogatories, requests for production or requests for admission shall comply with IN ST TRIAL P Rule 26(A.1)(a) or IN ST TRIAL P Rule 26(A.1)(b). IN ST TRIAL P Rule 26(A.1).

- The party shall serve the discovery request or response in an electronic format (either on a disk or as an electronic document attachment) in any commercially available word processing software system. If transmitted on disk, each disk shall be labeled, identifying the caption of the case, the document, and the word processing version in which it is being submitted. If more than one (1) disk is used for the same document, each disk shall be labeled and also shall be sequentially numbered. If transmitted by electronic mail, the document must be accompanied by electronic memorandum providing the forgoing identifying information; or

- The party shall serve the opposing party with a verified statement that the attorney or party appealing pro se lacks the equipment and is unable to transmit the discovery as required by IN ST TRIAL P Rule 26(A.1). IN ST TRIAL P Rule 26(A.1).

c. *Serving numerous defendants.* In any action in which there are unusually large numbers of defendants, the court, upon motion or of its own initiative, may order:

    i. That service of the pleadings of the defendants and replies thereto need not be made as between the defendants;

- That any cross-claim, counterclaim, or matter constituting an avoidance or affirmative defense contained therein shall be deemed to be denied or avoided by all other parties; and

- That the filing of any such pleading and service thereof upon the plaintiff constitutes due notice of it to the parties. IN ST TRIAL P Rule 5(D).

    ii. A copy of every such order shall be served upon the parties in such manner and form as the court directs. IN ST TRIAL P Rule 5(D).

d. *Service on parties in default for failure to appear.* No service need be made on parties in default for failure to appear, except that pleadings asserting new or additional claims for relief against them shall be served upon them in the manner provided by service of summons in IN ST TRIAL P Rule 4. IN ST TRIAL P Rule 5(A).

e. *Distribution.* Counsel or an unrepresented party submitting a motion, petition, notice, pleading or proposed order shall indicate the method of distribution desired on the Clerk's CCS entry form. The Clerk will not return or distribute copies of motions, petitions, pleadings, notices or proposed orders, other than those originated by the Court, by mail unless the Clerk is provided with stamped, addressed envelopes. IN ST ST JOSEPH CIV Rule 201(201.5.3).

f. *Mailbox.* As a matter of convenience to attorneys, each court provides a mailbox for the distribution filings and orders generated by the Court, and it is the responsibility of each attorney to periodically check these mailboxes for service and distribution of court-generated filings and orders. IN ST ST JOSEPH CIV Rule 201(201.5.3).

G. Hearings

1. The Indiana rules do not contemplate a hearing related to the filing and service of requests for production.

H. Forms

1. Request for Production of Documents Forms for Indiana

a. Request for production of documents. 5 INPRAC § 4:3.1.

b. Request for production of documents; Insurance company. 5 INPRAC § 4:3.2.

c. Request for production of documents; Medical records. 5 INPRAC § 4:3.3.

d. Request for production of documents; Non-party. 5 INPRAC § 4:3.4.

e. Motion to enlarge time to respond to request for production of documents. 5 INPRAC § 4:3.5.

f. Response to request for production of documents; General form with objections. 5 INPRAC § 4:3.6.

g. Request for production of documents; General form. 10 INPRAC § 67.6.

h. Request for entry upon land for inspection. 10 INPRAC § 67.7.

i. Request for production of documents; Products liability; Plaintiff to manufacturer. 10 INPRAC § 67.8.

j. Request for production of documents; Products liability; Property loss; Defendant. 10 INPRAC § 67.9.

k. Request for production of documents; Products liability; Vehicle; Plaintiff. 10 INPRAC § 67.10.

l. Products liability; Defendant to plaintiff regarding accident and injuries. 10 INPRAC § 67.11.

m. Request for production of documents; Action against insurance company. 10 INPRAC § 67.13.

n. Request for production of documents; Action against nursing home; Plaintiff. 10 INPRAC § 67.14.

o. Request for production of documents; Action against nursing home; Defendant. 10 INPRAC § 67.15.

p. Request for production of documents; Medical records. 10 INPRAC § 67.17.

q. Request for production of documents; To obtain corporate records. 10 INPRAC § 67.18.

r. Request for production of handwriting exemplars. 10 INPRAC § 67.19.

s. Response to request for production of documents; General form with objections. 10 INPRAC § 67.30.

t. Response to request for permission to enter upon land. 10 INPRAC § 67.31.

u. Motion to shorten time to respond to request for production. 10 INPRAC § 67.32.

v. Motion to enlarge time to respond to request for production. 10 INPRAC § 67.33.

w. Request for production of documents to nonparty; General form. 10 INPRAC § 67.40.

x. Request for production of documents to nonparty; Another form. 10 INPRAC § 67.41.

y. Request for production of documents to nonparty; Production of bank and financial records. 10 INPRAC § 67.42.

z. Request for production of documents to nonparty; Request that employer produce records relating to employee making personal injury claim. 10 INPRAC § 67.43.

I. Checklist

(I) ❏ Matters to be considered by the party serving the request for production

   (a) ❏ Required documents

      (1) ❏ Request for production of documents

      (2) ❏ Certificate of service

   (b) ❏ Supplemental documents

      (1) ❏ Stipulation regarding discovery procedure

      (2) ❏ Subpoena

      (3) ❏ Facsimile cover sheet

   (c) ❏ Timing

      (1) ❏ On parties: The request may, without leave of court, be served upon the plaintiff after commencement of the action and upon any other party with or after service of the summons and complaint upon that party

      (2) ❏ On non-parties: Neither a request nor subpoena to produce or permit as permitted by IN ST TRIAL P Rule 34 shall be served upon a non-party until at least fifteen (15) days after the date on which the party intending to serve such request or subpoena serves a copy of the proposed request and subpoena on all other parties

         (i) ❏ Provided, however, that if such request or subpoena relates to a matter set for hearing within such fifteen (15) day period or arises out of a bona fide emergency, such request or subpoena may be served upon a non-party one (1) day after receipt of the proposed request or subpoena by all other parties

(II) ❏ Matters to be considered by the responding party

   (a) ❏ Required documents

      (1) ❏ Response to request for production of documents

      (2) ❏ Certificate of service

   (b) ❏ Supplemental documents

      (1) ❏ Business records

      (2) ❏ Stipulation regarding discovery procedure

      (3) ❏ Facsimile cover sheet

   (c) ❏ Timing

      (1) ❏ The party upon whom the request is served shall serve a written response within a period

designated in the request, not less than thirty (30) days after the service thereof or within such shorter for longer time as the court may allow

Requests, Notices and Applications
Request for Admissions

Document Last Updated October 2013

A. **Applicable Rules**

1. *State rules*

    a. Appearance. IN ST TRIAL P Rule 3.1.

    b. Process. IN ST TRIAL P Rule 4.

    c. Service and filing of pleadings and other papers. IN ST TRIAL P Rule 5.

    d. Time. IN ST TRIAL P Rule 6.

    e. Pleadings. IN ST TRIAL P Rule 7; IN ST TRIAL P Rule 9.2; IN ST TRIAL P Rule 10.

    f. Signing and verification of pleadings. IN ST TRIAL P Rule 11.

    g. Pre-trial procedure; Formulating issues. IN ST TRIAL P Rule 16.

    h. General provisions governing discovery. IN ST TRIAL P Rule 26.

    i. Methods of discovery. IN ST TRIAL P Rule 27; IN ST TRIAL P Rule 29; IN ST TRIAL P Rule 30; IN ST TRIAL P Rule 31; IN ST TRIAL P Rule 33; IN ST TRIAL P Rule 34; IN ST TRIAL P Rule 35; IN ST TRIAL P Rule 36.

    j. Failure to make or cooperate in discovery; Sanctions. IN ST TRIAL P Rule 37.

    k. Judgment on the evidence (directed verdict). IN ST TRIAL P Rule 50.

    l. Findings by the court. IN ST TRIAL P Rule 52.

    m. Summary judgment. IN ST TRIAL P Rule 56.

    n. Motion to correct error. IN ST TRIAL P Rule 59.

    o. Relief from judgment or order. IN ST TRIAL P Rule 60.

    p. Access to court records. IN ST ADMIN Rule 9.

    q. Paper size. IN ST ADMIN Rule 11.

    r. Facsimile transmission. IN ST ADMIN Rule 12.

    s. Electronic filing and electronic service pilot projects. IN ST ADMIN Rule 16.

    t. Sealing of certain records by court; Hearing; Notice. IN ST 5-14-3-5.5.

    u. Sixtieth judicial circuit. IN ST 33-33-71-2.

    v. Privacy and confidentiality. IN ST 5-2-9-6; IN ST 5-14-3-4; IN ST 6-4.1-5-10; IN ST 6-4.1-12-12; IN ST 6-8.1-7-1; IN ST 11-13-1-8; IN ST 12-23-14-13; IN ST 16-39-3-10; IN ST 16-41-8-1; IN ST 22-4-19-6; IN ST 31-11-1-6; IN ST 31-19-5-23; IN ST 31-19-13-2; IN ST 31-19-19-1; IN ST 31-33-18-1; IN ST 31-39-1-1; IN ST 31-39-1-2; IN ST 33-23-16-16; IN ST 35-34-2-4; IN ST 35-38-1-13; IN ST 35-38-9-1; IN ST ADR Rule 2.11; IN ST ADR Rule 4.4; IN ST ADR Rule 5.6; IN ST JURY Rule 10.

2. *Local rules*

    a. Filing, pleading, and motions. IN ST ST JOSEPH CIV Rule 201.

    b. Uniform court and case number designation. IN ST ST JOSEPH CIV Rule 202.

    c. Discovery requests. IN ST ST JOSEPH CIV Rule 208.

    d. Pre-trial procedures. IN ST ST JOSEPH CIV Rule 209.

e.   Electronic filing of cases in St. Joseph County. IN ST ST JOSEPH ELECTRONIC Rule 701.

B. Timing

1.   *Time for service of request for admissions.* The request may, without leave of court, be served upon the plaintiff after commencement of the action and upon any other party with or after service of the summons and complaint upon that party. IN ST TRIAL P Rule 36(A).

2.   *Time for service of response.* The matter is admitted unless, within a period designated in the request, not less than thirty (30) days after service thereof or within such shorter or longer time as the court may allow, the party to whom the request is directed serves upon the party requesting the admission a written answer or objection addressed to the matter. IN ST TRIAL P Rule 36(A).

3.   *Completion of discovery pursuant to pretrial scheduling order.* In cases in which a preliminary pre-trial conference has been held under Rule 12(B) [Editor's note: this is likely supposed to be a reference to IN ST TRIAL P Rule 16(B)], discovery shall be made in accordance with the scheduling thereof then ordered. In cases in which no preliminary pre-trial conference has been held, all discovery shall be completed prior to the pre-trial conference and no discovery shall be conducted thereafter unless, upon motion or stipulation showing good cause therefore, an order is entered permitting further discovery within time to be prescribed by the Court. IN ST ST JOSEPH CIV Rule 209(209.5).

4.   *Computation of time*

   a.   *Generally; Days excluded.* In computing any period of time prescribed or allowed by the Indiana Rules of Trial Procedure, by order of the court, or by any applicable statute, the day of the act, event, or default from which the designated period of time begins to run shall not be included. The last day of the period so computed is to be included unless it is:

      i.   A Saturday,

      ii.   A Sunday,

      iii.   A legal holiday as defined by state statute, or

      iv.   A day the office in which the act is to be done is closed during regular business hours. IN ST TRIAL P Rule 6(A).

   b.   *Short periods.* In any event, the period runs until the end of the next day that is not a Saturday, a Sunday, a legal holiday, or a day on which the office is closed. When the period of time allowed is less than seven (7) days, intermediate Saturdays, Sundays, legal holidays, and days on which the office is closed shall be excluded from the computations. IN ST TRIAL P Rule 6(A).

   c.   *Additional time after service by United States mail.* Whenever a party has the right or is required to do some act or take some proceedings within a prescribed period after the service of a notice or other paper upon him and the notice or paper is served upon him by United States mail, three (3) days shall be added to the prescribed period. IN ST TRIAL P Rule 6(E).

   d.   *Enlargement of time.* When an act is required or allowed to be done at or within a specific time by the Indiana Rules of Trial Procedure, the court may at any time for cause shown:

      i.   Order the period enlarged, with or without motion or notice, if request therefor is made before the expiration of the period originally prescribed or extended by a previous order; or

      ii.   Upon motion made after the expiration of the specific period, permit the act to be done where the failure to act was the result of excusable neglect; but, the court may not extend the time for taking any action for judgment on the evidence under IN ST TRIAL P Rule 50(A), amendment of findings and judgment under IN ST TRIAL P Rule 52(B), to correct errors under IN ST TRIAL P Rule 59(C), statement in opposition to motion to correct error under IN ST TRIAL P Rule 59(E), or to obtain relief from final judgment under IN ST TRIAL P Rule 60(B), except to the extent and under the conditions stated in those rules. IN ST TRIAL P Rule 6(B).

      iii.   An initial written motion for enlargement of time pursuant to IN ST TRIAL P Rule 6(B)(1) to answer a claim shall be routinely granted for an additional thirty (30) days from the original due date or other period the assigned Judge deems reasonable by written order of the Court. The motion must be filed on or before the original due date or IN ST ST JOSEPH CIV Rule 201 shall be inapplicable. IN ST ST JOSEPH CIV Rule 201(201.9.5).

- Any motion for enlargement of time shall state the date when such response is due and the date to which time is requested to be enlarged. IN ST ST JOSEPH CIV Rule 201(201.9.5).

- All subsequent motions for enlargement of time shall be so designated and will only be granted for good cause shown or in the interest of justice. IN ST ST JOSEPH CIV Rule 201(201.9.5).

C. General Requirements

1. *Scope of discovery.* Unless otherwise limited by order of the court in accordance with the Indiana Rules of Trial Procedure, the scope of discovery is as follows:

   a. *In general.* Parties may obtain discovery regarding any matter, not privileged, which is relevant to the subject-matter involved in the pending action, whether it relates to the claim or defense of the party seeking discovery or the claim or defense of any other party, including the existence, description, nature, custody, condition and location of any books, documents, or other tangible things and the identity and location of persons having knowledge of any discoverable matter. It is not ground for objection that the information sought will be inadmissible at the trial if the information sought appears reasonably calculated to lead to the discovery of admissible evidence. IN ST TRIAL P Rule 26(B)(1).

      i. *Limiting discovery upon court determination.* The frequency or extent of use of the discovery methods otherwise permitted under the Indiana Rules of Trial Procedure and by any local rule shall be limited by the court if it determines that:

         - The discovery sought is unreasonably cumulative or duplicative, or is obtainable from some other source that is more convenient, less burdensome, or less expensive;

         - The party seeking discovery has had ample opportunity by discovery in the action to obtain the information sought or;

         - The burden or expense of the proposed discovery outweighs its likely benefit, taking into account the needs of the case, the amount in controversy, the parties' resources, the importance of the issues at stake in the litigation, and the importance of the proposed discovery in resolving the issues. IN ST TRIAL P Rule 26(B)(1).

         - The court may act upon its own initiative after reasonable notice or pursuant to a motion under IN ST TRIAL P Rule 26(C). IN ST TRIAL P Rule 26(B)(1). Refer to the Indiana KeyRules Motion for Protective Order document for more information.

      ii. *Relevancy in the discovery context.* When the word "relevancy" is used in IN ST TRIAL P Rule 26(B), it does not mean "relevancy" as that word in used to determine the admissibility of evidence in a trial court. It is much broader. It means "relevancy" to the "subject matter" of the litigation or pending action and it may relate to the claim or defense of any party. Pretrial discovery is available as to any nonprivileged matter relevant to the subject matter of the lawsuit or to obtain information reasonably calculated to lead to admissible evidence. 2A INPRAC R 26(26.4); Kaufmann v. Credithrift Financial, Inc., 465 N.E.2d 207, 210 (Ind.Ct.App. 1984).

      iii. *Tests for relevance.* Indiana case law has developed two (2) additional tests in this area. 2A INPRAC R 26(26.4).

         - The first test determines when a document or a request for information is actually relevant to the subject matter in the pending action. A document [or discovery request] is relevant to discovery if there is the possibility the information sought may be relevant to the subject matter of the action. 2A INPRAC R 26(26.4); CIGNA-INA/Aetna v. Hagerman-Shambaugh, 473 N.E.2d 1033, 1036 (Ind.Ct.App. 1985).

         - The second test speaks to appellate review of the trial court's determination that a document or discovery request is relevant to the subject matter of the pending action. The appellate court sees its review of the trial court's decision on relevancy to subject matter as being very limited. The court states: "Our review of the trial court's conclusion that the documents are relevant is limited. A trial court is vested with discretion in its rulings on discovery issues." 2A INPRAC R 26(26.4); Costanzi v. Ryan, 175 Ind.App. 257, 370 N.E.2d 1333 (Ind.Ct.App. 1978).

b. *Insurance agreements.* A party may obtain discovery of the existence and contents of any insurance agreement under which any person carrying on an insurance business may be liable to satisfy part or all of a judgment which may be entered in the action or to indemnify or reimburse for payments made to satisfy the judgment. Information concerning the insurance agreement is not by reason of disclosure admissible in evidence at trial. For purposes of IN ST TRIAL P Rule 26(B)(2), an application for insurance shall not be treated as part of an insurance agreement. IN ST TRIAL P Rule 26(B)(2).

c. *Trial preparation; Materials.* Subject to the provisions of IN ST TRIAL P Rule 26(B)(4), a party may obtain discovery of documents and tangible things otherwise discoverable under IN ST TRIAL P Rule 26(B)(1) and prepared in anticipation of litigation or for trial by or for another party or by or for that other party's representative (including his attorney, consultant, surety, indemnitor, insurer, or agent) only upon a showing that the party seeking discovery has substantial need of the materials in the preparation of his case and that he is unable without undue hardship to obtain the substantial equivalent of the materials by other means. In ordering discovery of such materials when the required showing has been made, the court shall protect against disclosure of the mental impressions, conclusions, opinions, or legal theories of an attorney or other representative of a party concerning the litigation. IN ST TRIAL P Rule 26(B)(3).

   i. A party may obtain without the required showing a statement concerning the action or its subject matter previously made by that party. Upon request, a person not a party may obtain without the required showing a statement concerning the action or its subject matter previously made by that person. If the request is refused, the person may move for a court order. The provisions of IN ST TRIAL P Rule 37(A)(4) apply to the award of expenses incurred in relation to the motion. For purposes of IN ST TRIAL P Rule 26(B)(3), a statement previously made is:

      - A written statement signed or otherwise adopted approved by the person making it, or

      - A stenographic, mechanical, electrical, or other recording, or a transcription thereof, which is a substantially verbatim recital of an oral statement by the person making it and contemporaneously recorded. IN ST TRIAL P Rule 26(B)(3).

   ii. The protection of IN ST TRIAL P Rule 26(B)(3) extends to material prepared or collected before litigation actually commences, but that some possibility of litigation must actually exist before the privilege and IN ST TRIAL P Rule 26(B)(3) become operative. 2A INPRAC R 26(26.9); CIGNA-INA/Aetna v. Hagerman-Shambaugh, 473 N.E.2d 1033, 1037 (Ind.Ct.App. 1985).

d. *Trial preparation; Experts.* Discovery of facts known and opinions held by experts, otherwise discoverable under the provisions of IN ST TRIAL P Rule 26(B)(1) and acquired or developed in anticipation of litigation or for trial, may be obtained as follows:

   i. A party may through interrogatories require any other party to identify each person whom the other party expects to call as an expert witness at trial, to state the subject matter on which the expert is expected to testify, and to state the substance of the facts and opinions to which the expert is expected to testify and a summary of the grounds for each opinion. IN ST TRIAL P Rule 26(B)(4)(a)(i).

   ii. Upon motion, the court may order further discovery by other means, subject to such restrictions as to scope and such provisions, pursuant to IN ST TRIAL P Rule 26(B)(4)(c), concerning fees and expenses as the court may deem appropriate. IN ST TRIAL P Rule 26(B)(4)(a)(ii).

   iii. A party may discover facts known or opinions held by an expert who has been retained or specially employed by another party in anticipation of litigation or preparation for trial and who is not expected to be called as a witness at trial, only as provided in IN ST TRIAL P Rule 35(B) or upon a showing of exceptional circumstances under which it is impracticable for the party seeking discovery to obtain facts or opinions on the same subject by other means. IN ST TRIAL P Rule 26(B)(4)(b).

    iv.   Unless manifest injustice would result,

- The court shall require that the party seeking discovery pay the expert a reasonable fee for time spent in responding to discovery under IN ST TRIAL P Rule 26(B)(4)(a)(ii) and IN ST TRIAL P Rule 26(B)(4)(b); and

- With respect to discovery obtained under IN ST TRIAL P Rule 26(B)(4)(a)(ii) the court may require, and with respect to discovery obtained under IN ST TRIAL P Rule 26(B)(4)(b) the court shall require, the party seeking discovery to pay the other party a fair portion of the fees and expenses reasonably incurred by the latter party in obtaining facts and opinions from the expert. IN ST TRIAL P Rule 26(B)(4)(c).

e.   *Claims of privilege or protection*

    i.   *Information withheld.* When a party withholds information otherwise discoverable under the Indiana Rules of Trial Procedure by claiming that it is privileged or subject to protection as trial preparation material, the party shall make the claim expressly and shall describe the nature of the documents, communications, or things not produced or disclosed in a manner that, without revealing information itself privileged or protected, will enable other parties to assess the applicability of the privilege or protection. IN ST TRIAL P Rule 26(B)(5)(a).

    ii.   *Information produced.* If information is produced in discovery that is subject to a claim of privilege or protection as trial-preparation material, the party making the claim may notify any party that received the information of the claim and the basis for it. After being notified, a party must promptly return, sequester, or destroy the specified information and any copies it has and may not use or disclose the information until the claim is resolved. A receiving party may promptly present the information to the court under seal for a determination of the claim. If the receiving party disclosed the information before being notified, it must take reasonable steps to retrieve it. The producing party must preserve the information until the claim is resolved. IN ST TRIAL P Rule 26(B)(5)(b).

    iii.   *Waiver.* The law of discovery has developed some holdings which indicate that "waiver" of a privileged communication in a discovery setting might be more exacting than "waiver" of a privileged communication when the only question at hand is an interpretation of the privilege itself. Thus, in litigation in which several documents are in issue, and some are released inadvertently, there is strong case law that holds that the "inadvertent production" of a privileged document does not constitute a waiver of the attorney-client privilege. 2A INPRAC R 26(26.5); Transamerica Computer Co. v. International Business Machines Corp., 573 F.2d 646 (9th Cir. 1978). Such a rule should be measured against the usual rule which suggests that a voluntary disclosure to a third person will generally suffice to show a waiver of the attorney-client privilege. 2A INPRAC R 26(26.5).

f.   *Use not limited.* Unless the court orders otherwise under IN ST TRIAL P Rule 26(C), the frequency of use of the methods listed in IN ST TRIAL P Rule 26(A) is not limited. IN ST TRIAL P Rule 26(A).

g.   *Sequence of discovery.* Unless the court upon motion, for the convenience of parties and witnesses and in the interests of justice, orders otherwise, methods of discovery may be used in any sequence and the fact that a party is conducting discovery, whether by deposition or otherwise, shall not operate to delay any other party's discovery. IN ST TRIAL P Rule 26(D).

h.   *Discovery disputes.* To promote the orderly and expeditious handling of cases to trial readiness, counsel shall attempt in good faith to resolve all disagreements between or among themselves concerning the necessity for and scope of discovery, the necessity to seek sanctions, and/or protection against discovery under IN ST TRIAL P Rule 26 through IN ST TRIAL P Rule 37. IN ST ST JOSEPH CIV Rule 208(208.5).

    i.   After personal consultation and good faith attempts to resolve differences as to the foregoing matters, counsel for any or all parties may move to compel discovery, invoke sanctions, or seek protection against discovery as aforesaid. IN ST ST JOSEPH CIV Rule 208(208.5).

    ii.   As a part of such motion, the party shall recite the date, time, and place of the personal consultations and the names of the participants. If counsel for any party advises the Court in writing that counsel for any other party has refused or delayed consultation hereby contemplated, the Court shall take such action as is appropriate to preclude, obviate, or avoid further delay. IN ST ST JOSEPH CIV Rule 208(208.5).

2. *Request for admissions.* A request for admission is a method of discovery which allows a party to establish facts and information during the discovery stage of the action so that evidence on those matters will not be required at trial. 22 INPRAC § 26.1; Walker v. Employers Ins. of Wausau, 846 N.E.2d 1098 (Ind.Ct.App. 2006); Brown v. Dobbs, 691 N.E.2d 907 (Ind.Ct.App. 1998). Requests for admission under IN ST TRIAL P Rule 36 are designed to simplify and clarify the issues, to cut trial preparation time, and to encourage settlement. 10 INPRAC § 69.1.

    a. *Request for admissions generally.* A party may serve upon any other party a written request for the admission, for purposes of the pending action only, of the truth of any matters within the scope of IN ST TRIAL P Rule 26(B) set forth in the request, including the genuineness of any documents described in the request. IN ST TRIAL P Rule 36(A).

    b. *Mutually known matters.* Requests for admissions as to matters within the mutual knowledge of both parties are proper. The function of IN ST TRIAL P Rule 36 is to establish admissions that will obviate the necessity of proof and expedite the trial, or to transform "mutual knowledge" into the established facts of a case. 3 INPRAC R 36(36.5).

    c. *Requests to be carefully drafted.* The burden on the requesting party is to carefully and artfully draft the statement of fact contained in the request for admission. The statement must be precise, unambiguous, and in no way mislead the answering party. 3 INPRAC R 36(36.2).

        i.   Fairness demands that any error arising out of inartful drafting be borne by the requesting party. The burden imposed on the answering party is unfairly "increased when the request for admission propounds a statement of fact which lacks clarity, is ambiguous, or which otherwise might mislead the answering party." 3 INPRAC R 36(36.2); F.W. Means & Co. v. Carstens, 428 N.E.2d 251, 257 (Ind.Ct.App. 1981).

    d. *Admissions by the requestor.* Propounding of requests for admissions admits nothing as to the requesting party. 3 INPRAC R 36(36.2); Indiana Construction Service v. Amoco Oil Company, 533 N.E.2d 1300 (Ind.Ct.App. 1989). This party in the action made an admission in the text of or during the request, to which the receiving party, of course, agreed. But it was not binding, as to the requesting party, the court held. Such a request is binding as to the party admitting the fact in response to a request. 3 INPRAC R 36(36.2); Indiana Construction Service v. Amoco Oil Company, 533 N.E.2d 1300 (Ind.Ct.App. 1989).

    e. *Motion to compel.* The party who has requested the admissions may move for an order with respect to the answers or objections. Unless the court determines that an objection is justified, it shall order that an answer be served. If the court determines that an answer does not comply with the requirements of IN ST TRIAL P Rule 36, it may order either that the matter is admitted or that an amended answer be served. The court may, in lieu of these orders, determine that final disposition of the request be made at a pre-trial conference or at a designated time prior to trial. IN ST TRIAL P Rule 36(A).

        i.   The provisions of IN ST TRIAL P Rule 37(A)(4) apply to the award of expenses incurred in relation to the motion. IN ST TRIAL P Rule 36(A).

        ii.   Refer to the Indiana KeyRules Motion to Compel Discovery document for more information.

3. *Response to request for admissions.* The matter is admitted unless, within a period designated in the request, not less than thirty (30) days after service thereof or within such shorter or longer time as the court may allow, the party to whom the request is directed serves upon the party requesting the admission a written answer or objection addressed to the matter, signed by the party or by his attorney. IN ST TRIAL P Rule 36(A).

    a. *Methods of response.* IN ST TRIAL P Rule 36 recognizes at least four (4) responses. The party:

        i.   May not respond, thereby admitting the request; or

    ii.   Answer; or

   iii.   Object to the request; or

   iv.   File a qualified response. 3 INPRAC R 36(36.4).

b.   *Effect of admission.* Any matter admitted under IN ST TRIAL P Rule 36 is conclusively established unless the court on motion permits withdrawal or amendment of the admission. IN ST TRIAL P Rule 36(B).

    i.   Any admission made by a party under IN ST TRIAL P Rule 36 is for the purpose of the pending action only and is not an admission by him for any other purpose nor may it be used against him in any other proceeding. IN ST TRIAL P Rule 36(B).

c.   *Denials.* The answer shall specifically deny the matter or set forth in detail the reasons why the answering party cannot truthfully admit or deny the matter. A denial shall fairly meet the substance of the requested admission, and when good faith requires that a party qualify his answer or deny only a part of the matter of which an admission is requested, he shall specify so much of it as is true and qualify or deny the remainder. IN ST TRIAL P Rule 36(A).

d.   *Lack of information or knowledge.* An answering party may not give lack of information or knowledge as a reason for failure to admit or deny unless he states that he has made reasonable inquiry and that the information known or readily obtainable by him is insufficient to enable him to admit or deny or that the inquiry would be unreasonably burdensome. IN ST TRIAL P Rule 36(A).

e.   *Objections.* If objection is made, the reasons therefor shall be stated. IN ST TRIAL P Rule 36(A).

    i.   A party who considers that a matter of which an admission has been requested presents a genuine issue for trial may not, on that ground alone, object to the request; he may, subject to the provisions of IN ST TRIAL P Rule 37(C), deny the matter or set forth reasons why he cannot admit or deny it. IN ST TRIAL P Rule 36(A).

    ii.   An objectionable request may not be properly attacked by a motion to strike, to dismiss, or to suppress. The party served must respond to the request and serve admissions or denials of all matters not deemed objectionable. 3 INPRAC R 36(36.4).

f.   *Withdrawal or amendment of admissions.* Subject to the provisions of IN ST TRIAL P Rule 16 governing amendment of a pre-trial order, the court may permit withdrawal or amendment when the presentation of the merits of the action will be subserved thereby and the party who obtained the admission fails to satisfy the court that withdrawal or amendment will prejudice him in maintaining his action or defense on the merits. IN ST TRIAL P Rule 36(B).

    i.   It is within sound discretion of trial court to permit or deny amendment of pretrial order, but trial court should amend or modify pretrial order when requested if modification is necessary to prevent manifest injustice. 2 INPRAC R 16(7); Hacienda Mexican Restaurant of Kalamazoo Corp. v. Hacienda Franchise Group, Inc., 641 N.E.2d 1036 (Ind.Ct.App. 1994).

g.   *Supplementation of responses.* A party who has responded to a request for discovery with a response that was complete when made is under no duty to supplement his response to include information thereafter acquired, except as follows:

    i.   A party is under a duty seasonably to supplement his response with respect to any question directly addressed to:

        •   The identity and location of persons having knowledge of discoverable matters, and

        •   The identity of each person expected to be called as an expert witness at trial, the subject-matter on which he is expected to testify, and the substance of his testimony. IN ST TRIAL P Rule 26(E)(1).

    ii.   A party is under a duty seasonably to amend a prior response if he obtains information upon the basis of which:

        •   He knows that the response was incorrect when made, or

        •   He knows that the response though correct when made is no longer true and the circumstances are such that a failure to amend the response is in substance a knowing concealment. IN ST TRIAL P Rule 26(E)(2).

iii. A duty to supplement responses may be imposed by order of the court, agreement of the parties, or at any time prior to trial through new requests for supplementation of prior responses. IN ST TRIAL P Rule 26(E)(3).

iv. The duty seasonably to supplement a discovery response is absolute and is not predicated on a court order. "It is a breach of a litigant's duty reasonably to supplement if the litigant postpones supplementing its response by not obtaining from its experts the information which is to be supplied in answer to interrogatories." 2A INPRAC R 26(26.27); Lucas v. Dorsey Corp., 609 N.E.2d 1191, 1196 (Ind.Ct.App. 1993).

D. Documents

1. *Required documents*

   a. *Request for admissions.* Refer to the General Requirements section of this document for information on the scope and content of a request for admissions.

   b. *Copies of documents.* Copies of documents shall be served with the request unless they have been or are otherwise furnished or made available for inspection and copying. IN ST TRIAL P Rule 36(A).

   c. *Certificate of service.* An attorney or unrepresented party tendering a document to the Clerk for filing shall certify that service has been made, list the parties served, and specify the date and means of service. The certificate of service shall be placed at the end of the document and shall not be separately filed. The separate filing of a certificate of service, however, shall not be grounds for rejecting a document for filing. The Clerk may permit documents to be filed without a certificate of service but shall require prompt filing of a separate certificate of service. IN ST TRIAL P Rule 5(C).

2. *Supplemental documents*

   a. *Stipulation regarding discovery procedure.* Unless the court orders otherwise, the parties may by written stipulation:

      i. Provide that depositions may be taken before any person, at any time or place, upon any notice, and in any manner and when so taken may be used like other depositions, and

      ii. Modify the procedures provided by the Indiana Rules of Trial Procedure for other methods of discovery. IN ST TRIAL P Rule 29.

   b. *Facsimile cover sheet.* Any document sent to the Clerk of the Circuit Court by electronic facsimile transmission shall be accompanied by a cover sheet which states the title of the document, case number, number of pages, identity and voice telephone number of the sending party and instructions for filing. The cover sheet shall contain the signature of the attorney or party, pro se, authorizing the filing. IN ST ADMIN Rule 12(D).

E. Format

1. *Form of requests for admissions.* The rules applicable to captions, and the signing and form of pleadings (IN ST TRIAL P Rule 8 through IN ST TRIAL P Rule 11), apply to all motions and other papers provided under the Indiana Rules of Trial Procedure. 22B INPRAC 7:2. Each matter of which an admission is requested shall be separately set forth. IN ST TRIAL P Rule 36(A).

   a. *Format of discovery requests.* Whenever agreed by the parties or otherwise ordered by the Court, a party shall forward simultaneously with the hard copy discovery request (interrogatories, requests for production, requests for admissions, or other requests for discovery) either a floppy disk or an electronic mail message with a copy of the request attached in digital format. Otherwise, an original and two (2) duplicate copies shall be prepared and served on the party required to answer. IN ST ST JOSEPH CIV Rule 208(208.2).

2. *Form of pleadings*

   a. *Caption; Names of parties.* Every pleading shall contain a caption setting forth the name of the court, the title of the action, the file number, and a designation as in IN ST TRIAL P Rule 7(A). In the complaint the title of the action shall include the names of all the parties, but in other pleadings it is sufficient to state the name of the first party on each side with an appropriate indication of other parties. IN ST TRIAL P Rule 10(A); IN ST ST JOSEPH CIV Rule 201(201.3.3). If a special judge has been assigned to the case, the pleading should also identify the special judge. IN ST ST JOSEPH CIV Rule 201(201.3.3).

    i.   *Title.* All pleadings or motions shall include a title, which shall delineate each topic included in the pleading. For example, where a pleading contains an answer, a motion to dismiss, and a jury request, each topic shall be set forth in the title. IN ST ST JOSEPH CIV Rule 201(201.3.4).

b.   *Paragraphs; Separate statements.* All averments of a claim or defense shall be made in numbered paragraphs, the contents of each of which shall be limited as far as practicable to a statement of a single set of circumstances, and a paragraph may be referred to by number in all succeeding pleadings. Each claim founded upon a separate transaction or occurrence and each defense other than denials may be stated in a separate count or defense whenever a separation facilitates the clear presentation of the matters set forth. IN ST TRIAL P Rule 10(B).

c.   *Adoption by reference; Exhibits.* Statements in a pleading may be adopted by reference in a different part of the same pleading or in another pleading or in any motion. A copy of any written instrument which is an exhibit to a pleading is a part thereof for all purposes. IN ST TRIAL P Rule 10(C).

d.   *Flat filing.* In order that the Clerk's files may be kept under the system commonly known as "flat filing," all papers presented to the Clerk for filing shall be flat and unfolded. Pleadings shall have no covers or backs and shall be fastened together at the top left-hand corner only. IN ST ST JOSEPH CIV Rule 201(201.1).

e.   *One side of page used.* Printing shall be on one (1) side of the paper. IN ST ST JOSEPH CIV Rule 201(201.3.2).

f.   *Copies.* All copies shall be on white paper of sufficient strength and durability to resist normal wear and tear. IN ST ST JOSEPH CIV Rule 201(201.3.1).

g.   *Margins.* Margins shall be at least one inch (1"). IN ST ST JOSEPH CIV Rule 201(201.3.2).

h.   *Double-spaced.* If typewritten, the lines shall be double spaced except for quotations, which shall be indented and single-spaced. IN ST ST JOSEPH CIV Rule 201(201.3.2).

i.   *Font size.* Type face shall be twelve (12) font size or larger within the body of the document and ten (10) font size or larger in the footnotes. IN ST ST JOSEPH CIV Rule 201(201.3.2).

j.   *Font type.* The font type must be legible and script type shall not be used. IN ST ST JOSEPH CIV Rule 201(201.3.2).

k.   *Italics.* Italicized type may be used for quotations, references, or case citations. IN ST ST JOSEPH CIV Rule 201(201.3.2).

l.   *Court and case designation.* All filings shall conform to the requirements for uniform court and case number designation set by IN ST ADMIN Rule 8. In addition, all filings shall contain the proper court and case designation as described below. IN ST ST JOSEPH CIV Rule 202.

    i.   *Court designation.* Pursuant to IN ST 33-33-71-2, St. Joseph County, Indiana, constitutes the Sixtieth Judicial Circuit. The legal names of the courts within the 60th Judicial Circuit are the St. Joseph Circuit Court, the St. Joseph Superior Court, and the St. Joseph Probate Court. All filings shall properly reflect the legal name of the applicable court. Any filing may be amended, rejected, or stricken if it does not contain the proper case name and/or the legal name of the court. IN ST ST JOSEPH CIV Rule 202(202.1).

m.   *Form of CCS entry.* Every written motion, petition, or other pleading subsequent to the original complaint presented to the Clerk for filing shall be accompanied by a Chronological Case Summary (CCS) entry form in duplicate which shall contain the title and cause number of the action, the date, and the proposed entry to appear on the docket. IN ST ST JOSEPH CIV Rule 201(201.4).

    i.   *Identification and signature.* The CCS entry form shall identify the party making the filing, designate each pleading being filed, and shall be signed by counsel of record or the unrepresented litigant. IN ST ST JOSEPH CIV Rule 201(201.4).

    ii.   *Date stamp.* The form shall be date stamped and presented to the Court Clerk, who shall initial the form and return the duplicate to the filing party. IN ST ST JOSEPH CIV Rule 201(201.4).

3. *Size of papers for filing.* Effective January 1, 1992, all pleadings, copies, motions and documents filed with any trial court or appellate level court, typed or printed, with the exception of exhibits and existing wills, shall be prepared on eight and one-half by eleven inch (8 1/2" x 11") size paper. IN ST ADMIN Rule 11.

   a. *Paper.* Pleadings, motions, and other papers shall be either legibly printed or typewritten on white opaque paper of good quality at least sixteen (16) pound weight, eight and one-half inches (8 1/2 ") in width and eleven inches (11") in length as required by IN ST ADMIN Rule 11. IN ST ST JOSEPH CIV Rule 201(201.3.1).

4. *Signature requirements*

   a. *Signature of attorney.* Every pleading or motion of a party represented by an attorney shall be signed by at least one (1) attorney of record in his individual name, whose address, telephone number, and attorney number shall be stated, except that this provision shall not apply to pleadings and motions made and transcribed at the trial or a hearing before the judge and received by him in such form. IN ST TRIAL P Rule 11(A).

      i. The signature of an attorney constitutes a certificate by him that he has read the pleadings; that to the best of his knowledge, information, and belief, there is good ground to support it; and that it is not interposed for delay. IN ST TRIAL P Rule 11(A).

      ii. If a pleading or motion is not signed or is signed with intent to defeat the purpose of the rule, it may be stricken as sham and false and the action may proceed as though the pleading had not been served. IN ST TRIAL P Rule 11(A).

      iii. For a willful violation of IN ST TRIAL P Rule 11 an attorney may be subjected to appropriate disciplinary action. Similar action may be taken if scandalous or indecent matter is inserted. IN ST TRIAL P Rule 11(A).

   b. *Signature of unrepresented party.* A party who is not represented by an attorney shall sign his pleading and state his address. IN ST TRIAL P Rule 11(A).

   c. *Verification not generally required.* Except when specifically required by rule, pleadings or motions need not be verified or accompanied by affidavit. The rule in equity that the averments of an answer under oath must be overcome by the testimony of two (2) witnesses or of one (1) witness sustained by corroborating circumstances is abolished. IN ST TRIAL P Rule 11(A).

   d. *Verification by affirmation or representation.* When in connection with any civil or special statutory proceeding it is required that any pleading, motion, petition, supporting affidavit, or other document of any kind, be verified, or that an oath be taken, it shall be sufficient if the subscriber simply affirms the truth of the matter to be verified by an affirmation or representation. IN ST TRIAL P Rule 11(B). IN ST TRIAL P Rule 11(B) states that the affirmation or representation should be in substantially the following language: "I (we) affirm, under the penalties for perjury, that the foregoing representation(s) is (are) true. (Signed) _____."

      i. Any person who falsifies an affirmation or representation of fact shall be subject to the same penalties as are prescribed by law for the making of a false affidavit. IN ST TRIAL P Rule 11(B).

   e. *Verified pleadings, motions, and affidavits as evidence.* Pleadings, motions and affidavits accompanying or in support of such pleadings or motions when required to be verified or under oath shall be accepted as a representation that the signer had personal knowledge thereof or reasonable cause to believe the existence of the facts or matters stated or alleged therein; and, if otherwise competent or acceptable as evidence, may be admitted as evidence of the facts or matters stated or alleged therein when it is so provided in the Indiana Rules of Trial Procedure, by statute or other law, or to the extent the writing or signature expressly purports to be made upon the signer's personal knowledge. When such pleadings, motions and affidavits are verified or under oath they shall not require other or greater proof on the part of the adverse party than if not verified or not under oath unless expressly provided otherwise by the Indiana Rules of Trial Procedure, statute or other law. Affidavits upon motions for summary judgment under IN ST TRIAL P Rule 56 and in denial of execution under IN ST TRIAL P Rule 9.2 shall be made upon personal knowledge. IN ST TRIAL P Rule 11(C).

f. *Signature, verification and other requirements.* Parties and their counsel are enjoined to comply with the verification requirements of IN ST TRIAL P Rule 11, and either the moving party or the party's attorney of record shall sign all pleadings and motions before filing with the Clerk of the Court. Every motion, petition, or other pleading filed with the Clerk shall contain the name, organization, physical address, telephone number, and facsimile number of the filing party or an attorney for that party. IN ST ST JOSEPH CIV Rule 201(201.3.6).

   i. The Clerk shall not accept any motion, petition, notice or other pleading or a CCS entry form for filing from an unrepresented litigant unless the unrepresented litigant's current address and phone number appear on the pleading, and an opposing party may service notices and responses on an unrepresented litigant at any address he or she has provided on a pleading. IN ST ST JOSEPH CIV Rule 201(201.3.6).

5. *Information excluded from public access.* Every document filed in a case shall separately identify information excluded from public access pursuant to IN ST ADMIN Rule 9(G)(1) as follows:

   a. Whole documents that are excluded from public access pursuant to IN ST ADMIN Rule 9(G)(1) shall be tendered on light green paper or have a light green coversheet attached to the document, marked "Not for Public Access" or "Confidential." IN ST TRIAL P Rule 5(G)(1).

   b. When only a portion of a document contains information excluded from public access pursuant to IN ST ADMIN Rule 9(G)(1), said information shall be omitted [or redacted] from the filed document, and set forth on a separate accompanying document on light green paper conspicuously marked "Not for Public Access" or "Confidential" and clearly designated [or identifying] the caption and number of the case and the document and location within the document to which the redacted material pertains. IN ST TRIAL P Rule 5(G)(2).

   c. With respect to documents filed in electronic format, the trial court, by local rule, may provide for compliance with IN ST TRIAL P Rule 5 in manner that separates and protects access to information excluded from public access. IN ST TRIAL P Rule 5(G)(3).

   d. IN ST TRIAL P Rule 5(G) does not apply to a record sealed by the court pursuant to IN ST 5-14-3-5.5 or otherwise, nor to records, documents, or information filed in cases to which public access is prohibited pursuant to IN ST ADMIN Rule 9(G). IN ST TRIAL P Rule 5(G)(4).

   e. The following information in case records is excluded from public access and is confidential:

      i. Information that is excluded from public access pursuant to federal law;

      ii. Information that is excluded from public access as declared confidential by Indiana statute or other court rule, including without limitation:

         • All adoption records created after July 8, 1941, as declared confidential by IN ST 31-19-19-1, et seq., except those specifically declared open by IN ST 31-19-13-2(2);

         • All records relating to chancroid, chlamydia, gonorrhea, hepatitis, human immunodeficiency virus (HIV), Lymphogranuloma venereum, syphilis, tuberculosis, as declared confidential by IN ST 16-41-8-1, et seq.;

         • All records relating to child abuse as declared confidential by IN ST 31-33-18-1, et seq.;

         • All records relating to drug tests as declared confidential by IN ST 5-14-3-4(a)(9);

         • Records of grand jury proceedings as declared confidential by IN ST 35-34-2-4;

         • Records of juvenile proceedings as declared confidential by IN ST 31-39-1-2, except those specifically open under statute;

         • All paternity records created after July 1, 1941 as declared confidential by IN ST 31-14-11-15, IN ST 31-19-5-23, IN ST 31-39-1-1 and IN ST 31-39-1-2 [Editor's note: IN ST 31-14-11-15 was repealed effective May 9, 2013];

         • All pre-sentence reports as declared confidential by IN ST 35-38-1-13;

         • Written petitions to permit marriages without consent and orders directing the Clerk of Court to issue a marriage license to underage persons, as declared confidential by IN ST 31-11-1-6;

- Only those arrest warrants, search warrants, indictments and informations ordered confidential by the trial judge, prior to return of duly executed service as declared confidential by IN ST 5-14-3-4(b)(1);

- All medical, mental health, or tax records unless determined by law or regulation of any governmental custodian not to be confidential, released by the subject of such records, or declared by a court of competent jurisdiction to be essential to the resolution of litigation as declared confidential by IN ST 16-39-3-10, IN ST 6-4.1-5-10, IN ST 6-4.1-12-12, and IN ST 6-8.1-7-1;

- Personal information relating to jurors or prospective jurors, other than for the use of the parties and counsel, pursuant to IN ST JURY Rule 10;

- Information relating to protection from abuse orders, no-contact orders and workplace violence restraining orders as declared confidential by IN ST 5-2-9-6, et seq.;

- Mediation proceedings pursuant to IN ST ADR Rule 2.11, Mini-Trial proceedings pursuant to IN ST ADR Rule 4.4(C), and Summary Jury Trials pursuant to IN ST ADR Rule 5.6;

- Information in probation files pursuant to the Probation Standards promulgated by the Judicial Conference of Indiana pursuant to IN ST 11-13-1-8(b);

- Information deemed confidential pursuant to the Rules for Court Administered Alcohol and Drug Programs promulgated by the Judicial Conference of Indiana pursuant to IN ST 12-23-14-13;

- Information deemed confidential pursuant to the Problem-Solving Court Rules promulgated by the Judicial Conference of Indiana pursuant to IN ST 33-23-16-16;

- All records of the Department of workforce Development as declared confidential by IN ST 22-4-19-6;

- Information regarding interception of electronic communications that is sealed or deemed confidential as set forth in IN ST 35-33.5-2-1, et seq.

iii. Information excluded from public access by specific court order;

iv. Complete Social Security Numbers of living persons;

v. With the exception of names, information such as addresses, phone numbers, and dates of birth which explicitly identifies:

- Natural persons who are witnesses or victims (not including defendants) in criminal, domestic violence, stalking, sexual assault, juvenile, or civil protection order proceedings, provided that juveniles who are victims of sex crimes shall be identified by initials only;

- Places of residence of judicial officers, clerks and other employees of courts and clerks of court, unless the person or persons about whom the information pertains waives confidentiality;

vi. Complete account numbers of specific assets, loans, bank accounts, credit cards, and personal identification numbers (PINs);

vii. All orders of expungement entered in criminal or juvenile proceedings, orders to restrict access to criminal history information pursuant to IN ST 35-38-5-5.5 or IN ST 35-38-8-5 and records excluded from public access by such orders, and information related to infractions that is excluded from public access pursuant to IN ST 34-28-5-15 or IN ST 34-28-5-16 [Editor's note: IN ST 35-38-5-5.5, IN ST 35-38-8-5 and IN ST 34-28-5-16 were repealed effective July 1, 2013; for information on orders restricting access to criminal history, refer to IN ST 35-38-9-1, et seq.];

viii. All personal notes and e-mail, and deliberative material, of judges, jurors, court staff and judicial agencies, and information recorded in personal data assistants (PDA's) or organizers and personal calendars. IN ST ADMIN Rule 9(G)(1).

F. Filing and Service Requirements

1. *Filing requirements.* Except as otherwise provided in IN ST TRIAL P Rule 5(E)(2), all pleadings and

papers subsequent to the complaint which are required to be served upon a party shall be filed with the Court either before service or within a reasonable period of time thereafter. IN ST TRIAL P Rule 5(E)(1).

a. *Non-filing of discovery until necessary*

    i. *Non-filing of discovery; Exceptions.* No deposition or request for discovery or response thereto under IN ST TRIAL P Rule 27, IN ST TRIAL P Rule 30, IN ST TRIAL P Rule 31, IN ST TRIAL P Rule 33, IN ST TRIAL P Rule 34 or IN ST TRIAL P Rule 36 shall be filed with the Court unless:

- A motion is filed pursuant to IN ST TRIAL P Rule 26(C) or IN ST TRIAL P Rule 37 and the original deposition or request for discovery or response thereto is necessary to enable the Court to rule; or

- A party desires to use the deposition or request for discovery or response thereto for evidentiary purposes at trial or in connection with a motion, and the Court, either upon its own motion or that of any party, or as a part of any pre-trial order, orders the filing of the original. IN ST TRIAL P Rule 5(E)(2).

    ii. *Custody of original and period of retention*

- The original of a deposition shall, subject to the provisions of IN ST TRIAL P Rule 30(E), be delivered by the reporter to the party taking it and shall be maintained by that party until filed with the Court pursuant to IN ST TRIAL P Rule 5(E)(2) or until the later of final judgment, agreed settlement of the litigation or all appellate rights have been exhausted. IN ST TRIAL P Rule 5(E)(3)(a).

- The original or any request for discovery or response thereto under IN ST TRIAL P Rule 27, IN ST TRIAL P Rule 30, IN ST TRIAL P Rule 31, IN ST TRIAL P Rule 33, IN ST TRIAL P Rule 34 and IN ST TRIAL P Rule 36 shall be maintained by the party originating the request or response until filed with the Court pursuant to IN ST TRIAL P Rule 5(E)(2) or until the later of final judgment, agreed settlement or all appellate rights have been exhausted. IN ST TRIAL P Rule 5(E)(3)(b).

    iii. *Original unavailable; Copies.* In the event it is made to appear to the satisfaction of the Court that the original of a deposition or request for discovery or response thereto cannot be filed with the Court when required, the Court may allow use of a copy instead of the original. IN ST TRIAL P Rule 5(E)(4).

    iv. *Filing as publication.* The filing of any deposition shall constitute publication. IN ST TRIAL P Rule 5(E)(5).

b. *Filing with the court defined.* The filing of pleadings, motions, and other papers with the court as required by the Indiana Rules of Trial Procedure shall be made by one of the following methods:

    i. Delivery to the clerk of the court;

    ii. Sending by electronic transmission under the procedure adopted pursuant to IN ST ADMIN Rule 12;

    iii. Mailing to the clerk by registered, certified or express mail return receipt requested;

    iv. Depositing with any third-party commercial carrier for delivery to the clerk within three (3) calendar days, cost prepaid, properly addressed;

    v. If the court so permits, filing with the judge, in which event the judge shall note thereon the filing date and forthwith transmit them to the office of the clerk; or

    vi. Electronic filing, as approved by the Division of State Court Administration pursuant to IN ST ADMIN Rule 16. IN ST TRIAL P Rule 5(F).

    vii. Filing by registered or certified mail and by third-party commercial carrier shall be complete upon mailing or deposit. IN ST TRIAL P Rule 5(F).

    viii. All pleadings shall be filed with the Clerk, not directly with the Court, unless otherwise required by the Indiana Rules of Court. The entry of appearances and the filing of pleadings or other matters not requiring immediate Court action shall be filed with the Clerk and not in open Court.

A Judge may permit papers to be filed in chambers, in which event he or she shall note thereon the filing date and transmit the papers to the Clerk. IN ST ST JOSEPH CIV Rule 201(201.2).

c. *Facsimile filing.* Unless otherwise authorized by IN ST ST JOSEPH ELECTRONIC Rule 701, electronic filing of pleadings by computerized or facsimile transmission is not permitted. IN ST ST JOSEPH CIV Rule 201(201.2).

d. *Additional copies.* In cases in which a party or counsel supplies the proposed order or decree, a sufficient number shall be prepared and filed as to provide the Clerk to retain two (2) copies, which shall be filed in the flat file and the record of judgments and orders. Should the party or counsel desire additional copies, a sufficient number of copies should be filed to effectuate that purpose. IN ST ST JOSEPH CIV Rule 201(201.6).

e. *Proof of filing.* Any party filing any paper by any method other than personal delivery to the clerk shall retain proof of filing. IN ST TRIAL P Rule 5(F).

2. *Service requirements.* Unless otherwise provided by the Indiana Rules of Trial Procedure or an order of the court, each party and special judge, if any, shall be served with: (1) every order required by its terms to be served; (2) every pleading subsequent to the original complaint; (3) every written motion except one which may be heard ex parte; (4) every brief submitted to the trial court; (5) every paper relating to discovery required to be served upon a party; and (6) every written notice, appearance, demand, offer of judgment, designation of record on appeal, or similar paper. IN ST TRIAL P Rule 5(A).

a. *Service generally.* Every motion, petition, notice, or other pleading required to be served by IN ST TRIAL P Rule 5 shall be served on all counsel of record or unrepresented parties either before it is filed or on the day it is filed with the Court, and the date of filing shall be indicated on the Certificate of Service. IN ST ST JOSEPH CIV Rule 201(201.5.1).

   i. *Copy.* A copy of the Clerk's CCS entry form of the filing shall also be served on all counsel of record or unrepresented parties whenever it contains an appearance of counsel or contains a date for Court hearing on the matter. IN ST ST JOSEPH CIV Rule 201(201.5.1).

b. *Methods of service*

   i. *Personal service.* Whenever a party is represented by an attorney of record, service shall be made upon such attorney unless service upon the party himself is ordered by the court. Service upon the attorney or party shall be made by delivering or mailing a copy of the papers to the last known address or where an attorney or party has consented to service by fax or e-mail, as provided in IN ST TRIAL P Rule 3.1(A)(4), by faxing or e-mailing a copy of the documents to the fax number or e-mail address set out in the appearance form or correction as required by IN ST TRIAL P Rule 3.1(E). IN ST TRIAL P Rule 5(B). Delivery of a copy within IN ST TRIAL P Rule 5 means:

   - Offering or tendering it to the attorney or party and stating the nature of the papers being served. Refusal to accept an offered or tendered document is a waiver of any objection to the sufficiency or adequacy of service of that document;

   - Leaving it at his office with a clerk or other person in charge thereof, or if there is no one in charge, leaving it in a conspicuous place therein; or

   - If the office is closed, by leaving it at his dwelling house or usual place of abode with some person of suitable age and discretion then residing therein; or,

   - Leaving it at some other suitable place, selected by the attorney upon whom service is being made, pursuant to duly promulgated local rule. IN ST TRIAL P Rule 5(B)(1).

   ii. *Service by the clerk.* Whenever the Clerk is required by rule or statute to give notice, the party or parties requesting such notice shall furnish the Clerk with sufficient copies of the notice to be given, along with stamped, addressed envelopes with the names and the addresses of the parties or their counsel to whom such notice is to be given. IN ST ST JOSEPH CIV Rule 201(201.5.4).

   iii. *Service on the court.* Service on a Judge may be made by delivering a copy to the Judge's secretary or mailing a copy to the Judge at his or her chambers. Service on a Judge may not be accomplished by facsimile transmission; however, a courtesy copy may be sent to the Judge's chambers by electronic mail or facsimile transmission contemporaneously with service by mail or otherwise. IN ST ST JOSEPH CIV Rule 201(201.5.5).

iv. *Service by mail.* If service is made by mail, the papers shall be deposited in the United States mail addressed to the person on whom they are being served, with postage prepaid. Service shall be deemed complete upon mailing. Proof of service of all papers permitted to be mailed may be made by written acknowledgment of service, by affidavit of the person who mailed the papers, or by certificate of an attorney. It shall be the duty of attorneys when entering their appearance in a cause or when filing pleadings or papers therein, to have noted in the Chronological Case Summary or said pleadings or papers so filed the address and telephone number of their office. Service by delivery or by mail at such address shall be deemed sufficient and complete. IN ST TRIAL P Rule 5(B)(2).

v. *Service by fax or e-mail.* A party who has consented to service by fax or e-mail may be served as follows:

- Service by e-mail shall be made by attaching the document being served in .pdf format. Discovery documents must also be served in accordance with IN ST TRIAL P Rule 26(A). IN ST TRIAL P Rule 5(B)(3)(a).

- Service by fax shall be deemed complete upon generation of a transmission record indicating the successful transmission of the entire document, except as provided in IN ST TRIAL P Rule 5(B)(3)(d). IN ST TRIAL P Rule 5(B)(3)(b).

- Service by e-mail shall be deemed complete upon transmission, except as provided in IN ST TRIAL P Rule 5(B)(3)(d). IN ST TRIAL P Rule 5(B)(3)(c).

- Service by fax or e-mail that occurs on a Saturday, Sunday, legal holiday, or day the court or agency in which the matter is pending is closed or after 5:00 PM local time of the recipient shall be deemed complete the next day that is not a Saturday, Sunday, legal holiday, or day that the court or agency in which the matter is pending is not closed. IN ST TRIAL P Rule 5(B)(3)(d).

vi. *Additional service of electronic discovery.* In addition to service under Rule IN ST TRIAL P Rule 5(B) or a .pdf format electronic copy, a party propounding or responding to interrogatories, requests for production or requests for admission shall comply with IN ST TRIAL P Rule 26(A.1)(a) or IN ST TRIAL P Rule 26(A.1)(b). IN ST TRIAL P Rule 26(A.1).

- The party shall serve the discovery request or response in an electronic format (either on a disk or as an electronic document attachment) in any commercially available word processing software system. If transmitted on disk, each disk shall be labeled, identifying the caption of the case, the document, and the word processing version in which it is being submitted. If more than one (1) disk is used for the same document, each disk shall be labeled and also shall be sequentially numbered. If transmitted by electronic mail, the document must be accompanied by electronic memorandum providing the forgoing identifying information; or

- The party shall serve the opposing party with a verified statement that the attorney or party appealing pro se lacks the equipment and is unable to transmit the discovery as required by IN ST TRIAL P Rule 26(A.1). IN ST TRIAL P Rule 26(A.1).

c. *Serving numerous defendants.* In any action in which there are unusually large numbers of defendants, the court, upon motion or of its own initiative, may order:

i. That service of the pleadings of the defendants and replies thereto need not be made as between the defendants;

- That any cross-claim, counterclaim, or matter constituting an avoidance or affirmative defense contained therein shall be deemed to be denied or avoided by all other parties; and

- That the filing of any such pleading and service thereof upon the plaintiff constitutes due notice of it to the parties. IN ST TRIAL P Rule 5(D).

ii. A copy of every such order shall be served upon the parties in such manner and form as the court directs. IN ST TRIAL P Rule 5(D).

d. *Service on parties in default for failure to appear.* No service need be made on parties in default for failure to appear, except that pleadings asserting new or additional claims for relief against them shall be served upon them in the manner provided by service of summons in IN ST TRIAL P Rule 4. IN ST TRIAL P Rule 5(A).

e. *Distribution.* Counsel or an unrepresented party submitting a motion, petition, notice, pleading or proposed order shall indicate the method of distribution desired on the Clerk's CCS entry form. The Clerk will not return or distribute copies of motions, petitions, pleadings, notices or proposed orders, other than those originated by the Court, by mail unless the Clerk is provided with stamped, addressed envelopes. IN ST ST JOSEPH CIV Rule 201(201.5.3).

f. *Mailbox.* As a matter of convenience to attorneys, each court provides a mailbox for the distribution filings and orders generated by the Court, and it is the responsibility of each attorney to periodically check these mailboxes for service and distribution of court-generated filings and orders. IN ST ST JOSEPH CIV Rule 201(201.5.3).

G. Hearings

1. The Indiana rules do not contemplate a hearing related to the filing and service of requests for admissions.

H. Forms

1. Request for Admissions Forms for Indiana

a. Request for admission. 5 INPRAC § 4:4.1.

b. Response to request for admission. 5 INPRAC § 4:4.2.

c. Response to request for admission; Alternative form. 5 INPRAC § 4:4.3.

d. Motion for order that matter be deemed admitted. 5 INPRAC § 4:4.4.

e. Requests for admission; General form. 10 INPRAC § 69.6.

f. Requests for admission; Genuineness of document. 10 INPRAC § 69.7.

g. Requests for admission; Specific document and matters related thereto; Insurance contract. 10 INPRAC § 69.8.

h. Requests for admission; Action against bank. 10 INPRAC § 69.9.

i. Requests for admission; Automobile accident. 10 INPRAC § 69.10.

j. Requests for admission; Automobile accident; Respondeat superior. 10 INPRAC § 69.11.

k. Requests for admission; Action on account stated. 10 INPRAC § 69.12.

l. Requests for admission; Action to foreclose on mortgage. 10 INPRAC § 69.13.

m. Requests for admission; Action for attorney malpractice. 10 INPRAC § 69.14.

n. Requests for admission; Products liability action; Defective hair products; Defendants. 10 INPRAC § 69.15.

o. Response to requests for admission; General form. 10 INPRAC § 69.20.

p. Alternative responses to requests for admission. 10 INPRAC § 69.21.

q. Motion for enlargement of time to respond to requests for admission. 10 INPRAC § 69.22.

r. Motion to withdraw and amend response to requests for admission. 10 INPRAC § 69.23.

s. Order granting motion to withdraw and amend responses. 10 INPRAC § 69.24.

t. Motion for order that matter be deemed admitted. 10 INPRAC § 69.25.

u. Motion for order requiring party to pay expenses for refusal to admit matters. 10 INPRAC § 69.26.

I. Checklist

(I) ❑ Matters to be considered by the party serving the request

    (a) ❑ Required documents

        (1) ❑ Request for admissions

    (2) ❑ Copies of documents

    (3) ❑ Certificate of service

 (b) ❑ Supplemental documents

    (1) ❑ Stipulation regarding discovery procedure

    (2) ❑ Facsimile cover sheet

 (c) ❑ Timing

    (1) ❑ The request may, without leave of court, be served upon the plaintiff after commencement of the action and upon any other party with or after service of the summons and complaint upon that party

(II) ❑ Matters to be considered by the responding party

 (a) ❑ Required documents

    (1) ❑ Response to request for admissions

    (2) ❑ Certificate of service

 (b) ❑ Supplemental documents

    (1) ❑ Stipulation regarding discovery procedure

    (2) ❑ Facsimile cover sheet

 (c) ❑ Timing

    (1) ❑ The matter is admitted unless, within a period designated in the request, not less than thirty (30) days after service thereof or within such shorter or longer time as the court may allow, the party to whom the request is directed serves upon the party requesting the admission a written answer or objection addressed to the matter

Requests, Notices and Applications
Notice of Deposition

Document Last Updated October 2013

A. Applicable Rules

1. *State rules*

   a. Appearance. IN ST TRIAL P Rule 3.1.

   b. Process. IN ST TRIAL P Rule 4.

   c. Service and filing of pleadings and other papers. IN ST TRIAL P Rule 5.

   d. Time. IN ST TRIAL P Rule 6.

   e. Pleadings. IN ST TRIAL P Rule 7; IN ST TRIAL P Rule 9.2; IN ST TRIAL P Rule 10.

   f. Signing and verification of pleadings. IN ST TRIAL P Rule 11.

   g. Parties plaintiff and defendant; Capacity. IN ST TRIAL P Rule 17.

   h. General provisions governing discovery. IN ST TRIAL P Rule 26.

   i. Discovery methods. IN ST TRIAL P Rule 27; IN ST TRIAL P Rule 28; IN ST TRIAL P Rule 29; IN ST TRIAL P Rule 30; IN ST TRIAL P Rule 31; IN ST TRIAL P Rule 32; IN ST TRIAL P Rule 33; IN ST TRIAL P Rule 34; IN ST TRIAL P Rule 35; IN ST TRIAL P Rule 36.

   j. Failure to make or cooperate in discovery; Sanctions. IN ST TRIAL P Rule 37.

   k. Evidence. IN ST TRIAL P Rule 43.

   l. Subpoena. IN ST TRIAL P Rule 45.

   m. Judgment on the evidence (directed verdict). IN ST TRIAL P Rule 50.

n. Findings by the court. IN ST TRIAL P Rule 52.

o. Summary judgment. IN ST TRIAL P Rule 56.

p. Motion to correct error. IN ST TRIAL P Rule 59.

q. Relief from judgment or order. IN ST TRIAL P Rule 60.

r. Recording machines; Court reports; Stenographic report or transcript as evidence. IN ST TRIAL P Rule 74.

s. Access to court records. IN ST ADMIN Rule 9.

t. Paper size. IN ST ADMIN Rule 11.

u. Facsimile transmission. IN ST ADMIN Rule 12.

v. Electronic filing and electronic service pilot projects. IN ST ADMIN Rule 16.

w. Sealing of certain records by court; Hearing; Notice. IN ST 5-14-3-5.5.

x. Sixtieth judicial circuit. IN ST 33-33-71-2.

y. Privacy and confidentiality. IN ST 5-2-9-6; IN ST 5-14-3-4; IN ST 6-4.1-5-10; IN ST 6-4.1-12-12; IN ST 6-8.1-7-1; IN ST 11-13-1-8; IN ST 12-23-14-13; IN ST 16-39-3-10; IN ST 16-41-8-1; IN ST 22-4-19-6; IN ST 31-11-1-6; IN ST 31-19-5-23; IN ST 31-19-13-2; IN ST 31-19-19-1; IN ST 31-33-18-1; IN ST 31-39-1-1; IN ST 31-39-1-2; IN ST 33-23-16-16; IN ST 35-34-2-4; IN ST 35-38-1-13; IN ST 35-38-9-1; IN ST ADR Rule 2.11; IN ST ADR Rule 4.4; IN ST ADR Rule 5.6; IN ST JURY Rule 10.

2. *Local rules*

a. Filing, pleading, and motions. IN ST ST JOSEPH CIV Rule 201.

b. Uniform court and case number designation. IN ST ST JOSEPH CIV Rule 202.

c. Discovery requests. IN ST ST JOSEPH CIV Rule 208.

d. Pre-trial procedures. IN ST ST JOSEPH CIV Rule 209.

e. Proposed order. IN ST ST JOSEPH CIV Rule 213.

f. Electronic filing of cases in St. Joseph County. IN ST ST JOSEPH ELECTRONIC Rule 701.

B. Timing

1. *Time for notice of deposition*

a. *Scheduling of depositions.* Pursuant to their obligations under the Indiana Rules of Professional Conduct and as officers of the St. Joseph Circuit, Superior or Probate courts, attorneys shall make a good faith effort to schedule depositions in a manner in which avoids scheduling conflicts. Unless agreed by counsel or otherwise authorized by the court, no deposition shall be scheduled on less than ten (10) days notice. IN ST ST JOSEPH CIV Rule 208(208.4).

b. *Depositions upon oral examination.* After commencement of the action, any party may take the testimony of any person, including a party, by deposition upon oral examination. IN ST TRIAL P Rule 30(A).

   i. A party desiring to take the deposition of any person upon oral examination shall give reasonable notice in writing to every other party to the action. IN ST TRIAL P Rule 30(B)(1).

   • The party who gives notice of taking a deposition must do so in a way which is sufficiently timely to permit the party who receives the notice to make arrangements to travel to the place where the deposition is to be taken, and the notice which is given must be in sufficient time to permit the party to seek a protective order under IN ST TRIAL P Rule 30(D) and IN ST TRIAL P Rule 26(C), if necessary. 2A INPRAC R 30(30.2).

   ii. Leave of court, granted with or without notice, must be obtained only if the plaintiff seeks to take a deposition prior to the expiration of twenty (20) days after service of summons and complaint upon any defendant except that leave is not required:

   • If a defendant has served a notice of taking deposition or otherwise sought discovery; or

- If special notice is given as provided in IN ST TRIAL P Rule 30(B)(2). IN ST TRIAL P Rule 30(A).

   iii.   The court may for cause shown enlarge or shorten the time for taking the deposition. IN ST TRIAL P Rule 30(B)(3).

  c. *Depositions upon written questions.* After commencement of the action, any party may take the testimony of any person, including a party, by deposition upon written questions. IN ST TRIAL P Rule 31(A).

    i.   *Service of cross questions.* Within twenty (20) days after the notice and written questions are served, a party may serve cross questions upon all other parties. IN ST TRIAL P Rule 31(A).

    ii.   *Service of redirect questions.* Within ten (10) days after being served with cross questions, a party may serve redirect questions upon all other parties. IN ST TRIAL P Rule 31(A).

   iii.   *Service of recross questions.* Within ten (10) days after being served with redirect questions, a party may serve recross questions upon all other parties. IN ST TRIAL P Rule 31(A).

   iv.   *Time to respond.* The court may for cause shown enlarge or shorten the time. IN ST TRIAL P Rule 31(A).

  d. *For deposition before action.* At least twenty (20) days before the date of hearing the notice shall be served in the manner provided in IN ST TRIAL P Rule 4 for service of summons; but if such service cannot with due diligence be made upon any expected adverse party named in the petition, the court may make such order as is just for service by publication or otherwise, and shall appoint, for persons not served in the manner provided in IN ST TRIAL P Rule 4, an attorney who shall represent them, and, in case they are not otherwise represented, shall cross-examine the deponent. If any expected adverse party is a minor or incompetent the provisions of IN ST TRIAL P Rule 17(C) apply. IN ST TRIAL P Rule 27(A)(2).

    i.   Refer to the Indiana KeyRules Complaint document for information regarding service under IN ST TRIAL P Rule 4.

  e. *For deposition pending appeal.* The party who desires to perpetuate the testimony may make a motion in the court for leave to take the depositions, upon the same notice and service thereof as if the action was pending in the court. IN ST TRIAL P Rule 27(B).

    i.   *Filing.* All pleadings and papers subsequent to the complaint which are required to be served upon a party shall be filed with the Court either before service or within a reasonable period of time thereafter. IN ST TRIAL P Rule 5(E)(1).

    ii.   *Service.* A written motion, other than one which may be heard ex parte, and notice of the hearing thereof shall be served not less than five (5) days before the time specified for the hearing, unless a different period is fixed by the Indiana Rules of Trial Procedure or by order of the court. IN ST TRIAL P Rule 6(D).

- *Of supporting affidavits.* When a motion is supported by affidavit, the affidavit shall be served with the motion. IN ST TRIAL P Rule 6(D).

2. *Completion of discovery pursuant to pretrial scheduling order.* In cases in which a preliminary pre-trial conference has been held under Rule 12(B) [Editor's note: this is likely supposed to be a reference to IN ST TRIAL P Rule 16(B)], discovery shall be made in accordance with the scheduling thereof then ordered. In cases in which no preliminary pre-trial conference has been held, all discovery shall be completed prior to the pre-trial conference and no discovery shall be conducted thereafter unless, upon motion or stipulation showing good cause therefore, an order is entered permitting further discovery within time to be prescribed by the Court. IN ST ST JOSEPH CIV Rule 209(209.5).

3. *Computation of time*

  a. *Generally; Days excluded.* In computing any period of time prescribed or allowed by the Indiana Rules of Trial Procedure, by order of the court, or by any applicable statute, the day of the act, event, or default from which the designated period of time begins to run shall not be included. The last day of the period so computed is to be included unless it is:

    i.   A Saturday,

    ii.   A Sunday,

    iii. A legal holiday as defined by state statute, or

    iv. A day the office in which the act is to be done is closed during regular business hours. IN ST TRIAL P Rule 6(A).

b.   *Short periods.* In any event, the period runs until the end of the next day that is not a Saturday, a Sunday, a legal holiday, or a day on which the office is closed. When the period of time allowed is less than seven (7) days, intermediate Saturdays, Sundays, legal holidays, and days on which the office is closed shall be excluded from the computations. IN ST TRIAL P Rule 6(A).

c.   *Additional time after service by United States mail.* Whenever a party has the right or is required to do some act or take some proceedings within a prescribed period after the service of a notice or other paper upon him and the notice or paper is served upon him by United States mail, three (3) days shall be added to the prescribed period. IN ST TRIAL P Rule 6(E).

d.   *Enlargement of time.* When an act is required or allowed to be done at or within a specific time by the Indiana Rules of Trial Procedure, the court may at any time for cause shown:

    i.   Order the period enlarged, with or without motion or notice, if request therefor is made before the expiration of the period originally prescribed or extended by a previous order; or

    ii. Upon motion made after the expiration of the specific period, permit the act to be done where the failure to act was the result of excusable neglect; but, the court may not extend the time for taking any action for judgment on the evidence under IN ST TRIAL P Rule 50(A), amendment of findings and judgment under IN ST TRIAL P Rule 52(B), to correct errors under IN ST TRIAL P Rule 59(C), statement in opposition to motion to correct error under IN ST TRIAL P Rule 59(E), or to obtain relief from final judgment under IN ST TRIAL P Rule 60(B), except to the extent and under the conditions stated in those rules. IN ST TRIAL P Rule 6(B).

    iii. An initial written motion for enlargement of time pursuant to IN ST TRIAL P Rule 6(B)(1) to answer a claim shall be routinely granted for an additional thirty (30) days from the original due date or other period the assigned Judge deems reasonable by written order of the Court. The motion must be filed on or before the original due date or IN ST ST JOSEPH CIV Rule 201 shall be inapplicable. IN ST ST JOSEPH CIV Rule 201(201.9.5).

- Any motion for enlargement of time shall state the date when such response is due and the date to which time is requested to be enlarged. IN ST ST JOSEPH CIV Rule 201(201.9.5).

- All subsequent motions for enlargement of time shall be so designated and will only be granted for good cause shown or in the interest of justice. IN ST ST JOSEPH CIV Rule 201(201.9.5).

C. General Requirements

1.   *Scope of discovery.* Unless otherwise limited by order of the court in accordance with the Indiana Rules of Trial Procedure, the scope of discovery is as follows:

a.   *In general.* Parties may obtain discovery regarding any matter, not privileged, which is relevant to the subject-matter involved in the pending action, whether it relates to the claim or defense of the party seeking discovery or the claim or defense of any other party, including the existence, description, nature, custody, condition and location of any books, documents, or other tangible things and the identity and location of persons having knowledge of any discoverable matter. It is not ground for objection that the information sought will be inadmissible at the trial if the information sought appears reasonably calculated to lead to the discovery of admissible evidence. IN ST TRIAL P Rule 26(B)(1).

    i.   *Limiting discovery upon court determination.* The frequency or extent of use of the discovery methods otherwise permitted under the Indiana Rules of Trial Procedure and by any local rule shall be limited by the court if it determines that:

- The discovery sought is unreasonably cumulative or duplicative, or is obtainable from some other source that is more convenient, less burdensome, or less expensive;

- The party seeking discovery has had ample opportunity by discovery in the action to obtain the information sought or;

- The burden or expense of the proposed discovery outweighs its likely benefit, taking into account the needs of the case, the amount in controversy, the parties' resources, the importance of the issues at stake in the litigation, and the importance of the proposed discovery in resolving the issues. IN ST TRIAL P Rule 26(B)(1).

- The court may act upon its own initiative after reasonable notice or pursuant to a motion under IN ST TRIAL P Rule 26(C). IN ST TRIAL P Rule 26(B)(1). Refer to the Indiana KeyRules Motion for Protective Order document for more information.

ii. *Relevancy in the discovery context.* When the word "relevancy" is used in IN ST TRIAL P Rule 26(B), it does not mean "relevancy" as that word in used to determine the admissibility of evidence in a trial court. It is much broader. It means "relevancy" to the "subject matter" of the litigation or pending action and it may relate to the claim or defense of any party. Pretrial discovery is available as to any nonprivileged matter relevant to the subject matter of the lawsuit or to obtain information reasonably calculated to lead to admissible evidence. 2A INPRAC R 26(26.4); Kaufmann v. Credithrift Financial, Inc., 465 N.E.2d 207, 210 (Ind.Ct.App. 1984).

iii. *Tests for relevance.* Indiana case law has developed two (2) additional tests in this area. 2A INPRAC R 26(26.4).

- The first test determines when a document or a request for information is actually relevant to the subject matter in the pending action. A document [or discovery request] is relevant to discovery if there is the possibility the information sought may be relevant to the subject matter of the action. 2A INPRAC R 26(26.4); CIGNA-INA/Aetna v. Hagerman-Shambaugh, 473 N.E.2d 1033, 1036 (Ind.Ct.App. 1985).

- The second test speaks to appellate review of the trial court's determination that a document or discovery request is relevant to the subject matter of the pending action. The appellate court sees its review of the trial court's decision on relevancy to subject matter as being very limited. The court states: "Our review of the trial court's conclusion that the documents are relevant is limited. A trial court is vested with discretion in its rulings on discovery issues." 2A INPRAC R 26(26.4); Costanzi v. Ryan, 175 Ind.App. 257, 370 N.E.2d 1333 (Ind.Ct.App. 1978).

b. *Insurance agreements.* A party may obtain discovery of the existence and contents of any insurance agreement under which any person carrying on an insurance business may be liable to satisfy part or all of a judgment which may be entered in the action or to indemnify or reimburse for payments made to satisfy the judgment. Information concerning the insurance agreement is not by reason of disclosure admissible in evidence at trial. For purposes of IN ST TRIAL P Rule 26(B)(2), an application for insurance shall not be treated as part of an insurance agreement. IN ST TRIAL P Rule 26(B)(2).

c. *Trial preparation; Materials.* Subject to the provisions of IN ST TRIAL P Rule 26(B)(4), a party may obtain discovery of documents and tangible things otherwise discoverable under IN ST TRIAL P Rule 26(B)(1) and prepared in anticipation of litigation or for trial by or for another party or by or for that other party's representative (including his attorney, consultant, surety, indemnitor, insurer, or agent) only upon a showing that the party seeking discovery has substantial need of the materials in the preparation of his case and that he is unable without undue hardship to obtain the substantial equivalent of the materials by other means. In ordering discovery of such materials when the required showing has been made, the court shall protect against disclosure of the mental impressions, conclusions, opinions, or legal theories of an attorney or other representative of a party concerning the litigation. IN ST TRIAL P Rule 26(B)(3).

i. A party may obtain without the required showing a statement concerning the action or its subject matter previously made by that party. Upon request, a person not a party may obtain without the required showing a statement concerning the action or its subject matter previously made by that person. If the request is refused, the person may move for a court order. The provisions of IN ST TRIAL P Rule 37(A)(4) apply to the award of expenses incurred in relation to the motion. For purposes of IN ST TRIAL P Rule 26(B)(3), a statement previously made is:

- A written statement signed or otherwise adopted approved by the person making it, or

- A stenographic, mechanical, electrical, or other recording, or a transcription thereof, which is a substantially verbatim recital of an oral statement by the person making it and contemporaneously recorded. IN ST TRIAL P Rule 26(B)(3).

ii. The protection of IN ST TRIAL P Rule 26(B)(3) extends to material prepared or collected before litigation actually commences, but that some possibility of litigation must actually exist before the privilege and IN ST TRIAL P Rule 26(B)(3) become operative. 2A INPRAC R 26(26.9).

d. *Trial preparation; Experts.* Discovery of facts known and opinions held by experts, otherwise discoverable under the provisions of IN ST TRIAL P Rule 26(B)(1) and acquired or developed in anticipation of litigation or for trial, may be obtained as follows:

  i. A party may through interrogatories require any other party to identify each person whom the other party expects to call as an expert witness at trial, to state the subject matter on which the expert is expected to testify, and to state the substance of the facts and opinions to which the expert is expected to testify and a summary of the grounds for each opinion. IN ST TRIAL P Rule 26(B)(4)(a)(i).

  ii. Upon motion, the court may order further discovery by other means, subject to such restrictions as to scope and such provisions, pursuant to IN ST TRIAL P Rule 26(B)(4)(c), concerning fees and expenses as the court may deem appropriate. IN ST TRIAL P Rule 26(B)(4)(a)(ii).

  iii. A party may discover facts known or opinions held by an expert who has been retained or specially employed by another party in anticipation of litigation or preparation for trial and who is not expected to be called as a witness at trial, only as provided in IN ST TRIAL P Rule 35(B) or upon a showing of exceptional circumstances under which it is impracticable for the party seeking discovery to obtain facts or opinions on the same subject by other means. IN ST TRIAL P Rule 26(B)(4)(b).

  iv. Unless manifest injustice would result,

    - The court shall require that the party seeking discovery pay the expert a reasonable fee for time spent in responding to discovery under IN ST TRIAL P Rule 26(B)(4)(a)(ii) and IN ST TRIAL P Rule 26(B)(4)(b); and

    - With respect to discovery obtained under IN ST TRIAL P Rule 26(B)(4)(a)(ii) the court may require, and with respect to discovery obtained under IN ST TRIAL P Rule 26(B)(4)(b) the court shall require, the party seeking discovery to pay the other party a fair portion of the fees and expenses reasonably incurred by the latter party in obtaining facts and opinions from the expert. IN ST TRIAL P Rule 26(B)(4).

e. *Claims of privilege or protection*

  i. *Information withheld.* When a party withholds information otherwise discoverable under the Indiana Rules of Trial Procedure by claiming that it is privileged or subject to protection as trial preparation material, the party shall make the claim expressly and shall describe the nature of the documents, communications, or things not produced or disclosed in a manner that, without revealing information itself privileged or protected, will enable other parties to assess the applicability of the privilege or protection. IN ST TRIAL P Rule 26(B)(5)(a).

  ii. *Information produced.* If information is produced in discovery that is subject to a claim of privilege or protection as trial-preparation material, the party making the claim may notify any party that received the information of the claim and the basis for it. After being notified, a party must promptly return, sequester, or destroy the specified information and any copies it has and may not use or disclose the information until the claim is resolved. A receiving party may promptly present the information to the court under seal for a determination of the claim. If the receiving party disclosed the information before being notified, it must take reasonable steps to retrieve it. The producing party must preserve the information until the claim is resolved. IN ST TRIAL P Rule 26(B)(5)(b).

  iii. *Waiver.* The law of discovery has developed some holdings which indicate that "waiver" of a privileged communication in a discovery setting might be more exacting than "waiver" of a privileged communication when the only question at hand is an interpretation of the privilege itself. Thus, in litigation in which several documents are in issue, and some are released inadvertently, there is strong case law that holds that the "inadvertent production" of a privileged document does not constitute a waiver of the attorney-client privilege. 2A INPRAC R 26(26.5); Transamerica Computer Co. v. International Business Machines Corp., 573 F.2d 646 (9th Cir. 1978). Such a rule should be measured against the usual rule which suggests that a voluntary disclosure to a third person will generally suffice to show a waiver of the attorney-client privilege. 2A INPRAC R 26(26.5).

f. *Use not limited.* Unless the court orders otherwise under IN ST TRIAL P Rule 26(C), the frequency of use of the methods listed in IN ST TRIAL P Rule 26(A) is not limited. IN ST TRIAL P Rule 26(A).

g. *Sequence of discovery.* Unless the court upon motion, for the convenience of parties and witnesses and in the interests of justice, orders otherwise, methods of discovery may be used in any sequence and the fact that a party is conducting discovery, whether by deposition or otherwise, shall not operate to delay any other party's discovery. IN ST TRIAL P Rule 26(D).

h. *Discovery disputes.* To promote the orderly and expeditious handling of cases to trial readiness, counsel shall attempt in good faith to resolve all disagreements between or among themselves concerning the necessity for and scope of discovery, the necessity to seek sanctions, and/or protection against discovery under IN ST TRIAL P Rule 26 through IN ST TRIAL P Rule 37. IN ST ST JOSEPH CIV Rule 208(208.5).

   i. After personal consultation and good faith attempts to resolve differences as to the foregoing matters, counsel for any or all parties may move to compel discovery, invoke sanctions, or seek protection against discovery as aforesaid. IN ST ST JOSEPH CIV Rule 208(208.5).

   ii. As a part of such motion, the party shall recite the date, time, and place of the personal consultations and the names of the participants. If counsel for any party advises the Court in writing that counsel for any other party has refused or delayed consultation hereby contemplated, the Court shall take such action as is appropriate to preclude, obviate, or avoid further delay. IN ST ST JOSEPH CIV Rule 208(208.5).

2. *Depositions upon oral examination.* IN ST TRIAL P Rule 30 provides for the pre-trial deposition on oral examination of a party, or a witness who is not a party. 2A INPRAC R 30(30.1).

a. *Generally.* The deposition may be used to narrow issues, or to create and enlarge them. It will eliminate matters that are not disputed among the parties; it might introduce new issues and questions which become disputed. The range and purpose of the deposition's use is almost limitless, as long as it is taken consistent with IN ST TRIAL P Rule 26 and IN ST TRIAL P Rule 30 and the principles of IN ST TRIAL P Rule 32. The deposition may obtain evidence that is admissible at trial; it may go quite beyond admissibility at trial if the area of investigation is relevant to the subject matter of the case under IN ST TRIAL P Rule 26. It can disclose the existence and availability of facts that may lead to evidence which may be used at trial. 2A INPRAC R 30(30.1).

b. *Notice*

   i. *Contents of notice.* The notice shall state the time and place for taking the deposition and the name and address of each person to be examined, if known, and if the name is not known, a general description sufficient to identify him or the particular class or group to which he belongs. If a subpoena duces tecum is to be served on the person to be examined, a designation of the materials to be produced thereunder shall be attached to or included in the notice. IN ST TRIAL P Rule 30(B)(1).

   ii. *Circumstances where leave of court required.* Leave of court, when required by IN ST TRIAL P Rule 30(A) is not required for the taking of a deposition by plaintiff if the notice:

   - States that the person to be examined is about to go out of the state or will be unavailable for examination unless his deposition is taken before expiration of the twenty (20) day period; and

   - Sets forth facts to support the statement. IN ST TRIAL P Rule 30(B)(2).

   iii. *Signature on notice.* The plaintiff's attorney shall sign the notice, and his signature constitutes a certification by him that to the best of his knowledge, information, and belief the statement and supporting facts are true. The sanctions provided by IN ST TRIAL P Rule 11 are applicable to the certification. IN ST TRIAL P Rule 30(B).

    iv. *Manner of recording.* If a party taking a deposition wishes to have the testimony recorded other than in a manner provided in IN ST TRIAL P Rule 74, the notice shall specify the manner of recording and preserving the deposition. The court may require stenographic taking or make any other order to assure that the recorded testimony will be accurate and trustworthy. IN ST TRIAL P Rule 30(B)(4).

    v. *Organization as deponent; Designation.* A party may in his notice name as the deponent an organization, including without limitation a governmental organization, or a partnership and designate with reasonable particularity the matters on which examination is requested. The organization so named shall designate one or more officers, directors, or managing agents, executive officers, or other persons duly authorized and consenting to testify on its behalf. The persons so designated shall testify as to matters known or available to the organization. IN ST TRIAL P Rule 30(B)(6) does not preclude taking a deposition by any other procedure authorized in the Indiana Rules of Trial Procedure. IN ST TRIAL P Rule 30(B)(6).

c. *Improper service of notice.* If any party shows that when he was served with notice under IN ST TRIAL P Rule 30(B)(2) he was unable through the exercise of diligence to obtain counsel to represent him at the taking of the deposition, the deposition may not be used against him. IN ST TRIAL P Rule 30(B).

d. *Examination and cross-examination; Record of examination; Oath; Objections.* Examination and cross-examination of witnesses may proceed as permitted at the trial under the provisions of IN ST TRIAL P Rule 43(B). The officer before whom the deposition is to be taken shall put the witness on oath and shall personally, or by someone acting under his direction and in his presence, record the testimony of the witness. The testimony shall be taken stenographically or recorded by any other means designated in accordance with IN ST TRIAL P Rule 30(B)(4). If requested by one of the parties, the testimony shall be transcribed. IN ST TRIAL P Rule 30(C).

    i. *Objections*

- All objections made at the time of the examination to the qualifications of the officer taking the deposition, or to the manner of taking it, or to the evidence presented, or to the conduct of any party, and any other objection to the proceedings, shall be noted by the officer upon the deposition. IN ST TRIAL P Rule 30(C).

- When there is an objection to a question, the objection and reason therefor shall be noted, and the question shall be answered unless the attorney instructs the deponent not to answer, or the deponent refuses to answer, in which case either party may have the question certified by the Reporter, and the question with the objection thereto when so certified shall be delivered to the party requesting the certification who may then proceed under IN ST TRIAL P Rule 37(A). IN ST TRIAL P Rule 30(C).

- In lieu of participating in the oral examination, parties may serve written questions on the party taking the deposition and require him to transmit them to the officer, who shall propound them to the witness and record the answers verbatim. IN ST TRIAL P Rule 30(C).

e. *Motion to terminate or limit examination.* At any time during the taking of the deposition, on motion of any party or of the deponent and upon a showing that the examination is being conducted in bad faith or in such manner as unreasonably to annoy, embarrass, or oppress the deponent or party, the court in which the action is pending or the court in the county where the deposition is being taken may order the officer conducting the examination to cease forthwith from taking the deposition, or may limit the scope and manner of the taking of the deposition as provided in IN ST TRIAL P Rule 26(C). IN ST TRIAL P Rule 30(D).

    i. If the order made terminates the examination, it shall be resumed thereafter only upon the order of the court in which the action is pending. IN ST TRIAL P Rule 30(D).

ii. Upon demand of the objecting party or deponent the taking of the deposition shall be suspended for the time necessary to make a motion for an order. The provisions of IN ST TRIAL P Rule 37(A)(4) apply to the award of expenses incurred in relation to the motion. IN ST TRIAL P Rule 30(D).

iii. Refer to the Indiana KeyRules Motion for Protective Order and Motion for Discovery Sanctions documents for more information.

f. *Submission to witness; Changes; Signing*

   i. When the testimony is fully transcribed, the deposition shall be submitted to the witness for reading and signing and shall be read to or by him, unless such reading and signing have been waived by the witness and by each party. "Submitted to the witness" as used in IN ST TRIAL P Rule 30(E)(1) shall mean:

      • Mailing of written notification by registered or certified mail to the witness and each attorney attending the deposition that the deposition can be read and examined in the office of the officer before whom the deposition was taken, or

      • Mailing the original deposition, by registered or certified mail, to the witness at an address designated by the witness or his attorney, if requested to do so by the witness, his attorney, or the party taking the deposition. IN ST TRIAL P Rule 30(E)(1).

   ii. If the witness desires to change any answer in the deposition submitted to him, each change, with a statement of the reason therefor, shall be made by the witness on a separate form provided by the officer, shall be signed by the witness and affixed to the original deposition by the officer. A copy of such changes shall be furnished by the officer to each party. IN ST TRIAL P Rule 30(E)(2).

   iii. If the reading and signing have not been waived by the witness and by each party the deposition shall be signed by the witness and returned by him to the officer within thirty (30) days after it is submitted to the witness. If the deposition has been returned to the officer and has not been signed by the witness, the officer shall execute a certificate of that fact, attach it to the original deposition and deliver it to the party taking it. In such event, the deposition may be used by any party with the same force and effect as though it had been signed by the witness. IN ST TRIAL P Rule 30(E)(3).

   iv. In the event the deposition is not returned to the officer within thirty (30) days after it has been submitted to the witness, the reporter shall execute a certificate of that fact and cause the certificate to be delivered to the party taking it. In such event, any party may use a copy of the deposition with the same force and effect as though the original had been signed by the witness. IN ST TRIAL P Rule 30(E)(4).

g. *Certification and filing; Exhibits; Copies*

   i. The officer shall certify on the deposition that the witness was duly sworn by him and that the deposition is a true record of the testimony given by the witness. He shall then securely seal the deposition in an envelope endorsed with the title of the action and marked "Deposition of (here insert name of witness)" and shall promptly deliver it to the party taking the deposition. IN ST TRIAL P Rule 30(F)(1). Documents and things, unless objection is made to their production for inspection during the examination of the witness, shall be marked for identification and annexed to and returned with the deposition, and may be inspected and copied by any party, except that:

      • The person producing the materials may substitute copies to be marked for identification, if he affords to all parties fair opportunity to verify the copies by comparison with the originals; and

      • If the person producing the materials requests their return the officer shall mark them, give each party an opportunity to inspect and copy them, and return them to the person producing them, and the materials may then be used in the same manner as if annexed to and returned with the deposition. IN ST TRIAL P Rule 30(F)(1).

   ii. Upon payment of reasonable charges therefor, the officer shall furnish a copy of the deposition to any party or the deponent. IN ST TRIAL P Rule 30(F)(2).

    iii. The officer taking the deposition shall give prompt notice to all parties of its delivery to the party taking the deposition. IN ST TRIAL P Rule 30(F)(3).

    iv. The filing of depositions shall be in accordance with the provisions of IN ST TRIAL P Rule 5(E). IN ST TRIAL P Rule 30(F)(4).

  h. *Failure to attend or to serve subpoena; Expenses*

    i. If the party giving the notice of the taking of a deposition fails to attend and proceed therewith and another party attends in person or by attorney pursuant to the notice, the court may order the party giving the notice to pay to such other party the amount of the reasonable expenses incurred by him and his attorney in so attending, including reasonable attorney's fees. IN ST TRIAL P Rule 30(G)(1).

    ii. If the party giving the notice of the taking of a deposition of a witness other than a party fails to serve a subpoena upon him and the witness because of such failure does not attend, and if another party attends in person or by attorney because he expects the deposition of that witness to be taken, the court may order the party giving the notice to pay to such other party the amount of the reasonable expenses incurred by him and his attorney in so attending, including reasonable attorney's fees. IN ST TRIAL P Rule 30(G)(2).

  i. *Depositions of prisoners.* The deposition of a person confined in prison may be taken only by leave of court on such terms as the court prescribes. IN ST TRIAL P Rule 30(A).

  j. *Cost of deposition.* In Indiana the rule is that the party who initiates a deposition pays for the cost necessarily incurred as a result of the deposition. Those costs are: (1) the stenographic reporter's fees, (2) the transcription and filing fees, and (3) transportation costs and perhaps other costs which might naturally arise in a particular situation. 2A INPRAC R 30(30.8); Briggs v. Clinton County Bank & Trust Co. of Frankfort, Ind., 452 N.E.2d 989, 1009 (Ind.Ct.App. 1983).

3. *Deposition upon written questions.* The use of written questions under IN ST TRIAL P Rule 31 is often not as effective as taking a deposition on oral examination, and is generally, as a practical matter, not suitable for complicated cases or where cross-examination is necessary, as in the case of a reluctant or hostile witness. Written questions are, however, an inexpensive device where simple or formal facts are sought. 2A INPRAC R 31(31.1).

  a. *Notice.* A party desiring to take a deposition upon written questions shall serve them upon every other party with a notice stating:

    i. The name and address of the person who is to answer them, if known, and if the name is not known, a general description sufficient to identify him or the particular class or group to which he belongs; and

    ii. The name or descriptive title and address of the officer before whom the deposition is to be taken. IN ST TRIAL P Rule 31(A).

  b. *Depositions of specific persons*

    i. *Prisoners.* The deposition of a person confined in prison may be taken only by leave of court on such terms as the court prescribes. IN ST TRIAL P Rule 31(A).

    ii. *Organization.* A deposition upon written questions may be taken of an organization, including a governmental organization, or a partnership in accordance with the provisions of IN ST TRIAL P Rule 30(B)(6). IN ST TRIAL P Rule 31(A).

  c. *Officer to take responses and prepare record.* A copy of the notice and copies of all questions served shall be delivered by the party taking the deposition to the officer designated in the notice, who shall proceed promptly, in the manner provided by IN ST TRIAL P Rule 30(C), IN ST TRIAL P Rule 30(E), and IN ST TRIAL P Rule 30(F), to take the testimony of the witness in response to the questions and to prepare, certify, and deliver the deposition, attaching thereto the copy of the notice and the questions received by him, in accordance with IN ST TRIAL P Rule 5(E). IN ST TRIAL P Rule 31(B).

  d. *Notice of filing.* When the deposition is filed the party taking it shall promptly give notice thereof to all other parties. IN ST TRIAL P Rule 31(C).

4. *Depositions before action or pending appeal*

a. *Use of deposition to perpetuate testimony.* IN ST TRIAL P Rule 27 does not exist to provide a method of discovery to determine whether a cause of action exists. Rather, the rule is intended to be used to "memorialize" evidence that is already known. Accordingly, a trial court should not grant a motion to perpetuate testimony by deposition on the mere possibility that witnesses may be transferred or leave current employment. 2A INPRAC R 27(27.2). IN ST TRIAL P Rule 27 is available for use "when a certain witness' testimony might become unavailable over time, and not to provide a method of discovery to determine whether a cause of action exits." 2A INPRAC R 27(27.2); Petition of Gary Construction, Inc., 96 F.R.D. 432 (D.C.Colo. 1983); Petition of Gurnsey, 223 F.Supp. 359 (D.D.C. 1963).

b. *Before action; Petition required*

i. *Petition.* A person who desires to perpetuate his own testimony or that of another person regarding any matter that may be cognizable in any court in which the action may be commenced, may file a verified petition in any such court of this state. IN ST TRIAL P Rule 27(A)(1). The petition shall be entitled in the name of the petitioner and shall state facts showing:

- That the petitioner expects to be a party to an action cognizable in a court of this or another state;

- The subject-matter of the expected action and his interest therein;

- The facts which he desires to establish by the proposed testimony and his reasons for desiring to perpetuate it;

- The names or a description of the persons he expects will be adverse parties and their addresses so far as known; and

- The names and addresses of the persons to be examined and the substance of the testimony which he expects to elicit from each, and shall ask for an order authorizing the petitioner to take the depositions of the persons to be examined named in the petition, for the purpose of perpetuating their testimony. IN ST TRIAL P Rule 27(A)(1).

ii. *Notice and service.* The petitioner shall thereafter serve a notice upon each person named in the petition as an expected adverse party, together with a copy of the petition, stating that the petitioner will apply to the court, at a time and place named therein, for the order described in the petition. IN ST TRIAL P Rule 27(A)(2).

iii. *Order and examination.* If the court is satisfied that the perpetuation of the testimony may prevent a failure or delay of justice, it shall make an order designating or describing the persons whose depositions may be taken and specifying the subject-matter of the examination or written interrogatories. The depositions may then be taken in accordance with the Indiana Rules of Trial Procedure; and the court may make orders of the character provided for by IN ST TRIAL P Rule 34 and IN ST TRIAL P Rule 35. For the purpose of applying the Indiana Rules of Trial Procedure to depositions for perpetuating testimony, each reference therein to the court in which the action is pending shall be deemed to refer to the court in which the petition for such deposition was filed. IN ST TRIAL P Rule 27(A)(3).

iv. *Use of deposition.* If a deposition to perpetuate testimony is taken under the Indiana Rules of Trial Procedure or if, although not so taken, it would be admissible in evidence in the court of the state in which it is taken, it may be used in any action involving the same subject-matter subsequently brought in a court of this state in accordance with the provision of IN ST TRIAL P Rule 32. IN ST TRIAL P Rule 27(A)(3).

c. *Pending appeal.* If an appeal has been taken from a judgment of any court or before the taking of an appeal if the time therefor has not expired, the court in which the judgment was rendered may allow the taking of the depositions of witnesses to perpetuate their testimony for use in the event of further proceedings in such court. In such case the party who desires to perpetuate the testimony may make a motion in the court for leave to take the depositions, upon the same notice and service thereof as if the action was pending in the court. IN ST TRIAL P Rule 27(B).

    i.   The motion shall show:

- The names and addresses of the persons to be examined and the substance of the testimony which he expects to elicit from each;
- The reasons for perpetuating their testimony. IN ST TRIAL P Rule 27(B).

    ii.   If the court finds that the perpetuation of the testimony is proper to avoid a failure or delay of justice, it may make an order allowing the depositions to be taken and may make orders of the character provided for by IN ST TRIAL P Rule 34 and IN ST TRIAL P Rule 35, and thereupon the depositions may be taken and used in the same manner and under the same conditions as are prescribed in the Indiana Rules of Trial Procedure for depositions taken in actions pending in the court. IN ST TRIAL P Rule 27(B).

  d.   *Perpetuation by action.* IN ST TRIAL P Rule 27 does not limit the power of a court to entertain an action to perpetuate testimony. IN ST TRIAL P Rule 27(C).

  e.   *Filing deposition.* The filing or custody of any deposition or evidence obtained under IN ST TRIAL P Rule 27 shall be in accordance with IN ST TRIAL P Rule 5(E). IN ST TRIAL P Rule 27(D).

5.   *Persons before whom depositions may be taken; Discovery across state lines; Before administrative agencies; And after judgment*

  a.   *Within the United States.* Within the United States or within a territory or insular possession subject to the dominion of the United States, depositions shall be taken before an officer authorized to administer oaths by the laws of the United States, or of the state of Indiana, or of the place where the examination is held, or before a person appointed by the court in which the action is pending. A person so appointed has power to administer oaths and take testimony. IN ST TRIAL P Rule 28(A).

  b.   *In foreign countries*

    i.   In a foreign country, depositions may be taken:

- On notice before a person authorized to administer oaths in the place in which the examination is held, either by the law thereof or by the law of the United States; or
- Before a person commissioned by the court, and a person so commissioned shall have the power by virtue of his commission to administer any necessary oath and take testimony; or
- Pursuant to a letter rogatory. IN ST TRIAL P Rule 28(B).

    ii.   A commission or a letter rogatory shall be issued on application and notice and on terms that are just and appropriate. It is not requisite to the issuance of a commission or a letter rogatory that the taking of the deposition in any other manner is impracticable or inconvenient; and both a commission and a letter rogatory may be issued in proper cases. A notice or commission may designate the person before whom the deposition is to be taken either by name or descriptive title. A letter rogatory may be addressed "To the Appropriate Authority in (here name the country)." Evidence obtained in response to a letter rogatory need not be excluded merely for the reason that it is not a verbatim transcript or that the testimony was not taken under oath or for any similar departure from the requirements for depositions taken within the United States under the Indiana Rules of Trial Procedure. IN ST TRIAL P Rule 28(B).

  c.   *Disqualification for interest.* Unless otherwise permitted by the Indiana Rules of Trial Procedure, no deposition shall be taken before a person who is a relative or employee or attorney or counsel of any of the parties, or is a relative or employee of such attorney or counsel, or is financially interested in the action. IN ST TRIAL P Rule 28(C).

    i.   Disqualification of the person before whom the deposition is taken is one of the matters which is waived under IN ST TRIAL P Rule 32(D)(3) unless objection is made as soon as the disqualification is known or could have been known by reasonable diligence. 2A INPRAC R 28(28.3).

  d.   *Scope of discovery outside state; Protective and enforcement orders.* A deposition may be taken outside the state as provided in IN ST TRIAL P Rule 28(A) and IN ST TRIAL P Rule 28(B), and the deponent may be requested to produce documents and things, and may also be requested to allow inspections and copies as provided in IN ST TRIAL P Rule 34 to submit to examination under IN ST TRIAL P Rule 35. Protective orders may be granted by the court in which the action is pending and by the court where discovery is being made. Enforcement orders may be made by the court where the discovery is sought, and enforcement orders and sanctions may be made by the court where the action is pending as against parties and as against witnesses subject to the jurisdiction of the court. When no action is pending, a court of this state may authorize a deposition to be taken outside this state of any person and upon any matters allowed by IN ST TRIAL P Rule 27. IN ST TRIAL P Rule 28(D).

e. *Assistance to tribunals and litigants outside this state.* A court of this state may order a person who is domiciled or is found within this state to give his testimony or statement or to produce documents or other things, allow inspections and copies and permit physical and mental examinations for use in a proceeding in a tribunal outside this state. The order may be made upon the application of any interested person or in response to a letter rogatory and may prescribe the practice and procedure, which may be wholly or in part the practice and procedure of the tribunal outside this state, for taking the testimony or statement or producing the documents or other things. To the extent that the order does not prescribe otherwise, the practice and procedure shall be in accordance with that of the court of this state issuing the order. The order may direct that the testimony or statement be given, or document or other thing produced, before a person appointed by the court. The person appointed shall have power to administer any necessary oath. A person within this state may voluntarily give his testimony or statement or produce documents or other things allowing inspections and copies and permit physical and mental examinations for use in a proceeding before a tribunal outside this state. IN ST TRIAL P Rule 28(E).

f. *Discovery proceedings before administrative agencies.* Whenever an adjudicatory hearing, including any hearing in any proceeding subject to judicial review, is held by or before an administrative agency, any party to that adjudicatory hearing shall be entitled to use the discovery provisions of IN ST TRIAL P Rule 26 through IN ST TRIAL P Rule 37. Such discovery may include any relevant matter in the custody and control of the administrative agency. IN ST TRIAL P Rule 28(F).

    i. Protective and other orders shall be obtained first from the administrative agency, and if enforcement of such orders or right of discovery is necessary, it may be obtained in a court of general jurisdiction in the county where discovery is being made or sought, or where the hearing is being held. IN ST TRIAL P Rule 28(F).

g. *Applicability of other laws.* IN ST TRIAL P Rule 28 does not repeal or modify any other law of this state permitting another procedure for obtaining discovery for use in this state or in a tribunal outside this state, except as expressly provided in the Indiana Rules of Trial Procedure. IN ST TRIAL P Rule 28(G).

h. *Discovery after judgment.* Discovery after judgment may be had in proceedings to enforce or to challenge the judgment. IN ST TRIAL P Rule 28(H).

6. *Supplementation of responses.* A party who has responded to a request for discovery with a response that was complete when made is under no duty to supplement his response to include information thereafter acquired, except as follows:

a. A party is under a duty seasonably to supplement his response with respect to any question directly addressed to:

    i. The identity and location of persons having knowledge of discoverable matters, and

    ii. The identity of each person expected to be called as an expert witness at trial, the subject-matter on which he is expected to testify, and the substance of his testimony. IN ST TRIAL P Rule 26(E)(1).

b. A party is under a duty seasonably to amend a prior response if he obtains information upon the basis of which:

    i. He knows that the response was incorrect when made, or

ii. He knows that the response though correct when made is no longer true and the circumstances are such that a failure to amend the response is in substance a knowing concealment. IN ST TRIAL P Rule 26(E)(2).

c. A duty to supplement responses may be imposed by order of the court, agreement of the parties, or at any time prior to trial through new requests for supplementation of prior responses. IN ST TRIAL P Rule 26(E)(3).

d. The duty seasonably to supplement a discovery response is absolute and is not predicated on a court order. "It is a breach of a litigant's duty reasonably to supplement if the litigant postpones supplementing its response by not obtaining from its experts the information which is to be supplied in answer to interrogatories." 2A INPRAC R 26(26.27); Lucas v. Dorsey Corp., 609 N.E.2d 1191, 1196 (Ind.Ct.App. 1993).

7. *Discovery disputes.* Where an objection is raised during the taking of a deposition which threatens to prevent the completion of the deposition and which counsel have a good faith belief is susceptible to resolution by the court without the submission of written materials, any party may recess the deposition for the purpose of submitting the objection by telephone to a judge for a ruling instanter, subject to the availability of and within the discretion of the judge. Prior to contacting a judge for such a ruling, all parties shall in good faith confer or attempt to confer in an effort to resolve the matter without court intervention and, if court action is still necessary, the parties shall inform the judge of the efforts taken to attempt to resolve the matter. IN ST ST JOSEPH CIV Rule 208(208.5).

D. Documents

1. *Deposition upon oral examination*

    a. *Required documents*

        i. *Notice of deposition.* Refer to the General Requirements section of this document for information on the content of a notice of deposition.

        ii. *Certificate of service.* An attorney or unrepresented party tendering a document to the Clerk for filing shall certify that service has been made, list the parties served, and specify the date and means of service. The certificate of service shall be placed at the end of the document and shall not be separately filed. The separate filing of a certificate of service, however, shall not be grounds for rejecting a document for filing. The Clerk may permit documents to be filed without a certificate of service but shall require prompt filing of a separate certificate of service. IN ST TRIAL P Rule 5(C).

    b. *Supplemental documents*

        i. *Subpoena/subpoena duces tecum.* The attendance of witnesses may be compelled by the use of subpoena as provided in IN ST TRIAL P Rule 45. IN ST TRIAL P Rule 30(A).

            • Proof of service of a notice to take a deposition as provided in IN ST TRIAL P Rule 30(B) and IN ST TRIAL P Rule 31(A) constitutes a sufficient authorization for the issuance by the clerk of court for the county in which the deposition is to be taken of subpoenas for the persons named or described therein. The subpoena may command the person to whom it is directed to produce designated books, papers, documents, or tangible things which constitute or contain matters within the scope of the examination permitted by IN ST TRIAL P Rule 26(B), but in that event the subpoena will be subject to the provisions of IN ST TRIAL P Rule 26(C) and IN ST TRIAL P Rule 45(B). IN ST TRIAL P Rule 45(D)(1).

            • An individual may be required to attend an examination only in the county wherein he resides or is employed or transacts his business in person, or at such other convenient place as is fixed by an order of court. A nonresident of the state may be required to attend only in the state and county wherein he is served with a subpoena, or within forty (40) miles from the place of service, or at such other convenient place as is fixed by an order of court. A non-resident plaintiff may be required to attend at his own expense an examination in the county of this state where the action is commenced or in a county fixed by the court. IN ST TRIAL P Rule 45(D)(2).

        ii. *Request for production.* The notice to a deponent may be accompanied by a request made in compliance with IN ST TRIAL P Rule 34 for the production of documents and tangible things at the taking of the deposition. IN ST TRIAL P Rule 30(B)(5).

   iii. *Stipulation regarding discovery procedure.* Unless the court orders otherwise, the parties may by written stipulation:

- Provide that depositions may be taken before any person, at any time or place, upon any notice, and in any manner and when so taken may be used like other depositions, and

- Modify the procedures provided by the Indiana Rules of Trial Procedure for other methods of discovery. IN ST TRIAL P Rule 29.

   iv. *Facsimile cover sheet.* Any document sent to the Clerk of the Circuit Court by electronic facsimile transmission shall be accompanied by a cover sheet which states the title of the document, case number, number of pages, identity and voice telephone number of the sending party and instructions for filing. The cover sheet shall contain the signature of the attorney or party, pro se, authorizing the filing. IN ST ADMIN Rule 12(D).

2. *Deposition upon written questions*

  a. *Required documents*

    i. *Notice of deposition.* Refer to the General Requirements section of this document for information on the content of a notice of deposition.

    ii. *Certificate of service.* An attorney or unrepresented party tendering a document to the Clerk for filing shall certify that service has been made, list the parties served, and specify the date and means of service. The certificate of service shall be placed at the end of the document and shall not be separately filed. The separate filing of a certificate of service, however, shall not be grounds for rejecting a document for filing. The Clerk may permit documents to be filed without a certificate of service but shall require prompt filing of a separate certificate of service. IN ST TRIAL P Rule 5(C).

  b. *Supplemental documents*

    i. *Subpoena.* The attendance of witnesses may be compelled by the use of subpoena as provided in IN ST TRIAL P Rule 45. IN ST TRIAL P Rule 31(A).

- Proof of service of a notice to take a deposition as provided in IN ST TRIAL P Rule 30(B) and IN ST TRIAL P Rule 31(A) constitutes a sufficient authorization for the issuance by the clerk of court for the county in which the deposition is to be taken of subpoenas for the persons named or described therein. The subpoena may command the person to whom it is directed to produce designated books, papers, documents, or tangible things which constitute or contain matters within the scope of the examination permitted by IN ST TRIAL P Rule 26(B), but in that event the subpoena will be subject to the provisions of IN ST TRIAL P Rule 26(C) and IN ST TRIAL P Rule 45(B). IN ST TRIAL P Rule 45(D)(1).

- An individual may be required to attend an examination only in the county wherein he resides or is employed or transacts his business in person, or at such other convenient place as is fixed by an order of court. A nonresident of the state may be required to attend only in the state and county wherein he is served with a subpoena, or within forty (40) miles from the place of service, or at such other convenient place as is fixed by an order of court. A non-resident plaintiff may be required to attend at his own expense an examination in the county of this state where the action is commenced or in a county fixed by the court. IN ST TRIAL P Rule 45(D)(2).

    ii. *Stipulation regarding discovery procedure.* Unless the court orders otherwise, the parties may by written stipulation:

- Provide that depositions may be taken before any person, at any time or place, upon any notice, and in any manner and when so taken may be used like other depositions, and

- Modify the procedures provided by the Indiana Rules of Trial Procedure for other methods of discovery. IN ST TRIAL P Rule 29.

    iii. *Facsimile cover sheet.* Any document sent to the Clerk of the Circuit Court by electronic facsimile transmission shall be accompanied by a cover sheet which states the title of the document, case number, number of pages, identity and voice telephone number of the sending party and instructions for filing. The cover sheet shall contain the signature of the attorney or party, pro se, authorizing the filing. IN ST ADMIN Rule 12(D).

3. *Deposition before action*

    a. *Required documents*

        i. *Notice of deposition.* Refer to the General Requirements section of this document for information on the contents of a notice of deposition.

        ii. *Petition.* Refer to the General Requirements section of this document for information on the content of a petition.

        iii. *Certificate of service.* An attorney or unrepresented party tendering a document to the Clerk for filing shall certify that service has been made, list the parties served, and specify the date and means of service. The certificate of service shall be placed at the end of the document and shall not be separately filed. The separate filing of a certificate of service, however, shall not be grounds for rejecting a document for filing. The Clerk may permit documents to be filed without a certificate of service but shall require prompt filing of a separate certificate of service. IN ST TRIAL P Rule 5(C).

    b. *Supplemental documents*

        i. *Stipulation regarding discovery procedure.* Unless the court orders otherwise, the parties may by written stipulation:

- Provide that depositions may be taken before any person, at any time or place, upon any notice, and in any manner and when so taken may be used like other depositions, and
- Modify the procedures provided by the Indiana Rules of Trial Procedure for other methods of discovery. IN ST TRIAL P Rule 29.

        ii. *Facsimile cover sheet.* Any document sent to the Clerk of the Circuit Court by electronic facsimile transmission shall be accompanied by a cover sheet which states the title of the document, case number, number of pages, identity and voice telephone number of the sending party and instructions for filing. The cover sheet shall contain the signature of the attorney or party, pro se, authorizing the filing. IN ST ADMIN Rule 12(D).

4. *Deposition pending appeal*

    a. *Required documents*

        i. *Motion for leave to take deposition and notice.* The requirement of notice is satisfied by service of the motion. IN ST TRIAL P Rule 7(B).

        ii. *Chronological Case Summary (CCS) entry form.* Every written motion, petition, or other pleading subsequent to the original complaint presented to the Clerk for filing shall be accompanied by a Chronological Case Summary (CCS) entry form in duplicate. IN ST ST JOSEPH CIV Rule 201(201.4). Refer to the Format section of this document for details on the format and filing requirements for the CCS entry form.

        iii. *Proposed order.* Unless local practice provides differently, a party should submit a proposed order with its written motion to be signed by the judge once the motion has been granted. 21 INPRAC § 13.8. All proposed orders shall be submitted in an original plus a number of copies equal to one more than the number of pro se parties and attorneys of record contained in the prepared proof of notice under IN ST TRIAL P Rule 72(D). IN ST ST JOSEPH CIV Rule 213(213.3); IN ST ST JOSEPH CIV Rule 201(201.5.2).

        iv. *Certificate of service.* An attorney or unrepresented party tendering a document to the Clerk for filing shall certify that service has been made, list the parties served, and specify the date and means of service. The certificate of service shall be placed at the end of the document and shall not be separately filed. The separate filing of a certificate of service, however, shall not be grounds for rejecting a document for filing. The Clerk may permit documents to be filed without a certificate of service but shall require prompt filing of a separate certificate of service. IN ST TRIAL P Rule 5(C).

    b.   *Supplemental documents*

        i.   *Stipulation regarding discovery procedure.* Unless the court orders otherwise, the parties may by written stipulation:

- Provide that depositions may be taken before any person, at any time or place, upon any notice, and in any manner and when so taken may be used like other depositions, and
- Modify the procedures provided by the Indiana Rules of Trial Procedure for other methods of discovery. IN ST TRIAL P Rule 29.

        ii.   *Supporting evidence.* When a motion is based on facts not appearing of record the court may hear the matter on affidavits presented by the respective parties, but the court may direct that the matter be heard wholly or partly on oral testimony or depositions. IN ST TRIAL P Rule 43(B).

        iii.   *Facsimile cover sheet.* Any document sent to the Clerk of the Circuit Court by electronic facsimile transmission shall be accompanied by a cover sheet which states the title of the document, case number, number of pages, identity and voice telephone number of the sending party and instructions for filing. The cover sheet shall contain the signature of the attorney or party, pro se, authorizing the filing. IN ST ADMIN Rule 12(D).

E. Format

1. *Form of notice.* The rules applicable to captions, and the signing and form of pleadings (IN ST TRIAL P Rule 8 through IN ST TRIAL P Rule 11), apply to all motions and other papers provided under the Indiana Rules of Trial Procedure. 22B INPRAC 7:2.

    a.   *Format of discovery requests.* Whenever agreed by the parties or otherwise ordered by the Court, a party shall forward simultaneously with the hard copy discovery request (interrogatories, requests for production, requests for admissions, or other requests for discovery) either a floppy disk or an electronic mail message with a copy of the request attached in digital format. Otherwise, an original and two (2) duplicate copies shall be prepared and served on the party required to answer. IN ST ST JOSEPH CIV Rule 208(208.2).

2. *Form of pleadings*

    a.   *Caption; Names of parties.* Every pleading shall contain a caption setting forth the name of the court, the title of the action, the file number, and a designation as in IN ST TRIAL P Rule 7(A). In the complaint the title of the action shall include the names of all the parties, but in other pleadings it is sufficient to state the name of the first party on each side with an appropriate indication of other parties. IN ST TRIAL P Rule 10(A); IN ST ST JOSEPH CIV Rule 201(201.3.3). If a special judge has been assigned to the case, the pleading should also identify the special judge. IN ST ST JOSEPH CIV Rule 201(201.3.3).

        i.   *Title.* All pleadings or motions shall include a title, which shall delineate each topic included in the pleading. For example, where a pleading contains an answer, a motion to dismiss, and a jury request, each topic shall be set forth in the title. IN ST ST JOSEPH CIV Rule 201(201.3.4).

    b.   *Paragraphs; Separate statements.* All averments of a claim or defense shall be made in numbered paragraphs, the contents of each of which shall be limited as far as practicable to a statement of a single set of circumstances, and a paragraph may be referred to by number in all succeeding pleadings. Each claim founded upon a separate transaction or occurrence and each defense other than denials may be stated in a separate count or defense whenever a separation facilitates the clear presentation of the matters set forth. IN ST TRIAL P Rule 10(B).

    c.   *Adoption by reference; Exhibits.* Statements in a pleading may be adopted by reference in a different part of the same pleading or in another pleading or in any motion. A copy of any written instrument which is an exhibit to a pleading is a part thereof for all purposes. IN ST TRIAL P Rule 10(C).

    d.   *Flat filing.* In order that the Clerk's files may be kept under the system commonly known as "flat filing," all papers presented to the Clerk for filing shall be flat and unfolded. Pleadings shall have no covers or backs and shall be fastened together at the top left-hand corner only. IN ST ST JOSEPH CIV Rule 201(201.1).

e. *One side of page used.* Printing shall be on one (1) side of the paper. IN ST ST JOSEPH CIV Rule 201(201.3.2).

f. *Copies.* All copies shall be on white paper of sufficient strength and durability to resist normal wear and tear. IN ST ST JOSEPH CIV Rule 201(201.3.1).

g. *Margins.* Margins shall be at least one inch (1"). IN ST ST JOSEPH CIV Rule 201(201.3.2).

h. *Double-spaced.* If typewritten, the lines shall be double spaced except for quotations, which shall be indented and single-spaced. IN ST ST JOSEPH CIV Rule 201(201.3.2).

i. *Font size.* Type face shall be twelve (12) font size or larger within the body of the document and ten (10) font size or larger in the footnotes. IN ST ST JOSEPH CIV Rule 201(201.3.2).

j. *Font type.* The font type must be legible and script type shall not be used. IN ST ST JOSEPH CIV Rule 201(201.3.2).

k. *Italics.* Italicized type may be used for quotations, references, or case citations. IN ST ST JOSEPH CIV Rule 201(201.3.2).

l. *Court and case designation.* All filings shall conform to the requirements for uniform court and case number designation set by IN ST ADMIN Rule 8. In addition, all filings shall contain the proper court and case designation as described below. IN ST ST JOSEPH CIV Rule 202.

   i. *Court designation.* Pursuant to IN ST 33-33-71-2, St. Joseph County, Indiana, constitutes the Sixtieth Judicial Circuit. The legal names of the courts within the 60th Judicial Circuit are the St. Joseph Circuit Court, the St. Joseph Superior Court, and the St. Joseph Probate Court. All filings shall properly reflect the legal name of the applicable court. Any filing may be amended, rejected, or stricken if it does not contain the proper case name and/or the legal name of the court. IN ST ST JOSEPH CIV Rule 202(202.1).

m. *Form of CCS entry.* Every written motion, petition, or other pleading subsequent to the original complaint presented to the Clerk for filing shall be accompanied by a Chronological Case Summary (CCS) entry form in duplicate which shall contain the title and cause number of the action, the date, and the proposed entry to appear on the docket. IN ST ST JOSEPH CIV Rule 201(201.4).

   i. *Identification and signature.* The CCS entry form shall identify the party making the filing, designate each pleading being filed, and shall be signed by counsel of record or the unrepresented litigant. IN ST ST JOSEPH CIV Rule 201(201.4).

   ii. *Date stamp.* The form shall be date stamped and presented to the Court Clerk, who shall initial the form and return the duplicate to the filing party. IN ST ST JOSEPH CIV Rule 201(201.4).

3. *Size of papers for filing.* Effective January 1, 1992, all pleadings, copies, motions and documents filed with any trial court or appellate level court, typed or printed, with the exception of exhibits and existing wills, shall be prepared on eight and one-half by eleven inch (8 1/2" x 11") size paper. IN ST ADMIN Rule 11.

   a. *Paper.* Pleadings, motions, and other papers shall be either legibly printed or typewritten on white opaque paper of good quality at least sixteen (16) pound weight, eight and one-half inches (8 1/2 ") in width and eleven inches (11") in length as required by IN ST ADMIN Rule 11. IN ST ST JOSEPH CIV Rule 201(201.3.1).

4. *Signature requirements*

   a. *Signature of attorney.* Every pleading or motion of a party represented by an attorney shall be signed by at least one (1) attorney of record in his individual name, whose address, telephone number, and attorney number shall be stated, except that this provision shall not apply to pleadings and motions made and transcribed at the trial or a hearing before the judge and received by him in such form. IN ST TRIAL P Rule 11(A).

      i. The signature of an attorney constitutes a certificate by him that he has read the pleadings; that to the best of his knowledge, information, and belief, there is good ground to support it; and that it is not interposed for delay. IN ST TRIAL P Rule 11(A).

      ii. If a pleading or motion is not signed or is signed with intent to defeat the purpose of the rule, it

may be stricken as sham and false and the action may proceed as though the pleading had not been served. IN ST TRIAL P Rule 11(A).

    iii. For a willful violation of IN ST TRIAL P Rule 11 an attorney may be subjected to appropriate disciplinary action. Similar action may be taken if scandalous or indecent matter is inserted. IN ST TRIAL P Rule 11(A).

b. *Signature of unrepresented party.* A party who is not represented by an attorney shall sign his pleading and state his address. IN ST TRIAL P Rule 11(A).

c. *Verification not generally required.* Except when specifically required by rule, pleadings or motions need not be verified or accompanied by affidavit. The rule in equity that the averments of an answer under oath must be overcome by the testimony of two (2) witnesses or of one (1) witness sustained by corroborating circumstances is abolished. IN ST TRIAL P Rule 11(A).

d. *Verification by affirmation or representation.* When in connection with any civil or special statutory proceeding it is required that any pleading, motion, petition, supporting affidavit, or other document of any kind, be verified, or that an oath be taken, it shall be sufficient if the subscriber simply affirms the truth of the matter to be verified by an affirmation or representation. IN ST TRIAL P Rule 11(B). IN ST TRIAL P Rule 11(B) states that the affirmation or representation should be in substantially the following language: "I (we) affirm, under the penalties for perjury, that the foregoing representation(s) is (are) true. (Signed) _____."

    i. Any person who falsifies an affirmation or representation of fact shall be subject to the same penalties as are prescribed by law for the making of a false affidavit. IN ST TRIAL P Rule 11(B).

e. *Verified pleadings, motions, and affidavits as evidence.* Pleadings, motions and affidavits accompanying or in support of such pleadings or motions when required to be verified or under oath shall be accepted as a representation that the signer had personal knowledge thereof or reasonable cause to believe the existence of the facts or matters stated or alleged therein; and, if otherwise competent or acceptable as evidence, may be admitted as evidence of the facts or matters stated or alleged therein when it is so provided in the Indiana Rules of Trial Procedure, by statute or other law, or to the extent the writing or signature expressly purports to be made upon the signer's personal knowledge. When such pleadings, motions and affidavits are verified or under oath they shall not require other or greater proof on the part of the adverse party than if not verified or not under oath unless expressly provided otherwise by the Indiana Rules of Trial Procedure, statute or other law. Affidavits upon motions for summary judgment under IN ST TRIAL P Rule 56 and in denial of execution under IN ST TRIAL P Rule 9.2 shall be made upon personal knowledge. IN ST TRIAL P Rule 11(C).

f. *Signature, verification and other requirements.* Parties and their counsel are enjoined to comply with the verification requirements of IN ST TRIAL P Rule 11, and either the moving party or the party's attorney of record shall sign all pleadings and motions before filing with the Clerk of the Court. Every motion, petition, or other pleading filed with the Clerk shall contain the name, organization, physical address, telephone number, and facsimile number of the filing party or an attorney for that party. IN ST ST JOSEPH CIV Rule 201(201.3.6).

    i. The Clerk shall not accept any motion, petition, notice or other pleading or a CCS entry form for filing from an unrepresented litigant unless the unrepresented litigant's current address and phone number appear on the pleading, and an opposing party may service notices and responses on an unrepresented litigant at any address he or she has provided on a pleading. IN ST ST JOSEPH CIV Rule 201(201.3.6).

5. *Information excluded from public access.* Every document filed in a case shall separately identify information excluded from public access pursuant to IN ST ADMIN Rule 9(G)(1) as follows:

a. Whole documents that are excluded from public access pursuant to IN ST ADMIN Rule 9(G)(1) shall be tendered on light green paper or have a light green coversheet attached to the document, marked "Not for Public Access" or "Confidential." IN ST TRIAL P Rule 5(G)(1).

b. When only a portion of a document contains information excluded from public access pursuant to IN ST ADMIN Rule 9(G)(1), said information shall be omitted [or redacted] from the filed document,

and set forth on a separate accompanying document on light green paper conspicuously marked "Not for Public Access" or "Confidential" and clearly designated [or identifying] the caption and number of the case and the document and location within the document to which the redacted material pertains. IN ST TRIAL P Rule 5(G)(2).

c. With respect to documents filed in electronic format, the trial court, by local rule, may provide for compliance with IN ST TRIAL P Rule 5 in manner that separates and protects access to information excluded from public access. IN ST TRIAL P Rule 5(G)(3).

d. IN ST TRIAL P Rule 5(G) does not apply to a record sealed by the court pursuant to IN ST 5-14-3-5.5 or otherwise, nor to records, documents, or information filed in cases to which public access is prohibited pursuant to IN ST ADMIN Rule 9(G). IN ST TRIAL P Rule 5(G)(4).

e. The following information in case records is excluded from public access and is confidential:

  i. Information that is excluded from public access pursuant to federal law;

  ii. Information that is excluded from public access as declared confidential by Indiana statute or other court rule, including without limitation:

  - All adoption records created after July 8, 1941, as declared confidential by IN ST 31-19-19-1, et seq., except those specifically declared open by IN ST 31-19-13-2(2);

  - All records relating to chancroid, chlamydia, gonorrhea, hepatitis, human immunodeficiency virus (HIV), Lymphogranuloma venereum, syphilis, tuberculosis, as declared confidential by IN ST 16-41-8-1, et seq.;

  - All records relating to child abuse as declared confidential by IN ST 31-33-18-1, et seq.;

  - All records relating to drug tests as declared confidential by IN ST 5-14-3-4(a)(9);

  - Records of grand jury proceedings as declared confidential by IN ST 35-34-2-4;

  - Records of juvenile proceedings as declared confidential by IN ST 31-39-1-2, except those specifically open under statute;

  - All paternity records created after July 1, 1941 as declared confidential by IN ST 31-14-11-15, IN ST 31-19-5-23, IN ST 31-39-1-1 and IN ST 31-39-1-2 [Editor's note: IN ST 31-14-11-15 was repealed effective May 9, 2013];

  - All pre-sentence reports as declared confidential by IN ST 35-38-1-13;

  - Written petitions to permit marriages without consent and orders directing the Clerk of Court to issue a marriage license to underage persons, as declared confidential by IN ST 31-11-1-6;

  - Only those arrest warrants, search warrants, indictments and informations ordered confidential by the trial judge, prior to return of duly executed service as declared confidential by IN ST 5-14-3-4(b)(1);

  - All medical, mental health, or tax records unless determined by law or regulation of any governmental custodian not to be confidential, released by the subject of such records, or declared by a court of competent jurisdiction to be essential to the resolution of litigation as declared confidential by IN ST 16-39-3-10, IN ST 6-4.1-5-10, IN ST 6-4.1-12-12, and IN ST 6-8.1-7-1;

  - Personal information relating to jurors or prospective jurors, other than for the use of the parties and counsel, pursuant to IN ST JURY Rule 10;

  - Information relating to protection from abuse orders, no-contact orders and workplace violence restraining orders as declared confidential by IN ST 5-2-9-6, et seq.;

  - Mediation proceedings pursuant to IN ST ADR Rule 2.11, Mini-Trial proceedings pursuant to IN ST ADR Rule 4.4(C), and Summary Jury Trials pursuant to IN ST ADR Rule 5.6;

  - Information in probation files pursuant to the Probation Standards promulgated by the Judicial Conference of Indiana pursuant to IN ST 11-13-1-8(b);

- Information deemed confidential pursuant to the Rules for Court Administered Alcohol and Drug Programs promulgated by the Judicial Conference of Indiana pursuant to IN ST 12-23-14-13;

- Information deemed confidential pursuant to the Problem-Solving Court Rules promulgated by the Judicial Conference of Indiana pursuant to IN ST 33-23-16-16;

- All records of the Department of workforce Development as declared confidential by IN ST 22-4-19-6;

- Information regarding interception of electronic communications that is sealed or deemed confidential as set forth in IN ST 35-33.5-2-1, et seq.

iii. Information excluded from public access by specific court order;

iv. Complete Social Security Numbers of living persons;

v. With the exception of names, information such as addresses, phone numbers, and dates of birth which explicitly identifies:

- Natural persons who are witnesses or victims (not including defendants) in criminal, domestic violence, stalking, sexual assault, juvenile, or civil protection order proceedings, provided that juveniles who are victims of sex crimes shall be identified by initials only;

- Places of residence of judicial officers, clerks and other employees of courts and clerks of court, unless the person or persons about whom the information pertains waives confidentiality;

vi. Complete account numbers of specific assets, loans, bank accounts, credit cards, and personal identification numbers (PINs);

vii. All orders of expungement entered in criminal or juvenile proceedings, orders to restrict access to criminal history information pursuant to IN ST 35-38-5-5.5 or IN ST 35-38-8-5 and records excluded from public access by such orders, and information related to infractions that is excluded from public access pursuant to IN ST 34-28-5-15 or IN ST 34-28-5-16 [Editor's note: IN ST 35-38-5-5.5, IN ST 35-38-8-5 and IN ST 34-28-5-16 were repealed effective July 1, 2013; for information on orders restricting access to criminal history, refer to IN ST 35-38-9-1, et seq.];

viii. All personal notes and e-mail, and deliberative material, of judges, jurors, court staff and judicial agencies, and information recorded in personal data assistants (PDA's) or organizers and personal calendars. IN ST ADMIN Rule 9(G)(1).

F. Filing and Service Requirements

1. *Filing requirements.* Except as otherwise provided in IN ST TRIAL P Rule 5(E)(2), all pleadings and papers subsequent to the complaint which are required to be served upon a party shall be filed with the Court either before service or within a reasonable period of time thereafter. IN ST TRIAL P Rule 5(E)(1).

   a. *Non-filing of discovery until necessary*

      i. *Non-filing of discovery; Exceptions.* No deposition or request for discovery or response thereto under IN ST TRIAL P Rule 27, IN ST TRIAL P Rule 30, IN ST TRIAL P Rule 31, IN ST TRIAL P Rule 33, IN ST TRIAL P Rule 34 or IN ST TRIAL P Rule 36 shall be filed with the Court unless:

         - A motion is filed pursuant to IN ST TRIAL P Rule 26(C) or IN ST TRIAL P Rule 37 and the original deposition or request for discovery or response thereto is necessary to enable the Court to rule; or

         - A party desires to use the deposition or request for discovery or response thereto for evidentiary purposes at trial or in connection with a motion, and the Court, either upon its own motion or that of any party, or as a part of any pre-trial order, orders the filing of the original. IN ST TRIAL P Rule 5(E)(2).

      ii. *Custody of original and period of retention*

         - The original of a deposition shall, subject to the provisions of IN ST TRIAL P Rule 30(E), be delivered by the reporter to the party taking it and shall be maintained by that party until filed with the Court pursuant to IN ST TRIAL P Rule 5(E)(2) or until the later of final judgment, agreed settlement of the litigation or all appellate rights have been exhausted. IN ST TRIAL P Rule 5(E)(3)(a).

- The original or any request for discovery or response thereto under IN ST TRIAL P Rule 27, IN ST TRIAL P Rule 30, IN ST TRIAL P Rule 31, IN ST TRIAL P Rule 33, IN ST TRIAL P Rule 34 and IN ST TRIAL P Rule 36 shall be maintained by the party originating the request or response until filed with the Court pursuant to IN ST TRIAL P Rule 5(E)(2) or until the later of final judgment, agreed settlement or all appellate rights have been exhausted. IN ST TRIAL P Rule 5(E)(3)(b).

   iii. *Original unavailable; Copies.* In the event it is made to appear to the satisfaction of the Court that the original of a deposition or request for discovery or response thereto cannot be filed with the Court when required, the Court may allow use of a copy instead of the original. IN ST TRIAL P Rule 5(E)(4).

   iv. *Filing as publication.* The filing of any deposition shall constitute publication. IN ST TRIAL P Rule 5(E)(5).

b. *Filing with the court defined.* The filing of pleadings, motions, and other papers with the court as required by the Indiana Rules of Trial Procedure shall be made by one of the following methods:

   i. Delivery to the clerk of the court;

   ii. Sending by electronic transmission under the procedure adopted pursuant to IN ST ADMIN Rule 12;

   iii. Mailing to the clerk by registered, certified or express mail return receipt requested;

   iv. Depositing with any third-party commercial carrier for delivery to the clerk within three (3) calendar days, cost prepaid, properly addressed;

   v. If the court so permits, filing with the judge, in which event the judge shall note thereon the filing date and forthwith transmit them to the office of the clerk; or

   vi. Electronic filing, as approved by the Division of State Court Administration pursuant to IN ST ADMIN Rule 16. IN ST TRIAL P Rule 5(F).

   vii. Filing by registered or certified mail and by third-party commercial carrier shall be complete upon mailing or deposit. IN ST TRIAL P Rule 5(F).

   viii. All pleadings shall be filed with the Clerk, not directly with the Court, unless otherwise required by the Indiana Rules of Court. The entry of appearances and the filing of pleadings or other matters not requiring immediate Court action shall be filed with the Clerk and not in open Court. A Judge may permit papers to be filed in chambers, in which event he or she shall note thereon the filing date and transmit the papers to the Clerk. IN ST ST JOSEPH CIV Rule 201(201.2).

c. *Facsimile filing.* Unless otherwise authorized by IN ST ST JOSEPH ELECTRONIC Rule 701, electronic filing of pleadings by computerized or facsimile transmission is not permitted. IN ST ST JOSEPH CIV Rule 201(201.2).

d. *Additional copies.* In cases in which a party or counsel supplies the proposed order or decree, a sufficient number shall be prepared and filed as to provide the Clerk to retain two (2) copies, which shall be filed in the flat file and the record of judgments and orders. Should the party or counsel desire additional copies, a sufficient number of copies should be filed to effectuate that purpose. IN ST ST JOSEPH CIV Rule 201(201.6).

e. *Proof of filing.* Any party filing any paper by any method other than personal delivery to the clerk shall retain proof of filing. IN ST TRIAL P Rule 5(F).

2. *Service requirements.* Unless otherwise provided by the Indiana Rules of Trial Procedure or an order of the court, each party and special judge, if any, shall be served with: (1) every order required by its terms to be served; (2) every pleading subsequent to the original complaint; (3) every written motion except one which may be heard ex parte; (4) every brief submitted to the trial court; (5) every paper relating to

discovery required to be served upon a party; and (6) every written notice, appearance, demand, offer of judgment, designation of record on appeal, or similar paper. IN ST TRIAL P Rule 5(A).

a. *Service generally.* Every motion, petition, notice, or other pleading required to be served by IN ST TRIAL P Rule 5 shall be served on all counsel of record or unrepresented parties either before it is filed or on the day it is filed with the Court, and the date of filing shall be indicated on the Certificate of Service. IN ST ST JOSEPH CIV Rule 201(201.5.1).

   i. *Copy.* A copy of the Clerk's CCS entry form of the filing shall also be served on all counsel of record or unrepresented parties whenever it contains an appearance of counsel or contains a date for Court hearing on the matter. IN ST ST JOSEPH CIV Rule 201(201.5.1).

b. *Methods of service*

   i. *Personal service.* Whenever a party is represented by an attorney of record, service shall be made upon such attorney unless service upon the party himself is ordered by the court. Service upon the attorney or party shall be made by delivering or mailing a copy of the papers to the last known address or where an attorney or party has consented to service by fax or e-mail, as provided in IN ST TRIAL P Rule 3.1(A)(4), by faxing or e-mailing a copy of the documents to the fax number or e-mail address set out in the appearance form or correction as required by IN ST TRIAL P Rule 3.1(E). IN ST TRIAL P Rule 5(B). Delivery of a copy within IN ST TRIAL P Rule 5 means:

   - Offering or tendering it to the attorney or party and stating the nature of the papers being served. Refusal to accept an offered or tendered document is a waiver of any objection to the sufficiency or adequacy of service of that document;

   - Leaving it at his office with a clerk or other person in charge thereof, or if there is no one in charge, leaving it in a conspicuous place therein; or

   - If the office is closed, by leaving it at his dwelling house or usual place of abode with some person of suitable age and discretion then residing therein; or,

   - Leaving it at some other suitable place, selected by the attorney upon whom service is being made, pursuant to duly promulgated local rule. IN ST TRIAL P Rule 5(B)(1).

   ii. *Service by the clerk.* Whenever the Clerk is required by rule or statute to give notice, the party or parties requesting such notice shall furnish the Clerk with sufficient copies of the notice to be given, along with stamped, addressed envelopes with the names and the addresses of the parties or their counsel to whom such notice is to be given. IN ST ST JOSEPH CIV Rule 201(201.5.4).

   iii. *Service on the court.* Service on a Judge may be made by delivering a copy to the Judge's secretary or mailing a copy to the Judge at his or her chambers. Service on a Judge may not be accomplished by facsimile transmission; however, a courtesy copy may be sent to the Judge's chambers by electronic mail or facsimile transmission contemporaneously with service by mail or otherwise. IN ST ST JOSEPH CIV Rule 201(201.5.5).

   iv. *Service by mail.* If service is made by mail, the papers shall be deposited in the United States mail addressed to the person on whom they are being served, with postage prepaid. Service shall be deemed complete upon mailing. Proof of service of all papers permitted to be mailed may be made by written acknowledgment of service, by affidavit of the person who mailed the papers, or by certificate of an attorney. It shall be the duty of attorneys when entering their appearance in a cause or when filing pleadings or papers therein, to have noted in the Chronological Case Summary or said pleadings or papers so filed the address and telephone number of their office. Service by delivery or by mail at such address shall be deemed sufficient and complete. IN ST TRIAL P Rule 5(B)(2).

   v. *Service by fax or e-mail.* A party who has consented to service by fax or e-mail may be served as follows:

   - Service by e-mail shall be made by attaching the document being served in .pdf format. Discovery documents must also be served in accordance with IN ST TRIAL P Rule 26(A). IN ST TRIAL P Rule 5(B)(3)(a).

- Service by fax shall be deemed complete upon generation of a transmission record indicating the successful transmission of the entire document, except as provided in IN ST TRIAL P Rule 5(B)(3)(d). IN ST TRIAL P Rule 5(B)(3)(b).

- Service by e-mail shall be deemed complete upon transmission, except as provided in IN ST TRIAL P Rule 5(B)(3)(d). IN ST TRIAL P Rule 5(B)(3)(c).

- Service by fax or e-mail that occurs on a Saturday, Sunday, legal holiday, or day the court or agency in which the matter is pending is closed or after 5:00 PM local time of the recipient shall be deemed complete the next day that is not a Saturday, Sunday, legal holiday, or day that the court or agency in which the matter is pending is not closed. IN ST TRIAL P Rule 5(B)(3)(d).

vi. *Additional service of electronic discovery.* In addition to service under Rule IN ST TRIAL P Rule 5(B) or a .pdf format electronic copy, a party propounding or responding to interrogatories, requests for production or requests for admission shall comply with IN ST TRIAL P Rule 26(A.1)(a) or IN ST TRIAL P Rule 26(A.1)(b). IN ST TRIAL P Rule 26(A.1).

- The party shall serve the discovery request or response in an electronic format (either on a disk or as an electronic document attachment) in any commercially available word processing software system. If transmitted on disk, each disk shall be labeled, identifying the caption of the case, the document, and the word processing version in which it is being submitted. If more than one (1) disk is used for the same document, each disk shall be labeled and also shall be sequentially numbered. If transmitted by electronic mail, the document must be accompanied by electronic memorandum providing the forgoing identifying information; or

- The party shall serve the opposing party with a verified statement that the attorney or party appealing pro se lacks the equipment and is unable to transmit the discovery as required by IN ST TRIAL P Rule 26(A.1). IN ST TRIAL P Rule 26(A.1).

c. *Serving numerous defendants.* In any action in which there are unusually large numbers of defendants, the court, upon motion or of its own initiative, may order:

i. That service of the pleadings of the defendants and replies thereto need not be made as between the defendants;

- That any cross-claim, counterclaim, or matter constituting an avoidance or affirmative defense contained therein shall be deemed to be denied or avoided by all other parties; and

- That the filing of any such pleading and service thereof upon the plaintiff constitutes due notice of it to the parties. IN ST TRIAL P Rule 5(D).

ii. A copy of every such order shall be served upon the parties in such manner and form as the court directs. IN ST TRIAL P Rule 5(D).

d. *Service on parties in default for failure to appear.* No service need be made on parties in default for failure to appear, except that pleadings asserting new or additional claims for relief against them shall be served upon them in the manner provided by service of summons in IN ST TRIAL P Rule 4. IN ST TRIAL P Rule 5(A).

e. *Distribution.* Counsel or an unrepresented party submitting a motion, petition, notice, pleading or proposed order shall indicate the method of distribution desired on the Clerk's CCS entry form. The Clerk will not return or distribute copies of motions, petitions, pleadings, notices or proposed orders, other than those originated by the Court, by mail unless the Clerk is provided with stamped, addressed envelopes. IN ST ST JOSEPH CIV Rule 201(201.5.3).

f. *Mailbox.* As a matter of convenience to attorneys, each court provides a mailbox for the distribution filings and orders generated by the Court, and it is the responsibility of each attorney to periodically check these mailboxes for service and distribution of court-generated filings and orders. IN ST ST JOSEPH CIV Rule 201(201.5.3).

G. Hearings

1. The Indiana rules do not contemplate a hearing related to the notice of deposition.

H. Forms

1. **Notice of Deposition Forms for Indiana**

    a. Notice of deposition; Individual. 5 INPRAC § 4:1.1.

    b. Notice of deposition; Deponent unknown. 5 INPRAC § 4:1.2.

    c. Notice of deposition; Corporation. 5 INPRAC § 4:1.3.

    d. Notice of deposition; With request for production of documents. 5 INPRAC § 4:1.4.

    e. Motion to limit scope of deposition. 5 INPRAC § 4:1.5.

    f. Motion to terminate deposition. 5 INPRAC § 4:1.6.

    g. Notice of hearing on petition for order to take deposition before action to perpetuate testimony. 5 INPRAC § 4:1.7.

    h. Petition to perpetuate testimony. 5 INPRAC § 4:1.7.30.

    i. Affidavit verifying petition to perpetuate testimony. 5 INPRAC § 4:1.7.70.

    j. Stipulation regarding deposition by remote electronic means. 5 INPRAC § 4:1.8.

    k. Petition to perpetuate testimony; Witness to automobile accident. 10 INPRAC § 59.3.

    l. Notice of hearing on petition to perpetuate testimony. 10 INPRAC § 59.6.

    m. Petition to perpetuate testimony pending appeal. 10 INPRAC § 59.13.

    n. Notice of deposition to perpetuate testimony pending appeal. 10 INPRAC § 59.15.

    o. Notice of deposition upon oral examination; Individual. 10 INPRAC § 62.3.

    p. Notice of deposition; Deponent unknown. 10 INPRAC § 62.4.

    q. Notice of deposition; Corporation. 10 INPRAC § 62.5.

    r. Notice of deposition; With request for production of documents. 10 INPRAC § 62.6.

    s. Motion for leave to take deposition within twenty days of service. 10 INPRAC § 62.7.

    t. Notice of deposition; Pursuant to order granting leave to take deposition. 10 INPRAC § 62.9.

    u. Stipulation for deposition upon written questions. 10 INPRAC § 63.2.

    v. Notice of deposition upon written questions. 10 INPRAC § 63.3.

    w. Direct questions. 10 INPRAC § 63.4.

    x. Cross questions. 10 INPRAC § 63.5.

    y. Redirect questions. 10 INPRAC § 63.6.

    z. Recross questions. 10 INPRAC § 63.7.

I. Checklist

(I) ❑ Matters to be considered by the party taking a deposition upon oral examination

    (a) ❑ Required documents

        (1) ❑ Notice of deposition

        (2) ❑ Certificate of service

    (b) ❑ Supplemental documents

        (1) ❑ Subpoena/subpoena duces tecum

        (2) ❑ Request for production

        (3) ❑ Stipulation regarding discovery procedure

        (4) ❑ Facsimile cover sheet

    (c) ❑ Timing

        (1) ❑ After commencement of the action, any party may take the testimony of any person, including a party, by deposition upon oral examination

(II) ❏ Matters to be considered by the party taking a deposition upon written questions

    (a) ❏ Required documents

        (1) ❏ Notice of deposition

        (2) ❏ Certificate of service

    (b) ❏ Supplemental documents

        (1) ❏ Subpoena

        (2) ❏ Stipulation regarding discovery procedure

        (3) ❏ Facsimile cover sheet

    (c) ❏ Timing

        (1) ❏ After commencement of the action, any party may take the testimony of any person, including a party, by deposition upon written questions

(III) ❏ Matters to be considered by the party taking a deposition before commencement of the action

    (a) ❏ Required documents

        (1) ❏ Notice of deposition

        (2) ❏ Petition

        (3) ❏ Certificate of service

    (b) ❏ Supplemental documents

        (1) ❏ Stipulation regarding discovery procedure

        (2) ❏ Facsimile cover sheet

    (c) ❏ Timing

        (1) ❏ At least twenty (20) days before the date of hearing the notice shall be served in the manner provided in IN ST TRIAL P Rule 4 for service of summons

(IV) ❏ Matters to be considered by the party taking a deposition pending appeal

    (a) ❏ Required documents

        (1) ❏ Motion for leave to take deposition and notice

        (2) ❏ Chronological Case Summary (CCS) entry form

        (3) ❏ Proposed order

        (4) ❏ Certificate of service

    (b) ❏ Supplemental documents

        (1) ❏ Stipulation regarding discovery procedure

        (2) ❏ Supporting evidence

        (3) ❏ Facsimile cover sheet

    (c) ❏ Timing

        (1) ❏ The party who desires to perpetuate the testimony may make a motion in the court for leave to take the depositions, upon the same notice and service thereof as if the action was pending in the court

        (2) ❏ A written motion, other than one which may be heard ex parte, and notice of the hearing thereof shall be served not less than five (5) days before the time specified for the hearing, unless a different period is fixed by the Indiana Rules of Trial Procedure or by order of the court

        (3) ❏ All pleadings and papers subsequent to the complaint which are required to be served upon a party shall be filed with the Court either before service or within a reasonable period of time thereafter

ST. JOSEPH COUNTY

Requests, Notices and Applications
Application for Temporary Restraining Order

Document Last Updated October 2013

A. Applicable Rules

1. *State rules*

   a. Appearance. IN ST TRIAL P Rule 3.1.

   b. Process. IN ST TRIAL P Rule 4.

   c. Service and filing of pleadings and other papers. IN ST TRIAL P Rule 5.

   d. Time. IN ST TRIAL P Rule 6.

   e. Pleadings. IN ST TRIAL P Rule 7; IN ST TRIAL P Rule 8; IN ST TRIAL P Rule 9.2; IN ST TRIAL P Rule 10.

   f. Signing and verification of pleadings. IN ST TRIAL P Rule 11.

   g. Evidence. IN ST TRIAL P Rule 43.

   h. Judgment on the evidence (directed verdict). IN ST TRIAL P Rule 50.

   i. Findings by the court. IN ST TRIAL P Rule 52.

   j. Summary judgment. IN ST TRIAL P Rule 56.

   k. Motion to correct error. IN ST TRIAL P Rule 59.

   l. Relief from judgment or order. IN ST TRIAL P Rule 60.

   m. Injunctions. IN ST TRIAL P Rule 65; IN ST 34-26-1-7; IN ST 34-26-1-8; IN ST 34-26-1-11.

   n. Security; Proceedings against sureties. IN ST TRIAL P Rule 65.1.

   o. Hearing of motions. IN ST TRIAL P Rule 73.

   p. Access to court records. IN ST ADMIN Rule 9.

   q. Paper size. IN ST ADMIN Rule 11.

   r. Facsimile transmission. IN ST ADMIN Rule 12.

   s. Electronic filing and electronic service pilot projects. IN ST ADMIN Rule 16.

   t. Sealing of certain records by court; Hearing; Notice. IN ST 5-14-3-5.5.

   u. Civil protection orders. IN ST 34-26-5-1; IN ST 34-26-5-20.

   v. Sixtieth judicial circuit. IN ST 33-33-71-2.

   w. Privacy and confidentiality. IN ST 5-2-9-6; IN ST 5-14-3-4; IN ST 6-4.1-5-10; IN ST 6-4.1-12-12; IN ST 6-8.1-7-1; IN ST 11-13-1-8; IN ST 12-23-14-13; IN ST 16-39-3-10; IN ST 16-41-8-1; IN ST 22-4-19-6; IN ST 31-11-1-6; IN ST 31-19-5-23; IN ST 31-19-13-2; IN ST 31-19-19-1; IN ST 31-33-18-1; IN ST 31-39-1-1; IN ST 31-39-1-2; IN ST 33-23-16-16; IN ST 35-34-2-4; IN ST 35-38-1-13; IN ST 35-38-9-1; IN ST ADR Rule 2.11; IN ST ADR Rule 4.4; IN ST ADR Rule 5.6; IN ST JURY Rule 10.

2. *Local rules*

   a. Court hours and scheduling. IN ST ST JOSEPH GEN AND ADMIN Rule 104.

   b. Filing, pleading, and motions. IN ST ST JOSEPH CIV Rule 201.

   c. Uniform court and case number designation. IN ST ST JOSEPH CIV Rule 202.

   d. Proposed order. IN ST ST JOSEPH CIV Rule 213.

   e. Electronic filing of cases in St. Joseph County. IN ST ST JOSEPH ELECTRONIC Rule 701.

B. Timing

1. *Temporary restraining order without notice.* There are no specific timing requirements for submitting an application for a temporary restraining order without notice.

    a. *Filing.* All pleadings and papers subsequent to the complaint which are required to be served upon a party shall be filed with the Court either before service or within a reasonable period of time thereafter. IN ST TRIAL P Rule 5(E)(1).

2. *Computation of time*

    a. *Generally; Days excluded.* In computing any period of time prescribed or allowed by the Indiana Rules of Trial Procedure, by order of the court, or by any applicable statute, the day of the act, event, or default from which the designated period of time begins to run shall not be included. The last day of the period so computed is to be included unless it is:

        i. A Saturday,

        ii. A Sunday,

        iii. A legal holiday as defined by state statute, or

        iv. A day the office in which the act is to be done is closed during regular business hours. IN ST TRIAL P Rule 6(A).

    b. *Short periods.* In any event, the period runs until the end of the next day that is not a Saturday, a Sunday, a legal holiday, or a day on which the office is closed. When the period of time allowed is less than seven (7) days, intermediate Saturdays, Sundays, legal holidays, and days on which the office is closed shall be excluded from the computations. IN ST TRIAL P Rule 6(A).

    c. *Additional time after service by United States mail.* Whenever a party has the right or is required to do some act or take some proceedings within a prescribed period after the service of a notice or other paper upon him and the notice or paper is served upon him by United States mail, three (3) days shall be added to the prescribed period. IN ST TRIAL P Rule 6(E).

    d. *Enlargement of time.* When an act is required or allowed to be done at or within a specific time by the Indiana Rules of Trial Procedure, the court may at any time for cause shown:

        i. Order the period enlarged, with or without motion or notice, if request therefor is made before the expiration of the period originally prescribed or extended by a previous order; or

        ii. Upon motion made after the expiration of the specific period, permit the act to be done where the failure to act was the result of excusable neglect; but, the court may not extend the time for taking any action for judgment on the evidence under IN ST TRIAL P Rule 50(A), amendment of findings and judgment under IN ST TRIAL P Rule 52(B), to correct errors under IN ST TRIAL P Rule 59(C), statement in opposition to motion to correct error under IN ST TRIAL P Rule 59(E), or to obtain relief from final judgment under IN ST TRIAL P Rule 60(B), except to the extent and under the conditions stated in those rules. IN ST TRIAL P Rule 6(B).

        iii. An initial written motion for enlargement of time pursuant to IN ST TRIAL P Rule 6(B)(1) to answer a claim shall be routinely granted for an additional thirty (30) days from the original due date or other period the assigned Judge deems reasonable by written order of the Court. The motion must be filed on or before the original due date or IN ST ST JOSEPH CIV Rule 201 shall be inapplicable. IN ST ST JOSEPH CIV Rule 201(201.9.5).

            • Any motion for enlargement of time shall state the date when such response is due and the date to which time is requested to be enlarged. IN ST ST JOSEPH CIV Rule 201(201.9.5).

            • All subsequent motions for enlargement of time shall be so designated and will only be granted for good cause shown or in the interest of justice. IN ST ST JOSEPH CIV Rule 201(201.9.5).

C. General Requirements

1. *Motions, generally.* Unless made during a hearing or trial, or otherwise ordered by the court, an application to the court for an order shall be made by written motion. The motion shall state the grounds therefor and the relief or order sought. IN ST TRIAL P Rule 7(B).

    a. *Motions as distinct from pleadings.* Motions and responses to motions are not pleadings, and

allegations contained in a motion are not admissions of a party. 22B INPRAC 7:2; Wachstetter v. County Properties, LLC, 832 N.E.2d 574 (Ind.Ct.App. 2005); Scott County Family YMCA, Inc. v. Hobbs, 817 N.E.2d 603 (Ind.Ct.App. 2004).

   b. *Unopposed motions generally granted.* It is common for a trial court to grant procedural motions, such as motions for enlargement of time, discovery motions, or motions for continuance, unless an objection is filed. 21 INPRAC § 13.8.

   c. *Proposed orders.* As directed by the Court, a party or an attorney for a party shall prepare a proposed order based on the decision rendered by the Court. The party so directed shall prepare the proposed order in a timely manner and, upon filing, shall advise the chambers of the applicable judge that the proposed order has been prepared and filed. IN ST ST JOSEPH CIV Rule 213(213.2).

      i. Prior to entry by the Court of orders granting motions or applications, the moving party or applicant (or his or her attorney) shall, unless the Court directs otherwise, furnish the Court with proposed orders in the matter of restraining orders, temporary, or permanent injunctions. IN ST ST JOSEPH CIV Rule 213(213.1(8)).

2. *Application for temporary restraining order.* Seeking a temporary restraining order should only be considered if there is a possibility that irreparable injury may occur before the hearing for a preliminary injunction can be held. 4 INPRAC R 65(65.4).

   a. *Without notice*

      i. *When notice not required.* A temporary restraining order may be granted without written or oral notice to the adverse party or his attorney only if:

         • It clearly appears from specific facts shown by affidavit or by the verified complaint that immediate and irreparable injury, loss, or damage will result to the applicant before the adverse party or his attorney can be heard in opposition; and

         • The applicant's attorney certifies to the court in writing the efforts, if any, which have been made to give notice and the reasons supporting his claim that notice should not be required. IN ST TRIAL P Rule 65(B).

      ii. *Motion for dissolution or modification of temporary restraining order.* On two (2) days' notice to the party who obtained the temporary restraining order without notice or on such shorter notice to that party as the court may prescribe, the adverse party may appear and move its dissolution or modification and in that event the court shall proceed to hear and determine such motion as expeditiously as the ends of justice require. IN ST TRIAL P Rule 65(B).

   b. *Temporary restraining orders with notice in Indiana.* IN ST TRIAL P Rule 65(B) in its entirety deals only with temporary restraining orders issued without notice. No mention is made of the issuance of temporary restraining orders with notice. 4 INPRAC R 65(65.4). Some Indiana cases have apparently held that there is no such thing as a temporary restraining order if the adverse party has notice and a hearing is held. 4 INPRAC R 65(65.4); Indiana State Dept. of Welfare v. Stagner, 410 N.E.2d 1348 (Ind.Ct.App. 1980); Szany v. City of Hammond, 170 Ind.App. 537, 352 N.E.2d 866 (Ind.Ct.App. 1976). Refer to the Indiana KeyRules Motion for Preliminary Injunction document for information on obtaining an injunction with notice to the opposing party.

   c. *Application without notice as ex parte communication with judge.* The failure to follow the requirements of IN ST TRIAL P Rule 65(B) may constitute, in some circumstances, an improper ex parte communication between attorney and judge. 4 INPRAC R 65(65.4.1); Ace Bail Bonds v. Government Payment Service, Inc., 892 N.E.2d 702 (Ind.Ct.App. 2008), transfer denied (Ind. Jan. 15, 2009).

      i. When a party knows of the presence of another party's attorney in litigation, because each is present at hearings or at trial, then, even if an ex parte T.R.O. arguably meets the criteria in IN ST TRIAL P Rule 65(B), it is not valid unless it meets the standards in Smith v. Johnston, 711 N.E.2d 1259 (Ind.1999). 4 INPRAC R 65(65.4.1).

      ii. Smith v. Johnston, was an appeal to set a default judgment aside. The court granted relief because the party who obtained the default did not give notice to the defaulted party, even though IN ST TRIAL P Rule 4 and IN ST TRIAL P Rule 5 do not require that notice be served on the opposite party's attorney. 4 INPRAC R 65(65.4.1). Smith v. Johnston's rationale clearly states that if an attorney "has knowledge of his opponent's representation, then the Rules of Professional Conduct establish a duty to provide notice 'before seeking any relief from the court.'" 4 INPRAC R 65(65.4.1); Smith v. Johnston, 711 N.E.2d 1259 (Ind.1999).

d. *Service of the temporary restraining order once issued.* Notice of the restraining order should be served upon the adverse party. The order may be served together with process in accordance with IN ST TRIAL P Rule 4, or, if obtained after service of process, then in accordance with IN ST TRIAL P Rule 5. 22 INPRAC § 29.2.

   i. IN ST 34-26-1-11 provides the "clerk shall issue a copy of the order of injunction, certified by the clerk, which shall be served promptly by delivering the order to the adverse party." 22 INPRAC § 29.2; IN ST 34-26-1-11.

   ii. However, service is not necessary to make the restraining order effective and binding, so long as the restrained party receives actual knowledge of the order. 22 INPRAC § 29.2; Reed Sign Service, Inc. v. Reid, 755 N.E.2d 690 (Ind.Ct.App. 2001).

e. *Form of order by judge*

   i. Every order granting temporary injunction and every restraining order shall include or be accompanied by findings as required by IN ST TRIAL P Rule 52; shall be specific in terms; shall describe in reasonable detail, and not by reference to the complaint or other document, the act or acts sought to be restrained; and is binding only upon the parties to the action, their officers, agents, servants, employees, and attorneys, and upon those persons in active concert or participation with them who receive actual notice of the order by personal service or otherwise. IN ST TRIAL P Rule 65(D).

   ii. Every temporary restraining order granted without notice shall be indorsed with the date and hour of issuance; shall be filed forthwith in the clerk's office and entered of record; shall define the injury and state why it is irreparable and why the order was granted without notice; and shall expire by its terms within such time after entry, not to exceed ten (10) days, as the court fixes, unless within the time so fixed the order, for good cause shown, is extended for a like period or unless the whereabouts of the party against whom the order is granted is unknown and cannot be determined by reasonable diligence or unless the party against whom the order is directed consents that it may be extended for a longer period. The reasons for the extension shall be entered of record. IN ST TRIAL P Rule 65(B).

f. *Temporary restraining orders; Domestic relations cases.* Parties wishing protection from domestic or family violence in Domestic Relations cases shall petition the court pursuant to IN ST 34-26-5-1 through IN ST 34-26-5-20. IN ST TRIAL P Rule 65(E). For more information refer to IN ST TRIAL P Rule 65(E) and IN ST 34-26-5-1, et seq.

3. *Security*

a. *Security requirement.* No restraining order or preliminary injunction shall issue except upon the giving of security by the applicant, in such sum as the court deems proper, for the payment of such costs and damages as may be incurred or suffered by any party who is found to have been wrongfully enjoined or restrained. No such security shall be required of a governmental organization, but such governmental organization shall be responsible for costs and damages as may be incurred or suffered by any party who is found to have been wrongfully enjoined or restrained. IN ST TRIAL P Rule 65(C).

   i. The provisions of IN ST TRIAL P Rule 65.1 apply to a surety upon a bond or undertaking under IN ST TRIAL P Rule 65. IN ST TRIAL P Rule 65(C).

b. *Proceedings against sureties.* Whenever the Indiana Rules of Trial Procedure or other laws require or permit the giving of security by a party to a court action or proceeding, and security is given in the form of a bond or stipulation or other undertaking with one or more sureties, each surety submits himself to the jurisdiction of the court and irrevocably appoints the clerk of the court as his agent upon whom any papers affecting his liability on the bond or undertaking may be served. His liability may be enforced on motion without the necessity of an independent action. The motion and such notice of the motion as the court prescribes may be served on the clerk of the court, who shall forthwith mail copies to the sureties if their addresses are known. IN ST TRIAL P Rule 65.1 applies to bonds or security furnished on appeal, and enforcement shall be in the court to which the case is returned after appeal. IN ST TRIAL P Rule 65.1.

    c. *Bond generally used as security.* IN ST TRIAL P Rule 65(C) speaks only of the giving of security and does not expressly require a surety on a bond. In practice, however, the giving of a bond with an insurance company as surety in the amount set by the court is typically the device used to satisfy this section. 4 INPRAC R 65(65.6).

D. Documents

  1. *Required documents*

    a. *Application for temporary restraining order.* Refer to the General Requirements section of this document for additional information on the contents of an application for a temporary restraining order.

    b. *Chronological Case Summary (CCS) entry form.* Every written motion, petition, or other pleading subsequent to the original complaint presented to the Clerk for filing shall be accompanied by a Chronological Case Summary (CCS) entry form in duplicate. IN ST ST JOSEPH CIV Rule 201(201.4). Refer to the Format section of this document for details on the format and filing requirements for the CCS entry form.

    c. *Security.* No restraining order or preliminary injunction shall issue except upon the giving of security by the applicant, in such sum as the court deems proper, for the payment of such costs and damages as may be incurred or suffered by any party who is found to have been wrongfully enjoined or restrained. IN ST TRIAL P Rule 65(C). Refer to the General Requirements section of this document for more information.

    d. *Proposed order.* Unless local practice provides differently, a party should submit a proposed order with its written motion to be signed by the judge once the motion has been granted. 21 INPRAC § 13.8. All proposed orders shall be submitted in an original plus a number of copies equal to one more than the number of pro se parties and attorneys of record contained in the prepared proof of notice under IN ST TRIAL P Rule 72(D). IN ST ST JOSEPH CIV Rule 213(213.3); IN ST ST JOSEPH CIV Rule 201(201.5.2).

  2. *Supplemental documents*

    a. *Supporting evidence.* When a motion is based on facts not appearing of record the court may hear the matter on affidavits presented by the respective parties, but the court may direct that the matter be heard wholly or partly on oral testimony or depositions. IN ST TRIAL P Rule 43(B).

    b. *Facsimile cover sheet.* Any document sent to the Clerk of the Circuit Court by electronic facsimile transmission shall be accompanied by a cover sheet which states the title of the document, case number, number of pages, identity and voice telephone number of the sending party and instructions for filing. The cover sheet shall contain the signature of the attorney or party, pro se, authorizing the filing. IN ST ADMIN Rule 12(D).

E. Format

  1. *Form of motions.* The rules applicable to captions, and the signing and form of pleadings (IN ST TRIAL P Rule 8 through IN ST TRIAL P Rule 11), apply to all motions and other papers provided under the Indiana Rules of Trial Procedure. 22B INPRAC 7:2.

    a. *Separate motions; Alternative motions.* Each motion shall be separate, while alternative motions filed together shall each be identified on the caption. IN ST ST JOSEPH CIV Rule 206(206.1).

  2. *Form of pleadings*

    a. *Caption; Names of parties.* Every pleading shall contain a caption setting forth the name of the court, the title of the action, the file number, and a designation as in IN ST TRIAL P Rule 7(A). In the complaint the title of the action shall include the names of all the parties, but in other pleadings it is sufficient to state the name of the first party on each side with an appropriate indication of other parties. IN ST TRIAL P Rule 10(A); IN ST ST JOSEPH CIV Rule 201(201.3.3). If a special judge has been assigned to the case, the pleading should also identify the special judge. IN ST ST JOSEPH CIV Rule 201(201.3.3).

    i. *Title.* All pleadings or motions shall include a title, which shall delineate each topic included in the pleading. For example, where a pleading contains an answer, a motion to dismiss, and a jury request, each topic shall be set forth in the title. IN ST ST JOSEPH CIV Rule 201(201.3.4).

b. *Paragraphs; Separate statements.* All averments of a claim or defense shall be made in numbered paragraphs, the contents of each of which shall be limited as far as practicable to a statement of a single set of circumstances, and a paragraph may be referred to by number in all succeeding pleadings. Each claim founded upon a separate transaction or occurrence and each defense other than denials may be stated in a separate count or defense whenever a separation facilitates the clear presentation of the matters set forth. IN ST TRIAL P Rule 10(B).

c. *Adoption by reference; Exhibits.* Statements in a pleading may be adopted by reference in a different part of the same pleading or in another pleading or in any motion. A copy of any written instrument which is an exhibit to a pleading is a part thereof for all purposes. IN ST TRIAL P Rule 10(C).

d. *Flat filing.* In order that the Clerk's files may be kept under the system commonly known as "flat filing," all papers presented to the Clerk for filing shall be flat and unfolded. Pleadings shall have no covers or backs and shall be fastened together at the top left-hand corner only. IN ST ST JOSEPH CIV Rule 201(201.1).

e. *One side of page used.* Printing shall be on one (1) side of the paper. IN ST ST JOSEPH CIV Rule 201(201.3.2).

f. *Copies.* All copies shall be on white paper of sufficient strength and durability to resist normal wear and tear. IN ST ST JOSEPH CIV Rule 201(201.3.1).

g. *Margins.* Margins shall be at least one inch (1"). IN ST ST JOSEPH CIV Rule 201(201.3.2).

h. *Double-spaced.* If typewritten, the lines shall be double spaced except for quotations, which shall be indented and single-spaced. IN ST ST JOSEPH CIV Rule 201(201.3.2).

i. *Font size.* Type face shall be twelve (12) font size or larger within the body of the document and ten (10) font size or larger in the footnotes. IN ST ST JOSEPH CIV Rule 201(201.3.2).

j. *Font type.* The font type must be legible and script type shall not be used. IN ST ST JOSEPH CIV Rule 201(201.3.2).

k. *Italics.* Italicized type may be used for quotations, references, or case citations. IN ST ST JOSEPH CIV Rule 201(201.3.2).

l. *Court and case designation.* All filings shall conform to the requirements for uniform court and case number designation set by IN ST ADMIN Rule 8. In addition, all filings shall contain the proper court and case designation as described below. IN ST ST JOSEPH CIV Rule 202.

    i. *Court designation.* Pursuant to IN ST 33-33-71-2, St. Joseph County, Indiana, constitutes the Sixtieth Judicial Circuit. The legal names of the courts within the 60th Judicial Circuit are the St. Joseph Circuit Court, the St. Joseph Superior Court, and the St. Joseph Probate Court. All filings shall properly reflect the legal name of the applicable court. Any filing may be amended, rejected, or stricken if it does not contain the proper case name and/or the legal name of the court. IN ST ST JOSEPH CIV Rule 202(202.1).

m. *Form of CCS entry.* Every written motion, petition, or other pleading subsequent to the original complaint presented to the Clerk for filing shall be accompanied by a Chronological Case Summary (CCS) entry form in duplicate which shall contain the title and cause number of the action, the date, and the proposed entry to appear on the docket. IN ST ST JOSEPH CIV Rule 201(201.4).

    i. *Identification and signature.* The CCS entry form shall identify the party making the filing, designate each pleading being filed, and shall be signed by counsel of record or the unrepresented litigant. IN ST ST JOSEPH CIV Rule 201(201.4).

    ii. *Date stamp.* The form shall be date stamped and presented to the Court Clerk, who shall initial the form and return the duplicate to the filing party. IN ST ST JOSEPH CIV Rule 201(201.4).

n. *Form of proposed order.* Any proposed order shall be a document that is separate and apart from the motion or application to which it relates and shall contain a caption showing the name of the court, the case number assigned to the case, and the title of the case as shown by the complaint pursuant to IN ST ST JOSEPH CIV Rule 201. IN ST ST JOSEPH CIV Rule 213(213.2).

    i. If there are multiple parties, the title may be shortened to include only the first name plaintiff and defendant with appropriate indication that there are additional parties. IN ST ST JOSEPH CIV Rule 213(213.2).

    ii. The proposed order shall be on white paper, eight and one-half by eleven inches (8 1/2" x 11") in size, and each page shall be numbered. IN ST ST JOSEPH CIV Rule 213(213.2).

    iii. The last page of the proposed order shall contain a line for the date, either "Dated _____" or "Signed on the date filemarked hereon." IN ST ST JOSEPH CIV Rule 213(213.2).

    iv. On the last page there also shall be a line for the signature of the Judge under which shall be typed "Judge, St. Joseph [Circuit or Superior or Probate] Court." IN ST ST JOSEPH CIV Rule 213(213.2).

    v. If the proposed order contains a recommendation from a Magistrate, the last page shall have a line for the signature of the Magistrate under which shall be typed "Magistrate, St. Joseph [Circuit or Superior or Probate] Court," to the left of which shall be the following, "So Recommended:" and beneath and to the left of which shall be typed, "Approved. So Ordered." IN ST ST JOSEPH CIV Rule 213(213.2).

    vi. To allow compliance with the notice requirements of IN ST TRIAL P Rule 72(D), the lower four (4) inches of the last page of the proposed order shall be left blank. The proposed order shall also include a prepared proof of notice under IN ST TRIAL P Rule 72(D), and in preparing such a notice the filing party shall complete all portions of the prepared proof of notice. IN ST ST JOSEPH CIV Rule 213(213.2).

3. *Size of papers for filing.* Effective January 1, 1992, all pleadings, copies, motions and documents filed with any trial court or appellate level court, typed or printed, with the exception of exhibits and existing wills, shall be prepared on eight and one-half by eleven inch (8 1/2" x 11") size paper. IN ST ADMIN Rule 11.

    a. *Paper.* Pleadings, motions, and other papers shall be either legibly printed or typewritten on white opaque paper of good quality at least sixteen (16) pound weight, eight and one-half inches (8 1/2 ") in width and eleven inches (11") in length as required by IN ST ADMIN Rule 11. IN ST ST JOSEPH CIV Rule 201(201.3.1).

4. *Signature requirements*

    a. *Signature of attorney.* Every pleading or motion of a party represented by an attorney shall be signed by at least one (1) attorney of record in his individual name, whose address, telephone number, and attorney number shall be stated, except that this provision shall not apply to pleadings and motions made and transcribed at the trial or a hearing before the judge and received by him in such form. IN ST TRIAL P Rule 11(A).

        i. The signature of an attorney constitutes a certificate by him that he has read the pleadings; that to the best of his knowledge, information, and belief, there is good ground to support it; and that it is not interposed for delay. IN ST TRIAL P Rule 11(A).

        ii. If a pleading or motion is not signed or is signed with intent to defeat the purpose of the rule, it may be stricken as sham and false and the action may proceed as though the pleading had not been served. IN ST TRIAL P Rule 11(A).

        iii. For a willful violation of IN ST TRIAL P Rule 11 an attorney may be subjected to appropriate disciplinary action. Similar action may be taken if scandalous or indecent matter is inserted. IN ST TRIAL P Rule 11(A).

    b. *Signature of unrepresented party.* A party who is not represented by an attorney shall sign his pleading and state his address. IN ST TRIAL P Rule 11(A).

    c. *Verification not generally required.* Except when specifically required by rule, pleadings or motions need not be verified or accompanied by affidavit. The rule in equity that the averments of an answer under oath must be overcome by the testimony of two (2) witnesses or of one (1) witness sustained by corroborating circumstances is abolished. IN ST TRIAL P Rule 11(A).

d. *Verification by affirmation or representation.* When in connection with any civil or special statutory proceeding it is required that any pleading, motion, petition, supporting affidavit, or other document of any kind, be verified, or that an oath be taken, it shall be sufficient if the subscriber simply affirms the truth of the matter to be verified by an affirmation or representation. IN ST TRIAL P Rule 11(B). IN ST TRIAL P Rule 11(B) states that the affirmation or representation should be in substantially the following language: "I (we) affirm, under the penalties for perjury, that the foregoing representation(s) is (are) true. (Signed) _____."

   i. Any person who falsifies an affirmation or representation of fact shall be subject to the same penalties as are prescribed by law for the making of a false affidavit. IN ST TRIAL P Rule 11(B).

e. *Verified pleadings, motions, and affidavits as evidence.* Pleadings, motions and affidavits accompanying or in support of such pleadings or motions when required to be verified or under oath shall be accepted as a representation that the signer had personal knowledge thereof or reasonable cause to believe the existence of the facts or matters stated or alleged therein; and, if otherwise competent or acceptable as evidence, may be admitted as evidence of the facts or matters stated or alleged therein when it is so provided in the Indiana Rules of Trial Procedure, by statute or other law, or to the extent the writing or signature expressly purports to be made upon the signer's personal knowledge. When such pleadings, motions and affidavits are verified or under oath they shall not require other or greater proof on the part of the adverse party than if not verified or not under oath unless expressly provided otherwise by the Indiana Rules of Trial Procedure, statute or other law. Affidavits upon motions for summary judgment under IN ST TRIAL P Rule 56 and in denial of execution under IN ST TRIAL P Rule 9.2 shall be made upon personal knowledge. IN ST TRIAL P Rule 11(C).

f. *Signature, verification and other requirements.* Parties and their counsel are enjoined to comply with the verification requirements of IN ST TRIAL P Rule 11, and either the moving party or the party's attorney of record shall sign all pleadings and motions before filing with the Clerk of the Court. Every motion, petition, or other pleading filed with the Clerk shall contain the name, organization, physical address, telephone number, and facsimile number of the filing party or an attorney for that party. IN ST ST JOSEPH CIV Rule 201(201.3.6).

   i. The Clerk shall not accept any motion, petition, notice or other pleading or a CCS entry form for filing from an unrepresented litigant unless the unrepresented litigant's current address and phone number appear on the pleading, and an opposing party may service notices and responses on an unrepresented litigant at any address he or she has provided on a pleading. IN ST ST JOSEPH CIV Rule 201(201.3.6).

5. *Information excluded from public access.* Every document filed in a case shall separately identify information excluded from public access pursuant to IN ST ADMIN Rule 9(G)(1) as follows:

   a. Whole documents that are excluded from public access pursuant to IN ST ADMIN Rule 9(G)(1) shall be tendered on light green paper or have a light green coversheet attached to the document, marked "Not for Public Access" or "Confidential." IN ST TRIAL P Rule 5(G)(1).

   b. When only a portion of a document contains information excluded from public access pursuant to IN ST ADMIN Rule 9(G)(1), said information shall be omitted [or redacted] from the filed document, and set forth on a separate accompanying document on light green paper conspicuously marked "Not for Public Access" or "Confidential" and clearly designated [or identifying] the caption and number of the case and the document and location within the document to which the redacted material pertains. IN ST TRIAL P Rule 5(G)(2).

   c. With respect to documents filed in electronic format, the trial court, by local rule, may provide for compliance with IN ST TRIAL P Rule 5 in manner that separates and protects access to information excluded from public access. IN ST TRIAL P Rule 5(G)(3).

   d. IN ST TRIAL P Rule 5(G) does not apply to a record sealed by the court pursuant to IN ST

5-14-3-5.5 or otherwise, nor to records, documents, or information filed in cases to which public access is prohibited pursuant to IN ST ADMIN Rule 9(G). IN ST TRIAL P Rule 5(G)(4).

e. The following information in case records is excluded from public access and is confidential:

i. Information that is excluded from public access pursuant to federal law;

ii. Information that is excluded from public access as declared confidential by Indiana statute or other court rule, including without limitation:

- All adoption records created after July 8, 1941, as declared confidential by IN ST 31-19-19-1, et seq., except those specifically declared open by IN ST 31-19-13-2(2);

- All records relating to chancroid, chlamydia, gonorrhea, hepatitis, human immunodeficiency virus (HIV), Lymphogranuloma venereum, syphilis, tuberculosis, as declared confidential by IN ST 16-41-8-1, et seq.;

- All records relating to child abuse as declared confidential by IN ST 31-33-18-1, et seq.;

- All records relating to drug tests as declared confidential by IN ST 5-14-3-4(a)(9);

- Records of grand jury proceedings as declared confidential by IN ST 35-34-2-4;

- Records of juvenile proceedings as declared confidential by IN ST 31-39-1-2, except those specifically open under statute;

- All paternity records created after July 1, 1941 as declared confidential by IN ST 31-14-11-15, IN ST 31-19-5-23, IN ST 31-39-1-1 and IN ST 31-39-1-2 [Editor's note: IN ST 31-14-11-15 was repealed effective May 9, 2013];

- All pre-sentence reports as declared confidential by IN ST 35-38-1-13;

- Written petitions to permit marriages without consent and orders directing the Clerk of Court to issue a marriage license to underage persons, as declared confidential by IN ST 31-11-1-6;

- Only those arrest warrants, search warrants, indictments and informations ordered confidential by the trial judge, prior to return of duly executed service as declared confidential by IN ST 5-14-3-4(b)(1);

- All medical, mental health, or tax records unless determined by law or regulation of any governmental custodian not to be confidential, released by the subject of such records, or declared by a court of competent jurisdiction to be essential to the resolution of litigation as declared confidential by IN ST 16-39-3-10, IN ST 6-4.1-5-10, IN ST 6-4.1-12-12, and IN ST 6-8.1-7-1;

- Personal information relating to jurors or prospective jurors, other than for the use of the parties and counsel, pursuant to IN ST JURY Rule 10;

- Information relating to protection from abuse orders, no-contact orders and workplace violence restraining orders as declared confidential by IN ST 5-2-9-6, et seq.;

- Mediation proceedings pursuant to IN ST ADR Rule 2.11, Mini-Trial proceedings pursuant to IN ST ADR Rule 4.4(C), and Summary Jury Trials pursuant to IN ST ADR Rule 5.6;

- Information in probation files pursuant to the Probation Standards promulgated by the Judicial Conference of Indiana pursuant to IN ST 11-13-1-8(b);

- Information deemed confidential pursuant to the Rules for Court Administered Alcohol and Drug Programs promulgated by the Judicial Conference of Indiana pursuant to IN ST 12-23-14-13;

- Information deemed confidential pursuant to the Problem-Solving Court Rules promulgated by the Judicial Conference of Indiana pursuant to IN ST 33-23-16-16;

- All records of the Department of workforce Development as declared confidential by IN ST 22-4-19-6;

- Information regarding interception of electronic communications that is sealed or deemed confidential as set forth in IN ST 35-33.5-2-1, et seq.

iii. Information excluded from public access by specific court order;

iv. Complete Social Security Numbers of living persons;

v. With the exception of names, information such as addresses, phone numbers, and dates of birth which explicitly identifies:

- Natural persons who are witnesses or victims (not including defendants) in criminal, domestic violence, stalking, sexual assault, juvenile, or civil protection order proceedings, provided that juveniles who are victims of sex crimes shall be identified by initials only;

- Places of residence of judicial officers, clerks and other employees of courts and clerks of court, unless the person or persons about whom the information pertains waives confidentiality;

vi. Complete account numbers of specific assets, loans, bank accounts, credit cards, and personal identification numbers (PINs);

vii. All orders of expungement entered in criminal or juvenile proceedings, orders to restrict access to criminal history information pursuant to IN ST 35-38-5-5.5 or IN ST 35-38-8-5 and records excluded from public access by such orders, and information related to infractions that is excluded from public access pursuant to IN ST 34-28-5-15 or IN ST 34-28-5-16 [Editor's note: IN ST 35-38-5-5.5, IN ST 35-38-8-5 and IN ST 34-28-5-16 were repealed effective July 1, 2013; for information on orders restricting access to criminal history, refer to IN ST 35-38-9-1, et seq.];

viii. All personal notes and e-mail, and deliberative material, of judges, jurors, court staff and judicial agencies, and information recorded in personal data assistants (PDA's) or organizers and personal calendars. IN ST ADMIN Rule 9(G)(1).

F. Filing and Service Requirements

1. *Filing requirements.* Except as otherwise provided in IN ST TRIAL P Rule 5(E)(2), all pleadings and papers subsequent to the complaint which are required to be served upon a party shall be filed with the Court either before service or within a reasonable period of time thereafter. IN ST TRIAL P Rule 5(E)(1).

a. *Filing with the court defined.* The filing of pleadings, motions, and other papers with the court as required by the Indiana Rules of Trial Procedure shall be made by one of the following methods:

i. Delivery to the clerk of the court;

ii. Sending by electronic transmission under the procedure adopted pursuant to IN ST ADMIN Rule 12;

iii. Mailing to the clerk by registered, certified or express mail return receipt requested;

iv. Depositing with any third-party commercial carrier for delivery to the clerk within three (3) calendar days, cost prepaid, properly addressed;

v. If the court so permits, filing with the judge, in which event the judge shall note thereon the filing date and forthwith transmit them to the office of the clerk; or

vi. Electronic filing, as approved by the Division of State Court Administration pursuant to IN ST ADMIN Rule 16. IN ST TRIAL P Rule 5(F).

vii. Filing by registered or certified mail and by third-party commercial carrier shall be complete upon mailing or deposit. IN ST TRIAL P Rule 5(F).

viii. All pleadings shall be filed with the Clerk, not directly with the Court, unless otherwise required by the Indiana Rules of Court. The entry of appearances and the filing of pleadings or other matters not requiring immediate Court action shall be filed with the Clerk and not in open Court. A Judge may permit papers to be filed in chambers, in which event he or she shall note thereon the filing date and transmit the papers to the Clerk. IN ST ST JOSEPH CIV Rule 201(201.2).

b. *Facsimile filing.* Unless otherwise authorized by IN ST ST JOSEPH ELECTRONIC Rule 701, electronic filing of pleadings by computerized or facsimile transmission is not permitted. IN ST ST JOSEPH CIV Rule 201(201.2).

c. *Additional copies.* In cases in which a party or counsel supplies the proposed order or decree, a sufficient number shall be prepared and filed as to provide the Clerk to retain two (2) copies, which shall be filed in the flat file and the record of judgments and orders. Should the party or counsel desire additional copies, a sufficient number of copies should be filed to effectuate that purpose. IN ST ST JOSEPH CIV Rule 201(201.6).

d. *Proof of filing.* Any party filing any paper by any method other than personal delivery to the clerk shall retain proof of filing. IN ST TRIAL P Rule 5(F).

2. *Service requirements.* Unless otherwise provided by the Indiana Rules of Trial Procedure or an order of the court, each party and special judge, if any, shall be served with: (1) every order required by its terms to be served; (2) every pleading subsequent to the original complaint; (3) every written motion except one which may be heard ex parte; (4) every brief submitted to the trial court; (5) every paper relating to discovery required to be served upon a party; and (6) every written notice, appearance, demand, offer of judgment, designation of record on appeal, or similar paper. IN ST TRIAL P Rule 5(A).

a. *Service generally.* Every motion, petition, notice, or other pleading required to be served by IN ST TRIAL P Rule 5 shall be served on all counsel of record or unrepresented parties either before it is filed or on the day it is filed with the Court, and the date of filing shall be indicated on the Certificate of Service. IN ST ST JOSEPH CIV Rule 201(201.5.1).

    i. *Copy.* A copy of the Clerk's CCS entry form of the filing shall also be served on all counsel of record or unrepresented parties whenever it contains an appearance of counsel or contains a date for Court hearing on the matter. IN ST ST JOSEPH CIV Rule 201(201.5.1).

b. *Methods of service*

    i. *Personal service.* Whenever a party is represented by an attorney of record, service shall be made upon such attorney unless service upon the party himself is ordered by the court. Service upon the attorney or party shall be made by delivering or mailing a copy of the papers to the last known address or where an attorney or party has consented to service by fax or e-mail, as provided in IN ST TRIAL P Rule 3.1(A)(4), by faxing or e-mailing a copy of the documents to the fax number or e-mail address set out in the appearance form or correction as required by IN ST TRIAL P Rule 3.1(E). IN ST TRIAL P Rule 5(B). Delivery of a copy within IN ST TRIAL P Rule 5 means:

- Offering or tendering it to the attorney or party and stating the nature of the papers being served. Refusal to accept an offered or tendered document is a waiver of any objection to the sufficiency or adequacy of service of that document;

- Leaving it at his office with a clerk or other person in charge thereof, or if there is no one in charge, leaving it in a conspicuous place therein; or

- If the office is closed, by leaving it at his dwelling house or usual place of abode with some person of suitable age and discretion then residing therein; or,

- Leaving it at some other suitable place, selected by the attorney upon whom service is being made, pursuant to duly promulgated local rule. IN ST TRIAL P Rule 5(B)(1).

    ii. *Service by the clerk.* Whenever the Clerk is required by rule or statute to give notice, the party or parties requesting such notice shall furnish the Clerk with sufficient copies of the notice to be given, along with stamped, addressed envelopes with the names and the addresses of the parties or their counsel to whom such notice is to be given. IN ST ST JOSEPH CIV Rule 201(201.5.4).

    iii. *Service on the court.* Service on a Judge may be made by delivering a copy to the Judge's secretary or mailing a copy to the Judge at his or her chambers. Service on a Judge may not be accomplished by facsimile transmission; however, a courtesy copy may be sent to the Judge's chambers by electronic mail or facsimile transmission contemporaneously with service by mail or otherwise. IN ST ST JOSEPH CIV Rule 201(201.5.5).

    iv. *Service by mail.* If service is made by mail, the papers shall be deposited in the United States mail addressed to the person on whom they are being served, with postage prepaid. Service shall be deemed complete upon mailing. Proof of service of all papers permitted to be mailed may be made by written acknowledgment of service, by affidavit of the person who mailed the papers, or by certificate of an attorney. It shall be the duty of attorneys when entering their appearance in a cause or when filing pleadings or papers therein, to have noted in the Chronological Case Summary or said pleadings or papers so filed the address and telephone number of their office. Service by delivery or by mail at such address shall be deemed sufficient and complete. IN ST TRIAL P Rule 5(B)(2).

    v. *Service by fax or e-mail.* A party who has consented to service by fax or e-mail may be served as follows:

- Service by e-mail shall be made by attaching the document being served in .pdf format. Discovery documents must also be served in accordance with IN ST TRIAL P Rule 26(A). IN ST TRIAL P Rule 5(B)(3)(a).

- Service by fax shall be deemed complete upon generation of a transmission record indicating the successful transmission of the entire document, except as provided in IN ST TRIAL P Rule 5(B)(3)(d). IN ST TRIAL P Rule 5(B)(3)(b).

- Service by e-mail shall be deemed complete upon transmission, except as provided in IN ST TRIAL P Rule 5(B)(3)(d). IN ST TRIAL P Rule 5(B)(3)(c).

- Service by fax or e-mail that occurs on a Saturday, Sunday, legal holiday, or day the court or agency in which the matter is pending is closed or after 5:00 PM local time of the recipient shall be deemed complete the next day that is not a Saturday, Sunday, legal holiday, or day that the court or agency in which the matter is pending is not closed. IN ST TRIAL P Rule 5(B)(3)(d).

c. *Serving numerous defendants.* In any action in which there are unusually large numbers of defendants, the court, upon motion or of its own initiative, may order:

    i. That service of the pleadings of the defendants and replies thereto need not be made as between the defendants;

- That any cross-claim, counterclaim, or matter constituting an avoidance or affirmative defense contained therein shall be deemed to be denied or avoided by all other parties; and

- That the filing of any such pleading and service thereof upon the plaintiff constitutes due notice of it to the parties. IN ST TRIAL P Rule 5(D).

    ii. A copy of every such order shall be served upon the parties in such manner and form as the court directs. IN ST TRIAL P Rule 5(D).

d. *Service on parties in default for failure to appear.* No service need be made on parties in default for failure to appear, except that pleadings asserting new or additional claims for relief against them shall be served upon them in the manner provided by service of summons in IN ST TRIAL P Rule 4. IN ST TRIAL P Rule 5(A).

e. *Distribution.* Counsel or an unrepresented party submitting a motion, petition, notice, pleading or proposed order shall indicate the method of distribution desired on the Clerk's CCS entry form. The Clerk will not return or distribute copies of motions, petitions, pleadings, notices or proposed orders, other than those originated by the Court, by mail unless the Clerk is provided with stamped, addressed envelopes. IN ST ST JOSEPH CIV Rule 201(201.5.3).

f. *Mailbox.* As a matter of convenience to attorneys, each court provides a mailbox for the distribution filings and orders generated by the Court, and it is the responsibility of each attorney to periodically check these mailboxes for service and distribution of court-generated filings and orders. IN ST ST JOSEPH CIV Rule 201(201.5.3).

G. Hearings

1. *Hearing on motion.* Unless local conditions make it impracticable, each judge shall establish regular times and places, at intervals sufficiently frequent for the prompt dispatch of business, at which motions requiring notice and hearing may be heard and disposed of; but the judge at any time or place and on such

notice, if any, as he considers reasonable may make order for the advancement, conduct, and hearing of actions. To expedite its business the court may direct the submission and determination of motions without oral hearing upon brief written statements of reasons in support and opposition, or direct or permit hearings by telephone conference call with all attorneys or other similar means of communication. IN ST TRIAL P Rule 73(A).

2. *Presentation of evidence.* On the hearing of an application for a restraining order or temporary injunction, each party may read affidavits or documentary or record evidence. IN ST 34-26-1-8.

3. *Hearing for preliminary injunction.* In case a temporary restraining order is granted without notice, the motion for a preliminary injunction shall be set down for hearing at the earliest possible time and takes precedence of all matters except older matters of the same character; and when the motion comes on for hearing the party who obtained the temporary restraining order shall proceed with the application for a preliminary injunction and, if he does not do so, the court shall dissolve the temporary restraining order. IN ST TRIAL P Rule 65(B). Refer to the Indiana KeyRules Motion for Preliminary Injunction document for more information.

4. *Hearing dates.* Hearing dates for filings requiring Court action shall be obtained from the Court Clerk and incorporated in the CCS entry at the time the motion or other pleading is filed. If no date is obtained prior to the filing, the fact of the hearing should be noted with the date and time left blank. IN ST ST JOSEPH CIV Rule 201(201.4).

5. *Hearing on matters other than trials.* Each Judge shall reserve periods of time for hearing matters other than contested trials, such as pre-trial and post-trial motions, rules to show cause, defaults, uncontested dissolutions of marriage, etc. As necessary to minimize conflicts in scheduling, the Judges shall set these schedules after consultation. Hearings shall be scheduled as follows:

   a. *Scheduling uncontested or routine matters.* Routine matters, procedural motions, domestic relations applications for provisional relief and contempt proceedings, uncontested petitions for dissolution of marriage, and all other matters appropriate for summary consideration and disposition will be heard on the daily calendar. IN ST ST JOSEPH GEN AND ADMIN Rule 104(104.3.1).

   b. *Scheduling contested or complicated matters.* Other matters that will require a hearing reasonably estimated to last in excess of twenty (20) minutes will be scheduled as the Court's calendar allows. Counsel or a party proceeding pro se should contact the chambers of the assigned judge to arrange for an appropriate hearing date and time. IN ST ST JOSEPH GEN AND ADMIN Rule 104(104.3.2).

   c. *Scheduling motions for hearings.* Except for motions to correct error or not likely to require a hearing (as described in IN ST ST JOSEPH CIV Rule 201), all motions shall be scheduled for hearing at the time they are filed. It shall the responsibility of the moving party or counsel for the moving party to secure the date and time of the hearing from the Clerk or Court personnel who maintain the calendar for each Judge or Magistrate Judge. It shall also be the responsibility of the moving party or counsel for the moving party to coordinate the hearing date with all opposing counsel or unrepresented parties. IN ST ST JOSEPH CIV Rule 201(201.9.1).

   d. *Oral arguments on motions and other pleadings.* Unless otherwise required by St. Joseph County Civil or Indiana Trial Rules, it is within the sound discretion of the assigned Judge whether to allow oral argument; however, any party may file a request for oral argument by filing a written request by separate motion contemporaneously or at any time before the Court has ruled upon the motion or pleadings to be argued. IN ST ST JOSEPH CIV Rule 201(201.9.4).

H. Forms

1. Application for Temporary Restraining Order Forms for Indiana

   a. Prayer in complaint for temporary restraining order. 5 INPRAC § 3:13.60.

   b. Motion for temporary restraining order; With notice. 5 INPRAC § 3:13.80.

   c. Notice of motion for temporary restraining order. 11 INPRAC § 97.2.

   d. Motion for temporary restraining order; Without notice. 11 INPRAC § 97.3.

   e. Affidavit in support of motion for temporary restraining order. 11 INPRAC § 97.4.

   f. Certificate of efforts of attorney to give notice of application for temporary restraining order. 11 INPRAC § 97.5.

g. Temporary restraining order without notice and order to show cause why preliminary injunction should not issue; Real estate. 11 INPRAC § 97.6.

h. Motion to extend temporary restraining order. 11 INPRAC § 97.7.

i. Order granting motion to extend temporary restraining order. 11 INPRAC § 97.8.

j. Stipulation extending temporary restraining order. 11 INPRAC § 97.9.

k. Order granting extension of temporary restraining order pursuant to stipulation. 11 INPRAC § 97.10.

l. Motion for judge of adjourning circuit to rule upon motion for temporary restraining order. 11 INPRAC § 97.11.

m. Affidavit in support of motion for judge of adjoining county to rule on motion for temporary restraining order. 11 INPRAC § 97.12.

n. Motion to advance trial on merits for consolidation with hearing on preliminary injunction. 11 INPRAC § 97.13.

I. Checklist

(I) ❑ Matters to be considered by the party filing the application without notice

    (a) ❑ Required documents

        (1) ❑ Application for temporary restraining order

        (2) ❑ Chronological Case Summary (CCS) entry form

        (3) ❑ Security

        (4) ❑ Proposed order

    (b) ❑ Supplemental documents

        (1) ❑ Supporting evidence

        (2) ❑ Facsimile cover sheet

    (c) ❑ Timing

        (1) ❑ There are no specific timing requirements for submitting an application for a temporary restraining order without notice

Requests, Notices and Applications
Pretrial Conferences, Scheduling, Management

Document Last Updated October 2013

A. Applicable Rules

1. *State rules*

    a. Appearance. IN ST TRIAL P Rule 3.1.

    b. Process. IN ST TRIAL P Rule 4.

    c. Service and filing of pleadings and other papers. IN ST TRIAL P Rule 5.

    d. Time. IN ST TRIAL P Rule 6.

    e. Pleadings. IN ST TRIAL P Rule 7; IN ST TRIAL P Rule 8; IN ST TRIAL P Rule 9.2; IN ST TRIAL P Rule 10.

    f. Signing and verification of pleadings. IN ST TRIAL P Rule 11.

    g. Pre-trial procedure; Formulating issues. IN ST TRIAL P Rule 16.

    h. Evidence. IN ST TRIAL P Rule 43.

    i. Judgment on the evidence (directed verdict). IN ST TRIAL P Rule 50.

j.   Findings by the court. IN ST TRIAL P Rule 52.

k.   Summary judgment. IN ST TRIAL P Rule 56.

l.   Motion to correct error. IN ST TRIAL P Rule 59.

m.   Relief from judgment or order. IN ST TRIAL P Rule 60.

n.   Access to court records. IN ST ADMIN Rule 9.

o.   Paper size. IN ST ADMIN Rule 11.

p.   Facsimile transmission. IN ST ADMIN Rule 12.

q.   Electronic filing and electronic service pilot projects. IN ST ADMIN Rule 16.

r.   Sealing of certain records by court; Hearing; Notice. IN ST 5-14-3-5.5.

s.   Sixtieth judicial circuit. IN ST 33-33-71-2.

t.   Privacy and confidentiality. IN ST 5-2-9-6; IN ST 5-14-3-4; IN ST 6-4.1-5-10; IN ST 6-4.1-12-12; IN ST 6-8.1-7-1; IN ST 11-13-1-8; IN ST 12-23-14-13; IN ST 16-39-3-10; IN ST 16-41-8-1; IN ST 22-4-19-6; IN ST 31-11-1-6; IN ST 31-19-5-23; IN ST 31-19-13-2; IN ST 31-19-19-1; IN ST 31-33-18-1; IN ST 31-39-1-1; IN ST 31-39-1-2; IN ST 33-23-16-16; IN ST 35-34-2-4; IN ST 35-38-1-13; IN ST 35-38-9-1; IN ST ADR Rule 2.11; IN ST ADR Rule 4.4; IN ST ADR Rule 5.6; IN ST JURY Rule 10.

2.   *Local rules*

a.   Case flow and disposition. IN ST ST JOSEPH GEN AND ADMIN Rule 106.

b.   Filing, pleading, and motions. IN ST ST JOSEPH CIV Rule 201.

c.   Uniform court and case number designation. IN ST ST JOSEPH CIV Rule 202.

d.   Pleading and motions under IN ST TRIAL P Rule 12 and IN ST TRIAL P Rule 56. IN ST ST JOSEPH CIV Rule 206.

e.   Pre-trial procedures. IN ST ST JOSEPH CIV Rule 209.

f.   Electronic filing of cases in St. Joseph County. IN ST ST JOSEPH ELECTRONIC Rule 701.

B.   Timing

1.   *Pretrial conference.* Unless otherwise ordered by the court the pretrial conference shall not be called until after reasonable opportunity for the completion of discovery. IN ST TRIAL P Rule 16(B). However, some Indiana courts will schedule a preliminary pretrial conference almost immediately after the case has been filed in order to establish the ground rules for discovery, discovery cut-off dates, and the procedures for filing additional pleadings, motions, and the like. In addition, some courts will only schedule a trial date at the pretrial conference. 22 INPRAC § 28.2.

a.   *Notice.* The clerks shall give at least thirty (30) days' notice of the pretrial conference unless otherwise directed by the court. IN ST TRIAL P Rule 16(B)(1); IN ST ST JOSEPH CIV Rule 209(209.2).

b.   *Pre-conference meeting.* Unless otherwise ordered by the court, at least ten (10) days prior to the pretrial conference, attorneys for each of the parties shall meet and confer. IN ST TRIAL P Rule 16(C). It shall be the duty of counsel for both plaintiff and defendant to arrange for the conference of attorneys at least ten (10) days in advance of the pretrial conference. IN ST TRIAL P Rule 16(E).

c.   *Pre-trial readiness conference.* At least ten (10) days prior to trial, the Court may set a Readiness Conference. IN ST ST JOSEPH CIV Rule 209(209.6).

2.   *Motion requesting pretrial conference*

a.   *Timing of motion for pretrial conference.* There is no specific timing requirement for filing a motion requesting a pretrial conference.

i.   *Filing.* All pleadings and papers subsequent to the complaint which are required to be served upon a party shall be filed with the Court either before service or within a reasonable period of time thereafter. IN ST TRIAL P Rule 5(E)(1).

b. *Service*

    i. *Of motion.* A written motion, other than one which may be heard ex parte, and notice of the hearing thereof shall be served not less than five (5) days before the time specified for the hearing, unless a different period is fixed by the Indiana Rules of Trial Procedure or by order of the court. IN ST TRIAL P Rule 6(D).

- *Of supporting affidavits.* When a motion is supported by affidavit, the affidavit shall be served with the motion. IN ST TRIAL P Rule 6(D).

    ii. *Of opposition.* Except as otherwise provided in IN ST TRIAL P Rule 59(D), opposing affidavits may be served not less than one (1) day before the hearing, unless the court permits them to be served at some other time. IN ST TRIAL P Rule 6(D).

- *Memorandum of law.* So long as consistent with Indiana Rules of Trial Procedure, an adverse party wishing to respond shall do so within fifteen (15) days of service. IN ST ST JOSEPH CIV Rule 206(206.1).

3. *Computation of time*

a. *Generally; Days excluded.* In computing any period of time prescribed or allowed by the Indiana Rules of Trial Procedure, by order of the court, or by any applicable statute, the day of the act, event, or default from which the designated period of time begins to run shall not be included. The last day of the period so computed is to be included unless it is:

    i. A Saturday,

    ii. A Sunday,

    iii. A legal holiday as defined by state statute, or

    iv. A day the office in which the act is to be done is closed during regular business hours. IN ST TRIAL P Rule 6(A).

b. *Short periods.* In any event, the period runs until the end of the next day that is not a Saturday, a Sunday, a legal holiday, or a day on which the office is closed. When the period of time allowed is less than seven (7) days, intermediate Saturdays, Sundays, legal holidays, and days on which the office is closed shall be excluded from the computations. IN ST TRIAL P Rule 6(A).

c. *Additional time after service by United States mail.* Whenever a party has the right or is required to do some act or take some proceedings within a prescribed period after the service of a notice or other paper upon him and the notice or paper is served upon him by United States mail, three (3) days shall be added to the prescribed period. IN ST TRIAL P Rule 6(E).

d. *Enlargement of time.* When an act is required or allowed to be done at or within a specific time by the Indiana Rules of Trial Procedure, the court may at any time for cause shown:

    i. Order the period enlarged, with or without motion or notice, if request therefor is made before the expiration of the period originally prescribed or extended by a previous order; or

    ii. Upon motion made after the expiration of the specific period, permit the act to be done where the failure to act was the result of excusable neglect; but, the court may not extend the time for taking any action for judgment on the evidence under IN ST TRIAL P Rule 50(A), amendment of findings and judgment under IN ST TRIAL P Rule 52(B), to correct errors under IN ST TRIAL P Rule 59(C), statement in opposition to motion to correct error under IN ST TRIAL P Rule 59(E), or to obtain relief from final judgment under IN ST TRIAL P Rule 60(B), except to the extent and under the conditions stated in those rules. IN ST TRIAL P Rule 6(B).

    iii. An initial written motion for enlargement of time pursuant to IN ST TRIAL P Rule 6(B)(1) to answer a claim shall be routinely granted for an additional thirty (30) days from the original due date or other period the assigned Judge deems reasonable by written order of the Court. The motion must be filed on or before the original due date or IN ST ST JOSEPH CIV Rule 201 shall be inapplicable. IN ST ST JOSEPH CIV Rule 201(201.9.5).

- Any motion for enlargement of time shall state the date when such response is due and the date to which time is requested to be enlarged. IN ST ST JOSEPH CIV Rule 201(201.9.5).

- All subsequent motions for enlargement of time shall be so designated and will only be granted for good cause shown or in the interest of justice. IN ST ST JOSEPH CIV Rule 201(201.9.5).

C. General Requirements

1. *Pretrial conference.* A pre-trial conference of Court and counsel may be scheduled by the Court on its own motion or at the request of counsel for any party in any civil case in which, in the discretion of the Court, possible problems can be identified, the course and progress of the case, the necessity, sequence, and scope of discovery should be anticipated, planned, scheduled, or estimated for the orderly and expeditious handling of it by Court and counsel. At the pre-trial conference, the Court may designate deadlines for discovery, dispositive motions, or alternative dispute resolution. The Court may also provide the parties with proposed dates for trial, additional pre-trial conferences, and/or require the filing of a pre-trial order. IN ST ST JOSEPH CIV Rule 209(209.2).

   a. *When required; Purpose.* IN ST ST JOSEPH CIV Rule 209 is intended to accomplish the original purpose of pre-trial procedure: to simplify the issues, make cases easier, quicker, and less expensive for the Court, lawyer, and litigant and to alleviate the burden of ceremonial detain and to aid the efficient preparation of a case. IN ST ST JOSEPH CIV Rule 209(209.1). In any action except criminal cases, the court may in its discretion and shall upon the motion of any party, direct the attorneys for the parties to appear before it for a conference to consider:

      i. The simplification of the issues;

      ii. The necessity or desirability of amendments to the pleadings;

      iii. The possibility of obtaining admissions of fact and of documents which will avoid unnecessary proof;

      iv. A limitation of the number of expert witnesses;

      v. An exchange of names of witnesses to be called during the trial and the general nature of their expected testimony;

      vi. The desirability of using one or more types of alternative dispute resolution under the rules therefor;

      vii. The desirability of setting deadlines for dispositive motions in light of the date set for trial; and

      viii. Such other matters as may aid in the disposition of the action. IN ST TRIAL P Rule 16(A).

   b. *Participants.* At least one (1) attorney planning to take part in the trial shall appear for each of the parties and participate in the pretrial conference. IN ST TRIAL P Rule 16(B)(2).

   c. *Conference of attorneys prior to pretrial conference*

      i. *Purpose of attorney conference.* In general, the purpose of the "pre-pretrial conference" is to ensure that the attorneys for both sides will be prepared to make maximum use of the pretrial conference itself. IN ST TRIAL P Rule 16 frees the pretrial conference itself from perfunctory matters; it is written to require that not only are attorneys very familiar with the case, but that routine matters are resolved before the pretrial conference so that it may be devoted to a determination of those issues and matters which will be litigated. 2 INPRAC R 16(16.3).

      ii. *Topics to be addressed at attorney conference.* Unless otherwise ordered by the court, at least ten (10) days prior to the pretrial conference, attorneys for each of the parties shall meet and confer for the following purposes:

         - *Exhibits.* Each attorney shall mark for identification and provide opposing counsel an opportunity to inspect and copy all exhibits which he expects to introduce at the trial. Numbers or marks placed on such exhibits shall be prefixed with the symbol "P/T", denoting its pretrial designation. When the exhibit is introduced at the trial of the case, the "P/T" designation will be stricken and the exhibits must also indicate the party identifying same. IN ST TRIAL P Rule 16(C)(1). Exhibits of the character which prohibit or make impracticable their production at conference shall be identified and notice given of their intended use. Necessary arrangements must be made to afford opposing counsel an opportunity to examine such exhibits. IN ST TRIAL P Rule 16(C)(1).

- *Exhibit stipulations.* Written stipulations shall be prepared with reference to all exhibits exchanged or identified. The stipulations shall contain all agreements of the parties with reference to the exchanged and identified exhibits, and shall include, but not be limited to, the agreement of the parties with reference to the authenticity of the exhibits, their admissibility in evidence, their use in opening statements, and the provisions made for the inspection of identified exhibits. The original of the exhibit stipulations shall be presented to the court at the pretrial conference. IN ST TRIAL P Rule 16(C)(2).

- *Fact stipulation.* The attorneys shall stipulate in writing with reference to all facts and issues not in genuine dispute. The original of the stipulations shall be presented to the court at the time of the pretrial conference. IN ST TRIAL P Rule 16(C)(3).

- *Exchange list of witnesses.* Attorneys for each of the parties shall furnish opposing counsel with the written list of the names and addresses of all witnesses then known. The original of each witness list shall be presented to the court at the time of the pretrial conference. IN ST TRIAL P Rule 16(C)(4).

- *Discuss settlement.* The possibility of compromise settlement shall be fully discussed and explored. IN ST TRIAL P Rule 16(C)(5).

d. *Readiness conference.* In addition to each party proceeding pro se and counsel for each of the parties, the Court may order that one or more of the parties themselves attend the Readiness Conference. The purpose of the Readiness Conference is to simplify the issues anticipated at trial, and the Conference will include a determination of the parties' readiness to proceed to trial, the progress of the parties in obtaining stipulations of fact and authenticity of exhibits and, if appropriate, the willingness of the parties to waive jury trial. Where the parties have filed a written stipulation signed by all parties addressing these issues and confirming the trial date, the Court in its discretion may vacate the Readiness Conference. IN ST ST JOSEPH CIV Rule 209(209.6).

e. *Preparation for conference of attorneys and pretrial.* Each attorney shall completely familiarize himself with all aspects of the case in advance of the conference of attorneys and be prepared to enter into stipulations with reference to as many facts and issues and exhibits as possible. IN ST TRIAL P Rule 16(D).

    i. *Adequate preparation for pre-trial conference.* The purpose of the pre-trial conference being to narrow and simplify the issues for trial and to expedite the trial, counsel shall report for such conference with the Judge after full preparation including an adequate meeting of counsel as contemplated by IN ST TRIAL P Rule 16(C). In all cases counsel shall be prepared to indicate to the Court whether the case may be tried to a jury of six (6) and whether the Judge may conduct all of the voir dire examination of prospective jurors or the initial voir dire examination with supplemental inquiry by counsel. IN ST ST JOSEPH CIV Rule 209(209.4).

f. *Refusal to stipulate.* If, following the conference of attorneys, either party determines that there are other facts or exhibits that should be stipulated and which opposing counsel refuses to stipulate upon, he shall compile a list of such facts or exhibits and furnish same to opposing counsel at least two (2) days in advance of the pretrial conference. The original of the list shall be presented to the court at the time of the pretrial conference. IN ST TRIAL P Rule 16(F).

g. *Witnesses or exhibits discovered subsequent to conference of attorneys and before a pretrial conference.* If, after the conference of the attorneys and before the pretrial conference, counsel discovers additional exhibits or names of additional witnesses, the same information required to be disclosed at the conference of the attorneys shall be immediately furnished opposing counsel. The original of any such disclosures shall be presented to the court at the time of the pretrial conference. IN ST TRIAL P Rule 16(G).

h. *More than one pretrial conference.* If necessary or advisable, the court may adjourn the pretrial conference from time to time or may order an additional pretrial conference. IN ST TRIAL P Rule 16(H).

i. *Witnesses or exhibits discovered subsequent to pretrial conference.* If, following the pretrial conference or during trial, counsel discovers additional exhibits or the names of additional witnesses, the same information required to be disclosed at the conference between attorneys shall be immediately furnished opposing counsel. The original of any such disclosure shall immediately be filed with the court and shall indicate the date it was furnished opposing counsel. IN ST TRIAL P Rule 16(I).

j. *Pretrial order.* The court shall make an order which recites the action taken at the conference, the amendments allowed to the pleading, and the agreements made by the parties as to any of the matters considered which limit the issues for trial to those not disposed of by admissions or agreement of counsel, and such order when entered shall control the subsequent course of action, unless modified thereafter to prevent manifest injustice. The court in its discretion may establish by rule a pretrial calendar on which actions may be placed for consideration as above provided, and may either confine the calendar to jury actions or non-jury actions or extend it to all actions. IN ST TRIAL P Rule 16(J).

   i. The pretrial order delineates the issues in the case and supplants allegations raised in the pleadings. All subsequent pleadings are then controlled by the order that the trial court enters in the case file, and court record. 2 INPRAC R 16(16.2); Dominguez v. Gallmeyer, 402 N.E.2d 1295, 1298 (Ind.Ct.App. 1980).

   ii. Civil cases may be set for trial at the pre-trial conference or as otherwise directed by the assigned Judge. IN ST ST JOSEPH CIV Rule 209(209.9).

   iii. In cases in which a preliminary pre-trial conference has been held under Rule 12(B) [Editor's note: this is likely supposed to be a reference to IN ST TRIAL P Rule 16(B)], discovery shall be made in accordance with the scheduling thereof then ordered. In cases in which no preliminary pre-trial conference has been held, all discovery shall be completed prior to the pre-trial conference and no discovery shall be conducted thereafter unless, upon motion or stipulation showing good cause therefore, an order is entered permitting further discovery within time to be prescribed by the Court. IN ST ST JOSEPH CIV Rule 209(209.5).

k. *Sanctions; Failure to appear.* If without just excuse or because of failure to give reasonable attention to the matter, no appearance is made on behalf of a party at a pre-trial conference, or if an attorney is grossly unprepared to participate in the conference, the court may order either one or both of the following:

   i. The payment by the delinquent attorney or party of the reasonable expenses, including attorney's fees, to the aggrieved party; or

   ii. Take such other action as may be appropriate. IN ST TRIAL P Rule 16(K).

   iii. Unless otherwise directed by the Court, each pre-trial conference shall be attended without exception by any party proceeding pro se and at least one (1) of the attorneys for each of the parties who will participate in the trial of the case and who shall be authorized to deal comprehensively with all subjects on the agenda. With prior approval of the presiding Judge, an attorney may appear telephonically. Sanctions for failure to comply with IN ST ST JOSEPH CIV Rule 209 shall be deemed appropriate. IN ST ST JOSEPH CIV Rule 209(209.7).

   iv. Failure to attend and adequately participate in pre-trial conferences as intended by IN ST TRIAL P Rule 16 may result in reassignment of the cause to the bottom of the appropriate assignment list, issuing an order pursuant to IN ST TRIAL P Rule 41(E), and/or the imposition of appropriate sanctions. IN ST ST JOSEPH CIV Rule 209(209.8).

   v. Refer to the Indiana KeyRules Motion for Sanctions document for more information.

l. *Listing of assigned cases.* After the filing of the first responsive pleading, the assigned Judge will cause the case to be placed upon a list to be kept by each Judge of the Court, in which noted cases are subject to call for trial pre-trial conference. Cases may be advanced upon this list by petition to the assigned Judge for good cause shown. IN ST ST JOSEPH GEN AND ADMIN Rule 106(106.4).

2. *Motions, generally.* Unless made during a hearing or trial, or otherwise ordered by the court, an application to the court for an order shall be made by written motion. The motion shall state the grounds therefor and the relief or order sought. IN ST TRIAL P Rule 7(B).

a. *Motions as distinct from pleadings.* Motions and responses to motions are not pleadings, and

allegations contained in a motion are not admissions of a party. 22B INPRAC 7:2; Wachstetter v. County Properties, LLC, 832 N.E.2d 574 (Ind.Ct.App. 2005); Scott County Family YMCA, Inc. v. Hobbs, 817 N.E.2d 603 (Ind.Ct.App. 2004).

b. *Unopposed motions generally granted.* It is common for a trial court to grant procedural motions, such as motions for enlargement of time, discovery motions, or motions for continuance, unless an objection is filed. 21 INPRAC § 13.8.

c. *Proposed orders.* As directed by the Court, a party or an attorney for a party shall prepare a proposed order based on the decision rendered by the Court. The party so directed shall prepare the proposed order in a timely manner and, upon filing, shall advise the chambers of the applicable judge that the proposed order has been prepared and filed. IN ST ST JOSEPH CIV Rule 213(213.2).

D. Documents

1. *Pretrial conference*

   a. *Documents to consider*

      i. *Exhibits and stipulations.* Refer to the General Requirements section of this document for information on exhibits and stipulations.

2. *Motion for pretrial conference*

   a. *Required documents*

      i. *Motion and notice.* The requirement of notice is satisfied by service of the motion. IN ST TRIAL P Rule 7(B). Refer to the General Requirements section of this document for information on the content of a motion for pretrial conference.

      ii. *Chronological Case Summary (CCS) entry form.* Every written motion, petition, or other pleading subsequent to the original complaint presented to the Clerk for filing shall be accompanied by a Chronological Case Summary (CCS) entry form in duplicate. IN ST ST JOSEPH CIV Rule 201(201.4). Refer to the Format section of this document for details on the format and filing requirements for the CCS entry form.

      iii. *Proposed order.* Unless local practice provides differently, a party should submit a proposed order with its written motion to be signed by the judge once the motion has been granted. 21 INPRAC § 13.8. All proposed orders shall be submitted in an original plus a number of copies equal to one more than the number of pro se parties and attorneys of record contained in the prepared proof of notice under IN ST TRIAL P Rule 72(D). IN ST ST JOSEPH CIV Rule 213(213.3); IN ST ST JOSEPH CIV Rule 201(201.5.2).

      iv. *Certificate of service.* An attorney or unrepresented party tendering a document to the Clerk for filing shall certify that service has been made, list the parties served, and specify the date and means of service. The certificate of service shall be placed at the end of the document and shall not be separately filed. The separate filing of a certificate of service, however, shall not be grounds for rejecting a document for filing. The Clerk may permit documents to be filed without a certificate of service but shall require prompt filing of a separate certificate of service. IN ST TRIAL P Rule 5(C).

   b. *Supplemental documents*

      i. *Supporting evidence.* When a motion is based on facts not appearing of record the court may hear the matter on affidavits presented by the respective parties, but the court may direct that the matter be heard wholly or partly on oral testimony or depositions. IN ST TRIAL P Rule 43(B).

      ii. *Facsimile cover sheet.* Any document sent to the Clerk of the Circuit Court by electronic facsimile transmission shall be accompanied by a cover sheet which states the title of the document, case number, number of pages, identity and voice telephone number of the sending party and instructions for filing. The cover sheet shall contain the signature of the attorney or party, pro se, authorizing the filing. IN ST ADMIN Rule 12(D).

E. Format

1. *Form of papers.* The rules applicable to captions, and the signing and form of pleadings (IN ST TRIAL

P Rule 8 through IN ST TRIAL P Rule 11), apply to all motions and other papers provided under the Indiana Rules of Trial Procedure. 22B INPRAC 7:2.

    a. *Separate motions; Alternative motions.* Each motion shall be separate, while alternative motions filed together shall each be identified on the caption. IN ST ST JOSEPH CIV Rule 206(206.1).

2. *Form of pleadings*

    a. *Caption; Names of parties.* Every pleading shall contain a caption setting forth the name of the court, the title of the action, the file number, and a designation as in IN ST TRIAL P Rule 7(A). In the complaint the title of the action shall include the names of all the parties, but in other pleadings it is sufficient to state the name of the first party on each side with an appropriate indication of other parties. IN ST TRIAL P Rule 10(A); IN ST ST JOSEPH CIV Rule 201(201.3.3). If a special judge has been assigned to the case, the pleading should also identify the special judge. IN ST ST JOSEPH CIV Rule 201(201.3.3).

        i. *Title.* All pleadings or motions shall include a title, which shall delineate each topic included in the pleading. For example, where a pleading contains an answer, a motion to dismiss, and a jury request, each topic shall be set forth in the title. IN ST ST JOSEPH CIV Rule 201(201.3.4).

    b. *Paragraphs; Separate statements.* All averments of a claim or defense shall be made in numbered paragraphs, the contents of each of which shall be limited as far as practicable to a statement of a single set of circumstances, and a paragraph may be referred to by number in all succeeding pleadings. Each claim founded upon a separate transaction or occurrence and each defense other than denials may be stated in a separate count or defense whenever a separation facilitates the clear presentation of the matters set forth. IN ST TRIAL P Rule 10(B).

    c. *Adoption by reference; Exhibits.* Statements in a pleading may be adopted by reference in a different part of the same pleading or in another pleading or in any motion. A copy of any written instrument which is an exhibit to a pleading is a part thereof for all purposes. IN ST TRIAL P Rule 10(C).

    d. *Flat filing.* In order that the Clerk's files may be kept under the system commonly known as "flat filing," all papers presented to the Clerk for filing shall be flat and unfolded. Pleadings shall have no covers or backs and shall be fastened together at the top left-hand corner only. IN ST ST JOSEPH CIV Rule 201(201.1).

    e. *One side of page used.* Printing shall be on one (1) side of the paper. IN ST ST JOSEPH CIV Rule 201(201.3.2).

    f. *Copies.* All copies shall be on white paper of sufficient strength and durability to resist normal wear and tear. IN ST ST JOSEPH CIV Rule 201(201.3.1).

    g. *Margins.* Margins shall be at least one inch (1"). IN ST ST JOSEPH CIV Rule 201(201.3.2).

    h. *Double-spaced.* If typewritten, the lines shall be double spaced except for quotations, which shall be indented and single-spaced. IN ST ST JOSEPH CIV Rule 201(201.3.2).

    i. *Font size.* Type face shall be twelve (12) font size or larger within the body of the document and ten (10) font size or larger in the footnotes. IN ST ST JOSEPH CIV Rule 201(201.3.2).

    j. *Font type.* The font type must be legible and script type shall not be used. IN ST ST JOSEPH CIV Rule 201(201.3.2).

    k. *Italics.* Italicized type may be used for quotations, references, or case citations. IN ST ST JOSEPH CIV Rule 201(201.3.2).

    l. *Court and case designation.* All filings shall conform to the requirements for uniform court and case number designation set by IN ST ADMIN Rule 8. In addition, all filings shall contain the proper court and case designation as described below. IN ST ST JOSEPH CIV Rule 202.

        i. *Court designation.* Pursuant to IN ST 33-33-71-2, St. Joseph County, Indiana, constitutes the Sixtieth Judicial Circuit. The legal names of the courts within the 60th Judicial Circuit are the St. Joseph Circuit Court, the St. Joseph Superior Court, and the St. Joseph Probate Court. All filings shall properly reflect the legal name of the applicable court. Any filing may be amended, rejected, or stricken if it does not contain the proper case name and/or the legal name of the court. IN ST ST JOSEPH CIV Rule 202(202.1).

m. *Form of CCS entry.* Every written motion, petition, or other pleading subsequent to the original complaint presented to the Clerk for filing shall be accompanied by a Chronological Case Summary (CCS) entry form in duplicate which shall contain the title and cause number of the action, the date, and the proposed entry to appear on the docket. IN ST ST JOSEPH CIV Rule 201(201.4).

    i. *Identification and signature.* The CCS entry form shall identify the party making the filing, designate each pleading being filed, and shall be signed by counsel of record or the unrepresented litigant. IN ST ST JOSEPH CIV Rule 201(201.4).

    ii. *Date stamp.* The form shall be date stamped and presented to the Court Clerk, who shall initial the form and return the duplicate to the filing party. IN ST ST JOSEPH CIV Rule 201(201.4).

n. *Form of proposed order.* Any proposed order shall be a document that is separate and apart from the motion or application to which it relates and shall contain a caption showing the name of the court, the case number assigned to the case, and the title of the case as shown by the complaint pursuant to IN ST ST JOSEPH CIV Rule 201. IN ST ST JOSEPH CIV Rule 213(213.2).

    i. If there are multiple parties, the title may be shortened to include only the first name plaintiff and defendant with appropriate indication that there are additional parties. IN ST ST JOSEPH CIV Rule 213(213.2).

    ii. The proposed order shall be on white paper, eight and one-half by eleven inches (8 1/2" x 11") in size, and each page shall be numbered. IN ST ST JOSEPH CIV Rule 213(213.2).

    iii. The last page of the proposed order shall contain a line for the date, either "Dated _____" or "Signed on the date filemarked hereon." IN ST ST JOSEPH CIV Rule 213(213.2).

    iv. On the last page there also shall be a line for the signature of the Judge under which shall be typed "Judge, St. Joseph [Circuit or Superior or Probate] Court." IN ST ST JOSEPH CIV Rule 213(213.2).

    v. If the proposed order contains a recommendation from a Magistrate, the last page shall have a line for the signature of the Magistrate under which shall be typed "Magistrate, St. Joseph [Circuit or Superior or Probate] Court," to the left of which shall be the following, "So Recommended:" and beneath and to the left of which shall be typed, "Approved. So Ordered." IN ST ST JOSEPH CIV Rule 213(213.2).

    vi. To allow compliance with the notice requirements of IN ST TRIAL P Rule 72(D), the lower four (4) inches of the last page of the proposed order shall be left blank. The proposed order shall also include a prepared proof of notice under IN ST TRIAL P Rule 72(D), and in preparing such a notice the filing party shall complete all portions of the prepared proof of notice. IN ST ST JOSEPH CIV Rule 213(213.2).

3. *Size of papers for filing.* Effective January 1, 1992, all pleadings, copies, motions and documents filed with any trial court or appellate level court, typed or printed, with the exception of exhibits and existing wills, shall be prepared on eight and one-half by eleven inch (8 1/2" x 11") size paper. IN ST ADMIN Rule 11.

a. *Paper.* Pleadings, motions, and other papers shall be either legibly printed or typewritten on white opaque paper of good quality at least sixteen (16) pound weight, eight and one-half inches (8 1/2 ") in width and eleven inches (11") in length as required by IN ST ADMIN Rule 11. IN ST ST JOSEPH CIV Rule 201(201.3.1).

4. *Signature requirements*

a. *Signature of attorney.* Every pleading or motion of a party represented by an attorney shall be signed by at least one (1) attorney of record in his individual name, whose address, telephone number, and attorney number shall be stated, except that this provision shall not apply to pleadings and motions made and transcribed at the trial or a hearing before the judge and received by him in such form. IN ST TRIAL P Rule 11(A).

    i. The signature of an attorney constitutes a certificate by him that he has read the pleadings; that to the best of his knowledge, information, and belief, there is good ground to support it; and that it is not interposed for delay. IN ST TRIAL P Rule 11(A).

ii. If a pleading or motion is not signed or is signed with intent to defeat the purpose of the rule, it may be stricken as sham and false and the action may proceed as though the pleading had not been served. IN ST TRIAL P Rule 11(A).

iii. For a willful violation of IN ST TRIAL P Rule 11 an attorney may be subjected to appropriate disciplinary action. Similar action may be taken if scandalous or indecent matter is inserted. IN ST TRIAL P Rule 11(A).

b. *Signature of unrepresented party.* A party who is not represented by an attorney shall sign his pleading and state his address. IN ST TRIAL P Rule 11(A).

c. *Verification not generally required.* Except when specifically required by rule, pleadings or motions need not be verified or accompanied by affidavit. The rule in equity that the averments of an answer under oath must be overcome by the testimony of two (2) witnesses or of one (1) witness sustained by corroborating circumstances is abolished. IN ST TRIAL P Rule 11(A).

d. *Verification by affirmation or representation.* When in connection with any civil or special statutory proceeding it is required that any pleading, motion, petition, supporting affidavit, or other document of any kind, be verified, or that an oath be taken, it shall be sufficient if the subscriber simply affirms the truth of the matter to be verified by an affirmation or representation. IN ST TRIAL P Rule 11(B). IN ST TRIAL P Rule 11(B) states that the affirmation or representation should be in substantially the following language: "I (we) affirm, under the penalties for perjury, that the foregoing representation(s) is (are) true. (Signed) _____."

i. Any person who falsifies an affirmation or representation of fact shall be subject to the same penalties as are prescribed by law for the making of a false affidavit. IN ST TRIAL P Rule 11(B).

e. *Verified pleadings, motions, and affidavits as evidence.* Pleadings, motions and affidavits accompanying or in support of such pleadings or motions when required to be verified or under oath shall be accepted as a representation that the signer had personal knowledge thereof or reasonable cause to believe the existence of the facts or matters stated or alleged therein; and, if otherwise competent or acceptable as evidence, may be admitted as evidence of the facts or matters stated or alleged therein when it is so provided in the Indiana Rules of Trial Procedure, by statute or other law, or to the extent the writing or signature expressly purports to be made upon the signer's personal knowledge. When such pleadings, motions and affidavits are verified or under oath they shall not require other or greater proof on the part of the adverse party than if not verified or not under oath unless expressly provided otherwise by the Indiana Rules of Trial Procedure, statute or other law. Affidavits upon motions for summary judgment under IN ST TRIAL P Rule 56 and in denial of execution under IN ST TRIAL P Rule 9.2 shall be made upon personal knowledge. IN ST TRIAL P Rule 11(C).

f. *Signature, verification and other requirements.* Parties and their counsel are enjoined to comply with the verification requirements of IN ST TRIAL P Rule 11, and either the moving party or the party's attorney of record shall sign all pleadings and motions before filing with the Clerk of the Court. Every motion, petition, or other pleading filed with the Clerk shall contain the name, organization, physical address, telephone number, and facsimile number of the filing party or an attorney for that party. IN ST ST JOSEPH CIV Rule 201(201.3.6).

i. The Clerk shall not accept any motion, petition, notice or other pleading or a CCS entry form for filing from an unrepresented litigant unless the unrepresented litigant's current address and phone number appear on the pleading, and an opposing party may service notices and responses on an unrepresented litigant at any address he or she has provided on a pleading. IN ST ST JOSEPH CIV Rule 201(201.3.6).

5. *Information excluded from public access.* Every document filed in a case shall separately identify information excluded from public access pursuant to IN ST ADMIN Rule 9(G)(1) as follows:

a. Whole documents that are excluded from public access pursuant to IN ST ADMIN Rule 9(G)(1) shall be tendered on light green paper or have a light green coversheet attached to the document, marked "Not for Public Access" or "Confidential." IN ST TRIAL P Rule 5(G)(1).

b. When only a portion of a document contains information excluded from public access pursuant to IN

ST ADMIN Rule 9(G)(1), said information shall be omitted [or redacted] from the filed document, and set forth on a separate accompanying document on light green paper conspicuously marked "Not for Public Access" or "Confidential" and clearly designated [or identifying] the caption and number of the case and the document and location within the document to which the redacted material pertains. IN ST TRIAL P Rule 5(G)(2).

c. With respect to documents filed in electronic format, the trial court, by local rule, may provide for compliance with IN ST TRIAL P Rule 5 in manner that separates and protects access to information excluded from public access. IN ST TRIAL P Rule 5(G)(3).

d. IN ST TRIAL P Rule 5(G) does not apply to a record sealed by the court pursuant to IN ST 5-14-3-5.5 or otherwise, nor to records, documents, or information filed in cases to which public access is prohibited pursuant to IN ST ADMIN Rule 9(G). IN ST TRIAL P Rule 5(G)(4).

e. The following information in case records is excluded from public access and is confidential:

   i. Information that is excluded from public access pursuant to federal law;

   ii. Information that is excluded from public access as declared confidential by Indiana statute or other court rule, including without limitation:

   - All adoption records created after July 8, 1941, as declared confidential by IN ST 31-19-19-1, et seq., except those specifically declared open by IN ST 31-19-13-2(2);

   - All records relating to chancroid, chlamydia, gonorrhea, hepatitis, human immunodeficiency virus (HIV), Lymphogranuloma venereum, syphilis, tuberculosis, as declared confidential by IN ST 16-41-8-1, et seq.;

   - All records relating to child abuse as declared confidential by IN ST 31-33-18-1, et seq.;

   - All records relating to drug tests as declared confidential by IN ST 5-14-3-4(a)(9);

   - Records of grand jury proceedings as declared confidential by IN ST 35-34-2-4;

   - Records of juvenile proceedings as declared confidential by IN ST 31-39-1-2, except those specifically open under statute;

   - All paternity records created after July 1, 1941 as declared confidential by IN ST 31-14-11-15, IN ST 31-19-5-23, IN ST 31-39-1-1 and IN ST 31-39-1-2 [Editor's note: IN ST 31-14-11-15 was repealed effective May 9, 2013];

   - All pre-sentence reports as declared confidential by IN ST 35-38-1-13;

   - Written petitions to permit marriages without consent and orders directing the Clerk of Court to issue a marriage license to underage persons, as declared confidential by IN ST 31-11-1-6;

   - Only those arrest warrants, search warrants, indictments and informations ordered confidential by the trial judge, prior to return of duly executed service as declared confidential by IN ST 5-14-3-4(b)(1);

   - All medical, mental health, or tax records unless determined by law or regulation of any governmental custodian not to be confidential, released by the subject of such records, or declared by a court of competent jurisdiction to be essential to the resolution of litigation as declared confidential by IN ST 16-39-3-10, IN ST 6-4.1-5-10, IN ST 6-4.1-12-12, and IN ST 6-8.1-7-1;

   - Personal information relating to jurors or prospective jurors, other than for the use of the parties and counsel, pursuant to IN ST JURY Rule 10;

   - Information relating to protection from abuse orders, no-contact orders and workplace violence restraining orders as declared confidential by IN ST 5-2-9-6, et seq.;

   - Mediation proceedings pursuant to IN ST ADR Rule 2.11, Mini-Trial proceedings pursuant to IN ST ADR Rule 4.4(C), and Summary Jury Trials pursuant to IN ST ADR Rule 5.6;

   - Information in probation files pursuant to the Probation Standards promulgated by the Judicial Conference of Indiana pursuant to IN ST 11-13-1-8(b);

- Information deemed confidential pursuant to the Rules for Court Administered Alcohol and Drug Programs promulgated by the Judicial Conference of Indiana pursuant to IN ST 12-23-14-13;
- Information deemed confidential pursuant to the Problem-Solving Court Rules promulgated by the Judicial Conference of Indiana pursuant to IN ST 33-23-16-16;
- All records of the Department of workforce Development as declared confidential by IN ST 22-4-19-6;
- Information regarding interception of electronic communications that is sealed or deemed confidential as set forth in IN ST 35-33.5-2-1, et seq.

iii. Information excluded from public access by specific court order;

iv. Complete Social Security Numbers of living persons;

v. With the exception of names, information such as addresses, phone numbers, and dates of birth which explicitly identifies:

- Natural persons who are witnesses or victims (not including defendants) in criminal, domestic violence, stalking, sexual assault, juvenile, or civil protection order proceedings, provided that juveniles who are victims of sex crimes shall be identified by initials only;
- Places of residence of judicial officers, clerks and other employees of courts and clerks of court, unless the person or persons about whom the information pertains waives confidentiality;

vi. Complete account numbers of specific assets, loans, bank accounts, credit cards, and personal identification numbers (PINs);

vii. All orders of expungement entered in criminal or juvenile proceedings, orders to restrict access to criminal history information pursuant to IN ST 35-38-5-5.5 or IN ST 35-38-8-5 and records excluded from public access by such orders, and information related to infractions that is excluded from public access pursuant to IN ST 34-28-5-15 or IN ST 34-28-5-16 [Editor's note: IN ST 35-38-5-5.5, IN ST 35-38-8-5 and IN ST 34-28-5-16 were repealed effective July 1, 2013; for information on orders restricting access to criminal history, refer to IN ST 35-38-9-1, et seq.];

viii. All personal notes and e-mail, and deliberative material, of judges, jurors, court staff and judicial agencies, and information recorded in personal data assistants (PDA's) or organizers and personal calendars. IN ST ADMIN Rule 9(G)(1).

F. Filing and Service Requirements

1. *Filing requirements.* Except as otherwise provided in IN ST TRIAL P Rule 5(E)(2), all pleadings and papers subsequent to the complaint which are required to be served upon a party shall be filed with the Court either before service or within a reasonable period of time thereafter. IN ST TRIAL P Rule 5(E)(1).

   a. *Filing with the court defined.* The filing of pleadings, motions, and other papers with the court as required by the Indiana Rules of Trial Procedure shall be made by one of the following methods:

   i. Delivery to the clerk of the court;

   ii. Sending by electronic transmission under the procedure adopted pursuant to IN ST ADMIN Rule 12;

   iii. Mailing to the clerk by registered, certified or express mail return receipt requested;

   iv. Depositing with any third-party commercial carrier for delivery to the clerk within three (3) calendar days, cost prepaid, properly addressed;

   v. If the court so permits, filing with the judge, in which event the judge shall note thereon the filing date and forthwith transmit them to the office of the clerk; or

   vi. Electronic filing, as approved by the Division of State Court Administration pursuant to IN ST ADMIN Rule 16. IN ST TRIAL P Rule 5(F).

   vii. Filing by registered or certified mail and by third-party commercial carrier shall be complete upon mailing or deposit. IN ST TRIAL P Rule 5(F).

viii. All pleadings shall be filed with the Clerk, not directly with the Court, unless otherwise required by the Indiana Rules of Court. The entry of appearances and the filing of pleadings or other matters not requiring immediate Court action shall be filed with the Clerk and not in open Court. A Judge may permit papers to be filed in chambers, in which event he or she shall note thereon the filing date and transmit the papers to the Clerk. IN ST ST JOSEPH CIV Rule 201(201.2).

b. *Facsimile filing.* Unless otherwise authorized by IN ST ST JOSEPH ELECTRONIC Rule 701, electronic filing of pleadings by computerized or facsimile transmission is not permitted. IN ST ST JOSEPH CIV Rule 201(201.2).

c. *Additional copies.* In cases in which a party or counsel supplies the proposed order or decree, a sufficient number shall be prepared and filed as to provide the Clerk to retain two (2) copies, which shall be filed in the flat file and the record of judgments and orders. Should the party or counsel desire additional copies, a sufficient number of copies should be filed to effectuate that purpose. IN ST ST JOSEPH CIV Rule 201(201.6).

d. *Proof of filing.* Any party filing any paper by any method other than personal delivery to the clerk shall retain proof of filing. IN ST TRIAL P Rule 5(F).

2. *Service requirements.* Unless otherwise provided by the Indiana Rules of Trial Procedure or an order of the court, each party and special judge, if any, shall be served with: (1) every order required by its terms to be served; (2) every pleading subsequent to the original complaint; (3) every written motion except one which may be heard ex parte; (4) every brief submitted to the trial court; (5) every paper relating to discovery required to be served upon a party; and (6) every written notice, appearance, demand, offer of judgment, designation of record on appeal, or similar paper. IN ST TRIAL P Rule 5(A).

a. *Service generally.* Every motion, petition, notice, or other pleading required to be served by IN ST TRIAL P Rule 5 shall be served on all counsel of record or unrepresented parties either before it is filed or on the day it is filed with the Court, and the date of filing shall be indicated on the Certificate of Service. IN ST ST JOSEPH CIV Rule 201(201.5.1).

   i. *Copy.* A copy of the Clerk's CCS entry form of the filing shall also be served on all counsel of record or unrepresented parties whenever it contains an appearance of counsel or contains a date for Court hearing on the matter. IN ST ST JOSEPH CIV Rule 201(201.5.1).

b. *Methods of service*

   i. *Personal service.* Whenever a party is represented by an attorney of record, service shall be made upon such attorney unless service upon the party himself is ordered by the court. Service upon the attorney or party shall be made by delivering or mailing a copy of the papers to the last known address or where an attorney or party has consented to service by fax or e-mail, as provided in IN ST TRIAL P Rule 3.1(A)(4), by faxing or e-mailing a copy of the documents to the fax number or e-mail address set out in the appearance form or correction as required by IN ST TRIAL P Rule 3.1(E). IN ST TRIAL P Rule 5(B). Delivery of a copy within IN ST TRIAL P Rule 5 means:

      • Offering or tendering it to the attorney or party and stating the nature of the papers being served. Refusal to accept an offered or tendered document is a waiver of any objection to the sufficiency or adequacy of service of that document;

      • Leaving it at his office with a clerk or other person in charge thereof, or if there is no one in charge, leaving it in a conspicuous place therein; or

      • If the office is closed, by leaving it at his dwelling house or usual place of abode with some person of suitable age and discretion then residing therein; or,

      • Leaving it at some other suitable place, selected by the attorney upon whom service is being made, pursuant to duly promulgated local rule. IN ST TRIAL P Rule 5(B)(1).

   ii. *Service by the clerk.* Whenever the Clerk is required by rule or statute to give notice, the party or parties requesting such notice shall furnish the Clerk with sufficient copies of the notice to be given, along with stamped, addressed envelopes with the names and the addresses of the parties or their counsel to whom such notice is to be given. IN ST ST JOSEPH CIV Rule 201(201.5.4).

iii. *Service on the court.* Service on a Judge may be made by delivering a copy to the Judge's secretary or mailing a copy to the Judge at his or her chambers. Service on a Judge may not be accomplished by facsimile transmission; however, a courtesy copy may be sent to the Judge's chambers by electronic mail or facsimile transmission contemporaneously with service by mail or otherwise. IN ST ST JOSEPH CIV Rule 201(201.5.5).

iv. *Service by mail.* If service is made by mail, the papers shall be deposited in the United States mail addressed to the person on whom they are being served, with postage prepaid. Service shall be deemed complete upon mailing. Proof of service of all papers permitted to be mailed may be made by written acknowledgment of service, by affidavit of the person who mailed the papers, or by certificate of an attorney. It shall be the duty of attorneys when entering their appearance in a cause or when filing pleadings or papers therein, to have noted in the Chronological Case Summary or said pleadings or papers so filed the address and telephone number of their office. Service by delivery or by mail at such address shall be deemed sufficient and complete. IN ST TRIAL P Rule 5(B)(2).

v. *Service by fax or e-mail.* A party who has consented to service by fax or e-mail may be served as follows:

- Service by e-mail shall be made by attaching the document being served in .pdf format. Discovery documents must also be served in accordance with IN ST TRIAL P Rule 26(A). IN ST TRIAL P Rule 5(B)(3)(a).

- Service by fax shall be deemed complete upon generation of a transmission record indicating the successful transmission of the entire document, except as provided in IN ST TRIAL P Rule 5(B)(3)(d). IN ST TRIAL P Rule 5(B)(3)(b).

- Service by e-mail shall be deemed complete upon transmission, except as provided in IN ST TRIAL P Rule 5(B)(3)(d). IN ST TRIAL P Rule 5(B)(3)(c).

- Service by fax or e-mail that occurs on a Saturday, Sunday, legal holiday, or day the court or agency in which the matter is pending is closed or after 5:00 PM local time of the recipient shall be deemed complete the next day that is not a Saturday, Sunday, legal holiday, or day that the court or agency in which the matter is pending is not closed. IN ST TRIAL P Rule 5(B)(3)(d).

c. *Serving numerous defendants.* In any action in which there are unusually large numbers of defendants, the court, upon motion or of its own initiative, may order:

i. That service of the pleadings of the defendants and replies thereto need not be made as between the defendants;

- That any cross-claim, counterclaim, or matter constituting an avoidance or affirmative defense contained therein shall be deemed to be denied or avoided by all other parties; and

- That the filing of any such pleading and service thereof upon the plaintiff constitutes due notice of it to the parties. IN ST TRIAL P Rule 5(D).

ii. A copy of every such order shall be served upon the parties in such manner and form as the court directs. IN ST TRIAL P Rule 5(D).

d. *Service on parties in default for failure to appear.* No service need be made on parties in default for failure to appear, except that pleadings asserting new or additional claims for relief against them shall be served upon them in the manner provided by service of summons in IN ST TRIAL P Rule 4. IN ST TRIAL P Rule 5(A).

e. *Distribution.* Counsel or an unrepresented party submitting a motion, petition, notice, pleading or proposed order shall indicate the method of distribution desired on the Clerk's CCS entry form. The Clerk will not return or distribute copies of motions, petitions, pleadings, notices or proposed orders, other than those originated by the Court, by mail unless the Clerk is provided with stamped, addressed envelopes. IN ST ST JOSEPH CIV Rule 201(201.5.3).

f. *Mailbox.* As a matter of convenience to attorneys, each court provides a mailbox for the distribution filings and orders generated by the Court, and it is the responsibility of each attorney to periodically

check these mailboxes for service and distribution of court-generated filings and orders. IN ST ST JOSEPH CIV Rule 201(201.5.3).

G. Hearings

1. The Indiana rules do not contemplate a hearing related to the pretrial conference.

H. Forms

1. Pretrial Conference, Scheduling, Management Forms for Indiana

a. Motion for pretrial conference. 5 INPRAC § 5:1.1.

b. Order for pretrial conference; Attorneys to hold preliminary conference. 5 INPRAC § 5:1.2.

c. Letter; To arrange preliminary conference of attorneys. 5 INPRAC § 5:1.3.

d. Letter; Documenting opposing counsel's failure to meet. 5 INPRAC § 5:1.4.

e. Letter; Request to stipulate to facts and exhibits. 5 INPRAC § 5:1.5.

f. Notice to court; Failure to stipulate. 5 INPRAC § 5:1.6.

g. Agenda; Pretrial conference. 5 INPRAC § 5:1.7.

h. Agenda for pretrial conference; Alternative. 5 INPRAC § 5:1.8.

i. Preliminary pretrial order. 5 INPRAC § 5:1.9.

j. Final pretrial order. 5 INPRAC § 5:1.10.

k. Motion to amend pretrial order. 5 INPRAC § 5:1.11.

l. Motion to extend discovery cutoff date. 5 INPRAC § 5:1.12.

m. Motion for pretrial conference. 10 INPRAC § 70.2.

n. Joint motion for pretrial conference. 10 INPRAC § 70.3.

o. Order for pretrial conference; Attorneys to hold preliminary conference. 10 INPRAC § 70.4.

p. Worksheet for preliminary conference of attorneys and pretrial conference. 10 INPRAC § 70.5.

q. Joint motion for continuance of pretrial conference. 10 INPRAC § 70.6.

r. Letter attempting to arrange preliminary conference of attorneys. 10 INPRAC § 70.7.

s. Notice of conference of attorneys. 10 INPRAC § 70.8.

t. Letter documenting opposing counsel's failure to meet for preliminary conference of attorneys. 10 INPRAC § 70.9.

u. Request that opposing party stipulate to facts and exhibits discovered after conference of attorneys. 10 INPRAC § 70.10.

v. Preliminary pretrial order. 10 INPRAC § 70.14.

w. Final pretrial order. 10 INPRAC § 70.15.

x. Motion to amend pretrial order; General form. 10 INPRAC § 70.16.

y. Motion to amend pretrial order; Party's contentions. 10 INPRAC § 70.17.

z. Motion for sanctions; Failure to attend pretrial conference. 10 INPRAC § 70.22.

I. Checklist

(I) ❑ Matters to be considered for the pretrial conference

    (a) ❑ Documents to consider

        (1) ❑ Exhibits and stipulations

    (b) ❑ Timing

        (1) ❑ Unless otherwise ordered by the court the pretrial conference shall not be called until after reasonable opportunity for the completion of discovery

        (2) ❑ The clerks shall give at least thirty (30) days' notice of the pretrial conference unless otherwise directed by the court

        (3) ❑ Unless otherwise ordered by the court, at least ten (10) days prior to the pretrial conference, attorneys for each of the parties shall meet and confer

(II) ❑ Matters to be considered by the party filing the motion for pretrial conference

    (a) ❑ Required documents

        (1) ❑ Motion and notice

        (2) ❑ Chronological Case Summary (CCS) entry form

        (3) ❑ Proposed order

        (4) ❑ Certificate of service

    (b) ❑ Supplemental documents

        (1) ❑ Supporting evidence

        (2) ❑ Facsimile cover sheet

    (c) ❑ Timing

        (1) ❑ There is no specific timing requirement for filing a motion requesting a pretrial conference

        (2) ❑ A written motion, other than one which may be heard ex parte, and notice of the hearing thereof shall be served not less than five (5) days before the time specified for the hearing, unless a different period is fixed by the Indiana Rules of Trial Procedure or by order of the court

        (3) ❑ All pleadings and papers subsequent to the complaint which are required to be served upon a party shall be filed with the Court either before service or within a reasonable period of time thereafter

Appendix - Related Court Documents

Complaint

2013 WL 5610421 (Ind.Cir.)

Westlaw Query>>

To find additional Complaint filings access the Indiana Civil Trial Court Filings Database (IN-FILING), choose Template Search, select Search Pleadings, then select Complaints.

Circuit Court of Indiana.

Adams County

Kerry GIROD and Barbara Rowland, Plaintiffs,

v.

RORICK ELECTRIC, INC., Thomas G. Rorick and Melissa K. Rorick, Defendants.

No. 01C0113096T0007.

September 4, 2013.

Complaint for Damages

Barrett & McNagny LLP.

Thomas M. Kimbrough #5414-02, 215 East Berry Street, P. O. Box 2263, Fort Wayne, Indiana 46801, Tele: (260) 423-9551, Fax (260) 423-8920, E-mail: tmk @barrettlaw.com.

Attorneys for Plaintiffs.

Keiry Girod and Barbara Rowland, by counsel, Barrett & McNagny LLP, and for their Complaint against Rorick Electric, Inc., Thomas G. Rorick and Melissa K. Rorick, allege and say as follows:

1. Kerry Girod is formerly an employee of Defendant and formerly resided in Decatur, County of Adams, Indiana.

2. Barbara Rowland is formerly an employee of Defendant and resides in Wilshire, Ohio.

3. Thomas G. Rorick is a resident of Adams County, Indiana.

4. Melissa K. Rorick is a resident of Adams County, Indiana.

5. Rorick Electric, Inc. does business in the State of Indiana and has its principal place of business and office in Adams County, Indiana.

6. In or around 2005 of 2006, Defendant offered its employees to be in a SEP IRA Plan with contributions being deducted from the employee's paychecks. A representative of the company's plan, Joel Cochran, had Melissa Rorick write checks for the amount that had been deducted from the employee's paychecks up to that date. Thereafter, contributions were deducted by Defendants on a regular basis.

7. During the course of their employment, Plaintiffs discovered that none of the contributions that had been deducted from the employee's paychecks had been put in to the SEP IRA Plan.

8. Upon discovering what had happened with their contributions, Plaintiffs informed Thomas and Melissa Rorick, plan administrators, concerning the problem but no action was taken to correct the problem.

9. Additionally, in May of 2011, Plaintiffs and other employees received letters from AFLAC Insurance that their premiums had not been paid and that the employees would be dropped if the employees did not personally pay the premiums to date. However, Defendants had represented to Plaintiffs, and other employees, that the premiums for the AFLAC Insurance would be deducted from their paychecks on a weekly basis, and in fact, sums of money which were supposed to be paid by Defendants for AFLAC Insurance had in fact been deducted from Plaintiffs' paychecks but had not been utilized to pay the AFLAC Insurance premiums.

10. As a result of the actions of Defendants, and each of them, the Plaintiffs' earnings and pay have been wrongfully and intentionally misappropriated and such actions forced Plaintiffs to exit the IRA and have caused them significant loss of income and benefits, loss of retirement dollars, loss of interest and destroyed such Plaintiffs' retirement plans.

COUNT I - CONVERSION

11. Defendants, and each of them, have wrongfully, knowingly and intentionally exerted unauthorized control over the earnings, wages and property belonging to Plaintiffs.

12. The acts of the Defendants, and each of them, constitute theft as defined by Ind. Code § 35-43-4-2 and other crimes against the person as defined by Indiana statute.

WHEREFORE, Plaintiffs demand judgment against Defendants, and each of them, in a sum equal to their actual damages, plus three times their actual damages, costs of this action, reasonable attorney fees, interest from the date of loss, and for other just and proper relief in the premises.

BARRETT & MCNAGNY LLP

By: <<signature>>

Thomas M. Kimbrough #5414-02

215 East Berry Street

P. O. Box 2263

Fort Wayne, Indiana 46801

Tele: (260) 423-9551

Fax (260) 423-8920

E-Mail: tmk@barrettlaw.com

Attorneys for Plaintiffs

Amended Complaint

2012 WL 7078163 (Ind.Super.)

Superior Court of Indiana.

Allen County

Rob STRAHM and Cindy Strahm, As next of friends Leonardo S. Strahm, Plaintiffs,

Westlaw Query>>

To find additional Amended Complaint filings access the Indiana Civil Trial Court Filings Database (IN-FILING), choose Terms and Connectors Search, then enter DT("amended complaint").

v.

THE FORT WAYNE SOUTH BEND DIOCESE, Alexandra Bergman, Principal, Sally Klotz, Temporary/Acting Principal, Most Precious Blood School, Sam Sroufe, Minor By his parents and next best friends, Randy Sroufe and Mary Sroufe, Cassandra Grey, Minor By her parents and next best friends Jeff Grey, and Kellie Grey, Tristen Yeager, Minor By his parents and next best friends, Tommy Yeager, and Mary Ann Yeager, Eddie Wene, Minor By his parents and next best friends, Chuck Wene, and Cheryl Wene, Defendants.

No. 02D01-1009-CT-389.

July 25, 2012.

Amended Complaint and Jury Demand

Konrad M. L. Urberg, ID #20414-02, Urberg Law Office, LLC, 2810 Beaver Avenue, Fort Wayne, IN 46807, (260) 456-9988 Fax: (260) 744-5411.

Come now the Plaintiffs, Rob Strahm and Cindy Strahm, and as next of friend Leonardo S. Strahm, by counsel, Konrad M.L. Urberg and files this Complaint and Jury Demand against Defendants, The Fort Wayne South Bend Diocese; Alexandra Bergman, Principal; Sally Klotz, acting /temporary Principal; Most Precious Blood School; Sam Sroufe, minor by his parents and next best friends, Randy Sroufe and Mary Sroufe; Cassandra Grey, minor by her parents and next best friends, Jeff Grey, Kellie Grey; Tristen Yeager, minor by his parents and next best friends, Tommy Yeager, and Mary Ann Yeager; Eddie Wene, minor by his parents and next best friends, Chuck Wene, and Cheryl Wene, and state and alleges as follows:

Count I

1. Plaintiff, Leonardo S. Strahm ("Leonardo") is a disabled minor suffering from cerebral palsey, who is a resident of Fort Wayne, Allen County, Indiana and a student with the Fort Wayne South Bend Diocese, Most Precious Blood School at the time of all incidents complained of herein.

2. Leonardo's disability requires him at all times relevant to wear leg braces to assist with walking and balance.

3. Rob Strahm and Cindy Strahm are the next friends and parents of Leonardo S. Strahm and are adults and residents of Fort Wayne, Allen County, Indiana at all times relevant.

4. Defendant, Most Precious Blood School is a parochial school of the Fort Wayne South Bend Diocese with said school being physically located at 1529 Barthold St., Fort Wayne, Indiana 46808.

5. The Fort Wayne-South Bend Diocese is headquartered in Fort Wayne, Indiana and has the ultimate responsibility for oversight of the Catholic parochial schools in Fort Wayne, including, but not limited to Most Precious Blood School.

6. Defendant, Sam Sroufe, minor by his parents and next best friends, Randy Sroufe and Mary Sroufe, are residents of Fort Wayne, Allen County, Indiana, and at all times relevant Sam Sroufe was enrolled as a student at Most Precious Blood School.

7. Defendant, Cassandra Grey, minor by her parents and next best friends, Jeff Grey, Kellie Grey are residents of Fort Wayne, Allen County, Indiana, and at all times relevant Cassandra Grey was enrolled as a student at Most Precious Blood School.

8. Defendant, Tristen Yeager, minor by his parents and next best friends, Tommy Yeager, and Mary Ann Yeager are residents of Fort Wayne, Allen County, Indiana, and at all times relevant Tristen Yeager was enrolled as a student at Most Precious Blood School.

9. Defendant, Eddie Wene, minor by his parents and next best friends, Chuck Wene, and Cheryl Wene are residents of Fort Wayne, Allen County, Indiana, and at an times relevant Eddie Wene was enrolled as a student at Most Precious Blood School.

10. Venue is proper in this Court, pursuant to Indiana Trial Rule 74(a) (5).

11. This is a claim for negligence and negligent supervision sustained by plaintiff, Leonardo S. Strahm. From the period of time of September 2008 through December 2009; there was a pattern of continuing and ongoing wrongs leading to the claim for negligence and negligent supervision.

12. Leonardo S. Strahm was a student in grades 6 and 7 during the periods of time September 2008 through December 2009.

13. Additionally this is a claim for assault, battery, false imprisonment, and negligent and or intentional infliction of emotional distress occurring from the period of September 2008 through December 2009.

14. Sam Sroufe was responsible for pushing the plaintiff up and down the stairs approximately twenty-five (25) times during the period of November 2008-January 2009, as well as defendants Tristian Yeager and Eddie Wene, jumped, pushed, punched and physically battered, Leonardo, as well as placed him in a headlock, assaulting and battering him between January 2009 and December 2009.

15. The separate and distinct incidents of assault, battery, false imprisonment, negligence and or intentional infliction of emotion distress involved Tristen Yeager and Eddie Wene as well as Sam Sroufe.

16. There is also conduct of verbal and emotional abuse including slanderous slurs regarding sexual orientation, physical abilities, and negative information regarding the parents of Leonardo all of which was inappropriate, slanderous and done intentionally and with negligence and/or intentionally for the infliction of emotion distress and constitutes bullying.

17. Such behavior was also carried out by Cassandra Grey and Tristen Yeager during the relevant time outlined herein.

18. All of the alleged conduct occurred under the supervision of class room teacher and or the assist and after the first incident and every incident thereafter Alexandra Bergman, principal; Sally Klotz, acting / temporary principal, Reverend Joseph Gaughan, Father of the Most Precious Blood Congregation and representative of the Fort Wayne-South Bend Diocese were all advised of said activities.

19. Any and all representatives of the Fort Wayne South Bend Diocese and Most Precious Blood School failed to take any action to prevent and or stop said conduct despite being made aware of said conduct repeatedly and on a regular basis and despite the pleas of Leonardo S. Strahm, Rob Strahm and Cindy Strahm for said conduct to stop.

20. All the incidents set forth occurred in the classrooms, hallways and or on the school grounds themselves.

21. While the aforesaid actions were occurring the plaintiff was powerless to resist and or escape.

22. Leonardo was in total fear and apprehension.

23. Said activities also caused plaintiff to become physically ill and affected his school performance, his physical health and required medical and psychological care to address said situation.

24. Said situation eventually lead to Leonardo withdrawing from Most Precious Blood School due to the environment created there.

25. After each attack Plaintiffs' Rob Strahm and or Cindy Strahm informed Principal Alexandra Bergman or other representatives of Most Precious Blood School including Sally Klotz and Reverend Joseph Gaughan and asked for repeated meetings with all said individuals.

26. That Leonardo at times was told to meet with Sally Klotz in the absence of Alexandra Bergman and one meeting with Klotz was held with Rob and Cindy Strahm.

27. Rob Strahm and Cindy Strahm requested meetings and held meetings with Reverend Joe Gaughan, who also made aware of it and offered no solution.

28. Plaintiffs Rob Strahm and or Cindy Strahm also attempted to meet with the Superintendent of the Fort Wayne South Bend Diocese and requests were not granted nor any meetings scheduled despite repeated requests to do so.

29. All the herein described conduct was in violation of defendant, Fort Wayne South Bend Diocese / Most Precious Blood School's policy and procedures.

30. Because of the continuation of unprovoked acts of bulling, verbal threats and harassment, plaintiff transferred to Lakeside Middle School to continue his education.

31. Under the Student's Rights and Responsibilities and Behavior Code, Leonardo and his parents were required to enter into an agreement with the Fort Wayne South Bend Diocese, which committed to provide a safe secure learning environment for all students. Additionally, the Fort Wayne-South Bend Diocese has a policy that prohibits injury to others, fighting, physical conduct pushing, shoving, or hitting, whether or not injury occurs is prohibited. The policy also addresses threatening harassing a student or other persons, threatening to strike, attack or harm any student or other person as well as battery, knowing and or intentionally knowing of touching of another person in a rude insolent or angry manner, causing or attempting to cause physical injury or behaving in such a way that could reasonably cause physical harm to students or others.

32. Plaintiff's safety was breached on the dates of the separate and distinct attacks at the Most Precious Blood School when it failed to provide him safety and protection as well as negligently supervised the children it was to care for.

33. Defendant, Most Precious Blood School's Principal acknowledged to Leonard's parents Rob Strahm and Cindy Strahm that she was aware of the incidents however she failed to take any action claiming there were "two sides to every story".

34. Plaintiff alleges that Defendant, Fort Wayne-South Bend Diocese, Most Precious Blood School, school's principal, security and administration were negligent in supervising the premises as to the student's safety because there was a complete failure to monitor the situation after being placed on notice of the attacks by the named Defendants.

35. Fort Wayne South Bend Diocese, Most Precious Blood School were in charge of the safety and education of Plaintiff Leonardo.

36. Despite plaintiffs repeated notification of these attacks by the other students, the fact the Fort Wayne --South Bend Diocese, Most Precious Blood School and Alexandra Bergman and other representatives of Most Precious Blood School were aware of the same, Defendants did not take any actions to prevent possible injury to Plaintiff Leonardo. No representatives of Most Precious Blood School took any action whatsoever, nor did they properly supervise the students it was responsible for.

37. Defendants had a duty to ensure the safety of the students attending its school, and owed such a duty to Plaintiff Leonardo during the periods of time of to this lawsuit.

38. Defendant, Most Precious Blood School, Fort Wayne South Bend Diocese breached its duty of care owed to plaintiff as and a result plaintiff suffered injuries from September 2008-December 2009.

39. There were approximately thirty (30) separate and distinct incidents of assault, battery, false imprisonment, negligent and/or intentional infliction of emotional distress during the period of time of September 2008 through December 2009. The bullying in the nature of slurs, intimidation and inappropriate comments and behavior

occurred nearly every day while Leonardo was present at Most Precious Blood School from September 2008-December 2009.

40. The parents of the minor defendants are financially responsible pursuant to Indiana law for the damages created by the conduct of their minor children.

Count II

41. Plaintiffs Rob Strahm and Cindy Strahm incorporate by reference rhetorical paragraphs 1 - 40 of Count I above and further state that the collective Defendants' conduct towards Leonardo S. Strahm resulted in him being injured.

42. Rob Strahm and Cindy Strahm suffered loss of companionship of their son, out of pocket expenses and loss of educational benefits as a result of said injury.

43. The direct and proximate cause of the collective Defendants' negligence and/or intentional conduct and negligent supervision and actions of the collective Defendants caused Plaintiff Leonardo S. Strahm to suffer personal injury.

WHEREFORE, Plaintiffs pray for judgment against Defendants as follows:

1. Expenses for past psychological counseling in an amount to be determined by a jury;

2. Expenses for future psychological counseling in an amount to be determined by a jury;

3. Past, present and future mental pain and suffering in an amount to be determined by a jury.

4. Expenses and costs for attending another school to receive an alternate method of education due to his injuries and refund of tuition paid to Most Precious Blood School.

5. Costs for said suit and other relief as the Court deems proper;

6. Pain and suffering, (embarrassment humiliation, mental stress and anxiety);

7. The costs of all medical or healthcare bills.

8. Punitive damages for any and all intentional conduct;

9. Court costs and for all other just and proper relief.

JURY DEMAND

Pursuant to I.R. 38, the Plaintiffs respectfully demand that this be tried to a jury.

Respectfully submitted:

_____

Konrad M. L. Urberg, ID #20414-02

URBERG LAW OFFICE, LLC

2810 Beaver Avenue

Fort Wayne, IN 46807

(260) 456-9988 Fax: (260) 744-5411

Answer

2013 WL 5565766 (Ind.Super.)

Superior Court of Indiana.

Allen County

REILLEY TRUCKING, INC., Plaintiff,

v.

J&L CONSTRUCTION & EXCAVATING, INC.,
Great Lakes Improvements of Indiana, Inc. and Allen County Community Development Corp.,
Defendants.

No. 02D01-1202-PL-46.

July 16, 2013.

Westlaw Query>>

To find additional Answer filings access the Indiana Civil Trial Court Filings Database (IN-FILING), choose Template Search, select Search Pleadings, then select Answers and Counterclaims.

Defendant J&L Construction & Excavating, Inc.'s Answer to Plaintiff's Complaint

April S. Grunden, #20150-02, Grunden Law Office, 9815 Dawson's Creek Blvd., Fort Wayne, in 46825, 260.969.1177, 260.497.9747 fax, Attorney for Defendants/Counterclaimants J&L.

COMES NOW Defendant J&L Construction & Excavating, Inc.(hereinafter "J&L"), by counsel, and submits its Answer to Plaintiff's Complaint for Damages and to Foreclose on Mechanic's Liens (hereinafter "Plaintiff's Complaint). J&L states to the Court as follows:

Parties

1. J&L lacks sufficient information and knowledge as to the statements and allegations set forth in paragraph 1 of Plaintiff's Complaint and therefore denies same.

2. J&L admits the statements set forth in paragraph 2 of Plaintiff's Complaint.

3. J&L lacks sufficient information and knowledge as to the statements and allegations set forth in paragraph 3 of Plaintiff's Complaint and therefore denies same.

4. J&L lacks sufficient information and knowledge as to the statements and allegations set forth in paragraph 4 of Plaintiff's Complaint and therefore denies same.

Jurisdiction

5. J&L admits the statements set forth in paragraph 5 of Plaintiff's Complaint.

6. J&L admits the statements set forth in paragraph 6 of Plaintiff's Complaint.

7. J&L admits the statements set forth in paragraph 7 of Plaintiff's Complaint.

COUNT I.

8. J&L admits the statements set forth in paragraph 8 of Plaintiff's Complaint.

9. J&L denies the statements and allegations set forth in paragraph 9 of Plaintiff's Complaint.

10. J&L admits the statements set forth in paragraph 10 of Plaintiff's Complaint.

11. J&L admits the statements set forth in paragraph 11 of Plaintiff's Complaint.

12. J&L admits the statements set forth in paragraph 12 of Plaintiff's Complaint.

13. J&L admits the statements set forth in paragraph 13 of Plaintiff's Complaint.

14. J&L admits the statements set forth in paragraph 14 of Plaintiff's Complaint.

15. J&L denies the statements and allegations set forth in paragraph 15 of Plaintiff's Complaint.

16. J&L denies the statements and allegations set forth in paragraph 16 of Plaintiff's Complaint.

COUNT II.

17. J&L reassert its responses to paragraphs 1 through 16 of Plaintiff's Complaint.

18. J&L admits the statements and allegations set forth in paragraph 18 of Plaintiff's Complaint.

19. J&L lacks sufficient information or knowledge as to the statements and allegations set forth in paragraph 19 of Plaintiff's Complaint and therefore denies same.

20. J J&L lacks sufficient information or knowledge as to the statements and allegations set forth in paragraph 20 of Plaintiff's Complaint and therefore denies same.

21. J&L lacks sufficient information or knowledge as to the statements and allegations set forth in paragraph 21 of Plaintiff's Complaint and therefore denies same.

22. J&L lacks sufficient information or knowledge as to the statements and allegations set forth in paragraph 22 of Plaintiff's Complaint and therefore denies same.

23. J&L lacks sufficient information or knowledge as to the statements and allegations set forth in paragraph 23 of Plaintiff's Complaint and therefore denies same.

COUNT III.

24. J&L reassert its responses to paragraphs 1 through 23 of Plaintiff's Complaint.

25. J&L lacks sufficient information or knowledge as to the statements and allegations set forth in paragraph 25 of Plaintiff's Complaint and therefore denies same.

26. J&L lacks sufficient information or knowledge as to the statements and allegations set forth in paragraph 26 of Plaintiff's Complaint and therefore denies same.

27. J&L lacks sufficient information or knowledge as to the statements and allegations set forth in paragraph 27 of Plaintiff's Complaint and therefore denies same.

28. J&L lacks sufficient information or knowledge as to the statements and allegations set forth in paragraph 28 of Plaintiff's Complaint and therefore denies same.

29. J&L lacks sufficient information or knowledge as to the statements and allegations set forth in paragraph 29 of Plaintiff's Complaint and therefore denies same.

DEFENDANTS' AFFIRMATIVE DEFENSES TO PLAINTIFF'S COMPLAINT

J&L assert and allege affirmative defenses as follows:

1. Plaintiff's Complaint fails to state any claim upon which relief may be granted.

2. Plaintiff's claims may be barred by applicable statutes of limitation.

3. Plaintiff's claims are barred by the doctrine of laches.

4. Plaintiff's claims are barred by the doctrine of equitable estoppel.

5. Defendants respectfully reserve the right to assert additional affirmative defenses in the course of this litigation.

DEFENDANT'S CROSS-CLAIM AGAINST GREAT LAKES IMPROVEMENTS OF INDIANA, INC.

1. Defendant/Cross-Claimant J&L is a corporation formed under the laws of the State of Indiana (hereinafter "J&L").

2. Defendant Great Lakes Improvements of Indiana, Inc. is a corporation formed under the laws of the State of Indiana ("Great Lakes").

3. On or about July 7, 2011, Great Lakes forwarded to J&L a bid request for demolition of residential structures in Fort Wayne, Indiana.

4. On or about October 26, 2011, Great Lakes entered into a contract with J&L for the demolition of four (4) residential structures in Fort Wayne, Indiana (hereinafter "the Contract"). A true and accurate copy of this contract is attached hereto as Exhibit "A".

5. Sometime in late 2011, Great Lakes requested services from J&L in addition to those provided for in the Contract.

6. The additional services referenced in paragraph 6 above included hauling of debris and brick from the four (4) residential lots and seeding of grass and straw on same lots.

7. Pursuant to a request from Great Lakes, J&L provided additional services in the form of the seeding of grass and straw on three (3) residential lots in Fort Wayne, Indiana, in late 2011/early 2012.

8. J&L subcontracted the services of hauling debris to Plaintiff.

9. J&L subcontracted the services of hauling brick to Dave Rice.

10. J&L completed all work requested by Great Lakes with the exception of the seeding of grass and straw of one (1) of the requested four (4) lots.

11. The services performed by J&L have been provided for the benefit of Great Lakes, and Great Lakes has made no complaints to J&L with regard to the quality of such services.

12. On or about November 8, 2011, J&L issued Invoice No. 3885 to Great Lakes for the services provided under the Contract and the additional services requested by Great Lakes. A true and accurate copy of this invoice is attached hereto as Exhibit "B".

13. On or about November 8, 2011, Great Lakes remitted payment in the amount of One Thousand and 00/100 Dollars ($1,000.00).

14. On or about December 12, 2011, Great Lakes remitted payment in the amount of Eighteen Thousand Six Hundred and 00/100 Dollars ($18,600).

15. Despite repeated request and demand, Great Lakes has failed to make any payment to Great Lakes for the amount due and owing as reflected by the invoice.

WHEREFORE, J&L respectfully requests that this Court enter Judgment in its favor and against the Cross-Defendant, Great Lakes, in the amount of Twenty-Six Thousand Nine Hundred Ninety-Two and 92/100 Dollars ($26,992.92), plus pre-judgment interest accruing thereon from the amount said payments were due and owing through the date of judgment, for costs, for any and all expenses, and for any and all other relief that this Court may deem to be just and proper in the premises.

Respectfully Submitted,

<<signature>>

April S. Grunden, #20150-02

Grunden Law Office

9815 Dawson's Creek Blvd.

Fort Wayne, IN 46825

260.969.1177

260.497.9747 fax

Attorney for Defendants/Counterclaimants J&L

Amended Answer

2012 WL 9297838 (Ind.Super.)

Superior Court of Indiana.

Allen County

REILLEY TRUCKING, INC., Plaintiff,

v.

J&L CONSTRUCTION & EXCAVATING, INC., Great Lakes Improvements of Indiana, Inc. and Allen County Community Development Corp., Defendants.

No. 02D01-1202-PL-46.

August 27, 2012.

Amended Answer to Plaintiff's Complaint

Jeremy W. Brown - 19284-01, Burry, Herman, Miller & Brown, P.C., 113 North Second Street, P.O. Box 470, Decatur, Indiana 46733, Telephone: (260) 724-2154, Fax: (260) 724-3127, Email: jbrown@burryherman.com.

Comes now the Defendant, Great Lakes Improvements of Indiana, Inc., by counsel, and files its Amended Answer to Plaintiffs Complaint. The Defendant, Great Lakes Improvements of Indiana, Inc., respectfully states as follows:

1. The Defendant is without sufficient knowledge or information to admit or deny the allegations contained in rhetorical paragraph 1 of Plaintiff's Complaint. Therefore, the Defendant respectfully denies the same.

2. The Defendant admits rhetorical paragraphs 2 and 3 of Plaintiff's Complaint.

3. The Defendant is without sufficient knowledge or information to admit or deny the allegations contained in rhetorical paragraph 4 of Plaintiff's Complaint. Therefore, the Defendant respectfully denies the same.

4. The Defendant admits rhetorical paragraphs 5, 6, and 7 of the Defendant's Complaint.

5. The Defendant is without sufficient knowledge or information to admit or deny the allegations contained in rhetorical paragraph 8 of Plaintiff's Complaint. Therefore, the Defendant respectfully denies the same.

6. The Defendant is without sufficient knowledge or information to admit or deny the allegations contained in rhetorical paragraph 9 of Plaintiff's Complaint. Therefore, the Defendant respectfully denies the same.

7. The Defendant is without sufficient knowledge or information to admit or deny the allegations contained in rhetorical paragraph 10 of Plaintiff's Complaint. Therefore, the Defendant respectfully denies the same.

8. The Defendant is without sufficient knowledge or information to admit or deny the allegations contained in rhetorical paragraph 11 of Plaintiff's Complaint. Therefore, the Defendant respectfully denies the same.

10. The Defendant is without sufficient knowledge or information to admit or deny the allegations contained in rhetorical paragraph 12 of Plaintiff's Complaint. Therefore, the Defendant respectfully denies the same.

11. The Defendant is without sufficient knowledge or information to admit or deny the allegations contained in rhetorical paragraph 13 of Plaintiff's Complaint. Therefore, the Defendant respectfully denies the same.

12. The Defendant is without sufficient knowledge or information to admit or deny the allegations contained in rhetorical paragraph 14 of Plaintiff's Complaint. Therefore, the Defendant respectfully denies the same.

13. The Defendant is without sufficient knowledge or information to admit or deny the allegations contained in rhetorical paragraph 15 of Plaintiff's Complaint. Therefore, the Defendant respectfully denies the same.

14. The Defendant is without sufficient knowledge or information to admit or deny the allegations contained in rhetorical paragraph 16 of Plaintiff's Complaint. Therefore, the Defendant respectfully denies the same.

15. The Defendant is without sufficient knowledge or information to admit or deny the allegations contained in rhetorical paragraph 17 of Plaintiff's Complaint. Therefore, the Defendant respectfully denies the same.

16. The Defendant admits rhetorical paragraph 18 of Plaintiff's Complaint.

17. The Defendant denies rhetorical paragraph 19 of Plaintiff's Complaint.

18. The Defendant denies rhetorical paragraph 20 of Plaintiff's Complaint.

19. The Defendant denies rhetorical paragraph 21 of Plaintiff's Complaint.

20. The Defendant denies rhetorical paragraph 22 of Plaintiff's Complaint.

21. The Defendant denies rhetorical paragraph 23 of Plaintiff's Complaint.

22. The Defendant is without sufficient knowledge or information to admit or deny the allegations contained in rhetorical paragraph 24 of Plaintiff's Complaint. Therefore, the Defendant respectfully denies the same.

23. The Defendant is without sufficient knowledge or information to admit or deny the allegations contained in rhetorical paragraph 25 of Plaintiff's Complaint. Therefore, the Defendant respectfully denies the same.

24. The Defendant is without sufficient knowledge or information to admit or deny the allegations contained in rhetorical paragraph 26 of Plaintiff's Complaint. Therefore, the Defendant respectfully denies the same.

25. The Defendant is without sufficient knowledge or information to admit or deny the allegations contained in rhetorical paragraph 27 of Plaintiff's Complaint. Therefore, the Defendant respectfully denies the same.

26. The Defendant is without sufficient knowledge or information to admit or deny the allegations contained in rhetorical paragraph 28 of Plaintiff's Complaint. Therefore, the Defendant respectfully denies the same.

27. The Defendant denies rhetorical paragraph 29 of Plaintiff's Complaint.

DEFENSES

28. The Plaintiff has failed to state a claim upon which relief can be granted. Therefore the Defendant, Great Lakes Improvements of Indiana, Inc. requests the Court to deny the relief sought by the Plaintiff.

29. The Service Agreement attached to Plaintiffs Complaint which was allegedly the contract between the Plaintiff and Defendant, J & L Construction & Excavating, Inc. is not signed by either party. Therefore, the Defendant contends there was no such written agreement between the Plaintiff and Defendant, J & L Construction & Excavating, Inc. As a result, the Plaintiffs claim should be denied in its entirety.

30. The Defendant, Great Lakes Improvements of Indiana, Inc., paid all subcontractors with whom it contracted for services in the performance if its obligations. Therefore, Defendant raises the affirmative defense of payment to the Plaintiffs Complaint.

31. The Defendant, Great Lakes Improvements of Indiana, Inc., at no time contracted with the Plaintiff nor made any representations to the Plaintiff that it would pay for any services provided by Plaintiff. The lack of contractual relationship precludes the relief sought by the Plaintiff against the Defendant, Great Lakes Improvements of Indiana, Inc.

COUNTERCLAIM

32. The Defendant Great Lakes Improvements of Indiana, Inc. has incurred attorney fees and other expenses associated with the defense of the groundless claim which the Plaintiff filed against the Defendant.

33. Pursuant to Indiana Code § 34-52-1-1, the court should order the Plaintiff to pay the reasonable costs of defense, including attorney fees, incurred by Defendant, Great Lakes Improvements of Indiana, Inc.

WHEREFORE, the Defendant respectfully requests the Court to issue a judgment finding the Defendant, Great Lakes Improvements of Indiana, Inc. owes nothing to the Plaintiff.

Furthermore, the Defendant requests a judgment against the Plaintiff and in favor of the Defendant, Great Lakes Improvements of Indiana, Inc. for an amount sufficient to compensate Defendant for the attorney fees and other expenses incurred in defense of this action.

Respectfully submitted,

<<signature>>

Jeremy W. Brown - 19284-01

BURRY, HERMAN, MILLER & BROWN, P.C.

113 North Second Street

P.O. Box 470

Decatur, Indiana 46733

Telephone: (260) 724-2154

Fax: (260) 724-3127

Email: *jbrown@burryherman.com*

Motion for Leave to Amend

2010 WL 8292365 (Ind.Super.)

Westlaw Query>>

To find additional Motion for Leave to Amend filings access the Indiana Civil Trial Court Filings Database (IN-FILING), choose Terms and Connectors Search, then enter DT("leave to amend").

Superior Court of Indiana.

Marion County

STATE OF INDIANA,

v.

INTERNATIONAL BUSINESS MACHINES CORPORATION.

No. 49D101005PL021451.

December 30, 2010.

State of Indiana's Motion for Leave to Amend Complaint

John R. Maley (14300-89), Peter J Rusthoven (6247-98), J. Curtis Greene (25600-29), Patrick W. Price (25058-49), Barnes & Thornburg LLP, 11 South Meridian Street, Indianapolis Indiana 46204, Telephone: 317.236.1313, Facsimile: 317.231.7433, E-mail: jmaley@btlaw.com, prusthoven@btlaw.com, cgreene@btlaw.com, pprice@btlaw.com, Counsel for Plaintiff State of Indiana.

Plaintiff State of Indiana ("State"), acting on behalf of the Family & Social Services Administration ("FSSA")), requests leave to amend its Amended Complaint for Damages and Declaratory Relief based on IBM's past and recent violations of publicity provisions within the Master Services Agreement ("MSA") as well as its abuse of judicial process. The basis for these additional claims includes conduct by IBM as late as December 3, 2010, when IBM submitted filings that once again - and contrary to prior warnings from this Court - contain scandalous, inaccurate, and impertinent material that attempts to use the auspices of the Court to disseminate what IBM is contractually prohibited from publicizing under the parties' contractual agreement. Claims for Breach of Publicity Obligations and Abuse of Process should be added to the State's Amended Complaint accordingly.

Indiana law dictates that "leave [to amend] shall be given when justice so requires." Ind. Trial Rule 15(A). "Consistent with an underlying purpose to facilitate decisions on the merits and to avoid pleading traps, the Indiana Trial Rules generally implement a policy of liberal amendment of pleadings, absent prejudice to an opponent." *Indiana Farmers Mut. Ins. Co. v. Richie,* 707 N.E.2d 992, 996 (Ind. 1999). Fairness and efficiency justify amendment here. The State's amendment will facilitate resolution of this case on the merits, and the parties will not be prejudiced as discovery remains open, documents have not been fully exchanged, and no depositions have occurred. Justice requires this amendment.

The State's proposed additional claims, which outline the factual considerations, have been attached as Exhibit A to serve as an addendum to its earlier pleading and in total constitute the State's Second Amended Complaint for Damages and Declaratory Relief. For the convenience of the Court and parties, the extensive allegations against IBM as well as the voluminous Master Services Agreement (consisting of several hundred pages) have not been reproduced.

WHEREFORE the State respectfully requests that the Court grant it leave to amend its Amended Complaint to include the attached Claims, which should be deemed filed as of the date of the Court's Order.

Respectfully submitted,

/s/ John R. Maley

John R. Maley (14300-89)

Peter J. Rusthoven (6247-98)

J. Curtis Greene (25600-29)

Patrick W. Price (25058-49)

BARNES AND THORNBURG LLP

11 South Meridian Street

Indianapolis, Indiana 46204

Telephone: 317.236.1313

Facsimile: 317.231.7433

E-mail: jmaley@btlaw.com

E-mail: prusthoven@btlaw.com

E-mail: cgreene@btlaw.com

E-mail: pprice@btlaw.com

Counsel for Plaintiff State of Indiana

Motion for Summary Judgment

2010 WL 6742931 (Ind.Super.)

Westlaw Query>>

To find additional Motion for Summary Judgment filings access the Indiana Civil Trial Court Filings Database (IN-FILING), choose Template Search, select Search Motions, then select Motion for Summary Judgment.

Superior Court of Indiana.

Lake County

Marjorie AUSTIN, as Mother and Next Friend of Mykel Austin, Deceased, Plaintiff,

v.

Marc A. CONNERY, M.D., Clark E. Kramer, M.D., Corporation A d/b/a Hospital A, and University of Chicago Hospitals d/b/a Child Life Center, Defendants.

No. 45D01-0508-CT-178.

February 16, 2010.

Defendant, Hospital A, Inc.'s Motion for Summary Judgment

Respectfully submitted by, Johnson & Bell, Ltd., Marian C. Drenth, #18639-64, 1435 East 85th Avenue, Merrillville, Indiana 46410, 219/791-1900, Attorneys for Defendant.

COMES NOW Defendant, Hospital A, Inc., by counsel, Johnson & Bell, Ltd., and pursuant to Indiana Trial Rule 56(C), respectfully prays and moves the Court for entry of summary judgment as a matter of law in its favor and against Plaintiff, Marjorie Austin, as Mother and Next Friend of Mykel Austin, Deceased. In support of the aforementioned, Hospital A, Inc. states the following:

1. This litigation involves claims for medical malpractice stemming from Plaintiff's claim that all named Defendants, including the staff and employees of Hospital A, Inc., were negligent in that it breached the standard of care that it owed Mykel Austin and that such treatment of the Mykel Austin was the proximate cause of his death.

2. However, the Plaintiff has failed to produce expert testimony establishing that Hospital A, Inc. breached the standard of care owed to Mykel Austin or that Hospital A, Inc.'s treatment of Mykel Austin was the proximate cause of Mykel Austin's death.

3. Rather, Plaintiff's experts, Dr. John Lindquist and Dr. Carol Miller, have both testified that Hospital A, Inc. did not breach the standard of care owed to Mykel Austin nor was Hospital A, Inc. the cause of Mykel Austin's death.

4. Additionally, the Plaintiff has agreed to dismiss Hospital A, Inc. from this matter; however, Co-Defendants, Dr. Marc A. Connery, Dr. Clark E. Kramer, and University of Chicago Hospital d/b/a Child Life Center have not yet agreed to a stipulation to dismiss Hospital A, Inc. from this matter.

5. Hospital A, Inc. has served Co-Defendants with written discovery. Co-Defendants have failed to provide any responses that controvert the present expert testimony stating that Hospital A, Inc. did not breach the standard of care owed to Mykel Austin nor was Hospital A, Inc. the proximate cause of or a contributing factor in causing Mykel Austin's death.

6. There are no genuine issues of material fact regarding whether the Defendant, Hospital A, Inc., met the applicable standard of care when providing care to Mykel Austin and there are no genuine issues of material fact regarding causation. Therefore, Defendant, Hospital A., Inc., is entitled to summary judgment as a matter of law on this matter.

7. That Defendant, Hospital A, Inc. files herewith its Memorandum of Law in Support of Motion for Summary Judgment pursuant to Trial Rule 56(C).

WHEREFORE, Defendant, Hospital A, Inc., respectfully prays and moves the Court for entry of summary judgment as a matter of law in its favor and against the Plaintiff on all claims asserted by the Plaintiff, for the Court to find that there exists no just reason for the delay in entry of final judgment upon said claim, for the Court to direct the Clerk to enter a final judgment upon said claim, and for all other just and proper relief in the premises.

Respectfully submitted by,

JOHNSON & BELL, LTD.

<<signature>>

Marian C. Drenth, #18639-64

1435 East 85th Avenue

Merrillville, Indiana 46410

219/791-1900

Attorneys for Defendant

Motion for Protective Order

2011 WL 9371091 (Ind.Cir.)

Circuit Court of Indiana.

St. Joseph County

George E. SMITH and Shari Smith, Plaintiffs,

Westlaw Query>>

To find additional Motion for Protective Order filings access the Indiana Civil Trial Court Filings Database (IN-FILING), choose Template Search, select Search Motions, then select Motion for Protective Order.

v.

KPL, INC., Defendant.

No. 71C01-0706-PL-00157.

December 14, 2011.

Plaintiffs' Motion For Protective Order and to Quash Subpoenas Duces Tecum

Michael J. Anderson (4004-71), Anderson ● Agostino & Keller, P.C., 131 South Taylor Street, South Bend, Indiana 46601, Telephone: (574) 288-1510, Attorney for Plaintiffs.

Plaintiffs, by counsel, file their Motion for Protective Order and to Quash Subpoenas Duces Tecum, and state as follows in support thereof:

1. On December 6, 2011, counsel for Defendant, KPL, Inc., (hereinafter referred to as "KPL") sent Notices to Plaintiffs' counsel of the Depositions of Dr. Robert Clemency and Dr. Charles Peterson set on December 29, 2011, along with Subpoenas Duces Tecum. (See Notices of Deposition of Dr. Robert Clemency and Dr. Charles Peterson, and accompanying Subpoena Duces Tecum, attached hereto as "Exhibit A" and "Exhibit B," respectively).

2. Pursuant to the Court's Order of June 2, 2011, the parties were ordered to complete discovery by September 30, 2011. (See Court's Order of June 2, 2011, attached hereto as "Exhibit C").

3. Prior to the setting of this Order of June 2, 2011, there have been multiple revisions of the Order and deadlines for this matter, including multiple extensions of the discovery deadline.

4. Counsel for Defendant has caused depositions to be set months outside the close of discovery, and less than a month prior to the scheduled January 24, 2012, trial setting. During the month of December, 2011, alone, the Court has further ordered the deadlines for the submissions of the Pretrial Order, agreed instructions, pretrial motions, proposed instructions and verdict forms.

5. This case is based upon an injury which occurred on June 22, 2005. On June 22, 2007, this case was filed with the Clerk in the St. Joseph County Circuit Court.

6. Counsel from the law firm of Bruce P. Clark & Associates entered appearance for Defendant KPL on July 11, 2007. Current attorney Jennifer Davis from the law firm of Bruce P. Clark & Associates entered her appearance on behalf of Defendant KPL on April 4, 2008.

7. Accordingly, counsel for Defendant KPL have had nearly four and a half years up to the current date in which to conduct and complete discovery and all necessary depositions prior to trial.

8. Indiana Trial Rule 26(B)(1) grants a trial court power over the frequency or extent of discovery methods otherwise permitted by the rules in situations where "the party seeking discovery has had ample opportunity by discovery in the action to obtain the information sought." In this case, counsel for Defendant KPL has had over forty-eight (48) months to obtain depositions of any necessary party.

9. Management of discovery is a litigation function particularly within the trial court's domain. It is within the discretion of the trial court to place bounds on the extent of discovery. *Coster v. Coster,* 452 N.E.2d 397, 400 (Ind. Ct. App. 1983). A trial court may require discovery be completed by a certain date to prevent delay of the trial. *Id.* In the *Coster* case, the trial court ordered the termination of all discovery fifty-three months (53) months after the initiation of the suit. *Id.* The court found that nearly five years of discovery during which necessary exhibits were provided to a party were a sufficient time frame. *Id.*

10. Furthermore, it is within the Court's discretion to quash subpoenas as untimely where they have been issued after the passing of the discovery deadline. *Bethlehem Steel Corp. v. Sercon Corp.,* 654 N.E.2d 1163, 1170 (Ind. Ct. App. 1995) *rehearing denied, transfer denied.* In the *Bethlehem* case, subpoenas were issued after the discovery deadline set by the Court had passed. *Id.* The court noted that the party issuing the subpoenas was always welcome to cross-examination of the opposing party's witnesses at trial if it so desired. *Id.*

11. The situation at hand is similar to that in the cases mentioned above. Counsel for Defendant KPL has had over four years and multiple extensions of the discovery deadline in order to obtain all needed and necessary discovery for trial. The fact that such depositions have not been taken leads to an inference that such depositions are likely to be irrelevant, duplicative of alternate discovery, and unnecessary. Even if such depositions were necessary, any failure to undertake necessary discovery over the course of four years of litigation by opposing counsel should not be seen as good cause for an extension of the discovery deadline validly entered in furtherance of the Court's interest in keeping its active docket moving.

12. Furthermore, without doubt opposing counsel has issued said notices and subpoenas more than two months after, and in violation of, the Court's designated discovery deadline of September 30, 2011. The defense failed to properly request and be granted an extension of the discovery deadline prior to its passing. This merely compounds the failure of the Defendant to properly prepare itself. Such actions should not be rewarded by this Court.

13. As such, the Plaintiffs pray that this Court enter an Order for Protection prohibiting Defendant KPL from taking the depositions of Drs. Clemency and Peterson. Pursuant to Indiana Trial Rule 26(C), the Court has the authority to order that discovery not be had. As the depositions of the doctors are untimely, unnecessary, wasteful, beyond the time limits imposed by this Court's Order, and in violation of said Order, the Plaintiffs move the Court for an Order of Protection preventing said depositions from being taken.

14. Furthermore, the Plaintiffs pray that this Court quash the respective subpoenas duces tecum issued simultaneously with the depositions at issue.

WHEREFORE, Plaintiffs, George and Shari Smith, by counsel, request the Court grant a Protective Order prohibiting Defendant KPL from taking the depositions of Drs. Clemency and Peterson, and an Order to Quash the respective subpoenas duces tecum.

Respectfully Submitted,

<<signature>>

Michael J. Anderson (4004-71)

Anderson • Agostino & Keller, P.C.

131 South Taylor Street

South Bend, Indiana 46601

Telephone: (574) 288-1510

Attorney for Plaintiffs

Motion for Discovery Sanctions

2011 WL 2913238 (Ind.Super.)

Westlaw Query>>

To find additional Motion for Discovery Sanctions filings access the Indiana Civil Trial Court Filings Database (IN-FILING), choose Terms and Connectors Search, then enter DT(discovery and sanction).

Superior Court of Indiana.

Marion County

Patricia J. MOWERY and Harold R. Mowery, Jr., Plaintiffs,

v.

Arron L. HOFMEISTER, Individually and as Employee/Agent of Marathon Petroleum Co, LLC and Marathon Petroleum Co, LLC, Defendants.

No. 49D12-0908-CT-038874.

January 28, 2011.

Defendants' Verified Motion for Discovery Abuse Sanctions

Gonzalez Saggio & Harlan, LLP, Miriam A. Rich, # 17138-49, Attorney for Defendants, Gonzalez Saggio & Harlan, LLP, 135 N. Pennsylvania Street, Suite 1740, Indianapolis, in 46204, (317) 686-9800, (31) 686-9821 [fax], richm @gshllp.com.

Defendants Arron Hofmeister and Marathon Petroleum Co., LP (f/k/a Marathon Petroleum Co., LLC), by Counsel Miriam A. Rich and Gonzalez Saggio & Harlan, LLP, hereby move the Court for an Order sanctioning Plaintiffs for discovery abuses and to bar the trial testimony of John R. Pinckney as the proper sanction for these abuses. In support of this Motion, Defendants would show the following:

1. Defendants served expert witness discovery, as set forth in their prior Motions in Limine, requiring service of all reports, including draft reports, of expert or opinion witnesses, as well as interrogatories requiring disclosure of opinions pursuant to Ind. T.R. 26(B)(4).

2. The duty to supplement discovery responses regarding the substance of expert witness opinions is automatic; and in addition, a party has a duty to supplement if the response is no longer true and failure to amend the prior response is in substance a knowing concealment. Ind. T.R. 26(E).

3. At the January 27, 2011, discovery deposition of John R. Pinckney, scheduled by leave of the Court after discovery closed due to the production of Mr. Pinckney's expert report less than one week prior to the discovery deposition cut-off, Plaintiffs produced a computer disk purportedly responsive to the *Subpoena Duces Tecum* served for records and documents relied upon by Mr. Pinckney ("Pinckney disk").

4. Contained on the Pinckney disk was a document titled "Brach Corrected Accident Analysis Report" dated September 13, 2010, ("Corrected Report") which had not been produced previously, and which Pinckney indicated he had not reviewed.

5. In this Corrected Report, Dr. Brach substantively and substantially altered the opinions that he gave in his prior report and to which he testified in his November 29, 2010, deposition.

6. Plaintiffs' failure to produce this Corrected Report to Defendants seasonably and production that appears to

have been inadvertent are violations of the spirit, the letter, and the intent of the Indiana law of discovery prohibiting trial by ambush and constitute a knowing concealment in violation of Ind. T.R. 26(E).

7. Additionally, Plaintiffs produced the report of John R. Pinckney ("Pinckney Report"), another alleged expert witness, with cover letter dated January 3, 2011, mailed via regular U.S. mail to the undersigned.

8. The Pinckney Report is dated December 20, 2010, and indicates that it was provided to Counsel for Plaintiffs via facsimile transmission on that date.

9. Instead of serving the Pinckney Report seasonably, Plaintiffs deposed Defendant Marathon's former DOT Coordinator on December 30, 2010, at which Plaintiffs' Counsel attempted to improperly elicit opinions from Defendant's employee on issues addressed in the Pinckney Report.

10. Plaintiffs are playing blind man's bluff with expert opinions in this case, a behavior reminiscent of that admonished by the Indiana Supreme Court in *Outback v. Markley,* 856 N.E.2d 65 (Ind. 2006), wherein an attorney failed to inform opposing counsel that a witness had given him a statement that conflicted with her deposition testimony, and that prior story formed the basis of her trial testimony. The Markley Court held that whether the omission was intentional or negligent, the failure to produce the information was misconduct. *Id.,* 856 N.E.2d 65 at 77.

11. In the Markley case, the trial court did not have an opportunity to pre-empt the resulting prejudice by appropriately sanctioning the party whose gamesmanship prejudiced the opposing party. Here, the Court has that opportunity.

12. Defendants are prejudiced, not only in the delay in obtaining Pinckney's opinions until the last few days of discovery, but in being lulled into reliance on the opinions given by Brach in his only produced report and his deposition testimony, completely unaware of the reversal of his opinions until eleven days before trial, the same day Counsel for Plaintiffs first disclosed that he no longer intended to call Brach as a witness.

13. Defendants should, due to the imminence of trial and the nature of the discovery abuses, be excused from the requirement that an informal attempt to resolve the discovery dispute be documented, as it is inconceivable that the only appropriate remedy short of dismissal - the exclusion of Pinckney's testimony - could result from any such attempt.

14. The Court should, pursuant to Trial Rule 37(B)(2)(b), bar the testimony of John R. Pinckney from evidence in this matter as a sanction for the cumulative prejudice of failing to seasonably produce the report of John R. Pinckney and the Corrected Report of R. Matthew Brach.

WHEREFORE, Defendants Arron Hofmeister and Marathon Petroleum Co., LP respectfully request that the Court enter an Order barring the testimony of John R. Pinckney as a sanction for failing to comply with discovery rules, for costs of this motion, and for all other relief just in the premises.

Respectfully submitted,

GONZALEZ SAGGIO & HARLAN, LLP

By: <<signature>>

Miriam A. Rich, # 17138-49

Attorney for Defendants

GONZALEZ SAGGIO & HARLAN, LLP

135 N. Pennsylvania Street, Suite 1740

Indianapolis, IN 46204

(317) 686-9800

(31) 686-9821 [fax]

richm@gshllp.com

Motion for Preliminary Injunction

2012 WL 463515 (Ind.Super.)

Westlaw Query>>

To find additional Motion for Preliminary Injunction filings access the Indiana Civil Trial Court Filings Database (IN-FILING), choose Template Search, select Search Motions, then select Motion for Preliminary Injunction.

Superior Court of Indiana.

Allen County

Steven CIMINO and Denise Cimino, Plaintiffs,

v.

KRUSE, INC. d/b/a Kruse International and Dean Kruse, Defendants,

v.

Edward L. Smith, Garnishee Defendant.

No. 02D01-0710-PL-490.

January 12, 2012.

Motion for Preliminary Injunction, Without Notice

Burt, Blee, Dixon, Sutton & Bloom, LLP, G. Martin Cole, #11164-49, Lindsay M. Hurni, #27886-49, 200 East Main Street, Suite 1000, Fort Wayne, IN 46802, (260) 426-1300.

COME NOW the Plaintiffs, Steven Cimino and Denise Cimino, by counsel, Burt, Blee, Dixon, Sutton & Bloom, LLP, and hereby move this Court for a Preliminary Injunction, Without Notice, enjoining Kruse, Inc., Dean Kruse and Edward L. Smith, and anyone in concert or participation with them, from moving the property that is subject of the Auction Brochure previously filed with this Court in Plaintiffs' Motion for Prejudgment Attachment and Affidavit in Support. In support of this Motion, Plaintiffs would show this Court as follows:

1. In order to give full force and effect to the prejudgment attachment Motion and hearing thereon set for Tuesday, January 17, 2012, at 3:00 p.m., the Ciminos seek an Order from this Court preliminarily enjoining Kruse, Inc., Dean V. Kruse and Edward L. Smith, and anyone in concert or participation with them, from moving any of the personal property equipment which is the subject of the Auction Brochure filed with this Court as part of its Motion for Prejudgment Attachment, With Notice. A hearing on the Preliminary Injunction, With Notice, can further be held on the same date as the Prejudgment Attachment hearing, Tuesday, January 17, 2012, at 3:00 p.m., so as to comport with due process. *Squibb v. State ex. rel. Davis,* 860 N.E.2d 904 (Ind.Ct.App. 2007).

2. There is in this action a substantial likelihood that the Plaintiffs are entitled to relief.

3. The auction, being held outside of the State of Indiana, shows a willingness to move the assets outside the State, and outside this Court's processes.

4. Public policy favors the entry of this Preliminary Injunction in that Dean V. Kruse and/or Edward L. Smith, are seeking to sell property of Dean V. Kruse subject to a pending claim, and such sale may, therefore, be considered to be a fraudulent conveyance.

5. Kruse, Inc., Mr. Kruse and Mr. Smith can contest this Court's Preliminary Injunction at the Prejudgment Attachment hearing set for Tuesday, January 17th, at 3:00 p.m.

6. This Motion for Preliminary Injunction, Without Notice, hereby incorporates by reference the Motion for Prejudgment Attachment, With Notice, and Affidavit in Support filed today, January 12, 2012.

WHEREFORE, Plaintiffs, Steven Cimino and Denise Cimino, by counsel, hereby pray for an Order preliminarily enjoining Kruse, Inc., Dean V. Kruse, Edward L. Smith, and anyone acting in concert or participation with them, to not move the property at issue, as set forth in the Auction Brochure, and that the property be kept and maintained in the State of Indiana until further Order of this Court, and for all other just and proper relief.

Respectfully submitted,

BURT, BLEE, DIXON, SUTTON & BLOOM, LLP

<<signature>>

G. Martin Cole, #11164-49

Lindsay M. Hurni, #27886-49

200 East Main Street, Suite 1000

Fort Wayne, IN 46802

(260) 426-1300

Motion to Dismiss for Lack of Subject Matter Jurisdiction

2007 WL 5355881 (Ind.Super.)

Westlaw Query>>

To find additional Motion to Dismiss for Lack of Subject Matter Jurisdiction filings access the Indiana Civil Trial Court Filings Database (IN-FILING), choose Terms and Connectors Search, then enter DT("subject matter jurisdiction").

Superior Court of Indiana,

Civil Division.

Lake County

THE METHODIST HOSPITALS, INC., Petitioner,

v.

Lori MERKNER, Arvid Merkner, Gregory Gordon, M.D., Larry Brazley, M.D., H. Carl Moultrie, II, M.D., Raied Abdullah, M.D., Dennis Streeter, D.O., Hamid Safavi, M.D., G. Anthony Bertig, and Jim Atterholt, Respondents.

No. 45D040706PL00065.

June 22, 2007.

Petition for Preliminary Determination and Motion to Dismiss for Lack of Subject Matter Jurisdiction

Douglas K. Walker, Attorney No. 21418-45, Attorney for the Petitioner, The Methodist Hospitals, Inc.

Katherine A. Brown-Henry, Attorney No. 26280-03, Attorney for the Petitioner, The Methodist Hospitals, Inc.

Blackmun, Bomberger, Tyler & Walker, 9006 Indianapolis Boulevard, Highland, Indiana 46322, Telephone: (219) 972-2200, Facsimile: (219) 972-2404.

Petitioner, The Methodist Hospitals, Inc., pursuant to Ind. Trial Rule 12(B)(1), the Indiana Medical Malpractice Act (Indiana Code, Title 34, Article 18), specifically Chapter 11 thereof (Ind. Code § 34-18-11-1 through Ind. Code § 34-18-11-5), and Indiana's Worker's Compensation Act (Indiana Code, Title 22, Article 3), specifically Chapter 2 thereof (Ind. Code § 22-3-2-1 through Indiana Code § 22-3-2-22), petitions the court for a preliminary determination of law for an order granting dismissal, with prejudice, of petitioner from the pending medical malpractice claim brought by respondents Lori and Arvid Merkner currently pending before the Indiana Department of Insurance for the reason that Indiana's Worker's Compensation Act provides the exclusive remedy of recovery for injuries arising out of and in the course of employment. The hospital incorporates herein by reference and submits its accompanying memorandum of law in support of its motion.

<<signature>>

Douglas K. Walker,

Attorney No. 21418-45

Attorney for the Petitioner

The Methodist Hospitals, Inc.

<<signature>>

Katherine A. Brown-Henry,

Attorney No. 26280-03

Attorney for the Petitioner

The Methodist Hospitals, Inc.

BLACKMUN, BOMBERGER, TYLER & WALKER

9006 Indianapolis Boulevard

Highland, Indiana 46322

Telephone: (219) 972-2200

Facsimile: (219) 972-2404

MEMORANDUM IN SUPPORT OF PETITION FOR PRELIMINARY DETERMINATION AND MOTION TO DISMISS FOR LACK OF SUBJECT MATTER JUDRISDICTION

Lori and Arvid Merkner, husband and wife, have filed a proposed complaint with the Indiana Department of Insurance alleging that her employer, The Methodist Hospitals, Inc., and other qualified healthcare providers, specifically Gregory Gordon, M.D.; Larry Brazley, M.D.; H. Carl Moultrie, II, M.D.; Raied Abdullah, M.D.; Dennis Streeter, D.O.; and Hamid Safavi, M.D., committed medical malpractice in providing Mrs. Merkner with health care in 2004. Jim Atterholt is joined as a party herein in his capacity as Commissioner of Insurance of the State of Indiana, and G. Anthony Bertig is joined as a party in his capacity as medical review panel chairman pursuant to I.C. § 34-18-11-2.

Mrs. Merkner complains of injuries in her medical malpractice action that arose out of and in the course and scope of her employment with The Methodist Hospitals, Inc. Her exclusive remedy against her employer for these injuries is Indiana's Worker's Compensation Act. The exclusivity provision of Indiana's Worker's Compensation Act bars her medical malpractice claim against The Methodist Hospitals, Inc.

Facts

At all times relevant herein, Lori Merkner was an employee of Petitioner, The Methodist Hospitals, Inc. (Ex. 1, p. 18; Ex. 4(B), Interrogatory Answer 1(g)) She worked as a registered nurse and nurse supervisor. (Ex. 1, pp. 5, 18)

On April 29, 2004, Mrs. Merkner presented herself to the emergency room at Methodist Hospital Southlake. (Ex. 1, p. 8) She complained of pain in the Achilles area of her right ankle which had worsened over the past 24 hours. *Id.* at 8, 9. She was found to have swelling and intractable pain in her right leg and was admitted to the hospital by Larry Brazley, M.D., for evaluation. *Id.* at 8-10.

Forty-eight hours prior to her admittance, Mrs. Merkner was in good health, but had noticed increasing pain and swelling in her right leg after working a 16 hour shift at the hospital. *Id.* at 5, 18, 26, 142. Mrs. Merkner was diagnosed with suspected compartment syndrome and a fasciotomy was done by Carl Moultrie, M.D. *Id.* at 18, 22. Following this surgery, Mrs. Merkner went into acute renal failure. *Id.* at 22-25.

Mr. Merkner was seen by Hamid Safavi, M.D., an infectious diseases specialist, who indicated her condition was indicative of an infection of the soft tissue of her right leg, possibly fasciitis or necrotizing fasciitis. *Id.* at 35. Her blood cultures were also positive for gram positive cocci, possibly Streptococcus toxic shock syndrome. *Id.* Mrs. Merkner also began to develop cellulitis in her groin area. *Id.* at 7, 38.

Due to her deteriorating leg condition, Mrs. Merkner was transferred to the University of Chicago for further treatment on May 5, 2004. *Id.* at 7, 393. When she was transferred, Mrs. Merkner's diagnosis was Strep A sepsis, sepsis, necrotizing fasciitis, rhabdomyolysis, and acute renal failure. *Id.* at 7.

On May 5, 2004, Mrs. Merkner's husband, Arvid Merkner, indicated that he felt Mrs. Merkner's condition was a worker's compensation claim. *Id.* at 538. He filled out an employee incident report on Mrs. Merkner's behalf indicating that she had contracted a Strep-A blood infection while working in the hospital's Southlake emergency room and that her injury was work related. (Ex. 2) As a result of this claim, Mrs. Merkner received worker's compensation benefits. (Ex. 3, p. 2) This compensation included 63.71 weeks of temporary total disability compensation for lost wages as well as coverage of her medical expenses. (Ex. 3; Ex. 4(A); Ex. 4(C)) Mrs. Merkner's worker's compensation ceased when she returned to work at the hospital. (Ex. 3, p. 2)

Mrs. Merkner continues to contend that her injury is compensable under Indiana's Worker's Compensation statute. (Ex. 3, pp. 3, 6) She acknowledges that she has received worker's compensation for her injury. (Ex. 3, p. 4; Ex. 4(C); Ex. 4(D)) Mr. and Mrs. Merkner now wrongfully continue to seek further compensation from the hospital for this work-related injury through a proposed complaint filed with the Indiana Department of Insurance in accordance with The Medical Malpractice Act. (Ex. 5)

Issue

Is Indiana Worker's Compensation Act the exclusive remedy for Mr. and Mrs. Merkner against her employer, The Methodist Hospitals, Inc.?

Discussion

Worker's Compensation is Mr. & Mrs. Merkner's Sole Remedy Against The Methodist Hospitals, Inc.

In this case, the Merkners' sole and exclusive remedy against the hospital is Indiana's Worker's Compensation Act. The exclusivity provision of the Worker's Compensation Act bars the medical review panel from hearing the Merkner's claim. Employer's challenges to employee's claims under the worker's compensation exclusivity provision are appropriately advanced through a motion to dismiss for lack of subject matter jurisdiction under T.R. 12(B)(1). *Foshee v. Shoney's,* 637 N.E.2d 1277, 1280 (Ind. 1994)

Indiana's Worker's Compensation Act (hereinafter "the Act") provides compensation to an employee for injuries which arise out of and occur in the course of the employee's employment. *Campbell v. Eckman/Freeman & Assoc.,* 670 N.E.2d 925, 929 (Ind.Ct.App. 1996). *See also* I.C. § 22-3-2-2 (2007). Under the Act, there is an "exclusive remedy provision," which states:

> The rights and remedies granted to an employee subject to IC 22-3-2 through IC 22-3-6 on account of personal injury or death by accident shall exclude all other rights and remedies of such employee, the employee's personal representatives, dependents, or next of kin, at common law or otherwise, on account of such injury or death, except for remedies available under IC 5-2-6.1 [which pertain to victims of violent crimes].

I.C. § 22-3-2-6 (2007). *See also Tarr v. Jablonski,* 569 N.E.2d 378, 379 (Ind.Ct.App. 1991); *Jennings v. St. Vincent Hospital & Health Care Center,* 832 N.E.2d 1104, 1050 (Ind.Ct.App. 2005).

The exclusive remedy provision limits an employee whose injury meets the jurisdictional requirements of the Act to the rights and remedies provided by the Act, to the exclusion of all other remedies. *Campbell* at 930. Thus, if an employee's injury arises out of and in the course of her employment, she is statutorily entitled to worker's compensation, and the exclusive remedy provision bars any other form of relief.[1] *Id.*

In *Campbell,* the plaintiff brought a medical negligence claim against her employer's insurance carrier for the care and treatment provided following a work-related injury. *Id.* at 927-928. The *Campbell* court held that the exclusive remedy provision barred the trial court from hearing any common law action brought against the employer for the same injuries for which the employee received worker's compensation benefits. *Id.* at 930.

Once an employer raises the issue of the exclusivity of the Act, the burden shifts to the employee to demonstrate some ground for taking the claim outside of the Act. *GKN Co. v. Magness,* 744 N.E.2d 397, 404 (Ind. 2001). An employee who has successfully collected worker's compensation on the premise that her injuries did arise out of and in the course of her employment is barred from denying that her injury and her claim are not work-related.

---

1. At the time of Mrs. Merkner's treatment for her work-related injury at the hospital, the hospital was a qualified health care provider in accordance with I.C. § 34-18-3-3. (Ex. 6). Under Indiana's Medical Malpractice Act, a plaintiff cannot commence a court action against a qualified health care provider until the claimant's proposed complaint has been presented to a medical review panel and an opinion has been given by that panel. I.C. § 34-18-8-4. The medical review panel process is a prerequisite to bringing a court action. *Hodge v. Johnson* 882 N.E.2d 650, 652-653 (Ind.Ct.App. 2006) and I.C. § 34-18-8-4.

Skinner v. Martin, 455 N.E.2d 1168, 1171 (Ind.Ct.App. 1983). Mrs. Merkner has collected worker's compensation benefits and is precluded from denying that her injuries and claim are not work related.

Although Mrs. Merkner cannot bring her medical malpractice claim against the hospital, this does not mean that she is without recourse. The *Campbell* court concluded that a medical malpractice claim arising from the treatment of a work-related injury precluded the plaintiff from bringing a claim against her employer or a co-employee, but she was not precluded from bringing the claim against a third-party tortfeasor. *Campbell* at 930 citing I.C. § 22-3-2-13. Therefore, the Merkners can still maintain their action against any other third-party tortfeasors.

In *Ross v. Shubert,* 388 N.E.2d 623 (Ind.Ct.App. 1979), a factory worker at International Harvester Company was allowed to bring medical malpractice claims against independent physicians working on a part-time basis at the company's clinic in the plant. *Id.* The court stated that, "since the act's inception, it has been the employment relationship which is to delineate its perimeters of immunity." *Id.* at 407. There was no question in that case that the worker could not sue International Harvester, his employer, for negligent healthcare provided at the employer's clinic. *Id.* However, the employee could sue the part time independent physicians working at the clinic. *Id.*

Similarly, there is no question that Mr. and Mrs. Merkner have no basis to sue Mrs. Merkner's employer, the hospital, under the Medical Malpractice Act, because their sole remedy is contained in the Worker's Compensation Act. However, their claims against the physicians may proceed.

Conclusion

Mrs. Merkner has collected worker's compensation benefits for the injury which is at issue in the medical malpractice case now before the Indiana Department of Insurance. The exclusive remedy provision of Indiana Worker's Compensation Act precludes the Merkners from seeking any other form of relief outside of the Act and bars Indiana's trial courts and any medical review panel from hearing any common law action brought against her employer, the hospital, regarding the same injuries for which the Mrs. Merkner received worker's compensation benefits.

Therefore, the trial court is without subject matter jurisdiction as to the Merkners' claims against Methodist Hospital, and the proposed complaint filed by the Merkners in the prerequisite Indiana Department of Insurance proceeding should be dismissed with prejudice pursuant to T.R. 12(B)(1).

WHEREFORE, the petitioner, The Methodist Hospitals, Inc., moves the Court to enter an order dismissing Arvid and Lori Merkner's claim now pending before the Indiana Department of Insurance, with prejudice.

<<signature>>

Douglas K. Walker,

Attorney No. 21418-45

Attorney for the Petitioner

The Methodist Hospitals, Inc.

<<signature>>

Katherine A. Brown-Henry,

Attorney No. 26280-03

Attorney for the Petitioner

The Methodist Hospitals, Inc.

BLACKMUN, BOMBERGER, TYLER & WALKER

9006 Indianapolis Boulevard

Highland, Indiana 46322

Telephone: (219) 972-2200

Facsimile: (219) 972-2404

Table of Laws and Rules

INDIANA CODE

TABLE OF LAWS AND RULES

INDIANA CODE—Continued

INDIANA CODE—Continued

INDIANA CODE—Continued

INDIANA CODE—Continued

INDIANA ADMINISTRATIVE RULES OF COURT

INDIANA ADMINISTRATIVE RULES OF COURT—Continued

INDIANA ADMINISTRATIVE RULES OF COURT—Continued

INDIANA RULES OF APPELLATE PROCEDURE

INDIANA RULES OF TRIAL PROCEDURE

INDIANA RULES OF TRIAL PROCEDURE—Continued

INDIANA RULES OF TRIAL PROCEDURE—Continued

INDIANA RULES OF TRIAL PROCEDURE—Continued

INDIANA RULES OF TRIAL PROCEDURE—Continued

INDIANA RULES OF TRIAL PROCEDURE—Continued

INDIANA RULES OF TRIAL PROCEDURE—Continued

INDIANA RULES OF TRIAL PROCEDURE—Continued

INDIANA RULES OF TRIAL PROCEDURE—Continued

INDIANA RULES OF TRIAL PROCEDURE—Continued

INDIANA RULES OF TRIAL PROCEDURE—Continued

INDIANA RULES OF TRIAL PROCEDURE—Continued

INDIANA RULES OF TRIAL PROCEDURE—Continued

INDIANA RULES OF TRIAL PROCEDURE—Continued

INDIANA RULES OF TRIAL PROCEDURE—Continued

INDIANA RULES OF TRIAL PROCEDURE—Continued

INDIANA RULES OF TRIAL PROCEDURE—Continued

INDIANA RULES OF TRIAL PROCEDURE—Continued

INDIANA RULES FOR ALTERNATIVE DISPUTE RESOLUTION

INDIANA RULES FOR ALTERNATIVE DISPUTE RESOLUTION—Continued

INDIANA JURY RULES

INDIANA JURY RULES—Continued

LOCAL CIVIL RULES OF THE ALLEN SUPERIOR AND CIRCUIT COURT

HAMILTON COUNTY LOCAL ADMINISTRATIVE AND TRIAL RULES

HAMILTON COUNTY LOCAL ADMINISTRATIVE AND TRIAL RULES—Continued

LAKE COUNTY RULES OF CIVIL PROCEDURE

LAKE COUNTY RULES OF CIVIL PROCEDURE—Continued

MARION CIRCUIT AND SUPERIOR COURT CIVIL DIVISION RULES

LOCAL GENERAL AND ADMINISTRATIVE, CIVIL, EMERGENCY, AND ELECTRONIC FILING RULES FOR ST JOSEPH COUNTY—Continued

INDIANA U.S. DISTRICT COURT ORDERS

Table of Cases

*

Index

References are to page number

INDEX

INDEX

†